D0181968

The Rough Guide to

Britain

written and researched by

**Robert Andrews, Jules Brown,
Rob Humphreys, Phil Lee** and **Donald Reid**

with additional contributions by

Matthew Teller

**ROUGH
GUIDES**

NEW YORK • LONDON • DELHI

www.roughguides.com

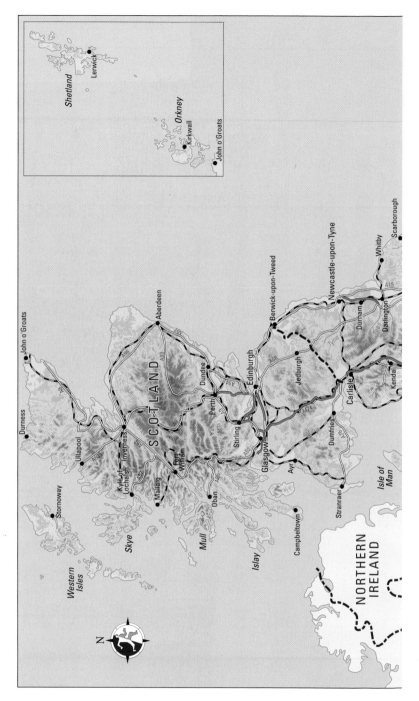

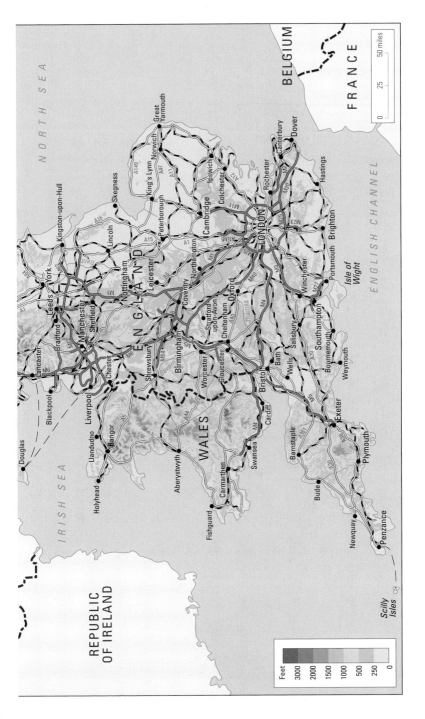

△ The Angel of the North, Gateshead

Introduction to

Britain

If ever a nation were both hostage to and beneficiary of its history, it's Britain. The most important thing to remember when travelling here is that you're visiting not one country, but three: England, Wales and Scotland. That means three capital cities (London, Cardiff and Edinburgh) and three sets of national identity – not to mention the myriad accent shifts as you move between them.

The truth is that were you to plan a country from scratch, you wouldn't even try to corral these three fiercely contradictory nations into a United Kingdom★. They've had centuries to get used to each other, but there's still little love lost: Wales has long been resentful of English dominance, Scotland is happiest as far away from both as possible, northern England is contemptuous of the south, and Londoners are convinced they're in a league of their own.

For visitors, this regional diversity means there's enough here for a lifetime's travels – from dynamic, cosmopolitan London to remote Scottish fishing villages; from the Welsh valleys to England's postindustrial heartland; from Land's End to John O'Groats; and the North Sea to the Irish Sea.

Travelling around Britain is not without its idiosyncrasies. The train system, infamously, is in disarray, with commuters and long-distance travellers in a semi-permanent state of delay and revolt. The arterial roads aren't much better, and are often gridlocked around major cities. And if

---

* "Britain" (or Great Britain) is a geographical term referring to the largest of the British Isles. "United Kingdom" is a political term, referring to the state comprising England, Scotland, Wales and Northern Ireland.

Fact file

• The **population** of Britain – which, at 93,000 square miles, is slightly smaller than the US state of Oregon – is about 58 million: 50 million in England, 5 million in Scotland and 3 million in Wales. The biggest city is London, with some 7.4 million inhabitants. **Ethnic minorities** represent about six percent of the total population, the largest groups being those of Caribbean or African descent (875,000 people), Indians (840,000) and Pakistanis and Bangladeshis (640,000). The official **language** is English, though Welsh also has official status in Wales. Scottish Gaelic is used in parts of Scotland.

• The **lowest point** is in the Fens of eastern England, at 13ft below sea level; the **highest point** is the summit of Ben Nevis at 4406ft. From the south coast of England to the extreme north of Scotland is about 600 miles; the **longest journey**, from Land's End to John O'Groats, is nearer 850 miles.

• The UK, comprising Britain and Northern Ireland, is a **constitutional monarchy**, whose head of state is Queen Elizabeth II. The bicameral parliament is composed of the directly elected **House of Commons** and the unelected **House of Lords**. There is no written constitution, and real power is concentrated in the hands of the **Prime Minister**, head of the largest party in the House of Commons.

you've just arrived clutching your euros from a tour of "The Continent", free of border controls and exchange rates, you'll swiftly be disabused of the notion that Britain is an integral part of Europe.

The country has dithered for decades about its postwar – and, more specifically, post-imperial – role: having ruled the roost for several hundred years, Brits are increasingly uncertain about their place in the new order. Paradoxically, it's the Welsh and the Scots, for so long under the English thumb, who have emerged with their national identities intact and tangible political power embodied in their own parliamentary assemblies. The English, still without a regional voice, are left unsure of how to modernize their institutions, ever-fearful of conflict erupting between town and country, north and south, rich and poor, blacks, Asians and whites, and increasingly lagging behind the social and political change that is being wrought as effectively in Edinburgh as in Brussels. England remains the dominant and most urbanized member of the British partnership, but crossing the border

▽ Notting Hill pub, London

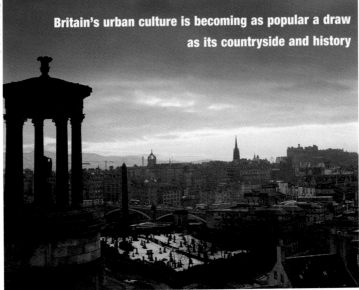

**Britain's urban culture is becoming as popular a draw
as its countryside and history**

into predominantly rural Wales brings you into an unmistakeably Celtic
land, while in Scotland (a nation whose absorption into the state was
rather more recent) the presence of a profoundly non-English world-view
is striking.

Across the country, virtually every town bears a mark of former wealth
and power, whether it be a Gothic cathedral financed from a monarch's
treasury, a parish church funded by the tycoons of medieval trade, or a
triumphalist Victorian civic building, raised on the income of the British
Empire. Elsewhere, you'll find old dockyards from which the Royal Navy
patrolled the oceans, and mills that employed whole town populations.
Meanwhile Britain's museums and galleries – several ranking among the
world's finest and most of the major ones with free admission – are full of
treasures trawled from its imperial conquests.

In London's and Bristol's vibrant music scene, in the fashionable restaurants and bars of Manchester and Glasgow, in the outstanding contemporary architecture in Cardiff and Newcastle, there's a buzz, a "feel-good"
factor, that is palpable. Indeed, there's always been an innovative flair to
British popular culture, which contrasts sharply with the bucolic view of
Britain that many tourist boards favour. The countryside may yield all
manner of delights, from walkers' trails around the hills and lakes, through
prehistoric stone circles, to traditional villages and their pubs, but Britain's
characterful and diverse urban culture is fast becoming as popular a draw
as its countryside and history.

The A to Z of fish and chips

Britain's one truly significant contribution to world cuisine emerges from the nation's fish-and-chip shops, or "chippies". A marriage made in nineteenth-century cities as cheap food for the working masses, battered fish and thick-cut potato chips – both deep-fried, salted and soused in vinegar – have conquered the world. These days, the traditional staples of cod and haddock are endangered species, so you're just as likely to see skate, hake, rock salmon (ie dogfish) and other coastal beasties on fish shop menus. In most places, ask for "fish and chips" if you want the works, though in Scotland it's a "fish supper". Mushy peas are the traditional accompaniment, while chips or fish in a bread-roll sandwich (with or, more often, without butter) is a "butty". Other available items range from battered sausages and saveloys to pickled eggs. After ordering all this, if you still feel that your meal hasn't got quite enough calories, you can always ask for a scoop of the leftover batter "bits" or "scraps" on top.

Where to go

England

L ondon is the place to start. Nowhere in the country can match the scope and innovation of the metropolis, a colossal, frenetic city, perhaps not as immediately attractive as its European counterparts, but with so much variety that the only obstacle to a great time is the shockingly high cost of everything. It's here that you'll find Britain's best spread of nightlife, cultural events, museums, galleries, pubs and restaurants. The other large cities, such as **Birmingham**, **Newcastle**, **Leeds**, **Manchester** and **Liverpool**, each have their strengths too. Birmingham has a resurgent arts scene, for example, while people travel for miles to sample Newcastle's nightlife, and **Manchester** these days can match the capital for glamour in cafés and clubs, and also boasts the inimitable draw of the world's best-known football team.

England's ancient cathedral cities, such as **Lincoln**, **York**, **Salisbury**, **Durham** and **Winchester**, cannot be equalled for sheer physical beauty, and wherever you're based, you're never more than a few miles from a ruined castle, a majestic country house, a secluded chapel or a monastery. In the southwest there are remnants of a Celtic culture that was all but eradicated elsewhere by the Romans, and everywhere you can find traces of prehistoric settlers – most famously the megalithic circles of **Stonehenge** and **Avebury**.

Most beguiling of all are the long-established villages of England, hundreds of which amount to nothing more than a pub, a shop, a gaggle of cottages and a farmhouse offering bed and breakfast. **Devon**, **Cornwall**, the **Cotswolds** and the **Yorkshire Dales** harbour some especially picturesque specimens, but every county can boast a decent showing. Then, of course, there's the English countryside, an extraordinarily diverse terrain from which Constable, Turner, Wordsworth, Emily Brontë and a host of other writers and artists took inspiration. **Exmoor**, **Dartmoor**, **Bodmin Moor**, the **North York Moors** and the **Lake District** are the most dramatic and best known of the national parks, each offering an array of landscapes crisscrossed with walking routes.

△ Shaftesbury, Dorset

Wales

Although **Cardiff** boasts most of Wales' national institutions, including the National Museum, the appeal of a visit lies outside the towns, where there's ample evidence of the warmongering which shaped the country's development. Castles are everywhere, from the little stone keeps of the early Welsh princes and the mighty **Carreg Cennen** to Edward I's doughty fortresses such as **Beaumaris**, **Conwy** and **Harlech**. Passage graves and stone circles (such as on **Holy Island**) offer a link to the pre-Roman era when the

△ Conwy Castle, North Wales

INTRODUCTION | WHERE TO GO | WHEN TO GO

Standing stones

Why the prehistoric peoples of Britain built circles of standing stones may never be fully known. The theories are as diverse as the sites themselves: perhaps they were places of sacrifice and celebration, or erected for an astronomical function. But two things remain obvious, even at a distance of five thousand years. Firstly, each series of standing stones represents a highly organized effort

by ancient peoples once thought of as unsophisticated. And secondly, whatever their function, the circles retain a powerful presence even today, recognized by the disparate bands of druids and New Age travellers who still seek solace in the stones. Mass tourism has dragged famous sites like Stonehenge into the embrace of the heritage industry, but there are other sites which retain their sense of mystery and isolation. At Castlerigg in the Lake District, Calanais in western Scotland, or Holy Island in North Wales, you can still wander alone, forming your own theories as the early morning mist rises above the stones.

priestly order of druids ruled over early Celtic peoples, and great medieval monastic houses, like ruined **Tintern Abbey**, are easily accessible.

All these attractions are enhanced by the beauty of the wild Welsh countryside. The backbone of the Cambrian Mountains terminates in the soaring peaks of **Snowdonia National Park** and the angular ridges of the **Brecon Beacons**; both are superb walking country, as is the **Pembrokeshire Coast** in the southwest. Much of the rest of the coast remains unspoilt, though long sweeps of sand are often backed by traditional British seaside resorts, such as **Llandudno** in the north or **Tenby** in the south.

Scotland

The Scottish capital, **Edinburgh**, is a handsome and ancient city, famous for its magnificent **castle** and **Palace of Holyroodhouse** as well as for an acclaimed international arts festival and some excellent museums – not least the outstanding **National Museum of Scotland**. A short journey west is **Glasgow**, a sprawling industrial metropolis that has done much to improve its image in recent years and can now boast a range of fine museums and galleries and dynamic nightlife to complement the impressive architectural legacy of its eighteenth- and nineteenth-century heyday.

Southern Scotland, often underrated, features some gorgeous scenery, but nothing quite to compare with the shadowy glens and well-walked

hills of the **Trossachs**, or with the **Highlands**, whose multitude of mountains, sea cliffs, glens and lochs cover the northern two-thirds of the country. **Inverness** is an obvious base here, although **Fort William**, near **Ben Nevis**, Britain's highest mountain, is an alternative.

Some of Britain's most thrilling wilderness experiences are to be had on the Scottish islands, the most accessible of which extend in a long rocky chain off the Atlantic coast, from **Arran** through **Skye** (the most visited of the Hebrides) to the **Western Isles**, where the remarkably hostile terrain harbours some of the last bastions of the Gaelic language. At Britain's northern extreme lie the sea- and wind-buffeted **Orkney** and **Shetland** islands, whose rich Norse heritage makes them distinct in dialect and culture from mainland Scotland, while their wild scenery offers some of Britain's finest bird-watching and some stunning archeological remains.

When to go

Considering the temperate nature of the British **climate**, it's amazing how much mileage the locals get out of the subject: a two-day cold snap is discussed as if it were the onset of a new Ice Age, and a week in the upper 70s starts rumours of a heatwave. The fact is that summers rarely get hot and the winters don't get very cold, except in the north of Scotland and on the highest points of the Welsh and Scottish uplands. Rainfall is fairly even, though again mountainous areas get higher quantities throughout the year (the west coast of Scotland is especially damp, and Llanberis, at the foot of Snowdon, gets more than twice as much rainfall as Caernarfon, seven miles away).

In general, the south is warmer and sunnier than the north, but the bottom line is that it's impossible to say with any degree of certainty what the weather will be like. May might be wet and grey one year and gloriously sunny the next; November stands an equal chance of being crisp and clear or foggy and grim. If you're planning to lie on a beach, or camp in the dry, you'll want to visit between June and September – a period when you shouldn't go anywhere without booking your accommodation in advance. Otherwise, if you're balancing the clemency of the weather against the density of the crowds, the best months to explore are April, May, September and October.

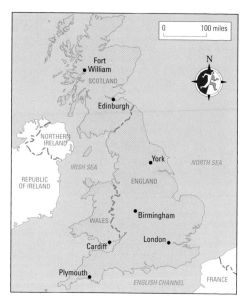

Average daily maximum temperatures

	Jan	Feb	Mar	Apr	May	June	July	Aug	Sept	Oct	Nov	Dec
Birmingham												
°F	42	43	48	54	61	66	68	68	63	55	48	44
°C	5	6	9	12	16	19	20	20	17	13	9	7
Cardiff												
°F	45	45	50	56	60	68	69	69	64	58	51	46
°C	7	7	10	13	16	20	21	21	18	14	11	8
Edinburgh												
°F	42	43	46	51	56	64	65	64	61	54	48	44
°C	5	6	8	11	13	18	18	18	16	12	9	7
Fort William												
°F	43	44	48	52	58	61	62	63	61	54	49	45
°C	6	7	9	11	14	16	17	17	16	12	9	7
London												
°F	43	44	50	56	62	69	71	71	65	58	50	45
°C	6	7	10	13	17	21	22	22	19	14	10	7
Plymouth												
°F	47	47	50	54	59	64	66	67	64	58	52	49
°C	8	8	10	12	15	18	19	19	18	14	11	9
York												
°F	43	44	49	55	61	67	70	69	64	57	49	45
°C	6	7	10	13	16	19	21	21	18	14	9	7

35
things not to miss

It's not possible to see everything that Britain has to offer in one trip – and we don't suggest you try. What follows is a selective taste of the highlights of England, Wales and Scotland: outstanding buildings, spectacular scenery, great festivals and unforgettable journeys. They're arranged in five colour-coded categories, which you can browse through to find the very best things to see and experience. All entries have a page reference to take you straight into the guide, where you can find out more.

01 **Tobermory** Page **1103** • Scotland's most picturesque fishing port, bar none.

02 Portmeirion Page **885** • Decidedly un-Welsh architecture makes this Italianate village a unique attraction.

03 A pint down the pub Page **43** • Whether supped in a trendy micro-brewery or an ancient coaching inn, a pint is an essential part of any visit to Britain.

04 Hillwalking Page **53** • The array of challenging but accessible hills makes walking one of the best ways to enjoy Britain.

05 Notting Hill Carnival Page 139 • Europe's biggest and loudest street festival takes place every August in the streets of west London.

06 Blackpool Page 605 • Britain's brashest seaside resort is given a touch of grace by its tower

07 Whisky Page 44 • Sampling varieties of the "water of life" is an undoubtedly pleasant part of any visit to Scotland.

08 Stately homes and castles Page 49 • For tangible proof of Britain's long and often violent past, the country's many stately homes and castles – like Alnwick in Northumberland – can't be bettered.

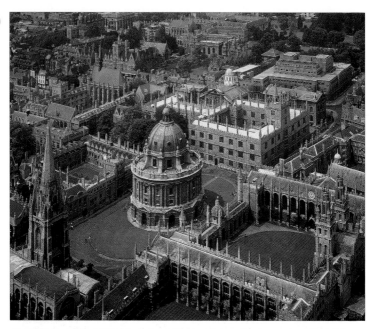

09 **Oxford** Page **288** • The famous old university town boasts many beautiful buildings, including the imposing Italianate rotunda, Radcliffe Camera.

10 **British Museum** Page **105** • In parts controversial and generally not British, the collections of the BM are still the greatest in the world.

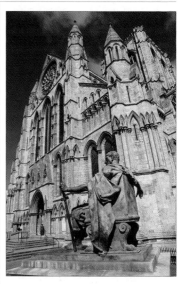

11 **York Minster** Page **696** • Britain's biggest Gothic church has a thousand-year history and treasures to match.

12 **Punting on the Cam** Page **468** ● The handsome university town of Cambridge is justifiably popular, and punting on the River Cam is *de rigueur*.

13 **Eden Project, Cornwall**
Page **398** ● Spectacular and refreshingly ungimmicky display of the planet's plant life, mainly housed in vast geodesic "biomes".

14 **Curry** Page **40** ● This very British take on traditional Indian cuisine has become as popular and ubiquitous as fish and chips.

15 **Kinloch Castle, Rùm** Page **1143** • Stay in the servants' quarters of this Edwardian Scottish-island hideaway or in one of its few remaining four-poster beds.

17 **Glasgow School of Art** Page **1023** • Finest example of the unique style of Glasgow architect and designer Charles Rennie Mackintosh.

16 **Skara Brae** Page **1268** • The extensive remains of this small fishing village offer a fascinating glimpse into Neolithic life.

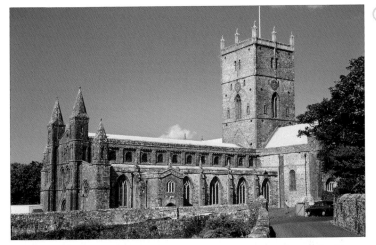

18 **St David's Cathedral** Page **814** • Serene cathedral set in a small, quiet village that has drawn pilgrims to this westernmost tip of Wales for well over a thousand years.

19 **Bonfire Night** Page **53** • Nationwide fireworks and bonfires commemorate the foiling of the 1605 Gunpowder Plot.

20 **St Ives Tate, Cornwall** Page **410** • Southwest England's best art collection occupies a superb site overlooking Porthmeor Beach.

21 **Loch Shiel** Page **1230** • Among Scotland's myriad lochs, Shiel stands out for its serene beauty and compelling history.

22 **West Highland Railway** Page **1204** • One of the great railway journeys of the world.

23 Iona Page **1107** • The home of Celtic Christian spirituality, an island of pilgrimage today as in antiquity.

24 Castle Arcade, Cardiff Page **785** • Some excellent shopping is to be had in the Victorian and Edwardian arcades occupying the centre of the Welsh capital.

25 Edinburgh Castle Page **921** • Dominating Scotland's capital, this fortress-cum-royal palace is intimately linked to the country's history.

26 Surfing, Newquay Page **415** • The beaches strung along the north coast of Devon and Cornwall offer some great breaks, and Newquay is still the top place to see and be seen.

27 National Museum of Wales Page **788** • Find out everything you ever wanted to know about Wales.

28 Avebury Page **275** • Avebury's stone circle rivals Stonehenge and its function is as hotly debated.

29 Snowdonia Page **869** • One of Britain's grandest national parks, a wedge of mountainous Welsh territory focused on the Snowdon massif.

30 **Glastonbury** Page **351** •
Established in the 1970s, the
Glastonbury Festival still attracts big names
and even bigger crowds.

31 **Harlech** Page **847** • An
evocative castle and twisting narrow
streets make this town a highlight of the
Cambrian Coast.

32 **Aberyswyth** Page **855** • Affirmedly Welsh and highly enjoyable, this lively seaside
resort makes a worthwhile stop.

33 **Bath**
Page **338**
• Whether you're
visiting the
Roman baths,
England's most
elegant
Georgian
terrace, or the
new high-tech
spa, Bath has it
all.

34 **Melrose Abbey** Page **974** • Melrose and its fine abbey ruins are reason enough for visiting the Scottish Borders region.

35 **Lizard Point, Cornwall** Page **404** • This south-coast headland has none of the razzmatazz of Land's End, but all the views – and some great beaches too.

Contents

Using this Rough Guide

We've tried to make this Rough Guide a good read and easy to use. The book is divided into five main sections, and you should be able to find whatever you want in one of them.

Colour section

The front colour section offers a quick tour of Britain. The **introduction** aims to give you a feel for the place, with suggestions on where to go. We also tell you what the weather is like and include a basic fact file. Next, our authors round up their favourite aspects of Britain in the **things not to miss** section – whether it's great food, an amazing sight or an unmissable festival. Right after this comes a full **contents** list.

Basics

The Basics section covers all the **pre-departure** nitty-gritty to help you plan your trip. This is where to find out which airlines fly to your destination, what paperwork you'll need, what to do about money and insurance, about Internet access, food, security, public transport, car rental – in fact just about every piece of **general practical information** you might need.

Guide

This is the heart of the Rough Guide, divided into user-friendly chapters, each of which covers a specific region. Every chapter starts with a list of

highlights and an **introduction** that helps you to decide where to go. Likewise, introductions to the various towns and smaller regions within each chapter should help you plan your itinerary. We start most town accounts with information on arrival and accommodation, followed by a tour of the sights, and finally reviews of places to eat and drink, and details of nightlife. Longer accounts also have a directory of practical listings. Each chapter concludes with **public transport** details for that region.

Contexts

Read Contexts to get a deeper understanding of what makes Britain tick. We include a brief **history** and a detailed further reading section that reviews dozens of **books** and **films** relating to Britain.

Index + small print

Apart from a **full index**, which includes maps as well as places, this section covers publishing information, credits and acknowledgements, and also has our contact details in case you want to send in updates and corrections to the book – or suggestions as to how we might improve it.

Map and chapter list

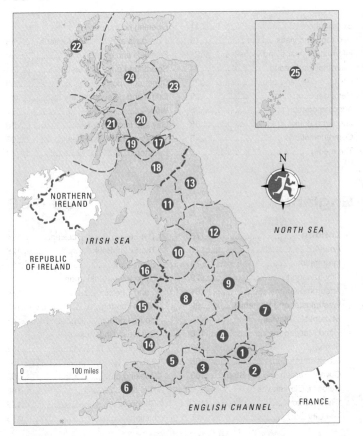

Contents

Scotland

907–1292

Contexts

small print and Index

Basics

Basics

✈ Getting there

BASICS | Getting there

For most travellers to Britain, the range of options will be greatest – and the fares usually the lowest – flying into London, one of the world's busiest transport hubs. However, if you're planning to tour the north of England or Scotland, you might do better on a nonstop flight into Manchester, Birmingham or Glasgow instead. It's also possible to connect in London to many other regional airports around England, Wales or Scotland on a domestic carrier.

London's biggest airports – **Heathrow** and **Gatwick** – take the bulk of transatlantic and long-haul flights into the UK, and are about equal in terms of convenient access to the capital. London's three smaller airports – **Stansted**, **Luton** and **City** – are well served by low-cost flights from mainland Europe, as are **Manchester**, **Glasgow** and other regional airports, including **Birmingham** in the West Midlands, **Bristol** in the West Country, **Leeds/Bradford** in Yorkshire, **Newcastle** in northeast England, and **Edinburgh** and **Aberdeen** in Scotland. There are no transatlantic flights into **Cardiff International Airport**, only a scattering of domestic services, but road and rail connections from London, Birmingham and Bristol are good.

Air fares depend on availability and also on the **season**, with the highest fares charged from mid-June to mid-September and around Christmas and New Year. Fares will ordinarily be cheaper during the rest of the year, which is considered low season, though some airlines also have a "shoulder" season – typically April to mid-June and mid-September to October.

You can often cut costs by going through a **specialist flight agent** – either a consolidator, who buys up blocks of tickets from the airlines and sells them at a discount, or a **discount agent**, who in addition to dealing with discounted flights may also offer special student and youth fares and a range of other travel-related services such as travel insurance, rail passes, car rentals, tours and the like. Some agents specialize in **charter flights**, which may be cheaper than anything available on a scheduled flight, but departure dates are fixed and withdrawal penalties are

high. You may even find it cheaper to pick up a bargain **package deal** from a tour operator and then find your own accommodation when you get there.

Travelling from mainland **Europe**, drivers and foot and rail passengers can either cross the Channel by **ferry** or go under it, thanks to **Eurotunnel** (the drive-on drive-off shuttle train for vehicles) or **Eurostar** (the high-speed passenger train from Paris and Brussels to London). If you're on a very tight budget, you might consider picking up a **bus** from any of the major European cities. **From Ireland**, it's quickest to fly, but there are also plenty of ferry crossings – especially useful if you're planning to tour around Scotland, Wales or the west of England.

Booking flights online

Many discount travel **websites** offer you the opportunity to book flight tickets and holiday packages online, cutting out the costs of agents and middlemen; these are worth going for, as long as you don't mind the inflexibility of non-refundable, non-changeable deals. There are some bargains to be had on auction sites too, if you're prepared to bid keenly. Almost all airlines have their own websites, offering flight tickets that can sometimes be just as cheap, and are often more flexible.

ⓦ **www.cheapflights.co.uk** (in UK & Ireland),
ⓦ **www.cheapflights.com** (in US),
ⓦ **www.cheapflights.ca** (in Canada),
ⓦ **www.cheapflights.com.au** (in Australia).
Flight deals, travel agents, plus links to other travel sites.
ⓦ **www.cheaptickets.com** Discount flight specialists (in US).

ⓦ www.ebookers.com Efficient, easy-to-use flight finder, with competitive fares.

ⓦ www.etn.nl/discount.htm A hub of consolidator and discount agent web links, maintained by the nonprofit European Travel Network.

ⓦ www.expedia.co.uk (in UK),
ⓦ www.expedia.com (in US),
ⓦ www.expedia.ca (in Canada). Discount air fares, all-airline search engine and daily deals.

ⓦ www.flyaow.com "Airlines of the Web" – online air travel info and reservations.

ⓦ www.lastminute.com (in UK),
ⓦ www.lastminute.com.au (in Australia),
ⓦ www.lastminute.co.nz (in New Zealand). Good last-minute holiday package and flight-only deals.

ⓦ www.priceline.co.uk (in UK),
ⓦ www.priceline.com (in US). Name-your-own-price website that has deals at around forty percent off standard fares.

ⓦ www.skyauction.com Bookings from the US only. Auctions tickets and travel packages to destinations worldwide.

ⓦ www.travelocity.co.uk (in UK),
ⓦ www.travelocity.com (in US),
ⓦ www.travelocity.ca (in Canada),
ⓦ www.zuji.com.au (in Australia). Destination guides, hot fares and great deals for car rental, accommodation and lodging.

ⓦ www.travelshop.com.au Australian site offering discounted flights, packages, insurance, and online bookings.

ⓦ travel.yahoo.com Incorporates some Rough Guides material in its coverage of destination countries and cities across the world, with information about places to eat and sleep.

Package holidays and organized tours

Though you'll want to see Britain at your own speed, you shouldn't dismiss the idea of a **package deal** out of hand. Many agents and airlines put together very flexible deals, sometimes amounting to nothing more restrictive than a flight plus accommodation and car or rail pass, and these can work out cheaper than the same arrangements made on arrival – especially car rental, which can be fairly expensive in Britain. A package can also be great for your peace of mind, if only to ensure a worry-free first week while you're finding your feet for a longer tour. It's worth checking, too, for last-minute deals, especially out of season.

There's no shortage of operators specializing in **tours** of Britain. Most can do packages of the standard highlights, but of greater interest are the outfits that help you explore Britain's unique points: many organize walking or cycling trips through the countryside, boat trips along canals and any number of theme tours based around literary heritage, history, pubs, gardens, theatre, golf – you name it. A few of the best operators are listed here, and a travel agent will be able to point out others. (Companies offering walking holidays are listed on p.55, and those specializing in cycling on p.56.) Note that as opposed to fully inclusive package operators, the UK-based companies listed below do not arrange flights into England, but only take care of itineraries, transport and accommodation once you've arrived. The advantage of booking with British tour operators is the greater range and flexibility of what's on offer, allowing you more freedom to join tours that fit your own schedule and interests. For a full listing of package and tour operators, contact Visit Britain (see p.21).

As a general rule, make sure that the tour operator adheres to an official association that guarantees minimum standards and the services offered, and be sure to examine the fine print of any deal.

Tour operators in the UK

Acorn Activities ☏0870/740 5055,
ⓦ www.acornactivities.co.uk. Diverse range of organized holidays for singles, couples and families, with the accent on activity breaks.

Capital Sport ☏01296/631671, ⓦ www .capitalsport.co.uk. Gentle cycling tours along the Thames, with stops at sights as well as all accommodation and luggage transfers arranged.

Contiki Holidays ☏020/8290 6777,
ⓦ www.contiki.com. Adventure trips and tours for 18–35s, going all over Britain.

Country Lanes ☏01425/655022,
ⓦ www.countrylanes.co.uk. Cycle tours and holidays, ranging from day-trips to week-long outings in the Cotswolds, Lake District and New Forest.

Discovery Travel ☏01904/766564,
ⓦ www.discoverytravel.co.uk. Tailor-made cycling and walking holidays in the Lake District, Yorkshire Dales and North York Moors, as well as coast-to-coast itineraries.

Drifters Club ☎ 020/7262 1292,
ⓦ www.driftersclub.com. Adventure trips aimed at
backpackers, offering good deals on flights to
London.
Holiday Lakeland ☎ 01697/371871,
ⓦ www.holiday-lakeland.co.uk. Offers 1-, 3- and
5-day cycle tours in the Lake District,
Northumberland and the Pennines.
Martin Randall Travel ☎ 020/8742 3355,
ⓦ www.martinrandall.com. Small-group cultural
tours, often timed to coincide with special events
such as music or opera festivals. Expert lecturers on
art, archeology, history or music give specialist
insight, and accommodation is always comfortable.
Outward Bound ☎ 0870/513 4227,
ⓦ www.outwardbound-uk.org. Courses and activity
holidays in the Lake District geared towards young
people and families, including climbing, caving and
canoeing.
Sunvil ☎ 020/8568 4499, ⓦ www.sunvil.co.uk.
Wide-ranging holiday options, focused on small-
group tours for a more independent-minded traveller,
as well as tailor-made trips.
Walking Women ☎ 0845/644 5335,
ⓦ www.walkingwomen.co.uk. Women-only walking
holidays and short breaks in the Lake District.
Wildlife Encounters ☎ 01737/218802,
ⓦ www.wildlife-encounters.co.uk. Top-rated
wildlife-watching tours, including whale-watching in
Scotland.
YHA ☎ 0870/770 8868, ⓦ www.yha.org.uk and
ⓦ www.hostelholidays.com. Hostel-based holidays
built around a range of activities, including walking,
climbing, biking, kayaking and caving.

Tour operators in North America

Abercrombie & Kent ☎ 1-800/323-7308 or
☎ 630/954-2944, ⓦ www.abercrombiekent.com.
Classy operator offering various packages including
cruises and rail tours around Scotland.
Adventures Abroad ☎ 1-800/665-3998 or
☎ 604/303-1099, ⓦ www.adventures-abroad.com.
Walking and sightseeing tours of Scotland.
Backroads ☎ 1-800/GO-ACTIVE or 510/527-
1555, ⓦ www.backroads.com. Cycling, hiking and
multi-sport tours designed for the young at heart,
with the emphasis on going at your own pace. Also
family-friendly options and singles trips.
BCT Scenic Walking ☎ 1-800/473-1210 or
760/944-4599, ⓦ www.bctwalk.com. Extensive
line-up of walking trips in the Cotswolds, Cornwall,
from coast to coast and in Scotland.
British Airways Holidays ☎ 1-877/4-A-
VACATION, ⓦ www.ba.com. Flight-inclusive
vacations and customized itineraries.

British Travel International ☎ 1-800/327-6097,
ⓦ www.britishtravel.com. Agent for all independent
arrangements: rail and bus passes, hotels and a
comprehensive B&B and vacation-homes reservation
service.
CBT Tours ☎ 1-800/736-2453 or 773/871-5510,
ⓦ www.cbttours.com. Bicycle tours through England
and Scotland.
CIE Tours ☎ 1-800/CIE-TOUR, ⓦ www.cietours
.com. Escorted coach tours and self-drive packages.
Classic Journeys ☎ 1-800/200-3887 or
858/454-5004, ⓦ www.classicjourneys.com.
Upmarket guided tours of classic English and
Scottish destinations, including the Cotswolds,
Cornwall and the Highlands.
Cross-Culture ☎ 1-800/491-1148 or 413/256-
6303, ⓦ www.crosscultureinc.com. Small-group
cultural tours, including all across Wales, Devon and
Cornwall, and the Scottish Highlands.
English Experience ☎ 1-800/892-9317,
ⓦ www.english-experience.com. Small-group
guided tours in homestays or hotels, covering
Sussex, Bath, the Cotswolds, the Lake District and
the Yorkshire Dales.
English Lakeland Ramblers ☎ 1-800/724-8801
or 212/505-1020, ⓦ www.ramblers.com. Walking
tours (usually seven or eight days) in the Lake
District and the Cotswolds.
Far and Wide ☎ 1-866/FAR-WIDE,
ⓦ www.farandwide.com. Very broad array of deals,
from customized trips and group tours to
independent travel.
gaytravel.com ☎ 1-800/724-8801,
ⓦ www.gaytravel.com. Gay and lesbian online travel
agent and tour operator, offering a nine-day tour of
"Haunted and Legendary England", including
London, the Cotswolds, Glastonbury, Dartmoor and
Cornwall.
Golf International Inc ☎ 1-800/833-1389,
ⓦ www.golfinternational.com. Scottish golf vacation
specialist.
Le Boat ☎ 1-800/922-0291 or 201/506-1941,
ⓦ www.leboat.com. Specializes in canal trips in
Cambridgeshire, Gloucestershire and on the River
Thames.
Lord Addison Travel ☎ 1-800/326-0170,
ⓦ www.lordaddison.com. Escorted coach tours.
Prestige Tours ☎ 1-800/890-7375,
ⓦ www.prestige-tours.com. Fly-drive, all-inclusive
coach tours and city breaks.
Rail Europe ☎ 1-877/EUROVAC,
ⓦ www.raileurope.com. Rail passes and advice,
plus good air fares, bookings for hotels and rental
cars, and flexible, multi-centre vacation packages.
REI Adventures ☎ 1-800/622-2236,
ⓦ www.rei.com. Climbing, cycling, hiking,

cruising and multisport tours around England and Scotland.

Select Travel Service ☏1-800/752-6787, ⊛www.selecttravel.com. Customized history, literature, theatre and horticulture tours.

Sterling Tours ☏1-800/727-4359, ⊛www.sterlingtours.com. Variety of independent itineraries, packages, country-house hotels and activity holidays.

Virgin Atlantic Vacations ☏1-800/862-8621, ⊛www.virgin-atlantic.com. Custom-made packages for independent travellers, including hotel, theatre and air-fare deals.

Wilderness Travel ☏1-800/368-2794 or 510/558-2488, ⊛www.wildernesstravel.com. Inn-to-inn hiking packages in the Lake District and from coast to coast, as well as Scottish trips.

Tour operators in Australia and New Zealand

Adventures Abroad Australia ☏1/800/147 827, New Zealand ☏0800/800 434, ⊛www.adventures-abroad.com. Trips round the south of England, taking in London, the university towns, Salisbury, Stonehenge and the Isle of Wight.

Adventure World Australia ☏02/8913 0755, ⊛www.adventureworld.com.au, New Zealand ☏09/524 5118, ⊛www.adventureworld.co.nz. Wide variety of independent, customized and escorted excursions around Britain.

CIT Australia ☏02/9267 1255, ⊛www.cittravel.com.au. Package deals around Britain, plus attractive stopover options in Asia.

Explore Holidays Australia ☏02/9423 8080, ⊛www.exploreholidays.com.au. Accommodation and package tours to prime destinations, with good Asian stopover options.

Kumuka Expeditions Australia ☏1800/804 277 or 02/9279 0491, ⊛www.kumuka.com. Independent tour operator specializing in local and private transport tours around Britain.

Martin Randall Travel Australia ☏1300/559 595, ⊛www.martinrandall.com. British company running small-group cultural tours. Expert lecturers on art, archeology, history or music give specialist insight, and accommodation is always comfortable.

YHA Travel Centre Australia ☏02/9261 1111 or 03/9670 9611, ⊛www.yha.com.au; New Zealand ☏09/379 4224, ⊛www.yha.co.nz. Organizes budget accommodation throughout Britain for YHA members.

From North America

Most eastbound flights **from North America** cross the Atlantic overnight, depositing you at your destination the next morning. Some London-bound flights from the East Coast depart at breakfast time, arriving late the same evening. These are useful for avoiding jet lag, but get you into the capital at approaching midnight – fine if you know your way around, but a recipe for a disorienting and possibly expensive first night if you're a newcomer.

Figure on six or seven hours' **flying time** from the East Coast nonstop to any British airport (it's an hour extra returning, due to headwinds). Add three or four hours more for travel from the West Coast. If you're switching planes in London for a connection to, say, Scotland, reckon on an extra hour and a quarter from London to Glasgow or Edinburgh (not including stopover time).

From the US, dozens of airlines fly from New York **to London**, and a few fly nonstop from other East Coast and Midwestern hubs. The best low-season return **fares** from New York to London hover around $338, with a similar price from Boston. In the same period you'll pay around $410 from Washington DC, $450 from Chicago or $520 from Houston. You can pick up flights from Los Angeles and San Francisco for under $500, but for other West Coast cities you're looking at paying $100 or so more. For high-season fares, add $150–250. Travelling late on a Saturday can considerably reduce the fare. As a comparison, equivalent low-season fares to Glasgow are $400–500 from New York, $500–600 from Chicago.

Several airlines fly **to Manchester** from some of the above cities; Manchester and **Birmingham** (direct flights with Continental from Newark) are "common rated" with London, which means that the Apex fare should be the same. If you fly to London on a discounted ticket, expect to pay about $100 each way for an onward connection within Britain. If you want to fly nonstop **to Scotland**, there's only a limited choice: American Airlines from Chicago to Glasgow, or Continental from New York to Glasgow or Edinburgh. Most other airlines, and all flights to other Scottish airports, route through London, Manchester or Dublin.

From Canada, you'll get the best deal flying to London from Toronto and Montréal, where low-season deals start from around Can$770 return; direct flights from Ottawa and Halifax will probably cost only slightly more. From Edmonton, Calgary and Vancouver to London the equivalent fare is Can$960. If you're travelling in high season, fares are likely to be about $300 higher. Air Canada flies nonstop from Toronto to Manchester or Glasgow (around Can$1000 low season), or you can pick up non-direct flights from many Canadian cities to Manchester, Birmingham and Newcastle (usually via London); from Vancouver, for instance, you're looking at around Can$1200 low season.

Airlines in North America

Aer Lingus ☎1-800/IRISH-AIR,
🖥 www.aerlingus.com
Air Canada ☎1-888/247-2262,
🖥 www.aircanada.com
American Airlines ☎1-800/624-6262,
🖥 www.aa.com
bmi ☎1-800/788-0555, 🖥 www.flybmi.com.
British Airways ☎1-800/AIRWAYS,
🖥 www.ba.com
Continental ☎1-800/231-0856,
🖥 www.continental.com
Delta ☎1-800/241-4141, 🖥 www.delta.com
Northwest/KLM ☎1-800/447-4747,
🖥 www.nwa.com
United Airlines ☎1-800/538-2929,
🖥 www.united.com
US Airways ☎1-800/622-1015,
🖥 www.usair.com
Virgin Atlantic ☎1-800/862-8621,
🖥 www.virgin-atlantic.com

Flight agents in North America

Air Brokers International ☎1-800/883-3273,
🖥 www.airbrokers.com. Consolidator.
Airtech ☎212/219-7000, 🖥 www.airtech.com.
Standby seat broker; also deals in consolidator fares.
Educational Travel Center ☎1-800/747-5551,
🖥 www.edtrav.com. Low-cost fares worldwide, student/youth discount offers, and Eurail passes, car rental and tours.
Flightcentre US ☎1-866/WORLD-51,
🖥 www.flightcentre.us, Canada ☎1-888/WORLD-55, 🖥 www.flightcentre.ca. Rock-bottom fares worldwide
New Frontiers/Nouvelles Frontières
☎1-800/677-0720, 🖥 www.newfrontiers.com.
Discount firm, specializing in travel from the US to Europe, with hotels, package deals.

STA Travel US ☎1-800/329-9537, Canada ☎1-888/427-5639, 🖥 www.statravel.com. Worldwide specialists in independent travel; also student IDs, travel insurance, car rental, rail passes, and so on.
Student Flights ☎1-800/255-8000,
🖥 www.isecard.com/studentflights. Student/youth fares, plus student IDs and European rail and bus passes.
TFI Tours International ☎1-800/745-8000,
🖥 www.lowestairprice.com. Consolidator with global fares.
Travel Avenue ☎1-800/333-3335,
🖥 www.travelavenue.com. Full-service travel agent that offers discounts in the form of rebates.
Travel Cuts US ☎1-800/592-CUTS, Canada ☎1-888/246-9762, 🖥 www.travelcuts.com.
Popular, long-established student-travel organization, with worldwide offers.
Travelers Advantage ☎1-877/259-2691,
🖥 www.travelersadvantage.com. Discount travel club, with cashback deals and discounted car rental. Membership required ($1 for 3 months' trial).
Travelosophy US ☎1-800/332-2687,
🖥 www.itravelosophy.com. Good range of discounted and student fares worldwide.

From Australia and New Zealand

Travel time from **Australia and New Zealand** to Britain is over twenty hours, and as long-haul flights can be very taxing you might want to consider taking advantage of a stopover and good night's sleep on the way.

The route to London is highly competitive, with the lowest **fares** starting from around A$1520/NZ$2200 with such airlines as Royal Brunei and Emirates Air. More expensive, but worth it for the extras such as fly-drive, accommodation packages and onward travel to other European destinations, are carriers such as Singapore Airlines, Qantas, British Airways and Air New Zealand, whose fares start at around A$1700/NZ$2500. To reach Scotland, you'll have to change planes either in London – the most popular choice – or in another European gateway such as Paris or Amsterdam.

From Australia the most direct flights to London are via Asia and Europe. In the low season, Qantas and BA charge around $1800 in low season from Melbourne, Sydney and Perth, rising in high season to around $3200.

It's usually slower and considerably more expensive to travel via the Americas.

From New Zealand the most direct route is via North America, with United Airlines charging around $3350 year-round, while Air New Zealand's fares are around $2820/$3075 in low and high season respectively. British Airways charge roughly $2250/$3500, but this does include onward connections to other destinations in Britain. All three journeys involve stops in Los Angeles. Garuda, Korean Air and Thai Airways fly to London via Asia with either a transfer or stopover in their home city for around $2880; Qantas fly via Sydney and either Singapore or Bangkok from $2510.

Airlines in Australia and New Zealand

Air New Zealand Australia ☏ 13 24 76, ⓦ www.airnz.com.au, New Zealand ☏ 0800/737 000, ⓦ www.airnz.co.nz
Britannia Airways Australia ☏ 02/9251 1299, New Zealand ☏ 0800/887 997, ⓦ www.britanniaairways.com
British Airways Australia ☏ 1300/767 177, New Zealand ☏ 0800/274 847, ⓦ www.ba.com
Cathay Pacific Australia ☏ 13 17 47, New Zealand ☏ 0508/800 454 or 09/379 0861, ⓦ www.cathaypacific.com
Emirates Australia ☏ 1300/303 777 or 02/9290 9700, New Zealand ☏ 09/377 6004, ⓦ www.emirates.com
Garuda Indonesia Australia ☏ 1300/365 330 or 02/9334 9944, New Zealand ☏ 09/366 1862, ⓦ www.garuda-indonesia.com
KLM Australia ☏ 1300/303 747, New Zealand ☏ 09/309 1782, ⓦ www.klm.com
Malaysia Airlines Australia ☏ 13 26 27, New Zealand ☏ 0800/777 747, ⓦ www .malaysia-airlines.com
Qantas Australia ☏ 13 13 13, New Zealand ☏ 0800/808 767 or 09/357 8900, ⓦ www.qantas.com
Royal Brunei Australia ☏ 07/3017 5000, New Zealand ☏ 09/977 2240, ⓦ www.bruneiair.com
Singapore Airlines Australia ☏ 13 10 11, New Zealand ☏ 0800/808 909, ⓦ www.singaporeair.com
Thai Airways Australia ☏ 1300/651 960, New Zealand ☏ 09/377 3886, ⓦ www.thaiair.com
United Airlines Australia ☏ 13 17 77, ⓦ www.united.com
Virgin Atlantic Airways Australia ☏ 02/9244 2747, ⓦ www.virgin-atlantic.com

Travel agents in Australia and New Zealand

Flight Centre Australia ☏ 13 31 33, ⓦ www.flightcentre.com.au; New Zealand ☏ 0800 243 544, ⓦ www.flightcentre.co.nz. Rock-bottom fares worldwide.
Holiday Shoppe New Zealand ☏ 0800/808 480, ⓦ www.holidayshoppe.co.nz. Great deals on flights, hotels and holidays.
OTC Australia ☏ 1300/855 118, ⓦ www.otctravel.com.au. Deals on flights, hotels and holidays.
Plan It Holidays Australia ☏ 03/9245 0747, ⓦ www.planit.com.au. Discounted air fares and accommodation packages in Southeast Asia.
STA Travel Australia ☏ 1300/733 035, New Zealand ☏ 0508/782 872, ⓦ www.statravel.com. Worldwide specialists in low-cost flights, overlands and holiday deals. Good discounts for students and under-26s.
Student Uni Travel Australia ☏ 02/9232 8444, ⓦ www.sut.com.au; New Zealand ☏ 09/379 4224, ⓦ www.sut.co.nz. Great deals for students.
Trailfinders Australia ☏ 02/9247 7666, ⓦ www.trailfinders.com.au. One of the best-informed and most efficient agents for independent travellers.
travel.com.au and **travel.co.nz** Australia ☏ 1300/130 482 or 02/9249 5444, ⓦ www.travel.com.au; New Zealand ☏ 0800/468 332, ⓦ www.travel.co.nz. Comprehensive online travel company, with discounted fares.

From Ireland

Stiff competition on routes **from Ireland** has kept the cost of flights relatively low. Ryanair flies to over a dozen destinations in England and Scotland **from Cork**, **Derry**, **Dublin**, **Kerry**, **Knock** and **Shannon**, and generally have the cheapest deals: for instance, Dublin to Glasgow Prestwick for as little as €30 return, if you book well in advance. If there are no special deals available, expect to pay around €50 for a return to London Stansted. Aer Lingus offers various deals from Dublin, Cork and Shannon, with fares from around €50–70 return, broadly similar to what you'll find on the no-frills carriers: bmibaby from Dublin and Cork to East Midlands, Cardiff or Manchester; flyBE from Cork and Shannon to Birmingham or Glasgow; MyTravelLite from Dublin and Knock to Birmingham; and Aer Arann from Cork, **Galway** and

Waterford to a range of British airports. British Airways often give good discounts on their published fares from Dublin, while Jetmagic flies from Cork to Edinburgh for around €100 return.

Flying **from Belfast** your best bet is easyJet, with return flights to London Luton, Gatwick, Stansted and an array of other English and Scottish airports from just £30. Flights into Heathrow with bmi cost from £64; BA are generally a little more expensive, with return fares from around £89, although you can pick up BA fares from Belfast or Derry to Glasgow from £60. The tiny Air Wales flies from Belfast and Dublin to both Cardiff and Swansea, as well as Cork to Plymouth and other routeings, from around £50 return, while you can pick up a bargain £30 return on bmibaby from Belfast to Teesside.

To keep costs to a minimum, you can always take the **coach**. Eurolines (Belfast ☏028/9033 7002, Dublin ☏01/836 6111, ⓦwww.eurolines.com) runs coaches to Birmingham and London from Belfast (£34) and Dublin (€62), with connections feeding in from around Ireland. These fares are great value; the downside is that the trip, which can involve an overnight ferry crossing to Holyhead, takes 10–12 hours. You can also travel for similar prices from Cork, Killarney, Limerick and Tralee to London via Fishguard and Bristol.

Bringing your **car** can be an expensive option. Fares fluctuate wildly depending on the time of year and the day of the week you travel, but expect to pay around €252 for a small vehicle and up to five adults on the ferry route between Dublin and Holyhead (€34–42 for a foot passenger), or €161–273 on the Cork–Swansea route (€35–50 foot passenger). Heading **to Scotland**, P&O Irish Sea runs several crossings daily from Larne to Cairnryan (takes 2hr by ferry, or 1hr by jet-liner). Stena Line operates conventional ferries and a high-speed service (HSS) daily from Belfast to Stranraer (takes between 1hr 45min and 3hr 15min), while SeaCat runs daily catamarans from Belfast to Troon, just outside Ayr (takes 2hr 30min). Peak period standard returns can cost over £250, though you can save £50 by booking in advance, and another £50 by travelling off-peak.

Passenger-only fares work out at around £50 return.

Airlines in Ireland

Aer Arann UK ☏0800/587 2324, Republic of Ireland ☏0818/210 210 or 01/814 1058, ⓦwww.aerarann.com
Aer Lingus UK ☏0845/084 4444, Republic of Ireland ☏0818/365 000, ⓦwww.aerlingus.com
Air Wales UK ☏0870/777 3131, Republic of Ireland ☏1800 654 193, ⓦwww.airwales.co.uk
bmi UK ☏0870/607 0555, Republic of Ireland ☏01/407 3036, ⓦwww.flybmi.com
bmibaby UK ☏0870/264 2229, Republic of Ireland ☏01/435 0011, ⓦwww.bmibaby.com
British Airways UK ☏0870/850 9850, Republic of Ireland ☏1800/626 747, ⓦwww.ba.com
easyJet UK ☏0871/750 0100, ⓦwww.easyjet.com
flyBE UK ☏0871/700 0535, Republic of Ireland ☏1890/925 532, ⓦwww.flybe.com
Jetmagic Republic of Ireland ☏0818/200 135, ⓦwww.jetmagic.com
MyTravelLite UK ☏0870/156 4564, Republic of Ireland ☏0818/300 012, ⓦwww.mytravellite.com
Ryanair UK ☏0871/246 0000, Republic of Ireland ☏0818/30 30 30, ⓦwww.ryanair.com

Travel agents in Ireland

Apex Travel Republic of Ireland ☏01/241 8000, ⓦwww.apextravel.ie. Consolidators for BA.
Aran Travel International Republic of Ireland ☏091/562 595, ⓦhomepages.iol.ie/~arantvl/aranmain.htm. Good-value flights.
ebookers Republic of Ireland ☏01/241 5689, ⓦwww.ebookers.ie. Low fares on an extensive selection of scheduled flights and package deals.
Go Holidays Republic of Ireland ☏01/874 4126, ⓦwww.goholidays.ie. City breaks and package tours.
Joe Walsh Tours Republic of Ireland ☏01/676 0991, ⓦwww.joewalshtours.ie. Long-established general budget fares and holidays agent.
Lee Travel Republic of Ireland ☏021/427 7111, ⓦwww.leetravel.ie. Flights and holidays.
McCarthys Travel Republic of Ireland ☏021/427 0127, ⓦwww.mccarthystravel.ie. General flight agent.
Neenan Travel Republic of Ireland ☏01/607 9900, ⓦwww.neenantrav.ie. Specialists in city breaks.
USIT Northern Ireland ☏028/9032 7111, ⓦwww.usitnow.com, Republic of Ireland

☏0818/200 020, ⒲www.usit.ie. Specialists in student, youth and independent travel.

Ferry companies in Ireland

Irish Ferries Britain ☏0870/517 1717, Northern Ireland ☏0800/018 2211, Republic of Ireland ☏1890/313 131, ⒲www.irishferries.com
Norse Merchant Ferries UK ☏0870/600 4321, Republic of Ireland ☏01/819 2999, ⒲www.norsemerchant.com
P&O Irish Sea UK ☏0870/242 4777, Republic of Ireland ☏1800/409 049, ⒲www.poirishsea.com
SeaCat UK ☏0870/552 3523, Republic of Ireland ☏1800/805055, ⒲www.seacat.co.uk
Stena Line Britain ☏0870/570 70 70, Northern Ireland ☏028/9074 7747, ⒲www.stenaline.co.uk, Republic of Ireland ☏01/204 7777, ⒲www.stenaline.ie
Swansea Cork Ferries UK ☏01792/456 116, Republic of Ireland ☏021/427 1166, ⒲www.swansea-cork.ie

By train

There are frequent **high-speed trains** from Paris, Brussels and Lille to London run by **Eurostar** (UK ☏0870/518 6186, France ☏08.92.35.35.39, Belgium ☏02/528 28 28, ⒲www.eurostar.com). Trains depart more or less hourly (roughly 6am–7.30pm) to London Waterloo through the Channel Tunnel from Paris Gare du Nord (2hr 40min) or Brussels-Midi/Zuid (2hr 20min) – up to 24 trains a day from Paris, up to 10 a day from Brussels. Some trains additionally stop at Ashford in Kent (40min before London), Calais (1hr 20min) and/or Lille (1hr 40min). Trains also serve London direct from Avignon (mid-May to mid-Oct: 1 train on Sat only; 6hr). The cheapest return ticket from Paris or Brussels is currently €69, though restrictions apply. You can take a bike – if it folds, it can go in the carriage with you; if not, you should register it as "Registered Baggage" a day in advance. Through-ticketing to stations around Britain is also possible – including the tube journey across London – from Eurostar. Inter-Rail, Eurail, Britrail and Eurodomino passes give discounts on Eurostar trains.

By car

There are many ways to drive **from mainland Europe** to Britain. Which service you

use will depend on where exactly you are coming from. The **Channel Tunnel** is the smoothest option by far, but **ferries** from Brittany, Normandy and Spain connect to southern England; those from northern France and Belgium serve Kent in southeast England; those from the Netherlands, Germany and Scandinavia cross the North Sea to the east coast and northeast of England as well as Scotland.

Eurotunnel

Eurotunnel (UK ☏0870/535 3535, France ☏03.21.00.61.00, ⒲www.eurotunnel.com) operates drive-on drive-off shuttle trains through the Channel Tunnel for vehicles and their passengers only. Trains run continuously between Coquelles, near Calais, and Folkestone. There are up to four departures per hour (only one per hour midnight–6am) and journey time is roughly 35min. It's possible to turn up and buy your ticket at the toll booths, though at busy times booking is advisable; if you've booked, you must arrive at least 30min before your scheduled departure. Fares depend on the time of year, time of day and length of stay; it's cheaper to travel between 10pm and 6am, while the highest fares apply at weekends and in July and August. A five-day fully flexible return for a car and passengers travelling off-peak costs €248, or €262 in high season. Bikes are carried on a specially adapted carriage that makes the crossing twice a day – see website for details.

By ferry

Tariffs on the **ferries from mainland Europe** to Britain are bewilderingly complex: prices vary with the month, day or even hour at certain times of the year, not to mention how long you're staying and the size of your car. Another thing to bear in mind is that some kind of sleeping accommodation is often obligatory on the longer crossings if made at night, pushing the price way above the basic rate. As an indication of cost, two people driving in a small car from Calais, Dieppe or Ostend to one of the English Channel ports by fast ferry or catamaran could expect to pay from about

€210 (the return fares are usually just twice the price); for a foot passenger the single fare is €36. On the Zeebrugge–Rosyth route, one of the longest crossings (17hr 30min), off-peak return fares start at around €110, plus €150 for a car, and another €50 for a cabin berth.

Ferry companies in Europe

Brittany Ferries UK ☏0870/366 5333, France ☏08.25.82.88.28, Spain ☏942 360 611, ⓦwww.brittanyferries.co.uk
Condor Ferries UK ☏0845/345 2000, France ☏08.25.16.03.00, ⓦwww.condorferries.co.uk
DFDS Seaways UK ☏0870/533 3000, Denmark ☏33 42 30 00, Germany ☏040/38 903-0, Netherlands ☏0255/54 66 66, Norway ☏23 10 68 00, Sweden ☏31 65 06 00, ⓦwww.dfdsseaways.co.uk
Fjord Line UK ☏0191/296 1313, Norway ☏815 33 500, ⓦwww.fjordline.no
Hoverspeed UK ☏0870/240 8070, France ☏00800/1211 1211, ⓦwww.hoverspeed.co.uk
Norfolk Line UK ☏0870/870 1020, France ☏03.28.28.95.50, ⓦwww.norfolkline.com
P&O Ferries UK ☏0870/520 2020, France ☏01.55.69.82.28, Netherlands ☏020/201 33 33, Belgium ☏02/710 64 44, Spain ☏912 702 332, ⓦwww.poferries.com

SeaFrance UK ☏0870/571 1711, France ☏08.03.04.40.45, ⓦwww.seafrance.com
Smyril Line UK ☏01595/690 845, Norway ☏55 59 65 20, ⓦwww.smyril-line.no
Stena Line UK ☏0870/570 70 70, Netherlands ☏0900/8123, ⓦwww.stenaline.nl
Superfast Ferries UK ☏0870/234 0870, Belgium ☏050/252 252, ⓦwww.superfast.com
Transmanche Ferries UK ☏0800/917 1201, France ☏0800 650 100, ⓦwww.transmancheferries.com

By bus

You can, of course, catch **buses** from a long list of European countries to Britain. Given the low cost of air fares from many cities, however, you'd have to be a masochist to want to travel by bus from, say, Athens to London – a journey of two nights and three days that costs more than the price of the flight. Eurolines (ⓦwww.eurolines.com) is a brand name under which thirty-plus companies operate international buses all round Europe, including services to London from Amsterdam, Brussels, Frankfurt, Hamburg, Madrid, Paris, Rome and dozens more cities. Compare price and service with Gullivers (ⓦwww.gullivers.de), part of the competing EuroBusExpress network.

Red tape and visas

Citizens of EU member countries have the right of free movement and residence throughout the European Economic Area (including the United Kingdom); for them and Swiss citizens there's just a brief passport/identity card check on arrival in the UK. Citizens of other European countries (with certain exceptions) can also enter Britain with just a passport, generally for up to three months. US, Canadian, Australian and New Zealand citizens don't need a visa and can enter the country for up to six months with just a passport.

All other nationalities require a **visa**, obtainable from the British Consular office in the country of application. For current details about entry and visa requirements, consult the UK's Foreign and Commonwealth Office's visa website ⓦwww.ukvisas.gov.uk.

An independent charity, the **Immigration Advisory Service** (IAS), based at County House, 190 Great Dover St, London SE1 4YB (☏020/7357 6917, ⓦwww.iasuk.org), offers free and confidential advice to anyone applying for entry clearance into the UK.

If you want to **extend your visa**, you should write, before its expiry date given in your passport, to the Immigration and Nationality Enquiry Bureau, Lunar House, Wellesley Road, Croydon CR9 2BY (℡0870/606 7766, ⊛www.ind.homeoffice .gov.uk).

UK embassies abroad

Australia British High Commission, Commonwealth Ave, Yarralumla, Canberra ACT 2600 ℡02/6270 6666, ⊛www.britaus.net
Canada British High Commission, 80 Elgin St, Ottawa, ON, K1P 5K7 ℡613/237-1530, ⊛www.britainincanada.org
Ireland British Embassy, 29 Merrion Rd, Ballsbridge, Dublin 4 ℡01/205 3700, ⊛www.britishembassy.ie
New Zealand British High Commission, 44 Hill St, Wellington 1 ℡04/924 2888, ⊛www.britain.org.nz
USA British Embassy, 3100 Massachusetts Ave NW, Washington, DC 20008 ℡202/588-6500, ⊛www.britainusa.com

Overseas embassies in Britain

American Embassy 24 Grosvenor Sq, London W1A 1AE ℡020/7499 9000, ⊛www.usembassy.org.uk
Australian High Commission Australia House, Strand, London WC2B 4LA ℡020/7379 4334, ⊛www.australia.org.uk
Canadian High Commission 1 Grosvenor Sq, London W1X 0AB ℡020/7250 6600, ⊛www.canadianembassy.co.uk/index.htm
Irish Embassy 17 Grosvenor Place, London SW1X 7HR ℡020/7235 2171, ⊛ireland.embassyhomepage.com
New Zealand High Commission New Zealand House, 80 Haymarket, London SW1Y 4TQ ℡020/7930 8422, ⊛www.nzembassy.com

Customs and tax

Travellers entering Britain directly from another EU country do not have to make a declaration to **customs** at their place of entry. If you've bought the goods in a normal shop or supermarket within the EU, the limits are 90 litres of wine (of which no more than 60 litres should be sparkling), 20 litres of fortified wine, 10 litres of spirits, 110 litres of beer, 800 cigarettes or 1kg of tobacco. If you are travelling from a non-EU country, you can still buy tax- or duty-free goods, but not within the EU. The **duty-free** allowances are as follows:

Tobacco 200 cigarettes, or 100 cigarillos, or 50 cigars, or 250 grams of loose tobacco.
Alcohol 2 litres of still wine plus 1 litre of spirits, or 2 litres of fortified, sparkling or still wine.
Perfumes 60cc of perfume plus 250cc of toilet water.
Other goods to the value of £145.

If you need any clarification on British import regulations, you should contact the **HM Customs and Excise** on ℡0870/010 9000, ⊛www.hmce.gov.uk. **Pets** from countries participating in the Pet Travel Scheme (PETS) are allowed into Britain, providing their owners follow certain procedures; for more information, check ⊛www.defra.gov.uk.

Most goods in Britain are subject to **Value Added Tax (VAT)**, which increases the cost of an item by 17.5 percent. Visitors from non-EU countries can save money through the Retail Export Scheme (tax-free shopping), which allows a refund of VAT on goods to be taken out of the country. Note that not all shops participate in this scheme (those doing so will display a sign to this effect) and that you cannot reclaim VAT charged on hotel bills or other services.

Following a devastating outbreak of Food & Mouth Disease in 2001, there are very strict controls on the import of meat, milk, fish, shellfish, plants, and their products, into the UK. For full details, see @www.defra .gov.uk.

Information, maps and websites

If you want to do a bit of research before arriving, you can either contact the overall British tourist authority "Visit Britain", which has offices worldwide, or one of the regional tourist boards in England, Wales or Scotland, which concentrate on particular areas. The tourist office websites are all useful, covering everything from local accommodation to festival dates, but there is also an almost limitless supply of other sites dedicated to Britain and its ways. We've picked out some of the best below, and some of the more offbeat, and also provided a review of the most useful maps you can buy for navigating your way around.

Tourist information

Virtually every town has its **tourist office** (usually called a Tourist Information Centre, or "**TIC**" for short). The average opening hours are much the same as standard shop hours, though they are also often open on Sundays, while hours are extended during the summer months and occasionally curtailed in the depths of winter, especially in more remote areas.

All centres offer information on local accommodation, public transport and attractions; note, though, that phone enquiries may be charged at a premium rate (numbers usually beginning with ☏09). Over the counter, staff will nearly always be able to **book accommodation** for you (for a fee of around £3), reserve space on guided tours, and sell you guides, maps and walk leaflets. You can ask for lists of local cafés, restaurants and pubs, and though the staff aren't really supposed to recommend particular places, you'll often be able to get a feel for the best local places to eat. It is worth being aware that staff may be reluctant to divulge information about local attractions or accommodation which are not paid-up members of the tourist board – and a number of perfectly decent guest houses and the like choose not to pay the fees. An increasing number of offices have **Internet access** for visitors too.

Areas designated as **national parks** (such as the Lake District, Yorkshire Dales or Snowdonia) tend to have their own information centres, which offer exactly the same services as TICs but are generally more expert in giving guidance on local walks and outdoor pursuits.

National tourist board

Ⓦ www.visitbritain.com
Australia Level 16, Gateway, 1 MacQuarie Place, Sydney, NSW 2000 ☏02/9377 4400,
Ⓦ www.visitbritain.com/au
Canada 5915 Airport Rd #120, Mississauga, ON, L4V 1T1 ☏905/405 1840,
Ⓦ www.visitbritain.com/ca
Ireland 18–19 College Green, Dublin 2 ☏01/670 8000, Ⓦ www.visitbritain.com/ie
New Zealand 17th Floor, 151 Queen St, Auckland 1 ☏09/303 1446, Ⓦ www.visitbritain.com/nz
USA 7th Floor, 551 Fifth Ave, New York, NY 10176 ☏1-800/GO 2 BRITAIN, Ⓦ www.travelbritain.org

Regional tourist boards

In England

Visit London ☏0906/866 3344 (premium rate), Ⓦ www.visitlondon.com
Tourism South East ☏01892/540766 or ☏023/8062 5400,
Ⓦ www.southeastengland.uk.com
East of England Tourist Board ☏0870/225 4800, Ⓦ www.eastofenglandtouristboard.com
South West Tourism ☏0870/442 0880,
Ⓦ www.visitsouthwest.co.uk
Visit Heart of England ☏01905/761100 or ☏0115/959 8383,
Ⓦ www.visitheartofengland.com
North West Tourist Board ☏01942/821222,
Ⓦ www.visitnorthwest.com
Yorkshire Tourist Board ☏01904/707961,
Ⓦ www.yorkshirevisitor.com

Cumbria Tourist Board ☎01539/444444,
🌐www.gocumbria.org
Northumbria Tourist Board ☎0191/375 3010,
🌐www.visitnorthumbria.com

In Wales

🌐www.visitwales.com
North Wales Tourism ☎01492/531731,
🌐www.nwt.co.uk
Mid & South Wales Tourism ☎0870/080 3436,
🌐www.mid-wales-tourism.gov.uk

In Scotland

🌐www.visitscotland.com
Aberdeen and Grampian ☎01224/288828,
🌐www.castlesandwhisky.com
Angus and Dundee ☎01382/527527,
🌐www.angusanddundee.co.uk
Argyll, the Isles, Loch Lomond, Stirling and
Trossachs ☎01786/470945,
🌐www.visitscottishheartlands.com
Ayrshire and Arran ☎01292/678100,
🌐www.ayrshire-arran.com
Dumfries and Galloway ☎01387/253862,
🌐www.dumfriesandgalloway.co.uk
Edinburgh and the Lothians
🌐www.edinburgh.org
Greater Glasgow and Clyde Valley
☎0141/204 4480, 🌐www.seeglasgow.com
Highlands of Scotland ☎01997/421160,
🌐www.host.co.uk
Kingdom of Fife ☎01592/750066,
🌐www.standrews.co.uk
Orkney ☎01856/872856,
🌐www.visitorkney.com
Perthshire ☎01738/627958,
🌐www.perthshire.co.uk
Scottish Borders ☎01750/20555, 🌐www
.scot-borders.co.uk
Shetland ☎01595/693434,
🌐www.visitshetland.com
Western Isles ☎01851/703088,
🌐www.witb.co.uk

Websites

There's a vast quantity of useful information
on the **Internet**. Apart from the national
and regional tourist authority websites
above, there are some excellent sites on
specific areas, which you'll find listed
throughout this book. Many tourist sights
have their own website, as do most hotels
and numerous B&Bs and shops – again,
we give them in the text where possible.

Below are a few of the more interesting
websites on Britain.

News and current affairs

🌐 **www.bbc.co.uk** The world's most respected
news organization, good for current affairs, sport
and weather. Check out "categories" for an
encyclopedic range of information on contemporary
life in Britain.

🌐 **www.guardian.co.uk** *The Guardian*, the UK's
main left-leaning broadsheet, has a website
particularly good for news and reviews.

🌐 **www.telegraph.co.uk** The *Daily Telegraph*
offers a right-leaning perspective on current affairs;
its website has particularly strong travel and sports
sections.

Maps, addresses and phone numbers

🌐 **www.multimap.com** Town plans and area
maps with scales up to 1:10,000, plus address
search, traffic info and more.

🌐 **www.visitmap.com** The Britain Visitor Atlas has
a clickable A–Z of town and city maps.

🌐 **www.yell.com** The Yellow Pages online –
search for any UK business.

🌐 **www.192.com** Free online resource for finding
out phone numbers of individuals and businesses.

Miscellaneous

🌐 **www.aboutscotland.com** Useful for
accommodation, easy to use and linked to holiday
activities.

🌐 **www.ceolas.org/ceolas.html** A very
informative Celtic music site, both historical and
contemporary, with lots of music to listen to.

🌐 **www.craptowns.com** England's "worst" towns,
vitriolically reviewed by *The Idler* magazine, whose
opinions are then attacked by outraged locals –
good, knockabout fun.

🌐 **www.clubconnexion.co.uk** All the gen on the
UK's club scene.

🌐 **www.geo.ed.ac.uk/home/scotland
/scotland.html** Produced by the Geography
Department of Edinburgh University – an introduction
to all things Scottish, history, geography and politics.

🌐 **www.goodguides.com** A combination of
information from the *Good Britain Guide* and *Good
Pub Guide*, both indispensable publications.

🌐 **www.icwales.com** First stop for the latest in
Welsh news, plus extensive links.

🌐 **www.information-britain.co.uk**
Comprehensive site with a county-by-county guide,
as well as listings on every conceivable subject.

Ⓦ www.knowhere.co.uk A self-styled user's guide to Britain incorporating scurrilous readers' comments, including best-of and worst-of sections.

Ⓦ www.londontheatreguide.co.uk What's on in the West End of London, and how to get tickets.

Ⓦ www.met-office.gov.uk Britain's favourite topic, the weather, discussed in detail with full regional forecasts.

Ⓦ www.ngs.org.uk The National Gardens Scheme details gardens, many of them private, open throughout the year for charity.

Ⓦ www.stonepages.com An offbeat though perfectly sane and informative website for those hooked on cairns and stone circles.

Ⓦ www.tylwythteg.com/dynionmwyn Welsh witchcraft homepage, with links to druidry, benign witchcraft and festival listings.

Ⓦ www.which.net Britain's biggest consumer organization provides reviews from its respected *Good Food Guide* alongside online access to its consumer reports on everything from electric toasters to holidays.

Maps

The most comprehensive **maps** of Britain are produced by the **Ordnance Survey** or OS (Ⓦ www.ordsvy.gov.uk), renowned for their accuracy and clarity. The 204 maps in their 1:50,000 (pink) Landranger series cover the whole of Britain and show enough detail to be useful for most walkers and cyclists. There's more detail still in the full-colour 1:25,000 (orange) Explorer series, which also covers the whole of Britain.

Coverage of the country at scales around 1:250,000 or 1:200,000 is provided by the Ordnance Survey, AA, Geographers' A-Z, Collins and others, either in a series of **folded maps** or combined into **atlases** for the whole of the UK. Among other publishers, Michelin covers England on three maps at 1:400,000, which highlight scenic routes. Estate Publications' *England and Wales* on one map (1:650,000) is produced in cooperation with various local tourist boards and is designed to highlight places of interest. Estate also has an extensive series of both regional and local maps at various scales, showing places of interest, recreational facilities, campsites, caravan parks and so forth. A similar series for popular holiday areas from Goldeneye includes additional altitude colouring, particularly useful for cyclists.

The **National Cycle Network** of cross-country routes along traffic-free roads is covered by a series of excellent waterproof maps (1:100,000) published by Sustrans. Ordnance Survey's new and expanding Touring series (also 1:100,000) can be disappointing, however: it's designed to carry plenty of tourist information, but the presentation of topography falls well short of the standard associated with the OS.

Map outlets

Australia and New Zealand

Map Centre Ⓦ www.mapcentre.co.nz.
Mapland 372 Little Bourke St, Melbourne ☏ 03/9670 4383, Ⓦ www.mapland.com.au
Map Shop 6–10 Peel St, Adelaide ☏ 08/8231 2033, Ⓦ www.mapshop.net.au
Map World 371 Pitt St, Sydney ☏ 02/9261 3601, Ⓦ www.mapworld.net.au. Also at 900 Hay St, Perth ☏ 08/9322 5733.
Map World 173 Gloucester St, Christchurch ☏ 0800/627 967, Ⓦ www.mapworld.co.nz

UK and Ireland

Stanfords 12–14 Long Acre, London WC2 ☏ 020/7836 1321, Ⓦ www.stanfords.co.uk. Also at 39 Spring Gardens, Manchester ☏ 0161/831 0250, and 29 Corn St, Bristol ☏ 0117/929 9966. One of the best travel bookshops in the world, with a global catalogue, expert knowledge and worldwide mail order.
Blackwell's Map Centre 50 Broad St, Oxford ☏ 01865/793 550, Ⓦ maps.blackwell.co.uk. Branches in Bristol, Cambridge, Cardiff, Leeds, Liverpool, Newcastle, Reading & Sheffield.
The Map Shop 30a Belvoir St, Leicester ☏ 0116/247 1400, Ⓦ www.mapshopleicester.co.uk
National Map Centre 22–24 Caxton St, London SW1 ☏ 020/7222 2466, Ⓦ www.mapsnmc.co.uk
National Map Centre Ireland 34 Aungier St, Dublin ☏ 01/476 0471, Ⓦ www.mapcentre.ie
Scotland's Map Centre 50 Couper St, Glasgow ☏ 0141/552 4394, Ⓦ www.johnsmith.co.uk
The Travel Bookshop 13–15 Blenheim Crescent, London W11 ☏ 020/7229 5260, Ⓦ www.thetravelbookshop.co.uk

North America

The giant US map wholesalers Map Link (Ⓦ www.maplink.com) has a useful list of specialist map/travel bookstores in every US state, as well as some worldwide; click on Retail Partners.

Book Passage 51 Tamal Vista Blvd, Corte Madera, CA 94925 ☎1-800/999-7909, ⓦwww.bookpassage.com
Globe Corner Bookstore 28 Church St, Cambridge, MA 02138 ☎1-800/358-6013, ⓦwww.globecorner.com
Longitude Books 115 W 30th St #1206, New York, NY 10001 ☎1-800/342-2164, ⓦwww.longitudebooks.com

Map Town 400 5 Ave SW #100, Calgary, AB, T2P 0L6 ☎1-877/921-6277, ⓦwww.maptown.com
Travel Bug Bookstore 3065 W Broadway, Vancouver, BC, V6K 2G9 ☎604/737-1122, ⓦwww.travelbugbooks.ca
World of Maps 1235 Wellington St, Ottawa, ON, K1Y 3A3 ☎1-800/214-8524, ⓦwww.worldofmaps.com

Insurance and health

Even though EU health care privileges apply in Britain, you'd do well to take out an insurance policy before travelling to cover against theft, loss and illness or injury. Before paying for a new policy, however, it's worth checking whether you are already covered: some all-risks home insurance policies may cover your possessions when overseas, and many private medical schemes include cover when abroad. In Canada, provincial health plans usually provide partial cover for medical mishaps overseas, while holders of official student/teacher/youth cards in Canada and the US are entitled to meagre accident coverage and hospital in-patient benefits. Students will often find that their student health coverage extends during the vacations and for one term beyond the date of last enrolment.

After exhausting the possibilities above, you'll probably want to contact a **specialist travel insurance company**, or consider the travel insurance deal we offer (see box). A typical travel insurance policy usually provides cover for the loss of baggage, tickets and – up to a certain limit – cash or cheques, as well as cancellation or curtailment of your journey. Most of them exclude so-called dangerous sports unless an extra premium is paid: in Britain this can mean scuba diving, windsurfing and skiing. Many policies can be chopped and changed to exclude coverage you don't need: for example, sickness and accident benefits can often be excluded or included at will. If you do take medical coverage, ascertain whether benefits will be paid as treatment proceeds or only after return home, and whether there is a 24-hour medical emergency number. When securing baggage cover, make sure that the per-article limit – typically under £500 – will cover your most valuable possession. If you need to make a claim, you should keep receipts for medicines and medical treatment, and in the event you have anything stolen, you must obtain an official statement from the police.

Health

No vaccinations are required for entry to the UK. EU citizens are entitled to free medical treatment at National Health Service hospitals on production of an **E111** form. Australia, New Zealand and several non-EU European countries have reciprocal healthcare arrangements with the UK. Citizens of other countries will be charged for all medical services except those administered by Accident and Emergency (A&E) units at National Health Service hospitals. Health insurance is therefore extremely advisable for all non-EU nationals.

Pharmacists (known as "chemists") can dispense only a limited range of drugs without a doctor's prescription. Most are open standard shop hours, though in large towns

Rough Guides travel insurance

Rough Guides offers its own low-cost **travel insurance**, especially customized for our statistically low-risk readers. There are five main plans: No Frills, the bare minimum for secure travel; Essential, which provides decent all-round cover; Premier, for comprehensive cover with a wide range of benefits; Extended Stay, for cover lasting between four months and a year; and Annual Multi-Trip, a cost-effective way of getting Premier cover if you travel more than once a year. Premier, Annual Multi-Trip and Extended Stay policies can be supplemented by a "Hazardous Pursuits Extension" if you plan to indulge in sports considered dangerous, such as scuba-diving or trekking.

For a quote, check ⓦ www.roughguides.com/insurance or call the Rough Guides Insurance Line: toll-free in the UK on ☎0800/015 0906, or at usual international rates from elsewhere on ☎+44 1392/314665. Rough Guides insurance is underwritten by a leading British broker, provided by the American International Group (AIG) and registered with the British regulatory body, GISC (the General Insurance Standards Council).

---

some may close as late as 10pm; local newspapers carry lists of late-opening pharmacies, or you can contact the local police for current details. **Doctors' surgeries** tend to be open from about 9am to noon and then for a couple of hours in the evening; outside surgery hours, you can turn up at the casualty department of the local hospital for complaints that require immediate attention – unless it's an emergency, in which case call for an ambulance on ☎999.

For free medical advice by phone you can call **NHS Direct** (☎0845/4647, ⓦwww .nhsdirect.nhs.uk), which also runs an increasing number of **walk-in centres** (usually daily 7.30am–9pm) in the bigger towns and cities.

Costs, money and banks

Britain is an expensive place to visit: transport, accommodation and restaurant prices are all above average compared with the rest of the EU, and much higher than in North America. There are, however, ways of cutting costs (see box p.28). The UK has not changed over to the euro, and for the foreseeable future looks unlikely to do so (for more information, visit ⓦwww.euro.gov.uk).

Currency and exchange

The UK's currency is the **pound** (£, known in slang as a "quid"), divided into 100 pence (p). Coins come in denominations of 1p, 2p, 5p, 10p, 20p, 50p, £1 and £2. Notes come as £5 (a "fiver"), £10 (a "tenner"), £20 and £50. Almost all banknotes are issued by the Bank of England, although in Scotland, the Clydesdale Bank, Bank of Scotland and Royal Bank of Scotland also issue their own banknotes in all the same denominations, plus a £100 note. All Scottish notes can be used throughout the UK, though you might find that some shopkeepers south of the border are unwilling to take them. Few people use £50 or £100 notes, and shopkeepers are likely to treat them with suspicion, since forgeries are widespread. At the time of going to press, £1 was worth around US$1.60, €1.45, Can$2.20, Aus$2.40 and

NZ$2.75; for the most up-to-date exchange rates, check ⓦ www.oanda.com.

There are **no exchange controls** in Britain, so you can bring in as much cash as you like and change travellers' cheques up to any amount. In every sizeable town and, surprisingly, in many small places too, you'll find a branch of at least one of the big high-street **banks**: Barclays, HSBC, Natwest, Lloyds TSB, Abbey, Halifax and so on. General **banking hours** are Monday to Friday from 9 or 9.30am to 4 or 5pm, though some branches are open until slightly later on Thursdays. Almost everywhere, banks are the best places in which to change money and travellers' cheques. Outside banking hours you'll have to use a **bureau de change**, found in most city centres and often at train stations or airports. Avoid changing money or cheques in hotels, where the rates are normally very poor.

Carrying money

Credit/debit cards are by far the most convenient way to carry your money. Most hotels, shops and restaurants in the UK accept major credit cards, although plastic is less useful in rural areas; smaller establishments all over the country, such as B&Bs, will often accept cash only. You can usually withdraw cash on your credit or debit card from bank **ATMs** (widely known as cash machines or cash points); you should contact your bank before you leave, to find out which banks you can use and how much you'll be charged for the service. You'll also find ATMs at all major points of arrival, train stations and motorway service areas, as well as at most large supermarkets, some petrol stations and even in some pubs and village shops.

Though a lot more hassle, old-fashioned **travellers' cheques** are still the safest way to carry your money. The usual fee for buying them is one or two percent, though this may be waived if you buy the cheques through a bank where you have an account. It pays to get a selection of denominations. Make sure to keep the purchase agreement and a record of cheque serial numbers safe and separate from the cheques themselves. Note that in the UK you are unlikely to be able to use your travellers' cheques as cash: you'll always have to cash them first, making them less reliable a source of funds if you intend to get far off the beaten track.

A compromise between travellers' cheques and plastic is **Visa TravelMoney**

Credit card safety

Credit card fraud is a growing problem in the UK. It takes no more than a second or two for a restaurant waiter to surreptitiously swipe your card through a palm-sized machine that will store your number: it's then easy to marry this up later on with your signature and go out on a midnight spending spree. Similarly, criminals have dozens of tricks with ATMs, including sliding plastic into the slot so that when you insert your card the ATM cannot read it: it seems like the machine has swallowed your card, you depart to phone customer service, and the fraudster pulls your card out of the slot and heads for the nearest department store.

The golden rule is to **never let your card out of your sight**: in some restaurants, waiters now bring a handheld device to the table in order to swipe your card in front of you. If they don't, you should get up and take your card to the till yourself – as you would in a shop – and watch carefully as the card is swiped through the machine; if you're faced with a turned back in a shadowy corner, you are quite entitled to ask to see the process with your own eyes. If you take money out of an ATM, choose one located safely – inside a bank, rather than out on the street if possible. Look around you to see who's nearby, and also look at the ATM to see if it's been obviously tampered with. As you type in your PIN, shield the keypad with your other hand: criminals have been known to monitor PIN numbers being typed in with a miniature camera stuck to the ATM's interior. And, of course, when the cash appears, don't stand around counting it: put card and notes away immediately, before turning round.

(⊛international.visa.com/ps), a disposable prepaid debit card with a PIN that works in all ATMs that take Visa cards. You load up your account with funds before leaving home, and when they run out, you simply throw the card away. You can buy up to nine cards to access the same funds – useful for couples or families travelling together – and it's a good idea to buy at least one extra as a back-up in case of loss or theft. The 24-hour toll-free customer assistance service centre is on ☎0800/963833 in the UK.

Costs

The minimum **expenditure**, if you're cycling or hitching, preparing most of your own food and camping, is in the region of £25–30 a day, rising to around £40 a day if you're staying at hostels, using some public transport and eating the odd meal out. Couples staying at budget B&Bs, eating at unpretentious restaurants and visiting a fair number of tourist attractions, are looking at around £50 each per day; if you're renting a car, staying in comfortable B&Bs or hotels and eating well, you should reckon on at least £100 a day per person. Single travellers should budget on spending around sixty percent of what a couple would spend (single rooms cost more than half the double-room rate). If you're visiting the big cities, which can be pricey, allow at least an extra £10 or so a day each, double that in London.

Taxes and tipping

Most goods (except books and food) are subject to a 17.5 percent tax called **Value Added Tax** (VAT). It's always included in the final price; you'll never have to add it on yourself before paying, though hotel bills and bills for other services are sometimes calculated with the tax added on separately at the end instead of item by item.

Some restaurants – usually the fancier kind, though not always – levy a "discretionary" or "optional" **service charge** of 10 or 12.5 percent. If they've done this, it should be clearly stated on the menu and on the bill. However, you are not obliged to pay the charge, and certainly not if the food or service wasn't what you expected. Otherwise, there are no fixed rules for **tipping**, although a ten to fifteen percent tip is expected by taxi drivers. In restaurants, if no service charge has been levied, you can either tip ten percent in cash on the table, or add an amount onto your credit card slip before signing. It's not normal to leave tips in pubs and bars, but you can, if you like, offer to buy the staff a drink; they'll either serve themselves with one there and then, or keep the money for later on (the assumption is they'll spend it on a drink after closing time). The only other occasions when you'll be expected to tip are in hairdressers, and in very upmarket city hotels where porters, bellboys and table waiters rely on being tipped to bump up their often dismal wages.

Youth/student discounts and money-wiring

Once obtained, various official and quasi-official youth/student ID cards soon pay for themselves in savings. Full-time students are eligible for the **International Student ID Card** (ISIC, ⊛www.isiccard.com), which entitles the bearer to special air, rail and bus fares and discounts at museums, theatres and other attractions. For Americans there's also a health benefit, providing up to $3000 in emergency medical coverage and $100 a day for 60 days in the hospital, plus a 24-hour hotline to call in the event of a medical, legal or financial emergency. The card costs $22 in the USA; Can$16 in Canada; Aus$16.50 in Australia; NZ$21 in New Zealand; £6 in the UK; and €12.70 in the Republic of Ireland. You only have to be 26 or younger to qualify for the **International Youth Travel Card**, which carries the same benefits. Teachers qualify for the **International Teacher Card**, offering similar discounts. Check the website for details of outlets selling the cards, which cost in the order of US$22, £7, Can$16, Aus$16.50 and NZ$21.

Wiring money from home using Thomas Cook (⊛www.thomascook.com), Travelers Express MoneyGram (⊛www.moneygram .com) or Western Union (⊛www .westernunion.com) is never convenient or cheap, and should only be considered a last resort. It's also possible to have money wired directly from a bank in your home country to a bank in London, although this is somewhat

Britain on a budget

Faced with another £2.50 pint, a £30 theatre ticket and a twenty-quid taxi ride back to your £100 a night hotel, Britain might seem like the most expensive country in Europe, but there are ways to stick to a **budget** and still live life to the full.

• Get advice from **tourist offices** – they exist to smooth your way, and can often give you tips on discounts and deals.

• Book **transport** tickets well in advance, and always ask about day rovers and other special deals. If you're flying, book online for the cheapest deals.

• Don't rule out **hostels** – many of them have cheap and very decent private rooms, often in beautiful buildings or handy locations, and always with prices a lot cheaper than a B&B or hotel.

• Don't drive – **walk**. In places like the Yorkshire Dales, the Lake District, Pembrokeshire, Cornwall, the Scottish Borders and more, the easiest and most enjoyable way to get from village to village is on your own two feet.

• Entry is free to many of Britain's showpiece **museums and galleries**, including some of the world's finest art and history collections in London, Birmingham, Manchester, Leeds, Liverpool, Cardiff, Edinburgh and Glasgow.

• Take every **discount card/ID** you're entitled to – students, young travellers, hostellers and seniors all get free or discounted entry to many sights and attractions.

• Set lunches can be a steal, even at the poshest of **restaurants**, where a limited-choice two- or three-course lunch might cost only 40 percent of what's charged in the evening.

• **Beer** is cheaper in Wales, Scotland and the north of England – cheapest of all in Lancashire, according to the peerless *Good Pub Guide*.

• Visit the **markets** – from grungy city-centre straggles of stalls to farmers' markets nationwide, you can browse for free (many have local crafts as well as food) and pick up some bargains along the way.

less reliable because it involves two separate institutions. If you go this route, your home bank will need the address of the "bank branch" where you want to pick up the money and the address and telex number of the head office, which will act as the clearing house; money wired this way normally takes two working days to arrive, and costs around £25/$40 per transaction. If you can last out the week, then arrange for friends or family to post you an **international money order**; these are exchangeable at any post office and are by far the cheapest way of sending money. If you're in really dire straits, you can get in touch with your embassy or High Commission, who will usually let you make one phone call home free of charge, and may – in worst cases only – repatriate you, but will never, under any circumstances, lend money.

Getting around

As you'd expect of such a small and densely populated country, just about every place in Britain is accessible by train or bus. However, costs are among the highest in Europe – London's commuters spend more on getting to work than any of their European counterparts – while cross-country travel can eat up a large part of your budget. It pays to plan ahead.

Make sure you're aware of all the passes and special deals on offer – note that some are only available outside Britain and must be purchased before you arrive. It's often cheaper to **drive** yourself around the country (certainly if you're sharing costs), though fuel and car rental tariffs again are among the highest in Europe and will seem prohibitive to North Americans. Congestion around the main cities can be bad, and even the motorways (notoriously the M25, London's orbital road, and the M6 between Birmingham and Manchester) are liable to jams, especially on public holidays when it seems like half the population is on the move. Given the congested state of the roads, **cycling** might not seem the most obvious (or safest) way to get around, but many people do bring bikes or rent once they arrive, and the country has a growing network of cycleways and traffic-free routes. For more on cycling, see "Sports and outdoor pursuits", p.53.

Domestic flights

Since the distances involved are small, **domestic flights** are not the most obvious choice for getting around Britain. However, with the rail system so inflexible and expensive, and several regional airports well served by no-frills airlines, flights can be a cost-effective as well as time-saving way of travelling.

There's a complex web of routeings across the country. **easyJet**, one of the major carriers, currently flies from several southern English airports to Scotland and Newcastle in the northeast of England, cutting out a long and potentially delay-ridden journey by road or rail. Similarly, **Ryanair** has budget flights from Stansted to Blackpool (near the Lake District) and Newquay in Cornwall (the latter mirrored by BA Gatwick–Plymouth). Fares on these, and other no-frills airlines, drop as low as £25 return, depending on when you book, although a more realistic average is around £50; their fare structure also means you can buy one-way tickets for half the cost, without penalties (the lowest fares are always online). You need to factor in both the time taken getting to and from the airport at both ends (no-frills carriers are notorious for flying to small, poorly connected airfields) and the impromptu delays these shoestring operations are prone to. **British Airways** is a more robust choice, offering fares as low as £60–70 for a Heathrow–Glasgow return. Odd but potentially very handy routeings are often flown by business-oriented carriers: **Eastern Airways**, for instance, flies Norwich–Aberdeen while **Scot Airways** flies London City–Dundee – but fares on both are at least double those on Ryanair and easyJet.

Flying comes into its own in the Scottish Highlands and Islands, where an outlay on a flight can save a day of travel by local bus and ferry. Scotland has numerous minor airports, many of them on the islands, some of which are little more than gravel airstrips. Fares are pretty high: a one-way fare from Glasgow to Islay will set you back around £80, and there are few discounted tickets available. A good alternative is British Airways' **Highland Rover**, which costs £169, and allows you to take any five flights within three months (flights to and between Orkney and Shetland are covered, but not inter-island flights within each). Most flights within Scotland are operated by British Airways or Loganair (a BA subsidiary), and the majority should be booked directly through BA, although competition is beginning to emerge, with Highland Airways flying a few routes from Glasgow and Inverness.

Airlines within Britain

Air Wales ☎0870/777 3131,
🌐 www.airwales.co.uk
bmi ☎0870/607 0555, 🌐 www.flybmi.com
bmibaby ☎0870/264 2229,
🌐 www.bmibaby.com
British Airways ☎0870/850 9850,
🌐 www.ba.com
Eastern Airways ☎01652/680600,
🌐 www.easternairways.com
easyJet ☎0871/750 0100, 🌐 www.easyjet.com
flyBE ☎0871/700 0535, 🌐 www.flybe.com
Highland Airways ☎0845/450 2245,
🌐 www.highlandairways.co.uk
Loganair ☎0870/850 9850,
🌐 www.loganair.co.uk
Ryanair ☎0871/246 0000, 🌐 www.ryanair.com
Scot Airways ☎0870/606 0707,
🌐 www.scotairways.com

By train

The British **rail network** has suffered chronic under-investment for decades, and the worsening situation was compounded in the 1990s by a foolhardy privatization. Nowadays, the track and the stations are run by one company, while dozens of other companies nationwide run the trains. Inevitably, this breakup has led to a severe decline in quality of service. Ongoing track repairs can still play havoc with official timetables, and you'll read endless horror stories in the newspapers about delayed services. However, it's fair to say that there are few major towns in **England** that cannot be reached by rail (Scotland and Wales are a different story). If you're travelling out of London, you have the pick of what are – most of the time – fast and frequent services: York or Exeter, for instance, can be reached in two hours. However if you're trying to make your way east–west across the country, things are much less easy: you're likely to find yourself forced to change trains and hang around for connecting services. **Scotland** has a modest rail network, at its densest in the central belt between Edinburgh and Glasgow, at its most skeletal in the Highlands, and all-but-nonexistent in the Islands. The West Highland Line, from Glasgow to Fort William, deserves a mention as probably the most scenic train ride in Britain. In **Wales**, the only two main lines (in the north from Chester to Holyhead, and the south from Newport to Fishguard) frame an array of thirty-odd volunteer-run private lines, often running vintage steam engines over short but scenic bits of track.

Rail information and tickets

In all instances (bar the private lines), an essential first call for information on timetables, routes and services throughout the country is **National Rail Enquiries** (see opposite). They can't make bookings, though: credit-card **reservations** are made through the rail companies themselves (National Rail Enquiries can supply the necessary contact name and number), or online via various agencies.

Given the huge variety of available options, it's almost impossible to give any meaningful advice about **ticket types** and costs, except to say that the earlier you book, the cheaper your ticket will be. Check 🌐 www .nationalrail.co.uk for full details. Travelling on a Friday, or just turning up at the station and buying a ticket, are the most expensive ways to go. The various train-operating companies have different names for different tickets, all with byzantine restrictions and arcane rules (for instance, it's often cheaper to travel return from the north to London, rather than from London to the north). Basically, the cheapest tickets need to be booked fourteen or seven days in advance and, as only limited numbers are issued, they sell out fast. A seat reservation is usually included with the ticket – always ask, because if it isn't, you may end up having to stand. To give an idea of the differing fares, travelling from London to Manchester on an open (fully flexible) return ticket costs £175-plus. Off-peak and with certain restrictions, this fare drops to around £50 return, while booking at least two weeks in advance (no refund, no changes) can bring the return fare as low as £20.

Children aged 5–15 inclusive pay half the adult fare on most journeys – but there are usually no discounts on advance-purchase tickets. Under-5s travel free, but are not entitled to a seat. At weekends and on public holidays, many long-distance services let you upgrade your ticket by buying a **first-class supplement** (£5–15), well worth paying if you're facing a five-hour journey on a packed train. If the station's ticket office is closed or does not have a vending machine, you may buy your ticket on the train. Otherwise, **boarding without a ticket** will render you liable to paying the full fare to your destination and, possibly, a penalty on top.

Rail passes

For foreign visitors who anticipate covering a lot of ground around Britain, a **rail pass** is a wise investment. For most this means a BritRail or Eurail pass, either of which must be bought before you enter the country. Any good travel agent or specialist operator can supply up-to-date information, as can Ⓦ www.raileurope.com, which has contact details of agents around the world.

The **BritRail Classic Pass** (Ⓦ www .britrail.com) gives unlimited travel in England, Scotland and Wales, comes in either a first or second-class version and is valid for four days (US$285/189), eight days (US$405/269), fifteen days (US$609/405), twenty-two days (US$769/515), or one month (US$915/609). **Youth Pass** (second-class only) and **Senior Pass** (first-class only) versions are also available, costing between twenty and thirty percent less than Classic Pass prices. In addition, you can buy a panoply of **other BritRail passes**, including a Flexi-Pass (good for travel on specified days in a time period), Family Pass, Party Pass (for three or four adults travelling together) and Pass'n'Drive (train travel plus car rental). A particularly useful one for London-bound visitors is the **London Visitor Travelcard** (US$32 for three days, US$43 for four days, US$64 for a week), giving unlimited bus and Tube travel in the capital including the ride from Heathrow. For information on rail passes on sale in England, see the box overleaf.

If you're planning to travel widely around Europe by train, then it may be worthwhile buying a **Eurail** pass (Ⓦ www.eurail.com), which allows unlimited free train travel in the UK and in sixteen other countries but is unlikely to pay for itself if you stick to Britain alone. The **Eurail Youthpass** (for under-26s) costs US$414 for fifteen days, US$534 for twenty-one days, or $664 for one month; if you're 26 or over you'll have to buy a first-class **Eurail Pass**, available in fifteen-day (US$588), twenty-one-day (US$762) and one-month (US$946) versions. There are also two- and three-month versions of both. You may stand a better chance of getting your money's worth out of a **Eurail Flexipass**, which is valid for a certain number of travel days in a two-month period. This, too, comes in under-26/first-class versions: ten days costs $488/$694, and fifteen days $642/$914.

Useful rail contacts

National Rail Enquiries ☎ 0845/748 4950, Ⓦ www.nationalrail.co.uk. Advice on timetables, routes, ticket types and services nationwide.
Ⓦ **www.qjump.co.uk** Ticket sales and seat reservations for any UK journey.
Ⓦ **www.seat61.com** The world's finest train travel website. It's almost nerdishly detailed, with more than you ever wanted to know about train travel in the UK (and worldwide), but full of useful tips and links.
Ⓦ **www.thetrainline.com** Ticket sales and seat reservations.

By coach and bus

Long-distance buses – known across Britain as **coaches** – duplicate many rail routes, very often at half the price of the train or less. Services between major towns and cities are frequent and the coaches are large and comfortable. Those plying longer routes often have drinks and sandwiches available on board. By far the biggest countrywide operator is **National Express**, whose network extends to every corner of England, as well as parts of Wales; their sister company **Scottish Citylink** takes over north of the border. On busy routes, and on any route at weekends and during holidays, it's advisable to book ahead, rather than just turn up. UK residents in full-time education, or those under 25 or over 50, can buy a National Express **Discount Coach Card** (£10 for one year, £19 for three), which entitles the holder

UK rail passes

Some rail passes are available only in Britain itself, to both locals and visitors; ⓦ www.nationalrail.co.uk has full information. All can be bought at main stations; take along two passport photographs and proof of age or status. These include the **Young Person's Railcard** (£18), available to full-time students and those aged between 16 and 25, and **Senior Citizens' Rail Card** for people over 60 (£18), both of which give a third off most fares. Families can make use of the **Family Railcard** (£20), which covers up to four adults who are entitled to a 33 percent discount, and up to four children who travel on a sixty percent reduction on the child's full fare. The most comprehensive pass for "free" travel that is buyable in the UK is the **All-Line Rover**, which starts at a whopping £325 for seven consecutive days' travel. There are also a number of localized passes, including the **Freedom of Scotland Travelpass**, which gives unlimited travel within Scotland on trains, most ferries and some buses; various versions are available, starting at £89 for four days' travel in an eight-day period. Other Scottish passes include the Highland Rover and the Central Scotland Rover. The **Freedom of Wales Flexipass** – for unlimited travel throughout Wales, starting at £55 for eight days' bus travel and any four days on the train – is backed up by eleven other Welsh passes.

to a thirty percent discount on travel. Anyone else, including foreign travellers of any age, can purchase a **Tourist Trail Pass**, which offers unlimited travel on the whole British network for two days within three (£49), five within thirty (£85), eight within thirty (£135), fifteen within thirty (£190) or fifteen within sixty (£205). Twenty percent discounts on these prices are available if you already hold a Discount Coach Card or (provided you would qualify for one) if you buy a Tourist Trail Pass from outside the UK.

Local bus services are run by a bewildering array of companies. In many cases, timetables and routes are well integrated, but it's increasingly the case that private companies duplicate the busiest routes in an attempt to undercut the commercial opposition, leaving the farther-flung spots neglected. Thus, if you want to get from one end of a big city to another, you'll probably have a choice of buses all offering cut-price fares, but to get out into the suburbs or to a satellite village, you may have to wait several hours. As a rule, the further away from urban areas you get, the less frequent and more expensive bus services become, but there are very few rural areas which aren't served by at least the occasional privately owned minibus.

In the summer, many national park areas support a network of **weekend and bank holiday buses**, taking visitors to beauty spots, villages, hiking trailheads and other out-of-the-way destinations. In addition, many rural areas not covered by other forms of public transport are served by **Postbuses** – minibuses that carry mail and three to ten fare-paying passengers. They set off in the morning (usually around 8am from the main post office) and head out to outlying areas. It's a sociable and cheap way to travel (£2–4 a journey), and can be a convenient way of getting to hidden-away B&Bs, although it is often excruciatingly slow.

The main difficulty is getting reliable **information** on schedules and routes: for this, the best (indeed, just about the only) source is **Traveline**, a publicly funded initiative providing detailed information from national long-distance services down to local buses.

Useful bus contacts

National Express ☎0870/580 8080,
ⓦ www.nationalexpress.com
Postbuses Contact Royal Mail Customer Service
☎0845/774 0740, ⓦ www.royalmail.com/postbus
Scottish Citylink ☎0870/550 5050,
ⓦ www.citylink.co.uk
Traveline ☎0870/608 2608,
ⓦ www.traveline.org.uk

Minibus and bus tours

Backpackers and travellers on a budget often prefer the flexibility of touring Britain on Stray

Travel's **"jump-on-jump-off" minibus** (£159; ☎020/7373 7737, ⊛www.straytravel.com), where you'll get the chance to travel with like-minded folk and see some off-the-beaten-track destinations. From London, the bus loops around the country (including Wales and Scotland), calling at all the major destinations before heading back to the capital. You can arrange your own accommodation or have Stray Travel do it for you; either way, it's a good-natured, budget-oriented trip. Other deals of theirs include Cornwall (three days £99) and the Get-a-Fix Day Trip to Stonehenge, Oxford and the Cotswolds (£34). Road Trip (☎0845/200 6791, ⊛www.roadtrip.co.uk) offers fully inclusive budget **bus tours** to a similar clientele, though you can't get on and off on their routes (three days from £69). If you're looking for something a bit more upmarket – **escorted coach tours** with an older target group – then any high street travel agency can provide brochures and recommend routes.

Similar companies operate out of Edinburgh. The current leader, Haggis (☎0131/557 9393, ⊛www.haggisadventures.com), has bright yellow minibuses setting off daily on whistlestop tours of various parts of Scotland lasting between one and six days, with food and accommodation included (three days £79). They also have a jump-on/jump-off deal (£69). Several other companies offer similar packages, including Macbackpackers (☎0131/558 9900, ⊛www.macbackpackers.com), who run tours linking up their own hostels round the country, and Wild in Scotland (☎0131/478 6500, ⊛www.wild-in-scotland.com), who unlike the others take in the Outer Hebrides or Orkney during their tours. The popular Rabbie's Trail Burners tours (☎0131/226 3133, ⊛www.rabbies.com) don't aim squarely at the backpacker market and have a rather more mellow approach.

By car

In order to **drive** in Britain you need a current full driving licence. If you're bringing your own vehicle into the country you should also carry your vehicle registration or ownership document at all times. Furthermore, you must be adequately insured: check your existing insurance policy.

In Britain you **drive on the left**. Motorways (prefixed with an "M") and most main "A" roads have either two lanes each way (called a "dual carriageway") or – motorways only – three each way, but you should still expect crowded roads and delays at peak travel times and around public holidays. In the deep countryside, "B" roads and minor roads may be only one car wide (known as "single track"), so you need to drive carefully – especially since locals tend to assume there's nothing else coming. Make use of passing places, both to let oncoming traffic pass and to let cars behind you overtake. Also, don't underestimate the weather: snow, ice, fog and wind cause havoc every year, and driving conditions on motorways as much as in rural areas can deteriorate quickly. Local radio stations and national BBC Radio Five Live (693 or 909 AM) feature frequently updated traffic bulletins.

Speed limits are 30 or 40mph (50 or 65kph) in built-up areas, 70mph (110kph) on motorways and dual carriageways, and 60mph (100kph) on most other roads. As a rule, assume that in any area with street lighting the speed limit is 30mph (50kph) unless otherwise stated. Prominent yellow **speed cameras** are increasingly used as a deterrent to speeding; if you're caught by one of these, the owner (or renter) of the vehicle will have to pay a fine. Aside from major bridges, such as across the Severn into Wales, the only significant **toll road** in the country is a section of the M6 motorway around Birmingham – but it splits off from the main route, so you can opt to drive on the untolled section for free. After years of gridlock, central London now has a so-called **congestion charge** (see p.81 for more): forcing drivers to pay has cut traffic levels in the city significantly.

Every petrol (gas) station has unleaded, diesel and leaded (known as "four-star") **fuels**, often in varying grades, and all very expensive compared to the rest of Europe and North America. You'll find the lowest prices at out-of-town superstores such as Asda, Sainsburys or Morrisons; suburban stations are usually fairly reasonable; and the highest prices are charged at motorway service areas.

Car parking in towns, cities and popular tourist spots can be a nightmare and will also cost you a small fortune. If you're in a tourist city for a day, look out for **park-and-ride schemes** where you can park your car on the outskirts and take a cheap or free bus to the centre. Parking in long- or short-stay **car parks** will be cheaper than using on-street meters, which restrict parking time to two or three hours at most. Some towns operate free **disc-zone parking**, which allows limited-hours town-centre parking in designated areas: if that's what roadside signs indicate, you need to pick up a cardboard disc from any local shop and display it in your windscreen. All over the country, a **yellow line** along the edge of the road indicates parking restrictions; check the nearest sign to see exactly what they are. A **double yellow line** means no parking at any time, though you can stop briefly to unload or pick up people or goods (maximum stop two minutes). A **double red line** means absolutely no stopping at all.

The three major British motoring organizations, the AA, RAC and Green Flag, all operate 24-hour emergency **breakdown** services, in addition to providing many other services, including a reciprocal arrangement for free assistance through many overseas motoring organizations; check the situation with your own before setting out. In remote areas, expect a long wait for assistance. You can make use of all three if you're not a member, but you will be required to join at the roadside and will incur a hefty surcharge as well.

Motoring organizations

Australia AAA ☎02/6247 7311, ⓦwww.aaa.asn.au
Canada CAA ☎613/247-0117, ⓦwww.caa.ca
Ireland AA Ireland ☎01/617 9999, ⓦwww.aaireland.ie
New Zealand AA ☎0800/500444, ⓦwww.nzaa.co.nz
UK AA ☎0870/600 0371, ⓦwww.theaa.com; RAC ☎0800/092 2222, ⓦwww.rac.co.uk; Green Flag ☎0800/328 8772, ⓦwww.greenflag.com
US AAA ☎1-800/222-4357, ⓦwww.aaa.com

Renting a car

Car rental is expensive, and you'll probably find it cheaper to arrange things from home

through one of the multinational chains, or by opting for a fly/drive deal. If you do rent a car locally, the least you can normally expect to pay is around £60 for a weekend or from £150 per week. You may find that you can save a considerable sum by using a local firm, particularly over the course of a week; tourist offices normally have details, or one budget option is easyCar (☎0906/333 3333 premium rate, ⓦwww.easycar.com), with multiple locations in and around Birmingham, Glasgow, Liverpool, London and Manchester. If you book far enough in advance, their rates can be as low as £10–15 per day, though there are only one or two small models on offer. For **camper van** (RV) rental, contact Just Go (☎0870/240 1918, ⓦwww.justgo.uk.com), which can supply quality vehicles sleeping four to six people, equipped with CD/DVD, full bathrooms and kitchen and bike racks. Rates range from £450 to £850 per week, depending on vehicle and season.

Most companies prefer you to pay with a **credit card**; otherwise, you may have to leave a deposit of over £100. There are very few **automatics** at the lower end of the price scale; if you want one, you should book well ahead. To rent, you need to show your **driving licence**; few companies will rent to drivers with less than a year's experience and most will only rent to customers between 21 and 75 years of age. Coverage by one of the breakdown services should be included automatically, but if you're renting from a smaller company it's worth checking that there is an arrangement in place.

International car rental companies

Avis Australia ☎136333, Canada ☎1-800/272-5871, Ireland ☎021/428 1111, New Zealand ☎0800/655111, UK ☎0870/606 0100, US ☎1-800/230-4898, ⓦwww.avis.com
Budget Australia ☎1300/362848, Canada ☎1-800/527-0700, Ireland ☎01/878 7814, UK ☎0800/181181, US & New Zealand ☎0800/652277, ⓦwww.budget-international.com
Hertz Australia ☎1800/550067, Canada ☎1-800/263-0600, Ireland ☎01/676 7476, New Zealand ☎0800/655955, UK ☎0870/844 8844, US ☎1-800/654-3001, ⓦwww.hertz.com.
Thrifty Australia ☎1300/367227, New Zealand ☎09/309 0111, UK ☎01494/751600, US & Canada ☎1-800/367-2277, ⓦwww.thrifty.com.

Taxis and minicabs

It would be a rich tourist who got around exclusively in **taxis**, but they can be a useful form of transport. In rural areas, there's often no alternative if you need to get to the next town in a hurry, and if you're in a group hiring a taxi can work out as cheap as taking a bus. Reckon on paying around £1.50 a mile in country districts. In towns and cities prices are higher for shorter distances, but there are wide regional variations: a cab home after a night out in Manchester, Newcastle or Glasgow is far less of a wallet-emptying experience than in London. In the capital, the famous black cabs are generally a little more expensive than minicabs, but are usually more reliable (the London cabbie's "knowledge" is such that he or she should know the location of every single street). You can hail a black cab on the street, but you must book minicabs by phone. The useful ⓦ**www.traintaxi.co.uk** can put you in touch with taxi firms serving all Britain's train, tram, metro and tube stations.

Accommodation

Accommodation in Britain is expensive. Budget travellers are well catered for with numerous hostels, and those with money to spend will relish the country's middle- and top-range hotels, many of which are former coaching inns or converted manor houses. In the middle market, however, the standard of many B&Bs, guesthouses and simple hotels is often disappointing, and it can be hard work finding places with the standards of taste, originality, efficiency and value which you might expect from a country with as well-developed a tourist market as Britain. Welcoming, comfortable, well-run places do, of course, exist in all parts of the country – but there are just not enough of them to go round.

Nearly all tourist offices will **book rooms** for you, although the fee for this service can vary. In some areas you will pay a deposit that's deducted from your first night's bill (usually ten percent), in others the office will take a percentage or flat-rate commission – usually around £3. Another useful service operated by the majority of tourist offices is the "Book-a-bed-ahead" service, which locates accommodation in your next port of

Accommodation price codes

Throughout this book, accommodation prices have been graded with the **codes** below, corresponding to the cost of the least expensive double room in high season. Bear in mind that many chain hotels slash their tariffs at the weekend, and that an upmarket establishment may also have a few less expensive rooms. Price codes are not given for **campsites**, most of which charge less than £10 per person. We've given the exact cost for **dorm beds** in hostels and student halls of residence, although for hostels that have both dorms and private double rooms, we've given a bed price and a code.

❶ under £40
❷ £41–50
❸ £51–60
❹ £61–70
❺ £71–90
❻ £91–110
❼ £111–150
❽ £151–200
❾ over £201

call – again for a charge of about £3, though the service is sometimes free.

Hotels, guest houses and B&Bs

A nationwide system exists for grading **hotels**, **guest houses** and **B&Bs**, with hotels graded by stars (five stars is the top rank), and guest houses and B&Bs by diamonds, with additional gold and silver awards for those that achieve distinction.

Although there's not a hard and fast correlation between standards and price, you'll pay in the region of £60 per night for a double room at a one-star **hotel** (breakfast included), rising to around £100 in a three-star and from around £200 for a five-star. In London and some tourist hotspots, rates are double that. In many towns and cities, larger hotels offer cut-price **weekend rates** to fill the rooms vacated by the weekday business trade. An increasing number of **budget hotel chains** – *Travel Inn*, *Travelodge*, *Holiday Inn Express*, *Ramada* and others – have properties usefully located in city centres across the country. The style at these tends towards the no-frills (with breakfast charged extra), but at £50–60 a room (often sleeping up to four) they're a good deal for families and people travelling in small groups.

At the lower end of the scale, it's sometimes difficult to differentiate between a hotel and a **B&B**. At their most basic, these places – often known as **guest houses** in resorts and other tourist towns – are ordinary private houses with a couple of bedrooms set aside for paying guests and a dining room for the consumption of a rudimentary breakfast. At their best, however, B&Bs offer rooms as well furnished as those in hotels costing twice as much, delicious home-prepared breakfasts and an informal hospitality that a larger place couldn't match. As a guideline on costs, you should be able to find a one-diamond place for under £40 per night for a double room and, though the sky is the limit at the top end of the scale, it is possible to stay in some four-diamond places for as little as £70 – farmhouse B&Bs are especially good value. As many B&Bs, even the pricier ones, have a very small number of rooms, you should certainly book a place as far in advance as possible, especially if you're travelling on your own. Finally, don't assume that a B&B is no good if it's ungraded. There are so many B&Bs in Britain that the grading inspectors can't possibly keep track of them all, and in the rural backwaters some of the most enjoyable accommodation is to be found in welcoming and beautifully set houses whose facilities may technically fall short of official standards. Check out ⓦ www.distinctlydifferent.co.uk for some unique converted buildings offering memorable B&B stays.

Hostels, student halls and bunkhouses

There's an ever-increasing number of **hostels** to cater for travellers – youthful or otherwise – who are unable or unwilling to pay the often exorbitant rates charged by hotels, guest houses and B&Bs. Many hostels are well equipped, clean and comfortable, sometimes offering doubles and even singles as well as dormitory accommodation. Others concentrate more on keeping the price as low as possible, simply providing a roof over your head and a few basic facilities. The Youth Hostels Association (**YHA**) network consists of over 230 properties in England and Wales, with the Scottish Youth Hostels Association (**SYHA**) responsible for around 80 properties in Scotland. Both are affiliated to **Hostelling International (HI)** and in cities the facilities are often every bit as good as some hotels: most boast cafés, laundry facilities, Internet access, entertainment and bike rental. Particularly in the popular city hostels, **advance booking** is recommended, and just about essential at Easter, Christmas and from May to August. We've given an email address for each place where possible, but you can also book by post, phone and sometimes fax, and your bed will be held until 6pm on the day of arrival. If you have a credit card, you can use either the YHA or SYHA website, or HI's **International Booking Network** (IBN) to book beds as far as six months in advance. Most hostels accept payment by Mastercard or Visa, and most are also closed from 10am to 5pm, with an 11.30pm curfew.

If you aren't already a member of Hostelling International through your home country's hostelling organization, you can join through the YHA or SYHA or in person at any affiliated hostel. **Membership** at a YHA hostel costs £6.75 per year for under-18s, £13.50 for others; at a SYHA hostel, it costs £9. **Bed prices** at most hostels are around £7 per night for under-18s and £10 for the over-18s, though in big cities (London, Oxford, York, Edinburgh) you could double that. Students aged 18–25 can get a £1 reduction on production of a valid student card. Length of stay is normally unlimited and the hostel warden will provide a linen sleeping bag for a small charge. Hostel **meals** are always good value (around £5). Nearly all hostels have kitchen facilities.

At best, **independent hostels** offer facilities similar to those of the YHA and SYHA places, and at a lower price. They are usually laid-back places with no membership, fewer rules and no curfew. Check out ⓦ www.backpackers.co.uk for more.

In university towns you should be able to find out-of-term accommodation in the **student halls**, usually one-bedded rooms either with their own or shared bathrooms. In some instances, this may be the only budget accommodation on offer in the centre of town. We've given details in relevant town accounts.

In the wilder parts of Britain, such as Snowdonia, Dartmoor and the Scottish islands, the YHA and SYHA also administer some basic accommodation for walkers (known in England as **camping barns**). Holding up to twenty people, these agricultural outbuildings are often unheated and are very sparsely furnished, with wooden sleeping platforms – or bunks if you're lucky – a couple of tables, a toilet and a cold-water supply, but they are weatherproof, extremely good value (from £4 a night) and perfectly situated for walking tours. Similar barns, often called **bunkhouses** (or **bothies** in Scotland), are usually run by private individuals.

Hostelling organizations

Australia ⓣ 02/9261 1111, ⓦ www.yha.com.au
Canada ⓣ 1-800/663-5777, ⓦ www.hihostels.ca
England & Wales ⓣ 0870/870 8808, ⓦ www.yha.org.uk
Ireland ⓣ 01/830 4555, ⓦ www.anoige.ie
Northern Ireland ⓣ 028/9032 4733, ⓦ www.hini.org.uk

New Zealand ⓣ 0800/278299, ⓦ www.yha.co.nz
Scotland ⓣ 0870/155 3255, ⓦ www.syha.org.uk
USA ⓣ 301/495-1240, ⓦ www.hiayh.org

Camping, caravanning and self-catering

There are hundreds of **campsites** in Britain, charging from £5 per tent per night to around £12 for the plushest sites, with amenities such as laundries, shops and sports facilities. Some hostels have small campsites on their property, charging half the indoor overnight fee. In addition to these official sites, farmers may offer pitches for as little as £3 per night, but don't expect tiled bathrooms and hair dryers for that kind of money. Even farmers without a reserved camping area may let you pitch in a field if you ask first, possibly for free; setting up a tent without asking is an act of trespass, which will not be well received. Free camping is illegal in national parks and nature reserves.

The problem with many campsites in the most popular parts of rural Britain – especially near the coast – is that tents have to share the space with **caravans**. Every summer the country's byways are clogged by migrations of these cumbersome trailers, which are still far more numerous than camper vans in Britain. The great majority of caravans, however, are permanently moored at their sites, where they are rented out to families for self-catering holidays, and the ranks of nose-to-tail trailers in the vicinity of most of Britain's best beaches might make you think that half the population shacks up in a caravan for the midsummer break.

If you're planning to do a lot of camping at official sites, it might be worthwhile joining the Camping and Caravanning Club (ⓣ 024/7669 4995, ⓦ www.campingandcaravanningclub.co.uk). Membership costs around £30 and entitles you to pay only a per-person fee, not a pitch fee, at CCC sites. Those coming from abroad can get the same benefits by buying an international camping carnet, available from home motoring organizations or a CCC equivalent.

Self-catering

A **self-catering** cottage or apartment is a good way to cut down on costs. In most cases, however, and particularly during summer, the minimum period of let is a week, and therefore isn't a valid option if you're aiming to tour round the country. The least you can expect to pay in the high season is around £200 per week for a place sleeping four, but something special – such as a well-sited coastal cottage – might cost two or three times that amount. Every regional tourist board has details of cottage rentals in its area. Alternatively, consult Ⓦ www.visitbritain.com, which has an exhaustive clickable list of self-catering rental agencies in every region. The weekend newspapers are another source of information on all types of self-catering accommodation, from canal boats to lighthouses.

Country Cottages in Scotland ☎ 0870/444 1133, Ⓦ www.countrycottagesinscotland.co.uk. Superior cottages with lots of character scattered across Scotland.

Country Holidays/English Country Cottages ☎ 0870/078 1200, Ⓦ www.country-holidays.co.uk. More than 3000 properties all over England.

Hoseasons ☎ 01502/502588, Ⓦ www .hoseasons.co.uk. Wide range of cottages and country lodges throughout the country.

Landmark Trust ☎ 01628/825925, Ⓦ www.landmarktrust.co.uk. Their handbook (£10) lists over 160 converted historic properties.

Mackay's Agency ☎ 0131/225 3539, Ⓦ www.mackays-scotland.co.uk. A whole range of properties across Scotland.

National Trust ☎ 0870/458 4422, Ⓦ www.nationaltrust.org.uk. The NT owns around 300 cottages and farmhouses, most set in their own gardens or grounds.

National Trust for Scotland ☎ 0131/243 9331, Ⓦ www.nts.org.uk. The NTS lets around forty of its converted historic cottages and houses.

Rural Retreats ☎ 01386/701177, Ⓦ www .ruralretreats.co.uk. Upmarket accommodation in restored old buildings, many of them listed.

Wales Cottage Holidays ☎ 01686/628200, Ⓦ www.wales-holidays.co.uk. A varied selection of 500 properties all over Wales.

Welcome Cottage Holidays ☎ 01756/696870, Ⓦ www.welcome.cottages.co.uk. A wide range of unpretentious cottages all over Scotland.

Food and drink

Though the British still tend to regard eating as a functional necessity rather than a sociable pleasure, things are getting better. In the last decade or so, changing tastes and greatly improved quality of local produce has led to something of a culinary revolution. As you might expect, London has been the epicentre of this, but today every large town and city has several very recommendable places along with an awakening café/bistro culture. "Modern British" cuisine – in effect anything inventive – has been at the core of this change, though wherever you go you'll find places serving Indian, Italian and Chinese food. This said, the pub is still the centre of British social life: a drink in a traditional "local" is often the best introduction to the life of a town.

Food

In many hotels and B&Bs you'll be offered what's termed an "**English breakfast**" – or Welsh or Scottish in the respective countries – which is basically sausage, bacon and eggs plus tea and toast. This used to be the typical working-class start to the day, but these days the British have adopted the healthier cereal alternative; most places will give you this option as well. Traditionally, a "**Scottish breakfast**" would include oatmeal porridge eaten with salt (though sugar is always on offer too). You may also be served kippers or Arbroath smokies (delicately smoked haddock with butter), or a large piece of haddock with a poached egg on

Restaurant prices

Our restaurant listings include a mix of high-quality and good-value establishments, but if you're intent on a culinary pilgrimage, you would do well to arm yourself with a copy of the *Good Food Guide* (£14.99), which is updated annually and includes nearly 1300 detailed recommendations.

Throughout this book, we've supplied the phone number for all restaurants where you may need to book a table. At places categorized as "**inexpensive**", you can expect to pay under £10 per head without drinks; "**moderate**" means £10–20, "**expensive**" £20–30, and "**very expensive**" over £30.

top. Oatcakes (plain savoury biscuits) and a "buttery" – not unlike a French croissant – will often feature.

For most overseas visitors the quintessential British meal is **fish and chips** (known in Scotland as a "fish supper", even at lunchtime), a dish that can vary from the succulently fresh to the indigestibly greasy – lashings of salt, vinegar and tomato ketchup or the fruitier brown sauce are common additions. The classier places have tables, but more often they serve **takeaway** (takeout) food only, sometimes supplying a disposable fork so that you can guzzle your roadside meal with a modicum of decorum. Fish-and-chip shops ("**chippies**") can be found on most high streets and main suburban thoroughfares throughout Britain, although they're frequently not as easy to spot as **pizza**, **kebab** and **burger** outlets. Other sources of straightforward food throughout the day are dowdy cafés or diners, known – tellingly – as "**greasy spoons**" (which tend to close at around 6–7pm), where you'll often find plain "meat-and-two-veg" dishes: steak-and-kidney pie, shepherd's pie (minced lamb or beef covered in mashed potato), chops and steaks, accompanied by boiled potatoes, carrots or some such vegetable. In Wales especially you'll come across dozens of small, inexpensive **wholefood cafés**, often doubling up as alternative resource centres. Also on the rise in the big towns are vaguely French **brasseries**, informal **bar/restaurants** offering simple meals from around £10–12 per head and often with a set lunchtime menu for around half that.

As far as eating goes, **pubs** have undergone something of a renaissance in recent years. A lot now take their food very seriously indeed, with separate dining areas, professional chefs and menus that can compete with better mid-range restaurants. And this "**gastro-pub**" revolution isn't confined to the ritzier city centres; it's not uncommon (especially in touristed areas like the Cotswolds or the Yorkshire Dales) to find that the old, lopsided pub in a sleepy rural hamlet – which may only boast a shop, a bus stop and a church – has a chic, contemporary-styled dining area, serving market-fresh ingredients on a broad, innovative menu.

The ranks of Britain's **gastronomic restaurants** grow with each passing year, with cordon-bleu chefs producing high-class French-style dishes, California-influenced menus, internationalist hybrid creations, and traditional British meat and fish dishes that are as delicious as the more arty creations of their cross-Channel counterparts. London of course has the highest concentration of top-notch places, but wherever you are in Britain you're never more than half an hour's drive from a really good meal – some of the very best dining rooms are to be found in the countryside hotels. The problem is that fine food costs more in Britain than it does anywhere else in Europe. If a place has any sort of reputation in foodie circles you're unlikely to be spending less than £30 per head, and for the services of the country's glamour chefs you could be paying up to a preposterous £120.

Vegetarians will rarely have difficulty, whatever their budget. Eating out in the towns and cities will present no problems: almost everywhere has at least one veggie option, a lot of Indian cooking is meat-free anyway, and there's a fair swathe of dedicated vegetarian restaurants around.

Eating ethnic

The most popular British meal these days isn't roast beef, nor even fish and chips – it's **chicken tikka masala**, a hybrid Anglo-Indian dish of marinated, lightly spiced chicken cooked in a tandoor oven, which was invented in Britain in the 1980s and is now the mainstay of menus at the innumerable **Indian** restaurants ("curry houses") up and down the land. ("Indian" has become a generic term, covering Pakistani and Bangladeshi food as well as the vast range of cuisines from India itself.) If you've never eaten Indian before, this is your big chance: Birmingham, Manchester, Bradford and the Brick Lane area of east London are renowned for the range and quality of Indian food on offer, although there are Indian restaurants in every town in Britain. When you sit down, order some popadoms (crisp discs of deep-fried lentil-flour dough, served with a range of chutneys) and get to grips with the menu; we've listed a few essential

Essential curry terms

Below are some basic terms to help you get to grips with a curry house menu. Each style is generally offered with chicken, lamb or prawns (sometimes king prawns); South Indian or Bangladeshi restaurants may include fish curries too. Vegetarians can either ask for veggie versions, or plump for a range of side-dishes which generally comprise mixtures of vegetables (such as *Sag Aloo*, *Chana Dal* or *Mutter Paneer*). We've gone for the most common spellings, and added a (subjective) idea of spiciness.

Cooking styles

Balti Despite its noble Pakistani origins, this term now applies to any curry cooked and served in a distinctive two-handled metal dish. The quintessential Birmingham curry, now popular nationwide. Traditionally eaten with naan bread rather than rice. Medium.

Biryani Curry – often vegetable – cooked with rice. Mild.

Bhuna Dry curry with onion, garlic, chilli and tomato. Medium.

Dhansak Sweet and sour, with aubergine, lentils and fruit. Mild.

Dopiaza Strongly flavoured, featuring both raw and cooked onion. Medium to hot.

Jalfrezi Red and highly spiced, often cooked with egg. Medium.

Korma A creamy coconut sauce. Mild.

Madras Fiery, with extra chilli. Hot.

Pathia Sweet and sour, with cream. Mild to medium.

Rogan Josh Full-flavoured, with tomatoes, onions and peppers in spiced oil. Hot.

Tikka Masala Flavourful and lightly spiced, with tomatoes. Very mild.

Vindaloo Beware! Lots of green chilis. Very hot.

Vegetables

Aloo Potato

Bhindi Okra

Brinjal Aubergine

Chana Chickpeas

Dal Lentils

Gobi Cauliflower

Mutter Peas

Onion bhaji Crisp ball of shredded, spiced onion. The classic starter.

Paneer Cheese

Sag Spinach

terms in the box. And remember, it's a scientific fact: curry tastes best accompanied by cold beer.

Other than Indian, you'll find good-value high-quality **Chinese** restaurants in every town of any size, and the larger cities have their own Chinatowns, complete with a range of tempting eating options. Other Asian restaurants, particularly **Thai**, are becoming more widespread, but are generally a shade more expensive, while further up the economic scale there's no shortage of **French** and **Italian** places – by far the most popular European cuisines, though most cities also have their share of **Spanish** tapas bars. **Japanese** food has been one of the success stories of recent years, with sushi bars joining the expense-account restaurants that have been established for some time in the business centres.

Regional cuisines

England is not particularly celebrated for its variety of regional cuisines, though most areas have a speciality or two. Lincolnshire and Cumberland (an old name for Cumbria) are known for their **sausages**, Lancashire for its **black pudding** (blood sausage), Yorkshire for its Yorkshire puddings (oven-baked batter cups, traditionally served with roast beef), Cornwall for its **pasty** (a chunky envelope of pastry filled with meat and potatoes), and Melton Mowbray for its hefty **pork pies**. England's traditional **cakes** – including Bath buns and Eccles cakes, both variations on the theme of flaky pastry with currants, and Bakewell tarts, a solid cake with a distinctively patterned almond-flavoured filling – can be found in bakeries on any high street, though they're at their most authentic in their place of origin. A few delicacies are seasonal, such as hot cross buns, available in the few weeks leading up to Easter, while other favourites such as scones, traditionally scoffed with jam and cream for afternoon tea, and biscuits, traditionally dunked in the tea, are popular year-round. More refined dishes are to be had along the coasts – the best **seafood** is found in Cornwall, while oysters are a speciality in Whitstable – and many English **cheeses**, notably Cheddar and Stilton, enjoy world recognition.

The quality of **Scottish food** has improved by leaps and bounds in recent years. Scottish produce – superb meat, fish and game, a wide range of dairy products and a bewildering variety of traditional baked goodies – is of outstanding quality and has to some extent been rediscovered of late. The quintessential Scottish dish is **haggis**, a sheep's stomach stuffed with spiced liver, offal, oatmeal and onion and traditionally eaten with bashed neeps (mashed turnips) and chappit tatties (mashed potatoes). Among other native staples is **stovies**, a tasty mash of onion and fried potato heated up with minced beef. Home-made soup is generally welcome in what can be a cold climate: try **Scots broth**, made with various combinations of lentil, split pea, mutton stock or vegetables and barley.

Welsh cooking is similarly in resurgence, as attested to by the many restaurants, hotels and pubs displaying the "Taste of Wales" (*Blas ar Cymru*) badge. Traditional dishes, such as the delicious native **lamb**, fresh **salmon** and **trout**, can be found on an increasing number of menus, frequently combined with the national vegetable, the **leek**. Particular Welsh specialities include **laver bread** (*bara lawr*), a thoroughly tasty seaweed and oatmeal cake often included in a traditional fried breakfast; **bara brith**, a fruit bread found in all teashops, **Glamorgan sausages**, a vegetarian combination of local cheese and spices; **cawl**, a chunky mutton broth; and **cockles**, trawled from the estuary north of the Gower. Dairy products feature highly in such a predominantly rural country, and there's a superb range of Welsh **cheeses**. The best known is Caerphilly, a soft crumbly white cheese that is mixed with beer and toasted on bread to form an authentic **Welsh Rarebit**.

Drink

The combination of an inclement climate and a British aversion to casual chat makes the simple **café** a rare phenomenon outside the big cities. A growing number of pubs now serve **tea and coffee** during the day, but in most places you'll attract consternation by asking for a cup; in the more genteel tourist towns – such as Stratford, Harrogate and York – you'll find plenty of **teashops**,

What's for afters?

Palate-tickling *hors d'oeuvres* aren't where the heart of British cooking lies. **Pudding**, however – a generic title for the sweet course at the end of a meal (also known as **dessert**, **afters** or just **sweet**, depending on region, custom and class) – is a much-loved part of the national culture. The variety is endless, but even so it's possible to pin down a few defining characteristics: pastry is thick and buttery, fillings are simple and satisfying, puddings are stodgy, cakes are plain, and there's lots of syrupy sauces, high-fat cream and rich yellow custard to help it all down. If you've chosen a Modern British restaurant, or you're just filling up at an ordinary café in any town in the country, try ditching the starter in order to leave room for a big pudding.

Though seen as quintessentially American, **apple pie** long predates the *Mayflower*. Familiar to the Elizabethans – who used a puree of apples, sugar, red wine, cinnamon and ginger – today there are myriad styles, invariably served with runny, whipped or **clotted cream** (the last a super-thick speciality of Devon and Cornwall), hot custard or ice cream. One variation is East Anglian apple cake, a substantial affair not unlike Dutch apple cake from across the sea. **Apple crumble** (or a crumble made with, for example, rhubarb or plums) is another classic, stewed fruit baked with a crunchy, sugary breadcrumb topping.

Treacle – the thick syrup left behind after sugar has crystallized – has been around since Britain started to refine sugarcane in the seventeenth century; it was replaced in the classic **treacle tart** by more refined "golden syrup" in the 1880s. You may also see **butterscotch tart** – its famous filling of butter and sugar boiled together originated in 1667 after the first cargo of sugarcane arrived for refining on Clydeside in Scotland (hence the name). **Cheesecake**, another dish that has been reinvented in the New World, is recorded as early as 1265; today, menus throughout northern England feature Yorkshire **curd tart** – sharp curd cheese baked in shortcrust pastry with cream, sugar and lemon zest.

Britain is famous for its steamed puddings, their high stodge value originating in the use of suet, or beef fat, an ingredient that is (thankfully) often dropped these days. **Sticky toffee pudding** is the national favourite, a wedge of steamed sponge drenched in a lip-smacking caramelized hot toffee sauce. Variations include chocolate, treacle and lemon pudding, while **spotted dick** – a steamed sponge dotted with currants – and **jam roly-poly** – steamed sponge with fruit jam – are both sauce-less. **Clootie dumpling** is a Scottish variation, served at Hogmanay (New Year). **Christmas pudding** is also steamed, but it's an even heavier dish, laden with lots more fruit, often alcoholic, and left to mature for at least six weeks. **Bread and butter pudding** is different again: slices of buttered white bread layered together, covered in milk or custard, sprinkled liberally with sugar and sultanas, and baked until golden.

Plenty of once-popular dishes are now cold-shouldered by virtually all "serious" restaurants but can still be found. **Trifle** – unfashionable now, but quite the thing in the eighteenth century – is a wobbly, semi-solid concoction of biscuits or cake soaked in brandy with layers of fruit jelly, everything topped with custard, crystallized fruits and sugary icing bits. Once ubiquitous items such as **death by chocolate** or **Mississippi mud pie** – favoured by child-friendly chain diners – are variations on the theme of chocolate cake with chocolate icing in chocolate sauce, while a **knickerbocker glory** is a super-size ice cream sundae. Perhaps the greatest loss is **rice pudding**, at its best a delectably mushy comfort dish of rice cooked in milk with sugar and sultanas, nowadays about as fashionable as a pipe and slippers.

unlicensed establishments where the normal procedure is to order a slice of cake or some other pastry with your tea or coffee. Increasingly common in the big cities are **brasseries** or equivalent establishments, where the majority of customers are there for a bite to eat, but where you're generally welcome to spend half an hour nursing a cappuccino or glass of wine.

Nothing, however, is likely to dislodge the **pub** from its status as the great British social institution. Originating as wayfarers' hostelries and coaching inns, pubs have outlived the church and marketplace as the focal points of communities, and at their best they can be as welcoming as the full name – "public house" – suggests. Pubs are as varied as the country's townscapes: in larger market towns you'll find huge oak-beamed inns with open fires and polished brass fittings; in the remoter upland villages there are stone-built pubs no larger than a two-bedroomed cottage; and in more inward-looking parts you'll come across no-nonsense pubs where something of the old division of the sexes and classes still holds sway – the "spit and sawdust" public bar is where working men can bond over a pint or two, the plusher saloon bar, with a separate entrance, is the preferred haunt of mutually preoccupied couples, the middle classes and unaccompanied women. Traditional **opening hours** (imposed during World War I to ensure factory workers got to their jobs on time and in a fit condition) are Mon–Sat 11am–11pm, Sun noon–10.30pm, with "last orders" called five minutes earlier: you then have twenty minutes to drink up before final closing. However, in most big towns and cities and across the whole of Scotland, late licences mean places often stay open until 1 or 2am, and special events (sports matches and New Year for example) often extend opening hours even further. The legal **drinking age** is eighteen and unless there's a special family room or a beer garden, children are not usually welcome.

Most pubs are owned by large breweries who favour their own **beers** and **lagers**, as well as some "guest beers", all dispensed by the pint or half-pint (a pint costs anything from £1.50 to £3.50, depending on the brew and the pub). **Cider**, the fermented produce

of apples, is a sweet, alcoholic beverage produced in the English West Country, where it's often preferred to beer; the far more potent and less refined **scrumpy** is the type consumed by aficionados of the apple. As with beer, the best scrumpy is available within a short radius of the factory, but the drink has nothing like the variety of beer. **Wines** sold in pubs are generally appalling, a strange situation in view of the excellent range of wine available in off-licences and supermarkets. The wine lists in brasseries and **wine bars** are nearly always better, but the mark-ups are often outrageous, and any members of the party who prefer beer will have to be content with bottled drinks. Nonetheless, many people are prepared to pay the extra in return for a less boozy and less male-dominated atmosphere.

Beer

The most widespread type of English beer is **bitter** (also known as **ale**), a dark, uncarbonated brew that should be pumped by hand from a cask in the cellar and served at room temperature; if it doesn't say "cask" or "cask-conditioned", it's not the real McCoy. Controversy exists over the head of foam on top: in southern England, people prefer their pint without a head, and brimming to the top of the glass; in the north and Scotland, flat beer is frowned on and drinkers prefer a short head of foam. Sweeter, darker **mild** and stronger **porter** are quite common in Welsh pubs, though virtually extinct in England. Traditional Scottish beer is a thick, dark ale known as **heavy**, graded by a shilling mark (/-) and served with a full head. Having said this, it's a fact that cold, blonde, fizzy **lager** is now more popular than bitter: every pub will have at least two or three brands on offer, but rarely is it a patch on bitter – as **CAMRA**, the Campaign for Real Ale (ⓦwww.camra.org.uk), has long been at pains to point out. Some of the beer touted as good English ale is nothing of the sort (if the stuff comes out of an electric pump, it isn't the real thing) but the big breweries do distribute some excellent brews, including Courage's Directors, a very classy strong bitter. Other names to look out for nationwide include Young's, Fuller's, Wadworth's,

Adnams, Greene King, Flowers and Tetley's. In Scotland, McEwan's Special and Tennent's Velvet are varieties of a 70/- ale, while the stronger, tastier 80/- varieties are slightly less widespread but do qualify as "real ales". Don't leave Wales without sampling Brains bitter, one of Britain's greatest pints, brewed in Cardiff.

However, if you really want to discover how good British beer can be, you should sample the products of the innumerable small local breweries producing ales to traditional recipes. Every region has its distinctive brew, frequently available at **free houses** – independently run establishments that sell what they please and are generally more characterful than so-called "tied pubs".

Guinness, a dark, creamy Irish stout, needs no introduction, and is on sale in virtually every pub in the land – though purists will tell you that it doesn't compare with the stuff sold in Ireland.

Whisky

Scotland's national drink is **whisky** – *uisge beatha*, the "water of life" in Gaelic (and almost never referred to as "scotch") – traditionally drunk in pubs with a half-pint of beer on the side, a combination known as a "nip and a hauf". Whisky has been produced in Scotland since the fifteenth century, and really took off in popularity after the 1780 tax on claret made wine too expensive for most people. The taxman soon caught up with illicit whisky distilling and drove the stills underground, and today many malt distilleries operate on the site of simple cottages that once distilled the stuff illegally. In 1823 Parliament revised its Excise Laws, in the process legalizing whisky production, and today the drink is Scotland's chief export. There are two types of whisky: **single malt**, made from malted barley; and grain whisky, which is made from maize and a little malted barley in a continuous still. **Blended whisky**, which accounts for more than ninety percent of all sales, is a mixture of the two types, with each brand's distinctive flavour coming from the malt whisky which is added to the grain in different quantities: the more expensive the blend, the higher the proportion of malts that have gone into it. Johnnie Walker, Bells, Teachers and The Famous Grouse are some of the best-known blended whiskies. All have a similar flavour, and are drunk neat or with water, sometimes with mixers such as soda or lemonade.

Single malt whisky is infinitely superior, and, as a result, a great deal more expensive. It is best drunk neat or with a splash of water to release its distinctive flavours. Single malts vary enormously depending on the amount of peat used for drying the barley, the water used for mashing, and the type of oak cask used in the maturing process. The two most important whisky regions are **Speyside**, which produces famous varieties such as Glenlivet, Glenfiddich and Macallan, and **Islay**, which produces distinctively peaty whiskies such as Laphroaig, Lagavulin and Ardbeg.

Communications

You should experience no problems with communications either within Britain or calling from abroad; the only difficulty you're likely to encounter is queues at the post office. The mail service is quick and generally efficient, public payphones are numerous, and outlets offering Internet access are ever-increasing.

Post

Virtually all **post offices** are open Mon–Fri 9am–5.30pm, Sat 9am–12.30 or 1pm; in small communities you'll find sub-post offices operating out of general stores; these are open standard post-office hours, even if the shop itself is open for longer. **Stamps** can be bought at supermarkets and newsagents, as well as from post office counters, in books of six or twelve. A first-class stamp for **letters** and **postcards** to anywhere in the British Isles currently costs 28p and should – in theory, at least – arrive the next day; second-class costs 20p and takes two to four days. Letters and post-cards weighing less than 20g (0.7oz) sent by **airmail** cost 38p within Europe and either 47p (under 10g) or 68p (10–20g) to anywhere else in the world. For more information, check out ⓦwww.royalmail.com.

Phones

Most public **payphones** are operated by British Telecom, known as BT (ⓦwww.bt.com) and, in towns at least, are widespread. Many BT payphones take all coins from 10p upwards, with a minimum charge of 20p. Prepaid cards are no longer available for payphones, but most accept credit and debit cards. Domestic calls are cheapest between 6pm and 8am Monday to Friday and all day on Saturday and Sunday.

Useful numbers

UK operator ☎100
UK directory assistance ☎118 500
International operator ☎155
International directory assistance ☎118 505

Throughout this guide, every phone number is prefixed by the area code, which is separated from the number by an oblique slash. You don't have to dial the code if you're calling from within the same area, unless you're using a mobile phone. Any number with the prefix ☎080 is toll-free (as is ☎0500); ☎0845 numbers are charged at local rate; ☎0870 at long-distance rate (☎0871 is similar); and all ☎09 numbers at very expensive premium rates. Most numbers beginning ☎07 are mobile phones.

If you want to use your **mobile/cellphone** in Britain, you'll need to check with your phone provider whether it will work abroad, and what the call charges are. Technology in the UK is GSM (ⓦwww.gsmworld.com). Unless you have a tri-band phone, it is unlikely that a cellphone bought for use in North America will work elsewhere. Most mobiles in Australia and New Zealand use GSM, but it pays to check before you leave home. To save yourself money and hassle, it might be worth simply picking up a "pay-as-you-go" deal once you've arrived in Britain.

Phoning home

To the US or Canada ☎001 + area code + number
To Ireland ☎00353 + area code without the zero + number
To Australia ☎0061 + area code without the zero + number
To New Zealand ☎0064 + area code without the zero + number

Telephone charge cards

One of the most convenient ways of phoning home from abroad is with a **telephone charge card**. Using a toll-free UK access code and a PIN number, you can make calls from most hotel, public and private phones that will be charged to your own account. While rates are always cheaper from a residential phone at off-peak rates, that's normally not an option when you're travelling. You may be able to use the card to minimize hotel phone surcharges, but don't depend on it. However, the benefit of calling cards is mainly one of convenience, as rates aren't necessarily cheaper than calling from a public phone while abroad and can't compete with discounted off-peak times many local phone companies offer. But since most major charge cards are free to obtain, it's certainly worth getting one at least for emergencies.

AT&T, MCI, Sprint, Canada Direct and other **North American** long-distance companies all enable their customers to make credit-card calls while overseas. Call your company's customer service line to find out what the toll-free access code is in the UK. Calls made from Scotland will automatically be billed to your home number, although you can also choose to make a collect call via the operator. Elsewhere, charge cards such as Telstra Telecard or Optus Calling Card in **Australia**, and Telecom NZ's Calling Card in **New Zealand**, can be used to make calls

abroad, which are charged back to a domestic account or credit card. Apply to Telstra (☎1800/038 000), Optus (☎1300/300 937), or Telecom NZ (☎04/801 9000).

Calling Britain from abroad

First dial your **international access code** (00 from Ireland and New Zealand; 011 from the US and Canada; 0011 from Australia), followed by **44** for the UK, then the area code minus its initial zero, then the number.

Email

An easy way to keep in touch while travelling is to sign up for a free web **email** address that can be accessed from anywhere, for example YahooMail (Ⓦwww.yahoo.com) or Hotmail (Ⓦwww.hotmail.com). Once you've set up an account, you can use these sites to pick up and send mail from any café, library or hotel with Internet access (which is most of them). The site Ⓦwww.kropla.com gives useful details of how to plug your laptop in when abroad, phone codes around the world, and information about electrical systems in different countries.

The media

Britain is well served with newspapers catering to all tastes; each city produces a local journal and newsagents' shelves are stacked floor to ceiling with magazines of every description. British television and radio remain among the most highly regarded in the world.

Newspapers and magazines

English daily newspapers come in two varieties, each named for their sheet-size: the "broadsheets" (self-dubbed the "quality press") are traditionally the repository of serious news, while the smaller-format "tabloids" are where the British press gets its world-famously bad reputation. The broadsheets

include the Murdoch-owned *Times* and the staunchly Conservative *Daily Telegraph*, which both outsell the high-quality journalism of the *Independent* and the left-of-centre *Guardian*. (You may see both *The Times* and *The Independent* available in tabloid editions, but the content is unchanged.) At the opposite end of the scale in terms of intellectual weight and volume of sales is the pernicious, reactionary *Sun*, the sleaziest

The Big Issue

In shopping streets and train stations all around Britain, you'll come across people selling **The Big Issue** magazine (Ⓦ www.bigissue.com) for £1.20. Buy it, if you can. The "big issue" of its title is homelessness, and the magazine represents an admirable way of combating social exclusion: vendors – who are all either homeless or at risk of becoming homeless – buy bundles of the magazine at 40–50 percent of the cover price. They then keep the difference, as a way to help themselves off the streets. Apart from helping out the disadvantaged, the magazine is consistently good, covering social and political stories with intelligence and insight, and often scooping big interviews.

occupant of the Murdoch stable; its chief rivals in the sex and scandal stakes are the *Daily Star* and self-consciously righteous *Daily Mirror*. The middle-brow arch-conservative daily tabloids – the *Daily Mail* and the *Daily Express* – show a depressing preoccupation with the royal family and TV celebrities. The scene is a little more varied on a Sunday, when the *Guardian*-owned *Observer*, England's oldest **Sunday newspaper**, supplements the Sunday editions of the dailies, whose ranks are also swelled by the popular *News of the World*, a smutty rag commonly known as the "News of the Screws".

All these are available in **Wales**, though they don't cover Welsh news in much depth. The only quality Welsh daily is the *Western Mail*, a mix of local, Welsh, British and token international news, though its attempts to give a Welsh slant to British stories can sometimes be ludicrous. The national Sunday paper, *Wales on Sunday*, is far superior.

In **Scotland**, the principal English papers are widely available, often as specific Scottish editions. The Scottish press produces two major daily papers, the liberal-left *Scotsman* and the slightly less-so *Herald*, published in Edinburgh and Glasgow respectively. Scotland's best selling daily paper is the downmarket *Daily Record*, from the same group as the *Daily Mirror*. Many national Sunday newspapers include a Scottish section, but Scotland's own Sunday "quality" is the wholly serious and somewhat dull *Scotland on Sunday*. Far more fun is the anachronistic *Sunday Post*, read by over half the population.

Every town in Britain seems to publish one or more **local papers**, ranging from quality regional news sheets to little more than a collection of adverts. Even these can, however, be a useful source for local events information.

British newsagents offer a range of **specialist periodicals** covering just about every subject, with motoring, music, sport, computers, gardening and home improvements all well served. One noticeably poor area is current events – the only high-selling weekly commentary magazine is the *Economist*, essential reading in boardrooms worldwide. The left-leaning alternative, the *New Statesman*, is subsidized by a few socialist millionaires. The satirical bi-weekly *Private Eye* is a much-loved institution that prides itself on printing the stories the rest of the press won't touch, and on surviving the consequent stream of libel suits. Scottish monthlies include the *Scottish Field*, a low-brow version of England's *Tatler*, covering the interests and pursuits of the landed gentry. In Wales, *Planet*, an English-language overview of the arts, history and politics, is the best of the bunch.

Australians and New Zealanders in London will be gratified to find the weekly free magazine *TNT*, which provides news from home as well as adverts for jobs, accommodation and events in the capital. For **North Americans**, *USA Today* and the *International Herald Tribune* are widely distributed, as are the magazines *Time* and *Newsweek*.

Television and radio

There are five main national **TV channels**: the publicly funded BBC1 and BBC2, and the independent commercial channels, ITV1, Channel 4, and Five. The **BBC** continues to maintain its worldwide reputation for in-house quality productions, ranging from expensive costume dramas to intelligent documentaries, split between the avowedly mainstream BBC1 and the more rarefied fare of BBC2. The commercial channel **ITV1** is divided between various regional companies, all producing light, generally undemanding fare, though its high-quality drama productions have proved increasingly successful. These are complemented by the quirkier **Channel 4**, which is replaced in Wales by the split Welsh- and English-language output of **S4C**. Eclectic **Five**, a mix of sport, TV movies and general-interest stuff, can't be received in some parts of the country. A plethora of satellite and, in the cities, cable channels are also available; the dominant force is Rupert Murdoch's **Sky** organization, which offers, among other channels, blanket sports coverage that plays wall-to-wall in pubs the length of the country. The satellite channel **BBC News 24** offers rolling news.

The **BBC radio** network broadcasts five main national channels, originating largely from London: Radio 1 (pop and dance music), Radio 2 (mainstream pop, rock and light music), Radio 3 (classical music), Radio 4 (current affairs, arts and drama) and Radio 5 Live (sports, news and talk). The award-winning BBC Radio Scotland and gentler BBC Radio Wales – both only available in their own countries – offer a refreshingly un-English perspective on news, politics, arts, music, travel and sport. National **commercial radio** stations include Virgin (pop music), TalkSport (phone-ins, not just about sport) and Classic FM (snippets of classical music with a DJ). There's a dense web of **local radio** stations – both BBC and commercial, on FM and AM – which vary from lively community mouthpieces to faceless CD-spinning operations.

The websites of **Voice of America** (ⓦ www.voa.gov) and **Radio Canada** (ⓦ www.rcinet.ca) list all the frequencies they broadcast on; they both stream material online, as does **Radio Australia** (ⓦ www.abc.net.au/ra), which doesn't broadcast to Europe.

Opening hours, public holidays and visitor attractions

General shop hours are Mon–Sat 9am–5.30 or 6pm, although you'll find some places open late one day a week in the larger towns. The big supermarkets tend to open earlier and close later, some staying open through the night. On Sundays, supermarkets and high-street stores can legally open for six hours – though in the case of the latter, this tends only to happen in larger centres and out-of-town shopping complexes; supermarkets tend to open from 10am to 4pm, while most stores choose to open from 11am to 5pm.

By contrast, many provincial towns still retain an **early-closing day**, when shops close at 1pm; Wednesday is the favourite. Bear in mind that in more traditionally minded areas, such as the Highlands and Islands of Scotland and parts of Wales, you'll find precious little open on a Sunday.

Not all motorway **service areas** are open 24 hours, although you can usually get fuel around the clock in larger towns and cities.

Most **visitor attractions** in England and Wales are open daily from Easter to October; many close all winter, and those that don't are often closed one or two days a week, though the major museums are open daily all year. In Scotland only the biggest museums and most popular indoor attractions are open in winter, although ruins and gardens are normally accessible year-round. We've given full details throughout the guide of opening hours for every attraction.

Public holidays

In **England and Wales** banks, businesses and most shops close on **public holidays**, though large supermarkets and many tourist attractions do not (although they may keep Sunday hours, as do most transport companies). Confusingly, several of England's public holidays are usually referred to as "**bank holidays**", and in most people's minds both terms mean the same.

In **Scotland**, "bank holidays" mean just that – they are literally days when the banks are closed, rather than general public holidays, and they vary from year to year (although cover much the same ground as in England).

Visitor attractions

Many of Britain's most treasured sites – from castles, abbeys and great houses to tracts of protected landscape – come under the control of the private **National Trust** and **National Trust for Scotland**. Both organizations charge an entry fee for the majority of their sites, and these can be quite high, especially for the more grandiose estates. If you think you'll be visiting more than half a dozen of their properties, denoted "**NT**" or "**NTS**" in the guide, it's worth taking out annual membership (NT £34; NTS £32), which allows free entry to both sets of properties, although you'll only receive mailings from the one that you join. A great many of Britain's other sites are controlled by the state-run **English Heritage**, **Historic Scotland**, and **CADW Welsh Historic Monuments**, which we've denoted as "**EH**", "**HS**" and "**CADW**" respectively. Annual membership of any one of the three (EH £34; HS £30; CADW £27) entitles you to half-price entry to properties run by the other two. All five also offer various deals on short-period season tickets and family passes.

A lot of **stately homes** remain in the hands of the landed gentry, who tend to charge in the region of £5 for admission to edited highlights of their domain – even more if, as at Longleat, they've added some theme-park attractions to the historic pile. Many other old buildings, albeit rarely the most momentous structures, are owned by the local authorities, which are generally more lenient with their admission charges, sometimes allowing free access. You may find that a history museum or a similar collection has been installed in the local castle or half-rebuilt ruin, and in these cases there's usually a modest entry charge. However, **municipal art galleries and museums** are often free, as are many of the great **state museums** – for example the British Museum and National Gallery in London, Cardiff's National Museum of Wales, and the National Museum of Scotland and National Gallery of Scotland in Edinburgh. On the other hand, many cash-starved institutions are nowadays obliged to request voluntary donations, as are several **cathedrals**. Most cathedrals charge a pound or two for admission to the most beautiful parts of the structure – usually the chapter-house or cloister. **Churches**, increasingly, are

Public holidays

January 1 (New Year's Day) England, Scotland, Wales

January 2 Scotland

Good Friday & **Easter Monday** (these bracket a weekend in late March or early April) England, Scotland, Wales

First Monday in May (May Day) England, Scotland, Wales

Last Monday in May (May Bank Holiday) England, Scotland, Wales

First Monday in August Scotland

Last Monday in August (August Bank Holiday) England, Scotland, Wales

December 25 & **26** (Christmas Day & Boxing Day) England, Scotland, Wales

Note that if Jan 1, Dec 25 or Dec 26 falls on a Saturday or Sunday, the holiday is shifted to the Monday immediately following.

kept locked except for services, but when they are open, entry is free.

You will certainly have to pay to visit any of Britain's burgeoning **heritage museums**, which in some instances are large multi-building sites staffed by people in period costume, but more often consist of interactive displays. Tickets for these can cost anywhere between £5 and £10, and expense is not necessarily an indication of quality. However, the most expensive attractions in Britain are those aimed squarely at tourists with cash to spend: Madame Tussaud's in London, the country's number one earner of foreign cash, now charges around £18 for basic admission.

The majority of fee-charging attractions have **reductions** for senior citizens, the unemployed, full-time students and children under 16, with under-5s being admitted free almost everywhere. Proof of eligibility will be required in most cases, though even the flintiest desk clerk will probably take on trust the age of a babe-in-arms. The entry charges given in the guide are the full adult charges; as a rule, adult reductions are in the range of 25–35 percent, while reductions for children are around 50 percent.

Finally, foreign visitors planning on seeing more than a dozen stately homes, monuments or gardens might find it worthwhile to buy a **Great British Heritage Pass** (Ⓦ www.visitbritain.com/heritagepass), which gives free admission to some six hundred sites, many of which are not run by the big five. Costing from £35/US$54 for seven days, it can be purchased through most travel agents at home, on arrival at any large UK airport, or from major tourist offices across Britain.

Heritage organizations

CADW ℡ 029/2050 0200,
Ⓦ www.cadw.wales.gov.uk
English Heritage ℡ 020/7973 3000,
Ⓦ www.english-heritage.org.uk
Historic Scotland ℡ 0131/668 8600,
Ⓦ www.historic-scotland.gov.uk
National Trust ℡ 020/7973 3000
Ⓦ www.nationaltrust.org.uk
National Trust for Scotland ℡ 0131/243 9330,
Ⓦ www.nts.org.uk

Festivals and events

Britain offers a huge range of organized annual events, reflecting both vibrant contemporary culture and well-marketed heritage.

In England, you'll often find grand spectacles such as the courtly pageant of Trooping the Colour or the annual rowing race between Oxford and Cambridge universities are given undue prominence by keen tourism marketers, while the riotous street party of the Notting Hill Carnival, or the summer Promenade concerts, Europe's most egalitarian high-class music season, are much better fun. In Scotland many visitors home straight in on Highland Games and other tartan-draped theatricals, but it's worth bearing in mind that there's more to Scotland than this – not least the fabulous Edinburgh Festival, an arts celebration unrivalled in size and variety in the world. Wales has a strong and alluring cultural identity: *eisteddfodau* – cultural festivals large and small that are held all over the country – are the most Welsh of events, incorporating theatre, dance, music (from rock to traditional choirs), debate, ceremony, readings of poetry and song and exhibitions.

In addition, every major town in Britain has its own local arts festival, the best of which, along with various other local fairs and commemorative shows, are mentioned in the main part of the guide; we've also listed the very biggest ones below.

To see Britain at its most idiosyncratic, take a look at one of the numerous regional celebrations that perpetuate **ancient customs**, the origins and meanings of which have often been lost or conveniently overlooked. The sight of the entire population of a village scrambling around a field after a barrel or chasing a cheese downhill is not easily forgotten. Some of these strange rituals are mentioned in the guide and included in the list below. Bear in mind that at a few of the smaller, more obscure events casual onlookers are not always welcome. If in doubt, check with the local tourist office. We've also included the main **sports events**, which may often be difficult to get tickets for, but are invariably televised.

Events calendar

Mid- to late Jan Celtic Connections, Glasgow. A major celebration of Celtic and folk music held in venues across the city.

Jan 25 Burns Night: Scots worldwide get stuck into haggis, whisky and vowel-grinding poetry to commemorate Scotland's greatest poet, Robert Burns.

Mid-Feb Chinese New Year. Festivities in London's and Manchester's Chinatown districts.

Feb–March Six Nations Rugby tournament between Scotland, England, Wales, Ireland, France and Italy.

March 1 St David's Day. Celebrations all over Wales.

March 1 Whuppity Scourie, Lanark. Local children race round the church beating each other with home-made paper weapons in a representation (it's thought) of the chasing away of winter or the warding off of evil spirits.

Mid-March Cheltenham Gold Cup meeting. England's premier national hunt horseracing event.

End of March or early April University Boat Race. Hugely popular rowing contest on the Thames, between Oxford and Cambridge.

Shrove Tuesday Purbeck Marblers and Stonecutters Day, Corfe Castle, Dorset. Ritual football game through the streets of the village. The rest of the country eats pancakes.

Maundy Thursday The Queen dispenses the Royal Maundy Money (at a different cathedral annually).

Easter Monday Hare Pie Scramble and Bottle-Kicking, Hallaton, Leicestershire.

Late March or early April Grand National meeting, Aintree, Liverpool. Cruelly testing steeplechase that entices most of Britain's population into the betting shops.

April Scottish Grand National, Ayr. Not quite as testing as the English equivalent steeplechase, but an important event on the Scottish racing calendar nonetheless.

April 6 Tartan Day. Over-hyped celebration of ancestry by North Americans of Scottish descent on the anniversary of the Declaration of Arbroath in 1320. Ignored by most Scots in Scotland, other than journalists.

May English FA Cup Final. The deciding contest in the country's premier football tournament is currently without a home of its own. For the time being, the English national game's most important fixture will be held in the Welsh capital, Cardiff.

May Scottish Cup Final in Glasgow. Scotland's premier football event.

May 1 Padstow Hobby Horse, Padstow, Cornwall. Processions, music and dancing through the streets.

May 8 Helston Furry Dance, Helston, Cornwall.

Last Monday in May Cheese Rolling, Brockworth, Gloucestershire. Pursuit of a cheese wheel down a murderous incline – one of the weirdest customs in England.

Late May Hay-on-Wye Festival of Literature. London's literati flock to the Welsh borders for a week.

Last week in May St David's Cathedral Festival. Superb setting for classical concerts and recitals.

Last week in May Chelsea Flower Show, Royal Hospital, Chelsea, London. Essential event for Britain's green-fingered legions.

Late May and early June Bath International Festival. International arts jamboree.

May–July Glyndebourne Opera Festival, East Sussex. The classiest and most snobbish arts festival in Britain.

June Aldeburgh Festival. Jamboree of classical music held on the Suffolk Coast. Established by Benjamin Britten.

June Shinty Camanachd Cup Final. The climax of the season for Scotland's own stick-and-ball game, normally held in one of the main Highland towns. Also marks the beginning of the Highland Games season across the Highlands, northeast and Argyll.

First week in June Eisteddfod Genedlaethol Urdd. The largest youth festival in Europe, alternating between North and South Wales.

First week in June Derby week, Epsom racecourse, Surrey. The world's most expensive horseflesh competing in the Derby, the Coronation Cup and the Oaks.

First Friday in June Cotswold Olimpicks, Chipping Campden, Gloucestershire. Rustic sports festival and torchlight procession.

First or second Saturday in June Trooping the Colour, Horse Guards Parade, London. Equestrian pageantry for the Queen's Official Birthday.

Mid-June Cardiff Singer of the World competition. Huge, televised week-long music festival, with a star-studded list of international competitors.

Mid-June Appleby Horse Fair, Appleby-in-Westmorland, Cumbria.

Mid-June Royal Ascot, Berkshire. High-class horseracing attended by high-class people.

End of June World Worm-Charming Championships, Willaston, Cheshire.

Last week of June Glastonbury Festival, Somerset. Hugely popular festival, with international bands, indie music and loads of hippies.

Last week of June and first week of July Lawn Tennis Championships, Wimbledon, London. Queues are phenomenal even for the early rounds, and you need to know a freemason or ex-champion to get in to the big games.

Late June Royal Highland Agricultural Show, at Ingliston near Edinburgh.

July Scottish Open Golf Championship, held at a different venue each year. Also Highland Games at Caithness, Elgin, Glengarry, North Uist, Inverness, Inveraray, Mull, Lewis, Durness, Lochaber, Dufftown, Halkirk.

Early July Llangollen International Music Eisteddfod. Over 12,000 participants from all over the world, including choirs, dancers, folk singers, groups and instrumentalists.

Early July Glasgow International Jazz Festival, and T in the Park – the latter Scotland's biggest outdoor music event, held in Glasgow's Strathclyde Park with a star-studded line-up of contemporary bands.

First week in July Henley Royal Regatta, Oxfordshire. Rowing event attended by much the same crew as populates the grandstands at Ascot.

First week of July Tynwald Ceremony, St Johns, Isle of Man.

Second weekend in July Gûyl Werin y Cnapan, Ffostrasol, near Lampeter, Ceredigion. The best folk and Celtic music festival in the world.

Second week in July York Early Music Festival. The premier early music festival lasts for ten days.

Second or Third Saturday in July Durham Miners' Gala, Durham.

Mid-July British Open Golf Championship, variable venue. The season's last Grand Slam golf tournament.

Third week in July Swan Upping, River Thames from Sunbury to Pangbourne. Ceremonial registering of the Thames cygnets.

Last week in July Royal Tournament, Earl's Court Exhibition Centre, London. Precision military displays.

Last week in July Cambridge Folk Festival. Biggest event of its kind in England.

Late July WOMAD, Reading. Three-day world music and dance festival.

Last week in July to first week in Aug Cardiff Festival. Incorporates music, art, drama, opera, literature and street entertainment.

July to early Sept The Promenade Concerts ("The Proms"), Royal Albert Hall, London. Classical music concerts ending in the fervently patriotic Last Night of the Proms.

Aug Edinburgh Festival. One of the world's great arts jamborees.

First week in Aug Royal National Eisteddfod. Wales's biggest single annual event: fun, very impressive and worth seeing if only for the overblown pageantry.

Early Aug The two-day Lammas Fair at St Andrews, the oldest medieval market in the country.

Early Aug Sidmouth Folk Festival. Folk and roots performers from around the world, plus theatre and dance.

Weekend in mid-Aug Bristol Balloon Fiesta. Hundreds of balloons take to the skies early morning and evening.

Aug Bank Hol Notting Hill Carnival, around Notting Hill, West London. Vivacious celebration by London's Caribbean community – plenty of music, food and floats.

Aug Bank Hol Reading Festival, Berkshire. Three-day hard rock jamboree.

Last Sun in Aug Plague Memorial, Eyam, Derbyshire.

Early Sept Ben Nevis Race (for amateurs), held on the first weekend in the month, running to the top of Scotland's highest mountain and back again. Also Highland Games at Braemar.

First Monday after Sept 4 Abbots Bromley Horn Dance, Abbots Bromley, Staffordshire. Vaguely pagan mass dance in mock-medieval costume – one of the most famous ancient customs.

Early Sept to early Nov Blackpool Illuminations, Lancashire. Five miles of extravagant light displays.

Oct Swansea Festival of Music and the Arts. Concerts, jazz, drama, opera, ballet and art events throughout the city.

Late Oct Glenfiddich Piping Championships at Blair Atholl for the world's top ten solo pipers.

Late Oct to early Nov Huddersfield Contemporary Music Festival. One of Europe's premier showcases for up-to-the-minute highbrow music.
First Sun in Nov London to Brighton Veteran Car Rally. Ancient machines lumbering down the A23 to the seafront.
Nov 5 Bonfire Night. Nationwide fireworks and bonfires commemorating the foiling of Guy Fawkes' Gunpowder Plot in 1605 – especially raucous celebrations at York (Fawkes' birthplace), Ottery St Mary in Devon and at Lewes, East Sussex.
Mid-Nov Lord Mayor's Procession and Show, the City of London. Cavalcade to mark the inauguration of the new mayor.

Nov 30 St Andrew's Day, celebrating Scotland's patron saint.
Dec 31 New Year Walk-In, Llanwrtyd Wells, Powys. A boozy stagger around the town.
Dec 31 Tar Barrels Parade, Allendale Town, Northumberland.
Dec 31 & Jan 1 Hogmanay and Ne'er Day: traditionally more important to the Scots than Christmas, known for the custom of "first-footing", when groups of revellers troop into neighbours' houses at midnight bearing gifts. More popular these days are huge and highly organized street parties, most notably in Edinburgh, but also in Aberdeen, Glasgow and other centres.

Sports and outdoor pursuits

No matter where you are in Britain, you're never far from a stretch of countryside where you can lose the crowds on a brief walk or cycle ride. For tougher specimens, there are numerous long-distance footpaths, as well as opportunities for the more extreme disciplines of rock climbing and potholing (caving). On the coast and many of the inland lakes you can follow the more urbane pursuits of sailing and windsurfing, and there are plenty of fine beaches for less structured fresh-air activities or just slobbing around.

Walking and climbing

Walking routes trace many of Britain's wilder areas, amid landscapes varied enough to suit anyone. More sedate walkers will be happy enough in England, where many of the footpaths traverse moorlands, but if you're after more demanding exercise, or a feeling of isolation, head for Wales or Scotland. Welsh Snowdonia and the Scottish Highlands offer Britain's best **climbing** and have acted as training grounds for some of the world's greatest mountaineers.

Numerous short walks and several major walks are covered in the guide – however, you should use these notes only as general outlines and always in conjunction with a good **map**. Where possible we have given details of the best maps to use – in most cases one of the Ordnance Survey (OS) series (see p.23) – along with advice, leaflets and specialist guidebooks from tourist offices and shops in walking areas. In England and Wales you need to keep to established routes as you'll often be crossing private land, even within the National Parks: all OS maps mark public rights of way. Scotland, in contrast, has a tradition of **free public access** to most of the countryside, restricted only at certain times of the year.

In England

England's finest **walking areas** are the granite moorlands and spectacular coastlines of **Devon and Cornwall** in the southwest, and the highlands of the north – the low limestone and millstone crags of the **Peak District**, between Sheffield and Manchester; the **Yorkshire Dales**, the stretch of the Pennines to the north of the **Peak District**; the **North York Moors**, a bleak, treeless

Safety in the mountains

British **mountains** are not high by European standards, but, due to rapid weather changes, they are potentially extremely dangerous and should be treated with respect. Every year, in every season, climbers and hill walkers die on mountains in Scotland, Wales and the English Lake District. If the weather looks as if it's closing in, get down fast. It is essential that you are properly equipped – even for what appears to be an easy expedition in apparently settled weather – with proper warm and waterproof layered clothing, supportive footwear and adequate maps, a compass (which you should know how to use) and food. Always leave word of your route and what time you expect to return; and remember to contact the person again to let them know that you are back. And don't rely on your mobile phone: coverage in the mountains can often be patchy.

upland to the east of the Pennines; and the glaciated Cumbrian Mountains, better known as the **Lake District**. On summer weekends the more accessible reaches of these regions can get very crowded with day-trippers, but at any time of the year you'll find yourself in relative isolation if you undertake one of the **Long Distance Footpaths (LDPs)**. Defined as any route over twenty miles long, LDPs exist all over the country – the most famous are the Pennine Way and the South West Coast Path – and are marked at frequent intervals with an acorn waymarker. **Youth hostels** are littered along most routes, though you may need a tent for some of the more heroic hikes.

In Scotland

The whole of **Scotland** offers good opportunities for gentle hill walking, from the smooth, grassy hills and moors of the **Southern Uplands** to the wild and rugged country of the northwest. Scotland has three **Long Distance Footpaths (LDPs)**, each of which takes days to walk, though you can of course just cover sections of them. The **Southern Upland Way** crosses Scotland from coast to coast in the south, and is the country's longest at 212 miles; the best known is the **West Highland Way**, a 95-mile hike from Glasgow to Fort William via Loch Lomond and Glen Coe; and the gentler **Speyside Way**, in Aberdeenshire, is a mere thirty miles. The green signposts of the Scottish Rights of Way Society point to these and many other cross-country routes; while in the wilder parts the accepted

freedom to roam allows extensive mountain walking, rock climbing, orienteering and allied activities.

Scotland's main **climbing areas** are in the Highlands, which boast many challenging peaks as well as great hill walks. There are 279 mountains over 3000ft (914m) in Scotland, known as **Munros** after the man who first classified them: many walkers "collect" them, and on a day of what is called "Munro-bagging", it's possible to conquer several. Serious climbers will probably head for **Glen Coe** or **Torridon** which offer difficult routes in spectacular surroundings. These and some of the other finest Highland areas (Lawers, Kintail, West Affric) are in the ownership of the National Trust for Scotland, while Blaven and Ladhar Bheinn (Knoydart) are John Muir Trust properties; both allow year-round access. Elsewhere there may be restricted access during lambing (dogs are particularly unwelcome during April and May) and deer-stalking seasons (mid-August to the third week in October). The **booklet** *Heading for the Scottish Hills* (published by the Scottish Mountaineering Club or "SMC") provides information on all areas.

In Wales

Wales's best **walking country** is to be found within its three national parks. Almost the whole of the northwestern corner of Wales is taken up with the **Snowdonia National Park**, a dozen of the country's highest peaks separated by dramatic glacial valleys and laced with hundreds of miles of ridge and moorland paths. From Snowdonia, the Cambrian Mountains stretch south to the

Brecon Beacons National Park, with its striking sandstone scarp at the head of the South Wales coalfield, and lush, cave-riddled limestone valleys to the south. One hundred and seventy miles of Wales's southwestern peninsula make up the third park – the **Pembrokeshire Coast National Park**, best explored by the **Pembrokeshire Coast Path** that traverses the cliff tops, frequently dipping down into secluded coves. This is only one of Wales's four frequently walked **Long Distance Paths** – the other three LDPs are the 168-mile-long **Offa's Dyke Path** that traces the England–Wales border; the 274-mile **Cambrian Way**, cutting north–south over the Cambrian Mountains, and **Glyndŵr's Way**, which weaves through mid-Wales for 120 miles.

As well as being superb walking country, Wales offers some of Britain's best **rock climbing** and some challenging scrambles – ascents that fall somewhere between walks and climbs, requiring some use of your hands. There are a couple of noted climbing spots around the Pembrokeshire coast and in the Brecon Beacons but the vast majority are in Snowdonia, with its predominance of low-lying crags and easy access. The best general **guide** for experienced climbers is *Rock Climbing in Snowdonia* by Paul Williams (Constable).

Walking holiday specialists

C-N-Do Scotland ☎01786/445703, ⓦwww.cndoscotland.com. Munro-bagging for novices and experts, in small groups and with qualified leaders, as well as day-long winter skills and navigation courses.
Explore Britain ☎01740/650900, ⓦwww.xplorebritain.com. Guided or independent walking holidays countrywide with luggage transfer.
Footpath Holidays ☎01985/840049, ⓦwww.footpath-holidays.com. Packages to various hill and coastal districts, with experienced group leaders.
Glen Coe Mountain Sport ☎01855/811472, ⓦwww.glencoe-mountain-sport.co.uk. Year-round programme of gentle walks and scrambles on Skye, and around Glen Coe and Ben Nevis.
HF Walking Holidays ☎020/8905 9556, ⓦwww.hfholidays.co.uk. A wide choice of locations and lodging in comfortable country houses.
Instep Walking Holidays ☎01903/766475,

ⓦwww.instephols.co.uk. Self-guided holidays with accommodation in small country hotels and guest houses.
Sherpa Expeditions ☎020/8577 2717, ⓦwww.sherpa-walking-holidays.co.uk. At-your-own-pace, self-guided walks between country pubs.
Walkabout Scotland ☎0131/661 7168, ⓦwww.walkaboutscotland.com. A great way to get a taste of hiking in the Highlands, with guided hillwalking day-trips from Edinburgh for £40 per person, with all transport included.

Cycling

There has been a boom in the sale of mountain **bikes** and a rise in the number of towns and cities that have incorporated designated cycle routes into their traffic schemes. However, cyclists may find that in some areas (especially the cities) motorists treat them with some disrespect. The organization Sustrans (ⓦwww.sustrans.co.uk) is going some way towards addressing this, and other problems, with public education programmes and campaigns for cycle paths and cyclists' rights.

Surprisingly, **helmets** are not compulsory in Britain – but if you're hellbent on tackling the congestion, pollution and aggression of city traffic, get one and a secure **lock** too: cycle theft is an organized and highly effective racket (it's always a good idea to make a note of your frame number in case you have to report a theft to the police). You do have to have a **rear reflector** and front and back **lights** when riding at night, and are not allowed to carry children without a special child seat. It's also illegal to cycle on pavements (sidewalks), and in most public parks.

Bike rental is available at cycle shops in most large towns, and at villages within national parks and other scenic areas; the addresses and telephone numbers of these appear in the relevant sections of the *Guide*. Expect to pay in the region of £10–20 per day for something sturdy, with discounts for longer periods.

Cycle routes

Britain already has several thousand miles of the **National Cycle Network** in place, with Sustrans dedicated to expanding that still more. A large proportion of the network is

Carrying your bike on public transport

The majority of **airlines** will carry bicycles as part of your luggage allowance on plane journeys, although protruding parts, such as pedals and handlebars, have to be removed, and the tyres deflated; some carriers also require you to stash the machine in a bike bag or cardboard cover. Check with your airline well in advance to find out exactly what their terms and conditions are, and bear in mind that you may have to pay excess baggage. Transporting cycles by **ferry** is also free, but a lot more straightforward; you just wheel them on and off, and reservations are not normally required.

Carrying your bike by **train** is a good way of getting to the interesting parts of Britain without a lot of stressful or boring pedalling. For some reason, however, rail companies seem determined on making life difficult for cyclists by slapping on hefty surcharges. Most suburban trains will carry cycles outside morning and evening rush hours (generally 7.30–9.30am & 4–7pm), but bikes are not allowed at all on some express trains, while those that do accept cycles charge between £1 and £3; this usually has to be paid at least 24 hours in advance, and for each separate leg of the trip, which can work out to be ridiculously expensive if your journey involves a couple of changes. See p.18 for details of **Eurostar**'s policy on transporting bikes.

made up of quiet backroads, dubbed "Cycleways", but more than half runs along disused railways and canal towpaths, including the showpiece section connecting the cities of Bath and Bristol. Aside from these, the backroads of rural Britain (those labelled with the prefix "B") make infinitely more enjoyable routes than trunk routes (or "A" roads), with generally amiable gradients and a sufficient density of pubs and B&Bs to keep the days manageable. Your main problem out in the countryside will be getting hold of any spare parts – only inner tubes and tyres are easy to find.

Off-road cycling is popular in the highland walking areas, but cyclists should remember to keep to rights of way designated on maps as Bridleways, BOATs ("Byways Open To All Traffic") or RUPFs ("Roads Used As Public Footpaths") and to pass walkers at considerate speeds. Footpaths, unless otherwise marked, are for pedestrian use only. Other rules of the road to bear in mind are that cycles are not permitted on motorways (labelled with the prefix "M").

Armed with a detailed OS **map** of any area, you can improvise scenic routes of your own that avoid the main roads – better still, most good bookshops stock a range of **cycling guides**, featuring suggestions for rides of varying length, with coloured maps and detailed route descriptions.

With more time, you may want to take on one of Britain's challenging **long-distance routes**. The Cyclists' Touring Club, or CTC (ⓦ www.ctc.org.uk), publishes special maps for some of these, and supplies members with touring and technical advice as well as insurance. The classic cross-Britain route is from Land's End, in the far southwest of England, to John O'Groats, on the northeast tip of Scotland – roughly a thousand miles that can be covered in two to three weeks, depending on which of the three CTC-recommended routes you choose. Other tempting long-distance tours could take you around the Yorkshire Dales, Pennines, and Peak District, around Dartmoor and the Cornish coast, or across the austere North York Moors.

Cycling holidays

For those who want a guaranteed hassle-free **cycling holiday**, there are various companies offering easy-going packages. These generally include transport of your gear to each night's halt, pre-booked accommodation, detailed route instructions, a packed lunch and back-up support. Most companies offer some budget cycling holidays, with hostels or B&Bs instead of hotels.
Acorn Activities ⓣ 0870/740 5055, ⓦ www.acornactivities.co.uk. Weekend and one-

week tours, with bikes, accommodation, luggage transportation and maps provided.

Bespoke Highland Tours ☏0141/342 4576, ⓦwww.scotland-inverness.co.uk/bht-main.htm. Organizes cycle touring in the Highlands and Islands, using a reliable and long-standing network of B&Bs and hostels, and arranges transport links and baggage transfer.

Bike Breaks ☏0151/722 8050, ⓦwww.byways-breaks.com. Tours of varying length in the Cheshire and Shropshire countryside.

Compass Holidays ☏01242/250642, ⓦwww.compass-holidays.com. Guided tours in the Cotswolds, the Lake District, Cornwall and Warwickshire.

Country Lanes ☏01590/622627, ⓦwww.countrylanes.co.uk. Tours in the New Forest, the Cotswolds and the Lake District.

Holiday Lakeland ☏016973/71871, ⓦwww.holiday-lakeland.co.uk. Guided and independent tours of two to five nights in the north of England, focused on the Pennines and the Lake District.

Rough Tracks ☏0700/056 0749, ⓦwww.rough-tracks.co.uk. Mountain bike and road weekend tours across the country, as well as bike maintenance weekends.

Saddle Skedaddle ☏0191/265 1110, ⓦwww.skedaddle.co.uk. Highly recommended cycle specialist offering a wide range of cycling holidays from weekend trips to the Peak District to week-long coast-to-coast expeditions.

Scottish Cycle Safaris ☏0131/556 5560, ⓦwww.cyclescotland.co.uk. Fully organized cycle tours at all levels, from camping to country house hotels, with a good range of bikes available for rent, from tandems to childrens' bikes.

Beaches

Britain is ringed by fine **beaches** and bays, the best of which are readily accessible by public transport – though of course that means they tend to get very busy in high summer. For a combination of decent climate and good sand, southwest **England** is the best area, especially the coast of north Cornwall and Devon. The beaches of England's southern coast become more pebbly as you approach the southeastern corner of the country – resorts round here are more garish than their southwestern counterparts. Moving up the east coast, the East Anglian shore is predominantly pebbly and very exposed, making it ideal for those who want to escape the crowds rather than

bask in the sun, while right up in the northeast there are some wonderful sandy strands and old-fashioned seaside resorts, though the North Sea breezes often require a degree of stoicism. Over in the northwest, the inland hills of Cumbria are a greater attraction than anything on the coast, though Blackpool has a certain appeal as the apotheosis of the "kiss-me-quick" holiday town.

Many of **Scotland's** beaches and bays are deserted even in high summer – perhaps hardly surprising given the bracing winds and icy water. Though you're unlikely to come here for a beach holiday, it's worth sampling one or two beaches, even if you never shed as much as a sweater. A rash of slightly melancholy seaside towns lies within easy reach of Glasgow, while on the east coast, the relatively low cliffs and miles of sandy beaches are ideal for walking. Despite the low temperature of the water, the beaches in the northeast figure on surfers' itineraries, attracting enthusiasts from all over Europe. Perhaps the most beautiful beaches of all are to be found on Scotland's islands: endless, isolated stretches that on a sunny day can seem the epitome of the Scottish Hebridean dream.

In **Wales** the best areas to head to for sunbathing and swimming are the Gower peninsula, the Pembrokeshire coast, the Lly̅n and the southwest coast of Anglesey. The southwest-facing beaches of Wales offer the best conditions for surfing, key spots being Rhossili, at the western tip of the Gower, and Whitesands Bay near St David's. Windsurfers tend to congregate at Barmouth, Borth, around the Pembrokeshire coast and at Mumbles. Though the north coast has more resorts than any other section of the Welsh coastline, its beaches are certainly not the most attractive, nor is it a good place to swim.

It has to be said that Britain's beaches are not the cleanest in Europe, and some of those that the British authorities declare to be acceptable actually fall below **EU standards**. The Marine Conservation Society (ⓦwww.goodbeachguide.co.uk) monitors bathing-water quality, as does ⓦwww.blueflag.org.

Surfing

For most people, **surfing** in Britain means surfing in Newquay, and while it's true that the southwest of England is the heartland of the British surf scene, it would be a mistake to think that there aren't decent waves elsewhere. You don't get the sunshine of Hawaii, and the waves are steely-grey rather than turquoise-blue, but there are world-class waves to be found if you know where to go. The major difference between Britain and the States or Australia is, of course, the water temperature, which even in midsummer rarely exceeds 15°C. For this reason, if you're planning to surf in the UK make sure you have a good wetsuit, and ideally a 5/3mm "steamer", wetsuit boots and, outside summer, gloves and a hood.

In **England**, the northeast coast, from Yorkshire to Northumberland, has a growing population of hardy surfers willing to endure low temperatures to surf clean northerly groundswells. The coastline here is often spectacular, and although the more popular breaks, such as Saltburn, are now crowded, you can find relative isolation off the beaten track. Nevertheless, the southwest, or more specifically Newquay, Cornwall, remains the country's undisputed surf Mecca. Visitors are often amazed to see the hype surrounding this self-styled "surf city". In summer, every other male seems to be a "surfie", sporting regulation bleached hair and designer gear, but the majority only turn up to cruise surf babes. It can still be hectic out in the water though, especially at the main break, Fistral, which regularly hosts international contests. Head out of town, however, and things quieten down noticeably. Try spots such as Perranporth or Polzeath, or travel up to Devon, which also gets decent waves, despite the overcrowding of its main break, Croyde.

Surfing in **Wales** tends to be concentrated on the south coast, around the Gower peninsula, which boasts a good variety of beach and reef breaks, and a lively social scene. One thing to bear in mind if you surf here, though, is the enormous tidal range of the Bristol Channel – it can be up to thirteen metres, and this can have a major effect on the surf. The tidal range drops as you head west towards Pembrokeshire, where the coastline becomes more scenic, and numbers in the water diminish considerably. This area, comprising Britain's only coastal national park, is where you'll find the most consistent surf beach in Wales, Freshwater West, as well as seals, porpoise, dolphins, basking sharks and sunfish in the water. Washed by the Irish Sea, the west coast gets much less surf than the south, with the waves breaking mostly in winter. Aberystwyth is the main centre hereabouts, and its local breaks tend to be pretty busy. Heading further north, you come to the Llŷn peninsula, in the shadow of Snowdonia, where Hell's Mouth has the best and most consistent waves in North Wales.

Scotland may not seem the most promising destination for surfers, but it is fast gaining a reputation for the high quality of its breaks. The number one spot is Thurso on the north coast, which has hosted the European Surfing Championships, and has what is widely acknowledged to be one of the finest reef breaks in Europe. Many other good breaks lie within easy reach of large cities (eg Pease Bay, near Edinburgh, and Fraserburgh, near Aberdeen), while the spectacular west coast has numerous possibilities: try Sandwood Bay, the most isolated beach in Britain, or the waves of the Outer Hebrides. All are surrounded by stunning scenery, and you'd be unlucky to encounter another surfer for miles, which is an important consideration in itself.

Top twenty British breaks

Bamburgh Northumberland, northeast England. A wonderfully scenic quiet beach, with seals in the water and a spectacular castle as a backdrop.
Constantine Cornwall, southwest England. Picks up a lot of swell.
Croyde Bay Devon, southwest England. Good beach breaks, but crowds can be a problem.
Fistral Newquay, Cornwall, southwest England. Hype, crowds, but still a good wave if you can get one to yourself.
Freshwater West Pembrokeshire, South Wales. Quality beach and reef breaks. Beware of currents.
Hell's Mouth Llŷn Peninsula, North Wales. Popular, quality break.
Llangennith Gower, South Wales. Long beach with peaks along its length. Busy.

Newgale Pembrokeshire. South Wales. Two-mile-long beach with peaks along its length.

Pease Bay Near Dunbar, 26 miles east of Edinburgh, Scotland. A popular break suited to all abilities.

*Pete's Reef Gower, South Wales. Picks up most swells. Popular.

*Porthleven Cornwall, southwest England. Heavy reef break, heavy locals.

Machrihanish Bay Mull of Kintyre. Four miles of beach breaks on one of Scotland's loneliest peninsulas.

Sandwood Bay A day's hike south of Cape Wrath in Sutherland. Beach breaks on one of the most scenic and remote shorelines in Britain, only accessible on foot.

Sennen Cove Cornwall, southwest England. Picks up any swell going.

Saltburn Cleveland, northeast England. Another good beach break, with atmosphere to match.

*Skirza Harbour three miles south of John O'Groats, northeast Scotland. An excellent left-hand reef break on the far northeast tip of Scotland.

*Staithes Yorkshire, northeast England. Excellent reef breaks, crowded and jealously guarded by locals.

*Thurso East Just below the castle, Thurso, northern Scotland. One of the best right-hand reef breaks in Europe.

*Torrisdale Bay Bettyhill, on the north coast of the Scottish Highlands. An excellent right-hand rivermouth break.

*Valtos On the Uig peninsula, Lewis, Outer Hebrides, Scotland. A break on one of the Outer Hebrides' most exquisite shell-sand beaches.

*Experienced surfers only

Golf

Though England and Wales have an array of international-quality golf courses – Royal Lytham & St Annes, Wentworth and Sunningdale, to name a few – **golf** enthusiasts looking to play a round or two should aim for the home of the game, Scotland, where the sport is less elitist and more accessible than anywhere else in the world. Golf in its present form took shape in the fifteenth century on the dunes of Scotland's east coast, and today you'll find some of the oldest courses in the world on these early coastal sites, known as "links". It's often possible just to turn up and play, though it's sensible to phone ahead; booking is essential for the championship courses.

Public courses are owned by the local council, while **private** courses belong to a club. You can play on both – occasionally the private courses require that you are a member of another club, and the odd one asks for introductions from a member, but these rules are often waived for overseas visitors and all you need to do is pay a one-off fee. The cost of a round will set you back around £10 on a small nine-hole course, and more than £40 for many good-quality eighteen-hole courses. In remote areas the courses are sometimes unstaffed; just put the admission fee into the honesty box. Most courses have **resident professionals** who give lessons, and some rent equipment at reasonable rates.

Scotland's **championship** courses, which often host the British Open, are renowned for their immaculately kept greens and challenging holes. **St Andrews** is the top destination: it's the home of the Royal and Ancient Golf Club, the worldwide controlling body that regulates the rules of the game. Of its six courses, the Old Course is probably the most famous in the world; unlike many exclusive courses it is possible for anyone with a valid handicap certificate (under 24 for men, or 36 for women) to play a round, either by booking a tee-time well in advance or striking lucky in the daily lottery, which allocates half of each day's tee-times. All the St Andrews courses are operated by the St Andrews Links Trust (℡01334/466666, ⓦwww.standrews.org.uk). One of the easiest championship courses to get into is the notoriously tough **Carnoustie** in Angus (ⓦwww.carnoustiegolflinks.co.uk), though you should still try to book as far ahead as possible. Other championship courses include **Gleneagles** in Perthshire (ⓦwww.gleneagles.com/golf), **Royal Dornoch** in Sutherland (ⓦwww.royal-dornoch.com), and **Turnberry** in Ayrshire (ⓦwww.turnberry.co.uk/golf). Professional players consider **Muirfield** in Gullane, near Edinburgh (℡01620/842123; Tues & Thurs only) to be one of the most testing courses in the world and it's also one of the most elitist – women can play only if accompanied by a man, and they aren't allowed into the clubhouse. ⓦwww.scotlands-golf-courses.com has contacts, scorecards and maps of signature holes for most main courses.

If you're coming to Scotland primarily to play golf, it's worth shelling out for a ticket that gives you access to a number of courses in any one region. There's more information at ⓦwww.scottishgolf.com and ⓦwww.visitscotland.com/golf.

Spectator sports

As a quick glance at the national press will tell you, sport in Britain is a serious business. Football, rugby and cricket are the major spectator sports, and horseracing also has a big following. The calendar is chock-full of one-off quality sports events, ranging from the massed masochism of the London Marathon to the Wimbledon championship, one of the world's greatest tennis tournaments.

For the top international events it can be almost impossible to track down a **ticket** without resorting to the services of a grossly overcharging ticket agency. You can, though, fall back on TV or radio coverage. BBC Radio 5 Live has live commentaries on almost every major sporting event, while big international rugby and cricket matches are broadcast live (or as recorded highlights) on one or other TV channel. Unfortunately, a lot of TV sport is bought up by satellite channels, which means the only realistic place to watch them is in a pub that is relaying the action live on a big screen.

Football

Football (soccer) is the most passionately supported sport in the land; if you have the slightest interest in the game then catching a league or FA Cup fixture is a must. There are four league divisons, covering England and Wales only: Third, Second, First and, at the top of the pyramid, the twenty-club "Premiership" or **Premier League** (ⓦwww.premierleague.com). By far the most famous English club is Manchester United, although the premiership is full of big names: the London clubs Arsenal, Tottenham and Chelsea; Aston Villa from the Midlands; Leeds, Liverpool and Newcastle from the north. **Wales**'s big three teams are Cardiff, Wrexham and Swansea, all of which play in lower divisions. **Scotland** has its own separate league,

smaller than south of the border: Second, First and the **Scottish Premier League** or SPL (ⓦwww.scotprem.com), which is dominated by the two Glasgow clubs, Celtic and Rangers. Running concurrently with both leagues are cup competitions – the big ones are the **FA Cup** and the **Scottish Cup**, which culminate in the razzmatazz finals of both competitions, played on consecutive weekends in May. Top British clubs also take part in cup matches against European club sides, generally played midweek.

The team with the biggest following is Manchester United, whose matches are almost always a sell-out, regardless of how the team is playing. Of the other glamorous English clubs, Liverpool and Newcastle United also command so ardent a following that tickets for their matches are like gold dust. It's easy enough to get tickets, if booked in advance, for most other Premier League games, unless two local sides are playing each other. In Scotland, only the "Old Firm" clash between Rangers and Celtic is a certain full house.

The **football season** runs from mid-August to early May. Most **fixtures** kick off at 3pm on Saturday, though there are generally a few midweek evening games, and a sprinkling on Sunday afternoons too. **Tickets** cost from about £25 for Premiership games, falling to less than £15 in the lower divisions. The stadiums of Premiership teams are all-seater and the number of women and children attending matches has increased dramatically in recent years. Nonetheless, watching a match is an intense business, with a lot of foul language and an edge to the atmosphere. Being stuck in the middle of several thousand supporters as their team goes 3–0 down is not one of life's more uplifting experiences.

Cricket

In the glory days of the Empire the **English** – and to a lesser extent the Welsh and Scottish – took cricket to the colonies as a means of instilling gentlemanly values of fair play while administering a sound thrashing to the natives. These days the former colonies, such as Australia, the West Indies and India, all beat England on a regular basis, so to see the game at its best you should try to get into one of the series – comprising three, five or six **Test matches** – that are played each summer between England and a touring international team. These fixtures are played in the middle of the cricket season, which runs from April to September. Two Test matches are always played in London – one at Lord's, the other at The Oval. Other Test grounds nationwide are Trent Bridge (Nottingham), Old Trafford (Manchester), Headingley (Leeds), Edgbaston (Birmingham) and Chester-le-Street (near Durham). In tandem with the full-blown five-day Tests, there's also a series of **one-day internationals**, again held in venues around England.

Getting to see England play one of the big teams may be difficult unless you book months in advance. If you can't wangle your way into a Test, you could watch it live on TV (the Test series is always televised), listen to ball-by-ball commentary on BBC radio, or settle instead for an inter-county match, either in the **county championship** (these are four-day games) or in one of the three fast and furious one-day competitions: the Benson and Hedges Cup and the NatWest Trophy (both knockout competitions), or the CGU National league.

Prices for Test matches cost £15–40 per day; for one-day internationals you can expect to pay £20–50, but tickets for the sparsely attended county games start at as little as £7.

Rugby

Rugby gets its name from Rugby public school, near Coventry, where the game mutated from football in the nineteenth century. A rugby match may at times look like a bunch of weightlifters grappling each other in the mud – as the old joke goes, rugby is a hooligan's game played by gentlemen, while football is a gentlemen's game played by hooligans – but it is in reality highly tactical and athletic. What's more, England's rugby teams have represented the country with rather more success in the last few years than the cricket and football squads – not least by winning the World Cup in Australia in 2003.

There are two types of rugby played in Britain, both professional. Fifteen-a-side **Rugby Union** is very strong in working-class Wales, especially in the valleys of the former South Wales coalfields, and across much of central and southern England and the Scottish Borders. The season, which runs from September to the end of April, concludes with the **Pilkington Cup**, and includes international "Test" matches and the acclaimed Six Nations (a tournament between England, Scotland, Wales, Ireland, France and Italy). Big international games are played at Twickenham in London, Murrayfield in Edinburgh and the Millennium Stadium in Cardiff.

Thirteen-a-side **Rugby League** – a remarkably different (some would say tougher) game – is played almost exclusively in the north of England, the season finishing with the **Challenge Cup** in May and also including some international games; rugby league is one of the few sports in which there's a Great Britain team, rather than individual nation sides.

Unless you are affiliated to one or other rugby club, or willing to pay well over the odds at a ticket agency, it is tough to get a ticket for a big international game. For Union and League club games, however, there should be no problem getting tickets at the gate; expect to pay from £5.

Tennis

Tennis in Britain is synonymous with **Wimbledon**, the only Grand Slam

The rules of cricket

The **rules of cricket** are so complex that the official book runs to some twenty pages. The basics, however, are by no means as byzantine as the game's detractors make out.

There are two teams of **eleven players**. A team wins by scoring more **runs** than the other team and dismissing all the opposition – in other words, a team could score many runs more than the opposition, but still not win if the last enemy batsman doggedly stays in (this would mean the match was drawn). The match is divided into **innings**, during which one team bats and the other fields. The number of innings varies depending on the type of competition.

In the middle of the ground is a rectangular length of closely cropped grass. This is the **wicket**. At either end of it are three vertical bits of wood (each known as a **stump**) topped by two small cross pieces (each known as a **bail**). Together, this set of stumps and bails is – confusingly – also known as a wicket.

The batsmen's aim is to score as many "runs" as possible. The aim of the fielding side is to limit the runs scored and get all eleven batsmen "out", one by one. Two **umpires**, one standing behind the stumps at the bowler's end and one square on to the play at the batting end, are responsible for adjudicating if a batsman is out.

Two players from the batting side are on the pitch at any one time. The fielding side has a **bowler** (who "bowls" the ball at one of the batsman with a distinctive overarm delivery), a **wicket keeper** (who squats behind the batsman in line with the bowler) and nine **fielders** spread around the ground. Each innings is divided into **overs**, which consist of six balls bowled. After each over, the batsmen stay where they are but the wicket keeper changes ends, a different bowler comes on to bowl and the fielders move positions.

The batsmen **score runs** either by running up and down from wicket to wicket (each time they cross in the middle is one "run"), or by hitting the ball over the boundary rope: they get four runs if the ball crosses the boundary after having touched the ground, and six runs if it flies straight over.

The main ways a batsman can be "got **out**" (or "dismissed") are: by being "bowled", in which the bowler bowls a ball that dislodges a bail; by being "run out", in which one of the fielding side dislodges a bail with the ball while the batsman is running between the wickets; by being caught, which is when any of the fielding side catches the ball after the batsman has hit it and before it touches the ground; or "LBW" (leg before wicket), where the batsman blocks with his leg a delivery that would otherwise have hit the stumps. In each case, the bowler is said to have "**got a wicket**" (ie got the batsman out).

These are the basics of a game whose beauty lies in the subtlety of its skills and tactics. The captain, for example, chooses which bowler to play and where to position his fielders to counter the strengths of the batsman, the condition of the pitch, and a dozen other variables – and must also concentrate on the long view: Test matches can take up to five days to complete. Cricket also has a beauty in its esoteric language, used to describe such things as fielding positions ("silly mid-off", "cover point", etc) and the various types of bowling delivery ("googly", "yorker", "chinaman" and so on). For beginners, some enlightenment may be gained by watching the TV coverage, or befriending a spectator – cricket fans tend to be congenial types, eager to introduce newcomers to the mysteries of the true faith.

tournament to be played on grass, and for many players the ultimate goal of their careers. The Wimbledon championship lasts for two weeks at the end of June and beginning of July. Most of the tickets, especially those with seats for the main courts (Centre and No. 1), are allocated in advance to Wimbledon's members, other tennis clubs and corporate "sponsors" – as well as by public ballot – and by the time these have taken their slice there's not a lot left for the general public. It is possible, however, to turn up on the day and buy tickets, and if you're rich enough you could buy through ticket agencies (although these sales are technically illegal). On tournament days, queues start to form around dawn and if you arrive by around 7am you have a reasonable chance of securing one of the limited number of Centre and No. 1 court tickets held back for sale on the day. If you're there by around 9am, you should get admission to the outside courts (where you'll catch some top players in the first week of the tournament). Either way, you then have a long wait until play commences at noon.

If you want to see big-name players, an easier opportunity is the **Stella Artois Championship** at Queen's Club in Hammersmith, London, which finishes a week before Wimbledon. Many of the stars use this tournament to acclimatize themselves to British grass-court conditions. As with Wimbledon, you have to apply for tickets in advance, although there are a limited number of returns on sale at 10am each day.

Horse racing

For most of the British population there is just one important day in the horseracing calendar – the last Saturday in March or the first in April, when the **Grand National**, the "World's Greatest Steeplechase", is run at Liverpool's Aintree course. Millions of people risk a quid or two on the race, and watch the proceedings anxiously on TV, where it's broadcast live and then repeated at least twice before the end of the day. The National is by far the most arduous (some would say

cruel) race of the **steeplechasing** and hurdling season, which runs from August to April, with races taking place on Saturdays and midweek at a vast array of courses, ranging from ovals of grass in the depths of the countryside to prestigious venues like Windsor. Ticket prices range from £5 to £40 or more.

The horses and the clientele are often more upmarket when it comes to **flat** racing, which is a summer sport, observing an April to October season. Whereas the big events in the steeplechasing season draw a broad-based crowd, the showcase races on the flat are largely about upper-crust networking. That said, thousands of Londoners treat themselves to a day out at **Epsom** on "Derby Day", the first Saturday in June. The Derby, a mile-and-a-half race for 3-year-old thoroughbreds, is the most prestigious of the five classics of the flat season, and is preceded in the three-day Epsom meeting by another classic, the **Oaks**, which is for fillies only. The other Classics are the **1000 Guineas**, **2000 Guineas** (both run at Newmarket) and the **St Leger** (run at Doncaster). For sheer snobbery nothing can match the **Royal Ascot** week in mid-June, when the Queen and selected members of the royal family are in attendance, along with half the nation's blue bloods. As with the Derby, the best seats are the preserve of the gentry, but the rabble are allowed into the public enclosure for a mere £8–10, and can get considerably closer to the action for around £40–50, providing they dress smartly. Prices are slightly lower at the country's other flat-racing meetings, many of which take place on courses used for steeplechasing in the winter, though some of the better courses – such as **Goodwood** – are reserved for the flat.

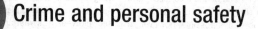

Crime and personal safety

Britain is a relatively safe country and for the visitor the likelihood of being a victim of crime is low. If the worst does happen, then the British police are, on the whole, helpful and professional, though the traditional image of the friendly "bobby" has been tarnished by stories of corruption, racism and crooked dealings.

As elsewhere, the major towns of Britain have their dangerous spots, but these tend to be inner-city housing estates where no tourist has any reason to be. The chief risk on Britain's streets is **pickpocketing**, and there are some virtuoso villains at work in the big cities, especially on the major shopping streets and public transport. Carry only as much money as you need, and keep all bags and pockets fastened.

A growing problem is the prevalence of random, **drink-related violence** after pub closing time at 11pm, especially on Friday and Saturday nights. If you're out and about at these times, stick to well-lit areas and keep your wits about you. Best of all, duck into a pub or club and phone for a taxi back to your hotel.

Should you have anything stolen or be involved in some incident that requires reporting, go to the local police station – we've given address and contact numbers throughout the guide for those in the bigger towns and cities. Only dial ☏999 if a crime is being committed or there's a life-threatening situation at hand (this is also the number for Fire Brigade, Ambulance and, in certain areas, Mountain Rescue or Coastguard).

Work

The kind of work you can expect to find in Britain as a visitor is generally unskilled employment in hotels, bars and restaurants, cleaning companies and on farms. As a casual employee you can expect poor pay of around £3–4 per hour and you may be fired at short notice. If you want to come to grips with the country a little more, you could also consider voluntary work, which can range from work camps, archeological digs and placements with service organizations, or even working holidays, whereby you may be required to contribute a small amount for food and lodging.

Visit Britain's **websites** can provide some information on working in Britain (see p.21), as can ⓦwww.hotrecruit.co.uk, an excellent resource for temporary and seasonal work. There are also several useful **publications**. *Working Holidays*, by the Central Bureau for Educational Visits and Exchanges (CBEVE; £9.99), can provide you with scores of ideas;

Summer Jobs in Britain by David Woodworth (£9.99) gives comprehensive information on paid seasonal work; and *Work Your Way Around the World* by Susan Griffith (£12.95) is also worth a try.

For **conservation work**, the British Trust for Conservation Volunteers (BTCV) can fix you up with schemes for improving footpaths or building dry-stone walls (around £70) and so on, as can the National Trust.

If you're aged between 17 and 27, you might also consider working as an **au pair**. This enables you to live for a maximum of two years with an English-speaking family. In return for your accommodation, food and a small amount of pocket money (say £50 per week), you'll be expected to help around the house and to look after the children for a maximum of five hours each day. The easiest way to find au pair work is through a licensed agency. The Recruitment and Employment Confederation (REC) has a list of reputable agents (ie those that are vetted annually by the government). Alternatively, look in the listings section of *The Lady* magazine.

Work permits

Unless you're a resident of an EU country, you need a **permit** to work legally in the UK, although without the backing of an established employer or company this can be very difficult to obtain. Those aged between 17 and 27 may, however, apply for a **Working Holiday-Maker Entry Certificate**, which entitles you to a two-year stay in the UK, during which time you are permitted to undertake work of a casual nature – in other words, not in a profession, or as a sportsperson or entertainer. The certificates are only available abroad, from British embassies and consulates, and when you apply you must be able to convince the officer you have a valid return or onward ticket, and the means to support yourself while you're in Britain. Note, too, that the certificates are valid from the date of entry into Britain – you won't be able to recoup time spent out of the country in the two-year period of validity.

In **North America**, full-time college students can get temporary work or study permits through BUNAC. Permits are valid for up to six months and cost $250; allow two to three weeks for processing of your application.

Other visitors entitled to work in Britain are **Commonwealth citizens**. Those who have a parent who was born in the UK can apply for a Certificate of Entitlement to the Right of Abode; if you have a grandparent who was born in the UK, or Ireland before 1922, you may be entitled to a UK Ancestry Employment Certificate, allowing you to work for up to four years in the UK. For further information contact your nearest British embassy (see p.20).

Useful addresses

BTCV 36 St Mary's St, Wallingford, Oxfordshire OX10 0EU ☎01491/839 766, ⓦ www.btcv.org.uk.
BUNAC PO Box 430, Southbury, CT 06488 ☎1-800/GO-BUNAC, ⓦ www.bunac.org.
National Trust (Enterprises) The Stable Block, Heywood House, Westbury, Wiltshire BA13 4NA ☎01225/7911199, ⓦ www.nationaltrust.org.uk.
The Recruitment and Employment Confederation (REC) 36–38 Mortimer St, London W1W 7RG ☎020/7462 3260, ⓦ www.rec.uk.com.

Gay and lesbian Britain

Britain offers one of the most diverse and accessible lesbian and gay scenes to be found anywhere in Europe. Nearly every town of any size has some kind of organized gay life – pubs, clubs, community groups, campaigning organizations, shops and phone lines – with the major scenes being found in London, Manchester and Brighton in England; Edinburgh and Glasgow in Scotland; and Cardiff, Swansea and Newport in Wales. Many gay and lesbian venues are listed in this book, and you'll find a free local listings sheet in virtually every one of them.

The age of consent in England, Scotland and Wales (for both homosexual and heterosexual acts) is 16. Attitudes are harder to gauge, but by and large the rest of society leaves the gay/lesbian scene to its own devices, a pragmatic tolerance – or intolerance soaked in indifference – that is occasionally rattled by the sensationalist trash published in the tabloid press. Of the nationwide publications, the weekly Pink Paper provides an outstanding summary of ongoing campaigns along with limited listings. The best bet for a comprehensive national directory of pubs, clubs, groups, gay accommodation and local lesbian and gay switchboards is the glossy monthly *Gay Times*, available from newsagents and alternative bookstores. First stop on the Internet is the encyclopedic ⓦwww.gaybritain.co.uk, with ⓦwww.scotsgay.co.uk and ⓦwww.gaywales.co.uk both useful.

Travellers with disabilities

In the last decade, the UK has made steady progress in improving its facilities for travellers with disabilities. There's still a long way to go, but all new public buildings – including museums and cinemas – are now obliged to provide wheelchair access, dropped kerbs are the rule in every city and town, and many buses have easy-access dropped boarding ramps. The railways have lagged behind, but are at least making moves in the right direction, and the number of accessible hotels and restaurants is increasing year on year. Reserved parking bays for blue-badge holders (ie people with disabilities) are available almost everywhere, from shopping malls to museums.

Britain has numerous specialist **tour operators** catering for disabled travellers, and the number of non-specialist operators who welcome clients with disabilities is increasing. For more information on these operators and on general facilities, you should get in touch with the organizations listed below. RADAR produces a useful annual holiday guide *Holidays in Britain and Ireland* (£8).

As for **accommodation** needs, disabled travellers will find that modified suites are available only at higher-priced establishments and perhaps at the odd B&B, where a ground-floor room has been adapted.

Wheelchair-users and visually impaired people are automatically given a third off the price of train fares, and people with other disabilities are eligible for the **Disabled Persons Railcard** (£14 a year; ⓦwww.disabledpersons-railcard.co.uk), which also gives a third off most tickets. Of the major **car rental** firms only Hertz is the leader in offering models with hand controls.

Contacts for travellers with disabilities

UK and Ireland

All Go Here ℡01923/840 463, ⓦwww.everybody.co.uk. Information on accommodation suitable for disabled travellers throughout the UK, including Northern Ireland.

Capability Scotland ℡0131/313 5510, ⓦwww.capability-scotland.org.uk. Well-run, well-connected organization for all disability issues and information.

Holiday Care 2nd floor, Imperial Building, Victoria Rd, Horley RH6 7PZ ℡0845/124 9971, minicom ℡0845/124 9976, ⓦwww.holidaycare.org.uk. Provides a list of accessible attractions in the UK.

Irish Wheelchair Association Blackheath Drive, Clontarf, Dublin 3 ℡01/818 6400, ⓦwww.iwa.ie. Useful information provided about travelling abroad with a wheelchair.

RADAR (Royal Association for Disability and Rehabilitation) 12 City Forum, 250 City Rd, London EC1V 8AF ℡020/7250 3222, minicom ℡020/7250 4119, ⓦwww.radar.org.uk. A good source of advice on holidays and travel in the UK. They produce an annual holiday guide called *Holidays in Britain and Ireland* for £8 in the UK, and have a dedicated accommodation website for Britain and Ireland, ⓦwww.radarsearch.org.

Tripscope Alexandra House, Albany Rd, Brentford TW8 0NE ℡0845/758 5641,

ⓦwww.tripscope.org.uk. This registered charity provides a national telephone information service offering free advice on UK and international transport for those with mobility problems.

North America

Access-Able ⓦwww.access-able.com. Online resource for travellers with disabilities.

Directions Unlimited 123 Green Lane, Bedford Hills, NY 10507 ℡1-800/533-5343 or 914/241-1700. Travel agency specializing in bookings for people with disabilities.

Mobility International USA 451 Broadway, Eugene, OR 97401 ℡541/343-1284, ⓦwww.miusa.org. Information and referral services, access guides, tours and exchange programmes. Annual membership $35 (includes quarterly newsletter).

Society for the Advancement of Travelers with Handicaps (SATH) 347 5th Ave, New York, NY 10016 ℡212/447-7284, ⓦwww.sath.org. Nonprofit educational organization that has actively represented travellers with disabilities since 1976.

Wheels Up! ℡1-888/38-WHEELS, ⓦwww.wheelsup.com. Provides discounted air fares, tour and cruise prices for disabled travellers, also publishes a free monthly newsletter and has a comprehensive website.

Australia and New Zealand

ACROD (Australian Council for Rehabilitation of the Disabled) ℡02/6282 4333, ⓦwww.acrod.org.au. Provides lists of travel agencies and tour operators for people with disabilities.

Disabled Persons Assembly ℡04/801 9100, ⓦwww.dpa.org.nz. New Zealand resource centre with lists of travel agencies and tour operators for people with disabilities.

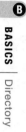

Directory

Drugs Being caught in possession of a small amount of hashish or grass may lead to a fine, but possession of larger quantities of "harder" narcotics could lead to imprisonment or deportation.

Electricity The current is 240v AC. North American appliances need a transformer and adapter; Australian and New Zealand appliances need only an adapter.

Laundry Coin-operated laundries are found in nearly all towns, and are open about twelve hours a day from Monday to Friday, less at weekends. A wash followed by a spin or tumble dry costs about £4; a "service wash" (having your laundry done for you in a few hours) costs about £2 extra.

Smoking Smoking is banned from just about all public buildings and on public transport. Many restaurants have non-smoking sections, some forbid it altogether. Most hotels limit smoking in their public areas and have nonsmoking rooms, but once again some operate a total ban. Pubs usually allow smoking everywhere.

Time From late October to late March, Britain is on Greenwich Mean Time (GMT). Over the summer, clocks go forward an hour for British Summer Time (BST). Either way, the changeover is well coordinated internationally, and the country is almost always five hours ahead of US Eastern Standard Time and ten hours behind Australian Eastern Standard Time.

Toilets Public loos, generally in a less than pristine condition, are found at all train and bus stations and signposted on town high streets; a fee of 10p or 20p is sometimes charged.

Videos British videotapes (in what's called the PAL format) will not play back on North American VCRs (which are NTSC format). However, North American video cameras are compatible with blank tapes purchased in Britain – the camera will format the tape while it records.

Guide

England

London

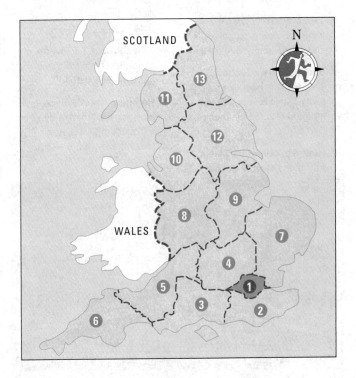

CHAPTER 1 # Highlights

* **British Museum** In time for its 250th anniversary, the BM reinvented itself with a wonderful new glass-covered courtyard. See p.105.

* **London Eye** The universally loved observation wheel is a graceful new addition to London's skyline. See p.129.

* **Tate Modern** London's biggest modern-art gallery is simply awesome. See p.131.

* **Shakespeare's Globe Theatre** Catch an open-air show in this amazing reconstructed Elizabethan theatre. See p.132.

* **Highgate cemetery** Take a tour of the steeply sloping terraces of the West Cemetery, whose overgrown graves are the last word in Victorian Gothic gloom. See p.146.

* **Greenwich** Picturesque riverside spot boasting a busy weekend market, the National Maritime Museum and the old Royal Observatory. See p.148.

* **Kew Gardens** Escape the city at London's superb botanic gardens. See p.154.

* **Hampton Court Palace** Tudor interiors, architecture by Wren, a maze and vast gardens make this a great day-out. See p.155.

△ The British Museum

London

What strikes visitors more than anything about **LONDON** is the sheer size of the place. With a population of just under eight million, it's Europe's largest city by far, stretching for more than thirty miles on either side of the **River Thames**. Ethnically, it's also Europe's most diverse metropolis, and for those without local roots the place can seem baffling. Londoners tend to cope with all this by compartmentalizing the city, identifying with the neighbourhoods in which they work or live, and just making occasional forays into the "centre of town" or "up West" – to the West End, London's shopping and entertainment heartland.

Despite Scottish, Welsh and Northern Irish devolution, London still dominates the national horizon, too: this is where the country's news and money are made, it's where the central government resides and, as far as its inhabitants are concerned, provincial life begins beyond the circuit of the city's orbital motorway. Londoners' sense of superiority causes enormous resentment in the regions, yet it's undeniable that the capital has a unique aura of excitement and success – in most walks of British life, if you want to get on, you've got to do it in London.

For the visitor, too, London is a thrilling place and since the beginning of the new millennium, the city has also been in a relatively buoyant mood. Thanks to the national lottery and the millennium-oriented funding frenzy, virtually every one of London's **world-class museums**, galleries and institutions has been reinvented, from the Royal Opera House to the British Museum. With Tate Modern and the London Eye, the city can now boast the world's largest modern art gallery and observation wheel, as well as two new pedestrian bridges, the first to cross the central section of the Thames for over a hundred years. And after sixteen years of being the only major city in the world not to have its own governing body, London now has an elected assembly again, housed in an eye-catching building within sight of Tower Bridge, and a mayor who's determined to try and solve one of London's biggest problems – transport.

In the meantime, **traditional sights** – Big Ben, Westminster Abbey, Buckingham Palace, St Paul's Cathedral and the Tower of London – continue to draw in millions of tourists every year. Monuments from the capital's more glorious past are everywhere to be seen, from medieval banqueting halls and the great churches of Christopher Wren to the eclectic Victorian architecture of the triumphalist British Empire. There is also much enjoyment to be had from the city's quiet Georgian squares, the narrow alleyways of the City of London, the riverside walks, and the quirks of what is still identifiably a collection of villages. Even London's traffic problems are offset by surprisingly large **expanses of greenery**: Hyde Park, Green Park and St James's Park

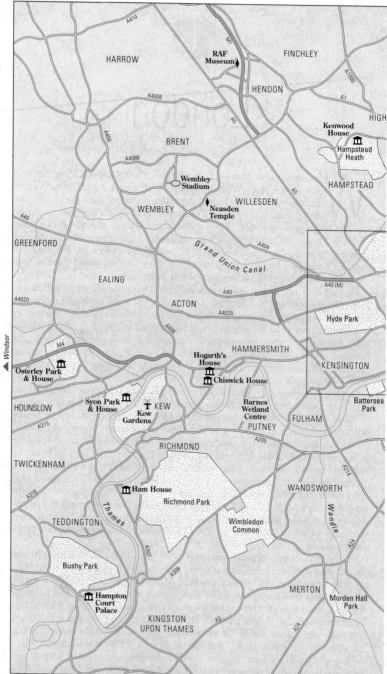

© Crown copyright

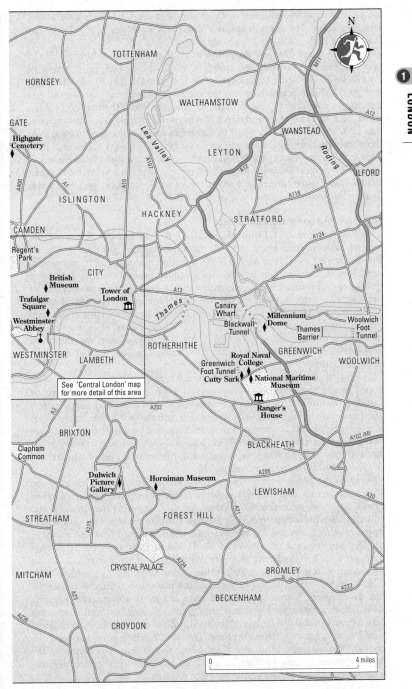

N

TOTTENHAM

HORNSEY

WALTHAMSTOW

GATE

Highgate
Cemetery

WANSTEAD

LEYTON

ILFORD

ISLINGTON

HACKNEY

STRATFORD

CAMDEN

Regent's
Park

CITY

British
Museum

Tower of
London

Trafalgar
Square

Westminster
Abbey

Thames

Canary
Wharf

Blackwall
Tunnel

Millennium
Dome

Thames
Barrier

Woolwich
Foot
Tunnel

ROTHERHITHE

GREENWICH

WESTMINSTER

LAMBETH

Royal Naval
College
Greenwich
Foot Tunnel

Cutty Sark

National Maritime
Museum

WOOLWICH

See 'Central London' map
for more detail of this area

Ranger's
House

BRIXTON

Clapham
Common

BLACKHEATH

Dulwich
Picture
Gallery

Horniman Museum

LEWISHAM

STREATHAM

FOREST HILL

MITCHAM

CRYSTAL PALACE

BROMLEY

BECKENHAM

CROYDON

0   4 miles

are all within a few minutes' walk of the West End, while, further afield, you can enjoy the more expansive parklands of Hampstead Heath and Richmond Park.

You could spend days just **shopping** in London too, hob-nobbing with the upper classes in Harrods, or sampling the offbeat weekend markets of Portobello Road, Brick Lane, Greenwich and Camden. The music, **clubbing** and **gay/lesbian scene** is second to none, and mainstream arts are no less exciting, with regular opportunities to catch brilliant **theatre** companies, dance troupes, exhibitions and opera. **Restaurants** these days, are an attraction, too. London has caught up with its European rivals, and offers a range from three-star Michelin establishments to low-cost, high-quality Chinese restaurants and Indian curry houses. Meanwhile, the city's **pubs** have heaps of atmosphere, especially away from the centre – and an exploration of the farther-flung communities is essential to get the complete picture of this dynamic metropolis.

A brief history of London

The Romans founded **Londinium** in 43 AD as a stores depot on the marshy banks of the Thames. Despite frequent attacks – not least by Queen Boudicca, who razed it in 61 AD – the port became secure in its position as capital of Roman Britain by the end of the century. London's expansion really began, however, in the eleventh century, when it became the seat of the last successful invader of Britain, the Norman duke who became **William I of England** (aka "the Conqueror"). Crowned king of England in Westminster Abbey, William built the White Tower – centrepiece of the Tower of London – to establish his dominance over the merchant population, the class that was soon to make London one of Europe's mightiest cities.

Little is left of medieval or Tudor London. Many of the finest buildings were wiped out in the course of a few days in 1666 when the **Great Fire of London** annihilated more than thirteen thousand houses and nearly ninety churches, completing a cycle of destruction begun the year before by the Great Plague, which killed as many as a hundred thousand people. Chief beneficiary of the blaze was Sir Christopher Wren, who was commissioned to redesign the city and rose to the challenge with such masterpieces as St Paul's Cathedral and the Royal Naval Hospital in Greenwich.

Much of the public architecture of London was built in the Georgian and Victorian periods covering the eighteenth and nineteenth centuries, when grand structures were raised to reflect the city's status as the financial and administrative hub of the invincible **British Empire**. However, in comparison to many other European capitals, much of London looks bland, due partly to the German bombing raids in World War II, and partly to some postwar development that has lumbered the city with the sort of concrete-and-glass mediocrity that gives modern architecture a bad name.

Yet London's special atmosphere comes not from its buildings, but from the life on its streets. A cosmopolitan city since at least the seventeenth century, when it was a haven for Huguenot immigrants escaping persecution in Louis XIV's France, today it is truly multicultural, with over a third of its permanent population originating from overseas. The last hundred years has seen the arrival of thousands from the Caribbean, the Indian subcontinent, the Mediterranean and the Far East, all of whom play an integral part in defining a metropolis that is unmatched in its sheer diversity.

Orientation, arrival and information

Stretching for more than thirty miles at its broadest point, **London** is a big place. The majority of its sights are situated to the north of the **River Thames**, which loops through the city from west to east. However, there is no single predominant focus of interest, since London has grown not through centralized planning but by a process of agglomeration – villages and urban developments that once surrounded the core are now lost within the amorphous mass of Greater London.

One of the few areas which is manageable on foot is **Westminster** and **Whitehall**, the city's royal, political and ecclesiastical power base, where you'll find the **National Gallery** and a host of other London landmarks from **Buckingham Palace** to **Westminster Abbey**. The grand streets and squares of **St James's**, **Mayfair** and **Marylebone**, to the north of Westminster, have been the playground of the rich since the Restoration, and now contain the city's busiest shopping zones.

East of Piccadilly Circus, **Soho** and **Covent Garden** are also easy to walk around and form the heart of the West End entertainment district, containing the largest concentration of theatres, cinemas, clubs, flashy shops, cafés and restaurants. To the north lie the university quarter of **Bloomsbury**, home to the ever-popular British Museum, and the secluded quadrangles of **Holborn**'s Inns of Court, London's legal heartland.

The City – the City of London, to give it its full title – is both the most ancient and the most modern part of London. Settled since Roman times, it's now one of the world's great financial centres, yet retains its share of historic sights, notably the **Tower of London** and a fine cache of Wren churches that includes **St Paul's Cathedral**. Despite creeping trendification, the **East End**, to the east of the City, is not conventional tourist territory, but to ignore it entirely is to miss out a crucial element of contemporary London. **Docklands** is the converse of the down-at-heel East End, with the Canary Wharf tower, still the country's tallest building, epitomizing the pretensions of the Thatcherite dream.

A small slice of central London south of the Thames is definitely worth exploring. First off, there's the **South Bank Centre**, London's little-loved concrete culture bunker, which is enjoying a new lease of life thanks to inspired artistic direction and its proximity to the **London Eye**, the world's biggest observation wheel. Further east along the river in Bankside is **Tate Modern**, one of the world's greatest modern art museums, now linked to the City by the funky pedestrian-only Millennium Bridge.

The largest segment of greenery in central London is Hyde Park, which separates wealthy **Kensington and Chelsea** from the city centre. The **museums** of South Kensington – the Victoria and Albert Museum, the Science Museum and the Natural History Museum – are a must; and if you have shopping on your agenda, you'll want to check out the hive of plush stores in the vicinity of Harrods.

The capital's most hectic weekend market takes place around Camden Lock in **North London**. Further out, in the literary suburbs of Hampstead and Highgate, there are unbeatable views across the city from half-wild **Hampstead Heath**, the favourite parkland of thousands of Londoners. The glory of **South London** is **Greenwich**, with its nautical associations, royal park and observatory. Finally, there are plenty of rewarding day-trips along the Thames from **Chiswick** to **Windsor**, most notably to Hampton Court Palace and Windsor Castle.

Arrival

Flying into London, you'll arrive at one of the capital's five **international airports**: Heathrow, Gatwick, Stansted, Luton or City Airport, all of which are less than an hour from the city centre.

Heathrow (℡08700/000123, ⓦwww.baa.co.uk), fifteen miles west of the centre, has four terminals, and two train/tube stations: one for terminals 1, 2 and 3, and a separate one for terminal 4. The high-speed **Heathrow Express** trains travel nonstop to Paddington Station (every 15min; 15–20min) for £13 each way or £23 return (less if you book online, more if you buy your ticket on board). A much cheaper alternative is to take the slow Piccadilly **Underground** line into central London (every 5–9min; 50min) for £3.70. If you plan to make several sightseeing journeys on your arrival day, buy a One-Day Travelcard (Zones 1–6) for £5.10 (see p.80). There is also a **National Express bus service** (℡08705/808080, ⓦwww.nationalexpress.com) from Heathrow direct to Victoria Coach Station (daily 6am–9.30pm), which departs every thirty minutes, takes approximately an hour depending on the traffic, and costs £8 single, £11 return. **Airbus** #2 also runs from outside all four Heathrow terminals to several destinations in the city (every 30min; 1hr) and costs £8 single, £12 return. From midnight, you'll have to take **Night Bus** #N9 to Trafalgar Square (every 30min; 1hr) for a bargain fare of £1. **Taxis** are plentiful, but cost at least £40 to central London, and take around an hour (longer in the rush hour).

Gatwick (℡08700/002468, ⓦwww.baa.co.uk), thirty miles to the south, has two terminals, North and South, connected by a monorail. The nonstop **Gatwick Express** train runs between the South Terminal and Victoria Station (every 15–30min; 30min) for £11. Other options include the **South Central** services to Victoria (every 15–20min; 40min) for £8.20, or **Thameslink** to King's Cross (every 15–30min; 50min) for around £10.

Stansted (℡08700/000303, ⓦwww.baa.co.uk), London's swankiest international airport, lies roughly 35 miles northeast of the capital, and is served by the **Stansted Express** to Liverpool Street (every 15min; 45min), which costs £13 single, £23 return. **Airbus** #6 also runs 24 hours a day to Victoria Coach Station (every 30min; 1hr 30min), and costs £8 single, £12 return.

Luton airport (℡01582/405100, ⓦwww.london-luton.com) is roughly thirty miles north of the city centre, and mostly handles charter flights. A **free shuttle bus** takes five minutes to transport passengers to Luton Airport Parkway station, connected by **rail** to King's Cross and other stations in central London, with **Thameslink** running trains every fifteen minutes, plus one or two throughout the night; the journey takes thirty to forty minutes and is £10 for a single fare. Alternatively, **Green Line** buses run from Luton to Victoria Station (every 30min; 1hr 30min), costing £8.50 single, £13.50 return.

London's smallest airport, **City Airport** (℡020/7646 0000, ⓦwww .londoncityairport.com), is situated in Docklands, nine miles east of central London. It handles European flights only, and is connected by shuttle bus with Canning Town (every 5min; 5min; £2.50), Canary Wharf (every 10min; 10min; £3), and Liverpool Street (every 10min; 30min; £6) tube stations.

Eurostar trains arrive at the central **Waterloo International**, south of the river. Arriving by train (℡08457/484950, ⓦwww.nationrail.co.uk) from elsewhere in Britain, you'll come into one of London's numerous main-line stations, all of which have adjacent Underground stations linking into the city centre's tube network. Coming into London **by coach** (℡08705/808080, ⓦwww.nationalexpress.com), you're most likely to arrive at **Victoria Coach**

Station, a couple of hundred yards south down Buckingham Palace Road from the train and Underground stations of the same name.

Information

The chief British Tourist Authority (BTA) office in London is the **Britain Visitor Centre**, near Piccadilly Circus at 1 Regent Street (Mon–Fri 9am–6.30pm, Sat & Sun 10am–4pm; Aug & Sept same times except Sat 9am–5pm; Ⓦwww.visitbritain.com). London also has its very own **London Tourist Board** or LTB with information online at Ⓦwww.visitlondon.com. Individual boroughs also run tourist offices; the most central one is on the south side of St Paul's Cathedral (April–Sept daily 9.30am–5pm; Oct–March Mon–Fri 9.30am–5pm, Sat 9.30am–12.30pm; Ⓣ020/7332 1456, Ⓦwww .cityoflondon.gov.uk).

Most tourist offices hand out a basic reference **map** of central London, plus plans of the public transport systems, and the maps in this chapter should be enough for most exploring, but to find your way around every nook and cranny you need to invest in either an *A–Z Atlas* or a *Nicholson Streetfinder*, both of which have a street index covering every street in the capital; you can get them at most bookshops and newsagents for under £5. The two best, simple, foldout maps are *London: The Rough Guide Map* – which also details hotels, restaurants, attraction opening hours and so on – and *Benson's London Mini Map*.

The only comprehensive and critical weekly **listings** magazine is *Time Out*, which costs £2.20 and comes out every Tuesday afternoon. In it you'll find details of all the latest exhibitions, shows, films, music, sport, guided walks and events in and around the capital.

City transport

London's transport network is among the most complex and expensive in the world. **Transport for London** (TfL) provides excellent free maps and details of bus and tube services from its **travel information** offices: the main one is at Piccadilly Circus tube station (daily 8.45am–6pm), and there are other desks at Heathrow and various tube and train stations. There's also a 24-hour phone line for information on all bus and tube services Ⓣ020/7222 1234 and a

---

The London Pass

If you're thinking of visiting a lot of fee-paying attractions in a short space of time, it's probably worth buying a **London Pass** (Ⓦwww.londonpass.com), which gives you entry to a mixed bag of attractions including Hampton Court Palace, Kensington Palace, London Aquarium, St Paul's Cathedral, the Tower of London and Windsor Castle, plus a whole host of lesser attractions, and various discounts at selected outlets. You can choose to buy the card with or without an All-Zone Travelcard thrown in; the saving is relatively small, but it does include free travel out to Windsor. The pass costs around £25 for one day (£16.50 for kids), rising to £70 for six days (£36.50 for kids); or £30 with a Travelcard (£19 for kids) rising to £107 (£56 for kids). The pass can be bought online or over the phone (Ⓣ08702/429988), or in person from Exchange International bureaux at Heathrow and Gatwick airports and London's mainline train or major Underground stations.

Travelcards

To get the best value out of the transport system, buy a **Travelcard**. Available from machines and booths at all tube and train stations, and at some newsagents (look for the sign), these are valid for the bus, tube, Docklands Light Railway, Tramlink and suburban rail networks. **Day Travelcards** come in two varieties: Off-Peak – which are valid after 9.30am on weekdays and all day during the weekend – and Peak. A Day Travelcard (Off-Peak) costs £4.10 for the central zones 1 and 2, rising to £5.10 for zones 1–6 (including Heathrow); the Day Travelcard (Peak) starts at £5.10 for zones 1 and 2. **Weekend Travelcards**, for unlimited travel on Saturdays and Sundays, start at £6.10 for zone 1 and 2. **Weekly Travelcards** are even more economical, beginning at £19.60 for zones 1 and 2; these cards can only be bought by holders of a **Photocard**, which you can get, free of charge, from tube and train station ticket booths on presentation of a passport photo.

website ⓦ www.tfl.gov.uk. One word of warning – avoid travelling during the **rush hour** (Mon–Fri 8–9.30am & 5–7pm), when tubes become unbearably crowded (and the lack of air-conditioning doesn't help), and some buses get so full they literally won't let you on.

Except for very short journeys, the fastest way of moving around the city is by **Underground** or tube (ⓦ www.thetube.com), as it's known to all Londoners. The eleven different tube lines cross much of the metropolis, although London south of the river is not very well covered. Each line has its own colour and name – all you need to know is which direction you're travelling in: northbound, eastbound, southbound or westbound. Services operate from around 5.30am Monday to Saturday, and from 7.30am on Sundays, and end just after midnight; you rarely have to wait more than five minutes for a train from central stations. **Tickets** must be bought in advance from the machines or booths in the station entrance hall; ticket inspectors operate throughout the system and if you cannot produce a valid ticket you'll be charged an on-the-spot Penalty Fare of £10. A single journey in the central zone costs an unbelievable £1.60, so if you're intending to travel about a bit, a Travelcard is a much better bet (see box above).

London's famous red **double-decker buses** are fun to ride on, but tend to get stuck in traffic jams, which prevent them running to a regular timetable. In central London, you must buy your ticket from one of the machines at the bus stop before boarding. Tickets for all bus journeys costs a flat fare of £1. In addition to the Travelcards mentioned above, a **One-Day Bus Pass** for zones 1–4, which can be used before 9.30am on weekdays costs £2 for adults and £1 for kids. Regular buses run between about 6am and midnight; **Night Buses** (prefixed with the letter "N") operate outside this period. Night bus routes radiate out from Trafalgar Square at approximately twenty to thirty-minute intervals, more frequently on some routes and on Friday and Saturday nights. Tickets are £1 and Travelcards (see box) are valid. All stops are treated as request stops.

Large areas of London's suburbs are best reached by the **suburban train** network (Travelcards valid). Wherever a sight can only be reached by over-ground train, we've indicated the nearest train station and the central terminus from which you must depart.

Boat services on the Thames do not form part of an integrated public transport system. Fares are expensive, and Travelcards currently only give the holders a 33 percent discount on tickets. All services are keenly affected by demand,

Congestion Charge

Given the traffic jams and the hassle, **driving in London** – especially central London – is by far the worst transport option available. The latest attempt to cut down on car usage in the capital is the controversial **congestion charge**, pioneered by Ken Livingstone in his first term as Mayor of London. Since early 2003, all vehicles entering central London on weekdays between 7am and 6.30pm are liable to a congestion charge of £5 per vehicle. Drivers can pay for the charge online, over the phone and at garages and shops, and must do so before 10pm the same day or incur a £5 surcharge. The congestion charging zone is bounded by Marylebone and Euston roads in the north, Commercial Street and Tower Bridge in the east, Kennington Lane and Elephant & Castle in the south and Edgware Road and Park Lane in the west.

tides and the weather, and tend to be drastically scaled down in the winter months. **Timetables and services** are complex, and there are numerous companies and small charter operators – for a full list pick up the Thames River Services booklet from an LT travel information office, phone ℡020/7222 1234 or visit ⓦwww.tfl.gov.uk.

Compared to most capital cities, London's metered **black cabs** are an expensive option unless there are three or more of you – a ride from Euston to Victoria, for example, costs around £10, more at the weekend, and after 8pm on weekdays. A yellow light over the windscreen tells you if the cab is available – just stick your arm out to hail it. If you want to book one in advance, call ℡020/7272 0272.

Minicabs look just like regular cars and are considerably cheaper than black cabs, but they are a bit of a law unto themselves. There are hundreds of minicab firms in the phone book, but the best way to pick one is to take the advice of the place you're at, unless you want to be certain of a woman driver, in which case call Ladycabs (℡020/7254 3501), or a gay/lesbian-friendly driver, in which case call Freedom Cars (℡020/7734 1313) or Liberty Cars (℡020/7739 9080).

Accommodation

There's no getting away from the fact that **accommodation** in London is expensive and compared with most European cities, you pay over the odds in every category. Rates at the city's hostels are among the highest in the world, while venerable institutions such as the *Ritz*, the *Dorchester* and the *Savoy* charge guests the very top international prices – up to £300 and more per luxurious night.

The cheapest places to stay are the dorm beds of the city's numerous independent **hostels**, followed closely behind by the official YHA hostels. Even the most basic **B&Bs** struggle to bring their tariffs down to £45 for a double with shared facilities, and you're more likely to find yourself paying £60 or more.

If you want to avoid the hassle of contacting individual hotels and B&Bs, you could turn to one of the various **accommodation agencies**. The British Hotel Reservation Centre (BHRC) desks at Heathrow, Gatwick and Victoria train and coach stations don't charge a fee for booking rooms, and most of their offices are open daily from 6am till midnight. You can also

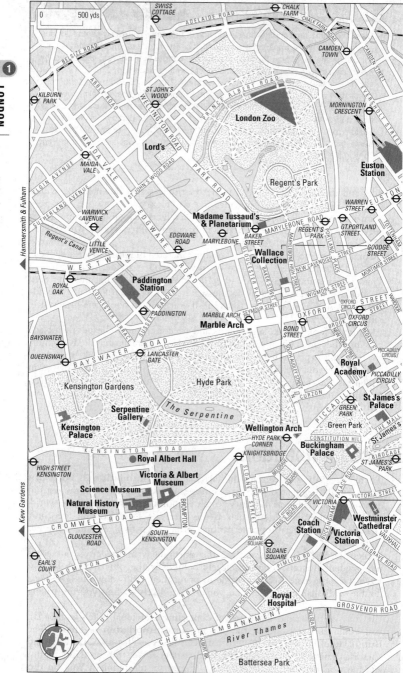

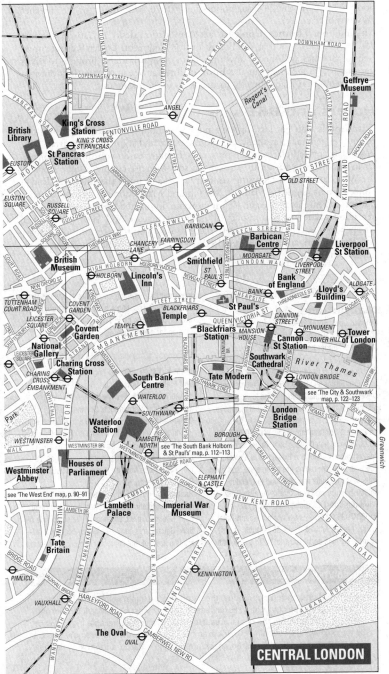

CENTRAL LONDON

83

© Crown copyright

▼ Lambeth

▼ Greenwich

see 'The City & Southwark' map, p. 122–123

see 'The South Bank Holborn & St Paul's' map, p. 112–113

see 'The West End' map, p. 90–91

book for free via the 24-hour phone line (☎020/7828 0601) or the Internet (Ⓦwww.bhrc.co.uk).

In addition, **Thomas Cook** has accommodation desks at Gatwick Airport (☎01293/529372) and at the British Visitor Centre on Lower Regent Street (see p.78) and will book anything from youth hostels through to five-star hotels (£5 fee). You can also **book online** for free at Ⓦwww.londontown.com; payment is made directly to the hotel on checking out.

Hotels and B&Bs

With **hotels** you get less for your money in London than elsewhere in the country – generally breakfasts are more meagre and rooms more spartan than in similarly priced places in the provinces. In high season you should phone as far in advance as you can if you want to stay within a couple of tube stops of the West End. When choosing your **area**, bear in mind that the West End – Soho, Covent Garden, St James's, Mayfair and Marylebone – and the western districts of Knightsbridge and Kensington, are dominated by expensive, upmarket hotels, whereas Bloomsbury is both inexpensive and very central. For cheaper rooms, the widest choice is close to the main train termini of Victoria and Paddington, and the budget B&Bs of Earl's Court. Where possible, we've marked the following on the maps in this chapter.

St James's, Mayfair and Marylebone

Edward Lear Hotel 28–30 Seymour St, W1 ☎020/7402 5401, Ⓦwww.edlear.com. Marble Arch tube. Former home of the famous poet and artist, decorated with lovely flower boxes, and boasting a plush foyer and a great location close to Oxford Street and Hyde Park. The rooms themselves are less remarkable, but the low prices reflect both this and the fact that most only have shared facilities. Kids free at weekends. ❹

La Place 17 Nottingham Place, W1 ☎020/7486 2323, Ⓦwww.hotellaplace.com. Baker Street tube. Just off busy Marylebone Road, this is a small, good-value place; rooms are all en suite, equipped with all the gadgets usually found in grander establishments, and comfortably furnished. ❼

Wigmore Court 23 Gloucester Place, W1 ☎020/7935 0928, Ⓦwww.wigmore-court-hotel.co.uk. Marble Arch or Baker Street tube. The relentlessly pink decor may not be to everyone's

taste, but this Georgian townhouse is a better than average B&B, boasting a high tally of returning clients. Unusually, there's also a laundry and basic kitchen for guests' use. ❺

Soho, Covent Garden and The Strand

The Fielding 4 Broad Court, Bow St, WC2 ☎020/7836 8305, Ⓦwww.the-fielding-hotel.co.uk. Covent Garden tube. See map, p.90. Quietly and perfectly situated on a traffic-free and gas-lit court, this excellent hotel is one of Covent Garden's hidden gems. Its en-suite rooms are a firm favourite with visiting performers, since it's just a few yards from the Royal Opera House. Breakfast is extra. ❻

Hazlitt's 6 Frith St, W1 ☎020/7434 1771, Ⓦwww.hazlittshotel.com. Tottenham Court Road tube. See map, p.90. Located off the south side of Soho Square, this early-eighteenth-century building is a hotel of real character and charm, offering

London postcodes

A brief word on **London postcodes**: the name of each street is followed by a letter giving the geographical location (E for "east", WC for "west central" and so on) and a number that specifies the postal area. However, this is not a reliable indication of the remoteness of the locale – W5, for example, lies beyond the more remote sounding NW10 – so it's always best to check a map before taking a room in what may sound like a fairly central area.

en-suite rooms decorated and furnished as close to period style as convenience and comfort allow. There's a small sitting room, but no dining room (although some of London's best restaurants are a stone's throw away); continental breakfast (served in the rooms) is available, but isn't included in the rates. **❾**

Manzi's 1–2 Leicester St, W1 ☎020/7734 0224, ⓦwww.manzis.co.uk. Leicester Square tube. See map, p.90. Set over the Italian and seafood restaurant of the same name, *Manzi's* is one of very few central hotels in this price range. It's certainly right in the thick of the West End, just off Leicester Square, meaning noise might prove to be a nuisance. Continental breakfast is included in the price. **❺**

St Martin's Lane 45 St Martin's Lane, WC2 ☎020/7300 5500 or ☎0800/634 5500, ⓦwww .ianschragerhotels.com. See map, p.90. Leicester Square tube. So cool you wouldn't know it was a hotel, this self-consciously chic "boutique hotel" from the New York-based Ian Schrager chain is a hit with the media crowd. From the fluorescent yellow and white minimalist lobby to the large Portuguese limestone bathrooms, the interior has been designed throughout by the mischievous Philippe Starck. Rooms currently start at around £250 a double, but rates come down at the weekend. **❾**

Bloomsbury

Cavendish 75 Gower St, WC1 ☎020/7636 9079, ⓦwww.hotelcavendish.com. Goodge Street tube. See map, p.90. Gower Street is very busy with traffic, but get a room at the back of the property and you'll have a peaceful night, and a real bargain, too, with lovely owners, two beautiful overrun gardens and some quite well-preserved original features. All rooms have shared facilities, and there are some good-value family rooms, too. **❸**

Crescent 49–50 Cartwright Gardens, WC1 ☎020/7387 1515, ⓦwww.crescenthoteloflondon .com. Euston or Russell Square tube. This very comfortable and tastefully decorated Regency B&B is definitely a cut above the rest. All doubles are en suite and have TVs, but there are a few basic singles with shared facilities. Guests also have use of tennis courts in the nearby gardens. **❺**

Garth 69 Gower Street, WC1 ☎020/7636 5761, ⓦwww.garthhotel-london.com; Goodge Street tube. See map, p.90. Gay-friendly, small, Georgian townhouse hotel, which prides itself on its friendly atmosphere and features many original antiques in its mostly en-suite bedrooms. **❸**

Jenkins 45 Cartwright Gardens, WC1 ☎020/7387 2067, ⓦwww.jenkinshotel.demon.co.uk. Euston or Russell Square tube. Smartly kept, family-run

place in this fine Regency crescent, with just fourteen fairly small but well-equipped and very clean rooms, most of which are en suite. **❹**

myhotel 11–13 Bayley St, WC1 ☎020/7667 6000, ⓦwww.myhotels.co.uk. Tottenham Court Road tube. See map, p.90.The aquarium in the lobby is the tell-tale sign that this is a feng shui hotel. Despite the positive vibes, and Conran-designed look, the double-glazed, air-conditioned rooms are on the small side for the price. Still, there's a gym, a very pleasant library, a restaurant attached and the location is great for the West End. **❽**

Ridgemount 65–67 Gower St, WC1 ☎020/7636 1141, ⓦwww.ridgemounthotel.co.uk. Goodge Street tube. See map, p.90. Old-fashioned, very friendly family-run place, with small rooms, half with shared facilities, a garden, free hot-drinks machine and a laundry service. Cash only, but a reliable, basic bargain for Bloomsbury. **❸**

Russell Russell Square, WC1 ☎020/7837 6470, ⓦwww.lemeridien.com. Russell Square tube. From its grand 1898 exterior to its opulent interiors of marble, wood and crystal, this late-Victorian landmark fully retains its period atmosphere in all its public areas. Thanks to a recent takeover – and makeover – by Le Meridien chain, the rooms now live up to the grandeur of the lobby, if not necessarily to its style. Expensive, but various deals are sometimes available. Breakfast not included. **❾**

Clerkwenwell and the City

City 12 Osborn St, E1 ☎020/7247 3313, ⓦwww.cityhotellondon.co.uk. Aldgate East tube. See map, p.122. Spacious, clean and modern inside, this hotel stands on the eastern edge of the City, and in the heart of the Bengali East End at the bottom of Brick Lane. The plainly decorated rooms are all en suite, and many have kitchens, too; four-person rooms are a bargain for those in a small group. **❻**

Great Eastern Liverpool St, EC2 ☎020/7618 5000, ⓦwww.great-eastern-hotel.co.uk. Liverpool Street tube. See map, p.122. Without doubt one of the best places to stay if you need or wish to be near the City. This venerable late-nineteenth-century station hotel has had a complete Conran makeover, yet manages to retain much of its clubby flavour. The rooms themselves are impeccably well appointed and tastefully furnished – to maximize your natural light, get a room facing out. Doubles start from around £200, but rates are cut at the weekend. **❾**

Jurys Inn 60 Pentonville Rd, N1 ☎020/7282 5500, ⓦwww.jurys.com. Angel tube. This modern

Irish chain hotel is decorated to a high, if bland, standard, and is geared up for business folk. Located on busy Pentonville Road, close to the tube, it's equally convenient for the City and for Islington and Clerkenwell's trendy bars and restaurants. Service is very friendly, and the fixed room-rate is a bargain for three adults sharing or for those with kids. **⑤**

The Rookery 12 Peter's Lane, Cowcross St EC1 ☏ 020/7336 0931, ⓦ www.rookeryhotel.com. Farringdon tube. Rambling Georgian townhouse on the edge of the City in trendy Clerkenwell that makes a fantastically discreet little hideaway. The rooms start at around £265 a double; each one has been individually designed in a deliciously camp, modern take on the Baroque period, and all have super bathrooms with lots of character. **⑧**

South Bank & Southwark

London County Hall Travel Inn Belvedere Rd, SE1 ☏ 020/7902 1619, ⓦ www.travelinn.co.uk. Waterloo or Westminster tube. See map, p.112. Don't expect river views at these prices, but the location in County Hall itself is pretty good if you're up for a bit of sightseeing. Decor and ambience is functional, but for those with kids, the flat-rate rooms are a bargain. **⑤**

Mad Hatter 3–7 Stamford St, SE1 ☏ 020/7401 9222, ⓦ www.fullers.co.uk. Southwark or Blackfriars tube. See map, p.112. Situated above a Fuller's pub – where breakfast is served – on the corner of Blackfriars Road, this place has a great location, a short walk from the Tate Modern and the South Bank. Ask about the weekend deals. **⑥**

Victoria

Melbourne House 79 Belgrave Rd, SW1 ☏ 020/7828 3516, ⓦ www.melbournehousehotel.co.uk. Victoria or Pimlico tube. One of the best B&Bs along Belgrave Road: family run, well furnished, offering clean and bright rooms, excellent communal areas and friendly service. All doubles have en-suite facilities, but there are a couple of very cheap singles without. **⑤**

Oxford House 92–94 Cambridge St, SW1 ☏ 020/7834 6467, ⓕ 020/7834 0225. Victoria tube. Probably the best-value rooms you can get in the vicinity of Victoria station. Showers and toilets are shared, but kept pristine. Full English breakfast is included in the price. **②**

Sanctuary House 33 Tothill St, SW1 ☏ 020/7799 4044, ⓦ www.fullers.co.uk. St James's Park tube. See map, p.90. Situated above a Fuller's pub, and decked out like one, too, in smart, pseudo-Victoriana. Breakfast is extra, and is served in the

pub, but the location right by St James's Park is very central. Ask about the weekend deals. **⑥**

Topham's 26 Ebury St, SW1 ☏ 020/7730 8147, ⓦ www.tophams.co.uk. Victoria tube. See map, p.136. Charming family-owned hotel in the English country-house style, just a couple of minutes' walk from Victoria main-line and tube station. Sumptuously furnished en-suite twins or doubles, including full English breakfast. **⑦**

Windermere 142–144 Warwick Way, SW1 ☏ 020/7834 5163, ⓦ www.windermere-hotel.co.uk. Sloane Square, Pimlico or Victoria tube. See map, p.136. Situated at the western end of Warwick Way, this is a tastefully decorated and quietly stylish place where most rooms are en suite. There's a tasty restaurant downstairs, too. **⑥**

Woodville House & Morgan House 107 & 120 Ebury St, SW1 ☏ 020/7730 1048, ⓦ www.woodvillehouse.co.uk. See map, p.136. Two above-average B&Bs, run by the same vivacious couple, with great breakfasts, patio gardens, and an iron and fridge for guests to use. All rooms at *Woodville* are with shared facilities; some at *Morgan* are en suite. Victoria tube. **④**

Paddington, Bayswater and Notting Hill

Columbia 95–99 Lancaster Gate, W2 ☏ 020/7402 0021, ⓦ www.columbiahotel.co.uk. Lancaster Gate tube. See map, p.136. The spacious public lounge, well-worn decor and useful 24-hour bar make this large white stucco hotel a rock-band favourite. The en-suite rooms themselves are actually very sober, and retain some original Victorian fittings. **⑤**

Garden Court 30–31 Kensington Garden Square, W2 ☏ 020/7229 2553, ⓦ www.gardencourthotel.co.uk. Queensway or Bayswater tube. See map, p.136. Presentable, family-run B&B on a quiet square close to Portobello market; half the rooms are with shared facilities, half are en suite. Full English breakfast included. **③**

The Gresham 116 Sussex Gardens, W2 ☏ 020/7402 2920, ⓦ www.the-gresham-hotel.co.uk. Paddington tube. See map, p.136. B&B with a touch more class than many in the area. Rooms are small but tastefully kitted out, and all have TV. Continental breakfast included. **⑤**

Pavilion 34–36 Sussex Gardens, W2 ☏ 020/7262 0905, ⓦ www.msi.com.mt/pavilion. Paddington tube. See map, p.136. The successful rock star's home-from-home, with outrageously over-the-top decor and every room individually themed. **⑥**

Pembridge Court 34 Pembridge Gardens, W11 ☏ 020/7229 9977, ⓦ www.pemct.co.uk. Notting Hill Gate or Holland Park tube. See map, p.136.

Attractively converted townhouse close to Portobello Market, with spacious, fully equipped rooms. Two cats add to the homely feel, as does the lively *Caps Restaurant and Bar.* **⑧**

Knightsbridge, Kensington and Chelsea

Abbey House 11 Vicarage Gate, W8 ☎020/7727 2594, ⓦwww.abbeyhousekensington.com. High Street Kensington or Notting Hill tube. See map, p.136. Inexpensive Victorian B&B in a quiet street just north of Kensington High Street. Rooms are large and bright – prices are kept down by sharing facilities rather than fitting the usual cramped bathroom unit. Full English breakfast, with free tea and coffee available all day. Cash only. **⑤**
Aster House 3 Sumner Place, SW7 ☎020/7581 5888, ⓦwww.asterhouse.com. South Kensington tube. See map, p.136. Pleasant, nonsmoking B&B in a luxurious white-stuccoed South Ken street; there's a lovely garden at the back and a large conservatory, where breakfast is served. **⑦**
Five Sumner Place 5 Sumner Place, SW7 ☎020/7584 7586, ⓦwww.sumnerplace.com. South Kensington tube. See map, p.136. Discreetly luxurious B&B in one of South Ken's prettiest white-stucco terraces. All rooms are en suite and breakfast is served in the house's lovely conservatory. **⑦**
The Gore 189 Queen's Gate, SW7 ☎020/7584 6601, ⓦwww.gorehotel.co.uk. South Kensington, Gloucester Road or High Street Kensington tube. See map, p.136. Popular, century-old hotel, awash with Oriental rugs, rich mahogany, walnut panelling and other Victoriana. A pricey, but excellent bistro restaurant adds to its allure, and it's only a step away from Hyde Park. **⑨**
The Hempel 31–35 Craven Hill Gardens, W2 ☎020/7298 9000, ⓦwww.the-hempel.co.uk. Lancaster Gate or Queensway tube. See map, p.136. Deeply fashionable minimalist hotel, designed by the actress turned designer Anouska Hempel, with a huge and very empty atrium entrance, and white-on-white rooms. **⑨**
Hotel 167 167 Old Brompton Rd, SW5 ☎020/7373 3221, ⓦwww.hotel167.com.

Gloucester Road tube. See map, p.136. Small, stylishly furnished B&B with en-suite facilities, double glazing and a fridge in all rooms. Continental buffet-style breakfast is served in the attractive morning room/reception. **⑦**
Vicarage 10 Vicarage Gate, W8 ☎020/7229 4030, ⓦwww.londonvicaragehotel.com. High Street Kensington or Notting Hill tube. See map, p.136. Ideally located B&B a step away from Hyde Park, with clean rooms – shared facilities – and a full English breakfast. Cash/travellers' cheques only. **⑤**

Earl's Court

Philbeach 30–31 Philbeach Gardens, SW5 ☎020/7373 1244, ⓦwww.philbeachhotel.freeserve.co.uk. Earl's Court tube. See map, p.136. Friendly, long-running gay/transvestite hotel, with basic and en-suite rooms, a pleasant TV lounge area, late bar and popular *Wilde About Oscar* garden restaurant. **③**
Rushmore 11 Trebovir Rd, SW5 ☎020/7370 3839, ⓕ020/7370 0274. Earl's Court tube. See map, p.136. A cut above the average, with its colourful murals, imaginative Italianate room decor and conservatory in this often dreary area. The attic rooms are especially spacious and comfortable. Full continental breakfast is included in the rates. **⑤**

Hampstead

La Gaffe 107–111 Heath St, NW3 ☎020/7435 4941, ⓦwww.lagaffe.co.uk. Hampstead tube. Small and warren-like but characterful hotel, situated over an Italian restaurant and bar in the heart of Hampstead village. All rooms are en suite and there's a roof terrace for use in fine weather. **⑥**
Hampstead Village Guest House 2 Kemplay Rd, NW3 ☎020/7435 8679, ⓦwww.HampsteadGuesthouse.com. Lovely B&B in an old house set in a quiet backstreet between Hampstead village and the Heath. Rooms (some en suite, all nonsmoking) have "lived-in" clutter, which makes a pleasant change from anodyne hotels and spartan B&Bs. Meals to order. Hampstead tube. **⑥**

Hostels and student accommodation

London's official **Youth Hostel Association (YHA) hostels** are generally the cleanest, most efficiently run hostels in the capital. There's no age limit, and if you're not already a member, you can join on the spot. You can book a bed over the phone with a credit card by ringing individual hostels, or by logging on to their **website** at ⓦwww.yha.org.uk. **Independent hostels** are cheaper and more relaxed, but can be less reliable in terms of facilities. Typical of this laid-back brand is the Astor chain of five hostels, run exclusively for the 18–30 age group. A good **website** for booking independent places online is ⓦwww.hostellondon.com. Outside term time, you also have the option of staying in **student halls of residence**: the quality of the rooms varies enormously, but tends to be fairly basic and prices are slightly higher than hostels. London's **campsites** are all on the perimeter of the city, though they are without doubt the cheapest accommodation available.

Where possible we've marked the location of the following on one of the maps in this chapter.

YHA hostels

City of London 36 Carter Lane, EC4 ☏020/7236 4965, ⓔcity@yha.org.uk. St Paul's tube. See map, p.112. Two-hundred-bed hostel in a great location opposite St Paul's Cathedral; some twins too (❸), but mostly four- to eight-bed dorms for £24 per person. No groups.

Earl's Court 38 Bolton Gardens, SW5 ☏020/7373 7083, ⓔearlscourt@yha.org.uk. Earl's Court tube. See map, p.136. Better than a lot of accommodation in Earl's Court, but only offering dorms of mostly ten beds at £16.80 per person – the triple-bunks take some getting used to. Kitchen, café and patio garden. No groups.

Hampstead Heath 4 Wellgarth Rd, NW11 ☏020/8458 9054, ⓔhampstead@yha.org.uk. Golders Green tube. One of London's biggest and best-appointed YHA hostels, with its own garden and the wilds of Hampstead Heath nearby. Beds cost £20.40 per person; rooms have three to six beds and family rooms have two to five beds.

Holland House Holland Walk, W8 ☏020/7937 0748, ⓔhollandhouse@yha.org.uk. Holland Park or High Street Kensington tube. See map, p.136. Idyllically situated in the wooded expanse of Holland Park and fairly convenient for the centre of town, this extensive dorm-only hostel offers a decent kitchen, an inexpensive café and beds for £21. Popular with school groups.

Oxford Street 14 Noel St, W1 ☏020/7734 1618, ⓔoxfordst@yha.org.uk. Oxford Circus or Tottenham Court Road tube. See map, p.90. The West End location and modest size mean that this hostel tends to be full even out of high season. No children under six, no groups, no café, but a large kitchen. Dorm bed £22 per person.

Rotherhithe Island Yard, Salter Rd, SE16 ☏020/7232 2114, ⓔrotherhithe@yha.org.uk. Rotherhithe or Canada Water tube. Large purpose-built hostel located in a Docklands area that has little going for it, though it's only a twenty-minute tube ride from the West End and often has space. Rooms have two, four, five or ten beds, and rates start at £15 per person.

St Pancras 79–81 Euston Road, NW1 ☏020/7388 9998, ⓔstpancras@yha.org.uk. King's Cross or Euston tube. Big hostel situated opposite the British Library, on busy Euston Road. Rooms are very clean, bright, triple-glazed and air-conditioned – some even have en-suite facilities and beds cost £24. There are a few en-suite doubles (❸) and family rooms available with TVs.

Private hostels

Ashlee House 261–265 Gray's Inn Rd WC1 ☏020/7833 9400, ⓦwww.ashleehouse.co.uk. King's Cross tube. Basic and a little cramped, but clean and friendly hostel in a converted office block near King's Cross Station. Laundry and kitchen facilities are provided. Dorms vary in size from four to sixteen beds, and there are also a few private rooms with bunk beds starting at £24 per person. Breakfast is included.

Generator Compton Place, off Tavistock Place, WC1 ☏020/7388 7666, ⓦwww.the-generator .co.uk. Russell Square or Euston tube. The neon- and UV-lighting and post-industrial decor may not be to everyone's taste, but with prices starting at just £12.50 a night for a dorm bed and breakfast, this is without doubt the best bargain in this part of town. Facilities include Internet access, a games room, movie nights, a bar open to residents only (till 2am) and a canteen.

Leinster Inn 7–12 Leinster Square, W2 ☏020/7229 9641, ⓦwww.astorhostels.com. Queensway or Notting Hill Gate tube. See map, p.136. The biggest and liveliest of the Astor hostels, with a party atmosphere, and two bars open until the small hours. Singles, doubles (❸) and dorm beds available from £15. Under 30s only.

Museum Inn 27 Montague St, WC1 ☏020/7580 5360, ⓦwww.astorhostels.com. Russell Square tube. See map, p.90. In a lovely Georgian house in Bloomsbury, this is the quietest of the Astor hostels. There's no bar, though it's still a sociable, laid-back place, and well situated. Small kitchen, TV lounge and Internet access. Under 30s only.

St Christopher's Village 161–165 Borough High St, SE1 ☎020/7407 1856, ⓦwww .st-christophers.co.uk. See map, p.112. London Bridge tube. Flagship of a chain of independent hostels, with no fewer than three properties on Borough High Street (and branches in Camden and Greenwich). The decor is upbeat and cheerful, the place is efficiently run and there's a party-animal ambience, fuelled by the neighbouring bar and the rooftop hot tub and sauna.

Student halls

Imperial College ☎020/7594 9507, ⓦwww.ic.ac.uk/conferences. Singles and twins available (with breakfast) in three halls of residence in South Kensington and Notting Hill. Open Easter & July to late-Sept. ❸
International Student House 229 Great Portland St, W1 ☎020/7631 8300, ⓦwww.ish.org.uk. Great Portland Street tube. Hundreds of singles, twins (❸), quads and dorm beds in a vast complex at the southern end of Regent's Park. Open year round; rates from £12.
King's College ☎020/7848 1700, ⓦwww.kcl.ac.uk/kcvb. King's College has a wide range of accommodation available in Bankside, Victoria and Hampstead from July to September. You can either contact the Vacation Bureau by phone or book online. Central rooms tend to be en suite but without breakfast; further afield, it's shared facilities but breakfast included. Rooms are

mostly singles from around £20 each; only Hampstead has twins (❷).
London School of Economics (LSE) ☎020/7955 7370, ⓦwww.lse.ac.uk/collections/vacations. The LSE offers singles, twins, triples and quads in five halls across London – en suite or with shared facilities. Singles start at £27, twins range from cheapies at Rosebery Hall in Clerkenwell (❶) to swanky en suite affairs on Bankside (❹). To find out about availability, you can ring the central office, or visit the website and book online.

Campsites

Abbey Wood Federation Rd, Abbey Wood, SE2 ☎020/8311 7708. Train from Charing Cross or London Bridge to Abbey Wood. Enormous, and well-equipped Caravan Club site, east of Greenwich and ten miles southeast of central London. Open all year.
Crystal Palace Crystal Palace Parade, SE19 ☎020/8778 7155. Train from Victoria or London Bridge to Crystal Palace. Caravan Club site, with maximum stays of two weeks in summer, three weeks in winter. Open all year.
Lea Valley Leisure Centre Caravan Park Meridian Way, N9 ☎020/8803 6900. Train from Liverpool Street to Ponders End. Well-equipped site, situated behind the leisure centre at Pickett's Lock, backing onto a vast reservoir. Open all year.

Westminster and Whitehall

Political, religious and regal power has emanated from **Westminster** and **Whitehall** for almost a millennium. It was Edward the Confessor who first established Westminster as London's royal and ecclesiastical power base, some three miles west of the City of London. The embryonic English parliament met in the abbey in the fourteenth century and eventually took over the old royal palace of Westminster. In the nineteenth century, Whitehall became the "heart of the Empire", its ministries ruling over a quarter of the world's population. Even now, though the UK's world status has diminished, the institutions that run the country inhabit roughly the same geographical area: Westminster for the politicians, Whitehall for the civil servants.

The monuments and buildings in and around Whitehall and Westminster also span the millennium, and include some of London's most famous landmarks – **Nelson's Column**, **Big Ben** and the **Houses of Parliament**, **Westminster Abbey** and **Buckingham Palace**, plus two of the city's finest permanent art collections, the **National Gallery** and **Tate Britain**. This is a well-trodden tourist circuit since it's also one of the easiest parts of London to walk round, with all the major sights within a mere half-mile of each other, linked by two of London's most triumphant avenues, **Whitehall** and **The Mall**.

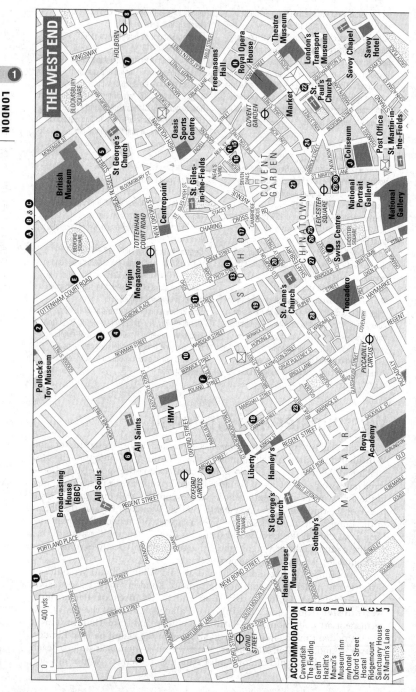

THE WEST END

ACCOMMODATION
Cavendish	A	
The Fielding	H	
Garth	B	
Hazlitt's	G	
Manzi's	I	
Museum Inn	D	
myhotel	E	
Oxford Street	F	
Hostel		
Ridgemount	C	
Sanctuary House	K	
St Martin's Lane	J	

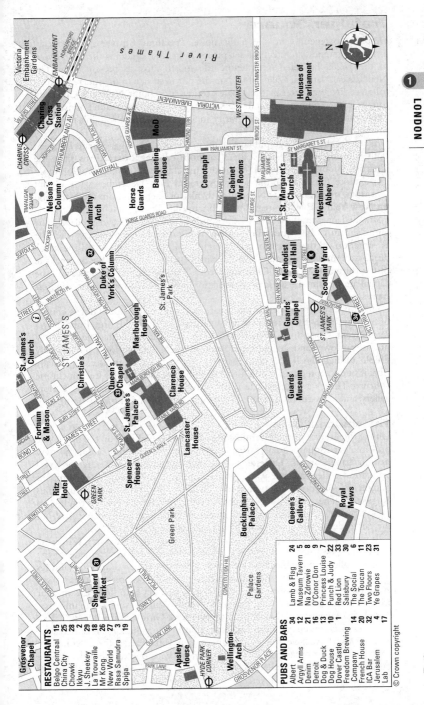

© Crown copyright

RESTAURANTS

Belgo Centraal	15
China City	25
Chowki	28
Ikkyu	2
J. Sheekey	29
La Trouvaille	18
Mr Kong	26
New World	27
Rasa Samudra	3
Spiga	19

PUBS AND BARS

Albert	34	Lamb & Flag	24	
Argyll Arms	12	Museum Tavern	5	
Denim	21	Na Zdrowie	8	
Detroit	16	O'Conor Don	9	
Dog & Duck	13	Princess Louise	7	
Dog House	10	Punch & Judy	22	
Dover Castle	1	Red Lion	33	
Freedom Brewing		Salisbury	30	
Company	14	The Social	6	
French House	20	The Toucan	11	
ICA Bar	32	Two Floors	23	
Jerusalem	4	Ye Grapes	31	
Lab	17			

Trafalgar Square

Despite the pigeons and the traffic noise, **Trafalgar Square** is still one of London's grandest architectural set-pieces. John Nash designed the basic layout in the 1820s, but died long before the square took its present form. The Neoclassical National Gallery filled up the northern side of the square in 1838, followed five years later by the square's central focal point, **Nelson's Column**, topped by the famous admiral; the very large bronze lions didn't arrive until 1868, and the fountains – a real rarity in a London square – didn't take their present shape until the late 1930s.

As one of the few large public squares in London, Trafalgar Square has been both a tourist attraction and a focus for **political demonstrations** since the Chartists assembled here in 1848 before marching to Kennington Common. On a more festive note, the square is graced each December with a giant Christmas tree, donated by Norway in thanks for liberation from the Nazis, and on **New Year's Eve**, thousands of inebriates sing in the New Year.

Stranded on a traffic island to the south of the column, and predating the entire square, is the **equestrian statue of Charles I**, erected shortly after the Restoration on the very spot where eight of those who had signed the king's death warrant were disembowelled. Charles's statue also marks the original site of the thirteenth-century **Charing Cross**, from where all distances from the capital are measured – a Victorian imitation now stands outside Charing Cross train station.

The northeastern corner of the square is occupied by James Gibbs's church of **St Martin-in-the-Fields** (ⓦ www.stmartin-in-the-fields.org), fronted by a magnificent Corinthian portico and topped by an elaborate and distinctly unclassical tower and steeple. Completed in 1726, the interior is purposefully simple, though the Italian plasterwork on the barrel vaulting is exceptionally rich; it's best appreciated while listening to one of the church's free lunchtime concerts. There's a licensed café in the roomy **crypt**, not to mention a shop, gallery and brass-rubbing centre (Mon–Sat 10am–6pm, Sun noon–6pm).

The National Gallery

Unlike the Louvre or the Hermitage, the **National Gallery**, on the north side of Trafalgar Square (daily 10am–6pm, Wed until 8pm; free; ⓦ www .nationalgallery.org.uk; Leicester Square or Charing Cross tube), is not based on a royal collection, but was begun as late as 1824 when the government bought 38 paintings belonging to a Russian emigré banker, John Julius Angerstein. The gallery's subsequent canny acquisition policy has resulted in more than 2300 paintings, but the collection's virtue is not so much its size, but the range, depth and sheer quality of its contents.

To view the collection chronologically, begin with the **Sainsbury Wing**, the softly-softly, postmodern 1980s adjunct that playfully imitates elements of the original gallery's Neoclassicism. However, with more than a thousand paintings on permanent display in the main galleries, you'll need real stamina to see everything in one day, so if time is tight your best bet is to home in on your areas of special interest, having picked up a gallery plan at one of the information desks. A welcome innovation is the **Gallery Guide Soundtrack**, with a brief audio commentary on a large selection of the paintings on display. The Soundtrack is available free of charge, though you're asked for a "voluntary contribution". Another possibility is to join up with one of the gallery's **free guided tours** (daily 11.30am & 2.30pm, plus Wed 6.30pm), which set off from the Sainsbury Wing foyer.

△ Trafalgar Square at night

Among the National's **Italian** masterpieces are Leonardo's melancholic *Virgin of the Rocks*, Uccello's *Battle of San Romano*, Botticelli's *Venus and Mars* (inspired by a Dante sonnet) and Piero della Francesca's beautifully composed *Baptism of Christ*, one of his earliest works. The fine collection of Venetian works includes Titian's colourful early masterpiece *Bacchus and Ariadne*, his very late, much gloomier *Death of Acteon*, and Veronese's lustrous *Family of Darius before Alexander*. Elsewhere, Bronzino's erotic *Venus, Cupid, Folly and Time* and Raphael's trenchant *Pope Julius II* keep company with Michelangelo's unfinished *Entombment*. Later Italian works to look out for include a couple by Caravaggio, a few splendid examples of Tiepolo's airy draughtsmanship and glittering vistas of Venice by Canaletto and Guardi.

From **Spain** there are dazzling pieces by El Greco, Goya, Murillo and Velázquez, among them the provocative *Rokeby Venus*. From the **Low Countries**, standouts include van Eyck's *Arnolfini Marriage*, Memlinc's perfectly poised *Donne Triptych*, and a couple of typically serene Vermeers. There are numerous genre paintings, such as Frans Hals' *Family Group in a Landscape*, and some superlative landscapes, most notably Hobbema's *Avenue, Middleharnis*. An array of Rembrandt paintings that features some of his most searching portraits – two of them self-portraits – is followed by abundant examples of Rubens' expansive, fleshy canvases.

Holbein's masterful *Ambassadors* and several of van Dyck's portraits were painted for the English court, and there's home-grown **British** art, too, represented by important works such as Hogarth's satirical *Marriage à la Mode*, Gainsborough's translucent *Morning Walk*, Constable's ever popular *Hay Wain*, and Turner's *Fighting Téméraire*. Highlights of the **French** contingent include superb works by Poussin, Claude, Fragonard, Boucher and Watteau, and the only two paintings in the country by David.

Finally, there's a particularly strong showing of **Impressionists** and **Post-Impressionists** in rooms 43–46 of the East Wing. Among the most famous works are Manet's unfinished *Execution of Maximilian*, Renoir's *Umbrellas*, Monet's *Thames below Westminster*, Van Gogh's *Sunflowers*, Seurat's pointillist *Bathers at Asnières*, a Rousseau junglescape, Cézanne's proto-Cubist *Bathers* and Picasso's Blue Period *Child with a Dove*.

The National Portrait Gallery

Around the east side of the National Gallery lurks the **National Portrait Gallery** (daily 10am–6pm, Thurs & Fri till 9pm; free; ⓦ www.npg.org.uk; Leicester Square or Charing Cross tube), founded in 1856 to house uplifting depictions of the good and the great. Though it has some fine works in its collection, many of the studies are of less interest than their subjects, and the overall impression is of an overstuffed shrine to famous Brits rather than a museum offering any insight into the history of portraiture. However, it's fascinating to trace who has been deemed worthy of admiration at any moment: aristocrats and artists in previous centuries, warmongers and imperialists in the early decades of the twentieth century, writers and poets in the 1930s and 1940s, and, latterly, retired footballers, and film and pop stars.

The NPG's millennial extension has proved a great success, providing a bigger Tudor section, and a new contemporary gallery to expand the section that's by far the most popular. There's also a computer gallery, lecture theatre and rooftop café/restaurant with a view over the cityscape. The NPG's **Sound Guide**, which gives useful biographical background information to some of the pictures, is provided free of charge, though you're strongly invited to give a "voluntary contribution" of £3.

The Mall and St James's Park

The tree-lined sweep of **The Mall** is at its best on Sundays, when it's closed to traffic. It was laid out in the first decade of the twentieth century as a memorial to Queen Victoria, and runs from Trafalgar Square to Buckingham Palace. The bombastic **Admiralty Arch** was erected to mark the entrance at the Trafalgar Square end of The Mall, while at the other end stands the ludicrous Victoria Memorial, Edward VII's overblown tribute to his mother.

Flanking nearly the whole length of the Mall, **St James's Park** is the oldest of the royal parks, having been drained and enclosed for hunting purposes by Henry VIII. It was landscaped by Nash in the 1820s, and today its tree-lined lake is a favourite picnic spot for the civil servants of Whitehall. Pelicans can still be seen at the eastern end of the lake, and there are ducks, swans and geese aplenty. From the bridge across the lake there's also a fine view over to Westminster and the jumble of domes and pinnacles along Whitehall.

Buckingham Palace

The graceless colossus of **Buckingham Palace** (Aug & Sept daily 9.30am–4.15pm; £12; ⓦ www.royal.gov.uk; Green Park tube), popularly known as "Buck House", has served as the monarch's permanent London residence only since the accession of Victoria. It began its days in 1702 as the Duke of Buckingham's city residence, built on the site of a notorious brothel, and was sold by the duke's son to George III in 1762. The building was overhauled in the late 1820s by Nash and again in 1913, producing a palace that's as bland as it's possible to be.

The Royal Family

Tourists may still flock to see London's royal palaces, but over the last decade the British public have become more critical of the huge tax bill that goes to support the **Royal Family** (ⓦ www.royal.gov.uk) in the style to which they are accustomed. This creeping republicanism can be traced back to 1992, which the Queen herself, in one of her few memorable Christmas Day speeches, accurately described as her *annus horribilis*. This was the year that saw the marriage break-ups of Charles and Di, and Andrew and Fergie, and the second marriage of divorcee Princess Anne.

Matters came to a head, though, over who should pay the estimated £50 million costs of repairs after the fire at Windsor Castle (p.156). Misjudging the public mood, the Conservative government offered taxpayers' money to foot the entire bill. After a furore, it was agreed that some of the cost would be raised by opening up Buckingham Palace to the public for the first time (and by cranking up the admission charges on the rest of London's royal palaces). In addition, under pressure from the media, the Queen also reduced the number of royals paid out of the Civil List, and, for the first time in her life, agreed to pay taxes on her enormous personal fortune.

Given the mounting resentment of the Royal Family, it was hardly surprising that public opinion tended to side with Princess Diana rather than Prince Charles during their various disputes. Diana's subsequent death, and the huge outpouring of grief that accompanied her funeral, further damaged the reputation of the royals, though her demise has also meant the loss of the Royal Family's most vociferous critic. Despite the low poll ratings, none of the political parties currently advocates abolishing the monarchy, and public appetite for stories about the antics of the princes (and their potential girlfriends), or the latest on Charles and Camilla, shows few signs of abating.

For two months of the year, the hallowed portals are grudgingly nudged open; timed tickets are sold from the marquee-like box office in Green Park at the western end of The Mall – to avoid queuing, you must book in advance on ☎020/7321 2233 or online. The interior, however, is a bit of an anticlimax: of the palace's 660 rooms, you're permitted to see twenty or so, and there's little sign of life, as the Queen decamps to Scotland every summer. For the other ten months of the year there's little to do here – not that this deters the crowds who mill around the railings, and gather in some force to watch the **Changing of the Guard** (see opposite), in which a detachment of the Queen's Foot Guards marches to appropriate martial music from St James's Palace (unless it rains, that is).

The public can also pay through the nose to view a small portion of the Royal Collection, at the rebuilt **Queen's Gallery** (daily 10am–5.30pm; £6.50), on the south side of the palace. Exhibitions change regularly, drawn from a collection which is three times larger than the National Gallery, and includes masterpieces by Michelangelo, Reynolds, Gainsborough, Vermeer, van Dyck, Rubens, Rembrandt and Canaletto, as well as the odd Fabergé egg and heaps of Sèvres china.

There's more pageantry on show at the Nash-built **Royal Mews** (March–July & Oct daily 11am–4pm; Aug & Sept Mon–Sat 10am–5pm; £5; Victoria tube), further along Buckingham Palace Road. The royal carriages, lined up under a glass canopy in the courtyard, are the main attraction, in particular the Gold Carriage, made for George III in 1762, smothered in 22-carat gilding and weighing four tons, its axles supporting four life-size figures.

Whitehall

Whitehall, the broad avenue connecting Trafalgar Square to Parliament Square, is synonymous with the faceless, pinstriped bureaucracy charged with the day-to-day running of the country. Since the sixteenth century, nearly all the key governmental ministries and offices have migrated here, rehousing themselves on an ever-increasing scale. The statues dotted about Whitehall recall the days when this street stood at the centre of an empire on which the sun never set.

During the sixteenth and seventeenth centuries Whitehall was the permanent residence of the kings and queens of England, and was synonymous with royalty. The original **Whitehall Palace** was the London seat of the Archbishop of York, confiscated and greatly extended by Henry VIII after a fire at Westminster forced him to find alternative accommodation. The chief section of the old palace to survive the fire of 1698 was the **Banqueting House** (Mon–Sat 10am–5pm; £4; ⓦ www.hrp.org.uk; Westminster tube), begun by Inigo Jones in 1619 and the first Palladian building to be built in England. The one room now open to the public has no original furnishings, but is well worth seeing for the superlative Rubens ceiling paintings glorifying the Stuart dynasty, commissioned by Charles I in the 1630s. Charles himself walked through the room for the last time in 1649 when he stepped onto the executioner's scaffold from one of its windows.

Across the road, two mounted sentries of the Queen's Household Cavalry and two horseless colleagues, all in ceremonial uniform, are posted daily from 10am to 4pm. Ostensibly they are protecting the **Horse Guards** building, originally built as the old palace guardhouse, but now guarding nothing in particular. The mounted guards are changed hourly; those standing every two hours. Try to coincide your visit with the Changing of the Guard (see box opposite), when a squad of twelve mounted troops arrive in full livery.

The Changing of the Guard

The Queen is colonel-in-chief of the seven **Household Regiments**: the Life Guards (who dress in red and white) and the Blues and Royals (who dress in blue and white) are the two Household Cavalry regiments; while the Grenadier, Coldstream, Scots, Irish and Welsh Guards make up the Foot Guards.

All these regiments still form part of the modern army as well as performing cere-monial functions such as the Changing of the Guard. If you're keen to find out more about the Foot Guards, pay a visit to the **Guards' Museum** (daily 10am–4pm; £2), in the Wellington Barracks on the south side of St James's Park.

The **Changing of the Guard** takes place at two separate locations in London: the two Household Cavalry regiments take it in turns to stand guard at Horse Guards on Whitehall (Mon–Sat 11am, Sun 10am, with inspection daily at 4pm), while the Foot Guards take care of Buckingham Palace (April–Aug daily 11.30am; Sept–March alternate days; no ceremony if it rains). A ceremony also takes place regularly at Windsor Castle (see p.156).

Further down this west side of Whitehall is London's most famous address, **Number 10 Downing Street** (ⓦ www.number-10.gov.uk; Westminster tube), the seventeenth-century terraced house that has been the residence of the prime minister since it was presented to Sir Robert Walpole, Britain's first PM, by George II in 1732. Facing the Downing Street gates, in the middle of the road, stands Edwin Lutyens' **Cenotaph**, eschewing any kind of Christian imagery, and inscribed simply with the words "The Glorious Dead". The memorial remains the focus of the Remembrance Sunday ceremony in November.

In 1938, in anticipation of Nazi air raids, the basements of the civil service buildings on the south side of King Charles Street, south of Downing Street, were converted into the **Cabinet War Rooms**, now open to the public (daily: April–Sept 9.30am–6pm; Oct–March 10am–6pm; £7; ⓦ www.iwm.org.uk; Westminster tube). It was here that Winston Churchill directed operations and held Cabinet meetings for the duration of World War II and the rooms have been left pretty much as they were when they were finally abandoned on VJ Day 1945, making for an atmospheric underground trot through wartime London. The museum's free audioguide helps bring the place to life and includes various eyewitness accounts by folk who worked there.

The Houses of Parliament

Clearly visible at the south end of Whitehall is one of London's best-known monuments, the Palace of Westminster, better known as the **Houses of Parliament** (ⓦ www.parliament.uk). The city's finest Victorian Gothic Revival building and symbol of a nation once confident of its place at the centre of the world, it's distinguished above all by the ornate, gilded clock tower popularly known as **Big Ben**, after the thirteen-ton main bell that strikes the hour (and is broadcast across the world by the BBC).

The original Westminster Palace was built by **Edward the Confessor** in the first half of the eleventh century, so that he could watch over the building of Westminster Abbey. It then served as the seat of all the English monarchs until a fire forced Henry VIII to decamp to Whitehall. The Lords have always convened at the palace, but it was only following Henry's death that the House of Commons moved from the abbey's Chapter House into the palace's St Stephen's Chapel, thus beginning the building's associations with parliament.

In 1834 the old palace burned down leaving the bare but impressive expanse of **Westminster Hall**, on the north side of the complex, as the chief relic of the medieval palace. Built by William Rufus in 1099, it's one of the most magnificent secular medieval halls in Europe – you get a glimpse of the hall en route to the public galleries. The **Jewel Tower** (daily: April–Sept 10am–6pm; Oct 10am–5pm; Nov–March 10am–4pm; £2; EH;), across the road from parliament, is another remnant of the medieval palace, now housing an excellent exhibition on the history of parliament – worth visiting before you queue up to get into the Houses of Parliament.

To watch the proceedings in either the House of Commons or the Lords, simply join the queue for the **public galleries** (known as Strangers' Galleries) outside St Stephen's Gate. The public are let in slowly from about 4pm onwards on Mondays, from 1pm Tuesday to Thursday, and from 10am on Fridays; the security checks are very tight, and the whole procedure can take an hour or more. If you want to avoid the queues, turn up an hour or more later, when the crowds have usually thinned. Recesses (holiday closures) of both Houses occur at Christmas, Easter, and from August to the middle of October; phone ☎020/7219 4272 for more information.

To see **Question Time** (Mon 2.30–3.30pm, Tues–Thurs 11.30am–12.30pm) – when the House is at its most raucous and entertaining and the prime minister usually present – you really need to book a **ticket** several weeks in advance from your local MP (if you're a UK citizen) or your embassy in London (if you're not). For part of the summer recess (Aug & Sept), there are public **guided tours** of the building (Mon, Tues, Fri & Sat 9.15am–4.30pm, Wed & Thurs 1.15–4.30pm; £7), lasting an hour and fifteen minutes. Visitors can book in advance by phoning ☎08709/063773, or simply head for the ticket office on Abingdon Green, opposite Victoria Tower. The rest of the year, it's still possible to organize a tour of the building through your MP or embassy. It's also possible to arrange a free guided tour up **Big Ben** (Mon–Fri only; no under-11s; free), again through your MP or embassy; to find out more about access requirements, phone ☎020/7219 4862.

Westminster Abbey

The Houses of Parliament dwarf their much older neighbour, **Westminster Abbey** (Mon–Fri 9.30am–4.45pm, Wed also 6–7pm, Sat 9.30am–2.45pm; £6; ⓦ www.westminster-abbey.org; Westminster or St James's Park tube), yet this single building embodies much of the history of England: it has been the venue for all coronations since the time of William the Conqueror, and the site of more or less every royal burial for some five hundred years between the reigns of Henry III and George II. Scores of the nation's most famous citizens are honoured here, too (though many of the stones commemorate people buried elsewhere), and the interior is crammed with hundreds of monuments, reliefs and statues.

Entry is unfortunately via the north transept, cluttered with monuments to politicians and traditionally known as **Statesmen's Aisle**, shortly after which you come to the abbey's most dazzling architectural set-piece, the **Lady Chapel**, added by Henry VII in 1503 as his future resting place. With its intricately carved vaulting and fan-shaped gilded pendants, the chapel represents the final spectacular gasp of the English Perpendicular style. The public are no longer admitted to the **Shrine of Edward the Confessor**, the sacred heart of the building (except on a guided verger tour; £3), though you do get to inspect Edward I's **Coronation Chair**, a decrepit oak throne dating from around 1300 and still used for coronations.

Nowadays, the abbey's royal tombs are upstaged by **Poets' Corner**, in the south transept, though the first occupant, Geoffrey Chaucer, was in fact buried here not because he was a poet, but because he lived nearby. By the eighteenth century this zone had become an artistic pantheon, and since then, the transept has been filled with tributes to all shades of talent. From the south transept, you can view the central sanctuary, site of the coronations, and the wonderful **Cosmati floor mosaic**, constructed in the thirteenth century by Italian craftsmen, and often covered by a carpet to protect it.

Doors in the south choir aisle lead to the **Great Cloisters** (daily 8am–6pm), rebuilt after a fire in 1298 and now home to a café. At the eastern end of the cloisters lies the octagonal **Chapter House** (daily: April–Sept 9.30am–5pm; Oct 10am–5pm; Nov–March 10am–4pm; EH; £1), where the House of Commons met from 1257. The thirteenth-century decorative paving-tiles and wall-paintings have survived intact. Chapter House tickets include entry to the **Undercroft Museum** (daily 10.30am–4pm), filled with generations of bald royal death masks and wax effigies.

It's only after exploring the cloisters that you get to see the **nave** itself: narrow, light and, at over a hundred feet in height, by far the tallest in the country. The most famous monument in this section is the **Tomb of the Unknown Soldier**, by the west door, which now serves as the main exit.

Tate Britain

Tate Britain (daily 10am–5.50pm; free; ⓦ www.tate.org.uk; Pimlico tube), the purpose-built gallery half a mile south of parliament, founded in 1897 with money from Henry Tate, inventor of the sugar cube, is now devoted exclusively to British art. As well as the collection covering from 1500 to the present and a whole wing devoted to Turner, Tate Britain also showcases contemporary British artists and continues to sponsor the Turner Prize, the country's most prestigious modern-art prize.

The galleries are rehung more or less annually, but always include a fair selection of works by British artists such as Hogarth, Constable, Gainsborough, Reynolds and Blake, plus foreign artists like van Dyck who spent much of their career over here. The ever-popular **Pre-Raphaelites** are always well represented, as are established twentieth-century greats such as Stanley Spencer and Francis Bacon alongside living artists such as David Hockney and Lucien Freud. Lastly, don't miss the Tate's outstanding **Turner collection**, displayed in the Clore Gallery.

Westminster Cathedral

Halfway down Victoria Street, which runs southwest from Westminster Abbey, you'll find one of London's most surprising churches, the stripy neo-Byzantine concoction of the Roman Catholic **Westminster Cathedral** (Mon–Fri & Sun 7am–7pm, Sat 8am–7pm; free; ⓦ www.rcdow.org.uk; Victoria tube). Begun in 1895, and thus one of the last and wildest monuments to the Victorian era, it's constructed from more than twelve million terracotta-coloured bricks, decorated with hoops of Portland stone, and culminating in a magnificent tapered campanile which rises to 274 feet, served by a lift (April–Nov daily 9.30am–12.30pm & 1–5pm; Dec–March Thurs–Sun only; £2). The **interior** is only half finished, so to get an idea of what the place will look like when it's finally completed, explore the series of **side chapels** whose rich, multicoloured decor makes use of over one hundred different marbles from around the world.

St James's, Mayfair and Marylebone

St James's, Mayfair and Marylebone emerged in the late seventeenth century as London's first real suburbs, characterized by grid-plan streets feeding into grand, formal squares. This expansion set the westward trend for middle-class migration, and as London's wealthier consumers moved west, so too did the city's more upmarket shops and luxury hotels, which are still a feature of the area.

Aristocratic St James's, the rectangle of land to the north of St James's Park, was one of the first areas to be developed and remains the preserve of the seriously rich. Piccadilly, which forms the border between St James's and Mayfair, is no longer the fashionable promenade it once was, but a whiff of exclusivity still pervades Bond Street and its tributaries. Regent Street was created as a new "Royal Mile", a tangible borderline to shore up these new fashionable suburbs against the chaotic maze of Soho and the City, where the working population still lived. Now, along with Oxford Street, it has become London's busiest shopping district – it's here that Londoners mean when they talk of "going shopping up the West End".

Marylebone, which lies to the north of Oxford Street, is another grid-plan Georgian development, a couple of social and real-estate leagues below Mayfair, but a wealthy area nevertheless. It boasts a very fine art gallery, the Wallace Collection, and, in its northern fringes, one of London's biggest tourist attractions, Madame Tussaud's, the oldest and largest wax museum in the world.

St James's

St James's, the exclusive little enclave sandwiched between The Mall and Piccadilly, was laid out in the 1670s close to St James's Palace. Royal and aristocratic residences predominate along its southern border, gentlemen's clubs cluster along Pall Mall and St James's Street, while jacket-and-tie restaurants and expense-account gentlemen's outfitters line Jermyn Street. Hardly surprising then that most Londoners rarely stray into this area. St James's does, however, contain some interesting architectural set pieces, such as Waterloo Place, at the centre of which stands the Guards' Crimean Memorial, fashioned from captured Russian cannon and featuring a statue of Florence Nightingale. Clearly visible, beyond, is the "Grand Old" Duke of York's Column, erected in 1833, ten years before Nelson's more famous one in Trafalgar Square.

Cutting across Waterloo Place, Pall Mall – named after the croquet-like game of *paglio a maglio* (literally "ball and mallet") that was popular at the time – leads west to St James's Palace, whose main red-brick gate-tower is pretty much all that remains of the Tudor palace erected here by Henry VIII. When Whitehall Palace burned down in 1698, St James's became the principal royal residence and, in keeping with tradition, an ambassador to the UK is still known as "Ambassador to the Court of St James", even though the court moved down the road to Buckingham Palace when Queen Victoria ascended the throne. The rambling, crenellated complex is off limits to the public, with the exception of the Chapel Royal (Oct to Good Friday Sun 8.30am & 11.15am; Green Park tube), situated within the palace, and the Queen's Chapel (Easter–July Sun 8.30am & 11.15am; Green Park tube), on the other side of Marlborough Road; both are open for services only.

Clarence House, connected to the palace's southwest wing, was home to the Queen Mother, and now provides a bachelor pad for Prince Charles

(ⓦ www.princeofwales.gov.uk); the public was allowed to view the five rooms on the ground floor used for official receptions for the first time in the summer of 2003, so it's worth enquiring about further public openings. An even more palatial St James's residence is Princess Diana's ancestral home, **Spencer House** (Feb–July & Sept–Dec Sun 10.30am–5.45pm; £6), a superb Palladian mansion erected in the 1750s. Inside, tour guides take you through nine of the state rooms, the most outrageous of which is Lord Spencer's Room, with its astonishing gilded palm-tree columns. Note that children under 10 are not admitted.

Piccadilly Circus and Regent Street

Anonymous and congested it may be, but **Piccadilly Circus** is, for many Londoners, the nearest their city comes to having a centre. A much-altered product of Nash's grand 1812 Regent Street plan and now a major traffic bottleneck, it may not be a picturesque place, but thanks to its celebrated aluminium statue, popularly known as **Eros**, it's prime tourist territory. The fountain's archer is one of the city's top attractions, a status that baffles all who live here. Despite the bow and arrow, it's not the god of love at all but the *Angel of Christian Charity*, erected to commemorate the Earl of Shaftesbury, a bible-thumping social reformer who campaigned against child labour.

Regent Street, leading north off Piccadilly Circus, is reminiscent of one of Haussmann's Parisian boulevards without the trees. Drawn up by John Nash in 1812 as both a luxury shopping street and a triumphal way between George IV's Carlton House and Regent's Park, it was the city's earliest attempt at dealing with traffic congestion, and also the first stab at slum clearance and planned social segregation, which would later be perfected by the Victorians.

Despite the subsequent destruction of much of Nash's work in the 1920s, it's still possible to admire the stately intentions of his original Regent Street plan. The increase in the purchasing power of the city's middle classes in the last century brought the tone of the street "down" and heavyweight stores catering for the masses now predominate. Among the best known are **Hamley's**, reputedly the world's largest toyshop, and **Liberty**, the department store that popularized Arts and Crafts designs in the early 1900s.

Piccadilly

Piccadilly apparently got its name from the ruffs or "pickadills" worn by the dandies who used to promenade here in the late seventeenth century. Despite its fashionable pedigree, it's no place for promenading in its current state, with traffic careering down it nose to tail most of the day and night. Infinitely more pleasant places to window-shop are the **nineteenth-century arcades**, originally built to protect shoppers from the mud and horse-dung on the streets, but now equally useful for escaping exhaust fumes.

Piccadilly may not be the shopping heaven it once was, but there are still several old firms here that proudly display their royal warrants. One of the oldest institutions is the food emporium of **Fortnum & Mason** (ⓦ www .fortnumandmason.com) at no. 181, established in the 1770s by one of George III's footmen, Charles Fortnum, and his partner, Hugh Mason. In a kitsch addition dating from 1964, the figures of Fortnum and Mason bow to each other on the hour every day as the clock over the main entrance clanks out the Eton school anthem.

Further along Piccadilly, with its best rooms overlooking Green Park, stands the **Ritz Hotel** (ⓦ www.theritzhotel.co.uk), a byword for decadence since it first wowed Edwardian society in 1906; the hotel's design, with its two-storey

French-style mansard roof and long arcade, was based on the buildings of Paris's Rue de Rivoli. For a prolonged look inside, you'll need to be in good appetite, dress appropriately, and book in advance, for the famous afternoon tea in the hotel's Palm Court.

Across the road from Fortnum & Mason, the **Royal Academy of Arts** (daily 10am–6pm, Fri until 10pm; £7–9; ⓦ www.royalacademy.org.uk; Green Park or Piccadilly Circus tube) occupies the enormous Burlington House, one of the few survivors from the ranks of aristocratic mansions that once lined the north side of Piccadilly. The Academy itself was the country's first-ever formal art school, founded in 1768 by a group of English painters including Thomas Gainsborough and Joshua Reynolds. The Academy hosts a wide range of art exhibitions, and an annual **Summer Exhibition** that remains a stop on the social calendar of upper middle-class England. Anyone can enter paintings in any style, and the lucky winners get hung, in rather close proximity, and sold. Supposed gravitas is added by the RA "Academicians", who are allowed to display six of their own works – no matter how awful. The result is a bewildering display, which gets panned annually by highbrow critics.

Along the west side of the Royal Academy runs **Burlington Arcade**, built in 1819 and Piccadilly's longest and most expensive nineteenth-century arcade, lined with mahogany-fronted jewellers, gentlemen's outfitters and the like. Upholding Regency decorum, it is still illegal to whistle, sing, hum, hurry or carry large packages or open umbrellas on this small stretch, and the arcade's beadles (known as Burlington Berties), in their Edwardian frock-coats and gold-braided top hats, take the prevention of such criminality very seriously.

Bond Street

While Oxford Street, Regent Street and Piccadilly have all gone downmarket, **Bond Street**, which runs parallel with Regent Street, has carefully maintained its exclusivity. It is, in fact, two streets rolled into one: the southern half, laid out in the 1680s, is known as Old Bond Street; its northern extension, which followed less than fifty years later, is known as New Bond Street. They are both pretty unassuming streets architecturally, yet the shops that line them, and those of neighbouring Conduit Street and South Molton Street, are among the flashiest in London, dominated by perfumeries, **jewellers** and designer clothing stores, including Versace, Gucci, Nicole Farhi and Yves St-Laurent. In addition to fashion, Bond Street is also renowned for its fine art galleries and its **auction houses**, the oldest of which is Sotheby's, 34–35 New Bond St (ⓦ www.sothebys.com), whose viewing galleries are open free of charge.

Handel House Museum

The German-born composer **George Frideric Handel** (1685–1759) spent the best part of his life in London, producing all the work for which he is now best known at 25 Brook Street, just west of New Bond Street, now the **Handel House Museum** (Tues–Sat 10am–6pm, Thurs till 8pm, Sun noon–6pm; £4.50; ⓦ www.handelhouse.org). The composer used the ground floor as a sort of shop where subscribers could buy scores, while the first floor was employed as a rehearsal room. Although containing few original artefacts, the house has been painstakingly reconstructed and redecorated to show how it would have looked in Handel's day. Further atmosphere is provided by the harpsichord in the rehearsal room, which gets played by music students throughout the week, and with more formal performances on Thursday evenings from 6pm. Access to the house is via the chic, cobbled yard at the back.

Oxford Street and around

As wealthy Londoners began to move out of the City in the eighteenth century in favour of the newly developed West End, so **Oxford Street** (Ⓦwww .oxfordstreet.co.uk) – the old Roman road to Oxford – gradually became London's main shopping thoroughfare. Today, despite successive recessions and sky-high rents, this scruffy, two-mile hotchpotch of shops is still probably England's busiest street, and is home to (often several) flagship branches of Britain's major retailers (see p.175). The street's only real landmark store is Selfridge's, opened in 1909 with a facade featuring the Queen of Time riding the ship of commerce and supporting an Art Deco clock.

The Wallace Collection

Immediately north of Oxford Street, on Manchester Square, stands Hertford House, a miniature eighteenth-century French chateau which holds the splendid **Wallace Collection** (Mon–Sat 10am–5pm, Sun noon–5pm; free; Ⓣ020/7563 9500, Ⓦwww.wallacecollection.org), a museum-gallery best known for its eighteenth-century French paintings (especially Watteau), Franz Hals' *Laughing Cavalier*, Titian's *Perseus and Andromeda*, Velázquez's *Lady with a Fan* and Rembrandt's affectionate portrait of his teenage son, Titus. There's a modern café in the newly glassed-over courtyard, but at heart, the Wallace Collection remains an old-fashioned place, with exhibits piled high in glass cabinets, and paintings covering every inch of wall space. The fact that these exhibits are set amidst period fittings – and a bloody great armoury – makes the place even more remarkable. If you're here for the paintings, head for the Great Gallery on the first floor, where the best of the works are hung.

Madame Tussaud's and the Planetarium

Madame Tussaud's (Mon–Fri 10am–6pm, Sat & Sun 9am–6pm; school holidays daily 9am–6pm; tickets from £14.99; Ⓣ08704/003000, Ⓦwww.madame-tussauds.co.uk; Baker Street tube), just up Marylebone Road from Baker Street tube, has been pulling in the crowds ever since the good lady arrived in London from Paris in 1802 bearing the sculpted heads of guillotined aristocrats (she herself only just managed to escape the same fate – her uncle, who started the family business, was less fortunate). The entrance fee might be extortionate, the likenesses occasionally dubious and the automated dummies inept, but you can still rely on finding London's biggest queues here. The only way to avoid joining the line is to pay extra and book a timed entry ticket in advance over the phone or on the Internet.

As well as the usual parade of wax figures, the tour ends with a manic five-minute "ride" through the history of London in a miniaturized taxi. Tickets for Madame Tussaud's also cover entry to the adjoining and equally crowded **London Planetarium** (Ⓦwww.london-planetarium.com), which features a twenty-minute high-tech presentation projected onto a giant dome: a quick romp through the cosmos accompanied by astro-babble commentary.

Soho

Soho gives you the best and worst of London: the porn joints that proliferated from the mid-1960s onwards still have a strong presence, but the area also boasts a lively fruit and vegetable market and a nightlife that has attracted writers and ravers of every sexual persuasion since the eighteenth century. The area's most recent transformation took place in the 1990s, when it became Europe's leading gay centre, with bars and cafés bursting out from the Old Compton Street area. Despite regeneration, it has retained an unorthodox and slightly raffish air, born of an immigrant history as rich as that of the East End (see p.124).

Bounded by Regent Street to the west, Oxford Street to the north and Charing Cross Road to the east, Soho remains very much the heart of London and one of the capital's most diverse and characterful areas. Conventional sights are few and far between, yet it's a great area to wander through, with probably more streetlife than anywhere else in London – whatever hour you wander through, there's always something going on. Most folk head here to visit one of the big movie houses on **Leicester Square**, to drink in the latest hip bar or to grab a bite to eat at the innumerable cafés and restaurants, ranging from the inexpensive Chinese places that pepper the tiny enclave of **Chinatown**, to exclusive, Michelin-starred establishments in the backstreets.

Leicester Square and Chinatown

By night, when the big cinemas and discos are doing good business, and the buskers are entertaining the crowds, **Leicester Square** is one of the most crowded places in London, particularly on a Friday or Saturday when huge numbers of tourists and half the youth of the suburbs seem to congregate here. It wasn't until the mid-nineteenth century that the square actually began to emerge as an entertainment zone; cinema moved in during the 1930s, a golden age evoked by the sleek black lines of the Odeon on the east side, and maintains its grip on the area. The Empire, on the north side, is the favourite for the big royal premieres and, in a rather half-hearted imitation of the Hollywood (and Cannes) tradition, there are hand prints visible in the pavement by the southwestern corner of the square.

Chinatown, hemmed in between Leicester Square and Shaftesbury Avenue, is a self-contained jumble of shops, cafés and restaurants that makes up one of London's most distinct and popular ethnic enclaves. **Gerrard Street**, Chinatown's main drag, has been endowed with ersatz touches – telephone kiosks rigged out as pagodas and fake Oriental gates – though few of London's 60,000 Chinese actually live in the three small blocks of Chinatown. Nonetheless, it remains a focus for the community, a place to do business or the weekly shopping, celebrate a wedding, or just meet up for meals, particularly on Sundays, when the restaurants overflow with Chinese families tucking into *dim sum*.

Old Compton Street

If Soho has a main drag, it has to be **Old Compton Street**, which runs parallel with Shaftesbury Avenue. The corner shops, peep shows, boutiques and trendy cafés here are typical of the area and a good barometer of the latest fads. Soho has been a permanent fixture on the **gay scene** for the better part of a century, but the approach is much more upfront nowadays, with gay bars, clubs and cafés jostling for position on Old Compton Street and round the corner in Wardour Street.

The streets round here are lined with Soho institutions past and present. One of the best known is London's longest-running jazz club, *Ronnie Scott's*, on Frith Street, founded in 1958 and still capable of pulling in the big names. Opposite is *Bar Italia*, an Italian café with late-night hours popular with Soho's clubbers. It was in this building, appropriately enough for such a media-saturated

Carnaby Street

Until the 1950s, **Carnaby Street** (ⓦwww.carnaby.co.uk) was a backstreet on Soho's western fringe, occupied, for the most part, by sweatshop tailors who used to make up the suits for nearby Savile Row. Then, sometime in the mid-1950s, several trendy boutiques opened catering for the new market in flamboyant men's clothing. In 1964 – the year of the official birth of the Carnaby Street myth – Mods, West Indian Rude Boys and other "switched-on people", as the *Daily Telegraph* noted, began to hang out here. The area quickly became the epicentre of Swinging Sixties' London, and its street sign London's most popular postcard. A victim of its own hype, Carnaby Street declined equally quickly into an avenue of overpriced tack. More recently, the street has been smartened up, along with neighbouring Newburgh Street, where contemporary London fashion now has a firm foothold, and the whole area is enjoying a new lease of life, though it's never going to recapture the excitement of the 1960s.

area, that John Logie Baird made the world's first public television transmission in 1926.

Bloomsbury

Bloomsbury gets its name from its medieval landowners, the Blemunds, though nothing was built here until the 1660s. Through marriage, the Russell family, the earls and later dukes of Bedford, acquired much of the land and established the many formal, bourgeois squares which are the main distinguishing feature of the area. The Russells named the grid-plan streets after their various titles and estates, and kept the pubs and shops to a minimum to maintain the tone of the neighbourhood.

In the twentieth century, Bloomsbury acquired a reputation as the city's most learned quarter, dominated by the dual institutions of the **British Museum** and **University of London**, and home to many of London's chief book publishers, but perhaps best known for its literary inhabitants. Today, the British Museum is clearly the star attraction, but there are other sights, such as the **Dickens House Museum**, that are high on many people's itineraries.

In its northern fringes, the character of the area changes dramatically, becoming steadily seedier as you near the two big train stations of **Euston** and **King's Cross**, where cheap B&Bs and run-down council estates provide fertile territory for prostitutes and drug dealers, and an unlikely location for the new **British Library**.

The British Museum

The **British Museum** (Mon–Wed, Sat & Sun 10am–5.30pm, Thurs & Fri 10am–8.30pm; free; ⓦwww.british-museum.ac.uk; Russell Square, Tottenham Court Road or Holborn tube) is one of the great museums of the world. With seventy thousand exhibits ranged over two and a half miles of galleries, the museum boasts one of the largest and most comprehensive collections of antiquities, prints and drawings to be housed under one roof – seven million at the last count (a number increasing daily with the stream of new acquisitions, discoveries and bequests). Its assortment of Roman and Greek art is unparalleled, its Egyptian collection is the most significant outside Egypt and, in addition, there are fabulous treasures from Anglo-Saxon and Roman Britain, from China, Japan, India and Mesopotamia – not to mention an enormous collection of prints and drawings, only a fraction of which can be displayed at any one time.

The building itself, begun in 1823, is the grandest of London's Greek Revival edifices, dominated by the giant Ionian colonnade and portico that forms the main entrance. The British Library's departure to St Pancras (see opposite) allowed the museum to open up and redevelop the building's **Great Court** (Mon–Wed, Sat & Sun 9am–6pm, Thurs & Fri 9am–11pm), which now features a remarkable, curving glass-and-steel roof, designed by Norman Foster. At the centre stands the copper-domed former **Round Reading Room**, built in the 1850s to house the British Library. It was here, reputedly at desk O7, beneath one of the largest domes in the world, that Karl Marx penned *Das Kapital*. The building is now a public study area, and features a multimedia guide to the museum's displays.

You'll never manage to see everything in one visit, so the best advice is to concentrate on one or two areas of interest, or else sign up with one of the museum's **guided tours**. One place you could start is the BM's collection of **Roman and Greek antiquities**, perhaps most famous for the Parthenon sculptures, better known as the **Elgin Marbles**, after the British aristocrat who walked off with the reliefs in 1801. Amidst the plethora of Greek and Roman statuary and vases, the only other single item with a similarly high profile is the **Portland Vase**, made from cobalt-blue blown glass around the beginning of the first century, and decorated with opaque white cameos.

The **Egyptian collection** ranges from monumental sculptures, such as the colossal granite head of Amenophis III, to the ever-popular **mummies** and their ornate outer caskets. Also on display is the **Rosetta Stone**, which finally unlocked the secret of Egyptian hieroglyphs. Close by the Egyptian Hall, you'll find a splendid series of **Assyrian reliefs** from Nineveh, depicting events such as the royal lion hunts of Ashurbanipal, in which the king slaughters one of the cats with his bare hands. Among the most extraordinary artefacts from **Mesopotamia** are the enigmatic Ram in the Thicket (a lapis lazuli and shell statuette of a goat) and an equally mysterious box known as the Standard of Ur.

The leathery half-corpse of the 2000-year-old **Lindow Man**, discovered in a Cheshire bog, and the Anglo-Saxon treasure from the **Sutton Hoo** ship burial are among the highlights of the prehistoric and Romano-British section. The medieval and modern collections, meanwhile, range from the twelfth-century Lewis chessmen, carved from walrus ivory, to twentieth-century exhibits such as a copper vase by Frank Lloyd Wright.

The dramatically-lit Mexican and North American galleries, plus the African galleries in the basement, mark the beginning of the return of the museum's **ethnographic collection** (formerly housed in the Museum of Mankind), while select works from the BM's enormous collection of **prints and drawings** can be seen in special exhibitions. In addition, there are fabulous **Oriental treasures** in the north wing, closest to the back entrance on Montague Place. The displays include ancient Chinese porcelain, ornate snuffboxes, miniature landscapes, a bewildering array of Buddhist and Hindu gods, and – the showpiece of the collection – dazzling limestone reliefs from the second-century stupa of Amaravati in south India.

Dickens House

Despite the plethora of blue plaques marking the residences of local luminaries, **Dickens' House** (Mon–Sat 10am–5pm, Sun 11am–5pm; £4;

@www.dickensmuseum.com), at 48 Doughty St, in Bloomsbury's eastern fringes, is the area's only literary museum. Dickens moved here in 1837 shortly after his marriage to Catherine Hogarth, and they lived here for two years, during which time he wrote *Nicholas Nickleby* and *Oliver Twist*. This is the only one of Dickens' fifteen London addresses to survive intact, but only the drawing room, in which Dickens entertained his literary friends, has been restored to its original Regency style. Letters, manuscripts and lots of memorabilia, including first editions, the earliest known portrait and the annotated books he used during extensive lecture tours, are the rewards for those with more than a passing interest in the novelist.

The University

London has more students than any other city in the world (over half a million at the last count), which isn't bad going for somewhere that only organized its own **University** in 1826 (@www.lon.ac.uk; Russell Square, Euston Square or Goodge Street tube), more than six hundred years after the likes of Oxford and Cambridge. The university started life in Bloomsbury, but it wasn't until after World War I that the institution really began to take over the area.

The university's piecemeal development means that its departments are spread over a wide area, though the main focus is between the 1930s **Senate House** skyscraper, behind the British Museum, and the Neoclassical **University College** (UCL; @www.ucl.ac.uk), near the top of Gower Street. UCL is home to London's most famous art school, the **Slade**, which puts on temporary exhibitions from its collection in the **Strang Print Room**, in the south cloister of the main quadrangle (term-time Wed–Fri 1–5pm; free). Also on display in the south cloisters is the fully-clothed skeleton of philosopher **Jeremy Bentham** (1748–1832), one of the university's founders, topped by a wax head and wide-brimmed hat.

The university also runs a couple of specialist museums. On the first floor of the D.M.S. Watson building on Malet Place, a tiny side street opposite Waterstone's bookshop on Torrington Place, the **Petrie Museum of Egyptian Archaeology** (Tues–Fri 1–5pm, Sat 10am–1pm; free; @www.petrie.ucl.ac.uk) has a couple of rooms jam-packed with antiquities, including the world's oldest dress. Further east down Torrington Place, tucked away in the southeast corner of Gordon Square, at no. 53, the **Percival David Foundation of Chinese Art** (Mon–Fri 10.30am–5pm; free; @www.pdfmuseum.org.uk) houses two floors of top-notch Chinese ceramics. Lastly, the temporary exhibitions of photography and art at the **Brunei Gallery** (Mon–Fri 10.30am–5pm; free), which is part of the School of Oriental and African Studies, east of Malet Street, are usually well worth visiting.

The British Library

The new **British Library** (Mon & Wed–Fri 9.30am–6pm, Tues 9.30am–8pm, Sat 9.30am–5pm, Sun 11am–5pm; free; @www.bl.uk; King's Cross or Euston tube), located on the busy Euston Road on the northern fringes of Bloomsbury, opened to the public in 1998. As the country's most expensive public building it was hardly surprising that the place drew fierce criticism from all sides. Architecturally the charge was led, predictably enough, by Prince Charles, who compared it to an academy for secret policemen. Yet while it's true that the building's red-brick brutalism is horribly out of fashion, and compares unfavourably with its cathedralesque Victorian neighbour, the former *Midland Grand Hotel*, the interior of the library has met with general approval, and the high-tech exhibition galleries are superb.

With the exception of the reading rooms, the library is open to the general public. The three exhibition galleries are to the left as you enter; straight ahead is the spiritual heart of the BL, a multistorey glass-walled tower housing the vast **King's Library**, collected by George III, and donated to the museum by George IV in 1823; to the side of the King's Library are the pull-out drawers of the **philatelic collection**. If you want to explore the parts of the building not normally open to the public, you must sign up for a **guided tour** (Mon, Wed & Fri 3pm, Sat 10.30am & 3pm; £6; or Sun 11.30am & 3pm if you want to see the reading rooms; £7).

The first of the three exhibition galleries to head for is the dimly lit **John Ritblat Gallery**, where a superlative selection of the BL's ancient manuscripts, maps, documents and precious books, including the richly illustrated Lindisfarne Gospels, are displayed. One of the most appealing innovations is "**Turning the Pages**", a small room off the main gallery, where you can turn the pages of selected texts "virtually" on a computer terminal. The **Workshop of Words, Sounds and Images** is a hands-on exhibition of more universal appeal, where you can design your own literary publication, while the **Pearson Gallery of Living Words** puts on excellent temporary exhibitions, for which there is sometimes an admission charge.

Covent Garden and the Strand

Covent Garden's transformation from a workaday fruit and vegetable market into a fashion-conscious *quartier* is one of the most miraculous and enduring developments of the 1980s. More sanitized and brazenly commercial than neighbouring Soho, it's a far cry from the district's heyday when the piazza was the great playground (and red-light district) of eighteenth-century London. The buskers in front of St Paul's Church, the theatres round about, and the **Royal Opera House** on Bow Street are survivors in this tradition, and on a balmy summer evening, **Covent Garden Piazza** is still an undeniably lively place to be. Another positive side-effect of the market development has been the renovation of the run-down warehouses to the north of the piazza, especially around the Neal Street area, which now boasts some of the most fashionable shops in the West End, selling everything from shoes to skateboards.

As its name suggests, the **Strand**, just to the south of Covent Garden, once lay along the riverbank: it achieved its present-day form when the Victorians shored up the banks of the Thames to create the Embankment. The Strand's most intriguing sight is **Somerset House,** the sole survivor of the street's grandiose river palaces, which now houses several museums and galleries as well as a lovely new fountain courtyard.

Covent Garden Piazza

London's oldest planned square, laid out in the 1630s by Inigo Jones, **Covent Garden Piazza** was initially a great success, its novelty value alone attracting a rich and aristocratic clientele, but over the next century the tone of the place fell as the fruit and vegetable market expanded, and theatres and coffee houses began to take over the peripheral buildings. When the market closed in 1974, the piazza narrowly survived being turned into an office development. Instead, the elegant Victorian market hall and its environs were restored to house shops, restaurants and arts-and-crafts stalls.

Of Jones's original piazza, the only remaining parts are the two rebuilt sections of north-side arcading, and **St Paul's Church**, facing the west side of the market building. The proximity of so many theatres has earned it the nickname of the "Actors' Church", and it's filled with memorials to international thespians from Boris Karloff to Gracie Fields. The space in front of the church's Tuscan portico – where Eliza Doolittle was discovered selling violets by Henry Higgins in George Bernard Shaw's *Pygmalion* – is now a legalized venue for buskers and street performers, who must audition for a slot months in advance.

The piazza's museums

A former flower-market shed on the piazza's east side is now home to the **London Transport Museum** (Mon–Thurs, Sat & Sun 10am–6pm, Fri 11am–6pm; £5.95; Ⓦ www.ltmuseum.co.uk). A herd of old buses, trains and trams make up the bulk of the exhibits, though there's enough interactive fun – touch-screen computers and the odd costumed conductor and vehicles to climb on – to keep most children amused. There's usually a good smattering of London Transport's stylish maps and posters on display, too, and you can buy reproductions, plus countless other LT paraphernalia, at the shop on the way out.

The rest of the old flower market now houses the **Theatre Museum** (Tues–Sun 10am–6pm; free; Ⓦ www.theatremuseum.org; entrance on Russell Street), displaying three centuries of memorabilia from every conceivable area of the performing arts in the West. The corridors of glass cases cluttered with props, programmes and costumes are not especially exciting, but the special exhibitions and long-term "temporary" shows tend to be a lot more fun, and usually have a performance, workshop or hands-on element to them. The museum also runs a booking service for West End shows and has an unusually good selection of cards and posters.

The Royal Opera House

The arcading on the northeast side of the piazza was rebuilt as part of the recent redevelopment of the **Royal Opera House** (Ⓦ www.royaloperahouse.org), whose main Neoclassical facade dates from 1811 and opens onto Bow Street. Now, however, you can reach the opera house from a passageway in the corner of the arcading. The spectacular wrought-iron **Floral Hall** (daily 10am–3pm) serves as the opera house's main foyer, and is open to the public, as is the *Amphitheatre* bar/restaurant (from one and a half hours before performance to the end of the last interval), which has a glorious terrace overlooking the piazza. Backstage tours of the opera house take place from Monday to Saturday (10.30am, 12.30 & 2.30pm; £7).

Strand

Once famous for its riverside mansions, and later its music halls, the **Strand** – the main road connecting Westminster to the City – is a shadow of its former self. Nowadays, it's best known for the young homeless who shelter in the shop doorways at night.

One such doorway, at no. 440, belongs to what was once London's largest private bank, **Coutts & Co** (Ⓦ www.coutts.com), whose customers include the Queen herself. It was founded in 1692 by the Scottish goldsmith, John

Campbell, a mock-up of whose original premises stands behind a screen in the bank's concrete and marble atrium. Today's male employees still sport anachronistic tail-coated suits, but the horse-drawn carriage which used to convey royal correspondence was sadly taken out of service in 1993.

Some way further east on the opposite side of the Strand, the blind side street of Savoy Court – the only street in the country where the traffic drives on the right – leads to **The Savoy**, London's grandest hotel, built in 1889 on the site of the medieval Savoy Palace. César Ritz was the original manager, Guccio Gucci started out as a dishwasher here, and the list of illustrious guests is endless: Monet painted the Thames from one of the south-facing rooms, Sarah Bernhardt nearly died here, and Strauss the Younger arrived with his own orchestra.

Victoria Embankment

The **Victoria Embankment**, built between 1868 and 1874, was the inspiration of French engineer Joseph Bazalgette, whose project simultaneously relieved congestion along the Strand, provided an extension to the underground railway and sewage systems, and created a new stretch of parkland with a riverside walk – no longer much fun due to the volume of traffic. The 1626 **York Watergate**, in the Victoria Embankment Gardens to the east of Villiers Street, gives you an idea of where the banks of the Thames used to be; the steps through the gateway once led down to the river.

London's oldest monument, **Cleopatra's Needle**, languishes little-noticed on the Thames side of the busy Victoria Embankment, guarded by two Victorian sphinxes. The 60-foot-high, 180-ton stick of granite in fact has nothing to do with Cleopatra – it's one of a pair erected in Heliopolis in 1475 BC (the other one is in New York's Central Park) and taken to Alexandria by the Emperor Augustus fifteen years after Cleopatra's suicide. This obelisk was presented to Britain in 1819 by the Turkish viceroy of Egypt, but nearly sixty years passed before it finally made its way to London.

The **Benjamin Franklin House** (Ⓦ www.rsa.org.uk/franklin), on the other side of Charing Cross Station at 36 Craven St, will probably attract more visitors than Cleopatra's Needle. Restored with the help of, among others, the nearby Royal Society of Arts, the museum should be open some time in 2005; for more information phone ☎020/7930 9121. The tenth son of a candle-maker, Franklin (1706–1790) had "genteel lodgings" here more or less continuously from 1757 to 1775. Whilst Franklin was espousing the cause of the British colonies (as the US then was), the house served as the first de facto American Embassy; eventually, he returned to America to help draft the Declaration of Independence, negotiate the peace treaty with Britain and frame the Constitution.

Somerset House

Somerset House (Ⓦ www.somerset-house.org.uk) is the sole survivor of the grand edifices which once lined the riverfront, its four wings enclosing a large **courtyard** (daily 10am–11pm; free) rather like a Parisian *hôtel*. From March to October, the courtyard features a wonderful 55-jet fountain that spouts straight from the cobbles; in winter, an ice rink is set up in its place. The present building was begun in 1776 by William Chambers as a purpose-built governmental office development, but now also houses a series of museums and galleries.

The south wing, overlooking the Thames, is home to the **Hermitage Rooms** (daily 10am–6pm; ticket prices vary; Ⓦ www.hermitagerooms.com), featuring changing displays drawn from St Petersburg's Hermitage Museum, and the magnificent **Gilbert Collection** (daily 10am–6pm; £5; ⓦwww .gilbert-collection.org.uk), a museum of decorative arts displaying European silver and gold, micro-mosaics, clocks, portrait miniatures and snuffboxes.

In the north wing are the **Courtauld Institute galleries** (daily 10am–6pm; £5; free Mon 10am–2pm; ⓦwww.courtauld.ac.uk), chiefly known for their dazzling collection of Impressionist and Post-Impressionist paintings. Among the most celebrated works is a small-scale version of Manet's *Déjeuner sur l'herbe*, Renoir's *La Loge*, and Degas's *Two Dancers*, plus a whole heap of Cézanne's canvases, including one of his series of *Card Players*. The Courtauld also boasts a fine selection of works by the likes of Rubens, van Dyck, Tiepolo and Cranach the Elder. The collection has recently been augmented by the long-term loan of a hundred top-notch twentieth-century paintings and sculptures by, among others, Kandinksy, Matisse, Dufy, Derain, Rodin and Henry Moore.

Holborn, Clerkenwell and Hoxton

Holborn, **Clerkenwell** and **Hoxton** lie on the periphery of the financial district of the City. **Holborn** (pronounced "Ho-bun") has long been associated with the law, and its **Inns of Court** make for an interesting stroll, their archaic, cobbled precincts exuding the rarefied atmosphere of an Oxbridge college, and sheltering one of the city's oldest churches, the twelfth-century **Temple Church**. Close by the Inns, in Lincoln's Inn Fields, is the **Sir John Soane's Museum**, one of the most memorable and enjoyable of London's small museums, packed with architectural illusions and an eclectic array of curios.

Clerkenwell, further to the northeast, is definitely off the conventional tourist trail with just a few minor sights. Since the 1990s, however, parts of the area have been transformed and, to a certain extent, gentrified, by an influx of young, loft-living designer and media types, whose arrival has had a marked effect on the choice and style of bars and restaurants on offer.

Neighbouring **Hoxton** (aka Shoreditch) to the east, has also acquired a certain caché, due to the high density of artists and architects who currently live and work here. Visually, Hoxton, a slum area badly damaged in the Blitz, remains harsher on the eye than Clerkenwell, though it, too, has more than its fair share of trendy bars and restaurants. Several of London's contemporary art dealers now have Hoxton outlets, and there's the excellent **Geffrye Museum** of furniture design to aim for too.

Temple and the Royal Courts of Justice

Temple (Temple or Blackfriars tube) is the largest and most complex of the Inns of Court, where every barrister in England must study before being called to the Bar. Temple itself is comprised of two Inns – **Middle Temple** (ⓦwww.middletemple.org.uk) and **Inner Temple** (ⓦwww.innertemple .org.uk) – both of which lie to the south of the Strand, and, strictly speaking, just within the boundaries of the City of London. A few very old buildings survive here, but the overall scene is dominated by the soulless neo-Georgian reconstructions that followed the devastation of the Blitz. Still, the maze of courtyards and passageways is fun to explore – especially after dark, when Temple is gas-lit – and there are several points of access, simplest of which is Devereux Court.

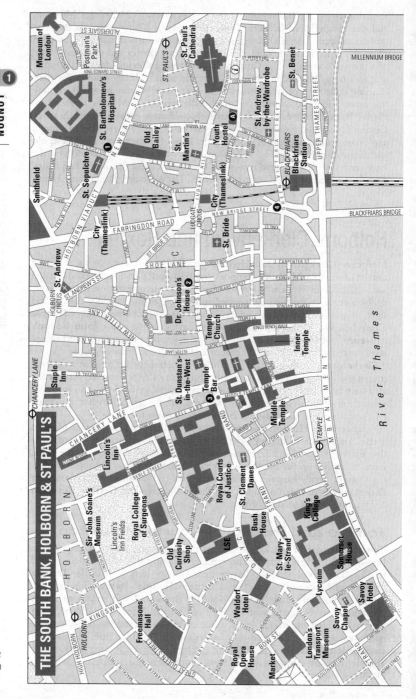

THE SOUTH BANK, HOLBORN & ST PAUL'S

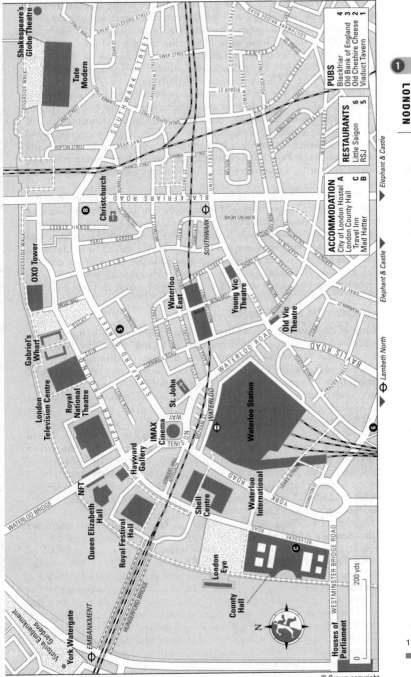

© Crown copyright

PUBS
Blackfriar 4
Old Bank of England 3
Old Cheshire Cheese 2
Viaduct Tavern 1

RESTAURANTS
Little Saigon 6
RSJ 5

ACCOMMODATION
City of London Hostel A
London County Hall C
Travel Inn B
Mad Hatter

Elephant & Castle
Elephant & Castle
Lambeth North

Shakespeare's
Globe Theatre

Tate Modern

OXO Tower

Gabriel's Wharf

London Television Centre

Royal National Theatre

Hayward Gallery

IMAX Cinema

Waterloo East

Young Vic Theatre

Old Vic Theatre

Christchurch

St. John

NFT

Queen Elizabeth Hall

Royal Festival Hall

Shell Centre

Waterloo Station

Waterloo International

London Eye

County Hall

Houses of Parliament

York Watergate

Victoria Embankment Gardens

N

0   200 yds

Medieval students ate, attended lectures and slept in the **Middle Temple Hall** (Mon–Fri 10am–noon & 3–4pm), across the courtyard, still the Inn's main dining room. The present building was constructed in the 1560s and provided the setting for many great Elizabethan masques and plays – probably including Shakespeare's *Twelfth Night*, which is believed to have been premiered here in 1602. The hall is worth a visit for its fine hammerbeam roof, wooden panelling and decorative Elizabethan screen.

The two Temple Inns share use of the complex's oldest building, **Temple Church** (Wed–Sun 11am–4pm; ⓦwww.templechurch.com), built in 1185 by the Knights Templar. An oblong chancel was added in the thirteenth century, and the whole building was damaged in the Blitz, but the original round church – modelled on the Church of the Holy Sepulchre in Jerusalem – still stands, with its striking Purbeck marble piers, recumbent marble effigies of knights, and tortured grotesques grimacing in the spandrels of the blind arcading.

Across the Strand from Temple, the **Royal Courts of Justice** (Mon–Fri 8.30am–4.30pm; Temple tube – Mon–Sat only – or Blackfriars) are home to the Court of Appeal and the High Court, where the most important civil cases are tried. Appeals and libel suits are heard here – it was from this building that the likes of the Guildford Four and Birmingham Six walked to freedom, and it is where countless pop and soap stars have battled it out with the tabloids. The fifty-odd courtrooms are open to the public, though you have to go through stringent security checks first (strictly no cameras allowed).

Lincoln's Inn Fields

North of the Law Courts lies **Lincoln's Inn Fields**, London's largest square, laid out in the early 1640s with **Lincoln's Inn** (Mon–Fri 9am–6pm; ⓦwww.lincolnsinn.org.uk; Holborn tube), the first – and in many ways the prettiest – of the Inns of Court, on its east side. The Inn's fifteenth-century **Old Hall** is open by appointment only (ⓣ020/7405 1393), but you can view the early seventeenth-century **chapel** (Mon–Fri noon–2pm), with its unusual fan-vaulted open undercroft and, on the first floor, its late Gothic nave, hit by a Zeppelin in World War I and much restored since.

The south side of Lincoln's Inn Fields is occupied by the gigantic **Royal College of Surgeons** (ⓦwww.rcseng.ac.uk), home to the **Hunterian Museum** (closed for refurbishment until 2005; Mon–Fri 10am–5pm; free; Holborn tube), a fascinating collection of pickled bits and bobs. Also on view are the skeletons of the Irish giant, O'Brien (1761–83), who was seven feet ten inches tall, and the Sicilian midget Caroline Crachami (1815–24), who was just one foot ten and a half inches when she died at the age of nine.

A group of buildings on the north side of Lincoln's Inn Fields house **Sir John Soane's Museum** (Tues–Sat 10am–5pm; first Tues of the month also 6–9pm; free; ⓦwww.soane.org; Holborn tube), one of London's best-kept secrets. The chief architect of the Bank of England, Soane (1753–1837) was an avid collector who designed this house not only as a home and office, but also as a place to stash his large collection of art and antiquities. Arranged much as it was in his lifetime, the ingeniously planned house has an informal, treasure-hunt atmosphere, with surprises in every alcove; the museum has also begun to exhibit contemporary art. At 2.30pm every Saturday, a fascinating, hour-long **guided tour** (£3) takes you round the museum and the enormous research library, next door, containing architectural drawings, books and exquisitely detailed cork and wood models.

Gray's Inn and Staple Inn

North of Lincoln's Inn, **Gray's Inn** (Mon–Fri 10am–4pm; @www
.graysinn.org.uk; Chancery Lane tube – Mon–Sat only – or Holborn), entered
from High Holborn, is named after the de Grey family, who owned the original mansion. The entrance is through an anonymous cream-coloured building
next door to the venerable *Cittie of Yorke* pub. Established in the fourteenth
century, most of what you see today was rebuilt after the Blitz, with the exception of the **hall** (by appointment only; ☎020/7458 7822), with its fabulous
Tudor screen and stained glass, where the premiere of Shakespeare's *Comedy of
Errors* is thought to have taken place in 1594.

Heading east along High Holborn, it's worth pausing to admire **Staple Inn**
on the right, not one of the Inns of Court, but one of the now defunct Inns
of Chancery, which used to provide a sort of foundation course for those aspiring to the Bar. Its overhanging half-timbered facade and gables date from the
sixteenth century and are the most extensive in the whole of London; they
survived the Great Fire, which stopped just short of Holborn Circus, but had
to be extensively rebuilt after the Blitz.

Clerkenwell

Poverty and overcrowding were the main features of nineteenth-century
Clerkenwell, and **Clerkenwell Green** became known in the press as "the
headquarters of republicanism, revolution and ultra-non-conformity". The
Green's connections with **radical politics** have continued and its oldest building, built as a Welsh Charity School in 1737, is now home to the **Marx
Memorial Library** (Mon, Tues & Thurs 1–6pm, Wed 1–8pm, & Sat
10am–1pm; @www.marxmemoriallibrary.sageweb.co.uk), at no. 37a. One-
time headquarters of the Social Democratic Federation press, this is where
Lenin edited seventeen editions of the Bolshevik paper *Iskra* in 1902–03. The
poky little back room where he worked is maintained as it was then, as a kind
of shrine – you can view it along with the workerist Hastings Mural
from 1935.

Of Clerkenwell's three medieval religious establishments, remnants of two
survive, hidden away to the southeast of Clerkenwell Green. The oldest is the
priory of the Order of St John of Jerusalem; the sixteenth-century **St John's
Gate** (Mon–Fri 10am–5pm, Sat 10am–4pm; free; @www.sja.org.uk), on the
south side of Clerkenwell Road, is the most visible survivor of the foundation.
Today, the gatehouse forms part of a **museum**, which traces the development
of the order before its dissolution in this country by Henry VIII, and its re-
establishment in the nineteenth century. In 1877, the St John Ambulance was
founded, to provide a voluntary first-aid service to the public. It's in this field
that the order is now best known in Britain – a splendid interactive gallery is
devoted to the history of the service. To get to see the rest of the gatehouse,
and to visit the Norman crypt of the Grand Priory Church over the road, you
must take a **guided tour** (Tues, Fri & Sat 11am & 2.30pm; £5 donation
requested).

A little to the southeast of St John's, on the edge of Smithfield, lies
Charterhouse (guided tours only April–Aug Wed 2.15pm; ☎020/7251 5002;
£5), founded in 1371 as a Carthusian monastery. The public school, with
which the foundation is now most closely associated, moved out to Surrey in
1872, but forty-odd pensioners – known, in the monastic tradition, as "brothers" – continue to be cared for here. The only way to visit the site is to join
one of the exhaustive two-hour **guided tours**, which start at the gatehouse

on Charterhouse Square. Very little remains of the original monastic buildings, but there's plenty of Tudor architecture to admire, dating from after the Dissolution when Charterhouse was rebuilt as a private residence.

Hoxton

Until recently, Shoreditch, on the northeastern edge of the City, was a none-too-savoury slice of London, an unpleasant amalgam of wholesale clothes and shoe shops, striptease pubs and roaring traffic. Over the last few years, however, it has been colonized by artists, designers and architects and rejacketed: what was once Shoreditch is now **Hoxton**, previously a much smaller neighbour-hood confined to the north of Old Street. Whatever its real name, the area is actually rich in literary and artistic associations. It was here that James Burbage established the country's first public theatre – called simply the Theatre – in 1576 (he subsequently took it down and reassembled it on Bankside as the Globe).

Just south of Old Street tube and roundabout – Hoxton's chief transport link with the rest of London – lie **Bunhill Fields**, the main burial ground for Dissenters or Nonconformists (practising Christians who were not members of the Church of England). The three most famous graves have been relocated in the central paved area: William Blake's simple tombstone stands next to a replica of Daniel Defoe's, while opposite lies John Bunyan's recumbent statue. Directly opposite Bunhill Fields on City Road stands the Georgian ensemble of **Wesley's Chapel and House** (Mon–Sat 10am–4pm; free). A place of pilgrimage for Methodists, the uncharacteristically ornate chapel, built in 1777, heralded the coming of age of Wesley's sect. Predictably enough, the **Museum of Methodism** in the basement has only a passing reference mention to the insanely jealous forty-year-old widow Wesley married, and who eventually left him. Wesley himself spent his last two years in the delightful Georgian house to the right of the main gates, and inside you can see his deathbed, plus an early shock-therapy machine he was particularly keen on.

The geographical focus of the area's current transformation is **Hoxton Square**, a strange and not altogether happy mixture of light industrial units and artists' studios arranged around a leafy, formal square. Despite the lack of aesthetic charm, the area has become an increasingly fashionable place to live and work and several leading West End **art galleries** have opened up prem-ises here, among them Victoria Miro, Jay Jopling's White Cube and Sadie Coles' Hoxton House. Other than cruising the bars (listed on p.164), and art galleries, there are no real sights as such, though you might want to take a peek at the **Prince's Foundation** (W www.princes-foundation.org), the institute of archi-tecture set up by Prince Charles, which has its headquarters on Charlotte Road, with a gallery that puts on temporary exhibitions of contemporary artists, photographers and designers.

Hoxton's one conventional tourist sight is the **Geffrye Museum** (Tues–Sat 10am–5pm, Sun noon–5pm; free; W www.geffrye-museum.org.uk), a museum of furniture design, set back from Kingsland Road in a peaceful little enclave of eighteenth-century ironmongers' almshouses. A series of period living rooms, ranging from the oak-panelled seventeenth century through refined Georgian and cluttered Victorian, leads to the state-of-the-art New Gallery Extension, housing the excellent twentieth-century section and a pleasant café/restaurant. To get to the museum, take bus #149 or #242 from Liverpool Street tube.

The City

The City is where London began. Long established as the financial district, it stretches from Temple Bar in the west to the Tower of London in the east – administrative boundaries that are only slightly larger than those marked by the Roman walls and their medieval successors. However, in this Square Mile (as the City is sometimes referred to), you'll find few leftovers of London's early days, since four-fifths of the area burnt down in the Great Fire of 1666. Rebuilt in brick and stone, the City gradually lost its centrality as London swelled westwards, though it has maintained its position as Britain's financial heartland. What you see on the ground is mostly the product of three fairly recent building phases: the Victorian construction boom of the latter half of the nineteenth century; the overzealous postwar reconstruction following the Blitz; and the building frenzy that began in the 1980s, during which nearly fifty percent of the City's office space has been rebuilt.

When you consider what has happened here, it's amazing that so much has survived to pay witness to the City's two-thousand-year history. Wren's spires still punctuate the skyline here and there and his masterpiece, **St Paul's Cathedral**, remains one of London's geographical pivots. At the eastern edge of the City, the **Tower of London** still stands protected by some of the best-preserved medieval fortifications in Europe. Other relics, such as the City's few surviving medieval alleyways, Wren's **Monument** to the Great Fire and London's oldest synagogue and church, are less conspicuous, and even locals have problems finding the more modern attractions of the **Museum of London** and the **Barbican** arts complex.

Perhaps the biggest change of all, though, has been in the City's population. Up until the eighteenth century the majority of Londoners lived and worked in or around the City; nowadays 300,000 commuters spend the best part of Monday to Friday here, but only 5000 people remain at night and at weekends. The result of this demographic shift is that the City is fully alive only during office hours. This means that weekdays are by far the best time to visit; many pubs, restaurants and even some tube stations and tourist sights close down at the weekend.

Fleet Street

In 1500 a certain Wynkyn de Worde, a pupil of William Caxton, moved the Caxton presses from Westminster to **Fleet Street**, to be close to the lawyers of

---

The Corporation of London

The one unchanging aspect of the City is its special status, conferred on it by William the Conqueror and extended and reaffirmed by successive monarchs and governments ever since. Nowadays, with its Lord Mayor, its Beadles, Sheriffs and Aldermen, its separate police force and its select electorate of freemen and liverymen, the City is an anachronism of the worst kind. **The Corporation** (ⓦ www .corpoflondon.gov.uk), which runs the City like a one-party mini-state, is an unreconstructed old boys' network whose medievalist pageantry camouflages the very real power and wealth which it holds – the Corporation owns nearly a third of the Square Mile (and several tracts of land elsewhere in and around London). Its anomalous status is all the more baffling when you consider that the City was once the cradle of British democracy: it was the City that traditionally stood up to bullying sovereigns.

the Inns of Court and to the clergy of St Paul's. However, the street really boomed two hundred years later when, in 1702, the now-defunct *Daily Courant*, Britain's first daily newspaper, was published here. By the nineteenth century all the major national and provincial dailies had their offices and printing presses in the Fleet Street district, a situation that prevailed until the 1980s, when the press barons relocated their operations elsewhere. The best source of information about the old-style Fleet Street is the so-called "journalists' and printers' cathedral", the church of **St Bride's** (Mon–Sat 9am–5pm; Ⓦwww.stbrides.com; Blackfriars tube), which boasts Wren's tallest and most exquisite spire (said to be the inspiration for the tiered wedding cake), and whose crypt contains a little museum of Fleet Street history.

The western section of Fleet Street was spared the Great Fire, which stopped just short of **Prince Henry's Room** (Mon–Sat 11am–2pm; free; Ⓦwww.cityoflondon.gov.uk/phr), a fine Jacobean house with timber-framed bay windows. The first-floor room now contains material relating to the diarist **Samuel Pepys**, who was born nearby in Salisbury Court in 1633 and baptized in St Bride's. Even if you've no interest in Pepys, the wooden-panelled room is worth a look – it contains one of the finest Jacobean plasterwork ceilings in London, and a lot of original stained glass.

Numerous narrow alleyways lead off the north side of Fleet Street, two of which – Bolt Court and Hind Court – eventually open out into Gough Square, on which stands **Dr Johnson's House** (May–Sept Mon–Sat 11am–5.30pm; Oct–April Mon–Sat 11am–5pm; £4; Ⓦwww.drjh.dircon.co.uk). The great savant, writer and lexicographer lived here from 1747 to 1759, whilst compiling the 41,000 entries for the first dictionary of the English language, two first editions of which can be seen in the grey-panelled rooms

The City churches

The City of London boasts over forty churches (Ⓦwww.london-city-churches.org), the majority of them built or rebuilt by Wren after the Great Fire. As a general rule, weekday lunchtimes are the best time to visit these churches, many of which put on free lunchtime concerts for the local wage slaves.

On the surface, many of the City churches appear quite similar: plain, light-filled interiors, in white, gold and dark wood furnishings. Below is a list of six of the most varied and interesting churches within the Square Mile:

St Bartholomew-the-Great Cloth Fair; Barbican tube. The oldest surviving church in the City and by far the most atmospheric; a fascinating building. St Paul's aside, if you visit just one church in the City, it should be this one.

St Mary Abchurch Abchurch Lane, Cannon Street; Cannon Street or Bank tube. Uniquely for Wren's City churches, the interior features a huge painted domed ceiling, plus the only authenticated Gibbons reredos.

St Mary Aldermary Queen Victoria Street; Mansion House tube. Wren's most successful stab at Gothic, with fan vaulting in the aisles and a panelled ceiling in the nave.

St Mary Woolnoth Lombard Street; Bank tube. Hawksmoor's only City church, sporting an unusually broad, bulky tower and a Baroque clerestory that floods the church with light from its semicircular windows.

St Olave Hart Street; Tower Hill tube. Built in the fifteenth century, and one of the few pre-Fire Gothic churches in the City.

St Stephen Walbrook Walbrook; Bank tube. Wren's dress rehearsal for St Paul's, with a wonderful central dome and plenty of original woodcarving.

of the house. You can also view the open-plan attic, in which Johnson and his six helpers put together the dictionary.

St Paul's Cathedral

St Paul's Cathedral (Mon–Sat 8.30am–5pm; £6; Ⓦ www.stpauls.co.uk; St Paul's tube), topped by an enormous lead-covered dome that's second in size only to St Peter's in Rome, has been a London icon since the Blitz, when it stood defiantly unscathed amid the carnage (as in the famous wartime propaganda photo). It remains a dominating presence in the City, despite the encroaching tower blocks – its showpiece west facade is particularly magnificent, and is at its most impressive at night when bathed in sea-green arc lights. Westminster Abbey has the edge, however, when it comes to celebrity corpses, pre-Reformation sculpture, royal connections and sheer atmosphere. St Paul's, by contrast, is a soulless but perfectly calculated architectural set piece, a burial place for captains rather than kings, though it does contain more artists than Westminster Abbey. The cathedral's services, featuring the renowned St Paul's choir, are held from Monday to Saturday at 5pm and on Sunday at 10am, 11.30am and 3.15pm.

The best place from which to appreciate the glory of St Paul's is beneath the **dome**, decorated (against Wren's wishes) with Thornhill's trompe l'oeil frescoes. The most richly decorated section of the cathedral, however, is the Quire or **chancel**, where the mosaics of birds, fish, animals and greenery, dating from the 1890s, are particularly spectacular. The intricately carved oak and limewood **choir stalls**, and the imposing organ case, are the work of Wren's master carver, Grinling Gibbons. Meanwhile, in the south-choir aisle is the only complete effigy to have survived from Old St Paul's, the upstanding shroud of **John Donne**, poet, preacher and one-time dean of St Paul's.

A series of stairs, beginning in the south aisle, lead to the dome's three **galleries**, the first of which is the internal **Whispering Gallery**, so called because of its acoustic properties – words whispered to the wall on one side are distinctly audible over one hundred feet away on the other, though the place is often so busy you can't hear much above the hubbub. The other two galleries are exterior: the wide **Stone Gallery**, around the balustrade at the base of the dome, and ultimately the tiny **Golden Gallery**, below the golden ball and cross which top the cathedral.

Although the nave is crammed full of overblown monuments to military types, burials in St Paul's are confined to the **crypt**, reputedly the largest in Europe. The whitewashed walls and bright lighting, however, make this one of the least atmospheric mausoleums you could imagine. Immediately to your right is Artists' Corner, which boasts as many painters and architects as Westminster Abbey has poets, including Christopher Wren himself, who was commissioned to build the cathedral after its Gothic predecessor, Old St Paul's, was destroyed in the Great Fire. The crypt's two other star tombs are those of **Nelson** and **Wellington**, both occupying centre stage and both with more fanciful monuments upstairs.

Museum of London and the Barbican

Despite London's long pedigree, very few of its ancient structures are now standing. However, numerous Roman, Saxon and Elizabethan remains have been discovered during the City's various rebuildings, and many of these finds are now displayed at the **Museum of London** (Mon–Sat 10am–5.50pm, Sun noon–5.50pm; free; Ⓦ www.museumoflondon.org.uk; St Paul's or Barbican tube), hidden above the western end of London Wall, in the southwestern corner of the Barbican complex. The museum's permanent exhibition is basically an educational trot through London's past from prehistory to the present day. This is interesting enough (and understandably attracts a lot of school groups), but the real strength of the museum lies in the excellent temporary exhibitions, gallery tours, lectures, walks and videos it organizes throughout the year – visit the website or pick up a programme of exhibitions and events from the information desk before you set out.

The City's only large residential complex is the **Barbican**, a phenomenally ugly and expensive concrete ghetto built on the heavily bombed Cripplegate area. The zone's solitary prewar building is the heavily restored sixteenth-century church of **St Giles Cripplegate** (Mon–Fri 11am–4pm), situated across from the infamously user-repellent **Barbican Arts Centre** (Ⓦwww .barbican.org.uk), London's supposed answer to Paris's Pompidou Centre, which was formally opened in 1982. The complex, which is at least traffic-free, serves as home to the London Symphony Orchestra and the London chapter of the Royal Shakespeare Company, and holds free gigs in the foyer area.

Guildhall

Situated at the geographical centre of the City, **Guildhall** (May–Sept daily 10am–5pm; Oct–April Mon–Sat 10am–5pm; free; Ⓦwww.cityoflondon .gov.uk; St Paul's or Bank tube) has been the ancient seat of the City administration for over eight hundred years. It remains the headquarters of the Corporation of London (see p.117), and is still used for many of the City's formal civic occasions. Architecturally, however, it is not quite the beauty it once was, having been badly damaged in both the Great Fire and the Blitz, and scarred by the addition of a grotesque 1970s concrete cloister and wing.

Nonetheless, the **Great Hall**, basically a postwar reconstruction of the fifteenth-century original, is worth a brief look, as is the **Clockmakers' Museum** (Mon–Fri 9.30am–4.30pm; free), a collection of over six hundred timepieces, including one of the clocks that won John Harrison the Longitude prize (see p.150). Also worth a visit is the purpose-built **Guildhall Art Gallery** (Mon–Sat 10am–5pm, Sun noon–4pm; £2.50), which contains one or two exceptional works, such as Rossetti's *La Ghirlandata*, and Holman Hunt's *The Eve of St Agnes*, plus a massive painting depicting the 1782 Siege of Gibraltar, commissioned by the Corporation.

The financial centre

Bank is the finest architectural arena in the City. Heart of the finance sector and the busy meeting point of eight streets, it's overlooked by a handsome collection of Neoclassical buildings – among them, the Bank of England, the Royal Exchange and Mansion House (the Lord Mayor's official residence) – each one faced in Portland Stone.

Sadly, only the **Bank of England** (Ⓦwww.bankofengland.co.uk), which stores the nation's vast gold reserves in its vaults, actually encourages visitors. Established in 1694 by William III to raise funds for the war against France, the so-called "Grand Old Lady of Threadneedle Street" wasn't erected on its present site until 1734. All that remains of the building on which Sir John Soane spent the best part of his career from 1788 onwards is the windowless, outer curtain wall, which wraps itself round the three-and-a-half-acre island site. However, you can view a reconstruction of Soane's Bank Stock Office, with its characteristic domed skylight, in the **museum** (Mon–Fri 10am–5pm; free; Bank tube), which has its entrance on Bartholomew Lane.

East of Bank, beyond Bishopsgate, stands Richard Rogers' glitzy **Lloyd's Building**, completed in 1984. A startling array of glass and blue steel pipes – a vertical version of Rogers' own Pompidou Centre – this is easily the most popular of the modern City buildings, at least with the general public. Its closest rival is Norman Foster's giant "erotic gherkin" building for **Swiss Re**, just completed to the north on the site of the old Baltic Exchange which was blown up by the IRA in the early 1990s.

Hidden away behind a modern red-brick office block in a little courtyard off Bevis Marks, north up St Mary Axe from the Lloyd's building, the **Bevis Marks Synagogue** (guided tours Mon–Wed, Fri & Sun noon; £2) was built in 1701 by Sephardic Jews who had fled the Inquisition in Spain and Portugal. This is the country's oldest surviving synagogue, and its roomy, rich interior gives an idea of just how wealthy the congregation was at the time. Nowadays, the Sephardic community has dispersed across London and the congregation has dwindled, though the magnificent array of chandeliers makes it popular for candle-lit Jewish weddings.

Just south of the Lloyd's building you'll find the picturesque **Leadenhall Market**, whose richly painted, graceful Victorian cast-ironwork dates from 1881. Inside, the traders cater mostly for the lunchtime City crowd, their barrows laden with exotic seafood and game, fine wines, champagne and caviar.

London Bridge and Monument

Until 1750, **London Bridge** was the only bridge across the Thames. The Romans were the first to build a permanent crossing here, but it was the medieval bridge that achieved world fame: built of stone and crowded with timber-framed houses, it became one of the great attractions of London – there's a model in the nearby church of St Magnus the Martyr (Tues–Fri 10am–4pm, Sun 10am–1pm). The houses were finally removed in the mid-eighteenth century, and a new stone bridge erected in 1831; that one now stands in the middle of the Arizona desert, having been bought for $2.4 million in the late 1960s by a gentleman who, so the story goes, was under the impression he had purchased Tower Bridge. The present concrete structure, without doubt the ugliest yet, dates from 1972.

The only reason to go anywhere near London Bridge is to see the **Monument** (daily 10am–6pm; £1.50), which was designed by Wren to commemorate the Great Fire of 1666. Crowned with spiky gilded flames, this plain Doric column stands 202 feet high, making it the tallest isolated stone column in the world; if it were laid out flat it would touch the bakery where the Fire started, east of Monument. The bas-relief on the base, now in very bad shape, depicts Charles II and the Duke of York in Roman garb conducting the emergency relief operation. The 311 steps to the viewing gallery once guaranteed an incredible view; nowadays it is somewhat dwarfed by the buildings around it.

The Tower of London

One of Britain's main tourist attractions, the **Tower of London** (March–Oct Mon–Sat 9am–6pm, Sun 10am–6pm; Nov–Feb Mon & Sun 10am–5pm, Tues–Sat 9am–5pm; £12; ⓦ www.hrp.org.uk; Tower Hill tube) overlooks the river at the eastern boundary of the old city walls. Despite all the hype and heritage claptrap, it remains one of London's most remarkable buildings, site of some of the goriest events in the nation's history, and somewhere all visitors and Londoners should explore at least once. Chiefly famous as a place of

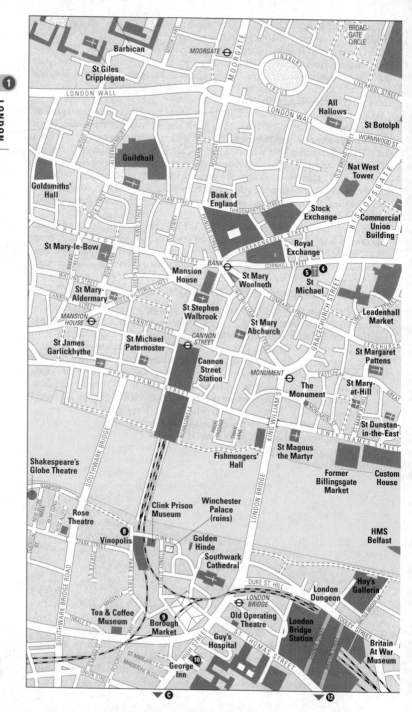

BROADGATE CIRCLE

Barbican

St Giles Cripplegate

MOORGATE ⊖ MOORGATE

FINSBURY CIRCUS

LIVERPOOL STREET

LONDON WALL

LONDON WALL

All Hallows

St Botolph

WORMWOOD ST

MOOR LANE

MOORGATE

WOOD STREET

ALDERMANBURY

Guildhall

COLEMAN STREET

OLD BROAD STREET

Nat West Tower

BISHOPSGATE

Goldsmiths' Hall

GRESHAM STREET

Bank of England

THROGMORTON STREET

Stock Exchange

Commercial Union Building

MILK STREET

KING STREET

OLD JEWRY

PRINCES STREET

St Mary-le-Bow

CHEAPSIDE

POULTRY

BANK

Royal Exchange

5 4

BREAD STREET

BOW LANE

QUEEN STREET

Mansion House

St Mary Woolnoth

CORNHILL STREET

St Michael

WATLING STREET

St Mary-Aldermary

QUEEN VICTORIA STREET

St Stephen Walbrook

KING WILLIAM STREET

LOMBARD STREET

GRACECHURCH STREET

Leadenhall Market

CANNON STREET

MANSION HOUSE ⊖

CANNON STREET

St Mary Abchurch

FENCHURCH

St Margaret Pattens

St James Garlickhythe

St Michael Paternoster

CANNON STREET

Cannon Street Station

MONUMENT

EASTCHEAP

St Mary-at-Hill

GREAT

UPPER THAMES STREET

The Monument

MONUMENT ST

ST MARY AT HILL

St Dunstan-in-the-East

MONUMENT ⊖

LOWER THAMES STREET

ALLHALLOWS LA

ANGEL PASSAGE

SWAN LANE

KING WILLIAM ST

St Magnus the Martyr

Custom House

Shakespeare's Globe Theatre

BANKSIDE

Fishmongers' Hall

LONDON BRIDGE

Former Billingsate Market

NEW GLOBE WALK

BEAR GDNS

Rose Theatre

ROSE ALLEY

Clink Prison Museum

Winchester Palace (ruins)

HMS Belfast

EMERSON ST

8

Vinopolis

PARK STREET

CLINK ST

Golden Hinde

Southwark Cathedral

PARK STREET

PORTER STREET

STONEY STREET

DUKE ST HILL

Hay's Galleria

SOUTHWARK BRIDGE ROAD

Tea & Coffee Museum

9

Borough Market

MAIDEN LANE

LONDON BRIDGE ⊖

London Dungeon

London Bridge Station

TOOLEY STREET

BATTLE BRIDGE LA

IRRALE ST

HIGH STREET

Old Operating Theatre

London Bridge Station

Britain At War Museum

ST MARGARETS CT

MAIDSTONE BLDGS

10

George Inn

Guy's Hospital

ST THOMAS STREET

UNION STREET

REDCROSS

⊽ C

⊽ 12

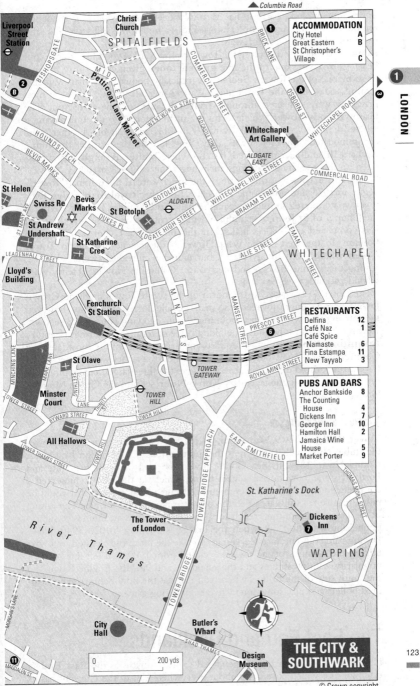

▲ Columbia Road

ACCOMMODATION
City Hotel	A
Great Eastern	B
St Christopher's Village	C

Liverpool Street Station

Christ Church

SPITALFIELDS

BRICK LANE

OSBORN ST

WHITECHAPEL ROAD

BISHOPSGATE

MIDDLESEX STREET

Petticoat Lane Market

WENTWORTH STREET

COMMERCIAL STREET

GOULSTON STREET

Whitechapel Art Gallery

HOUNDSDITCH

ALDGATE EAST

WHITECHAPEL HIGH STREET

LEMAN STREET

COMMERCIAL ROAD

BEVIS MARKS

St Helen

Swiss Re

Bevis Marks

ST BOTOLPH ST

ALDGATE

BRAHAM STREET

St Botolph

St Andrew Undershaft

DUKES PI

ALDGATE

ST MARY AXE

ALDGATE HIGH STREET

ALIE STREET

WHITECHAPEL

St Katharine Cree

LEADENHALL STREET

Lloyd's Building

MANSELL STREET

MINORIES

Fenchurch St Station

PRESCOT STREET

RESTAURANTS
Delfina	12
Café Naz	1
Café Spice Namaste	6
Fina Estampa	11
New Tayyab	3

MINCING LANE

St Olave

MARK LANE

SEETHING LANE

TOWER GATEWAY

ROYAL MINT STREET

PUBS AND BARS
Anchor Bankside	8
The Counting House	4
Dickens Inn	7
George Inn	10
Hamilton Hall	2
Jamaica Wine House	5
Market Porter	9

Minster Court

TOWER STREET

CRUTCHED FRIARS

BYWARD STREET

TOWER HILL

TOWER HILL

All Hallows

TOWER HILL

TOWER THAMES STREET

EAST SMITHFIELD

TOWER BRIDGE APPROACH

THOMAS MORE STREET

St. Katharine's Dock

Dickens Inn

River Thames

WAPPING

The Tower of London

TOWER BRIDGE

N

MORGAN'S LANE

City Hall

Butler's Wharf

SHAD THAMES

Design Museum

MAGDALEN ST

0   200 yds

THE CITY & SOUTHWARK

© Crown copyright

imprisonment and death, it has variously been used as a royal residence, armoury, mint, menagerie, observatory and – a function it still serves – a safe-deposit box for the Crown Jewels.

Before you set off to explore the Tower complex, it's a good idea to get your bearings by taking one of the free **guided tours**, given every thirty minutes or so by one of the Tower's **Beefeaters** (officially known as Yeoman Warders). Visitors today enter the Tower along Water Lane, but in times gone by most prisoners were delivered through **Traitors' Gate**, on the waterfront. The nearby **Bloody Tower**, which forms the main entrance to the Inner Ward, is where the twelve-year-old Edward V and his ten-year-old brother were accommodated "for their own safety" in 1483 by their uncle, the future Richard III, and later murdered. It's also where **Walter Raleigh** was imprisoned on three separate occasions, including a thirteen-year stretch.

The **White Tower**, at the centre of the Inner Ward, is the original "Tower", begun in 1076, and now home to displays from the **Royal Armouries**. Even if you've no interest in military paraphernalia, you should at least pay a visit to the **Chapel of St John**, a beautiful Norman structure on the second floor that was completed in 1080 – making it the oldest intact church building in London. To the west of the White Tower is the execution spot on **Tower Green** where seven highly placed but unlucky individuals were beheaded, among them Anne Boleyn and her cousin Catherine Howard (Henry VIII's second and fifth wives).

The Waterloo Barracks, to the north of the White Tower, hold the **Crown Jewels**, perhaps the major reason so many people flock to the Tower; however, the moving walkways are disappointingly swift, allowing you just 28 seconds' viewing during peak periods. The oldest piece of regalia is the twelfth-century **Anointing Spoon**, but the vast majority of exhibits postdate the Commonwealth (1649–60), when many of the royal riches were melted down for coinage or sold off. Among the jewels are the three largest cut diamonds in the world, including the legendary **Koh-i-Noor**, set into the Queen Mother's Crown in 1937.

Tower Bridge

Tower Bridge (daily 9.30am–6pm; £4.50; ⊛ www.towerbridge.org.uk; Tower Hill tube) ranks with Big Ben as the most famous of all London landmarks. Completed in 1894, its neo-Gothic towers are clad in Cornish granite and Portland stone, but conceal a steel frame, which, at the time, represented a considerable engineering achievement, allowing a road crossing that could be raised to give tall ships access to the upper reaches of the Thames. The raising of the bascules (from the French for "see-saw") remains an impressive sight – phone ahead to find out when the bridge is opening (☎020/7940 3984). Having paid your entrance fee, you get to take the lift to the elevated walkways linking the summits of the towers – closed from 1909 to 1982 due to their popularity with prostitutes and the suicidal – and visit the Engine Room, on the south side of the bridge, where you can see the now defunct giant coal-fired boilers and play some interactive engineering games.

The East End and Docklands

Few places in London have engendered so many myths as the **East End** (a catch-all title which covers just about everywhere east of the City, but has its heart closest to the latter). Its name is synonymous with slums, sweatshops and crime, as epitomized by antiheroes such as Jack the Ripper and the Kray Twins, but also with the rags-to-riches careers of the likes of Harold Pinter and Vidal Sassoon, and whole generations of Jews who were born in the most notorious of London's cholera-ridden quarters and have now moved to wealthier pastures. Old East Enders will tell you that the area's not what it was – and it's true, as it always has been. The East End is constantly changing as newly arrived immigrants assimilate and move out.

The area's first immigrants were French Protestant Huguenots, fleeing religious persecution in the late seventeenth century. Within three generations the Huguenots were entirely assimilated, and the Irish became the new immigrant population, but it was the influx of Jews escaping pogroms in eastern Europe and Russia that defined the character of the East End in the second half of the nineteenth century. The area's Jewish population has now dispersed throughout London, though the East End remains at the bottom of the pile; even the millions poured into the **Docklands** development have failed to make much impression on local unemployment and housing problems. Unfortunately, racism is still rife, and is directed, for the most part, against the extensive Bengali community, who came here from the poor rural area of Sylhet in Bangladesh in the 1960s and 1970s.

As the area is not an obvious place for sightseeing, and certainly no beauty spot – Victorian slum clearances, Hitler's bombs and postwar tower blocks have all left their mark – most visitors to the East End come for its famous **Sunday markets**. However, there's plenty more to get out of a visit, including a trio of **Hawksmoor churches**, and the vast **Canary Wharf** redevelopment, which has to be seen to be believed.

Whitechapel and Spitalfields

The districts of **Whitechapel**, and in particular **Spitalfields**, within sight of the sleek tower blocks of the financial sector, represent the old heart of the East End, where the French Huguenots settled in the seventeenth century, where the Jewish community was at its strongest in the late nineteenth century, and where today's Bengali community eats, sleeps, works and prays. If you visit just one area in the East End, it should be this zone, which preserves mementos from each wave of immigration.

The easiest approach is from Liverpool Street Station, a short stroll west of **Spitalfields Market**, the red-brick and green-gabled market hall built in 1893, half of which was recently demolished in order to make way for yet more City offices. The dominant architectural presence in Spitalfields, however, is **Christ Church** (Mon–Fri 12.30–2.30pm), built in 1714–29 to a characteristically bold design by Nicholas Hawksmoor, and now facing the market hall. Best viewed from Brushfield Street, the church's main features are its huge 225-foot-high spire and a giant Tuscan portico, raised on steps and shaped like a Venetian window (a central arched opening flanked by two smaller rectangles), a motif repeated in the tower and doors.

Whitechapel Road – as Whitechapel High Street and the Mile End Road are collectively known – is still the East End's main street, shared by all the many races who live in the borough of Tower Hamlets. The East End institution that draws in more outsiders than any other here is the **Whitechapel Art Gallery** (Tues & Thurs–Sun 11am–6pm, Wed 11am–8pm; free; ⓦ www.whitechapel .org), housed in a beautiful crenellated 1899 Arts and Crafts building by Charles Harrison Townsend, architect of the similarly audacious Horniman Museum

East End Sunday markets

Most visitors to the East End come here for the **Sunday markets** (@www
.eastlondonmarkets.com). Approaching from Liverpool Street, the first one you
come to, on the east side of Bishopsgate, is **Petticoat Lane** (Sun 9am–2pm;
Liverpool Street or Aldgate East tube), not one of London's prettiest streets, but one
of its longest-running Sunday markets, specializing in cheap (and often pretty tacky)
clothing. The authorities renamed the street Middlesex Street in 1830 to avoid the
mention of ladies' underwear, but the original name has stuck.

Two blocks north of Middlesex Street, down Brushfield Street, lies **Spitalfields
Market** (organic market Fri & Sun 10am–5pm; general market Mon–Fri 11am–3pm
& Sun 10am–5pm; Liverpool Street tube), once the capital's premier wholesale fruit
and vegetable market, now specializing in organic food, plus clothes, crafts and
jewellery. Further east lies **Brick Lane** (Sun 8am–1pm; Aldgate East, Shoreditch or
Liverpool Street tube), heart of the Bengali community, famous for its bric-a-brac
Sunday market, wonderful curry houses and non-stop bagel bakery, and now also
something of a magnet for young designers. From Brick Lane's northernmost end,
it's a short walk to **Columbia Road** (Sun 8am–1pm), the city's best market for flowers and plants, though you'll need to ask the way, or head in direction of the folk
bearing plants.

(p.151). The gallery stages some of London's most innovative exhibitions of
contemporary art, as well as hosting the biennial Whitechapel Open, a chance
for local artists to get their work shown to a wider audience.

Bethnal Green Museum of Childhood

The East End's most popular museum is the **Bethnal Green Museum of
Childhood** (daily except Fri 10am–5pm; free; @www.museumofchildhood
.org.uk), situated opposite Bethnal Green tube station. The open-plan,
wrought-iron hall, originally part of (and still a branch of) the V&A museum
(see p.140), was transported here in the 1860s to bring art to the East End. The
variety of exhibits means that there's something here for everyone from 3 to
93, but the museum's most frequent visitors are children – that said, the
displays are not very hands-on. The ground floor is best known for its unique
collection of antique dolls' houses dating back to 1673. You'll need a pile of
20p pieces with you to work the automata – Wallace the Lion gobbling up
Albert is always a favourite. Elsewhere, there are puppets, a jumble of toys, a
vast doll collection and excellent temporary exhibitions.

Docklands

The architectural embodiment of Thatcherism, a symbol of 1980s smash-and-
grab culture according to its critics, or a blueprint for inner-city regeneration
to its free-market supporters – the **Docklands** redevelopment provokes
extreme reactions. Despite its catch-all name, however, Docklands is far from
homogeneous. Canary Wharf, with its Manhattan-style skyscrapers, is only its
most visible landmark; industrial-estate sheds and riverside flats of dubious
architectural merit are more indicative of the area. **Wapping**, the westernmost
district, has retained much of its old Victorian warehouse architecture, while
the **Royal Docks**, further east, are only just beginning to be transformed from
an industrial wasteland.

The docks were originally built from 1802 onwards to relieve congestion on
the Thames quays, and eventually became the largest enclosed cargo-dock

Docklands transport

Although Canary Wharf is on the Jubilee line, the best way to view Docklands is either from one of the boats that course up and down the Thames (see p.80), or from the driverless, overhead **Docklands Light Railway** or DLR (ⓦwww .tfl.gov.uk/dlr), which sets off from Bank, or from Tower Gateway, close to Tower Hill tube. Travelcards are valid on the DLR, or you can buy a variety of DLR-only day passes giving you unlimited travel on certain sections of the network. Tour guides give a free running commentary on DLR trains that set off on the hour from Tower Gateway (daily 10am–2pm) and Bank (Mon–Fri 11am–2pm, Sat & Sun 10am–2pm) as far as Cutty Sark; passengers and guides starting at Tower Gateway and heading for Canary Wharf or Greenwich must change at Westferry (except Sat & Sun 11am–5pm). If you're heading for Greenwich, and fancy taking a boat back into town, it might be worth considering a Rail River Rover ticket (£8.30), which gives you unlimited travel on the DLR and City Cruises services between Greenwich and Westminster.

system in the world. However, competition from the railways, and later, the development of container ships, forced the closure of most of the docks in the 1960s. Then, at the height of the recession in the 1980s, regeneration began in earnest. No one thought the old docks could ever be rejuvenated, but twenty years on, more has been achieved than many thought possible (though less than some had hoped). Travelling through on the overhead railway, Docklands comes over as an intriguing open-air design museum, not a place one would choose to live or work – most people stationed here still see it as a bleak business-oriented outpost – but a spectacular sight nevertheless.

Wapping to Limehouse

From the DLR overhead railway, you get a good view of two of Hawksmoor's landmark East End churches; the first one is **St George-in-the-East**, built in 1726 and visible to the south just before you reach Shadwell station. It's easy to spot thanks to its four domed corner towers and distinctive west-end tower topped by an octagonal lantern. You're missing nothing by staying on the train, though, as the interior was devastated in the Blitz. As the DLR leaves Limehouse station and skirts Limehouse Basin marina, Hawksmoor's **St Anne's Church** is visible to the north. Begun in 1714 and dominated again by a gargantuan west tower, the church is topped by an octagonal lantern and adorned with the highest church clock in London. Again, the interior isn't worth the effort as it was badly damaged by fire in 1850.

An alternative to the DLR is to walk from Wapping to Limehouse, along the Thames Path, which sticks to, or close to, the riverbank. You begin at **St Katharine's Dock**, immediately east of the Tower of London, and the first of the old docks to be renovated way back in the 1970s. St Katharine's redeeming qualities are the old swing bridges and the boats themselves, many of which are beautiful old sailing ships. Continue along **Wapping High Street**, lined with tall brick-built warehouses, most now tastefully converted into yuppie flats, and you will eventually find yourself in Limehouse, beyond which lies the Isle of Dogs (see below). The fairly well-signposted walk is about two miles in length, and will bring you eventually to Westferry DLR station.

The Isle of Dogs: Canary Wharf

The Thames begins a dramatic horseshoe bend at Limehouse, thus creating the **Isle of Dogs**, the geographical and ideological heart of the new Docklands.

The area reaches its apotheosis in **Canary Wharf** (W www.canarywharf.com), the strip of land in the middle of the former West India Docks, previously a destination for rum and mahogany, later tomatoes and bananas (from the Canary Islands – hence the name).

The only really busy bit of the new Docklands, Canary Wharf is best known as the home of Britain's tallest building, Cesar Pelli's landmark tower, officially known as **One Canada Square**. The world's first skyscraper to be clad in stainless steel, it's an undeniably impressive sight, both from a distance (its flashing pinnacle is a feature of the horizon at numerous points in London) and close up. However, it no longer stands alone, having been joined by several other skyscrapers that stop just short of Pelli's stumpy pinnacle.

The warehouses to the north of Canary Wharf have been converted into flats, bars, restaurants and the **Museum in Docklands** (daily 10am–6pm; £5; W www.museumindocklands.org.uk), which charts the history of the area from Roman times to the development of Canary Wharf via interactive displays, a reconstructed sailor town and numerous paintings and photographs. Unless you're keen to visit the museum, there's little point in getting off the DLR as it cuts right through the middle of the Canary Wharf office buildings under a parabolic steel-and-glass canopy.

The South Bank

The **South Bank** (W www.southbanklondon.com) – the area immediately opposite Victoria Embankment – is best known for the **London Eye**, the world's largest observation wheel and one of the capital's most popular millennium projects. The arrival of the Eye helped kick-start the renovation of the **South Bank Centre**, London's much unloved concrete culture bunker of theatres and galleries, built, for the most part, in the 1960s. After decades in the doldrums, the centre is currently under inspired artistic direction and the whole area is enjoying something of a renaissance.

The wheel's success has rubbed off on the rest of the area too, prompting a major refurbishment programme beginning with the transformation of **Hungerford Bridge**, connecting the South Bank to Embankment, into a gleaming double suspension footbridge. What's more, you can now happily explore the whole area on foot, free from the traffic noise and fumes that blight so much of central London, thanks to the well-marked **Thames Path** which runs along the riverside.

Further afield, in what used to be the village of **Lambeth**, there are one or two places worth visiting, in particular the **Imperial War Museum**, which contains the most detailed exhibition on the Holocaust in Britain.

The South Bank Centre

The modern development of the South Bank dates back to the 1951 **Festival of Britain**, when the South Bank Exhibition was held on derelict land south of the Thames. The festival was a fairly successful attempt to revive postwar morale by celebrating the centenary of the Great Exhibition (when Britain really did rule over half the world). The most striking features of the site were the Royal Festival Hall (which still stands), the ferris wheel (inspiration for the current London Eye), the saucer-shaped Dome of Discovery (disastrously revisited in the guise of the Millennium Dome), and the cigar-shaped Skylon tower.

The Festival of Britain's success provided the impetus for the eventual creation of the **South Bank Centre** (Ⓦwww.sbc.org.uk), now home to artistic institutions such as the Royal Festival Hall (Ⓦwww.rfh.org.uk), the Hayward Gallery (Ⓦwww.hayward.org.uk), the National Film Theatre (NFT), the high-tech BFI London IMAX Cinema, and lastly Denys Lasdun's Royal National Theatre (Ⓦwww.nt-online.org), popularly known as "the National" or NT, which boasts three separate theatres. Its unprepossessing appearance is softened, too, by its riverside location, its avenue of trees, its fluttering banners, its occasional buskers and skateboarders and the secondhand bookstalls and café outside the National Film Theatre.

The London Eye and County Hall

South of the South Bank Centre proper, beside County Hall, is London's most prominent new landmark, the **London Eye** (daily: April–Sept 9.30am–10pm; Oct–March 9am–8pm; £11; ☎08705/000600, Ⓦwww.ba-londoneye.com; Waterloo or Westminster tube), British Airways' magnificently graceful millennium wheel which spins slowly and silently over the Thames. Standing 443ft high, the wheel is the largest ever built, and it's constantly in slow motion – a full-circle "flight" in one of its 32 pods takes around thirty minutes, and lifts you high above the city. It's one of the few places (apart from a plane window) from which London looks a manageable size, as you can see right out to where the suburbs slip into the countryside. Ticket prices are outrageously high, and queues can be very bad at the weekend, so book in advance over the phone or online.

The colonnaded crescent of **County Hall** is the only truly monumental building in this part of town. Designed to house the LCC (London County Council), it was completed in 1933 and enjoyed its greatest moment of fame as the headquarters of the GLC (Greater London Council), abolished by Margaret Thatcher in 1986, leaving London as the only European city without an elected authority. In 2000, the former GLC leader Ken Livingstone was elected as Mayor of London, and moved into the new GLA (Greater London Authority) building near Tower Bridge (see p.134).

County Hall, meanwhile, is in the hands of a Japanese property company, and of the various attractions that have shaped the complex's redevelopment the most popular is the **London Aquarium** (daily 10am–6pm or later; £8.75; Ⓦwww.londonaquarium.co.uk; Waterloo or Westminster tube), laid out across three floors of the basement. With some super-large, multi-floor tanks, and everything from dog-face puffers to piranhas, this is somewhere that's pretty much guaranteed to please younger kids. The "**Beach**", where children can actually stroke the (non-sting) rays, is particularly popular. Though impressive in scale, the aquarium is fairly conservative in design, however, with no walk-through tanks and only the very briefest of information on any of the fish.

Three giant Surrealist sculptures on the riverside walkway in front of County Hall advertise another of the building's attractions, **Dalí Universe** (daily 10am–6pm or later; £8.50; Ⓦwww.daliuniverse.com). There's no denying Salvador Dalí was an accomplished and prolific artist, but you'll be disappointed if you're expecting to see his "greatest hits" – those are scattered across the globe. Most of the works here are little-known bronze and glass sculptures, and various drawings from the many illustrated books that he published, ranging from works by Ovid to the Marquis de Sade. Aside from these, there's one of the numerous Lobster Telephones, which Edward James commissioned for his London home, a copy of his famous Mae West lips sofa, and the oil painting from the dream sequence in Hitchcock's movie *Spellbound*.

△ The London Eye

The latest recruit to the County Hall complex is the **Saatchi Gallery** (Mon–Thurs & Sun 10am–6pm, Fri & Sat 10am–10pm; £8.50; ⓦwww .saatchi-gallery.co.uk) of contemporary art, which now occupies the imposing former council chamber on the first floor. Charles Saatchi, the Jewish Iraqi-born art collector behind the gallery, was, in fact, the man whose advertising for the Tory government helped topple County Hall's original incumbents, the GLC. Saatchi broke with the Tate in the 1980s, after he was accused of including too many items he owned in Tate exhibitions, and went on to help promote the Young British Artists of the 1980s and 1990s, snapping up such seminal Turner Prize-nominated works as Damien Hirst's pickled shark and Tracey Emin's soiled and crumpled bed. The gallery puts on changing exhibitions drawn from Saatchi's vast collection.

Imperial War Museum

The domed building at the east end of Lambeth Road, formerly the infamous lunatic asylum "Bedlam", is now the **Imperial War Museum** (daily 10am–6pm; free; ⓦwww.iwm.org.uk), by far the best military museum in the capital. The treatment of the subject is impressively wide-ranging and fairly sober, with the main hall's militaristic display offset by the lower-ground-floor array of documents and images attesting to the human damage of war. The museum also has a harrowing **Holocaust Exhibition** (not recommended for children under 14), which you enter from the third floor. The exhibition pulls few punches, and has made a valiant attempt to avoid depicting the victims of the Holocaust as nameless masses by focusing on individual cases, and interspersing the archive footage with eyewitness accounts from contemporary survivors.

Southwark

Until well into the seventeenth century, the only reason for north-bank residents to cross the Thames, to what is now **Southwark**, was to visit the infamous Bankside entertainment district around the south end of London Bridge, which lay outside the jurisdiction of the City. What started out as a red-light district under the Romans, reached its peak as the pleasure quarter of Tudor and Stuart London, where disreputable institutions banned in the City – most notably theatres – continued to flourish until the Puritan purges of the 1640s.

Thanks to wholesale regeneration in the last few years, Southwark's riverfront is once more somewhere to head for. The area is linked to St Paul's and the City by the fabulous new Norman Foster-designed **Millennium Bridge**, the first to cross the Thames for over a century, and London's first pedestrian-only bridge. At the end of the bridge, a whole cluster of sights vie for attention, most notably the **Tate Modern** art gallery, housed in a converted power station, and next to it, a reconstruction of Shakespeare's **Globe Theatre**. The **Thames Path** connects the district with the South Bank to the west, and allows you to walk east along Clink Street and Tooley Street, home to a further rash of popular sights such as the **London Dungeon**. Further east still, Butler's Wharf is a thriving little warehouse development centred on the excellent **Design Museum**.

Tate Modern

The masterful conversion of the austere Bankside power station into the **Tate Modern** (daily 10am–6pm; Fri & Sat open until 10pm; free;

ⓦwww.tate.org.uk) has left plenty of the original, industrial feel, while providing wonderfully light and spacious galleries in which to show off the Tate's vast international twentieth-century art collection. The best way to enter is down the ramp from the west, so you get the full effect of the stupendously large turbine hall. It's easy enough to find your way around the galleries, with levels 3 and 5 displaying the permanent collection, level 4 used for fee-paying temporary exhibitions, and level 7 home to a café with a great view over the Thames.

Given that Tate Modern is the largest modern art gallery in the world, you need to spend the best part of a day here to do justice to the place, or be very selective. Pick up a plan (and, for an extra £1, an audioguide), and take the escalator to level 3. The curators have eschewed the usual chronological approach through the "isms", preferring to group works together thematically: Landscape/Matter/Environment, Still Life/Object/Real Life, History /Memory/Society and Nude/Action/Body. On the whole this works very well, though the early twentieth-century canvases, in their gilded frames do struggle when made to compete with contemporary installations.

Although the displays change every six months or so, you're still pretty much guaranteed to see at least some works by **Monet** and Bonnard, Cubist pioneers **Picasso** and Braque, Surrealists such as **Dalí**, abstract artists like **Mondrian**, Bridget Riley and Pollock, and Pop supremos **Warhol** and Lichtenstein. There are seminal works such as a replica of **Duchamp**'s urinal, entitled *Fountain* and signed "R. Mutt", Yves Klein's totally blue paintings and Carl André's trademark piles of bricks. And such is the space here that several artists get whole rooms to themselves, among them the painter Francis Bacon, Joseph Beuys and his shamanistic wax and furs, and **Mark Rothko**, whose abstract "Seagram Murals", originally destined for a posh restaurant in New York, have their own shrine-like room in the heart of the collection.

From the Globe to the Cathedral

Seriously dwarfed by the Tate Modern but equally spectacular is **Shakespeare's Globe Theatre** (ⓦwww.shakespeares-globe.org; Southwark or Blackfriars tube), a reconstruction of the polygonal playhouse where most of the Bard's later works were first performed, and which was originally erected on nearby Park Street in 1598. To find out more about Shakespeare and the history of Bankside, the Globe's pricey but stylish **exhibition** (daily: May–Sept 9am–noon & 12.30–4pm; Oct–April 10am–5pm; £8) is well worth a visit. It begins by detailing the long campaign by American actor Sam Wanamaker to have the Globe rebuilt, but it's the imaginative hands-on exhibits that really hit the spot. You can have a virtual play on medieval instruments such as the crumhorn or sackbut, prepare your own edition of Shakespeare, and feel the thatch, hazelnut-shell and daub used to build the theatre. Visitors also get taken on an informative **guided tour** round the theatre itself, except in the afternoons during the summer season, when you can only visit the exhibition (for a reduced entrance fee).

East of Bankside, beyond Southwark Bridge, lies **Vinopolis** (Mon, Fri & Sat noon–9pm; Tues–Thurs & Sun noon–6pm; £12.50; ⓦwww.vinopolis.co.uk), discreetly housed in former wine vaults under the railway arches on Clink Street. The focus of the complex is the "**Wine Odyssey**", a light-hearted trot through the world's wine regions, equipped with an audioguide. There are plenty of visual gags – you get to tour round the Italian vineyards on a Vespa – but the most appealing and educative aspect of the tour is the **wine-tasting**.

Visitors get five generous samples – from champagne to vintage port – with the option of buying more if you've the head for it.

Further down the suitably gloomy confines of dark and narrow Clink Street is the **Clink Prison Museum** (Map 7, D8; daily 10am–6pm, until 9pm in summer; £4; ℗ www.clink.co.uk), built on the site of the former Clink Prison, origin of the expression "in the clink". The prison began as a dungeon for disobedient clerics, built under the Bishop of Winchester's Palace – the rose window of the palace's Great Hall survives just east of the museum – and later became a dumping ground for heretics, prostitutes and a motley assortment of Bankside lowlife. Today's exhibition features a handful of prison-life tableaux, and dwells on the torture and grim conditions within, but, given the rich history of the place, this is a disappointingly lacklustre museum.

An exact replica of the **Golden Hinde** (phone for times ℗08700/118700; £2.75; ℗ www.goldenhinde.co.uk), the galleon in which Francis Drake sailed around the world from 1577 to 1580, nestles in St Mary Overie Dock, at the eastern end of Clink Street. The ship is surprisingly small, and its original crew of eighty-plus must have been cramped to say the least. There's a refreshing lack of interpretive panels, so it's worth paying the little bit extra and getting a guided tour from one of the folk in period garb – ring ahead to check a group hasn't booked the place up.

Close by the *Golden Hinde* stands **Southwark Cathedral** (Mon–Sat 10am–6pm, Sun 11am–5pm; ℗ www.dswark.org/cathedral), built as the medieval Augustinian priory church of St Mary Overie, and given cathedral status only in 1905. Of the original thirteenth-century church, only the choir and retrochoir now remain, separated by a tall and beautiful stone Tudor screen, making them probably the oldest Gothic structures left in London. The nave was entirely rebuilt in the nineteenth century, but the cathedral contains numerous interesting monuments, from a thirteenth-century oak effigy of a knight to an early twentieth-century memorial to Shakespeare. If you're feeling peckish, the cathedral refectory serves tasty food, but the new multimedia **exhibition** (£3) that whizzes through Southwark's history can be happily skipped.

Borough Market (℗ www.boroughmarket.org.uk), squeezed underneath the railway arches by the cathedral, is one of the few wholesale fruit and vegetable markets still trading under its original Victorian wrought-iron shed. It's recently undergone a transformation from scruffy obscurity to a small foodie haven, with permanent outlets such as Neal's Yard Dairy and Konditor & Cook, joined by gourmet market stalls on Fridays and, particularly, Saturdays.

The **Bramah Tea and Coffee Museum** has recently moved to 40 Southwark Street, a couple of blocks southwest of the cathedral. The place is endearingly ramshackle and well worth a visit. Founded in 1992 by Edward Bramah, who began his career on an African tea garden in 1950, the museum's emphasis is firmly on tea, though the café also serves a seriously good cup of coffee. There's an impressive array of teapots from Meissen to the world's largest, plus plenty of novelty ones, and coffee machines spanning the twentieth century, from huge percolator siphons to espresso machines.

From London Bridge to Butler's Wharf

The most educative and strangest of Southwark's museums, the **Old Operating Theatre, Museum and Herb Garret** on St Thomas Street (daily 10.30am–5pm; £4; ℗ www.thegarret.org.uk; London Bridge tube) is located to the east of the cathedral on St Thomas Street, on the other side of Borough High Street. Built in 1821 at the top of a church tower, where the hospital apothecary's herbs were stored, this women's operating theatre dates from the pre-anaesthetic era. Despite being entirely gore-free, the museum is as stomach-churning as the London Dungeon (see below). The surgeons who used this room would have concentrated on speed and accuracy (most amputations took less than a minute), but there was still a thirty percent mortality rate, with many patients simply dying of shock, and many more from bacterial infection, about which very little was known.

The vaults beneath the railway arches of London Bridge train station, on the south side of **Tooley Street**, are now occupied by two museums. Young teenagers and the credulous probably get the most out of the ever-popular **London Dungeon** (daily: March to mid-July, Sept & Oct 10am–5.30pm; mid-July to Aug 9.30am–7.30pm; Nov–Feb 10.30am–5pm; £12.95; ⓦwww.thedungeons.com; London Bridge tube) – to avoid the inevitable queue, buy your ticket online. The life-sized waxwork tableaux inside include a man being hung, drawn and quartered and one being boiled alive, the general hysteria being boosted by actors, dressed as top-hatted Victorian vampires, pouncing out of the darkness. Visitors are then herded into a court room, condemned to the "River of Death" boat ride, and forced to endure the "Jack the Ripper Experience", an exploitative trawl through post-mortem photos and wax mock-ups of the victims, followed by the "Great Fire of London", in which you experience the heat and the smell of the plague-ridden city, before walking through a revolving tunnel of flames.

A little further east on Tooley Street is **Winston Churchill's Britain at War** (daily: April–Sept 10am–5.30pm; Oct–March 10am–4.30pm; £7.50; ⓦwww.britainatwar.co.uk), an illuminating insight into the stiff-upper-lip London mentality during the Blitz. The museum contains hundreds of wartime artefacts, including an Anderson shelter, where you can hear the chilling sound of the V1 "doodlebugs" and tune in to contemporary radio broadcasts. The grand finale is a walk through the chaos of a just-bombed street.

There's more World War II history, from a more aggressive angle, at **HMS Belfast** (daily: March–Oct 10am–6pm; Nov–Feb 10am–5pm; £6; ⓦwww.iwm.org.uk), a World War II cruiser, permanently moored between London Bridge and Tower Bridge. Armed with six torpedoes, and six-inch guns with a range of over fourteen miles, the *Belfast* spent over two years of the war in the Royal Naval shipyards after being hit by a mine in the Firth of Forth at the beginning of hostilities. It later saw action in the Barents Sea during World War II and during the Korean War, before being decommissioned. The maze of cabins is fun to explore but if you want to find out more about the *Belfast*, head for the exhibition rooms in zone 5.

A short stroll east of the *Belfast* is Norman Foster's startling glass-encased **City Hall** (Mon–Fri 8am–8pm; ⓦwww.london.gov.uk), the new Greater London Authority headquarters that looks like a giant car headlight. Visitors are welcome to stroll around the building and watch the London Assembly proceedings from the second floor.

In contrast to the brash offices on Tooley Street, **Butler's Wharf**, east of Tower Bridge, has retained its historical character. **Shad Thames**, the narrow street at the back of Butler's Wharf, has kept the wrought-iron overhead gangways by which the porters used to transport goods from the wharves to the warehouses further back from the river, and is one of the most atmospheric alleyways in the whole of Bermondsey. The chief attraction of Butler's Wharf is the superb riverside **Design Museum** (daily 10am–5.45pm, Fri until 9pm;

£6; ⓦ www.designmuseum.org; Bermondsey or Tower Hill tube), a stylish, Bauhaus-like conversion of a 1950s warehouse at the eastern end of Shad Thames. The excellent temporary **exhibitions** on important designers, movements or single products are staged on the first floor, while the **galleries** on the top floor offer a brief overview of mass-produced industrial design from TVs to Tupperware. The small coffee bar in the foyer is a great place to relax, and there's a pricier restaurant on the top floor.

Hyde Park, Kensington and Chelsea

Hyde Park, together with its westerly extension, Kensington Gardens, covers a distance of two miles from Oxford Street in the northeast to Kensington Palace in the southwest. At the end of your journey, you've made it to one of London's most exclusive districts, the Royal Borough of **Kensington** and **Chelsea**, which makes up the bulk of this chapter. Other districts go in and out of fashion, but this area has been in vogue ever since royalty moved into **Kensington Palace** in the late seventeenth century.

Aside from the shops around Harrods in Knightsbridge, however, the popular tourist attractions lie in **South Kensington**, where three of London's top (and currently free) **museums** – the Victoria and Albert, Natural History and Science museums – stand on land bought with the proceeds of the Great Exhibition of 1851. Chelsea, to the south, has a slightly more bohemian pedigree. In the 1960s, the **King's Road** carved out its reputation as London's catwalk, while in the late 1970s it was the epicentre of the punk explosion. Nothing so rebellious goes on in Chelsea now, though its residents like to think of themselves as rather more artistic and intellectual than the purely moneyed types of Kensington.

Once slummy, now swanky, **Bayswater** and **Notting Hill**, to the north of Hyde Park, were the bad boys of the borough for many years, dens of vice and crime comparable to Soho. Despite gentrification over the last 25 years, they remain the borough's most cosmopolitan districts, with a strong Arab presence and vestiges of the African-Caribbean community who initiated and still run the city's (and Europe's) largest street **carnival**, which takes place every August Bank Holiday.

Hyde Park and Kensington Gardens

Seized from the Church by Henry VIII to satisfy his desire for yet more hunting grounds, **Hyde Park** (ⓦ www.royalparks.gov.uk) was first opened to the public by James I, and soon became a fashionable gathering place for the beau monde, who rode round the circular drive known as the Ring, pausing to gossip and admire each other's *équipage*. Hangings, muggings and duels, the Great Exhibition of 1851 and numerous public events have all taken place in Hyde Park and even today it's still a popular gathering point or destination for political demonstrations. For most of the time, however, the park is simply a leisure ground – a wonderful open space that allows you to lose all sight of the city beyond a few persistent tower blocks.

Located at the treeless northeastern corner of the park, **Marble Arch** was originally erected in 1828 as a triumphal entry to Buckingham Palace, but is now stranded on a ferociously busy traffic island at the west end of Oxford Street. This is the most historically charged spot in Hyde Park as it marks the site of **Tyburn gallows**, the city's main public execution spot until 1783. It's

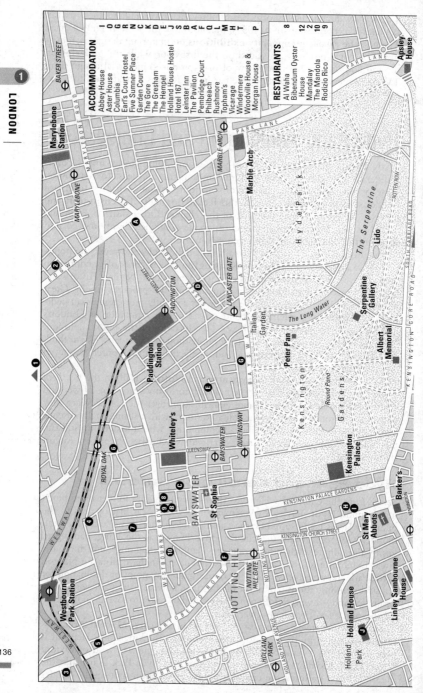

ACCOMMODATION

I	Abbey House
O	Aster House
G	Columbia
R	Earl's Court Hostel
N	Five Summer Place
C	Garden Court
K	The Gore
D	The Gresham
E	The Hempel
J	Holland House Hostel
S	Hotel 167
B	Leinster Inn
A	The Pavilion
F	Pembridge Court
Q	Philbeach
L	Rushmore
M	Topham's
H	Vicarage
T	Windermere
P	Woodville House & Morgan House

RESTAURANTS

8	Al Waha
12	Bibendum Oyster House
2	Mandalay
10	The Mandola
9	Rodizio Rico

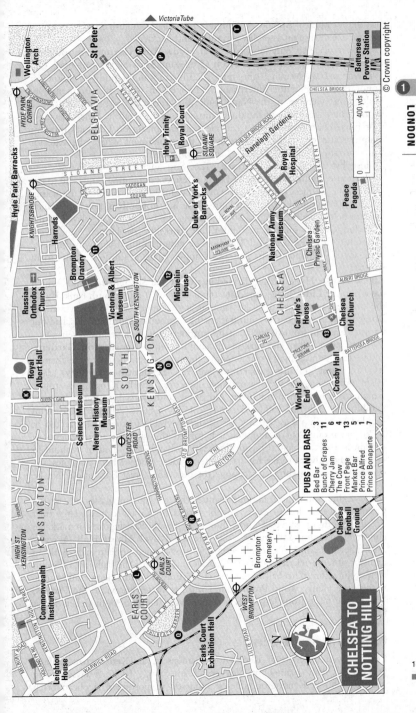

▲ Victoria Tube

© Crown copyright

PUBS AND BARS

Bed Bar	3
Bunch of Grapes	11
Cherry Jam	6
The Cow	4
Front Page	13
Market Bar	5
Prince Alfred	1
Prince Bonaparte	7

CHELSEA TO NOTTING HILL

also the location of **Speakers' Corner**, a peculiarly English Sunday morning tradition, featuring an assembly of ranters and hecklers.

A better place to enter the park is at **Hyde Park Corner**, the southeast corner, where the **Wellington Arch** (Wed–Sun: April–Sept 10am–6pm; Oct 10am–5pm; Nov–March 10am–4pm; £2.50) stands in the midst of another of London's busiest traffic interchanges. Erected in 1828 to commemorate Wellington's victories in the Napoleonic Wars, the arch was originally topped by an equestrian statue of the duke himself, later replaced by Peace driving a four-horse chariot. Inside, you can view an exhibition on London's outdoor sculpture and take a lift to the top of the monument where the exterior balconies offer a bird's eye view of the swirling traffic.

Close by stands **Apsley House** (Tues–Sun 11am–5pm; £4.50; ⓦwww .apsleyhouse.org.uk), Wellington's London residence and now a museum to the "Iron Duke". Unless you're a keen fan of the duke (or the architect, Benjamin Wyatt), the highlight of the museum is the **art collection**, much of which used to belong to the king of Spain. Among the best pieces, displayed in the Waterloo Gallery on the first floor, are works by de Hooch, van Dyck, Velázquez, Goya, Rubens and Murillo. The famous, more than twice life-size, nude statue of Napoleon by Antonio Canova stands at the foot of the main staircase.

Back outside, Hyde Park is divided in two by the **Serpentine Lake**, which has a popular **Lido** (June–Aug daily 10am–6pm; £3) on its south bank. By far the prettiest section of the lake, though, is the upper section known as the **Long Water**, which narrows until it reaches a group of four fountains, laid out symmetrically in front of an Italianate summerhouse designed by Wren.

The western half of the park is officially known as **Kensington Gardens**, and is, strictly speaking, a separate entity, though you hardly notice the change. Its two most popular attractions are the **Serpentine Gallery** (daily 10am–6pm; free; ⓦwww.serpentinegallery.org; South Kensington tube), which has a reputation for lively, and often controversial, contemporary art exhibitions, and the richly decorated, High Gothic **Albert Memorial** (guided tours Sun 2 & 3pm; £3.50), clearly visible to the west. Erected in 1876, the monument is as much a hymn to the glorious achievements of Britain as to its subject, Queen Victoria's husband (who died of typhoid in 1861). Recently restored to his former gilded glory, Albert occupies the central canopy, clutching a catalogue for the 1851 Great Exhibition that he helped to organize.

The Exhibition's most famous feature, the gargantuan glasshouse of the Crystal Palace, no longer exists, but the profits were used to buy a large tract of land south of the park, now home to South Kensington's remarkable cluster of museums and colleges, plus the vast **Royal Albert Hall** (ⓦwww .royalalberthall.com), a splendid iron-and-glass-domed concert hall, with an exterior of red brick, terracotta and marble that became the hallmark of South Ken architecture. The hall is the venue for Europe's most democratic music festival, the Henry Wood Promenade Concerts, better known as the **Proms**, which take place from July to September, with standing-room tickets for as little as £3.

Kensington Palace

On the western edge of Kensington Gardens stands **Kensington Palace** (March–Oct daily 10am–6pm; Nov–Feb 10am–5pm; £10.50; ⓦwww.hrp.org .uk; High Street Kensington tube), a modestly proportioned Jacobean brick mansion bought by William and Mary in 1689, and the chief royal residence for the next fifty years. KP, as it's fondly known in royal circles, is best known today as the place where **Princess Diana** lived until her death in 1997. It was, in fact, the official London residence of both Charles and Di until the couple formally separated. In the weeks following Diana's death, literally millions of flowers, mementos, poems and gifts were deposited at the gates to the south of the palace.

Visitors don't get to see Diana's apartments, which were on the west side of the palace, where various minor royals still live. Instead, they get to view some of Diana's frocks – and also several worn by the Queen – and then the sparsely furnished state apartments. The highlights are the trompe l'oeil ceiling paintings by William Kent, in particular the Cupola Room, and the oil paintings in the King's Gallery. En route, you also get to see the tastelessly decorated rooms in which the future Queen Victoria spent her unhappy childhood. To recover from the above, take tea in the exquisite **Orangery** (times as for palace).

Kensington High Street

Shopper-thronged **Kensington High Street** is dominated architecturally by the twin presences of Sir George Gilbert Scott's neo-Gothic church of St Mary Abbots, whose 250-foot spire makes it London's tallest parish church, and the Art Deco colossus of Barkers department store, remodelled in the 1930s.

Hidden away in the backstreets to the north of High Street Kensington is the densely wooded **Holland Park**, the former grounds of a Jacobean mansion (only the east wing still stands), where theatrical and musical performances are staged throughout the summer and several **formal gardens** surround the house – most notably the Japanese-style Kyoto Gardens – while the rest of the park is dotted with a series of abstract sculptures.

A number of wealthy Victorian artists rather self-consciously founded an artists' colony in the streets that lie between the High Street and Holland Park. It's possible to visit one of the most remarkable of these artist pads, **Leighton House**, at 12 Holland Park Rd (daily except Tues 11am–5.30pm; free; ⓦwww.rbkc.gov.uk/leightonhousemuseum). "It will be opulence, it will be sincerity," Lord Leighton opined before starting work on the house in the 1860s – he later became president of the Royal Academy and was ennobled on his deathbed. The big attraction is the domed Arab Hall, decorated with Saracen tiles, gilded mosaics and woodwork drawn from all over the Islamic world. The other rooms are less spectacular but, in compensation, are hung with paintings by Lord Leighton and his Pre-Raphaelite chums.

Notting Hill

Epicentre of the country's first race riots, when bus-loads of whites attacked West Indian homes in the area, **Notting Hill** is now more famous for its annual **Carnival**, which began life in direct response to the riots. These days, it's the world's biggest street festival outside Rio, with an estimated two million revellers turning up on the last weekend of August for the two-day extravaganza of parades, steel bands and deafening sound systems.

The rest of the year, Notting Hill is a lot quieter, though its cafés and restaurants are cool enough places to pull in folk from all over. On Saturdays, big crowds of Londoners and tourists alike descend on the mile-long **Portobello Road Market**, which is lined with stalls selling everything from antiques to cheap secondhand clothes and fruit and vegetables.

Within easy walking distance of Portobello Road, on the other side of the railway tracks, gasworks and canal, is **Kensal Green Cemetery**

(Ⓦwww.kensalgreen.co.uk; Kensal Green tube), opened in 1833 and still a functioning burial ground. Graves of the more famous incumbents – Thackeray, Trollope and Brunel – are less interesting architecturally than those arranged on either side of the Centre Avenue, which leads from the easternmost entrance on Harrow Road. Guided tours of the cemetery take place every Sunday at 2pm (£5); on the first and third Sunday of the month, the tour includes a trip down the catacombs (bring a torch).

Knightsbridge and Harrods

South of Hyde Park lies the irredeemably snobbish **Knightsbridge**, revelling in its reputation as the swankiest shopping area in London, a status epitomized by **Harrods** (Mon–Sat 10am–7pm; Ⓦwww.harrods.com) on Brompton Road. London's most famous department store started out as a family-run grocery store in 1849, with a staff of two. The current 1905 terracotta building is owned by the Egyptian Mohammed Al Fayed and employs in excess of 3000 staff. Tourists flock to Harrods – it's thought to be one of the city's top-ranking tourist attractions – though if you can do without the Harrods carrier bag, you can buy most of what the shop stocks more cheaply elsewhere.

The store does, however, have a few sections that are architectural sights in their own right: the Food Hall, with its exquisite Arts and Crafts tiling, and the Egyptian Hall, with its pseudo-hieroglyphs and sphinxes, are particularly striking. Now that a fountain dedicated to Di and Dodi is in place, the Egyptian Escalators are an added attraction, and will whisk you to the first floor "luxury washrooms", where you can splash on free perfume after relieving yourself. Note, too, that the store has a draconian dress code: no shorts, no vest T-shirts and backpacks must be carried in the hand.

Victoria and Albert Museum (V&A)

In terms of sheer variety and scale, the **Victoria and Albert Museum**, on Cromwell Road (daily 10am–5.45pm, Wed & last Fri of month until 10pm; free; Ⓦwww.vam.ac.uk; South Kensington tube), popularly known as the V&A, is the greatest museum of applied arts in the world. The range of exhibits on display here means that, whatever your taste, there's bound to be something to grab your attention among the beautifully but haphazardly displayed seven miles of halls and corridors. With such a large collection, the V&A's treasures are impossible to survey in a single visit so a floor plan from the information desks is useful to help you decide which areas to concentrate on. If you're flagging, there's a restaurant in the basement of the Henry Cole Wing, or a more edifying, snacky café in the museum's period-piece **Poynter, Morris and Gamble** refreshment rooms.

The most celebrated of the V&A's numerous exhibits are the **Raphael Cartoons**, seven vast biblical paintings that served as designs for a set of tapestries destined for the Sistine Chapel. Close by, you can view highlights from the country's largest dress collection, and the world's largest collection of Indian art outside India. In addition, there are galleries devoted to British, Chinese, Islamic, Japanese and Korean art, as well as costume jewellery, glassware, metalwork and photography. Wading through the huge collection of European sculpture, you come to the surreal **Plaster Casts** gallery, filled with copies of European art's greatest hits, from Michelangelo's *David* to Trajan's Column (sawn in half to make it fit). There's even a gallery of twentieth-century objets d'art – everything from Bauhaus furniture to Swatch watches – to rival that of the Design Museum.

Over in the **Henry Cole Wing**, meanwhile, you'll find an entire office interior by Frank Lloyd Wright, a collection of sixteenth-century portrait miniatures, more Constable paintings than the Tate, and a goodly collection of sculptures by Rodin. As if all this were not enough, the V&A's temporary shows are among the best in Britain, ranging over vast areas of art, craft and technology.

If you've energy left after your visit, stop by London's most flamboyant Roman Catholic church, the **Brompton Oratory**, built in Neo-Baroque style in the 1880s, which lies just next door to the museum on Brompton Road.

Science Museum

Established as a technological counterpart to the V&A, the **Science Museum**, on Exhibition Road (daily 10am–6pm; free; Ⓦwww .sciencemuseum.org.uk; South Kensington tube), on Exhibition Road, is undeniably impressive, filling seven floors with items drawn from every conceivable area of science, including space travel, telecommunications, time measurement, chemistry, computing, photography and medicine. Keen to dispel the enduring image of museums devoted to its subject as boring and full of dusty glass cabinets, the Science Museum has been busy updating its galleries with more interactive displays, and puts on daily demonstrations to show that not all science teaching has to be deathly dry.

First off, head for the **information desk** in the Power Hall and find out what events and demonstrations are taking place; you can also sign up for a guided tour on a specific subject. Most people will want to head for the **Wellcome Wing**, full of state-of-the-art interactive computers and an IMAX cinema, and geared to appeal to even the most museum-phobic teenager. To get there, go past the info desk, and through the Space gallery, to the far side of the Making of the Modern World, a display of iconic inventions from Robert Stephenson's *Rocket* train of 1829 to the Ford Model T, the world's first mass-produced car.

The **Launch Pad**, one of the first hands-on displays aimed at kids, remains as popular and enjoyable as ever, as do the **Garden** and **Things** galleries, all of which are in the basement. The **Materials** gallery, on the first floor, is aimed more at adults, and is an extremely stylish exhibition covering the use of materials ranging from aluminium to zerodur (used for making laser gyroscopes).

Natural History Museum

Alfred Waterhouse's purpose-built mock-Romanesque colossus ensures the **Natural History Museum** (Mon–Sat 10am–5.50pm, Sun 11am–5.50pm; free; Ⓦwww.nhm.ac.uk; South Kensington tube) its status as London's most handsome museum. Caught up, without huge public funds, in the current enthusiasm for museum redesign and accessibility, the contents are a mishmash of truly imaginative exhibits peppered amongst others little changed since the museum's opening in 1881. The museum is caught in a genuine conundrum, for its collections are important resources for serious zoologists, while its collection of real dinosaurs is a big hit with the kids.

The **main entrance**, in the middle of the 675-foot terracotta facade, leads to what are now known as the **Life Galleries**. Just off the vast Central Hall, dominated by an 85ft-long plaster cast of a Diplodocus skeleton, you'll find the Dinosaur gallery, where a team of animatronic deinonychi feast on a half-dead tenontosaurus. Other popular sections include the Creepy-Crawlies Room, the Mammals gallery with its life-size model of a blue whale, and the high-tech Ecology Gallery, plus the somewhat ancient displays of stuffed creatures.

Visitors can view more of the museum's millions of zoological specimens in the collections store of the new **Darwin Centre**, Phase One of which opened in 2002. To see the rest of the building, however, you need to sign up for a **guided tour** (book ahead either online or by phone ☎020/7942 6128; free). These set off roughly every half an hour and last about 35 minutes, allowing visitors to get a closer look at the specimens, including the larger ones which have to be preserved in tanks. You also get to see behind the scenes at the labs, and even talk to one of the museum's 350 scientists about their work.

If the queues for the museum are long (as they can be at weekends and during school holidays), you might be better off heading for the side entrance on Exhibition Road, which leads into the former Geology Museum, now known as the **Earth Galleries**, an expensively revamped and visually exciting romp through the earth's evolution. The most popular sections are the slightly tasteless Kobe earthquake simulator, and the spectacular display of gems and crystals in the Earth's Treasury.

Chelsea

It wasn't until the latter part of the nineteenth century that **Chelsea** began to earn its reputation as London's very own Left Bank. Its household fame, however, came through the **King's Road**'s role as the unofficial catwalk of the "Swinging Sixties". The road remained a fashion parade for hippies too, and in the Jubilee Year of 1977 it witnessed the birth of punk, masterminded from a shop called Sex, run by Vivienne Westwood and Malcolm McLaren. These days, the area is better known for its young, upper-class residents – the original Sloane Rangers – and is lined with the usual chain stores and interior design shops.

Among the most nattily attired of all those parading down the King's Road are the scarlet or navy-blue clad Chelsea Pensioners, army veterans from the nearby **Royal Hospital** (Mon–Fri 9am–noon & 2–4.30pm, Sat & Sun closes 3pm; free; Sloane Square tube), founded by Charles II in 1681. The hospital's majestic red-brick wings and grassy courtyards became a blueprint for institutional and collegiate architecture all over the English-speaking world. The public are allowed to view the austere hospital chapel, and the equally grand, wood-panelled dining hall, opposite, which has a vast allegorical mural of Charles II.

The concrete bunker next door to the Royal Hospital, on Royal Hospital Road, houses the **National Army Museum** (daily 10am–5.30pm; free; ⓦwww.national-army-museum.ac.uk). The militarily obsessed are unlikely to be disappointed by the succession of uniforms and medals, but there's little here for non-enthusiasts. The temporary exhibitions staged on the ground floor are the museum's strong point, but it's rather disappointing overall – you're better off visiting the infinitely superior Imperial War Museum (see p.131).

Cheyne Walk and Cheyne Row

The quiet riverside locale of **Cheyne Walk** (pronounced "chainy") drew artists and writers in great numbers during the nineteenth century. Since the building of the Embankment and the increase in the volume of traffic, however, the character of this peaceful haven has been lost. Novelist Henry James, who lived at no. 21, used to take "beguiling drives" in his wheelchair along the Embankment; today, he'd be hospitalized in the process.

The chief reason to come here nowadays is to visit the **Chelsea Physic Garden** (April–Oct Wed noon–5pm, Sun 2–6pm; £4; ⓦwww

.chelseaphysicgarden.co.uk; Sloane Square tube), which marks the beginning of Cheyne Walk. Founded in 1673, this small walled garden is the second oldest botanic garden in the country. At the entrance (on Swan Walk) you can pick up a map of the garden with a list of the month's most interesting flowers and shrubs, whose labels are slightly more forthcoming than the usual terse Latinate tags. The garden also has an excellent teahouse, where you can get delicious home-made cakes.

It's also worth popping into the nearby **Chelsea Old Church** (daily 9.30am–1pm & 2–4.30pm; Sloane Square tube), halfway down Cheyne Walk, where Thomas More built his own private chapel in the south aisle. The church was badly bombed in the last war, but an impressive number of monuments were retrieved from the rubble and continue to adorn the church's interior.

A short distance inland from Cheyne Walk, at 24 Cheyne Row, is **Carlyle's House** (April–Oct Wed–Sun 11am–5pm; £3.50; NT; Sloane Square tube), where the historian Thomas Carlyle set up home, having moved down from his native Scotland in 1834. The house became a museum just fifteen years after Carlyle's death and is a typically dour Victorian abode, kept much as the Carlyles would have had it: the historian's hat still hanging in the hall, his socks in the chest of drawers.

North London

Almost all of **North London**'s suburbs are easily accessible by tube from the centre – indeed it was the expansion of the tube which encouraged the forward march of bricks and mortar into many of these areas – though just a handful of these satellite villages, now subsumed into the general mass of the city, are worth bothering with.

The first section covers one of London's finest parks, **Regent's Park**, framed by Nash-designed architecture and home of London Zoo. Close by is **Camden Town**, where the weekend market is one of the city's big attractions – a warren of stalls selling street fashion, books, records and ethnic goods.

The real highlights of north London, though, for visitors and residents alike, are **Hampstead** and **Highgate**, elegant, largely eighteenth-century developments which still reflect their village origins. They have the added advantage of proximity to one of London's wildest patches of greenery, **Hampstead Heath**, where you can enjoy stupendous views, kite-flying and outdoor bathing, as well as outdoor concerts and high art in the setting of **Kenwood House**.

Regent's Park

As with almost all of London's royal parks, we have Henry VIII to thank for **Regent's Park** (Ⓦwww.royalparks.org.uk; Regent's Park, Baker Street or Great Portland Street tube), which he confiscated from the Church for yet more hunting grounds. However, it wasn't until the reign of the Prince Regent (later George IV) that the park began to take its current form. According to the masterplan, devised by John Nash in 1811, the park was to be girded by a continuous belt of terraces, and sprinkled with a total of 56 villas, including a magnificent pleasure palace for the prince himself, which would be linked by Regent Street to Carlton House in St James's. The plan was never fully realized, due to lack of funds, but enough was built to create something of the idealized garden city that Nash and the Prince Regent envisaged.

Regent's Canal by boat

Three companies run **boat services** on the Regent's Canal between Camden Lock (Camden Town tube) and Little Venice (Warwick Avenue tube), passing through the Maida Hill tunnel and stopping off at London Zoo on the way. The narrowboat *Jenny Wren* (⊤020/7485 4433) starts off at Camden Lock, at the top of Camden High Street, while Jason's narrowboats (⊤020/7286 3428, ⓦwww.jasons.co.uk) start off at Little Venice, opposite 60 Blomfield Rd; the London Waterbus Company (⊤020/7482 2660) sets off from both places. Jason's and the London Waterbus Company run all year round, though at weekends only during winter. Whichever you choose, you can board at either end; **tickets** cost around £5–6 one-way (and only a little more return) and journey time is 50 minutes one-way.

To appreciate the special quality of Regent's Park, take a closer look at the architecture, starting with the Nash terraces, which form a near-unbroken horseshoe of cream-coloured stucco around the Outer Circle. Within the Inner Circle is the **Open Air Theatre** (ⓦwww.openairtheatre.org), which puts on summer performances of Shakespeare, opera and ballet, and **Queen Mary's Gardens**, by far the prettiest section of the park. A large slice of the gardens is taken up with a glorious rose garden, featuring some four hundred varieties, surrounded by a ring of ramblers.

The northeastern corner of the park is occupied by **London Zoo** (March–Oct 10am–5.30pm; Nov–Feb 10am–4pm; £12; ⓦwww.londonzoo .co.uk; Camden tube), founded in 1826. It may not be the most uplifting place for animal lovers, but kids love it – smaller ones are particularly taken with the children's enclosure, where they can actually handle the animals, and the regular "Animals in Action" live shows. The zoo boasts some striking architectural features, too, most notably the modernist, spiral-ramped 1930s concrete penguin pool (where Penguin Books' original colophon was sketched); it was designed by the Tecton partnership, led by Russian émigré Berthold Lubetkin. Other zoo landmarks include the colossal tetrahedral aluminium-framed tent of the Snowdon Aviary, and the eco-conscious invertebrate-filled Web of Life.

Camden Town

For all the gentrification of the last twenty years, **Camden Town** retains a gritty aspect, compounded by the various railway lines that plough through the area, the canal, and the large shelter for the homeless on Arlington Street. The market, however, gives the area a positive lift at the weekend, and is now the district's best-known attribute.

Having started out as a tiny crafts market in the cobbled courtyard by the lock, **Camden Market** has since mushroomed out of all proportion. More than 100,000 shoppers turn up here each weekend, and parts of the market now stay open week-long, alongside a similarly oriented crop of shops, cafés and bistros. The sheer variety of what's on offer, from bootleg tapes to furniture, along with a mass of street fashion and clubwear, and plenty of foodstalls, is what makes Camden so special. To avoid the crowds, which can be overpowering on a summer Sunday afternoon, you'll need to get here by 10am – by 4pm many of the stalls will be packing up.

Despite having no significant Jewish associations, Camden is home to London's **Jewish Museum** (Mon–Thurs 10am–4pm, Sun 10am–5pm; £3.50; ⓦwww.jewishmuseum.org.uk), at 129 Albert St, just off Parkway. The purpose-built premises are smartly designed, but the conventional style and contents of the museum are disappointing: apart from the usual displays of Judaica, there's a video and exhibition explaining Jewish religious practices and the history of the Jewish community in Britain. More challenging temporary exhibitions are held in the museum's Finchley branch at 80 East End Road, N3 (☎020/8349 1143; Finchley Central tube).

Hampstead

Perched on a hill above Camden Town, **Hampstead** village developed into a fashionable spa in the eighteenth century, after a celebrated physician declared the waters of its spring as being of great medicinal value. Its sloping site, which deterred Victorian property speculators and put off the railway companies, saved much of the Georgian village from destruction, and it's little altered to this day. Later, it became one of the city's most celebrated literary *quartiers* and even now it retains its reputation as a bolt hole of the high-profile intelligentsia. You can get some idea of its tone from the fact that the local Labour MP is currently the actress-turned-politician Glenda Jackson.

Whichever route you take north of Hampstead tube, you'll probably end up at the small triangular green on Holly Bush Hill, on the north side of which stands the late seventeenth-century **Fenton House** (mid-March to Oct Wed–Fri 2–5pm, Sat & Sun 11am–5pm; NT; £4.50; Hampstead tube). As well as housing a collection of European and Oriental ceramics, this National Trust house contains the superb Benton-Fletcher collection of early musical instruments, chiefly displayed on the top floor. Among the many spinets, virginals and clavichords are the earliest extant English grand piano, and an Unverdorben lute from 1580 (one of only three in the world). For an extra £1, you can hire a tape of music played on the above instruments, to listen to while you walk round.

For a fascinating insight into the modernist mindset, take a look inside **2 Willow Road** (March & Nov Sat noon–5pm; April–Oct Thurs–Sat noon–5pm; NT; £4.50; Hampstead tube), an unassuming red-brick terraced house at the far end of Flask Walk, which leads east off the High Street. Built in the 1930s by the Hungarian-born architect Ernö Goldfinger, this was a state-of-the-art pad, its open-plan rooms flooded with natural light and much of the furniture designed by Goldfinger himself. Strangely for a modernist, Goldfinger changed little in the house in the following sixty years, so what you see is a 1930s avant-garde dwelling preserved in aspic, a house at once both modern and old-fashioned. An added bonus is that the rooms are packed with *objets trouvés* and works of art by the likes of Max Ernst, Marcel Duchamp, Henry Moore and Man Ray. Before 3pm, visits are by hour-long guided tour only (noon, 1 & 2pm), for which you must book in advance; after 3pm the public has unguided, unrestricted access.

Hampstead's most lustrous figure is celebrated at **Keats' House** (Tues–Sun: April–Oct noon–5pm; Nov–March noon–4pm; £3; ⓦwww.cityoflondon .gov.uk/keats; Hampstead tube), an elegant, whitewashed Regency double villa on Keats Grove, a short walk south of Willow Road. Inspired by the peacefulness of Hampstead and by his passion for girl-next-door Fanny Brawne (whose house is also part of the museum), Keats wrote some of his most famous works here before leaving for Rome, where he died of consumption in 1821. The neat, rather staid interior contains books and letters, Fanny's engagement ring and the four-poster bed in which the poet first coughed up blood, confiding to his companion, Charles Brown, "that drop of blood is my death warrant".

One of the most poignant of London's house museums is the **Freud Museum** (Wed–Sun noon–5pm; £5; Ⓦ www.freud.org.uk; Finchley Road tube), hidden away in the leafy streets of south Hampstead at 20 Maresfield Gardens. Having lived in Vienna for his entire adult life, Freud, by now semi-disabled with only a year to live, was forced to flee the Nazis, arriving in London in the summer of 1938. The ground-floor study and library look exactly as they did when Freud lived here; the collection of erotic antiquities and the famous couch, sumptuously draped in Persian carpets, were all brought here from Vienna. Upstairs, home movies of family life in Vienna are shown continually, and a small room is dedicated to his daughter, Anna, herself an influential child analyst, who lived in the house until her death in 1982.

Hampstead Heath and Kenwood

North London's "green lung", **Hampstead Heath** is the city's most enjoyable public park. It may not have much of its original heathland left, but it packs a wonderful variety of bucolic scenery into its 800 acres. At its southern end are the rolling green pastures of **Parliament Hill**, north London's premier spot for kite-flying. On either side are numerous ponds, three of which – one for men, one for women and one mixed – you can swim in for free. The thickest woodland is to be found in the **West Heath**, beyond Whitestone Pond, also the site of the most formal section, **Hill Garden**, a secretive and romantic little gem with eccentric balustraded terraces and a ruined pergola. Beyond lies **Golders Hill Park**, where you can gaze at pygmy goats and fallow deer, and inspect the impeccably maintained aviaries, home to flamingos, cranes and other exotic birds.

Finally, don't miss the landscaped grounds of Kenwood, in the north of the Heath, which are focused on the whitewashed Neoclassical mansion of **Kenwood House** (daily: April–Sept 10am–6pm; Oct 10am–5pm; Nov–March 10am–4pm; free; EH; Hampstead tube or bus #210 from Archway tube). The house is now home to the **Iveagh Bequest**, a collection of seventeenth- and eighteenth-century art, including a handful of real masterpieces by the likes of Vermeer, Rembrandt, Boucher, Gainsborough and Reynolds. Of the house's period interiors, the most spectacular is Robert Adam's sky-blue and gold **library**, its book-filled apses separated from the central entertaining area by paired columns. To the south of the house, a grassy amphitheatre slopes down to a lake where outdoor classical concerts are held on summer evenings.

Highgate

Northeast of the Heath, and fractionally lower than Hampstead (appearances notwithstanding), **Highgate** lacks the literary cachet of its neighbour, but makes up for it with London's most famous cemetery, resting place of Karl Marx. It also retains more of its village origins, especially around **The Grove**, Highgate's finest row of houses, the oldest dating as far back as 1685.

To get to the cemetery, head south down Highgate High Street and **Highgate Hill**, with its amazing views towards the City. When you get to the copper dome of "Holy Joe", the Roman Catholic Church which stands on Highgate Hill, pop into the pleasantly landscaped **Waterlow Park**, next door, with its fine café and restaurant.

The park provides a through route to **Highgate Cemetery** (Ⓦ www .highgate-cemetery.org), which is ranged on both sides of Swain's Lane. Highgate's most famous corpse, that of **Karl Marx**, lies in the **East Cemetery** (April–Oct Mon–Fri 10am–5pm, Sat & Sun 11am–5pm; Nov–March closes

4pm; £2). Marx himself asked for a simple grave topped by a headstone, but by 1954 the Communist movement decided to move his grave to a more prominent position and erect the vulgar bronze bust that now surmounts a granite plinth. Close by lies the much simpler grave of the author George Eliot.

What the East Cemetery lacks in atmosphere is in part compensated for by the fact that you can wander at will through its maze of circuitous paths, whereas to visit the more atmospheric and overgrown **West Cemetery**, with its spooky Egyptian Avenue and sunken catacombs, you must go round with a guided tour (March–Nov Mon–Fri 2pm, Sat & Sun hourly 11am–4pm; Dec–Feb Sat & Sun hourly 11am–3pm; £3). Among the prominent graves usually visited are those of artist Dante Gabriel Rossetti, and lesbian novelist Radclyffe Hall.

Hendon: The RAF Museum

A world-class assembly of historic military aircraft can be seen at the **RAF Museum** (daily 10am–6pm; free; Ⓦ www.rafmuseum.org.uk; Colindale tube), located in a godforsaken part of north London beside the M1 motorway. Enthusiasts won't be disappointed, but those looking for a balanced account of modern aerial warfare will – the overall tone is unashamedly militaristic, not to say jingoistic. Those with children should head for the hands-on Fun 'n' Flight gallery; those without might prefer to explore the often overlooked display galleries, ranged around the edge of the Main Aircraft Hall, which contain an art gallery and an exhibition on the history of flight, accompanied by replicas of some of the death-traps of early aviation.

Neasden: the Shri Swaminarayan temple

Perhaps the most remarkable building in the whole of London lies just off the North Circular, in the glum suburb of **Neasden**. Here, rising majestically above the surrounding semidetached houses like a mirage, is the **Shri Swaminarayan Mandir** (daily 9am–6pm; free, Ⓦ www.swaminarayan.org; Stonebridge Park or Neasden tube), a traditional Hindu temple topped with domes and shikharas, erected in 1995 in a style and scale unseen outside of India for more than a millennium. To reach the temple, you must enter through the adjacent Haveli, or cultural complex, with its carved wooden portico and balcony. After taking off your shoes, you can proceed to the **Mandir** (temple) itself, carved entirely out of Carrara marble, with every possible surface transformed into a honeycomb of arabesques, flowers and seated gods. Beneath the Mandir, an **exhibition** (£2) explains the basic tenets of Hinduism and details the life of Lord Swaminarayan, and includes a video about the history of the building.

South London

Now largely built up into a patchwork of Victorian terraces, one area of **South London** stands head and shoulders above all the others in terms of sightseeing, and that is **Greenwich**, with its outstanding ensemble of the Royal Naval College and the Queen's House, courtesy of Christopher Wren and Inigo Jones respectively. Most visitors, it has to be said, come to see the National Maritime Museum, the Royal Observatory, and the beautifully landscaped royal park, though Greenwich also pulls in an ever-increasing volume of Londoners in search of bargains at its Sunday **market**.

Greenwich is, of course, also famous as the "home of time", thanks to its status as the **Prime Meridian of the World**, from where time all over the globe is measured. It's partly for this reason that Greenwich was chosen as the centrepiece of the country's millennium celebrations, though the **Dome** is, in fact, situated in the reclaimed industrial wasteland of North Greenwich, a mile or so northeast of Greenwich town centre.

The only other suburban sights that stand out are the **Dulwich Picture Gallery**, a public art gallery even older than the National Gallery, and the eclectic **Horniman Museum**, in neighbouring Forest Hill.

Greenwich

Greenwich is one of London's most beguiling spots, and the one place in southeast London that draws large numbers of visitors. At its heart stands one of the capital's finest architectural set pieces, the former Royal Naval College overlooking the Thames. To the west lies Greenwich town centre, while to the south, you'll find Greenwich's two prime tourist sights, the National Maritime Museum and the Royal Observatory.

If you're heading straight for the National Maritime Museum from central London, the quickest way to get there is to take the **train** from London Bridge (every 30min) to Maze Hill, on the eastern edge of Greenwich Park. Those wanting to start with the town or the *Cutty Sark* should alight at Greenwich station. A more scenic way of getting to Greenwich is to take a **boat** from one of the piers in central London. A third possible option is to take the **Docklands Light Railway** (DLR) to Cutty Sark station. For the best view of the Wren buildings, though, get off the DLR at Island Gardens, and then take the Greenwich Foot Tunnel under the Thames.

The town centre

Greenwich town centre, laid out in the 1820s with Nash-style terraces, is nowadays plagued with heavy traffic. To escape the busy streets, head for the old covered market, now at the centre of the weekend **Greenwich Market** (Thurs–Sun 9am–5pm), a lively place full of antiques, crafts and clothes stalls that have spilled out up the High Road, Stockwell Road and Royal Hill. A short distance in from the old covered market, on the opposite side of Greenwich Church Street, rises Nicholas Hawksmoor's **St Alfege's Church** (Mon–Sat 10am–4pm, Sun noon–4pm; Ⓦwww.st-alfege.org), built in 1712–18, flattened in the Blitz, but now magnificently restored to its former glory.

Wedged in a dry dock by the Greenwich Foot Tunnel is the majestic **Cutty Sark** (daily 10am–5pm; £3.95; Ⓦwww.cuttysark.org.uk), the world's last surviving tea clipper, built in 1869. The *Cutty Sark* spent just eight years in the China tea trade, and it was as a wool clipper that it actually made its name, making a return journey to Australia in just 72 days. Inside, there's little to see beyond the exhibition in the main hold which tells the ship's story from its inception to its arrival in Greenwich in 1954.

It's entirely appropriate that the one London building that makes the most of its riverbank location should be the **Old Royal Naval College** (daily 10am–5pm; free; Ⓦwww.greenwichfoundation.org.uk), Wren's beautifully symmetrical Baroque ensemble, initially built as a royal palace, but eventually converted into a hospital for disabled seamen. From 1873 until 1998 it was home to the Royal Naval College, but now houses the University of Greenwich and the Trinity College of Music. The two grandest rooms, situated underneath Wren's twin domes, are open to the public and well worth visiting. The

Chapel, in the east wing, has exquisite pastel-shaded plasterwork and spectacular, decorative detailing on the ceiling, all designed by James "Athenian" Stuart after a fire in 1799 destroyed the original interior. From the chapel, you can take the underground Chalk Walk to gain access to the magnificent **Painted Hall** in the west wing, which is dominated by James Thornhill's gargantuan allegorical ceiling painting, and his trompe l'oeil fluted pilasters.

National Maritime Museum

The main entrance to the excellent **National Maritime Museum** (daily 10am–5pm; free; ⓦ www.nmm.ac.uk), which occupies the old Naval Asylum, is on Romney Road. From here, you enter the spectacular glass-roofed central courtyard, which houses the museum's largest artefacts, among them the splendid 63ft-long gilded **Royal Barge**, designed in Rococo style by William Kent for Prince Frederick, the much unloved eldest son of George II.

The various themed galleries are superbly designed to appeal to visitors of all ages. In **Explorers**, on Level 1, you get to view some of the museum's most highly prized relics, such as **Captain Cook**'s sextant and K1 marine clock, Shackleton's compass, and **Captain Scott**'s furry sleeping bag and sledging goggles. Sponsors P&O get to display their wares in **Passengers**, which traces the history of modern passenger liners, and **Cargoes**, which concentrates on containerization. On Level 2, there's a large maritime **art gallery**, a contemporary section on the future of the sea, and a gallery devoted to the legacy of the British Empire, warts and all.

Level 3 boasts two hands-on galleries: **The Bridge**, where you can attempt to navigate a catamaran, a paddle steamer and a rowing boat to shore; and **All Hands**, where children can have a go at radio transmission, loading miniature cargo, firing a cannon and so forth. Finally, you reach the **Nelson Gallery**, which contains the museum's vast collection of Nelson-related memorabilia, including Turner's *Battle of Trafalgar, 21st October, 1805*, his largest work and only royal commission.

Inigo Jones's **Queen's House**, originally built amidst a rambling Tudor royal palace, is now the focal point of the Greenwich ensemble, and is an integral part of the Maritime Museum. As royal residences go, it's an unassuming

Greenwich Mean Time

One of Greenwich's many claims to fame is as the home of **GMT** and the **Prime Meridian** – a meridian being any north–south line used as a basis for astronomical observations, and therefore also for the calculation of longitude and time. In 1852, Britain adopted "London time", which meant, in effect, Greenwich Mean Time (GMT), though, in fact, this wasn't formally acknowledged until 1880. Three years later the USA adopted Greenwich as the Prime Meridian, and in 1884 persuaded an international convention in Washington DC to agree to make Greenwich the Prime Meridian of the World – in other words, zero longitude. As a result, the entire world sets its clocks in relation to GMT.

The red strip in the main courtyard lies along the Greenwich Prime Meridian, which is still used as an absolute today. However, what the Royal Observatory don't tell you is that, as a result of communications problems encountered during the Vietnam War, the Americans starting using satellites to work out longitude in the 1980s. The global standard for air navigation, and used widely by the military, is now the **Global Positioning System** or GPS, which bases its calculations on the centre of the earth not the surface, and places the meridian approximately 336ft to the east of the red strip.

country house, but as the first Neoclassical building in the country, it has enormous architectural significance. The interior is currently used for temporary exhibitions. Nevertheless, one or two features survive (or have been reinstated) from Stuart times. Off the Great Hall, a perfect cube, lies the beautiful Tulip Staircase, Britain's earliest cantilevered spiral staircase – its name derives from the floral patterning in the wrought-iron balustrade.

Royal Observatory

Crowning the hill in Greenwich Park, behind the National Maritime Museum, the **Royal Observatory** (daily: April–Sept 10am–6pm; Oct–March 10am–5pm; free; Ⓦ www.rog.nmm.ac.uk) was established in 1675 by Charles II to house the first Astronomer Royal, John Flamsteed. Flamsteed's chief task was to study the night sky in order to discover an astronomical method of finding the longitude of a ship at sea, the lack of which was causing enormous problems for the emerging British Empire. Astronomers continued to work here at Greenwich until the postwar smog forced them to decamp to Herstmonceux Castle and the clearer skies of Sussex (they've since moved to the Pacific); the old observatory, meanwhile, is now a very popular museum.

The oldest part of the observatory is the Wren-built **Flamsteed House**, whose northeastern turret sports a bright red time-ball that climbs the mast at 12.58pm and drops at 1pm GMT precisely; it was added in 1833 to allow ships on the Thames to set their clocks. Passing through Flamsteed's restored apartments and the Octagon Room, where the king used to show off to his guests, you reach the Chronometer Gallery, which focuses on the search for the precise measurement of longitude, and displays four of the clocks designed by **John Harrison**, including "H4", which helped win the Longitude Prize in 1763.

The exhibition ends on a soothing note in the Telescope Dome of the octagonal **Great Equatorial Building**, home to Britain's largest telescope. In addition, there are regular presentations in the **Planetarium** (daily 2.30 & 3.30pm; £4), housed in the adjoining South Building.

The Ranger's House and the Fan Museum

Southwest of the observatory, and backing onto Greenwich Park's rose garden, is the **Ranger's House** (Wed–Sun: April–Sept 10am–6pm; Oct 10am–5pm;

The Dome

London's controversial **Millennium Dome** (North Greenwich tube) is clearly visible from the riverside at Greenwich and from the upper parts of Greenwich Park. Built at a cost approaching £800 million of public money, and designed by Richard Rogers (of Lloyd's Building and Pompidou Centre fame), it is by far the world's largest dome – over half a mile in circumference and 160ft in height – held up by a dozen, 300ft-tall yellow steel masts. In 2000, for one year only, it housed the nation's chief millennium extravaganza: an array of high-tech themed zones set around a stage, on which a circus-style performance took place twice a day.

Like most grand projects, the Dome had a rough ride from the press right from the beginning. The hiccups and headaches continued into the new millennium, with bad reviews and over-optimistic estimates of visitor numbers. Nevertheless, millions paid up £20 each to visit the Dome, and millions went away happy.

With the empty Dome eating up £28 million of public money on maintenance costs in 2001 alone, the government were no doubt relieved the following year when entertainment giants, AEG, agreed to spend £135 million of their own money turning the Dome into a 26,000-seater venue.

Nov, Dec & March 10am–4pm; closed Christmas to Feb; £4.50; EH), a red-brick Georgian villa that houses an art collection amassed by Julius Wernher, the German-born millionaire who made his money by exploiting the diamond deposits of South Africa. His taste in art is eclectic, ranging from medieval ivory miniatures to Iznik pottery, though he was definitely a man who placed technical virtuosity above artistic merit. The high points of the collection are Memlinc's *Virgin and Child*, the pair of sixteenth-century majolica dishes decorated with mythological scenes for Isabella d'Este, both located upstairs, and the Reynolds portraits and de Hooch interior, located downstairs.

Croom's Hill, running down the west side of the park, boasts some of Greenwich's finest Georgian buildings, one of which houses the **Fan Museum** at no. 12 (Tues–Sat 11am–5pm, Sun noon–5pm; £3.50; Ⓦwww.fan-museum.org). It's a fascinating little place (and an extremely beautiful house), revealing the importance of the fan as a social and political document. The permanent exhibition on the ground floor traces the history of the materials employed, from peacock feathers to straw, while temporary exhibitions on the first floor explore such subjects as techniques of production and changing fashion.

Dulwich Picture Gallery and the Horniman Museum

Dulwich Picture Gallery (Tues–Fri 10am–5pm, Sat & Sun 11am–5pm; £4, free on Fri; Ⓦwww.dulwichpicturegallery.org.uk; West Dulwich train station from Victoria), on College Road, is the nation's oldest public art gallery, designed by John Soane and opened in 1817. Soane created a beautifully spacious building, awash with natural light and crammed with superb paintings – elegiac landscapes by Cuyp, one of the world's finest Poussin series, and splendid works by Hogarth, Gainsborough, van Dyck, Canaletto and Rubens, plus **Rembrandt**'s tiny *Portrait of a Young Man*, a top-class portrait of poet, playwright and Royalist, the future Earl of Bristol. At the centre of the museum is a tiny mausoleum designed by Soane for the sarcophagi of the gallery's founders.

To the southeast of Dulwich Park, on the busy South Circular road, is the wacky **Horniman Museum** (daily 10.30am–5.30pm; free; Ⓦwww.horniman.ac.uk; Forest Hill train station from Victoria or London Bridge), purpose-built in 1901 by Frederick Horniman, a tea trader with a passion for collecting. The museum is principally a monument to its creator's freewheeling eclecticism: in addition to its small aquarium and its large collection of stuffed creatures, there's a wide-ranging anthropology section, and a musical department with more than 1500 instruments from Chinese gongs to electric guitars. The museum also has a lovely **park** (daily 8am–dusk), around the back, where you'll find turkeys, goats and rabbits, a sunken water garden, a bandstand and a graceful Victorian conservatory.

Out west: Chiswick to Windsor

Most people experience west London en route to or from Heathrow airport, either from the confines of the train or tube (which runs overground at this point), or the motorway. The city and its satellites seem to continue unabated, with only fleeting glimpses of the countryside. However, in the five-mile stretch from Chiswick to Osterley there are several former country retreats, now surrounded by suburbia, which are definitely worth digging out.

The Palladian villa of **Chiswick House** is perhaps the best known of these attractions. However, it draws nothing like as many visitors as **Syon House**, most of whom come for the gardening centre rather than for the **house** itself, a showcase for the talents of Robert Adam, who also worked at **Osterley House**, another Elizabethan conversion, now owned by the National Trust.

Running through much of the area is the **River Thames**, once known as the "Great Highway of London" and still the most pleasant way to travel in these parts during the summer. Boats plough up the Thames all the way from central London via the **Royal Botanic Gardens** at **Kew** and the picturesque riverside at **Richmond**, as far as **Hampton Court**, home of the country's largest royal residence and the famous maze. To reach the heavily touristed royal outpost of **Windsor Castle**, however, you need to take the train.

Chiswick

Chiswick House (daily: April–Sept 10am–6pm; Oct 10am–5pm; £3.50; EH; Chiswick train station from Waterloo), is a perfect little Neoclassical villa, designed in the 1720s by the Earl of Burlington, and set in one of the most beautifully landscaped gardens in London. Like its prototype, Palladio's Villa Rotonda near Vicenza, the house was purpose-built as a "temple to the arts" where, amid his fine-art collection, Burlington could entertain artistic friends such as Swift, Handel and Pope. Visitors enter via the **lower floor**, where you can pick up an audio guide, before heading to the **upper floor**, a series of cleverly interconnecting rooms, each enjoying a wonderful view out onto the gardens – all, that is, except the Tribunal, the central octagonal hall, where the earl's finest paintings and sculptures would have been displayed.

If you leave Chiswick House gardens by the northernmost exit, beyond the Italian garden, it's just a short walk along the thunderous A4 road to **Hogarth's House** (April–Oct Tues–Fri 1–5pm, Sat & Sun 1–6pm; Nov–March Tues–Fri 1–4pm, Sat & Sun 1–5pm; closed Jan; free), where the artist spent each summer with his wife, sister and mother-in-law from 1749 until his death in 1764. Nowadays it's difficult to believe Hogarth came here for "peace and quiet", but in the eighteenth century the house was almost entirely surrounded by countryside. In addition to scores of Hogarth's engravings, you can see copies of his satirical series *An Election*, *Marriage à la Mode* and *A Harlot's Progress*, and compare the modern view from the parlour with the more idyllic scene in *Mr Ranby's House*.

Barnes: the Wetland Centre

For anyone even remotely interested in wildlife, the **Wetland Centre** (Mon–Sat: summer 9.30am–6pm; winter 9.30am–5pm; £6.75; ⓦ www.wwt.org.uk; bus #283 from Hammersmith tube, or walk from Barnes train station) in well-to-do Barnes, across the river from Chiswick, is something of an unexpected boon. On the site of four disused reservoirs, the Wildfowl & Wetland Trust (WWT) has created a high-tech 105-acre mosaic of wetland habitats. Heading north from the visitor centre, you enter **World Wetlands**, where a variety of extremely rare wildfowl – from White-faced Whistling Ducks to Blue Ducks – are breeding in captivity in miniature versions of their own endangered wetland habitats. Beyond, in the **Wildside**, are the reedbeds and pools that attract native species, such as lapwing, tufted ducks, grebes and even the odd bittern. **Waterlife**, east of the visitor centre, includes a chance for younger children to get near some domesticated wild-fowl, and, best of all, do some pond-dipping. At the far end is the mother of all hides: a triple-decker octagonal one with a lift, allowing views over the whole of the reserve.

Around Kew Bridge

Difficult to miss thanks to its stylish Italianate standpipe tower, **Kew Bridge Steam Museum** (11am–5pm; Mon–Fri £3.50, Sat & Sun £4.60; Ⓦ www.kbsm.org; Kew Bridge train station from Waterloo; or bus #237 or #267 from Gunnersbury tube) occupies a former pumping station, on the corner of Kew Bridge Road and Green Dragon Lane, 100m west of the bridge itself. At the heart of the museum is the Steam Hall, which contains a triple expansion steam engine and four gigantic nineteenth-century Cornish beam engines. The museum also has a hands-on **Water for Life** gallery in the basement, devoted to the history of the capital's water supply. The best time to visit is at weekends, when each of the museum's industrial dinosaurs is put through its paces, and the small narrow-gauge steam railway runs back and forth round the yard.

Just west of the Steam Museum along Kew Bridge Road and Brentford High Street is the superb **Musical Museum** (Ⓦ www.musicalmuseum.co.uk), packed with musical automata and run by wildly enthusiastic and engaging volunteers. The museum has recently moved into new purpose-built premises and is due to reopen sometime in 2004. When it does, it will definitely be worth a visit for the noisy ninety-minute demonstrations, during which you get to hear every kind of mechanical music-making machine, from cleverly crafted music boxes to the huge orchestrions that were once a feature of London's swish cafés. The museum also boasts one of the world's finest collections of player-pianos, and an enormous Art Deco Wurlitzer cinema organ.

Syon House

Across the water from Kew stands **Syon Park** (Ⓦ www.syonpark.co.uk), seat of the Duke of Northumberland since Elizabethan times, now as much a working commercial concern as a family home, embracing a garden centre, a wholefood shop, an aquatic centre stocked with tropical fish, a mini-zoo and a butterfly house, as well as the old aristocratic mansion and its gardens.

From its rather plain castellated exterior, you'd never guess that **Syon House** (April–Oct Wed, Thurs & Sun 11am–5pm; £6.95, including entry to the gardens; bus #237 or #267 from Gunnersbury tube or Kew Bridge train station) contains the most opulent eighteenth-century interiors in the whole of London. The splendour of Robert Adam's refurbishment is immediately revealed, however, in the pristine **Great Hall**, an apsed double cube with a screen of Doric columns at one end and classical statuary dotted around the

---

River transport

Westminster Passenger Services (☎ 020/7930 2062, Ⓦ www.wpsa.co.uk) runs four boats from Westminster Pier to Kew, and two boats to Richmond and Hampton Court daily from April to September. The full trip takes 3hr 30min one-way, and costs £12 single, £18 return. In addition, Turks (☎ 020/8546 2434, Ⓦ www.turks.co.uk) run a regular service from Richmond to Hampton Court (April to mid-Sept) which costs £5.50 single or £7 return.

edges. There are several more Adam-designed rooms to admire in the house, plus a smattering of works by van Dyck, Lely, Gainsborough and Reynolds.

While Adam beautified Syon House, Capability Brown laid out its **gardens** (daily 10.30am–5.30pm; £3.50) around an artificial lake, surrounding it with oaks, beeches, limes and cedars. The gardens' chief focus now, however, is the crescent-shaped **Great Conservatory**, an early nineteenth-century addition which is said to have inspired Joseph Paxton, architect of the Crystal Palace. Those with young children will be compelled to make use of the **miniature steam train**, which runs through the park at weekends from April to October, and on Wednesdays during the school holidays.

Another plus point for kids is Syon's **Butterfly House** (daily: May–Sept 10am–5pm; Oct–April 10am–3pm; £3.50; ⓦwww.butterflies.org.uk), a small, mesh-covered hothouse, where you can walk amid hundreds of exotic butterflies from all over the world, as they flit about the foliage. If your kids show more enthusiasm for life-threatening reptiles than delicate insects, then you could skip the butterflies and go instead for the adjacent **London Aquatic Experience** (daily: April–Sept 10am–6pm; Oct–March 10am–5pm; £4; ⓦwww.aquatic-experience.org), a purpose-built centre with a mixed range of aquatic creatures from the mysterious basilisk, which can walk on water, to the perennially popular piranhas.

Osterley Park and House

Robert Adam redesigned another colossal Elizabethan mansion three miles northwest of Syon at **Osterley Park** (daily 9am–7.30pm or dusk; free), which maintains the impression of being in the middle of the countryside, despite the presence of the M4 to the north of the house. The park itself is well worth exploring, and there's a great café in the Tudor stables, but anyone with a passing interest in Adam's work should pay a visit to **Osterley House** (March Sat & Sun 1–4.30pm; April–Oct Wed–Sun 1–4.30pm; £4.50; NT; Osterley tube). From the outside, Osterley bears some similarity to Syon, the big difference being Adam's grand entrance portico, with its tall, Ionic colonnade. From here, you enter a characteristically cool **Entrance Hall**, followed by the so-called State Rooms of the south wing. Highlights include the **Drawing Room**, with Reynolds portraits on the damask walls and a coffered ceiling centred on a giant marigold, and the **Etruscan Dressing Room**, in which every surface is covered in delicate painted trelliswork, sphinxes and urns, a style that Adam (and Wedgwood) dubbed "Etruscan", though it is in fact derived from Greek vases found at Pompeii.

Kew Gardens

Established in 1759, the **Royal Botanic Gardens** (daily 9.30am to 7.30pm or dusk; £7.50; ⓦwww.kew.org; Kew Gardens tube) have grown from their original eight acres into a three-hundred-acre site in which more than 33,000 species are grown in plantations and glasshouses, a display that attracts over a million visitors every year, most of them with no specialist interest at all. There's always something to see, whatever the season, but to get the most out of the place, come sometime between spring and autumn, bring a picnic and stay for the day. The only drawback to Kew is that it lies on a frequently used (and very noisy) flight path to Heathrow. Of all the glasshouses, by far the most celebrated is the **Palm House**, a curvaceous mound of glass and wrought-iron, designed by Decimus Burton in the 1840s. Its drippingly humid atmosphere nurtures most of the known palm species, while in the basement there's a small but excellent tropical aquarium. Kew's origins as an eighteenth-century royal pleasure garden are evident in the numerous follies dotted about Kew, the most conspicuous of which is the ten-storey 163-foot-high **Pagoda**.

Richmond Park and Ham House

Richmond, upriver from Kew, basked for centuries in the glow of royal patronage, with Plantagenet kings and Tudor monarchs frequenting the riverside palace. Although most of the courtiers and aristocrats have gone, **Richmond** is still a wealthy district, with two theatres and highbrow pretensions. Richmond's greatest attraction though, is the enormous **Richmond Park** (daily: March–Sept 7am–dusk; Oct–Feb 7.30am–dusk; free; Ⓦ www .royalparks.gov.uk), at the top of Richmond Hill – 2500 acres of undulating grassland and bracken, dotted with coppiced woodland and as wild as anything in London. Eight miles across at its widest point, this is Europe's largest city park, famed for its red and fallow deer, which roam freely, and for its ancient oaks. For the most part untamed, the park does have a couple of deliberately landscaped plantations that feature splendid springtime azaleas and rhododendrons, in particular the Isabella Plantation.

Back down the hill, if you continue along the towpath beyond Richmond Bridge, after a mile or so, you leave the rest of London far behind and arrive at **Ham House** (April–Oct Mon–Wed, Sat & Sun 1–5pm; £7; NT; bus #371 or walk from Richmond tube), home to the earls of Dysart for nearly three hundred years. Expensively furnished in the seventeenth century, but little altered since then, the house boasts one of the finest Stuart interiors in the country, from the stupendously ornate Great Staircase to the Long Gallery, featuring six "Court Beauties" by Peter Lely. Elsewhere, there are several fine Verrio ceiling paintings, some exquisite parquet flooring and works by van Dyck and Reynolds. Another bonus is the formal seventeenth-century **gardens** (Mon–Wed, Sat & Sun 10.30am–6pm; £3), especially the Cherry Garden, laid out with a pungent lavender parterre, surrounded by yew hedges and pleached hornbeam arbours. The Orangery, overlooking the original kitchen garden, currently serves as a tea room.

Hampton Court

Hampton Court Palace (April–Oct Mon 10.15am–6pm, Tues–Sun 9.30am–6pm; Nov–March closes 4.30pm; £11.50; Ⓦ www.hrp.org.uk; Hampton Court train station from Waterloo), a sprawling red-brick ensemble on the banks of the Thames, thirteen miles southwest of London, is the finest of England's royal abodes. Built in 1516 by the upwardly mobile **Cardinal Wolsey**, Henry VIII's Lord Chancellor, it was purloined by Henry himself after Wolsey fell from favour. In the second half of the seventeenth century, Charles II laid out the gardens, inspired by what he had seen at Versailles, while William and Mary had large sections of the palace remodelled by Wren a few years later.

The **Royal Apartments** are divided into six thematic walking tours. There's not a lot of information in any of the rooms, but guided tours, each lasting 45 minutes, are available at no extra charge for Henry VIII's and the King's apartments; all are led by period-costumed historians, who do a fine job of bringing the place to life. If your energy is lacking – and Hampton Court is huge – the most rewarding sections are: **Henry VIII's State Apartments**, which feature the glorious double hammer-beamed Great Hall; the **King's Apartments** (remodelled by William III); and the vast **Tudor Kitchens**. The last two are also served by audio tours. Part of the Royal Collection is housed in the **Renaissance Picture Gallery** and is chock-full of treasures, among them paintings by Tintoretto, Lotto, Titian, Cranach, Bruegel and Holbein.

Tickets to the Royal Apartments cover entry to the rest of the sites in the grounds. Those who don't wish to visit the apartments are free to wander around the gardens, but have to pay extra to visit the curious **Royal Tennis Courts** (50p), the palace's famously tricky yew-hedge **Maze** (£3), and the **Privy Garden** (£3), where you can view Andrea Mantegna's colourful, heroic canvases, *The Triumphs of Caesar*, housed in the Lower Orangery, and the celebrated **Great Vine**, whose grapes are sold at the palace each year in September.

Windsor and Eton

Every weekend trains from Waterloo and Paddington are packed with people heading for **WINDSOR**, the royal enclave 21 miles west of London, where they join the human conveyor belt round **Windsor Castle** (March–Oct 9.45am–5.15pm; Nov–Feb 9.45am–4.15pm; £11.50; ⓦwww.royal.gov.uk; Paddington to Windsor & Eton Central via Slough, or Waterloo to Windsor & Eton Riverside – note that you must arrive and depart from the same station, as tickets are not interchangeable). Towering above the town on a steep chalk bluff, the castle is an undeniably awesome sight, its chilly grey walls, punctuated by mighty medieval bastions, continuing as far as the eye can see. Inside, most visitors just gape in awe at the monotonous, gilded grandeur of the **State Apartments**, while the real highlights – the paintings from the Royal Collection that line the walls – are rarely given a second glance. More impressive is **St George's Chapel** (Mon–Sat 10am–4pm), a glorious Perpendicular structure ranking with Henry VII's chapel in Westminster Abbey (see p.98), and the second most important resting place for royal corpses after the Abbey. On a fine day, it pays to put aside some time for exploring Windsor Great Park, which stretches for several miles to the south of the castle.

Crossing the bridge at the end of Thames Avenue in Windsor town brings you to **ETON**, a one-street village lined with bookshops and antique dealers, but famous all over the world for **Eton College** (Easter, July & Aug daily 10.30am–4.30pm; after Easter to June & Sept daily 2–4.30pm; £3.50; guided tours daily 2.15pm & 3.15pm; £4.50; ⓦwww.etoncollege.com), a ten-minute walk from the river. When the school was founded in 1440, its aim was to give free education to seventy poor scholars and choristers; how times have changed. The original fifteenth-century **schoolroom**, gnarled with centuries of graffiti, survives, but the real highlight is the **College Chapel**, completed in 1482, a wonderful example of English Perpendicular architecture. The self-congratulatory **Museum of Eton Life**, where you're deposited at the end of the tour, is well worth missing unless you have a fascination with flogging, fagging and bragging about the school's facilities and alumni – Percy Bysshe Shelley is a rare rebellious figure in the roll call of Establishment greats.

Among younger kids, the attractions of Windsor Castle are overshadowed by the town's **Legoland** (daily 10am–5pm, later in school holidays; adults £18.95, under 15s £15.95, under 3s free; ⓦwww.legoland.co.uk) theme park aimed at pre-teenage children (the perfect age is around 5 to 8). Whatever you do, though, try not to go at the weekend or during the school holidays, when the queues for the various rides become grievously long and the tickets cost £4 more. On arrival, a funicular railway takes visitors down into the park, disgorging them close to Miniland, with its miniature Lego depictions of various European landmarks. The rest of the park is really just a series of rides, most of them very gentle. There are numerous places to eat, though it makes sense to take a picnic and save yourself some money.

Eating

London is an exciting (though often expensive) place in which to eat out. It's home to people from all over the globe, and you can pretty much sample any kind of cuisine here, from Georgian to Peruvian. Indeed, London is now home to some of the best **Cantonese** restaurants in the whole of Europe, is a noted centre for **Indian** and **Bangladeshi** food, and has numerous French, Greek, Italian, Japanese, Spanish and Thai restaurants; and within all these cuisines, you can choose anything from simple meals to gourmet spreads. Traditional and modern **British** food is available all over town, and some of the best venues are reviewed below.

Cafés and snacks

There are plenty of **cafés** and small, basic restaurants all over London that can fill you up for under £10, including tea or coffee. A huge number of them are run by Anglo-Italians, which means you're guaranteed proper coffee and decent sandwiches. Several of the places listed are also open in the evening, but the turnover is fast, so don't expect to linger; they're best seen as fuel stops before – or in a few cases, after – a night out. It's worth bearing in mind that most **pubs** (which are covered in the following section) serve meals, and some take their food quite seriously.

Mayfair and Marylebone

Mô 25 Heddon St, W1. Piccadilly Circus tube. The ultimate Arabic pastiche. The adjacent restaurant is pricey, but the tearoom serves delicious snacks and is a great place to hang out, with tables and hookahs spilling out onto the pavement of this little alleyway off Regent Street. Closed Sun.
Patisserie Valerie at Sagne 105 Marylebone High St, W1. Bond Street tube. Founded as *Maison Sagne* in the 1920s, and preserving its wonderful decor from those days, this café is Marylebone's finest without doubt.

Soho

Bar Italia 22 Frith St, W1. Leicester Square tube. A tiny café that's a Soho institution, serving coffee, croissants and sandwiches more or less around the clock – as it has done since 1949.
Bar du Marché 19 Berwick St, W1. Tottenham Court Road, Piccadilly Circus or Leicester Square tube. A weird find in the middle of raucous Berwick Street market: a licensed French café serving brasserie staples for under £10. Closed Sun.
Beatroot 92 Berwick St, W1. Piccadilly Circus tube. Great little veggie café by the market, doling

out hot savoury bakes, stews and salads (plus delicious cakes) in boxes of varying sizes – all under £5. Closed Sun.
Centrale 16 Moor St, W1. Leicester Square tube. Tiny, friendly Italian café that serves up huge plates of steaming, garlicky pasta, as well as omelettes, chicken and chops for around £5. Closed Sun.
Maison Bertaux 28 Greek St, W1. Leicester Square tube. Long-standing, old-fashioned and downbeat Soho patisserie, with tables on two floors (and one or two outside) and a loyal clientele that keeps things busy.
Patisserie Valerie 44 Old Compton St, W1. Leicester Square or Piccadilly Circus tube. Popular 1920s coffee, croissant and cake emporium attracting a loud-talking, arty Soho crowd.
Red Veg 95 Dean St, W1. Tottenham Court Rd tube. Simple veggie junk food outlet, which doles out a short list of cheap, classic munchies-fodder: veggie burgers, noodles and felafel.

Chinatown

Lee Ho Fook 4 Macclesfield St, W1. Leicester Square tube. Very difficult to find, but a genuine

Chinese barbecue house – small, spartan and cheap.

Kopi-Tiam 9 Wardour St, W1. Leicester Square tube. Bright, cheap Malaysian café serving up curries, coconut rice, juices and "herbal soups" to local Malays, all for around a fiver.

Tokyo Diner 2 Newport Place, WC2. Leicester Square tube. Friendly place on the edge of Chinatown that shuns elaboration for fast food, Tokyo style. Minimalist decor lets the sushi and sumo do the talking.

Covent Garden and Bloomsbury

Café in the Crypt St Martin-in-the-Fields, Duncannon St, WC2. Charing Cross tube. The self-service buffet food is nothing special, but there are regular veggie dishes, and the handy location makes this an ideal spot to fill up before hitting the West End.

Food for Thought 31 Neal St, WC2. Covent Garden tube. Long-established but minuscule, bargain veggie restaurant and takeaway counter – the food is good, with the menu changing twice daily. Expect to queue and don't expect to linger at peak times.

Gaby's 30 Charing Cross Rd, WC2. Leicester Square tube. Busy café and takeaway joint serving a wide range of home-cooked veggie and Middle Eastern specialities.

Monmouth Coffee Company 27 Monmouth St, WC2. Covent Garden or Leicester Square tube. The marvellous aroma is the first thing you notice here, while the cramped wooden booths and daily newspapers on hand evoke an eighteenth-century coffee-house atmosphere. No smoking. Closed Sun.

Paul 29 Bedford St, WC2. Covent Garden tube.

Seriously French, classy boulangerie with a wood-panelled café at the back. Try one of the chewy *fougasses*, quiches or tarts, before launching into the exquisite patisserie.

Rock & Sole Plaice 47 Endell St, WC2. Covent Garden tube. A rare survivor: a no-nonsense traditional fish and chip shop in central London. Takeaway, eat in or out at one of the pavement tables.

Wagamama 4 Streatham St, WC1. Tottenham Court Road tube. Much copied since, *Wagamama* was the pioneer when it comes to austere, minimalist, canteen-style noodle bars. Branches around central London.

World Food Café 14 Neal's Yard, WC2. Covent Garden tube. First-floor veggie café that comes into its own in summer, when the windows are flung open and you can gaze down upon trendy humanity as you tuck into pricey but tasty dishes from all corners of the globe.

Clerkenwell & Hoxton

Clark & Sons 46 Exmouth Market, EC1. Angel or Farringdon tube. Exmouth Market is currently undergoing something of a transformation, so it's all the more surprising to find this genuine eel and pie shop still going strong. Closed Sun.

Feast 86 St John St, EC1. Farringdon or Barbican tube. Delicious tortilla-wrapped sandwiches made to order; takeaway or eat-in in this small, trendy, designer Clerkenwell café. Closed Sat & Sun.

Ktchn 35 Charlotte Rd, EC2. Old Street tube. Tiny, vowel-free Hoxton/Shoreditch café with just four stools, serving delicious upmarket lunch options: big soups, grilled tuna, rare-roast beef, exotic salads and great pastries all freshly prepared. Closed Sat & Sun.

London for veggies

Most cafés and restaurants in London will make some attempt to cater for **vegetarians**. Below is a list of exclusively vegetarian places recommended in the "Eating" section.

Beatroot 92 Berwick St, W1 (see p.157)

Food for Thought 31 Neal St, WC2 (see above)

The Gate 2 72 Belsize Lane, NW3 (see p.162)

The Gate 51 Queen Caroline St, W4 (see p.162)

Manna 4 Erskine Rd, NW3 (see p.162)

The Place Below Church of St Mary-le-Bow, Cheapside, EC2 (see p.159)

Rasa 6 Dering St, W1 (see p.161)

Red Veg 95 Dean St, W1 (see p.157)

World Food Café 14 Neal's Yard, WC2 (see above)

The City and the East End

Arkansas Café Unit 12, Old Spitalfields Market, E1. Liverpool Street tube. American barbecue fuel stop, using only the very best free-range ingredients.

Brick Lane Beigel Bake 159 Brick Lane, E1. Shoreditch or Whitechapel tube. The bagels at this no-frills 24-hour takeaway in the heart of the East End are freshly made and unbelievably cheap, even when stuffed with smoked salmon and cream cheese.

Café 1001 1 Dray's Lane, E1. Off Brick Lane, tucked in by the Truman Brewery, this smoky café has a beaten-up studenty look, with lots of sofas to crash in, and dishes out simple sandwiches and delicious cakes. Whitechapel tube.

The Place Below St Mary-le-Bow, Cheapside, EC2. St Paul's or Bank tube. City café serving imaginative (albeit slightly pricey) vegetarian dishes in a wonderful Norman crypt. Closed Sat & Sun.

The South Bank & Southwark

Konditor & Cook 22 Cornwall Rd, SE1. Waterloo tube. A cut above your average bakery, *Konditor & Cook* make wonderful cakes and biscuits, as well as offering a choice of sandwiches and coffee and tea. There are branches elsewhere on the south side of the Thames at 10 Stoney St by Borough Market, in the Design Museum and in the Young Vic Theatre. Closed Sun.

Kensington, Chelsea and Notting Hill

Books for Cooks 4 Blenheim Crescent, W11. Ladbroke Grove or Notting Hill Gate tube. Tiny café/restaurant within London's top cookery bookshop – just wander in and have a coffee while browsing, or get there in time to grab a table for the set menu lunch. No smoking.

Daquise 20 Thurloe St, SW7. South Kensington tube. This old-fashioned Polish café right by the tube is something of a South Ken institution, serving Polish home cooking or simple coffee, tea and cakes depending on the time of day.

Gloriette 128 Brompton Rd, SW7. South Kensington or Knightsbridge tube. Long-established Viennese café that makes a perfect post-museum halt for coffee and outrageous cakes; also serves sandwiches, Wiener Schnitzel, pasta dishes, goulash and fish and chips.

Lisboa Patisserie 57 Golborne Rd, W10. Ladbroke Grove tube. Authentic and friendly Portuguese pastelaria, with coffee and cakes including the best custard tarts this side of Lisbon. The *Oporto*, at 62a Golborne Rd, is a good fallback if this place is full.

Afternoon tea

The classic English **afternoon tea** – assorted sandwiches, scones and cream, cakes and tarts and, of course, lashings of tea – is available all over London. The best venues are the capital's top hotels and most fashionable department stores; a selection of the best is picked out below. To avoid disappointment it's best to book ahead. Expect to spend £15–25 a head, and leave your jeans and trainers at home – most hotels will expect men to wear a jacket of some sort, though only the *Ritz* insists on jacket and tie.

Brown's 33–34 Albemarle St, W1 ℡020/7493 6020, ⊛www.brownshotel.com. Green Park tube. Daily 2–6pm.

Claridge's Brook St, W1 ℡020/7629 8860, ⊛www.savoy-group.co.uk. Bond Street tube. Daily 3–5.30pm.

The Dorchester 54 Park Lane, W1 ℡020/7629 8888, ⊛www.dorchesterhotel .co.uk. Hyde Park Corner tube. Daily 3–6pm.

Fortnum & Mason 181 Piccadilly, W1 ℡020/7734 8040, ⊛www.fortnumandmason .com. Green Park or Piccadilly Circus tube. Daily 3–5.45pm.

Lanesborough Hyde Park Corner, SW1 ℡020/7259 5599, ⊛www.lanesborough .com. Hyde Park Corner tube. Daily 3.30–6pm.

The Ritz Piccadilly, W1 ℡020/7493 8181, ⊛www.theritzhotel.co.uk. Green Park tube. Daily 1.30, 3.30 & 5.30pm.

The Savoy Strand, WC2 ℡020/7836 4343, ⊛www.savoy-group.co.uk. Charing Cross tube. Daily 3–5.30pm.

Camden and Hampstead

Brew House Kenwood, Hampstead Lane, NW3. Bus #210 from Archway tube or a walk across the Heath. Everything from full English breakfast to lunches, cakes and teas, all served in the old laundry at Kenwood, or enjoyed on the terrace overlooking the lake.

Café Mozart 17 Swains Lane, N6. Gospel Oak train station or bus #C2 from Kentish Town tube. Viennese café that's usefully close to the southeast side of Hampstead Heath, and also serves a few hearty Austrian dishes.

Louis Patisserie 32 Heath St, NW3. Hampstead tube. Popular central-European tea room in Hampstead village serving sticky cakes to a mix of Heath-bound hordes and elderly locals.

Marine Ices 8 Haverstock Hill, NW3. Situated halfway between Camden and Hampstead, this is a splendid and justly famous old-fashioned Italian ice-cream parlour; pizza and pasta are served in the adjacent restaurant. Chalk Farm tube.

Greenwich

Pistachio's Café 15 Nelson Rd, SE10. Cutty Sark DLR or Greenwich DLR and train station. Just about the only decent sandwich café in the centre of Greenwich, serving excellent coffee, and with a small garden out back.

Tai Won Mein 39 Greenwich Church St, SE10. Cutty Sark DLR or Greenwich DLR and train station. Good quality fast-food noodle bar that gets very busy at weekends. Decor is functional and minimalist; choose between rice, soup or various fried noodles, all for under a fiver.

Restaurants

Many of the restaurants we've listed will be busy on most nights of the week, particularly on Thursday, Friday and Saturday, and it's best to **reserve a table**. As for **prices**, you can pay an awful lot for a meal in London, and if you're used to North American portions, you're not going to be particularly impressed by the volume in most places. For cheaper eats, see the section above. For an explanation of the pricing system, see Basics, p.39. Where possible we've marked the following options on the maps in this chapter.

St James's, Mayfair and Marylebone

Fairuz 3 Blandford St, W1 ☎020/7486 8108. Bond Street tube. One of London's more accessible Middle Eastern restaurants, with an epic list of meze, a selection of charcoal grills and one or two oven-baked dishes. Moderate.

La Galette 56 Paddington St, W1 ☎020/7935 1554. Baker Street tube. Bright modern pancake place. The hors d'oeuvres are very simple and very French and the savoury and sweet buckwheat galettes are generous. Inexpensive.

Mandalay 444 Edgware Rd, W2 ☎020/7258 3696. Edgware Road tube. See map, p.136. Small nonsmoking restaurant that serves Burmese cuisine – a melange of Thai, Malaysian, a lot of Indian and a few things that are unique. The portions are huge and the flavours hit the mark. Closed Sun. Inexpensive.

The Providores 109 Marylebone High St, W1 ☎020/7935 6175. Green Park tube. Outstanding fusion restaurant run by an amiable New Zealander and split into two: snacky tapas bar downstairs and full-on restaurant upstairs. The food at both is original and wholly satisfying. Inexpensive–Moderate.

Soho and Chinatown

China City White Bear Yard, WC2 ☎020/7734 3388. Leicester Square tube. See map, p.90. Large restaurant tucked into a little courtyard off Lisle Street; fresh and bright, with *dim sum* that's up there with the best, service that's "Chinatown brusque". Moderate.

Chowki 2–3 Denman St, W1 ☎020/7439 1330. Piccadilly Circus tube. See map, p.90. Large, cheap Indian restaurant serving authentic food in stylish surroundings. The menu changes every month in order to feature three different regions of India – the regional feast for around £10 is great value. Inexpensive.

Mr Kong 21 Lisle St, WC2 ☎020/7437 7923. Leicester Square tube. See map, p.90. One of Chinatown's finest. To sample the restaurant's more unusual dishes order from the "Today's" and "Chef's Specials" menu, and don't miss the mussels in black-bean sauce or the fresh razor clam with garlic. Moderate.

New World 1 Gerrard Place, W1 ☎020/7734 0396. Leicester Square tube. See map, p.90. Another reasonable stab at an overblown Hong Kong dining palace – all red, gold and dragons. Best deal here is the lunchtime *dim sum*, served by indefatigable trolley-pushers. Inexpensive.

Spiga 84–86 Wardour St, W1 ☎ 020/7734 3444. Leicester Square tube. See map, p.90. A pleasantly casual Italian affair, with a lively atmosphere, a serious wood-fired oven and a cool look about it. Moderate.

La Trouvaille 12a Newburgh St, W1 ☎ 020/7287 8488. Oxford Circus tube. See map, p.90. Here, they understand the English need for really French Frenchness and if you hanker after a "dangerously French" dish, try the tripe terrine. Closed Sun lunch. Moderate.

Covent Garden & Bloomsbury

Belgo Centraal 50 Earlham St, WC2 t020/7813 2233. Covent Garden tube. See map, p.90. Massive metal-minimalist cavern off Neal Street, serving excellent kilo buckets of moules marinière, with *frites* and mayonnaise, a bewildering array of Belgian beers to choose from, and waffles for dessert. The lunchtime specials are a bargain for central London. Inexpensive to Moderate.

Ikkyu 67a Tottenham Court Rd, W1 ☎ 020/7636 9280. Goodge Street tube. See map, p.90. Busy, basic basement Japanese restaurant, good enough for a quick lunch or a more elaborate dinner. Be warned, however: it's hard to find and, when you do, shockingly popular. Closed all Sat & Sun lunch. Moderate.

J. Sheekey 28–32 St Martin's Court, WC2 ☎ 020/7240 2565. Leicester Square tube. See map, p.90. Long-established stylish place whose menu is focused on fish, from traditional fare such as grilled Dover sole, to modernist dishes like grilled cuttlefish with creamed *brandade*. Expensive.

Rasa Samudra 5 Charlotte St, W1 ☎ 020/7637 0222. Goodge Street tube. See map, p.90. Sophisticated Southern Indian fish dishes that are a million miles from the usual London curry-house staples. *Rasa* also has an exclusively vegetarian branch at 6 Dering St, W1 (☎ 020/7629 1346; Bond Street tube). Closed Sun. Moderate to Expensive.

Clerkenwell & Hoxton

Cicada 132 St John St, EC1 ☎ 020/7608 1550. Farringdon tube. Bar-restaurant set back from the street with alfresco eating and an unusual Thai-based menu. Closed Sat lunch & Sun. Moderate.

Real Greek 15 Hoxton Market, N1 ☎ 020/7739 8212. Old Street tube. Small, modern and comfortable place where the menu has authentic Greek dishes, and the service is excellent. Set lunch and early doors dinner are a bargain. Closed Sun. Moderate.

St John 26 St John St, EC1 ☎ 020/7251 0848. Farringdon tube. A genuinely English restaurant, specializing in all those strange and unfashionable cuts of meat that were once commonplace in rural England – brains, bone marrow. Closed Sat lunch & Sun. Expensive.

Viet Hoa Café 72 Kingsland Rd, E2 ☎ 020/7729 8293. Old Street tube. Large, light and airy Vietnamese café not far from the Geffrye Museum, serving splendid "meals in a bowl" – soups and noodle dishes with everything from spring rolls to tofu.

East End

Café Naz 46–48 Brick Lane, E1 ☎ 020/7247 0234. Aldgate East tube. See map, p.122. Self-proclaimed contemporary Bangladeshi restaurant with an open-plan kitchen offering all the standards plus a load of "baltis". Inexpensive.

Café Spice Namaste 16 Prescott St, E1 ☎ 020/7488 9242. Tower Hill tube. See map, p.122. Very popular Indian on the fringe of the City that is definitely not your average curry house. Parsee delicacies rub shoulders with dishes from Goa, Hyderabad and Kashmir, and the tandoori specialities are awesome. Closed Sat lunch & Sun. Moderate.

New Tayyab 83 Fieldgate St, E1 ☎ 020/7247 9543. Aldgate East or Whitechapel tube. See map, p.122. Smart, designer restaurant serving straight-forward Pakistani fare: good, freshly cooked and served without pretension. Booking is essential and service is speedy and slick. Cash or cheque only. Inexpensive.

South Bank and Southwark

Delfina 50 Bermondsey St, SE1 ☎ 020/7357 0244. London Bridge tube. See map, p.122. This adjunct to the Delfina art gallery is a serious Modern British restaurant and a great place to go for lunch if you're in the area. The prices have moved well beyond café norms, but the quality justifies a bit of a splurge. Closed Sat & Sun. Expensive.

Fina Estampa 150 Tooley St, SE1 ☎ 020/7403 1342. London Bridge tube. See map, p.122. One of London's few Peruvian restaurants, which also happens to be very good, bringing a little of down-town Lima to London Bridge. The menu is traditional Peruvian, with a big emphasis on seafood. Closed Sat lunch & all Sun. Moderate.

Little Saigon 139 Westminster Bridge Rd, SE1 ☎ 020/7207 9747. Waterloo tube. See map, p.122. Great Vietnamese spring rolls, grilled squid-cake and crystal pancakes, all served with a wonderful array of sauces, plus crispy fried noodles. Closed Sat & Sun lunch. Moderate.

RSJ 13a Coin St, SE1 ☎020/7928 4554, ⓦwww.rsj.uk.com. Waterloo tube. Regularly high standards of Anglo-French cooking make this a good spot for a meal after or before an evening at a South Bank theatre or concert hall. The set meals for around £15 are particularly popular. Closed Sat lunch & Sun. Expensive.

Kensington and Chelsea

Bibendum Oyster House Michelin House, 81 Fulham Rd, SW3 ☎020/7589 1480, ⓦwww.bibendum.co.uk. South Kensington tube. See map, p.136. A glorious tiled affair built in 1911, this former garage is one of the prettiest places to eat shellfish in London – if you're really hungry, go for the "Plateau de Fruits de Mer". Moderate.

Boisdale 15 Ecclestone St, SW1 ☎020/7730 6922, ⓦwww.boisdale.co.uk. Victoria tube. Owned by Ranald MacDonald, son of the Chief of Clanranald, this is a very Scottish place, strong on hospitality, and fresh Scottish produce. Closed Sun. Moderate to Expensive.

Hunan 51 Pimlico Rd, SW1 ☎020/7730 5712. Sloane Square tube. Probably England's only restaurant serving Hunan food, a relative of Sichuan cuisine, with the same spicy kick to most dishes. Closed Sun. Expensive.

Bayswater and Notting Hill

Al Waha 75 Westbourne Grove, W2 ☎020/7229 0806. Queensway or Bayswater tube. See map, p.136. Arguably London's best Lebanese restaurant; meze-obsessed, but also painstaking in its preparation of the main-course dishes, where spanking fresh and accurately cooked grills predominate. Moderate.

The Mandola 139–141 Westbourne Grove, W11 ☎020/7229 4734. Notting Hill Gate tube. See map, p.136. Small, seriously informal, supremely popular, unlicensed neighbourhood restaurant serving strikingly delicious "urban Sudanese"

food at sensible prices. Closed Mon lunch. Moderate.

Rodizio Rico 111 Westbourne Grove, W11 ☎020/7792 4035. Notting Hill Gate or Queensway tube. See map, p.136. No menu, no prices, but no problem either as this Brazilian eatery specializes in smoky, grilled meat. Carvers come round and lop off chunks of freshly grilled meats, while you help yourself from the salad bar and hot buffet to prime your plate. Closed Mon–Fri lunch. Moderate.

Camden and Hampstead

Cucina 45a South End Rd, NW3 ☎020/7435 7814. Belsize Park tube. Brightly painted, wooden-floored, Modern British restaurant that's very contemporary, very fashionable and very Hampstead. Expensive.

The Gate 2 72 Belsize Lane, NW3 ☎020/7435 7733. Belsize Park tube. The modern, minimalist *Gate 2* serves excellent and original veggie dishes with intense and satisfying tastes and textures, ranging from wild mushroom terrine to root vegetable tagine. Moderate.

Manna 4 Erskine Rd, NW3 ☎020/7722 8028. Chalk Farm tube. Old-fashioned, casual vegetarian restaurant with 1970s decor, serving large portions of very good veggie food. Don't show up here in a hurry or without a serious appetite. Closed Mon–Fri lunch & Sat & Sun eve. Moderate.

Chiswick to Richmond

Chez Lindsay 11 Hill Rise, Richmond ☎020/8948 7473. Richmond tube. Small, bright, authentic Breton creperie, offering galettes, crepes or more formal French main courses, including lots of fresh fish and shellfish, all washed down with Breton cider in traditional earthenware *bolées*. Inexpensive to Moderate.

The Gate 51 Queen Caroline St, W4 ☎020/8748 6932. Hammersmith tube. Tucked away behind the Hammersmith Apollo, this is a vegetarian restaurant that eschews healthy, wholefood eating. It's as rich, colourful, calorific and naughty as anywhere in town, just without meat. Moderate.

Drinking

London's **drinking** establishments run the whole gamut from grand Victorian gin palaces to funky modern bars with resident DJs catering to a pre-club crowd. The emergence in the last decade or so of gastropubs, where the food is as important as the drink, has had a huge impact on the rest of the pub trade.

Where possible we've marked the places below on the maps in this chapter.

Whitehall and Westminster

Albert 52 Victoria St, SW1. St James's Park or Victoria tube. See map, p.90. Roomy High-Victorian pub with big bay windows, glass partitions, good bar food and an excellent carvery upstairs.

ICA Bar 94 The Mall, SW1. Piccadilly Circus or Charing Cross tube. See map, p.90. You have to be a member (or be visiting an exhibition or cinema/theatre/talk event) to drink at the late-opening *ICA Bar* – but anyone can join on the door (Mon–Fri £1.50; Sat & Sun £2.50). It's a cool drinking venue, with a *noir* dress code observed by the arty crowd and staff, but beware the weekend DJ nights.

Paviour's Arms Page St, SW1. Pimlico tube. A unique survivor, this large, stylish 1930s Art Deco pub, in the backstreets close to the Tate Gallery, has much of its original decor intact; you can also get decent Thai food with your beer. Closed Sat & Sun.

St James's, Mayfair and Marylebone

Dover Castle 43 Weymouth Mews, W1. Regent's Park or Oxford Circus tube. See map, p.90. A traditional, quiet boozer hidden away down a labyrinthine Marylebone mews. Green upholstery, dark wood and a nicotine-stained lincrusta ceiling add to the ambience. Closed Sun.

O'Conor Don 88 Marylebone Lane, W1. Bond Street tube. See map, p.90. A stripped bare, anti-theme Irish pub that's a cut above the average, with excellent Guinness, a pleasantly measured pace and Irish food on offer. Closed Sat & Sun.

Red Lion 23 Crown Passage, SW1. Green Park tube. See map, p.90. Not to be confused with the nearby pub of the same name, this is a small, local, wood-panelled place hidden away in a passageway off Pall Mall. Closed Sun.

The Social 5 Little Portland St, W1. Oxford Circus tube. See map, p.90. Industrial club-bar with great DJs playing everything from rock to rap, a truly hedonistic-cum-alcoholic crowd and the ultimate snacks – beans on toast and soup in a mug. Closed Sun.

Ye Grapes 16 Shepherd Market, W1. Green Park or Hyde Park Corner tube. See map, p.90. A great local in the heart of Mayfair, this busy Victorian free house has a good selection of real ales and an open fire.

Soho

Argyll Arms 18 Argyll St, W1. Oxford Circus tube. See map, p.90. A stone's throw from Oxford Circus, this is a great Victorian pub, which has preserved many of its original features and serves good real ales.

Dog & Duck 18 Bateman St, W1. Leicester Square or Tottenham Court Road tube. See map, p.90. Tiny Soho pub that retains much of its old character, beautiful Victorian tiling and mosaics, and a loyal clientele. Closed Sat & Sun lunch.

Dog House 187 Wardour St, W1. Leicester Square or Tottenham Court Road tube. See map, p.90. Colourful basement bar, popular for hip-hop, funk and acid jazz, that draws a friendly mix of office types, students and film runners. Mon–Sat eve only.

French House 49 Dean St, W1. Leicester Square tube. See map, p.90. Soho institution since before World War I. Free French and literary associations galore, half pints only at the bar and a fine little restaurant upstairs (book ahead on ☏ 020/7437 2799).

Lab 12 Old Compton St, W1. Tottenham Court Road or Leicester Square tube. See map, p.90. Chic, multicoloured former strip joint that stirs up some of the best cocktails in town for its style-conscious crowd of beautiful Soho-ites.

The Toucan 19 Carlisle St. Tottenham Court Road tube. See map, p.90. Small bar serving excellent Guinness and a wide range of Irish whiskeys, plus cheap, wholesome and filling food. So popular it can get mobbed. Closed Sun.

Two Floors 3 Kingly St, W1. Oxford Circus or Piccadilly Circus tube. See map, p.90. Laid-back, designer-style Soho bar, laid out, unsurprisingly, on two floors, attracting a mixed media crowd. Closed Sun.

Covent Garden

Denim 4a Upper St Martin's Lane, WC2. Leicester Square tube. See map, p.90. The retro orange and purple decor goes down a treat with the young after-work punters, who don't seem to flinch at the outrageous bar prices. Eve only.

Detroit 35 Earlham St, WC2. Covent Garden tube. See map, p.90. Cavernous underground venue with an open-plan bar area, secluded Gaudíesque booths and a huge range of spirits. DJs take over at the weekends. Closed Sun.

Freedom Brewing Company 41 Earlham St, WC2. Covent Garden tube. See map, p.90. Busy, brick-vaulted basement brewery bar with wrought-iron pillars, lots of brushed steel and pricey, strong brews, made on the premises – in particular, there's a very fine organic honey wheat beer.

Lamb & Flag 33 Rose St, WC2. Leicester Square tube. See map, p.90. Busy, tiny and highly atmospheric pub, tucked away down an alley between

Garrick Street and Floral Street, where John Dryden was attacked in 1679 for writing scurrilous verses about one of Charles II's mistresses.

Punch & Judy 40 The Market, WC2. Covent Garden tube. See map, p.90. Horribly mobbed and loud, but this Covent Garden Market pub does boast an unbeatable location with a very popular balcony overlooking the Piazza.

Salisbury 90 St Martin's Lane, WC2. Leicester Square tube. See map, p.90. Easily one of the most beautifully preserved Victorian pubs in the capital – and certainly the most central – with cut, etched and engraved windows, bronze figures, red velvet seating and a fine lincrusta ceiling.

Bloomsbury & Holborn

Jerusalem 33–34 Rathbone Place, W1. Tottenham Court Road tube. See map, p.90. Chandeliers and velvet drapes set the tone, and there's an especially good mix of music on Thursday nights, though it does attract a large proportion of local office workers. Closed Sun.

Lamb 94 Lamb's Conduit St, WC1. Russell Square tube. Pleasant pub with a marvellously well-preserved Victorian interior of mirrors, old wood and snob screens.

Museum Tavern 49 Great Russell St, WC1. Tottenham Court Road or Russell Square tube. See map, p.90. Large and characterful old pub, right opposite the British Museum, erstwhile drinking hole of Karl Marx.

Na Zdrowie 11 Little Turnstile, WC1. Holborn tube. See map, p.90. Great Polish bar hidden in an alleyway behind Holborn tube, with a wicked selection of flavoured vodkas and cheap Polish food.

Princess Louise 208 High Holborn, WC1. Holborn tube. See map, p.90. Old-fashioned place, with highly decorated ceilings, lots of glass, brass and mahogany, and a good range of real ales. Closed Sun.

Clerkenwell

Café Kick 43 Exmouth Market, EC1. Farringdon or Angel tube. Stylish take on a local French-style café-bar in the heart of fashionable Exmouth Market, with table football to complete the retro theme. Closed Sun.

Clerkenwell House 23–27 Hatton Wall, EC1. Farringdon tube. The Med food is good, there are four American pool tables in the basement bar and the retro 1970s furniture includes some seriously comfy semicircular sofas. Closed Sat lunch.

Eagle 159 Farringdon Rd, EC1. Farringdon tube. The first of London's pubs to go foody, this place is heaving at lunch and dinnertimes, as *Guardian*

workers tuck into Med dishes, but you should be able to find a seat at other times. Closed Sun eve.

Fox & Anchor 115 Charterhouse St, EC1. Farringdon or Barbican tube. Handsome Smithfield market pub famous for its early opening hours (from 7am) and huge breakfasts. Closed Sat & Sun.

Jerusalem Tavern 55 Britton St, EC1. Farringdon tube. Cosy converted Georgian parlour, stripped bare and slightly "distressed", serving tasty food along with an excellent range of draught beers from St Peter's Brewery in Suffolk. Closed Sat & Sun.

Lifthouse 85 Charterhouse St, EC1. Farringdon tube. Next door to *Fabric*, this three-floored New York-style club-bar-restaurant houses a cocktail bar and club space upstairs.

Hoxton

Bricklayer's Arms 63 Charlotte Rd, EC2. Old Street tube. An appealingly ramshackle Shoreditch pub (serving Thai food) that predates the area's trendification, and is therefore all the more popular with its new arty residents. Closed Sun.

Dragon 5 Leonard St, EC2. Old Street tube. Discreetly signed clubby pub with bare-brick walls and crumbling leather sofas, that attracts a mixed crowd happy to listen to whatever takes the resident DJ's fancy.

Shoreditch Electricity Showrooms 39A Hoxton Square, N1. Old Street tube. The upstairs bar mixes kitsch artwork with digital boards flashing ironic weather and text messages, while the intimate club downstairs hosts weekend parties. Good Modern European food available too. Closed Mon.

The City: Fleet Street to St Paul's

Blackfriar 174 Queen Victoria St, EC4. Blackfriars tube. See map, p.112. A gorgeous, utterly original pub, with Art Nouveau marble friezes of boozy monks and a wonderful highly decorated alcove, all dating from 1905. Closed Sat & Sun.

Old Bank of England 194 Fleet St, EC4. Temple or Chancery Lane tube. See map, p.112. Not the actual Bank of England, but the former Law Courts' branch, this imposing High Victorian banking hall is now a magnificently opulent ale and pie pub. Closed Sat & Sun.

Old Cheshire Cheese Wine Office Court, 145 Fleet St, EC4. Blackfriars tube. See map, p.112. A famous seventeenth-century watering hole, with several snug, dark panelled bars and real fires. Popular with tourists, but by no means exclusively so. Closed Sun eve.

Viaduct Tavern 126 Newgate St, EC1. St Paul's tube. See map, p.112. Glorious gin palace built in 1869 opposite what was then Newgate Prison and is now the Old Bailey. Ask to see the old cells now used for storing beer. The walls are adorned with oils of faded ladies representing Commerce, Agriculture and the Arts.

The City: Bank to Bishopsgate

The Counting House 50 Cornhill, EC2. Bank tube. See map, p.122. Another City bank conversion, with fantastic high ceilings a glass dome, chandeliers and a central oval bar. Naturally enough, given the location, it's wall-to-wall suits. Closed Sat & Sun.

Hamilton Hall Liverpool Street Station, EC2. Liverpool Street tube. See map, p.122. Cavernous, gilded, former ballroom of the *Great Eastern* hotel, adorned with nudes and chandeliers. Packed out with City commuters tanking up before the train home, but a great place nonetheless.

Jamaica Wine House St Michael's Alley, EC3. Bank tube. See map, p.122. An old City institution tucked away down a narrow alleyway. Despite the name, this is really just a pub, divided into four large snugs by high wood-panelled partitions. Closed Sat & Sun.

East End and Docklands

Dickens Inn St Katharine's Way, E1. Tower Hill tube. See map, p.122. Eighteenth-century timber-framed warehouse transported on wheels from its original site, with a great view over the docks, but very firmly on the tourist trail.

The Gun 27 Cold Harbour, E14. South Quay or Blackwall DLR, or Canary Wharf tube. An old dockers' pub with lots of maritime memorabilia, and – the main attraction – an unrivalled view of the Millennium Dome.

Prospect of Whitby 57 Wapping Wall, E1. Wapping tube. London's most famous riverside pub with a flagstone floor, a cobbled courtyard and great views over the Thames.

Town of Ramsgate 62 Wapping High St, E1. Wapping tube. Dark, narrow medieval pub located by Wapping Old Stairs, which once led down to Execution Dock. Captain Blood was discovered here with the crown jewels under his cloak, and Admiral Bligh and Fletcher Christian were regular drinking partners in pre-mutiny days.

South Bank and Southwark

Anchor Bankside 34 Park St, SE1. London Bridge, Southwark or Blackfriars tube. See map, p.122. While the rest of Bankside has changed almost beyond all recognition, this pub still looks much as it did when first built in 1770 (on the inside, at least). Good for alfresco drinking by the river.

George Inn 77 Borough High St, SE1. Borough or London Bridge tube. See map, p.122. London's only surviving coaching inn – dating from the seventeenth century and now owned by the National Trust – serving a good range of real ales.

Market Porter 9 Stoney St, SE1 ☎ 020/7407 2495. London Bridge tube. See map, p.122. Handsome semicircular pub with early opening hours for workers at the Borough Market, and a seriously huge range of real ales.

Kensington & Chelsea

Bed Bar 310 Portobello Rd, W10. Westbourne Park tube. See map, p.136. Despite Moroccan-theme, low-level lighting and cushioned seating areas, *Bed Bar* is crammed with hedonistic locals Wed–Sun, standing on the sofas, arms aloft while the DJs spin funky house and Latin-tinged beats.

Bunch of Grapes 207 Brompton Rd, SW3. South Kensington tube. See map, p.136. This popular High-Victorian pub, complete with snob screens, is the perfect place for a post-V&A (or post-Harrods) pint, pie and chips.

Front Page 35 Old Church St, SW3. Sloane Square tube. See map, p.136. Tucked away in the centre of villagey, bohemian Chelsea and infinitely preferable to anything on offer on the King's Road, the *Front Page* is small and snug, and serves very good Mediterranean food.

Notting Hill

Cherry Jam 52 Porchester Rd, W2. Royal Oak tube. See map, p.136. Owned by Ben Watt (house DJ and half of pop group Everything But The Girl), this smart intimate basement place mixes a decadent cocktail bar with top-end West London DJs. Eve only.

The Cow 89 Westbourne Park Rd, W2. Westbourne Park or Royal Oak tube. See map, p.136. Vaguely Irish-themed pub that pulls in the beautiful W11 types thanks to its spectacular food, including a daily supply of fresh oysters, and excellent Guinness.

Market Bar 240a Portobello Rd, W11. Ladbroke Grove tube. See map, p.136. Self-consciously bohemian pub divided by gilded mirrors and ruched curtains and scattered with weird *objets* – all very Portobello Road. Occasional live music and DJs.

Prince Bonaparte 80 Chepstow Rd, W2. Royal Oak tube. See map, p.136. Pared-down, minimalist pub, with acres of space for sitting and supping or enjoying the excellent Mediterranean food. Notting Hill Gate or Royal Oak tube.

St John's Wood and Maida Vale

Prince Alfred 9 Formosa St, W9. Warwick Avenue tube. See map, p.136. A fantastic period-piece Victorian pub with all its original 1862 fittings intact, right down to the glazed snob screens that divide the bar into a series of snugs, and a surprisingly young and funky clientele.

Warrington Hotel 93 Warrington Crescent, W9. Warwick Avenue or Maida Vale tube. Yet another architectural gem – this time flamboyant Art Nouveau – in an area replete with them. The interior is rich and satisfying, as are the draught beers and the Thai restaurant upstairs.

Camden Town

Bar Vinyl 6 Inverness St, NW1. Camden Town tube. Tiny, funky glass-bricked place with a breakbeat and trip-hop vibe, and a record shop downstairs.

Bartok 78–79 Chalk Farm Rd, NW1. Chalk Farm or Camden Town tube. Unusual bar where punters sink into the sofas and sup beer or wine while listening to classical music and live jazz instead of the usual muzak. Closed Mon–Fri lunch.

The Engineer 65 Gloucester Ave, NW1. Chalk Farm tube. One of a number of gastropubs in the much sought-after residential area of Primrose Hill, *The Engineer* is a smart, grandiose place which serves exceptional but pricey Modern Brit/Med food.

Hampstead and Highgate

The Flask 14 Flask Walk, NW3. Hampstead tube. Convivial Hampstead local, hidden away along the pedestrianized Flask Walk, that retains its original Victorian snob screen and serves above-average food and Young's ale.

The Flask 77 Highgate West Hill, N6. Highgate tube. Ideally situated at the heart of Highgate village green, with a rambling low-ceilinged interior and a summer terrace. The range of beers is good, but the food is nothing special.

Freemason's Arms 32 Downshire Hill, NW3. Hampstead tube. Big, smart pub close to the Heath, popular on sunny days primarily for its large beer garden; also does comfort pub food, has a basement skittle alley, and an outdoor pell mell pitch.

Holly Bush 22 Holly Mount, NW3. Hampstead tube. A lovely old wood-panelled, gas-lit pub, tucked away in the steep backstreets of Hampstead village. Mobbed at the weekend.

Dulwich and Greenwich

Crown & Greyhound 73 Dulwich Village, SE21. West Dulwich train station from Victoria. Grand, spacious Victorian pub with an ornate plasterwork ceiling and a nice summer beer garden. Convenient for the Picture Gallery, but be prepared for the Sunday lunchtime crowds.

Cutty Sark Ballast Quay, off Lassell St, SE10. Cutty Sark DLR or Maze Hill train station. The nicest riverside pub in Greenwich, spacious, more of a local and much less touristy than the more famous *Trafalgar Tavern* (it's a couple of minutes walk further east, following the river). The views are great, as is the draught beer, and the bar food is a cut above the norm.

Trafalgar Tavern 5 Park Row, SE10. Cutty Sark DLR or Maze Hill train station. A great riverside position and a mention in Dickens' *Our Mutual Friend* have made this Regency-style inn a firm tourist favourite, which is fair enough really, as it's a convivial period piece, and serves good food.

Chiswick to Richmond

Dove 19 Upper Mall, W6. Ravenscourt Park tube. A short walk from Hammersmith Bridge, this old riverside pub is known for its literary associations and the smallest back bar in the UK (4ft by 7ft).

White Cross Hotel Water Lane, Richmond. Richmond tube. With a longer pedigree and more character than its clinical chain rivals nearby, the *White Cross* is also much closer to the river (its front garden regularly gets flooded).

White Swan Riverside, Twickenham. Twickenham train station from Waterloo. Filling pub food, draught beer and a quiet riverside location – with a beer pontoon on the Thames if you want to get even closer to the water – make this a good halt on any towpath ramble.

Nightlife

On any night of the week London offers a bewildering range of things to do after dark, from top-flight opera and theatre to clubs with a life span of a couple of nights. The **listings magazine** *Time Out*, which comes out every Tuesday afternoon, is essential if you want to get the most out of this city, giving full details of prices and access, plus previews and reviews.

Live music venues

Over the past five years London has established itself as the music capital of not just Europe, but the world. Rio may be sunnier, Paris prettier and Madrid madder but for sheer range and diversity there's nowhere to beat London. The **live music** scene remains extremely diverse, encompassing all variations of rock, blues, roots and world music; and although London's jazz clubs aren't on a par with those in the big American cities, there's a highly individual scene of home-based artists, supplemented by top-name visiting players.

Rock and blues clubs and pubs

Astoria 157 Charing Cross Rd, WC2 ⓦwww.meanfiddler.com. Tottenham Court Road tube. This central, large, balconied one-time theatre tends to host slightly alternative bands, with club nights on Fri & Sat.

Borderline Orange Yard, off Manette St, W1 ⓦwww.borderline.co.uk. Tottenham Court Road tube. Intimate basement joint and a good place to catch new bands, although big names sometimes turn up under a pseudonym.

Brixton Academy 211 Stockwell Rd, SW9. Brixton tube. This refurbished Victorian hall, complete with Neoclassical decorations, can hold 4000 but still manages to seem small and friendly.

Forum 9–17 Highgate Rd, NW5 ⓦwww .meanfiddler.com. Kentish Town tube. The Forum is North London's best medium-sized venue, and is still a frequent stopoff point for established jazz-funk and rock bands.

Mean Fiddler 24–28a Harlesden High St, NW10 ⓦwww.meanfiddler.com. Willesden Junction tube. An excellent – if inconveniently located – small venue with a main hall and smaller acoustic room. The bands veer from rock to world to folk.

Orange 3 North End Crescent, North End Rd W14. West Kensington tube. Pub-like venue for serious-minded jazz-funkers. There are also varying club nights (call ahead on ☏020/7371 4317).

Roadhouse Jubilee Hall, 35 The Piazza, WC2 ⓦwww.roadhouse.co.uk. Covent Garden tube. American food, 1950s US-style decor and a line-up of mainly blues and rock'n'roll bands performing to a mature, nostalgic crowd.

Shepherd's Bush Empire Shepherds Bush Green, W12 ⓦwww.shepherds-bush-empire .co.uk. Shepherd's Bush tube. Grand old West London theatre that regularly draws the cream of the crop of non-stadium-rocking bands.

Station Tavern 41 Bramley Rd, W10. Latimer Road tube. Arguably London's best blues venue, with free – and occasionally great – blues six nights a week.

Subterania 12 Acklam Rd, W10 ⓦwww .meanfiddler.com. Ladbroke Grove tube. One of the original live music/club crossover venues, set in an arch under a bridge. The crowd is as clued up as the music, which is often dance-oriented.

Underworld 174 Camden High St, NW1 ⓦwww.theunderworldcamden.co.uk. Camden Town tube. Labyrinthine venue that's good for new bands, and has sporadic club nights.

Jazz, world music and roots

100 Club 100 Oxford St, W1. Tottenham Court Road tube. Unpretentious and inexpensive jazz venue – in a very central location.

606 Club 90 Lots Rd, SW10. Fulham Broadway tube. A rare all-jazz venue, located just off the less trendy end of King's Road.

Africa Centre 38 King St, WC2 ⓦwww .africacentre.org.uk. Covent Garden tube. Small place hosting African bands and nights like Saturday's P-funk-heavy Funkin Pussy drawing a vibrantly enthusiastic crowd.

Cargo 83 Rivington St, EC2 ⓦwww.cargo-london .com. Old St tube. Great live music venue for modern genre mix-ups that blend jazz with Brazilian, Latin and African music, from young, vibrant bands, often complemented by DJs.

Jazz Café 5 Parkway, NW1 ⓦwww.jazzcafe.co.uk. Camden Town tube. Futuristic, white-walled venue with an adventurous booking policy exploring Latin, rap, funk, hip-hop and musical fusions. Diehard trad-jazz fans won't be happy, despite the fact that there's a rather good restaurant upstairs with a few prime view tables overlooking the stage.

Pizza Express 10 Dean St, W1. Oxford Street tube. Enjoy a good pizza, then listen to the resident band or highly skilled guest players – late night session on Saturdays.

Ronnie Scott's 47 Frith St, W1 ⓦwww .ronniescotts.co.uk. Leicester Square tube. The most famous jazz club in London: small and smoky and still going strong. Top-line names play two sets – one at around 10pm, the other after midnight. Book a table, or you'll have to stand.

Clubs

More than fifteen years after acid-house irreversibly shook up British clubs, London remains *the* place to come if you want to party after dark. The sheer diversity of dance music has enabled the city to maintain its status as **Europe's dance capital** – and it's still a port of call for DJs from around the globe. Nearly all of London's **dance clubs** open their doors between 10pm and midnight. Some are open six or seven nights a week, some keep irregular days, others just open at the weekend – and very often a venue will host a different club on each night of the week; for up-to-the-minute listings, pop into one of Soho's many record shops to pick up flyers or check *Time Out*.

Admission charges vary wildly, with small midweek sessions starting at around £3 and large weekend events charging as much as £15; around £10 is the average for a Friday or Saturday night, but bear in mind that profit margins at the bar are often more outrageous than at live music venues.

Clubs

333 333 Old St, EC1. Old Street tube. Three floors of drum'n'bass, twisted disco and breakbeat madness.

93 Feet East 150 Brick Lane, E2 Ⓦ www.93feeteast.co.uk. Old St tube. An old East End brewery with four rooms across two levels, as well as an excellent rooftop balcony and outdoor space that's well worth a visit in the summer.

Bagley's Studios King's Cross Goods Yard, off York Way, N1. King's Cross tube. Vast warehouse-style venue, making it the perfect place for enormous raves, with a different DJ in each of the three rooms, and a chill-out bar complete with sofas.

Bar Rumba 36 Shaftesbury Ave, W1 Ⓦ www.barrumba.co.uk. Piccadilly Circus tube. Fun, smallish West End venue with an adventurous mix of nights ranging from the future-jazz to top-notch house and R&B at weekends.

Café de Paris 3 Coventry St, W1. Leicester Square tube. Elegantly restored ballroom that plays house, garage and disco to a smartly dressed crowd of wannabes – no jeans or trainers.

Camden Palace 1 Camden High St, NW1 Ⓦ www.camdenpalace.com. Camden Town tube. Home to popular Saturday garage nights with great lights, great sounds and heaving crowds.

The Cross Goods Way Depot, off York Way, N1 Ⓦ www.the-cross.co.uk. King's Cross tube. House and garage club hidden underneath railway arches, that's bigger than you imagine, but always crammed with Balearic clubby types.

Cuba 11–13 Kensington High St, W8. High Street Kensington tube. Grab a cocktail upstairs in the sociable bar before heading below for club nights that focus around Latin, salsa and Brazilian bossanova.

Electric Ballroom 184 Camden High St, NW1 Ⓦ www.electricballroom.co.uk. Camden Town tube. This place attracts a truly mixed crowd of Camden regulars from punks to b-boys who come for the wide range of sounds: rock, hip-hop, jazz and house.

The End 18 West Central St, WC1 Ⓦ www.the-end.co.uk. Tottenham Court Road or Holborn tube. Designed for clubbers by clubbers, *The End* is large and spacious, with chrome minimalist decor and a devastating sound system.

Fabric 77a Charterhouse St, EC1 Ⓦ www.fabriclondon.com. Farringdon tube. If you're a serious dance music fan then there really isn't a better weekend venue in London than *Fabric*, a cavernous, underground brewery-like space with three rooms, holding 2500 people. Get there early to avoid a night of queuing.

Fridge Town Hall Parade, Brixton Hill, SW2 Ⓦ www.fridge.co.uk. Brixton tube. Weekends alternate between pumping mixed/gay nights, and nights with a psychedelic, trancey vibe.

Gardening Club 4 The Piazza, WC2 Ⓦ www.rockgarden.co.uk. Covent Garden tube. A popular choice for house and garage, but be warned – you could well find yourself sharing the dance floor with beer-boys and bemused tourists.

Gossips 69 Dean St, W1 Ⓦ www.gossips.co.uk. Tottenham Court Road tube. Cave-like basement club that seems to have been around for aeons. Located deep in the heart of Soho, it's a popular stop for swing and hip-hop fans.

Herbal 12–14 Kingsland Rd, E2 Ⓦ www.herbaluk.com. Old Street tube. An intimate two-floored venue that's often home to big-name DJs for the entrance price of a packet of cigarettes.

HQs West Yard, Camden Lock, NW1. Camden Town tube. Smallish venue by the canal with a range of nights, though the emphasis is on hip-hop and jazz-fusion. Friendly vibe, good cocktails and free entry if you arrive early on weekdays.

ICA The Mall, SW1 ⓦ www.ica.org.uk. Piccadilly Circus or Charing Cross tube. Weekends at the ICA play host to some of the most cutting-edge audio-visual collaborations in town.

Ministry of Sound 103 Gaunt St, SE1 ⓦ www.ministryofsound.co.uk. Elephant & Castle tube. A vast, state-of-the-art club based on New York's legendary *Paradise Garage*, with an exceptional sound system. Corporate clubbing and full of tourists, but it still draws the top talent.

Notting Hill Arts Club 21 Notting Hill Gate, W11. Notting Hill Gate tube. Basement club that's popular for everything from Latin-inspired funk, jazz and disco through to soul, house and garage, and famed for Ben Watt's Sunday night deep house session, Lazy Dog.

Office 3–5 Rathbone Place W1. Tottenham Court Road tube. Various music styles, often focusing on swing and hip-hop, but best known as home to a midweek session where you can play silly board games like Ker-Plunk. Booking a table in advance is advised.

Salsa! 96 Charing Cross Rd, WC2. Leicester Square tube. Funky and fun salsa-based club-cum-restaurant that's a popular choice for group birthday bookings; you can book a table to eat as you mambo.

Scala 278 Pentonville Rd, N1 ⓦ www .scala-london.co.uk. King's Cross tube. One of London's best clubs, holding unusual and multi-faceted nights that take in film, live bands and music ranging from quirky hip-hop to drum'n'bass and deep house.

Subterania 12 Acklam Rd, W10 ⓦ www .meanfiddler.com. Ladbroke Grove tube. Worth a visit for its diverse club nights at weekends, including the superior hip-hop and R&B-heavy Rotation every Friday.

Turnmills 63 Clerkenwell Rd, EC1 ⓦ www .turnmills.com. Farringdon tube. The place to come if you want to sweat to trance and house from dusk till dawn, with an alien-invasion-style bar and funky split-level dance floor in the main room.

Gay and lesbian London

London's **lesbian and gay scene** is so huge, diverse and well established that it's easy to forget just how much – and how fast – it has grown over the last few years. **Soho** is the obvious place to start exploring, with a mix of traditional gay pubs, designer café-bars and a range of gay-run services. Details of most events appear in *Time Out*, while another excellent source of information is the London **Lesbian and Gay Switchboard** (☎020/7837 7324, ⓦ www.llgs.org.uk), which operates around the clock. The **outdoor event** of the year is **Mardi Gras** (ⓦ www.londonmardigras.com) in July, a colourful, whistleblowing march through the city streets followed by a huge, ticketed party in a central London park.

Bars and clubs

There are loads of lesbian and gay **cafés, bars and pubs** in London, many of which have been around for years while some pop up and disappear within months, such is the fickle nature of the scene. Our list is by no means exhaustive as every corner of London has its own gay local. Many cafés and bars transform themselves into **drinking dens** at night and, as some open beyond licensing hours, they can be a cheap alternative to some **clubs**, which open up and shut down with surreal frequency – it's a good idea to check the gay press and listings mags before you set out. Bear in mind that although more and more lesbian bars admit gay men, mixed, as ever, tends to mean mostly men.

Mixed bars

Bar Aquda 13–14 Maiden Lane, WC2. Leicester Square or Covent Garden tube. Bright, modern and fashionable café-bar with good food. Mixed, but mostly boys.

The Black Cap 171 Camden High St, NW1. Camden Town tube. Venerable North London institution offering cabaret of wildly varying quality almost every night. Laugh, sing and lip-synch along, and then dance to 80s tunes until the early hours.

The Box 32–34 Monmouth St, WC2. Covent Garden or Leicester Square tube. Popular, bright café/bar serving good food for a mixed gay/straight crowd during the day, and becoming queerer as the night draws in.

The Edge 11 Soho Square, W1. Tottenham Court Road tube. Busy, style-conscious and pricey Soho café/bar spread over several floors, and (in summer) onto the pavement. Food daily, good art exhibitions and DJs most nights.

First Out 52 St Giles High St, WC2. Tottenham Court Road tube. The West End's original gay café/bar, and still permanently packed, serving good veggie food at reasonable prices. *Girl Friday* is a busy pre-club Friday session for grrrls; gay men are welcome as guests.

Freedom 60–66 Wardour St, W1. Piccadilly Circus tube. Hip, busy, late-opening café/bar, popular with a mixed straight/gay crowd. Great juices and healthy food in the daytime, cocktails and over-priced beer in the evening.

Old Compton Café 34 Old Compton St, W1. Tottenham Court Road or Leicester Square tube. This enduringly busy Soho institution never closes. Strong coffee and a cosmopolitan range of cakes and snacks make it the obvious solution to sudden mid- or post-party wooziness.

Ted's Place 305a North End Rd, W14. West Kensington or West Brompton tube. Friendly, late-opening local with a gay/lesbian/bi and TV/TS clientele, long-running lesbian Blind Date contest and assorted outbreaks of frivolity.

The Yard 57 Rupert St, W1. Piccadilly Circus tube. Attractive café/bar with courtyard and loft areas. Good food, weekly cabaret and regular fortune tellers.

Lesbian bars

Candy Bar 4 Carlisle St, WC2. Tottenham Court Road tube. Now re-established at its original venue but still with the same crucial, cruisey vibe that made it the hottest girl bar in central London.

The Glass Bar West Lodge, Euston Square Gardens, 190 Euston Rd, NW1. Euston tube. Difficult to find (and hard to forget), you knock on the door and become a member to enter this friendly and intimate late-opening women-only bar. Closed Sun.

Vespa Lounge The Conservatory, Centrepoint House, 15 St Giles High St, WC1. Tottenham Court Road tube. This centrally located girls' bar gets super-busy at weekends. Pool table, video screen, cute bar staff and a predominantly young crowd. Gay men welcome as guests.

Gay men's bars

79CXR 79 Charing Cross Rd, WC2. Leicester Square tube. Busy, cruisey men's den on two floors, with industrial decor, late licence and a no-messing atmosphere.

Site 41–43 St Martin's Lane, WC2. Leicester Square tube. Formerly *Brief Encounter*, this is one of the oldest men's bars in London and still hard at it. A popular pre-*Heaven* or post-opera hangout; the front bar is bright, the back bar dark, both are busy.

Central Station 37 Wharfdale Rd, N1. King's Cross tube. Award-winning, late-opening community pub on three floors, offering cabaret, cruisey club nights, and the UK's only gay sports bar. Not strictly men-only, but mostly so.

Compton's of Soho 53 Old Compton St, W1. Leicester Square or Piccadilly tube. This large, traditional-style pub is a Soho institution, always busy with a youngish crowd, but still a relaxed place to cruise or just hang out.

Clubs

Crash 66 Goding St, SE11. Vauxhall tube. Four bars, two dance floors, chill-out areas and hard bodies make this weekly Saturday club night busy, buzzy, sexy and mostly boyzy.

DTPM *Fabric*, 77a Charterhouse St, EC1 ⓦwww.dtpm-online.net. Farringdon Road tube. This long-running Sunday-nighter can now be found in *Fabric*'s chic surroundings, with three dance floors offering soul, jazz, funk, R&B, hip-hop, Latino house and progressive to hard house.

Duckie *The Royal Vauxhall Tavern*, 372 Kennington Lane, SE11 ⓦwww.duckie.co.uk. Vauxhall tube. Modern, rock-based hurdy-gurdy provides a creative and cheerfully ridiculous anti-dote to the dreary forces of gay house domination.

Exilio Latino 229 Great Portland St, W1. Great Portland Street tube. Every Saturday night, *Exilio* erupts in a lesbian & gay Latin frenzy, spinning salsa, cumbias and merengue, and also featuring live acts.

G.A.Y. *The Astoria*, 157 Charing Cross Rd, WC2. Tottenham Court Road tube. Widely considered as the launch venue for new (and ailing) boy and girl bands, this huge, unpretentious and fun-loving dance night is where the young crowd gathers.

Heaven under The Arches Villiers St, WC2. Charing Cross or Embankment tube. Widely regarded as the UK's most popular gay club, this legendary, 2000-capacity venue continues to reign supreme. More Muscle Mary than Diesel Doris.

Popstarz *Scala*, 27 Pentonville Rd, N1. King's Cross tube. A groundbreaking Friday night indie club, *Popstarz* has had to enforce a gay and lesbian majority door policy as its winning formula of alternative toons, 70s and 80s trash, cheap beer and no attitude attracts a growing straight, studenty crowd.

Queer Nation *Substation South*, 9 Brighton Terrace, SW9. Brixton tube. Long-running and popular New York-style house and garage weekly Saturday night club for funksters.

Trade *Turnmills*, 63b Clerkenwell Rd, EC1, @www.turnmills.com. Farringdon tube. Legendary techno and hard house Saturday all-nighter (4am to Sunday lunchtime) that features some of the best DJs in the country, plus lots of lasers and special effects.

Theatre

The **West End** is the heart of London's "Theatreland", with Shaftesbury Avenue its most congested drag, but the term is more of a conceptual pigeon-hole than a geographical term. West End theatres tend to be dominated by tourist-magnet musicals (more often than not by Andrew Lloyd Webber) or similarly unchallenging shows, but others offer more intriguing productions. The government-subsidized **Royal Shakespeare Company** and the **National Theatre** often put on extremely original productions of mainstream masterpieces. while some of the most exciting work is performed in what have become known as the **Off-West End** theatres, which consistently stage interesting and often challenging productions. Further down the financial ladder still are the **Fringe** theatres, more often than not pub venues, where ticket prices are low, and quality variable.

Tickets under £10 are restricted to the Fringe; the box-office average is closer to £15–25, with £30–40 the usual top whack. Ticket agencies such as Ticketmaster (℡020/7344 4444, @www.ticketmaster.co.uk) or First Call (℡020/7497 9977, @www.firstcalltickets.com) can get seats for most West End shows, but add up to ten percent on the ticket price. The cheapest way to buy your ticket is to go to the theatre box office in person; if you book over the phone, you're likely to be charged a booking fee. Students, senior citizens and the unemployed can get **concessionary rates** on tickets for many shows, and several theatres offer reductions on standby tickets to these groups. Whatever you do, avoid the touts and the dodgy-looking ticket agencies that abound in the West End – there's no guarantee that the tickets are genuine.

The Society of London Theatre (@www.officiallondontheatre.co.uk) runs the **tkts ticket booth** in Leicester Square (Mon–Sat 10am–7pm, Sun noon–3pm), which sells on-the-day tickets for all the West End shows at discounts of up to fifty percent, though they tend to be in the top end of the price range, are limited to four per person, and carry a service charge of £2.50 per ticket.

Venues

What follows is a list of those West End theatres that offer a changing roster of good plays, along with the most consistent of the Off-West End and Fringe venues. This by no means represents the full tally of London's stages, as there are scores of fringe places that present work on an intermittent basis – the weekly listings mag *Time Out* provides the most comprehensive and detailed up-to-the-minute survey.

Almeida Almeida St, N1 ℡020/7359 4404, @www.almeida.co.uk. Angel or Highbury & Islington tube. A deservedly popular Off-West End venue in Islington, which premieres excellent new plays and excitingly reworked classics, attracting some big Hollywood names in the process.

Barbican Centre Silk St, EC2 ℡020/7638 8891, @www.barbican.org.uk. Barbican or Moorgate tube. The Barbican's two venues – the excellently designed Barbican Theatre and the much smaller Pit – put on a wide variety of theatrical spectacles from puppetry and musicals to new drama works, and, of course, Shakespeare, courtesy of the Royal Shakespeare Company who perform here (and elsewhere in London) on and off from autumn to spring each year.

Battersea Arts Centre 176 Lavender Hill, SW11 ℡020/7223 2223, ⊛www.bac.org.uk. Clapham Junction train station from Victoria or Waterloo. The BAC is a triple-stage building, housed in an old town hall in south London, and has acquired a reputation for excellent fringe productions, from straight theatre to comedy and cabaret.

Bush Shepherd's Bush Green, W12 ℡020/7610 4224. Goldhawk Road or Shepherd's Bush tube. This minuscule above-pub theatre is London's most reliable venue for new writing after the Royal Court, and it has turned out some real crackers.

Donmar Warehouse Thomas Neal's, Earlham St, WC2 ℡020/7369 1732, ⊛www .donmarwarehouse.com. Covent Garden tube. A performance space that's noted for new plays and top-quality reappraisals of the classics, and whose former artistic director, Sam Mendes, managed to entice several Hollywood stars to take to the stage.

Drill Hall 16 Chenies St, WC1 ℡020/7307 5060, ⊛www.drillhall.co.uk. Goodge Street tube. This studio-style venue specializes in gay, lesbian, feminist and all-round politically correct new work. Monday evenings are women only; Thursdays are no smoking.

National Theatre South Bank Centre, South Bank, SE1 ℡020/7452 3000, ⊛www.nationaltheatre.org.uk. Waterloo tube. National Theatre, as it's now officially known, consists of three separate theatres: the 1100-seater Olivier, the proscenium-arched Lyttelton and the experimental Cottesloe. Standards set by the late Laurence Olivier, founding artistic director, are maintained by the country's top actors and directors in a programme ranging from Greek tragedies to Broadway musicals. Some productions sell out months in advance, but 20–30 of the cheapest tickets go on sale on the morning of each performance – get there by 8am for the popular shows.

The Royal Hampstead Theatre Eton Avenue, NW3 ℡020/7722 9301, ⊛www .hampstead-theatre.co.uk. Swiss Cottage tube. A spanking new zinc and glass-fronted theatre in Swiss Cottage (not in Hampstead proper) whose productions often move on to the West End. Such

is its prestige that the likes of John Malkovich have been seduced into performing here.

ICA Nash House, The Mall, SW1 ℡020/7930 3647, ⊛www.ica.org.uk. Piccadilly Circus or Charing Cross tube. The Institute of Contemporary Arts attracts the most innovative practitioners in all areas of performance. It also attracts a fair quantity of modish junk, but the hits generally outweigh the misses.

Open Air Theatre Regent's Park, Inner Circle, NW1 ℡020/7486 2431, ⊛www.openairtheatre.org. Baker Street tube. If the weather's good, there's nothing quite like a dose of alfresco drama. This beautiful space in Regent's Park hosts a tourist-friendly summer programme of Shakespeare, musicals, plays and concerts.

Royal Court Sloane Square, SW1 ℡020/7565 5000, ⊛www.royalcourttheatre.com. Sloane Square tube. The refurbished Royal Court is one of the best places in London to catch radical new writing, either in the proscenium arch Theatre Downstairs, or the smaller-scale Theatre Upstairs studio space.

Shakespeare's Globe New Globe Walk, SE1 ℡020/7902 1400, ⊛www .shakespeares-globe.org. London Bridge, Blackfriars or Southwark tube. This thatch-roofed replica Elizabethan theatre uses only natural light and the minimum of scenery, and currently puts on Shakespearean shows and other period pieces from mid-May to mid-September, with "groundling" tickets (standing only) for around £5.

Tricycle Theatre & Cinema 269 Kilburn High Rd, NW6 ℡020/7328 1000, ⊛www.tricycle.co.uk. Kilburn tube. One of London's most dynamic fringe venues, showcasing a mixed bag of new plays, with an emphasis on black and Irish issues, and international productions of the core repertoire.

Young Vic The Cut, SE1 ℡020/7928 6363, ⊛www.youngvic.org. Waterloo tube. A large "in-the-round" space, perfect for Shakespeare, which is something of a speciality, as well as a studio for variable Fringe productions. Big names have appeared at the main stage over the years – Vanessa Redgrave's version of Ibsen's *Ghosts* is near-legendary.

Comedy and cabaret

London's **comedy scene** continues to live up to its status as the new rock-'n'roll with the leading comedians catapulted to unlikely stardom on both stage and screen. The Comedy Store is the best-known and most central venue on the circuit, but just about every London suburb has a venue giving a platform to young hopefuls (full listings appear on ⊛www.chortle.co.uk, and in the weekly *Time Out*). Note that many venues operate only on Friday and Saturday nights, and that August is a lean month, as much of London's talent heads north for the Edinburgh Festival. **Tickets** at smaller venues can be had for around £5, but in the more established places, you're looking at £10 or more.

Venues

Backyard Comedy Club 231 Cambridge Heath Rd, E2 ☏ 020/7739 3122, ⓦ www.leehurst.com. Bethnal Green tube. Purpose-built club in Bethnal Green established by comedian Lee Hurst, who has successfully managed to attract a consistently strong line-up. Fri & Sat.

Banana Cabaret *The Bedford*, 77 Bedford Hill, SW12 ☏ 020/8673 8904, ⓦ www.bananacabaret.co.uk. Balham tube. This double-stage pub has become one of London's most welcoming comedy venues – well worth the trip out from the centre of town. Fri & Sat from 9pm, followed by a DJ.

Canal Café Theatre *The Bridge House*, Delamere Terrace, W2 ☏ 020/7289 6054, ⓦ www.chortle.co.uk/venues/canal.html. Warwick Avenue tube. Perched on the water's edge in Little Venice, this venue is good for improvisation acts and is home to the Newsrevue team of topical gagsters; there's usually something going on from Thursday to Sunday.

Comedy Café 66 Rivington St, EC2 ☏ 020/7739 5706, ⓦ www.comedycafe.co.uk. Old Street tube. Long-established, purpose-built club in Shoreditch/Hoxton, often with impressive line-ups,

and free admission for the new-acts slot on Wednesday nights. Wed–Sat.

Comedy Store Haymarket House, 1a Oxendon St, SW1 ☏ 020/7344 0234, ⓦ www.thecomedystore.co.uk. Piccadilly Circus tube. Widely regarded as the birthplace of alternative comedy, though no longer in its original venue, the Comedy Store has catapulted many a stand-up onto primetime TV. Improvisation by in-house comics on Wednesdays and Sundays, in addition to a stand-up bill; Friday and Saturday are the busiest nights, with two shows, at 8pm and midnight – book ahead.

Jongleurs Camden Lock, Dingwalls Building, 36 Camden Lock Place, Chalk Farm Road, NW1; box office ☏ 020/7564 2500, information ☏ 08707/870707, ⓦ www.jongleurs.com. Camden tube. Jongleurs is the chain store of comedy, doling out high quality stand-up and post-revelry disco-dancing nightly on Fridays. Book well in advance.

Meccano Club Dove Regent, 65 Graham St, N1 ☏ 020/7813 4478, ⓦ www.themeccanoclub.co.uk. Angel tube. Popular, intimate, pub-based Islington venue that features consistently strong line-ups. Fri & Sat.

Cinema

There are an awful lot of **cinemas** in the West End, but very few places committed to independent films, and even fewer repertory cinemas programming serious movies from the back catalogue. November's **London Film Festival** (ⓦ www.lff.org.uk), which occupies half a dozen West End cinemas, is now a huge event, and so popular that many of the films sell out soon after publication of the festival's programme. Below is a selection of the cinemas that put on the most interesting programmes.

Cinemas

Ciné Lumière 17 Queensberry Place, SW7 ☏ 020/7073 1350, ⓦ www.institut-francais.org.uk. South Kensington tube. Predominantly, but by no means exclusively, French films, both old and new (sometimes with subtitles), put on by the Institut Français.

Electric 191 Portobello Rd, W11 ☏ 20/7299 8688, ⓦ www.the-electric.co.uk. Notting Hill Gate or Ladbroke Grove tube. One of the oldest cinemas in the country (opened 1910), the Electric has been restored and refurbished as the most luxurious cinema in London with leather armchairs and sofas, and a bar.

ICA Cinema Nash House, The Mall, SW1 ☏ 020/7930 3647, ⓦ www.ica.org.uk. Piccadilly Circus or Charing Cross tube. Vintage and underground movies shown on one of two tiny screens in the avant-garde HQ of the Institute of Contemporary Arts.

BFI London Imax South Bank Centre, SE1 ☏ 020/7902 1234, ⓦ www.bfi.org.uk/imax. Waterloo tube. The British Film Institute's remarkable glazed drum has the largest screen in Europe. It's stunning, state-of-the-art stuff all right, showing 2D and 3D films on a massive screen, but like all IMAX cinemas, it suffers from the paucity of good material that's been shot in the format.

National Film Theatre South Bank, SE1
☎020/7928 3232, ⓦwww.bfi.org.uk/nft. Waterloo tube. Known for its attentive audiences and an exhaustive, eclectic programme that includes directors' seasons and thematic series. Around six films daily are shown in the vast NFT1 and the smaller NFT2.
Prince Charles 2–7 Leicester Place, WC2

☎020/7494 3654, ⓦwww .princecharlescinema.com. Leicester Square or Piccadilly Circus tube. The bargain basement of London's cinemas (entry for most shows is just £3.50), with a programme of new movies, classics and cult favourites – the *Sing-Along-A-Sound-of-Music* (as well as other participatory romps) is a regular.

Classical music, opera and dance

London is spoilt for choice when it comes to **orchestras**. On most days you'll be able to catch a concert by either the London Symphony Orchestra, the London Philharmonic, the Royal Philharmonic, the Philharmonia or the BBC Symphony Orchestra, or a smaller-scale performance from the English Chamber Orchestra, London Sinfonietta or the Academy of St Martin-in-the-Fields. During the week, there are also **free lunchtime concerts** by students or professionals in many of London's churches, particularly in the City; performances in the Royal College of Music and Royal Academy of Music are of an amazingly high standard, and the choice of work a lot riskier than the commercial venues can manage.

The principal **large-scale venue** is the South Bank Centre (☎020/7960 4242, ⓦwww.sbc.org.uk), where the biggest names appear at the Royal Festival Hall, with more specialized programmes staged in the Queen Elizabeth Hall and Purcell Room. With the outstanding London Symphony Orchestra as its resident orchestra, and with top foreign orchestras and big-name soloists in regular attendance, the Barbican (☎020/7638 8891, ⓦwww.barbican .org.uk) is one of the capital's best arenas for classical music. Programming is much more adventurous than it was, and free music in the foyer is often very good. For **chamber music**, the intimate and elegant Wigmore Hall, 36 Wigmore St, W1 (☎020/7935 2141, ⓦwww.wigmore-hall.org.uk), is many a Londoner's favourite.

From July to September each year, **the Proms** at the Royal Albert Hall (☎020/7589 8212, ⓦwww.bbc.co.uk/proms) feature at least one concert daily, with hundreds of standing tickets sold for just £3 on the night. The acoustics aren't the world's best, but the calibre of the performers is unbeatable and the programme is a fascinating mix of standards and new or obscure works. The hall is so vast that if you turn up half an hour before the show starts there should be little risk of being turned away.

Despite its elitist image, **opera** in the capital continues to attract new audiences. Of the two main companies, the **Royal Opera House** (☎020/7304 4000, ⓦwww.royaloperahouse.org), is undergoing a new lease of life since its refurbishment and the appointment of a new music director. Meanwhile **English National Opera** on St Martin's Lane (☎020/7632 8300, ⓦwww.eno.org), has started renovating its theatre, the vast London Coliseum, while continuing to show what can be achieved with young, home-grown talent and lively, radical productions.

From the time-honoured showpieces of the **Royal Ballet** (☎020/7304 4000, ⓦwww.royaloperahouse.org) to the diverse and exciting range of British and international dance that goes on at the newly rebuilt Sadler's Wells (☎020/7863 8000, ⓦwww.sadlers-wells.com), and at the much smaller venue, The Place (☎020/7387 0031, ⓦwww.theplace.org.uk), there's always a **dance performance** of some kind afoot in London, and the city also has a good reputation for international dance festivals showcasing the work of a spread of ensembles. The biggest of the annual events is the **Dance Umbrella** (T020/8741 5881, W www.danceumbrella.co.uk), a six-week season (Sept–Nov) of new work from bright young choreographers and performance artists at venues across the city.

Shopping

Whether it's time or money you've got to burn, London is one big shoppers' playground, and although chains and superstores predominate along the high streets, you're still never too far from the kind of oddball, one-off establishment that makes shopping an adventure rather than a chore. From the *folie de grandeur* that is Harrods to the frantic street markets of the East End, there's nothing you can't find in some corner of the capital.

In the centre of town, **Oxford Street** is the city's most frantic chain store mecca, and together with **Regent Street**, which crosses it halfway, offers pretty much every mainstream clothing label you could wish for. Just off Oxford Street, high-end designer outlets line **St Christopher's Place** and **South Molton Street**, and you'll find even pricier designers and jewellers along the very chic **Bond Street**.

Tottenham Court Road, which heads north from the east end of Oxford Street, is the place to go for electrical goods and furniture and design shops. **Charing Cross Road**, heading south, is the centre of London's book trade, both new and secondhand. At its north end, and particularly on **Denmark Street**, you can find music shops selling everything from instruments to sound equipment and sheet music. **Soho** offers an offbeat mix of sex boutiques, records and silks, while the streets surrounding **Covent Garden** yield art and design shops, mainstream fashion stores, designer wear and outdoor pursuits gear.

Just off Piccadilly, **St James's** is the natural habitat of the quintessential English gentleman, with **Jermyn Street** in particular harbouring shops dedicated to his grooming. **Knightsbridge**, further west, is home to Harrods and Harvey Nichols, and the big-name fashion stores of **Sloane Street** and **Brompton Road**.

Books

The biggest bookstore in the capital is Waterstones' Piccadilly branch (Piccadilly Circus tube), but the largest choice of bookshops is still on **Charing Cross Road**, where you'll not only find all the **chain stores** – Borders at no. 120, and Blackwell's at no. 100 – but also Foyles at nos. 113–119, and other smaller **independent shops** such as Islamic bookshop Al-hoda at nos. 76–78, art specialists Zwemmer at no. 80, crime specialists Murder One at nos. 71–73 and numerous **secondhand stores**, including Any Amount of Books at no. 62.

Department stores

Fortnum & Mason, 181 Piccadilly (Green Park or Piccadilly Circus tube), is the place to go for fabulous, gorgeously presented and pricey food, plus upmarket clothes, furniture and stationery. **Harrods**, Knightsbridge (Knightsbridge tube), is famous for its fantastic Art Nouveau tiled food hall, obscenely huge toy department and supremely tasteless memorial to Diana and Dodi; beware the draconian dress code (see p.140). Nearby, **Harvey Nichols**, 109–125 Knightsbridge, offers all the latest designer collections and famously frivolous and pricey luxury foods. Over at Oxford Circus, several major stores are close at hand, among them: **John Lewis**, 278–306 Oxford St (Oxford Circus tube), which offers everything from buttons to stockings to furniture and household goods; **Liberty**, 210–220 Regent St (Oxford Circus tube), founded as a retail outlet for the Victorian Arts and Crafts Movement, and still the place to go for regal fabrics and decorative household goods; and **Selfridge's**, 400 Oxford St (Bond Street tube), London's first great department store, which has a wide range of clothing, food and furnishings.

Markets

Camden, running from Camden High Street to Chalk Farm Road (daily; Camden Town tube), is top of the list for market shopping on most tourist itineraries; the atmosphere is a studenty mix of clubby and grungey and the stuff on sale is mainly cheap clothes and jewellery, though the stalls around Camden Lock are generally more interesting; weekends are the best – and busiest – times to visit. **Spitalfields**, Commercial Street (Sun; Liverpool Street tube), is an arty-crafty market similar to Camden, but on a much smaller scale, which also offers organic fruit and veg. Nearby, **Brick Lane** (Sun; Aldgate East, Shoreditch or Liverpool Street tube) has everything from sofas and antiques to cheap junk; and **Petticoat Lane**, Middlesex Street and Goulston Street (Sun; Aldgate East or Liverpool Street tube), offers cheap and cheerful clothes. **Bermondsey** (New Caledonian) Market, Bermondsey Square (Fri; Borough, London Bridge or Bermondsey tube), is a huge, unglamorous but highly regarded antique market that kicks off at 5am; while **Portobello**, Portobello Rd (Fri–Sun; Notting Hill or Ladbroke Grove tube), is mostly boho-chic clothes and (Sat only) portable antiques. South of the river, **Greenwich**, Market Square (Sat & Sun; Cutty Sark DLR or Greenwich train station), is another small arty-crafty market, with secondhand clothing and antiques on sale, too.

Music

The **megastores** are: HMV, 150 Oxford St (Oxford Circus tube); Tower Records, 1 Piccadilly Circus (Piccadilly Circus tube); Virgin Megastore, 14–16 Oxford St (Tottenham Court Road tube). For **jazz**, try Ray's on the first floor of Foyles, 113–119 Charing Cross Rd (Tottenham Court Road tube). For **indie music**, there's Sister Ray, 94 Berwick St (Oxford Circus or Piccadilly Circus tube). For **reggae**, **ragga** and **drum'n'bass**, head to Daddy Kool, 12 Berwick St (Oxford Circus or Tottenham Court Road tube). **Hip-hop** is available at Mr Bongo 44 Poland St (Oxford Circus tube). For **house**, **techno** and **trance** go to Eukatech, 49 Endell St (Covent Garden tube).

Listings

Airport enquiries Gatwick ☎08700/002468, ⓦwww.baa.co.uk; Heathrow ☎08700/000123, ⓦwww.baa.co.uk; London City Airport ☎020/7646 0000, ⓦwww.londoncityairport.com; Luton ☎01582/405100, ⓦwww .london-luton.com; Stansted ☎08700/000303, ⓦwww.baa.co.uk.

American Express 30–31 Haymarket, SW1 ☎020/7484 9600 (and other branches); ⓦwww.americanexpress.com. Mon–Sat 9am–6pm, Sun 10am–5pm. Piccadilly Circus tube.

Bike rental On Your Bike, 52–54 Tooley St, SE1 ☎020/7378 6669, ⓦwww.onyourbike.net.

Mon–Fri 8am–7pm, Sat 9.30am–5.30pm. London Bridge tube.

Car rental For the most competitive rates, ring round a few local firms from the *Yellow Pages* (ⓦwww.yell.com) before you try your luck with the usual suspects. Europcar, 12 Semley Place, SW1 (ⓣ020/7259 1600, ⓦwww.europcar.co.uk; Victoria tube) and at Heathrow, Gatwick, Stansted and City airports; Hertz, 156 Southampton Row, WC1 (ⓣ020/7278 1588, ⓦwww.hertz.co.uk; Russell Square tube) and at Heathrow, Gatwick and City airports; Easycar, Euston Station car park, Level 5, NW1 (ⓣ09063/333333, ⓦwww.easycar.com).

Cricket Two Test matches are played in London each summer: one at Lord's (ⓣ020/7432 1000, ⓦwww.lords.org), the home of English cricket, in St John's Wood; the other at The Oval (ⓣ020/7582 6660, ⓦwww.surreycricket.com), in Kennington. In tandem with the full-blown five-day Tests, there's also a series of one-day internationals, two of which are usually held in London.

Consulates and Embassies Australia, Australia House, Strand, WC2 ⓣ020/7379 4334, ⓦwww.australia.org.uk; Canada, Canada House, Trafalgar Square, WC2 ⓣ020/7528 6533 ⓦwww.canada.org.uk; Ireland, 17 Grosvenor Place, SW1 ⓣ020/7235 2171; New Zealand, New Zealand House, 80 Haymarket, SW1 ⓣ020/7930 8422, ⓦwww.nzembassy.com; South Africa, South Africa House, Trafalgar Square, WC2 ⓣ020/7451 7299, ⓦwww.southafricahouse.com; USA, 24 Grosvenor Square, W1 ⓣ020/7499 9000, ⓦwww.usembassy.org.uk.

Dentist Emergency treatment: Guy's Hospital, St Thomas St, SE1 ⓣ020/7955 4317 (Mon–Fri 9am–3pm).

Football London's top club at the moment is Arsenal (ⓣ020/7704 4000, ⓦwww.arsenal.com); their closest rivals (geographically) are Tottenham Hotspur (ⓣ08700/112222, ⓦwww.spurs.co.uk). Meanwhile, in west London, Chelsea (ⓣ020/7915 2951, ⓦwww.chelseafc.co.uk) have recently had millions pumped into them by a Russian billionaire. Tickets for most Premiership games start at £20–25 and are virtually impossible to get hold of on a casual basis: you need to book in advance, or try and see one of the European or knock-out cup fixtures.

Hospitals For 24hr accident and emergency: St Mary's Hospital, Praed St, W2 ⓣ020/7886 6666; University College Hospital, Grafton Way, WC1 ⓣ020/7387 9300.

Internet cafés easyInternetcafe (ⓦwww.easy.everything.com) has 24hr branches at 456 Strand, off Trafalgar Square (Charing Cross

tube), 9–16 Tottenham Court Rd (Tottenham Court Road tube) and 9–13 Wilton Rd (Victoria tube).

Left luggage AIRPORTS Gatwick: North Terminal (daily 6am–10pm); South Terminal (24hr). Heathrow: Terminal 1 (daily 6am–11pm); Terminal 2 (daily 5.30am–11pm); Terminal 3 (daily 5am–11pm); Terminal 4 (daily 5.30am–11pm). London City Airport (daily 5.30am–9.30pm). Stansted Airport (24hr).TRAIN STATIONS Charing Cross (daily 7am–11pm); Euston (Mon–Sat 6.45am–11.15pm, Sun 7.15am–11pm); Victoria (daily 7am–10.15pm); Waterloo International (daily 7am–10pm).

Lost property AIRPORTS Gatwick ⓣ01293/503162 (Mon–Sat 8am–7pm, Sun 8am–4pm); Heathrow ⓣ020/8745 7727 (daily 8am–4pm); London City Airport ⓣ020/7646 0000 (Mon–Fri 5.30am–10pm, Sat 5.30am–1am, Sun 10am–10pm); Stansted ⓣ01279/680500 (daily 6am–midnight).
BUSES ⓣ020/7222 1234 (24hr).
HEATHROW EXPRESS ⓣ020/8745 7727, ⓦwww.heathrowexpress.co.uk (daily 8am–4pm).
TAXIS (black cabs only) ⓣ07918/2000 (Mon–Fri 9am–4pm).
TRAIN STATIONS Euston ⓣ020/7387 8699 (Mon–Fri 9am–5.30pm); King's Cross ⓣ020/7278 3310 (Mon–Fri 9am–5.30pm); Liverpool Street ⓣ020/7247 4297 (Mon–Fri 9am–5.30pm); Paddington ⓣ020/7313 1514 (Mon–Fri 9am–5.30pm); Victoria ⓣ020/7922 9887 (daily 7am–midnight); Waterloo ⓣ020/7401 7861 (Mon–Fri 7.30am–8pm).
TUBE TRAINS Transport for London ⓣ020/7486 2496, ⓦwww.tfl.gov.uk.

Police Central police stations include: Charing Cross, Agar St, WC2 ⓣ020/7240 1212; Holborn, 70 Theobalds Rd, WC1 ⓣ020/7404 1212; King's Cross, 76 King's Cross Rd, WC1 ⓣ020/7704 1212; West End Central, 10 Vine St, W1 ⓣ020/7437 1212; City of London Police, Bishopsgate, EC2 ⓣ020/7601 2222.

Post offices The only (vaguely) late-opening post office is the Trafalgar Square branch at 24–28 William IV St, WC2 4DL ⓣ020/7484 9304 (Mon–Fri 8.30am–6.30pm, Sat 9am–5.30pm); it's also the city's poste restante collection point. For general postal enquiries phone ⓣ08457/740740 (Mon–Fri 8am–7.30pm, Sat 8am–6pm), or visit the website ⓦwww.royalmail.co.uk.

Tennis Tennis in England is synonymous with Wimbledon (ⓣ020/8946 2244, ⓦwww .wimbledon.com), the only Grand Slam tournament in the world to be played on grass, and for many players the ultimate goal of their careers. To buy tickets on the day, you must arrive by around 7am for tickets on Centre and No. 1 courts, or by around 9am for the outside courts (and avoid the middle Saturday of the tournament).

Train stations and information As a rough guide, Euston handles services to northwest England and Glasgow; King's Cross northeast England and Edinburgh; Liverpool Street eastern England; Paddington western England; Victoria and Waterloo southeast England. For information, contact national rail enquiries ☏ 08457/484950, ⓦ www.nationalrail.co.uk.

Travel agents STA Travel, 33 Bedford St, WC1 ☏ 020/7240 9821, ⓦ www.statravel.co.uk; Trailfinders, Lower Ground Floor, Waterstone's, 203–205 Piccadilly, W1 ☏ 020/7292 1888, ⓦ www.trailfinders.co.uk.

Travel details

Buses

For information on all local and national bus services, contact Traveline ☏ 08706/082608 (daily 7am–9pm), ⓦ www.traveline.org.uk.

London Victoria Coach Station to: Bath (every 1–2hr; 3hr 15min); Bristol (hourly; 2hr 30min); Birmingham (hourly; 2hr 40min); Brighton (every 30min; 2hr); Cambridge (every 30min; 2hr); Canterbury (hourly; 1hr 50min); Dover (hourly; 2hr 25min); Exeter (every 1–2hr; 4hr 10min); Gloucester (hourly; 3hr 15min); Liverpool (5 daily; 4hr 30min–5hr); Manchester (8 daily; 4hr 30min–5hr); Newcastle (4 daily; 6hr 30min–7hr); Oxford (every 20min; 1hr 40min); Plymouth (8 daily; 4hr 50min–5hr 15min); Stratford (3 daily; 3hr).

Trains

For information on all local and national rail services, contact National Rail Enquiries ☏ 08457/484950, ⓦ www.nationalrail.co.uk.

London Charing Cross to: Canterbury (hourly; 1hr 25min); Dover Priory (every 30min; 1hr 45min).

London Euston to: Birmingham New St (every 30min; 1hr 45min); Carlisle (every 2hr; 4hr); Lancaster (hourly; 3hr–3hr 20min); Liverpool Lime St (hourly; 3hr); Manchester Piccadilly (hourly; 2hr 30min).

London King's Cross to: Brighton (every 15–30min; 1hr 15min); Cambridge (every 30min; 45min–1hr); Durham (every 1–2hr; 2hr 40min–3hr); Leeds (hourly; 2hr 20min); Newcastle (every 30min; 3hr); Peterborough (every 30min; 45min); York (every 30min; 2hr).

London Liverpool Street to: Cambridge (Mon–Sat every 30min; 1hr 20min); Norwich (every 30min–hourly; 1hr 50min); Stansted Airport (every 15–30min; 45min).

London Paddington to: Bath (every 30min–hourly; 1hr 30min); Bristol (every 30–45min; 1hr 20min); Cheltenham (every 2hr; 2hr); Exeter (every 1–2hr; 2hr 5min); Gloucester (every 2hr; 1hr 45min); Oxford (every 30min–hourly; 1hr); Penzance (8–9 daily; 5hr); Plymouth (hourly; 3hr–3hr 40min); Windsor (change at Slough; Mon–Fri every 20min; Sat & Sun every 30min; journey time 30–40min); Worcester (hourly; 2hr 20min).

London St Pancras to: Leicester (every 30min; 1hr 30min); Nottingham (hourly; 2hr 10min); Sheffield (hourly; 2hr 20min).

London Victoria to: Brighton (every 30min; 1hr); Gatwick (every 15min; 30min).

London Waterloo to: Portsmouth Harbour (every 30min; 1hr 30min); Southampton Central (every 30min; 1hr 15min); Winchester (every 30min; 1hr 10min); Windsor (Mon–Sat every 30min, Sun hourly; 50min).

Surrey, Kent and Sussex

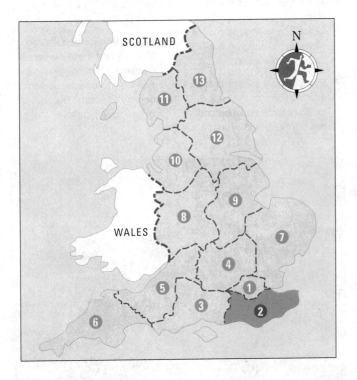

CHAPTER 2 # Highlights

* **Canterbury Cathedral** An essential, tourist stop that lives up to the hype, the cathedral was the destination of pilgrims in Chaucer's *Canterbury Tales* and the magnificent sixteenth-century interior includes a shrine to the murdered Thomas à Becket. See p.194.

* **The white cliffs of Dover** Best seen from a boat, the famed chalky cliffs also offer walks and vistas over the Channel. See p.200.

* **Rye** Superbly set hilltop town offering some of the best meals, accommodation and pubs in Sussex. See p.210.

* **The Royal Pavilion, Brighton** George IV's pleasure dome, designed by Nash, is the supreme (and only) example of Oriental-Gothic architecture. See p.221.

* **Petworth House** As well as being one of the country's most attractive stately homes, this place is home to a splendid art collection. See p.227.

* **Fishbourne Roman Palace** Mosaics and a well-preserved heating system are among the treasures to be seen at the country's greatest Roman palace. See p.228.

△ Brighton Pier

Surrey, Kent and Sussex

The southeast corner of England was traditionally where London went on holiday. In the past, trainloads of Eastenders were shuttled to the hop fields and orchards of **Kent** for a working break from the city; boats ferried people down the Thames to the beach at Margate; and everyone from royalty to cuckolding couples enjoyed the seaside at Brighton, a blot of decadence in the otherwise sedate county of **Sussex**. **Surrey** is the least pastoral and historically significant of the three counties – the home of wealthy metropolitan professionals prepared to commute from what has become known as the "stockbroker belt".

The late twentieth century brought big changes to the southeast region. In purely administrative terms the three counties have become four, since local government reorganization split Sussex into East and West. More significantly, many of the old seaside resorts struggled to keep their tourist custom in the face of ever more accessible foreign destinations. To make matters worse, **Brighton**, long known as "London beside the sea", now matches the capital with one of the highest proportions of homeless people in the country. On the positive side, there has been something of a renaissance in recent years, with celebrities and big-city refugees settling in more congenial surroundings away from the metropolitan hubbub, while the whole region has maintained consistently high standards of both accommodation and gourmet dining. Narrow country lanes and verdant meadows preserve their picturesque charm, and there are even pockets of comparative wilderness, not to mention the miles of bleak and cliffy coastline.

The proximity of Kent and Sussex to the continent has dictated the history of this region, which has served as a gateway for an array of invaders. **Roman** remains dot the coastal area – most spectacularly at **Bignor** in Sussex and **Lullingstone** in Kent – and many roads, including the main A2 London to Dover road, follow the arrow-straight tracks laid by the legionaries. When **Christianity** spread through Europe, it arrived in Britain on the **Isle of Thanet** – the northeast tip of Kent, since rejoined to the mainland by silting and subsiding sea levels. In 597 AD Augustine moved inland and established a monastery at **Canterbury**, still the home of the Church of England and the county's prime historic attraction.

The last successful invasion of England took place in 1066, when the **Normans** overran King Harold's army near **Hastings**, on a site now marked

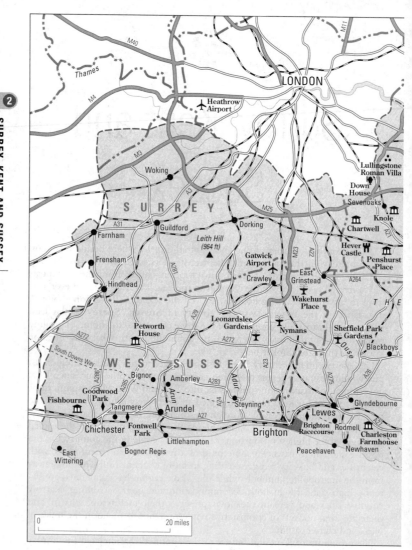

by **Battle Abbey**. The Normans left their mark all over this corner of the kingdom, and Kent remains unmatched in its profusion of medieval castles, among them **Dover**'s sprawling cliff-top fortress guarding against continental invasion and **Rochester**'s huge, box-like citadel, close to the old dockyards of **Chatham**, power base of the formerly invincible British navy.

Away from the great historic sites, you can spend unhurried days in elegant old towns such as **Royal Tunbridge Wells**, **Rye** and **Lewes**, or enjoy the less elevated charms of the traditional resorts, of which **Brighton** is far and away the best, combining the buzz of a university town with a good-time

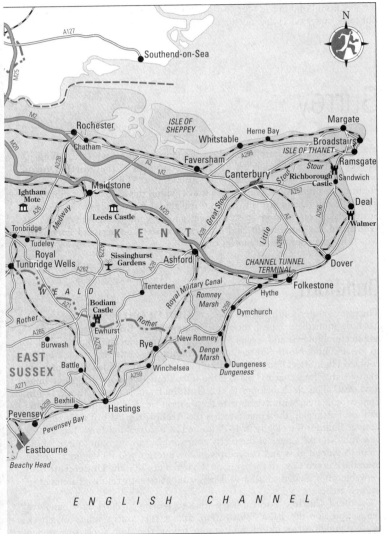

© Crown copyright

atmosphere and an excellent range of eating options. Dramatic scenery may be in short supply, but in places the **South Downs Way** offers an expanse of rolling chalk uplands that, as much as anywhere in the crowded southeast, gets you away from it all. And of course Kent, Sussex and Surrey harbour some of the country's finest **gardens**, ranging from the lush flowerbeds of **Sissinghurst** to the great landscaped estates of **Sheffield Park** and **Petworth**.

The commuter traffic in this corner of England is the heaviest in Europe, so almost everywhere of interest is close to a **train** station. National Express services from London and other parts of England to the region are pretty good, but local **bus** services are much less impressive.

2 Surrey

Effectively a rural suburb of southern London for those who can afford it, **Surrey** is bisected laterally by the chalk escarpment of the **North Downs** which rise west of Guildford, peak around Box Hill near Dorking, and continue east into Kent. The satellite towns within the M25 orbital motorway hold little natural and virtually no historical appeal, but outside the M25's ring, Surrey takes on a more pastoral demeanour, with the county town of **Guildford**, the open heath land of Surrey's western borders and **Farnham**, which has the county's only intact castle.

Guildford

Thirty-five miles southwest of London, **GUILDFORD**, the county capital, has little immediate appeal, though its sloping **High Street** retains plenty of architectural interest and several picturesque narrow lanes and courts lead off it to the adjoining North Street, and south towards the castle. As you look up the cobbled High Street you can't fail to spot the wonderful gilded clock projecting over the street that has marked the town's time for more than three hundred years. The clock belongs to the **Guildhall** (guided tours Tues & Thurs 2pm & 3pm; free) with its elaborate Restoration facade disguising Tudor foundations. Further up the High Street is the **Archbishop Abbot's Hospital**, a hospice built for the elderly in 1619 fronted by a palatial red-brick Tudor gateway. You can take a peek at the pretty courtyard, but if you want to inspect the Flemish stained glass and oak beams of the interior you must join a guided tour. Back down towards the river, on the left at no. 72 is the **Undercroft** (also viewable on a guided tour), a well-preserved thirteenth-century basement of vaulted arches.

Guildford **Castle**'s Norman keep (due to reopen in 2004 after extensive renovation; for the latest information, ask at the tourist office or check Ⓦ www.guildford.gov.uk) sits on its motte behind the High Street, surrounded by flower-filled gardens. Beneath the castle, **Guildford Museum** (Mon–Sat 11am–5pm; free) displays mementoes of the writer Lewis Carroll (aka the Reverend Charles Dodgson), author of the children's classics, *Alice's Adventures in Wonderland* and *Alice through the Looking Glass*. An imaginative sculpture of Alice is to be found in the Castle Gardens, and Dodgson's grave can be visited in the cemetery off the Mount, on the other side of the river.

At the bottom of the High Street runs the **River Wey**, a rather neglected feature of the town, although the once-crucial River Wey and Godalming Navigation Canal has been restored into a picturesque waterway. From Easter to October, you can **rent canoes** (swimmers only) and **rowing boats** (Mon–Sat 9am–5.30pm, Sun 10am–6pm; canoes £4 an hour; rowing boats £6 an hour; £20 deposit) from Guildford Boat House, based in the Millbrook car park, and in summer take the same company's **pleasure cruises** up the river from the town wharf, at the bottom of the High Street (☎01483/504494 or 536186 for timetable information; ⓦwww.guildfordboats.co.uk). Half a mile further north up the river is **Dapdune Wharf** (March–Oct Thurs–Mon 11am–5pm; £3; NT), whose buildings house an interactive museum recounting the story of what is claimed to be Britain's oldest working waterway, while outside you can visit the restored barge *Reliance*.

Ostentatiously perched on Stag Hill by the university, a mile northwest of the centre, Guildford's unremarkable red-brick **Cathedral** (daily 8.30am–5.30pm) is one of only four Anglican cathedrals built in England in the twentieth century. Resembling an outsized crematorium and consecrated in 1961 following wartime delays, the cathedral's plain, bright interior, with its concrete vaulting, has all the spirituality of a concert hall, but without the acoustics. Its most notable claim to fame is having been a location in the film *The Omen*.

Practicalities

Guildford's main **train station** lies just over the river to the west of the town centre, and the **bus station** is between the town centre and the train station, at the western end of North Street. The county's main **tourist office** is at 14 Tunsgate, near the Guildhall, just off the High Street (May–Sept Mon–Sat 9am–5.30pm, Sun 10am–4.30pm; Oct–April Mon–Sat 9.30am–5.30pm; ☎01483/444333, ⓦwww.guildford.gov.uk).

Guildford's less expensive **accommodation** options are all some distance from the town centre and include the homely *Atkinsons Guest House*, 129 Stoke Rd (☎01483/538260, ⓦwww.s-h-systems.co.uk; ❷), with four rooms, ten minutes' walk up the A320 Woking road. Plusher lodgings can be found at the *Jarvis Guildford Hotel*, 253 Upper High St (☎01483/564511, ⓦwww.jarvis.co.uk; ❺) and at the timber-beamed, 500-year-old *Angel Posting House and Livery*, 91 High St (☎01483/564555, ⓦwww.johansens.com; ❼).

For **eating** options, head for *Zinfandel*, 4–5 Chapel St (☎01483/455155; closed Sun), which dishes up Californian and Pacific-rim cooking plus good-value pizzas, or *Olivo*, housed in the town's sixteenth-century dispensary at 53 Quarry St (☎01483/303535; closed Sun), and specializing in delicious regional Italian dishes. Virtually next door is one of Guildford's better **pubs**, the *King's Head*, serving real ales and inexpensive meals, while Guildford's oldest hostelry, *Ye Olde Ship Inn* on Portsmouth Road, boasts open fires.

Farnham

Tucked into Surrey's southwestern corner, ten miles west of Guildford along the exposed ridge-top of the Hog's Back, lies **FARNHAM**. Smaller and, in parts, more charming than Guildford, the town moves at a slower pace. Notwithstanding its thousand-year history, the majority of Farnham's architecture dates from the eighteenth century, when it enjoyed a boom period based on hop farming.

Farnham is also home to Surrey's only intact **castle**, built around 1138 by Henry de Blois, Bishop of Winchester, as a convenient residence halfway between his diocese and London. The castle was continuously occupied until 1927, but now houses a conference venue. The **keep** (April–Sept daily 10am–6pm; Oct daily 10am–5pm; £2.50; EH), from where there are good views over the rooftops to the Downs beyond, is the only part of the castle that is open to the public.

Farnham **train station** is five minutes from the centre, over the river on the southern edge of town, down South Street and over the bypass. The **tourist office** is in the council offices on South Street, midway between the station and the centre (Mon–Thurs 9.30am–5.15pm, Fri 9.30am–4.45pm, Sat 9am–noon; ⓣ01252/715109, ⓦwww.waverley.gov.uk). **Accommodation** includes *Meads Guest House*, 48 West St (ⓣ01252/715298; no credit cards; ❸), and the excellent *Stafford House Hotel*, 22 Firgrove Hill (ⓣ01252/724336; ❸), close to the station. On Castle Street, the oak-beamed *Nelson Arms* offers reasonable bar **meals**; for Italian, the best bet is the friendly *Caffe Piccolo*, 84 West St (ⓣ01252/723277).

The North Kent coast

It's a commonly held view that the northern part of Kent is a scenic and cultural wasteland, a prejudice that stems partly from the fact that most visitors only glimpse the area as they race to or from the Channel ports. However, the region has its fair share of attractions, all of which are easily accessible from London. **Rochester** and **Chatham** have both historic and literary interest, while the seaside resorts of **Whitstable**, **Margate** and **Broadstairs**, ranging from genteel to seedy, have a growing cachet among weekenders from the capital.

Rochester and around

ROCHESTER was first settled by the Romans, who built a fortress on the site of the present **castle** (daily: April–Sept 10am–6pm; Oct–March 10am–4pm; £3.90), at the northwest end of the High Street; some kind of fortification has remained here ever since. In 1077, William I gave Gundulf – architect of the White Tower at the Tower of London – the See of Rochester and the job of improving the defences on the River Medway's northernmost bridge on Watling Street. The resulting castle remains one of the best-preserved examples of a Norman fortress in England, with the stark hundred-foot-high keep glowering over the town, while the interior is all the better for having lost its floors, allowing clear views up and down the dank interior. It has three square towers and a cylindrical one, the southwest tower, which was rebuilt following its collapse during the siege of 1215, when the bankrupt King John eventually wrested the castle from its archbishop. The outer walls and two of the towers retain their corridors and spiral stairwells, allowing access to the uppermost battlements.

The foundations of the adjacent **cathedral** (daily 7.30am–6pm; suggested donation £3) were also Gundulf's work, but the building has been much modified over the past nine hundred years. Plenty of Norman touches have endured, however, particularly in the cathedral's west front, with pencil-shaped towers, blind arcading and a richly carved portal and tympanum. Norman round arches, decorated with zigzags and made from lovely honey-coloured Caen stone, also line the nave. Some fine paintings survived the Dissolution, most notably the thirteenth-century depiction of the Wheel of Fortune on the walls of the choir (only half of which survives); shown as a treadmill, it's a trenchant image of medieval life's relentless slog.

Rochester's most famous son, **Charles Dickens**, spent his youth here, but would seem to have been less than impressed by the place – it appears as

"Mudfog" in *The Mudfog Papers*, and "Dullborough" in *The Uncommercial Traveller*. Many of the buildings feature in his novels: the *Royal Victoria and Bull Hotel*, at the top of the High Street, became the *Bull* in *Pickwick Papers* and the *Blue Boar* in *Great Expectations*, while most of his last book, the unfinished *Mystery of Edwin Drood*, was set in the town. A gritty picture of Victorian life is conjured up by the tableaux at the **Charles Dickens Centre** in the distinctive red-brick and timber-framed Eastgate House at the southeast end of the High Street (daily: April–Sept 10am–6pm; Oct–March 10am–4pm; £3.90). High-tech audiovisual displays, including the "Dickens' Dream" sequence, depict key scenes and characters from his well-known books, and the whole place is entertaining and informative. Round the back of the building, you can see **Dickens' Chalet**, a two-storey wooden structure that was removed from his house at Gad Hill Place. The chalet was used by Dickens as his summer study and it was here that he was working on *The Mystery of Edwin Drood* just before he died in 1870. Back up the High Street stands **Watts' Charity** (March–Oct Tues–Sat 2–5pm; free), a sixteenth-century almshouse featuring galleried Elizabethan bedrooms and immortalized in Dickens' short story *The Seven Poor Travellers*.

At the northwest end of the High Street, Rochester's excellent **Guildhall Museum** (daily 10am–4.30pm; free) holds a vivid model of King John's siege of the castle and a chilling exhibition on the prison ships or hulks that were used to house convicts and prisoners of war at the end of the eighteenth century.

Practicalities

Rochester **train station** is at the southeastern end of the High Street, and the **tourist office** is halfway along the High Street, opposite the cathedral at no. 95 (Mon–Sat 10am–5pm, Sun 10.30am–5pm; ℡01634/843666, ⓦwww.medway.gov.uk). You could **spend the night** with some Dickensian ghosts at the ancient *Royal Victoria and Bull Hotel*, 16–18 High St (℡01634/846266, ⓦwww.rvandb.co.uk; ❸), or at the plush *Gordon House Hotel* at no. 91 (℡01634/831000, ⓦwww.gordonhousehotel.net; ❹). Decent B&Bs include the *Grayling House*, 54 St Margaret's St (℡01634/826593, ⓔgraylinghouse @aol.com; no credit cards; ❷), further up the hill behind the castle. The nearest **youth hostel** (℡0870/770 5964, ⓔmedway@yha.org.uk; £11.50, ❶) is at Capstone Farm, Gillingham, two miles southeast of Chatham (bus #114). The best **places to eat** include two Italians, both on the High Street, *Casa Lina,* at no. 146 (℡01634/844993; closed Sun & Mon), and the more expensive *Don Vincenzo* (℡01634/408373) at no. 108, while at no. 188 the *Cumin Club* (℡01634/400880) offers contemporary Indian cuisine. Alternatively, try the *Coopers Arms* on St Margaret's Street, which serves good lunches in its small beer garden.

Chatham

CHATHAM, less than two miles east of Rochester, has none of the charms of its neighbour. Its chief attraction is its **Historic Dockyard** (mid-Feb to Oct daily 10am–6pm or dusk; Nov Sat & Sun 10am–dusk, last entry 2 hours before closing; £9.50), originally founded by Henry VIII, and once the major base of the Royal Navy, many of whose vessels were built, stationed and victualled here. Well sheltered, yet close to London and the sea, and lined with tidal mud flats that helped support ships' keels during construction, the port expanded quickly and by the time of Charles II it had become England's largest naval base. This era of shipbuilding came to an ignominious end when the dockyards were closed in 1984, reopening soon afterwards as a tourist attraction.

The dockyard occupies a vast eighty-acre site about one mile north of the town centre along the Dock Road (ask at the tourist office in Rochester for bus times). Once there, take advantage of the free vintage-bus service to take you around the array of historically and architecturally fascinating buildings dating back to the early eighteenth century. In addition to an impressive display of fifteen historic RNLI lifeboats, there's the "**Wooden Walls**" gallery, where you can experience life as an apprentice in the eighteenth-century dockyards. Here too lies the **Ocelot Submarine**, the last warship built at Chatham, whose crew endured unbelievably cramped conditions – a major deterrent to visiting claustrophobes – and a newly restored Victorian sloop, the *Gannet*. The main part of the exhibition, however, consists of the Ropery complex, including the former rope-making room – at a quarter of a mile long, it's the longest room in the country.

Whitstable

Peculiarities of silt and salinity have made **WHITSTABLE** an oyster-friendly environment since classical times, when the Romans feasted on the region's marine delicacies. Indeed, production grew to such levels during the Middle Ages that **oysters** were exported all over Europe, but the whole industry collapsed during the twentieth century. Oysters are once more farmed in the area, but Whitstable is now more dependent on its commercial port, fishing and seaside tourism, while small-scale boat-building and a mildly bohemian ambience have made this one of the most agreeable spots along the north Kent coast to spend any time.

Follow the signs at the top of Whitstable's busy High Street to reach the seafront, a quiet shingle beach backed by some pretty weatherboard cottages. Local maritime history is illustrated in the **Whitstable Museum and Gallery** (July & Aug Mon–Sat 10am–4pm, Sun 1–4pm; Sept–June closed Sun; free), housed in the former Foresters' Hall, heralded by its eye-catching entrance on Oxford Street, with displays on diving and some good photographs and old film footage of the town's heyday.

Whitstable's **train station** is five minutes' walk along Cromwell Road, east of Oxford Street, the southern continuation of the High Street, while the **tourist office** is next to the museum at 7 Oxford St (July & Aug Mon–Sat 10am–5pm; Sept–June Mon–Sat 10am–4pm; ℡01227/275482, ⓦwww .canterbury.co.uk). For **accommodation** along the seafront, try *Copeland House*, 4 Island Wall (℡01227/266207, ⓦwww.copelandhouse.co.uk; no credit cards; ➋), west of the High Street, with a garden that backs onto the beach, or *The Cherry Garden*, 62 Joy Lane (℡01227/266497; no credit cards; ➋), ten minutes' stroll along Seasalter Road. For **campsites**, you're best off heading to *Seaview Caravan Park* (℡01227/792246; closed Nov–March), which backs onto the beach towards Herne Bay.

Whitstable's fishing background is reflected in its **eating** places, from any number of fish-and-chip outlets along the High Street and Harbour Street to the very popular *Royal Native Oyster Stores*, The Horsebridge (℡01227/276856; closed Sun eve & Mon), one of the town's best restaurants. Opposite, *Pearson's Crab and Oyster House* (℡01227/272005) offers bar meals downstairs and has a pricier restaurant upstairs. For top-notch Italian food, head for *Giovanni's*, 49–55 Canterbury Rd (℡01227/273034: closed Sun eve & all Mon), while for a **drink** and excellent atmosphere check out the *Old Neptune*, standing alone in its white weatherboards on the shore.

The Thanet resorts

The **Isle of Thanet**, a featureless plain fringed by low chalk cliffs and the odd sandy bay, became part of the mainland when the navigable Wantsum Channel began silting up around the time of the first Roman invasion. In 43 AD, nearly a century after Julius Caesar's exploratory visit, the Romans got into their stride when they landed near Pegwell Bay and established Richborough port in preparation for the march inland. The Saxons followed them four hundred years later – the island is named after the "tenets", or fire beacons, which used to warn local residents of the Saxons' raids – and Augustine arrived here in 597 on a divine mission to end Anglo-Saxon paganism. The evangelist is supposed to have met King Ethelbert of Kent and preached his first sermon at a spot three miles west of Ramsgate – a cross marks the location at Ebbsfleet, next to St Augustine's Golf Club.

Over the next thousand years or so, civilization advanced to the point at which, in 1751, a resident of Margate, one Mr Benjamin Beale, invented the bathing machine, a wheeled cubicle that enabled people to slip into the sea without undue exhibitionism. It heralded the birth of sea bathing as a recreational and recuperative activity, and led to the growth of **seaside resorts**. By the mid-twentieth century the Isle's intermittent expanses of sand had become fully colonized as the "bucket and spade" resorts of the capital's leisure-seeking proletariat. That heyday has passed, but these earliest of resorts still cling to their traditional attractions to varying degrees.

Margate

MARGATE – memorably summarized by Oscar Wilde as "the nom-de-plume of Ramsgate" – is a ragged assortment of cafés, shops and amusement arcades wrapped around a broad bay. At the town's peak thousands of Londoners were ferried down the Thames every summer's day, to be disgorged at the pier – the functional precursor of all such seaside structures.

Other than the agreeable, if small, sandy beach, the main attraction is the intriguing **Shell Grotto** on Grotto Hill, off Northdown Road (Easter–Oct daily 10am–5pm; Nov–Easter Sat & Sun 11am–4pm; £2), claiming to be the world's only underground shell temple. It has been open to the public since it was discovered by some schoolkids in 1835, but its origin is open to continued dispute. The **Margate Museum** on the Market Place (April–Sept Tues–Sun 10am–5pm; Oct–March Thurs–Sun 11am–4.30pm; £1) allows you to take a trip down memory lane; the building also served as the town's police station from 1858 to 1959 and there are several surviving police cells. A new centre for the visual arts to be located on the pier, the Turner Centre, is promised for 2007.

Margate's **tourist office** is at 12–13 The Parade (Easter–Sept Mon–Fri 9am–5pm, Sat 9am–4pm, Sun 10am–4pm; Oct–Easter Mon–Sat 9am–4pm; ☎01843/583333, ⓦwww.tourism.thanet.gov.uk) and the **train station** is on All Saints' Avenue. Lining the Regency squares and crescents of the Cliftonville area, Margate's best **accommodation** choices include the family-run *Malvern Hotel*, 29 Eastern Esplanade (☎01843/290192, ⓦwww.malvern-hotel.co.uk; ❸), the *Innsbruck Hotel*, Dalby Square (☎01843/298946; no credit cards; ❶), and the grand 1920s-style *Walpole Bay Hotel*, Fifth Avenue (☎01843/221703, ⓦwww.walpolebayhotel.co.uk; ❹). There's a YHA **hostel** at 3–4 Royal Esplanade, by Westbrook Bay to the west of the train station (☎0870/770 5956, Ⓔmargate@yha.org.uk; £11.50, ❶). Prosaic seaside **food** is on offer at the seafront greasy spoons and fish-and-chip outlets, but you can dine well at

Greenfields Bistro (℡01843/224347; closed Sun & Mon) at 4 Hawley Square, near the Regency theatre. The *Walpole Bay Hotel* is the place for afternoon tea or a Sunday lunch with piano accompaniment; book for lunches. It's worth steering away from the **pubs** around the seafront in favour of the tiny Victorian *Rose in June* on Trinity Square, or for real ales (and pizzas), the *Spread Eagle*, at the top of Victoria Road.

Broadstairs

Said to have been established on the profits of shipbuilding and smuggling, today **BROADSTAIRS** is the smallest, quietest and, undoubtedly, the most pleasant of Thanet's resort towns, overlooking the pretty little Viking Bay from its cliff-top setting. Its main claim to fame is as Dickens' holiday retreat: throughout his most productive years he stayed in various hostelries here, and eventually rented an "airy nest" overlooking Viking Bay from Fort Road, since renamed **Bleak House** and opened to the public (daily: July & Aug 10am–9pm; Sept to mid-Dec & mid-Feb to June 10am–6pm; mid-Dec to mid-Jan 11am–4pm; £3). It was here that he planned the eponymous novel as well as finishing *David Copperfield*, and three rooms in the house have been pre-served as the author would have known them. There's more of the same on the main cliff-top seafront at the **Dickens House Museum**, 2 Victoria Parade (daily: Easter to mid-June and Sept & Oct 2–5pm; mid-June to Aug daily 10.30am–5pm; £2), in the house Dickens used as a model for Betsy Trotwood's House. The town's **Dickens Festival**, held annually since 1937, takes place in June and features lectures, dramatizations of the author's works and a nightly Victorian music hall.

It's a ten-minute walk from the **train station** to Broadstairs' seafront along the High Street, where you'll find the **tourist office** at no. 6b (April–Sept daily 9am–5pm; Oct–March Mon–Sat 9am–4.30pm; ℡01843/583334, Ⓦwww.tourism.thanet.gov.uk). Among the ivy-covered Georgian **B&Bs** in Belvedere Road, behind the High Street, try *Dundonald House* at no. 43 (℡01843/862236, Ⓦwww.dundonaldhousehotel.co.uk; ❸) and the *Hanson Hotel* next door (℡01843/868936, Ⓔhotelhanson@aol.com; ❷). The *Royal Albion Hotel*, 6–12 Albion St (℡01843/868071, Ⓦwww.marchesi.co.uk; ❻), where Dickens wrote part of *Nicholas Nickleby*, is a comfortable but pricey treat for literary fans. There's a **youth hostel** housed in a Victorian villa at 3 Osborne Rd, just two minutes' walk south from the train station (℡0870/770 5730, Ⓔbroadstairs@yha.org.uk; £10.25, ❶).

For **food**, there are plenty of fish-and-chip outlets and cafés along Albion Street and down Harbour Street, but for a more congenial setting, head for *Harpers Wine Bar*, also on Harbour Street (℡01843/602494; eve only), which serves moderately priced seafood dishes. Broadstairs' top restaurant is the Swiss-run *Marchesi Brothers* restaurant, 18 Albion St (℡01843/862481). As for **pubs**, *Ballard's Lounge* at the *Royal Albion Hotel* has bay views from its garden, while the popular and friendly *Neptune's Hall*, at the top of Harbour Street, serves great beer.

Ramsgate

If Thanet had a capital, it would be **RAMSGATE**, a handsome resort, rich in robust Victorian red-brick. Most of the town is set high on a cliff linked to the seafront and harbour by broad, sweeping ramps, with the villas on the seaward side displaying wrought-iron verandas and bricked-in windows – a legacy of the tax on glazed windows. A large-scale regeneration project in the harbour and along the seafront is breathing some new life into the area.

Currently, the most entertaining sight in Ramsgate is the subterranean **Motor Museum** at West Cliff Hall, on The Paragon just by the ferry terminal (April–Oct daily 10.30am–5.30pm; Nov–Easter Sun 10am–5pm; £3.50), which spices up its eclectic collection of cars and motorbikes by placing each vehicle in historical context. A predictable chronicle of municipal life from Roman times onwards is presented at the **Ramsgate Maritime Museum**, in the harbour's nineteenth century Clock House (Easter–Sept Tues–Sun 10am–5pm; Oct–Easter Thurs–Sun 11am–4pm; £1.50); the display is brightened by an illuminating section on the Goodwin Sands sandbanks – six miles southeast of Ramsgate – the occasional playing field of the eccentric Goodwin Sands Cricket Club.

Ramsgate's **train station** is about a mile northwest of the centre, at the end of Wilfred Road, at the top of the High Street. The **tourist office** is at 17 Albert Court, York St (daily 9.30am–4.30pm; ☎01843/583333, ⓦwww.tourism.thanet .gov.uk). For an overnight **stay**, the *Spencer Court Hotel*, 37 Spencer Square (☎01843/594582, ⓦwww.s-h-systems.co.uk; ❶), offers comfortable accommodation in a listed Regency building, directly above the ferry terminal; while, just east of the harbour, the Victorian *Eastwood Guest House*, 28 Augusta Rd (☎01843/591505; no credit cards; ❷), has some rooms with balconies. *The Crescent*, 19 Wellington Crescent (☎01843/591419, ⓦwww.ramsgate-uk.com; ❷), is an attractive seafront option in a Georgian terrace originally built to house the duke's officers. The nearest **campsite** is *Nethercourt Touring Park*, just two miles southwest of the town centre (☎01843/595485; closed Nov–March). For **food** the reasonably priced *Surin Thai* at 30 Harbour St (☎01843/592001; closed Mon) specializes in quality Cambodian, Lao and Thai food. The relaxed *Ocean Lounge Bar* at 62 Harbour Parade serves Mediterranean snacks all day. Best for fish and chips is the gaudy *Peter's Fish Factory* at 96 Harbour Parade. For traditional **pubs** try the ornately tiled *Queen's Head* on Harbour Parade and for cliff-top views, real ales and live music (Sun), head for the *Churchill Tavern* on The Paragon, overlooking the harbour.

Canterbury

One of England's most venerable cities, **CANTERBURY** offers a rich slice through two thousand years of history, with Roman and early Christian ruins, a Norman castle and a famous cathedral that dominates a medieval warren of time-skewed Tudor dwellings. The city began as a Belgic settlement that was overrun by the Romans and renamed **Durovernum**, which they established as a garrison and supply base. With the empire's collapse came the Saxons, who renamed the town **Cantwarabyrig**; it was a Saxon king, Ethelbert, who in 597 welcomed Augustine, despatched by the pope to convert the British Isles to Christianity. By the time of his death, Augustine had founded two Benedictine monasteries, one of which – Christ Church, raised on the site of the Roman basilica – was to become the first cathedral in England.

At the turn of the first millennium Canterbury suffered repeated sackings by the Danes until Canute, a recent Christian convert, restored the ruined Christ Church, only for it to be destroyed by fire a year before the Norman invasion. As Christianity became a tool of control, a struggle for power developed between the archbishops, the abbots from the nearby Benedictine abbey and King Henry II, culminating in the assassination of Archbishop Thomas à Becket in 1170, a martyrdom that effectively established the autonomy of the archbishops and made this one of Christendom's greatest shrines. Geoffrey Chaucer's *Canterbury Tales*, written towards the end of the fourteenth century, portrays the unexpectedly festive nature of pilgrimages to Becket's tomb, which was later plundered and destroyed on the orders of Henry VIII.

In 1830 a pioneering passenger railway service linked Canterbury to the sea and prosperity grew until the city suffered extensive German bombing on June 1, 1942, in one of the notorious **Baedeker Raids** – the Nazi plan to destroy Britain's most treasured historic sites as described in the eponymous German travel guides. Today the cathedral and compact town centre, enclosed on three sides by medieval walls, remain the focus for leisure-motivated pilgrims from across the globe.

Arrival, information and accommodation

Canterbury's two **train stations** – Canterbury East for services from London Victoria and Dover Priory, and Canterbury West for services from London

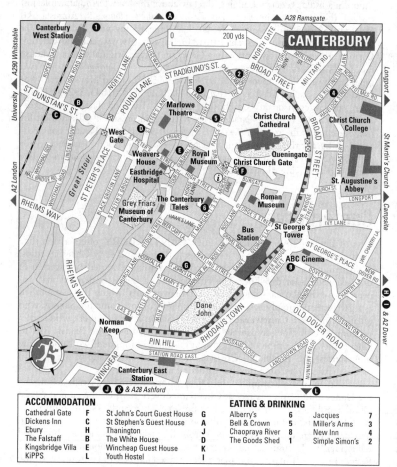

ACCOMMODATION				EATING & DRINKING			
Cathedral Gate	F	St John's Court Guest House	G	Alberry's	6	Jacques	7
Dickens Inn	C	St Stephen's Guest House	A	Bell & Crown	5	Miller's Arms	3
Ebury	H	Thanington	J	Chaopraya River	8	New Inn	4
The Falstaff	B	The White House	D	The Goods Shed	1	Simple Simon's	2
Kingsbridge Villa	E	Wincheap Guest House	K				
KiPPS	L	Youth Hostel	I				

Charing Cross and the Isle of Thanet – are south and northwest of the centre respectively, each a ten-minute walk from the cathedral. National Express services and local **buses** use the bus station just inside the city walls on St George's Lane. The busy **tourist office** is at the Butter Market at 12–13 Sun St (Jan–Easter Mon–Sat 10am–4pm; Easter–Oct Mon–Sat 9.30am–5pm, Sun 10am–4pm; Nov–Dec daily 10am–4pm; ☎01227/378100, ⊛www .canterbury.co.uk), opposite the main entrance to the cathedral. You can access the **Internet** at Dot Café, 21 St Dunstan's St (Mon–Sat 10am–7pm, Sun 11am–7pm).

Accommodation consists mostly of B&Bs and small hotels and can be difficult to secure in July and August – the tourist office can help, though they charge for the service.

Hotels and B&Bs

Cathedral Gate 36 Burgate ☎01227/464381, ⊛www.cathgate.co.uk. Built in 1438, this venerable pilgrims' hostelry has crooked floors and exposed beams alongside more modern amenities. ❸

The Dickens Inn 71 St Dunstan's St ☎01227/472185, ⊛www.dickens-inn.co.uk. Originally a thirteenth-century yeoman's house, this timbered inn has colourful rooms and a pleasant walled garden. ❸

Ebury 65–67 New Dover Rd ☎01227/768433, ⊛www.eburyhotel.co.uk. Very comfortable and spacious family-owned Victorian hotel, fifteen minutes' walk from the centre, with an indoor pool. ❺

The Falstaff 8–10 St Dunstan's St ☎01227/462138, ⊛www.corushotels .co.uk/thefalstaff. Fifteenth-century coaching inn with four-poster beds and an award-winning restaurant. ❺

Kingsbridge Villa 15 Best Lane ☎01227/766415, ⊛www .canterburykingsbridgevilla.co.uk. Two of the rooms in this well-furnished Victorian house have views of the cathedral. Vegan and vegetarian breakfasts on offer too. ❷

St John's Court Guest House St John's Lane ☎01227/456425, ℮nigelnrw@aol.com. Obliging and good-value guest house in a quiet but central location, just south of the old town. No credit cards. ❶

St Stephen's Guest House 100 St Stephen's Rd ☎01227/767644, ⊛www.st-stephens.fsnet.co.uk. A mock Tudor house on the northern side of the

city, ten minutes' walk along the Stour, offering excellent value en-suite accommodation. No credit cards. ❸

Thanington 140 Wincheap ☎01227/453227, ⊛www.thanington-hotel.co.uk. Comfortably converted Georgian building, with an indoor pool and a games room. ❺

The White House 6 St Peter's Lane ☎01227/761836, ⊛www.sh-systems.co.uk. Small and friendly guest house offering en-suite accommodation in a fine Regency building, midway between the cathedral and Canterbury West station. ❸

Wincheap Guest House 94 Wincheap ☎01227/ 762309, ⊛www.wincheapguesthouse.co.uk. Good-value Victorian B&B, with shared facilities, close to Canterbury East station. ❶

Hostels and campsites

The Caravan and Camping Club Site Bekesbourne Lane ☎01227/463216. Large year-round caravan park, one and a half miles east of the city off the A257 road to Sandwich.

KiPPS 40 Nunnery Fields ☎01227/786121, ⊛www.kipps-hostel.com. Self-catering hostel offering single and double rooms (❶) and dormitory (£12) accommodation a few minutes' walk from Canterbury East station.

Youth Hostel 54 New Dover Rd ☎0870/770 5744 ℮canterbury@yha.org.uk. Half a mile out of town, and 15min on foot from Canterbury East station, this friendly hostel is set in a Victorian villa. Dorm bed £14.50. Closed Jan. ❶

The City

Despite the presence of a university and art and teacher-training college, England's second most visited city is a surprisingly small place with a population of just 40,000. The town centre, partly ringed by ancient walls, is virtually car free, but this doesn't stop the High Street seizing up all too frequently with tourists.

The cathedral

Mother Church of the Church of England and seat of the Primate of All England, **Canterbury Cathedral** (Mon–Sat 9am–6.30pm, Sun 12.30–2.30pm & 4.30–5.30pm; closes Mon–Sat 5pm in winter; also closed on some days in mid-July for university graduation ceremonies; £4, free on Sun; ⓦ www.canterbury-cathedral.org) fills the northeast quadrant of the city with a befitting sense of authority, even if architecturally it's not the country's most impressive. A cathedral has stood here since 602, but in 1070 the first Norman archbishop, Lanfranc, levelled the original Saxon structure to build a new cathedral. Over successive centuries the masterpiece was heavily modified, and with the puritanical lines of the Perpendicular style gaining ascendancy in late medieval times, the cathedral now derives its distinctiveness from the thrust of the 235-foot-high Bell Harry Tower, completed in 1505. The precincts (daily 7am–9pm) are entered through the superbly ornate early sixteenth-century **Christ Church Gate**, where Burgate and St Margaret's Street meet. This junction, the city's medieval core, is known as the Butter Market, where religious relics were once sold to pilgrims hoping to prevent an eternity in damnation. Having paid your entrance fee, you pass through the gatehouse and get one of the finest views of the cathedral, foreshortened and crowned with soaring towers and pinnacles.

Once in the magnificent **interior**, look for the tomb of Henry IV and his wife, Joan of Navarre, and for the gilded effigy of Edward III's son, the Black Prince, all of them in the Trinity Chapel, behind the main altar. Also here, until demolished in 1538, was the shrine of Thomas à Becket; the actual spot where he died is marked by the **Altar of the Sword's Point**, in the "Martyrdom" in the northwest transept, where a jagged sculpture of the assassins' weapons is suspended on the wall. Steps from here descend to the low, Romanesque arches of the **crypt**, one of the few remaining relics of the Norman cathedral and considered the finest such structure in the country, with some amazingly well-preserved carvings on the capitals of the columns. Particularly vivid is the medieval **stained glass**, much of which dates back to the twelfth and thirteenth centuries, notably in the Trinity chapel, where the life and miraculous works of Thomas à Becket are depicted. Look out too for Adam delving, girt about with an animal skin, in the west window and Jonah and the whale in the Corona (beyond the Trinity Chapel). Contemporary with the windows (1220) is the white marble **St Augustine's Chair** on which all archbishops of Canterbury are enthroned; it's located in the choir at the top of the steps beyond the high altar.

On the cathedral's north flank are the fan-vaulted colonnades of the **Great Cloister**, from where you enter the **Chapter House**, with its intricate web of fourteenth-century tracery supporting the roof and a wall of stained glass. In 1935 it was a fitting venue for the inaugural performance of T.S. Eliot's *Murder in the Cathedral*.

The rest of the city

Exiting the cathedral grounds at the Queningate, you come to the vestigial remains of **St Augustine's Abbey** (daily: April–Sept 10am–6pm; Oct 10am–5pm; Nov–March 10am–4pm; £3; EH), occupying the site of the church founded by Augustine in 598. Built outside the city because of a Christian tradition forbidding burials within the walls, it became the final resting place of Augustine, Ethelbert and successive archbishops and kings of Kent, although no trace remains either of them or of the original Saxon church. Shortly after the Normans arrived, the church was demolished and replaced by a much larger abbey, most of which was destroyed in the Dissolution so that today only the ruins and foundations remain. Nearby, on the corner of North Holmes Road and St Martin's Lane, **St Martin's Church** (Tues & Thurs 10am–3pm, Sat 10am–1pm; free) is one of England's oldest churches, built on the site of a Roman villa or temple and used by the earliest Christians. Although medieval additions obscure the original Saxon structure, this is perhaps the earliest Christian site in Canterbury – it was here that Queen Bertha welcomed St Augustine in 597, and her husband King Ethelbert was baptized.

South of the Cathedral, the redevelopment of the Longmarket area between Burgate and the High Street in the early 1990s exposed Roman foundations and mosaics that are now part of the **Roman Museum** (June–Oct Mon–Sat 10am–5pm, Sun 1.30–5pm; Nov–May closed Sun; £2.70). The extant remnants of the larger building are pretty dull, and better mosaics can be seen at Lullingstone (see p.206), but the display of recovered artefacts and general design of the museum are tasteful, with Roman domestic scenes re-created, as well as a computer-generated view of Durovernum.

St Margaret's Street holds the former church that's now **The Canterbury Tales** (daily: mid-Feb to June, 10am–5pm; July–Oct 9.30am–5.30pm; Nov to mid-Feb 10am–4.30pm; £6.75), a quasi-educational show based on Geoffrey Chaucer's book, in which visitors equipped with headsets wander through odour-enhanced galleries in which mannequins occupy idealized fourteenth-century tableaux and recount five of Chaucer's tales. Genuinely educational and better value is the **Museum of Canterbury**, round the corner in Stour Street (June–Oct Mon–Sat 10.30am–5pm, Sun 1.30–5pm; Nov–May Mon–Sat 10.30am–5pm; £3), an interactive exhibition spanning local history from the splendour of Durovernum through to the more recent literary figures of Joseph Conrad (buried in the cemetery on London Road) and local-born Mary Tourtel, creator of the check-trousered philanthropist Rupert Bear. An excellent thirty-minute video on the Becket story details the intriguing personalities and events that led up to his assassination.

Eastbridge Hospital, standing where the High Street passes over a branch of the River Stour (Mon–Sat 10am–4.45pm; £1), was founded in the twelfth century to provide poor pilgrims with shelter. Downstairs is an exhibition on Chaucer's life, while storytellers in feudal garb recite parts of his book. Over the road is the wonky, half-timbered **Weavers' House**, built around 1500 – once inhabited by Huguenot textile workers, it's now a café.

Just before High Street becomes St Peter's Street, the **Royal Museum and Art Gallery** (Mon–Sat 10am–5pm; free) is housed on the first floor of an awesome mock-Tudor building. There's lots of military memorabilia in the Buffs regimental gallery, and the art gallery holds the odd Henry Moore and Gainsborough too. St Peter's Street terminates at the massive crenellated towers of the medieval **West Gate**, the only one of the town's seven city gates to have survived intact. Its prison cells and guard chambers house a small **museum** (Mon–Sat 11am–12.30pm & 1.30–3.30pm; £1), which displays contemporary armaments and weaponry used by the medieval city guard, as well as giving access to the battlements.

Eating, drinking and nightlife

The combination of a large student population and the tourist trade means Canterbury has a good selection of **places to eat**, many of them in old and atmospheric settings. At Canterbury West Station, *The Goods Shed* offers everything from a bowl of soup or sandwich to a first-class full meal, with ingredients fresh from the adjacent farmers' market (℡01227/459153; closed Sun eve & all day Mon). *Alberry's*, a lively wine bar on St Margaret's Street (℡01227/452378), has snacks, pastas, fish and meat dishes, and *Lloyds*, 89–90 St Dunstans St (℡01227/768222), has a contemporary style in a beamed barn setting, fairly expensive but with a good-value set dinner (Sun–Thurs). For a change from English fare, *Chaopraya River*, 2 Dover St (℡01227/462876), serves refined Thai cuisine at reasonable prices (closed Mon**)**, while *Jacques*, 71 Castle St (℡01227/781000; closed Sun eve), is a homely little French bistro.

Nightlife in Canterbury keeps a low profile, though there are some good **pubs** such as the *Miller's Arms* on Mill Lane, a pleasant weir-side spot, and the *New Inn*, 19 Havelock St, one of Canterbury's tiniest pubs, popular for its real ales. At 10 Palace St, the *Bell & Crown* is another cramped medieval hostelry, while *Simple Simon's*, 3 Church Lane, attracts the university crowd and has **live music**. The university also stages gigs, and is the place for a good range of arty **films** at Cinema 3, and for **plays** at the Gulbenkian Theatre (℡01227/769075, Ⓦwww.kent.ac.uk/gulbenkian). In town, the Marlowe Theatre in The Friars (℡01227/787787, Ⓦwww.marlowetheatre.com) is the main venue for drama. Finally, there's the **Canterbury Festival** (℡01227/452853, Ⓦwww.canterburyfestival.co.uk), an international mix of music, theatre and arts over two weeks in October. For all events, see the free *What, Where and When* **listings magazine** available at the tourist office.

The Channel ports

Dover, just 21 miles from mainland Europe (Calais's low cliffs are visible on a clear day), is the southeast's principal cross-Channel port. As a town it is not immensely appealing, even though its key position has left it with a clutch of historic attractions. To the north lie **Sandwich**, once the most important of the Cinque Ports but now no longer even on the coast, and the pleasant resort

---

The Cinque Ports

In 1278 Dover, Hythe, Sandwich, New Romney and Hastings – already part of a long-established but unofficial confederation of defensive coastal settlements – were formalized under Edward I's charter as the **Cinque Ports** (pronounced "sink", despite its French origin). In return for providing England with maritime support when necessary, chiefly in the transportation of troops and supplies to the Continent during times of war, the five ports were given trading privileges and other liberties, which enabled them to prosper while neighbouring ports struggled to survive. Some took advantage of this during peacetime, boosting their wealth by various nefarious activities such as piracy and the smuggling of tax-free contraband.

Later, Rye and Winchelsea were added to the confederation along with several other "limb" ports on the southeast coast which joined up at various times. The confederation continued until 1685, when the ports' privileges were revoked. Their maritime services had become increasingly unnecessary after Henry VIII had founded a professional navy and, due to a shifting coastline, several of the ports' harbours had silted up anyway, leaving some of them several miles inland. Nowadays, only Dover is still a major working port, though the post of Lord Warden of the Cinque Ports still exists as an honorary title bestowed by the presiding monarch.

towns of **Deal** and **Walmer**, each with its own set of distinctive fortifications as well as a smattering of traditional seaside B&Bs.

Sandwich and around

SANDWICH, situated on the River Stour four miles north of Deal, is best known nowadays for giving rise to England's favourite culinary contribution when, in 1762, the Fourth Earl of Sandwich, passionately absorbed in a game of cards, ate his meat between two bits of bread for a quick snack. Aside from this incident, the town's main interest lies in its maritime connections – it was chief among the Cinque Ports (see box opposite) until the Stour silted up. Unlike other former harbour inlets, however, the Stour hasn't silted up completely and still flows through town, its grassy willow-lined banks adding to the once great medieval port's present charm.

By the bridge over the Stour stands Sandwich's best-known feature, the sixteenth-century **Barbican**, a stone gateway where tolls were once collected. Running parallel to the river is **Strand Street**, whose crooked half-timbered facades front antique shops and private homes while, back in the town centre, another fine sixteenth-century edifice, the **Guildhall**, houses both the tourist office (see below) and a small **museum** recounting the town's history (April–Sept Tues, Wed & Fri 10.30am–12.30pm & 2–4pm, Thurs & Sat 10.30am–4pm, Sun 2–4pm; Oct to mid-Dec & March Tues, Wed, Fri & Sun 2–4pm, Thurs & Sat 10.30am–4pm; £1). The genteel town is separated from the sandy beaches of Sandwich Bay by the **Royal St George Golf Course** – frequent venue of the British Open tournament – and a mile of nature reserves. The reserve that most ornithologists make for is the **Gazen Salts Nature Reserve**, three miles north of town, across the Stour.

Overlooking the doleful expanse of Pegwell Bay, two miles northwest of Sandwich, is **Richborough Fort** (April–Sept daily 10am–6pm; Oct daily 10am–5pm; Nov–Feb Sat & Sun 10am–4pm; March Wed–Sun 10am–4pm; £3; EH), one of the earliest coastal strongholds built by the Romans along what later became known as the Saxon Shore on account of the frequent raids by the Germanic tribe. The castle guarded the southern entrance to the Wantsum Channel, which then isolated the Isle of Thanet from the mainland. Rumour has it that Emperor Claudius, on his way to London, once rode on an elephant through a triumphal arch erected inside the castle, but all that remains within the well-preserved Roman walls are the relics of an early Saxon church. Richborough's historical significance far outshines its present appearance, especially as Pegwell Bay is now blighted by an ugly chemical works. The nicest way of reaching the fort is to take the **river bus** up the Stour from Sandwich Quay (T07958/376183; £3).

Finding **accommodation** in Sandwich shouldn't be much of a problem – the local **tourist office**, housed in the Guildhall (April–Oct daily 10am–4pm; T01304/613565, Wwww.whitecliffscountry.org.uk), will provide you with a list of local **hotels** and **guest houses**. Try the *Fleur de Lis*, an old coaching inn near the Guildhall at 6–8 Delf St (T01304/611131, Wwww.verinitaverns.co.uk; ❹), or the more modest *Le Trayas* bungalow, 10 Poulders Rd (T01304/611056, Wwww.letrayas.co.uk; closed Oct; no credit cards; ❶), a ten-minute walk from The Quay. Your best choice for top-class **food** is the pricey *Fishermans Wharf* on the quayside (T01304/613636), which serves excellent seafood. For something less expensive, try one of the pubs by the Barbican or *The Haven*, 20a King St, for good coffee, snacks and light meals. For the definitive Sandwich sandwich, head for the twee *Little Cottage Tearooms*, on The Quay.

Deal and Walmer Castle

One of the most unusual of Henry VIII's forts is the diminutive castle at **DEAL**, six miles southeast of Sandwich and site of Julius Caesar's first successful landfall in Britain in 55 BC. The **castle** (April–Sept daily 10am–6pm; Oct daily 10am–5pm; Nov–March Wed–Sun 10am–4pm; £3.50; EH) is situated off The Strand at the south end of town. Its unusual shape – viewed from the air it looks like a Tudor rose – is as much an affectation as a defensive design, though the premise was that the rounded walls would be better at deflecting missiles; inside, the comprehensive display on the other similar forts built during Henry VIII's reign is well worth a visit.

A mile south of Deal, reachable either on hourly buses or, if the weather's good, on foot along the seafront, **Walmer Castle** (April–Sept daily 10am–6pm; Oct daily 10am–5pm; Nov, Dec & March Wed–Sun 10am–4pm; Jan & Feb Sat & Sun 10am–4pm; £5.50; EH) is another rotund Tudor-rose-shaped affair, commissioned when the castle became the official residence of the Lord Warden of the Cinque Ports in 1730. Now it resembles a heavily fortified stately home more than a military stronghold. The best-known resident was the Duke of Wellington, who died here in 1842, and not surprisingly, the house is devoted primarily to his life and times. Busts and portraits of the Iron Duke crowd the rooms and corridors, where you'll also find the armchair in which he expired and the original Wellington boots in which he triumphed at Waterloo.

Deal's **tourist office** is situated in the library on Broad Street near the Quarterdeck car park (Mon, Tues & Thurs–Sat 9.30am–5pm, Wed 9.30am–1pm; ☎01304/369576, ⓦwww.whitecliffscountry.org.uk). There's a whole host of places offering **accommodation** on Beach Street: try the winsome *King's Head* pub at no. 9 (☎01304/368194, ⓦwww.kingsheaddeal.co.uk; ❸), or the nearby townhouse of *Channel View* at no. 17 (☎01304/368194; ❸), run by the same proprietor. Another option is *Dunkerley's*, next door at no. 19 (☎01304/375016, ⓦwww.dunkerleys.co.uk; ❻), whose **restaurant** is one of Deal's finest (and priciest). For more affordable seafood try the *Lobster Pot* (☎01304/374713), 81–83 Beach St, opposite the pier.

Dover

Badly bombed during the war, **DOVER**'s town centre and seafront just don't have what it takes to induce many travellers to linger. Although the town authorities have put a lot of effort and money into sprucing the place up, particularly the early Victorian New Bridge development along the Esplanade, Dover Castle is still by far the most interesting of the numerous attractions in the port. Entertainment of a saltier nature is offered by Dover's legendary White Cliffs, which dominate the town and have long been a source of inspiration for lovers, travellers and soldiers sailing off to war.

It was in 1168, a century after the Conquest, that the Normans constructed the keep that now presides over the bulk of **Dover Castle** (daily: April–Sept 10am–6pm; Oct 10am–5pm; Nov–March 10am–4pm; £8; EH), a superbly positioned defensive complex that was in continuous use as some sort of military installation from then right up to the 1980s. Much earlier, the Romans had put Dover on the map when they chose the harbour as the base for their northern fleet, and erected a **lighthouse** (*pharos*) here to guide the ships into the river mouth. Beside the chunky hexagonal remains of this stands a Saxon-built church, **St Mary-in-Castro**, dating from the seventh century, with motifs graffitied by irreverent Crusaders still visible near the pulpit. Further up

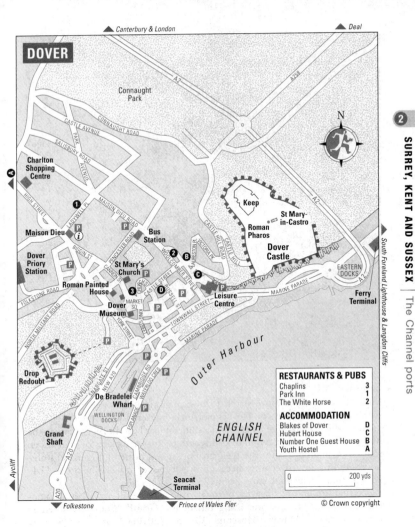

the hill is the impressive, well-preserved **Norman Keep**, built by Henry II as a palace. Inside, there's an interactive exhibition on spying, and you can also climb its spiral stairs to the lofty battlements for views over the sea to France. The castle's other main attraction is its network of **Secret Wartime Tunnels** dug during the Napoleonic Wars. Extended during World War II, you can tour "Hellfire Corner" – the tunnels' wartime nickname – on a fifty-minute guided tour (leaving every 20min). The tour is spiced up with a little gore, and reveals the quaintly low-tech communications systems and war rooms of the navy's command post.

Postwar rebuilding has made Dover **town centre** a rather unprepossessing place, though the **Roman Painted House** (April–Sept Tues–Sun 10am–5pm; £2), once a hotel for official guests, possesses some reasonable Roman wall paintings, the remains of an underground Roman heating system and some mosaics. The nearby **Dover Museum** on the Market Square (April–Oct

Mon–Sat 10am–6pm; Nov–March 10am–5.30pm; £2) has three floors packed with informative displays on Dover's past, including a restored Bronze Age boat discovered in the town in 1992 – and a stuffed polar bear. In Biggin Street, the **Maison Dieu** was founded in the thirteenth century as a place for pilgrims en route to Canterbury. After the Reformation, it was turned into a naval storehouse, and in the last century became part of the town hall. The Stone Hall, with its fine timber roof, dates from 1253.

The high ground to the west of town, originally the site of a Napoleonic-era fortress, retains one interesting oddity, the **Grand Shaft** (for opening times contact Dover Museum ☎01304/201066 or see Ⓦwww.dover-western-heights.org), a 140-foot triple staircase, entered on Snargate Street, by which troops could go down at speed to defend the port in case of attack. Looming above the Grand Shaft is the formidable **Drop Redoubt** (as above for opening information), a sunken fortress built in 1808, from which guns could fire in all directions.

There are some great **walks** to be had along Dover's cliffs: to reach **Shakespeare Cliff**, catch bus #D2A from Worthington Street towards Aycliff, alternatively, there's a steep two-and-a-half-mile climb from North Military Road, off York Street, taking you by the **Western Heights**, a series of defensive battlements built into the cliff in the nineteenth century.

Practicalities

Dover Priory **train station** is situated off Folkestone Road, a ten-minute walk west of the centre; there are regular shuttle buses to the Eastern and Western

△ The White Cliffs of Dover

Docks. Buses from London run to the Eastern Docks and the town-centre **bus station** on Pencester Road. The **tourist office**, in the Town Hall in Biggin Street (June–Aug daily 9am–5.30pm; Sept–May Mon–Fri 9am–5.30pm & Sat 10am–4pm; ☎01304/205108, ⓦwww.whitecliffscountry.org.uk), has a free *White Cliffs Trails* pamphlet that outlines coastal and inland walks near Dover. *Café En-route* provides **Internet** access at 8 Bench St (Mon–Sat 9am–9pm, Sun 11am–9pm), near Market Square.

Dover's best **B&Bs** include *Hubert House*, 9 Castle Hill Rd (☎01304/202253, ⓦwww.huberthouse.co.uk; ❷), convenient for the Eastern Dock, the smart, good-value *Number One Guesthouse*, opposite, at 1 Castle St (☎01304/202007, ⓦwww.number1guesthouse.co.uk; ❷), and *Blakes of Dover*, 52 Castle St (☎01304/202194, ⓦwww.blakesofdover.co.uk; ❷), which has a very genial owner. There's a very busy **youth hostel** in a listed Georgian house at 306 London Rd (☎0870/770 5798, ⓔdover@yha.org.uk; £14.50, ❶), a mile up the High Street from Dover Priory station. The most convenient **campsite** is *Hawthorn Farm* (☎01304/852658; closed Dec–Feb) close to Martin Mill train station, one stop up the line towards Ramsgate.

Given the town's uninspiring appearance, Dover's **pubs** are surprisingly characterful: try *Park Inn*, a big revamped old boozer at 1–2 Park Place, Ladywell, with plenty of real ales, and *The White Horse* on St James Street, a nice old eighteenth-century pub at the foot of the castle. Dover's culinary offerings are poor, though *Blakes* (see above) has a lovely wood-panelled wine bar and restaurant, and *Chaplins*, 2 Church St, serves excellent-value **breakfasts** and **lunches**.

Hythe to Dungeness: the Romney and Denge marshes

In Roman times, the **Romney and Denge marshes** – now the southern-most part of Kent – were submerged beneath the English Channel. The lowering of the sea levels in the Middle Ages and later reclamation created a forty-square-mile area of shingle and marshland which, until the nineteenth century, was afflicted by malaria and various other malaises. Contrasting strongly with the wooded pastures of Kent's interior, the sheep-speckled marshes have an eerie, forlorn appearance, as if still unassimilated with the mainland and haunted by their maritime origins. The ancient town of **Hythe** is on the eastern edge of the reclaimed marshes and is linked with Rye in East Sussex (see p.210), on the marsh's western edge, by the arc of the 23-mile Napoleonic-era **Royal Military Canal**.

Hythe

Separated from the drab port of Folkestone by the massive earthworks of the Channel Tunnel, **HYTHE** is a sedate seaside resort bisected by the disused waterway of the Royal Military Canal, which was built as a defensive obstacle during the perceived threat of Napoleonic invasion. Hythe's receding shoreline reduced its usefulness as a port and the nearby coast is now just a sweep of beach punctuated by **Martello Towers**, part of the chain of 74 such towers built along the south and east coasts in the early nineteenth century as a defence against potential French invasion.

The most rewarding area of Hythe for a wander is the quiet back alleys to the north of the High Street, where you might drop in to the macabre collection of ancient bones and skulls in the **crypt** (May–Sept Mon–Sat 10.30am–noon & 2.30–4pm, Sun noon–4.30pm; 50p) of the eleventh-century St Leonard's Church. A ride on the **Romney, Hythe and Dymchurch Railway** (R, H & DR), a fifteen-inch-gauge line which runs the fourteen miles from Hythe to Dungeness (April–Sept daily; March & Oct Sat & Sun; plus school holidays throughout the year; ☎01797/362353, ⓦwww.rhdr.demon.co.uk), is also a must. The station is to the west of the town centre, on the south bank of the canal by Station Bridge. A return ticket from Hythe to Dungeness currently costs £9.60.

Hythe's **tourist office** is, bizarrely, situated in the old public toilets in Red Lion Square (Mon–Fri 9am–5.30pm Sat 9am–5pm; ☎01303/267799, ⓦwww.shepway.gov.uk). For **accommodation** check out the Tudor-style *Seabrook House* (☎01303/269282; ❸), with pleasing light and airy rooms; the *Swan Hotel*, a friendly pub on the High Street (☎01303/266236, ⓦwww.theswanhotelhythe.co.uk; ❷), which has a Nepalese restaurant; the Edwardian *Fern Lodge*, a mile east of the town centre at 87 Seabrook Rd (☎01303/267315; no credit cards; ❸), or if you've got more money to spend, the very superior *Hythe Imperial*, Prince's Parade (☎01303/267441, ⓦwww.marstonhotels.com; ❼). For **food** there's high-class fish and chips, eat-in or takeaway at *Torbay of Hythe*, 81 High St (closed Sun & Mon); alternatively, there's sensibly priced home cooking at the *King's Head*, 117 High St (☎01303/266283; closed Sun eve), which serves quality meat and fish dishes.

Dungeness

DUNGENESS, fifteen miles south of Hythe and the southern terminus for the R, H & DR, is set in a spooky wasteland, part of which, at the edge of the

Denge Marsh, was chosen as the site of a nuclear power station in the 1960s. Another landmark, right by the station, is the **Old Lighthouse** (May–Oct Sat & Sun 11am–5pm, call ahead for winter hours; £2.50; ☎01797/321300, ⓦwww.dungenesslighthouse.com), built in 1904 and the fourth one on the site since 1615 – the present one is visible half a mile away. The shingle-swathed expanse of Dungeness has become the abode of eccentric and reclusive characters living in basic fishermen's cabins or disused railway carriages, apparently relishing the area's bleak austerity and carcinogenic threat. The barren environment of the Denge Marsh also supports a unique floral ecology and all around you'll see tiny communities of wildflowers struggling against the unrelenting breeze. On the road back towards Lydd, past the two lighthouses, the flotsam sculptures and flora in the shingle garden of **Prospect Cottage** (not open to the public), home of the late avant-garde director, writer and artist, Derek Jarman, make an eye-catching sight.

The Dungeness shingle bank attracts huge colonies of gulls and terns, as well as smews and gadwalls, information on which can be found at the **RSPB visitor centre** (daily: March–Oct 10am–5pm; Nov–Feb 10am–4pm; £3), off the road from Dungeness to Lydd.

The Kent Weald

The Weald is usually taken to refer to the region around the spa town of **Royal Tunbridge Wells**, but in fact it stretches across a much larger area between the North and South Downs and includes parts of both Kent and Sussex, though the majority of its attractions are in Kent. During Saxon times, much of the Weald was covered in thick forest – the word itself derives from the Germanic word *Wald*, meaning forest, and the suffixes -hurst (meaning wood) and -den (meaning clearing) are commonly found in Wealden village names. Now, however, the region is epitomized by gentle hills, sunken country lanes and somnolent villages as well as some of England's most beautiful gardens – **Sissinghurst**, fifteen miles east of Tunbridge Wells, being the best known – and a scattering of highly picturesque historical sites, including **Leeds Castle**, north of Sissinghurst, and **Hever Castle**, northwest of Tunbridge Wells.

Royal Tunbridge Wells and around

ROYAL TUNBRIDGE WELLS – not to be confused with the more mundane Tonbridge, a few miles to the north – is the home of the mythical whingeing right-wing letter-writer known as "Disgusted of Tunbridge Wells". Most British people, therefore, view it with derision, but don't be misled – this prosperous spa town, surrounded by gorgeous countryside, is an elegant and diverting place. After a bubbling spring discovered here in 1606 was claimed to have curative properties, a spa resort evolved, reaching its height of popularity during the Regency period when such restorative cures were in vogue. The distinctively well-mannered architecture of that period, generously surrounded by parklands in which the rejuvenated gentry exercised, gives the southern and western part of town its special character. The architecture also has an effect on the locals.

The icon of those genteel times is the **Pantiles**, an elegant colonnaded parade of shops, ten minutes' walk south of the train station, where the fashionable once gathered to promenade and take the waters. The name stems from the chunky Kent tiles made of baked clay, which were put down as paving during Queen Anne's reign. Hub of the Pantiles is the original **Chalybeate Spring** (pronounced with the emphasis on the "be") in the Bath House (Easter–Sept daily 10am–5pm), where a "Dipper" has been employed since the late eighteenth century to serve the ferrous waters. A period-dressed incumbent will fetch you a glass from the cool spring for 40p – or, if you bring your own cup, you can help yourself for free from the adjacent source. The Bath House itself was built in 1804, but failed as an enterprise as the water turns a nasty colour when heated; it closed in 1847 and now houses a pharmacy.

You can view one of the original "pantiles" in the exhibition, **A Day at the Wells** (daily: April–Oct 10am–5pm; Nov–March 10am–4pm; £5.50), situated in the basement of the nearby Corn Exchange. An audio tour, narrated as if by Richard "Beau" Nash – self-appointed arbiter of good taste (see box on p.341) – attempts to re-create, with the help of various historical tableaux, spa life in the eighteenth century. Apart from tiles, Tunbridge also produced domestic ceramics, on view with other local relics and historical artefacts in the **Museum and Art Gallery** built in the 1950s at the top of Mount Pleasant Road (Mon–Sat 9.30am–5pm; free), a fifteen-minute walk up the High Street, from the Pantiles.

The Tunbridge Wells **tourist office** is housed in the Old Fish Market, in the Pantiles (June–August Mon–Sat 9am–6pm, & Sun 10am–5pm; Sept–May Mon–Sat 9am–5pm & Sun 10am–4pm; ☏01892/515675, ⓦwww .visittunbridgewells.com). The **train station** is south of the town centre, where High Street becomes Mount Pleasant Road. **B&Bs** include the elegant *Ephraim Lodge* on The Common (☏01892/523053, ⓔjohnandglyn @freenet.co.uk; no credit cards; ❹), and the large Victorian *Clarken Guest House*, nearby at 61 Frant Rd (☏01892/533397, ⓔbarry.kench@virgin.net; no credit cards; ❷). On the Pantiles, the plush *Swan Hotel* makes a memorable splurge (☏01892/543319, ⓦwww.the-swan-hotel.com; ❺).

Among the cluster of top-notch **restaurants** are *Thackeray's House*, one-time home of the writer, at 85 London Rd (☏01892/511921, ⓦwww .thackeraysrestaurant.com; closed Sun eve & Mon), which offers a bargain three-course set menu at lunchtime, and *Sankey's*, 39 Mount Ephraim (☏01892/511422, ⓦwww.sankeys.co.uk; main restaurant closed Sun), specializing in seafood but it also has a great selection of specialist beers in a cosy cellar wine bar, where, again, you'll find a good deal at lunchtime. There are great veggie options both at the *Trinity Arts Centre Café* in a converted church on Church Road (lunch & pre-theatre deals only; closed Sun) and at *Continental Flavour*, 14 Mount Pleasant, a wholefood restaurant and shop (open daytime only; closed Sun). You're unlikely to miss the popular *Opera House* **pub**, in the town's former 1902 theatre on Mount Pleasant Road – you can sit in the foyer, the stalls or even on stage and gaze up at the balconies.

Penshurst Place and Hever Castle

Tudor timber-framed houses and shops line the high street of the attractive village of **PENSHURST**, five miles northwest of Tunbridge Wells (bus #231 or #233; not Sun). Its village church, **St John the Baptist**, is capped by an unusual four-spired tower and is entered under a beamed archway that conceals a rustic post office. However, the main reason for coming here is to visit **Penshurst Place** (March Sat & Sun noon–5.30pm; April–Oct daily noon–5.30pm; grounds same days 10.30am–6pm; £6.50, grounds only £5), home to the Sidney family since 1552 and birthplace of the Elizabethan soldier and poet, Sir Philip Sidney. The fourteenth-century Barons Hall, built for Sir John de Pulteney, four times Mayor of London, is the chief glory of the interior, with its sixty-foot-high chestnut roof still in place. The ten acres of grounds include a formal Italian garden with clipped box hedges, and double herbaceous borders mixed with an abundance of yew hedges.

The moated and much-altered **Hever Castle**, three miles further west (daily: March–Nov noon–5pm; £8.40, gardens only £6.70), is where Anne Boleyn, second wife of Henry VIII, grew up, and where Anne of Cleves, Henry's fourth wife, lived after their divorce. In 1903, having fallen into disrepair, the castle was bought by William Waldorf-Astor, American millionaire owner of *The Times*, who had the house assiduously restored, panelling the rooms with worthy reproductions of Tudor woodcarvings. In the Inner Hall hangs a fine portrait of Henry VIII by Holbein; a further Holbein painting of Elizabeth I hangs on the middle floor. Upstairs, in Anne of Cleves' room, there's an unusually well-preserved tapestry, illustrating the marriage of Henry's sister to King Louis XII of France, with Anne Boleyn as one of the ladies-in-waiting.

Outside in the grounds, next to the gift shop, is the absorbing **Guthrie Miniature Model Houses Collection**, showing the development of aristocratic seats from feudal times on. However, the best feature of the grounds is Waldorf-Astor's beautiful **Italian Garden**, built on reclaimed marshland and decorated with Roman statuary.

Sissinghurst and Leeds Castle

Sissinghurst, twelve miles east of Tunbridge Wells (late March to Oct Mon, Tues & Fri 11am–6.30pm or dusk, Sat & Sun 10am–6.30pm or dusk; £6.50; NT), was described by Vita Sackville-West as "a garden crying out for rescue" when she and her husband took it over in the 1920s. Gradually, they transformed the five-acre plot into one of England's greatest and most popular modern gardens. Spread over the site of a medieval moated manor (which was rebuilt into an Elizabethan mansion of which only one wing remains today), the gardens were designed around the linear pattern of the former buildings' walls. A major part of Sissinghurst's appeal derives from the way that the flowers are allowed to spill over onto the narrow walkways, defying the classical formality of the great gardens that preceded it. The brick tower that Vita had restored and used as her study acts as a focal point and offers the best views of the walled gardens. Most impressive are the **White Garden**, composed solely of white flowers and silvery-grey foliage, and the **Cottage Garden**, featuring flora in shades of orange, yellow and red. **Bus** #297 from Royal Tunbridge Wells takes you within two miles of the gardens.

Leeds Castle, fifteen miles north of Sissinghurst off the A20 (daily: April–Oct 10am–5pm; Nov–March 10am–3pm; grounds close 2hr later; castle, park & gardens £12; park & gardens £9.50), more closely resembles a fairy-tale palace than a defensively efficient fortress. Work on the castle began around 1120, half on an island in the middle of a lake and half on the mainland surrounded by landscaped parkland. Following centuries of regal and noble ownership (and, less glamorously, service as a prison) the castle is now run as a commercial concern, hosting conferences and sporting and cultural events. Its interior fails to match the castle's stunning external appearance and, in places, modern renovations have quashed its historical charm. The most unusual feature inside is the dog collar museum in the gatehouse, while the grounds hold a fine aviary with some superb and colourful exotic specimens, as well as manicured gardens and a mildly challenging maze.

Sevenoaks and around

Set among the green sand ridges of west Kent, 25 miles from London, **SEVENOAKS** lost all but one of the ageing oaks from which it derives its name in a freakish storm that struck southern England in October 1987. With mere saplings having taken their place, the only real reason to visit the town is for the immense baronial estate of **Knole** (late March to Oct Wed–Sun 11am–4pm; garden May–Sept first Wed of month 11am–4pm; £5.50, garden £2; NT), entered from the south end of the Sevenoaks High Street. The house was created in 1456 by Archbishop Thomas Bourchier, who transformed the existing dwelling into a palace for himself and succeeding archbishops of Canterbury. The palace, numerically designed to match the calendar with 365 rooms, 7 courtyards and 52 staircases, was appropriated by Henry VIII, who lavished further expense on it and hunted in the thousand acres of **parkland** (free access throughout the year), still home to several hundred deer. Henry's daughter, Elizabeth I, passed the estate on to her cousin, Thomas Sackville, who remodelled the house in 1605. Part of Knole's allure is that it has preserved its Jacobean exterior and remained in the family's hands ever since. Vita Sackville-West, who in 1923 penned a definitive history of her family entitled *Knole and the Sackvilles*, was brought up here, and her one-time lover Virginia Woolf derived inspiration for her novel *Orlando* from her frequent visits to the house. The thirteen rooms open to the public feature an array of fine, if well-worn, furnishings and tapestries. Paintings by Gainsborough and Van Dyck are on display, as are Reynolds's depictions of George III and of Queen Charlotte – between them hangs a painting of their strutting, dandified progeny, George IV, one of the fifteen children she bore the king.

Sevenoaks' **tourist office** is in the library building (April–Sept Mon–Sat 9.30am–5pm; Oct–March Mon–Fri 9.30am–5pm, Sat 9.30am–4.30pm; ☎01732/450305, ⓦwww.heartofkent.org.uk), just beyond the **bus station** in Buckhurst Lane; the **train station** is north of the centre on London Road. Reasonable **accommodation** options include *Burley Lodge*, Rockdale Road (☎01732/455761; no credit cards; ❷), close to the entrance to Knole, and *4 Old Timber Top Cottages*, Bethel Road (☎01732/460506, ⓔanthony @ruddassociates.ndo.co.uk; ❹), where you can have a timber-clad cottage to yourself. The nearest **youth hostel** (☎0870/770 5890; £10.25) is an imposing Victorian vicarage in Kemsing, four miles northeast of Sevenoaks and a two-mile hike from Kemsing station; take bus #425/6 or #433 from Sevenoaks to Kemsing post office (not Sun).

For truly delicious (and expensive) food, go to *No. 5* (☎01732/455555), the restaurant at the *Royal Oak Hotel* at the south end of the High Street. For an inexpensive evening meal, head for the hotel's bistro (in other words the bar), which is also good – and half the price – or try the *Dorset Arms*, a better-than-average **pub** on Dorset Street.

Around Sevenoaks

Seven miles north of Sevenoaks and three quarters of a mile along the river west of the village of Eynsford, **Lullingstone Roman Villa** (daily: April–Sept 10am–6pm; Oct 10am–5pm; Nov–March 10am–4pm; £3; EH) has some of the best-preserved Roman mosaics in southeast England on show, in a pleasant location alongside the trickle of the River Darent. Believed to have been the first-century residence of a farmer, the site has yielded some fine marble busts now on display in the British Museum in London, but a superb floor remains depicting the killing of the Chimera, a mythical fire-breathing beast with a lion's head, goat's body and a serpent's tail. Excavation in a nearby chamber has revealed early Christian iconography, which suggests that the villa may have become a Romano-Christian chapel in the third century, pre-empting the official arrival of that religion by three hundred years and making Lullingstone one of the earliest sites of clandestine Christian worship in England. From Sevenoaks there are hourly trains to Eynsford, from where it's a fifteen-minute walk.

Down House (Wed–Sun: April–Sept 10am–6pm; Oct 10am–5pm; Nov, Dec, Feb & March 10am–4pm; £6; EH), home of the scientist Charles Darwin, is located ten miles northwest of Sevenoaks in the village of Downe, overlooking the southeastern suburbs of London. Darwin moved here in 1842, shortly after his marriage to his cousin Emma Wedgwood, who nursed the hypochondriac scientist here until his death forty years later. The house is set in lovely grounds, and is stuffed with Darwin memorabilia, though there's no sign (nor smell) of the barnacles which Darwin spent eight years dissecting – he later moved on to the study of orchids, to the relief, no doubt, of his wife and children. Trains connect Sevenoaks with Orpington station, from where bus #R2 runs twice hourly (not Sun).

Six miles west of Sevenoaks, **Chartwell** (late March to June & Sept to early Nov Wed–Sun 11am–5pm; July & Aug Tues–Sun 11am–5pm; £6.50; NT) was the residence of Winston Churchill from 1924 until his death in 1965. It's an unremarkable, heavily restored Tudor building whose main appeal is the wartime premier's memorabilia, including his paintings, which show an unexpectedly contemplative side to the famously gruff statesman. Entry to the house is by timed ticket at peak times – expect long queues. A direct bus service runs to Chartwell from Sevenoaks bus station four times daily on Sundays and public holidays.

The secluded, moated manor house of **Ightham Mote** (pronounced "I-tam"), six miles southeast of Sevenoaks just off the A227 (late March to early Nov Mon, Wed–Fri, Sun & public holidays 10.30am–5pm; £6; NT), originates from the fourteenth century and is one of the southeast's most picturesque National Trust properties, though the original defensive appearance of this half-timbered ragstone building has been muted by Tudor alterations. A tour of the interior reveals a mixture of architectural styles ranging from the fourteenth-century Old Chapel and crypt, through a barrel-vaulted Tudor chapel with a painted ceiling to an eighteenth-century Palladian window. By bus, take the infrequent #404 from Sevenoaks (not Sun) to reach Ightham.

Hastings and around

During the twelfth and thirteenth centuries, **Hastings** flourished as an influential Cinque Port (see p.196), but in 1287 its harbour creek was silted up by the same storm that washed away nearby Winchelsea (see p.210). These days, Hastings is a curious mixture of unpretentious fishing port, traditional seaside resort and arty retreat popular with painters (there's even a street and quarter named Bohemia). In 1066, William, Duke of Normandy, landed at Pevensey Bay, a few miles west of town, and made Hastings his base, but his forces met

Harold's army – exhausted after quelling a Nordic invasion near York – at **Battle**, six miles northwest of Hastings. Battle today boasts a magnificent abbey built by William in thanks for his victory, which makes a good afternoon's excursion from Hastings. Further north, **Batemans**, once the home of Rudyard Kipling, and the classic **Bodiam Castle** are both easily reached from Hastings in a day-trip, as are the ancient Cinque Ports of **Rye** and **Winchelsea**, to the east.

Hastings

Hastings **old town**, east of the pier, holds most of the appeal of this part tacky, part pretty seaside resort. With the exception of the oddly neglected Regency architecture of **Pelham Crescent**, directly beneath the castle ruins, **All Saints Street** is by far the most evocative thoroughfare, punctuated with the odd, rickety, timber-framed dwelling from the fifteenth century. The thirteenth-century **St Clement's Church** stands in the High Street, which runs parallel to All Saints Street, on the other side of The Bourne. By a louvred window at the top of the church's tower rests a cannonball that was lodged there by a Dutch galleon in the 1600s – its poignancy rather dispelled by a companion fitted in the eighteenth century for the sake of symmetry.

Down by the seafront, the area known as **The Stade** is characterized by its tall, black weatherboard **net shops**, most dating from the mid-nineteenth century (and still in use), but which first appeared here in Tudor times. Hastings still boasts a working fishing fleet, the boats being dragged up onto the shingle, and you can still buy fresh fish from several of the net shops. There's a trio of nautical attractions on nearby Rock-a-Nore Road. The **Fisherman's Museum** (daily: April–Oct 10am–5pm; Nov–March 11am–4pm; free), a converted seaman's chapel, offers an account of the port's commercial activities and displays one of Hastings' last clinker-built luggers – exceptionally stout trawlers able to withstand being winched up and down the shingle beach. The neighbouring **Shipwreck Heritage Centre** (daily: 10.30am–5pm; free) details the dramas of unfortunate mariners, focusing on the wreck of the *Amsterdam*, beached in 1749 and now embedded in the sand three miles west of town awaiting excavation.

Castle Hill, separating the old town from the visually less interesting modern quarter, can be ascended by the **West Hill Cliff Railway**, from George Street, off Marine Parade, one of two Victorian funicular railways in Hastings (daily: April–Oct 10.30am–5.30pm; Nov–March 11am–4.30pm; 90p), the other being the **East Cliff Railway**, on Rock-a-Nore Road (same times and price). Castle Hill is where William the Conqueror erected his first **Castle** in 1066, one of several prefabricated wooden structures brought over from Normandy in sections. Built on the site of an existing fort, probably of Saxon origins, it was soon replaced by a more permanent stone structure, but in the thirteenth century storms caused the cliffs to subside, tipping most of the castle into the sea; the surviving ruins, however, offer an excellent prospect of the town. The castle is home to **The 1066 Story** (daily: Easter–Sept 10am–5pm; Oct–Easter 11am–3pm; £3.20), in which the events of the last successful invasion of the British mainland are described inside a mock-up of a siege tent. The twenty-minute audiovisual details the history of the castle and corrects a few myths about the famous battle.

More fun is the **Smugglers' Adventure**, over the hill (daily: Easter–Sept 10am–5.30pm; Oct–Easter 11am–4.30pm; £5.75), where the labyrinthine St Clement's caves – named after a carving resembling St Clement but probably predating Christianity – have been converted to house a number of amusing and educational dioramas depicting the town's long history of duty-dodging.

Practicalities

Hastings' **train station** is a ten-minute walk from the seafront along Havelock Road; National Express **bus** services operate from the station at the junction of Havelock and Queen's roads. The **tourist office** is located within the Town Hall on Queen's Road (Mon–Fri 8.30am–6.15pm, Sat 9am–5pm, Sun 10am–4.30pm; ℡01424/781111, ⊛www.hastings.gov.uk); there's also a smaller seafront office (Easter–Oct daily 10am–5pm, Nov–Easter Sat & Sun 11am–4pm; ℡01424/781120) near the Boating Lake on East Parade by the old town. You'll find **Internet** access at *Revolver Internet Café*, 26 George St (℡01424/439899).

As for **accommodation**, the best choices are in the old town, where you'll find the cosy, timber-framed *Lavender and Lace*, 106 All Saints St (℡01424/716290; closed Jan & Feb; no credit cards; ❷), and *Lionsdown House*, 116 High St (℡01424/420802, ⊛www.lionsdownhouse.co.uk; no smoking; ❷), an authentic Wealden house with homemade bread and organic produce for breakfast. *Argyle Guest House*, 32 Cambridge Gardens (℡01424/421294, ⊛www.argyleguesthouse.com; no credit cards; ❶), offers good-value rooms near the station. The nearest **youth hostel** is at Guestling Hall (℡0870/770 5850; £10.25), three miles east of Hastings on the road to Rye (bus #711), where you can also camp. Hastings has a good range of affordable places for a **meal**, for example *Harris*, 58 High St (℡01424/437221; closed Sun & Mon), where you can enjoy tapas in a wood-panelled setting, and *Pissarro's*, 10 South Terrace ℡01424/421363), offering a variety of bistro food with live jazz and blues accompaniment. The best fish and chips in town are served at *Mermaid*, 2 Rock-a-Nore, right by the beach, while for something more special, head out to St Leonard's-on-Sea, where *Bonaparte's*, on the seafront at 64 Eversfield Place, specializes in classy seafood (℡01424/712218; closed Sun & Mon; expensive).

Among the **pubs**, the local fishermen's favourite is the *Lord Nelson*, right by the front on The Bourne; others to check out are the ever-popular *First In Last Out*, 15 High St, and the clubby bar, *The Street*, 53 Robertson St. *The Hastings Arms*, at 3 George St, offers great food alongside the ales and has blues every Monday, while you can hear jazz on Tuesdays at *The Anchor*, further up George Street.

Battle

The town of **BATTLE** – a ten-minute train ride from Hastings – occupies the site of the most famous land battle in British history. Here, on October 14, 1066, the invading Normans swarmed up the hillside from Senlac Moor and overcame the Anglo-Saxon army of King Harold, who is thought to have been killed not by an arrow through the eye – a myth resulting from the misinterpretation of the Bayeux Tapestry – but by a workaday clubbing about the head. Before the battle took place, William vowed that, should he win the engagement, he would build a religious foundation on the very spot of Harold's slaying to atone for the bloodshed, and, true to his word, **Battle Abbey** (daily: April–Sept 10am–6pm; Oct 10am–5pm; Nov–March 10am–4pm; £5; EH) was built four years later and subsequently occupied by a fraternity of Benedictines. The magnificent structure, though partially destroyed in the Dissolution and much rebuilt and revised over the centuries, still dominates the town, with the huge gatehouse, added in 1338, containing a good audiovisual exhibition on the battle. You can also wander through the ruins of the abbey to the spot where Harold was killed – the site of the high altar of William's abbey, now marked by a memorial stone.

Though nothing can match the resonance of the abbey, the rest of the town is worth a stroll. At the far end of High Street, the fourteenth-century **Almonry** – the present town hall – holds a **museum** (April–Oct Mon–Sat 10am–4.30pm, Sun 2–5pm; £1) that contains the only battle-axe discovered at Battle and the oldest Guy Fawkes in the country. Every year, on the Saturday nearest to November 5, this 300-year-old effigy is paraded along High Street at the head of a torch-lit procession culminating at a huge bonfire in front of the abbey gates – similar celebrations occur in Lewes (see p.213).

The **tourist office** is situated in the Gatehouse at Battle Abbey (daily: April–Sept 9.30am–5.30pm; Oct 9am–5pm; Nov–March 10am–4pm; ☎01424/773721, ⓦwww.battletown.co.uk). Battle's **accommodation** tends to be expensive; less pricey B&Bs include the obliging *High Hedges*, 28 North Trade Rd (☎01424/774140, ⓔgloria.jones@btinternet.com; no credit cards; ❷), a few minutes, walk north of High Street, or the *Gateway Café*, 78 High St (☎01424/772856; ❷). Among the town-centre **pubs** serving decent meals, try the fifteenth-century *Old King's Head* on Mount St or the *Chequers Inn* at Lower Lake, on High St.

Rye and Winchelsea

Ten miles northeast of Hastings, perched on a hill overlooking the Romney Marshes, the ancient town of **RYE** was added as a "limb" to the original Cinque Ports (see p.196), but was subsequently marooned two miles inland by the retreat of the sea and the silting-up of the River Rother. It is now one of the most popular places in East Sussex – half-timbered, skew-roofed and quintessentially English, but also very commercialized.

From Strand Quay, head up The Deals to Rye's most picturesque street, the sloping cobbled lane of **Mermaid Street**, which will bring you eventually to the peaceful oasis of Church Square. Henry James, who strangely suggested that "Rye would … remind you of Granada", lived from 1898 until his death in 1916 in **Lamb House** at the east end of Mermaid Street (April–Oct Wed & Sat 2pm–6pm; £2.60; NT). The house's three rooms and garden are of interest chiefly to fans of James's novels, or to admirers of E.F. Benson, who lived here after James. A blue plaque in the High Street also testifies that Radclyffe Hall, author of the seminal lesbian novel, *The Well of Loneliness*, was also once a resident of the town. At the centre of Church Square, **St Mary's Church** boasts the oldest functioning pendulum clock in the country; the ascent of the church tower – whose bells were looted by French raiders in 1377 and then retrieved with similar audacity – offers fine views over the clay-tiled roofs. In the far corner of the square stands the **Ypres Tower** (April–Oct Mon, Thurs & Fri 10am–1pm & 2–5pm, Sat & Sun 10.30am–1pm & 2–5pm; Nov–March Sat & Sun 10.30am–3.30pm; £1.90), formerly used to keep watch for cross-Channel invaders, and now a part of the **Rye Castle Museum** on nearby East Street (April–Oct Mon, Thurs & Fri 10am–1pm & 2–5pm, Sat & Sun 10.30am–1pm & 2–5pm; £1.90; combined ticket for both sites £2.90). Both sites house a number of relics from Rye's past, including an eighteenth-century fire-engine.

WINCHELSEA, sited on a hill two miles southwest of Rye and easily reached by train, bus, foot or bike, shares Rye's indignity of having become detached from the sea, but has a very different character. Rye gets all the visitors, whereas Winchelsea feels positively deserted, an impression augmented as you pass through the medieval Strand Gate and see the ghostly ruined **Church**

of St Thomas à Becket. Pillaged by the French in the fourteenth and fifteenth centuries, the church still constitutes the county's finest example of the Decorated style. Head south for a mile and a half and you get to **Winchelsea beach**, a long expanse of pebbly sand.

Practicalities

Rye's **train station** is at the bottom of Station Approach, off Cinque Ports Street, while Winchelsea's is a mile north of the town. **Bus #711** runs into the centre of both towns from Hastings. Rye's **tourist office is** on Strand Quay (April–Oct Mon–Sat 10am–5pm, Sun 10am–4pm; Nov–March Mon–Sat 10am–4pm; ☎01797/226696, ⓦwww.visitrye.co.uk). The town's popularity with weekending Londoners gives it an excellent, but pricey, choice of **accommodation**. Try the handsomely furnished *Jeake's House* on Mermaid Street (☎01797/222828, ⓦwww.jeakeshouse.com; ❺), or the *Durrant House Hotel*, 2 Market St (☎01797/223182, ⓦwww.durranthouse.com; ❹), a friendly and well-equipped Georgian house with a garden looking out towards Dungeness and the marshes. In Winchelsea the best option is the fourteenth-century *Strand House* (☎01797/226276, ⓦwww.s-h-systems.co.uk; ❸), at the foot of the cliff below Strand Gate. Rye's **restaurants** offer excellent seafood, for example at the *Old Forge*, 24 Wish St (☎01797/223227), or the *Flushing Inn* on Market Street (☎01797/223292; closed Mon eve & all Tues). *The Peacock*, 8 Lion St (☎01797/226702), serves up snacks, cream teas and full meals in a suitably ancient setting. The fifteenth-century *Mermaid* on Mermaid Street is Rye's most atmospheric **pub**, with heavy exposed timbers throughout, though an excellent alternative is the *Ypres Castle* in Gun Gardens, down the steps behind the Ypres Tower.

Bodiam Castle

Bodiam Castle, nine miles north of Hastings (late Feb to Oct daily 10am–6pm or dusk; Nov–Feb Sat & Sun 10am–4pm or dusk; £4; NT), is a classically stout square block with rounded corner turrets, battlements and a wide moat. When it was built in 1385 to guard what were the lower reaches of the River Rother, Bodiam was state-of-the-art military architecture, but during the Civil War, a company of Roundheads breached the fortress and removed its roof to reduce its effectiveness as a possible stronghold for the king. Over the next 250 years Bodiam fell into neglect until restoration in the last century by Lord Curzon. The extremely steep spiral staircases, leading to the crenellated battlements, will test all but the strongest of thighs. An absorbing fifteen-minute video portrays medieval life in a castle. You can get here from Hastings by regular buses #4 and #5.

For **accommodation** and **food**, head a couple of miles southeast of Bodiam to the quaint *White Dog Inn* (☎01580/830264, ❷), in the lovely village of Ewhurst.

Burwash and Bateman's

Fifteen miles northwest of Hastings on the A265, halfway to Tunbridge Wells, **BURWASH**, with its red-brick and weatherboarded cottages and Norman church tower, exemplifies the pastoral idyll of inland Sussex. Half a mile south of the village lies the main attraction, **Bateman's** (house & garden: April–Oct Mon–Wed, Sat, Sun & public holidays 11am–5pm; £5.20; garden only March Sat & Sun 11am–4pm; £2.60; NT), home of the writer and journalist Rudyard Kipling from 1902 until his death in 1936. Built by a local ironmaster in the seventeenth century and set amid attractive gardens, the house features a working watermill converted by Kipling to generate electricity. Inside, the house is laid out as Kipling left it, with letters, early editions of his work and mementoes from his travels on display. Next to the house, a garage houses the last of Kipling's Rolls-Royces, one of the many that he owned during his lifetime, although he never actually drove them himself. Getting to Bateman's without your own transport involves a three-mile walk from Etchingham Station, which is served by regular trains from Hastings.

Eastbourne and around

Like so many of the southeast's seaside resorts, **EASTBOURNE** was kick-started into life in the 1840s, when the Brighton, Lewes and Hastings Rail Company built a branch line from Lewes to the sea. Past holiday-makers include George Orwell and the composer Claude Debussy, who finished writing *La Mer* here, as well as Marx and Engels. Nowadays Eastbourne has a solid reputation as a retirement town by the sea, with one of the grandest piers on the south coast jutting out from its long Promenade. The one lively exception to the prevailing sedateness is the **Towner Art Gallery and Museum** (Tues–Sat noon–5pm, Sun 2–5pm; Nov–March Tues–Sat noon–4pm, Sun 2–5pm; free), a ten-minute walk northwest of the train station. Its display of refreshingly contemporary works of art is complemented by the **"How We Lived Then" Museum of Shops** at 20 Cornfield Terrace (daily 10am–5.30pm; £3.50), just down from the tourist office, where a range of artefacts – old packages, coronation cups, toys – from the last hundred years of consumerism is crammed into mock-up shops spread over several floors. A more serious attempt to tackle the history of the town is made at the **Eastbourne Heritage Centre** (May–Sept Mon–Fri & Sun 2–5pm; £1), in a distinctive corner house opposite the Winter Gardens.

The real reason to visit Eastbourne, however, is for expeditions onto the **South Downs**. A short walk west from Eastbourne takes you out along the

The South Downs Way

Following the undulating crest of the South Downs, between the city of Winchester and the spectacular cliffs at Beachy Head, the **South Downs Way** extends over eighty miles along the chalk uplands, offering the southeast's finest walks. If undertaken in its entirety, the bridle-path is best traversed from west to east, taking advantage of the prevailing wind, Eastbourne's better transport services and accommodation, and the psychological appeal of ending at the sea. **Steyning**, the halfway-point, marks a transition between predominantly wooded sections and more exposed chalk uplands – to the east of here you'll pass the modern **youth hostel** at Truleigh Hill (℡0870/770 6078, ✉truleigh@yha.org.uk; dorm bed £10.25, ➊). Other hostels along the way are at Telscombe and at Alfriston, where a southern loop can be taken which brings you to Eastbourne along the cliffs of the Seven Sisters, and there's a bunkhouse at Gumber Farm (℡01243/814484; closed Nov–Easter), near Bignor Hill.

The OS Landranger **maps** #198 and #199 cover the eastern end of the route; you'll need #185 and #197 as well to cover the lot. Half a dozen guides are available, the best being *South Downs Way* by Miles Jebb (Cicerone Press), or the more detailed *South Downs Way* by Paul Millmore (Aurum Press). You can also check the website ⓦwww.nationaltrails.gov.uk.

most dramatic stretch of coastline in Sussex, where the chalk uplands are cut by the sea into a sequence of splendid cliffs. The most spectacular of all, **Beachy Head**, is 575ft high, with a diminutive-looking lighthouse, but no beach – the headland's name derives from the French *beau chef* meaning "beautiful head". The beauty certainly went to Friedrich Engels' head; he insisted his ashes be scattered here, and depressed individuals regularly try to join him by leaping to their doom from this well-known suicide spot. An open-top bus runs half-hourly (late May to Sept; £6) from Eastbourne Pier to the top of Beachy Head.

West of the headland the scenery softens into a diminishing series of chalk cliffs, a landmark known as the **Seven Sisters**. The eponymous country park provides some of the most impressive walks in the county, taking in the cliff-top path and the lower valley of the meandering River Cuckmere, into which the Seven Sisters subside.

Practicalities

Eastbourne's **train station** is a splendid Italianate terminus ten minutes' walk from the seafront up Terminus Road; the **bus station is** on Cavendish Place right by the pier. The **tourist office** is at 3 Cornfield Rd, just off Terminus Road (July to early Sept Mon–Sat 9.30am–5.30pm, Sun 10am–1pm; rest of year closed Sun; ☎01323/411400, ⓦwww.eastbourne.org). There are a couple of good **accommodation** choices: *Sea Breeze Guest House*, 6 Marine Rd (☎01323/725440, ⓦwww.seabreezeguesthouse.co.uk; no credit cards; ❷), just a hundred yards from the sea, and *Sea Beach House Hotel*, 39–40 Marine Parade (☎01323/410458, ⓦwww.seabeachhousehotel.com; ❸), on the seafront. A mile and a half west along the A259 to East Dean there's a **youth hostel** (☎0870/770 5806, ⓔeastbourne@yha.org.uk; £10.25) with spectacular views across Eastbourne; take buses #710, #712, #713 from the train station. If you'd rather stay near the South Downs Way, check in at the *Birling Gap Hotel* (☎01323/423197; ❸), a Victorian villa overlooking the dramatic cliffs between Seven Sisters and Beachy Head, or bed down at the Frog Firle youth hostel (☎0870/770 5666, ⓔalfriston@yha.org.uk; £10.25) in a traditional Sussex flint building a couple of miles south of Alfriston. You can camp right by a sandy beach at the secluded *Bay View* **campsite** (☎01323/768688; closed Oct–March), off the A259 east to Pevensey.

The best **restaurant** option is the *Café Belge* on the seafront at 11–23 Grand Parade, good for *moules et frites* and snack lunches. Otherwise head for the concentration of moderately priced places in the Terminus Road area, between the train station and the sea. If you're in need of a large ice-cream sundae, go to *Fusciardi's* opposite the Winter Gardens on Carlyle Road. The most amenable **pubs** are some distance from the seafront: the capacious Wetherspoon's bar at 21–23 Cornfield Rd, and the *Hurst Arms* at 76 Willingdon Rd, a ten-minute walk inland from the station up Upperton Road, which has locally brewed beers on tap.

Lewes and around

East Sussex's county town, **LEWES** straddles the River Ouse as it carves a gap through the South Downs on its final stretch to the sea. Though there's been some rebuilding in the riverside Cliffe area (the place where Lewes started), and new housing estates are spreading from the town's fringes, the core of

The bonfire societies

Each November 5, while the rest of Britain lights small domestic bonfires or attends municipal firework displays to commemorate the 1605 foiling of a Catholic plot to blow up the Houses of Parliament (see p.97), Lewes puts on a more dramatic show, whose origins lie in the deaths of the town's Protestant martyrs. By the end of the eighteenth century, Lewes's **Bonfire Boys** had become notorious for the boisterousness of their anti-Catholic demonstrations, in which they set off fireworks indiscriminately and dragged rolling tar barrels through the streets – a tradition still practised today, although with a little more caution. In 1845 events came to a head when the incorrigible pyromaniacs of Lewes had to be read the Riot Act, instigating a night of violence between the police and Bonfire Boys. Lewes's first **bonfire societies** were established soon afterwards, to try to get a bit more discipline into the proceedings, and in the early part of the last century they were persuaded to move their street fires to the town's perimeters.

Today's tightly knit bonfire societies, each with its quasi-militaristic motto ("Death or Glory", "True to Each Other", etc), spend much of the year organizing the Bonfire Night shenanigans, when their members dress up in traditional costumes and parade through the town carrying flaming torches, before marching off onto the Downs for their society's big fire. At each of the fires, effigies of Guy Fawkes and the pope are burned alongside contemporary, but equally reviled, figures – chancellors of the exchequer and prime ministers are popular choices.

Lewes remains remarkably good-looking: Georgian and crooked older dwellings still line the High Street and the narrow lanes – or "Twittens" – lead off this main street and its continuations, with views onto the Downs. With some of England's most appealing chalkland right on its doorstep, and numerous traces of a history that stretches back to the Saxons, Lewes is a worthwhile stopover on any tour of the southeast – and an easy one, with good rail connections with London and along the coast.

Following the Norman Conquest, William's son-in-law, William de Warenne, built a priory and castle here, the latter still dominating the High Street. In 1264 Henry III's incompetence caused a baronial revolt led by Simon de Montfort which culminated in the king's surrender at the Battle of Lewes, although de Montfort and his reduced force were annihilated within a year at the Battle of Evesham. De Montfort's name crops up all over the town, as do references to the Lewes Martyrs, the seventeen Protestants burned here in 1556, at the height of Mary Tudor's militant revival of Catholicism – an event commemorated in spectacular fashion every November 5 (see box above). Intellectual non-conformity is something of a Lewes trademark, its roll call of free-thinkers featuring pioneer paleontologist Gideon Mantell and the radical humanist Tom Paine, whose *Common Sense* and *The Rights of Man* inspired or supported the revolutions in France and America. The conservative spirit triumphed in 1914, however, after a pair of local enthusiasts commissioned a version of Rodin's majestic sculpture *The Kiss*, depicting Paolo and Francesca – lovers from Dante's *Inferno* – clinched in a full-on embrace. Local sentiment was outraged when the piece was unveiled in Lewes town hall, leading to its rapid removal amid a flurry of controversy (the sculpture was re-exhibited in the town hall in 1999, 85 years after the scandal).

Within a few miles of Lewes lies a trio of places worth visiting: two houses associated with the Bloomsbury group – **Rodmell** and **Charleston** – and the mecca for picnicking opera lovers, **Glyndebourne**.

The Town

The best way to begin a tour of the town from the train station is to walk up Station Road, then left down the High Street. Lewes's **Castle** (Mon–Sat 10am–5.30pm, Sun 11am–5.30pm; closed Mon in Jan; winter closes at dusk; £4.20) is hidden from view behind the houses on your right. Inside the castle complex – unusual for being built on two mottes, or mounds – the shell of the eleventh-century keep remains, and both the towers can be climbed for excellent views over the town to the surrounding Downs. Tickets for the castle include admission to the **museum** (same hours as castle), by the castle entrance, which is much better than the usual stuffy town museum.

A few minutes' walk further west along the High Street, past St Michael's Church with its unusual twin towers, one wooden and the other flint, brings you to the steep cobbled and much photographed **Keere Street**, down which the reckless Prince Regent is alleged to have driven his carriage. Keere Street leads to **Southover Grange** (Mon–Sat 8am–dusk, Sun 9am–dusk; free), with its lovely gardens. Built in 1572 from the priory's remains, the Grange was also the childhood home of the diarist John Evelyn and now houses the local Registry Office. Past the gardens, a right turn down Southover High Street leads to the Tudor-built **Anne of Cleves House** (Tues–Sat 10am–5pm, Mon, Sun & public holidays 11am–5pm; Nov–Feb closed Mon; £2.80; combined ticket with the castle £5.80), given to her in settlement after her divorce from Henry VIII – though she never actually lived there. The magnificent oak-beamed Tudor bedroom is impressive, with its cumbersome "bed wagon", a bed-warming brazier which would fail the slackest of fire regulations and which the 400-year-old Flemish four-poster has managed to survive. The house's decor dates from the sixteenth century when the Wealden iron industry was flourishing and Sussex produced most of England's iron, with Lewes being a centre of cannon manufacture.

On the opposite side of the road and closer to the train station is the church of **St John the Baptist**, with its squat, brick tower capped by a six-foot shark for a weather vane; inside there's some superb stained glass and a tiny chapel with the lead coffins of William de Warenne and his wife Gundrada, William I's daughter. De Warenne was one of the six barons presiding over the new administrative provinces – known as the **Rapes of Sussex** – created by the Normans soon after the Conquest. Behind the church are the ruins of de Warenne's **St Pancras Priory**, once one of Europe's principal Cluniac institutions, with a church the size of Westminster Abbey. Sadly it was dismantled to build townhouses following the Dissolution and is now an evocative ruin surrounded by playing fields.

At the east end of the High Street, School Hill descends towards **Cliffe Bridge**, built in 1727 and entrance to the commercial centre of the medieval settlement. For the energetic, a path leads up onto the Downs from the end of Cliffe High Street – site of England's worst avalanche disaster in 1836, when a bank of snow slid onto Cliffe village, killing eight people. The path passes close to an obelisk, commemorating the town's seventeen Protestant martyrs.

Practicalities

The **train station** lies south of High Street down Station Road, and the **bus station** is on Eastgate Street, near the foot of School Hill. The **tourist office** is at the junction of the High Street and Fisher Street (April–Sept Mon–Fri 9am–5pm, Sat 10am–5pm, Sun 10am–2pm; Oct–March Mon–Fri 9am–5pm, Sat 10am–2pm; ℡01273/483448, ⓦwww.lewes.gov.uk). For **accommodation**, try

Castle Banks Cottage, 4 Castle Banks (℡01273/476291, ⓦwww
.s-h-systems.co.uk; no smoking; no credit cards; ❸), a beamed period house with
great views, tucked away off West Street, or, failing that, *The Crown
Inn*, 191 High St, close to the tourist office (℡01273/480670, ⓦwww
.s-h-systems.co.uk; ❸). The nearest **youth hostel** is in the village of Telscombe,
six miles south of Lewes (see below); there's another – a rustic wooden cabin
with basic facilities – eleven miles northeast of town at Blackboys, near Uckfield
(℡0870/770 5698; £10.25, ❶).

Lewes is home of the excellent Harvey's brewery and most of the **pubs** serve
its wares – try the *Brewers' Arms* opposite St John the Baptist, or the *Lewes Arms*
tucked behind the Star Brewery Studio. On the outskirts of town, the lively
Snowdrop Inn at South Street also serves excellent **food** including vegetarian
and vegan options, while *Stoyan*, at 13 Station St (℡01273/476707; closed Sun
and Mon lunch), provides moderately priced Mediterranean dishes. For an
inexpensive snack, you could do a lot worse than the café in the gardens at
Southover Grange (March–Oct daily 9am–5pm).

Around Lewes: Glyndebourne, Rodmell and Charleston

Glyndebourne, Britain's only unsubsidized opera house, is situated near the
village of Glynde, three miles east of Lewes. Founded in 1934, the
Glyndebourne season (mid-May to Aug) is an indispensable part of the high-
society calendar, with ticket prices and a distribution system that excludes all
but the most devoted opera-lovers. While the spectacle of lawns thronged with
gentry and corporate bigwigs ingesting champagne and smoked salmon may
put you off, the musical values at Glyndebourne are the highest in the country, using young talent rather than expensive star names, and taking the sort of
risks Covent Garden wouldn't dream of. A new, award-winning theatre (seating 1200) has broadened the appeal of this exclusive venue to a wider
audience, and there are tickets available at reduced prices for dress rehearsals
or for standing-room-only; call ℡01273/813813 or check ⓦwww
.glyndebourne.com.

Three miles south of Lewes, the main source of interest at the village of
RODMELL is the **Monk's House** (April–Oct Wed & Sat 2–5.30pm; £2.60;
NT), former home of Virginia Woolf, a leading figure of the Bloomsbury
Group (see box opposite). She and her husband, Leonard, moved to the weatherboarded cottage in 1919 and Leonard stayed there until his death in 1969;
both Virginia's and Leonard's remains are interred in the gardens. Nearby, you
can see the River Ouse where Virginia killed herself in 1941 by walking into
the water with her pockets full of stones. The house's interior is nothing special and will only really be of interest to ardent Bloomsbury fans; admirers can
look round the study where Virginia wrote several of her novels, and her bedroom which is laid out with period editions of her work. To get there, catch a
train to Southease, from where it's a mile northwest to Rodmell village, across
the river.

Three miles south of Rodmell, in the village of **TELSCOMBE**, is a quiet
youth hostel (℡0870/770 6062; £10.25), whose simple accommodation is in
200-year-old cottages; take bus #123 from Lewes.

Six miles east of Lewes, off the A27, is another Bloomsbury Group shrine,
Charleston Farmhouse (March–June, Sept & Oct Wed–Sun and public
holidays 2–6pm; July & Aug Wed–Sat 11am–6pm, Sun & public holidays
2–6pm; £6; guided tours Wed–Sat; last entry 5pm), home to Virginia Woolf's

The Bloomsbury Group

The **Bloomsbury Group** were essentially a bevy of upper-middle-class friends, who took their name from the Bloomsbury area of London, where most of them lived before acquiring houses in the Sussex countryside. The Group revolved around Virginia, Vanessa, Thoby and Adrian Stephen, who lived at 46 Gordon Square, the London base of the Bloomsbury Group. Thoby's Thursday evening gatherings and Vanessa's Friday Club for painters attracted a whole host of Cambridge-educated snobs who subscribed to Oscar Wilde's theory that "aesthetics are higher than ethics". Their diet of "human intercourse and the enjoyment of beautiful things" was hardly revolutionary, but their behaviour, particularly that of the two sisters (unmarried, unchaperoned, intellectual and artistic), succeeded in shocking London society, especially through their louche sexual practices (most of the group swung both ways).

All this, though interesting, would be forgotten were it not for their individual work. In 1922 Virginia declared, without too much exaggeration, "Everyone in Gordon Square has become famous": Lytton Strachey had been the first to make his name with *Eminent Victorians*, a series of unprecedentedly frank biographies; Vanessa, now married to the art critic Clive Bell, had become involved in Roger Fry's prolific design firm, Omega Workshop; and the economist John Maynard Keynes had become an adviser to the Treasury (he later went on to become the leading economic theorist of his day). The Group's most celebrated figure, Virginia, married Leonard Woolf and became an established novelist; she and Leonard also founded the Hogarth Press, which published T.S. Eliot's *Waste Land* in 1922.

Eliot was just one of a number of writers, such as Aldous Huxley, Bertrand Russell and E.M. Forster, who were drawn to the interwar Bloomsbury set, but others, notably D.H. Lawrence, were repelled by the clan's narcissism and snobbish narrow-mindedness. Whatever their limitations, the Bloomsbury Group were Britain's most influential intellectual coterie of the interwar years, and their appeal shows little sign of waning – even now, scarcely a year goes by without the publication of the biography or memoirs of some Bloomsbury peripheral.

sister Vanessa Bell, Vanessa's husband, Clive Bell, and her lover, Duncan Grant. As conscientious objectors, the trio moved here during World War I so that the men could work on local farms (farm labourers were exempted from military service). The farmhouse became a gathering point for other members of the Bloomsbury Group, including the biographer Lytton Strachey, the economist Maynard Keynes and the novelist E.M. Forster. Duncan Grant continued to live in the house until his death in 1978. Almost every surface of the farmhouse interior is painted and the walls are hung with paintings by Picasso, Renoir and Augustus John, alongside the work of the markedly less talented residents. Many of the fabrics, lampshades and other artefacts bear the unmistakeable mark of the Omega Workshop, the Bloomsbury equivalent of William Morris's artistic movement.

Brighton

Recorded as the tiny fishing village of Brithelmeston in the Domesday Book, **BRIGHTON** seems to have slipped unnoticed through history until the mid-eighteenth-century sea-bathing trend established it as a resort that has never looked back since. The fad received royal approval in the 1780s

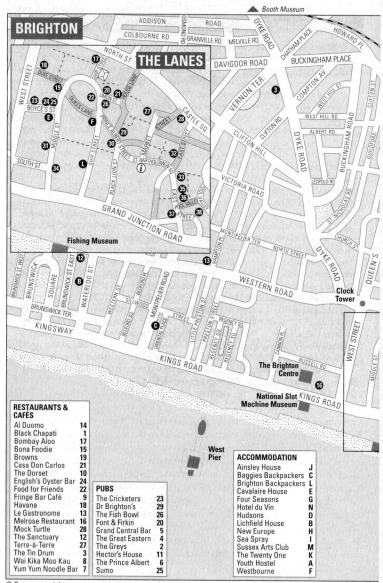

▲ Booth Museum

BRIGHTON

THE LANES

ADDISON ROAD
COLBOURNE RD.
OSMOND RD.
GRANVILLE RD.
MELVILLE RD.
DYKE ROAD
CHATHAM PLACE
HOWARD PL.
BUCKINGHAM PLACE
COMPTON AV.
WEST HILL ST.
CLIFTON ST.
WEST HILL RD.
ALBERT RD.
BUCKINGHAM ROAD
GUILDFORD RD.
LEOPOLD RD.
ST. NICHOLAS RD.
CHURCH ST.
QUEEN'S
DAVIGDOR ROAD
VERNON TER.
CLIFTON RD.
CLIFTON HILL
CLIFTON RD.
DYKE ROAD
VICTORIA ROAD
MONTPELIER TER.
NORTH STREET
DYKE ROAD
Clock Tower
WESTERN ROAD
NORTH ST.
WEST STREET
DUKE STREET
BOYCE'S ST.
DUKES LANE
MIDDLE ST.
SOUTH ST.
SHIP STREET
PRINCE ALBERT STREET
BLACK LION ST.
ST. BARTHOLOMEWS
MARKET STREET
SHIP LANE
UNION ST.
EAST STREET
CASTLE SQ.
CASTLE SQUARE
POOL VALLEY
EAST STREET
MANCHESTER ST.
GRAND JUNCTION ROAD

Fishing Museum

BRUNSWICK STREET WEST
BRUNSWICK STREET EAST
BRUNSWICK SQUARE
BRUNSWICK TER.
KINGSWAY
WATERLOO ST.
WESTERN ST.
SILLWOOD STREET
BEDFORD PL.
BEDFORD SQ.
MONTPELIER ROAD
ORIENTAL PLACE
LITTLE PRESTON ST.
PRESTON STREET
REGENCY SQ.
REGENCY SQUARE
CANNON PL.
HAMPTON PL.
MONTPELIER TER.
NORTH STREET
WESTERN ROAD
KINGS ROAD

RUSSELL RD.
WEST STREET
MIDDLE ST.

The Brighton Centre

National Slot Machine Museum
KINGS ROAD

West Pier

RESTAURANTS & CAFÉS	
Al Duomo	14
Black Chapati	1
Bombay Aloo	17
Bona Foodie	15
Browns	19
Casa Don Carlos	21
The Dorset	10
English's Oyster Bar	24
Food for Friends	22
Fringe Bar Café	9
Havana	18
Le Gastronome	13
Melrose Restaurant	16
Mock Turtle	28
The Sanctuary	12
Terre-à-Terre	27
The Tin Drum	3
Wai Kika Moo Kau	8
Yum Yum Noodle Bar	7

PUBS	
The Cricketers	23
Dr Brighton's	29
The Fish Bowl	26
Font & Firkin	20
Grand Central Bar	5
The Great Eastern	4
The Greys	2
Hector's House	11
The Prince Albert	6
Sumo	25

ACCOMMODATION	
Ainsley House	J
Baggies Backpackers	C
Brighton Backpackers	L
Cavalaire House	E
Four Seasons	G
Hotel du Vin	N
Hudsons	D
Lichfield House	B
New Europe	H
Sea Spray	I
Sussex Arts Club	M
The Twenty One	K
Youth Hostel	A
Westbourne	F

© Crown copyright

when the decadent Prince of Wales (the future George IV) began patronizing the town in the company of his mistress, thus setting a precedent for the "dirty weekend", Brighton's major contribution to the English collective consciousness. Trying to shake off this blowsy reputation, Brighton now highlights its Georgian charm, its upmarket shops and classy restaurants, and its thriving conference industry. Yet, however much it tries to present itself

as a comfortable middle-class town (granted city status in 2000), the essence of Brighton's appeal is its faintly bohemian vitality, a buzz that comes from a mix of English holiday-makers, thousands of young foreign students from the town's innumerable language schools, a thriving gay community and an energetic local student population from the art college and two universities.

Arrival, information and accommodation

Brighton **train station** is at the head of Queen's Road, which descends to the Clocktower and then becomes West Street, eventually leading to the seafront – a distance of about half a mile. The **bus station** is tucked just in from the seafront on the south side of the Old Steine. The **tourist office** is at 10 Bartholomew Square (June–Sept Mon–Fri 9am–5.30pm, Sat 10am–5pm, Sun 10am–4pm; Oct–May Mon–Sat 9am–5pm, Sun 10am–4pm, closed Sun Nov–Feb; ℡0906/7112255, ₩www.visitbrighton.com), behind the town hall on the southern side of the Lanes – the maze of narrow alleyways marking Brighton's old town. There's **Internet access** at Curve, 45 Gardner St, and Sumo, 8–12 Middle St.

You'll find most budget **accommodation** clustered around the **Kemp Town** district, to the east of the Palace Pier, with the more elegant and expensive hotels west of the town centre around Regency Square. Brighton's official **campsite** is the *Sheepcote Valley* site (℡01273/626546), just north of Brighton Marina; take bus #1 or #7 to Wilson Ave, or take the Volks railway and walk up Arundel Road to Wilson Avenue.

Hotels and B&Bs

Ainsley House 28 New Steine ℡01273/605310, ₩www.ainsleyhotel.com. Friendly, upmarket guest house in an attractive Regency terrace. **❸**

Cavalaire House 34 Upper Rock Gardens ℡01273/696899, ₩www.cavalaire.co.uk. Just off Marine Parade, with contemporary iron beds and triples and quads. No smoking. **❹**

Four Seasons 3 Upper Rock Gardens ℡01273/673574, ₩www.hotel4seasons.co.uk. Bright and light B&B in the Kemp Town area, offering good vegetarian breakfast options. No smoking. **❹**

Hotel du Vin Ship St ℡01273/718588, ₩www.hotelduvin.com. A Gothic revival building in a contemporary style, luxuriously furnished in subtle seaside colours with an excellent bar and bistro. **❼**

Hudsons 22 Devonshire Place ℡01273/683642, ₩www.hudsonshotel.demon.co.uk. Relaxed and exclusively gay and lesbian guest house east of the centre off St James St. **❹**

Lichfield House 30 Waterloo St ℡01273/777740, ₩www.lichfieldhouse.freeserve.co.uk. Stylishly and colourfully furnished townhouse. **❸**

New Europe 31–32 Marine Parade ℡01273/624462, ₩www.neweuropehotel.co.uk. Large, buzzing, gay hotel on the seafront, with late bar and regular cabaret nights. **❹**

Sea Spray 25 New Steine ℡01273/680332, ₩www.seaspraybrighton.co.uk. Boutique hotel with themed rooms, breakfast in bed, and veggie and vegan options. **❺**

Sussex Arts Club 7 Ship St ℡01273/727371, ₩www.sussexarts.com. Laid-back and lively hotel, though with just seven rooms, in a Regency house right in the centre of town. There's a pub on the ground floor and a club in the basement. **❺**

The Twenty One 21 Charlotte St, off Marine Parade ℡01273/686450, ₩www.s-h-systems.co.uk. Classy Kemp Town B&B with very comfortable rooms in an ornate, early Victorian house. **❹**

Westbourne 46 Upper Rock Gardens ℡01273/686920, ₩www.s-h-systems.co.uk. Traditional well-appointed B&B close to the seafront and all amenities. **❸**

Hostels

Baggies Backpackers 33 Oriental Place ℡01273/733740. Spacious house a little west of the West Pier with large bright dorms, starting at £12 a night, and decent showers. No credit cards. **❶**

Brighton Backpackers 75 Middle St ℡01273/777717, ₩www.brightonbackpackers.com. Established independent hostel with a lively, easy-going atmosphere. An annexe just round the corner overlooks the seafront and offers a quieter alternative; dorm beds £11. No credit cards. **❶**

Youth Hostel Patcham Place, London Rd ℡0870/770 5724, ℮brighton@yha.org.uk. Brighton's YHA hostel is housed in a splendid Queen Anne mansion four miles north of the sea, close to the junction of the roads to Lewes and London. Bus #5 or #5A from the town centre Dorm bed £13.25.

The City

Any visit to Brighton inevitably begins with a visit to its two most famous landmarks – the exuberant **Royal Pavilion** and the wonderfully tacky **Palace Pier**, a few minutes away – followed by a stroll along the seafront promenade or the pebbly beach. Just as interesting, though, is an exploration of Brighton's car-free **Lanes**, where some of the town's diverse restaurants, bars and tiny bric-a-brac, jewellery and antique shops can be found, or an idle meander through the quaint, but more bohemian streets of **North Laine**.

The Royal Pavilion and the Brighton Museum

In any survey to find England's most loved building, there's always a bucketful of votes for Brighton's exotic extravaganza, the **Royal Pavilion** (daily: April–Sept 10am–5.45pm; Oct–March 10am–5.15pm; £5.80), which flaunts itself in the middle of the main thoroughfare of Old Steine. The building was a conventional farmhouse until 1787, when the fun-loving Prince of Wales converted it into something more regal, and for a couple of decades the prince's south-coast pied-à-terre was a Palladian villa, with mildly Oriental embellishments. Upon becoming Prince Regent, however, George commissioned John Nash, architect of London's Regent Street, to build an extraordinary confection of slender minarets, twirling domes, pagodas, balconies and miscellaneous motifs imported from India and China. Supported on an innovative cast-iron frame, the result defined a genre of its own – Oriental-Gothic. The dour Queen Victoria was not amused by George's taste in architecture, however, and all the Pavilion's valuable fittings were carted off to her London palaces. Having been sold to the town, the gutted building was pressed into a series of humdrum roles, but has now been brilliantly restored, its exuberant compendium of Regency exotica enhanced by the return of many of the objects that Victoria had taken away.

One of the highlights – approached via the restrained Long Gallery – is the **Banqueting Room**, which erupts with ornate splendour and is dominated by a one-ton chandelier hung from the jaws of a massive dragon cowering in a plantain tree. Next door, the huge, high-ceilinged kitchen, fitted with the most modern appliances of its time, has iron columns disguised as palm trees. The stunning **Music Room**, the first sight of which reduced George to tears of joy, has a huge dome lined with more than twenty-six thousand individually gilded scales and hung with exquisite umbrella-like glass lamps. After climbing the famous cast-iron staircase with its bamboo-look banisters, you can go into Victoria's sober and seldom-used bedroom and the North Gallery where the king's portrait hangs, along with a selection of satirical cartoons. More notable, though, is the **South Gallery**, decorated in sky blue with trompe l'oeil bamboo trellises and a carpet that appears to be strewn with flowers.

Across the gardens from the Pavilion stands the **Dome**, once the royal stables and now the town's main concert hall. Adjoining it is the refurbished **Brighton Museum and Art Gallery** (Tues 10am–7pm, Wed–Sat & public holidays 10am–5pm, Sun 2–5pm; free), which is entered just around the corner on Church Street. It houses an eclectic mix of modern fashion and design, archeology, painting and local history, including a large collection of pottery from basic Neolithic earthenware to delicate eighteenth-century porcelain figurines. The highlight of the collection of classic Art Deco and Art Nouveau furniture is Dalí's famous sofa based on Mae West's lips. The *Balcony Café* is the perfect setting for a coffee or tea.

The rest of the town

Tucked between the Pavilion and the seafront is a warren of narrow, pedestrianized thoroughfares known as **the Lanes** – the core of the old fishing village from which Brighton evolved. Long-established antiques shops, designer outlets and several bars, pubs and restaurants generate a lively and intimate atmosphere in this part of town. **North Laine**, which spreads north of North Street along Kensington, Sydney, Gardner and Bond streets, is more bohemian, with its hub along pedestrianized Kensington Gardens. Here the shops are more eclectic, selling secondhand records, clothes, bric-a-brac and New Age objects, and mingle with earthy coffee shops and downbeat cafés. Slightly to the north of here is the **Sussex Toy and Model Museum** (Tues–Fri 10am–5pm, Sat 11am–5pm; £3.50), housed in an old stables underneath the train station, whose collection ranges from an entire cabinet full of Smurfs to a set of Pelham puppets, and a set of working model railways.

Much of Brighton's **seafront** is an ugly mix of shops, entertainment complexes and such hotels as the impressively pompous *Grand Hotel* – scene of the IRA's attempted assassination of the Conservative Cabinet in October 1984. To soak up the tackier side of Brighton, take a stroll along the **Palace Pier**, completed in 1899, whose every inch is devoted to cacophonous fun and money-making. Brighton's architecturally superior West Pier, built in 1866 half a mile west along the seafront, was damaged in World War II and then fell into disrepair, though is due to be restored to its former glory by 2006. From near the Palace Pier, the antiquated locomotives of **Volk's Electric Railway** (Easter to mid-Sept Mon–Fri 11am–5pm, Sat & Sun 11am–6pm; £2.40 return) – the first electric train in the country – run eastward towards the Marina and the nudist beach, usually the preserve of just a few thick-skinned souls.

In Brighton's northern suburbs, the **Booth Museum of Natural History** (Mon–Wed, Fri & Sat 10am–5pm, Sun 2–5pm; free), a mile up Dyke Road from the centre of town (bus #26 or #26A), is worth seeking out. Purpose-built to house a prodigious collection of stuffed birds, it's a wonderfully fusty old Victorian museum with beetles, butterflies and animal skeletons galore, but which also displays very imaginative temporary shows.

Eating, drinking and nightlife

Brighton has the greatest concentration of **restaurants** in the southeast after London. Around North Laine are some great, inexpensive cafés, while for classier establishments head to the Lanes and out towards Hove. Many of the cheaper places offer discounts of around ten percent to students, so bring ID. **Nightlife** is hectic and compulsively pursued throughout the year: as well as the mainstream **theatre** and **concert** venues, there are myriad **clubs**, lots of **live music** and plenty of cinemas. Brighton has one of Britain's longest-established and most thriving **gay communities**, with a variety of lively clubs and bars drawing people from all over. It also hosts a number of gay events including the annual **Gay Pride Festival**, held over two weeks at the beginning of July – check out ⓦwww.gay.brighton.co.uk. In May, the three-week-long **Brighton Festival** (ⓣ01273/709709, ⓦwww.brighton-festival.org.uk) includes funfairs, exhibitions, street theatre and concerts from classical to jazz. For up-to-date details of **what's on**, there's an array of free listings magazines available from the tourist office, or check out the website ⓦwww.brighton.co.uk.

Cafés

Bona Foodie 21 St James's St, Kemp Town. Delicatessen with colourful, cosy café at the back, serving excellent baguettes; choose from the speciality patés and cheeses or come early for lunching in.

The Dorset corner of Gardner St and North Rd. Bar, café and restaurant rolled into one, with delicious international vegetarian dishes and real cream teas.

Fringe Bar Café 10 Kensington Gardens. Small, smart bar, with a terrace for watching life in the North Laine go by, serving good breakfasts, homemade burgers and salads. There's a restaurant below as well.

Mock Turtle 4 Pool Valley. Old-fashioned tea shop crammed with bric-a-brac and inexpensive homemade cakes. Closed Sun & Mon.

The Sanctuary 51–55 Brunswick St East, Hove ✆01273/770002. Cool and arty vegetarian café with a relaxed ambience and cellar performance venue.

Restaurants

Al Duomo 7 Pavilion Buildings ✆01273/326741. Brilliant pizzeria, with a wood-burning oven. There's a more intimate sister restaurant, *Al Forno*, at 36 East St (✆01273/324905). Inexpensive.

Black Chapati 12 Circus Parade ✆01273/699011. Innovative Asian cooking with Japanese and Thai influences as well as more conventional Indian dishes. Something of a Brighton landmark despite its out-of-the-way location, more than a mile inland, at the point where the London road enters town. Moderate.

Bombay Aloo 39 Ship St ✆01273/776038. No flock wallpaper and an all-you-can-eat veggie buffet for a fiver – what more could you ask for? Inexpensive.

Browns 3–4 Duke St ✆01273/323501. A mixture of meat, seafood and pasta dishes as well as traditional favourites like Guinness-marinated steak-and-mushroom pie, served in a Continental setting. Moderate.

Casa Don Carlos 5 Union St ✆01273/327177. Small, long-established tapas bar in the Lanes with outdoor seating and daily specials. Also serves more substantial Spanish dishes and drinks. Inexpensive.

English's Oyster Bar 29–31 East St ✆01273/327980. Three fishermen's cottages knocked together to house a marble and brass oyster bar and a red velvet dining room. Seafood's the speciality with a mouthwatering menu and better value than you might expect, especially the set menus. Expensive.

Food for Friends 17 Prince Albert St ✆01273/202310. Brighton's ever-popular wholefood veggie eatery is imaginative enough to please die-hard meat-eaters too. It's usually busy, but well worth the squeeze. Moderate.

Le Gastronome 3 Hampton Place ✆01273/777399. Well known for its good-value classic French cuisine, friendly service and outstanding selection of wines. Closed Sun & Mon. Moderate.

Havana 32 Duke St ✆01273/773388. Very stylish continental brasserie with just a hint of tropical ambience. The menu is French influenced – the lunchtime deal is particularly good value. Expensive.

Melrose Restaurant 132 King's Rd ✆01273/326520. Traditional and decent seafront establishment that has been serving seafood, roasts and custard-covered puddings for over forty years. Inexpensive.

Terre-à-Terre 71 East St ✆01273/729051. Imaginative, global, veggie cuisine in a modern arty setting. Closed Mon lunch. Moderate–Expensive.

The Tin Drum 95–97 Dyke Rd ✆01273/777575. Buzzing Continental-style café-bar and restaurant with a taste for Baltic-rim cooking and a blend of Eastern European influences; fresh seasonal ingredients and speciality vodkas. Moderate.

Wai Kika Moo Kau 11 Kensington Gardens ✆01273/671117. Slightly distressed decor at this funky global veggie café/restaurant with everything from Thai curry to aubergine bake – all for around £5. Inexpensive.

Yum Yum Noodle Bar 22–23 Sydney St ✆01273/606777. Serves anything Southeast Asian – Chinese, Thai, Indonesian and Malaysian noodle dishes – situated above a Chinese supermarket. Lunch only. Inexpensive.

Pubs and bars

The Cricketers 15 Black Lion St. Just west of the Lanes, this is Brighton's oldest pub and it looks it too; very popular with good daytime pub grub served in its Courtyard Bar.

Dr Brighton's 16 King's Rd. Popular gay venue.

The Fish Bowl 74 East St. A popular pre-club choice for its range of music – sometimes better than the clubs themselves – and a good daytime menu.

Font & Firkin Union St. Spacious converted chapel with a bar in place of the altar and occasional live music.

Grand Central Bar 29–30 Surrey St. Cool, light and comfy bar opposite the station. Exemplary, well-priced breakfasts and snacks; live jazz and funk at weekends.

The Great Eastern 103 Trafalgar St. Relaxing pub with bare boards and bookshelves, lots of real ales and malt whiskies, and no fruit machines or TV.

The Greys 105 Southover St. Old-fashioned pub with an open fire, stone floors and wooden benches, plus good food and Belgian beers. Frequent live bands.

Hector's House 52 Grand Parade. Big bare-boards-and-sofa student pub that has nightly pre-club music (except Mon) with in-house DJs.

The Prince Albert 48 Trafalgar St. A listed lbuilding, right by the train station, popular with students. Live rock upstairs, real ale downstairs; regular theme nights.

Sumo 8–12 Middle St. Designer-cool Pacific-rim bar with DJs spinning R&B and hip-hop, plus Internet access.

Nightlife

Club New York 11 Dyke Rd ☎01273/208678. Salsa seven nights a week upstairs and a mixture of everything from Sixties nights to highlife downstairs.

Concorde 2 Madeira Shelter, Madeira Drive ☎01273/772770, ⓦwww .concorde2.co.uk. Live music venue, with an

admirably eclectic booking policy; also has club nights at the weekend.

Escape 10 Marine Parade ☎01273/606906, ⓦwww.theescapeclub.co.uk. Brighton's trendiest nightclub packs them in night after night, specializing in funk and house.

Funky Buddha Lounge 169 King's Road Arches ☎01273/ 725541. Tiny venue renowned for progressive house, breakbeats and soul.

Hanbury Ballroom St George's Rd, ☎01273/605789. Kemp Town's answer to mainstream clubs – anything from Japanese manga music to jamming on laptops, plus party nights.

Pool 8–9 Marine Parade ☎01273/624.091. Small, smart gay club that puts on special nights and cabaret. Women's night on first and third Fri of month.

Revenge 32 Old Steine ☎01273/606064, ⓦwww.revenge.co.uk. The south's largest gay club with Mon night cabarets plus upfront dance and retro boogie on two floors.

The Zap 180–192 Kings Rd Arches ☎01273/202407. Brighton's most durable club, right on the seafront spanning Seventies and Eighties disco and funky house; dress up.

Mid-Sussex

The principal attraction of **Mid-Sussex** is its wealth of fine gardens, ranging from the majestic **Sheffield Park** to the luscious flowerbeds of **Nymans** and the landscaped lakes of **Leonardslee**. Exploring this region by public transport isn't really feasible unless you take your bike on the train; tourist information is thin on the ground too – it's best to get clued up at Brighton's tourist office beforehand.

Sheffield Park and the Bluebell Railway

Around twenty miles northeast of Brighton the centrepiece of the country estate of **Sheffield Park** is a Gothic mansion built for Lord Sheffield by James Wyatt. The house is closed to the public, but you can roam around the hundred-acre **gardens** (Jan & Feb Sat & Sun 10.30am–4pm; March–Oct Tues–Sun & public holidays 10.30am–6pm; Nov & Dec Tues–Sun 10.30am–4pm; £5; combined ticket with Bluebell Railway £11; NT), which were laid out by Capability Brown. A mile southwest of the gardens lies the southern terminus of the **Bluebell Railway** (May–Sept daily; Oct–April Sat, Sun & school holidays; day ticket £8.50; ☎01825/722370 24hr information line; ⓦwww.bluebell-railway.co.uk), whose vintage steam locomotives chuff nine miles north via Horsted Keynes to Kingscote. Although the service gets extremely crowded at weekends – especially in May, when the bluebells blossom in the woods through which the line passes – it's an entertaining and nostalgic way of travelling through the Sussex countryside and your day ticket lets you go to and fro as often as you like.

Nymans and Leonardslee

Fifteen miles north of Brighton, **Nymans** (March to early Nov Wed–Sun 11am–6pm; early Nov to Feb Sat & Sun 11am–4pm; £6.20; NT), near the village of Handcross (bus #273), is one of the southeast's greatest gardens. Created by Ludwig Messel, an inspired gardener and plant collector, the gardens contain a valuable collection of exotic trees and shrubs as well as more everyday plants, of which the colourful rhododendrons are particularly prolific. The highlight of the series of enclosures and gardens is the large, romantic walled garden, almost hidden from sight by an abundance of climbing plants and housing a collection of rare Himalayan magnolia trees. The gardens are centred on the picturesque ruins of a mock-Tudor manor house, now covered in wisteria, roses and honeysuckle, and are laced with gently sloping paths linking the huge beds of rhododendrons, azaleas and roses.

Four miles southwest of Nymans, the highly picturesque gardens at **Leonardslee** (daily: April–Oct 9.30am–6pm, last admission 4.30pm; £5, £7/£8 in May) lie near the village of Crabtree (bus #107). Set in a wooded valley, the seventy-acre site is crisscrossed by steep paths, which link six lakes created – like those at Sheffield Park – in the sixteenth century to power waterwheels for iron foundries. The range of flora is especially impressive, featuring many hybrid species of rhododendron that were created specifically for this garden and are at their best in May. Wallabies, sika and fallow deer roam freely, adding to the Edenic atmosphere.

Arundel and around

The hilltop town of **ARUNDEL**, eighteen miles west of Brighton, has for seven centuries been the seat of the dukes of Norfolk, whose fine castle looks over the valley of the River Arun. The medieval town's well-preserved appearance and picturesque setting draws in the crowds on summer weekends, but at any other time a visit reveals one of West Sussex's least spoilt old towns. Arundel also has a unique place in English cricket: traditionally, the first match of every touring side is played against the Duke of Norfolk's XI on the ground beneath the castle and other matches are played regularly throughout the summer. North of here lie two contrasting sites: **Bignor Roman Villa**, containing some of the best Roman mosaics in the country, and the grand seventeenth-century **Petworth House**, replete with an impressive collection of paintings.

Arundel Castle, towering over the High Street (April–Oct Mon–Fri & Sun noon–5pm; castle, grounds & chapel £9; grounds & chapel £3.50), is what first catches the eye and, despite its medieval appearance, most of what you see is little more than a century old. The structure dates from Norman times, but was ruined during the Civil War, then lavishly reconstructed from 1718 onwards. From the top of the keep, you can see the current duke's spacious residence and the pristine castle grounds. Inside the castle, the renovated quarters include the impressive **Barons Hall** and the **library**, which boasts paintings by Gainsborough, Holbein and Van Dyck. On the edge of the castle grounds, the fourteenth-century **Fitzalan Chapel** houses tombs of past dukes of Norfolk including twin effigies of the seventh duke – one as he looked when he died and, underneath, one of his emaciated corpse. The Catholic chapel belongs to the Norfolk estate, but is actually physically joined to the **Church of St Nicholas**, the parish church, whose entrance is in London Road. It is separated from the altar of the main Anglican church by an iron grille and a glass screen. Although traditionally Catholics, the dukes of Norfolk have shrewdly played down their papal allegiance in sensitive times – such as during the Tudor era when two of the third duke's nieces, Anne Boleyn and Catherine Howard, became Henry VIII's wives.

West of the parish church, further along London Road, is Arundel's other major landmark, the towering Gothic bulk of **Arundel Cathedral** (April–Oct daily 9am–6pm; Nov–March 9am–dusk). Constructed in the 1870s by the fifteenth duke of Norfolk over the town's former Catholic church, the cathedral's spire was designed by John Hansom, inventor of the hansom cab, the earliest taxi. Inside are the enshrined remains of St Philip Howard, the fourth duke's son, exhumed from the Fitzalan Chapel after his canonization in 1970. Following his wayward youth, Howard returned to the Catholic fold at a time when the Armada's defeat saw anti-Catholic feelings soar. Caught fleeing overseas and sentenced to death for praying for Spanish victory, he spent the next decade in the Tower of London, where he died. The cathedral's impressive outline is more appealing than the interior, but it fits in well with the townscape of the medieval seaport. The rest of Arundel is pleasant to wander round, with the antique shop-lined Maltravers and Arun streets being the most attractive thoroughfares.

Practicalities

Arundel is served by regular trains from London Victoria, Portsmouth, Brighton and Chichester. The **train station** is half a mile south of the town centre over the river on the A27, with **buses** arriving either on High Street or River Road. The **tourist office** is at 61 High St (April–Oct Mon–Sat 10am–6pm, Sun 10am–4pm; Nov–March daily 10am–3pm; ☎01903/882268, Ⓦwww.sussexbythesea.com). The best **accommodation** options are the ornate rooms of the genial Georgian *Town House*, 65 High St (☎01903/883847, Ⓦwww.thetownhouse.co.uk; ❹), the elegant eighteenth-century *Byass House*, 59 Maltravers St (☎01903/882129, Ⓦwww.byasshouse.co .uk; no credit cards; ❹), or the less expensive *Woodpeckers*, 15 Dallaway Rd (☎01903/883948; no smoking; no credit cards; ❷), a modern house on the outskirts of town. Arundel's **youth hostel** (☎0870/770 5676; £11.50) is in a large Georgian house by the river at Warningcamp, a mile and a half northeast of town. You can **camp** here, or try the *Maynards* site (☎01903/882075) at the top of the hill on the A27 two miles southeast of town.

If your pocket is up to it, first choice for **food** is the *Town House* (see above; closed Mon) where you dine under a spectacular Italian gilded ceiling. Otherwise try *The Muse* (☎01903/883477; closed Sun eve & Mon) at 2–8 Castle Mews, or the restaurant attached to the *White Hart* pub over the river at 3 Queen St (☎01903/882374). *Butlers Wine Bar*, 25 Tarrant St (☎01903/882222; closed Sun eve), complete with an indoor vine, is a popular choice for steak-lovers, while further down the same road at no. 41, *The Eagle* is the best real-ale **pub** in town.

Bignor and Petworth

Six miles north of Arundel, the excavated second-century ruins of the **Bignor Roman Villa** (March & April Tues–Sun 10am–5pm; May & Oct daily 10am–5pm; June–Sept daily 10am–6pm; £3.50) include some well-preserved mosaics, of which the Ganymede is the most outstanding. The site, first excavated between 1811 and 1819, is superbly situated at the base of the South Downs and features the longest extant section of mosaic in England, as well as the remains of a hypocaust, the underfloor heating system developed by the Romans.

Adjoining the pretty little village of **PETWORTH**, eleven miles north of Arundel, **Petworth House** (April–Oct Mon–Wed, Sat & Sun 11am–5.30pm; park daily 8am–dusk; £7, park free; NT) is one of the southeast's most impressive stately homes. Built in the late seventeenth century, the house contains an outstanding art collection, with paintings by Van Dyck, Titian, Gainsborough, Bosch, Reynolds, Blake and Turner – the last a frequent guest here. Highlights of the interior decor are Louis Laguerre's murals around the **Grand Staircase** and the **Carved Room**, where work by Grinling Gibbons and Holbein's full-length portrait of Henry VIII can be seen. The seven-hundred-acre grounds were landscaped by Capability Brown and are considered one of his finest achievements. The extensive **Servants' Quarters**, connected by a tunnel to the main house, contain an impressive series of kitchens bearing the latest technological kitchenware of the 1870s.

To get to Petworth by **public transport** from Arundel involves a train journey to Pulborough station from where you can pick up the regular Stagecoach Coastline #1 bus. Petworth's **tourist office** is on the Market Square (April–Sept Mon–Sat 10am–5pm, Sun 11am–4pm; March & Oct Mon–Sat 10am–4pm; Nov & Dec Wed–Sat 10am–3pm; Jan & Feb Fri–Sat 10am–4pm; ☎01798/343523, ⓦwww.chichester.gov.uk). For a memorable night's **stay**, book in at the converted *Old Railway Station* (☎01798/342346, ⓦwww .old-station.co.uk; ❺), two miles south of Petworth on the A285 Chichester road.

Chichester and around

The county town of West Sussex and its only city, **CHICHESTER** is an attractive, if stuffy, market town, which began life as a Roman settlement – the Roman cruciform street plan is still evident in the four-quadrant symmetry of the town centre, spread around the Market Cross. The city has built itself up as one of southern England's cultural centres, hosting the **Chichester Festival** (ⓦwww.chifest.org.uk) for two weeks in July; its focus is a fairly safe programme of middlebrow plays, though the studio theatre is a bit more adventurous; for the latest details check their website. The racecourse at **Goodwood Park**, north of the city, hosts one of England's most fashionable racing events at the same time. The Gothic cathedral is the chief permanent attraction in the city, but two miles west of the town are the restored Roman ruins of **Fishbourne**, one of the most visited ancient sites in the county.

The City

The main streets lead off to the compass's cardinal points from the Gothic **Market Cross**, a bulky octagonal rotunda topped by ornate finials and a crown lantern spire, and built in 1501 to provide shelter for the market traders, although it appears far too small for its function.

A short stroll down West Street brings you to the neat form of the **Cathedral** (daily: Easter to mid-Sept 7.30am–7pm; mid-Sept to Easter 7.30am–5pm), whose slender spire – a nineteenth-century addition – is visible out at sea. Building began in the 1070s, but the church was extensively rebuilt following a fire a century later and has been only minimally modified since about 1300, except for the spire and the unique, freestanding fifteenth-century bell tower, which now houses the cathedral shop. The **interior** is renowned for its contemporary devotional art, which includes a stained glass window by Marc Chagall and an enormous altar-screen tapestry by John Piper. Other points of interest are the sixteenth-century painting in the north transept of the past bishops of Chichester, and the fourteenth-century Fitzalan tomb which inspired a poem by Philip Larkin, *An Arundel Tomb*. However, the highlight is a pair of reliefs in the south aisle, close to the tapestry – created around 1140, they show the raising of Lazarus and Christ at the gate of Bethany. Originally highly coloured, the reliefs once featured semiprecious stones set in the figures' eyes and are among the finest Romanesque stone carvings in England.

Off South Street, in the well-preserved Georgian quadrant of the city known as the Pallants, you'll find **Pallant House Gallery**, 9 North Pallant (Tues–Sat 10am–5pm; Sun & public holidays 12.30–5pm; £4). Stone dodos stand guard over the gates of this fine mansion, which houses artefacts and furniture from the early eighteenth century. Modern works of art are also included, among them pieces by Henry Moore, Barbara Hepworth and Graham Sutherland.

Crossing East Street and heading north up Little London brings you to the **Chichester District Museum** (Tues–Sat 10am–5.30pm; free), housed in an old white weatherboarded corn store. Inside, the modest but entertaining display on local life includes a portable oven carried by Joe Faro, the city pieman, as well as the portable stocks used for the ritual humiliation of petty criminals. The **Guildhall** (June to mid-Sept Sat noon–4pm; free), a branch museum within a thirteenth-century Franciscan church in the middle of Priory Park, at the north end of Little London, has some well-preserved medieval frescoes. It was formerly a town hall and court of law, where the poet, painter and visionary William Blake was tried for sedition in 1804.

Practicalities

Chichester's **train station** lies on Stockbridge Road, with the **bus station** across the road at South Street. From either station it's a ten-minute walk north to the Market Cross, passing the **tourist office** at 29a South St (April–Sept Mon–Sat 9.15am–5.15pm, Sun 10am–4pm; Oct–March closed Sun; ☎01243/775888, ⓦwww.chichester.gov.uk).

There should be no problem finding **accommodation** except during the festival. Central B&B options include the brick and flint *Riverside Lodge*, 7 Market Ave, outside the Pallants quarter (☎01243/783164, ⓦwww .riverside-lodge-chichester.co.uk; no smoking; no credit cards; ❷), and the 200-year-old *Friary Close*, Friary Lane (☎01243/527294, ⓦwww .tuckedup.com; ❸), just inside the city wall. You can **camp** at the *Red House Farm*, Brookers Lane, Earnley (☎01243/512959; closed Nov–Easter), six miles southwest of town, a mile or so from the beach.

For something to **eat**, both the *Toad* pub, formerly a church in West Street and a lively spot for snacks and meals, and the intimate and more expensive *Café Coco*, 13 South St (☎01243/786989; closed Sun), specializing in French cuisine, are close to the cathedral. *Purchase's Wine Bar*, 31 North St (☎01243/537532; closed Sun), serves a good selection of Danish open sand-wiches, pâtés and salads, while *The Ship*, also on North Street, is a good place for a **drink**, as is *The Park Tavern*, a convivial pub serving excellent Gale's ales on Priory Lane, overlooking Priory Park.

Fishbourne Roman Palace

Fishbourne, two miles west of Chichester and easily accessible by bus and train, is the largest and best-preserved Roman palace in the country

(March–July, Sept & Oct daily 10am–5pm; Aug daily 10am–6pm; Nov, Dec & Feb Sat & Sun 10am–4pm; £5). Roman relics have long been turning up hereabouts, and in 1960 a workman unearthed their source – the site of a depot used by the invading Romans in 43 AD which is thought later to have become the vast, hundred-room palace of the Romanized Celtic aristocrat, Cogidubnus. A pavilion has been built over the north wing of the excavated remains, where floor mosaics depict Fishbourne's famous dolphin-riding cupid as well as the more usual geometric patterns.

Like the more evocative remains at Bignor (see p.226), only the residential wing of the former quadrangle has been excavated – other parts of the dwelling fulfilled mundane service roles and probably lacked the mosaics that give both sites their singular appeal. The underfloor heating system has also been well restored and an audiovisual programme gives a fuller picture of the palace as it was in Roman times. The extensive gardens attempt to re-create the appearance of the palace grounds as they would have been then.

Travel details

Buses

For information on all local and national bus services, contact Traveline ☎0870/608 2608 (daily 7am–9pm), ⊕www.traveline.org.uk.

Arundel to: Chichester (Mon–Sat, hourly; 1hr 5min); Brighton (Mon–Sat every 30min, 1hr 55min).

Battle to: Hastings (Mon–Sat hourly; 30mins).

Brighton to: Chichester (Mon–Sat every 30min, Sun hourly; 2hr 30min); Eastbourne (Mon–Sat every 20min, Sun every 30min; 1hr 20min–1hr 30min); Lewes (Mon–Sat every 15min, Sun hourly; 30–40min); London Victoria (hourly; 2hr 5min); Portsmouth (Mon–Sat every 30min, Sun hourly; 3hr 30min); Tunbridge Wells Mon–Sat hourly, Sun 7; 1hr 45min).

Broadstairs to: Dover (Mon–Sat hourly; 40min); Margate (Mon–Fri 8 daily; 1hr); Ramsgate (every 20–30min; 15min).

Canterbury to: Deal (Mon–Sat hourly, Sun 4; 1hr 5min); Dover (Mon–Sat hourly; 40min); London Victoria (hourly; 2hr); Margate (Mon–Sat hourly; 1hr 25min); Ramsgate Mon–Sat hourly; 40min); Sandwich (Mon–Sat hourly, Sun 4; 45min); Whitstable (Mon–Sat every 15min, Sun hourly; 35min).

Chatham to: Rochester (every 10min; 5min).

Chichester to: Arundel (Mon–Sat, hourly; 1hr 55min), Brighton (Mon–Sat every 30min, Sun hourly; 2hr 30min); Portsmouth (Mon–Sat every 30min, Sun hourly; 1hr 5min).

Deal to: Canterbury (Mon–Sat hourly, Sun 4; 1hr 5min); Dover (Mon–Sat hourly, Sun 6; 30min);

Sandwich (Mon–Sat hourly, Sun 4; 25min).

Dover to: Canterbury (Mon–Sat hourly; 40min); Deal Mon–Sat hourly, Sun 6; 30min); Hastings (Mon–Sat hourly, Sun 6; 2hr 40min); London Victoria (hourly; 2hr 40min–3hr 20min); Sandwich (Mon–Sat 8 daily; 55min).

Eastbourne to: Brighton (Mon–Sat every 20min, Sun every 30min; 1hr 20min–1hr 30min); Hastings (Mon–Sat every 30min, Sun hourly; 1hr 10min–1hr 55min).

Farnham to: Guildford (Mon–Sat 1–2 hourly, Sun hourly; 35min).

Gatwick Airport to: Brighton (every 30min; 45min); London Victoria (hourly; 1hr 20min).

Guildford to: Farnham (Mon–Sat 1–2 hourly, Sun hourly; 35min); London Victoria (6 daily; 1hr).

Hastings to: Eastbourne (Mon–Sat every 30min, Sun hourly; 1hr 10min–1hr 55min); Dover (Mon–Sat hourly, Sun 6; 2hr 40min); London Victoria (2 daily; 2hr 50min–3hr 50min); Rye (Mon–Sat hourly, Sun 6; 45 min).

Hythe to: Rye (Mon–Sat hourly, Sun 6; 1hr 10min).

Lewes to: Brighton (Mon–Sat every 15 min, Sun hourly; 30–40min); Tunbridge Wells (Mon–Sat hourly, Sun 7; 1hr 30min).

Margate to: Broadstairs (Mon–Fri 8 daily; 1hr); Canterbury (Mon–Sat hourly; 1hr 25min); London Victoria (5 daily; 2hr 30min); Ramsgate (Mon–Sat every 30min; 40min).

Ramsgate to: Broadstairs (every 20–30min; 15min); Canterbury (Mon–Sat hourly; 40min); London Victoria (5 daily; 3hr); Margate (Mon–Sat every 30min; 40min).

Rochester to: Chatham (every 10min; 5min).
Rye to: Hastings Mon–Sat hourly, Sun 6; 45 min); Hythe (Mon–Sat hourly, Sun 6; 1hr 10min).
Sandwich to: Canterbury (Mon–Sat hourly, Sun 4; 45min); Deal (Mon–Sat hourly, Sun 4; 25min); Dover (Mon–Sat 8 daily; 55min).
Sevenoaks to: Tunbridge Wells (Mon–Sat hourly; 50min).
Tunbridge Wells to: Brighton Mon–Sat hourly, Sun 7; 1hr 45min); Lewes (Mon–Sat hourly, Sun 7; 1hr 30min); Sevenoaks (Mon–Sat hourly; 50min).
Whitstable to: Canterbury (Mon–Sat, every 15min, Sun hourly; 30min).

Trains

For information on all local and national rail services, contact National Rail Enquiries ☎ 08457/48 49 50, ⓦ www.nationalrail.co.uk.
Arundel to: London Victoria (Mon–Sat every 30min, Sun hourly; 1hr 20min).
Battle to: Hastings (Mon–Sat every 30min, Sun hourly; 15min); London Charing Cross (every 30min; 1hr 20min); Sevenoaks (Mon–Sat every 30min, Sun hourly; 45min); Tunbridge Wells (Mon–Sat every 30min, Sun hourly; 30min).
Brighton to: Chichester (Mon–Sat every 30min, Sun hourly; 50min); Gatwick Airport (every 15min; 25–40min); Hastings (Mon–Sat every 30min, Sun hourly; 1hr 10min); Lewes (Mon–Sat every 15min, Sun every 30min; 15min); London Victoria (every 30min; 1hr–1hr 20min); London King's Cross (Mon–Sat every 15min, Sun every 30min; 1hr 15min); London Bridge (Mon–Sat every 15min, Sun every 30min; 1hr); Portsmouth Harbour (hourly; 1hr 30min).
Broadstairs to: London Victoria (Mon–Sat every 30min, Sun hourly; 1hr 50min); Ramsgate (every 20–30min; 5min).
Canterbury East to: Dover Priory (Mon–Fri every 30min, Sat & Sun hourly; 40min); London Victoria (Mon–Sat every 30min, Sun hourly; 1hr 20min).
Canterbury West to: London Charing Cross (hourly; 1hr 40min); Ramsgate (hourly; 20min).
Chatham to: Dover Priory (Mon–Sat every 30min, Sun hourly; 1hr 10min); London Victoria (every 30min; 1hr).

Chichester to: London Victoria (Mon–Sat every 30min, Sun hourly; 1hr 45min); Portsmouth Harbour (Mon–Sat every 30min, Sun hourly; 40min).
Dover Priory to: London Charing Cross (Mon–Fri every 30min, Sat & Sun hourly; 1hr 40min); London Victoria (Mon–Fri every 30min, Sat & Sun hourly; 1hr 50min).
Eastbourne to: Gatwick Airport (every 30min; 1hr); Hastings (Mon–Sat every 30min, Sun hourly; 30min); Lewes (Mon–Sat every 20min, Sun hourly; 20min); London Victoria (Mon–Sat every 30min, Sun hourly; 1hr 35min).
Farnham to: Aldershot (for connections to London Waterloo; Mon–Sat 1–2 hourly, Sun hourly; 10min); Guildford (Mon–Sat 1–2 hourly, Sun hourly; 35min).
Gatwick Airport to: Brighton (every 15min; 30min); London Victoria (very frequent; 30min).
Guildford to: Farnham (Mon–Sat 1–2 hourly, Sun hourly; 35min); London Waterloo (Mon–Sat every 20min, Sun hourly; 35min).
Hastings to: London Victoria (hourly; 2hr); Rye (hourly; 30min).
Lewes to: Brighton (Mon–Sat every 15min, Sun every 30min; 15min); London Victoria (Mon–Sat every 30min, Sun hourly; 1hr 10min).
Margate to: Canterbury West (hourly; 30min); London Victoria (Mon–Sat every 30min, Sun hourly; 1hr 50min).
Ramsgate to: London Victoria (Mon–Sat every 30min, Sun hourly; 1hr 50min).
Rochester to: Dover Priory (Mon–Sat every 30min, Sun hourly; 1hr 10min); London Charing Cross (every 30min; 1hr 15min); London Victoria (Mon–Sat every 15–20min, Sun every 30min; 45min).
Rye to: Hastings (hourly; 20min).
Sandwich to: Dover Priory (hourly; 30min); Ramsgate (hourly; 15min).
Sevenoaks to: London Charing Cross (Mon–Sat every 20min; 30min).
Tunbridge Wells to: London Charing Cross (Mon–Sat every 30min, Sun hourly; 55min).
Whitstable to: London Victoria (hourly; 1hr 20min); Ramsgate (Mon–Sat every 30min, Sun hourly; 30min).

Hampshire, Dorset and Wiltshire

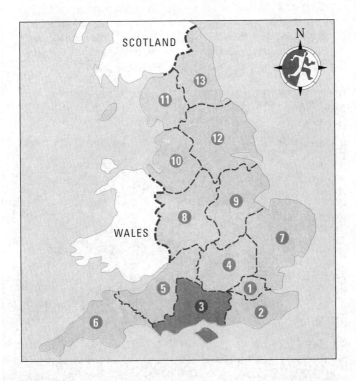

CHAPTER 3

Highlights

* **Cowes Week, Isle of Wight** This yachting jamboree draws thousands, infecting even the staunchest landlubbers. **See p.245**

* **Wykeham Arms, Winchester** Ancient tavern serving gourmet-standard food alongside the real ales. **See p.250**

* **The New Forest** William the Conqueror's old hunting ground, and home to wild ponies and deer, the New Forest is ideal for walking, biking and riding. **See p.251**

* **Corfe Castle** Picturesque ruins with a weathered, romantic charm. **See p.258**

* **Durdle Door** This crumbling natural arch stands at the end of a splendid beach – a great place for walkers and swimmers alike. **See p.259**

* **Avebury** This crude stone circle has a more powerful appeal than nearby Stonehenge, not least for its great size and easy accessibility, in a peaceful village setting. **See p.275**

△ New Forest Ponies

3

Hampshire, Dorset and Wiltshire

T he distant past is perhaps more tangible in **Hampshire** (often abbreviated to "Hants"), **Dorset** and **Wiltshire** than in any other part of England. Predominantly rural, these three counties overlap substantially with the ancient kingdom of **Wessex**, whose most famous ruler, Alfred, repulsed the Danes in the ninth century and came close to establishing the first unified state in England. Before Wessex came into being, however, many earlier civilizations had left their stamp on the region. The chalky uplands of Wiltshire boast several of Europe's greatest Neolithic sites, including **Stonehenge** and **Avebury**, while in Dorset you'll find **Maiden Castle**, the most striking Iron Age hill fort in the country, and the **Cerne Abbas Giant**, source of many a legend. The Romans tramped all over these southern counties, leaving the most conspicuous signs of their occupation at the amphitheatre of **Dorchester** – though that town is more closely associated with the novels of Thomas Hardy and his distinctively gloomy vision of Wessex.

None of the landscapes of this region could be described as grand or wild, but the countryside is consistently seductive, not least the crumbling fossil-bearing cliffs around **Lyme Regis**, the managed woodlands of the **New Forest** and the gentle, open curves of **Salisbury Plain**. Its towns are also generally modest and slow-paced, with the notable exceptions of the two great maritime bases of **Portsmouth** and, to a lesser extent, **Southampton**, a fair proportion of whose visitors are simply passing through on their way to the more genteel pleasures of the **Isle of Wight**. The two great cathedral cities in these parts, **Salisbury** and **Winchester**, and the seaside resort of **Bournemouth** see most tourist traffic, and the great houses of **Wilton**, **Stourhead**, **Longleat** and **Kingston Lacy** also attract the crowds, but you don't have to wander far off the beaten track to encounter medieval churches, manor houses and unspoilt country inns a-plenty – there are few parts of England in which an aimless meander can be so rewarding.

Portsmouth

Britain's foremost naval station, **PORTSMOUTH** occupies the bulbous peninsula of Portsea Island, on the eastern flank of a huge, easily defended

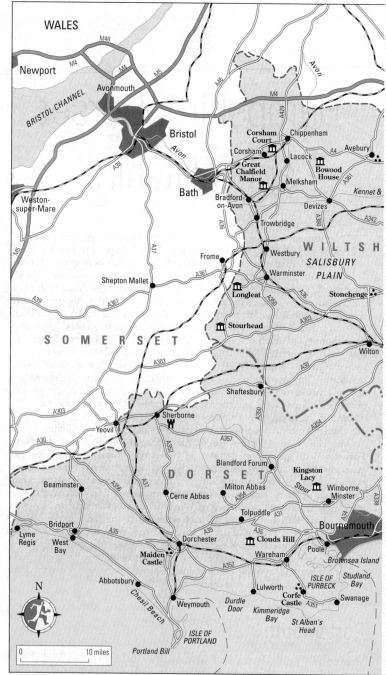

WALES

Newport

M48

M4

M4

M5

Avonmouth

BRISTOL CHANNEL

Bristol

Avon

A46

A429

M4

Avon

Corsham Court

Chippenham

Corsham

Lacock

A4

Avebury

Great Chalfield Manor

Bowood House

A361

Bath

Melksham

Kennet &

Weston-super-Mare

A38

Bradford-on-Avon

A361

Devizes

A342

A36

Trowbridge

A360

A37

Frome

Westbury

WILTSH

A5

Shepton Mallet

A361

Warminster

SALISBURY PLAIN

A39

A361

Longleat

A350

A36

Stonehenge

A303

Stourhead

A303

Wilton

SOMERSET

A303

A30

A303

Shaftesbury

A354

A30

Sherborne

A350

Yeovil

A352

A357

Beaminster

A356

Blandford Forum

Kingston Lacy

Wimborne Minster

A338

A37

DORSET

Cerne Abbas

Milton Abbas

A354

Stour

A324

Bridport

A35

Tolpuddle

A31

Bournemouth

Lyme Regis

West Bay

Dorchester

A35

A35

Clouds Hill

Poole

Maiden Castle

Wareham

Brownsea Island

Abbotsbury

A352

ISLE OF PURBECK

Studland Bay

Chesil Beach

Lulworth

Corfe Castle

A351

Swanage

Weymouth

Durdle Door

Kimmeridge Bay

St Alban's Head

N

ISLE OF PORTLAND

Portland Bill

0   10 miles

Channel Islands ▼

Channel Islands & Cherbourg ▼

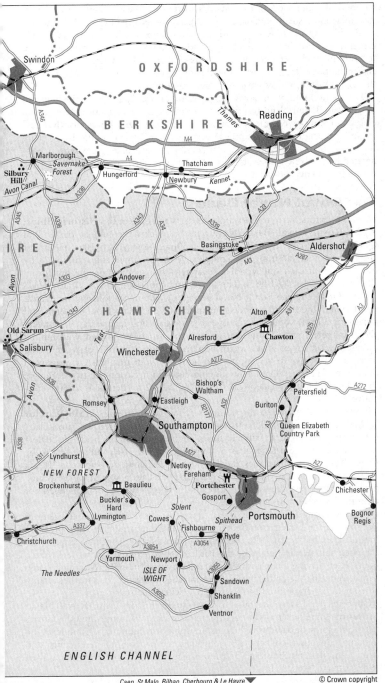

3

ENGLISH CHANNEL

Caen, St Malo, Bilbao, Cherbourg & Le Havre ▼

© Crown copyright

harbour. The ancient Romans raised a fortress on the northernmost edge of this inlet, and a small port developed during the Norman era, but this strategic location wasn't fully exploited until Tudor times, when Henry VII established the world's first dry dock here and made Portsmouth a royal dockyard. It has flourished ever since and nowadays Portsmouth is a large industrialized city, its harbour clogged with naval frigates, ferries bound for the continent or the Isle of Wight, and swarms of dredgers and tugs.

Due to its military importance, Portsmouth was heavily bombed during World War II, and bland tower blocks from the nadir of British architectural endeavour now give the city an ugly profile. Only **Old Portsmouth**, based around the original harbour, preserves some Georgian and a little Tudor character. East of here is **Southsea**, a residential suburb of terraces with a half-hearted resort strewn along its shingle beach, where a mass of B&Bs face stoic naval monuments and tawdry seaside amusements.

The Royal Naval Base

For most visitors, a trip to Portsmouth begins and ends at the **Historic Ships**, in the **Royal Naval Base** (ⓦwww.historicdockyard.co.uk) at the end of Queen Street (daily: April–Oct 10am–5.30pm; Nov–March 10am–5pm; last entry 1hr before closing). The complex comprises three ships and as many museums, with each ship visitable separately, though most people opt for an all-inclusive ticket (£14.85). The main attractions are *HMS Victory*, *HMS Warrior* (including the Royal Naval Museum), Action Stations (an interactive simulation of life aboard a modern naval frigate), the Mary Rose Museum, and a harbour tour. If you don't manage to do everything in one day, your ticket allows for return visits. Note that visits to the *Victory* are guided, with limited numbers at set times, so it's worth booking early to ensure a place, and even then you may have to wait up to two hours for your turn. Also, visitors with disabilities will have a hard time moving between decks on the two complete ships; a virtual tour by video (call ☎023/9272 2562 for details) is a good alternative.

Nearest the entrance to the complex is the youngest ship, **HMS Warrior** (£9.50), dating from 1860. It was Britain's first armoured, or "iron-clad" battleship, complete with sails and steam engines, and the pride of the fleet in its day. Longer and faster than any previous naval vessel, and the first to be fitted with washing machines, the *Warrior* was described by Napoleon III as a "black snake amongst the rabbits". The ship displays a wealth of weaponry, including rifles, pistols and sabres, though the *Warrior* was never challenged nor even fired a cannon in her 22 years at sea.

HMS Victory (£9.50) was already forty years old when she set sail from Portsmouth for Trafalgar on September 14, 1805, returning in triumph three months later, but bearing the corpse of Admiral Nelson. Shot by a sniper from a French ship at the height of the battle, Nelson expired below decks three hours later, having been assured that victory was in sight. Although badly damaged during the battle, the *Victory* continued in service for a further twenty years, before being retired to the dry dock where she rests today.

Opposite the *Victory*, various buildings house the exhaustive **Royal Naval Museum** (same ticket as *Warrior*). Tracing naval history from Alfred the Great's fleet to the present day, this is the most resistible attraction in the complex. One building contains a collection of jolly figureheads, Nelson memorabilia and nautical models, but coverage of a more recent conflict, the Falklands War of 1982, is treated very lightly.

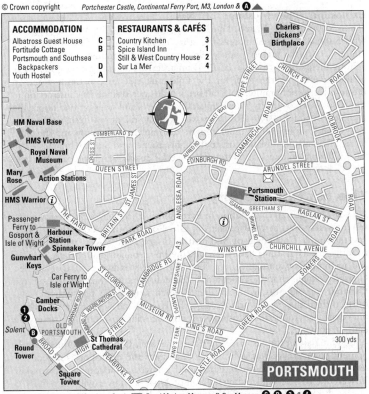

ACCOMMODATION

Albatross Guest House	C
Fortitude Cottage	B
Portsmouth and Southsea Backpackers	D
Youth Hostel	A

RESTAURANTS & CAFÉS

Country Kitchen	3
Spice Island Inn	1
Still & West Country House	2
Sur La Mer	4

Charles
Dickens'
Birthplace

N

HM Naval Base
HMS Victory
Royal Naval Museum
Mary Rose   Action Stations
HMS Warrior ⓘ
Passenger Ferry to Gosport & Isle of Wight   Harbour Station
Spinnaker Tower
Gunwharf Keys
Car Ferry to Isle of Wight
Camber Docks
Solent   OLD PORTSMOUTH
St Thomas Cathedral
Round Tower
Square Tower

CUMBERLAND ST
HOPE STREET   MARKET WAY   CHURCH ST   ROAD   LAKE   HOLBROOK
CROSS ST   ALFRED RD   EDINBURGH RD   COMMERCIAL   ROAD
QUEEN STREET   ST JAMES ST   ARUNDEL STREET
BRITAIN ST   ANGLESEA ROAD   ISAMBARD   GREETHAM ST   RAGLAN ST   ROAD
THE HARD   PARK ROAD   BRUNEL RD
WINSTON   CHURCHILL AVENUE   ROAD
ST GEORGE'S RD   CAMBRIDGE RD   HAMPSHIRE   A3   SOMERS
WARBLINGTON RD   MUSEUM RD   DAD ROAD   KING'S ROAD   GREEN ROAD
GUNWHARF ROAD   STREET   KING'S TERR
OLD   PORTSMOUTH   HIGH   CASTLE ROAD
BROAD ST   PEMBROKE RD

ⓘ

0   300 yds

PORTSMOUTH

Southsea, IoW Hovercraft, Southsea Castle, ▼ Royal Marines Museum, D-Day Museum, **C**, **D**, **3** & **4**

In a shed behind the *Victory* are the remains of the **Mary Rose** (£9.50), HenryVIII's flagship, which capsized before his eyes off Spithead in 1545 while engaging French intruders, sinking swiftly with almost all her seven-hundred-strong crew. In 1982 a massive conservation project successfully raised the remains of the hull, which silt had preserved beneath the seabed. The ship itself is less absorbing than the thousands of objects retrieved near the wreck, displayed in an exhibition close to the *Warrior*. Videos of the recovery operation are shown, as well as depictions of life aboard a sixteenth-century warship.

From the harbour

The naval theme is continued at the **Submarine Museum** on Haslar Jetty in Gosport (daily: April–Oct 10am–5.30pm; Nov–March 10am–4.30pm; last tour 1hr before closing; £4, or £7.20 with Explosion Museum), reached by taking the passenger ferry from Harbour train station jetty (daily 5.30am–midnight; £1.60 return), or, from the same place, the water-bus, which gives you a half-hour tour of the harbour before dropping you in Gosport (Easter–Oct 10.30am–5pm; £4). Allow yourself a couple of hours to explore these slightly creepy vessels – a guided tour inside *HMS Alliance* gives you an insight into life on board and the museum elaborates evocatively on the long history of submersible craft. Nearby, housed in the old armaments depot at Priddy's Hard,

Explosion! The Museum of Naval Firepower (April–Oct daily 10am–5.30pm; Nov–March, Thurs, Sat & Sun 10am–4.30pm; £5, or £7.20 with Submarine Museum) tells the story of naval warfare from the days of gunpowder to the present, much helped by computer animations.

From the pontoon beside *HMS Warrior*, ferries depart (Sun 2.45pm; £8, including entry to the fort) for the mile-long ride to **Spitbank Fort**, an offshore bastion of granite, iron and brick little altered since its construction in the 1860s. With over fifty rooms linked by passages and steps on two floors, the complex includes a 400-foot-deep well, which still draws fresh water from below the seafloor, and an inner courtyard complete with a café and sheltered terrace. The artificial island hosts pub nights, parties and Sunday lunches – call ☎01329/664286 or ask at the tourist office for details – and you can also sleep here (see opposite).

The rest of the city

Back at the Harbour train station in Portsmouth, it's a well-signposted twenty-minute walk south to what remains of **Old Portsmouth**. Along the way, you pass the simple **Cathedral of St Thomas** on the High Street, whose original twelfth-century features have been obscured by rebuilding after the Civil War and again in the twentieth century. The High Street ends at a maze of cobbled Georgian streets huddling behind a fifteenth-century wall protecting the **Camber**, or old port, where Walter Raleigh landed the first potatoes and tobacco from the New World. Nearby, the Round and Square Towers, which punctuate the Tudor fortifications, are popular vantage points for observing nautical activities.

Stretching along the historic waterfront, the sleek **Gunwharf Quays** development hosts a myriad of stylish cafés, restaurants and nightspots alongside the retail outlets. It's also the site of Portsmouth's newest attraction, the **Spinnaker Tower**, due to be completed by the end of 2004. The tower will rise a full 165 metres above the harbour, offering views over Portsmouth and up to twenty miles beyond from three viewing decks.

The only other point of interest in Portsmouth itself is **Charles Dickens' Birthplace** at 393 Old Commercial Rd (daily: April–Sept 10am–5pm; £2.50), but there are more sites of military interest a mile or so east in **Southsea**. The main attraction here is the **D-Day Museum** on Clarence Esplanade (daily: April–Sept 10am–5.30pm; Oct–March 10am–5pm; last entry 1hr before closing; £5), focusing on Portsmouth's role as the main assembly point for the D-Day invasion in World War II, code-named "Operation Overlord". The museum's most striking exhibit is the 270-foot long *Overlord Embroidery*, which illustrates the Normandy landings. Next door to the museum, the squat profile of **Southsea Castle** (April–Oct daily 10am–5pm; £2.50), built from the remains of Beaulieu Abbey (see p.252), may have been the spot from where Henry VIII watched the *Mary Rose* sink in 1545. A mile further along the shoreside South Parade, just past South Parade pier, the **Royal Marines Museum** (daily: June–Sept 10am–5pm; Oct–May 10am–4.30pm; last entry 1hr before closing; £4.75) describes the origins and greatest campaigns of the navy's elite fighting force.

More compelling is **Portchester Castle** (daily: April–Sept 10am–6pm; Oct 10am–5pm; Nov–March 10am–4pm; £3.50; EH), six miles out of the centre, just past the marina development at Port Solent. Built by the Romans in the third century this fortification boasts the finest surviving example of Roman walls in northern Europe – still over twenty feet high and incorporating some twenty bastions. The Normans felt no need to make any substantial alterations when they moved in, but a castle was later built within Portchester's precincts by Henry II, which Richard II extended and Henry V used as his garrison when assembling the army that was to fight the Battle of Agincourt. Today its grassy enclosure makes a sheltered spot for a congenial game of cricket or a kickabout with a football.

Practicalities

Portsmouth's main **train station** is in the city centre, but the line continues to **Harbour Station**, the most convenient stop for the main sights and old town. Passenger **ferries** leave from the jetty at Harbour Station for Ryde, on the Isle of Wight (see p.242), and Gosport, on the other side of Portsmouth Harbour. Wightlink car ferries depart from the ferry port off Gunwharf Road for Fishbourne on the Isle of Wight (see p.242). There are three **tourist offices** (all ☎023/9282 6722, ⓦwww.visitportsmouth.co.uk) in Portsmouth, one on The Hard, by the entrance to the dockyards (daily: Easter–Sept 9.30am–5.45pm; Oct–Easter 9.30am–5.15pm); another in the library at Guildhall Square, near the main train station (Mon–Sat 10am–5pm); and a third on Southsea's seafront, next to the Sea Life Centre (daily 9.30am–5.45pm).

The main concentration of **hotels and B&Bs** is south of the centre in Southsea, where you'll find the *Albatross Guest House*, 51 Waverley Rd (☎023/9282 8325; no smoking; no credit cards; ❶), dating from the 1860s and with nautically themed rooms. In Old Portsmouth, *Fortitude Cottage* overlooks the quayside at 51 Broad St (☎023/9282 3748, ⓦwww.fortitudecottage.co.uk; no smoking; ❷). There's a YHA **hostel** at Wymering Manor, Old Wymering Lane, Cosham (☎023/9237 5661, ⓔportsmouth@yha.org.uk; £10.25), ten minutes west of Cosham train station (or take bus #5 or #57), and an independent hostel, *Portsmouth and Southsea Backpackers*, at 4 Florence Rd, Southsea (☎023/9283 2495 or 9282 2963, ⓦwww.portsmouthbackpackers.co.uk; £12), with full facilities and some en-suite doubles (❶). Campers should head to *Southsea Leisure Park*, Melville Rd, Southsea (☎023/9273 5070, ⓔinfo@southsea-caravans-ltd.co.uk). More unusual accommodation is available at *Spitbank Fort* (☎023/9250 4207, ⓦwww.spitbankfort.co.uk; no credit cards; ❷), a man-made island one mile from Portsmouth Harbour in the middle of the Solent, accessible by ferry; the two very basic rooms here are available (weather permitting) between April and September.

Places to eat are surprisingly scarce in the old town, though you'll find a good range of hot and cold dishes at a couple of adjacent waterside hostelries in Bath Square, the *Spice Island Inn* and the *Still & West Country House*. In Southsea, try *Sur La Mer*, 69 Palmerston Rd (☎023/9287 6678; closed Sun), serving inexpensive French and seafood dishes, and *Country Kitchen*, 59 Marmion Rd, a vegetarian and vegan restaurant with newspapers on hand and free coffee refills (daytime only; closed Sun).

Southampton

A glance at the map gives some idea of the strategic maritime importance of **SOUTHAMPTON**, which stands on a triangular peninsula formed at the place where the rivers Itchen and Test flow into Southampton Water, an eight-mile inlet from the Solent. Sure enough, Southampton has figured in numerous stirring events: it witnessed the exodus of Henry V's Agincourt-bound army, the Pilgrim Fathers' departure in the *Mayflower* in 1620 and the maiden voyages of such ships as the *Queen Mary* and the *Titanic*. Unfortunately, since its pummelling by the Luftwaffe and some disastrous postwar planning, the thousand-year-old city is now a sprawling conurbation, with little to justify more than a fleeting visit.

Core of the modern town is the **Civic Centre**, a short walk east of the train station. Its clock tower is the most distinctive feature of the skyline, and it houses an excellent **art gallery** that's particularly strong on twentieth-century British artists such as Sutherland, Piper and Spencer (Tues–Sat 10am–5pm, Sun 1–4pm; free). The **Western Esplanade**, curving southward from the station, runs alongside the best remaining bits of the old city **walls**. Rebuilt after a French attack in 1338, they feature towers with evocatively chilly names – Windwhistle, Catchcold and **God's House Tower** – the last of these, at the southern end of the old town in Winkle Street, houses a **Museum of Archeology** (Tues–Fri 10am–5pm, Sat 10am–4pm, Sun 2–5pm; free). Best preserved of the city's seven gates is **Bargate**, at the opposite end of the old town, at the head of the High Street; an elaborate structure, cluttered with lions, classical figures and machicolations (defensive apertures through which missiles could be dropped), it was formerly the guildhall and court house.

Other ancient buildings survive amid the piecemeal redevelopment of the High Street area. The oldest church is **St Michael's**, to the west of the High Street, with a twelfth-century font of black Tournai marble. The nearby **Tudor House Museum**, in Bugle Street, is an impressive fifteenth-century timber-framed building, its grand banqueting hall and reconstructed Tudor garden outshining the sundry exhibits of Georgian, Victorian and early twentieth-century social history (the site is due to reopen after refurbishment in 2004: call ☎023 8063 5904 for opening times). Down at the southwest corner of the old town, by the seafront, the **Wool House** is a fine fourteenth-century stone warehouse; formerly used as a jail for Napoleonic prisoners, it now houses a **Maritime Museum** (Tues–Fri 10am–5pm, Sat 10am–4pm, Sun 2–5pm; free) with accounts of the heyday of ocean liners, and includes a huge model of the *Queen Mary* and various mementoes from the *Titanic*. The museum also offers the opportunity to listen to the recorded voices of various survivors of the *Titanic* tragedy relating their experiences.

Practicalities

Southampton's central **train station** is in Blechynden Terrace, west of the Civic Centre; the **bus** and **coach stations** are immediately south and north of the Civic Centre. The **tourist office** is at 9 Civic Centre Rd (Mon, Tues & Thurs–Sat 8.30am–5.30pm, Wed 10am–5.30pm; ☎023/8083 3333, Ⓦwww.southampton.gov.uk).

Southampton isn't a wildly attractive **place to stay**, but you can soak up the antique atmosphere at the four-hundred-year-old *Star* (☎023/8033 9939, Ⓦwww.thestarhotel.com; ❺) or the slightly younger *Dolphin* (☎023/8033 9955, Ⓔenquiries@thedolphin.co.uk; ❹), both halfway down the High Street. B&Bs include *Linden*, just north of the train station on the Polygon (☎023/8022 5653; no credit cards; ❶), and *Argyle Lodge*, 13 Landguard Road (☎023/8022 4063; ❶), also close to the station, where evening meals are available. The best **eating** places are clustered on Oxford Street, off Bernard Street from the High Street, for example *The Olive Tree* at no. 29 (☎023/8034 3333), serving moderately priced Mediterranean dishes, and with pavement seating and live music on Sundays, and the *Oxford Brasserie* at no. 35 (☎023/8063

5043), a relaxed place for baguettes, salads, pastas and fuller evening meals. As for **pubs**, try the tiny old *Platform Tavern* in Winkle Street, at the south end of the High Street, or the twelfth-century *Red Lion*, complete with minstrels' gallery at 55 High Street.

The Isle of Wight

Though a separate county since 1974, the lozenge-shaped **ISLE OF WIGHT** still has difficulty shaking off its image as a mere adjunct of rural southern England – comfortably off, scrupulously tidy and desperately unadventurous. Yet the island, which measures less than 23 miles at its widest point, packs a surprising variety of landscapes and coastal scenery within its bounds. North of the chalk ridge that runs across its centre, the terrain is low-lying woodland and pasture, deeply cut by meandering rivers, while southwards lies open chalky downland fringed by high cliffs. Two **Heritage Coast** paths follow the best of the shoreline, and a splendid array of well-preserved Victoriana provides added interest. Chief of these is **Osborne House**, near Cowes, originally designed as a summer retreat for the royal family, later Queen Victoria's permanent home after Albert died. Several other eminent Victorians also had close associations with the island: Tennyson lived at Freshwater, Dickens stayed and wrote in Winterbourne House (now also a hotel) in Bonchurch – the town where the poet and critic Swinburne grew up and is now buried – while Julia Margaret Cameron resided at Dimbola Lodge, where a museum commemorates her photographic work.

If you're dependent upon **public transport**, pick up the Southern Vectis bus route map and timetable (50p) from the tourist office, ferry office or bus

---

Sea routes to the Isle of Wight

Hovertravel ☏ 023/9281 1000 or 01983/811000, ⓦ www.hovertravel.co.uk. Year-round hovercraft service from Southsea to Ryde Mon–Fri 7.10am–8.45pm, Sat & Sun 8.15am–8.45pm (early Oct to early April last sailing at 8.10pm); every 15–30min; 10min; £11.60 for foot passengers only.

Red Funnel ☏ 023/8033 4010, ⓦ www.redfunnel.co.uk. Year-round ferries on two routes, one of them a high-speed service: **Southampton–East Cowes** 2 hourly; 55min; £9.80 for foot passengers; £69.50 for car and driver plus £9.80 per passenger. **Southampton–West Cowes** high-speed service daily 5.50am–11pm (Mon–Wed & Sun) or 11.40pm (Thurs–Sat); every 30min; 22min; £14 for foot passengers only.

Wightlink Ferries ☏ 0870/582 7744, ⓦ www.wightlink.co.uk. Three year-round ferry routes, including a faster but more expensive catamaran service to Ryde: **Portsmouth–Ryde** catamaran; 1–2 hourly; 15min; £13 for foot passengers only. **Portsmouth–Fishbourne** ferry runs once or twice every two hours; 35min; £10.60 for foot passengers; £71.90–93.80 according to season and day for car and driver, plus £10.60 per passenger. **Lymington–Yarmouth** ferry (June–Dec) midnight–10.15pm; 2 hourly; 30min; £10.60 for foot passengers; £71.90–93.80 according to season and day for car and driver plus £10.60 per passenger.

All the prices quoted are for a ninety-day (Wightlink and Red Funnel) or one-year (Hovertravel) standard return ticket. Wightlink and Red Funnel offer day and half-day returns as well as a range of other short-break deals for cars, with discounts of around 35 percent.

station at your point of arrival. The company's hourly Island Explorer buses (routes #7 and #7A) run all round the island in about four hours. The **rail line** is a short east-coast stretch linking Ryde, Brading, Sandown and Shanklin. A Rover Ticket allows you unlimited travel on the bus and train networks, costing £7.50 for a Day Rover, £13 for a Two-Day Rover and £30 for a Weekly Rover. **Cycling** is a very popular way of getting around the Isle of Wight, especially as bikes are carried free on all ferry services, but beware that in summer the narrow lanes can get very busy. For **information about the whole island**, call ☎01983/813818, consult ⓦwww.islandbreaks.co.uk, or call in at the tourist offices detailed below.

Ryde and around

As a major ferry terminal, **RYDE** is the first landfall many visitors make on the island, but one where few choose to linger, despite some grand nineteenth-century architecture and decent beach amusements. The **tourist office** (March–Oct Mon–Sat 9am–5.30pm, Sun 9am–5pm; Nov–Feb daily 9am–4.30pm; ☎01983/813818), **bus station**, **Hovercraft terminal** and **Esplanade train station** (the northern terminus of the Island Line train line) are all located near the base of the pier. **Boat trips** to the Solent forts leave from Ryde jetty; for details contact Solent & Wight Line Cruises (☎01983/564602).

Accommodation is available over the road from the jetty in St Thomas Street, where the *Biskra House Hotel and Restaurant* at no. 17 (☎01983/567913; ⑤) offers balconied rooms, a sea-facing terrace, and a fine restaurant. Just south of the Esplanade, the *Trentham Guest House*, 38 The Strand (☎01983/563418; no credit cards; ❶) and the *Vine Guest House*, 16 Castle St (☎01983/566633; ❶; closed Nov & Dec) offer great value. Good, central **eating** opportunities include the Continental-style *Joe Daflo's Café Bar* at 24 Union St, and on Castle Street, the coolly sophisticated *Blue Moon* (closed lunch, plus all Sun & Mon).

As elsewhere on the island, just a couple of miles can remove you from an undistinguished urban setting into one of idyllic rusticity. Two miles west of Ryde, outside the village of Binstead, one of the island's earliest Christian relics, **Quarr Abbey**, was founded in 1132 by Richard de Redvers for Savigny monks; its name was derived from the quarries nearby, where stone was mined for use in the construction of Winchester and Chichester cathedrals. Only stunted ruins survived the Dissolution and ensuing plunder of ready-cut stone, although an ivy-clad archway still hangs picturesquely over a farm track. In 1907 a new abbey was founded just west of the ruins, a striking rose-brick building with Byzantine overtones (daily 9am–9pm; Vespers 5pm).

Just south of the ancient village of **Brading**, on the busy Ryde-to-Sandown A3055 (bus #7, #7A, or #7B), the remains of **Brading Roman Villa** lie on Morton Old Road (April–Oct daily 9.30am–5pm; £2.95). It's one of two such villas on the island (the other is in Newport; see p.248), both of which were probably sites of bacchanalian worship. The Brading site is renowned for its superbly preserved mosaics, including intact images of Medusa and depictions of Orpheus, associated with the cult of Bacchus.

Nunwell House (July to early Sept Mon–Wed 1–5pm; £4), signposted off the A3055 less than a mile northwest of Brading, was where, in 1647, Charles I spent his last night of freedom before being taken to Carisbrooke Castle (see p.247) and thence to his eventual execution in Whitehall. The house has been in the Oglander family for nearly nine hundred years, with the present building blending Jacobean, Georgian and Victorian styles. There are guided tours of the house, and five acres of lovely gardens.

Sandown and Shanklin

The two eastern resorts of Sandown and Shanklin merge into each other across the sandy reach of Sandown Bay, representing the island's holiday-making epicentre. **SANDOWN**, a traditional Sixties bucket-and-spade resort, appropriately possesses the island's only surviving pleasure **pier**, bedecked with amusement arcades, cafeterias, dodgems and a large theatre with nightly entertainment in season. At the northern end of the Esplanade, the **Tiger and Big Cat Sanctuary and Isle of Wight Zoological Gardens** (April–Sept daily 10am–6pm; March & Oct daily 10am–4pm; Nov open weekends weather permitting, call ☎01983/403883; £5.95) is the best of the family entertainments, containing several species of tigers, panthers and other big cats, some of which are heading for extinction in the wild. There are also some frisky lemurs and monkeys, and an exhaustive selection of spiders and snakes.

SHANKLIN, with its auburn cliffs, Old Village and scenic Chine, has a marginally more sophisticated aura than its northern neighbour. The rose-clad, thatched **Old Village** may be syrupy, but the adjacent **Shanklin Chine** (daily: late March to May & Oct 10am–5pm; June–Sept 10am–10pm; £3.50), a twisting pathway descending a mossy ravine and decorated on summer nights with fairy lights, is undeniably picturesque, popular since early Victorian times when local resident John Keats drew his Romantic imagery from the environs.

Sandown's **tourist office** is located at 8 High St (Easter–Oct Mon–Sat 9am–5.30pm, Sun 9am–5pm; Nov–Easter irregular hours; ☎01983/813818); Shanklin's is at 67 High St (same hours and telephone number). Both towns have Island Line train stations about half a mile inland from their beachfront centres. For **accommodation in Shanklin**, try *Pink Beach*, 20 Esplanade (☎01983/862501, ⓦwww.pink-beach-hotel.co.uk; ❸), a shocking-pink Victorian hotel, a stone's throw from the beach, or *Luccombe Hall*, Luccombe Rd (☎01983/862719, ⓦwww.luccombehall.co.uk; ❺), originally built as the summer palace for the Bishop of Portsmouth, now a secluded and finely situated hotel with two pools, a mile from the Old Village. In **Sandown**, *Grange Hall*, 2 Grange Rd (☎01983/403531, ⓔgrangehall@C4.com; ❸), is a good-value Victorian cliff-top hotel, and *Mount Brocas*, 15 Beachfield Rd (☎01983/406276, ⓔbrocas@netguides.co.uk; ❷), offers comfortable B&B at the west end of High Street, very close to the beach. There's a **youth hostel** right in Sandown's town centre, on Fitzroy Street (☎0870/770 6020, ⓔsandown@yha.org.uk; £11.50).

The Continental-style *King's House Café*, 43 High St, Sandown, offers **meals and refreshment**, with great views over the sea; on Shanklin's Appley Beach, the *Fisherman's Cottage*, an atmospheric seafaring pub at the southern end of the Esplanade, serves wholesome food (closed Nov–Feb).

Ventnor and around

The seaside resort of **VENTNOR** and its two village suburbs of **Bonchurch** and **St Lawrence** sit at the foot of St Boniface Down, the island's highest point at 787ft. The Down periodically disintegrates into landslides, creating the jumbled terraces known locally as the **Undercliff**, whose sheltered, south-facing aspect, mild winter temperatures and thick carpet of undergrowth have contributed to the former fishing village becoming a fashionable health spa. Thanks to these unique factors, the town possesses rather more character than the island's other resorts, its Gothic Revival buildings clinging dizzily to zigzagging bends.

The floral terraces of the Cascade curve down to the slender Esplanade and narrow beach, where former boat builders' cottages now provide more recreational services. From the Esplanade, it's a pleasant mile-long stroll to Ventnor's famous Botanical Gardens, where 22 landscaped acres of subtropical vegetation flourish. Ventnor's tourist office is at 34 High St (Easter–Oct Mon–Sat 9.30am–5.30pm, Sun 10am–3pm; ☎01983/813818). For accommodation, try the *Spyglass Inn* on Ventnor's Esplanade (☎01983/855338; ❸), which has a few self-contained rooms and balconies, or, a few doors down, *St Martin's* (☎01983/852345; no credit cards; ❸), whose comfortable rooms with sea views lie next to the cottage where Turgenev started his novel *Fathers and Sons* in 1860. East of Ventnor, in the quaint village of Bonchurch, the *Horseshoe Bay House Café*, Horseshoe Bay, offers B&B right on the beach (☎01983/856800, ✉howard@horseshoebayhouse.com. There's also an excellent café here, serving seafood from its outdoor tables with 180-degree views (closed eve & weekdays in winter; no credit cards). In Ventnor town centre, *Merlin's Bistro* (☎01983/731173) on Blackgang Road serves tasty and inexpensive home-cooked snacks in a mellow atmosphere.

Appuldurcombe House and St Catherine's Point

Follow the B3327 for a couple of miles inland, over St Boniface Down, through arable farmland and past market gardens, to Wroxall, where a track leads left for half a mile to the ruins of **Appuldurcombe House** (☎01983/852484 daily: May–Sept 10am–5pm; mid-Feb to April & Oct to mid-Dec 10am–4pm; £2.50; EH), the island's grandest pre-Victorian house. The present mansion was built in the late eighteenth century in the Palladian style, with gardens landscaped by Capability Brown. Semi-abandoned in the early twentieth century, Appuldurcombe has been preserved in a picturesque state of decay, a partially roofed but intact shell with a stately eastern facade, a spring-fed fountain and an impressive outlook over a fold in the downs.

The western Undercliff begins to recede at the village of Niton, where a footpath continues to the most southerly tip of the island, **St Catherine's Point**, marked by a modern lighthouse. A prominent landmark on the downs behind is **St Catherine's Oratory**, known locally as the "Pepper Pot", and originally a lighthouse, reputedly built in 1325 as an act of expiation by Walter de Goditon who had attempted to pilfer a cargo of wine owned by a monastic community. A short distance west, **Blackgang Chine** (daily: end March to June & early Sept to Oct 10am–5pm; July to early Sept 10am–10pm; £7.50) opened as a landscaped garden in 1843 and gradually evolved into a theme park – possibly the world's first – that now offers a half-dozen exhibits from Cowboy Town to Jungleland.

Yarmouth and the western tip

Linked to Lymington in the New Forest by car ferry, the pleasant town of **YARMOUTH**, on the northern coast of the Isle of Wight, makes an appealing arrival or departure point, and is also the best base for exploring the western tip of the island. Although razed by the French in 1377, the port prospered after **Yarmouth Castle** (April–Sept daily 10am–6pm; Oct 10am–5pm; £2.50; EH), tucked between the quay and the pier, was commissioned by Henry VIII. The top attractions hereabouts, however, lie four miles west of Yarmouth, around the isle's western tip. From the multichrome cliffs at **Alum Bay**, a chair lift (£3.50 return) runs down to ochre-hued sands, which were used as pigments for painting local landscapes in the Victorian era. From here, it's a twenty-minute walk to the lookout on top of the three tall chalk stacks known as **The Needles**, best seen from a boat trip leaving from Alum Bay (Needles Pleasure Cruises; ☎01983/754477; 25min).

Between the Needles and Freshwater Bay, the breezy four-mile ridge of **Tennyson Down** is one of the island's most satisfying walks, with vistas onto rolling downs and vales. There's a monument here to the poet and local resident after whom it's named – one of the many reminders of the venerable Victorians who were drawn to the area. On the coastal road at Freshwater Bay, on the corner with Terrace Lane, **Dimbola Lodge** (Tues–Sun 10am–5pm, also Mon during school holidays; £3.50) was the home of pioneer photographer Julia Margaret Cameron, who settled here after visiting Tennyson in 1860. The building now houses a gallery of her work and changing exhibitions, as well as a bookshop, tearoom and vegetarian restaurant.

Yarmouth's **tourist office** is on the Quay (Easter–Oct Mon–Sat 9am–5.30pm, Sun 9am–5pm; Nov–Easter daily 10am–4pm; ☎01983/813818). Affordable **accommodation** in town includes *Jireh House* in St James's Square (☎01983/760513; ❸), a pretty seventeenth-century stone guest house and tearoom, serving evening meals in summer, and *Wavell's*, a grocer's shop also on the square (☎01983/760738; ❷). If you're on the Tennyson trail, you can lodge in style at the pricey *Farringford Hotel*, on Bedbury Lane (☎01983/752500, ⓦ www.farringford.co.uk; ❻), the poet's former home, where facilities include an outdoor pool, putting green and tennis courts. There's a **youth hostel** a short walk northeast from the Needles, at Totland Bay (☎0870/770 6070, ⓔ totland@yha.org.uk; closed Sun in winter; £11.50).

Yarmouth's *Bugle Hotel* in St James's Square offers bar **meals** and has a separate restaurant. Alternatively, try nearby *Fender's Bistro* – its ceiling plastered with board games – in Bridge Road.

Cowes and around

COWES, at the island's northern tip, is inextricably associated with sailing craft and boat building: Henry VIII installed a castle here to defend the Solent's expanding naval dockyards from the French and Spanish, and in the 1950s the world's first hovercraft made its test runs here. In 1820 the Prince Regent's patronage of the yacht club gave the port its cachet with the Royal Yacht Squadron, now one of the world's most exclusive sailing clubs. The first week of August sees the international yachting festival known as **Cowes Week**, which visiting royalty turns into a high-society gala, although the presence of serious sailors helps to lift the event above the merely ceremonial. There are dozens of organized events, including a spectacular fireworks display on the Friday night, and a great party atmosphere. In addition to Cowes Week, most summer weekends see some form of nautical event taking place in or around town.

The town is bisected by the River Medina, with West Cowes being the older, more interesting half, and holding most of the facilities, including the **tourist office**, at the Arcade, Fountain Quay (April–Oct Mon–Sat 9am–5pm, Sun 10am–4pm, with extended hours during Cowes Week; Nov–March Tues–Sat 9.30am–4.30pm; ☎01983/813818). At the bottom of the meandering High Street, **boat trips** upriver and around the harbour leave from the Parade; for details contact Solent & Wight Line Cruises (☎01983/564602, ⓦwww .solentcruises.co.uk).

△ Cowes Week, Isle of Wight

The more affordable **accommodation** options include the *Union Inn* in Watch House Lane, off High Street (☎01983/293163; ❸), and *Halcyone Villa*, Grove Road, up Mill Hill Road from the east end of the High Street (☎01983/291334, ✉halcyonevilla@bigfoot.com; ❷); in East Cowes, there's the *Doghouse* (☎01983/293677; no credit cards; ❸), Crossways Rd, opposite Osborne House. The town has some decent **places to eat**: the *Octopus's Garden*, 63 High St, is a café and bistro filled with Beatles memorabilia and serving all-day breakfasts as well as baguettes and pies. *Cats*, 15 Shooters' Hill (☎01983/298754), offers an eclectic and innovative menu and has *The Kitten Club* downstairs, good for a late-night drink. Bar meals are served at the *Anchor* **pub** on the High Street, which also has rooms (☎01983/292823; ❷) and a garden.

Osborne House and Whippingham

A "floating bridge", or chain ferry (Mon–Sat 5am–midnight, Sun 6.35am–midnight; pedestrians free, cars £1.30) connects West Cowes to the more industrial East Cowes, where the only place of interest is Queen Victoria's family home, **Osborne House** (daily: April–Oct 10am–5pm; grounds April–Sept 10am–6pm; Oct 10am–5pm; last admission 1hr before closing; £8; EH), signposted one mile southeast of town (bus #4 from Ryde or #5 from Newport). The house was built in the late 1840s by Prince Albert and Thomas Cubitt as an Italianate villa, with balconies and large terraces overlooking the landscaped gardens towards the Solent. The state rooms, used for entertaining visiting dignitaries, exude an expected formality, while the private apartments feel more homely, like the affluent family holiday residence that Osborne was – far removed from the pomp and ceremony of state affairs in London. Following Albert's death, the desolate Victoria spent much of her time here, and it's where she eventually died in 1901. Since then, according to her wishes, the house has remained virtually unaltered, allowing an unexpectedly intimate glimpse into Victoria's family life.

At **WHIPPINGHAM**, a mile south of Osborne, there's another of Albert's architectural extravaganzas, the Gothic Revival **Royal Church of St Mildred** (Easter–Sept Mon–Fri 10am–5pm; Oct closes 4pm). The German Battenberg family, who later adopted the anglicized name Mountbatten, have a chapel here, and the parents of the present Queen's late uncle, Earl Mountbatten, the island's last governor, are buried in the churchyard.

Newport and Carisbrooke Castle

NEWPORT, the capital of the Isle of Wight, sits at the centre of the island at a point where the River Medina's commercial navigability ends. Apart from a few pleasant old quays dating from its days as an inland port, the town isn't particularly engaging, content to fulfil its role as the island's municipal and commercial centre. Newport's main attraction lies in the hilltop fortress of **Carisbrooke Castle** (daily: April–Sept 10am–6pm; Oct 10am–5pm; Nov–March 10am–4pm; £5; EH), on the southwest outskirts (buses #7, #7A or #7B from Newport). This austere Norman keep's most famous visitor was Charles I, detained here (and caught one night ignominiously jammed between his room's bars while attempting escape) prior to his execution in London. The **museum** in the centre of the castle features many relics from his incarceration, as well as those of the last royal resident, Princess Beatrice, Queen Victoria's youngest daughter. The castle's other notable curiosity is the sixteenth-century well-house, where donkeys still trudge inside a huge treadmill to raise a barrel 160ft up the well shaft. The remains of a **Roman villa** stand a well-signposted ten-minute walk southeast of the town centre in Cypress Road (April–Nov Mon–Sat 10am–4.30pm, July & Aug also Sun noon–4pm; £2), but frankly you'd be better off visiting its sister villa in Brading (see p.242).

❸ Winchester

Nowadays a tranquil, handsome market town, **WINCHESTER** was once one of the mightiest settlements in England. Under the Romans it was Venta Belgarum, the fifth largest town in Britain, but it was **Alfred the Great** who really put Winchester on the map when he made it the capital of his Wessex kingdom in the ninth century. For the next couple of centuries Winchester ranked alongside London, its status affirmed by William the Conqueror's coronation in both cities and by his commissioning of the local monks to prepare the **Domesday Book**. It wasn't until after the Battle of Naseby in 1645, when Cromwell took the city, that Winchester began its decline into provinciality.

Hampshire's county town now has a scholarly and slightly anachronistic air, embodied by the ancient almshouses that still provide shelter for senior citizens of "noble poverty" – the pensioners can be seen wandering round the town in medieval black or mulberry-coloured gowns with silver badges. A trip to this secluded old city is a must – not only for the magnificent **cathedral**, chief relic of Winchester's medieval glory, but for the all-round well-preserved ambience of England's one-time capital.

The City

The first minster to be built in Winchester was raised by Cenwalh, the Saxon king of Wessex in the mid-seventh century, and traces of this building have been unearthed near the present **cathedral** (daily 8.30am–6pm; £3.50 donation requested), which was begun in 1079 and completed some three hundred years later, producing a church whose elements range from early Norman to Perpendicular styles. The exterior is not its best feature – squat and massive, the cathedral crouches stumpily over the tidy lawns of the Cathedral Close. The interior is rich and complex, however, and its 556-foot **nave** makes this Europe's longest medieval church. Outstanding features include its carved Norman font of black Tournai marble, the fourteenth-century misericords (the choir stalls are the oldest complete set in the country) and some amazing monuments – **William of Wykeham's Chantry**, halfway down the nave on the right, is one of the best. Jane Austen, who died in Winchester, is commemorated close to the font by a memorial brass and slab beneath which she's interred, though she's recorded simply as the daughter of a local clergyman. Above the high altar lie the mortuary chests of pre-Conquest kings, including Canute (though the bones were mixed up after Cromwell's Roundheads broke up the chests in 1645); William Rufus, killed while hunting in the New Forest in 1100, lies in the presbytery. Behind the impressive Victorian screen at the end of the presbytery, look out for the memorial shrine to St Swithun. Originally buried outside in the churchyard, his remains were later interred inside the cathedral where the "rain of heaven" could no longer fall on him, whereupon he took revenge and the heavens opened for forty days – hence the legend that if it rains on St Swithun's Day (July 15) it will continue for another forty. His exact burial place is unknown. Accessible from

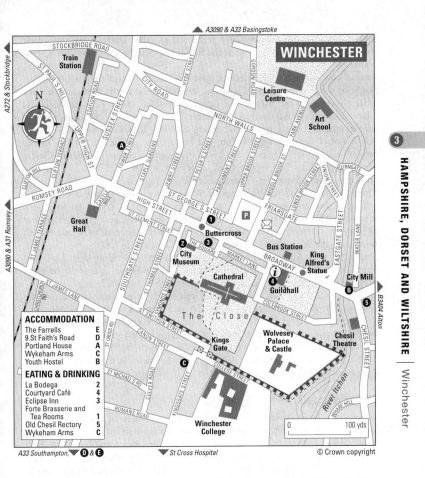

A3090 & A33 Basingstoke

WINCHESTER

STOCKBRIDGE ROAD
Train Station
Leisure Centre
Art School
A272 & Stockbridge
ST PAUL'S HILL
CITY ROAD
HYDE STREET
GORDON ROAD
PARK AVENUE
STATION ROAD
SUSSEX STREET
UPPER HIGH ST
CLIFTON TERRACE
CLIFTON HILL
NORTH WALLS
TOWER STREET
STAPLE GARDENS
JEWRY STREET
ST PETER'S STREET
PARCHMENT STREET
UPPER BROCK STREET
MIDDLE BROCK ST
LOWER BROCK STREET
UNION STREET
DURNGATE
ROMSEY ROAD
A3090 & A31 Romsey
HIGH STREET
ST GEORGE'S STREET
FRIARSGATE
EASTGATE STREET
WATER LANE
Great Hall
CASTLE HILL
ST CLEMENT STREET
Buttercross
THE SQUARE
City Museum
MARKET LANE
Bus Station
BROADWAY
King Alfred's Statue
City Mill
B3404 Alton
ST JAMES TERRACE
ST JAMES LANE
CHRISTCHURCH RD
SOUTHGATE STREET
ST THOMAS STREET
SYMONDS STREET
Cathedral
Guildhall
COLEBROOK STREET
The Close
ST SWITHUN STREET
CANON STREET
ST CROSS RD
Kings Gate
Wolvesey Palace & Castle
Chesil Theatre
CHESIL STREET
ST MICHAEL'S RD
CULVER ROAD
KINGSGATE STREET
College Street
Winchester College
ROMANS ROAD
River Itchen
WHARF HILL

ACCOMMODATION

The Farrells	E
9 St Faith's Road	D
Portland House	A
Wykeham Arms	C
Youth Hostel	B

EATING & DRINKING

La Bodega	2
Courtyard Café	4
Eclipse Inn	3
Forte Brasserie and Tea Rooms	1
Old Chesil Rectory	5
Wykeham Arms	C

0 — 100 yds

© Crown copyright

A33 Southampton, D & E   St Cross Hospital

the north transept, the Norman **crypt** is only rarely open, since it's flooded for much of the time – the cathedral's original foundations were dug in marshy ground, and at the beginning of last century a steadfast diver, William Walker, spent five years replacing the rotten timber foundations with concrete (Deep Sea Adventure in Weymouth gives you the full story; see p.262). If it's open, you can see inside two fourteenth-century statues of William of Wykeham, and Antony Gormley's standing figure, "Sound II".

Outside the cathedral, the **City Museum**, a basic local history display, sits on the Square (April–Oct Mon–Sat 10am–5pm; Sun noon–5pm Nov–March Tues–Sat 10am–4pm Sun noon–4pm; free). Walk west along the High Street from here to reach the **Great Hall** on Castle Street (summer daily 10am–5pm; winter Mon–Fri 10am–5pm, Sat & Sun 10am–4pm; free), the vestigial remains of a thirteenth-century castle destroyed by Cromwell. Sir Walter Raleigh heard his death sentence here in 1603, though he wasn't finally dispatched until 1618, and Judge Jeffreys held one of his Bloody Assizes in the castle after Monmouth's rebellion in 1685. The main interest now, however, is a large, brightly painted disc slung on one wall like some curious antique dartboard. This is alleged to be King Arthur's Round Table, but the woodwork is probably fourteenth-century, later repainted as a PR exercise for the Tudor dynasty – the portrait of Arthur at the top of the table bears an uncanny resemblance to Henry VIII.

Head east along the High Street, past the Guildhall and the august bronze statue of King Alfred on the Broadway, to reach the River Itchen and the **City Mill** (March Sat & Sun 11am–5pm; April–June, Sept & Oct Wed–Sun 11am–5pm; July & Aug daily 11am–5pm; £2; NT), where you can see restored mill machinery; the eighteenth-century building is now part-occupied by a youth hostel. Turning right before the bridge you pass what remains of the Saxon walls, which bracket the ruins of the twelfth-century **Wolvesey Castle** (April–Sept daily 10am–6pm; Oct daily 10am–5pm; £2.20; EH) and the Bishop's Palace, built by Christopher Wren. Immediately to the west up College Street stand the buildings of **Winchester College**, the oldest public school in England – established in 1382 by William of Wykeham for "poor scholars", it now educates few but the wealthy and privileged. The cloisters and chantry are open during term time and the chapel is open all year. Jane Austen moved to the house at 8 College St from Chawton in 1817, when she was already ill with Addison's Disease, dying there later the same year. The thirteenth-century **Kings Gate**, at the top of College Street, is one of the city's original medieval gateways, housing the tiny St Swithun's Church.

About a mile south of College Walk, reached by a pleasant stroll across the watermeadows of the Itchen, lies **St Cross Hospital** (Easter–Sept Mon–Sat 9.30am–5pm; Oct–Easter 10.30am–3.30pm; £2). Founded in 1136 as a hostel for poor brethren, it boasts a fine church, begun in that year and completed a century or so later, where you can see a triptych by the Flemish painter Mabuse. Needy wayfarers may still apply for the "dole" at the Porter's Lodge – a tiny portion of bread and beer.

Practicalities

Winchester **train station** is about a mile northwest of the cathedral on Stockbridge Road. If you arrive by **bus**, you'll find yourself on the Broadway, conveniently opposite the **tourist office** in the imposing Guildhall (May–Sept Mon–Sat 9.30am–5.30pm, Sun 11am–4pm; Oct–April Mon–Sat 10am–5pm; ℡01962/840500, ⓦwww.visitwinchester.co.uk). Pleasant **accommodation** options include *Portland House*, 63 Tower St (℡01962/865195, Ⓔtony@knightworld.com; no credit cards; ❸), in a quiet mews between the cathedral and train station, and a pair of B&Bs off St Cross Road, *The Farrells*, 5 Ranelagh Rd (℡01962/869555; no smoking; no credit cards; ❷), and *9 St Faith's Road* (℡01962/877522 or 07811/952618; no credit cards; ❷), offering organic breakfasts overlooking the garden. For character and location, however, it's hard to beat the *Wykeham Arms*, 75 Kingsgate St (℡01962/ 853834; ❺), a fine old hostelry with beamed, quirkily shaped rooms. Winchester's **youth hostel** is perfectly sited in the City Mill, 1 Water Lane (℡0870/770 6092, Ⓔwinchester@yha.org.uk; £10.25).

You can have **snacks and full meals** at the animated and central *Forte Brasserie and Tea Rooms*, 78 Parchment St (℡01962/856840; open daytime and Thurs & Fri eves only; closed Sun), and *La Bodega*, 9 The Square (℡01962/864004), a wine and tapas bar with a restaurant upstairs, right across from the cathedral. Behind the Guildhall, the daytime-only *Courtyard Café* has a relaxed snack bar and bistro. For quality dining, choose the *Old Chesil Rectory*, 1 Chesil St (℡01962/851555), a fifteenth-century oak-beamed restaurant serving traditional English cooking, or the richly atmospheric *Wykeham Arms*

(☎01962/853838), which is also the best place for a drink. Other worthy **pubs** include the sixteenth-century *Eclipse Inn*, 25 The Square, which has pavement seating and serves pies and casseroles.

The Watercress Line and Chawton

ALRESFORD, six miles east of Winchester, is the departure-point for the **Mid-Hants Watercress Line** (March, April & Oct Sat & Sun; May–Sept & school holidays daily; ☎01962/733810, ⓦwww.watercressline.co.uk; £9), a jolly, steam-powered train, so named because it passes through the former watercress beds that once flourished here. The train chuffs ten miles to Alton, with gourmet dinners on Saturday evenings and traditional Sunday lunches served on board.

A mile southwest of Alton lies the village of **CHAWTON**, where Jane Austen lived from 1809 to 1817, during the last and most prolific years of her life, and where she wrote or revised almost all her six books, including *Sense and Sensibility* and *Pride and Prejudice*. **Jane Austen's House** (March–Nov daily 11am–4pm; Dec–Feb Sat & Sun 11am–4pm; £4), in the centre of the village, is a plain red-brick building, containing first editions of some of her greatest works.

The New Forest

Covering about 144 square miles – a third now in private ownership, the rest administered by the Forestry Commission – the **NEW FOREST** is misleadingly named, for much of this region's woodland was cleared for agriculture and settlement long before the Normans arrived, and its poor sandy soils support only a meagre covering of heather and gorse in many areas. The forest was requisitioned by William the Conqueror in 1079 as a game reserve, and the rights of its inhabitants soon became subservient to those of his precious deer. Fences to impede their progress were forbidden and terrible punishments were meted out to those who disturbed the animals – hands were lopped off, eyes put out. Later monarchs less passionate about hunting than the Normans gradually restored the forest-dwellers' rights, and today the New Forest enjoys a unique patchwork of ancient laws and privileges, enveloped in an arcane vocabulary dating from feudal times. The forest boundary is the "perambulation", and owner-occupiers of forest land have common rights to obscure practices such as "turbary" (peat-cutting), "estover" (firewood collecting) and "mast" (letting pigs forage for acorns and beech nuts), as well as the more readily comprehensible right of pasture, permitting domestic animals to graze freely.

The **trees** of the forest are now much more varied than they were in pre-Norman times, with birch, holly, yew, Scots pine and other conifers interspersed with the ancient oaks and beeches. One of the most venerable trees is the much-visited **Knightwood Oak**, just a few hundred yards north of the A35 three miles southwest of Lyndhurst, which measures about 22ft in circumference at shoulder height. The most obvious species of New Forest **fauna** is the New Forest **ponies** – you'll see them grazing nonchalantly by the roadsides and ambling through some villages. The local deer are less visible now that some of the faster roads are fenced, although several species still roam the woods, including the tiny **sika deer**, descendants of a pair that escaped from nearby Beaulieu in 1904. Deer numbers are carefully surveyed and an annual cull keeps numbers at a steady 2000, helping to prevent damage to the woodland and the habitats of other New Forest species.

To get the best from the region, you need to **walk** or **ride** through it, avoiding the places cars can reach. There are 150 miles of car-free gravel roads in the forest, making cycling an appealing prospect – pick up a book of route maps from tourist offices or bike rental shops. The Ordnance Survey Leisure Map 22 of the New Forest is best for exploring, and in Lyndhurst you'll find numerous specialist walking books and natural history guides. Lyndhurst and nearby Brockenhurst, both on train lines, have bus connections to most parts of the forest, and both have plenty of reasonably priced accommodation. The forest has ten **campsites** run by the Forestry Commission, most closed between October and Easter – to get the full list, write to 231 Corstorphine Rd, Edinburgh EH12 7AT (℡0131/334 0066) – and there's a **youth hostel** in Cottesmore House, Cott Lane, Burley, in the west of the Forest (℡0870/770 5734, ✉burley@yha.org.uk; closed early Oct–March, limited opening April & Sept to early Oct; £10.25).

Lyndhurst and Brockenhurst

LYNDHURST, its town centre skewered by an agonizing one-way system, isn't a particularly interesting place, though the brick **parish church** is worth a glance for its William Morris glass, a fresco by Lord Leighton and the grave of one Mrs Reginald Hargreaves, better known as Alice Liddell, Lewis Carroll's model for Alice. The town is of most interest to visitors for the **New Forest Museum and Visitor Centre** in the central car park off the High Street (March–Oct daily 10am–5pm; Nov–Feb Mon–Fri 10am–4pm, Sat & Sun 10am–5pm; ℡023/8028 2269, ⓦwww.thenewforest.co.uk), where you can buy bus passes and route maps. The **museum** (£2.75) focuses on the history, wildlife and industries of the forest. Nearby in Gosport Lane, AA Bike Hire (℡023/80283349) rents **bikes**. For **accommodation** try *Forest Cottage*, at the west end of the High Street (℡023/8028 3461, ⓦwww.forestcottage.co.uk; no credit cards; no smoking; ❷), where you can consult a natural history library, or *Burwood Lodge*, 27 Romsey Rd (℡023/8028 2445, ⓦwww .burwoodlodge.co.uk; ❸), a large old house a few minutes from the High Street. *Le Café Parisien* at 64 High St sells **snacks** that you can eat in its small garden in summer; for larger **meals**, head for the nearby *Crown Hotel*.

The forest's most visited site, the **Rufus Stone**, stands three miles northwest of Lyndhurst. Erected in 1745, it marks the putative spot where the Conqueror's son and heir, **William II** – aka William Rufus after his ruddy complexion – was killed by a crossbow bolt in 1100.

BROCKENHURST, four miles south of Lyndhurst, also has **bikes for rent** at New Forest Cycle Experience, by the level-crossing (℡01590/624204). Local **accommodation** choices include the *Cottage Hotel* on Sway Road (℡01590/622296; ✉terry_eisner@compuserve.com; ❺; closed Dec–Feb) with evening meals on request, and, a short distance further south in Sway, *Little Purley Farm*, a quiet B&B in Chapel Lane (℡01590/682707; no credit cards; no smoking; ❶), with views over to the Isle of Wight. The *Snakecatcher* on Lyndhurst Road is a good **pub** that also serves terrific bar food.

Beaulieu and Buckler's Hard

The village of **BEAULIEU** (whose name originates from the French meaning "Beautiful Place", but is pronounced "Bewley"), in the southeast corner of the New Forest, was the site of one of England's most influential monasteries, a Cistercian house founded in 1204 by King John – in remorse, it is said, for ordering a group of supplicating Cistercian monks to be trampled to death. Built using stone ferried from Caen in northern France and Quarr on the Isle of Wight, the **abbey** managed a self-sufficient estate of ten thousand acres, but was dismantled soon after the Dissolution. Its refectory now forms the parish church, which, like everything else in Beaulieu, has been subsumed by the Montagu family who have owned a large chunk of the New Forest since one of Charles II's illegitimate progeny was created duke of the estate.

The estate has been transformed with a prodigious commercial vigour into **Beaulieu** (daily: May–Sept 10am–6pm; Oct–April 10am–5pm; £13; ⓦ www.beaulieu.co.uk), a tourist complex comprising **Palace House**, the attractive if unexceptional family home, the abbey and the main attraction, Lord Montagu's **National Motor Museum**. An undersized monorail and an old London bus ease the ten-minute walk between the entry point and Palace House. The latter, formerly the abbey's gatehouse, contains masses of Montagu-related memorabilia while the undercroft of the adjacent abbey houses an exhibition depicting medieval monastic life. Inside the celebrated Motor Museum, a collection of 250 cars and motorcycles, includes a McLaren F1, spindly antiques and recent classics, as well as a couple of svelte land-speed racers, including the record-breaking *Bluebird*. The entertaining "Wheels", a dizzying ride-through display, takes you on a trip through the history of motoring. You can also **rent bikes** from the museum (April–Sept; ⓣ01590/611029).

If Beaulieu amply deserves its visit, **Buckler's Hard**, a couple of miles downstream on the River Beaulieu (daily: Easter–Sept 10.30am–5pm; Oct–Easter 11am–4pm; £5), has an even more wonderful setting. It doesn't look much like a shipyard now, but from Elizabethan times onwards dozens of men o' war were assembled here from giant New Forest oaks. Several of Nelson's ships were launched here, to be towed carefully by rowing boats past the sandbanks and across the Solent to Portsmouth. The largest house in this hamlet of shipwrights' cottages, which forms part of the Montagu estate, belonged to Henry Adams, the master builder responsible for most of the Trafalgar fleet; it's now an upmarket hotel and restaurant. At the top of the village, the **Maritime Museum** traces the history of the great ships and incorporates buildings preserved in their eighteenth-century form.

Lymington

The most pleasant point of access for the Isle of Wight (for ferry details, see p.241) is **LYMINGTON**, a sheltered haven that has become one of the busiest leisure harbours on the south coast. Rising from the quay area, the old town is full of cobbled streets and Georgian houses and has one unusual building – the partly thirteenth-century church of **St Thomas the Apostle**, with a cupola-topped tower built in 1670.

Information is available in summer from the local **visitor centre** in New Street, off the High Street (May–Sept Mon–Sat 10am–5pm, Sun 2–5pm; Oct–April Mon–Sat 10am–4pm; ⓣ01590/689000). Places to **stay** in town include *The Monks Pool*, 22 Waterford Lane (ⓣ01590/678850, ⓦ www.camandjohn.com; ❸), a pleasant family home with a private lake, and *Dolphins*, 6 Emsworth Rd (ⓣ01590/676108, ⓦ www.dolphinsnewforestbandb.co.uk; ❷), which rents out bikes and offers use of a chalet by the beach. For **snacks**, try the cheap and cheerful *Coffee Mill*, opposite the visitor centre on New Street, or head for Lymington's excellent **pubs**: the *Chequers* on

Ridgeway Lane, on the west side of town, the *Bosun's Chair*, on Station Road, and the harbourfront *Ship Inn*, with seats outside looking over the water.

Signposted two miles east of Lymington, the **Sammy Miller Museum**, in New Milton (daily 10am–4.30pm; £3.50), gives classic motorcycles the "Beaulieu" treatment. Many of the once-eminent British marques from Ariel to Vincent are displayed, as well as several acclaimed trials bikes ridden by Sammy Miller himself, one of Britain's most successful trials riders.

Bournemouth and around

Renowned for its clean sandy beaches, the resort of **Bournemouth** has a single-minded holiday-making atmosphere, though neighbouring **Poole** and **Christchurch** are more interesting historically. North of this unbroken coastal sprawl, the pleasant old market town of **Wimborne** has one of the area's most striking churches, while the stately home of **Kingston Lacy** contains an outstanding collection of old masters and other paintings.

The City

BOURNEMOUTH dates only from 1811, when a local squire, Louis Tregonwell, built a summer house on the wild, unpopulated heathland that once occupied this stretch of coast, and planted the first of the pine trees that now characterize the area. The mild climate, sheltered site and glorious sandy beach encouraged the rapid growth of the resort, though today Bournemouth has acquired an unshakably genteel, elderly image. However, its geriatric nursing homes are counterbalanced by burgeoning numbers of language schools and a nightclub scene fuelled by a transient youthful population.

Apart from its pristine sandy beach (one of southern England's cleanest) Bournemouth is famed for its unusually high proportion of green space – a sixth of the town is given over to horticultural displays. Its most enthralling attraction, however, is the **Russell-Cotes Art Gallery and Museum** on East Cliff Promenade (Tues–Sun 10am–5pm; free), one of the region's best collections of Victoriana. The motley assortment of artworks and Oriental souvenirs was gathered from around the world by the Russell-Cotes family, hoteliers who grew wealthy during Bournemouth's late-Victorian tourist boom. The lavishly decorated building is jam-packed with their eclectic collections, of which the Japanese artefacts and the Pre-Raphaelite and other British art are especially striking. There's also a cliff-top landscaped garden.

In the centre of town, you might visit the graveyard of **St Peter's** church, just east of the Square, where Mary Shelley, author of the Gothic horror tale *Frankenstein*, is buried, together with the heart belonging to her husband, the Romantic poet Percy Bysshe Shelley. The tombs of Mary's parents – radical thinker William Godwin and early feminist Mary Wollstonecraft – are also here.

Arrival, information and accommodation

The **train station** and **bus station** opposite lie about a mile east of the centre, connected by frequent buses. The **tourist office** is centrally located on Westover Road (mid-July to mid-Sept Mon–Sat 9.30am–7pm, Sun 10.30am–5pm; mid-Sept to mid-July Mon–Sat 9.30am–5.30pm; ☎0906/8020234, ⊛www.bournemouth.co.uk). The town has **accommodation** to suit all budgets: try *Tudor Grange*, 31 Gervis Rd, East Cliff

(℡01202/291472; **④**), with attractive interior and gardens, or *Earlham Lodge*, 91 Alumhurst Rd, Alum Chine (℡01202/761943, **ⓦ**www.earlhamlodge.com; **❸**), a friendly guest house near the beach. The small, friendly *Bournemouth Backpackers*, 3 Frances Rd (℡01202/299491, **ⓦ**www.bournemouthbackpackers.co.uk; £16), three minutes from the train and bus stations, has some doubles available (**❷**).

Centrally located on the Promenade by the pier, *West Beach* (℡01202/587785) is a good seafood **restaurant** that's also a takeaway in summer and has weekly live jazz, while *Bistro on the Beach*, at the Southbourne end of the Esplanade (℡01202/431473), is right on the beach (closed Mon, Tues & Sun). The *Goat and Tricycle* **pub**, 27 West Hill Rd, is worth the uphill trek for the real ales and homemade food.

The biggest and best known of Bournemouth's **nightclubs** is *Elements*, right in the centre of town on Firvale Road, playing mainstream R&B and house sounds, and there's an adjoining pub/club, *Circo*, which takes in the pre-club crowds. The *Triangle Club*, Bournemouth's biggest **gay** club, is located at the top of Commercial Road from The Square. The flamboyant *Opera House*, 570 Christchurch Rd, offers something a little different. On a more sedate note, the **Bournemouth International Festival** takes place over a fortnight between June and July, drawing performers of every musical genre.

Christchurch

CHRISTCHURCH, five miles east of Bournemouth, is best known for its colossal parish church, **Christchurch Priory** (Mon–Sat 10am–5pm, Sun 2.15–5.30pm; £1 donation requested), bigger than most cathedrals. Built on the site of a Saxon minster dating from 650 AD, but exhibiting chiefly Norman and Perpendicular features, the church is the longest in England, at 311ft, and its fan-vaulted North Porch is the country's biggest. Fine views can be gained from the top of the 120-foot tower (ask at desk; £1).

The area round the old town quay has a carefully preserved charm. The **Red House Museum and Gardens** on Quay Road (Tues–Sat 10am–5pm, Sun 2–5pm; £1.50) contain an affectionate collection of local memorabilia, and **boat trips** (Easter to mid-Oct daily; ℡01202/429119) can be taken from the grassy banks of the riverside quay east to Mudeford (30min; £4.50 return) or up the river to the *Tuckton Tea Rooms* outside Bournemouth (15 min; £2 return).

The **tourist office** is at 23 High St (June–Sept Mon–Fri 9.30am–5.30pm, Sat 9.30am–5pm; July & Aug also Sun 10am–2pm; Oct–May Mon–Fri 9.30am–5pm, Sat 9.30am–4.30pm; ℡01202/471780, **ⓦ**www.resort-guide.co.uk/christchurch). Christchurch's **accommodation** options can be fairly pricey, though Barrack and Stour roads, northwest of the centre, have a selection of less expensive if unexciting guest houses, such as *Grosvenor Lodge*, 53 Stour Rd (℡01202/499008, **ⓦ**www.grosvenorlodge.co.uk; **❸**). *The Three Gables*, 11 Wickfield Avenue (℡01202/481166, **ⓦ**www.3gables-christchurch.co.uk; **❷**), is convenient for the centre and beaches. For something **to eat**, try *La Mamma*, 51 Bridge St (℡01202/471608; closed Sun lunch & Mon in winter), where you can enjoy candle-lit Italian classics (including pizzas) at moderate prices, with alfresco eating in summer; or the *Bistro on the Bridge*, 3 Bridge St (℡01202/482522; closed Mon & Tues), where you can have inexpensive lunches, afternoon tea, or pricier evening meals, and there's riverside seating on a veranda. Recommended **pubs** include the *King's Arms Hotel*, right by the priory, and Christchurch's oldest pub, *Ye Olde George Inn*, 2a Castle St – both have beer gardens and food.

Poole

West of Bournemouth, **POOLE** is an ancient seaport on a huge, almost land-locked harbour. The town developed in the thirteenth century and was successively colonized by pirates, fishermen and timber traders, more recently replaced by companies prospecting for oil in the shallow waters. The old quarter by the quayside is worth exploring, containing over a hundred historic buildings, of which the old Custom House, Scaplen's Court and Guildhall are the most striking.

At the bottom of Old High Street, **Scaplen's Court** (Aug Mon–Sat 10am–5pm, Sun noon–5pm; free) is a late medieval building where Cromwell's troops were once billeted (you can see their graffiti around the fireplace). It has now been restored as an educational centre, with reconstructions of a Victorian kitchen, pharmacy and school room. Over the road, local history is elaborated at the **Waterfront Museum** (April–Oct Mon–Sat 10am–5pm, Sun noon–5pm; Nov–March Mon–Sat 10am–3pm, Sun noon–3pm; free), tracing Poole's development over the centuries and featuring well-displayed local ceramics and tiles and a rare Iron Age log boat.

From Poole's harbour, you can catch one of the frequent ferries (£5.50 return) to **Brownsea Island** (April–June & Sept to early Oct daily 10am–5pm; July & Aug daily 10am–6pm; £3.70; NT), famed for its red squirrels, wading birds and other wildlife, which you can spot along themed trails that reveal a surprisingly diverse landscape.

One of the area's most famous gardens lies on the outskirts of Poole, **Compton Acres** (March–Oct daily 10am–6pm; £5.95), signposted off the A35 Poole Road, towards Bournemouth (buses #150, #151 or the summer-only open-top #12). Each of the seven gardens here has a different international theme, the best of which is the elegantly understated Japanese Garden.

Poole's **tourist office** is in the Waterfront Museum (April, May & Oct Mon–Sat 10am–5pm, Sun noon–5pm; June, July & Sept Mon–Fri 10am–5.30pm, Sat & Sun 10am–5pm; Aug daily 10am–6pm; Nov–March Mon–Fri 10am–5pm, Sat 10am–3pm, Sun noon–3pm; ℡01202/253253, ⓦ www.pooletourism.com). Central **accommodation** choices include the *Antelope Hotel* at 8 High Street (℡01202/672029; ❻), a handsome old hostelry, and the eighteenth-century *Mansion House*, Thames Street (℡01202/685666, ⓦ themansionhouse.co.uk; ❻). A mile or so north of the centre, the more economical *Harbour Lights Hotel*, 121 North Rd, Parkstone (℡01202/748417; no credit cards; ❷), has basic but comfortable rooms with shared bathrooms.

There's a collection of good **restaurants** on the High Street, for example *Storm*, a moderately priced seafood restaurant at no. 16 (℡01202/674970; closed lunchtime), right next to *Hardy's* (closed Sun), which is good for light lunches and sandwiches. At the top end of the street, *Alcatraz* is a lively Italian brasserie with outdoor tables. Good **pubs** include the *King Charles* on Thames Street, with leather armchairs.

Wimborne Minster and Kingston Lacy

An ancient town on the banks of the Stour, just a few minutes' drive north from the suburbs of Bournemouth, **WIMBORNE MINSTER**, as the name suggests, is mainly of interest for its great church, the **Minster of St Cuthberga** (Mon–Sat 9.30am–5.30pm). Built on the site of an eighth-century monastery, its massive twin towers of mottled grey and tawny stone dwarf the rest of the town, and at one time the church was even more imposing – its spire crashed down during morning service in 1602. What remains today is basically Norman with later features added such as the Perpendicular west tower, which bears a figure dressed as a grenadier of the Napoleonic era, who strikes every quarter-hour with a hammer. Inside, the church is crowded with memorials and eye-catching details – look out for the orrery clock inside the west tower, with the sun marking the hours and the moon marking the days of the month, and for the organ with trumpets pointing out towards the congregation instead of pipes. The **Chained Library** above the choir vestry (Easter–Oct Mon–Thurs 10.30am–12.30pm & 2–4pm, Fri 10.30am–12.30pm), dating from 1686, is Wimborne's most prized possession and one of the oldest public libraries in the country.

Wimborne's older buildings stand around the main square near the minster, and are mostly from the late eighteenth or early nineteenth century. The **Priest's House** on the High Street started life as lodgings for the clergy, then became a stationer's shop. Now it is a **museum** (April–Nov 10am–4.30pm; also open two weeks after Christmas; £2.70), with each room furnished in the style of a different period, such as a working Victorian kitchen, a Georgian parlour and an ironmonger's shop. There's also a display of items relating to local archeology and history, while the walled garden at the rear provides an excellent spot for summer teas.

Kingston Lacy (house: late March to Oct Wed–Sun 11am–5pm; grounds: Feb to mid-March Sat & Sun 10.30am–4pm; late March to Oct daily 10.30am–6pm or dusk if earlier; Nov–Dec Fri & Sun 10.30am–4pm, Sat 10am–12.30pm; house & grounds £6.80, grounds only £3.50; NT), one of the country's finest seventeenth-century country houses, lies two miles northwest of Wimborne Minster, in 250 acres of parkland grazed by a herd of Red Devon cattle. Designed for the Bankes family, who were exiled from Corfe Castle (see p.258) after the Roundheads reduced it to rubble, the brick building was clad in grey stone during the nineteenth century by Sir Charles Barry, co-architect of the Houses of Parliament. William Bankes, then owner of the house, was a great traveller and collector, and the **Spanish Room** is a superb scrapbook of his Grand Tour souvenirs, lined with gilded leather and surmounted by a Venetian ceiling. Kingston Lacy's **picture collection** is also outstanding, featuring Titian, Rubens, Velázquez and many other old masters. Be warned, though, that this place gets so swamped with visitors that timed tickets are issued on busy weekends.

The Isle of Purbeck

Though not actually an island, the **ISLE OF PURBECK** – a promontory of low hills and heathland jutting out beyond Poole Harbour – does have an insular and distinctive feel. Reached from the east by the **ferry from Sandbanks**, at the narrow mouth of Poole harbour, or by a long and congested landward journey via the bottleneck of **Wareham**, Purbeck can be a difficult destination to reach, but its villages are immensely pretty, none more so than **Corfe Castle**, with its majestic ruins. From **Swanage**, a low-key seaside resort, the Dorset Coast Path provides access to the oily shales of Kimmeridge Bay, the spectacular cove at Lulworth and the much-photographed natural arch of **Durdle Door**.

Wareham and around

The grid pattern of its streets indicates the Saxon origins of **WAREHAM**, and the town is surrounded by even older earth ramparts known as the Walls. A riverside setting adds greatly to its charms, though the major road junction at its heart causes horrible traffic queues in summer, and the scenic stretch along the Quay also gets fairly overrun. Nearby lies an enclave of quaint houses around **Lady St Mary's Church**, which contains the marble coffin of Edward the Martyr, murdered at Corfe Castle in 978 by his stepmother, to make way for her son Ethelred. **St Martin's Church**, at the north end of town, dates from Saxon times and the chancel contains a faded twelfth-century mural of St Martin offering his cloak to a beggar, but the church's most striking feature is a romantic effigy of T.E. Lawrence in Arab dress, which was originally destined for Salisbury Cathedral, but was rejected by the dean there who disapproved of Lawrence's sexual proclivities. Lawrence was killed in 1935 in a motorbike accident on the road from Bovington (6 miles west); his simply furnished cottage is at **Clouds Hill**, seven miles northwest of Wareham (April–Oct Thurs–Sun noon–5pm or dusk; £2.90; NT). The small **museum** next to Wareham's town hall in East Street (Easter–Oct Mon–Sat 11am–1pm & 2–4pm; free) displays some of Lawrence's memorabilia, as does the **Tank Museum** in Bovington Camp, five miles west of town (daily 10am–5pm; £7.50), whose main exhibits are some 150 military vehicles.

Holy Trinity Church, on South Street, contains Wareham's **tourist office** (June to mid-Sept Mon–Sat 9.30am–5pm, Sun 10am–1pm; mid-Sept to May Mon–Sat 9.30am–1pm & 1.45–5pm; ⓣ01929/552740). Boats can be rented from the nearby Quay. The best **accommodation** options are *Anglebury House*, 15 North St (ⓣ01929/552988; ❸), whose previous guests have included Thomas Hardy and T.E. Lawrence, and the *Old Granary* on the Quay (ⓣ01929/552010; ❷), which also has a **restaurant** with views over the river.

Corfe Castle

The romantic ruins crowning the hill behind the village of **CORFE CASTLE** (daily: March 10am–5pm; April–Oct 10am–6pm; Nov–Feb 10am–4pm; £4.40; NT) are perhaps the most evocative in England. The family seat of Sir John Bankes, Attorney General to Charles I, this Royalist stronghold withstood a Cromwellian siege for six weeks, gallantly defended by Lady Bankes. One of her own men, Colonel Pitman, eventually betrayed the castle to the Roundheads, after which it was reduced to its present gap-toothed state by gunpowder. Apparently the victorious Roundheads were so impressed by Lady Bankes's courage that they allowed her to take the keys to the castle with her – they can still be seen in the library at the Bankes's subsequent home, Kingston Lacy (see p.257).

The village is well stocked with tearooms and gift shops and has a couple of good **pubs** too: the *Fox* on West Street, and, below the castle ramparts, the *Greyhound*. There's moderately priced **accommodation** at *The Old Curatage*, 30 East St (ⓣ01929/481441, ⓔoldcuratage@aol.com; no smoking; no credit cards; ❷), and at the *Bankes Arms Hotel* (ⓣ01929/480206, ⓦwww.dorset-hotel.co.uk; ❷), an old inn outside the castle entrance.

Swanage and around

Purbeck's largest town, **SWANAGE**, is a traditional seaside resort with a pleasant sandy beach and an ornate town hall. The town's station is the southern terminus of the **Swanage Steam Railway** (April–Oct daily; Nov, Dec & late Feb to March Sat & Sun; £7 return), which runs as far as Norden, just north of Corfe Castle. For timetables, call ☎01929/425800, check at ⓦwww .swanagerailway.co.uk or pick up a leaflet from the tourist office. On foot, you can walk north out of Swanage, past the Foreland promontory to the broad sweep of **Studland Bay**. Its most northerly stretch, **Shell Bay**, is a magnificent beach of icing-sugar sand backed by a remarkable heathland ecosystem that's home to all six British species of reptile – adders are quite common, so be careful. At the top end of the beach a chain **ferry** (daily 7am–11pm every 20min) connects the Isle of Purbeck with Sandbanks in Poole.

Swanage's **tourist office** is by the beach on Shore Road (Easter–Oct daily 10am–5pm; Nov–Easter Mon–Thurs 10am–5pm, Fri 10am–4pm; ☎01929/ 420680, ⓦwww.swanage.gov.uk), and there's a **youth hostel**, with good views across the bay, on Cluny Crescent (☎0870/770 6058, ⓔswanage@yha.org.uk; open Fri–Sun during school terms and daily during school holidays; £11.50). The town's numerous **accommodation** options include the *Purbeck Hotel,* 19 High St (☎01929/425160, ⓦwww.purbeckhotel.co.uk; ❷), which also has a decent pub, and there are clusters of B&Bs on King's Road near the train station, and along Park Road off the High Street. For a **meal**, head for the cosy *Trattoria*, 12 High St (☎01929/423784; closed daytime), a popular, moderately priced Italian restaurant; during the day, cappuccinos and baguettes are served next door at *Forte's Caffè Tratt*, under the same management.

Durlstone Head to Durdle Door

Highlights of the coast beyond Swanage are the cliffs of **Durlstone Head** and the coastal path to **St Alban's Head**. West of this headland, **Kimmeridge Bay** shelters a remarkable marine wildlife reserve much appreciated by divers – there's a Dorset Wildlife Trust **information centre** by the slipway (daily 10am–5pm; ☎01929/481044). The quaint thatch-and-stone villages of East and West Lulworth form a prelude to **Lulworth Cove**, a perfect shell-shaped bite formed when the sea broke through a weakness in the cliffs and then gnawed away at them from behind, forming a circular cave which eventually collapsed to leave a bay enclosed by sandstone cliffs. The mysteries of the local geology are explained at the **Lulworth Heritage Centre** (daily: March–Oct 10am–6pm, Nov–Feb 10am–4pm; free).

Immediately west of the cove, **Stair Hole** is a roofless sea cave riddled with arches that will eventually collapse to form another Lulworth. A couple of miles west, the famous limestone arch of **Durdle Door** appeals to serious geologist and casual sightseer alike. Most people take the uphill route to the arch which starts from the car park at Lulworth Cove but you can avoid the steep climb by walking from the *Durdle Door Holiday Park*, on the road to East Chaldon from West Lulworth.

WEST LULWORTH is the obvious **place to stay** or eat hereabouts. The *Castle Inn* (☎01929/400311, ⓦwww.thecastleinn-lulworthcove.co.uk; ❸), *Cromwell House Hotel* (☎01929/400253, ⓦwww.lulworthcove.co.uk; ❹), right on the coast path, and the seventeenth-century *Ivy Cottage* (☎01929/400509; no credit cards; ❶) all make for good stopoffs. There's a **youth hostel** at the end of School Lane West (☎0870/770 5940, ⓔlulworth@yha.org.uk; sporadic opening in winter; £10.25), a stone's throw from the Dorset Coast Path. **Campers** can find a pitch at the above-mentioned *Durdle Door Holiday Park* (☎01929/400200; closed Nov–Feb). In East Chaldon, four miles northwest of Lulworth Cove, the *Sailor's Return* has mouthwatering **pub food**.

Dorchester and around

The county town of Dorset, **DORCHESTER** still functions as the main agricultural centre for the region, and if you catch it on a Wednesday when the market is in full swing you'll find it livelier than usual. For the local tourist authorities, however, this is essentially **Thomas Hardy**'s town; he was born at Higher Bockhampton, three miles east of here, his heart is buried in Stinsford, a couple of miles northeast (the rest of him is in Westminster Abbey), and he spent much of his life in Dorchester itself, where his statue now stands on High West Street. The town appears in his novels as Casterbridge, and the countryside all around is evocatively depicted, notably the wild heathland fo the east (Egdon Heath) and the eerie yew forest of Cranborne Chase. The real Dorchester has a pleasant central core of mostly seventeenth-century and Georgian buildings, though the town's origins go back to the Romans, who founded "Durnovaria" in about 70 AD. The Roman walls were replaced in the eighteenth century by tree-lined avenues called "Walks" (Bowling Alley Walk, West Walk and Colliton Walk), but some traces of the Roman period have survived. At the back of County Hall excavations have uncovered a fine Roman villa with a well-preserved mosaic floor, and on the southeast edge of town you'll find **Maumbury Rings**, where the Romans held vast gladiatorial combats in an amphitheatre adapted from a Stone Age site. The gruesome traditions continued into the Middle Ages, when gladiators were replaced by bear-baiting and public executions or "hanging fairs".

Dorchester is also associated with the notorious **Judge Jeffreys**, who, after the ill-fated rebellion of the Duke of Monmouth (another of Charles II's illegitimate offspring) against James II, held his "Bloody Assizes" in the Oak Room of the **Antelope Hotel** on Cornhill in 1685. A total of 292 men were sentenced to death, though most got away with a flogging and transportation to the West Indies, while 74 were hung, drawn and quartered, their heads stuck on pikes throughout Dorset and Somerset. Judge Jeffreys lodged just round the corner from the *Antelope* in High West Street, where a half-timbered restaurant now capitalizes on the lurid association.

In 1834 the **Shire Hall**, further down High West Street, witnessed another *cause célèbre*, when six men from the nearby village of Tolpuddle were sentenced to transportation for banding together to form the Friendly Society of Agricultural Labourers, in order to petition for a small wage increase on the grounds that their families were starving. After a public outcry the men were pardoned, and the **Tolpuddle Martyrs** passed into history as founders of the trade union movement. The room in which they were tried is preserved as a memorial to the martyrs, and you can find out more about them in Tolpuddle itself, eight miles east on the A35, where there's a fine little **museum** (April–Oct Tues–Sat 10am–5.30pm, Sun 11am–5.30pm; Nov–March closes at 4pm; free).

The best place to find out about Dorchester's history is the engrossing **Dorset County Museum** on High West Street (May–Oct daily 10am–5pm; Nov–April Mon–Sat 10am–5pm; £3.90), where archeological and geological displays trace Celtic and Roman history, including a section on Maiden Castle. Pride of place goes to the re-creation of Thomas Hardy's study, where his pens are inscribed with the names of the books he wrote with them. Other museums in town include the formidably turreted **Keep Military Museum** (July & Aug Mon–Sat 9.30am–5pm, Sun 10am–4pm; rest of year closed Sun; £3), at the top of High West Street, which traces the fortunes of the Dorset and

Devonshire regiments over three hundred years and offers sweeping views over the town, and **Tutankhamun: The Exhibition**, lower down High West Street (daily 9.30am–5.30pm; £5.50), a fascinating and thorough exploration of the young pharaoh's life and afterlife through to the eventual discovery of his tomb in 1922. Everything from the mummified remains, complete burial chamber and the celebrated golden mask has been carefully and atmospherically re-created with painstaking detail.

Practicalities

Dorchester has two **train stations**, both of them to the south of the centre: trains from Weymouth and London arrive at Dorchester South, while Bath and Bristol trains use the Dorchester West station. Most **buses** stop around the car park on Acland Road, to the east of South Street. The **tourist office** is in Antelope Walk (April & Oct Mon–Sat 9am–5pm; May–Sept Mon–Sat 9am–5pm, Sun 10am–3pm; Nov–March Mon–Sat 9am–4pm; ℡01305/267992, ⓦwww.westdorset.com).

Dorchester's **accommodation** ranges from the superior Georgian *Casterbridge Hotel*, 49 High East St (℡01305/264043, ⓦwww.casterbridgehotel.co.uk; ❺), to such budget options as the *King's Arms*, also on High East St (℡01305/265353; ❷), and *Maumbury Cottage*, 9 Maumbury Rd (℡01305/266726; no credit cards; ❶), near the Rings and the stations. The nearest **youth hostel** is at Litton Cheney (℡0870/770 5922; closed Sept–March; £10.25), halfway between Dorchester and Bridport.

When it comes to **food**, your best bet is a pub meal; try the *King's Arms* (see above), or, on High West Street, the *Royal Oak* or *Old Ship Inn*.

Maiden Castle

One of southern England's finest prehistoric sites, **Maiden Castle** (free access) stands on a hill two miles or so southwest of Dorchester. Covering about 115 acres, it was first developed around 3000 BC by a Stone Age farming community and then used during the Bronze Age as a funeral mound. Iron Age dwellers expanded it into a populous settlement and fortified it with a daunting series of ramparts and ditches, just in time for the arrival of Vespasian's Second Legion. The ancient Britons' slingstones were no match for the more sophisticated weapons of the Roman invaders, however, and Maiden Castle was stormed in a bloody massacre in 43 AD.

What you see today is a massive series of grassy concentric ridges about sixty feet high, creasing the surface of the hill. The main finds from the site are displayed in the Dorset County Museum (see opposite).

Weymouth to Bridport

Whether George III's passion for sea bathing was a symptom of his eventual madness is uncertain, but it was at the bay of **Weymouth** that in 1789 he became the first reigning monarch to follow the craze. Sycophantic gentry rushed into the waves behind him, and soon the town, formerly a workaday harbour, took on the elegant Georgian stamp which it bears today. A likeness of the monarch on horseback is even carved into the chalk downs northwest of the town, like some guardian spirit. Weymouth nowadays is a lively family holiday destination in summer, reverting to a more sedate rhythm out of season.

Just south of the town stretch the giant arms of Portland Harbour, and a long causeway links Weymouth to the odd excrescence of the **Isle of Portland**. West of the causeway, the eighteen-mile bank of pebbles known as **Chesil Beach** runs northwest towards **Bridport**.

Weymouth

WEYMOUTH had long been a port before the Georgians popularized it as a resort. It's possible that a ship unloading a cargo here in 1348 first brought the Black Death to English shores, and it was from Weymouth that John Endicott sailed in 1628 to found Salem in Massachusetts. A few buildings survive from these pre-Georgian times: the restored **Tudor House** on Trinity Street (June–Sept Tues–Fri 1pm–3.45pm; Oct–May first Sun of month 2–4pm; £2.50) and the ruins of **Sandsfoot Castle** (free access), built by Henry VIII, overlooking Portland Harbour. But Weymouth's most imposing architectural heritage stands along the Esplanade, a dignified range of bow-fronted and porticoed buildings gazing out across the graceful bay, an ensemble rather disrupted by the garish **Clock Tower** commemorating Victoria's jubilee. The more intimate quayside of the Old Harbour, linked to the Esplanade by the main pedestrianized thoroughfare St Mary's Street, is lined with waterfront pubs from where you can view the passing yachts, trawlers and ferries.

Weymouth's faded gentility is now counterbalanced by a number of "all-weather" attractions, the most high-profile of which is the **Sea Life Park** in Lodmoor Country Park, east of the Esplanade (daily: 10am–5pm; winter week-days closes at 4pm; last admission 1hr before closing; £8.95, £6.50 from tourist office; ☎01305/761070), where you can get close to sharks and rays and wander among multichrome birds in the tropical house. Other attractions include the **Deep Sea Adventure** at the Old Harbour (daily 9.30am–7pm; last entry 90min before closing; £3.75), which describes the origins of modern diving and the sobering story of the *Titanic* disaster. Over the river on Hope Square, **The Timewalk**, housed in Brewer's Quay (Mon–Sat 10am–5.30pm, Sun 11am–4.30pm; school holidays open until 9pm; last entry 1hr before closing; £4.25), contains an entertaining and educational walk-through exhibition of Weymouth's maritime and brewing past. A fifteen-minute walk southwards leads to **Nothe Fort** (May to mid-Sept daily 10.30am–5.30pm; rest of year hours are variable; ☎01305/766626; £3.50), built 1860–72 to defend Portland Harbour, where there are displays on military themes and a museum describing garrison life and the castle's role in coastal defence.

Practicalities

Weymouth's **train station** is a couple of blocks west of the King's Statue on the Esplanade, which is where you'll find the town's **tourist office** (daily: April–Sept 9.30am–5pm; Oct–March 10.30am–3pm; ☎01305/785747, ⓦwww.weymouth.gov.uk). A cluster of the town's **accommodation** options lies at the south end of the Esplanade, for instance *Chatsworth*, at no. 14 (☎01305/785012, ⓦwww.thechatsworth.co.uk; ❺), which has a garden terrace, and the Georgian *Cavendish House*, at no. 5 (☎01305/782039; no credit cards; ❷), overlooking the bay with harbour views at the back. Nearer the train station but just a few steps from the seafront, the *Wilton Guest House* (☎01305/783317, ⓦwww.weymouthwilton-gh.co.uk; ❶), on Gloucester Street, also offers good value. As for **restaurants**, you can't do better than *Perry's* for seafood, overlooking the quayside at 4 Trinity Rd (☎01305/785799; closed Sat lunch & Mon lunch, also Sun eve in winter). You can gaze out to sea through the large windows of the *Statue House*, 109 St Mary's St, a popular tapas bar. Amenable **pubs** include, the *Old Rooms Inn*, at the northern end of Trinity Road, an inexpensive lunch venue with a strong maritime theme, and the *Nothe Tavern*, buried among Nothe Gardens, south of the harbour on Barrack Road, which has bar meals and views from the garden.

Portland

Stark, wind-battered and treeless, the **Isle of Portland** is famed above all for its hard white limestone, which has been quarried here for centuries – Wren used it for St Paul's Cathedral, and it clads the UN headquarters in New York. It was also used for the six-thousand-foot breakwater that protects Portland Harbour – the largest artificial harbour in Britain, which was built by convicts in the mid-nineteenth century.

The causeway road by which the Isle is approached stands on the easternmost section of the Chesil shingle. To the east you get a good view of the huge harbour, a naval base since 1872. The first settlement you come to, **FORTUNESWELL**, overlooks the huge harbour and is itself surveyed by a 460-year-old Tudor fortress, **Portland Castle** (April–Sept daily 10am–6pm; Oct daily 10am–5pm; Nov–March Fri–Sun 10am–4pm; £3.50; EH), commissioned by Henry VIII. The craggy limestone of the Isle rises to 496 feet at Verne Hill, to the southeast of here. South of **EASTON**, the main village on the island, Wakeham Road holds **Pennsylvania Castle** (now a private house), built in 1800 for John Penn, governor of the island and a grandson of the founder of Pennsylvania. A couple of hundred yards beyond the house, the seventeenth-century **Avice's Cottage** is home to a small **museum** with exhibitions on local shipwrecks, smuggling and quarrying (Easter–July, Sept & Oct Mon, Tues & Fri–Sun 10.30am–1pm & 1.30–5pm; Aug & school holidays daily 10.30am–1pm & 1.30–5pm; £2). The cottage owes its name to Thomas Hardy, who described it in his novel, *The Well-Beloved*. Nearby, in **Church Ope Cove**, you can see the ruins of St Andrew's Church and those of Rufus Castle, associated with William II (William Rufus, son of William the Conqueror), though the visible remains probably belong to a reconstruction after the Norman castle was destroyed in 1142.

At **Portland Bill**, the southern tip of the island, a lighthouse has guarded the promontory since the eighteenth century. You can climb the 153 steps of the present one, dating from 1906, for the views (Easter–Sept Mon–Fri & Sun 11am–5pm; tours £2), and it also houses Portland's **tourist office** (Easter–Sept Mon, Tues & Thurs–Sun 10am–4pm, Wed 11am–4pm; ☎01305/861233). **Accommodation** options in the area include *Sturt Corner* (☎01305/822846; no credit cards; ❶) and the *Pulpit Inn* (☎01305/821237; ❷), both nearby on Portland Bill, and there's a **youth hostel** just south of Portland Castle, on Castle Road (☎0870/770 6000; closed Oct to mid-April; £11.50).

Chesil Beach to Bridport

Chesil Beach is the strangest feature of the Dorset coast, a two-hundred-yard-wide, fifty-foot-high bank of pebbles that extends for eighteen miles, its component stones gradually decreasing in size from fist-like pebbles at Portland to "pea gravel" at Burton Bradstock in the west. This sorting is an effect of the powerful coastal currents, which make this one of the most dangerous beaches in Europe – churchyards in the local villages display plenty of evidence of wrecks and drownings. Though not a swimming beach, Chesil is popular with sea anglers, and its wild, uncommercialized atmosphere makes an appealing antidote to the south coast resorts. Behind the beach, **The Fleet**, a brackish lagoon, was the setting for J. Meade Faulkner's classic smuggling tale, *Moonfleet*.

At the point where the shingle beach attaches itself to the shore is the pretty village of **ABBOTSBURY**, all tawny ironstone and thatch. Its fifteenth-century Tithe Barn is the last remnant of the village's Benedictine abbey, and today holds the **Smuggler's Barn** (daily: Easter–Oct 10am–6pm; Nov–Easter Sat & Sun 11am–dusk; last admissions 1hr before closing; £4.80), which examines the ins and outs of contrabanding. The village **Swannery** (mid-March to Sept daily 10am–6pm; Oct daily 10am–5pm; last admission 1hr before closing; £5.80), a wetland reserve for mute swans, dates back to medieval times, when presumably it formed part of the abbot's larder. Other attractions include the **Subtropical Gardens** (daily: March–Oct 10am–6pm; Nov–Feb 10am–dusk; last admission 1hr before closing; £5.80), where delicate species thrive in the micro-climate created by Chesil's stones, which act as a giant radiator to keep out all but the worst frosts. Up on the downs a couple of miles inland from Abbotsbury is a monument to Thomas Hardy, not the usual one associated with Dorset, but the flag captain in whose arms Admiral Nelson expired. If you want to **stay** in Abbotsbury try *Swan Lodge*, 1 Rodden Row (℡01305/871249; **❸**), or the *Ilchester Arms* in the village centre, a handsome stone inn with fine food (℡01305/871243, ⓦwww.ilchesterarms.co.uk; **❷**).

BRIDPORT, just beyond the far end of Chesil Beach, is a pleasant old town of brick rather than stone, with unusually wide streets, a hangover from its rope-making days when cords made of locally grown hemp and flax were stretched between the houses. You can find out about the rope and net industry at **West Bay**, Bridport's access to the sea, where the **Harbour Life Exhibition** (April–Oct daily 10am–5pm; £1) will fill you in about "Bridport daggers" (hangman's nooses) and more besides. West Bay also has the area's best place to **eat**, the *Riverside Restaurant*, a renowned but informal fish place with views over the river (℡01308/422011; moderate–expensive). Across the harbour, the *Bridport Arms Hotel* (℡01308/422994; **❹**) offers good **accommodation** near the beach; in the centre of Bridport, try *Cranston Cottage*, 27 Church St (℡01308/456240; no credit cards; **❶**). The town's **tourist office** is at 32 South St (April–Oct Mon–Sat 9am–5pm; Nov–March Mon–Sat 10am–3pm; ℡01308/424901, ⓦwww.bridportandwestbay.co.uk), and there's a seasonal office at West Bay's Harbour Life Exhibition (April–Oct daily 10am–5pm; ℡01308/422807).

Lyme Regis and around

LYME REGIS, Dorset's most westerly town, shelters snugly between steep hills, just before the grey, fossil-filled cliffs lurch into Devon. Its intimate size and undeniable photogenic qualities make Lyme so popular that in high summer car-borne crowds jostle with pedestrians for the limited space along its narrow streets. For all that, the town lives up to the classy impression created by its regal name, which it owes to a royal charter granted by Edward I in 1284. It has some upmarket literary associations to further bolster its self-esteem – Jane Austen summered in a seafront cottage and set part of *Persuasion* in Lyme (and the town appears in the 1995 film adaptation), while novelist John Fowles is the town's most famous current resident. It was the film adaptation of Fowles' book, *The French Lieutenant's Woman*, shot on location here, that did more than any tourist board production ever could to place the resort firmly on the map.

Colourwashed cottages and elegant Regency and Victorian villas line its seafront and flanking streets, but Lyme's best-known feature is a briskly practical reminder of its commercial origins. **The Cobb**, the curving harbour wall, was first constructed in the thirteenth century but has suffered many alterations since, most notably in the nineteenth century, when its massive boulders were clad in neater blocks of Portland stone.

As you walk along the seafront and out towards The Cobb, look for the outlines of ammonites in the walls and paving stones. The cliffs around Lyme are made up of a complex layer of limestone, greensand and unstable clay, a perfect medium for preserving fossils, which are exposed by landslips of the waterlogged clays. In 1811, after a fierce storm caused parts of the cliffs to collapse, 12-year-old Mary Anning, a keen fossil-hunter, discovered an almost complete dinosaur skeleton, a 30-foot ichthyosaurus now displayed in London's Natural History Museum (see p.141).

Hammering fossils out of the cliffs is frowned on by today's conservationists, and in any case is rather hazardous. Hands-off inspection of the area's complex geology can be enjoyed on both sides of town: to the west lies the **Undercliff**, a fascinating jumble of overgrown landslips, now a nature reserve. East of Lyme, the Dorset Coast Path is closed as far as jaded **Charmouth** (Jane Austen's favourite resort), but at low tide you can walk for two miles along the beach, then, just past Charmouth, rejoin the coastal path to the headland of **Golden Cap**, whose brilliant outcrop of auburn sandstone is crowned with gorse.

Lyme's excellent **Philpot Museum** on Bridge Street (April–Oct Mon–Sat 10am–5pm, Sun 11am–5pm; Nov–March Sat 10am–5pm, Sun 11am–5pm, also open Christmas & school half-terms at same times; £2) provides a crash course in local history and geology, while **Dinosaurland** on Coombe Street (daily 10am–5pm, Aug until 6pm; £4) fills out the story on ammonites and other local fossils. Also worth seeing is the small **marine aquarium** on The Cobb (Easter–Oct 10am–5pm, with later closing in July & Aug; £2), where local fishermen bring unusual catches, and the fifteenth-century **parish church** of St Michael the Archangel, up Church Street, which contains a seventeenth-century pulpit and a massive chained Bible.

Practicalities

Lyme's nearest **train station** is in Axminster, five miles north (bus #31). National Express runs a daily service from Exeter (see p.363). The **tourist office** is on Church Street (May–Oct Mon–Sat 10am–5am, Sun 10am–4pm; Nov–April Mon–Sat 10am–2pm; ☎01297/442138, ⊛www.lymeregistourism.co.uk).

Central accommodation choices in Lyme include *Coombe House,* 41 Coombe St (☎01297/443849; no credit cards; ❷), a friendly place, with large rooms and a self-catering studio; the *Old Monmouth Hotel*, 12 Church St (☎01297/442456, ⊛www.lyme-regis-hotel.co.uk; ❷); and *Cliff Cottage* on Cobb Road (☎01297/443334; no credit cards; closed Nov–March; ❶), which has harbour views, a garden chalet and a fish restaurant. For a daytime snack or inexpensive **meal**, try the *Bell Cliff Restaurant* at 5–6 Broad St, occasionally staying open on summer evenings, while *Café Clemence*, a courtyard bistro on Mill Lane (☎01297/445757; closed Mon daytime), makes a pleasant spot for something fancier. The best **pubs** are the *Royal Standard* on Ozone Parade, and the *Pilot Boat* on Bridge Street, which also does excellent seafood and vegetarian meals.

Inland Dorset and southern Wiltshire

The main pleasures of inland Dorset come from unscheduled meandering through its ancient landscapes and tiny rural settlements. The rumbustious chalk-carved giant outside the village of **Cerne Abbas** is the county's most photographed site, but the major tourist honeypots are the towns of **Blandford Forum**, **Shaftesbury** and **Sherborne**, and, across the county boundary in Wiltshire, the landscaped garden at **Stourhead** and the brasher stately home at **Longleat**, an unlikely hybrid of safari park and historic monument.

Blandford Forum

BLANDFORD FORUM, the gateway into mid-Dorset from Bournemouth, owes its latinate name not to the Romans but to medieval pedantry – the original Saxon name Cheping, meaning "market", was translated as Forum by Latin-speaking tax officials in the thirteenth century. In 1731 Blandford was all but destroyed by fire, the fourth such conflagration since the end of the sixteenth century. The phoenix that rose from these ashes – as the Fire Monument near the church puts it – was designed by the unfortunately named Bastard brothers, John and William, whose "Blandford School" produced buildings characterized by mellow dapplings of brick and stone. Sleepy Blandford still boasts one of the most harmonious and complete Georgian townscapes in England, with its centrepieces being the **Town Hall** and the **Church of St Peter and St Paul**, built in 1739. Outside, the church's distinguishing feature is the cupola perched on its handsome square tower; inside, it has fine box pews and huge Ionic columns. The town **museum** in Bere's Yard, opposite the church (Easter–Sept daily 10am–4pm; £1.50), offers a pithy account of local history, while **Mrs Penny's Cavalcade of Costume** at Lime Tree House, The Plocks (Easter–Sept Mon & Thurs–Sun 11am–5pm; Oct–Easter same days 11am–4pm; £3.40), presents over five hundred items of costume and accoutrements from 1730 to the 1950s, collected throughout the lifetime of a local woman, Mrs Penny.

Blandford's **tourist office** is in the car park on West Street (Mon–Sat: April–Oct 10am–5pm; Nov–March 10am–1pm; ☎01258/454770, ⓦwww.ruraldorset.com). For local **accommodation**, try *Gone Walkabout*, at 3 Alexandra St (☎01258/455699, ⓔgonewalkabout@talk21.com; no smoking; no credit cards; ❶), a Georgian house close to the town centre and welcoming to walkers and cyclists. The *Greyhound*, in quiet Greyhound Place (off Market Place), is a good-looking **pub** with outdoor seating and great food.

Cerne Abbas

Sixteen miles west of Blandford, just off the A352, on the #216 bus route between Dorchester and Sherborne, **CERNE ABBAS** has bags of charm, with gorgeous Tudor cottages and abbey ruins, but its main attraction is the enormously priapic **giant** carved in the chalk hillside just north of the village, standing 180-feet high and flourishing a club over his disproportionately small head. The age of the monument is disputed, some authorities believing it to be pre-Roman, others thinking it might be a Romano-British figure of Hercules. Either way, in view of his prominent feature it's probable that the giant originated as some primeval fertility symbol. Folklore has it that lying on the outsize member will induce conception, but the National Trust, who now own the site, do their best to stop people wandering over it and eroding the two-foot trenches that form the outlines.

Shaftesbury

Ten miles north of Blandford, **SHAFTESBURY** perches on a spur of lumpy green-gold hills, with severe gradients on three sides of the town. On a clear day, views from the town are terrific – one of the best vantage points is **Gold Hill**, quaint, cobbled and very steep. The local history **museum** at the top of Gold Hill (Mon–Tues & Thurs–Sun 10.30am–4.30pm; £1) is worth a glance – its contents include a collection of locally made buttons, for which the area was once renowned.

Pilgrims used to flock to Shaftesbury to pay homage to the bones of Edward the Martyr, which were brought to the **Abbey** in 978, though now only the footings of the abbey church survive, just off the main street (April–Nov daily 10am–5pm; £2). **St Peter's Church** on the market place is one of the few reminders of Shaftesbury's medieval grandeur, when it boasted a castle, twelve churches and four market crosses.

The **tourist office** is on Bell Street (April–Sept daily 10am–5pm; Oct–March Mon–Sat 10am–3pm, ☎01747/853514, ⓦwww.ruraldorset.com). If you're looking for **somewhere to stay**, try *Maple Lodge* on Christy's Lane, with modern, fully-equipped rooms (☎01747/853945, ⓦwww.maplelodgebb .com; no credit cards; ❸), or the *Knoll* in Bleke Street (☎01747/855243, ⓦwww.pick-art.org.uk; ❸), which boasts views over three counties. The *Salt Cellar* at the top of Gold Hill makes a great place for a **snack** or **meal**.

Stourhead

Landscape gardening was a favoured mode of display among the grandest eighteenth-century landowners, and **Stourhead**, ten miles northwest of Shaftesbury, is one of the most accomplished examples of the genre (April–Oct Mon, Tues & Fri–Sun 11am–5pm or dusk; garden: daily 9am–7pm or dusk; house & garden £8.90; house £5.10; garden £5.10 or £3.95 in winter; NT). The Stourton estate was bought in 1717 by Henry Hoare, who commissioned Colen Campbell to build a new villa in the Palladian style. Hoare's heir, another Henry, returned from his Grand Tour in 1741 with his head full of the paintings of Claude and Poussin, and determined to translate their images of well-ordered, wistful classicism into real life. He dammed the Stour to create a lake, then planted the terrain with blocks of trees, domed temples, stone bridges, grottoes and statues, all mirrored vividly in the water. In 1772 the folly of **King Alfred's Tower** (April–Nov daily noon–5pm or dusk; £1.85) was added and today affords fine views across the estate and into neighbouring counties. The house, in contrast, is fairly run-of-the-mill, though it has some good Chippendale furniture.

A mile to the southeast, in the showpiece village of **STOURTON**, the *Spread Eagle Inn* has five en-suite **rooms** available (☎01747/840587; ❺), with prices halving in winter, and is also a good place to have **lunch**.

Longleat

If Stourhead is an unexpected outcrop of Italy in Wiltshire, the African savannah intrudes even more bizarrely at **Longleat** (house April–Sept daily 10am–5.30pm; Oct–March guided tours at set times 10am–3pm, check at ☎01985/844400 or ⓦwww.longleat.co.uk; safari park Easter–Oct Mon–Fri

10am–4pm, Sat, Sun & school holidays 10am–5pm; house £9; safari park £9; combined ticket £16), two and a half miles south of the road from Warminster to Frome. In 1946 the sixth marquess of Bath raised eyebrows among his peers as the first stately-home owner to open his house to the paying public on a regular basis to help make ends meet. In 1966 he caused even more amazement when Longleat's Capability Brown landscapes were turned into a drive-through **safari park** – the first in the country. Once committed to such commercial enterprise, the bosses of Longleat knew no limits: other attractions now include the world's largest hedge maze, a Doctor Who exhibition, a hi-tech simulation of the world's most dangerous modes of travel and the seventh marquess's steamy murals encapsulating his interpretation of life and the universe (children not admitted). Beyond the brazen razzmatazz, though, there's an exquisitely furnished Elizabethan house, built for Sir John Thynne, Elizabeth's High Treasurer, with the largest private library in Britain and a fine collection of pictures, including Titian's *Holy Family*.

Longleat is about four miles from the train stations of Frome and Warminster and is currently served by a Lion-Link bus (Easter–Oct only) that leaves Warminster train station at 11.10am and returns from the Information Centre at Longleat at 5.15pm – the service is provided free to coach- and rail-ticket holders, and otherwise costs £1.50. Alternatively, there's the #53 bus (Mon–Sat) which shuttles roughly every hour between Warminster and Frome train stations – though be prepared to walk the two and a half miles to the house from the entrance of the grounds.

Sherborne

Tucked away in the northwest corner of Dorset, the pretty town of **SHER-BORNE** was once the capital of Wessex, its church having cathedral status until Old Sarum (see p.272) usurped the bishopric in 1075. This former glory is embodied by the magnificent **Abbey Church** (daily: April–Oct 8.30am–6pm; Nov–March 8.30am–4pm), which was founded in 705, later becoming a Benedictine abbey. Most of its extant parts date from a rebuilding in the fifteenth century, and it is one of the best examples of Perpendicular architecture in Britain, particularly noted for its outstanding **fan vaulting**. The church also has a famously weighty peal of bells, led by "Great Tom", a tenor bell presented to the abbey by Cardinal Wolsey. Among the abbey church's many tombs are those of Alfred the Great's two brothers, Ethelred and Ethelbert, and the Elizabethan poet Thomas Wyatt, all located in the northeast corner. The **almshouse** on the opposite side of the Abbey Close was built in 1437 and is a rare example of a medieval hospital; another wing provides accommodation for Sherborne's well-known public school.

The town also has two "castles", both associated with Sir Walter Raleigh. Queen Elizabeth I first leased, then gave, Raleigh the twelfth-century **Old Castle** (April–Sept daily 10am–6pm; Oct daily 10am–1pm & 2–5pm; £2; EH), but it seems that he despaired of feudal accommodation and built himself a more comfortably domesticated house, **Sherborne Castle**, in adjacent parkland (April–Oct Tues, Thurs & Sun 11am–4.30pm, Sat 2.30–5pm; gardens closed Sat; castle & gardens £6, gardens only £3.25). When Sir Walter fell from the queen's favour by seducing her maid of honour, the Digby family acquired the house and have lived there ever since; portraits, furniture and books are displayed in a whimsically Gothic interior, remodelled in the nineteenth century. The Old Castle fared less happily, and was pulverized by Cromwellian cannon fire for the obstinately Royalist leanings of its occupants. The **museum** near the abbey on Church Lane (April–Oct Tues, & Thurs–Sat 10.30am–4.30pm, Sun 2.30–4.30pm; last admission 4pm; £1) includes a model of the Old Castle and photographs of parts of the fifteenth-century Sherborne Missal, a richly illuminated tome weighing nearly fifty pounds, now housed in the British Library.

The **tourist office** is at 3 Tilton Court, Digby Rd (Mon–Sat: April–Oct 9am–5pm; Nov–Easter 10am–3pm; ☎01935/815341). For an **overnight stay** try the *Britannia Inn*, on Westbury, just down from the abbey (☎01935/813300; ❷), or the *Cross Keys Hotel*, 88 Cheap St (☎01935/812492; ❷), a cosy **pub** which has a few tables out front for drinks and meals. *Oliver's*, 19 Cheap St, and the *Church House Gallery*, close to the abbey on Half Moon Street, are both good for teas and light lunches.

Salisbury

SALISBURY, huddled below Wiltshire's chalky plain in the converging valleys of the Avon and Nadder, looks from a distance very much as it did when Constable painted his celebrated view of it from across the water meadows. Wiltshire's only city is designed on a pleasantly human scale, with no sprawling suburbs or high-rise buildings to challenge the supremacy of the cathedral's immense spire.

The town sprang into existence in the early thirteenth century, when the bishopric was moved from **Old Sarum**, an ancient Iron Age hillfort settled by the Romans and their successors. The deserted remnant of Salisbury's precursor now stands on the northern fringe of the town, just a bit closer in than **Wilton House** to the west, one of Wiltshire's great houses.

The City

Begun in 1220, **Salisbury Cathedral** (June–Aug Mon–Sat 7.15am–7.15pm, Sun 7.15am–6.15pm; Sept–May daily 7am–6.15pm; £3.80 suggested donation) was mostly completed within forty years and is thus unusually consistent in its style, with one extremely prominent exception – the **spire**, which was added a century later and at 404ft is the highest in England. Its survival is something of a miracle, for the foundations penetrate only about six feet into marshy ground, and when Christopher Wren surveyed it he found the spire to be leaning almost two and a half feet out of true. He added further tie-rods, which finally arrested the movement.

The interior is over-austere after James Wyatt's brisk eighteenth-century tidying, but there's an amazing sense of space and light in its high nave, despite the sombre pillars of grey Purbeck marble, which are visibly bowing beneath the weight they bear. Monuments and carved tombs line the walls, where they were neatly placed by Wyatt, and in the north aisle there's a fascinating clock dating from 1386, one of the oldest functioning clock mechanisms in Europe. Other features not to miss are the vaulted colonnades of the **cloisters**, and the octagonal **chapter house** (June–Aug Mon–Sat 9.30am–6.45pm, Sun noon–5.30pm; Sept–May Mon–Sat 9.30am–5.30pm, Sun noon–5.30pm), which displays a rare original copy of the Magna Carta, and whose walls are decorated with a frieze of scenes from the Old Testament. On most days, you can join a free 45-minute **tour** of the church leaving two or more times a day, and there are also tours to the roof and spires (£4).

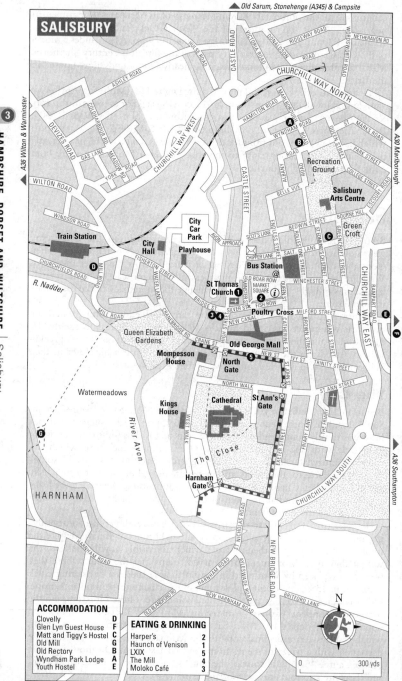

SALISBURY

Old Sarum, Stonehenge (A345) & Campsite

A36 Wilton & Warminster

A30 Marlborough

A30 Southampton

A36 Southampton

A338 Bournemouth

Train Station

City Hall

Playhouse

City Car Park

St Thomas Church

Bus Station

Poultry Cross

Old George Mall

Mompesson House

North Gate

Queen Elizabeth Gardens

Watermeadows

Kings House

Cathedral

St Ann's Gate

The Close

Harnham Gate

HARNHAM

Salisbury Arts Centre

Recreation Ground

Green Croft

R. Nadder

River Avon

N

ACCOMMODATION

Clovelly	D
Glen Lyn Guest House	F
Matt and Tiggy's Hostel	C
Old Mill	G
Old Rectory	B
Wyndham Park Lodge	A
Youth Hostel	E

EATING & DRINKING

Harper's	2
Haunch of Venison	1
LXIX	5
The Mill	4
Moloko Café	3

0   300 yds

© Crown copyright

Surrounding the cathedral is the **Close**, the largest and most impressive in the country, a peaceful precinct of lawns and mellow old buildings. Most of the houses have seemly Georgian facades, though some, like the Bishop's Palace and the deanery, date from the thirteenth century. **Mompesson House** (April–Oct Mon–Wed, Sat & Sun 11am–5.30pm, last entry 4.30pm; £3.90, garden only 80p; NT), built by a wealthy merchant in 1701, contains some beautifully furnished eighteenth-century rooms and a superbly carved staircase, as displayed to great effect in the film *Sense and Sensibility*. Also in the Close is the **King's House**, home to the **Salisbury and South Wiltshire Museum** (July & Aug Mon–Sat 10am–5pm, Sun 2–5pm; rest of year closed Sun; £3.50) – an absorbing account of local history. It includes a good section on Stonehenge and also focuses on the life and times of General Pitt-Rivers, the father of modern archeology, who excavated many of Wiltshire's prehistoric sites, including Avebury (see p.275).

The Close's **North Gate** opens onto the centre's older streets, where narrow pedestrianized alleyways bear names like Fish Row and Salt Lane, indicative of their trading origin. Many half-timbered houses and inns have survived all over the centre, and the last of four market crosses, **Poultry Cross**, stands on stilts in Silver Street, near the Market Square. The market, held on Tuesdays and Saturdays, still serves a large agricultural area, as it did in earlier times when the city grew wealthy on wool. Nearby, the church of **St Thomas** – named after Thomas à Becket – is worth a look inside for its carved timber roof and "Doom painting" over the chancel arch, depicting Christ presiding over the Last Judgment. Dating from 1475, it's the largest of its kind in England.

Lastly, to best appreciate the city's inspiring silhouette – the view made famous by Constable – take a twenty-minute walk through the water meadows southwest of the centre to **HARNHAM**; the *Old Mill* here serves drinks and meals.

Practicalities

Trains from London arrive half a mile west of Salisbury's centre, on South Western Road; the bus station is a short way north of the Market Place, on Endless Street. The **tourist office** is on Fish Row, just off the Market Square (May Mon–Sat 9.30am–5pm, Sun 10.30am–4.30pm; June–Sept Mon–Sat 9.30am–6pm, Sun 10.30am–4.30pm; Oct–April Mon–Sat 9.30am–5pm; ☎01722/334956, ⓦ www.visitsalisbury.com) and is the starting point for informative and inexpensive **guided walks** of the city. There's **Internet access** at Starlight Internet Café, 1a Endless Street.

Salisbury has numerous **accommodation** possibilities to suit all pockets. One of the best is the *Old Mill*, Town Path, Harnham (☎01722/327517; ❺), a riverside inn boasting great views across the meadows to the cathedral about a mile away. There are two comfortable B&Bs near each other a short walk north of the centre: the *Old Rectory*, 75 Belle Vue Rd (☎01722/502702, ⓦ www.theoldrectory-bb.co.uk; no smoking; no credit cards; ❸), with light, airy rooms, and the Victorian *Wyndham Park Lodge*, 51 Wyndham Rd (☎01722/416517, ⓦ www.wyndhamparklodge.co.uk; no smoking; ❷), with period furnishings. *Clovelly*, at 17 Mill Rd (☎01722/322055, ⓦ www .clovellyhotel.co.uk; no smoking; ❹), is a useful choice close to the train station, and offers homemade yoghurt for breakfast. A ten-minute walk east of the centre, *Glen Lyn*, 6 Bellamy Lane (☎01722/327880, ⓦ www .glenlynbandbatsalisbury.co.uk; ❸), is an elegant Victorian guest house in a quiet lane off Milford Hill, which is the site of Salisbury's **youth hostel**

(☎0870/770 6018, ✉salisbury@yha.org.uk; £14.50), where separate lodges accommodate couples or smaller groups (❶). More centrally, there's also the independent *Matt and Tiggy's Hostel*, 51 Salt Lane (☎01722/327443; £12), small, friendly and clean. There's a **campsite** a mile and a half north of Salisbury close to Old Sarum, *Salisbury Camping and Caravanning Club*, Hudson's Field (☎01722/320713; closed Oct to mid-March).

You can enjoy good-value, traditional English lunches and evening **meals** at *Harper's*, Market Square (☎01722/333118; closed Sun eve in winter), or savour the elegant, modern style and upmarket local cooking at *LXIX*, 69 New St (☎01722/340000; closed Sun), close to the cathedral. **Pub** grub and drinks are dispensed at *The Mill*, Bridge St, with riverside seating, and at the atmospheric *Haunch of Venison*, Minster St, whose curiosities include the mummified hand of a nineteenth-century card player still clutching his cards. *Moloko Café*, 5 Bridge St, serves coffees and vodkas until late.

Old Sarum

The ruins of **Old Sarum** (daily: April–June & Sept 10am–6pm; July & Aug 9am–6pm; Oct 10am–5pm; Nov–March 10am–4pm; £2.20; EH) occupy a bleak hilltop site two miles north of the city centre – an easy walk, but there are frequent local bus connections. Possibly occupied up to five thousand years ago, then developed as an Iron Age fort whose double protective ditches remain, it was settled by Romans and Saxons before the Norman bishopric of Sherborne was moved here in the 1070s. Within a couple of decades a new cathedral had been consecrated at Old Sarum, and a large religious community was living alongside the soldiers in the central castle. Old Sarum was an uncomfortable place, parched and windswept, and in 1220 the dissatisfied clergy – additionally at loggerheads with the castle's occupants – appealed to the pope for permission to decamp to Salisbury (still known officially as New Sarum). When permission was granted, the stone from the cathedral was commandeered for Salisbury's gateways, and once the church had gone the population waned. By the nineteenth century Old Sarum was deserted, but it continued to exist as a political constituency – William Pitt was one of its representatives – and became notorious as a so-called "rotten borough", returning two MPs at a time to Westminster until the 1832 Reform Act put a stop to it. Huge earthworks, banks and ditches are the dominant features of the site today, with a broad trench encircling the rudimentary remains of the Norman palace, castle and cathedral.

Wilton

WILTON, five miles west of Salisbury, is renowned for its carpet industry and the splendid **Wilton House** (mid-April to Oct daily 10.30am–5.30pm; last entry 1hr before closing; £9.25, grounds only £4.75), of which Daniel Defoe wrote: "One cannot be said to have seen any thing that a man of curiosity would think worth seeing in this county, and not have been at Wilton House." The Tudor house, built for the First Earl of Pembroke on the site of a dissolved Benedictine abbey, was ruined by fire in 1647 and rebuilt by Inigo Jones, whose classic hallmarks can be seen in the sumptuous Single Cube and Double Cube rooms, so called because of their precise dimensions. Sir Philip Sidney, illustrious Elizabethan courtier and poet, wrote part of his magnum opus *Arcadia* here – the dado round the Single Cube Room illustrates scenes from the book – and the Double Cube room was the setting for the ballroom scene in Ang Lee's film, *Sense and Sensibility*. The easel **paintings** are what makes Wilton really special, however – the collection includes paintings by Van Dyck, Rembrandt, two of the Brueghel family, Poussin, Andrea del Sarto and Tintoretto. In the grounds, the famous **Palladian Bridge** has been joined by various ancillary attractions including an adventure playground and an audiovisual show on the colourful earls of Pembroke.

Salisbury Plain and northwards

The Ministry of Defence is the landlord of much of **Salisbury Plain**, the hundred thousand acres of chalky upland to the north of Salisbury. Flags warn casual trespassers away from MoD firing ranges and tank training grounds, while rather stricter security cordons off such secretive establishments as the research centre at Porton Down, Britain's centre for chemical and biological warfare. As elsewhere, the army's presence has ironically saved much of the plain from modern agricultural chemicals, thereby inadvertently nurturing species that are all but extinct in more trampled landscapes.

Though now largely deserted except by forces families living in ugly barracks quarters, Salisbury Plain once positively throbbed with communities. Stone Age, Bronze Age and Iron Age settlements left hundreds of burial mounds scattered over the chalklands, as well as major complexes at Danebury, Badbury, Figsbury, Old Sarum, and, of course, the great circle of **Stonehenge**. North of Salisbury Plain lies the softer Vale of Pewsey, traversed by the Kennet canal. **Marlborough**, to the north of the Vale, is the centre for another cluster of ancient sites, including the huge stone circle of **Avebury**, the mysterious grassy mound of **Silbury Hill** and the chamber graves of **West Kennet**.

Stonehenge

No ancient structure in England arouses more controversy than **Stonehenge** (daily: mid-March to May & Sept to mid-Oct 9.30am–6pm; June–Aug 9am–7pm; mid-Oct to end Oct 9.30am–5pm; end Oct to mid-March 9.30am–4pm; £5; NT & EH; ⓦ www.stonehengemasterplan.org), a mysterious ring of monoliths nine miles north of Salisbury. While archeologists argue over whether it was a place of ritual sacrifice and sun-worship, an astronomical calculator or a royal palace, the guardians of the site struggle to accommodate its year-round crowds and improve the facilities. Conservation of Stonehenge is obviously an urgent priority, and unless you prearrange a supervised tour (by calling ahead on ☏01980/626267), you must be content with walking round rather than among the stones, equipped with handsets that dispense a range of information on the site – some of the soundtrack is interesting, but much is misleading and patronizing. The current dissatisfaction that many feel on visiting the landmark may be allayed by the projected rerouteing of the nearby roads, and by the new visitors' centre planned two miles east of the stones at the Amesbury roundabout (scheduled to open 2005).

What exists today is only a small part of the original prehistoric complex, as many of the outlying stones were probably plundered by medieval and later farmers for building materials. The **construction** of Stonehenge is thought to have taken place in several stages. In about 3000 BC the outer circular bank and ditch were constructed, just inside which was dug a ring of 56 pits, which at a later date were filled with a mixture of earth and human ash. Around 2500 BC the first stones were raised within the earthworks, comprising approximately forty great blocks of dolerite (bluestone), whose ultimate source was

Preseli in Wales. Some archeologists have suggested that these monoliths were found lying on Salisbury Plain, having been borne down from the Welsh mountains by a glacier in the last Ice Age, but the lack of any other glacial debris on the plain would seem to disprove this theory. It really does seem to be the case that the stones were cut from quarries in Preseli and dragged or floated here on rafts, a prodigious task which has defeated recent attempts to emulate it.

The crucial phase in the creation of the site came during the next six hundred years, when the incomplete bluestone circle was transformed by the construction of a circle of twenty-five **trilithons** (two uprights crossed by a lintel) and an inner horseshoe formation of five trilithons. Hewn from Marlborough Downs sandstone, these colossal stones (called sarsens), ranging from 13ft to 21ft in height and weighing up to thirty tons, were carefully dressed and worked – for example, to compensate for perspectival distortion the uprights have a slight swelling in the middle, the same trick as the builders of the Parthenon were to employ hundreds of years later. More bluestones were arranged in various patterns within the outer circle over this period. The purpose of all this work remains baffling, however. The symmetry and location of the site (a slight rise in a flat valley with even views of the horizon in all directions) as well as its alignment towards the points of sunrise and sunset on the summer and winter solstices tend to support the supposition that it was some sort of observatory or time-measuring device. The site ceased to be used at around 1600 BC, and by the Middle Ages it had become a "landmark".

There's a lot less charisma about the reputedly significant Bronze Age site of **Woodhenge** (dawn–dusk; free), two miles northeast of Stonehenge. The site consists of a circular bank about 220ft in diameter enclosing a ditch and six concentric rings of post holes, which would originally have held timber uprights, possibly supporting a roofed building of some kind. The holes are now marked more durably if less romantically by concrete pillars. A child's grave was found at the centre of the rings, suggesting that it may have been a place of ritual sacrifice.

Marlborough

An obvious base from which to explore Salisbury Plain is **MARLBOROUGH**, a handsome old stagecoach stop on the London-to-Bath route, with a dignified assembly of Georgian buildings. Its wide High Street has a fine Perpendicular church standing at each end and half-timbered cottages rambling up the alleyways behind. The famous public school is not especially old – it was established in 1843 – but incorporates an ancient coaching inn among its red-brick buildings.

Marlborough **tourist office** is in the car park on George Lane, accessible from the High Street via Hilliers Yard (Easter–Oct Mon–Sat 10am–5pm; Nov–Easter Mon–Sat 10am–4.30pm; ☏01672/513989, ⓦwww.kennet.gov .uk). There are several inns and guest houses offering **accommodation** along the High Street, including the *Merlin* pub at nos. 36–39 (☏01672/512151; ❹). Less expensive central options include the B&B at 63 George Lane (☏01672/512771; no credit cards; ❶), which overlooks water meadows, while with your own transport you could stay at the eighteenth-century *Clench Farmhouse* (☏01672/810264; no credit cards; ❸), four miles south near Wootton Rivers and equipped with a tennis court and pool. Good bistro **food** is served at *Ivy House*, at the top of the High Street, while *Polly Tea Rooms* serves snacks and ice cream.

Silbury Hill, West Kennet and Avebury

The neat green mound of **Silbury Hill**, five miles west of Marlborough, is probably overlooked by the majority of drivers whizzing by on the A4. At 130ft it's no great height, but when you realize it's the largest prehistoric artificial mound in Europe, and was made by a people using nothing more than primitive spades, it commands more respect. It was probably constructed around 2600 BC, but like so many of the sites of Salisbury Plain, no one knows quite what it was for, though the likelihood is that it was a burial mound. You can't actually walk on the hill – so having admired it briefly from the car park, cross the road to the footpath that leads half a mile to the **West Kennet Long Barrow** (free access; NT & EH). Dating from about 3250 BC, this was definitely a chamber tomb – nearly fifty burials have been discovered at West Kennet.

Immediately to the west, the village of **AVEBURY** stands in the midst of a **stone circle** (free access; NT & EH) that rivals Stonehenge – the individual stones are generally smaller, but the circle itself is much wider and more complex. A massive earthwork 20ft high and 1400ft across encloses the main circle, which is approached by four causeways across the inner ditch, two of them leading into wide avenues stretching over a mile beyond the circle. The best guess is that it was built soon after 2500 BC, and presumably had a similar ritual or religious function to Stonehenge. The structure of Avebury's diffuse circle is quite difficult to grasp, but there are plans on the site, and you can get an excellent overview at the **Alexander Keiller Museum**, at the western entrance to the site (daily: April–Oct 10am–6pm or dusk if earlier; Nov–March 10am–4pm; £4 also for Barn Gallery; NT & EH), which displays excavated material and explanatory information. Nearby, the **Barn Gallery** (same times and prices) holds a permanent exhibition of Avebury and the surrounding country, and shows clips from recently discovered home-movies of Keiller excavating the stones aided by a bevy of nubile assistants. Having absorbed the contents of the various collections, you can wander round the peaceful circle, accompanied by sheep and cattle grazing unconcernedly among the stones. To the southeast, an avenue of standing stones leads half a mile beyond West Kennet towards a spot known as the Sanctuary, though there is little left to see here.

Back in the placid **village** of Avebury, you can have a **snack** or cream tea at *The Circles* vegetarian restaurant, or a drink in the *Red Lion* **pub**, which also serves reasonable **meals** as well as providing a few rather down-at-heel rooms should you wish to **stay** over (℡01672/539266; ❸). A preferable choice would be *The Lodge* (℡01672/539023, ✉avebury@email.com; no smoking; ❺) on the High Street, a Georgian B&B with strictly vegetarian or vegan breakfasts and views towards the stones. There's a **tourist office** (daily: summer 10am–5.30pm; winter 10am–4.30pm; ℡01672/539425) in the Avebury Chapel Centre on Green Street.

Devizes and around

DEVIZES, seven miles down the A361 from Avebury at the mouth of the Vale of Pewsey, is a pleasant place, with some attractive eighteenth-century houses, a stately semicircular market place and a couple of fine churches, St Mary's and St John's. It's chiefly worth a stop, however, for the excellent **Museum** at 41 Long St (Mon–Sat 10am–5pm, Sun noon–4pm; £3, free Sun & Mon), housing an exceptional collection of prehistoric finds from barrows and henges throughout the county. Star exhibit is the so-called Marlborough Bucket, decorated with bronze reliefs from the first century BC.

The town offers some appealing nooks to explore: seek out the timbered and jettied row of Elizabethan-era houses on the cobbled St John's Alley, tucked away behind St John's Street. Out of town, you can enjoy a pleasant canalside stroll along the **Kennet and Avon Canal**, which boasts 29 locks at Caen Hill, roughly an hour-and-a-half's walk westwards, but easily cyclable too.

Devizes' very helpful **tourist office** is on Market Place (Mon–Sat 9.30am–5pm; ☏01380/729408). The cushiest place to **stay** is the *Castle Hotel*, on New Park Street, a former coaching inn (☏01380/729300; ❹); cheaper choices include the *Craven House* B&B, Station Rd (☏01380/723514; no credit cards; ❶), and the *White Bear Inn*, Monday Market St (☏01380/727588; no credit cards; ❷). For **eating**, try *Quintessence*, St John's St, which serves light lunches and snacks (closed eves), or *The Bistro* on The Little Brittox, a quiet lane off the High Street, specializing in organic and vegetarian dishes (closed daytime & Mon; moderate).

Lacock

LACOCK, ten miles northwest of Devizes, is the perfect English feudal village, albeit one gentrified by the National Trust to within a hair's breadth of natural life, and besieged by tourists all summer. Appropriately for so photogenic a spot, it has a fascinating museum dedicated to the founding father of photography, Henry Fox Talbot, a member of the dynasty which has lived in the local **abbey** since it passed to Sir William Sharington on the Dissolution of the Monasteries in 1539. Sir William's descendant, William Henry Fox Talbot, was the first to produce a photographic negative, and the **Fox Talbot Museum**, in a sixteenth-century barn by the abbey gates (March–Oct daily 11am–5.30pm; £4.20; NT), captures something of the excitement he must have experienced as the dim outline of an oriel window in the abbey steadily imprinted itself on a piece of silver nitrate paper. A copy of the postage-stamp-sized result is on display in the museum (the original is in Bradford's National Museum of Photography, Film and Television, see p.671). The **abbey** itself (April–Oct Mon & Wed–Sun 1–5.30pm; £5.30; £6.50 including museum; NT) preserves a few monastic fragments amid the eighteenth-century Gothic, while the church of **St Cyriac** (free access) contains the opulent tomb of Sir William Sharington, buried beneath a splendid barrel-vaulted roof.

The village's delightfully Chaucerian-sounding hostelry, *At the Sign of the Angel*, is a good, if expensive, **hotel** and **restaurant** (☏01249/730230; Ⓦwww.lacock.co.uk; ❼).

Corsham Court and Bowood House

The main sight within a short drive of Lacock is **Corsham Court** (mid-March to Oct Sat, Sun & Tues–Thurs 2–5.30pm; Nov to mid-March Sat & Sun 2–4.30pm; £5, garden only £2), three miles west. It dates from Elizabethan times, though what you see now bears the Georgian stamp of Nash and Capability Brown, and the house, furnished by Robert Adam and Thomas Chippendale among others, contains a fine collection of art, including pieces by Caravaggio, Rubens, Reynolds and Michelangelo. The village of **CORSHAM** is another dignified little cloth-making town of Bath stone, riddled with underground limestone quarries and a long railway tunnel engineered by Brunel.

Ten miles east of Corsham, off the A342 Chippenham–Devizes road and just outside the village of Calne, **Bowood House** (April–Oct daily 11am–5.30pm;

£6.25) was designed in the eighteenth century by the likes of Henry Keene, Charles Barry and – again – Robert Adam. Adam was primarily responsible for the great south front and the Orangery, and, inside the house, the library – though the present appearance of this owes more to Charles Robert Cockerell, architect of Oxford's Ashmolean Museum, who also built the Neoclassical chapel. But it is the magnificent grounds of Bowood that are the real draw, with rhododendron gardens, a Doric temple on the banks of its placid lake and a waterfall in the woods.

Bradford-on-Avon

With its buildings of mellow auburn stone, reminiscent of the townscapes just over the county border in Bath and the Cotswolds, **BRADFORD-ON-AVON** is the most appealing town in the northwest corner of Wiltshire. Sheltering against a steep wooded slope, it takes its name from its "broad ford" across the Avon, though the original fording place was replaced in the thirteenth century by a **bridge** that was in turn largely rebuilt in the seventeenth century. The domed structure at one end is a quaint old jail converted from a chapel.

The local industry, based on textiles like that of its Yorkshire namesake, was revolutionized with the arrival of Flemish weavers in 1659, and many of the town's handsome buildings reflect the prosperity of this period. Yet Bradford's most significant building is the tiny **St Lawrence Church** on Church Street, an outstanding example of Saxon architecture dating from about 700 AD. Wrecked by Viking invaders, and later used as a school and a simple dwelling, it was rehabilitated by a local vicar in 1856. Its distinctive features are the carved angels over the chancel arch.

Bradford's **train station** is close to the town centre on St Margaret's Street, where you'll find the **tourist office** at no. 50 (daily: April–Dec 10am–5pm; Jan–March 10am–4pm; ☎01225/865797, ⓦwww.bradfordonavontown .com). Local **accommodation** choices include *Bradford Old Windmill*, a B&B up the hill at 4 Mason's Lane (☎01225/866842, ⓔtic@bradfordoldwindmill .co.uk; ❸–❺; may be closed in winter), brimming with character and offering imaginative vegetarian food (evening meals currently on Mon, Thurs & Sat). The *Riverside Inn,* 49 St Margaret's St (☎01225/863526; ❷), lives up to its name, with private facilities in all rooms. For light lunches or cakes, try the excellent *Scribbling Horse* at 34 Silver St or *The Cottage Cooperative,* just around the corner at no. 33, which serves good coffee and light vegetarian meals and has a garden (**Internet access** is also available here). The *Bunch of Grapes* **pub** on Silver Street has food and drink, and weekly jazz, folk and blues gigs.

Great Chalfield

Great Chalfield Manor (guided tours: April–Oct Tues–Thurs 12.15pm, 2.15pm, 3pm, 3.45pm & 4.30pm; £4.20; NT), two and a half miles northeast of Bradford, is a splendid moated complex of house, church and outbuildings dating from about 1470, sensitively restored at the beginning of the twentieth century as a family home. The exterior looks like a typical Cotswold manor, all gables and mullions; inside, the Great Hall is overlooked by a minstrels' gallery from which three gargoyle-like masks gaze down into the hall, the eyes cut away so that the womenfolk could inspect the proceedings below without jeopardizing their modesty. The interior of the church features some fifteenth-century wall paintings.

Travel details

Buses

For information on all local and national bus services, contact **Traveline** ☎0870/608 2608 (daily 7am–9pm), ⊛www.traveline.org.uk.

Bournemouth to: Dorchester (3 daily; 1hr 15min–1hr 35min); London (every 30min; 2hr 35min–4hr 10min); Southampton (10 daily; 45min–2hr); Weymouth (3 daily; 1hr 15min–1hr 30min); Winchester (6 daily; 1hr 15min–2hr).

Dorchester to: Bournemouth (3 daily; 1hr 10min–1hr 40min); London (1 daily; 4hr); Weymouth (every 20–30min; 20min–1hr).

Portsmouth to: London (13 daily; 2hr 20min–3hr 45min); Salisbury (1 daily; 1hr 25min); Southampton (9 daily; 40min–1hr), Winchester (hourly; 1hr 10min–2hr).

Salisbury to: London (3 daily; 2hr 45min–3hr 40min); Portsmouth (1 daily; 1hr 30min); Southampton (every 30min; 35min–1hr 30min).

Southampton to: Bournemouth (10 daily; 50min–1hr 30min); Bristol (1 daily; 2hr 40min), London (every 30min; 2hr 20min–3hr); Portsmouth (10 daily; 40min–55min); Salisbury (every 30min; 35min–1hr 30min); Weymouth (2 daily; 3hr–3hr 15min); Winchester (every 30min; 25min–1hr).

Winchester to: Bournemouth (5 daily; 1hr 15min–2hr); London (11 daily; 2hr–2hr 35min); Portsmouth (every 30min; 1hr 15min–2hr); Southampton (every 30min; 25min–1hr).

Trains

For information on all local and national rail services, contact **National Rail Enquiries** ☎08457/48 49 50, ⊛www.nationalrail.co.uk.

Bournemouth to: Brockenhurst (every 20min; 15–25min); Dorchester (hourly; 45min); London (every 30min; 1hr 45min–2hr); Poole (1–4 hourly; 10–15min); Southampton (every 20min; 30min–1hr 20min); Weymouth (hourly; 55min); Winchester (1–3 hourly; 45min–1hr 15min).

Dorchester to: Bournemouth (hourly; 40min); Brockenhurst (hourly; 1hr); London (hourly; 2hr 30min); Weymouth (1–2 hourly; 10–15min).

Portsmouth to: London (every 20min; 1hr 35min–1hr 50min); Salisbury (hourly; 1hr 15min); Southampton (every 30min; 40–55min); Winchester (hourly; 1hr).

Ryde (Isle of Wight) to: Shanklin (every 30min; 20–25min).

Salisbury to: Exeter (every 2hr; 1hr 45min–2hr); London (every 20–30min; 1hr 25min); Portsmouth (hourly; 1hr 25min); Southampton (1–2 hourly; 30–40min).

Southampton to: Bournemouth (every 20min; 35–50min); Bristol (1–2 hourly; 1hr 35min–1hr 55min); Brockenhurst (every 15min; 20–45min); London (every 15min; 1hr 15min–1hr 30min); Portsmouth (every 30min; 40min–1hr); Salisbury (every 30min; 30–40min); Weymouth (hourly; 1hr 30min); Winchester (every 15min; 20min).

Winchester to: Bournemouth (every 20min; 45min–1hr); London (every 15–30min; 1hr–1hr 10min); Portsmouth (hourly; 55min); Southampton (every 15min; 15–20min).

Ferries and Hovercraft

Lymington to: Yarmouth, Isle of Wight (1–2 hourly; 30min).

Portsmouth to: Fishbourne, Isle of Wight (1–2 hourly; 35min); Ryde, Isle of Wight (1–2 hourly; 15min).

Southampton to: East Cowes, Isle of Wight (hourly; 55min); West Cowes, Isle of Wight (hourly; 22min).

Southsea to: Ryde, Isle Of Wight (every 10min).

3

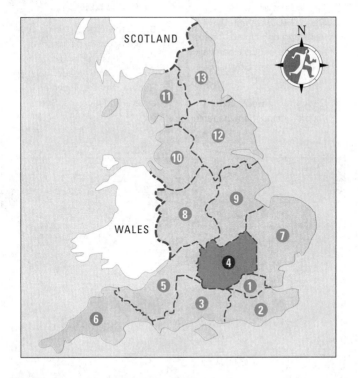

Oxford and around

4

OXFORD AND AROUND

SCOTLAND

WALES

N

CHAPTER 4

Highlights

* **Chiltern Hills** Stretching southwest from Luton to the River Thames near Reading, the Chiltern Hills offer lovely wooded scenery. Henley-on-Thames, site of the famous Henley Regatta, is the best base for further explorations. See p.283

* **The Vale of White Horse** Tranquil spot with pretty villages and eponymous prehistoric horse cut into the chalk of the Berkshire Downs. See p.286

* **Radcliffe Camera, Oxford** Oxford boasts many beautiful old buildings, but the most imposing is the Italianate rotunda, Radcliffe Camera. See p.296

* **Le Petit Blanc restaurant, Oxford** Oxford has several excellent restaurants, but the pick is *Le Petit Blanc*, creation of the French chef, Raymond Blanc. See p.299

* **St Albans** This appealing city on the northern periphery of London has a splendid cathedral and some wonderful Roman remains, including several fine mosaics. See p.304

△ Roman mosaic, St Albans

Oxford and around

A rching around the peripheries of London, beyond the orbital M25, the "Home Counties" of England form London's commuter belt. Beyond the suburban sprawl, however, there is plenty to entice. The northwestern Home Counties – **Berkshire**, **Buckinghamshire** and **Hertfordshire** – are at their most appealing amidst the **Chiltern Hills**, a picturesque band of chalk uplands with **Henley-on-Thames** the most obvious target, a good-looking old town famous for its Regatta and with a good supply of accommodation.

The Chilterns are traversed by the **Ridgeway**, a prehistoric track – and now a national trail – that offers excellent hiking, though its finest portion is further to the west, across the Thames, on **the downs** straddling the Berkshire-Oxfordshire border. Here, the Ridgeway visits a string of prehistoric sites, the most extraordinary being the gigantic chalk horse that gives the **Vale of White Horse** its name. The Vale is dotted with pleasant little villages, and both **Woolstone** and plainer **Uffington** have places to stay; but neither is it far to the university city of **Oxford**, which can keep you busy for several days. Oxford is this region's star turn and it's also close to **Woodstock**, the handsome little town abutting one of England's most imposing country homes, **Blenheim Palace**.

To the northeast of Oxford, well beyond the Chilterns, the plain landscapes of north Buckinghamshire hardly fire the soul, though modest **Buckingham** is pleasant enough and is also within easy striking distance of **Stowe Gardens**, which hold a remarkable collection of outdoor sculptures, monuments and follies. Travel east from Buckingham and you soon reach Bedfordshire, mostly flat agricultural land with a hint of industrial Midlands. It's not a county you'd cross England to visit, but **Bedford** is of interest for its John Bunyan connection and possibly useful for its hotels and restaurants.

In Bedfordshire you're on the edge of the East Midlands (see chapter 7), but travel back towards London and you'll cross Hertfordshire, where the prime target is **St Albans**, an ancient and dignified town with Roman remains and a superb cathedral.

The area covered in this chapter is threaded by five **motorways**, the M25, M4, M40, M1 and A1(M). These give swift access from all directions, though drivers will need a detailed map to successfully explore the rural nooks and crannies. Long-distance **buses** mostly stick to the motorways, too, providing an efficient service to all the larger towns, but local services between the villages are patchy, sometimes nonexistent. There are mainline **train** services from London's Paddington station to Oxford, Henley-on-Thames and Reading, and from London's St Pancras to St Albans and Bedford. These main routes are supplemented by a number of branch lines, the most useful of which links Henley-on-Thames with Cookham.

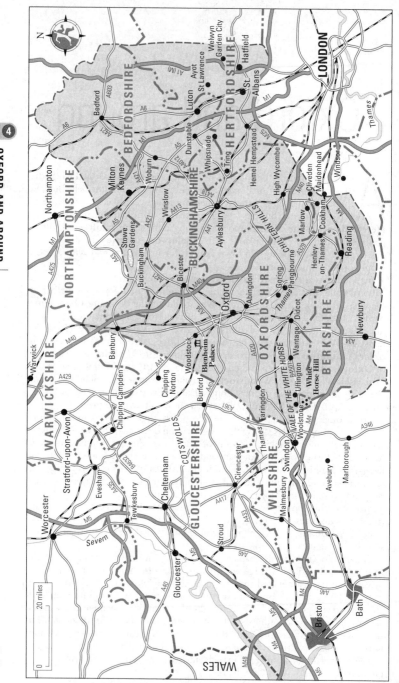

© Crown copyright

4

Thames passenger boat services

Salter's Steamers run **passenger boats** along the River Thames from mid-May to late September, with services between Oxford and Abingdon, Reading and Henley, Henley and Marlow, and between Marlow, Cookham and Windsor. Prices are reasonable – Oxford to Abingdon costs £7.60, Henley to Marlow £7.50 – and there are one or two boats daily on the more popular routes, three weekly on others. For further details contact local tourist offices or Salter Brothers direct on ℡01865/243421, ⊛www.salterssteamers.co.uk.

The Chiltern Hills and the Vale of White Horse

The **Chiltern Hills** extend southwest from the workaday town of Luton, beside the M1, bumping across Buckinghamshire and Oxfordshire as far as the River Thames, just to the west of Reading. At their best, the hills offer handsome countryside, comprising a band of forested chalk hills with steep ridges and deep valleys interrupted by easy, rolling farmland. The Chilterns are also one of the country's wealthiest areas, liberally sprinkled with exclusive commuter hideaways-cum-country homes – though there are unappetising suburban blotches too. For nonresidents, the obvious target is **Henley-on-Thames**, a pleasant riverside town within easy striking distance of the area's key attractions and with a reasonable range of accommodation. The particular target to aim for is the village of **Cookham**, home to the fascinating Stanley Spencer gallery. Spare a thought also for Thameside **Reading**, not so much for itself (it's brusquely modern), but for its two big **music festivals**, Reading Rock Festival and the World Music extravaganza, WOMAD.

Crossing the Chilterns to the north and west of Henley, the **Ridgeway National Trail** offers splendid hiking, though the most diverting part of the trail is further to the west, beyond the Chilterns and the Thames, where, on the edge of the **Vale of White Horse**, the trail sticks to a chalky ridge that provides magnificent views of the surrounding countryside and skirts the giant prehistoric figure after which the Vale is named. Here, you might opt to stay locally in the attractive YHA hostel on the ridge above **Wantage**, in the humdrum town itself or in one of the Vale's quaint villages – tiny **Woolstone** is perhaps the most appealing – though the Vale most readily lends itself to day-trips.

As regards public transport, Henley and Reading are easy to reach by **train** and **bus**, but for the smaller towns and the Vale of White Horse you have to cope with intermittent local bus services. The only good news is the **Ridgeway Explorer bus**, which links Reading and Swindon via Wantage and the Vale of White Horse on Saturdays and Sundays from mid-April to late October (see p.306).

Henley-on-Thames

Three counties – Oxfordshire, Berkshire and Buckinghamshire – meet at **HENLEY-ON-THAMES**, a long-established stopping place for travellers between London and Oxford. Henley is a good-looking, affluent commuter town that is at its prettiest among the old brick and stone buildings that flank the short main drag, **Hart Street**. At one end of Hart Street is the Market

Place and its large and fetching **Town Hall**, at the other stands the easy Georgian curves of **Henley Bridge**. Overlooking the bridge is the **parish church of St Mary**, whose sturdy square tower sports a set of little turrets worked in chequerboard flint and stone, a popular decorative motif in the fifteenth and sixteenth centuries. Several operators run **boat trips** out along the Thames from the jetties just south of the bridge, including Hobbs & Sons (☎01491/572035, ⓦwww.hobbs-of-henley.com), who offer frequent, hour-long jaunts from April to September for £4.75. There's also an imaginative **River and Rowing Museum** (daily 10am–5pm; £4.95), a ten-minute walk south along the riverbank from the foot of Hart Street via Thames Side. This focuses on three main themes: the history of the town, the development of rowing from the Greeks onwards, and the Thames both as a wildlife habitat and as a trading link.

Henley is, however, best known for its **Royal Regatta**, the world's most important amateur rowing tournament, when the town gets all puffed up. Established in 1839, the Regatta is the boating equivalent of the Ascot races, a quintessentially English parade ground for the rich, aristocratic and aspiring, whose champagne-swilling antics are inexplicably found thrilling by larger numbers of the hoi polloi. The Regatta, featuring past and potential Olympic rowers, begins on the Wednesday before the first weekend in July and runs for five days. Further information is available from the Regatta Headquarters on the east side of the Henley Bridge (☎01491/572153, ⓦwww.hrr.co.uk).

Practicalities

Two or three times daily a direct train runs from London's Paddington station to Henley, but mostly you have to change at Twyford. From Henley **train station**, it's a five-minute walk north to Hart Street, along Station Road and its continuation Thames Side. Henley is easy to reach by bus, too, with regular services from Oxford, Reading and London. **Buses** from Reading and points south and west mostly pull in on Hart Street, while those from the north and east – including Marlow and Cookham – stop on Bell Street, immediately to the north of Hart Street. The **tourist office** (Mon–Sat 9.30am–5pm, Sun 11am–4pm; ☎01491/578034, ⓦwww.visit-henley.org.uk) is located in a refurbished old barn, in a courtyard across from the Town Hall – it's clearly signed.

Henley has several first-rate **B&Bs**. One especially good option is the smart and tastefully furnished *Alftrudis*, 8 Norman Ave (☎01491/573099, ⓦwww.alftrudis.co.uk; no credit cards; ❸), which occupies a handsome Victorian townhouse in a quiet, leafy residential street. There are three guest rooms here, all en suite. Another excellent choice is *Lenwade*, 3 Western Rd (☎01491/573468, ⓔlenwadeuk@aol.com; no credit cards; ❹), an attractive Edwardian house with three en-suite guest rooms, comfortable furnishings and fittings and an unusual stained glass window in the hallway. **Hotels** are thin on the ground here, but pick of the bunch is the delightful, wisteria-clad old coaching inn, the *Red Lion*, beside Henley Bridge, with over twenty well-appointed bedrooms, individually decorated in period style (☎01491/572161, ⓦwww.redlionhenley.co.uk; ❼).

The *Red Lion* has the best **restaurant** in town, but there are other more informal – and inexpensive – places on Hart Street, including the *Thai Orchard* at no. 8 (☎01491/412227). **Pubs** line up on Hart Street, but the *Angel*, by the bridge, has the advantage of an outside deck overlooking the river.

Marlow

Heading north and then east out of Henley along the A4155, it's eight leafy miles to bustling **MARLOW**, another pleasant Thames-side town, its centre dotted with comely Georgian buildings. Here, you can while away an hour or two watching boats go through the lock, or tracing Marlow's literary connections. In 1817 Shelley and his wife Mary moved to a cottage on West Street, just along from the Sir William Borlase School, and stayed for a year – just long enough for him to compose the *Revolt of Islam* and for her to write *Frankenstein*. T.S. Eliot lived down the road at no. 31 in 1918, and Jerome K. Jerome wrote a chunk of *Three Men in a Boat* in the *Two Brewers* on St Peter's Street, Marlow's best pub.

There are regular **buses** from Henley to Marlow; they are also linked by **train** – though you do have to change twice and it takes about an hour. Buses drop passengers close to Marlow High Street, a couple of minutes walk from the **tourist office**, at no. 31 (Mon–Fri 9am–5pm, Sat 9.30am–5pm; winter closes 4pm; ☎01628/483597). From the train station, it's a short walk west along Station Road to the tourist office.

Cookham

Tiny **COOKHAM**, on the other side of the Thames just three miles southeast of Marlow – and not to be confused with neighbouring Cookham Dean and Cookham Rise – is noteworthy as the former home of **Stanley Spencer** (1891–1959), one of Britain's greatest – and most eccentric – artists. The Bible fired Spencer's imagination and many of his paintings depict biblical tales transposed into his Cookham surroundings – remarkable, visionary works in which the village is turned into a sort of earthly paradise. Spencer made his artistic name in the 1920s, firstly as an official war artist and then for his *Resurrection: Cookham*, which attracted rave reviews when it was exhibited in London in 1927. No one minded much that his brand of Christianity was extremely unorthodox – he called his religious system the "Church of Me" – but in the 1930s his reputation temporarily dipped and he took endless critical flak when his work took an erotic turn. In part, this reflected his own changing circumstances; in 1937, he divorced his first wife, Hilda, in order to marry his mistress, Patricia Preece, but the latter exploited him financially and, so most contemporaries thought, regularly humiliated him.

Much of Spencer's most acclaimed work is displayed at Tate Britain in London (see p.99), but there's a fine sample here at the **Stanley Spencer Gallery** (Easter–Oct daily 10.30am–5.30pm; Nov–Easter Sat & Sun 11am–5pm; £1), which occupies the old Methodist Chapel on the High Street. Three prime exhibits are *The Last Supper*, *Christ Preaching at Cookham Regatta: Listening from Punts* and another wonderful (but unfinished) *Christ Preaching at Cookham Regatta*.

There's an hourly **train** service from Marlow to Cookham and from the station it's a pleasant ten-minute walk east across the common to the Spencer Gallery. Cookham's *Bel & Dragon* **pub**, directly opposite the gallery, has ancient beams and ample leather chairs, pulls a good pint and serves decent home-made food.

Reading

READING is a modern, prosperous town on the south bank of the River Thames, ten miles south of Henley. Guarding the western approaches to the capital, it has always been important, long a stopping-off point for kings and queens and once home to one of the country's richest abbeys. Henry VIII took care of the abbey, seizing its lands and hanging the abbot from the main gate, and today almost nothing remains of the old town except the shattered remains of the aforementioned abbey, a short walk to the east of the pedestrianized shopping centre.

There's a flourishing **arts scene** here however, with both the Reading Film Theatre (℡0118/9868497, 🌐www.readingfilmtheatre.co.uk) and the Hexagon Theatre (℡0118/9606060, 🌐www.readingarts.com) offering a good programme of shows, but you wouldn't make a beeline for the place were it not for its two big summertime **music festivals**. The first, the three-day **WOMAD** festival (🌐www.womad.org; tickets ℡0118/9390930), held each July, is a celebration of World Music, Arts and Dance, originally inspired by Peter Gabriel. Since the first WOMAD in 1982, there have been about a hundred spin-off events in twenty countries, but the Reading festival remains the focus, held at the Rivermead Leisure Complex, Richfield Avenue, just to the north of the town centre. At the same venue, but a little later in the summer, the **Reading Festival** (🌐www.readingfestival.com) is a three-day event featuring many of the big names of contemporary music. Details of who is performing are published in the music press at least a couple of months in advance and tickets are available from record shops and ticket outlets across the country. The vast majority of festival-goers **camp on site** and special buses run there in their hundreds, or you can walk in fifteen minutes from Reading train station.

Reading can be reached by train from London Paddington and Waterloo. The **tourist office**, in the town centre in Church House, on Chain Street (Mon–Fri 10am–5pm, Sat 9.30am–4pm; ℡0118/9566226, 🌐www.readingtourism .org.uk), operates an accommodation-booking service; be sure to reserve a room months in advance if you're planning on being here for either festival.

The Vale of White Horse

The **Vale of White Horse**, falling between Wantage, a modest market town about thirty miles west of Henley, and Faringdon, seventeen miles southwest of Oxford, is a shallow valley, whose fertile farmland is studded with tiny villages. It takes its name from the prehistoric figure cut into the chalk downs above two of its smaller hamlets – **Uffington** and **Woolstone**. Carved in the first century BC, the horse is the most conspicuous of a string of prehistoric remains that punctuates the downs and includes burial mounds and Iron Age forts. The **Ridgeway National Trail** (🌐www.nationaltrails.gov.uk), running along – or near – the top of the downs, links several of these sites and offers wonderful, breezy views over the Vale. Originally a prehistoric footpath, the Ridgeway was long used as a drove road, with sheep taken over the downs to market. Nowadays, horses are more common, the well-drained turf providing an ideal training ground for racehorses.

Wantage

Workaday **WANTAGE** is an unassuming, somewhat careworn market town, whose crowded Market Place is overseen by a statue of its most famous son, Alfred the Great (849–99), the most distinguished of England's Saxon kings. Unveiled in 1877, the statue doesn't do Alfred any favours – though he must have been very strong to stand any chance of lifting his over-large axe. From the south side of the Market Place – which is where long-distance buses pull in – a couple of alleys lead through to Church Street. This is the location of the **tourist office** (☏01235/760176), which shares its premises – and times – with the modest **Vale and Downland Museum** (Mon–Sat 10am–4.30pm, Sun 2.30–5pm; £1.50).

Wantage is handy for the finest portion of the **Ridgeway** and the tourist office is the place to pick up local hiking maps and bus timetables. The quickest way to reach the Ridgeway direct from Wantage is to take **bus #38** (Mon–Sat only, hourly; 20min) from the Market Place to **Letcombe Bassett**, less than a mile from the path, but be aware that not all of these buses follow the same route so check with the driver. Excellent walking along the Ridgeway takes you westwards from Letcombe Bassett to the White Horse (see below), a distance of about seven miles.

There's no strong reason to stay in Wantage, but there are several **B&Bs**, the most recommendable of which is the well-kept *Alfred's Lodge*, in a detached Victorian house about five minutes' walk southeast of the centre at 23 Ormond Rd (☏01235/762409; no credit cards; ❶). To get there from the east end of the Market Place, take Newbury Street and watch for Ormond on the left. Alternatively, the **Ridgeway youth hostel** (☏0870/770 6064, ✉ridgeway@yha.org.uk; dorm beds £11.50) occupies a prime position just off the A338 a couple of miles south of Wantage – watch for the sign. The hostel consists of several sympathetically converted old timber barns set around a courtyard, with the Ridgeway a stone's throw away. On weekdays, the nearest you'll get by public transport is bus #38 from Wantage to Letcombe Regis, from where it's a mile or so uphill to the hostel. At the weekend, **The Ridgeway Explorer** bus (see p.306) stops right outside.

Wantage has one excellent **restaurant**, *Thyme and Plaice*, near the east end of the Market Place at 8 Newbury St (☏01235/760568), serving imaginatively prepared contemporary dishes featuring local ingredients, but it's expensive – a two-course set meal costs around £20 – so for a much less pricey deal, try the *Cornucopia Coffee Shop*, which serves tasty snacks and lunches from its premises at Unit 13, Post Office Vaults, at the east end of the Market Place.

White Horse Hill

White Horse Hill, six miles west of Wantage along the B4507, follows close behind Stonehenge (see p.273) and Avebury (see p.275) in the hierarchy of Britain's ancient sites, though it attracts nothing like the same number of visitors. Carved into the north-facing slope of the downs above the villages of Uffington and Woolstone, the 374-foot-long **horse** looks like something created with a few swift strokes of an immense brush, and there's been no lack of weird and wonderful theories as to its origins. Some have suggested it was a glorified signpost, created to show travellers where to join the Ridgeway, others that it represented the horse (or even the dragon) of St George. In fact, burial sites excavated in the surrounding area point to the horse having some kind of sacred function, though frankly noone knows quite what. The first written record of the horse's existence dates from the time of Henry II, but it was cut much earlier, probably in the first century BC, making it one of the oldest chalk figures in Britain. A detailed 1994 study showed that its creators dug out the soil to a depth of a metre and then filled the hollow with clear white chalk taken from a nearby hilltop. Here also, at the top of the hill, is the Iron Age earthwork of **Uffington Castle**, which provides wonderful views over the Vale.

The Ridgeway runs alongside the horse and continues west to reach, after one-and-a-half miles, **Wayland's Smithy**, a 5000-year-old burial mound encircled by trees. It's one of the best Neolithic remains along the Ridgeway, though heavy restoration has rather detracted from its mystery. In ignorance of its original function, the invading Saxons named it after Wayland Smith, an invisible smith who, according to their legends, made invincible armour and shoed horses without ever being seen.

Woolstone and Uffington

About three quarters of a mile below the White Horse car park, on the north side of the B4057, is the minuscule hamlet of **WOOLSTONE** where the attractive *White Horse Inn* (℡01367/820726; ❸) occupies a half-timbered, partly thatched building and offers both good-quality pub food and **accommodation**, mostly in a modern annexe. A second option is the *Hickory House* (℡01367/820303; no credit cards; ❷), offering two en-suite guest rooms in a spick-and-span modern house close to the pub. A mile or two to the north of Woolstone, the much larger (and plainer) village of **UFFINGTON** has a couple of **B&Bs**, notably the well-kept and unassuming *Norton House*, next to the post office on the main street (℡01367/820230; no credit cards; ❷).

Oxford

When they think of **OXFORD**, visitors almost always think of its **university**, revered as one of the world's great academic institutions, inhabiting honey-coloured stone buildings set around ivy-clad quadrangles. Much of this is accurate enough, but although the university dominates central Oxford both physically and mentally, the wider city has an entirely different character, its economy built on the **car plants** of Cowley to the south of the centre. It was here that Britain's first mass-produced cars were produced in the 1920s and, although there have been more downs than ups in recent years, the plants are still vitally important to the area.

Oxford started late, in Anglo-Saxon times, and blossomed even later, under the Normans, when the cathedral was constructed and Oxford was chosen as a royal residence. The origins of the university are obscure, but it seems that the reputation of **Henry I**, the so-called "Scholar King", helped attract students in the early twelfth century, their numbers increasing with the expulsion of English students from the Sorbonne in 1167. The first colleges, founded mostly by rich bishops, were essentially ecclesiastical institutions and this was reflected in collegiate rules and regulations – until 1877 lecturers were not allowed to marry and women were not granted degrees until 1920. There are common architectural features, too, with the private rooms of the students arranged around quadrangles (quads), as are most of the communal rooms – the chapels, halls (dining rooms) and libraries.

Arrival

From Oxford **train station**, it's a five- to ten-minute walk east to the centre along Park End Street and Hythe Bridge Street. Long-distance and many county-wide buses terminate at the Gloucester Green **bus station**, in the centre adjoining George Street. The Oxford Bus Company (℡01865/785400) operates most local and city buses, many of which pull in on the High Street and St Giles. They also run the city's **Park-and-Ride** scheme, with buses (daily Mon–Sat 5.30am–11pm, Sun 8.30am–6.30pm) travelling into the centre every thirty minutes – fifteen at peak periods – from four large and clearly signed car parks on the main approach roads into the city. Parking costs are minimal, whereas parking in the city centre is – by municipal design – both inordinately expensive and hard to find.

Information and guided tours

The **tourist office** is plum in the centre of town at 15 Broad St (Mon–Sat 9.30am–5pm, plus late April to late Oct Sun 10am–3.30pm; ☎01865/726871, ⓦwww.visitoxford.org). They have a wealth of information about the city and its sights, though little of it is issued free, with the notable exception of two free **listings booklets** – *This Month in Oxford* and *In Oxford*. The tourist office also operates an accommodation-booking service and offers excellent **guided walking tours**; a two-hour stroll round the city centre costs £6.50. There are several tours daily, but it's still a good idea to book in advance.

Accommodation

With supply struggling to keep pace with demand, Oxford's central **hotels** are almost invariably expensive. There are one or two cheaper places in or near the centre, but by and large they are far from inspiring and, at the budget end of the market, you're better off choosing a **guest house** or **B&B**, of which there is a healthy supply. The problem is that the majority (but certainly not all) of these establishments are scattered on the edge of town – and Oxford is much better appreciated if you stay in the centre. Wherever you stay, book ahead in high season either direct or through the tourist office, which operates an efficient accommodation-booking service and compiles a comprehensive accommodation listings booklet, *Staying in Oxford* (£1).

Hotels

Bath Place 4 Bath Place ☎01865/791812, ⓦwww.bathplace.co.uk. Unusual, pink and blue hotel, down an old cobbled courtyard, with just thirteen rooms, all of them reasonably attractive. The location is excellent – in the centre, off Holywell Street. ❻

Old Bank 92 High St ☎01865/799599, ⓦwww.oxford-hotels-restaurants.co.uk. Great location for a first-rate hotel. Over twenty immaculate bedrooms are decorated in smart, modern style and some have great views over All Souls college. The *Quod* bistro is on the ground floor. ❽

Parklands 100 Banbury Rd ☎01865/554374, ⓔtheparklands@freenet.co.uk. Pleasant fourteen-room hotel in a Victorian house with a garden, licensed restaurant and bar. North of the centre, but connected to it by a frequent bus service. Good value. ❺

Guest houses and B&Bs

Becket Guest House 5 Becket St ☎01865/724675. Modest bay-windowed guest house in a plain terrace close to the train station. Most rooms en suite. ❸

Brown's Guest House 281 Iffley Rd ☎01865/246822, ⓦwww.brownsguesthouse.co.uk. Well-maintained and recently revamped guest house in a pleasing Victorian property with ten rooms, all en suite. ❸

College Guest House 103 Woodstock Rd ☎01865/552579, ⓦwww.oxfordcity.co.uk. About ten minutes' walk north of the centre, this pleasant guest house occupies a distinctive older, high-gabled building. There are eight rooms, four en suite. ❸

Cotswold House 363 Banbury Rd ☎01865/310558, ⓦwww.house363.freeserve.co.uk. Top-notch B&B, two miles north of the centre, in a bright and breezy modern house, offering excellent breakfasts and comfortable, well-appointed en-suite rooms. ❹

St Michael's Guest House 26 St Michael's St ☎01865/242101. Often full, this friendly, well-kept B&B, in a cosy three-storey terraced house, has unsurprising furnishings and fittings, but a charming, central location. A real snip. ❸

Hostels

Oxford Backpackers Hostel 9A Hythe Bridge St ☎01865/721761, ⓔoxford@hostels.co.uk. Independent hostel with quads and dorms, holding up to eighteen people each. Fully equipped kitchen

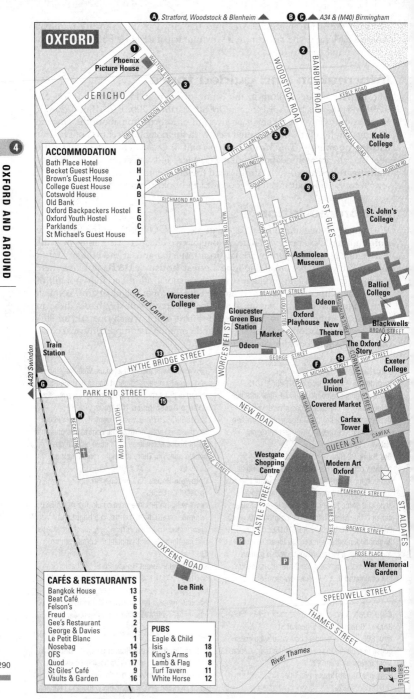

OXFORD

A, Stratford, Woodstock & Blenheim ▲   B, C, ▲ A34 & (M40) Birmingham

Phoenix Picture House

① ② ③ ④ ⑤ ⑥ ⑦ ⑧ ⑨

JERICHO

WALTON STREET

GREAT CLARENDON STREET

WOODSTOCK ROAD

BANBURY ROAD

KEBLE ROAD

BLACKHALL ROAD

MUSEUM RD.

Keble College

LITTLE CLARENDON STREET

WELLINGTON SQUARE

WALTON CRESCENT

RICHMOND ROAD

ST. JOHN'S STREET

PUSEY STREET

PUSEY LANE

ST. GILES

St. John's College

ACCOMMODATION

Bath Place Hotel	D
Becket Guest House	H
Brown's Guest House	J
College Guest House	A
Cotswold House	B
Old Bank	I
Oxford Backpackers Hostel	E
Oxford Youth Hostel	G
Parklands	C
St Michael's Guest House	F

WALTON STREET

Oxford Canal

Worcester College

BEAUMONT STREET

Ashmolean Museum

Balliol College

GLOUCESTER STREET

MAGDALEN STREET

Odeon

Gloucester Green Bus Station

Oxford Playhouse

New Theatre

Blackwells

BROAD STREET

ⓘ

Market

Odeon

GEORGE STREET

SHIP STREET

The Oxford Story

Exeter College

Train Station

HYTHE BRIDGE STREET

⑬

E

WORCESTER ST.

F ⑭

ST. MICHAEL'S STREET

CORNMARKET STREET

MARKET STREET

A420 Swindon

G

PARK END STREET

H

BECKET STREET

HOLLYBUSH ROW

⑮

NEW INN HALL STREET

Oxford Union

Covered Market

NEW ROAD

PARADISE STREET

Carfax Tower ⋔

QUEEN ST.

CARFAX

Westgate Shopping Centre

CASTLE STREET

Modern Art Oxford

✉

ST. EBBE'S STREET

ST. ALDATES

PEMBROKE STREET

BREWER STREET

P

P

OXPENS ROAD

ROSE PLACE

War Memorial Garden

Ice Rink

SPEEDWELL STREET

THAMES STREET

River Thames

Punts

FOLLY BRIDGE

CAFÉS & RESTAURANTS

Bangkok House	13
Beat Café	5
Felson's	6
Freud	3
Gee's Restaurant	2
George & Davies	4
Le Petit Blanc	1
Nosebag	14
OFS	15
Quod	17
St Giles' Café	9
Vaults & Garden	16

PUBS

Eagle & Child	7
Isis	18
King's Arms	10
Lamb & Flag	8
Turf Tavern	11
White Horse	12

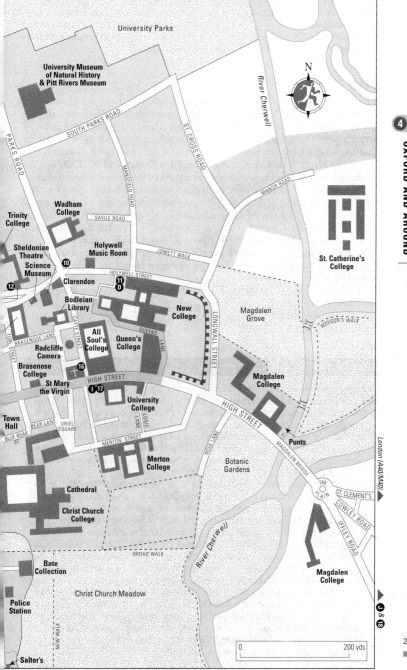

University Parks

River Cherwell

N

University Museum
of Natural History
& Pitt Rivers Museum

SOUTH PARKS ROAD

ST. CROSS ROAD

MANSFIELD ROAD

MANOR ROAD

PARKS ROAD

Trinity
College

Wadham
College

SAVILE ROAD

St. Catherine's
College

Sheldonian
Theatre
Science
Museum

Holywell
Music Room

JOWETT WALK

10

12

Clarendon

HOLYWELL STREET

11
D

Bodleian
Library

New
College

Magdalen
Grove

ADDISON'S WALK

CATTE STREET

All
Soul's
College

Queen's
College

QUEENS

LONGWALL STREET

Radcliffe
Camera

16

Magdalen
College

TURL STREET

BRASENOSE LANE

Brasenose
College

St Mary
the Virgin

HIGH STREET

I **17**

QUEENS

LANE

London (A40/M40)

Town
Hall

BEAR LANE

University
College

LOGIC

LANE

HIGH STREET

BLUE BOAR ST

ORIEL
SQUARE

MAGDALEN BRIDGE

Punts

MERTON STREET

ROSE LANE

Merton
College

Botanic
Gardens

THE
PLAIN

ST. CLEMENT'S

Cathedral

COWLEY ROAD

Christ Church
College

IFFLEY ROAD

Magdalen
College

BROAD WALK

River Cherwell

J & **18**

Bate
Collection

Christ Church Meadow

Police
Station

NEW WALK

0   200 yds

Salter's

Abingdon

© Crown copyright

and laundry plus Internet facilities. Handy location between the train station and the centre; 24-hour access. Dorm beds £13.

Oxford Youth Hostel 2A Botley Rd ☎0870/770 5970, ©oxford@yha.org.uk. Next door to the train station, this popular YHA hostel has 184 beds divided up into two-, four- and six-bedded rooms. There's 24-hour access, good self-catering facilities and an inexpensive café. Dorm beds including breakfast £19.50.

The City

The compact centre of Oxford is wedged in between the rivers Thames and Cherwell, just to the north of the point where they join. In theory, and on most maps, the Thames is known within the city as the "Isis", but few locals actually use the term. Central Oxford's principal point of reference is **Carfax**, a busy junction from where three of the city's main thoroughfares begin: the **High Street** runs east to Magdalen Bridge and the Cherwell; **St Aldates** south to the Thames; and **Cornmarket** north to the broad avenue of St Giles. Many of the oldest **colleges** face onto the High Street or the side streets adjoining it, their mellow stonework combining to create one of the most beautiful parts of Oxford, though the most stunning college of them all is **Christ Church**. Here, as elsewhere in the city, all of the more visited colleges have restricted opening hours and some impose an admission charge, while others permit no regular public access at all. Of those that do open their doors, **college opening times** are fairly consistent throughout the year, but there are sporadic term-time variations, especially at weekends. It's also worth noting that during the exam season, which stretches from late April to early June, all the colleges have periods when they are closed to the public. For more specific information, call the relevant college.

On the river

Punting is a favourite summer pastime among both students and visitors, but handling a punt – a flat-bottomed boat ideal for the shallow waters of the Thames and Cherwell rivers – requires some practice. The punt is propelled and steered with a long pole, which beginners inevitably get stuck in riverbed mud: if this happens, let go and paddle back, otherwise you're likely to be pulled overboard. The Cherwell, though much narrower than the Thames and therefore trickier to navigate, provides more opportunities for pulling to the side for a picnic, an essential part of the punting experience.

As regards **boat rental**, there are two fairly central places. The first is the Magdalen Bridge boathouse (☎01865/202643), beside the Cherwell at the east end of the High Street; the second is the Thames boat station at Folly Bridge (☎01865/243421), a five- to ten-minute stroll south of the centre along St Aldates. However, in summer the queues soon build up at both, so either get there early in the morning – at around 10am – or head off to the Cherwell Boat House (☎01865/515978), a mile or so north of the centre: to get there, head out of the centre on Banbury Road, turn right along Linton Road and the boat house is at the end, behind Wolfson College. At all three boathouses, expect **to pay** about £12 per hour for a boat plus a £30 deposit, and remember that sometimes ID is required. Punts can take a maximum of five passengers – four sitting and one punting. Call the boathouses for opening times – which vary – or if there are any doubts about the weather. If you're determined not to do any actual punting yourself, you might consider hiring a **chauffeured punt** (£25 for 30min). The boathouses also rent out pedaloes, which cost less, but aren't as much fun.

South from Carfax to Modern Art Oxford

Too busy to be comfortable and too modern to be pretty, the **Carfax** is not a place to hang around, but it's overlooked by an interesting remnant of the medieval town, a chunky fourteenth-century **tower**, adorned by a pair of clocktower jacks dressed in vaguely Roman gear. The tower is all that remains of St Martin's church, where legend asserts that William Shakespeare stood sponsor at the baptism of one of his friend's children. You can climb the **tower** (daily: April–Oct 10am–5.30pm; Nov–March 10am–3.30pm; £1.40) for wide views over the centre, though other vantage points have the edge.

Spreading down St Aldates from the Carfax, Oxford's **Town Hall** is an ostentatious Victorian confection that reflects a municipal determination not to be overwhelmed by the university. A staircase on its south side gives access to the **Museum of Oxford** (Tues–Fri 10am–4pm, Sat 10am–5pm, Sun noon–4pm; £2), which makes good use of photographs to tell the history of the city.

From the Town Hall, cross St Aldates and it's a few paces to Pembroke Street, which possesses the city's best contemporary art gallery, **Modern Art Oxford** (Tues–Sat 10am–5pm, Sun noon–5pm; free; ⓦ www.modernartoxford.org.uk). The gallery has an excellent programme of temporary exhibitions, featuring international contemporary art in a wide variety of media, along with lectures, films, workshops and multimedia performances (not all of which are free).

Christ Church College

Doubling back along Pembroke Street, turn right down St Aldates for the main facade of **Christ Church College** (Mon–Sat 9.30am–5.30pm, Sun noon–5.30pm; £4; ☎01865/276492), whose distinctive Tom Tower was added by Christopher Wren in 1681 to house the weighty "Great Tom" bell. The tower lords it over the main entrance of what is Oxford's largest and arguably most prestigious college, but visitors have to enter from the south, a signed five-minute walk away – just past the tiny War Memorial Garden and from the top of Christ Church Meadow. Albert Einstein, William Gladstone and no fewer than twelve other British prime ministers were educated here and the college also claims the distinction of having been founded three times, lastly in 1545, when it assumed its present name.

Entering the college from the south, it's a short step to the striking **Tom Quad**, the largest quad in Oxford, so large in fact that the Royalists penned up their mobile larder of cattle here during the Civil War. Guarded by the Tom Tower, the Quad's soft, honey-coloured stone makes a harmonious whole, but it was built in two main phases with the southern side dating back to Wolsey, the north finally finished in the 1660s. A wide stone staircase in the southeast corner of the Quad leads up to the **Dining Hall**, the grandest refectory in Oxford with a fanciful hammer-beam roof and a set of stern portraits of past scholars by a roll-call of well-known artists.

Just to the rear of the Tom Quad stands the **Cathedral**, which is also – in a most unusual arrangement – the college chapel. The Anglo-Saxons built a church on this site in the seventh century as part of St Frideswide Priory. The priory was suppressed in 1524, but the church survived, becoming a cathedral forty years later, though in between Wolsey knocked down the west end to make space for the Tom Quad. It's an unusually discordant church, with all sorts of bits and bobs from different periods, but it's fascinating all the same. The dominant feature is the sturdy circular columns and rounded arches of the Normans, but there are also early Gothic pointed arches and the chancel ceiling is a particularly fine example of fifteenth-century stone vaulting. The battered **shrine of St Frideswide**, in the Latin Chapel – to the far right of the entrance – was destroyed during the Dissolution, but the pieces were found down an old well and gamely assembled by the Victorians. Today, it exhibits some of the earliest natural foliage in English sculpture, a splendid confection of leaves dating from around 1290.

A passage at the northeast corner of the Tom Quad leads through to the **Peckwater Quad**, whose pleasantries are overwhelmed by the whopping Neoclassical library. A few steps more and you're in the pocket-sized **Canterbury Quad**, where the **Picture Gallery** (Mon–Sat 10.30am–5.30pm, Sun 2–5pm; £2) is home to works by many of Italy's finest artists from the fifteenth to eighteenth centuries, including Leonardo da Vinci and Michelangelo. There's also a good showing by the Dutch –Van Dyck, Frans Hals and so forth. The Canterbury Quad abuts Oriel Square and Merton College.

Merton College

Next door to Christ Church, **Merton College** (Mon–Fri 2–4pm, Sat & Sun 10am–4pm; free; ☎01865/276310) is historically the city's most important college. Balliol and University colleges may have been founded earlier, but it was Merton – opened in 1264 – which set the model for colleges in both Oxford and Cambridge, being the first to gather its students and tutors together in one place. Furthermore, unlike the other two, Merton retains some of its original medieval buildings, with the best of the thirteenth-century architecture clustered around **Mob Quad**, a charming courtyard with mullioned windows and Gothic doorways to the right of the Front Quad. From the Mob Quad, an archway leads through to the **Chapel**, which dates from 1290. Notice the curious funerary plaque of Thomas Bodley – founder of Oxford's most important library – his bust surrounded by ungainly, boyish-looking women in classical garb. Apart from Bodley, famous Merton alumni include T.S. Eliot, Angus Wilson, Louis MacNeice and Kris Kristofferson.

University and Queen's colleges

From Merton, narrow Logic Lane threads to the east end of **University College** (no set opening times; ☎01865/276602), whose long curved facade and twin gateway towers spread along the High Street. Known as "Univ", the college claims Alfred the Great as its founder, but things really got going with a formal endowment in 1249, making it Oxford's oldest college – though nothing of that period survives. The college's most famous recent alumnus was Bill Clinton, the non-inhaling Rhodes Scholar; former Australian premier Bob Hawke also studied here.

Across the High Street from Univ stands **Queen's College** (no set opening times; ☎01865/279120), whose handsome Baroque buildings cut an impressive dash. The only Oxford college to have been built in one period (1682–1765), Queen's benefited from the skills of several talented architects, most notably Nicholas Hawksmoor and Christopher Wren. Wren designed (or at least influenced the design of) the college's most diverting building, the **Chapel**, whose ceiling is filled with cherubs amidst dense foliage.

St Mary the Virgin

From Queen's, it's a couple of minutes' walk west along the High Street to **St Mary the Virgin** (daily 9am–5pm; free), a hotchpotch of architectural styles, but mostly dating from the fifteenth century. The church's saving graces are its elaborate, thirteenth-century pinnacled spire and its distinctive Baroque porch, flanked by chunky corkscrewed pillars – and paid for by a Charles I loyalist, Archbishop Laud, who came to a sticky end at the hands of the

Parliamentarians. The other diversion is the church **tower** (same times; £2), whose views can't be bettered, both across to the Radcliffe Camera (see p.296) and east over **All Souls College** (Mon–Fri 2–4pm; free; ℡01865/279379), with its twin mock-Gothic towers (the work of Hawksmoor) and conspicuous, brightly decorated sundial designed by Wren. The tower can also be entered round the back of the church.

Magdalen College and the University Botanic Gardens

Heading east along the High Street, it's a short walk to **Magdalen College** (pronounced "Maudlin"; Mon–Fri noon–6pm, Sat & Sun 2–6pm; £3; ℡01865/276000), whose gaggle of stone buildings is overshadowed by its chunky medieval bell tower. Steer right from the entrance and you soon reach the **Chapel**, which has a handsome reredos – though you have to admire it from a distance, through the windows of an ungainly stone screen. The adjacent **cloisters**, arguably the finest in Oxford, are adorned by standing figures, some of which are biblical and others folkloric – most notably the cacophony of bizarre grotesques. Magdalen's alumni include Oscar Wilde, C.S. Lewis, John Betjeman, Julian Barnes, A.J.P. Taylor and Dudley Moore.

Across the High Street from Magdalen lie the **University of Oxford Botanic Gardens** (daily: April–Sept 9am–5pm; Oct–March 9am–4.30pm; £2.50), whose greenery is bounded by a graceful curve of the Cherwell. First planted in 1621, the gardens comprise several different zones, from a lily pond, a bog garden and a rock garden through to borders of bearded irises and variegated plants. There are also eight large **glasshouses** featuring tropical and desert species (daily: April–Sept 10am–4.30pm; Oct–March 10–4pm; no extra charge).

The gardens are next to **Magdalen Bridge**, where you can rent punts (see box on p.292).

New College

Retracing your steps back along the High Street to Queen's, cut up **Queen's Lane** and you'll dog-leg your way north to **New College** (daily: April–Oct 11am–5pm; Nov–March 2–4pm; £2; ℡01865/279555). Founded in 1379, the college kicks off with an attractive **Front Quad,** though the splendid Perpendicular Gothic architecture of the original was spoiled by the addition of an extra storey in 1674. The adjoining **Chapel** has been mucked about, too, yet it can still lay claim to being the finest in Oxford, not so much for its design as its contents. The ante-chapel contains some superb fourteenth-century stained glass and the west window – of 1778 – holds an intriguing (if somewhat unsuccessful) Nativity scene based on a design by Sir Joshua Reynolds. Beneath it stands the wonderful *Lazarus* by Jacob Epstein; Khrushchev, after a visit to the college, claimed that the memory of this haunting sculpture kept him awake at night. An archway on the east side of the Front Quad leads through to the modest **Garden Quad**, with the thick flower beds of the **College Garden** beckoning beyond. The north side of the garden is flanked by the largest and best-preserved section of Oxford's medieval **city wall**, but the conspicuous earthen **mound** in the middle is a later decorative addition and not, disappointingly, medieval at all. Notable New College alumni include politicians Hugh Gaitskell and Tony Benn, and the author John Fowles.

The Sheldonian Theatre and the Bodleian Library

The east end of Broad Street abuts some of Oxford's most monumental architecture, beginning with the **Sheldonian Theatre** (Mon–Sat

10am–12.30pm & 2–4.30pm; winter closes 3.30pm; £1.50), ringed by a series of glum-looking, pop-eyed classical heads. The Sheldonian was Christopher Wren's first major work, a reworking of the Theatre of Marcellus in Rome, semicircular at the back and rectangular at the front. It was conceived in 1663, when the 31-year-old Wren's main job was as professor of astronomy. Designed as a stage for university ceremonies, nowadays it also functions as a concert hall, but the interior lacks any sense of drama, and even the views from the cupola are disappointing.

Wren's colleague, Nicholas Hawksmoor, designed the **Clarendon Building**, a domineering, solidly symmetrical edifice topped by allegorical figures that is set at right angles to – and lies immediately east of – the Sheldonian. The Clarendon was erected to house the University Press, but is now part of the **Bodleian Library** – the UK's largest after the British Library in London – which has an estimated eighty miles of shelves distributed among various buildings. The heart of the Bodleian is located straight across from the Clarendon in the **Old Library**, which inhabits the beautifully proportioned **Old Schools Quadrangle**, built in the early seventeenth century in the ornate Jacobean-Gothic style that distinguishes many of the city's finest buildings. On the quad's east side is the handsome **Tower of the Five Orders**, which gives a lesson in architectural design, with tiers of columns built according to the five classical styles – Tuscan, Doric, Ionic, Corinthian and Composite. On the west side is the library's main entrance and, although most of the complex is out of bounds to the general public, you can pop into the **Divinity School** (Mon–Fri 9am–4.45pm, Sat 9am–12.30pm; free), one large room where, until the nineteenth century, degree candidates were questioned in detail about their subject by two interlocutors, with a professor acting as umpire. Begun in 1424, and sixty years in the making, the Divinity School boasts an extravagant vaulted ceiling, a riot of pendants and decorative bosses that comprises an exquisite example of late Gothic architecture. However, this elaborate design was never carried right through – funding was a constant problem – and parts of the school were finished off in a much plainer style with the change being especially pronounced on the south wall.

The Radcliffe Camera

Behind the Old Schools Quadrangle rises Oxford's most imposing – or vainglorious – building, the Bodleian's **Radcliffe Camera** (formerly the Radcliffe Library; no public access), a mighty rotunda, built between 1737 and 1748 by James Gibbs, architect of London's St Martin-in-the-Fields church. There's no false modesty here. Dr John Radcliffe was, according to a contemporary diarist, "very ambitious of glory" and when he died in 1714 he bequeathed a mountain of money for the construction of a library – the "Radcliffe Mausoleum" as one wag termed it. Gibbs was one of the few British architects of the period to have been trained in Rome and his rotunda was thoroughly Italian in style, its limestone columns ascending to a delicate balustrade, decorated with pinprick urns and encircling a lead-sheathed dome.

Cornmarket and the Ashmolean

Broad Street leads into the **Cornmarket**, a busy shopping strip lined by major stores. There's precious little here to fire the imagination, but it's only a few yards more to the **Ashmolean** (Tues–Sat 10am–5pm, Sun 2–5pm, plus late opening one evening a week in summer; free), the university's principal museum, occupying a mammoth Neoclassical building on the corner of Beaumont Street and St Giles. The museum grew up around the collections of

△ Radcliffe Camera, Oxford

the magpie-like **John Tradescant**, gardener to Charles I and an energetic traveller. During his wanderings, Tradescant built up a huge assortment of artefacts and natural specimens, which became known as Tradescant's Ark. He bequeathed all this to his friend and sponsor, the lawyer Elias Ashmole, who in turn gave it to the university. Tradescant's Ark has been added to ever since and today the Ashmolean is far too large to absorb in one visit, so either allow for several or stick to the highlights. Plans are available at reception and the museum shop sells a useful introductory guide.

Beginning on the ground floor, the **Egyptian** rooms should not be missed: in addition to well-preserved mummies and sarcophagi, there are unusual frescoes, rare textiles from the Roman and Byzantine periods and several fine examples of relief carving, such as on the shrine of Taharqa. Nearby, the **Islamic Art** room includes superb Islamic ceramics, while the six **Chinese Art** rooms contain some remarkable early Chinese pottery with the simple monochrome pots of the Sung dynasty (960–1279) looking surprisingly modern.

On the first floor, a selection from Tradescant's Ark is gathered together in **Room 27**. Amongst the assorted curiosities, a particular highlight is Powhatan's mantle, a handsome garment made of deerskin and decorated with shells. Powhatan was the father of Pocahontas, and this mantle therefore dates back to the earliest contacts between English colonists and the Native Americans of modern-day Virginia. In this room also are Guy Fawkes' lantern, Oliver Cromwell's death mask and the peculiar armour-plated hat that Bradshaw, the president of the board of regicides, thought it prudent to wear when he condemned Charles I to death.

Archeologist Arthur Evans' stunning collection of Minoan finds from his years working at Knossos in Crete (1900–06) are displayed in the **Ancient Crete & Aegean Room** and pride of place goes to the storage jars, sumptuously decorated with sea creatures and marine plants. Close by, in **Room 35**, is the extraordinary Alfred Jewel, a tiny gold, enamel and rock crystal piece of uncertain purpose. The inscription reads "Alfred ordered me to be made" – almost certainly a reference to King Alfred the Great. Most of the rest of the first floor is devoted to European painting from the Italian Renaissance to the early twentieth century with a series of clearly labelled galleries arranged in roughly chronological order. There's a strong showing of **French paintings**, with Pissarro, Monet, Manet and Renoir featuring alongside Cézanne and Bonnard.

Up on the second floor, one room each is devoted to eighteenth- and nineteenth-century **British art**: Samuel Palmer's visionary paintings run rings around the rest, though there are lashings of Pre-Raphaelite stuff from Rossetti and Holman Hunt to assorted cohorts.

Eating and drinking

With so many students and tourists to cater for, Oxford has developed a wide choice of places to eat and drink. For a midday bite, the numerous **sandwich bars** are ideal – some of the best are listed below and you'll find several others in the **Covered Market**, between the High Street and Cornmarket, an Oxford institution as essential to local shoppers as the Bodleian is to academics. There's also a sprinkling of first-rate (and pricey) **restaurants**, but the majority cater for the less expensive end of the market with varying degrees of success. Reasonable food is served at most **pubs**, but those listed have been singled out for their ambience or selection of beers rather than for their menus.

Snacks and cafés

Beat Café Little Clarendon St. Hippified café with fancy decor and stained-glass windows. Sells a good line in inexpensive sandwiches, salads and smoothies.

Felson's 32 Little Clarendon St. Another hot contender for Oxford's best sandwich bar, this tiny, friendly place has a huge range of fillings for its baguettes and rolls.

George & Davies Little Clarendon St. An established ice-cream parlour that stays open well after the pubs and cinemas. The cow mural is good fun too.

Nosebag 6 St Michael's St. A civilized but unassuming place, with chintzy decor and classical background music. The hot and cold food attracts queues at lunchtime; not so in the evening, when it's a good place for a quick but wholesome meal. Good selection of veggie food.

St Giles' Café 52 St Giles. Oxford's favourite greasy spoon. The huge fry-ups and strong coffee pull an interesting mix of people, from poets to punks.

Vaults & Garden Radcliffe Square. Attached to the church of St Mary the Virgin, this inexpensive café occupies an atmospheric stone-vaulted room and serves up good-quality coffee and cake and quiche-and-salad lunches. Daily 10am–6pm.

Restaurants

Bangkok House 42a Hythe Bridge St ☏01865/200705. Best Oriental restaurant in town, with superb Thai food and excellent service. The mixed starter and the coconut-milk curries are particularly good. Moderate.

Freud Walton St ☏01865/311171. Occupying a grand building in the style of a Roman temple, this fashionable café-bar serves Italian food with a twist. Located about five minutes' walk north of Worcester College, opposite Great Clarendon St. Open Mon & Tues 11am–midnight, Wed–Sat 11am–2am, Sun 11am–10.30pm.

Gee's Restaurant 61 Banbury Rd ☏01865/553540. Chic conservatory setting, but not as expensive as it looks. The inventive menu includes such items as chargrilled vegetables with polenta, roasted beetroot, a variety of steaks and a wide choice of breads. Open daily for lunch and dinner plus brunch at weekends. Moderate.

Le Petit Blanc 71–72 Walton St ☏01865/510999. Renowned French chef Raymond Blanc's affordable, and much praised, alternative to his famous *Manoir aux Quat' Saisons* in Great Milton, some seven miles east of Oxford (☏01844/278881). The food is a refreshing mix of French gourmet (corn-fed quail with lime leaf and ginger) and traditional English (pan-fried Gloucester old spot pork). If you want to splash out, this is the place to do it; main courses are a very reasonable £15–18.

Quod 92 High St ☏01865/202505. Slick restaurant-cum-bar, all angular furnishings and fittings and serving a good line in Italian food – from pizzas and pastas through to char-grilled meats and seafood. A popular spot with moderate prices.

Pubs

Eagle & Child 49 St Giles. Known variously as the "Bird & Baby", "Bird & Brat" or "Bird & Bastard", this pub was once the haunt of J.R.R. Tolkien and C.S. Lewis, and still attracts a comparatively genteel mix of professionals and academics.

Isis By Iffley Lock. Agreeable pub in a lovely setting, amid the flood meadows just under two miles southeast of Folly Bridge at the west edge of Iffley village. The best way to get there is along the Thames Path, which runs along the river from Folly Bridge.

King's Arms 40 Holywell St. Prone to student overkill on term-time weekends, but otherwise very pleasant, with snug rooms at the back and a reasonably good choice of beers.

Lamb & Flag St Giles. Generations of university students have hung out in this old pub, which comes complete with low-beamed ceilings and a series of cramped but cosy rooms. Good range of ales.

Turf Tavern Bath Place, off Holywell St. Small, extraordinarily atmospheric seventeenth-century pub with a fine range of beers, abundant seating outside in summer and mulled wine in winter.

White Horse 52 Broad St. A tiny, old pub with snug rooms, pictures of old university sports teams on the walls and real ales. It was used as a set for the *Inspector Morse* TV series.

Entertainment and nightlife

The home town of both Supergrass and Radiohead, Oxford is nonetheless far from a popular music hot spot, the star quality of its local heroes not reflected in either the **live-music** or **club scene** which are, aside from a couple of noteworthy venues, comparatively lame. Part of the reason for this is that the city's students tend to fall back on college music dos, an option closed to the rest. By comparison, devotees of **classical music** are well catered for, with concert halls and certain college chapels – primarily Christ Church, Merton and New College – offering a wide-ranging programme of concerts and recitals. As regards **theatre**, student productions dominate the city repertoire, but the quality of acting varies, particularly when they tackle Shakespeare, the favourite for the open-air college productions put on for tourists during the summer.

For jazz, classical music and theatre **listings**, consult either *This Month in Oxford* or *In Oxford*, both free and available at the tourist office. The daily *Oxford Mail* newspaper and the weekly *Oxford Times* also both carry information on up-coming gigs and events. For more adventurous stuff – special club nights etc – watch out for wall-posted flyers.

Live music and clubs

Old Fire Station (OFS) 40 George St.
Multipurpose venue with musicals and theatre (box office ☎01865/297170), plus a separate café-bar featuring one-off DJ club nights.
Park End Club Cantay House, 37 Park End St ☎01865/250181. A slick outfit, currently the most popular mainstream club in Oxford, with heavies on the door and a cattle-market atmosphere at weekends.
Zodiac 190 Cowley Rd ☎01865/420042, ⓦwww.thezodiac.co.uk. Far and away Oxford's most respected indie and dance venue, with a fast-moving programme of live bands and guest DJs.

Classical music and theatre

Holywell Music Room 32 Holywell St. Small, plain, Georgian building – opened in 1748 as the first public music hall in England – offering a

varied programme, from straight classical to experimental, with occasional bouts of jazz. Programme details are posted outside and are available at the Oxford Playhouse (see below), which also sells its tickets.
New Theatre George St ☎0870/6063500. Popular – and populist – programme of theatre, dance, pop music, musicals and opera.
Oxford Playhouse Beaumont St ☎01865/305305, ⓦwww.oxfordplayhouse.com. Professional touring companies perform a mixture of plays, opera and concerts at what is generally regarded as the city's best theatre.
Pegasus Theatre Magdalen Rd ☎01865/722851, ⓦwww.pegasustheatre.org.uk. Low-budget, avant-garde productions dominate the programme of this east Oxford theatre.
Sheldonian Theatre Broad St ☎01865/277299. Some have criticized the acoustics here, but this is still Oxford's top concert hall and its resident symphony orchestra is the Oxford Philomusica (☎01865/798600, ⓦwww.oxfordphil.com).

Listings

Bike rental Bikezone, 6 Lincoln House, Market St, off Cornmarket ☎01865/728877.
Bookshops The leading university bookshop is Blackwells. They have several outlets including three shops a stone's throw from each other on Broad St: Blackwells Music, Blackwells Art & Posters and the main bookshop, at 50 Broad St (☎01865/792792).
Buses Most local buses, including Park-and-Ride, are operated by the Oxford Bus Company (☎01865/785400), which also – amongst several companies – offers fast and frequent services to

London and Gatwick and Heathrow airports. Most other long-distance services are in the hands of National Express (☎08705/808080).
Internet & email Mices, Gloucester Green and 118 High St (both Mon–Sat 9am–11pm, Sun 10am–11pm).
Post office At the top of St Aldates, near the corner with High St.
Taxis Ranks are liberally distributed across the city centre, including at the train station and on the High St and St Giles. Alternatively, call City Taxis ☎01865/201201.

Around Oxford

As a base for exploring some of the more delightful parts of central England, Oxford is hard to beat. It's a short drive west to the Cotswolds (see Chapter 5) and near at hand also are the Vale of White Horse (see p.286) and the Chiltern

Hills (see pp.283–286). If, on the other hand, you're using public transport, the options are much more limited, the best choice being the short and easy bus ride north to the charming little town of **Woodstock** and its imperious neighbour, **Blenheim Palace**.

Woodstock

WOODSTOCK, eight miles north of Oxford, has royal associations going back to Saxon times, with a string of kings attracted by its excellent hunting. Henry I built a royal lodge here and his successor, Henry II, enlarged it to create a grand manor house-cum-palace, where, incidentally, the Black Prince was born in 1330. The Royalists used Woodstock as a base during the Civil War, but, after their defeat, Cromwell never got round to destroying either the town or the palace; the latter was ultimately given to (and flattened by) the Duke of Marlborough, in 1704. Long dependent on royal and then ducal patronage, Woodstock is now both a well-heeled commuter town for Oxford and a provider of food, drink and beds for visitors to Blenheim. It's also an extremely pretty little place, its handsome stone buildings gathered around the main square, at the junction of Market and High streets, which is also where you'll find the town's one specific sight, the **Oxfordshire Museum** (Tues–Sat 10am–5pm, Sun 2–5pm; £2.50), a well-composed review of the archeology, social history and industry of the county.

The museum shares its premises with the town's **tourist office** (March–Oct Mon–Sat 9.30am–5.30pm, Sun 1–5pm; Nov–Feb Mon–Sat 10am–5pm; ☏01993/813276, ⓦwww.oxfordshirecotswolds.org), which has a useful range of information on the nearby Cotswolds. Woodstock has several good **pubs**, the best being the *Bear*, a delightful old coaching inn across from the museum with low-beamed ceilings and antique furnishings; it offers a varied menu and serves a good range of beers. **Buses** from Oxford run every thirty minutes or so (reduced service on Sun), with some continuing on to Stratford-upon-Avon.

Blenheim Palace

Nowadays, successful British commanders get medals and titles, but in 1704, as a thank-you for his victory over the French at the battle of Blenheim, Queen Anne gave **John Churchill**, **Duke of Marlborough** (1650–1722), the royal estate of Woodstock, along with the promise of enough cash to build himself a gargantuan palace.

Work started promptly on **Blenheim Palace** (mid-March to Oct daily 10.30am–4.45pm; £10.50 including park & gardens) with the principal archi-tect being Sir John Vanbrugh, who was also responsible for Castle Howard in Yorkshire (see p.700). All seemed set fair, but things went downhill fast. The duke's formidable wife, Sarah Jennings, who had wanted Christopher Wren as architect, was soon at loggerheads with Vanbrugh, while Queen Anne had second thoughts, stifling the flow of money. Construction work was halted and the house was only finished after the duke's death at the instigation of his widow, who ended up paying most of the bills and designing much of the inte-rior herself. The end result is the country's grandest example of Baroque civic architecture, an Italianate palace that is more a monument than a house – just as Vanbrugh intended.

The **interior** is stuffed with paintings and tapestries, plus all manner of objets d'art, including furniture from Versailles, and stone and marble carvings by Grinling Gibbons. The ceiling of the Great Hall sports painted allegories celebrating Marlborough's martial skills and the Dining Saloon holds murals by Louis Laguerre, but frankly it's hard to warm to all this conspicuous consumption. Horace Walpole, the eighteenth-century wit and social commentator, had it about right when he wrote that Blenheim resembled "the palace of an auctioneer who had been chosen King of Poland". As for the Marlboroughs, John Churchill was one of the few members of the clan to have made anything but a poor impression, the spectacular exception being **Sir Winston Churchill**, born here in 1874. Several rooms are dedicated to the wartime prime minister, who is buried with his wife in the graveyard of **Bladon Church**, visible from the palace.

Formal **gardens** (same times; £3.50 gardens only) flank the house, but the open **parkland** (daily 9am–4.45pm; £2.50 pedestrians, £7.50 for cars, including passengers) is more enticing, especially just north of the house, where the ground falls away dramatically to an exquisite artificial lake, Queen Pool.

There are two entrances to Blenheim, one just south of Woodstock on the Oxford road and another through the Triumphal Arch at the end of Park Street in Woodstock itself.

North Buckinghamshire and Bedfordshire

The untidy landscapes of **north Buckinghamshire** and **Bedfordshire** herald a transition between the satellite towns of London and the Midlands. Since the war, the character of the region has been transformed by the attempt to solve London's overcrowding. Sprawling suburbs now festoon many of the small country towns of yesteryear and, in the 1960s, Milton Keynes swallowed thirteen existing villages to become the country's largest new town. Nonetheless, there are several interesting targets, beginning in north Buckinghamshire with the National Trust's **Stowe Gardens**, dotted with a remarkable assortment of outdoor sculptures and follies. Over in Bedfordshire, the county's most distinctive feature is the wriggling **River Ouse**, whose banks were once lined with dozens of watermills, though these were not nearly as important as the brickworks that long underpinned the local economy. For the casual visitor, the county might not warrant a major detour, but **Bedford** itself deserves more than just a sideward glance, if for no other reason than for its links with John Bunyan.

Buckingham and around

Unassuming **BUCKINGHAM** is tucked into a sharp bend in the River Ouse about 25 miles northeast of Oxford. It became the county town of Buckinghamshire in the tenth century and flourished during medieval times, but was bypassed by the Industrial Revolution and remained a forgotten backwater until a recent wave of incomers created the modern suburbs that surround it today. The town centre is at its prettiest along the wide, sloping Market Hill, standing in the middle of which is the **Old Gaol**, a chunky, stone structure that is home to the tourist office (see below) and a modest, local history **museum** (Mon–Sat 10am–4pm; £1.50). Otherwise, Buckingham is short on sights, though you might take a peek inside the sombre **church of St Peter and St Paul**, which perches on the hill where the castle once stood – take Castle Street from the west end of Market Hill and you can't miss it.

There's no train service to Buckingham, but there are **bus** links from neighbouring towns, principally Milton Keynes. Buses stop on the High Street a few yards from the **tourist office** in the Old Gaol (July & Aug Mon–Sat 10am–4pm, Sun noon–4pm; rest of year closed Sun; ☎01280/823020). They have a small supply of **B&Bs**, which they will book on your behalf, or you can target Buckingham's best **hotel**, the *Villiers*, which occupies an imaginatively modernized old inn bang in the centre of town at 3 Castle St (☎01280/822444; ❼). The best spot for **food** is the *Dipalee Indian Restaurant* (☎01280/813151), just along Castle Street from the hotel and with a good range of dishes; main courses average about £8.

Northwest of Buckingham: Stowe Gardens

Just three miles northwest of Buckingham off the A422, the extensive **Stowe Landscape Gardens** (Wed–Sun: March–Oct 10am–5.30pm; Nov–Dec 10am–4pm; £5; NT) contain an extraordinary collection of outdoor sculptures, monuments and decorative buildings by some of the greatest designers and architects of the eighteenth century. They worked at the behest of the prodigiously wealthy Temple and Grenville families, and later the dukes of Buckingham and Chandos. The thirty-odd structures that comprise this ornamental miscellany are spread over a sequence of separate, carefully planned landscapes, from the lake views of the Western and Eastern gardens to the wooded delights of the Elysian Fields and the gentle folds of the Grecian Valley, Capability Brown's first large-scale design. The gardens were planned in detail, but the romantic rural idyll they represented was a fundamental break with the strictly formal garden tradition that had dominated Europe for decades. Several of the buildings are of particular interest too, most memorably the neo-Romanesque **Hermitage**, the eccentric **Gothic Temple**, and the beautifully composed **Palladian Bridge**, one of only three such bridges in the country.

Finally, at the heart of the gardens, the **main house**, with its whopping Neoclassical facade, is separate from the gardens, as it is used by Stowe School, who offer fairly regular guided tours (£3) – ring ☎01280/818282 for the schedule.

Bedford

BEDFORD, some thirty miles east of Buckingham, has struggled to retain a modicum of character in the face of redevelopment, but the end result is pleasant enough, the town's neat and tidy centre hugging the north bank of the River Ouse. Bedford also makes the most of its connections with **John Bunyan** (1628–88), a blaspheming tinker turned Nonconformist preacher, who lived most of his life in and around the town. Bunyan fought for Parliament in the Civil War and became a well-known public speaker during Cromwell's Protectorate, but the Restoration proved disastrous for him. In 1660, he was arrested for breaking Charles II's new religious legislation, which restricted the activities of Nonconformist preachers, and he spent most of the next seventeen years in Bedford prison. During his incarceration, he wrote *The Pilgrim's Progress*, a seminal text whose simple language and powerful allegories were to have a profound influence on generations of Nonconformists – and it was they who championed a raft of progressive causes, most notably the campaign for the abolition of slavery.

Built in 1850 on the spot where Bunyan founded his first Independent Congregation, the **Bunyan Meeting Free Church** (Tues–Sat 10am–4pm), just east of the High Street on Mill Street, is still a Nonconformist church. It bears several memorials to Bunyan, beginning with the splendid bronze doors, decorated with ten finely worked panels depicting scenes from *The Pilgrim's Progress*. Inside, the stained-glass windows develop the theme, again depicting scenes from the book, plus one showing Bunyan scribbling away in prison. Next door, the homely **Bunyan Museum** (March–Nov Tues–Sat 11am–4pm; free) features extracts from his book and tracks through the author's life and times.

Bedford's other noteworthy attraction is the **Cecil Higgins Art Gallery**, just to the south of Mill Street on Castle Lane (Tues–Sat 11am–5pm & Sun 2–5pm; £2.20, free on Fri). The gallery holds strong collections of ceramics, glass and local lace as well as a competent range of watercolours and prints, though these are not always on display due to their sensitivity to light. There are also several period rooms, done out in high Victorian style, including the eccentrically flamboyant **Burges Room**. The gallery's admission charge covers the adjacent **Bedford Museum** (same hours), a ponderous trawl through the city's history.

Practicalities

Bedford is on the London St Pancras–Sheffield rail line with **trains** arriving at Midland Station, from where it's a ten-minute walk east to the centre – just follow the signs. The **bus station** is on All Hallows and from here it's a couple of minutes' walk east to the short High Street, which runs north–south and spans the River Ouse. The **tourist office** (Mon–Sat 9.30am–5pm; ☎01234/215226, ⓦwww.bedford.gov.uk/tourism) is in the old Town Hall, just off the High Street on St Paul's Square.

The town's best **hotel** is *The Swan* (☎01234/346565, ⓦwww .bedfordswanhotel.co.uk; ❼), whose Georgian stonework conceals a lavish and tastefully modernized interior; it's down by the river on The Embankment at the foot of the High Street. As a second choice, the *Embankment Hotel* (☎01234/261332, ⓦwww.embankmenthotelbedford.co.uk; ❸), just along the river from the Swan, has twenty comfortable en-suite rooms behind an extravagant mock-Tudor facade; it shares its premises with a real ale pub. Alternatively, the tourist office has a small cache of **B&Bs**.

Bedford's large Italian community adds a bit of zip to the local **restaurant** scene. Pick of the bunch, serving the tastiest pizzas and pastas in town, is *Pizzeria Santaniello*, 9 Newnham St, immediately to the east of Mill Street's Bunyan Meeting Free Church. Further down Newnham Street, at no. 36, *Bar Cappuccino* chips in with authentic coffee, ice cream, pizzas and snacks. In between the two, *The Castle* has bar food and real ales, and occupies ancient (but heavily modernized) premises.

St Albans

ST ALBANS is one of the most appealing towns on the peripheries of London, its well-blended medley of medieval and modern features grafted onto the site of Verulamium, the town founded by the Romans soon after their successful invasion of 43 AD. Boudicca and her followers burned this settlement to the ground eighteen years later, but reconstruction was swift and the town grew into a major administrative base. It was here, in 209 AD, that a Roman soldier by the name of Alban became the country's first Christian martyr, when he was beheaded for giving shelter to a priest. Pilgrims later flocked to the town that had come to bear his name, with the place of execution marked by a hilltop cathedral that was once one of the largest churches in the Christian world.

Not just a religious centre, St Albans also flourished as a trading town and a staging post on the route to London from the north, its economy further buttressed by two local industries, brewing and straw-hat-making. In the nineteenth century, the coaching trade faded away with the coming of the railways, but when St Albans was connected to London by train in 1868, it rapidly reinvented itself as a prosperous and pleasant commuter town, a description that fits well today.

St Albans' best-known attraction is its **cathedral**, but the town also possesses the outstanding **Verulamium Museum**, home to several breathtaking Roman mosaics, as well as a likeable riverside park and a number of charming old streets. All the town's main sights are within easy walking distance of each other, making St Albans an ideal day-trip, but if you do decide to stay the night be sure to try out some of the excellent pubs.

The City

One good way to start a tour of the city is by climbing to the top of the fifteenth-century **Clock Tower**, plumb in the centre of town where the High Street and Market Place meet (Easter–Oct Sat & Sun 10.30am–5pm; 30p). The climb is a tight squeeze, but worth it for the view over the **Cathedral** (daily 8am–5.45pm; donation requested), a vast brick and flint edifice immediately to the south – and reached down a narrow passageway across from the foot of the tower. An abbey was constructed here in 1077, on the site of a Saxon abbey founded by King Offa of Mercia, and despite subsequent alterations – including the ugly nineteenth-century west front – the legacy of the Normans remains the most impressive aspect. The sheer scale of their design is breathtaking: the **nave**, almost 300-foot long, is the longest medieval nave in Britain, even if it isn't the most harmonious – the massive Norman **pillars** on the north side stand out from those in the later Early English style opposite.

Behind the high altar an elaborate stone **reredos** hides the fourteenth-century **shrine** of St Alban. The tomb was smashed up during the Dissolution, but the Victorians discovered the pieces and gamely put them all together again. Some of the carving on the Purbeck marble is now remarkably clear – look out for the scene on the west end depicting the saint's martyrdom.

A few yards to the west of the cathedral's main entrance, the **abbey gateway** is the only other part of the original complex to have survived the Dissolution.

Verulamium

From the abbey gateway, Abbey Mill Lane leads down past the *Fighting Cocks* (one of the oldest pubs in the country) and across the trickle of the River Ver to **Verulamium Park**, whose sloping lawns and duck-happy ponds occupy the site of the Roman city. The park holds a scattering of Roman remains, including fragments of the old city wall and the foundations of a townhouse complete with an in situ mosaic and the original underfloor heating system or **hypocaust** of the bath suite. However, this is small beer in comparison with the **Verulamium Museum** (Mon–Sat 10am–5.30pm, Sun 2–5.30pm; £3.30), which occupies an attractive circular building on the northern edge of the park. Inside, a series of well-conceived displays illustrate and explain life in Roman Britain, but these are eclipsed by the **mosaics**, five wonderful floor examples exhibited in one gallery and unearthed hereabouts in the 1930s and 1950s and dated to about 200 AD.

Just to the west, across busy Bluehouse Hill, the **Roman Theatre of Verulamium** (daily: March–Oct 10am–5pm; Nov–April 10am–4pm; £1.50) was built around 140 AD, but was reduced to the status of a municipal rubbish dump by the fifth century. Little more than a small hollow now, the site is still impressive enough and gives a real sense of how these theatres would once have looked. Further excavation nearby has revealed a house and several workshops.

From the theatre, it's a five- to ten-minute walk back to the centre via **St Michael's** and **Fishpool** streets.

Practicalities

Trains on the Bedford to London King's Cross line call at **St Albans station**, from where it's a ten-minute walk west up the hill along Victoria street to the main drag – at a point just north of the Clock Tower. Trains from Watford Junction (for London Euston and the north) serve the small **St Albans Abbey Station**, a similar distance from the centre, but this time to the south at the bottom of Holywell Hill. Almost all **buses** pull in on the main street, again to the north of the Clock Tower, and some continue on to St Albans station.

The **main street** comprises Chequer Street, which begins at the Clock Tower, and its northern continuation St Peter's Street. At the intersection of the two is the Market Place, home of the **tourist office**, in the Town Hall (Easter–Oct Mon–Sat 9.30am–5.30pm, Sun 10am–4pm; Nov–Easter Mon–Sat 10am–4pm; ☎01727/864511, ⓦ www.stalbans.gov.uk). St Albans has a good supply of **B&Bs**, with several clustered near St Albans station, including the first-rate *Wren Lodge*, 24 Beaconsfield Rd (☎01727/855540; no credit cards; ❸), a well-maintained Edwardian house with four comfortable and attractively furnished bedrooms – two en suite. Fishpool Street is, however, a much prettier spot to head for and it's here you'll find the splendid *St Michael's Manor Hotel* (☎01727/864444, ⓦ www.stmichaelsmanor.com; ❾), a family-run establishment in a handsome Georgian house down by the river.

When it comes to **food**, the *St Michael's Manor Hotel* (see above) has a first-class restaurant featuring Modern British cuisine, but it's pricey. Less expensively, several pubs serve up tasty bar food, with *The Goat*, on Sopwell Lane off Holywell Hill (☎01727/833934), leading the way. St Albans is the headquarters of CAMRA, the real ale campaigners, so it's gratifying to see the excellent quality of the local **pubs**. The *Blue Anchor*, on Fishpool Street, is a good, solid old pub with an open fire in winter and garden seating in summer, whilst the *Farmer's Boy*, a short stroll east of the Clock Tower at 134 London Rd, brews its own beers on site and also stocks a superb range of German and Belgian bottled beers.

Travel details

Buses

For information on all local and national bus services, contact Traveline ☎ 0870/608 2 608, ⓦ www.traveline.org.uk.
The Ridgeway Explorer bus service operates on Saturdays, Sundays and bank holidays from mid-April to late October. It links Swindon bus station with Reading rail station (4 daily; 2hrs 15min) via Woolstone, the Ridgeway Centre YHA and Wantage. A one-day Rover ticket costs £5, and timetable details are on ☎ 0870/608 2608.

Bedford to: Buckingham (hourly; 2hr 30min).
Buckingham to: Bedford (hourly; 2hr 30min); Oxford (hourly; 1hr 30min).
Henley to: Oxford (hourly; 50min); Reading (hourly; 20min); Wantage (hourly; 1hr 40min).
Oxford to: Buckingham (hourly; 1hr 30min); Burford (hourly; 30min); Chipping Norton (hourly; 50min); Cirencester (every 2hr; 2hr); Henley (hourly; 50min); Lechlade (hourly; 1hr 40min); Reading (every 2hrs; 1hr 30min); Wantage (hourly; 1hr).
Reading to: Henley (hourly; 20min); Oxford (every 2hrs; 1hr 30min).

Wantage to: Henley (hourly; 1hr 40min); Oxford (hourly; 1hr).

Trains

For information on all local and national rail services, contact National Rail Enquiries ☏08457/48 49 50, ⓦ www.nationalrail.co.uk.

Bedford to: London (1–2 hourly; 30min–1hr); Oxford (hourly; 2hr 30min); St Albans (1–2 hourly; 40min).
Hatfield to: London (1–2 hourly; 20min).
Henley to: London (3 daily; 1hr).
Oxford to: Bedford (hourly; 2hr 30min); Birmingham (hourly; 1hr 30min); London (1–2 hourly; 1hr).
St Albans to: Bedford (1–2 hourly; 40min); London (14 daily; 20–40min).

OXFORD AND AROUND | Travel details

5

The Cotswolds and Somerset

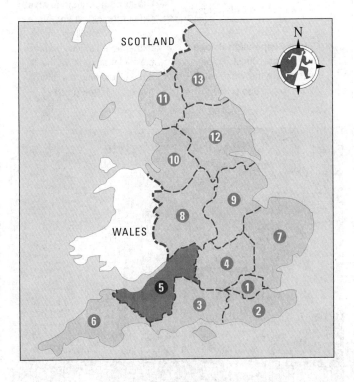

CHAPTER 5

Highlights

✳ **Chipping Campden, Gloucestershire** Perhaps the most handsome of the Cotswolds towns, with honey-coloured stone houses flanking the superb church of St James. **See p.316**

✳ **Falkland Arms, Great Tew** Wonderful pub in the most charming of hamlets, deep in the heart of the Cotswolds. **See p.316.**

✳ **Clifton Suspension Bridge** Brunel's lofty construction rears above the impressive Avon Gorge. **See p.337**

✳ **Bath** Beautifully preserved Roman baths and wonderful Georgian architecture make a visit to Bath a must. **See p.338**

✳ **Wells Cathedral** A gem of medieval masonry, not least for its richly ornamented west front. **See p.345**

✳ **Glastonbury music festival** One of the oldest and biggest rock festivals still retains its authentic aura, less commercialized than most of the ilk, and still drawing the alternative crowd. **See p.351**

△ Royal Crescent, Bath

5

The Cotswolds and Somerset

The rolling green swards of **Gloucestershire** and **Somerset**, a wedge of land linking the Midlands with the West Country, encapsulate a vision of rural England which has very largely survived the inroads of modern urban culture. The relatively remote settlements may not, for the most part, be peopled by shepherds and farmers, but the landscape has preserved its slumberous charm, and wears a mellow tranquillity which has even seeped into the towns which grew rich on its wealth. Occupying the eastern side of Gloucestershire, the **Cotswolds**, in particular, show plenty of evidence of past prosperity, not least in the beautiful old mansions and churches endowed from the fortunes made through the medieval wool trade. Moreover, the remarkable continuity of Cotswold architecture has created villages as picturesque as any in England, though the resulting tourist deluge makes some spots nightmarish in summer. Tourism is less of a nuisance in the south of this region, around the busy market town of **Cirencester**, once a major Roman stronghold and still an important transport hub.

To the west, the land drops sharply from the Cotswold escarpment down to **Cheltenham**, an elegant Regency spa town most famous these days for its horse racing. The town's reputation as a bastion of blue-stockinged conservatism is fairly passé now, and it has developed a more sophisticated veneer in recent years, boasting some of the best restaurants and nightlife in the region. Cheltenham would also make a good base for visits to **Gloucester**, with its superb cathedral and rejuvenated harbour area, and **Stroud**, where the much-praised Museum in the Park has recently opened. The Vale of Gloucester follows the route of the **River Severn** northeast towards Worcestershire, the stone cottages of the Cotswolds giving way to the thatched, half-timbered and red-brick houses which are characteristic of **Tewkesbury**, a solidly provincial town with a magnificent abbey.

South down the M5, **Bristol** is the biggest city in these parts, and one of the most go-ahead, cosmopolitan places outside London. Its dynamism and flare have saddled it with dense traffic and some pretty hideous postwar architecture, but all is compensated for by its surviving traces of every phase in its long maritime history. Bristol is only a few miles from Georgian **Bath**, whose symmetrical honey-toned terraces contribute to its operatic setting. The proximity of urban grace to panoramic splendour is characteristic of much of **Somerset**, as in the exquisite cathedral city of **Wells**, lying on the edge of the

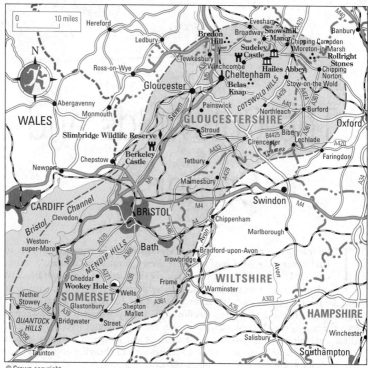

© Crown copyright

Mendip Hills. The landscape assumes more dramatic lines west of here, where the hills are pocked by cave systems, as at **Wookey Hole**, and sliced through by the **Cheddar Gorge**. The ancient town of **Glastonbury** lies close at hand, a site steeped in Christian lore and Arthurian legend, and popular with New Age mystics. To the west, **Bridgwater** and **Taunton** lie at the southern end of the **Quantock Hills**, where Coleridge and Wordsworth roamed, a time recalled in Coleridge's old house at **Nether Stowey**.

The line between London's Paddington Station and Bristol provides the backbone of the **rail network** through this region, though you could also make use of the London–Oxford–Worcester line that runs through Moreton-in-Marsh, in the middle of the Cotswolds. There are also direct lines to Cheltenham and Gloucester, and these towns form the hubs of **bus routes** which connect nearly all the places covered here – though beware that services in the Cotswolds can be extremely sketchy, with little running at all on a Sunday. Your own transport would be ideal for exploring this area, while the M4 and M5 motorways are useful through-routes for longer-distance jaunts.

The Cotswolds

The limestone hills of the **Cotswolds** are preposterously photogenic, strewn with countless picture-book villages built by wealthy cloth merchants. Wool was important here as far back as the Roman era, but the greatest fortunes were made between the fourteenth and sixteenth centuries, and at this time many of the region's fine manors and churches were built. Largely bypassed by the Industrial Revolution, which heralded the area's commercial decline, much of the Cotswolds is technically speaking a relic, its architecture preserved in often immaculate condition. Numerous churches are decorated with beautiful Norman carving, for which the local limestone was ideal: soft and easy to carve when first quarried, but hardening after long exposure to the sunlight. The use of this local stone is a strong unifying characteristic, though its colour modulates as subtly as the shape of the hills, ranging from a deep golden tone in **Chipping Campden** to a silvery grey in **Painswick**.

The consequence is that the Cotswolds have become one of the country's main tourist attractions, with many towns afflicted by plagues of tearooms and souvenir and antiques shops – this is Morris Dancing country. To see the Cotswolds at their best, you should visit off-season or perhaps avoid the most popular towns and instead escape into the hills themselves, though really it's churlish to avoid the charms of **Chipping Campden** and **Northleach** at any time of the year. As for walking, this might be a tamed landscape, but there is good scope for exploring the byways, either in the gentler valleys that are most typical of the Cotswolds or along the dramatic escarpment which marks the boundary with the Severn Valley. A long-distance path called the **Cotswold Way** runs along the top of the ridge, stretching about one hundred miles from Chipping Campden past Cheltenham, Gloucester and Stroud as far as Bath. A number of prehistoric sites provide added interest along the route, with some – such as **Belas Knap** near Winchcombe – being well worth a diversion.

There are a few large settlements in this region, the biggest true Cotswold town being **Cirencester**, a buzzing community dating back to the Romans.

Lechlade and around

Marking the westernmost navigable point of the Thames, **LECHLADE**, some twenty miles west of Oxford, teems with pleasure boats, but for most people it's handier as a springboard for exploring the southern fringe of the Cotswolds. For **overnight stops** easily the best place is the modern and stylish *Cambrai Lodge* (℡01367/253173; no credit cards; ❸) in Oak Street. You can pitch a tent either at the St John's Priory **campsite** (℡01367/252360), a mile southeast along the A417 (follow the signs for Faringdon), or in the field by the *Trout* pub (℡01367/252313) next door. The *Trout*, reachable by footpath across the meadow from by the church, is a real anglers' pub, with stuffed fish on the wall, and on Tuesday and Sunday there's live jazz. From Easter to October the *Trout* rents out **rowing boats** and motors boats.

Isolated among fields just three miles east of Lechlade, **KELMSCOTT** has become a place of pilgrimage for devotees of **William Morris** (see box on p.314), who used the Tudor manor as a summer home from 1871 to his death in 1896. The simple beauty of the **house** (April–Sept Wed & third Sat of month 11am–5pm; July & Aug also first Sat of month 11am–5pm; £7; ℡01367/252486, ⓦwww.kelmscottmanor.co.uk) is enhanced by the furniture, fabrics, wallpapers and tapestries – some rescued from dog baskets – that were created by Morris and his Pre-Raphaelite friends, including Burne-Jones and Rossetti. Entry is by timed ticket and it's wise to call first to confirm the opening hours, which are erratic. You can't reach Kelmscott on public transport, but it's a pleasant stroll along the north bank of the Thames from

William Morris (1834–1896), the socialist, writer and craftsman, had a profound influence on his contemporaries and on subsequent generations. In some respects he was an ally of Karl Marx, railing against the iniquities of private property and the squalor of industrialized society. Where he differed from Marx, however, was in his belief that machines necessarily enslave the individual, and in his vision of a world in which each person would be liberated through a sort of communistic, crafts-based economy. His prose/poem story *News from Nowhere* vaguely described his Utopian society, but his main legacy was the **Arts and Crafts Movement**, a direct offshoot of his work and a lasting influence on British crafts.

His career as an artist began at Oxford, where he met **Edward Burne-Jones**, who shared his admiration for the arts of the Middle Ages. After graduating they both ended up in London, painting under the direction of Dante Gabriel Rossetti, the leading light of the **Pre-Raphaelites** – a loose grouping of artists intent on regaining the spiritual purity characteristic of art before Raphael and the Renaissance "tainted" the world with humanism. In 1861 Morris founded **Morris & Co** ("The Firm"), whose designs came to embody the ideas of the Arts and Crafts Movement, one of whose basic tenets was formulated by its founder: "Have nothing in your houses that you do not know to be useful or believe to be beautiful." Rossetti and Burne-Jones were among the designers, though the former remains better known for his paintings of Jane Morris, his friend's wife and his own mistress, whom he turned into the archetypal Pre-Raphaelite woman. Morris's own designs for fabrics, wallpapers and numerous other products were to prove a massive – some would say negative – influence in Britain, as evidenced by the success of the Laura Ashley aesthetic, a lineal descendant of Morris's rustic nostalgia.

Morris's energy was not exhausted by his work for The Firm. In 1890 he set up the **Kelmscott Press**, named after but not located at his summer home, whose masterpiece was the so-called *Kelmscott Chaucer*, the collected poems of one of the Pre-Raphaelites' great heroes, with woodcuts by Burne-Jones. Morris also pioneered interest in the architecture of the Cotswolds – it was in response to hideous restoration work in this region that Morris instigated the **Society for the Protection of Ancient Buildings**, still an active force in preserving the country's architectural heritage.

Lechlade, and, should you need **to stay**, there are eight en-suite rooms in the modernized *Plough Inn* (℡01367/253543; ❾), which dates from the seventeenth century and also serves **meals**.

Burford and the Windrush Valley

Eight miles north of Lechlade you get your first real taste of the Cotswolds at **BURFORD**, where the magnificent High Street, which slopes down to the bridge over the **River Windrush**, holds every variety of golden Cotswold stone. Try to avoid visiting the town in summer, when cars battle for space and tourists fight it out on the pavements and in the antique shops, though the huge **parish church of St John**, originally Norman but remodelled in the fifteenth century, is a delight at any time. An unusual monument to Henry VIII's barber, Edmund Harman, shows four Amazonian Indians, said to be the first representation of Native Americans in Britain.

Burford straddles several main Cotswold routes. **Buses** along the A40 between Oxford and Cheltenham stop several times a day; buses along other routes are mostly once-a-week market-day services. The **tourist office** is situated in Sheep Street (April–Sept Mon–Sat 9.30am–5.30pm,

Sun 10am–3pm; Oct–March Mon–Sat 10am–4.30pm; ☎01993/823558, Ⓦwww.oxfordshirecotswolds.org). Many of Burford's old inns have metamorphosed into expensive **hotels**, but the unassuming *Highway Hotel* at 117 High St (☎01993/822136; ❸) is good value. There are several **B&Bs**, including the discreetly signed *Tudor Cottage* at 40 Witney St, off the main High Street, beautifully furnished with antiques (☎01993/823251, Ⓔbunkered@ compuserve.com; no credit cards; ❸). For good **food** *The Angel Brasserie* (☎01993/822714, Ⓦwww.theangel-uk.com; closed Sun & Mon eve, plus late Jan to early Feb) at 14 Witney St should satisfy; there are three themed bedrooms as well (❺). For the obligatory tea and cakes, head for *Huffkins*, on the High Street.

Chipping Norton and around

The bustling market town of **CHIPPING NORTON**, eleven miles north of Burford, presides over one of the least explored, but most scenic, corners of the Cotswolds – a region of rambling limestone uplands latticed by long dry-stone walls and dotted with picturesque villages. The western approach to the town, via the A44 from Moreton-in-Marsh, is dominated by the extraordinary chimney stack of the **Bliss Tweed Mill**, mounted on a domed tower and the quirkiest of a crop of monuments dating from the boom of the textile trade. Granted a charter in the twelfth century by King John to hold a wool fair, Chipping Norton reached its peak three hundred years later, when it acquired most of the stalwart stone houses and half-timber-framed coaching inns that now line up along the market square. Also paid for by wealthy wool merchants, **St Mary's Parish Church**, just below the square in Church Street, harbours a fine fifteenth-century Perpendicular nave, in addition to some well-preserved brasses and tombs. More remnants of the town's former prominence are housed in the small **museum** at the top of the square above the Westgate Centre (Easter–Oct Tues–Sun 2–4pm; £1). Among the exhibits is a carved head of a Roman river god unearthed by a local farmer, equipment salvaged from the Victorian wool mill, and a display on Fred Lewis, who founded the English Baseball Club in 1920.

Buses to Chipping Norton drop passengers in front of the town hall, at the opposite end of the square to the **tourist office** (March–Oct Mon–Sat 9.30am–5.30pm; Nov–Feb Mon–Sat 10am–3pm; ☎01608/644379), which is good for local information. **Accommodation** is thin on the ground, but there are pleasant rooms behind the imposing facade of the *Crown and Cushion* (☎01608/642533, Ⓦwww.thecrownandcushion.com; ❸), which is handily located on the High Street – and was once owned by Keith Moon. Three miles southwest of town along the B4450 in the hamlet of **Churchill**, there's also *The Forge* (☎01608/658173, Ⓦwww.cotswolds-accommodation.com; ❸), an excellent country house B&B offering en suite rooms in tastefully converted old stone premises.

The best **pubs** are both in Goddards Lane, on the square: the stone-tiled *Blue Boar* serves imaginative bar food and real ales, as does the *Chequers* close by. If you prefer the **café-bar** atmosphere, try *Whistlers* (☎01608/643363; closed Sun eve) just along from the tourist office at 9 Middle Row, where a set lunch will cost £12.

Great Tew and the Rollright Stones

A labyrinth of country lanes spreads east of Chipping Norton through a string of well-manicured villages and valleys to tiny **GREAT TEW**, the perfect target for a pub walk. Hidden deep amid woodland, this hamlet of honey-coloured thatched houses contains one of England's most idyllic pubs, the **Falkland Arms**, which rotates half a dozen guest beers (including the legendary local bitter, Hook Norton), and sells a fine selection of single malts, herbal wines, snuff, and clay pipes you can fill with tobacco for a smoke in the flower-filled garden. Little has changed in the flagstone-floored bar since the sixteenth century, although the adjacent snug was recently converted into a small restaurant serving snacks and evening meals. It's also a popular place to stay (☎01608/683653, ⓦwww.falklandarms.org.uk; ❹), but at weekends is booked up months ahead.

Another local expedition takes in the **Rollright Stones**, high up on the wolds about five miles northwest of Chipping Norton, and the third most important **stone circle** in Britain after Stonehenge and Avebury. Legend recounts that these gnarled Bronze Age rocks are a king and his army (of unknown identity), petrified by a witch while on a campaign to conquer England.

Moreton-in-Marsh

MORETON-IN-MARSH, eight miles west of Chipping Norton, has more of a buzz than most Cotswold towns, particularly on Tuesdays, when the High Street disappears beneath a huge market. But the thing not to miss is the **Batsford Arboretum** (March to mid-Nov daily 10am–5pm; mid-Nov to Feb Sat & Sun 10am–4pm; £4, joint ticket with Falconry Centre £6.50), a fifteen-minute walk from the High Street. The largest private collection of rare trees in the country, it was planted in the 1880s by Lord Redesdale following his return from a posting in Tokyo. The hilly gardens have a distinctly Japanese flavour, and you can sit here amid magnolias and Chinese pocket-handkerchief trees enjoying wonderful views.

Moreton has better **public transport** services than most other towns in the region, with daily **buses** (except Sun) to Stow-on-the-Wold, Chipping Campden, Evesham, Malvern, Stratford and Cheltenham. In addition, Moreton is on the London–Oxford–Worcester **train** line. There's a useful **tourist office** in the High Street (Mon 8.45am–5pm, Tues–Thurs 8.45am–5.15pm, Fri 8.45am–4.45pm, Sat 10am–12.30pm; ☎01608/650881, ⓦwww.cotswold.gov .uk) and **bike rental** is available from the toyshop on the High Street (☎01608/650756). Best value of the **hotels** is the lively *Bell Inn*, ☎01608/652195, ⓦwww.bellinncotswold.com; ❸), also on the High Street. For **B&B**, try *Acacia*, in a fetching stone terrace house at 2 New Rd, on the way to the station (☎01608/650130; no credit cards; ❶); or the luxurious *Windy Ridge* (☎01451/832328, ⓦwww.windy-ridge.co.uk; ❺), in an attractive thatched house a couple of miles southwest of town towards Longborough and with its own arboretum and indoor pool.

Places to eat line the High Street, but the pick of the bunch is the *Redesdale Arms*, whose forte is game and seafood – all at affordable prices.

Chipping Campden

CHIPPING CAMPDEN, six miles northwest of Moreton-in-Marsh, gives a better idea than anywhere else in the Cotswolds as to what a prosperous wool town might have looked like in the Middle Ages. The houses have undulating, weather-beaten roofs and many retain their original mullioned windows, while the fine Perpendicular **Church of St James** (March–Oct Mon–Sat 10am–5pm, Sun 2–5pm; Nov–Feb Mon–Sat 11am–3pm, Sun 2–4pm; free) dates from the fifteenth century, the zenith of the town's wool-trading days. Inside, an ostentatious monument commemorates the family of Sir Baptist Hicks, a local benefactor who built the nearby almshouses and the market hall in the High Street. His own home was burnt down during the Civil War, but you can glimpse the ruins over the wall beside the church.

A fine panoramic view rewards those who make the short but severe hike up the Cotswold Way northwest to **Dover's Hill** (follow Hoo Lane north off the High Street). Since 1610 this natural amphitheatre has been the stage for an Olympics of rural sports, though the event was suspended last century when games such as shin-kicking became little more than licensed thuggery. A more civilized version, the **Cotswold Olimpick Games**, has been staged each June since 1951: no shin-kicking, but still the odd bit of hammer-throwing and tug-of-war pulling.

Such a museum-piece as Chipping Campden must inevitably cope with a bevy of visitors in summer. Try to stay overnight and explore in the evening or at dawn, when the streets are empty and the golden hues of the stone at their richest. **Public transport** to the area is good, with frequent bus services to Moreton, Evesham and Stratford. You can't move for **guest houses** along the High Street and most of them can be booked through the **tourist office** (daily 10am–5.30pm; ☎01386/841206, ⓦwww.chippingcampden.net). Recommendable places include the *Dragon House*, on the High Street (☎01386/840734, ⓦwww.dragonhouse-chipping-camden.co.uk; no credit cards; ❸), a tastefully converted former coaching inn with delightful gardens whose various old stone buildings are mostly given over to self-catering, though there's B&B in two neat and trim, en-suite rooms as well. Most of the **pubs** have rooms, with one of the classiest establishments being the *Noel Arms*, which occupies a handsome old stone building on the High Street (☎01386/840317, ⓦwww.cotswold-inns-hotels.co.uk; ❼). The *Noel* is good for a pint as well, but the best **pub** in town is the *Eight Bells Inn*, a particularly cosy spot around the corner from the church. Curiously, there's a window in the floor showing the passage once used by Catholic priests escaping from the church.

Winchcombe and around

The journey to **WINCHCOMBE**, twelve miles southwest of Chipping Campden, is stunning, an exhilarating ride down the B4632, which weaves along the lower folds of the escarpment. Winchcombe was an important Saxon town, one-time capital of the kingdom of **Mercia**, and the possessor of a large Saxon abbey. The town lost its importance centuries ago – and the abbey didn't survive the Dissolution – but it's a pleasant spot all the same, even if its fetching blend of stone and half-timbered buildings play second fiddle to a quartet of neighbouring attractions – **Sudeley Castle**, **Hailes Abbey**, **Snowshill Manor** and **Belas Knap**.

Winchcombe is easy to reach by **bus** from Cheltenham, though services are spasmodic on Sundays. The **tourist office** (April–Oct Mon–Sat 10am–1pm & 2–5pm, Sun 10am–1pm & 2–4pm; Nov–March Sat & Sun 10am–1pm & 2–4pm; ☎01242/602925, ⓦwww.visitcotswoldsandsevernvale.gov.uk) is in the Town Hall, next to the modest **Police and Folk Museum** (April–Oct Mon-Sat 10am–5pm; £1), which displays examples of 1829 Peeler, Japanese and Nazi uniforms. Of the many **B&Bs**, one of the best is the Jacobean *Great House* on Castle St (☎01242/602490; no credit cards; ❷), full of old family furniture and one lovely four-poster room. Alternatively, the excellent *Gower House*, 16 North St (☎01242/602616; no credit cards; ❷), offers three extremely comfortable en-suite rooms, whilst the unassuming *Cleevely*, three miles south of the village on Corndean Lane (℡01242/602059; no credit cards; ❷), is the least expensive option in the area.

There's little to choose between the town's two main **pubs**, the *White Hart* and the *Plaisterers Arms*, which are both on the main street and serve food.

Sudeley Castle

A short walk east of Winchcombe, **SUDELEY CASTLE** (April–Oct daily 11am–5pm; gardens March–Oct daily 10.30am–5.30pm; £6.70, gardens only £5; ⓦwww.sudeleycastle.co.uk) was once a favourite country retreat of Tudor and Stuart monarchs. It has a particularly strong connection with Catherine Parr, the sixth wife of Henry VIII, who came to live here with her second husband, Thomas Seymour, Lord of Sudeley, shortly after the king's death. During the Civil War the house became a base for the Royalists and suffered the consequences when the New Model Army smashed the place up. What remained stood empty until 1830, when the ruins were bought by the Dent family, who restored much – but not all – of the exterior. Inside, the uneven collection includes paintings by Turner and Constable, a bed Charles I once slept in and one of Catherine Parr's teeth – her tomb is in the chapel. The real joy of Sudeley lies outside: in the **Queen's Garden**, with its huge yew hedges cut like masonry; in the creeper-covered ruins of the banqueting hall; and, above all, in the setting, with the green slopes of the escarpment behind.

Hailes Abbey and Snowshill Manor

HAILES ABBEY (April–Sept daily 10am–6pm; Oct daily 10am–5pm; £3; EH), a two-mile stroll northeast of Winchcombe, was once one of England's great Cistercian monasteries. Pilgrims came here from all over the country to pray before the abbey's phial of Christ's blood, a relic shown to be a fake at the time of the Dissolution, when the thirteenth-century monastery was demolished. Not much of the original complex remains beyond the foundations, but some cloister arches survive, worn by wind and rain. The ruins may lack drama, but Hailes is still worth visiting for its **museum**, where you can examine thirteenth-century bosses at close quarters, and for the nearby **church**, which is older than the abbey and contains beautiful wall paintings dating from around 1300.

Three miles northeast of Hailes Abbey, **SNOWSHILL MANOR** is a good-looking Cotswold manor house that invites a detour (April–June & Sept-Oct Wed–Sun noon–5pm; July & Aug Mon & Wed–Sun noon–5pm; garden same months & days 11am–5.30pm; £6.40, gardens only £3.60; NT). Inspired as a boy by his grandmother's "wonderful" Chinese cabinet (now in the Zenith room of the house), the architect, craftsman and poet Charles Paget Wade (1883–1956) spent decades hunting down objects which were not "rare or valuable" but "of interest as records of various vanished handicrafts". The results of his forays – model carts, boneshaker bicycles, children's prams, wooden toys, beds, beetles, all kinds of musical instruments – were crammed into the house, while he himself lived in a cottage in the garden. It's an endlessly diverting collection, a veritable trove of exotic curiosities. Most dramatic is the arrangement of 26 Samurai warriors dating from the seventeenth to the nineteenth centuries in the Green Room. Note that there is a ten-minute walk to the house from the entrance to the grounds.

Belas Knap

Up on the ridge overlooking Winchcombe, the Neolithic long barrow of **BELAS KNAP** occupies one of the most breathtaking spots in the Cotswolds. Dating from around 3000 BC, this is the best-preserved burial chamber in England, stretching out like a strange sleeping beast cloaked in green velvet. The two-mile climb up the Cotswold Way from Winchcombe contributes to the fun, giving good views back over Sudeley Castle. The path strikes off to the right near the entrance to Sudeley; when you reach the road at the top, turn right and then left up into the woods, from where it's a ten-minute hike to Belas Knap.

Stow-on-the-Wold

Straddling eight roads, including the Roman Fosse Way (now the A429) some four miles south of Moreton-in-Marsh – and eleven from Winchcombe – windswept **STOW-ON-THE-WOLD** sucks in a disproportionate number of visitors for its size and attractions, which essentially comprise an old marketplace surrounded by brassy pubs, antiques shops and souvenir boutiques. The narrow walled alleyways, or "tunes", running into the square were designed for funnelling sheep into the market, which is itself dominated by an imposing Victorian hall and, just to the south, a medieval cross allegedly raised to instil honesty among the traders.

Stow is the logical springboard for trips deeper into the region with its good bus connections from Moreton-in-Marsh and Cheltenham, and its healthy supply of hotels and B&Bs. The **tourist office** on the Market Square (April–Oct Mon–Sat 9.30am–5.30pm; Nov–March Mon–Sat 9.30am–4.30pm; ☏01451/831082, ⓦwww.cotswold.gov.uk) sells National Express bus tickets and keeps a list of local accommodation. Among the **B&Bs**, one very recommendable spot is the secluded and pretty *Honeysuckle Cottage* (☏01451/830973; no credit cards; closed Nov & Jan; ❸), which is tucked away on Union Street – take the short-cut passage through the *King's Arms* pub from the square; or you could try *Tall Trees* (☏01451/831296; no credit cards; ❸), on the edge of town off the Oddington road (A436), which has sweeping views and a cosy wood burner in its modern sitting room annexe. Close to the tourist office stands the popular **youth hostel** (☏0870/7706050, ⓔstow@yha.org.uk; restricted opening Oct–March; £13), which has fifty beds in four- to eight-bedded rooms. Also central, on the corner of Park and Digbeth streets, is *The Royalist* (☏01451/830670, ⓦwww.theroyalisthotel .co.uk; ❼), an upmarket hotel that bills itself as England's oldest inn, a claim partly substantiated by wooden beams carbon-dated at around one thousand years old.

For **food**, *The Royalist* offers tasty light meals in its *Eagle & Child* bar and also possesses the more formal but extremely good *947AD* restaurant, where a three-course meal will rush you about £30. Alternatively, the *Cotswold Garden Tearoom*, next to the church on Sheep Street, offers mouthwatering homemade cakes and snacks in a delightful walled garden.

Northleach

NORTHLEACH, secluded in a shallow depression nine miles south of Stow, is one of the most appealing and least developed villages in the Cotswolds. This, together with its location at the heart of the plateau, within easy reach of Oxford, Stratford and the picturesque Windrush Valley, makes it a perfect base from which to explore the region. Rows of immaculate late-medieval cottages cluster around the village's spacious central square, but the most outstanding feature is its handsome Perpendicular **Church of St Peter and St Paul,**

erected in the fifteenth-century at the height of the wool boom, when the surrounding fields supported a vast population of sheep. Inside, the floor of the beautifully proportioned nave, lit by wide clerestory windows, is inlaid with an exceptional collection of **memorial brasses** marking the tombs of the merchants whose endowments paid for the church. On several, you can make out the woolsacks laid out beneath the corpse's feet – a symbol of wealth and power that features to this day in the House of Lords, where a woolsack is placed on the Lord Chancellor's seat.

Excellent **accommodation** can be enjoyed right in the centre at the *Cotteswold House*, a wonderfully well-preserved Tudor cottage with exposed stone arches and antique oak panelling on the Market Place (℡01451/860493, Ⓦwww.cotteswoldhouse.com; ❸). A recommendable second choice is the *Wheatsheaf Hotel* (℡01451/860244, Ⓦwww.wheatsheafatnorthleach.com; ❸), a former coaching inn just down from the square on West End with eight, spick-and-span, en-suite modern rooms. The best **restaurant** in Northleach is the *Old Woolhouse*, on the Market Place (℡01451/860366; reservations recommended), where you can expect to spend around £40 per head for top-notch French cuisine. Less expensively, the *Wheatsheaf* offers restaurant meals and the *Sherborne Arms*, on the Market Place, supplies good bar food.

Cirencester

Ten miles from Northleach, on the southern fringes of the Cotswolds, **CIRENCESTER** makes a refreshing change from its more gentrified neighbours. Here, the "olde-worlde" image in which many Cotswold towns indulge has been exchanged for an endearingly old-fashioned atmosphere, generated partly by shops that haven't changed for decades. Under the **Romans**, the town was called Corinium and ranked second only to Londinium in size and importance. A provincial capital and a centre of trade, it flourished for three centuries and had one of the largest forums north of the Alps. However, the Saxons polished off almost all of the Roman city and the town's prosperity was only restored with the wool boom of the Middle Ages. Nowadays, Cirencester, with its handsome stone buildings, is one of the most affluent towns in the area and lays claim to be the "Capital of the Cotswolds".

Cirencester's heart is the delightful swirling **Market Place**, on Mondays and Fridays packed by traders' stalls. An irregular line of eighteenth-century facades along the north side contrasts with the heavier Victorian structures opposite, but the parish church of **St John the Baptist**, built in stages during the fifteenth century, dominates. The extraordinary flying buttresses that support the tower had to be added when it transpired that the church had been constructed upon a filled-in ditch. Its grand three-tiered south porch, the largest in England – big enough to function as the one-time town hall – leads to the nave, where slender piers and soaring arches create a superb sense of space, enhanced by clerestory windows that bathe the nave in a warm light. The church contains much of interest, including a colourful wineglass **pulpit**, carved in stone in around 1450 and one of the few pre-Reformation pulpits to have survived in Britain. North of the chancel, superb fan vaulting hangs overhead in the **chapel of St Catherine**, who appears in a still vivid fragment of a fifteenth-century wall painting. In the adjacent **Lady Chapel** are two good seventeenth-century monuments, to Humphrey Bridges and his family and to the dandified Sir William Master.

Few medieval buildings other than the church have survived in Cirencester. The houses along the town's most handsome streets – Park, Thomas and

Coxwell – date mostly from the seventeenth and eighteenth centuries. One of those on Park Street houses the **Corinium Museum** (closed till July 2004), which mostly devotes itself to Roman and Saxon artefacts, including several wonderful **mosaic pavements**. A yew hedge the height of telegraph poles runs along Park Street, concealing **Cirencester House**, the home of the Earl of Bathurst. At no point can you see the building (it's plain anyway), but the attached three-thousand-acre park is open to the public: you enter it from Cecily Hill, a lovely street except for the eccentric Victorian barracks.

Finally, the **Brewery Arts Centre** (Mon–Sat 10am–5pm; free; ℡01285/657181), off Cricklade Street, is occupied by more than a dozen resident artists, whose studios you can visit and whose work you can buy in the shop. The centre's theatre hosts high-calibre plays and concerts (from jazz to classical), and there is a buzzing café on the first floor.

Practicalities

Nine roads radiate from Cirencester, five of them Roman, but **bus** services to the town could be better, though there are at least daily connections from Swindon, fourteen miles southeast, and Cheltenham, fifteen miles north. All services stop in the Market Place. The **tourist office** (April–Dec Mon–Sat 9.30am–5.30pm; Jan–March Mon–Sat 9.30am–5pm; ℡01285/654180, Ⓦwww.thecotswolds.org), in the Corn Hall on the Market Place, covers the whole of the Cotswolds and has a list of local **accommodation** pinned outside. A string of **B&Bs** lines Victoria Road, a short walk east: two good options here are *The Ivy House*, in high-gabled Victorian premises at no. 2 (℡01285/656626, Ⓦwww.ivyhousecotswolds.com; ❷), and similarly appointed *The Leauses*, at no. 101 (℡01285/653643, Ⓦwww.theleauses.co.uk; no credit cards; ❷). For a little more luxury, stay at the *Crown of Crucis Hotel* in Ampney Crucis (℡01285/851806, Ⓦwww.thecrownofcrucis.co.uk; ❺), a sixteenth-century former coaching inn with riverside gardens, a good restaurant and a no-smoking rule; to reach it, head two-and-a-half miles east on the A417. The most accessible **campsite** is at the *Mayfield Touring Park* at Perrotts Brook (℡01285/831301), two miles north on the A435; any Cheltenham-bound bus will drop you there.

For **snacks** you can't do much better than *Keith's Coffee Shop* on Blackjack Street, which also serves the best coffee in town. The *Café Bar* **restaurant**, next to the Brewery Centre, is inexpensive and goes out of its way to make its vegetarian dishes interesting (no credit cards; closed Sun). The best choice for a relaxing evening meal, however, is *Harry Hare's* at 3 Gosditch St (℡01285/652375), just behind the church, which specializes in classy renditions of down-to-earth English dishes for under £20. If you're splashing out and have transport, the *Crown of Crucis* in Ampney Crucis (see accommodation, above) is another option also worth considering.

Cirencester has plenty of **pubs**, their clientele swollen by tweedy students from the nearby Royal Agricultural College. Try the *Kings Head* on the Market Place or, for **bar meals**, the *Waggon & Horses* on London Road, and the *Butcher's Arms* in Ampney Crucis.

Malmesbury

The striking half-ruin of a Norman abbey presides over the small hill-town of **MALMESBURY**, one of the oldest boroughs in England. Lying twelve miles south of Cirencester (and only five miles north off the M4 motorway), it's not part of the Cotswolds geologically, though the town's early wealth was based on wool. Malmesbury certainly lacks the tweeness of the Cotswold towns to the north, with new housing estates encircling the centre, and modern developments marring views over the Avon. But none of this can detract from the splendour of the abbey, a majestic structure with some of the finest Romanesque sculpture in the country.

The High Street begins at the bottom of the hill by the old silk mills and heads north across the river and up past a jagged row of ancient cottages on its way to the octagonal **Market Cross**, built in around 1490 to provide shelter from the rain. Nearby, the eighteenth-century **Tolsey Gate** leads through to the **Abbey** (daily: April–Oct 10am–5pm; Nov–March 10am–4pm; free), which was once a rich and powerful Benedictine monastery. The first abbey burnt down in about 1050, the second was roughed up during the Dissolution, but the beautiful Norman **nave** has survived, its south porch sporting a multitude of exquisite if badly worn figures. To the left of the high altar, the pulpit virtually hides the **tomb of King Athelstan**, grandson of Alfred the Great and the first Saxon to be recognized as king of England; the tomb, however, is empty, the location of the king's remains unknown. The abbey's greatest surviving treasures are housed in the parvise (room above the porch), reached via a narrow spiral staircase right of the main doorway, where pride of place is given to four Flemish **medieval Bibles**, written on parchment and sumptuously illuminated with gilt ink and exquisite miniature paintings.

Practicalities

Buses to Malmesbury – including services from Cirencester and Chippenham – pull into the Market Place, a short walk from the **tourist office**, in the town hall off Cross Hayes car park (Mon–Thurs 9am–4.50pm, Fri 9am–4.20pm, Sat 10am–4pm; ☎01666/823748, Ⓦwww.wiltshiretourism.co.uk). There's no strong reason to stay the night here, but the *Old Bell* (☎01666/822344, Ⓦwww.oldbellhotel.com; ❻), in Abbey Row, originally built as a guest house for the abbey, has plush and extremely comfortable rooms. For **food**, stick to either the *Whole Hog*, a stone-walled tearoom-cum-pub overlooking the Market Place, or the *Summer Café* on the High St, which does a good line in sandwiches.

Cheltenham

Until the eighteenth century **CHELTENHAM** was like any other Cotswold town, but then the discovery of a spring in 1716 transformed it into Britain's most popular **spa**. During Cheltenham's prime, a century or so later, the royal, the rich and the famous descended in hordes to take the waters, which were said to cure anything from constipation to worms. These days, while a fair proportion of Cheltenham's hundred thousand-odd inhabitants are undoubtedly well-heeled, of Conservative persuasion (true of the Cotswolds in general) and above retirement age, the town saves itself from too smug an image by a lively and increasingly cosmopolitan atmosphere. Its various **festivals** are established highlights of the cultural calendar – folk (Feb), jazz (April), science (June), classical music (July) and literature (October) – while Cheltenham's famous races (see box opposite) and a fairly spirited nightlife complete the picture.

The focus of Cheltenham, the broad **Promenade**, sweeps majestically south from the High Street, lined with the town's grandest houses, smartest shops and most genteel public gardens. A short walk north of the High Street brings you to **Pittville**, which, planned as a spa town to rival Cheltenham, was never completed and is now mostly parkland. Here you can stroll along a few solitary

Cheltenham races

Cheltenham racecourse, a ten-minute walk north of Pittville Park at the foot of Cleeve Hill, is Britain's main steeplechasing venue. The principal event of the season, the three-day **National Hunt Festival** in March, attracts forty thousand people each day. Other meetings take place in January, April, October, November and December: a list of fixtures is posted up at the tourist office. For the cheapest but arguably the best view, pay £5 (rising to £15 during the Festival) for entry to the Courage Best Enclosure, as the pen in the middle is known. For schedules and other information, call ☎01242/513014 or access the website at ⓦwww.cheltenham .co.uk. For the National Hunt Festival it's essential to buy tickets in advance.

A popular pre-meet watering hole is the *King's Arms*, a short walk east of the racecourse in **Prestbury**, an old Cotswold village with a reputation for being the most haunted village in England, and which has now been subsumed into the town. **Fred Archer**, considered by many to have been the finest Flat jockey of all time, was brought up here, and he features prominently among the pub's racing memorabilia. The pub has sadly lost much of its character since becoming part of a chain, and you might find the nearby *Royal Oak* more congenial.

Regency avenues and visit the grandest spa building, the domed **Pump Room** (Mon & Wed–Sun 11am–4pm), where you can sample England's only naturally alkaline water for free, though the building's chief function nowadays is as a concert hall. On your return route, the **Holst Birthplace Museum** is worth a glance, at 4 Clarence Rd (Tues–Sat 10am–4pm; £2.50). Once the home of the composer of *The Planets*, the intimate rooms hold plenty of Holst memorabilia – including his piano – and also give a good insight into Victorian family life. Back in the centre, the well-set-out **Art Gallery and Museum** on Clarence St (Mon–Sat 10am–5.20pm, Sun 2–4.20pm; free) marks the high point of Cheltenham. It's very good on social history, with different eras represented by table displays of personal belongings and a typical dinner of the time. There's also a fine room dedicated to the Arts and Crafts Movement, containing several pieces by Charles Voysey and Ernest Gimson, two of the period's most graceful designers. Also on display is an array of rare Chinese ceramics, and works by Cotswold artists such as Stanley Spencer and Vanessa Bell.

Practicalities

All long-distance **buses** arrive at the station in Royal Well Road, just west off the Promenade. The **train station** is on Queen's Road, southwest of the centre, a twenty-minute walk (or take buses #D or #E). The **tourist office**, at 77 Promenade (Mon–Sat 9.30am–5.15pm; ☎01242/522878, ⓦwww .visitcheltenham.com), can provide information on bus tours in the Cotswolds.

Accommodation is plentiful, but availability will be limited during the races and festivals. Many options are in fine Regency houses, for example *Brennan*, on a quiet square at 21 St Luke's Rd (☎01242/525904; ❷), and *Crossways*, 57 Bath Rd (☎01242/527683, ⓦwww.crosswaysguesthouse.com; no smoking; ❸), only two minutes' walk from the centre. More upmarket are *Lypiatt House*, Lypiatt Road (☎01242/224994, ⓦwww.lypiatt.co.uk; ❺), set in its own grounds, with open fires and a conservatory with a small bar, and *Lawn*, 5 Pittville Lawn (☎01242/526638; no credit cards; no smoking; ❹), near the park, catering for vegetarians and vegans only and also housing an art gallery.

Cheltenham's **restaurants** draw in foodies from far and wide. At the top end, *Le Champignon Sauvage*, Suffolk Road (☎01242/573449), and *Le Petit Blanc*, The Promenade (☎01242/266800), an outpost of Raymond Blanc's famed

Manoir Aux Quat' Saisons, both serve superlative French cuisine, with fixed-price lunches offsetting the otherwise high prices. Marginally less expensive, *The Daffodil*, 18–20 Suffolk Parade (℡01242/700060), also offers gourmet choices in a former cinema, where the screen has been replaced with a hubbub of chefs. More affordably, the *Orange Tree*, 317 High St (℡01242/234232), has a range of vegetarian and vegan dishes, including breakfasts, which you can eat in a pleasant courtyard (closed Mon eve & all Sun), and you can munch on salads and sandwiches in the relaxed sofa basement or the upstairs rooms and at *Boogaloos*, 16 Regent St (closed eves).

Cheltenham also has the area's best **pubs and bars**, for example *The Beehive*, 1–3 Montpellier Villas, which has a games shed, courtyard garden and cosy snug, and *Tailor's Wine Bar*, 4 Cambray Place, just off the High Street, where you can relax in old leather armchairs or sit in the courtyard. *J's Vodka Bar*, 6 Regent St, dispenses a range of vodkas to a house and funk accompaniment, while the town's most popular **clubs** include *Subtone*, 115–117 The Promenade (Ⓦwww.subtone.co.uk; closed Sun), and *Time*, 33–35 Albion St (℡01242/570583).

Stroud and around

Five heavily populated valleys converge at **STROUD**, twelve miles west of Cirencester, creating an exhausting jumble of hills and a sense of high activity atypical of the Cotswolds. The bustle is not a new phenomenon. During the heyday of the wool trade the Frome River powered 150 mills, turning Stroud into the centre of the local cloth industry. Even now, the town is very much a working place, and one that doesn't need to peddle its heritage to the tourists in order to survive. While some of the old mills have been converted into flats, others contain factories, but only two continue to make cloth – no longer the so-called Stroudwater Scarlet used for military uniforms, but high-quality felt for tennis balls and snooker tables. In recent years, Stroud has become a thriving alternative centre, containing one of the country's first eco-housing projects, and with communities of artists and New Agers in the nearby valleys. Sadly, however, in spite of its scenic setting, the town remains the dowdiest of the region.

For visitors, the main point of interest is the excellent and family-friendly **Museum in the Park**, housed in an eighteenth-century mansion in Stratford Park, half a mile from the centre of town on the Gloucester road (April–Sept Tues–Fri 10am–5pm, Sat & Sun 11am–5pm; Oct–March Tues–Fri 10am–5pm, Sat & Sun 11am–4.30pm; free). Beautifully laid out, the collection demonstrates the history of the town through imaginatively themed rooms such as "Clean, Fit and Tidy" and "Industry and Invention". Look out for the lovely eighteenth-century paintings showing the tentering (hanging out) of Stroud's scarlet cloth on the hillsides.

Industrial archeology is strewn the length of the Frome Valley – the so-called Golden Valley. Council offices occupy one of the valley's finest mills, **Ebley Mill**, a twenty-minute walk west of the centre along the old Stroudwater Canal – for the best view you should then walk south across the field to the village of **Selsley**.

The unused **Severn and Thames Canal** east of Stroud cuts a more picturesque route, particularly beyond Chalford, three miles east, where houses perch precariously on the hillside. Walk thirty minutes along the towpath from here and you'll end up at the mouth of the **Sapperton tunnel**, more than two miles long and a great feat of eighteenth-century engineering. It's unsafe to go inside,

5

so seek sustenance at the nearby *Daneway Inn* instead, or head for the hilltop village of Sapperton, a world away from the hurly-burly of the Frome Valley.

Trains from London and Gloucester and **buses** from Cirencester, among other places, arrive at the station on Merrywalks. The **tourist office** is in the Subscription Rooms on Kendrick Street (Mon–Sat 10am–5pm; ☏01453/760960, ⓦwww.visitthecotswolds.co.uk). The most central place to **stay** is the *London Hotel*, 30–31 London Rd (☏01453/759992, ⓦwww.s-h-systems.co.uk; ❸), otherwise head for the *Downfield Hotel* at 134 Cainscross Rd (☏01453/764496, ⓦwww.downfieldhotel.co.uk; ❸), in a Georgian building five minutes from the High Street. You'll find the nearest **youth hostel** and **campsite** at Slimbridge (see below).

For **food** in the daytime go straight to *Mills Café* in Withey's Yard off High Street, which sells delicious cakes, homemade soups and other wholesome concoctions, or to the smartish *Retreat* wine bar in Church Street – in the evenings, the choice narrows down to Indian or Chinese.

Uley

The B4066 cuts a glorious route along the valley ridge southwest of Stroud, passing through **ULEY**, six miles from town. Boasting one of the best settings in the region, the village **church** lords it over the small green and the *Old Crown* pub. **Uley Bury**, among the largest hill forts in Britain, extends along the ridge above the village. The path from the church takes you up the shortest and steepest route (drivers can park right by the fort). Fences prevent you from clambering on top of the bury, but you can walk around the edge – a distance of about two miles altogether – and take in some staggering views. The atmosphere peaks on a winter's day, when bracing winds blow across the ridge while mist gathers in the valley below.

Slimbridge

Eight miles southwest of Stroud, **SLIMBRIDGE** sits in a narrow corridor between the M5 and the Severn – a surprising location for the **Slimbridge Wildfowl and Wetlands Centre** (daily: April–Oct 9.30am–6pm; Nov–March 9.30am–5pm; last entry 1hr before closing; £6.40; ⓦwww.wwt.org.uk), covering 120 acres between Sharpness Canal and the river. Since ornithologist Sir Peter Scott created it in 1946, the centre has become Britain's largest **wildfowl sanctuary**, and a breeding ground with an important conservation role. Geese, swans, ducks and a huge gathering of flamingos make up the bulk of the birdlife. While some birds are resident all year round, many are migratory: the greatest numbers congregate in the winter months, when Bewick swans, for example, migrate from Russia. There's an extensive network of trails around the sanctuary, with hides for observation.

Slimbridge has a **youth hostel** (☏0870/770 6036, ⓔslimbridge @yha.org.uk; £10.25) accessible from a lane opposite the *Tudor Arms* pub in the village, and a **campsite**, the *Tudor Caravan Park* (☏01453/890483, ⓦwww.tudorcaravanpark.co.uk), midway between the village and the wildfowl centre, about half a mile from each. The only useful **buses** are those between Gloucester and Bristol or Dursley, which stop by the turn-off on the A38, just over a mile east of Slimbridge.

Berkeley

Though quite secluded within a swathe of meadows and neat gardens, **Berkeley Castle** (April–Aug Tues–Sat 11am–4pm, Sun 2–5pm; Sept Wed–Sat 11am–4pm, Sun 2–5pm; Oct Sun 2–5pm; £6.25, grounds only £3) dominates the little village of **BERKELEY**, five miles southwest of Slimbridge on the A38. The fortress has an agreeably turreted medieval look, the robust twelfth-century walls softened by later accretions acquired in its gradual transformation into a family home. The interior is packed with mementoes of its long history, including its grisliest moment in 1327, when Edward II was murdered here – apparently by a red-hot iron thrust into his bowels. You can view the cell where the event took place, along with dungeons, dining room, kitchen, picture gallery and the Great Hall. Outside, the grounds include an Elizabethan terraced garden and a Butterfly Farm (£2), and within easy walking distance, in the village itself, is the **Jenner Museum** (April–Sept Tues–Sat 12.30–5.30pm, Sun 1–5.30pm; Oct Sun 1–5.30pm; £3), dedicated to Edward Jenner, son of a local vicar and discoverer of the principle of vaccination.

For a lunchtime stop near Berkeley, follow the narrow High Street out of the centre of the village for about a mile to reach the *Salutation*, an unpretentious country **pub** with a garden. To reach Berkeley by public transport, Beaumont Travel (℡01452/309770, ⓦwww.beaumont-travel.com) operates coaches from Gloucester.

Painswick

The A46 and the B4070 are equally attractive routes linking Stroud and Cheltenham, but the former has the edge because after four miles you reach the old wool town of **PAINSWICK**, where ancient buildings jostle for space on narrow streets running downhill off the busy main street. The fame of Painswick's **church** stems not so much from the building itself as from the surrounding **graveyard**, where 99 yew trees, cut into bizarre bulbous shapes resembling lollipops, surround a collection of eighteenth-century table-tombs unrivalled in the Cotswolds. However, it's the **Rococo Garden** (mid-Jan to Oct daily 11am–5pm; £3.60), about half a mile north up the Gloucester road and attached to Painswick House (not open to the public), that ranks as the town's main attraction. Created in the early eighteenth century and later abandoned, the garden has been restored to its original form with the aid of a painting dated 1748. Although there's usually some restoration in progress, it's a beautiful example – and the country's only one – of Rococo garden design, a short-lived fashion typified by a mix of formal geometrical shapes and more naturalistic, curving lines. With a vegetable patch as an unusual centrepiece, the Painswick garden spreads across a sheltered gully – for the best vistas, walk around anticlockwise.

Painswick's **tourist office** is housed in the library on the main street (April–Oct Tues–Fri 10am–4pm, Sat 10am–1pm; ℡01452/813552). The best local **accommodation** choices include *Thorne Guest House* on Friday Street (℡01452/812476; no credit cards; closed Dec & Jan; ❸), one of the oldest houses in the village, and *Cardynham House* on St Mary's Street (℡01452/814006, ⓦwww.cardynham.co.uk; ❺), with beautifully themed rooms, one with a lounge and private pool. The *March Hare* Thai **restaurant**, attached to *Cardynham House* (℡01452/813452; closed Sun & Mon), is almost the only place to eat in Painswick – not counting the nearby *Royal Oak*, reckoned to be the best **pub** hereabouts.

Gloucester

For centuries life was good for **GLOUCESTER**. The Romans chose the spot for a garrison to guard the Severn and spy on Wales, and later for a *colonia* or home for retired soldiers – the highest status for a provincial Roman town. Commercial prestige came with trade up the River Severn, which developed into one of the busiest trade routes in Europe. The city's political importance peaked under the Normans, when William the Conqueror met here frequently with his council of nobles. The Middle Ages saw Gloucester's rise as a religious centre, and the construction of what is now the cathedral, but also witnessed its political and economic decline: navigating the Severn as far up as Gloucester was so difficult that most trade gradually shifted south to Bristol. In a brave attempt to reverse the city's fortunes, a canal was opened in 1827 to link Gloucester to Sharpness, on a broader stretch of the Severn further south. Trade picked up for a time, but it was only a temporary remedy.

Today, the canal is busy once again, though this time with pleasure boats, while the Victorian dockyards have undergone a facelift. Gloucester's most magnificent possession, however, remains its **cathedral**, whose tower is visible for miles around. Otherwise, little of the city has survived the ravages of history and the twentieth century, with the centre a mishmash of medieval ruins swallowed up by ugly new buildings, and surrounded by a web of roads.

The City

Gloucester lies on the east bank of the Severn, its centre spread around a curve in the river. **The Cross**, once the entrance to the Roman forum, marks the heart of the city and the meeting-point of Northgate, Southgate, Eastgate and Westgate streets, all Roman roads. **St Michael's Tower**, the remains of an old church, over-looks it. The **cathedral** and the **docks** lie west of the Northgate–Southgate axis.

Southgate and Westgate streets

The most interesting parish church in Gloucester is **St Mary de Crypt** on Southgate Street, mostly late medieval but with some of its original Norman features; fragments of a sixteenth-century wall painting of the Adoration of the Magi in the chancel show unusual detail for work of that period. The church is kept locked, but you can get the key from the tourist office across the road. Greyfriars runs alongside St Mary's, past the ruins of a Franciscan church and the Eastgate Market to the **City Museum** on Brunswick Road (Tues–Sat 10am–5pm; £2; combined ticket with Folk Museum £3), with a good arche-ological collection including a fragment of the Roman city wall, preserved *in situ* below ground level (viewable from the museum on summer Saturdays only, or at any time from Eastgate Street). Westgate Street, quieter and many times more pleasant than its three Roman counterparts, retains several medieval buildings. One of them, a creaking timber-framed house at the bottom of the street, contains the **Folk Museum** (Tues–Sat 10am–5pm; £2; combined ticket with City Museum £3), which illustrates the social history of the Gloucester area using an impressive collection of objects, from huge wrought-iron cheese presses to salt-filled rolling pins used to scare off witches. College Court Alley leads from Westgate Street to the haven of the cathedral, passing the Beatrix Potter shop and museum – the house sketched by the children's artist and author while she was on holiday here in 1897 and subse-quently appearing in every copy of *The Tailor of Gloucester*.

The Cathedral

The superb condition of Gloucester **Cathedral** (daily 7.30am–6pm; sug-gested donation £2.50; ⓦ www.gloucestercathedral.uk.com) is striking in a city that has lost so much of its past. An abbey was founded on this spot by the Saxons, but four centuries later Benedictine monks came and built their own church, begun in 1069. As a place of worship it shot to importance after the murder at Berkeley Castle of Edward II in 1327: Bristol and Malmesbury wouldn't take his body, but Gloucester did, and the king's shrine became a major place of pilgrimage. The money generated helped to finance the conversion of the church into the country's first and greatest example of the **Perpendicular style**: the magnificent 225-foot tower crowns the achievement. Henry VIII recognized the church's prestige by conferring on it the status of cathedral.

Beneath the reconstructions of the fourteenth and fifteenth centuries, some Norman aspects remain, best seen in the **nave**, flanked by sturdy pillars and arches adorned with immaculate zigzag mouldings. Only when you reach the choir and transepts can you see how skilfully the new church was built inside the old, the Norman masonry hidden beneath the finer lines of the Perpendicular panelling and tracery. The **choir** has extraordinary fourteenth-century misericords, and also provides the best vantage point for admiring the **east window** completed in around 1350 and – at almost 80 feet tall – the largest medieval window in Britain. Beneath it, to the left (as you're facing the east window) is the **tomb of Edward II**, immortalized in alabaster and marble and in good fettle apart from some graffiti. In the nearby **Lady Chapel**, delicate carved tracery holds a staggering patchwork of windows, virtually creating walls of stained glass. There are well-preserved monuments here, too, but the tomb of Robert II, in the **south ambulatory**, is far more unusual. Robert, eldest son of William the Conqueror, died in 1134, but the painted wooden effigy dates from around 1290. Dressed as a crusader, he lies in a curious pose, with his arms and legs crossed, his right hand gripping his sword ready to do battle with the infidel.

The innovative nature of the cathedral's design can perhaps be best appreciated in the beautiful **cloisters**, completed in 1367 and featuring the first fan vaulting in the country. The fine quality of the work is outdone perhaps only by Henry VII's Chapel in Westminster Abbey, which it inspired. The setting was used to represent the corridors of Hogwart's School of Witchcraft and Wizardry in the *Harry Potter* films. Back inside, an **exhibition** in the upstairs galleries, reached from the north transept (April–Oct Mon–Fri 10.30am–4pm, Sat 10.30am–3pm; £1.50) gives the low-down on the east window and allows you to view it at close quarters. Here, you can try out the **Whispering Gallery**, where you can pick up the tiniest sounds from across the vaulting. Lastly, you can climb the cathedral's **tower** for the best views of Gloucester (April–Oct Wed, Thurs, Fri 2.30pm, Sat 2pm & 3pm; £2.50).

The Docks

The **Docks** complex was developed during the fifty years following the opening of the Sharpness canal in 1827. The import of corn represented the bulk of the port's business at that time, and huge **warehouses** were built for storing the grain. Fourteen of them have survived, mostly now converted into municipal offices and shops as well as a museum, a redevelopment at its most crudely commercial in the **Merchants' Quay** shopping centre.

The **National Waterways Museum** (daily 10am–5pm, last admission 4pm; £5; ⓦ www.nwm.org.uk), in the southernmost Llanthony Warehouse, completely immerses you in the canal mania that swept Britain in the eighteenth and nineteenth centuries, touching on everything from the engineering of the locks to the lives of the horses that trod the towpaths. The three floors contain plenty of atmospheric noises off, videos, accessible information and interactive displays. In the old customs house, the **Regiments of Gloucestershire Museum** (June–Sept daily 10am–5pm; Oct–May Tues–Sun 10am–5pm; £4.25) makes a potentially dull or alienating subject fascinating, with its focus on all aspects of life as a soldier, both in war and during peacetime.

Practicalities

Gloucester's **bus and train stations** are opposite one another across Bruton Way, five minutes' walk east of the Cross. The **tourist office** is at 28 Southgate St (Mon–Sat 10am–5pm, also Sun in July & Aug 11am–3pm; ☎01452/396572, ⓦwww.gloucester.gov.uk/tourism). Of the few **hotels** within easy walking distance of the train station and centre, the *Albert* at 56–60 Worcester St (☎01452/502081, ⓦwww.alberthotel.com; ❷), a listed red-brick building from the 1830s, and the Victorian *Edward* at 88–92 London Rd (☎01452/525865, ⓦwww.edwardhotel-gloucester.co.uk; ❸) offer the best value. Central, inexpensive **B&Bs** include *Spalite* (☎01452/380828, ⓦwww.spalitehotel.com; ❷), at the bottom of Southgate Street near the docks and prone to traffic noise, and the four-storey *Lulworth* at 12 Midland Rd (☎01452/521881, ⓦwww.s-h-systems.co.uk; ❷), in a quiet location behind the park.

The selection of **restaurants** is only slightly more remarkable than the hotels, and many places are open only during the day. You'll find reliable if rather unimaginative fare in the *Orchids at the Undercroft* restaurant in the cathedral, open until 5pm, and at the café-bar in the Guildhall on Eastgate Street – open until 11pm and always lively. *Ye Olde Fish Shoppe* on Hare Lane, even more of a Gloucester institution, occupies a sixteenth-century building and serves excellent crispy takeaway fish until 6.30pm, though the attached restaurant stays open later (☎01452/255502; no credit cards; closed all Sun & Mon eve). In the evenings, choice extends to the vaulted *Cellars* (closed Sun & Mon) in Longsmith Street or the *Café René*, Greyfriars, Southgate Street, where walls and ceilings are smothered with bottles. For pizzas go to *Pizza Piazza* at Merchants' Quay – the only reason to venture to the docks in the evening.

There isn't a huge choice of **pubs** either, though the best are all within spitting distance of the Cross. The rambling fifteenth-century *New Inn* in Northgate Street has a good atmosphere, a splendid galleried courtyard and cheap meals, but for really tasty hot food at rock-bottom prices go to the *Fountain Inn*, down a narrow alley off Westgate Street, which also pulls a sublime pint of Abbot ale and has tables in an adjacent courtyard. For **clubbers**, *Innteraction* on Bruton Way (Wed–Sat; ☎01452/302222, ⓦwww.innteraction.com) covers most tastes and has theme nights.

Tewkesbury and around

The small market town of **TEWKESBURY**, ten miles north of Gloucester, stands hemmed in by the Avon and Severn rivers, which converge nearby. Pressure of space accounts for the narrow alleys and courts leading off from the main streets, of which thirty of the original ninety still survive. The comparatively unchanging face of Tewkesbury is also due to the fact that it almost completely missed out on the Industrial Revolution. Elegant Georgian houses and medieval timber-framed buildings still line several of the town's main streets – especially Church Street – and the Norman abbey has survived as one of the greatest in England.

The site of **Tewkesbury Abbey** (daily 7.30am–6pm; suggested donation £2) was first selected for a Benedictine monastery in the eighth century, but virtually nothing of the Saxon complex survived a sacking by the Danes, and a new abbey was founded by a Norman nobleman in 1092. The work took about sixty years to complete, with some additions made in the fourteenth century. Two hundred years later the Dissolution brought about the destruction of most of the monastic buildings, but the abbey itself survived. The sheer scale of the exterior makes a lasting impact: its colossal **tower** is the largest Norman tower in the world, while the west front's soaring recessed arch – 65 feet high – is the only exterior arch in the country to boast such impressive proportions. In the nave, fourteen stout Norman pillars steal the show, graceful despite their size, and topped by a fourteenth-century ribbed and vaulted ceiling, studded with gilded bosses (look for the musical angels). On the blue and scarlet **choir** roof, the bosses include a ring of shining suns (emblem of the Yorkist cause), said to have been put there by Edward IV after the defeat of the Lancastrians at Tewkesbury in 1471. (The battlefield, known as Bloody Meadow, is off Lincoln Green Lane, southwest of the abbey.) The abbey's medieval tombs celebrate Tewkesbury's greatest patrons, the Fitzhamons, De Clares, Beauchamps and Despensers, who turned the building into something of a mausoleum for themselves. The Despensers have the best monuments, particularly Sir Edward, standard-bearer to the Black Prince, who died in 1375 and is shown as a kneeling figure on the roof of the **Trinity Chapel** to the right of the high altar: you can see it best from beside the Warwick Chantry Chapel in the north aisle. Nearby, in the ambulatory, the macabre so-called **Wakeman Cenotaph**, carved in the fifteenth century but of otherwise uncertain origin, represents a decaying corpse being consumed by snakes and other creatures.

Practicalities

Tewkesbury's **tourist office** at 64 Barton St (April–Oct Mon–Sat 9.30am–5pm, Sun 10am–4pm; Nov–March closed Sun; ☎01684/295027, ⓦwww.visitcotswoldsandsevernvale.gov.uk) holds a small museum (£1) upstairs. You won't have to look far to find a **room**: almost opposite the abbey at 62 Church Street, *Abbey Antiques Guest House* (☎01684/298145; no credit cards; ❸) is colourfully furnished with antiques, while *Barton House*, 5 Barton Rd (☎01684/292049 or 07946/460601, ⓦwww.s-h-systems.co.uk; no credit cards; ❷) has an eclectic mix of furniture, and plain rooms. Best of Tewkesbury's **hotels** are the *Royal Hop Pole*, Church Street (☎01684/293236, ⓦwww .regalhotels.co.uk; ❺), whose annexe has a loggia facing the garden, and the black and white *Tudor House*, High Street (☎01684/297755; ❹).

For daytime **snacks** or **lunches**, choose between the chrome of the *Aubergine* café-bar (closed Sun) at 25 Church St for good salads and sandwiches, *My Great Grandfathers*, 84 Church St (closed Mon), which is excellent for traditional puddings, and the ancient *Berkeley Arms* **pub** at 8 Church St, which serves astoundingly cheap meals. In the evenings, the *Rendezvous*, 78 Church St (☎01684/290357; closed Mon) concentrates on Mediterranean-style fish and meat dishes and has a cellar bar for snacks; it also opens for Sunday lunch.

Bredon Hill

The most important Iron Age fort in the area once crowned **Bredon Hill**, six miles northeast of Tewkesbury and visible for miles around in the flat Severn Vale. Excavation of the site revealed more than fifty bodies, all hacked to pieces, seemingly the victims of a final assault by unknown attackers in the first century AD. Inside the rampart, a huge expanse covering eleven acres, an eighteenth-century tower called Parson's Folly is an incongruous centrepiece, but the views are supreme, with deer often grazing on the slopes.

The site can be approached from various places around the southern foot of the hill. From **Overbury**, one of the prettier villages, the climb takes less than an hour. If you're relying on public transport, buses bound for Evesham from Tewkesbury pass through the village of **Bredon** (not Sun), from where you should allow about three hours to walk to the hill and back.

Bristol and around

On the borders of Gloucestershire and Somerset, **BRISTOL** has harmoniously blended its mercantile roots with a progressive, modern outlook, stimulated in recent years by fast money, new technology and a large student population. As a centre for the arts and media, the city has a vibrant youth culture and can boast some of the region's best restaurants and nightlife.

Weaving through its centre, the River Avon forms part of a system of waterways that made Bristol a great inland port, in later years booming on the transatlantic trafficking of such goods as rum, tobacco and slaves. In the nineteenth century the illustrious **Isambard Kingdom Brunel** laid the foundations of a tradition of engineering, creating two of Bristol's greatest monuments – the SS *Great Britain* and the lofty Clifton Suspension Bridge. More recently, spin-offs from the aerospace industry have placed the city at the forefront of the fields of communications, computing, design and finance. Beneath the prosperous surface, Bristol has its negative aspects – one of England's highest populations of homeless people, some of the most notorious housing estates and the highest proportion of cars to inhabitants. Nonetheless, it remains an attractive city, predominantly hilly, and surrounded by rolling countryside.

Arrival, information and accommodation

Bristol's **bus station** is centrally located off Marlborough Street, and Temple Meads **train station** is a twenty-minute walk east of the centre, and served by frequent buses #8 and #9, which pass through the centre on their way to Cotham (#9 only) and Clifton. If you arrive at Bristol Parkway station, on the outskirts of town, take bus #73 (on Sundays, #73, #82, #573 or #584). The **tourist office** is in the at-Bristol complex, on Wildscreen Walk, Harbourside (March–Oct daily 10am–6pm; Nov–Feb Mon–Sat 10am–5pm, Sun 11am–4pm; ℡0906/586 2313, ⓦwww.visitbristol.co.uk).

Most of Bristol's **accommodation** is in the leafy areas of Cotham and Clifton, which are also the districts where the majority of the city's students live. Price-wise, it's hard to beat *St Michael's Guest House*, 145 St Michael's Hill (℡0117/907 7820; ❷), offering simple rooms with shared bathrooms over one of Cotham's most popular cafés. In Clifton, choices range from the *Sunderland Guest House*, 4 Sunderland Place (℡0117/973 7249 or 0797/624 9108, ⓔsunderland.gh@blueyonder.co.uk; no credit cards; ❷), basic, but quiet, clean and very near the centre; *Downs View*, 38 Upper Belgrave Rd (℡0117/973 7046, ⓦwww.downsviewguesthouse.co.uk; ❸), with views over Clifton Downs and the city from the back; *Naseby House*, 105 Pembroke Rd (℡0117/973 7859, ⓦwww.nasebyhousehotel.co.uk; ❹), a plush Victorian guest house, beautifully furnished; and *Victoria Square*, Victoria Square (℡0117/973 9058, ⓦwww.vicsquare.com; ❻), in a choice location near Clifton Village.

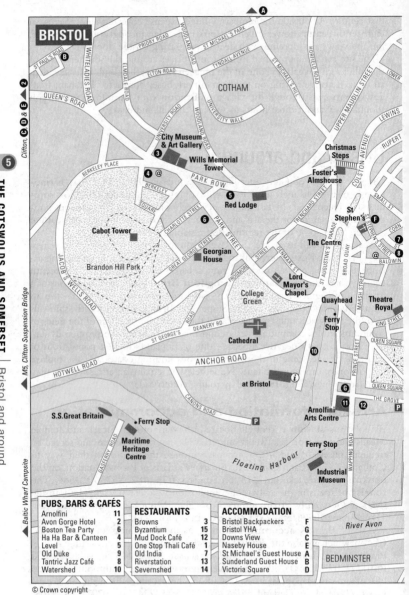

PUBS, BARS & CAFÉS

Arnolfini	11
Avon Gorge Hotel	2
Boston Tea Party	6
Ha Ha Bar & Canteen	4
Level	5
Old Duke	9
Tantric Jazz Café	8
Watershed	10

RESTAURANTS

Browns	3
Byzantium	15
Mud Dock Café	12
One Stop Thali Café	1
Old India	7
Riverstation	13
Severnshed	14

ACCOMMODATION

Bristol Backpackers	F
Bristol YHA	G
Downs View	C
Naseby House	E
St Michael's Guest House	A
Sunderland Guest House	B
Victoria Square	D

Bristol has two **hostels**: the modern and central **YHA**, 14 Narrow Quay (℡0870/770 5726, 🖂bristol@yha.org.uk; £16), located in a refurbished warehouse, with some twin rooms (❶), and the central and friendly *Bristol Backpackers*, 17 St Stephen's St (℡0117/925 7900, 🌐www .bristolbackpackers.co.uk; £14), housed in a lovely old building with a late bar, first-class showers and cheap Internet access, though it can be noisy.

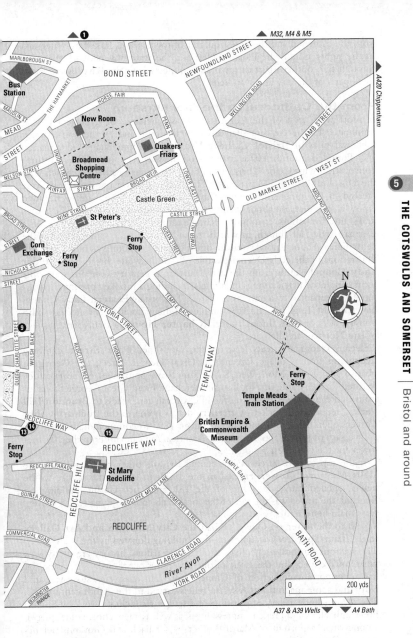

The City

A good place to start exploring, **the Centre** was once a quay-lined dock but is now the traffic-ridden nucleus of the city, with cars swirling round the statues of Edmund Burke, MP for Bristol from 1774 to 1780, and local merchant and benefactor Edward Colston (1636–1721). The Centre is just a few steps from the cathedral and the oldest quarter of town, and is linked by water-taxi to the sights around the Floating Harbour, the waterway network that runs through the southern part of town and connects with the River Avon. Buses to all parts of the city also stop here.

From the Cathedral to the City Museum

A short walk west of the Centre, the grassy expanse of College Green is dominated by the crescent-shaped Council House and by the contrastingly medieval lines of **Bristol Cathedral** (daily 8am–6pm; suggested donation £2). Founded around 1140 as an abbey on the supposed spot of St Augustine's convocation with Celtic Christians in 603, it became a cathedral church with the Dissolution of the Monasteries. The two towers on the west front were erected in the nineteenth century in a faithful act of homage to Edmund Knowle, architect and abbot at the start of the fourteenth century. The cathedral's interior offers a unique example among Britain's cathedrals of a German-style hall church, in which the aisles rise to the same height as the central area. Abbot Knowle's **choir** offers one of the country's most exquisite illustrations of the early Decorated style of Gothic, while the adjoining **Elder Lady Chapel**, dating from the early thirteenth century, contains some fine tombs and eccentric carvings of animals, including a monkey playing the bagpipes accompanied by a ram on the violin. The ornate **Eastern Lady Chapel** has some of England's finest examples of heraldic glass. From the south transept, a door leads through to the **Chapter House**, a richly carved piece of late Norman architecture.

Elegant Georgian streets lead off the shop-lined **Park Street**, climbing steeply up from College Green. On Great George Street, the **Georgian House** (April–Oct Mon–Wed, Sat & Sun 10am–5pm; free), is the faithfully restored former home of a local sugar merchant. From Great George Street, or from Berkeley Square further up the hill, you can gain access to **Brandon Hill Park**, a sequestered pocket of greenery that is home to the landmark **Cabot Tower** (open daily until dusk; free), built in 1897 to commemorate the 400th anniversary of John Cabot's voyage to America. You can climb up the 105-foot tower for the city's best panorama.

At the top of Park Street stands central Bristol's other chief landmark, the **Wills Memorial Tower**, erected in the 1920s to lend some stature to the newly opened university. One of the last great neo-Gothic buildings in England, the tower was the gift of the local Wills tobacco dynasty, the university's main benefactors.

Next to the tower, on Queen's Road, the **City Museum and Art Gallery** (daily 10am–5pm; free) occupies another building donated by the Wills family. The sections on local archeology, geology and natural history are pretty well what you'd expect, but the scope of the museum is occasionally surprising – it has an important collection of Chinese porcelain, glassware, stoneware and ivory, and some magnificent Assyrian reliefs carved in the eighth century BC. The second-floor gallery of paintings and sculptures includes work by English Pre-Raphaelites and French Impressionists, as well as a few choice older pieces, among them a portrait of Martin Luther by Cranach and Giovanni Bellini's unusual *Descent into Limbo*.

From the Centre to Broadmead

One of Bristol's oldest churches, **St Stephen's**, stands just east of the Centre. Established in the thirteenth century, rebuilt in the fifteenth and thoroughly restored with plenty of neo-Gothic trimmings in 1875, the parish church has some flamboyant tombs inside. On nearby **Corn Street**, the Georgian Corn Exchange was designed by John Wood of Bath and now holds the covered St Nicholas markets. The four engraved bronze pillars outside the entrance date from the sixteenth and seventeenth centuries and were transferred from a nearby arcade where they served as trading tables – thought to be the "nails" from which the expression "pay on the nail" is derived.

Beyond the market, Wine Street runs along the site of the old **Bristol Castle**, now a park, and the modern **Broadmead** shopping centre, an uninspiring development laid out on the ruins left by wartime bombing. In the midst of the chain stores, the **New Room** (Mon–Sat 10am–4pm; free), the country's first Methodist chapel, is accessible from both the central strip of Broadmead and the Horsefair. Established by John Wesley in 1739, it looks very much as he left it, with a double-deck pulpit in the chapel, beneath a hidden upstairs window from which the evangelist could observe the progress of his trainee preachers.

King Street to St Mary Redcliffe

King Street, a short walk east from the Centre, was laid out in 1633 and still holds a cluster of historic buildings, among them the **Theatre Royal**, the oldest working theatre in the country, opened in 1766 and preserving many of its original Georgian features. The theatre hosted most of the famous names of its time, including Sarah Siddons, whose ghost is said to stalk the building. Further down, and in a very different architectural style, stands the timber-framed **Llandoger Trow** pub, its name taken from the flat-bottomed boats that traded between Bristol and the Welsh coast. Traditionally the haunt of seafarers, it is reputed to have been the meeting place of Daniel Defoe and Alexander Selkirk, the model for Robinson Crusoe.

South of King Street, **Queen Square** is an elegant grassy area with a statue of William III by Rysbrack at its centre, reckoned to be the best equestrian statue in the country. The square was the site of some of the worst civil disturbances ever seen in England when the Bristolians rioted in support of the Reform Bill of 1832, burning houses on two sides of the square; among the survivors was no. 37, where the first American consulate was established in 1792.

From the southeast corner of the square, cross Redcliffe Bridge to reach **St Mary Redcliffe** (Mon–Sat 9am–5pm, or 9am–4pm in winter, Sun 8am–8pm; requested donation £1), whose spire provides one of the distinctive features of the city's skyline. Described by Elizabeth I as "the goodliest, fairest, and most famous parish church in England", the church was largely paid for and used by merchants and mariners who prayed here for a safe voyage. The present building was begun at the end of the thirteenth century, though it was added to in subsequent centuries and the spire was constructed in 1872. Inside, memorials and tombs recall some of the figures associated with the building, including the arms and armour of Sir William Penn, admiral and father of the founder of Pennsylvania, on the north wall of the nave, and the Handel Window in the North Choir aisle, installed in 1859 on the centenary of the death of Handel, who composed on the organ here. The whale bone above the entrance to the Chapel of St John the Baptist is thought to have been brought back from Newfoundland by John Cabot.

Above the church's north porch is the muniment room, where **Thomas Chatterton** claimed to have found a trove of medieval manuscripts; the poems, distributed as the work of a fifteenth-century monk named Thomas Rowley, were in fact dazzling fakes. The young poet committed suicide after his forgery was exposed, thereby supplying English literature with one of its most glamorous stories of self-destructive genius. The "Marvellous Boy" is remembered by a memorial stone in the south transept.

A few minutes' walk east, Bristol's **Old Station** stands outside Temple Meads Station, the original terminus of the Great Western Railway linking London and Bristol. The terminus, like the line itself, was designed by Brunel in 1840, and was the first great piece of railway architecture. Part of the original building now houses the **British Empire and Commonwealth Museum** (daily 10am–5pm; £5.95), which focuses on the history of the empire and the Commonwealth that succeeded it, covering trade, slavery and culture.

Around Bristol's waterways

At the southern end of the Centre, the River Frome disappears underground at the **Quayhead**, a spot marked by a statue of Neptune and a memorial plaque to Samuel Plimsoll, inventor of the eponymous line that's painted on the hulls of merchant ships. **St Augustine's Reach**, the central part of the Floating Harbour, is flanked by the **Arnolfini** and **Watershed** arts centres, bastions of Bristol's cultural scene and both housed in refurbished Victorian warehouses. Outside the Arnolfini is a statue of **John Cabot**, the Genoan-born explorer licensed by Henry VII to sail from Bristol in 1497; his landing at Newfoundland formed the basis of England's later claims on the New World.

Beyond the Watershed, Bristol's Harbourside is the home of **at-Bristol** (daily 10am–6pm; Explore £7.50, Wildwalk £6.50, IMAX £6.50, or £16.50 for all three, valid for a week; Ⓦ www.at-bristol.org.uk), a complex made up of three principal attractions: Explore, an interactive science centre; Wildwalk, a multimedia wildlife complex, including an indoor "tropical forest"; and an IMAX cinema (film screenings need to be booked in advance). Although chiefly aimed at families and schoolkids, there's enough here to occupy everyone for a whole day or more. The wildlife displays and scientific wizardry are most impressive, and subsidiary attractions include the Imaginarium (£2), a metal-clad spherical planetarium.

To explore further afield, take advantage of the **ferry service**, which connects the various parts of the Floating Harbour, and which leaves every forty minutes from near Neptune's statue at the Quayhead (10.30am–5.50pm; £1.20 single fare; £3.50 forty-minute round trip; £4 one-hour round trip; £5 all-day ticket; Ⓣ0117/927 3416, Ⓦwww .bristolferryboat.co.uk). Across from the Arnolfini, the **Industrial Museum** features a diverse collection of vehicles, mostly with Bristol connections, and a display of maritime models and reconstructions (Mon–Wed, Sat & Sun 10am–5pm; free). Moored off the Floating Harbour west of here, the **SS Great Britain** (daily: April–Oct 10am–5.30pm; Nov–March 10am–4.30pm; £6.25) was the first propeller-driven, ocean-going iron ship, built in 1843 by Brunel. It was used initially between Liverpool and New York, then between Liverpool and Melbourne, circumnavigating the globe 32 times over a period of 26 years. Her ocean-going days ended in 1886 when she was caught in a storm off Cape Horn, and abandoned in the Falkland Islands, from where she was finally recovered and returned to Bristol in 1968. Some cabins have been restored, the bunks occupied by eerily breathing mannequins, and you can peer into the immense engine room. The same ticket allows you admission to the much smaller **Matthew**, moored close by – a replica of the vessel in which John Cabot sailed to America in 1497 – and to the adjoining **Maritime Heritage Centre**, which gives the background of both vessels, of Cabot and his exploits, and of Bristol's long ship-building history.

Clifton

North and west of the Wills Tower (see p.334) extends **Clifton**, once an aloof spa resort, now Bristol's most elegant quarter. Clifton Village, its select enclave, is centred on the Mall, close to **Royal York Crescent**, the longest Georgian crescent in the country, offering splendid views over the steep drop to the River Avon below.

A few minutes' walk behind the Crescent is Bristol's most famous symbol, **Clifton Suspension Bridge**, 702ft long and poised 245ft above high water. Money was first put forward for a bridge to span the Avon Gorge by a Bristol wine merchant in 1753, though it was not until 1829 that a competition was held for a design, won by Isambard Brunel on a second round, and not until 1864 that the bridge was completed, five years after Brunel's death. Hampered by financial difficulties, the bridge never quite matched the engineer's original ambitious design, which included Egyptian-style towers topped by sphinxes at each end. You can see copies of his plans in the **Visitor Centre**, due to reopen right next to the bridge in late 2004 (check for opening hours at ☎0117/974 4664, ⓦwww.clifton-suspension-bridge.org.uk). Some of the designs proposed by Brunel's rivals are also displayed here, some of them frankly bizarre, alongside explanatory panels.

Just above the bridge in Clifton, a small **Observatory** containing a working camera obscura sits on an arm of Clifton Downs overlooking the gorge (daily: summer 11am–5pm; rest of year noon–4pm; £1). You can also buy a ticket (£1) for the 190-foot tunnel leading from here to the "Giant's Cave" set in the cliffs overlooking the gorge, once housing a Roman Catholic chapel. Both attractions may be closed in bad weather. Adjoining the downs is **Bristol Zoo** (daily: June–Aug 9am–5.30pm; Sept–May 9am–4.30pm; £8.90), renowned for its animal conservation work, and also featuring a collection of rare trees and shrubs.

Eating, drinking and nightlife

Bristol's numerous **pubs** and **restaurants** are nearly always buzzing – especially those around King Street. Nightlife is equally lively; if you want to check out the **clubs**, pick up a copy of *Venue*, the Bristol and Bath weekly listings magazine (£1.20), or look up the website ⓦwww.thisisbristol.com, for details of what's on where.

Restaurants

Browns 38 Queen's Rd ☎0117/930 4777. Spacious and relaxed place for a cocktail, hamburger or delicious fisherman's pie, housed in the Venetian-style former university refectory. Moderate.

Byzantium 2 Portwall Lane ☎0117/922 1883. Opposite St Mary Redcliffe, a warehouse that's been transformed into a highly theatrical dining area, themed along the lines of a Beirut hotel circa 1930. There's an equally exotic bar downstairs that stays open late. Closed Sun. Expensive.

Mud Dock Café 40 The Grove. A winning if unlikely combination of bike shop and café-

bar/restaurant by the river. There's good food and a barbecue on the balcony in summer. Moderate.

Old India 34 St Nicholas St ☎0117/922 1136. Housed in the old Stock Exchange building, this Indian restaurant has classy dishes to match the sumptuous surroundings. Moderate.

One Stop Thali Café 12 York Rd ☎0117/942 6687. Dhaba-style Asian food in the Montpelier quarter. There's no menu, but a combination of dishes are served on a steel plate. Live music currently on Wed. Closed Mon. Inexpensive.

riverstation The Grove ☎0117/914 4424. A former river-police station now houses *The Deck*, where you can chew on deli-type snacks, and a

more formal upstairs restaurant which has a range of international dishes. Inexpensive to moderate.
Severnshed The Grove ☎0117/925 1212. Right next to *riverstation* in a harbour setting with a waterside terrace, this serves light, tasty food, ranging from fish and chips "with Yorkshire caviar" (mushy peas) to vegetarian risotto. There's a good-value fixed-price menu between noon and 7pm on weekdays. Inexpensive to moderate.

Pubs, bars and cafés

Arnolfini Narrow Quay. This arts centre serves excellent vegetarian and meat dishes, plus drinks at the bar or outside on the cobbled quayside.
Avon Gorge Hotel Sion Hill. On the edge of the Gorge in Clifton Village, this mediocre bar has a broad terrace from which to contemplate the magnificent views. Snacks available.
Boston Tea Party 75 Park St. Cosy place in the centre of town for teas and coffees as well as soups and pies, with seating on two floors and a heated terrace garden.
Ha! Ha! Bar & Canteen Berkeley Square. Sofas, a mellow vibe and cool sounds, with a chilled-out DJ on Sun. Food served until 10pm, and there's courtyard seating.
Level 24 Park Row. Late bar with a 1960s airport feel and good city views. Drum'n'bass and hip-hop predominate on the turntables.
Old Duke King St. Jolly, trad jazz pub with live bands nightly and tables outside.
Tantric Jazz Café 39–41 St Nicholas St ☎0117/940 2304. Relaxed coffee stop that offers full Mediterranean-style meals in the evenings, when there are live jazz and blues performances until late. Closed Sun.

Watershed 1 Canons Rd, St Augustine's Reach. A great bar and café in the arts complex overlooking the boats, with food available until 9pm.

Clubs and venues

The Academy Frogmore St ☎0117/927 9227, ⓦwww.bristol-academy.co.uk. Near the Centre, this spacious, popular place stages live gigs as well as mainstream and hard-house parties.
Bierkeller All Saints St, off Broadmead ☎0117/926 8514, ⓦwww.bristolbierkeller.co.uk. Live music from thrash metal to revival bands in this sweaty cellar venue.
Colston Hall Colston Ave ☎0117/922 3686, ⓦwww.colstonhall.org. Major names appear in this stalwart of mainstream venues. Most of the events in the classical Proms Festival, at the end of May, take place here.
Creation 13–21 Baldwin St ☎0117/922 7177. Central clubbers' club, for banging house tunes from top-flight DJs. Dress up, and expect a crowd.
Fiddlers Willway St, Bedminster ☎0117/987 3403, ⓦwww.fiddlers.co.uk. Mainly live folk and world music at this relaxed and well-run club on the south side of the river, off Bedminster Parade.
Fleece and Firkin 12 St Thomas St ☎0117/945 0996. Stone-flagged ex-wool warehouse, now a loud and sweaty pub putting on live rock and comedy six nights a week.
The Station Silver St ☎0117/904 3336, ⓦwww.screamtheclub.co.uk. Central, multistorey club in an old fire station, better than most mainstream places and with occasional live music.
Thekla Phoenix Wharf, off Queen Square ☎0117/929 3301, ⓦwww.thekla.co.uk. A riverboat venue staging regular club nights and occasional live shows, popular with students. Food available.

Bath and around

Though only twelve miles from Bristol, **BATH** has a very different feel from its neighbour – more harmonious, compact, leisurely and complacent. The city's elegant crescents and Georgian buildings are studded with plaques naming Bath's eminent inhabitants from its heyday as a spa resort; it was here that Jane Austen set *Persuasion* and *Northanger Abbey*, and where Gainsborough established himself as a portraitist and landscape painter. Nowadays Bath ranks as one of Britain's top tourist cities, yet the place has never lost the exclusive air those names evoke.

Bath owes its name and fame to its **hot springs** – the only ones in the country – which made it a place of reverence for the local Celtic population, though it had to wait for Roman technology to create a fully fledged bathing establishment. The baths fell into decline with the departure of the Romans,

5

but the town later regained its importance under the Saxons, its abbey seeing the coronation of the **first king of all England**, Edgar, in 973. A new bathing complex was built in the sixteenth century, popularized by the visit of Elizabeth I in 1574, and the city reached its fashionable zenith in the eighteenth century, when **Beau Nash** ruled the town's social scene. It was at this time that Bath acquired its ranks of Palladian mansions and townhouses, all of them built in the local **Bath stone**, which is still the city's leitmotif today. Three miles southeast of the centre, **Claverton** holds a museum of Americana amid gorgeous rolling countryside.

The swathes of parkland between Bath's Georgian terraces lend the city a spacious feel, but the sheer weight of traffic pouring through the central streets can be a major turn-off. Drivers are advised to use one of the **Park-and-Ride** car parks around the periphery – and if you're coming from Bristol, note that you can **cycle** all the way along a cycle-path that follows the route of a disused railway line and the course of the Avon.

Arrival, information and accommodation

Bath Spa **train station** and the city's **bus station** are both on Manvers Street, a short walk from the centre. The **tourist office**, right next to the abbey on Abbey Churchyard (May–Sept Mon–Sat 9.30am–6pm, Sun 10am–4pm; Oct–May Mon–Sat 9.30am–5pm, Sun 10am–4pm; ℡0906/711 2000, ⓦwww.visitbath.co.uk), can supply a detailed list of **accommodation**. Most establishments are small, so always phone ahead; most places demand a two-night minimum stay at weekends in high season.

Hotels and B&Bs

Belmont 7 Belmont, Lansdown Rd ℡01225/423082. Huge rooms – apart from a poky single – some with en-suite shower, in a house designed by John Wood. No credit cards. ❷

Cranleigh 159 Newbridge Hill ℡01225/310197, ⓦwww.cranleighguesthouse.com. A mile or so west of the centre, this period Victorian house has fine views from the back rooms, four-posters and multiple breakfast options. Buses #17, #319 and #332 (#632 Sun). No smoking. ❺

Henry Guest House 6 Henry St ℡01225/424052, ⓦwww.thehenry.com. Excellent budget choice just round the corner from the abbey, with large rooms (none en suite) and friendly owners, but limited availability. No credit cards. ❸

Holly Villa 14 Pulteney Gardens ℡01225/310331, ⓦwww.hollyvilla.com. Neat and friendly B&B, close to the Kennet and Avon Canal, with a small, flower-filled front garden and six rooms with en-suite or private facilities. No smoking and no credit cards. Closed 2wks in March & in Nov. ❹

Koryu 7 Pulteney Gardens ℡01225/337642, ⓔjapanesekoryu.@aol.com. The name means "Sunshine" in Japanese – the mother-tongue of the landlady, who offers brightly painted rooms, small but clean. No shoes inside and no smoking. No credit cards. ❸

Paradise House 88 Holloway ℡01225/317723,

ⓦwww.paradise-house.co.uk. The wonderful view justifies the ten-minute uphill trudge from the centre to this lovely Georgian villa. Croquet or boules in the lush garden and open fires in the winter are further attractions. No smoking. ❻

Hostels

Bath Backpackers Hostel 13 Pierrepoint St ℡01225/446787, ⓦwww.hostels.co.uk. Aussie-run place right in the centre of things. There's no curfew or lockout, a kitchen, bar, pool room and Internet access, but no breakfast. Dorm beds are £12, doubles with bath ❶.

Bath YHA Bathwick Hill ℡0870/770 5688, ⓔbath@yha.org.uk. An Italianate mansion a mile from the centre, with gardens and panoramic views. Dorm beds (£11.50) and double rooms with evening snacks also available. Buses #18 or #418 from the station. ❶

White Hart Widcombe Hill ℡01225/313985, ⓦwww.whitehartbath.co.uk. The comfiest of Bath's hostels has a kitchen, a licensed café and a sunny courtyard. Dorms mainly have four beds (at £12.50 each), and doubles and twins are available. ❶

YMCA International House, Broad St ℡01225 /460471, ⓦwww.bathymca.co.uk. Clean, central, with dorm beds (£10–12), singles and doubles. All prices include breakfast, and there are reductions for weekly stays, but there's no kitchen. ❶

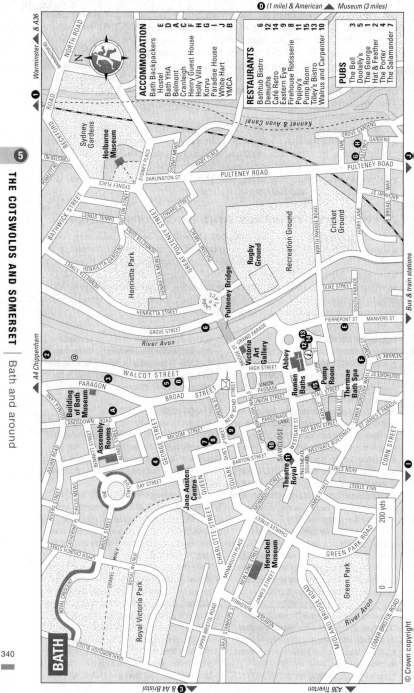

BATH

D (1 mile) & American ▲ Museum (3 miles)

Warminster ▲ & A36

NORTH ROAD

ACCOMMODATION
Bath Backpackers
Hostel   E
Bath YHA   D
Belmont   A
Cranleigh   C
Henry Guest House   F
Holly Villa   H
Koryu   G
Paradise House   I
White Hart   J
YMCA   B

RESTAURANTS
Bathtub Bistro   6
Demuths   12
Café Retro   14
Eastern Eve   9
Firehouse Rotisserie   8
Popjoy's   11
Pump Room   15
Tilley's Bistro   13
Walrus and Carpenter   10

PUBS
The Bell   3
Doolally's   5
The George   1
Hat & Feather   2
The Porter   4
The Salamander   7

A4 Chippenham ▲

▲ A4 Bristol

A36 Tiverton ▲

Bus & train stations ▲

Kennet & Avon Canal

Sydney Gardens

Holburne Museum

Building of Bath Museum

Assembly Rooms

Jane Austen Centre

Herschel Museum

Royal Victoria Park

Green Park

Pulteney Bridge

Victoria Art Gallery

Abbey

Roman Baths

Pump Room

Thermae Bath Spa

Theatre Royal

River Avon

0   200 yds

© Crown copyright

The City

Although Bath could easily be seen on a day-trip from Bristol, it really deserves a stay of a couple of days. The city itself is chock-full of museums, but some of the greatest enjoyment comes simply from the streets, with their pale gold architecture and sweeping vistas.

The Baths and the Abbey

Bath's focal point is the pedestrianized Abbey Church Yard, two interlocking squares usually milling with buskers, tourists and traders, and site of both the Baths and the Abbey. Although ticket prices are high for the **Roman Baths** (daily: March–June, Sept & Oct 9am–6pm; July & Aug 9am–10pm; Nov–Feb 9.30am–5.30pm; £7.50, £9.50 combined ticket with Museum of Costume), there's two or three hours' worth of well-balanced, informative entertainment here, with a taped commentary provided on handsets allowing you to wander at your own pace around the temple and bathing complex, where a spring still

---

Beau Nash and Bath's Golden Age

Richard "Beau" Nash was an ex-army officer, ex-lawyer, dandy and gambler, who became Bath's Master of Ceremonies in 1704, conducting public balls of an unprecedented splendour. Wielding dictatorial powers over dress and behaviour, Nash orchestrated the social manners of the city and even extended his influence to cover road improvements and the design of buildings. In an early example of health awareness, he banned smoking in Bath's public rooms at a time when pipe-smoking was a general pastime among men, women and children. Less philanthropically, he also encouraged gambling and even took a percentage of the bank's takings. Nonetheless, he was generally held in high esteem and succeeded in establishing rules such as the setting of specific hours and procedure for all social functions. Balls were to begin at six and end at eleven and every ball had to open with a minuet "danced by two persons of the highest distinction present". White aprons were banned, gossipers and scandalmongers were shunned, and, most radical of all, the wearing of swords in public places was forbidden, a ruling referred to in Sheridan's play *The Rivals*, in which Captain Absolute declares, "A sword seen in the streets of Bath would raise as great an alarm as a mad dog."

As for Bath's distinctive Georgian style of architecture, this was largely the work of **John Wood** ("the elder", c.1704–54) and his son, also called John Wood ("the younger", 1727–81), both champions of the NeoClassical Palladianism that originated in Renaissance Italy. Their "speculative developments", designed to cater to the seasonal floods of fashionable visitors, were constructed in the soft oolitic limestone from local quarries belonging to **Ralph Allen** (c.1694–1764), another prominent figure of the period. A deputy postmaster who made a fortune by improving England's postal routes, and later from Bath's building boom, Allen was nicknamed "the man of Bath", and is best remembered for Prior Park, the mansion he built outside the city based on the elder Wood's designs, and for his association with Pope, Fielding and other luminaries who were frequent visitors.

Next to the innovations of Nash and the creations of Allen and the two John Woods, the name of **William Oliver** should not be forgotten in the story of Georgian Bath. A physician and philanthropist, Oliver did more than anyone to boost the city's profile as a therapeutic centre, thanks to publications such as his *Practical Essay on the Use and Abuse of Warm Bathing in Gouty Cases* (1751), and by founding the Bath General Hospital to enable the poor to make use of the waters. He is remembered today by the Bath Oliver biscuit, which he invented, and by the use of Olivers as the exchange currency in a local community bartering scheme.

issues water at a constant 46.5°C. Highlights of the remains are the open-air (but originally covered) Great Bath, its vaporous waters surrounded by nineteenth-century pillars, terraces and statues of famous Romans; the Circular Bath, where bathers cooled off; the Norman King's Bath; and part of the temple of Minerva. Among a quantity of coins, jewellery and sculpture exhibited are the gilt bronze head of Sulis Minerva, the local deity, and a grand, Celtic-inspired gorgon's head from the temple's pediment. Models of the complex at its greatest extent give some idea of the awe which it must have inspired, while the graffiti salvaged from the Roman era – mainly curses and boasts – give a nice personal slant on this antique leisure centre. You can get a free glimpse into the baths from the next-door **Pump Room**, the social hub of the Georgian spa community and still redolent of that era, housing an excellent tearoom and restaurant.

Although there has been a church on the site since the seventh century, **Bath Abbey** (daily 9am–6pm; closes 4pm in winter; requested donation £2.50) did not take its present form until the end of the fifteenth century, when Bishop Oliver King began work on the ruins of the previous Norman building, some of which were incorporated into the new church. The bishop was said to have been inspired by a vision of angels ascending and descending a ladder to heaven, which the present facade recalls on the turrets flanking the central window. The west front also features the founder's signature in the form of carvings of olive trees surmounted by crowns, a play on his name.

The interior is in a restrained Perpendicular style, and boasts splendid fan vaulting on the ceiling, which was not properly completed until the nineteenth century. The floor and walls are crammed with elaborate monuments and memorials, and traces of the grander Norman building are visible in the Norman Chapel.

To the Circus and the Royal Crescent

Present-day visitors to Bath can take the waters at the city's newest attraction, **Thermae Bath Spa**, a state-of-the-art spa complex at the bottom of the elegantly colonnaded Bath Street, leading west from Abbey Church Yard (daily 7am–10pm; ☎01225/331234, ⓦwww.thermaebathspa.com). Utilizing the city's thermal waters (also used for heating), the spa offers everything from massages to dry flotation, and includes two open-air pools, one on the roof of its centrepiece, the New Royal Bath, Nicholas Grimshaw's sleekly futuristic "glass cube". No membership is required to use the facilities; prices start at £10 (for 1hr 30min), rising to £35 (full day).

North of Hot Bath Street, Westgate Street and Sawclose are presided over by the **Theatre Royal**, opened in 1805 and one of the country's finest surviving Georgian theatres. Next door is the house where Beau Nash spent his last years, now a restaurant. Up from the Theatre Royal, off Barton Street, the gracious **Queen Square** was the first Bath venture of the architect **John Wood**, who with his son (see box p.341) was chiefly responsible for the Roman-inspired developments of the areas outside the confines of the medieval city. Wood himself lived at no. 24, giving him a vista of the northern terrace's palatial facade.

West of Queen Square, the small **Herschel Museum** here (mid-Feb to Nov Mon, Tues, Thurs & Fri 2–5pm; Sat & Sun 11am–5pm; £3.50) at 19 New King St was the former home of the musician and astronomer Sir William Herschel and his sister Caroline, who together discovered the planet Uranus in 1781. Among the contemporary furnishings, musical instruments and various knick-knacks from the Herschels' life, you can see a replica of the telescope with which

Uranus was identified. Just north of the square, at 40 Gay St, the **Jane Austen Centre** (Mon–Sat 10am–5.30pm, Sun 10.30am–5.30pm; £4.45) provides an overview of the author's connections with the city, illustrated by extracts from her writings, contemporary costumes, furnishings and household items.

At the top of Gay Street, the elder John Wood's masterpiece, **The Circus**, consists of three crescents arranged in a tight circle of three-storey houses, with a carved frieze running round the entire circle. Wood died soon after laying the foundation stone for this enterprise, and the job was finished by his son. The painter Thomas Gainsborough lived at no. 17 from 1760 to 1774.

The Circus is connected by Brock Street to the **Royal Crescent**, grandest of Bath's crescents, begun by the younger John Wood in 1767. The stately arc of thirty houses is set off by a spacious sloping lawn from which a magnificent vista extends to green hills and distant ribbons of honey-coloured stone. The interior of **No. 1 Royal Crescent**, on the corner with Brock Street, has been restored to reflect as nearly as possible its original Georgian appearance (mid-Feb to Oct Tues–Sun 10.30am–5pm; Nov Tues–Sun 10.30am–4pm; last entry 30min before closing; £4).

At the bottom of the Crescent, Royal Avenue leads onto **Royal Victoria Park**, the city's largest open space, containing an aviary and botanical gardens.

The Assembly Rooms, the Paragon and Milsom Street

The younger John Wood's **Assembly Rooms**, east of the Circus on Bennett Street, were, with the Pump Room, the centre of Bath's social scene. A fire virtually destroyed the building in 1942, but it has now been perfectly restored and houses a **Museum of Costume** (daily 10am–5pm; £4.20, or £9.50 with Baths), an entertaining collection of clothing from the Stuart era to the latest Japanese designs.

From the Assembly Rooms, Alfred Street leads to the area known as the **Paragon**. Here, accessed from the raised pavement, the Georgian-Gothic Countess of Huntingdon's Chapel houses the **Building of Bath Museum** (mid-Feb to Nov Tues–Sun 10.30am–5pm; £4), a fascinating exhibition on the construction and architecture of Bath. At the bottom of the Paragon, off George Street, lies **Milsom Street**, a wide shopping strand designed by the elder Wood as the main thoroughfare of Georgian Bath.

The river and Great Pulteney Street

East of the abbey, Grand Parade looks down onto the formal Parade Gardens and the River Avon. The flow of the river here is interrupted by a graceful V-shaped weir just below the shop-lined **Pulteney Bridge**, an Italianate structure designed by Robert Adam. The bridge was intended to link the city centre with **Great Pulteney Street**, a handsome avenue originally planned as the nucleus of a large residential quarter on the eastern bank. The work ran into financial difficulties, however, so the roads running off it now stop short after a few yards, though there is a lengthy vista to the imposing classical facade of the **Holburne Museum** at the end of the street (Feb to mid-Dec Tues–Sat 10am–5pm, Sun 2.30–5.30pm; £4.50). The three-storey building contains an impressive range of decorative and fine art, mostly furniture, silverware, porcelain and paintings, including work by Stubbs and the famous *Byam Family* by Gainsborough. When Holburne House was a bustling hotel, the pleasure gardens behind it, now **Sydney Gardens**, were the venue for concerts and fireworks, as witnessed by Jane Austen, a frequent visitor here – the family had lodgings across the street at 4 Sydney Place. Today, the slopes are cut through by the railway and the Kennet and Avon Canal. From here, it's a pleasant one-and-a-half mile saunter along the canal to the *George* pub (see opposite).

If you want to explore the river itself, rent a skiff, punt or canoe from the **Victorian Bath Boating Station** at the end of Forester Road, behind the Holburne Museum (April–Sept; £5 per person per hour). Organized river trips can be made from Pulteney Bridge and weir, and there are cruises on the Kennet and Avon Canal from Sydney Wharf, near Bathwick Bridge. A two-mile **nature trail** winds along the banks of the restored canal, which itself extends east as far as Reading.

Eating, drinking and nightlife

Bath has a good range of **restaurants** – though many over-exploit the twee period trappings. Coffee shops and snack bars are ubiquitous in the centre, as are pubs offering lunchtime fare.

For concerts and other events, refer to *Venue*, the weekly listings magazine (£1.20), or to *This Month in Bath*, a free monthly listings guide available from the tourist office. **Theatre** and ballet fans should check out what's showing at the Theatre Royal on Sawclose (℡01225/448844), which stages more experimental productions in the Ustinov Studio. There's a great range of festivals throughout the year, notably the **Bath International Music Festival** (ⓦwww.bathmusicfest.org.uk), held between mid-May and June and featuring jazz, classical and World Music; the **Bath Fringe Festival** (ⓦwww.bathfringe.co.uk), running from late May to early June, with the accent on art and performance; and **Bath Literature Festival** (ⓦwww.bathlitfest.org.uk), taking place over ten days in February/March. For further information on these and other festivals, call ℡01225/463362, ⓦwww.bathfestivals.org.uk, or check out the individual websites above.

Best of Bath's **clubs** is *Moles* (℡01225/404445, ⓦwww.moles.co.uk) on George Street, a local institution which has live music and DJs; the Moroccan-style *Fez Club*, The Paragon (℡01225/444162), playing funk, trance and old skool; and *Po Na Na*, 8 North Parade (℡01225/401115), also Moroccan-themed, with a largely student crowd.

Restaurants

Bathtub Bistro 2 Grove St ℡01225/460593. Off Pulteney Bridge, this tiny-looking place reveals several eating areas on three levels. The international menu includes pure beef hamburgers and innovative vegetarian dishes. BYO Mon & Tues. Inexpensive to moderate.

Demuths 2 North Parade Passage ℡01225/446059. Bath's favourite eating place for veggies and vegans, offering original and delicious dishes, as well as organic beers, wines and coffees. No smoking. Moderate to expensive.

Café Retro 18 York St. A laid-back place near the Abbey for a cappuccino break, lunch or full evening meal, all to mellow sounds. There's also the *Retro-to-Go* takeaway next door. Moderate.

Eastern Eye 8 Quiet St ℡01225/422323. Designer curry house occupying a Georgian bank, with a spectacular vaulted ceiling. The food's notable too. Moderate.

Firehouse Rotisserie 2 John St ℡01225/482070. Delicious, outsized Californian pizzas and grills are the main items in this busy place with a pleasant woody interior on two floors. Closed Sun. Moderate.

Popjoy's Sawclose ℡01225/460494. Though somewhat touristy, this restaurant is still worth sampling for its prime location next to the Theatre Royal, and for the curiosity value of being Beau Nash's house (it's named after his mistress). The food is high-quality, and there's a good-value pre-theatre menu. Closed Sun. Expensive.

Pump Room Abbey Church Yard ℡01225/444477. If you don't want to splash out on an Eggs Benedict brunch, you might succumb to a Bath bun, cream tea, or the excellent lunch-time menu, all to the accompaniment of a pianist or a classical trio. You get a good view of the baths, and a chance to sample the waters, though be prepared to queue for a table. Open daytime only, plus evenings during the Bath Festival, Aug and Christmas. Inexpensive to moderate.

Tilley's Bistro 3 North Parade Passage ☏01225/484200. Informal, cramped French restaurant with starter-sized and -priced portions to allow more samplings, good set-price lunchtime menus and a separate vegetarian menu. Closed Sun. Moderate.

Walrus and Carpenter 28 Barton St ☏01225/314864. Relaxed spot serving steaks, burgers, poultry dishes and a full vegetarian menu in a warren of small rooms. Moderate.

Pubs and cafés

The Bell 103 Walcot St. Excellent, easy-going pub with a beer garden and live music three times a week (Mon & Wed eve, plus Sun lunchtime).

Doolally's 51 Walcot St. Friendly place to extend a coffee or lunch break. Spicy teas, mochas and lassis are specialities, and there's dinner with live world or folk accompaniment Thursday–Saturday.

The George Mill Lane, Bathampton. Popular canal-side pub twenty minutes' walk from the centre and with better than average bar food.

Hat & Feather 14 London St. At the top of Walcot Street, this grungy drinking hole continues the quarter's alternative theme, with table football, pool and regular DJs and live music.

The Porter Miles Buildings, George St. Part of *Moles* club (see opposite page), serving good beer and veggie food in a funky setting. There are tables outside and pool and table football in the Cellar Bar, where there's free live music (Mon–Thurs), DJs (Fri & Sat) and comedy (Sun).

The Salamander 3 John St. Real ale pub with a woody decor, a laid-back atmosphere and good food available (Tues–Sat) at the bar or in the renowned upstairs restaurant. The pub has a no-smoking area.

Claverton

For a quick sample of the lovely countryside around Bath you could make an easy excursion to **CLAVERTON**, on the eastern edge of Bath, site of the **American Museum** (late March to July & Sept–Nov Tues–Sun 2–5pm; Aug daily 2–5pm; grounds Tues–Thurs 1–6pm, Fri–Sun noon–6pm; £6, grounds only £3.50). Occupying the early nineteenth-century Claverton Manor, where Winston Churchill made his maiden political speech in 1897, the museum shows reconstructed rooms illustrating life in the New World from the seventeenth to the nineteenth centuries, and has sections devoted to textiles, whaling, the opening of the West, Native Americans and Hispano-American culture. The glorious **grounds** contain a replica of George Washington's garden, an arboretum and assorted relics resembling items from a movie set. University buses #18 and #418 run throughout the year to the Avenue (the stop before the campus), from where it's a ten-minute walk to the museum.

Wells, the Mendips and Glastonbury

Wells, twenty miles south of Bristol across the Somerset border and the same distance southwest from Bath, is a miniature cathedral city that has not signif-icantly altered in eight hundred years. You might decide to make it an accom-modation stop for visiting nearby attractions in the **Mendip Hills**, such as the **Wookey Hole** caves and the **Cheddar Gorge**. On the southern edge of the range, the town of **Glastonbury** has for centuries been one of the main Arthurian sites of the West Country, and is now the country's most enthusias-tic centre of New Age cults.

Wells

Technically England's smallest city, **WELLS** owes its celebrity entirely to its **cathedral** (daily: April–Sept 7am–7pm; Oct–March 7am–6pm; suggested donation £4.50). Hidden from sight until you pass into its spacious close from the central Market Place, the building presents a majestic spectacle, the broad lawn of the former graveyard providing a perfect foreground. The west front teems with some three hundred thirteenth-century figures of saints and kings, once brightly painted and gilded, though their present honey tint has a subtle splendour of its own. Close up, the impact is slightly lessened, as most of the statuary is badly eroded and many figures were damaged by Puritans in the seventeenth century. The facade was constructed about fifty years after work on the main building was begun in 1180. The **interior** is a supreme example of early English Gothic, the long nave punctuated by a dramatic "scissor arch", one of three that were constructed in 1338 to take the extra weight of the newly built tower. Beyond the arch, there are some gnarled old tombs to be seen in the aisles of the **Quire**, at the end of which is the richly coloured stained glass of the fourteenth-century **Lady Chapel**. The **capitals and corbels** of the transepts hold some amusing narrative carvings – look out for the men with toothache and an old man caught pilfering an orchard – and, in the north transept, there's a 24-hour astronomical clock dating from 1390. From his seat high up on the right of the clock, a figure known as Jack Blandiver kicks a couple of bells every quarter-hour, heralding the appearance of a pair of jousting knights charging at each other, and on the hour he strikes the bell in front of him. Opposite the clock, a doorway leads to a graceful, much-worn flight of steps rising to the **Chapter House** (closes 4.30pm), an octagonal room elaborately ribbed in the Decorated style.

The row of clerical houses on the north side of the cathedral green are mainly seventeenth- and eighteenth-century, though one, the **Old Deanery**, shows traces of its fifteenth-century origins. The chancellor's house is now a **museum** (Easter–July & mid-Sept to Oct Mon–Sat 10am–5.30pm, Sun 10am–4pm; Aug to mid-Sept daily 10am–8pm; Nov–Easter Mon & Wed–Sun 11am–4pm; £2.50), displaying, among other items, some of the cathedral's original statuary, placed here for conservation reasons (and replaced by replicas), as well as a good geological section with fossils from the surrounding area, including Wookey Hole.

Beyond the arch, a little further along the street, the cobbled medieval **Vicars' Close** holds more clerical dwellings, linked to the cathedral by the Chain Gate and fronted by small gardens. The cottages were built in the mid-fourteenth century – though only no. 22 has not undergone outward alterations – and have been continuously occupied by members of the cathedral clergy ever since.

On the other side of the cathedral – and accessible through the cathedral shop – are the cloisters, from which you can enter the tranquil grounds of the **Bishop's Palace** (April–July, Sept & Oct Mon–Fri 10.30am–6pm, Sun 1–6pm; Aug daily 10.30am–6pm, though occasionally closed for functions; last entry at 5pm; £3.50), also reachable from Market Place through the Bishop's Eye archway. The residence of the Bishop of Bath and Wells, the palace was walled and moated as a result of a rift with the borough in the fourteenth century, and the imposing gatehouse still displays the grooves of the portcullis and a chute for pouring oil and molten lead on would-be assailants. Its tranquil gardens contain the springs from which the city takes its name and the scanty but impressive remains of the **Great Hall**, built at the end of the thirteenth century and despoiled during the Reformation. Across the lawn stands the square **Bishop's Chapel** and the **Undercroft**, holding displays relating to the history of the site, state rooms and a café.

Practicalities

Wells **bus station** is off Market Street; the city is not connected to the rail network. The **tourist office** is on Market Place (daily: April–Oct 9.30am–5.30pm; Nov–March 10am–4pm; ☏01749/672552, ⓦwww.wells-uk.com).

Good **accommodation** choices include the central *Canon Grange*, its spacious rooms facing the cathedral's west front (☏01749/671800, ⓦwww.canongrange.co.uk; ❷), and *Bekynton House*, a little further out at 7 St Thomas St (☏01749/672222, ⓦwww.bekynton-house.co.uk; no smoking; ❸). Alternatively, soak up the authentically antique flavour in either of the old coaching inns in the centre of town: the *Crown Hotel*, Market Place (☏01749/673457, ⓦcrownatwells.co.uk; ❹), where William Penn was arrested in 1695 for illegal preaching, and the *Swan*, on Sadler Street (☏01749/836300; ❻), with limited views of the cathedral.

For **food**, head for *Bekynton Brasserie*, close to the cathedral on Market Place, open for daytime snacks and full evening meals (☏01749/675993; closed Mon–Wed eves). Round the corner on Sadler Street, the Italian-run *Ancient Gate House* (☏01749/672029) and *Ritcher's* (☏01749/679085) are more formal places with fairly expensive prices, though the latter also has a downstairs bar/patisserie selling coffees and panini. Excellent wholefood is on hand at the *Good Earth* on Priory Rd, near the bus station (closed daytime & Sun), also with delicious takeaway items. The *City Arms* on Cuthbert Street, formerly the gaol, is the best central **pub**, with a flower-filled courtyard and meals in an upstairs restaurant.

The Mendips

The **Mendip Hills**, rising to the north of Wells, are chiefly famous for Wookey Hole – the most impressive of many caves in this narrow limestone chain – and for the **Cheddar Gorge**, where a walk through the narrow cleft might make a starting point for more adventurous trips across the Mendips. From Wells, take buses #172 or #670 to Wookey Hole (#972 on Sun), and #126 or #826 to the gorge.

Wookey Hole

Hollowed out by the River Axe a couple of miles outside Wells, **Wookey Hole** is an impressive cave complex of deep pools and intricate rock formations, but it's folklore rather than geology that takes precedence on the guided tours (daily: April–Oct 10am–5pm; Nov–March 10.30am–4.30pm; closed Dec 17–25; £8.80). Highlight of the tour is the alleged petrified remains of the Witch of Wookey, a "blear-eyed hag" who was said to turn her evil eye on crops, young lovers and local farmers until the Abbot of Glastonbury intervened; he dispatched a monk who drove the witch into the inner cave, sprinkled her with holy water and turned her into stone. Some substance was lent to the legend when an ancient skeleton – in fact Romano-British – was unearthed here in 1912, together with a dagger, sacrificial knife and a big rounded ball of pure stalagmite, the so-called witch's ball. Beside her were found two skeletons, the remains of goats tied to a stake. At the end of the hour-long tour, you can visit a functioning Victorian paper mill, rooms containing speleological exhibits and, on a less earnest note, a range of amusements including a collection of Edwardian fairground pieces.

Cheddar Gorge

Six miles west of Wookey on the A371, the rather plain village of Cheddar has given its name to Britain's best-known cheese – most of it now mass-produced far from here – and is also renowned for the **Cheddar Gorge**, lying beyond the neighbourhood of Tweentown about a mile to the north.

Cutting a jagged gash across the Mendip Hills, the limestone gorge is an impressive geological phenomenon, though its natural beauty is undermined by the minor road running through it and by the Lower Gorge's mile of shops, coach park and **tourist office** (June–Sept daily 10am–5pm; Oct daily 10.30am–4.30pm; Nov–March Sun 11am–4pm; ☎01934/744071, Ⓦwww.somersetbythesea.co.uk). Few trippers venture further than the first few curves of the gorge, which admittedly holds its most dramatic scenery, though each turn of the two-mile length presents new, sometimes startling vistas. At its narrowest the path squeezes between cliffs towering almost five hundred feet above, and if you don't want to follow the road as far as **Priddy**, the highest village in the Mendips, you can reach more dramatic destinations by branching off onto marked paths to such secluded spots as **Black Rock**, just two miles from Cheddar, or **Black Down**, at 1067ft the Mendips' highest peak. Cliff-top paths winding along the rim of the gorge provide an alternative to walking next to the road. The tourist office can give you details of a two-and-a-half-hour circular walk and of the **West Mendip Way**, a forty-mile route extending from Uphill, near Weston-super-Mare, to Wells and Shepton Mallet.

Beneath the gorge, the **Cheddar Caves** (daily: July & Aug 10am–5pm; Sept–June 10.30am–4.30pm; £9.50) were scooped out by underground rivers in the wake of the Ice Age, and subsequently occupied by primitive communities. Today the caves are floodlit to pick out the subtle pinks, greys, greens and whites in the rock, and the array of tortuous rock formations that resemble organ pipes, waterfalls and giant birds. Close to Cox's Caves, the 274 steps of **Jacob's Ladder** (same ticket as caves) lead to a cliff-top viewpoint looking towards Glastonbury Tor, Exmoor and the sea. It's a muscle-wrenching climb – anyone not in a state of honed fitness can reach the same spot with a great deal more ease via the narrow lane winding up behind the cliffs. You can also survey the panorama from **Pavey's Lookout Tower** nearby.

Among Cheddar's handful of **B&Bs**, try *Chedwell Cottage*, Redcliffe St (☎01934/743268; no credit cards; ❷), which has two en-suite rooms and a garden, and, on the outskirts, *Wossells House*, Upper New Rd (☎01934/744317; no credit cards; ❷), where huge breakfasts are served; both are nonsmoking. Other options include a **youth hostel**, off the Hayes (☎0870/770 5760; closed Jan & very limited opening mid-Nov to Dec & Feb; £11.50), and, a hundred yards past the church in the village centre, *Froglands* (☎01934/742058; closed mid-Oct to Easter), one of four **campsites** in the neighbourhood.

Glastonbury

Six miles south of Wells, **GLASTONBURY** lies at the centre of the so-called **Isle of Avalon**, a region rich with mystical associations. At the heart of it all is the early Christian legend that the young Christ once visited this site, a story that is not as far-fetched as it sounds. The Romans had a heavy presence in the area, mining lead in the Mendips, and one of these mines was owned by **Joseph of Arimathea**, a well-to-do merchant said to have been related to Mary. It's not completely impossible that the merchant took his kinsman on one of his many visits to his property, in a period of Christ's life of which nothing is recorded. It was this possibility to which William Blake referred in his

△ Glastonbury Tor

Glastonbury Hymn, better known as *Jerusalem*: – "And did those feet in ancient times/Walk upon England's mountains green?"

Another legend relates how Joseph was imprisoned for twelve years after the Crucifixion, miraculously kept alive by the **Holy Grail**, the chalice of the Last Supper, in which the blood was gathered from the wound in Christ's side. The Grail, along with the spear which had caused the wound, were later taken by Joseph to Glastonbury, where he founded the abbey and commenced the conversion of Britain.

More verifiably, a Celtic monastery was founded here in the fourth or fifth century – making this the oldest Christian foundation in England. Enlarged by St Dunstan in the tenth century, **Glastonbury Abbey** (daily: Feb 10am–5pm; March 9.30am–5.30pm; April–Sept 9.30am–6pm; Oct 9.30am–5pm; Nov 9.30am–4.30pm; Dec & Jan 10am–4.30pm; £4) became the richest Benedictine abbey in the country. Three Anglo-Saxon kings (Edmund, Edgar and Edmund Ironside) were buried here, the library had a far-reaching fame, and the church had the longest known nave of any monastic church at the time of the Dissolution (580ft – Wells Cathedral's nave reaches 415ft). The original building was destroyed by fire in 1184 and the ruins are the rather scanty remains of what took its place, reduced to their present state at the Dissolution. Hidden behind walls at the centre of town, surrounded by grassy parkland and shaded by trees, the ruins only hint at the extent of the building, which was financed largely by a constant procession of medieval pilgrims. The most prominent and photogenic remains are the transept piers and the shell of the Lady Chapel, with its carved figures of the Annunciation, the Magi and Herod.

The abbey's **choir** introduces another strand to the Glastonbury story, for it holds what is alleged to be the tomb of **Arthur and Guinevere**. As told by William of Malmesbury and Thomas Malory, the story relates how, after being mortally wounded in battle, King Arthur sailed to Avalon where he was buried alongside his queen. The discovery of two bodies in an ancient cemetery outside the abbey in 1191 – from which they were transferred here in 1278 – was taken to confirm the popular identification of Glastonbury with Avalon. In the grounds, the fourteenth-century **abbot's kitchen** is the only monastic building to survive intact, with four huge corner fireplaces and a great central lantern above. Behind the main entrance to the grounds, look out for the thorn-tree that is supposedly from the original **Glastonbury Thorn** said to have sprouted from the staff of Joseph of Arimathea when he landed here to convert the country. The plant grew for centuries on a nearby hill known as Wyrral, or Weary-All, and despite being hacked down by Puritans, lived long enough to provide numerous cuttings whose descendants still bloom twice a year (Easter & Dec) – only at Glastonbury do they flourish, it is claimed.

On the edge of the abbey grounds, the fourteenth-century Abbey Barn is the centrepiece of the engaging **Somerset Rural Life Museum** (April–Oct Tues–Fri 10am–5pm, Sat & Sun 2–6pm; Nov–March Tues–Sat 10am–5pm; free), illustrating a range of local rural occupations, from cheese- and cider-making to peat-digging, thatching and farming.

From the museum it's about a mile's hike to **Glastonbury Tor**, at 521ft a landmark for miles around. The conical hill – topped by the dilapidated **St Michael's Tower**, sole remnant of a fourteenth-century church – commands stupendous views encompassing Wells, the Quantocks, the Mendips, the once-marshy peat moors rolling out to the sea, and, on very clear days, the Welsh mountains. Pilgrims once embarked on the stiff climb here with hard peas in their shoes as penance – nowadays people come to feel the vibrations of crossing ley-lines. If you don't fancy the steep ascent, take the easier path further up

THE COTSWOLDS AND SOMERSET | Wells, the Mendips and Glastonbury

Wellhouse Lane, the road that leads to the Tor Park from the centre of town. You can also save some legwork by taking advantage of the **Glastonbury Tor Bus** (May to mid-Sept), which ferries people from the High Street to the base of the Tor every thirty minutes; your £1 ticket can be used all day.

At the bottom of Wellhouse Lane, in the middle of a lush garden intended for quiet contemplation, the **Chalice Well** (daily: Feb, March & Nov 11am–5pm; April–Oct 10am–6pm; Dec & Jan noon–4pm; £2.70) is alleged to be the hiding-place of the Holy Grail. The iron-red waters were considered to have curative properties, making the town a spa for a brief period in the eighteenth century, and they are still prized – there's a tap in Wellhouse Lane.

Back in town, you might take a glance at the fifteenth-century church of **St John the Baptist**, halfway along the High Street. The tower is reckoned to be one of Somerset's finest, and the **interior** has a fine oak roof and stained glass illustrating the legend of St Joseph of Arimathea, both from the period of the church's construction. The Glastonbury thorn in the churchyard is the biggest in town.

Further down the street, the fourteenth-century **Tribunal** was where the abbots presided over legal cases; it later became a hotel for pilgrims, and now holds the small **Glastonbury Lake Village Museum** of finds from the Iron Age lake villages that once fringed the marshland below the Tor (April–Sept Mon–Thurs & Sun 10am–5pm, Fri & Sat 10am–5.30pm; Oct–March closes 1hr earlier; £2).

Practicalities

Buses #376 and #377 (on Sun #977 and #929) run once or twice an hour from Wells. Glastonbury's **tourist office** is housed in the Tribunal on the High St (April–Sept Mon–Thurs & Sun 10am–5pm, Fri & Sat 10am–5.30pm; Oct–March closes 1hr earlier; ☎01458/832954 or 832020 for information on tickets for the festival, ⊛www.glastonburytic.co.uk).

Accommodation

Glastonbury has a rich assortment of good-value **accommodation** ranging from medieval hostelries to hostels. Most places are within a brief walk of the Tor and town centre.

Hotels and guest houses

1 Park Terrace Street Road ☎01458/835845, ⊛www.no1parkterrace.co.uk. Large Victorian house, five minutes' walk from the centre, where all rooms are en suite or have private facilities. ❷

3 Magdalene St ☎01458/832129. Beautifully furnished bedrooms make for a stylish stay in this listed Georgian house with a large walled garden, right next to the abbey. ❻

George & Pilgrims High Street ☎01458/831146, ⊛www.georgeandpilgrims.activehotels.com. This fifteenth-century oak-panelled inn overflows with antique atmosphere. ❸

Little Orchard Ashwell Lane ℡01458/831620. At the foot of the Tor, on the A361 Shepton Mallet road, this good-value B&B offers panoramic views. No credit cards. ❷

Hostels and campsite

Glastonbury Backpackers 4 Market Place ℡01458/833353, ⓦwww .backpackers-online.com/glastonbury. Very centrally located old coaching inn with café,

restaurant, pool room and no curfew, plus occasional bands playing in the bar. Dorm beds £12, doubles ❶.

Isle of Avalon Campsite ℡01458/833618. Decent campsite within sight of the Tor, ten minutes' walk up Northload Street on Godney Road.

YHA hostel Ivythorn Hill, Street ℡0870/770 6056. The nearest YHA lies a couple of miles south of Glastonbury (bus #376 or #377, on Sun #977; alight at Marshalls Elm crossroads and follow signs). Dorm beds are £10.25. Open Wed & Thurs only Oct–March.

Eating, drinking and entertainment

Wedged between the esoteric shops of Glastonbury's High Street are several decent **cafés** serving inexpensive meals, including the *Blue Note Café* at no. 4, with some outside seating and evening meals on Fridays and Saturdays when there's live music, and *Olly's Café/Bar* at no. 52, which has some meat dishes among the predominantly vegetarian choices, and also stays open on Friday and Saturday evenings (℡01458/834521). Just off Market Place, *Mocha Berry* has a buzzy feel and serves up organic sausages and mash and Homity Pie. The best **pubs** are the *Market House Inn*, almost opposite the abbey entrance, which has snacks, a garden and occasional bands, and *Glastonbury Backpackers* (see above). Halfway up the High Street, the Assembly Rooms has a wholefood café, but is better known as the venue for talks and musical and theatrical **performances**. You can also buy tickets for concerts and miracle plays staged in the abbey grounds in summer – call ℡01458/832267 for details, or view the abbey's website, ⓦwww.glastonburyabbey.com.

Bridgwater, Taunton and the Quantocks

Travelling west from Glastonbury, your route could take you through both **Bridgwater** and **Taunton**, each of which would make a handy starting point for excursions into the gently undulating **Quantock Hills**, a mellow landscape of snug villages set in scenic wooded valleys or "combes". Public transport is fairly minimal round here, but you can see quite a lot on the **West Somerset Railway** between Bishops Lydeard and the coastal resort of Minehead, with stops at some of the thatched, typically English villages along the west flank of the Quantocks.

Bridgwater

Sedate **BRIDGWATER** has seen little excitement since it was embroiled in the Civil War and its aftermath, in particular the events surrounding the **Monmouth Rebellion** of 1685. Having landed from his base in Holland, the Protestant Duke of Monmouth, an illegitimate son of Charles II, was enthusiastically proclaimed king at Taunton, and was only prevented from taking Bristol by the encampment of the Catholic James II's army there. Monmouth turned round and attempted to surprise the king's forces on **Sedgemoor**, three miles outside Bridgwater. The disorganized rebel army was mown down by the royal artillery, Monmouth himself was captured and later beheaded, and a period of repression was unleashed under the infamous Judge Jeffreys, whose

Bloody Assizes created a folk-memory in Somerset of gibbets and gutted carcasses displayed around the county.

The town was once one of Somerset's major ports and, despite some ugly outskirts, still has some handsome red-brick buildings around its centre. The thirteenth- to fourteenth-century **St Mary's Church** (Tues–Sun 10.30am–noon; free), immediately identifiable by its polygonal, acutely angled steeple soaring above the town centre, has an oak pulpit and a seventeenth-century Italian altarpiece. By the River Parrett on Blake Street – round the corner from the red-brick Christ Church where Coleridge preached in 1797 and 1798 – Bridgwater's **Blake Museum** (Tues–Sat 10am–4pm; free) shows relics, models and a video-documentary relating to the Battle of Sedgemoor. The sixteenth-century building is reputedly the birthplace of local hero Robert Blake, admiral under Oliver Cromwell, whose swashbuckling career is chronicled and illustrated here.

Bridgwater's **tourist office** is on the High Street (Easter–Oct Mon–Fri 10am–5pm, Sat 10am–4.30pm; Nov–Easter Mon, Wed & Fri 10am–1pm & 1.45–4pm; ℡01278/427652, ⓦwww.somersetbythesea.co.uk). Local **B&Bs** include the *Castle Bar* on West Quay (℡01278/423847; no smoking; ❸), which has fairly basic en-suite rooms, the best ones overlooking the river, and *Acorns*, 61 Taunton Rd (℡01278/445577; no credit cards; ❷), on the banks of the Bridgwater–Taunton canal south of the centre. For **snacks** head for the *Nutmeg House* in Angel Crescent, behind the shopping centre off the High Street, offering good pastas, soups and grills at outdoor tables (closed Sun), or the nearby *Great Escape* **pub**, also with tables outside, and with a full bar menu and DJs on Fridays and Saturdays. On Castle Street, the Bridgwater Arts Centre (℡01278/422700) has concerts, plays, comedy and a bar.

A good time to be in Bridgwater would be for the **carnival** celebrations, which usually take place on the nearest Thursday or Friday to Bonfire Night. Grandly festooned floats of the local Carnival Clubs roll through town before heading off to do the same in various other Somerset towns and villages, including Glastonbury and Wells.

Taunton

Twelve miles from Bridgwater, Somerset's county town of **TAUNTON** lies in the fertile Vale of Taunton, wedged between the Quantock, Brendon and Blackdown hills. The region is famed for its production of cider and scrumpy (cider's less refined cousin), while Taunton itself is host to one of the country's biggest cattle markets.

Most of Taunton's **castle**, started in the twelfth century, was pulled down in 1662, but a part of it now houses the **County Museum** (Tues–Sat 10am–5pm; free), which includes a portrait of Judge Jeffreys among other memorabilia of local interest. Overlooking the county cricket ground are the pinnacled and battlemented towers of the town's two most important churches: **St James** and **St Mary Magdalene**, both fifteenth-century though remodelled by the Victorians. St Mary's is worth a look inside for its roof-bosses carved with medieval masks.

Otherwise Taunton should only detain you as a base to visit the Quantock villages or Exmoor. Information is on hand at the **tourist office** in the library building on Paul Street (April–Oct Mon–Thurs 9.30am–5.30pm, Fri 9.30am–7pm, Sat 9.30am–5pm; Nov–March Mon–Fri 9.30am–5.30pm, Sat 9.30am–5pm; ℡01823/336344, ⓦwww.heartofsomerset.com). There are three central **B&Bs** within a few steps of each other on Wellington Road: *Brookfield* at no. 16 (☎01823/272786; no credit cards; ❷), *Beaufort Lodge* at no. 18 (☎01823/326420; no credit cards; ❷) – both with all rooms en suite and non-smoking – and *Acorn Lodge* at no. 22 (☎01823/337613; no credit cards; ❶), with shared bathrooms. For a snack or **meal**, head down East Street from Fore Street to *Brettons*, a congenial wine bar and restaurant at 49 East Reach (closed lunchtime Sat & Mon, and all day Sun). Vegetarian dishes are served at the *Brewhouse Theatre and Arts Centre* on Coal Orchard, where there's usually something going on in the evening.

The Quantock Hills

The **Quantock Hills** are a cultivated outpost of Exmoor, just twelve miles in length and mostly between 800 and 900 feet high. Watered by clear streams and grazed by red deer, the range is enclosed by a triangle of roads leading up from Bridgwater and Taunton, within which a tangle of narrow lanes connect the secluded hamlets.

North of Taunton, the first villages you pass through on the A358 give you an immediate introduction to the flavour of the Quantocks. **BISHOPS LYDEARD**, four miles up, has a splendid church tower in the Perpendicular style; the church's interior is also worth a look for its carved bench-ends. Linked by bus #28 (on Sun, #928) from Taunton's train station, the village is the terminus of the **West Somerset Railway**, with steam and diesel trains departing up to seven times daily between March and November (plus some dates in Dec & Jan), stopping at renovated stations on the way to Minehead, some twenty miles away (see p.392). For a talking timetable call ☎01643/707650, for other enquiries call ☎01643/704996, or log on at ⓦ www.west-somerset-railway.co.uk.

A couple of miles north, **COMBE FLOREY** is almost exclusively built of the pink-red sandstone characteristic of Quantock villages. For over fifteen years (1829–45), the local rector was the unconventional cleric Sydney Smith, called "the greatest master of ridicule since Swift" by Macaulay; more recently it's been home to Evelyn Waugh. A little over three miles further or so along the A358, **CROWCOMBE** is another typical cob-and-thatch Quantock village, with a well-preserved Church House from 1515. Opposite, the parish church has some pagan-looking carved bench-ends from around the same time that are worth a look. There's a **youth hostel** signposted southeast of the village (☎0870/770 5782; closed Oct to mid-March; £10.25), where evening meals are available.

Eight miles west of Bridgwater on the A39, on the edge of the hills, the pretty village of **NETHER STOWEY** is best known for its association with **Samuel Taylor Coleridge**, who walked here from Bristol at the end of 1796, to join his wife and child at their new home. This "miserable cottage", as Sara Coleridge called it, was visited six months later by William Wordsworth and his sister Dorothy, who soon afterwards moved into Alfoxden House, a couple of miles down the road near Holford. The year that Coleridge and Wordsworth spent as neighbours was extraordinarily productive – Coleridge composed some of his best poetry at this time, including *The Rime of the Ancient Mariner* and *Kubla Khan*, and the two poets collaborated on the *Lyrical Ballads*, the poetic manifesto of early English Romanticism. In **Coleridge Cottage** (April–Sept Thurs–Sun 2–5pm; £3; NT), not such an "old hovel" now, you can see the man's parlour and reading room, and, upstairs, his bedroom and an exhibition room containing various letters and first editions.

The village library in nearby Castle Street has a **Quantock Information Centre** (Mon, Wed & Fri 10am–12.30pm & 2–5pm, Sat 10am–1pm & 2–4pm; ℡01278/732845, ⓦwww.quantockhills.com), which can provide walking itineraries and some local information. As for **accommodation**, the best choices locally are the handsomely furnished *Stowey Brooke House*, 18 Castle St (℡01278/733356, ⓦwww.stoweybrookehouse.co.uk; ❷), and, across the street, the *Old Cider House* at no. 25 (℡01278/732228, ⓦwww.theoldciderhouse.co.uk; ❷), which also serves evening meals. The *Rose & Crown* on St Mary Street has standard inn accommodation (℡01278/732265; ❶), and provides sustenance in the form of ales and bar meals – as does the *George* next door. **Campers** should head for *Mill Farm* (℡01278/732286), a couple of miles east of Nether Stowey on the A39, outside the village of Fiddington, which also has a stables and two pools. There's a **youth hostel** two miles west of the village of Holford, itself five miles west of Nether Stowey along the A39, where you can **camp** in the grounds (℡0870/770 6006; closed early Sept to mid-April; £10.25).

South of Nether Stowey, a minor road winds off the A39 to the highest point on the Quantocks at **Wills Neck** (1260ft); drivers can park at Triscombe Stone, on the edge of Quantock Forest, from where a footpath leads to the summit about a mile distant. Stretching between Wills Neck and the village of Aisholt, the moorland plateau of **Aisholt Common** is the heart of the Quantocks, best explored from **West Bagborough**, where a five-mile path starts at Birches Corner. Lower down the slopes, outside Aisholt, the banks of **Hawkridge Reservoir** make a lovely picnic stop.

The Quantock seaboard can be seen at its best at **Kilve Beach**, signposted off the A39 below Holford. Not so much a beach as a grand shale-studded foreshore, it's perfect for messing about in the rock pools and roaming the seaweedy shore.

Six miles to the west, **WATCHET** is Somerset's only port of any consequence, and the place from which Coleridge's Ancient Mariner set sail. Watchet is only a stop away on the West Somerset Railway from **Washford**, from where it's a ten-minute walk to **Cleeve Abbey** (daily: April–Sept 10am–6pm; Oct 10am–5pm; Nov–March 10am–1pm & 2–4pm; £3; EH), a Cistercian house founded in 1198. Although the church itself has been mostly destroyed, the convent buildings are in excellent condition, providing the country's most complete collection of domestic buildings belonging to this austere order. An exhibition on the premises illustrates how the monks lived and how the local population pleaded in vain with Henry VIII for the abbey's survival.

Travel details

Buses

For information on all local and national bus services, contact Traveline ℡0870/608 2608 (daily 7am–9pm), ⓦwww.traveline.org.uk. For details of services from Oxford to the Cotswolds see p.307.
Bath to: Bristol (every 15–30min; 50min); London (11 daily; 2hr 50min–3hr 50min); Salisbury 1 daily; 1hr 25min); Wells (Mon–Sat hourly, Sun 7; 1hr 15min).

Bridgwater to: Glastonbury (Mon–Sat hourly, 1hr 10min); Minehead (4–6 daily; 1hr 30min); Taunton (Mon–Sat every 30min, Sun every 2hr; 45min); Wells (Mon–Sat hourly; 1hr 25min).
Bristol to: Bath (every 15–30min; 50min); Birmingham (5–8 daily; 2hr–2hr 30min); Cheltenham (3–5 daily; 1hr–1hr 25min); Exeter (4–5 daily; 1hr 45min–2hr); Gloucester (3–5 daily; 1hr–1hr 25min); London (hourly; 2hr 30min); Wells (hourly; 1hr).

Burford to: Chipping Norton (4 daily; 2hr); Cirencester (4 daily; 1hr 30min); Lechlade (2 daily; 1hr); Oxford (hourly; 30min).

Chipping Campden to Moreton-in-Marsh (3 daily; 30min).

Chipping Norton to: Burford (4 daily; 2hr); Cirencester (every 2–3hr; 2hr); Lechlade (every 3hr; 2hr 30min); Oxford (hourly; 50min).

Cheltenham to: Gloucester (Mon–Sat every 20min, Sun hourly; 40min); London (11 daily; 2hr 50min–3hr 20min); Painswick (Mon–Sat hourly; Sun 3 daily; 30min); Stroud (Mon–Sat hourly, Sun 3 daily; 45min); Tewkesbury (Mon–Sat every 20min, Sun 6 daily; 30min).

Cirencester to: Burford (4 daily; 1hr 30min); Chipping Norton (every 2–3hr; 2hr); Lechlade (every 2–3hr; 1hr); Moreton-in-Marsh (every 2hr; 1hr); Oxford (every 2hr; 2hr).

Glastonbury to: Bridgwater (Mon–Sat hourly, 1hr 10min); Taunton (5–6 daily; 50min); Wells (1–2 hourly; 15min).

Gloucester to: Bristol (3–5 daily; 50min–1hr); Cheltenham (Mon–Sat every 20min, Sun hourly; 40min); Tewkesbury (Mon–Sat hourly, Sun 5 daily 20min); London (11 daily; 3hr 20min).

Lechlade to: Burford (2 daily; 1hr); Chipping Norton (every 3hr; 2hr 30min); Cirencester (every 2–3hr; 1hr); Oxford (hourly; 1hr 40min).

Moreton-in-Marsh to: Chipping Campden (3 daily; 30min); Cirencester (every 2hr; 1hr).

Taunton to: Bridgwater (Mon–Sat every 30min, Sun every 2hr; 45min); Exeter (Mon–Sat 5 daily; 1hr 20min); Glastonbury (5–6 daily; 50min);

Minehead (Mon–Sat hourly, Sun 9; 1hr 10min).

Tewkesbury to: Cheltenham (Mon–Sat every 20min, Sun 6; 30min); Gloucester (Mon–Sat hourly, Sun 5; 20min).

Wells to: Bath (Mon–Sat hourly, Sun 7 daily; 1hr 15min); Bridgwater (Mon–Sat hourly, 1hr 25min); Bristol (hourly; 1hr); Glastonbury (1–2 hourly; 15min).

Trains

For information on all local and national rail services, contact National Rail Enquiries ☎ 08457/48 49 50, ⓦ www.nationalrail.co.uk.

Bath to: Bristol (every 20min; 20min); Dorchester (Mon–Sat 6–7 daily, Sun 1 daily; 2hr); London (1–2 hourly; 1hr 30min); Salisbury (hourly; 1hr); Southampton (hourly; 1hr 30min).

Bristol to: Bath (every 20min; 20min); Birmingham (every 30min; 1hr 30min); Cheltenham (every 30min; 50min); Exeter (1–2 hourly; 1hr 15min–1hr 45min); Gloucester (1–2 hourly; 50min–1hr 20min); London (every 30min; 1hr 45min); Penzance (5 daily; 4hr–4hr 30min); Plymouth (1–2 hourly; 2hr–2hr 30min); Truro (5 daily; 3hr 15min–4hr 15min).

Cheltenham to: Bristol (2 hourly; 45min); Gloucester (1–2 hourly; 10min); London (1–2 hourly; 2hr–2hr 40min); Worcester (hourly; 30min).

Gloucester to: Bristol (1–2 hourly; 50min–1hr 20min); Cheltenham (1–2 hourly; 10min); London (1–2 hourly; 1hr 50min–2hr 15min); Stroud (hourly; 15–20min).

Devon and Cornwall

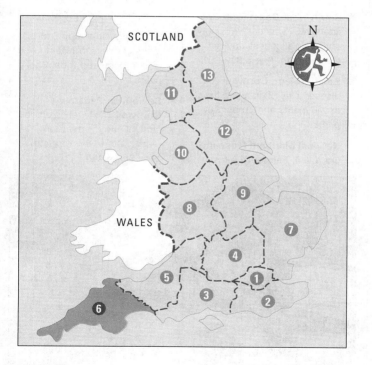

SCOTLAND

N

11

13

12

10

9

8

WALES

7

4

5

1

3

2

6

Highlights

* **Sidmouth International Festival** Folk and world music predominate at this annual festival. See p.369

* **A hike on Dartmoor** Rugged tors, bleak moorland and pockets of tangled forest make this ideal walking terrain. See p.379

* **South West Coast Path** Ever-changing vistas ensure variety on Britain's longest way-marked path. See p.392

* **Eden Project, Cornwall** A disused clay pit is home to exotic plants and crops. See p.398

* **National Maritime Museum Cornwall, Falmouth** A fascinating, all-round exhibition of sea-related items. See p.402

* **Lizard Point, Cornwall** Battered by waves, this unspoiled headland is the starting point for some inspiring walks. See p.403

* **Tate St Ives, Cornwall** This modern gallery showcases local artists. See p.410

* **Surfing in Newquay** Endless ranks of rollers draw enthusiasts from far and wide. See p.415

* **Seafood in Padstow, Cornwall** The local catch goes straight into the excellent restaurants of this bustling port. See p.418

△ Fishing harbour

6

Devon and Cornwall

At the western extremity of England, the counties of **Devon and Cornwall** encompass everything from genteel, cosy villages to vast Atlantic-facing strands of golden sand and wild expanses of granite moorland. The combination of rural peace and first-class beaches has made the peninsula perennially popular with tourists, so much so that tourism has replaced the traditional occupations of fishing and farming as the main source of employment and income. Enough remains of these beleaguered communities to preserve the region's authentic character, however – even if this can be occasionally obscured during the summer season. Avoid the peak periods and you'll be seduced by the genuine appeal of this area, which beckons ever westwards into rural backwaters where increasingly exotic place-names and idiosyncratic pronunciations recall that this was once England's last bastion of Celtic culture.

Although the human history of the region has left its stamp, it's the natural landscape which exerts the strongest pull, and not just in the beauty of the long, deeply indented seaboard. Straddling the border between Devon and Somerset, **Exmoor** is one of the peninsula's three great moors, its heathery slopes much favoured by hunting parties as well as by hikers. For wilderness, however, nothing can beat the remoter tracts of **Dartmoor**, which takes up much of the southern half of inland Devon. The greatest of the West Country's granite massifs, most of Dartmoor retains its solitude in spite of its proximity to the only major cities at this end of the country, either of which would make a good touring base. Of the two, **Exeter** is by far the more interesting, dominated by the twin towers of its medieval cathedral and offering a rich selection of restaurants and nightlife. Much of the city was destroyed by bombing during World War II, though the region's largest city, **Plymouth**, suffered even worse, the consequence of its historic role as a great naval port. Bland postwar development inflicted almost as much damage as the Luftwaffe, although enough of Plymouth's Elizabethan core has survived to merit a visit, and the city, by capitalizing on its maritime associations, has succeeded in reviving its port area.

The coastline on either side of Exeter and Plymouth is within easy reach. Warmed by the Gulf Stream, and enjoying more hours of sunshine than virtually anywhere else in England, this part of the country can sometimes come fairly close to the atmosphere of the Mediterranean, and indeed Devon's principal resort, **Torquay**, styles itself the capital of the "English Riviera". St Tropez it ain't, but there's no denying a certain glamour, far removed from the old-fashioned charm of the seaside towns of **East Devon**, or the cliff-backed resorts of the county's northern littoral.

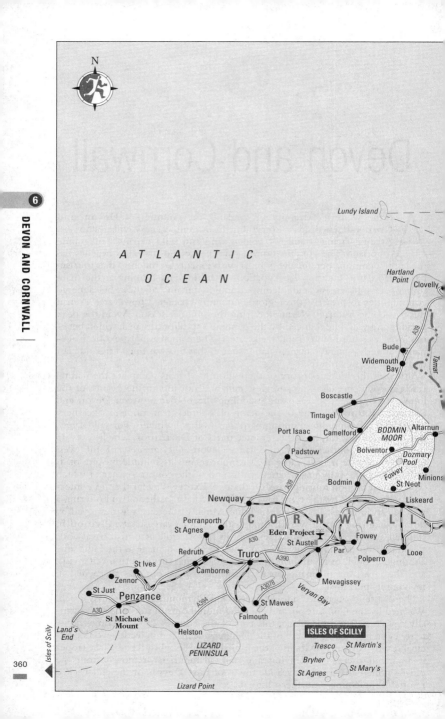

N

ATLANTIC
OCEAN

Lundy Island

Hartland
Point

Clovelly

Bude

Widemouth
Bay

Tamar

Boscastle

Tintagel

Port Isaac   Camelford

BODMIN
MOOR   Altarnun

Padstow

Bolventor

Dozmary
Pool

Fowey   Minions

Bodmin   St Neot

A39

Newquay   Liskeard

Perranporth

St Agnes   C O R N W A L L

Eden Project

Redruth   St Austell   Fowey

A30   Par

Truro   A390   Polperro   Looe

St Ives   Camborne

Zennor   Mevagissey

St Just   A3078

Penzance   Veryan Bay

A394   St Mawes

St Michael's
Mount   Falmouth

Land's
End   Helston

LIZARD
PENINSULA

ISLES OF SCILLY

Tresco   St Martin's

Bryher

St Agnes   St Mary's

Lizard Point

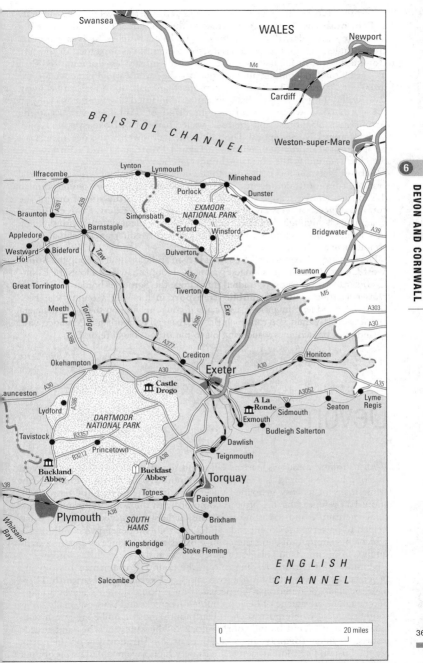

© Crown copyright

Cornwall too has its pockets of concentrated tourist development – chiefly at **Falmouth** and **Newquay**, the first of these a sailing centre, the second a mecca for surfers drawn to its choice of west-facing beaches. **St Ives** is another crowd-puller, though the town has a separate identity as a magnet for the arts. Despite the tourist incursions, this county is essentially less domesticated than its agricultural neighbour, in part due to the overbearing presence of the turbulent Atlantic, which is never more than half an hour's drive away. Cornwall's old fishing ports have an almost embattled character, especially on the north coast, where the fortified headland of **Tintagel**, with its strong Arthurian associations – and the rock-walled harbour of **Boscastle** are typical of the county's craggy appeal. The full elemental power of the ocean can best be appreciated on the twin pincers of **Lizard Point** and **Land's End**, where the cliffs resound to the constant thunder of the waves.

Cornwall's starker feel is also due to the ubiquitous reminders of its industrial past, the ruins of its defunct mine-works presenting a salutary counterpoint to the tourist-centred seaside towns. A disused clay pit is the site of one of the county's biggest success stories of recent times, the **Eden Project**, which imaginatively highlights the diversity of the planet's plant systems with the help of science-fiction "biomes", where tropical and Mediterranean climates and conditions have been re-created.

The best way of exploring the coast of Devon and Cornwall is along the **South West Coast Path**, Britain's longest waymarked footpath, which allows the dauntless hiker to cover over six hundred miles from the Somerset border to Poole in Dorset. Getting around by **public transport** in the West Country can be a convoluted and lengthy process, especially if you're relying on the often deficient bus network. By train, you can reach Bristol, Exeter, Plymouth and Penzance, with a handful of branch lines wandering off to the major coastal resorts.

Devon

With its rolling meadows, narrow lanes and remote thatched cottages, **Devon** has long been idealized as a vision of a preindustrial, "authentic" England. But while many of its cosy, gentrified villages are inhabited largely by retired folk and urban refugees, having little in common with the county's strong agricultural, mercantile and maritime traditions, at least the stereotyped image has helped to preserve the countryside and coast in the undeveloped condition for which they are famous, and the county offers an abundance of genuine tranquillity, from moorland villages to quiet coves on the spectacular coastline.

Reminders of Devon's leading role in the country's **maritime history** are never far away, particularly in the two cities of **Exeter** and **Plymouth**. These days the nautical tradition is perpetuated on a domesticated scale by yachtspeople taking advantage of Devon's numerous creeks and bays, especially on its southern coast, where ports such as Dartmouth and Salcombe are awash with amateur sailors. Land-bound tourists flock to the sandy beaches and seaside resorts, of which **Torquay**, on the south coast, and **Ilfracombe**, on the north, are the busiest. The most attractive are those which have retained traces of their nineteenth-century elegance, such as **Sidmouth**, in East Devon. **Inland**, Devon is characterized by swards of lush pasture and a scattering of sheltered villages, the county's low population density dropping to almost zero on **Dartmoor**, the wildest and bleakest of the West's moors, and **Exmoor**, whose seaboard constitutes one of the West Country's most scenic littorals.

Exeter and Plymouth are on the main **rail** lines from London and the Midlands, with branch lines from Exeter linking the north coast at Barnstaple and the south-coast towns of Exmouth and Torquay. **Buses** from the chief stations fan out along the coasts and into the interior, though the service can be extremely rudimentary for the smaller villages.

Exeter

EXETER's sights are richer than those of any other town in Devon or Cornwall, the legacy of an eventful history since its Celtic foundation and the establishment here of the most westerly Roman outpost. After the Roman withdrawal, Exeter was refounded by Alfred the Great and by the time of the Norman Conquest had become one of the largest towns in England, profiting from its position on the banks of the River Exe. The expansion of the wool trade in the Tudor period sustained the city until the eighteenth century, and Exeter has maintained its status as commercial centre and county town, and, despite having much of its ancient centre gutted by World War II bombing, enough has survived to justify a lengthy exploration.

The coast around Exeter holds an architectural oddity, **A La Ronde**, and a string of old-fashioned seaside resorts – **Sidmouth** would be a good overnight stop, as would the neighbouring villages of **Beer** and **Seaton**.

Arrival, information and accommodation

Exeter has two **train stations**, Exeter Central and St David's, the latter a little further out from the centre of town, and connected by frequent city buses. South West trains from Salisbury stop at both, as do trains on the branch lines to Barnstaple and Exmouth, but most long-distance trains stop at St David's only. The **bus station** is on Paris Street, right across from the main **tourist office** (July & Aug Mon–Sat 9am–5pm, Sun 10am–4pm; Sept–June Mon–Sat 9am–5pm; ℡01392/265700, ⊛www.exeter.gov.uk). There's an **Internet point** at the St Sidwell Centre, Sidwell Street (℡01392/666222).

Most of Exeter's cheaper **accommodation** lies north of the centre, near the two stations, including two B&Bs close to each other in a quiet location: *Park View*, 8 Howell Rd ℡01392/271772, ⊛www.parkviewhotel.freeserve.co.uk; **❷**), a Georgian building overlooking a park, and *Raffles*, 11 Blackall Rd (℡01392/270200, ⊛www.raffles-exeter.co.uk; **❸**), an elegant Victorian house with period furnishings and organic garden produce for breakfasts. More centrally, *Bendene*, 15 Richmond Rd (℡01392/213526, ⊛www .bendene.co.uk; no credit cards; **❷**), with a heated outdoor swimming pool, and *Maurice*, 5 Bystock Terrace (℡01392/213079, ⊛www.hotelmaurice .eclipse.co.uk; nonsmoking; **❶**), have bright, smallish but comfortable rooms. For a stylish splurge, check into *Hotel Barcelona*, Magdalen Street (℡01392/281000, ⊛www.hotelbarcelona-uk.com; **❻**), in a red-brick former Victorian eye hospital, with light, spacious rooms and a Mediterranean-style bistro. Exeter has two **hostels**: *Exeter YHA*, 47 Countess Wear Rd ℡0870/770 5826, ⓔexeter@yha.org.uk; £11.50), in a country house two miles outside the

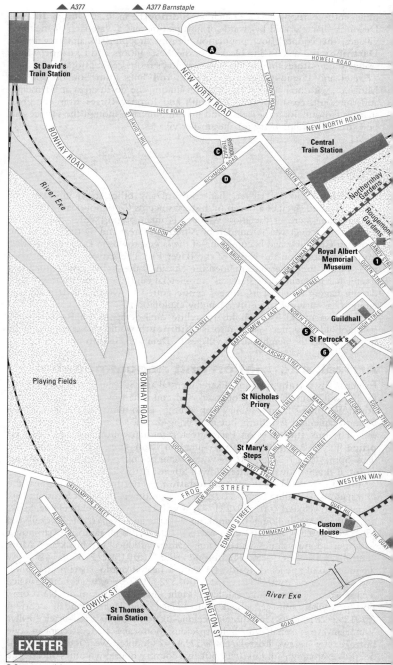

© Crown copyright

EXETER

▲ A377   ▲ A377 Barnstaple

▼ M5, A30 Okehampton & A38 Plymouth

St David's
Train Station

NEW NORTH ROAD

HOWELL ROAD

ELMGROVE ROAD

HELE ROAD

NEW NORTH ROAD

BONHAY ROAD

ST DAVID'S HILL

Central
Train Station

BISTOCK TERRACE

RICHMOND ROAD

HALDON ROAD

QUEEN'S STREET

Northernhay
Gardens

Rougemont
Gardens

River Exe

IRON BRIDGE

EXE STREET

NORTHERNHAY STREET

Royal Albert
Memorial
Museum

GANDY STREET

QUEEN STREET

PAUL STREET

NORTH STREET

BARTHOLOMEW ST EAST

Guildhall

HIGH STREET

St Petrock's

Playing Fields

BONHAY ROAD

BARTHOLOMEW ST WEST

MARY ARCHES STREET

St Nicholas
Priory

FORE STREET

SMYTHEN STREET

MARKET STREET

ST GEORGE'S ST

SOUTH STREET

TUDOR STREET

St Mary's
Steps

KING STREET

STEPCOTE HILL

PRESTON STREET

WEST STREET

WESTERN WAY

OKEHAMPTON STREET

ALBION STREET

BUTTS ROAD

FROG STREET

NEW BRIDGE STREET

EDMUND STREET

COMMERCIAL ROAD

QUAY HILL

Custom
House

THE QUAY

COWICK ST

St Thomas
Train Station

ALPHINGTON ST

River Exe

HAVEN ROAD

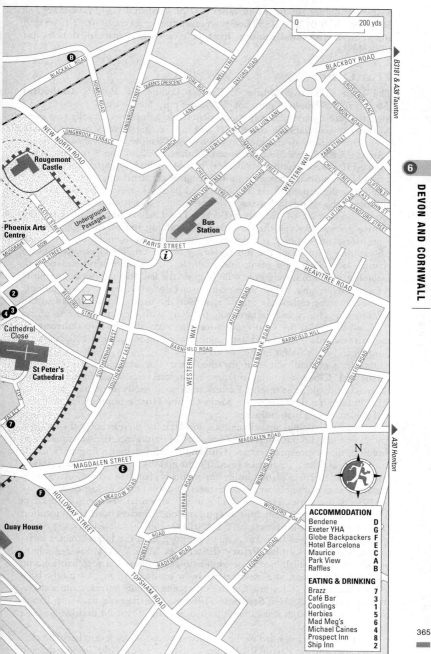

▶ B3181 & A30 Taunton

▶ A30 Honiton

BLACKBOY ROAD

BLACKALL ROAD

HOWELL ROAD

NEW NORTH ROAD

LONGBROOK TERRACE

LONGBROOK STREET

QUEEN'S CRESCENT

YORK ROAD

WELL STREET

OXFORD ROAD

RED LION LANE

GROSVENOR PLACE

BELMONT ROAD

PARR STREET

LANE

CHURCH

SIDWELL STREET

SUMMERLAND STREET

VERNEY STREET

WESTERN WAY

CHUTE STREET

CLIFTON ST

EAST JOHN ST

CLIFTON ROAD

SANDFORD STREET

Rougemont
Castle

CHEEKE STREET

BAMPFYLDE STREET

BELGRAVE ROAD

Bus
Station

Underground
Passages

CASTLE STREET

MUSGRAVE ROW

Phoenix Arts
Centre

HIGH STREET

PARIS STREET

ⓘ

HEAVITREE ROAD

❷

ⓐ❸

BEDFORD STREET

✉

Cathedral
Close

ATHELSTAN ROAD

BARNFIELD HILL

DENMARK ROAD

SPICER ROAD

St Peter's
Cathedral

SOUTHERNHAY WEST

SOUTHERNHAY EAST

BARNFIELD ROAD

WESTERN WAY

COLLEGE ROAD

PALACE GATE

❼

N

MAGDALEN ROAD

Ⓔ

MAGDALEN STREET

WONFORD ROAD

Ⓕ

HOLLOWAY STREET

BULL MEADOW ROAD

FAIRPARK ROAD

WONFORD ROAD

Quay House

❽

ROBERTS ROAD

RADFORD ROAD

ST LEONARD'S ROAD

TOPSHAM ROAD

0 — 200 yds

ACCOMMODATION
Bendene	**D**
Exeter YHA	**G**
Globe Backpackers	**F**
Hotel Barcelona	**E**
Maurice	**C**
Park View	**A**
Raffles	**B**

EATING & DRINKING
Brazz	**7**
Café Bar	**3**
Coolings	**1**
Herbies	**5**
Mad Meg's	**6**
Michael Caines	**4**
Prospect Inn	**8**
Ship Inn	**2**

▼ Ⓖ, M5 & A376 Exmouth

centre (minibuses #K or #T, or buses #57 or #85), and *Globe Backpackers*, 71 Holloway St ☎01392/215521, ⓦwww.exeterbackpackers.co.uk; £12), clean and central, with good showers, Internet access and a spacious double also available (❶).

The City

The most distinctive feature of Exeter's skyline, **St Peter's Cathedral** (Mon–Fri 7.30am–6.30pm, Sat 7.30am–5pm, Sun 8am–7.30pm; £3.50 suggested donation) is a stately monument made conspicuous by the two great Norman towers flanking the nave. Close up, it's the facade's ornate Gothic screen that commands attention: its three tiers of sculpted (and very weathered) figures – including Alfred, Athelstan, Canute, William the Conqueror and Richard II – were begun around 1360, part of a rebuilding programme which left only the Norman towers from the original construction.

Entering the cathedral, you're confronted by the longest unbroken **Gothic ceiling** in the world, its **bosses** vividly painted – one, towards the west front, shows the murder of Thomas à Becket. The **Lady Chapel** and **Chapter House** – respectively at the far end of the building and off the right transept – are thirteenth-century, but the main part of the nave, including the lavish rib-vaulting, dates from the full flowering of the English Decorated style, a century later. There are many fine examples of sculpture from this period, including, in the minstrels' gallery high up on the left side, angels playing musical instruments, and, below them, figures of Edward III and Queen Philippa. Dominating the cathedral's central space are the organ pipes installed in the seventeenth century and harmonizing perfectly with the linear patterns of the roof and arches. In the **Choir** don't miss the sixty-foot **bishop's throne** or the **misericords** – decorated with mythological figures around 1260, they are thought to be the oldest in the country.

Outside, a graceful statue of the theologian Richard Hooker surveys the **Cathedral Close**, a motley mixture of architectural styles from Tudor to Regency, though most display Exeter's trademark red-brickwork. One of the finest buildings is the Elizabethan **Mol's Coffee House**, impressively timbered and gabled, now a map shop.

Some older buildings are still standing amid the banal concrete of the modern town centre, including, on the pedestrianized High Street, Exeter's finest civic building, the fourteenth-century **Guildhall**, claimed to be England's oldest municipal building in regular use. It's fronted by an elegant Renaissance portico, and merits a glance inside for its main chamber, whose arched roof timbers rest on carved bears holding staves, symbols of the Yorkist cause during the Wars of the Roses. The Guildhall is usually **open to visitors** on weekdays from 10.30am to 1pm and 2pm to 4pm, and on Saturdays from 10am to noon (but may be closed for functions, call ☎01392/265500 to check).

On the west side of Fore Street, the continuation of the High Street, a turning leads to **St Nicholas Priory** (Easter–Oct Mon, Wed & Sat 2–4.30pm; 50p), part of a small Benedictine foundation that became a merchant's home after the Dissolution; the interior has been restored to what it might have looked like in the Tudor era. On the other side of Fore Street, trailing down towards the river, cobbled **Stepcote Hill** was once the main road into Exeter from the west, though it is difficult to imagine this steep and narrow lane as a main thoroughfare.

Exeter's centre is bounded to the southwest by the River Exe, where the port area is now mostly devoted to leisure activities, particularly around the old

Quayside. Pubs, shops and cafés share the space with handsomely restored nineteenth-century warehouses and the smart **Custom House**, built in 1681, its opulence reflecting the former importance of the cloth trade. Next door, the Quay House from the same period has an information desk and, upstairs, a video on Exeter's history (Easter–Oct). The area comes into its own at night, but is worth a wander at any time, and you can **rent bikes** and **canoes** at Saddles & Paddles on the quayside (℡01392/424241,ⓦwww.saddlepaddle .co.uk) to explore the **Exeter Canal**, which runs five miles to Topsham and beyond.

Back at the north end of the High Street, Romansgate Passage (next to Boots) holds the entrance to a network of **underground passages** first excavated in the thirteenth century to bring water to the cathedral precincts. The passages can be visited as part of a fascinating 50-minute guided **tour** (June–Sept & school holidays Mon–Sat 10am–noon & 2–5pm; Oct–May Tues–Fri noon–5pm, Sat 10am–5pm; last tour at 4.30pm; June–Sept £3.75, rest of year £3) – not recommended to claustrophobes, however. Nearby, Castle Street leads to what remains of **Rougemont Castle**, now little more than a perimeter of red-stone walls that are best appreciated from the surrounding Rougemont and Northernhay Gardens. Following the path through this park, exit at Queen Street to drop in at the excellent **Royal Albert Memorial Museum** (Mon–Sat 10am–5pm; free), a motley assortment including everything from a menagerie of stuffed animals to mock-ups of the various building styles used at different periods in the city. The collections of silverware, watches and clocks contrast nicely with the colourful ethnography section, and the picture gallery has some good specimens of West Country art alongside work by other artists associated with Devon.

Eating, drinking and entertainment

The café inside the Royal Albert Memorial Museum is handy and congenial for wholesome **snacks**, while round the corner from the museum, in medieval Gandy Street, *Coolings* is a popular wine bar and bistro serving tasty lunches – it's also open until late with DJs on Tuesday and Wednesday evenings and a cellar bar open Fridays and Saturdays. Opposite the cathedral, the *Café Bar* is a casually modish spot for a coffee or lunch, serving toasties, salads, burgers and pastas, and full meals in the evenings, with themed nights and live jazz on Fridays (for which booking is advised; ℡01392/310130). It's part of the next-door *Michael Caines* (℡01392/31003; closed Sun), one of Exeter's classiest **restaurants**, where you'll find sophisticated modern European cuisine in sleek surroundings; prices are fairly high, though there are reasonable fixed-price menus at lunchtime. In total contrast, the Olde Worlde atmosphere is laid on thickly at *Mad Meg's* (closed Mon–Wed lunch & Sun eve; ℡01392/221225) – once a nunnery, now staffed by waitresses in wench costume – but there are some good-value traditional dishes here; it's tucked away near the top of Fore Street, below a bike shop. Nearby *Herbie's*, 15 North St (℡01392/258473; closed all day Sun & Mon eve), is a cosy wholefood restaurant, with organic ice cream on the menu. *Brazz*, at 10–12 Palace Gate, off South Street, is a stylish bar/bistro with a sparkly ceiling and an aquarium.

Among the **pubs**, the *Ship Inn*, in St Martin's Lane, serves reasonably priced lunches and prides itself on the claim that it was once Francis Drake's local. The pubs and clubs on Exeter's Quay make this a lively spot to while away an evening. You can eat and drink sitting outside at the seventeenth-century *Prospect Inn*, followed up with a bop at one of the two biggest **club complexes** in town: the *Warehouse*, *Boxes* and *Boogies*, and *Volts* and *Hothouse*, playing a mix of mainstream and retro sounds. In the centre, the *Timepiece*, Little Castle Street, occupies a former prison and has a good daytime bar with a garden. For **live music**, especially post-punk bands, head for the *Cavern Club* (℡01392/495370, ⊛www.cavernclub.co.uk), with entrances in Queen and Gandy streets (also open 10.30am–4pm for snacks). The **Phoenix Arts Centre**, off Gandy Street (℡01392/667080, ⊛www.exeterphoenix.org.uk), has films, exhibitions and gigs, as well as a great café/bistro. During the first three weeks of July, the **Exeter Festival** (℡01392/265198) features jazz, blues and classical concerts at various venues around town.

A La Ronde

Five miles south of Exeter off the A376 (bus #57), the Gothic folly of **A La Ronde** (April–Oct Mon–Thurs & Sun 11am–5.30pm; £3.80; NT) was the creation of two cousins, Jane and Mary Parminter, who in the 1790s were inspired by their European Grand Tour to construct a sixteen-sided house possibly based on the Byzantine basilica of San Vitale in Ravenna. The end product is filled with mementos of the Parminters' tour as well as a number of their more offbeat creations, such as a frieze made of feathers culled from game birds and chickens. In the upper rooms are a gallery and staircase completely covered in shells, too fragile to be visited, though part can be glimpsed from the completely enclosed octagonal room on the first floor – a closed-circuit TV system enables visitors to home in on details.

The women intended that the house should be inherited only by female descendants, though the conditions of Mary Parminter's will were broken at the end of the nineteenth century when the building was inherited by the Reverend Oswald Reichel, who added dormer windows on the second floor, which afford superb views over the Exe Estuary to Haldon Hill and Dawlish Warren.

Exmouth and around

Originating as a Roman port, **EXMOUTH** went on to become the first of Devon's resorts to be popularized by holiday-makers in the late eighteenth century. Overlooking lawns, rock pools and a respectable two miles of beach, the town's Georgian terraces once accommodated such folk as the wives of Nelson and Byron – installed at nos. 6 and 19 The Beacon respectively. **Hotels and B&Bs** for present-day visitors range from the nonsmoking *Blenheim Guest House*, 39 Morton Rd (℡01395/223123, ⊛www.come.to/freesunshine; no credit cards; ❷), near the tourist office and the beach, to the more atmospheric *Manor Hotel*, The Beacon (℡01395/274477, ⊛www.manorexmouth .co.uk; ❹), whose rooms enjoy wonderful panoramic views. The **tourist office** is on Alexandra Terrace (mid-March to June, Sept & Oct Mon–Sat 9.30am–5pm; July & Aug Mon–Sat 9.30am–5pm, Sun 10am–3pm; Nov to mid-March Mon–Sat 9.30am–2pm; ℡01395/222299, ⊛www .exmouthguide.co.uk).

Exmouth is reachable from Exeter by train or on the frequent bus #57, which also serves **BUDLEIGH SALTERTON**, four miles east of Exmouth. Bounded on each side by red sandstone cliffs, Budleigh's thatched and white-washed cottages have attracted such figures as Noël Coward and P.G. Wodehouse, and John Millais painted his famous *Boyhood of Raleigh* on the shingle beach here. (Sir Walter Raleigh was born in East Budleigh, a couple of miles inland.) The **tourist office** on Fore Street (Easter–June, Sept & Oct Mon–Sat 10am–5pm; July & Aug Mon–Sat 10am–5pm, Sun 11am–5pm;

Nov–Easter Mon–Sat 10am–12.30pm; ☏01395/445275, ⓦwww.eastdevon .net/tourism) can advise you on local excursions, for example to **Ladram Bay**, a popular pebbly beach sheltered by woods and beautiful eroded cliffs three miles east of Budleigh.

Sidmouth and around

Set amidst a shelf of crumbling red sandstone, **SIDMOUTH** is the chief resort on the east Devon coast (bus #52, #52A or #52B from Exeter). The cream-and-white town boasts nearly five hundred buildings listed as having special historic or architectural interest, among them the stately Georgian homes of **York Terrace** behind the Esplanade. Both the mile-long main town beach and Jacob's Ladder, a cliff-backed shingle and sand strip to the west of town, are easily accessible and well tended. To the east, the coast path climbs steep Salcombe Hill to follow cliffs that give sanctuary to a range of birdlife including yellowhammers and green woodpeckers, as well as the rarer grasshopper warbler. Further on, the path descends to meet one of the most isolated and attractive beaches in the area, **Weston Mouth**.

The **tourist office** is on Ham Lane, off the eastern end of the Esplanade (March & April Mon–Thurs 10am–4pm, Fri & Sat 10am–5pm, Sun 10am–1pm; May–July & Sept–Oct Mon–Sat 10am–5pm, Sun 10am–4pm; Aug Mon–Sat 10am–6pm, Sun 10am–5pm; Nov–Feb Mon–Sat 10am–1.30pm; ☏01395/516441, ⓦwww.visitsidmouth.co.uk). Of the **B&Bs**, *Rock Cottage* on Peak Hill Road (☏01395/514253; no smoking; ❹) offers unrivalled sea views and access to the beach at the quieter, western end of the Esplanade. Further from the seafront, the *Old Farmhouse*, on Hillside Road (☏01395/512284; no smoking; no credit cards; ❹; closed Nov–Jan), has plenty of atmosphere and offers delicious meals on request. There's more choice in the string of decent guest houses along Salcombe Road, including *Berwick Guest House* at 4 Albert Terrace (☏01395/513621, ⓦwww.berwick-house.co.uk; no under-12s; no smoking; no credit cards; ❸). For **meals** in town, try the seafood at *Mocha Restaurant* on The Esplanade (daytime only, eves in summer), and the daily specials (including vegetarian dishes) at *Brown's Wine Bar & Bistro* at 33 Fore St (closed Sun). On Old Fore Street, the *Old Ship* and *Anchor* **pubs** provide excellent bar meals and suppers as well as a good range of ales.

Sidmouth hosts what many consider to be the country's best **folk festival** over eight days at the beginning of August. For details, contact the tourist office, call ☏01629/827010 or check out the website ⓦwww.sidmouthfestival.com. Book early for the main acts.

Beer

Eight miles east along the coast, the fishing village of **BEER** lies huddled within a small sheltered cove between gleaming white headlands. A stream rushes along a deep channel dug into Beer's main street, and if you can ignore the crowds in high summer much of the village looks unchanged since the time when it was a smugglers' eyrie, its inlets used by such characters as Jack Rattenbury, who published his *Memoirs of a Smuggler* in 1837. The village is best known for its quarries, which were worked from Roman times until the nineteenth century: **Beer Stone** was used in many of Devon's churches and houses, and as far afield as London. You can visit the complex of **underground quarries** (Easter–Sept 10am–5pm; Oct 11am–4pm; last entry 1hr before closing; £4.25) a mile or so west of the village on a guided tour, along with a small exhibition of pieces carved by medieval masons, among others. Take something warm to wear. *Bay View* (☏01297/20489; no credit cards; ❶; closed

Nov–Easter), overlooking the sea on Fore Street, is the best of the **B&Bs**, and there's a **youth hostel** half a mile northwest, at Bovey Combe, Townsend (☎0870/770 5690, ✉beer@yha.org.uk; closed Wed–Sun Nov–Feb; £11.50). For **food**, head for the *Barrel of Beer* pub, on the main street, where the superb menu includes local delicacies such as Devon oysters and home-smoked fish; there are imaginative vegetarian options, too.

The "English Riviera" region

The wedge of land between Dartmoor and the sea contains some of Devon's most fertile pastures, backing onto some of the West's most popular coastal resorts. Chief of these is **Torbay**, an amalgam of **Torquay**, **Paignton** and **Brixham**, together forming the nucleus of an area optimistically known as "**The English Riviera**". To the south, the estuary port of **Dartmouth** is linked by riverboat to historic and almost unspoiled **Totnes**. West of the River Dart, the rich agricultural district of **South Hams** extends as far as Plymouth, cleft by a web of rivers flowing off Dartmoor. The main town here is **Kingsbridge**, at the head of an estuary down which you can ferry to the sailing resort of **Salcombe**.

Torquay

Sporting a mini-corniche and promenades landscaped with flowerbeds, **TORQUAY**, the largest of the **Torbay** resorts, comes closest to living up to the self-styled "English Riviera" sobriquet. The much-vaunted palm trees (actually New Zealand cabbage trees) and the coloured lights that festoon the harbour by night contribute to the town's unique flavour, a blend of the mildly exotic with classic English provincialism. Torquay's transformation from a fishing village began with its establishment as a fashionable haven for invalids, among them the consumptive Elizabeth Barrett Browning, who spent three years here. In more recent years the most famous figures associated with Torquay – crimewriter Agatha Christie and traveller Freya Stark – have been joined by the fictional TV hotelier Basil Fawlty, whose jingoism and injured pride perfectly encapsulate the town's adaptation to the demands of mass tourism.

The town is focused on the small **harbour** and marina, separated by limestone cliffs from Torquay's main beach, **Abbey Sands**. Good for chucking a frisbee about but too busy in summer for serious relaxation, it takes its name from **Torre Abbey**, sited in ornamental gardens behind the beachside road. The Norman church that once stood here was razed by Henry VIII, though a gatehouse, tithe barn, chapterhouse and tower escaped demolition. The present **Abbey Mansion** (Easter–Oct daily 9.30am–6pm, last entry 5pm; £3) is a seventeenth- and eighteenth-century construction, now containing the mayor's office, a suite of period rooms with collections of paintings, silver and glass, and one devoted to Agatha Christie, who was born and raised in Torquay. There's more material relating to the Mistress of Murder at the main **Torquay Museum**, 529 Babbacombe Rd (Mon–Sat 10am–5pm, also Sun in summer 1.30–5pm; £3), but most of the space is given over to the local history and natural history collections.

Walking north round the promontory from the harbour, you'll reach some good sand beaches, the nearest of which, **Meadfoot**, lies at the end of a pretty half-mile coastal walk that takes you through Daddyhole Plain, a large chasm in the cliff caused by a landslide locally attributed to the devil ("Daddy"). Round the point, a string of beaches extends along the coast as far as the cliff-backed coves of **Watcombe** and **Maidencombe**.

Practicalities

Torquay's main **train station** is off Rathmore Road, southwest of Torre Abbey Gardens; most **buses**, including the #X46 from Exeter, stop near the marina, close to the **tourist office** on Vaughan Parade (late May to Sept Mon–Sat 9.30am–6pm, Sun 10am–6pm; Oct to late May Mon–Sat 9.30am–5pm; ℡0906/680 1268, ⓦwww.theenglishriviera.co.uk). There's plenty of **accommodation** in town, most of the budget choices lying around Belgrave Road and Avenue Road, for example *The Exton*, 12 Bridge Rd (℡01803/293561, ⓦwww.extonhotel.co.uk; ❷), a small and quiet hotel, ten minutes from the train station. Nonsmokers with a yen for antique pine furnishings and crisp bed linen should head for *Mulberry House*, 1 Scarborough Rd (℡01803/213639; ❹), with a superb wholefood restaurant on the premises (see below). For views and stately surroundings, try the *Allerdale Hotel*, Croft Road (℡01803/292667, ⓦwww.allerdalehotel.co.uk; ❹), which has a long, lawned garden. *Torquay Backpackers*, 119 Abbey Rd (℡01803/299924, ⓦwww.torquaybackpackers.co.uk; £12), offers cheap and friendly **hostel** accommodation, and doubles are available (❶). It's a ten-minute walk from the station, and there's a free pick-up service with advance notice.

One of the best **restaurants** in Torquay is the *Mulberry House Restaurant*, 1 Scarborough Rd (℡01803/213639; open lunchtime Fri & Sat, eves Wed–Sat, also Mon & Tues to residents), where the accent is on healthy and low-cholesterol dishes, at fairly high prices. Cheaper places on the harbourside include the *Sea Spray* at 8 Victoria Parade (closed Mon–Wed eves), offering everything from toasties to swordfish steaks. Strong on atmosphere, the cobbled *Hole in the Wall* **pub** on Park Lane serves some vegetarian dishes and has sing-songs round the piano – it was the Irish playwright Sean O'Casey's boozer when he lived in Torquay.

Paignton

Not so much a rival to Torquay as its complement, **PAIGNTON** lacks the gloss of its neighbour. Activity is concentrated at the southern end of the wide town beach, around the small harbour that nestles in the lee of the appropriately named Redcliffe headland. Otherwise, diversion-seekers could wander over to **Paignton Zoo** (daily summer 10am–6pm, last entry 5pm, winter 10am–5pm or dusk if earlier, last entry 3pm; £8.25), a mile out on Totnes Road, or board the **Paignton & Dartmouth Steam Railway** at Paignton's Queen's Park train station near the harbour (℡01803/555872, ⓦwww.paignton-steamrailway.co.uk). Running daily from June to September, with a patchy service in April, May, October and December, the line connects with Paignton's other main beach – **Goodrington Sands** – before trundling alongside the Dart estuary to Kingswear, seven miles south. You could make a day of it by taking the ferry connection from Kingswear to Dartmouth (see p.374), then taking a riverboat up the Dart to Totnes, from where you can take any bus back to Paignton – a "Round Robin" ticket (£12) lets you do this.

Paignton's bus and train stations are next to each other off Sands Road. Five minutes away, the seafront has a **tourist office** (late May to Sept Mon–Sat 9.30am–6pm, Sun 10am–6pm; Oct to late May Mon–Sat 9.30am–1pm & 2–5pm; ℡0906/680 1268).

Brixham

From Paignton, it's a fifteen-minute bus ride down to **BRIXHAM**, the prettiest of the Torbay towns. For centuries fishing has been the port's lifeblood, and it still supplies fish to restaurants as far away as London. Among the trawlers on Brixham's quayside is moored a full-size reconstruction of the **Golden Hind** (daily: July–Aug 9am–10pm, Sept–June 10am–5pm; £2.50), the surprisingly small vessel in which Francis Drake circumnavigated the world, and where you can see the extremely cramped crew's quarters – it has no real connection with the port, however. The harbour is overlooked by an unflattering statue of William III, a reminder of his landing in Brixham to claim the crown of England in 1688. From here, steep lanes and stairways thread up to the older centre around Fore Street, where buses pull in.

From the harbour, you can reach the promontory of **Berry Head** along a path winding up from the *Berry Head House Hotel*. Fortifications built during the Napoleonic Wars are still standing on this southern limit of Torbay, which is now a conservation area, attracting colonies of nesting seabirds and affording fabulous views.

Brixham's **tourist office** (June to Sept daily 9.30am–6pm, Sun 10am–6pm; Oct Mon–Sat 9.30am–5pm; Nov–May Mon–Fri 9.30am–5pm; ☎0906/680 1268) is on the quayside, next to William's statue. For the views, the best **accommodation** is on King Street, overlooking the harbour, such as the *Harbour View Hotel*, at no. 65 (☎01803/853052, ⓦwww.s-h-systems.co.uk; ❷), with all rooms en suite, and the classier *Quayside Hotel* two doors down (☎01803/855751, ⓦwww.quaysidehotel.co.uk; ❺), which has two bars and a restaurant. Away from the harbour, the reputedly ghost-ridden *Smugglers' Haunt* on Church Hill (☎01803/853050, ⓦwww.smugglershaunt-hotel-devon .co.uk; ❸) is creaky and cramped, but useful if everywhere else is full; all rooms are en suite. There's a YHA **hostel** four miles away outside the village of Galmpton, on the banks of the Dart (☎0870/770 5962, Ⓔmaypool@yha.org.uk; closed Nov to mid-Feb; £10.25), a two-mile walk from Churston Bridge (bus #12 or #12A) – you can also get there on the Paignton & Dartmouth Steam Railway (see p.371), which passes right through the hostel's grounds.

When it comes to **eating options**, Brixham offers fish and more fish – from the harbourside stalls selling cockles, whelks and mussels to the moderately expensive *YardArms* (☎01803/858266; closed lunch & all Mon, plus all Tues in winter; no kids), on Beach Approach off the quayside, one of Brixham's top choices for seafood; there's also a wine bar here for cheaper lunchtime eats. For a relaxed pint, try the *Blue Anchor* on Fore Street, with coal fires and low beams.

Totnes

Most of the Plymouth buses from Paignton and Torquay make a stop at **TOTNES**, on the west bank of the River Dart. The town has an ancient pedigree, its period of greatest prosperity occurring in the sixteenth century when this inland port exported cloth to France and brought back wine. Some handsome structures from that era remain, and there is still a working port down on the river, but these days Totnes has mellowed into a residential market town, popular with the alternative and New Age crowd.

The town centres on the long main street that starts off as Fore Street, site of the town's **museum** (mid-March to Oct Mon–Fri 10.30am–5pm; £1.50), occupying a four-storey Elizabethan house at no. 70. Showing how wealthy clothiers lived at the peak of Totnes's fortunes, it's packed with domestic objects and furniture, and also has a room devoted to local mathematician Charles Babbage, whose "analytical engine" was the forerunner of the computer. Fore Street becomes the **High Street** at the East Gate, a much retouched medieval arch. Beneath it, Rampart Walk trails off along the old city walls, curving round the fifteenth-century church of **St Mary**, a red sandstone building inside which you can see an exquisitely carved rood screen. Behind the church, the eleventh-century **Guildhall** (April–Sept Mon–Wed 10.30am–3.30pm; £1) was originally the refectory and kitchen of a Benedictine priory. Granted to the city corporation in 1553, the building still houses the town's Council Chamber, which you can see together with the former jail cells and court-room.

Totnes **Castle** (April–Sept daily 10am–6pm; Oct daily 10am–5pm; £1.80; EH) on Castle Street – leading off the High Street – is a classic Norman structure of the motte and bailey design, its simple crenellated keep atop a grassy mound offering wide views of the town and Dart valley. Totnes assumes a much livelier air at the bottom of Fore Street, at river level. This is the highest navigable point on the **River Dart** for seagoing vessels, and there's constant activity around the craft arriving from and leaving for European destinations. There are also **cruises to Dartmouth** between Easter and October, leaving from the far bank at Steamer Quay (1hr 15min; £7 return; ☎01803/834488, ⓦwww.riverlink.co.uk). Riverside walks in either direction pass some congenial pubs, and near the railway bridge you can board a steam train of the **South Devon Railway** on its run along the course of the Dart to Buckfastleigh, adjacent to Buckfast Abbey (see p.382).

Practicalities

Totnes's **tourist office** is signposted off The Plains near the Safeway car park (Mon–Sat 9.30am–5pm; ☎01803/863168, ⓦwww.totnesinformation .co.uk). You'll find a range of **accommodation** in and around town. Opposite the castle car park on North Street, the *Elbow Room* (☎01803/863480, ⓔelbowroomtotnes@aol.com; no smoking; no credit cards; ❸) occupies a 200-year-old cottage and cider press, while the *Old Forge*, just over the river in Seymour Place (☎01803/862174; nonsmoking; ❸), is a medieval former forge with modernized rooms and a secluded walled garden. Above the town, *Acacias*, a ten-minute walk from the centre at 7 Cherry Cross (☎01803/867306; no smoking; no credit cards; ❷), offers views and organic, vegetarian and vegan breakfasts. The local **youth hostel** (☎0870/770 5788; closed Sept to mid-April; £10.25) is in a sixteenth-century cottage next to the River Bidwell, two miles from Totnes and half a mile from Shinner's Bridge (bus #X80).

You don't need to stray off the Fore Street/High Street axis to find a good place to **eat** in Totnes. *Willow*, 87 High St (☎01803/862605; closed Sun), has inexpensive vegetarian snacks, evening meals (Wed, Fri & Sat) and live music (Fri). Indonesian food is on offer at *Rickshaws*, 98 High St (☎01803/866171; closed Tues eve, plus all Sun & Mon), while *Rumour*, 30 High St, serves coffees, snacks and good-value full meals including pizzas (☎01803/864682; closed Sun lunch; no credit cards). Two of the nicest **pubs** are on the town's outskirts: the *Kingsbridge Inn* on Leechwell Street (off Kingsbridge Hill), and the *Steampacket*, by the riverside on St Peter's Quay (reached by walking west along The Plains), which is also good for evening meals.

A walkable couple of miles out of Totnes, **Dartington Hall** features a constant programme of films, performances and workshops – for details, call ☎01803/847870, or see ⓦwww.dartingtonarts.org.uk.

Dartmouth and around

South of Torbay, and eight miles downstream from Totnes, **DARTMOUTH** has thrived since the Normans recognized the trading potential of this deep-water port. Today its activities embrace fishing, freight, and a booming leisure industry, as well as the education of the senior service's officer class at the Royal Naval College, built at the start of this century on a hill overlooking the port. Coming from Torbay, visitors to Dartmouth can save time and a long detour through Totnes by using the frequent ferries crossing over the Dart's estuary from Kingswear (75p, £2.50 for cars), the last one at around 10.45pm (11.45pm Fri–Sun).

Behind the enclosed boat basin at the heart of town, the four-storey **Butterwalk**, built in the seventeenth century for a local merchant, is richly decorated with wood carvings. The timber-framed construction was restored after bombing in World War II, though still looks precarious as it overhangs the street on eleven granite columns. This arcade now holds shops and Dartmouth's small **museum** (Mon–Sat: April–Sept 11am–4.30pm; Oct–March noon–3pm; £1.50), mainly devoted to maritime curios, including old maps, prints and models of ships. Nearby **St Saviour's**, rebuilt in the 1630s from a fourteenth-century church, has long been a landmark for boats sailing upriver. The building stands at the head of Higher Street, the old town's central thoroughfare and the site of another tottering medieval structure, the *Cherub* inn. More impressive is **Agincourt House** on the parallel Lower Street, built by a merchant after the battle after which it is named, then restored in the seventeenth century and again in the twentieth.

Lower Street leads down to **Bayard's Cove**, a short cobbled quay lined with well-restored eighteenth-century houses, where the Pilgrim Fathers stopped en route to the New World. A twenty-minute walk from here along the river takes you to **Dartmouth Castle** (April–Sept daily 10am–6pm; Oct daily 10am–5pm; Nov–March Wed–Sun 10am–1pm & 2–4pm; £3.20; EH), one of two fortifications on opposite sides of the estuary. The site includes coastal defence works from the nineteenth century and from World War II, though the main interest is in the fifteenth-century castle, the first in England to be constructed specifically to withstand artillery. The castle was never actually tested in action, and consequently is excellently preserved. If you don't relish the return walk, you can take advantage of a ferry back to town, leaving roughly every fifteen minutes from Easter to October (£1).

Continuing south along the coastal path brings you through the pretty hill-top village of **Stoke Fleming** to **Blackpool Sands** (45min from the castle), the best and most popular beach in the area. The unspoilt cove, flanked by steep, wooded cliffs, was the site of a battle in 1404 in which Devon archers repulsed a Breton invasion force sent to punish the privateers of Dartmouth for their cross-Channel raiding.

From Dartmouth there are regular ferries across the river to **Kingswear**, terminus of the Paignton & Dartmouth Steam Railway (see p.371). There are various **cruises** from Dartmouth's quay up the River Dart, the best way to see the river's deep creeks and the various houses overlooking the river, among them the **Royal Naval College** and **Greenway House**, birthplace of Walter Raleigh's three seafaring half-brothers, the Gilberts, and later rebuilt for Agatha Christie.

Practicalities

Dartmouth's **tourist office** is opposite the car park at Mayor's Avenue (Jan & Feb Mon–Sat 9.30am–4pm; March–June & Sept to mid-Oct Mon–Sat

9.30am–5.30pm; July & Aug Mon–Sat 9.30am–5.30pm, Sun 10am–2pm; mid-Oct to Dec Mon–Sat 9.30am–5pm; ℡01803/834224, ⓦwww .dartmouth-information.co.uk).The less expensive **accommodation** is either at the top of steep hills or strung along Victoria Road, a continuation of Duke Street. The hill-top choices are preferable for their views, such as the spacious and elegant *Avondale* at 5 Vicarage Hill (℡01803/835831, ⓦwww .avondaledartmouth.co.uk; no credit cards; ❸), while good choices lower down include *Sunnybanks* at 1 Vicarage Hill (℡01803/832766, ⓦwww.sunnybanks .com; no credit cards; ❷), and, more centrally, *Café Caché*, 24 Duke St (℡01803/833804, ⓦwww.cafecache.co.uk; ❸), which has rooms above a café/restaurant. For something a little different, book a berth on the *Res Nova Inn* (℡07770/628967, ⓦwww.res-nova.co.uk; no credit cards; closed Nov–Easter; ❷), a barge moored in mid-river, to which guests are ferried from the quayside.

Dartmouth has a wide choice of **restaurants**, ranging from the relaxed *Café Alf Resco* on Lower Street, good for breakfasts and coffees and with out-door tables (daytime only, and evenings in summer; closed Mon & Tues), to the formal (and very expensive) *Carved Angel*, at 2 South Embankment (℡01803/832465; closed Sun eve, Mon lunch), a high-class seafood restaurant that also excels in game in winter, and has great harbourside views. If you're put off by the prices and ambience, drop into its inexpensive off-shoot, the *Carved Angel Café* at 7 Foss St (℡01803/834842; no smoking; closed Mon–Wed eve & all Sun). The *Res Nova Inn* (see above) also offers excellent fish suppers, including fresh lobster; call to be picked up (closed Nov–Easter).

Salcombe and around

The area between the Dart and Plym estuaries, the **South Hams**, holds some of Devon's comeliest villages and most striking coastline.The "capital" of the region, **Kingsbridge**, is a useful transport hub but lacks the appeal of **SALCOMBE**, almost at the mouth of the Kingsbridge estuary and Devon's southernmost resort, reachable on a summer ferry from Kingsbridge. Once a nondescript fishing village, Salcombe is now a full-blown sailing and holiday centre, its calm waters strewn with small pleasure craft. Enough fishing activity and working boatyards remain to give the place a sense of purpose, while the ruined Fort Charles at the harbour entrance injects a touch of romance amid the villas and hotels. You can bone up on boating and local history at **Salcombe Maritime Museum** on Market Street, off the north end of the central Fore Street (Easter–Oct 10.30am–12.30pm & 2.30–4.30pm; £1). From a quay off Fore Street, you can take a **ferry** down to the beach at South Sands (Easter–Oct every 30min; £2.20), from where it's a fifteen-minute climb to the excellent **Overbecks Museum** (April–July & Sept Mon–Fri & Sun 11am–5.30pm; Aug daily 11am–5.30pm; Oct Mon–Thurs & Sun 11am–5pm; garden open daily all year 10am–7pm; £4.40; NT), which focuses on the area's natural history. There's great coastal walking south and west of here, eventually leading to sandy **beaches** at Thurlestone and, across the Avon estuary, Bigbury-on-Sea, while the path eastwards from **East Portlemouth** – accessible by ferry from Salcombe's quay – takes in some craggily photogenic scenery around Gammon Point and Prawle Point.

Salcombe's **tourist office** is on Market Street (Easter to mid-July, Sept & Oct daily 10am–5pm; mid-July to Aug Mon–Sat 9am–5pm, Sun 10am–5pm; Nov–March Mon–Thurs 10am–3pm, Fri & Sat 10am–5pm; ℡01548/843927,

@ www.salcombeinformation.co.uk). Many of the town's **B&Bs** enjoy excellent estuary views, for example *Rocarno* on Grenville Road (℡01548/842732, @ rocarno@aol.com; no credit cards; ➋). Near the car park on Shadycombe Road, there's the timber-framed *Old Tree House* (℡01548/843670, @ suehobbs1@aol.com; ➌) and *The Old Porch House* (℡01548/842157; ➌), which dates back to 1660. Part of Overbeck's Museum (see above) houses a capacious **youth hostel** (℡0870/770 6016; closed Nov to mid-April; £11.50), while local **campsites** include *Alston Farm* (℡01548/561260, @ www.welcome.to/alstonfarm), signposted off the A381 Marlborough road.

Plymouth and around

PLYMOUTH's predominantly bland and modern face belies its great historic role as a naval base and, in the sixteenth century, the stamping ground of such national heroes as John Hawkins and Francis Drake. It was from here that Drake sailed to defeat the Spanish Armada in 1588, and 32 years later the port was the last embarkation point for the Pilgrim Fathers, whose New Plymouth colony became the nucleus for the English settlement of North America. The importance of the city's Devonport dockyards made the city a target in World War II, when the Luftwaffe reduced most of the old centre to rubble. Subsequent reconstruction has done little to improve the place, though it would be difficult to spoil the glorious vista over **Plymouth Sound**, the basin of calm water at the mouth of the combined Plym, Tavy and Tamar estuaries, largely unchanged since Drake played his famous game of bowls on the Hoe before joining battle with the Armada.

One of the best local excursions from Plymouth is to **Mount Edgcumbe**, where woods and meadows provide a welcome antidote to the urban bustle, and are within easy reach of some fabulous sand. East of Plymouth, the aristocratic opulence of **Saltram House** includes some fine art and furniture, while to the north you can visit Drake's old residence at **Buckland Abbey**.

The City

A good place to start a tour of the city is **Plymouth Hoe**, an immense esplanade studded with reminders of the great events in the city's history, and with glorious views over the sea. Approaching from the town centre, the most distinctive landmark is a tall white naval war memorial, standing alongside smaller monuments to the defeat of the Spanish Armada and to the airmen who defended the city during the wartime blitz, and a rather portly statue of Sir Francis Drake, gazing grandly out to the sea. Appropriately, there's a bowling green back from the brow.

In front of the memorials, the red-and-white-striped **Smeaton's Tower** (Easter–Sept 10.30am–4.30pm; £2, combined ticket with Plymouth Dome £6) was erected in 1759 by John Smeaton on the treacherous Eddystone Rocks, fourteen miles out to sea. When replaced by a larger lighthouse in 1882, it was reassembled here, where it gives the loftiest view over Plymouth Sound. Below Smeaton's Tower, **Plymouth Dome** (April–Oct daily 10am–5pm, Nov–March Tues–Sat 10am–4pm; last entry 1hr before closing; £4.50, combined ticket with Smeaton's Tower £6) has audiovisual exhibitions on Plymouth's history, Drake, the Mayflower Pilgrims and Captain Cook. On the seafront, Plymouth's **Royal Citadel** (June–Sept tours at 2.30pm; £3; EH) is an uncompromising fortress constructed in 1666, whose older sections, including

Francis Drake

Born around 1540 near Tavistock, **Francis Drake** worked in the domestic coastal trade from the age of 13, but was soon taking part in the first English slaving expeditions between Africa and the West Indies, led by his Plymouth kinsman John Hawkins. Later, Drake was active in the secret war against Spain, raiding and looting merchant ships in actions unofficially sanctioned by Elizabeth I. In 1572 he became the first Englishman to sight the Pacific, and soon afterwards, on board the *Golden Hind*, became the first one to **circumnavigate the world**, for which he received a knighthood on his return in 1580. The following year Drake was made mayor of Plymouth, settling in Buckland Abbey (see p.379), but was back in action before long – in 1587 he "singed the king of Spain's beard" by entering Cadiz harbour and destroying 33 vessels that were to have formed part of Philip II's **armada**. When the replacement invasion fleet appeared in the English Channel in 1588, Drake – along with Raleigh, Hawkins and Frobisher – played a leading role in wrecking it. The following year he set off on an unsuccessful expedition to help the Portuguese against Spain, but otherwise most of the next decade was spent in relative inactivity in Plymouth, Exeter and London. Finally, in 1596 Drake left with Hawkins for a raid on Panama, a venture that cost the lives of both captains.

Drake has come to personify the Elizabethan Age's swashbuckling expansionism and patriotism, but England's naval triumphs were as much the result of John Hawkins' humbler work in building and maintaining a new generation of warships as they were of the skill and bravery of their captains. Drake was simply the most flamboyant of a generation of reckless and brilliant mariners who broke the Spanish hegemony on the high seas, laying the foundations for England's later imperialist pursuits.

the Governor's House and the Royal Chapel of St Katherine, can be seen on 90-minute tours (tickets from the Plymouth Dome and the tourist office).

Round the corner, the old town's quay at **Sutton Harbour** is still used by the trawler fleet. The **Mayflower Steps** here commemorate the sailing of the Pilgrim Fathers and a nearby plaque lists the names and professions of the 102 Puritans on board. Captain Cook's voyages to the South Seas, Australia and the Antarctic also started from here, as did the nineteenth-century transport ships to Australia, carrying thousands of convicts and colonists. Edging the harbour, the **Barbican** district is the heart of old Plymouth. Most of the buildings are now shops and restaurants, but off the quayside, New Street holds most of the oldest buildings, among them the **Elizabethan House** (April–Sept Wed–Sun 10am–5pm; £1.10), a captain's dwelling retaining most of the original architectural features. Cross the bridge over Sutton Harbour to reach the **National Marine Aquarium** (daily: April–Oct 10am–6pm; Nov–March 10am–5pm; last entry 1hr before closing; £8), a grand complex on three levels where a range of marine environments have been re-created, from moorland stream to coral reef and deep-sea ocean. The live exhibits include everything from sea horses to sharks.

Practicalities

Plymouth's **train station** is off Saltash Road (connected to the centre by bus #25a), the **bus station** is at Bretonside, just over St Andrew's Cross from Royal Parade, and the **tourist office** is off Sutton Harbour at 9 The Barbican (April–Oct Mon–Sat 9am–5pm, Sun 10am–4pm; Nov–March Mon–Fri 9am–5pm, Sat 10am–4pm; ☎0870/225 4950, ⓦwww.visitplymouth.co.uk).

Internet access is available from the Carp Internet Café, 32 Franfort Gate (Mon–Sat 9am–5pm; ☎01752/221777).

The city's **accommodation** includes a row of B&Bs edging the Hoe on Citadel Road, for example *Acorns and Lawns*, at no. 171 (☎01752/229474; no credit cards; ❶), and *The Beeches*, at no. 175 (☎01752/266475; no credit cards; ❶). On the west side of the Hoe, the smart *Bowling Green Hotel*, 9–10 Osborne Place, Lockyer Street (☎01752/209090, ⊛www.bowlinggreenhotel.com; ❸), overlooks Francis Drake's fabled haunt, while *Osmond Guest House*, 42 Pier St (☎01752/229705, ✉mike@osmondgh.freeserve.co.uk; no smoking; ❷), is nearer the Great Western Docks and offers a pick-up service from the bus and train stations. There's also an independent **hostel** on the hotel strip near the Hoe and Royal Parade, *Plymouth Backpackers*, 172 Citadel Rd (☎01752/225158, ⊛www.backpackers.co.uk/plymouth; £10), with double rooms available (❶).

You'll find a wildly eclectic range of **restaurants** in Plymouth's Barbican area. One of the best seafood places is *Piermaster's*, 3 Southside St (☎01752/229345; closed Sun), whose kitchen is supplied straight from the nearby harbour, while tasty Italian dishes draw the crowds at the more casual *Pasta Bar* across the road. At the top of Southside, the inexpensive *Barbican Revival* on Notte Street is a Mexican/Italian/American diner with lots of jazzy ambience. Plymouth Arts Centre, 38 Looe St, has a vegetarian restaurant (closed all Sun & Mon eve), useful for anyone coming here for its exhibitions, films and live performances (☎01752/206114, ⊛www.plymouthac.org.uk).

The *Dolphin* **pub** on Southside Street serves simple lunchtime snacks and good ales, while *The Cooperage*, 134 Vauxhall St (☎01752/229275, ⊛www .thecooperage.co.uk), has **live bands** and club nights.

Mount Edgcumbe, Saltram House and Buckland Abbey

Lying on the Cornish side of Plymouth Sound and visible from the Hoe, **MOUNT EDGCUMBE** features richly landscaped gardens and acres of rolling parkland and coastal paths. The **house** (April to Sept Mon–Thurs & Sun 11am–4.30pm; £4.50) is a reconstruction of the bomb-damaged Tudor original, though inside the predominant note is eighteenth-century, the rooms elegantly restored with authentic Regency furniture. Far more enticing are the impeccable **gardens** divided into French, Italian and English sections – the first two a blaze of flowerbeds adorned with classical statuary, the last an acre of sweeping lawn shaded by exotic trees – while the **park**, which is free and open all year, gives access to the coastal path. You can reach Edgcumbe by passenger **ferry** to Cremyll, leaving at least hourly from Admiral's Hard, a small mooring in Plymouth's Stonehouse district (bus #34 from the Guildhall), or, in summer, by direct motor launch from the Mayflower Steps to **Cawsand**, an old smugglers' haunt two hours' walk from the house. Cawsand itself is just a mile from the southern tip of the huge **Whitsand Bay**, the best bathing beach for miles around.

The remodelled Tudor mansion **SALTRAM HOUSE** (open Mon–Thurs, Sat & Sun: April–Sept noon–4.30pm: Oct 11.30am–3.30pm; garden same days April–Sept 11am–5pm; Nov–March 11am–4pm; £6.30, garden only £3.30, less in winter; NT), two miles east of Plymouth off the A38, is Devon's largest country house, featuring work by the great architect Robert Adam and fourteen portraits by **Joshua Reynolds**, who was born nearby in Plympton. Showpiece is the Saloon, a fussy but exquisitely furnished room dripping with gilt and plaster, and set off by a huge Axminster carpet especially woven for it in 1770. Saltram's landscaped park provides a breather from this riot of interior design, though it's marred by the proximity of the road. You can get here on the hourly #22 bus (not Sun) from Royal Parade to Merafield Road, from where it's a fifteen-minute signposted walk.

Six miles north of Plymouth, close to the River Tavy and on the edge of Dartmoor, **BUCKLAND ABBEY** (mid-April to Oct Mon–Wed & Fri–Sun 10.30am–5.30pm; Nov to late Dec & mid-Feb to March Sat & Sun 2–5pm; £5, grounds only £2.70; NT) was once the most westerly of England's Cistercian abbeys. After its dissolution Buckland was converted to a family home by the privateer Richard Grenville (cousin of Walter Raleigh), from whom the estate was acquired by Sir Francis Drake in 1582, the year after he became mayor of Plymouth. It remained his home until his death, though the house reveals few traces of Drake's residence. There are, however, numerous maps, portraits and mementoes of his buccaneering exploits on show, most famous of which is Drake's Drum, which was said to beat a supernatural warning of impending danger to the country. The house stands in majestic grounds which contain a fine fourteenth-century **Great Barn**, buttressed and gabled and larger than the abbey itself. To get here, take bus #84, #85 or #86 from Plymouth to Tavistock, changing at Yelverton for the hourly #55a minibus (not Sun).

Dartmoor

Occupying the main part of the county between Exeter and Plymouth, **DARTMOOR** is southern England's greatest expanse of wilderness, some 365 square miles of raw granite, barren bogland, sparse grass and heather-grown moor. It was not always so desolate, as testified by the remnants of scattered Stone Age settlements and the ruined relics of the area's nineteenth-century tin-mining industry. Today desultory flocks of sheep and groups of ponies are virtually the only living creatures to be seen wandering over the central fastnesses of the National Park, with solitary birds – buzzards, kestrels, pipits, stonechats and wagtails – wheeling and hovering high above.

The core of Dartmoor, characterized by tumbling streams and high tors chiselled by the elements, is **Dartmoor Forest**, which has belonged to the Duchy of Cornwall since 1307, though there is almost unlimited public access. Networks of signposts or painted stones exist to guide **walkers**, but map-reading abilities are a prerequisite for any but the shortest walks, and a good deal of experience is essential for longer distances. Note that it is not allowed to park overnight in unauthorized places, and no vehicles are permitted beyond fifteen yards from the road; camping should be out of sight of houses and roads, but fires are strictly forbidden. Information on **guided walks** and riding facilities is available from National Park Visitor Centres in Dartmoor's major towns and villages, and from information points in smaller villages.

Much to the irritation of locals and visitors alike, the **Ministry of Defence** has appropriated a significant portion of northern Dartmoor, an area that contains its highest tors and some of its most famous beauty spots. The MoD firing ranges are marked by red and white posts; when firing is in progress, red flags or red lights signify that entry is prohibited. As a general rule, you can assume that if no warning flags are flying by 9am between April and September, or by 10am from October to March, there is to be no firing

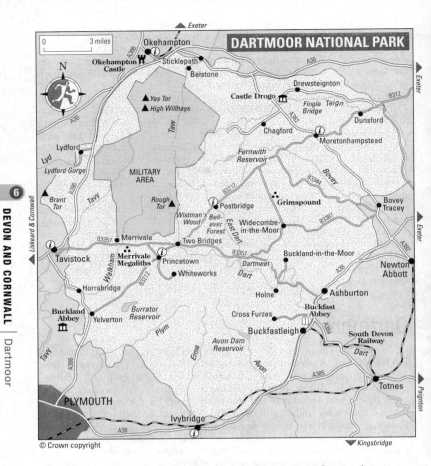

on that day; alternatively, check at ☎0800/458 4868 or ⓦwww.dartmoor-ranges.co.uk.

Princetown and the central moor

PRINCETOWN owes its growth to the proximity of Dartmoor Prison, a high-security jail originally constructed for POWs captured in the Napoleonic Wars. The grim presence seeps into the village, which has a somewhat oppressed air and functional grey stone houses, some of them – like the parish church of St Michael – built by French and American prisoners. What Princetown lacks in beauty is amply compensated for by the surrounding countryside, the best of which lies immediately to the north.

Information on all of Dartmoor is given by the main **National Park information centre**, on the village's central green (daily: Easter–Oct 10am–5pm; Nov–March 10am–4pm; ☎01822/890414, ⓦwww.dartmoor-npa.gov.uk). One of the best **places to stay** locally is the nonsmoking *Duchy House* on Tavistock Road (☎01822/890552, ⓔduchyhouse@aol.com; ❾; closed Nov), while two pubs in Princetown's central square also offer accommodation, the

Railway Inn (℡01822/890232; ②) and the *Plume of Feathers* (℡01822/890240; ①), claimed to be the oldest building in town, and also offering dormitory accommodation in two bunkhouses as well as a convenient **campsite**. Standard bar food is available from both pubs.

Northeast of Princetown, two miles north of the crossroads at Two Bridges, the dwarfed and misshapen oaks of **Wistman's Wood** are an evocative relic of the original Dartmoor Forest, cluttered with lichen-covered boulders and a dense undergrowth of ferns. The gnarled old trees are alleged to have been the site of druidic gatherings, a story unsupported by any evidence but quite plausible in this solitary spot.

Three miles northeast of Two Bridges, the largest and best preserved of Dartmoor's **clapper bridges** crosses the East Dart river at **POSTBRIDGE**. Used by tin miners and farmers since medieval times, these simple structures consist of huge slabs of granite supported by piers of the same material; another more basic example is at Two Bridges. Postbridge has a useful tourist office in the car park near the bridge (Easter–Oct 10am–5pm, Nov & Dec Sat & Sun 10am–4pm; ℡01822/880213). If you're not content with strolling up and down the river here, you might decide to venture south through **Bellever Forest** to the open moor where **Bellever Tor** (1453ft) affords outstanding views. On the edge of the forest, a mile or so south of Postbridge on the banks of the East Dart river, lies one of Dartmoor's three **youth hostels** (℡0870/770 5692, ✉bellever@yha.org.uk; closed Nov–Feb; £10.25) – it's on a minor road from Postbridge, accessible on Plymouth Citybus #98 from Tavistock, or else walk from Postbridge. There's also a **camping barn** close to Bellever Forest at Runnage Farm, with a bunkhouse and outdoor camping facilities alongside and bikes available for hire (for this and any of Dartmoor's other camping barns, it's wise to book ahead, particularly at weekends: ℡0870/770 6113, ✉campingbarns@yha.org.uk). You'll find a lot more luxury in the riverside *Lydgate House Hotel*, signposted off the main road half a mile southwest of Postbridge and offering easy access to Bellever Forest and the moor (℡01822/880209, ⊛www.lydgatehouse.co.uk; no under-12s and no smoking; ⑤). Two miles northeast of Postbridge, the solitary *Warren House Inn* offers warm, firelit comfort and **meals** in an unutterably bleak tract of moorland.

To the east of the B3212, reachable on a right turn towards Widecombe-in-the-Moor, the Bronze Age village of **Grimspound** lies below Hameldown Tor, about a mile off the road. Inhabited some three thousand years ago, this is the most complete example of Dartmoor's prehistoric settlements, consisting of 24 circular huts scattered within a four-acre enclosure. The site is thought to have been the model for the Stone Age settlement in which Sherlock Holmes camped in *The Hound of the Baskervilles*, while **Hound Tor**, an outcrop three miles to the southwest, was the inspiration for Conan Doyle's tale – according to local legend, phantom hounds were sighted racing across the moor to hurl themselves on the tomb of a hated squire following his death in 1677. There's a **camping barn** here, *Great Houndtor*, with two upstairs sleeping areas, a cooking area and showers (℡0870/770 6113 or ℡01647/221202).

Widecombe-in-the-Moor and the southeastern moor

Four miles east of the crossroads at Two Bridges, **Dartmeet** marks the place where the East and West Dart rivers merge after tortuous journeys from their remote sources. Crowds home in on this beauty spot, but the valley is memorably lush and you don't need to walk far to leave the car park and ice-cream vans behind. From here the Dart pursues a more leisurely course, joined by the River Webburn near the pretty moorland village of **BUCK-LAND-IN-THE-MOOR**, one of a cluster of moorstone-and-thatched hamlets on this southeastern side of the moor.

Four miles north, **WIDECOMBE-IN-THE-MOOR** is set in a hollow amid high granite-strewn ridges. Its church of **St Pancras** provides a famous local landmark, its pinnacled tower dwarfing the fourteenth-century main building, whose interior boasts a beautiful painted rood screen. The nearby **Church House** was built in the fifteenth century for weary churchgoers from outlying districts, and was later converted into almshouses. Widecombe's other claim to fame is the traditional song, *Widdicombe Fair*: the **fair** is still held annually on the second Tuesday of September, but is now primarily a tourist attraction. You could **stay** in Widecombe at the elegant *Old Rectory* (☎01364/621231, ✉rachel.belgrave@care4free.net; no credit cards; ❷), opposite the post office and set in a lovely garden; or try *Manor Cottage* (☎01364/621218; no credit cards; ❷), next to the post office.

South of Buckland, the village of **HOLNE** is another rustic idyll surrounded on three sides by wooded valleys. The vicarage here was the birthplace of Charles Kingsley, author of *The Water Babies* and such Devon-based tales as *Westward Ho!*. A couple of miles east, the Dart weaves through a wooded green valley to enter the grounds of **Buckfast Abbey** (daily: May–Oct 9am–5.30pm; Nov–April 10am–4pm; free), a modern monastic complex on the site of an abbey founded in the eleventh century by Canute, abandoned two hundred years later, refounded, and finally dissolved by Henry VIII. The present buildings were the work of a handful of French Benedictine monks who consecrated their new abbey in 1932. The traditional Anglo-Norman style follows the design of the Cistercian building razed in 1535.

The northeastern moor

On the northeastern edge of the moor, the market town of **MORETON-HAMPSTEAD** makes an attractive entry point from Exeter. Local **information** is handled by a Visitor Information Point at 10 The Square (Easter–Oct daily 10am–5pm; Nov–Easter Fri–Sun 10am–5pm; ☎01647/440043). There's classy **accommodation** on the western edge of the village in the *Old Post House* in Court Street (☎01647/440900, ⓦwww.theoldposthouse.com; no credit cards; nonsmoking; ❷), a friendly B&B which welcomes walkers and will set you up with a packed lunch if required, and at *Cookshayes*, a little further out at 33 Court St (☎01647/440374, ⓦwww.cookshayes.co.uk; ❷; closed Nov–Feb), offering good home cooking. The village also has a first-rate independent **hostel**, *Sparrowhawk Backpackers*, at 45 Ford St (☎01647/440318, ⓦwww.sparrowhawkbackpackers.co.uk; £11), which has some private rooms (❶), and there's the *Steps Bridge* youth hostel (☎0870/770 6048, ✉bellever@yha.org.uk; closed Sept–March; dorm beds £9) on the outskirts of **Dunsford**, three miles northeast of Moretonhampstead on the boundary of the National Park – buses #359 (not Sun) and #82 stop nearby. Its woodland setting overlooking the Teign Gorge makes it a popular overnight stop for hikers.

Moretonhampstead has a historic rivalry with neighbouring **CHAGFORD**, a Stannary town (a chartered centre of the tin trade) that also enjoyed prosperity as a centre of the wool industry. It stands on a hillside overlooking the River Teign, with a fine fifteenth-century church and some good **accommo-**

dation possibilities – such as the ancient *Three Crowns Hotel* (℡01647/433444, Ⓦwww.chagford-accom.co.uk; ❹), facing the church, or the sixteenth-century *Cyprian's Cot*, 47 New St (℡01647/432256, Ⓦwww.dartmooraccommodation .co.uk; no credit cards; no smoking; ❸). There's also a renowned and very expensive **restaurant** here, the nonsmoking *22 Mill Street* (℡01647/432244, Ⓦwww.22millstreet.co.uk; closed Sun and lunchtime Mon & Tues), which offers pricey, but top-quality modern cuisine. For diners only, there are also two en-suite rooms available (❸).

Numerous **walks** can be made in the immediate vicinity, for instance downstream along the Teign to the twentieth-century extravaganza of **Castle Drogo** (April–Oct Mon & Wed–Sun 11am–5.30pm; grounds daily 10.30am–dusk; £5.90, grounds only £3; NT), stupendously sited overlooking the Teign gorge. Having retired at the age of 33, grocery magnate Julius Drewe unearthed a link that suggested his descent from a Norman baron, and set about creating a castle befitting his pedigree. Begun in 1910, to a design by **Edwin Lutyens**, it was not completed until 1930, but the result was an unsurpassed synthesis of medieval and modern elements. Paths lead from Drogo east to **Fingle Bridge**, a noted beauty spot, where shaded green pools hold trout and the occasional salmon. The *Fingle Bridge Inn* here has an adjoining **restaurant**.

The north and northwestern moor

The main centre on the northern fringes of Dartmoor, **OKEHAMPTON** grew prosperous as a market town for the medieval wool trade, and some fine old buildings survive between the two branches of the River Okement that meet here, among them the prominent fifteenth-century tower of the **Chapel of St James**. Across the road from the seventeenth-century town hall, a granite archway leads into the **Museum of Dartmoor Life** (Easter–Sept Mon–Sat 10am–5pm, Sun 10am–4.30pm; Oct–Easter Mon–Sat 10am–5pm; £2.50), an excellent overview of habitation on the moor since earliest times. Perched above the West Okement southwest of the centre, **Okehampton Castle** (April–Sept daily 10am–6pm; Oct daily 10am–5pm; £2.60; EH) is the shattered hulk of a stronghold laid waste by Henry VIII; its ruins include a gatehouse, Norman keep and the remains of the Great Hall, buttery and kitchens.

Okehampton's station, which provides a useful Sunday **rail** connection with Exeter between late May and late September, lies a fifteen-minute walk up Station Road from Fore Street, where the **tourist office** (April, May & mid-Sept to Oct Mon–Sat 10am–4.30pm; June to mid-Sept daily 10am–5pm; Nov–March Mon, Fri & Sat 10am–4.30pm; ℡01837/53020, Ⓦwww .okehamptondevon.co.uk) sits next to the museum. Nearby on Fore Street, the beamed *Fountain Hotel* (℡01837/53900; no smoking; ❹), an old coaching inn, offers rooms with character, though cheaper **B&B** can be found a short walk north of here towards the station at *Meadowlea*, 65 Station Rd (℡01837/53200; no credit cards; ❷). If you prefer rural surroundings, the comfortable and spacious *Upcott House* lies half a mile north of the centre on Upcott Hill (℡01837/53743, Ⓦwww.upcotthouse.com; no credit cards; ❷). Okehampton's **youth hostel** (℡0870/770 5978, Ⓔokehampton@yha.org.uk; closed Dec & Jan; £13) is housed in a converted goods shed at the station, and offers a range of outdoor activities. The nicest **campsites** locally are the small *Yertiz* (℡01837/52281), less than a mile east of Okehampton on the B3260, and *Olditch Caravan and Camping Park*, Sticklepath (℡01837/840734, Ⓦwww.olditch.co.uk; closed mid-Nov to mid-March), which has walking access to the moor.

Okehampton has no great choice when it comes to **eating**, though the *Coffee Pot*, tucked away behind the museum in Fairplace Terrace, can be relied upon for breakfasts, coffees and meals (closed eve & Mon), while *Cellars Bistro*, a candlelit basement beside the river at 25 Fore St (℡01837/54242; no smoking; closed Sun & Mon), offers light lunches and moderately priced evening meals, with Mediterranean specialities.

Lydford

Five miles southwest of Okehampton, the village of **LYDFORD** boasts the sturdy but small-scale Lydford Castle, a Saxon outpost, then a Norman keep and later used as a prison. The chief attraction here, though, is **Lydford Gorge** (April–Sept 10am–5.30pm; Oct 10am–4pm; Nov–March 10.30am–3pm; £3.80; NT), whose main entrance is a five-minute walk downhill. Two routes – one above, one along the banks – follow the ravine burrowed through by the River Lyd as far as the hundred-foot White Lady Waterfall, coming back on the opposite bank. Overgrown with thick woods, the one-and-a-half-mile gorge is alive with butterflies, spotted woodpeckers, dippers, herons and clouds of insects. The full course would take you roughly two hours at a leisurely pace, though there is a separate entrance at the south end of the gorge if you only want to visit the waterfall. In winter months, when the river can flood, the waterfall is the only part of the gorge open.

Back in the village, the picturesque *Castle Inn*, right next to the castle, provides a beer garden and a fire-lit sixteenth-century bar for drinks and snacks, a quality **restaurant** in a curio-cluttered back room, and **accommodation** in oak-beamed rooms (℡01822/820242, @castleinnlyd@aol.com; ❹). Cheaper rooms are available at the family-run *Moorlands* (℡01822/820229; no credit cards; ❸), 300yds from the A386 on the Lydford turning.

Tavistock

The main town of the western moor, **TAVISTOCK** owes its distinctive Victorian appearance to the building boom that followed the discovery of copper deposits here in 1844. Originally, however, this market and Stannary town on the River Tavy grew around what was once the West Country's most important Benedictine abbey, established in the eleventh century. Some scant remnants survive in the churchyard of **St Eustace**, a mainly fifteenth-century building with stained glass from William Morris's studio in the south aisle.

Tavistock's **tourist office** is in the town hall on Bedford Square (Easter to late July & early Sept to Oct Mon–Sat 9.30am–5pm; late July to early Sept daily 9.30am–5pm; Nov–Easter Mon, Tues, Fri & Sat 10am–4.30pm; ℡01822/612938). Local **accommodation** choices include *Kingfisher Cottage*, Mount Tavy Road (℡01822/613801028, @kingfisher.cott@btopenworld.com; no smoking; no credit cards; ❷), and, about half a mile east of Tavistock off the B3357 Princetown Road, *Mount Tavy Cottage* (℡01822/614253, @www.mounttavy.freeserve.co.uk; ❸), set in a lush garden and offering organic breakfasts. Two miles east of Tavistock on the same road, campers can find a pitch at *Higher Longford*, near Merrivale (℡01822/613360, @www.higherlongford.co.uk).

North of Tavistock, a four-mile lane wanders up to **Brent Tor**, 1130 feet high and dominating Dartmoor's western fringes. Access to its conical summit is easiest along a path gently ascending through gorse on its southwestern side, leading to the small church of St Michael at the top. Bleak, treeless moorland extends in every direction, wrapped in silence that's occasionally pierced by the shrill cries of stonechats and wheatears. A couple of miles eastwards, **Gibbet**

Hill looms over Black Down and the ruined stack of the abandoned Wheal Betsy silver and lead mine.

North Devon

From Exeter the A377 runs alongside the scenic Tarka Line railway to **North Devon**'s major town, **Barnstaple**. Within easy reach of here, the resorts of **Ilfracombe** and **Woolacombe** draw the crowds, though the fine sandy beaches surrounding the latter give ample opportunity to find your own space. The river port of **Bideford** gives its name to a long bay that holds the precipitous village of **Clovelly**, a famous beauty spot. Away from the coast, there is plenty of scope for walking and cycling along the Tarka Trail, passing through some of the region's loveliest countryside. For a complete break, the tiny island of **Lundy** provides further opportunities for stretching the legs and clearing the lungs.

Barnstaple

BARNSTAPLE, at the head of the Taw estuary, makes an excellent North Devon base, being well connected to the resorts of Bideford Bay, Ilfracombe and Woolacombe, as well as to the western fringes of Exmoor. The town's centuries-old role as a marketplace is perpetuated in the daily bustle around the huge timber-framed **Pannier Market** off the High Street, alongside which runs **Butchers Row**, its 33 archways now converted to a variety of uses. Also off the High Street, in the pedestrianized area between it and Boutport Street, lies Barnstaple's **parish church**, itself worth a look, and the fourteenth-century

---

The Tarka Line and the Tarka Trail

North Devon makes no secret of its association with Henry Williamson's *Tarka the Otter* (1927), rated by some as one of the finest pieces of nature writing in the English language. With parts of the book set in the Taw valley, it was inevitable that the Exeter to Barnstaple rail route – which follows the Taw for half of its length – should be dubbed the **Tarka Line**. Leaving almost hourly from Exeter St David's station, trains on this branch line cut through the sparsely populated heart of Devon, the biggest town en route being **Crediton**, ancient birthplace of St Boniface (patron saint of Germany and the Netherlands) and site of the bishopric before its transfer to Exeter in the eleventh century.

Barnstaple forms the centre of the figure-of-eight traced by the **Tarka Trail**, which tracks the otter's wanderings for a distance of over 180 miles. To the north, the trail penetrates Exmoor then follows the coast back, passing through Williamson's home village of **Georgeham** on its return to Barnstaple. South, the path takes in Bideford (see p.387), and continues as far as Okehampton (see p.383), before swooping up via Eggesford, the point at which the Tarka Line joins the Taw valley.

Twenty-three miles of the trail follow a former rail line that's ideally suited to **bicycles**, and there are rental shops at Barnstaple and Bideford. Sculptures have been placed along the route to mark its inclusion in the National Cycle Network. A good ride from Barnstaple is to **Torrington** (fifteen miles south), where you can eat at the *Puffing Billy* pub, formerly the train station.

Tourist offices give out leaflets on individual sections of the trail, but the best overall book is *The Tarka Trail: A Walker's Guide* (Devon Books; £4.95), available from tourist offices or bookshops.

St Anne's Chapel, converted into a grammar school in 1549 and later numbering among its pupils John Gay, author of *The Beggar's Opera*; it's now closed to the public. At the end of Boutport Street, the **Museum of North Devon** (Tues–Sat 10am–4.30pm; free) is a lively miscellany and includes a collection of the eighteenth-century pottery for which the region was famous. The museum lies alongside the Taw, where footpaths make for a pleasant riverside stroll, with the colonnaded eighteenth-century **Queen Anne's Walk** – built as a merchants' exchange – providing some architectural interest and housing the **Barnstaple Heritage Centre** (April–Oct Mon–Sat 10am–5pm; Nov–March Mon–Fri 10am–4.30pm, Sat 10am–3.30pm; £2.50), which traces the town's social history by means of reconstructions and touch-screen computers.

Barnstaple's well-equipped **tourist office** is at the Museum of North Devon (Mon–Sat 9.30am–5pm; ℡01271/375000, ⓦwww.staynorthdevon .co.uk). Local accommodation choices include, five hundred yards south of Long Bridge, *Ivy House*, Victoria Road, off Newport Road (℡01271/325167, ⓔivy.grundy@btopenworld.com; no smoking; no credit cards; ❷), an elegant, sometimes noisy, B&B. A little further out, on Landkey Road – a continuation of Newport Road – is the first-rate *Mount Sandford* (℡01271/342354; no credit cards; ❷), a Regency building with a beautiful garden. With your own transport, you could stay at *Broomhill Art Hotel*, Muddiford, signposted two miles north of Barnstaple off the A39, a striking combination of gallery, restaurant and hotel (℡01271/850262, ⓦwww.broomhillart.co.uk; no credit cards; ❹).

You can pick up coffees and **snacks** at the *Old School Coffee House*, a building dating from 1659 on Church Lane, near St Anne's Chapel, while the coolly modern *PV*, 70 Boutport St (closed Sun), has a moderately priced upstairs **restaurant** and the ground floor becomes a wine bar in the evening. On Butchers Row, *Jan's Kitchen* and *Marshford Organic Produce* both sell baguettes, pasties, pies, and wholefoods to take away.

Ilfracombe and around

The most popular resort on Devon's northern coast, **ILFRACOMBE** is essentially little changed since its evolution into a Victorian and Edwardian tourist centre, large-scale development having been restricted by the surrounding cliffs. Nonetheless, the relentless pressure to have fun and the ubiquitous smell of chips can become oppressive, though in summer you can always pop down to the small harbour and escape on a coastal tour, a fishing trip or a cruise to Lundy Island (see p.389). An attractive stretch of coast runs east out of Ilfracombe, beyond the grassy cliffs of Hillsborough, where a succession of undeveloped coves and inlets is surrounded by jagged slanting rocks and heather-covered hills. There are sandy **beaches** here, though many prefer those beyond **Morte Point**, five miles west of Ilfracombe, from which the view takes in the island of Lundy, fifteen miles out to sea. Below the promontory stretches a rocky shore whose menacing sunken reef inspired the Normans to give it the name Morte Stone. A break in the rocks makes space for the pocket-sized **Barricane Beach**, famous for the tropical shells washed here from the Caribbean by the Atlantic currents, and a popular swimming spot. There's more space on the two miles of **Woolacombe Sands**, a broad, west-facing expanse much favoured by surfers and families alike. The beach can get crowded towards its northern end, where a cluster of hotels, villas and retirement homes makes up the summer resort of **WOOLACOMBE**. At the quieter southern end, **Putsborough Sands** is a choice swimming spot bracketed by **Baggy Point**, where from September to November the air is a swirl of gannets, shags, cormorants and shearwaters. South of this promontory, **Croyde Bay** is another surfers' delight, more compact than Woolacombe, with stalls on the sand renting surfboards and wet suits, while **Saunton Sands** is a magnificent long stretch of coast pummelled by endless ranks of classic breakers.

Practicalities

Ilfracombe's **tourist office** is at the Landmark on the seafront (Easter–July & Oct Mon–Sat 10am–5pm, Sun 10am–4pm; Aug & Sept daily 10am–5.30pm; Nov–Easter Mon–Sat 10am–5pm, Sat 10am–4pm; ☎01271/863001, ⓦwww.ilfracombe-tourism.co.uk). The town's numerous **accommodation** choices include *Wentworth House*, a Victorian B&B at the top of Church Hill on Belmont Road (☎01271/863048; no credit cards; ❷), *Sherborne Lodge Hotel*, Torrs Park (☎01271/862297; ❷), a roomy villa in a quiet area of town west of the centre, and *Ocean Backpackers*, an excellent independent **hostel** near the bus station and harbour at 29 St James Place (☎01271/867835, ⓦwww .oceanbackpackers.co.uk; £11), also offering double rooms (❶). Local **campsites** include *North Morte Farm*, near Morte Point (☎01271/870381, ⓦwww.northmortefarm.co.uk; closed Oct–Easter). *Ocean Backpackers* has a relaxed international **restaurant**, the *Atlantis*, with ambient, world and jazz musical background (closed Oct–Easter).

In **Woolacombe**, *Sandunes* is one of a number of B&Bs on Beach Road (☎01271/870661; no smoking; no credit cards; ❷), minutes from the beach and with views. Surfers and others gather at the *Red Barn*, a popular **bar** and **restaurant** just behind the beach (closed Sun eve). Woolacombe's **tourist office** is on the Esplanade (Easter–Oct Mon–Sat 10am–5pm, Sun 10am–3pm; Nov–Easter Mon–Sat 10am–4pm; ☎01271/870553, ⓦwww .woolacombetourism.co.uk).

Bideford Bay

BIDEFORD BAY (sometimes called Barnstaple Bay) encapsulates the variety of Devon, encompassing the photogenic village of **Clovelly** and the savage windlashed rocks of **Hartland Point**. Bideford itself is mainly a transit centre, with regular boats for Lundy Island, though the old port of **Appledore** makes an attractive place to spend some time.

Bideford and Appledore

Like Barnstaple, nine miles to the east, the estuary town of **BIDEFORD** formed an important link in north Devon's trade network in the Middle Ages, mainly due to its **bridge**, which still straddles the River Torridge. From the Norman era until the eighteenth century, the port was the property of the Grenville family, whose most celebrated member was **Richard Grenville**, commander of the ships that carried the first settlers to Virginia, and later a major player in the defeat of the Spanish Armada. The town's greatest prosperity came in the seventeenth and eighteenth centuries, when it enjoyed a flourishing trade with the New World.

A couple of miles downstream from Bideford, the old shipbuilding port of **APPLEDORE** is worth a wander and a drink in one of its cosy pubs. There are still several operating boatyards, but the peaceful, pastel-coloured Georgian houses give little hint of the extent of the industry in earlier times.

Bideford's **tourist office** is next to Victoria Park at the northern end of town (Easter–June & Sept Mon–Sat 10am–5pm, Sun 10am–1pm; July & Aug Mon–Sat 10am–5pm, Sun 10am–4pm; Oct–Easter Mon, Tues, Thurs & Fri 10am–4.30pm, Wed & Sat 10am–1pm; ☎01237/477676, ⓦwww.torridge .gov.uk). Useful **B&Bs** nearby are the *Cornerhouse*, 14 The Strand, (☎01237/473722, ⓦwww.cornerhouse-guesthouse.co.uk; no credit cards; ❷), and the *Mount* (☎01237/473748, ⓦwww.themount1.cjb.net; ❸), further out on Northdown Road, but linked to the centre by a footpath; both are non-smoking. For a **meal** or a drink, head up Bridge Street to Market Place, where the porticoed *Old Coach Inn* provides ales and hearty snacks.

Clovelly

The impossibly picturesque village of **CLOVELLY** must have featured on more calendars, biscuit boxes and tourist posters than anywhere else in the West Country. It was put on the map in the second half of the nineteenth century by two books: Charles Dickens' *A Message From the Sea* and *Westward Ho!* by Charles Kingsley, whose father was rector here for six years. To an extent, the tone of the village has been preserved by limiting hotel accommodation and holiday homes, and restricting coach parties, though there's still a fairly regular stream of sightseers and it's best avoided altogether during school summer holidays.

Past the **visitor centre** (daily: April–Oct 9am–5pm; Nov–March 10am–4pm; ⓦwww.clovelly.co.uk; £4) – walkers, cyclists and users of public transport have free access to the village via a separate entrance to the right – the cobbled, traffic-free main street plunges down past neat, flower-smothered cottages where sledges are tethered for transporting goods – the only way to carry supplies since the use of donkeys ended. At the bottom, Clovelly's stony beach and tiny harbour snuggle under a cleft in the cliff wall. If you can't face the return climb to the top of the village, there's a Land Rover service leaving every fifteen minutes or so from behind the *Red Lion* (Easter–Oct 9am–5.30pm; £2, or £3 return). From the visitor centre, a more level walk is possible along **Hobby Drive**, through woods of sycamore, oak, beech, rowan and holly, with grand views over the village.

Clovelly has just two **hotels**, both pricey: the *New Inn*, halfway down the High Street (☎01237/431303, ⓔnewinn@clovelly.co.uk; ❼), and the *Red Lion* at the harbour (☎01237/431237, ⓔredlion@clovelly.co.uk; ❽). Below the *New Inn* is a small **B&B**, *Donkey Shoe Cottage* (☎01237/431601; no credit cards; ❷), and there's a greater selection of guest houses a twenty-minute walk up from the visitor centre in Higher Clovelly: try *Boat House Cottage*, on the main road (☎01237/431209; no credit cards; ❷).

Hartland Point and around

You could drive along minor roads to **Hartland Point**, ten miles west of Clovelly, but the best approach is on foot along the coastal path. The headland presents one of Devon's most dramatic sights, its jagged black rocks battered by the sea and overlooked by a solitary lighthouse 350ft up. South of Hartland Point, the saw-toothed rocks and near-vertical escarpments defiantly confront the waves, with spectacular waterfalls tumbling over the cliffs. This sheer stretch of coast has seen dozens of shipwrecks over the centuries, though many must have been prevented by the sight of the tower of fourteenth-century **St Nectan's** – a couple of miles south of the Point in the village of **STOKE** – which acted as a landmark to sailors before the construction of the lighthouse. At 128ft, it is the tallest church tower in north Devon, and inside the church boasts a finely carved rood screen and a Norman font beneath a wagon-type roof. Tea and scones are served at *Stoke Barton Farm*, just opposite (Easter–Sept Tues–Thurs, Sat & Sun).

Half a mile east of the church, gardens and lush woodland surround **Hartland Abbey** (May, June & Sept Wed, Thurs & Sun 2–5.30pm; July & Aug also Tues 2–5.30pm; gardens April–Sept daily except Sat 2–5.30pm; £6), an eighteenth-century country house incorporating the ruins of an abbey dissolved in 1539, and displaying fine furniture, old photographs and recently uncovered frescoes. **HARTLAND** itself, further inland, holds little appeal beyond its three pubs and café, but on the coast, **Hartland Quay** deserves a linger: once a busy port, financed in part by the mariners Raleigh, Drake and Hawkins, it was mostly destroyed by storms in the nineteenth century, and now holds a solitary pub and hotel, surrounded by beautiful slate cliffs.

Among Hartland's **accommodation** options, try the small, friendly B&B, at 2 Harton Manor, North St, off Fore St (℡01237/441670; no credit cards; **2**). For proximity to the sea, you can't do better than the *Hartland Quay Hotel*, Hartland Quay (℡01237/441218; **3**), but if you want to be nearer Hartland Point, try *West Titchberry Farm* (℡01237/441287; no credit cards; **2**), for which you should follow signs for Hartland Lighthouse. In nearby Stoke, *Stoke Barton Farm* (see above) also provides basic **camping** facilities (℡01237/441238), while further south, at Elmscott, at the end of a three-and-a-half-mile sign-posted footpath from Hartland, and about half a mile from the sea, there's a **youth hostel** in a converted Victorian schoolhouse (℡0870/770 5814; closed mid-Sept to mid-April; £10.25). The only public transport is bus #319 from Barnstaple; alight at Hartland.

Lundy Island

There are fewer than twenty full-time residents on **Lundy**, a tiny windswept island twelve miles north of Hartland Point. Now a refuge for thousands of marine birds, Lundy has no cars, just one pub and one shop – indeed little has changed since the Marisco family established itself here in the twelfth century, making use of the shingle beaches and coves to terrorize shipping along the Bristol Channel. Later, Lundy's most famous inhabitants included **William Hudson Heaven**, who bought the island in 1834 and established what became known as the "Kingdom of Heaven". His home, **Millcombe House**, an incongruous piece of Georgian architecture in the desolate surroundings, is one of many relics of former habitation scattered around the island, though a recent addition compared with the thirteenth-century **castle** standing on Lundy's southern end.

Today, **walking** along the interweaving tracks and footpaths is about the only thing to do here. Inland, the grass, heather and bog is crossed by dry-stone walls and grazed by ponies, goats, deer and the rare soay sheep. The shores – mainly cliffy on the west, softer and undulating on the east – shelter a rich variety of **birdlife**, including kittiwakes, fulmars, shags and Manx shearwaters, which often nest in rabbit burrows. The most famous birds, though, are the **puffins** after which Lundy is named – from the Norse *Lunde* (puffin) and *ey* (island). They can only be sighted in April and May, when they come ashore to mate. Offshore, **grey seals** can be seen all the year round.

Practicalities

The *MS Oldenburg* sails to Lundy up to six times a week from Bideford or Ilfracombe between April and October, taking around two hours from both places. Day return tickets cost around £25, period returns £42; to reserve a place, call ☏01271/863636 (day returns can also be booked from local tourist offices). Between November and March, a helicopter service from Hartland Point (see p.388) takes over, taking just seven minutes (currently Mon & Fri at midday, £69 return).

Accommodation on the island is managed by the Landmark Trust and can be booked up for weekly rentals months in advance. As shorter B&B bookings can only be made within two weeks of the proposed visit, this limits the options, though outside the holiday season it is still possible to find a double room for under £50 per night – contact the Landmark Trust to make a booking (☏01628/825925). Options range from the remote *Admiralty Lookout* (lacking electricity and with only hand-pumped water), through the two-storey granite *Barn*, a hostel sleeping fourteen, to the comfortable *Old House*, where Charles Kingsley stayed in 1849, and the *Old Light*, a lighthouse built in 1820 by the architect of Dartmoor Prison. There's also a **campsite** open throughout the year, though it can get pretty rainy and windswept in winter. More information on transport and accommodation can be found on the island's website, ⓦwww.lundyisland.co.uk.

Exmoor

A high bare plateau sliced by wooded combes and splashing streams, **EXMOOR** can be one of the most forbidding landscapes in England, especially when shrouded in a sea mist. When it's clear, though, the moorland of this National Park reveals rich swathes of colour and an amazing diversity of wildlife, from buzzards to the unique **Exmoor ponies**, a species closely related to prehistoric horses. In the treeless heartland of the moor in particular, it's not difficult to spot these short and stocky animals, though fewer than twelve hundred are registered, and of these only about two hundred are free-living on the moor. Much more elusive are the **red deer**, England's largest native wild animal, of which Exmoor supports the country's only wild population, currently around two and half thousand.

Endless permutations of **walking routes** are possible along a network of some six hundred miles of footpaths and bridleways, and **horseback riding** is another option for getting the most out of Exmoor's desolate beauty – visitor centres can supply details of guided walks and local stables. Whether walking or riding, bear in mind that over seventy percent of the National Park is privately owned and that access is theoretically restricted to public rights of way; special permission should certainly be sought before camping, canoeing, fishing or similar.

Inland, there are four obvious bases for walks, all on the Somerset side of the county border: **Dulverton** in the southeast, site of the main information facilities; **Simonsbath** in the centre; **Exford**, near Exmoor's highest point of Dunkery Beacon; and the attractive village of **Winsford**, close to the A396 on the east of the moor. Exmoor's coastline offers an alluring alternative to the open moorland, all of it accessible via the **South West Coast Path**, which embarks on its long coastal journey at **Minehead**, though there is more charm to be found further west at the sister villages of **Lynmouth** and **Lynton**, just over the Devon border.

Dulverton

The village of **DULVERTON**, on the southern edge of the National Park, is the Park Authority's headquarters and so makes a good introduction to

Exmoor. Information on the whole moor is available at the **visitor centre**, 7 Fore St (daily: April–Oct 10am–1.15pm & 1.45–5pm; Nov–March 11am–3pm; ℡01398/323841, Ⓦwww.exmoor-nationalpark.gov.uk). Dulverton's best **accommodation** choice is *Town Mills* (℡01398/323124; ❸), an old mill house in the centre of the village; alternatively try the *Lion Hotel* in Bank Square (℡01398/323444; ❹) or the relaxed *Crispin's* off 26 High St (℡01398/323397; ❷), which has one double and a self-catering suite. With its small garden, this is also the place to come for snacks and full evening **meals**. Moorland **horse riding** is offered at West Anstey Farm (℡01398/341354), a couple of miles west of Dulverton; there's also a **camping barn** here.

Winsford, Exford and Dunkery Beacon

Just west of the A396 five miles north of Dulverton, **WINSFORD** lays good claim to being the moor's prettiest village. A scattering of thatched cottages ranged around a sleepy green, it is watered by a confluence of streams and rivers – one of them the Exe – giving it no fewer than seven bridges. The *Royal Oak*, a thatched and rambling old inn on the village green, offers drinks, snacks and full restaurant **meals**, though room rates are high (℡01643/851455, Ⓦwww.royaloak-somerset.co.uk; ❻). *Larcombe Foot* (℡01643/851306; no credit cards; ❷; closed Dec–Feb), a mile north, offers excellent **B&B** overlooking the Exe, and there's a well-equipped **campsite** a mile southwest of the village at *Halse Farm* (℡01643/851259, Ⓦwww.halsefarm.co.uk; closed Nov to mid-March).

The hamlet of **EXFORD**, an ancient crossing point on the River Exe, is popular with hunting folk as well as with walkers here for the four-mile hike to **Dunkery Beacon**, Exmoor's highest point at 1700ft. Local **accommodation** includes *Exmoor Lodge*, a friendly B&B on Chapel Street (℡01643/831694, Ⓦwww.smoothhound.co.uk; no smoking; ❷), and Exmoor's main **youth hostel**, a rambling Victorian house in the centre (℡0870/770 5820; limited opening Nov–Feb; £11.50).

Exmoor Forest and Simonsbath

At the heart of the National Park stands **Exmoor Forest**, the barest part of the moor, scarcely populated except by roaming sheep and a few red deer – the word "forest" denotes simply that it was a hunting reserve. In the middle of it stands the village of **SIMONSBATH** (pronounced "Simmonsbath"), home to the Knight family, who bought the forest in 1818 and, by introducing tenant farmers, building roads and importing sheep, brought systematic agriculture to an area that had never before produced any income. The Knights also built a wall round their land – parts of which can still be seen – as well as the intriguing Pinkworthy (pronounced "Pinkery") Pond, four miles to the northwest, whose exact function remains unexplained.

Simonsbath would make a good base for hikes on the moor, but there are only two **accommodation** possibilities: the *Exmoor Forest Hotel* (℡01643/831341; ❹; closed Jan) and the posher *Simonsbath House Hotel* (℡01643/831259, Ⓦwww.simonsbathhouse.co.uk; ❺), former home of the Knights, where there's a good but expensive **restaurant**. In a converted barn next to the hotel, *Boevey's* offers coffees and snack lunches, while a couple of miles outside the village on the Brayford Road, the *Poltimore Arms* at **Yarde Down** is a classic country **pub** serving excellent **food**, including vegetarian dishes.

Minehead and Dunster

The Somerset port of **MINEHEAD** quickly became a favourite Victorian watering hole with the arrival of the railway, and it has preserved an upbeat holiday-town atmosphere ever since. Steep lanes link the two quarters of **Higher Town**, on North Hill, containing some of the oldest houses, and **Quay Town**, the harbour area. It's in Quay Town that the **Hobby Horse** performs its dance in the town's three-day May Day celebrations, snaring maidens under its prancing skirt and tail in a fertility ritual resembling the more famous festivities at the Cornish port of Padstow (see p.417).

The **tourist office** is midway between Higher Town and Quay Town at 17 Friday St, off the Parade (April–June, Sept & Oct Mon–Sat 9.30am–5pm; July & Aug Mon–Sat 9.30am–5.30pm, Sun 10am–1pm; Nov–March Mon–Sat 10am–4pm; ☏01643/702624). If you want to **stay** in Minehead, try the *Old Ship Aground* right by the harbour on Quay Road (☏01643/702087; ❷), or, nearer the centre, a few minutes' walk up from the tourist office, *Kildare Lodge* on Tudor Road (☏01643/702009; ❹), a comfortable, reconstructed Tudor inn designed by a pupil of Lutyens. There's a **youth hostel** a couple of miles southeast, outside the village of Alcombe (☏0870/770 5968; £10.25; limited opening Sept–March), in a secluded combe on the edge of Exmoor.

Minehead is a terminus for the **West Somerset Railway**, which curves eastwards into the Quantocks as far as Bishops Lydeard (see p.354). The Minehead area's major attraction, the old village of **DUNSTER**, is about a mile from the line's first stop, three miles inland. Dunster's main street is dominated by the towers and turrets of its **castle** (April–Sept Mon–Wed, Sat & Sun 11am–5pm; Oct Mon–Wed, Sat & Sun 11am–4pm; grounds daily: April–Oct 10am–5pm; Nov–March 11am–4pm; £6.40, grounds only £3.50; NT), most of whose fortifications were demolished after the Civil War, after which time the castle became something of an architectural showpiece, and subject to a thorough Victorian restoration. A tour of the castle takes in various portraits of the Luttrells, owners of the house for six hundred years before the National Trust took over in the 1970s; a bedroom once occupied by Charles I; a fine seventeenth-century carved staircase; and a richly decorated banqueting hall. The grounds include terraced gardens and riverside walks – and drama productions

---

The South West Coast Path

The South West Coast Path, the longest footpath in Britain, starts at Minehead and tracks the coastline as closely as it possibly can along Devon's northern seaboard, round Cornwall, back into Devon, and on to Dorset, where it finishes close to the entrance to Poole Harbour. The path was conceived in the 1940s, but it was just over 25 years ago that – barring a few significant gaps – the full **630-mile route** opened, much of it on land owned by the National Trust, and all of it well signposted.

The relevant Ordnance Survey **maps** can be found at most village shops on the route, while many newsagents, bookshops and tourist offices will stock books or pamphlets containing route plans and details of local flora and fauna. Aurum Press (ⓦwww.aurumpress.co.uk) publishes four National Trail Guides using Ordnance Survey maps, while the **South West Coast Path Association** publishes an annual guide (£7) to the whole path, including accommodation lists, ferry timetables and transport details; there's also a supplement, the *Other Way Round* (£3.50), for those travelling in the Poole-to-Minehead direction. You can contact the Association at Windlestraw, Penquit, Devon PL21 0LU (☏01752/896237, ⓦwww.swcp.org.uk).

and other events are staged here in the summer. The nearby hilltop tower is a folly, **Conygar Tower**, dating from 1776.

Below the castle, relics of Dunster's wool-making heyday include the octagonal **Yarn Market** in the High Street, dating from 1609, while the three-hundred-year-old **water mill** at the end of Mill Lane is still used commercially for milling the various grains which go to make the flour and muesli sold in the shop (April, May & Oct daily except Fri 10.30am–5pm, June–Sept daily 10.30am–5pm; £2.30; NT) – the café, overlooking its riverside garden, is a good spot for lunch. For somewhere to **stay**, try the traditional *Yarn Market Hotel*, 25–31 High St (☎01643/821425, ⓦwww.yarnmarkethotel.co.uk; ❹), which has rooms overlooking the Yarn Market and a restaurant. There's a **visitor centre** at the top of Dunster Steep by the main car park (Easter–Oct daily 10am–5pm; Nov–Easter some weekends 11am–3pm; ☎01643/821835).

Porlock

The real enticement of **PORLOCK**, six miles west of Minehead, is its extraordinary position in a deep hollow, cupped on three sides by the hog-backed hills of Exmoor. The thatch-and-cob houses and dripping charm of the village's long main street have drawn armies of tourists, though others come in search of the place's literary links. According to Coleridge's own less than reliable testimony, it was a "man from Porlock" who broke the opium trance in which he was composing *Kubla Khan*, while the High Street's beamed *Ship Inn* prides itself on featuring prominently in the Exmoor romance *Lorna Doone* and, in real life, having sheltered the poet Robert Southey, who staggered in rain-soaked after an Exmoor ramble.

Porlock's **tourist office** is at West End, High St (Easter–Oct Mon–Fri 10am–1pm & 2–5pm, Sat 10am–5pm, Sun 10am–1pm; Nov–Easter Mon–Fri 10am–1pm, Sat 10am–2pm; ☎01643/863150, ⓦwww.porlock.co.uk). The best **accommodation** is on the High Street, where you'll find the Victorian *Lorna Doone Hotel* (☎01643/862404; ❷) and *The Cottage*, a smaller and quainter B&B (☎01643/862996; ❸). Both places serve snacks, meals and teas – as does the *Whortleberry Tearoom* (closed Mon), also on the High Street. Porlock has a central **campsite**, *Sparkhayes Farm* (☎01643/862470; closed Jan & Feb), signposted off the main road near the *Lorna Doone*.

Two miles west over the reclaimed marshland, the tiny harbour of **PORLOCK WEIR** gives little inkling of its former role as a hard-working port trafficking with Wales. It's a peaceful spot, and there's a top-notch – and very expensive – **restaurant**, *Andrews on the Weir* (☎01643/863300, ⓦwww.andrewsontheweir.co.uk), which cooks up local lamb and seafood to perfection and also offers luxury **accommodation** (❺). An easy two-mile stroll west from Porlock Weir along the South West Coast Path brings you to **St Culbone**, a tiny church – claimed to be the country's smallest – sheltered within woods once inhabited by a leper colony.

Lynton and Lynmouth

West from Porlock, the road climbs 1350ft in less than three miles, though cyclists and drivers might prefer the gentler and more scenic toll-road alternative to the direct uphill trawl. Nine miles along the coast, on the Devon side of the county line, the Victorian resort of **LYNTON** perches above a lofty gorge with splendid views over the sea. Almost completely cut off from the rest of the country for most of its history, the village struck lucky during the Napoleonic Wars, when frustrated Grand Tourists – unable to visit their usual

In addition to the coastal path, there are several popular walks inland in this region. The one-and-a-half-mile tramp to **Watersmeet**, for example, follows the East Lyn River to where it's joined by Hoar Oak Water, a tranquil spot transformed into a roaring torrent after a bout of rain. From the fishing lodge here – now open as a café and shop in summer – you can branch off on a range of less-trodden paths, such as the three-quarters-of-a-mile route south to **Hillsford Bridge**, the confluence of Hoar Oak and Farley Water.

North of Watersmeet, a path climbs up **Countisbury Hill** and the higher **Butter Hill** (nearly 1000ft), affording riveting views of Lynton, Lynmouth and the north Devon coast, and there's also a track leading to the lighthouse at **Foreland Point**, close to the coastal path. East from Lynmouth you can reach the point via a fine sheltered shingle beach at the foot of Countisbury Hill – one of a number of tiny coves that are easily accessible on either side of the estuary.

From Lynton, an undemanding expedition takes you west along the North Walk, a mile-long path leading to the **Valley of the Rocks**, where the steep heathland is dominated by rugged rock formations and grazed by herds of wild goats.

continental haunts – discovered in Lynton a domestic piece of Swiss landscape. Coleridge and Hazlitt trudged over to Lynton from the Quantocks, but the greatest spur to the village's popularity came with the publication in 1869 of R.D. Blackmore's Exmoor melodrama *Lorna Doone*, a book based on the outlaw clans who inhabited these parts in the seventeenth century. Lynton's imposing **town hall** on Lee Road epitomizes the Victorian–Edwardian accent of the village. It was the gift of publisher George Newnes, who also donated the nearby **cliff railway** connecting Lynton with Lynmouth (March to mid-July & mid-Sept to Nov daily 9am–7pm; mid-July to mid-Sept daily 9am–9pm; £2.75 return).

Five hundred feet below, **LYNMOUTH** lies at the junction and estuary of the East and West Lyn rivers, in a spot described by Gainsborough as "the most delightful place for a landscape painter this country can boast". Shelley spent his honeymoon here with his 16-year-old bride Harriet Westbrook, during which time he wrote his polemical *Queen Mab* – two different houses claim to have been the Shelleys' love nest. In summer, the harbour offers boat trips and fishing expeditions, and, at the top of the village, you can explore the walks, waterfalls and displays of the uses and dangers of waterpower in the **Glen Lyn Gorge** (daily 10am–dusk; exhibition Easter–Oct 10am–dusk; £3, gorge only £2). The wooded gorge was the course taken by the destructive floods of 1952, when Lynmouth was almost washed away by floodwaters coming off Exmoor, a disaster of which there are many reminders around the village.

Practicalities

Lynton's **tourist office** is in the town hall (Easter–Oct Mon–Sat 9.30am–5.30pm, Sun 10am–4pm; Nov–Easter Mon–Sat 10am–4pm, Sun 10am–2pm; ☎01598/752225 or 0845/660 3232, ⓦwww.lyntourism.co.uk), while Lynmouth has a **National Park Visitor Centre** on the seafront (Easter–Oct daily 10am–5pm; Nov, Dec & Feb–Easter Sat & Sun 11am–4pm; ☎01598/752509).

Lynton has the better choice of cheaper **accommodation**, including *The Turret*, 33 Lee Rd (☎01598/753284, ⓦwww.turrethotel.co.uk; no smoking; no under-14s; ❷), a friendly Victorian B&B built by the same engineer who constructed the cliff railway, and *St Vincent House* (☎01598/752244,

@ stvincenthotel@aol.com; no smoking; ❸), a whitewashed, Georgian house on Castle Hill with beautifully furnished rooms. There's a **youth hostel** in a homely Victorian house about one mile inland from Lynton's centre, signposted off Lynbridge Road (☎0870/770 5942; limited opening Nov–Easter; £10.25). **Meals** are served at the small, nonsmoking *Lily May's*, 1 Castle Hill (☎01598/753591; closed all day Wed, also eves in winter).

In **Lynmouth**, central choices include *Riverside Cottage*, above a busy tea shop on Riverside Road (☎01598/752390, ⓦwww.riversidecottage.co.uk; ❸), and the posh *Shelley's*, next to the Glen Lyn Gorge (☎01598/753219, ⓦwww.shelleyshotel.co.uk; ❹), where you can stay in the room supposed to have been occupied by the poet – he apparently left without paying his bill. Splendidly sited across the river at the harbour entrance, the *Rock House Hotel* (☎01598/753508, ⓦwww.rock-house.co.uk; ❹) has chintzy, nonsmoking rooms with views, as well as a tea-garden, snacks at the bar and meals in its **restaurant**.

Cornwall

When D.H. Lawrence wrote that being in **Cornwall** was "like being at a window and looking out of England", he wasn't just thinking of its geographical extremity. Virtually unaffected by the Roman conquest, Cornwall was for centuries the last haven for a **Celtic culture** elsewhere eradicated by the Saxons – a land where princes communed with Breton troubadours, where chroniclers and scribes composed the epic tales of Arthurian heroism, and where itinerant monks from Welsh and Irish monasteries disseminated an elemental and visionary Christianity. Primitive granite crosses and a crop of Celtic saints remain as traces of this formative period, and though the Cornish language had ebbed away by the eighteenth century, it is recalled in Celtic place names that in many cases have grown more exotic as they have mutated over time.

Another strand of Cornwall's folkloric character comes from the **smugglers** who thrived here right up until the nineteenth century, exploiting the sheltered creeks and hidden anchorages of the southern coasts. For many fishing villages, contraband provided an important secondary income, as did the looting of the ships that regularly came to grief on the reefs and rocks. Cornwall has also had a strong **industrial economy**, based mainly on the mining of **copper** and **tin** in the north, centred on the towns of Redruth and St Agnes, and in the south on the deposits of **china clay**, which are still being mined in the area around St Austell.

Nowadays, of course, Cornwall's most flourishing industry is tourism. The repercussions of the holiday business have been uneven, for instance cluttering **Land's End** with a tacky leisure complex but leaving Cornwall's other great headland, **Lizard Point**, undeveloped. The thronged resorts of **Falmouth**, site of the impressive new National Maritime Museum, and **Newquay**, the West's chief surfing centre, have successfully adapted to the demands of mass tourism, but its effects have been more destructive in smaller, quainter places, such as

Mevagissey, **Polperro** and **Padstow**, whose genuine charms can be hard to make out in full season. Other villages, such as **Fowey**, **Charlestown**, **Port Isaac** and **Boscastle**, still preserve an authentic feel, however, while you couldn't wish for anything more remote than **Bodmin Moor**, a tract of wilderness in the heart of Cornwall, or the **Isles of Scilly**, idyllically free of development. It would be hard to compromise the sense of desolation surrounding **Tintagel**, site of what is fondly known as King Arthur's castle, or the appeal of the seaside resorts of **St Ives** and **Bude** – both with great surfing beaches – while, near **St Austell**, the spectacular **Eden Project**, located in an abandoned clay pit, celebrates environmental diversity with visionary style.

6 From Looe to Veryan Bay

The southeast strip of the Cornish coast holds a string of medieval harbour towns interspersed with long stretches of magnificent coastline. The main rail stop is **St Austell**, the capital of Cornwall's china clay industry, though there is a branch line connecting nearby **Par** with the north coast at Newquay. To the east of St Austell Bay, the touristy **Polperro** and **Looe** are easily accessible by bus from Plymouth, and there's a rail link to Looe from Liskeard. The estuary town of **Fowey**, in a niche of Cornwall closely associated with the author Daphne Du Maurier, is most easily reached by bus from St Austell and Par, as is **Mevagissey**, to the west.

Looe and Polperro

LOOE was drawing crowds as early as 1800, when the first "bathing-machines" were wheeled out, but the arrival of the railway in 1879 was what really packed its beaches. Though the river-divided town now touts itself as something of a shark-fishing centre, most people come here for the sand, the handiest stretch being the beach in front of East Looe. Away from the river mouth, you'll find cleaner water a mile eastwards at **Millendreath**. Most of Looe's attractions are in boating and bathing, so it's hardly surprising that the **Old Guildhall Museum** on Higher Market Street (Easter & late May to Sept Mon–Fri & Sun 11.30am–4.30pm; £1.50) includes a collection of maritime models among its exhibits; equally interesting are the fifteenth-century building's preserved prison cells and raised magistrates' benches.

East Looe's **tourist office** is at the New Guildhall, on Fore Street (Easter & May to mid-Sept daily 10am–5pm; April & mid-Sept to Oct daily 10am–2pm; ☎01503/262072, ⓦwww.looecornwall.com). **Accommodation** in East Looe includes the *Sea Breeze*, a three-storey B&B close to the beach and harbour in Lower Chapel Street (☎01503/263131, ⓦwww.cornwallexplore.co.uk/seabreeze; ❶); in **West Looe**, there's the nonsmoking *St Aubyn's* on Marine Drive (☎01503/264351, ⓦwww.staubyns.co.uk; no under-5s; ❸; closed Nov–March), a mile west of the centre in the Hannafore district, with great sea views. The town abounds in inexpensive places to eat; try the *Golden Guinea* on Fore Street, a seventeenth-century building that does a brisk trade in staple seaside meals as well as cream teas.

Looe is linked by frequent buses with neighbouring **POLPERRO**, a smaller and quainter place, but with a similar feel. From the bus stop and car park at the top of the village, it's a five- or ten-minute walk alongside the River Pol to the pretty harbour. The surrounding cliffs and the tightly packed houses rising on each side of the stream have an undeniable charm, and the tangle of lanes is little changed since the village's heyday of smuggling and pilchard fishing, but the "discovery" of Polperro has almost ruined it, and its straggling main street – the Coombes – is now an unbroken row of tourist shops and fast-food outlets. The best places to **stay** include *The House on Props*, Talland Street (☎01503/272310; no credit cards; ❹), and the central but relatively secluded *Old Mill House*, an agreeable pub on Mill Hill (☎01503/272362, ⓦwww .oldmillhouse.i12.com; ❸). There's a separate **restaurant** at the *Old Mill*, though vegetarian and seafood fans will do better at the nonsmoking *Kitchen* on the Coombes (☎01503/272780; eves only; closed Oct–Easter).

Fowey

The ten miles west from Polperro to Polruan are among south Cornwall's best stretches of the coastal path, giving access to some beautiful secluded sand beaches. There are frequent ferries across the River Fowey from Polruan, affording a fine prospect of the quintessential Cornish port of **FOWEY** (pronounced "Foy"), a cascade of neat, pale terraces at the mouth of one of the peninsula's greatest rivers. The major port on the county's south coast in the fourteenth century, Fowey finally became so ambitious that it provoked Edward IV to strip the town of its military capability, though it continued to thrive commercially, coming into its own as the leading port for china clay shipments in the nineteenth century. In addition to the bulkier freighters sailing from wharves north of the town, the harbour today is crowded with trawlers and yachts, giving the town a brisk, purposeful character lacking in many of Cornwall's south-coast ports.

Fowey's steep layout centres on the church of **St Fimbarrus**, a distinctive fifteenth-century construction. Beside it, the **Literary Centre** on South Street is a small exhibition including a twelve-minute video of Daphne Du Maurier's life and work (daily summer 10.30am–5pm, closes 7.30pm in Aug, winter 10.30am–4pm; free). Behind the church stands **Place House**, an extravagance belonging to the local Treffry family, with a Victorian Gothic tower grafted onto the fifteenth- and sixteenth-century fortified building. Below the church, the **Ship Inn**, sporting some fine Elizabethan panelling and plaster ceilings, held the local Roundhead HQ during the Civil War. From here, Fore Street, Lostwithiel Street and the Esplanade fan out, the **Esplanade** leading to a footpath that gives access to some splendid coastal walks. Past the remains of a blockhouse that once supported a defensive chain hung across the river's mouth, the small beach of **Readymoney Cove** is soon reached, close to the ruins of **St Catherine's Castle**, built by Thomas Treffry on the orders of Henry VIII and offering fine views across the estuary.

Practicalities

Separated from eastern routes by its river, Fowey is most accessible by #24 **buses** from St Austell. The **tourist office** is in the town's post office on Custom House Hill (Easter–Oct Mon–Fri 9am–5.30pm, Sat & Sun 9am–5pm; Nov–Easter Mon–Fri 9am–5.30pm, Sat 9am–5pm, Sun 9am–1pm; ☎01726/833616, ⓦwww.fowey.co.uk). All of the central pubs offer **accommodation**; on Lostwithiel Street, try the *Ship* (☎01726/832230; ❷) or the *Safe Harbour* (☎01726/833379; ❸), both offering en-suite rooms and parking. Near the top of the town, the B&B *Pendower*, 11 Park Rd (☎01726/833559; no smoking; no credit cards; ❷), has river vistas. There's a **youth hostel** outside Golant, two miles north, at *Penquite House*, a Georgian mansion with views over the valley (☏0870/770 5832, ℮golant@yha.org.uk; closed Dec & Jan; £13).

Fowey has some quality seafood **restaurants**; among the best are the elegant but relaxed *Q*, by the waterside at the sumptuous *Old Quay House Hotel* at 28 Fore Street (☏01726/83302), and *Food For Thought* on the Quay (☏01726/832221; eves only, also lunchtime June–Aug; closed Sun & Dec–March), both expensive. The area is also well provided with good **pubs**, some of which can be sampled on walkabouts, such as Golant's *Fisherman's Arms*, the *Old Ferry Inn* at Bodinnick, which also has comfortable rooms (☏01726/870237, ⓦwww.oldferryinn.co.uk; ❸), and Polruan's excellent *Lugger Inn*.

St Austell and around

It was the discovery of china clay, or kaolin, in the downs to the north of **ST AUSTELL** that spurred the town's growth in the eighteenth century. An essential ingredient in the production of porcelain, kaolin had until then only been produced in northern China, where a high ridge, or *kao-lin*, was the sole known source of the raw material. Still a vital part of Cornwall's economy, the clay is now mostly exported for use in the manufacture of paper, as well as paint and medicines. The conical spoil heaps left by the mines are a feature of the local landscape, especially on Hensbarrow Downs to the north, the great green and white mounds making an eerie sight.

St Austell's nearest link to the sea is at **CHARLESTOWN**, an easy downhill walk from the centre of town. This unassuming and unspoilt port is named after the entrepreneur Charles Rashleigh, who in 1791 began work on the harbour in what was then a small fishing community two miles south of St Austell, widening its streets to accommodate the clay wagons daily passing through. The wharves are still used, loading clay onto vessels that appear over-sized beside the tiny jetties, and also providing a backdrop for the location filming that frequently takes place here. Behind the harbour, the **Shipwreck & Heritage Centre** (March–Oct daily 10am–5pm, closes 6pm in peak season; £5) is entered through tunnels once used to convey the clay to the docks, and shows a good collection of photos and relics as well as tableaux of historical scenes.

On each side of the dock the coarse sand and stone **beaches** have small rock pools, above which cliff walks lead around St Austell Bay. Eastwards, you soon arrive at overdeveloped **Carlyon Bay**, whose main resort is **Par**. The beaches here get clogged with clay – the best swimming is to be found by pressing on to the sheltered crescent of **Polkerris**. The easternmost limit of St Austell Bay is marked by **Gribbin Head**, near which stands Menabilly House, where Daphne Du Maurier lived for 24 years – it was the model for the "Manderley" of *Rebecca*. The house is not open to the public, but you can walk down to Polridmouth Cove, where Rebecca met her watery end.

Eden Project

A disused clay pit four miles northeast of St Austell holds the newest and highest-profile of Cornwall's attractions, the **Eden Project** (daily: April–Oct 10am–6pm, closes 8pm Tues–Thurs late July to early Sept; Nov–March 10am–4.30pm; last entry 90min before closing; £11; ⓦwww.edenproject.com), reachable on bus #T9 from St Austell station and #T10 from Newquay. Occupying a 160-foot-deep crater whose awesome scale only reveals itself once you have passed the entrance at its lip, the project showcases the diversity of the planet's plant life in an imaginative, sometimes wacky, but refreshingly ungimmicky style. The whole site is stunningly landscaped with an array of various crops and flowerbeds, but at centre stage are the vast geodesic "biomes", or conservatories made up of ecofriendly Teflon-coated, hexagonal panels. One cluster holds groves of olive and citrus trees, cacti and other plants more usually found in the warm, temperate zones of the Mediterranean, southern Africa and southwestern USA, while the larger group contains plants from the tropics, including teak and mahogany trees, and there's a waterfall and river gushing through. Equally impressive are the external grounds (described as "Picasso meeting the Aztecs"), where plantations of bamboo, tea, hops, hemp and tobacco are interspersed with brilliant swathes of flowers. The whole "living theatre" presents a constantly changing spectacle, and should ideally be visited in different seasons. Allow at least half a day for a full exploration, but arrive early – or take advantage of the extended opening in summer – to avoid congestion. There are timed "story-telling" sessions, a lawn-carpeted arena where world, jazz and other music is performed, and abundant good food on hand – consult the website for events.

Note that anyone arriving at the site by bike or on foot is entitled to a £3 discount and can skip the queues by going straight to the fast track ticket window. See below for bike rental and accommodation in the area.

Practicalities

St Austell makes an unexciting place to stay, but there are good **accommodation** options near the Eden Project at *Treberthan*, a farmhouse at Bodelva, halfway between Par and the site and just fifteen minutes from Eden via a footpath (℡01726/817711; no smoking; ❸), and in Charlestown at *T'Gallants* (℡01726/70203; ❸), a smart Georgian B&B at the back of the harbour, and *Broad Meadow House*, behind the Shipwreck Centre on Quay Road (℡01726/76636, ✉best.tribe@btopenworld.com, no credit cards; ❸), which, in addition to B&B, also offers "tent and breakfast" (£15 per person), with family-size tents provided in a meadow by the sea. Behind *T'Gallants*, the *Rashleigh Arms* offers real ale and a range of **food**, though the most highly commended **pub** in the area is the *Rashleigh Inn* at Polkerris. The best **campsite** hereabouts is *Carlyon Bay* (℡01726/812735, ⓦwww.chycor.co.uk; closed Nov–March), at Bethesda, near the beach at Carlyon Bay, and just a mile and a half from the Eden Project.

To **rent a bike** locally, contact Bugle Bike Hire in the village of Bugle, five miles north of St Austell on the A391 and a little less than that west of the Eden Project (Easter–Oct; ℡01726/852285, ⓦwww.buglecyclehire.co.uk). Happy Trails Bike Rides (℡01726/852058, ⓦwww.happytrailsbikerides.com) arranges accompanied bike rides to the Eden Project from surrounding villages between April and September (£15 including Eden entry).

Mevagissey to Veryan Bay

MEVAGISSEY was once known for the construction of fast vessels, used for carrying contraband as well as pilchards. Today the tiny port might display a few stacks of lobster pots, but the real business is tourism, and in summer the maze of back streets is saturated with day-trippers, converging on the inner harbour and overflowing onto the large sand beach at **Pentewan** a mile to the north. A couple of miles north of Mevagissey lie the **Lost Gardens of Heligan** (daily: April–Oct 10am–6pm, last entry 4.30pm; Nov–March 10am–5pm, last entry 3.30pm; £6; ⓦwww.heligan.com), a fascinating

Victorian garden which had fallen into neglect and was resurrected by Tim Smit, the visionary instigator of the Eden Project (see p.398). A boardwalk takes you through a jungle and under a canopy of bamboo and ferns down to the Lost Valley, where there are lakes, woods and wild flower meadows. You can get here on #526 **buses** from St Austell and Mevagissey.

Four miles south of Mevagissey juts the striking headland of **Dodman Point**, cause of many a wreck and topped by a stark granite cross built by a local parson as a seamark in 1896. The promontory holds the substantial remains of an Iron Age fort, with an earthwork bulwark cutting right across the point. Curving away to the west, the elegant parabola of **Veryan Bay** holds a string of exquisite inlets and coves, such as **Hemmick Beach**, a fine place for a dip with rocky outcrops affording a measure of privacy, and **Porthluney Cove**, a crescent of sand whose centrepiece is the battlemented **Caerhays Castle** (mid-March to May Mon–Fri 1–4pm; gardens mid-Feb to May daily 10am–5.30pm, last entry 4.30pm; house £5.50, garden £5.50, combined ticket £9.50), built in 1808 by John Nash and surrounded by beautiful gardens. A little further on, minuscule and whitewashed **Portloe** is fronted by jagged black rocks that throw up fountains of seaspray, giving it a good, end-of-the-road feel.

Sequestered inland, **VERYAN** has a pretty village green and pond, but is best known for its curious circular white houses built in the 19th century by one Reverend Jeremiah Trist. A lane from Veryan leads down to one of the cleanest swimming spots on Cornwall's southern coast, **Pendower Beach**. Two-thirds of a mile long and backed by dunes, Pendower joins with the neighbouring **Carne Beach** at low tide to create a long sandy continuum.

Practicalities

From St Austell's train station or Trinity Street, **buses** #25 and #526 run to Mevagissey; Veryan and Portloe are reachable on #51 from Truro. In the heart of Mevagissey, the best **accommodation** option is the fifteenth-century *Fountain Inn* (℡01726/842320, ＠www.fountain.inn.cwc.net; ❷), on Cliff Street, off East Quay; alternatively try *Lawn House*, set back from the harbour at 1 Church Lane (℡01726/842754; no credit cards; ❹; phone ahead Nov–Easter), a spacious Queen Anne construction. The nearest **youth hostel** (℡0870/770 5712; closed Nov–March; £11.50) is at **Boswinger**, a remote spot half a mile from Hemmick Beach and about a mile from Gorran Church Town, which is served infrequently by bus #526. Boswinger also has a **campsite**, *Seaview* (℡01726/843425, ＠www.seaviewinternational.com; closed Oct–March), overlooking Veryan Bay. In **Veryan**, head for the *Elerkey Guest House* (℡01872/501261, ＠www.elerkey-guest-house.co.uk; ❸), with a spacious garden and adjoining art gallery; it's the first on the left after the church. The *New Inn* serves pub meals and also provides B&B (℡01872/501362; ❸).

Mevagissey's **restaurants** specialize in fish: for example the large harbourfront *Sharksfin Hotel* (℡01726/843241; moderate). The *Fountain Inn* and the *Ship Inn* on Fore Street both offer pub grub.

Truro, Falmouth and St Mawes

Lush tranquillity collides with frantic tourist activity around **Carrick Roads**, the complex estuary basin to the south of **Truro**, the region's main centre for transport and accommodation. At the mouth of the Carrick Roads, **Falmouth** is the major resort around here, and the site of one of Cornwall's mightiest castles, Pendennis. Its sister fort lies across the Carrick Roads in **St Mawes**, the main settlement on the **Roseland** peninsula, a luxuriant backwater of woods and sheltered creeks between the River Fal and the sea.

Truro

TRURO, seat of Cornwall's law courts and other county bureaucracies, has a distinctly small-scale provincial feel, even if its Georgian houses do reflect the prosperity that came with the tin-mining boom of the 1800s. Blurring the town's overall identity, its modern shopping centre stands alongside the powerful but chronologically confused **Cathedral** (daily 7.30am–6pm; £4 donation requested), at the bottom of Pydar Street. Completed in 1910, this was the first Anglican cathedral to be built in England since St Paul's in London, but it incorporates part of the fabric of the old parish church that previously occupied the site. The airy interior's best feature is its neo-Gothic baptistry, complete with emphatically pointed arches and elaborate roof vaulting. To the right of the choir, St Mary's aisle is a relic of the original Perpendicular building, other fragments of which adorn the walls, including – in the north transept – a colourful Jacobean memorial to local Parliamentarian John Robartes and his wife.

Truro's other unmissable attraction is the **Royal Cornwall Museum** (Mon–Sat 10am–5pm; £4), housed in an elegant Georgian building on River Street. The exhibits include minerals, Celtic inscriptions and paintings by Cornish artists.

Truro's **tourist office** is on Boscawen Street (April–May & Sept Mon–Fri 9am–5.30pm, Sat 9am–1pm; June–Aug Mon–Fri 9am–5.30pm, Sat 9am–5pm; Oct Mon–Fri 9am–5pm, Sat 9am–1pm; Nov–March Mon–Fri 9am–5pm; ☎01872/274555, Ⓦwww.truro.gov.uk). Buses stop nearby at Lemon Quay, or near the train station on Richmond Hill. Best **accommodation** near the train station is the *Gables*, at the bottom of Station Road at 49 Treyew Rd (☎01872/242318; no credit cards; ❶), while the Georgian *Bay Tree* lies halfway between the station and the centre at 28 Ferris Town (☎01872/240274; ❶). At the bottom of Lemon Street, the very central *Royal Hotel* (☎01872/270345, Ⓦwww.royalhotelcornwall.co.uk; ❺) has a bright, modern feel.

You'll find a cluster of Truro's **restaurants** around Kenwyn Street, including *Number Ten* at no. 10 (☎01872/272363), serving coffees and healthy fruit drinks as well as full meals, and *The Feast*, at no. 15, which has excellent wholefood, organic wines and Belgian beers (☎01872/272546; daytime only; closed Sun); both places have outdoor eating areas. Elsewhere in town, the *Pizza Express* on Boscawen Street is housed in the imposing old Coinage Hall, which sports portraits of George II and other notables. On the corner of Frances and Castle streets, the *Wig and Pen* is a decent **pub** with bar food, real ale and patio seating, and the next-door *Globe Inn* also serves hot meals as well as a range of coffees.

Falmouth

The construction of Pendennis Castle on the southern point of Carrick Roads in the sixteenth century prepared the ground for the growth of **FALMOUTH**, then no more than a fishing village. The building of its deep-water harbour was proposed a century later by Sir John Killigrew, and Falmouth's prosperity was assured when in 1689 it became chief base of the fast Falmouth Packets, which sped mail to the Americas. Recent years, however, have seen the town increasingly overwhelmed by waves of tourist traffic, attracted to the lush beaches to the south of town, and the long **High Street** and its continuations Market and Church streets are crammed with humdrum bars and cafés. The southern end, Arwenack Street, though, does have the Tudor remains of the Killigrews' **Arwenack House** (closed to the public). Falmouth's newest attraction, the **National Maritime Museum Cornwall**, stands on the quayside just opposite (Feb–Dec daily 10am–5pm; £6). The large, purpose-built exhibition centre holds diverse examples of vessels from all over the world, many of them suspended in midair in the Flotilla Gallery, the museum's cavernous centrepiece. In addition, numerous smaller galleries examine specific aspects of boat-building, seafaring history, Falmouth's packet ships and Cornwall's various other links with the sea, including fishing.

A few minutes' walk west of the museum, **Pendennis Castle** stands sentinel at the tip of the promontory that separates Carrick Roads from Falmouth Bay (daily: April–Sept 10am–6pm; Oct 10am–5pm; Nov–March 10am–4pm; £4.20; EH). The extensive fortification shows little evidence of its five-month siege by the Parliamentarians during the Civil War, which ended only when half its defenders had died and the rest had been starved into submission. Though this is a less-refined contemporary of the castle at St Mawes (see opposite), its site wins hands down, facing right out to sea on its own pointed peninsula, the stout ramparts offering the best all-round views of Carrick Roads and Falmouth Bay. Round Pendennis Point, south of the centre, a long sandy bay holds a succession of sheltered **beaches**: from the popular **Gyllyngvase Beach**, you can reach the more attractive **Swanpool Beach** by cliff path, or walk a couple of miles further on to **Maenporth**, from where there are some fine cliff-top walks.

Practicalities

Falmouth's **tourist office** is off the Moor, on Killigrew Street (April–Sept Mon–Sat 9.30am–5.30pm; July & Aug also Sun 10am–2pm; Oct–March Mon–Fri 9.30am–4.30pm, Sat 10am–4pm; ☎01326/312300, ⓦwww.go-cornwall.com). Most of the town's **accommodation** is near the train station and beach area, including the Victorian *Melvill House Hotel*, 52 Melvill Rd (☎01326/316645, ⓦwww.melvill-house-falmouth.co.uk; no smoking; ❸), with sea or harbour views, and the steeply gabled *Chellowdene* (☎01326/314950; no credit cards; ❸; closed Oct–April) on Gyllyngvase Hill. The very clean and friendly *Falmouth Lodge* backpackers' **hostel** is also near the beach at 9 Gyllyngvase Terrace (☎01326/319996, ⓦwww.falmouthbackpackers.co.uk; no smoking; £12), with use of kitchen and Internet access. On the coast south of Falmouth, the **campsite** at *Tregedna Farm* is more tent-friendly than most hereabouts, two and a half miles from town and half a mile from Maenporth Beach and the coast path (☎01326/250529; closed Oct–April).

Arwenack Street has two cool and contemporary **café/restaurants**, *Blue South* at nos. 35–37 (☎01326/212122) and *Hunky Dory* at no. 46 (☎01326/212997); both get very busy. On Gyllyngvase Beach, you can tuck in to grills and pizzas at the *Gyllyngvase Beach Café-Bar*, which has a lively feel and is open in the evenings in summer. The *Quayside Inn*, on Arwenack Street, is the pick of the **pubs**, with outdoor tables overlooking the harbour.

St Mawes and the Roseland peninsula

Stuck at the very end of a prong of land at the bottom of Carrick Roads, the secluded, unhurried town of **ST MAWES**, accessible on the frequent **ferries** from Falmouth's Prince of Wales Pier, has an attractive walled seafront lying below a hillside of villas and abundant gardens. Just out of sight at the end of the seafront stands the small and pristine **St Mawes Castle** (April–Sept daily 10am–6pm; Oct daily 10am–5pm; Nov–March Wed–Sun 10am–1pm & 2–4pm; £3; EH). Built during the reign of Henry VIII to a cloverleaf design, the castle owes its excellent condition to its early surrender during the Civil War when it was besieged by Parliamentary forces in 1646. The dungeons and gun installations contain various artillery exhibits as well as some background on local social history.

Outside St Mawes, you could spend a pleasant afternoon poking around the Roseland peninsula between the Percuil River and the eastern shore of Carrick Roads. Two and a half miles north, the scattered hamlet of **ST JUST-IN-ROSELAND** holds the strikingly picturesque church of St Just standing right next to the creek, surrounded by palms and subtropical shrubbery, its gravestones tumbling down to the water's edge. In summer, there's a **ferry** from St Mawes to the southern arm of the Roseland Peninsula, which holds the equally charming twelfth- to thirteenth-century church of **St Anthony-in-Roseland**.

Practicalities

St Mawes makes an attractive – if pricey – **place to stay**. The best budget choices are a ten-minute walk up from the seafront on Newton Road: *Little Newton* (℡01326/270664; ❸) and *Newton Farm*, next door (℡01326/270427; ❸), both are nonsmoking establishments, with spacious rooms and friendly hosts. For location – and steep rates – book in at the *St Mawes Hotel*, right on the seafront with glorious views over the estuary (℡01326/270266, ⓦwww.stmaweshotel.co.uk; ❻; closed Jan). There's a **campsite** at Trethem Mill, three miles north, outside St-Just-in-Roseland (℡01872/580504; closed mid-Oct to March). In St Mawes, the bar and brasserie at the *St Mawes Hotel* offers great views, while the *Victory Inn* is a fine old oak-beamed **pub** just off the seafront, which also serves seafood meals.

The Lizard peninsula

The **Lizard peninsula** – from the Celtic *lys ardh*, or "high point" – preserves a thankfully undeveloped appearance. If this flat and treeless expanse can be said to have a centre, it is **Helston**, a junction for buses running from Falmouth and Truro to the spartan villages of the peninsula's interior and coast. The most useful services are Truronian **buses** #T1, #T2 and the #T3 "Lizard Rambler", which links all the villages.

The east coast to Lizard Point

To the north of the peninsula, the snug hamlets dotted around the **River Helford** are a complete contrast to the rugged character of most of the Lizard. At the river's mouth stands **MAWNAN**, whose granite church of St Mawnan-in-Meneage is dedicated to the sixth-century Welsh missionary St Maunanus – Meneage means "land of monks". Upstream, outside the village of Gweek, lies the **Gweek Seal Sanctuary** (daily: summer 10am–5pm, winter 10am–4pm; £7.50), a rehabilitation and release centre for injured seals. On the south side of the estuary, **Frenchman's Creek**, one of a splay of creeks and arcane inlets running off the river, was the inspiration for Daphne Du

Maurier's novel of the same name – her evocation of it holds true: "still and soundless, surrounded by the trees, hidden from the eyes of men".

You can get over to the south bank by the seasonal ferry from Helford Passage to **Helford**, an agreeable old smugglers' haunt worth a snack stop – pub lunches are available in the *Shipwright's Arms*, whose garden overlooks the river. South of here, on the B3293, the broad, windswept plateau of Goonhilly Downs is interrupted by the futuristic saucers of Goonhilly Satellite Station and the nearby ranks of wind turbines. East, the road splits: left to **ST KEVERNE**, an inland village whose tidy square is flanked by two pubs and a church, right to meet the sea at **COVERACK**, a fishing port at one end of a sheltered bay. There's a handful of **places to stay** here, including the friendly *Fernleigh* (☎01326/280626; no credit cards; ❸) on Chymbloth Way, a turn-off from Harbour Road, which has wonderful bay views, and the smaller *Bakery Cottage* (☎01326/280474; no credit cards; ❶), right by the seafront. There's a **youth hostel** just west of Coverack overlooking the bay (☎0870/770 5780; closed Nov–Feb; £10.25), and a campsite, *Little Trevothan* (☎01326/280260, ⓦwww.littletrevothan.com; closed Oct–Easter). For **eating**, the *Lifeboat House Seafood Restaurant* (☎01326/280899; closed Mon & Oct–Easter) is pricey and often fully booked, but the fish is superb, and you can pick up first-class fish and chips from the attached takeaway.

Beyond the safe and clean swimming spot of **Kennack Sands**, the south tip of the promontory and mainland Britain's southernmost point, **Lizard Point**, is marked by a plain lighthouse and a couple of low-key cafés and gift shops. Sheltered from the ceaselessly churning sea, a tiny cove holds a disused lifeboat station. From the point, a road and footpath lead a mile inland to the nondescript village called simply **THE LIZARD**, holding several **accommodation** options, for example the nonsmoking *Caerthillian*, a comfortable Victorian B&B in the centre of the village (☎01326/290019; no credit cards; ❷), and, on Penmenner Road *Parc Brawse House* (☎01326/290466, ⓦwww .cornwall-online.co.uk/parcbrawsehouse; ❷) and the nonsmoking *Penmenner House* (☎01326/290370; ❸), both a twenty-minute walk from Lizard Point and forty minutes from Kynance Cove. Signposted from the village, a Victorian villa houses a **youth hostel** right on the coast, with majestic views (☎0870/770 6120, ⓔcoverack@yha.org.uk; closed Nov–March; £11.50). In the village, the *Top House* pub provides **snacks**.

A mile west, the peninsula's best-known beach, **Kynance Cove**, has sheer hundred-foot cliffs, stacks and arches of serpentine rock and offshore outcrops. The water quality here is excellent – but take care not to be stranded by the tide.

The west coast

Four miles north of Kynance Cove, the inland village of **MULLION** has a fifteenth- to sixteenth-century church dedicated to the Breton **St Mellane** (or Malo), with a dog-door for canine churchgoers. In the centre of the village, behind an enclosed garden at the top of Nansmellyon Road, *The Old Vicarage* (☎01326/240898, ⓦwww.s-h-systems.co.uk; no credit cards; ❹) provides elegant **B&B**, or there's *Campden House*, just outside Mullion on The Commons (☎01326/240365; no credit cards; ❶), ten minutes' walk from the sea and with snacks and evening meals available. There's a small beach at tiny **Mullion Cove**, sheltered behind a lovely harbour and more rock stacks, though the neighbouring sands at **Polurrian** and **Poldhu**, to the north, are better and attract surfers. At the cliff edge, the Marconi Monument marks the spot from which the first transatlantic radio transmission was made in 1901. Three miles further north, strong currents make it unsafe to swim at the beautiful beach at **Loe Bar**, a strip of shingle which separates the freshwater **Loe Pool** from the sea. The elongated Pool is one of two places claiming to be where the sword Excalibur was restored to its watery source (the other is on Bodmin Moor), and the path running along its western shore as far as Helston, five miles north, makes a fine **walk**.

Another three or four miles up the coast, **PORTHLEVEN** is a sizeable port that once served to export tin ore from the inland Stannary town of **HELSTON**, the main transport junction and centre for the Lizard peninsula. The town is best known for its **Furry Dance** (or Flora Dance), which dates from the seventeenth century. Held on May 8 (unless this falls on a Sun or Mon, when the procession takes place on the nearest Sat), it's a stately procession of top-hatted men and summer-frocked women performing a solemn dance through the town's streets and gardens. You can learn something about it and absorb plenty of other local history in the eclectic **Helston Folk Museum** (Mon–Sat 10am–1pm, closes 4pm school holidays; £2), housed in former market buildings behind the Guildhall on Church Street. Helston has the peninsula's only **tourist office** at 79 Meneage St (Aug Mon–Fri 10am–1pm & 2–4.30pm, Sat 10am–4pm; rest of year closes 1pm on Sat; ☎01326/565431). For a drink or a **pub** snack, check out the *Blue Anchor*, 50 Coinagehall St, a fifteenth-century monastery rest house, now a cramped pub with flagstone floors and mellow Spingo beer brewed on the premises in three strengths. Next door to the pub, the **B&B** at 52 Coinagehall St makes a smart night-stop, with solid old furnishings (☎01326/569334; no credit cards; ❷).

The Penwith peninsula

Though more densely populated than the Lizard, the **Penwith peninsula** is a more rugged landscape, with a raw appeal that is still encapsulated by **Land's End**, despite the commercial paraphernalia superimposed on that headland. The seascapes, the quality of the light and the slow tempo of the local fishing communities made this area a hotbed of artistic activity towards the end of the nineteenth century, when the painters of **Newlyn**, near **Penzance**, established a distinctive school of painting. More innovative figures – among them Ben Nicholson, Barbara Hepworth and Naum Gabo – were soon afterwards to make **St Ives** one of England's liveliest cultural communities, and their enduring influence is illustrated in the St Ives branch of the Tate Gallery, showcasing the Modern artists associated with the locality.

Penwith is far more easily toured than the Lizard, with a road circling its coastline and a better network of public transport from the two main towns, St Ives and Penzance, which also have most of the accommodation.

Penzance and around

Occupying a sheltered position at the northwest corner of Mount's Bay, **PENZANCE** has always been a major port, but most traces of the medieval town were obliterated at the end of the sixteenth century by a Spanish raiding party. Today the dominant style of Penzance is Georgian, particularly at the top of **Market Jew Street** (from *Marghas Jew*, meaning "Thursday Market"), which climbs from the harbour and the train and bus stations. At the top of the street stands the green-domed Victorian **Market House** before which stands a statue of **Humphry Davy** (1778–1829), the local woodcarver's son who pioneered the science of electrochemistry and invented the life-saving miners' safety-lamp which his statue holds.

Turn left here into **Chapel Street**, which has some of the town's finest buildings, including the flamboyant **Egyptian House**, built in 1835 to contain a geological museum but subsequently abandoned until its restoration 25 years ago. Across the street, the **Union Hotel** dates from the seventeenth century, and originally housed the town's assembly rooms: news of Admiral Nelson's victory at Trafalgar and the death of Nelson himself was first announced from the minstrels' gallery here in 1805.

West of Chapel Street on Morrab Road, the excellent **Penlee House Gallery and Museum** (Mon–Sat: May–Sept 10am–5pm; Oct–April 10.30am–4.30pm; £2, free on Sat) features works of the Newlyn School – impressionistic harbour scenes, frequently sentimentalized but often bathed in an evocatively luminous light. There are frequent exhibitions, and also displays on local history. **NEWLYN** itself, Cornwall's biggest fishing port, lies immediately south of Penzance, protected behind two long piers. The absorbing **Pilchard Works** here (Easter–October Mon–Fri 10am–6pm; £3.25) provides an insight into Cornwall's fishing industry and incorporates a working salt pilchard factory.

Practicalities

Penzance's **tourist office** (May–Sept Mon–Fri 9.30am–5pm, Sat 9am–5pm, Sun 10am–1pm; Oct–April Mon–Fri 9am–5pm, Sat 10am–1pm; ℡01736/362207, Ⓦwww.go-cornwall.com) is right next to the train and bus stations on the seafront. Penzance Computer Centre, 76 Market Jew St, provides **Internet access**.

Accommodation choices on Chapel Street include the historic *Union Hotel* (℡01736/362319; ❸), but most of the B&Bs are west of the centre along Morrab Road, where you'll find *Kimberley House* at no. 10 (℡01736/362727, Ⓦwww.s-h-systems.co.uk; no smoking; no credit cards; ❸), and on the parallel Alexandra Road, where there's *Holbein House* (℡01736/332625; no credit cards; ❶). On the seafront, the nonsmoking *Camilla House Hotel* is useful for the harbour at 12 Regent Terrace, off the Promenade (℡01736/363771, Ⓦwww.camillahouse-hotel.co.uk; ❸). The tidy and friendly *Penzance Backpackers* **hostel** (℡01736/363836, Ⓦwww.pzbackpack.com; £10), which also has private rooms (❶), is on Alexandra Road. There's a YHA hostel in a Georgian mansion at Castle Horneck, Alverton (℡0870/770 5992, Ⓔpenzance@yha.org.uk; closed Jan; £11.50), a two-mile walk or take bus #5 or #6 from Penzance station as far as the *Pirate Inn*, from which it's signposted.

Bar Coco's on Chapel Street is good for coffees, cakes, beers and tapas. Vegetarians and wholefoodies will feel at home in the spacious and relaxed *Brown's*, above a health shop in Bread Street, open daytime and on Friday evenings for a buffet (closed Sun). The *Blue Snappa*, 18 Market Place (at the top of Chapel Street), and the *Boatshed*, facing the harbour on the Promenade, are congenial café-bars serving ciabattas, salads, wraps and evening meals. Also on the Promenade, *The Olive Farm* sells delicious rolls and other takeaway snacks. Chapel Street has a couple of characterful **pubs**, the *Admiral Benbow*, crammed with gaudy ships' figureheads and other nautical items, and the *Turk's Head*, the town's oldest inn, reputed to date back to the thirteenth century.

St Michael's Mount

Frequent buses from Penzance leave for Marazion, five miles east, the access point to **St Michael's Mount** (April–Oct Mon–Fri 10.30am–5.30pm, plus most weekends; Nov–March guided tours Mon, Wed & Fri, phone for times ℡01736/710507; £4.80; NT), a couple of hundred yards offshore. A vision of the archangel Michael led to the building of a church on this granite pile around the fifth century, and within three centuries a Celtic monastery had been founded here. The present building derives from a chapel raised in the eleventh century by Edward the Confessor, who handed over the abbey to the Benedictine monks of Brittany's Mont St Michel, whose island abbey was the model for this one. After the Civil War, when it was used to store arms for the Royalist forces, it became the residence of the St Aubyn family, who still inhabit the castle. Some of the buildings date from the twelfth century, but the later additions are more interesting, such as the battlemented **chapel** and the seventeenth-century decorations of the **Chevy Chase Room**, the former refectory. At low tide the promontory can be approached on foot via a cobbled causeway; at high tide there are boats from Marazion (£1).

Mousehole to Land's End

Accounts vary as to the derivation of the name of **MOUSEHOLE** (pronounced "Mowzle"), though it may be from a smugglers' cave just south of town. In any case, the name evokes perfectly this minuscule harbour, cradled in the arms of a granite breakwater three miles south of Penzance. The village attracts more visitors than it can handle, so hang around until the crowds have departed before you walk through its tight tangle of lanes to take in Mousehole's oldest house, the fourteenth-century Keigwin House (a survival of a Spanish raid in 1595, when the village was set on fire), and a drink at the *Ship Inn*, which also has **rooms** (℡01736/731234; ❸). Half a mile inland, the churchyard wall at **Paul** holds a monument to Dolly Pentreath, a local resident who, at her death in 1777, was supposedly the last person to speak solely in Cornish.

Eight miles west, one of Penwith's best beaches lies at **PORTHCURNO**. Steep steps lead up from the beach of tiny white shells to the **Minack Theatre**, hewn out of the cliff in the 1930s and since enlarged to hold 750 seats, though retaining the basic Greek-inspired design. The spectacular backdrop of Porthcurno Bay makes this one of the country's most inspiring theatres – providing the weather holds. From May to September, a range of plays, operas and musicals are presented, with tickets at £5.50–7 (box office Mon–Fri from 9.30am; ℡01736/810181, ⓦwww.minack.com). Bring a cushion and a rug. You can also visit the **Exhibition Centre** (daily: April–Sept 9.30am–5.30pm; Oct–March 10am–4pm; closed during performances; £2.50), which allows you to see the theatre and follow the story of its creation through photographs and audiovisual displays.

On the shore to the east of Porthcurno, a white pyramid marks the spot where the first transatlantic cables were laid in 1880. On the headland beyond lies an Iron Age fort, **Treryn Dinas**, close to the famous rocking stone called **Logan's Rock**, a seventy-ton monster that was knocked off its perch by a nephew of playwright Oliver Goldsmith and a gang of sailors in 1824. Somehow they replaced the stone, but it never rocked again.

The extreme western tip of England, **Land's End**, lies four miles west of Porthcurno. Best approached on foot along the coastal path, the 60ft turf-covered cliffs provide a platform to view the Irish Lady, the Armed Knight, Dr Syntax Head and the rest of the Land's End outcrops, beyond which you can spot the Longships lighthouse, a mile and a half out to sea, and sometimes the

Wolf Rock lighthouse, nine miles southwest, or even the Isles of Scilly, twenty-eight miles away. Although nothing can completely destroy the potency of this majestic headland, the **Land's End Experience** theme park (daily: Easter–Oct 10am–6pm; Oct–Easter 10am–5pm, or earlier at quiet times; ℡0870/458 0099; £10), on an extensive site just behind, violates the spirit of the place, offering a trivializing panoply of lasers and unconvincing sound effects in place of the real open-air experience.

Whitesand Bay to Zennor

To the north of Land's End the rounded granite cliffs fall away at **Whitesand Bay** to reveal a glistening mile-long shelf of beach that offers the best swimming on the Penwith peninsula. The rollers make for good surfing and boards can be rented at **Sennen Cove**, the more popular southern end of the beach. There are a few places to **stay** around here, including *Myrtle Cottage* (℡01736/871698; no credit cards; ❷), which also has a cosy café open to non-residents, and nearby *Polwyn Cottage* on Old Coastguard Row (℡01736/871349; no credit cards; ❷). If you don't mind being a few minutes' walk inland, the *Whitesands Lodge* **hostel** makes a good local base (℡01736/871776, ⓦwww.whitesandslodge.co.uk; £12.50), with some private rooms (❷) as well as **camping** space.

Cape Cornwall, a highly scenic headland three miles northwards, is dominated by the chimney of the Cape Cornwall Mine, which closed in 1870. Half a mile inland the grimly grey village of **ST JUST-IN-PENWITH** was a centre of the tin and copper industry, and the rows of trim cottages radiating out from Bank Square are redolent of the close-knit community that once existed here. The tone is somewhat lightened by the grassy open-air theatre where the old Cornish miracle plays were staged; it was later used by Methodist preachers as well as Cornish wrestlers. Most of the local pubs have **accommodation**, for example the traditional *Star Inn* off Bank Square (℡01736/788767; no credit cards; ❷), and there's a **youth hostel** (℡0870/770 5906; closed Nov–March; £11.50) three-quarters of a mile south – take the left fork past the post office – and close to an excellent secluded **campsite**, *Kelynack Caravan and Camping Park* (℡01736/787633), which also has bunks (£8). For good **snacks**, *The Cook Book*, 3 Cape Cornwall Rd (closed Mon; no smoking), should satisfy, with tables outside and secondhand books on sale upstairs, or step into *Kegen Teg*, 12 Market Square, for a moderately priced **dinner** (℡01736/788562; no smoking at lunchtime; closed Sun).

Eight miles northeast of St Just, set in a landscape of rolling granite moorland, **ZENNOR** is associated with D.H. Lawrence, who came to live here with his wife Frieda in 1916. "It is a most beautiful place," he wrote, "lovelier even than the Mediterranean." The Lawrences stayed a year and a half in the village – long enough for him to write *Women in Love* – before being given notice to quit by the local constabulary, who suspected them of unpatriotic sympathies (their Cornish experiences were later described in *Kangaroo*). Zennor's fascinating **Wayside Museum** is dedicated to Cornish life from prehistoric times (April to late July, Sept & Oct daily 11am–5pm; late July to Aug daily 10.30am–5.30pm; £2.75). At the top of the lane, the church of **St Sennen** displays a sixteenth-century bench-carving of a mermaid who, according to local legend, was so entranced by the singing of a chorister that she lured him down to the sea, from where he never returned – though his singing can still occasionally be heard. Nearby, the *Tinners Arms* is a cosy place to **drink** and

△ Surfing in Carnwall

eat. If you don't mind sleeping up to six to a room, the *Old Chapel Backpackers Hostel* makes a fun place **to stay**, right next to the Wayside Museum (☎01736/798307, ⓦwww.backpackers.co.uk/zennor; £12); there's a family room (❷), and a café provides breakfast and evening meals.

The Iron Age village of **Chysauster** (April–Sept daily 10am–6pm; Oct daily 10am–5pm; £2; EH), located on a windy hillside a couple of miles inland from Zennor, off the minor road to Penzance, is the best-preserved ancient settlement in the southwest. Dating from about the first century BC, it contains two rows of four buildings, each consisting of a courtyard with small chambers leading off it, and a garden that was presumably used for growing vegetables.

St Ives

East of Zennor, the road runs four hilly miles on to the steeply built town of **ST IVES**, a place that has smoothly undergone the transition to holiday haunt from its previous role as a centre of the fishing industry. So productive were the offshore waters that a record sixteen and a half million fish were caught in one net on a single day in 1868, and the diarist Francis Kilvert was told by the local vicar that the smell was sometimes so great as to stop the church clock. By the time the pilchard reserves dried up around the early 1900s, the town was beginning to attract a vibrant **artists' colony**, precursors of the wave later headed by Ben Nicholson, Barbara Hepworth, Naum Gabo and the potter Bernard Leach, who in the 1960s were followed by a third wave including Terry Frost and Patrick Heron.

Sunday painters dominate the dozens of galleries sandwiched between the town's restaurants and bars; the place to view the best work created in St Ives is the **Tate St Ives**, overlooking Porthmeor Beach on the north side of town (March–Oct daily 10am–5.30pm; Nov–Feb Tues–Sun 10am–4.30pm; £4.75; combined ticket with Barbara Hepworth Museum £7.50). Most of the paintings, sculptures and ceramics displayed within the airy, gleaming-white building date from the period 1925 to 1975, and there are specially commissioned contemporary works on view as well as exhibitions. The gallery's rooftop **café** is one of the best places in town for a break.

A short distance away on Barnoon Hill, the **Barbara Hepworth Museum** (March–October daily 10am–5.30pm; Nov–Feb Tues–Sun 10am–4.30pm or dusk; £4.25; combined ticket with the Tate £7.50) provides a further insight into the local arts scene. One of the foremost non-figurative sculptors of her time, Hepworth lived in the building from 1949 until her death in a studio fire in 1975. Apart from the sculptures, which are arranged in positions chosen by Hepworth in the house and garden, the museum has background on her art, from photos and letters to catalogues and reviews.

Porthmeor Beach dominates the northern side of St Ives, its excellent water quality and surfer-friendly rollers drawing a regular crowd, while the broader **Porthminster Beach**, south of the station, is usually less crowded. East of town, there's a string of magnificent golden beaches lining **St Ives Bay** – especially fine on the far side of the port of Hayle, at the mouth of the eponymous river.

Practicalities

St Ives **train station** is off Porthminster Beach, just below the **bus station** on Station Hill. The **tourist office** is in the narrow Street-an-Pol, two minutes' walk away (mid-May to June Mon–Sat 9.30am–5.30pm, Sun 10am–1pm; July

& Aug Mon–Sat 9am–6pm, Sun 10am–4pm; Sept Mon–Fri 9.30am–5pm, Sat 9am–1pm; Oct to mid-May Mon–Fri 9am–5pm, Sat 10am–1pm; ℡01736/796297, ⓦwww.go-cornwall.com).

Among the numerous **accommodation** choices near Porthminster Beach and the stations, try either of the two quiet B&Bs, *Chy-Roma*, 2 Seaview Terrace (℡01736/797539, ⓦwww.connexions.co.uk/chyroma; no credit cards; ❷), and *Starfish*, 6 Porthminster Terrace ℡01736/799575, ⓦwww.starfishbandb.co.uk; no smoking; no credit cards; ❷), or the Edwardian *Primrose Valley* hotel, Porthminster Beach (℡01736/794939, ⓦwww.primroseonline.co.uk; ❺). Alternatively, *Cornerways*, The Square ℡01736/796706; no credit cards; ❸), offers tasteful B&B in a modern cottage conversion above Porthmeor Beach. The *St Ives Backpackers* **hostel** at The Stennack (℡01736/799444, ⓦwww.backpackers.co.uk/st-ives; £14, double rooms ❶) occupies an old Wesleyan chapel school, while the nearest **campsite**, *Ayr*, at Higher Ayr (℡01736/795855, ⓦwww.ayrholidaypark.co.uk), lies half a mile west of the centre above Porthmeor Beach.

St Ives has a dazzling range of **restaurants**. With its sun deck and beach location, *Porthminster Beach Café*, on Porthminster Beach (℡01736/795352; closed Nov to mid-March), makes a superb spot for coffees, lunches, cream teas and fairly expensive evening meals. Under the same management, the *Porthgwidden Beach Café* in the Downalong area of town offers a smaller range of similar fare. On the harbourfront, *Alba* (℡01736/797222; closed Sun eve & all Mon in winter; moderate–expensive) is a sleekly modern restaurant in a converted lifeboat house, while the *Harbour Kitchen* café downstairs serves some of the same locally sourced dishes at lower prices. For a simple pizza or pasta in mellow surroundings, try *Peppers*, 22 Fore St (℡01736/794014). On Tregenna Place, *Isobar* is a cocktail and tapas bar with DJs on the decks and a separate club upstairs.

The Isles of Scilly

The **Isles of Scilly** are a compact archipelago of about a hundred islands 28 miles southwest of Land's End, none of them bigger than three miles across, and only five of them inhabited – **St Mary's**, **Tresco**, **Bryher**, **St Martin's** and **St Agnes**. In the annals of folklore, the Scillies are the peaks of the submerged land of Lyonesse, though in fact they form part of the same granite mass as Land's End, Bodmin Moor and Dartmoor. Despite rarely rising above a hundred feet, they possess a remarkable variety of landscape. All are swept by an energizing briny air filled with the cries of seabirds, and the beaches are well-nigh irresistible, ranging from small coves to vast untrammelled strands – though the water is very cold. Along with Cornwall's greatest concentration of prehistoric remains and some fabulous rock formations, you'll also see masses of **flowers** here; along with tourism, the main source of income is flower-growing, for which the equable climate and the long hours of sunshine – their name means "Sun Isles" – make the islands ideal.

Free of traffic, theme parks and amusement arcades, the Scillies are a welcome respite from the tourist trail, the main drawbacks being the high cost of reaching the islands and the shortage of accommodation – making advance booking essential at any time. If you're coming between May and September, try to time your visit to be here on a Wednesday or Friday evening to witness the **gig races** performed by six-oared vessels around thirty feet in length.

Getting to the islands

The islands are accessible by sea or air. **Boats from Penzance to St Mary's**, operated by the Isles of Scilly Steamship Group (℡0845/710 5555, ⓦwww .ios-travel.co.uk), depart from the South Pier, where there's a ticket office. Sailings, which can be nauseatingly rough, take place daily between April and October and last about two and three-quarter hours; single tickets cost £38, day returns £32, short-break returns (travelling on Mon, Tues or Wed) £60, and period returns £78, with discounts for children. There are ferries between each of the inhabited islands (about £6.50 return fare), though these are sporadic in winter.

The main departure points for **flights** (also operated by the Isles of Scilly Steamship Company) are **Land's End**, near St Just (Mon–Sat; 15min; £80–103 return), **Newquay** (Mon–Sat; 30min; £100–125 return), **Exeter** (Mon–Sat; 50min; £199 return), **Bristol** (Mon–Sat; 1hr 10min; £245 return) and **Southampton** (Mon–Wed & Fri; 90min; £260 return). In winter, there are departures only from Land's End and Newquay. British International also runs **helicopter** flights (℡01736/363871, ⓦwww.scillyhelicopter.co.uk) from the heliport a mile east of Penzance to St Mary's (not Sun) and Tresco (not Sun) taking twenty minutes, with return fares currently at £117 – though you can get discounted day returns, advance returns and short-break returns.

St Mary's

The island of **ST MARY'S** holds the overwhelming majority of the archipelago's population and most of its tourist accommodation. From the airport there are buses to shuttle passengers the mile to **HUGH TOWN**, straddling a neck of land at the southwestern end of the island. Ferries from Penzance dock on the north side of town, under a knob of land still known as the Garrison, where the eight-pointed **Star Castle**, built in Elizabeth I's reign, has been converted into a hotel. The nearby rampart walk is a good place to get your bearings, affording views over all the islands. On Church Street, the engaging **Isles of Scilly Museum** (April–Oct daily 10am–noon, 1.30–4.30pm & 7.30–9pm; Nov–March Mon–Sat 10am–noon; £1.50) shows relics salvaged from the many ships foundered on or around the islands. Hugh Town's best bathing **beach** is in the sheltered bay of Porthcressa, from which a path wanders south to skirt the **Peninnis Headland**, passing some impressive sea-sculpted granite rocks. The path follows the coast to **Old Town Bay**, around which the modern houses of **OLD TOWN** give little hint of its former role as the island's chief port. There are cafés and a sheltered south-facing beach, where Underwater Diving Safari offers diving trips and rents out equipment (℡01720/422732; closed Nov–Easter).

Three-quarters of a mile east, **Porth Hellick** is the next major inlet on the island's southern coast, marked by a rugged quartz monument to the fantastically named Sir Cloudesley Shovell, who in 1707 was washed up here from a shipwreck which claimed four ships and nearly 1700 lives. Near the rock shape known as the **Loaded Camel**, a gate leads to a 4000-year-old **barrow**, probably used by Bronze Age people from the Iberian peninsula who were the Scillies' first colonists.

Pelistry Bay, on the northeastern side of St Mary's, less than two miles from Hugh Town, is one of the most secluded spots on the island, its sandy beach and crystal-clear waters sheltered by the outlying **Toll's Island**, joined to St Mary's at low tide by a slender strand. The best remnants of early human settlement on the Scillies are to be found at **Halangy Down**, a mile or so north of Hugh Town, overlooking the sea. Dating from around 200 BC, it's an extensive complex of stone huts, chief of them a structure built around a courtyard with interconnecting buildings. Most complete is **Bant's Carn**, part of a much earlier site, probably contemporaneous with the one at Porth Hellick, comprising a long rectangular roofed chamber where cremations were carried out.

Hugh Town's **tourist office**, on Hugh Street (Easter to Oct Mon–Fri 8.30am–5.30pm, Sat 8.30am–5pm; Nov–Easter Mon–Fri 9am–5pm; ☎01720/422536, ⓦwww.simplyscilly.co.uk), has information on available accommodation for all the Scillies. Though availability can be scarce in peak season, the town is well supplied with **B&Bs**: The Strand has the friendly, nonsmoking *Lyonesse Guest House* (☎01720/422458; no credit cards; ❸; closed Nov–March), right on the harbourfront, while *The Boathouse*, on the Thoroughfare, also enjoys a good view over the harbour (☎01720/422688; ❸; closed Nov to mid-April). High up on the Garrison, *Veronica Lodge* (☎01720/422585; no credit cards; ❸) has a spacious garden and excellent views, while close by is the island's most atmospheric hotel, the *Star Castle* (☎01720/422317, ⓦwww.starcastlescilly.demon.co.uk; ❽; closed 6wks Jan–Feb), and a **campsite**, *Garrison Campsite* (☎01720/422670). Camping elsewhere on the island is not allowed.

In the middle of the main Hugh Street, the *Kavorna Bakery* is a handy spot for daytime refreshment, while the *Pilot's Gig*, at the end of the street below the Garrison Gate, offers simple lunchtime snacks and fish suppers (both closed Oct–Easter).

Tresco

After St Mary's, **TRESCO** is the most visited island of the Scillies, yet the boatloads of visitors somehow manage to lose themselves on the two-miles-by-one island, the second largest in the group. Once the private estate of Devon's Tavistock Abbey, Tresco still retains a cloistered, slightly privileged air, and it has no budget accommodation.

The centrepiece of the island is the **Abbey Gardens** (daily 10am–4pm; £6.50), where subtropical gardens first laid out in 1834 are set amid the ruins of the priory. Many of the plants were grown from seeds taken from London's Kew Gardens, others were brought here from Africa, South America and the Antipodes. The entry ticket also admits you to a collection of figureheads and name plates taken from local shipwrecks. There are alluring sandy beaches southwest of the Abbey at **Appletree Bay**, north and south of **Old Grimsby**, on the island's eastern side, and around the cluster of cottages that make up **New Grimsby**, on the island's western shore. North of here, Tresco's tidy fields give way to an untended heathland of heather and gorse, while a narrow path traces the coast to **Charles' Castle**, built in the 1550s. Strategically positioned on a height to cover the lagoon-like channel separating Tresco from Bryher, the castle was in fact badly designed, its guns unable to depress far enough to be effective, and it was superseded in 1651 by the much better-preserved **Cromwell's Castle**, actually no more than a gun-tower, built at sea level next to a pretty sandy cove. The shore path winds northwest from here, round to **Piper's Hole**, a deep underground cave accessible from the cliff edge on the northern coast.

Apart from properties for weekly rental, Tresco's only **accommodation** is at the *Island Hotel* at the centre of the island (☎01720/422883, ⓦwww.tresco.co.uk; ❾; closed Nov to mid-March), and the *New Inn* at New Grimsby

(☎01720/422844, ⓦwww.tresco.co.uk; ❸). Both have gourmet **restaurants**, and the *New Inn* also serves quality pub snacks in its bar and garden.

Bryher and Samson

Covered with a thick carpet of bracken, heather and bramble, **BRYHER** is the wildest of the inhabited islands, but the seventy-odd inhabitants have introduced some pockets of order in the form of flower plantations. These are mostly confined to the small settlement around the quay and climbing up the slopes of **Watch Hill** on Bryher's eastern side. The exposed western seaboard takes the full brunt of the Atlantic, most spectacularly at the aptly named **Hell Bay**, worth catching when the wind's up. In contrast to this sound and fury, peace reigns in the southern cove of **Rushy Bay**, one of the best beaches on the island. From the quay, there are frequent tours to seal and bird colonies, and to the small isle of **SAMSON**, deserted since 1855. Most of the famous **gig races** start off from Nut Rock, to the east of Samson, finishing at St Mary's quay.

Among Bryher's tiny choice of **B&Bs** are *Soleil D'Or*, on the eastern side of the island with views over to Tresco (☎01720/422003; ❷), and *Bank Cottage*, on the western side near Gweal Pool (☎01720/422612; ❸) – both of which offer meals, and both are closed November–March. There's a **campsite** at Jenford Farm on Watch Hill (☎01720/422886; closed Nov–March). The island's one hotel, the *Hell Bay* (☎01720/422947; ❽; closed Nov–Feb), below Gweal Hill, has a **bar** and **restaurant**, and you can also eat inexpensively at the *Vine Café*, below Watch Hill (no credit cards; closed Nov–Feb, Fri eve & Sat eve), and the *Fraggle Rock*, near the post office.

St Martin's

The main landing stage at **ST MARTIN'S** is on the southern promontory, at the head of the majestic sweep of **Par Beach** – a fitting entry to the island that boasts the best of the Scillies' beaches. From the quay, a road leads up to **HIGHER TOWN**, the main concentration of houses and location of the only shop as well as St Martin's Diving Centre (☎01720/422848, ⓦwww .scillydiving.com). Beyond the church, follow the road westwards along the island's long, narrow ridge to **LOWER TOWN**, little more than a cluster of cottages on the western extremity, overlooking the uninhabited isles of **Teän** and **St Helen's**. The latter holds the remains of a tenth-century oratory, monks' dwellings and a chapel, as well as a pest house, erected in 1756 to house plague-carriers entering British waters.

Along the gentler southern shore, you'll find the long strand of **Lawrence's Bay** and large areas of flowerbeds. On the northern side, the coast is rougher, with the exception of **Great Bay**, a beautiful half-mile recess of sand, utterly secluded and ideal for swimming. From its western end, you can climb across boulders at low tide to the hilly and wild **White Island**, on the northeastern side of which is a vast cave, **Underland Girt**, accessible at low tide. Below **St Martin's Head** on the northeastern tip of the main island, site of a red and white Daymark erected in 1683 (not 1637 as inscribed) as a warning to shipping, another fine beach, **Perpitch**, looks out to the scattered Eastern Isles, slivers of rock to which boats take trippers to view puffins and grey seals.

St Martin's has just one **B&B**, *Polreath* (☎01720/422046; ❺; closed Nov to mid-March), in Higher Town, with all-round views and a café/restaurant, and there's also a select **hotel**, *St Martin's on the Isle*, Lower Town (☎01720/422092; closed Nov–Feb; ❽), consisting of a cluster of cottages looking onto a sandy beach. There's a relatively sheltered **campsite** (℡01720/422888, ⓦwww.stmartinscampsite.co.uk; closed mid–Oct to March), just off the road near Lawrence's Bay. **Snacks** are available at the *Seven Stones Inn* in Lower Town.

St Agnes

Visitors to the southernmost inhabited island of the Scillies, **ST AGNES**, disembark at **Porth Conger**, from where a road leads to the western side of the island, on the way passing the disused **Old Lighthouse**, one of the oldest in the country, dating from 1680. From here the right-hand fork leads to **Periglis Cove**, a mooring for boats on the western side of the island, while the left-hand fork goes to **St Warna's Cove**, where the patron saint of shipwrecks is reputed to have landed from Ireland, the exact spot being marked by a holy well. Between the two coves the coastal path passes the miniature **Troy Town Maze**, thought to have been created a couple of centuries ago, but possibly much older. Beyond St Warna's Cove, the path continues down over Wingletang Down to the southern headland of **Horse Point**, where there are some tortuous wind-eroded rocks. The eastern side of St Agnes has one of the best beaches, the small, sheltered **Covean**, and at low tide you can cross a sand bar to reach the islet of **Gugh**, where there's a scattering of untended Bronze Age remains. St Agnes's western side looks out onto the **Western Rocks**, a horseshoe of islets rich in birdlife that can be explored on boat tours.

Best of the **B&B**s on St Agnes are the *Coastguards*, past the Old Lighthouse on the island's western side (℡01720/422373; ❸; closed Nov–March), and *Covean Cottage*, above Porth Conger (℡01720/422620; ❸; closed Oct–Easter). Both have **café/restaurants** open to all. There's a good **campsite** at *Troy Town Farm* near Periglis Cove (℡01720/422360; closed Nov–Feb). Above the jetty at Porth Conger, the *Turk's Head* serves beer and superb pasties.

The north Cornish coast to Bude

Though generally harsher than the county's southern seaboard, the north Cornish coast is punctuated by some of the finest beaches in England, the most popular of which are to be found around **Newquay**, the surfers' capital, and **Padstow**, also renowned for its gourmet seafood restaurants. North of the Camel estuary, the coast is an almost unbroken line of cliffs as far as the Devon border, the gaunt, exposed terrain making a melodramatic setting for **Tintagel**, though there are more beaches at **Bude**, attracting both surfers and families. The more westerly stretches of this coast are littered with the derelict stacks and castle-like ruins of the engine-houses that once powered the region's **copper** and **tin mines**, industries that at one time led the world.

Newquay and around

It is difficult to imagine a lineage for **NEWQUAY** that extends more than a few decades, but the "new quay" was built in the fifteenth century in what was already a long-established fishing port. Up to then it had been more colourfully known as Towan Blistra, and was concentrated in the sheltered west end of the bay. The town was given a boost in the nineteenth century when its harbour was expanded for coal import and a railway was constructed across the peninsula for china clay shipments. With the trains came a swelling stream of seasonal visitors, drawn to the town's superb position on a knuckle of cliffs overlooking fine golden sands and Atlantic rollers, natural advantages which have made Newquay the premier resort of north Cornwall. Try to coincide your visit to Newquay with one of the **surfing competitions** and events that run right through the summer – contact the tourist office for details.

The centre of town is a somewhat tacky parade of shops and restaurants, partly pedestrianized, from which lanes lead to ornamental gardens and sloping lawns on the cliff-tops. At the bottom of Beach Road, adjacent to the small harbour, the **Blue Reef Aquarium** (daily 10am–5pm; £5.50) provides some distraction, allowing you to admire tropical fish from an underwater tunnel. Below the aquarium, in the crook of the massive Towan Head, **Towan Beach** is the most central of the seven miles of firm sandy beaches that follow in an almost unbroken succession. You can reach all of them on foot, though for some of the further ones, such as **Porth Beach**, with its grassy headland, or the extensive **Watergate Bay**, you might prefer to make use of bus #556 to Padstow (not Sun in winter). The beaches can all be unbearably crowded in full season, and all are popular with surfers, particularly Watergate and – west of Towan Head – **Fistral Bay**, the largest of the town beaches. On the other side of East Pentire Head from Fistral, **Crantock Beach** – reachable over the Gannel River by ferry or upstream footbridge – is usually less crowded, and has a lovely backdrop of dunes and undulating grassland. South of Crantock, **Holywell Bay** and the three-mile expanse of **Perran Beach**, enhanced by caves and natural rock arches, are also very popular with surfers.

Practicalities

Newquay's **train station** is off Cliff Road, a couple of hundred yards from the **bus station** on East Street, which itself lies opposite the **tourist office** on Marcus Hill (mid-May to mid-Sept Mon–Sat 9.30am–5.30pm, Sun 9.30am–1pm; Oct–April Mon–Fri 9.30am–4.30pm, Sat 9.30am–12.30pm; ℡01637/854020, ⓦwww.newquay.co.uk). Ask here about places offering **surfing courses** as well as kite-surfing, paragliding, land yachting and wave-skiing sessions. You can rent or buy surfing equipment from beach stalls or from various outlets around town. There's an **Internet** café, *Tad & Nick's*, at 72 Fore St.

Newquay's **accommodation** is plentiful but can still be booked solid in July and August. Phone ahead for the beautifully furnished *Rockpool Cottage*, 92 Fore St (℡07971/594485, ⓦwww.rockpoolcottage.co.uk; ❷; closed Jan–Easter), convenient for Fistral Beach, or the nonsmoking *Trewinda Lodge*, 17 Eliot Gardens (℡01637/877533, ⓦwww.trewindalodge.co.uk; ❷), a few minutes' walk from Tolcarne Beach; both B&Bs can give informed advice to surfers, and neither accepts credit cards. Among the town's plethora of independent **hostels**, there's the fully equipped *Escape Hotel*, near the tourist office at 1 Mount Wise (℡01637/851736, ⓦwww.escape2newquay.co.uk; £18–20); *St Christopher's*, overlooking the harbour above *Belushi's* bar at 35 Fore St (℡01637/859111, ⓦwww.st-christophers.co.uk/newquay_hostel; £18–25); and *Safi*, Narrowcliff Seafront (℡01637/872800, ⓦwww.mysafi.com; £15–30), a gigantic place facing Tolcarne Beach with a 24-hour bar. On the cliff-top outside **Perranporth**, at the southern end of Perran Beach, there's a **youth hostel** housed in a former coastguard station (℡0870/770 5994; closed Oct to mid-April; £10.25). Newquay's **campsites** include *Trevelgue* (℡01637/851851, ⓦwww.trevelgue.co.uk; closed Nov–Easter), a mile east of Porth Beach on Trevelgue Road.

Although most of Newquay's numerous **eateries** are pretty bland, recent years have seen an influx of more stylish places, for example *Finn's*, right on the harbour (☏01637/874062; closed Mon & Tues; expensive), where you can watch the fish being landed just yards away and cooked in the outdoor kitchen. You can eat more cheaply in one of the town's good choice of **cafés**, such as *The Chy*, a sleekly modern place on Beach Road, with a spacious terrace for seafood lunches by day, and DJs in the evenings, and the laid-back *Café Irie*, 38 Fore St, which serves snacks, teas and evening meals accompanied by world music sounds and live folk (closed Tues & Wed). At **Watergate Bay**, *The Beach Hut* provides surf food and fish specials all day.

For a **night out**, have a drink in the Aussie-themed *Walkabout Inn* on Beachfield Avenue, with great waterside views, before hitting one of the town's **clubs**; the current hot spots are *Berties* on East Street (☏01637/872255, ⓦwww.bertiesclub.com), *Sailors* on Fore Street (☏01637/872838), *The Beach* (☏01637/872194, ⓦwww.beachclubnewquay.com) and the *Koola Club* on Beach Road (☏01637/870240, ⓦwww.thekoola.com), and *Tall Trees* on Tolcarne Road (☏01637/850313, ⓦwww.talltreesclub.co.uk).

Padstow and around

The small fishing port of **PADSTOW** is nearly as popular as Newquay, but has a very different feel. Enclosed within the estuary of the Camel – the only river of any size that empties on Cornwall's north coast – the town has long retained its position as the principal fishing port on this stretch, and can boast the best seafood restaurants. Padstow is also known for its annual **Obby Oss** festival, a May Day romp when a local in horse costume prances through the town preceded by a masked and club-wielding "teaser", in a spirited re-enactment of an old fertility rite.

On the hill overlooking Padstow, the church of **St Petroc** is dedicated to Cornwall's most important saint, a Welsh or Irish monk who landed here in the sixth century, died in the area and gave his name to the town – "Petrock's Stow". The building has a fine fifteenth-century font, an Elizabethan pulpit and some amusing carved bench-ends. The walls are lined with monuments to the local Prideaux family, who still occupy nearby **Prideaux Place**, an Elizabethan manor house with grand staircases, richly furnished rooms full of portraits, fantastically ornate ceilings and formal gardens (Easter & mid-May to early Oct Mon–Thurs & Sun 1.30–5pm, last tour at 4pm; £6, grounds only £2), all of which have been used as settings for various films, including *Twelfth Night* and *Oscar and Lucinda*.

The harbour is jammed with launches and boats offering cruises in Padstow Bay, while a regular **ferry** (summer daily 8am–7.30pm; winter Mon–Sat 8am–4.30pm; £2 return) carries people across the river to **ROCK** – close to the low-slung church of **St Enodoc** (John Betjeman's burial place) and to the good beaches around Polzeath (see p.418). At low water, the ferry leaves from near the war memorial downstream.

The coast on the **west side** of the estuary offers more beaches, as well as some terrific walks. The river mouth is clogged by **Doom Bar**, a sand bar that was allegedly the curse of a mermaid who had been mortally wounded by a fisherman who mistook her for a seal. Apart from thwarting the growth of Padstow as a busy commercial port, the bar has scuppered some three hundred vessels, with great loss of life. Round **Stepper Point** you can reach the sandy and secluded Harlyn Bay and, turning the corner southwards, **Constantine Bay**, the area's best surfing beach. The dunes backing the beach and the rock pools skirting it make this one of the most appealing bays on this coast, more-over it boasts the best water quality, though the tides can be treacherous and bathing hazardous near the rocks. Three or four miles further south, the slate outcrops of **Bedruthan Steps** were traditionally held to be the stepping-stones of a giant called Bedruthan; they can be readily viewed from the cliff-top path – at a point which drivers can reach on the B3276 – and steps lead down to the broad beach below (not advised for swimming).

Padstow is also the start of an excellent **cycle-track** converted from the old rail line to Wadebridge, forming part of the **Camel Trail**, a fifteen-mile traf-fic-free path that follows the river up as far as Bodmin Moor. You can **rent bikes** from Brinham's (℡01841/532594) and Padstow Cycle Hire (℡01841/533533), both on South Quay, by the start of the Trail.

Practicalities

Padstow's **tourist office** is on the harbour (Easter–Oct daily 9.30am–5pm; Nov–Easter Mon–Fri 9am–4pm; ℡01841/533449, Ⓦwww.padstowlive.com). Central **accommodation** includes the B&B at 4 Riverside (℡01841/532383; no credit cards; ❷), also on the harbour, and *Armside*, 10 Cross St (℡01841/532271; ❸), an elegant eighteenth-century townhouse. The nearest **youth hostel** is well sited at Treyarnon Bay (℡0870/770 6076, Ⓔtreyarnon@yha.org.uk; closed Nov–March; £10.25), for which you can take the #556 Newquay bus to Constantine, then walk half a mile. The *Dennis Cove* **campsite** (℡01841/532349; closed Oct–Easter) is alongside the estuary, about a ten-minute walk south of town.

Padstow's quayside is lined with pasty shops, snack bars and pubs, but foodies know the town best for its **restaurants**, particularly those associated with star chef Rick Stein, whose *Seafood Restaurant*, at Riverside (℡01841/532700), is one of England's top places for fish. Its success has led to the opening of two offshoots, *St Petroc's Bistro* at 4 New St (℡01841/532700), offering a lighter, cheaper but more restricted version of its parent's menu, and, nearby at 10 Middle St, the cool and casual *Rick Stein's Café* (closed Sun). All three places also have classy accommodation (❺–❻). Plainer pizzas and pastas can be had at *Rojano's* on Mill Square (closed Sun and all Dec & Jan), while the *London Inn* on Lanadwell Street does **pub** grub. Picnickers can sample some of Stein's creations from his **delicatessen** on South Quay.

Polzeath and Port Isaac

Facing west into Padstow Bay, the beaches of and around **POLZEATH** are the finest in the vicinity, pelted by rollers which make this one of the best surf-ing sites in the West Country (tuition and gear to rent are available from stalls and shops). The *Seascape Hotel* offers about the only solid-walled **accommo-dation** around here (℡01208/863638, Ⓦwww.seascapehotel.co.uk; ❺), while the popular *Tristram* **campsite** (℡01208/862215; closed Nov–Feb) is on a cliff overlooking the beach. On the seafront, the *Galleon* does various snacks and takeaways, *Finn's* serves full meals, and the *Oyster Catcher* bar is a lively evening hangout.

The next settlement of any size is **PORT ISAAC**, wedged in a gap in the precipitous cliff wall and dedicated to the crab and lobster trade. Narrow lanes lead down to the seafront, where there are a couple of pubs and a pebble beach and rock pools exposed by the low tide. The village offers a range of **accommodation**, notably the *Slipway Hotel* (℡01208/880264, Ⓦwww .portisaac.com; ❻), a sixteenth-century building right opposite the harbour, the *Old School Hotel*, higher up on Fore Street (℡01208/880721, Ⓦwww .cornwall-online.co.uk/old-school-hotel; ❸), and *Anchorage Guest House*, 12

The Terrace (℡01208/880629; nonsmoking; no credit cards; ❷) – the last two with wonderful views.

You can sample the local crab from stalls at the harbour or from either of the excellent **restaurants** at the *Slipway Hotel* and the *Old School* (closed Tues in winter), which is also open for snacks and teas. The *Golden Lion* **pub** has an adjoining bistro and balcony seating overlooking the harbour.

Tintagel

East of Port Isaac, the coast is wild and unspoiled, making for some steep and strenuous walking, and providing an appropriate backdrop for the forsaken ruins of **Tintagel Castle** (daily: April to mid-July & late Aug to Sept 10am–6pm; mid-July to late Aug 10am–7pm; Oct 10am–5pm; Nov–March 10am–4pm; £3.20; EH). It was the twelfth-century chronicler Geoffrey of Monmouth who first popularized the notion that this was the **birthplace of King Arthur**, son of Uther Pendragon and Ygrayne. Tintagel is certainly a

King Arthur in Cornwall

Did **King Arthur** really exist? If he did, it's likely that he was an amalgam of two people: a sixth-century Celtic warlord who united the local tribes in a series of successful battles against the invading Anglo-Saxons, and a local Cornish saint. Whatever his origins, his role was recounted and inflated by poets and troubadours in later centuries. There is no mention of him in the ninth- to twelfth-century *Anglo-Saxon Chronicle*, but his exploits were elaborated by the medieval chroniclers Geoffrey of Monmouth, who made Arthur the conqueror of western Europe, and William of Malmesbury, who narrated the legend that, after being mortally wounded in battle, Arthur sailed to Avalon (Glastonbury), where he was buried alongside Guinevere. The Arthurian legends were crystallized in Thomas Malory's epic, *Morte d'Arthur* (1485), further romanticized in Tennyson's *Idylls of the King* (1859–85) and resurrected in T.H. White's saga, *The Once and Future King* (1937–58).

Although there are places throughout Britain and Europe which claim some association with Arthur, it's England's West Country, and **Cornwall** in particular, that has the greatest concentration of places boasting a link. Here, the legends, fertilized by fellow Celts from Brittany and Wales, have established deep roots, so that, for example, the spirit of Arthur is said to be embodied in the Cornish chough – a bird now almost extinct. Cornwall's most famous Arthurian site is **Tintagel**, which is said to be his birthplace, and where Merlin is thought to have lived in a cave under the castle (and also on a rock near Mousehole, south of Penzance, according to some). Nearby **Bodmin Moor** is full of places with associated names such as "King Arthur's Bed" and "King Arthur's Downs", while Camlan, the battlefield where Arthur was mortally wounded fighting against his nephew Mordred, is thought to lie on the northern reaches of the moor at Slaughterbridge, near **Camelford** (which is also sometimes identified as Camelot itself). At **Dozmary Pool**, the knight Bedivere was dispatched by the dying Arthur to return the sword Excalibur to the mysterious hand emerging from the water – though Loe Pool in Mount's Bay also claims this honour. According to some, Arthur's body was transported after the battle to **Boscastle**, on Cornwall's northern coast, from where a funeral barge transported the body to Avalon.

Cornwall is also the presumed home of King Mark, who sent the knight Tristan to Ireland to fetch his betrothed, Iseult; his headquarters is supposed to have been at Castle Dore, north of Fowey. Out beyond Land's End, the fabled, vanished country of Lyonesse is also said to be the original home of Arthur, as well as being (according to Spenser's *Faerie Queene*) the birthplace of Tristan.

plausibly resonant candidate for the abode of the Once and Future King, but the **castle** ruins in fact belong to a Norman stronghold occupied by the earls of Cornwall, who after sporadic spurts of rebuilding allowed it to decay, most of it having been washed into the sea by the sixteenth century. The remains of a sixth-century **Celtic monastery** are also visible on the headland, and have provided important insights into how the country's earliest monastic houses were organized.

The easiest access to the site is from the village of **TINTAGEL**, a dreary collection of cafés and B&Bs where the only item of note is the **Old Post Office** (April–Sept daily 11am–5.30pm; Oct daily 11am–4pm; £2.40; NT), a rickety-roofed slate-built construction dating from the fourteenth century, now restored to its appearance in the Victorian era when it was used as a post office.

The **tourist office** is in the car park on the road from Camelford (daily: March–Oct 10am–5pm; Nov–Feb 10.30am–4pm; ☎01840/779084). Most of the local **accommodation** is fairly basic, but you'll find a pair of comfortable B&Bs at the end of the sea-facing Atlantic Road: *Pendrin House* (☎01840/770560, ⓦwww.pendrinhouse.co.uk; ❷; closed Nov–Feb) and the nonsmoking *Bosayne* (☎01840/770514, ⓦwww.bosayne.co.uk; ❸). Nearer the castle, and within sight of it, is *Castle View*, 2 King Arthur's Terrace (☎01840/770421, ⓔcastleviewbandb@aol.com; no smoking; no credit cards; ❶), small and plain and offering a no-breakfast option. Three-quarters of a mile west of the village at Dunderhole Point, the offices of a former slate quarry now house a **youth hostel** with great coastal views (☎0870/770 6068; closed Nov to mid-April; £10.25). Scenic **camping** is available at the *Headland* on Atlantic Road (☎01840/770239, ⓦwww.headlandcaravanpark.co.uk; closed Oct–Easter). Both the *Old Malt House* and the *Tintagel Arms Hotel* on Fore Street have **restaurants**.

Boscastle

Three miles east of Tintagel, the port of **BOSCASTLE** lies compressed within a narrow ravine drilled by the rivers Jordan and Valency, its tidy riverfront bordered by thatched and lime-washed houses. Above and behind, a collection of seventeenth- and eighteenth-century cottages can be seen on a circular walk that traces the valley of the Valency for about a mile to reach Boscastle's graceful **parish church**, tucked away in a peaceful glen. A mile and a half further up the valley lies another church, **St Juliot's**, restored by Thomas Hardy when he was plying his trade as a young architect.

Boscastle's **tourist office** is situated in the car park at the bottom of the main road into the village (daily: March–Oct 10am–5pm; Nov–Feb 10.30am–4pm; ☎01840/250010). *St Christopher's Hotel* (☎01840/250412, ⓦwww.stchristophershotel.co.uk; ❷; closed Dec–Feb), a restored Georgian manor house at the top of the High Street, offers first-rate accommodation, but for a real Thomas Hardy experience, head for the *Old Rectory*, on the road to St Juliot (☎01840/250225, ⓦwww.stjuliot.com; no smoking; no under-12s; ❸; closed Dec–March), where you can stay in the author's bedroom and roam the extensive grounds. There's also a fine old **youth hostel** on the harbourside (☎0870/770 5710; closed mid-Oct to mid-March; £10.25). Nearby, you can eat at the *Harbour Restaurant* (☎01840/250380; closed Nov to Easter, also eves Easter–May & Oct), serving sandwiches and teas as well as organic, Asian-influenced food. Village **pubs** include the *Napoleon*, in the upper part of Boscastle, which has a seafood bistro and a spacious lawned garden, and the *Cobweb* down near the harbour, with bar food and good atmosphere; both have live music evenings.

Bude and around

There is little distinctively Cornish in Cornwall's northernmost town of **BUDE**, four miles west of the Devon border. Built around an estuary surrounded by a fine expanse of sands, the town has sprouted a crop of holiday homes and hotels, though these have not unduly spoilt the place nor the magnificent cliffy coast surrounding it.

Of the excellent beaches hereabouts, the central **Summerleaze** is clean and wide, while the mile-long **Widemouth Bay**, south of town, is the main focus of the holiday hordes, with the cleanest water monitored between Bude and Polzeath (though bathing can be dangerous near the rocks at low tide). Surfers also congregate five miles down the coast at **Crackington Haven**, wonderfully situated between 430-foot crags at the mouth of a lush valley. The cliffs on this stretch are characterized by remarkable zigzagging strata of shale, limestone and sandstone, a mixture which erodes into vividly contorted detached formations. To the **north** of Bude, acres-wide **Crooklets** is the scene of **surfing** and life-saving demonstrations and competitions. A couple of miles further on, **Sandy Mouth** holds a pristine expanse of sand with rock pools beneath the encircling cliffs. It's a short walk from here to another surfers' delight, **Duckpool**, a tiny sandy cove flanked by jagged reefs at low tide, and dominated by the three-hundred-foot **Steeple Point**.

Bude's **tourist office** is in the car park off the Crescent (April–Sept Mon–Fri 9.30am–5pm, Sat & Sun 10am–4pm; Oct–March Mon–Fri 10am–4pm, Sat 10am–2pm; ☏01288/354240, ⓦwww.visitbude.info). The town's cheaper **accommodation** includes a cluster of B&Bs overlooking the golf course on Burn View, among them *Sunrise* at no. 6 (☏01288/353214; no credit cards; ❷), and *Palms* at no. 17 (☏01288/353962; no credit cards; ❷). Near Summerleaze Beach, the *Falcon Hotel* on Breakwater Road is an old coaching inn (☏01288/352005, ⓦwww.falconhotel.com; ❻). There's a backpackers' **hostel** at 57 Killerton Rd (☏01288/354256, ⓦwww.northshorebude.com; £12), with a large garden, Internet access and some double rooms (❶). The nearest of the numerous **campsites** around Bude is *Upper Lynstone* (☏01288/352017, ⓦwww.upperlynstone.co.uk; closed Nov–Easter), three-quarters of a mile south of the centre on the coastal road to Widemouth Bay.

For style, location and cuisine, Bude's best **restaurant** is *Life's a Beach*, right on Summerleaze Beach, a café by day and a romantic (and expensive) bistro in the evening, worth reserving ahead for (☏01288/355222). In town, try the *Atlantic Diner*, 5–7 Belle Vue (closed Mon, also eves Tues–Thurs & Sun in winter; inexpensive–moderate), popular with shoppers and surfers alike for its burgers, steaks, curries and ice creams. **Surfing equipment** can be rented from various outlets in town.

Bodmin and Bodmin Moor

Bodmin Moor, the smallest of the West Country's great moors, has some beautiful tors, torrents and rock formations, but much of its fascination lies in the strong human imprint, particularly the wealth of relics left behind by its **Bronze Age** population. Separated from these by some three millennia, the churches in the villages of **St Neot's**, **Blisland** and **Altarnun** are among the region's finest examples of fifteenth-century art and architecture.

Bodmin

BODMIN's position on the western edge of Bodmin Moor, equidistant from the north and south Cornish coasts and the Fowey and Camel rivers, encouraged its growth as a trading town. It was also an important ecclesiastical centre after the establishment of a priory by St Petroc, who moved here from Padstow in the sixth century. The priory disappeared but Bodmin retained its prestige through its church of **St Petroc**, at the end of Fore Street, built in the fifteenth century and still the largest in Cornwall (April–Sept daily 10am–3pm; at other times call ☎01208/73867). Inside, there's an extravagantly carved twelfth-century font and an ivory casket that once held the bones of the saint, while the southwest corner of the churchyard holds a sacred well. Close by, the notorious **Bodmin Jail** (Mon–Fri & Sun 10am–6pm, Sat 11am–5pm; £4.25) on Berrycombe Road is redolent of the public executions that were once guaranteed crowd-pullers here. You can visit part of the original eighteenth-century structure, including the condemned cell and some grisly exhibits chronicling the lives of the inmates.

From Bodmin Parkway, the train station three miles southeast of the centre, it's less than two miles' walk to one of Cornwall's most celebrated country houses, **Lanhydrock** (April–Sept Tues–Sun 11am–5.30pm; Oct Tues–Sun 11am–5pm; garden open daily 10am–6pm or dusk; £7.20, grounds only £3.90; NT), originally seventeenth-century but totally rebuilt after a fire in 1881. The granite exterior remains true to its original form, but the 42 rooms show a very different style, including a long picture gallery with a plaster ceiling depicting scenes from the Old Testament and servants' quarters that reveal the daily workings of a Victorian manor house. The grounds have magnificent beds of magnolias, azaleas and rhododendrons, and a huge area of wooded parkland bordering onto the River Fowey.

Practicalities

Bodmin's **tourist office** (Easter–Sept Mon–Sat 10am–5pm; Oct–Easter Mon–Fri 10am–5pm; ☎01208/76616) is near the main car park at the bottom of St Nicholas Street. Comfortable **B&B** is available at *Higher Windsor Cottage*, 18 Castle St (☎01208/76474, ⊛www.higherwindsorcottage.co.uk; no credit cards; ➋), and the beflowered, seventeenth-century *Priory Cottage*, near St Petroc's church at 34 Rhind St (☎01208/73064, ⊛www.stayanite.com; no smoking; no credit cards; ➋). A couple of miles south of town, *Bokiddick Farm* is convenient for Lanhydrock and boasts magnificent views (☎01208/831481, ⊛www.bokiddickfarm.co.uk; no smoking; ➌). There's a **campsite** on Old Callywith Road, a fifteen-minute walk from Castle Street (☎01208/73834; closed Nov–Feb).

Off Fore Street, the *Hole in the Wall* **pub** in Crockwell Street has bar lunches, an upstairs **restaurant** and a courtyard. Wholesome snacks are also served at the *Maple Leaf*, a tiny café just across from St Petroc's at 14 Honey St (closed Sun).

Blisland and the western moor

BLISLAND stands in the Camel valley on the western slopes of Bodmin Moor, three miles northeast of Bodmin. Georgian and Victorian houses cluster around a village green and a church whose well-restored interior has an Italianate altar and a startlingly painted screen. On **Pendrift Common** above the village, the gigantic **Jubilee Rock** is inscribed with various patriotic insignia commemorating the jubilee of George III's coronation in 1809. From this seven-hundred-foot vantage point you look eastward over the De Lank gorge and the boulder-crowned knoll of **Hawk's Tor**, three miles away. On the shoulder of the tor stand the Neolithic **Stripple Stones**, a circular platform once holding 28 standing stones, of which just four are still upright. If you're looking for a **place to stay** in the area, try *Lavethan* (℡01208/850487, Ⓦwww.cornwall-online.co.uk/lavethan; no credit cards; ❺), a beautiful sixteenth-century manor house set in thirty acres of park-like fields and gardens sloping to a small river; it's ten minutes' walk from the village towards St Mabyn. On Blisland's village green, you can sample good **ales and food** at the *Blisland Inn*, with outdoor tables.

Bolventor and Dozmary Pool

The village of **BOLVENTOR**, lying at the centre of the moor midway between Bodmin and Launceston, is an uninspiring place close to one of the moor's chief focuses for walkers and sightseers alike – **Jamaica Inn** (℡01566/86250, Ⓦwww.jamaicainn.co.uk; ❹). A staging post even before the precursor of the A30 road was laid here in 1769, the inn was described as being "alone in glory, four square to the winds" by Daphne Du Maurier, who stayed here in 1930, soaking up inspiration for her smugglers' yarn, *Jamaica Inn*. Adjacent to the hotel, the **Smuggler's Museum** (daily 10am–5pm; £2.50) shows the diverse ruses used for concealing contraband.

Bolventor is not on any public transport route. If you're driving, the inn's car park is a useful place to leave your vehicle and venture forth on foot. Just a mile away, **Dozmary Pool** is another link in the West Country's Arthurian mythologies – after Arthur's death Sir Bedevere hurled Excalibur, the king's sword, into the pool, where it was seized by an arm raised from the depths. Despite its proximity to the A30, the diamond-shaped lake usually preserves an ethereal air, though it's been known to run dry in summer, dealing a bit of a blow to the legend that the pool is bottomless.

The lake is also the source of another, more obviously Cornish legend, that of John Tregeagle, a steward at Lanhydrock, whose unjust dealings with the local tenant farmers in the seventeenth century brought upon his spirit the curse of endlessly baling out the pool with a perforated limpet shell. As if this were not enough, his ghost is further tormented by a swarm of devils pursuing him as he flies across the moor in search of sanctuary; their infernal howling is sometimes audible on windy nights.

Liskeard and St Neot

LISKEARD, a bus and rail junction just off the southern limits of the moor, makes a good overnight stop, with **accommodation** at two decent B&Bs: *Elnor*, 1 Russell St (℡01579/342472; no credit cards; ❷), located on the way to the train station, and the immaculately kept *Hyvue* just north of the centre at Barras Cross (℡01579/348175; nonsmoking; no credit cards; ❶). From here, buses go on to **ST NEOT**, one of Bodmin Moor's prettiest villages, approached through a lush wooded valley. Its fifteenth-century **church** contains some of the most impressive stained-glass windows of any parish church in the country, the oldest glass being the fifteenth-century **Creation Window**, at the east end of the south aisle. For **accommodation** in St Neot's, head for the seventeenth-century *Dye Cottage* (℡01579/321394, Ⓦwww.cornwall-info.co.uk/dye-cottage; no credit cards; ❶), which offers home-grown produce for breakfast and has a garden sloping down to a stream.

This southern edge of the moor is far greener and more thickly wooded than the northern reaches, due to the confluence of a web of rivers into the Fowey. One of the moor's best-known beauty spots is a couple of miles east, below Draynes Bridge, where the Fowey tumbles through the **Golitha Falls**, less a waterfall than a series of rapids. Dippers and wagtails flit through the trees, and there's a pleasant woodland walk you can take to Siblyback Lake reservoir just over a mile away.

Camelford and the northern tors

The northern half of Bodmin Moor is dominated by its two highest tors, both of them easily accessible from **CAMELFORD**, which offers a couple of diverting museums: the **British Cycling Museum** (daily: Mon–Thurs & Sun 10am–5pm, phone ahead for Fri & Sat ☎01840/212811; £2.90), housed in the old station one mile north of town on the Boscastle Road, a cyclophile's dream, containing some four hundred examples of bikes through the ages and a library, and the more conventional **North Cornwall Museum** (April–Sept Mon–Sat 10am–5pm; £2) in the village itself, displaying domestic items and exhibits relating to the local slate industry – and it also has a **tourist office** (same hours; ☎01840/212954). Among Camelford's **accommodation**, try the *Mason's Arms* on Market Place (☎01840/213309; no credit cards; ❶) and the thirteenth-century, slate-hung *Darlington Inn* on Fore Street (☎01840/213314; ❶). *King's Acre* (☎01840/213561; ❷), on the B3266 between the village and the cycling museum, provides both B&B and **camping** (campsite closed Nov–Easter). Both the *Mason's Arms*, which has a beer garden, and the *Darlington Inn* make good **refreshment** stops.

Rough Tor, the second highest peak on Bodmin Moor at 1311ft, is four miles' walk southeast from Camelford. The hill presents a different aspect from every angle: from the south an ungainly mass, from the west a nobly proportioned mountain. A short distance to the east stand the Little Rough Tor, where there are the remains of an Iron Age camp, and Showery Tor, capped by a prominent formation of piled rocks. Easily visible to the southeast, **Brown Willy** is, at 1375ft, the highest peak in Cornwall, as its original name signified – Bronewhella, or "highest hill". Like Rough Tor, Brown Willy shows various faces, its sugarloaf appearance from the north sharpening into a long multipeaked crest as you approach. The tor is accessible by continuing from the summit of Rough Tor across the valley of the De Lank, or, from the south, by footpath from Bolventor.

Altarnun and the eastern moor

ALTARNUN is a pleasant, granite-grey village snugly sheltered beneath the eastern heights of the moor. Its prominent **church**, dedicated to St Nonna (mother of David, patron saint of Wales) contains a fine Norman font and 79 bench-ends carved at the beginning of the sixteenth century, depicting saints, musicians and clowns. Accessed by a private gate from St Nonna's (and also from the road), *Penhallow Manor* (☎01566/86206, ⓦwww.penhallow-manor.co.uk; no smoking; ❺), originally the vicarage, now offers tasteful **accommodation** in spacious, old-fashioned rooms. Cheaper rooms can be found 500yds towards the A30, where the *King's Head* (☎01566/86241; no credit cards; ❷) has beams, saggy ceilings and **meals** from around a fiver.

South of Altarnun, **Withey Brook** tumbles four hundred feet in less than a mile of gushing cascades before meeting up with the River Lynher, which bounds Bodmin Moor to the east. Beyond the brook, on **Twelve Men's Moor**, lie some of Bodmin Moor's grandest landscapes. The quite modest elevations of Hawk's Tor (1079ft) and the lower Trewartha Tor appear enormous from the north, though they are overtopped by **Kilmar**, highest of the hills on the moor's eastern flank at 1280ft.

Withey Brook starts life about six miles from Altarnun on **Stowe's Hill**, site of the moor's most famous stone pile, **The Cheesewring**, a precarious pillar of balancing granite slabs, marvellously eroded by the wind. A mile or so south down Stowe's Hill stands an artificial rock phenomenon, **The Hurlers**, a wide complex of three circles dating from about 1500 BC. The purpose of these stark upright stones is not known, though they owe their name to the legend that they were men turned to stone for playing the Celtic game of hurling on the Sabbath.

The Hurlers are easily accessible just outside **MINIONS**, Cornwall's highest village, three miles south of which stands another Stone Age survival, **Trethevy Quoit**, a chamber tomb nearly nine feet high, surmounted by a massive capstone. Originally enclosed in earth, the stones have been stripped by centuries of weathering to create Cornwall's most impressive megalithic monument. Buses #267 and #269 from Liskeard call at St Cleer and Darite (not Sun), both of which are close to Trethevy Quoit; alternatively, it's a three-mile walk from Liskeard.

Travel details

Buses

For information on all local and national bus services, contact Traveline: ☎0870/608 2608 (daily 7am–9pm), ⓦ www.traveline.org.uk.

Bodmin to: Newquay (1–2 daily; 30–45min); Plymouth (2 daily; 1hr); St Austell (hourly; 50min–1hr); Truro (Mon–Sat 5 daily; 1hr 30min).

Exeter to: Bristol (4 daily; 1hr 45min–2hr); Falmouth (1 daily; 3hr 50min); Newquay (Mon–Sat 6 daily; 3hr); Plymouth (hourly; 1hr 15min); Sidmouth (Mon–Sat 2 hourly, Sun hourly; 45min); St Austell (1 daily; 2hr 25min); Torquay (hourly; 1hr–1hr 20min); Truro (1 daily; 3hr).

Falmouth to: Exeter (1 daily; 4hr); Helston (Mon–Sat every 30min, Sun in summer 4 daily; 35min); Penzance (Mon–Sat hourly; 1hr 5min); Plymouth (1–2 daily; 2hr 30min); St Austell (Mon–Sat hourly; 1hr 10min); Truro (Mon–Sat every 30min; 30min–1hr 15min).

Newquay to: Bodmin (2 daily; 50min); Exeter (Mon–Sat 7 daily; 3hr); Plymouth (2–3 daily; 1hr 30min–2hr); St Austell (hourly; 1hr).

Penzance to: Falmouth (Mon–Sat hourly; 1hr 10min); Helston (Mon–Sat every 30min, Sun hourly; 45min); Plymouth (5 daily; 3hr 30min); St Austell (Mon–Sat hourly, Sun 3 daily; 2hr 15min); St Ives (every 20–30min; 35–45min); Truro (1–2 hourly, Sun 8 daily; 1hr 35min).

Plymouth to: Bodmin (2 daily; 1hr); Exeter (hourly; 1hr 15min); Falmouth (2 daily; 2hr 15min); Newquay (2–3 daily; 1hr 20min–1hr 45min); Penzance (5 daily; 3hr–3hr 20min); St Austell (4 daily; 1hr 15min); St Ives (3 daily; 2hr 40min–3hr); Torquay (hourly; 1hr 45min); Truro (4 daily; 1hr 50min).

St Austell to: Bodmin (hourly; 50min); Exeter (1 daily; 2hr 35min; Falmouth (Mon–Sat hourly; 1hr 10min); Newquay (hourly; 1hr); Penzance (Mon–Sat hourly, Sun 3 daily; 2hr–2hr 15min); Plymouth (4 daily; 1hr 20min); St Ives (2 daily; 1hr 30min); Truro (1–2 hourly; 30–40min).

St Ives to: Penzance (every 20–30min; 35min); Plymouth (3 daily; 3hr–3hr 20min); St Austell (1 daily; 1hr 50min); Truro (Mon–Sat hourly, Sun 1 daily; 1hr 25min).

Torquay to: Exeter (hourly; 1hr–1hr 20min); Plymouth (hourly; 1hr 45min).

Truro to: Bodmin (Mon–Sat 6 daily; 1hr 30min); Exeter (1 daily; 3hr 35min); Falmouth (Mon–Sat 1–2 hourly; 25min); Penzance (Mon–Sat every 30min, Sun 9 daily; 1hr 30min); Plymouth (1–2 daily; 2hr); St Austell (1–2 hourly; 35min); St Ives (Mon–Sat hourly, Sun 1 daily; 1hr–1hr 25min).

Trains

For information on all local and national rail services, contact National Rail Enquiries ☎ 08457/48 49 50, ⓦ www.nationalrail.co.uk.

Barnstaple to: Exeter (Mon–Sat 9–14 daily, Sun 4–5 daily; 1hr–1hr 15min).

Bodmin to: Exeter (1–2 hourly; 1hr 35min–1hr 50min); London (8–10 daily; 4hr); Penzance (1–2 hourly; 1hr 25min); Plymouth (1–2 hourly; 40min–1hr 15min).

Exeter to: Barnstaple (Mon–Sat 9–14 daily, Sun 4–5 daily; 1hr–1hr 10min); Birmingham (hourly; 2hr 45min); Bodmin (1–2 hourly; 1hr 45min); Bristol (1–2 hourly; 1hr 10min–1hr 25min); Exmouth (Mon–Sat every 30min, Sun 7–13 daily; 25min); Liskeard (1–2 hourly; 1hr 30min); London (8–10 daily; 2hr 30min); Par (hourly; 2hr); Penzance (hourly; 3hr 15min); Plymouth (1–2 hourly; 1hr–1hr 20min); Salisbury (every 2hr; 2hr); Torquay (hourly; 45min); Totnes (1–2 hourly; 40min); Truro (hourly; 2hr 15min).

Falmouth to: Truro (10–12 daily; 25min).

Honiton to: Exeter (hourly; 30min); Salisbury (every 1–2hr; 1hr 20min).

Liskeard to: Exeter (1–2 hourly; 1hr 30min); London (9–11 daily; 3hr 45min–4hr 20min); Looe (8–10 daily, not Sun in winter; 30min); Penzance (hourly; 1hr 30min); Plymouth (1–2 hourly; 25min); Truro (hourly; 1hr 30min).

Newquay to: Par (4–6 daily, not Sun in winter; 50min).

Par to: Exeter (hourly; 1hr 50min); Newquay (4–6 daily, not Sun in winter; 50min); Penzance (hourly; 1hr 15min); Plymouth (1–2 hourly; 50min).

Penzance to: Bodmin (hourly; 1hr 20min); Bristol (5 daily; 4hr); Exeter (hourly; 3hr); Liskeard (hourly; 1hr 30min); London (7 daily; 5–6hr); Par (hourly; 1hr 10min); Plymouth (hourly; 2hr); St Ives (4–6 daily, not Sun in winter; 20min); Truro (1–2 hourly; 40min).

Plymouth to: Birmingham (11 daily; 3hr 45min); Bodmin (1–2 hourly; 40min); Bristol (8 daily; 2hr–2hr 45min); Exeter (2 hourly; 1hr); Liskeard (1–2 hourly; 30min); London (8 daily; 3–4hr); Par (1–2 hourly; 45min–1hr); Penzance (hourly; 2hr); St Erth (hourly; 1hr 50min); Truro (hourly; 1hr 15min).

St Ives to: Penzance (4–6 daily, not Sun in winter; 20min); St Erth (every 30min; 15min).

Torquay to: Exeter (hourly; 45min).

Truro to: Bristol (5 daily; 3–4hr); Exeter (hourly; 2hr 15min); Falmouth (10–12 daily; 25min); Liskeard (hourly; 50min); London (9 daily; 4hr 40min); Penzance (1–2 hourly; 40min); Plymouth (hourly; 1hr 15min).

7

East Anglia

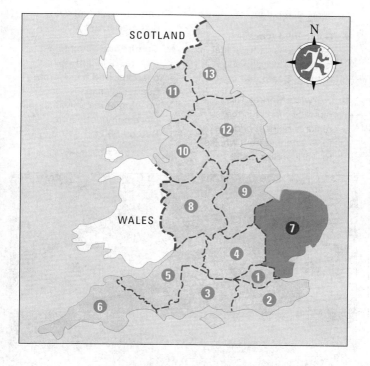

CHAPTER 7

Highlights

* **Orford** Remote and peaceful hamlet, hidden away on the Suffolk coast. See p.443

* **The Aldeburgh Festival** The region's prime classical music festival takes place for three weeks in June. See p.445

* **Southwold** A picture-perfect seaside town that is ideal for walking and bathing. See p.446

* **Norwich Market** This open-air market is the region's biggest and best for everything from whelks to wellies. See p.452

* **Holkham Bay** Wide bay with Norfolk's finest beach, acres of golden sand set against hilly dunes. See p.461

* **Ely** An isolated Cambridgeshire town, Ely has a true fenland flavour and a magnificent cathedral. See p.463

* **Cambridge** Fine architecture, dignified churches and handsome quadrangles jostle for position in the university city's compact centre. See p.465

△ Southwold beach and huts

East Anglia

S trictly speaking, **East Anglia** is made up of just three counties – Suffolk, Norfolk and Cambridgeshire – which were settled by Angles from Holstein in the fifth century, though in more recent times it's come to be loosely applied to parts of Essex too. As a region it's renowned for its wide skies and flat landscapes, and of course such generalizations always contain more than a grain of truth – if you're looking for mountains, you've come to the wrong place. That said, East Anglia often fails to conform to its stereotype: parts of Suffolk are positively hilly, and its coastline can induce vertigo; the north Norfolk coast holds steep cliffs as well as wide sandy beaches; and even the pancake-flat fenlands are broken by wide, muddy rivers and hilly mounds, on one of which perches Ely's magnificent cathedral. Indeed, the whole region is sprinkled with fine medieval churches, the legacy of the days when this was England's most progressive and prosperous region.

Of all the region's counties, **Suffolk** is the most varied. Its undulating southern reaches, straddling the River Stour, are home to a string of picturesque, well-preserved little towns – **Lavenham** and **Kersey** are two excellent examples – which enjoyed immense prosperity during the thirteenth to sixteenth centuries, the heyday of the wool trade. Elsewhere, **Bury St Edmunds** boasts not just the ruins of its once-prestigious abbey, but also some fine Georgian architecture, while even the much maligned county town of **Ipswich** has more to offer than it's generally given credit for. Nevertheless, for many visitors it's the north Suffolk coast that steals the show. In **Southwold**, with its comely Georgian high street, Suffolk possesses a delightful seaside resort, elegant and relaxing in equal measure, and neighbouring **Aldeburgh** hosts one of the best music festivals in the country.

Norfolk, as everyone knows thanks to Noël Coward, is very flat. It's also one of the most sparsely populated and tranquil counties in England, a remarkable turnaround from the days when it was an economic and political powerhouse – until, that is, the Industrial Revolution simply passed it by. Its capital, **Norwich**, is still East Anglia's largest city, renowned for its Norman cathedral and castle, and for its high-tech Sainsbury Centre, exhibiting a challenging collection of twentieth-century art. The most visited part of Norfolk is, however, the **Broads**, a unique landscape of reed-ridden waterways that has been intensively exploited by boat-rental companies for the last twenty years. Similarly popular, the **Norfolk coast** holds a string of busy, very English seaside resorts – **Cromer**, **Sheringham** and **Hunstanton** to name but three – but for the most part it's a charmingly unspoilt region of tiny flintstone villages with **Blakeney Point** and the

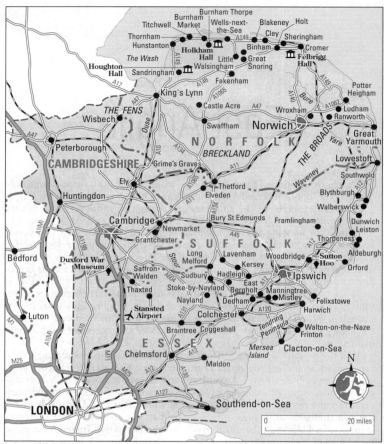

surrounding marshes among the country's top nature reserves. Meanwhile, sheltering inland, are several outstanding stately homes, most memorably **Felbrigg Hall** and **Holkham**.

Cambridge is the one place in East Anglia everyone visits, largely on account of its world-renowned university, whose ancient colleges boast some of the finest medieval and early modern architecture in the country. The rest of Cambridgeshire is dominated by the landscape of the **Fens**, for centuries an inhospitable marshland, which was eventually drained to provide rich alluvial farming land. The one star turn here is the cathedral town of **Ely**, settled on one of the few areas of raised ground in the fens and an easy and popular day-trip from Cambridge.

Heading into the region from the south almost inevitably takes you through **Essex**, whose proximity to London has turned much of the county into an unappetizing commuter strip with only the historic town of **Colchester** really worth a detour.

The **train** network is at its best to and from London, with quick and frequent services from the capital to all of East Anglia's major towns, though it's also relatively easy to move from one to another. However, once you get away from the major towns, you're going to have to rely on local **buses**, whose services, run by a multitude of companies, are very patchy – especially on Sundays and in winter. Indeed, in parts of north Norfolk and inland Suffolk, you may find the only way to get about is by your own transport. The largest regional bus operator is **First Eastern Counties**, who sell Ranger tickets (£7) providing unlimited travel for one day or more on their buses. These are available either in advance or from their drivers.

Colchester

If you visit anywhere in Essex, it should be **COLCHESTER**, an agreeable town with a castle, a university and a large army base, fifty miles northeast of London. Colchester prides itself on being England's oldest town and there is indeed documentary evidence of a settlement here as early as the fifth century BC. By the first century AD, the town was the region's capital under **King Cunobelin** – better known as Shakespeare's Cymbeline – and when the **Romans** invaded Britain in 43 AD they initially chose Colchester (Camulodunum) as their new capital. A millennium later, the conquering Normans built one of their mightiest strongholds in Colchester, but the conflict that most marked the town was the **Civil War**. In 1648, Colchester was subjected to a gruelling siege by the Parliamentarian army led by Lord Fairfax; after three months, during which the population ate every living creature within the walls, the town finally surrendered and the Royalist leaders were promptly executed for their pains.

Today, Colchester makes a potential base for further explorations of the surrounding countryside – particularly the Stour valley towns of Constable country (see pp.433–439), within easy reach to the north.

Arrival, information and accommodation

Colchester has two **train stations**. Services from London, Ipswich and Harwich arrive at the mainline Colchester North Station, from where it's a fifteen-minute walk south into town – follow North Station Road and its continuation North Hill until you reach the west end of the High Street. Trains from Frinton, Walton and Clacton-on-Sea arrive at Colchester Town Station, to the south of the centre at the bottom of St Botolph's Street. The **bus station** is off Queen Street, the northerly continuation of St Botolph's Street, and a couple of minutes' walk from the east end of High Street. You can get bus timetables here from the First Eastern National office (Mon–Fri 9am–5pm, Sat 9am–1pm; ☎01206/572478), which also sells Bus Ranger tickets (see above).

The **tourist office** is at 1 Queen St (April–Oct Mon–Sat 9.30am–6pm, Sun 10am–5pm; Nov–March Mon–Sat 10am–5pm; ☎01206/282920, ⓦ www.colchesterwhatson.co.uk), at the east end of High Street, just behind the castle. As well as helping with accommodation, they sell leaflets detailing local walks and coordinate daily **guided walks** around town (May–Sept; £2.50). You can rent a **bike** from Action Bikes, beside the Odeon Cinema on Crouch St (☎01206/541744) – one way of getting out to see the nearby "Constable Country" (see pp.433–439).

For **accommodation**, Colchester has more than its fair share of old hotels as well as pleasant, well-located B&Bs. The *Rose & Crown Hotel*, East St (℡01206/866677, Ⓦwww.rose-and-crown.com; ❹), occupies a tastefully refurbished Tudor inn – the oldest in town – while the *George Hotel*, 116 High St (℡01206/578494, Ⓦwww.bestwestern.co.uk;❺), is an attractive old coaching inn, whose rooms come with all mod cons. The *Red Lion*, 43 High St (℡01206/577986, Ⓦwww.brook-hotels.co.uk; ❺), is another old-timer, a fifteenth-century timber building containing 24 modernized en-suite rooms. The *Old Manse*, 15 Roman Rd (℡01206/545154, Ⓦwww.doveuk .com/oldmanse; ❸), is the best of the many B&B options along Roman Road, with three pleasant guest rooms; Roman Road is on the east side of the Castle.

The Town

Most visitors start off at the town's rugged, honey-coloured **castle** (Mon–Sat 10am–5pm, Sun 11am–5pm; £4.25), the perfect introduction to Colchester's long history, set in attractive parkland, which stretches down to the River Colne. Begun less than ten years after the Battle of Hastings, it boasts a phenomenally large keep – the largest in Europe at the time – built on the site of the defunct Roman temple. The castle's **museum** contains the best of the region's Romano-British archeological finds, although, apart from a fine bronze of Mercury, the messenger of the gods, this amounts to little more than a smattering of coins, tombstones, statues and mosaics. The museum also covers the 1648 siege, and you can sign up for a **guided tour** of the underground tunnels (45min; £1.50), which give access to the foundations of the Roman temple and the Norman chapel and walls – parts not otherwise accessible to regular visitors. Outside, down towards the river in Castle Park is a section of the old **Roman walls**, whose battered remains are still visible around much of the town centre.

The castle stands at the eastern end of the wide and largely pedestrianized **High Street**, which lies pretty much along the same route as it did in Roman times. The most arresting building here is the flamboyant **Town Hall**, built in 1902 and topped by a statue of St Helena, mother of Constantine the Great and daughter of "Old King Cole" of nursery-rhyme fame – after whom, some say, the town was named. Immediately north of the High Street is the so-called **Dutch Quarter**, where Flemish refugees settled in the sixteenth century giving a boost to the town's ailing cloth trade. The area's lofty buildings still make this a pleasant place to stroll, particularly along West and East Stockwell streets. South of the High Street, much of the medieval street plan has been subsumed within a vast shopping precinct and an open-air **market** held every Friday and Saturday in Vineyard Street.

With a little time to spare, it's worth strolling down **East Hill**, a continuation of the High Street east of the castle. Splendid Georgian houses line the top end of the hill, one of which – opposite the tourist office – is now the **Hollytrees Museum** (Mon–Sat 10am–5pm, Sun 11am–5pm; free), containing a modest collection of costumes, toys, domestic items and decorative arts from the eighteenth to the twentieth century. Over the road at the **Minories** (April–Sept Mon–Sat 10am–5pm, Sun 11am–5pm; Oct–March closed Sun; free) another Georgian exterior conceals a contemporary arts centre, with a changing exhibition programme, a garden and a great café.

Eating, drinking and nightlife

Colchester's **oysters** have been highly prized since Roman times and the local vineyards have an equally long heritage, so it's no surprise to find the town has a good choice of first-rate **restaurants**. Probably the best place in town is the *The Hub*, 19 Head St (℡01206/564977), which offers tasty dishes at moderate prices from a broadly Mediterranean menu. Alternatively, try *Ruan Thai*, 82a East Hill (℡01206/870770), an excellent and moderately priced Thai restaurant near the top of East Hill; *Tilly's*, 22 Trinity St (closed Sun), a Victorian tearoom that serves snacks and full English meals; or the garden café at the Minories (closed Sun in winter), where the lunches are delicious. *The Lemon Tree*, 48 St John's St (℡01206/767337; closed Sun), is a moderately priced option, popular for its lunch specials and sunny courtyard seating. To get top-quality oysters you do, however, have to venture out of town to the oyster fisheries at **West Mersea**, home of *The Company Shed*, 129 Coast Road (℡01206/382700), where the freshest of oysters are served without any frills at rickety tables. Mersea Island, home to both West and East Merseas, is located about six miles south of Colchester; the season runs from September to May.

Colchester's town centre is crowded with **pubs**, with three of the best being the *Red Lion*, 43 High St; the *Foresters Arms*, a nice backstreet local on Castle Road; and the *Goat & Boot*, just one of several lively spots down East Hill. And, as you'd expect in a university town, the town rates reasonably well when it comes to **arts and nightlife**. The Colchester Arts Centre, on Church St next to the Balkerne Gate (℡01206/500900, ⓦwww.colchesterartscentre .com), puts on a good programme of rock, folk, jazz, theatre and dance, plus some club nights – all in a converted Victorian church. Nearby is the Mercury Theatre (℡01206/573948, ⓦwww.mercurytheatre.co.uk), the town's main drama venue.

The Stour Valley and the old wool towns of south Suffolk

Five miles or so north of Colchester, the **Stour River Valley** forms the border between Essex and Suffolk, and signals the beginning of East Anglia proper. Compared with much of the region it is positively hilly, a handsome landscape of farms and woodland latticed by dense, well-kept hedges and thick grassy banks that once kept the Stour in check. The valley is dotted with lovely little villages, where rickety, half-timbered Tudor houses and elegant Georgian dwellings cluster around medieval churches. The Stour's prettiest villages are concentrated along its lower reaches – to the east of the A134 – in Dedham Vale, with **Stoke-by-Nayland** and **Dedham** arguably the most appealing of them all. The vale is also known as "**Constable Country**", as it was the home of John Constable (1776–1837), one of England's greatest artists, and the subject of his most famous works. Inevitably, there's a Constable shrine – the much-visited complex of old buildings down by the river at **Flatford Mill**.

The villages along the River Stour and its tributaries were once busy little places at the heart of East Anglia's weaving trade, which boomed from the thirteenth to the fifteenth century. By the 1490s, the region produced more cloth than any other part of the country, but in Tudor times production shifted to Colchester, Ipswich and Norwich. Bypassed by the Industrial Revolution, south Suffolk had, by the late nineteenth century, become a remote rural backwater, an impoverished area whose decline had one unforeseen consequence. With few exceptions, the towns and villages were never well enough off to modernize, and the architectural legacy of medieval and Tudor times survived. The two best-preserved villages are **Lavenham** and **Kersey**, both of which heave with sightseers on summer weekends, but there are other attractive spots too, notably **Sudbury**. The latter boasts an excellent museum devoted to the work of Thomas Gainsborough, another great English artist and a native of the town.

Seeing the region by **public transport** is problematic – distances are small (Dedham Vale is only about ten miles long), but buses between the villages are infrequent and you'll find it difficult to get away from the towns. Several rail lines cross south Suffolk, the most useful being the London–Colchester–Sudbury route. More positively, the area is crisscrossed by **footpaths**, some of the most enjoyable of which are in the vicinity of Dedham village.

East Bergholt, Flatford Mill – and John Constable

"I associate my careless boyhood to all that lies on the banks of the Stour" wrote **John Constable**, who was born the son of a miller in **EAST BERGHOLT**, nine miles northeast of Colchester in 1776. The house in which he was born has long since disappeared, so it has been left to **Flatford Mill**, a mile or so to the south, to take up the painter's cause. The mill was owned by his father and was where Constable painted his most famous canvas, *The Hay Wain* (now in the National Gallery, London), which created a sensation when it was exhibited in 1824. To the chagrin of many of his contemporaries, Constable turned away from the landscape-painting conventions of the day, rendering his scenery with a realistic directness that harked back to the Dutch landscape painters of the seventeenth century. Typically, he justified this approach in unpretentious terms, observing that, after all "no two days are alike, nor even two hours; neither were there ever two leaves of a tree alike since the creation of the world." The mill itself – not the one he painted, but a Victorian replacement – is not open to the public, but the sixteenth-century thatched **Bridge Cottage** (March & April Wed–Sun 11am–5.30pm; May–Sept daily 10am–5.30pm; Oct daily 11am–4.30pm; Nov & Dec Wed–Sun 11am–3.30pm; Jan & Feb Sat & Sun 11am–3.30pm; free, but parking £1.50; NT), which overlooks the scene, has been painstakingly restored and stuffed full of Constabilia. Unfortunately, none of the artist's paintings are displayed here, but there's a pleasant riverside tearoom to take in the view. Beyond stands **Willy Lott's Cottage** (also closed to the public), which does actually feature in *The Hay Wain*.

In summer, the National Trust organizes **guided walks** around the sites of Constable's paintings (call ☎01206/298260 for details), but there are many other pleasant walks to be had along this deeply rural bend in the Stour. One footpath connects the mill to the **train station** at Manningtree, two miles to the east, and another runs over to the village of Dedham, a mile and a half to the west. It's also possible to hire a **rowing boat** (£5 per hour) from beside the bridge and potter peacefully along the river. There's a **B&B** here too, the *Flatford Granary* (☎01206/298111; ❷), where the comfortable rooms, with their beamed ceilings, are pleasant, and the views idyllic.

Dedham

Constable went to school in **DEDHAM**, just upriver from Flatford Mill and one of the region's most attractive villages, with a scattering of ancient timber-framed houses strung along the wide main street. The only sights as such are

435

△ Flatford mill

St Mary's Church, an early sixteenth-century structure that Constable painted on several occasions, and the **Sir Alfred Munnings Art Museum**, in Castle House (Easter–July & Sept Wed & Sun 2–5pm; Aug Wed, Thurs, Sat & Sun 2–5pm; £4), just south of the village on the road to Ardleigh. A locally born academician, Munnings is barely remembered today, but in his time he was well known for his portraits of horses. In the 1940s, Munnings became a controversial figure when, as President of the Royal Academy, he savaged almost every form of modern art there was. Few would say his paintings were inspiring, but seeing them is a pleasant way to fill a rainy afternoon. It is, however, the general flavour of Dedham which appeals most.

There's a **bus** service from Colchester to Dedham, but this only runs in the morning and in the early afternoon on weekdays with an even scantier service at the weekend. Dedham has one of the smartest **hotels** in the area, *Maison Talbooth* (℡01206/322367, Ⓦwww.talbooth.com; ❽), which occupies a good-looking Victorian country house about fifteen minutes' walk southwest of the village on the road to Stratford St Mary. All of the hotel's ten large bedrooms are individually decorated in sumptuous style and dinner can be had close by at *Le Talbooth* (℡01206/323150), an expensive, but top-notch **restaurant** in an ancient timber-framed house. Alternatively, there's *Dedham Hall* (℡01206/323027, Ⓦwww.dedhamhall.demon.co.uk; ❺), an old manor house set in its own grounds off Brook Street – be sure to ask for a room in the house itself. The restaurant here is very good too (closed Mon). You can also stay in the heart of Dedham itself at the *Marlborough Head* pub (℡01206/323250; ❹), where a handful of very pleasant rooms are available above the bar, and excellent, moderately priced **food** can be had from an inventive and wide-ranging menu.

Stoke-by-Nayland and Nayland

Heading northwest from Dedham, the B1029 dips beneath the A12 to reach the byroad to Higham, an unremarkable hamlet where you pick up the road to **STOKE-BY-NAYLAND**, four miles to the west. This is the most picturesque of villages, where a knot of half-timbered, pastel-painted cottages snuggle up to **St Mary's Church** (daily 9am–5pm; free), which, with its pretty brick and stone-trimmed tower, was one of Constable's favourite subjects. The doors of the south porch are sumptuously covered by the carved figures of a medieval Jesse Tree and the sombre interior boasts a magnificent, soaring tower arch. The village also has a great old **pub**, the *Angel Inn* (℡01206/263245; ❹), known for its adventurous food (eat in the bar or book for the restaurant) and cosy **rooms**. There are several other good places to stay, including *Thorington Hall* (℡01206/337329; Easter–Sept; ❸), which offers four bedrooms in a seventeenth-century house. The hall is located a little over a mile east of the village on the road to Higham.

Southwest from here, it's two miles back to the River Stour at **NAYLAND**, a workaday little place that is chiefly remarkable for its church's altar painting, *Christ Blessing the Bread and Wine*. It's one of only two attempts by Constable at a religious theme – and, dated to 1809, it was completed long before he found his artistic rhythm. While you're here, you can wet your whistle and sample quality bar food at the venerable *White Hart*, 11 High Street. Local **accommodation** is available at *Hill House*, Gravel Hill (℡01206/262782; ❷), on the edge of the village, and at *Gladwins Farm*, Harper's Hill (℡01206/262261, Ⓦwww.gladwinsfarm.co.uk; ❹), a secluded timber-framed farmhouse with its own indoor pool.

Sudbury

SUDBURY is the most important town in this part of the Stour Valley. A handful of timber-framed houses hark back to its days of wool-trade prosperity, but its three Perpendicular churches were underwritten by another local industry, **silk weaving**, which survives on a small scale to this day. Sudbury's most famous export, however, is **Thomas Gainsborough** (1727–1788), the leading English portraitist of the eighteenth century, whose statue, with brush and palette, stands on Market Hill. A superb collection of the artist's work is on display a few yards away in the house where he was born – **Gainsborough's House**, at 46 Gainsborough St (April–Oct Tues–Sat 10am–5pm, Sun 2–5pm; Nov–March Tues–Sat 10am–4pm, Sun 2–4pm; £3.50). Gainsborough moved to London when he was 13 and was apprenticed to an engraver, but it seems he was soon moonlighting and the earliest of his surviving portrait paintings – his *Boy and Girl*, a remarkably self-assured work dated to 1744 – is displayed here. In 1752, Gainsborough moved on to Ipswich, where he quickly established himself as a portrait painter to the Suffolk gentry with one of his specialities being wonderful "conversation pieces", so-called because the sitters engage in polite chitchat with a landscape as the backdrop. Seven years in Ipswich were followed by a move upmarket to Bath, where he painted high-society figures, as he did when he moved back to London in 1774. Examples of Gainsborough's later work exhibited here include the *Portrait of Harriet, Viscountess Tracy* (1763) and the particularly striking *Portrait of Abel Moysey, MP* (1771). In his later years, the artist also dabbled with romantic paintings of country scenes – as in *A Wooded Landscape with Cattle by a Pool* – a playful variation of the serious landscaping painting he loved to do best; the rest, he often said, just earned him money.

Sudbury is just seven miles northwest of Nayland – and twice that from Colchester – along the A134. It's accessible by **train** from Colchester (for some services, change at Marks Tey) and is the hub of **bus** services to and from neighbouring towns and villages including Colchester and Ipswich. The **tourist office** in the town hall on Market Hill (April–Sept Mon–Fri 9am–5pm & Sat 10am–4.45pm; Oct–March Mon–Fri 9am–5pm & Sat 10am–2.45pm; ☎01787/881320, ⊛www.visit-suffolk.org.uk) can provide **accommodation** details.

Lavenham

Seven miles from Sudbury, off the A134, lies **LAVENHAM**, formerly a centre of the region's wool trade and today one of the most visited villages in Suffolk, thanks to its unrivalled ensemble of perfectly preserved half-timbered houses. The whole place has changed little since the demise of the wool industry, owing in part to a zealous local preservation society that has carefully maintained the village's antique appearance.

The village is at its most beguiling in the triangular **Market Place**, an airy spot flanked by pastel-painted, medieval dwellings whose beams have been bent into all sorts of wonky angles by the passing of the years. It's here you'll find Lavenham's most celebrated building, the pale-white, timber-framed **Corpus Christi Guildhall** (March & Nov Sat & Sun 11am–4pm; April Wed-Sun 11am–5pm; May-Oct daily 11am–5pm; £3; NT), erected in the sixteenth century as the headquarters of one of Lavenham's four guilds. In the much-altered interior (used successively as a prison and workhouse), there's an exhibition on the wool industry, but most visitors quickly reach the walled garden and the teashop. Just to the east across the square is the mostly fifteenth-century **Little Hall** (April–Oct Wed, Thurs, Sat & Sun 2–5.30pm; £1.50), which contains a modest collection of furniture and objets d'art, but the view down Prentice Street from beside the neighbouring *Angel Hotel* is much more arresting – a line of creaky timber-framed dwellings dipping into the deep green countryside beyond. The other building worthy of special notice is the Perpendicular **church of St Peter and St Paul** (daily: May–Sept 8.30am–5.30pm; Oct–April 8.30am–3.30pm; free), a short walk southwest of the centre, at the top of Church Street. Local merchants endowed the church with a nave of majestic proportions and a mighty flint tower, at 141ft the highest for miles around, partly to celebrate the Tudor victory at the Battle of Bosworth in 1485 (see p.1303), but mainly to show off their wealth.

Practicalities

There are fairly frequent **buses** to Lavenham from Colchester via Sudbury and Long Melford, with the service continuing on to Bury St Edmunds. The **tourist office** is on Lady Street (April–Oct daily 10am–5pm; Nov–March Sat & Sun 11am–4pm; ℡01787/248207, ⓦwww.visit-suffolk.org.uk), just south of Market Place. They can help with **accommodation** and sell a detailed, street-by-street walking guide. Rooms at the *Swan Hotel* (℡08704/008116, ⓦwww.macdonald-hotels.co.uk; ❻), a splendid old inn on High Street, are some of the most comfortable in town; the building incorporates part of the Elizabethan Wool Hall and is a warren of cosy lounges and courtyard gardens. There's more luxurious accommodation at *Lavenham Priory*, on Water St (℡01787/247404, ⓦwww.lavenhampriory.co.uk; ❺), where four immaculate rooms are contained within the old Benedictine priory. Less expensive options on the Market Place include the ancient *Angel Hotel* (℡01787/247388, ⓦwww.lavenham.co.uk/angel; ❹), which has eight pleasant rooms above its bar, and the dinky *Angel Gallery* (℡01787/248417, ⓦwww.lavenham.co .uk/angelgallery/; ❸), where the three guest rooms are situated above a pocket-sized art shop. For cheaper B&B options, you'll probably end up staying outside Lavenham itself; the tourist office can provide details.

For **food**, the *Angel Hotel* serves up excellent, moderately priced bar meals, as does the *Swan*. The other choice in Market Place is the *Great House* (℡01787/247431; closed Sun & Mon), whose outstanding restaurant serves reasonably priced food.

Kersey and Hadleigh

Seven miles southeast off the A1141, **KERSEY** vies with Lavenham as the most photographed village in Suffolk. Another old wool town, Kersey seems to have dodged just about every historical bullet since the seventeenth century and now comprises little more than one exquisite street of timber-framed houses, which dips in the middle to cross a ford that's inhabited by a family of fearless ducks. Prime real estate today, Kersey's more populous past is recalled by its large and austere parish **church**, visible for miles around, perched on high ground above the village. There's nowhere to stay, but there is one good **pub**, the *White Horse*, which serves good, reasonably priced bar food.

Another couple of miles southeast, the market town of **HADLEIGH** is a positive metropolis compared to Kersey, but nonetheless everything of interest is within a stone's throw of the parish church of **St Mary's** (daily: May–Sept 9am–5.30pm, Oct–April 9am–3.30pm). The church, one block west of the elongated High Street, is mainly fifteenth century, a good-looking replacement for several earlier versions. Legend asserts that Guthrum, the Danish chieftain and arch-rival of **Alfred the Great**, was buried underneath the south aisle in 889, but his remains have never been definitively identified. Opposite the church, across the graveyard, is the half-timbered **Guildhall** (guided tours June–Sept Thurs & Sun 2–4.30pm; donation), every bit as immaculate as Lavenham's, with the earliest sections dating from 1438 – and offering very English cream teas in the garden from June to September (Mon–Fri & Sun 2.30–5pm). At the back of the church is the extravagantly ornate **Deanery Tower**, a fifteenth-century gatehouse whose palace was never completed. In the garret room at the top of the tower, the Oxford Movement, which opposed liberal tendencies within the Anglican Church and sought to promote Anglo-Catholicism, was founded in 1833 by local rector Hugh Rose.

Hadleigh is easy to reach by **bus** with regular services from Sudbury, Lavenham, Ipswich and Colchester, though Sundays can be a bit tricky. Several Hadleigh-bound buses pass through Kersey too. For a bite to **eat**, *Ferguson's Delicatessen*, 48 High St (closed Sun), sells delicious sandwiches.

Bury St Edmunds

Appealing **BURY ST EDMUNDS** started out as a Benedictine monastery, founded to house the remains of Edmund, the last Saxon king of East Anglia, who was tortured and beheaded by the marauding Danes in 869. Almost two centuries later, England was briefly ruled by the kings of Denmark and the shrewdest of them, **King Canute**, made a gesture of reconciliation to his Saxon subjects by conferring on the monastery the status of abbey. It was a popular move and the abbey prospered, so much so that before its dissolution in 1539, it had become the richest religious house in the country. Most of the abbey disappeared long ago, and nowadays Bury is better known for its graceful Georgian streets, its flower gardens and its sugar-beet plant than for its ancient monuments. Nonetheless, it's an amiable, eminently likeable place, and, with good transport connections on to Cambridge, Colchester, Ipswich and Norwich, it demands at least half a day of anyone's time.

The Town

The town centre has preserved its Norman street plan, a gridiron in which Churchgate was aligned with the abbey's high altar. It was the first planned town of Norman Britain and, for that matter, the first example of urban planning in England since the departure of the Romans. Beside the abbey grounds is **Angel Hill**, a broad, spacious square partly framed by Georgian buildings, the most distinguished being the ivy-covered **Angel Hotel**, which features in Dickens' *Pickwick Papers*. Dickens also gave readings of his work in the **Athenaeum**, the Georgian assembly rooms at the far end of the square. A twelfth-century wall runs along the east side of Angel Hill, with the bulky fourteenth-century **Abbey Gate** forming the entrance to the abbey gardens and ruins.

The **abbey ruins** themselves (open access) are like nothing so much as petrified porridge, with little to remind you of the grandiose Norman complex that dominated the town. Thousands of medieval pilgrims once sought solace at St Edmund's altar and the cult was of such significance that the barons of England gathered here to swear that they would make King John sign their petition – the Magna Carta of 1215. Today, the only significant remnants are on the far side of the abbey gardens, behind the more modern cathedral, and they comprise the rubbled remains of a small part of the old **abbey church** integrated into a set of unusual Georgian houses. In front, across the green, is the imposing **Norman Tower**, once the main gateway into the abbey and now a solitary monument with dragon gargoyles and fancily decorated capitals.

Incongruously, the tower is next to the front part of Bury's Anglican **Cathedral of St James** (daily: 8.30am–6pm; £2 donation requested), with chancel and transepts added as recently as the 1960s. It was a toss-up between this place and **St Mary's Church** (Mon–Sat 10am–4pm, 3pm in winter; free), further down Crown Street, as to which would be given cathedral status in 1914. The presence of the tomb of the resolutely Catholic Mary Tudor in the latter was probably the clinching factor.

The town's main **commercial area** is on the west side of the centre, a five-minute walk up Abbeygate Street from Angel Hill. There's been some intrusive modern planning here, but dignified Victorian buildings flank both **Cornhill** and **Buttermarket**, the two short main streets, as well as the narrower streets in between. Also in between the two is **Bury St Edmunds Art Gallery** (Tues–Sat 10am–5pm; £1; @ www.burystedmundsartgallery.org), which features a lively programme of temporary exhibitions focusing on contemporary fine and applied art. Older still is the Cornhill's flint-walled **Moyse's Hall**, one of the few surviving Norman houses in England, while the streets to the south are lined by an attractive medley of architectural styles, from elegant Georgian townhouses to Victorian brick terraces. You'll see the best by strolling along Guildhall Street and turning left down Churchgate, which brings you back to Angel Hill.

Practicalities

From Bury St Edmunds' **train station**, it's ten minutes' walk south to Angel Hill via Northgate Street. The **bus station** is on St Andrew Street North, near Cornhill. The town's **tourist office**, at 6 Angel Hill (Easter–Sept Mon–Sat 9.30am–5.30pm, Sun 10am–3pm; Oct–Easter Mon–Fri 10am–4pm, Sat 10am–1pm; ℡01284/764667, @ www.stedmundsbury.gov.uk), provides free town maps and has a useful range of leaflets.

The pick of the town's **hotels** is the *Angel*, on Angel Hill (℡01284/714000, @ www.theangel.co.uk; ❻), an immaculately maintained hotel with thick carpets, oodles of wood panelling and suitably luxurious rooms. A good alternative is the *Chantry Hotel*, 8 Sparhawk St (℡01284/767427; ❹), which has sixteen comfortable rooms in a converted Georgian building. The town has a good supply of **B&Bs**, including the excellent *South Hill House*, 43 Southgate St (℡01284/755650, @ www.southill.freeserve.co.uk; ❷), a handsome old townhouse with many Georgian features and three large en-suite bedrooms.

For **restaurants**, *Maison Bleue*, 31 Churchgate St (℡01284/760623; closed Sun & Mon), serves wonderfully fresh seafood at moderate prices. *The Vaults*, inside the medieval undercroft at the *Angel Hotel*, is also first-rate, with tasty main dishes from £8. Otherwise, aim for coffee, cakes and **snacks** in either the Cathedral *Refectory* (closed Sun) or the *Scandinavia Coffee House*, 30 Abbeygate Street. Of the **pubs**, the one you shouldn't miss is the *Nutshell* (closed Sun), on The Traverse at the top of Abbeygate, which, at sixteen feet by seven and a half, claims to be Britain's smallest. For entertainment, there's a year-round programme of cultural events held at the **Theatre Royal**, on Westgate St. (℡01284/755127, @ www.theatreroyal.org).

Ipswich

Situated at the head of the Orwell estuary, **IPSWICH** was a rich trading port in the Middle Ages, but its appearance today is mainly the result of a revival of fortunes in the Victorian era – give or take some clumsy postwar development. The two surviving reminders of old Ipswich – **Christchurch Mansion** and the splendid **Ancient House** – plus the recently renovated quayside are all reason enough to spend at least an afternoon here. Ipswich also boasts a wealth of medieval flint churches, one of which now houses the tourist office, from where **guided walks** depart a couple of times a week during the season (May–Sept Tues & Thurs 2.15pm; £2) – perhaps the best way to see the town on a short visit.

The Town

The ancient Saxon market place, **Cornhill**, is still the town's focal point, a likeable urban space flanked by a bevy of imposing Victorian edifices – the Italianate town hall, the old Neoclassical Post Office and the pseudo-Jacobean Lloyds building. From here, it's just a couple of minutes' walk to the Buttermarket and Ipswich's most famous building, the **Ancient House**, whose exterior was decorated around 1670 in extravagant style, a riot of pargeting and stucco work that together make one of the finest examples of Restoration artistry in the country. Europe is symbolized by a Gothic church, America a tobacco pipe, Asia an Oriental dome and Africa, eccentrically enough, by an African astride a crocodile. Since the house is now a shop, you're free to take a peek inside to view yet more of the decor.

From the Ancient House, head up Dial Lane past the fifteenth-century church of **St Lawrence** and you're soon on Tavern Street, where two wonderful mock-Tudor shops, built in the 1930s, face the **Great White Horse Hotel**, the "overgrown tavern" which appears in Dickens' *Pickwick Papers*. Heading north from here up Northgate Street takes you past the much-restored sixteenth-century, half-timbered **Oak House**, once an inn and now housing office space, to busy St Margaret's Plain and the gates of **Christchurch Mansion** (Tues–Sat 10am–5pm, 4pm from Nov–March, Sun 2.30–4.30pm; free). This handsome, if much-restored Tudor building, sporting seventeenth-century Dutch gables, is set in 65 acres of parkland, an area larger than the town centre itself. The mansion's labyrinthine interior is well worth exploring, with period furnishings and a good collection of paintings by Constable and Gainsborough.

On the south side of the centre, follow Key Street and you'll soon reach the Neptune Quay marking the northern edge of the **Wet Dock**, the largest in Europe when it opened in 1845 and looking much as it did then, apart from the rash of yachts in the marina. The smell of malt and barley still wafts across the quayside, and several of the granaries continue to function, though other warehouses have been turned into pubs, restaurants and offices. Halfway along the Neptune Quay stands the proud Neoclassical **Customs House**, built for the opening of the dock.

Practicalities

Ipswich **train station** is on the south bank of the river, ten minutes' walk from Cornhill along Princes Street. The **bus station** is more central, occupying part of the old cattle market, a short walk south of Cornhill and close to the **tourist**

office (Mon–Sat 9am–5pm; ☎01473/258070, ⓌＷwww.suffolk.org
.uk/tourism), in the converted St Stephen's Church off St Stephen's Lane.

There's no overriding reason **to stay**, especially with the Suffolk coast so
close, but a full list of B&Bs is available from the tourist office. One of the best
is *Burlington Lodge*, 30 Burlington Rd (☎01473/251868, ⓔburlingtonlodge
@bigfoot.com; no cards; ❷), an attractive Victorian detached house with five
comfortable en-suite bedrooms, ten minutes' walk west of Cornhill.
Alternatively, try the ultramodern *Novotel Hotel*, in the centre near Wolsey's
Gateway, on Grey Friars Rd (☎01473/232400, Ⓦwww.novotel.com; ❸) or,
even better, the newly converted *Salthouse Harbour Hotel*, 82 Fore St
(☎01473/257677, Ⓦwww.salthouseharbour.com; ❼), with views over the
harbour and stylish rooms.

There are several good **restaurants** down by the Wet Dock. *Il Punto*, on
Neptune Quay (☎01473/289748), offers good-quality French cuisine at
moderate prices, on board a Dutch pleasure boat. Opposite, there's also the
more expensive *Bistro On The Quay* (☎01473/286677; closed Sun), located in
one of the old red-brick quayside warehouses and specializing in seafood.
Cafés in town include *Pickwick's*, 1 Dial Lane, with courtyard seating next to
St Lawrence's Church.

For a **drink**, try either the *Black Horse* on Black Horse Lane, near the Civic
Centre, or the *Glasshouse* on the Buttermarket. For **entertainment**, head for
the Ipswich Film Theatre, in the Corn Exchange complex (☎01473/433100,
Ⓦwww.ipswich-ents.co.uk), behind the town hall on King Street, which
shows mainstream and art movies.

Sutton Hoo and Framlingham

Beyond Ipswich, the obvious destination is the Suffolk coast (see opposite), but
on the way it's worth considering a short stop at **Sutton Hoo**, where a
National Trust visitor centre has been built beside an Anglo-Saxon burial site
unearthed in 1939. Near here also, a short detour to the north, is the tranquil
village of **Framlingham**, a delightful place with a gaunt, ruined castle.

Sutton Hoo

In the fearful summer of 1939, at **SUTTON HOO**, about ten miles northeast
of Ipswich, a local landowner stumbled across an Anglo-Saxon royal burial site
belonging to Raedwald, king of East Anglia, who died around 625 AD. It was
the richest single archeological find in Britain, comprising a forty-oar open
ship containing a wooden tomb stuffed with gold and jewelled ornaments.
Further archeological research was conducted on the site in the 1980s, and in
November 1991 a second undisturbed grave was uncovered. Most of the artefacts are displayed in London's British Museum (see p.105), but some (along
with replicas of others) have been returned to Sutton Hoo, where the National
Trust has an immaculate **exhibition hall** (late March to May & Oct Wed–Sun
10am–5pm; June–Sept daily 10am–5pm; Nov–Feb Sat & Sun 11am–4pm; £4;
NT). The latter holds a full-size reconstruction of the burial chamber and
explains the history and significance of the finds. Afterwards, you can wander
the burial site itself, about 500 yards away.

To get to Sutton Hoo, head for **Woodbridge**, a few miles northeast of
Ipswich and from there take the Melton Road – the B1438 – turning right
onto the A1152 and watch for the signs.

Framlingham

FRAMLINGHAM, ten miles north of Woodbridge, boasts a magnificent **castle** (daily: April–Oct 10am–6pm; Nov–March 10am–4pm; £4; EH), whose severe, turreted walls date from the twelfth century. The original seat of the dukes of Norfolk, the fortress is little more than a shell inside, but the curtain-wall, with its thirteen towers, has survived almost intact, a splendid example of medieval military architecture. Footpaths crisscross the earthen banks encircling the castle, and from the internal wall walkways there are sweeping views across town to the imposing red-brick mass of Framlingham College. Unfortunately nothing remains of the castle's Great Hall where Mary Tudor was proclaimed Queen of England in 1553.

The drowsy little village next to the castle is a real pleasure, its elongated main street, **Market Hill**, flanked by a harmonious ensemble of sedate old buildings, including the *Crown Hotel* (☎01728/723521, ⓦwww.framlingham-crown .com; ❺), a traditional seventeenth-century inn with roaring fires, wood panelling and snug bedrooms. The parish **Church of St Michael** is also intriguing, its finely crafted hammer-beam roof sheltering several wonderful, sixteenth-century tombs belonging to the Howard family, who owned the castle at the time.

The Suffolk coast

The **Suffolk coast** feels detached from the rest of the county: the road and rail lines from Ipswich to Lowestoft funnel traffic five miles inland for most of the way, and patches of marsh and woodland make the separation still more complete. The coast has long been plagued by erosion and this has contributed to the virtual extinction of the local fishing industry, and, in the case of **Dunwich**, destroyed virtually the entire town. What is left, however, is undoubtedly one of the most unspoilt shorelines in the country – if, that is, you set aside the **Sizewell** nuclear power station. Highlights include the sleepy isolation of minuscule **Orford** and several genteel resorts, most notably **Southwold**. There are scores of delightful **walks** hereabouts, easy routes along the coast that are best followed with either OS map #156 or #0169, or the simplified *Footpath Maps* available at most tourist offices. The Suffolk coast is also host to East Anglia's most compelling cultural gathering, the three-week-long **Aldeburgh Festival**.

Orford and Orford Ness

Twelve miles east of Woodbridge, on the far side of Rendlesham Forest, the tiny village of **ORFORD** is dominated by two buildings, both of them medieval. The more impressive is the twelfth-century **castle** (April–Oct daily 10am–6pm; Nov–March Wed–Sun 10am–1pm & 2–4pm; £4; EH), built on high ground to the southwest of the village by Henry II, and under siege within months of its completion from Henry's rebellious sons. Most of the castle disappeared centuries ago, but the lofty keep remains, its impressive stature hinting at the scale of the original fortifications. Orford's other medieval edifice, on the far side of the main square, is **St Bartholomew's Church**, where Benjamin Britten premiered his most successful children's work, *Noye's Fludde*, as part of the 1958 Aldeburgh Festival (see box on p.445).

From the top of the castle keep, there's a great view across **Orford Ness**, a six-mile-long shingle spit that has all but blocked off Orford from the sea since Tudor times. Its mud flats and marshes harbour sea lavender beds, which act as feeding and roosting areas for wildfowl and waders. The National Trust offers **boat trips** (July–Sept Tues–Sat outward boats 10am–2pm; last ferry back 5pm; mid-April to June & Oct Sat only; £5.70; NT members £3.70; ☏01394/450057) across to the Ness from Orford Quay, four hundred yards down the road from the church, and a five-mile hiking trail threads its way along the spit. En route, the trail passes the occasional, abandoned **military building**. Some of the pioneer research on radar was carried out here, but the radar station was closed at the beginning of World War II because of the threat of German bombing. There are also plenty of **walks** to be had around Orford itself. One of the best is the five-mile hike north along the river wall that guards the west bank of the River Alde, returning via Ferry Road, a narrow country lane.

Orford's gentle, unhurried air is best experienced on a night's stay. **Rooms** are available at the *Crown & Castle* (☏01394/450205, ⓦwww.crownandcastlehotel.co.uk; ❻), an attractive inn across from the castle with chic bedrooms kitted out with all mod cons, and at the marginally less enticing *King's Head* (☏01394/450271; ❸), on Market Hill, the main square. For **meals**, don't miss the *Butley Orford Oysterage* (☏01394/450277; closed Oct–April) also on Market Hill. This has a very reasonably priced café/restaurant, whose menu focuses on fresh oysters and oak-wood smoked fish. Its main rival is the top-notch restaurant at the *Crown & Castle*, which again features local produce – main courses average around £12. For a **pint**, it's the *Crown & Castle* again or the *Jolly Sailor Inn*, down near the quay.

Aldeburgh and around

ALDEBURGH is best known for its annual arts festival, the brainchild of composer **Benjamin Britten** (1913–76), who is buried in the village churchyard alongside the tenor Peter Pears, his lover and musical collaborator. They lived by the seafront in Crag House on Crabbe Street – the street named after the poet who provided Britten with his greatest inspiration (see box opposite). Outside of June, when the festival takes place, and November, when the three-day international poetry festival fills the town, Aldeburgh is the quietest of places, with just a small fishing fleet selling its daily catch from wooden shacks along the pebbled shore.

The wide **High Street** and its narrow sidestreets run close to the beach, but this was not always the case – hence their garbled appearance. The sea swallowed most of what was once an extensive medieval town long ago and today Aldeburgh's oldest remaining building, the sixteenth-century **Moot Hall** (Easter–May & Oct Sat & Sun 2.30–5pm; June & Sept daily 2.30–5pm; July & Aug daily 10.30am–12.30pm & 2.30–5pm; £1), which began its days in the centre of town, now finds itself on the seashore. It's a handsome building made out of a mixture of red brick, flint and timber and holding a modest local museum. One of Aldeburgh's newest buildings, the **RNLI Lifeboat Station**, is situated bang in the middle of the seafront and from the public viewing deck you can look at the town's lifeboat and inspect the tractor used to drag it out to sea.

Several **footpaths** radiate out from Aldeburgh, with the most obvious trail leading north along the seashore to Thorpeness, with others leading southwest to the winding estuary of the **River Alde**, an area rich in wildfowl.

Practicalities

Aldeburgh's festival box office (see box, below) shares its High Street premises with the local **tourist office** (daily 9am–5.30pm, till 5.15pm in winter; ℡01728/453637, Ⓦwww.suffolkcoastal.gov.uk/leisure), which has a useful range of leaflets. They also book **accommodation**, though things get very tight during the main festivals when you should book months in advance. The town boasts several splendidly sited **hotels**, including the comfortable *Wentworth* (℡01728/452312, Ⓦwww.wentworth-aldeburgh.com; ❻), a family-owned hotel along the seafront from the Moot Hall. Of the **B&Bs**, the *Ocean House*, 25 Crag Path (℡01728/452094; ❹), is probably the best. An immaculately maintained Victorian dwelling right on the seafront in the centre of town, it's decorated in period style; dinner is available by prior arrangement. Also in the town centre is *East Cottage*, 55 King St (℡01728/453010; ❷; closed Sept–April), a brightly painted Victorian cottage a block back from the sea. Another option is *Wateringfield*, on Golf Lane (℡01728/453163; ❷), a spacious 1930s house overlooking the golf course on the edge of town. There's also a forty-bed YHA **youth hostel** on Heath Walk in the hamlet of Blaxhall (℡08707/705702, Ⓔblaxhall@yha.org.uk; closed Nov–Feb; dorm beds £11.50), a couple of miles west of the concert facilities at Snape Maltings.

There are tearooms and fish-and-chip shops on the High Street, but Aldeburgh does much better than that with the town's highbrow leanings

---

Benjamin Britten and the Aldeburgh Festival

Benjamin Britten was born in Lowestoft in 1913, and was closely associated with Suffolk for most of his life. The main break was during World War II when, as a conscientious objector, Britten exiled himself to the USA. Ironically enough, it was here that Britten first read the work of the nineteenth-century Suffolk poet, George Crabbe, whose *The Borough*, a grisly portrait of the life of the fishermen of Aldeburgh, was the basis of the libretto of Britten's best-known opera, *Peter Grimes*. The latter was premiered in London in 1945 to great acclaim.

In 1947 Britten founded the English Opera Group and the following year launched the **Aldeburgh Festival** as a showpiece for his own works and those of his contemporaries. He lived in the town for the next ten years and it was during this period that he completed much of his best work as a conductor and pianist. For the rest of his life he composed many works specifically for the festival, including his masterpiece for children, *Noye's Fludde,* and the last of his fifteen operas, *Death in Venice*.

By the mid-1960s, the festival had outgrown the parish churches in which it began, and moved into a collection of disused malthouses, five miles west of Aldeburgh on the River Alde, just south of the small village of **Snape** along the B1069. **Snape Maltings** were subsequently converted into one of the finest concert venues in the country. In addition to the concert hall, there's now a recording studio, a music school, various craft shops and galleries, a tearoom, and a nice pub, the *Plough & Sail*.

For more information on the Aldeburgh Festival, contact the **festival box office**, 152 Aldeburgh High Street (April–Sept Mon–Sat 9.30am–4.30pm, Oct–March Mon–Sat 10am–1pm & 2–4pm; ℡01728/687110, Ⓦwww.aldeburgh.co.uk). Tickets for the concerts, talks, exhibitions and other special events go on sale to the public towards the end of March, and usually sell out fast for the big-name recitals; prices range from £9 to £50. There are all sorts of concerts and performances at other times of the year too – again details are available from the booking office – with showcase events including the Proms season in August and the three-day Britten Festival in late October.

sustaining a glut of terrific **restaurants**. *152 Aldeburgh*, 152 High St (℡01728/454594), is one of the best, offering reasonably priced and stylishly prepared fresh fish in elegant surroundings. There are more Mediterranean flavours and adventurous use of local ingredients at both the *Lighthouse*, 77 High St (℡01728/453377), and the *Regatta*, 171–173 High St (℡01728/452011; closed Mon & Tues in winter), each moderately priced. For **drinks**, head for the *White Lion Hotel*, just along the seafront from the Moot Hall.

Dunwich

Seat of the kings of East Anglia, a bishopric and once the largest port on the Suffolk coast, the ancient city of **DUNWICH**, about twelve miles up the coast from Aldeburgh, reached its peak of prosperity in the twelfth century. Over the last millennium, however, something like a mile of land has been lost to the sea, a process that continues at the rate of about a yard a year. As a result, the whole of the medieval city now lies underwater, including all twelve churches, the last of which toppled over the cliffs in 1919. All that survives today are fragments of the Greyfriars monastery, which originally lay to the west of the city and now dangles at the sea's edge. For a potted history of the lost city, head for the **museum** (April–Sept daily 11.30am–4.30pm; Oct daily noon–4pm; free) in what's left of Dunwich – little more than one small street of terraced houses built by the local landowner in the nineteenth century.

A sprawling, coastline **car park** gives ready access to this part of the seashore and is also where fishing boats still sell their daily catch off the shingle beach. From the car park, it's a short stroll west to the village and south to Greyfriars. Or you can hike further south, out along the beach to **Dunwich Heath**, where the coastguard cottages have been turned into a National Trust shop and tearoom (mid-July to mid-Sept daily 10am-5pm; rest of year varies, but always open Sat & Sun from 10am; ℡01728/648505). The heath is itself next to the **Minsmere RSPB Nature Reserve**, whose star turn is a colony of avocets. You can rent binoculars from the RSPB **visitor centre** (for times, call ℡01728/648281) and strike out on the trails to the birdwatching hides.

The coastline and its heaths have an eerie quality that is best appreciated by **staying** at Dunwich's one and only pub, the *Ship Inn* (℡01728/648219; ❸). With its low wooden beams and open fire, the bar here is a great place for a drink and the **food** is both moderately priced and very tasty.

Southwold

Perched on robust cliffs just to the north of the River Blyth, **SOUTHWOLD** gained what Dunwich lost, and by the sixteenth century it had overtaken all its local rivals. Its days as a busy fishing port are, however, long gone and today it's a genteel seaside resort, an eminently appealing little town with none of the crassness of many of its competitors. There are fine old buildings, a long sandy beach, open heathland, a dinky harbour and even a little industry – in the shape of the Adnams brewery – but no burger bars and certainly no amusement arcades. This gentility was not to the liking of **George Orwell**, who lived for a time at his parents' house at 36 High St (a plaque marks the spot). Orwell heartily disliked the town's airs and graces, and has left no trace of his time here – apart from disguised slights in a couple of early novels.

The town

Southwold's breezy **High Street** is framed by attractive, mainly Georgian buildings, which culminate in the pocket-sized Market Place. From here, it's a brief stroll along East Street to the curious **Sailors' Reading Room** (daily 9am–5pm; free), decked out with model ships and nautical texts, and the bluff above the **beach**, where row upon row of candy-coloured huts march across the sands. Queen Street begins at the Market Place too, quickly leading to **South Green**, the prettiest of several greens dotted across town. In 1659, a calamitous fire razed much of Southwold and when the town was rebuilt the greens were left to act as firebreaks. Beyond, both Ferry Road and the ferry footpath lead down to the **harbour**, at the mouth of the River Blyth, an idyllic spot, where fishing smacks rest against old wooden jetties. There's a footpath along the harbourside that leads to a tiny **ferry** (Easter–May Sat & Sun 10am–12.30pm & 2–4.30pm; June–Aug daily 10am–12.30pm & 2–4.30pm; 40p), which pops across the river to Walberswick. Turn right after the *Harbour Inn* and right again to walk back into town across **Southwold Common**. The whole circular walk takes about thirty minutes.

Back on the Market Place, it's a couple of hundred yards north along Church Street to East Green, with Adnams Brewery on one side and the stumpy lighthouse on another. Close by is Southwold's architectural pride and joy, the **Church of St Edmund** (daily: June–Aug 9am–6pm; Sept–May 9am–4pm; free), a handsome fifteenth-century structure whose solid symmetries are balanced by its long and elegantly carved windows. Inside, the slender, beautifully proportioned nave is distinguished by its panelled roof, embellished with praying angels, and its intricate rood screen. Look out also for "**Southwold Jack**", a brightly painted, medieval effigy of a man in armour nailed to the wall beside the font. No one knows when or why this very military carving was moved into the church – it certainly doesn't fit in – but the betting is that he was once part of a clock, nodding belligerently as he struck the hours. From the church, it's a short walk north to the **pier**, the latest incarnation of a structure that dates from 1899. Built as a landing stage for passenger ferries, the pier has had a troubled history: it has been repeatedly damaged by storms, was hit by a sea-mine and then partly chopped up by the army as a protection against German invasion in World War II.

Practicalities

With frequent services from other towns along the coast, Southwold is easy to reach by **bus**. These stop on the Market Place, yards from the **tourist office**, at 69 High St (April–Sept Mon–Fri 10am–5pm, Sat 10am–5.30pm, Sun 11am–4pm; Oct–March Mon–Fri 10.30am–3.30pm, Sat 10am–4.30pm; ☎01502/724729, ⓦwww.visit-southwold.co.uk), which has details of local attractions and sells walking maps. The town has two well-known **hotels** beside the Market Place, both owned and operated by Adnams. The smarter of the two is *The Swan* (☎01502/722186, ⓦwww.adnams.co.uk; ➏), which occupies a splendid Georgian building with lovely period rooms, though the bedrooms are a little small. *The Crown,* just along the High Street (☎01502/722275, ⓦwww.adnams.co.uk; ➎), has twelve simple bedrooms, all en suite. The best **B&B** in town is the delightful *Acton Lodge*, 18 South Green (☎01502/723217; no credit cards; ➎), which occupies a grand Victorian house complete with its own neo-Gothic tower. The interior is decorated in period style and the three comfortable bedrooms are all en suite. Alternatively, there's a string of **guest houses** down along the seafront on North Parade: try the *North Parade*, at no. 21 (☎01502/722573; ➋), a well-tended Victorian house with sprucely decorated bedrooms; or the attractive *Dunburgh*, at no. 28 (☎01502/723253, ⓦwww.southwold.ws/dunburgh/; ➌), housed in a rambling building with its own mini-tower.

Southwold has two outstanding **places to eat**. *The Crown*'s front bar provides superb informal meals, encompassing daily fish and meat specials combined with an enlightened wine list. Expect to pay £15 or so for two courses. *The Swan*'s more formal dining room is the place for a gourmet blow-out, offering a choice of set dinners at £20–30 a head. For a **drink**, sample Adnams' brews in the *Crown*'s wood-panelled back-bar or stroll along to the *Red Lion* on South Green.

Norwich

One of the five largest cities in Norman England, **NORWICH** once served a vast hinterland of East Anglian cloth producers, whose work was brought here by river and exported to the continent. Its isolated position beyond the Fens meant that it enjoyed closer links with the Low Countries than with the rest of England – it was, after all, quicker to cross the North Sea than to go cross-country to London. The local textile industry, based on worsted cloth (named after the nearby village of Worstead), was further enhanced by an influx of Flemish and Huguenot weavers, who made up more than a third of the population in Tudor times. By 1700, Norwich was the second richest city in the country after London.

With the onset of the Industrial Revolution, however, Norwich lost ground to the northern manufacturing towns – the city's famous mustard company, Colman's, is one of its few industrial success stories – and this, together with its continuing geographical isolation, has helped preserve much of the ancient street plan and many of the older buildings. Pride of place goes to the beautiful cathedral and the castle, but the city's hallmark is its medieval **churches**, thirty or so squat flintstone structures with sturdy towers and sinuous stone tracery round the windows. Isolation has also meant that the population has never swelled to any great extent and today, with just 170,000 inhabitants, Norwich remains an easy and enjoyable city to negotiate. Yet Norwich is no provincial backwater. In the 1960s, the foundation of the University of East Anglia (UEA) made it more **cosmopolitan** and bolstered its arts scene, while in the 1980s it attracted new high-tech companies, who created something of a mini-boom, making the city again one of England's wealthiest. As East Anglia's unofficial capital, Norwich also lies at the hub of the region's **transport** network and serves as a useful base for visiting the Broads, and even as a springboard for the north Norfolk coast.

Arrival and information

Norwich's grandiose **train station** is on the east bank of the River Wensum, ten minutes' walk from the city centre along Prince of Wales Road. Long-distance **buses** terminate at the Surrey Street station, also ten minutes' walk from the town centre, but this time to the south off Surrey Street (though some stop in the centre on Castle Meadow too). Information on local and regional bus services is provided by **NORBIC**, 17–19 Castle Meadow (Mon–Sat 8.30am–5pm; T08453/006116). The First Eastern Counties' Bus Tourist Ticket (£7), valid for a day's unlimited travel on most East Anglian bus routes, is available here, as is the three-day ticket for unlimited travel on three days in seven (£16). The **tourist office** is in The Forum, a gleamingly new, glassy building beside the Market Place (June–Sept Mon–Sat 10am–6pm & Sun 10.30am–4.30pm; Oct–May Mon–Sat 10am–5.30pm; T01603/666071,

@ www.norwich.gov.uk). The **Broads Authority Office**, 18 Colegate (Mon–Fri 9.30am–5pm; ℡01603/610734, @ www.broads-authority.gov.uk), is a useful source of information for those heading for the Broads (see p.455).

The best way to see the city is on **foot** and the tourist office's **city walking tours** (April, May & Oct Sat 1 daily; June & Sept 4 weekly; July & Aug Mon–Sat 1–2 daily; 1hr 30min; £2.50) are a good way of getting the lie of the land. It's also worth bearing in mind the **riverbus** (May–Oct 5 daily; 15min; £1.50), which runs from the Elm Hill Quay to the Thorpe Road Quay, opposite the train station. It is operated by City Boats (℡01603/701701, @ www.cityboats.co.uk), who also offer a limited range of longer cruises out into the surrounding countryside and to the Norfolk Broads from both the Elm Hill and Thorpe Road quays.

Accommodation

Norwich has **accommodation** to suit all budgets, but there's precious little in the town centre. Most **B&Bs** and **guest houses** are strung along the Earlham Road, a tedious, mostly Victorian street running west towards the university, which itself offers **rooms**, during summer and Easter holidays.

Hotels and guest houses

The Beeches 2–6 Earlham Rd ℡01603/621167, @ www.beeches.co.uk. This medium-sized hotel occupies three fully modernized Victorian townhouses and has 36 en-suite rooms. Popular with business folk. **5**

Earlham Guest House 147 Earlham Rd ℡01603/454169, @ www.earlhamguesthouse .co.uk. Spick-and-span lodgings at this family-run guest house, a good ten minutes walk from the centre. Seven bedrooms, each with a TV. **2**

Maid's Head Tombland ℡01603/209955, @ www.regalhotels.co.uk/maidshead. Bang in the centre, this smart hotel incorporates all sorts of architectural bits and pieces from Art Deco flourishes through to heavy Victorian-style wood panelling. The end result is quite pleasing and the bedrooms come complete with modern furnishings and fittings. **6**

Rosedale Guest House 145 Earlham Rd ℡01603/453743. Typical Victorian guest house

containing six frugal but perfectly adequate bedrooms, each with a TV. A ten-minute walk from town centre. **2**

Swallow Nelson Prince of Wales Rd ℡01603/760260 @ www.swallownelsonhotel.co.uk. This modern, riverside hotel, directly opposite the train station, caters to a mainly business clientele. It offers spick-and-span rooms, an indoor pool and a health club. **7**

Student halls

University of East Anglia ℡01603/593297. There are sixty en-suite rooms available year-round in Nelson Court (£52.50 per double), and also single student rooms with shared bathrooms (£25) and en suite (£35) available during Easter and summer vacations. The campus is four miles west of the centre along Earlham Road; buses #25, #26 and #27 from Castle Meadow run here frequently.

The City

Tucked into a sweeping bend of the River Wensum, Norwich's irregular street plan, a Saxon legacy, can make orientation difficult. There are, however, three obvious landmarks to help you find your way – the **cathedral** with its giant spire, the Norman **castle** on its commanding mound and the distinctive **clocktower** of City Hall. Finally, note that most museums and attractions are closed on Sundays, as are many restaurants.

The Cathedral

Norwich **Cathedral** (daily: May–Sept 7.30am–7pm; Oct–April 7.30am–6pm; free tours Mon–Sat; £3 donation requested) is distinguished by its prickly

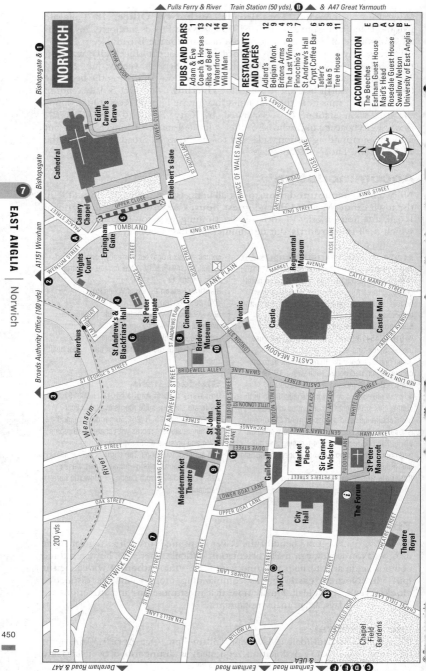

NORWICH

PUBS AND BARS

Adam & Eve	1
Coach & Horses	13
Ribs of Beef	2
Waterfront	14
Wild Man	10

RESTAURANTS AND CAFES

Adlard's	12
Belgian Monk	9
Britons Arms	4
The Last Wine Bar	3
Pinocchio's	7
St Andrew's Hall Crypt Coffee Bar	6
Tatler's	5
Take 5	8
Tree House	11

ACCOMMODATION

The Beeches	E
Earlham Guest House	D
Maid's Head	A
Rosedale Guest House	C
Swallow Nelson	B
University of East Anglia	F

Pulls Ferry & River   Train Station (50 yds), **B** & A47 Great Yarmouth

Bishopsgate & **1**

Bishopsgate

A1151 Wroxham

Broads Authority Office (100 yds)

Dereham Road & A47

Earlham Road   Earlham Road   **C D E F** & UEA

200 yds

octagonal spire which rises to a height of 315ft, second only to Salisbury. It's best viewed from the Lower Close to the west, where the thick curves of the flying buttresses, the rounded excrescences of the ambulatory chapels – unusual in an English cathedral – and the straight symmetries of the main trunk can all be seen to perfection.

The **interior** is pleasantly light thanks to a creamy tint in the stone and the clear glass windows of much of the nave, where the thick pillars are a powerful legacy of the Norman builders who began the cathedral in 1096. Look up to spy the nave's fan vaulting, delicate and geometrically precise carving adorned by several hundred roof **bosses** recounting – from east to west – the story of the Old and New Testaments from the Creation to the Last Judgement. Moving on down the south side of the ambulatory, you reach **St Luke's Chapel** where the cathedral's finest work of art, the *Despenser Reredos*, is a superb painted panel commissioned to celebrate the crushing of the Peasants' Revolt of 1381. Accessible from the south aisle of the nave are the cathedral's unique **cloisters**. Built between 1297 and 1450, and the only two-storey cloisters left standing in England, they contain a remarkable set of sculpted **bosses**, similar to the ones in the main nave, but here they are close enough to be scrutinized without binoculars. The carving is fabulously intricate and the dominant theme is the **Apocalypse**, but look out also for the bosses depicting green men, pagan fertility symbols.

The cathedral precincts

Outside, beside the main entrance, stands the medieval **Canary Chapel**, the original building of Norwich School, whose blue-blazered pupils are often visible during term time. A statue of the school's most famous boy, Horatio Nelson, faces the chapel, standing on the green of the **Upper Close**, which is guarded by two ornate and imposing medieval gates, **Erpingham** and, a few yards to the south, **Ethelbert**. Beside the Erpingham gate is a memorial to **Edith Cavell**, a local nurse shot by the Germans in 1915 in occupied Brussels for helping allied prisoners to escape, a fate that made her an instant folk hero; her grave is beside the cathedral ambulatory. Both gates lead onto the old Saxon market place, **Tombland**, a wide and busy thoroughfare whose name derives from the Saxon word for an open space.

Tombland is a convenient place to start an exploration of the rest of the city centre, but instead you might prefer to wander pedestrianized **Cathedral Close**, which extends east to the river from – and including – the Upper Close. Just beyond the Upper Close is the **Lower Close**, where a scattering of silver birches is flanked by attractive Georgian and Victorian houses. Keeping straight, the footpath continues east to **Pull's Ferry**, a landing stage at the city's medieval watergate, named after the last ferryman to work this stretch. It's a picturesque spot from where you can wander along the riverbank either south to the railway station or north to Bishopgate.

From Tombland to Elm Hill and Bridewell

At the north end of Tombland, fork left into Wensum Street and cobbled **Elm Hill** soon appears on the left. Priestley, in his *English Journey* of 1933, thought this part of Norwich to be overbearingly Dickensian, proclaiming "it difficult to believe that behind those bowed and twisted fronts there did not live an assortment of misers, mad spinsters, saintly clergymen, eccentric comic clerks, and lunatic sextons". Since then, the tourist crowds have sucked the atmosphere, but the quirky half-timbered houses still appeal and while you're here take a look at **Wright's Court**, down a passageway at no. 43, one of the few remaining enclosed courtyards which were once a feature of the city. Elm Hill quickly opens out into a triangular square centred on a plane tree, planted on the spot where the eponymous elm tree from Henry VIII's time once stood. It then veers left up to **St Peter Hungate**, a good-looking, fifteenth-century flint church equipped with a solid square tower and gentle stone tracery round its windows.

Turn right at the church and it's just a few yards to **St Andrew's Hall** and **Blackfriars Hall**, two adjoining buildings that were originally the nave and chancel, respectively, of a Dominican monastery church. Imaginatively recycled, the two halls are now used for a variety of public events; the crypt of the former is a café (Mon–Sat 10am–4.30pm). South of here, off St Andrews Street and along Bridewell Alley, stands the **Bridewell Museum** (April–Sept Mon–Sat 10am–4.30pm, but closed Mon during school terms; £2), one of the city's more enjoyable museums. Formerly the city jail, it holds a pot-pourri of old machines, adverts, signs, and reconstructed shops celebrating Norwich's old trades and industry. Inevitably, there's a lot on the all-important mustard industry, which did much to keep the city's economy afloat in its more troubled times.

Maddermarket

From the top of Bridewell Alley, Bedford Street and then Lobster Lane lead west to Pottergate's **St John Maddermarket** (June–Sept Tues–Sat 10.30am–5pm; free), one of thirty medieval churches standing within the boundaries of the old city walls. Apart from the stone trimmings, the church is almost entirely composed of flint rubble, the traditional building material of east Norfolk, an area chronically short of decent stone. It's a good example of the Perpendicular style, a subdivision of English Gothic which flourished from the middle of the fourteenth to the early sixteenth century and is characterized by straight vertical lines and large windows framed by flowing, but plain, tracery. By comparison, the interior is something of a disappointment, its furnishings and fittings thoroughly remodelled at the start of the twentieth century. The church also has a good selection of **brasses** and the volunteers will kit you out so you can rub away to your heart's content. Back outside, the arch under the church tower leads through to the **Maddermarket Theatre**, built in 1921 in the style of an Elizabethan playhouse.

The Market Place

From Pottergate, several narrow alleys lead through to the city's **Market Place**, site of one of the country's largest open-air markets (closed Sun), with stalls selling everything from bargain-basement clothes to local mussels and whelks. Four very different but equally distinctive buildings oversee the market's stripy awnings, the oldest of them being the fifteenth-century **Guildhall**, an attractive flint and stone structure begun in 1407. Opposite, commanding the heights of the marketplace, are the austere **City Hall**, a lumbering brick pile with a landmark clocktower built in the 1930s in a Scandinavian style – it bears a striking resemblance to Oslo's city hall – and **The Forum**, a flashy, glassy structure completed in 2001. The latter is home to the tourist office and the three-floor interactive **Origins** (Mon–Sat 10am–6pm, Sun 10.30am–4.30pm; £4.95) exploring everything to do with Norwich and Norfolk from its history to a feature on the local accent. On the south side of the Market Place is the finest of the four buildings, **St Peter Mancroft** (Mon–Fri 9.30am–4.30pm, Sat 10am–3pm; free), whose long and graceful nave leads to a mighty stone tower, surmounted by a spiky little spire. The church once delighted John Wesley, who declared "I scarcely ever remember to have seen a more beautiful parish church," a fair description of what remains an exquisite example of the Perpendicular style.

Back outside and just below the church is the **Sir Garnet Wolseley** pub, sole survivor of the 44 ale houses that once crowded the Market Place – and stirred the local bourgeoisie into endless discussions about the drunken fecklessness of the working class. Opposite the pub, across **Gentlemen's Walk**, the town's main promenade, which runs along the bottom of the market place, is the **Royal Arcade**, an Art Nouveau extravagance from 1899. The arcade has been beautifully restored to reveal the swirl and blob of the tiling, ironwork and stained glass, though it's actually the eastern entrance, further from Gentlemen's Walk, which is the most appealing section.

The Castle

Perched high on a grassy mound in the centre of town, and imaginatively tailored into a modern shopping mall down below, the stern walls of **Norwich Castle**, replete with blind arcading and dating from the twelfth century, were built to intimidate the local population. To begin with they were a reminder of Norman power and then, when the castle was turned into a prison, they served as a grim warning to potential law-breakers. Recently refurbished in lavish style, the castle now holds an excellent **Museum and Art Gallery** (July & Aug Mon–Sat 10am–6pm, Sun 1–5pm; Sept–June Mon–Sat 10.30am–4.30pm, Sun 1–5pm; £4.95 all zones), which is divided into three colour-coded zones – yellow for Art and Exhibitions, green for Natural History, and pink for the Castle Keep. The **Natural History** section holds a fairly routine collection of stuffed and mounted wildlife, but **Art and Exhibitions** scores well with its temporary displays and boasts an outstanding selection of work by the **Norwich School**. Founded in 1803, and in existence for just thirty years, this school of landscape painters produced richly coloured, formally composed land- and seascapes in oil and watercolour, paintings whose realism harked back to the Dutch landscape painters of the seventeenth century. The leading figures were John Crome – aka "Old Crome" – and more particularly John Sell Cotman, who is generally acknowledged as one of England's finest water-colourists. Both have a gallery to themselves and, helpfully, there's also a gallery given over to those Dutch painters who influenced them.

Moving on, the **Castle Keep** is no more than a shell, its gloomy walls towering above a scattering of local archeological finds and exhibits that illustrate traditional forms of punishment. The gibbet and its instruments of torture attract most attention, but more unusual is a bloated model **dragon**, known as Snap, which was paraded round town on the annual guilds' day procession – a folkloric hand-me-down from the dragon St George had so much trouble finishing off. To see more of the keep, join one of the regular **guided tours** (an extra £2.50) that explore the battlements and the dungeons.

Finally, a long and dark (and one-way) tunnel leads down from the Castle Museum to the **Royal Norfolk Regimental Museum** (Mon–Sat 10am–4.30pm, closed Mon during school terms), which tracks through the history of the regiment with remarkable candour – including an even-handed account of the Norfolks' policing role in Northern Ireland. The exit leaves you below the castle on Market Avenue.

The University

The **University of East Anglia** (UEA) occupies a sprawling campus on the western outskirts of the city beside the B1108. Its buildings are resolutely modern concrete-and-glass blocks of varying designs – some quite ordinary, others like the prize-winning "ziggurat" halls of residence, designed by Denys Lasdun, eminently memorable. The main reason to visit is the flashy, high-tech **Sainsbury Centre for Visual Arts** (Tues–Sun 11am–5pm, mid-May to mid-Sept Wed till 8pm; £2; ⓦ www.uea.ac.uk/scva), built by Norman Foster in the 1970s. The interior houses one of the most varied collections of sculpture and painting in the country, donated by the family which founded the Sainsbury supermarket chain, in which the likes of Degas, Seurat, Picasso, Giacometti, Bacon and Henry Moore rub shoulders with Mayan and Egyptian antiquities. The centre also runs a first-rate programme of temporary exhibitions. **Buses** #25, #26 and #27 run frequently to UEA from Castle Meadow.

Eating and drinking

There are plenty of **cafés and restaurants** in the city centre – most of them very good value. Decent **pubs**, though, are harder to find, maybe because previously serviceable places have been turned into ersatz "traditional" drinking dens for students.

Cafés and restaurants

Adlard's 79 Upper Giles St ☏ 01603/633522. Engaging Modern-British restaurant with accomplished seasonal cooking from a brief but enticing menu. Closed all Sun & Mon lunch. Expensive.

Belgian Monk 7 Pottergate ☏ 01603/767222. Perhaps too theme-ish for some tastes, this bar and restaurant specializes in all-things Flemish – from beers through to soup and, of course, mussels and chips. Moderate.

Britons Arms 9 Elm Hill. Home-made quiches, tarts, cakes and scones plus pies and salads in a quaint Elm Hill thatched house with a terraced garden. Open Mon–Sat 9.30am–5pm. Inexpensive.

The Last Wine Bar 70–76 St George's St ☏ 01603/626626. Converted factory building holding a smart wine bar, which serves up tasty bistro-style dishes. A couple of minutes' walk north of the river. Closed Sun. Moderate.

Pinocchio's 11 St Benedict's St ☏ 01603/613318. Relaxed Italian restaurant in a pleasantly converted old general store, with inventive food combinations and live music a couple of times a week. Closed Sun. Moderate.

St Andrew's Hall Crypt Coffee Bar St Andrew's Plain at St George's St. Bargain spot for budget meals or just a coffee and cake. Open Mon–Sat 9am–4.30pm. Inexpensive.

Tatler's 21 Tombland ☏ 01603/766670. Brasserie in an elegantly converted Georgian townhouse with modern French cooking and an excellent wine list. Moderate.

Take 5 Cinema City, St Andrew's Plain. Imaginative, budget bistro food served in amenable surroundings. Mon–Sat 11am–11pm. Inexpensive.

Tree House 14 Dove St, above the Rainbow wholefood shop. Vegetarian café-restaurant offering a daily changing menu of soups, salads and main courses, plus organic wines and beers. Closed Sun. Inexpensive.

Pubs, bars and clubs

Adam & Eve Bishopgate. There's been a pub on this site for seven hundred years and it's still the top spot in town for the discerning drinker with a changing range of real ales and an eclectic wine list supplied by Adnams.

Coach & Horses Bethel St. Pleasant city-centre pub – across the street from City Hall – with lived-in furnishings and fittings. Good for a quiet drink.

Ribs of Beef Wensum St. Boisterous riverside drinking haunt, popular with students and townies alike. Well-kept ales and inexpensive bar food.

Waterfront 139–141 King's St ☏ 01603/632717. Norwich's principal club and alternative music venue, with gigs and DJs most nights. Sponsored by UEA.

Wild Man Bedford St. Long-established, popular city-centre watering hole that has greased many a student wheel.

Entertainment

Predictably, Norwich has its fair share of multi-screen **cinemas** showing Hollywood blockbusters, but it also has the excellent art-house **Cinema City**, in Suckling House on St Andrew's Plain (☏ 01603/622047, ⓦ www

.cinemacity.co.uk). The **arts scene** here is perhaps a tad self-conscious, but the city does possess several first-rate **theatres**. The Theatre Royal, on Theatre Street (℡01603/630000, www.theatreroyalnorwich.co.uk), has a wide-ranging programme of mainstream and more adventurous plays and dance, while the amateur Maddermarket, St John's Alley, off Pottergate (℡01603/620917, www.maddermarket.co.uk), offers an interesting range of modern theatre. Predictably enough, **UEA** is a major source of entertainment for students and locals alike, with gigs at the Union and classical concerts at the Music Centre. The annual **Norfolk and Norwich Festival** each October (℡01603/766400, www.n-joy.org) features music, film, theatre, comedy, dance, walks and talks at venues all over the city.

The Norfolk Broads

Three rivers – the Yare, Waveney and Bure – meander across the flatlands to the east of Norwich, converging on Breydon Water before flowing into the sea at **Great Yarmouth**. In places these rivers swell into wide expanses of water known as "broads", which for years were thought to be natural lakes. In fact they're the result of extensive peat cutting, several centuries of accumulated diggings made in a region where wood was scarce and peat a valuable source of energy. The pits flooded when sea levels rose in the thirteenth and fourteenth centuries to create the **Norfolk Broads**, now one of the most important wetlands in Europe – a haven for many birds – and the county's major tourist attraction.

The Broads' delicate ecological balance suffered badly during the 1970s and 1980s. The careless use of fertilizers poisoned the water with phosphates and nitrates, encouraging the spread of algae; the decline in reed cutting – previously in great demand for thatching – made the Broads partly unnavigable; and the enormous increase in pleasure-boat traffic began to erode the banks. National Park status was, however, accorded to the area in 1988, and efforts are now under way to clear the waters and protect the ecosystem. Coordinating the clean up is the **Broads Authority** (℡01603/610734, www.broads-authority.gov.uk), which maintains a series of information centres throughout the region. At any of these, you can pick up a free copy of the *Broadcaster*, a useful newspaper guide to the Broads as a whole.

The region is crossed by several **train** lines, with connections from Norwich to Wroxham, Acle and Reedham, as well as Berney Arms, near Breydon Water, one of the few places in England that can be reached by rail but not road. However, the best – really the only – way to see the Broads themselves is **by boat**, and you could happily spend a week or so exploring the 125 miles of lock-free navigable waterways, visiting the various churches, pubs and windmills en route. Among many **boat rental** companies, two of the more established are Blakes Holiday Boating (℡01603/739400, www.blakes.co.uk) and Broads Tours Ltd (℡01603/782207, www.broads.co.uk), both of whom operate out of Wroxham (see p.456). Prices for cruisers start at around £700 a week for four people in peak season, but less expensive, short-term rentals are widely available too. Houseboats are much cheaper than cruisers, but they are, of course, static.

Trying to explore the Broads by car is pretty much a waste of time, but cyclists and walkers have it much better, taking advantage of the region's network of footpaths and cycling trails. There are eight Broads Authority **bike rental** points dotted around (£9 per day; ℡01603/782281).

Wroxham and Ludham

The easiest boating centre to reach from Norwich is **WROXHAM**, seven miles to the northeast and accessible by train, bus and car. Wroxham is itself short on charm, but it has a useful **information centre**, on Station Road (Easter–Oct daily 9am–1pm & 2–5pm; ☎01603/782281), and plenty of places where you can stock up with food before heading out on a cruise.

Some six miles east of Wroxham, the village of **LUDHAM** straggles along the roadside at the tip of the Womack Water, an offshoot of the River Thurne. Just north of the village is How Hill, where the Broads Authority maintain **Toad Hole Cottage** (June–Sept daily 10am–6pm; April, May & Oct Mon–Fri 11am–1pm & 1.30–5pm; free), an old eel-catcher's cottage housing a small exhibit on the history of the trade, which was common hereabouts until the 1940s. Behind the cottage is the narrow River Ant, where there are hour-long, wildlife-viewing boat trips in the *Electric Eel* from Easter to October – call ☎01692/678763 for schedule and reservations; trips cost £4.

Potter Heigham and Ranworth

A couple of miles east of Ludham, **POTTER HEIGHAM** is the nominal capital of the Broads, taking its name from the pottery which once stood here on the River Thurne and from the Saxon lord of Heacham who founded the first settlement. Again, there's not much to keep your attention, though you can watch boaters struggling with the village's fourteenth-century bridge, regarded as one of the most difficult passages in the Broads. All the major boat rental companies have outlets here and there's also an **information centre** (Easter–Oct daily 9am–1pm & 2–5pm; ☎01692/670779). The only public transport to Potter Heigham is by bus from Great Yarmouth, on the coast to the southeast.

Tiny **RANWORTH**, around twelve miles east of Norwich via the B1140, is a quieter spot altogether, though in the evening the place does fill up with boaters, who moor up in Ranworth Staithe and then pop into the local for a pint. There's no point in coming here if you're after hiring a boat, but the village does have its own **information office** (Easter–Oct daily 9am–5pm; ☎01603/270453), with stacks of stuff on local walking and wildlife. Ranworth also possesses a good-looking **church**, which is graced by a much-admired fifteenth-century rood screen, and there are regular **boat trips** to the isolated ruins of **St Benet's Abbey**, a couple of miles downstream along the River Bure (April–Oct Mon–Sat 1 daily; £5.50). There's also a **ferry** (April–Oct 2–4 daily; 30min; 80p) service to the **Broadland Conservation Centre**, a floating information centre and nature reserve just across Ranworth Staithe.

The north Norfolk coast

The first place of any note on the **north Norfolk coast** is **Cromer**, a workaday seaside town some twenty miles north of Norwich whose bleak and blustery cliffs have drawn tourists for over a century. A few miles to the west is another well-established resort, **Sheringham**, but thereafter the shoreline becomes a ragged patchwork of salt marshes, dunes and shingle spits which form an almost unbroken series of nature reserves, supporting a fascinating range of flora and fauna. It's a lovely stretch of coast and the villages bordering it, principally **Cley**, **Blakeney** and **Wells–next–the–Sea**, are prime targets for an overnight stay. The other major attractions hereabouts are the string of stately homes that lie a short distance inland.

Cromer and Sheringham are the only places reachable by **train**, with an hourly service from Norwich on the Bittern Line. Local **bus** services fill in (most of) the gaps, connecting all of the towns and many of the villages. There's also the **Coasthopper bus** (June–Sept Mon–Sat hourly, Sun 4 daily; ☏ 08453/006116), which provides regular services along the whole length of the coast from Cromer to Hunstanton, with some buses continuing to Great Yarmouth and King's Lynn. The Coasthopper Rover ticket (£5) gives a day's unlimited travel on the route.

Cromer and around

Dramatically poised on a high bluff, **CROMER** should be the most memorable of the Norfolk coastal resorts, but its fine aspect is partly undermined by a shabbiness in the streets and shopfronts – an "atrophied charm" as Paul Theroux called it. The tower of **St Peter and St Paul**, at 160ft the tallest in Norfolk, attests to the port's medieval wealth, but it was the advent of the railway in the 1880s that heralded the most frenetic flurry of building activity. A bevy of grand Edwardian hotels was constructed along the seafront and for a moment Cromer became the most fashionable of resorts, but the gloss soon wore off and only the dishevelled **Hotel de Paris** has survived. While you're here, be sure to take a stroll out onto the **pier**, which was badly damaged in a storm in November 1993, but has since been repaired and struggles gamely on, and, of course, don't forget to grab a **crab** – JWH Jonas, 7 New Street, has some fine specimens.

Somewhat miraculously Cromer has managed to retain its rail link with Norwich; the **train station** is a five-minute walk west of the centre. **Buses** terminate on Cadogan Road, next to the **tourist office** (April to late July, Sept & Oct Mon–Sat 10am–5pm & Sun 10am–4pm; late July to Aug daily 9.30am–5pm; Nov–March daily 10am–1pm & 2–4pm; ☏ 08702/254853), which is just 200 yards from the cliff-top promenade. An hour or two in Cromer is probably enough, though the **beach** is first-rate and the cliff-top walk exhilarating. There's no shortage of inexpensive **accommodation** – the tourist office has all the details – but it's hard to beat the enticing *Beachcomber B&B*, a cosy place with six en-suite rooms, near the centre at 17 Macdonald Road (☏ 01263/513398, ⓦ www.beachcomber-guesthouse .co.uk; no cards; ❷).

Felbrigg Hall

Just a couple of miles southwest of Cromer off the A148, **Felbrigg Hall** (April–Oct Mon–Wed, Sat & Sun 1–5pm; £6; NT) is a charming Jacobean mansion. The main facade is particularly appealing, the soft hues of the ageing limestone and brick intercepted by three bay windows, which together sport a large, cleverly carved inscription – Gloria Deo in Excelsis – in celebration of the reviving fortunes of the family who once owned the place, the Windhams. The interior is splendid too, with the studied informality of both the dining room and the drawing room enlivened by some magnificent seventeenth-century plasterwork ceilings and sundry objets d'art. Many of the **paintings** in Felbrigg were purchased by William Windham II, who did his Grand Tour in the 1740s.

The surrounding **parkland** (daily dawn to dusk) divides into two, with woods to the north and open pasture to the south. Footpaths crisscross the park and a popular spot to head for is the medieval church of **St Margaret's** in the southeastern corner, which contains a fine set of brasses and a fancy memorial to William Windham I and his wife by Grinling Gibbons. Nearer the house there's the extensive **walled garden**, which features flowering borders and an octagonal dove house, and the **stables**, which have been converted into very pleasant **tearooms**.

Sheringham

SHERINGHAM, a popular seaside town four miles west of Cromer, has an amiable, easy-going air and makes a reasonable overnight stop, though frankly you're only marking time until you hit the more appealing places further west. One of the distinctive features of the town is the smooth local beach pebbles that face and decorate the houses, a **flinting technique** used frequently in this part of Norfolk – the best examples here are off the High Street. The downside is that the power of the waves which makes the pebbles smooth has also forced the local council to spend thousands rebuilding the sea defences. The resultant mass of reinforced concrete makes for a less than pleasing seafront – all the more reason to head, instead, for **Sheringham Park**, the 770-acre woodland park a couple of miles southwest of the town, laid out by Humphry Repton in the early 1800s. The park boasts a wonderful array of rhododendrons and azaleas, at their best in late May to early June, and a series of look-out posts from which you can admire the view down to the coast. The other out-of-town jaunt is on the **North Norfolk Railway**, whose steam trains operate along the five miles of track southwest from Sheringham to the modest market town of Holt (May–Sept daily, frequent services in April & Oct; all-day ticket £8; ☎01263/820800, ⓦwww.nnrailway.co.uk).

Sheringham's two **train stations** are opposite each other on either side of Station Road. The main station, the terminus of the Bittern Line from Norwich, is just to the east, the North Norfolk Railway station to the west. The **tourist office** (April–Oct Mon–Sat 10am–5pm, Sun 10am–4pm; ☎08702/554854) is in between them on Station Approach. From the tourist office, it's a five-minute walk north to the seafront, straight down Station Road and its continuation, the High Street.

There are plenty of **B&B** options, with one of the best being *Oak Lodge* at 2 Morris St (☎01263/823158, ⓦwww.oak-lodge.co.uk; ❸), a smart Edwardian house with four attractive bedrooms. A reasonable alternative is the unassuming *Two Lifeboats*, 2 High St (☎01263/822401, ⓦwww.twolifeboats.co.uk; ❹), a small hotel on the promenade offering sea views from most of its bedrooms. The **youth hostel** is a short, five-minute walk south of the main train station at 1 Cremer's Drift (☎08707/706024; closed Dec–Jan; £11.50), set in its own grounds just off Cromer Road.

For a bite to **eat**, *Dave's*, 50 High Street, serves the best fish and chips for miles around and for dessert try a homemade ice cream from *Ronaldo's*, 14 High Street, with flavours ranging from chocolate and ginger to cinnamon and lavender.

Cley-next-the-Sea and Blakeney Point

Travelling west from Sheringham, the **A149** meanders through a pretty rural landscape offering occasional glimpses of the sea and a shoreline protected by a giant shingle barrier erected after the catastrophic flood of 1953, a disaster which claimed over one thousand lives. After seven miles you reach **CLEY-NEXT-THE-SEA**, once a busy wool port but now little more than a row of flint cottages and Georgian mansions. The original village was destroyed in a fire in 1612, which explains why Cley's fine medieval **Church of St Margaret** is located half a mile inland at the very southern edge of the current village, overlooking the green. Plague brought church construction to a sudden halt, hence the contrast between the stunted, unfinished chancel and the splendid nave, which boasts several fine medieval brasses and some folksy fifteenth-century bench ends depicting animals and grotesques. Cley's other great draw – housed in an old forge on the main street – is the excellent **Cley Smoke House**, selling local smoked fish and other delicacies, while nearby **Picnic Fayre** has long been one of the finest delis in East Anglia.

It's about 400 yards east from the village to the mile-long byroad that leads to the shingle mounds of **Cley beach**, the starting point for the four-mile hike west out along the spit to **Blakeney Point**, a nature reserve famed for its colonies of terns and seals. The seal colony is made up of several hundred common and grey seals, and the old lifeboat house, at the end of the spit, is now a National Trust information centre. The shifting shingle can, however, make the going difficult, so keep to the low-water mark – which also means that you won't accidentally trample any nests. The easier alternative is to take one of the boat trips to the point from Blakeney or Morston (see below). The Norfolk Coast Path passes close to the beach too and then continues along the edge of the **Cley Marshes**, which attract a bewildering variety of waders – and, of course, "twitchers".

As for a **place to stay**, Cley holds the outstanding *Cley Mill B&B* (℡01263/740209, Ⓦwww.cleymill.co.uk; ❺), housed in a converted windmill complete with sails and a balcony offering wonderful views. Another recommendable place is the *Three Swallows* pub (℡01263/740526; ❸), on the green by the church, which has several pleasant en-suite rooms. For **food**, *The Café at Whalebone House* (℡01263/740336, Ⓦwww.thecafe.org.uk), on the main street, is an intimate vegetarian restaurant offering an innovative menu at affordable prices. They also have a couple of stylish **rooms** (❺) for stays of two nights or more.

Blakeney

BLAKENEY is delightful. Once a bustling port exporting fish, corn and salt, it's now a lovely little place of pebble-covered cottages sloping up from a narrow harbour just a mile west of Cley. Crab sandwiches are sold from stalls at the quayside, the meandering high street is flanked by family-run shops, and footpaths stretch out along the sea wall to east and west, allowing long, lingering looks over the salt marshes. The only sight as such is the **Church of St Nicholas**, beside the A149 at the south end of the village, whose sturdy tower and nave are made of flint rubble with stone trimmings.

Blakeney **harbour** is linked to the sea by a narrow channel, which wriggles its way through the salt marshes but is only navigable for a few hours at high tide. Depending on the tides, there are **boat trips** from Blakeney or Morston quay, a mile or two to the west, to both Blakeney Point (see above) – where passengers have a couple of hours at the point before being ferried back – and to the seal colony just off the point. The main operators advertise departure times on blackboards by the quayside or you can reserve in advance with Beans Boats (℡01263/740505) or Bishop's Boats (℡01263/740753). Both the seal trips and those to Blakeney Point cost about £6.

For **accommodation**, the quayside *Blakeney Hotel* (℡01263/740797, Ⓦwww.blakeney-hotel.co.uk; ❼) is one of the most charming hotels in

Norfolk, a rambling building with high-pitched gables and pebble-covered walls. The hotel has an indoor pool, secluded garden, cosy lounges and outstanding **food**. The cheaper rooms can be poky and somewhat airless, but pay a little more and you'll be rewarded with splendid views across the harbour and the marshes. A good alternative is the *Manor Hotel* (℡01263/740376, Ⓦwww.blakeneymanor.co.uk; ❺), which occupies a low-lying courtyard complex a few yards to the east of the harbour; or you might try the excellent *King's Arms*, just back from the quay on Westgate (℡01263/740341; ❹), a traditional pub, with low, beamed ceilings and seven en-suite bedrooms. The latter also serves up delicious, reasonably priced **bar food**. For longer stays, contact *Quayside Cottages* (℡01462/768627, Ⓦwww.blakeneycottages.co.uk), who rent some charming local cottages. Finally, *Morston Hall*, a couple of miles west of Blakeney on the A149 (℡01263/741041, Ⓦwww.morstonhall.com; ❻), occupies an attractive old house with beautiful gardens and tastefully decorated rooms; they also have a top-flight but relaxed restaurant where the emphasis is on seafood.

Wells-next-the-Sea and around

Despite its name, **WELLS–NEXT–THE–SEA**, some eight miles west of Blakeney, is situated a good mile or so from open water. In Tudor times, when it enjoyed much easier access to the North Sea, it was one of the great ports of eastern England, a major player in the trade with the Netherlands. Those heady days are long gone and although today it's the only commercially viable port on the north Norfolk coast, this is hardly a huge advantage. More importantly, Wells is also one of the county's more attractive towns, and though there are no specific sights among its narrow lanes, it makes a good base for exploring the surrounding coastline.

The town divides into three distinct areas, starting with **The Buttlands**, a broad rectangular green on the south side of town, lined with oak and beech trees and framed by a string of fine Georgian houses; it takes its unusual name from the years it was used for archery practice – a butt being the earthen mound behind the target. North from here, across Station Road, lie the narrow lanes of the town centre, with **Staithe Street**, the minuscule main drag, flanked by quaint old-fashioned shops. Staithe Street leads down to the **quay**, a somewhat forlorn affair inhabited by a couple of amusement arcades and fish-and-chip shops, and the mile-long byroad that scuttles north to the **beach**, a handsome sandy tract backed by pine-clad dunes. The beach road is shadowed by a high flood defence and a tiny narrow-gauge **railway**, which scoots down to the beach every twenty minutes or so from 10.30am, Easter to October (90p each way).

Buses to Wells stop on The Buttlands, a short stroll from the **tourist office** at the foot of Staithe Street (April–Oct Mon–Sat 10am–5pm, Sun 10am–4pm; ℡08702/254857). The steam **trains** of the Wells & Walsingham Light Railway (℡01328/710631) use the train station on the southeast edge of town beside the A149. Several of the best **guest houses** are along Standard Road, which runs up from the eastern end of the quayside. First choice should be the elegant *Normans* (℡01328/710657; ❸), whose five spacious and tastefully decorated rooms are all en suite; the TV lounge has a log fire and racks of games and the first-floor look-out window provides a wide view over the marshes – binoculars are provided. Other options include *Mill House*, a dignified old millowner's home on Northfield Lane (℡01328/710739, Ⓦwww.broadland.com/millhouse; ❸), and *Ilex House* on Bases Lane

(℡01328/710556, 🌐www.broadland.com/ilexhouse; ❸). The last is a good-looking Georgian villa with three guest rooms that sits in its own grounds, just to the west of the centre. There's also a **campsite**, the sprawling *Pinewoods Caravan and Camping Park*, by the beach (℡01328/710439; closed Nov to mid-March).

For **pub food**, head straight for the *Crown* on The Buttlands, the best pub in town. Alternatively, *Nelson's*, 21 Staithe St, is a pleasant tea and coffee shop that serves inexpensive meals.

Holkham Hall

One of the most popular outings from Wells is to **Holkham Hall** (June–Sept Mon & Thurs–Sun 1–5pm; £6.50; 🌐www.holkham.co.uk), three miles to the west and a stop on the Coasthopper bus (see p.457). This grand and self-assured stately home was designed by the eighteenth-century architect William Kent for the first earl of Leicester and is still owned by the family. The severe sandy-coloured Palladian exterior belies the warmth and richness of the interior, which retains much of its original decoration, notably the marble hall, with its fluted columns and intricate reliefs. The rich colours of the state rooms are an appropriate backdrop for a fabulous selection of **paintings**, including canvases by Van Dyck, Rubens, Gainsborough and Gaspar Poussin. One real treat is the Landscape Room where around twenty landscape paintings are displayed in the cabinet style of the eighteenth century.

The **grounds** (dawn to dusk; free) are laid out on sandy, saline land, much of it originally salt marsh. The focal point is an 80-foot-high obelisk, atop a grassy knoll, from where you can view both the hall to the north and the triumphal arch to the south. In common with the rest of the north Norfolk coast, there's plenty of **birdlife** to observe in and around the park – Holkham's lake attracts Canada geese, herons and grebes – and several hundred deer graze the open pastures.

The footpaths latticing the estate stretch as far as the A149, from where a half-mile byroad – Lady Anne's Drive – leads north across the marshes from opposite the *Victoria Hotel* to **Holkham Bay**, which boasts one of the finest sandy beaches on this stretch of coast, golden sand flexed against pine-studded sand dunes. Warblers, flycatchers and redstarts inhabit the drier coastal reaches, while waders paddle about the mud and salt flats.

Little Walsingham

For centuries **LITTLE WALSINGHAM**, five miles south of Wells (and not to be confused with adjoining Great Walsingham), rivalled Bury St Edmunds and Canterbury as the foremost pilgrimage site in England. It all began in 1061 when the Lady of the Manor, a certain Richeldis de Faverches, was prompted to build a replica of the **Santa Casa** (Mary's home in Nazareth) here – inspired, it is said, by visions of the Virgin Mary. Whatever the reason for her actions, it brought instant fame and fortune to this little Norfolk village and every medieval king from Henry III onwards made at least one trip, walking the last mile barefoot. Both the Augustinians and the Franciscans established themselves here and all seemed set fair when Henry VIII followed in his predecessors' footsteps in 1511. However, pilgrim or not, it didn't stop Henry from destroying the shrine in the Dissolution of the 1530s, and at a stroke the village's principal trade came to an abrupt halt. Pilgrimages resumed in earnest after 1922, when the local vicar, one Alfred Hope Patten, organized an Anglo-Catholic pilgrimage, the prelude to the building of an Anglican shrine in the

1930s to the chagrin of the diocesan authorities. Today the village does good business out of its holy connections and the narrow-gauge **steam railway** from Wells (Easter–Oct daily 4–5 daily each way; 30mins; £6 return; ☎01328/710631).

Little Walsingham now has a number of **shrines** catering to a variety of denominations – there's even a Russian Orthodox Church – though the main one is the **Anglican shrine**, beside the road from Holt, a few yards from the main square, **Common Place**. It's a strange-looking building – a cross between an English village hall and an Orthodox church – and inside the candle-lit Santa Casa contains the statue of Our Lady of Walsingham.

Shrines apart, Little Walsingham has an attractive centre, beginning with the Common Place, whose half-timbered buildings surround a quaint octagonal structure built to protect the village **pump** in the sixteenth century. The **High Street** extends south from here, overlooked by handsome Georgian and half-timbered houses, several of which are given over to shrine shops and religious bookstores. The High Street is also flanked by the impressive fifteenth-century **Abbey gatehouse** of the old Augustinian Priory, though the **ruins** beyond (April–Oct daily 10am–4.30pm; March, Nov & Dec Sat & Sun 10am–4pm; closed Jan; £3), whose landscaped grounds stretch east to the River Stiffkey, are inconsequential. Footsteps from the south end of the High Street is the town's second square, **Friday Market Place**, which backs onto the village's second set of ecclesiastical **ruins** (open access; free) – those of the old Franciscan Friary.

Practicalities

The Coasthopper **bus** – as well as the fairly frequent Wells to Fakenham (for Norwich) bus – stops outside the Anglican shrine. The **train station** (for the steam train from Wells, see above) is a five-minute walk from Common Place: from the station, turn left along Egmere Road and take the second major right down Bridewell Street. The **tourist office** is on Common Place (April–Oct daily 10am–4.30pm; ☎01328/820510). It's difficult to find accommodation during major **pilgrimages** – the main ones are the national pilgrimage on the late May Bank Holiday and the pilgrimage for the sick and disabled on August 30. That said, the *Black Lion Hotel* on Friday Market (☎01328/820235; ❺) has comfortable en-suite rooms and a restaurant, as does the more modest *Bull Inn* on Common Place (☎01328/820333; ❹). Even better is *The Manor House*, on Barsham Road in the neighbouring hamlet of **Great Snoring** (☎01328/820597, ⓦwww.norfolkcountryhouse.co.uk; ❻). This family-run hotel occupies a very distinctive house, whose towers and turrets date back to the fifteenth century. The gardens are splendid and each of the six en-suite rooms is pleasantly furnished in homely style; dinners are by prior arrangement only.

Burnham Deepdale and Hunstanton

Back on the A149, it's eight miles west from Wells-next-the-Sea to the hamlet of **BURNHAM DEEPDALE**, where *Deepdale Farm* (☎01485/210156, ⓦwww.deepdalefarm.co.uk; dorm beds £10.50, ❶), situated just off the road, is a lively and very friendly setup, operating a combined campsite, café and hostel in inventively renovated former stables. From here, it's a further nine miles to **HUNSTANTON**, a Victorian seaside resort that pretty much marks the end of The Norfolk coast. Hunstanton grew up to the southwest of the original fishing village – now **Old Hunstanton** – but although it has its fair share of amusement arcades and so forth, the resort has hung on to its genteel origins – and its sandy, cliff-backed beaches, which are among the cleanest in the county.

The **tourist office** is in the town hall (daily: April–Sept 9.30am–5pm; Oct–March 10.30am–4pm; ☎01485/532610) on the wide sloping green, which serves as the focal point of the town. They can help out with **accommodation**, though it's easy enough to find. The nicest and priciest places are among the cottages of Old Hunstanton. One particular recommendation is *Le Strange Arms*, Golf Course Rd (☎01485/534411, ⓦwww.abacushotels.co.uk; ⑥), a large mansion dating from the nineteenth century and with gardens running down to the beach. At the other end of the market, the **youth hostel** occupies a pair of Victorian townhouses at 15 Avenue Rd (☎08707/705872, ⓔhunstanton@yha.org.uk; closed Nov–Easter; dorm beds £10.25), south of Hunstanton green.

Sandringham House

It's about eight miles south from Hunstanton along the A149 to the turnings that lead into the seven-thousand-acre estate of **Sandringham House** (mid-April to Oct daily 11am–4.45pm; closed for two weeks late-July or early Aug; £6.50; ⓦwww.sandringhamestate.co.uk), bought in 1861 by Queen Victoria for her son, the future Edward VII. The house is billed as a private home, but few families have a drawing room crammed with Russian silver and Chinese jade. The **museum**, housed in the old coach and stable block, contains an exhibition of royal memorabilia from dolls to cars, but much more arresting are the beautifully maintained **grounds** (10.30am–5pm), a mass of rhododendrons and azaleas in spring and early summer. The estate's sandy soil is also ideal for game birds, which was the attraction of the place for the terminally bored Edward, whose tradition of shooting parties is still followed by the royals.

Ely and around

Perched on a mound of clay above the River Great Ouse, **ELY** – literally "eel island" – was to all intents and purposes a true island until the draining of the fens in the seventeenth century. Up until then, the town was encircled by treacherous marshland, which could only be crossed with the help of the local "fen-slodgers" who knew the firm tussock paths. In 1070, **Hereward the Wake** turned this inaccessibility to military advantage, holding out against the Normans and forcing William the Conqueror to undertake a prolonged siege – and finally to build an improvised road floated on bundles of sticks.

Since then, Ely has always been associated with Hereward, which is really rather ridiculous as Ely is, above all else, an ecclesiastical town and a Norman one to boot. The Normans built the **cathedral**, a towering structure visible for miles across the flat landscape and Ely's only significant sight. Though easy to see on a day-trip from Cambridge, Ely does make a pleasant night's stop in its own right.

The Town

Ely **Cathedral** (June–Sept daily 7am–7pm; Oct–May Mon–Sat 7.30am–6pm, Sun 7.30am–5pm; Mon–Sat £4.80, free on Sun) is seen to best advantage from the south, the crenellated towers of the west side perfectly balanced by the prickly finials to the east with the distinctive timber lantern rising above them both. To approach from this direction, follow the footpath leading up the hill into the cathedral precincts from **Broad Street** – also the second turning on the right as you walk up Station Road from the train station. At the top of the footpath, pass through the medieval **Porta**, once the principal entrance to the monastery complex, and turn right to reach the main entrance on the lopsided **west front** – one of the transepts collapsed in a storm in 1701.

The first things to strike you as you enter the **nave** are the sheer length of the building and the lively nineteenth-century painted ceiling, largely the work of amateur volunteers. The nave's procession of plain late-Norman arches, built around the same time as those at Peterborough, leads to the architectural feature that makes Ely so special, the **octagon** – the only one of its kind in England – built in 1322 to replace the collapsed central tower. Its construction, employing the largest oaks available in England to support some four hundred tons of glass and lead, remains one of the wonders of the medieval world, and the effect, as you look up into this Gothic dome, is simply breathtaking. From March to October, **Octagon tours** (£3; reservations & schedule ☏01353/667735) depart two to four times daily from the desk at the entrance, venturing up into the octagon itself.

When the central tower collapsed, it fell eastwards, onto the **choir**, the first three bays of which were rebuilt at the same time as the octagon in the Decorated style – in contrast to the plainer Early English of the choir bays beyond. Further east still is the thirteenth-century **presbytery**, which houses the relics of **St Ethelreda**, founder of the abbey in 673, who, despite being twice married, is honoured liturgically as a virgin. Also at the east end are three **chantry chapels**, the most charming of which (on the left) is an elaborate Renaissance affair dated to 1533. The other marvel at Ely is the **Lady Chapel**, a separate building accessible via the north transept. It lost its sculpture and its stained glass during the Reformation, but its fan vaulting remains, an exquisite example of English Gothic. Retracing your steps, the south triforium near the main entrance holds the **Stained Glass Museum** (Easter–Oct Mon–Sat 10.30am–5pm, Sun noon–6pm; Nov–Easter Mon–Sat 10.30am–4.30pm, Sun noon–4.30pm; £3.50), an Anglican money-spinner exhibiting examples of this applied art from 1240 to the present day.

The rest of Ely is pretty enough, but hardly compelling after the wonders of the cathedral. To the north, the **High Street**, with its Georgian buildings and old-fashioned shops, makes for an enjoyable browse and, if you push on past the Market Place down Forehill and then Waterside, you'll soon reach the **Babylon Gallery** (Tues–Sun 10am–4pm; free), where an imaginative programme of temporary exhibitions featuring contemporary art and craft is displayed in a renovated old brewery warehouse. Alternatively, head west from the cathedral entrance across the Palace Green, to **Oliver Cromwell's House** at 29 St Mary's St (April–Oct daily 10am–5.30pm; Nov–March Mon–Fri & Sun 11am–4pm, Sat 10am–5pm; £3.50), a timber-framed former vicarage, which holds a small exhibition on the Protector's ten-year sojourn in Ely, when he was employed as a tithe collector.

Practicalities

Ely lies on a major rail intersection, with direct **trains** from as far afield as Liverpool, Norwich and London, as well as from Cambridge, just twenty minutes to the south. The **train station** is a ten-minute walk from the cathedral straight up Station Road and its continuation Back Hill. **Buses** (from King's Lynn and Cambridge) stop on Market Street immediately to the north of the cathedral. The **tourist office** is in Oliver Cromwell's House (April–Oct daily 10am–5.30pm; Nov–March Mon–Fri & Sun 11am–4pm, Sat 10am–5pm; ℡01353/662062, ⓦwww.eastcambs.gov.uk).

Ely has several appealing **B&Bs**, the best being the handy *Cathedral House*, 17 St Mary's St (℡01353/662124, ⓦwww.cathedralhouse.co.uk; no credit cards; ❸), an attractive Georgian townhouse with three comfortable, en-suite bedrooms. Several other good options are concentrated along Egremont Street, about five minutes' walk north from the cathedral via Lynn Road. Possibilities here include the spacious *Old Egremont House* at no. 31 (℡01353/663118; no cards; ❸), with cathedral views and a walled garden, and the more modern, spick and span *Posthouse* at no. 12a (℡01353/667184; no cards; ❷).

Of the numerous **tearooms** in town, *The Almonry* (daily 10am–5pm), on the north side of the cathedral, is by far the best sited, with garden seats granting great views of the octagon. A good reserve is the *Steeplegate Tea Rooms* at 16–18 High St (closed Sun), backing onto the cathedral grounds. The pick of the town's **restaurants** is the *Old Fire Engine House*, 25 St Mary's St (℡01353/662582; closes 9pm, 5pm on Sun), a gourmet English restaurant of some local repute with main courses averaging £9. Two excellent **pubs** are on Silver Street, just south of the cathedral – the relaxed and welcoming *Fountain* at no. 1, which comes complete with a goodly set of stuffed animals, and the *Prince Albert*, at no. 62, which squeezes in a little book-selling to help you along with your pint.

Cambridge

On the whole, **CAMBRIDGE** is a much quieter and more secluded place than Oxford, though for the visitor what really sets it apart from its scholarly rival is "**the Backs**" – the green swathe of land that straddles the languid River Cam, providing exquisite views over the backs of the old colleges. At the front, the handsome facades of these same colleges dominate the layout of the town centre, lining up along the main streets. Most of the older colleges date back to the late thirteenth and early fourteenth centuries and are designed to a **similar plan** with the main gate leading through to a series of "courts", typically a carefully manicured slab of lawn surrounded on all four sides by college residences or offices. Many of the buildings are extraordinarily beautiful, but the most famous is **King's College**, whose magnificent **King's College Chapel** is one of the great statements of late Gothic architecture. There are 31 university colleges in total, each an independent, self-governing body, proud of its achievements and attracting a close loyalty from its students, amongst whom privately educated boys remain hopelessly over-represented despite decades of perfectly adequate state education.

Cambridge is an extremely compact place, and you can **walk** round the centre, visiting the most interesting colleges, in an afternoon. A more thorough exploration will, however, take at least a couple of days. If possible, avoid coming in high summer, when the students are replaced by hordes of sightseers. Faced with such crowds, the more popular colleges have restricted their opening times and several have introduced admission charges. Bear in mind, too, that during the exam period (late April to early June), most colleges close their doors to the public at least some of the time. There are **three terms** – Michaelmas (Oct–Dec), Lent (Jan–March) and Easter (April–June) – and the students' biggest annual knees-up, the "May balls", are held in June.

Some history

Tradition has it that Cambridge was founded in the late 1220s by scholastic refugees from Oxford, who fled the town after one of their number was lynched by hostile townsfolk – though the first proper college wasn't founded until 1271. Rivalry has existed between the two institutions ever since while internal tensions between "**town and gown**" have inevitably plagued a place where, from the late fourteenth century onwards, the university has tended to control local life.

In the sixteenth century, Cambridge became a centre of **church reformism**, educating some of the most famous Protestant preachers in the country. Later, during the Civil War, Cambridge once again found itself at the centre of events: **Oliver Cromwell** was both a graduate of Sidney Sussex and the local MP, though the university itself was largely Royalist. After the Restoration, the university regained most of its privileges, but by the eighteenth century it was in the doldrums, better known, as Byron put it, for its "din and drunkenness" than for its academic record.

In Victorian times, the university finally lost its ancient **privileges** over the town, which was expanding rapidly thanks to the arrival of the railway. The town's population quadrupled between 1800 and 1900 and meanwhile the university expanded too, with the number of students increasing by leaps and bounds following the broadening of the curriculum to include new subjects such as natural science and history. More recently, change has been much slower in coming, particularly when it comes to **equality of the sexes**. The first two women's colleges were founded in the 1870s, but it was only in 1947 that women were actually awarded degrees and one or two colleges held out against accepting women students until the 1980s. In the meantime, the city and university had been acquiring a reputation as a **high-tech centre** of excellence, what locals refer to half-seriously as "Silicon Fen". Cambridge has always been in the vanguard of scientific research – its alumni have garnered no less than ninety Nobel prizes – and it has now become a major international player in the lucrative electronic communications industry.

Arrival

Cambridge **train station** is a mile or so southeast of the city centre, off Hills Road. It's an easy but tedious twenty-minute walk into the centre, or take shuttle bus #3, which runs to downtown Emmanuel Road every ten minutes or so (less frequently on Sun). The **bus station** is centrally located on Drummer Street, right by Christ's Pieces. **Stansted**, London's third airport, is just thirty miles south of Cambridge on the M11; there are hourly trains from the airport to the city, and regular bus services too. Arriving by **car**, you'll find much of the city centre closed to traffic and on-street parking well-nigh impossible – for a day-trip, at least, the best option is a **Park-and-Ride** car park; they are signposted on all major approaches.

Information and getting around

Cambridge **tourist office** is conveniently situated in the ornate former public library on Wheeler Street, off King's Parade (April–Oct Mon–Fri 10am–5.30pm, Sat 10am–5pm, Sun 11am–4pm; Nov–March Mon–Fri 10am–5.30pm, Sat 10am–5pm; ℡09065/862526 premium rate, ⓦwww.tourismcambridge.com). They issue city maps, have lots of leaflets on local attractions and sell an in-depth guide to the city (£5) as well as a mini-guide for just 50p. They can also help with accommodation. The best source of

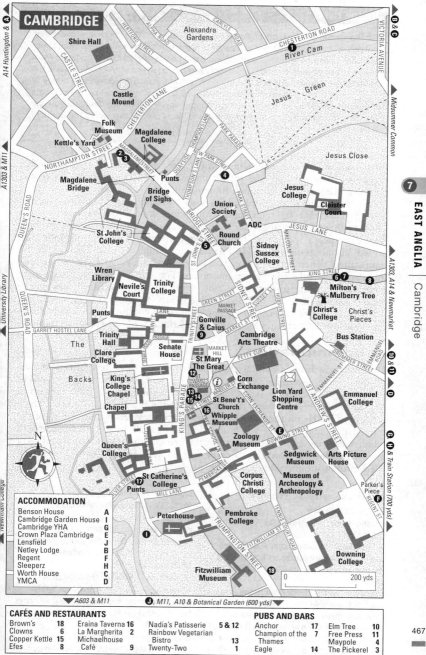

CAMBRIDGE

Shire Hall

Alexandra Gardens

CHESTERTON ROAD

River Cam

Jesus Green

Castle Mound

Jesus Close

Folk Museum

Kettle's Yard

Magdalene College

NORTHAMPTON STREET

Punts

Magdalene Bridge

Bridge of Sighs

Union Society

Jesus College

Cloister Court

ADC

St John's College

Round Church

Sidney Sussex College

Wren Library

Nevile's Court

Trinity College

KING STREET

Milton's Mulberry Tree

Christ's College

Christ's Pieces

Punts

Trinity Hall

Gonville & Caius

MARKET PASSAGE

Bus Station

Senate House

Clare College

King's College Chapel

St Mary The Great

Cambridge Arts Theatre

Emmanuel College

Market Hill

Corn Exchange

Lion Yard Shopping Centre

St Bene't's Church

The Backs

Chapel

St Edward's Passage

Whipple Museum

Queen's College

Zoology Museum

Sedgwick Museum

Arts Picture House

St Catherine's College

Corpus Christi College

Museum of Archeology & Anthropology

Punts

Parker's Piece

Peterhouse

Pembroke College

Downing College

Fitzwilliam Museum

A603 & M11

M11, A10 & Botanical Garden (600 yds)

0 — 200 yds

© Crown copyright

7

EAST ANGLIA | Cambridge

A14 Huntingdon & A

B & C

Midsummer Common

A1303 & M11

A1303, A14 & Newmarket

University Library

Queen's Road

D

E

G H & Train Station (700 yds)

F

J

467

ACCOMMODATION

Benson House	A
Cambridge Garden House	I
Cambridge YHA	G
Crown Plaza Cambridge	E
Lensfield	J
Netley Lodge	B
Regent	F
Sleeperz	H
Worth House	C
YMCA	D

CAFÉS AND RESTAURANTS

Brown's	18	Eraina Taverna	16	Nadia's Patisserie	5 & 12
Clowns	6	La Margherita	2	Rainbow Vegetarian	
Copper Kettle	15	Michaelhouse		Bistro	13
Efes	8	Café	9	Twenty-Two	1

PUBS AND BARS

Anchor	17	Elm Tree	10
Champion of the	7	Free Press	11
Thames		Maypole	4
Eagle	14	The Pickerel	3

On the river

Punting is the quintessential Cambridge activity, though it's a good deal harder than it looks. First-timers find themselves zigzagging across the water and "punt jams" are very common on the stretch of the Cam beside the Backs in summer. **Punt rental** is available at several points, including the boatyard at Mill Lane (beside the Silver Street bridge), at Magdalene Bridge, and at the Garret Hostel Lane bridge at the back of Trinity College. It costs around £10 an hour (and most places charge a deposit), with up to six people in each punt. If you find it all too daunting you can always hire a **chauffeur punt** from any of the rental places; this works out at about a fiver a head.

information on entertainment is the *Cambridge Agenda*, a free bimonthly magazine; it's available at the tourist office and larger bookshops. There are, however, plans to launch a much more detailed listings magazine.

The city centre is small enough to walk round comfortably, so apart from getting to and from the train station, you shouldn't have to use the city's buses. On the other hand, cycling is an enjoyable way of getting around and has long been extremely popular with locals and students alike. **Bike rental** outlets are dotted all over town (see p.476), including a couple of places handy for the train station. When and wherever you leave your bike, padlock it to something immoveable as bike theft is commonplace. For a more focused direction to your roamings, the tourist office runs very popular **walking tours** of the centre (1–4 daily; 2hr; £7.85; guided tours number ☏01223/457574). Admittedly, they're expensive but they do include entrance to at least one college that normally charges for the privilege. Book well in advance in summer.

Accommodation

Cambridge is short of central accommodation and those few **hotels** that do occupy prime locations are expensive. That said, Chesterton Lane and its continuation Chesterton Road, the busy street running east from the top of Magdalene Street, has several reasonably priced hotels and guest houses. There are lots of **B&Bs** on the outskirts of town, with several in the vicinity of the train station, and it's here you'll also find the **youth hostel**. In high season, when vacant rooms are often thin on the ground, the tourist office's efficient **accommodation booking service** can be very useful (☏01223/457581, Ⓔ accommodationbookings@cambridge.gov.uk).

Hotels, guest houses and B&Bs

Benson House 24 Huntingdon Rd
☏01223/311594
Ⓔ bensonhouse@btconnect.com. Pleasant, well-kept guest house in a demure brick house about five minutes' walk north from the Magdalene Bridge. ❸

Cambridge Garden House Moat House Granta Place, Mill Lane ☏01223/259988,
Ⓦ www.moathousehotels.com. Disregard the clumsy name, for this is arguably Cambridge's best central hotel, set in its own gardens with a fine riverside location and excellent facilities. ❽

Crowne Plaza Cambridge Downing St
☏01223/464466, Ⓦ www.cambridge
.crowneplaza.com. The dignified facade, hides a sleek and slick hotel. The foyer is adventurously designed and the rooms are resolutely modern in efficient chain-hotel style. Great central location too. ❻

Lensfield 53 Lensfield Rd ☏01223/355017,
Ⓦ www.lensfieldhotel.co.uk. Well-kept, family-owned hotel on the ring road, just round the corner from the Fitzwilliam Museum, with thirty unassuming rooms. ❻

Netley Lodge 112 Chesterton Rd
☏01223/363845. Cosy B&B in a Victorian town-

house, a manageable one-mile walk from the centre. Three attractively furnished bedrooms, one en suite. No credit cards. ❷

Regent 41 Regent St ☏ 01223/351470, ⓦ www.regenthotel.co.uk. Small-scale hotel in an old brick townhouse within easy walking distance of the centre. The thirty-odd rooms are decorated in an efficient modern style. ❻

Sleeperz Station Rd ☏ 01223/304050, ⓦ www .sleeperz.com. Popular hotel in an imaginatively converted granary warehouse, right outside the train station. Most of the rooms are bunk-style affairs done out in the manner of a ship's cabin, and there are a few doubles too. All rooms are en suite. ❷

Worth House 152 Chesterton Rd ☏ 01223/316074, ⓦ www.worth-house.co.uk. Pleasant B&B in a tastefully upgraded Victorian house, about twenty minutes' walk from the

centre. Two bedrooms only, both en suite. Highly recommended. ❸

Hostels and campsites

Cambridge YHA 97 Tenison Rd ☏ 0870/7705742, ⓔ cambridge@yha.org.uk. This well-equipped hostel has laundry and self-catering facilities, a cycle store, a games room and a small courtyard garden. It's close to the train station – Tenison Road is a right turn a couple of hundred yards down Station Road. Dorm beds £16.

YMCA Queen Anne House, Gonville Place ☏ 01223/356998. Central location on the south side of Parker's Piece – about a quarter of a mile east from the junction of Drummer Street and Emmanuel Road, then hang a right. Offers singles and twins, with breakfast included in the price, but very busy during summer – book well in advance. ❶

The City

Cambridge's main shopping street is Bridge Street, which becomes Sidney Street, St Andrew's Street and finally Regent Street; the other main thoroughfare is the procession of St John's Street, Trinity Street, King's Parade and Trumpington Street. The university developed on the land west of this latter route along the banks of the Cam, and now forms a continuous half-mile parade of **colleges** from Magdalene to Peterhouse, with sundry others scattered about the periphery. The **Fitzwilliam Museum**, with easily the city's finest art collection, is on Trumpington Street. The account below starts with **King's College**, whose chapel is the university's most celebrated attraction, and covers the rest of the town in a broadly clockwise direction.

King's College

Henry VI founded **King's College** (☏ 01223/331212) in 1441, but he was disappointed with his initial efforts, so four years later he cleared away half of medieval Cambridge to make room for a much grander foundation. His plans were ambitious, but the Wars of the Roses – and bouts of royal insanity – intervened and by the time of his death in 1471 very little had been finished. Indeed, work on Henry's **Great Court** hadn't even started and the site remained empty for three hundred years. The present complex – facing King's Parade from behind a long stone screen – is largely neo-Gothic, built in the 1820s to a design by William Wilkins. However, Henry's workmen did start on the college's finest building, the much celebrated **King's College Chapel** (term time Mon–Fri 9.30am–3.30pm, Sat 9.30am–3.15pm, Sun 1.15–2.15pm; rest of year Mon–Sat 9.30am–4.30pm, Sun 10am–5pm; £3.50), on the north side of today's Great Court. Committed to canvas by Turner and Canaletto, and eulogized in three sonnets by Wordsworth, it's now best known for its **boys' choir**, whose members process across the college grounds during term time in their antiquated garb to sing evensong (Tues–Sat at 5.30pm) and carols on Christmas Eve. Begun in 1446 and over sixty years in the making, the chapel is an extraordinary building. **From the outside**, it seems impossibly slender, its streamlined buttresses channelling up to a dainty balustrade and four spiky turrets, but the exterior was, in a sense at least, a happy accident – its design predicated by the carefully composed interior. Here, in the final flowering of the Gothic style, the mystery of the Christian faith was expressed by a long, uninterrupted **nave** flooded with kaleidoscopic patterns of light filtering in through copious stained-glass windows. Paid for by Henry VIII, the **stained glass** was largely the work of Flemish glaziers, with the lower windows portraying scenes from the New Testament and the Apocrypha, and the upper windows displaying the Old Testament. Henry VIII also paid for the intricately carved wooden **choir screen**, one of the earliest examples of Italian Renaissance woodcarving in England, but the **choir stalls** beyond date from the 1670s. Above the **altar** hangs Rubens' *Adoration of the Magi*. Finally, an exhibition in the **chantries** puts more historical flesh on Henry's grand plans.

Like Oxford's New College, King's enjoyed an exclusive supply of students from one of the country's public schools – in this case, Eton – and until 1851 claimed the right to award its students degrees without taking any examinations. The first non-Etonians were only accepted in 1873. Times have changed since those days, and, if anything, King's is now one of the more progressive colleges, having been one of the first to admit women in 1972. Among its most famous alumni are E.M. Forster, who described his experiences in *Maurice*, film director Derek Jarman, poet Rupert Brooke and John Maynard Keynes, whose economic theories did much to improve the college's finances when he became the college bursar.

From King's Parade to Clare College

King's Parade, originally the medieval High Street, is inevitably dominated by King's College and Chapel, but the higgledy-piggledy shops opposite are an attractive foil to William Wilkins's architectural screen. At the northern end of King's Parade is **St Mary the Great** (daily 9am–6pm except during services; free), the university's pet church, a sturdy Gothic structure dating from the fifteenth century. Its tower (Mon–Sat 9.30am–4.30pm, Sun 12–4.30pm; £2) offers a good overall view of the colleges and a bird's-eye view of **Market Hill**, east of the church, where food and bric-a-brac stalls are set out daily. Opposite the church stands **Senate House**, an exercise in Palladian classicism by James Gibbs, and the scene of graduation ceremonies on the last Saturday in June. It's not usually open to the public, though you can wander around the quad if the gate is open.

The northern continuation of King's Parade is Trinity Street, a short way along which, on the left, is the main entrance to **Gonville and Caius College** (☎01223/332400), known simply as Caius (pronounced "keys"), after the sixteenth-century co-founder John Keys, who latinized his name, as was then the custom with men of learning. The design of the college owes much to Keys, who placed a gate on three sides of two adjoining courts, each representing a different stage on the path to academic enlightenment: the **Gate of Humility**, through which the student entered the college, now stands in the Fellows' Garden; the **Gate of Virtue**, sporting the female figures of Fame and Wealth, marks the entrance to Caius Court; while the exquisite **Gate of Honour**, capped with sundials and decorated with classical motifs, leads to Senate House Passage and on to Senate House.

Senate House Passage continues west beyond the Gate of Honour to Trinity Lane and **Trinity Hall** (☎01223/332500) – not to be confused with Trinity College – where the Elizabethan library retains several of its original chains, designed to prevent students from purloining the texts. A few metres to the south is the much more diverting **Clare College** (daily 10am–5pm; £2; ☎01223/333200). One of seven colleges founded, rather surprisingly, by women, its plain period-piece courtyards, completed in the early eighteenth century, lead to one of the most picturesque of all the bridges over the Cam, **Clare Bridge**. Beyond lies the Fellows' Garden, one of the loveliest college gardens open to the public (times as college). Back at the entrance to Clare, it's a few metres more to the North Gate of King's College, beside the chapel (see p.469).

Trinity

Trinity College, on Trinity Street (daily 10am–4.30pm; £2; ☎01223/338400), is the largest of the Cambridge colleges and to ram home the point it also has the largest courtyard. It comes as little surprise then that its list of famous alumni is longer than any other college: literary greats, including Dryden, Byron, Tennyson and Vladimir Nabokov; the Cambridge spies Blunt, Burgess and Philby; two prime ministers, Balfour and Baldwin; William Thackeray, Isaac Newton, Lord Rutherford, Vaughan Williams, Pandit Nehru, Bertrand Russell and Ludwig Wittgenstein, not to mention a trio of (much less talented) royals, Edward VII, George VI and Prince Charles.

A statue of Henry VIII, who founded the college in 1546, sits in majesty over Trinity's **Great Gate**, his sceptre replaced with a chair leg by a student wit. Beyond lies the vast asymmetrical expanse of **Great Court**, which displays a fine range of Tudor buildings, the oldest of which is the fifteenth-century clock tower – the annual race against its midnight chimes is now common currency thanks to the film *Chariots of Fire*. The centrepiece of the court is the delicate fountain, in which, legend has it, Lord Byron used to bathe naked with his pet bear – the college forbade students from keeping dogs.

To get through to **Nevile's Court** – where Newton first calculated the speed of sound – you must pass through "the screens", a passage separating the Hall from the kitchens, a common feature of Oxbridge colleges. The west end of Nevile's Court is enclosed by the university's most famous building after King's College Chapel, the **Wren Library** (term time Mon–Fri noon–2pm, Sat 10.30am–12.30pm; rest of year Mon–Fri noon–2pm; free). Viewed from the outside, it's impossible to appreciate the scale of the interior thanks to Wren's clever device of concealing the internal floor level. In contrast to many modern libraries, natural light pours into the white stuccoed interior, which contrasts wonderfully with the dark lime-wood bookcases, also Wren-designed and housing numerous valuable manuscripts including Milton's *Lycidas*, Wittgenstein's journals and A.A. Milne's *Winnie the Pooh*.

St John's

Next door, **St John's College**, on St John's St (daily 10am–5pm; £2; ☎01223/338600), sports a grandiloquent Tudor gatehouse, distinguished by the coat of arms of the founder, Lady Margaret Beaufort, the mother of Henry VII, held aloft by two spotted, mythical beasts. Beyond, three successive courts lead to the river, but there's an excess of dull reddish brickwork here – enough for Wordsworth, who lived above the kitchens on F staircase, to describe the place as "gloomy". The arcade on the far side of Third Court leads through to the **Bridge of Sighs**, a chunky, covered bridge built in 1831 but in most respects very unlike its Venetian namesake. The bridge is best viewed either from a punt or from the much older, more stylish Wren-designed bridge a few metres to the south. The Bridge of Sighs links the old college with the fanciful nineteenth-century **New Court**, a crenellated neo-Gothic extravaganza topped by a feast of pinnacles and a central tower – hence its nickname "the wedding cake".

From the Round Church to Magdalene

Back on St John's Street, it's a few seconds' walk to Bridge Street and the **Round Church** (June–Sept Tues–Sat 10am–5pm, Sun & Mon 1–5pm; Oct–May daily 1–4pm; free), built in the twelfth century on the model of the Holy Sepulchre in Jerusalem. It's a curious-looking structure, squat with an ill-considered late medieval extension to the rear, but the Norman pillars of the original church remain. The church is also the starting point for Christian heritage walks around the city (Feb–Nov Wed 11am, Sun 2.30pm; £3 recommended donation; ℡01223/311602).

Saving nearby Jesus College till later (see below), it only takes a minute or two to stroll up from the Round Church to **Magdalene Bridge**, the site of the old Roman ford. Just beyond is **Magdalene College** (℡01223/332100) – pronounced "maudlin" – which was founded as a hostel by the Benedictines, became a university college in 1542 and was the last of the colleges to admit women, finally succumbing in 1988. Here, the main focus of attention is the **Pepys Building** (Nov & mid-Jan to mid-March Mon–Sat 2.30–3.30pm; late April to Aug Mon–Sat 11.30am–12.30pm & 2.30–3.30pm; free), in the second of the college's ancient courtyards. Samuel Pepys, a Magdalene student, bequeathed his entire library to the college, where it has been displayed ever since in its original red-oak bookshelves – though his famous diary, which also now resides here, was only discovered in the nineteenth century.

Jesus

Back down Magdalene Street and Bridge Street, the first left after the Round Church takes you to **Jesus College** (℡01223/339339), whose intimate cloisters are reminiscent of a monastery. This is not too surprising as the Bishop of Ely founded the college on the grounds of a suppressed Benedictine nunnery in 1496. The main red-brick gateway is approached via a distinctive walled walkway known as "the Chimney". Beyond, much of the ground plan of the nunnery has been preserved, especially around **Cloister Court**, the prettiest of the college's courtyards, dripping with ivy and overflowing hanging baskets. Entered from the court, the college **chapel** occupies the former priory chancel and looks like a medieval parish church; it was imaginatively restored in the nineteenth century, using ceiling designs by William Morris and Pre-Raphaelite stained glass. The poet Samuel Taylor Coleridge was the college's most famously bad student, absconding in his first year to join the Light Dragoons, and returning only to be kicked out for a combination of bad debts and unconventional opinions.

Sidney Sussex and Christ's colleges

Near Jesus, Malcolm Street cuts off Jesus Lane to reach King Street, from where it's a short stroll through to **Sidney Sussex College** (℡01223/338800), whose sombre, mostly mock-Gothic facade glowers over Sidney Street. Oliver Cromwell studied here and, in 1960, his skull was brought to the college and buried in a secret location in the pint-sized ante-chapel. The adjacent **chapel** is long and slender with a fancy marble floor, a hooped roof and oodles of Baroque wood panelling.

Just to the south of Sidney Sussex, on St Andrew's Street, you hit the hustle and bustle of the town's central shopping area, dominated by the **Lion Yard** shopping centre. This was one of the few town-planning mistakes in the centre of Cambridge, a clumsy modern structure that rumbles along **Petty Cury**, formerly a cobbled curve of leaning half-timbered houses. Aesthetic relief is, however, close at hand, just opposite Lion Yard, in the turreted gateway of

Christ's College (☏01223/334900), which features the coat of arms of the founder, Lady Margaret Beaufort, who also founded St John's. Passing through First Court you come to the Fellows' Building, attributed to Inigo Jones, whose central arch gives access to the **Fellows' Garden** (Mon–Fri 10am–noon; free). The poet John Milton is said to have either painted or composed beneath the garden's elderly mulberry tree, though there's no definite proof that he did either; Christ's other famous undergraduate was Charles Darwin, who showed little academic promise and spent most of his time hunting. If you continue walking through the college, you come to its modern adjunct, Denys Lasdun's concrete pyramidal accommodation block, dubbed "the typewriter".

Emmanuel College

A little further along St Andrew's Street is **Emmanuel College** (☏01223/334200), whose stolid Neoclassical facade hides a neat and trim Front Court, where the college **chapel** was designed by Wren in a simple Classical style, its wood-panelled nave set beneath a fancy stucco ceiling. The college was founded in 1584 to train a new generation of Protestant clergy following the Reformation. Emmanuel men were numbered among the Pilgrims who settled New England, which not only explains the derivation of the place name Cambridge in Massachusetts but also accounts for Harvard University – **John Harvard**, another alumnus, is remembered by a memorial window in the chapel.

Corpus Christi and Queens'

Opposite Emmanuel, Downing Street leads into **Pembroke Street**, at the west end of which, around the foot of King's Parade, are two more noteworthy town-centre colleges, the first being **Corpus Christi** (☏01223/338000), founded by two of the town's guilds in 1352. Ignore the first court and instead head north into **Old Court**, which dates from the foundation of the college and is where Christopher Marlowe wrote *Tamburlaine* before graduating in 1587. The college library, on the south side, contains a priceless collection of Anglo-Saxon manuscripts, while the north side is linked by a gallery to **St Bene't's Church**, which served as the college chapel, but is of much earlier Saxon origin. Inside, Thomas Hobson's Bible is exhibited in a glass case; Hobson was the owner of a Cambridge livery stable, where he would only allow customers to take the horse nearest the door – hence "Hobson's choice".

Nearby **Queens' College** (daily 10am–4.30pm; £1.30; ☏01223/335511), accessed through the gate on Queens' Lane, just off Silver Street, is the most popular college with university applicants, and it's not difficult to see why. In the **Old Court** and the **Cloister Court**, Queens' possesses two fairy-tale Tudor courtyards, with the first of the two the perfect illustration of the original collegiate ideal with kitchens, library, chapel, hall and rooms all set around a tiny green. Cloister Court is flanked by the Long Gallery of the President's Lodge, the last remaining half-timbered building in the university, and, in its southeast corner, by the tower where Erasmus is thought to have beavered away during his four years here, probably from 1510 to 1514. Be sure to pay a visit to the college **Hall**, off the screens passage between the two courts, which holds mantel tiles by William Morris, and portraits of Erasmus and one of the college's co-founders, Elizabeth Woodville, wife of Edward IV. Equally eye-catching is the wooden **Mathematical Bridge** over the Cam (visible for free from the Silver Street Bridge), a copy of the mid-eighteenth-century original which, it was claimed, would stay in place even if the nuts and bolts were removed.

The Fitzwilliam Museum

Of all the museums in Cambridge, the **Fitzwilliam Museum**, on Trumpington Street (Tues–Sat 10am–5pm, Sun 2.15–5pm; free), stands head and shoulders above the rest. The building itself is a splendidly grandiloquent interpretation of Neoclassicism, built in the mid-nineteenth century to house the vast collection bequeathed by Viscount Fitzwilliam in 1816. Since then, the museum has been bequeathed a string of private collections, most of which are focused on a particular specialism. Consequently, the Fitzwilliam says much about the changing tastes of the British upper class. The **Lower Galleries** contain a wealth of antiquities including Egyptian sarcophagi and black- and red-figure Greek vases, plus a bewildering display of European ceramics. Further on, there are sections dedicated to armour, glass and pewterware, medals, portrait miniatures and illuminated manuscripts, and – right at the far end – galleries devoted to Far Eastern applied arts and Korean ceramics.

The **Upper Galleries** concentrate on painting and sculpture with three of the first five rooms containing an eclectic assortment of mostly nineteenth- and early twentieth-century European paintings, including works by Picasso, Matisse, Monet, Renoir and Degas. The other two rooms feature British painting, with works by William Blake, Constable and Turner, amongst others. Moving on, the Italian section displays paintings by Titian and Veronese, while Frans Hals and Ruisdael feature in the Flemish section. The post-1945 gallery is packed with a fascinating selection including pieces by Lucian Freud, David Hockney and Henry Moore.

To the University Botanic Gardens

Past the Fitzwilliam Museum, turn left along busy Lensfield Road for the **Scott Polar Research Institute** (Tues–Sat 2.30–4pm; free), founded in 1920 in memory of the explorer, Captain Robert Falcon Scott (1868-1912), with displays from the expeditions of various polar adventurers, plus exhibitions on native cultures of the Arctic. There's more general interest near at hand in the shape of the **University Botanic Gardens** (daily: Feb–Oct gardens 10am–6pm, glasshouses 10am–4.30pm; Nov–Jan gardens 10am–4pm, glasshouses 10am–3.30pm; £2.50), whose entrance is on Bateman Street. Founded in 1760 and covering forty acres, the gardens are second only to Kew with glasshouses as well as bountiful outdoor displays. The outdoor beds are mostly arranged by natural order, but there is also a particularly unusual series of chronological beds, showing when different plants were introduced into Britain.

Eating and drinking

Even at Cambridge, students are not the world's greatest restaurant-goers, so although the downtown **takeaway** and **café** scene is fine, decent **restaurants** are a little thin on the ground. On any kind of budget, the myriad Italian places – courtesy of Cambridge's large Italian population – will stand you in good stead; otherwise, choose carefully, particularly in the more touristy areas, where quality isn't always all it should be. Happily, Cambridge abounds in excellent **pubs**, and our list rounds up some of the best traditional student and local drinking haunts.

Cafés and restaurants

Brown's 23 Trumpington St. Breezy brasserie with a fairly wide-ranging menu housed in a former hospital outpatients department. The grand setting – all plants and fans – sets the meal off a treat. Inordinately popular, but no reservations – wait in line or at the bar. Moderate.

Clowns 54 King St. Italian-style cappuccino and cakes, sandwiches and snacks, plus newspapers to browse. Off the tourist route and not part of a chain – bonuses in anyone's books.

Copper Kettle 4 King's Parade. Generations of students have whiled away the hours in this resolutely old-fashioned café opposite King's College, sipping coffee, eating pastries and putting the world to rights.

Efes 80 King St ☏ 01223/350491. Intimate Turkish restaurant, with chargrilled meats prepared under your nose and a decent meze selection. Moderate.

Eraina Taverna 2 Free School Lane ☏ 01223/368786. Packed Greek taverna, which satisfies the hungry hordes with huge platefuls of stews and grills, as well as pizzas, curries and a whole host of other menu madness. Inexpensive.

La Margherita 15 Magdalene St ☏ 01223/315232. Cheapish and cheerful Italian outfit offering pizzas and pastas as well as standard meat and fish dishes. Inexpensive to moderate.

Michaelhouse Café Trinity St. Vegetarian café serving homemade snacks, salads and sandwiches in the converted St Michael's church, opposite Caius College. Inexpensive.

Nadia's Patisserie 11 St John's St. Good sandwich and cake takeaway in the centre, opposite St John's. One of several outlets – there's another at 20 King's Parade.

Rainbow Vegetarian Bistro 9a King's Parade ☏ 01223/321551. Vegetarian restaurant with main courses – ranging from couscous to Indonesian gado-gado – all for around £7. Good-value breakfasts, and organic wines served with meals. Closed Sun. Inexpensive.

Twenty-Two 22 Chesterton Rd ☏ 01223/351880. Consistently the best restaurant in Cambridge, a

candlelit townhouse in which the good-value, fixed-price menu (at around £25) touches all the modern bases. Closed Sun & Mon. Expensive.

Pubs and bars

Anchor Silver St. Very popular riverside tourist haunt with views of the Backs, adjacent punt rental and an outdoor deck.

Champion of the Thames 68 King St. Gratifyingly old-fashioned central pub with decent beer and a student/academic clientele.

Eagle Bene't St. An ancient inn with a cobbled courtyard where Crick and Watson sought inspiration in the 1950s, at the time of their discovery of DNA. It's been tarted up since and gets horribly crowded, but is still worth a pint of anyone's time.

Elm Tree 42 Orchard St. Cosy local with frequent live music, mainly jazz. Just to the north of Parker's Piece and full of furiously smoking refugees from the nearby *Free Press* (see below). To get here, follow Emmanuel Road north off Drummer Street, near the bus station, and take the third turning on the right – it's on the corner with Eden Street.

Free Press 7 Prospect Row. Classic, superbly maintained backstreet local with an admirable no-smoking policy, good beer and fine food. It's located a few yards along the street from the *Elm Tree* – for directions, see above.

Maypole 20a Park St. Small, well-kept pub in the centre near the Round Church, with an invigorating atmosphere.

The Pickerel 30 Magdalene St. Once a brothel and one of several pubs competing for the title of the oldest in town, the *Pickerel* has a lively atmosphere and offers a good range of beers beneath its low beams.

Entertainment

The **performing arts** scene is at its best during term time, with numerous student **drama** productions, **classical concerts** and **gigs** culminating in the traditional whizzerama of excess following the exam season. That said, the more firmly town-based venues, such as the Corn Exchange, do put on events throughout the year. Each college and several churches contribute to the performing arts scene too, with the **King's College choir** being the most famous attraction (see p.469), though the choral scholars who perform at St John's and Trinity are also exceptionally good. For upcoming events, ask for details at the tourist office (see p.466), who issue various listings leaflets and also stock the *Cambridge Agenda*, a free bimonthly listings magazine. For advance tickets for most events, pop into the Corn Exchange.

June and July are the busiest times in Cambridge's calendar of **events**. The fortnight of post-exam celebrations, which take place in the first two weeks of June – and are confusingly known as **May Week** – herald the ball and garden-party season, and include boat races, known as the "May Bumps", on the Cam by Midsummer Common. The vaguely hippified **Midsummer Fair** takes place in mid-June on Midsummer Common, with bands, theatre and much more besides – all for free. By contrast, you'll have to pay out around £50 for a tent pitch and entry into the three-day **Cambridge Folk Festival** (Ⓦ www.cam-folkfest.co.uk), held annually at the end of July at neighbouring Cherry Hinton, and attracting a wide variety of loosely folk-based acts.

Venues

Arts Picture House 38–39 St Andrew's St
Ⓣ 01223/504444, Ⓦ www.picturehouses.co.uk.
Art-house cinema with an excellent, wide-ranging programme.
Boat Race 170 East Rd Ⓣ 01223/508533,
Ⓦ www.boatrace.co.uk. Lively pub venue for all kinds of music, with gigs every night.
Cambridge Arts Theatre 6 St Edward's Passage, off King's Parade Ⓣ 01223/503333, Ⓦ www .cambridgeartstheatre.com. The city's main repertory theatre, founded by John Maynard Keynes, and launch pad of a thousand-and-one famous careers, offers a top-notch range of cutting-edge and classic productions.

Cambridge Corn Exchange Wheeler St
Ⓣ 01223/357851, Ⓦ www.cornex.co.uk. Revamped nineteenth-century trading hall, now the main city-centre venue for opera, ballet, musicals and comedy as well as regular rock and folk gigs.
Cambridge Modern Jazz Club at Sophbeck Sessions, 14 Tredgold Lane, Napier St
Ⓣ 01223/722811, Ⓦ www.cambridgejazz.org. Attracts top-ranking artists from around the world. East of the city centre, near the Grafton Centre shopping mall, off Newmarket Road.
Junction Clifton Rd Ⓣ 01223/511511, Ⓦ www .junction.co.uk. Rock, Indie, jazz, reggae or soul gigs, plus occasional comedy acts and dance groups at this popular arts and entertainments venue.

Listings

Bike rental Station Cycles, outside the train station Ⓣ 01223/307125; Mikes Bikes, 28 Mill Rd Ⓣ 01223/312591; and H. Drake, near the train station at 56–60 Hills Rd Ⓣ 01223/363468.
Bookshops Heffers has several outlets with its main branch at 20 Trinity St; Cambridge University Press has a shop at 1 Trinity St; Borders are at 12–13 Market St; and Waterstones at 22 Sidney St. For secondhand books try the shops down St Edward's Passage off King's Parade.
Buses Most city buses use the stops along Emmanuel Street. Close by, at the top of Emmanuel Street, the Drummer Street bus station is for long-distance services. For information call Ⓣ 0870/608 2608, or drop by the Premier Travel Agency, beside the Drummer Street station (Ⓣ 01223/572300). In addition, Airlinks (Ⓣ 0870/574 7777) operates direct services to the

London airports; and National Express (Ⓣ 0870/580 8080) runs services to London and other major cities.
Car rental Avis, 245 Mill Rd Ⓣ 01223/212551; Budget, 303–305 Newmarket Rd
Ⓣ 01223/323838; Europcar, 22 Cambridge Rd Ⓣ 01223/233644; National, 264 Newmarket Rd Ⓣ 01223/365438.
Internet Internet Exchange, opposite St Mary the Great church
Pharmacies Boots, 28 Petty Cury
Ⓣ 01223/350213; Lloyds, 30 Trumpington St Ⓣ 01223/359449.
Post office The main office is at 9–11 St Andrew's St (Mon–Sat 9am–5.30pm).
Taxis There are ranks at the train and bus stations. To book, call Diamond Ⓣ 01223/523523; or Panther Ⓣ 01223/715715.

Around Cambridge – the Imperial War Museum at Duxford

Eight miles south of Cambridge, and visible from the M11 – it's next to junction #10 – are the giant hangars of the **Imperial War Museum** (daily: mid-March to late Oct 10am–6pm; late Oct to mid-March 10am–4pm; £8.50; Ⓦ www.iwm.org.uk/duxford), based at Duxford airfield. Throughout World War II, East Anglia was a centre of operations for the RAF and the USAF, with the flat, unobstructed landscape dotted by dozens of airfields. Duxford itself was a Battle of Britain station, equipped with Spitfires, and there's a reconstructed Operations Room in one of the control towers. In total, Duxford holds over 150 historic aircraft, a wide-ranging collection of civil and military planes from the Sunderland flying boat to Concorde, though the Spitfires remain the most enduringly popular. Most of the planes are kept in full working order and are taken out for a spin several times a year at **Duxford Air Shows**, which attract thousands of visitors. There are usually four Air Shows a year and tickets cost from £18 to £22.50; advance bookings are strongly recommended (℡01223/499353).

For details of the free courtesy bus service linking Duxford with Cambridge, call ℡01223/835000.

Travel details

Buses

For information on all local and national bus services, contact Traveline ℡0870/608 2 608, ⓦwww.traveline.org.uk.
The **Norfolk Coasthopper** runs from Cromer to King's Lynn – or Hunstanton – via a whole gaggle of towns and villages, including Blakeney, Sheringham and Wells. Frequencies vary on different stretches of the route and there are more buses in the summer, but on the more popular stretches are mostly every half-hour or hour. The operator is Norfolk Green ℡01553/776980, ⓦwww.norfolkgreen.co.uk.
Cambridge to: Birmingham (3 daily; 3hr 45min); Bury St Edmunds (hourly; 55mins); Colchester (7 daily; 2hr 30min); Ely (every 30min; 45min); Ipswich (daily; 2hr); London (hourly; 2hr); Manchester (2 daily; 2hr 20min); Norwich (1 daily; 2hr 50min); Peterborough (hourly; 2hr 20min); Stansted airport (hourly; 50min).
Colchester to: Bury St. Edmunds (7 daily; 1hr 30min); Cambridge (7 daily; 2hr 30min); Ipswich (hourly; 1 hour); London (3 daily; 2hr 20min).
Ely to: Cambridge (every 30min; 45min).
Ipswich to: Bury St. Edmunds (2 daily; 1hr 30min); Colchester (hourly; 1hr); London (2 daily; 3hr); Aldeburgh (hourly; 1hr 30min); Woodbridge (every 15min; 30min)

Norwich to: Bury St. Edmunds (5 daily; 1hr 30min); Cambridge (1 daily; 2hr 50min); Great Yarmouth (every 15min; 30min); London (5 daily; 3hr); Sheringham (every 30min; 1hr 20min).

Trains

For information on all local and national rail services, contact National Rail Enquiries ℡08457/48 49 50, ⓦwww.nationalrail.co.uk.
Cambridge to: Bury St Edmunds (8 daily; 40min); Ely (hourly; 15min); Ipswich (6 daily; 1hr 20min); London (every 30min; 1hr); Norwich (hourly; 1hr); Stansted (10 daily; 40min).
Colchester to: Ipswich (every 30min; 25min); London (every 30min; 50min); Norwich (hourly; 1hr).
Ely to: Cambridge (hourly; 15min); Manchester (hourly; 3hr 30min); Nottingham (hourly 1hr 45min).
Ipswich to: Bury St Edmunds (10 daily; 30min); Ely (7 daily; 1hr); London (every 30min; 1hr 10min); Norwich (hourly; 45min); Woodbridge (every 1–2hr; 15min).
Norwich to: Ely (hourly; 50min); Cromer (every 1–2hr; 50min); Great Yarmouth (hourly; 30min); London (hourly; 2hr); Manchester (hourly; 4hr 30min); Nottingham (hourly; 2hr 30min); Sheringham (every 1–2hr; 1hr).

8

The West Midlands and the Peak District

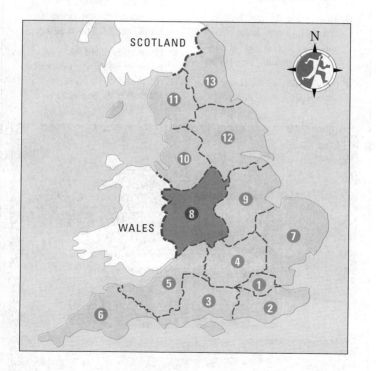

CHAPTER 8

Highlights

* **The theatres, Stratford-upon-Avon** *The* place to see Shakespeare's plays. **See p.487**

* **Mappa Mundi, Hereford Cathedral** The complex iconography of this antique map provides a powerful insight into the medieval mind. **See p.493**

* **Ironbridge Gorge** The first iron bridge ever to be constructed arches high above the River Severn. **See p.498**

* **Hay-on-Wye** This dinky little town has more secondhand bookshops per person than anywhere else in the world. **See p.496**

* **Ludlow** A postcard-pretty country town with wonderful half-timbered houses and a gaggle of chi-chi restaurants. **See p.503**

* **Buxton** This good-looking former spa town is the ideal base for exploring the Peak District. **See p.520**

* **Hassop Hall Hotel, Hassop** The Peak District's most charming hotel *Hassop Hall*. **See p.531**

△ Hassop Hall

The West Midlands
and the Peak District

The factories of the **West Midlands** were the powerhouse of the Industrial Revolution and **Birmingham**, Britain's second city, was once the world's greatest industrial metropolis. Long saddled with a reputation as a culture-hating, car-loving backwater, Birmingham has redefined its image in recent years, initiating some ambitious architectural and environmental schemes, jazzing up its museums and industrial heritage sites and giving itself a higher profile on the nation's cultural map than it's ever had before. Admittedly it's not an especially good-looking city, but it does hold several excellent attractions and has a nightlife encompassing everything from Royal Ballet productions to all-night grooves, and a great spread of restaurants and pubs in between.

The **counties** to the south and west of Birmingham and beyond the Black Country – Warwickshire, Worcestershire, Herefordshire and Shropshire – comprise a rural stronghold that maintains an emotional and political distance from the conurbation. For the most part, the four counties constitute a quiet, unassuming stretch of pastoral England whose beauty is rarely dramatic, but whose charms become more evident the longer you stay. Of the four counties, **Warwickshire** is the least obviously scenic, but draws by far the largest number of visitors, for – as the road-signs declare at every entry point – this is "Shakespeare Country". The prime target is, of course, **Stratford-upon-Avon**, with its handful of Shakespeare-related sites and world-class theatre, but spare time also for the diverting town of **Warwick**, which has a superb church and a whopping castle.

Neighbouring **Worcestershire** holds two principal places of interest: **Worcester**, which is graced by a mighty cathedral, and **Great Malvern**, a mannered inland resort spread along the rolling contours of the **Malvern Hills**. From here, it's west again for **Herefordshire**, a large and sparsely populated county that's home to several charming market towns, most notably picture-postcard **Ledbury** and **Hay-on-Wye**; the latter has the largest concentration of secondhand bookshops in the world. There's also **Hereford**, where the remarkable medieval Mappa Mundi map is displayed, and pocket-sized **Ross-on-Wye**, which is within easy striking distance of an especially scenic stretch of the **Wye River Valley**. To the north, rural **Shropshire** weighs in with **Ludlow**, one of the region's prettiest towns, and the amiable county

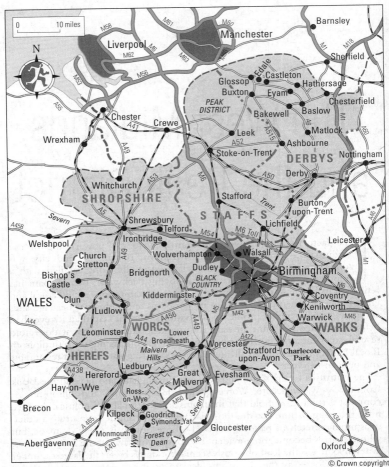

© Crown copyright

town of **Shrewsbury**. Shropshire has a fascinating industrial history, too, for it was here in the **Ironbridge Gorge** that British industrialists built the world's first iron bridge and pioneered the use of coal as a smelting fuel. These were two key events in the Industrial Revolution and, appropriately, the Gorge's industrial heyday is recalled by a phalanx of museums.

To the east of Shropshire is **Staffordshire**, where **Lichfield** highlights its links with **Samuel Johnson**. Beyond lies **Derbyshire**, whose northern reaches incorporate the region's finest scenery in the rough landscapes of the **Peak District National Park**, as well as the former spa town of **Buxton**, the limestone caverns of **Castleton** and the so-called "Plague Village" of **Eyam**. In addition, there's the grandiose stately pile of **Chatsworth House** and **Haddon Hall**, an exceptionally intact old manor house.

Birmingham, the region's **public transport hub**, is easily accessible by **train** from London Euston, Liverpool, Manchester, Leeds, York and a score of other towns. It is also well served by the National Express **bus** network, with dozens of buses leaving every hour for destinations all over Britain. Local **bus** services are excellent around the West Midlands conurbation and very good in the Peak District, but fade away badly in amongst the villages of Herefordshire and Shropshire.

Stratford-upon-Avon and around

Despite its worldwide fame, **STRATFORD-UPON-AVON** is, at heart, an unassuming market town. Its first settlers forded, and later bridged, the River Avon, and developed commercial links with the farmers who tilled the surrounding flatlands. A charter for Stratford's weekly market was granted in the twelfth century and the town later became an important stopping-off point for stagecoaches between London, Oxford and the north. Like all such places, Stratford had its clearly defined class system within which John and Mary **Shakespeare** occupied the middle rank and would have been forgotten long ago had their first son, **William**, not turned out to be the greatest writer ever to use the English language. A consequence of their good fortune is that nowadays the streets of this little town groan under the weight of thousands of tourists, but dodging the multitudes is possible by visiting the busiest attractions early or late in the day, and the town is also worth a visit for the outstanding **Royal Shakespeare Company**.

Arrival and information

Stratford's **train station** is on the northwestern edge of town, ten minutes' walk from the centre. Local **bus services** arrive and depart from central Bridge Street; National Express services and most other long-distance and regional buses pull into the Riverside station on the east side of the town centre, off Bridgeway.

The **tourist office** (Mon–Sat 9.30am–5pm, Sun 10.30am–4.30pm; ☎01789/293127, ⓦwww.shakespeare-country.co.uk) is located a couple of minutes' walk from the bus station by the bridge at the junction of Bridgeway and Bridgefoot. They operate an accommodation-booking service, issue bus timetables and sell bus tickets and, in addition, sell the all-in ticket for all five **Shakespeare Birthplace Trust** properties (£13), or a **Three In-Town Shakespeare Property Ticket** (£9) for the three Trust properties in the town centre; both tickets are also available from the sites themselves.

Accommodation

Stratford's **accommodation** is a tad pricey and gets booked up well in advance. In peak months, and during the Shakespeare birthday celebrations around April 23, it's pretty much essential to book ahead. The town has a couple of dozen **hotels**, but most visitors choose to stay in a **B&B**, of which there's a particular concentration to the southwest of the centre around Grove Road, Evesham Place and Broad Walk.

Hotels

Falcon Chapel St ☎01789/279953, ⓦwww .regalhotels.co.uk/thefalcon. In the middle of town, this place has a half-timbered facade dating from

the sixteenth century, though most of the rest is an unremarkable modern rebuild. ❺
Grosvenor Warwick Rd ☎01789/269213, ⓦwww.groshotelstratford.co.uk. A couple of

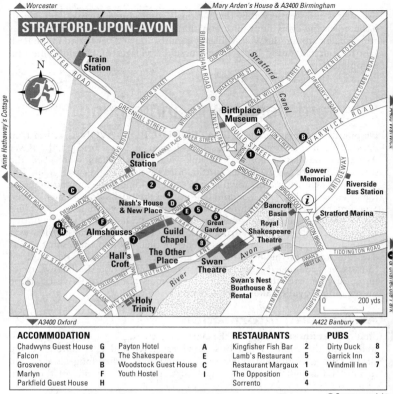

Map of Stratford-upon-Avon

Worcester ▲   Mary Arden's House & A3400 Birmingham ▲

STRATFORD-UPON-AVON

Train Station

Birthplace Museum

Police Station

Nash's House & New Place

Almshouses

Guild Chapel

Hall's Croft

The Other Place

Swan Theatre

Holy Trinity

Great Garden

Bancroft Basin

Royal Shakespeare Theatre

Gower Memorial

Riverside Bus Station

Stratford Marina

Swan's Nest Boathouse & Rental

Anne Hathaway's Cottage ◄

A3400 Oxford ▼   A422 Banbury ▼

0   200 yds

© Crown copyright

ACCOMMODATION				RESTAURANTS		PUBS	
Chadwyns Guest House	G	Payton Hotel	A	Kingfisher Fish Bar	2	Dirty Duck	8
Falcon	D	The Shakespeare	E	Lamb's Restaurant	5	Garrick Inn	3
Grosvenor	B	Woodstock Guest House	C	Restaurant Margaux	1	Windmill Inn	7
Marlyn	F	Youth Hostel	I	The Opposition	6		
Parkfield Guest House	H			Sorrento	4		

minutes' walk from the town centre, the *Grosvenor* occupies a row of pleasant, two-storey Georgian houses. The interior is crisp and modern and there's ample parking at the back. ❹

Marlyn 3 Chestnut Walk ☎01789/293752, ⓦwww.marlynhotel.co.uk. In a pleasant two-storey brick house with sash windows, this small hotel is good value and has comfortable rooms. ❸

Payton 6 John St ☎01789/266442, ⓦwww.payton.co.uk. This comfortable hotel occupies an attractive Georgian townhouse on a quiet residential street. Family-run, there are five comfortable rooms, all en suite. ❸

The Shakespeare Chapel St ☎0870/4008182, ⓦwww.shakespearehotel.net. Now part of a chain, this old hotel, with its mullion windows and half-timbered facade, is one of Stratford's best known. The interior has low beams and open fires and represents a fairly successful amalgamation of the old and new. ❽

Guest Houses and B&Bs
Chadwyns 6 Broad Walk ☎01789/269077, ⓦwww.chadwyns.co.uk. This unassuming guest house occupies a two-storey Victorian terrace house and offers seven en-suite rooms. Great breakfasts with vegetarian options. ❷

Parkfield 3 Broad Walk ☎01789/293313, ⓦwww.parkfieldbandb.co.uk. Very pleasant B&B in a rambling Victorian house in a residential street off Evesham Place. Most rooms are en suite. ❷

Woodstock 30 Grove Rd ☎01789/299881, ⓔwoodstockhouse@compuserve.com. A smart and neatly kept B&B five minutes' walk from the centre, with five extremely comfortable bedrooms, all en suite. No credit cards. ❷

Hostels and camping
Stratford-upon-Avon Youth Hostel
Hemmingford House, Alveston ☎0870/7706052, ⓔstratford@yha.org.uk. Rambling Georgian mansion on the edge of the pretty village of Alveston,

with dormitories and family rooms, some of which are en suite, plus laundry, Internet access, car parking and self-catering facilities. It's located two miles east of the town centre on the B4086 and served by regular bus from Stratford's Riverside bus station. Open all year. Dorm beds £16.

Stratford-on-Avon Racecourse Camp Site
Luddington Rd ☎ 01789/267949. Well-equipped camping and caravan site one mile or so to the southwest of the town centre. Regular buses into town (not Sun). Closed Oct–March. Tent pitches from £5, caravans from £9.

The Town

Spreading back from the River Avon, Stratford's **town centre** is flat and compact, its mostly modern buildings filling out a simple gridiron. Running along the northern edge of the centre is **Bridge Street**, the main thoroughfare lined with shops and chock-a-block with local buses. At its west end Bridge Street divides into Henley Street, home of the **Birthplace Museum**, and Wood Street, which leads up to the marketplace. It also intersects with High Street. This, and its continuations Chapel and Church streets, cuts south to pass most of the old buildings that the town still possesses, most notably **Nash's House** and **Hall's Croft**. From here, it's a short hop to the charming **Holy Trinity Church**, where Shakespeare lies buried, and then only a few minutes back along the river past the **theatres** to Bridge Street. In addition, there are two outlying Shakespearean properties, **Anne Hathaway's Cottage** in Shottery and **Mary Arden's House** in Wilmcote – though you have to be a really serious sightseer to want to see them all.

The Birthplace Museum

Top of everyone's Bardic itinerary is the **Birthplace Museum**, on Henley Street (June–Aug Mon–Sat 9am–5pm, Sun 9.30am–5pm; April–May & Sept–Oct Mon–Sat 10am–5pm, Sun 10.30am–5pm; Nov–March Mon–Sat 10am–4pm, Sun 10.30am–4pm; £6.50; ⓦ www.shakespeare.org.uk), comprising an ugly modern visitor centre and the heavily restored half-timbered building where the great man was born. The visitor centre pokes into every corner of Shakespeare's life and times, making the most of what little hard evidence there is. His will is interesting in so far as he passed all sorts of goodies to his daughter, but precious little to his wife. Next door, the half-timbered dwelling is actually two buildings knocked into one. The northern half was the business premises of the poet's father, who is thought to have worked as a glover; the south half – bought by John Shakespeare in 1556 – displays a modest range of period artefacts.

Nash's House and New Place

Follow **High Street** south from the junction of Bridge and Henley streets, and you'll soon come to another Birthplace Trust property, **Nash's House** on Chapel Street (June–Aug Mon–Sat 9.30am–5pm, Sun 10am–5pm; April–May & Sept–Oct daily 11am–5pm; Nov–March daily 11am–4pm; £3.50). Once the property of Thomas Nash, first husband of Shakespeare's granddaughter, Elizabeth Hall, the house's ground floor is now kitted out with a pleasant assortment of period furnishings. Upstairs, one display provides a potted history of Stratford, while another focuses on the house with a cabinet of woodcarvings made from the **mulberry tree** that once stood outside. Reputedly planted by Shakespeare, the tree was chopped down in the 1750s by the owner, a certain Reverend Francis Gastrell, because he was fed up with all the pilgrims. An enterprising woodcarver bought the wood and carved Shakespearean mementoes from it.

The adjacent gardens contain the bare foundations of **New Place** (same hours), Shakespeare's last residence, which was demolished by the same Reverend Gastrell, but for different reasons – Gastrell was in bitter dispute with the town council over taxation. A replacement mulberry tree has been planted beside the foundations of New Place and there are others in the adjacent **Great Garden** (March–Oct Mon–Sat 9am–dusk, Sun 10am–dusk; Nov–Feb Mon–Sat 9am–4pm, Sun noon–4pm; free), a formal affair of topiary, lawns and flowerbeds. A path leads into the Great Garden from New Place, but the main entrance is on Chapel Lane.

On the other side of Chapel Lane stands the **Guild Chapel**, adjoining King Edward VI **Grammar School**, where it's assumed Shakespeare was educated.

Hall's Croft

Chapel Street continues south as Church Street. At the end, turn left along Old Town Street for Stratford's most impressive medieval house, the Birthplace Trust's **Hall's Croft** (June–Aug Mon–Sat 9.30am–5pm, Sun 10am–5pm; April–May & Sept–Oct daily 11am–5pm; Nov–March daily 11am–4pm; £3.50). The former home of Shakespeare's elder daughter, Susanna, and her doctor husband, John Hall, the immaculately maintained Croft, with its creaking wooden floors, beamed ceilings and fine kitchen range, holds a good-looking medley of period furniture and a fascinating display on **Elizabethan medicine**.

Holy Trinity Church

Beyond Hall's Croft, Old Town Street steers right to reach the handsome **Holy Trinity Church** (April–Sept Mon–Sat 8.30am–6pm & Sun 12.15–5pm; March & Oct Mon–Sat 9am–5pm & Sun 12.15–5pm; Nov–Feb Mon–Sat 9am–4pm & Sun 12.15–5pm; free), whose mellow, honey-coloured stonework dates from the thirteenth century. Enhanced by its riverside setting, the church's dignified proportions are the result of several centuries of chopping and changing. Inside, the nave is bathed in light from the clerestory **windows**, some of whose stained glass dates back to the fourteenth century. In the north aisle, beside the transept, is the **Clopton Chapel**, where the large wall-tomb of George Carew is a Renaissance extravagance, but poor old George is long forgotten, unlike William Shakespeare, who lies buried in the **chancel** (£1), his remains overseen by a sedate and studious memorial plaque and effigy added seven years after his death.

The theatres

Doubling back from the church, turn right along Southern Lane and its continuation, Waterside, to reach the town's two Royal Shakespeare Company **theatres** – the Swan Theatre and the Royal Shakespeare Theatre. There was no theatre in Stratford in Shakespeare's day and indeed the first home-town festival in his honour was only held in 1769 at the behest of London-based David Garrick. Thereafter, the idea of building a permanent home in which to perform Shakespeare's works slowly gained momentum, and finally, in 1879, the first Memorial Theatre was opened on land donated by local beer baron Charles Flower. A fire in 1926 necessitated the construction of a new theatre, and the ensuing architectural competition, won by Elisabeth Scott, produced today's **Royal Shakespeare Theatre**. In the 1980s, the burnt-out original theatre round the back was turned into a replica "in-the-round" Elizabethan stage – the **Swan**. A third RSC auditorium, **The Other Place**, on Southern Lane, is currently closed except for special events.

Anne Hathaway's Cottage and Mary Arden's House

Anne Hathaway's Cottage (June–Aug Mon–Sat 9am–5pm, Sun 9.30am–5pm; April, May, Sept & Oct Mon–Sat 9.30am–5pm, Sun 10am–5pm; Nov–March daily 10am–4pm; £5), also operated by the Birthplace Trust, is located just over a mile west of the centre in the well-heeled suburb of Shottery. The cottage – actually an old farmhouse – is an immaculately maintained, half-timbered affair with a thatched roof and dinky little chimneys. This was the home of Anne Hathaway before she married Shakespeare in 1582, and the interior now holds a comely combination of period furniture, including a superb, finely carved four-poster bed. The garden is splendid too, crowded with bursting blooms in the summertime, and the adjacent **Shakespeare Tree Garden** features a scattering of modern sculptures and over forty trees, shrubs and roses mentioned in the plays.

The Birthplace Trust also keeps **Mary Arden's House** (June–Aug Mon–Sat 9.30am–5pm, Sun 10am–5pm; April, May, Sept & Oct Mon–Sat 10am–5pm, Sun 10.30am–5pm; Nov–March daily 10am–4pm; £5.50), three miles northwest of the town centre in the village of Wilmcote. Mary was Shakespeare's mother who, when her father died in 1556, inherited the house and land, thus becoming one of the neighbourhood's most eligible women – John Shakespeare, eager for self-improvement, married her within a year. The house is a well-furnished example of an Elizabethan farmhouse and, though the labelling is rather scant, a platoon of guides fills in the details of family life and traditions.

Eating and drinking

Stratford is used to feeding and watering thousands of visitors, so finding refreshment is never difficult. Standards aren't great, though there is a scattering of very good **restaurants** and a handful of **pubs** and **cafés**, too. The best restaurants are concentrated along Sheep Street, running up from Waterside near the theatres.

Restaurants and cafés

Kingfisher Fish Bar 13 Ely St. The best fish-and-chip shop in town. Closed Sun.

Lamb's Restaurant 12 Sheep St ☎01789/292554. Smart restaurant serving a mouthwatering range of stylish English and continental dishes in antique premises. Expensive.

The Opposition 13 Sheep St ☏ 01789/269980. Top-quality, imaginative international cuisine in a busy but amiable atmosphere. Moderate.

Restaurant Margaux 6 Union St ☏ 01789/269106. Smart and intimate restaurant serving top-quality seafood and meat dishes, often with a Mediterranean slant. Expensive.

Sorrento 8 Ely St ☏ 01789/297999. Smart-verging-on-formal Italian restaurant offering great meat and seafood along with pizzas and pastas. Expensive.

Pubs

Dirty Duck 53 Waterside. The archetypal actors' pub, stuffed to the gunwales every night with a vocal entourage of RSC employees and hangers-on.

The Garrick Inn 25 High St. Arguably the town's most photogenic and best-preserved old ale house: exposed beams, real ales and good bar food.

Windmill Inn Church St. Popular pub of cosy little rooms with low-beamed ceilings. A good range of Flowers beers too.

Warwick

WARWICK, just eight miles northeast of Stratford and easily reached by bus and train, is famous for its massive castle, but it also possesses several charming streetscapes erected in the aftermath of a great fire in 1694, as well as an especially fine church chancel.

The Castle

Towering above the River Avon at the foot of the town centre, **Warwick Castle** (daily: April–Sept 10am–6pm; Oct–March 10am–5pm; £13.50; parking £2.50) is locally proclaimed the "greatest medieval castle in Britain" and, if bulk equals greatness, then the claim is certainly valid, though much of the existing structure is the result of extensive nineteenth-century restoration. It's likely that the first fortress here was raised by Ethelfleda, daughter of Alfred the Great, in about 915 AD, but things really took off with the Normans, who built a large motte and bailey towards the end of the eleventh century. Almost three hundred years later, the eleventh Earl of Warwick turned the stronghold into a formidable stone castle, complete with elaborate gatehouses, multiple turrets and a keep.

The **entrance** is through the old stable block, beyond which a footpath leads round to the imposing **East Gate**. Over the footbridge – and beyond the protective towers – is the main **courtyard**. You can stroll along the ramparts and climb the towers, but most visitors head straight for one or other of the special displays installed inside by the present owners, Madame Tussauds. The most popular of these displays is the "Royal Weekend Party, 1898", an extravaganza of waxwork nobility hobnobbing in the private apartments which were rebuilt in the 1870s after fire damage. Rather less obviously commercial are the **Great Hall** and neighbouring **Chapel**, though both are drably Victorian, the only saving grace being the former's assorted suits of armour. The **grounds** are much more enjoyable, acres of woodland and lawn inhabited by peacocks and including a large glass **conservatory**.

The town centre

Re-emerging from the castle at the stables, **Castle Street** leads up the hill to the High Street. Turn left and it's a brief stroll to the **Lord Leycester Hospital** (April–Oct Tues–Sat 10am–5pm & Sun 11am–5pm; Nov–March Tues–Sun 10am–4pm; £3.20), a tangle of half-timbered buildings that lean at fairy-tale angles against the old West Gate. The complex represents one of Britain's best-preserved examples of domestic Elizabethan architecture and was established as a hostel for old soldiers by the Earl of Leicester, a favourite of Queen Elizabeth I.

Doubling back along the High Street, turn left up Church Street for **St Mary's church** (daily 10am–5pm, 4pm in winter; £1 donation suggested), which was rebuilt in a weird Gothic-Renaissance amalgam after the fire of 1694. One part remained untouched, however – the **chancel**, a glorious illustration of the Perpendicular style with a splendid vaulted ceiling of flying and fronded ribs. On the right-hand side of the chancel, the **Beauchamp Chapel** contains several beautiful tombs, exquisite works of art beginning with that of Richard Beauchamp, Earl of Warwick, who is depicted in an elaborate suit of Italian armour. The adjacent tomb of Ambrose Dudley is of finely carved alabaster, as is that of Robert Dudley, Earl of Leicester.

Practicalities

From Warwick **train station**, on the northern edge of town, it's about ten minutes' walk to the centre via Station and Coventry Road. More conveniently, **buses** stop on Market Street, just off the Market Square, from where it's a couple of minutes' walk east to St Mary's church. The **tourist office** is in the Courthouse at the corner of Castle and Jury streets (daily 9.30am–4.30pm; ☏01926/492212, ⓦwww.warwick-uk.co.uk). They have a list of local hotels and B&Bs, but with Stratford so near and easy to reach, there's no special reason to stay.

For a bite to **eat**, head for the reasonably-priced *Vanilla Restaurant*, a slick modern place just along from the tourist office at 6 Jury St (☏01926/498930). The light bites here are actually more tempting than the full meals. For a **drink**, try the amiable *Zetland Arms*, nearby at 11 Church St.

Worcestershire

In geographical terms, **Worcestershire** can be compared to a huge saucer, with the low-lying plains of the Severn Valley and the Vale of Evesham rising to a lip of hills, principally the Malverns in the west and the Cotswolds to the south (see pp.312–326). To the north lie the industrial and overspill towns that have much in common with the Birmingham conurbation, while the south is predominantly rural. Marking the transition between the two is **Worcester**, whose main claim to fame is its splendid cathedral. The south holds the county's finest scenery in the **Malvern Hills**, excellent walking territory and home to the amiable former spa town of **Great Malvern**.

The proximity of Birmingham ensures Worcestershire has a good network of **trains** and **buses**, though services are spasmodic amongst the villages in the south of the county.

Worcester

Right at the geographical heart of the county **WORCESTER** is something of an architectural hotchpotch, its half-timbered Tudor and stone Georgian buildings standing cheek by jowl with some fairly charmless modern developments. Postwar clumsiness apart, the biggest single influence on the city has always been the **River Severn**, which flows along Worcester's west flank. The river's major drawback is its propensity to breach its banks, though this has at least limited development along the riverside, where a leafy footpath passes below the mighty bulk of the **cathedral**, Worcester's star turn.

The Cathedral

Worcester's riverside is dominated by the sandstone bulk of the **cathedral** (daily 8.30am–5.30pm; free), a rich stew of architectural styles dating from 1084. The bulk of the church is firmly medieval, from the Norman transepts through to the late Gothic cloister, though the Victorians did have a good old hack at the exterior. Inside, the cavernous **nave** is unexceptional except for its two west bays, which are an unusual – and unusually fine – example of the transitional period, when the rounded Norman arch was being supplanted by the pointed arches of Early English Gothic. They date to the 1160s. Moving on, the **choir**, built between 1220 and 1260, is a beautiful illustration of the Early English style, while in front of the high altar is the **table-tomb** of England's most reviled monarch, **King John**, who died in 1216. Just beyond the tomb – on the right – is **Prince Arthur's Chantry**, a delicate lacy confection of carved stonework built in 1504 to commemorate Arthur, King Henry VII's son, who died at the age of 15 in Ludlow. He was on his honeymoon with Catherine of Aragon, who was soon passed on – with such momentous consequences – to his younger brother, Henry. A stairway beside the chantry leads down to the **crypt**, the oldest part of the cathedral and the largest Norman crypt in the country. In addition, a doorway on the south side of the nave leads to the **Cloisters** and the circular, largely Norman **Chapter House**, which has the distinction of being the first such building constructed with the use of a central supporting pillar.

The rest of the city

Tucked away behind the cathedral on Severn Street, the **Royal Worcester Porcelain** complex (Mon–Sat 9am–5.30pm, Sun 11am–5pm) contains factory shops, a visitor centre, a substantial porcelain museum (same times; £3.50), and the factory itself (tours Mon–Fri only, reservations required on ℡01905/746000; £5.50). Beginning in the mid-eighteenth century, porcelain manufacture was long the city's main industry and Royal Worcester its leading light.

From here, it's a brief walk north via Severn Street to the **Commandery** (Mon–Sat 10am–5pm & Sun 1.30–5pm; £3.95), on the far side of the busy Sidbury dual carriageway. This is the oldest building in the city, a rambling, half-timbered and smartly panelled structure dating from the early sixteenth century. Its moment of fame came when **King Charles II** used the building as his headquarters during the battle-cum-siege of Worcester in 1651, and to celebrate the connection, the building holds the large and detailed **Civil War Exhibition**.

It's a short step northwest from the Commandery along the dual carriageway to **Friar Street**, whose pedestrianized upper reaches hold an attractive sequence of antique half-timbered buildings. Amongst them is **Greyfriars** (April–Oct Wed–Fri 2–5pm, Sat 1–5pm; £3.10; NT), a largely fifteenth-century townhouse, whose wonky timbers and dark-stained panelling shelter a charming collection of antiques bequeathed to the National Trust by the last owner-occupiers, the Moores, in the 1980s.

Practicalities

Worcester has two **train stations**. Foregate Street is about half a mile south of the cathedral along Foregate Street, while Shrub Hill is about a mile to the northeast of the cathedral. The **bus station** is at the back of the sprawling Crowngate shopping mall, on The Butts. The **tourist office** (Mon–Sat 9.30am–5pm; ☎01905/726311, Ⓦwww.visitworcester.com) is in the 1720s Guildhall on the High Street.

One of the city's most appealing **hotels** is the likeable *Diglis House Hotel*, in an attractive Georgian building beside the river on Severn Street (☎01905/353518, Ⓦwww.diglishousehotel.co.uk; ❺). Amongst several central **B&Bs**, the pick is *Burgage House*, 4 College Precincts (☎01905/25396, Ⓦwww.burgagehouse.co.uk; no credit cards; ❸), which occupies a narrow Georgian townhouse on a cobbled lane beside the cathedral.

For **food**, recommendable cafés and restaurants include *Puccini's*, opposite Greyfriars at 12 Friar St, a moderately priced restaurant serving pastas and pizzas from £5, and the rather better *Saffron's Bistro*, 15 New St (☎01905/610505), which has an imaginative menu including vegetarian dishes. Friar Street possesses a cosy, traditional **pub** too, the *Cardinal's Hat*, at no. 23.

Great Malvern and the Malvern Hills

One of the most exclusive and prosperous areas of the Midlands, **The Malverns** is the generic name for a string of towns and villages stretched along the eastern lower slopes of the **Malvern Hills**, which rise spectacularly out of the flat plains a few miles to the southwest of Worcester. Of ancient granite rock, the hills are punctuated by over twenty summits, mostly around 1000-feet-high, and in between lie innumerable dips and hollows. Nonetheless, it's easy if energetic walking country, with great views, and there's an excellent network of hiking trails, most of which can be completed in a day or half-day.

Amongst The Malverns, it's **GREAT MALVERN** that grabs the attention, its pocket-sized centre clambering up the hillside with the crags of North Hill beckoning beyond. The Benedictines chose this hilly setting for one of their abbeys and although Henry VIII closed the place down in 1538, the **Priory Church** (daily: April–Sept 9am–6.30pm; Oct–March 9am–4.30pm) has survived, the crisp symmetries and elaborate decoration of its exterior witnessing the priory's former wealth. Inside, the high and mighty nave is sternly Norman and it sweeps down to the chancel, a fine example of the Perpendicular, its sinuous tracery serving to frame a simply fabulous set of **stained-glass windows** dating from the end of the fifteenth century.

A couple of minutes' walk away, hard by the top of Church Street, the modest **Malvern Museum** (Easter–Oct daily 10.30am–5pm; £1) is housed in the delicately proportioned Priory Gatehouse, but it concentrates on Great Malvern's days as a spa town. The spring waters hereabouts became popular at the end of the eighteenth century, but it was to be the Victorians who packed the place out – and built the grand stone houses that still line the town's streets. You can still sample the waters at **St Ann's Well** (Sat & Sun 10am–5pm, plus Easter–Sept Mon–Fri 10am–5pm or dusk), a cosy Victorian building (and café) situated a steep fifteen-minute walk up the wooded hillside from the top of town; the signposted path begins on the far side of the main road across from the Foley Arms Hotel.

Back at the museum, it's a short walk down the hill to Grange Road, where the **Malvern Theatres** (☎01684/892277 Ⓦwww.malvern-theatres.co.uk) is the key venue for the wide range of special events the town puts on each year.

Hiking The Malverns

Great Malvern tourist office (see below) sells hiking maps and issues half a dozen free **Trail Guide leaflets**, which describe circular routes up to and along the hills that rise behind the town. The shortest trail is just one and a half miles, the longest four. One of the most appealing is the 2.5-mile hoof up to the top – and back – of **North Hill** (1307ft), from where there are panoramic views over the surrounding countryside; this hike takes in St Ann's Well (see p.491). Alternatively, the one-way hike along the top of the ridge is a sterner test that takes all day and is ten miles long. On the way, you'll pass through the vague remains of a brace of Iron Age hill forts. It's best to start at the southern end – at **Chase End Hill** – and work your way north.

Practicalities

Great Malvern's rustic **train station** has fast and frequent connections with Birmingham and Worcester. It's located half a mile or so from the town centre via Avenue Road and then **Church Street**, the steeply sloping main drag. The **tourist office** is at the top of Church Street, across from the Priory Church (daily 10am–5pm; ☏01684/892289, ⓦwww.malvernhills.gov.uk).

Amongst the **hotels**, the pick is *The Abbey* (☏01684/892332, ⓦwww.sarova.com; ❼), a rambling, creeper-clad Victorian hotel with plush rooms behind the Priory Church on Abbey Road – the modern wing is less appetizing. A second choice is the *Foley Arms Hotel* at 14 Worcester Rd (☏01684/573397, ⓦwww.foleyarmshotel.com; ❻), though the rooms don't match up to the attractive Georgian facade. One very recommendable **B&B** is the *Wyche Keep*, an impressive Edwardian house with garden access to the Hills. It's located one mile south from the top of Church Street along the A449 at 22 Wyche Rd (☏01684/567018; no credit cards; ❹). A more central choice is *The Red Gate B&B*, in a large Victorian house near the train station at 32 Avenue Road (☏01684/565013; ❹) and offering well-appointed en-suite rooms. The **youth hostel**, 18 Peachfield Rd, (☏0870/770 5948, ⓦwww.yha.org.uk; dorm beds £10.25), occupies a rambling Edwardian house just one mile south of the train station.

The **restaurant** scene in Great Malvern is not as varied as you might expect. Nonetheless, *The Abbey Hotel* has a very competent if pricey restaurant, or you could try the *White Season Restaurant*, at the top of Church St (☏01684/575954; closed Sun), a crisply decorated modern place with a good line in seafood. The town also possesses the curious *Lady Foley's Tea Room* (Mon–Sat 9am–6pm), a **café** with character – in a converted waiting room down at the train station.

Herefordshire

Over the Hills from Worcestershire, the rolling agricultural landscapes of **Herefordshire** have an easy-going charm, but the finest scenery hereabouts is along the banks of the **River Wye**, which wriggles and worms its way across the county linking most of the places of interest. Plonked in the middle is **Hereford**, a sleepy, rather old-fashioned sort of place whose proudest possession is the cathedral's remarkable Mappa Mundi map. Hereford is also close to the delightful little town of **Ledbury**, distinguished by its Tudor and Stuart half-timbered buildings. The southeast corner of the county has one attractive town, **Ross-on-Wye**, a genial little place that is also an ideal base for explorations into one of the wilder portions of the **Wye River Valley**. To the west of Hereford, hard by the Welsh border, the key attraction is **Hay-on-Wye**, which has become the world's largest repository of secondhand books.

Herefordshire possesses one **rail line**, linking Ledbury and Hereford and running north to Shrewsbury. Otherwise, you'll be restricted to the tender mercies of the county's **buses**, which provide a reasonable service between the villages and towns, except on Sundays when there's almost nothing at all.

Hereford

Founded by the Saxons in the seventh century, **HEREFORD** – literally "army ford" – was long a border garrison town against the Welsh, its military importance guaranteed by its strategic position beside the River Wye. It also became a religious centre after the Welsh murdered the Saxon king Ethelbert near here in 794. Legend asserts that Ethelbert's ghost kept on turning up to insist his remains be interred here in Hereford – and eventually it got its way. Ethelbert's posthumous antics made him a military martyr and a Saxon cult soon grew up around his name, prompting the construction of the first cathedral. The Welsh were, however, having none of this and, in 1055, they attacked Hereford and burnt the cathedral to the ground. Today it's the second **cathedral**, dating from the eleventh century, which forms the main focus of architectural interest.

The Cathedral and the Mappa Mundi

Hereford **Cathedral** (daily 8.30am–5.30pm; £2 donation suggested) is a curious building, an uncomfortable amalgamation of architectural styles, from the eleventh to the nineteenth century. From the outside, the sandstone **tower** is the dominant feature, constructed in the early fourteenth century to eclipse the Norman western tower, which subsequently collapsed under its own weight in 1786. The tumbling masonry mauled the **nave** and its replacement lacks the grandeur of most other English cathedrals, though the forceful symmetries of the long rank of surviving Norman arches and piers more than hints at what went before. The **north transept** is, however, a flawless exercise in thirteenth-century taste, its soaring windows a classic example of Early English architecture. Across the church, the **south transept** is largely Norman, its chunky stonework interrupted by an old fireplace, one of the few still surviving within an English church, and decorated by an intricately carved *Adoration of the Magi*, a sixteenth-century, bas-relief triptych from Germany.

In the 1980s, financial difficulties prompted the cathedral authorities to plan the sale of their most treasured possession, the **Mappa Mundi**. There was an awful lot of cultural huffing and puffing about this controversial proposal, but the government and John Paul Getty Jnr rode to the rescue, with the oil tycoon stumping up a million pounds to keep the map here and install it in a brand new building. Made of sandstone, this New Library blends in seamlessly. It contains the immaculate **Mappa Mundi and Chained Library Exhibition** (April–Sept Mon–Sat 10am–5pm, Sun 11am–4pm; Oct–March Mon–Sat 11am–4pm; last admission 45min before closing; £4.50), which begins with a series of interpretative panels that lead to the Mappa, displayed in a dimly lit room. Dating to about 1300, and measuring 62 by 52 inches, the map is quite simply remarkable, depicting not only the general geography of the world – with Asia at the top and Europe and Africa below – but also squeezing in history, mythology and theology. The New Library also holds the **Chained Library**, a remarkably extensive collection of books and manuscripts dating from the eighth to the eighteenth century. The Cathedral also owns a copy of the **Magna Carta** which is frequently on display in the Chained Library too.

The rest of the city

After the Mappa, Hereford's other attractions can't help but seem rather pedestrian. Nonetheless, the **Hereford Museum and Art Gallery** on Broad Street (April–Sept Tues–Sat 10am–5pm, Sun 10am–4pm; Oct–March Tues–Sat 10am–5pm; free), does hold a mildly diverting collection of geological remains, local history and Victorian art. From the gallery, Broad Street continues up and round into the main square, **High Town**, which is fringed by several good-looking Georgian buildings.

Set amidst rolling countryside, Hereford's economy is still largely dependent on its agricultural base and the local **cider** industry is one of the city's biggest trades. Cider enthusiasts should make their way to the **Cider Museum and King Offa Distillery**, 21 Ryelands St (April–Oct daily 10am–5.30pm; Nov–March Tues–Sun 11am–3pm; £2.70), which tracks through the history of cider-making and offers samples of King Offa ciders. The museum is, however, a dull fifteen-minute walk west of the centre, off the A438. To get there, take Eign Gate west from High Town, cross the ring road onto Eign Street and watch for Ryelands Street on the left.

Practicalities

From Hereford **train station**, it's about half a mile southwest to the main square, High Town. The long-distance **bus station** is just off Commercial Road, but most local buses stop in St Peter's Square, at the east end of High Town. The **tourist office** is directly opposite the cathedral, at 1 King St (Mon–Sat 9am–5pm; ℡01432/268430, ⓦwww.visitorlinks.com).

Easily the best **hotel** in town is the *Castle House*, a truly immaculate hotel in an elegantly refurbished Georgian mansion just a couple of minutes' walk from the Cathedral on Castle St (℡01432/356321, ⓦwww.castlehse.co.uk; ❽). Pick of the **B&Bs** is *Charades*, 34 Southbank Rd (℡01432/269444; ❷), with six comfortable, mostly en-suite guest rooms in a large Victorian house. To get there, take Commercial Street and then Commercial Road, cross the railway bridge and Southbank is the second on the right.

As regards **eating**, there are several appealing places near the Cathedral on pedestrianized Church Street, including two very good and inexpensive cafés, *Rendez-vous* (Mon–Tues 9.30am–5pm & Wed–Sat 9.30am–5pm & 7–10pm) and *Nutters* (Mon–Sat 9am–5pm), a vegetarian place just off Church St on Capuchin Yard. There's also *Cafe@allsaints*, in the old church at the top of Broad St (Mon–Sat 8.30am–5.30pm), where they serve a tasty range of well-conceived dishes for around £6. The best restaurant in town is the pricey *La Rive*, at the *Castle House Hotel* (see above), offering French cuisine at its finest.

When it comes to **drinking**, don't leave town without sampling the favourite local tipple, **cider**. Every pub in town serves the stuff with one of the most enjoyable being *The Barrels*, five minutes' walk southeast of High Town, on St Owen's Street. *The Barrels* is also the home pub of the local Wye Valley Brewery, whose trademark **bitters** are much acclaimed.

Ledbury

Heading east from Hereford, it's an easy fifteen miles along the A438 to **LEDBURY**, a good-looking little town glued to the western edge of the Malvern Hills. The focus of the town is the Market Place, home to the dinky

Market House, a Tudor beamed building raised on oak columns and with herringbone pattern beams. From beside it, narrow **Church Lane** – not to be confused with adjacent Church Street – runs up the slope to **St Michael's parish church**, whose strong and angular detached spire pokes high into the sky. The nucleus of the church is Norman but there are early Gothic flourishes too, most importantly the nave's long and slender windows. Otherwise, the most interesting features are the funerary monuments, including the spectacular seventeenth-century **Skynner Tomb**, where five sons and five daughters kneel in honour of their parents, beneath the canopied slab on which their parents also kneel, she in a hat that looks fancy enough to wear at Ascot.

Ledbury **train station** is inconveniently situated on the northern edge of town, about three-quarters of a mile from the Market Place – straight down the A438. **Buses** stop on the Market Place, across from the **tourist office** (March to mid-July & mid-Sept to Nov Mon–Sat 10am–5pm, mid-July to mid-Sept daily 10am–5pm; ℡01531/636147). **Accommodation** is thin on the ground, but the *Feathers Hotel* (℡01531/635266, Ⓦwww.feathers–ledbury .co.uk; ❻) on the High Street has nineteen very comfortable rooms. For **food**, the *Malthouse Restaurant*, on Church Lane (℡01531/634443; closed Sun), is exemplary, with a creative menu featuring local ingredients – main courses average around £15 in the evening, lunches around £7. Also on Church Lane, the charming *Prince of Wales* **pub** is a great place to sink a beer amidst its snug, low-beamed rooms.

Ross-on-Wye and around

Pocket-sized **ROSS-ON-WYE**, perched above a loop in the river sixteen miles southeast of Hereford, is a relaxed, easy-going town with an artsy/New Age undertow. It's also the obvious base for exploring one of the more dramatic sections of the **Wye River Valley**.

Ross's jumble of narrow streets zeroes in on the **Market Place**, which is shadowed by the seventeenth-century **Market House**, a sturdy two-storey sandstone structure that now accommodates a modest **Heritage Centre** (April–Oct Mon–Sat 10am–5pm, Sun 10.30am–4pm; Nov–March Mon–Sat 10am–4pm; free), exploring the town's history. Veer right at the top of the Market Place, then turn left up Church Street to reach Ross's other noteworthy building, the mostly thirteenth century **St Mary's church**, whose sturdy stonework culminates in a slender, tapering spire. In front of the church, at the foot of the graveyard, is a plain but rare **Plague Cross**, commemorating the three hundred or so townsfolk who were buried here by night without coffins during a savage outbreak of the plague in 1637. Inside, the church holds two distinctive **table-tombs**, one of which – that of a certain William Rudhall – is a late example of the wonderful alabaster sculptures created by the specialist masons of Nottingham, whose work was prized right across medieval Europe. Beside the church, to the right of the entrance, **The Prospect** is a neat public garden offering pleasant views over the river.

Practicalities

There are no trains to Ross, but the **bus station** is handily located on Cantilupe Road, from where it's a couple of minutes' walk west to the Market Place. The **tourist office** is equally convenient, located a few yards west of the Market Place on the corner of High and Edde Cross streets (Mon–Sat 9.30am–5pm, plus mid-July to mid-Sept Sun 10am–4pm; ℡01989/562768). **Bikes** can be rented from Revolutions on Broad Street (℡01989/562639).

The main cultural event is the **Ross International Festival** (℡01989/562562, ⓦwww.rossonwye-intfestival.co.uk), a mixed bag of music, theatre and dance held over two weeks in August.

Ross is strong on **B&Bs** with one of the best being the *Linden House*, in a three-storey Georgian building at 14 Church St (℡01989/565373, ⓦwww.lindenguesthouse.com; ❷). The seven rooms are cosily decorated in modern style and the breakfasts are delicious. Another excellent choice is the *Old Court House*, across from the tourist office at 53 High St (℡01989/762275, ⓦwww.visitorlinks.com; ❸). This is sited in a sympathetically modernized, half-timbered townhouse with grand fireplaces and a warren-like layout.

For **food**, *Oat Cuisine*, a daytime café at 41 Broad St, sells an unusual range of whole and health foods. Alternatively, there's *Meaders Hungarian Restaurant* (℡01989/562803; closed Sun), just along the High Street from the Market Place and offering delicious Hungarian dishes at moderate prices. Of the **pubs**, the *Crown & Sceptre,* on Broad Street, offers a good range of brews, but the traditional *Man of Ross*, at the top of Wye Street across from the tourist office, wins on atmosphere.

The Wye River Valley

Heading **south from Ross** along the B4234, it's just five miles to the sullen sandstone mass of **Goodrich Castle** (April–Oct daily 10am–6pm; Nov–March Wed–Sun 10am–1pm & 2–4pm; £3.70; EH), which commands wide views over the hills and woods of the **Wye River Valley**. Dating from the twelfth century, the castle's strategic location beside a busy river crossing point guaranteed its importance as a border stronghold from the twelfth century onwards. Today, the substantial ruins incorporate a Norman keep, a maze of later rooms and passageways and walkable ramparts.

The castle stands next to tiny **GOODRICH VILLAGE**, which is on the Ross to Monmouth bus route – Stagecoach **bus** #34 (every 2hr, not Sun). From the village, it's around a mile and a half southeast along narrow country lanes to the solitary **Welsh Bicknor hostel** (℡0870/770 6086, ⓔwelshbicknor @yha.org; £11.50; restricted opening Sept–March; closed 10am–5pm), in a Victorian riverside rectory. The hostel, in 25-acre grounds, has 76 beds and provides evening meals on request. Given the hostel's seclusion, booking ahead is strongly recommended.

Symonds Yat Rock and Symonds Yat East

Beyond Goodrich – and beyond all hope of a bus – it's a couple of miles south along narrow roads to the signposted turning that wriggles its way up to the top of **Symonds Yat Rock**, rising high above a wooded, hilly loop in the Wye. This is one of the region's most celebrated views and you'll probably share it with the birdwatchers who come here to spy the raptors gliding below. At the foot of the rock – a two-mile drive away – is **SYMONDS YAT EAST**, a pretty little hamlet that straggles along the east bank of the river. It's a popular spot, with canoe rental and forty-minute cruises operated by Kingfisher (℡01600/891063; March–Oct only), and there are several places to stay. The most appealing **hotel** is the bright and cheerful *Forest View* (℡01600/890210; ❺).

The road to the village is a dead end, so you have to double back to regain the main local road, the **B4432**.

Hay-on-Wye

Straddling the Anglo-Welsh border some twenty miles west of Hereford, the hilly little town of **HAY-ON-WYE** is known to most people for one thing –

books. Hay saw its first bookshop open in 1961, courtesy of the entrepreneurial Richard Booth, who remains the leading bookman hereabouts. Since then, it has become a bibliophile's paradise, with just about every spare inch of the town given over to the trade, including the old cinema and the ramshackle stone castle.

Hay has an attractive setting, amidst rolling forested hills, and its narrow, bendy streets are lined with a particularly engaging assortment of old stone houses. In summer, the town plays host to a succession of riverside parties and travelling fairs, the pick of which is the **Hay Festival of Literature and the Arts** (☏01497/821066, Ⓦwww.hayfestival.co.uk), held over ten days at the back end of May, when London's literary world decamps here.

Before you start ambling round the town, visit the tourist office (see below) to pick up the free leaflet that gives the low-down on all of Hay's bookshops together with a street plan. Across the street from the tourist office, a signed footpath leads up the slope to the **castle**, a careworn Jacobean mansion built into the walls of an earlier medieval fortress. Richard Booth lives in part of the castle, but its southern extremities are given over to a pair of bookshops: **Castle Drive Books** (daily 10.30am–5pm; ☏01568/780707), which has a large stock of remaindered books, and **Hay Castle Bookshop** (daily 9.30am–5.30pm; ☏01497/820503, Ⓦwww.boothbooks.co.uk), a trusty collection focused on fine art, cinema, antiquarian and photography. From here, the footpath twists its way round the western flank of the castle to meet the steps that lead down to Castle Street, home to **Bookends**, at no. 9 (April–Oct Sun–Wed 11am–5.30pm, Thurs–Sat 9am–8pm; Nov–March daily 9am–5.30pm; ☏01497/821341, Ⓦwww.bookspostfree.com), where all the books cost £1.

Castle Street slopes up to the main square, High Town, from where it's straight on for Lion Street and **Booth Books** at no. 44 (April–Oct Mon–Sat 9am–8pm, Sun 11.30am–5.30pm, Nov–March Mon–Sat 9am–5.30pm, Sun 11.30am–5.30pm; ☏01497/820322, Ⓦwww.richardbooth.demon.co.uk), a huge, draughty warehouse of almost unlimited browsing potential.

Practicalities

Buses to Hay stop in the centre of town on Oxford Road beside the main car park. The adjacent **tourist office** (daily: Easter–Oct 10am–1pm & 2–5pm; Nov–Easter 11am–1pm & 2–4pm; ☏01497/820144, Ⓦwww.hay-on-wye .co.uk) stocks an exhaustive range of hiking books and maps.

Accommodation in town is plentiful. Amongst the town's many **B&Bs** and **guest houses**, one excellent option is the *Seven Stars*, plum in the centre across from the Victorian Clock Tower at 11 Broad St (☏01497/820886, Ⓦwww.hay-on-wye.co.uk/sevenstars; no cards; ❸), and occupying an attractive ivy-clad stone house. Another good bet is the *Belmont House*, Belmont Rd

---

Canoeing in Hay-on-Wye

Scores of visitors come to Hay-on-Wye to hike and cycle, but the district is just as pleasantly explored by kayak or canoe on the River Wye. For rental, Paddles & Peddles, 15 Castle St (☏01497/820604, Ⓦwww.canoehire.co.uk), is a reputable outfit, full of good ideas and advice. Rental of life jackets and other essential equipment (such as waterproof canisters to carry your gear) is included in the price, which works out at around £40 per canoe for a full 24 hours, with discounts for longer trips. In addition, Paddles & Peddles will transport their customers to the departure and from the finishing points by minibus.

(☎01497/820718; no credit cards; ❷), a well-kept B&B in a good-looking Georgian villa. There's also *20 Lion Street B&B*, a cosy and carefully tended little stone cottage on the east side of the centre (☎01497/821901; no cards; ❶). The nearest **campsite** to Hay is *Radnors End* (☎01497/820780), in a pleasant setting five minutes' walk from the town centre across the Wye bridge on the Clyro road.

For **food**, *Shepherds*, 9 High Town (Mon–Sat 9.30am–5.30pm, Sun 11am–5.30pm), is an appealing café with a good line in snacks and mouth-watering, locally made ice cream. There's also the hard-to-beat *Granary* (daily till 9pm; ☎01497/820790), a combined café, bar and restaurant on Broad Street, offering wholefood snacks and soups as well as filling main meals (£6–8) with the emphasis on local organic produce. For a more formal meal, head for the *Famous Old Black Lion*, Lion St (☎01497/820841), an antique inn serving moderately priced first-rate food.

Shropshire

One of England's largest and least populated counties, **Shropshire** stretches from its long and winding border with Wales to the very edge of the urban Black Country. It was here that the Industrial Revolution made a huge stride forward with the spanning of the River Severn by the very first **iron bridge**. The assorted industries that subsequently squeezed into the gorge are long gone, but a series of **museums** celebrate their craftsmanship – from tiles and iron through to porcelain. The River Severn also flows through the county town of **Shrewsbury**, whose antique centre holds dozens of old half-timbered buildings, though **Ludlow**, further to the south, has the edge when it comes to handsome Tudor and Jacobean architecture. In between lie the beautiful twin ridges of **Wenlock Edge** and the **Long Mynd**, both of which are prime hiking areas, best explored from the attractive little town of **Church Stretton**.

For all its attractions, Shropshire remains well off the main tourist routes, one factor protecting the county's isolation being the paucity of its **public transport**. Shrewsbury and Telford are connected to Birmingham, whilst Ludlow and Church Stretton are connected to Shrewsbury, but that's the limit of the **train** services, whilst rural **buses** tend to connect outlying villages on just a few days of the week. One recent step forward has been the creation of the **Shropshire Hills Shuttle bus** service (Ⓦ www.shropshirehillsshuttles.co.uk) aimed at the tourist market and operating every weekend from April to November. The shuttle has five main routes and there are buses every hour or two. An Adult Day Rover ticket costs just £3.

Ironbridge Gorge

Both geographically and culturally, **Ironbridge Gorge**, the collective title for a cluster of small villages huddled in the wooded Severn valley to the south of new-town Telford, looks to the towns of the West Midlands rather than rural Shropshire. Ironbridge Gorge was the crucible of the Industrial Revolution, a process encapsulated by its famous span across the Severn – the world's first **iron bridge**, engineered by Abraham Darby and opened on New Year's Day, 1781. Darby was the third innovative industrialist of that name – the first Abraham Darby started iron-smelting here back in 1709 and the second invented the forging process that made it possible to produce massive single beams in iron. Under the guidance of such creative figures as the Darbys and Thomas Telford, the area's factories once churned out engines, rails, wheels and other heavy-duty iron pieces in quantities unmatched anywhere else in the world. Manufacturing has now all but vanished, but the surviving monuments make the gorge the most extensive industrial heritage sight in England – and one that has been granted World Heritage Site status by UNESCO.

Arrival, getting around and information

Monday to Friday just one **bus** runs from Shrewsbury to Ironbridge village via Telford train station, from where there's a second Mon–Fri only bus to the village. On Saturdays and Sundays, the **Gorge Connect bus** (part of the Shropshire Hills Shuttle service) runs along the Gorge from Coalbrookdale in the west to Coalport in the east every half hour or so. A Day Rover ticket costs just £3.

A thorough exploration of the gorge takes a couple of days, but the **highlights** – the Museum of Iron and the Coalport China Works Museum – are easily manageable on a day trip. If you're intending to visit several of the museums and attractions, a **passport ticket** (£13) allows access to each of them once in any calendar year and is available at all the main sights. **Parking** is free at most of the sights, but not in Ironbridge village itself. Pick up local maps and information from the **Ironbridge Visitor Information Centre** (Mon–Fri 9am–5pm, Sat & Sun 10am–5pm; ☎01952/432166, ⓦwww .ironbridge.org.uk), in the old toll house at the south end of the bridge.

Accommodation

Most visitors to the gorge come for the day, but there are several pleasant **B&Bs** in Ironbridge village, which is where you want to be. Two of the best are *The Library House*, which occupies a charming Georgian villa just yards from the iron bridge at 11 Severn Bank (☎01952/432299, ⓦwww .libraryhouse.com; no credit cards; ❸); and *Bridge View*, whose neat and trim rooms are also a stone's throw from the bridge at 10 Tontine Hill (☎01952/432541, ⓦwww.ironbridgeview.co.uk; ❷). Alternatively, *Coalbrookdale Villa* occupies an attractive Victorian ironmasters' house about half a mile up the hill from the west end of Ironbridge village in tiny Paradise (☎01952/433450, ⓦwww.coalbrookdalevilla.co.uk; no credit cards; ❸). It's metres from one of the gorge's two **youth hostels**, *Coalbrookdale*, in the old Literary and Scientific Institute building, a Victorian whopper with eighty beds parcelled up into two- to eight-bedded rooms (☎0870/770 5882, ⒺIronbridge@yha.org.uk; dorm beds £11.50). Breakfasts and evening meals are provided here, but pre-booking is required. A second hostel, *Coalport* (same details), is three miles east along the gorge in the former Coalport China factory, and no advance booking is required.

Ironbridge village

There must have been an awful lot of nervous sweat during the construction of the **iron bridge** over the River Severn in the late 1770s. The first of its kind, no one was quite sure how the new material would wear and although the single-span design looked sound, many feared the bridge would simply tumble into the river. To compensate, Abraham Darby used more iron than was strictly necessary, but the end result still manages to appear stunningly graceful, arching between the steep banks with the river far below. The settlement at the north end of the span was promptly renamed **IRON-BRIDGE**, and today its brown-brick houses climb prettily up the hill. The village is home to the **Museum of the Gorge** (daily 10am–5pm; £2.10), located in a church-like, neo-Gothic old riverside warehouse about 500 yards west of the bridge along the main road. This provides an introduction to the industrial history of the gorge and provides a few environmental pointers too.

The rest of the Gorge

At the roundabout just to the west of the Museum of the Gorge, turn right for the half-mile trip up to what was once the gorge's big industrial deal, the **COALBROOKDALE iron foundry**, which boomed throughout the eighteenth and early nineteenth centuries, employing up to four thousand men and boys. The foundry has been imaginatively converted into the **Museum of Iron** (daily 10am–5pm; £5.15, including Darby Houses), with a wide range of displays on iron-making in general and the history of the company in particular. There are superb examples of Victorian and Edwardian ironwork here, as well as the ruins of the **furnace** where Abraham Darby pioneered the use of coke as a smelting fuel in place of charcoal.

From the foundry, it's about 100 yards up to the **Darby Houses** (daily 10am–5pm; £3) – Dale House and Rosehill – a pair of attractively restored, old ironmaster's homes with Georgian period rooms and a scattering of items that once belonged to the Darby family.

Heading east from the iron bridge, it's just over a mile to the turning for Blists Hill (see below) and another 500 yards or so to the **Tar Tunnel** (April–Oct daily 10am–5pm; £1.15), built to transport coal from one part of the gorge to another, but named for the bitumen that oozes naturally from its walls. Beside the tunnel, a footbridge crosses the river to reach **JACKFIELD**, a sleepy little place that once hummed to the tune of its tile factory. The factory has now been turned into the **Jackfield Tile Museum** (daily 10am–5pm; £4.50), which features an excellent collection of brightly coloured tiles.

Back at the tunnel, a canal towpath leads east in a couple of minutes to **COALPORT China works**, a large brick complex holding a youth hostel (see p.499) and the **Coalport China Museum** (daily 10am–5pm; £4.30), crammed full with Coalport wares, the particular highlight being the gaudy and ornate pieces manufactured in the company's Victorian heyday, from around 1820 to 1890. There's also a workshop, where potters demonstrate their skills, a Social History Gallery, which explores the hard life of the factory's workers, and two **bottle-kilns**, whose distinctive conical structures were long the hallmark of the pottery industry.

Doubling back along the river, it's a third of a mile west from Coalport to the clearly signed, mile-long road that cuts up to the gorge's most popular attraction, the rambling **Blists Hill Victorian Town** (daily 10am–5pm; £8.25). This encloses a substantial number of reconstructed Victorian buildings, most notably a school, a candle-makers, a doctor's surgery complete with horrific instruments, a gas-lit pub, and a wrought-iron works. Jam-packed on most summer days, it's especially popular with school parties, who keep the period-dressed employees very busy.

Eating and drinking

There are two excellent **pubs** in the gorge – the *Boat Inn*, a cosy little place with a riverside setting across the footbridge from the tar tunnel, and the *Coalbrookdale Inn*, a smashing traditional pub on the main road above the Museum of Iron. Both serve inexpensive **food,** but the *Coalbrookdale Inn* does it much better.

Shrewsbury

SHREWSBURY, the county town of Shropshire, sits in a narrow loop of the River Severn, a three-hundred-yard spit of land being all that keeps the town centre from becoming an island. It would be difficult to design a better defensive site and the Britons were quick to erect a fort here once the Roman legions had hot-footed in the fifth century. In Georgian times, Shrewsbury became a fashionable staging post on the busy London to Holyhead route and since then it has evolved into an easy-going, middling market town, whose appealing centre is made up of narrow lanes, courtyards and alleys.

Arrival and information

Shrewsbury is well connected by **train** to the rest of the country, and its station lies at the northeast edge of the centre off Castle Gates. **Buses** from London, Birmingham and beyond pull into the National Express stand at the Raven Meadows bus station, off the Smithfield Road, five minutes' walk west of the train station. The **tourist office** is a five-minute walk south up the hill from the train station, on The Square (May–Sept Mon–Sat 9.30am–5.30pm, Sun 10am–4pm; Oct–April Mon–Sat 10am–5pm; ☎01743/281200, ⓦwww.shrewsburytourism.co.uk).

Accommodation

Shrewsbury has one particularly good **hotel**, the *Prince Rupert*, which occupies a cannily converted old building, right in the centre of town off Pride Hill on Butcher Row and offers comfortable, slightly fancy rooms (☎01743/499955, ⓦwww.prince-rupert-hotel.co.uk; ❻). A second option is *The Lion*, a former coaching inn on the Wyle Cop (☎0870/609 6167, ⓦwww.regalhotels.co.uk/the lion; ❻). The pick of the central **B&Bs** is the *College Hill Guest House*, a well-maintained Georgian townhouse at 11 College Hill, just south of The Square (☎01743/365744; no credit cards; ❷). Further afield, one mile east of the centre across the English Bridge, is another quality B&B, the *Fieldside*, in a large Victorian property with eight neat and trim mostly en-suite guest rooms, next to St Giles's church at 38 London Road (☎01743/353143, ⓦwww.fieldsideguesthouse.co.uk; no cards; ❸).

The Town

Poking up above the mansion-like train station, the careworn ramparts of Shrewsbury **castle** are but a pale reminder of the mighty medieval fortress that once dominated the town, largely because the illustrious Thomas Telford turned the castle into the private home of a local bigwig in the 1780s. **Castle Gates** winds up the hill from the station into the heart of the river loop where the medieval town took root. Here, off Pride Hill, several half-timbered buildings are dotted along **Butcher Row**, which leads into the quiet precincts of **St Alkmund's church**, from where there's a charming view of the fine old buildings of **Fish Street**. Close by is the most interesting of the town's churches, **St Mary the Virgin** (Mon–Fri 10am–5pm, Sat 10am–4pm; free), whose sombre exterior is partly redeemed by its slender spire. Inside, the church is unusual in so far as it exhibits both the rounded arches beloved of the Normans in the nave and the pointed arches of Early English Gothic in the choir and the transepts. The nave also boasts a splendid panelled roof, featuring angels with musical instruments, while the east window of the chancel, with its filigree tracery rising above the high altar, represents the apogee of the Decorated style and dates to the 1330s.

Doubling back, it's the briefest of walks from St Mary's to the High Street, on the far side of which, in the narrow confines of **The Square**, is the **Old Market House**, a heavy-duty stone structure built in 1596. High Street snakes down the hill from The Square to become **Wyle Cop**, lined with higgledy-piggledy ancient buildings and leading to the **English Bridge**, which sweeps across the Severn in grand Georgian style. Beyond the bridge, on Abbey Foregate, is the stumpy redstone mass of the **Abbey church** (daily: April–Oct 9.30am–5.30pm; Nov–March 10.30am–3pm; free), all that remains of the Benedictine abbey that was a major political and religious force hereabouts until the Dissolution. The church is still in use as a place of worship, hence its good condition, but the interior is fairly pedestrian.

Eating and drinking

For **daytime food**, try the inexpensive *Goodlife Wholefood Restaurant* (Mon–Fri 9.30am–3.30pm & Sat 9.30am–4.30pm), on Barracks Passage, just off – and about halfway along – Wyle Cop; they specialize in salads and vegetarian dishes. Another good bet is *Philpotts Quality Sandwiches*, which deserves its name and is located at 15 Butcher Row. In the **evening**, there's tasty tandoori at *Shalimar*, by the Abbey church at 23 Abbey Foregate, and a wide range of snacks and meals just along the street in the modern and inexpensive *Peach Tree* café-bar at 21 Abbey Foregate (daily 9am–10pm). Another good bet is the authentic, moderately priced Asian cuisine of *Thai Orchids* (℡01743/353117) right in the centre of town, off Pride Hill on Butchers Row. However, many locals think that the best restaurant in town is *Osteria da Paolo*, a homely Italian place offering mouthwatering cuisine from its premises down a narrow alley off Hills Lane near the Welsh Bridge (℡01743/243336).

Amongst Shrewsbury's many **pubs**, one of the most distinctive is the *Loggerheads*, an ancient place with four small rooms and great real ales; it's located near St Alkmund's Place at 1 Church Street. Other recommendable **pubs** include the smoke-free *Three Fishes*, in an ancient building on Fish Street, and the cosy *Coach & Horses*, on Swan Hill just south of The Square.

Church Stretton - and the Long Mynd

Beginning about ten miles south of Shrewsbury, the upland heaths of the **Long Mynd**, some ten miles long and between two and four miles wide, run parallel to and just to the west of the A49. This is prime walking territory and the heathlands are latticed with footpaths, the pick of which offer sweeping views over the border to the Black Mountains of Wales. Nestled at the foot of the Mynd beside the A49 is **CHURCH STRETTON**, a tidy little village and popular day-trippers' destination that makes it the ideal base for hiking the area. The village also possesses the dinky parish **church of St Laurence**, parts of which – especially the nave and transepts – are Norman.

As for practicalities, Church Stretton is easy to reach from Shrewsbury and Ludlow by **train** and **bus**. Most buses stop in the centre of the village along the High Street, but some pull in beside the train station, which is close to the A49 – and about 600 yards east of the High Street. The **tourist office**, on Church St (Easter–Sept Mon–Sat 10am–1pm & 2–5pm; ℡01694/723133), is yards from St Laurence, one street to the west of the High Street. They stock an excellent range of hiking leaflets, have information on off-road cycle routes and will book accommodation. Of the many **hikes** beginning in the village, one good choice is the six-mile circular hike to the top of **Caer Caradoc**, the steep hill to the northeast of the village, and back again. The hill is crowned by the scant remains of an Iron Age fort and affords superb views.

There's no shortage of good-value **accommodation** in and around Church Stretton. One particularly recommended **B&B** is *Acton Scott Farm* (℡01694/781260, ⓦwww.actonscottfarm.co.uk; no credit cards; ❷; closed Nov–Jan), a seventeenth-century farmhouse with log fires and three well-appointed rooms; it's located some three miles south of Church Stretton, east off the A49 in Acton Scott. There's also the first-rate *Jinlye Guest House* (℡01694/723243, ⓦwww.jinlye.co.uk; ❹), in an attractively modernized and extended stone cottage on Castle Hill in All Stretton, one mile north of Church Stretton. **Campers** have a choice of several sites, including *Ley Hill Farm* (℡01694/771366; tents £6), deep in the countryside a couple of miles to the northeast of Church Stretton, near the hamlet of Cardington. **Hostellers** have choices too – between **Wilderhope Manor** (℡0870/770 6090, ⓔwilderhope@yha.org.uk; call ahead for opening dates & reservations; dorm beds £11.50) in Longville-in-the-Dale, about six miles east along the B4371, and **Bridges Long Mynd** (℡01588/650656; Mon–Sat only; dorm beds £9), five miles west from Church Stretton near Ratlinghope.

Ludlow

LUDLOW, perched on a hill nearly thirty miles south of Shrewsbury, is one of the most picturesque towns in the West Midlands, if not in England – a cluster of beautifully preserved black-and-white half-timbered buildings packed around a craggy stone castle, with rural Shropshire forming a drowsy backdrop. Close to the Welsh border, the Saxons were the first to recognize the site's defensive qualities, but it was the Normans who got down to business when Roger Montgomery turned up here with his men in 1085. Over the next few decades, Montgomery's fortifications were elaborated into an immense **castle** (Jan Sat & Sun 10am–4pm; Feb, March & Oct–Dec daily 10am–4pm; April–July & Sept daily 10am–5pm; Aug daily 10am–7pm; £3.50), strong enough to keep the Welsh at bay. Surviving the attentions of the Parliamentary troops in the Civil War, the rambling and imposing ruins that remain today include towers and turrets, gatehouses and concentric walls as well as the remains of the 110-foot Norman **keep** and an unusual **Round Chapel** built in 1120. With its spectacular setting above the rivers Teme and Corve, the castle also makes a fine open-air auditorium during the **Ludlow Festival** (℡01584/872150, ⓦwww.ludlowfestival.co.uk), three weeks of assorted musical and theatrical fun running from the end of June to early July.

The castle gates open out onto **Castle Square**, an airy rectangle, whose eastern side abuts four narrow lanes – take the one on the left, Church Street and then King Street, to reach the gracefully proportioned **church of St Laurence** (daily 10am–5.30pm; £1 suggested donation). The church's interior is distinguished by its stained-glass windows and oak misericords, which run the gamut from royal emblems and religious scenes to the folkloric and seemingly profane. More serene are the church's several table-tombs, including, in the south transept, the delicately carved alabaster memorial to a certain Dame Mary Evre. Back outside the church, King Street leads into the **Bull Ring**, home of the **Feathers Hotel** (see p.504), a beautiful Jacobean building with the fanciest wooden facade imaginable.

To the south of Castle Square, the gridiron of streets laid out by the Normans has survived intact, though most of the buildings date from the eighteenth century. It's the general appearance that appeals rather than any special sight, but steeply sloping **Broad Street** is particularly attractive, flanked by many of Ludlow's five hundred half-timbered Tudor and red-brick Georgian listed buildings, its north end framed by the high and mighty **Butter Cross**, a Neoclassical extravagance from 1744. At the foot of Broad Street is Ludlow's only surviving medieval **gate**, which was turned into a house in the eighteenth century.

Practicalities

From Ludlow **train station**, on the Shrewsbury–Hereford line, it's a five- to ten-minute walk southwest to the castle – just follow the signs. Most **buses** stop on Mill Street, just off Castle Square. Ludlow's **tourist office**, on Castle Square (April–Sept Mon–Sat 10am–5pm, Sun 10.30am–5pm; Oct–March Mon–Sat 10am–5pm; ☎01584/875053, ⓦwww.ludlow.org.uk), has a wide range of maps and books for walkers, as well as a selection of inexpensive leaflets detailing day hikes in the area. **Accommodation** is plentiful, though rooms can get scarce during the festival. First choice has to be the beautiful *Feathers Hotel* on the Bull Ring (☎01584/875261, ⓦwww.feathersatludlow .co.uk; ❺), an intricately decorated Jacobean townhouse with luxury rooms and period furnishings. Two other options in the town centre are the *Wheatsheaf Inn*, a quaint little pub at the foot of Broad Street (☎01584/872980; ❷), and, just beyond at 28 Lower Broad Street, the excellent *Number Twenty Eight B&B*, in an attractive Georgian house with four smart en-suite guest rooms (☎01584/875466, ⓦwww.ludlowno28.com; ❺).

Ludlow has a string of fine **restaurants** with one of the best being the *Merchant House* (☎01584/875438; closed Sun & Mon), in a good-looking half-timbered building about half a mile from the centre on Corve Street, a northerly continuation of the Bull Ring. A second outstanding restaurant is the *Hibiscus*, much closer to the centre at 17 Corve Street (☎01584/872325; closed Sun), where they serve expensive, classic French cuisine with vim and gusto. Cheaper is the popular *Olive Branch*, on the Bull Ring (daily 10am–3pm), whose speciality is inexpensive light meals and salads, or the *Ego Café-Bar*, just north off Castle Square on Quality Square, which serves everything from snacks to filling meals at moderate prices.

Birmingham

If anywhere can be described as the first purely industrial conurbation, it has to be **BIRMINGHAM**. Unlike the more specialist industrial towns that grew up across the north and Midlands, "Brum" – and its "Brummies" – turned its hand to every kind of manufacturing, gaining the epithet "the city of 1001 trades". It was here also that the pioneers of the Industrial Revolution – James Watt, Matthew Boulton, William Murdock, Josiah Wedgwood, Joseph Priestley and Erasmus Darwin (grandfather of Charles) – formed the **Lunar Society**, an extraordinary melting-pot of scientific and industrial ideas. They conceived the world's first purpose-built factory, invented gas lighting and pioneered both the distillation of oxygen and the mass production of the steam engine. Thus, a modest Midlands market town mushroomed into the nation's economic dynamo – in the fifty years up to 1830 the population more than trebled to 130,000.

Now the second largest city in Britain, with a population of over one million, Birmingham has long outgrown the squalor and misery of its boom years and today its industrial supremacy is recalled in a crop of excellent **heritage museums** and an extensive network of **canals**. It also boasts a thoroughly multiracial population that makes this one of Britain's most cosmopolitan cities. An intelligent and far-reaching revamp of the city centre included the construction of a glitzy **Convention Centre**, while the enormous **National Exhibition Centre** (NEC) inhabits the outskirts near the international airport. In addition, Birmingham has launched a veritable raft of cultural initiatives, enticing a division of the **Royal Ballet** to take up residence here, and building a fabulous new concert hall for the **City of Birmingham Symphony Orchestra**. Nonetheless, there's no pretending that Birmingham is packed with interesting sights – it isn't – though along with its first-rate restaurant scene and nightlife, it's well worth at least a day or two.

Arrival, information and city transport

Birmingham's **international airport** is eight miles east of the city centre off the A45 and near the M42 (Junction 6); the main terminal is beside Birmingham International train station, from where there are regular services into the centre. **New Street train station**, to which all InterCity and the vast majority of local services go, is right in the heart of the city. However, trains on the Stratford-upon-Avon, Warwick, Worcester and Malvern lines usually use **Snow Hill** and **Moor Street stations**, both about ten minutes' signposted walk from New Street. National Express **coach** travellers are dumped in the grim surroundings of **Digbeth coach station**, from where it's a ten-minute uphill walk to the centre.

Maps, loads of local leaflets and transport information are provided by all the city's **tourist offices**. The main office is located in the city centre in the base of the Rotunda at the east end of New Street (Mon–Sat 9.30am–5.30pm & Sun 10.30am–4.30pm; ℡0121/202 5099, ⓦwww.birmingham.org.uk). A second, smaller office occupies a large glass kiosk also in New Street (Mon–Sat 9.30am–5.30pm; same number). In addition, there are tourist offices at the International Convention Centre, Centenary Square (ICC; same number), and next to the airport in the National Exhibition Centre (NEC; same number). All of the tourist offices operate a hotel bed booking service at no charge.

Birmingham's excellent **trains**, **metro** and **buses** delve into almost every urban nook and cranny. Various companies provide these services, but they are coordinated by **Centro**, which operates a regional public transport information line, ℡0121/200 2700, ⓦwww.centro.org.uk. A one-day **Centrocard**, valid on all services, can be purchased from bus drivers and at train and metro stations; it costs £5 (£4 after 9.30am and at the weekend).

Accommodation

As you might expect, Birmingham has a wide range of **accommodation**. All of the city's tourist offices have the full details and there's a selection of hotels in both their *Pocket Guide to Birmingham* (free) and the *Night & Day Essential Visitor Guide* (£1.25). All the tourist offices operate a **hotel room booking service** at no charge and are often aware of special deals and discounts.

Ashdale House 39 Broad Road, Acocks Green ℡0121/706 3598, ⓦwww.ashdalehouse.co.uk. Pleasant Victorian townhouse with nine smartly furnished, mostly en-suite guest rooms. Full English or vegetarian breakfasts. Take the train from Moor Street to Spring Road station and walk the half-mile from there. ➋

Burlington 6 Burlington Arcade, 126 New St

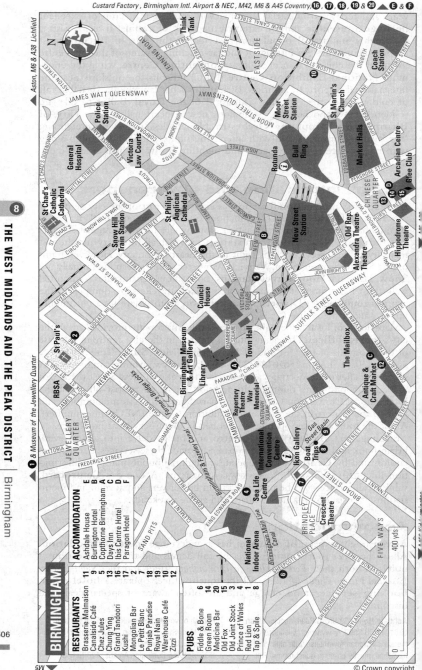

Custard Factory , Birmingham Intl. Airport & NEC , M42, M6 & A45 Coventry. 16 , 17 , 18 , 19 & 20 ▲ E & F

Aston, M6 & A38 Lichfield

1 & Museum of the Jewellery Quarter

M5 ▼

BIRMINGHAM

RESTAURANTS
Brasserie Malmaison	11
Canalside Café	9
Chez Jules	5
Chung Ying	13
Grand Tandoori	16
Kushi	1
Mongolian Bar	2
Le Petit Blanc	7
Punjab Paradise	18
Royal Nain	19
Warehouse Café	10
Zizzi	12

ACCOMMODATION
Ashdale House	E
Burlington Hotel	B
Copthorne Birmingham	A
Days Inn	C
Ibis Centre Hotel	D
Paragon Hotel	F

PUBS
Fiddle & Bone	6
Green Room	14
Medicine Bar	20
Old Fox	15
Old Joint Stock	3
Prince of Wales	4
Red Lion	19
Tap & Spile	8

400 yds

© Crown copyright

①0121/643 9191, ⓦwww.burlingtonhotel.com. Handsomely refurbished Victorian red-brick hotel with over one hundred bright and well-appointed rooms. Fitness facilities, too. ❽

Copthorne Birmingham Paradise Circus ①0121/200 2727, ⓦwww.milleniumhotels.com. It may look like a Rubik cube from outside, but this is a great hotel, partly because its 212 modern bedrooms are neat and trim, and partly because of its central location. Weekend prices drop a few codes. ❽

Days Inn 160 Wharfside Street, The Mailbox ①0121/643 9344, ⓦwww.daysinn.com. Modest chain hotel in a trendy setting – the newly devel- oped Mailbox complex has shops, restaurants and bars. ❹

Ibis Centre Ladywell Walk, Arcadian Centre ①0121/622 6010, ⓦwww.ibishotel.com. Rather characterless, but well-situated chain hotel, bang in the Chinese Quarter, near the major theatres and nightclubs. ❸

Paragon 145 Alcester St ①0121/627 0627, ⓦwww.paragonhotel.net. Splendid conversion of a Victorian workhouse about fifteen minutes' walk from New Street station out along Digbeth and its continuation High Street. Excellent-value doubles, though the surrounding area hardly inspires confidence. ❸

The City Centre

Many visitors get their first taste of central Birmingham at **New Street station**, whose unreconstructed ugliness – piles of modern concrete – makes a dispiriting start, though there are plans afoot to give the place a thorough facelift. Things soon get better west along pedestrianized **New Street**, one of the city's principal shopping streets, to the elegantly revamped **Victoria Square**. The adjacent **Chamberlain Square** has been refurbished too and holds the **Birmingham Museum and Art Gallery**, the city's finest museum. Further west still, is the glossy **International Convention Centre**, from where it's another short hop to the **Gas Street Basin**, the prettiest part of the city's serpentine canal system. Close by is canalside **Brindley Place**, a smart, brick and glass complex with slick cafés and bars and the enterprising **Ikon Gallery** of contemporary art.

From Brindley Place, it's a short walk southeast to the **Mailbox**, the immaculately rehabilitated former postal sorting office with yet more chic bars and restaurants, or you can head north along the old towpath of the **Birmingham and Fazeley canal** as far as Newhall Street. The latter is within easy walking distance of both **St Philip's Cathedral**, back in the centre on Colmore Row, and – in the opposite direction – the **Jewellery Quarter**, which holds an excellent museum and scores of workshops and retail outlets. Finally, the **Bullring**, at the east end of New Street, has been redeveloped with panache, while the nearby **Eastside** district is in the throes of massive regeneration, the first fruits of which are the **Think Tank** museum of science and discovery

Victoria and Chamberlain squares

At its west end, New Street opens out into the handsomely refurbished **Victoria Square**, whose centrepiece is a large and particularly engaging water fountain designed by Dhruva Mistry. The fountain's large and distinctive female figure is affectionately known as "the floozy in the jacuzzi" by the locals – but there's no such term of endearment for Anthony Gormley's rusting *Iron Man* lurking nearby, and leaning at a precarious angle like a Saturday-night drunk. The waterfall out-does poor old Queen Victoria, whose **statue** is glum and uninspired, though the thrusting self-confidence of her bourgeoisie is very apparent in the flamboyant buildings that frame the adjacent **Chamberlain Square**. Amongst the assorted ornate gables and cupolas, columns and towers, the **Council House** is the most impressive edifice, opened in 1879 and complete with a pair of proud lions.

Very different is Chamberlain Square's **Town Hall** of 1834, whose classical design – by Joseph Hansom, who went on to design Hansom cabs – was based on the Roman temple in Nîmes. In the middle of the square is a dinky neo-Gothic memorial in honour of **Joseph Chamberlain** (1836–1914), who made himself immensely popular by taking the city's gas and water supplies into public ownership.

The Birmingham Museum and Art Gallery

The **Birmingham Museum and Art Gallery** occupies a rambling, Edwardian building on Chamberlain Square (Mon–Thurs & Sat 10am–5pm, Fri 10.30am–5pm, Sun 12.30–5pm; free). Its several sections are spread over Floors 2 and 3, but the pick is the **art section**, which contains one of the world's most comprehensive collections of **Pre-Raphaelite** work, concentrated on Floor 2, in Rooms 14 and 17–19. Founded in 1848, the Pre-Raphaelite Brotherhood consisted of seven young artists, of whom Rossetti, Holman Hunt, Millais and Madox Brown are best known. The name of the group was selected to express their commitment to honest observation, which they thought had been lost with the Renaissance. Many of the Brotherhood's most important paintings are displayed here, including **Dante Gabriel Rossetti**'s (1828–1882) seminal *First Anniversary of the Death of Beatrice* (1849), inspired by Dante, and **Ford Madox Brown**'s (1821–1893) powerful image of emigration, *The Last of England* (1855). By 1853, the Brotherhood had effectively disbanded, but a second wave of artists carried on in its footsteps. The most prominent of them was **Edward Burne-Jones** (1833–98), who has an entire room to himself (Room 14) – his *Star of Bethlehem* is one of the largest watercolours ever painted, a mysterious, almost magical piece with earnest Magi and a film-star-like Virgin Mary. The rest of the art section, though not as memorable, contains a first-rate collection of eighteenth- to twentieth-century British art, and there's also a significant sample of **European** paintings.

Sharing Floor 2 is the **industrial art section**, kicking off with the **Industrial Gallery** and its locally produced stained glass, ceramics, metalwork – especially silver – and jewellery that amply illustrates the city's industrial prowess. Here also is the **Edwardian Tea Room**, one of the more pleasant places in Birmingham for a cuppa.

Moving on, Floor 1's cavernous **Gas Hall** is an impressive venue for touring art exhibitions, while the newly opened **Waterhall Gallery** (same times), just across Chamberlain Square from the main museum building, showcases modern and contemporary art including the likes of Francis Bacon and Bridget Riley.

To Gas Street Basin

From the north side of Chamberlain Square, walk through the hideously kitsch **Paradise Forum** shopping and fast-food complex to get to **Centenary Square**, where there's an unusual World War I war memorial. The square was entirely revamped to complement the showpiece **International Convention Centre** (ICC) and the **Birmingham Repertory Theatre**, but the sculpture that was designed as the centrepiece – *Forward* by Raymond Mason – has recently been burnt down

From the square, it's a brief stroll along Broad Street to the bridge over – and steps down to – **Gas Street Basin**, the hub of Birmingham's intricate **canal system**. There are eight canals within the city's boundaries, comprising no less than thirty-two miles of canal. The highpoint of canal construction was the late eighteenth century, when almost all heavy goods were transported by water. In the middle of the nineteenth century, the railways made the canals uneconomic, but they struggled on until the 1970s when tourism – and narrow boats – gave them a new lease of life. Much of Birmingham's surviving canal network slices through the city's grimy, industrial bowels, but certain sections have been immaculately restored, with Gas Street Basin leading the way. At the junction of the Worcester and Birmingham and Birmingham Main Line canals, the Basin, with its herd of brightly painted narrow boats, is edged by a delightful medley of old brick buildings. There's a good pub here – the *Tap & Spile* – and regular **boat trips** leave to explore the prettier parts of the system. There are several operators, but Second City Canal Cruises are as good as any (☎0121/236 9811; £3 per person). In summer, there's also a **water taxi** service between several stops along the central part of the canal system (July & Aug daily 10am–5pm; May, June & Sept Sat & Sun 10am–5pm; every 45mins; day pass £3.50).

Brindley Place and the Ikon Gallery

From the Basin, it's a short walk north along the canal towpath to the bars, shops and clubs of waterside **Brindley Place**, named after James Brindley the eighteenth-century engineer who was responsible for many of Britain's early canals. It's an extraordinarily successful – and aesthetically pleasing – development where you'll also find the city's celebrated **Ikon Gallery** (Tues–Sun 11am–6pm; free; ⓦwww.ikon-gallery.co.uk), housed in a lovely old Victorian building and one of the country's most imaginative venues for touring exhibitions of contemporary art.

Along the Birmingham & Fazeley canal to St Paul's Square

Just beyond Brindley Place, in front of the huge dome of the National Indoor Arena (NIA), the **canal forks**: the Birmingham & Fazeley leads northeast (to the right) and the Birmingham Main Line canal cuts west (to the left), though to complicate matters the latter has a spur loop here, going under Sheepcote Street. Also beside the main canal junction is the shell-like **National Sea Life Centre** (daily 10am–5pm, last admission 1hr before closing; £9; ☎0121/633 4700, ⓦwww.sealife.co.uk), which can't help but raise a few eyebrows, given the city's inland location. Nevertheless, it's an enterprising educational venture, offering Birmingham's landlubbers an opportunity to view and even touch many unusual varieties of fish and sea life – it's so popular with kids that bookings are advised during school holidays.

Beyond the main canal fork, the first part of the **Birmingham & Fazeley canal** has been attractively restored, its antique brick buildings cleaned of accumulated grime and leading to the quaint **Farmer's Bridge Locks**. Further on, however, things take a grittier aspect as the canal bores beneath the city centre amidst its industrial tangle. Emerging at **Newhall Street** (it's signed), about half a mile from the main canal junction, you're a stone's throw from **St Paul's Square**, flanked by sturdy Georgian buildings and one of the more agreeable parts of the centre. Here, beside the square in Dakota House, on Brook Street, the **Royal Birmingham Society of Artists** (RBSA; Mon–Wed & Fri 10.30am–5.30pm, Thurs 10.30am–7pm, Sat 10.30am–5pm; donation) offers an inventive range of fine art exhibitions.

St Philip's Cathedral

Also near at hand is **Colmore Row**, a busy shopping strip where pride of architectural place goes to **St Philip's Cathedral** (Mon–Fri 7am–7pm, Sat &

Sun 9am–5pm; free), a bijou example of English Baroque. Consecrated in 1715, St Philip's was initially a parish church that served as an overspill for St Martin's (see below). It was, however, in a more genteel location than the older church and when, in 1905, the Church of England decided to establish a new diocese in Birmingham, they made St Philip's the cathedral. The church was extended in the 1880s, when four new stained-glass windows were commissioned from local boy **Edward Burne-Jones**, a leading light of the Pre-Raphaelite movement (see p.508).

The Bullring – and the new Selfridges

Colmore Row lies just to the west of the city centre's pedestrianized core with chain stores and shopping precincts lining up along Corporation, New and High streets. At the intersection of New and High streets is the distinctive Modernism of the whopping **Rotunda**, but mercifully its neighbour, the notorious **Bullring** indoor shopping centre, which fulfilled every miserable cliché of 1960s town planning, has been demolished. The new Bullring shopping centre that has sprung up in its place would be a textbook example of safe contemporary planning were it not for the billowing organic swell of **Selfridges** protruding from its east side. Reminiscent of an inside-out octopus, Selfridges shimmers with an architectural chain mail of thousands of silver discs, altogether a bold and hugely successful attempt to create a popular city landmark. It was designed by Future Systems to resemble a sequinned dress, hence its nickname – the "Bobbles Building".

Nestling at the foot of the Bullring, **St Martin's church** has recently been cleared of its accumulated grime and now reveals itself to be a rather fetching amalgamation of the Gothic and the neo-Gothic, with fancifully carved decoration and a delightful Burne-Jones stained-glass window. Just to the south are the **Market Halls** (daily 7.30am–4pm), jam-packed with every conceivable knick-knack, all sold at bargain basement prices and supplemented by a **Rag Market** on Tuesdays, Thursdays and Saturdays (same times).

Digbeth's Custard Factory

From the Bullring, **Digbeth** – once the main thoroughfare through medieval Birmingham – falls away to the southeast. Jammed with traffic and jostled by decrepit industrial buildings, there are only two reasons to venture out here – the first is the bus station on the right, the second – on the left just along and off Gibb Street – is the arts complex that occupies the old **Alfred Bird Custard Factory**. The factory is a homely affair set around a friendly little courtyard and the **arts complex** offers a variety of workshops and has gallery space for temporary exhibitions of modern art. There are a couple of cafés and bars here, too (see p.513).

Eastside

Long a neglected corner of the city, **Eastside**, the grid of streets to the east of Moor Street Queensway – and north of Digbeth – is currently undergoing a major, pedestrian-friendly regeneration. First off the blocks has been the **Think Tank** (daily 10am–5pm; £6.95; ☎0121/202 2222, ⊛www.thinktank.ac), a brand new museum of science and discovery at the Millennium Point complex on Curzon street. The museum rambles over four floors with hands-on exhibits for all ages, a Lego robotics lab, and an imaginative exploration of the history of Birmingham. It's an excellent museum and made even more appealing by its neighbour, the **Imax theatre** (show times on ☎0121/202 2222, ⊛www.imax.ac; £6.00), where you can explore away in 3-D.

△ St Martin's Church and Selfridges

The Jewellery Quarter

Birmingham's long-established **Jewellery Quarter** lies just to the northwest of the city centre, about half a mile from Colmore Row via Newhall Street. Buckle-makers and toy-makers first colonized the area in the 1750s, opening the way for hundreds of silversmiths, jewellers and goldsmiths. There are still around five hundred jewellery-related companies in the district with most of the **jewellery shops** concentrated along Vittoria Street and the adjacent Frederick Street and Warstone Lane. The prime attraction hereabouts is the engrossing **Museum of the Jewellery Quarter**, 75–79 Vyse St (Mon–Fri 10am–4pm; Sat 11am–5pm; £3), a short walk north of the Frederick Street/Warstone Lane intersection. A visitor centre starts proceedings, detailing the growth and decline of the trade in Birmingham, but it's the old factory that steals the show. Here, the atmosphere and conditions of the old works are superbly re-created – the jewellers were wedged into tiny, hot and noisy spaces to churn out hundreds of earrings, brooches and rings. Their modern counterparts use the old machines to show how some of the most common designs were produced.

Eating and drinking

Central Birmingham has a bevy of first-rate **restaurants** with a string of smart, new venues springing up in the slipstream of the burgeoning conference and trade-fair business, particularly along Broad Street, near the ICC. There's also a concentration of decent, reasonably priced restaurants in the Chinese Quarter, just south of New Street station, on and around Hurst Street. Birmingham's gastronomic speciality is the **balti**, a delicious and astoundingly inexpensive Kashmiri stew cooked and served in a small wok-like dish called a *karahi*, with nan bread instead of cutlery. Although balti houses have opened up within the city centre, the original and arguably the best are in the gritty suburbs of **Balsall Heath**, a couple of miles to the south of the centre, and **Sparkhill**, about three miles to the southeast. Some of these are listed here – but note that many are unlicensed, so you may want to take your own booze.

The liveliest city centre **pubs**, catering for a mixed bag of conference delegates and Brummies-out-on-the-ale, are liberally sprinkled along Broad Street, in the immediate vicinity of the Convention Centre, and in Brindley Place.

Cafés and restaurants

Brasserie de Malmaison The Mailbox, Royal Mail St ☎0121/246 5000. Delicious French cuisine with a menu that concentrates on a particular – and changing – region of France. Moderate.

Canalside Café Gas St ☎0121/248 7979. Cosy café on the Gas Street Basin serving homemade snacks, cakes and fantastic cherry pies. Inexpensive.

Chez Jules 5a Ethel St, off New Street ☎0121/633 4664. Recommendable medium-priced French restaurant in the city centre, with especially good lunchtime deals. Moderate.

Chung Ying 16–18 Wrottesley St ☎0121/622 1793. Arguably the best Cantonese dishes in the Chinese Quarter, and always busy. Moderate.

Grand Tandoori 343 Stratford Rd, Sparkhill ☎0121/773 9244. Extensive balti menu in a concentration of other balti houses. Buses #4, #31 and #41 from the centre. Inexpensive.

Kushi 558 Moseley Rd, Balsall Heath ☎0121/449 2311. Excellent, award-winning balti house that's unlicensed, very inexpensive, and deservedly popular. Bus #50 from the centre.

Mongolian Bar 24 Ludgate Hill ☎0121/236 3842. Lively and enjoyable curry house, where you choose your ingredients and see them flash-fried before you. Just off the inner ring road. Moderate.

Le Petit Blanc 9 Brindley Place ☎0121/633 7333. Directly opposite the Ikon Gallery, this swish restaurant, with its slick modern furnishings and fittings, offers first-rate French cuisine with a touch of Asia thrown in. Reservations advised. Expensive.

Punjab Paradise 377 Ladypool Rd, Balsall Heath ☎0121/449 4110. One of the city's classic balti houses, specializing in milder dishes. Inexpensive.

Royal Nain 417 Stratford Rd, Sparkhill ☎0121/766 7849. Twice named Brum's best balti house – as good as it gets. Bus #6 from Corporation St. Inexpensive.

Warehouse Café 54 Allison St, Digbeth ☎0121/633 0261. Imaginative vegan and vegetarian café – ring for times and bring your own wine. Inexpensive.

Zizzi The Mailbox, Royal Mail St ☎0121/632 1333. Canalside restaurant that does great stone-baked pizzas. Good spot to nurse a drink too. Moderate.

Pubs and bars

Fiddle and Bone 4 Sheepcote St ☎0121/200 2223. Canalside pub-cum-restaurant with good old-fashioned decor and regular live music, often to a very high standard.

The Green Room Hurst St. Busy and very amenable bar opposite the Hippodrome. A good range of ales.

Medicine Bar Custard Factory, Gibb Street, off Digbeth. Great bar located in a laid-back arts complex that was once a custard factory. Turns into a club late at night – see *Medicine Bar*, below.

The Old Fox Arcadian Centre, Hurst Street. Over-modernized but popular pub, with an excellent selection of beers and a boisterous atmosphere.

Old Joint Stock 4 Temple Row West. Lively bar in an attractively reworked old bank.

Prince of Wales 84 Cambridge St. Old-fashioned haunt with long-standing custom from the Repertory Theatre, now pulling them in from the neighbouring ICC too. Very recommendable.

Red Lion 94 Warstone Lane. Appealing, traditional Brummie pub in the Jewellery Quarter.

Tap & Spile 10 Gas St. Charming traditional pub with low-beamed ceilings beside the canal on Gas Street Basin. Once the hangout of weathered canal men, it now attracts tourists and locals in equal measure.

Nightlife and entertainment

Nightlife in Birmingham is thriving, and the **club scene** is recognized as one of Britain's best, spanning everything from word-of-mouth underground parties to meat-market mainstream clubs. **Live music** is strong in the city, too, with big-name concerts at several major venues and other, often local bands appearing at some clubs and pubs. Birmingham's showpiece **Symphony Orchestra** and **Royal Ballet** are the spearheads of the city's resurgent classical scene. The social calendar also gets an added fillip from a wide range of up-market **festivals**, including the **Film and TV Festival** (☎0121/212 0999, ⓦ www.film-tv-festival.org.uk) in March, the **Jazz Festival** (☎0121/454 7020, ⓦ www.bigbearmusic.com) in the first two weeks of July and the three-day **Artsfest** (ⓦ www.artsfest.org.uk) of film, dance, theatre and music in September.

For current **information** on all events, performances and exhibitions, pick up a free copy of the excellent, fortnightly **What's On**, Birmingham's definitive listings guide. It's available at all of the tourist offices and many public venues.

Clubs

Air Heath Mill Lane, off Digbeth ☎0121/693 2633, ⓦ www.godskitchen.com. Shiny, high-tech superclub host to God's Kitchen and hundreds of house- and trance-hungry clubbers.

Baker's 162 Broad St ☎0121/633 3839. Intimate and energetic hard-house venue.

Bobby Brown's 52 Gas St ☎0121/643 2573. Chart sounds plus speciality nights. Popular with students.

House of God Various venues monthly. Birmingham's ever-popular techno night is still going strong and loud. This is the sound of the city.

The Jam House 1 St Paul's Square ☎0121/200 3030, ⓦ www.thejamhouse.co.uk. With Jools Holland as the musical director, there's nightly piano jams and a bluesy-jazz focus at this fashionable restaurant-club.

Medicine Bar Custard Factory, Gibb St, off Digbeth ☎0121/604 7777, ⓦ www .medicinebarbirmingham.co.uk. Eclectic and frequently impeccable music policy, plus juicy live events. One of the best nights out in town.

The Nightingale Essex House, Kent St ☎0121/622 1718, ⓦ www.nightingaleclub.co.uk. The king of Brum's gay clubs, but popular with straights too. Five bars, three levels, two discos, a café bar and even a garden. About ten minutes' walk south of New Street station, along Hurst Street.

Snob's 30 Paradise Circle ☏0121/643 5551, ⊛www.snobsnightclub.co.uk. Unashamed mosh pit heaving with indie and rock fans and abandonment galore.

Waterworks Jazz Club Gough St ☏0121/354 6059. Specialist jazz joint just off the inner ring road near Holloway Circus.

Classical music, theatre, comedy and dance

Alexandra Theatre Suffolk Street, Queensway ☏0870/607 7544. Mainstream pop concerts, musicals and plays.

Birmingham Repertory Theatre Broad St ☏0121/236 4455, ⊛www.birmingham-rep.co.uk. Mixed diet of classics and new work, featuring local and experimental writing.

The Crescent Theatre Sheepcote Street, Brindley Place ☏0121/643 5858, ⊛www.crescent -theatre.co.uk. Adventurous theatre group and venue for visiting companies.

Glee Club Arcadian Centre, Hurst St ☏0121/693 2248, ⊛www.glee.co.uk. Dedicated comedy club, with top national names and up-and-coming stars.

Hippodrome Theatre Hurst St ☏0870/7301234, ⊛www.birmingham -hippodrome.co.uk. Home to the Birmingham Royal Ballet and regularly hosts the Welsh National Opera. Also features touring plays and big pre- and post-West End productions, plus a splendiferous Christmas pantomime.

National Exhibition Centre (NEC) Bickenhill Parkway ☏0870/909 4133, ⊛www.necgroup.co.uk. The NEC's arena hosts major pop concerts. Ten miles east of the centre beside the M42; train from New Street to Birmingham International station.

Old Rep Theatre Station St ☏0121/236 5622. Britain's oldest repertory theatre, with regular performances by the imaginative Birmingham Stage Company.

Symphony Hall International Convention Centre, Broad St ☏0121/780 3333, ⊛www .symphonyhall.co.uk. Acoustically one of the most advanced concert halls in Europe, home of the acclaimed City of Birmingham Symphony Orchestra (CBSO), as well as a venue for touring music and opera.

Listings

Bookshops Waterstone's, 24 High St and 128 New St.

Bus enquiries Centro Hotline ☏0121/200 2700, ⊛www.centro.org.uk.

Car rental Avis, 17 Horse Fair ☏0121/622 5666 and at the airport ☏0121/782 6183; Europcar, at the airport ☏0121/782 6507; National, Bristol St ☏0121/622 6131 and at the airport ☏0121/782 5481.

Internet At the main Library, in the city centre on

Chamberlain Square. Free access for the first hour.

Laundry Clean & Care, 758 Alum Rock Rd.

Pharmacy Boots, 65 High St ☏0121/212 1631. Late-night opening roster posted in the window here and at the tourist office.

Post office 1 Pinfold St, on the corner with Victoria Square (Mon–Fri 9am–5.30pm, Sat 9am–6pm).

Taxis Toa Taxis ☏0121/427 8888, Radio Taxis ☏0121/764 6464.

Staffordshire

Spreading north from the Birmingham conurbation, the miscellaneous and low-key landscapes of **Staffordshire** don't enthral too many people. Nonetheless, the county packs in coachloads of visitors on account of **Alton Towers** (☏0870/4444455, ⊛www.altontowers.com; closed Nov–March; day pass £26, under-12s £21), the nation's most popular amusement park, with several million visitors annually howling and screaming on attractions with names that include *Nemesis* and *Ripsaw*. The white-knuckle rides take much more money than do the hoteliers in the cathedral city of **Lichfield**, at the southern end of Staffordshire, both the main historic attraction and the county's most agreeable town.

Lichfield

Some eighteen miles to the north of Birmingham, the pocket-sized town of **LICHFIELD** is a slow-moving, amiable kind of place that demands a visit for one reason – its magnificent sandstone **Cathedral** (daily 8am–6.30pm; £3 donation requested). Begun in 1085, but substantially rebuilt in the thirteenth and fourteenth centuries, the cathedral is unique in possessing three spires – an appropriate distinction for a bishopric that once extended over virtually all of the Midlands.

The **west front** is adorned by over one hundred statues of biblical figures, English kings and the supposed ancestors of Christ, some of them dating back to the thirteenth century, but mostly Victorian replacements of originals destroyed by Cromwell's troops.

Inside, the **nave** is graced by a long line of slender pointed arches, whose decorated capitals are set beneath an elaborately carved clerestory and a soaring vaulted roof that, taken together, resemble the ribcage of a giant beast. The transept's **St Michael's Chapel** is dedicated to the Staffordshire Regiment and its railings are decorated with replica Zulu shields to celebrate their involvement in the Zulu War; the sphinx does the same for another vainglorious campaign in Egypt, the 1882 suppression of the proto-nationalist uprising of Arabi Pasha. Beyond the transepts, the first three bays of the **choir** are the oldest part of the church, completed in the Early English style of the twelfth century, but thereafter the choir is resolutely middle Gothic. On the south side of the choir a narrow stone stairway leads up to a fine **minstrels' gallery** and the **St Chad's Head Chapel**, where the head of the saint associated with the cathedral was once displayed to cheer up the faithful. Most impressive of all, however, is the **Lady Chapel**, at the far end of the choir, which boasts a set of magnificent sixteenth-century windows, purchased from the Cistercian abbey at Herkenrode in Belgium in 1802.

The cathedral's greatest treasure, the **Lichfield Gospels**, are displayed in the **chapter house**, off the north side of the choir. A rare and exquisite example of Anglo-Saxon artistry dating to the eighth century, this illuminated manuscript contains the complete Gospels of Matthew and Mark, and a fragment of the Gospel of Luke, written in Latin and embellished with elaborate decoration. No one knows who wrote it, but it's likely it was produced locally. Different pages are exhibited at different times, but a particular favourite is the gorgeous Carpet Page, showing a decorative cross whose decorative blend of Coptic, Celtic and Oriental influences make it the equal of the more famous Irish *Book of Kells* and Lindisfarne Gospels (see p.761).

The rest of the town centre

The Cathedral is flanked by **The Close**, which, with its good-looking medley of Tudor, Georgian and Victorian buildings, is the prettiest place in town. From the Close, it's a short walk along **Dam Street** – past the gloomy waters of the Minster Pool – to the **Market Place**, where there's a peculiar little statue of a puck-nosed Boswell and a much better one honouring **Samuel Johnson**, who looks suitably intellectual.

At the back of the Market Place stands **St Mary's church**, home to the **Lichfield Heritage Centre** (Mon–Sat 10am–5pm, Sun 10.30am–5pm; £3.50), which tracks through the city's history, with an illuminating section on the Civil War. On the outside wall of the church several **plaques** commemorate noteworthy incidents. One of them is a memorial to the unfortunate Edward Wightman, who was burnt at the stake for heresy on this very spot in 1612 – the last Englishman to be so punished for this particular crime.

Also on the Market Place, is the **Samuel Johnson Birthplace Museum** (April–Sept daily 10.30am–4.30pm; Oct–March daily noon–4.30pm; £2.20).

Samuel Johnson

Eighteenth-century England's most celebrated wit and critic, **Samuel Johnson**, was born above his father's bookshop in Lichfield's Market Place in 1709. From Lichfield he went to Pembroke College, Oxford, which he left in 1731 without having completed his degree. Disgruntled with academia, Johnson returned to Staffordshire as a teacher, before settling in Birmingham for three years, a period that saw his first pieces published in the *Birmingham Journal*.

In 1735 Johnson married Elizabeth Porter, a Birmingham friend's widow twenty years his senior, returning to his home district to open a private school in the village of Edial, just outside Lichfield. The school was no great success, so after two years the Johnsons abandoned the project and went to London with the young **David Garrick**, their star pupil. Journalism and essays were the mainstay of the Johnsons' penurious existence until publisher Robert Dodsley asked Samuel to consider compiling a **Dictionary of the English Language**, a project that nobody had undertaken before, and which was to occupy him for eight years prior to its publication in 1755. Massively learned and full of mordant wit ("lexicographer: a writer of dictionaries; a harmless drudge"), the Dictionary is one of Johnson's greatest legacies, although he was financially and emotionally stretched to breaking point by the workload it imposed. The dictionary was widely acclaimed, but, despite his increasing celebrity, money problems continued to dog him – in 1759 he wrote the novel *Rasselas* in one week, in order to raise money for his mother's funeral. Nevertheless, Johnson's financial bacon was saved shortly afterwards when, in the early 1760s, the new king, George III, granted him a bursary of £300 per year.

In 1763 Johnson met James Boswell, a pushy young Scot who clung tenaciously to the cantankerous older man until he learned to like him. Their journey to Scotland resulted in one of the finest travel books ever written, **A Journey to the Western Isles of Scotland** (1775), in which Johnson's fascinated incredulity at the native way of life makes for utterly absorbing reading. Other publications from his final decade included a preface to Shakespeare's plays, a series of political tracts and the magnificent **Lives of the English Poets**. However, the work by which he is now best known is not one that he wrote himself – it's Boswell's **Life of Johnson**, commenced on its subject's death in 1784, published in 1791 and arguably still the English language's most full-blooded biography. Johnson was buried in Westminster Abbey.

The great man's father – Michael – was a bookseller and this house, a narrow four-storey affair, was both the family home and a bookshop. The museum's ground floor still serves as a bookshop – with copies of Boswell's biography and many of Johnson's works – whilst up above, on the first floor, a video provides a well-considered potted introduction to its subject.

Practicalities

Lichfield has two **train stations** – Lichfield City, with regular connections to and from Birmingham, is about five minutes' walk south of the centre, while Lichfield Trent Valley, served by mainline trains from London Euston, is on the eastern fringe of the city, about twenty minutes' walk from the centre. The **bus station** is opposite Lichfield City station. Clearly signed from all three stations, the city centre is dominated by the sprawling Three Spires Shopping Mall. The **tourist office** is currently on Bore Street, just off the Market Place, though there are plans to move to the west edge of Minster Pool, on Bird Street (April–Sept Mon–Sat 9am–5pm; Oct–March Mon–Fri 9am–4.45pm & Sat 9am–2pm; ☎01543/308209, ⓦ www.lichfield-tourist.co.uk).

Lichfield has a healthy selection of **cafés** and **restaurants**. The *Cathedral Coffee Shop*, on the south side of the Cathedral at 19 The Close (Mon–Sat

9.30am–5pm, Sun noon–5pm), is an old-fashioned café with inexpensive homemade food; or you could try the *Garrick Coffee Shop*, at 14 Dam Street, another inexpensive café serving a tasty line in pies. Bird Street, a brief walk west of the Market Place, holds a string of restaurants. These include *Don Paco*, a Spanish place at no. 28 (☎01543/300789; closed Sun), and a smart, modern Mongolian joint, the *Llama Palor*, at no. 17 (☎01543/411911). The **Lichfield Garrick Theatre** (☎01543/412121, ⊛www.lichfieldgarrick.com), right in the centre on Castle Dyke, offers a lively contemporary programme.

Derby and the Peak District

In 1951, the hills and dales of the **Peak District**, at the southern tip of the Pennine range, became Britain's first National Park. Wedged between **Derby**, Manchester and Sheffield, it's effectively the backyard for the fifteen million people who live within an hour's drive of its boundaries, though somehow it accommodates the huge influx with minimum fuss.

Landscapes in the Peak District come in two forms. The brooding high moorland tops of **Dark Peak**, fifteen miles east of central Manchester, take their name from the underlying gritstone, known as millstone grit for its former use – a function commemorated in the millstones demarcating the park boundary. Windswept, mist-shrouded and inhospitable, the flat tops of these peaks are nevertheless a firm favourite with walkers on the **Pennine Way**, which meanders north from the tiny village of **Edale** to the Scottish border. Altogether more forgiving, the southern limestone hills of the **White Peak** have been eroded into deep forested dales populated by small stone villages and often threaded by walking trails, some of which follow former rail routes. The limestone is riddled with complex cave systems around **Castleton** and under the region's largest centre, **Buxton**, a charming former spa town just outside the park's boundaries and at the end of an industrialized corridor that reaches out from Manchester. Two of the country's most distinctive manorial piles, **Chatsworth House** and **Haddon Hall**, stand near **Bakewell**, a town famed locally not just for its cakes but also for its **well-dressing**, a possibly pagan ritual of thanksgiving for fresh water that takes place in about thirty local villages each summer. The well-dressing season starts in early April and continues through to mid-September; a specialist leaflet, available at most tourist offices, gives the low-down on when and where.

There's no obvious **route** around the Peaks, but the one outlined below comes in from the south – from Derby – and then cuts up to Buxton before looping round in a clockwise direction to Castleton, Hathersage, Baslow, Bakewell and points in between. As for a **base**, you're spoiled for choice, but Buxton probably wins out with Eyam and Castleton coming a close second.

Public transport

There are frequent **trains** south from Manchester to end-of-the-line Buxton and Manchester–Sheffield trains cut through Edale and Hathersage. The main **bus access** is via the Trent Barton bus company's TransPeak service from Nottingham to Manchester via Derby, Matlock, Bakewell and Buxton; otherwise First Mainline's bus #272 runs regularly from Sheffield to Castleton, via Hathersage and Hope, and Stagecoach's bus #65 connects Sheffield to Buxton every hour or so. If you're not planning on walking or driving between towns and villages, you'll need the essential, encyclopedic **Peak District Bus**

Timetable (60p) as well as the free **Derbyshire Train Times booklet**, both of which are available at local tourist and National Park information offices. Various one-day **bus passes** allow unlimited travel to and within specified zones. The South Yorkshire Peak Explorer (£5.25) covers the chunk of the park in Yorkshire, the Wayfarer (£7) and the Derbyshire Wayfarer (£7.50) covers the rest. For all Peak District bus **timetable information** call ☎0870/608 2608.

The Peaks has a wide network of dedicated cycle lanes, tracks and old railway lines – and the National Park Authority provides a series of **cycle rental** outlets from which to make use of them (£12.50 per day, plus £20 deposit; 10 percent discount for YHA members). The centres are located at Ashbourne (☎01335/343156); Derwent (☎01433/651261); Hayfield (☎01663/746222); Middleton Top (☎01629/823204); Parsley Hay, Buxton (☎01298/84493); and Waterhouses (☎01538/308609).

Information and accommodation

The main **Peak District National Park Authority office** is at Aldern House, Baslow Road, Bakewell DE45 1AE (☎01629/816200, ⓦwww.peakdistrict.org). They operate a string of **information centres**, whose services supplement a host of town and village tourist offices. A variety of **maps** and **trail guides** are widely available, but for the non-specialist it's hard to beat the **Grate Little Guides**, a series of leaflets which provide hiking suggestions and trail descriptions for a dozen or so localities in a clear and straightforward style. They cost £1.80 each and are on sale at almost every tourist office and information centres, but note that the maps printed on the leaflets are best used in conjunction with an OS map. Finally, be sure to pick up a copy of the free and official **Peak District paper**, crammed with useful information and local news.

There's plenty of **accommodation** in and around the national park, mostly in B&Bs, though one of the area's distinctive features is the quality of its **country hotels** – like the ones in Ashford in the Water, Baslow and Hassop. The greatest concentration of first-rate hotels and B&Bs is, however, in the town of Buxton. The Peak District also holds numerous campsites and a dozen or so youth hostels as well as a network of YHA-operated **camping barns**. For further details, contact the YHA Camping Barns Reservation Office on ☎0870/770 6113 or ⓔcampingbarns@yha.org.uk.

Derby

The proximity of the Peak District might lead you to think that **DERBY**, forty miles northeast of Birmingham, could prove to be an interesting stopping-off point. Sadly, the city – a status conferred as recently as 1977 – is an unexciting place, though its workaday centre is partly redeemed by several long and handsome nineteenth-century stone terraces. There's also a fine **Cathedral** (daily 8.30am–6pm; free), whose pinnacled tower soars high above its modest, mostly Victorian surroundings on Queen Street – just north along Irongate from the spacious, central Market Place. The church's interior is of equal appeal, the wide and graceful Georgian nave sweeping down to a splendidly ornate wrought-iron rood screen.

Of the city's several museums, easily the best is the attractively laid-out **Derby Museum and Art Gallery** at the top of the Strand (Mon 11am–5pm, Tues–Sat 10am–5pm, Sun 2–5pm; free), a couple of minutes walk west from the Cathedral via Irongate and Sadlergate. Amongst a string of separate displays,

8

the museum exhibits a splendid collection of Derby **porcelain**, several hundred pieces tracking through the different phases and styles from the mid-eighteenth century until today. In addition, the museum possesses a first-rate collection of the work of **Joseph Wright** (1734–97), a local artist generally regarded as one of the most talented English painters of his generation. Wright's bread and butter came from portraiture, though his attempt to fill the boots of Gainsborough, when the latter moved from Bath to London, came unstuck – his more forceful style did not satisfy his genteel customers and Wright soon hightailed it back to Derby. Typical of his style is his portrait of *Sir Richard Arkwright*, looking uncompromising and very porky. Wright was one of the few artists of his period to find inspiration in technology and his depictions of the scientific world were hugely influential – as in his *The Alchemist Discovering Phosphorus* and *A Philosopher Lecturing on the Orrery*.

Practicalities

There are fast and frequent connections to many major cities – including Sheffield and Birmingham – from Derby **train station**, a mile to the south-east of the city centre: follow Midland Road and turn right onto London Road at the end, though it's a dreary walk, so best advice is to take a taxi. The **bus station** is more convenient, just off the inner ring road about five minutes' walk southeast of the Market Place, which is where you'll find the **tourist office** (Mon–Fri 9.30am–5.30pm, Sat 9.30am–5pm, Sun 10.30am–2.30pm; ☏01332/255802, ⓦwww.visitderby.co.uk). For a bite to **eat**, there are several good places on Sadler Gate including *Café B*, across from the Derby Museum and serving the best coffee in town.

Ashbourne

Sitting pretty on the edge of the Peaks twelve miles northwest of Derby, **ASH-BOURNE** is an amiable little town, whose stubby, cobbled **Market Place** is flanked by a happy ensemble of old stone buildings. Hikers tramp into town from the neighbouring dales to hang around the square's cafés and pubs, and stroll down the hill to take a peek at the suspended wooden beam spanning Church Street. Once a common feature of English towns, but now a rarity, these **gallows** were not warnings to malcontents, but advertising hoardings. Walk west along Church Street from here and you soon leave the bustling centre for a quieter part of town, all set beneath the soaring spire of **St Oswald's church**, an imposing lime- and ironstone structure dating from the thirteenth century. Something of an architectural muddle, the interior of the church is intriguing nonetheless, its columns decorated with all sorts of weathered sculptures and graced by handsome stained-glass windows, the best of which are exquisite examples of early twentieth-century Arts and Crafts design.

Practicalities

There are no trains to Ashbourne, but the town is easy to reach by bus from Derby, Buxton and Manchester. From Ashbourne **bus station**, it's a short walk to the Market Place – turn right out of the station, left at the T-junction and follow Dig Street over the river. The **tourist office**, on the Market Place (March–June, Sept & Oct Mon–Sat 9.30am–5pm; July & Aug Mon–Sat 9.30am–5pm, Sun 10am–4pm; Nov–Feb Mon–Sat 10am–4pm; ☏01335/343666), has oodles of hiking maps and guides and can also advise on **accommodation**, though Ashbourne is perhaps best regarded as a pit-stop rather than as a base for further wanderings. For **food**, *Ye Olde Vaults*, on the Market Place, serves competent bar meals, whilst the *Patrick & Brooksbank* delicatessen, 22 Market Place, has a superb selection of takeaway food, including local cheeses and hams.

Buxton

BUXTON, twenty miles north of Ashbourne, is now on the way up, its centre revamped with imagination and flair and a string of excellent hotels and B&Bs making it a perfect base for exploring much of the Peaks National Park. Additionally, it boasts the outstanding **Buxton Festival** (brochure line ☎01298/70395, tickets ☎0845/1272190; ⓦwww.buxtonfestival.co.uk), running for two weeks in July. It features a full programme of classical music, opera and literary readings, and has spawned the first-rate **Buxton Festival Fringe** (ⓦwww.buxtonfringe.com), with the emphasis on contemporary music, theatre and film.

Buxton has a long history as a **spa**, beginning with the Romans, but its salad days came at the end of the eighteenth century with the **fifth duke of Devonshire**'s grand design to create a northern answer to Bath or Cheltenham, a plan ultimately thwarted by the climate, but not before some distinguished buildings had been erected, most memorably The Crescent. Neither was Victorian Buxton a laggard, for although it may not have had quite the elan of its more southerly rivals, it still flourished, creating the raft of handsome stone houses that edge the town centre today.

Arrival and information

There's an hourly train service from Manchester Piccadilly to Buxton, terminating two minutes' walk from The Crescent at the **train station** on Station Road. The **TransPeak bus**, running every two hours between Manchester (Chorlton Street Coach Station) and Nottingham, stops in Buxton's Market Place, as do the regular buses from Sheffield. Buxton **tourist office** is in The Crescent (March–Oct daily 9.30am–5pm; Nov–Feb daily 10am–4pm; ☎01298/25106, ⓦwww.visitbuxton.co.uk) in what used to be the old Mineral Baths – hence the small display on Buxton's mineral water. They operate an accommodation booking service and have oodles of information on the town in particular and the Peaks in general.

Accommodation

The town centre is liberally sprinkled with first-rate **B&Bs** and **hotels**. Several of the best choices are located on the pedestrianized Broad Walk, where a string of distinguished Edwardian and Victorian stone houses face out onto the Pavilion Gardens. Finding somewhere is rarely a problem, except during the Buxton Festival in July (see above), when advance reservations are well-nigh essential.

Buxton's Victorian Guest House 3a Broad Walk ☎01298/78759, ⓦwww.buxtonvictorian.co.uk. Cosy B&B occupying one of the grand Victorian houses flanking Broad Walk and offering a handful of well-appointed rooms decorated in crossover traditional/modern style. Breakfasts feature local produce wherever possible. ❹

Grosvenor House Hotel 1 Broad Walk ☎01298/72439. There are eight en-suite guest rooms here in this well-appointed Victorian townhouse beside the Pavilion Gardens, each decorated in a modern rendition of period style. Tasty breakfasts plus evening meals by prior arrangement. ❸

Old Hall Hotel The Square ☎01298/22841, ⓦwww.oldhallhotelbuxton.co.uk. Nowhere in Buxton boasts more history than this hotel – Mary, Queen of Scots stayed here and so did Daniel Defoe. The building itself, with its fetching, ivy-clad

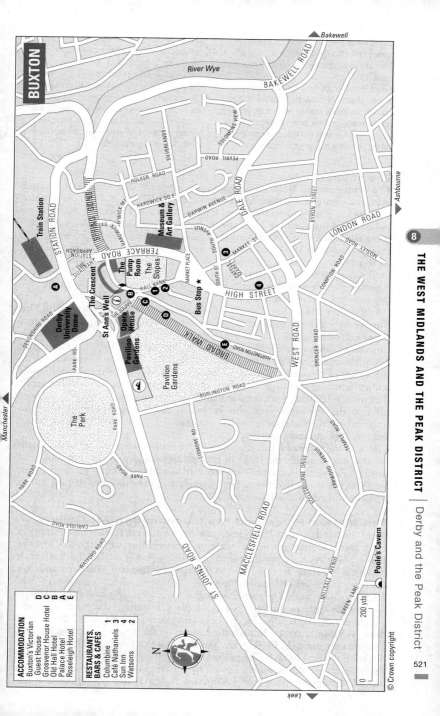

BUXTON

▲ Bakewell

River Wye

BAKEWELL ROAD

Train Station

SILVERLANDS

SOLOMONS VIEW

HOLKER ROAD

PEVRIL ROAD

HARDWICK MT

DALE ROAD

HARDWICK SQ E

Museum & Art Gallery

DARWIN AVENUE

BYRON STREET

STATION ROAD

THE QUADRANT

STATION APPROACH

HARDWICK ST

TERRACE ROAD

SOUTH AVENUE

SPRING GARDENS

Ⓐ

The Pump Room

The Crescent

The Slopes

SOUTH ST

MARKET ST

Ⓐ

LONDON ROAD

St Ann's Well

HALL BANK

MARKET PLACE

Ⓑ

①②

CAVENDISH CIRCUS

Opera House

ⓘ

Ⓒ

★ Bus Stop

Ⓓ

HIGH STREET

Ⓐ

COMPTON ROAD

MOSLEY ROAD

Derby University Dome

Pavilion Gardens

Ⓓ

HARTINGTON ROAD

BURTON MARKET

Ⓔ

WEST ROAD

SPENCER ROAD

PARK RD.

Pavilion Gardens

BURLINGTON ROAD

The Park

PARK ROAD

LISMORE RD

ECCLESBOURNE DRIVE

FERNWOOD AVENUE

FAIRFIELD ROAD

PARK ROAD

MACCLESFIELD ROAD

ST JOHNS ROAD

GREEN LANE

MILLDALE AVENUE

Poole's Cavern

◀ Manchester

CARLISLE ROAD

WATFORD ROAD

N

© Crown copyright

▼ Leek

▼ Ashbourne

8

THE WEST MIDLANDS AND THE PEAK DISTRICT | Derby and the Peak District

521

ACCOMMODATION
Buxton's Victorian Guest House D
Grosvenor House Hotel C
Old Hall Hotel B
Palace Hotel A
Roseleigh Hotel E

RESTAURANTS, BARS & CAFÉS
Columbine 1
Café Nathaniels 3
Sun Inn 4
Watsons 2

200 yds

0

facade, dates from the middle of the sixteenth century and, although the interior is much later, it maintains an appealingly antique air in its public rooms. **6**

Palace Hotel Palace Road ☎01298/22001, ⓦwww.paramount-hotels.co.uk/palace. Built to impress, the *Palace* was the pride of the Victorian spa, its sweeping stone facade lording it over the town centre. The hotel is a little careworn today, but the bedrooms are very comfortable and although the decor is modern, many have a quirky antique charm. Substantial discounts are commonplace – ring ahead to check. **7**

Roseleigh Hotel 19 Broad Walk ☎01298/24904, ⓦwww.roseleighhotel.co.uk. This classic three-storey gritstone Victorian townhouse is an excellent place to stay, its neat and trim public rooms decorated in attractive modern style, the en-suite bedrooms beyond similarly well appointed. **3**

The town centre

The centrepiece of Buxton's hilly, compact centre is **The Crescent**, a broad sweep of Georgian stonework commissioned by the 5th Duke of Devonshire in 1780 and modelled on the Royal Crescent in Bath. It's recently been refurbished, but remains empty while the townsfolk discuss its future, one good idea being the creation of a brand new thermal baths. Facing The Crescent, the old **Pump Room** of 1894 provides space for art and crafts exhibitions, while the adjacent water **fountain**, supplied by St Ann's Well, is still used to fill many a local water bottle. For a better view of The Crescent, clamber up **The Slopes**, a narrow slice of park that rises behind the Pump Room dotted with decorative urns and a war memorial.

At the west end of The Crescent, the appealing old stone buildings of **The Square** – though square it isn't – nudge up to the grandly refurbished **Buxton Opera House** (guided tours £3; ring ☎0845/127 2190 for schedule), an Edwardian extravagance whose twin towers, cherubs and tiffany glass date from 1903. Stretching back from the Opera House is the **Pavilion Gardens**, a slender string of connected buildings distinguished by their wrought-iron work and culminating in a large and glassy dome. The pavilions are actually a good deal more interesting from outside than from within, reason enough to wander off into the adjoining park, also known as the **Pavilion Gardens**, whose immaculate lawns and neat borders are graced by a bandstand, ponds, dinky little footbridges and fountains.

Back at the Opera House, it's impossible not to notice the enormous **dome** of what was originally the Duke of Devonshire's stables and riding school, built in 1789. For decades, the building was used as a hospital, but it's recently been purchased by the University of Derby, who are in the process of turning it into a leisure and educational complex.

The Market Place and the Museum and Art Gallery

From the south end of The Square, the fetching stone terrace that comprises **Hall Bank** scuttles up to the wide and breezy but traffic-choked **Market Place**. There's nothing much here to hold the eye, but it's only a few yards back down the hill along Terrace Road to the first-rate **Buxton Museum and Art Gallery** (Tues–Fri 9.30am–5.30pm, Sat 9.30am–5pm & Easter–Sept Sun 10.30am–5pm; free). The museum begins well with its ground floor largely devoted to enterprising temporary displays featuring the work of local contemporary artists. Upstairs, the large and extremely proficient "Wonders of the Peak" display tracks through the history of the region from its geological construction through the Romans and on to the Victorians. One of the most diverting sections looks at the prehistoric hilltop forts that lie dotted over the Peaks, another examines the relics left by the Anglo-Saxons, most notably the incised Crosses at Eyam (see p.528) and Bakewell (see p.530). Best of all, however, is the section dealing with the **petrifactioners**, who turned local semiprecious stones into ornaments and jewellery designed to tickle the fancy of the visitors who arrived here in numbers after the duke had put Buxton on the tourist map.

Eating and drinking

Buxton has several great places to eat, with one of the best **restaurants** in town being the *Columbine*, a small and intimate place in the centre at 7 Hall Bank (℡01298/78752; closed Sun & Tues in winter). The menu here is short but imaginative with main courses averaging £12. An excellent second choice is the *Sun Inn*, a fine old pub with antique beamed rooms just south of the Market Place at 33 High Street. They offer fine ales and first-rate bar food – beef in ale, for instance, at £7.50. A third very recommendable spot is *Café Nathaniel's*, just off the Market Place at 11 Market Street, where, amidst the stripped wood interior, they serve an excellent range of moderately priced seafood. The best place for a **pint** is the *Sun Inn* (see above), but you could also check out *Watsons*, on Hall Bank, a café-bar with frequent live music, especially jazz.

Castleton

The agreeable little village of **CASTLETON**, ten miles northeast of Buxton, lies on the northern edge of the White Peak, its huddle of old stone cottages ringed by hills and set beside a babbling brook. As a base for local walks, the place is hard to beat and the hikers resting up in the quiet Market Place, just off the main drag behind the church, have the choice of a healthy spread of local accommodation and services. Overseeing the whole ensemble is **Peveril Castle** (April–Oct daily 10am–6pm; Nov–March Wed–Sun 10am–4pm; £2.50; EH), from which the village takes its name. William the Conqueror's illegitimate son William Peveril raised the first fortifications here to protect the king's rights to the forest that then covered the district, but most of the remains – principally the ruinous square keep – date to the 1170s. After a stiff climb up to the keep, you can trace much of the surviving curtain wall, which commands great views of the Hope Valley down below with the swollen mass of Mam Tor rising to the west.

The Peak and Speedwell caverns

The limestone hills pressing in on Castleton are riddled with water-worn **cave systems** and four of them have been developed as tourist attractions. They can all be reached by car or on foot – a three and a half mile circular trail that begins in the village and takes two hours; the tourist office (see p.524) has the leaflet and sells the maps. **Peak Cavern** is the handiest (April–Oct daily 10am–5pm; Nov–March Sat & Sun 10am–5pm; £5.50; ℡01433/620285), tucked in a gully at the back of the village, its gaping mouth once providing shelter for a rope factory and a small village. Daniel Defoe, visiting in the eighteenth century, noted the cavern's colourful local name, the **Devil's Arse**, after the fiendish fashion in which the interior contours twisted and turned – hence the signs of today. Most visitors settle for just one set of caves – and either the Peak or the Treak Cliff Cavern (see p.524) will do very nicely – but it's only six hundred yards or so west from the village along the main road to **Speedwell Cavern** (daily: April–Oct 9.30am–6pm; Nov–March 10am–4.30pm; last entry 1hr before closing; £6; ℡01433/620512). At 600 feet below ground, this is the deepest of the four cave systems, but the main drama comes with the means of access – down a hundred dripping steps and then by boat through a quarter-mile-long claustrophobic tunnel that was blasted out in search of lead. At the end lies the Bottomless Pit, a pool where 40,000 tons of mining rubble were dumped without raising the water level one iota.

The Treak Cliff and Blue John caverns

The other two caves are the world's only source of the sparkling fluorspar known as **Blue John**. Highly prized for ornaments and jewellery since Georgian times, this semiprecious stone comes in a multitude of hues from blue through deep red to yellow, depending on its hydrocarbon impurities. Before being cut and polished, it is soaked in pine resin, a process originally carried out in France, where the term *bleu et jaune* (after its primary colours) provided its English name. The **Treak Cliff Cavern** (daily: March–Oct 10am–5pm; Nov–Feb 10am–4pm; last entry 40min before closing; £5.60; ☎01433/620571), across the main road some four hundred yards from Speedwell, contains the best examples of the stone *in situ* and a good deal more in the shop. This is also the best cave to visit in its own right, dripping – literally – with stalactites (some up to 100,000 years old), flowstone and bizarre rock formations, all visible on an entertaining forty-minute walking tour through the main cave system. Water collected in one of the caves is used to make tea in the café at the entrance – it's much purer than the stuff that pours from local taps.

Further afield, just two miles or so west of Castleton off the B6061, tours of **Blue John Cavern** (daily: April–Oct 9.30am–5.30pm; Nov–March 9.30am–dusk; £6.50; ☎01433/620638) dive deep into the rock, with narrow steps and sloping paths following an ancient watercourse. The tour leads through whirlpool-hollowed chambers to Lord Mulgrave's Dining Room, a cavern where the eponymous lord and owner once put on a banquet for his miners. A goodly sample of Blue John is on sale at the cavern gift shop.

Practicalities

Easily the most scenic approach to Castleton is from the west, either along the A625 or the A623/B6061, though they merge just to the west of the village to wiggle through the dramatic Winnats Pass. However, the principal **bus** service to Castleton arrives from the east from Sheffield and Hathersage. It's First Mainline's bus #272 and it runs hourly. The only bus from Buxton to Castleton is Stagecoach's bus #203, but this only operates on summer weekends and even then only once daily. The nearest **train station** is at Hope, a couple of miles or so to the east of Castleton along the valley. The station is on the Manchester Piccadilly, Hope Valley and Sheffield line and there are trains every hour or two; bus #272 links Hope station with Castleton. The brand new **Castleton Centre** (daily: April–Sept 9.30am–5.30pm, Oct–March 10am–5pm; ☎01433/621656), a combined museum, visitor centre and tourist office, stands beside the car park on the west side of the village, just off the main street, which dog-legs through Castleton doubling as the A625. They sell hiking leaflets and maps and operate an accommodation booking service.

Accommodation is plentiful, but should be booked in advance at holiday times. Cream of the **B&B** crop is *Bargate Cottage*, in a modernized old cottage at the top end of the Market Place (☎01433/620201, ⓦwww.bargatecottage.co.uk; no credit cards; ❷). They have three, well-kept en-suite rooms, each kitted out in frilly modern style, and the breakfasts are first-rate. Another inexpensive option is the *Cryer House*, just off the Market Place opposite the church on Castle St (☎01433/620244; no credit cards; ❷). This B&B occupies an older building as well and has just two guest rooms – plus a pleasant conservatory. The best pub lodgings are at *Ye Olde Nag's Head* (℡01433/620248; ❺), a heavily revamped old coaching inn on the main street. Finally, the lively **youth hostel** (℡0870/770 5758, ⓦwww.yha.org.uk; closed Jan; dorm beds £11.50) is housed in Castleton Hall, a capacious old stone mansion on the Market Place. The hostel is well equipped with a self-catering kitchen, a café, cycle store and drying room, and its 150 beds are parcelled up among two- to eight-bedded rooms, many of which are en suite.

For **food**, Castleton's pubs are its gastronomic mainstay and there's nowhere better than the *Castle*, opposite the church on Castle Street, which offers tasty bar food at very affordable prices. Alternatively, *Ye Olde Nag's Head*, on the main street, offers more-than-competent bar food (6–9pm), including home-made steak and Guinness pies, and also holds the *Stables Tearoom* (daily 9am–5.30pm), good for snacks and light meals.

Edale village

There's almost nothing to **EDALE village**, some seven miles by road from Castleton, except for a slender, half-mile trail of stone houses, which march up the main street from the train station with a couple of pubs, an old stone church and a scattering of B&Bs on the way – and it's this somnambulant air that is of immediate appeal. Walkers arrive in droves throughout the year to set off on the 250-mile **Pennine Way** (see box, p.526) across England's backbone to Kirk Yetholm on the Scottish border; the route's starting-point is signposted from outside the Old Nag's Head at the head of the village.

An excellent **circular walk** (9 miles; 5hr) uses the first part of the Pennine Way, leading up onto the bleak gritstone, table-top of **Kinder Scout** (2088ft), below which Edale cowers. The route cuts west from the Old Nag's Head – along a packhorse route once used by Cheshire's salt exporters – to reach the campsite and **camping barn** at Upper Booth Farm (℡0870/770 6113). From here, you climb the path called Jacob's Ladder and then continue half a mile west to the carved medieval **Edale Cross**. Backtracking a couple of hundred yards, the Pennine Way branches north along the broken edge of the plateau to **Kinder Downfall**, Derbyshire's highest cascade. This was the site of the Kinder Scout Trespass of 1932, when dozens of protesters walked onto unused but private land, five subsequently receiving prison sentences. It was the turning point in the fight for public access to open moorland, leading, three years later, to the formation of the Ramblers' Association. At Kinder Downfall, turn east then southeast across the often boggy peat towards the wind-sculpted **Wool Pack** rocks, then across to the eastern rim, where a path to the south along Grindslow Knoll and down into Edale avoids Grindsbrook Clough, the highly eroded route of the original Pennine Way. It can be extremely wet up here among the bare furrows of peat – as long-distance walker John Hillaby recorded on his *Journey Through Britain*. Hillaby had to resort to removing his footwear to make his way across the sodden top of Kinder Scout, which to his appalled mind looked as if it was "entirely covered in the droppings of dinosaurs".

Practicalities

Edale village is about five miles northwest of Castleton by road, slightly more by footpath. Hourly **trains** from Manchester, Sheffield and Hathersage provide surprisingly easy access. **Buses** #200 and #260 supplement the trains with a reasonably frequent service from Castleton. From Edale train station, it's 400 yards or so up the road to the **Peak District National Park Information Centre** (daily 9am–1pm & 2–5pm; ℡01433/670207). They sell all manner of trail leaflets and hiking guides and can advise about local accommodation. The nearest **youth hostel**, the extremely popular *Edale YHA Activity Centre* (℡0870/770 5808, ✉edale@yha.org.uk; dorm beds £11.50), lies two miles east of Edale station, in an old country house at Rowland Cote, Nether Booth. It's clearly signed from the road into Edale or you can hoof it there across the fields from behind the information centre. There are 150 beds in two- to twelve-bedded rooms and a good range of facilities from a laundry and a café through to a self-catering kitchen. Naturally enough, the hostel is popular with Pennine Way walkers – as is the YHA **camping barn** at Cotefield Farm, Ollerbrook (℡0870/770 6113), which lies on the path from the village to the hostel. There are two village **campsites**, *Fieldhead* (℡01433/670386), behind the information centre, and *Cooper's* at Newfold Farm (℡01433/670372), in the centre of Edale near the *Old Nag's Head*.

Those without hair shirts, or with more money, will do better at Edale's **B&Bs**, starting with *Stonecroft*, a detached Victorian house with two pleasantly comfortable guest rooms in the village near the church (℡01433/670262, Ⓦwww.stonecroftguesthouse.co.uk; ③). Nearby, in another old stone house, is *Mam Tor B&B* (℡01433/670253, Ⓦwww.edale-valley.co.uk/mamtor.htm; no credit cards; ①), which offers three pleasant guest rooms. As for **food**, there are only two options – the *Rambler*, yards from the train station at the bottom of the village, and the *Old Nag's Head*, at the top. Both are hiker-friendly and both serve bar food, though the *Rambler* has the edge.

Hathersage

Hilly **HATHERSAGE**, five miles east of Castleton and just eleven from Sheffield on the A625, has a hard time persuading people not to pass straight through into the heart of the Peaks. This little town is, however, worth at least an hour of anyone's time, the prime target being the much restored **church of St Michael and All Angels**, a good-looking stone structure perched high on the hill on its eastern edge. The views out over the surrounding countryside are delightful and, enclosed within a miniature iron fence in the churchyard opposite the porch, is the grave – or at least what legend asserts to be the grave – of Robin Hood's old sparring partner, **Little John**. Hathersage's other claim to fame is its association with Charlotte Brontë's **Jane Eyre**. The title of the book was borrowed from a certain James Eyre, a former landlord of the *George Hotel*, and the book's "Morton" takes its name from the landlord – James Morton – who met Charlotte off the stagecoach from Haworth when she came to stay here in 1845. Charlotte was visiting a friend, whose brother was the local vicar, and Charlotte was doubtless shown the Eyre brasses, inside the church beside the table-tomb of Robert Eyre (d.1459) – another prompt for the title.

In the 1800s, Hathersage became a needle-making centre with a string of factories billowing out dust and dirt. The needle grinders were the best paid factory workers, but most of them didn't last very long – the metallic dust simply killed them off. Those dangerous days are long gone, but the metalworking tradition has been revived by the Sheffield designer David Mellor, who has set up his factory in the distinctive **Round Building**, a comely gritstone edifice with a sweeping lead roof. The attached Country Shop (Mon–Sat 10am–5pm, Sun 11am–5pm; ☎01433/650220, ⓦwww.davidmellordesign.com) sells the full range of Mellor cutlery, tableware and kitchenware – but you pay for the quality. The factory is about half a mile south of town on the B6001, beyond the train station.

Practicalities

Hathersage is on the Manchester–Sheffield rail line and from the town **train station** it's about five hundred yards north to the scattering of shops, banks and pubs that comprise the centre, strung along the main street, which doubles as the A625. Among several **buses** to Hathersage, one of the most useful is the frequent First Mainline bus #272 linking Sheffield and Castleton. In Hathersage, it stops on the main street outside the *Best Western George Hotel* (☎0845/456 0581, ⓦwww.george-hotel.net; ❼), a one-time coaching inn with an immaculate interior that remains very much *the* place to stay – don't be deterred by the discordant stone facade. Hathersage **youth hostel** (☎0870/770 5852, ⓦwww.yha.org.uk; dorm beds £10.25) occupies a rambling Victorian house on the main road just to the west of the *George*. It has forty beds, in two- to six-bedded rooms, and a good range of facilities, including a self-catering kitchen.

The *George* has a first-rate **restaurant** featuring a canny amalgamation of traditional and modern dishes with main courses averaging around £14. A second good choice is the inexpensive *Longland's Eating House*, (Mon 11am–5pm, Tues–Fri 10am–5pm, Sat & Sun 9am–6pm), a laid-back, vegetarian café above a hiking/outdoors shop across from the *George*.

Eyam

Within a year of September 7, 1665, the lonely lead-mining settlement of **EYAM** (pronounced "Eem"), five miles south of Hathersage, had lost almost half of its population of 750 to the bubonic plague, a calamity that earned it the enduring epithet "The Plague Village". The first victim was one George Vicars, a journeyman tailor who is said to have released some infected fleas into his lodgings from a package of cloth he had brought here from London. Acutely conscious of the danger to neighbouring villages, William Mompesson, the village rector, speedily organized a self-imposed quarantine, arranging for food to be left at places on the parish boundary. Payment was made with coins left in pools of disinfecting vinegar in holes chiselled into the old boundary stones – and these can still be seen at **Mompesson's Well**, half a mile up the hill to the north of the village and accessible by footpath. The rector closed the church and held services in the open air at a natural rock arch to the south of the village – and every year since 1906, on the last Sunday in August, a commemorative service has been held here, at Cucklet Delph. Mompesson himself survived the plague, though his wife did not – poor reward for a man whose endeavours prevented the plague from spreading across the Peaks.

Long, thin and hilly, Eyam is little more than one main street – Church and then Main Street – that trails west up from **The Square**, which is really no more than a crossroads overlooked by a few old stone houses. First up of interest along Church Street is the comely **church of St Lawrence** (Easter–Sept Mon–Sat 9am–6pm, Sun 1–5.30pm; Oct–Easter Mon–Sat 9am–4pm, Sun 1–5.30pm; free), of medieval foundation but extensively revamped in the nineteenth century. In the church graveyard a few feet from the entrance stands a conspicuous, eighth-century carved **Celtic cross** and close by is the distinctive **table-tomb** of Mompesson's wife, whose sterling work nursing sick villagers is recalled every Remembrance Day when red roses are left beside her tomb. Inside the church, informative panels reveal more of the village's plague history, highlighting a number of associated sites in and around the village. The most harrowing of these is the **Riley Graves**, in open country half a mile east of The Square, where a certain Elizabeth Hancock buried her husband, three sons and three daughters within the space of six days in 1666.

Much nearer at hand, immediately to the west of the church, are the so-called **plague cottages**, where plaques explain who died where and when – it was here that Vicars met his maker. Another short hop brings you to **Eyam Hall** (guided tours late May to Aug Wed, Thurs & Sun 11am–4pm; £4.50), which was built for Thomas Wright a few years after the plague ended, possibly in an attempt to secure his position as the squire of the depleted village. Wright's heirs have lived in it ever since, building up a mildly diverting collection of furnishings, family portraits, tapestries, costumes and incidental bygones. Some of the adjacent farm buildings have been turned into a **Craft Centre** (Tues–Sun 10.30am–5pm; free) with a restaurant and gift shop.

Practicalities

Buses to Eyam – from Sheffield, Manchester, Buxton, Hathersage, Bakewell and Baslow – all stop on The Square, and one or two also run along Main/Church Street. Amongst a handful of **B&Bs**, the pick is the *Delf View House* (①01433/631533, Ⓦwww.delfviewhouse.co.uk; no credit cards; ❺), a beautifully kept Georgian villa set in its own grounds just along and across the street from the church; breakfast is served in a superb old dining room with a flagstone floor, imposing fireplace and beamed ceiling. A second choice is the *Miner's Arms*, in antique premises just off The Square on Water Lane (①01433/630853; ❹), which has seven perfectly adequate, en-suite rooms of a modern disposition. Finally, there's the well-equipped **youth hostel** (①0870/7705830, Ⓔeyam@yha.org.uk; £11.50), which occupies an idiosyncratic Victorian house whose ersatz medieval towers and turrets overlook Eyam from amidst wooded grounds on Hawkhill Road, a stiff, half-mile walk up from the museum. There are sixty beds here in two- to eight-bedded rooms, but note that opening dates and times vary – ring ahead for details.

The best place **to eat** is the *Miner's Arms*, which serves delicious bar meals as well as very enjoyable and moderately priced, traditional British dinners in its restaurant every evening except Sunday and Monday.

Baslow

BASLOW, on the north edge of the Chatsworth estate (see below) some four miles southeast of Eyam, is a little village, whose oldest stone cottages string prettily along the River Derwent. The village possesses several **B&Bs**, the best of which is *The Old School House*, in attractive Victorian premises in the centre on School Lane (℡01246/582488; ❹). Even better – and one of the Peak's greatest luxuries – is *Fischer's Baslow Hall* (℡01246/583259, ⓦwww.fischers-baslowhall .co.uk; ❼), a mile or so out of the village back towards Eyam along the A623. In its own grounds, the hall is picture-postcard perfect, a handsome Edwardian building made of local stone with matching gables and a dinky canopy over the front door. The interior is suitably lavish and the service attentive with rooms both in the main building and in the Garden House annexe next door. The **restaurant** is superb too, and has won several awards for its imaginative cuisine – or you can pop back into Baslow for a bite at the excellent *Avant Garde Café* (daily 9am–5pm), where they serve a delicious range of salads and light meals in bright, modern surroundings; the café is opposite St Anne's church.

Chatsworth House

Fantastically popular, **Chatsworth House** (April to late Dec daily 11am–5.30pm, last admission 4.30pm; gardens till 6pm, last admission 5pm; house & gardens £8.50, gardens only £5), just south of Baslow via the A619, was built in the seventeenth century by the first duke of Devonshire. It has been owned by the family ever since and several of them have done a bit of tinkering – the sixth duke, for instance, added the north wing in the 1820s – but the end result is remarkably harmonious. The house is seen to best advantage from the **B6012**, which meanders across the estate to the west of the house, giving a full view of its vast Palladian frontage, whose clean lines are perfectly balanced by the undulating partly wooded **parkland**, which rolls in from the south and west. The B6012 also gives access to the immaculately maintained estate village of **EDENSOR**, whose sturdy stone houses are well worth a look in their own right, and a signed turning off it leads to the house itself.

Many visitors forgo the house altogether, concentrating on the gardens instead, and this is understandable given the predictability of the assorted baubles accumulated by the family over the centuries. Nonetheless, amongst the maze of grand staircases and grandiose rooms, there are several noteworthy highlights, including the ornate ceilings of the **State Apartments**, daubed with strikingly energetic cherubs. In the apartments is the **State Bedroom**, where pride of place goes to the four-poster in which King George II breathed his last, and the anachronistic **Oak Room**, kitted out with overpoweringly heavy oak panelling in the 1840s. There's also the showpiece **Great Dining Room**, which has its table set as it was for the visit of George V and Queen Mary in 1933. And then there are the paintings. Amongst many, Frans Hals, Tintoretto, Veronese and Van Dyck all have a showing and there's even a Rembrandt – *A Portrait of an Old Man* – hanging in the chapel. The sixth duke also added a **Sculpture Gallery** to show all the tackle he had acquired on his travels, mostly large-scale Italian sculptures, but here also is the Chatsworth tazza, probably the largest Blue John vase in the world; for more on this semi-precious stone, see p.524.

Back outside, the **gardens** are a real treat and owe much to the combined efforts of Capability Brown, who designed them in the 1750s, and Joseph Paxton (designer of London's Crystal Palace), who had a bash seventy years later. Amongst all sorts of fripperies, there are water fountains, a rock garden, an artificial waterfall, a grotto and a folly as well as a nursery and greenhouses. Afterwards, you can wend your way to the **café** in the handsomely converted former Stables.

The best way to get to Chatsworth House is **on foot** along one of the footpaths that lattice the estate. It's easy walking and the obvious departure point is Baslow on the northern edge of the estate. The "Grate Little Guide" (see p.518) to Chatsworth describes an especially pleasant four-mile loop through the estate, taking in the house and beginning and ending in Baslow. By **bus**, take any Bakewell–Baslow bus and ask to be put off at Edensor, from where it's about one mile east across the park to the house.

Bakewell and around

BAKEWELL, flanking the banks of the River Wye four miles southwest of Baslow – and twelve miles east of Buxton – is famous for its **Bakewell Pudding**. Known throughout the rest of the country as a Bakewell Tart, this is a wonderful slippery, flaky, almond-flavoured confection – now with a dab of jam – invented here around 1860 when a cook botched a recipe for strawberry tart. Almost a century before this fortuitous mishap, the duke of Rutland set out to turn what was then a remote village into a prestigious spa, thereby trumping the work of his rival, the duke of Devonshire, in Buxton. The frigidity of the water made failure inevitable, leaving only the prettiness of **Bath Gardens** at the heart of the town centre, beside the crossroads Rutland Square, as a reminder of the venture.

Famous tart apart, Bakewell is an undemanding place today, its main streets too crowded by traffic – and tourists – to be much fun, though it is within easy striking distance of several first-rate attractions. In town, there is some interest in the web of narrow shopping streets around **Water Street**, just off the main drag near Rutland Square, as well as in the nearby **riverside walkway**, but the most agreeable part of Bakewell trails up the hill at the west end of the centre. Here, strolling up North Church Street, with its line of comely stone cottages, you soon reach **All Saints church**, the result of centuries of architectural fiddling from the Normans onwards. Outside, in the churchyard, is a rare **Saxon cross**, carved with decorative circles and scrolls, and inside in the south transept's Vernon Chapel are the **tombs** of the Vernons/Manners, local bigwigs who long ruled the Bakewell roost. The finest is that of George Manners, whose alabaster effigy is set above his kneeling children plus the baby he lost at birth, all wrapped up in swaddling clothes.

Practicalities

Bakewell doesn't have a train station, but there are regular **buses** from a string of towns and villages including Baslow, Buxton, Manchester, Derby, Sheffield and Nottingham. All services stop on – or very close to – central Rutland Square. The **tourist office** is just a couple of hundred yards along the main drag, Bridge Street, from the square in the recycled Old Market Hall (daily: Easter–Oct 9.30am–5.30pm; Nov–Easter 10am–5pm; ☎01629/813227). They are very well equipped with public transport timetables as well as local biking and hiking leaflets and guides.

There's no overriding reason to stay the night in Bakewell, but there are several appealing **B&Bs**. One good choice is *Avenue House*, whose three attractively furnished, en-suite rooms are in a spacious Victorian building just south of the centre on Haddon Road (℡01629/812467; no credit cards; ❷). A second option is the homely *Castle Inn* (℡01629/812103; ❸), a sympathetically modernized old inn set plum in the centre at the foot of busy Castle Street, yards from the main bridge into town and with four straightforward, comfortable rooms. The **youth hostel**, with just 28 beds in two- to six-bedded rooms, is in a modest, modern building on Fly Hill (℡0870/770 5682, ⓔbakewell@yha.org.uk; dorm beds £10.25; call for days & dates of opening). It has self-catering facilities and serves evening meals. Fly Hill is near the church – just follow North Church Street round and you'll hit it. There's also pedestrian-only access up a steep lane from Buxton Road – the A6 – just north of the centre.

Bakeries all over town claim to make Bakewell Pudding to the original recipe, but arguably the most authentic is the Old Original Bakewell Pudding Shop, on the main street a few yards from Rutland Square. They sell the pudding in several sizes, from the small and handy to the gargantuan version, enough to keep the average family going for a whole day. Alternatively, *Bloomer's*, just off the main drag on Water Street, is an excellent café, deli and bakery with a special line in homemade sweet and savoury pies. There are several good **restaurants** too, most notably *Renaissance*, on Bath St immediately north of the main street (℡01629/812687), where the emphasis is on French cuisine with a la carte and set meals – a three-courser costs about £20.

Hassop

Hidden away in the heart of the Peaks, about three miles north of Bakewell on the B6001, the tiny hamlet of **HASSOP** has a rugged, solitary feeling. It is also home to one of the region's finest **hotels**, the wonderful *Hassop Hall* (℡01629/640488; ❺), a handsome Neoclassical manor house whose long stone facade ripples with elegant bay windows. The interior has kept faith with the Georgian architecture too – modernization has been kept to a subtle minimum – and the views out over the surrounding parkland are perfectly delightful. Neither should you leave the hotel to eat as the **restaurant** (closed Sun eve) is first class, with a two-course set meal costing £21, considerably more on Saturday.

Haddon Hall

Haddon Hall (April–Sept daily 10.30am–5pm; Oct Thurs–Sun 10.30am–4.30pm; £7.25, plus £1 parking), perched on a hill above the River Wye two miles south of Bakewell along the A6, is one of the finest medieval manor houses in the Midlands. The original Norman manor house passed to the Vernons in the middle of the twelfth century and they held on to it until 1558 when the sole heir, one **Dorothy Vernon**, married John Manners, scion of another powerful family, who were later ennobled as the dukes of Rutland. All might have been well but for antics of the Devonshires, whose construction of Chatsworth in the eighteenth century made neighbouring Haddon Hall look very paltry indeed. Partly as a consequence, the Rutlands left the hall to its own devices, preferring to live elsewhere – and thereby sparing it from Georgian and Victorian meddling.

A Lord Manners still owns the place and today the hall is immaculately maintained, the soft yellow stonework of its main buildings set around a wonky, paved courtyard. Inside, a veritable rabbit warren of ancient rooms incorporates an appealing hotchpotch of architectural features dating from the fourteenth to the seventeenth century. The kitchen is one of the oldest parts of the complex, a rare survivor of a typical medieval kitchen complete with its original fireplace and mullion windows. The Dining Room is also of special interest for its splendid painted chequerboard ceiling, while the Long Gallery, built by John Manners himself, is encased by rich oak panelling with walnut inlays. Even more fascinating is the **chapel**, whose murals sport a jungle of foliage and a herd of exotic animals as well as pictures of the saints – most strikingly St Christopher fording a stream. The paintings were plastered over at the Reformation and only uncovered at the beginning of the twentieth century. After you've finished in the house, be sure to allow time for the terraced **gardens**, which tumble down towards the river.

Haddon Hall is on the TransPeak **bus** route, but be sure to ask the driver to put you off.

Travel details

Buses

For information on all local and national bus services, contact Traveline ☎0870/608 2608, Ⓦ www.traveline.org.uk.

Operated by the Trent Barton bus company, the **TransPeak** bus service runs from Nottingham to Manchester via Derby, Matlock, Bakewell and Buxton 5 times daily. The whole journey takes 3 hours.

Birmingham to: Buxton (2 daily; 4hr); Cambridge (3 daily; 3hr 25min); Great Malvern (2 daily; 1hr 30min); Hereford (2 daily; 2hr 20min); Liverpool (6 daily; 3hr); London (hourly; 3hr); Ludlow (hourly; 2hr 10min); Manchester (hourly; 2hr 30min); Nottingham (6 daily; 1hr 30min); Oxford (5 daily; 1hr 30min); Ross-on-Wye (2 daily; 1hr 30min); Shrewsbury (2 daily; 1hr 20min); Stratford-upon-Avon (every 2hr; 1hr).

Buxton to: Ashbourne (4 daily; 2hr); Birmingham (2 daily; 4hr); Derby (3 daily; 1hr 30min).

Derby to: Buxton (3 daily; 1hr 30min).

Hay-on-Wye to: Hereford (4 daily; 1hr); Ross-on-Wye (5 daily; 2hr).

Hereford to: Birmingham (2 daily; 2hr 20min); Hay-on-Wye (4 daily; 1hr); Ludlow (4 daily; 4hr); Ross-on-Wye (hourly; 40min); Shrewsbury (2 daily; 3hr 30min).

Ludlow to: Birmingham (hourly; 2hr 10min); Hereford (4 daily; 4hr); Shrewsbury (6 daily; 1hr 20min).

Ross-on-Wye to: Birmingham (2 daily; 1hr 30min); Hay-on-Wye (5 daily; 2hr); Hereford (hourly; 40min).

Shrewsbury to: Birmingham (2 daily; 1hr 20min); Hereford (2 daily; 3hr 30min); Ludlow (6 daily; 1hr 20min); Stratford-upon-Avon (2 daily; 2hr 30min).

Stratford-upon-Avon to: Birmingham (every 2 hr; 1hr); Shrewsbury (2 daily; 2hr 30min).

Worcester to: Birmingham (hourly; 1hr 30min); Great Malvern (7 daily; 35min); Hereford (2 daily; 1hr); Ludlow (2 daily; 2hr 15min).

Trains

For information on all local and national rail services, contact **National Rail Enquiries** ☎08457/48 49 50, Ⓦ www.nationalrail.co.uk.

Birmingham New Street to: Birmingham International (every 15–30min; 15min); Derby (hourly; 45min); Hereford (10 daily; 1hr 50min); Leicester (hourly; 50min); London (every 30min; 1hr 40min); Shrewsbury (hourly; 1hr 20min).

Birmingham Snow Hill to: Stratford-upon-Avon (Mon–Sat hourly; 50min); Warwick (Mon–Sat hourly; 40min).

Derby to: Birmingham (every 20min; 45min); Leicester (hourly; 30min); London (hourly; 1hr 50min); Nottingham (every 20min; 35min).

Hereford to: Birmingham (hourly; 1hr 40min); London (5 daily; 2hr 45min); Ludlow (hourly; 30min); Shrewsbury (hourly; 1hr).

Shrewsbury to: Birmingham (2–4 hourly; 1hr 10min); Church Stretton (every 30min; 15min); Craven Arms (hourly; 30min); Hereford (2–3 hourly; 1hr); Ludlow (hourly; 30min); Telford (every 30min; 20min).

Stratford-upon-Avon to: Birmingham (Mon–Sat hourly; 1hr); Oxford (4 daily; 1hr 10min); Warwick (Mon–Sat 8 daily; 30min).

Worcester to: Birmingham (every 30min; 40min–1hr); Great Malvern (every 30min; 15min); Hereford (13 daily; 40min).

The East Midlands

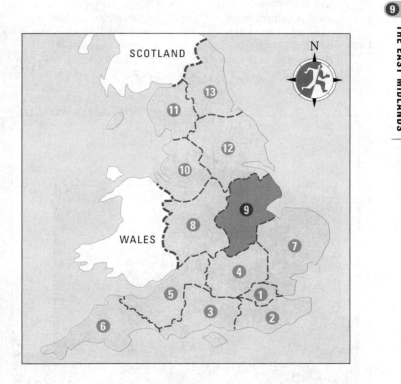

CHAPTER 9

Highlights

* **The Bomb, Nottingham**
Nottingham is proud of its
nightclubs, with good
reason – it's cutting edge
stuff and *The Bomb* continues the story. See p.541

* **Hardwick Hall** Elizabeth I
was formidable – and so
was her contemporary,
Bess of Hardwick. Her
beautiful Elizabethan mansion survives in fine fettle.
See p.542

* **Rufford Country Park** Well
off the usual tourist track,
Rufford offers a ceramic
gallery, a bird sanctuary, a
mill and a sculpture garden
with lots of relaxed strolling
in between. See p.543

* **Lincoln Cathedral** One of
the finest medieval cathedrals in the land, seen to
great advantage on a
rooftop guided tour. See
p.559

△ Hardwick Hall

9

The East Midlands

M any tourists bypass the four major counties of the **East Midlands** – Nottinghamshire, Leicestershire, Northamptonshire and Lincolnshire – on their way to more obvious destinations, an understandable mistake given that the region is short on star attractions. The most obvious targets are **Nottingham**, **Leicester** and **Northampton** – three of the four county towns – but although they share a long and eventful history, all have been badly bruised by postwar town planning and industrial development. Nevertheless, embedded in the modernity are a few historical landmarks – an especially fine church in Northampton, the castle in Nottingham, and traces of Roman baths in Leicester – and even though these are the frills rather than the substance, Nottingham does have enough character to give it an aesthetic edge. Furthermore, if few would actually describe this trio of towns as especially good-looking, the countryside surrounding them can be very engaging, with rolling farmland punctuated by wooded ridges and flowing hills, all sprinkled with fascinating country homes, pretty villages and old market towns. In Nottinghamshire, Byron's **Newstead Abbey** is intriguing, though **Hardwick Hall**, just over the border in Derbyshire, is even better, an especially beautiful Elizabethan country home built by the redoubtable Bess of Hardwick. In addition, the eastern reaches of Nottinghamshire hold two appealing market towns – **Southwell** and **Newark** – whilst west Leicestershire weighs in with the fascinating mansion of **Calke Abbey**. East of Leicestershire, the easy countryside rolls over into **Rutland**, the region's fifth and smallest county, and here you'll find two more pleasant country towns, **Oakham** and **Uppingham**. Rutland benefits from the use of limestone as the traditional building material, as does **Northamptonshire**. Here, the rural parts of the county are studded with handsome, old stone villages and small towns – most notably **Fotheringhay** and **Oundle** – plus large country estates, the best known of which is **Althorp**, the final resting place of Princess Diana.

Lincolnshire is very different in character from the rest of the region, an agricultural backwater that remains surprisingly remote – locals sometimes call it the "forgotten" county. This was not always the case: throughout medieval times the county flourished as a centre of the wool trade with Flanders, its merchants and landowners becoming some of the wealthiest in England. Reminders of the high times are legion, beginning with the majestic cathedral that graces **Lincoln**, a dignified old city which, with its cobbled lanes and ancient buildings, well deserves an overnight stay. Equally enticing is the splendidly intact stone town of **Stamford**, but the county's urban attractions pretty much end there. Out in the sticks, the most distinctive feature is **The Fens**,

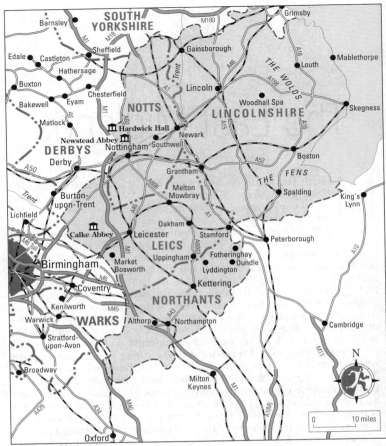
© Crown copyright

whose pancake-flat fields, filling out much of the south of the county and extending deep into East Anglia (see Chapter 7), have been regained from the marshes and the sea. Fenland villages are generally short of charm, but the **parish churches**, whose spires regularly interrupt the wide-skied landscape, are simply stunning, the most impressive of the lot being St Botolph's in **Boston**.

In north Lincolnshire, the gentle chalky hills of the **Lincolnshire Wolds** contain the county's most diverse scenery, including a string of sheltered valleys concentrated in the vicinity of **Louth**, an especially fetching country town. To the east of the Wolds is the **coast**, whose long sandy beach extends, with a few marshy interruptions, from Mablethorpe to **Skegness**, the main resort. The coast has long attracted thousands of holiday-makers from the big cities of the East Midlands and Yorkshire, hence its trail of bungalows, camp-sites and caravan parks – though, to be fair, significant chunks of the seashore are now protected as nature reserves.

As for public transport, travelling between the cities of the East Midlands by **train** or **bus** is simple and most of the larger towns have good regional links, too; but things are very different in the country with bus services very patchy.

Nottinghamshire

With a population of 270,000, **Nottingham** is one of England's big cities, a long-time manufacturing centre for bikes, cigarettes, pharmaceuticals and lace, though it's much more famous for its association with **Robin Hood**, the legendary thirteenth-century outlaw. Hood's bitter enemy was, of course, the Sheriff of Nottingham, but unfortunately his home and lair – the city's imposing medieval castle – is long gone, and today Nottingham is at its most diverting in the Lace Market, whose cramped streets are crowded with the mansion-like warehouses of the Victorian lacemakers.

The county town is flanked to the south by the commuter villages of the Nottinghamshire Wolds and to the north by the gritty towns and villages of what was, until Thatcher and her cronies decimated it in the late 1980s, the Nottinghamshire coalfield. Both are unremarkable, but encrusted within the old coalfield are the thin remains of **Sherwood Forest**, the bulk of which is contained within **The Dukeries**, named after the five dukes who owned most of this area and preserved at least part of the ancient broad-leaved forest. Three of the four remaining estates – Worksop, Welbeck and Thoresby – are still in private hands, but the fourth estate, **Clumber Park**, is now owned by the National Trust and offers charming woodland walks. Also within the confines of the former coalfield are two fascinating country houses, **Newstead Abbey**, one-time home of Byron, and, even better, the wonderful Elizabethan extravagance of **Hardwick Hall**. Moving on, eastern Nottinghamshire is agricultural, its most important town being **Newark**, an agreeable, low-key kind of place straddling the River Trent. Newark has a castle, but the main attraction hereabouts is the fine Norman church at nearby **Southwell**.

Fast and frequent **trains** connect Nottingham with, among many destinations, London, Birmingham, Newark, Lincoln and Leicester. County-wide **bus** services radiate out from the city, too, making Nottingham the obvious base for a visit.

Nottingham

Controlling a strategic crossing point over the River Trent, the Saxon town of **NOTTINGHAM** was built on one of a pair of sandstone hills whose 130-foot cliffs looked out over the river valley. In 1068, William the Conqueror built a castle on the other hill, and the Saxons and Normans traded on the low ground in between, the **Market Square**. The castle was a military stronghold and royal palace, the equal of the great castles of Windsor and Dover, and every medieval king of England paid regular visits.

After the Civil War, the Parliamentarians slighted the castle and, in the 1670s, the ruins were cleared by the duke of Newcastle to make way for a **palace**, whose continental – and, in English terms, novel – design he chose from a pattern book, probably by Rubens. Beneath the castle lay a market town which, according to contemporaries, was handsome and well kept – "One of the most beautiful towns in England," commented Daniel Defoe. But in the second half of the eighteenth century, it was transformed by the expansion of the lace and hosiery industries, and within the space of fifty years, Nottingham's population increased from ten thousand to fifty thousand, the resulting slums becoming a hotbed of radicalism.

The worst of these were cleared in the late nineteenth century, when the city centre assumed its present structure, with the main commercial area ringed by alternating industrial and residential districts. Crass **postwar development**, adding tower blocks, shopping centres and a ring road has, however, ensconced the remnants of the city's past in a townscape that will be dishearteningly familiar if you've seen a few other English commercial centres.

Arrival and information

Nottingham **train station** is on the south side of the city centre, a five- to ten-minute walk from the Market Square – just follow the signs. Most long-distance buses arrive at the Broad Marsh **bus station**, down the street from the train station on the way to the centre, but some – including services to north Nottinghamshire – pull in at the Victoria Bus Station, a five-minute walk north of the Market Square. If you spend any time in the centre, you can't miss the new **tram**, but it serves the suburbs rather than any of the city's attractions. The city's **tourist office** is on the Market Square, on the ground floor of the Council House, 1 Smithy Row (Easter–July Mon–Fri 9am–5.30pm, Sat 9am–5pm; Sept & Oct Mon–Fri 9am–5.30pm, Sat 9am–5pm, Sun 10am–3pm; Nov–Easter Mon–Sat 9am–5.30pm; ℡0115/9155330, ⊛www.nottinghamcity.gov.uk).

Accommodation

As you might expect of a big city, Nottingham has a good range of accommodation, with the more expensive **hotels** concentrated in the centre, the cheaper places and the **B&Bs** mostly located on the outskirts and the main approach roads. Finding a room is rarely difficult, but the tourist office can always help out.

Hotels and guest houses

Best Western Westminster 312 Mansfield Rd ℡0115/955 5000, ⊛www.westminster-hotel .co.uk. Comfortable, popular mid-range hotel in a big old red-brick mansion complete with turret and high gables. On a main road about one mile north of the city centre. ❺

Greenwood City Lodge 5 Third Ave, off Sherwood Rise ℡0115/962 1206, ⊛www .greenwoodlodgecityguesthouse.co.uk. Attractive guest house in a quiet corner of the city, down a narrow lane about a mile north of the city centre. Six bedrooms decorated in smart Victorian style. Highly recommended. ❼

Lace Market 29 High Pavement ℡0115/852 3232, ⊛www.lacemarkethotel.co.uk. Great loca-

tion, footsteps from St Mary's church, this smart hotel has thirty individually decorated rooms within a tastefully modernized Georgian house. ❻

Rutland Square Rutland St, off St James' St ℡0115/941 1114, ⊛www.forestdale.com. Enticing and tastefully furnished modern hotel in a good location, just by the castle. ❻

Hostels

Igloo Tourist Hostel 110 Mansfield Rd ℡0115/947 5250, ⊛www.igloohostel.co.uk. Backpackers' haven in a large Victorian house in the town centre, opposite the *Golden Fleece* pub, with a convivial atmosphere, good showers and free tea and coffee. Bunk-beds in mixed or single-sex dorms for £13 per person.

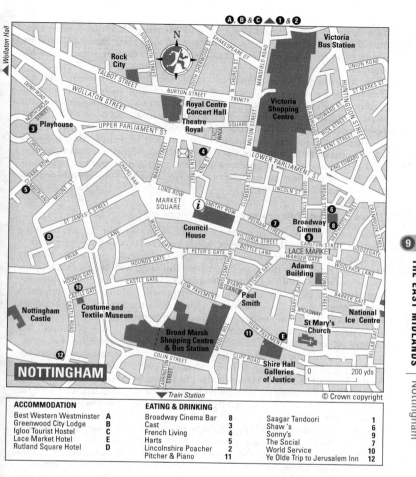

NOTTINGHAM

© Crown copyright

▼ Train Station

ACCOMMODATION		EATING & DRINKING			
Best Western Westminster	A	Broadway Cinema Bar	8	Saagar Tandoori	1
Greenwood City Lodge	B	Cast	3	Shaw 's	6
Igloo Tourist Hostel	C	French Living	4	Sonny's	9
Lace Market Hotel	E	Harts	5	The Social	7
Rutland Square Hotel	D	Lincolnshire Poacher	2	World Service	10
		Pitcher & Piano	11	Ye Olde Trip to Jerusalem Inn	12

The Old Market Square and the Castle

The **Old Market Square** is still the heart of the city, an airy open plaza whose shops, offices and fountains are watched over by the grand neo-Baroque **Council House**, completed as part of a make-work scheme in 1928. From here, it's a five-minute walk west up Friar Lane to **Nottingham Castle** (daily 10am–5pm, grounds daily 9am–dusk; Sat & Sun £2, free at other times), whose heavily restored gateway stands above a folkloric bronze of Robin Hood, with plaques depicting legendary scenes from his life on the wall behind. Beyond the gateway, lawns slope up to the squat ducal **palace**, which – after remaining a charred shell for forty years – was opened as the country's first provincial museum in 1878. The mansion occupies the site of the castle's upper bailey; round the back, just outside the main entrance, two sets of steps lead down into the maze of ancient caves that honeycomb the cliff beneath. One set is currently open for guided tours only (1–2 daily; call

☎0115/915 3700; £2), and this leads into **Mortimer's Hole**, a three-hundred-foot shaft along which, so the story goes, the young Edward III and his chums crept in October 1330 to capture the queen mother, Isabella, and her lover, Roger Mortimer.

The interior of the ducal mansion holds the **Castle Museum and Art Gallery**, which makes a dull start on the ground floor with a series of small, piecemeal exhibitions. Much better is the "Story of Nottingham" on the lower level, a lively, well-presented and entertaining account of the city's development. In particular, look out for a small but exquisite collection of late medieval **alabaster carvings**, an art form for which Nottingham once had an international reputation. It's worth walking up to the top floor, too, for a turn round the main **picture gallery**, a handsome and spacious room that has a curious assortment of mostly English nineteenth-century romantic paintings.

The Lace Market

A few minutes' walk away, on the east side of the Market Square up along Victoria Street, is the **Lace Market**, whose narrow lanes and alleys are flanked by an attractive assortment of Victorian factories and warehouses. **Stoney Street**, for one, holds the imposing Adams Building, with its handsome stone and brick facade, whilst adjoining **Broadway** chips in with a line of especially homogeneous red-brick and sandstone-trimmed buildings that perform a neat swerve halfway along the street. One feature that many of the buildings share is long attic windows designed to light what were once the mending and inspection rooms. Intruding into the Lace Market is the **National Ice Centre** (Ⓦwww.wayahead.com/icecentre), a whopping spaceship-like structure that's both the home of the Panthers ice-hockey team and a trainee skaters' paradise. To arrange lessons, call ☎0115/853 3036 (£13 for 30min). At the heart of the Lace Market is the church of **St Mary**, a good-looking, mostly fifteenth-century structure built on top of the hill that was once the Saxon town. The church abuts High Pavement, the administrative centre of Nottingham in Georgian times, and here you'll find **Shire Hall**, whose Neoclassical columns, pilasters and dome date from 1770. Now accommodating the **Galleries of Justice** (Tues–Sat 10am–5pm, plus Mon 10am–5pm in school holidays; £6.95), the Shire Hall boasts two superbly preserved Victorian courtrooms as well as an Edwardian police station, some spectacularly unpleasant old cells, a women's prison with bath house and a prisoners' exercise yard. Most visitors opt for the "Crime and Punishment" tour, which includes role play – on arrival you're issued with a criminal identity number, and so it continues – but it's possible to wander round under your own steam, which takes about an hour.

Nearby, on Byard Lane, is the first shop of local lad **Paul Smith**, a major success story of recent British fashion.

Eating

Nottingham's **restaurant** scene has improved immeasurably in the last decade, and the city now boasts at least a dozen first-rate places. Most of the smarter restaurants feature fairly elaborate menus which attempt to balance unusual ingredients, but there are more straightforward joints too – primarily French, Italian and Asian. Like every other city in the UK, Nottingham is now awash with **cafés** and **café-bars**. Almost without exception, they've adopted the same formula – angular and ultramodern furnishings and fittings – but the vast majority stick to coffees and snacks rather than more substantial offerings.

French Living 27 King St ⓉⓅ0115/958 5885. Authentic French cuisine served in cosy basement surroundings. Daytime snacks and baguettes on the ground floor too. Moderate

Harts Standard Court, Park Row ⓉⓅ0115/911 0666. One of the city's most acclaimed restaurants, featuring an international menu of carefully presented (and expensive) meals. Attractive pastel/Modernist decor and attentive service in part of the old general hospital. Many locals swear by the place. Expensive.

Saagar Tandoori Restaurant 473 Mansfield Rd ⓉⓅ0115/962 2014. Excellent Indian restaurant, a mile or so north of the city centre. The decor is very homely – you feel as if you're in someone's living room – but it's a very popular spot. Moderate.

Shaw's 20 Broad St ⓉⓅ0115/950 0009. Informal,

pleasantly decorated basement restaurant serving an imaginative, well-considered menu supplemented by an outstanding selection of daily specials – the sardines, when they're on, are simply superb. Customers can eat in the ground-floor bar too. Very reasonable prices; highly recommended. Moderate.

Sonny's Restaurant 3 Carlton St ⓉⓅ0115/947 3041. Well-established restaurant with a pleasant atmosphere and crisp, bright decor. A thoughtful menu whets the appetite and each dish is well-prepared, filling and tasty. Moderate.

World Service Newdigate House, Castle Gate ⓉⓅ0115/847 5587. Chic restaurant with bags of flair in charming premises up near the Castle. An international menu done with imagination. Expensive.

Pubs and nightlife

Nottingham's **nightclub** scene is boisterous, with places moving in and out of cool all the time. The **pubs** around Old Market Square have a tough edge to them, especially at the weekend, but within a few minutes' walk there's a selection of equally lively and more enjoyable drinking-holes. For **live music**, both popular and classical, most big names play at the Royal Centre Concert Hall on Wollaton Street (ⓉⓅ0115/989 5555, Ⓦwww.royalcentre-nottingham.co.uk; nearby *Rock City* (see below) also pulls in some star turns. The Broadway, in the Lace Market at 14 Broad St (ⓉⓅ0115/952 6611, Ⓦwww.broadway.org.uk), is far and away the best **cinema** in town, featuring the pick of mainstream and avant-garde films.

Pubs and bars

Broadway Cinema Bar Broadway Cinema, 14 Broad St. Informal, fashionable bar serving an eclectic assortment of bottled beers to a cinema-keen clientele. Can get too smoky for comfort, so they have a smaller, smoke-free café-bar upstairs.

Cast Wellington Circus. The bar of the Nottingham Playhouse is a popular, easy-going spot with courtyard seating on summer nights. Good supply of real ales.

Lincolnshire Poacher 161 Mansfield Rd. Very popular and relaxed pub, with a wide selection of bottled and real ales. An older clientele than in the – very youthful – city centre a five- to ten-minute walk away.

Pitcher & Piano High Pavement. Lively, fashionable pub in an imaginatively converted Victorian church on the edge of the Lace Market. Good fun; very young.

The Social Pelham St. Just up from the Market Square, this packed and popular bar is very much à la mode. Spartan, modern furnishing and fittings

plus frequent DJ sounds.

Ye Olde Trip to Jerusalem Inn below the castle in Brewhouse Yard. Carved into the castle rock, this ancient inn may well have been a meeting point for soldiers gathering for the Third Crusade. Its cave-like bars, with their rough sandstone ceilings, are delightfully secretive.

Clubs

The Bomb 45 Bridlesmith Gate ⓉⓅ0115/950 6667, Ⓦwww.thebomb.twelveten.com. A front-runner in the club scene with regular house, techno and garage nights.

Media Queen St ⓉⓅ0115/910 1101, Ⓦwww.meanfiddler.com. One of the grooviest places in town with grand decor and great sounds. Leading DJs are its forte.

Rock City 8 Talbot St ⓉⓅ0115/958 8484, Ⓦwww.rock-city.co.uk. Giant-sized, crowded nightclub/music venue, with different sounds and crowds each night, from Goth to metal to Indie. Regularly hosts name bands on UK tours.

Northern Nottinghamshire

Rural **northern Nottinghamshire**, with its easy rolling landscapes and large ducal estates, was transformed in the nineteenth century by **coal** – deep, wide seams of the stuff that spawned dozens of collieries, and colliery towns, stretching north across the county and on into Yorkshire. Almost without exception, the mines have closed, their passing marked only by the old pit-head winding wheels left, bleak and solitary, to commemorate the thousands of men who laboured here. The suddenness of the pit closure programme imposed by the Conservative government in the 1980s knocked the stuffing out of the area and only now is it beginning to revive. One prop has been the tourist industry, for the countryside in between these mining communities holds several enjoyable attractions, the best known of which is **Sherwood Forest** – or at least the patchy remains of it – one-time haunt (allegedly) of Robin Hood. Byron is a pipsqueak in the celebrity stakes by comparison, but his family home, **Newstead Abbey**, is here too, there are some pleasant woodland walks in the NT's **Clumber Park** and, last but certainly not least, there's **Hardwick Hall**, a stunningly handsome Elizabethan mansion.

Reaching this quartet of attractions by **bus** from Nottingham is easy enough – with the exception of Hardwick Hall, for which you'll need your own transport.

Hardwick Hall

Born the daughter of a minor Derbyshire squire, Elizabeth, Countess of Shrewsbury (1527–1608) – aka **Bess of Hardwick** – became one of the leading figures of Elizabethan England, renowned for her political and business acumen. She also had a penchant for building and her major achievement, **Hardwick Hall** (April–Oct Wed, Thurs, Sat & Sun 12.30–5pm; plus July & Aug Mon 12.30–5pm; gardens same months daily 11am–5.30pm; house & gardens £6.60, gardens only £3.50; NT), begun when she was 62, has survived in amazingly good condition. The house was the epitome of fashionable taste, a balance of symmetry and ingenious detail in which the rectangular lines of the building are offset by line upon line of windows – there's actually more glass than stone – whilst, up above, her giant-sized initials – E.S. – hog every roof line. Inside, the ground floor is relatively routine, but it's here that Hardwick's extensive collection of sixteenth- and seventeenth-century needlework is displayed, including several pieces by Mary, Queen of Scots, who was held in custody by the Earl of Shrewsbury for years.

On the top floor, the **High Great Chamber**, where Bess received her most distinguished guests, boasts an extraordinary plaster frieze, a brightly painted, finely worked affair celebrating the goddess Diana, the virgin huntress – it was, of course, designed to please the virgin queen herself. Next door, the **Long Gallery** is simply breathtaking, like an indoor cricket pitch only with exquisite furnishings and fittings from the splendid chimneypieces and tapestries through to a set of portraits, including one each of the queen and Bess. The gallery was where Bess and her chums could exercise – and keep out of the sun at a time when any hint of a tan was considered peasant-plebeian.

Outside, the **garden** makes for a pleasant wander and, beyond the ha-ha, rare breeds of cattle and sheep graze the surrounding **parkland** (daily 8am–6pm; free). Finally – and rather confusingly – Hardwick Hall is next to **Hardwick Old Hall** (April–Oct Mon, Wed, Thurs, Sat & Sun 11am–6pm; £3; EH),

Bess's previous home, but now little more than a broken-down if substantial ruin.

The easiest way to reach Hardwick is along the M1; come off at Junction #29 and follow the signs from the roundabout at the top of the slip road – a three-mile trip. Note, however, that Hardwick is not signed from the motorway itself.

Newstead Abbey

In 1539, Henry VIII granted **Newstead Abbey** (house April–Sept daily noon–5pm; grounds daily 9am–dusk; £5, grounds only £2.50), ten miles north of Nottingham on the A60, to Sir John Byron, who demolished most of the church and converted the monastic buildings into a family home. In 1798, **Lord Byron** inherited Newstead, then little more than a ruin. He restored part of the complex during his six-year residence (1808–14), but most of the present structure dates from later renovations, which maintained much of the shape and feel of the medieval original while creating the warren-like mansion that exists today. **Inside**, a string of intriguing period rooms includes everything from a neo-Gothic Great Hall to the Henry VII bedroom, fitted with carved panels and painted house screens imported from Japan. Some of the rooms are pretty much as they were when Byron lived here – notably his bedroom and dressing room – and in the library is a small collection of the poet's possessions, from letters and manuscripts through to his pistols and boxing gloves. The surrounding **gardens** are simply delightful, a secretive and subtle combination of walled garden, lake, Gothic waterfalls, yew tunnels and Japanese-style rockeries, complete with eccentric pagodas.

There's a fast and frequent **bus** service leaving every twenty minutes or so from Nottingham's Victoria Centre bus station to the gates of Newstead Abbey, a mile from the house; the journey takes about twenty-five minutes.

Rufford Country Park

Council-run country parks may be ten a penny, but **Rufford Country Park** (daily dawn–dusk; main facilities daily 10.30am–5pm; free) shows just how things should be done. The remains of the original twelfth-century Cistercian Abbey and the country house built in its stead – but largely demolished in 1956 – are neither very substantial nor especially interesting, but the old buildings are all pleasantly maintained and the former stable block now holds a café, a better-than-average craft shop and a first-rate ceramics gallery. At the back of the stables are the gardens, both informal and formal, and an outstanding **Sculpture Garden**, which manages to be both very accessible and very contemporary. Further afield is a lake and a mill, a bird sanctuary and a wetland area, all reachable by footpath. There's a lively programme of special events and temporary art exhibitions too.

Rufford is right beside the A614 about eighteen miles north of Nottingham and reached on hourly Stagecoach **bus** #33 from Nottingham's Victoria Centre bus station.

Robin Hood – and Sherwood Forest Country Park

Most of **Sherwood Forest**, once a vast royal woodland of oak, birch and bracken covering all of northern Nottinghamshire, was cleared in the eighteenth century – nowadays it's difficult to imagine the protection it provided for generations of outlaws, the most famous of whom was **Robin Hood**.

There's no "true story" of Robin's life – the earliest reference to him, in Langland's *Piers Plowman* of 1377, treats him as fiction – but to the balladeers of fifteenth-century England, who invented most of the folklore, this was hardly the point. For them, Robin was a symbol of yeoman decency, a semi-mythological opponent of corrupt clergymen and evil officers of the law; in the early tales, although Robin shows sympathy for the peasant, he has rather more respect for the decent nobleman, and he's never credited with robbing the rich to give to the poor. This and other parts of the legend, such as Maid Marion and Friar Tuck, were added later.

Robin Hood may lack historical authenticity, but it hasn't discouraged the county council from spending thousands of pounds sustaining the **Major Oak**, the creaky tree where Maid Marion and Robin are supposed to have "plighted their troth". The Major Oak is on a pleasant one-mile trail that begins beside the visitor centre at the main entrance to **Sherwood Forest Country Park** (daily dawn–dusk; free), which comprises 450 acres of oak and silver birch crisscrossed with footpaths. The visitor centre is half a mile north of the village of Edwinstowe, itself just two miles northwest of Rufford Park and twenty-odd miles north of Nottingham via the A614.

There's a regular **bus** service on Stagecoach bus #33 from Nottingham's Victoria Centre bus station to Edwinstowe via Rufford.

Clumber Park

North of Ollerton, Edwinstowe's immediate neighbour, the A614 trims the edge of Thoresby Park, to reach, after six miles, the eastern entrance to the NT's **Clumber Park** (daily dawn–dusk; free, but parking for non-NT members £3.60), four thousand acres of park and woodland lying to the south of industrial Worksop. The estate was once the country seat of the dukes of Newcastle, and it was here in the 1770s that they constructed a grand mansion overlooking Clumber Lake. The house was dismantled in 1938, when the duke sold the estate, and today the most interesting survivor of the lakeside buildings – located about two and a half miles from the A614 – is the Gothic Revival **Chapel** (daily: April–Sept 10.30am–5.30pm; Oct–March 10.30am–4pm; free; NT), an imposing edifice with a soaring spire and an intricately carved interior built for the seventh duke in the 1880s. Close by, the old **stable block** now houses a National Trust office, shop and **café** (daily: April–Sept 10.30am–5.30pm; Oct–March 10.30am–4pm), and there's **bike rental** (April–Sept) immediately behind the chapel. The woods around the lake offer some delightful strolls and rides through planted woodland interspersed with the occasional patch of original forest.

Departing Nottingham's Victoria Centre bus station, Stagecoach East Midlands, hourly **bus** #33 runs to Rufford and Edwinstowe, from where it travels on up the west side of Clumber Park en route to Worksop; get off at Carburton for the 2.5-mile walk to the Clumber Park NT office. The excursion is best done as a day-trip from Nottingham, but there is a **campsite** (℡01909/482303; closed Nov–April) in Clumber Park's walled garden, a few minutes' walk north of the chapel.

Eastern Nottinghamshire

Without coal, **eastern Nottinghamshire** escaped the heavy-duty industrialization that fell upon its county neighbours in the late nineteenth century. It remains a largely rural area, its undulating farmland, punctuated by dozens of pint-sized villages, rolling seamlessly over to the River Trent, the boundary with Lincolnshire. By and large, it's a prosperous part of the county and by no means unpleasant, but for the casual visitor the attractions are distinctly low-key, being essentially confined to **Southwell** and **Newark**, both of which are easy to reach by regular **buses** from Queen Street in the centre of Nottingham.

Southwell

SOUTHWELL, some fourteen miles northeast of Nottingham, is a sedate backwater distinguished by **Southwell Minster** (April–Sept Mon-Sat 8am–7pm; Oct–March Mon–Sat 8am–dusk; Sun same hours, but depending on services; free but £3 donation suggested), whose twin towers are visible for miles around, and the fine Georgian mansions facing it along Church Street. The Normans built the Minster at the beginning of the twelfth century and, although some elements were added later, their design predominates, from the imposing west towers through to the dog-tooth-decorated doorways. Inside, the proud and forceful arcaded stonework of the **nave** ends abruptly at the transepts with the inelegance of the fourteenth-century **rood screen**, beyond which lies the Early English **choir** and the extraordinary **chapterhouse**. The latter is embellished with naturalistic foliage dating from the late thirteenth century, some of the earliest carving of its type in England.

For a bite to **eat**, the daytime *Deli* (Mon–Sat 9am–5pm), a five-minute walk from the Minster on the main drag through the village at 85a King St, sells a tasty range of baguettes. Alternatively, the *Saracen's Head*, across from the Minster, does a good line in afternoon teas.

Newark

From Southwell, it's eight miles east to **NEWARK**, an amiable, low-key river port and market town that was once a major staging point on the Great North Road. Fronting the town as you approach from the west are the gaunt riverside ruins of **Newark Castle** (daily dawn–dusk; free), all that's left of the mighty medieval fortress that was pounded to pieces during the Civil War. From here, it's just a couple of minutes walk east to the expansive **Market Place**, surrounded by a network of narrow and ancient alleys and framed by a sequence of attractive Georgian and Victorian facades. It's also overlooked by the mostly thirteenth-century church of **St Mary Magdalene** (Mon–Sat 8.30am–4.30pm), whose massive spire, at 236ft, towers over the town centre. It's a handsome church, its well-proportioned nave cheered by some brightly restored roof paintings and a fancy reredos.

There's a regular **bus** service from Nottingham to Newark via Southwell, and Newark is also on the Nottingham–Lincoln **train** line. The Newark Castle **train station** (there is another, so be sure to get off at the right one) is on the west side of the River Trent, a five-minute walk from both the castle and the adjacent **tourist office**, on Castlegate (daily 9am–5pm; ☎01636/655765). The **bus station** is on Lombard Street, a couple of minutes' walk south from the tourist office along Castlegate. Newark has a small supply of **hotels** and **B&Bs**, which the tourist office will book on your behalf at no extra charge, but remember that rooms are well-nigh impossible to find during the Newark International Antiques Fair, Europe's biggest such event, held six times a year. For **food**, make for the excellent *Gannets*, 35 Castlegate (Mon–Fri 9am–4pm, Sat 9am–5pm & Sun 9.30am–4pm), an astoundingly good coffee bar serving daytime snacks and meals, or the simply superb *Café Bleu*, opposite at 14 Castlegate (℗01636/610141), a brilliant French restaurant serving top-class meals from an inventive menu. It's one of the best restaurants in the county, with an outside terrace and live jazz; the decor – all pastel-painted cheerfulness – is appealing too.

Leicestershire and Rutland

The compact county of **Leicestershire** is one of the more anonymous of the English shires, though **Leicester** itself is saved from mediocrity by its role as a focal point for Britain's Asian community. West Leicestershire has rather more to offer, for although its rolling landscape is blemished by a series of industrial settlements, things pick up at **Ashby-de-la-Zouch**, a pleasing little town graced by the substantial remains of its medieval castle, and at **Calke Abbey**, a dishevelled country house set in its own estate just over the border in Derbyshire. In east Leicestershire, the farmland is studded with long-established market towns. None of them are particularly enthralling, but genial **Market Harborough** does hold several attractive old buildings and an interesting museum.

To the east of Leicestershire lies England's smallest county, **Rutland**, reinstated in 1997 following 23 unpopular years of merger with its larger neighbour. Rutland has two places of special note, **Oakham**, the county town, and **Uppingham**, with its elegant Georgian architecture.

Getting around Leicestershire and Rutland can be problematic. **Train** lines radiate out from Leicester, most usefully to Market Harborough and Oakham, and there's a good network of **bus** services between the market towns, but these fade away in the villages where, if there is a bus at all, it only runs once or twice a day.

Leicester

On first impression, **LEICESTER** is a resolutely modern city, but further inspection reveals traces of its medieval and Roman past, situated immediately to the west of the downtown shopping area near the River Soar. The Romans, choosing this site in the middle of the rebellious Coritani, developed Leicester's precursor, Ratae Coritanorum, as a fortified town on the Fosse Way, the military road running from Lincoln to Cirencester, and **Emperor Hadrian** kitted it out with huge public buildings. Subsequently, in the eighth century, the Danes colonized the town and later still its medieval castle became the base of the earls of Leicester. Since the late seventeenth century, Leicester has been a centre of the hosiery trade and it was this industry that attracted hundreds of Asian immigrants to settle here in the 1950s and 1960s. Today, about one third of Leicester's population is **Asian** and the city elected the country's first Asian MP, Keith Vaz, in 1987. Leicester's Hindus put on two massive and internationally famous festivals in October and November,

Navrati and **Diwali**, the Festival of Light (Ⓦ www.discoverleicester.com). In addition, the city's sizeable Afro-Caribbean community celebrates its culture in a whirl of colour and music on the first weekend in August. This, the **Leicester Caribbean Carnival** (Ⓦ www.lccarnival.org.uk), is the country's second biggest street festival after the Notting Hill Carnival (see p.139).

Arrival and information and accommodation

On the line from London's St Pancras station, Leicester **train station** is situated on London Road just to the southeast of the city centre. The **bus station** is on the north side of the centre, just off Gravel Street. The centre is signed from both – the large Haymarket Shopping Centre in between the two is an easy landmark. The **tourist office** is a short walk to the south of the Haymarket at 7–9 Every St, on Town Hall Square (Mon–Wed & Fri 9am–5.30pm, Thurs 10am–5.30pm, Sat 9am–5pm; premium-rated line ℡0906/294 1113, Ⓦ www.discoverleicester.com).

With other more enticing cities near at hand – Nottingham being a case in point – there's no strong reason to overnight here, but Leicester does have a good crop of business **hotels** close to the centre, within walking distance of the train station, including the *Best Western Belmont House Hotel,* De Montfort St (℡0116/254 4773, Ⓦ www.belmonthotel.co.uk; ❺), a proficient chain hotel in an efficiently modernized and extended Georgian property. The *Holiday Inn* at 129 St Nicholas Circle (℡0116/253 1161, Ⓦ www.leicester.holiday-inn .com; ❺) manages to counteract its motorized setting – in the middle of the ring road – by creating a relaxed environment, with comfortable rooms, indoor pool and extensive fitness facilities, while *Spindle Lodge Hotel,* 2 West Walk (℡0116/233 8801; ❸) is a well-maintained, medium-sized place in a pleasantly converted Victorian townhouse, ten minutes' walk from the train station. The tourist office also has a substantial list of competitively priced **B&Bs**, though most are not central. They will help fix you up with somewhere to stay, but things rarely get difficult except during Navrati and Diwali.

The city centre

The most conspicuous building in Leicester's crowded centre is undoubtedly the modern Haymarket Shopping Centre, but the proper landmark is the Victorian **clocktower** of 1868, standing in front of the Haymarket and marking the spot where seven streets meet. One of the seven is Cheapside, which leads south in a few yards to Leicester's open-air produce **market** (Mon–Sat), arguably the best in the land. Alternatively, from back at the clocktower, East Gates and then the old High Street run west with Silver Street (subsequently Guildhall Lane), soon branching off to reach **St Martin's Cathedral**, a much-modified eleventh-century structure that incorporates a fine, ornately carved medieval wooden entrance porch. Next door is the **Guildhall** (Mon–Sat 10am–5pm & Sun 1–5pm, Oct–March till 4pm; free), a half-timbered building that has served, variously, as the town hall, prison and police station.

West to the Jewry Wall

From the Guildhall, it's a short walk west to St Nicholas Place and then St Nicholas Circle, a large roundabout that is part of the ring road. Go round it to the right – there's a walkway – and on the right behind the church is the **Jewry Wall**, a chunk of Roman masonry some 18ft high and 73ft long that was originally part of Hadrian's public baths. The project was a real irritation to the emperor. Hadrian's grand scheme was spoilt by the engineers, who miscalculated the line of the aqueduct that was to pipe in the water, and so bathers had to rely on a hand-filled cistern replenished from the river – which wasn't what he had in mind at all. The adjacent **Jewry Wall Museum** (April–Sept Mon–Sat 10am–5pm, Sun 1–5pm; Oct–March Mon–Sat 10am–4pm, Sun 1–4pm; free) charts Leicester's history from prehistoric to medieval times. The most interesting artefacts are Roman, a hotchpotch of archeological finds from Fosse Way milestones to two splendid mosaics.

South to New Walk Museum and Art Gallery

From the city centre, it's about ten minutes' walk south to the **New Walk Museum and Art Gallery** (April–Sept Mon–Sat 10am–5pm, Sun 1–5pm; Oct–March Mon–Sat 10am–4pm, Sun 1–4pm; free), easily the best of the city's museums, on **New Walk**, a pedestrianized promenade that runs out to Victoria Park. On the museum's ground floor is a real surprise – an outstanding collection of work by German Expressionists, mostly sketches, woodcuts and lithographs by the likes of Otto Dix and George Grosz. In particular, look out for the latter's 1919 rallying-call sketch of the coffins of the two murdered leftists, Rosa Luxembourg and Karl Liebknecht. The Germans share the ground floor with the Ancient Egypt Gallery, featuring mummies and hieroglyphic tablets brought from Egypt as souvenirs in the 1880s. The Victorian Gallery is fascinating too, dominated by extravagant, often mawkish romantic paintings, amongst which is Charles Green's iconic *The Girl I left behind Me* of 1880.

From the museum, it takes about ten minutes to walk back to the Haymarket.

Belgrave

Beginning about a mile to the northeast of the centre, the gritty **Belgrave** neighbourhood is the focus of Leicester's Asian community. Both Belgrave Road and its northerly continuation, Melton Road, are lined with Indian and Pakistani goldsmiths and jewellers, sari shops, Hindi music stores and curry houses. It's never dull down here, but Sunday afternoons are particularly enjoyable, when locals have time to stroll the streets in their finest gear. Belgrave celebrates two major Hindu festivals: **Diwali**, the Festival of Light, held in October or November, when six thousand lamps are strung out along the Belgrave Road and 20,000 come to watch the switch-on alone; and **Navrati**, an eight-day celebration in October held in honour of the goddess Ambaji.

Eating, drinking, nightlife and entertainment

People come from miles around to eat at the **Indian restaurants** along Belgrave Road. The pick are clustered just beyond the flyover to the northeast of the centre, and it's here you'll find the most famous, *Bobby's*, at nos. 154–156 (☏0116/266 0106). Run by Gujaratis, this moderately priced, unassuming place is strictly vegetarian and uses no garlic or onions; try their delicious house speciality, *undhyu*, or the multi-flavoured Bobby's Special Chaat. Excellent alternatives include the *Sayonara Thali*, at no. 49 (☏0116/266 5888), which specializes in set thali meals, where several different dishes, breads and pickles are served together on large steel plates, and the *Chaat House* (☏0116/266 0513), south of *Bobby's* on the same side of the road at no. 108. The latter does wonderful masala dosas and other south Indian snacks – legendary cricket captain Kapil Dev and his Indian team ate here when they were on tour. In the city centre, and diversifying from the Asian restaurants, the cream of the crop is the *Opera House*, 10 Guildhall Lane (℡0116/223 6666), in lovely old premises and with an imaginative, wide-ranging menu.

The city's **pubs** have taken a pounding from the boom in cafés and café-bars, but *The Globe*, 43 Silver St, supplies a goodly range of ales in traditional surroundings, while the much slicker *Watsons Restaurant & Bar*, 5 Upper Brown St, is – with its crisply modern furnishings and fittings – one of the most popular places in town.

The **performing arts** come up trumps in Leicester at the excellent Phoenix Arts Centre, Newarke St (℡0116/255 4854, ⓦwww.phoenix.org.uk), which features a first-rate mix of comedy, music, theatre and dance, whilst doubling up as an independent cinema. The city's main concert arena is De Montfort Hall, on Granville Road (℡0116/233 3111, ⓦwww.demontforthall.co.uk), adjoining Victoria Park at the far end of New Walk.

West Leicestershire

Give or take the odd industrial blip, most of **west Leicestershire** – to the west of the A6 – is rural, its small towns and villages dotted over undulating countryside. The key attractions here are best visited as day-trips, beginning with **Calke Abbey**, technically over the boundary in Derbyshire and not an abbey at all, but an intriguing country house whose faded charms witness the declining fortunes of the landed gentry. There's also a good castle, at **Ashby-de-la-Zouch**, and a fine church, perched on top of one of the few hills hereabouts at **Breedon-on-the-Hill**.

With the notable exception of Calke Abbey, the places mentioned above are easy to reach by **bus** from Leicester – and Ashby can readily be reached by bus from Nottingham, too.

Ashby-de-la-Zouch

ASHBY-DE-LA-ZOUCH, fourteen miles northwest of Leicester, takes its fanciful name from two sources – the town's first Norman overlord was Alain de Parrhoet la Souche and the rest means "place by the ash trees". Nowadays, Ashby is far from rustic, but it's an amiable little place. A short walk off main drag Market Street stands its principal attraction, the **castle** (April–Oct daily 10am–6pm; Nov–March Wed–Sun 10am–4pm; £3.20; EH), whose rambling ruins mostly date from the fifteenth century. The star turn is the hundred-foot-high **Hastings Tower**, a self-contained four-storey stronghold which, dating from the 1470s, represented the latest thinking in castle design. It provided a secure inner fastness and much better accommodation than was previously available. Improved living quarters reflecting the power and pride of the nobility were built all over England at this time and this is a rare survivor – witness the large windows on the upper floors, accessible via the tower's well-worn spiral staircase.

Breedon-on-the-Hill

It's five miles northeast from Ashby to the village of **BREEDON-ON-THE-HILL**, which sits in the shadow of the large but partly quarried hill from which it takes its name. A steep footpath and a winding, half-mile lane lead up from the village to the summit, where the fascinating church of **St Mary and St Hardulph** (daily 9.30am–6.30pm or dusk; free) occupies the site of an Iron Age hillfort and an eighth-century Anglo-Saxon monastery. Mostly dating from the thirteenth century, the church is kitted out with Georgian pulpit and pews as well as a large and distinctly rickety box pew. Much rarer are a number of **Anglo-Saxon carvings**, both individual saints and prophets and wall friezes, where a dense foliage of vines is inhabited by a tangle of animals and humans. The friezes are quite extraordinary, and the fact that the figures look Byzantine rather than Anglo-Saxon has fuelled much academic debate. The church has something else too, in the form of a set of fine alabaster tombs occupied by members of the Shirley family, who long ruled the local roost. One is an especially imposing affair with the kneeling family up above and a skeleton down below.

Calke Abbey

The eighteenth-century facade of **Calke Abbey House** (April–Oct Mon–Wed, Sat & Sun 1–5.30pm; garden same days 11am–5.30pm; £5.60, garden only £3.20; NT) is all self-confidence, its acres of dressed stone and three long lines of windows polished off with an imposing Victorian Greek Revival portico. This all cost oodles of money and the Harpurs and then the Harpur-Crewes, who owned the estate, were doing very well until the economics of the English country estate changed after World War I. Then, at a time when country houses were being demolished by the score, the Harpur-Crewes simply hung on, becoming the epitome of faded gentility and refusing to make all but the smallest of changes to the house – though they did finally install electricity in 1962. The last Harpur-Crewe to live here, Charles, died in 1981 and the estate passed in its entirety to the National Trust. Very much to their credit, the Trust decided not to bring in the restorers and have kept the house in its dishevelled state – and this is its real charm.

A visit starts in one of the old agricultural outbuildings, from where it's a short stroll to the **house**, whose Entrance Hall adroitly sets the scene, its walls decorated with ancient and distinctly moth-eaten stuffed heads from the family's herd of prize cattle. Beyond is the Caricature Room, whose walls are lined (up to three or four deep) with satirical cartoons, some of which were executed by the leading cartoonists of their day, including Gillray and Cruikshank. Further on is an intensely cluttered Mrs Faversham-like Drawing Room and a state bed given to the Harpurs by the daughter of George II in 1734 and then left packed until the National Trust arrived. It's displayed on its own in one of the first-floor rooms viewable towards the end of the self-guided tour. After you've finished in the house, you can wander out into the **gardens** and pop into the Victorian estate **church**.

There's no public transport to Calke Abbey, and motorists must follow a long-winded one-way system: to get there from Ashby, take the B587 Melbourne Road and follow the signs – the entrance is at the village of Ticknall to the north of the house; the exit is to the south.

East Leicestershire and Rutland

For the casual visitor at least, there's nothing compelling about **east Leicestershire**, though the scenery is pleasant enough, with open farmland broken up by hills and ridges, and the middling town of **Market Harborough** is well worth a visit. Things do, however, improve over in neighbouring **Rutland** with a pair of attractive country towns – **Oakham** and **Uppingham**. Market Harborough is on the Leicester–London main train line and there are reasonably frequent **buses** to and between all the destinations mentioned.

Market Harborough

MARKET HARBOROUGH, fifteen miles southeast of Leicester, is an unassuming provincial town that once prospered from its position at the junction of the turnpike roads to Leicester, Nottingham and London. Consequently, the predominantly Georgian High Street's *Three Swans* and *Angel* hotels were originally coaching inns, and the square and solid old **Town Hall**, opposite the *Three Swans*, was designed to help local traders sell their wares, with butchers on the ground floor and cloth merchants up above. Just off the High Street, the triangular **Market Place** is overlooked by the church of **St Dionysius**, whose striking tower is in stark contrast to the dumpy ironstone nave down below. Here, also, is the **Old Grammar School**, an early seventeenth-century, half-timbered structure mounted on stilts to protect locals from the rain. From 1908 to 1974, the large Victorian building standing directly behind the grammar school on Adam & Eve Street was a factory owned by the Symington family, who designed the world's best-selling corsets. The factory has been redeveloped and now houses both the council offices and the **town museum** (Mon–Sat 10am–4.30pm, Sun 2–5pm; free), which has a small but intriguing display on Symington corsetry. In particular, look out for the adverts attempting to sell bodices to kids and the 1937 poster advertising the full range of Avro corsets – a mind-boggling selection designed to cover every occasion and eventuality. Market Harborough's **tourist office** (Mon–Fri 9am–5pm & Sat 9.30am–12.30pm; ☏01858/821270) is here too.

Market Harborough's **train station** is fifteen minutes' walk east of the town centre. More conveniently, **buses** stop a couple of minutes' walk from the Market Place at the top of Northampton Road, a southerly continuation of the High Street. For **food**, *Aldin's Tea Rooms*, across from St Dionysius, is a spick and span café serving tasty homemade food at reasonable prices.

Oakham

Some twenty miles east from Leicester and twenty northeast of Market Harborough, well-heeled **OAKHAM**, Rutland's county town, has a long history as a commercial centre, its prosperity bolstered by Oakham School, a late sixteenth-century foundation that's become one of the country's more exclusive private schools. The town's stone terraces and Georgian villas are too often interrupted by the mundanely modern to assume much grace, but Oakham does have its architectural moments – particularly in the L-shaped **Market Place**, where a brace of sturdy awnings shelter the old water pump and town stocks. Footsteps from the north side of the Market Place stands **Oakham Castle** (Mon–Sat 10.30am–1pm & 1.30–5pm, Sun 1–5pm; free), comprising a banqueting hall that was originally part of a fortified house dating back to 1191. The hall is a good example of Norman domestic architecture, and inside the whitewashed walls are covered with horseshoes, the result of an ancient custom by which every lord or lady, king or queen, is obliged to present an ornamental horseshoe when they first set foot in the town.

Oakham School is housed in a series of impressive ironstone buildings that frame the west edge of the Market Place. On the right-hand side of the school, a narrow lane allows you to see a little more of the buildings on the way to **All**

Saints' church, whose heavy tower and spire rise high above the town. Dating from the thirteenth century, the church is an architectural hybrid, but the airy interior is distinguished by the intense medieval carvings along the columns of the nave and choir, with Christian scenes and symbols set alongside dragons, grotesques, devils and demons.

Practicalities

With regular services from Leicester and Peterborough, Oakham **train station** lies on the west side of town, five minutes' walk from the Market Place. **Buses** pull in on John Street, close to the Market Place, just behind the Somerfield supermarket. A thorough exploration of Oakham only takes a couple of hours, but if you do decide to stay the **tourist office** in Victoria Hall, 41 High St (Tues–Sat 11am–3pm; ☎01572/724329, ⓦwww.rutnet.co.uk), will help you find **accommodation**. Options include the *Whipper-In Hotel*, on the Market Place (☎01572/756971, ⓦwww.brook-hotels.co.uk; ❺), whose smartly decorated modern rooms are set behind an attractive old facade, and the more distinctive *Lord Nelson's House Hotel*, just along the street (☎01572/723199, ⓦwww.nelsons-house.com; ❻), which has a handful of elegant bedrooms, each with its own decorative theme. For **food**, stick to the excellent and affordably priced *Nicks Restaurant*, part of the Lord Nelson Hotel, where they serve a tasty modern menu featuring local ingredients. For a **drink**, head off to the *Wheatsheaf*, a traditional pub with a good range of brews across from All Saints' church at 2–4 Northgate.

Uppingham

The town of **UPPINGHAM**, six miles south of Oakham, has the uniformity of style Oakham lacks, its narrow, meandering High Street flanked by bow-fronted shops and ironstone houses, mostly dating from the eighteenth century. It's the general appearance that pleases, rather than any individual sight, but the town is famous as the home of **Uppingham School**, a bastion of privilege whose imposing fortress-like building stands at the west end of the High Street. Founded in 1587, the school was distinctly second-rate until the middle of the nineteenth century, when a dynamic headmaster, the Reverend Edward Thring, grabbed enough land to lay out some of the biggest playing fields in England – fitness being, of course, an essential attribute of the rulers of the British Empire.

Uppingham has one especially good **hotel**, the *Lake Isle*, in a tastefully modernized eighteenth-century townhouse at 16 High St East (☎01572/822951, ⓦwww.lakeislehotel.com; ❺). The hotel **restaurant** is outstanding, offering a superb and varied menu from guinea fowl to local venison, with main courses averaging around £14. For a **drink**, head for *The Vaults*, on the minuscule Market Place.

Northamptonshire

Northamptonshire is one of the region's most diverse counties – so diverse in fact that even many Midlanders can't recall what is actually in it and what isn't. With justification, its superabundance of stately homes and historic churches enables it to style itself as the "County of Spires and Squires". It also holds a scattering of charming villages, the most picturesque of which, untouched by all but the vaguest sniff of modernity, are built of local limestone. By contrast, however, three of the county's four big towns – Wellingborough, Corby and Kettering – are primarily industrial and whatever charms they offer to their inhabitants, there's not much to attract the regular tourist. Yet the fourth town, **Northampton**, does something to bridge the gap, its busy centre possessed of several fine old buildings and an excellent museum devoted to shoe-making, the industry that has long made the place tick.

Gentle hills, farmland and patchy woodland stretch right across the county with the **A508** forming an easy if arbitrary dividing line between west and east Northamptonshire. The prime target in the former is **Althorp**, family home of the Spencers and the burial place of Diana, Princess of Wales. East Northamptonshire's star turn is the good-looking town of **Oundle**, which makes the best base for visiting the delightful hamlet of **Fotheringhay**. The county also has a notable **long-distance footpath**, the seventy-mile Nene Way, which follows the looping course of the river right across the county. Nene Way brochures are available at or from Northampton Tourist Office.

Getting to Northampton by **public transport** is no problem, but to reach the villages and stately homes, you'll mostly need your own vehicle – or some careful planning around patchy bus services.

Northampton

Spreading north from the banks of the River Nene, **NORTHAMPTON** is a workaday modern town whose appearance largely belies its ancient past. Throughout the Middle Ages, this was one of central England's most important towns, a flourishing commercial centre whose now demolished castle was a popular stopping-off point for travelling royalty. A fire in 1675 burnt most of the medieval city to a cinder, and the Georgian town that grew up in its stead was itself swamped by the Industrial Revolution, when Northampton swarmed with boot and shoe makers. Their products shod almost everyone in the Empire – from Australia to Canada – as well as the British army.

Northampton's compact **centre** is at its most appealing on and around its main plaza, Market Square, which is where you'll find the town's finest buildings, notably All Saints' Church and the Guildhall. Half a day is enough for a quick gambol round the sights, but if you're tempted to stay the night there's a reasonable supply of hotel accommodation and a scattering of B&Bs. The only times of the year when finding a room can be difficult are during the annual **Balloon Festival** in August, which attracts thousands of visitors, and over the weekend of the British Grand Prix, held in July at the nearby **Silverstone** race-track.

The Town

Northampton's expansive, cobbled **Market Square** has a busy, self-confident air, its sides flanked by a comparatively harmonious mixture of the old and the new. From here, either of a couple of narrow lanes leads through to the church of **All Saints** (Mon–Sat 9am–2pm; free), whose unusually secular appearance stems from its finely proportioned, pillared portico as well as its towered cupola. A statue of a bewigged Charles II in Roman attire surmounts the portico, a (flattering) thank you for his donation of a thousand tons of timber after the Great Fire of 1675 had incinerated the earlier church. Inside, the elegant interior looks more like a ballroom than a church, from the sweep of its timber galleries through to its Neoclassical pillars and a ceiling coated in delicately sculpted plasterwork.

Behind the church is one of Lutyens's less inspiring monuments, a plain, blunt **war memorial** dating from 1926, and, just beyond that, in St Giles' Square, is the **Guildhall**, a flamboyant Victorian edifice constructed in the 1860s to a design by Edward Godwin. Godwin was one of the period's most inventive architects and his Gothic exterior, with its high-pointed windows and dinky turrets and towers, sports kings and queens plus scenes central to the county's history.

The **Northampton Museum and Art Gallery** (Mon–Sat 10am–5pm, Sun 2–5pm; free), a few yards south on Guildhall Road, celebrates the town's industrial heritage with a fabulous collection of **shoes**. Along with silk slippers, clogs and high-heeled nineteenth-century court shoes, there's one of the four boots worn by an elephant during the British Expedition of 1959, which retraced Hannibal's putative route over the Alps into Italy. There's celebrity footwear too – almost inevitably, a pair of Elton John shoes (the giant DMs he wore in *Tommy*) – plus whole cabinets of heavy-duty riding boots, pearl-inlaid raised wooden sandals from Ottoman Turkey and a couple of cabinets showing just how long high heels have been in fashion. Moving on, the next floor up focuses on ceramics, glass and fine art, whilst the top floor is given over to an excellent display charting the town's history from its Roman days to the present, paying particular attention to the significance of the shoe industry, which employed no less than half the town's population in 1920.

Practicalities

From Northampton **train station**, which has regular services to London Euston and Birmingham, it's a ten-minute walk east to the Market Square – just follow the signs. Buses pull into the **bus station** on Lady's Lane, behind the hideous Grosvenor Shopping Centre, immediately to the north of the Market Square; motorists aiming for the centre should follow the signs for the Grosvenor. The **tourist office** (Mon–Sat 10am–5pm, Sun 2–5pm; ☎01604/622677, ⓦwww.northampton.gov.uk/tourism) shares premises with the Northampton museum (see above). Staff operate an accommodation-booking service, have oodles of information on the county and issue bus timetables.

Amongst a light scattering of downtown **hotels**, the *Northampton Moat House* is a dependable chain hotel in a large modern block on Silver Street (☎01604/739988, ⓦwww.moathousehotels.com; ❼). More distinctive is the *Lime Trees Hotel*, 8 Langham Place, Barrack Road (☎01604/632188, ⓦwww.limetreeshotel.co.uk; ❺), in pleasant Georgian premises half a mile north of the centre. The pick of the more central **B&Bs** is the *St George's Private Hotel*, 128 St George's Ave (☎01604/792755, ⓦwww.stgeorgeshotel.co.uk; ❷). This attractive place has ten spacious, comfortable en-suite guest rooms and occupies a large Victorian house about a mile and a half from the centre, overlooking Racecourse Park.

A good spot for daytime **snacks** and coffee is *Ask*, opposite the Guildhall on St Giles Square, where you can get pizzas (£5–8) as well as more substantial Italian meals averaging around £7.

The rest of Northamptonshire

The slice of easy countryside that comprises **west Northamptonshire**, falling to the west of the A508, is dotted with stately homes, amongst which the most diverting is **Althorp**, the last resting place of Diana, Princess of Wales. **East Northamptonshire** – that part of the county east of the A508 – is dissected by the River Nene, which wriggles its way through a string of little villages and towns, amongst which **Oundle** and **Fotheringhay** offer most interest.

Althorp

Some six miles northwest of Northampton off the A428, the ritzy mansion of **Althorp** is the focus of the Spencer estate. The Spencers have lived here for centuries, but this was no big deal until one of the tribe, **Diana**, married Prince Charles in 1981. The disintegration of the marriage and Diana's elevation to popular sainthood is a story known to millions. The public outpouring of grief following Diana's death in 1997 was quite astounding, and Althorp became the focus of massive media attention as the coffin was brought up the M1 motorway from London to be buried on an island in the grounds of the family estate. Today, visitors troop round the **Diana exhibition**, in the old stable block, as well as the adjacent Althorp house, where there's a large collection of priceless paintings, including works by Gainsborough, Van Dyck and Rubens. From the house, a footpath leads round a lake in the middle of which is the islet (no access) on which Diana is buried. The estate is open from July to September (daily 10am–2pm & 1–5pm, last admission 4pm; £10.50 in advance, £11.50 on the gate; ℡08700/679000, ⓦwww.visitalthorp.com) and advance reservations are strongly advised.

There are occasional **buses** from Northampton to Althorp, and sometimes special coaches – contact Northampton tourist office for details.

Oundle

Arguably Northamptonshire's prettiest town, pocket-sized **OUNDLE** slopes up gently from the River Nene, its congregation of old limestone houses zeroing in on the congenial **Market Place**. Preserving much of its medieval layout, Oundle boasts some of the finest seventeenth- and eighteenth-century streetscapes in the Midlands, and is a suitably exclusive setting for one of England's better-known private schools, **Oundle School**, which has been running since 1556 and owns many of the town's most prized buildings. Above all it's the general appearance of the place that appeals rather than anything in particular, the exception being the parish church of **St Peter**, whose magnificent two-hundred-foot Decorated spire soars high above the centre, though the interior – give or take the odd stained-glass window – is unremarkable.

Buses from Peterborough and Northampton stop on the Market Place, a short walk from the **tourist office**, at 14 West St (Easter to Aug Mon–Sat 9am–5pm, Sun 1–4pm; rest of year closed Sun; ℡01832/274333). They issue maps and bus timetables, have comprehensive details of local attractions and operate an **accommodation** service. One recommended place to stay is the *Talbot Hotel*, just along from the Market Place on New Street (℡01832/273621, ⓦwww.oldenglish.co.uk; ❻). This hotel dates from 1626 and comes complete with what is thought to be the very oak staircase Mary, Queen of Scots used on the way to her execution at Fotheringhay Castle (see p.556). Apparently the queen's executioner stayed at the *Talbot* and both his and

Mary's ghost are said to wander the upper floor. For somewhere less expensive, head for the immaculate *Ashworth House*, a modest little stone house with two en-suite guest rooms, five minutes walk from the Market Place at 75 West St (℡01832/275312, Ⓦwww.ashworthhouse.co.uk; ❷). The best place to **eat** is at the *Talbot*, unless you want a takeaway or picnic, in which case *Trendalls* (closed Sun), on the Market Place, is just dandy for baguettes and sandwiches of all descriptions.

Fotheringhay

Nestling by the River Nene just four miles northeast of Oundle, the tiny hamlet of **FOTHERINGHAY** has long been left to its own devices, but its medieval heyday is recalled by its magnificent church of **St Mary and All Saints** (dawn–dusk; free), rising mirage-like above the green riverine meadows. Begun in 1411 and a hundred and fifty years in the making, the church is a paradigm of the Perpendicular, its exterior sporting wonderful arching buttresses, its nave lit by soaring windows and the whole caboodle topped by a splendid octagonal lantern tower. The interior is a tad bare, but there are two fancily carved medieval pieces to look for – a painted pulpit and a sturdy stone font.

Fotheringhay **castle** witnessed two key events – the birth of Richard III in 1452 and the beheading of Mary, Queen of Scots in 1587. On the orders of Elizabeth I, Mary was executed in the castle's Great Hall with no one to stand in her defence – apart, that is, from her dog, who is said to have rushed from beneath her skirts as her head dropped off. Not long afterwards, the castle fell into disrepair and nowadays only a grassy **mound** and ditch remain to mark its position; it's signposted down a short and narrow lane on the bend of the road as you come into the village from Oundle.

Fotheringhay has an excellent **pub-restaurant**, *The Falcon* (℡01832/226254), in a neat stone building with modern patio, and offering a delicious and imaginative menu with main courses averaging around £10.

Lincolnshire

The obvious place to start a visit to **Lincolnshire** is **Lincoln** itself, an old and easy-paced city where the cathedral, the third largest church in England, remains the county's outstanding attraction. Northeast and east of here, the Lincolnshire **Wolds** band the county, their gentle green hills harbouring the pleasant market town of **Louth**, where conscientious objectors were sent to dig potatoes during World War II. The Wolds are flanked by the coast, so different from the rest of Lincolnshire, its brashness encapsulated by the mega resort of **Skegness**, though there are unspoilt stretches, too, most notably at the **Gibraltar Point Nature Reserve**.

Beguiling **Stamford**, in the southwest corner of the county, is an alternative base, an attractive town where the narrow streets are flanked by a handsome ensemble of antique stone buildings, and next door stands one of the great monuments of Elizabethan England, **Burghley House**. From Stamford, it's a short hop east into **The Fens**, whose most diverting villages lie along the A17, a road that runs close to the old fenland port of **Boston**, now Lincolnshire's second town. On any tour of the Fens you'll pass some of the county's most imposing medieval **churches**. Several are worth a special visit, especially **St Botolph's** in Boston and **St Andrew's** in Heckington – seen to best advantage, like all the other churches of this area, in the pale, watery sunlight of the fenland evening.

Getting around Lincolnshire by public transport can be difficult. Lincoln is the hub of the county's limited **rail** network, with regular services south to Sleaford and Spalding and east via Sleaford to Heckington, Boston and Skegness. There are also links northwest to Gainsborough and west to Grantham and Newark, in Nottinghamshire, both of which are on the main line from London to the Northeast. In addition, there are reasonable **bus** services between Lincoln and the county's larger market towns, like Louth and Boston, but amongst the villages you'll be struggling without your own transport.

Lincoln

Reaching high into the sky from the top of a steep hill, the triple towers of the mighty cathedral of **LINCOLN** are visible for miles across the flatlands. This conspicuous spot was first fortified by the Celts, who called their settlement Lindon, "hillfort by the lake", a reference to the pools formed by the River Witham in the marshy ground below. In 47 AD the Romans occupied Lindon and built a fortified town that subsequently became, as Lindum Colonia, one of the four regional capitals of Roman Britain.

Today, only fragments of the Roman city survive, mostly pieces of the third-century town wall, and these are outdone by reminders of Lincoln's medieval heyday, which began during the reign of William the Conqueror with the building of the **castle** and **cathedral**. Lincoln flourished, first as a Norman power base and then as a centre of the wool trade with Flanders, until 1369, when the wool market was transferred to neighbouring Boston. It was almost five hundred years before the town revived, the recovery based upon its manufacture of agricultural machinery and drainage equipment for the fenlands. As the nineteenth-century town spread south down the hill and out along the old Roman road – the Fosse Way – so Lincoln became a place of precise class distinctions: the "**Uphill**" area, spreading north from the cathedral, became synonymous with middle-class respectability, "**Downhill**" with the proletariat. It's a distinction that remains – locals selling anything from secondhand cars to settees still put "Uphill" in brackets to signify a better quality of merchandise. For the visitor, almost everything of interest is confined to the "Uphill" part of town, and it's here also you'll find the best **pubs** and **restaurants**.

Arrival and information

Both Lincoln's **train station**, on St Mary's Street, and its **bus station**, close by off Broadgate, are located "Downhill" in the city centre. From either, it's a very steep, twenty-minute walk to the cathedral, which can also be reached by the city's **Walk & Ride bus** service (Mon–Sat 10am–5pm & Sun noon–5pm; 3 hourly; 70p each way) – the nearest stop to the bus and train stations is at the junction of Mint and Silver streets. There are two **tourist offices**. One is in the shopping centre on Cornhill, close to the train and bus stations

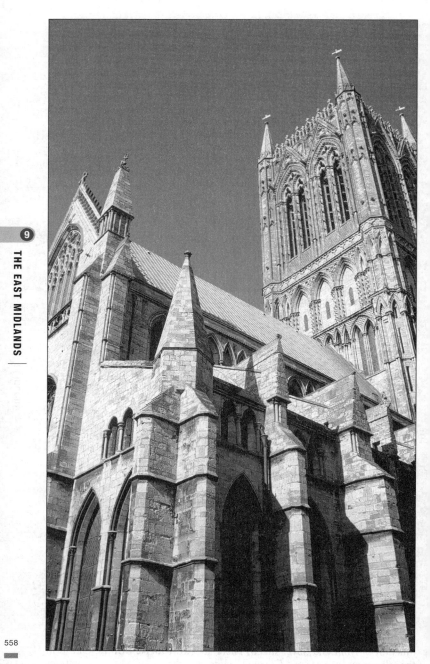

△ Lincoln Cathedral

(Mon–Thurs 9.30am–5.30pm, Fri 9.30am–5pm, Sat 10am–5pm; ☎01522/873256, ⓦwww.lincoln.gov.uk); the other is at 9 Castle Hill, between the cathedral and the castle (Mon–Thurs 9.30am–5.30pm, Fri 9.30am–5pm, Sat & Sun 10am–5pm; ☎01522/873213, same website). Both have a useful range of literature on Lincoln and its surroundings, take bookings for guided tours of the city, and operate an accommodation-booking service.

Accommodation

Lincoln has a good supply of competitively priced **hotels** and **B&Bs**, though surprisingly few of them are in the vicinity of the Cathedral – "Uphill" – and this is precisely where you want to be. All the places below are "Uphill," unless otherwise indicated. On occasion, demand can exceed supply, in which case head for the tourist office.

Hotels, guest houses and B&Bs

Carline Guest House 1–3 Carline Rd ☎01522/530422, ⓦwww.carlineguesthouse .co.uk. One of the best B&Bs in the city, *Carline* occupies a spick-and-span Edwardian house about ten minutes' walk down from the cathedral. Breakfasts are first-rate, and the rooms smart and tastefully furnished. No credit cards. ②

D'Isney Place Eastgate ☎01522/538881, ⓦwww.disneyplacehotel.co.uk. This delightful hotel occupies a lovely eighteenth-century building close to the cathedral. Breakfast is served in the bedrooms, some of which have four-poster beds and spa baths. Highly recommended. ⑤

Edward King House The Old Palace, Minster Yard ☎01522/528778, ⓦwww.ekhs.org.uk. For something a little different, head for this unusual B&B in a former residence of the Bishops of Lincoln, immediately below the cathedral. The exterior is a good bit grander than the rooms, but these are perfectly adequate and some have fine views over the city. ②

Hillcrest 15 Lindum Terrace ☎01522/510182, ⓦwww.hillcrest-hotel.com. Traditional, very English hotel in a large red-brick house that was originally a Victorian rectory. Sixteen comfortable rooms with all mod cons plus a large, sloping garden. The owner, who is often in attendance, has loads of ideas about what to visit. ⑤

St Clements Lodge 21 Langworth Gate ☎01522/521532. In a brisk, modern house a short walk from the cathedral, this comfortable B&B offers a handful of pleasant, en-suite guest rooms. No credit cards. ③

Hostel

Lincoln Youth Hostel 77 South Park ☎0870/770 5918, ⓔlincoln@yha.org.uk. The town's YHA hostel occupies a Victorian house beside South Common Park, one mile south of the train station. There are 46 beds in 2- to 8-bedded rooms. To get there from the centre, head south along Canwick Rd and South Park is on the right opposite the cemetery. Closed Nov–Jan. Dorm beds £10.25.

The Cathedral

Not a hill at all, **Castle Hill** is a wide, short and level cobbled street that links Lincoln's castle and cathedral. It's a charming spot and its east end is marked by the arch of the medieval **Exchequergate**, beyond which soars the glorious

---

Guided tours of Lincoln cathedral

Monday to Saturday, the cathedral offers two sorts of **guided tour** free with the price of admission. The first – the **Floor Tour** (Mon–Sat 1–2 daily) – is a quick gambol round the cathedral's salient features, while the second, the **Roof Tour** (Mon–Sat 2–3 daily), takes in parts of the church otherwise out of bounds. Both are very popular, so it's a good idea to book in advance – call ☎01522/544544 or see ⓦwww.lincolncathedral.com.

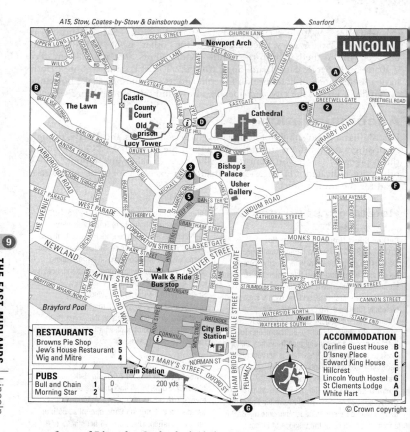

LINCOLN

CHURCH LANE
CECIL STREET
Newport Arch
EAST BIGHT
UPPER LONG LEYS ROAD
BURTON ROAD
OCCUPATION RD
WILLIS'S
CHAPEL LANE
BAILGATE
NORTHGATE
NETTLEHAM ROAD

WESTGATE
ST PAUL'S LANE
BAILGATE
A
LANGWORTHGATE
1
GREETWELLGATE
GREETWELL ROAD
B
BELLE VUE RD
UNION ROAD
Castle
County
Court
Old
prison
EASTGATE
Cathedral
C
MINNA
2
STY LANE
WRAGBY ROAD
SWELL ROAD
GREETWELL ROAD

The Lawn
CARLINE ROAD
i
D
CASTLE HILL
EASTGATE
POTTERGATE
UPPER LINDUM ST
EASTGATE ROAD

ALEXANDRA TERRACE
Lucy Tower
DRURY LANE
LINDUM TERRACE

YARBOROUGH ROAD
SPRING HILL
BEAUMONT FEE
MICHAELGATE
GREESTONE PLACE
LINDUM AVENUE
F

VICTORIA TERRACE
3
Bishop's
Palace
LINDUM ROAD
VINE STREET
CHEVIOT STREET

WEST PARADE
VICTORIA STREET
4
Usher
Gallery
CATHEDRAL STREET
ST HIGH STREET

THE AVENUE
ORCHARD ROAD
WEST PARADE
MOTHERBY LA.
ST MARTIN'S
STEEP HILL
DANES TER
DANESGATE
GATE
MONKS ROAD
MONTAGUE STREET
BAGHOME ROAD
JOHN STREET
THOMAS STREET
AVONDALE STREET

NEWLAND
CORPORATION STREET
HUNGATE
GRANTHAM STREET
FRIARS LANE
ROSEMARY LANE
CROFT ST

MINT LA.
PARK STREET
CLASKETGATE
BROADGATE
WINN STREET

BRAYFORD WHARF NORTH
LUCY TOWER STREET
MINT STREET
SILVER STREET
FREE SCHOOL LANE
ST RUMBOLDS STREET
CROFT STREET
CANNON STREET

WIGFORD WAY
★ **Walk & Ride**
Bus stop
SALTERGATE
WATERSIDE NORTH
STAMP END

Brayford Pool
HIGH STREET
WATERSIDE
MELVILLE STREET
City Bus
Station
WATERSIDE SOUTH
River Witham

RESTAURANTS
Browns Pie Shop   3
Jew's House Restaurant   5
Wig and Mitre   4

PUBS
Bull and Chain   1
Morning Star   2

i
CORNHILL
SINCIL STREET
★ P
N

ACCOMMODATION
Carline Guest House   **B**
D'Isney Place   **C**
Edward King House   **E**
Hillcrest   **F**
Lincoln Youth Hostel   **G**
St Clements Lodge   **A**
White Hart   **D**

Train Station
ST MARY'S STREET
NORMAN ST
OXFORD ST
PELHAM BRIDGE
PELHAM ST
0   200 yds

G

© Crown copyright

west front of **Lincoln Cathedral** (daily: May–Sept 7.15am–8pm, Oct–April 7am–6pm, except during services when access is restricted; £4 including guided tour – see previous page), a sheer cliff-face of blind arcading mobbed by decorative carving. Most striking of all is the extraordinary band of twelfth-century carved panels depicting biblical themes with passionate intimacy, their inspiration being a similar frieze at Modena cathedral in Italy. The west front's apparent homogeneity is, however, deceptive, and further inspection reveals two phases of construction – the small stones and thick mortar of much of the facade belong to the original church, completed in 1092, whereas the longer stones and finer courses date from the early thirteenth century. These were enforced modifications, for in 1185 an earthquake shattered much of the Norman church, which was then rebuilt under the auspices of **Bishop Hugh of Avalon**, the man responsible for most of the present cathedral, with the notable exception of the (largely) fourteenth-century central tower.

The cavernous **interior** is a fine example of Early English architecture, with the nave's pillars conforming to the same general design yet differing slightly, their varied columns and bands of dark Purbeck marble contrasting with the oolitic limestone that is the building's main material. Looking back up the nave from beneath the central tower, you can also observe a major medieval cock-up: Bishop Hugh's roof is out of alignment with the earlier west front, and the point where they meet has all the wrong angles. It's possible to pick out other irregularities, too – the pillars have bases of different heights, and there are ten windows in the nave's north wall and nine in the south – but these are deliberate features, reflecting a medieval aversion to the vanity of symmetry.

Beyond the rood screen lies **St Hugh's Choir**, its fourteenth-century misericords carrying an eccentric range of carvings, with scenes from the life of Alexander the Great and King Arthur mixed up with biblical characters and folkloric parables. Further on is the open and airy Gothic **Angel Choir**, completed in 1280, dotted with stone table-tombs and its roof embellished by dozens of finely carved statuettes, including the tiny Lincoln Imp (see p.562). Finally, a corridor off the choir's north aisle leads to the wooden-roofed **cloisters** and the polygonal **chapter house**, where Edward I and Edward II convened gatherings that prefigured the creation of the English Parliament.

Hidden behind a wall immediately below (and to the south of) the cathedral on Minster Yard are the ruins of what would, in its day, have been the city's most impressive building. This, the medieval **Bishop's Palace** (April–Oct daily 10am–6pm; Nov–March Sat & Sun 10am–4pm; £3.20; EH), once consisted of two grand halls, a lavish chapel, kitchens and ritzy private chambers, but today the most coherent survivor is the battered and bruised Alnwick Tower – where the entrance is. The damage was done during the Civil War when a troupe of Roundheads occupied the palace until they themselves had to evacuate the place after a fierce fire.

The Castle

From the west front of the cathedral, it's a quick stroll across Castle Hill to **Lincoln Castle** (April–Sept Mon–Sat 9.30am–5.30pm, Sun 11am–5.30pm; Oct–March Mon–Sat 9.30am–4pm, Sun 11am–4pm; £3.50). Intact and forbidding, the castle walls incorporate bits and pieces from the twelfth to the nineteenth century and the wall walkway offers great views over town. The earliest remains are those of the **Lucy Tower**, built on the steep grassy mound to the left of the main entrance and once the site of one of the two original Norman mottes. The castle was turned into a prison in the 1820s and some of the prisoners were unceremoniously buried here at the top of the mound – a sad and lonely spot if ever there was one, especially as the tombs were only allowed to carry the prisoners' initials. The spacious grounds enclosed by the castle walls hold the old **prison**, a dour red-brick structure with multiple turrets that holds one of the four surviving copies of the **Magna Carta** (see p.1299) as well as a truly remarkable **prison chapel**. Here, the prisoners were locked in high-sided cubicles, where they could see the preacher and his pulpit but not their fellow internees. Neither was this approach just applied to chapel visits: the prisoners were kept in perpetual solitary confinement, and were compelled to wear masks when they took to the exercise yard. This system was founded on the pseudo-scientific theory that defined crime as a contagious disease, but unfortunately for the theorists, their so-called Pentonville System of "Separation and Silence", which was introduced here in 1846, drove many prisoners crazy, and it had to be abandoned thirty years later; nobody ever bothered to dismantle the chapel.

The rest of the city

As for the rest of "**Uphill**" **Lincoln**, it's scattered with historic remains, notably several chunks of Roman wall, the most prominent of which is the second-century **Newport Arch** straddling Bailgate and once the main north gate into the city. There's also a bevy of medieval stone houses, at their best on and around the aptly named **Steep Hill** as it cuts down to the city centre. In particular, look out for the tidily restored twelfth-century **Jew's House**, a reminder of the Jewish community that flourished in medieval Lincoln. A rare and superb example of domestic Norman architecture, it now houses the *Jew's House* restaurant (see below).

The **Usher Gallery**, Lindum Rd (Tues–Sat 10am–5.30pm, Sun 2.30–5pm; £2), is on the hillside too, its well-presented displays featuring some fine paintings of the cathedral and its environs, the best being those of William Logsdail (1859–1944). There's also a *Lincoln* view by Lowry as well as memorabilia celebrating Lincolnshire's own Alfred Tennyson (1809–1892), one of Victorian England's favourite poets. In addition, the gallery holds an eclectic collection of coins, porcelain, and watches and clocks dating from the seventeenth century. The timepieces were given to the gallery by its benefactor, James Ward Usher, a local jeweller and watchmaker who made a fortune by devising the legend of the **Lincoln Imp**, which he turned into the city's emblem in the 1880s. His story has a couple of imps hopping around the cathedral, until one of them is turned to stone for trying to talk to the angels carved into the roof of the Angel Choir. His chum made a hasty exit on the back of a witch, but the wind is still supposed to haunt the cathedral awaiting their return.

Eating and drinking

Lincoln's **café** and **restaurant** scene is a little patchy – with lots of places offering mundane food geared to the day-tripping trade – but there are excellent places too, mostly within shouting distance of the Cathedral. First stop must be *Browns Pie Shop*, 33 Steep Hill – at the top – which has a creative menu where the emphasis is on British ingredients; a main course here will cost you about £10. Next door, and similarly enticing, is the *Wig and Mitre*, with a restaurant upstairs and a bar-restaurant below. Another recommendable spot on Steep Hill is the more expensive – and more formal – *The Restaurant in the Jew's House* (℡01522/524851), where again much emphasis is placed on local ingredients.

As for **pubs**, there is a pair of amiable and traditional locals near the cathedral – the *Bull & Chain*, on Langworthgate, and the *Morning Star*, close by on Greetwellgate. The former has a garden.

The Wolds and the coast

The rolling hills and gentle valleys of the **Lincolnshire Wolds**, a narrow band of chalky land running southeast from Caistor to just outside Skegness, stand out amidst the more mundane agricultural landscapes of north Lincolnshire. A string of particularly appealing valleys is concentrated in the vicinity of **Louth**, which, with its striking church and antique centre, is easily the most enticing of the region's towns – with the added advantage of being fairly close to the coast. A few miles to the south of Louth, the Wolds dip down to the fens, pancake-flat and creating a wide and deep arch around the intrusive stump of The Wash. In the other direction, east of the Wolds, lies the coast, whose bungalows, campsites and caravans are parked beside a sandy beach that extends, with a few marshy interruptions, north from **Skegness**, the main resort, to Mablethorpe and ultimately Cleethorpes. Near Skegness, the

Gibraltar Point Nature Reserve is a welcome diversion from the bucket-and-spade/amusement-arcade commercialism.

Louth and around

Henry VIII described the county of Lincolnshire as "one of the most brutal and beestlie of the whole realm", his contempt based on the events of 1536, when thousands of northern peasants rebelled against his religious reforms. In Lincolnshire, this insurrection, the **Pilgrimage of Grace**, began in the north-east of the county at **LOUTH**, twenty-three miles from Lincoln, under the leadership of the local vicar, who was subsequently hung, drawn and quartered. There's a commemorative plaque in honour of the rebels beside Louth's church of **St James** (Easter to mid-Dec Mon–Sat 10.30am–4pm; free), which is the town's one outstanding building, its soaring Perpendicular spire, buttresses, battlements and pinnacles set on a grassy knoll just to the west of the centre. The interior is delightful too, the sweeping symmetries of the nave illuminated by slender windows and capped by a handsome Georgian wooden roof decorated with dinky little angels. The roof of the tower vault is, if anything, even finer, its intricate stonework an exercise in geometrical precision. Finally, don't forget the café and its homemade cakes – locals set out early to get a slice of lemon-drizzle cake.

Next to the church, the well-tended gardens and Georgian houses of **Westgate** make it one of Louth's prettiest streets; you can grab a drink here at the antique *Wheatsheaf Inn*. Afterwards, it doesn't take long to explore the rest of the town centre, whose cramped lanes and alleys – focusing on the **Cornmarket** – are flanked by red-brick buildings mostly dating from the nineteenth century.

Practicalities

With reasonably regular weekday services from Boston and Lincoln, Louth's **bus station** is at the east end of Queen Street, a couple of minutes' walk from the Cornmarket – walk west along Queen Street and turn right onto the Market Place. The **tourist office**, in the Market Hall off Cornmarket (Mon–Sat 9am–5pm; ☏01507/609289), has a competent range of local information including accommodation details. The best **hotel** is the *Priory*, on Eastgate (☏01507/602930, ⓦwww.theprioryhotel.com; ❹), an excellent family-run place in a Georgian villa of 1818 with an idiosyncratic neo-Gothic facade and extensive gardens; it's located at the east end of the centre, about ten minutes' walk from the Cornmarket.

For **food**, the antique *Ye Olde Whyte Swanne*, at 45 Eastgate on the corner of Market Place, sells tasty bar snacks, including home-made game and pork pies as well as the illustrious (and extremely large) Lincolnshire sausage.

The Saltfleetby-Theddlethorpe dunes

An enjoyable short excursion from Louth takes you east along the **B1200** across about nine miles of fen farmland to the coast. This byroad is built on an old Roman road that was used to transport salt inland from the seashore salt pans, once a lucrative source of income for local traders. On the coast, at the end of the B1200, turn right along the main A1031 and, after about half a mile, take the (poorly signed) gravel track on the left through the dunes of the **Saltfleetby–Theddlethorpe Dunes National Nature Reserve**. Comprising over five miles of sand dune, salt and freshwater marsh, the reserve is at its prettiest in midsummer, when the dunes sprout buckthorn bushes and sea heather flowers, forming a carpet of violet spreading down towards the sea. A network of trails navigates the dunes and lagoons, with the latter attracting hundreds of migratory wildfowl in spring and autumn.

Skegness and around

SKEGNESS, south along the coast from the Saltfleetby-Theddlethorpe reserve, has been a busy resort ever since the railways reached the Lincolnshire coast in 1875. Its heyday was before the 1960s, when the Brits began to take themselves off to sunnier climes, but it still attracts tens of thousands of city-dwellers who come for the wide, sandy beaches and for a host of attractions ranging from nightclubs to bowling greens. Every inch the traditional English seaside town, Skegness gets the edge over many of its rivals by keeping its beaches sparklingly clean and its parks spick-and-span, whilst a massive leisure complex in neighbouring Ingoldmells has a whopping indoor "fun pool". Indeed, Skegness has a tradition of keeping ahead of its competitors: in 1908 it came up with the ground-breaking "Skegness is So Bracing" slogan beneath a picture of a "Jolly Fisherman", and it was here in 1936 that ex-showman Billy Butlin opened the first Butlin's Holiday Camp. All that said, the seafront, with its rows of souvenir shops and amusement arcades, can be dismal, especially on rainy days, and you may well decide to sidestep the whole caboodle by heading south three miles along the coastal road to the **Gibraltar Point National Nature Reserve** (daily dawn–dusk). Here, a network of clearly signed footpaths patterns a narrow strip of salt and freshwater marsh, sand dune and beach that attracts an inordinate number of birds, both resident and migratory.

As for practicalities, Skegness **bus** and **train stations** are next door to each other about ten minutes' walk from the seashore – cut across Lumley Square and go straight up the High Street to the landmark clock tower. The **tourist office** (daily: April–Sept 9.30am–5pm; Oct–March 10am–4pm; ℡01754/899887, Ⓦwww.funcoast.co.uk) is yards from the clock tower, opposite the Embassy Centre on Grand Parade. They can provide a colossal list of accommodation, including scores of **hotels**, **B&Bs** and **guest houses**. Several good ones are strung along South Parade, which runs south from the Clock Tower, behind the large park that fronts onto the beach. Options here include the unassuming *Palm Court Hotel* (℡01754/767711; ❷), a tidy little place in a modern building, and the comparable *South Parade Hotel* (℡01754/764113; ❷). Moving upmarket, the *Best Western Vine Hotel*, Vine Road (℡01754/763018; ❻), is located on a quiet residential street about three quarters of a mile from the clocktower, and occupies a rambling, ivy-clad old house set in its own grounds.

The Lincolnshire Fens

The Lincolnshire section of **The Fens**, the great chunk of eastern England extending from Boston to Cambridge, encompasses some of the most productive farmland in Europe. With the exception of the occasional hillock, this pancake-flat, treeless terrain has been painstakingly reclaimed from the marshes and swamps that once drained into the Wash, a process that has taken almost two thousand years. In earlier times, outsiders were often amazed by the dreadful conditions hereabouts, but they did spawn the distinctive culture of the so-called **fen slodgers**. The latter embanked small portions of marsh to create pastureland and fields, supplementing their diets by catching fish and fowl, and gathering reed and sedge for thatching and fuel. Their economy was threatened by the large-scale land reclamation schemes of the late fifteenth and sixteenth centuries, and time and again the fenlanders sabotaged progress by breaking down the banks and dams. But the odds were stacked against the saboteurs, and a succession of great landowners eventually drained huge tracts of the fenland; by the end of the eighteenth century the fen slodgers' way of life had all but disappeared. Nonetheless, the Lincolnshire fens remain a distinctive area of introverted little villages, with just one major settlement, the old port of **Boston**.

Boston

As it nears The Wash, the muddy River Witham weaves its way through **BOSTON** (a corruption of Botolf's stone, or Botolph's town), which was named after the Anglo-Saxon monk-saint who first established a monastery here, overlooking the main river crossing point in 645 AD. In the thirteenth and fourteenth centuries, the settlement expanded to become England's second largest seaport, its flourishing economy dependent on the wool trade with Flanders. Local merchants, revelling in their success, decided to build a church that demonstrated their wealth, the result being the magnificent medieval church of St Botolph, whose 272-foot tower still presides over the town and surrounding fenland. The church was completed in the early sixteenth century, but by then Boston was in decline as trade drifted west towards the Atlantic and the Witham silted up. The town's fortunes only revived in the late eighteenth century when, after the nearby fens had been drained, it became a minor agricultural centre with a modest port that has, in recent times, been modernized for trade with the EU. A singular mix of fenland town and seaport, Boston is an unusual little place that is at its liveliest on **market days** – Wednesday and Saturday.

The town

Mostly edged by Victorian red-brick buildings, the mazy streets of Boston's cramped and compact centre, on the east side of the Witham, radiate out from the **Market Place**, a dishevelled square of irregular shape. Just to the west looms the massive bulk of **St Botolph's** (daily 8.30am–4.30pm, Sun 8.30am–12.30pm; free), whose exterior masonry is embellished by the high-pointed windows and elaborate tracery of the Decorated style. Most of the structure dates from the fourteenth century, but the huge and distinctive **tower**, whose lack of a spire earned the church the nickname the "Boston Stump", is of later construction. The octagonal lantern is later still, added in the sixteenth century and graced by flying buttresses and pointy pinnacles. A tortuous 365-step spiral staircase (closed on Sun) leads to a balcony near the top, from where the panoramic views over Boston and the fens amply repay both the price of the ticket (£2) and the effort of the climb. Down below, St Botolph's light and airy **nave** is an exercise in the Perpendicular, all soaring columns and high windows. The sheer purity of design is stunning, its virtuos-ity heightened by the narrowness of the annexe-like chancel and the elegance of the Decorated arch that partly screens it from view.

The church's most famous vicar was **John Cotton** (1584–1652), who helped stir the Puritan stew during his twenty-year tenure, encouraging a stream of Lincolnshire dissidents to head off to the colonies of New England to found their "New Jerusalem". Cotton emigrated himself in 1633 and soon became the leading light among the Puritans of Boston, Massachusetts. The Cotton connection was finally commemorated here in the Stump by the creation of the **Cotton Chapel**, at the west end of the nave, in 1857. The most interesting relic from Cotton's sojourn here is not in the chapel at all, but in the nave in the form of the ornate **pulpit** from which he pounded out his three-hour sermons.

Boston had been alive to religious dissent before Cotton arrived and, in 1607, several of the **Pilgrim Fathers** were incarcerated here after their failed attempt to escape religious persecution by slipping across to Holland. They were imprisoned for thirty days in the old **Guildhall** (closed for refurbishment), on South Street – a brief walk south from St Botolph's back through the Market Place. A creaky affair, the Guildhall spreads over three levels and incorporates an antique Council Chamber, the court where the Pilgrim Fathers were tried and sentenced, as well as the cells where they were locked up.

Practicalities

It's ten minutes' walk east from Boston **train station** to the town centre – head straight out of the station along Station Street and keep going until you hit the river. The **bus station** is also to the west of the centre, just five minutes' walk away on Lincoln Lane. The **tourist office** (Mon–Sat 9am–5pm; ☎01205/356656, ⊛www.boston.gov.uk) is in the Market Place beneath the Assembly Rooms. Staff have oodles of local information and a list of **B&Bs**, among which one good option is the *Bramley House* (☎01205/354538; no cards; ❷), in an attractively converted eighteenth-century farmhouse about one mile west of the train station at 267 Sleaford Rd. Another good choice is *Fairfield Guest House*, in a much-enlarged Victorian property about three miles to the south of the centre at 101 London Rd (☎01205/362869; no cards; ❷). There are fifteen guest rooms here (seven en-suite); each is decorated in bright and cheerful style. Town-centre accommodation is limited and the best you'll do is the *New England Hotel*, Wide Bargate (☎01205/365255, ⊛www.thenewengland.co.uk; ❺), an unassuming mid-range place of thirty bedrooms with modern furnishings and fittings.

For **food**, cosy *Goodbarns Yard*, just to the north of the Stump on Wormgate, serves copious pub meals inside or out in a back garden overlooking the river. Vegetarians should make a beeline for *Maud's Tea Rooms*, inside the Maud Foster Windmill, on Willoughby Road (open 3 to 5 days a week, 10am or 11am–5pm; ☎01205/352188). Built to grind corn in 1819, the windmill, with its five whopping sails, is still in full working order. You can inspect its grinding gears and buy the organic flour it churns out at the tea room, which serves a range of vegetarian and vegan meals and a good selection of delicious cakes. The windmill is about ten minutes' walk northeast of the Market Place, beside the road to Horncastle.

Heckington

The village of **HECKINGTON**, thirteen miles west of Boston and five east of Sleaford, has a tidy little centre that drapes around the church of **St Andrew** (Mon–Sat 9am–5pm or dusk in winter; free), a splendid example of the Decorated style, with a pinnacled spire and elaborate canopied buttresses framing the flowing tracery of the windows. Inside, the original fourteenth-century chancel fittings have survived, including the battered tomb of the founder, Richard de Potesgrave, and an **Easter Sepulchre**, whose folksy and energetic carved figures are set against a dense undergrowth of foliage. The sepulchre, one of the finest in England, was built to accommodate the Host between Good Friday and Easter morning. The **sedilia** is intriguing, too, boasting a cartoon strip of domestic scenes on the subject of food – a man eating fruit, a woman feeding the birds and suchlike. Heckington has one other attraction, its unique eight-sailed **windmill**, located a short stroll from the church and worth visiting when it's in operation (call ☎ 01529/461919 for times). In between the wind-mill and the church, on the High Street, is the village's best pub, the *Nag's Head*.

On the Skegness–Grantham line, Heckington **train station** is in the centre opposite the windmill.

Stamford

STAMFORD, some thirty miles south of Heckington, is delightful. A hand-some little limestone town of yellow–grey seventeenth- and eighteenth-cen-tury buildings edging narrow streets that slope up from the River Welland. It was here that the Romans forded this important river, establishing a fortified outpost that the Danes subsequently selected for one of their regional capitals. Later the town became a centre of the medieval wool and cloth trade, its wealthy merchants funding a series of almshouses known as "**callises**" – after Calais, the English-occupied port through which most of them traded. Indeed, Stamford **cloth** became famous throughout Europe for its quality and dura-bility. Stamford was also the home of **William Cecil**, Elizabeth's chief minis-ter, who built his splendid mansion, Burghley House, close by. The town survived the collapse of the wool trade, prospering as an inland port after the Welland was made navigable to the sea in 1570, and, in the eighteenth century, as a staging post on the Great North Road from London. More recently, Stamford escaped the three main threats to old English towns – the Industrial Revolution, wartime bombing and postwar development – and was designated the country's first Conservation Area in 1967.

The town centre

Above all, it's the harmony of Stamford's architecture that pleases, rather than any specific sight. There are, nevertheless, a handful of buildings of some special interest amongst the web of narrow streets that make up the town's compact centre, beginning with the church of **St Mary** (no regular opening hours), set beside a pristine close of proud Georgian buildings on St Mary's Place. The church, with its splendid spire, has a small, airy interior, which incorporates the Corpus Christi chapel, whose intricately embossed, painted and panelled roof dates from the 1480s.

Across the street from St Mary's, several lanes thread through to the carefully preserved **High Street**, from where Ironmonger Street leads north again to the wide and handsome Broad Street, the site of the **Stamford Museum** (April–Sept Mon–Sat 10am–5pm, Sun 2–5pm; Oct–March Mon–Sat 10am–5pm; free). This features a tasteless exhibit comparing the American midget Tom Thumb with **Daniel Lambert**, the Leicester fat man who died at Stamford in 1809, aged 39 and weighing 52st 11lb (336kg). After Lambert's death his clothes were displayed in a local inn, which Tom Thumb, otherwise Charles Stratton, visited several times to perform a few party tricks, such as standing in Lambert's waistcoat armhole.

Nearby, also on Broad Street, is **Browne's Hospital** (May–Sept Sat & Sun 11am–4pm; £2.50), the most extensive of the town's almshouses, dating from the late fifteenth century. Not all of the complex is open to the public, but it's still worth visiting with the first room – the old dormitory – capped by a splendid wood-panelled ceiling. The adjacent chapel holds some delightfully folksy misericords, and upstairs, the audit room is illuminated by a handsome set of stained-glass windows.

From Browne's, it's a few paces more to Red Lion Square, which is over-looked by **All Saints'** (daily dawn–dusk; free). Several centuries in the making, this church is a happy amalgamation of Early English and Perpendicular features that takes full advantage of its position, perched on a small hillock. Entry is via the south porch, itself an ornate structure with a fine – if badly weathered – crocketted gable, and, although most of the interior is routinely Victorian, the carved capitals are of great delicacy. There's also an engaging folkloric carving of the Last Supper behind the high altar.

High Street St Martin's

Down the slope from St Mary's, across the reedy River Welland on High Street St Martin's, is the **George Hotel**, a splendid old coaching inn whose Georgian facade supports one end of the gallows that span the street – not a warning to criminals, but an advertising hoarding. Just along – and across – the street, the plain and sombre, late fifteenth-century church of **St Martin** (daily 9.30am–4pm; free) shelters the magnificent tombs of the lords Burghley, with a recumbent William Cecil carved beneath twin canopies, holding his rod of office and with a lion at his feet. Just behind, the early eighteenth-century effigies of John Cecil and his wife show the couple as Roman aristocrats, propped up on their elbows, she to gaze at him, John to stare across the nave commandingly.

Burghley House

Burghley House (April–Oct daily 11am–4.30pm; viewing by guided tours only every 10–20mins, except Sat & Sun pm; £7.50; ⓦwww.burghley.co .uk), an extravagant Elizabethan mansion standing in landscaped parkland, is located a mile and a half or so to the east of Stamford, out along the Barnack Road from High Street St Martin's. Completed in 1587, the house sports a mellow-yellow ragstone exterior, embellished by dainty cupolas, a pyramidal clock tower and skeletal balustrading, all to a plan by **William Cecil**, the long-serving adviser to Elizabeth I.

With the notable exception of the Tudor kitchen, little remains of Burghley's Elizabethan interior. Instead, the house bears the heavy hand of John, fifth Lord Burghley, who toured France and Italy in the late seventeenth century, commissioning furniture, statuary and tapestries, as well as buying up old Florentine and Venetian paintings, such as Paolo Veronese's *Zebedee's Wife Petitioning our Lord*. To provide a suitable setting for his old masters, John brought in Antonio Verrio and his assistant Louis Laguerre, who between them covered many of Burghley's walls and ceilings with frolicking gods and goddesses. These gaudy and gargantuan murals are at their most engulfing in the **Heaven Room**, an artfully painted classical temple that adjoins the **Hell Staircase**, where the entrance to the inferno is through the gaping mouth of a cat. Have a close look also at the fine portraits in the **Pagoda Room**, in particular the querulous Elizabeth I and a sublimely self-confident Henry VIII by Joos van Cleve.

Practicalities

With frequent services from Peterborough and Oakham, Stamford **train station** is five minutes' walk from the town centre, which lies just to the north across the river. The **bus station** is on the west side of the centre, on Sheepmarket, off All Saints' Street. The **tourist office** is in the centre inside Stamford Arts Centre at 27 St Mary's St (April–Oct Mon–Sat 9.30am–5pm, Sun 10am–4pm; Nov–March closed Sun; ☎01780/755611, ⓦwww.stamfordonline.co.uk).

Stamford has several charming **hotels**, the most celebrated of which is the beguiling *George*, 71 High Street St Martin's (☎01780/750750, ⓦwww.georgehotelofstamford.com; ❻), an old and cleverly remodelled coaching inn with flagstone floors and antique furnishings, where the most appealing rooms overlook the cobbled courtyard. Just along the street is the attractive *Garden House* (☎01780/763359, ⓦwww.gardenhousehotel.com; ❻), which occupies a tastefully modernized eighteenth-century building with twenty smart bedrooms. Stamford also possesses a clutch of **B&Bs** and the tourist office has the full list, but the majority are on the town's outskirts.

For **food**, it has to be the *George Hotel* – either in the formal and expensive restaurant, where the emphasis is on British ingredients served in imaginative ways, or in the moderately priced and informal *Garden Lounge*. There's delicious and inexpensive bar food, too, served in the *York Bar* at lunchtimes.

Travel Details

Buses

For information on all local and national bus services, contact Traveline on ☎0870/608 2608, ⓦwww.traveline.org.uk.

Leicester to: Lincoln (hourly; 1hr 40min); Market Harborough (every 15min; 40min); Northampton (hourly; 1hr); Nottingham (every 30min; 1hr 40min); Oakham (hourly; 1hr 10min); Stamford (hourly; 2hr).

Lincoln to: Boston (hourly; 1hr 30min); Leicester (hourly; 1hr 30min); Louth (every 1–2hr; 40min); Northampton (hourly; 3hr); Nottingham (hourly; 2hr 30min); Oakham (hourly; 2hr 20min); Skegness (hourly; 1hr 45min).

Northampton to: Leicester (hourly; 1hr); Lincoln (hourly; 3hr); Nottingham (hourly; 2hr); Stamford (hourly; 2hr 30).

Nottingham to: Leicester (every 30min; 1hr 40min); Lincoln (hourly; 2hr 30min); Newark (hourly; 30min); Northampton (hourly; 2hr).

Oakham to: Leicester (hourly; 1hr 10min); Lincoln (hourly; 2hr 20min); Stamford (every 30min; 20min).

Stamford to: Leicester (hourly; 2hr); Northampton (hourly; 2hr 30min–2hr 50min); Oakham (every 30min; 20min).

Trains

For information on all local and national rail services, contact National Rail Enquiries ☎08457/484950, ⓦwww.nationalrail.co.uk.

Leicester to: Birmingham (every 30min; 1hr); Coventry (hourly; 45min); Derby (hourly; 35min); Lincoln (hourly; 1hr 40min); London (every 30min; 1hr 30min); Market Harborough (every 1–2 hours; 15min); Nottingham (every 30min; 20min); Oakham (hourly; 30min); Stamford (hourly; 50min).

Lincoln to: Birmingham (hourly; 3hr); Boston (hourly; 1hr); Cambridge (hourly; 1hr); Leicester (hourly; 1hr 30min); London (hourly; 2hr 15min); Newark (hourly; 25min); Nottingham (hourly; 45min); Peterborough (hourly; 1hr 20min); Skegness (hourly; 1hr 40min); Spalding (every 1–2hr; 1hr).

Northampton to: Birmingham (every 30min; 1hr); Coventry (every 30min; 40min); London Euston (every 30min; 1hr 10min–1hr 40min).

Nottingham to: Leicester (every 30min; 30min); Lincoln (hourly; 1hr 15min); London (hourly; 1hr 40min); Newark (hourly; 30min).

Stamford to: Cambridge (hourly; 1hr 20min); Leicester (hourly; 40min); Oakham (hourly; 10min); Peterborough (hourly; 15min).

The Northwest

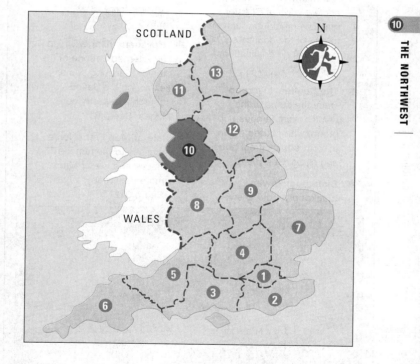

Highlights

✳ Café society, Manchester From breakfast croissant to late-night drinks, Manchester's café-bars set the tone for this happening city. **See p.587**

✳ City walls, Chester A two-mile walk around the ancient walls of Chester makes a great introduction to one of the country's most historic destinations. **See p.592**

✳ The Beatles, Liverpool Trace the steps of the world's most famous pop group, who started out in this city's backstreet pubs and clubs. **See p.599**

✳ Blackpool Tower Blackpool's bold answer to the Eiffel Tower lights up the skyline of the UK's favourite resort. **See p.607**

✳ Lancaster Castle From the dungeons to the ornate court rooms, the castle tour is a historical tour-de-force. **See p.610**

✳ Heysham Village Spend an afternoon at one of the region's unsung gems, exploring the Saxon church and pretty cottages. **See p.612**

✳ Isle of Man From Norse crosses to the famous TT Races, the Isle of Man more than repays a visit. **See p.612**

△ Blackpool Tower

⑩

The Northwest

ithin the **northwest** of England lie some of the ugliest and some of the most beautiful parts of the country. The least attractive zones are found in the sprawl connecting the country's third and sixth largest conurbations, Manchester and Liverpool, but even here the picture isn't unrelievedly bleak, as the cities themselves have an ingratiating appeal. **Manchester**, in particular, surprises many who don't expect to see beyond its dour, industrial heritage. Where once only a handful of Victorian Gothic buildings lent any grace to the cityscape, Manchester today has been completely transformed by a rebuilding programme that puts it in the vanguard of modern British urban design. Quite apart from a clutch of top-class visitor attractions, where Manchester really scores is in the buzz of its thriving café and club scene. **Liverpool**, set on the Mersey estuary, is perhaps less appealing at first glance, though Georgian townhouses, grand civic buildings, its twin cathedrals and a burgeoning café scene soon change perceptions. At the redundant docks that once made the city's fortune, many of the old warehouses and buildings have been redeveloped as part of the Albert Dock scheme, housing a fine swathe of museums, including the northern outpost of the Tate Gallery.

The hills, which form the southern tip of the Pennine range, melt away to the west into undulating, pastoral **Cheshire**, whose county town, **Chester**, with its circuit of town walls and partly Tudor centre, is as alluring as any of the country's northern towns.

Lancashire, which historically lay directly to the north of Cheshire, reached industrial prominence in the nineteenth century primarily due to the cotton-mill towns around Manchester and to the thriving port of Liverpool. Today, substantially reduced in size and having lost its two biggest cities, the county's oldest town and major commercial and administrative centre is **Preston** – home of the national museum of England's national game, football – though tourists are perhaps more inclined to linger in the charming towns and villages of the nearby **Ribble Valley**. Meanwhile, along the coast to the west and north of the major cities stretches a line of **resorts** that once formed the mainstay of the northern British holiday trade. Only **Blackpool** is really worth visiting for its own sake, however, a rip-roaring resort which has stayed at the top of its game by supplying undemanding entertainment with more panache than its neighbours. For anything more culturally invigorating you'll have to continue north to the historically important city of **Lancaster**, with its Tudor castle. Finally, the semi-autonomous **Isle of Man**, only twenty-five miles off the coast and served by ferries from Liverpool and Heysham (or short flights from various regional airports), provides a terrain almost as rewarding as that of the Lake District but without the seasonal overcrowding.

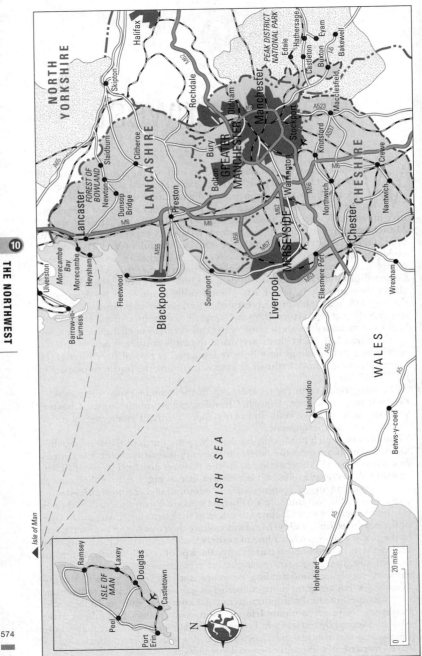

© Crown copyright

Manchester's international **airport** picks the city out as a major UK point of arrival, and there are direct train services from the airport to Liverpool, Blackpool, Lancaster, Leeds and York, as well as to Manchester itself. Both Manchester and Liverpool are well served by **trains**, with plentiful connections to the Midlands and London, and up the west coast to Scotland. There's also a frequent rail and bus service between both cities, and from each to Chester, allowing an easy triangular loop between Greater Manchester, Merseyside and Cheshire. The major east–west rail lines in the region are the direct routes between Manchester, Leeds and York, and between Blackpool, Bradford, Leeds and York. In addition, the Morecambe/Lancaster–Leeds line slips through the Yorkshire Dales (with possible connections at Skipton for the famous Settle–Carlisle line; see p.679); further south, the Manchester–Sheffield line provides a rail approach to the Peak District. Regional **rover tickets** are available for a week's unlimited travel in the northwest or in the "coast and peaks" region (basically between Liverpool, Manchester, the Peak District and North Wales).

Manchester

Few cities in the world have embraced social change so heartily as **MANCHESTER**. From engine of the Industrial Revolution to test-bed of contemporary urban design, the city has no realistic provincial English rival. Its domestic dominance expresses itself in various ways, most swaggeringly in the success of Manchester United, the richest football club in Britain, but also in a thriving music and cultural scene that has given birth to world-beaters as diverse as the Hallé Orchestra and Oasis. Moreover, the city's cutting-edge concert halls, theatres, clubs and café society are boosted by one of England's largest student populations and a blooming gay community, whose spending power has created a pioneering **Gay Village**. For inspiration, Manchester's planners look to Barcelona – another revitalized industrial powerhouse – and scoff at many of their northern rivals.

Manchester is first and foremost a Victorian manufacturing city with the imposing streets and buildings to match. Its rapid growth was the equal of any flowering of the Industrial Revolution – from little more than a village in 1750 to the world's major cotton-milling centre in only a hundred years. The spectacular rise of **Cottonopolis**, as it became known, came from the production of vast quantities of competitively priced imitations of expensive Indian calicoes, using machines evolved from Arkwright's first steam-powered cotton mill, which opened in 1783. The rapid industrialization of the area brought prosperity for a few but a life of misery for the majority. The discontent this engendered amongst the working class came to a head in 1819 when eleven people were killed at **Peterloo**, in what began as a peaceful demonstration against the oppressive Corn Laws. Things were, however, even worse when the 23-year-old Friedrich Engels came here in 1842 to work in his father's cotton plant, and the suffering he witnessed – recorded in his *Condition of the Working Class in England* – was a seminal influence on his later collaboration with Karl Marx in the *Communist Manifesto*.

Waterways and railway viaducts form the matrix into which the city's principal buildings have been bedded – as early as 1772 the Duke of Bridgewater had a canal cut to connect the city to the coal mines at Worsley, and in 1830 the Manchester–Liverpool railway opened. The **Manchester Ship Canal**, constructed to entice ocean-going vessels into Manchester and away from burgeoning Liverpool, was completed in 1894, and played a crucial part in sustaining Manchester's competitiveness. Within sixty years, though, the city was in trouble, with the docks, mills and canals in dangerous decline. Sporadic efforts were made to pull Manchester out of the economic doldrums of the 1960s and 1970s, but the main engine of change turned out to be the devastating **IRA bomb**, which exploded in June 1996 and wiped out much of the city's commercial infrastructure. The largest explosion on the mainland since World War II, it devastated the area around the Arndale Centre and the Royal Exchange. Rather than simply patch up the buildings, however, the planning authorities embarked on an ambitious rebuilding scheme with entire new districts taking shape as once-blighted areas along the canals were reclaimed for retail and residential use.

Arrival and information

A direct rail link into the city makes **Manchester Airport**, ten miles south of the city, an increasingly popular point of entry into Britain. Trains to Piccadilly (every 10min 5.15am–10.15pm, reduced service through the night; 25min) cost £2.35, £2.80 on weekdays before 9.30am. A taxi from the airport to the centre costs £12–15. There are tourist information offices in the arrivals halls of Terminal 1 (daily 8am–9pm; ☎0161/436 3344) and Terminal 2 (daily 7.30am–12.30am; same number); and a Travel Shop for public-transport enquiries in Terminal 1 (Mon–Sat 5.30am–9pm, Sun 7am–9pm).

Manchester's three main **train stations** form the points of a triangle that encloses much of the city centre. National mainline trains all pull into **Piccadilly Station**, facing London Road, on the east side, from where you can walk a few hundred yards west into the city's core, via Piccadilly Gardens (or catch the free Centreline bus #4 from outside the station, every 10min, not Sunday, to all main city-centre locations).

Regional train routes to points south, east and west call both at Piccadilly and at **Oxford Road Station**, south of the centre, while **Victoria Station**, in the north, services the northern hinterland and Bradford. The city's Metrolink **tram** service connects Piccadilly station (the platform is underneath the train station) to Victoria and G-Mex – the latter being the best stop if you're heading straight for Castlefield. National Express and most long-distance buses use **Chorlton Street Coach Station**, a few hundred yards west of Piccadilly train station. Local and some regional buses might drop you instead in nearby Piccadilly Gardens.

The **Manchester Visitor Centre** in the town hall extension on Lloyd Street, facing central St Peter's Square (Mon–Sat 10am–5.30pm, Sun 10.30am–4.30pm; ☎0161/234 3157, ⓦwww.manchester.gov.uk/visitor -centre/), offers a free map of the city centre, the handy *City Guide*, various other useful leaflets and brochures and a National Express tickets service, and can book guided tours and accommodation too. There are direct trams to the Visitor Centre (St Peter's Square stop) from Piccadilly and Victoria stations. To find out **what's on** in the city, buy the weekly *City Life* listings and reviews magazine (ⓦwww.citylife.co.uk), from any newsstand, or check out the Friday edition of the *Manchester Evening News* (ⓦwww.manchesteronline.co.uk).

City transport

The city centre is compact enough to cover on **foot**, though buses will be needed for Oxford Road and you'll have to take the tram out to Salford

Quays. **Piccadilly Gardens Bus Station** is the hub of the urban bus network, though a new transport interchange at **Shudehill** (north of the Arndale Centre; due for completion by 2006) may affect some routes. For Oxford Road, use the stops at the top by the Palace Hotel. **Information** about all services is available from the Travel Shop in Piccadilly Gardens (Mon–Sat 7am–6pm, Sun 10am–6pm); or call the GMPTE Travel Line (☎0161/228 7811, Ⓦwww.gmpte.gov.uk; daily 8am–8pm). Various bus companies ply the city-centre and suburban routes, though they are all accessible with a **Day Saver** ticket (£3.30), which gives unlimited travel on any city bus.

Metrolink (☎0161/205 2000) – the electric tram service – whisks through the city centre and out to the suburbs, linking Manchester with Bury, Salford Quays, Eccles and Altrincham (every 6–15min 6am–11.30pm). New stations are planned for the Shudehill transport interchange and the airport. Tickets for short hops run from 50p to £1.90, though (trips to Salford Quays aside) you're unlikely to use the system for getting around unless you simply fancy the ride.

Accommodation

There's been a boom in the number of city-centre **hotels**, particularly among the budget chains, which means you have a good chance of finding a smart, en-suite, motel-style room in central Manchester for around £50–60. Almost all the plusher places offer weekend reductions too – note that, during the week, breakfast isn't included at most of the pricier hotels. Cheaper **guesthouse** accommodation is concentrated some way out of the centre, mainly on the southern routes into the city, and **B&B** accommodation in private houses is easy to arrange, too. The city's well-located **YHA**, in Castlefield, is a first-choice for most budget travellers – book well in advance. If you use the Visitor Centre's **accommodation booking service**, you'll pay a small fee, though their free *Accommodation Guide* lists most of the city's possibilities. There's no real peak **accommodation season**, though the city fills up during the many festivals and major events; it's also difficult to get a city-centre hotel room when Manchester United play at home.

Hotels, guest houses and B&Bs

Castlefield Liverpool Rd ☎0161/832 7073, Ⓦwww.castlefield-hotel.co.uk. Red-brick, warehouse-style development in the Castlefield basin, opposite the Science and Industry museum. Nicely appointed rooms, and attached leisure club and pool (free to guests). ❹

Holiday Inn Express Waterfront Quay, Salford Quays ☎0161/868 1000 or 0800/897121, Ⓦwww.hiexpress.co.uk. Reasonably sized rooms in a great Quays location, convenient for The Lowry or even Old Trafford. Continental breakfast included. ❹

Jury's Inn 56 Great Bridgewater St ☎0161/953 8888, Ⓦwww.jurys.com. Very handy location for this large, 265-room, no-fuss budget hotel. Rates are room only, but you're close to any number of decent cafés; special weekend deals bring the price down a code or two. ❺

The Lowry 50 Dearman's Place, Chapel Wharf, Salford ☎0161/827 4000, Ⓦwww.rfhotels.com.

Manchester's first five-star hotel sits, exuding class, on the banks of the River Irwell, resplendent in its contemporary finery. Room rates are hideously expensive (up to £500 for a riverside view), but you get all mod cons, excellent levels of service, health centre, sauna and gym, and a Marco Pierre White dining room. ❾

Malmaison Piccadilly ☎0161/278 1000, Ⓦwww.malmaison.com. The ornate Edwardian facade of this place hides sleek interior lines and contemporary design from the Malmaison group. There's a gym, sauna, bar and brasserie, though breakfast costs extra. Weekend discounts depend on availability. ❼

Midland Crowne Plaza Peter St ☎0161/236 3333, Ⓦwww.crowneplaza.com. Once the terminus hotel for Central Station (now G-Mex) and the place where Rolls first met Royce, this building is the apotheosis of Edwardian style. The bars and public rooms impress most, though there's a full raft of leisure facilities and weekend reductions are sometimes available. ❽

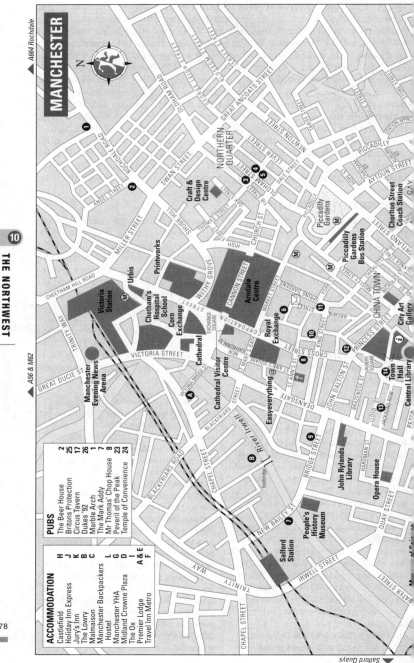

MANCHESTER

▲ A664 Rochdale

▲ A56 & M62

▼ Salford Quays

ACCOMMODATION

Castlefield	H
Holiday Inn Express	J
Jury's Inn	K
The Lowry	B
Malmaison	C
Manchester Backpackers Hostel	L
Manchester YHA	G
Midland Crowne Plaza	D
The Ox	I
Premier Lodge	A & E
Travel Inn Metro	F

PUBS

The Beer House	2
Britons Protection	25
Circus Tavern	17
Dukes '92	26
Marble Arch	1
The Mark Addy	7
Mr Thomas' Chop House	8
Peveril of the Peak	23
Temple of Convenience	24

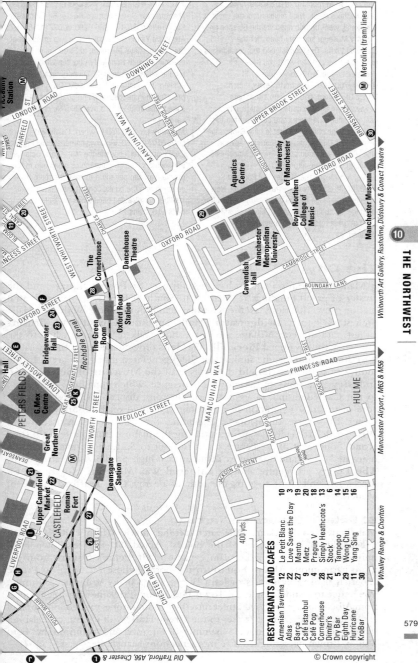

RESTAURANTS AND CAFÉS

Armenian Taverna	12	Le Petit Blanc	10
Atlas	22	Love Saves the Day	3
Barça	27	Manto	19
Café Istanbul	9	Metz	20
Café Pop	4	Prague V	18
Cornerhouse	28	Simply Heathcote's	13
Dimitri's	21	Stock	6
Dry Bar	5	Tampopo	14
Eighth Day	7	Wong Chu	15
Hurricane	11	Yang Sing	16
KroBar	16		

0 ———— 400 yds

© Crown copyright

Whitworth Art Gallery, Rusholme, Didsbury & Conact Theatre ▶

Manchester Airport, M63 & M56 ▶

Whalley Range & Chorlton ▶

Old Trafford, A56, Chester & ◀

The Ox 71 Liverpool Rd ⓣ0161/839 7740, ⓦwww.theox.co.uk. Nine pleasant rooms above a traditional, well-run pub opposite the Science and Industry Museum and very handy for the Castlefield bars. The food is good too; breakfast is extra (£3–6, depending what you have). ❷

Premier Lodge 7–11 Lower Mosley St ⓣ0870/700 1476; and North Tower, Victoria Bridge St, Salford, ⓣ0870/700 1488; both ⓦwww.premierlodge.com. Good-value, city-centre, motel-style rooms and comfort from the Premier Lodge chain. The first is near G-Mex, the second near Deansgate, and there are several other lodges scattered about Greater Manchester, including one at the airport. ❷

Travel Inn Metro The Circus, 112 Portland St ⓣ0870/238 3315, ⓦwww.travelinn.co.uk. New city-centre location for the budget *Travel Inn*, offering decently equipped rooms (2 adults plus 2 children) at great rates, though breakfast is not included. ❷

Hostels and student halls

Manchester Backpackers Hostel 64 Cromwell Rd, Stretford ⓣ0161/865 9296 or 07711/556157. Attractive Victorian terrace house two miles out of the centre – take Metrolink to Stretford, or it's a ten-minute walk from leafy Chorlton which has regular buses into the city. Laundry facilities, kitchen, TV lounge and pool table. The small dorm provides the cheapest accommodation at £15; en-suite twins/doubles also available. No credit cards. ❶

Manchester YHA Potato Wharf, Castlefield ⓣ0870/770 5950, ⓦwww.yhamanchester.org.uk. Excellent hostel, opposite the Museum of Science and Industry. The en-suite rooms sleep one to four people (you can pay more to have the room to yourself) and the bunks convert into double beds; facilities for disabled people are available. Dorm beds £19, twins ❷

The City

If Manchester can be said to have a centre, it's **St Peter's Square** and the cluster of grand buildings focused on it. South of here, the former Central Station now functions as the **G-Mex** exhibition centre, with the Hallé orchestra's home, **Bridgewater Hall**, opposite; **Chinatown** (Britain's largest) and the **Gay Village** are just a short walk to the east; while to the northeast, the revamped **Piccadilly Gardens** provides access to the so-called **Northern Quarter**, the funkiest of the regenerated inner-city areas. To the southwest is the **Castlefield** district, site of the **Museum of Science and Industry**. The spine of the city is **Deansgate**, which runs from Castlefield to the Cathedral and, in its northern environs, displays the most dramatic core of urban regeneration in the country, centred on **Exchange Square**. Other city-centre diversions – including the Manchester Museum and Whitworth Art Gallery – string out along the main southern artery **Oxford Road**. Southwest of the centre, trams run out to **Salford Quays** where the renovated docks and quays now maintain two high-profile visitor attractions, **The Lowry** arts centre and the **Imperial War Museum North**; and no soccer fan will want to miss the tour of nearby **Old Trafford**, home of Manchester United.

St Peter's Square and around

Manchester could claim little architectural merit without its Victorian neo-Gothic buildings. One of the boldest, Alfred Waterhouse's Town Hall, finished in 1877, divides the plain expanse of **St Peter's Square** from the more harmonious **Albert Square** to the north (whose memorial to Prince Albert is flanked by statues of John Bright and a perky William Gladstone). You're free to wander inside the **Town Hall** (Mon–Fri 9am–5pm; free) – enter from Albert Square or Lloyd Street into the echoing stone-vaulted interior and climb one of the grand staircases to the **Great Hall**, with its iron candelabras, stained-glass windows, double hammer-beam roof and paintings by Ford Madox Brown depicting decisive moments from Manchester's past.

On the south side of the Town Hall, the circular **Central Library** (Mon–Thurs 10am–8pm, Fri & Sat 10am–5pm) faces St Peter's Square. Built in 1934 as the largest municipal library in the world, it's an elegant classical construction with a domed reading room. The library building is still an impressive sight, but modern construction work has dwarfed adjacent landmarks – Lutyens' **Cenotaph** in St Peter's Square passes virtually unnoticed these days amid the swooshing trams.

South of St Peter's Square, Lower Mosley Street runs past the **G-Mex** exhibition and conference centre, in use as a train station until 1969; pop your head into the huge vaulted interior for a quick goggle at its proportions. Adjacent is the **International Convention Centre**, while on the other side of G-Mex rises the **Bridgewater Hall**, at the junction of Bridgewater Street. This – Britain's finest purpose-built concert hall – is, uniquely, balanced on shock-absorbing springs to guarantee clarity of sound. Moving on, the flashy apartment block at the corner of Lower Mosley Street and Whitworth Street West bears the name of the site's previous occupant, the fabulously famous – and musically seminal – **Hacienda** club, the spiritual home of Factory Records, which opened in 1982 and finally closed in 1997. In its 1980s heyday, the club showcased live performances by an army of important bands, many from Manchester, including the likes of the Happy Mondays and The Smiths, and pioneered and popularized a new dance craze – "House"; the rest, as they say, is history.

The City Art Gallery and around

The other way up Mosley Street, north of St Peter's Square, rises Charles Barry's porticoed **City Art Gallery** (Tues–Sun 10am–5pm; free; ⓦwww.manchestergalleries.org), where a comprehensive collection of high Victorian art includes the country's finest public collection of works by the Pre-Raphaelite Brotherhood and possibly the best decorative art collection outside London. Following extensive refurbishment, the gallery has doubled in size and has a new extension linked by a glass public area to the original gallery. A top-floor space for special exhibitions concentrates on visual art and design, while the separate Gallery of Craft and Design provides space to display many items from the permanent collection for the first time. The Manchester Gallery is devoted to the visual history of the city and there's also a dedicated children's gallery, plus a theatre for decorative arts, a café and a restaurant.

Around the corner from here, the grid of streets between Princess and Charlotte streets marks the boundaries of Britain's largest **Chinatown**, heralded by the inevitable Dragon Arch, focus of the city's annual Chinese New Year celebrations. To the southeast, the roads off Portland Street lead down to the Rochdale Canal, where Canal Street is the heart of Manchester's thriving **Gay Village**. The pink pound has transformed this part of the city and canalside cafés, clubs, bars and businesses have turned a formerly abandoned warehouse district into something with the verve of San Francisco.

Castlefield and the Museum of Science and Industry

Fifteen minutes' walk southwest of St Peter's Square lies **Castlefield**. The country's first man-made canal, the Bridgewater Canal, brought coal and other goods to the warehouses here in the eighteenth century; the railway followed fifty years later, cementing Castlefield's pre-eminent position, which only declined after World War II. Since the early 1980s, an influx of money allied to a fair amount of speculative vision has resulted in a cobbled canalside, cleaned-up water, outdoor events arena and some attractive café-bars.

The **Museum of Science and Industry**, on Liverpool Road (daily 10am–5pm; last admission 4pm; free, admission charge for special exhibitions; ☎0161/832 2244, ⓦwww.msim.org.uk), is one of the most impressive museums of its type in the country. It occupies various connected buildings and mixes technological displays with trenchant analysis of the social impact of industrialization. With Manchester at the forefront of the Industrial Revolution, it's hardly surprising that the museum trumpets the region's massive technological contribution – starting with the Lancashire-made steam engines, some of which are fired daily in the **Power Hall**. Pride of place goes to a working replica of Robert Stephenson's *Planet* – for which his father George's *Rocket* was the prototype. Built in 1830, the *Planet* reliably attained a scorching 30mph but had no brakes; the museum's version does, and uses them at weekends (call for times), dropping passengers a quarter-mile away at the **world's oldest passenger railway station**. It was here that the *Rocket* arrived on a rainy September 15, 1830, after fatally injuring Liverpool MP William Huskisson at the start of the inaugural passenger journey from Liverpool.

A reconstructed Victorian **sewer** below the station illustrates the problems of sanitation in the 1870s, when poor areas were still using street-end standpipes. The improvements brought about by domestic electrification are brought home in a suite of rooms that includes a wonderfully kitsch Fifties' living room. There's also a hands-on science centre and interactive gallery, where the kids hog all the best experiments, and displays dealing with fibres, fabrics and fashion, while the museum's comprehensive selection of carding machines, bobbin threaders and cotton looms crashes into action at weekends in the **Textile Gallery**.

Along Deansgate

Deansgate cuts through the city from the canal to the cathedral, its architectural reference points ranging from Victorian industrialism to post-millennium posturing. South of Peter Street, the **Peter's Fields** development has transformed a magnificent sweep of late-nineteenth-century warehousing into the **Great Northern** commercial and leisure complex, offset by glass walls, a campanile, open-air amphitheatre and grassy lawn. The inevitable café-bars, restaurants and shops provide a social focus; a pattern repeated a few minutes' further south down Deansgate where **Deansgate Locks** (stretching along Whitworth St) house a run of café-bars in the old railway arches along a section of the Rochdale Canal.

North along Deansgate, opposite Brazenose Street, is the beautifully detailed **John Rylands Library** (closed for refurbishment till 2005), the city's supreme example of Victorian Gothic. It was founded in 1890 by Enriqueta Ryland to house the theological works collected by her late husband, and has in the past displayed Bibles in more than three hundred languages among its million-strong general collection. Books are sure to be the main focus when the library reopens, but it's the interior detail that catches the eye – all carved and burnished wood, Art Nouveau metalwork, delicately crafted stone and stained glass.

St Ann's Square is tucked away off the eastern side of Deansgate, a couple of blocks up from the library. Squat **St Ann's Church** (daily 9.30am–5pm) – baptismal church of Thomas De Quincey – flanks its southern side. Built in 1712, its lovely Renaissance interior was restored under the masterful direction of Alfred Waterhouse at the end of the nineteenth century, from when the striking stained glass dates. Crowning glory of St Ann's Square is the **Royal Exchange**, which houses the famous **Royal Exchange Theatre**, the country's largest theatre-in-the-round, whose steel-and-glass cat's cradle sits plonked under the building's immense glass-vaulted roof. Formerly the Cotton

Exchange, this building employed seven thousand people until trading finished on December 31, 1968 – the old trading board still shows the last day's prices for American and Egyptian cotton.

The Cathedral

At the far end of Deansgate stands the small, Perpendicular **cathedral** (daily 8am–5.30pm; free), the third church on this site since its foundation in the ninth century. A fragment of stone by the choir and a fourteenth-century arch by the tower are all that remain of the earlier structures, and in truth it's been hacked about too much to have any real coherence. Indeed, the famed widest nave in England (114ft, as opposed to York Minster's 106ft) is entirely a result of rich families adding side chapels to the fifteenth-century church, which were later opened out to provide space for Manchester's burgeoning nineteenth-century church-goers.

The area around the cathedral is being refashioned as the city's **Millennium Quarter**, with the six-storey **Urbis** (daily 10am–6pm; £5; ⓦ www .urbis.org.uk) at its core. This hi-tech visitor centre explores the experience of six of the planet's cities – Manchester, naturally, claimed as the world's first industrial city – through a whole series of interactive exhibits; the other cities are São Paulo, Los Angeles, Tokyo, Paris and Singapore. If that doesn't draw you in, perhaps the SkyGlide indoor funicular (apparently the world's first) will, or you might be tempted by the top-floor restaurant, which offers splendid city views.

Exchange Square and around

Just to the north of St Ann's Square, **Exchange Square** sits at the heart of the ambitious city-centre rebuilding programme launched following the devastating bomb of 1996. A pedestrian boulevard – **New Cathedral Street** – runs from St Ann's Square to the Cathedral, skirting the flanks of the flagship **Marks & Spencer** store whose gigantic glazed facade makes up the south side of Exchange Square. The landscaped square, with its water features and public sculpture, plus Selfridges and Harvey Nichols stores, has quickly become a much-frequented, if not exactly loved, urban space, buzzed by skateboarders.

To the east, the Sixties' eyesore that was the **Arndale Centre** has been enlarged, modernized and clad in glass. To the north, the old **Corn Exchange** has been refurbished completely, while retaining its historic facade and glass dome. Relaunched as the **Triangle** (reflecting the unusual shape of its interior), this is a rare wrong foot in the brave new Manchester: gone is any sense of the building's tradition, replaced by yet another batch of retail outlets selling expensive shoes and Japanese rice bowls. Across Withy Grove, meanwhile, the former Mirror Building contains the futuristic **Printworks**, an adult "entertainment centre", complete with IMAX screen, cinema megaplex and various themed bars and restaurants. Step inside and you're confronted by a theme-park style re-creation of a New York street, though some of the building's original features have survived.

Piccadilly Gardens and the Northern Quarter

For years, the bleak expanse of **Piccadilly Gardens** divided rather than united the city, but a recent beautification project by Japanese architects has dramatically restyled the area. The gardens remain a major local transport hub and gateway to the still shabby but improving Oldham Street, which has been adopted by "alternative" entrepreneurs who have dubbed it the **Northern Quarter**. Traditionally, this is Manchester's garment district and you'll still find shops and wholesalers selling high-street fashions, shop fittings, mannequins and hosiery, but there are also new design outlets, lots of music stores, and some funky bars and cafés. Loft-style apartments change hands around here for serious money; the renovated **Smithfield Buildings** are an example of what can be done with Oldham Street's fine old buildings. There are more skills and crafts on display in the excellent **Manchester Craft and Design Centre**, 17 Oak St (Mon–Sat 10am–5.30pm; free; Ⓦ www.craftanddesign.com) – a great place to pick up ceramics, fabrics, earthenware, jewellery and decorative art, or just sip a drink in the cosy café.

Oxford Road and points south

From St Peter's Square, **Oxford Road** – initially Oxford Street – stretches through a ragged mile of faculty buildings to Rusholme and the leafy suburbs beyond. Oxford Road Station lurks behind the **Cornerhouse**, the dynamo of the Manchester arts scene. In addition to screening art-house films, the Cornerhouse has three floors of gallery space (Tues–Sat 11am–6pm, Sun 2–6pm; free) devoted to contemporary and local artists' work. The café and bar are popular, too. Across the road, Alfred Waterhouse's majestic **Refuge Assurance** building of 1891 is one of Manchester's joys, its soaring clocktower, dome and terracotta facade now hiding the bulk of the *Palace Hotel*. An endless stream of buses runs down Oxford Road from here, passing the buildings and sights detailed below.

A mile or so from the Cornerhouse is the city's modern art collection, housed in the red-brick **Whitworth Gallery** (Mon–Sat 10am–5pm, Sun 2–5pm; free; Ⓦ www.whitworth.man.ac.uk). The gallery forms two distinct halves, pre-1880s and modern, with the former collection incorporating a strong assembly of watercolours by Turner, Constable, Cox and Blake as well as Gillray engravings and Hogarth prints. The modern collection concentrates on post-1880 British staples, with Moore, Frink and Hepworth setting off contributions from lesser-known artists. Look for works by Paul Nash (one of the organizers of the London Surrealist exhibition of 1936), the World War II artist John Piper and those of Stephen Conroy, a contemporary figurative painter whose subjects resonate with Victorian images. With Manchester's cotton connections it's perhaps not surprising that the gallery also displays the country's widest range of textiles outside London's Victoria and Albert Museum.

Salford Quays – The Lowry and the Imperial War Museum North

The Metrolink extension to **Salford Quays** provides easy access to one of the city's first urban development projects. For ninety years, from 1894 when the Manchester Ship Canal opened, the Salford docks turned the city into one of Britain's busiest ports. Trade declined in the 1970s and the docks eventually closed in 1982, since which time the Salford Quays development has transformed the run-down quays on the western edge of the city centre into a hugely popular waterfront residential and leisure complex.

Various Metrolink stations serve the area: for the **Salford Quays tourist information office** (Mon–Fri 8.30am–4.30pm, Sun 10am–4pm; ☎0161/848 8601, Ⓦ www.visitsalford.com) get off at Salford Quays station. You can pick up a map here and wander down the Centenary Walkway quayside, studded with commemorative discs whose engraved words and snippets reflect the area's history. This ends at the promontory taken up by **The Lowry** (daily from 9.30am; free; Ⓦ www.thelowry.com), the Quays' striking, shining steel arts centre whose theatres, galleries (Sun–Wed 11am–5pm, Thurs–Sat 11am–8pm; free) and creative ArtWorks exhibition (Mon–Fri 10am–3pm, Sat & Sun 10am–4pm; suggested

585

△ Imperial War Museum North

donation £3) have quickly become one of Manchester's leading attractions; to travel straight here, stay on the Metrolink until Broadway. The building itself is a great piece of art and you're free to wander around or grab a bite to eat in the café or restaurant. The centre, of course, takes its name from L.S. Lowry and no artist is more closely linked with an English city than Lowry is with Manchester. There's always a selection of **Lowry paintings** on show for free, illustrating both his early views on the desolation and sadness of Manchester's millworkers and his changing outlook in later life when he repeated earlier paintings changing the greys and sullen browns for lively reds and pinks.

A footbridge runs from The Lowry across to the Trafford side of the docks where the startling **Imperial War Museum North** (daily 10am–6pm; free; W www.iwm.org.uk/north) raises a giant steel fin into the air, all to the design of Daniel Libeskind. The museum's three steel "shards" represent war on land and sea and in the air. The interior is just as striking, its angular lines serving as a dramatic backdrop to the displays, which kick off with the Big Picture, when the walls of the main hall are transformed into giant screens to show three rotated, fifteen-minute, surround-sound films. Among the hundreds of artefacts displayed in the main hall are five so-called "iconic objects", including the artillery piece that fired the first British shell in World War I and a fire pump used when Manchester was blitzed in World War II. In addition, there are all sorts of themed displays in six separate exhibition areas – the Silos – focusing on everything from women's work in the two world wars to war reporting and the build up to the Iraq conflict of 2003.

Old Trafford

Looming in the near distance from the Salford Quays is **Old Trafford**, the self-styled "Theatre of Dreams" and home of **Manchester United**, arguably the most famous football team in the world. The club's following is such that only season ticket holders can ever attend games, but **tours** of Old Trafford and its museum (daily 9.30am–5pm; museum & tour £8.50, museum only £5.50; advance booking essential, T 0870/442 1994, W www.manutd.com) placate out-of-town fans who want to gawp at the silverware, sit in the dug-out and visit the *Red Café*. To get here, take the Metrolink to Old Trafford station and walk up Warwick Road to Sir Matt Busby Way.

Eating, drinking and nightlife

Second only to London in the breadth and scope of its **cafés** and **restaurants**, Manchester has something to suit everyone and your money goes a lot further than it does in the capital. The bulk of Manchester's eating and drinking places are scattered around the city centre, while out at Rusholme you'll find the best range of curries this side of the Pennines. Most city **pubs** dish up something filling at lunchtime, but for a more modish snack or drink, European-style **café-bars** are everywhere, especially in the new city-centre developments, in the Northern Quarter, and in the Gay Village on the Rochdale Canal.

For the last twenty years Manchester has been vying with London as Britain's capital of **youth culture**. Banks of flyposters advertise what's going on in the numerous **clubs** which, as elsewhere, frequently change names and styles on different nights of the week. The most enduring places are listed below and you can expect to pay £3–15 cover depending on what's on. The city also has an excellent **live music** scene in pubs, clubs and larger venues, with tickets from £5–15. For details of Manchester's musical happenings, check the weekly *City Life* magazine or Friday's *Manchester Evening News*.

Cafés and café-bars

Atlas 376 Deansgate. One of the best café-bars in the city, justly known for its quality focaccia sandwiches, and also the place for Sunday brunch, a bottle of beer or a decent glass of wine.

Barça Arch 8 & 9, Catalan Square. Trendy Castlefield bar/restaurant tucked into the restored railway arches, with a lovely canalside terrace, cosy lounge with fire, and upstairs dining room and deck for fashionable Mediterranean flavours.

Café Pop 34–36 Oldham St. Retro café full of 70s kitsch and pop collectables, with the emphasis on veggie fry-ups, hefty sandwiches (including the famous triple-decker Scooby Snax), omelettes and the like. Service can be a bit chaotic but portions are enormous and prices very fair. Closed Sun.

Cornerhouse 70 Oxford St. The place to sip a cappuccino after viewing the galleries or catching a movie. The first-floor café (daily until 11pm) dishes up meze and pizzas, and there's also a good bar downstairs.

Dry Bar 28–30 Oldham St. The earliest of the designer café-bars on the scene, started by Factory records and the catalyst for much of what has happened since in the Northern Quarter. *Dry* is still as cool as they come.

Eighth Day 107–111 Oxford Rd. Manchester's oldest organic-vegetarian café has got spanking new premises on its old Oxford Road site – shop, takeaway and juice bar upstairs, café/restaurant downstairs.

Kro Bar 325 Oxford Rd. Half the students in Manchester seem to crowd into this huge good-natured café-bar, sited in what was once a men-only teetotallers' club. Offers value-for-money food, caffeine and a vast range of on-tap beers; on a sunny day, you'll struggle to find table space outside.

Kro 2 Oxford House, Oxford Rd. Sister to the *Kro Bar*, this stylish bar-restaurant is in the gleamingly new National Computing Centre. It offers a first-rate selection of drinks and meals in an easy-going, informal atmosphere.

Love Saves the Day Smithfield Building, Tib St. New York style and sass in this Northern Quarter deli-café, where a daily changing menu of platters, salads, pasta and sandwiches keeps the locals happy – and there's very good coffee too. Closed Sun.

Manto 46 Canal St. Gay Village stalwart whose chic crowd laps up the cool sounds and club nights. A canalside Sunday brunch is a treat here, or hop upstairs to *Sarasota* for fusion cooking and the city's only retractable roof for alfresco dining.

Metz 3 Brazil St. Classy converted warehouse bar and restaurant. It's great for a pre-club drink or two and its Eastern European food's not bad either.

Prague V 40 Chorlton St. Gay-friendly hangout on the Canal Street corner, with Czech beer, Mediterranean-inspired meals and snacks, and a late weekend drinks licence.

Restaurants

Armenian Taverna Albert Square ☏ 0161/834 9025. Filling meze platters (for vegetarians too) bring in many, who then find they wish they'd plumped for a halibut kebab or grilled spring chicken, or one of a dozen other mighty main courses. Closed Mon. Moderate.

Café Istanbul 79 Bridge St ☏ 0161/833 9942. Delicious Turkish dishes, including a great meze selection, and an extensive wine list (try the powerful Turkish red). Closed Sun. Inexpensive to moderate.

Dimitri's 1 Campfield Arcade, Deansgate ☏ 0161/839 3319. Pick and mix from the Greek/Spanish/Italian menu (particularly good for vegetarians), or grab a sandwich, an arcade table and sip a drink (Greek coffee to Lebanese wine). Moderate.

Hurricane King St, Spring Gardens ☏ 0161/839 9966. The city's great and good have adopted this former haunt of the Reform Club as their pet restaurant, revelling in its oh-so-glamorous Venetian-Gothic exterior and spiffing French-inspired food. Closed Sun. Expensive.

Le Petit Blanc 55 King St ☏ 0161/832 1001. Best place in the city for reasonably priced classic and regional French cooking is Raymond Blanc's mid-range brasserie operation – fish soup to a roast poussin off the a la carte menu or good-value, three-course, *prix fixe* for around £18. Real food for children too. Moderate.

Simply Heathcote's Jackson Row ☏ 0161/835 3536. Massive, minimalist dining rooms operated by Lancastrian chef Paul Heathcote. Mixes Mediterranean and local flavours, so expect updated working-class dishes alongside the parmesan shavings. The set lunch/early-bird menu is one of the city's best deals for food of this stature. Expensive.

Stock 4 Norfolk St ☏ 0161/839 6644. Superior Italian cooking – the fish Is renowned – accompanied by a wine list of serious intent. It's housed In the city's old stock exchange, hence the name. Closed Sun. Expensive.

Tampopo 16 Albert Square ☏ 0161/819 1966. Basement noodle bar with long benches and a fast turnover. Noodle dishes are Japanese, Thai, Malaysian or Indonesian with most dishes under £7. Inexpensive.

Wong Chu 63 Faulkner St ☎0161/236 2346.
Simply the best of the budget Chinatown eateries,
this no-frills, paper-tablecloth joint serves up enormous portions of Cantonese staples. Highlights are
the deep-bowl noodle soups or piled-high rice-
and-meat plates, at bargain prices. Inexpensive.

Yang Sing 34 Princess St ☎0161/236 2200. The
Yang Sing is one of the best Cantonese restaurants
in the country, with thoroughly authentic food,
from a lunchtime plate of fried noodles to the full
works. Stray from the printed menu for the most
interesting dishes; ask the friendly staff for advice.
Moderate to Expensive.

Pubs

The Beer House 6 Angel St. The best place for
ale-tasting, with a constant stock of more than
thirty brews.

Britons Protection 50 Great Bridgewater St.
Elegantly decorated traditional pub opposite
Bridgewater Hall, with a couple of cosy, smoky
rooms and a brickyard beer garden. The homemade
pies are good, and there are comedy nights too.

Circus Tavern 86 Portland St. Manchester's
smallest pub – a Victorian drinking-hole that's
many people's favourite city-centre pit stop. You
may have to knock on the door to get in; once you
do, you're confronted by the landlord in the corridor pulling pints.

Dukes '92 Castle St. Classily revamped former
stable block (for canal horses) with art on the
walls, terrace seating and a fine selection of beers.
Serves great-value food too, including a wide
range of pâtés and cheeses.

Marble Arch 73 Rochdale Rd. Curious real ale
house with a sloping floor, whose in-house Marble
Brewery produces some fine brews – the seasonal
"Ginger Marble" or the strong "Chocolate Heavy"
among them.

The Mark Addy 2 Stanley St. Mainly known for its
food, the Mark Addy – named after a local
Victorian character – serves a choice of fifty
cheeses and eight pâtés (including vegetarian). Eat
inside, or outside by the River Irwell.

Mr Thomas' Chop House 52 Cross St. Victorian
classic with a Dickensian feel to its nooks and
crannies. Office workers, hardcore daytime
drinkers, old goats and students all call it home.
There's good-value, traditional English "chop-
house" food (oysters, bubble and squeak, etc)
served in the ornate dining-and-drinking room at
the rear.

Peveril of the Peak 127 Great Bridgewater St.
The pub that time forgot – one of Manchester's
best real ale houses, with a youthful crowd and
some superb Victorian glazed tilework outside.

Temple of Convenience Great Bridgewater St. A
tiny converted public toilet – yes that's right –
stocking a wide selection of Belgian beers.

Clubs and small live venues

The Attic above the *Thirsty Scholar*, 50 New
Wakefield St ☎0161/236 6071. Regular weekend
blasts of funk, soul and dance for a student crowd.

Band on the Wall 25 Swan St ☎0161/834 1786,
Ⓦwww.bandonthewall.org. Cosy Northern Quarter
joint with a great reputation for its live bands –
from world and folk to jazz and reggae – and club
nights.

The Brickhouse 6 Whitworth St West
☎0161/236 4418. Rotating indie and pop in a
relaxed atmosphere geared up for an older
crowd.

Manchester Academy 269 Oxford Rd, on the
university campus ☎0161/275 2930,
Ⓦwww.umu.man.ac.uk. Popular student venue for
new and established bands.

Manchester Roadhouse 8–10 Newton St
☎0161/237 9789, Ⓦwww.theroadhouse
.u-net.com. Regular and varied gigs by local
bands plus a succession of fine club nights.

The Music Box 65 Oxford St ☎0161/236 9971,
Ⓦwww.jillys.co.uk/musicbox. The astute clubber's
venue of choice, host to the wildly popular monthly
Electric Chair with Mr Scruff keeping it unreal on
many a night. Recommended.

Paradise Factory 112–116 Princess St
☎0161/273 5422, Ⓦwww.paradisefactory.com.
One of the hottest clubs on the scene, featuring a
varied diet of DJ nights with soulful funk a speciality.

Sankey's Soap Beehive Mill, Jersey St, Ancoats
☎0161/661 9668, Ⓦwww.tribalgathering.co.uk.
Many people's favourite night out, brought to you
by the legendary Tribal Gathering crew – Friday's
Tribal Sessions and Saturday's The Red Light, playing sleazy house music – in newly revamped
premises.

Stadium venues

G-Mex Centre Windmill St ☎0161/834 2700,
Ⓦwww.g-mex.co.uk. Mid-sized city-centre indoor
stadium.

The Manchester Apollo Stockport Rd, Ardwick
Green ☎0161/242 2560,
Ⓦwww.alive.co.uk/apollo. Huge theatre auditorium
for all kinds of concerts.

Manchester Evening News Arena Victoria
Station, 21 Hunts Bank ☎0161/950 5000,
Ⓦwww.men-arena.com. Indoor stadium that seats
20,000 and hosts all the big names.

Arts and culture

Manchester is blessed with the North's most highly regarded **orchestra**, the Hallé, which is resident at Bridgewater Hall. The Cornerhouse is the local **arts** mainstay, and there's a decent selection of **comedy** on offer in the city too. For **film**, the **Printworks** entertainment complex contains the twenty-screen **Filmworks** cinema as well as an IMAX cinema, though there are plenty of other places to catch movies, too. The biggest annual event is August's **Manchester Festival** (Ⓦ www.festivalmanchester.com), an arts and TV extravaganza, while October's **x.traxonthestreets** (Ⓦ www.xtrax.org.uk) festival, showcasing live street theatre, music and entertainment, is the other highlight of a varied festival programme.

Concerts and music

Bridgewater Hall Lower Mosley St ☎0161/907 9000, Ⓦ www.bridgewater-hall.co.uk. Home of the Hallé (founded 1857) and the Manchester Camerata; also sponsors a full programme of chamber, classical and jazz concerts.

The Lowry Pier 8, Salford Quays ☎0161/876 2000, Ⓦ www.thelowry.com. Full, year-round programme of music events, from opera to country.

Royal Northern College of Music (RNCM) 124 Oxford Rd ☎0161/907 5278, Ⓦ www.rncm.ac.uk. Stages top-quality classical and modern-jazz concerts, including performances by Manchester Camerata.

Opera House Quay St ☎0161/242 2509, Ⓦ www.manchestertheatres.co.uk. Major venue for touring West End musicals, drama and concerts.

Theatre and the arts

Contact Theatre 15 Oxford Rd ☎0161/274 0600, Ⓦ www.contact-theatre.org. One of the most innovative theatre companies in town, housed in provocatively designed premises and putting on predominantly modern works.

Cornerhouse 70 Oxford St ☎0161/200 1500, Ⓦ www.cornerhouse.org. Engaging centre for contemporary arts, with three cinema screens, changing art exhibitions, recitals, talks, bookshop, café and bar.

Dancehouse Theatre 10 Oxford Rd ☎0161/237 9753, Ⓦ www.thedancehouse.co.uk. Home of the Northern Ballet School, and venue for dance, drama and comedy.

Royal Exchange Theatre St Ann's Square ☎0161/833 9833, Ⓦ www.royalexchange.co.uk. The theatre-in-the-round in the Royal Exchange is the most famous stage in the city; and there's a Studio Theatre (for works by new writers) alongside the main stage.

Cinemas

Cornerhouse 70 Oxford St ☎0161/200 1500, wwww.cornerhouse.org. The three screens at the Cornerhouse are your best bet for art-house releases, special screenings and cinema-related talks and events.

The Filmworks Printworks, Exchange Square ☎08700/102030, Ⓦ www.thefilmworks.co.uk. State-of-the-art cinema with twenty screens, IMAX movies, digital projection and comfortable seating.

Odeon 1 Oxford St ☎0870/505 0007, Ⓦ www.odeon.co.uk. Seven-screen city-centre cinema showing mainstream movies at cut-price rates.

Listings

Bookshops The main chains have outlets on Deansgate and around St Ann's Square. Blackwell's academic bookshop is in the Precinct Centre, Oxford Rd; Sportspages, the sports specialist, is in Barton Square, off St Ann's Square; and Gibb's Bookshop, 10 Charlotte St, is great for secondhand books and classical music.

Bus information For all city services, call GMPTE on ☎0161/228 7811 or visit Ⓦ www.gmpte.gov.uk; for intercity services, call

National Express on ☎08705/808080.

Internet easyEverything, 18 Exchange St, St Ann's Square; Net-Works Centre at the Central Library.

Pharmacy Boots, 11–13 Piccadilly Gardens and 20 St Ann's St.

Post Office 29 Spring Gardens; 63 Newton St.

Taxis Mantax ☎0161/230 3333; Taxifone ☎0161/236 9974. Airtax (for the airport) ☎0161/499 9000.

Chester

In 1779 Boswell wrote to Samuel Johnson: "Chester pleases me more than any town I ever saw" – and although **CHESTER**, forty miles southwest of Manchester, has changed since then, it's not by much. A glorious two-mile ring of medieval and Roman walls encircles a neat kernel of Tudor and Victorian buildings, including the unique raised arcades called the "Rows". Very much the commercial hub of its county, Chester has enough in the way of sights, restaurants and atmosphere to make it an enjoyable base for a couple of days, though admittedly it can get very crowded.

The fabric of the town is riddled with two thousand years of history. In 79 AD the Romans built Deva Castra here, their largest known fortress in Britain. Later, Ethelfleda, the daughter of King Alfred the Great, extended and refortified the place, only for it to be brutally sacked by William the Conqueror. Trade routes to Ireland made Chester the most prosperous port in the northwest, a status it recovered after the English Civil War, during which its enthusiasm for Charles I saw it subjected to a two-year siege by the Parliamentarians. By the middle of the eighteenth century, however, silting of the port had forced the Irish trade to be rerouted first through Parkgate on the Dee estuary, and then to Liverpool. Things improved a little with the Industrial Revolution, as the canal and railway networks made Chester an important regional trading centre, a function it still retains.

Arrival and information

National Express and most regional bus services arrive at **Chester bus station**, between Delamere and George streets. Close by are the northern city walls and Northgate Street. Most other local buses use the **bus exchange** just behind the town hall, off Princess Street. Merseyrail **trains** from Liverpool (every 20–30min 6am–11pm; 45min) and all other regional and national services call at the **train station**, northeast of the centre, from where it's a ten-minute walk down City Road and along Foregate Street to the central Eastgate Clock. The City-Rail Link bus from the station to the centre (every 12min, 30min on Sun) is free to anyone with a valid train ticket.

There's a **tourist office** in the Town Hall (April–Sept Mon–Sat 9.30am–5.30pm, Sun 10am–4pm; Oct–March Mon–Sat 10am–5pm) and also the **Chester Visitor Centre**, on Vicars Lane opposite the amphitheatre (May–Oct Mon–Sat 9am–5.30pm, Sun 10am–4pm; Nov–April Mon–Sat 10am–5pm, Sun 10am–4pm), both with the same telephone enquiries number and website (℡01244/402111, Ⓦwww.chestertourism.com). At either, you can book accommodation and guided tours, and pick up a copy of the *Chester Visitor Guide*. Central city **parking** is scarce, so drivers should use the Park and Ride scheme, catching a bus from one of the car parks scattered around the ring road.

Accommodation

Chester's popularity is apparent as soon as you arrive, and in high summer **B&B accommodation** can be in short supply, as can space in the more characterful old inns. The places reviewed below are the best of the central choices. If you arrive late, or strike out in the centre, there are lots of budget-rated B&Bs along Brook Street, just a couple of minutes from the train station, and several moderate hotels down City Road, also near the station.

Hotels and B&Bs

Castle House 23 Castle St ☎01244/350354. B&B in a sixteenth-century house with good facilities; bang in the centre and excellent value for money. No credit cards. ②

The Chester Grosvenor Eastgate St ☎01244/324024, Ⓦ www.chestergrosvenor.co.uk. Superbly appointed luxury hotel bristling with liveried staff, very comfortable bedrooms and a whole host of facilities, not least two fine restaurants. Parking available. One price code less at weekends. ⑨

Chester Town House 23 King St ☎01244/350021, Ⓦ www.chestertownhouse.co.uk. A very high-standard B&B in a comfortably furnished seventeenth-century townhouse, on a curving, cobbled central street off Northgate Street. There are five en-suite rooms and private parking. ③

Commercial St Peter's Church Yard ☎01244/320749. Friendly Georgian inn with good beer and half-a-dozen pleasant rooms in a brick-walled churchyard. ②

The Mill Milton St ☎01244/350035, Ⓦ www.millhotel.com. Sensitive warehouse conversion on the canal, between St Oswald's Way and Hooley Way, not far from the train station. Has its own car park and a nice waterside bar and café-bar; rooms with balcony attract a small supplement. ⑤

Pied Bull Northgate St ☎01244/325829. Characterful old coaching inn, close to the walls and cathedral. ②

Youth Hostel

Youth Hostel Hough Green House, 40 Hough Green ☎0870/770 5672, Ⓔ chester@yha.org.uk. Twenty minutes' walk southwest of the centre, this Victorian house has a cafeteria, self-catering and laundry facilities, and a shop. Over 100 beds in two- to ten-bedded rooms; dorm beds £15.

The City

Central Chester is a delightful spot, its easy charms readily explored on foot. There are two special highlights: **The Rows**, the picturesque galleries that run above the central shops, and the ancient **city wall**, from the top of which there are fetching views of Chester's environs.

The Rows – and Eastgate Street

Intersecting at **The Cross**, where the town crier welcomes visitors to the city (May–Aug Tues–Sat at noon), the four main thoroughfares of central Chester are lined by **The Rows**, unique galleried arcades running on top of the ground-floor shops. This engaging black-and-white tableau is a blend of genuine Tudor houses and Victorian half-timbered imitations, with the finest Tudor buildings on Watergate Street – though **Eastgate Street** is perhaps the most picturesque, leading to the filigree **Eastgate Clock**, erected atop a sandstone arch to commemorate Victoria's Diamond Jubilee. There's no clear explanation of the origin of The Rows – they were first recorded soon after the fire that wrecked Chester in 1278, and may originally have been built on top of the heaped rubble left after the blaze.

The Town Hall and the Cathedral

North of The Cross, along Northgate Street, rises the neo-Gothic **Town Hall**, whose acres of red and grey sandstone look over to the **Cathedral** (daily 7.30am–6pm; free tours Mon–Sat at 2.30pm, donation requested), a much modified structure dating back to the Normans, but dedicated to St Werburgh, an Anglo-Saxon princess who became Chester's patron saint. Parts of the original eleventh-century structure can still be seen in the north transept, but the highlight of an otherwise simple interior is the fourteenth-century choir stalls, with their intricately carved misericords. Doors in the north wall of the nave lead into the shady sixteenth-century cloisters, encircling a small garden whose focal point is an imaginative and striking bronze sculpture by Stephen Broadbent of the Woman of Samaria offering Jesus water at the well.

Around the walls

East of the cathedral, steps provide access to the top of the two-mile girdle of medieval and Roman **city walls** – the most complete in Britain, though in places the wall is barely above street level. You can walk past all its towers, turrets and gateways in an hour or two, and most have a tale to tell. The fifteenth-century **King Charles Tower** in the northeast corner is so named because Charles I stood here in 1645 watching his troops being beaten on Rowton Moor, two miles to the southeast. The earlier **Water Tower** at the northwest corner, meanwhile, once stood in the river – evidence of the changes brought about by the gradual silting of the River Dee.

The Grosvenor Museum and Chester Castle

Scores of sculpted tomb panels and engraved headstones once propped up the wall to either side of the Water Tower, evidence of some nervous repair work undertaken when the Roman Empire was in retreat. Much of this stonework was retrieved by the Victorians and is now on display at the **Grosvenor Museum** at 27 Grosvenor St (Mon–Sat 10.30am–5pm, Sun 2–5pm; free). This is the best investigation of Roman Chester, with good displays about the legionary system, city buildings, grave sites, defences, daily life and culture. The tombstones themselves form the largest collection from a single Roman site in Britain, the finest being the carving of a wounded barbarian – the surviving piece of a memorial to a Roman cavalryman. The back of the museum opens into a preserved Georgian house complete with furnished kitchen, parlour, bedrooms, rickety floors and sloping stairs.

Close by, on Castle Street, the **Cheshire Military Museum** (daily 10am–4.30pm; £2) inhabits part of the same complex as **Chester Castle** (no public access), built by William the Conqueror, though most of what you see today is resolutely Georgian and used as courts and offices.

The Roman Amphitheatre and the Church of St John the Baptist

East of the castle, the city wall is buried under the street, but it rises again alongside the **Roman Gardens** (open access) on Souters Lane at Little John Street, where Roman foundations and columns dug up during redevelopment are on display. Across the road stands the half-excavated remains of the **Roman Amphitheatre** (open access); it is estimated to have held seven thousand spectators, making it the largest amphitheatre in Britain, but the stonework is barely head-high now. The garrison at Roman Deva was 6000 strong in its heyday, and the amphitheatre was used by soldiers of the Twentieth Legion for weapons training as well as for entertainment.

The partly ruined pink-stone **Church of St John the Baptist** (daily 9.15am–6pm; free), a little to the east in Grosvenor Park, was founded by the Saxon king Ethelred in 689 and briefly served as the cathedral of Mercia. Rebuilt in its entirety by the Normans, it's an impressive structure, the solid Norman pillars of the nave rising to a Transitional triforium and Early English clerestory. The east portion of the church was abandoned at the Reformation and left to crumble, creating the romantic ruins of today – look out for what purports to be a thirteenth-century coffin emblazoned with the inscription "Dust to Dust" set into an arch.

Eating, drinking and entertainment

You can't walk more than a few paces in downtown Chester without coming across somewhere to **eat and drink**, as often as not housed in a medieval crypt or Tudor building. Given the number of day-trippers, it's not surprising that some places serve up some pretty mediocre stuff, but standards are generally high and several of the **pubs** are delightful. The cafés and restaurants listed below are open for lunch and dinner unless otherwise stated.

A batch of annual **festivals** keeps the town's concert halls and churches busy. The most renowned is the **Summer Music Festival** (Ⓦ www.chesterfestivals .co.uk), held every July, which sees outdoor concerts and fireworks in Grosvenor Park, as well as a simultaneous Fringe Festival.

Cafés and restaurants

Boulevard de la Bastille Bridge St Row. One of the nicest of the arcade cafés, with tables looking over the street, doing a roaring trade in breakfasts, pastries and sandwiches. Inexpensive.

Chez Jules 69 Northgate St ☏ 01244/400014. Classic brasserie menu (salad niçoise to vegetable cassoulet, Toulouse sausage to rib-eye steak) including a terrific value two-course lunch. Inexpensive.

Francs 14 Cuppin St ☏ 01244/317952. An excellent and very French bistro with good-value set meals. You can also just drop in for a coffee and cake. Moderate.

Hattie's Tea Shop 5 Rufus Court. Pleasant café with homemade soups, sandwiches and cakes. Inexpensive.

La Tasca 6–12 Cuppin St ☏ 01244/400887. Huge tapas selection – Spanish cheeses to grilled prawns – and paella too. Nice spot in the summer when they throw the windows wide open. Inexpensive to moderate.

The Mediterranean Restaurant 1 Rufus Court,

off Northgate St ☏ 01244/320004. Georgian house by the walls, with a sunny courtyard garden, serving tapas, pasta, fish, paella and meze. Moderate.

Ruan Orchid 14 Lower Bridge St ☏ 01244/400661. This place's huge menu ranges across all the Thai regions – good for red and green curries, duck dishes and noodles. Moderate.

Pubs and bars

Albion Inn corner of Albion and Park streets. A true English Victorian terraced pub in the shadow of the city wall – no fruit machines or muzak. Good bar food and a great range of ales.

The Falcon Lower Bridge St. This half-timbered pub was once a townhouse built by the Grosvenor family by enclosing part of a Row.

Mill Hotel Milton St. Ale lovers flock to this converted Victorian corn mill to sample an excellent range of brews in a lively atmosphere.

Old Harkers Arms 1 Russell St, below the City Road bridge. Canalside real ale pub imaginatively sited in a former warehouse.

Liverpool and around

LIVERPOOL spent too many of the twentieth-century postwar years struggling against adversity. Things are looking up at last, as economic and social regeneration brightens the centre and old docks, while the city's successful bid to be European Capital of Culture for 2008 promises to transform the way outsiders see the city. Some may sneer at the very concept of Liverpudlian "culture", but this is already a city with a Tate Gallery of its own, as well as a series of stand-out museums tracing its fascinating social history. Liverpool also makes great play of its musical heritage, which is reasonable enough from the city that produced The Beatles.

Although it gained its charter from King John in 1207, Liverpool remained a humble fishing village for half a millennium until the silting-up of Chester and the booming slave trade prompted the building of the first dock in 1715. From then until the abolition of slavery in Britain in 1807, Liverpool was the apex of the **slaving triangle** in which firearms, alcohol and textiles were traded for African slaves, who were shipped to the Caribbean and America. The holds were then filled with tobacco, raw cotton and sugar for the return journey. After the abolition of the trade, the port continued to grow into a seven-mile chain of docks, not only for freight but also to cope with wholesale European **emigration**, which saw nine million people from half of Europe leave for the Americas and Australasia between 1830 and 1930.

The docks lost their pre-eminence by the middle of the twentieth century and, although the arrival of car manufacturing plants in the 1960s stemmed the decline for a while, during the 1970s and 1980s Liverpool became a byword for British economic malaise. However, over the last decade there's been a concerted effort to transform Liverpool's economy and reputation, with major investment by blue-chip companies, plus a move away from traditional industries into financial services, information technology and biotechnology. There's a welcome new confidence about the city, as plans are laid to redevelop the waterfront, rebuild parts of the city centre and refurbish its magnificent municipal and industrial buildings. Visitors, meanwhile, have to plan ahead if they are to get around the sights in two or three days. The **River Mersey** provides one focus, whether crossing on the famous ferry to the **Wirral** peninsula or on a tour of the attractions in the rejuvenated warehouses of **Albert Dock**. If you want a **cathedral**, they've "got one to spare" as the song goes; plus there's a fine showing of British art in the celebrated **Walker Art Gallery**, and a revitalized arts and nightlife urban quarter centred on **FACT**, Liverpool's showcase for film and the media arts.

Arrival, information and city transport

Mainline trains pull in to **Lime Street** station, while the suburban **Merseyrail** system (for trains from Chester) calls at four underground stations in the city, including Lime Street. National Express **buses** use the station on Norton Street, just northeast of Lime Street. Local buses depart from Queen Square (for city centre, Pier Head and Chester services), Paradise Street Bus Station (southbound and a few northbound services), and St Thomas Street (eastbound and cross-river). Liverpool **airport** – officially named after John Lennon – is eight miles southeast of the city centre. From outside the main entrance, the **Airport Express #500 bus** (every 30min; 5.15am–1.35am; £2) runs directly into the city centre, stopping at all major bus terminals and at Lime Street. The slower, cheaper local bus #80A (every 15–30min; 6am–11pm) makes the same journey, or a **taxi** to Lime Street costs around £12. Most **ferry** arrivals – from the Isle of Man, Dublin and Belfast – dock at the terminals just north of Pier Head, not far from James Street Merseyrail station, though Norse Merchant arrivals are over the water on the Wirral at Twelve Quays, near Woodside ferry terminal (ferry or Merseyrail to Liverpool).

Tourist information is available from either the **Queen's Square Centre**, centrally located in Queen Square (Mon–Sat 9am–5.30pm, Sun 10.30am–4.30pm), or the **Albert Dock Centre** at the Atlantic Pavilion (daily 10am–5.30pm), which share the same telephone enquiries number and Website (Ⓣ09066/806886, Ⓦwww.visitliverpool.com).

Liverpool city centre is surprisingly compact and you'll easily be able to get around on foot. The local transport authority is **Merseytravel** (Ⓦwww.merseytravel.gov.uk), which coordinates all buses, trains and ferries. There's a telephone enquiry line (Ⓣ0151/236 7676; daily 8am–8pm) or visit the Merseytravel information centre inside the Queen's Square Centre. Daily off-peak, zonal **Saveaway tickets** (£2–3.50) for unlimited use on most city buses, trains and ferries are available from post offices, newsagents and the Merseytravel office. The amphibious half-truck-half-boat **Yellow Duckmarine** (mid-Feb to Christmas, daily every hour from 11am; £9.95;

☏0151/708 7799, ⓦwww.theyellowduckmarine.co.uk) departs from Gower Street, in front of Albert Dock, and trundles around the city centre before splashing down into the docks themselves for a spot of aquatic sightseeing.

Accommodation

There's a fair choice of **accommodation**, from budget chains and small-scale guest houses to boutique hotels and business-oriented four-stars, plus a wide range of hostels and halls of residence. Both tourist offices book rooms for free; call ☏0845/601 1125 for their details of special-offer weekend breaks and packages.

Hotels and guest houses

Aachen 89–91 Mount Pleasant ☏0151/709 3477, ⓦwww.aachenhotel.co.uk. A range of value-for-money rooms (with and without en-suite showers) and big "eat-as-much-as-you-like" breakfasts. ❺

Alicia 3 Aigburth Drive, Sefton Park ☏0151/727 4411, ⓦwww.feathers.uk.com. Restored townhouse with park views and a variety of inviting rooms, plus Edwardian-style bar, restaurant, conservatory and garden. ❺

Britannia Adelphi Ranelagh Place ☏0151/709 7200, ⓦwww.britannia-hotels.co.uk. The *Adelphi* catered to passenger-liner customers in its heyday, but it's lost its lustre since then. However, weekend discounts and special-break rates are always available. ❺

Campanile Wapping and Chaloner St ☏0151/709 8104. Purpose-built budget motel-style property near Albert Dock, overlooking the Mersey, and offering all-one-price rooms. ❸

Crowne Plaza Liverpool St Nicholas Place, Princes Dock, Pier Head ☏0151/243 8000, ⓦwww.cpliverpool.com. Great dockside location plus pool, sauna and gym, brasserie and bar. ❺–❼

Express by Holiday Inn Britannia Pavilion, Albert Dock ☏0151/709 1133, ⓦwww.hiexpress.com. All of the en-suite dockside rooms go for the same bargain price, with continental buffet breakfast and parking included. ❹

Feathers 117–125 Mount Pleasant ☏0151/709 9655, ⓦwww.feathers.uk.com. A converted terrace of Georgian houses, with a variety of rooms in warm crimson tones, all en suite. Buffet breakfast included. ❺

Hope Street 40 Hope St (entrance on Hope Place) ☏0151/709 3000, ⓦwww.hopestreethotel.co.uk. Victorian warehouse given a contemporary makeover – hardwood floors, huge beds and widescreen TVs. Breakfast not included. ❼

Liverpool Moat House Paradise St ☏0151/471 9988, ⓦwww.moathousehotels.com. Well-equipped, modern hotel a short walk from the Albert Dock, with comfortable rooms and good sports facilities including indoor pool and spa. ❻–❼

Marriott 1 Queen Square ☏0151/476 8000, ⓦwww.marriott.com. Stylish city-centre hotel, featuring a leisure club (with indoor pool and hot tub), restaurant and bar. ❻–❼

Premier Lodge 45 Victoria St ☏08709/906584, ⓦwww.premierlodge.co.uk. Motel-style comfort near the Cavern Quarter at pretty much unbeatable prices. Family rooms available. Breakfast not included. ❸

Racquet Club Hargreaves Building, 5 Chapel St ☏0151/236 6676, ⓦwww.racquetclub.org.uk. Boutique-style townhouse hotel, mixing good linen and traditional furniture with contemporary art and all mod cons. Breakfast costs £6–10 extra. ❻

Travel Inn Vernon St ☏08702/383323, ⓦwww.travelinn.co.uk. Bang in the city centre, offering decent-sized en-suite rooms with big beds; a good deal for families. Breakfast not included. ❸

Trials 56 Castle St ☏0151/227 1021, ⓦwww.trialshotel.com. Classy nineteenth-century building with Victorian-styled public areas and modernized rooms. ❼

Hostels and halls of residence

International Inn 4 South Hunter St, off Hardman St ☏0151/709 8135, ⓦwww.internationalinn.co.uk. Converted Victorian warehouse with modern accommodation for 100 in heated, en-suite rooms sleeping two to ten people. Lounge, kitchen, laundry and baggage storage, bedding provided and no curfew. Dorm £15, twin rooms. ❶

John Moores University ☏0151/231 3511, ⓦwww.livjm.ac.uk. Single rooms available with or without continental breakfast. Mid-June to early Sept only. Room only £17.50, B&B £19.50

Liverpool YHA Wapping ☏0870/770 5924, ⓔliverpool@yha.org.uk. Accommodation (the price

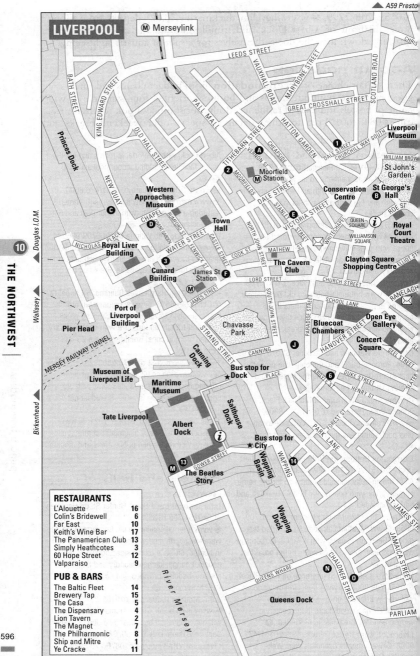

RESTAURANTS

L'Alouette	16
Colin's Bridewell	6
Far East	10
Keith's Wine Bar	17
The Panamerican Club	13
Simply Heathcotes	3
60 Hope Street	12
Valparaiso	9

PUB & BARS

The Baltic Fleet	14
Brewery Tap	15
The Casa	5
The Dispensary	4
Lion Tavern	2
The Magnet	7
The Philharmonic	8
Ship and Mitre	1
Ye Cracke	11

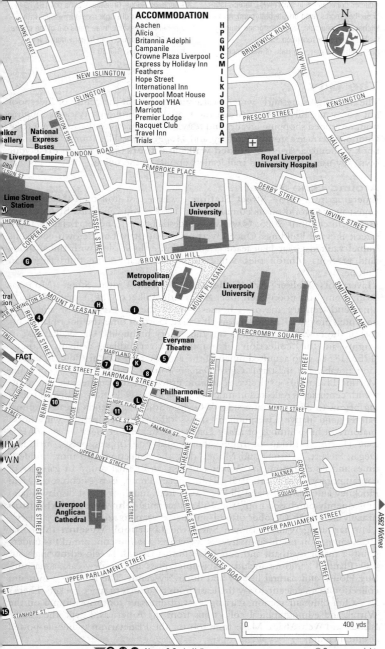

ACCOMMODATION

Aachen	H
Alicia	P
Britannia Adelphi	G
Campanile	N
Crowne Plaza Liverpool	C
Express by Holiday Inn	M
Feathers	I
Hope Street	L
International Inn	K
Liverpool Moat House	J
Liverpool YHA	O
Marriott	B
Premier Lodge	E
Racquet Club	D
Travel Inn	A
Trials	F

N

ST ANNE STREET

NEW ISLINGTON

ISLINGTON

NORTON STREET

LONDON ROAD

BRUNSWICK ROAD

LOW HILL

KENSINGTON

ary

alker
allery

National
Express
Buses

Liverpool Empire

ORD
ELSON ST

PEMBROKE PLACE

PRESCOT STREET

HALL LANE

Royal Liverpool
University Hospital

Lime Street
Station
M

LHORNE ST

COPPERAS HILL

RUSSELL STREET

DERBY STREET

MINSHULL ST

IRVINE STREET

Liverpool
University

G

BROWNLOW HILL

central
ion

UPPER NEWINGTON ST

RENSHAW STREET

MOUNT PLEASANT

Metropolitan
Cathedral

MOUNT PLEASANT

Liverpool
University

H

I

SMITHDOWN LANE

4

ABERCROMBY SQUARE

FACT

COLQUITT STREET

STREET

BERRY STREET

LEECE STREET

RODNEY STREET

MARYLAND ST

SOUTH HUNTER ST

Everyman
Theatre

7

K

5

HARDMAN STREET

8

9

MULBERRY STREET

GROVE STREET

RUSCOE STREET

10

PILGRIM STREET

HOPE PLACE

L

Philharmonic
Hall

CATHERINE STREET

MYRTLE STREET

INA

WN

11

RICE ST

HOPE STREET

12

FALKNER ST

GREAT GEORGE STREET

UPPER DUKE STREET

HOPE STREET

CATHERINE STREET

FALKNER
SQUARE

GROVE STREET

A562 Widnes

Liverpool
Anglican
Cathedral

UPPER PARLIAMENT STREET

PRINCES ROAD

UPPER PARLIAMENT STREET

MULGRAVE STREET

ET

15

STANHOPE ST

0   400 yds

P, 16, 17, Airport & Speke Hall

© Crown copyright

includes breakfast) is in smart two-, three-, four- or six-bed rooms (with private bathroom). Also a kitchen, licensed café, luggage storage, laundry facilities and 24hr reception. £19
University of Liverpool Halls of Residence, Greenbank House, Greenbank Lane ☎0151/794 6402. Hundreds of single rooms available, with continental breakfast, three miles out of the centre (bus #80). Open mid-April to early May & mid-June to mid-Sept. £17.50

The City

The main sights are fairly widely scattered throughout the centre of Liverpool but you can easily walk between most of them, through cityscapes ranging from revamped shopping arcades and restyled city squares to the surviving regal Georgian terraces around Rodney and Hope streets. The tourist offices can book you onto a variety of **guided walks and tours** (from £3), or make your own way using the themed trail leaflets on sale in the offices.

Around Lime Street

Emerging from **Lime Street Station** – whose cast-iron train shed was the largest in the world on its completion in 1867 – you can't miss **St George's Hall** (closed until 2005; ⓦwww.stgeorgeshall.com), one of Britain's finest Greek Revival buildings. Once Liverpool's concert hall and crown courts, its tunnel-vaulted Great Hall features an exquisite floor, tiled with thirty thousand precious Minton tiles, while the Willis organ is the third largest in Europe.

Liverpool's **Walker Art Gallery** on William Brown Street (Mon–Sat 10am–5pm, Sun noon–5pm; free; ⓦwww.thewalker.org.uk) – named after a nineteenth-century mayor – houses one of the country's finest and best-presented provincial art collections. If you're short on time, the floor plan available at the entrance desk picks out the gallery highlights. The Walker had its origins in the collection of eminent Liverpudlian William Roscoe (1753–1831), who acquired much of the early Renaissance art now on display, most notably the masterful *Christ Discovered in the Temple* (1342) by Simeone Martini. Liverpool's explosive economic growth in the eighteenth and nineteenth centuries is reflected in much of the Walker's collection, as British painting begins to occupy centre stage – George Stubbs, England's greatest animal painter (and native Liverpudlian) shows off his preoccupation with horse anatomy in his paintings of *Molly Longlegs* (1762) and *A Horse Frightened by a Lion* (1770). A group of Impressionists and post-Impressionists, including Degas, Sickert, Cézanne and Monet, drag the collection into more modern times and tastes, before the Walker embarks on its final round of galleries of contemporary British art. Paul Nash, Lucian Freud, Ben Nicholson, David Hockney and John Hoyland all have work here, much of it first displayed (and subsequently purchased from) the Walker's biennial **John Moores Exhibition** (usually held from October of odd-numbered years to the following January).

Further along William Brown Street the **Liverpool Museum** (Mon–Sat 10am–5pm, Sun noon–5pm; free; ⓦwww.liverpoolmuseum.org.uk) is undergoing a major overhaul and certain sections may still be closed during your visit. Planned additions include a six-storey glass atrium, new café, aquarium, Bug House, and natural history and discovery centre. The result is a museum collection that's eclectic to say the least, from tarantulas to space rockets. There's also a full dinosaur section, starring a set of dinosaur footprints found on the Wirral, and ethnographical collections from the Americas, Egypt, the Pacific Islands and West Africa. Make time too for the Planetarium (schedule posted at entrance desk; £1).

The Beatles in Liverpool

No Liverpool band is ever likely to eclipse **The Beatles**. Mathew Street, ten minutes' walk west of Lime Street station, is where *The Cavern* used to be – once the womb of Merseybeat, it's become a little enclave of Beatles nostalgia. *The Cavern* itself was where the band was first spotted by Brian Epstein; the club closed in 1966 and was partly demolished in 1973, though a latterday successor, the **Cavern Club** at 10 Mathew St (ⓦwww.cavern-liverpool.co.uk), complete with souvenir shop, was rebuilt on half of the original site, using, it's claimed, the original bricks. The **Cavern Pub**, immediately across the way, boasts a coiffed Lennon lounging against the wall and an exterior "Wall of Fame", highlighting both the names of all the bands who appeared at the club between 1957 and 1973 (etched into the bricks) and brass discs commemorating every Liverpool No. 1 chart-topper since 1952.

At Albert Dock **The Beatles Story** in the Britannia Vaults (daily: March–Oct 10am–6pm; Nov–Feb 10am–5pm; £7.95; ⓦwww.beatlesstory.com) traces The Beatles' rise from the early days to their disparate solo careers. Then it's on to the two houses where John Lennon and Paul McCartney grew up, both now saved for the nation by the National Trust. At **20 Forthlin Rd**, home of the McCartney family from 1955–1964, visitors don headphones and tramp round the 1950s terraced house where John and Paul wrote songs and where Paul's mother Mary died. **Mendips**, the rather more genteel house where John Lennon lived between 1945 and 1963 with his Aunt Mimi and Uncle George, has been similarly preserved. The houses are only accessible on a pre-booked minibus tour (Easter–Oct Wed–Sun; booking essential; £10; NT members £5), departing at 10.30am and 11.20am from Albert Dock (ⓣ0151/708 8574) and at 1.50pm and 3.55pm from Speke Hall (ⓣ0151 427 7231; see p.601). The price also includes free access to Speke Hall garden and grounds. Dedicated pilgrims will undoubtedly want to see all the other famous Beatles' landmarks, like Strawberry Fields (a Salvation Army home) and Penny Lane (an ordinary suburban street). This is best done on an **organized Beatles tour**, though note that these tours only show you the exteriors of the Lennon and McCartney homes.

Beatles Tours

Phil Hughes ⓣ0151/228 4565 or 07961 511223, ⓦwww.tourliverpool.co.uk. Small (8-seater) minibus tours with a guide well versed in The Beatles and Liverpool life. Three-and-a-half-hour tours daily on demand, £11 per person (private tour £65); city-centre pick-ups/drop-offs, plus free refreshments.

Magical Mystery Tour Book through Cavern City Tours ⓣ08712/221967, ⓦwww.cavern-liverpool.co.uk, or Mersey Tourism ⓣ0151/709 3285. Two-hour tours (£10.95 or £15 with the Beatles Story) on board a multicoloured Mystery Bus, departing daily throughout the year from Queen Square and Albert Dock.

The cathedrals

On the hill behind Lime Street, off Mount Pleasant, rises the funnel-shaped Catholic **Metropolitan Cathedral** of Christ the King (Mon–Sat 8am–6pm, Sun 8am–5pm; free), denigratingly known as "Paddy's Wigwam" and the "Mersey Funnel". Built in the 1960s in the wake of the revitalizing Second Vatican Council, it was raised on top of the tentative beginnings of Sir Edwin Lutyens's grandiose project to outdo St Peter's in Rome. Bits of Lutyens's cathedral can be seen in the crypt. At the other end of the aptly named Hope Street, the Anglican **Liverpool Cathedral** (daily 8am–6pm; donation requested) looks much more ancient but was actually completed eleven years later, in 1978, after 74 years in construction. The last of the great neo-Gothic structures, Sir Giles Gilbert Scott's masterwork claims a smattering of superlatives: Britain's largest and the world's fifth largest cathedral, the world's tallest Gothic arches and the highest and heaviest bells. On a clear day, a trip up the 330ft **tower** (11am–4pm; £2) through the cavernous belfry is rewarded by views to the Welsh hills.

The city centre

In the former warehouse and factory district between **Bold Street** and **Duke Street** (sometimes called the Ropewalks), new apartments, urban spaces, café-bars and shops have sprouted in recent years. There's an increasing number of places in which you can sip a latte, or shop for punk records and vintage clothing, while **Concert Square**, just off Bold Street occupies space once taken up by a factory which was levelled to provide room for warehouse-style bar developments. **FACT** at 88 Wood St (Ⓦ www.fact.co.uk) – that's "Film, Art and Creative Technology" – provides a cultural anchor for the neighbourhood with its galleries for art, video and new media exhibitions (Tues & Wed 11am–6pm, Thurs–Sat 11am–8pm, Sun noon–5pm; free), community projects, cinema screens (see p.604), café and bar. Further down Wood Street, the **Open Eye Gallery**, at nos. 28–32 (Tues–Fri 10.30am–5.30pm, Sat 10.30am–5pm; free; Ⓦ www.openeye.org.uk), features several temporary exhibitions a year, concentrating on photography, installation and video work.

Bold Street ends at Hanover Street, with the pedestrianized shopping street, Church Street continuing beyond. To the left, School Lane throws up the beautifully proportioned **Bluecoat Chambers**, built in 1717 as an Anglican boarding school for orphans and now a contemporary art gallery (Tues–Sat 9.30am–5.30pm; free) with a decent café, bookstore and crafts centre (Mon–Sat 9.30am–5pm; Ⓦ www.bluecoatdisplaycentre.com). From School Lane turn right on Paradise Street and walk down Whitechapel towards **Queen Square**, where one of the neighbourhood's surviving Victorian warehouses, on the corner of Whitechapel and Queen Square, is occupied by the **Conservation Centre** (Mon–Sat 10am–5pm, Sun noon–5pm; free, tours £2 on Wed at 2pm & 3pm, Sat 2pm; Ⓦ www.conservationcentre.org.uk). This is where Merseyside's museums and galleries undertake their restoration work and give visitors a hands-on, behind-the-scenes look.

Pier Head, Mersey Ferry and the Graces

Though the tumult of shipping which once fought the current here has gone, the **Pier Head** landing stage remains the embarkation point for the **Mersey Ferry** (Ⓣ 0151/330 1444, Ⓦ www.merseyferries.co.uk) to Woodside (for Birkenhead) and Seacombe (Wallasey). Straightforward ferry shuttles (£2 return) operate during the morning and evening rush hours, but at other times the boats run circular fifty-minute **cruises** (hourly: Mon–Fri 10am–3pm, Sat & Sun 10am–6pm; £4.30). The view back across the Mersey to the Liverpool skyline is one of the city's glories. Dominating the waterfront are the so-called **Three Graces** – namely the Port of Liverpool Building (1907), Cunard Building (1913) and, most prominently, the 322-foot high **Royal Liver Building** (1910), topped by the "Liver Birds", a couple of cormorants which have become the symbol of the city. A "Fourth Grace" – Will Alsop's controversial "Cloud" building – is due to be completed by 2007, the centrepiece of a planned 70-mile-long Mersey Waterfront Regional Park.

Albert Dock

Albert Dock, five minutes' walk south of Pier Head, was built in 1846 when Liverpool's port was a world leader. It started to decline at the beginning of the twentieth century, as the new deep-draught ships were unable to berth here, and last saw service in 1972. A decade later the site was given a complete refit, emerging as a type of rescued urban heritage that's been copied throughout the country, but rarely as successfully as here. There's free **parking** – follow the city-centre signs – and **buses** every twenty minutes during the day from Queen Square bus station.

A trip through the **Merseyside Maritime Museum** (daily 10am–5pm; free; ⓦ www.liverpoolmuseums.org.uk), filling one wing of the Albert Dock, can easily take two hours. It has sections on the history of Liverpool's evolution as a port and shipbuilding centre, plus an illuminating display detailing Liverpool's pivotal role as a springboard for over nine million emigrants. The Irish potato famine and a multiplicity of European wars, combined with the lure of gold and free land, brought people scurrying here to buy their passage to North America or Australia, and to cater for them, short-stay lodging houses sprang up all over the centre, as illustrated in an 1854 street scene. The museum is at its best, however, in its "Transatlantic Slavery" exhibit, which banishes years of Eurocentric excuses to expose the true horror of the exploitation of African slaves, who were kidnapped, abused and sold as property. The conditions they endured on the transatlantic voyage are illustrated by a reconstruction of a slave ship, echoing with haunting voices reading from diaries of slaves and slavers.

The neighbouring **Tate Liverpool** (Tues–Sun 10am–6pm; free, special exhibitions usually £3–5; ⓦ www.tate.org.uk/liverpool) is the country's national collection of modern art in the north of England. Popular retrospectives and an ever-changing display of individual works are its bread and butter, and there's also a full programme of events, talks and tours – the daily half-hour gallery talk at 2pm is free. There couldn't be a bigger contrast between the Tate and the Dock's latest attraction, **Fingerprints of Elvis** (daily 10am–6pm; £7.95; ⓦ www.fingerprintsofelvis.com), which does indeed display the only known set of the King's fingerprints (taken for his gun licence) alongside other Elvis-related ephemera and memorabilia.

The **Museum of Liverpool Life** (daily 10am–5pm; free; ⓦ www .museumofliverpoollife.org.uk) lies across the dock and is particularly revealing about the hardships that have moulded the resilient Scouse character. It has excellent sections on the city's traditional work, with investigations of the lives of ordinary shipwrights, stevedores, carters and seamen. "City Lives", meanwhile, homes in on Liverpool's cultural diversity, examining the experiences of immigrants and the former living conditions of ordinary Scousers. This might all sound a bit worthy, but it's utterly engrossing, with other equally illuminating sections spreading light on the history of the River Mersey and on the city's own King's Regiment – the last section heralded by a big-screen cacophonous blood-and-guts Napoleonic battle.

Speke Hall

Located near Liverpool's airport, six miles southeast of the centre, **Speke Hall** (Easter–Oct Wed–Sun 1–5.30pm; Nov to mid-Dec Sat & Sun 1–4.30pm; gardens Easter–Oct daily 11am–5.30pm, Nov–Easter daily 11am–4.30pm; house & gardens £5.50, gardens only £2.50; NT; ⓦ www.spekehall.org.uk) is one of the country's finest examples of Elizabethan timbered architecture. Highlights of the interior are the Jacobean plasterwork in the Great Parlour and the Great Hall's carved oak panel. There are ornamental gardens and woodland walks, a model Victorian farm, and horse-drawn carriage rides through the estate most Sundays. Any bus to the airport from Paradise Street in the city centre runs within half a mile of the entrance.

The Wirral

Across the Mersey lies the **Wirral**, the peninsula that sits between Liverpool and Chester, flanked by the Irish Sea and the River Dee. There's plenty to tempt you off the Mersey Ferry from Liverpool, and local information is available from **Birkenhead tourist office**, inside Woodside ferry terminal (daily 10am–5pm; ℡0151/647 6780, ⓦwww.wirral.gov.uk).

From the ferry at Woodside terminal it's a ten-minute walk (or bus #E1) to **Birkenhead Priory** (Easter–Oct Tues–Sun 1–5pm; Nov–Easter Tues–Sun noon–4pm; free), dating from 1150, the oldest building on Merseyside. The Benedictine foundation is a peaceful haven, and there are magnificent river views from the church tower. The other major draws are Birkenhead's **Historic Warships**, moored at the East Float Dock on Dock Road (Easter–Oct daily 10am–5pm, Nov–Easter closes at 4pm, and closed weekdays Jan & Feb; £5.50; ⓦwww.warships.freeserve.co.uk); bus #401 runs there from Woodside ferry terminal. Both the Type 12 frigate HMS Plymouth and the O-class sub HMS Onyx saw action in the Falklands War – indeed, the surrender of South Georgia was signed in the Plymouth's wardroom. A self-guided tour takes you through both vessels, clambering around bunk rooms, cabins, galleys, engine rooms and bomb bays.

For a glimpse of one of the more benign aspects of Merseyside's industrial past, take the Merseyrail under the river to **Port Sunlight**, a garden village created in 1888 by industrialist William Hesketh Lever for the workers at his soap factory. The project is explained at the **Port Sunlight Heritage Centre**, 95 Greendale Rd (April–Oct daily 10am–4pm; Nov–March Sat & Sun 11am–4pm; 70p; ⓦwww.portsunlightvillage.com), from where a self-guided trail runs through the housing estates. Off Greendale Road, a little further from Port Sunlight station, the **Lady Lever Art Gallery** (Mon–Sat 10am–5pm, Sun noon–5pm; free; ⓦwww.ladyleverartgallery.org.uk) houses a small collection of English eighteenth-century furniture, Pre-Raphaelite paintings by artists such as Rossetti and Ford Madox Brown, Wedgwood china, porcelain and assorted Greek and Roman artefacts.

This sporting life

Liverpool's most popular recreational activity, bar none, is football. **Liverpool** football club plays at **Anfield** (ticket office ℡08702/202345, ⓦwww.liverpoolfc.net) in front of some of the nation's most loyal supporters. There's a popular tour around the well-stocked museum, trophy room and dressing rooms (daily 10am–5pm; museum and tour £8.50, museum only £5; booking essential ℡0151/260 6677). **Everton**, the city's less glamorous side, commands equally intense devotion at **Goodison Park** (ticket office ℡0151/330 2300; tours Mon, Wed, Fri & Sun 11am & 2pm; booking advised on ℡0151/330 2277; ⓦwww.evertonfc.com). The first Saturday in April is **Grand National Day** at **Aintree** – the "World's Greatest Steeplechase". The race is the culmination of a meeting that starts on the previous Thursday, with prices for entry into the grounds ranging from £7 to £65. Catch the Merseyrail to Aintree and buy a ticket on the gate or book on ℡0151/523 2600. The "Grand National Experience" (May–Oct Tues–Fri 11am–2pm; £7, booking advised on ℡0151/522 2921, ⓦwww.aintree.co.uk) shows you the stables, weighing room and museum, before letting you ride the National on a race simulator.

Eating, drinking and nightlife

Liverpool's dining scene is slowly shifting up a gear and there's now a good choice of classy **restaurants** alongside a fine selection of cafés and budget places to eat. Liverpool's **pubs and bars** stay open later than most, with many serving until 1am or 2am. Fleet Street, Slater Street and Wood Street have seen most development, with the action centred on Concert Square, where drinkers spill out onto the terraces until the small hours from a variety of cafés, dance bars and theme pubs. Victoria Street in the business district is another fast-developing area for bars and nightlife. You'll catch regular gigs at any of the **live music** venues detailed below. The evening paper, the *Liverpool Echo*, has **listings** of what's going on, or pick up flyers in the shops, bars and cafés.

Cafés

Bluecoat Café Bar Bluecoat Chambers, School Lane. Mainly vegetarian food – salad bar, baked potatoes and dips – served throughout the day. Closed Sun.

Caffe Latte.net 4 South Hunter St. Fast Internet access, good coffee, big sandwiches, cheap café food and friendly service. Closes at 9pm, weekends 5.30pm.

Espresso Exchange 6 Victoria St. Locally owned espresso bar with great coffee, snacks and sandwiches. Open until 8pm, Thurs–Sat until 1am; closed Sun.

Number Seven Café 7 Falkner St. Daytime deli and coffee shop, with some seats outside on the Georgian terrace. Closed Sun.

Café-bars

Beluga Bar 40 Wood St. Hip basement space that's great for a drink or something to eat from the changing, seasonal menu. Opens at 5pm.

Blue Bar Edward Pavilion, Albert Dock. Brick-vaulted café-bar with dockside tables, big sofas and upstairs grill – a useful stop for lunch, dinner or a late-night drink.

Everyman Bistro and Bar 9–11 Hope St. Long-standing theatre-basement hangout with home-made quiche, pies and bakes, pizza and salad-type meals. Bar closes at midnight or 2am at weekends. Closed Sun.

The Living Room 15 Victoria St. Classy piano bar ambience and a fusion menu, plus a simply huge range of cocktails.

The Platinum Lounge Beetham Plaza, 25 The Strand. Feeling smooth? Come right on in to the Liverpool lounge scene where you'll need a bulging wallet and a taste for cocktails.

Tabac 126 Bold St. Café-bar serving a wide-ranging menu from breakfast until 10pm. Thai curry, risotto and Italian-style pot roasts are particular favourites.

Tea Factory 79 Wood St. Very cool, very chic "bar and kitchen" in the Ropewalks neighbourhood.

Restaurants

L'Alouette 2 Lark Lane ☎0151/727 2142. Contemporary French cuisine in intimate surroundings. Closed Sat lunch and all Mon. Moderate.

Colin's Bridewell Campbell St, off Duke St ☎0151/707 8003. Drink and dine in the cells of the old police lock-up, where big banquettes along the brick walls fill up with a lunch and after-work crowd. Lunch moderate, dinner expensive.

Far East 27–35 Berry St ☎0151/709 6072. One of the longest-serving and most reliable of Liverpool's Cantonese eating houses, with authentic *dim sum* (noon–6pm) and superb roast duck among other classics. Moderate.

Keith's Wine Bar 107 Lark Lane ☎0151/728 7688. An old favourite, as much for its good-value bistro food as its wine selection. Inexpensive.

The Panamerican Club Britannia Pavilion, Albert Dock ☎0151/709 7097. Extraordinarily handsome warehouse conversion that brings snappy North American style and service to its cavernous bar and restaurant. Expensive.

Simply Heathcotes Beetham Plaza, 25 The Strand ☎0151/236 3536. Many people's favourite Liverpool restaurant. Come Fri–Sun lunch, and before 7pm Fri & Sat, and you'll get a three-course meal for £15. Expensive.

60 Hope Street 60 Hope St ☎0151/707 6060. Currently Liverpool's best, with gourmet sandwiches and bistro-style dishes in the café-bar (open all day; closed Sun), and Modern British food of distinction in the restaurant (closed Sat lunch and all Sun). Café moderate, restaurant expensive.

Valparaiso 4 Hardman St ☎0151/708 6036. Latin-American dishes, with wines to match, like a Chilean-style *bouillabaisse* or serious steaks. Good vegetarian selection too. Closed Sun & Mon. Moderate.

Pubs and bars

The Baltic Fleet 33a Wapping. Restored pub with age-old shipping connections, known for its fine food and local beer.

Brewery Tap Stanhope St. Enjoyable Victorian brewery pub where you can sample Liverpool's own Cains beers. There are brewery tours if you're interested in the process (call ☎ 0151/709 8734, ⓦ www.cainsbeer.com; £3.75).

The Casa 29 Hope St. A good, cheap meeting place for drinks (until 2am at weekends) and bistro food (Mon–Wed noon–3pm, Thurs & Fri noon–7pm).

The Dispensary 87 Renshaw St. Highly sympathetic re-creation of a Victorian pub using rescued and antique wood, glass and tiles.

Lion Tavern 67 Moorfields. Real ale in superbly restored Victorian surroundings, from the tiles to the stained-glass rotunda. Also excellent cheese and pâté lunches (Mon–Fri).

The Magnet 45 Hardman St. Booth seating, blood-red decor, a bit of Barry White – it's groovy all right, plus there's a funky club downstairs and a great diner next door that stays open until 2am.

The Philharmonic 36 Hope St. A superb, traditional watering-hole where the main attractions – the beer aside – are the mosaic floors, tiling, gilded wrought-iron gates and the marble decor in the gents.

Ship and Mitre 133 Dale St. For the biggest real ale choice in Liverpool – ten guest beers, plus ciders and imported lagers.

Ye Cracke 13 Rice St. Crusty backstreet pub off Hope Street, much loved by the young Lennon, and with a great jukebox.

Clubs and live music

The Cavern Club 10 Mathew St ☎ 08712/221957, ⓦ www.cavern-liverpool.co.uk. The self-styled "most famous club in the world" puts on live bands Thurs to Sun.

Liverpool Academy 160 Mount Pleasant ☎ 0151/794 6868, ⓦ www.liverpoolacademy.co.uk. Local bands, touring acts and club nights playing to a mostly student audience, though open to all.

Masque Venue 90 Seel St ☎ 0151/708 8708, ⓦ www.masquevenue.fsnet.co.uk. Varied club nights and live bands, plus a bar-bistro (open until 2am Thurs–Sat). Closed Sun & Mon.

The Picket 24 Hardman St ☎ 0151/708 5318, ⓦ www.thepicket.co.uk. One of the best venues for local bands (Thurs–Sat nights), with two bars and a beer garden.

Arts, concerts and entertainment

The Royal Liverpool Philharmonic Orchestra, ranked with Manchester's Hallé as the northwest's best, dominates the city's **classical music** scene and often plays at the Philharmonic Hall and the Everyman Theatre. **Theatre** is well entrenched in the city, at a variety of venues, while independent **cinema** has found a home at FACT, the city's creative technology centre.

Annual **festivals** include ship visits and events at the Mersey Maritime Festival (June); a celebration of African arts and music in Africa Oye (June); the Summer Pops (July), when the Royal Philharmonic and top pop names perform beneath a huge marquee on King's Dock; Party at the Pier (August) for big-name pop and rock; the Merseyside International Street Festival (August; ⓦ www.brouhaha.uk.com), which involves performances by a host of European theatre groups; the Mathew Street Festival (August; ⓦ www .mathewstreetfestival.com), a free shindig, with local and national street performers playing the best of The Beatles; and Liverpool Now (October) which sees local bands playing in various venues around the city.

Bluecoat Arts Centre School Lane ☎ 0151/709 5297, ⓦ www.bluecoatartscentre.com. Eclectic mix of events – drama, dance, poetry, comedy, music and art exhibitions.

Everyman Theatre and Playhouse Hope St ☎ 0151/709 4776, ⓦ www.everymanplayhouse .com. Presents everything from Shakespeare to Jarman, as well as concerts, exhibitions, dance and musical performances.

Liverpool Empire Lime St ☎ 0870/606 3536, ⓦ www.liverpool-empire.co.uk. The city's largest theatre, a venue for touring West End shows, opera, ballet and music.

Philharmonic Hall Hope St ☎ 0151/709 3789, ⓦ www.liverpoolphil.com. Home of the Royal Liverpool Philharmonic Orchestra. Shows classic films once a month.

Picturehouse at FACT Wood St ☎ 0151/707 4460, ⓦ www.picturehouses.co.uk. A great programme of new films, reruns, festivals and a Saturday morning kids' club. Cheaper tickets weekdays before 6pm, and cheapest Tues to Thurs before 4pm.

Royal Court Theatre Roe St ☏0151/709 4321, ⓦwww.royalcourttheatre.net. Art Deco theatre and concert hall, which sees regular pop and rock concerts.

Listings

Airport ☏0151/288 4000, ⓦwww .liverpooljohnlennonairport.com.
Banks and exchange ATMs are ubiquitous. American Express, 54 Lord St ☏0870/600 1060; Thomas Cook, 75 Church St ☏0151/552 1340. You can also change money at the two tourist offices, the main post office (see below) and at the airport.
Books Most of the bookshops are along Bold Street: Dillons at no. 14, Waterstones at no. 52 and the more radical News from Nowhere at no. 112.
Buses Merseytravel ☏0151/236 7676, National Express ☏08705/808080.
Car rental Avis ☏0151/709 4737; easyRentacar ☏09063/333333; Europcar ☏0151/709 7563; Hertz ☏0151/486 7444.
Ferries Isle of Man Steam-Packet Company for ferries/Sea Cats to Isle of Man ☏08705/523523,

ⓦwww.seacat.co.uk; Mersey Ferries ☏0151/330 1444, ⓦwww.merseyferries.co.uk.
Hospital Royal Liverpool University Hospital, Prescot Street ☏0151/706 2000.
Internet Planet Electra, 36 London Rd (daily 10am–6pm); Caffe Latte.net, 4 South Hunter St (Mon–Fri 9am–9pm, Sat & Sun 9am–5.30pm).
Laundry Liver Launderette, 80 & 170 Aigburth Rd & 104 Prescot Rd.
Pharmacy Boots, Clayton Sq Shopping Centre ☏0151/709 4711; Moss Pharmacy, 68–70 London Rd ☏0151/709 5271 (daily until 11pm).
Police Canning Place ☏0151/777 4545.
Post office City-centre office at The Lyceum, 1 Bold St. Open Mon–Sat 8.30am–6pm.
Taxis Mersey Cabs ☏0151/298 2222; Davy Liver ☏0151/709 4646.
Travel agent Discounted and student tickets from STA Travel, 78 Bold St ☏0151/707 1123.

Blackpool

Shamelessly brash **BLACKPOOL** is the archetypal British seaside resort, its "Golden Mile" of piers, fortune-tellers, amusement arcades, tram and donkey rides, fish-and-chip shops, candyfloss stalls, fun pubs and bingo halls making no concessions to anything but low-brow fun-seeking of the finest kind. There are seven miles of wide sandy beach backed by an unbroken chain of hotels and guest houses, attracting sixteen million people each year. It was the coming of the railway in 1846 that made Blackpool what it is today: within thirty years, there were piers, promenades and theatres for the thousands who descended. The Winter Gardens, with its barrel-vaulted ballroom, the Baroque Grand Theatre on Church Street, Blackpool's own "Eiffel Tower" on the seafront and other refined diversions were built to cater to the tastes of the first influx, but it was the Central Pier's "open air dancing for the working classes" that heralded the crucial change of accent. Suddenly Blackpool was favoured destination for the "Wakes Weeks", when whole Lancashire mill towns descended for their annual seven days' holiday.

Where other British holiday resorts have suffered from the rivalry of cheap foreign packages, Blackpool has simply gone from strength to strength by shrewdly providing exactly what its visitors want. Underneath the populist veneer there's a sophisticated marketing approach, which balances ever more elaborate rides and attractions with well-grounded traditional entertainment. When other resorts begin to close up for the winter, Blackpool's main season is just beginning, as over half a million light bulbs are used to create **the Illuminations** which decorate the promenade from the beginning of September to early November. Lately, Blackpool has been looking to extend its attractions further, with plans laid to build a series of casino resorts, entertainment complexes and leisure parks. Development is expected to take up to twenty years and cost around £1 billion, though the master plan shies away from the inevitable comparisons with Las Vegas – laser shows, glass domes and resort-style hotels might all follow, but they will complement, not supplant, the town's Victorian heritage.

Arrival, information and accommodation

Blackpool's main train station is **Blackpool North** (direct trains from Manchester and Preston), half a dozen blocks up Talbot Road from North Pier. A few steps down Talbot Road, towards the sea, stands the combined National Express and local **bus station**. Some trains from Preston also run to **Blackpool South**, near the Pleasure Beach. There are **car parks** signposted all over town (including on Albert Road, Talbot Road, Bank Street and Central Drive), and it's best to use them since on-street parking is only short-term. Blackpool's **airport** lies two miles south of the centre; there are buses from the bus station or it's a £5 taxi ride. The main **tourist office** at 1 Clifton St (Mon–Sat 9am–5pm, Wed from 9.30am; ☎01253/478222, ⊛www.blackpooltourism .com) is on the corner of Talbot Road; a second office sits on the promenade opposite Blackpool Tower (summer only: Mon–Sat 9.15am–5pm, Wed from 9.30am, Sun 10.15am–4.15pm). You can pick up maps and hefty accommodation brochures; they also sell Travel Cards (one-day £4.95; three-day £12.75; five-day £16.25; seven-day £17.25) for use on all local buses and trams.

Bed-and-breakfast prices are generally low (from £15 per person, even less on a room-only basis or out of season), but rise at weekends and during the Illuminations. Anything cheap between North and Central piers is guaranteed to be noisy; for more peace and quiet (an unusual request in Blackpool, it has to be said), look for places along the more restful North Shore, beyond North Pier.

Guest houses and hotels

The Big Blue Ocean Boulevard, Blackpool Pleasure Beach ☎0845/367 3333, ⊛www.bigbluehotel.com. Family suites with DVDs, games consoles and separate children's area. Rates are room-only, and rise slightly during the Illuminations. ❹

Boltonia 124–126 Albert Rd ☎01253/620248, ⊛www.boltoniahotel.co.uk. Not far from the Winter Gardens, on a corner plot that lets in lots of light – superior rooms are a bit more spacious and have large TVs. ❷

Clifton Talbot Square ☎01253/621481, ⨏01253/627345. On the North Pier prom, this traditional beauty – a Grade 2 listed building – has fine sea views from many rooms. Check for special offers. ❻

Dutchman 269 The Promenade ☎01253/404812, ⊛www.dutchmanhotel.com. A great budget seafront choice between Central and South piers, whose small, cheery rooms have showers. It's probably the only Blackpool B&B to offer a cream-cheese bagel for breakfast. Two-night minimum stay at weekends. ❷

Grosvenor View 7–9 King Edward Ave ☎01253/352851. Rooms in this detached property are larger and better equipped than most – and

you're in the care of an award-winning landlady. ❷

The Imperial North Promenade ☎01253/623971, ⊛www.paramount-hotels.co.uk. The politicians' conference favourite, a four-star hotel with excellent sea-facing rooms, pool and gym. It's a short tram ride away from the Tower and the rest of the sights. ❼

The Old Coach House 50 Dean St ☎01253/349195, ⊛www.theoldcoachhouse .freeserve.co.uk. Detached Tudor-style villa near the Pleasure Beach and South Prom offering a rare Blackpool commodity – peace and quiet. The eleven bedrooms have crisp decor, king-sized beds and high-spec bathrooms. ❺

Raffles 73–77 Hornby Rd ☎01253/294713, ⊛www.raffleshotelblackpool.co.uk. Nice place back from Central Pier and away from the bustle, with seventeen well-kept rooms. ❹

Ruskin Albert Rd ☎01253/624063, ⊛www.ruskinhotel.com. At the prom end of Albert Road, the *Ruskin* offers smart rooms with decent bathrooms, all individually decorated. ❺

Wildlife 39 Woodfield Rd ☎01253/346143. Non-smoking, animal-friendly place, just off the promenade, between Central and South piers. Twelve simple rooms with showers and toilets. No credit cards. ❶

The Town

With seven miles of beach – the tide ebb is half a mile, leaving plenty of sand at low tide – and accompanying promenade, you'll want to jump on and off the electric **trams** if you plan to get up and down much between the piers. South Pier to North Pier – between which lies most of what there is to see and do – costs £1.10.

The major event in town is **Blackpool Pleasure Beach** on the South Promenade (March–Easter Sat & Sun 10am–8pm; Easter–June Mon–Fri 2–8pm, Sat & Sun 10am–10pm; July to Nov 5 daily 10am–11pm; hours can vary, call ☎0870/444 5566, ⓦwww.blackpoolpleasurebeach.com), just south of South Pier. Entrance to the amusement park is free, but you'll have to fork out for the superb array of "white knuckle" rides including "The Big One", which involves a terrifying near-vertical drop from 235ft. After this, the Pleasure Beach's wonderful antique wooden rollercoasters – "woodies" to aficionados – seem like kids' stuff, but each is unique. The original "Big Dipper" was invented at Blackpool in 1923 and still thrills. Individual rides cost from £1 to £5, but if you're not leaving until you've been on everything buy an unlimited ride wristband (£26, usually cheaper in the off-season).

Jump a tram for the ride up to **Central Pier** with its 108-foot-high revolving Big Wheel. The **Sea-Life Centre** (July & Aug Mon–Thurs & Sun 10am–6pm, Fri & Sat 10am–10pm; Sept–June daily 10am–6pm; £7.50; ⓦwww.sealife.co.uk) nearby is one of the country's best, with eight-foot sharks looming at you as you march through a glass tunnel and a very large, lurking Giant Pacific octopus. For a taste of what Blackpool attractions used to be like, you could then hit **Louis Tussauds Waxworks**, 87–89 Central Promenade (daily 10am–10pm; £6) – these days, more Posh and Becks than Churchill and Margaret Thatcher.

Blackpool's elegant cast-iron **piers** also strike a traditional note. They're covered with arcades and amusements, while much of what passes for evening family entertainment – TV comics and variety shows – takes place in the various pier theatres. Between Central and North piers stands the 518-foot **Blackpool Tower** (June–Oct daily 10am–11pm; Nov–May daily 10am–6pm; £11.50; ⓦwww.theblackpooltower.co.uk), erected in 1894 when it was thought that the northwest really ought not to be outdone by Paris. It provides the skyline's sole touch of grace, but paying the hefty entrance fee is the only way to ride up to the top (where there's a postbox) for the stunning view and an unnerving walk on the see-through glass floor. From the very early days, there's been a Moorish-inspired **circus** (shows also included in the entry ticket; up to three daily performances) between the tower's legs, which still functions, though in the spirit of the times it's now animal-free.

Eating

Eating out revolves around the typical British seaside fare of fish and chips, available all over town. Given the sheer volume of customers, other restaurants don't have to try too hard: you'll have no trouble finding cheap roasts, pizzas, Chinese or Indian food, but might struggle if you're seeking a bit more sophistication.

Cafés

Barista 24 Birley St. Seattle-style coffee house, with grilled sandwiches, muffins and croissants. Closes 5.30pm.
Dress Circle Café Grand Theatre, Church St. Dine in the ornate bar (a daily roast, steak, scampi and lasagna) to the accompaniment of show tunes. Closes 5.30pm.
Robert's Oyster Bar 92 The Promenade. Glorious, wood-panelled, 130-year-old café where you can

buy oysters, cockles and mussels, or seafood platters. Closes 5pm in winter.

Restaurants

Harry Ramsden's 60–63 The Promenade, corner of Church St ☎01253/294386. The celebrated Yorkshire chippie chain has the town's pre-eminent (and priciest) sit-down fish and chips – there's a takeaway counter too. Moderate.

Kwizeen 47 King St ☎01253/290045. Anglo-Med bistro, with a bargain two-course weekday lunch (£5.95) and a seasonally changing menu. Closed Sun. Moderate.

Lagoonda 37 Queen St ☎01253/293837. Party-time Afro-Caribbean restaurant. Choose from jerk or ginger pork, stuffed plantain, fruity curry and other such dishes. Moderate.

September Brasserie 15–17 Queen St ☎01253/623282. The restaurant with the best reputation in town – set prices for two- and three-course meals with a menu ranging from locally potted shrimps to king prawn tempura. Closed Sun, & Mon lunch. Moderate.

White Tower Ocean Blvd, Blackpool Pleasure Beach ☎01253/346710. The closest the town gets to Vegas – a lounge-style restaurant with prom views, snappy service and Modern British food. Closed Mon, & Sat lunch. Expensive.

Drinking, nightlife and entertainment

If you like your **nightlife** late, loud and libidinous, summertime Blackpool has few English peers. *Yates' Wine Lodge* has two popular branches, in Talbot Square and between Central and South piers, where you can sip an amontillado sherry or champagne on draught. There's also a plethora of Irish theme bars, notably *O'Neill's* on the corner of Talbot Road and Abingdon Street, *Finn's* in the *Clifton Hotel* on Talbot Square and *Scruffy Murphy's*, 32 Corporation St. *The Wheatsheaf* on Talbot Road, opposite Blackpool North station, features real ales from local breweries, an open fire and beat-era memorabilia. For **dancing**, local opinion favours *Blue*, on Corporation Street, near the Grand Theatre, or *The Syndicate* on Church Street (the UK's biggest club). *Bar Red* on Church Street, next to the Winter Gardens, is the pre-club party venue. *Funny Girls*, a transvestite cabaret bar at 9 The Strand (☎01253/624901), has nightly shows that attract long (gay and straight) queues. Otherwise, entertainment is based very heavily on family shows, musicals, veteran TV comedians, crooners and stage spectaculars put on at a variety of end-of-pier and Pleasure Beach theatres or historic venues such as the **Grand Theatre** (☎01253/290190, ⓦwww.blackpoolgrand.co.uk), **Winter Gardens** (☎01253/292029, ⓦwww.blackpoollive.co.uk) and **Opera House** (☎01253/292029), all on Church Street.

Preston and around

With the siren draws of the Lakes, the Peak District and the Yorkshire Dales so close, the rest of Lancashire often gets bypassed in the rush to the surrounding national parks, and more's the pity. In **Preston,** 25 miles northwest of Manchester, the county has one of England's oldest towns, containing two fine museums and some appealing Georgian and Victorian remnants. North of the town, rural Lancashire is at its most bucolic in the villages of the **Ribble Valley**, particularly in the **Forest of Bowland**, whose gateway is the small market town of **Clitheroe**.

Preston

Strategically placed on the banks of the River Ribble, **PRESTON** (possibly a contraction of "Priest's Town") was already an important market town in Anglo-Saxon times and received its royal charter in 1179 – origin of the famous

Preston Guild celebrations, which since 1542 have taken place every twenty years (the next in 2012). The town was attacked by Robert the Bruce, changed hands in the Civil War and saw action during the Jacobite rebellions, while Charles Dickens gathered material here for *Hard Times*, his coruscating attack on the factory system. Some handsome Victorian public buildings do survive, most notably the majestic Greek-Revival-style **Harris Museum and Art Gallery** (Mon–Sat 10am–5pm; free), in the central Market Square. The permanent collection focuses on fine art (particularly British landscape and portraiture, and contemporary photography) and decorative art, while temporary exhibitions often explore links with the town's significant Asian population. On either side of the Harris lies the modern shopping area, converging on Fishergate, the main street through town: the Victorian **Miller Arcade** (facing Fishergate) and outdoor and indoor **markets** (up Market Street; closed Sun) are the main draw. For a change in emphasis, cross Fishergate to explore the handsome Georgian development of **Winckley Square**, once home to the town's richest cotton magnates. If you needed any more incentive to stop it would be to make your way to the ground of Preston North End – one of Britain's oldest football clubs and winners of the first Football League championship – for the marvellous **National Football Museum**, Sir Tom Finney Way, Deepdale Stadium (Tues–Sat 10am–5pm, midweek matchday 10am–7.30pm, Sun 11am–5pm; free; ⓦwww.nationalfootballmuseum.com). On one level, this is simply an unparalleled collection of football memorabilia: those who know about such things will relish the chance to see items as diverse as the Geoff Hurst crossbar from the 1966 World Cup Final. But you really don't have to know anything about football to enjoy the museum, since "the true story of the world's greatest game" is backed by fascinating archive material on football's origins, its social importance, the experience of fans through the ages, and other relevant themes.

For the football museum, it's a ten-minute ride on bus #19 from Preston **bus station**, right in the centre of town. The **train station**, on the west coast main line, has regular services to Lancaster, Manchester and Blackpool. The **tourist office** is in the Guild Hall, on Lancaster Road (Mon–Sat 10am–5.30pm; ☎01772/253731, ⓦwww.visitpreston.com), just round the corner from the Harris Museum.

The Ribble Valley

When the nineteenth-century Lancashire cotton weavers enjoyed a rare break from their industry they took to the bucolic retreats of the **Ribble Valley**, north of Preston, which cuts through the heart of northern Lancashire to the River Ribble's source in the Yorkshire Dales. **Public transport** is limited to the train service from Manchester and Blackburn, or buses from Preston, to the market town of Clitheroe; from there, buses run out to Slaidburn (with connections on to Settle in Yorkshire), the tiny village in the heart of the region.

A tidy market town on the banks of the River Ribble, **CLITHEROE** is best seen from the terrace of its empty Norman keep which towers above the Ribble Valley floor. From here, the small centre is laid out before you and, if there's little else specific to see – save a **Castle Museum** (11am–4.30pm; Easter–Oct daily; Nov–Dec & Feb weekends only; March–Easter closed Thurs & Fri; £1.65) in the extensive grounds – you can at least spend an hour or two browsing around the shops and old pubs. One obvious target is Pendle Hill, a couple of miles to the east, where the ten **Pendle Witches** allegedly held the diabolic rites that led to their hanging in 1612. The evidence against them came mainly from one small child, but nonetheless a considerable mythology has grown up around the witches, whose memory is perpetuated by a hilltop gathering each Halloween. You can sort out transport connections at the **bus and rail interchange** at the train station; a **Ribble Valley Day Ranger** ticket (£3, available on board any bus) is the best local deal. Pedal Power on Waddington Road (℡01200/422066) can sort you out with a **mountain bike** (£12 a day) for in-depth exploration of the nearby Forest of Bowland.

Heading northwest from Clitheroe on the B6478 brings you to the **Forest of Bowland** – the name "forest" is used in its traditional sense of a "royal hunting ground", and much of the land still belongs to the Crown. **SLAIDBURN** is the most substantial and attractive of the Forest's settlements. Hoary stone cottages fronted by a strip of aged cobbles set the tone – a truly ancient **inn**, the *Hark to Bounty* (℡01200/446246, ⓦwww.hark-to-bounty.co.uk; ❸), and a popular **youth hostel** (℡0870/770 6034, Ⓔslaidburn@yha.org.uk; £10.25; closed Nov–Easter), itself a former inn, complete the picture.

Lancaster and around

LANCASTER, Lancashire's county town, dates back at least as far as the Roman occupation, though only the scant remains of a bath-house and traces of the fort wall survive from that period. It later became an important port on the slave triangle, and it's the legacy of predominantly Georgian buildings from that time that gives the town its character, particularly in the leafy areas around the castle. It's no surprise that many people choose to spend a night here on the way to the Lakes or Dales to the north, and it's an easy side-trip the few miles west to the resort of Morecambe and to neighbouring Heysham village and its ancient churches.

Lancaster Castle (daily tours, every 30min, 10.30am–4pm; £4; ⓦwww .lancastercastle.com) has been the city's focal point since Roman times, when there was a fort on this site. Currently, about a quarter of the battlemented building can be visited on an entertaining hour-long tour, though court sittings sometimes affect the schedules. The castle's neighbour, the former Benedictine **Priory Church of St Mary** (daily 10am–4.30pm; free), has a (possibly) Saxon doorway at the west end and some finely carved fourteenth-century choir stalls. A two-minute walk down the steps between the castle and church brings you to the seventeenth-century **Judges' Lodgings** (Easter–June & Oct Mon–Fri 1–4pm, Sat & Sun noon–4pm; July–Sept Mon–Fri 10am–4pm, Sat & Sun noon–4pm; £2), once used by visiting magistrates and now home to two museums. Rooms on the ground and first floors house furniture by Gillows of Lancaster, one-time boat builders who, in the early eighteenth century, took to cabinet-making with the tropical timber which came back as ballast in their boats. The top floor is given over to a **Museum of Childhood**, with memory-jogging displays of toys and games, and a period (1900) schoolroom.

Continuing down the hill and left onto Damside Street, you arrive on the banks of the **River Lune** whose navigable lengths inspired the growth of the port. The river was first bridged in Roman times: the latest span, an eye-catching steel suspension bridge for pedestrians, follows the line of the medieval wooden, later stone, bridge. The top floor of one of the eighteenth-century warehouses here is taken up by part of the **Maritime Museum**, St George's Quay (daily: Easter–Oct 11am–5pm; Nov–Easter 12.30–4pm; £2), entered through the Old Custom House on the riverside.

For a panorama of the town, Morecambe Bay and the Cumbrian fells, take a bus from the bus station (or a steep 25-minute walk up Moor Lane) to **Williamson Park** (Easter–Oct daily 10am–5pm; Nov–Easter Mon–Fri

11am–4pm, Sat & Sun 10am–4pm; free), Lancaster's highest point. Funded by local statesman and lino magnate Lord Ashton, the park's centrepiece is the 220-foot-high **Ashton Memorial** (same hours as park; free), a Baroque folly raised by his son in memory of his second wife. The other local excursion is to the **Crook O'Lune**, a beauty spot made famous by J.M.W. Turner. It's four miles northeast of the city, reached by a path/cycle-way along the River Lune.

Practicalities

Lancaster is a regular stop on the West Coast rail line from London to Scotland; there are also hourly trains from Manchester and even more frequently from Preston. From either the **train station** on Meeting House Lane, or the combined local **bus** and National Express station on Cable Street in town, it's a five-minute walk to the **tourist office** at 29 Castle Hill (March–Sept Mon–Sat 10am–5pm, Tues closes at 4pm; Oct–Feb Mon–Sat 10am–4pm; ℡01524/32878, ⓦwww.lancaster.gov.uk), in front of the castle. Annual **events and festivals** include an Easter maritime festival, the Worldbeat weekend for global music and crafts (Aug), Georgian festival (Aug bank holiday), and spectacular Bonfire Night celebrations (Saturday nearest Nov 5). For other cultural affairs, visit **Dukes** on Moor Lane (℡01524/598500, ⓦwww.dukes -lancaster.org), the city's main arts centre, which has a cinema and theatre.

Accommodation

Edenbreck House Sunnyside Lane ℡01524/32464. Large Victorian house ten minutes' walk out of the centre, set in its own grounds at the end of Ashfield Avenue, off Meeting House Lane. No credit cards. ❷

Old Station House 25 Meeting House Lane ℡01524/381060. Amiable, nonsmoking accommodation, each room with shower or private bathroom. No credit cards. ❸

Royal King's Arms Market St ℡01524/32451, ⓦwww.bookmenzies.com. Lancaster's best-sited

hotel has fifty prettily furnished rooms with smart bathrooms, plus a bar and brasserie. Ask for a castle view. ❻

Shakespeare 96 St Leonardsgate ℡01524/841041. Eight cosy rooms in this popular nonsmoking townhouse hotel on a central street. Advance reservations advised. No credit cards. ❸

Wagon & Horses 27 St George's Quay ℡01524/846094. Pleasant rooms above a riverside pub, just past the Maritime Museum. No credit cards. ❷

Cafés and restaurants

Il Bistro Morini 26 Sun St ℡01524/846252. The best Italian in town, with a veggie-friendly Mediterranean menu. Best to book in advance. Closed Sun. Moderate.

Pizza Margherita 2 Moor Lane ℡01524/36333. Friendly pizza place, with sixteen choices on the menu (and Lancashire cheese on a couple of them). You can fill up for around £10. Inexpensive.

Simply French 27 St George's Quay ℡01524/843199. Riverside brasserie in a con-

verted warehouse close to the Maritime Museum. Closed Mon, also Tues & Wed lunch. Moderate.

Sun Café 25 Sun St ℡01524/845599. The contemporary bistro cooking is the draw in this stylish café/restaurant. Closed Sun evening. Inexpensive to moderate.

The Whale Tail 78a Penny St. Veggie and wholefood café, serving salads, burgers, sandwiches and baked potatoes. Closes 5pm, 3pm on Sun. Inexpensive

Pubs

Ye Olde John O'Gaunt 53 Market St, near the City Museum. City-centre local with home-cooked food, special beers, tea and coffee on request, live trad jazz and R&B, plus a small beer garden.

Water Witch Aldcliffe Rd (across the canal bridge). Canalside pub named after an old canal packet boat, with posh pub food and an impressive range of real ales and continental lagers.

Morecambe and Heysham

Although the name **MORECAMBE**, meaning "Great Bay", dates from Celtic times, the seaside town five miles west of Lancaster only took it in the nineteenth century when it rapidly expanded from a small fishing village into a full-blown resort. The sweep of the bay is still the major attraction, with the lakeland fells visible beyond and the local sunsets a renowned phenomenon. The **Stone Jetty**, all that remains of the former harbour, has been remodelled by sculptors and stonemasons and now features bird sculptures, games and motifs – recognizing Morecambe Bay as Britain's most important wintering site for wildfowl and wading birds. A little way along the prom stands the most popular statue of all, of one of Britain's most treasured comedians – Eric Bartholomew, who took the stage name **Eric Morecambe** when he met his comedy partner, Ernie Wise. Regular buses or trains from Lancaster make the ten-minute trip to Morecambe: from the **bus** or **train stations**, on either side of Central Drive, it's five minutes' walk to the Stone Jetty.

The main historic interest on this side of Morecambe Bay is at **HEYSHAM**, three miles southwest of Morecambe and best approached on foot, along the promenade from Morecambe. Heysham's hidden gem is the shoreside **Heysham Village**, centred on a group of charming seventeenth-century cottages and barns, one of which is now the local **Heritage Centre** (April–Sept daily 11am–4pm; Oct–March Sat & Sun only 12.30–3pm; free). Settlement here can be traced back to prehistoric times, though proudest relic is the well-preserved Viking hog's-back tombstone in Saxon **St Peter's** church, set in a romantic churchyard below the headland. Just up the lane, on the headland itself, the earlier ruins of **St Patrick's Chapel** occupy a superb vantage-point over the bay and to the lakeland hills beyond.

The Isle of Man

The **Isle of Man**, almost equidistant from Ireland, England, Wales and Scotland, is one of the most beautiful spots in Britain, a mountainous, cliff-fringed island just thirty-three miles by thirteen, into which are shoehorned austere moorlands and wooded glens, sandy beaches, fine castles, beguiling narrow-gauge railways and scores of standing stones and Celtic crosses. It takes some effort to reach, and the weather is hardly reliable, factors that have seen tourist numbers fall since its Victorian heyday. This means, though, that the Isle of Man has been spared the worst excesses of the British tourist trade: there's peace and quiet in abundance, walks around the unspoilt hundred-mile coastline, picket fences and picnic spots, rural villages straight out of a 1950s picture-book, steam trains and cream teas – a yesteryear ensemble if ever there was one.

St Patrick is said to have come here in the fifth century AD bringing Christianity, which struggled for a while when the **Vikings** established garrisons here in the eleventh century, though they converted while they reigned as **Kings of Mann** – the name derived from that of the island's ancient sea-god, Mannannan Mac Lir (Son of the Sea). The Scots under Alexander wrested power from the Norsemen in 1275, the beginning of an ultimately unsuccessful 130-year struggle with the English for control of the island. The distinct identity of the island remained intact, however, and many true Manx inhabitants insist that the Isle of Man is not part of England, nor even of the UK. Indeed, although a Crown dependency, the island has its own government, **Tynwald**, arguably the world's oldest democratic parliament, which has run continuously since 979 AD. To further complicate matters, the island maintains a unique associate status in the EU, neither contributing nor receiving funds but enjoying the same trading rights. The island has its own sterling currency, worth the same as the mainland currency; its own laws, though they generally follow Westminster's; an independent postal service; and a Gaelic-based language which is taught in schools (and visible on dual-language road signs throughout the island). The island, of course, also produces its own tail-less version of the domestic cat, as well as famously good kippers and queenies (scallops).

The first regular steamship service from England commenced in 1819, and **tourism** began to flourish during the late-Victorian and Edwardian eras with the influx of northwestern factory workers. In recent times the real money-spinner has been the **offshore finance industry**, exploiting the island's low income tax and absence of capital gains tax and death duties. Given its financial expertise, the Isle of Man is also playing a major role in the development of **e-banking and e-commerce**, while the low-tax island has provided incentives for the **filming** of an increasing number of movies.

Although the landscapes are wonderful, the island's main tourist draw is the **TT (Tourist Trophy) motorcycle races** (held in the two weeks after the late-May bank holiday), a frenzy of speed and burning rubber that's shattered the island's peace annually since 1907. This is only the most famous of a summer-long list of **rallies and races** on the island's roads, from the Manx Rally, International Rally and Manx Classic to the Manx Kart Grand Prix, when go-carts buzz through the streets of Peel. If you want to stay on the island at these times (exact dates available from the Isle of Man tourist office), you must book your accommodation well in advance.

Getting to the island

Ferries or the quicker **Sea Cats**, both run by the Isle of Man Steam Packet Company (℡08705/523523, ⓦwww.seacat.co.uk), run from either Heysham (near Lancaster) or Liverpool to Douglas, the capital. Heysham (Sea Cat 2hr, ferry 3hr 30min) has the most frequent service, with two or three sailings a day throughout the year. Liverpool manages two Sea Cat services a day (2hr 30min) between April and September, with a much-reduced ferry service (4hr) at other times (between October and March, down to 1 daily at weekends). One-way **fares** start at £19 for foot passengers and £89 for drivers, but advance-purchase tickets, special offers, short breaks and night-time sailings offer substantial savings. An increasing number of airlines offer **flights** to the island from almost twenty British and Irish regional airports. Services are with British Airways (from Birmingham, Dublin, Glasgow, Leeds Bradford, Liverpool, London Gatwick, London Luton and Manchester; ℡0845/773 3377, ⓦwww.ba.com); Eastern Airways (Liverpool; ℡01652/680600, ⓦwww.easternairways.com); EuroManx (Dublin, East Midlands, Edinburgh, Liverpool; ℡01624/822123, ⓦwww.euromanx.com); Flybe (Belfast, Bristol, London City and Newcastle; ℡08705/676676, ⓦwww.flybe.com); and Fly Keenair (Belfast, Blackpool; ℡08000/837783, ⓦwww.keenair.co.uk). Prices start at £79 return on all routes, sometimes less, though you should book well in advance for the best fares.

Douglas

A mere market town as late as 1850, with one pier and an undeveloped seafront, **DOUGLAS** was a product of Victorian mass tourism and displays many similarities to Blackpool, just across the water. However, where once half a million people a year sported on the sands, package tourism to hotter climates has long since burst the bubble. As long as you put aside thoughts of Blackpool-style state-of-the-art entertainment, you can still have a thoroughly enjoyable time here, but it's likely to consist largely of pulling up a candy-striped deckchair and enjoying the extensive beach, with a ride on the horse-drawn tram thrown in for variety.

The town is at its oldest, and most interesting, in the streets near the **harbour**, where an attempt has been made to preserve Douglas's "historic quayside". There's not much to it, save a few old pubs and the odd teetering building, and you're soon pushed up Victoria Street, past the Manx Legislative Building, to the **Manx Museum**, on the corner of Kingswood Grove and Crellin's Hill (Mon–Sat 10am–5pm; free). The museum makes a good start for anyone wanting to get to grips with Manx culture and heritage before setting off around the island. Various rooms provide an absorbing synopsis of the island's history, packed with Neolithic standing stones, Celtic grave markers and other artefacts, notably some excellent displays relating to Viking burials and runic crosses.

Arrival, orientation and information

Ronaldsway airport is at Ballasalla, ten miles south of Douglas, close to Castletown. Buses (every 30min–1hr, 7am–11pm) connect the airport with Douglas as well as Castletown/Port St Mary. A taxi costs around £16 to Douglas, £20 to Peel. Ferries and Sea Cats dock by the **Sea Terminal** at the southern end of the Douglas waterfront. Fifty yards beyond the forecourt taxi rank, the Lord Street **bus terminal** is the hub of the island's dozen or so bus routes; the **Travel Shop** here (Mon 10am–12.30pm & 1.30–5.45pm, Tues 8am–12.30pm & 1.30–4pm, Wed–Fri 8am–5.45pm, Sat 8am–12.30pm & 1.30–5.45pm; ☎01624/662525) has timetable information and sells Island Explorer **travel tickets** for buses and trains – see "The rest of the island" for details.

North Quay runs 300 yards west from the bus terminal alongside the river and fishing port to Douglas Station, the northern terminus of the **steam railway** to Port Erin. The waterfront (progressively Loch, Central and Queen's promenades) runs two miles north to Derby Castle Station for the **electric railway** to Laxey and Ramsey – take the horse-drawn tram along the promenade or bus #24, #24a, #26 or #26a from North Quay.

The **tourist office** is in the Sea Terminal building (mid-May to Sept daily 9.15am–7pm; April to mid-May & Oct daily 9am–5pm; Nov–March Mon–Thurs 9am–5.30pm, Fri 9am–5pm, Sat 9.30am–12.30pm); ☎01624/686766). The main **websites** for information are ⓦwww.gov.im, ⓦwww.isleofman.com and ⓦwww.visitisleofman.com. The island's twelve heritage sites and museums have individual admission charges, though a **4 Site Pass** (£10, available from any attraction) will save you some money.

Accommodation

B&Bs are packed in along Douglas's front and up the roads immediately off Harris Promenade, particularly along Broadway, Castle Mona Avenue, Empress Drive and Empire Terrace. Note that many places demand a two-night minimum stay in the summer. The **campsites** listed below are the ones nearest to Douglas, but for a full list of rural sites contact the tourist office.

B&Bs, guest houses and hotels

Admiral House Loch Promenade
T01624/629551, W www.admiralhouse.com. At the ferry terminal end of the prom, with very comfortable rooms equipped with elegant bathrooms, café-bar and Italian restaurant. **5**

Blossoms 4 The Esplanade T01624/673360. One of the better choices at the cheaper end of the market – the sea-view rooms tend to go early. No credit cards. **1**

Claremont 18–19 Loch Promenade
T01624/698800, W www.sleepwellhotels.com. Sympathetically renovated promenade hotel with a good bar and restaurant. Rooms have all the latest gadgets, while executive suite upgrades get you a separate lounge area. **5**

Cubbon House 48 Loch Promenade
T01624/670799. Unpretentious and good value place, with comfortable beds and quiet rooms at the rear. **3**

Dreem Ard Ballanard Rd, 2 miles west of the centre T01624/621491. Tranquil, out-of-town B&B with three en-suite rooms, including a large garden suite with its own dressing room and sitting area. No credit cards. **3**

Regency Queen's Promenade T01624/680680, W www.regency.iom-1.net. A contemporary facelift has retained this place's Victorian features while kitting out guest quarters in style. Rooms also available in the associated *Hotel Penta* further down the prom (book through the *Regency*). Breakfast not included. **5**

Sefton Harris Promenade T01624/645500, W www.seftonhotel.co.im. Spacious rooms offering a sea view or a balcony over the impressive internal water garden. It's the only four-star hotel in Douglas, with pool, gym, Internet access, bike rental, bar and restaurant. **6**

St Heliers Hotel Central Promenade
T01624/624355. Reasonably priced guest house on the front with a friendly welcome and a variety of simply furnished rooms, some with tiled shower and loo, and a few with sea views. No credit cards. **2**

Welbeck Hotel Mona Drive, off Central Promenade T01624/675663, W www.welbeckhotel.com. Mid-sized family-run hotel 100 yards up the hill off the seafront – some rooms have a sea view. Six two-person self-catering apartments also available (breakfast not included in the apartments). **5**

Campsites

Grandstand T01624/621132. Closest to Douglas, this backs onto Noble's Park Grandstand on Glencrutchery Road, a mile north of the tourist office. Closed Oct–May and during TT and Manx Grand Prix races.

Glenlough Farm T01624/851326. Three miles west at Union Mills on the Peel road. Closed Oct–April.

Glendhoo International Campsite
T01624/621254. In a sheltered valley, two miles north at the Cronk ny Mona crossroads on the A18. Closed Oct–Easter.

Eating and drinking

Douglas has the best choice of **cafés and restaurants** on the island, with plenty of inexpensive places to grab a bite to eat as well as some more sophisticated dining options. Manx-brewed beer is on sale at most **pubs** and brews such as "Old Bushy Tail" soon revive flagging spirits, while for a more fashionable night out, the **bar scene** in Douglas is ever improving.

Cafés and restaurants

Café Tanroagan 9 Ridgeway St
T07624/472411. The best fish and seafood on the island, in a relaxed, contemporary restaurant with the kitchen open to view. Reservations essential. Closed Sat lunch & all Sun. Expensive.

C'est La Vie 28 Victoria St. Good-looking café-bar that's well known for its globally inspired food – bangers and mash to spicy Indonesian noodles. Inexpensive.

Greens Douglas Station, North Quay. Vegetarian café in the ticket office serving drinks and snacks until 5pm, with hot lunches and a veggie buffet from noon to 2.30pm.

Paparazzi 26 Loch Promenade T01624/673222. Pizzeria-trattoria with Sicilian beer and a few more unusual specialities alongside the traditional pizzas, pastas and Italian dishes. Moderate.

Scotts Bistro 7 John St T01624/623764. Housed in Douglas's oldest (seventeenth-century) building and has queenies (scallops) in garlic sauce and Manx trout on its bistro menu. Closed Sun. Moderate.

Spill the Beans 1 Market Hill. Douglas' best coffee house, with a choice of brews plus muffins, croissants, cakes and pastries. Closes at 5pm, and all Sun. Inexpensive.

Pubs and bars

Bar George Hill St. A fashionable haunt housed in a converted Sunday School.

Colours *Hilton Hotel*, Central Promenade. Outdoor sea-view tables make for a nice coffee stop, while it's more of a party venue at night.

Fiesta Havana 7–17 Wellington St. For drinks and cocktails, Latin American food, salsa nights and club sounds; open until 3am Fri and Sat.

Rovers Return 11 Church St. Cosy old local around the corner from *Scotts Bistro*.

Listings

Airport Ronaldsway airport, flight enquiries ℡01624/821600, Ⓦwww.iom-airport.com.

Banks ATMs at Barclays, Victoria St; NatWest, Prospect Hill; Lloyds-TSB, Prospect Hill; HSBC, Ridgeway St; Isle of Man Bank, Sea Terminal.

Bicycle rental Eurocycles, 8a Victoria Rd, off Broadway ℡01624/624909. Rental from £12 a day; closed Sun.

Buses All bus enquiries ℡01624/662525.

Car rental Most outfits have offices at the airport or can arrange to deliver cars to the Sea Terminal. Contact: Athol, Athol Garage, Peel Rd and at the airport ℡01624/822481, Ⓦwww.athol.co.im; Isle of Man Rent-a-Car, at the airport and deliveries to your hotel or Sea Terminal ℡01624/825855; Mylchreests, at the airport and deliveries to Sea Terminal ℡08000/190355.

Cruises Seasonal cruises, from Villier steps, Douglas Promenade, to Port Soderick or Laxey on the *MV Karina*. Departures daily April–Sept, weather permitting; tickets £10; call ℡01624/861724 or ℡07624/493592.

Ferries and Sea Cats Isle of Man Steam Packet Company ℡01624/661661, Ⓦwww.seacat.co.uk.

Hospital Noble's Hospital, Strang ℡01624/650000.

Internet Feegan's Lounge, 22 Duke St, off Victoria St (Mon–Fri 9am–6pm, Sat 9am–5pm).

Pharmacies Boots, 14 Strand St; John Atkinson, 2 Granville St.

Police Douglas Police Station, Glencrutchery Rd ℡01624/631212.

Post office Main post office is at 6 Regent St ℡01624/686141.

Trains Steam Railway enquiries ℡01624/673623; Electric Railway and Snaefell Mountain Railway enquiries ℡01624/663366.

The rest of the island

Don't miss a trip on one of the two century-old rail services which still provide the best public transport to all the major towns and sights except for Peel. The carriages of the **Steam Railway** (Easter–Oct daily 10am–5pm; £7 return to Port Erin) rock their fifteen-mile course from Douglas to Castletown, Port St Mary and Port Erin at a spirited pace. The rolling terrain due north of Douglas was too steep for conventional trains, but by 1893 fledgling technology was available to construct the **Manx Electric Railway** (Easter–May, Sept & Oct daily 9.40am–5.20pm; June–Aug 9.40am–6.40pm; £6 return to Ramsey) which runs for seventeen miles from Douglas's Derby Castle Station to Ramsey via Laxey. There's also the **Snaefell Mountain Railway** from Laxey to the top of the island's highest mountain, Snaefell. The "**Island Explorer**" ticket gives one (£8), three (£18), five (£26) or seven (£32) days' unlimited travel on all bus services, plus steam and electric train routes, the trip to Snaefell and horse-tram rides in Douglas. Tickets are available from the Travel Shop, the tourist office in Douglas, and main train and tram stations.

Laxey

The straggling village of **LAXEY**, seven miles north of Douglas, spills down from its train station to a small harbour and long, pebbly beach, squeezed between two bulky headlands. The Manx Electric Railway drops you at the station used by the Snaefell Mountain Railway. Shops and a couple of cafés here attempt to divert the crowds who disembark and then head inland and uphill to Laxey's pride, the **"Lady Isabella" Great Laxey Wheel** (Easter–Oct daily 10am–5pm; £3), said

The island's glorious countryside encourages all sorts of **outdoor activities**, from farm-based horse or quad-bike rides to clambering up waterfalls in a wetsuit. Individuals and families are welcome at all the places listed below, but it's essential to make bookings in advance. Bring along clothes and trainers you don't mind getting dirty/wet. There are also two main long-distance footpaths, the shortest being the 28-mile **Millennium Way**, from Castletown to Ramsey. It splits into three day-hikes, though serious hikers do it in one day. The greatest challenge, however, is the round-island **Raad ny Foillan (Road of the Gull)**, a well-signposted (white gull on a blue background) 100-mile coastal walk which takes most people around five days to complete. OS Landranger map 95 covers the entire island, while the free small guide *Walks on the Isle of Man*, available from Douglas tourist office, spells out all the other options.

Abbeylands Equestrian Centre Lower Sulby Farm, Scollag Rd, Onchan ☏01624/676717; closed Fri afternoon. Off-road pony trekking, riding and jumping lessons, for all levels of ability, from £15.

Gemini Charter Boat ☏01624/832761 or 07624/483328. Fishing trips, and bird- or seal-watching trips out of Port St Mary, all year, weather permitting. From £5 an hour per person, plus £4 for rod hire.

Quad Bike Trail Rides Ballacraine Farm, A1 road, St John's ☏01624/801219. An hour and a half's exhilarating quad-bike ride on farmland and open moorside; full instruction and protective clothing provided; £35 per person.

The Venture Centre Lewaigue Farm, Maughold ☏01624/814240, ⓦwww.adventure-centre.co.uk. Canoeing, sea-kayaking, abseiling, gorge-climbing, powerboat training, sailing and archery, from around £30 a session.

10

to be the largest working waterwheel in the world. Otherwise Laxey is at its best down in **Old Laxey**, around the harbour, half a mile below the station, where large car parks attest to the popularity of the beach and river. Hourly **buses** #3 and #3A run to Laxey from Douglas; the #3B and #3C run directly to Old Laxey four times a day (not Sun). The *Mines Tavern*, by the station, has some shaded outdoor seats and serves **meals** (lunch and dinner). Down at the harbour, the *Shore Hotel* is a nice pub by the bridge, which brews its own bitter.

Snaefell

Every thirty minutes, the tramcars of the **Snaefell Mountain Railway** (Easter–Oct daily 10.30am–3.30pm; £6 return, £7.50 from Douglas) begin their thirty-minute wind from Laxey through increasingly denuded moorland to the island's highest point, the top of **Snaefell** (2036ft) – the Vikings' "Snow Mountain" – from where you can see England, Wales, Scotland and Ireland on a clear day. The four-and-a-half miles of track were built in seven months over the winter of 1895 by two hundred men; one gang worked down from the summit, the other up from Laxey, an unimaginable effort in bitter conditions. At the summit, most people are content to pop into the inelegant café and bar and then soak up the views until the return journey, but with a decent map and a clear day, you could walk back instead, following trails down the mountain to Laxey, Sulby Glen or the Peel–Ramsey road.

Maughold, Ramsey and the north

The Manx Electric Railway trains stop within a mile and a half of **MAUGH-OLD**, seven miles northeast of Laxey, a tiny hamlet just inland from the cliff-side lighthouse at **Maughold Head**. It's an isolated spot which only adds to the attraction of Maughold's parish church, in whose grounds is maintained an outstanding collection of early Christian and Norse **carved crosses** – 44 pieces, dating from the sixth to the thirteenth century, and ranging from fragments of runic carving to a six-foot-high rectangular slab.

RAMSEY marks the northern terminus of the Electric Railway, 45 minutes beyond Laxey, where the Victorian tourist boom left behind the island's only iron pier and a solitary grand terrace along the front. You'll really need a car to see any more of the island beyond Ramsey. Due north at the end of the A16 is the **Point of Ayre** lighthouse, at the northeastern tip of the island, built in 1818, where you could leave your vehicle and walk west along the coastal footpath the two miles to the **Ayres Visitor Centre** (end of May–Sept Wed–Sun & bank hol Mon 2–5pm; free), which acts as an interpretation centre for the surrounding Ayres National Nature Reserve. For **accommodation** in the north, nonsmoking Victorian *Hillcrest House* on May Hill (℡01624/817215, Ⓦwww.HillcrestHouse.co.uk; no credit cards; ❸), five minutes' walk from the centre of Ramsey, makes an excellent base.

St John's

The trans-island A1 (and hourly bus #5 or #6 from Douglas) follows a deep twelve-mile-long furrow between the northern and southern ranges from Douglas to Peel. A hill at the crossroads settlement of **ST JOHN'S**, nine miles along it, is the original site of **Tynwald**, the ancient Manx government, which derives its name from the Norse *Thing Völlr*, meaning "Assembly Field". Nowadays the word refers to the Douglas-based House of Keys and Legislative Council, but acts passed in the capital only become law once they have been proclaimed here on July 5 (ancient Midsummer's Day) in an annual open-air parliament that also hears the grievances of the islanders. Tynwald's four-tiered grass mound – made from soil collected from each of the island's parishes – stands at the other end of a processional path from the stone **St John's Church**, which traditionally doubled as the courthouse.

Peel

The main settlement on the west coast, **PEEL** immediately captivates, with its fine castle rising above the harbour and a sandy beach running the length of its eastern promenade. It's a town of some antiquity and its enduring appeal is as one of the most "Manx" of all the island's towns. Archeological evidence indicates that **St Patrick's Isle**, which guards the harbour, has had a significant population since Mesolithic times. What probably started out as a flint-working village on a naturally protected spot gained significance with the foundation of a monastery in the seventh or eighth century, parts of which remain inside the ramparts of the red sandstone **Peel Castle** (Easter–Oct daily 10am–5pm; £3). The Vikings built the first fortifications and the site became the residence of the Kings of Mann until 1220, when they moved to Castle Rushen in Castletown.

It's a fifteen-minute walk from the town around the river harbour and over the bridge to the castle. On the way, you'll have passed the excellent harbourside House of Mannannan **heritage centre** (daily 10am–5pm; £5, combined ticket with Peel Castle £7) named after the island's ancient sea-god. You should allow at least two hours to get around the museum, which concentrates strongly on participatory exhibits – whether it's listening to Celtic legends in a replica roundhouse, examining the contents and occupants of a life-sized Viking ship, walking through a kipper factory or steering a steamer.

The most regular **bus** service to Peel is the hourly #5 or #6 from Douglas; this service continues to Ramsey via Kirk Michael and Sulby. The much less frequent #8 (not Sun) connects Peel to Port Erin, via St John's and Castletown. When it comes to **eating**, if you're looking for something more than the seafront cafés and fish-and-chip shops, then head for the pub opposite the House of Mannannan: the *Creek Inn* serves a delicious array of specials, from seafood platters to scallops mornay.

Port Erin

Plans for the southern branch of the steam railway beyond Castletown included the speculative construction of the new resort of **PORT ERIN**, at the southwestern tip of the island, an hour and a quarter's ride from Douglas. The aspect certainly demanded a resort: a wide, fine sand beach backing a deeply indented bay sits beneath green hills, which climb to the tower-topped headland of **Bradda Head** to the northwest. Families relish the beach and nearby coves, and the time-warped atmosphere, which appears to have altered little in fifty years.

The **train station** is on Station Road, a couple of hundred yards above and back from the beach. **Buses** #1 and #2 from Douglas/Castletown, and #8 from Peel/St John's, stop on Bridson Street, across Station Road and opposite the *Cherry Orchard* hotel. For **accommodation**, the best B&B is *Rowany Cottier* (☏01624/832287; no credit cards; ❸), a detached, nonsmoking house overlooking the bay, opposite the entrance to Bradda Glen. The nicest hotel rooms are at the *Cherry Orchard* on Bridson Street (☏01624/833811, ⓦwww.cherry-orchard.com; ❻), a couple of hundred yards back from the promenade, which has a range of self-catering or serviced **apartments** sleeping up to six people. These are available by the night, and guests also have the use of a pool, Jacuzzi, gym, sauna, restaurant and bar. For **eating**, your choice is between the *Whistlestop Café* at the train station for a light lunch or afternoon tea; bistro meals at the *Bay Hotel* down by the beach; or the restaurant at the *Cherry Orchard*, which also has a popular Sunday buffet lunch.

Port St Mary and around

Two miles east of Port Erin, the fishing harbour still dominates little **PORT ST MARY**, with its houses strung out in a chain above the busy dockside. From Port St Mary, a minor road runs out along the Meayll Peninsula towards Cregneash, the oldest village on the island, part of which now forms the **Cregneash Village Folk Museum** (Easter–Oct daily 10am–5pm; £3), a picturesque cluster of nineteenth-century thatched crofts. It's peopled at weekends with spinners, weavers, turners and smiths dressed in period costumes; there's a café, an information centre with introductory video, demonstrations of thatching and dry-stone walling, and a chance to walk through the seasonal crops in the field and watch the horses at work. A footpath continues around **Spanish Head**, the island's southern tip, to **The Sound Visitor Centre** (daily 10am–5pm; free), which also marks the end of the road from Port St Mary. Across the narrows lies the **Calf of Man**, a small islet now preserved as a bird sanctuary. Boat trips run out here, departing either from the pier at Port Erin (April–Oct daily; £10; usually at 10.15am, 11.30am and 1.30pm, weather permitting; ☏01624/832339) or from Port St Mary (year-round, weather permitting; £10; ☏01624/832761 or ☏07624/483328). It's best to call in advance in either case for information.

Regular **steam trains** run to Port Erin or back to Douglas from Port St Mary, with the station a ten-minute walk from the harbour along High Street, Bay View Road and Station Road; hourly **buses** from the harbour serve the same places. Nicest **accommodation** is at *Aaron House*, The Promenade (☏01624/835702; ❹), a lovingly re-created Victorian experience combining brass beds and clawfoot bathtubs with doilies and cake in the parlour. For tasty home-cooked pub **meals**, you can't beat *The Albert* on Athol Street (no food Sun night or Mon; ☏01624/832118), by the harbour – it's a nice place for a pint of Manx beer, though you should book for evening meals at the weekend.

Castletown and around

From the twelfth century until 1869, **CASTLETOWN** was the island's capital, but then the influx of tourists and the increase in trade required a bigger harbour and Douglas took over. So much the better for Castletown, which is a much more pleasant place than it might otherwise have been. Its sleepy harbour and low-roofed cottages are all dominated by **Castle Rushen** (Easter–Oct daily 10am–5pm; £4.25), one of the most complete and compact medieval castles in Britain. The heavy defences, comprising three concentric rings of stone-clad ramparts, fosses and a complex series of doors and portcullises, must have made entry a forbidding objective. Across Market Square and down Castle Street in tiny Parliament Square you'll find the **Old House of Keys**. Built in 1821, this was the site of the Manx parliament, the Keys, until 1874 when it was moved to Douglas. The frock-coated Secretary of the House meets you at the door and shows you into the restored debating chamber, where visitors are included in a highly entertaining participatory session of the House, guided by a hologram Speaker. The visits are conducted on the hour (Easter–Oct daily 10am–noon & 2–5pm; £3) and advance tickets are available from the **Old Grammar School** on nearby Quay Lane, which was the former capital's first church, built around 1200, and used as a school from 1570. There's not a lot to see here, save a few information boards, but it does house a handy **tourist office** (Easter–Oct daily 10am–5pm).

The island's most important medieval religious site, **Rushen Abbey** (Easter–Oct daily 10am–5pm; £3), lies two miles north of Castletown at Ballasalla ("place of the willows"). The excavated remains themselves – low walls, grass-covered banks and a sole church tower from the fifteenth century – would hold only specialist appeal were it not for the excellent interpretation centre, which explains much about daily life in a Cistercian abbey. The **Silverburn Trail** runs from Castletown to the abbey, and there are pleasant walks in the surrounding area too, including a crossing of the fourteenth-century packhorse bridge known as the **Monks' Bridge**, just upstream of the abbey gardens.

The **steam train station** is five minutes' walk from the centre of Castletown, out along Victoria Road from the harbour; **buses** #8 (from Peel/Port Erin) and #1 (from Douglas) stop in the main square. The only central **accommodation** is the *George Hotel* in the square (☏01624/822533; ❷). Best place for **food** is *The Garrison*, across from the hotel at 5 Castle St (☏01624/824885; closes Sun at 5pm), a tapas bar with a sunny courtyard. Out of town, at **Santon**, about 5 miles northeast of Castletown, the *Mount Murray Hotel and Country Club* (☏01624/661111, ⓦwww.mountmurray.com; ❼) is the highest-rated rural hotel on the island, with its own golf course, pool and health club.

Travel details

Buses

For information on all local and national bus services, contact Traveline ☏ 0870/608 2608, ⓦ www.traveline.org.uk.

Blackpool to: London (4–6 daily; 6hr); Manchester (every 2hr; 1hr 50min); Preston (every 2hr; 40min).

Chester to: Liverpool (every 20min; 1hr 20min).

Lancaster to: Carlisle (4–5 daily; 1hr 10min); Kendal (hourly; 1hr); Leeds (1 daily; 3hr); London (2–3 daily; 5hr 30min); Manchester (2 daily; 2hr); Windermere (hourly; 1hr 45min).

Liverpool to: Blackpool (1 daily; 2hr); Chester (hourly; 1hr); Leeds (hourly; 2hr 40min); London (5 daily; 4hr); Manchester (hourly; 1hr); Preston (2 daily; 1hr).

Manchester to: Birmingham (6 daily; 3hr); Blackpool (5 daily; 1hr 40min); Leeds (6 daily; 2hr); Liverpool (hourly; 40min); London (every 1–2hr; 4hr 30min–6hr 45min); Newcastle (6 daily; 5hr); Sheffield (4 daily; 2hr 40min).

Trains

For information on all local and national rail services, contact National Rail Enquiries ☏ 08457/484950, ⓦ www.nationalrail.co.uk.

Blackpool to: Manchester (hourly; 1hr 10min); Preston (hourly; 30min).

Chester to: Birmingham (5 daily; 2hr); Knutsford (hourly; 50min); Liverpool (2 hourly; 45min); London (3 daily; 3hr 30min); Manchester (2 hourly; 1hr–1hr 20min); Northwich (hourly; 30min).

Lancaster to: Barrow-in-Furness (hourly; 1hr); Carlisle (every 30–60min; 1hr); Heysham (2–3 daily; 30min); Manchester (every 30–60min; 1hr); Morecambe (every 30–60min; 10min); Preston (every 20–30min; 20min).

Liverpool to: Birmingham (hourly; 1hr 40min); Chester (2 hourly; 45min); Leeds (hourly; 2hr); London (hourly; 2hr 40min); Manchester (hourly; 50min); Newcastle (8 daily; 4–5hr); Oxford (12 daily; 3–4hr); Preston (14 daily; 1hr 5min); Sheffield (hourly; 1hr 45min); York (hourly; 2hr 20min).

Manchester to: Barrow-in-Furness (Mon–Sat 7 daily, Sun 3 daily; 2hr 15min); Birmingham (hourly; 1hr 30min); Blackpool (hourly; 1hr 10min); Buxton (hourly; 50min); Carlisle (8 daily; 1hr 50min); Chester (every 30min; 1hr–1hr 20min); Lancaster (hourly; 1hr); Leeds (hourly; 1hr); Liverpool (every 30min; 50min); London (hourly; 2hr 40min); Newcastle (10 daily; 3hr); Oxenholme (4–6 daily; 40min–1hr 10min); Penrith (2–4 daily; 2hr); Preston (every 20min; 55min); Sheffield (hourly; 1hr); York (hourly; 1hr 35min).

11

Cumbria and the Lakes

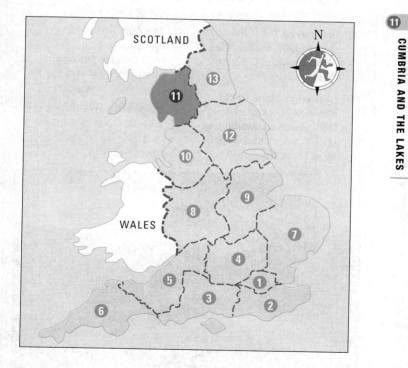

* **Windermere** England's largest lake never disappoints. Take a cruise – jumping off to hike, to picnic, or even to swim. See p.629

* **Old Dungeon Ghyll, Langdale** The very picture of a classic lakeland inn – cosy rooms, stone-flagged floors, open fires and real ale. See p.634

* **Brantwood** The home of John Ruskin, sited on the placid shores of Coniston Water. See p.638

* **Castlerigg Stone Circle, Keswick** These prehistoric stones have a powerful presence in this most spectacular of spots. See p.640

* **Borrowdale** Most people's choice for prettiest valley in the Lakes – falls, hamlets and woods in abundance. See p.642

* **Church of St Mary and St Michael, Cartmel** This twelfth-century priory church is a magnificent reminder of the wealth of the medieval Church. See p.649

* **The Rum Story, Whitehaven** West Cumbria's most intriguing museum attraction, dedicated to the "dark stuff". See p.651

* **Carlisle Castle** Cumbria's mightiest fortification dominates the region's county town. See p.653

△ Castlerigg Stone Circle

Cumbria and the Lakes

The Lake District is England's most hyped scenic area, and for good reasons. Within an area a mere thirty miles across, sixteen major lakes are squeezed between the steeply pitched faces of the country's highest mountains, an almost alpine landscape that's augmented by waterfalls and picturesque stone-built villages packed into the valleys. Most of what people refer to as the Lake District – or simply the Lakes – lies within the **Lake District National Park**. This, in turn, falls entirely within the north-western county of **Cumbria**, formed in 1974 from the historic counties of Cumberland and Westmorland, and the northern part of Lancashire. Consequently Cumbria contains more than just its lakes, stretching south and west to the **coast**, and north to its county town of **Carlisle**, a place bearing traces of a pedigree that stretches back beyond the construction of Hadrian's Wall. To the east, **Penrith** and the Eden Valley separate the lakes from the near wilderness of the northern Pennines.

National Express **coaches** connect London and Manchester with Windermere, Ambleside, Grasmere, Keswick and Carlisle, while **trains** leave the West Coast main line at **Oxenholme**, north of Lancaster, for the branch line service to Kendal and Windermere. The only other places directly accessible by train are Penrith and Carlisle, further north on the West Coast line, and the towns along the Cumbrian coast. A **Lakes Ranger** (one day, £10) gives unlimited train travel between Lancaster, the Cumbrian coast and Windermere, plus free bus travel south of Keswick and a Windermere cruise. Stagecoach is Cumbria's biggest **local bus** operator and their **Explorer Tickets** (one-day £7.50, four-day £17, seven-day £25) can be bought on the bus. The two main bus services are the #555 (Kendal–Windermere–Ambleside–Grasmere–Keswick) and the open-top #599 (Kendal–Windermere–Bowness–Ambleside–Grasmere), but all routes are detailed in the free *Lakeland Explorer* timetable or the *Getting Around Cumbria and the Lake District* timetable book, both available from tourist offices throughout the region.

For more **information** about all aspects of the National Park, visit ⓦwww.lake-district.gov.uk; while the official site of the Cumbria Tourist Board is ⓦwww.golakes.co.uk. All the background information you could possibly want on **outdoor sports and activities** can be found on ⓦwww.lakedistrictoutdoors.co.uk.

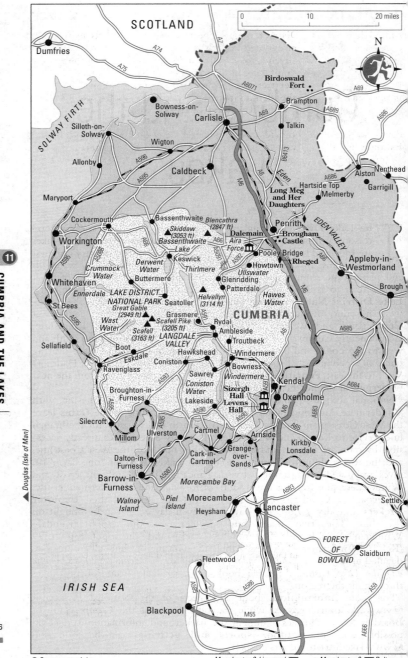

SCOTLAND

N

0   10   20 miles

Dumfries

A74

A75

SOLWAY FIRTH

Bowness-on-Solway

A6071

Birdoswald Fort

Brampton

A689

A69

Silloth-on-Solway

Carlisle

A69

Talkin

A7

A596

Wigton

A6

Eden

B6413

M6

Hartside Top

A686

Alston

Nenthead

Garrigill

Allonby

Caldbeck

Melmerby

Long Meg and Her Daughters

Maryport

A595

A596

Penrith

Hartside Top

Eden Valley

Appleby-in-Westmorland

Cockermouth

Bassenthwaite

Skiddaw (3053 ft)

Blencathra (2847 ft)

Dalemain

Brougham Castle

Brough

Workington

A66

Bassenthwaite Lake

Keswick

Aira Force

Pooley Bridge

Rheged

A5086

A66

Derwent Water

Thirlmere

Howtown

A592

Ullswater

Whitehaven

Crummock Water

Buttermere

LAKE DISTRICT

Glenridding

Patterdale

Hawes Water

St Bees

Ennerdale

NATIONAL PARK

Seatoller

Helvellyn (3114 ft)

CUMBRIA

A685

Great Gable (2949 ft)

Scafell Pike (3205 ft)

Grasmere

Rydal

Sellafield

Wast Water

Scafell (3163 ft)

LANGDALE VALLEY

Ambleside

Troutbeck

A591

A684

Boot

Eskdale

Hawkshead

Windermere

Kendal

Ravenglass

Coniston

Bowness

Windermere

A593

Sawrey

Oxenholme

M6

A683

Broughton-in-Furness

Coniston Water

Lakeside

Sizergh Hall

Levens Hall

A590

A65

Silecroft

Ulverston

Cartmel

Arnside

Kirkby Lonsdale

Millom

Cark-in-Cartmel

Grange-over-Sands

Dalton-in-Furness

A5087

A65

Barrow-in-Furness

Morecambe Bay

Settle

Walney Island

Piel Island

Morecambe

A683

Heysham

Lancaster

A65

Douglas (Isle of Man)

IRISH SEA

Fleetwood

FOREST OF BOWLAND

Slaidburn

A585

M6

Blackpool

M55

A586

A59

A666

© Crown copyright

Manchester & Liverpool ▼   Manchester & ▼ Bolton

The Lake District

Although the **Lake District** might appear too popular for its own good, tourist numbers are concentrated in fairly specific areas, and it's relatively easy to escape the crowds. Given a week you could see most of the famous settlements and lakes – a circuit taking in the towns of Ambleside, Windermere and Bowness, all on **Windermere**, the Wordsworth houses and sites in pretty villages such as **Hawkshead** and **Grasmere**, and the more dramatic northern scenery near **Keswick** and **Ullswater** would give you a fair sample of the whole. But it's away from the crowds that the Lakes really begin to pay dividends, so aim if you can to steer by central valleys such as **Langdale** and **Eskdale**, and the less-visited lakes of **Wast Water** and **Buttermere**.

Human interaction has played a significant part in the shaping of the Lake District. As the first settlers, five thousand years ago, learned to shape flints into axes, they began to clear the upland forests, a process accelerated by the road-building Romans. An even greater impact was made by the Norse Vikings in the ninth and tenth centuries, who farmed the land extensively and left their mark on the local dialect: a mountain here is referred to as a "fell", a waterfall is a "force", streams are "becks", a mountain lake is a "tarn", while the suffix "-thwaite" indicates a clearing. Two factors spurred the first waves of **tourism**: the reappraisal of landscape brought about by such painters as Constable and the writings of Wordsworth and his contemporaries, and the outbreak of the French Revolution and its subsequent turmoil, which put paid to the idea of the continental Grand Tour. At the same time, as the war pushed food prices higher, farmers began to reclaim the hillsides, a tendency sanctioned by the General Enclosure Act of 1801. Most of the characteristic dry-stone walls were built at this time, a development that alarmed Wordsworth, who wrote in his *Guide to the Lakes* that he desired "a sort of national property, in which every man has a right and interest who has an eye to perceive and a heart to enjoy." His wish finally came to fruition in 1951 when the government designated 880 square miles of the Lake District as England's largest national park.

Kendal and around

The limestone-grey town of **KENDAL** might be billed as the "Gateway to the Lakes", but it's nearly ten miles from Windermere – the true start of the lakes – and has more in common with the market towns to the east. Nonetheless, it offers rewarding rambles around the "yards" and "ginnels" which make an

---

Walking in the Lakes

It's only when you start to **walk around the Lakes** that you can really say you've explored the region. Four peaks top out at over 3000ft – including Scafell Pike, the highest in England – but there are literally hundreds of other mountains, crags, fells and valleys to roam. If you are planning to walk, you should always be properly equipped: wear strong-soled, supportive shoes or boots, carry water, and take a map (and know how to use it). Bad weather can move in quickly, even in the height of summer, so before starting out you should check the **weather forecast** – many hotels and outdoor shops post a daily forecast – or call ☏017687/75757 (24-hour line). Essential are the 1:50,000 OS Landranger **maps** 89, 90, 96 and 97, or, better, the yellow 1:25,000 OS Outdoor Leisure series, which cover the whole Lake District.

engaging maze on both sides of Highgate and Stricklandgate, the main streets. The old **Market Place** has long since succumbed to development, with the market hall now converted to the Westmorland Shopping Centre, but traditional stalls still do business outside every Wednesday and Saturday.

The **Kendal Museum**, on Station Road (Mon–Sat: Easter–Oct 10.30am–5pm; Nov, Dec & mid-Feb to Easter 10.30am–4pm; £3.50; Ⓦ www.kendalmuseum.org.uk), holds the district's natural history and archeological finds, bolstered by the preserved office, pen-and-ink drawings and personal effects of **Alfred Wainwright** (1907–91), Kendal's former borough treasurer (and honorary clerk at the museum). Wainwright moved to Kendal in 1941, and by 1952, dissatisfied with the accuracy of existing maps of the paths and ancient tracks across the fells, he embarked on what became a series of highly personal walking guides, painstakingly handwritten with mapped routes and delicately drawn views. They have been hugely popular guidebooks ever since, which many treat as gospel in their attempts to "bag" ascents of the 214 fells he recorded.

The town's other two museums are in the Georgian **Abbot Hall** (Ⓦ www.abbothall.org.uk) and its stable block, by the river to the south. The main hall houses the **Art Gallery** (Mon–Sat: Easter–Oct 10.30am–5pm; Nov, Dec & mid-Feb to Easter 10.30am–4pm; £3.75), where cherubic portraits by society painter George Romney line the walls. Across the way, the former stables contain the **Museum of Lakeland Life and Industry** (Mon–Sat: Easter–Oct 10.30am–5pm; Nov, Dec & mid-Feb to Easter 10.30am–4pm; £2.75, joint admission with Art Gallery £4.50; Ⓦ www.lakelandmuseum .org.uk). Here, reconstructed seventeenth-, eighteenth- and nineteenth-century house interiors stand alongside workshops which exhibit rural trades and crafts, from spinning and weaving to tanning – medieval Kendal was on the main north–south cattle-trade routes and leather production was once an important local industry. Just behind Abbott Hall, the wide aisles of the Early English **parish church** house a number of family chapels, including that of the Parr family, who once owned **Kendal Castle**, on a hillock to the east across the river.

Practicalities

Kendal's **train station** is the first stop on the Windermere branch line, five minutes from the **Oxenholme** main-line station. All buses (including National Express services) stop at the **bus station** on Blackhall Road (off Stramongate). The **tourist office** (July & Aug Mon–Sat 9am–6pm, Sun 10am–5pm; Sept–June Mon–Sat 9am–5pm, Sun 10am–4pm; Jan & Feb closed Sun; ☏ 01539/725758, Ⓦ www.kendaltown.org) is in the town hall on Highgate. There's **Internet** access at Kendal library on Stricklandgate (closed Sun) and at *Dot Café*, inside the Westmorland Shopping Centre.

Best local **B&B** is *Lakeland Natural Vegetarian Guesthouse* at Low Slack, Queen's Road (☏ 01539/733011, Ⓦ www.lakelandnatural.co.uk; ❹), five minutes' walk west of the centre – breakfasts incorporate homemade muffins, organic yoghurt and fresh fruit salad. Or look along Milnthorpe Road, a few minutes' south of the centre – straight down Highgate and Kirkland – where several places cluster together, including *The Headlands*, 53 Milnthorpe Rd (☏ 01539/732464; ❷). There's a **youth hostel** at 118 Highgate (☏ 0870/770 5982, Ⓔ kendal@yha.org.uk; dorm beds £14; closed 1–2 days of the week Oct–Easter), which is attached to The Brewery arts centre.

For inexpensive veggie wholefood **meals** and riverside seating, visit the *Waterside Café* on Gulfs Road, by the river at the bottom of Lowther Street.

Best **restaurant** is the highly regarded *Moon*, 129 Highgate (☎01539/729254; dinner only, closed Mon & Tues), an easy-going contemporary bistro using locally sourced ingredients, or eat Thai at the *Chiang Thai*, 54 Stramongate (☎01539/720387; dinner only, closed Mon), which is more moderately priced. For evening entertainment, the **Brewery Arts Centre**, on Highgate (☎01539/725133, ⓦwww.breweryarts.co.uk), is the town's central focus. Its *Green Room Restaurant* and lively *Vats Bar* serve light lunches and pizzas, pastas and stir-fries for dinner; the centre also has two cinema screens, a theatre and concert hall.

Sizergh Castle and Levens Hall

Three miles south of Kendal stands **Sizergh Castle** (Easter–Oct Mon–Thurs & Sun 1.30–5.30pm; gardens same days 12.30–5.30pm; £5, gardens only £2.50; NT), tucked away off the A591 amid acres of parkland and reached on bus #555. Sizergh is more of a grand manor house than a castle, but owes its epithet to the fourteenth-century peel tower at its core, one of the best examples of the towers built throughout the region as safe havens during the protracted border raids of the Middle Ages. Like much of the rest of the house, the Great Hall underwent significant changes in Elizabethan times, when extensions were added to the house and most of its rooms were panelled in oak, with their ceilings layered in elaborate plasterwork.

Two miles south of Sizergh, just off the A590 and on the #555 bus route, **Levens Hall** (Easter to mid-Oct Mon–Thurs & Sun noon–5pm; gardens same days 10am–5pm; £7, gardens only £5.50; ⓦwww.levenshall.co.uk), also built around an early peel tower, is more uniform in style than Sizergh, since the bulk of it was built or refurbished in classic Elizabethan style between 1570 and 1640. The main entrance opens into the spacious Great Hall, its panelled walls lined with coats of arms; to the left of the hall are the large and small drawing rooms. The other end of the Great Hall leads to the most splendid apartment, the dining room, panelled not with oak but with goat's leather, printed with a deep green floral design – one goat was needed for every forty or so squares.

Windermere town and Brockhole

WINDERMERE town was all but nonexistent until 1847 when a railway terminal was built here, making England's longest lake (after which the town is named) an easily accessible resort. Windermere town remains the transport hub for the southern lakes, but there's precious little else to keep you in the slate-grey streets. Instead, all the traffic pours a mile downhill to Windermere's older twin town, Bowness; buses leave Windermere train station every twenty minutes for the ten-minute run down to the lakeside piers.

It's understandable to want to rush straight to Bowness and the lake, but you should certainly make time for the **Lake District Visitor Centre at Brockhole** (Easter–Oct daily 10am–5pm; grounds & gardens open all year; free, parking £3), set in landscaped grounds on the shores of the lake, three miles northwest of Windermere. It's the headquarters and main information point for the Lake District National Park, and besides the natural history and geological displays, the centre hosts a full programme of guided walks, children's activities, garden tours and special exhibitions. The #555 and #559 **buses** between Windermere and Ambleside run past the visitor centre, or you can get there by Windermere Lake Cruises **launch** from Waterhead (Ambleside) or from Bowness.

Practicalities

National Express and all local **bus** services stop outside Windermere **train station**. With a Bus & Boat ticket (£6) you can travel from Windermere to Bowness and Ambleside on the open-top #599 and return by boat down the lake. A hundred yards away from the station at the top of Victoria Street stands the **tourist office** (daily: July & Aug 9am–7.30pm; Sept–June 9am–6pm; ☎015394/46499). There's free **Internet** access at the library, in the park off Broad Street. For **bike rental**, contact Country Lanes, The Railway Station, Windermere (☎015394/44544, Ⓦwww.countrylanes.co.uk). Mountain Goat, near the tourist office on Victoria Street (☎015394/45161, Ⓦwww .mountain-goat.com) offers daily **minibus tours** (half-day from £14, full-day £26) that get off the beaten track.

Windermere doesn't have the waterside advantages of Bowness, but it does have a lot more **accommodation** – good places to look for B&Bs are on High Street and neighbouring Victoria Street, with other concentrations on College Road, Oak and Broad streets. **Eating and drinking** is generally better done down in Bowness, but it is worth seeking out the *Miller Howe Café* inside Lakeland Ltd, behind the train station, which serves up superior snacks, sandwiches and daily specials. At night, the *Lamplighter Bar* at the *Oakthorpe Hotel* on High Street provides bistro meals (gammon, fresh fish, rack of lamb) at value-for-money prices.

B&Bs, guest houses and hotels

Archway 13 College Rd ☎015394/45613, Ⓦwww.communiken.com/archway. Victorian house known for its special breakfasts – pancakes, kippers and homemade yoghurt and granola. No credit cards. ❸

Ashleigh 11 College Rd ☎015394/42292 Ⓦwww.ashleighhouse.com. Smart nonsmoking house whose tasteful rooms have been furnished in welcoming country pine. No credit cards. ❷

Boston House The Terrace ☎015394/43654, Ⓦwww.bostonhouse.co.uk. Beautifully restored nonsmoking Victorian Gothic house, a minute's walk from the tourist office. ❺

Brendan Chase 1–3 College Rd ☎015394/45638. Spick-and-span place with a budget room-only option, and other inexpensive rooms, either standard or en-suite. No credit cards. ❶

The Coach House Lake Rd ☎015394/44494, Ⓦwww.lakedistrictbandb.com. Five classy rooms with wrought-iron beds, gleaming bathrooms and elegant touches. ❹

Miller Howe Rayrigg Rd, the A592 ☎015394/42536, Ⓦwww.millerhowe.com. A candidate for best in the Lakes, this gorgeous Edwardian house occupies an elevated position above Windermere. Rates include dinner. Closed Jan. ❾

Hostel

Lake District Backpackers' Lodge High St ☎015394/46374, Ⓦwww.lakedistrictbackpackers.co.uk. Small dorms (£13), plus Internet access, satellite TV, bike storage and lockers. The price includes a tea, toast and cereal breakfast. No credit cards.

Bowness and the lake

BOWNESS-ON-WINDERMERE – to give it its full title – spills up from its lakeside piers in a series of terraces lined with guest houses and hotels. Set back from the thumbprint indent of Bowness Bay, there's been a village here since the fifteenth century and a ferry service across the lake for almost as long. On a hot summer's day, crowds swirl around the trinket shops, cafés, ice cream stalls and lakeside seats, but you can escape onto the lake or into the hills easily enough. Most tourists, though, bypass everything in Bowness, bar the lake, for the chance to visit **The World of Beatrix Potter** in the Old Laundry on Crag Brow (daily: Easter–Sept 10am–5.30pm; Oct–Easter 10am–4.30pm;

Windermere Lake Cruises (☎015394/31188, ⓦwww.windermere-lakecruises .co.uk) operates services to Lakeside at the southern tip (£4.40 one-way, £6.60 return) or to the Lake District Visitor Centre at Brockhole and Waterhead (for Ambleside) at the northern end (£4.30 one-way, £6.40 return). There's also a direct hourly service from Ambleside to Brockhole (£5 return) and a shuttle service between Bowness pier and Sawrey (£1.60 one-way, £2.80 return), saving pedestrians the walk down to the car ferry. A 24-hour **Freedom-of-the-Lake** ticket costs £11.50. Services on all routes are frequent between Easter and October (every 30min–1hr at peak times), but much reduced during the winter. The company also operates an enjoyable 45-minute circular **cruise around the islands** (departs several times daily from Bowness; £5).

£3.75; ⓦwww.hop-skip-jump.com). It's unfair to be judgemental – you either like Beatrix Potter or you don't – but it's safe to say that the displays here find more favour with children than the more formal Potter attractions at Hill Top and Hawkshead. Five hundred yards north of Bowness, on Rayrigg Road, the **Windermere Steamboat Museum** (Easter–Oct daily 10am–5pm; £3.50, steam-launch cruises £5; ⓦwww.steamboat.co.uk) has as its star exhibit the 1850 *Dolly*, claimed to be the world's oldest mechanically driven boat, and extremely well preserved after spending 65 years in the mud at the bottom of Ullswater.

The lake itself – simply **Windermere** (from the Norse, "Vinandr's Lake", and thus never "*Lake* Windermere") – is the heavyweight of Lake District waters, at ten and a half miles long, a mile wide in parts and a shade over two hundred feet deep. Rowing boats are available for rent by the lakeside piers, while Windermere Lake Cruises (see box above) operates modern cruisers and vintage steamers throughout the year. The traditional **ferry service** is the chain-guided contraption across the water from Ferry Nab on the Bowness side to Ferry House, Sawrey (Mon–Sat 7am–10pm, Sun 9am–10pm; departures every 20min; 40p; cars £2), providing access to Beatrix Potter's former home at Hill Top and to Hawkshead beyond.

Practicalities

The **bus** from Windermere train station stops at the lakeside piers, with the **Bowness Bay Information Centre** nearby on Glebe Road (Easter–Oct daily 9.30am–5pm, July & Aug until 6pm; Nov–Easter Fri–Sun 10am–4pm; ☎015394/42895). Crag Brow and then Lake Road is the main thoroughfare up from the lake towards Windermere, on and off which you'll find much of the accommodation, cafés and restaurants. T2, 4 Windermere Bank, on Lake Road, is the local **Internet** outlet.

Accommodation is plentiful, though note that most places with even a glimpse of the water set their prices accordingly. The nicest **café** is *2 Eggcups*, 6a Ash St. Pizza and pasta is on offer at *Rastelli's*, Lake Road (☎015394/44227; dinner only, closed Wed), while the Anglo-Italian *Porthole*, 3 Ash St (☎015394/42793; closed Tues and mid-Dec to mid-Feb), is the most respected quality **restaurant** – lunch is available Thursday, Friday and Sunday, otherwise it's dinner only. For a drink, you can't beat the *Hole in't Wall* **pub**, the town's oldest hostelry, on Fallbarrow Road behind Bowness church.

B&Bs, guest houses and hotels

Above The Bay 5 Brackenfield ☏015394/88658, ⓦwww.abovethebay.co.uk. An elevated house, just off the Kendal road. Three spacious rooms open onto a private terrace with stunning lake views. No credit cards. ❸

Gilpin Lodge Crook Rd ☏015394/88818, ⓦwww.gilpin-lodge.co.uk. A country-house retreat a couple of miles east on the Kendal road (B5284). Fourteen elegant rooms – rates include dinner. ❾

Laurel Cottage St Martin's Square ☏015394/45594, ⓦwww.laurelcottage-bnb.co.uk. Pretty rooms in a seventeenth-century cottage, or more space – for a few extra pounds – in the adjacent Victorian building. No credit cards. ❸

Montclare House Crag Brow ☏015394/42723. Simple B&B accommodation that's about the best value in Bowness. No credit cards. ❷

New Hall Bank Fallbarrow Rd ☏015394/43558, ⓦwww.newhallbank.com. Detached Victorian house with a lake view and a central location (a few yards from the *Hole in't Wall* pub). ❺

Old England Church St ☏015394/42444, ⓦwww.heritage-hotels.com. Opposite the church, with heated outdoor pool and terraced lakeside gardens. Prices drop in winter. ❼

Campsite

Braithwaite Fold Glebe Rd ☏015394/42177. Closest site to the lakeshore for tents, near the ferry to Sawrey, half a mile from Bowness; closed Nov–March.

Around Bowness

Mackay Hugh Baillie Scott's **Blackwell** (mid-Feb to Dec daily 10am–5pm, closes 4pm in winter; £4.50; ⓦwww.blackwell.org.uk) was built in 1900 as a lakeside holiday home for Edward Holt, of the Manchester brewing family, and selected rooms of its restored Arts and Crafts interior can be viewed. Lakeland motifs (particularly trees, flowers, birds and berries) are visible in virtually every nook and cranny, from the stonework to the stained glass. There's a tearoom and gardens, though no bus – the walk south from Bowness is about a mile and a half (25min).

From Bowness piers cruises (see p.631) head south down the lake the five or so miles to **Lakeside**, on Windermere's quieter southern reaches and the terminus of the **Lakeside and Haverthwaite Railway** (Easter–Oct 6–7 daily; £4.30 return; ☏015395/31594), whose steam-powered engines chuff along four miles of track through the forests of Backbarrow Gorge. The boat arrivals at Lakeside connect with train departures throughout the day, and you can buy a joint boat-and-train ticket (£10.50 return) at Bowness. Also on the quay at Lakeside is the **Aquarium of the Lakes** (daily: April–Sept 9am–6pm; Oct–May 9am–5pm; £5.95; ⓦwww.aquariumofthelakes.co.uk), an entertaining natural history exhibit centred on the fish and animals found in and along a lakeland river, including a pair of captive otters and a walk-through-tunnel aquarium. Again, there's a joint ticket available with the boat ride from Bowness (£11.30 return).

Troubeck

Troutbeck Bridge, a mile northwest of Windermere along the A591, heralds the start of a gentle valley where you'll find Windermere's local **youth hostel** at Bridge Lane (☏0870/770 6094, ⓔwindermere@yha.org.uk; dorm beds £11.50; weekends only in Dec), almost a mile uphill from the bridge. A YHA shuttle-bus service (£2) operates to the hostel from Windermere train station (meeting arriving trains) and from Ambleside youth hostel, or there's a fine cross-country walking route (3 miles; 1hr 30min) via **Orrest Head** (784ft), whose summit gives a 360-degree panorama – the path branches off the main road a hundred yards south of Windermere train station, by the *Windermere Hotel* on the A591.

A little further up the minor valley road from the hostel, **Townend** (Easter–Oct Tues–Fri & Sun 1–5pm; £3; NT) has been preserved as a seventeenth-century yeoman-farmer's house, complete with original furniture and decorative woodwork. Troutbeck's **inn**, the *Mortal Man* (☎015394/33193, Ⓦwww.themortalman.co.uk; ❺, ❻ with dinner; closed mid-Nov to mid-Feb), has terrific valley views from its rooms and beer garden, while the *Queen's Head*, down on the main A592 (☎015394/32174, Ⓦwww.queensheadhotel .com; ❺; two-night minimum stay at weekends), serves very good food. The *Queen's Head* is a stop on the summer weekend #517 bus route from Bowness and Windermere.

Ambleside

Five miles northwest of Windermere, **AMBLESIDE** is at the heart of the southern lakes region, making it a first-class base for walkers. The town centre consists of a cluster of grey-green stone houses, shops and B&Bs hugging a circular one-way system, which loops round just south of the narrow gully of stony Stock Ghyll. The rest of town lies a mile (15min walk) south at **Waterhead** (referred to as Ambleside on ferry timetables), a harbour on the shores of Windermere that's filled with ducks, swans and rowing boats. In Ambleside itself, spare a few minutes for the mural of the rush-bearing ceremony – when fresh rushes were strewn on the church floor – in **St Mary's Church**, whose spire is visible from all over town. For some background on Ambleside's history, stroll a couple of minutes along Rydal Road to the **Ambleside Armitt Museum** (daily 10am–5pm; £2.50; Ⓦwww.armitt.com), whose collection catalogues the very distinct contribution to lakeland society made by John Ruskin, Beatrix Potter and longtime Ambleside resident, writer Harriet Martineau. Finally, soccer fans shouldn't miss the **Homes of Football** (daily 10am–5pm, until 7pm in July and Aug; free; Ⓦwww.homesoffootball.co.uk), 100 Lake Rd. The gallery of football photographer Stuart Clarke, it's a permanent archive of over 60,000 images of the country's stadiums and fans.

A good **walk** (6 miles; around 4hr) is possible straight from the town centre. Stock Ghyll Lane runs up the left bank of the tumbling stream to one of the more attractive waterfalls in the region, **Stock Ghyll Force**. The path then rises steeply to **Wansfell Pike** (1581ft) and down into Troutbeck village, with the *Mortal Man* inn a short detour to the left. Head south down the minor road through the village, towards Townend, just before which a track leads west onto the flanks of Wansfell and around past the viewpoint at **Jenkin Crag** back to Ambleside.

Practicalities

Buses (including National Express) stop on Kelsick Road, opposite the library. The **tourist office** is just up the road, in Central Buildings on Market Cross (daily 9am–5.30pm; ☎015394/32582); for **online information**, consult Ⓦwww.ambleside.u-k.org, a useful community website. For **bike rental**, try Biketreks on Compston Road (☎015394/31505), or Ghyllside Cycles on The Slack (☎015394/33592, Ⓦwww.ghyllside.co.uk).

B&Bs, guest houses and hotels

3 Cambridge Villas Church St ☎015394/32307. The well-kept house hides a variety of agreeably furnished rooms. No credit cards ❷

Compston House Compston Rd ☎015394/32305, Ⓦwww.compstonhouse.co.uk.

There's a New York welcome here, with American-style themed rooms and breakfasts of pancakes and maple syrup. ❸

Grey Friar Lodge Clappersgate ☎015394/33158, Ⓦwww.cumbria-hotels.co.uk. A mile southwest of town, the lodge makes the most of its commanding position over the River Brathay. Closed mid-Dec to mid-Feb. ❺

Linda's B&B Shirland, Compston Rd
℡ 015394/32999. The cheapest rates in town.
Two of the rooms (all share a bathroom) can
sleep three or four. No credit cards. **❶**
Mill Cottage Rydal Rd ℡ 015394/34830. Housed
in a sixteenth-century mill building, with a riverside café underneath. **❷**

Hostels

Ambleside Backpackers Old Lake Rd ℡ 015394/
32340, ⓦ www.englishlakesbackpackers.co.uk.
Midway between lake and town, this secluded
independent backpackers' hostel has free breakfasts of tea, toast and cereal, a barbecue area and
mountain bikes for rent. Dorm beds cost £13.75.
Ambleside YHA Waterhead, A591, 1 mile south
℡ 0870/770 5672, ⓔ ambleside@yha.org.uk. The
YHA's flagship regional hostel, a huge lakeside
affair with dorms (£14), doubles (**❶**) and family
rooms, bike rental and Internet access.

Campsite

Low Wray National Trust Campsite Wray,
three miles south of town ℡ 015394/32810.
Nearest campsite to Ambleside, by the lake –
an hourly bus on the Ambleside to
Hawkshead/Coniston route passes within a mile.
Closed Nov–Easter.

Cafés and restaurants

Apple Pie Rydal Rd ℡ 015394/33679. Busy day-
time café with a range of dishes from homemade
pies to BLTs. Inexpensive.
Glass House Rydal Rd ℡ 015394/32137.
Renovated mill with waterwheel, serving accom-
plished Mediterranean/Modern British cooking.
Closed Tues in winter. Expensive.
Lucy's on a Plate Church St ℡ 015394/31191.
Enjoyable bistro offering a daily changing menu
with tons of choice. *Lucy 4*, 2 St Mary's Lane, just
over the way, is its tapas offshoot. Moderate.
Zeffirelli's Compston Rd ℡ 015394/33845.
Specializes in vegetarian food, either in the day-
time *Garden Café* or upstairs in the restaurant
(closed Mon–Fri lunch) for pizzas and pasta.
Moderate.

Langdale

Three miles west of Ambleside along the A593, Skelwith Bridge marks the start
of **Great Langdale**, a U-shaped glacial valley overlooked by the prominent
rocky summits of the **Langdale Pikes**, the most popular of the central
Lakeland fells. Between April and October, the #516 Langdale Rambler **bus**
from Ambleside's Kelsick Road runs to Elterwater and the *Old Dungeon Ghyll
Hotel* at the head of the valley.

Half a mile northwest of its namesake water, **ELTERWATER** is an attractive
settlement fringed by sheep-filled common land and centred on a tiny village
green. It sees its fair share of Langdale-bound hikers, not least because of its two
local **youth hostels**: *Elterwater*, just across the bridge from the village
(℡ 0870/770 5816, ⓔ elterwater@yha.org.uk; dorm beds £10.25), is the most
convenient; *Langdale High Close*, a mile from Elterwater (℡ 0870/770 5908,
ⓔ langdale@yha.org.uk; dorm beds £10.25; closed Nov–Feb), has a more
spectacular setting, high on the road over Red Bank from Skelwith Bridge to
Grasmere. There's traditional hospitality at the *Britannia Inn* (℡ 015394/37210,
ⓦ www.britinn.co.uk; **❺**), an old lakeland pub on the green.

The riverside **Cumbria Way footpath** runs as far as the *New Dungeon Ghyll
Hotel*, three miles from Elterwater. A path indicated by the "Stickle Ghyll" sign
follows the beck straight up to **Stickle Tarn**, around to the right then left up
to **Pavey Ark** (2297ft). It is fairly easy from then on to **Harrison Stickle**
(2414ft), down to the stream forming the headwaters of Dungeon Ghyll and
slowly up to **Pike of Stickle** (2326ft). Backtracking a short distance, a path
leads to the right almost parallel with Dungeon Ghyll, back to the start (4
miles; 2400ft ascent; 4hr).

The traditional **accommodation** in the valley is the peerless *Old Dungeon
Ghyll Hotel* (℡ 015394/37272, ⓦ www.odg.co.uk; **❺**, **❼** with dinner), at the
end of the B5343, seven miles northwest of Ambleside; it offers three-course
dinners in its restaurant (£19.50, book in advance) and has a stone-flagged

hikers' bar with roaring range and filling food. In the evening, the bar fills up with refugees from the nearby *Great Langdale* **campsite** (☎015394/37668). A mile or so back down the road the rooms at the *New Dungeon Ghyll Hotel* (☎015394/37213, ⓦwww.dungeon-ghyll.com; ❻) feature dramatic fell views. You can also eat here, or at the adjacent *Sticklebarn Tavern* (☎015394/37356), which has big breakfasts served every day and inexpensive bar meals available year-round, as well as **bunk–barn accommodation** (£10 per night).

Grasmere and around

Four miles northwest of Ambleside, the village of **GRASMERE** consists of an intimate cluster of grey-stone houses on the old packhorse road that runs beside the babbling River Rothay. It's an eminently pleasing ensemble, set back from one of the most alluring of the region's small lakes, but it loses some of its charm in summer thanks to the hordes who descend on the trail of the village's most famous former resident, **William Wordsworth** (1770–1850). The poet, his wife Mary, sister Dorothy and other members of his family are buried beneath the yews in **St Oswald's churchyard**, around which the river makes a sinuous curl.

On Grasmere's southeastern outskirts, on the main A591, stands **Dove Cottage** (daily 9.30am–5.30pm; closed mid-Jan to mid-Feb; £5.80; ⓦwww.wordsworth.org.uk), home to William and Dorothy Wordsworth from 1799 to 1808 and where Wordsworth wrote some of his best poetry. Most of the furniture in the cottage belonged to the Wordsworths, while in the upper rooms are various other possessions, including a pair of William's ice skates. In good weather, the garden is open for visits as well (same hours as cottage).

Another mile and a half southeast along the A591 from Grasmere, the hamlet of **RYDAL** consists of an inn, a few houses and **Rydal Mount** (March–Oct daily 9.30am–5pm; Nov–Feb Wed–Mon 10am–4pm, closed for three weeks in Jan; £4.50, gardens only £2; ⓦwww.rydalmount.co.uk), home of William Wordsworth from 1813 until his death in 1850. Parts of the house have been redecorated, but furniture and portraits give a good sense of its former occupants: in the drawing room and library is the only known portrait of Dorothy, while memorabilia includes William's black leather sofa, his ink stand and despatch box. For many, the highlight is the **garden**, which has been preserved as Wordsworth designed it, complete with terraces where he used to declaim his poetry. Buses #555 and #599 pass the house on the way to Grasmere from Windermere and Ambleside.

Practicalities

Grasmere is on the main #555 and #599 **bus** routes, which both stop on the village green. The Lakes Day Rider bus ticket (£5.50) allows unlimited travel between Windermere, Bowness or Ambleside and the Wordsworth houses and Grasmere. The **tourist office** (Easter–Oct daily 9.30am–5pm; Nov–Easter Fri, Sat & Sun 10am–3.30pm; ☎015394/35245) is by the main car park on Red Bank Road at the southern end of the village.

Bed and breakfast **accommodation** can be hard to come by in summer, so book well in advance, but Grasmere does have three very popular youth hostels. Of the many **tea rooms and cafés**, picnic necessities are best from *Newby's Deli & Bakery* in Red Lion Square (underneath the *Harwood Hotel*), while across the road, *Baldry's* (closed Tues–Thurs in winter) offers home-made cakes, puddings, pies and quiches. The *Jumble Room Café* on Langdale Road (☎015394/35188; closed Mon & Tues) is a funky, reasonably priced café–restaurant with an organic touch to its ethnically diverse menu; or there's the *Dove Cottage Tea Rooms and Restaurant*, at Town End near Dove Cottage, open during the day for tearoom favourites and in the evening (℡015394/35268; closed Mon May–Oct, plus Tues & Sun rest of year) for moderately priced dinners.

B&Bs, guest houses and hotels

Banerigg House One mile south of Grasmere on A591 ℡015394/35204. Nonsmoking lakeside property, with rooms offering lake views (though no TVs). No credit cards. ❸

Harwood Red Lion Square ℡015394/35248, ⓦwww.harwoodhotel.co.uk. Genial, nonsmoking family-run hotel with eight rooms. Two-night minimum stay at weekends. ❸

How Foot Lodge Town End ℡015394/35366, ⓦwww.howfoot.co.uk. A spacious Victorian villa, just yards from Dove Cottage, with six nonsmoking rooms. Closed Jan. ❸

Lancrigg Vegetarian Country House Hotel Easedale Rd ℡015394/35317, ⓦwww.lancrigg.co.uk. Gourmet vegetarian retreat half a mile northwest of the village. A dozen variously sized rooms, plus an inventive four-course dinner included in the price. ❽

Titteringdales Pye Lane ℡015394/35439. Cosy detached house five minutes' walk from the centre. No single-night advance reservations. ❷

White Moss House Rydal Water, one mile south on the A591 ℡015394/35295, ⓦwww.whitemoss.com. Once owned by Wordsworth, the ivy-clad house has antique-filled rooms in the main house and two more in a cottage suite. The food (dinner included in room rate) is wonderful. Closed Dec & Jan. ❽

Wordsworth Hotel College St ℡015394/35592, ⓦwww.grasmere-hotels.co.uk/wordsworth. The plum choice in the village itself – relaxed, attractive and comfortable, with a heated pool, conservatory and terrace. ❼

Hostels

Butterlip How Easedale Rd ℡0870/770 5836, Ⓔgrasmere@yha.org.uk. Closest YHA hostel to the centre, 150 yards north of the green. Closed Mon–Thurs in winter. Dorm beds £13.

Grasmere Independent Hostel Broadrayne Farm ℡015394/35055, ⓦwww.grasmerehostel.co.uk. Just north of town on the A591, past the *Travellers' Rest* pub. Rooms here sleep three to six people (£12.50 per bed) and facilities include kitchen, laundry, sauna, and common room.

Thorney How ℡0870/770 5836, Ⓔgrasmere@yha.org.uk. Grasmere's smaller, simpler YHA hostel, a characterful former farmhouse, is just under a mile further along the unlit road past Butterlip How. Closed Nov–Easter. Dorm beds £10.25

Coniston

Coniston Water is not one of the most immediately imposing of the lakes, yet it has a quiet beauty that sets it apart from the more popular destinations. The nineteenth-century art critic and social reformer **John Ruskin** made the lake his home, and today his isolated house, Brantwood, on the northeastern shore, provides the most obvious target for a day-trip. Some come here, too, on the *Swallows and Amazons* trail. **Arthur Ransome** was a frequent visitor, his memories and experiences providing much of the detail in his famous children's books. In the mid-1960s, the glass-like surface of Coniston Water attracted the attention of national hero **Donald Campbell**, who in 1955 had set a world water-speed record of 202mph on Ullswater, bumping it up to 276mph nine years later in Australia. On January 4, 1967, he set out to better his own mark on Coniston Water, but just as his jet-powered *Bluebird* hit an estimated 320mph, a patch of turbulence sent it into a somersault. Campbell was killed immediately and his body and boat lay undisturbed at the bottom of the lake until both were retrieved in 2001.

Coniston Village, Water and Brantwood

A memorial seat and plaque to Donald Campbell decorates the green in the slate-grey village of **CONISTON** (a derivation of "King's Town"), hunkered

Writers in the Lake District

William Wordsworth was not the first to praise the Lake District – Thomas Gray wrote appreciatively of his visit in 1769 – but it is Wordsworth who dominates its literary landscape, not solely through his poetry but also through his still-useful *Guide to the Lakes* (1810). Born in Cockermouth in 1770, he was sent to school in Hawkshead before a stint at Cambridge, a year in France and two in Somerset. In 1799 he returned to the Lake District, settling in the Grasmere district, where he spent the last two-thirds of his life with his sister Dorothy, who not only transcribed his poems but was an accomplished diarist as well.

Wordsworth and fellow poets **Samuel Taylor Coleridge** and **Robert Southey** formed a clique that became known as the "Lake Poets", a label based more on their fluctuating friendships and their shared passion for the region than on any common subject matter in their writings. A fourth member of the Cumbrian literary elite was the critic and essayist **Thomas De Quincey**, chiefly known today for his *Confessions of an English Opium-Eater*. One of the first to fully appreciate the revolutionary nature of Wordsworth's and Coleridge's collaborative *Lyrical Ballads*, De Quincey became a long-term guest of the Wordsworths in 1807, taking over Dove Cottage from them in 1809. He stayed there until 1820, but it was only in the 1830s that he started writing his *Lake Reminiscences*, offending Wordsworth and Coleridge in the process.

Inspired by Wordsworth's writings and by the terrain itself, the social philosopher and art critic **John Ruskin** also made the Lake District his home, settling at Brantwood, outside Coniston, in 1872. His letters and watercolours reflect a deep love of the area, also demonstrated by his unsuccessful fight to prevent the damming of Thirlmere. Much of Ruskin's feeling for the countryside permeated through to two other literary immigrants, **Arthur Ransome**, also a Coniston resident and writer of the children's classic *Swallows and Amazons*, and **Beatrix Potter**, whose favourite Lakeland spots feature in her children's stories.

below the craggy and copper-mine-riddled bulk of **The Old Man of Coniston** (2628ft). Campbell's grave is nearby, in the new cemetery behind the *Crown Hotel*. Having studied this and Ruskin's grave, which lies in St Andrew's original churchyard beneath a beautifully worked Celtic cross, you've seen all that Coniston has to offer, save for the excellent **Ruskin Museum** on Yewdale Road (Easter to mid-Nov daily 10am–5.30pm; mid-Nov to Easter Wed–Sun 10am–3.30pm; £3.50; ⓦ www.ruskinmuseum.com), which combines local history and geology exhibits with a fascinating look at Ruskin's life and work through his watercolours, manuscripts and personal memorabilia.

Coniston Water is half a mile southeast of the village. Here, the *Bluebird Café* sells ices and drinks, while the adjacent **Coniston Boating Centre** (ⓣ015394/41366) rents out rowing boats, sailing dinghies, canoes, electric launches and motorboats. From the nearby pier, the sumptuously upholstered **Steam Yacht Gondola** (ⓣ015394/63856, ⓦ www.nationaltrust.org .uk/gondola), built in 1859, leaves on the hour (Easter–Oct 11am–4pm, not 1pm; £5 round trip) for Ruskin's Brantwood. The wooden **Coniston Launch** (Easter–Oct hourly; Nov–Easter up to 4 daily depending on the weather; ⓣ015394/36216, ⓦ www.conistonlaunch.co.uk) operates a year-round service to Brantwood on two routes, north (£3.80 return) or south (£5.80) around the lake. Special **cruises** (Easter–Oct; call for times) concentrate on the various sites associated with *Swallows and Amazons* (£7.50) and Donald Campbell (£6.50).

Nestling among trees on a hillside above the eastern shore of Coniston Water, **Brantwood** (mid-March to mid-Nov daily 11am–5.30pm; mid-Nov to mid-March Wed–Sun 11am–4.30pm; house & gardens £4.75, gardens only £3; 50p discount if you arrive by Gondola or Coniston Launch; ⓦwww .brantwood.org.uk) was where art critic and moralist John Ruskin lived from 1872 until his death in 1900. Champion of J.M.W. Turner and the Pre-Raphaelites and proponent of the supremacy of Gothic architecture, Ruskin insisted upon the indivisibility of ethics and aesthetics, and was appalled by the conditions in which the captains of industry made their labourers work and live, while expecting him to applaud their patronage of the arts. A twenty-minute video expands on his philosophy and whets the appetite for rooms full of his watercolours. His study – hung with handmade paper to his own design – and dining room boast superlative lake views, bettered only by those from the Turret Room where he used to sit in later life in his bathchair. Various other exhibition rooms and galleries display Ruskin-related arts and crafts, while the *Jumping Jenny Tearooms* – named after Ruskin's boat – has outdoor terrace seating for meals and drinks.

Practicalities

Buses stop on the main road through Coniston village, though some of the services also run down to the ferry pier at the lake. A Ruskin Explorer ticket (£10.40) gets you return bus travel between Bowness and Coniston, plus use of the Coniston Launch and free entry to Ruskin's house – buy the ticket on the bus. The **tourist office** (Easter–Oct daily 9.30am–5.30pm; Nov–March Fri–Sun 10am–3.30pm; ☎015394/41533) is right in the centre on Ruskin Avenue. You can **rent bikes** from Summitreks on Yewdale Road (☎015394/41212, ⓦwww.summitreks.co.uk).

B&Bs are plentiful in and around Coniston, and all the pubs have rooms available too. The **hostels** are popular with walkers, so book early if you need a budget bed. The closest **campsite** is *Coniston Hall* (☎015394/41223; closed Nov–Easter), a mile south of town by the lake at Haws Bank; booking is essential. **Eating** opportunities outside the pubs are limited, but in any case you shouldn't look much further than the *Sun Hotel*, whose cosy bar has filling meals and real ales as well as photographs and newspaper accounts of the famous Campbell crash. For sandwiches, homemade pies, all-day breakfasts and **Internet** access, visit the *Village Pantry* on Yewdale Road.

B&Bs, guest houses and hotels

Beech Tree Guesthouse Yewdale Rd
☎015394/41717. Friendly vegetarian place 150 yards north of the village on the Ambleside road. No credit cards. ❷

Lakeland House Tilberthwaite Ave
☎015394/41303, ⓦwww.lakelandhouse.com. Friendly place, accustomed to walkers and their ways and with an attached café. No credit cards. ❷

Shepherds Villa Tilberthwaite Ave
☎015394/41337. One of the village's most popular B&Bs, with ten comfortable rooms, some ensuite. ❷

Sun Hotel ☎015394/41248, ⓦwww .thesunconiston.com. Coniston's best pub rooms

are at this fine old inn, 200 yards uphill from the bridge in the centre of the village. Minimum two-night stay at weekends. ❺

Thwaite Cottage Waterhead, half a mile from Coniston on the Hawkshead road
☎015394/41367,
ⓦwww.thwaitcot.freeserve.co.uk. Slate-flagged, seventeenth-century cottage with three peaceful rooms with oak beams and panelled walls. No credit cards. ❸

Hostels

Coniston Coppermines ☎0870/770 5772, ⓔcoppermines@yha.org.uk. Dramatic mountain setting a mile or so from the village. Dorms cost £10.25; closed Nov–March, & Sun & Mon in April, May, Sept & Oct.

Coniston Holly How Ambleside Rd ☎0870/770 5770, ©conistonhh@yha.org.uk. Closest hostel to the village (just a few minutes' walk north). Dorm beds cost £10.25; limited weekend opening outside summer holiday period. Closed Nov to mid-Jan.

Hawkshead and around

Greystone **HAWKSHEAD**, between Coniston and Ambleside, wears its beauty well, its patchwork of cottages and cobbles backed by woods and fells and barely affected by modern intrusions. This is partly due to the enlightened policy of banning traffic in the centre – huge car parks at the village edge take the strain, and when the crowds of day-trippers leave, Hawkshead regains its natural tranquillity.

The village was an important wool market at the time Wordsworth was studying at **Hawkshead Grammar School** (Easter–Oct Mon–Sat 10am–12.30pm & 1.30–5pm, Sun 1–5pm; £2), founded in 1585, whose entrance lies opposite the tourist office – pride of place is given to the desk on which William carved his signature. While there he attended the fifteenth-century **Church of St Michael** above the school, which harks back to Norman designs in its rounded pillars and patterned arches. From its knoll the churchyard gives a good view over the village's twin central squares, and of Main Street, housing the **Beatrix Potter Gallery** (Easter–Oct Mon–Wed, Sat & Sun 10.30am–4.30pm; £3, joint ticket with Hill Top £7; NT), occupying rooms once used by her solicitor husband. Fans get bustled into rooms full of Potter's original illustrations, though the less devoted might find displays on her life as keen naturalist, conservationist and early supporter of the National Trust more diverting.

It's two miles from Hawkshead, down the eastern side of Esthwaite Water on the B5285 to the pretty twin hamlets of Near and Far Sawrey, the first the site of Beatrix Potter's beloved **Hill Top** (Easter–Oct Mon–Wed, Sat & Sun 10.30am–4.30pm; £4.50, joint ticket with Beatrix Potter Gallery £7; NT). A Londoner by birth, Potter bought the farmhouse here with the proceeds from her first book, *The Tale of Peter Rabbit*, and retained it as her study long after she moved out following her marriage in 1913. Its furnishings and contents have been kept as they were during her occupancy and the small house is always busy with visitors; so much so that numbers are often limited. In summer, expect to have to queue. From April to October, you can travel to Hill Top directly from Bowness on a combined "boat-and-goat" **ferry-and-minibus service** (10am–4.30pm every 40min; ☎015394/45161, ⓦwww.mountain -goat.com), which runs on from Hill Top to Hawkshead and back.

The other local diversion is to take the minor road off the Hawkshead–Coniston B5285, which winds the couple of miles northwest to the highly popular **Tarn Hows**, a body of water circled by paths and picnic spots. It takes an hour to walk around the tarn, during which you can ponder on the fact that this miniature idyll is in fact almost entirely artificial – the original owners enlarged two small tarns to make the one you see today. A free National Trust Tarn Hows **bus service** runs between Hawkshead and Coniston on Sundays between Easter and the end of October. Otherwise, you can walk the two miles up from Coniston or Hawkshead on country paths and lanes.

Practicalities

The main **bus service** to Hawkshead is the #505 between Windermere, Bowness, Ambleside and Coniston; on reaching Hawkshead it loops down to

Hill Top and back. The **tourist office** is at the main car park (Easter–Oct daily 9.30am–5.30pm; Nov–Easter Fri, Sat & Sun 10am–3.30pm; ☎015394/36525).

Book a long way ahead if you want to **stay** in Hawkshead during the peak summer season. The tourist office can help with finding accommodation if the places listed below are full. Both the *King's Arms* and *Queen's Head* have bar **meals** as well as a more formal restaurant, and the *King's Arms* has a snug little bar with a fire and a fine beer selection.

B&Bs, guest houses and hotels

Ann Tyson's Cottage Wordsworth St ☎015394/36405, ⓦwww.anntysons.co.uk. Some contend that Wordsworth briefly boarded here, and today there are B&B rooms in the barn conversion or two cottages to rent. ❸

Ivy House Main St ☎015394/36204, ⓦwww.ivy-househotel.com. Eighteenth-century elegance – six rooms in the main house, five more in the lodge behind; rates include dinner. ❻

King's Arms Market Square ☎015394/36372, ⓦwww.kingsarmshawkshead.co.uk. Old inn whose nine rooms retain their oak beams and idiosyncratic proportions (bathrooms are up to date, though). ❺

Queen's Head Main St ☎015394/36271, ⓦwww.queensheadhotel.co.uk. Guest rooms here have been thoroughly modernized; family rooms sleep three or four. ❺

Yewfield Hawkshead Hill, 2 miles west off B5285 ☎015394/36765, ⓦwww.yewfield.co.uk. Vegetarian guest house set amongst organic vegetable gardens. Closed mid-Nov to Jan. ❸

Hostel

Esthwaite Lodge YHA ☎0870/770 5836, ⓔhawkshead@yha.org.uk. A mile to the south down the Newby Bridge road, housed in a Regency mansion. Dorm beds cost £11.50. Closed Nov–Jan, plus other days in winter.

Campsites

Croft Caravan and Campsite North Lonsdale Rd ☎015394/36374, ⓦwww.hawkshead-croft.com. Busy site, right by the village, with bike rental available. Closed Nov to mid-March.

Hawkshead Hall Farm Half a mile north of the village on the Ambleside road ☎015394/36221. An inexpensive tap-and-toilet affair. Closed Dec–Feb.

Keswick and Derwent Water

Standing on the shores of Derwent Water at the junction of the main north–south and east–west routes through the Lake District, **KESWICK** makes a good base for exploring delightful Borrowdale – the start of many walking routes to the central peaks around Scafell Pike – or Skiddaw and Blencathra, which loom over the town. For those not up to a day on the fells, Keswick remains a popular place throughout the year, with a big enough population (around five thousand) to warrant a bevy of local museums and sights.

Granted its market charter by Edward I in 1276 – **market day** is Saturday – Keswick was an important wool and leather centre until around 1500, when these trades were supplanted by the discovery of local graphite. Northwest of the centre up Main Street, the **Cumberland Pencil Museum** at Greta Bridge (daily 9.30am–4pm; £2.50; ⓦwww.pencils.co.uk) tells the whole story entertainingly. On the edge of Fitz Park, on Station Road, you'll find the **Keswick Museum and Art Gallery** (Easter–Oct daily 10am–4pm; £1), a quirky Victorian collection of ancient dental tools, fossils and some prized manuscripts and letters written by the Lakeland Poets. Make time, too, for a couple of churches: **St John's**, on St John's Street in the centre, where the novelist Sir Hugh Walpole (of Herries novels fame) is buried; and **Crosthwaite Church**, a fifteen-minute walk northwest of town over Greta Bridge, resting place of the poet Robert Southey.

Keswick's most celebrated landmark, **Castlerigg Stone Circle**, is made especially resonant by its magnificent mountain backdrop. From the end of Station

Road, take the Threlkeld rail line path (signposted by the *Keswick Country House Hotel*) and follow the signs. Thirty-eight hunks of Borrowdale volcanic stone, the largest almost eight feet tall, form a circle a hundred feet in diameter; another ten blocks delineate a rectangular enclosure within. The array probably had an astronomical or timekeeping function when it was erected four or five thousand years ago. Back on the rail path, you can easily continue all the way to **Threlkeld** itself, three miles from town, on a delightful riverside walk with the promise of a drink in one of Threlkeld's old pubs at the end.

On any reasonably decent day, the best move in Keswick is down to the shores of **Derwent Water**, five minutes' walk south of the centre along Lake Road and through the pedestrian underpass. It's among the most attractive of the lakes, ringed by crags and studded with islets, and is most easily seen by hopping on the **Keswick Launch** (Easter–Nov daily 10am–6pm, until 8pm in July & Aug; Dec–Easter Sat & Sun 10am–6pm; £5.40 round-trip, 85p per stage; ☏017687/772263, ⓦwww.keswick-launch.co.uk), which runs right around the lake calling at several points en route. There's also an enjoyable one-hour evening **cruise** (£6) from May Day bank holiday until mid-September; phone or pop down during the day to reserve a place. Best launch excursion is up **Cat Bells** (get off at Hawes End), a renowned vantage-point (1481ft) above the lake's western shore – allow two and a half hours for the scramble to the top and a return to Keswick along the wooded lake shore.

Practicalities

All **buses**, including National Express services, use the terminal behind Lakes Foodstore, off Main Street. The **tourist office** is in the Moot Hall on Market Square (daily: April–Oct 9.30am–5.30pm; Nov–March 9.30am–4.30pm; ☏017687/72645, ⓦwww.keswick.org). George Fisher, at 2 Borrowdale Rd (☏017687/772178), is one of the most celebrated **outdoors stores** on the Lakes, with a full range of equipment and maps and a daily weather information service. For **bike rental**, try Keswick Mountain Bikes on Southey Hill (☏017687/775202, ⓦwww.keswickmountainbikes.co.uk). There's **Internet** access at U-Compute, above the post office at 48 Main St (daily 9am–5.30pm, sometimes later in summer; ☏017687/775127).

There's a fair amount of entertainment on offer in Keswick throughout the year: a **cinema** on St John's Street which hosts an annual film festival (times vary), the **jazz festival** each May, **beer festival** in June, and traditional country shows in the locality during the summer. The **Theatre by the Lake** on Lake Road (☏017687/774411, ⓦwww.theatrebythelake.com) hosts a full programme of drama, concerts, exhibitions, readings and talks.

B&Bs, guest houses and hotels

Bluestones 7 Southey St ☏017687/774237. Well-kept guest house used to walkers, with a variety of rooms (some sleeping three or four). ❷

Bridgedale Guesthouse 101 Main St ☏017687/773914. Caters for all requirements: whether you're looking for a room-only deal, en-suite facilities or long-stay discount, you'll find it here – mention *Rough Guides* for a better deal. No credit cards. ❶–❷

Fitz House 47 Brundholme Terrace, Station Rd ☏017687/774488, ⓦwww.fitzhouse.co.uk.

Stylish Victorian villa overlooking the park. Two-night minimum weekend stay. ❷

George Hotel St John's Street ☏017687/772076, ⓦwww.georgehotelkeswick.co.uk. Keswick's oldest coaching inn, with bags of character. The food is good, eaten in the bar or more formal restaurant. ❹

Greystones Ambleside Rd ☏017687/773108, ⓦwww.greystones.tv. Nonsmoking Victorian terraced house close to the centre at the end of St John's Street. ❸

Highfield Hotel The Heads ☏017687/772508, ⓦwww.highfieldkeswick.co.uk. Beautifully restored hotel whose stylish "feature rooms" include two turret rooms and a converted chapel. Dinner included in the price. **❻**, **❼** for feature rooms.

Howe Keld 5–7 The Heads ☎017687/772417, ⓦwww.howekeld.co.uk. Welcoming, nonsmoking, guest house with a reputation for great breakfasts and cosy rooms. **❸**

Morrels 34 Lake Rd ☎017687/772666, ⓦwww.morrels.co.uk. Reputable restaurant-with-rooms operation, where residents get ten percent off dinner. **❹**

Youth hostels

Derwentwater Barrow House, Borrowdale ☎0870/770 5792, Ⓔderwentwater@yha.org.uk. Old mansion with fifteen acres of grounds sloping down to the lake, a couple of miles south of Keswick along the B5289. Closed Nov & Dec, and open weekends only in Jan. Dorm beds £11.50.

Keswick Station Rd ☎0870/770 5894, Ⓔkeswick@yha.org.uk. A converted wool mill by the river in town. Dorm beds cost £11.50, you get free tea and coffee on arrival, and there's Internet access. Open all year.

Campsites

Castlerigg Hall Rakefoot Lane, off the A591, Castlerigg ☎017687/772437, ⓦwww.castlerigg.co.uk. Out-of-town campsite, a mile and a half southeast of Keswick; you can reach the nearby stone circle by footpath. Closed Nov–Easter.

Derwentwater Caravan Club and Camping Site Derwent Water ☎017687/772392. Less than ten minutes' walk from the centre, down by the lake; turn left off Main St beside the supermarket. Closed Dec & Jan.

Cafés, pubs and restaurants

Abraham's Tea Rooms George Fisher's, 2 Borrowdale Rd. The top-floor tearoom in the outdoors store comes to your aid with warming mugs of *glühwein*, homemade soups, big breakfasts and daily specials. No credit cards. Inexpensive.

The Four in Hand Lake Rd, opposite George Fisher's. Popular pub food – grilled Cumberland ham and eggs, local trout and other lakeland specialities. Inexpensive.

Lakeland Pedlar Henderson's Yard, Bell Close, off Main St. Keswick's best café serves inventive veggie food – from breakfast burritos to veg crumble. Open evenings July & Aug. Inexpensive.

Lake Road Inn Lake Rd. Intimate Jenning's pub known for its good-value food, particularly the homemade pies and Borrowdale trout. Inexpensive.

Loose Box Pizzeria King's Arms Courtyard, Main St ☎017687/72083. Popular pizza-and-pasta joint – the house special is *spaghetti rustica* (tomato, garlic, chilli and prawns). Moderate.

Luca's Greta Bridge ☎017687/774621. Classic pastas and pizzas, and pricier main meals (such as monkfish wrapped in pancetta) in a riverside Italian bistro; closed Mon. Expensive.

Mayson's 33 Lake Rd ☎☎017687/774104. Licensed, self-service restaurant serving lasagna, moussaka, pies, curries and stir-fries (until 9pm in summer). No credit cards. Inexpensive

Borrowdale

It's difficult to overstate the beauty of **Borrowdale**, with its river flats and yew trees, lying at the head of Derwent Water and overshadowed by the peaks of Scafell and Scafell Pike, the highest in England. Climbs up these, as well as up Great Gable, one of the finest-looking mountains in England, start from the head of the valley, accessible on the #77/77A and #79 **buses** from Keswick.

Just before the *Derwentwater* youth hostel, a narrow road branches left for a steep climb to the photogenic **Ashness Bridge**. The minor road ends two miles further south at **Watendlath**, an idyllic little tarn and tearooms which can be hopelessly overrun at times in summer – the National Trust's free Watendlath Wanderer bus runs here every couple of hours from Keswick on summer Sundays, via Ashness. Back on the B5289, a signposted path heads to the **Lodore Falls**, only really worth the diversion after sustained wet weather. Further south, there's a slight detour across an old packhorse bridge to **GRANGE**, a peaceful riverside hamlet peered down upon by Borrowdale's forested crags. At Grange, it's under a mile south to the 1900-ton **Bowder Stone**, a house-sized lump of rock scaled by way of a wooden ladder and worn to a shine on top by thousands of pairs of feet.

Shaded paths through the wood, and the B5289, lead in around a mile to the straggling hamlet of **ROSTHWAITE**. As well as two or three B&Bs, there are comfortable **rooms** at the hiker-friendly *Royal Oak Hotel* (℡017687/777214, ⓦwww.royaloakhotel.co.uk; ❺, includes dinner) and the smarter, neighbouring *Scafell Hotel* (℡017687/777208, ⓦwww.scafell.co.uk; ❺, ❼ with dinner), whose attached *Riverside Inn* − the only local pub − serves popular bar food. A nice **youth hostel**, *Borrowdale Longthwaite* (℡0870/770 5706, Ⓔborrowdale@yha.org.uk; dorm beds £11.50; closed Jan–March), is a mile south of Rosthwaite, on the riverside footpath to Seatoller; while across the river, on the eastern side of the B5289, is the *Chapel House Farm* **campsite** (℡017687/777602).

Another mile on, **SEATOLLER** and the **Seatoller Barn National Park Information Centre** (Easter–Nov daily 10am–5pm; limited weekend opening in winter; ℡017687/777294) marks the end of the #79 bus route from Keswick. *Seatoller House* (℡017687/777218, ⓦwww.seatollerhouse.co.uk; ❹, ❻ with dinner; no dinner Tues, closed Dec–Feb) has rooms in an atmospheric seventeenth-century farmhouse right by the road. There's also an informal **campsite** in a small field by the beck along the minor road south to **SEATHWAITE**, twenty minutes' walk away. This is a popular base for walks up the likes of **Great Gable** (2949ft), **Scafell** (3163ft) and **Scafell Pike** (3205ft). The trout farm at the foot of the valley has a fine café (Easter–Sept daily 10am–6.30pm), serving fresh grilled trout or sandwiches, as well as another informal and basic campsite (no phone) used extensively by climbers.

Buttermere, Crummock Water and Loweswater

Overlooked by the steep Borrowdale Fells, the B5289 cuts west at Seatoller, up and over the dramatic **Honister Pass**. Bus #77/77A comes this way, making the initial, and steep, mile-and-a-quarter grind from Borrowdale to the car park at the top of Honister Pass, by the *Honister Hause* **youth hostel** (℡0870/770 5870, Ⓔhonister@yha.org.uk; dorm beds £10.25; closed mid-Nov to Easter).

From Honister Pass, the B5289 follows Gatesgarthdale Beck for three miles and makes a dramatic descent into the **Buttermere valley**, passing another **youth hostel** (℡0870/770 5736, Ⓔbuttermere@yha.org.uk; dorm beds £11.50; Sept–Easter closed certain days of the week) just before **BUTTERMERE** village. The village itself has two hotels: the *Bridge Hotel* (℡017687/770252, ⓦwww.bridge-hotel.com; ❼, includes dinner) and the smaller *Fish Hotel* (℡017687/770253, ⓦwww.fish-hotel.co.uk; ❹) − both serve reasonable meals, while the *Bridge* has a popular bar. There's also **camping** right by the lake at *Syke Farm* (℡01768/770222; closed Nov–March). To get to Buttermere directly from Keswick, take the #77/77A bus.

The village − set between the two expanses of Buttermere and neighbouring **Crummock Water** − makes a good walking base, with a particularly easy two-mile hike out along Crummock Water's southwestern edge to the 125ft **Scale Force** falls. The four-mile, **round-lake** stroll circling Buttermere itself shouldn't take more than a couple of hours. The scenery flattens out as the road heads north from Crummock Water and into the pastoral **Lorton Vale**, with Cockermouth just a few miles beyond. A minor road south just beyond Brackenthwaite leads directly to minuscule **Loweswater**, around which there's a gentle, four-mile (2hr) walk. En route, you'll pass the *Kirkstile Inn* (℡01900/85219, ⓦwww.kirkstile.com; ❹), where there are bistro-style meals available in the cosy bar or restaurant, and a relaxed beer garden.

Wast Water

The awesome sight of the peaks crowding slim, deep **Wast Water** impresses most visitors who venture to this remote lake. The highest slopes in England frame the northern shores, while on the wild southeastern banks rise the impassable screes which separate the lake from Eskdale to the south. The only road (there's no public transport) winds from the main coastal A595, through remote settlements, before meeting the lake at its southwestern tip, at the *Wasdale Hall* **youth hostel** (☎0870/770 6082, ✉wastwater@yha.org.uk; dorm beds £10.25; Sept–Easter closed 1–2 days a week), a country house set in its own lakeside grounds. The minor road then hugs the shore of the lake, ending four miles away at **Wasdale Head**, a Shangri-la-like clearing between the mountain ranges, where you'll find the marvellous *Wasdale Head Inn* (☎019467/26229, ⓦwww.wasdale.com; ❻), one of the most celebrated of all lakeland inns. Nearby, there's **B&B**, friendly advice and packed lunches from hiker-friendly *Lingmell House* (☎019467/26261, ⓦwww.lingmellhouse.com; no credit cards; ❸; closed Jan), on the track to the church, or **camping** at the National Trust's *Wasdale Head* campsite (☎019467/26220; closed Nov–March).

Eskdale

Eskdale is accessed either by the Ravenglass and Eskdale Railway (see p.651), which drops you right in the heart of superb walking country around the hamlet of Boot; or by the east–west minor road route between the coast, via Eskdale Green and Little Langdale, just west of Skelwith Bridge. The attractive rural ride by road or train through the valley from the west begins to peter out as you approach **Dalegarth station** (terminus of the Ravenglass and Eskdale Railway), just beyond which nestles the dead-end hamlet of **BOOT**. Three miles beyond, and 800 feet up, the remains of granaries, bath houses and the commandant's quarters for **Hardknott Roman Fort** (always open; free access) command a strategic and panoramic position.

Boot has a fair smattering of **accommodation and services**, which makes it the obvious base for extended walks in the valley. The nearest place to Dalegarth station is *Brook House Inn* (☎019467/23288, ⓦwww.brookhouseinn.co.uk; ❹), which serves meals in its *Poachers Bar* and has a separate restaurant, too. In Boot itself, the *Burnmoor Inn* (☎019467/23224, ⓦwww.burnmoor.co.uk; ❸) is the traditional hikers' choice. Further up the road past the turn-off to Boot, it's 500 yards to *Hollins Farm* **campsite** (☎019467/23253), and another three-quarters of a mile to the *Woolpack Inn* (☎019467/23230; ❸–❹), which as well as rooms has a purpose-built **bunkhouse** (£16.50 including breakfast). Another 400 yards beyond the pub you'll find Eskdale **youth hostel** (☎0870/770 5824, ✉eskdale@yha.org.uk; dorm beds £10.25; closed Nov–Feb).

Cockermouth

The farming community of **COCKERMOUTH**, midway between the coast and Keswick at the confluence of the Cocker and Derwent rivers, is yet another station on the Wordsworth trail: the **Wordsworth House** on Main Street (Easter–May & Sept Mon–Fri 10.30am–4.30pm; Jun–Aug Mon–Sat

10.30am–4.30pm; £3.50; NT) is where William and Dorothy were born and spent their first few years. Some of the original features remain and there are occasional Wordsworthian relics – a chest of drawers here, a pair of candlesticks there – but on a warm day the walled garden beside the river is more pleasurable than the house. There's certainly no shortage of rainy day attractions ranged elsewhere along Main Street – including museums of printing, toys and models, and motoring – while if you follow your nose, you're likely to stumble upon **Jennings Brewery**, on Brewery Lane near the river. The hour-and-a-half-long Jenning's Brewery Tour (£4.50; booking advisable; ☏0845/129 7190; ⊛www.jenningsbrewery.co.uk) culminates with a tasting. Finally, at the **Lakeland Sheep and Wool Centre** (daily 10am–6pm; ☏01900/822673, ⊛www.sheep-woolcentre.co.uk), a mile south of town on the Egremont road, indoor sheepdog trials, sheep-shearing displays and related exhibits introduce visitors to the complexities of country life. The sheepdog show costs £4 (March–Oct 4 Mon–Thurs & Sun, call for current times), but access to the visitor centre, shop and café is free.

All **buses**, including National Express services, stop on Main Street, from where you follow the signs east to the **tourist office** in the Town Hall, off Market Place (April–June & Oct Mon–Sat 9.30am–4.30pm; July–Sept Mon–Sat 9.30am–5pm, Sun 10am–2pm; Nov–March Mon–Fri 9.30am–4pm, Sat 10am–2pm; ☏01900/822634). Most appealing **B&B** is *Pumpkin House*, 3 Challoner St (☏01900/828269, ⊛www.lakesnw.co.uk/pumpkinhouse; no credit cards; ❷), a vegetarian-friendly place where you can also get a packed lunch for the fells or an evening meal. The *Trout Hotel* on Crown Street (☏01900/823591, ⊛www.trouthotel.co.uk; ❼), by the river, is the top choice, and there are also rooms available in the *Shepherd's Hotel*, out at the Lakeland Sheep and Wool Centre (☏01900/822673, ⊛www.shepherdshotel.co.uk; ❸). Ten minutes' walk south along Station Road, Fern Bank brings you to the Double Mills **youth hostel** (☏0870/770 5768; dorm beds £9; closed Nov–Easter).

Best **pub** by far is *The Bitter End* on Kirkgate, housing Cumbria's smallest brewery. Of the **cafés**, *Over The Top*, 36 Kirkgate (☏01900/827016; closed Sun–Tues), has an eclectic menu of home-cooked dishes from around the world; it's open during the day and for dinner, and also has **Internet** access. The *Quince & Medlar*, 12 Castlegate (☏01900/823579; dinner only; closed Sun & Mon), meanwhile, serves gourmet vegetarian dishes in a wood-panelled Georgian house. **Market day** in Cockermouth is Monday.

Ullswater

Wordsworth declared **Ullswater** "the happiest combination of beauty and grandeur, which any of the Lakes affords" – a judgement that still holds good. At over seven miles long, Ullswater is the second longest lake in Cumbria and much of its appeal derives from its serpentine shape. The chief lakeside settlements, Patterdale and Glenridding, are less than a mile apart at the southern tip of Ullswater, each with a smattering of cafés and B&Bs. The main **public transport to Ullswater** is the #108 bus service (Easter–Oct) from Penrith, which runs via Pooley Bridge, Aira Force and Glenridding to Patterdale. On summer weekends, the #517 Kirkstone Rambler bus continues south over the Kirkstone Pass to Bowness.

In **GLENRIDDING** the *Fairlight Guest House* (☏017684/82397; ❷) is by the hamlet's main car park, though it's at the *Inn on the Lake* (☏017684/82444, ⊛www.innonthelakeullswater.com; ❻–❼) that you really

△ Ullswater

begin to appreciate Ullswater's charms; its *Ramblers Bar* is *the* place for a beer and a bar meal. *Gillside Caravan & Camping* (☏01768/482346, ⊛www .gillsidecaravanandcampingsite.co.uk; closed Nov–Feb) is half a mile away up the valley behind the helpful **tourist office** (Easter–Oct daily 9am–6pm; Nov–Easter Fri–Sun 9.30am–3.30pm; ☏017684/82414) in the main car park. You can get a bite to eat at *Fellbites*, opposite the tourist office. Climbers wanting an early start on Helvellyn (see below) stay at the Helvellyn **youth hostel** (☏0870/770 6110, ✉helvellyn@yha.org.uk; dorm beds £10.25; closed certain days of the week except in July & Aug), a mile and a half up the valley track from Glenridding. In **PATTERDALE**, the cheapest place to stay is the rustic **youth hostel** (☏0870/770 5986, ✉patterdale@yha.org.uk; dorm beds £11.50; closed certain days of the week except Sept–March), just south of the hamlet on the A592, which serves good food and has Internet access. Patterdale's only **pub**, the *White Lion* (☏017684/82214; ❸), has a few rooms available and decent beer. There's **camping** at *Side Farm* (☏017684/82338; closed Nov–Easter), and a small post office/village **shop** opposite the pub.

The climb to the summit of **Helvellyn** (3114ft; 2hr 30min from Ullswater), the most popular of the four 3000ft mountains in Cumbria, is challenging enough for most visitors, who tend to make a day-long circuit from either Glenridding or Patterdale. The most frequently chosen approach is via the infamous **Striding Edge**, an alarming, undulating rocky ridge offering the most direct access to the summit. With **Red Tarn** – the highest Lake District tarn – a dizzying drop below, purists negotiate the very ridge top of Striding Edge; slightly safer, but no less precipitous tracks follow the line of the ridge, just off the crest. The classic return is to the northeast via the less demanding **Swirral Edge**, where a route leads down to Red Tarn, then follows the beck to the disused slate quarry workings and Helvellyn youth hostel, a mile and a half from Glenridding.

Around the lake

On busy summer days the A592 up the western side of the lake is packed with traffic, all looking for space in one of the few designated car parks. Busiest is usually that below **Gowbarrow Park**, three miles north of Glenridding, where the A5091 meets the A592. The hillside still blazes green and gold in spring, as it was doing when the Wordsworths visited; it's thought that Dorothy's recollections of the visit in her diary inspired William to write his famous "Daffodils" poem. The car park at Gowbarrow is also the start of an easy, brief walk up to **Aira Force**, a bush-cloaked seventy-foot fall that's spectacular in spate and can be viewed from bridges spanning the top and bottom of the drop.

The lake itself is traversed by the **Ullswater Steamer** (☏017684/82229, ⊛www.ullswater-steamers.co.uk), which has year-round services from Glenridding to Howtown, halfway up the lake's eastern side (£3.90 one way; 35min), and from Howtown to Pooley Bridge, at the northern end of the lake (£3.90; 20min). Alternatively, you can buy a ticket between Glenridding and Pooley Bridge that effectively makes a two-hour round-the-lake cruise (£8.80). **HOWTOWN** is tucked into a little clearing at the foot of beautiful Fusedale, where the *Howtown Hotel* makes a great spot for lunch or a drink. A minor road from here hugs the eastern shore of the lake the four miles to **POOLEY BRIDGE**, passing the incomparable *Sharrow Bay* (☏017684/ 86301, ⊛www.sharrow-bay.com; ❾ with dinner) on the way, one of England's finest hotel-restaurants.

Penrith and around

Once a thriving market town on the main north–south trading route, **PENRITH** today suffers from undue comparisons with the improbably pretty settlements of the nearby Lakes. The brisk streets, filled with no-nonsense shops and shoppers, have more in common with the towns of the North Pennines than the stone villages of south Cumbria, and even the local building materials emphasize the geographic shift. Its deep-red buildings were erected from the same rust-red sandstone used to construct **Penrith Castle** (daily: June–Sept 8am–9pm; Oct–May 8am–4.30pm; free) in the fourteenth century, as a bastion against raids from the north; it's now a romantic, crumbling ruin, opposite the train station. The town itself is at its best in the narrow streets, arcades and alleys off **Market Square**, and around **St Andrew's** churchyard, whose so-called "Giant's Grave" is actually a collection of pre-Norman crosses and "hogsback" tombstones.

Penrith **train station** is five minutes' walk south of Market Square and Middlegate. The **bus station** is on Albert Street, behind Middlegate, and has regular services to Patterdale, Keswick, Cockermouth, Carlisle and Alston. The **tourist office** on Middlegate (April–July & Sept Mon–Sat 9.30am–5pm, Sun 1–4.45pm; Aug Mon–Sat 9.30am–6pm, Sun 1–5.45pm; Oct–March Mon–Fri 10am–4pm, Sat 10.30am–4pm; ☎01768/867466, ⊕www.visiteden.co.uk) can help you find **accommodation**. The bulk of the B&Bs line Victoria Road, the continuation of King Street running south from Market Square: *Victoria Guest House*, at no. 3 (☎01768/863823, ⊕www.vicguesthouse.co.uk; no credit cards; ➋), and *Blue Swallow*, at no. 11 (☎01768/866335, ⊕www.blueswallow.co.uk; no credit cards; ➋), are the two most convenient choices. Or try *The Limes* at Redhills (☎01768/863343; ➌), one and a half miles west of town, a comfortable Victorian house in a rural setting. For **food**, the fantastically stocked J. & J. Graham's deli-grocery in Market Square can't be beaten. Otherwise, there's inexpensive tapas at *Costa's*, 9 Queen St (☎01768/895550), while *Ruhm*, 15 Victoria Rd, combines a gallery displaying art and ceramics with a cheery continental café.

Around Penrith

Several attractions lie close to town, the nearest being **Brougham Castle** (daily: April–Sept 10am–6pm; Oct 10am–5pm; £2.50; EH), a mile and a half south of Penrith by the River Eamont. Slightly further out, three miles southwest of town, reached from either the A66 or A592, is **Dalemain** (Easter to mid-Oct Mon–Thurs & Sun 10.30am–5pm; £5.50; gardens only £3.50; ⊕www.dalemain.com), a country house set in ample grounds. There's the usual run of imposing public rooms, while the medieval courtyard and Elizabethan great barn doubled as the grim schoolroom and dormitory of Lowood School in the TV adaptation of Charlotte Brontë's *Jane Eyre*. However, top local attraction is undoubtedly **Rheged** (daily 10am–5.30pm; ⊕www.rheged.com; free) at Redhills on the A66, a couple of minutes' drive from the M6 (junction 40); bus #X4/X5/X50 between Penrith and Keswick stops outside. Billed as Britain's largest earth-covered building, it takes its name from the ancient kingdom of Cumbria and features a spectacular atrium-lit underground visitor centre, which fills you in on the region's culture and history by way of exhibitions, local art and craft displays and family activities. There's also a giant-format cinema screen showing *Rheged: The Movie*, documenting a Cumbrian journey through time, plus other big-screen presentations (£5.50 each, though discounted combo tickets available); as well as the separate **National Mountaineering Exhibition** (same times; £5.50; Ⓦ www.mountain-exhibition.co.uk), presenting an entertaining history of mountain-climbers and climbing, from the Lake District to Everest.

The Cumbrian coast

South and west of the national park, the **Cumbrian coast** attracts much less attention than the spectacular scenery inland, but it would be a mistake to write it off. It splits into two distinct sections, the most accessible being the **Furness peninsulas** area (Ⓦ www.lake-district-peninsulas.co.uk), just a few miles from Windermere's Lakeside, where varied attractions include the monastic priory at **Cartmel** and the enjoyable market town of **Ulverston**. In addition, the dramatic ruins of nearby **Furness Abbey** have been attracting visitors for almost two hundred years. The **Cumbrian coast** itself is generally judged to begin at Silecroft and stretches for more than sixty miles to the small resort of Silloth, on the shores of the Solway Firth. In between lie isolated beaches and the headland of St Bees as well as the delights of the **Ravenglass and Eskdale Railway** and the attractive Georgian port of **Whitehaven**.

Cartmel and Holker Hall

Sheltered several miles inland from Morecambe Bay, **CARTMEL** grew up around its twelfth-century Augustinian priory and is still dominated by the proud **Church of St Mary and St Michael** (daily: June–Sept 9am–5.30pm; Oct–May 9am–3.30pm; tours Easter–Oct Wed 11am & 2pm; free), the only substantial remnant to survive the Dissolution. A diagonally crowned tower is the most distinctive feature outside, while the light and spacious Norman-transitional interior climaxes at a splendid chancel, illuminated by the 45-foot-high **East Window**. Everything else in the village is modest in scale, centred on the attractive **market square**, beyond the church, with its Elizabethan cobbles, water pump and fish slabs.

Trains stop at Cark-in-Cartmel, two miles southwest of the village proper; **buses** from there or from Grange-over-Sands train station run to the village. There's no tourist office, but the local **website**, Ⓦ www.cartmelvillage.com, can fill you in on history, sights, events and businesses. On Market Square, *Market Cross Cottage* (℡ 015395/36143, Ⓔ burgess@marketcross.freeserve .co.uk; no credit cards; ❸) is a cosy, seventeenth-century **B&B**. Up a notch, the celebrated *Cavendish Arms* on Cavendish Street (℡ 015395/36240, Ⓦ www .thecavendisharms.co.uk; ❹), just off the square, is a sixteenth-century inn, which retains many of its original features and offers good (if pricey) food. Otherwise, there's the *King's Arms* (℡ 015395/36220; ❸) on the square, which has attractive rooms, outdoor tables and bar meals.

One of Cumbria's most interesting country estates, **Holker Hall** (Easter–Oct Mon–Fri & Sun 10am–6pm; last admission 4.30pm; hall, gardens, grounds & motor museum £8.75; various cheaper combination tickets also available; Ⓦ www.holker-hall.co.uk) lies just over a mile north of Cark-in-Cartmel station. The vast, sandstone hall, which is made up of a pleasing combination of Victorian, Elizabethan and older styles, overlooks acres of beautifully designed gardens, woods and nature trails. Next to the house, the **Lakeland Motor Museum** (Easter–Oct Mon–Fri & Sun 10.30am–4.45pm) displays more than a hundred vehicles, from wartime ambulances to 1980s MGs. A special exhibition concentrates on the speed-freak Campbells – Sir Malcolm and son Donald.

Ulverston

The railway line winds westwards to **ULVERSTON**, a close-knit market town, which formerly prospered on the cotton, tanning and iron-ore industries. It's an attractive place, enhanced by its dappled grey limestone cottages and a jumble of cobbled alleys and traditional shops zigzagging off the central **Market Place**. Stalls are still set up here and in the surrounding streets every Thursday and Saturday; on other days (not Wed or Sun), the **market hall** on New Market Street is the centre of commercial life.

Ulverston's most famous son is Stan Laurel (born Arthur Stanley Jefferson), the whimpering, head-scratching half of the comic duo, celebrated in a mind-boggling collection of memorabilia at the **Laurel and Hardy Museum** (Feb–Dec daily 10am–4.30pm; £2; ⓦ www.laurel-and-hardy-museum.co.uk), up an alley at 4c Upper Brook St, near Market Place. It's also worth checking to see what's on at the **Lanternhouse**, on The Ellers (exhibitions, when on, Wed–Sat 11am–4pm; free; ⓦ www.welfare-state.org), just off the A590 at the bottom of Market Street and across Tank Square (a traffic roundabout). A group of multimedia artists known as Welfare State International occupy this award-winning conversion of an old school, presenting imaginative exhibitions relating to the "celebratory arts".

Ulverston **train station** is only a few minutes' walk from the town centre – head down Prince's Street and turn right at the main road for County Square. **Buses** arrive on nearby Victoria Road. The **tourist office** is in Coronation Hall on County Square (Mon–Sat 9am–5pm; ☏01229/587120, ⓦ www.ulverston.net). The 70-mile **Cumbria Way** long-distance footpath from Ulverston to Carlisle starts from The Gill, at the top of Upper Brook Street. **Bike rental** is available from Gill Cycles, on The Gill (☏01229/581116). Pick of the **B&Bs** is *Dyker Bank* (☏01229/582423; no credit cards; ❷), a Georgian house near the station at 2 Springfield Rd, while *Trinity House Hotel*, 200 yards downhill from the station, on the corner of Prince's Street and the main A590 (☏01229/588889 ⓦ www.traininghotel.co.uk; ❹, weekend room-only rate ❷), has spacious rooms in a handsome old building. There's also a great *Walker's Hostel* on Oubas Hill (☏01229/585588, ⓦ www.walkershostel.freeserve.co.uk; no credit cards; £13; closed Nov & Dec), fifteen minutes' walk from the centre on the A590 near Canal Head: there are thirty beds in small rooms (you won't have to share with strangers), with vegetarian breakfasts (included) and evening meals available (£7). **Cafés** include the funky *Hot Mango*, 27 King St, or the Buddhist-run (and organic vegetarian) *Peace Café* at 5 Cavendish Street (closed Sun & Mon), which has **Internet** access. Most of the **pubs** serve food, best being the *Farmers Arms* in Market Place.

Furness Abbey

Furness Abbey (April–Sept daily 10am–6pm; Oct daily 10am–5pm; Nov–March Wed–Sun 10am–4pm; £3; EH), a set of roofless sandstone arcades and pillars hidden in a wooded vale – the so-called "Valley of Deadly Nightshade", lies a mile and a half out of Barrow-in-Furness on the Ulverston road (local buses to Dalton-in-Furness and Ulverston pass close by). Now one of Cumbria's finest ruins, it was once the most powerful abbey in the north-west, possessing much of southern Cumbria as well as land in Ireland and the Isle of Man. By the fourteenth century it had become such a prize that the Scots raided it twice, though it survived until April 1536, when Henry VIII chose it to be the first of the large abbeys to be dissolved. The transepts stand virtually at their original height, while the massive slabs of stone-ribbed vaulting, richly embellished arcades and intricately carved *sedilia* in the presbytery are the equal of any of Yorkshire's far busier abbey ruins. The *Abbey Tavern* at the entrance serves drinks at tables scattered about some of the ruined outbuildings.

Ravenglass and Muncaster

On its way between Barrow-in-Furness and Whitehaven, the Cumbrian coast railway stops at **RAVENGLASS**, which preserves a row of characterful nineteenth-century cottages facing out across the mud flats and dunes. Despite appearances, the village dates back to the arrival of the Romans, who established a supply post here in the first century AD for the northern legions manning Hadrian's Wall. Look for the sign to the "Roman Bath House", just past the station: 500 yards up a single-track lane lie the fairly extensive remains of a fort which survived in Ravenglass until the fourth century.

Ravenglass station is the starting point for the **Ravenglass & Eskdale Railway** (Easter week & May–Oct daily; rest of year Sat & Sun; £7.80 return; ☎01229/717171, Ⓦ www.ravenglass-railway.co.uk), known affectionately as La'al Ratty. Opened in 1875 to carry ore from the Eskdale mines to the coastal railway, the tiny train, running on a 15-inch gauge track, takes forty minutes to wind its way through seven miles of forests and fields between the fell sides of the Eskdale Valley to Dalegarth station (see p.644). From the first stop on the line, Muncaster Mill, there's a path south through the woods to **Muncaster Castle**, where – apart from the rooms of the castle itself (Mon–Fri & Sun noon–5pm; £2.10) – there are also spectacular **gardens**, as well as an **owl centre** and **meadowvole maze** (both daily 10.30am–6pm, closing at dusk in winter; £5.70). There are B&Bs in Ravenglass, but the best **accommodation** hereabouts is at Muncaster Castle, where rooms (☎01229/717614, Ⓦ www.muncaster.co.uk; ❷, en suite ❸) in the converted stable block offer a comfortable night.

Whitehaven

Some fine Georgian houses mark out the centre of **WHITEHAVEN**, one of the few grid-planned towns in England. The economic expansion that forced this planning was as much due to the booming slave trade as to the more widely recognized coal traffic. Whitehaven spent a brief period during the eighteenth century as Britain's third busiest port (after London and Bristol), making it a prime target for an abortive raid led by Scottish-born American lieutenant **John Paul Jones**. Disgusted with the slave trade he witnessed while ship's mate in America, Jones returned to the port of his apprenticeship to rebel, but, let down by a drunk and potentially mutinous crew, he damaged only one of the two hundred boats in dock and his mini-crusade fell flat. All this and more is explained in **The Beacon** (Easter–Oct Tues–Sun 10am–5.30pm; Nov–Easter 10am–4.30pm; £4.25), an enterprising heritage centre on the harbour. After seeing this, stroll up Lowther Street to the **Rum Story** (daily: April–Sept 10am–5pm; Oct–March 10am–4pm; £4.50; Ⓦ www.rumstory.co.uk), housed in the eighteenth-century shop, courtyard and warehouses of the rum-producing Jefferson family. This is another place you could easily spend an hour or so, discovering Whitehaven's links with the Caribbean and learning all about rum, the Navy, temperance and the hideousness of the slaves' Middle Passage, amongst other matters. Also on Lowther Street, don't miss Michael Moon's secondhand **bookshop** at no. 19 (closed Sun), a bookworm's treasure trove.

From the **train station** you can walk around the harbour to The Beacon in less than ten minutes; the **bus station** is just across the Tesco supermarket's car park from the train station. The helpful **tourist office** is in the Market Hall on Market Place (Easter–Oct Mon–Sat 9.30am–5pm, plus July & Aug Sun 11am–3pm; Nov–Easter Mon–Sat 10am–4.30pm; ℡01946/852939, ⓌWwww.copelandbc.gov.uk), just back from the harbour. For **accommodation**, the best central B&B is the very comfortable *Corcickle Guest House*, 1 Corcickle (℡01946/692073, Ⓔcorcickle@tinyworld.co.uk; no credit cards; ❷), five minutes' walk from the centre – keep on up Lowther Street, past *Safeway* and *McDonald's* to find the row of Georgian townhouses. For **meals**, the *Courtyard Café* in the *Rum Story* serves wraps, sandwiches, baked potatoes and snacks under a glass roof. For something a bit more modish, there's *Zest Harbourside* on West Strand, a waterside café-bar doing tapas-style dishes. The sister restaurant, *Zest*, on Low Road (℡01946/692848; dinner only Wed–Sat), three-quarters of a mile out of the centre (on the B5349 Whitehaven–St Bees road), offers moderately priced Modern British cuisine.

Carlisle and around

The county capital of Cumbria and its only city, **CARLISLE** is also the repository of much of the region's history, its strategic location having been fought over for more than 2000 years. The original Celtic settlement was superseded by a Roman town, whose first fort was raised here in 72 AD. Carlisle thrived during the construction of Hadrian's Wall and then, long after the Romans had gone, the Saxon settlement was repeatedly fought over by the Danes and the Scots – the latter losing it eventually to the Normans. The struggle with the Scots defined the very nature of Carlisle as a border city: William Wallace was repelled in 1297 and Robert the Bruce eighteen years later, but Bonnie Prince Charlie's troops took Carlisle in 1745 after a six-day siege, holding it for only six weeks before surrendering to the Duke of Cumberland, who bombarded the city with cannon dragged from Whitehaven.

The main thoroughfare of English Street is pedestrianized as far as the expansive **Green Market** square, formerly heart of the medieval city, though a huge fire in 1392 destroyed its buildings and layout. The only historic survivors are the **market cross** (1682), the Elizabethan former **Town Hall** behind it, which now houses the tourist office and, at the southern end of Fisher Street, the timber-framed **Guildhall** (1405). It's only a few steps along to **Carlisle Cathedral** (Mon–Sat 7.30am–6.15pm, Sun 7.30am–5pm; £2 donation requested), founded in 1122 but embracing a considerably older heritage. Christianity was established in sixth-century Carlisle by St Kentigern (often known as St Mungo), who became the first bishop and patron saint of Glasgow. The cathedral's sandstone bulk has endured the ravages of time and siege: Parliamentarian troops during the Civil War destroyed all but two powerful arches of the original eight bays of the Norman nave, but there's still much to admire in the ornate fifteenth-century choir stalls and the glorious **East Window**, which features some of the finest pieces of fourteenth-century stained glass in the country. Opposite the main entrance, the reconstructed **Fratry**, or monastic building, houses the cathedral library, while its undercroft doubles as the *Prior's Kitchen*, a daytime café (Mon–Sat 10am–4pm) aptly using space that was once the monks' dining hall.

For more on Carlisle's history, head for the **Tullie House Museum and Art Gallery** (Mon–Sat 10am–5pm, Sun noon–5pm; Nov–March closes at 4pm; £5.20; ⓦwww.tulliehouse.co.uk), reached up Castle Street or through the cathedral grounds, via Abbey Street. This takes a highly imaginative approach to Carlisle's turbulent past, with special emphasis put on life on the edge of the Roman Empire – climbing a reconstruction of part of Hadrian's Wall, you learn about catapults and stone-throwers, while other sections elaborate on domestic life, work and burial practices. There's also plenty on the Jacobite siege of 1745, as well as a dramatic attempt to convey the intensity of the feuds between the "Reivers" – border families who, from the fourteenth to the seventeenth century, lived beyond the jurisdiction of the Scottish and English authorities in the so-called "Debatable Lands". A public walkway from outside Tullie House crosses Castle Way to **Carlisle Castle** (daily: Easter–Oct 9.30am–6pm; Nov–Easter 10am–4pm; £3.50; EH). This was originally built by William Rufus on the site of a Celtic hillfort, though having now clocked up over nine hundred years of continuous military use, the castle has undergone considerable changes. These are most evident in its outer bailey, which is filled with fairly modern buildings named after battles from the Napoleonic Wars and World War I. Apart from the gatehouse, with its reconstructed warden's quarters, it's the **inner bailey** surrounding the keep that's the real draw. It was here, in 1568, that Elizabeth I kept Mary Queen of Scots as her "guest". There's a **Military Museum** located in the former armoury, but much more interesting are the excellent displays in the **Keep**, and the elegant heraldic carvings made by prisoners in a second-floor alcove. **Guided tours** of the castle (Easter–Oct daily; ask at the entrance; an extra £1.60) help bring the history to life.

Practicalities

From either the **train station** (just off Botchergate) or the **bus station** (off Lowther Street, parallel to English Street), it's a five-minute walk to the **tourist office** in the Old Town Hall on Green Market (June–Aug Mon–Sat 9.30am–5.30pm, Sun 10.30am–4pm; March–May, Sept–Oct Mon–Sat 9.30am–5pm, Sun 10.30am–4pm; Nov–Feb Mon–Sat 10am–4pm; ☏01228/625600, ⓦwww.historic-carlisle.org.uk). Most of the budget **accommodation** is east of the tourist office, concentrated in a conservation area in the streets between Victoria Place and Warwick Road. Cultural **entertainment** revolves around the concerts, plays, performances, talks, exhibitions and workshops at Tullie House or the associated Stanwix Arts Theatre on Brampton Road (box office ☏01228/534664). The *Sportsman Inn* on Heads Lane (at the back of Marks and Spencer) is a cosy old **pub** – one of the oldest in the city – backing onto St Cuthbert's churchyard. Or there's the *Near Boot* at Tarraby, a mile and a half east of Carlisle, which serves Cumbrian real ales and good pub food.

B&Bs, guest houses and hotels

Aldingham House 1 Eden Mount, Stanwix ☏01228/522554, ⓦwww.aldinghamhouse.co.uk. Superior B&B accommodation, a 10min walk from the centre over Eden Bridge. Breakfasts include local sausages and bacon, pancakes and fruit smoothies. ⑤

Crown and Mitre English St, Green Market ☏01228/525491, ⓦwww.crownandmitre-hotel-carlisle.com. Refurbished Edwardian hotel with indoor pool and whirlpool spa. Reduced weekend rates available. ⑥

Lakes Court Hotel Court Square ☏01228/531951, ⓦwww.lakescourthotel.co.uk. Smart and spacious rooms in a renovated Victorian building. Weekend rates typically knock off about ten percent. **⑤**

Langleigh House 6 Howard Place ☎01228/530440, ⓦwww.langleighhouse.co.uk. Modest townhouse B&B with eight rooms, including a family room that sleeps four. No credit cards. **②**

Number Thirty One 31 Howard Place ☎01228/597080, ⓦwww.number31.freeservers.com. Grand Victorian house offering comfort in three well-appointed rooms. Dinner (£20) by arrangement. **⑤**

Youth hostel

Old Brewery Residences Bridge Lane, Caldewgate ☎0870/770 5752, ⓔdee.carruthers @unn.ac.uk. Summer-only (July & Aug) YHA accommodation, just west of the town centre (take the A595, and it's on the right past the castle), in university halls of residence. Dorm beds £14

Cafés and restaurants

Alexandros 68 Warwick Rd ☎01228/592227. Greek specialities, from dips, salads and stuffed vegetables to chargrilled meats and seafood. Closed all Sun, plus Mon lunch. Moderate.

Café Courtyard Treasury Court. Enter through the gates on Scotch or Fisher streets to find this hidden-away café, serving sandwiches, salads and light meals. Inexpensive.

Café Sol Castle St, opposite the cathedral. Funky little café-bar serving good-value breakfasts, gourmet sandwiches and *panini* melts. Inexpensive.

The Lemon Lounge 18 Fisher St ☎01228/546363. Easygoing cellar bistro with a sun-trap outdoor terrace, where you can roam the gastronomic world. It's inexpensive at lunch; prices rise slightly at night. Moderate.

Meat and Two Veg Laughingstock, Crosby, 4 miles east of Carlisle ☎01228/573111. A refined contemporary British restaurant (menu changes monthly) in a minimalist setting – the name reflects the laidback atmosphere and warm service. Dinner only, closed Sun & Mon. Expensive.

Number 10 10 Eden Mount ☎01228/524183. Townhouse restaurant that many rate as the best in the city, serving a seasonally changing Modern English menu. Dinner only, closed Sun & Mon. Expensive.

The Weary Sportsman Castle Carrock, Brampton, 8 miles east of Carlisle ☎01228/670230. Traditional eighteenth-century inn on the outside, utterly contemporary inside, with fashionable food, from steak and ale pie to chilli prawns with Thai spices. No lunch Mon. Moderate.

Around Carlisle

Eight miles east of Carlisle, the market town of **BRAMPTON** is at the centre of several outlying attractions that can make a fine day's tour from the city. Two miles south of Brampton, on the B6413 (Castle Carrock road), **Talkin Tarn** is the city's traditional bolthole, a pretty lake set within 120 acres of farm and woodland. A similar distance to the northeast of Brampton (just north of the A69, at Low Row), the ruins of **Lanercost Priory** (Easter–Sept daily 10am–6pm; Oct daily 10am–5pm; £2.50; EH) occupy a lovely spot in deep countryside. The Augustinian priory dates from 1166 – though carved stones found here date back to Roman times – and you can view the remains of a medieval undercroft and the Prior's Tower; the nearby *Abbey Bridge Inn* is the local hostelry.

A little further east, signposted from the A69 five miles beyond Brampton and fifteen from Carlisle – **Birdoswald Fort** (March–Nov daily 10am–5.30pm; £3; half-price for EH members; ⓦwww.birdoswaldromanfort .org.uk) is the area's real highlight. One of sixteen forts along Hadrian's Wall, it has all tiers of the Roman structure intact, the defences comprising an earth ditch, a large section of masonry wall, and the trench and mound foundations behind. An informative visitor centre fleshes out the historic background, and then you can walk the third of a mile to the nearby **Harrow's Scar Milecastle** for some spectacular views. There's a tearoom and picnic area at the fort, while the fort's residential study centre is available to overnight hikers and others as a summer-only **youth hostel** (☎0870/770 6124, ⓔgreenhead@yha.org.uk; dorm beds £11.50), open mid-July to first week of September only.

The **Hadrian's Wall Bus** (see p.748) leaves Carlisle three times daily in summer (June to mid-Sept, plus Sun in April, May & Oct), calling at Brampton (20min), Lanercost (30min) and Birdoswald (40min). The rest of the year, the #685 from Carlisle runs to Brampton and Gilsland (the latter a two-mile walk from Birdoswald).

Travel details

Buses

For information on all local and national bus services, contact Traveline ☎0870/608 2608 (daily 7am–9pm), ⓦ www.traveline.org.uk.

Carlisle to: Keswick (4 daily; 1hr 30min); Lancaster (4 daily; 1hr 10min); London (3 daily; 5hr 30min); Manchester (2 daily; 2hr 30min); Newcastle (hourly; 2hr 30min); Whitehaven (hourly; 1hr 30min); Windermere/Bowness (3 daily; 2hr 20min).

Kendal to: Ambleside (hourly; 40min); Cartmel (7 daily; 1hr); Grasmere (hourly; 1hr); Keswick (hourly; 1hr 30min); Lancaster (hourly; 1hr); Windermere/Bowness (hourly; 30min).

Keswick to: Ambleside (hourly; 1hr); Buttermere (2 daily; 30min); Carlisle (4 daily; 1hr 30min); Cockermouth (7 daily; 35min); Grasmere (hourly; 40min); Kendal (hourly; 1hr 30min); Manchester (1–3 daily; 3hr); Seatoller (9 daily; 30min); Whitehaven (5 daily; 1hr 30min); Windermere (hourly; 1hr).

Windermere to: Ambleside (up to 3 hourly; 15min); Carlisle (3 daily; 2hr 20min); Grasmere (hourly; 30min); Kendal (hourly; 30min); Keswick (hourly; 1hr); Lancaster (hourly; 1hr 45min); Manchester (3 daily; 3hr).

Trains

For information on all local and national rail services, contact National Rail Enquiries ☎08457/484950, ⓦ www.nationalrail.co.uk.

Carlisle to: Barrow-in-Furness (5 daily; 2hr 20min); Lancaster (every 30min; 1hr); Manchester (5 daily; 2hr 30min); Newcastle (hourly; 1hr 20min); Preston (21 daily; 1hr 20min–1hr 40min); Whitehaven (hourly; 1hr 10min).

Oxenholme (Lake District) to: Carlisle (14 daily; 40–50min); Manchester (1–5 daily; 1hr 40min); Penrith (14 daily; 30min); Preston (hourly; 30–40 min).

Windermere to: Kendal (hourly; 15min); Oxenholme (hourly; 20min).

Yorkshire

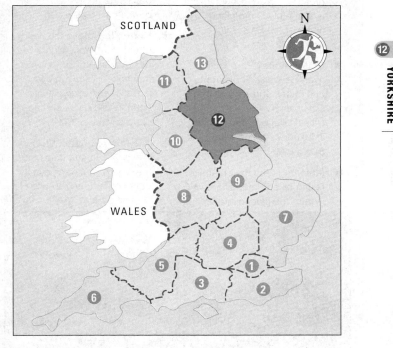

✳ **National Museum of Photography, Film and Television, Bradford** The north's most hands-on museum has all there is to know about film, photography and TV. **See p.671**

✳ **Haworth** One of England's greatest literary pilgrimages is to the bleak moorland home of the Brontë sisters. **See p.672**

✳ **Bolton Abbey** Priory ruins, riverside walks and sumptuous rooms and food at the *Devonshire Arms* – this Dales' village is the ultimate in luxury weekend getaways. **See p.676**

✳ **Malham** Make the breathtaking hike from Malham village to the glorious natural amphitheatre of Malham Cove and the glassy expanse of Malham Tarn. **See p.678**

✳ **York** From historic York Minster to the award-winning National Railway Museum, there's never a dull day in the north's most compelling city. **See p.690**

✳ **Hutton le Hole** In the heart of the North York Moors lies this quintessential English moorland village – grassy lanes, sheep everywhere, comfortable B&Bs and an old pub. **See p.707**

✳ **The Magpie Café, Whitby** The best fish and chips in the world? You decide at Whitby's famous fish-and-chip emporium. **See p.716**

△ Malham Cove

Yorkshire

F ew visitors pass through **Yorkshire**, England's largest county, without spending time in history-soaked **York**, for centuries England's second city. Famed primarily for its minster, the city is an ensemble of tiny medieval alleys, castle ruins, tucked-away churches, riverside gardens and topnotch museums. York's mixture of medieval, Georgian and Victorian architecture is mirrored in miniature in the prosperous north and east of the county by towns such as **Beverley**, centred on another soaring minster; **Richmond**, banked under a crag-bound castle; and **Ripon**, gathered around its honey-stoned cathedral. **Knaresborough** shares similar attributes, but is overshadowed by the faded spa-town gentility of neighbouring **Harrogate**. The Yorkshire coast, too, retains something of the grandeur of the days when its towns were the first to promote themselves as resorts: places such as **Bridlington** and **Scarborough** boomed in the nineteenth century and again in the postwar period, though the best of the Yorkshire coast is found in characterful, historic places such as **Whitby** and **Robin Hood's Bay**.

The engine of growth during the Industrial Revolution was not in the north of the county, but in the south and west. By the nineteenth century, Leeds, Bradford, Sheffield and their satellites were the world's mightiest producers of textiles and steel. Ruthless economic logic devastated the area in the last century, leaving only disused mills, abandoned works and great soot-covered civic buildings. However, a new vigour has infused South and West Yorkshire during the last decade, and the city-centre transformations of **Leeds** and **Sheffield** in particular have been remarkable. Both are now making open play for tourists with a series of high-profile attractions, while **Bradford** and its National Museum of Photography, Film and Television waylays people on their way to **Haworth**, birthplace of the Brontë sisters.

During even the worst of times, broad swathes of moorland survived above the slum- and factory-choked valleys, and it can come as a surprise to discover the amount of open countryside on Leeds' and Bradford's doorsteps. The **Yorkshire Dales**, to the northwest, form a lovely patchwork of stone-built villages, limestone hills and serene valleys. To the northeast lie the **North York Moors**, the county's other National Park, whose bleak upland areas are tempered by a tremendous rugged coastline. Of the predictable roster of stately homes, **Castle Howard** stands supreme, while from an earlier age, before the Reformation, survive many beautifully situated **monastic ruins** – at Fountains, Rievaulx, Bolton Abbey, Whitby and elsewhere. These are graceful counterpoints to the more solid remains of the **castles** at York, Richmond, Scarborough and Pickering, the foremost of more than twenty castles raised in Yorkshire by the Normans.

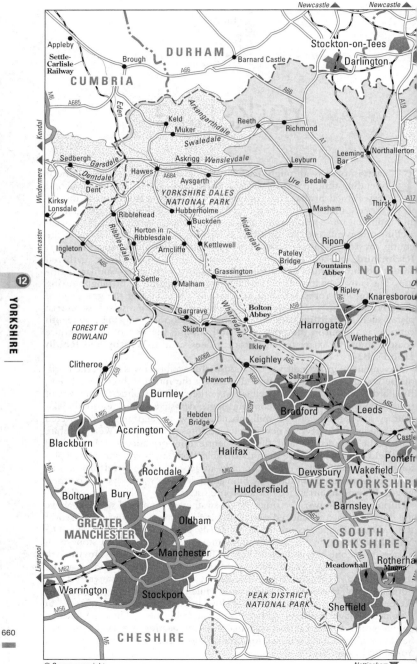

© Crown copyright

Newcastle ▲   Newcastle ▲

Nottingham ▼

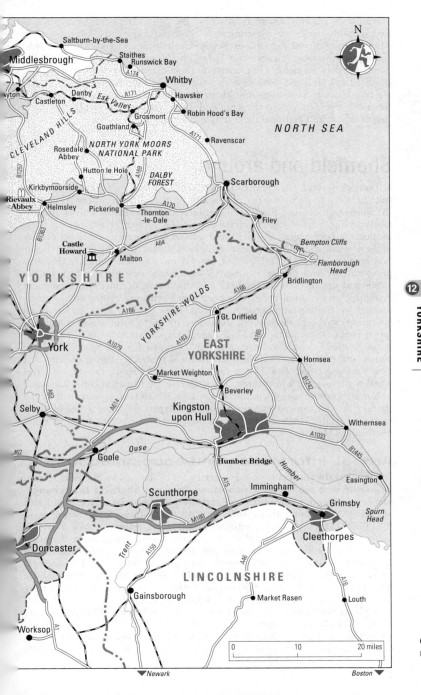

Trains are a useful way of approaching the Moors, Yorkshire coast and the Dales, with lines to Scarborough (from York) and Whitby (from Middlesbrough), and the famous **Settle–Carlisle** line (accessed from Leeds) running to the southern and west Dales. The **North Country Rover** ticket (any four days in eight; £59) covers unlimited train travel north of Leeds, Bradford and Hull and south of Newcastle and Carlisle. **Bus** services – including post buses and summer-only **Moorsbus** shuttles – are collected in special timetable booklets (*Moors Explorer* and *Dales Explorer*), available free from tourist offices and National Park information centres.

Sheffield and around

Yorkshire's second city, **SHEFFIELD** remains inextricably linked with its steel industry, in particular the production of high-quality cutlery. As early as the fourteenth century, the carefully fashioned, hard-wearing knives of hard-working Sheffield enjoyed national repute. Technological advances in steel production later turned Sheffield into one of the country's foremost centres of heavy and specialist engineering, which meant the city suffered heavy bombing in World War II. However, more damaging than bombs to the city's pre-eminence was the steel industry's subsequent downturn, which by the 1980s had tipped parts of Sheffield into dispiriting decline. The subsequent economic and cultural revival has been rapid, with the centre utterly transformed by flagship architectural projects, from gardens to galleries. As an emerging city-break destination, Sheffield can't fail to surprise, while a glut of sports facilities (including the Ski Village, Europe's largest artificial ski resort) backs Sheffield's claim to be considered "National City of Sport". Steel, of course, still underpins much of what Sheffield is about – this is the city that gave the world *The Full Monty*, the black comedy about five former steel workers carving out a new career as a striptease act. Museum collections tend to home in on the region's industrial heritage, which is complemented by the startling science-and-adventure exhibits at **Magna** built on a disused steel works at nearby **Rotherham**, the former coal and iron town a few miles northeast of the city.

Arrival, information and accommodation

Sheffield's **train station** is on the eastern edge of the city, by Sheffield Hallam University, with the bus and coach station, known as **Sheffield Interchange**, two hundred yards to the north on Pond Street. The **tourist office** is on Tudor Square (Mon–Thurs 10am–4pm, Fri 10.30am–4pm, Sat 9.30am–4pm; ☎0114/221 1900, ⊛www.sheffieldcity.co.uk), five minutes' walk from the stations, near the Winter Gardens. Most local **buses** depart from the High Street, while the **Supertram** system connects the city centre with Meadowhall (northeast), Middlewood (northwest) and Halfway (southeast). For fare and timetable information, visit the **Travel Information Centre** at the Interchange (Mon–Fri 8am–5.30pm, Sat 8.30am–5pm, Sun 9am–5pm). A one-day TravelMaster Pass (£4.95) gives unlimited travel on buses, trains and trams throughout South Yorkshire. **Internet** access is available at Havana Internet Café, 32–34 Division St, and – free – at the City Library.

Sheffield has a fair amount of mid-range central **accommodation** – even so, the tourist office's free room-booking service can come in handy (☎0114/201 1011).

Hotels and guest houses

Hotel Bristol Blonk St ☎0114/220 4000, ⓦ www.hotel-bristol.co.uk. Breezy, informal business hotel near the river, quays and markets. ❺

Cutlers George St ☎0114/273 9939, ⓦ www.cutlershotel.co.uk. Handily located city-centre inn, close to the theatres, with budget en-suite rooms, bistro and bar. ❹

Hilton Victoria Quays, Furnival Rd ☎0114/252 5500, ⓦ www.hilton.com. Four-star hotel that makes superb use of its revitalized canalside site, with a range of leisure facilities. ❺

Houseboat Hotels Victoria Quays ☎0114/244 4136 or 07974 590264, ⓦ www.houseboathotels.com. Two moored houseboats, available by the night, both with en-suite bathrooms, kitchens, TV and video. They're rented exclusively, for two people ❹ or four people ❺

Travel Inn Metro Angel St ☎0870/238 3324, ⓦ www.travelinn.co.uk. Few frills in this standard chain hotel, but you can't beat the price for convenient room-only accommodation. ❸

Whitley Hall Elliott Lane, Grenoside, 4 miles north ☎0114/245 4444, ⓦ www.whitleyhall.com. Country house hotel with Elizabethan roots, accessible from the motorways or the city centre (A61 out of Sheffield; call for directions). ❻

University accommodation

University of Sheffield ☎0114/222 6059, ⓦ www.sheffield.ac.uk. Single rooms from £15 per person in the various student halls of residence. Available mid-June to mid-Sept only. Reservations essential.

The City

New-look Sheffield is at its best around the landmark **Town Hall**, at the junction of Pinstone and Surrey streets. Completed in 1897, it's topped by the figure of Vulcan, the Roman god of fire and metalworking, and the facade sports a fine frieze depicting traditional Sheffield industries. The adjacent **Peace Gardens** feature central water jets that whoosh up intermittently to send children giddy with delight. Rising to the east, a minute's walk away, is the main symbol of the city regeneration, the **Winter Gardens** (daily 8am–6pm; free), an arched steel-and-wood glasshouse almost 200 feet long and over 60 feet high – inside, the central Norfolk pines will eventually touch the roof. Sheffield's **Millennium Galleries** (Mon–Sat 10am–5pm, Sun 11am–5pm; free, visiting exhibitions £4; ⓦ www.sheffieldgalleries.org.uk) back onto the gardens where, in the **Metalworks Gallery**, you can discover why the eighteenth-century city's natural endowments (a fast water supply, forests for charcoal, and gritstone deposits) ensured the rapid development of the cutlery industry. There's also the highly diverting **Ruskin Gallery**, based on the collection founded by John Ruskin in 1875 to improve the working people of Sheffield. A library of classic nineteenth-century texts ("the working man's Bodleian") is complemented by an intriguing selection of watercolours, sketches, minerals, paintings, casts and medieval illuminated manuscripts.

Southeast of the Winter Gardens, clubs and galleries exist alongside arts and media businesses in the **Cultural Industries Quarter**, while north of the stations, near the River Don, **Castlegate** and its traditional markets are still undergoing redevelopment. Closer to the Town Hall, at the end of Fargate, the city's **Cathedral of St Peter and St Paul** retains elements of its fifteenth-century origins, though it's been restored on many occasions. Across from here sits the **Cutler's Hall** of 1832, an imposing reminder of Sheffield's traditions. The Company of Cutlers was first established in 1624 to regulate the affairs of the cutlery industry, and this is the third hall on the site. South of the Town Hall, the pedestrianized **Moor Quarter** draws in shoppers, though it's the nearby **Devonshire Quarter**, centred on Division Street, that is the trendiest shopping area.

On the city's western outskirts, the **Mappin Art Gallery** in Weston Park and adjacent **City Museum** are currently under long-term restoration (due to reopen in 2005), though you could still make a case for coming out this side of the city to visit the lovely **Botanical Gardens** (Mon–Fri 8am–dusk, Sat & Sun 10am–dusk; free). Closer in, fifteen minutes' walk north of the cathedral, the **Kelham Island Museum** on Alma Street (Mon–Thurs 10am–4pm, Sun 11am–4.45pm; £3.50), reveals the breadth of the city's industrial output, where exhibits range from a colossal twelve-thousand horsepower steam engine to a silver-plated penny-farthing made for the tsar of Russia.

Rotherham: Magna

About six miles northeast of Sheffield, across the M1, **ROTHERHAM** sees itself as just as much a gateway to Yorkshire as its bigger neighbour. Its churches are its proudest feature and, in the Chapel of Our Lady on Rotherham Bridge, the town has one of only four surviving examples in England of a medieval bridge chantry. For most visitors to the region, however, this pales in comparison with **Magna** (daily 10am–5pm; £8; ⓦ www.magnatrust.org.uk), the UK's first science adventure centre, housed in the building of a former steelworks on Sheffield Road (A6178), Templeborough, just off the M1 a mile from the Meadowhall shopping complex (bus #69 from either Sheffield or Rotherham Interchanges, or a ten-minute taxi ride from Meadowhall's supertram station). The massive building offers four gadget-packed, themed **pavilions** around the four basic elements of earth, air, fire and water, and although most of the centre is aimed at children, the half-hourly *Big Melt* will have everyone gripping onto the railings. An original arc furnace is used in a bone-shaking light and sound show, showing the moment when metal is transformed into white molten steel.

Eating, drinking and nightlife

Sheffield has plenty of great **café-bars** and good-value **restaurants**, while the **pubs** listed below are those with a bit of character and staying power. Sheffield's Crucible, Lyceum and Studio **theatres** on Tudor Square (ⓣ 0114/249 6000, ⓦ www.sheffieldtheatres.co.uk) put on a full programme of theatre, dance, comedy and concerts. The Showroom, 7 Paternoster Row (ⓣ 0114/275 7727, ⓦ www.showroom.org.uk), is the biggest independent **cinema** outside London. Friday's *Sheffield Telegraph* lists the week's theatre performances, concerts and films. Also look out for the *Dirty Stop Out's Guide* (£2.50; ⓦ www.dirtystopoutsguide.co.uk), a comprehensive tell-it-like-it-is listings-and-reviews booklet, available at the tourist office.

Cafés and café-bars

Blue Moon Café 2 St James St. Relax in the skylit dining room, next to the cathedral, and tuck into homemade vegetarian/vegan food. Closes 8pm; closed Sun.

The Forum 127–129 Division St. Long the main-stay of the Devonshire Quarter, the *Forum* has a great menu and laid-back clientele. Closed Sun.

Jules & Giovanna 1 Brown St. Deli-café by the Site Gallery, serving Mediterranean snacks, pastas and breakfast. Closes 5pm; closed Sun.

Showroom 7 Paternoster Row. Café-restaurant on one side and a great bar on the other. Check out their weeknight film-and-food offers.

Twenty Two A 22a Norfolk Row. This little café is a nice find for breakfast, inventive sandwiches or more substantial meals like *mee goreng* (fried noodles) or sesame prawns. Closes 5pm; closed Sun.

Restaurants

Nonna's 539–541 Eccleshall Rd ⓣ 0114/268 6166. Where the Sheffield beautiful hang out, a combination Italian café, wine bar and restaurant. Moderate.

Pizza Volante 255 Glossop Rd ⓣ 0114/273 9056. Rumbustious pasta and pizza place that's a hit with locals and students. Inexpensive to Moderate.

Slammers 625 Eccleshall Rd ☏0114/268 0999. Seafood (and pretty much only seafood) is what's on offer in Sheffield's buzziest restaurant. Bring your own wine allowed Mon–Wed, but fully licensed. Expensive.

Trippet's Wine Bar 89 Trippets Lane ☏0114/278 0198. There's always a nice atmosphere in this unstuffy wine bar behind West St. Moderate.

Vietnamese Noodle Bar 200–202 London Rd ☏0114/258 3608. BYO place that's hugely popular for cheap Oriental eats – it pays to book ahead. Inexpensive.

Pubs, clubs and live music

The Boardwalk 39 Snig Hill ☏0114/279 9090, ⓦwww.theboardwalklive.co.uk. Popular venue for indie bands, rock, folk and comedy.

The Casbah 1 Wellington St ☏0114/275 6077. As in "Rock the . . .", which tells you what to expect – a stroll down punk/rock memory lane.

Demspey's 1 Hereford St ☏0114/275 4616. Bar and club with the most reliable gay scene in the city.

Devonshire Cat 49 Wellington St, Devonshire Green. A big pub where there's a beer menu on every table and good cheap food. Or take a walk out (15min from the centre) to the *Fat Cat* 23 Alma St, the *Devonshire Cat*'s cosier, older sister.

Gatecrasher One 112 Arundel St ☏0114/276 6777. Formerly *The Republic*, now relaunched as flagship of the Gatecrasher clubbing brand.

Leadmill 6–7 Leadmill Rd ☏0114/221 2828, ⓦwww.leadmill.co.uk. Hosts live bands and DJs most nights of the week.

Sheffield Hallam University Nelson Mandela Building, Pond St ☏0114/253 4122. Regular gigs and club nights.

University of Sheffield Students' Union Western Bank ☏0114/222 8777. Regular indie/rock gigs and a varied programme of club nights, including the city's biggest gay/lesbian night, *Climax*.

The Washington 79 Fitzwilliam St. A favoured muso's pub, just two minutes across the green from Division St.

Leeds and around

Yorkshire's commercial capital, and one of the fastest-growing cities in the country, **LEEDS** has undergone a radical transformation in recent years. There's still a true northern grit to its character, and in many of its dilapidated suburbs, but the grime has been removed from the Victorian centre and the city is revelling in its renaissance as a financial, administrative and cultural boom town. The most obvious manifestation of change has been the advent of late-opening cafés, bars, clubs and eclectic restaurants, and the arrival of the swanky department store, Harvey Nichols. It's also long been the region's **cultural** centre, home to Opera North, the noted West Yorkshire Playhouse and a triennial international piano competition that ranks among the world's top musical events. Museums start with the hugely impressive **Royal Armouries**, which hold the national arms and armour collection, while the **City Art Gallery** has one of the best collections of British twentieth-century art outside London. **Leeds Industrial Museum** and **Abbey House Museum** take care of the city's historical legacy, while further from the city you might try to see one of the country's great Georgian piles, **Harewood House**.

Arrival, information and accommodation

Leeds Station is off City Square on the southern flank of the city centre, and houses the Gateway Yorkshire **tourist office** in the Arcade (Mon 10am–5.30pm, Tues–Sat 9.30am–5.30pm, Sun 10am–4pm; ☏0113/242 5242, ⓦwww.leeds.gov.uk). The **bus station** occupies a site to the east, behind Kirkgate Market, on St Peter's Street, close to the West Yorkshire Playhouse. The **Metro Travel Centre** at the bus station has up-to-date service details (Mon–Fri 8.30am–5.30pm, Sat 9am–4.30pm; ⓦwww.wymetro.com), or call **Metroline** (daily 8am–8pm; ☏0113/245 7676). Bus/train day rover (£4.50),

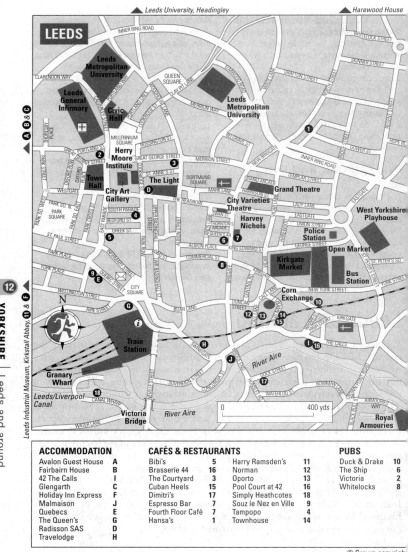

ACCOMMODATION

Avalon Guest House	A
Fairbairn House	B
42 The Calls	I
Glengarth	C
Holiday Inn Express	F
Malmaison	J
Quebecs	E
The Queen's	G
Radisson SAS	D
Travelodge	H

CAFÉS & RESTAURANTS

Bibi's	5	Harry Ramsden's	11
Brasserie 44	16	Norman	12
The Courtyard	3	Oporto	13
Cuban Heels	15	Pool Court at 42	16
Dimitri's	17	Simply Heathcotes	18
Espresso Bar	7	Souz le Nez en Ville	9
Fourth Floor Café	7	Tampopo	4
Hansa's	1	Townhouse	14

PUBS

Duck & Drake	10
The Ship	6
Victoria	2
Whitelocks	8

separate bus or train day rovers (£3.80 each) and a family day rover (£6) are all valid for use on local buses and trains. **Taxis** are available at the train station, outside the bus station, and on New Briggate. The best places for **Internet** access are Internet Exchange, 29 Boar Lane (☎0113/242 1093) and at the Central Library, Calverley St (☎0113/247 8274).

The recent growth in **accommodation** has been in stylish designer hotels, many located in revamped old buildings, while plenty of cheaper B&Bs lie out to the northwest in the student area of Headingley, a bus or taxi ride away. For **short breaks** and weekends away contact the tourist office's special booking line on ⓣ0800/808050. There's no city youth hostel; the nearest one is at Haworth.

Guest houses and hotels

Avalon Guest House 132 Woodsley Rd ⓣ0113/243 2545. Decent budget B&B near the university in a large Victorian house. ❷

Fairbairn House 71–75 Clarendon Rd ⓣ0113/343 6633. Victorian house owned by the university. Quiet setting and good value. ❷

42 The Calls 42 The Calls ⓣ0113/244 0099, ⓦwww.42thecalls.co.uk. Converted riverside grain mill, where rooms come with great beds, sharp bathrooms, filter coffee machine and CD player, though the cheapest rates are for the smallest "studio" rooms. Breakfast not included. ❼

Glengarth Hotel 162 Woodsley Rd ⓣ0113/245 7940. Homely B&B with a variety of single and double rooms. No credit cards. ❷

Holiday Inn Express Cavendish St ⓣ0113/242 6200, ⓦwww.ichotelsgroup.com. On the western edge of the centre, but only a 15min walk from the shops, bars and restaurants. The one-size-fits-all room rate includes continental breakfast. ❹

Malmaison Sovereign Quay ⓣ0113/398 1000, ⓦwww.malmaison.com. Classy waterside premises, with big beds, power showers, CD players and cable TV in the rooms. Breakfast not included. ❼

Quebecs 9 Quebec St ⓣ0113/244 8989, ⓦwww.theetongroup.com. A five-star boutique makeover for the former Leeds and County Liberal Club. Weekend rates from £99. ❼

The Queen's City Square ⓣ0113/243 1323, ⓦwww.paramount-hotels.co.uk. Refurbished four-star Art Deco landmark. Even during the week you can sometimes get a room from £70 (the code given is the official rate). ❼

Radisson SAS No.1 The Light, The Headrow ⓣ0113/236 6000, ⓦwww.radissonsas.com. Snazzy rooms and suites reflect high-tech, Art Deco or modern Italian design. Breakfast not normally included, though it is with weekend rates (from £110), while deals booked through the website sometimes offer rooms for around £75. ❽

Travelodge Blayds Court, off Swinegate ⓣ0870/191 1655 or 08700/850950, ⓦwww.travelodge.co.uk. Reasonable centrally located accommodation. Set price per room, breakfast not included. ❸

Student accommodation

Clarence Dock Holiday Apartments Clarence Dock ⓣ0113/233 6100. Near the Royal Armouries, available mid-July to the beginning of September. Single en-suite rooms (£25 per person per night for the first night, or £30 for two nights and £15 a night thereafter) in shared five-bed flats.

The City

Opposite the train station, a prancing statue of Edward, the Black Prince, welcomes you to **City Square**, a smartened-up space that still retains its bronze nymph gas-lamps. It's a short walk to the top of East Parade where you can't miss **Leeds Town Hall**, one of the finest expressions of nineteenth-century civic pride in the country. The masterpiece of local architect Cuthbert Broderick, it's colonnaded on all sides, guarded by white lions and topped by a perky clocktower. East from the Town Hall and you're on **The Headrow**, the city's central spine, with Leeds' **City Art Gallery** (Mon–Sat 10am–5pm, Wed 10am–8pm, Sun 1–5pm; free; ⓦwww.leeds.gov.uk/artgallery) the major draw. Changing selections from the permanent collection of nineteenth- and twentieth-century art and sculpture are presented, with an understandable bias towards pieces by Henry Moore and Barbara Hepworth, both former students at the Leeds School of Art; Moore's *Reclining Woman* lounges at the top of the steps outside the gallery. From the gallery, a slender bridge connects to the adjacent **Henry Moore Institute** (daily 10am–5.30pm, Wed until 9pm; free; ⓦwww.henry-moore-fdn.co.uk), devoted to showcasing temporary exhibitions of sculpture from all periods and nationalities.

Most visitors make a beeline for the brimming, shop-filled arcades on either side of pedestrianized **Briggate**. These nineteenth-century palaces of marble, mahogany, stained glass and mosaics have been magnificently restored and perhaps the most splendidly decorated of all is the light-flooded **Victoria Quarter**, with Harvey Nichols as its designer lodestone. Across Vicar Lane, **Kirkgate Market** (closed Wed afternoon & Sun) is the largest market in the north of England. Housed in a superb Edwardian building, it's a descendant of the medieval woollen markets that were instrumental in making Leeds the early focus of the region's textile industry. On the corner of Vicar Lane and Duncan Street, the elliptical, domed **Corn Exchange** (open daily) was built in 1863, and is now a hip market for jewellery, retro clothes, furnishings, music and other bits and bobs.

The biggest transformation in Leeds has been along the **Leeds–Liverpool Canal** and **River Aire**, formerly a stagnant relic of industrial decline. At **Granary Wharf**, a couple of minutes' walk from the train station, stores, restaurants and craft shops fill the extensive cobbled, vaulted arches (the "Dark Arches"), while every weekend (and bank holiday) a market with stalls, bands and entertainers spills out onto the canal basin. Further east along the river (10min walk, or bus #752 runs from Eastgate to Clarence Dock) beckons the gun-metal grey bulk of the **Royal Armouries** (daily 10am–5pm; free; ⓦ www.armouries.org.uk), purpose-built to house the arms and armour collection from the Tower of London. Themed galleries cover concepts such as "War" and "Hunting", with displays – ranging from gun emplacements to Mughal Indian elephant armour – backed up by intelligent commentary, video exhibits and documentary evidence. Interpretations and demonstrations take place throughout the day (you're handed a schedule on entering), so you might learn smallsword techniques from a Georgian swordsmaster or sixteenth-century javelin skills in the outdoor Tiltyard.

Out of the city

The nearest of the outlying sights is the **Thackray Museum** on Beckett Street (daily 10am–5pm, last admission 3pm; £4.90; ⓦ www.thackraymuseum .org), a mile east of the city centre next to St James' Hospital; buses #4, #22, #42, #49, #50 and #88 all run past. Essentially a medical history museum, it's a hugely popular and entertaining place – ghoulish too at times when it delves into topics like surgery before anaesthetics, and the workings of the human intestine. For Leeds' industrial past, visit the vast **Leeds Industrial Museum**, two miles west of the centre off Canal Road (Tues–Sat 10am–5pm, Sun 1–5pm; £2; ⓦ www.leeds.gov.uk/armleymills), which runs between Armley and Kirkstall Road – take bus #5a, #14, #66 or #67. There's been a mill on the site since at least the seventeenth century, and the present building was one of the world's largest woollen mills until its closure in 1969. You should also see the bucolic ruins and cloisters of **Kirkstall Abbey** (dawn to dusk; free), the city's most important medieval relic. Built between 1152 and 1182 by Cistercian monks from Fountains Abbey, it was the site of 400 years of monastic life before being surrendered to Henry VIII in 1539. The abbey lies about three miles northwest of the city centre on Abbey Road; take bus #732, #733, #734, #735 or #736. The former gatehouse now provides the setting for the **Abbey House Museum** (Tues–Fri & Sun 10am–5pm, Sat noon–5pm; £3), with two floors dedicated to Victorian Leeds. Four miles east of the city, the Tudor-Jacobean house of **Temple Newsam** (April–Oct Tues–Sun 10.30am–5pm; Nov–March Tues–Sun 10.30am–4pm; £3) contains many of the paintings and much of the decorative art owned by Leeds City Art Gallery. The house has recently been restored, and new displays installed, though many still come out solely for the splendid park, walled gardens and estate grounds (daily 10am–dusk; free), laid out by Capability Brown in 1762. There's an hourly Sunday bus service to the house; otherwise, parking costs £1.50.

If you were to see just one stately home in the area, though, it should be **Harewood House**, seven miles north of Leeds (Easter–Oct daily 11am–4.30pm, grounds & bird garden 10am–6pm; Nov–Easter Sat & Sun only; £9.50, grounds & bird garden only £6.75, plus £1 extra on Sun and bank hols; ⓦwww.harewood.org). Conceived in 1759 by York architect John Carr, the building was finished by Robert Adam, the furniture made by Thomas Chippendale and the landscaped gardens laid out by Capability Brown. To cap it all a sweeping terrace designed by Sir Charles Barry (architect of the Houses of Parliament) overlooks the garden, with the ensemble enhanced inside by paintings by Turner, Gainsborough, Reynolds, El Greco and a whole host of Italian masters. There are frequent buses from Leeds (including the #36, every 20min, 30min on Sun), and if you come on the bus, you'll get a fifty-percent discount on admission (keep your bus ticket).

Eating, drinking and nightlife

Leeds rivals Manchester in the number of continental-style **café-bars** and excellent **restaurants** which dot the centre. The best of the city's **pubs** are the ornate, spruced-up Victorian ale-houses in which Leeds specializes, and when these close you can move on to one of the city's DJ bars or **clubs**, many of which have a nationwide reputation – not least because Leeds lets you dance until 5 or 6am most weekends. For information about **what's on**, the *Yorkshire Evening Post* is your best bet, or pick up a copy of the fortnightly *Leeds Guide* (£1.70) for listings and features on the city. Best **website** is ⓦwww.itchyleeds.co.uk, for insightful club, bar and entertainment listings.

Cafés and café-bars

The Courtyard 25–37 Cookridge St. Slip in during the day for snacks, coffee and drinks in the brick-paved courtyard (heated in winter). Fresh and funky club sounds until 2am at weekends.

Cuban Heels The Arches, 28–30 Assembley St. A vibrant salsa café under the railway arches, opposite the Corn Exchange.

Espresso Bar Harvey Nichols, Victoria Quarter, Briggate. Domain of the high-fashion shopper.

Norman 36 Call Lane. Industrial-chic juice-and-booze bar, plus Asian noodle-curry-and-satay menu, club nights and Monday Latin jazz. The "Daily Norman" (all Mon & Tues–Fri noon–3pm) provides a meal and a beer for a fiver.

Townhouse Assembley St. Café-bar grill and restaurant, serving fashionable food, all-day drinks, cocktails, and with weekend club nights.

Restaurants

Bibi's Minerva House, 16 Greek St ☎0113/243 0905. Classic old-time Italian, with pizzas and

pastas alongside pricier meat and fish dishes. Moderate.

Brasserie 44 44 The Calls ☎0113/234 3232. Modern British brasserie, with some temptingly priced lunch and early-bird deals, serving everything from Whitby cod to Middle Eastern meze. Closed Sat lunch & Sun. Expensive.

Dimitri's Simpson's Fold, 20 Dock St ☎0113/246 0339. Pick and mix dishes and flavours in this Greek-Mediterranean tapas-style diner. Inexpensive.

Fourth Floor Café Harvey Nichols, Victoria Quarter, Briggate ☎0113/204 8000. Light lunches, British classics and exotic flavours. And great views over the rooftops of central Leeds. Closed Mon–Wed eve & all Sun. Moderate (lunch) to expensive (dinner).

Hansa's 72–74 North St ☎0113/244 4408. This Gujarati vegetarian restaurant serves aromatic Indian food with a choice of Indian, vegetarian or organic wines. Inexpensive.

Harry Ramsden's White Cross, Otley Rd, Guiseley

⌖ 01943/874641. If you feel like making the pilgrimage to the world's most famous fish-and-chip restaurant (best done in a taxi) then expect to wait in line. Moderate.

Oporto 31–33 Call Lane ⌖0113/245 4444. Funky bistro-bar serving gourmet sandwiches, home-made burgers and risottos during the day, and Asian-influenced Modern British meals at night. Lunch moderate, dinner expensive.

Pool Court at 42 42–44 The Calls ⌖0113/244 4242. Cutting-edge cuisine with a seasonally changing menu, and a sought-after riverside balcony. Closed Sat lunch & Sun. Very Expensive.

Simply Heathcotes Canal Wharf, Water Lane ⌖0113/244 6611. A tiny spot of gourmet Lancashire in Yorkshire's grittiest city. Very stylish, with a great interior and canal views. Lunch moderate, dinner expensive.

Souz le Nez en Ville Basement, Quebec House, 9 Quebec St ⌖0113/244 0108. Basement wine bar/restaurant that's strong on fish – there are always half a dozen special starters and mains. Closed Sun. Expensive.

Tampopo 15 South Parade ⌖0113/245 1816. Best of the central noodle bars, this is the place to sort out your *ramen* from your *pho*. Inexpensive.

Pubs

Duck & Drake 43 Kirkgate, by the railway bridge. Real-ale pub with local bands performing for free two or three nights a week.

The Ship Ship Inn Yard, off Briggate. The yard tables – crammed into a space about three feet wide – take the city's obsession with continental outdoor ways to extremes.

Victoria Great George St. Ornate Victorian "family and commercial hotel", restored to its former glory, with proper pub food and a period feel.

Whitelocks Turk's Head Yard, off Briggate. Leeds' oldest and most atmospheric pub retains its traditional decor, though you'll be hard pushed to see any of it at peak times.

DJ bars, clubs and live music

Atrium 6–9 The Grand Arcade ⌖0113/242 6116. Relaxed vibe upstairs and a funky basement club for the diehard clubbers.

Cockpit Bridge House, Swinegate ⌖0113/244 1573, ⓦ www.thecockpit.co.uk. The city's best live music venue, plus assorted club nights including the popular gay night "Poptastic" on Thursdays.

Creation 55 Cookridge St ⌖0113/242 7272, ⓦ www.creation-leeds.co.uk. Hosts high profile live bands as well as regular club nights.

The Elbow Room 64 Call Lane ⌖0113/245 7011, ⓦ www.theelbowroom.co.uk. Funk and food, and a place to play pool.

Fibre 168 Lower Briggate ⌖0113/234 1304, ⓦ www.barfibre.com. Leeds' coolest gay café-bar with dancing until midnight, 2am at weekends. It's the pre-club bar for club night "Federation" (first Sat of month) at the Blank Canvas, Dark Arches, Granary Wharf.

Hifi 2 Central Rd ⌖0113/242 7353, ⓦ www.thehificlub.co.uk. Smart and stylish club, playing everything from Stax and Motown to hip-hop or drum 'n' bass.

Milo 10–12 Call Lane ⌖0113/245 7101. Unpretentious bar with DJs most evenings, ringing the changes from old soul and reggae to electronica.

Rehab 2 Waterloo House, Assembley St ⌖0113/223 7644. Where it's currently at in Leeds – including Friday night's "Sleaze" and the legendary "Basics" house night every Saturday.

The Wardrobe St Peter's Sq ⌖0113/383 8800, ⓦ www.the-wardrobe.co.uk. Live jazz and soul acts, and DJs playing the best funk, jazz and hip hop.

The Warehouse 19–21 Somers St ⌖0113/246 8287. One of the biggest clubs in the city, with house, garage and techno sounds bringing in clubbers from all over the country.

Arts, festivals and entertainment

Opera North (ⓦ www.operanorth.co.uk) gives a free performance each summer at Temple Newsam, as does the **Northern Ballet Theatre** – details from the tourist office. Temple Newsam also hosts concerts and events, from plays to rock gigs, while at Kirkstall Abbey every summer there's a Shakespeare Festival (ⓦ www.openairshakespeare.com). An international **film festival** is held in the city each October (programmes from the tourist office), and August heralds another festival in the **West Indian Carnival**.

Venues

City Varieties Swan St, Briggate
☎ 08456/441881, ⓦ www.cityvarieties.co.uk. One of the country's last surviving music halls, though it's less music-hall fare these days and more tribute bands, comedians and cabaret.

Grand Theatre and Opera House 46 New Briggate ☎ 0113/222 6222,
ⓦ www.leeds.gov.uk/grandtheatre. The regular base of Opera North and Northern Ballet.

Hyde Park Picture House Brudenell Rd, Headingley
☎ 0113/275 2045, ⓦ www.leeds.gov.uk/hydepark. The place to come for classic cinema; bus #56, #57 or #63 from the city centre.

Leeds Town Hall The Headrow ☎ 0113/224 3801, ⓦ www.leedsconcertseason.com. Supports an annual international concert season of great distinction and is the venue for Leeds' internationally renowned piano competition.

Ster Century Cinema The Light, The Headrow ☎ 0870/240 3696, ⓦ www.stercentury.co.uk. The only cinema in Leeds' city centre, with 13 screens showing mainstream releases.

West Yorkshire Playhouse Quarry Hill Mount ☎ 0113/213 7700, ⓦ www.wyplayhouse.com. The city's most innovative playhouse hosts a wide range of productions and premieres of local works.

Bradford

BRADFORD has always been a working town, booming in tandem with the Industrial Revolution, when it changed in decades from a rural seat of woollen manufacture to a polluted metropolis. In its Victorian heyday it was the world's biggest producer of worsted cloth, its skyline etched black with mill chimneys, and its hills clogged with some of the foulest back-to-back houses of any northern city. Contemporary Bradford is valiantly rinsing away its associations with urban decrepitude, and a few spruced-up buildings and the rejuvenation of the late-Victorian woollen warehouse quarter, Little Germany, signify an attempt to beautify the city centre. Most visitors hang around at least long enough to sample one of Bradford's famous curry houses, but with Haworth the indisputable local draw, and York and the heart of the Yorkshire Dales only an hour away, few stay longer.

The main interest is provided by the superb **National Museum of Photography, Film and Television** (Tues–Sun & public holidays 10am–6pm; free; ⓦ www.nmpft.org.uk), whose daily **IMAX** and 3-D film screenings (£5.95; ⓦ www.imaxnorth.co.uk) are billed as "so real you'll think you're there". The museum's ground floor kicks off with the Kodak Gallery, a museum-within-a-museum which houses the contents of Kodak's private collection and traces the story of popular photography. Successive exhibitions are devoted to every nuance of film and television, including state-of-the-art topics like digital imaging and computer animation, and detours into advertising and news-gathering.

A walk past the Venetian-Gothic **Wool Exchange** building on Market Street provides ample evidence of the wealth of nineteenth-century Bradford. The building has been splendidly restored and is now almost entirely taken up by a *Waterstone's*. Over to the east, north of Leeds Road, the tight grid of streets that is **Little Germany** retains an enclave of warehouse and office buildings in which transplanted German and Jewish merchants once plied their wool trade. At the **Design Exchange**, 34 Peckover St (Mon–Fri 9am–5pm; free), the temporary art and design exhibitions are usually worth a peek.

Three miles out of Bradford towards Keighley, along the A650 to the north, lies **SALTAIRE**, a model industrial village and textile mill built by the industrialist Sir Titus Salt. **Salt's Mill**, built to emulate an Italian palazzo and larger than St Paul's Cathedral in London, was the biggest factory in the world when it opened in 1853. Its 1200 looms produced over 30,000 yards of cloth a day, and the mill was surrounded by schools, hospitals, a train station, parks, baths and wash-houses, plus 45 almshouses and around 850 homes. Salt's Mill remains the fulcrum of the village, its several floors now housing art, craft and furniture shops, and a craft centre, but its enterprising centrepiece is the **1853 Gallery** (daily 10am–6pm; free; Ⓦwww.saltsmill.org.uk), an entire floor of the old spinning shed given over to the world's largest retrospective collection of the works of Bradford-born **David Hockney**. Trains run to Saltaire station from Bradford Forster Square, or take bus #679 from the Interchange, which stops in Saltaire village.

Practicalities

Trains and buses both arrive at **Bradford Interchange** off Bridge Street, a little to the south of the city-centre grid. There's also a much smaller station at **Forster Square**, across the city, for trains to Keighley. The **tourist office** (Mon–Sat 9am–5.30pm; ℡01274/433678, Ⓦwww.visitbradford.com), located in Centenary Square's City Hall, is three minutes' signposted walk from the Interchange or five minutes from Forster Square.

Bradford's large Asian population has made the city famous for its **curry houses**. The *Kashmir*, 27 Morley St (℡01274/726513; open until 3am) – two minutes up the road that runs between the Alhambra and the National Museum – claims to be Bradford's first curry house: like many others in town it's unlicensed, though you can take your own booze. At the *Mumtaz*, 386–400 Great Horton Rd (℡01274/571861; no alcohol allowed), the food is sold by weight – a half-pound dish feeds two and the sweet lassi is legendary. It may be a twenty-minute walk up towards the university, but you won't be disappointed.

Haworth

Of English literary shrines, probably only Stratford sees more visitors than the quarter of a million who swarm annually into the village of **HAWORTH** to tramp the cobbles once trodden by the Brontë sisters. Quite why the sheltered life of the Brontës should exert such a powerful fascination is a puzzle, though the contrast of their pinched provincial existences with the brooding moors and tumultuous passions of *Wuthering Heights* may well form part of the answer. Whatever the reasons, during the summer the village's steep, cobbled Main Street is lost under huge crowds, herded by multilingual signs around the various stations on the Brontë trail.

Of these, the **Brontë Parsonage Museum**, at the top of the main street (April–Sept daily 10am–5.30pm; Oct–March daily 11am–5pm; £4.80, Ⓦwww.bronte.info), is the obvious focus, a modest Georgian house bought by Patrick Brontë in 1820 to bring up his family. After the tragic early loss of his wife and two eldest daughters, the surviving four children – Anne, Emily, Charlotte and their dissipated brother, Branwell – spent most of their short lives in the place, which is furnished as it was in their day, and filled with the sisters' pictures, books, manuscripts and personal treasures. The **parish church** in front of the parsonage – substantially rebuilt since the Brontës lived here – contains the family vault; Charlotte was married here in 1854. At the **Sunday School**, between the parsonage and the church, Charlotte, Anne and even Branwell did weekly teaching stints; Branwell, however, was undoubtedly more at home in the **Black Bull**, a

Patrick Prunty or Bronty (it's unclear which) was born in Ireland and became a schoolmaster at the age of sixteen. He later won a place at St John's, Cambridge, where he changed his name to **Brontë**, perhaps influenced by naval hero Lord Nelson, who was made the Duke of Brontë. Later ordained, the Reverend Brontë, and his wife Maria, took up a living at Thornton, just outside Bradford, where the four youngest of their six children – Maria, Elizabeth, Charlotte, Branwell, Emily and Anne – were born between 1816 and 1820. Later that year, the Brontë family moved into the draughty **parsonage** in nearby Haworth.

Mrs Brontë died within the year and the four oldest girls were sent away to school, but withdrawn after first Maria, then Elizabeth, died after falling ill. The surviving daughters, and the cosseted Branwell, were kept at home, where they amused themselves by making up stories and writing miniature books. As they successively came of age, the girls took up short-lived jobs as governesses at various local schools. **Branwell**, meanwhile, acquired a certain talent for art, but failed to apply to study at the Royal Academy, got into debt, and then spent two years as a junior stationmaster near Halifax but was later dismissed in disgrace. He retreated to Haworth, made himself overly familiar with the beer in the *Black Bull* and began experimenting with drugs.

Charlotte's, Emily's and Anne's continuing attempts to amuse themselves with their writings led to the private publication, in 1846, of a series of poems. They used the (male) pseudonyms Currer, Ellis and Acton Bell – corresponding to their own initials – and though few copies of the collection were ever sold, the little volume acted as a catalyst. Keeping the pseudonym, **Charlotte** wrote a novel the same year, which was rejected by various publishers; but her *Jane Eyre*, submitted in 1847, was an instant success. **Emily**'s *Wuthering Heights* and **Anne**'s *Agnes Grey* received similar acclaim the same year; Anne's second novel, the better-known *Tenant of Wildfell Hall*, was published in 1848.

But the next two years destroyed the family, as it was ravaged by consumption. First Branwell, who had sunk ever deeper into addictive misery and ill health, died in September 1848, followed by Emily in December of that year, and Anne in May of the following year. Charlotte lived on for another six years, writing two more novels – *Shirley* (1849) and *Villette* (1853) – and becoming something of a literary figure once she had revealed her identity. Charlotte finally **married** Reverend Brontë's curate, Arthur Bell Nicholls, who moved into the parsonage, but she died after nine months of marriage in the early stages of pregnancy. The Reverend Brontë lived on until 1861 – the entire family, except Anne (who is buried in Scarborough), lies in the **Brontë vault** in the village church, next to the house.

pub within staggering distance of the parsonage near the top of Main Street. He got his opium at the pharmacist's over the road (now a lace shop).

The most popular local walk runs to **Brontë Falls** and **Bridge**, reached via West Lane and a track from the village, and to **Top Withens**, a mile beyond, a ruin fancifully thought to be the model for Wuthering Heights (3hr round trip). The moorland setting beautifully evokes the flavour of the book, and to enjoy it further you could walk on another two and a half miles to **Ponden Hall**, perhaps the Thrushcross Grange of *Wuthering Heights*.

Practicalities

Haworth is eight miles northwest of Bradford. To get there by **bus**, take the #662 from Bradford Interchange to Keighley (every 10min), and change there for the #663, #664 or #665 (every 20min), which drop at various points in the streets immediately below the cobbled Main Street. On Sundays, only the #663 and #665 operate (every 30min). Alternatively, you can use the steam trains of the **Keighley and Worth Valley Railway** (Easter week, school holidays, July & Aug daily; rest of the year Sat & Sun); day rover ticket £10; recorded information ☎01535/647777, ⓦwww.kwvr.co.uk). Regular trains from Leeds or Bradford's Forster Square run to Keighley station, while on arrival at Haworth, cross the footbridge from the station and follow Butt Lane up the side of the park to the bottom of Main Street.

Haworth **tourist office** is at the top of Main Street at 2–4 West Lane (daily 9.30am–5.30pm; closes at 5pm Oct–March; ☎01535/642329, ⓦwww.visithaworth.com). You'll need to book **accommodation** ahead at most times of the year. There are any number of teashops and **cafés** along Main Street, while *Aitches* guest house has a **restaurant** (dinner from around £20 plus drinks) that serves meals to residents (Tues–Thurs), and is open to the public on Friday and Saturday evenings. Otherwise, *Weaver's* (Tues–Sat dinner only, plus Sun lunch; reservations essential) serves good modern northern cuisine using local ingredients from around £25 a head.

Guest houses and hotels

Aitches 11 West Lane ☎01535/642501, ⓦwww.aitches.co.uk. This place offers a few comfortable, cottage-style en-suite rooms. ❸
Apothecary 86 Main St ☎01535/643642. Traditional guest house opposite the church. ❷
Moorfield Guest House 80 West Lane ☎01535/643689, ⓦwww.moorfieldgh.demon.co.uk. Victorian house 5min walk from the village centre that makes the most of its elevated position. ❷
Old White Lion Main St ☎01535/642313, ⓦwww.oldwhitelionhotel.com. Old coaching inn at the top of Main St, offering pub-style accommodation. ❹

Weaver's 15 West Lane ☎01535/643822, ⓦwww.weaversmallhotel.co.uk. A renowned restaurant-with-rooms operation housed in a converted row of weavers' cottages. ❺

Youth hostel

Haworth YHA Longlands Hall, Longlands Drive, Lees Lane ☎0870/770 5858, ⓔhaworth@yha.org.uk. Dorm beds (£10.25) in a Victorian mansion, a mile from the centre, off the Keighley road. The Bradford buses stop on the main road nearby. Weekends only Nov to mid-Dec, closed mid-Dec to Jan.

The Yorkshire Dales

The **Yorkshire Dales** – "dales" from the Viking word *dalr* (valley) – form a lovely and varied upland area of limestone hills and pastoral valleys at the heart of the Pennines, wedged between the Lake District to the west and the North York Moors to the east. Most approaches are from the south, via the superbly engineered **Settle to Carlisle Railway**, or along the main A65 road from towns such as **Skipton**, **Settle** and **Ingleton**. This makes southern dales like **Wharfedale** the most visited, while neighbouring **Malhamdale** is also immensely popular, thanks to the fascinating scenery squeezed into its narrow confines around **Malham** village. **Ribblesdale** is more sombre, its villages popular with hikers intent on tackling the Dales' famous **Three Peaks** – the mountains of Pen-y-ghent, Ingleborough and Whernside. To the northwest lies the more remote **Dentdale**, one of the least known but most beautiful of the valleys. Moving north, there are two parallel dales, **Wensleydale** and **Swaledale**, with Swaledale's lower stretches encompassing the appealing historic town of **Richmond**.

Public transport is surprisingly good, with special summer Sunday and bank holiday services (usually between May and Sept, peaking in school holidays) connecting almost everywhere. Pick up the invaluable, free *Dales Explorer* timetable (W www.dalesbus.org) from tourist offices and from the **National Park information centres** at Grassington, Aysgarth Falls, Malham, Reeth, Hawes and Clapham. For any kind of serious hiking, you'll need the OS Outdoor Leisure **maps** #2, #10 and #30. The **Pennine Way** cuts right through the heart of the Dales, and the region is crossed by the Coast-to-Coast Walk, but the principal local route is the **Dales Way**, an 84-mile footpath from Ilkley to Bowness on Windermere in the Lake District, which takes around a week to walk.

Skipton

SKIPTON, southernmost town of the Dales, is best visited on one of its four weekly **market** days (Mon, Wed, Fri & Sat), when the streets and pubs are filled with what seems like half the Dales population, milling around and determined to enjoy themselves. *Sceptone*, or "Sheeptown", was a settlement long before the arrival of the battling Normans, whose **Castle**, located at the top of the High Street (March–Sept Mon–Sat 10am–6pm, Sun noon–6pm; Oct–Feb Mon–Sat 10am–4pm, Sun noon–4pm; £4.80; W www.skiptoncastle.co.uk), provided the basis for the present fortress, among England's best preserved. Little survives in the way of furniture or fittings, but it very much looks the part and a self-guided tour leads you through the original Norman gateway to see the banqueting hall, spacious kitchens and storerooms. The **Church of the Holy Trinity**, which stands in front of the castle at the top of the High Street (summer daily 9am–4.30pm; winter daily 9am–dusk; £1 donation requested), has a fine bossed fifteenth-century roof, beautiful chancel screen (dating from 1533) and a twelfth-century font crowned with a towering wooden Jacobean cover. The alleys on the western side of the High Street emerge onto the banks of the **Leeds–Liverpool Canal**, which runs right through the centre of Skipton. Pennine Boat Trips at Waterside Court (T01756/790829), next to the George Fisher outdoor store, offers daily **canal cruises** (Easter–Oct; £4).

Practicalities

The **train station** is on Broughton Road, a ten-minute walk from the centre. Note that if you're heading for the Settle–Carlisle Railway (p.679), most trains from Skipton are direct – you shouldn't need to change at Settle unless you want to break your journey. The **bus station** is on Keighley Road, just shy of Devonshire Place at the bottom of the High Street. Local services run to Settle (not Sun) for connections on to Ingleton and Horton; Malham (Mon–Fri only); and Grassington (not Sun). The **tourist office**, 35 Coach St (Mon–Sat 10am–5pm, Sun 11am–3pm; T01756/792809, W www.skiptononline.co.uk), offers a friendly service and details of local and seasonal events. You can **rent bikes** for £15 a day from The Bicycle Shop on Water Street (T01756/794386).

Accommodation is plentiful, with a host of central pubs offering rooms, as well as several B&Bs a few minutes' walk out of the centre, either on Gargrave (west) or Keighley (south) roads. **Eating** is better in Skipton than in most Dales towns, and there is one outstanding **pub** too. There's even a **cinema**, the Plaza, on Sackville Street off Keighley Road.

Accommodation

Carlton House 46 Keighley Rd ☎01756/700921. A small, nonsmoking Victorian townhouse, a couple of minutes from the centre. ❷

Craven Heifer Grassington Rd ☎01756/792521, ⓦwww.cravenheifer.co.uk. Stone-built Dales inn, a mile out of town (2min drive), with en-suite rooms fashioned from an old barn. No single Saturday-night bookings. ❷

Dalesgate Lodge 69 Gargrave Rd ☎01756/790672, ⓔdalesgatelodge@hotmail.com. Three en-suite doubles and one twin available in this family-run, nonsmoking B&B. No credit cards. ❷

Woolly Sheep Inn 38 Sheep St ☎01756/700966. A restored seventeenth-century inn at the bottom of the High Street with nine pine-furnished rooms. Downstairs there are Timothy Taylor's beers and meals served daily, lunch and dinner. Parking available. ❸

Eating and drinking

Aagrah Devonshire Place, off Keighley Rd ☎01756/790807. Has a loyal local following for its fresh, tasty Indian dishes. Dinner only. Inexpensive.

Le Caveau 86 High St ☎01756/794274. Skipton's top spot, an Anglo-Med cellar restaurant with lunchtime specials and a seasonal menu. Closed Sun & Mon. Expensive.

Coffee House Coach St Car Park. Known for its coffee, but also the place for warm, filled herb baguettes, stuffed ciabattas, toasted bagels, homemade soups and the like. Closed Sun. Inexpensive.

The Narrow Boat 38 Victoria St. All you want from a pub – varied cask ales, a multitude of Belgian and German beers, and good, inexpensive food (lunch daily, dinner until 8pm, not Fri or Sat; Moderate) from Cumberland sausage to grilled salmon.

Wharfedale

The best of **Wharfedale** starts just east of Skipton at **Bolton Abbey**, and then continues north in a broad, pastoral swathe scattered with villages as picture-perfect as any in northern England. **Grassington** is the main village, a popular walking centre, though smaller hamlets in Upper Wharfedale, like **Kettlewell**, make less frenetic bases. **Buses** run roughly hourly (not Sun) to Grassington from Skipton (via Cracoe and Threshfield), and then half a dozen times a day on up the B6160 to Kettlewell and beyond. This is augmented by the #800/805/806 weekend services (Sun all year, plus extra summer services on Sat & Sun) from Leeds and Bradford, running through Wharfedale and on to Wensleydale.

Bolton Abbey

BOLTON ABBEY, five miles east of Skipton, is the name of a whole village rather than an abbey, a confusion compounded by the fact that the place's main monastic ruin is known as **Bolton Priory** (daily 9am to dusk; free), founded here in the 1150s. Turner painted the site, and Ruskin described it as the most beautiful in England, though the priory is now mostly ruined. The priory is the starting point for several popular riverside walks, including a section of the **Dales Way** footpath that follows the river's west bank to take in Bolton Woods and the **Strid** (from "stride"), an extraordinary piece of white water two miles north of the abbey, where softer rock has allowed the river to funnel into a cleft just a few feet wide. Beyond the Strid, the path emerges at **Barden Bridge**, four miles from the priory, where the fortified **Barden Tower** has a tearoom.

To get here without your own transport, you're reliant upon the weekend-only #800/805/806 bus service, or a taxi from Skipton (around £8 each way). Alternatively, steam locomotives run from **Embsay**, two miles east of Skipton (up to 5 daily in summer; rest of year runs at least on Sun; 11am–4pm, £6 return; call ☎01756/795189 or 710614 for information), to Bolton Abbey station, which is a mile and a half from the priory ruins – there's a signposted footpath. The main **hotel** is the sumptuous *Devonshire Arms* (☎01756/710441, ⓦwww.thedevonshirearms.co.uk; ❾), just south of the village, owned by the duke and duchess of Devonshire and furnished with antiques from their ancestral pile at Chatsworth; there's a brasserie and bar open to the public. Considerably easier on the pocket are two **B&Bs**, one at *Hesketh Farm*, a mile west of the village (℡01756/710541; no credit cards; **❶**), the other at *Holme House Farm*, a quarter of a mile south of Barden, overlooking the river (℡01756/720661; no credit cards; **❶**; closed Nov–March). *Bolton Abbey Tea Cottage*, next to the priory, offers traditional **afternoon teas**.

Grassington and around

GRASSINGTON, the dale's popular main village, is nine miles from Bolton Abbey. It has a cobbled Market Square, home to several inns and a small local museum, though the surroundings are at their best by the river, where the shallow Linton Falls thunder after rain; a waterside path leads a mile upstream to the Grass Wood nature reserve. The **National Park information centre** on Hebden Road (April–Oct daily 10am–5pm; Nov–March Wed & Fri–Sun 10am–4pm; ℡01756/752774) stands across from the **bus stop**, while Grassington also has the bulk of the dale's services – a bank with ATM, small supermarket and post office.

There's a fair amount of **accommodation** in the village, but even so, at busy times you may have to look further afield – no hardship since Grassington is surrounded by tiny scenic villages, all connected by minor country roads and footpaths (both Burnsall and Appletreewick are on the Dales Way). The nearest hostels are at Malham (7 miles) or Kettlewell (8 miles).

Hotels, inns and B&Bs

Ashfield House Summers Fold, Grassington ℡01756/752584, ⓦwww.ashfieldhouse.co.uk. Lovely seventeenth-century house, 50yds off the square, boasting a walled garden and good breakfasts. Dinner available (£17). Closed Dec & Jan. **❺**

Devonshire Fell Burnsall, 3 miles southeast of Grassington ℡01756/729000, ⓦwww.devonshirefell.co.uk. Although this is a country house retreat, it's definitely not "country" in feel. There's a classy bar and bistro, while guests can use Bolton Abbey's *Devonshire Arms'* leisure facilities. Weekend two-night minimum. **❼**

Devonshire Hotel Main St, Grassington ℡01756/752525, ⓕ01756/753748. The old inn on the square has plenty of character, well-priced rooms, a cosy bar, open fire and real ales. **❹**

Grassington Lodge 8 Wood Lane, Grassington ℡01756/752518, ⓦwww.grassingtonlodge.co.uk. Quiet village house whose seven en-suite rooms, furnished in country pine, have a really airy feel. No credit cards. **❹**

Kirkfield Hebden Rd, Grassington ℡01756/752385. A detached house with dale views, set in its own grounds, 100 yards from the National Park Centre. No credit cards. **❷**

Red Lion Burnsall, 3 miles southeast of Grassington ℡01756/720204, ⓦwww.redlion.co.uk. A real old country inn, with log fires, oak beams, a cosy bar, and river views from its comfortable, traditionally furnished rooms. **❼**

Campsites

Bell Bank Skirethorns Lane, Threshfield ℡01756/752321. Nearest campsite to Grassington, a little over a mile to the west – milk and eggs are available to buy. Closed Nov–Easter.

Mason's Ainhams Farm, Appletreewick ℡01756/720236. Farm camping, 4 miles south-east of Grassington. Closed Nov–Easter.

Eating and drinking

Angel Inn Hetton, 4 miles southwest of Grassington ℡01756/730263. Gastropub *par excellence*, with renowned food served either in the bar-brasserie (lunch & dinner) or more formal restaurant (Mon–Sat dinner & Sun lunch) – best to book for either. Expensive.

Dales Kitchen 51 Main St, Grassington ℡01756/753208. Serving traditional tearoom dishes during the day – including homemade fruitcake with Wensleydale cheese. Inexpensive.

Fountaine Inn Linton, 1 mile southwest of Grassington ℡01756/752210. The old pub on the green makes a nice target for a walk across the river from Grassington. Inexpensive.

Old Hall Inn Threshfield, 1 mile west of Grassington ℡01756/752441. Stone-flagged inn with great food: expect to have to wait for a table. Closed Mon lunch. Moderate.

Upper Wharfedale

KETTLEWELL (Norse for "bubbling spring") is the main centre for the upper dale, with a **National Park information point** in the Over and Under outdoor shop, a campsite (℡01756/760886) just to the north at Fold Farm, and **youth hostel** (℡0870/770 5896, ℮kettlewell@yha.org.uk; £10.25; closed Sun April–June, Sept & Oct, & closed other days during winter) in the centre of the village. The *Racehorses* (℡01756/760233; ❹), on the bridge, is an eighteenth-century hotel with twelve en-suite rooms and views of the River Wharfe; or there's *Chestnut Cottage* by the stream (℡01756/760804; no credit cards; ❷). The village **pubs**, the *Bluebell* and the *King's Head*, are both cosy places for a drink.

It's lovely country north of Kettlewell, accessed either via the dale's single lonely road (B6160) or the Dales Way path. At **STARBOTTON**, two miles away, the *Fox & Hounds* (closed Mon & all Jan) has ancient flagged floors, a huge fire and popular food. There's also a great pub in **BUCKDEN**, another couple of miles to the north, the *Buck Inn* (℡01756/760228; ❺), which has good food and beer. A mile upstream, the river flows through Langstrothdale to **HUBBERHOLME** and the stone-flagged, whitewashed *George* (℡01756/760223; ❸), the favourite pub of archetypal Yorkshireman J.B. Priestley, who is buried in the churchyard of the nearby small chapel of St Michael and All Angels.

Malhamdale

A few miles west of Wharfedale lies **Malhamdale**, one of the National Park's most heavily visited regions, thanks to its three outstanding natural features: Malham Cove, Malham Tarn and Gordale Scar. The approach by **public transport** is on the #210 bus from Skipton (not weekends) or the summer Sunday #820 from Grassington.

Unless you're here off-season, some idea of what to expect in **MALHAM** village comes at the vast peripheral car park, likely to be packed solid with hikers and day-trippers. The village is home to barely a couple of hundred people, who inhabit the huddled stone houses on either side of a bubbling river, but this microscopic gem attracts perhaps half a million visitors a year. Your first stop should be the **National Park information centre** on the southern edge of the village (Easter–Oct daily 10am–5pm; Nov–Easter Fri–Sun 10am–4pm; ℡01729/830363). In summer, you'll need to book ahead to get a bed at the **youth hostel** (℡01729/830321, ℮malham@yha.org.uk; £11.50; closed Sun–Wed Nov–Jan). However, there's also a **bunkhouse barn** at *Hill Top Farm* (℡01729/830320; £8, groups only at weekends), immediately north of the National Park information centre, and several good village **B&Bs**, among them *Beck Hall* (℡01729/830332, ⓌＷwww.beckhallmalham.com; ❸); the excellent *Miresfield Farm* (℡01729/830414; ❸); or comfortable *Riverhouse Hotel* (℡01729/830315, Ｗwww.riverhousehotel.co.uk; ❸). There are pub rooms at the welcoming *Buck Inn* (℡01729/830317; ❸), almost next door. You can **camp** under Gordale Scar at *Gordale Scar House Campsite* (℡01729/830333; closed Nov–March). Meals are served in the **pubs**, notably at the *Buck Inn*, with a popular walkers' back bar, but also at the fancier *Lister Arms* (℡01729/830330, Ｗwww.listerarms.co.uk; ❸), which has a good range of beers.

There's a classic circuit which takes in cove, tarn and scar in a clockwise **walk from Malham** (8 miles; 3hr 30min). Appearing first in spectacular fashion, a mile north of Malham, **Malham Cove** is a white-walled limestone amphitheatre rising three hundred feet above its surroundings. There's a breath-sapping haul to the top, where the rewards are fine views and the famous limestone pavement, an expanse of clints (slabs) and grykes (clefts) created by water seeping through weaker lines in the limestone rock. A simple walk over the moors, either via the Pennine Way or the more interesting dry valley to the west, abruptly brings **Malham Tarn** into sight, a lake created by an impervious layer of glacial debris. Meanwhile, at **Gordale Scar** (also easily approached direct from Malham village), the cliffs are if anything more spectacular than at Malham Cove, complemented by a deep ravine to the rear caused by the collapse of a cavern roof. A little to the south of the scar, off the road, lies **Janet's Foss**, a peach of a waterfall set amidst green–damp rocks and overarching trees.

Ribblesdale

The scenery of **Ribblesdale**, west of Malhamdale, is more dour and brooding than the bucolic valleys to the east. It's entered from Settle, starting point of the **Settle–Carlisle Railway**, among the most scenic rail routes in the country (see box below), with daily **trains** heading north through Horton in Ribblesdale to Carlisle and south to Skipton, Keighley and Leeds; a limited service operates on Sundays. The hourly #580/581 **bus** (not Sun) connects Skipton with Settle, from where it runs three or four times daily (not Sun) to Horton but no further, and northwest to Ingleton in the western dales. There's also the summer Sunday and bank holiday bus #807 from Skipton to Settle, Horton and Ribblehead, continuing on to Wensleydale and Richmond.

Nestled under the wooded knoll of Castleberg, **SETTLE** is well placed for upper Ribblesdale and a pleasant enough base if you haven't the time to find a more intimate overnight stop within the National Park. The **tourist office** is in the town hall on Cheapside, just off Market Place (daily 9.30am–4.30pm; ℡01729/825192), with the **train station** less than five minutes' signposted walk away, down Station Road. Two comfortable old town **inns**, the *Royal Oak* on Market Place (℡01729/822561; ❸), and the *Golden Lion*, just off Market Place along Duke Street (℡01729/822203, ⓦwww.goldenlionhotel.net; ❸), are the most atmospheric places to stay, though there's also **B&B** at the

The Settle to Carlisle railway

In the six years between 1869 and 1875, when the 72-mile **Settle to Carlisle** line opened, herculean efforts were made by thousands of navvies to blast a route through the unforgiving Dales mountainsides. Living in squalid shanty towns by the sides of the track, six thousand men built twenty viaducts and bored fourteen tunnels in a feat of Victorian engineering that has few equals in Britain.

The attraction in riding the line is the chance to experience what the operators – with no hint of hype – dub "**England's most scenic railway**". Between Horton and Ribblehead the line climbs two hundred feet in five miles, before crossing the famous 24-arched Ribblehead viaduct, while the station at Dent Head is the highest, and bleakest, main-line station in England. The journey from Settle to Carlisle takes just under an hour and forty minutes, so it's easy to make a **return trip** (£16.40 adult day return) along the whole length of the line. Two **rover tickets** are also available: for three consecutive days (£30) or three days in seven (£35). There are connections to Settle from Skipton (20min) and Leeds (1hr); full **timetable** details are available from National Rail Enquiries, ℡08457/484950, or from the website, ⓦwww.settle-carlisle.co.uk. If you only have time for a short trip, the best section is that between Settle and Garsdale (30min), though note that you'll typically have a very short or very long wait for the return train.

Georgian *Liverpool Guest House* on Chapel Square (℡01729/822247; no credit cards; ❷) among others. During the day, it's hard to see anyone resisting the lure of *Ye Olde Naked Man Café* (closed Wed), serving breakfasts, proper coffee and good homemade food. **STAINFORTH**, two miles north of Settle, has the local **youth hostel** (℡0870/770 6046, ✉stainforth@yha.org.uk; £11.50; open most weekends and daily in school holidays), located in an old Georgian country house about a quarter of mile south of the village.

The noted walking centre of **HORTON IN RIBBLESDALE** dates from Norman times but the village gained a new lease of life in the nineteenth century with the arrival of the Settle–Carlisle Railway. The celebrated **Pen-y-ghent Café** here is a **National Park information point** (Mon & Wed–Fri 9am–6pm, Sat & Sun 8am–6pm; ℡01729/860333) and an unofficial headquarters for the famous **Three Peaks Walk**, a twenty-five-mile, twelve-hour circuit of Pen-y-ghent (2273ft), Whernside (2416ft) and Ingleborough (2373ft). As well as providing food, maps, guides and weather reports, the *Pen-y-ghent Café* operates a "safety service" for walkers, enabling hikers to register in and out (not Tues or Fri). Horton straggles along an L-shaped mile of the Settle–Ribblehead road (B6479), with the **train station** at the northern end and the church at the southern end. In between are the café, a post office/store, and a couple of **B&Bs**. The *Crown Hotel* (℡01729/860209, ⓦwww.crown-hotel.co.uk; ❷), by the bridge, is a popular walkers' haunt with bar food served until 8.30pm. The *Golden Lion* (℡01729/860206), by the church, has both B&B rooms (❷) and bunk-room beds (£8; breakfast and packed lunches available). There's a **campsite** at *Holme Farm* (℡01729/860281), near the church.

The western Dales

The **western Dales** is a term of convenience for a couple of tiny dales running north from **Ingleton**, a village perfectly poised for walks up Ingleborough and Whernside, and for **Dentdale**, one of the loveliest valleys in the National Park. Meanwhile, just outside the park and county boundary to the west, the interesting market town of **Kirby Lonsdale** sports a graceful medieval bridge spanning the River Lune. Ingleton is linked by **bus** to Kirby Lonsdale, Settle (for Skipton) and Horton, and the Settle–Carlisle Railway offers access to upper Dentdale.

Ingleton and around

INGLETON sits upon a ridge at the confluence of two streams, the Twiss and the Doe, whose beautifully wooded valleys are easily the area's best features. The four-and-a-half mile **Falls' Walk** (daily 9am–dusk; entrance fee £3, parking – including fee – £6; ⓦwww.ingletonwaterfallswalk.co.uk) is the main local attraction, a lovely circular walk up the tree-hung Twiss Valley, past viewing points over the Pecca Falls and Thornton Force.

The Inglesport **hiking store** on Main Street (℡015242/41146, ⓦwww.inglesport.com) in the village is the place for maps, equipment and weather forecasts. Ingleton's **tourist office** is in the community centre car park, just off Main Street (April–Oct daily 10am–4pm; ℡015242/41049), with the main **bus stop** just outside. The **youth hostel** (℡0870/770 5880, ✉ingleton@yha.org.uk; £11.50; closed certain days of the week Sept–Feb) is an old stone house in its own gardens, located centrally in a lane between the market square and the swimming pool. There are also a dozen local **B&Bs and guest houses**, most lying along Main Street, five minutes' walk south of the tourist office. *Ingleborough View* (℡015242/41523; no credit cards; ❷) has a patio overlooking the river, or try nearby *Riverside Lodge* (℡015242/41359, @info@riversideingleton.co.uk; ❸), where breakfast is served in the valley-view conservatory. You can **camp** at *Stackstead Farm*, a mile south off the minor road to High Bentham (℡015242/41386, @enquiries@stacksteadfarm.co.uk), which has tent space and a **bunkhouse barn** (£10, groups only at weekends). Ingleton has a bank, bakery and grocery stores – making it a good place to stock up for the hiking to come. The *Inglesport Café* on the first floor of the store on Main Street (daily 9am–6pm) serves hearty soups and chips with everything, or in the evening there's *La Tavernetta*, 23 Main St (℡015242/42465) for inexpensive Italian meals.

Just one and a half miles out of Ingleton on the Ribblehead/Hawes road (B6255) is the entrance to the **White Scar Caves** (daily 10am–5pm, tours hourly; £6.50; ℡015242/41244, Ⓦwww.whitescarcave.co.uk), the longest show cave in England. Don't be put off by the steep price – it's worth every penny for the eighty-minute tour of dank underground chambers, contorted cave formations and glistening stalactites.

Dentdale

Any rail or road route to **Dentdale** has plenty of scenic rewards, but the most breathtaking is the minor-road route from Ingleton up Kingsdale and down Deepdale, with the vast whalebacks of Gragareth and Whernside rising to each side of the windswept little road. As you might expect, there's next to nothing to do locally except walk or revel in the scenery, but there are few better spots to do either, with **DENT** village an unbeatable base. Here, the main road gives way to grassy cobbles, while the huddled stone cottages sport blooming window-boxes trailing over ancient lintels. You can stay at either of the village's two **pubs**, the *Sun Inn* (℡01539/625208, @thesun@dentbrewery.co.uk; ❶) and the *George & Dragon* (℡01539/625256, @thedragon@dentbrewery.co.uk; ❸), which are virtually next to each other in the centre. Otherwise, *Stone Close Guest House* (℡01539/625231, @heather@stoneclose.com; ❷) has a good café (10.30am–5.30pm; Nov–Easter weekends only), doubling as a National Park information point.

Confusion is caused by Dent's **train station** (on the Settle–Carlisle line) not being in Dent at all, but four miles to the east. A Wednesday and Saturday bus service runs between the station, Dent, Sedburgh and Kendal in the Lakes. Dentdale **youth hostel** (℡0870/770 5790, @dentdale@yha.org.uk; £11.50; closed: Sun Easter–Aug, Sun & Mon Sept & Oct, and all Dec & Jan; weekends only Nov & Feb) is a couple of miles south of here down the Dales Way.

Kirkby Lonsdale

Close to the point where Yorkshire, Cumbria and Lancashire meet, the flint and limestone houses of quaint **KIRKBY LONSDALE** sit on a rise above the River Lune. Ten minutes' walk south of town on the A683, the three-arched **Devil's Bridge** dates from medieval times and once formed the main route into Yorkshire from the Lakes. A path from here follows the river to the base of a steep flight of steps that re-enters the town behind St Mary's Church at a point called **Ruskin's View**. Turner painted the famous view of the Lune valley from here but it was John Ruskin who, with typical overstatement, declared that "I do not know in all my own country, still less in France or Italy, a place more naturally divine."

The #567 **bus** from Ingleton runs here four times daily (not Sun), a fifteen-minute ride. The local **tourist office** is at 24 Main St (March–Oct daily 9.30am–5pm; Nov–Feb Thurs–Sun 10am–1pm & 2–5pm; ℡015242/71437,

@www.kirkbylonsdale.co.uk). The *Snooty Fox* on Main St (☎015242/71308, @www.mortal-man-inns.co.uk; ❸) is a country **inn** with flair, serving Mediterranean-inspired food. Or there's the *Sun Hotel*, 6 Market St (☎015242 /71965; ❹), which backs onto the churchyard, and several cheaper B&Bs.

Wensleydale

Best known of the Dales, if only for its cheese, **Wensleydale** is the largest, least varied and most serene of the National Park's dales. Known in medieval times as Yoredale, after its river (the Ure), the dale takes its present name from an easterly village, and while there are towns to detain you – including one of the area's biggest in Hawes, to the west – it's Wensleydale's rural attractions that linger longest in the mind. Many will be familiar to devotees of the **James Herriott** books and TV series, set and filmed in the dale. Year-round **public transport** is provided by a combination of post and service buses (#156 and #157) from Hawes, while there are also summer weekend and bank holiday services connecting Hawes to Wharfedale (#800/801/805/806), Masham and Ripon (#803), and Richmond or Ribblesdale (#807).

Hawes

HAWES – from the Anglo-Saxon *haus*, a mountain pass – is head of Wensleydale in all respects: it's the chief town, main hiking centre, and home to its tourism, cheese and rope-making industries. It received its market charter in 1699; the weekly **Tuesday market** – crammed with farmers and market traders – is still going strong. The cheese trail invariably leads to the **Wensleydale Creamery** on Gayle Lane (Mon–Sat 9am–5pm, Sun 10am–4.30pm; £2; @www.wensleydale.co.uk), a few hundred yards (signposted) south of the centre. The first cheese in Wensleydale was made by medieval Cistercian monks from ewes' milk, and after the Dissolution local farmers made a version from cows' milk which, by the 1840s, was being marketed as "Wensleydale" cheese. The Creamery's "Cheese Experience" tours tell you all this and more, with plenty of opportunity to see the stuff being made, and to sample and purchase in the shop. All three of Wensleydale's industries come together in the **Dales Countryside Museum** (daily 10am–5pm; £3), housed in Station Yard's former train station and warehouses, on the Aysgarth side of town. Alongside it, in a long shed, the **Hawes Ropemakers Museum** (July–Oct Mon–Fri 9am–5.30pm, Sat 10am–5.30pm; Nov–June Mon–Fri 9am–5.30pm; free) presents popular demonstrations of traditional rope-making. A mile and a half out of town to the north, people cough up the £1 toll at the *Green Dragon* pub to walk to **Hardraw Force**. It's about all the fall is worth for much of the year, for although this is the highest above-ground waterfall in the country there's often barely a trickle dribbling over the edge.

The **National Park information centre** shares the same building as the Dales Countryside Museum (daily 10am–5pm; ☎01969/667450). **Buses** stop in Market Place except for the special summer-only services, which pull up outside the museum, and the post buses, which depart from outside the post office (over the road from the information centre car park). **Accommodation** is plentiful in local B&Bs, while all the pubs in and around the market square – the *Board*, *Crown*, *Fountain*, *Bull's Head* and *White Hart* – have rooms, too, so you shouldn't be stuck for choice. Traditional English meals – game a speciality – are served in the *Cocketts Hotel* **restaurant**, though Hawes' best dining experience is at *Herriot's Hotel*, whose restaurant (no lunch Wed & Thurs) features a wide-ranging continental menu.

B&Bs, guest houses and hotels

Cocketts Market Place ☎01969/667312, ⓦwww.cocketts.co.uk. The smartest choice in town, offering traditionally decorated rooms in a seventeenth-century building. ❹

Green Dragon 1.5 miles north of Hawes ☎01969/667392, ⓦwww.greendragoninn .fsnet.co.uk. Country inn with hotel rooms or self-catering apartments. Home-cooked food, real ales and live folk/rock/blues/R&B every Sat. ❸

Herriot's Main St ☎01969/667536, ⓦwww .herriotshotel.com. Small hotel with restaurant, just off Market Place, where a couple of the rooms have fell views. ❹

Laburnum House The Holme ☎01969/667717, ⓦwww.stayatlaburnumhouse.co.uk. At the turn-off from the main road to the museum, this tearoom/B&B has four simple rooms available. No credit cards. ❷

Steppe Haugh Guest House Town Head ☎01969/667645, ⓦwww.steppehaugh.co.uk. Nonsmoking seventeenth-century cottage with cosy rooms, a few minutes' walk from the centre. No credit cards. ❸

Youth hostel and campsite

Bainbridge Ings ☎01969/667354, ⓦwww .bainbridge-ings.co.uk. Half a mile east (10min walk) of the centre, just off the A684 (Aysgarth road). Milk and eggs available.

Hawes YHA Lancaster Terrace ☎0870/770 5854, ⓔhawes@yha.org.uk. Modern hostel on the edge of town, at the junction of the main A684 and B6255. Some twin and family rooms available (❶), otherwise dorm beds cost £10.25. Sept–March closed certain days of the week.

Askrigg

The mantle of "Herriot country" lies heavy on **ASKRIGG**, six miles east of Hawes, as the TV series *All Creatures Great and Small* was filmed in and around the village. There is, however, little to see or do, though the pubs and Georgian houses have their charms, and you might stroll to a couple of nearby falls, **Whitfield Force** and **Mill Gill Force**, both a mile or so to the west of the village. The market at Askrigg has its origins in medieval times, and predates that of Hawes – notice the bull-ring set outside the church here, a relic of bull-baiting days. There's an **information point** in the village shop in the Market Place. The *King's Arms* has stills from the *All Creatures* TV series, and it's a cosy old haunt with wood panelling, good beer and bar meals.

Aysgarth and around

The ribbon-village of **AYSGARTH**, straggling along and off the A684, is the vortex that sucks in Wensleydale's largest number of visitors, courtesy of the twin Aysgarth Falls, half a mile below the village (there's a path through the fields). A marked nature trail runs through the surrounding woodlands and there's a big car park and excellent **information centre** on the north bank (Easter–Oct daily 10am–5pm; Nov–Easter Fri, Sat & Sun 10am–4pm; ☎01969/663424). The **Upper Falls** and picnic grounds lie just back from here, by the bridge and church; the more spectacular **Lower Falls** are a half-mile stroll to the east through shaded woodland. The only local **pub**, the *George & Dragon* (☎01969/663358; ❺), has pleasant en-suite rooms (cheaper out of season) and a bar-meal menu with plenty of choice. Down by the falls, you'll find the **youth hostel** (☎0870/770 5678, ⓔaysgarth@yha.org.uk; £10.25; under refurbishment, call for opening details), and there's a **campsite**, *Westholme Caravan Park* (☎01969/663268; closed Nov–Easter), half a mile east on the A684.

There's a superb **circular walk** northeast from Aysgarth (6 miles; 4hr), which starts at the falls themselves and climbs up through Thoresby, with the foursquare battlements of **Castle Bolton** (March–Nov daily 10am–5pm; restricted winter opening, call for details; ☎01969/623981, ⓦwww.boltoncastle.co.uk; £4) a magnetic lure from miles away across the fields. Built in 1379 by Richard le Scrope, lord chancellor to Richard II, it's a massive defensive structure in which Mary, Queen of Scots was imprisoned for six months in 1568.

Swaledale

Narrow and steep-sided in its upper reaches, **Swaledale** emerges rocky and rugged in its central tract, which takes in the remote villages of **Keld**, **Thwaite** and **Muker**, before more typically pastoral scenery cuts in at the main village of **Reeth**. Unless you're hiking, it's Reeth that provides the best overnight stop, with the best choice of accommodation in the dale. From Richmond, **bus #30** (not Sun) runs up the valley along the B6270 as far as Keld. The only other public transport access is with the summer-only #801 (Sat, from Leeds/Bradford and Wharfedale) to Keld, or the #803 (Sun, from Hawes) to Muker and Reeth.

KELD, eight miles north of Hawes, is at the crossroads of the Pennine Way and the Coast-to-Coast path, making it an ideal hiking centre. The busy **youth hostel** is at Keld Lodge, an old shooting lodge near the telephone kiosk (℡0870/770 5888, Ⓔkeld@yha.org.uk; £10.25; closed Nov–Feb and certain days in winter). North and west of here, the upper reaches of Swaledale are wild indeed, with an atmosphere bordering on desolate even in summer. The Pennine Way shadows the very minor Stonesdale road for the three or four miles across **Stonesdale Moor** to the splendid *Tan Hill Inn* (℡01833/628246; ❷), reputedly the highest pub in Britain (1732ft above sea level).

THWAITE is the first hamlet south of Keld, just a two-mile walk away. Some of the loveliest scenery follows beyond the little village of **MUKER** (the name derives from the Norse for "meadow"), a mile or so to the east, distinguished by tiny side-valleys such as Oxnop Beck, south of Oxnop. Muker has a National Park **information point** in the village store, and there's a nice **pub**, the *Farmers Arms*, serving good food.

Further east lies **REETH**, the dale's main village and market centre (market day is Friday), set in a dramatic moorland bowl. Reeth has the biggest range of facilities in the dale, including a petrol station, a post office, the only bank, and a National Park **information centre** on the green (daily 10am–5pm; ℡01748/884059). Some cottages around the green post **B&B** signs in their windows, while the three central **pubs** also have rooms, most notably the *King's Arms* (℡01748/884259, Ⓦwww.thekingsarms.com; ❹; weekend 2-night minimum), on the green. The *Arkleside Hotel* (℡01748/884200, Ⓦwww.arklesidehotel.co.uk; ❺), just off the top of the green, was converted from a row of old miners' cottages and is a very cosy place to stay; or there's the superior *Burgoyne Hotel* (Ⓦwww.theburgoyne.co.uk; ❻), lording it over the top of the green.

Numerous paths across the fields on the south side of the river let you complete a circular walk from Reeth via **GRINTON**, whose attractive bridge, church and riverside inn, *The Bridge*, are just a mile away by road. The local **youth hostel**, *Grinton Lodge* (℡0870/770 5844, Ⓔgrinton@yha.org.uk; £11.50; winter closed 1–2 days a week), is housed in a former shooting lodge spectacularly sited in the hills above, ten minutes' walk from Grinton. You can rent mountain bikes here (book in advance), and the hostel can provide route details for local rides.

Richmond

Although marginalized on the National Park's northeasternmost borders, **RICHMOND** is the Dales' single most tempting historical town, thanks mainly to its magnificent castle, whose extensive walls and colossal keep cling to a precipice above the River Swale. Indeed, the entire town is an absolute gem, centred on a huge cobbled market square backed onto by hidden alleys and gardens housing mainly Georgian buildings of great refinement. The town itself is much older, having been dubbed *Riche-Mont* ("noble hill") by the Normans who first built a castle here in 1071.

There's no better place to start than **Richmond Castle** (daily: April–Oct 10am–6pm; Nov–March 10am–4pm; £3; EH), reached by signposted alleys from the market square. Originally built by Alan Rufus, first Norman earl of Richmond, it retains many features from its earliest incarnation, principally the gatehouse, curtain wall and Scolland's Hall, the oldest Norman great hall in the country. Most of medieval Richmond sprouted around the castle, but much of the town now radiates from the vast **Market Place**, with the Market Hall alongside (markets on Tues, Thurs, Fri & Sat). The most unusual structure here is the defunct **Holy Trinity** church, built in 1135 and now serving as the **Green Howards Museum** (April–Oct Mon–Sat 9.30am–4.30pm; Nov, Dec & March Mon–Fri 10am–4pm; closed Jan & Feb; £2.50). This honours North Yorkshire's Green Howards regiment, and contains a lot more than just uniforms and medals. The keenest interest of all, however, is in the town's **Theatre Royal**, dating from 1788, making it one of England's oldest extant theatres. Unassuming from the outside, the theatre's tiny interior is one of England's finest pieces of Georgian architecture. The theatre is open for both performances (box office ☏01748/823021) and tours (☏01748/823710), though as it's been under refurbishment recently, it's best to call first.

Below the castle, a signposted walk runs along the north bank of the **River Swale** out to the beautifully situated church of St Agatha and adjacent **Easby Abbey** (dawn to dusk; free; EH), whose golden stone walls stand a mile southeast of the town centre. The evocative remains are extensive, and in places – notably the thirteenth-century refectory – still remarkably intact.

Practicalities

Buses stop in the Market Place; there are regular services into Wensleydale and Swaledale, and to Darlington, ten miles to the northeast, which is on the main East Coast train line. The **tourist office**, at Friary Gardens, Victoria Road (summer daily 9.30am–5.30pm; winter Mon–Sat 9.30am–4.30pm; ☏01748/850252, ⓦwww.richmond.org.uk), organizes **guided walking tours** around the town in summer (free, donations welcome). **Accommodation** is plentiful, with central Frenchgate in particular boasting small B&Bs and guest houses in historic buildings.

Accommodation

Frenchgate Hotel 59–61 Frenchgate ☏01748/822087, ⓦwww.frenchgatehotel.com. Georgian townhouse with brightly furnished rooms, patio garden, bar and restaurant. ❺

King's Head Hotel Market Place ☏01748/850220, ⓦwww.kingshearichmond.co.uk. The town's principal hotel. Bar meals available, or eat in the restaurant for around £20 (excluding drinks). ❻

Restaurant on the Green 5–7 Bridge St ☏01748/826229. Seventeenth-century house below the castle, with a couple of nice B&B rooms available. A good place for bistro food at moderate prices (Fri & Sat dinner only), though you'll need to book. ❷

West End Guest House 45 Reeth Rd ☏01748/824783, ⓦwww.stayatwestend.com. Ten minutes' walk out of the centre (along and beyond Victoria Road). The tranquil gardens also contain four self-catering cottages. No credit cards. ❸

Willance House 24 Frenchgate ☏01748/824467. Characterful seventeenth-century cottage with three rooms. No credit cards. ❷

Cafés and restaurants

Frenchgate Café 29 Frenchgate
☎01748/824949. Open from 10am for coffee and breakfast, followed by light lunches and bistro-style dinners. Closed Mon. Inexpensive to Moderate.
Latino's 2 Trinity Church Sq ☎01748/825008.

Italian restaurant and pizzeria, next to Holy Trinity church on the square. Dinner only, closed Sun & Mon. Moderate.
A Taste of Thailand 15 King St
☎01748/829696. Just as it says, with a menu to satisfy most. You can bring your own wine. Moderate.

Ripon

The unassuming market town of **RIPON**, eleven miles north of Harrogate, is centred upon its relatively small but vital **Cathedral** (daily 7.30am–6.30pm; donation requested), which can trace its ancestry back to its foundation by St Wilfrid in 672; the original crypt is still extant below the central tower. Despite a rather plain exterior, there's plenty that pleases here, from the subtle, twin-towered, thirteenth-century west front to the choir's misericords, full of painted figures of miserable clergymen. The town's other focus is its **market-place**, linked by Kirkgate to the cathedral; market day is Thursday. Meanwhile, three restored buildings show a different side of Ripon's heritage, under the banner of the Yorkshire Law and Order Museums (all open April–Oct daily: July, Aug & school hols 11am–4pm, other times 1–4pm; combined ticket £4). At the **Prison and Police Museum** (otherwise £2.50), on St Marygate behind the cathedral, the old cells serve as the backdrop for an informative exhibition on policing since Anglo-Saxon times. Cases were heard at the 1830s **Courthouse** on Minster Road (£1), while the "undeserving" poor were incarcerated in the nearby **Ripon Workhouse**, on Allhallowgate (£1.50), for such heinous crimes as being unable to pay their bills.

The **bus station** (regular services from Masham, Harrogate, Knaresborough and Leeds) is just off the Market Place, while the town's **tourist office** is on Minster Road opposite the cathedral (July & Aug Mon–Sat 10am–6pm, Sun 10am–1pm; April, May, June & Sept Mon–Sat closes 5/5.30pm, Sun 10am–1pm; Oct Mon–Sat closes 4pm & closed Sun; Nov–March Tues–Sat 10am–1pm & 1.30–4.30pm; ☎01765/604625, Ⓦwww.riponcity.info). Ripon is the nearest base from which to visit Fountains Abbey (see below) and local **accommodation** options include *Bishopton Grove House*, Bishopton (☎01765/600888; no credit cards; ➊), a Georgian house in a peaceful corner of the town; and the *Unicorn Hotel*, Market Place (☎01765/602202, Ⓦwww.unicorn-hotel.co.uk; ➍), an old coaching inn and central Ripon's finest. There are several **restaurants** along Kirkgate across from the cathedral, including *Cibo*, 25 Kirkgate (☎01765/602722), an unpretentious Italian place, open daily for lunch and dinner.

Fountains Abbey and Studley Royal

It's tantalizing to imagine how the English landscape might have appeared had Henry VIII not dissolved the monasteries, with all the artistic ruin precipitated by that act. **Fountains Abbey** (April–Sept daily 10am–6pm; Oct–March daily 10am–4pm; last admission 1hr before closing; £5; NT), four miles southwest of Ripon off the B6265, gives a good idea of what might have been, and is the one ruin amongst Yorkshire's many monastic fragments you should make a

△ Fountains Abbey

point of seeing. The estate is owned by the National Trust, which organizes an ambitious range of activities and events – from opera and firework displays to **free guided tours** (April–Oct daily; call ☏01765/608888 for details). There are regular **buses** to Ripon from Harrogate and York (amongst other places), but the onward service to the abbey is patchy in summer (Sundays and bank holidays only), paltry in winter. Ring Ripon tourist office or the abbey for the latest.

Beautifully set in a narrow, wooded valley, the abbey was founded in 1133 by thirteen dissident Benedictine monks from the wealthy abbey of St Mary's in York. Within a hundred years, Fountains had become the wealthiest Cistercian foundation in England and it is to this century that the three main phases of the abbey's structural development belong: the church's nave and transepts, the domestic buildings, and the church's east end. Most immediately eye-catching is the **abbey church**, in particular the **Chapel of the Nine Altars** at its eastern end, whose delicacy is in marked contrast to the austerity of the rest of the nave. A great sixty-foot-high window rises over the chapel, complemented by a similar window at the nave's western doorway, over 370ft away. The **Perpendicular Tower**, almost 180ft high, looms over the whole ensemble, added by the eminent early sixteenth-century Abbot Marmaduke Huby, who presided over perhaps the abbey's greatest period of prosperity. Equally grandiose in scale is the undercroft of the **Lay Brothers' Dormitory** off the cloister, a stunningly vaulted space over three hundred feet long that was used to store the monastery's annual harvest of fleeces. The size of the lay buildings – including a substantial **Lay Brothers' Infirmary** – gives an idea of the number of lay brothers at the abbey. All are considerably larger than the corresponding monks' buildings, of which the most prepossessing are the **Chapter House** and **Refectory** – notice the huge fireplace of the tiny **Warming Room** alongside the refectory, the only heated space in the entire complex. Outside the abbey perimeter, between the gatehouse and the bridge, are the Abbey Mill and **Fountains Hall** (same times; NT), the latter a fine example of early seventeenth-century domestic architecture.

A riverside walk, marked from the visitor centre car park, takes you to a series of ponds and ornamental gardens, harbingers of **Studley Royal** (same times as the abbey; NT). This lush medley of lawns, lake, woodland and **Deer Park** (daily dawn to dusk; free) was laid out in 1720 and there are some scintillating views of the abbey from the gardens, though it's the cascades and water gardens that command most attention. The full circuit, from visitor centre to abbey and gardens and then back, is a good couple of miles' walk.

Harrogate

HARROGATE – the very picture of genteel Yorkshire respectability – owes its airy, planned appearance and early prosperity to the discovery of Tewit Well in 1571. This was the first of over eighty ferrous and sulphurous springs that, by the nineteenth century, were to turn the town into one of the country's leading spas. Tours of Harrogate's spa heritage begin with the **Royal Baths Assembly Rooms**, built in 1897, where you can still take a Turkish bath in the tiled Victorian surroundings (call ☏01423/556746 for hours; from £10.50 a session); the public entrance is on Parliament Street. Just around the corner in Crown Place stands the **Royal Pump Room**, built in 1842 over the

sulphur well that feeds the Royal Baths. The **museum** here (April–Oct Mon–Sat 10am–5pm, Sun 2–5pm; Nov–March Mon–Sat 10am–4pm, Sun 2–4pm; £2.50) re-creates something of the town's health-fixated past and also lets you sample the water; free hour-long **guided walks** leave here several times a week between July and October (information from the tourist office). Harrogate deserves much credit for the preservation of its green spaces, most prominent of which is **The Stray**, a jealously guarded green belt that curves around the south of the town centre. To the southwest, the 120-acre **Valley Gardens** are the venue for the annual Spring Flower Show and Sunday band concerts in summer, while many visitors also make for the **Harlow Carr Botanical Gardens** (daily 9am–6pm or dusk if earlier; £4.50; Ⓦ www.rhs.org.uk), the main showpiece of the Northern Horticultural Society. These lie one and a half miles out, on the town's western edge; take the B6162 Otley road, or walk beyond the Valley Gardens, through the Pine Woods.

Practicalities

Bus and **train** stations are on Station Parade, just a few minutes' walk from all the central sights. Harrogate's **tourist office** (April–Sept Mon–Sat 9am–6pm, Sun 10am–1pm; Oct–March Mon–Sat 9am–5pm; ☎01423/537300, Ⓦ www.harrogate.gov.uk) is in the Royal Baths on Crescent Road. You shouldn't have any problem finding somewhere to stay, other than during one of Harrogate's many festivals. Of these the most famous are the **flower shows** (second weeks of April and Sept), but there's also the **Great Yorkshire Show** (second week in July) and the Northern Antiques Fair (second half of Sept).

Accommodation

Cavendish Hotel 3 Valley Drive ☎01423/509637. A comfortable, friendly place, whose best rooms overlook the Valley Gardens. ❸

Cutlers on the Stray 19 West Park ☎01423/524471, Ⓦ www.cutlers-web.co.uk. Former coaching inn, now contemporary brasserie with rooms (some with views across The Stray). ❻

Fountains Hotel 27 King's Rd ☎01423/530483, Ⓦ www.fountains.fsworld.co.uk. Nonsmoking rooms with trim little bathrooms; it's quieter at the side, where the rooms look over a shady copse. ❸

Hotel du Vin Prospect Place ☎01423/856800, Ⓦ www.hotelduvin.com. Fashionable townhouse hotel and bistro overlooking The Stray, with variously sized boutique-style rooms featuring trademark big beds and bathrooms. ❻

Rudding Park Hotel Rudding Park, Follifoot ☎01423/871350, Ⓦ www.ruddingpark.com. Stylish country-house hotel located three miles southeast of town (down the A661). Fine bar and brasserie, and attached gardens and golf course. ❽

with spacious en-suite rooms (one a four-poster), terraced bar and charming garden. ❻

Restaurants and pubs

Betty's 1 Parliament St ☎01423/502746. Very much a Harrogate institution, established in the 1920s. The cakes and tarts are to die for, but full meals are also served. Closes at 9pm. Inexpensive.

Drum and Monkey 5 Montpellier Gardens ☎01423/502650. Long-standing fish and seafood restaurant, a firm favourite with locals and out-of-towners alike. Closed Sun. Moderate to Expensive.

Old Bell Tavern 6 Royal Parade ☎01423/507930. Treat it as a pub – it's the best in town – or come to eat, since there are bar meals and sandwiches served daily (lunchtime and 6–7pm) and a nonsmoking brasserie upstairs. Moderate.

Orchid 28 Swan Rd ☎01423/560425. Wok-wielding chefs conjure up specialities from all corners of Southeast Asia. Closed Mon & Sat lunch. Moderate.

Salsa Posada 4 Mayfield Grove ☎01423/565151. Funky Mexican restaurant

Knaresborough

A four-mile hop east from Harrogate, **KNARESBOROUGH** rises spectacularly above the River Nidd's limestone gorge, its old townhouses, pubs, shops and gardens clustered together on the wooded northern bank, with the river itself crossed by two bridges ("High" and "Low") and an eye-opener of a rail viaduct. The rocky crag above the town is crowned by the stump of a **Castle** (Easter–Sept daily 10.30am–5pm; £2.50) dating back to Norman times. It was here that Henry II's knights fled after the murder of Thomas à Becket in Canterbury Cathedral; here, too, that Richard II was held before being removed to Pontefract, where he was murdered in 1400.

The town's two novelty acts are to be found on the west side of the river. **Mother Shipton's Cave** (daily: March–Oct 9.30am–5.45pm; Nov & Feb 10am–4.45pm; closed Dec & Jan; £4.95; ⓦ www.mothershipton.co.uk) was home to a sixteenth-century soothsayer who predicted the defeat of the Armada, the Great Fire of London, world wars, cars, planes, iron ships – falling short, however, in the most important oracular chestnut of them all, predicting the End of the World: "The world to an end will come," she prophesied, "in eighteen hundred and eighty one." Close by is the **Petrifying Well**, where dripping, lime-soaked waters coat everyday objects – gloves, hats, coats, toys – in a brownish veneer that sets rock-hard in a few weeks. Both cave and well are contained within a riverside estate, reached along a fine eighteenth-century wooded "Long Walk"; the main entrance is just over the High Bridge, north of the town.

Regular **trains** and **buses** (every 10min) from Harrogate are frequent enough to make Knaresborough an easy side trip. Signs point you to the **tourist office** at 9 Castle Courtyard, around the back of Market Place (Easter–Oct Mon–Sat 10am–5.30pm, July & Aug until 6pm, Sun 10am–1pm; ℡01423/866886), from where free **guided walks** depart on Tuesday afternoons in summer (July–Sept).

York

YORK is the north's most compelling city, a place whose history, said George VI, "is the history of England". This is perhaps overstating things a little, but it reflects the significance of a metropolis that until the Industrial Revolution was second only to London in population and importance, not only at the heart of the country's religious life, but also a key player in some of the major events that have shaped the nation. These days a more provincial air hangs over the city, except in summer when York feels like a heritage site for the benefit of tourists. That said, no trip to this part of the country is complete without a visit to York, while the city is well placed for any number of day-trips, the most essential being to **Castle Howard**, the gem amongst English stately homes.

A brief history of York

The **Romans** chose York as the site of a military camp during their campaigns against the Brigantes in 71 AD, and in time this fortress became a city – **Eboracum**, capital of the empire's northern European territories. The base for Hadrian's northern campaigns, it was also ruled for three years by Septimius founder of Constantinople; at Chlorus' death, his son was proclaimed Roman emperor here – the only occasion an emperor was enthroned in Britain.

Much fought over after the decline of Rome, the city later became the fulcrum of Christianity in northern England. It was here, on Easter Day in 627, that Bishop Paulinus, on a mission to establish the Roman Church, baptized King Edwin of Northumbria in a small timber chapel built for the purpose. Six years later the church became the first minster and Paulinus the first archbishop of York. In 867 the city fell to the **Danes**, who renamed it **Jorvik**, and later made it the capital of eastern England (Danelaw). Later Viking raids culminated in the decisive **Battle of Stamford Bridge** (1066) six miles east of the city, where English King Harold defeated Norse King Harald – a Pyrrhic victory in the event, for his weakened army was defeated by the Normans just a few days later at the Battle of Hastings, with well-known consequences for all concerned. In York, aside from the physical remains left by the Vikings on show in several of the museums, the very street names tell of their profound influence – the suffix "-gate" is derived from an old Norse word for street.

The **Normans** devastated much of York's hinterland in their infamous "Harrying of the North", building two castles in the city itself. Stone walls were thrown up during the thirteenth century, when the city became a favoured Plantagenet retreat and commercial capital of the north, its importance reflected in the new title of Duke of York, bestowed ever since on the monarch's second son. Although Henry VIII's Dissolution of the Monasteries took its toll on a city crammed with religious houses, York remained strongly wedded to the Catholic cause, and the most famous of the Gunpowder Plot conspirators, **Guy Fawkes**, was born here. During the **Civil War** Charles I established his court in the city, which was strongly pro-Royalist, inviting a Parliamentarian siege that was eventually lifted by Prince Rupert of the Rhine, a nephew of the king. Rupert's troops, however, were routed by Cromwell and Sir Thomas Fairfax at the **Battle of Marston Moor** in 1644, another seminal battle in England's history, which took place six miles west of York.

While the Industrial Revolution largely passed it by, the arrival of the **railways** brought renewed prosperity, thanks largely to the enterprise of pioneering "Railway King" George Hudson, lord mayor during the 1830s and 1840s. The railway is still a major employer, as is the confectionery industry – in the shape of companies such as Terry Suchard and Nestlé – together with the proceeds from new service and bioscience industries – and not forgetting, of course, the income from four million annual tourists.

Arrival, information, transport and tours

Trains arrive at **York Station**, just outside the city walls, a 750-yard walk from the historic core. National Express **buses** and most other regional bus services drop off and pick up on Rougier Street, two hundred yards north of the train station, just before Lendal Bridge, though National Express services call at the train station, too. There's a **tourist office** at the train station (April–Oct Mon–Sat 9am–6pm, Sun 9.30am–4.30pm; Nov–March Mon–Sat 9am–5pm, Sun 10am–4pm), though the main office is over Lendal Bridge, two hundred yards west of the Minster in the De Grey Rooms, on Exhibition Square (April–Oct Mon–Sat 9am–6pm, Sun 10am–5pm; Nov–March Mon–Sat 9am–5pm, Sun 10am–4pm). Each office shares the same telephone number and website (☎01904/621756, ⓦ www.visityork.org).

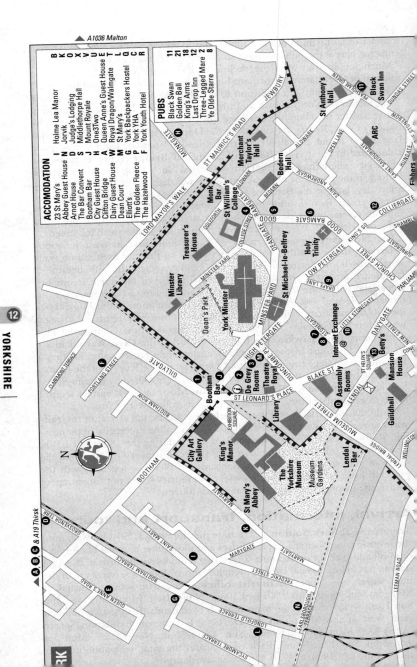

▲ A1036 Malton

▲ A B C & A19 Thirsk

ACCOMMODATION

23 St Mary's	I	Holme Lea Manor	B
Abbey Guest House	N	Jorvik	K
Arnot House	D	Judge's Lodging	X
The Bar Convent	S	Middlethorpe Hall	V
Bootham Bar	J	Mount Royale	U
City Guest House	H	One3Two	E
Clifton Bridge	A	Queen Anne's Guest House	L
Dairy Guest House	W	Royal Dragon/Walmgate	T
Dean Court	M	St Mary's	Q
Elliot's	G	York Backpackers Hostel	C
The Golden Fleece	P	York YHA	R
The Hazelwood	F	York Youth Hotel	

PUBS

Black Swan	11
Golden Ball	21
King's Arms	18
Last Drop Inn	12
Three-Legged Mare	2
Ye Olde Starre	8

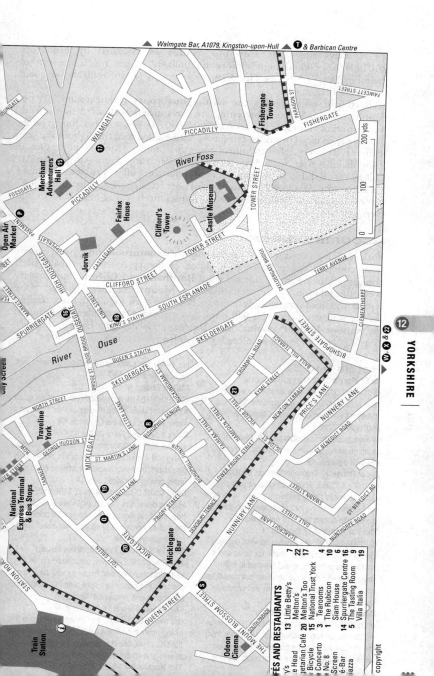

▲ Walmgate Bar, A1079, Kingston-upon-Hull ▲ ● & Barbican Centre

YORKSHIRE

12

CAFÉS AND RESTAURANTS

y's	13	Little Betty's	7
e Head		Melton's	22
etarian Café	20	Melton's Too	17
Bicycle	15	National Trust York	4
Concerto	3	Tearooms	10
No. 8	1	The Rubicon	6
Screen		Siam House	14
é-Bar		Spurriergate Centre	16
iazza		The Tasting Room	9
	5	Villa Italia	19

copyright

streets, alleys and yards. City **bus routes** are operated by First York (℡01904/622992), though visitors are unlikely to get much use out of their FirstDay (£2.10) or FirstWeek rover tickets (£10), available on board the buses.

The tourist office pushes the various **bus tours** (from around £8 per person), but much more interesting are the **guided walks** led by the York Association of Voluntary Guides (℡01904/640780, ⓦwww.york.touristguides .btinternet.co.uk). They offer a free, two-hour guided tour throughout the year (daily at 10.15am), plus additional tours in summer (April, Sept & Oct at 2.15pm; June–Aug at 2.15pm & 6.45pm), departing from outside the Art Gallery in Exhibition Square. Several operators offer **cruises**, including YorkBoat (℡01904/628324, ⓦwww.yorkboat.co.uk), sailing daily from King's Staith and Lendal Bridge (Feb–Nov; cruises from £6, £6.50/7.50 in the evening).

Accommodation

York is a busy tourist town, with the range of **accommodation** you'd expect, from countless cheap B&Bs to a clutch of luxury hotels. The main B&B concentrations are in the sidestreets off **Bootham and Clifton** (immediately west of Exhibition Square), as well as in the **Mount** area (turn right out of the station and head down Blossom Street. If you're stuck for a bed, make straight for the tourist offices, who will book you a room. Or consider the rooms at the various **budget chains**, like *Travelodge, Holiday Inn Express, Ramada, Novotel, Quality Hotel*, and so on, which all have hotels in York.

Hotels and B&Bs

23 St Mary's 23 St Mary's, Bootham
℡01904/622738. Amiable family-house hotel just west of St Mary's Abbey and gardens. ❹

Abbey 14 Earlsborough Terrace, Marygate
℡01904/627782,
ⓦwww.bedandbreakfastyork.co.uk. Riverside terraced guest house with pretty rooms, two of which overlook the river. ❸

Arnot House 17 Grosvenor Terrace, Bootham
℡01904/641966, ⓦwww.arnothouseyork.co.uk.
Victorian family house preserving many of its original features, offering four no-smoking en-suite rooms with distant views of the Minster. ❸

The Bar Convent 17 Blossom St
℡01904/643238, ⓦwww.bar-convent.org.uk.
Eleven single rooms (£26 each), six twins and a double; one of the twins and the double is en suite, otherwise there are separate bathrooms and access to a self-catering kitchen and guest lounge. ❷

Bootham Bar 4 High Petergate
℡01904/658516. Petite townhouse rooms in an eighteenth-century building, just 100 yards from the Minster. All en-suite except for three basic singles (£25) which share a bathroom. Parking

ing, family-run guest house with budget rates, not far from the Minster. ❸

Clifton Bridge Water End, Clifton
℡01904/610510, ⓦwww.cliftonbridgehotel.co.uk.
A mile northwest of the Minster beyond Bootham, nicely situated in its own grounds. ❺

Dairy 3 Scarcroft Rd ℡01904/639367,
ⓦwww.dairyguesthouse.co.uk. Charming Victorian house half a mile south of the station, retaining its pine doors, cast-iron fireplaces, stained glass and pretty courtyard. Closed Jan. ❹

Dean Court Duncombe Place ℡01904/625082,
ⓦwww.deancourt-york.co.uk. Views of the Minster from the front rooms, which means it's pricey, but the facilities come up to scratch. Ask about special-break prices. ❼

Elliott's Sycamore Place, Bootham Terrace
℡01904/623333, ⓦwww.elliottshotel.co.uk. A large detached Victorian house tucked away in a peaceful and convenient spot, with big breakfasts, bar snacks and restaurant. ❹

The Golden Fleece 16 Pavement
℡01904/625171. Just four rooms available in this historic pub, but what a collection – one overlooks the Shambles, one has views to the Minster towers and all are haunted (well, maybe). ❺

The Hazelwood 24–25 Portland St, Gillygate

Tea and coffee always available in the lounge; also a pleasant garden. **⑤**

Holme Lea Manor 18 St Peter's Grove, Clifton ☎01904/623529, ⓦwww.holmelea.co.uk. Comfortable en-suite rooms with period touches in a quiet, tree-lined Victorian cul-de-sac just ten minutes from the centre. **④**

Jorvik 52 Marygate, Bootham ☎01904/653511, ⓦwww.jorvikhotel.co.uk. Family-run townhouse hotel with a variety of rooms – you'll pay a little more to overlook the abbey gardens. **④**

Judge's Lodging 9 Lendal ☎01904/638733, ⓔjudgeshotel@aol.com. One of the top central, historic choices, located in the eighteenth-century Georgian residence of the former assize court judges. There's a restaurant and a good cellar bar. **⑦**

Middlethorpe Hall Bishopsthorpe Rd ☎01904/641241, ⓦwww.middlethorpe.com. York's most celebrated spot, a grand eighteenth-century mansion a couple of miles south of the city, next to the racecourse. **⑧**

Mount Royale The Mount ☎01904/628856, ⓦwww.mountroyale.co.uk. Luxurious, antique-filled retreat with garden suites set around a private garden, together with a heated outdoor pool (open summer only), sauna and steam room. **⑥**

One3Two 132 The Mount ☎01904/600060, ⓦwww.one3two.co.uk. Indulge yourself in one of five beautifully furnished rooms in a sympathetically restored Georgian townhouse, 10min from the city centre. Enormous teak beds, spacious marble bathrooms and champagne breakfast hampers. **⑦**

Queen Anne's 24–26 Queen Anne's Rd ☎01904/629389, ⓦwww.s-h-systems.co.uk/hotels/queenann.html. Budget-rated Bootham B&B with seven bright rooms. **②**

Royal Dragon/Walmgate 16 Barbican Rd ☎01904/623134. Clean, simple rooms attached to a very reasonably priced Chinese restaurant close to the Barbican Centre. **②**

St Mary's 17 Longfield Terrace ☎01904/626972, ⓦwww.stmaryshotel.co.uk. Homely, flower-draped, no-smoking hotel in a peaceful railway-cutting backstreet south of Bootham. **③**

Hostels and student halls

University of York ☎01904/432222, ⓦwww.york.ac.uk. University accommodation available at four separate sites during Easter and summer holidays, either B&B in well-equipped rooms (single and twins **③**), or three-night stays (from £250) and week-long breaks (from £450) in self-contained flats/houses (sleeping 6–12).

York Backpackers Hostel Micklegate House, 88–90 Micklegate ☎01904/627720, ⓦwww.yorkbackpackers.mcmail.com. Dorm space (£13), doubles and family rooms in a Grade I listed building. There's a self-catering kitchen, laundry, Internet access, TV and games room, café and licensed cellar bar. Prices include breakfast. **②**

York YHA Water End, Clifton ☎0870/770 6102, ⓔyork@yha.org.uk. Large Victorian mansion 20min walk from the centre. Beds mostly in four-bedded dorms (£16.50), though private rooms also available with TV, towels and kettle. Facilities include a café, Internet access and large garden. **①**

York Youth Hotel 11–13 Bishophill Senior ☎01904/625904, ⓦwww.yorkyouthhotel.demon.co.uk. Variously priced 4-, 8- and 20-bed dorms available (£11–16), plus single and twin rooms. Also a kitchen, laundry, games room, TV lounge and Internet access. Breakfast available Sun only (£2–3.50). **①**

The City

If the city council and tourist office are to be believed, there are around sixty churches, museums and historic buildings crammed within York's walls. In fact the tally of things you really want to see is surprisingly limited, with most sights within easy walking distance of one another. Even so, it's hard to get round everything in less than two days, and equally difficult to stick to any rigid itinerary. The **Minster** is the obvious place to start, followed by the cluster of buildings that circle it; then you might cut south to the **Shambles**, central to the city's old centre and pedestrianized grid, or walk around **the walls** from the Minster to Exhibition Square and Museum Street for the **City Art Gallery**, **Yorkshire Museum** and **St Mary's Abbey**, evocative ruins surrounded by the city's loveliest gardens. Thereafter you could walk through

Tower and the nearby **Jorvik Viking Centre** and **Castle Museum**. Lastly, be sure to leave time to take in the **National Railway Museum**, a superb museum whose appeal goes way beyond railway memorabilia.

York Minster

York Minster (daily: June–Sept 7am–8.30pm; Oct–May 7am–6pm; £4.50, minster and all its attractions £6; Ⓦ www.yorkminster.org) ranks as one of the country's most important sights. Seat of the Archbishop of York, it is Britain's largest Gothic building and home to countless treasures, not least of which is the world's largest medieval stained-glass window and an estimated half of all the medieval stained glass in England. In its earliest incarnation the Minster was probably the wooden chapel used to baptize King Edwin of Northumbria in 627. After its stone successors were destroyed by the Danes, the first significant foundations were laid around 1080 and it was from the germ of this Norman church that the present structure emerged.

Nothing else in the Minster can match the magnificence of the stained glass in the nave and transepts. The **West Window** (1338) contains distinctive heart-shaped upper tracery (the "Heart of Yorkshire"), whilst in the nave's north aisle, the second bay window (1155) contains slivers of the oldest stained glass in the country. The north transept's **Five Sisters Window** is named after the five fifty-foot lancets, each glazed with thirteenth-century grisaille, a distinctive frosted, silvery-grey glass. Opposite, the south transept contains a sixteenth-century, 17,000-piece **Rose Window**, commemorating the 1486 marriage of Henry VII and Elizabeth of York, an alliance that marked the end of the Wars of the Roses. The greatest of the church's 128 windows, however, is the majestic **East Window** (1405), at 78ft by 31ft the world's largest area of medieval stained glass in a single window. Its themes are the beginning and the end of the world, the upper panels showing scenes from the Old Testament, the lower sections mainly episodes from the book of Revelation.

Before leaving the main body of the interior, give some time to the north transept's 400-year-old wooden clock with its oak knights, and the stone **choir screen**, knotted with incredibly intricate carvings and decorated with life-size figures of English monarchs from William I to Henry VI – all except the latter carved in the last quarter of the fifteenth century. Amongst the many **tombs**, those of most interest are the monument in the south transept to Walter de Grey, a beautiful grey-green canopy protecting a recumbent stone figure, and the tomb of the 10-year-old William, second son of Edward III, in the choir aisle.

The foundations, or **undercroft** (Mon–Sat 9am–5.15pm, Sun 12.30–5.15pm; £2.50), have been turned into a museum, while amongst precious church relics in the adjoining **treasury** are silver plate found in Walter de Grey's tomb and the eleventh-century *Horn of Ulf*, presented to the Minster by a relative of the tide-turning King Canute. There's also access from the undercroft to the **crypt**, the spot that transmits the most powerful sense of antiquity, as it contains portions of Archbishop Roger's choir and sections of the 1080 church, including pillars with fine Romanesque capitals. Access to the undercroft, treasury and crypt is from the south transept, also the entrance to the **central tower** (£2.50), which you can climb for rooftop views over the city. Finally pop into the **Chapter House**, an architectural novelty whose buttressed octagonal walls remove the need for a central pillar, otherwise a common feature of this type of building.

The walls

gates (or "bars"), whilst the northern sections still follow the line of the Roman ramparts. **Monk Bar** at the northern end of Goodramgate is as good a point of access as any, tallest of the city's four main gates and host to a small **Richard III Museum** (daily: March–Oct 9am–5pm; Nov–Feb 9.30am–4pm; £2; ⓦ www.richardiiimuseum.co.uk), where you're invited to decide on the guilt or innocence of England's most maligned king. For a taste of the walls' best section, take the ten-minute stroll west from Monk Bar to **Bootham Bar**, the only gate on the site of a Roman gateway and marking the traditional northern entrance to the city. A stroll round the walls' entire two-and-a-half-mile length will take you past the southwestern **Micklegate Bar**, long considered the most important of the gates since it, in turn, marked the start of the road to London. It was built to a Norman design reputedly using ancient stone coffins as building stone, and was later used to exhibit the heads of executed criminals and rebels. The engaging **Micklegate Bar Museum** (daily 9am–5pm; £2) occupies a surviving fortified tower.

The Shambles

The Shambles, off King's Square at the southern end of Goodramgate, could be taken as the epitome of medieval York. Flagstoned, almost impossibly narrow and lined with perilously leaning timber-framed houses, it was the home of York's butchers, its erstwhile stench and squalor now difficult to imagine, though old meat hooks still adorn the odd house. At no. 35, there's a **shrine** (closed to the public) to Margaret Clitherow, the Catholic wife of a butcher, martyred in 1586 for allegedly sheltering priests; she was pressed to death with rocks piled on top of a board on the city's Ouse Bridge. Newgate **market** (daily 8am–5pm) lies off the Shambles, together with the core of the city's shopping streets.

The Yorkshire Museum and St Mary's Abbey

South of Exhibition Square on Museum Street stands the entrance to the **Yorkshire Museum** (daily 10am–5pm; £4), which lies within the beautifully laid-out grounds of St Mary's Abbey, itself now in ruins. It's one of York's better museums, strong on archeological remains which it presents in a series of rooms examining the Roman presence in the city. There are impressive displays of Viking and Anglo-Saxon artefacts, too, though chief exhibit is the fifteenth-century Middleham Jewel, found in 1985 – a diamond-shaped jewel with an oblong sapphire, claimed as the finest piece of Gothic jewellery in England.

Part of the museum basement incorporates the fireplace and chapter house of **St Mary's Abbey** (dawn to dusk; free), whose ruins lie around the Museum Gardens, the abbey's former grounds. Founded around 1080, the abbey later became an important Benedictine foundation, additionally significant as it was from here that disenchanted monks fled to found Fountains Abbey.

South to Jorvik

At the **Merchant Adventurers' Hall**, off Fossgate (Easter–Sept Mon–Thurs 9am–5pm, Fri & Sat 9am–3pm, Sun noon–4pm; Oct–Easter Mon–Sat 9am–3pm; £2), the overpowering whiff of wood polish prepares you for one of the finest medieval timber-framed halls in Europe. The beautiful building was raised by the city's most powerful guild, dealers in wool from the Wolds, woollens from the Dales and lead from the Pennines, commodities that were

Fairfax House, on nearby Castlegate (Mon–Thurs & Sat 11am–5pm, Sun 1.30–5pm; guided tours only on Fri at 11am & 2pm; closed Jan & Feb; £4.50; ⓦ www.fairfaxhouse.co.uk), celebrates the wealth of a later period. This elegant Georgian townhouse was restored to house the collection of fine arts left by Noel Terry, scion of one of the city's chocolate dynasties. The bulk of the collection consists of eighteenth-century furniture and clocks, while every December the popular "Keeping of Christmas" exhibition re-creates a Georgian Christmas in the house.

Around the corner, in the Coppergate shopping centre, the crowds descend upon the city's blockbuster Viking exhibit – **Jorvik** (daily: April–Oct 10am–5pm; Nov–March 10am–4pm; £7.20; ⓦ www.vikingjorvik.com). This multimillion-pound affair flies visitors back in "time capsules" to the tenth-century city of York, presenting not just the sights but the sounds and even the smells of a riverside Viking settlement, complete with costumed villagers, street scenes and panoramic views of the re-created city. Not surprisingly, it's a hugely popular exhibit, and great for children. Queues form early, but you can avoid queues by pre-booking your entrance ticket online (though this costs £1 more). It's worth noting that the museum organizes York's annual **Viking Festival** every February when themed events take place throughout the city – details from the Festival Office at the centre.

York Castle and the Castle Museum

Despite the rich architectural heritage elsewhere in the city, there's precious little left of **York Castle**, one of two established by William the Conqueror. Only the perilously leaning **Clifford's Tower** (daily: Easter–June & Sept 10am–6pm; July & Aug 10am–7.30pm; Oct 10am–5pm; Nov–Easter 10am–4pm or dusk; £2.50; EH) remains, as evocative a piece of military engineering as you could wish for: a stark and isolated stone keep built on one of William's mottes between 1245 and 1262.

Immediately east of the tower lies the excellent **Castle Museum** (daily 9.30am–5pm; £6), a remarkable collection founded by a Dr Kirk of Pickering, who in the 1920s realized that many of the everyday items used in rural areas were in danger of disappearing. He took the unusual step of accepting bric-a-brac from his patients in lieu of fees. A whole range of early craft, folk and agricultural ephemera is complemented by costumes, militaria, workshops, two entire reconstructed streets and special exhibitions on subjects as diverse as chocolate, burials and fire engines. Pride of place is given to a dazzling Viking helmet, discovered during the Coppergate excavations and the only one of its kind ever found.

The National Railway Museum

The **National Railway Museum** on Leeman Road (daily 10am–6pm; free; ⓦ www.nrm.org.uk), ten minutes' walk (600 yards) from the station, is a must if you have even the slightest interest in railways, history, engineering or Victoriana. The Great Hall alone features some fifty restored locomotives dating from 1829 onwards, among them the Mallard, at 126mph the world's fastest steam engine. The Station Hall, a former goods station, complete with tracks and platforms, holds the major permanent exhibitions, where you can see the plush splendour of the royal carriages ("Palaces on Wheels") and the bleak segregation of classes in the Victorian coaches. A separate wing, "The Works", provides access to the engineering workshop where conservation work is undertaken; to a walk-round backstage warehouse area, showcasing the

Eating and drinking

In keeping with much else in the city, many establishments are relentlessly and self-consciously old-fashioned, though there are some real highlights – truly historic **pubs**, the remarkable *Betty's*, the ultimate **teashop** experience, and a scattering of well-regarded **restaurants**. The **coffee and café-bar** scene has flourished too, with the main chain-names (Starbucks, Coffee Republic, Bar 38, Pitcher & Piano) all represented, alongside some honourable independents.

Tearooms, cafés and café-bars

Betty's 6–8 St Helen's Square. If there are tea-shops in heaven they'll be like *Betty's*. There are a dozen or so fish and meat hot dishes, some extraordinary puddings, and specialities like pikelets and Yorkshire fat rascals. Daily 9am–9pm.

Blake Head Vegetarian Café 104 Micklegate. Bookstore café with patio for freshly baked cakes, pâtés, quiche, brunch, salads and soups. Mon–Sat 9.30am–5pm, Sun 10am–5pm.

Café Concerto 27 High Petergate. A good all-rounder in the heart of the city that's café by day and bistro by night. Daily 10am–10pm.

Café No. 8 8 Gillygate. Caesar salads, inventive ciabatta sarnies and cool sounds in this funky little café-bar, just outside Bootham Bar. Mon–Fri 11am–3pm, Thurs & Fri also 5–11pm, Sat 11am–11pm, Sun 11am–5pm.

City Screen Café-Bar 13–17 Coney St. York's independent cinema has a riverside café-bar, serving food until 9pm and boasting a whole host of events. Daily 11am–11pm.

Little Betty's 46 Stonegate. Owned by *Betty's* and in the same league; over 100 years old, it's the picture of a classic tearooms. Daily 9am–5.30pm.

Melton's Too 25 Walmgate. Exposed brickwork, cushions scattered on armchairs and the daily papers set the tone for this relaxed café-bar and bistro. Drop in for superior tapas, Thai green curries (a house speciality), salads, steaks and more. Mon–Sat 10.30am–10.30pm, Sun 10.30am–9.30pm.

National Trust York Tearooms 30 Goodramgate. A slickly run place just 200 yards from the Minster, serving snacks and light meals. Mon–Sat 10am–5pm.

Spurriergate Centre St Michael's Church, Spurriergate. Quiche, salads and baked potatoes served in the impressive interior of twelfth-century St Michael's. Mon–Fri 10am–4.30pm, Sat 9.30am–5pm.

Restaurants

Blue Bicycle 34 Fossgate ☎01904/673990.

from innovation. Reservations advised. Expensive.

Melton's 7 Scarcroft Rd ☎01904/634341. Simple, classy cooking, including very good fish dishes, and imaginative vegetarian food. Closed Mon lunch & Sun dinner. Reservations advised. Expensive.

La Piazza 45 Goodramgate ☎01904/642641. Authentic Italian coffee bar out front, courtyard restaurant out back, tucked into a nice Tudor building. Moderate.

The Rubicon 5–7 Little Stonegate ☎01904/676076. Contemporary style and vegetarian world flavours, so there's moussaka and veggie lasagne but also Thai red curry and cinnamon couscous on offer. Moderate.

Siam House 63a Goodramgate ☎01904/624677. This prettily furnished Thai restaurant rarely disappoints – the menu is huge enough to cater for any tastes, and lunch for £6.95 is good value. Closed Sun lunch. Moderate.

The Tasting Room 13 Swinegate Court East, off Grape Lane ☎01904/627879. Plenty of choice from a light lunch menu (omelettes, pasta, oak-smoked salmon salad) to more elaborate meals in the evening. Closed Sun & Mon. Lunch inexpensive, dinner moderate.

Villa Italia 69 Micklegate ☎01904/670501. York's premier Italian, where delights on offer include good pizzas, Sardinian fish stew, garlic-and-lime-marinated tuna or roast duck with rosemary and celery. Closed Sun. Expensive.

Pubs

Black Swan Peasholme Green. York's oldest (sixteenth-century) pub with some superb stone flagging and wood panelling. Home of the city's folk club.

Golden Ball Cromwell Rd, Bishophill. Perhaps the city centre's nicest and most archetypal "local", with an attractive beer garden tucked away at the back.

King's Arms King's Staithe. Close to the Ouse Bridge, this pub has a fine riverside setting with outdoor tables.

Last Drop Inn 27 Colliergate. A friendly, bare-

Three-Legged Mare 15 High Petergate. York Brewery's cosy outlet for its own quality beer and definitely a pub for grown-ups – no juke box, no video games and no kids.

Ye Olde Starre 40 Stonegate. Vies with the *Black Swan* for historic precedence; good beer, a beer garden and plenty of atmosphere.

Nightlife, culture and entertainment

There are healthy helpings of **live music**, culture and **nightlife** in York, much of it detailed in the local *Evening Press* (and on their useful website, ⓦwww .thisisyork.co.uk). Most bigger bands bypass the city in favour of Leeds, though the Barbican Centre pulls in its fair share of major mainstream artists. The annual **Early Music Festival**, held in July, is perhaps the best of its kind in Britain, with dozens of events spread over ten days – details are available on ⓣ01904/658338, ⓦwww.ncem.co.uk, or from the tourist office. The famous **York Mystery Plays** have traditionally been held every four years, though funding and organizational problems have taken their toll – the next performances are now not envisaged until 2010.

Live music venues

Barbican Centre Barbican Rd ⓣ01904/656688. Country, rock, folk and MOR stalwarts all appear here sooner or later.

Black Swan Peasholme Green ⓣ01904/632922, ⓦwww.freeweb.telco4u.net/blackswanfolk. Regular folk nights with quality bands and singer-songwriters, plus jam sessions once or twice a week.

Fibbers Stonebow House, Stonebow ⓣ01904/466148, ⓦwww.fibbers.co.uk. Indie and guitar-pop bands (local and national) play most nights of the week.

Cinema, theatre and the arts

Cinema: City Screen 13–17 Coney St ⓣ01904 /541155, ⓦwww.picturehouses.co.uk. The choice for art-house cinema, with a riverside café-bar.

Grand Opera House Cumberland St, at Clifford St ⓣ01904/671818. Musicals, ballet and family entertainment in all its guises.

Theatre Royal St Leonard's Place ⓣ01904/623568, ⓦwww.theatre-royal-york .co.uk. Musicals, pantos and mainstream theatre, as well as a café-bar.

Listings

Banks and exchange Most main banks are in and around St Helen's Square. American Express, 6 Stonegate; Thomas Cook, 4 Nessgate, and inside HSBC, 13 Parliament St.

Bike rental Bob Trotter, 13–15 Lord Mayor's Walk, at Monkgate ⓣ01904/622868, ⓦwww .bobtrottercycles.com. Rates from £10 per day, plus a deposit.

Bus information Traveline York, 20 George Hudson St (office Mon–Fri 8.30am–5pm; telephone enquiries Mon–Sat 8am–8pm, Sun 8am–2pm; ⓣ01904/551400) can advise about all local and regional bus (and train) information.

Car rental Avis ⓣ01904/610460; Budget ⓣ01904/644919; Europcar ⓣ01904/656161; Hertz ⓣ01904/612586; Practical ⓣ01904/624277.

Hospital York District Hospital, Wigginton Road (24hr emergency number ⓣ01904/631313); bus #1, #2 or #3. Also York Walk-in Centre, 31 Monkgate (ⓣ01904/674557) offers care, advice and treatment without an appointment.

Internet Internet Exchange, 13 Stonegate ⓣ01904/638808; Gateway, 26 Swinegate ⓣ01904/646446; access also available at the youth hostels.

Pharmacy Boots, Coney St ⓣ01904/653657.

Police Fulford Rd ⓣ01904/631321.

Post Office The main office is at 22 Lendal ⓣ01904/617285.

Taxis Ranks at Rougier Street, Duncombe Place, Exhibition Square, and the train station; or call Station Taxis ⓣ01904/623332; Castle Taxis ⓣ01904/611511.

Castle Howard

Immersed in the deep countryside of the Howardian Hills, fifteen miles northeast open at 10am; £9; grounds only £6; Ⓦ www.castlehoward.co.uk) is the seat of one of England's leading aristocratic families and among the country's grandest stately homes. Since providing the setting for the television version of *Brideshead Revisited*, the house's car parks have been packed every weekend, but fitting it into a public transport itinerary is something of a problem. In summer there are two Yorkshire Coastliner buses a day (one on Sun) from York, Malton or Pickering, but daily bus tours from York can bring you out and back, too, or take the train to Malton (regular services on the York–Scarborough line) and then a taxi the five miles from the station to the house.

The colossal main house was designed by **Sir John Vanbrugh** in 1699 and was almost forty years in the making – remarkable enough, were it not for the fact that Vanbrugh was, at the start of the commission at least, best known as a playwright and had no formal architectural training. Shrewdly, Vanbrugh recognized his limitations and called upon the assistance of Nicholas Hawksmoor, who had a major part in the house's structural design – the pair later worked successfully together on Blenheim Palace. If Hawksmoor's guiding hand can be seen throughout, Vanbrugh's influence is clear in the very theatricality of the building, notably in the palatial **Great Hall**. This was gutted by fire in the 1940s, but has subsequently been restored from old etchings and photographs to something approaching its original state.

Vanbrugh soon turned his attention to the estate's thousand-acre **grounds** where he could indulge his playful inclinations to excess, and the formal gardens, clipped parkland, towers, obelisks and blunt sandstone follies stretch in all directions, sloping gently to a large artifical lake. He completed the **Temple of the Four Winds** before his death in 1726, leaving Hawksmoor to design the Howard family **Mausoleum**, which is taller than the house itself. Take a look, too, at the fine **stables** which have been converted into the Costume and Regalia Gallery, Britain's largest private collection of period clothes. There are **cafés** here, one in the main house and another by the lake, as well as a children's playground, nature trails, plant centre and gift shop.

Hull

HULL – officially Kingston upon Hull – has a maritime pre-eminence that dates back to 1299, when it was laid out as a seaport by Edward I. It quickly became England's leading harbour, and was still a vital garrison when the gates were closed against Charles I in 1642, the first serious act of rebellion of what was to become the English Civil War. Fishing and seafaring have always been important here, and today's city maintains a firm grip on its heritage while bolstering its attractions for visitors – the dramatic aquarium known as The Deep joins a superior set of free local museums and a revived Old Town area that provide scope for a good couple of days' worth of sightseeing.

First stop for the maritime legacy should be the **Maritime Museum** (Mon–Sat 10am–5pm, Sun 1.30–4.30pm; free) on Queen Victoria Square, immediately north of Princes Quay. The main boost to the town's coffers in the eighteenth and nineteenth centuries was whaling, and the museum tells the story well, displaying a blubber pot cauldron, alongside model ships, old photographs, Inuit relics and a whale skeleton. Leave Queen Victoria Square

9.30am–noon; Oct–March Tues–Fri 11am–2pm, Sat 9.30am–noon; free), among the most pleasing parish churches in the country. A couple of blocks to the east, over towards the River Hull, you reach the **High Street**, whose crop of former merchants' houses and narrow cobbled alleys have seen it designated a **Museums Quarter** (all attractions Mon–Sat 10am–5pm, Sun 1.30–4.30pm; free). At its northern end stands **Wilberforce House**, the former home of William and containing some fascinating exhibits on slavery and its abolition to which cause he dedicated much of his life. Next door is **Streetlife**, devoted to the history of transport in the region and centred on a 1930s street scene of reconstructed shops, railway goods yard, and cycle and motor works. If this is good, then the adjacent **Hull and East Riding Museum** is even better, a life-size mammoth and a walk-through Iron Age village setting you up for the showpiece attractions, namely vivid displays of Celtic burials, medieval battles and spectacular Roman mosaics retrieved from the East Yorkshire countryside.

Protruding from a promontory overlooking the River Humber looms **The Deep** (daily 10am–6pm, last entry 5pm; £6.50; Ⓦwww.thedeep.co.uk), ten minutes' walk from the old town across a pedestrian footbridge that spans the River Hull. Its educational displays and videos wrap around an immense thirty-foot-deep, 2.3-million-gallon viewing tank filled with sharks, rays, octopuses and any number of other deep-sea denizens. It's very entertaining, and features a café overlooking the Humber estuary.

Practicalities

The **train station** is on the west side of town, on the main drag of Ferensway, with the **bus station** just to the north. The main **tourist office** is on Paragon Street at Queen Victoria Square (Mon–Sat 10am–5pm, Sun 11–3pm; Ⓣ01482/223559, Ⓦwww.hullcc.gov.uk), and they coordinate richly anecdotal **guided tours** around the old town (April–Oct, Mon–Sat at 2pm, Sun 11am; £2.50).

The tourist office can help with **accommodation** – and offers special weekend hotel rates (from around £25 per person per night; call Ⓣ01482/615744). Amongst several reasonably central B&Bs is *Clyde House Hotel*, 13 John St (Ⓣ01482/214981; ❷), five minutes' walk north of Princes Quay, near Hull New Theatre. There are also decent rooms and rates at the *Quality Hotel Royal*, 170 Ferensway (Ⓣ01482/325087; ❸), by the station; *Comfort Inn*, just south of the train station at 11 Anlaby Rd (Ⓣ01482/323299, Ⓦwww.choicehotels.com; ❸); and the *Hotel Ibis*, Osborne St, Ferensway (Ⓣ01482/387500, Ⓦwww.ibishotel.com; ❷), over the road. Of the **cafés**, *McCoy's* in Colonial Chambers, Princes Dock Street, serves wraps, sandwiches and pasta on three floors. Or there's *Studio 101/2* (closed Sun), opposite Holy Trinity church on King Street, for tasty veggie specials. **Restaurants** include *Venn*, 21 Scale Lane (Ⓣ01482/224004), in the old town, a contemporary brasserie-restaurant, and *Mimosa*, 406–408 Beverley Rd (Ⓣ01482/474748), a friendly Turkish restaurant with an open charcoal grill.

Hull has dozens of **pubs**, the best of which are picked out in a "Hull Ale Trail" leaflet available from the tourist office. The venerable *George* is found on the curiously named street The Land of Green Ginger, while *Green Bricks*, 9 Humber Dock St, offers real ales from its prize waterside location. The excellent **Hull Truck Theatre Company**, on Spring Street (Ⓣ01482/323638,

Beverley

BEVERLEY, nine miles north of Hull, ranks as one of northern England's premier towns, its minster the superior of many an English cathedral, its tangle of old streets, cobbled lanes and elegant Georgian and Victorian terraces the very picture of a traditional market town. Indeed, over 350 buildings are listed as possessing historical or architectural merit. Approaches to the town are dominated by the twin towers of **Beverley Minster** (March–Oct Mon–Sat 9am–5pm; Nov–Feb Mon–Sat 9am–4pm; plus Sun year round, depending on services, but usually noon–4.30pm; donation requested; Ⓦ www.beverleyminster .co.uk), visible for miles across the local flatlands. Initiated as a modest chapel, the minster later became a monastery under John of Beverley, who was buried here in 721 and canonized in 1037 – his body lies under the crossing at the top of the nave. Fires and the collapse of the central tower in 1213 paved the way for two centuries of rebuilding, funded by bequests from pilgrims paying homage to the saint, and the result was one of the finest Gothic creations in the country. The **west front** (1420) is widely considered without equal, its survival due in large part to Baroque architect Nicholas Hawksmoor, who restored much of the church in the eighteenth century. Similar outstanding work awaits in the interior, most notably the fourteenth-century **Percy Tomb** on the north side of the altar, its carved canopy one of the masterpieces of medieval European ecclesiastical art. Other incidental carving throughout the church is magnificent, particularly the 68 misericords of the oak **choir** (1520–24), where much of the decorative work is on a musical theme. Beverley had a renowned guild of itinerant minstrels, which provided funds in the sixteenth century for the carvings on the transept aisle capitals, where you'll be able to pick out players of lutes, bagpipes, horns and tambourines.

Beverley's **train station** is just a couple of minutes' walk from the Minster. The **bus station** is at the junction of Walkergate and Sow Hill Road, with the main street just a minute's walk away. The **tourist office** is at 34 Butcher Row in the main shopping area (June–Aug Mon–Fri 9.30am–5.15pm, Sat 10am–4.45pm, Sun 10am–2pm; Sept–May closed Sun; ℡ 01482/391672). There's plenty of local **accommodation**, including the *Eastgate*, 7 Eastgate (℡ 01482/868464; no credit cards; ❷), a few minutes' from the Minster, and *Number One*, 1 Woodlands (℡ 01482/862752, Ⓦ www.number-one-bedandbreakfast-beverley.co.uk; no credit cards; ❷), a B&B in a quiet Victorian house two minutes' walk from the market place. Top town-centre hotel is the *Beverley Arms*, North Bar Within (℡ 01482/869241, Ⓦ www.regalhotels.co.uk; ❻). The **youth hostel** (℡ 0870/770 5696, Ⓔ beverleyfriary@yha.org.uk; £10.25; closed Nov–Easter, and closed Sun & Mon) occupies a restored Dominican friary that was mentioned in the Canterbury Tales. It's located in Friar's Lane, off Eastgate, just a hundred yards southeast of the Minster. For **food**, *Courts*, 1 Sow Hill Rd, is the place for good coffee, bagels and sandwiches, while *Cerutti 2*, in Station Square (℡ 01482/866700; closed Sun), serves fresh fish. Best **pub** is the celebrated *White Horse* on Hengate, near St Mary's, a thoroughly atmospheric traditional drinking den.

The East Yorkshire coast

constant erosion and shifting currents that scour much of England's eastern shores. Between the two lie a handful of tranquil villages and miles of windswept dunes and mud flats, noted bird sanctuaries, and superbly lonely retreats accessible to anyone prepared to cycle or walk the paths and lanes that fan out amidst the dunes. The two main resorts, Bridlington and Filey, are linked by the regular **train** service between Hull and Scarborough. There's also an hourly bus service between Bridlington, Filey and Scarborough.

The southernmost major resort on the Yorkshire coast, **BRIDLINGTON** has maintained its harbour for almost a thousand years. The seafront promenade looks down upon the town's best asset – its sweeping sandy **beach**. It's an out-and-out family resort, which means plenty of candy floss, amusement arcades, rides, boat trips and other diversions – a paddle in the sea and fish and chips eaten on the milling harbourfront are traditional pursuits. The **tourist office** is close to the harbour at 25 Prince St (Easter–Oct daily 9.30am–5.30pm; Nov–Easter Mon–Sat 9.30am–5.30pm, Sun 11am–4pm; ☎01262/673474) and has full lists of local accommodation.

Around fourteen miles of precipitous four-hundred-foot cliffs gird **Flamborough Head**, just to the northeast of Bridlington. The Heritage Coast path, a grassy cliff-top track, negotiates most of the headland and from **BEMPTON**, two miles north of Bridlington, you can follow the path all the way round to Flamborough Head. Alternatively, you can reach the RSPB sanctuary at **Bempton Cliffs** along a quiet lane from Bempton. This is the only mainland gannetry in England, while Bempton also boasts the second-largest puffin colony in the country, with several thousand returning to the cliffs each year – late March and April is the best time to see them. The **Visitor Centre** (March–Nov daily 10am–5pm; Dec & Feb weekends only 9.30am–4pm; ☎01262/851179) here can rent you a pair of binoculars (£2.50).

FILEY, half a dozen miles further north up the coast, has a good deal more class as a resort than Bridlington, retaining many of its Edwardian features, including some splendid panoramic gardens. It, too, claims miles of wide sandy beach, stretching most of the way south to Flamborough Head and north the mile or so to the jutting rocks of **Filey Brigg**. If you're going to clamber around on the Brigg, check the tide tables first at the tourist office since people do get caught unawares by the incoming waters. **Bus** and **train** stations are just west of the centre on Station Avenue; walk down Station Avenue and Murray Street to **Filey Visitor Centre** on John Street (May–Sept daily 10am–5.30pm; Oct–April Sat & Sun 10am–4.30pm; ☎01723/518000). A few **hotels** sit down on the beachfront, with *Downcliffe House* (☎01723/513310; ❺) the pick of them, boasting a seaview restaurant serving fresh fish.

The North York Moors

Virtually the whole of the **North York Moors**, from the Hambleton and Cleveland hills in the west to the cliff-edged coastline to the east, is protected by one of the country's finest National Parks. The moors are heather-covered, flat-topped hills cut by steep-sided valleys, and views here stretch for miles, interrupted only by giant cultivated forests. Barrows and ancient forts provide memorials of early settlers, mingling on the high moorland with the battered

Helmsley is the best starting point for any exploration of the western and central moors, **Pickering** (actually just outside the National Park), for the eastern moors and northern Esk Valley. The central moors offer the best walking and the most noted landscapes, with **Hutton le Hole** perhaps the most picture-perfect village in the region. Any exploration of the district should also include the religious ruins of **Rievaulx Abbey**, the views from **Sutton Bank**, and the gentle landscapes of the **Esk Valley**. The main southern artery linking the western, central and eastern divisions is the A170, which runs from Thirsk, through Helmsley and Pickering to Scarborough. Two trans-moor roads, the Helmsley–Stokesley B1257 (west side) and the Pickering–Whitby A169 (east), offer access into the very heart of the moors. The steam trains of the **North Yorkshire Moors Railway** run between Pickering and Grosmont (even more popular since being used as the *Hogwarts Express* in the *Harry Potter* films). At Grosmont you can connect with the regular trains on the Esk Valley line, running east to Whitby or west through more remote settlements (and ultimately to Middlesbrough). The main **bus** approaches to the moors are from Scarborough and York to Helmsley and Pickering, and there are also summer **Moorsbus** services, running between points not usually served by public transport. You'll need the free *Moors Explorer* booklet, available from tourist offices and park information centres.

Thirsk and around

The small market town of **THIRSK**, 23 miles north of York and just outside the park boundary, made the most of its strategic crossroads position on the ancient drove road between Scotland and York and on the historic east–west route from dales to coast. Its medieval prosperity is clear from the large, cobbled **Market Place** (market days are Monday and Saturday), while later well-to-do citizens endowed the town with a bevy of commendable Georgian houses. However, Thirsk's main draw is its attachment to the legacy of local vet Alf Wight, better known as **James Herriott**. Thirsk was the "Darrowby" of the Herriott books, and the vet's former surgery, at 23 Kirkgate, is now the hugely popular **World of James Herriott** (daily: Easter–Oct 10am–6pm; Nov–Easter 11am–4pm, last admission 1hr before closing; £4.70), crammed with period pieces and Herriott memorabilia.

Eleven miles north of Thirsk, straight up the A19, the fourteenth-century **Mount Grace Priory** (Easter–Oct daily 10am–6pm; Nov–March Wed–Sun 10am–1pm & 2–4pm; £3.20; NT & EH) is the most important of England's nine Carthusian ruins. The Carthusians took a vow of silence and lived, ate and prayed alone in their two-storey cells, each separated from its neighbour by a small garden and high walls. The foundations of the cells are still clearly visible, together with one that has been reconstructed to suggest its original layout and the monks' way of life.

Thirsk is only a half-hour drive from York, making an easy day-trip; **buses** stop in the Market Place while the **train station** is a mile west of town on the A61 (Ripon road), connected to the centre by minibus. The **tourist office** is at 49 Market Place (daily: Easter–Oct 10am–5pm; Nov–Easter 11am–4pm; ☎01845/522755, ⓦwww.hambleton.gov.uk), and can help with **accommodation**. There are B&Bs on Kirkgate, on the road up to the parish church, while the **pubs** in the Market Place offer rooms as well.

Sutton Bank, Coxwold and Byland Abbey

The main A170 road enters the National Park from Thirsk as it climbs five hundred feet in half a mile to **Sutton Bank** (960ft), a phenomenal viewpoint whose panorama extends across the Vale of York to the Pennines on the far horizon. At the top of the climb stands the North York Moors National Park **Visitor Centre** (Easter–Oct daily 10am–5pm; Nov, Dec & March daily 11am–4pm; Jan & Feb Sat & Sun 11am–4pm; ☎01845/597426, ⓦwww.moors.uk.net), full of background on the short waymarked walks you can make from here, and with a café too.

A diversion off the A170 takes you into **COXWOLD**, as attractive a little village as they come. The majority of its many visitors come to pay homage to the novelist **Laurence Sterne**, who is buried by the south wall (close to the porch) in the churchyard of **St Michael's**, where he was vicar from 1760 until his death in 1768. **Shandy Hall**, 150 yards further up the road past the church (May–Sept Wed 2–4.30pm, Sun 2.30–4.30pm; gardens May–Sept Mon–Fri & Sun 2–4.30pm; house & gardens £4.50, gardens only £2.50), was Sterne's home, now a museum crammed with literary memorabilia. A mile and a half northeast of the village lies twelfth-century **Byland Abbey** (June–Sept daily 10am–1pm & 2–6pm; Oct–May closed Tues & Wed; £2; EH), which, though larger in ground area than the Cistercian houses at Fountains and Rievaulx, is far less well preserved, leaving the haunting location and stark west front as the abbey's most memorable aspects. Back in Coxwold, the *Fauconberg Arms* (☎01347/868214, ⓦwww.fauconbergarms.co.uk; ●) is a superb old **inn** on Main Street, with a cosy bar serving good food and a more formal restaurant. **Buses** run from Thirsk to Coxwold (and on to Helmsley) on Mondays, Fridays and Saturdays, and the Moorsbus runs here daily from Thirsk and Helmsley in summer.

Helmsley

One of the moors' most appealing towns, **HELMSLEY** makes a perfect base for visiting the western moors and Rievaulx Abbey. Local life revolves around a large cobbled market square (market day is Friday), dominated by a vaunting monument to the second earl of Feversham, whose family was responsible for rebuilding most of the village in the nineteenth century. The old **market cross** marks the start of the 110-mile Cleveland Way (see opposite page). Close to the square is **Helmsley Castle** (April–Sept daily 10am–6pm; Oct daily 10am–5pm, Nov–March Wed–Sun 10am–1pm & 2–4pm; £2.60; EH), its unique twelfth-century D-shaped keep ringed by massive earthworks. To the southwest of the town, overlooking a wooded meander of the Rye, stands the Fevershams' country seat, **Duncombe Park** (April–Oct Mon–Thurs & Sun: house, tours 12.30–3.30pm; garden, parkland & visitor centre 11am–5.30pm; house, gardens & parkland £6, gardens £3, parkland £2; ⓦwww.duncombepark.com), built in 1713. The grounds are more appealing than the house (which was extensively rebuilt after a fire in 1879), boasting swathes of landscaped gardens, which include Britain's tallest ash and lime trees, and a brace of artfully sited temples.

Helmsley is a hub for the **Moorsbus** and you can pick up timetables in the useful **tourist office** in the town hall on Market Place (Easter–Oct daily 9.30am–5pm; Nov–Easter Fri–Sun 10am–4pm; ℡01439/770173, Ⓦ www.ryedale.gov.uk). The office also has full information about walking the 110-mile **Cleveland Way**, which embraces both the northern rim of the moors and Cleveland Hills and the cliff scenery of the North Yorkshire coast. Of the **hotels** ringing Market Place, the best mid-range place is the *Crown* (℡01439/770297; ❺), a family-run inn serving very good-value evening meals. Finest of all is the *Black Swan* (℡0870/400 8112; ❼), a gorgeous Elizabethan-Georgian hybrid, while the classy *Feversham Arms*, behind the church at 1 High St (℡01439/770766; ❼), combines hip styling with spacious rooms, brasserie, pool and gym. The **youth hostel** (℡0870/770 5860, Ⓔ helmsley@yha.org.uk; £10.25; closed Nov–Easter, and closed Sun & Mon Sept & Oct) is a few hundred yards east of Market Place – follow Bondgate to Carlton Road and turn left. **Market** day in Helmsley is Friday. The old **pubs** in the Market Place – the *Royal Oak* and the *Feathers* – are both atmospheric places for a drink and a bite to eat, though for a drive out into the country and a fine meal you can't do better than the *Star Inn* (℡01439/770397, Ⓦ www.thestaratharome.co.uk; no food Sun eve & Mon; ❼) at **Harome**, a thatched pub a couple of miles south of the A170, where Michelin-rated food and comfortable rooms await.

Rievaulx Abbey and Terrace

From Helmsley you can easily hike across country to **Rievaulx Abbey** (daily: April–Sept 10am–6pm; Oct 10am–5pm; Nov–March 10am–4pm; £3.80; EH). The signposted path takes around an hour and a half. Founded in 1132, the abbey became the mother church of the Cistercians in England, quickly developing to become a flourishing community with interests in fishing, mining, agriculture and the woollen industry. At its height, 140 monks and up to 500 lay brothers lived and worked at the abbey, though numbers fell dramatically once the Black Death (1348–49) had done its worst. The end came with the Dissolution, when many of the walls were razed and the roof lead stripped – the beautiful ruins, however, still suggest the abbey's former splendour.

Although they form some sort of ensemble with the abbey, there's no access between the ruins and **Rievaulx Terrace and Temples** (Easter–Oct daily 10.30am–6pm; £3.30; NT), a site entered from the B1257, a couple of miles northwest of Helmsley. This half-mile stretch of grass-covered terraces and woodland was laid out as part of Duncombe Park in the 1750s, and engineered partly to enhance the views of the abbey. The resulting panorama over the ruins and the valley below is superb, and this makes a great spot for a picnic or simply for strolls along the lawns and woodland trail.

Hutton le Hole, Farndale and Rosedale

Lying eight miles northeast of Helmsley, one of Yorkshire's quaintest villages, **HUTTON LE HOLE**, has become so great a tourist attraction that you'll have to come off-season to get much pleasure from its tidy gardens, its stream-crossed village green and the sight of sheep wandering freely through the lanes. The big draw is the **Ryedale Folk Museum** (Easter–Oct daily 10am–5.30pm; £3.25; Ⓦ www.ryedalefolkmuseum.co.uk), an ever-expanding set of displays over a two-acre site. Special events and displays throughout the season mean there's always something going on. The museum houses a **National Park information centre** (same hours as museum; ☎01751/417367), while **accommodation** is zealously fought for: try *Moorlands* (☎01751/417548, ⓦwww.moorlandshouse.com; ❹), a Georgian house with streamside garden; the *Barn Hotel* (☎01751/417311; ❹), just down from the museum; or the *Hammer and Hand* (☎01751/417300; ❸), a comfortable B&B on the village green. If you stay the night you'll have plenty of time to become acquainted with the *Crown*, the friendly local pub.

FARNDALE is entered from the south by a minor road from **Gillamoor**, a little to the west of Hutton le Hole. Further up the vale the country lanes are packed in spring with tourists here to see the area's wild daffodils, protected by the two-thousand-acre **Farndale nature reserve**. The Moorsbus runs a special "Daffodil" service every Sunday in April and over Easter, shuttling visitors from Hutton le Hole.

Trim and tidy **ROSEDALE ABBEY**, four miles northeast of Hutton le Hole, preserves only a few fragments of the Cistercian priory (1158) that gave it its name, most of them incorporated into **St Lawrence's** parish church. It's hard to believe now, but the village once had a population of over five thousand, most employed in the ironstone workings whose remnants lie scattered all over the high moors round about. Rosedale village itself gets packed on summer weekends, many of the visitors sitting outside the *Milburn Arms* (☎01751/417312, ⓦwww.milburnarms.co.uk; ❺; closed Jan), overlooking the small green. There's a popular **campsite** at *Rosedale Caravan Park* (☎01751/417272) down by the river, while north of Rosedale Abbey is the windswept *Lion Inn* (☎01751/417320, ⓦwww.lionblakey.co.uk; ❸) on Blakey Ridge, a couple of miles south of the junction with the Hutton le Hole–Castleton road (along which the Moorsbus travels).

Pickering

The biggest centre for miles around, the thriving market town of **PICKERING** takes for itself the title "Gateway to the Moors", which is pushing it a bit, though it's certainly a handy place to stay if you're touring the villages and dales of the eastern moors. **Market** day is Monday, but otherwise its most attractive feature is the **castle** on the hill north of the market place (Easter–Sept daily 10am–6pm; Oct daily 10am–5pm; Nov–March Wed–Sun 10am–4pm; £2.60; EH), reputedly used by every English monarch up to 1400 as a base for hunting in nearby Blandsby Park. Eight monarchs certainly put up here, including Edward II after his trouncing by the Scots at the Battle of Byland Abbey in 1322, and possibly a ninth, Richard II, was kept here as a prisoner shortly before his murder in Pontefract.

Pickering's biggest plus, if you're using public transport, is the **North Yorkshire Moors Railway** (NYMR; see box opposite). Otherwise, you could make use of the **Moorsbus** services, which radiate from Pickering, and the regular bus services to and from Helmsley, Scarborough, York and Leeds. **Buses** stop outside the library and **tourist office** on The Ropery (Easter–Oct Mon–Sat 9.30am–5pm, Sun 9.30am–4pm; Nov–Easter Mon–Sat 10am–4.30pm; ☎01751/473791, ⓦwww.ryedale.gov.uk), opposite Safeway in the centre of town; the **NYMR train station** is less than five minutes' signposted walk away. For **B&B**, tree-lined Eastgate (the Scarborough road) has the tastefully presented *Eden House* at no. 120 (☎01751/472289, ⓦwww.edenhousebandb.co.uk;

The **North Yorkshire Moors Railway** (NYMR) connects **Pickering** with the Esk Valley (Middlesbrough–Whitby) line at **Grosmont**, 18 miles to the north. The line was completed by George Stephenson in 1835, just ten years after the opening of the Stockton and Darlington Railway, making it one of the earliest lines in the country. Even by the standards of later projects it was a remarkable feat of engineering, navigating 1-in-15 gradients and using thousands of tons of brushwood and heather-stuffed sheepskins to provide bedding for the track through the dale's extensive bogs.

Services
Scheduled **services** operate between mid-March and early November (plus Christmas specials), with trains running hourly to three times daily depending on the time of year. For **advance bookings and information**, call ☏01751/472508 (Mon–Fri 9am–5pm, Sat & Sun 10am–2.30pm); for the talking timetables call ☏01751/473535; or check the website at ⓦwww.nymr.demon.co.uk. A day-return **ticket** for the whole line costs £12. Part of the line's attraction, of course, is the **steam trains**, though be warned that diesels are pulled into service when the fire risk in the forests is high.

Walks from the NYMR
The first station stop is **Levisham**, perfect for walks to the village of **LEVISHAM**, a mile and a half to the east, where the *Horseshoe Inn* is a favourite target, especially for Sunday lunch. A steep winding road continues another mile beyond Levisham, down across the beck and then up to **LOCKTON**, where there's a path due north to the **Hole of Horcum**, a bizarre natural hollow gouged by glacial meltwaters. Paths run back to Levisham station from here, a seven-mile circuit all told. The second train stop, **Newtondale Halt**, is only a couple of miles northwest of the Hole of Horcum, or you can head off through the extensive woods of **Cropton Forest** to the west on trails specially marked by the Forestry Commission. The best-preserved stretch of Roman road in Europe, **Wheeldale Roman Road**, is signposted off the untarred road from Stape to **Goathland** (the third stop on the railway line), though anyone equipped with a decent map will also be able to find their way to the Roman road direct by track (3 miles) from Newtondale Halt.

⑫

no credit cards; ❸), and there are more modest places on the same road. A couple of the **pubs** have rooms, top choice easily being the *White Swan*, on Market Place (☏01751/472288, ⓦwww.white-swan.co.uk; ❻), which serves fine Modern British food at moderate prices. The nearest **youth hostel** is a simple affair at the Old School, Lockton (☏0870/770 5938; £8; closed Oct–Easter), five miles northeast off the A169 – ask to be dropped at the turn-off by the Whitby bus. The local **campsite** is *Upper Carr* (☏01751/473115, ⓦwww.uppercarr.demon.co.uk; closed Nov–Feb), a mile and half south of town on the Malton Road.

The Esk Valley

The northernmost reaches of the National Park are crossed by the east–west **Esk Valley**, whose pretty river flows into the sea at Whitby. Access is easy, either by road from Whitby via the A169 through Sleights, or more attractively by train: the North Yorkshire Moors Railway connects at Grosmont, where you're on the Esk Valley line, which runs between Middlesbrough and Whitby.

GROSMONT, little more than a level-crossing, station and a couple of tearooms, sees plenty of summer traffic, as does EGTON BRIDGE - similarly tiny but with the bonus of a beautifully sited riverside pub, the *Horseshoe* (℡01947/895245; ❷), with a spacious beer garden and terrific food. Further west, the scenery becomes tinged by the looming moors until, at the isolated stone village of DANBY, you're once again within striking distance of some excellent walks, all detailed on trail leaflets available from the **Moors Centre** (Easter–Oct daily 10am–5pm; Nov, Dec & March daily 11am–4pm; Jan & Feb Sat & Sun 11am–4pm; ℡01439/772737, Ⓦwww.moors.uk.net). The *Stonehouse Bakery & Tea Shop* is great for daytime snacks, while a mile out of the village at **Ainthorpe**, the *Fox & Hounds* (℡01287/660218, Ⓦwww .foxandhounds-ainthorpe.com; ❹) has rooms, moderately priced meals and views over the moors.

South of Grosmont, train, footpath and beck climb out of the Esk Valley towards Goathland. Only on foot will you be able to stop at BECK HOLE, after a couple of miles, an idyllic bridgeside hamlet focused on the *Birch Hall Inn*, one of the finest rural pubs in all England. A gentle path from the hamlet runs the mile through the fields up to GOATHLAND, set in open moorland beneath the great expanses of Wheeldale and Goathland moors. If it seems oddly familiar – and unduly crowded – it's because it's widely known as "Aidensfield", the fictional village at the centre of the *Heartbeat* TV series. Signposts point you to the local sight, the **Mallyan Spout**, a seventy-foot-high waterfall. This lies half a mile or so from the imposing *Mallyan Spout Hotel* on the common (℡01947/896486; ❺), the best place to stay, and certainly the best place to eat and drink.

The North Yorkshire coast

A bracing change after the flattened seascapes of East Anglia and much of East Yorkshire, the **North Yorkshire coast** is the southernmost stretch of a cliff-edged shore that stretches almost unbroken to the Scottish border. **Scarborough** is the biggest town and resort, and the terminus for bus and rail links from York and beyond. Cute **Robin Hood's Bay** is the most popular of the many Yorkshire villages with fishing and smuggling traditions, while **Staithes** – a fishing harbour on the far edge of North Yorkshire – has yet to tip over into full-blown tourist mode. **Whitby**, in between the two, is the best stopover, its fine sands and resort facilities tempered by its abbey ruins, cobbled streets, Georgian buildings and maritime heritage. For those who want to sample the most dizzying cliff-tops, the **Cleveland Way** provides a marked path along virtually the entire length of the coast.

Hourly **buses** (fewer on Sun) run along the A171 between Scarborough and Whitby, and a similarly frequent service operates to Robin Hood's Bay, and north between Whitby and Staithes. The Yorkshire Coastliner service connects Leeds and York with Scarborough (hourly) or Whitby (2–5 daily). You can also reach Scarborough direct by **train** from York or Hull, and Whitby from Middlesbrough.

Scarborough

The oldest resort in the country, **SCARBOROUGH** first attracted early seventeenth-century visitors to its newly discovered mineral springs. Fashionable among the Victorians – to whom it was "the Queen of the

Watering Places" – Scarborough saw its biggest transformation after World War II, when it (and many other resorts) became a holiday haven for workers from the industrial heartlands. All the traditional ingredients of a beach resort are still here in force, from superb, clean sands, kitsch amusement arcades and Kiss-Me-Quick hats to the more refined pleasures of its tightknit old-town streets and a genteel round of quiet parks and gardens.

There's no better place to acquaint yourself with the local layout than from the walls of **Scarborough Castle** (daily: April–Sept 10am–6pm; Oct 10am–5pm; Nov–March 10am–4pm; £3; EH), mounted on a jutting headland between two golden-sanded bays east of the town centre. The present castle consists mainly of a three-storey keep dating from the twelfth century, and a thirteenth-century barbican and raking buttressed walls that trace the cliff edge. Although besieged many times, the fortifications were never taken by assault, its only fall coming in the Civil War when the Parliamentarians starved the garrison into surrender. As you leave, drop into the church of **St Mary** (1180), immediately below on Castle Road, whose graveyard contains the tomb of Anne Brontë, who died here in 1849.

The town museums are clustered around Valley Road, south of the train station. An "Annual Pass" (£3; valid for a year) gets you into **Wood End** on The Crescent (June–Sept Tues–Sun 10am–5pm; Oct–May Wed, Sat & Sun 11am–4pm), holiday home of the Sitwell family of writers and aesthetes, the adjacent **Art Gallery** (June–Sept Tues–Sun 10am–5pm; Oct–May Thurs, Fri & Sat 11am–4pm), and the nearby **Rotunda Museum** on Vernon Road (June–Sept Tues–Sun 10am–5pm; Oct–April Tues, Sat & Sun 11am–4pm; £2), which holds the local archeological and historic finds.

Most of what passes for family entertainment takes place on the **North Bay** – massive water slides at Atlantis, the kids' amusements at Kinderland, and the miniature North Bay Railway (daily Easter–Sept), which runs up to the **Sea Life Centre**, with its pools of flounders, rock-pool habitats and fishy exhibits. The **South Bay** is more refined, backed by the pleasant Valley Gardens and the Italianate meanderings of the South Cliff Gardens, and topped by an esplanade from which a **hydraulic lift** (daily 10am–4pm, till 10pm July & Aug) potters down to the beach.

Practicalities

The **train station** is at the top of town facing Westborough; **buses** pull up outside or in the surrounding streets, though the National Express services (direct from London) stop in the car park behind the station. Scarborough's **tourist office** is in Pavilion House, Valley Bridge Rd (daily: May–Sept 9.30am–6pm; Oct–April 10am–4.30pm; ℡01723/373333, Ⓦwww.discoveryorkshirecoast.com), just over the road from the station. Open-top **seafront buses** (April–Sept daily from 9.30am, March weekends only; £1) run throughout the season from the *Corner Café* in North Bay to the Spa Complex in South Bay.

Scarborough is crammed with inexpensive **accommodation**, though in high season, if you arrive without a reservation, you'd do best to let the tourist office find you something. Happy hunting grounds include North Bay's Queen's Parade and its continuation, Blenheim Terrace. The cheapest places in town are those without sea views – try along central Aberdeen Walk (off Westborough), or on North Marine Road and Trafalgar Square, behind Queen's Parade. Above South Bay, hotels tend to be pricier, though there's a clutch of B&Bs around West Street.

Hotels and guest houses

Crown Esplanade ☎01723/357426, ⓦwww
.chariethotels.co.uk. The *Crown* makes the most
of its Edwardian features, views and genteel feel.
D, B&B rates offer the best deal. ❻

Interludes 32 Princess St ☎01723/360513,
ⓦwww.interludeshotel.co.uk. Quiet, nonsmoking,
Georgian townhouse in the old-town streets
behind the harbour. It's a gay-friendly place,
though all (except children) are welcome. ❸

Paragon 123 Queen's Parade ☎01723/372676,
ⓦwww.paragon-hotel.demon.co.uk. Traditional,
family-run B&B (some rooms with sea views). ❸

Riviera St Nicholas Cliff ☎01723/372277,
ⓦwww.rivierahotel.scarborough.co.uk. Restored
Victorian hotel with super bay views and comfortable en-suite rooms. ❹

Whiteley 99 Queen's Parade ☎01723/373514,
ⓔwhiteleyhotel@bigfoot.com. Formerly a Victorian
merchant's house, this is one of the best Queen's
Parade options. ❷

Windmill Mill St, off Victoria Rd
☎01723/372735, ⓦwww.windmill-hotel.co.uk.
Eighteenth-century windmill sited incongruously
in the town centre with its country-style rooms
(upper-floor ones with veranda) ranged around a
cobbled courtyard. ❸

Wrea Head Country House Hotel Barmoor Lane,
Scalby, 2 miles north of town ☎01723/378211,
ⓦwww.englishrosehotels.co.uk. Peaceful country
house where traditionally furnished rooms come
with glorious rural views – the seaside bustle seems
an age away. The room rate includes dinner. ❼

Youth hostel and camp-sites

Scalby Close Park Burniston Rd, 2 miles north of
town ☎01723/365908. Tents and caravans.
Closed Nov–Easter.

Scalby Manor Caravan Park Burniston Rd, 2
miles north of town ☎01723/366212. There are
tent spaces at this huge site, handy for the North
Bay. Closed Nov–Easter.

Scarborough YHA Burniston Rd, Scalby Mills,
2 miles north of town ☎0870/770 6022,
ⓔscarborough@yha.org.uk. Occupies a converted
watermill, off the A165, 10min walk from the Sea
Life Centre and the sea. Dorm beds cost £10.25;
closed Sun & Mon in Sept & Oct, and closed
Nov–Easter.

Cafés, restaurants and pubs

The Alma 1 Alma Parade, at the top of
Westborough. A thoroughly decent local, just right
for a quiet pint.

Café Italia 36 St Nicholas Cliff. Microscopic Italian
coffee bar where genuine coffee, focaccia slices
and ice cream keep a battery of regulars happy.
Closes 5pm.

Il Castello 34–36 Castle Rd ☎01723/377312.
The town's best pizzas, and some inventive home-
made pastas and other Italian dishes. Closed Mon
& Tues. Moderate.

Gianni's 13 Victoria Rd ☎01723/507388. The
most immediately welcoming of the town's Italian
restaurants, whose good-natured staff bustle up
and down stairs, delivering quality pizzas, pastas
and quaffable wine. Moderate.

The Golden Grid 4 Sandside ☎01723/360922.
The harbourside's choicest fish-and-chip establishment, "catering for the promenader since
1883". Closed Mon–Thurs dinner in winter.
Inexpensive to Moderate.

Hole in the Wall 26 Vernon Rd. Cosy, real-ale
haunt with beer-knowledgeable staff and good
food (served noon–2pm).

Peppers 11 York Place ☎01723/500642.
Specialities range from a grilled red mullet and
roast pepper salad to tuna steak with a *salsa
romesco*. Dinner only; closed Sun. Expensive.

Stephen Joseph Theatre Restaurant
Westborough ☎01723/356655. Fashionable food
in the theatre restaurant – sandwiches, pastas,
fish cakes, noodles and salads at lunch, and seasonally changing Modern Brit dinners. Lunch
Mon–Sat, dinner Thurs–Sat. Moderate.

Theatre

Stephen Joseph Theatre Westborough
☎01723/370541, ⓦwww.sjt.uk.com. Housed in a
former Art Deco cinema, this premieres every new
play of local playwright Alan Ayckbourn and pro-
motes strong seasons of theatre and film.

Robin Hood's Bay

Although known as Robbyn Huddes Bay as early as Tudor times, there's nothing except half-remembered myth to link **ROBIN HOOD'S BAY** with
Sherwood's legendary bowman – locals anyway prefer the old name, Bay Town
or simply Bay. Among the best-known and most heavily visited spot on the
coast, the village fully lives up to its reputation, with narrow streets and

pink-tiled cottages toppling down the cliff-edge site, evoking the romance of a time when this was both a hard-bitten fishing community and smugglers' den *par excellence*. From the upper village, lined with Victorian villas, now mostly B&Bs, it's a very steep walk down the hill to the harbour. The **Old Coastguard Station** (June–Sept daily 10am–5pm; Oct–May weekends only; free; ☎01947/885900) has been turned into a visitor centre with displays relating to the area's geology and sealife. When the tide is out, the massive rock beds below are exposed, split by a geological fault line and studded with fossil remains. There's an easy circular walk (2.5 miles) to **Boggle Hole**, a mile south, returning inland via the path along the old Scarborough–Whitby railway line.

Buses from Scarborough or Whitby, seven miles north, drop you at the top of the village. Whitby has the nearest train station, and the nearest tourist office; walkers, along the coastal Cleveland Way, can make Whitby to Robin Hood's Bay in around three hours. **Accommodation** is plentiful, but often in short supply during high season, though many people see the village as a day-trip from Whitby. *York House* on King St (☎01947/880088, ⓦwww.robinhoodsbay.uk.com; ❷) is typical of what's on offer, a cosy Georgian house close to the harbour. There are also three good **pubs** in the lower village, two of which have rooms: the tiny *Laurel*, on Main Street (☎01947/880400; ❶; two-night minimum); and the *Bay Hotel*, right on the harbour (☎01947/880278; ❸), where the food is pretty good. The *Old Chapel* bookshop has a vegetarian **café** and great coastal views from its terrace tables. Boggle Hole's **youth hostel** is one of Yorkshire's most popular, a former mill located in a wooded ravine about a mile south of Robin Hood's Bay at Mill Beck (☎0870/770 5704, ⓔbogglehole@yha.org.uk; £10.25). Note that a torch is essential after dark. A couple of miles northwest of Robin Hood's Bay at **Hawsker**, on the A171, Trailways (☎01947/820207, ⓦwww.trailways.fsnet.co.uk) is a bike-rental outfit based in the old Hawsker train station, perfectly placed for day-trips along the largely flat railway line in either direction. They'll deliver or pick up from local addresses (including Boggle Hole youth hostel).

Whitby

If there's one essential stop on the North Yorkshire coast it's **WHITBY**, whose historical associations, atmospheric ruins, fishing harbour and intrinsic charm make it many people's favourite northern resort. The seventh-century abbey here made Whitby one of the key foundations of the early Christian period, and a centre of great learning, though little interfered with the fishing community that scraped together a living on the harbour banks of the River Esk below. For a thousand years, the local herring boats landed their catch until the great whaling boom of the eighteenth century transformed the fortunes of the town. Melville's *Moby Dick* makes much of Whitby whalers such as William Scoresby, while James Cook took his first seafaring steps from the town in 1746, on his way to becoming a national hero. All four of Captain Cook's ships of discovery – the *Endeavour*, *Resolution*, *Adventure* and *Discovery* – were built in Whitby, and a stunning replica *Endeavour* moors in the harbour most summers for guided visits (schedule available at ⓦwww.barkendeavour.com.au) The town splits into two distinct halves joined by a swing bridge: the **old town** to the east, centred on a curving cobbled street of great character, and the newer (though mostly eighteenth- and nineteenth-century) town across the bridge, generally known as **West Cliff**.

Bram Stoker and Dracula

Bram Stoker was born in Dublin in 1847 and wrote his first stories while working in the Irish civil service. A meeting with Sir Henry Irving in 1877 led him to quit his job and move to London, where he became Irving's manager and close friend. Forgettable adventure novels followed, until in 1890, on holiday in Whitby, Stoker began to become interested in writing a story of vampires and the undead, already popularized in "Gothic" novels earlier that century. Using first-hand observation of a town he knew well – he stayed at a house on the West Cliff, now marked by a plaque – Stoker built a story which mixed real locations, legend, myth and historical fact: the grounding of Count Dracula's ship on Tate Hill Sands was based on an actual event reported in the local papers. The novel was published in 1897 and became synonymous with Stoker's name.

With many of the early chapters recognizably set in Whitby, it's hardly surprising that the town has cashed in on its **Dracula Trail**. The various sites – Tate Hill Sands, the abbey, church and steps, the graveyard, Stoker's house – can all be visited, while down on the harbourside the Dracula Experience attempts to pull in punters to its rather lame horror-show antics. Keen interest has also been sparked amongst the **Goth** fraternity, who now come to town en masse a couple of times a year (usually in late spring and around Halloween) for a vampire's ball, concerts and readings; their unofficial headquarters is the otherwise sedate *Elsinore* pub on Flowergate.

Cobbled **Church Street** is the old town's main thoroughfare, barely changed in aspect since the eighteenth century, though now lined with tearooms and gift shops. Parallel **Sandgate** has more of the same, the two streets meeting at the small marketplace where souvenirs and trinkets are sold; there's a farmers' market here every Thursday. Whitby, understandably, likes to make a fuss of Captain Cook who served an apprenticeship here from 1746–49 under John Walker, a Quaker shipowner. The **Captain Cook Memorial Museum** (Easter–Oct daily 9.45am–5pm; March Sat & Sun 11am–3pm; £3; ⓦ www.cookmuseumwhitby.co.uk), housed in Walker's rickety old house in Grape Lane (on the east side of the swing bridge), contains an impressive amount of memorabilia, including ships' models, letters and paintings by artists seconded to Cook's voyages.

At the end of Church Street, you climb the famous **199 steps** of the Church Stairs – now paved, but originally a wide wooden staircase built for pallbearers carrying coffins to the church of St Mary above. The parish church of **St Mary** at the top of the steps, loftily removed from the town it served, is an architectural dog's dinner dating back to 1110, boasting a Norman chancel arch, a profusion of eighteenth-century panelling, box pews unequalled in England and a triple-decker pulpit – note the built-in ear trumpets, added for the benefit of a nineteenth-century rector's deaf wife. The cliff-top ruins of **Whitby Abbey** (daily: April–Sept 10am–6pm; Oct 10am–5pm, Nov–March 10am–4pm; £3.80; EH), beyond St Mary's, are some of the most evocative in England, the nave, soaring north transept and lancets of the east end giving a hint of the building's former delicacy and splendour. Its monastery was founded in 657 by St Hilda of Hartlepool, daughter of King Oswy of Northumberland, and by 664 had become important enough to host the **Synod of Whitby**, an event of seminal importance in the development of English Christianity. It settled once and for all the question of determining the date of Easter, and adopted the rites and authority of the Roman rather than the Celtic Church. **Caedmon**, one of the brothers at the abbey during its earliest years, has a twenty-foot cross to his memory which stands in front of St Mary's, at the top of the steps. His nine-line *Song of Creation* is the earliest surviving poem in English, making the abbey not only the cradle of English Christianity, but also the birthplace of English literature. You'll discover all this and more in the **Visitor Centre** (hours as above), housed in the shell of the adjacent mansion, built after the Dissolution using material from the plundered abbey. Audio-visual displays concentrate on life both at the medieval abbey and at the house, whose seventeenth-century geometric "hard" garden has been restored.

Final port of call should be **Whitby Museum** in Pannett Park (May–Sept Mon–Sat 9.30am–5.30pm, Sun 2–5pm; Oct–April Tues 10am–1pm, Wed–Sat 10am–4pm, Sun 2–4pm; £2.50), up the hill from the train station on West Cliff. There's more Cook memorabilia, including various objects and stuffed animals brought back as souvenirs by his crew, as well as casefuls of exhibits devoted to Whitby's seafaring tradition, its whaling industry in particular. Some of the best and largest fossils of Jurassic period reptiles unearthed on the east coast are also preserved here.

Practicalities

Trains arrive in Station Square, a couple of hundred yards south of the bridge to the old town. Most local buses leave from the adjacent **bus station**, though the Yorkshire Coastliner services (from Leeds, York and Pickering) and National Express buses (from London and York) sometimes stop around the corner on Langborne Road, just down from the tourist office. There's a **Travel Centre** (℡01947/602146) in the train station for all local transport enquiries. Whitby's **tourist office** (daily: May–Sept 9.30am–6pm; Oct–April 10am–12.30pm & 1–4.30pm; ℡01947/602674, ⓦwww.discoveryorkshirecoast.com, ⓦwww.visitwhitby.com) is a right turn outside the train station to the corner of Langborne Road and New Quay Road.

The main **B&B** concentrations are on West Cliff, in the streets stretching back from Royal Crescent. For superior **holiday cottages** in town, contact Shoreline Cottages (℡0113/289 3539, ⓦwww.shoreline-cottages.com) or Coast Cottages (℡01947/821390, ⓦwww.coastcottages.co.uk). Whitby is at the centre of the local music scene, which comes to a head during the annual **Whitby Folk Week** in August (the week immediately preceding the bank holiday), when the town's streets, pubs and concert halls are filled day and night with singers, bands, traditional dancers, storytellers and music workshops. Best place to find out what's on is at The Port Hole, 16 Skinner St, a fair-trade craft shop with excellent attached world/folk CD store called Folk Devils.

Hotels, B&Bs and guest houses

Bramblewick 3 Havelock Place ℡01947/604504, ⓦwww.bramblewick.co.uk. Victorian house which retains its original fireplaces and wrought-iron balconies. The old attic rooms at the top have the best views. Two-night minimum stay. ❷

Duke of York Church St ℡01947/600324. At the bottom of the 199 steps, this popular pub has en-suite rooms overlooking the harbour. ❷

Dunsley Hall Dunsley ℡01947/893437. Quite the grandest retreat in the locality, this stately oak-panelled pile has all the trimmings, including a pool, good restaurant and cosy bar. It's a couple of miles inland (west) of town. ❼

Estbek House Sandsend ℡01947/893424, ⓦwww.fastfix.com/estbek. Georgian house with five rooms, restaurant and tea garden, overlooking the stream at Sandsend, a couple of miles from Whitby. ❹

Number Five 5 Havelock Place ℡01947/606361. Amiable West Cliff B&B that provides a good breakfast (veggie options available). No credit cards. ❷

Shepherd's Purse 95 Church St ℡01947/820228. Popular wholefood shop and restaurant with its best rooms set around a galleried courtyard. Vegetarian breakfast available. ❸

White Horse & Griffin 87 Church St ℡01947/604857, ⓦwww.whitehorseandgriffin.co.uk. Easily the most atmospheric place to stay in the old town – a welcoming eighteenth-century coaching inn with stylishly decorated en-suite rooms, open fires and a good restaurant. ❹

White Linen 24 Bagdale ☎01947/603635. Superior B&B in a restored Georgian house, not far from the train station. ❹

Hostels

Whitby Backpackers 28 Hudson St ☎01947/601794, ⓦwww.thewhitbybackpack-ers.co.uk. Easygoing West Cliff hostel with 19 beds (from £10) in a variety of rooms, including a couple of twin/double rooms and en-suite family rooms (both ❶). There's a kitchen and lounge, lovely garden, free tea and coffee, and no curfew. Closed Jan & Feb.

Whitby YHA East Cliff ☎0870/770 6088, Ⓔwhitby@yha.org.uk. A converted stable a stone's throw from the abbey, with superb views over the town. One room sleeps two (❶), otherwise beds (£10.25) in variously sized dorms. Open weekends only Nov–March

Café-bars and restaurants

Finley's 22 Flowergate ☎01947/606660. Easy-going café-bar with deep sofas, dishing up gourmet sandwiches, *nachos*, pasta, fish cakes and the like. Inexpensive.

Grapevine 2 Grape Lane ☎01947/820275. Tiny, funky, dinner-only place serving tapas-style meals. Closed Sun & Mon. Inexpensive.

Green's 13 Bridge St ☎01947/600284. Whitby's best and most relaxed restaurant, producing stylish meals with contemporary flavours. Reservations essential. Expensive.

Magpie Café 14 Pier Rd ☎01947/602058. The traditional fish-and-chip choice in town for over forty years. In summer you'll have to wait in long queues to get through the doors. Closes 9pm. Moderate.

North Beach Café Sea Wall ☎01947/602066. The roof terrace has the best sea views in town, and serves a summer grill menu (day and night). Downstairs, there are sandwiches and light meals by day, and Mediterranean-style fish and meat mains at dinner (winter open during the day and on selected evenings). Moderate.

Trenchers New Quay Rd ☎01947/603212. Highly rated fish-and-chip restaurant, near the tourist office, with snappy service and mountainous portions. Closes 9pm & all Nov–March. Moderate.

Pubs and live music

Duke of York Church St. Classic Whitby pub, at the bottom of the 199 steps, with harbour views, good-value food and occasional music.

Huntsman Inn Aislaby. It's well worth driving (or cabbing) out the couple of miles to Aislaby for the home-cooked pub food here – steaks a speciality.

Middle Earth 26 Church St. Regular music nights at this local, down by the marina – outdoor seats provide harbour views.

Tap & Spile New Quay Rd. The town's real-ale haunt, with a changing selection of guest beers and live music nearly every night.

Staithes

At first sight **STAITHES** is an improbably beautiful grouping of huddled stone houses around a small harbour, backed by the severe outcrop of Cowbar Nab, a sheer cliff face which protects the northern flank of the village. Storms and floods have battered Staithes for centuries: the *Cod and Lobster*, the pub on the harbour, has been rebuilt three times and is shuttered against the wind, while the draper's shop in which James Cook first worked before moving to Whitby collapsed completely in 1745 – its rebuilt successor is now marked by a plaque. Cook is remembered in the **Captain Cook and Staithes Heritage Centre**, on the High Street (daily 10am–5.30pm; £2.50), which re-creates an eighteenth-century street among other interesting exhibits.

You could stay at one of the B&Bs in the houses at the top of the village, but better **accommodation** is available down below, either at *Brooklyn* (☎01947/841396; ❷), a comfortable B&B in a former sea captain's house on Brown's Terrace – just off the steep road down, on the right – or at the *Endeavour Restaurant* (☎01947/840825, ⓦwww.endeavour-restaurant.co.uk; ❹). The latter, incidentally, is the best place to eat for miles around, with superb (but pricey) fresh fish meals (dinner only; closed Sun & Mon, except bank holidays). Alternatively, drive the three miles south (back towards Whitby) to

Runswick Bay, a tiny little one-pub village and beach, where the *Cliffemount Hotel* (☎01947/840103, ⓦwww.cliffemounthotel.co.uk; ❺) glories in its elevated position.

Travel details

Buses

Details of minor and seasonal local bus services are frequently given in the text. It's essential to pick up either the Dales Explorer or Moors Explorer timetable booklets from a local tourist office if visiting those parts of the county. For details of the Moorsbus in the North York Moors National Park see p.705. For information on all other local and national bus services, contact Traveline: ☎0870/608 2608 (daily 7am–9pm), ⓦwww.traveline.org.uk.

Helmsley to: Pickering (hourly; 40min); Scarborough (hourly; 1hr 30min); York (3 daily; 1hr 30min).

Harrogate to: Knaresborough (every 10min; 15min); Leeds (every 30–60min; 40min); Ripon (every 30min; 30min); York (hourly; 1hr 15min).

Pickering to: Helmsley (3–7 daily; 40min); Scarborough (hourly; 1hr); Whitby (5 daily; 1hr); York (hourly; 1hr 20min).

Richmond to: Ripon (Mon–Sat hourly; 1hr 15min).

Scarborough to: Bridlington (hourly; 1hr 15min); Filey (hourly; 30min); Helmsley (hourly; 1hr 30min); Hull (1 daily; 2hr); Leeds (hourly; 3hr); Pickering (hourly; 1hr); Robin Hood's Bay (hourly; 45min); Whitby (hourly; 1hr); York (hourly; 1hr 45min).

Skipton to: Grassington (Mon-Sat hourly; 30min); Malham (4 daily; 35min); Settle (Mon-Sat hourly; 40min).

Whitby to: Robin Hood's Bay (hourly; 25min); Staithes (hourly; 30min); York (4–5 daily; 2hr).

York to: Beverley (4 daily; 1hr 15min); Harrogate (hourly; 1hr 15min); Hull (5 daily; 1hr 30min); Pickering (hourly; 1hr 15min); Whitby (4–5 daily; 2hr).

Trains

For information on all local and national rail services, contact National Rail Enquiries ☎08457/484950, ⓦwww.nationalrail.co.uk.

For more detailed information about specific lines, turn to the following pages: Settle to Carlisle Railway p.679; North Yorkshire Moors Railway p.709; Keighley and Worth Valley Railway p.674.

Harrogate to: Knaresborough (every 30min; 15min); Leeds (every 30min; 45min); York (hourly; 30min).

Hull to: Beverley (Mon–Sat hourly, Sun 4 daily; 15min); Leeds (hourly; 1hr); London (3–4 daily; 2hr 45min); Scarborough (every 2hr; 1hr 30min); York (10 daily; 1hr 15min).

Knaresborough to: Harrogate (every 30min; 15min); Leeds (every 30min; 45min); York (hourly; 30min).

Leeds to: Bradford (every 15min; 20min); Carlisle (3–9 daily; 2hr 40min); Harrogate (every 30min; 45min); Hull (hourly; 1hr); Knaresborough (every 30min; 45min); Lancaster (3 daily; 2hr); Liverpool (hourly; 2hr); London (every 30min; 2hr); Manchester (every 30min; 35min); Scarborough (every 30–60min; 1hr 15min); Settle (3–8 daily; 1hr); Sheffield (every 30min; 45min–1hr 15min); Skipton (hourly; 40min); York (every 30min; 40min).

Pickering to: Grosmont (April–Oct 5–8 daily, plus limited winter service; 1hr).

Scarborough to: Hull (every 2hr; 1hr 30min); Leeds (hourly; 1hr 15min); York (every 30–60min; 45min).

Sheffield to: Leeds (every 30min; 45min–1hr 15min); London (every 45min; 2hr 30min); York (hourly; 1hr 20min).

Whitby to: Danby (4–5 daily; 35min); Egton Bridge (4–5 daily; 20min); Grosmont (4–5 daily; 15min); Middlesbrough (4–5 daily; 1hr 30min).

York to: Bradford (every 45min; 1hr); Durham (every 30min; 40min); Edinburgh (hourly; 2hr); Harrogate (hourly; 30min); Hull (hourly; 1hr 15min); Leeds (every 30min; 40min); London (every 30min; 2hr); Manchester (hourly; 1hr 45min); Newcastle (every 30min; 1hr); Scarborough (8–15 daily; 45min); Sheffield (hourly; 1hr 20min).

The Northeast

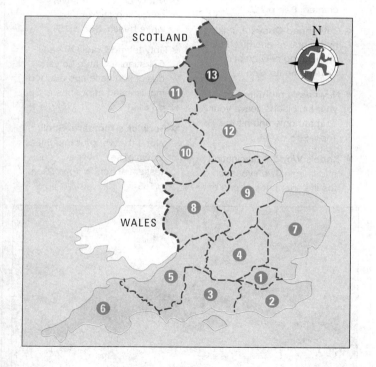

CHAPTER 13

Highlights

* **Durham Cathedral** Awe-inspiring Romanesque church towering above the wooded banks of the River Wear. **See p.727**

* **Beamish Museum** The everyday details of the northeast's industrial past poignantly re-created. **See p.729**

* **Gateshead Quays** A striking riverscape re-energized by challenging new artistic developments. **See p.741**

* **Newcastle nightlife** Lock up your inhibitions, leave your coat at home and hit the Toon. **See p.744**

* **Bede's World** A fascinating and imaginative evocation of the life and times of one of Europe's greatest scholars. **See p.746**

* **Hadrian's Wall** Put your walking boots on to make the most of this extraordinary monument and its wild landscape. **See p.748**

* **Warkworth** Ruined riverside castle and miles of lonely white beach. **See p.757**

* **Holy Island** Cradle of early Christianity, with a Lutyens-designed castle and a brooding, isolated atmosphere. **See p.761**

* **Berwick's ramparts** Stroll along the walls for matchless views of sea, river and quintessential frontier town. **See p.763**

△ Hadrian's Wall

The Northeast

For England's northeastern region – in particular the counties of Northumberland and Durham – the period between the Roman invasion and the 1603 union of the English and Scottish crowns was one of almost incessant turbulence. To mark the Roman Empire's limit **Hadrian's Wall** was built along the 76 miles between the North Sea and the west coast, an extraordinary military structure that is now one of the country's most evocative ruins – easily visited from the appealing abbey-town of **Hexham**. When the Romans departed, the northeast was divided into unstable Saxon principalities until order was restored by the kings of Northumbria, who dominated the region from 600 until the 870s. It was they who nourished the region's early Christian tradition, which achieved its finest flowering with the creation of the **Lindisfarne Gospels** on what is now known as **Holy Island**. The monks abandoned their island at the end of the ninth century, in advance of the Vikings' destruction of the Northumbrian kingdom, and only after the Norman Conquest did the northeast again become part of a greater England. The Norman kings and their successors repeatedly attempted to subdue Scotland, passing effective regional control to powerful local lords, whose authority is recalled by a sequence of formidable **fortresses** dotted along the Northumbrian coast.

Long after the northeast had ceased to be a critical military zone, its character and appearance were transformed by the **Industrial Revolution**. Coal had been mined here for hundreds of years, but exploitation only began in earnest towards the end of the eighteenth century, when two main coalfields were established, in County Durham and along the Northumberland coast from the Tyne. The world's **first railway**, the Darlington and Stockton line, was opened in 1825 to move coal to the nearest port for export, while local coal and ore also fuelled the foundries that supplied the shipbuilding and heavy-engineering companies of Tyneside.

Most visitors dodge the industrial areas, bypassing the towns along the **Tees Valley** – Darlington, Stockton, Middlesbrough and Hartlepool – on the way to **Durham**, a handsome university city, dominated by its cathedral. From Durham it's a short hop to **Newcastle upon Tyne**, distinguished by some fine Victorian buildings, the revitalized Quayside, and a vibrant cultural scene and nightlife. The **Northumberland coast** to the north boasts some superb castles – most impressively at Warkworth, Dunstanburgh and Bamburgh – as well as a string of superb dune-backed beaches. **Alnwick**, four miles inland from the sea, features another stunning castle and northern England's finest new garden, while the extravagant ramparts of **Berwick-upon-Tweed** signal the imminence of the Scottish border. Inland, the Durham dales of **Teesdale**

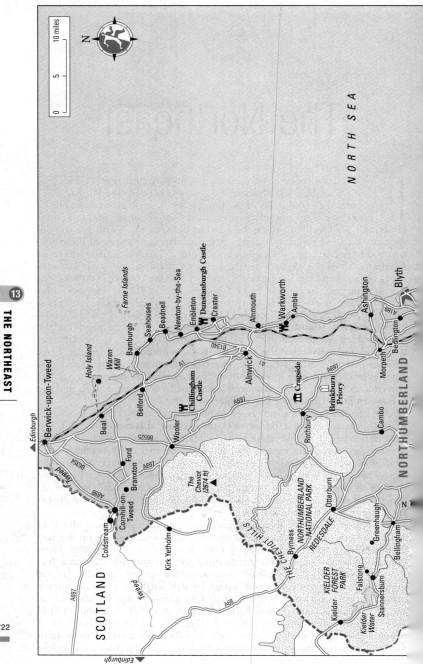

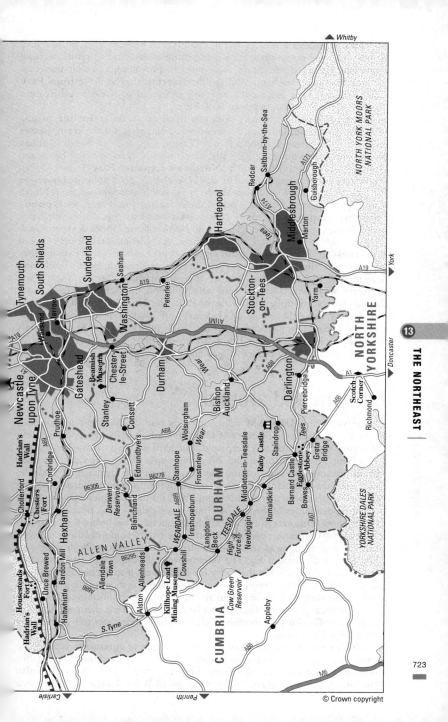

13

© Crown copyright

and **Weardale** offer a mix of scenic countryside, heritage attractions, stately homes and rural pubs, while it's worth setting aside a day to ramble around **Beamish Museum**, England's most thought-provoking open-air museum. Northwest, beyond Hadrian's Wall, lies the **Northumberland National Park** – at its most remote around the reservoir and forest of Kielder and its most graceful in the Victorian streets of Rothbury.

Getting to the region is easy with the main east coast **train line** passing through Darlington, Durham, Newcastle and Berwick. Useful **train passes** include the Northeast Regional Rover (7 days; £73) and the North Country Rover (any 4 days out of 8; £61.50), which is valid as far south as Leeds and Hull and west as far as Preston. The **Northeast Explorer Pass** (1-day; £5.75), valid after 9am on weekdays and all day at weekends, gives unlimited travel on local buses from Berwick-upon-Tweed as far south as Scarborough in North Yorkshire or west to Carlisle – buy it on board any bus. For all local **public transport enquiries** log onto Nexus (Ⓦwww.nexus.org.uk), which has a useful journey-planner option. The useful *Northumberland Public Transport Guide* (£1) is sold at most local tourist offices. A Northumbria Tourist Board **Powerpass** (£2), from any of the region's tourist offices, gives two-for-the-price-of-one entry to many attractions, including Beamish, Bede's World and Segedunum. The main long-distance footpath through the northeast is the **Pennine Way**, which crosses Hadrian's Wall and then climaxes in a climb through the Northumberland National Park. The **Hadrian's Wall Path** provides access along the whole of Hadrian's Wall, from near Newcastle to the Cumbrian coast. Less well known is the 63-mile pilgrim's route, **St Cuthbert's Way**, which links Holy Island with Melrose, where St Cuthbert started his ministry, just across the border in Scotland.

Durham and around

The view from **DURHAM** train station is one of the finest in northern England – a panoramic prospect of Durham Cathedral, its towers dominating the skyline from the top of a steep sandstone bluff within a narrow bend of the River Wear. This dramatic site has been the resting place of St Cuthbert since 995, his hallowed remains making Durham a place of pilgrimage for both the Saxons and the Normans, who began work on the present cathedral at the end of the eleventh century. In the meantime, William the Conqueror, aware of the defensive possibilities of the site, had built a castle that was to be the precursor of ever more elaborate fortifications. Subsequently, the bishops of Durham were granted extensive powers to control the troublesome northern marches of the kingdom, ruling as semi-independent **prince bishops**, with their own army, mint and courts of law. The bishops were at the peak of their power in the fourteenth century, but thereafter the office went into decline, especially in the wake of the Reformation, yet they clung to the vestiges of their authority until 1836, when they ceded them to the Crown. They abandoned Durham Castle for their palace in Bishop Auckland and transferred their old home to the fledgling **Durham University**, England's third oldest seat of learning after Oxford and Cambridge.

Within easy striking distance of the city are a host of attractions recalling the county's past and some scenic and largely crowd-free countryside. Most people troop off to the reconstructed colliery village (and much more) at the **Beamish Museum**, north of Durham. To the west, there's **Raby Castle**, a stately home near the market town of **Barnard Castle**, itself the setting for the opulent art collection of the Bowes Museum. Further west lie the Pennine valleys of **Teesdale** and **Weardale**, whose upper reaches boast some enjoyable moorland scenery, most dramatically at Teesdale's **High Force** waterfall. If you have your own transport, you can move on north from Weardale via **Blanchland**, a delightful stone village tucked away in the valley of the Derwent River across the border in Northumberland. Durham County Council Environment Department (℡0191/383 4144) offers a year-round programme of **guided walks** (£2), ranging from rural rambles to industrial heritage trails.

Arrival, information and accommodation

From either Durham **train station,** or the **bus station** on North Road, it's ten minutes' walk to the city centre, across the river. The "Cathedral" **bus** (#40) links train and bus stations with the Market Place (for the tourist office) and the cathedral (every 20min; 50p for all-day ticket). Arriving by car, park in one of the designated **car parks**, signposted as you enter town, as on-street parking is difficult to find; and note that the peninsula road (to the castle and cathedral) is a toll road (Mon–Sat 10am–4pm; £2). The **tourist office** (℡0191/384 3720, ⓦwww.durhamtourism.co.uk) is located at **Millennium Place**, off Claypath, a development which also incorporates a cinema showing a forty-minute large-format film presentation on Durham (twice daily; £2.50), plus theatre, public library, bar and café. **Guided walks** (£2) depart regularly from the tourist office, while to get out onto the river, either rent a **rowing boat** (£2.50/person; 1hr) from Brown's Boathouse, Elvet Bridge, or take a summer **cruise** aboard the *Prince Bishop* (℡0191/386 9525; £4.50; 1hr; from Elvet Bridge). **Bike rental** is available from Cycle Force 2000, 87 Claypath (℡0191/384 0319; £12 a day). Free **Internet** access can be had at the City Library, Millennium Place.

Apart from the **accommodation** listed below, Durham also provides rooms at the colleges of **Durham University** (Christmas, Easter and July–Sept), all within walking distance of the centre; the tourist office has a full list, or call the Conference and Tourism Office for a brochure (℡0800/289970, ⓦwww.dur.ac.uk/conference_tourism; from £20 per person, or £30 in en-suite rooms, breakfast included).

Guest houses and hotels

Castle View Guest House 4 Crossgate ℡0191/386 8852. Pretty townhouse, on a cobbled terrace next to St Margaret's Church. ❸

Georgian Town House 10 Crossgate ℡0191/386 8070, ⓦwww.thegeorgiantownhouse.co.uk. Good breakfasts, plus some rooms with cathedral views. No credit cards. ❹

Green Grove 99 Gilesgate ℡0191/384 4361. Suburban B&B, a 20min walk from the centre. No credit cards. ❷

Marriott Royal County Old Elvet ℡0191/386 6821, ⓦwww.marriotthotels.com. Durham's top hotel, with indoor swimming pool, restaurant, brasserie and bar. Breakfast not included except when booked as special/weekend rate. ❼

Seaham Hall Lord Byron's Walk, Seaham, 10 miles northeast of Durham ℡0191/516 1400, ⓦwww.seaham-hall.com. Hip, holistic spa hotel that makes a great coastal base for city sightseeing – Durham is a 20min drive away. ❽

Swallow Three Tuns New Elvet ℡0191/386 4326, ⓦwww.swallowhotels.com. A former sixteenth-century coaching inn with access to the *Royal County*'s leisure centre. ❻

Travelodge Durham Station Rd, Gilesgate ℡08700/850950, ⓦwww.travelodge.co.uk. Motel-style accommodation on the edge of town that's a good deal for families (breakfast not included). ❸

Campsite

Grange Camping and Caravan Site Meadow Lane, Carrville ℡0191/384 4778. By the junction of the A1(M) and the A690, two miles northeast of the city; take bus #220 or #222 for Sunderland from the bus station.

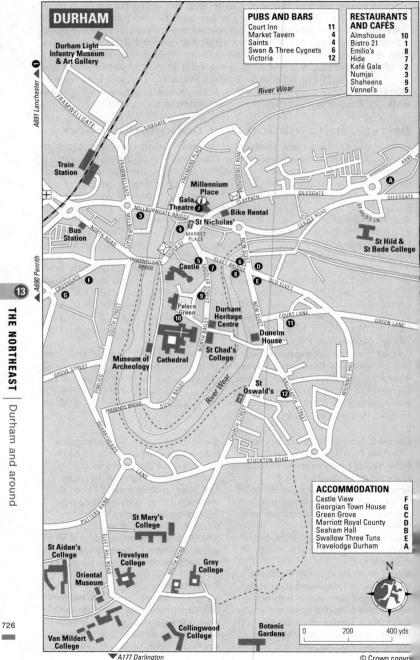

DURHAM

PUBS AND BARS

Court Inn	11
Market Tavern	4
Saints	4
Swan & Three Cygnets	6
Victoria	12

RESTAURANTS AND CAFÉS

Almshouse	10
Bistro 21	1
Emilio's	8
Hide	7
Kafé Gala	2
Numjai	3
Shaheens	9
Vennel's	5

ACCOMMODATION

Castle View	F
Georgian Town House	G
Green Grove	C
Marriott Royal County	D
Seaham Hall	B
Swallow Three Tuns	A
Travelodge Durham	E

A691 Lanchester

A690 Penrith

River Wear

Durham Light Infantry Museum & Art Gallery

FRAMWELLGATE

SIDEGATE

Train Station

FRAMWELLGATE

MILLBURNGATE

NORTH ROAD

Bus Station

FRAMWELLGATE BRIDGE

CROSSGATE

SOUTH STREET

PIMLICO

GROVE STREET

FREEMANS PLACE

PROVIDENCE ROW

Millennium Place

Gala Theatre

St Nicholas'

MARKET PLACE

SILVER ST

Castle

SADDLER STREET

ELVET BRIDGE

Palace Green

NORTH BAILEY

Museum of Archeology

Cathedral

Durham Heritage Centre

St Chad's College

SOUTH BAILEY

PREBENDS BRIDGE

River Wear

CLAYPATH

GILESGATE

A690

GILESGATE

ST HILD'S LN

St Hild & St Bede College

LEAZES ROAD

NEW ELVET

OLD ELVET

NEW ELVET

COURT LANE

Dunelm House

GREEN LANE

St Oswald's

HALLGARTH STREET

WHINNEY HILL

Bike Rental

QUARRY HEADS LANE

POTTERS BANK

ELVET HILL ROAD

St Aidan's College

Oriental Museum

St Mary's College

Trevelyan College

SOUTH ROAD

CHURCH STREET

Grey College

STOCKTON ROAD

Collingwood College

Botanic Gardens

Van Mildert College

A177 Darlington

N

0	200	400 yds

© Crown copyri

The City

Surrounded on three sides by the River Wear, Durham's surprisingly compact centre is approached by two road bridges that lead from the western, modern part of town across the river to the spur containing castle and cathedral. The commercial heart of this "old town" area is the triangular **Market Place**, inappropriately dominated by an equestrian statue of the third marquis of Londonderry, a much-hated nineteenth-century colliery owner. The Victorian **Market Hall** (closed Sun) hosts a lively outdoor market every Saturday, as well as farmers' markets, held on the third Thursday of the month.

The Cathedral

From Market Place, it's a five-minute walk up cobbled Saddler Street to **Durham Cathedral** (July–Sept Mon–Sat 9.30am–8pm, Sun 12.30–8pm; Oct–June Mon–Sat 9.30am–6.15pm, Sun 12.30–5pm; guided tours Easter–Sept Sat at 11am & 2.30pm, plus July & Aug Sat 6.15pm, Sun 5pm; access sometimes restricted, call ☏0191/386 4266 to check; £3 suggested donation; tours £3.50; ⓦ www.durhamcathedral.co.uk), completed in 1133 by French master masons and a supreme example of the Norman-Romanesque style. The awe-inspiring **nave** used pointed arches for the first time in England, raising the vaulted ceiling to new and dizzying heights. The weight of the stone is borne by massive pillars, their heaviness relieved by striking Moorish-influenced geometric patterns – chevrons, diamonds and vertical fluting. A door gives access to the **tower** (Mon–Sat 10am–4pm; £2) and from the top there are gut-wrenching views of the city. Separated from the nave by a Victorian marble screen is the **choir**, where the dark-stained Restoration stalls are overshadowed by the vainglorious **bishop's throne**, reputedly the highest in medieval Christendom. Beyond, the **Chapel of the Nine Altars** dates from the thirteenth century, its Early English stonework distinguished by its delicacy of detail. Here, and around the adjoining **Shrine of St Cuthbert**, much of the stonework is Frosterley marble, each dark shaft bearing its own fancy pattern of fossils. Cuthbert himself lies beneath a plain marble slab, his shrine having gained a reputation over the centuries for its curative powers. The legend was given credence in 1104, when the saint's body was exhumed for reburial here, and was found to be completely uncorrupted, more than four hundred years after his death on Lindisfarne. Almost certainly, this was the result of his fellow monks having (unintentionally) preserved the body by laying it in sand containing salt crystals – though to medieval eyes, here was testament enough to the saint's potency.

Back near the entrance, at the west end of the church, the **Galilee Chapel** was begun in the 1170s, its light and exotic decoration in imitation of the Great Mosque of Cordoba, a contrast to the forcefulness of the nave. Subdivided by twelve slender columns, each surrounded by a medley of geometric patterns, the chapel contains the simple tombstone of the **Venerable Bede**, the Northumbrian monk credited with being England's first historian. Bede died at the monastery of Jarrow in 735, and his remains were first transferred to the cathedral in 1020. An ancient wooden doorway opposite the main entrance leads into the spacious **cloisters**, which are flanked by what remains of the monastic buildings. These include the **monks' dormitory** (Mon–Sat 10am–3.30pm, Sun 12.30–3.15pm; 80p) and the **Treasures of St Cuthbert** exhibition in the undercroft (Mon–Sat 10am–4.30pm, Sun 2–4.30pm; £2), where you can see some striking relics of the saint, including the reassembled fragments of his delicately carved oak coffin. There's also a splendid facsimile copy of the Lindisfarne Gospels (the originals are in the British Library in London), whose pages are turned at regular intervals.

The rest of the city

Across Palace Green from the cathedral, **Durham Castle** (Easter & July–Sept daily 10am–12.30pm & 2–4pm; rest of the year Mon, Wed, Sat & Sun 2–4pm; £3; ☎191/374 3800, ⓦwww.durhamcastle.com) lost its medieval appearance long ago during refurbishments arranged by a succession of prince bishops. It's only possible to visit the castle on a 45-minute guided tour, highlights of which include rapid visits to the fifteenth-century kitchen, a climb up the enormous hanging staircase and the jog down to the Norman chapel, notable for its lively Romanesque carved capitals. The castle is sometimes closed for functions during its regular opening hours, so it's best to call ahead to check.

Below the castle and the cathedral are the wooded banks of the **River Wear**, where a pleasant footpath runs right round the peninsula. It takes about thirty minutes to complete the circuit, passing a succession of elegant bridges with fine vantage points over town and cathedral. Just along from **Framwellgate Bridge**, on the riverbank, the university's **Museum of Archeology** (April–Oct daily 11am–4pm; Nov–March Mon & Fri–Sun 11.30am–3.30pm; £1) occupies an old stone fulling mill, its displays a mixture of permanent archeological relics and temporary exhibitions. Eighteenth-century **Prebends Bridge** boasts celebrated views of the cathedral, and the path then continues round to the handsome **Elvet Bridge**.

The university's **Oriental Museum** (Mon–Fri 10am–5pm, Sat & Sun noon–5pm; £1.50; ⓦwww.dur.ac.uk/oriental.museum) is set among college buildings a couple of miles south of the city centre on Elvet Hill Road (take bus #5 or #6 to South Rd). Highlights of its wide-ranging collection include outstanding displays of Chinese ceramics and Arabic calligraphy, a magnificent Chinese bed and Japanese wood-block prints, complemented by temporary exhibitions and events. After the museum, you may as well continue on foot to the nearby **Botanic Garden** (daily: March–Oct 10am–5pm; Nov–Feb 11am–4pm; £1.50), whose glasshouses, café and visitor centre are set in eighteen acres near Collingwood College; buses run back to the centre from either Elvet Hill Road or South Road. North of the centre, a ten-minute walk from the train station takes you to the **Durham Light Infantry Museum and Art Gallery**, at Aykley Heads (daily: April–Oct 10am–5pm; Nov–March 10am–4pm; £2.50; ⓦwww.durham.gov.uk/dli). Downstairs, it tells the story of World War I, in which 12,000 men of the DLI died; the less compelling first floor traces the history of the regiment through World War II to its last parade in 1968. The art gallery plays host to an indefinable variety of temporary exhibitions.

Eating, drinking and entertainment

Durham has plenty of **restaurants**, cafés, tearooms and budget eateries, and you don't have to look far for inexpensive pizza, pasta or bar meals. Regular **classical concerts** are held at various venues around the city, including the cathedral, while Durham is lucky enough to have two **arts–centre venues**, namely the DLI Museum and Art Gallery and the Gala Theatre, which between them host a full annual programme of music, theatre, dance, comedy and cinema. June sees the university's **arts week**, and in the same month the **Durham Regatta** packs the riverbanks and river. Over the first weekend in July, the **Durham Summer Festival** encompasses all manner of musical entertainments, as well as historical re-enactments on Palace Green; on the following Saturday, the **Miners' Gala** – when the traditional lodge banners are paraded through the streets – has been revived as a celebration of the international labour movement.

Cafés and restaurants

Almshouse Palace Green. Inventive bistro meals for around £5–6 in the shadow of the cathedral. In summer (May–Aug) open until 8pm. Inexpensive.

Bistro 21 Aykley Heads ☎0191/384 4354. Excellent Modern British cuisine in a converted farmhouse north of the centre, 10min walk from the DLI museum and art gallery. Closed Sun. Expensive.

Emilio's 96 Elvet Bridge ☎0191/384 0096. The city's Italian of choice. Happy-hour pizza and pasta deals are a steal. Closed Sun lunch. Moderate.

Hide 39 Saddler St ☎0191/384 1999. Best of the café-bars with foodie pretensions, serving a daytime brunch-style menu with prices rising at night for a funky Modern British tour of world cuisine. Inexpensive to Moderate.

Kafé Gala Millennium Place. Drinks, muffins and light meals with sunny courtyard seating. Open until 9pm. Inexpensive.

Numjai 19 Millburngate Centre ☎0191/386 2020. Authentic Thai restaurant that dishes up plenty of seafood and veggie options. Expensive.

Shaheens 48 North Bailey ☎0191/386 0960. The place to head for the best curry in town. Closed Mon. Moderate.

Vennel's Saddler's Yard, Saddler St. Drinks, sandwiches, salads, quiche and pastas served in its hidden sixteenth-century courtyard. Closes 5pm, though upstairs bar open after 7pm. Inexpensive.

Bars and pubs

Court Inn Court Lane. Best pub dining in town, a favourite with students and locals, with a classic pub menu, plus dip-and-share tapas.

Market Tavern Market Place. Bleary-eyed old socialists will want to make time for a quick pint in the place where the influential Durham Miners' Association was founded in 1871.

Saints Market Vaults, Back Silver St. Student vaults bar, below Millburngate bridge, with real ales, drinks deals, and budget meals and grills.

Swan & Three Cygnets Elvet Bridge. Town and gown converge in this popular riverside pub.

Victoria 86 Hallgarth St. Once, all pubs were like this – Victorian feel and decor, half-a-dozen well-kept ales, no food, no music, and closed between 2 and 6pm (7pm on Sun).

Live music and arts venues

DLI Museum and Art Gallery Aykley Heads ☎0191/384 2214, ⊛www.durham.gov.uk/dli. Lunchtime recitals, special exhibitions, summertime brass band concerts, ceilidhs and other events.

Durham Students' Union Dunelm House, New Elvet ☎0191/374 2000. Gigs during term time, and regular rock, jazz and comedy.

Gala Theatre and Cinema Millennium Place ☎0191/332 4041, ⊛www.galadurham.co.uk. Live music, theatre, cinema (outdoor classic movies in summer), and Comedy Store gigs on the first Sun of every month.

Beamish Museum

The open-air **Beamish Museum** (Easter–Oct 10am–5pm; Nov & Dec daily 10am–4pm; Jan–Easter Tues–Thurs, Sat & Sun 10am–4pm; last admission 3pm; admission £12, £4 in winter; ☎0191/370 4000, ⊛www.beamish.org.uk) spreads out over 300 acres beside the A693, about ten miles north of Durham. It's the one County Durham attraction you really shouldn't miss, as popular with tourists as it is with local people, who come to chew the fat with the costumed guides, many of whom are recruited for their real-life experience.

Buildings from all over the region have been reassembled in six main sections, linked by restored trams and buses and all painstakingly kitted out with period furnishings and fittings. Costumed shopkeepers, workers and householders can answer your questions about daily life a century or two ago. Four of the sections show life in 1913, before the upheavals brought about by World War I, notably a pint-sized **colliery village**, complete with drift mine (regular tours throughout the day), old stone winding house, cottages, Methodist chapel and school. This was a period when County Durham produced 41 million tons of coal each year, raised from three hundred pits by 170,000 miners. In retrospect, it was the heyday of the Durham coalfield: just 127 mines were left when the industry was nationalized in 1947, only 34 in 1969, and today not a single working pit remains. There's also a large-scale re-creation of a market **town**, its High Street lined by shops, bank, pub, dentist's surgery, newspaper office, garage, stables, sweet factory and solicitor's office. Two areas date to 1825, at the beginning of the northeast's industrial development: a **manor house**, with horse yard, formal gardens, vegetable plots and orchards; and the **Pockerley Waggonway**, where you can ride behind a replica of George Stephenson's *Locomotion*, the first passenger-carrying steam train in the world. There's a great deal to see and most people make a day of it – reckon on at least four hours to get round the lot in summer, two in winter when only the town and train station are usually open. Call ahead to check on **special events** held throughout the summer, from craft displays to whippet racing.

Drivers should follow signs to the museum off the A1(M) Chester-le-Street exit, then follow the signs along the A693 to Stanley. By **bus**, take the #720 from Durham bus station (hourly) or the #709 from Newcastle's Eldon Square (hourly), which drop you close to the main entrance. In summer, hang on to your bus ticket and you'll get a discount on entrance to the museum.

Bishop Auckland and around

Eleven miles southwest of Durham city, **BISHOP AUCKLAND** has been the country home of the bishops of Durham since the twelfth century and their official residence for more than a hundred and fifty years. Their palace, the gracious **Auckland Castle** (Easter–Sept Sun & Mon 2–5pm; £4; Ⓦ www.auckland-castle.co.uk), standing in eight-hundred-acre grounds, is approached through an imposing gatehouse just off the town's large Market Place. The palace has been extensively remodelled since its medieval incarnation, redesigned to satisfy the whims of such occupants as the seventeenth-century Bishop Cosin who refurbished the original banqueting hall to create today's splendid marble and limestone chapel. Here, the stained-glass windows relate the stories of early Christian saints familiar throughout the northeast, especially Cuthbert, Bede and Aidan. After you've seen the castle you can stroll into the adjacent **Bishop's Deer Park** (daily dawn–dusk; free), where an eighteenth-century deer house survives.

The town itself plays second fiddle to the castle, though don't leave until you've followed the mile-long lane from behind the Town Hall (signposted by the *Sportsman Inn*) to the remains of **Binchester Roman Fort** (Easter & May–Sept daily 11am–5pm; £1.60). Only a small portion of the ten-acre site – Roman Vinovia – has been excavated, but this includes the country's best example of a hypocaust, built to warm the private bath suite of the garrison's commanding officer.

Southeast of town the A688 (between Bishop Auckland and Barnard Castle) provides access to the sprawling battlements of **Raby Castle** (May & Sept Wed & Sun 1–5pm; June–Aug Mon–Fri & Sun 1–5pm; gardens same days 11am–5.30pm; castle & gardens £6, gardens only £4; Ⓦ www.rabycastle.com), roughly halfway between the two towns. The castle mostly dates from the fourteenth century, reflecting the power of the Neville family, who ruled the local roost until 1569. It was then that Charles Neville helped plan the "Rising of the North", the abortive attempt to replace Elizabeth I with Mary Queen of Scots. The revolt was a dismal failure, and Neville's estates were confiscated, with Raby subsequently passing to the Vane family in 1626. The Vanes, now the lords Barnard, still live in the castle, the interior of which was extensively renovated in the eighteenth and nineteenth centuries, though the medieval kitchen remains intact. Raby's focal point is the first-floor Baron's Hall, still of cathedral-like dimensions in spite of the floor being raised ten feet in 1787 to let carriages pass through the neo-Gothic entrance below. Outside in the two-hundred-acre **deer park** are the walled **gardens**, where peaches, apricots and pineapples once flourished under the careful gaze of forty Victorian gardeners. Meanwhile, a tearoom in the former stables has seats in the old horse stalls.

Practicalities

Buses drop you centrally, near Market Place, where the Town Hall, library (free Internet access) and **tourist office** share the same premises (April–Sept Mon–Fri 10am–5pm, Sat 9am–4pm Sun 1–4pm; Oct–March closed Sun; ☎01388/602610). A mile east of town, along the A688 (Spennymoor/Durham road), there's courtyard **accommodation**, a bar and restaurant at the *Park Head Hotel*, at New Coundon (☎01388/661727, Ⓦwww.parkheadhotel.com; ❹). A mile further up, just off the A688 in Binchester is *Five Gables Guest House*, in the former colliery manager's house (☎01388/608204, Ⓦwww.five-gables.co.uk; ❸). The best **restaurant** hereabouts is the *Fox & Hounds* in Newfield (☎01388/662787; closed Sun dinner & all Mon), a gastro-pub two miles beyond *Five Gables*.

Barnard Castle

Fifteen miles southwest of Bishop Auckland, the skeletal remains of **Barnard Castle** (April–Sept daily 10am–6pm; Oct daily 10am–5pm; Nov–March Wed–Sun 10am–4pm; often closed 1–2pm for lunch; £2.60; EH), poking out from a cliff high above the River Tees, overlook the town that grew up in its shadow. First fortified in the eleventh century, the castle was long a stronghold of the Balliols, a Norman family interminably embroiled in the struggle for the Scottish crown. It was one of this clan, Bernard, who built the circular tower, which survives to this day, an impressive thirteenth-century fortification just to the right of the later Round Tower, where a beautiful oriel window carries the emblematic boar of Richard III, one of the subsequent owners.

Castle aside, the prime attraction is the grand French-style chateau that constitutes the **Bowes Museum** (daily 11am–5pm; £6; Ⓦwww.bowesmuseum .org.uk), half a mile east of the centre, signposted along Newgate. Begun in 1869, the chateau was commissioned by John and Josephine Bowes, a local businessman and MP and his French actress wife, who spent much of their time in Paris collecting the ostentatious treasures and antiques. It's a hugely rewarding collection, ranging from furniture, paintings, tapestries and ceramics to incidental curiosities, notably a late eighteenth-century mechanical silver swan in the lobby which still performs daily at 2pm, preening to a brief forty-second melodic burst. There's a café, too, and a stroll in the grounds on a nice day is no bad thing with various marked routes along a "Tree Trail". Otherwise, from the town centre, it's a pleasant mile-and-a-half walk from the castle, southeast (downriver) through the fields above the banks of the Tees, to the glorious shattered ruins of **Egglestone Abbey** (dawn–dusk; free), a minor Premonstratensian foundation dating from 1195.

Practicalities

Buses stop on either side of central Galgate, with the **tourist office** on Flatts Road, at the end of Galgate by the castle (April–Oct daily 10am–6pm;

Nov–March Mon–Sat 11am–4pm; ☎01833/690909). Among several convenient **B&Bs** along the upper reaches of Galgate are the welcoming *Homelands*, 85 Galgate (☎01833/638757, ⊛www.homelandsguesthouse .co.uk; no credit cards; ❸), and the similar *Marwood House*, opposite at no. 98 (☎01833/637493, ⊛www.kilgarriff.demon.co.uk; no credit cards; ❷). The *Old Well Inn*, 21 The Bank (☎01833/690130, ⊛www.oldwellinn.co.uk; ❹), originally a Tudor coaching inn, has huge en-suite rooms and weekend half-board deals. *Stables*, in Horsemarket between Galgate and the Market Place (part of the Hayloft indoor craft market), provides inexpensive **café** meals and all-day breakfasts, while the town's top **restaurant** is *Blagraves House* at 30–32 The Bank (☎01833/637668; closed Sun & Mon), a sixteenth-century former inn, with set menus (£16.95) that change monthly. For a quiet **drink**, try the *Old Well Inn*, which has a beer garden backing onto the castle walls.

Teesdale

Extending twenty-odd miles northwest from Barnard Castle, **Teesdale** begins calmly enough, though the pastoral landscapes of its lower reaches are soon replaced by wilder Pennine scenery. There's a regular **bus service** as far as Middleton-in-Teesdale, the valley's main settlement, with infrequent (Tues, Wed, Fri & Sat) services on to High Force waterfall.

MIDDLETON-IN-TEESDALE was once the archetypal "company town", owned lock, stock and barrel by the Quaker-run London Lead Company, which began mining here in 1753. A heritage centre – known as Meet the Middletons – based around the life and work of a mining family, is scheduled to open here in 2004. The **tourist office** in the central Market Place (daily 10am–1pm & 2–5pm, closes 4pm in winter; ☎01833/641001) can tell you more about this and provide details of local **accommodation**. The best B&B is at *Cornforth & Cornforth*, a genial continental café at 16 Market Place (☎01833/640300, ⊜cornjohnviv@aol.com; ❷) with three brightly painted en-suite rooms, daytime meals in the café (closed Mon & Wed), and dinner (£10) by arrangement. Three miles back down the road towards Barnard Castle, the *Rose & Crown* (☎01833/650213, ⊛www.rose -and-crown.co.uk; ❻) at pretty **ROMALDKIRK** is an ivy-clad eighteenth-century inn, with highly accomplished Modern British cooking in the bar or restaurant (prices moderate to expensive).

Past Middleton, the countryside becomes harsher and the Tees more vigorous as the B6277 travels the three miles on to **Bowlees Visitor Centre** (April–Sept daily 10.30am–5pm; Oct–March Sat & Sun 10.30am–4pm; 50p), the halt for the short walk to the rapids of **Low Force**. A mile further up the road is the altogether more compelling **High Force**, a seventy-foot cascade that rumbles over an outcrop of the Whin Sill, a black dolerite ridge that pokes up in various parts of northern England. The waterfall is on private Raby land, and visitors must pay £1 to view the falls and £1.50 to use the nearby car park, by the B6277.

Weardale

Seeing the dramatic high-dale scenery of **Weardale** by public transport can be a frustrating business. Bus #101 runs roughly hourly between Bishop Auckland and Stanhope, the main village, with less frequent extensions up the valley to Cowshill; however, to get the bus to take you to the fascinating lead-mining museum at Killhope, two miles further on, you'll have to ask the driver (or arrange it in advance with the bus company; ☎01388/528235). It's better on foot, as the **Weardale Way** runs the length of the valley.

Lead and iron-ore mining flourished in and around Weardale from the 1840s to the 1880s, leaving today's landscape scarred with old workings. One of the bigger mines, situated about three miles west of Cowshill, at the head of the valley, has been turned into the **Killhope Lead Mining Museum** (April–July & Sept daily 10.30am–5pm; Aug until 5.30pm; Oct Sat & Sun 10.30am–5pm; £3.40, £5 including mine visit; ⓦ www.durham.gov.uk/killhope), whose 34-foot-high waterwheel still turns, using six thousand gallons of water per minute from a string of diverted streams. Descending Park Level Mine with hard-hat and lamp gives you a taste of the miserable mining life. Two miles east of Cowshill (the *Cowshill Hotel* here does bar meals), tiny **IRESHOPEBURN** is the home of the **Weardale Museum** (Easter, May–July & Sept Wed–Sun 2–5pm; Aug daily 2–5pm; £1.50), an excellent small folk museum with displays on lead mining, the railways and Methodism, the faith of the majority of Durham's lead miners; entry to the museum also allows you access to the adjacent **High House Chapel**, the oldest Methodist chapel in the world in continuous use.

About nine miles downstream from Ireshopeburn lies **STANHOPE**, an elongated village that makes a useful base for hikes on the moors. It has a castle (closed to the public), built for a local MP in 1798, whose walled gardens now house the **Durham Dales Centre** – on the main road through Stanhope – in which you'll find the **tourist office** (Easter–Oct daily 10am–5pm; Nov–Easter Mon–Fri 10am–4pm, Sat & Sun 11am–4pm; ☎01388/527650). **Accommodation** is available in several local B&Bs, but you may not want to pass up the chance to stay at *Stanhope Old Hall* (☎01388/528451; ❹), a twelfth-century fortified hunting lodge of the prince bishops of Durham. It's on the main road just west of the town centre, opposite the swimming pool.

Blanchland

The trans-moorland B6278, which cuts north from Weardale at Stanhope for ten extraordinarily wild miles, runs to tiny **BLANCHLAND**. Little more than a handful of ancient, lichen-stained stone cottages huddled round an L-shaped square, the hamlet was once the site of a Premonstratensian abbey, founded in the twelfth century. The village has been preserved and protected since 1721, when Lord Crewe, the childless bishop of Durham, bequeathed his estate to trustees on condition that they rebuilt the old conventual buildings, as Blanchland had slowly fallen into disrepair after the abbey's dissolution. The original trustees obliged and their successors have allowed but the faintest whiff of subsequent centuries to intrude. Consequently, the village bears many reminders of its monastic past, from the sturdy gatehouse that now accommodates the post office to the L-shaped parish church. But it's the *Lord Crewe Arms Hotel* (☎01434/675251, ⓦ www.crewearms.freeserve.co.uk; ❼) that steals the show, boasting dark vaulted basements, two big fireplaces left over from the canons' kitchen and a priest's hideaway stuck inside the chimney. The restaurant serves table d'hôte dinners for around £30, or there are cheaper meals in the fine public bar in the undercroft.

The Tees Valley

The **River Tees**, along with the Tyne further north, was one of the great engines of British economic power in the late nineteenth century. That it's so far off the contemporary tourist map as to be invisible is hardly the fault of towns whose livelihood largely disappeared once iron- and steel-making and shipbuilding became things of the past in England. But once there were rich pickings here, in places such as **Darlington**, twenty miles south of Durham city, where the first public passenger-carrying steam train, George Stephenson's *Locomotion*, made its inaugural run and is now on permanent display. The line ran first to **Stockton-on-Tees** and was then extended to ports at **Middlesbrough** and **Hartlepool**, to enable ever-increasing amounts of Durham coal to be unloaded and exported.

Darlington

DARLINGTON hit the big time in 1825, when George Stephenson's *Locomotion* hurtled from here to nearby Stockton-on-Tees, with the inventor at the controls, at the terrifying speed of fifteen miles per hour. This novel form of transport soon proved popular with passengers, an unlooked-for bonus for Edward Pease, the line's instigator: he had simply wanted a fast and economical way to transport coal from the Durham pits to the docks at Stockton. Subsequently, Darlington grew into a rail-engineering centre, and didn't look back till the pruning of the network and the closure of the works in 1966.

It's little surprise, then, that all signs in town point to the **Darlington Railway Centre and Museum** (daily 10am–5pm; £2.10; Ⓦwww.drcm.org.uk), housed in North Road station, a twenty-minute walk up Northgate from the central Market Place. The museum's pride and joy is the original *Locomotion*, actually built in Newcastle, which continued in service until 1841 – other locally made engines superseded it, and some of these are on show, too. The origins of the rest of Darlington lie deep in Saxon times, following which it enjoyed a long history as an agricultural centre and staging post on the Great North Road. The monks carrying St Cuthbert's body from Ripon to Durham stopped here, the saint lending his name to the graceful central, riverside church of **St Cuthbert** (Easter–Sept Mon–Sat 11am–2pm; Oct–Easter Fri 11am–1pm), where the needle-like spire and decorative turrets herald the delicate Early English stonework inside. One of England's largest market squares spreads beyond the church up to the restored Victorian covered **market** (Mon–Sat 8am–5pm, with a large outdoor market Mon & Sat) and prominent clocktower.

Darlington's **train station** is on the main line from London to Scotland. From the station, walk up Victoria Road to the roundabout and turn right down Feethams for the central Market Place. You'll pass the Town Hall on Feethams, opposite which most **buses** stop. The **tourist office** on the south side of Market Place at 13 Horsemarket (Mon–Fri 9am–5pm, Sat 10am–4pm; ☎01325/388666, Ⓦwww.visitdarlington.net) can help with **accommodation**. Cheap and basic board (separate bathrooms, no breakfast) is available at the town's Arts Centre (☎01325/483271; ❶), in Vane Terrace, ten minutes' walk west of the centre, where guests can use the centre's bars and lunchtime bistro – follow Duke Street from central Skinnergate. Best central **restaurant** is *Sardis* (☎01325/61222), at 196 Northgate, just north of the town centre near the cinema, serving Mediterranean-influenced food fit for the England football team (they came here after an international friendly match). Other options include *Joe Rigatoni's* (☎01325/464642), a busy Italian place on the corner of Grange and Coniscliffe roads, just up from Market Place, and *Number Twenty 2*, 22 Coniscliffe Rd, a self-professed "alehouse" with guest beers on tap and gastropub-style lunches (not Sun).

Middlesbrough

MIDDLESBROUGH, Teesside's largest town, fifteen miles east of Darlington, is entirely a product of the early industrial age, with nineteenth-century iron and steel barons throwing up factories and housing almost as fast as they could ship their products out of the docks. What was a hamlet at the turn of the nineteenth century was a thriving industrial town of 100,000 people by the turn of the twentieth. When iron and steel declined in importance and the local shipbuilding industry collapsed, Middlesbrough took to the chemical industry. Add to this a contemporary renaissance in light engineering and it seems that, compared to many of its neighbours, Middlesbrough can boast relative success in keeping its economic head above water. For visitors, however, none of these enterprises lend themselves easily to the celebration of industrial heritage so much in evidence further west, in the coalfields. The modern centre is unremarkable in every way and the town prefers to trumpet its position as "Gateway to Captain Cook Country", fair enough given that he was born a mile and a half south of the centre in Marton in 1728. Here, the **Captain Cook Birthplace Museum** in Stewart Park (Tues–Sun: Easter–Oct 10am–5.30pm; Nov–Easter 9am–3.30pm; £2.40) covers the life and times of Britain's greatest seaman and explorer, Captain James Cook, and does it very well by way of good interpretative and interactive displays. Buses run from the bus station every fifteen minutes or so to Marton – ask the driver for the stop. For more on the captain and the local area, see ⓦ www.captaincook.org.uk.

From Middlesbrough **train station**, it's just a short walk up Albert Road to the main Corporation Road. Turn right for the **bus station** – five minutes further up on its continuation, Newport Road – and carry straight on for the **tourist office**, 99 Albert Rd (Mon–Thurs 9am–5pm, Fri 9am–4.30pm, Sat 9am–1.30pm; ☎ 01642/358086, ⓦ www.middlesbrough.gov.uk). The *Purple Onion*, 80 Corporation Rd (☎ 01642/222250), is the best **restaurant** in Middlesbrough, serving bitingly trendy food at middling-to-high prices.

Stockton-on-Tees

To complete the Captain Cook trail through this part of the country, you'll need to hop across the river from Middlesbrough to **STOCKTON-ON-TEES**. Tied up at Castlegate Quay is a detailed full-sized replica of **HM Bark Endeavour**, the converted collier in which Cook set sail in 1768 on his first scientific and surveying expedition to Tahiti, New Zealand and Australia. The ship's taken over by youth groups for part of the week, but from Sundays to Wednesdays (April–Oct 11am–5pm; £3) enthusiastic and knowledgeable volunteer guides recount the rigours of life on board during this hazardous voyage. Stockton's **train station** is five minute's walk northwest of the High Street, where numerous **buses** from Middlesbrough will drop you. Off the east side of the High Street in Theatre Yard is the **tourist office** (Mon–Sat 9am–5pm; ☎ 01642/393936), with the river and Castlegate Quay just beyond.

Hartlepool

HARTLEPOOL, ten miles north of Middlesbrough, was England's third largest port in the nineteenth century and once a noted shipbuilding centre. After years in the doldrums, its image has been transformed by the renaissance of its once decaying dockland area, now spruced up as the popular **Hartlepool Historic Quay** off Marina Way (daily 10am–5pm; last admission 2hr before closing; £5.50). The entrance fee gets you onto the bustling eighteenth-century quayside where active attractions based around press gangs, the Royal Navy, seaport life and fighting ships stir the senses. There are also period shops, a replica eighteenth-century maritime pub, games and play area, coffee shop and market, while a separate fee is charged if you want to take a guided tour of **HMS Trincomalee** (daily: April–Oct 10.30am–5pm; Nov–March 10.30am–4pm; £3.50), a navy training ship built in 1817 and now berthed here. On the edge of the quay in the entertaining **Museum of Hartlepool** at Jackson Dock (daily 10am–5pm; free), you can climb the port's original lighthouse, board a restored paddle steamer and trace the town's history.

Newcastle upon Tyne and around

At first glance **NEWCASTLE UPON TYNE** – virtual capital of the area between Yorkshire and Scotland – may appear to be just another northern industrial conurbation, but the banks of the Tyne have been settled for nearly two thousand years and the city consequently has a greater breadth of attractions than many of its rivals. The Romans were the first to bridge the river here, and the "new castle" appeared as long ago as 1080. In the seventeenth century a regional monopoly on coal export brought wealth and power to Newcastle and – as well as giving a new expression to the English language – engendered its other great industry, shipbuilding. In its nineteenth-century heyday, Newcastle's engineers and builders gave the city an elegance that has survived today in the impressive buildings of Grainger Town – indeed, only London and Bath have more listed classical buildings. Industrial decline hit the area early, as highlighted by the Jarrow Crusade of 1936, but there's been an extraordinary revival over the last decade as the city has shed its dowdy provincial coat to emerge as a vibrant European arts and nightlife destination. The pre-eminent artistic symbol of this renewal is Antony Gormley's **Angel of the North**, a magnificent steel sculpture the size of a jumbo jet that welcomes anyone approaching from the south by rail or road. Newcastle's city centre has been transformed, particularly along the banks of the River Tyne, whose famous series of bridges acts as a backdrop to the ever-developing cultural and entertainment scene. On **Gateshead Quays** are the BALTIC contemporary arts centre and Norman Foster's Sage music centre, while Newcastle's **Quayside** is scene of much of the city's contemporary nightlife. Add to these the lure of some impressive museums and galleries, including the unique Life Science Centre and the best traditional art gallery in the Northeast, the Laing, and there's a case for taking whatever time you were going to spend in the city and doubling it.

You'll certainly need to stay an extra day or so if you plan on seeing any of the nearby attractions, notably the Roman fort at **Wallsend** and the early Christian site of **Jarrow**, while both Sunderland and Washington are easily seen from the city too.

Arrival, information and city transport

Central Station, on Neville Street, is a five-minute walk from the city centre. National Express services arrive at the **coach station** on St James's Boulevard, not far from Central Station, while most regional **bus** services use the **Haymarket** bus station on Percy Street on the north side of the centre (Haymarket Metro). Many other city and local bus services arrive at and depart from the underground bus station a hundred yards down the same street in

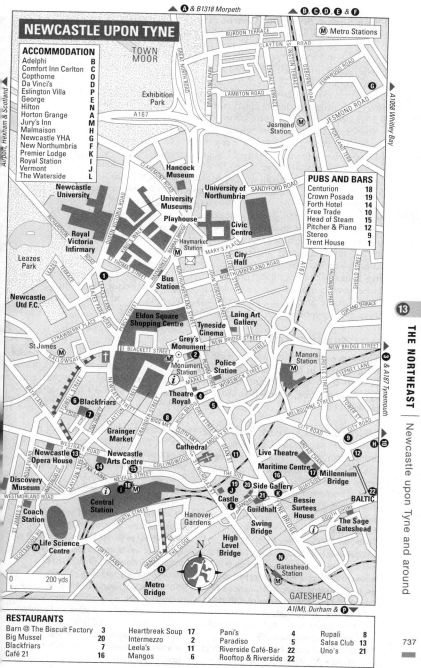

NEWCASTLE UPON TYNE

TOWN MOOR

BURDON TERRACE
CLAYTON ROAD

ACCOMMODATION

Adelphi	B
Comfort Inn Carlton	C
Copthorne	O
Da Vinci's	D
Eslington Villa	P
George	E
Hilton	N
Horton Grange	A
Jury's Inn	M
Malmaison	H
Newcastle YHA	G
New Northumbria	F
Premier Lodge	K
Royal Station	I
Vermont	J
The Waterside	L

Exhibition Park

A167

Newcastle University

Hancock Museum

University Museums

Playhouse

University of Northumbria

SANDYFORD ROAD

Jesmond Station

Civic Centre

Royal Victoria Infirmary

Leazes Park

City Hall

Haymarket Station

St. MARY'S PLACE

NORTHUMBERLAND ROAD

Newcastle Utd F.C.

Bus Station

PUBS AND BARS

Centurion	18
Crown Posada	19
Forth Hotel	14
Free Trade	10
Head of Steam	15
Pitcher & Piano	12
Stereo	9
Trent House	1

Eldon Square Shopping Centre

Laing Art Gallery

Tyneside Cinema

Grey's Monument

Monument Station

Police Station

Manors Station

St James

BLACKETT STREET

NEW BRIDGE STREET

Theatre Royal

Blackfriars

Grainger Market

Cathedral

Live Theatre

Newcastle Opera House

Newcastle Arts Centre

Maritime Centre

Millennium Bridge

Discovery Museum

Side Gallery

Castle

BALTIC

WESTMORLAND ROAD

Central Station

Hanover Gardens

Guildhall

Bessie Surtees House

The Sage Gateshead

Coach Station

High Level Bridge

Swing Bridge

Life Science Centre

Metro Bridge

N

Gateshead Station

GATESHEAD

0   200 yds

RESTAURANTS

Barn @ The Biscuit Factory	3	Heartbreak Soup	17	Pani's	4	Rupali	8
Big Mussel	20	Intermezzo	2	Paradiso	5	Salsa Club	13
Blackfriars	7	Leela's	11	Riverside Café-Bar	22	Uno's	21
Café 21	16	Mangos	6	Rooftop & Riverside	22		

Eldon Square Shopping Centre. Newcastle's **airport**, six miles north of the city, is linked by Metro to Central Station (5.50am–11.10pm, every 7–15min; 20min; £1.80) and beyond. **Ferry arrivals** from Scandinavia and Holland dock at Royal Quays, North Shields, seven miles east of the city. Connecting bus services run you to Central Station. There are **tourist offices** at 132 Grainger St (Mon–Wed & Fri 9.30am–5.30pm, Thurs 9.30am–7.30pm, Sat 9am–5pm, Sun 10am–4pm; Oct–May closed Sun; ☏0191/277 8000, ⒲www.visitnewcastlegateshead.com), and in Central Station (Mon–Fri 9.30am–5pm, Sat 9am–5pm; same contact details).

You can walk around the whole of central Newcastle easily enough, but for journeys further afield you'll need to get to grips with the conurbation's **Metro** system (daily 5.15am–11.30pm, services every 3–15min). The most useful discount pass is the Metro Day Saver for unlimited rides (£3 after 9am Mon, Tues, Thurs & Fri, all day Sat & Sun; £2 after 9.30am Wed; or £1.50 after 6.30pm any day), available from ticket machines at every station. For all public transport enquiries, call **Nexus Traveline** (☏0870/608 2608, ⒲www.nexus.org.uk), or visit the Nexus Travelshops at Haymarket, Monument or Gateshead Metro stations.

Three-hour **sightseeing cruises** (£10; ☏0191/296 6740, ⒲www .tyneleisureline.co.uk) depart most weekends throughout the year, and Tuesdays and Thursdays in summer, from Newcastle's Quayside. Guided **walking tours** of the city centre (June–Sept daily; £2) are arranged by the Grainger Street tourist office. There's also an open-top **sightseeing bus**, which departs from Central Station (Easter–Sept daily 10am–4pm, until 5pm in Aug, departures every 30–60min; £5; ⒲www.city-sightseeing.com).

Accommodation

The biggest concentration of small hotels and guest houses is a mile north of the centre in Jesmond, along and off Osborne Road: take bus #30B, #31B or #80 from Central Station or Haymarket. Save yourself time and effort by using the free **room-booking service** available at the tourist offices to personal callers.

Hotels and guest houses

Adelphi Hotel 63 Fern Ave, off Osborne Rd, Jesmond ☏0191/281 3109. Cheery family-run B&B with a variety of acceptable rooms, some big enough to sleep three. ❸

Comfort Inn Carlton 82–86 Osborne Rd, Jesmond ☏0191/281 3361. Decent value motel-style rooms, with everything you need for a comfortable night. ❺

Copthorne The Close, Quayside ☏0191/222 0333, ⒲www.millenniumhotels.com. This stylish four-star hotel has Tyne views from most of its well-appointed rooms. Breakfast not included except for weekend packages. ❽, weekend ❼

Da Vinci's 73 Osborne Rd, Jesmond ☏0191/281 5284, ⒲www.davincis.co.uk. The sixteen well-priced rooms, most of them fairly large and light, are a popular Jesmond choice. ❹

Eslington Villa 8 Station Rd, Low Fell, Gateshead ☏0191/487 6017, ☏0191/420 0667. Only practicable with your own transport, this small, quiet hotel has stylishly decorated rooms, well-tended gardens and a top-class restaurant. ❺

George 88 Osborne Rd, Jesmond ☏0191/281 4442, ⒲www.thegeorgehotel.org. Victorian town-house hotel with a dozen of the city's least expensive en-suite rooms. ❷

Hilton Newcastle Gateshead Bottle Bank, Gateshead Quays ☏08705/515151, ⒲www.hilton.co.uk. The four-star *Hilton*, near the Tyne Bridge, sports terrific views, pool, gym, health club, bar and restaurant. ❽, weekend ❼

Horton Grange 2 miles north of Dinnington ☏01661/860686, ⒲www.horton-grange.co.uk. Relaxed and welcoming country-house hotel with an excellent conservatory restaurant, five miles north of the city centre off the A1(M). ❻

Jury's Inn Scotswood Rd ☏0191/201 4400, ⒲www.bookajurysinn.com. Fixed-rate rooms accommodate up to three adults or a family, there's a pub and restaurant on site, and 24hr reception. ❹

Malmaison Quayside ☎0191/245 5000, ⓦwww.malmaison.com. Chic lodgings in the former Co-op building, right on the Quayside. ❼

New Northumbria 61–69 Osborne Rd, Jesmond ☎0191/281 4961, ⓦwww.newnorthumbriahotel.co.uk. Contemporary boutique-style rooms, big beds, warm decor, and lovely panelled bathrooms. ❺

Premier Lodge Quayside ☎0870/990 6530, ⓦwww.premierlodge.com. An unbeatable location for this no-frills chain: in the nineteenth-century Exchange Buildings under the Tyne Bridge. ❸

Royal Station Neville St ☎0191/232 0781, ⓦwww.royalstationhotel.com. The city's original Victorian station hotel has an indoor pool, Jacuzzi and gym, while rooms are often available at discounted rates. Breakfast not included. ❻, weekend ❺

Vermont Castle Garth ☎0191/233 1010, ⓦwww.vermont-hotel.com. High-class twelve-storey business hotel, with good views and facili-ties, including a fitness centre, three bars and restaurant. ❽, weekend ❼

The Waterside 48–52 Sandhill ☎0191/230 0111, ⓦwww.watersidehotel.com. Small, luxury hotel in a listed building right in the centre of the Quayside night-time action. Breakfast not included. ❺

Hostel and university accommodation

Newcastle YHA 107 Jesmond Rd ☎0870/770 5972, ⒺNewcastle@yha.org.uk. Popular town-house hostel with sixty beds (£11.50), including five twin rooms (❶), near Jesmond Metro station – reserve in advance in summer. Closed Christmas to mid-Jan.

University of Newcastle ☎0191/222 6296. Hundreds of rooms available during Easter holidays and from July to September. From £22 per person.

University of Northumbria ☎0191/227 4024. Call for details of single rooms available during Easter holidays and from July to September. From £22.50 per person.

The City

The city splits into several distinct areas, though it's only a matter of minutes to walk between them. Castle and cathedral occupy the heights immediately above the River Tyne, whose Newcastle and Gateshead quaysides now form the biggest single attraction in the city. North of the cathedral lies Grainger Town, the city-centre district of listed Victorian buildings that is at its most dramatic along Grey Street. West of here is Chinatown and the two big draws of the Discovery Museum and Life Science Centre; east is the renowned Laing Gallery; and north the university museums.

Castle and cathedral

Anyone arriving by train from the north will get a sneak preview of the **Castle** (daily: April–Sept 9.30am–5.30pm; Oct–March Tues–Sun 9.30am–4.30pm; £1.50), which dates from the twelfth century and is everything a castle should be: thick, square and labyrinthine. Staircases and rooms, including a bare Norman chapel, lie off a draughty Great Hall, where displays relate to the Civil War siege of 1644 by a Scottish army supporting the Parliamentarian cause; a small museum room shows various archeological finds. Down in the garrison room, prisoners were incarcerated during the sixteenth to eighteenth centuries.

Further along St Nicholas' Street stands the **Cathedral** (Mon–Fri 7am–6pm, Sat 8.30am–4pm, Sun 7.30am–noon & 4–7pm; guided tours Easter–Sept Wed 11am; free), dating mainly from the fourteenth and fifteenth centuries and remarkable chiefly for its tower – erected in 1470, it is topped with a crown-like structure of turrets and arches supporting a lantern. Inside, behind the high altar, is one of the largest funerary brasses in England; it was commissioned by Roger Thornton, the Dick Whittington of Newcastle, who arrived in the city penniless and died its richest merchant in 1430. The brass is etched with near life-size figures of Thornton and his wife. Much of the interior was given a

△ Tyne Bridges, Newcastle

neo-Gothic remodelling in the late nineteenth century under Sir George Gilbert Scott.

Along the River Tyne

On Newcastle's **Quayside** there have been fixed river crossings since Roman times and today the Tyne is spanned by seven bridges in close proximity, the most prominent being the looming **Tyne Bridge** of 1928, symbol of the city. To the west of it, road and rail lines cross the river on the **High Level Bridge**, built by Robert Stephenson in 1849. Protected by the towering castle, the Quayside became the commercial heart of the city and in the sixteenth and seventeenth centuries its half-timbered houses were the homes of Newcastle's wealthiest merchants. One is **Bessie Surtees' House**, at 41–44 Sandhill (Mon–Fri 10am–4pm; free), the residence of an eighteenth-century woman who scandalously eloped to Scotland with her beau; all ended well and the groom in question went on to become Lord Eldon, Chancellor of England. Directly opposite is the **Guildhall**, rebuilt many times since its foundation in 1316, where court sessions were held; John Wesley preached here in 1742 and had to be rescued from a volatile crowd by a hefty fishwife. On Sundays a busy morning **market** spreads around the nearby hydraulic **Swing Bridge**, which was erected in 1876 by Lord Armstrong to replace the old Tyne Bridge, so that larger vessels could reach his shipyards upriver.

Beyond the Tyne Bridge, the modern-day regeneration of the Quayside is in full swing. Riverside apartments, a landscaped promenade, public sculpture and pedestrianized squares have paved the way for a series of fashionable new bars and restaurants, centred on the supremely graceful **Millennium Bridge**, the world's first tilting span, which is designed to pivot to allow ships to pass. Locals, who chose the design in a public vote, call it the "blinking eye".

The bridge allows pedestrians and cyclists to cross the Tyne to the **Gateshead Quays**, to visit **BALTIC**, the dramatic Centre for Contemporary Art (Mon–Wed & Sat 10am–7pm, Thurs 10am–8pm, Sun 10am–5pm; free; Ⓦ www.balticmill.com), fashioned from a brick flour mill built in the 1940s. This has been converted into a huge visual "art factory", second only in scale to London's Tate Modern. There's no permanent collection here, though the galleries display a robust series of specially commissioned or invited art exhibitions, as well as local community projects and other displays. The BALTIC has been joined on the Gateshead side by **The Sage Gateshead** (Ⓦ www .thesagegateshead.org), a billowing steel, aluminium and glass structure that's home to the Northern Sinfonia and Folkworks, an organization promoting British and international traditional music. The inaugural 2005 season will see The Sage's main concert hall and studio space in use, along with a public concourse offering marvellous river and city views, a café-bar and bistro.

Grainger Town and the city centre

By the mid-nineteenth century, Newcastle's centre of balance had shifted away from the river, uphill to the rapidly expanding Victorian town. In a few short years, businessmen-builders and architects such as Richard Grainger, Thomas Oliver and John Dobson fashioned the best-designed Victorian town in England, with classical facades of stone lining splendid new streets, most notably **Grey Street** – "that descending, subtle curve", as John Betjeman described it. The street takes its name from the Northumberland dynasty of political heavyweights whose most illustrious member was the second Earl Grey, prime minister from 1830 to 1834. In the middle of his term in office he carried the Reform Bill through parliament, an act commemorated by

Grey's Monument at the top of the street. **Grainger Market** (Mon–Sat 8am–5pm) near Grey's Monument, was Europe's largest undercover market when built in the 1830s.

West of here, behind Gallowgate, is the most complete stretch of the old **city walls**, leading down to Westgate Road. On the south side of Westgate Road, the **Discovery Museum** in Blandford Square (Mon–Sat 10am–5pm, Sun 2–5pm; free; ⓦ www.twmuseums.org.uk) puts into context the city's history in a series of extremely impressive displays housed in the former headquarters of the Co-operative Wholesale Society. Standout attractions include the "Newcastle Story", a walk through the city's past with tales from animated characters along the way, and the interactive "Science Maze" which focuses on Newcastle's pioneering inventors (including one Joseph Swan who, according to locals at least, beat Edison to the invention of the light bulb).

Heading back towards the Central Station along Westmorland Street, you can't miss the sleek, contemporary lines of the **International Centre for Life**, whose buildings reach around the sweeping expanse of Times Square. This ambitious "science village" project combines bioscience and genetics centres with the **Life Science Centre** (Mon–Sat 10am–6pm, Sun 11am–6pm, last admission 4pm; £6.95; ⓦ www.lifesciencecentre.co.uk), which aims to convey the scientific secrets of life using the latest entertainment technology. The centre is always adding new attractions, from science experiments to virtual reality experiences, so expect to spend a good three hours here, if not more, with the *Times Square Café* on hand to provide a break.

Laing Gallery and the university museums

Newcastle's – indeed, the northeast's – premier art collection is the **Laing Gallery** on New Bridge St (Mon–Sat 10am–5pm, Sun 2–5pm; free; ⓦ www.twmuseums.org.uk), off John Dobson Street, behind the library. It's a splendidly organized museum, in which local pottery, glassware, costume and sculpture play their part, while on permanent display is a sweep through British art from Reynolds to John Hoyland, with a smattering of Pre-Raphaelites, so admired by English industrial barons. The real treat though is the lashings of John Martin (1789–1854), a self-taught Northumberland painter with a penchant for massive biblical and mythical scenes inspired by the dramatic northeastern scenery. The other must-see in the gallery is the Art on Tyneside exhibition, which romps through the history of art and applied art in the region since the seventeenth century with considerable gusto, highlighting the contribution of Thomas Bewick, whose pastoral works were also inspired by the surrounding countryside. Outside the Laing's front door don't miss a stroll over the notorious **Blue Carpet** – a public art installation whose tiles fold back on themselves to form unusual benches, lit from underneath.

Newcastle University, opposite Haymarket Metro, also contains a knot of fine museums and galleries, located off King's Walk: the **Museum of Antiquities** (Mon–Sat 10am–5pm; free) makes a good place to get to grips with the history of Hadrian's Wall; the **Shefton Museum of Greek Art and Archeology** (Mon–Fri 10am–4pm; free) contains a valuable collection of armour, sculpture and pottery; while the celebrated **Hatton Gallery** (Mon–Fri 10am–5.30pm, Sat 10am–4.30pm; free) features a collection of African sculpture, the only surviving example of Kurt Schwitters' Merzbau (a sort of architectural collage) and a wide variety of temporary exhibitions. Also attached to the university is the **Hancock Museum** on Barras Bridge

(Mon–Sat 10am–5pm, Sun 2–5pm; £4.50; ⓦwww.twmuseums.org.uk), based on an eighteenth-century natural history collection, which hosts annual blockbuster exhibitions.

Eating, drinking and nightlife

At the budget end of the market, Italian, Indian and Chinese food dominates the scene, while at the top end of the scale the city has attracted some inventive chefs. For Chinese food, check out Stowell Street in **Chinatown** where you'll find cheap all-you-can-eat buffets as well as more refined Cantonese restaurants. If you're counting the pennies, aim to eat early – many city-centre restaurants offer **early bird/happy hour** deals before 7pm, while others serve **set lunches** at often ludicrously low prices.

Newcastle's boisterous nightlife centres on the pubs and clubs in the older parts of town: between Grainger Street and the cathedral in the area called the **Bigg Market** – spiritual home of Sid the Sexist and the Fat Slags from *Viz* magazine – and around the **Quayside**, where the bars tend to be slightly more sophisticated. The grandiosely named "**Gay Quarter**" of mostly mixed gay and lesbian bars and clubs centres on the International Centre for Life, spreading out to Waterloo Street and Westmorland and Scotswood roads – the scene is chronicled exhaustively in *The Crack*, the city's free monthly listings magazine. Top brew is, of course, **Newcastle Brown** – an ale known locally as "Dog" – produced in the city since 1927.

Cafés and café-bars

Intermezzo 10–12 Pilgrim St. Café-bar (open daily until 11pm) attached to the Tyneside Cinema, with Italian pastries, sandwiches, pizza slices and salads.

Pani's 61–65 High Bridge St, off Grey St. Come for stuffed sandwiches, *antipasti*, pasta and salads – open until 10pm for authentic cheap eats. Closed Sun.

Paradiso 1 Market Lane. Mellow café-bar-restaurant with great food (Thai-style mussels to handmade pasta), indoor booths and a sun-deck. *Popolo* lounge bar downstairs mops up post-diners and drinkers. Closes Sun at 7pm.

Riverside Café-Bar BALTIC, South Shore Rd, Gateshead. The BALTIC's ground-floor café-bar is a handy spot for a coffee and gourmet sandwich (food served until 7pm).

Restaurants

Barn @ The Biscuit Factory Stoddart St ☎0191/230 3338. Superbly creative cooking in the contemporary surroundings of the old biscuit factory-now-art gallery. Café menu served at lunchtime, a la carte at dinner. It's a bit of a way out; take a taxi. Closed Sun dinner. Expensive.

Big Mussel 15 The Side ☎0191/232 1057. Mussels, chips and mayo served seven ways for a tenner, though there are other fish and seafood choices on the menu. Moderate.

Blackfriars Friar St ☎0191/261 5945. Stylishly updated twelfth-century monks' refectory, where the food trips around the world with confidence, from liver and mash to Thai curry. Closed Sun dinner and all Mon. Moderate to expensive.

Café 21 21 Queen St ☎0191/222 0755. Stylish Parisian-influenced bistro with a classic menu – confit of duck, smoked haddock with bubble and squeak, steak with herb butter. Closed Sun. Expensive.

Heartbreak Soup Baltic Chambers, 77 Quayside ☎0191/222 1701. Good-value global food – jerk pork, crab risotto or Catalan-style chicken. Dinner only, closed Sun. Moderate.

Leela's 20 Dean St ☎0191/230 1261. High-quality South Indian cuisine, with plenty of vegetarian options. Closed Sun. Expensive.

Mangos 43 Stowell St ☎0191/232 6522. A bit more stylish and a bit more authentic than most Chinatown eateries, *Mangos* offers traditional and new-wave Cantonese dishes, from *dim sum* to sizzling plate specials. Moderate.

Rooftop & Riverside Restaurants BALTIC, South Shore Rd, Gateshead ☎0191/440 4949. The cheaper *Riverside* has a popular outdoor terrace and serves light meals until 4pm and a bistro menu in the evening. Up at the *Rooftop*, the food is well regarded and the views sublime. Rooftop closed Sun dinner. Moderate to expensive.

Rupali 6 Bigg Market ⊕0191/232 8629. Budget Indian restaurant owned by the self-styled Lord of Harpole – eat a plate of the hottest curry on the menu and you get it for free. Inexpensive.

Salsa Club 89 Westgate Rd ⊕0191/221 1022. A cosy, bare-boards place with people dropping in for a coffee, sandwich and *tapas*. Closed Sun lunch. Inexpensive.

Uno's 18 Sandhill ⊕0191/261 5264. Come weekdays before 7pm, or Saturdays before 5pm, and pizzas or pastas are a staggering £2.45. The party (and price) picks up at night. Moderate.

Pubs and bars

Centurion Central Station, Neville St. The station's former first-class waiting rooms, now revived as an extraordinary bar, brasserie and deli.

Crown Posada 31 The Side. Local beers and guest ales in a wood-and-glass-panelled Victorian pub down by the Quayside.

Forth Hotel Pink Lane. City-centre boozer with a fine juke box, a lively, varied crowd and good lunchtime food.

Free Trade St Lawrence Rd. Walk along the Newcastle Quayside past the Millennium Bridge and look for the shabby pub on the hill, where you are invited to "drink beer, smoke tabs" with the city's pub *cognoscenti*.

Head of Steam 2 Neville St. Relaxed drinking den boasting a big range of real ales, imported bottles, good sounds and big sofas.

Pitcher & Piano 108 Quayside. The riverfront's most spectacular bar.

Stereo Sandgate, Quayside. Sharp designer style, plus an outdoor deck with Millennium Bridge views.

Trent House 1–2 Leazes Lane. Good beer, not to mention a surviving Space Invaders machine.

Clubs

The Cooperage 32 The Close, Quayside ⊕0191/233 2941. Quayside pub, whose upstairs club hosts indie, funk, African and dance nights, local bands and monthly salsa sessions.

Foundation 57–59 Melbourne St ⊕0191/261 8985. Stylish venue hosting club nights (Mon & Wed–Sat), with Shindig (ⓦwww.shindiguk.com) the long-running Saturday special.

Tuxedo Princess Hillgate Quay, Gateshead ⊕0191/477 8899. Floating nightclub, on the south side of the river below the Tyne Bridge, serving up scantily clad dancers and seven different styles of music in seven bars. Closed Sun.

World Headquarters Carliol Square ⊕07775/848 358, ⓦwww.theworldheadquarters.com. Newcastle's mellowest bar and club, playing funk, soul and hip-hop every Friday and Saturday.

Arts, culture and music

There's a varied theatrical and cultural life in the city, from the offerings at the splendid Victorian Theatre Royal and Newcastle Opera House to those of smaller contemporary **theatre** companies and local **arts centres**. The Sage and City Hall are the main classical music **concert venues**. There's a full **festival calendar**, with particular emphasis on outdoor concerts and sports – in October, Europe's biggest half-marathon, the Great orth Run, sees 50,000 competitors running across the Tyne Bridge. Undoubted highlight is the New Year's Eve celebration on the Quayside, an exuberantly good-natured rival to the traditional gatherings in London.

Live music

Black Swan Newcastle Arts Centre, 69 Westgate Rd ⊕0191/261 9959. Cellar-bar with live music up to five nights a week – rock, folk, world and jazz – and a Friday-night salsa session.

City Hall Northumberland Rd ⊕0191/261 2606, ⓦwww.newcastle.gov.uk/cityhall. The city centre's main concert venue, hosting orchestras from around the world, plus mainstream rock, pop and comedy.

The Cluny 36 Lime St, Ouseburn ⊕0191/230 4474. The best small venue in the city is a 20min walk from Quayside if you know where you're going (otherwise take a taxi), with gigs almost every night from 7.30pm.

Jazz Café 23 Pink Lane ⊕0191/232 6505. Intimate jazz club with a late licence. Live music from 8pm; salsa nights Thurs–Sat. Closed Sun.

Newcastle Opera House 111 Westgate Rd ⊕0191/232 0899, ⓦwww.newcastleopera house.com. Beautifully restored Victorian theatre with a wide range of shows, comedy and gigs.

The Sage Gateshead South Shore Rd, Gateshead Quays ☏0191/443 4555, ✆www .thesagegateshead.org. Stunning international music centre, hosting classical, folk, world and jazz music.

Theatres and arts centres

BALTIC South Shore Rd, Gateshead ☏0191/478 1810, ✆www.balticmill.com. Studio sessions and classes, films, artists' talks, community projects, dance and concerts.

Live Theatre 27 Broad Chare ☏0191/232 1232, ✆www.live.org.uk. Regular productions promoting local actors and writers (Lee Hall gave his boy-ballet movie, *Billy Elliot*, its first reading here). Also has live music at its regular *Jumpin' Hot Club*, plus espresso

bar and restaurant (courtesy of the *Café 21* people).

Newcastle Arts Centre 69 Westgate Rd ☏0191/261 5618, ✆www.newcastle-arts-centre.co.uk. Art gallery, workshops, and concert, drama and club venue.

Newcastle Playhouse Barras Bridge ☏0191/230 5151. Home of Newcastle's own Northern Stage company (✆www.northernstage.com) and co-host of the annual RSC season in Nov.

Theatre Royal Grey St ☏0870/905 5060, ✆www.theatre-royal-newcastle.co.uk. Drama, opera, dance, musicals and comedy; also co-host of the annual RSC season in Nov.

Tyneside Cinema 10 Pilgrim St ☏0191/232 1507, ✆www.tynecine.org. The city's premier art-house cinema, with a wide-ranging international programme, and a good café.

Listings

Airport 24hr enquiry line ☏0191/286 0966, ✆www.newcastleairport.com.

Banks and exchanges Banks are concentrated around Grey and Northumberland streets. There's a bureau de change at the airport, in the main post office and in Thomas Cook travel agency.

Car rental Avis, 7 George St ☏0191/232 5283 and at the airport ☏0191/214 0116; Europcar, 90 Westmorland Rd ☏0191/261 0833 and at the airport ☏0191/286 5070; and Hertz, 2 Forth Banks ☏0191/232 5313 and at the airport ☏0191/286 6748.

Football Newcastle United play at St James' Park (ticket office ☏0191/261 1571, ✆www.nufc .co.uk) in front of the country's most fanatical supporters. You're unlikely to get a ticket for the big matches against major rivals, but seats do go on general sale for some games.

Hospital Royal Victoria Infirmary, Queen Victoria Rd ☏0191/232 5131, behind the university.

Internet Internet Exchange, 26–30 Market St (Mon–Fri 9.30am–8pm, Sat 10am–8pm, Sun 11am–6pm). There's free access at the Library and at the Live Wires Centre in the Discovery Museum.

Pharmacies Boots, Monument Mall, Grey St ☏0191/232 4423.

Police Corner of Market and Pilgrim streets ☏0191/214 6555.

Post office St Mary's Place, near the Civic Centre, at Haymarket.

Taxis Ranks at Haymarket, Bigg Market, and outside Central Station. Call Noda Taxis (☏0191/222 1888 or 232 7777) at Central Station for advance bookings.

Travel agents STA, 9 St Mary's Place ☏0191/233 2111 and University of Northumbria, 2 Sandyford Rd ☏0870/160 6070; Thomas Cook, 79 Grainger St ☏0191/232 5809; Trailfinders, 7–9 Ridley Place ☏0191/261 2345.

Around Newcastle

The Metro runs east along both banks of the River Tyne, connecting Newcastle with several historic attractions, and southeast to Sunderland. A Metro Day Saver ticket (see p.738) enables you to get the best out of the local transport system, and it's also valid for most buses in the county of Tyne and Wear.

Wallsend and Segedunum

As the name tells you, **WALLSEND**, four miles east of Newcastle, was the last outpost of Hadrian's great border defence. **Segedunum**, the "strong fort" a couple of minutes' signposted walk from the Metro station (daily: April–Oct 10am–5pm; Nov–March 10am–3.30pm; £3.50;

A range of activities and events takes place year-round (including summer re-enactments of Roman drill and equipment) and, besides the extensive excavations, the grounds contain a fully reconstructed bathhouse, complete with steaming pools and colourful frescoes, and a rebuilt section of the Wall itself. To complete the picture, climb the 110-foot tower for a spectacular overview of the remains and the adjacent ship-repair yards. The "wall's end" itself is visible at the edge of the site, close to the river and Swan Hunter shipyard, and it's from here that the **Hadrian's Wall Path** (see p.749) runs for 84 miles to Bowness on Solway in Cumbria; you can get your walk "passport" stamped inside the museum.

Jarrow

JARROW, five miles east of Newcastle, and south of the Tyne, has been ingrained on the national consciousness since the 1936 **Jarrow Crusade**, a march to London by unemployed protesters, which became the most potent image of the hardships of 1930s Britain. However, the town made a mark rather earlier, as the seventh-century St Paul's church and monastery were one of the region's early cradles of Christianity. The first Saxon church here was built in 681 AD, and its monastic buildings soon attracted a reputation for scholastic learning. It was here that the **Venerable Bede** (673–735 AD) came to live as a boy, growing to become one of Europe's greatest scholars and England's first historian – his *History of the English Church and People*, describing the struggles of the island's early Christians, was completed at Jarrow in 731. Access to the tranquil stone church of **St Paul's** and the adjacent monastery ruins (Mon–Sat 10am–4.30pm, Sun 2.30–4.30pm) is free, although they stand within the wider development that is **Bede's World** (April–Oct Mon–Sat 10am–5.30pm, Sun noon–5.30pm; Nov–March Mon–Sat 10am–4.30pm, Sun noon–4.30pm; £4.50; @ www.bedesworld.co.uk), a fascinating exploration of early medieval Northumbria. The multimedia **museum** traces the development of Northumbria and England through the use of extracts from Bede's writings, set alongside archeological finds and vivid re-creations of monastic life. After this you can take a turn through Gyrwe, the eleven-acre **farm** which features reconstructed timber buildings from the early Christian period, as well as demonstrating contemporary agricultural methods. St Paul's and Bede's World are at Church Bank in Jarrow, a signposted fifteen-minute walk from **Bede Metro station**. Alternatively, buses #526 or #527 run roughly every 30 minutes from Neville Street (Central Station) in Newcastle or Jarrow Metro station.

Sunderland

SUNDERLAND, bisected by the River Wear and elevated in 1992 to the ranks of Britain's cities, shares Newcastle's long history, river setting and industrial heritage but cannot match its architectural splendour. Formed from three medieval villages flanking the Wear, it was one of the wealthiest towns in England by 1500, and later supported the Parliamentary cause in the Civil War. The twentieth century made and broke the town: from being the largest shipbuilding centre in the world, supporting a dozen shipyards, Sunderland slumped after ferocious bombing during World War II. However, the city centre has seen a revival of late and now has a couple of visitor attractions to rival anything in nearby Newcastle.

First stop should be the **Sunderland Museum** (Mon 10am–4pm, Tues–Sat 10am–5pm, Sun 2–5pm; free; @ www.twmuseums.org.uk), straight down

Fawcett Street from the tourist office, at the junction with Borough Road, which does a very good, multimedia job of telling the city's history. The attached **Winter Gardens**, housed in an impressive steel and glass hothouse, replace the original Victorian glasshouses bombed by the Germans in 1941. The main interest in Sunderland lies across the River Wear, whose landscaped **Riverside** is actually the oldest settled part of the city. Along the north bank, in front of the university campus buildings, the early Christian church of **St Peter** (Easter–Oct daily 2–4pm), built in 674 AD, is the elder sibling of St Paul's church at Jarrow. Walk from the church down to the waterside to find the city's extraordinary **National Glass Centre** (daily 10am–5pm; £5; Ⓦ www.nationalglasscentre.com), which tells the story of glass-making – a traditional industry in Sunderland since the seventh century, when work-shops turned out stained glass for the north's monastic houses. Regular tours throughout the day (£5) include a glass-making demonstration in the on-site workshop.

The main stop for **Metros** from Newcastle is in the central **train station** opposite the Bridges Shopping Centre, but get off at the previous stop, St Peter's, to walk along the north side of the river to the National Glass Centre or St Peter's Church. The **tourist office** is behind the central station on the main shopping drag, at 50 Fawcett Street (Mon–Sat 9am–5pm, Sun 10am–4pm; Ⓣ0191/553 2000, Ⓦwww.sunderland.gov.uk). All buses use the **Park Lane Bus Station** (also on the Metro), a five-minute walk south of the train station. At *Eden* **café-brasserie** in the museum, you can take your cappuccino and muffin out onto the wonderful terrace overlooking the lake in Mowbray Park. Alternatively, head for the *Throwing Stones* restaurant in the National Glass Centre (Ⓣ0191/565 3939; lunch daily, dinner Fri & Sat), where a sandwich or stuffed-tortilla lunch can be had for around a fiver.

Washington

Five miles west of Sunderland, the River Wear keeps to the south of the New Town of **WASHINGTON**, focus of much of the area's contemporary invest-ment and manufacture. Split into planned, numbered districts and organized on American lines, it's not an obvious stop, although the original **Old Village** has been zealously preserved as a conservation area and boasts a couple of pubs and tea rooms. Just off the village green stands the ancestral home of the family that spawned the first **US president**. The "de Wessyngtons" – later the Washingtons – originally came over with William the Conqueror, and by 1183 were based at the **Old Hall** (April–Oct Mon–Wed & Sun 11am–5pm; £3; NT), where they lived until 1613. Carefully preserved as a Jacobean showpiece, the echo-ing, stone-flagged house has a fine kitchen, Great Hall and garden, and some exemplary wood panelling, and although none of the furniture is original to the Washington family, it is contemporaneous. Every Fourth of July, the raising of the US flag at the house heralds Independence Day celebrations and entry to the Old Hall is free for the occasion.

The other main attraction in the area is the **Washington Wildfowl and Wetlands Centre** (daily: April–Oct 9.30am–5pm; Nov–March 9.30am–4pm; £5.50, Ⓦwww.wwt.org.uk), east of town and north of the River Wear in District 15, its hundred acres designed by Sir Peter Scott and home to swans, geese, ducks, herons and flamingos. It's signposted off most local roads, four miles from the A1(M).

For Washington Village and the Old Hall, take the #185 bus from Sunderland Park Lane Bus Station (not Sun). The Wildfowl Centre is reached on the #56A from Newcastle's Market Street (not Sun) or the #X4 from either Newcastle's Eldon Square or Sunderland Park Lane (not Sun).

Along Hadrian's Wall

Emperor Hadrian, who toured Roman Britain in 122 AD, wanted the empire to live at peace within stable frontiers, most of which were defined by geographical features. In northern Britain, however, with no natural barrier, Hadrian decided to create his own by constructing a 76-mile **wall** from the Tyne to the Solway Firth. It was not intended to be an impenetrable fortification, but rather a base for patrols that could push out into hostile territory. Built up to a height of fifteen feet in places, it was punctuated by **milecastles**, which served as gates, depots and mini-barracks, and by observation **turrets**, two of which were stood between each pair of milecastles. A chain of **forts** straddled the Wall at six- to nine-mile intervals, concentrating the Wall's garrison in a handful of key points, making it possible to respond quickly to any threat. The structure remained in operation until the late fourth century AD, though centralized Roman rule in Britain had all but broken down by then.

Most of Hadrian's Wall disappeared centuries ago, yet walking its length remains a popular pastime, made easier by an official waymarked **Hadrian's Wall Path** (see box opposite). In the east, the prosperous-looking market town of **Hexham** makes a good base, with **Haltwhistle**, further west, offering another overnight option. Scattered in between is a variety of key archeological sites and museums, notably **Chesters Roman Fort and Museum** near Chollerford, the remains of **Housesteads** and **Vindolanda forts**, and the milecastle remains at **Cawfields**, north of Haltwhistle.

A special **Hadrian's Wall bus**, the cutely tagged #AD122, runs from Wallsend and Newcastle to Corbridge, Hexham, and all the wall sites, and then on to Carlisle and Bowness-on-Solway (the end of the Hadrian's Wall Path). This operates between Easter and October, up to five times a day in each direction in high summer (Sun only in April and October); a typical one-way ticket, from Hexham to Vindolanda, costs £2.30, though Day Rover tickets (£6 one day, £10 three days) offer better value. There's also a year-round service on the #685 bus between Newcastle and Carlisle. The nearest **train** stations are on the Newcastle–Carlisle line at Corbridge, Hexham, Haydon Bridge, Bardon Mill and Haltwhistle. Hexham, Bardon Mill and Haltwhistle will leave you a fair walk to Chesters, Vindolanda/Once Brewed and Cawfields/Greenhead respectively. Holders of Northeast Explorer and Stagecoach Cumberland Explorer bus **passes** get free travel on the Hadrian's Wall bus. There's also a Hadrian's Wall Rail Rover Ticket (£12.50, available from train stations), valid for two days in any three-day period (after 9am weekdays), covering travel on the

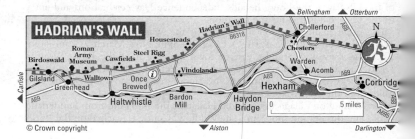

© Crown copyright

Newcastle–Carlisle train line, the #AD122 and the Tyne & Wear Metro. You can pick up a comprehensive Hadrian's Wall **public transport timetable** from local tourist offices, or contact the **Hadrian's Wall information line** on ☎01434/322002, ⊛www.hadrians-wall.org.

Corbridge

CORBRIDGE is a quiet and well-heeled commuter town overlooking the River Tyne from the top of a steep ridge. One mile to the west of its Market Place, accessible either by road or along the riverside footpath, lies **Corbridge Roman Site** (Easter–Sept daily 10am–6pm; Oct daily 10am–5pm; Nov–March Wed–Sun 10am–1pm & 2–4pm; £3.10; EH), the location of the garrison town of Corstopitum. This is the oldest fortified site in the region, first established as a supply base for the Roman advance into Scotland in 80 AD (and thus predating the Wall itself). It remained in regular military use until the end of the second century, after which it became surrounded by a fast-developing town – most of the visible archeological remains date from this period, when Corstopitum served as the nerve centre of Hadrian's Wall. The clearly labelled remains provide an insight into the layout of the civilian town, showing the foundations of temples, public baths, garrison headquarters, workshops and houses as well as the best-preserved Roman granaries in Britain. In the site **museum** the celebrated *Lion and Stag* fountainhead – the so-called "Corbridge Lion" – gets pride of place; to the Romans, the lion and its prey symbolized the triumph of life over death.

The **train station** is half a mile outside town, across the river, while Corbridge **tourist office** is on Hill Street, at the library (mid-May to Sept Mon–Sat 10am–1pm & 2–6pm, Sun 1–5pm; Easter to mid-May & Oct Mon–Sat 10am–1pm & 2–5pm, Sun 1–5pm; ☎01434/632815). The *Riverside Guest House* on Main Street (☎01434/632942, ⊛www.theriversideguesthouse.co.uk; ❸) is a comfortable eighteenth-century house with fine views of the Tyne. You'll need to book in advance for the *Angel Inn* on Main Street (☎01434/632119, ⊛www.theangelofcorbridge.co.uk; ❺, ❼ with dinner), which has had a contemporary makeover – this is now also the best place to eat in town, with classy lunches and dinners served daily. At the *Wheatsheaf* **pub**, on Watling Street, a couple of Roman stones stand in the former stableyard.

Hexham and around

In 671, on a bluff above the Tyne, four miles west of Corbridge, St Wilfrid founded a Benedictine monastery whose church was, according to contemporary accounts, the finest to be seen north of the Alps. Unfortunately, its gold

---

The Hadrian's Wall Path

The **Hadrian's Wall Path**, an 84-mile waymarked National Trail, runs from Wallsend in the east to Bowness-on-Solway in the west, shadowing the line of the Wall. You could walk the main route in four days, but that's allowing little or no time to explore the archeological sites, remains, towns and villages on the way, so a week is a more realistic timescale. To prove you made it, a "path passport" is available, which you get stamped at six locations along the way. Contact Haltwhistle tourist office for an official free **walking and accommodation guide**; there's also the *Hadrian's Wall Path: National Trail Guide* (Aurum Press), which details the route in exhaustive detail.

and silver proved irresistible to the Vikings, who savaged the place in 876, but the church was rebuilt in the eleventh century as part of an Augustinian priory, and the town of **HEXHAM**, governed by the Archbishop of York, grew up in its shadow.

The stately exterior of **Hexham Abbey** (daily: May–Sept 9am–7pm; Oct–April 9am–5pm; free) still dominates the west side of the Market Place. Entry is through the south transept, where there's a bruised but impressive first-century tombstone honouring Flavinus, a standard-bearer in the Roman cavalry, who's shown riding down his bearded enemy. The memorial lies at the foot of the broad, well-worn steps of the canons' **night stair**, one of the few such staircases – providing access from the monastery to the church – to have survived the Dissolution. Beyond, most of the high-arched nave dates from an Edwardian restoration and it's here that you gain access to the **crypt**, a Saxon structure made out of old Roman stones, where pilgrims once viewed the abbey's reliquaries. The nave's architect also used Roman stonework, sticking various sculptural fragments in the walls, many of which he had unearthed during the rebuilding.

The rest of Hexham's large and irregularly shaped **Market Place** (main market day is Tuesday) is peppered with remains of its medieval past. The massive walls of the fourteenth-century **Moot Hall** were built to serve as the gatehouse to "The Hall", a well-protected enclosure that was garrisoned against the Scots. Nearby, the archbishops also built their own prison, a formidable fortified tower dating from 1330 and now accommodating the **Border History Museum** (April–Oct daily 10am–4.30pm; Feb, March & Nov Mon, Tues & Sat 10am–4.30pm; £2), which provides information and displays concerning the border-raiding Reivers.

Around four miles north of Hexham, and half a mile west of present-day Chollerford, **Chesters Roman Fort** (daily: Easter–Sept 10am–6pm; Oct 10am–5pm; Nov–Easter 10am–4pm; £3.10; EH), otherwise known as *Cilurnum*, was built to guard a Roman bridge over the river. Enough remains of the original structure to pick out the design of the fort, and each section has been clearly labelled, but the highlight is down by the river where the vestibule, changing room and steam range of the garrison's **bath house** are still visible, along with the furnace and the latrines. The **museum** at the entrance has an excellent collection of Roman stonework, including Juno (now headless) in a delicately pleated dress standing on a cow, one of the finest pieces of statuary found along the Wall.

Practicalities

Hexham's **train station** sits on the northeastern edge of the town centre, a ten-minute walk from the abbey; the **tourist office** is halfway between the two, in the main Wentworth **car park**, near the Safeway superstore (Easter to mid-May & Oct Mon–Sat 9am–5pm, Sun 10am–5pm; mid-May to Sept Mon–Sat 9am–6pm, Sun 10am–5pm; Nov to Easter Mon–Sat 9am–5pm; ☎01434/652220, ⓦ www.tynedale.gov.uk). The **bus station** is off Priestpopple, a few minutes' stroll east of the abbey. There's **Internet** access in the library, inside Queen's Hall on Beaumont Street.

Accommodation is usually pretty easy to come by, though the tourist office can make other suggestions if our choices are full. There are four Indian and a couple of Italian **restaurants** in town, but the only place that really stands out is *Danielle's*, an unpretentious bistro at 12 Eastgate (☎01434/601122; closed Sun & Mon). On Dipton Mill Road, two miles south of the centre (45min walk), *Dipton Mill Inn* serves wholesome **bar meals** (until 8.30pm) and own-brewed beer, in a lovely streamside setting. Or a similar distance to the northeast is the *Rat* at Anick (pronounced Ay-nick), on a glorious hillside location. The main focus of entertainment in town is the **Queen's Hall Arts Centre** on Beaumont Street (℡01434/652477), which puts on a year-round programme of theatre, dance, music and art exhibitions.

Guest houses and hotels
Beaumont Beaumont St ℡01434/602331, ⓦwww.beaumont-hotel.co.uk. Old-fashioned family-run hotel with spacious doubles overlooking the abbey; breakfast not included. **⑤**
Kitty Frisk House Corbridge Rd ℡01434/601533, ⓦwww.kittyfriskhouse.co.uk. Welcoming Edwardian retreat, half a mile from the centre down the Corbridge road (past the hospital) in a residential area. No credit cards. **❸**
Royal Priestpopple ℡01434/602270, ⓦwww.hexham-royal-hotel.co.uk. Restored coaching house near the bus station, offering a dozen modern-styled en-suite rooms. **❹**
Topsy Turvy 9 Leazes Lane ℡01434/603152. Bright and breezy central B&B. No credit cards. **❷**
West Close House Hextol Terrace, off B6305, Allendale Rd ℡01434/603307. Quiet, secluded and very friendly, with a delightful garden and

wholefood continental breakfasts. No credit cards. **❸**

Youth hostel
Acomb YHA Main St, Acomb ℡0870/770 5664. Small, simple, 36-bed hostel (£8 per night), two miles from Hexham – take bus #880 or #882, which pass Hexham train station. Closed Nov & Dec, and Mon & Tues April–June, Sept & Oct; open weekends only Jan–March.

Campsites
Fallowfield Dene Caravan Park Acomb ℡01434/603553. A tranquil place with laundry facilities. See hostel above for transport details. Closed Nov–March
Riverside Leisure Campsite Tyne Green Rd ℡01434/604705. Beside the River Tyne, half a mile north of the abbey. Closed Nov–Feb

Housesteads to Cawfields

Overlooking the bleak Northumbrian moors from the top of the Whin Sill, **Housesteads Roman Fort** (daily: Easter–Sept 10am–6pm; Oct 10am–5pm; Nov–Easter 10am–4pm; £3.10; EH & NT), eight miles west of Chesters, has long been the most popular site on the Wall. The fort is of standard design but for one enforced modification – forts were supposed to straddle the line of the Wall, but here the original stonework tracked along the very edge of the cliff, so Housesteads was built on the steeply sloping ridge to the south. Access is via the tiny **museum**, from where you stroll across to the south gate, beside which lie the remains of the civilian settlement that was dependent on the one thousand infantrymen stationed within. You don't need to pay for entrance to Housesteads if you simply intend to walk west along the Wall from here. The three-mile hike past the lovely wooded **Crag Lough** to **Steel Rigg** (car park) offers the most fantastic views, especially when you spy the course of the Wall as it threads over the crags ahead. Leaving the Wall at Steel Rigg, it's roughly half a mile south to the main road (B6318) and the visitor centre at **Once Brewed**, where there's also a youth hostel, pub and access road to the Vindolanda excavations (see p.752). Otherwise, Wall walkers can continue another three miles west from Steel Rigg to **Cawfields** (free access). This was the site of a temporary Roman camp that again pre-dated the Wall, and there are also the remains of another milecastle, this one perched on one of the most rugged crags on this section.

Practicalities

The very informative **Once Brewed National Park Visitor Centre** (June–Aug daily 9.30am–5.30pm; mid-March to May, Sept & Oct daily 9.30am–5pm; much reduced hours in winter, usually Sat & Sun only, call for details; ☎01434/344396) has exhibitions and information on both the Wall and the National Park.

Accommodation

Gibbs Hill Farm Once Brewed ☎01434/344030. Working farm with en-suite rooms, two miles north of Steel Rigg. Closed Nov–Feb. ❷

Hadrian's Wall Camping and Caravan Site 2 miles north of Melkridge, just south of B6318 ☎01434/320495. Friendly, family-run site just half a mile from the Wall, with showers, washing machine and dryer; breakfast available. Open all year.

Langley Castle A686, 2 miles south of Haydon Bridge ☎01434/688888, ⓦwww.langleycastle.com. You don't get many chances to spend the night in a genuine medieval castle – nor many chances to spend this kind of money in Northumberland. ❼

Once Brewed YHA Military Rd, B6318, Once Brewed ☎0870/770 5980, ⓔoncebrewed@yha.org.uk. Next to the visitor centre, providing cheap three-course dinners (£5.10), kitchen and lounge. Dorms (£11.50) are small (mostly four-bed). Closed Dec & Jan, and Sun Feb, March & Nov.

Twice Brewed Inn Military Rd, B6318 ☎01434/344534, ⓦwww.twicebrewedinn.co.uk. Friendly pub, 50 yards up from Once Brewed visitor centre, with simple rooms (en-suite available in next price category), food served all day until 8.30pm, local beers on tap and Internet access. Closed Jan. ❶

Vindolanda

The excavated garrison fort of **Vindolanda** actually predates the Wall itself though most of what you see today survives from the second and third centuries AD, when the fort was a thriving metropolis of five hundred soldiers with its own civilian settlement attached. The site (daily: May & June 10am–6pm; July & Aug 10am–6.30pm; April & Sept 10am–5.30pm; March & Oct 10am–5pm; Nov, Dec & Feb 10am–4pm; £4.10, ⓦwww.vindolanda.com) is operated by the private Vindolanda Trust, which has done an excellent job of imaginatively presenting its finds. Note that the Trust also administers the Roman Army Museum at Greenhead; if you're visiting both sites, request a discounted joint-admission ticket (£6).

The ongoing **excavations** are spread over a wide area, with civilian houses, inn, guest quarters, administrative building, commander's house and main gates all clearly visible. The path through the excavations descends to what's termed the **open-air museum**, where you can walk into reconstructions of a shrine of the water nymphs, a shop and a house, all with lively sound commentaries. Beyond lies the café, shop and **museum**, the latter housing the largest collection of Roman leather items ever discovered on a single site – dozens of shoes, belts, even a pair of baby boots – which were preserved in the black silt of waterlogged ditches. The most intriguing sections are concerned with the excavated hoard of **writing tablets**, now in the British Museum. The writings depict graphically the realities of military life in Northumberland, under the prefecture of Flavius Cerialis: soldiers' requests for more beer, birthday party invitations, court reports on banishments for unspecified wrongdoings, even letters from home containing gifts of underwear for freezing frontline grunts.

Haltwhistle

There's not much to the small town of **HALTWHISTLE**, and it's a couple of miles off the Wall itself, but it makes a useful overnight stop, and features the only full set of amenities (ATMs, supermarket, shops and cafés) this side of Hexham. The town also claims to be the very centre of Britain, something you could debate with the **tourist office** (Easter to mid-May & Oct Mon–Sat 9.30am–1pm & 2–5pm, Sun 1–5pm; mid-May to Sept Mon–Sat 9.30am–1pm & 2–5.30pm, Sun 1–5pm; Nov to Easter Mon, Tues & Thurs–Sat 10am–noon & 1–3.30pm; ☎01434/322002) in the train station, at the western edge of town, close to the A69. From here, walk up to Westgate, which becomes Main Street. **Mountain bikes** can be rented for £12 a day from Edens Lawn petrol station on the eastern edge of town (☎01434/320443). The best **hotel**, the *Centre of Britain* (☎01434/322422, ⓦwww.centre-of-britain.org.uk; ❸–❺), is on Main Street. Close by is *Hall Meadows*, also on Main Street (☎01434/321021; no credit cards; ❷), or there's *Ashcroft* in an elegant former vicarage on Lantys Lonnen (☎01434/320213, ⓦwww.ashcroftguesthouse.co.uk; ❸) – a turn off Main Street just after the *Centre of Britain*. The local **campsite** is in Burnfoot Park (☎01434/320106; closed Nov–Feb), beside the Tyne on the southeast edge of town.

Roman Army Museum and Greenhead

A further four-mile trek west from Cawfields takes you past the remains of **Great Chesters Fort** before reaching a spectacular section of the Wall, known as the **Walltown Crags**, where a turret from a signal system predating the Wall still survives. Adjacent to the crags, at Carvoran, call into the Vindolanda Trust's **Roman Army Museum** (daily: May & June 10am–6pm; July & Aug 10am–6.30pm; April & Sept 10am–5.30pm; March & Oct 10am–5pm; early Nov & late Feb 10am–4pm; £3.30; joint ticket with Vindolanda £6), which tells you everything there is to know about life in the Roman army by way of exhibits, dioramas, reconstructions and games. There's also a virtual-reality aerial "flight" along the Wall.

Push on just a mile southwest, and you're soon in minuscule **GREENHEAD**, where the **youth hostel** (☎0870/770 5842, ⓔgreenhead@yha.org.uk; £10.25; closed Nov–Easter) is located in a converted Methodist chapel. *Holmhead Guest House* (☎016977/47402, ⓦwww.bandbhadrianswall.com; ❸), an old stone farmhouse sporting exposed beams, is up a track behind the hostel. There are also two **camping** spaces here, and a small bunk barn (£8 per person), handy for Wall walkers. Heading west, the next section of Hadrian's Wall worth exploring is at Birdoswald, in Cumbria (see p.654), a four-mile walk or ten-minute ride on the bus.

Northumberland National Park

Northwest Northumberland, the great triangular chunk of land between Hadrian's Wall and the coastal plain, is dominated by the wide-skied landscapes of the **Northumberland National Park** (ⓦwww.northumberland-national-park.org.uk), whose four hundred windswept square miles rise to the Cheviot Hills on the Scottish border. These uplands are interrupted by great slabs of forest, mostly the conifer plantations of the Forestry Commission, and a string of river valleys, of which Coquetdale, Tynedale and Redesdale are the longest. Remote from lowland law and order, these dales were once the homelands of the **Border Reivers**, turbulent clans who ruled these parts from the thirteenth to the sixteenth century. The Reivers took advantage of the struggles between England and Scotland to engage in endless cross-border rustling and general brigandage, activities recalled by the ruined **bastles** (fortified farmhouses) and **peels** (defensive tower-houses) that dot the landscape.

The most popular hiking trail is the **Pennine Way**, which, entering the National Park at Hadrian's Wall, cuts up through Bellingham on its way to **The Cheviot**, the park's highest peak at 2674ft, and finishes at Kirk Yetholm, over the border in Scotland. As an introduction, it's hard to beat the lovely moorland scenery of the fifteen-mile stretch from Housesteads at Hadrian's Wall to **Bellingham**, a pleasant town on the banks of the North Tyne. Bellingham is also on the road to **Kielder Water**, a massive pine-surrounded reservoir, watersports centre and nature reserve. Further north, **Rothbury**, in Coquetdale, is close to **Cragside**, the nineteenth-century country home of Lord Armstrong, whilst at **Wooler**, footpaths lead into the Cheviot Hills.

Bellingham

The stone terraces of **BELLINGHAM** (pronounced Bellinjum) slope up from the banks of the Tyne on the eastern edge of the Northumberland National Park. There's nothing outstanding about the place, but it's a restful spot set in splendid rural surroundings, and it does contain the medieval church of **St Cuthbert**, which has an unusual stone-vaulted roof – designed (successfully) to prevent raiding Border Reivers from burning the church to the ground.

Buses from Hexham and Otterburn (also direct from Newcastle's Eldon Square on summer Wed, Sun & bank holidays) stop in the centre on Market Place, a few hundred yards down from the tourist office. There are onward services to Kielder most days. The helpful **tourist office** on Main Street (Easter–Oct Mon–Sat 9.30am–1pm & 2–5pm, Sun 1–5pm; Nov–Easter Mon–Fri 2–5pm; ☎01434/220616) is housed in Bellingham's former Poor House building and is well stocked with local information. The **youth hostel** (☎0870/770 5694; £9; closed Nov–Easter, & closed Sun & Mon April–June, Sept & Oct) has simple self-catering facilities six hundred yards from the centre of the village on Woodburn Road (signposted from Main Street). All other lodgings are within a hundred yards or so of each other, including the rooms at *Lyndale Guest House* (☎01434/220361, ⓦwww.lyndaleguesthouse.co.uk; ❸), just past the *Rose & Crown* **pub**. The local **campsite** is at Demesne Farm (☎01434/220258; closed Nov–Feb), right in the centre near the police station. Bellingham has a bank with a cash machine, small supermarket and a couple of **cafés**, though otherwise you're dependent on the bar meals served at the pubs.

Kielder Water and Forest

West of Bellingham the road follows the North Tyne River and skirts the forested edge of **Kielder Water** (ⓦwww.kielder.org), passing the assorted visitor centres, waterside parks, picnic areas and anchorages that fringe its southern shore. First stop is the Visitor Centre at **Tower Knowe** (daily: July & Aug 9am–6pm; April–June, Sept & Oct 10am–5pm; ☎0870/240 3549), eight miles from Bellingham, with a café and an exhibition on the history of the valley and lake. Another four miles west, at **Leaplish**, the waterside park (daily: April & Oct 9am–6pm; May–Sept 9am–11pm; Nov–March call to check times on ☎0870/240 3549), bar and restaurant are the focus of most of Kielder's outdoor activities. A ten-mile, hour-and-a-half's cruise on the **Osprey ferry** (Easter–Oct 5 daily; £5) is always a pleasure; departures are from the piers at either Tower Knowe or Leaplish.

Five miles from Leaplish at the top of the reservoir and just three miles from the Scottish border, **KIELDER VILLAGE** is dominated by Kielder Castle, built in 1775 as the hunting lodge of the Duke of Northumberland and now the **Forest Park Visitor Centre** (Easter–Oct daily 10am–5pm; Nov & Dec

Sat & Sun 11am–4pm; ℡01434/250209). The castle is surrounded by the **Kielder Forest Park**, comprising several million spruce trees, crisscrossed by trails and home to red squirrels, deer and countless birds. Several easy and clearly marked footpaths, dotted with arresting modern sculptures, lead from the castle into the forest. There's **mountain bike rental** available from Kielder Bikes (℡01434/250392; £17.50 per day) at the castle, with thirteen way-marked trails and two off-road routes through the forest to choose from.

On Sundays and bank holidays from the end of May to mid-October, the **Kielder Bus** (day rover ticket £5) runs once daily in the morning from Gateshead Metro, Newcastle Central Station and Newcastle Haymarket to Kielder Castle, and then provides a shuttle service to Kielder attractions before returning to the city in the late afternoon. At other times, you're dependent on the local bus **from Bellingham**, which calls at Tower Knowe, Leaplish and Kielder, and less regularly at Stannersburn and Falstone. As well as the **accommodation** options listed below, there are several B&Bs in Kielder village and the surrounding area – the Tower Knowe and Kielder visitor centres can assist. The **Kielder Campsite** (℡01434/250291; closed Oct–Easter) is in Kielder Village, about half a mile north of the castle on the banks of the Tyne.

Accommodation

Blackcock Inn Falstone, 1 mile north of Stannersburn ℡01434/240200. Small inn located in a riverside hamlet. ❸

Kielder YHA Butteryhaugh, Kielder Village ℡0870/770 5898, ✉kielder@yha.org.uk. Activity-based hostel, with some two- and three-bedded rooms plus small dorms (£10.25). It has a self-catering kitchen, and a restaurant offering breakfast and dinner. Closed Nov–Easter.

Leaplish Waterside Park Information ℡0870/240 3549, reservations through

Hoseasons ℡0870/333 2000. Bunk-barn accommodation (dorms £10–12) and three en-suite rooms (double £25, family £40), plus a drying room, kitchen, laundry and showers. Lodges also available, from £230–620 per week depending on season (cheaper 3-day stays available all year).

Pheasant Inn Stannersburn ℡01434/240382, ✉thepheasantinn@kielderwater.demon.co.uk. On the road in from Bellingham, this early seventeenth-century inn has eight comfortable rooms and decent meals. ❹

Rothbury and around

ROTHBURY, straddling the River Coquet, prospered as a late Victorian resort because it gave ready access to the forests, burns and ridges of the Simonside Hills. Rothbury remains a popular spot for walkers, and the **Tourist Information and National Park Visitor Centre**, near the Cross on Church Street (April–Oct daily 10am–5pm; June–Aug until 6pm; Nov–March Sat & Sun 10am–5pm; ℡01669/620887, ⟨W⟩www.visit-rothbury.co.uk), offers exhibitions related to the national park and can provide advice on local trails.

Buses stop at the bottom of Rothbury's High Street, outside the *Queen's Head*. There are several convenient **B&Bs**, including *Katerina's Guest House* up the High Street (℡01669/620691, ⟨W⟩www.katerinasguesthouse.co.uk; ❸), and the comfortable Georgian *Orchard Guest House*, further up the same street (℡01669/620684, ⟨W⟩www.orchardguesthouse.co.uk; ❸). Most of the places to **eat and drink** – two or three cafés, a deli and a couple of pubs – are strung out along the High Street. There's **Internet** access at Rothbury Computer Services, opposite the *Queens' Head*.

Cragside

Victorian Rothbury was dominated by Sir William, later the first **Lord Armstrong**, the immensely wealthy nineteenth-century arms manufacturer, shipbuilder and engineer who built his country home at **Cragside** (Easter–Sept

Tues–Sun 1–5.30pm, Oct until 4.30pm; £7.20, gardens only £4.80; NT), on the steep, forested slopes of Debdon Burn, a mile to the east of the village. He hired Richard Norman Shaw, one of the period's top architects, and work continued until the mid-1880s, culminating in a grandiose, and utterly romantic, Tudor-style mansion. The interior is stuffed with Armstrong's furnishings and fittings, heavy dark pieces enlivened by his art collection and by the William Morris stained glass in the library and the dining-room inglenook. House **tours** are usually available on Friday and Sunday mornings. Armstrong was an avid innovator, fascinated by hydraulic engineering and by hydroelectric power. At Cragside he could indulge himself, damming the Debdon Burn to power several domestic appliances, such as the spit and the dumb waiter in the massive kitchen, as well as heating his personal Turkish-style plunge bath and steam room. In 1880, he also managed to supply Cragside with electricity, making this the first house in the world to be lit by hydroelectric power. The remains of the original system are still visible in the grounds, which, together with the splendid **formal gardens**, have longer opening hours (Easter–Oct Tues–Sun 10.30am–7pm or dusk; Nov to mid-Dec Wed–Sun 11am–4pm).

Wooler and around

Stone-terraced **WOOLER**, a grey one-street market town twenty miles north of Rothbury, was wholly rebuilt after a calamitous fire in the 1860s, though its hillside setting high above Harthope Burn and its proximity to the **Cheviot Hills** do much to lift the spirits. Local walks provide an introduction to the range, with a particular favourite being the one-mile hike to the top of Humbleton Hill, site of a battle in 1402 in which Hotspur inflicted heavy casualties on forces of the Douglas clan. But to get into the heart of the Cheviots you'll have to tackle the trek to **The Cheviot** itself, seven miles to the southwest and 2674ft above sea level. Starting out from Wooler youth hostel, count on four hours up, a little less back – your reward, an utterly bleak spot with views, on a clear day, to the coast, the castles at Bamburgh and Dunstanburgh, and over to Holy Island. Wooler is also a staging post on **St Cuthbert's Way**, the trans-Cheviot route, which runs west from the town to the Scottish village of Kirk Yetholm and beyond or northeast to Holy Island.

Frequent buses link Wooler with Berwick-upon-Tweed and Alnwick, the two nearest towns, and the **bus station** is set back off the High Street. At the other end of the High Street, off Burnhouse Road (by the free **car park**), you'll find the **tourist office** in the Cheviot Centre at Padgepool Place (Easter–Oct Mon–Sat 10am–1.30pm & 2–5pm, Sun 10am–1.30pm & 2–6pm; T01668/282123). *Tilldale House*, 34 High St (T01668/281450, E tilldalehouse@freezone.co.uk; **②**), has spacious en-suite **rooms** and serves evening meals; while *Winton House*, just off the High Street at 39 Glendale Rd (T01668/281362, W www.wintonhouse.ntb.org.uk; no credit cards; **②**; closed Dec–Feb), is a stone-built Edwardian house with garden. Wooler also has a comfortable **youth hostel** – the most northerly in England – at 30 Cheviot St (T0870/770 6100; £10.25; closed Nov–Feb & closed various days March–June, Sept & Oct), a five-minute walk up the hill from the bus station, as well as a **campsite**, Highburn House on Burnhouse Road (T01668/281344; closed Nov–Feb), just north of town, about half a mile from the bus station.

Chillingham

Six miles southeast of Wooler, and served by bus #470 towards Alnwick, the eccentricities of **Chillingham Castle** (Easter–Sept daily except Sat 1–5pm;

£5; ⓦwww.chillingham-castle.com) provide a refreshing counterpoint to the high-minded tidiness of National Trust-restored stately homes. Starting from an eleventh-century tower, the castle was augmented at regular intervals until 1873, though it keeps the essential structure of its mid-fourteenth-century incarnation, a grand, heavily walled courtyard with four impressive corner towers. For fifty years from 1933, however, Chillingham was largely left to the elements, until the present owner set about restoring it in his own individualistic way: bedrooms, living rooms and even a grisly torture chamber are stuffed and decorated with all manner of historical flotsam. Several self-catering **apartments** within the castle, including the Elizabethan Long Gallery, are available, either by the night (ⓣ01668/215359; breakfast not included, ❻) or by the week.

In 1220, the adjoining 365 acres of parkland were enclosed to protect the local wild cattle for hunting and food. And so the **Chillingham Wild Cattle**, a fierce, primeval herd with white coats, black muzzles and black tips to their horns, have remained to this day, cut off from mixing with domesticated breeds. It's possible to visit these unique relics, but only in the company of a warden and from a safe distance – bring binoculars if you can – as the animals are potentially dangerous and need to be protected from outside infection (April–Oct Mon & Wed–Sat 10am–noon & 2–5pm, Sun 2–5pm; £3; ⓣ01668/215250, ⓦwww.chillingham-wildcattle.org.uk). The visit takes about an hour and a half.

The Northumberland coast

The low-lying **Northumberland coast**, stretching 64 miles north from Newcastle to the Scottish border, boasts many of the region's principal attractions, not least a succession of mighty fortresses, beginning with **Warkworth Castle** and **Alnwick Castle**, former and present strongholds of the Percys, the county's biggest landowners. Further along, there's the formidable fastness of **Bamburgh** and then, last of all, the magnificent Elizabethan ramparts surrounding **Berwick-upon-Tweed**. In between you'll find splendid sandy beaches – notably at Warkworth, Bamburgh and the tiny seaside resort of **Alnmouth** – as well as the site of the Lindisfarne monastery on **Holy Island** and the seabird and nature reserve of the **Farne Islands**, reached by boat from Seahouses.

Warkworth

WARKWORTH, a coastal hamlet set in a loop of the River Coquet, is best seen from the north, from where the grey stone terraces of the long main street slope up towards the commanding remains of **Warkworth Castle** (daily: April–Sept 10am–6pm; Oct 10am–5pm; Nov–March 10am–1pm & 2–4pm; £3; EH), which perch on top of an immense grassy mound at the far end of the village. Mostly built in the fourteenth century, the three-storeyed keep has a honeycomb-like interior, a fine example of the designs developed by the castle-builders of Plantagenet England. It was here that most of the Percy family, earls of Northumberland, chose to live throughout the fourteenth and fifteenth centuries. The main street sweeps down into the attractive village, flattening out at Dial Place before curving right to cross the River Coquet; just over the bridge – a modern affair flanked by a splendid medieval turreted span – a signposted quarter-mile lane leads to the **beach**, which stretches for five miles from Amble to Alnmouth. Back in Dial Place stands the church of **St Lawrence**, whose many Norman features include the impressive ribbed vaulting of the chancel. From the churchyard (or, further up, from below the castle), a delightful path heads the half-mile inland along the peaceful right bank of the Coquet to the little boat that shuttles visitors across to **Warkworth Hermitage** (April–Sept Wed & Sun 11am–5pm; £2; EH), a series of simple rooms and a claustrophobic chapel that were hewn out of the cliff above the river sometime in the fourteenth century.

Warkworth is on the route of the bus service linking Alnwick, Alnmouth and Newcastle, and **buses** stop in Dial Place, near the church. Top **accommodation** is the *Sun Hotel*, 6 Castle Terrace (℡01665/711259, Ⓦwww.rytonpark-sun.co.uk; ❺), which commands fine views from its perch between the castle and the river. Good rooms are also available down the hill at the *Hermitage Inn* (℡01665/711258; ❸), a cosy place with well-kept beers and bar meals. At the *Greenhouse*, opposite on the corner of Dial Place (closed Tues & Sun eves), coffee and cakes, salmon kebabs, *cassoulet*, and other bistro favourites are served on stripped pine tables.

Alnmouth

It's just three miles north from Warkworth to the resort of **ALNMOUTH**, whose narrow, mostly nineteenth-century centre is strikingly situated on a steep spur of land between the sea and the estuary of the Aln. It's a lovely setting, and there's a wide sandy beach and rolling dunes. Alnmouth was a busy and prosperous port up until 1806, when the sea, driven by a freakish gale, broke through to the river and changed its course, moving the estuary from the south to the north side of Church Hill and rendering the original harbour useless. Alnmouth never really recovered, though it has been a low-key holiday spot since Victorian times, as attested by the elegant seaside villas.

There are local **bus services** from Alnwick and Warkworth, while the regular Newcastle to Alnwick bus also passes through Alnmouth and calls at its **train station** at Hipsburn, a mile and a half west of the centre. Most of the **accommodation** lies along or just off the main Northumberland Street. Best central B&B is *The Grange* opposite the church (℡01665/830401, Ⓔenquiries@thegrange-alnmouth.com; no credit cards; ❹), overlooking the river. A few yards further down Northumberland Street, at no. 56, *Beaches* (℡01665/830443, Ⓦwww.beachesbyo.co.uk; no credit cards; ❸) has a variety of highly individual en-suite rooms attached to a good **restaurant** (Tues–Sat dinner only), where meals of local cod, Northumbrian game casserole and the like go for around £15 a head; you can take your own wine.

Alnwick

The unassuming town of **ALNWICK** (pronounced "Annick"), thirty miles north of Newcastle and four miles inland from Alnmouth, is renowned for its castle and gardens – seat of the dukes of Northumberland – which overlook the River Aln. You'll need a full day to do these justice while, as the biggest town between Hadrian's Wall and the Scottish border, Alnwick itself warrants an overnight stop in any case. It's an appealing town of cobbled streets and Georgian houses, centred on the old cross in Market Place, site of weekly markets (Thursdays and Saturdays) since the thirteenth century (and a farmers' market on the last Friday of the month). Other than catching the market in full swing, the best time to visit is during the week-long **Alnwick Fair**, a medieval re-enactment which starts on the last Sunday in June.

Alnwick castle, gardens and town

The Percys – who were raised to the dukedom of Northumberland in 1750 – have owned **Alnwick Castle** (Easter–Oct daily 11am–5pm; £7.50; joint ticket with gardens £10; ⓦ www.alnwickcastle.com) since 1309, when Henry de Percy reinforced the original Norman keep and remodelled its curtain wall. His successor, another Henry, built the imposing barbican and connecting gatehouse. In the eighteenth century, the castle was badly in need of a refit, so the first duke had the interior refurbished by Robert Adam in an extravagant Gothic style – which in turn was supplanted by the gaudy Italianate decoration preferred by the fourth duke in the 1850s. There's plenty to see inside, though the interior is not to everyone's taste and it can be crowded at times – not least with families on the *Harry Potter* film trail, since the castle doubled as Hogwarts School. Each room displays part of the duke's extensive collection of paintings, including pieces by Canaletto, Titian, Tintoretto, Van Dyck and Turner. Three of the perimeter towers contain **museum** collections – the Regimental Museum of the Royal Northumberland Fusiliers in the Abbot's Tower, early British and Roman finds in the Postern Tower, and an exhibition dedicated to the Percy Tenantry Volunteers, a private force raised by the second duke during the Napoleonic Wars, in the Constable's Tower.

Signs lead you out of the grounds for the short walk to **Alnwick Garden** (daily 10am–dusk; £4, joint admission with castle £10; ⓦ www.alnwick garden.com), which is still to be established fully but already draws crowds to marvel at its sheer scale. At its heart is the computerized Grand Cascade, which shoots water jets in a regular synchronized display, while the rose garden is a particular favourite with many, sporting its own variety, the "Alnwick Castle".

Once you've dealt with the castle and gardens, the main sight in town is the **Bailiffgate Museum**, 14 Bailiffgate (Easter–Oct daily 10am–5pm, Nov–Easter Tues–Sun 10am–4pm; £2.20, ⓦ www.bailiffgatemuseum.co.uk), housed in the former church of St Mary, just around the corner from the castle's main entrance. This tells the history of the town and its trades in an entertaining fashion, mixing archive film and traditional music with buttons to press, armour to try on and a coal seam to crawl through.

Practicalities

Alnwick **bus station** is on Clayport Street, a couple of minutes' walk west of the Market Place, where you'll find the **tourist office**, in the arcaded Shambles (Easter–Sept Mon–Fri 9am–6pm, Sat 9am–5pm, Sun 10am–4pm; Oct–March Mon–Fri 9am–5pm, Sat 10am–4pm; ☏01665/510665, ⓦ www.alnwick.gov.uk). Several **accommodation** options cluster round the gatehouse at the end of Bondgate. Inside the gate, the welcoming *Tower Restaurant & Accommodation*, 10 Bondgate Within (☏01665/603888, ⓦ www.tower-alnwick.co.uk; ❺), stands out, while Alnwick's main hotel is the *White Swan*, also on Bondgate Within (☏01665/602109, ⓦ www.macdonald-hotels.co.uk; ❼). If you'd prefer to stay in the countryside, consider the *Masons' Arms* at **Rennington** (☏01665/577275, ⓦ www.masonsarms.net; ❹), four miles northeast of town on the Seahouses (B1340) road, an old coaching inn with good bar food, as well as six en-suite bedrooms.

There are traditional **cafés** and coffee shops throughout town, but the nicest is the *Grapevine Café*, just up from the tourist office on the corner of Market Place, serving *panini*, salads and drinks until 10pm (Sun until 5pm). For more of a **restaurant** experience, there's *Bibbi's*, 14 Bondgate Within (☏01665/602607; closed lunch Mon–Wed) – up a side alley next to the *White Swan Hotel* – a Modern British café/restaurant with a tempting menu.

Benvenuti on Narrowgate (☎01665/604465; closed Sun) is a reliable, traditional Italian occupying an atmospheric eighteenth-century townhouse. Check to see what's on at the **Alnwick Playhouse**, just through the arch on Bondgate Without (☎01665/510785, ⓦwww.alnwickplayhouse.co.uk), a venue for theatre, music and film throughout the year.

Craster and Dunstanburgh Castle

Heading northeast out of Alnwick along the B1340, it's a six-mile hop to the region's kipper capital, the tiny fishing village of **CRASTER**, perched above its minuscule harbour. There's not a great deal to make you stop long, but you can buy wonderful kippers here at Robson's factory and have a pot of tea in the *Bark Pots*. Even better is the *Jolly Fisherman*, the **pub** above the harbour, with sea views from its back window and garden and famously good crab meat, whisky and cream soup, crab sandwiches and kipper pâté. Most spectacularly, however, the village provides access to **Dunstanburgh Castle** (April–Sept daily 10am–6pm; Oct daily 10am–5pm; Nov–March Wed–Sun 10am–4pm; £2.20; NT & EH), whose shattered medieval ruins occupy a magnificent promontory about thirty minutes' windy walk up the coast.

Half a dozen **buses** a day run to Craster from Alnwick, a half-hour journey; the service continues to Seahouses and Bamburgh. There's a small **tourist office** in the village car park (Easter–Oct daily 9.30am–4.30pm; Nov–Easter Sat & Sun 10am–4pm; ☎01665/576007).

⑬ Seahouses and the Farne Islands

SEAHOUSES, otherwise a desultory fishing-port-cum-resort, is the embarkation point for boat trips to the windswept and treeless **Farne Islands**, a rocky archipelago lying a few miles offshore. Owned by the National Trust and maintained as a nature reserve, the Farnes are the summer home of many species of migrating seabirds, especially puffins, guillemots, terns, eider ducks and kittiwakes, and home to the only grey seal colony on the English coastline. To protect the wildlife, only two of the islands are open to visitors: **Inner Farne** (April–Sept daily; landing fee £4.50 May–July, £3.50 at other times) and **Staple Island** (same months & prices). Weather permitting, several boat owners operate daily **excursions**, usually starting at around 10am: Billy Shiel (☎01665/720308, ⓦwww.farne-islands.com), the best of the bunch, runs a varied programme, from two-and-a-half-hour **cruises** round either island (£10), to all-day trips landing at both (£20). Note that if you land on the islands, you'll have to pay the separate NT landing fee (members free). For more information, contact the **National Trust Shop**, 16 Main St, Seahouses (☎01665/721099), across from the *Olde Ship* (☎01665/720200, ⓦwww.seahouses.co.uk; ❺), easily the most atmospheric place in Seahouses to stay, eat and drink.

Bamburgh

Flanking a triangular green in the lee of its castle, three miles north of Seahouses, the tiny village of **BAMBURGH** is only a five-minute walk from two splendid sandy beaches, backed by rolling, tufted dunes. From the sands **Bamburgh Castle** (April–Oct daily 11am–5pm; £5; ⓦwww.bamburghcastle.com) is a spectacular sight, its elongated battlements crowning a formidable basalt crag high above the beach. This beautiful spot was first fortified by the Celts, but its heyday was as an Anglo-Saxon stronghold, one-time capital of Northumbria and the protector of the preserved head and hand of St Oswald, the seventh-century king who invited St Aidan over from Iona to convert his subjects. Rotted by seaspray and buffeted by winter storms, Bamburgh Castle struggled on until 1894, when it was bought by Lord Armstrong, who demolished most of the structure to replace it with a cumbersome hybrid castle-mansion. The focal point of the new building was the King's Hall, a teak-ceilinged affair of colossal dimensions, whose main redeeming feature is an exquisite collection of Fabergé stone animal carvings. In the ground floor of the keep, the stone-vaulted ceiling maintains its Norman appearance, making a suitable arena for a display of fetters and man-traps.

Bamburgh is also the home of the **Grace Darling Museum** (Easter–Oct Mon–Sat 10am–5pm, Sun noon–5pm; donation requested), which celebrates the daring sea rescue accomplished by Grace and her lighthouseman father, William, in September, 1838. When a gale dashed the steamship *Forfarshire* against the rocks of the Farne Islands, nine passengers struggled onto a reef, where they were subsequently saved by the Darlings, who left the safety of the lighthouse to row out to them. The museum details the rescue and displays the fragile boat the Darlings used; in the churchyard of thirteenth-century **St Aidan's** opposite is the pompous Gothic Revival memorial that covers Grace's body (she died of tuberculosis aged 26 in 1842).

A regular **bus** service links Alnwick and Berwick-upon-Tweed with Bamburgh, stopping on Front Street by the green. At the top of the village green, the *Victoria Hotel* (☎01668/214431, ⓦwww.victoriahotel.net; ❻) has been tastefully refurbished, and operates a brasserie with a Modern British menu. *The Greenhouse*, a few doors down at 5 Front St (☎01668/214513, ⓦwww.thegreenhouseguesthouse.co.uk; ❸) has en-suite **rooms** and serves daytime meals (not Tues), or further down the green there's the *Lord Crewe Arms Hotel*, Front St (☎01668/214243; ❻, winter ❺; closed Jan, weekends only Dec & Feb), a comfortable old inn with oak beams, open fires, public bar and restaurant.

Holy Island

There's something rather menacing about the approach to **Holy Island**, past the barnacle-encrusted marker poles that line the causeway. The danger of drowning is real enough if you ignore the safe crossing times posted at the start of the three-mile trip across the tidal flats. (The island is cut off for about five hours every day, so to avoid a tedious delay it's best to consult the **tide timetables** at one of the region's tourist offices or in the local newspapers.) Once here, it's easy to picture the furious Viking hordes sweeping across Holy Island, giving no quarter to the monks at this quiet outpost of early Christianity. Today's sole village is plain in the extreme, which doesn't deter summer day-trippers from clogging the car parks as soon as the causeway is open. But Holy Island has a distinctive and isolated atmosphere, especially out of season.

Once known as **Lindisfarne**, Holy Island has an illustrious history. It was here that St Aidan of Iona founded a monastery at the invitation of King Oswald of Northumbria in 634. The monks quickly evangelized the northeast and established a reputation for scholarship and artistry, the latter exemplified by the **Lindisfarne Gospels**, the apotheosis of Celtic religious art, now kept in the British Library. The monastery had sixteen bishops in all, the most celebrated being **St Cuthbert**, who only accepted the job after Ecgfrith, another Northumbrian king, pleaded with him. But Cuthbert never settled here and within two years he was back in his hermit's cell on the Farne Islands, where he died in 687. His colleagues rowed the body back to Lindisfarne, which became a place of pilgrimage until 875, when the monks abandoned the island in fear of marauding Vikings, taking Cuthbert's remains with them.

The pinkish sandstone ruins of **Lindisfarne Priory** (daily: Easter–Sept 10am–6pm; Oct 10am–5pm; Nov–Easter 10am–4pm; £3; EH) date from a later Benedictine foundation, which lasted here until the Dissolution. Behind lie the scant remains of the original monastic buildings while adjacent is the mostly thirteenth-century church of **St Mary the Virgin**, whose delightful churchyard overlooks the ruins. The **museum** (same times as priory; entrance included in priory fee) features a collection of incised stones that constitute all that remains of the first monastery. The finest of them is a round-headed tombstone showing armed Northumbrians on one side, and kneeling figures before the Cross on the other – presumably a propagandist's view of the beneficial effects of Christianity.

The **Lindisfarne Heritage Centre** (daily 10am–5.30pm, though times may vary according to the tides; £2.50; ⓦwww.lindisfarne-heritage-centre.org), occupying a former coaching inn on the main street, holds computer terminals giving you a virtual opportunity to see the major illustrated pages of the Lindisfarne Gospels and details the wildlife as well as the former living and working conditions on the island. Everyone then decants into **St Aidan's Winery**, just up from the green, sole producer of Lindisfarne Mead, a sickly beverage on sale all over the northeast.

Stuck on a small pyramid of rock half a mile away from the village, **Lindisfarne Castle** (Easter–Oct Mon–Thurs, Sat & Sun, hours vary according to tide but always include noon–3pm; £4.20; NT) was built in the middle of the sixteenth century to protect the island's harbour from the Scots. It was, however, merely a decaying shell when Edward Hudson, the founder of *Country Life* magazine, stumbled across it in 1901. Hudson bought the castle and turned it into a holiday home to designs by Edwin Lutyens.

The historic sites are all that most people bother with, but a **walk** around the island's perimeter is a fine way to spend a couple of hours. Most of the northwestern portion of the island is maintained as a **nature reserve**: from a bird hide you can spot terns and plovers, and then plod through the dunes and grasses to your heart's content.

Practicalities

The #477 **bus** from Berwick-upon-Tweed to Holy Island is something of a law unto itself given the interfering tides, but basically service is daily in August and twice weekly (Wed & Sat) the rest of the year. Departure times (and sometimes days) vary with the tides, and the journey takes thirty minutes. The island is short on **accommodation** and you should make an advance booking, whenever you visit. Two good places are the *Open Gate*, on Marygate (ⓣ01289/389222; ➌), which offers comfortable rooms in a sixteenth-century listed building; or the cheaper *Castlereigh* (ⓣ01289/389218; ➋; closed Nov–Feb), just by the green. Among the **pubs**, best is the *Ship* on Marygate (ⓣ01289/389311; ➋; closed Jan). **Camping** isn't allowed anywhere on the island. Options for **eating and drinking** are limited to a couple of tearooms and the hostelries, of which the *Ship* is the pick.

Berwick-upon-Tweed

Before the union of the English and Scottish crowns in 1603, **BERWICK-UPON-TWEED**, twelve miles north of Holy Island, was the quintessential frontier town, changing hands no fewer than fourteen times between 1174 and 1482, when the Scots finally ceded the stronghold to the English. Interminable cross-border warfare ruined Berwick's economy, turning the prosperous Scottish port of the thirteenth century into an impoverished garrison town, which the English forcibly cut off from its natural trading hinterland up the River Tweed. By the late sixteenth century, Berwick's fortifications were in a dreadful state of repair and Elizabeth I, apprehensive of the resurgent alliance between France and Scotland, had the place rebuilt in line with the latest principles of military architecture. The ramparts are now the town's major attraction, and you'll want to stop at least long enough to take a walk around the walls. A set of interesting local museums, and the town's attractive riverside location, warrant a night's stay, especially as Berwick is a useful staging post between England and Scotland.

The Town

Berwick's **walls** – protected by ditches on three sides and the Tweed on the fourth – are strengthened by immense bastions, whose arrowhead-shape ensured that every part of the wall could be covered by fire. Begun in 1558, the defences were completed after eleven years at a cost of £128,000, more than Elizabeth paid for all her other fortifications put together. And, as it turned out, it was all a waste of time and money: the French didn't attack and, once England and Scotland were united, Berwick was stuck with a white elephant. Today, the easy mile circuit along the top of the walls and ramparts (say an hour) offers a succession of fine views out to sea, across the Tweed and over the orange-tiled rooftops of a town that's distinguished by its elegant **Georgian mansions**. These, dating from Berwick's resurgence as a seaport between 1750 and 1820, are the town's most attractive feature, with the tapering **Lions' House**, on Windmill Hill, and the daintily decorated facades of **Quay Walls**, beside the river, of particular note.

Within the ramparts, the Berwick skyline is punctured by the stumpy spire of the eighteenth-century **Town Hall** (Easter–Oct Mon–Fri tours at 10.30am & 2pm; £1.50) at the bottom of Marygate, right at the heart of the compact centre. This retains its original jailhouse on the upper floor, now housing the **Cell Block Museum**, entertaining tours of which dwell on tales of crime and punishment in Berwick.

Opposite **Holy Trinity** church, the finely proportioned **Barracks** (Easter–Sept daily 10am–6pm; Oct daily 10am–4pm; Nov–Easter Wed–Sun 10am–4pm; £3; EH) date from the early eighteenth century and were in use until 1964, when the King's Own Scottish Borderers regiment decamped. Inside, the *By Beat of Drum* exhibition traces the life of the British infantryman from the sixteenth to the nineteenth century, while a superior borough museum and art gallery are sited in the **Clock Block**. Geared up for school parties, the museum features imaginative dioramas, recordings and displays of local traditional life, even a model of a local clergyman haranguing visitors from his pulpit.

Practicalities

From Berwick **train station** it's about ten minutes' walk down Castlegate and Marygate to the town centre. Most regional **buses** stop on Golden Square (where Castlegate meets Marygate), though some may also stop in front of the station. The **tourist office** at 106 Marygate (Easter–Oct Mon–Sat 10am–5pm, Sun 11am–3pm; Nov–Easter Mon–Sat 10am–4pm; ☎01289/330733, ⊛www.berwickonline.org.uk, ⊛www.exploreberwick.co

.uk) can book you onto informative one-hour **walking tours** of town (Easter–Oct Mon–Fri, 4 daily; £3). For **bike rental**, contact Tweed Cycles, 17a Bridge St (☎01289/331476) – you can get details of a scenic route to Holy Island (24 miles return) here. There's free **Internet** access in the library, behind the tourist office on the corner of Walkergate and Chapel Street.

Berwick has plenty of **accommodation** and the tourist office offers a room-booking service – local hotels and B&Bs post pictures and adverts inside the office. There are plenty of local **campsites**, though only *Marshalls Meadows Farm*, off the A1, two miles north (☎01289/307375; closed Nov–Feb) has space for tents.

B&Bs, guest houses and hotels

Berwick Backpackers 56–58 Bridge St ☎01289/331481. Townhouse backpackers with a six-bed dorm (£10), one single (£12) and three cheap twins/doubles (❶). Also a kitchen, Internet access and bike rental. No credit cards.

Dervaig Guest House 1 North Rd ☎01289/307378, ⓦwww.dervaig-guesthouse .co.uk. Spacious, well-appointed rooms, a large walled garden and parking, 5min walk from the centre. ❸

King's Arms Hide Hill ☎01289/307454, ⓦwww.kings-arms-hotel.com. The best central hotel, with a contemporary café, Italian restaurant and summer dining in the walled garden. ❻

No.1 Sallyport Bridge St ☎01289/308827, ⓦwww.1sallyport-bedandbreakfast.com. Berwick's most luxurious B&B, with three sensa-tional rooms in a seventeenth-century house next to the city walls. Master bedroom, suite (sleeps four) or "Manhattan loft" (with widescreen TV and DVD) are all elegantly furnished. Reservations essential. ❺

Old Vicarage Guest House 24 Church Rd, Tweedmouth ☎01289/306909, ⓦwww .oldvicarageberwick.co.uk. The finest choice in nearby Tweedmouth, a delightful Victorian villa with a range of rooms, some sharing bathrooms. No credit cards. ❷

Whyteside House 46 Castlegate ☎01289/331019. Victorian splendour at the top end of Castlegate – the house retains many origi-nal features, and rooms are spacious and nicely furnished. No credit cards. ❸

Cafés and restaurants

Café 52 50–52 Bridge St ☎01289/306796. Funky café-bistro with coffee and ciabatta sandwiches during the day, and a Mediterranean menu served until 10pm. Closed Sun eve and all Mon. Moderate.

Foxton's 26 Hide Hill ☎01289/303939. Bar-brasserie serving an inexpensive menu of sand-wiches, light meals and traditional main courses. Closed Sun. Moderate.

Queen's Head 6 Sandgate ☎01289/307852. Old Berwick inn that's gone for the gastropub look and menu – Craster crab with sweet chilli, rack of Northumbrian lamb, or ostrich fillet are typical dishes. Expensive.

Royal Garden 35 Marygate ☎01289/331411. Chinese restaurant whose menu raises it above the ordinary – tofu, *char siu*, oyster dishes included. Moderate.

Drinking and entertainment

Barrels Ale House 59–61 Bridge St ☎01289/308013, ⓦwww.thebarrelsalehouse.com. Chilled-out inde-pendent pub at the foot of Berwick Bridge, with guest beers, tapas lunches (Wed–Sun) and an interesting programme of live music and DJs in the basement.

The Maltings Eastern Lane ☎01289/330999, ⓦwww.maltingsberwick.co.uk. Berwick's arts centre with a year-round programme of music, theatre, comedy, film and dance, and river views from its licensed café.

Travel details

Buses

For more information on all local and national bus services, contact Traveline ⓣ 0870/608 2608, Ⓦ www.traveline.org.uk.

Alnwick to: Bamburgh (4–6 daily; 1hr 5min); Berwick-upon-Tweed (3 daily; 2hr).

Bamburgh to: Alnwick (4–6 daily; 1hr 5min); Craster (4–5 daily; 30–40min); Seahouses (Mon–Sat 9 daily, Sun 4; 10min).

Barnard Castle to: Bishop Auckland (Mon–Sat 9 daily, Sun 6; 50min); Darlington (hourly; 35min); Middleton-in-Teesdale (hourly; 35min); Raby Castle (9 daily; 15min).

Berwick-upon-Tweed to: Holy Island (Aug 2 daily, rest of the year 2 weekly; 30min); Newcastle (Mon–Sat 6 daily, Sun 3; 2hr 30min); Wooler (Mon–Sat 4–7 daily; 50min).

Bishop Auckland to: Barnard Castle (Mon–Sat 9 daily, Sun 6; 50min); Cowshill (Mon–Sat 7 daily, Sun 4; 1hr 10min); Darlington (Mon–Sat hourly; 35min); Newcastle (hourly; 1hr 15min); Stanhope (Mon–Sat 7 daily, Sun 4; 45min); Sunderland (Mon–Sat 4 daily; 2hr).

Darlington to: Barnard Castle (hourly; 35min); Bishop Auckland (Mon–Sat hourly; 35min); Carlisle (1 daily; 3hr); Durham (every 30min; 1hr); Middleton-in-Teesdale (Mon–Sat 9 daily, Sun 3; 1hr 20min); Newcastle (every 30min; 2hr).

Durham to: Barnard Castle (1 daily; 1hr); Beamish (May–Sept 1–3 daily; 25min); Bishop Auckland (every 30min; 30min); Darlington (every 30min; 1hr); Newcastle (hourly; 1hr); Stanhope (June–Sept 1–2 weekly; 45min); Sunderland (every 15–30min; 50min).

Haltwhistle to: Hexham (hourly; 45min).

Hexham to: Bellingham (Mon–Sat 5 daily; 40min); Haltwhistle (hourly; 40min).

Middlesbrough to: Newcastle (hourly; 1hr).

Newcastle to: Alnmouth (hourly; 1hr 30min); Alnwick (Mon–Sat 6 daily, Sun 3; 1hr 15min); Bamburgh (3 daily; 2hr 30min); Barnard Castle (1 daily; 1hr 25min); Berwick-upon-Tweed (Mon–Sat 6 daily, Sun 3; 3hr); Carlisle (hourly; 2hr); Craster (3 daily; 1hr 50min); Darlington (every 30min; 2hr); Durham (hourly; 1hr); Hexham (every 30min; 1hr 15min); Leeds (10 daily; 3hr); Middlesbrough (hourly; 1hr); Rothbury (Mon–Sat 7 daily, Sun 2; 1hr 15min); Seahouses (3 daily; 2hr 10min); Warkworth (hourly; 1hr 20min); Wooler (Mon–Fri 1–2 daily, Sat 4 (2hr 15min).

Wooler to: Alnwick (Mon–Sat 4 daily; 45min); Berwick-upon-Tweed (Mon–Sat 4–7 daily; 50min).

Trains

For information on all local and national rail services, contact National Rail Enquiries ⓣ 08457/484950, Ⓦ www.nationalrail.co.uk.

Darlington to: Bishop Auckland (every 1–2hr; 30min); Durham (every 30min; 20min); Newcastle (every 30min; 35min).

Durham to: Darlington (every 30min; 20min); London (hourly; 3hr); Newcastle (every 30min; 15min); York (hourly; 50min).

Hexham to: Carlisle (hourly; 1hr); Haltwhistle (hourly; 20min); Newcastle (hourly; 40min).

Middlesbrough to: Durham (hourly; 50min); Grosmont, for North Yorkshire Moors Railway (see p.709: Mon–Sat 4 daily; 1hr); Newcastle (hourly; 1hr 10min); Whitby (Mon–Sat 4 daily; 1hr 30min).

Newcastle to: Alnmouth (Mon–Sat 9–10 daily, Sun 3 daily; 30min); Berwick-upon-Tweed (hourly; 45min); Carlisle (hourly; 1hr 30min); Corbridge (hourly; 40min); Darlington (every 30min; 35min); Durham (every 30min; 15min); Edinburgh (hourly; 1hr 30min); Haltwhistle (hourly; 1hr); Hexham (hourly; 40min); London (hourly; 2hr 45min–3hr 30min); York (hourly; 1hr).

Wales

Wales

South Wales

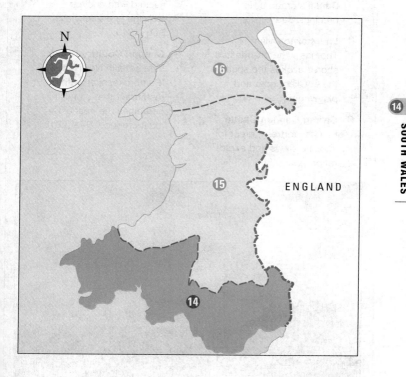

CHAPTER 14

Highlights

* **Blaenafon** Fascinating ironworks town plus deep mine museum. See p.779

* **National Museum of Wales** From exquisite art to rugged tales of Welsh history, all housed in Cardiff's grand civic precinct. See p.783

* **Laugharne** Dylan Thomas's "heron-priested shore" evokes the spirit of the ebullient poet and playwright. See p.802

* **Carreg Cennan Castle** Fantasy fortress, great for sublime views and exploration. See p.805

* **St David's** Inspirational village with a splendid cathedral and heart-racing boat trips out to offshore islands. See p.814

* **Mynydd Preseli** Mysterious mountains flecked with ancient remains and trackways. See p.818

* **Cnapan Country House** Fine hotel in Newport (Pembrokeshire), with a restaurant that exquisitely combines the freshest local produce. See p.818

△ Carreg Cennan Castle

14

South Wales

T he most heavily populated, and by far the most anglicized, part of Wales is the **south**. This is a region of distinct character, whether in the resurgent seaport cities of Cardiff and Swansea, the mining-scarred Valleys or the beauty of the Glamorgan, Carmarthenshire and Pembrokeshire coasts. Unlike the rest of Wales, transport connections are fast and frequent, making this region by far the easiest Welsh stop for those on a limited itinerary.

Monmouthshire, the easternmost county in Wales, abuts the English border and contains the full span of south Welsh life, from the bucolic charms of the **River Wye** and **Tintern Abbey** to **Newport**, Wales's third largest conurbation, near the remains of an extensive Roman settlement at **Caerleon**. West and north are the world-famous **Valleys**. Although all but one of the coal mines have closed, the area is still one of tight-knit towns, with a rich working-class heritage that displays itself in some excellent museums and colliery tours, such as **Big Pit** at Blaenafon and the **Rhondda Heritage Park** in Trehafod. The valleys course down to the great ports of the coast, which once shipped Wales's products all over the world. The greatest of them all was **Cardiff**, now Wales's upbeat capital and an essential stop. Further west is Wales's second city, **Swansea** – rougher, tougher and less anglicized than the capital. It sits on an impressive arc of coast that shelves round to the delightful **Gower Peninsula**, one of the country's favourite playgrounds, that juts out into the sea like a mini-Wales of grand beaches, rocky headlands, bracken heaths and ruined castles.

Too many people rush from here straight to the coastal national park of Pembrokeshire, missing out **Carmarthenshire**. Of all the routes that spoke out of the county town of **Carmarthen**, the most glorious is the winding road to **Llandeilo** along the **Tywi Valley**, past ruined hilltop forts and two of the country's finest gardens. Immediately west sits Wales's most impressively sited castle at **Carreg Cennen**, high up on the dizzy rock plug of the Black Mountain.

The wide sands fringing Carmarthen Bay stretch towards the popular seaside resort of **Tenby**, a major stop on the 186-mile **Pembrokeshire Coast Path**. The rutted coastline of **St Bride's Bay** is the most glorious part of the coastal walk, which leads north to brush past the impeccable mini-city of **St David's**, whose exquisite cathedral shelters in its own protective hollow. Nearby are plenty of opportunities for spectacular coast and hill walks, dinghy crossings to local islands and numerous other outdoor activities.

The main road route into South Wales from England is the M4 motorway, which divides at Junction 21 near Bristol: the old **Severn Bridge** carries the M48 loop, while the M4 itself forms the Second (or **New**) **Severn Crossing** a little downstream. Both impose a **toll** on westbound traffic, payable by cash or cheque only (Ⓦ www.severnbridge.co.uk): a hefty £4.50 for a car, free for

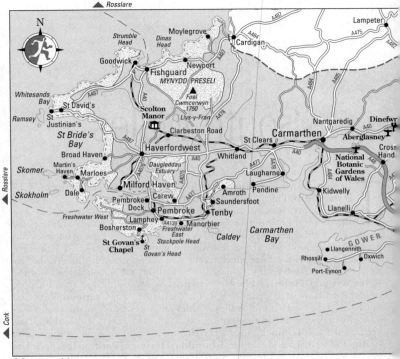

© Crown copyright

a motorbike. Cyclists and pedestrians can follow a dedicated path on the old Severn Bridge for free. The frequent **trains** along the London–Bristol–Cardiff route duck under the water courtesy of the Severn Rail Tunnel.

The Wye Valley

The **Wye Valley** (ⓦ www.visitwyevalley.com), along with the rest of Monmouthshire, was finally recognized as part of Wales only in the local government reorganization of 1974. Before then, the county was officially included as part of neither England nor Wales, so that maps were frequently headlined "Wales and Monmouthshire". Most of the rest of Monmouthshire is firmly and redoubtably Welsh, but the woodlands and hills by the meandering River Wye have more in common with the landscape over the border. The two main centres are **Chepstow**, with its massive castle, and the spruce, old-fashioned town of **Monmouth**, sixteen miles upstream. Six miles north of Chepstow lie the inspirational ruins of the Cistercian **Tintern Abbey**.

Chepstow and around

Of all the places that call themselves "the gateway to Wales", **CHEPSTOW** (Cas-Gwent) has probably the greatest claim, situated on the western bank of

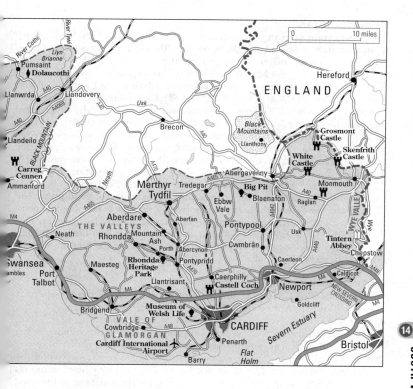

the River Wye just over a mile from where its tidal waters flow out into the muddy Severn estuary. Chepstow is a sturdy place robbed of the immediate charm of many other Welsh market towns by soulless modern developments. Nonetheless, there's an identifiably medieval street plan hemmed in by the thirteenth-century **Port Wall**, which encases a tight loop of the River Wye and the strategically sited **Chepstow Castle** (June–Sept daily 9.30am–6pm; April, May & Oct daily 9.30am–5pm; Nov–March Mon–Sat 9.30am–4pm, Sun 11am–4pm; £3; CADW). Guarding one of the most important routes into Wales, Chepstow was the first stone castle to be built in Britain, the Great Tower keep being built in 1067 to help subdue the restless Welsh. The Lower Ward is the largest of the three enclosures and dates mainly from the thirteenth century. Here you'll find the **Great Hall**, the home of a wide-ranging exhibition on the history of the castle, with particular emphasis on the English Civil War years, when Royalist Chepstow was twice besieged. Twelfth-century defences separate the Lower Ward from the Middle Ward, which is dominated by the still imposing ruins of the **Great Tower**. Beyond this is the far narrower Upper Ward, which leads up to the Barbican **watchtower** from where there are superb views looking down the cliff to the river estuary.

Opposite is the **Chepstow Museum** (Mon–Sat 11am–5pm, Sun 2–5pm; £1) containing nostalgic photographs and paintings of the trades supported in the past by the River Wye, and recording Chepstow's brief life in the early part of last century as a shipbuilding centre.

Practicalities

Chepstow's **train station** is five minutes' walk to the south of the High Street; its **bus station** is behind the shops on the other side of the western Town Gate. The **tourist office** is located in the castle car park, off Bridge Street (daily: Easter–Oct 10am–5.30pm; Nov–Easter 10am–3.30pm; ℡01291/623772). Inexpensive B&B **accommodation** can be found at *Mrs Batchelor*, 7 Lancaster Way (℡01291/626344; ❶), fifteen minutes' walk from the centre of town towards Tintern, and, a mile east of town over the Wye, at the wonderful *Upper Sedbury House*, Sedbury Lane (℡01291/627173, ⓦwww.smoothhound.co.uk/hotels/uppersed; ❶). *The George Hotel* (℡01291/625363, ⓦwww.bw-royalgeorgehotel.co.uk; ❺) is a grand old coaching inn next to the medieval gate on Moor Street. The nearest YHA **hostel**, *St Briavels Castle* (℡0870/770 6040, ⓔstbriavels@yha.org.uk; dorm £11.50; ❶), is seven miles northeast, over the border in England.

Chepstow has a handful of decent **restaurants** and a host of good **pubs**. *The Grape Escape*, on St Mary's Street, by the river, is best for reasonably inexpensive dining. For gourmet meals, try the moderately priced *Wye Knot*, on The Back (℡01291/622929); nearby on the same street is the *Boat Inn*, a waterside tavern with a good veggie-friendly menu. The *Five Alls*, at the bottom of High Street, is an earthy local pub.

Tintern Abbey

Six miles north of Chepstow, along one of the River Wye's most spectacular stretches, **Tintern Abbey** (June–Sept daily 9.30am–6pm; April, May & Oct daily 9.30am–5pm; Nov–March Mon–Sat 9.30am–4pm, Sun 11am–4pm; £2.50; CADW) has inspired writers and painters for over two hundred years – Wordsworth and Turner among them. Such is the place's popularity, however, that it's advisable to go out of season or at either end of the day when the hordes have thinned out. The abbey was founded in 1131 by Cistercian monks from Normandy, though most of the remaining buildings date from the massive rebuilding and expansion plan in the fourteenth century, when Tintern was at its mightiest. Its survival after the depredations of the Dissolution is largely thanks to its remoteness, as there were no nearby villages ready to use the abbey stone for rebuilding.

The centrepiece of the complex is the magnificent Gothic **church**, whose remarkable tracery and intricate stonework remains intact. Around the church are the less substantial ruins of the monks' domestic quarters and cloister, mostly reduced to one-storey rubble. The course of the abbey's waste disposal system can be seen in the Great Drain, an irregular channel that links kitchens, toilets and the infirmary with the nearby Wye. The **Novices' Hall** lies handily close to the Warming House, which together with the kitchen and infirmary would have been the only heated parts of the abbey, suggesting that novices might have gained a falsely favourable impression of monastic life before taking their final vows.

Monmouth and around

Enclosed on three sides by the rivers Wye and Monnow, **MONMOUTH** (Trefynwy), fifteen miles north of Chepstow, retains some of its quiet charm as an important border post and county town, and makes a good base for a drive – or a long hike – around the **Three Castles** of the pastoral border country to the north.

The centre of the town is **Agincourt Square**, a handsome open space at the top of the wide, shop-lined Monnow Street, which descends gently to the thirteenth-century bridge over the River Monnow. The cobbled square is dominated by the arched, Georgian **Shire Hall**, in which is embedded an eighteenth-century statue of the Monmouth-born King Henry V, victor of the Battle of Agincourt, in 1415. In front is the pompous statue of another local, the Honourable Charles Stewart Rolls, co-founder of Rolls-Royce and, in 1910, the first man to pilot a double flight over the English Channel. Almost opposite Shire Hall is **Castle Hill**, which you can walk up to glimpse some of the scant ruins of the **castle**, founded in 1068. A small **regimental museum** (April–Oct daily 2–5pm; Nov–March Sat & Sun 2–4pm; free) is the only part that can be visited. Priory Street leads north from Agincourt Square to the market hall, where the **Nelson Museum** (Mon–Sat 10am–1pm & 2–5pm, Sun 2–5pm; £1) attempts to portray the life of one of the most successful sea-going Britons through use of the Admiral's personal artefacts, collected by Charles Rolls' mother, who was an admirer. At the bottom of Monnow Street, the road narrows to squeeze into the confines of the seven-hundred-year-old **Monnow bridge**, crowned with its hulking stone gate of 1262, that served both as a means of defence for the town and a toll-collection point. To burn off some energy, you could **rent a canoe** for a trip up the Wye from the Monmouth Canoe & Activity Centre (℡01600/713461, ⓦwww.monmouthcanoehire.20m.com) in Castle Yard, Old Dixton Road, which also does accompanied abseiling and caving trips.

The **bus station** is behind the Kwik Save supermarket, at the bottom of Monnow Street. The **tourist office** is in the Shire Hall, Agincourt Square (daily: April–Oct 10am–5.30pm; Nov–March 10am–4pm; ℡01600/713899). **Accommodation** in town is thin on the ground. Try the simple but good *Burton Guesthouse*, on St James Square (℡01600/714958, ⓦwww .burtonhousemonmouth.co.uk; ❶), the intimate *Riverside Hotel* on Cinderhill Street, over the Monnow Bridge (℡01600/715577, ⓦwww .compass-rose.org.uk; ❸), or the excellent *Church Farm Guesthouse*, two miles south in the village of Mitchel Troy (℡01600/712176; ❷). The nearest tent-friendly **campsites** are both on Drybridge Street (over Monnow Bridge then right): the *Monnow Bridge* (℡01600/714004), behind the *Three Horseshoes* pub, and the slightly pricier *Monmouth Caravan Park* (℡01600/714745), a quarter of a mile beyond.

Inexpensive daytime **eating** can be had at either *Maltsters Coffee Shop*, 14 St Mary's St, or at *Cygnet's Kitchen* in White Swan Court, off Church Street, which serves more substantial soups and casseroles and has outside seating. The *French Horn* (℡01600/772733), handsomely situated at 24 Church St, serves moderately priced French fare for lunch and dinner. You can opt for inexpensive pub grub at the *Punch House*, in Agincourt Square, or the *Green Dragon*, in St Thomas Square, down by the Monnow Bridge.

Raglan

RAGLAN (Rhaglan), seven miles west of Monmouth, is an unassuming village worth visiting for its glorious **castle** (June–Sept daily 9.30am–6pm; April, May & Oct daily 9am–5pm; Nov–March Mon–Sat 9.30am–4pm, Sun 11am–4pm; £2.50; CADW), whose fussy and comparatively intact style makes it stand out from so many other crumbling Welsh fortresses. The last medieval fortification built in Britain, the design of which combines practical strength with ostentatious style, Raglan was begun on the site of a Norman motte in 1435 by Sir William ap Thomas. The **gatehouse**, still used as the main entrance, houses the best examples of the castle's showy decoration in its heraldic shields, intricate stonework edging and gargoyles. In the mid-fifteenth century, ap Thomas's grandson, William Herbert II, was responsible for the two inner courts, built around his grandfather's original gatehouse, hall and keep. The first is the cobbled **Pitched Stone Court**, designed to house the functional rooms like the kitchen, with its two vast, double-flued chimneys, and the servants' quarters. To the left is **Fountain Court**, a well-proportioned grassy space surrounded by opulent residences that once included grand apartments and state rooms. Separating the two are the original hall, from 1435, the buttery, the remains of the chapel and the dank, cold cellars below.

The Three Castles

The fertile, low-lying land between the Monnow and Usk rivers was important as an easy access route into the agricultural lands of South Wales, and in the eleventh century the Norman invaders built a trio of strongholds here to protect their interests. In 1201, Skenfrith, Grosmont and White castles were presented by King John to Hubert de Burgh, who employed sophisticated new ideas on castle design to replace the earlier, square-keeped castles. In 1260, the advancing army of Llywelyn ap Gruffydd began to threaten the king's supremacy in South Wales, and the three castles were refortified in readiness. Gradually, the castles were adapted as living quarters and royal administration centres, and the only return to military usage came in 1404–05, when Owain Glyndŵr's army pressed down to Grosmont, only to be defeated by the future King Henry V. The castles slipped into disrepair and were finally sold separately in 1902, the first time since 1138 that the three had fallen out of single ownership.

White Castle (Easter–Sept daily 10am–5pm; £2; CADW), eight miles northwest of Monmouth and six miles east of Abergavenny (see p.831), is the most awesome of the three, sited in rolling countryside with some superb views over to the hills surrounding the River Monnow. A few patches of the white rendering that gave the castle its name can be seen on the exterior walls. The grassy Outer Ward is enclosed by a curtain wall with four towers, divided by a moat from the brooding mass of the Inner Ward. A bridge leads to the dual-towered Inner Gatehouse, where you can climb the western tower for its sublime vantage point. At the back of the Inner Ward are the massive foundations of the Norman keep, demolished in about 1260.

Seven miles northeast of White Castle, in the attractive border village of Skenfrith (Ynysgynwraidd), is the thirteenth-century **Skenfrith Castle** (free access), dominated by the circular keep that replaced an earlier Norman structure. Whilst not as impressive as White Castle, Skenfrith has a pretty riverside setting, its castle walls built of a sturdy red sandstone arranged in an irregular rectangle. In the centre of the ward is a low, round keep, raised slightly on an earth mound, containing the vestiges of the private apartments of the castle's lord on the upper floors.

Five miles upstream of Skenfrith, right on the English border, the most dilapidated of the Three Castles, **Grosmont Castle** (free access), sits on a small hill above its village. Entering over the wooden bridge above the dry moat brings you into the small central courtyard, dominated on the right-hand side by the ruins of a large Great Hall dating from the first decade of the thirteenth century.

Newport and Caerleon

Dominating the once industrious valley towns of southern Monmouthshire, **Newport**, Wales's third largest town, is a downbeat, working-class place that grew up around the docks at the mouth of the River Usk. Its rich history was largely swept away by the twentieth century, but isolated nuggets remain, most notably at Roman **Caerleon** – the "old port" on the River Usk – now a northern suburb of Newport, but predating the town by about a thousand years.

Newport

NEWPORT (Casnewydd), fifteen miles west of Chepstow, is hardly the most prepossessing of towns, with its modern city centre strung along the banks of the foul and muddy River Usk. Overlooking these waters stand both the pathetic remains of **Newport Castle**, and Peter Fink's giant red sculpture *Steel Wave*, a nod to one of Newport's great industries. The place does have a tremendous energy, however, and can be well worth a night's stop.

The central High Street leads to Newport and Westgate squares, and the ornate, Victorian **Westgate Hotel** where, in 1839, soldiers sprayed a crowd of Chartist protesters with gunfire (see box) – the hotel's original pillars still show bullet marks. A hundred yards along Commercial Street, in John Frost Square, the quirky **Newport clock** shudders, shakes, spits smoke and comes near to apparent collapse every hour, usually drawing an appreciative crowd. In front of the clock is the town's library, tourist office and inspiring civic **museum** (Mon–Thurs 9.30am–5pm, Fri 9.30am–4.30pm, Sat 9.30am–4pm; free). Starting with the origins of the county of Monmouthshire, the displays examine the county's original occupations and early lifestyles, and include a section on mining, with a roll call of those killed in local pit accidents – 3,508 men between 1837 and 1927. Newport's spectacular growth from 1000 townspeople in 1801 to a grimy port town of 70,000 people a century later is well charted, but the two most interesting sections deal with the Chartist uprising and a fine Roman mosaic.

Dominating the Newport skyline with its comical, spidery legs is the **Transporter Bridge** (May–Sept Mon–Sat 8am–8.50pm, Sun 1–9pm; Oct–April Mon–Sat 8am–5.50pm, Sun 1–5pm; car toll 50p, cyclists and pedestrians free), built in 1906 to enable cars and people to cross the river without disturbing the shipping channel, gliding them across the Usk on a dangling platform. A visitor centre (April–Sept Wed–Sat 10am–5pm, Sun 1–5pm; Oct–March Sat 10am–5pm, Sun 1–5pm) on the west bank tells its story.

Newport's **tourist office** is in the museum complex in John Frost Square (Mon–Sat 9.30am–5pm; ☎01633/842962), a hundred yards from Kingsway **bus station** and five minutes' walk south of the **train station**. Staying in Caerleon is a more amenable option, but there are some decent **B&Bs**,

including *Craignair*, 44 Corporation Rd (☎01633/259903, ✉ruthuen-craig-nair@ntlworld.com; **❶**), and the genteel *St Etienne*, 162 Stow Hill (☎01633/262341, ✉etienneguesthouse@hotmail.com; **❸**). At the western end of Bridge Street, Caerau Road rises up sharply to the south, passing the relaxed, hospitable *Kepe Lodge* at no. 46a (☎01633/262351; **❸**). There's a **campsite** at *Tredegar House* (☎01633/815600), a couple of miles west – take bus #315 or #30 from the town centre. For **food**, make for the *Oriel* café on the top floor of the museum, the vegetarian *Hunky Dory's* at 17 Charles St, or *Ristorante Vittorio* up by the cathedral at 113 Stow Hill (☎01633/840261). With **rock music** buoyant in Newport, the best place to catch the vibe is at the legendary *TJ's*, 14 Clarence Place, where it's said that Kurt Cobain proposed to Courtney Love.

Caerleon

Compact **CAERLEON** (Caerllion), three miles north of central Newport (bus #2; every 15min), but still within the city limits, is peppered with the remnants of the major Roman town of Isca, named after the River Usk (Wysg). The settlement was built to provide administrative and military services for the smaller, outlying camps in the rest of South Wales and grew to a size and importance on a par with the better-known York and Chester in the north of England. Although the town fell gradually into decay after the Romans had left, there were still some massive remains standing when, in 1188, episcopal envoy Giraldus Cambrensis noted with evident relish the "immense palaces, which, with the gilded gables of their roofs, once rivalled the magnificence of ancient Rome".

Although time has had an inevitably corrosive effect on the remains since Giraldus's time, there's a powerful sense of history running through the Roman **fortress baths** (April–Oct daily 9.30am–5pm; Nov–March Mon–Sat 9.30am–5pm, Sun 2–5pm; £2.50; CADW). The bathing houses, cold hall and communal pool area are remarkably intact and beautifully presented, with highly imaginative use of audiovisual equipment, sound commentary and models. On the High Street, a Victorian Neoclassical portico is the sole survivor of the original **Legionary Museum** (Mon–Sat 10am–5pm, Sun 2–5pm; free; ⓦwww.nmgw.ac.uk), now housed in a modern building behind and laden with artefacts unearthed here. Opposite the Legionary Museum, Fosse Lane leads down to the hugely atmospheric Roman **amphitheatre** (free access), the only one of its kind preserved in Britain. Hidden under a grassy mound until the 1920s, the amphitheatre was built around 80 AD, at the same time as the Colosseum in Rome. Up to six thousand could watch animal baiting, military exercises or the gory combat of gladiators.

Caerleon's **tourist office** (daily 10am–5pm; Nov–March closes 4pm; ☎01633/422656) lies next to the legionary museum, or there's more informal information in the delightful Ffwrrwm craft centre, down the main street. There's central, shared-bathroom **B&B** at *Pendragon*, 18 Cross St (☎01633/430871; **❷**), and *Great House*, Isca Road (☎01633/420216; **❷**). The best place to **eat** is *Oriel*, a bistro in the courtyard of the Ffwrrwm centre.

The Valleys

No other part of Wales is as instantly recognizable as the **Valleys**, a generic name for the string of settlements packed into the narrow gashes in the mountainous terrain to the north of Newport and Cardiff. Arriving from England, the change from rolling countryside to sharp contours and a post-industrial landscape is almost instantaneous. Each of the valleys depended almost solely on coal-mining which, although nearly defunct as an industry, has left its mark on the staunchly working-class towns: row upon row of brightly painted terraced housing, tipped along the slopes at some incredible angles, are broken only by austere chapels, the occasional remaining pithead and the dignified memorials to those who died underground.

This is not traditional tourist country, but it's one of the most interesting and distinctive corners of Wales, full of sociological and human interest. Some of the former mines have reopened as gutsy and hard-hitting museums – **Big Pit** at Blaenafon and the **Rhondda Heritage Park** at Trehafod being the best – while other excellent civic museums include those at **Pontypridd** and **Merthyr Tydfil**. A few older sites, such as vast **Caerphilly Castle** and the six-teenth-century manor house of **Llancaiach Fawr**, have been attracting visitors for hundreds of years.

Blaenafon and Big Pit

Fourteen miles north of Newport, the valley of the Llwyd opens out at the airy iron and coal town of **BLAENAFON** (sometimes Blaenavon), whose popu-lation has shrunk to five thousand, a quarter of its nineteenth-century size. It's a fascinating and evocative place, a fact recognized by UNESCO, who granted it World Heritage Site status in 2000. The town's boom kicked off at the Blaenafon **ironworks**, just off the Brynmawr road (April–Oct daily 9.30am–4.30pm; call ☎01633/648081 for winter hours; £2; CADW), founded

Working the black seam

The land beneath the inhospitable South Wales Valleys had some of the most abun-dant and accessible natural seams of **coal** and **iron ore** to be found, readily milked in the boom years of the nineteenth and early twentieth centuries. Wealthy, predomi-nantly English capitalists came to Wales and ruthlessly stripped the land of its natural assets, while simultaneously exploiting those who risked life and limb underground. The mine owners were in a formidably strong position as thousands flocked to the Valleys in search of work and some sort of sustainable life. By the turn of the twenti-eth century, the Valleys – virtually unpopulated a century earlier – became packed with pits, chapels and immigrant workers from Ireland, Scotland, Italy and all over Wales.

In 1920, there were 256,000 men working in the 620 mines of the South Wales coalfield, providing one-third of the world's coal. Vast Miners' Institutes jostled for position with the Nonconformist chapels, whose fervent brand of Christianity was matched by the zeal of the region's politics – trade-union-led and avowedly left-wing. Great socialist orators rose to national prominence, cementing the Valleys' reputation as a world apart from the rest of Britain, let alone Wales. Even Britain's pioneering National Health Service, founded by a radical Labour government in the years following World War II, was based on a Valleys' community scheme devised by locally born politician Aneurin Bevan.

Over half of the original pits closed in the harsh economic climate of the 1930s as coal seams became exhausted and the political climate changed. In the 1980s, further closures threatened to bring the number of men employed in the South Wales coalfields down to four figures, and the miners went on strike from 1984–1985. No coalfield was as solidly behind the strike as South Wales but today all of the deep pits – bar one reprieved and taken over in a workers' buy-out in 1994 – have closed.

in 1788. Limestone, coal and iron ore – ingredients for successful iron-smelting – were abundant locally, and the Blaenafon works was one of the largest in Britain until it closed in 1900. The line of Georgian blast furnaces, the water-balance lift and the **museum** in the workers' cottages offer a thorough picture of both the process and the lifestyle that went with it. The ironworks also contains the town's **tourist office** (same hours; ☎01495/792615).

Just as it is now possible to visit the home of Blaenafon's iron industry, the town's defunct coal trade has also been transformed smoothly into the site that most clearly evokes the experience of a miner's work and life. At the **Big Pit National Mining Museum** (mid-Feb to Nov daily 9.30am–5pm; last underground tour 3.30pm; free; ⓦ www.nmgw.ac.uk), a mile west of the town and reached by a half-hourly shuttle bus from Blaenafon, you're kitted out with lamp, helmet and very heavy battery pack and lowered three hundred feet into the labyrinth of shafts and coal faces for a guided tour. The guides – most of whom are ex-miners – lead you through explanations and examples of the different types of coal mining, while constant streams of rust-coloured water flow by, adding to the dank and chilly atmosphere that must have terrified the small children who were once paid twopence – of which one penny was taken out for the cost of their candles – for a six-day week pulling the coal wagons along the tracks. Back on the surface, the old pithead baths, smithy, miners' canteen and winding engine house have all been preserved and filled with some fascinating displays about the local mining industry.

The Taff and Cynon valleys

The River Taff flows out into the Bristol Channel at Cardiff, after passing through a condensed couple of dozen miles of industry and population. The first town in the Taff vale is **Pontypridd**, one of the most cheerful in the Valleys, and probably the best base. Continuing north, the river splits again at Abercynon, where the River Cynon flows in from Aberdare, site of Wales's only remaining deep mine. Just outside Abercynon is the enjoyable, sixteenth-century **Llancaiach Fawr** manor house. To the north, the Taff is packed into one of the tightest of all the Valleys, passing Aberfan five miles short of the imposing valley head town of **Merthyr Tydfil**.

Pontypridd

PONTYPRIDD, twelve miles north of Cardiff, is built up around its quirky arched **bridge**. Once the largest single-span stone bridge in Europe, it was built in 1775 by local amateur stonemason William Edwards, whose previous attempts had crumbled into the river below. Across the river is **Ynysangharad Park**, where Sir W. Goscombe John's gooey statue honours Pontypridd weaver Evan James, who composed the stirringly nationalistic song *Hen Wlad fy Nhadau (Land of My Fathers)*, that has become the Welsh national anthem. By the bridge at the end of Taff Street, a lovingly restored church houses the **Pontypridd Museum** (Mon–Sat 10am–5pm; free), one of the best museums in the Valleys. A treasure trove of photographs, videos, models and exhibits succeeds in painting a warm and human picture of the town and its outlying valleys, as well as paying homage to the town's famous sons, singer Tom Jones and opera star and actor Sir Geraint Evans.

Pontypridd is well connected to bus, train and road networks. The **tourist office** (Mon–Sat 10am–5pm; ☎01443/490748) is in the museum, on Bridge Street. **Accommodation** is rather scarce: in the town centre, try the lively *Millfield Hotel*, Mill Street, near the station (☎01443/480111; ❷), or, right in the thick of the action, the bustling *Market Tavern*, Market Street (℡01443/485331, Ⓦwww.markettavernhotel.fsbusiness.co.uk; ❷). Better bets are a few miles out, notably the well-kept and extremely friendly *Fairmead* guest house (℡01443/411174; ❸), almost opposite Llancaiach Fawr (see below), and the floral *Llechwen Hall* (℡01443/742050, Ⓦwww.llechwen.com; ❹), signposted off the A470 a couple of miles north of Pontypridd.

Llancaiach Fawr

Five miles north of Pontypridd, the river divides at **Abercynon**, a stark, typical valley town of punishingly steep streets lined with terraced houses that fade out into a coniferous hillside. Two miles east, just north of the village of Nelson, is the sixteenth-century **Llancaiach Fawr** (Mon–Fri 10am–5pm, Sat & Sun 10am–6pm; Nov–Feb closed Mon; last admission 90min before closing; £4.50), a Tudor house, built around 1530, that has been transformed into a living history museum set in 1645, the time of the Civil War, with all of the guides dressed as house servants, speaking the language of seventeenth-century Britain. Although potentially tacky, it is quite deftly done, with well-researched period authenticity and numerous fascinating anecdotes from the staff; visitors are even encouraged to try on the master of the household's armour. Regular **buses** from Pontypridd and Cardiff pass the entrance.

Merthyr Tydfil

Downtown **MERTHYR TYDFIL** (or Tudful), ten miles north of Pontypridd, is a robust place whose main glory is its location at the top of the Taff Valley, on the cusp of the industrial coal country to the south and the grand, windy heights of the Brecon Beacons to the north. In the eighteenth century it became the largest iron-producing town in the world, as well as by far the most populous town in Wales, with four massive ironworks exploiting the local abundance of the key ingredients. A century earlier, what was then a village became a rallying point for Dissenter and Radical movements, which gained adherents as the profits from growing industrialization lined the pockets of the works owners, with little cash finding its way to the workers. Merthyr's radicalism bubbled furiously, breaking out into occasional riots and prompting the election of Britain's first socialist MP, Keir Hardie, in 1900.

Half a mile northwest of the town centre, just off Nant-y-Gwenith Street, the lower end of Neath Road, is **Chapel Row**, a line of skilled ironworkers'

Aberfan

North of Abercynon, the Taff Valley contains one sight that is hard to forget. Two neat lines of distant arches mark the graves of 144 people killed in October 1966 by an unsecured slag heap collapsing on Pantglas primary school in the village of **Aberfan**. Thousands of people still make the pilgrimage to the village graveyard, to stand silent and bemused by the enormity of the disaster. Among the dead were 116 children, who died huddled in panic at the beginning of their school day. A humbling and beautiful valediction can be seen on one of the gravestones, that of a ten-year-old boy, who, it simply records, "loved light, freedom and animals". Official enquiries all told the sorry tale that this disaster was almost inevitable, given the cavalier approach to safety so often displayed by the coal bosses. Gwynfor Evans, then newly elected as the first Plaid Cymru (Welsh Nationalist) MP in Westminster, spoke with well-founded bitterness when he said: "Let us suppose that such a monstrous mountain had been built above Hampstead or Eton, where the children of the men of power and wealth are at school...". But that, of course, would never have happened.

cottages built in the 1820s, one of which holds composer **Joseph Parry's Birthplace** (April–Sept Thurs–Sun 2–5pm; Oct–March enquire in advance at the castle, see below; free). Parry wrote the national favourite, *Myfanwy*, which is now piped into the rooms, some of which are given over to a display on his life and music.

Back across the other side of the river, just beyond the Brecon Road, is a home in absolute contrast to Parry's humble and cramped birthplace. **Cyfartha Castle** (April–Sept daily 10am–5.30pm; Oct–March Tues–Fri 10am–4pm, Sat & Sun noon–4pm; free) was built in 1825 as an ostentatious mock-Gothic castle for William Crawshay II, boss of the town's original ironworks. The castle is set within vast, attractive parkland which slopes down to the river and once afforded Crawshay a view over his iron empire. The old wine cellars contain a varied and enjoyable walk through the history of Merthyr, with the political turmoil and massive exploitation of the past couple of centuries picked over in gory detail. Upstairs, the castle's grand main rooms house an **art gallery** with an impressive collection of Welsh pieces, including works by Augustus John, Cedric Morris, Vanessa Bell, Jack Yeats and Kyffin Williams.

The **train station** is a minute's walk from the High Street. North from here is Glebeland Street, with the **bus** station and, at no. 14a, the **tourist office** (Mon–Sat: April–Sept 9.30am–5.30pm, Oct–March 9am–5pm; ☎01685/379884). Municipal **bike rental** (April–Oct; ☎01685/376940) is available at the Cyfartha Castle Visitor Centre. **Accommodation** is varied and includes the unpretentious *Tregenna Hotel*, in Park Terrace, next to Penydarren Park (☎01685/723627; ❸), as well as the humbler surroundings of the *Hanover Guest House*, 31 Hanover St (☎01685/379303; ❶), and *Penylan*, 12 Courtland Terrace (☎01685/723179; ❶). There's a **campsite** four miles north of town in the beautiful surroundings of *Grawen Farm*, Cwmtaf, near Cefn-Coed (☎01685/723740).

The Rhondda

Pointing northwest from Pontypridd, the **Rhondda Fawr** – sixteen miles long and never as much as a mile wide – is undoubtedly the most famous of all the Welsh valleys, as well as being the heart of the massive South Wales coal industry. For many it immediately conjures up Richard Llewellyn's 1939 book – and subsequent Oscar-winning weepie – *How Green Was My Valley*, although this was, strictly speaking, based on the author's early life in nearby Gilfach Goch,

Male voice choirs

Fiercely protective of its reputation as a land of song, the voice of Wales is most commonly heard amongst the ranks of **male voice choirs**. Although found all over the country, it is in the southern, industrial heartland that they are loudest and strongest. Their roots lie in the Nonconformist religious traditions of the seventeenth and eighteenth centuries, when Methodism in particular swept the country, and singing was a free and potent way of cherishing the frequently persecuted faith. Classic hymns like *Cwm Rhondda* and the Welsh national anthem, *Hen Wlad Fy Nhadau* (*Land of My Fathers*), are synonymous with the choirs, whose full-blooded interpretation of them continues to render all others insipid. Each valleys' town still has its own, often depleted choir, most of whom happily accept visitors to sit in on rehearsals. A leaflet, available from tourist offices, gives contact phone numbers for each choir's secretary. Contact them directly, and take the chance to hear one of the world's most distinctive choral traditions in full, roof-raising splendour.

outside the valley. Between 1860 and 1910 the Rhondda's population grew from 3000 to nearly 160,000, squeezed into ranks of houses grouped around sixty or so pitheads. The Rhondda, more than any other of the valleys, became a self-reliant, hard-living, chapel-going, poor and terrifically spirited breeding ground for radical religion and firebrand politics. For decades, the Communist Party ran the town of Maerdy (nicknamed "Little Moscow" by Fleet Street in the 1930s). The last pit in the Rhondda closed in 1990, but what was left behind was not some dispiriting ragbag of depressing towns, but a range of new attractions, cleaned-up hillsides and some of the friendliest pubs and working men's clubs to be found anywhere in Britain.

Specific attractions are few, however. The only one which really stands out is the colliery museum of the **Rhondda Heritage Park** (daily 10am–6pm, last admission 4.30pm; Oct–Easter closed Mon; £5.60; ⓦwww .rhonddaheritagepark.com), at **TREHAFOD**, formed by locals when the Lewis Merthyr pit closed in 1983. You can explore the engine-winding houses, lamp room and fan house, and take a simulated "trip underground", with stunning visuals and sound effects, re-creating 1950s and late nineteenth-century life through the eyes of colliers. The display concludes with a chilling roll call of pit deaths and a moving final narration by Neil Kinnock, once leader of the Labour Party, about the human cost of mining.

A **train** line from Cardiff, punctuated with stops every mile or so, runs the entire length of the Rhondda, stopping at Trehafod, a few minutes' walk from the Heritage Park. **Buses** also cover the route, continuing up into the mountains and the Brecon Beacons. **Accommodation** is scarce: by the Heritage Park on Coed Cae Road in Trehafod is the business-oriented *Heritage Park Hotel* (☏01443/687057, ⓦwww.heritageparkhotel.co.uk; ❺), while nearby is the *Bertie*, 1–3 Phillips Terrace (☏01443/688204; ❷), a decent bar-cum-B&B. Also nearby is the *Rickards*, Trebanoy Road, Porth (☏01443/688023; ❶).

Cardiff and around

Official capital of Wales since only 1955 (hence the ubiquitous "Europe's Youngest Capital" slogan), the buoyant city of **CARDIFF** (Caerdydd) has swiftly grown into its new status. A number of progressive developments, not least the sixty-member Welsh National Assembly, are giving the city the feel of an international capital, if not always with a very Welsh flavour – compared with Swansea, Cardiff is noticeably anglicized.

The second marquis of Bute built Cardiff's first dock in 1839, opening others in swift succession. The Butes, who owned massive swathes of the rapidly industrializing South Wales valleys, insisted that all coal and iron exports use the family docks in Cardiff, and it became one of the busiest ports in the world. In the hundred years up to the turn of the twentieth century, Cardiff's population soared from almost nothing to 170,000, and the spacious and ambitious new civic centre in Cathays Park was well under way. The twentieth century saw varying fortunes: the dock trade slumped in the 1930s and the city suffered heavy bombing in World War II, but with the creation of Cardiff as capital in 1955, optimism and confidence in the city blossomed. Many large governmental and media institutions have moved here from London, and the development of the dock areas around the new Assembly building being built in Cardiff Bay has given a largely positive boost to the cityscape.

Arrival, information and accommodation

The main **bus station** is off Wood Street, on the southwestern side of the city centre. Across the forecourt is Cardiff Central **train station**, for all intercity services as well as many suburban and Valley Line services. Queen Street station, at the eastern edge of the centre, is for local trains only. The city **tourist office**, at 16 Wood St, opposite Cardiff Central (Mon–Sat 10am–6pm, Sun 10am–4pm; ☎029/2022 7281, ⊛www.visitcardiff.info), provides good free maps of the city and plenty of information on accommodation and entertainment in the city. There's a branch on Harbour Drive at Cardiff Bay (Mon–Fri 9.30am–6pm, Sat & Sun 10.30am–6pm; Nov–March closes daily 5pm; no accommodation booking).

Cardiff is compact enough to walk around, as even the bay area is within thirty minutes' stroll of Central station. Once you're out of the centre, however, it's best to fall back on the extensive **bus** network, most reliably operated by the garish-orange-liveried Cardiff Bus Company (⊛www.cardiffbus.com). Information and passes are available from the counter next to the tourist office (Mon–Fri 8.30am–5.30pm, Sat 9am–4.30pm). A couple of useful **travel passes**, which can also be bought on board buses, are the City Rider ticket (£3.20), which gives unlimited travel around Cardiff and Penarth for a day, and the Network Rider (£5), which extends the range to Caerphilly and Newport; ask about family deals.

The main belt of guest houses and **hotels** lies along the genteel and leafy Cathedral Road, fifteen minutes' walk northwest of the city centre. You also have the option of a couple of budget **hostels** and two **campsites**.

Hotels, guest houses and B&Bs

Acorn Lodge 182 Cathedral Rd, Pontcanna ☎029/2022 1373. One of the least expensive B&Bs on this street, yet pleasant and quiet. Some en-suite rooms. ❶

Arosa House 24 Plasturton Gardens, Pontcanna ☎029/2039 5342. Very friendly and reasonably priced B&B in a quiet street just off Cathedral Road. ❶

Big Sleep Bute Terrace ☎029/2063 6363, ⊛www.thebigsleephotel.com. This trendy designer hotel is a refreshing antidote to the brocade and floral fabric palaces elsewhere. The ground floor bar is worth seeing in itself. Voted one of the 25 coolest hotels in the world by Condé Nast Traveller. Cut-price bargains on Sundays. ❷–❹

Churchills Cardiff Rd, Llandaff ☎029/2040 1300, ⊛www.churchillshotel.co.uk. Mock-Edwardian hotel in a quiet part of the city near the cathedral. ❹

Courtfield 101 Cathedral Rd, Pontcanna ☎029/2022 7701, ⊛www.courtfieldhotel.co.uk. Popular, comfortable and nicely furnished hotel with a sizeable gay clientele. ❸

Lincoln House 118 Cathedral Rd ☎029/2039 5558, ⊛www.lincolnhotel.co.uk. Elegant, small hotel restored in Victorian style, with heavy brocade and even a couple of four-poster beds. ❺

Scott's of St Fagans Greenwood Lane, St Fagans ☎029/2056 5400. Four miles from Cardiff, this old post office has been completely remodelled in minimalist style: all white walls, blond ash furniture, chic spotlighting and top quality fittings. ❹

St David's Hotel and Spa Havannah St, Cardiff Bay ☎029/2045 4045, ⊛www.rfhotels.com. The most luxurious hotel in Cardiff: a tall postmodern structure right on the waterfront that's all clean lines and elegant, understated decor. Rooms come with superb views and access to gorgeous spa facilities. ❾

Town House 70 Cathedral Rd, Pontcanna ☎029/2023 9399, ⊛www.thetownhousecardiff.co.uk. Restored Victorian house with en-suite rooms, a comfortable lounge and better-than-average facilities. ❸

Hostels

Cardiff Backpacker 98 Neville St ☎029/2034 5577, ⊛www.cardiffbackpacker.com. Spotlessly well-kept hostel with Internet access, bike rental, roof garden, pool table and on-site café and bar. Some private rooms, plus single-sex and mixed dorms (4–10 beds). Dorms £15 (cheaper if you stay three nights or more). ❶

YHA hostel 2 Wedal Rd, Roath Park ☎0870/770 5750, ⓔcardiff@yha.org.uk. Large, purpose-built, red-brick building, situated just underneath the

A48 Eastern Avenue flyover at the top of Roath Park, almost two miles from the city centre. Buses #78, #80 or #82 go from the central bus station. No curfew. Dorms £14.50. ❶

Campsites

Cardiff Caravan Park Pontcanna Fields ☎029/2039 8362. Closest campsite to the city centre, off Cathedral Road near the Sophia Gardens cricket ground. Well equipped and open year-round.

Lavernock Point Holiday Estate Lavernock Point, Fort Road, near Penarth ☎029/2070 7310, ⓦwww.lavernockpoint.com. Back-up option if the *Cardiff Caravan Park* is full. Located over five miles out of the city, off the B4267 near Penarth; buses #P4, #P5 and #P8 pass within a mile of the site. Also with bungalows.

The City

Cardiff's sights are clustered around fairly small, distinct districts. The compact commercial centre is bounded by the **River Taff**, which flows past the tremendous **Millennium Stadium**; in this rugby-mad city, the atmosphere in the pubs and streets when Wales have a home match – particularly against the old enemy, England – is charged with good-natured, beery fervour. Just upstream, the Taff is flanked by the wall of Cardiff's extraordinary **castle**, an amalgam of Roman remains, Norman keep and Victorian fantasy. North of the castle is a series of white Edwardian buildings grouped around **Cathays Park**: the City Hall, Cardiff University and the superb **National Museum**. A mile south of the commercial centre, the area around **Cardiff Bay** is striving to become one of the city's liveliest quarters, home to the National Assembly of Wales and a welter of new waterfront developments that make it an ideal place for eating, drinking or just ambling about. A couple of miles north of the city centre, **Llandaff Cathedral** warrants a visit for its strange clash of Norman and modern styles.

The city centre

Cardiff **city centre** forms a rough square bounded by the castle, Queen Street and Central stations and the Cardiff International Arena. Dominating the skyline, on the other side of Wood Street from Central Station, is the simply magnificent **Millennium Stadium** (tours hourly Mon–Sat 10am–5pm, Sun 10am–4pm, subject to events; book on ☎029/2082 2228, ⓦwww .cardiff-stadium.co.uk; £5), which has swiftly become an iconic symbol not only of Cardiff but of Wales as a whole. Built to an incredibly tight deadline in order to be ready for the Rugby World Cup of 1999, the stadium – with its trademark retractable roof – can seat 72,500 people and has hosted sporting matches of every description (including, with the lack of a national stadium in England, the FA Cup football final), as well as an array of huge rock gigs and other spectaculars. The tours include walking the players' tunnel, visiting the dressing rooms, VIP areas and a rugby museum. They start from the **stadium shop** at Entrance Gate 3 on Westgate Street. Don't forget to stroll the walkway along the river that was specially built out on ramps to accommodate the huge swell of the stadium walls.

The districts to the east are Cardiff's main shopping areas. **Queen Street**, running from the castle to Queen Street station, is a pedestrianized thoroughfare containing a predictable clutch of big-name chain stores and covered modern malls. Far more interesting are the **Arcades**, a series of Victorian and Edwardian galleries where you'll find all of the city centre's most alluring little independent shops and cafés – great for picking up flyers and information on gigs, club nights and other such events. Particularly impressive are the **High Street** and **Castle arcades**, either side of the High Street near the castle. A few

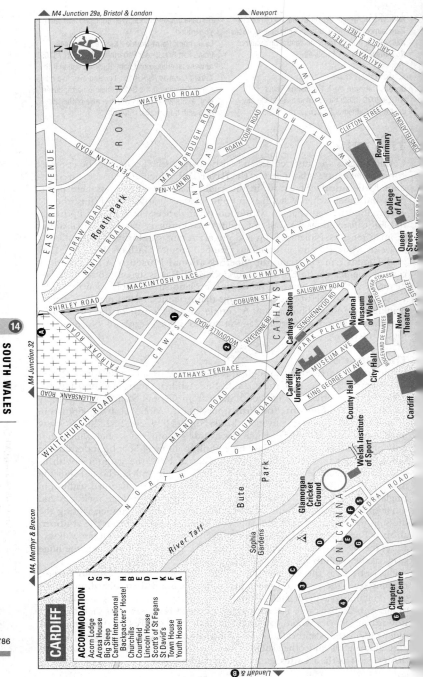

▲ M4 Junction 29a, Bristol & London   ▲ Newport

WATERLOO ROAD

R O A T H

Roath Park

EASTERN AVENUE

PEN-Y-LAN ROAD
TY-DRAW ROAD
NINIAN ROAD

MARLBOROUGH ROAD
PEN-Y-LAN RD
ALBANY ROAD
ROATH COURT ROAD

NEWPORT ROAD
BROADWAY
CLIFTON STREET
RAILWAY STREET
CARLISLE STREET
CONSTELLATIONS

Royal Infirmary

College of Art

Queen Street Station

▲ M4 Junction 32

SHIRLEY ROAD
MACKINTOSH PLACE
CITY ROAD
RICHMOND ROAD

C R W Y S   R O A D
WOODVILLE ROAD
COBURN ST
WYEVERNE RD
SALISBURY ROAD
SENGHENNYDD RD

CATHAYS
Cathays Station
STUTTGARTER STRASSE
BOULEVARD DE NANTES
QUEEN STREET

FAIROAK ROAD

A

❶
❷

CATHAYS TERRACE

ALLENSBANK ROAD
WHITCHURCH ROAD

M A E N D Y   R O A D
COLUM ROAD

PARK PLACE
MUSEUM AVE
KING GEORGE VII AVE

National Museum of Wales

City Hall

New Theatre

Cardiff University

County Hall

Cardiff

N O R T H   R O A D

B u t e   P a r k

River Taff

Sophia Gardens

Glamorgan Cricket Ground

Welsh Institute of Sport

P O N T C A N N A
CATHEDRAL ROAD

❸
❹
❻

Ⓒ
Ⓓ
Ⓔ Ⓕ ❺
Ⓖ

Chapter Arts Centre

▲ M4, Merthyr & Brecon

▲ Llandaff & B

▼ Llandaff & B

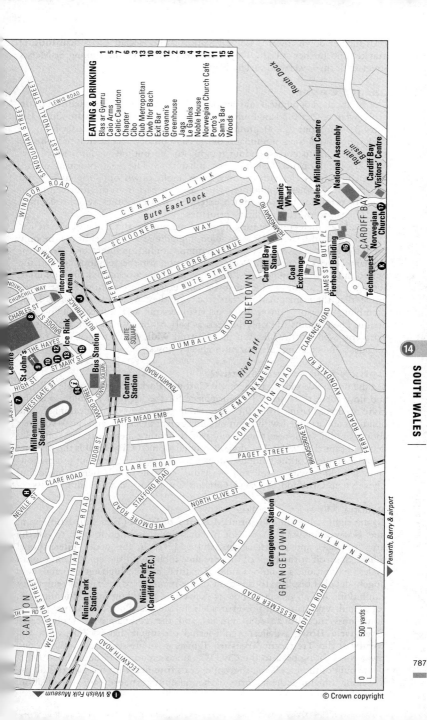

EATING & DRINKING

Bias ar Gymru	1
Caio Arms	5
Celtic Cauldron	7
Chapter	6
Cibo	3
Club Metropolitan	13
Clwb Ifor Bach	10
Exit Bar	8
Giovanni's	12
Greenhouse	2
Jags	9
Le Gallois	4
Noble House	14
Norwegian Church Café	17
Porto's	11
Sam's Bar	15
Woods	16

© Crown copyright

▼ Penarth, Barry & airport

▼ & Welsh Folk Museum

yards further down towards Central Station is the elegant Edwardian **indoor market** and further still the **Royal** and **Morgan arcades**, linking St Mary's Street with the lower end of The Hayes.

Cardiff Castle

The political, geographical and historical heart of the city is **Cardiff Castle** (daily: March–Oct 9.30am–6pm, last entry 5pm; Nov–Feb 9.30am–5pm, last entry 3.30pm; tour £5.80, grounds only £2.90; Ⓦ www.cardiffcastle.com), an intriguing hotchpotch of remnants of the city's history. The fortress hides inside a vast walled yard corresponding roughly to the outline of the original fort built by the Romans, Cardiff's first inhabitants. The neat Norman motte, crowned with its eleventh-century **keep**, looks down onto the turrets and towers of the domestic buildings, which date in part from the fourteenth and fifteenth centuries, but were much extended in Tudor times, when residential needs began to overtake military priorities.

In the late nineteenth century, the third marquis of Bute, one of the richest men in the world, lavished a fortune on upgrading his pile – although he only lived there for six weeks a year – commissioning architect and decorator William Burges to aid him. With their passion for the religious art and the symbolism of the Middle Ages, they systematically overhauled the buildings, adding a spire to the octagonal tower and erecting a clocktower. But it was inside that their imaginations ran free, and they radically transformed the crumbling interiors into palaces of vivid colour and intricate, high-camp design. These rooms can only be seen as part of the guided tour, making the extra cost well worthwhile. On the **Animal Wall**, visible from Castle Street, outside, stone creatures are frozen in cheeky poses.

Cathays Park and around

On the north side of the city centre is **Cathays Park**, a large rectangle of lawns and flowerbeds that forms the centrepiece for the impressive buildings of the **civic centre**. Dating from the early twentieth century, the gleaming white buildings are arranged with pompous Edwardian precision, and speak volumes about Cardiff's self-assertion, even half a century before it was officially declared capital of Wales. The dragon-topped, domed **City Hall** is the magnificent centrepiece of the complex, an exercise in every cliché about ostentatious civic self-glory, with a roll call of statues of male Welsh heroes, including Llywelyn ap Gruffudd, St David, Giraldus Cambrensis and Owain Glyndŵr.

National Museum of Wales

To the right stands the **National Museum of Wales** (Tues–Sun 10am–5pm; free; Ⓦ www.nmgw.ac.uk), one of Britain's finest, attempting both to tell the story of Wales and to reflect the nation's place in the wider, international sphere. Start off at the back of the entrance lobby with the epic "Evolution of Wales" exhibition, a fabulous mix of natural history, high-tech gizmos and hugely detailed displays. To the right of the main lobby are various temporary exhibitions and an extensive botany collection, including some stunning silk, paper and wax plant and flower models. In the first-floor archeology gallery, don't miss the Bronze Age remains and the comparatively sophisticated **Caergwrle Bowl**, a delicate, gold-leafed ornament that is 3000 years old. Nearby is the **Tregwynt Treasure Trove**, an impressive cache of gold and silver coins dating back to the Civil War, uncovered near Fishguard in 1996.

The bulk of the East Wing is given over to **fine art**, with ten galleries on the first floor containing the majority of the museum's extraordinary art collection.

The oldest part of the collection starts with the fifteenth- and sixteenth-century **Italian schools**, pushing on to seventeenth-century galleries rich in **Flemish** and **Dutch** work, including Rembrandt's coolly aloof portrait of *Catrina Hooghsaet* and Jacob van Ruisdael's mesmerizing *Waterfall*. The most famous, or perhaps infamous, pieces here are the **Cardiff Cartoons**, four monumental tapestries bought at great expense in 1979 and, at the time, presumed to be the work of Rubens. The first of the great Welsh artists is shown to maximum effect in the **eighteenth-century** galleries, where landscapes by Richard Wilson include *Caernarfon Castle* and *Dolbadarn Castle*. The **nineteenth-century** galleries include a round-up of some of the century's greater painters, including J.M.W. Turner, whose *Thames Backwater, with Windsor Castle* is a characteristic wash of diffuse colour and light.

The most exciting art works are contained in galleries eleven to fifteen, kicking off with a fabulous **sculpture collection**, including many by the one-man Victorian Welsh statue industry, Goscombe John, that contrast with the more delicate Rodin pieces nearby. Gallery Thirteen is home to the National Museum's pride, the Davies collection of **Impressionist paintings**. Cézanne, Monet and Degas figure predominantly, alongside Corot's legendary *Distant view of Corbeil, morning*, Pissarro's classic views of Rouen and Paris, and Renoir's chirpy portrait of *La Parisienne*. Gallery Fourteen houses a hearty collection of Post-Impressionists, Futurists and Surrealists, while Gallery Fifteen showcases abstract work with a strong Welsh bent.

Cardiff Bay

The parallel Lloyd George Avenue and Bute Street connect the city centre with **Cardiff Bay**, a thirty-minute walk south (alternatively, use bus #8 or the half-hourly train to Cardiff Bay station from Queen Street station). Like much of the Bay area, Lloyd George Avenue is a grand example of sweeping recent redevelopment; also like much of the Bay area, it feels soulless and imposed from on high. After all, this area used to be one of Cardiff's spiciest quarters, a multicultural stew of colour and vibrancy, immortalized by local lass Shirley Bassey under its more pithy epithet of Tiger Bay. Big money has changed it utterly, and the jury is still out as to whether that's for the better.

For those who love these sorts of wholesale regeneration projects, Cardiff Bay is nirvana. Gone is the seedy dereliction of the old docks in favour of an area of landscaped walkways, some audacious modern public art, gardens and public attractions. Whatever your opinion, it's hard to disagree that this is a fascinating corner of Cardiff, where ostentatious Victorian shipping company headquarters rub shoulders with spruced-up ex-dockers' housing, and sleek restaurants lurk in the shadow of glittering, postmodern corporate headquarters. Central to the whole project is the **Cardiff Bay Barrage**, across the Ely and Taff estuaries, which has transformed a vast mud flat into a freshwater lake, controversially depriving the wading bird population of a prime habitat.

First stop is the modern, tubular **Cardiff Bay Visitor Centre** (Mon–Fri 9.30am–6pm, Sat & Sun 10.30am–6pm; Nov–March closes daily 5pm; free), looking out onto the bay like a giant eye. It's a thinly disguised PR job, but at least it contains a scale model of the entire docks area, which is well worth seeing. The adjacent park is graced by the gleaming witch's-hat spire of the **Norwegian church arts centre** (daily 10am–4pm and for evening performances; ☎029/2045 4899), an old seamen's chapel in which the writer Roald Dahl was christened, now converted to a excellent café (see p.791) and exhibition space. Alongside is the site of the new **National Assembly of Wales** building, due to open in August 2005 – a stunning glass creation that will greatly enhance the Bay's skyline. In the meanwhile, you'll have to content yourself with the undistinguished current Assembly building that lies behind, the red-brick Crickhowell House, and the magnificent **Pierhead Building**, a typically rich, neo-Gothic terracotta pile that now serves as the National Assembly's **Visitor and Education Centre** (Mon–Thurs 9.30am–4.30pm, Fri 10am–4.30pm, Sat & Sun 10am–5pm; free; ⓦ www.wales.gov.uk).

On the other side of a newly landscaped basin and the mammoth Exchange Building, built in the 1880s as Britain's central Coal Exchange, is **Techniquest** (Mon–Fri 9.30am–4.30pm, Sat & Sun 10.30am–5pm; £6.50; ⓦ www .techniquest.org), a fun, hands-on science gallery – perfect for kids. Backing the whole area you'll see the sweeping wavy roofline and vast glass-brick wall of the **Atlantic Wharf**, which makes a striking impression for what is essentially just a big box filled with a twelve-screen cinema, a bowling alley and a few restaurants.

Llandaff Cathedral

Two miles northwest of the city centre along Cathedral Road, the small, quiet suburb of **Llandaff** is home to a church that has now grown up into the city's **cathedral** (daily 10am–7pm; free). It's believed to have been founded in the sixth century by St Teilo, but was rebuilt in Norman style in around 1120, and worked on well into the thirteenth century. From the late fourteenth century onwards, it declined into an advanced state of disrepair, and one of the twin towers and the nave roof eventually collapsed. Restoration only began in earnest in the early 1840s, when **Pre-Raphaelite** artists such as Edward Burne-Jones, Dante Gabriel Rossetti and the firm of William Morris were commissioned to make colourful new windows and decorative panels. Their work is best seen in the south aisle.

The fusion of different styles and ages is evident from outside, especially in the mismatched western towers. Inside, the nave is dominated by Jacob Epstein's overwhelming *Christ in Majesty*, a concrete parabola topped with a soaring Christ figure. At the west end of the north aisle, the **St Illtyd Chapel** features Rossetti's cloying triptych *The Seed of David*. In the south presbytery is a tenth-century Celtic cross, the only survivor of the pre-Norman cathedral.

Eating, drinking and nightlife

Cardiff's long-standing internationalism has paid handsome dividends in the range of **restaurants**, with the influence of Italian immigrants particularly evident in the number of cafés, bistros and trattorias. There are numerous places right in the centre, most notably in the "café quarter" along Mill Lane. Most other places are within easy walking distance; there are good hunting grounds in the cheaper quarters of Cathays and Roath, particularly the curry houses along Crwys, Albany and City roads, a stone's throw from the centre beyond the university. Cardiff's **pub** life has expanded exponentially over recent years, and there are some wonderful Edwardian palaces of etched, smoky glass and deep red wood, where you'll find Cardiff's very own Brains bitter.

Top-flight concert venues such as St David's Hall and the Cardiff International Arena have brought internationally acclaimed orchestras and **musical** performers to the city, although these sterile environments are no match for the sweatier gigs and traditional rock found in some of Cardiff's earthier pubs and clubs. The burgeoning Welsh rock scene, both English- and Welsh-language, breaks out regularly in the capital. Cardiff also has a modest **gay and lesbian scene**, centred on Charles Street, just off Queen Street; the best information source is South Wales Friend (Tues–Thurs 7.30–9.30pm; ☏029/2034 0101).

Cafés and restaurants

Blas ar Gymru 48 Crwys Rd, Cathays ☏029/2038 2132. Meaning "Taste of Wales", this is a comfortable restaurant with a highly imaginative, moderately priced menu made up of delicious traditional recipes from every corner of Wales. Leave room for the selection of Welsh cheeses. Closed Sun. Moderate to expensive.

Celtic Cauldron Castle Arcade. A friendly daytime café, dedicated to bringing a range of simple Welsh food – soups, stews, laver bread, cakes – to an appreciative public. Inexpensive.

Cibo 83 Pontcanna St, off Cathedral Rd ☏029/2223 2226. A slice of Italy in Cardiff: a small, inexpensive and welcoming trattoria serving ciabatta sandwiches and simple, well-cooked food. No credit cards. Moderate.

Giovanni's 38 The Hayes ☏029/2022 0077. One of Cardiff's best Italian restaurants, lively and enormously friendly, with a wide menu of old favourites and some unusual house specialities. Closed Sun. Moderate.

Greenhouse 38 Woodville Rd, Cathays ☏029/2023 5731. Licensed vegetarian restaurant with a modern take on traditional dishes. Closed Sun & Mon. Moderate.

Jags 4 Church St. Eat-in and take-out sandwich bar serving stuffed baguettes and good coffee. Inexpensive.

Le Gallois 8 Romily Crescent, Canton ☏029/2034 1264. Fantastic modern French cuisine in a cheerful environment. Moderate.

Noble House 9–10 St David's House, Wood St ☏029/2038 8430. Excellent Chinese restaurant, with a good range of Peking and Szechuan dishes. Moderate.

Norwegian Church Café Harbour Drive. Cosy spot for Norwegian open sandwiches, salads, some scrumptious cakes and filter coffee. Inexpensive.

Porto's 40 St Mary's St ☏029/2022 0060. Authentic restaurant in a dark, wood-beamed room serving massive portions of Portuguese and Madeiran favourites, including endless variations on dried cod. Moderate.

Woods Brasserie Stuart St, Cardiff Bay ☏029/2049 2400. One of Cardiff's most stylish establishments, where you'll definitely need to book in advance to sample the excellent Modern British cuisine. Moderate (lunch); expensive (evening).

Bars, pubs and clubs

Caio Arms Cathedral Road. Great pub, airy and comfortable. Popular with Welsh speakers.

Chapter Market Rd, Canton ☏029/2030 4400, ⓦwww.chapter.org. A smart and popular bar in this arts complex with a good choice of real ales, guest beers and whiskies.

Club Metropolitan Bakers Row ☏029/2037 1549. Slightly scruffy venue for some of the best indie dance nights in town, with plenty of students drawn by the drink specials.

Clwb Ifor Bach Womanby St ☏029/2023 2199. A sweaty and enjoyable live-music and DJ club with nightly gigs and sessions, many featuring Welsh-language bands.

Exit Bar 48 Charles St. Frantic, noisy disco-bar, popular among the gay community for pre-club drinks before heading to *Club X*, opposite. Open until midnight.

Sam's Bar 63 St Mary St ☏029/2034 5189. Lively club-bar, with everything from live heavy metal through comedy and drag shows to house DJs. A good place to check the pulse of the Mill Lane "café quarter".

Theatre, cinema and classical music

Cardiff International Arena Bute Terrace ☏029/2022 4488. For mega concerts, both rock and classical.

Chapter Arts Centre Market Rd, Canton ☏029/2030 4400, ⓦwww.chapter.org. Multi-use arts complex that hosts British and touring theatre and dance companies, as well as Cardiff's main art-house cinema.

New Theatre Park Place ☏029/2087 8889, ⓦwww.newtheatrecardiff.co.uk. Splendid Edwardian city-centre theatre that plays host to big London shows. Currently the home of the Welsh National Opera.

The Point West Bute St, Cardiff Bay ☏029/2049 9979, ⓦwww.thepointcardiffbay.com. Experimental performance space in an old church.

Sherman Theatre Senghenydd Rd, Cathays ☏029/2064 6900, ⓦwww.shermantheatre.co.uk. An excellent, two-auditorium repertory theatre hosting a mixed bag of classic Welsh-language pieces (both original and translated), stand-up comedy, children's entertainment, drama classics, music and dance.

St David's Hall The Hayes ☏029/2087 8444, ⓦwww.stdavidshallcardiff.co.uk. Part of the massive St David's shopping centre, this large and glamorous venue is possibly the most architecturally exciting building in town. Home to visiting orchestras and musicians from jazz to opera, it's frequently used by the excellent BBC Welsh Symphony Orchestra and Chorus.

Listings

Airport Cardiff International Airport (☎01446/711111, ⓦwww.cial.co.uk) is at Rhoose, ten miles southwest of the city centre in the Vale of Glamorgan. Hourly buses operate into the city.

Banks and exchange All major banks have branches along High Street or Queen Street. American Express is at 3 Queen St (Mon–Fri 9am–5.30pm, Sat 9am–5pm; ☎029/2064 9305), Thomas Cook at 16 Queen St (Mon–Sat 9am–5.30pm, July & Aug also Sun noon–6pm; ☎029/2042 2500).

Bike rental Waterfront Bike Hire (☎029/2048 4110) rent decent machines from their stand in Britannia Park, right by the Cardiff Bay Visitor Centre.

Bus information Traveline (☎0870/608 2608, ⓦwww.traveline.org.uk) has details of Cardiff Bus and National Express services.

Health University of Wales Hospital, Heath ☎029/2074 7747. For emergency dental work: Riverside Health Centre, Wellington St, Canton ☎029/2037 1221.

Laundries Drift Inn, 104 Salisbury Rd, Cathays Park; GP, 244 Cowbridge Rd, Canton; Launderama 60 Lower Cathedral Rd.

Left luggage At Central Station (Mon–Sat 9.30am–5.30pm, Sun noon–5.30pm; £5 per day).

Pharmacy Boots, 5 Wood St (Mon–Sat 8am–8pm Sun 6–7pm; ☎029/2023 4043).

Police Central Police Station, King Edward VII Ave, Cathays Park ☎029/2022 2111.

Post office The Hayes (Mon–Fri 9am–5.30pm, Sa 9am–12.30pm; ☎029/2022 7363).

Around Cardiff

On the edge of the northern Cardiff suburbs, the thirteenth-century fairy-tal castle of **Castell Coch** stands on a hillside in the woods, while just furthe north is the massive **Caerphilly Castle**. West of the city, the massively popular **Museum of Welsh Life**, in the grounds of the rambling Elizabethan country house of **St Fagans Castle**, tells the country's history through a collection of buildings salvaged from all over Wales.

Castell Coch

Four miles north of Llandaff, the turreted **Castell Coch** (June–Sept dail 9.30am–6pm; April, May & Oct daily 9.30am–5pm; Nov–March Mon–Sa 9.30am–4pm, Sun 11am–4pm; £3; CADW) was once a ruined thirteenth-century fortress. Like Cardiff Castle, it was rebuilt and transformed into a fantasy structure in the late 1870s by William Burges for the third marquess of Bute With its working portcullis and drawbridge, Castell Coch is the ultimate wealthy man's medieval fantasy, isolated on its almost alpine hillside, yet only few hundred yards from the motorway and Cardiff suburbs. There are man similarities with Cardiff Castle, notably the outrageously lavish decor, culled from religious and moral fables, which dazzles in each room. **Bus #136** from Central Station turns round at the castle gates, while bus #26 drops in Tongwynlais village, ten minutes' walk away.

Caerphilly

Caerphilly (Caerffili), seven miles north of Cardiff, is a flattened and colour less town, notable mainly for its **castle** (June–Sept daily 9.30am–6pm; April May & Oct daily 9.30am–5pm; Nov–March Mon–Sat 9.30am–4pm, Su 11am–4pm; £3; CADW), the first in Britain built concentrically, with an inne system of defences overlooking the outer ring. Looming out of its vast sur rounding moat, the medieval fortress with its cock-eyed tower occupies ove thirty acres, presenting an awesome promise not entirely fulfilled inside. The castle was begun in 1268 by Gilbert de Clare as a defence against Llywelyn the Last. Two years later, Llywelyn largely destroyed the castle. It was swiftly rebuilt, but for the next few hundred years Caerphilly was little more than a decaying toy, given at whim by kings to their favourites. By the turn of the twentieth century, it was in a sorry state, sitting amidst a growing industrial town that saw fit to build in the then-dry moat and castle precincts. Houses and shops were demolished in order to allow the moat to be reflooded in 1958.

You enter the castle through the much-restored **gatehouse**, where there's an exhibition on the castle's history. A platform behind the barbican wall exhibits medieval war and siege engines, overlooked on the left by the southeastern tower, out-leaning its rival in Pisa. Of the rest of the castle, the most interesting section is the massive eastern gatehouse, which includes an impressive upper hall and oratory and, to its left, the wholly restored and re-roofed **Great Hall**.

Caerphilly is also known for its crumbly white **cheese**, made in dairies around the town, and available in a ploughman's lunch at the *Courthouse* pub, on Cardiff Road, right by the castle and a five minute stroll from the **bus** and **train** stations.

The Museum of Welsh Life and St Fagans Castle

St Fagans (Sain Ffagan), four miles west of Cardiff city centre, has a rural feel that is only partially disturbed by the bus-loads of tourists that roll in regularly to visit the excellent **Museum of Welsh Life** (daily 10am–5pm; free; ⓦwww.nmgw.ac.uk), built around St Fagans Castle, a country house erected in 1580 and furnished in early nineteenth-century style. The most impressive part of the museum is the fifty-acre outdoor collection of buildings from all corners of Wales that have been carefully dismantled and rebuilt on this site since the museum's inception in 1946. There are particular highlights, including the diminutive, whitewashed Pen-Rhiw Chapel, built in Dyfed in 1777; the pristine and evocative St Mary's Board School, built in Lampeter in Victorian times; and the stern mini-fortress of a tollhouse that once guarded the southern approach to Aberystwyth, from 1772. The superb Rhyd-y-car **ironworkers' cottages**, from Merthyr Tydfil, were originally built in around 1800. Each of the six houses, with its accompanying strip of garden, has been furnished in the style of a different period, stretching from 1805 to 1985. **Buses** #32 (hourly) and #C1 (variable times) run to the museum from Cardiff Central station.

Swansea and Gower

Dylan Thomas called **SWANSEA** (Abertawe) – his birthplace – an "ugly, lovely town", an epithet which poet Paul Durcan updated to "pretty, shitty city". Both ring true. Large, sprawling and boisterous, it is the second city of Wales, with around 200,000 people, and has great aspirations to be the first; it's certainly far more Welsh than Cardiff. The city centre was massively rebuilt after devastating bomb attacks in World War II, and a jumble of tower blocks now dot the horizon. But closer inspection reveals Swansea's multifarious charms: some intact old corners of the city centre, the spacious and graceful suburb of Uplands, a wide **seafront** overlooking Swansea Bay and a bold marina development around the old docks, while spread throughout are some of the best-funded **museums** in Wales. Situated on the edge of the **Gower peninsula**, which holds some of the country's most popular and inspirational

△ Gower Peninsula

coastal and rural scenery, Swansea makes a logical base: transport out into the surrounding areas is good, and beds tend to be less expensive in the city than in the more picturesque parts of Gower.

The city's Welsh name, Abertawe, means the settlement at the mouth of the River Tawe, a grimy ditch that is slowly being teased back to life after centuries of use as a sewer for Swansea's metal trades. The first reliable mention of Swansea dates from 1099, when a Norman castle was built here as an outpost of William the Conqueror's empire. A small settlement grew near the coalfields and the sea, developing into a mining and shipbuilding centre that, by 1700, was the largest coal port in Wales. Copper smelting became the area's dominant industry in the eighteenth century, soon attracting other metal trades to pack out the lower Tawe Valley, making it one of the world's most prolific metal-bashing centres. Over the years, the valley became a five-mile stretch of rusting, stagnant land and water that has only recently begun to be re-landscaped.

Arrival, information and accommodation

Swansea is the main interchange station for trains out to the west of Wales, and for the slow line across to Shrewsbury in England. The **train station** is at the top end of the High Street, a ten-minute hike from the **bus station**, which lies adjacent to the Quadrant Shopping Centre. Nearby, on Plymouth Street, is the **tourist office** (Mon–Sat 9.30am–5.30pm, May–Sept also Sun 10am–4pm; ☎01792/468321). Most of the sights are within walking distance of each other; popular suburbs, such as Uplands and Sketty, near the university, are a bracing thirty-minute walk from the centre, though buses get you there easily. **Ferries** to Cork in Ireland leave roughly once a day from the docks, around a mile east of the town centre (☎01792/456116, ⓦwww.swansea-cork.ie).

There are dozens of dirt-cheap **hotels** and **B&Bs** stretched out along the seafront Oystermouth Road, whose trade is largely pitched at those catching the Swansea–Cork ferry. Better places congregate in leafy Uplands, a thirty-minute walk from town. There are no campsites or hostels in the city itself, although nearby places in Gower are easily reached.

Hotels and guest houses

Crescent 132 Eaton Crescent, Uplands ☎01792/466814, ⓦwww.crescentguesthouse .co.uk. Large, pleasant Edwardian guest house. All rooms have en-suite showers, and half have superb views over the city and the bay. ❸

Harlton 89 King Edward Rd, Brynmill ☎01792/466938, ⓦwww.harltonguesthouse .co.uk. Budget guest house that is a little yellow around the edges but perfectly adequate – and very inexpensive. ❶

Morgans Somerset Place ☎01792/484848, ⓦwww.morganshotel.co.uk. A well-run, five-star hotel occupying a historic building bang in the heart of town. Rooms feature fresh, modern styling, with nice touches like plasma screens and double showers, and there's a sophisticated restaurant and bar downstairs. ❻

Oyster 262 Oystermouth Rd ☎01792/654345. Small and friendly hotel with some en-suite rooms and serving great local cuisine. ❶

St James 76b Walter Rd, Uplands ☎01792/649984. Small, welcoming hotel in an airy Victorian house. ❷

Uplands Court 134 Eaton Crescent, Uplands ☎01792/473046. Appealing guest house in a gracious Victorian villa situated in a pleasant area. ❶

White House 4 Nyanza Terrace, Uplands ☎01792/473856, ⓦwww.thewhitehousehotel .co.uk. Excellent-value and extremely well-kept guest house: all the well-appointed rooms have satellite TV and some have en-suite facilities. Great breakfasts, and good three-course evening meals for £10. Also email and Internet access. ❷

Windsor Lodge Mount Pleasant ☎01792/642158, ⓦwww.windsor-lodge.co.uk. A two-century-old house like a country hotel in the city, with nicely decorated en-suite rooms and elegant but comfortable lounges. British and French cuisine served in the evenings. Cheaper rates at the weekend. ❹

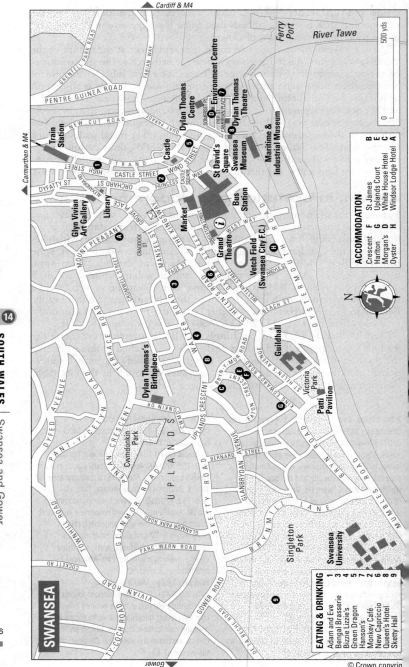

SWANSEA

▲ Cardiff & M4

River Tawe

Ferry Port

500 yds

0

Gower ▼

© Crown copyrig

PENTRE GUINEA ROAD

GRENFELL PARK ROAD

FABIAN WAY

QUAY PARADE

NEW CUT ROAD

▲ Carmarthen & M4

Train Station

HIGH STREET

DYFATTY ST

ALEXANDRA RD

ORCHARD ST

CASTLE STREET

CASTLE STREET

STRAND

WIND ST

PRINCESS

CASTLE SQUARE WAY

Castle

Dylan Thomas Centre

SOMERSET PL

PIER ST

CAMBRIAN PLACE

Environment Centre

Dylan Thomas Theatre

St David's Square

Swansea Museum

Maritime & Industrial Museum

Glyn Vivian Art Gallery

Library

GROVE PLACE

MOUNT PLEASANT

CROMWELL STREET

CRADDOCK ST

MANSEL ST

PAGE ST

THE KINGSWAY

ST HELEN'S ROAD

SINGLETON STREET

Market

Grand Theatre

Bus Station

i

Vetch Field (Swansea City F.C.)

WEST WAY

ORCHARD ST

WALTER ROAD

ST HELEN'S ROAD

WESTERN STREET

ARGYLE ST

BEACH ST

OYSTERMOUTH ROAD

Guildhall

Dylan Thomas's Birthplace

UPLANDS CRESCENT

CWMDONKIN DR

BRYN-Y-MOR ROAD

KING EDWARDS ROAD

ST HELEN'S AVENUE

EATON CRES

Victoria Park

Patti Pavilion

TERRACE ROAD

ENLAN CRESCENT

CWMDONKIN ROAD

Cwmdonkin Park

DYFED AVENUE

PANT-Y-CELYN ROAD

GLANMOR ROAD

TOWNHILL ROAD

GLANMOR PARK ROAD

PARC WERN ROAD

UPLANDS

SKETTY ROAD

UPLANDS CRESCENT

BERNARD STREET

GLANBRYDAN AVENUE

BRYNMILL LANE

BRYN ROAD

MUMBLES ROAD

Singleton Park

Swansea University

COCKETT RD

VIVIAN ROAD

GOWER ROAD

DE-LA-BECHE ROAD

N

ACCOMMODATION

Crescent	F
Harlton	G
Morgan's	D
Oyster	H
St James	E
Uplands Court	C
White House Hotel	B
Windsor Lodge Hotel	A

EATING & DRINKING

Adam and Eve	1
Bengal Brasserie	3
Bizzie Lizzie's	4
Green Dragon	5
Hanson's	7
Monkey Café	2
New Capriccio	6
Queen's Hotel	8
Sketty Hall	9

The City

Swansea's train station faces out onto the morose High Street, which heads south past the remains of the Norman **castle**, which enjoys an improved setting against the revamped Castle Square. Alexandra Road forks right off the High Street immediately south of the train station, leading down to the **Glynn Vivian Art Gallery** (Tues–Sun 10am–5pm; free; Ⓦwww.swansea.gov.uk /glynnvivian), a delightful Edwardian showcase of inspiring Welsh art including the huge, frantic canvases of Ceri Richards, Wales' most respected twentieth-century painter, and works by Gwen John and her brother, Augustus, whose mesmerizing portrait of Caitlin Thomas, Dylan's wife, is a real highlight. The gallery also houses a large collection of fine porcelain – of which Swansea was a noted centre in the early nineteenth century – together with contemporary works from Nantgarw, near Cardiff.

The main shopping streets lie to the south, notably underneath the Quadrant Centre where the curving-roofed **market** makes a lively sight, with traditional and long-standing stalls selling local delicacies such as laver bread (a delicious savoury made from seaweed), as well as cockles trawled from the nearby Loughor estuary, typical Welsh cakes, fish and cheeses. If you're a Dylan Thomas fan, or just keen on books, it's worth popping down Wind Street to Salubrious Passage for the **Dylan Thomas Bookshop**, filled to the rafters with material on the poet. Wind Street has become something of a magnet for bars and restaurants recently, and it's fast become one of the city's more pleasant places to hang out and watch the world drift by.

Hourly buses leave the Quadrant depot for **Uplands**, a twenty- to thirty-minute walk from the city centre. North of the main road, leafy avenues rise up the slopes past the sharp terraces of **Cwmdonkin Park**, at the centre of which is a memorial to Dylan Thomas inscribed with lines from *Fern Hill*, one of his best-known poems. On the eastern side of the park is Cwmdonkin Drive, a sharply rising set of solid Victorian semis, notable only for the blue plaque on no. 5, birthplace of the poet in 1914.

The spit of land between Oystermouth Road, the sea and the Tawe estuary has been christened the **Maritime Quarter** – tourist-board-speak for the old docks – built around a vast marina surrounded by legions of modern flats. The city's old South Dock, now cleaned and spruced up, features the enticingly old-fashioned **Swansea Museum** (Tues–Sun 10am–5pm; free). A small grid of nineteenth-century streets around the museum has been thoughtfully cleaned up and now houses some enjoyable cafés, pubs and restaurants.

Behind the museum, in Somerset Place, is the airy **Dylan Thomas Centre**, the national literature centre of Wales (Tues–Sun 10am–4.30pm; free), complete with theatre space, book and craft shops, a great café, and two galleries. One of these is devoted to Dylan Thomas, and includes a mock-up of the shed in which he wrote, where you can see a fascinating video on his life and work. From here, Burrows Place leads down to the **marina**, where the new National Waterfront Museum is due to open in 2005.

Eating, drinking and nightlife

Swansea's metamorphosis from a working-class, industrial city into a would-be tourist centre is well demonstrated in the **pubs**, **restaurants** and **entertainment** venues of the city. For nightlife, the city is well placed, with most passing theatre, opera and music of all sorts being obliged to make a stop here. The BBC Welsh Symphony Orchestra appears at the Brangwyn Hall in the Art

Deco Civic Centre. Thomas's classics get a regular airing at the Dylan Thomas Theatre, by the marina, while the Taliesin Arts Centre, in the university, is the city's more offbeat venue.

Cafés and restaurants

Bengal Brasserie 47 Walter Rd ☎01792/643747. Best of the many Indian restaurants in Swansea, well worth the ten-minute hike from the city centre. Moderate.

Bizzie Lizzie's 55 Walter Rd ☎01792/473379. Relaxed and informal cellar-bar bistro, with a good range of Welsh, international and vegetarian dishes. Reservations recommended. Inexpensive to moderate.

Hanson's Pilot House Wharf ☎01792/466200. Low-key restaurant on the far side of the marina, at the end of Bathurst Street, serving tasty and well-presented British and Mediterranean dishes. Closed Sun eve. Moderate.

Monkey Café 13 Castle St, ⓦwww.monkeycafe.co.uk. Groovy, mosaic-floored café with a relaxed atmosphere, great sandwiches and cakes, and a selection of Mexican and Italian dishes, including many vegetarian options. Inexpensive.

New Capriccio 89 St Helen's Rd ☎01792/648804. Popular Italian restaurant, with a bargain lunch menu. Closed Mon & Sun eve. Inexpensive.

Queen's Hotel Gloucester Place, near the marina. Large old seafaring hotel and pub, with good ales, snack lunches and Sunday roasts. Inexpensive.

Sketty Hall Singleton Park ☎01792/284011. Catering academy in beautiful surroundings, where you can sample the excellent student cuisine for bargain prices. Booking essential. Inexpensive.

Pubs and clubs

Adam and Eve 205 High St. Traditional pub, with a great atmosphere and varied clientele. Well known for the excellence of its beer.

Duke of York Princess Way. Home of *Ellington's* club (small cover charge), Swansea's best venue for jazz and blues music, which hosts nightly gigs.

Escape Club Northampton Lane, off Kingsway ☎01792/652854. Enormous and glitzy mainstream dance club.

Green Dragon Green Dragon Lane, off Wind St ☎01792/641437. Decent pub in the café quarter of town, good for Sunday lunch carvery.

Po Na Na 22 Wind St. Thriving chain club with Moroccan "souk" decor, playing mostly garage and hip-hop. Small cover charge on Sat & DJ nights.

Gower

A fifteen-mile-long peninsula of undulating limestone, **Gower** (Gŵyr) points down into the Bristol Channel to the west of Swansea. The area is fringed by sweeping yellow bays and precipitous cliffs, with caves and blowholes to the south, and wide, flat marshes and cockle beds to the north. Bracken heaths dotted with prehistoric remains and tiny villages lie between, and there are numerous castle ruins and curious churches to be found. Out of season, the winding lanes afford wonderful opportunities for exploration, but in the height of summer – July and August especially – they are congested with caravans shuffling between one overpriced car park and the next. Buses from Swansea serve the whole peninsula, with frequent services to Mumbles, Port Eynon and even out to Rhossili.

Gower can be said to start in Swansea's western suburbs, along the coast of Swansea Bay that curves round to a point at the pleasantly old-fashioned resort of **Mumbles**. It finishes with **Rhossili Bay**, a spectacular four-mile yawn of sand backed by the village of Rhossili and occupying the entire western end of the peninsula. The southern coast is punctuated by the village of **PORT EYNON**, home to an excellent YHA **hostel** (☎0870/770 5998, ⓔporteynon@yha.org.uk; April–Oct; dorms £10.25; ❶) and a beautiful beach. West of Port Eynon, the coast becomes a wild, frilly series of inlets and cliffs, topped by a five-mile path that stretches all the way to the peninsula's glorious westernmost point, **Worms Head**. The northern coast merges into the tidal flats of the estuary.

Mumbles and Oystermouth

At the far westernmost end of Swansea Bay, **Mumbles** (Mwmbwls) derives its name from the French *mamelles*, or breasts, a reference to the twin islets off the end of Mumbles Head, and is now used as the name for all of the loose sprawl around **OYSTERMOUTH** (Ystumllwynarth). Here, the seafront is an unbroken curve of budget hotels, breezy pubs and cafés, leading down to the refurbished pier and the rocky plug of Mumbles Head. Around the headland, reached either by the longer, barren coast road or by a short walk over the hill, is the district of **Langland Bay**, whose sandy beach is fairly popular with surfers. The small **tourist office** (April–Oct Mon–Sat 9.30am–5.30pm, June–Aug also Sun same hours; ☏01792/361302) is in Oystermouth Square, near the hilltop ruins of **Oystermouth Castle** (April–Sept daily 11am–5.30pm; £1.20). Founded as a Norman watchtower, the castle was strengthened to withstand attacks by the Welsh before being converted for more amenable residential purposes during the fourteenth century. Today you can see the remains of a late thirteenth-century keep next to a more ornate three-storey ruin incorporating an impressive banqueting hall and state rooms.

Mumbles is a lively and enjoyable base for the southern Gower coast, with a good clutch of typically tacky seaside entertainment on offer. **Accommodation** is plentiful: try *Henfaes Guesthouse*, 4 Rotherslade Rd (☏01792/366003; ❶); the Victorian shorefront *Tides Reach*, 388 Mumbles Rd (☏01792/404877; ❸); the superb *Alexandra House*, 366 Mumbles Rd (☏01792/406406; ❸); or the sumptuous *Osborne Hotel* (☏01792/366274; ❻), high on a cliff top on Rotherslade Road in Langland Bay. There are several good **places to eat** including the inexpensive *Coffee Denn*, 34 Newton Rd, which is good for light lunches and imaginative ice cream sundaes. *Seafront 604*, 604 Mumbles Rd, does moderately priced light meals, while the expensive, fairly formal *Patricks*, 636 Mumbles Rd (☏01792/360199; closed Sun eve), serves an eclectic range of wonderful modern dishes. *Verdi's*, overlooking the sea at Knab Rock near the pier, is a Mumbles institution for its lively Welsh–Italian atmosphere and superb pizzas and ice creams. The scores of pubs along the seafront constitute the **Mumbles Mile**, one of Wales's most notorious pub crawls. The ones to linger in are the *Antelope*, the *Oystercatcher* and the *White Rose*.

Rhossili and Worms Head

The village of **RHOSSILI** (Rhosili), at the western end of Gower, is a centre for walkers and beach loungers alike. Dylan Thomas described the terrain to the west of the village as "rubbery, gull-limed grass, the sheep-pilled stones, the pieces of bones and feathers", and you can tread in his footsteps to **Worms Head**, an isolated string of rocks, accessible for only five hours, at low tide. At the head of the road, near the village, is a well-stocked National Trust **information centre** (April–Oct daily 10.30am–5.30pm; Jan–March Sat & Sun 11am–4pm; Nov & Dec Wed–Sun 11am–4pm; ☏01792/390707). They post the tide times outside for those heading for Worms Head, and hold details of local companies renting surfing and hang-gliding equipment.

Below the village, a great curve of white sand stretches away into the distance, a dazzling coastline vast enough to absorb the crowds, especially if you are prepared to head north towards **Burry Holms**, an islet that is cut off at high tide. The northern end of the beach can also be reached along the small lane that runs from Reynoldston, in the middle of the peninsula, to **LLANGENNITH**, on the other side of the towering, 633-foot **Rhossili Down**. In the village, PJ's Surfshop (☏01792/386669, ⓦwww.pjsurfshop.co.uk) rents **surfboards** and boogie boards; a mile away at the *Hillend* campsite (see below) is another Surf School (℡01792/386426), which runs half-day (£20) and full-day (£30) **surfing courses**.

In Rhossili village, there are some great **B&Bs**, including the very friendly *Meadow View*, a mile from the beach (℡01792/390518; ❶), with small but nicely furnished rooms. **Campsites** can be found at *Pitton Cross Park* (℡01792/390593, ⓦ www.pittoncross.co.uk), close to *Meadow View*, at the foot of the northern slopes of Rhossili Down; and at *Hillend* (℡01792/386204), at the end of the southern lane from Llangennith, behind the dunes that bump down to the glorious beach. There's a rather dingy **restaurant** and bar in Rhossili, but you're better off at the *King Arthur*, in nearby Reynoldston, which serves hearty meals and hosts live folk and rock music nights. If you're feeling particularly flush, exquisite food and accommodation can be found at *Fairyhill* (℡01792/390139, ⓦ www.fairyhill.net; ❼), just north of Reynoldston, which hikes its prices at the weekend.

Southern Carmarthenshire

Frequently overlooked in the stampede towards the resorts of Pembrokeshire, **southern Carmarthenshire** is a quiet part of the world, with few of the problems of mass tourism suffered by more popular parts of Wales. **Kidwelly**, with its dramatically sited castle, is the only reason to stop before **Carmarthen**, the unquestioned capital of its region but one which fails to live up to the promise of its status. There's little of great interest in town, but it does make a good enough base for forays up the Tywi Valley (see p.803). On the western side of the Taf estuary, the village of **Laugharne** has become a place of pilgrimage for Dylan Thomas devotees.

Kidwelly

The sleepy little town of **KIDWELLY** (Cydweli) is dominated by its imposing **castle** (June–Sept daily 9.30am–6pm; April, May & Oct daily 9.30am–5pm; Nov–March Mon–Sat 9.30am–4pm, Sun 11am–4pm; £2.50; CADW). Established around 1106 by the bishop of Salisbury as a satellite of Sherborne Abbey in Dorset, the castle is situated at a strategic point overlooking the River Gwendraeth and vast tracts of coast. On entering through the massive fourteenth-century gatehouse, you can still see portcullis slats and murder holes, through which noxious substances could be tipped onto unwelcome visitors. The gatehouse forms the centrepiece of the impressively intact outer ward walls, which can be climbed for some great views over the grassy courtyard and rectangular inner ward to the river. This is the oldest surviving part of the castle, dating from around 1275. The upper storeys were added in the fourteenth century by the nephew of Edward I. On the northwest edge of the town is the small-scale **Industrial Museum**, on Priory Street (Easter–Sept Mon–Fri 10am–5pm, Sat & Sun 2–5pm; free), housed in an old tin-plate works. Many of the original features have been preserved, including the rolling mills where long lines of tin were rolled and spun into wafer-thin slices.

There's superb B&B **accommodation** at *Penlan Isaf Farm* (℡1554/890084, ⓔ penlan@talk21.com; ❷), on a dairy farm overlooking the town. You can **camp** at *Tanylan Farm* (℡01267/267306), which perches alongside the estuary west of Kidwelly. Good **food** and **drink** are available at the cosy *Boot &*

14

Shoe, 2 Castle St, or at the excellent *King's Arms* in the village of Llansaint, up in the hills a couple of miles west of town.

Carmarthen and around

CARMARTHEN (Caerfyrddin), the ancient capital of the region, is a solid, if hardly thrilling, sort of place. It remains the major town in west Wales where the native language is heard at all times, and was once – in the early eighteenth century – the largest town in the country. Founded as a Roman fort, it is now best known as the supposed birthplace of the wizard Merlin (Myrddin in Welsh gives the town its name). A good place to catch up on the town's past is the small **Heritage Centre** (Wed–Sat 11am–4pm; free), tucked away down on the Quay Side, by the river.

The most picturesque part of town lies spread out at the base of Edward I's uninspiring **castle** (a reworking of an earlier Norman fortress), around King Street and Nott Square, the main shopping hub. The town's handsome eighteenth-century **Guildhall** sits just off Nott Square, from the bottom of which Darkgate leads to Lammas Street, a wide Georgian thoroughfare flanked by coaching inns. From the top of Nott Square, King Street heads northeast towards the undistinguished **St Peter's Church** and the Victorian School of Art, which has now metamorphosed into **Oriel Myrddin** (Mon–Sat 10am–5pm; free), a craft centre and excellent gallery that acts as an imaginative showcase for local artists.

The severe grey Bishop's Palace at **Abergwili**, two miles east of Carmarthen, was the seat of the Bishop of St David's between 1542 and 1974, and now houses the **Carmarthenshire County Museum** (Mon–Sat 10am–4.30pm; free), a spirited amble through the history of the area. This surprisingly interesting exhibition covers the history of Welsh translations of the New Testament and Book of Common Prayer – both first translated here, in 1567. Local pottery, archeological finds, wooden dressers and a lively history of local castles are presented in well-annotated displays. The upstairs section examines a number of topics including geology, the local coracle industry and the origins of one of Wales' first *eisteddfodau* (Welsh cultural festivals), held in Carmarthen in 1450.

The **train station** lies over Carmarthen Bridge, on the south side of the river. All **buses** terminate at the bus station on Blue Street, just on the north side of the bridge, and many connect with trains. The town's **tourist office** is on Lammas Street, close to the Crimea Monument (Mon–Sat 10am–5pm; Oct–Easter closes 4.15pm; ℡01267/231557). For **bike rental**, go to Ar Dy Feic (On Yer Bike), over the river on Llangunnor Road (℡01267/221182). There's lots of **accommodation** in town, especially on Lammas Street, where you'll find the *Boar's Head* (℡01267/222789; ❷), one of the town's grandest old coaching inns, and the *Drovers Arms* (℡01267/237646; ❸). The best B&Bs are *Y Dderwen Fach*, 98 Priory St (℡01267/234193, ⓔannbowyer47@hotmail.com; ❶), and the *Old Priory* guest house, 20 Priory St (℡01267/237471; ❶), both out along the main road to Lampeter and Llandeilo. If you're looking for something a little more remote, don't pass up *Tŷ Mawr* (℡01267/202332, ⓦwww.tymawrhotel.co.uk; ❺), an oak-beamed country-house hotel in the entirely unspoilt village of **BRECHFA**, some twelve miles northeast of Carmarthen. You can find good snack **food** at the old-fashioned *Morris Tea Rooms*, almost opposite the Lyric Theatre in King Street, and at the vegetarian café in the Waverley Stores health-food shop, on 23 Lammas St. The best meals in town can be found at the wonderful *Quayside Brasserie*, on the Tywi quay (℡01267/223000; closed Sun).

Laugharne

The village of **LAUGHARNE** (Talacharn), on the western side of the Taf estuary, is a delightful spot, with its ragged castle looming over the reeds and tidal flats and narrow lanes snuggling in behind. Catch it in high season though and you're immediately aware that Laugharne is increasingly being taken over by the legend of the poet **Dylan Thomas**.

At the end of a narrow lane bumping along the estuary is the **Dylan Thomas Boathouse** (daily: Easter & May–Oct 10am–5.30pm; Nov–Easter 10.30am–3.30pm; £3; ⓦ www.dylanthomasboathouse.com), the simple home of the Thomas family from 1949 until Dylan's death in 1953. It's an enchanting museum, with views of the peaceful, ever-changing water and light of the estuary and its "heron-priested shore". Inside, a period wireless set in the intact living room regales you with the rich tones of the poet reading his own work, while contemporary newspaper reports of his demise show how he was, while alive, a fairly minor literary figure. Back along the narrow lane, you can peer into the blue garage where he wrote: curled photographs of literary heroes, a pen collection and numerous scrunched-up balls of paper on the cheap desk suggest quite effectively that he is about to return at any minute. Thomas is buried in the graveyard of the parish church in the village centre, his grave marked by a simple white cross.

Laugharne has numerous Thomas connections, and plays them with curiously disgruntled aplomb – none more so than the great alcoholic's old boozing hole, **Brown's Hotel** on the main street where, in the nicotine-crusted front bar, Thomas's cast-iron table still sits in a window alcove. At the bottom of the

Dylan Thomas

Dylan Thomas was the stereotypical Celt – fiery, verbose, richly talented and habitually drunk. Born in 1914 into a snugly middle-class family in Swansea's Uplands district, Dylan's first glimmers of literary greatness came when he was posted, as a young reporter, to the *South Wales Evening Post* in Swansea. Some of his most popular tales in the *Portrait of the Artist as a Young Dog* were inspired during this period.

Rejecting the coarse provincialism of Swansea and Welsh life, Thomas arrived in London as a broke twenty-year-old in 1934, weeks before the appearance of his first volume of poetry, which was published as the first prize in a *Sunday Referee* competition. Another volume followed shortly afterwards, cementing the engaging young Welshman's reputation in the British literary establishment. He married in 1937, and the newlyweds returned to Wales, settling in the hushed, provincial backwater of Laugharne. Short stories – crackling with rich and melancholy humour – tumbled out as swiftly as poems, further widening his base of admirers, though, like so many other writers, Thomas has only gained star status posthumously. Perhaps better than anyone, he writes in an identifiably Welsh, rhythmic wallow in the language.

Thomas, especially in public, liked to adopt the persona of what he perceived to be an archetypal stage Welshman: sonorous tones, loquacious, romantic and inclined towards a stiff tipple. This role was particularly popular in the United States, where he journeyed on lucrative lecture tours. It was on one of these that he died, in 1953, poisoned by a massive whisky overdose. Just one month earlier, he had put the finishing touches to what many regard as his masterpiece: *Under Milk Wood*, a "play for voices". Describing the dreams, thoughts and lives of a straggling Welsh seaside community called Llareggub – misspelt Llaregyb by the po-faced BBC, who couldn't sanction the usage of the expression "bugger all" backwards, it is based loosely on Laugharne, New Quay in Cardiganshire and a vast dose of Thomas's own imagination.

main street, the gloomy hulk of **Laugharne Castle** (Easter–Sept 10am–5pm; £2.50; CADW) broods over the estuary. Two of the early medieval towers survive, although most of the ruins are those of the Tudor mansion built over the original for Sir John Perrot. The views from the domed roof over the tight, huddled little town are sublime.

Laugharne has recently upped its hitherto meagre selection of tourist **accommodation**. *Castle House*, on Market Lane in the village centre (T01994/427616, Wwww.laugharne.co.uk; ❸), has large en-suite rooms and gorgeous estuary views from some rooms; while *Swan Cottage*, 20 Gosport St (T01994/427409; ❷), is very welcoming. A little out of town, you can do no better than the delightful *Brunant Farm* B&B (T01994/240421; ❷), high on the hills two miles southeast of Whitland. The nearest **campsite** is *Ants Hill Camping Park*, just north of Laugharne (T01994/427293). For **eating**, try the moderately priced *Stable Door* (closed Mon & Tues), near the central town hall, or the *Under Milk Wood Inn*, on the square. If your budget's a little more generous, treat yourself at *The Cors* (T01994/427219; Thurs–Sat; ❹) on Newbridge Road, which serves wonderful food in a genteel country-house atmosphere, and also has rooms.

The Tywi Valley

The **River Tywi** curves and darts its way east from Carmarthen through some of the most magical scenery in south Wales. The thirty-mile trip to Llandovery is punctuated by gentle, impossibly green hills topped with ruined castles, notably the wonderful **Carreg Cennen**. It's not hard to see why the Merlin legend has taken such a hold in these parts – the landscape does seem infused with a kind of eerie splendour. Along the way, a couple of budding gardens have sprung up in the last couple of years: one completely new in the form of the **National Botanic Garden of Wales**, the other a faithful reconstruction of linked walled gardens around the long-abandoned house of **Aberglasney**. Further upstream, the market town of **Llandovery** makes a good base for visiting the Roman gold mine at **Dolaucothi**.

The National Botanic Garden and around

The **National Botanic Garden of Wales**, nine miles west of Carmarthen (daily 10am–6pm; Oct–Easter closes 4.30pm; £6.95; Wwww.gardenofwales .org.uk) is a fine attraction and has huge potential, but has been under severe financial pressure. At the time of writing funding had been withdrawn and the garden's future was uncertain; you should phone ahead or check the website before making a journey out here. Buses #165 and #166 run every two hours from Carmarthen train station to the garden, where, at the entrance, you'll find a fully functioning **tourist office** (same hours; T01558/669084).

From the entrance, you head along the central broadwalk, past lakes, sculpture and geological outcrops from all over Wales. On the other side of the broadwalk, the double-walled garden is being teased back to life, while on the estate's outer edges are re-creations of moorland, spring wood, prairie and native Welsh habitats.

At the top of the hill is the garden's most audacious feature: the vast oval **glasshouse** designed by Norman Foster, a truly stunning piece of architecture that justifies a visit on its own. Inside are plants from regions with a Mediterranean climate: the Cape region of South Africa, southwestern

Australia, Chile, California and the Mediterranean itself. Near the glasshouse lie the remains of **Middleton Hall**, whose old estate forms the centrepiece of the gardens. A nearby group of buildings house the restaurant, an excellent exhibition about the Welsh herbalists known as the Physicians of Myddfai and the new Theatre Botanica, all focused around **Millennium Square**, the venue for open-air concerts and performances. The entire garden has been designed around principles of sustainability: rainwater is caught and used for irrigation; the glasshouses are heated by burning wood coppiced on the grounds; and human waste is transformed into essentially pure water by means of a series of reed beds. The theme runs through to a large section of the surrounding land which is being turned over to organic farming using Welsh breeds of cattle and sheep – which eventually end up on a plate in the visitors' restaurant.

Aberglasney

A complementary and much older garden is open a few miles to the east, around the dilapidated stately home of **Aberglasney** (April–Oct daily 10am–6pm; Nov–March 10.30am–4pm; £5; Ⓦ www.aberglasney.org), half a mile south of the A40 near Broad Oak. There's little to see in the stabilized shell of the house itself, but archeological work has pretty much peeled back half a century of neglect to reveal a set of interlinking walled gardens mostly constructed between the sixteenth and eighteenth centuries. The basic framework – the walls, ponds and outline of the beds – is largely intact, but detailed digging continues to uncover more about the site, and extensive restoration is under way in the kitchen garden and secular cloister garden – thought to be the only one in Britain. A walkway leads around the top of the cloister, giving access to a set of six Victorian aviaries from where there are great views over the Jacobean pool garden. The highlight of the garden, however, is the **yew tunnel**, planted around three hundred years ago and trained over to root on the far side.

Llandeilo and around

Fifteen miles east of Carmarthen, the main street – Rhosmaen Street – of the handsome small market town of **LLANDEILO** climbs up from the Tywi bridge. Although there's little in the way of actual sights in the town, Llandeilo is brilliantly situated in a bowl of hills, a quiet, rustic place whose few streets cluster around the main thoroughfare. Behind the main street are the **tourist office** (Easter–Oct Mon–Sat 9am–4pm; Nov–Easter Mon–Fri 9am–5pm; ⓣ01558/824226) in the principal car park and, a couple of blocks to the north, the **train station**. **Accommodation** in town includes the very decent *Glynceirch* B&B (ⓣ01558/823378; ❶), near the station at the northern end of Rhosmaen Street, or, further down the same street into the town centre, the relatively plush *Cawdor Arms* (ⓣ01558/823500, Ⓦ www.cawdorarms.com; ❸), which serves expensive but beautifully cooked evening meals. *Y Capel Bach* bistro, a couple of doors down, serves tasty, moderately priced **meals**, and there is good drinking to be had across the road at the *Castle Hotel*.

A mile west of Llandeilo is the gorgeous parkland of **Plas Dinefwr**, site also of two splendid castles. On a wooded bluff above the Tywi sits the tumbledown shell of **Dinefwr Old Castle** which became ill-suited to the needs of the landowning Rhys family, who aspired to something a little more luxurious. The "new" castle, now named **Newton House** (April–Oct Mon & Thurs–Sun 11am–5pm; £3.30, park only £2.30; NT), was built in 1523, and given a limestone facade in the 1860s.

Carreg Cennen

Isolated in rural hinterland, four miles southeast of Llandeilo, is one of the most magnificently sited castles in the whole of Wales, **Carreg Cennen Castle** (daily: April–Oct 9.30am–7.30pm; Nov–March 9.30am–dusk; £3; CADW), just beyond the tiny hamlet of Trap. Sir Urien, one of King Arthur's knights, is said to have built his fortress on the fearsome rocky outcrop, although the first known construction dates from 1248. Carreg Cennen fell to the English in 1277, during Edward I's initial invasion of Wales, and was finally abandoned after being partially destroyed in 1462 by the earl of Pembroke, who believed it to be the base of a group of lawless rebels. The most astounding aspect of the castle is its commanding position, 300ft above a sheer drop down into the green valley of the small River Cennen. The highlights of a visit are the views down into the river valley and the long descent down into a watery, pitch-black **cave** that is said to have served as a well. Torches are essential (rented from the excellent tearoom near the car park) – it's worth continuing as far as possible and then turning them off to experience absolute darkness.

Llandovery and around

Twelve miles beyond Llandeilo, the town of **LLANDOVERY** (Llanymddyfri) has architecture and a layout that have changed little for centuries. As with so many mid-Wales settlements to the north, an influx of New Agers since the 1960s has had a discernible effect on the town: there's a thriving independent theatre, and bookshops and wholefood stores abound. Alongside this more alternative flavour, Llandovery is still a major centre for its cattle market, held every other Tuesday.

On the south side of the main Broad Street, a grassy mound holds the scant remains of the town's **castle**. Just in front, an eerie stainless-steel sculpture commemorates the gruesome death here, in 1401, of Llywelyn ap Gruffydd Fychan at the hands of Henry IV's men in Owain Glyndŵr's war of independence.

Broad Street has been Llandovery's thoroughfare for years, as can be seen from the solid early nineteenth-century townhouses and earlier inns that line the road as it widens towards the cobbled, rectangular Market Square. Above the tourist office on Kings Road, the excellent **Llandovery Heritage Centre** (Easter–Sept daily 10am–5.30pm; Oct–Easter Mon–Sat 10am–4pm, Sun 2–4pm; donation appreciated) depicts some powerful local legends and tales. Stone Street heads north from the Market Square to the **Llandovery Theatre**, a shadow of its former self but worth keeping an eye on for an update on events in the area.

Llandovery **train station** sits on the main A40 just before Broad Street; **buses** leave from Broad Street and Market Square. The joint **tourist office** and **Brecon Beacons National Park office** (Easter–Sept daily 10am–5.30pm; Oct–Easter Mon–Sat 10am–4pm, Sun 2–4pm; ☏01550/720693) is on Kings Road, the continuation of Broad Street. The best central **accommodation** is at *The Drovers*, 9 Market Square (☏01550/721115; ❶), an eighteenth-century townhouse full of antique furniture. Less central B&Bs include *Pencerrig*, New Road, on the way out of town towards Llandeilo (☏01550/721259; ❶); the superb Gothic-styled en-suites at *Cwm Rhuddan Mansion* (☏01550/721414, ✉mikeandjan@cwmrhuddan .fsnet.co.uk; ❷), a mile southwest on the A4069; and, a mile further out on the same road, *Cwmgwyn Farm*, Llangadog Road (☏01550/720410; ❷). The nearest **campsite**, a mile east off the A40, is the *Erwlon* (☏01550/720332).

Llandovery has precious few good **places to eat**, though there are a number of daytime cafés and tearooms, mainly around the Market Square, and the *Castle Hotel*, on Broad Street, offers delicious, moderately priced lunchtime and evening food. For **drinking**, the eccentric and bizarrely old-fashioned *Red Lion*, a red, colonnaded house nestled in an easy-to-miss corner at 2 Market Square, can't be beaten.

The Dolaucothi Gold Mine

The countryside to the west of Llandovery is blissfully quiet, with just a handful of main roads and lanes that rarely contain traffic of any volume. The principal route off the A40 between Llandeilo and Llandovery, the A482, heads towards the straggling village of **PUMSAINT** (Five Saints). The origin of the name is explained by a stone found near the entrance of the **Dolaucothi Gold Mine** (April–Oct daily 10am–5pm; £2.90; NT), half a mile off the main road. Indentations in the rock are said to be the marks left by five sleeping saints, who rested here one night. Pumsaint is the only place in Britain where it's certain that the Romans mined gold, laying complicated and astoundingly advanced systems to extract the precious metal from the rock. The remains of Roman workings – a few water channels and an open cast mine – can still be seen around the site. An underground **tour** (for an extra £3.80) goes deep into the mine workings and usually allows visitors to prospect for gold themselves.

Tenby and Caldey Island

On a natural promontory of great strategic importance, the beguilingly old-fashioned resort of **TENBY** (Dinbych-y-Pysgod), wedged between two sweeping beaches fronting an island-studded seascape, is everything a seaside resort should be. Narrow streets wind down from the medieval centre to the harbour past miniature gardens fashioned to catch the afternoon sun. Steps lead down the steeper slopes to dockside arches which still house fishmongers selling the morning's catch.

Tenby has a long pedigree. First mentioned in a ninth-century bardic poem, the town grew under the twelfth-century Normans, who erected a castle on the headland in their attempt to colonize south Pembrokeshire and create a **"Little England beyond Wales"** – an appellation by which the area is still known today. Three times in the twelfth and thirteenth centuries the town was ransacked by the Welsh. In response, the castle was fortified once more and the stout town walls – largely still intact – were built. Tenby prospered as a major port for a wide variety of foodstuffs and fine goods between the fourteenth and sixteenth centuries, and although decline followed, the arrival of the railway brought renewed wealth as the town became a fashionable resort. Lines of neat, prosperous hotels and expensive shops still stand haughtily along the seafront.

Although the town is extremely conservative, with a large population of retired people, there's plenty of entertainment and a huge number of pubs and restaurants. Not for nothing has the town become one of Britain's most fashionable venues for hen and stag parties – something the authorities are keen to discourage – and in summer it can seem full to bursting point, with heavy traffic restrictions and a considerable rush on decent accommodation. Tenby is also one of the major stopping-off points along the **Pembrokeshire Coast Path**, a welcome burst of glitter and excitement amidst mile upon mile of undulating cliff scenery. The **National Park** boundary skirts around the edge of the town, while a couple of miles offshore, the old monastic ruins of **Caldey Island** make for a pleasant day-trip.

The Town

Tenby is shaped like a triangle, with two sides formed by the coast meeting at Castle Hill. The third side is formed by the remains of the twenty-foot-high town **walls**, first built in the late thirteenth century and massively strengthened by Jasper Tudor, earl of Pembroke and uncle of Henry VII, in 1457. Further refortification came in the 1580s, when Tenby was considered to be in the frontline against a possible attack by the Spanish Armada. In the middle of the remaining stretch is the only town gate still standing, at **Five Arches**, a semicircular barbican that combined practical day-to-day usage with hidden look-outs and angles acute enough to surprise invaders.

The centrepiece and most notable landmark of the town centre is the 152-foot spire of the largely fifteenth-century **St Mary's Church**, between St George's Street and Tudor Square. A pleasantly light interior shows the elaborate ceiling bosses in the chancel to good effect, and fifteenth-century tombs of local barons demonstrate Tenby's important mercantile tradition.

Wedged between the town walls and the two bays, the **old town** is a great place to wander, with many of the original medieval lanes still intact in the immediate area around the parish church. **Sun Alley** is a tiny crack between overhanging whitewashed stone houses that connects Crackwell and High streets. Due east, on the other side of the church, **Quay Hill** runs parallel, a narrow set of steps and cobbles tumbling down past some of the town's oldest houses to the top of the harbour. Wedged in a corner of Quay Hill is the **Tudor Merchant's House** (April–Sept Mon, Tues & Thurs–Sat 10am–5pm, Sun 1–5pm; Oct Mon, Tues, Thurs & Fri 10am–3pm, Sun noon–3pm; £2; NT), built in the late fifteenth century for a wealthy local merchant at the time when Tenby was second only to Bristol as an important west-coast port. The rambling house is on three floors, packed with period furniture from the sixteenth century, although more notable are the tapering Flemish-style chimney pieces, a prominent local fashion.

During the day, the **harbour** is the scene of considerable activity as the departure point for numerous excursion boats, the most popular being the short trip over to Caldey Island (see p.808). Above the harbour is the headland and **Castle Hill**, where paths and flower beds have been planted around the remaining **gatehouse** of the Norman castle. Here, the town **museum** (daily 10am–5pm; Nov–Easter closed Sat & Sun; £2; @ www.tenbymuseum .free-online.co.uk) doubles as a small art gallery and is typical of Tenby: slightly ponderous and municipally minded, but still interesting.

Practicalities

Tenby's **train station** is at the western end of the town centre, at the bottom of Warren Street. Some **buses** stop at South Parade, at the top of Trafalgar Road, although most call at the bus shelter on Upper Park Road. The **tourist office** faces the North Beach, on The Croft (Easter–Oct daily 10am–5.30pm; Nov–Easter Mon–Sat 10am–4pm; ☎01834/842402).

As a major resort, Tenby has dozens of **hotels** and **guest houses**, all pressed from pretty much the same mould, though paying more gets you a wider range of facilities and a sea view. The best budget place is the spotless *Boulston Cottage*, 29 Trafalgar Rd (☎01834/843289; ❶). *Lyndale Guest House*, Warren Street (☎01834/842836; ❶), is a welcoming B&B near the station, happy to cater for vegetarians; and *Ashby House*, 24 Victoria St (☎01834/842867, ⓦwww .ashbyhousetenby.co.uk; ❷), is good too. The *Atlantic*, The Esplanade (☎01834/842881, ⓦwww.atlantic-hotel.uk.com; ❻), is at the top of the range, with a couple of good restaurants and even a small indoor pool. Four miles west of Tenby, overlooking the cliffs, is the bright and modern *Manorbier* YHA **hostel**, at Skrinkle Haven (☎0870/770 5954, ⓔmanorbier@yha.org.uk; dorms £11.50; ❶; March–Oct). You can **camp** there, and at the small and semi-official *Meadow Farm*, Northcliff, on the northern fringes of town (☎01834/844829; April–Sept).

There are dozens of **cafés** and **restaurants** around town. For ice cream and Italian snacks, try *Fecci and Sons*, Upper Frog Street. *Quay Room*, on Quay Hill, is good for coffee and snacks, while the moderately priced *Paxton's Bistro* at the *Tenby House Hotel*, Tudor Square (☎01834/842000), and the more expensive *Plantagenet House*, Quay Hill (☎01834/842350), offer well-cooked local specialities; the latter is said to be the oldest house in Tenby, complete with massive twelfth-century Flemish chimney breast. For **pubs**, head for the *Lifeboat Tavern*, Tudor Square, or the *Coach and Horses*, Upper Frog Street. The *Three Mariners*, on St George's Street, has good beer and live music.

Caldey Island

Looming large over Tenby's seascape is **Caldey Island** (Ynys Pyr; ⓦwww.caldey-island.co.uk), a couple of miles offshore and where Celtic monks first settled in the sixth century. Little is then known of the island until 1136, when it was given to the Benedictine monks of St Dogmael's at Cardigan, who founded their priory here. Upon the Dissolution of the monasteries in 1536, the Benedictine monks left the island and a fanciful succession of owners bought and sold it on a whim, until it was, once again, sold to a Benedictine monastic order in 1906 and subsequently to an order of Reformed Cistercians. The island has been a monastic home almost constantly ever since.

Boats leave Tenby Harbour (mid–May to mid–Sept Mon–Sat 10am–4pm every 15min; Easter to mid–May & mid–Sept to Oct Mon–Fri 10am–3pm every 30min; weather permitting; ☎01834/842296 or 844453; £8). Tickets for the twenty-minute journey are sold at the kiosk in Castle Square, directly above the harbour. On landing at Caldey's jetty, a short walk leads through the woods to the island's main settlement.

The village itself is the main hub of Caldey life. As well as a tiny post office and popular tearoom, there's a **perfume shop** selling the herbal fragrances distilled by the monks from Caldey's abundant flora. The narrow road going to the left leads down to the heavily restored **chapel of St David**, whose most impressive feature is its round-arched Norman door. Opposite is the gathering point for men-only tours of the garish twentieth-century **monastery** (July & Aug every 2hr; rest of year 1 daily), a white, turreted heap that resembles a Disney castle. A lane leads south from the village to the old **priory**, abandoned at the Dissolution and restored at the turn of the twentieth century. The centrepiece of the complex is the remarkable, twelfth-century **St Illtud's Church**, which houses one of the most significant pre-Norman finds in Wales, the sandstone **Ogham Cross**, found under the stained-glass window on the south side of the nave. It is carved with an inscription from the sixth century which was added to, in Latin, during the ninth. The lane continues south from the site, climbing up to the gleaming white island **lighthouse**, built in 1828, from which there are memorable views.

Southern Pembrokeshire

The southern zigzag of coast that darts west from Tenby is a strange mix of caravan parks, Ministry of Defence shooting ranges, spectacularly beautiful bays and gull-covered cliffs. From Tenby, the A4139 passes through **Penally**, with its wonderful beach, and continues past idyllic coves, the lily ponds at **Bosherston** and the remarkable and ancient **St Govan's Chapel**, squeezed into a rock cleft above the crashing waves. The ancient town of **Pembroke** really only warrants a visit to its impressive castle before pressing on to neighbouring **Lamphey**, with its fine Bishop's Palace. **Buses** to most corners of the peninsula radiate out from Haverfordwest (see p.812).

Penally to Bosherston

Just over a mile down the A4139 from Tenby, the dormitory village of **PENALLY** is unremarkable save for its vast beach. The coastal path hugs the cliff top from the viewpoint at Giltar Point, just below Penally, reaching the glorious privately owned beach at the headland of **Lydstep Haven** after two miles (fee charged for the sands). A mile further west is the cove of **Skrinkle Haven**, and above it the excellent *Manorbier* YHA **hostel** (T0870/770 5954, E manorbier@yha.org.uk; dorms £11.50; March–Oct), where you can also **camp**.

The next part of the coast path heads inland to avoid the artillery range that occupies the beautiful outcrop of **Old Castle Head**, then leads straight into the quaint village of **MANORBIER** (Maenorbŷr), pronounced "mannerbeer", birthplace in 1146 of the Welsh-Norman historian, writer and ecclesiastical reformer Giraldus Cambrensis. Manorbier's **castle** (April–Sept daily 10.30am–5.30pm; £2.50), founded in the early twelfth century as an impressive baronial residence, sits above the village and its beach on a hill of wild

The Pembrokeshire National Park and Coast Path

The **Pembrokeshire Coast** is Britain's only predominantly sea-based national park (W www.pembrokeshirecoast.org.uk), hugging the rippled coast around the entire western section of Wales. Established in 1952, the park is not one easily identifiable mass, rather a series of occasionally unconnected coastal and inland scenic patches.

Crawling around almost every wriggle of the coastline, the **Pembrokeshire Coast Path** winds 186 miles from St Dogmael's near Cardigan in the north to its southern point at Amroth, near Tenby. For the vast majority of the way, the path clings precariously to cliff-top routes, overlooking seal-basking rocks, craggy offshore islands, unexpected gashes of sand and shrieking clouds of sea birds. The most popular and ruggedly inspiring segments of the coast path are: either side of St Bride's Bay, around St David's Head and the Marloes Peninsula; the stretch along the southern coast from the castle at Manorbier to the tiny cliff chapel at Bosherston; and the generally quieter northern coast either side of Fishguard, past undulating contours, massive cliffs, bays and old ports.

Of all the seasons, spring is perhaps the finest for walking as the crowds are yet to arrive and the cliff-top flora is at its most vivid. There are numerous publications available about the coast path, of which the best is Brian John's *National Trail Guide* (£11), which includes sections of 1:25,000 maps of the route. The National Park publishes a handy *Coast Path Accommodation* guide (£2.25), detailing B&Bs and campsites along its entire length.

gorse. The Norman walls are in a good state of repair, surrounding an inner grass courtyard in which the extensive remains of the castle's chapel and state rooms jostle for position with the nineteenth-century domestic residence. In the walls and buildings are a warren of dark passageways to explore, occasionally opening out into little cells with lacklustre wax figures purporting to illustrate the castle's history.

The rocky little harbour at **Stackpole Quay**, reached via the small lane from Freshwater East through East Trewent, is a good starting point for walks along the breathtaking cliffs to the north. Another walk leads half a mile south to one of the finest beaches in Pembrokeshire, **Barafundle Bay**, with its soft beach fringed by wooded cliffs at either end. The path continues around the coast, through the dunes of **Stackpole Warren**, to **BROAD HAVEN**, where a pleasant small beach overlooks several rocky islets, now managed by the National Trust. Basing yourself here gives good access to the nearby **Bosherston Lakes** inland, three artificial fingers of water beautifully landscaped in the late eighteenth century. The westernmost lake is the most scenic, especially in late spring and early summer when the lilies that form a carpet across its surface are in full bloom.

Another lane dips south from the village of **BOSHERSTON**, across the MoD training grounds, to a spot overlooking the cliffs where tiny **St Govan's Chapel** is wedged: it's a remarkable building, known to be at least eight hundred years old. Steps descend straight into the sandy-floored chapel, now devoid of any furnishings save for the simple stone altar.

Pembroke and around

The old county town of **PEMBROKE** (Penfro) and its fearsome castle sit on the southern side of the River Pembroke, a continuation of the massive Milford Haven waterway, described by Nelson as the greatest natural harbour in the world. Despite its location, Pembroke is surprisingly dull, with one long main street of attractive Georgian and Victorian houses, some intact stretches of medieval town wall but little else to catch the eye. The town grew up solely to serve the castle, the mightiest link in the chain of Norman strongholds built across southern Wales. The walled town, drawn out along a hilltop ridge, flourished as a port for Pembrokeshire goods, which were sold throughout Britain and exported to Ireland, France and Spain. The castle was attacked by Cromwell during the Civil War, and though the town developed as a centre of leather-making, weaving, dyeing and tailoring, it never really regained its former importance.

Pembroke's history is inextricably bound up with that of its impregnable **castle** (daily: April–Sept 9.30am–6pm; March & Oct 10am–5pm; Nov–Feb 10am–4pm; £3; ⓦ www.pembrokecastle.co.uk), founded by the Normans, but rebuilt between 1189 and 1245. During the Civil War, Pembroke was a Parliamentarian stronghold until the town's military governor suddenly switched allegiance to the king, whereupon Cromwell's troops sacked the castle after a 48-day siege. Yet despite Cromwell's battering, and centuries of subsequent neglect, Pembroke Castle still inspires feelings of awe at its sheer, bloody-minded bulk, even if it is largely due to extensive restoration over the last century. The soaring gatehouse leads into the large, grassy courtyard around the vast, round Norman **keep**, 75ft high and with walls 18ft thick, crowned by a dome. In the domestic quarters, there's a dungeon tower, a Norman hall where the period arch has been disappointingly over-restored and reinforced, and the Oriel or Northern hall, a Tudor re-creation of an earlier antechamber. The intact towers and battlements contain many heavily restored communal rooms, now empty of furniture and, to a large extent, atmosphere too, although some of them, mainly in the gatehouse, are used to house excellent displays on the history of the castle and the Tudor empire.

Opposite the castle walls is the delightfully eccentric **Museum of the Home**, at 7 Westgate Hill, the northward continuation of Main Street (May–Sept Mon–Thurs 11am–5pm; £1.50). Packed into the steep townhouse is a collection of utterly ordinary items dating from the eighteenth to the twentieth century. The objects are loosely gathered into themes, including toiletries, bedroom accessories and children's games – all demonstrated with great enthusiasm.

Practicalities

Pembroke's **train station** is east of the town centre on Station Road. The **tourist office**, on Commons Road, parallel to Main Street (Easter–Oct daily 10am–5.30pm; ☏01646/622388), provides a useful, free town guide and has limited information on the Pembrokeshire National Park. If you decide to **stay**, head straight for *Beech House B&B*, 78 Main St (☏01646/683746; ❶), which easily outdoes places charging twice as much – one room even boasts a four-poster. If it's full, try the slightly pricier *Merton Place House*, a few doors up at 3 East Back (☏01646/684796; ❶), which has a pleasant walled garden at the back. More expensive places in town aren't great shakes, but you could stay in Lamphey (see below), a couple of miles away. Trains continue from Pembroke to Pembroke Dock, two miles northwest, where **Irish Ferries** (☏0870/517 1717, ⓦwww.irishferries.com) operates two daily services to Rosslare in Ireland.

For **food**, try the *Pantry*, 4 Main St, during the daytime and early evening, or the well-cooked bar food at the *King's Arms Hotel*, 13 Main St. Further along, at no. 63, the expensive *Left Bank* (☏01646/622333) serves well-thought-out French cuisine in stylish surroundings. The best of the dozens of **pubs** is the *Old Cross Saws*, 109 Main St, although it's hard to beat a summer evening on the veranda overlooking the Mill Pond at the *Waterman's Arms*, over the bridge on Northgate Street.

Lamphey

The pleasant village of **LAMPHEY** (Llandyfai), two miles southeast of Pembroke, is best known for the ruined **Bishop's Palace** (daily 10am–5pm; £2.50; CADW), off a quiet lane to the north of the village. A country retreat for the bishops of St David's, the palace dates from around the thirteenth century, but was abandoned following the Reformation. Stout walls surround the ruins, which are scattered over a large area. Many of the palace buildings have long been lost under grassy banks. Most impressive are the remains of the Great Hall, extending across the entire eastern end of the complex. You can still see Bishop Gower's hallmark arcaded parapets running along the top, similar to those he built in the Bishop's Palace of St David's.

One of the area's swankiest **hotels** is here, in the shape of the Neoclassical *Lamphey Court Hotel* (☏01646/672273, ⓦwww.lampheycourt.co.uk; ❼), opposite the Bishop's Palace. Otherwise, there's the more modest *Lamphey Hall Hotel* (☏01646/672394; ❸) by the church, or great bunkhouse **dorms** at the *Barn at the Back of Beyond* (☏01646/672047; from £9.50), half a mile east of the village along The Ridgeway.

Carew

A tiny village that can become unbearably packed in high season, **CAREW**, four miles east of Pembroke, by the River Carew, is a pretty place. Just south of the river crossing, by the main road, is the village's **Celtic cross**, the graceful, remarkably intact taper of the shaft covered in fine tracery of ancient Welsh designs. A small hut beyond the cross serves as the ticket office for **Carew Castle and Mill** (Easter–Oct daily 10am–5pm; £2.80; castle or mill only £1.90; Ⓦ www.carewcastle.com). The castle, a hybrid of Elizabethan fancy and earlier defensive necessity, is reached across a field. A few hundred yards to the west is the **Carew French Mill**, used commercially until 1937 and now the only tide-powered mill in Wales. The impressive eighteenth-century exterior belies the rather pedestrian exhibitions and audiovisual displays inside, which describe the milling process.

Mid- and Northern Pembrokeshire

The most westerly point of Wales is one of the country's most enchanting areas. The chief town of the region, **Haverfordwest**, remains rather soulless despite some handsome architecture, but it's useful as a jumping-off point for **St Bride's Bay**. The coast here is broken into rocky outcrops, islands and broad, sweeping beaches curving between two headlands that sit like giant crab pincers facing out into the warm Gulf Stream. The southernmost headland winds around every conceivable angle, offering calm, east-facing sands at **Dale** and sunny expanses of south-facing beach at **Marloes**. Near **Martin's Haven**, boats depart for the offshore islands of **Skomer**, **Skokholm** and **Grassholm**. To the north, the spectacularly lacerated coast veers to the left and the **St David's peninsula**, along stunning cliffs interrupted only by occasional strips of sand. Just north of **St Non's Bay**, the tiny cathedral city of **St David's** is definitely a highlight. Rooks and crows circle above the impressive ruins of the huge Bishop's Palace, sitting beneath the delicate bulk of the cathedral, the most impressive in Wales.

The north-facing coast that forms the very southern tip of Cardigan Bay is noticeably less commercialized and far more Welsh than the touristy shores of south and mid-Pembrokeshire. From the crags and cairns above St David's Head, the coast path perches precariously on the cliffs where only the thousands of sea birds have access. There are only the modest charms of small bays and desolate coves to detain you en route to the charming town of **Newport** – unless you're heading for **Fishguard** and the ferries to Ireland.

Haverfordwest

In the seventeenth and eighteenth centuries, the town of **HAVERFORD-WEST** (Hwlffordd), ten miles north of Pembroke, prospered as a port and trading centre, but despite its natural advantages, it is scarcely a place to linger. A cursory look at the dingy shell of the thirteenth-century **castle** and the less-than-exciting **town museum** (Easter–Oct Mon–Sat 10am–4pm; £1) is enough, though as the main transport hub and shopping centre for western Pembrokeshire, you are likely to pass through.

The **tourist office** (Mon–Sat 10am–5.30pm; Oct–April closes 4pm; ☎01437/763110) is next to the bus terminus, at the end of the Old Bridge. There's also a highly informative **National Park office** at 40 High St (open limited hours). Next to the tourist office, the Holiday Information Centre includes an excellent booking agency for self-catering cottages in Pembrokeshire (☎01437/765765, Ⓦ www.coastalcottages.co.uk). Low-cost

accommodation is provided at *College Guest House*, 93 Hill St (℡01437/763710; ❶) and there are slightly pricier rooms at the solidly Georgian *Castle Hotel*, in Castle Square (℡01437/769322; ❸). For **lunch**, duck into *Morillo's*, on the pedestrian Bridge Street, a successful combination of Italian café and chippy. Evening meals are best at *The George's* pub, at the top of town on Market Street (closed Sun).

Four miles northeast of town, along the B4329, **Scolton Manor** (April–Oct Tues–Sun 10.30am–5.30pm; £2) is a modest stately home that now forms the nucleus of the diverting **Pembrokeshire County Museum**. Aside from the enchanting period rooms indoors, outhouses showcase all manner of quirky exhibits, and there's a good café and an environmentally aware visitor centre on site.

Dale and around

DALE, fourteen miles west of Haverfordwest, can be unbearably crowded in peak season, but it's a pleasant enough village, whose east-facing shore makes it excellent for water sports in the lighter seas. All the activity happens around the beachside shack of West Wales Wind, Surf and Sailing (℡01646/636642, Ⓦwww.surfdale.co.uk), who give instruction in power-boating, windsurfing, surfing, sailing and kayaking (£30–50 per half-day) and offer B&B **accommodation** on the Dale waterfront (❶) – breakfast is usually taken at *Planet Dale*, a good-value café open summer only. The *Post House Hotel* (℡01646/636201; ❷) is in the middle of the village just behind the real-ale *Griffin Inn*, which has en-suite rooms and optional evening meals; and for a touch of comfort, there's *Allenbrook* (℡01646/636254, Ⓦwww.ukworld.net /allenbrook; ❹; closed Dec), a charming country house close to the beach.

The calm waters of Dale are deceptive, and as soon as you head further south towards **St Ann's Head**, an invigoratingly desolate place, the wind speed whips up, with waves and tides to match. The coast path sticks tight to the undulating coastline, passing tiny bays en route to the St Ann's lighthouse.

The most useful **bus** for accessing the central Pembrokeshire coast is the #400 summer service (2 daily) which runs from Milford Haven to Dale (25min), Martin's Haven (40min), Broad Haven (1hr 15min) and St David's (2hr).

Marloes

The coast turns and heads north from St Ann's Head to the unexciting hamlet of **MARLOES**. Only a mile away from the village, the broad, deserted beach is a safe place to swim, and looks out towards the island of Skokholm. From here, the coast path and a narrow road continue for two miles to the National Trust-owned swathe of **Deer Park** – which has no deer but is the name given to the grassy far tip of the southern peninsula of St Bride's Bay – and **Martin's Haven**, from where you can take a **boat** out to the islands of Skomer, Skokholm and Grassholm.

Marloes is tolerably well off for **accommodation**, with the excellent *Foxdale Guesthouse*, Glebe Lane, opposite the church (℡01646/636243, Ⓦwww .foxdale.guest.house.8m.com; ❷), and the en-suite *Lobster Pot* (℡01646/636233; ❸), nearby in the centre of the village, above the village's only real restaurant. You can pitch a **tent** behind *Foxdale*, up the street at the field-and-toilets *Greenacre* site, and at *Runwayskiln* (℡01646/636257), close to the *Marloes Sands* YHA **hostel** (℡01646/636667, Ⓔreservations@yha.org.uk; dorms £8; April–Sept), which consists of a series of converted farm buildings overlooking the northern end of the beach. *West Hook Farm*, near Martin's Haven (☎01646/636424), also has **camping**.

Skomer, Skokholm and Grassholm islands

Weather permitting, **boats** (April–Oct Tues–Sun 10am, 11am & noon; £13) run from Martin's Haven to **Skomer Island**, a 722-acre flat-topped island rich in sea birds and spectacular carpets of wild flowers, perfect for birdwatching and walking. You can also cross to **Skokholm Island** (June–Aug Mon 10am; £16; booking essential on ☎01646/636234), a couple of miles south of Skomer and far smaller, more rugged and remote, noted for its cliffs of warm red sandstone. Britain's first bird observatory was founded here as far back as the seventeenth century, and there are still a huge number of petrels, gulls, puffins, oystercatchers and rare Manx shearwaters. The trip includes a guided tour by the island's warden. Boat trips also head out even further, to the tiny outpost of **Grassholm Island**, over five miles west of Skomer (boats June–Sept; landing trip Fri noon; guided trip Thurs 5pm; £20; ☎01646/603123). Visiting the island is an unforgettable experience, largely due to the 70,000 or so screaming gannets who call it home. No booking is required for Skomer trips or the guided trips to Grassholm on Thursdays, although these can be arranged via National Park centres.

St David's and around

ST DAVID'S (Tyddewi) is one of the most enchanting spots in Britain. This miniature city sits back from its purple- and gold-flecked cathedral at the very westernmost point of Wales in bleak, treeless countryside. Spiritually, it's the centre of Welsh ecclesiasticism. Traditionally founded by the Welsh patron saint himself in 550 AD, the see of St David's has drawn pilgrims for a millennium and a half – William the Conqueror included – and by 1120, Pope Calixtus II decreed that two journeys to St David's were the spiritual equivalent of one to Rome. The surrounding city – in reality, never much more than a large village – grew up in the shadow cast by the cathedral, and St David's today still relies on the imported wealth of pilgrims and visitors to the area, attracted by its savage beauty.

The City

From the central square of St David's, ranged around a **Celtic cross**, the main street continues under the thirteenth-century **Tower Gate**, which forms the entrance to the serene **Cathedral Close**, backed by a windswept landscape of treeless heathland. The cathedral lies down to the right, hidden in a hollow by the River Alun. This apparent modesty is explained by reasons of defence, as a towering cathedral, visible from the sea on all sides, would have been vulnerable to attack. On the other side of the babbling Alun lie the ruins of the Bishop's Palace.

The Cathedral

From beyond the powerfully solid Tower Gate, the Thirty-Nine Articles – steps named after Thomas Cranmer's key tenets of Anglicanism – approach the purple and golden stone **cathedral** (Ⓦwww.stdavidscathedral.org.uk). The 125-foot tower, topped by pert golden pinnacles, has clocks on only three sides – the people of the northern part of the parish couldn't raise enough money for one to be constructed facing them. You enter through the south side of the low, twelfth-century nave in full view of its most striking feature, the intricate latticed oak **roof**. This was added to hide emergency restoration work carried out in the sixteenth century, when the nave was in danger of collapse. The nave floor still has a discernible slope and the support buttresses inserted in the northern aisle look incongruously new and temporary. At the crossing, an elaborate **rood screen** was constructed under the orders of fourteenth-century Bishop Gower, who envisaged it as his own tomb. Behind the screen and the organ, the choir sits directly under the magnificently bold and bright lantern ceiling of the tower, another addition by Gower. At the back of the south choir stalls is a unique **monarch's stall**, complete with royal crest, for, unlike any other British cathedral, the Queen is an automatic member of the St David's Cathedral Chapter.

Separating the choir and the presbytery is a finely traced, rare **parclose screen**. The back wall of the **presbytery** was once the eastern extremity of the cathedral, as can be seen from the two lines of windows. The upper row has been left intact, while the lower three were blocked up and filled with delicate gold mosaics in the nineteenth century. The colourful fifteenth-century roof, a deceptively simple repeating medieval pattern, was extensively restored by Gilbert Scott in the mid-nineteenth century. At the back of the presbytery, around the altar, the **sanctuary** has a few fragmented fifteenth-century tiles still in place. On the south side is a beautifully carved sedilla, a seat for the priest and deacon celebrating mass. To its right are the thirteenth-century tombs of bishops Iorwerth and Anselm de la Grace, and on the other side of the sanctuary is the also thirteenth-century but disappointingly plain tomb of St David, largely destroyed in the Reformation.

The Bishop's Palace

From the cathedral, a path leads to the splendid **Bishops' Palace** (June–Sept daily 9.30am–6pm; April, May & Oct daily 9.30am–5pm; Nov–March Mon–Sat 9.30am–4pm, Sun 11am–4pm; £2.50; CADW), built by bishops Beck and Gower around the turn of the fourteenth century. The huge central quadrangle is fringed by a neat jigsaw of ruined buildings built in extraordinarily richly tinted stone. The **arched parapets** that run along the top of most of the walls were a favourite feature of Gower, who did more than any of his predecessors or successors to transform the palace into an architectural and political powerhouse. Two ruined but still impressive halls – the **Bishops' Hall** and the enormous **Great Hall**, with its glorious rose window – lie off the main quadrangle, above and around a myriad of rooms adorned by some eerily eroded corbels. Underneath the Great Hall are dank vaults containing an interesting exhibition about the palace and the indulgent lifestyles of its occupants. The destruction of the palace is largely due to sixteenth-century Bishop Barlow, who supposedly stripped the buildings of their lead roofs to provide dowries for his five daughters' marriages to bishops.

Practicalities

The main road from Haverfordwest enters St David's past the attractive **tourist office** (Easter–Oct daily 9.30am–5.30pm; Nov–Easter Mon–Sat 10am–4pm; ☏01437/720392), and continues for two hundred yards down High Street to the **bus station** in New Street. You can **rent bikes** at Ramsey Island Cruises, located behind TYF No Limits, 1 High St (☏01437/721611, ⓦwww.tyf.com), who rent surf gear and kayaks as well as running various **outdoor courses**. The best among these is "coasteering" (full day £60; half-day £35), which involves scrambling over rocks, jumping off cliffs and swimming across the narrow bays of St David's Peninsula.

There are numerous places to **stay**. Good, inexpensive options in town are *Pen Albro*, 18 Goat St (℡01437/721865; ❶), and *Y Glennydd*, 51 Nun St (℡01437/720576; ❶), which has some en-suite rooms. *The Waterings* (℡01437/720876, ⓦwww.stdavids.co.uk/waterings; ❹), on High Street by the tourist office, has luxurious suites in a former marine research establishment, while *Twr-y-Felin*, High Street (℡01437/721678; ❹), offers B&B, camping and a lively bar in a converted windmill. *Ramsey House*, Lower Moor (℡01437/720321, ⓦwww.ramseyhouse.co.uk; ❺), is an excellent small hotel a quarter of a mile out on the road to Porth Clais; from June to September, room prices rise but include a superb Welsh evening meal.

Apart from *Twr-y-Felin*, St Davids' nearest **campsite** is at *Caerfai Farm*, Caerfai Bay (℡01437/720548; May–Sept), a fifteen-minute walk from the city. A delightful thirty-minute walk west of town are the cliff-top camping fields of *Pencarnon Farm* (℡01437/720324), just short of St Justinian's, with amazing views and a virtually private beach below; and there's a YHA **hostel** in a former farmhouse two miles northwest, near Whitesands Bay (℡0870/770 6042; April–Oct).

For inexpensive **eating**, there are a number of adequate tearooms and the traveller-oriented *Low Pressure Café*, at 1 High St. For more of a treat, *Morgan's Brasserie*, 20 Nun St (℡01437/720508), serves meals made with wonderfully fresh local produce. **Nightlife** boils down to the lively *Farmers Arms*, Goat Street, the city's only real pub, with a terrace overlooking the cathedral.

The St David's peninsula

Surrounded on three sides by inlets, coves and rocky stacks, St David's is an easy base for some excellent walking around the headland of the same name. A mile due south, accessed along the signposted lane from the main Haverfordwest road just near the school, popular **Caerfai Bay** provides a sandy gash in the purple sandstone cliffs, rock which was used in the construction of the cathedral. To the immediate west is the craggy indentation of **St Non's Bay**, reached from Goat Street in St David's down the tiny rhododendron-flooded lane signposted to the *Warpool Court Hotel*. St Non reputedly gave birth to St David at this spot during a tumultuous storm around 500 AD, when a spring opened up between Non's feet, and despite the crashing thunder all around, an eerily calm light filtered down onto the scene. St Non's Bay has received pilgrims for centuries, resulting in the foundation of a tiny, isolated chapel in the pre-Norman age. The ruins of the subsequent thirteenth-century chapel now lie in a field to the right of the car park, beyond the sadly dingy well and coy shrine where the nation's patron saint is said to have been born.

The road from St David's to St Non's branches at the *St Non's Hotel*, where Catherine Street becomes a winding lane that leads a mile down the tiny valley of the River Alun to its mouth at **Porth Clais**. Supposedly the place at which St David was baptized, Porth Clais was the city's main harbour, the spruced-up remains of which can still be seen at the bottom of the turquoise river creek. Today, commercial traffic has long gone, replaced by a boaties' haven.

Running due west out of St David's, Goat Street ducks past the ruins of the Bishop's Palace and over the rocky plateau for two miles to the harbour at **St Justinian's**, little more than a lifeboat station and ticket hut for the boats over to **Ramsey Island** (ⓦwww.ramseyisland.co.uk). This dual-humped plateau, less than two miles long, has been under the able stewardship of the RSPB since 1992 and is quite enchanting. Birds of prey circle the skies above the island, but it's better known for the tens of thousands of sea birds that noisily crowd the sheer cliffs on its western side. On the beaches, seals laze sloppily below the paths beaten out by a herd of red deer. Two companies run boats – weather permitting – around Ramsey, but the only ones that land are Thousand Islands Expeditions' trips (April–Oct daily; ☎01437/721721, ⓦwww.thousandislands.co.uk; £11); you can stay up to five hours. During the springtime nesting season you actually see more from boats which circle the island but don't land: try Ramsey Island Cruises (year-round daily; ☎01437/720285 or 0800/854367; £17), who also operate longer whale-watching trips (£45). Thousand Island Expeditions operate a similar Ramsey circumnavigation from **Whitesands Bay** (Porth Mawr), two miles to the north and reached from St David's via the B4583 off the Fishguard road.

Fishguard

From St David's, the coast road runs northeast, parallel to numerous small and less-commercialized bays, to **Strumble Head**, which protects the harbour at **FISHGUARD** (Abergwaun), an attractive, hilltop town seldom seen as anything more than a brief stopoff to or from the Stena Line **ferries** (☎0870/570 7070, ⓦwww.stenaline.com), which leave regularly for Rosslare in Ireland.

Near the town hall is the **Royal Oak Inn**, where a bizarre Franco-Irish attempt to conquer Britain in 1797 at nearby Carregwastad Point is remembered. The hapless forces arrived to negotiate a cease-fire, which was turned by the assembled British into an unconditional surrender. Part of the invaders' low morale – apart from the drunken farce in which they'd become embroiled – is said to have been sparked off by the sight of a hundred local women marching towards them. The troops mistook their stovepipe hats and red flannel dresses for the outfit of a British infantry troop and instantly capitulated. Even if this is not true, it is an undisputed fact that 47-year-old cobbler Jemima Nicholas, the "Welsh Heroine", single-handedly captured fourteen French soldiers. Her grave can be seen next to the uninspiring Victorian parish church, St Mary's, behind the pub. At the time of writing, the fabulous **Fishguard Tapestry**, which tells the story of this ramshackle invasion, is out of public view – a new, more permanent home is being sought.

Buses stop by the town hall in the central Market Square, right outside Fishguard's **tourist office** (April–Oct daily 10am–5.30pm; Nov–March Mon–Sat 10am–4pm; ☎01348/873484). There's a subsidiary tourist office in the foyer of the Ocean Lab in Goodwick (daily 10am–6pm; Nov–Easter closes 4pm; ☎01348/872037), around half a mile from the Rosslare ferry terminus. Local **boat trips** aboard *The Sea Spirit* (Easter–Oct; ☎01348/874864; £15) go from Goodwick up and down the coast. The **train station** is next to the ferry terminal on Quay Road. Buses usually meet ferries, though seldom the more frequent catamarans; a **taxi** (☎01348/874491) into town costs around £3.

Accommodation is plentiful and cheap, with most places well used to visitors coming and going at odd times. Next to the port is the faded elegance of the *Fishguard Bay Hotel*, on Quay Road (☎01348/873571, ⓔmhr177485@aol.com; ❹); and you'll find comfortable rooms at *Glanmoy Lodge*, on Trefwrgi Road, ten minutes' walk from the port (☎01348/874333, ⓦwww.glanmoylodge.co.uk; ❷). In Fishguard proper is *Three Main Street* (☎01348/874275; ❸), easy to find and with an expensive and highly praised restaurant; or there are **dorms** at *Hamilton Backpackers Lodge*, 21–23 Hamilton St (☎01348/874797; dorms from £10; ❶), just a minute's walk from the tourist office. The nearest **camping** is at *Tregroes Touring Park* (☎01348/872316), a mile southwest of Fishguard just off the A40.

Newport

NEWPORT (Trefdraeth) is an ancient and proud little town set on a gentle slope that courses down to the estuary of the Afon Nyfer. There's little to do except stroll around, but you'd be hard pressed to find a better place to do it. Just short of the Nevern estuary bridge, on the town side, **Carreg Coetan Arthur**, a well-preserved, capped Neolithic burial chamber, can be seen behind the holiday bungalows. The footpath that runs along the river either side of the bridge is marked as the Pilgrims' Way; follow it eastwards for a delightful riverbank stroll to Nevern, a couple of miles away. Another popular local walk is up to the craggy and magical peak of **Carn Ingli**, the Hill of Angels, behind the town. On Lower St Mary Street, the old school has metamorphosed into the excellent **West Wales Eco Centre** (Mon–Fri 9.30am–4.30pm; variable extended hours in summer; free), a venue for exhibitions, advice and resources on various aspects of sustainable living.

Newport's nearest beach, the **Parrog**, is complete with sandy stretches at low tide. On the other side of the estuary is the vast dune-backed **Traethmawr beach**, reached over the town bridge down Feidr Pen-y-Bont. Newport also makes a good jumping-off point for exploring the wooded vales and gnarled hills of **Mynydd Preseli**, just inland, which are scattered with prehistoric remains, notably the four-thousand-year-old capstone at **Pentre Ifan**, a couple of miles south of Newport.

The **tourist office** (April–Sept Mon–Sat 10am–5.30pm; ☏01239/820912) is on Long Street, just off the main road. **Bike rental** is available in town from the *Llysmeddyg* guesthouse, on East Street. There's plenty of **accommodation**: the *Golden Lion* pub, on the main street (☏01239/820321, ⓔgoldenlionpembs @aol.com; ❷), does inexpensive B&B, as does *Trewarren*, half a mile to the north (☏01239/820455; ❷), overlooking the estuary and with great views – follow Feidr Pen-y-Bont from town. For more luxury, try the superb *Cnapan Country House*, on East Street (☏01239/820575, ⓦwww.online-holidays.net /cnapan; ❹; closed Jan & Feb). The *Trefdraeth* YHA **hostel** is tucked in behind the Eco Centre (☏01239/820080; dorms £10.25; ❶; April–Sept); and a mile south of town, there's a great independent bunkhouse at *Brithdir Mawr*, on Ffordd Cilgwyn, at the bottom of the slopes of Carn Ingli (☏01239/820164, ⓦwww.brithdirmawr.freeserve.co.uk; dorms £5). The nearest **campsite** is the *Morawelon* (☏01239/820565), just west of town, at the Parrog, with nice gardens and its own café. For **food**, the *Cnapan Country House* serves exquisite meals, or there are solid pub classics, including a good veggie menu, at the *Royal Oak*, on Bridge Street. Great snacks can be found at the *Fountain House Foods* deli, and *Fronlas Café*, both on Market Street.

Travel details

Buses

For information on all local and national bus services, contact Traveline ☏0870/608 2608, ⓦwww.traveline.org.uk.
Cardiff to: Abergavenny (hourly; 1hr 20min); Aberystwyth (2 daily; 4hr); Blaenafon (hourly; 1hr 40min); Brecon (1 daily; 1hr 20min); Caerphilly (every 30min; 40min); Cardiff International Airport (hourly; 30min); Chepstow (hourly; 1hr 20min); London (8 daily; 3hr 10min); Merthyr Tydfil (every 30min; 45min); Newport, Monmouthshire (every 30min; 30min); Swansea (every 30min; 1hr).
Carmarthen to: Aberystwyth (2 daily; 1hr 45min); Haverfordwest (5 daily; 1hr); Kidwelly (hourly; 25min); Laugharne (hourly; 30min); Llandeilo (15

daily; 40min); National Botanic Garden (4 daily; 20min); Swansea (hourly; 1hr 30min); Tenby (2 daily; 1hr).

Chepstow to: Monmouth (16 daily; 50min); Newport (hourly; 50min); Tintern (8 daily; 20min); Usk (6 daily; 45min).

Fishguard to: Cardigan (hourly; 50min); Haverfordwest (hourly; 40min); Newport, Pembrokeshire (hourly; 20min); St David's (7 daily; 50min).

Haverfordwest to: Carmarthen (5 daily; 1hr); Fishguard (hourly; 40min); Manorbier (hourly; 1hr 10min); Newport, Pembrokeshire (hourly; 1hr 10min); Pembroke (hourly; 50min); St David's (hourly; 40min); Tenby (hourly; 1hr 20min).

Llandovery to: Brecon (Mon–Sat 5 daily, none on Sun; 40min); Llandeilo (9 daily; 45min).

Merthyr Tydfil to: Abergavenny (hourly; 1hr 30min); Brecon (10 daily; 40min); Cardiff (every 30min; 45min).

Monmouth to: Abergavenny (6 daily; 40min); Chepstow (16 daily; 50min); Raglan (8 daily; 20min); Tintern (8 daily; 30min).

Newport (Monmouthshire) to: Abergavenny (hourly; 1hr 10min); Blaenafon (every 30min; 1hr 10min); Cardiff (every 20min; 40min); Chepstow (hourly; 50min).

Newport (Pembrokeshire) to: Fishguard (hourly; 20min); Haverfordwest (hourly; 1hr 10min).

Pembroke to: Bosherston (Mon–Fri 2 daily; 1hr); Haverfordwest (hourly; 50min); Manorbier (hourly; 20min); Pembroke Dock (every 10min; 10min); Stackpole (Mon–Fri 2 daily; 50min); Tenby (hourly; 40min).

St David's to: Broad Haven (2 daily; 40min); Fishguard (7 daily; 50min); Haverfordwest (hourly; 40min).

Swansea to: Brecon (3 daily; 1hr 30min); Cardiff (every 30min; 1hr); Dan-yr-ogof (4 daily; 1hr); Merthyr Tydfil (hourly; 1hr); Mumbles (every 10min; 15min); Port Eynon (7 daily; 50min); Rhossili (Mon–Sat 10 daily; 1hr).

Tenby to: Carmarthen (2 daily; 1hr); Haverfordwest (hourly; 1hr 20min); Manorbier (hourly; 20min); Pembroke (hourly; 40min).

Trains

For information on all local and national rail services, contact National Rail Enquiries ℡ 08457/484950, Ⓦ www.nationalrail.co.uk.

Cardiff to: Abergavenny (hourly; 40min); Birmingham (8 daily; 2hr); Bristol (every 30min; 50min); Caerphilly (every 20min; 20min); Carmarthen (7 daily; 1hr 30min); Chepstow (hourly; 30min); Fishguard Harbour (2 daily; 2hr 20min); Haverfordwest (5 daily; 2hr 40min); London (every 30min; 2hr); Merthyr Tydfil (hourly; 1hr); Newport (every 15–30min; 10min); Pontypool (hourly; 30min); Swansea (hourly; 50min); Tenby (4 daily; 2hr 30min); Ystrad Rhondda (every 30min; 50min).

Carmarthen to: Cardiff (7 daily; 1hr 30min); Fishguard (2 daily; 1hr); Haverfordwest (9 daily; 40min); Pembroke (8 daily; 1hr 10min); Swansea (hourly; 50min); Tenby (8 daily; 40min).

Haverfordwest to: Carmarthen (9 daily; 40min); Swansea (7 daily; 1hr 30min).

Newport (Monmouthshire) to: Abergavenny (hourly; 30min); Cardiff (every 15–30min; 10min); Chepstow (hourly; 20min); London (every 30min; 1hr 50min).

Pembroke to: Lamphey (7 daily; 3min); Manorbier (7 daily; 10min); Pembroke Dock (7 daily; 10min); Tenby (7 daily; 20min).

Swansea to: Cardiff (hourly; 50min); Carmarthen (hourly; 50min); Fishguard (2 daily; 1hr 30min); Haverfordwest (7 daily; 1hr 30min); Llandrindod Wells (5 daily; 2hr 20min); London (hourly; 3hr); Newport (hourly; 1hr 20min); Pembroke (6 daily; 2hr); Tenby (7 daily; 1hr 40min).

Tenby to: Carmarthen (8 daily; 40min); Pembroke (7 daily; 20min); Swansea (7 daily; 1hr 40min).

Mid-Wales

ENGLAND

Highlights

* **Sgwd yr Eira waterfall** A waterfall you can dive through, in the midst of the Brecon Beacons National Park. **See p.829**

* **Bear Hotel, Crickhowell** The quality of food here is top-notch, garnering awards by the barrow-load. **See p.831**

* **Llangollen** Robust and enjoyable riverside town, with an internationally famous eisteddfod. **See p.842**

* **Harlech** A perfect castle and beautiful town wedged between the mountains and the sea. **See p.847**

* **Ardudwy Beach** Eight miles of one of the best beaches in Wales, with wide sands and a warm sea. **See p.849**

* **Mawddach Estuary** Sublime estuary crossed by the rickety rail bridge to Barmouth. **See p.849**

* **Centre for Alternative Technology** Imaginative showcase for sustainable and community development. **See p.854**

* **Aberystwyth** Lively seaside resort town that is rooted firmly in Welsh culture and language, and hosts the fine National Library of Wales. **See p.855**

△ Llangollen Eisteddfod

Mid-Wales

Mid-Wales is a huge, beautiful region, crisscrossed by breathtaking mountain passes, dotted with characterful little towns and never far from water – whether sparkling rivers, great lakes or the sea of the Cambrian coast. This is certainly the least-known part of Wales, and that is, perhaps, to its advantage, for it's here that you'll find Welsh culture at its most beguiling and most natural, folded into the contours of the land as it has been for centuries.

A quarter of the area of Wales is occupied by the inland county of **Powys**, whose name harks back to a fifth-century Welsh kingdom. By far the most popular attraction is **Brecon Beacons National Park**, stretching from the dramatic limestone country of Fforest Fawr in the west through to the English border beyond the Black Mountains. The best bases are the tiny city of **Brecon** or the market town of **Abergavenny**.

North of the Beacons lie the old spa towns of Radnorshire, among them twee **Llandrindod Wells**. The quiet countryside to the north, crossed by spectacular mountain roads such as the **Abergwesyn Pass** from Llanwrtyd, is barely populated, dotted with ancient churches and introspective villages. In the east, the border town of **Knighton** is the home of the flourishing **Offa's Dyke path** industry. **Montgomeryshire** is the northern portion of Powys, similarly underpopulated and remote. Like many country towns in mid-Wales, beautiful **Llanidloes** has a healthy stock of old hippies amongst its population, contributing to a thriving arts and crafts community and a relaxed atmosphere. It's also a great base for the mountains, forests and boggy heathland that surround it.

Continuing north are the mountains that course down into the **Dee Valley**, a fertile landscape much fought over between the English and the Welsh. With the language still thriving hereabouts, there's more of a tangibly Welsh feel to towns like the fabulous **Llangollen**, a great base for a variety of ruins, rides and rambles, as well as the venue each summer for the colourful International Eisteddfod festival. Further west is the old county of **Meirionydd**, which stretches to the enduringly popular Cambrian Coast, peppered with coastal resorts. Between the towns of **Harlech** and **Barmouth** lie some great beaches, backed by burbling rivers and stunning mountains.

The southern tranche of Meirionydd is dominated by mountain scenery, most notably around the massif of **Cadair Idris**. South of the great mountain is **Machynlleth**, a great base for beaches, mountains, shopping and the **Centre for Alternative Technology**, an impressive showpiece for community living and renewable energy resources.

Between Meirionydd and Pembrokeshire is the county of **Ceredigion**, firmly Welsh but surprisingly cosmopolitan with it. This is especially so in the

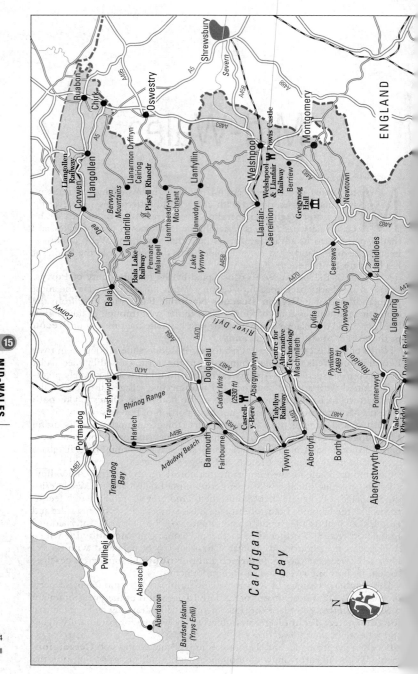

ENGLAND

Shrewsbury

Severn

A5

Oswestry

A495

Ruabon

Chirk

A5

A483

Welshpool

Powis Castle

Montgomery

A490

Llangollen Railway

Llangollen

Corwen

Llanarmon Dyffryn Ceiriog

Llanfair-Caereinion

Welshpool & Llanfair Railway

Berriew

Gregynog Hall

Newtown

Dee

Berwyn Mountains

Pistyll Rhaedr

Llanrhaeadr-ym-Mochnant

Llanfyllin

A483

Landrillo

Pennant Melangell

Llanwddyn

Lake Vyrnwy

A458

Caersws

Llanidloes

A470

Bala Lake Railway

Bala

A494

A47

Conwy

A470

A487

Llyn Clywedog

Dyfi

Llangurig

A44

A483

Rhinog Range

River Dyfi

Centre for Alternative Technology

Machynlleth

Plynlimon (2469 ft)

Rheidol

Devil's Bridge

Portmadog

Trawsfynydd

A470

Dolgellau

A487

Cadair Idris (2930 ft)

Abergynolwyn

A489

Ponterwyd

A487

Tremadog Bay

Harlech

A496

Barmouth

Fairbourne

Castell-y-Bere

Talyllyn Railway

Tywyn

Aberdyfi

Vale of Rheidol

Pwllheli

Ardudwy Beach

A493

Borth

Abersoch

Aberdaron

Bardsey Island (Ynys Enlli)

Cardigan Bay

Aberystwyth

N

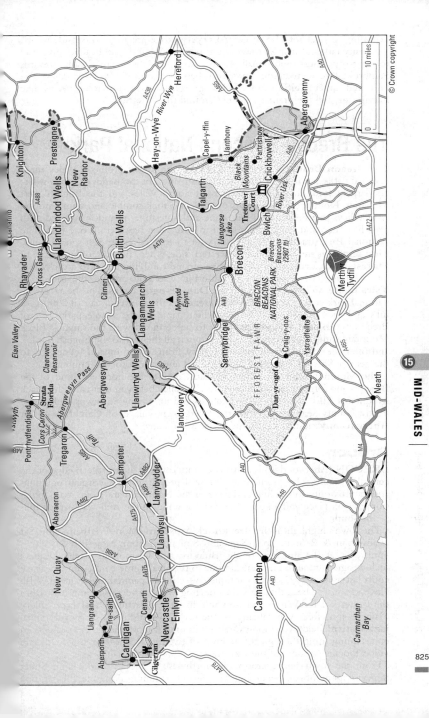

© Crown copyright

beguiling "capital" of Mid-Wales, **Aberystwyth**, a great mix of seaside resort, university city and market town. From here, wide sands and beaches give way to cliff-top paths and small sandy coves, as the coast heads towards Pembrokeshire. Ceredigion's interior is best seen around two river valleys: the lush and quiet **Teifi**, running through old-fashioned market towns like **Lampeter**, and the dramatic ravines around the **Rheidol**.

The Brecon Beacons National Park

The **Brecon Beacons National Park** has the lowest profile of Wales' three national parks, but it is nonetheless the destination of thousands of urban walkers, largely from the industrial areas of South Wales and the English West Midlands. Rounded, spongy hills of grass and rock tumble and climb around river valleys that lie between sandstone and limestone uplands, peppered with glass-like lakes and villages that seem to have been hewn from one rock. The National Park straddles Powys from west to east, covering 520 square miles. Most remote is the area at the far western side, where the vast, open terrain of **Fforest Fawr** forms miles of tufted moorland tumbling down to a rocky terrain of rivers, deep caves and spluttering waterfalls around the village of **Ystradfellte** and the chasms of the **Dan-yr-ogof caves**. The heart of the national park comprises the **Brecon Beacons** themselves, a pair of 2900-foot hills and their satellites which lend their name to the whole park. East of Brecon, the **Black Mountains** – not to be confused with the singular Black Mountain some distance to the west – stretch all the way to the English border, and offer the region's most varied scenery, from rolling upland wilderness to the gentler **Vale of Ewyas**, with its ruined abbey and isolated churches.

The Monmouthshire and Brecon Canal defines the northern limit of the Beacons and forges a passage along the Usk Valley between them and the Black Mountains. This is where you're likely to end up staying; in towns such as the sturdy county seat of **Brecon**, the overgrown village of **Crickhowell**, or **Abergavenny**, nestled below the Black Mountains.

Brecon

BRECON (Aberhonddu) is a sturdy county town at the northern edge of the central Beacons. The proliferation of well-proportioned Georgian buildings and its proximity to the hills and lakes of the National Park make it a popular stopping-off place and a good base for day-walks in the well-waymarked hills to the south.

The town's highlight is the **Brecknock Museum** (Mon–Fri 10am–5pm, Sat 10am–1pm & 2–5pm; April–Sept also Sun noon–5pm; Nov–Feb Sat closes 4pm; £1), at the junction of the Bulwark and Glamorgan Street. Displays include agricultural implements unique to the area, a nineteenth-century assize court last used in 1971, and an antique collection of painstakingly carved Welsh "love spoons" – betrothal gifts for courting Welsh lovers. Running east from the Bulwark is the Watton, where you'll find the diverting **Oriel Jazz** gallery (daily 1–4pm; free). Capitalizing on the town's astonishingly successful annual **jazz festival**, held over a long weekend in mid-August, the gallery presents an entertaining romp through the archives of twentieth-century music, with rare video footage of some of the jazz greats.

From the town-centre crossroads, northwest of the Bulwark, High Street Superior goes north, becoming The Struet, running alongside the rushing

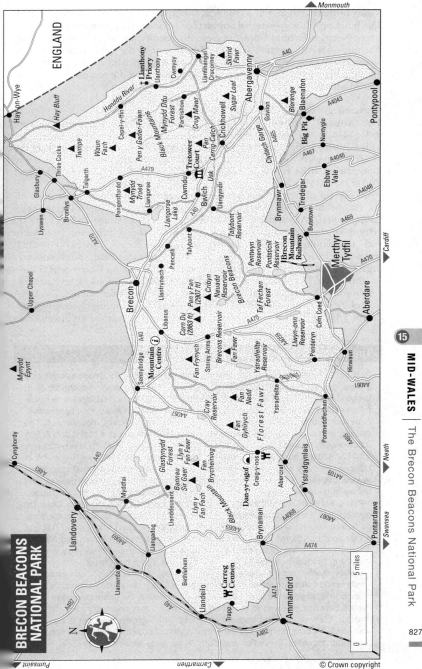

BRECON BEACONS NATIONAL PARK

ENGLAND

Monmouth

Pontypool

Cardiff

Aberdare

Neath

Swansea

Pontardawe

Ammanford

Carmarthen

Pumsaint

N

5 miles

0

© Crown copyright

waters of the Honddu. Off to the left, a footpath climbs up to the **cathedral**. The building's dumpy external appearance belies its lofty interior, graced with a few Norman features from the eleventh century, including a hulking font. The mid-sixteenth-century **Games Monument**, in the southern aisle, is made of three oak beds and depicts an unknown woman whose hands, clasped in prayer, remain intact, but whose arms and nose have been unceremoniously hacked off.

Practicalities

The **tourist office** (daily 9.30am–5pm; Nov–Easter closed Sun; ☏01874/622485) and **Brecon Beacons National Park office** (Easter–Oct daily 9.30am–5.30pm; ☏01874/623156, ⓦwww.breconbeacons.org) share the same building in the Market car park off Lion Street, next to the Safeway supermarket. **Bike rental** is available at the Brecon Cycle Centre, Ship Street (☏01874/622557).

Brecon and adjacent Llanfaes bulge with **accommodation** to suit all pockets, except during the August jazz festival. Best bets are the budget *Tirbach Guest House*, 13 Alexandra Rd (☏01874/624551, ⓦwww.tirbach.co.uk; ❶), up behind Safeway, and a couple of lovely places costing a little more: the warm and welcoming *Pickwick House*, St John's Road (☏01874/624322, ⓦwww.pickwick-house.brecon.co.uk; ❸), with excellent, predominantly organic breakfasts and evening meals; and the nonsmoking *Cantre Selyf*, 5 Lion St (☏01874/622904, ⓦwww.cantreselyf.co.uk; ❸), an imposing seventeenth-century townhouse, all creaking floors and moulded plaster ceilings. The YHA **hostel** *Ty'n-y-Caeau*, Groesffordd (☏0870/770 5718, ⓔbrecon@yha.org.uk; ❶; dorms £10.25), is two miles east of the town. It can be reached via Slwch Lane,

The central Beacons near Brecon

Popular for walking and pony trekking, the central **Brecon Beacons**, grouped around the two highest peaks in the National Park, are easily accessible from Brecon, which lies just six miles to the north. This is classic old red sandstone country, sweeping peaks rising up out of glacial scoops of land. Although the peaks never quite reach 3000ft, the terrain is unmistakeably, and dramatically, mountainous. The panorama fans out from the **Brecon Beacons Mountain Centre** (daily: July & Aug 9.30am–6pm; March–June, Sept & Oct 9.30am–5pm; Nov–Feb 10.30am–4.30pm; ☏01874/623366; small parking fee), on a windy ridge just off the A470 turn-off at Libanus, six miles southwest of Brecon. As well as a fantastic café that specializes in local ingredients, there are interesting displays on the flora, fauna, geology and history of the area, together with a well-stocked shop of maps, books and guides.

Pen y Fan (2907ft) is the highest peak in the Beacons. Together with **Corn Du** (2863ft), half a mile to the west, they form the most popular ascents in the park, particularly along the well-trampled muddy red path that starts from Pont ar Daf, half a mile south of Storey Arms, on the A470, midway between Brecon and Merthyr Tydfil. This is the most direct route from a road, where a comparatively easy five-mile round trip gradually climbs up the southern flank of the two peaks. A longer and generally quieter ascent leads up to the two peaks along the "Gap" route, the ancient road that winds its way north from the Neuadd reservoirs, immediately south of Brecon. This passes through the only natural break in the sandstone ridge of the central Beacons, heading to the bottom of the lane that eventually joins the main street in Llanfaes, Brecon, as Bailihelig Road. Although the old road is no longer accessible for cars, car parks at either end open out onto the track for an eight-mile round-trip ascent up Pen y Fan and Corn Du from the east.

a path from Cerrigcochion Road in Brecon, or it's a one-mile walk from the bus stops at either Cefn Brynich lock (Brecon–Abergavenny buses) or Troedyrharn Farm (Brecon–Hereford buses). *Brynich Caravan and Camping Park*, Brynich (℡01874/623325), is situated a mile east of town, just off the A470, overlooking the town and the river.

For **eating**, the inexpensive *Waterfront Bistro* in the Theatr Brycheiniog on the Canal Basin is open in the daytime for tasty café food and until 7.30pm for superb pre-theatre suppers; the *Beacons Guest House* (℡01874/623339), over the river at 16 Bridge St, Llanfaes, is open to nonresidents for excellent meals, many of which are inspired by local produce and traditional Welsh recipes. The *Bull's Head*, 86 The Struet, is the pick of the town's **pubs**, or you could make your way four miles north along the B4520 to the *Seland Newydd* at Pwllgloyw, a peaceful country pub that offers much the best eating around Brecon.

The Fforest Fawr

Covering a vast expanse of hilly landscape west of the central Brecon Beacons, the **Fforest Fawr** (Great Forest) seems something of a misnomer for an area of largely unforested sandstone hills dropping down to a porous limestone belt in the south. The name, however, refers to its former status as a hunting area. The hills rise up to the south of the A40, west of Brecon, with the A4067 piercing the western side of the range and the A470 defining the Fforest's eastern limit. Between the two, a twisting mountain road crosses a bleak plateau and descends into one of Britain's classic limestone landscapes, around the hamlet of **YSTRADFELLTE**. With a dazzling countryside of lush, deep ravines on its doorstep, Ystradfellte has become a phenomenally popular centre for its walks over great pavements of bone-white rock next to cradling potholes, disappearing rivers and crashing waterfalls.

A mile to the south, the River Mellte tumbles into the dark mouth of the **Porth-yr-ogof** (White Horse Cave), emerging into daylight a few hundred yards further south. A signposted path heads south from the Porth-yr-ogof car park and into the green gorge of the River Mellte. After little more than a mile, the first of three waterfalls is reached at **Sgwd Clun Gwyn** (White Meadow Fall), where the river crashes fifty feet over two huge, angular steps of rock before hurtling down the course for a few hundred yards to the other two falls – the impressive **Sgwd Isaf Clun Gwyn** (Lower White Meadow Fall) and, around the wooded corner, the **Sgwd y Pannwr** (Fall of the Fuller). The path continues to the confluence of the rivers Mellte and Hepste, half a mile further on. A quarter of a mile along the Hepste is the most popular of the area's falls, the **Sgwd yr Eira** (Fall of Snow), whose rock below the main tumble has eroded back six feet, allowing you to walk directly behind a dramatic twenty-foot curtain of water. A shorter two-mile walk to Sgwd yr Eira leads from **PENDERYN** village, off the A4059, three miles north of Hirwaun: to get there, catch **bus** #9 (hourly) from Merthyr Tydfil to Hirwaun and change to bus #15 to Penderyn (every 30min). For **accommodation** in Ystradfellte, there's the cosy *Tai'r Heol* YHA hostel (℡0870/770 6106; March–Oct; £9), half a mile south, and just a short walk from Porth-yr-ogof, plus numerous informal **camping** spots in the woods.

Dan-yr-ogof Showcaves

Six miles of upland forest and squelchy moor lie between Ystradfellte and the **Dan-yr-ogof Showcaves** (April–Oct daily 10am–3pm; call ℡01639/730801 for winter hours; £8.50; ⊛www.dan-yr-ogof-showcaves.co.uk), off the A4067 to the west. Only discovered in 1912, they are claimed to form the largest system of subterranean caverns in northern Europe, and, although relentless marketing has turned them into something of an overdone theme park, the caverns are truly awesome in their size. A concrete path leads into the first of three caverns, the **Dan-yr-ogof** cave, and a bewildering subterranean warren, the crags and walls framed by stalactites and frothy limestone deposits. Emerging back outside, you pass a downbeat re-created Iron Age "village" and a hideous park of fibreglass dinosaurs, and walk through a succession of spookily lit caverns, where water cascades relentlessly down the walls. A swelling classical soundtrack and a dancing light show come together in the final 150-foot-long **Cathedral Cave** – impressive despite its tawdriness. A precarious path leads to the **Bone Cave**, where so far 42 human skeletons have been found (most dating from the Bronze Age), as well as animal bones. Here, the owners have fenced off an assortment of dressed-up mannequins that make Bronze Age woman look like a reject from TopShop. **Camping** is available just up the road at the *Tafarn-y-Garreg* pub (✆01639/730236).

The Black Mountains

The easternmost section of the National Park centres on the **Black Mountains**, far quieter than the central belt of the Brecon Beacons and skirted by the wide valley of the River Usk. The only exception to the Black Mountains' unremitting sandstone is an isolated outcrop of limestone, long divorced from the southern belt, that peaks due north of Crickhowell at Pen Cerrig-calch (2302ft). The Black Mountains have the feel of a landscape only partly tamed by human habitation: tiny villages, isolated churches and delightful lanes are folded into an undulating green landscape which levels out to the south around the pretty villages of **Tretower** and **Crickhowell**.

Tretower

Rising out of the valley floor, dominating the view from both the A40 and the A479 mountain road, the solid round tower of the **Castle and Court** (March–Oct daily 9.30am–5pm; £2.50; CADW) at **TRETOWER** (Tre-tûr), ten miles southeast of Brecon, was built to guard the pass. The bleak, thirteenth-century round tower replaced an earlier Norman fortification, and in the late fourteenth century was supplemented by a comparatively luxurious manor house, itself being gradually expanded over the ensuing years. An enjoyable audioguide tour takes you around an open-air gallery and wall walk, and explains late medieval building methods using the exposed plaster and beams where work is still under way. In the summer, contemporary and Shakespeare **plays** are performed in the inspirational surroundings of the fully restored court (box office ✆01874/730279), with its ostentatious, beam-ceilinged Great Hall facing in on the central cobbled courtyard and square sandstone gatehouse.

Crickhowell

Compact **CRICKHOWELL** (Crucywel), four miles southeast of Tretower, on the northern bank of the wide and shallow Usk, makes for a lively base from which to explore the surrounding area. There isn't much to see in town, however, apart from a grand seventeenth-century **bridge**, with thirteen arches visible from the eastern end and only twelve from the west, spawning many a local myth. **Table Mountain** (1481ft) provides a spectacular northern backdrop, topped by the remains of the 2500-year-old hill fort (*crug*) of Hywel, accessed on a path past The Wern, off Llanbedr Road. Many walkers follow a route north from Table Mountain, climbing two miles up to the plateau-topped limestone hump of **Pen Cerrig-calch** (2302ft).

The **tourist office** (April–Sept daily 9.30am–5pm; ☎01873/812105) is in Beaufort Chambers, on Beaufort Street, and you can **rent bikes** from Mountain and Water, in the Riverside Centre, on New Road (☎01873/831825). **Accommodation** is abundant, with a grandiose coaching inn, the *Bear Hotel*, on Beaufort Street (☎01873/810408, ⓦwww.bearhotel .co.uk; ❹), and the *Dragon*, on High Street (☎01873/810362, ⓦwww .dragonhotel.co.uk; ❸); for cheaper B&B, try *Greenhill Villas*, Beaufort Street (☎01873/811177; ❶). The town-centre *Riverside Park* **campsite** lies on New Road (☎01873/810397). Across the river from the delightful nearby village of Llanbedr, *Gellirhydd Farm* (☎01873/810466; ❶) offers great B&B and wood-craft classes.

For straightforward snacks and **lunches** at low, low prices you can't beat the *Queen Coffee Tavern* on Standard Street, just off High Street, even if you're not immediately drawn by the strains of Cliff Richard and being overlooked by floor-to-ceiling Cliff photos and memorabilia. If you really can't bear it, visit the *Cheese Press* teashop on the High Street. The *Bear Hotel* wins legions of awards for its delectable, pricier-than-average bar and inexpensive to moder-ately priced restaurant food. The *Bridge End* pub, by the town bridge, offers inexpensive local delicacies and veggie specialities. A couple of miles out on the Brecon road, by the A40/A479 junction, the lovely *Nantyffin Cider Mill Inn* (☎01873/810775) is great for real ales and ciders, as well as tasty food.

Abergavenny and around

Flanking the Brecon Beacons National Park, the lively market town of **ABER-GAVENNY** (Y Fenni), seven miles southeast of Crickhowell, makes one of the best bases for an extended stay. There's not a whole lot to do, but there's a fine range of places to eat, drink and sleep, and the town is a magnet to walk-ers bound for the local mountains: **Sugar Loaf** and the legend-infused **Holy Mountain** (Skirrid Fawr). Stretching north from town, the **Vale of Ewyas** runs along the foot of the Black Mountains, where the astounding churches at Partrishow and Cwmyoy are lost in rural isolation. Abergavenny also makes a good base for visiting Monmouthshire's "Three Castles" (see p.776), set in the pastoral border country to the east.

Although only a couple of miles and a few hills away from the iron and coal towns of the Valleys (see p.778), Abergavenny grew on the basis of its weaving and tanning trades, giving it an entirely different feel. These industries pros-pered alongside a flourishing market, which is still the focal point for a wide area, drawing many people up from the Valleys every Tuesday. In World War II, Hitler's deputy, Rudolf Hess, was kept in the town's mental asylum as a pris-oner, after his plane crash-landed in Scotland in 1941. He was allowed a weekly walk in the nearby hills, growing, it is said, to love the Welsh countryside.

From the train station, Monmouth Road rises gently, eventually becoming High Street, off which you'll find the fragmented remains of the medieval **castle**, whose ugly Victorian keep houses the **town museum** (March–Oct Mon–Sat 11am–1pm & 2–5pm, Sun 2–5pm; Nov–Feb Mon–Sat 11am–1pm & 2–4pm; £1), which displays ephemera from the town's history and a recon-struction of Basil Jones' grocery shop, once on Main Street. After the death of Jones' son in 1989, the contents of the shop were transported to the museum lock, stock and biscuit barrel. Some goods are of recent origin, but much dates from the 1930s and 1940s – some even from the nineteenth century. Abergavenny's parish church of **St Mary**, on Monk Street, contains some superb tombs that span the entire medieval period. There are effigies of members of the notorious de Braose family, along with the tomb and figure of Sir William ap Thomas, founder of Raglan Castle (see p.775). Look out for the **Jesse Tree**, a recumbent, twice-life-size statue of King David's father that would once have formed part of an altarpiece tracing the family lineage from Jesse to Jesus.

Practicalities

Abergavenny's **train station** lies on the well-used line between Newport and Hereford. Buses depart from Swan Meadow **bus station**, right by the joint **tourist office** (daily 10am–5.30pm; Nov–March closes 4.30pm; ☎01873/857588) and **Brecon Beacons National Park office** (Easter–Sept daily 9.30am–5.30pm; ☎01873/853254, ⓦwww.breconbeacons.org). You can **rent bikes** from Abergavenny Mountain Bike Hire (☎01873/850910), and from Pedalabikeaway (☎01873/830219), who are based out of town but deliver.

   Accommodation comes in the form of B&Bs, many on the Monmouth Road between the town centre and the train station: *Maes Glas*, Raglan Terrace, Monmouth Road (☎01873/854494; ❶), is the best. Nearby, the Georgian *Park Guest House*, 36 Hereford Rd (☎01873/853715, ⓔparkguesthouse@hotmail.com; ❶), is also very good, while the central *King's Arms* pub, on Neville Street (☎01873/855074; ❷), has inexpensive and well-appointed rooms. If you've got transport, *Glangrwney Court* (☎01873/811288; ❷), off the A40 midway to Crickhowell, is an excellent option. The nearest place to pitch a **tent** is *Pyscodlyn Farm Caravan and Camping Site* (☎01873/853271), two miles west of town, off the A40. There are plenty of **places to eat** in Abergavenny, including the moderately priced *Greyhound Vaults*, Market Street, great for a wide range of tasty Welsh and English specialities, including the best vegetarian dishes in town. The very expensive *Walnut Tree Inn* (☎01873/852797), on the B4521 at Llanddewi Sgyrrid, two miles north of town, is a legendary foodies' paradise for superb Italian and Mediterranean cuisine. Of Abergavenny's **pubs**, the best is the staunchly traditional *Hen & Chickens*, Flannel Street, just off the High Street, with a separate dining room for inexpensive food.

The Vale of Ewyas

In total contrast to the urban blights in the northern Valleys, just a few miles to the south, the northern finger of Monmouthshire, stretching along the English border, is one of the most enchanting and reclusive parts of Wales. The main A465 Hereford road leads six miles north out of Abergavenny to Llanfihangel Crucorney, where the B4423 diverges off to the north into the beautiful **Vale of Ewyas**, along the banks of the Honddu River.

   After a mile, a lane heads west towards the enchanting valley of Gwyrne Fawr, and the delightful church and well of St Issui in the hamlet of **Partrishow**. First founded in the eleventh century, the tiny church was refashioned in the thirteenth and fourteenth centuries. In the 1500s it acquired a lacy rood screen, carved out of solid Irish oak and adorned with crude symbols of good and evil – most notably in the corner, where an evil dragon consumes a vine, a symbol of hope and wellbeing. The rest of the whitewashed church breathes simplicity by comparison. Of special note are the wall texts painted over the picture of a skeleton and scythe. Before the Reformation, such pictures were widely used to teach an illiterate population about the scriptures, until King James I ordered that such "popish devices" be whitewashed over and repainted with scripture texts.

Back on the main B4423, the road winds its way up the valley's western side, past the fork at the *Queen's Head* pub (☎01873/890241), a bargain place to **camp**. In the adjacent village of **Cwmyoy**, the parish church of St Martin has substantially subsided due to geological twists in the underlying rock. Nothing squares up: the tower leans at a severe angle from the bulging body of the church, and the view inside from the back of the nave towards the sloping altar, askew roof and straining windows is unforgettable.

Llanthony and around

Four miles further up this most remote of valleys is the hamlet of **LLAN-THONY**, little more than a small cluster of houses, an inn and a few outlying farms around the wide open ruins of **Llanthony Priory** – a grander setting, and certainly a quieter one, than Tintern, though the buildings are far more modest in scale. It was founded in around 1100 by the Norman knight William de Lacy, who, it is said, was so captivated by the spiritual beauty of the site that he renounced worldly living and founded a hermitage, attracting like-minded recluses and forming Wales' first Augustinian priory. The roofless church, with its pointed transitional arches and squat tower, was constructed in the latter half of the twelfth century and retains a real sense of spirituality and peace. There are two good places to **stay**: the *Abbey Hotel* (☎01873/890487, ⓦwww .llanthonypriory.supanet.com; ❸; Nov–March weekends only), fashioned out of part of the tumbledown priory, was built in the eighteenth century as a hunting lodge; while along the road is the *Half Moon Inn* (☎01873/890611; ❷), serving superb beer and good-value meals.

From Llanthony, the road slowly climbs four miles alongside the narrowing Honddu River to the isolated hamlet of **CAPEL-Y-FFIN**, from where it's a further mile to the YHA **hostel** (☎0870/770 5748; ❶; March–Oct; dorms £9), which also has pony trekking and **camping**. The road then weaves a tortuous route up over **Gospel Pass** and onto the howling, windy moor of **Hay Bluff**, on the glorious roof of the Black Mountains, before descending five miles to the border town of Hay-on-Wye (see p.496).

The Wells towns

The **spa towns** of mid-Wales, strung out along the Heart of Wales rail line between Swansea and Shrewsbury, were once all obscure villages, but with the arrival of the great craze for spas in the early eighteenth century, anywhere with a decent supply of apparently healing water joined in on the act. Royalty and nobility spearheaded the fashion, but the arrival of the railways opened them to all. The westernmost, **Llanwrtyd Wells**, was a popular haunt of the Welsh middle classes, some of whom arrived over the bleak moors by the **Abergwesyn Pass**, a narrow road still connecting the area to the Cambrian Coast. Far prettier – although considerably more twee and anglicized – is **Llandrindod Wells** to the north, whose spa is the only one of the four in any state of decent repair. In between, the larger town of Builth Wells was very much the spa of the Welsh working classes and there's no reason to stop other than to change buses. The fourth spa town, Llangammarch Wells, warrants even less attention.

Llanwrtyd Wells and around

Of the four spa towns, **LLANWRTYD WELLS**, twenty miles northwest of Brecon, is the most appealing. It's more Welsh, less spoilt and in more beautiful surroundings than the other three. This was the spa to which the Welsh – farmers of Dyfed alongside the Nonconformist middle classes from Glamorgan – came to the great *eisteddfodau* (festivals of Welsh music, dance and poetry) in the valley of the River Irfon.

South of where the Main Street crosses the turbulent Irfon, a lane winds for half a mile along the river to the *Dolecoed Hotel*, built near the original sulphurous spring. Although the distinctive aroma had been noted in the area for centuries, it was truly "discovered" in 1732 by the local priest, Theophilus Evans, who drank from an evil-smelling spring after seeing a rudely healthy frog pop out of it. The spring, named **Ffynon Droellwyd** (Stinking Well), can still be sniffed out in the fields beyond the hotel, now erupting around a dome-shaped extension behind the dilapidated red-and-white spa buildings. The *Neuadd Arms* pub is the base for a wide range of bizarre and entertaining annual events, including a Man-versus-Horse race and a Drovers' Walk (both in June); a town festival (first weekend in Aug); a snorkelling competition in a local bog (end of Aug); a beer festival (Nov); and a torchlight procession through the town (New Year's Eve).

Llanwrtyd's **tourist office** is in *Tŷ Barcud*, on the main square (June–Aug daily 10am–5pm; Sept–May Mon–Sat 10am–5pm; ☏01591/610666). **Accommodation** includes the *Neuadd Arms*, on the square (☏01591/610236, ⓦwww.neuaddarmshotel.co.uk; ❸), which also rents out **bikes**; the solidly Victorian *Belle Vue Hotel*, a few yards away (☏01591/610237; ❶); and *Oakfield House*, Dol-y-coed Road (☏1591/610605; ❷). The *Stonecroft Inn*, also on Dol-y-coed Road (☏01591/610332, ⓦwww.stonecroft.co.uk; ❶; dorms £13.50), is a superb pub with great food and regular live music, plus a self-catering **hostel** with bunks. Both the *Neuadd Arms* and the *Belle Vue* provide cheap, hearty **food**. The moderately priced *Drovers* restaurant (☏01591/610264), by the bridge, serves wholesome and highly acclaimed traditional Welsh dishes.

The Abergwesyn Pass

A lane from Llanwrtyd meets up with another road from Beulah at the riverside hamlet of **ABERGWESYN**, five miles north of Llanwrtyd. From here, you can drive the quite magnificent winding thread of an ancient cattle drovers' road – the **Abergwesyn Pass** – up the perilous **Devil's Staircase** and through dense conifer forests to miles of wide, desolate valleys where sheep graze unhurriedly. At the little bridge over the tiny Tywi River, a track heads south past an isolated, gas-lit YHA **hostel** at **DOLGOCH** (☏01974/298680; May–Sept; dorms £8; ❶). Remote paths lead from the hostel through the forests and hillsides to the tiny chapel at **Soar-y-Mynydd** and over the mountains to the next, and equally primitive, YHA **hostel** at **TYNCORNEL** (☏0870/770 6113; April–Sept; dorms £8; ❶), five miles from Dolgoch. Although the Abergwesyn Pass, which ends in the market square of Tregaron in Ceredigion, is less than twenty miles long, it takes a good hour in a car to negotiate the twisting, narrow road safely. The old drovers, driving their cattle to Shrewsbury or Hereford, would have taken a day or two to cover the same stretch.

Llandrindod Wells

If anything can sum up a town succinctly, it is the plaque at **LLAN-DRINDOD WELLS** station, commemorating the 1990 "Revictorianisation of Llandrindod railway station". The town, fifteen miles northeast of Llanwrtyd, has not been slow to follow suit, peddling itself furiously as Wales' most upmarket Victorian inland resort, despite its one-time reputation for licentiousness. It was the railway that made Llandrindod, bringing carriages full of well-to-do Victorians to the fledgling spa from 1864 onwards. The town blossomed, new hotels were built, neat parks were laid out and it came to rival many of the more fashionable spas and resorts over the border. Even now, Llandrindod can seem like a breath of fresh air, with its finer buildings swabbed and sandblasted, its ornate cast-iron railings restored, and the spa brought back to some kind of life.

Llandrindod's Victorian opulence is still very much in evidence in the town's grandiose public buildings, especially the lavishly restored **spa pump room** in the pleasant **Rock Park**, with its trickling streams and well-manicured glens. EU regulations sanction the use of only one of Llandrindod's spa taps in the café inside: a tiny – but more than ample – glass costs 10p, or you can step outside for a free gulp from the chalybeate fountain outside. The architecture around the park entrance is Llandrindod at its most confidently Victorian, with elaborately carved terracotta frontages and expansive gabling.

The High Street, running from here to the centre, contains antique, junk and bookshops. The tourist office, on Temple Street, behind, houses the small **Radnorshire Museum** (Tues–Thurs 10am–1pm & 2–5pm, Fri 10am–1pm & 2–4.30pm, Sat & Sun 11am–5pm; £1), which is largely dedicated to excavated remains from the Roman fort at Castellcollen, a mile northwest of Llandrindod. Kitsch Victoriana makes up the bulk of the rest of the collection, although there's also one of the better red-kite galleries, including a video with stunning footage. The **National Cycle Exhibition**, on the corner of Temple Street and Spa Road (March–Oct daily 10am–4pm; call ☏01597/825531 for winter hours; £2.95), is a nostalgic collection of over 250 bikes, from a reproduction 1818 Hobbyhorse to relatively modern folding bikes and choppers, including styles that look far too uncomfortable to have been a success.

Practicalities

Buses pull in by the **train station** in the heart of town, between High Street and Station Crescent. The **tourist office** is on Temple Street (April–Sept daily 9.30am–5pm; Oct–March Mon–Sat 9.30am–5.30pm; ☏01597/822600). **Bikes** can be rented from the Greenstiles Bike Shed (☏01597/824594), next to the Cycle Exhibition.

As mid-Wales' major tourist centre for the past 130 years, Llandrindod is well served for **accommodation**. For something smart and reasonably close to the station, try *Greylands*, High Street (☏01597/822253; ➊), or nearby *Rhydithon*, Dyffryn Road (☏01597/822624; ➊). The *Kincoed Hotel*, Temple Street (☏01597/822656; ➊), is well appointed but not a patch on the Edwardian elegance of the *Metropole Hotel*, on the same street (☏01597/822881, ⓦwww.metropole.co.uk; ➎), an old spa hotel with a pool, the centrepiece of the town. Well worth a visit, for nonresidents too, is their superb *Radnor* **restaurant**, with some dazzling interpretations of local cuisine. For reasonably priced food, head for the *Herb Garden*, Spa Road, a welcoming veggie and wholefood restaurant, or the *Llanerch Inn*, Llanerch Lane, central Llandrindod's only **pub**, and an excellent one at that – a cosy sixteenth-century inn that predates most of the surrounding town, serving a solid menu of good-value, well-cooked classics. Even nicer is the *Drovers' Arms* (☏01597/822508, ⓦwww.drovers-arms.co.uk; ➋), a couple of miles south of town in the village of Howey, a cosy foodies' pub with decent rooms.

North and East Radnorshire

Radnorshire has long been one of the most sparsely populated counties in England and Wales, its north and east still being especially remote. In the northwest, Rhayader is the only settlement of any size, a gateway to the four interlocking reservoirs of the **Elan Valley** and the surrounding wild, spartan countryside of waterfalls, bogland and bare peaks. The countryside to the northeast of Rhayader is tamer, and lanes and bridle paths delve in and around the woods and farms, occasionally brushing through minute settlements like the village of **Abbeycwmhir**, whose name is taken from its deserted Cistercian abbey. The hills roll eastwards towards the handsome town of **Knighton**, perched right on the English border, beside some of the most intact parts of **Offa's Dyke**.

Elan Valley and around

The poet Shelley spent his honeymoon in buildings now submerged by the waters of the **Elan Valley** reservoirs, a nine-mile-long string of four lakes built between 1892 and 1903 to supply water to the rapidly growing industrial city of Birmingham, 75 miles east. Although the lakes enhance an already beautiful and idyllic part of the world, the way in which Welsh valleys, villages and farmsteads were seized and flooded to provide water for English cities is something that Welsh nationalists have long protested. The tourist board prefers to advertise the profusion of rare plants and birds that resulted, notably the red kites.

From the workaday market town of **RHAYADER**, ten miles west of Llandrindod Wells, the B4518 heads southwest four miles to **ELAN** village, a curious collection of stone houses built in 1909 to replace the reservoir constructors' village that had grown up on the site. Just below the dam of the first reservoir, Caban Coch, the **Elan Valley Visitor Centre** (mid-March to Oct daily 10am–6pm; ☏01597/810898) incorporates a tourist office and a permanent exhibition stressing just how awful conditions were in nineteenth-century Birmingham, how rich the wildlife and flora around the lakes is and even how some of the water is now drunk in Wales. Frequent guided **walks** head off from the centre, and a road tucks in along the bank of Caban Coch to the **Garreg Ddu** viaduct, where it winds along for four spectacular miles to the vast, rather chilling 1952 dam on **Claerwen Reservoir**. More remote and less popular than the Elan lakes, Claerwen is a good base for a serious **walk** from the far end of the dam across eight or so harsh but beautiful miles to the monastery of Strata Florida (see p.862). Alternatively, you can follow the path that skirts around the northern shore of Claerwen to the lonely **Teifi Pools**, glacial lakes from which the River Teifi springs.

Back at the Garreg Ddu viaduct, a more popular road continues north along the long, glassy finger of Garreg Ddu reservoir, before doubling back on itself just below the awesome **Pen-y-garreg** dam and reservoir; if the dam is overflowing, the vast wall of foaming water is mesmerizing. At the top of Pen-y-garreg lake, it's possible to drive over the final dam on the system, at **Craig Goch**. Thanks to its gracious curve, elegant Edwardian arches and neat little green cupola, this is the most photographed of all the dams.

ABBEYCWMHIR (Abaty Cwm Hir), seven miles northeast of Rhayader, takes its name from the **abbey** whose sombre ruins (free access) lie behind the village. Cistercian monks founded the site in 1146, planning one of the largest churches in Britain. Destruction by Henry III's troops in 1231 scuppered plans to continue building, but the sparse ruins – a rocky outline of the floor plan – lie in a conifer-carpeted valley alongside a gloomy green lake, lending weight to the site's melancholic associations. Llywelyn ap Gruffydd's body was rumoured to have been buried here, and a new granite slab carved with a Celtic sword lies on the altar to commemorate this last native prince of Wales.

Practicalities

Bus #103 runs to the Elan Valley Visitor Centre from Llandrindod and Rhayader (Mon–Fri 2 daily). The main **accommodation** base in the area is the *Elan Valley Hotel* (℡01597/810448, ⓦwww.elanvalleyhotel.co.uk; ❸), an imposing, neocolonial pile on the Rhayader side of Elan village. It's also very good for eating, drinking and entertainment. Otherwise, you may want to make use of Rhayader, where buses stop opposite the **tourist office** (April–Oct daily 9.30am–5.30pm; Nov–March Mon–Sat 10am–5.30pm; ℡01597/810591), housed in the leisure centre. Eighteenth-century coaching inns still line Rhayader's main streets, including the *Elan Hotel*, West Street (℡01597/810373; ❷), or there's more modern accommodation at the *Bryncoed* B&B, opposite the tourist office on Dark Lane (℡01597/811082; ❶); or *The Mount*, East Street (℡01597/810585; ❶), a friendly B&B and the base for Clive Powell Mountain Bikes (℡01597/811343), from whom you can **rent bikes** or join one of his organized trips around the tracks of mid-Wales. There's a **campsite** (℡01597/810183) at Wyeside, off the A44 north of Rhayader.

Knighton

A town that straddles King Offa's eighth-century border as well as the modern Wales–England divide, **KNIGHTON** (Tref-y-clawdd, the "Town on the Dyke"), twenty miles northeast of Llandrindod, has come into its own as the most obvious centre for those walking the **Offa's Dyke Path**. Located almost exactly halfway along the route, it's a lively, attractive place that easily warrants a visit, although it has few specific sights. The town is so close to the border that its **train station** is actually in England. From here, Station Road crosses the River Teme into Wales and climbs a couple of hundred yards to Brookside Square. Further up the hill is the town's alpine-looking Victorian clocktower, at the point where Broad Street becomes West Street and the steep High Street soars off up to the left, past rickety Tudor buildings and up to the mound of the old **castle**.

Offa's Dyke

Offa's Dyke has provided a potent symbol of Welsh–English antipathy ever since it was created in the eighth century as a demarcation line by King Offa of Mercia, ruler of central England. George Borrow, in his classic *Wild Wales*, notes that, once, "it was customary for the English to cut off the ears of every Welshman who was found to the east of the dyke, and for the Welsh to hang every Englishman whom they found to the west of it".

The earthwork – up to 20ft high and 60ft wide – made use of natural boundaries like rivers in its run north to south, and is best seen in the sections near **Knighton**. Today's England–Wales border crosses the dyke many times, although the basic boundary has changed little since Offa's day. A glorious, 177-mile **long-distance footpath**, opened in 1971, runs the length of the dyke from Prestatyn in the north to Chepstow, and is one of the most rewarding walks in Britain.

In West Street, the excellent **Offa's Dyke Centre** also houses the **tourist office** (Easter–Oct daily 9am–5.30pm; Nov–Easter Mon–Fri 9am–5pm; ℡01547/529424). **Accommodation** is plentiful: try *Fleece House*, Market Street (℡01547/520168, Ⓦwww.fleecehouse.co.uk; ❷), the basic but cheerful *Red Lion*, West Street (℡01547/528231; ❶), or the bargain *Jenny Stothert's*, down towards the river at 15 Mill Green (℡01547/520075; ❶), where you can also **camp**. For **eating** and drinking, it's hard to beat the comfortable *Horse & Jockey*, at the town end of Station Road. There's folk and jazz **music** in *The Plough* on Market Street.

Montgomeryshire

The northern part of Powys is made up of the old county of **Montgomeryshire** (Maldwyn), an area of enormously varying landscapes and few inhabitants. The solid little town of **Llanidloes** is a base for ageing hippies on the River Severn (Afon Hafren). To the east, the muted old county town of **Montgomery**, with its fine Georgian architecture, perches amid gentle, green hills above the border and Offa's Dyke. Further north, **Welshpool**, the only major settlement, is packed in above the wide flood plain of the Severn; an excellent local museum, toy rail line, good pubs and reasonable hotels make it a fair stop. On the southern side of Welshpool is Montgomeryshire's one unmissable sight, the sumptuous **Powis Castle** and its exquisite terraced gardens.

Llanidloes and around

Thriving when so many other small market towns seem in danger of atrophying, the secret of success for **LLANIDLOES**, twelve miles north of Rhayader, seems to be in its adaptability. It has developed from a rural village to a weaving town, and has latterly become a centre for artists, craftspeople and assorted alternative lifestylers. One of mid-Wales's prettiest towns, the four main streets meet at the black and white **market hall**, built on timber stilts in 1600 to allow the market – which has long since moved – to take place on the cobbles beneath. Running parallel with the length of the market hall are China Street and Longbridge Street, the latter good for some interesting little shops, including the very browsable Nature Gallery art store. Off Longbridge Street is Church Street, which opens out into a yard surrounding the dumpy parish church of **St Idloes**, the impressive fifteenth-century hammerbeam roof of which is said to have been poached from Abbeycwmhir. The fantastic **millennium window** in the church was designed and built by two local stained-glass artists.

From the market hall, the broad Great Oak Street heads west to the **Town Hall**, originally built as a temperance hotel to challenge the boozy *Trewythen Arms* opposite. A plaque on the hotel commemorates Llanidloes as an unlikely-seeming place of industrial and political unrest, when, in April 1839, Chartists stormed the hotel, dragging out and beating up special constables who had been despatched to the town in a futile attempt to suppress political activism amongst the town's flannel weavers. In the town hall, you'll also find the wonderfully eclectic and much revamped town **museum** (Easter–Sept daily except Wed 11am–1pm & 2–5pm; Oct–Easter Mon, Tues, Thurs & Fri 11am–1pm & 2–5pm, Sat 10am–1pm; £1), featuring an exhibition on red kites (the birds, that is) and live transmission from nests in the nearby Hafren Forest. China Street curves down to the car park, from where all **bus** services operate. The **tourist office** (April–Sept daily 9.30am–5pm, Oct–March

Mon–Sat 10am–5pm; ☎01686/412605) is just north of the market hall, on Longbridge Street. **Accommodation** includes the *Red Lion Hotel*, Longbridge Street (☎01686/412270; ❷) and the genteel *Unicorn*, on the same street (☎01686/413167; ❶). You can **camp** at *Dol-llys Farm* (☎01686/412694), on the northern fringe of town. Among the many options for **food**, the best bet is the wholesome fare in the laid-back *Great Oak Café*, on Great Oak Street. The lively *Red Lion* **pub** also does good food. One event worth investigating is the annual **Fancy Dress Night**, held on the first Friday of July, when the pubs open late, the streets are cordoned off and virtually the whole town gets kitted out.

Montgomery and around

Tiny **MONTGOMERY** (Trefaldwyn), around twenty miles northeast of Llanidloes, is Montgomeryshire at its most anglicized. From the mound of its **castle**, situated just on the Welsh side of Offa's Dyke, there are wonderful views over the lofty church tower and the handsome Georgian streets, notably the impressively symmetrical main street – well-named Broad Street – which swoops up to the perfect little red-brick **Town Hall**, crowned by a pert clock-tower. The rebuilt tower of Montgomery's parish **Church of St Nicholas** dominates the snug proportions of the buildings around it. Largely thirteenth-century, the highlights of its spacious interior include a 1600 monument to local landowner Sir Richard Herbert and his wife. Their eight children – who included prominent Elizabethan poet George – have been carved in beatific kneeling positions behind them. Call in too at the engaging **Old Bell Museum**, just by the town hall (July & Aug Mon–Fri & Sun 1.30–5pm, Sat 10.30am–5pm; April–June & Sept Wed–Fri & Sun 1.30–5pm, Sat 10.30am–5pm; £1), an enjoyable collection of excavated artefacts, scale models of local castles and mementoes from Montgomery civic life.

Montgomery is within striking distance of one of the best-preserved sections of **Offa's Dyke**, traced by the long-distance footpath (see box on p.837), which runs on either side of the B4386. Ditches almost twenty feet high give one of the best indications of the dyke's original appearance. To the south of the main road, the England–Wales border still runs along the line of the dyke, twelve hundred years after it was built. If you want to **stay** here, *Little Brompton Farm*, two miles north on the B4385 (☎01686/668371, ⓦwww .littlebromptonfarm.co.uk; ❷), is handily close to the Offa's Dyke Path or, in town, the *Brynwylfa*, Broad Street (☎01686/668555; ❷), is a beautiful townhouse at 4 Bishops Castle St. For **food** and **drink** head for the *Checkers* pub on Broad Street.

Berriew

Three miles northwest of Montgomery, the neat village of **BERRIEW** (Aberrhiw) is more redolent of the Tudor settlements over the English border than anywhere in Wales. Its black and white houses are grouped picturesquely around a small church, the shallow waters of the River Rhiw and the slightly twee *Lion Hotel* (☎01686/640452, ⓕ640604; ❺), excellent nonetheless for food. Just over the river bridge, the **Andrew Logan Museum of Sculpture** (May–Oct Wed–Sat noon–6pm; Nov–Christmas Sat & Sun noon–4pm; £2.50) makes for an incongruous attraction in such a setting, with a good selection of the notable modern sculptor's work. Logan inaugurated the great 1970s drag-and-grunge ball known as the "Alternative Miss World Contest", astounding costumes and memorabilia from which form a large part of the exhibits at the museum. Logan's oversized horticultural sculpture, including giant lilies encrusted with shattered mirrors and vast metal irises, rises to scrape the roof, while his smaller-scale jewellery and model goddesses only add to the sublime camp of the exhibition.

Welshpool and around

Eastern Montgomeryshire's chief town of **WELSHPOOL** (Y Trallwng), seven miles north of Montgomery, was formerly known as just Pool, its prefix added in 1835 to distinguish it from the English seaside town of Poole in Dorset. Welshpool lies in the valley of the River Severn, just three miles from the English border, and was dependent largely upon the patronage of English landlords and kings. As a result, the town never developed a very Welsh character, but it's an attractive place to visit, with a number of fine Tudor, Georgian and Victorian buildings in the centre, and the sumptuous Powis Castle nearby.

Along Severn Street from the **train station**, a hump-backed bridge over the much-restored **Montgomery Canal** hides the wharf, from where gaudily painted **boats** will chug you up the navigable section for a few miles and a couple of hours (℡01938/553271; £4.50). Nearby, a carefully restored warehouse contains the **Powysland Museum** (Mon, Tues, Thurs & Fri 11am–1pm & 2–5pm, Sat & Sun 2–5pm; May–Sept Sat & Sun also 10am–1pm; £1). The impressive local history collection includes archeological nuggets such as those from an old local woodhenge and displays medieval remains from the now obliterated local Cistercian abbey of Strata Marcella.

From the *Royal Oak Hotel*, at the centre of town, follow Broad Street – which changes name five times as it rises up the hill – towards the tiny Raven Square terminus station of the **Welshpool and Llanfair Light Railway** (April–Oct weekends; Easter, Whitsun week and June–Aug daily; generally 2 trains a day; return ticket £9.50; ℡01938/810441, ⓦwww.wllr.org.uk). The eight-mile narrow-gauge rail line was open to passengers for less than thirty years prior to its closure in 1931. Now, scaled-down engines once more chuff their way along to the peaceful little village of **Llanfair Caereinion**, a good base for daytime walks, with good pub food at the *Goat Hotel*. The post office, opposite the church, stocks free leaflets on some good local circular walks.

Practicalities

The pompous neo-Gothic turrets of Welshpool's old Victorian **train station** (its modern replacement is directly behind) sit at the top of Severn Street, which leads down into the town centre – the intersection of Severn, Berriew, Broad and Church streets. The **tourist office** (daily: March–Oct 9am–5.30pm; Nov–Feb 9.30am–5pm; ℡01938/552043) is fifty yards up Church Street in the Vicarage Gardens car park. There's plenty of **accommodation** in town, including the central *Royal Oak* (℡01938/552217, ⓦwww.s-h-systems.co.uk; ❺), a traditional coaching inn at the main crossroads. Dozens of **B&Bs** line Salop Road; *Montgomery House* (℡01938/552693; ❶) is the surest bet. Further from the centre are a couple of options: the beautiful *Lower Trelydan Farm* (℡01938/553105, ⓦwww.lowertrelydan.com; ❷), out towards the village of Guilsfield (Cegidfa); and *Severn Farm*, on Leighton Road (℡01938/553098; ❶), just beyond the industrial estate to the east of the station, which allows **camping**. The best **eating** in town is at the *Royal Oak* pub, which has managed to retain its old-world grandiosity while including a superb all-day café-bar. Failing that, up the High Street, the *Talbot* pub serves excellent lunchtime and evening meals, and there are numerous stodgy cafés around town.

Powis Castle

In a land of ruined castles, the sheer scale and beauty of **Powis Castle** (April–Oct Wed–Sun castle 1–5pm, gardens 11am–6pm; July & Aug also Tues same hours; castle £8; gardens only £5.50; NT), a mile from Welshpool up Park Lane, is reason enough for coming to the town. On the site of an earlier Norman fort, the castle was started in the reign of Edward I by the Gwenwynwyn family; to qualify for the site and the barony of De la Pole, they had to renounce all claims to Welsh princedom. In 1587, Sir Edward Herbert bought the castle and began to transform it into the Elizabethan palace that survives today. Inside, the **Clive Museum** – named after Edward Clive, son of Clive of India, who married into the family in 1784 – forms a lively account of the British in India, through diaries, letters, paintings, tapestries, weapons and jewels. But it is the sumptuous period rooms that impress most, from the vast, kitsch frescoes by Lanscroon above the balustraded staircase, to the mahogany bed, brass and enamel toilets and decorative wall hangings of the state bedroom. The elegant **Long Gallery** has a rich sixteenth-century plasterwork ceiling overlooking winsome busts and marble statuettes of the four elements, placed between the glowering family portraits. The **gardens**, designed by Welsh architect William Winde, are spectacular. Dropping down from the castle in four huge stepped terraces, the design has barely changed since the seventeenth century, with a charmingly precise orangery and topiary that looks as if it is shaved daily. In summer, outdoor **concerts**, frequently with firework finales, take place in the gardens.

Llanfyllin and around

The hills and plains of northern Montgomeryshire conceal a maze of deserted lanes and farm outposts along the contours that swell up towards the north and the foothills of the Berwyn Mountains. The only real settlement of any size is **Llanfyllin**, ten miles northwest of Welshpool, a peaceful but friendly hillside town with a Thursday market. There is really nothing to do though, and you'd do better continuing on to the hiking and nature-communing around **Lake Vyrnwy**, or pressing north to **Pistyll Rhaeadr**, Wales' highest waterfall.

The Rhaeadr valley

For a place so near the English border, **LLANRHAEADR-YM-MOCHNANT**, six miles north of Llanfyllin, is surprisingly Welsh in its language and appearance. The small, low-roofed village is remembered as the serving parish of Bishop William Morgan, who translated the Bible into Welsh in 1588, but it's mostly visited as a base for **Pistyll Rhaeadr**, Wales' highest waterfall, at 240ft. The village lies at the foot of a lane that runs four miles northwest from the village alongside the River Rhaeadr through an increasingly rocky valley to the falls. The river tumbles down the crags in two stages, flowing furiously under a natural stone arch that has been christened the Fairy Bridge. When it's quiet, tame chaffinches swoop and settle all around this enchanting spot, although the charms are a little hard to appreciate amid the tourists on a warm summer Sunday.

The summer-only *Tan-y-Pistyll* licensed café, by the waterfall car park, is tolerable and they run a decent **B&B** (℡01691/780392; ❷) with a **campsite** in the back field. The village has a bargain B&B, *Powys House*, on the central square (℡01691/780201; ❶), and two great **pubs** – the *Three Tuns* and the *Wynnstay Arms*.

Lake Vyrnwy

A monument to the self-aggrandizement of the Victorian age, **Lake Vyrnwy** (Llyn Efyrnwy) combines its functional role as a water supply for Liverpool with a touch of architectural genius in the shape of the huge nineteenth-century dam at its southern end and the Disneyesque turreted straining tower that edges out into the icy waters. It's a magnificent spot, and a popular centre for walking and birdwatching, with nature trails. The village of **LLANWD-DYN** was flattened and rebuilt at the eastern end, the inhabitants receiving compensation of just £5 for losing their homes. The story is told, somewhat apologetically, in the RSPB **Vyrnwy Visitor Centre** (Jan–March Sat & Sun 10am–4.30pm; April–Dec daily 10am–5.30pm; free), which includes a whizzy 3D film presentation on local wildlife. Down the lane are the **tourist office** (Easter–Oct daily 10am–5pm; Nov–Easter Sat & Sun 10am–4pm; ☎01691/870346) and a **birdwatching centre**, in the cluster of buildings on the western side of the dam. **Bikes** can be rented from *Mandy's Tea Shop*, next door.

Lake Vyrnwy's immediate surroundings have some of the best **accommodation** in the region, notably the grand *Lake Vyrnwy Hotel* (☎01691/870692, Ⓦwww.lakevyrnwy.com; ❼), overlooking the waters above the southeastern shore. If you just want a look, the hotel serves a full afternoon tea in a chintzy lounge overlooking the lake. Close by, *Tŷ Uchaf* (☎01691/870286; ❷) has B&B and a good tearoom. Farmhouse B&B is available not far away at *Tynymaes* (☎01691/870216; ❶), a couple of miles east of Llanwddyn on the B4393. If you're **camping**, there are five tent pitches at *Fronheulog* (☎01691/870662), at the top of the hairpin bends on the road to Llanfyllin, or in Llanwddyn itself at *Bryn Fedwen* (☎01691/870288).

The Dee Valley

Llangollen, along with the smaller town of Bala (see p.846), grew up partly as a market centre, but also served the needs of cattle drovers who used the passage carved by the **River Dee** (Afon Dyfrdwy) through the hills – the easiest route from the fattening grounds of northwest Wales to the markets in England. Long before rail and road transport pushed the dwindling numbers of drovers out of business at the end of the nineteenth century, they had already been joined by early tourists. Most made straight for Llangollen, where the ruins of both a Welsh castle and a Cistercian abbey lent a gaunt Romantic charm to a dramatic gorge naturally blessed with surging rapids. The arrival of the railway, in the middle of the nineteenth century, made Llangollen a firm favourite with tourists from the mill towns of northwest England. Between Llangollen and the English border, the Dee is joined by one of its major tributaries, the Ceiriog, which flows down its peaceful valley to the Marcher fortress of **Chirk Castle**.

Llangollen and around

LLANGOLLEN, thirty miles north of Welshpool, is the embodiment of a Welsh town in both setting and character, clasped tightly in the narrow Dee Valley between the shoulders of the Berwyn and Eglwyseg mountains. Along the valley's floor, the waters of the River Dee run down to the town, licking the angled buttresses of the weighty Gothic bridge, which has spanned the river since the fourteenth century. On its south bank, half a dozen streets, their houses harmoniously straggling up the rugged hillsides, are labelled in both Welsh and English, and form the core of the scattered settlement flung out across the low hills. Every July, the town comes alive for the **International Music Eisteddfod**.

As the only river crossing point for miles, Llangollen was an important town long before the early Romantics arrived at the end of the eighteenth century, when they were cut off from their European Grand Tours by the Napoleonic Wars. Turner came to paint the swollen river and the Cistercian ruin of **Valle Crucis**, a couple of miles up the valley; John Ruskin found the town "entirely lovely in its gentle wildness"; and writer George Borrow made Llangollen his base for the early part of his 1854 tour detailed in *Wild Wales*. The rich and famous came not just for the scenery, but to visit the "Ladies of Llangollen", an eccentric couple who became the toast of society from their house, Plas Newydd. But by this stage some of the town's rural charm had been eaten up by the works of one of the century's finest engineers, Thomas Telford, who squeezed both his London–Holyhead trunk road and the **Llangollen Canal** alongside the river.

The Town

Standing in twelve acres of formal gardens, half a mile up Hill Street from the southern end of Castle Street, the two-storeyed mock-Tudor **Plas Newydd** (Easter–Oct daily 10am–5pm; £2.75) was, for almost fifty years, home to the celebrated **Ladies of Llangollen**. Lady Eleanor Butler and Sarah Ponsonby were a couple from Anglo-Irish aristocratic backgrounds, and tried to elope together at the end of the eighteenth century. After two botched attempts dressed in men's clothes, they were grudgingly allowed to leave their family seats in 1778 with an annual allowance of £280, enough to settle in Llangollen, where they became celebrated hosts and legendary local characters. Despite their desire for a "life of sweet and delicious retirement", they didn't seem to mind the constant stream of gentry who called on them. Walter Scott was well received, though he found them "a couple of hazy or crazy old sailors" in manner, and like "two respectable superannuated clergymen" in their mode of dress. Visitors' gifts of sculpted **wood panelling** formed the basis of the riotous friezes of gloomy woodwork that weigh on your every step around the modest black and white timbered house. Most of the rooms have been left almost empty, so as not to hide the panelling; only one upper room has been devoted to a few of the ladies' possessions and panels detailing their life story. Llangollen takes its name from the **Church of St Collen**, on Bridge Street (May–Sept daily 1.30–6pm; free), outside which is a triangular railed-off monument to the Ladies and their devoted maid.

The hills around Llangollen echo to the shrill cry of steam engines easing along the **Llangollen Steam Railway** (Easter–Oct daily; plus weekends and holidays throughout the year; ☎01978/860979, ⓦwww .llangollen-railway.co.uk), shoe-horned into the north side of the valley. From Llangollen's time-warped station it runs along a restored section of the disused Ruabon–Barmouth line, the belching steam engines creeping west along the riverbank, hauling ancient carriages which proudly sport the liveries of their erstwhile owners. The restored line currently runs the eight miles to Carrog, although plans to push through to Corwen are well in hand.

A short riverside walk from the station leads to the **Llangollen Exhibition Centre** on Mill Street (daily 10am–5pm; combined ticket valid all day £9.75; ⓦwww.dapol.co.uk), an ugly light-industrial building converted to house two wildly divergent museums: the **Doctor Who Exhibition** (individually £5.95), an endearing homage to this much-loved British TV sci-fi drama, and **Model Railway World** (individually £5.95), with plenty of layouts and engines to play with. Entry to either gives you the opportunity to watch model-making in progress in the parent Dapol toy factory.

Across the street is the Llangollen Canal, one of the finest feats of British canal building. Its architect, Thomas Telford, succeeded in building a canal without locks through fourteen miles of hilly terrain, most spectacularly by means of the thousand-foot-long **Pontcysyllte Aqueduct**, passing 127ft over the River Dee at Froncysyllte, four miles east. **Canal trips** (Easter–Oct daily; horse-drawn trip £4, aqueduct trip £7; ☎01978/860702) over the aqueduct leave from Llangollen Wharf, just above the steam train station on Wharf Hill.

Walking west from the town bridge, you'll soon come to the site of the International Eisteddfod, crowned by the extraordinary **Royal International Pavilion**, which – especially from the walk up the hill to Dinas Brân – resembles some giant armoured reptile dropped from a great height into the valley. Outside the Eisteddfod season, the auditorium acts as a concert venue and sports hall, with temporary exhibitions in the foyer (Mon–Fri 10am–4pm; free).

Practicalities

Buses stop on Market Street, while the nearest **train station** is five miles away at Ruabon, which is passed by frequent buses on the Llangollen–Wrexham run. The **tourist office**, on Castle Street (Easter–Oct daily 10am–6pm; Nov–Easter Mon–Sat 9.30am–4.30pm; ☎01978/860828), is fifty yards from the bridge and less than a hundred yards from the bus stop on Market Street. There's **bike rental** from the town's hostel – you don't have to be staying there.

Finding **rooms** in Llangollen can be a chore in summer, especially during the Eisteddfod. Low-cost B&Bs worth checking out include the bright, simply furnished rooms at *Greenbank Guesthouse*, Victoria Square (T01978/861835, Wwww.greenbank.uk.com; ❶); *Bryant Rose*, 31 Regent St (T01978/860389; ❶), a central B&B with large, airy rooms; and *Jonkers*, 9 Chapel St (T01978/861158; ❶), which has a couple of compact, low-beamed rooms in an ancient house with uneven floors and narrow stairways. Moving upmarket, go for *Gales*, 18 Bridge St (T01978/860089, Wwww.galesofllangollen.co.uk; ❸), a comfortable guesthouse above a wine bar; or *Bodidris Hall* (T01978/790434, Wwww.bodidrishall.com; ❻), seven miles north of Llangollen on the A5104, which offers secluded luxury in a largely Tudor building with log fires, oak beams and an award-winning restaurant. The excellent YHA **hostel**, on Tyndwr Road (T0870/770 5932, Ellangollen @yha.org.uk; ❶, dorms £10.25), is a mile and a half from town – go along the A5 towards Shrewsbury, turn right up Birch Hill, then right again. *Eirianfa* (T01978/860919), a mile west of the town on the A5, is the closest **campsite** – they also rent out bikes.

Though not extensive by city standards, Llangollen boasts a fairly good selection of **restaurants** and no shortage of cafés around town. *The Gallery*, 15 Chapel St (T01978/860076), is a good start for moderately priced pizza and pasta dishes. *Jonkers* (see above; closed Sun & Mon), is well worth the extra pound or two for its classy meals, and there's outside seating in summer. *Gales Wine Bar* (see above; closed Sun), has great old church pews and an extensive cellar, and serves decent bistro-style food. The *Hand Hotel*, 26 Bridge St, is a straightforward local **pub** where you can listen to a male voice choir in full song (Mon & Fri 7.30pm) or sink a pint in their gorgeous riverside garden. Another good watering hole is *Jenny Jones*, Abbey Road, with live country and western music (Wed) and jazz (Thurs). Top no-nonsense boozing haunt is the youthful *Bull Hotel* on Castle Street.

Around Llangollen

The panoramic view, especially at sunset, justifies the 45-minute slog up to **Castell Dinas Brân** (Crow's Fortress Castle), perched on a hill 800ft above the town, and reached by a path beginning near Llangollen Wharf. The lure certainly isn't the few sad – if powerfully evocative – stumps which stand as a poor testament to what was once the district's largest and most important Welsh fortress. Built in the 1230s by the ruler of northern Powys, Prince Madog ap Gruffydd Maelor, the castle rose on the site of an earlier Iron Age fort. Edward I soon captured it as part of his first campaign against Llywelyn ap Gruffydd, but the castle was left to decay. In 1540, John Leland, Henry VIII's antiquarian, found it "all in ruin".

The gaunt ruin of **Valle Crucis Abbey** (Easter–Sept daily 10am–5pm, £2; all other times free access; CADW), a mile or so west of Llangollen, greets you with its best side, the largely intact west wall of the church pierced by the frame of a rose window. Though one of the last Cistercian foundations in Wales, and the first Gothic abbey in Britain, it is no match for Tintern Abbey (see p.774), but nevertheless stands majestically in a pastoral – and much less-visited – setting. Despite a devastating fire in its first century, and a complement of far from pious monks, it survived until the Dissolution, in 1535. The church fell into disrepair, after which the monastic buildings, in particular the monks' dormitory, were employed as farm buildings. Now they hold displays on monastic life, reached by a detour through the mostly ruined cloister and past the weighty vaulting of the chapterhouse.

Seven miles southeast of Llangollen, the busy Dee Valley contrasts with the parallel valley of the River Ceiriog, its entrance guarded by the massive, drum-towered **Chirk Castle** (April–Sept Wed–Sun noon–5pm, garden 11am–6pm; Oct same days, closes 1hr earlier; castle £5.80, garden only £3.60; NT), squatting ominously on a rise half a mile to the west of **CHIRK** (Y Waun). Construction was begun in the thirteenth century, at the behest of Edward I, who wanted to control the borderlands between England and Wales. The structure is designed to mimic Beaumaris Castle, although it lacks its purity and symmetry. At the end of a long avenue of oaks, the approach is guarded by a magnificent Baroque gate screen, the finest work done by the Davies brothers of Bersham, who wrought it between 1712 and 1719. The ebullient floral designs are capped by the coat of arms of the Myddletons who have lived here for the past four hundred years. The exterior has been extensively remodelled, as have the interiors, leaving a legacy of sumptuous rooms reflecting sixteenth- to nineteenth-century tastes, many now returned to their former states after some Victorian meddling by Pugin in the 1840s.

Meirionydd

Containing stunning scenery and precious few people, the old county of **Meirionydd** (now part of Gwynedd) covers an enormous area from the lushness of the upper Dee Valley, through harsh mountain landscape to the gentle beaches of the west coast. Traditionally, Meirionydd was known as the most remote, and poorest, area in all of Wales, cut off behind the peaks of the Rhinog range. But the landscape tells an even older story: here lie some of Wales' greatest concentrations of Neolithic remains, many from early Irish and Celtic settlers.

Bala was one of Meirionydd's major market towns. Although its agricultural base has waned, the town is a fine place for visitors, especially watersports enthusiasts, who are well catered for on the shores of **Llyn Tegid**, next to the town. Crossing the moors and mountains brings you to the coast, in particular the hilltop fortress of **Harlech**, the bucket-and-spade resort of **Barmouth** and the fabulous stretch of **Ardudwy beach** between them. Barmouth sits at the head of the beautiful **Mawddach estuary**, which snakes its way inland to the old county town of **Dolgellau**, sheltering beneath the northern flank of **Cadair Idris** (2930ft), one of Wales' most inspirational mountains.

Bala

The little town of **BALA** (Y Bala), twenty miles west of Llangollen, is set at the northern end of Wales' largest natural lake, **Llyn Tegid** (Bala Lake). The town was renowned for its piety in the nineteenth century, but these days it has become a major **water-sports** centre, and there's little else to do here now. The lake is perfect for windsurfing in particular, due to the winds buffeting up the Talyllyn valley, which slices thirty miles northeast from the coast, along the Bala geological fault.

Slalom kayak fans can make for the **Canolfan Tryweryn** white-water course, four miles west up the A4212. When water is released from the dam, around two hundred days a year, it crashes down a mile and a half through the slalom site, the venue for frequent summer-weekend competitions and commercial **white-water rafting** trips (℡01678/521083, ⓦwww .welsh-canoeing.org.uk). It costs a fairly steep £10 for a single heart-stopping run down the roughest part, but for a minimum of £150 a group of up to seven can rent a raft and instructor for two hours, or about four runs. Down on the shores of Llyn Tegid, by the tourist office, the Bala Adventure and Watersports Centre (☎01678/521059) runs courses and rents equipment for **windsurfing**, **kayaking** and **sailing**.

The only public transport access is on **bus** #94, which runs from Llangollen to Dolgellau, stopping on Bala's High Street. The **tourist office** (Easter–Oct daily 10am–6pm; Nov–March Mon–Fri 10am–4.30pm; ☎01678/521021) is on Pensarn Road on the lakeside, five minutes' walk away. Bala has plenty of **places to stay**, or you can make the most of the surrounding countryside by staying in the Vale of Edeirnion, northeast of the town. Centrally, try the welcoming and good-value *Trem Aran House* B&B, 1 Tegid St (☎01678/520848; ❶). A little further out there's *Abercelyn*, a fine country house half a mile south of Bala on the A494 (☎01678/521109, ⓦwww.abercelyn.co.uk; ❷), and *Fron Feuno Hall* (☎01678/521115, ⓕ52115; ❹), a gracious place with lots of thoughtful touches. One and a half miles north on the A494, there's a great independent **hostel**, the *Coach House*, at Tomen Y Castell (☎01678/520738, ⓦwww.balawales.com/coach-house; ❶; dorms £8.50). *Pen-y-Bont*, just by the lakeside steam railway station off the B4391 Llandrillo back road (☎01678/520549; April–Oct), is the nearest **campsite**.

Harlech

One of the undoubted highlights of the Cambrian Coast is charming **HARLECH**, 25 miles due west of Bala, with its time-worn castle dramatically clinging to its rocky outcrop, and the town cloaking the ridge behind, commanding one of Wales' finest views over Cardigan Bay to the Llŷn. There are good beaches nearby, and the town's twisting, narrow streets harbour places where you can eat and sleep surprisingly well for such a small place.

Harlech's substantially complete **castle** (June–Sept daily 9.30am–6pm, April, May & Oct daily 9.30am–5pm, Nov–March Mon–Sat 9.30am–4pm, Sun 11am–4pm; £3; CADW) sits on its 200-foot-high bluff, a site chosen by Edward I for one more link in his magnificent chain of fortresses. Begun in 1285, it was built of a hard Cambrian rock, known as Harlech grit, hewn from the moat. The sea, which originally protected one side of the fortress, has now receded, leaving the castle dominating a stretch of duned coastline. Harlech withstood a siege in 1295, but was taken by Owain Glyndŵr in 1404. The young Henry VII withstood a seven-year siege at the hands of the Yorkists until 1468, when the castle was again taken. It fell into ruin, but was put back into service for Charles I during the Civil War; in March 1647, it was the last Royalist castle to fall. The first defensive line comprised the three successive pairs of gates and portcullises built between the two massive half-round towers of the **gatehouse**, where an **exhibition** now outlines the castle's history. Much of the castle's outermost ring has been destroyed, leaving only the twelve-foot-thick curtain walls rising up forty feet to the exposed **battlements**. Only the towering gatehouse prevents you from walking the full circuit.

Harlech's **train station** is below the castle on the main A496. Most **buses** call both here and on High Street, a few yards from the **tourist office** (April–Oct daily 10am–6pm; ☎01766/780658). The pick of the local places to **stay** is the cosy, informal *Castle Cottage* hotel, on Pen Llech near the castle (☎01766/780479, ⓦwww.castlecottageharlech.co.uk; ❻), which has the

△ Harlech Castle

trappings of a place charging twice as much. Other possibilities include the *Plas Newydd* **hostel** (℡0870/770 5926, ⓔllanbedr@yha.org.uk; ❶, dorms £10.25), three miles south in Llanbedr (buses #38 & #94), where the lane also heads west to the sprawling **camping** resort at *Shell Island* (℡01341/241453, ⓦwww.shellisland.co.uk), great for camp fires in the dunes and walks on the splendid **Ardudwy Beach** (part of which, near the village of Dyffryn Ardudwy, is officially naturist). If you want to camp in Harlech itself, head for the *Min y Don* campsite, Beach Road (℡01766/780286; Easter–Sept), three minutes' walk from the beach; take the first right out of the station. There are some wonderful places to **eat** on High Street, including the inexpensive but licensed *Plas Café*, with a good range of food and fabulous views from the garden and conservatory; the bistro-style *Yr Ogof*, where you'll find a good-value range of inventive vegetarian and meat dishes; and the classy, modern *Castle Cottage*.

Barmouth and around

Continuing along the coast, the best approach to **BARMOUTH** (Abermaw) is from the south, where the Cambrian Coast rail line sweeps across the Mawddach River from tiny **Fairbourne**, over 113 rickety-looking wooden spans. It's still the haunt of English holidaymakers from the Midlands, who fashioned Barmouth as a sea-bathing resort in the nineteenth century, but also warrants some attention for breezy rambles on the cliffs of **Dinas Oleu**, above the town, and a great walk around the mouth of the estuary (see box). Central attractions don't extend beyond the **Tŷ Gwyn Museum** (July–Sept Tues–Sun 10.30am–5pm; free), a medieval tower house – now a Tudor museum – where Henry VII's uncle, Jasper Tudor, is thought to have plotted Richard III's downfall; and the **Tŷ Crwn Roundhouse**, on the hill behind (same times) which once acted as a lockup for drunken sailors.

Buses from Harlech and Dolgellau stop in the leisure centre car park by the train station, just a few yards from the **tourist office** in the Old Library on Station Road (Easter–Oct daily 10am–6pm; ℡01341/280787). **Accommodation** is plentiful, and best at *The Gables*, Mynach Road (℡01341/280553; ❷), ten minutes' walk north of town and particularly welcoming to walkers, or the seafront *Wavecrest Hotel*, 8 North Parade (℡01341/280330, ⓦwww.lokalink.co.uk/wavecrest; ❷). The closest of a long string of **campsites** is *Hendre Mynach*, Llanaber Road (℡1341/280262; March–Oct), a mile north of town and just off the beach. Basic **cafés** are plentiful, though for just a little more money you can get mammoth French sticks,

---

Walking the Barmouth–Fairbourne Loop

The best lowland walk in the Cambrian Coast region, the **Barmouth–Fairbourne Loop** (5 miles; 300ft ascent; 2–3hr) is a fine way to spend an afternoon with impressive mountain scenery, and estuarine and coastal views all the way. The walking component can be virtually eradicated by using both the mainline and Fairbourne railways. The route first crosses the estuary rail bridge (50p) to Morfa Mawddach mainline station, then follows the lane to the main road, crossing it onto a footpath that loops behind a small wooded hill to Pant Einion Hall, then follows another lane back to the main road near Fairbourne. In Fairbourne, turn north, either walking along the beach to the quay at the end of the spit or catching the **Fairbourne Railway** (Easter–Oct 3–6 daily) to the **passenger ferry** (Easter–Oct; hourly) across the estuary mouth back to Barmouth.

good pizzas and decent veggie meals at *Isis* on The Quay. Nearby, in Church Street, *The Last Inn*, in a former cobbler's shop, serves good **pub** meals, while its outside tables catch the afternoon sun.

Dolgellau

Its distance from England and its historical position in the heartland of Welsh nationalism should make **DOLGELLAU** (pronounced "dol-geth-lye") the most Welsh of towns, but the town's granite architecture draws more from nineteenth-century England, with a dour series of small neo-Georgian squares all bearing English names. Victorian tourists came to marvel at **Cadair Idris** and the Mawddach Estuary – still the best policy, as the town has little to offer beyond the **Quaker Interpretive Centre**, above the tourist office (Easter–Oct daily 10am–6pm; Nov–Easter Mon & Thurs–Sun 10am–5pm). This details the lives of Quakers forced by persecution to seek a better life in Pennsylvania, where some towns still bear Welsh names: Bangor, Bryn Mawr and others.

Walks around Dolgellau

Dolgellau is a good base for **walks**, whether fairly easy rambles, like the first two described here, or more strenuous mountain hiking. For the **Cadair Idris** ascent, you'll need a map and walking equipment and the 1:25,000 OS *Explorer* map OL23, "Cadair Idris & Llyn Tegid", though the 1:50,000 *Landranger* map #124, "Porthmadog & Dolgellau", will do.

Torrent Walk

Victorians seldom missed the lowland, beechwood **Torrent Walk** (2 miles; 100ft ascent; 1hr) which follows the course of the River Clywedog as it carves its way through bedrock to the *Clywedog Tea Garden*, where home-baked scones are served beside the river. Bus #2 takes the two miles east along the A470 to the start, by the junction of the B4416 road to Brithdir.

Precipice Walk

Nowadays, more people head for the not-remotely-precipitous **Precipice Walk** (3–4 miles; negligible ascent; 2hr), a circuit around the bracken and heather-covered Foel Cynach, with great views along the Mawddach Estuary and towards the thousand-foot ramparts of Cadair Idris. Best done in the late afternoon, when the sun is low on the estuary, the walk is fairly well signposted from the start, three miles north of Dolgellau along the Llanfachreth road, which turns off the A494 by Big Bridge. Bus #33 (Tues & Fri 3 daily) runs to the start.

Cadair Idris ascents

More ambitious Victorians climbed **Cadair Idris** on the since-eroded Fox's Path, now widely ignored in favour of the straightforward, classic **Pony Path** (6–7 miles; 2500ft ascent; 4–5hr), starting three miles up Cadair Road in the car park at Ty Nant. As you begin by the sign near the telephone box, the view to the craggy flanks of the massif are tremendous, but they disappear as you climb steeply to the col, where a left turn leads to the summit shelter on **Penygadair** (2930ft). The most impressive ascent of Cadair Idris, however, is up the **Minffordd Path** (6 miles; 2900ft ascent; 5hr), which leads up to and then around the glacial lake of Cwm Cau before reaching the summit. The path starts from the car park just west of the *Minffordd Hotel* where the A487 meets the B4405; buses between Dolgellau and Machynlleth pass the spot.

Dolgellau has no train station but is well served by **buses**, all of which pull into the central Eldon Square, close to the **tourist office** (Easter–Oct daily 10am–6pm; Nov–Easter Mon & Thurs–Sun 10am–5pm; ☎01341/422888). Central **accommodation** is best found at the *Ivy House*, Finsbury Square (☎01341/422535, ⓦwww.ukworld.net/ivyhouse; ❷). Outside town, the eighteenth-century *Tyddyn Mawr Farmhouse*, Islawrdref (☎01341/422331; ❸), stands on the slopes of Cadair Idris at the foot of the Pony Path, while the superb seventeenth-century *George III Hotel*, Penmaenpool (☎01341/422525, ⓦwww.george-3rd.co.uk; ❺), overlooks the Mawddach Estuary, two miles west of Dolgellau. There's a decent town-centre independent **hostel** in the shape of *Plas Isa* on Lion Street (☎01341/440666 or ☎01766/540569; ❶, minimum £50 for 4-bunk room). The tent-only *Bryn-y-Gwyn* **campsite**, Cader Road (☎01341/422733), is less than a mile southeast of town. There's a fair choice for **eating** in Dolgellau: the best bet is the *Tyn-y-Groes Hotel*, Glanllwyd (☎01341/440275), four miles north of town in the Coed y Brenin forest, with good beer, fine bar meals and a la carte dinners, while *Y Sospan* (☎01341/423174), on Queen Square behind the tourist office, is a dependable central bistro for good lunches and bookable dinners. The *Tafarn Caetanws*, Smithfield Street, is a great **pub** for food and occasional music and comedy. Dolgellau's mid-July festival of folk and rock, **Sesiwn Fawr** (ⓦwww .sesiwnfawr.demon.co.uk), has rapidly grown into one of Wales' finest.

Tywyn and around

TYWYN is primarily of interest as a base for the Talyllyn and Dysynni valleys, although the town does have miles of sandy beach and the five-foot-high **Ynysmaengwyn**, or St Cadfan's Stone, within the Norman nave of the **Church of St Cadfan** (daily 9am–5pm; hours extended in summer; tours Wed 5pm), which bears the earliest example of written Welsh, dating back to around 650 AD.

Tywyn's three main roads meet at the joint **train station** and main **bus stop**, a short walk from the **tourist office**, opposite the entrance to the leisure centre on High Street (Easter–Oct daily 9.30am–5.30pm; ☎01654/710070), and, two hundred yards to the south, the Talyllyn narrow-gauge train station (Tywyn Wharf). The Talyllyn Valley is served by **bus** #30, running from Tywyn to Abergynolwyn, continuing to Minffordd (where you can catch bus #2 to Dolgellau) and Machynlleth. Decent **accommodation** can be found at the *Ivy Guest House*, High Street (☎01654/711058; ❷), opposite the tourist office, or the cheaper, nonsmoking *Glenydd Guest House*, 2 Maes Newydd (☎01654/711373; ❷), two hundred yards from the beach off Pier Road. The handiest **campsite** is *Ynysmaengwyn Caravan Park*, a mile out on the Dolgellau road (☎01654/710684; April–Sept). The best **eating** in town is upstairs at the moderately priced, nonsmoking *Proper Gander*, High Street.

The Talyllyn and Dysynni valleys

The **Talyllyn narrow-gauge railway** (April–Oct 2–8 daily; also at Christmas; £10 day rover; ☎01654/710472, ⓦwww.talyllyn.co.uk) belches seven miles inland through the delightful wooded Talyllyn Valley to Nant Gwernol. From 1866 to 1946, the rail line was used to haul slate to Tywyn Wharf station. Just four years after its closure, enthusiasts restarted services, making this the world's first volunteer-run railway. At a leisurely 15mph, the round trip takes two hours, longer if you get off to take in some fine broadleaf forest walks. The best of these starts at Dolgoch Falls station, where three well-marked trails (maximum 1hr) lead off to the lower, mid- and upper falls. At the end of the line, more woodland walks take you around the site of the old slate quarries.

From Tywyn, the road runs parallel to the Talyllyn Railway, meeting it at Dolgoch Falls, a couple of miles short of the valleys' largest settlement, **Abergynolwyn**, comprising a few dozen quarry workers' houses, a shop and a pub, the excellent *Railway Inn*. The Dysynni Valley branches northwest here, but Talyllyn Valley continues northeast to **Tal-y-llyn Lake** (Llyn Mwyngil) and the fifteenth-century **St Mary's**, a fine example of a small Welsh parish church, unusual because of its chancel arch painted with an alternating grid of red and white roses, separated by grotesque bosses.

The **Dysynni Valley** has more to offer in the way of sights, though the lack of public transport makes it difficult to get to. A mile and a half northwest of Abergynolwyn, a side road cuts northeast to the hamlet of **Llanfihangel-y-Pennant** and the scant, but impressive, ruins of **Castell-y-Bere** (free access; CADW), a fortress built by Llywelyn the Great in 1221 to protect the mountain passes. One of the most massive of the Welsh castles, it was besieged twice before being consigned to seven centuries of obscurity and decay. There's still plenty to poke around, with large slabs of the main towers still standing, but it's primarily a great place just to sit gazing at Cadair Idris, or three miles seaward to **Craig yr Aderyn** (Birds' Rock), a 760-foot-high cliff where thirty breeding pairs of cormorants have remained loyal to the spot as, over the centuries, the sea has receded. Also worth seeing is the fabulous three-dimensional patchwork map of the Dysynni Valley that can be found just up the road in the vestry of Llanfihangel-y-Pennant church.

Good places to **stay** include *Tan-y-Coed-Uchaf* (℡01654/782228; ❷; March–Oct), a superb farmhouse B&B close to Dolgoch Falls; the excellent *Riverside Guesthouse* in Abergynolwyn (℡01654/782235, ⓦwww .snowdonia-wales.co.uk; ❶); or the *Minffordd Hotel* (℡01654/761665, ⓦwww.minffordd.com; ❻; closed Jan), an eighteenth-century farmhouse and coaching inn by Tal-y-llyn Lake, open to nonresidents for moderately priced traditional British **dinners** (Thurs–Sat). There's a basic **campsite** at *Cedris Farm*, a mile northeast of Abergynolwyn (℡01654/782280), and plenty of others dotted about the two valleys.

Machynlleth

A finger of Montgomeryshire poking out between Meirionydd and Ceredigion, the flat river plain and rolling hills of **Dyfi Valley** lay justifiable claim to being one of the greenest corners of Europe, an area replete with B&Bs and other businesses started up by idealistic New Agers who have flocked to this corner of Wales since the late 1960s. The focal point is the genial town of **MACHYNLLETH** (pronounced "ma-hun-thleth"), eighteen miles northeast of Aberystwyth, a candidate for the Welsh capital in the 1950s and site of Owain Glyndŵr's embryonic fifteenth-century Welsh parliament. In the hills to the north, the renowned, self-contained **Centre for Alternative Technology** runs on cooperative lines and makes for one of the most interesting days out in Wales.

The town that might have been the nation's capital consists essentially of just two streets. The wide main street, **Heol Maengwyn**, is busiest on Wednesdays, when a lively market springs up out of nowhere; **Heol Penrallt** intersects at the fussy clocktower. Glyndŵr's partly fifteenth-century **Parliament House**

Owain Glyndŵr

No name is so frequently invoked in Wales as that of **Owain Glyndŵr**, a potent figurehead of Welsh nationalism since he rose up against the occupying English in the early fifteenth century. Little is known about the real Glyndŵr, although he is described in Shakespeare's *Henry IV, Part I* as "not in the roll of common men". There's little doubt that the charismatic Owain fulfilled many of the mystical medieval prophecies about the rising up of the red dragon. Born in the late fourteenth century to an aristocratic family, he had a conventional upbringing, part of it studying English in London, where he became a loyal and distinguished soldier of the English king. He returned to Wales to take up his claim as Prince of Wales, being directly descended from the princes of Powys and Cyfeiliog, but became the focus of a rebellion born of discontent simmering since Edward I's stringent policies of subordinating Wales.

Goaded by a parochial land dispute in North Wales in which the courts failed to back him, Glyndŵr garnered four thousand supporters and declared anew that he was Prince of Wales. He attacked Ruthin, and then Denbigh, Rhuddlan, Flint, Hawarden and Oswestry, before encountering English resistance at Welshpool, but whole swathes of North Wales were his for the taking. The English king, Henry IV, dispatched troops and rapidly drew up a range of severely punitive laws against the Welsh, even outlawing Welsh-language bards and singers. Battles continued to rage until, by the end of 1403, Glyndŵr controlled most of Wales.

In 1404, Glyndŵr assembled a parliament at Machynlleth, drawing up mutual recognition treaties with France and Spain, and being crowned king of a free Wales. A second parliament in Harlech took place a year later, with Glyndŵr making plans to carve up England and Wales into three as part of an alliance against the English king. The English army, however, attacked the Welsh uprising with increased vigour, and the Tripartite Indenture was never realized. From then on, Glyndŵyr lost battles, ground and castles, and was forced into hiding, dying, it is thought, in Herefordshire. The draconian anti-Welsh laws stayed in place until the accession to the English throne of Henry VII, who had Welsh origins, in 1485. Wales became subsumed into English custom and law, and Glyndŵr's uprising became an increasingly powerful symbol of frustrated Welsh independence. Even in the 1980s, a shadowy organization that razed several English holiday homes took the name Meibion Glyndŵr – the Sons of Glyndŵr.

(Easter–Sept Mon–Sat 10am–5pm; other times by arrangement on ☎01654/702827; free) sits halfway along Heol Maengwyn, a modest-looking black and white fronted building, concealing a large interior. Displays chart the course of Glyndŵr's life, his military campaign, his downfall and the 1404 parliament, when he controlled almost all of what we now know as Wales. The sorriest tales are from 1405 onwards when tactical errors and the sheer brute might of the English forced a swift retreat and an ignominious end to the greatest Welsh uprising.

On the Aberystwyth road, at Y Plas, the **Celtica** exhibition (daily 10am–6pm; last admission 4.40pm; £4.95; ⓦwww.celticawales.com) combines audiovisual trickery with tales of the Celtic peoples in a thunderous romp through history. The overall effect is certainly impressive, even if the old Welsh addiction to sentimentality is evident on occasion. Upstairs are more detailed exhibitions relating to Celtic history and language. On the other side of the central clocktower, housed in the beautifully serene old chapel Y Tabernacl on Heol Penrallt, is the **Museum of Modern Art Wales** (MOMA Cymru; Mon–Sat 10am–4pm; free), which hosts an ongoing programme of temporary exhibitions. It's also the place to go for films, theatre, comedy, concerts and the August Gûyl Machynlleth **festival**, which combines classical and some folk music with drama and debating.

Practicalities

The old Victorian **train station** and **bus stop** are both a five-minute walk from the clocktower, up Heol Penrallt and its continuation, Heol Doll. The **tourist office** (daily: Easter–Sept 10am–6pm; Oct–Easter 9.30am–5pm; ℡01654/702401) is next to the Glyndŵr Parliament House on Heol Maengwyn. **Bike rental** is available from Greenstyles Cycles, 4 Heol Maengwyn near the clocktower (℡01654/703543).

B&B **accommodation** includes the *Maenllwyd*, on Newtown Road, the eastern extension of Heol Maengwyn (℡01654/702928, Ⓦwww .maenllwyd.co.uk; ❷), and *Gwelfryn*, in the town centre at 6 Greenfields, Bank Street (℡01654/702532; ❶). Best of the hotels is the wonderful, if slightly pricey, *Wynnstay Arms,* on Heol Maengwyn (℡01654/702941; ❹). There's a lovely **campsite** three miles north, opposite the Centre for Alternative Technology, at *Llwyngwern Farm* (℡01654/702492), or a very simple tent site at *Plas Forge* (℡01654/703228), a mile or so out on the road to Dylife. There's a great YHA **hostel** (℡0870/770 5778; ❶; March–Oct daily, Nov–Feb weekends only; dorms £10.25) six miles north in the slate village of Corris, easily reached by regular bus. There are plenty of **cafés**, **restaurants** and **pubs** in town, including a great wholefood shop and café at *Siop y Chwarel*, opposite the *Wynnstay Arms* on Heol Maengwyn. The *Wynnstay Arms* does fantastic lunches and evening meals, and the *Glyndŵr*, on Heol Doll, has live music at the weekend. The bar at *Y Tabernacl* is the most arty hangout in town.

Centre for Alternative Technology

Since its foundation in the middle of the oil crisis of 1974, the **Centre for Alternative Technology**, or Canolfan y Dechnoleg Amgen (daily: Aug 9.30am–6pm; Easter–July, Sept & Oct 10am–5.30pm; Nov–Easter 10am–4.30pm; summer £7, winter £5; discounts to those arriving by bike or public transport; Ⓦwww.cat.org.uk) – just over two miles north of Machynlleth off the A487 – has become one of the biggest attractions in Wales. A former derelict slate quarry covering seven acres, over the last 25 years the centre has become an entirely self-sufficient community, generating its own power and water from on-site equipment. It's not a museum, but it is open to the public. It's a fascinating place to visit, combining earnest education about renewable resources and practices with flashes of pizzazz, such as the water-powered cliff rail line (April–Oct) that whisks you 197ft up from the car park. Whole houses have been constructed to showcase energy-saving ideas and the fifty-strong staff – who all live communally and receive identical (very low) wages – are ebullient and helpful in explaining the ideas. There are also organic gardens, beehives, a water wheel, an adventure playground and numerous hands-on exhibits. Two new buildings are the stunning straw-bale theatre and the superb shop, which stocks a vast range of eco-related literature and all sorts of gadgetry. Don't miss the wholefood **restaurant**, which is excellent.

Ceredigion

South of Machynlleth is the county of **Ceredigion**, formerly known as Cardiganshire. Lying as it does between the two national parks of the

Pembrokeshire Coast and Snowdonia, Ceredigion is often overlooked by visitors, but it shouldn't be. In many ways, it combines the best of both national parks – the stunning mountain scenery of southern Snowdonia with the little ports and sandy coves of Pembrokeshire, and all soaked in a relaxed, upbeat and firmly Welsh culture. The county's main town is ebullient **Aberystwyth**, a top spot for everything from serious study and exhibitions in the National Library to student-oriented raves and bar culture. It's also a great base for the luscious countryside inland, especially the waterfalls and woods of the **Vale of Rheidol** out towards mythical **Devil's Bridge**.

The southern Ceredigion coast is broken by some spirited little ports: most notably Georgian **Aberaeron**, higgledy-piggledy **New Quay** and the old county town of **Cardigan**, where the **River Teifi** flows into the sea. Towns and sights inland along the Teifi are worth exploring, especially the mighty castle at **Cilgerran** and the charming little university town of **Lampeter**. Near the source of the Teifi is the atmospheric **Strata Florida Abbey**.

Aberystwyth and around

The liveliest seaside resort in Wales, **ABERYSTWYTH** is an essential stop along the Ceredigion coast. Being rooted in all aspects of Welsh culture, it is possibly the most enjoyable and relaxed place to gain an insight into the national psyche. As the capital of sparsely populated mid-Wales, and with one of the most prestigious colleges of the University of Wales in the town, there are plenty of cultural and entertainment diversions, as well as an array of Victorian and Edwardian seaside trappings. In 1907, the National Library was inaugurated here, and Cymdeithas yr Iaith (the Welsh Language Society) was founded here in 1963. Aberystwyth's politics are firmly radical Welsh, and in a country that still struggles with its inherent conservatism, the town is a blast of fresh air.

The Town

With two long, gentle bays curving around between rocky heads, Aberystwyth's position is hard to beat. **Constitution Hill** (430ft), at the north end of the long Promenade, rises sharply away from the rocky beach. It's a favourite jaunt, crowned with a tatty jumble of amenities – café, picnic area, millennium beacon, telescopes and an octagonal **camera obscura** (Easter–Oct daily 10am–5.30pm; free) – reached on foot or by the clanking 1896 **cliff railway** (Easter–Oct daily 10am–6pm; £2.25 return) from the grand terminus building at the top of Queen's Road, behind the Promenade. South along the Promenade – officially called Marine Terrace – and off to the left on Terrace Road, the **Ceredigion Museum** (Mon–Sat 10am–5pm; free) houses cosy reconstructed cottages, a dairy and a nineteenth-century pharmacy in the atmospherically ornate Edwardian music hall, the Coliseum.

Marine Terrace continues past the spindly **pier** to the dazzling **Old College**, all turrets, friezes and mosaics. Originally a John Nash-designed villa, it was later converted to a hotel to soak up the anticipated masses arriving on the new railway line. When the venture failed, the building was sold to the fledgling university. The Promenade cuts around the front of the building to the ruins of Edward I's thirteenth-century **castle** (free access), a fine place for a picnic, but notable more for its breezy position than for the buildings themselves.

To the east of town, Penglais Road climbs the hill northwards towards the **university**'s main campus and the **National Library of Wales** (Mon–Sat

Glan-y-Mor Leisure Park (3 miles), Borth (5 miles) & Machynlleth (20 miles)

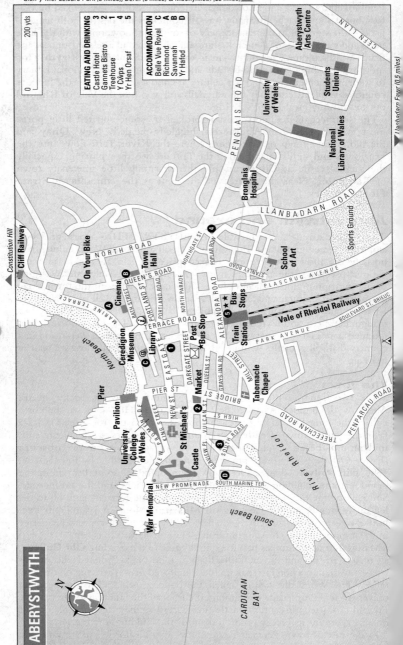

ABERYSTWYTH

EATING AND DRINKING
Castle Hotel 3
Gannets Bistro 2
Treehouse 1
Y Cŵps 4
Yr Hen Orsaf 5

ACCOMMODATION
Belle Vue Royal C
Richmond A
Savannah B
Yr Hafod D

0   200 yds

N

CARDIGAN BAY

© Crown copyright

9.30am–5pm; free; Ⓦwww.llgc.org.uk), which has excellent temporary exhibitions and **A Nation's Heritage**, a well-rounded introduction to the history of the written word and printing in Wales, shown in an absorbing range of old texts, maps, photos, and the Morgan's 1588 Welsh Bible. Above the National Library is the University campus, which includes the superb **Aberystwyth Arts Centre**, always a sure bet for a couple of decent exhibitions.

Practicalities

Aberystwyth's mainline and Vale of Rheidol **train stations** are adjacent on Alexandra Road, a ten-minute walk from the seafront on the southern side of the town centre. Local **buses** stop outside the station, with long-distance ones using the depot immediately next door, by the entrance to the park. The busy **tourist office** (March–Oct daily 10am–6pm, Nov–Feb Mon–Sat 10am–5pm; ℡01970/612125) is a ten-minute stroll from the station, straight down Terrace Road towards the seafront. On Your Bike, in the Old Police Yard, Queens Road (℡01970/626996), does **bike rental**.

There are hundreds of places to **stay**, mostly in the streets around the station and along South Marine Terrace, where you'll find *Yr Hafod*, at no. 1 (℡01970/617579, Ⓕ636835; ❷). The well-priced *Savannah* guest house, 27 Queens Road (℡01970/615131, Ⓔterrysadler@hotmail.com; ❸), is another good choice. On the Marine Terrace good bets are the *Richmond Hotel* at nos. 44–45 (℡01970/612201, Ⓦwww.richmondhotel.uk.com; ❹) and the smart *Belle Vue Royal* (℡01970/617558, Ⓦwww.bellevueroyal.co.uk; ❻). Outside term-time, B&B is also available on the Penglais and seafront sites of the University College of Wales (℡01970/621960, Ⓦwww.aber.ac.uk/visitors; ❷). The nearest place to pitch a **tent** is the *Aberystwyth Holiday Village* (℡01970/624211), off the main Penparcau Road to the south of town, a twenty-minute walk from the station.

Aberystwyth's cultural and gastronomic life is an ebullient, year-round affair, thriving on students in term-time and visitors in the summer. Just behind the market, *Gannets Bistro*, at 7 St James Square (closed Tues), creates imaginative, inexpensive dishes from local farm and sea produce. *JD's* on Northgate Street, is a small and brightly painted café specializing in pancakes and Internet access, while the organic *Treehouse* (℡01970/615791) is a warming veggie café in the daytime and superb evening option (Thurs–Sat) for all tastes. For decent and very reasonable **pub food**, you're best off at *Yr Hen Orsaf*, which, as its name implies, is in the old station buildings on Alexandra Road – you can even have a pint or a meal under a stunning glass canopy on the platform. For no-nonsense **drinking**, Aberystwyth has scores of options, and many pubs stay open until 1am in the summer: try the *Castle Hotel* on South Road, a harbourside pub that's built in the style of an ornate Victorian gin palace, and which has regular gigs. *Y Cŵps* (Coopers Arms), Llanbadarn Road, is fun and friendly, with regular Welsh folk and jazz nights. For a slice of Edwardian gentility, take afternoon tea in any of the seafront hotels along the Promenade. The Aberystwyth Arts Centre, at the university's Penglais site (℡01970/623232), has art-house **cinema** and touring **theatre**.

The Vale of Rheidol

Inland from Aberystwyth, the River Rheidol winds its way up to a secluded, wooded valley, where occasional old industrial workings have moulded themselves into the contours, rising up past waterfalls and hamlets to Devil's Bridge. It's a glorious route, and by far the best way to see it is on board one of the trains of the **Vale of Rheidol railway** (April–Oct; £11 return;

@ www.rheidolrailway.co.uk), a narrow-gauge steam train that wheezes its way along sheer rock faces from the terminus in Aberystwyth to Devil's Bridge. It was built in 1902, ostensibly for the valley's lead mines but with a canny eye on its tourist potential as well, and has run ever since. Partway along, a punishing path on the north side of the river from the Rhiwfron halt scrambles up over the mines for a mile to the sombre little village of Ystumtuen, a former lead-mining community. From here it's a couple of miles' walk to Devil's Bridge.

Folk legend, idyllic beauty and travellers' lore combine at **DEVIL'S BRIDGE** (Pontarfynach), twelve miles east of Aberystwyth, a tiny settlement built solely for the growing visitor trade of the last few hundred years. Be warned, however, that Devil's Bridge is a seriously popular day excursion: in order to escape some of the inevitable congestion, it's wisest to come here at the beginning or end of the day, or out of season.

The main attraction here is the **bridge** itself, which is actually three stacked bridges spanning the chasm of the churning River Mynach, yards upstream from its confluence with the Rheidol. The road bridge in front of the striking *Hafod Arms* **hotel** (℡01970/890232, @ www.hafodarms.co.uk; ❸) is the most modern of the three, dating from 1901. Immediately below it, wedged between the rock faces, are the stone bridge from 1753 and, at the bottom, the original bridge, dating from the eleventh century and reputedly built by the monks of Strata Florida Abbey (see p.862). For a remarkable view of the bridges, you have to enter the turnstile (£1) downstream of the bridge and head down slippery steps to the deep cleft of the **Punch Bowl**, where the water pounds and hurtles through the gap crowned by the bridges. More dramatic still, the gate on the other side (Easter–Oct daily 9.30am–5.30pm; £2.50; at other times access through turnstiles; £2) leads west to a path that tumbles down into the valley below the bridges, descending ultimately to the crashing **Mynach Falls**. The scenery here is magnificent: sharp, wooded slopes rise away from the frothing river and distant mountain peaks surface on the horizon. Platforms overlook the series of falls, from where a set of steep steps takes you further down to a footbridge dramatically spanning the river at the bottom of the falls.

There's a **campsite** – *Woodlands Caravan Park* (℡01970/890233) – by the petrol station, just beyond the bridges.

Aberaeron

ABERAERON, sixteen miles along the coast from Aberystwyth, is a handsome place, even if it is almost unique amongst the Ceredigion resorts for being on an unappealing stretch of coastline. Nonetheless, the town, with its pastel-shaded houses encasing a large harbour inlet, has a rare unity of design, the result of a complete nineteenth-century rebuilding by the Reverend Alban Gwynne. He spent his way through his wife's inheritance by dredging the Aeron Estuary and constructing a formally planned town around it as a new port for mid-Wales.

The A487 runs straight through the heart of town, down Bridge Street and past the large **Alban Square**, named after the rich rector. On the north side of the town bridge, a grid of streets stretches down to a neat line of ordered, colourful houses on the seafront. Quay Parade runs down the side of the seafront past some of the old fisherman's houses and pubs to the fairly humdrum **Sea Aquarium** (Easter–Oct daily 10am–5pm; £3.95). A trip to the exquisite kitchen gardens at **Llanerchaeron**, three miles east of Aberaeron (April–Oct Wed–Sun 11.30am–4.30pm; £4; NT), makes for a better excursion. Once an integrated smallholding typical of this region, the estate is currently undergoing restoration; occasional open days allow access to the Nash-designed main house.

Aberaeron's **tourist office** is on Quay Parade, the seafront road (Mon–Sat 10am–6pm; Oct–April closes 5pm; ☎01545/570602). One town-centre **B&B** overlooking the harbour on Cadwgan Place is *Coedmor* (☎01545/571615, ⓦwww.coedmorbandb.co.uk; ❷). A B&B that's better than most small hotels can be found nearby on South Road: the *Hazeldene* (☎01545/570652, ⓦwww.aberaeron.co.uk/hazeldene; ❷). The nearest local **campsite** is the *Aeron Coast*, on the A487 just north of town (☎01545/570349). For **food**, the best place to eat is the relaxed café/bistro at the *Harbourmaster Hotel* on Pen Cei. Daytime alternatives include the *Hive on the Quay*, Cadwgan Place (April to mid-Sept), which serves fine local seafood in its conservatory, and has scrumptious **honey ice cream** to eat in or take away.

New Quay and around

Along with Laugharne in Carmarthenshire (see p.802), **NEW QUAY** (Cei Newydd), seven miles from Aberaeron, lays claim to being the original Llareggub in Dylan Thomas's *Under Milk Wood*. Certainly, it has the little tumbling streets, prim Victorian terraces, cobbled stone harbour and air of dreamy isolation that Thomas evoked in his play but, in the height of summer, the quiet isolation can be hard to find. Although there is a singular lack of excitement in New Quay, it's a truly pleasant base for good beaches, walking, surfing, eating and drinking.

The pretty **harbour** and small, curving beach are backed by a higgledy-piggledy line of multicoloured shops and houses. The beachfront streets comprise the **lower town** – the more traditionally "seaside" part of New Quay, full of cafés, pubs and beach shops. Tucked away down the slipway above the beach is the interesting **Marine Wildlife Centre** (April–Sept daily 10am–5pm; donation requested), with some good displays on the dolphins, seals and sea birds of Cardigan Bay. Sharply inclined streets lead to the residential **upper town**, with some delightful views over the sweeping shoreline below. The northern beach soon gives way to a rocky headland, **New Quay Head**, where an invigorating path steers along the top of aptly named **Bird Rock**.

Buses stop on Park Street, from where it's a walk down any of the steep streets to the seafront, where you'll find the **tourist office**, centrally located at the junction of Church Street and Wellington Place (April–Sept daily 10am–6pm; ☎01545/560865). **Accommodation** includes the welcoming *Dolau House* on Church Street (☎01545/561029; ❷), one of whose rooms has a sea view, and the chintzy luxury of *Ffynnon Feddyg*, out towards Cei Bach on the eastern edge of town (☎01545/560222; ❷; March–Oct). The nearest **campsite** is the *Neuadd* (☎01545/560709), fifteen minutes' walk away, behind the *Penrhiwllan Inn*, at the top of the hill on the way to Synod Inn. New Quay contains innumerable cheap **cafés**, amongst which the *Mariner's Café*, by the harbour wall, is a sure bet. Most of the **pubs** serve food, the best being the *Seahorse*, Margaret Street, and the *Wellington*, by the tourist office on the seafront.

Tre-Saith and Llangranog

The most popular stopping-off point on the stretch of coast south of New Quay is Aberporth, an elderly resort built around two less than appealing bays, easily shown up by the neighbouring hamlet of **TRE-SAITH**, a mile to the east, which staggers down the tiny valley to a delightful beach. There are **dinghy races** from the beach every Sunday in summer. Around the rocks to the right of the beach, the River Saith plummets over the mossy black rocks in a waterfall. You can **camp** right above the beach in one of the quieter outlying fields of the *Llety Caravan Park*, reached by road en route to Aberporth (℡01239/810354).

Three miles north of the A487, **LLANGRANOG** is the most attractive village on the Ceredigion coast, wedged in between bracken and gorse-beaten hills, the main streets winding to the tiny seafront. The beach can become horribly congested in midsummer, when it's better to follow the cliff path to **Cilborth Beach**, and on to the glorious NT-owned headland, **Ynys Lochtyn**. In Llangranog, you can **stay** on the seafront either at the excellent *Ship Inn* (℡01239/654423; ❸) or the earthier *Pentre Arms* (℡01239/654345; ❷); both do good **food**. Between Penbryn and Llangranog is the *Maesglas* caravan park (℡01239/654268), which takes **tents**.

Cardigan

An ancient borough and fomer port at the lowest bridging point of the Teifi Estuary, **CARDIGAN** (Aberteifi) was founded by the Norman lord Roger de Montgomery around a castle in 1093. From the castle mound by the bridge, Bridge Street sweeps through High Street to the turreted oddity of the **Guildhall**, with the Welsh flag skewered adamantly to its grey frontage. Through the Guildhall courtyard is the town's **covered market**, a typically eclectic mix of fresh food, local crafts and secondhand stalls. Across the bridge from the town centre, the **Cardigan Heritage Centre** (Canolfan Hanes Aberteifi; March–Oct daily 10am–5pm; call ℡01239/614404 for winter hours; £2), housed in an old granary, tells the story of the port's rise and fall.

The helpful **tourist office** (June–Aug daily 10am–6pm; Sept–May Mon–Sat 10am–5pm; ℡01239/613230) is in the foyer of Theatr Mwldan, Bath House Road. There's limited **accommodation**, with a few B&Bs along the Gwbert Road, off North Road, including the *Brynhyfryd*, at the town end (℡01239/612861; ❷). On the High Street, the old-fashioned *Black Lion* pub (℡01239/612532; ❸) does good B&B and evening meals. There's a YHA **hostel** four miles away at Poppit Sands, at the end of the Pembrokeshire Coast Path (℡0870/770 5996, ✉poppit@yha.org.uk; March–Oct; dorms £10.25); buses connect in July and August, but for the rest of the year they terminate at St Dogmael's, two miles short. For **food**, try the inexpensive Theatr Mwldan café or *Jackets*, 58 North Rd, which serves pizzas, potatoes, kebabs and pies. The best pub food is at the *Eagle*, at the southern end of the town bridge.

The Teifi Valley

The Teifi is one of Wales' most eulogized rivers, for its rich spawn of fresh fish, its meandering rural charm and the coracles that were a regular feature from pre-Roman times. On the way to its estuary at Cardigan, it flows through some gloriously green and undulating countryside, winding its way over the falls at **Cenarth** and passing the massive ramparts of **Cilgerran Castle**. Further upstream, the river also takes in the proudly Welsh university town of **Lampeter**, and the river's infancy can be seen near the ruins of **Strata Florida Abbey**, beyond which the river emerges from the dark and remote **Teifi Pools**.

Cilgerran Castle

Just a couple of miles up the Teifi River from Cardigan, the attractive village of **CILGERRAN** clusters around its wide main street. Behind is the bulk of the **castle** (daily 9.30am–6.30pm; Nov–March closes 4pm; £2.50; CADW), founded in 1100 at a commanding vantage point on a high wooded bluff above the river, then still navigable for sea-going ships. This is the legendary site of the 1109 abduction of Nest (the "Welsh Helen of Troy") by a love-struck Prince Owain of Powys. Her husband, Gerald of Pembroke, escaped by slithering down a toilet waste chute through the castle walls. The two massive drum towers still dominate the castle, and the outer walls, some four feet thicker than those facing the inner courtyard, are traced by vertiginously high walkways. The outer ward, over which a modern path now runs from the entrance, is a good example of the keepless castle that evolved throughout the thirteenth century. The views over the forested valley towards the pink and grey Georgian fantasy castle of **Coedmore**, on the opposite bank, are inspiring.

A footpath runs down from the castle to the river's edge; an exhibition at the quay about local industries – coracles included – also covers the story of America-bound emigrants leaving from Cardigan. Guided two-hour **canoe trips** leave from the quay in summer.

Cenarth and around

A tourist magnet since it was swooped on by nineteenth-century Romantics and artists, **CENARTH**, five miles east of Cilgerran, is a pleasant spot but hardly merits the mass interest that it receives. The village's main asset, its **waterfalls**, are close to the main road, connected by a path from opposite the *White Hart* pub. This runs past the **National Coracle Centre** (Easter–Oct daily except Sat 10am–5.30pm; other times by arrangement ☎01239/710980; £3), a small museum with displays of these curiously designed boats from all over the world, before continuing to a restored seventeenth-century flour mill by the falls' edge.

The area's prolific past as a weaving centre is best seen at the **Museum of the Welsh Woollen Industry** (due to reopen in mid-2004 after renovations; ⓦ www.nmgw.ac.uk), in the village of **Dre-Fach Felindre**, eight miles southeast of Cenarth, which once had over forty working mills.

Lampeter

Twenty miles east of Cenarth, **LAMPETER** (Llanbedr Pont Steffan or, popularly, Lambed) is the home of possibly the most remote university in Britain. St David's University College, now a constituent of the University of Wales, was Wales' first university college, founded in 1822 by the bishop of St David's to aid Welsh students who couldn't afford the trip to England to receive a full education. With a healthy student population and large numbers of resident hippies, the small town is well geared up for young people and visitors.

There's not a great deal to see, and what you are able to visit is fairly low-key. **Harford Square** forms the hub of the town. Around the corner, at 2 Bridge St, is **Celtic Edge**, a showcase for local artists' work at the back of the Mulberry Bush health-food shop, which has a good bulletin board. The main buildings of the **University College** lie off College Street, and include a quadrangle modelled on an Oxbridge college and the motte of Lampeter's long-vanished castle – a strange sight amidst such order. The High Street is the most architecturally distinguished part of town, its eighteenth-century coaching inn, the *Black Lion*, dominating the streetscape; you can see its old stables and coach house through an archway.

Leaflets in the town library – through the archway of the old town hall and past the supermarket – and the noticeboards in the Mulberry Bush health-food shop (see above) are the closest Lampeter get to a tourist office. *Haulfan*, 6 Station Terrace, behind University College (℡01570/422718; ❷), is the best **B&B**, or you could try the *Black Lion*, High Street (℡01570/422172; ❹). Just off the B4343 is one of the area's best farmhouse B&Bs, at *Pentre Farm*, near Llanfair Clydogau, five miles from Lampeter (℡01570/493313; ❸). The nearest **campsite** is five miles northeast, at Moorlands, near Llangybi (℡01570/493543).

In-town **eating** can be fairly lacklustre. *Lloyds* is an upmarket fish-and-chip restaurant in Bridge Street; *Sosban Fach*, 1 New St, does good daytime meals; and *Shapla* on College Street does the best curries for miles around. Stick your head into *Conti's Café*, on Harford Square – the food is cheap and not that great, but the decor is wonderfully time-warped, plastered with ageing accolades for the café's homemade ice cream. Just south of town, where the A485 joins the A482, the *Cwmann Tavern* is the best bet for catching the beery local **music** scene.

Strata Florida Abbey and the Teifi Pools

Twenty miles northeast of Lampeter, the mighty **Strata Florida Abbey** (Easter–Sept daily 10am–5pm; £2; CADW) dominates the bucolic Ystrad Fflur, the Valley of the Flowers. This Cistercian abbey was founded in 1164, swiftly growing into a centre for milling, farming and weaving, and becoming an important political centre for Wales. In 1238, Llywelyn the Great, whose conquering exploits throughout the rest of Wales had brought him to the peak of the Welsh feudal pyramid, summoned the lesser Welsh princes here. He was near death, and worried that his work of unifying Wales under one ruler would disintegrate, so he commanded the assembled princes to pay homage not just to him but also to his son, Dafydd, so sealing the succession. The church here was vast – larger than the cathedral at St David's – and, although very little survived Henry VIII's dissolution of the monasteries, the huge Norman west doorway gives some idea of its dimensions. Fragments of one-time side chapels include beautifully tiled medieval floors, and there's also a serene cemetery, but it's really the abbey's position that impresses most, in glorious rural solitude amongst wide open skies and fringed with a scoop of sheep-flecked hills. A sinewy yew tree reputedly shades the spot where Dafydd ap Gwilym, fourteenth-century bard and contemporary of Chaucer, is buried.

The narrow lane running due east from Strata Florida leads to Tyncwm, a farm with bridleways to the drenched grass and craggy outcrops around the **Teifi Pools**, a series of sombre lakes where the Teifi River rises, set in stern, but rewarding, walking country.

Travel details

Buses

For information on all local and national bus services, contact Traveline ℡ 0870/608 2608, Ⓦ www.traveline.org.uk.
Aberaeron to: Aberystwyth (hourly; 40min); Cardigan (6 daily; 1hr 10min); Carmarthen (7 daily; 1hr 40min); Lampeter (7 daily; 35min); New Quay (hourly; 20min).

Abergavenny to: Brecon (Mon–Sat 7 daily, none on Sun; 1hr); Cardiff (hourly; 1hr 20min); Crickhowell (Mon–Sat 7 daily, none on Sun; 20min); Llanfihangel Crucorney (6 daily; 15min); Merthyr Tydfil (hourly; 1hr 30min); Monmouth (6 daily; 40min); Raglan (6 daily; 20min).
Aberystwyth to: Aberaeron (hourly; 40min); Caernarfon (1 daily; 2hr 40min); Cardiff (2 daily; 3hr 50min); Cardigan (9 daily, most change at

Synod Inn; 1hr 50min); Carmarthen (2 daily; 1hr 40min); Devil's Bridge (2 daily; 40min); Dolgellau (6 daily; 1hr 15min); Lampeter (5 daily; 1hr 30min); Machynlleth (8 daily; 45min); New Quay (hourly; 1hr); Swansea (2 daily; 2hr 45min).

Bala to: Dolgellau (9 daily; 40min); Llangollen (8 daily; 1hr).

Barmouth to: Bala (8 daily; 1hr); Blaenau Ffestiniog (4 daily; 1hr); Dolgellau (8 daily; 20min); Harlech (9 daily; 30min); Llangollen (7 daily; 1hr 50min); Wrexham (7 daily; 2hr 20min).

Brecon to: Abergavenny (Mon–Sat 7 daily, none on Sun; 1hr); Cardiff (1 daily; 1hr 20min); Craig-y-nos/Dan-yr-ogof (2 daily; 30min); Crickhowell (Mon–Sat 7 daily, none on Sun; 25min); Hay-on-Wye (6 daily; 50min); Libanus (9 daily; 10min); Llandrindod Wells (Mon–Sat 2 daily, none on Sun; 1hr); Merthyr Tydfil (10 daily; 40min); Swansea (2–3 daily; 1hr 30min).

Cardigan to: Aberaeron (10 daily; 1hr 10min); Aberporth (hourly; 30min); Aberystwyth (9 daily, most change at Synod Inn; 1hr 50min); Carmarthen (hourly; 1hr 30min); Fishguard (hourly; 50min); Newcastle Emlyn (hourly; 30min); Newport, Pembrokeshire (hourly; 30min); New Quay (hourly; 1hr).

Dolgellau to: Aberystwyth (6 daily; 1hr 15min); Bala (9 daily; 40min); Barmouth (8 daily; 20min); Blaenau Ffestiniog (3 daily; 50min); Caernarfon (5 daily; 1hr 40min); Llangollen (8 daily; 1hr 30min); Machynlleth (10 daily; 40min); Porthmadog (6 daily; 50min); Tywyn (6 daily; 50min); Wrexham (8 daily; 2hr).

Harlech to: Barmouth (9 daily; 30min); Blaenau Ffestiniog (4 daily; 40min).

Knighton to: Ludlow (3 daily; 1hr 10min); Presteigne (5 daily; 30min).

Lampeter to: Aberaeron (7 daily; 40min); Aberystwyth (5 daily; 1hr 30min); Carmarthen (8 daily; 1hr 10min); Machynlleth (1 daily; 2hr 30min).

Llandrindod Wells to: Abbeycwmhir (Mon–Fri 1 postbus daily; 2hr); Aberystwyth (1 daily; 1hr 40min); Brecon (Mon–Sat 2 daily, none on Sun; 1hr); Elan Village (Mon–Fri 1 postbus daily; 40min); Hay-on-Wye (Wed & Sat 1 daily; 1hr); Rhayader (3 daily; 30min).

Llanfyllin to: Llanwddyn for Lake Vyrnwy (Mon–Sat 3 daily, none on Sun; 30min); Welshpool (Mon–Sat 1 daily; 40min).

Llangollen to: Bala (8 daily; 1hr); Chirk (7 daily; 20min); Wrexham (at least hourly; 30min).

Llanidloes to: Aberystwyth (1 daily; 1hr); Welshpool (5 daily; 1hr 10min).

Llanwrtyd Wells to: Abergwesyn (Mon–Fri 1 postbus daily; 20min); Builth Wells (2 daily; 50min).

Machynlleth to: Aberystwyth (8 daily; 45min); Bala (4 daily; 1hr 20min); Cardiff (1 daily; 5hr 15min); Dolgellau (6 daily; 40min); Lampeter (1 daily; 2hr 30min); Llangollen (6 daily; 3hr); Porthmadog (4 daily; 1hr 45min); Tywyn (4–6 daily; 40min).

New Quay to: Aberaeron (hourly; 20min); Aberporth (hourly; 40min); Aberystwyth (hourly; 1hr); Cardigan (hourly; 1hr).

Welshpool to: Berriew (Mon–Sat 6 daily, none on Sun; 20min); Llanfyllin (Mon–Sat 1 daily, none on Sun; 40min); Llanidloes (5 daily; 1hr 10min); Montgomery (school bus; 25min).

Trains

For information on all local and national rail services, contact **National Rail Enquiries** ⓣ 08457/48 49 50, ⓦ www.nationalrail.co.uk.

Abergavenny to: Cardiff (hourly; 40min); Hereford (hourly; 20min); Newport (hourly; 30min).

Aberystwyth to: Birmingham (8 daily; 3hr); Machynlleth (10 daily; 30min); Shrewsbury (8 daily; 2hr); Welshpool (8 daily; 1hr 30min).

Barmouth to: Harlech (6 daily; 30min); Machynlleth (6 daily; 1hr); Porthmadog (6 daily; 45min).

Harlech to: Barmouth (6 daily; 30min); Birmingham (5 daily; 4hr 15min); Machynlleth (6 daily; 1hr 20min); Porthmadog (7 daily; 20min).

Knighton to: Llandrindod Wells (4 daily; 40min); Llanwrtyd Wells (4 daily; 1hr 10min); Swansea (4 daily; 3hr 10min).

Llandrindod Wells to: Knighton (4 daily; 40min); Llanwrtyd Wells (4 daily; 30min); Shrewsbury (4 daily; 1hr 40min); Swansea (4 daily; 2hr 20min).

Machynlleth to: Aberystwyth (10 daily; 30min); Barmouth (6 daily; 1hr); Birmingham (9 daily; 2hr 30min); Harlech (6 daily; 1hr 20min); Porthmadog (6 daily; 1hr 45min); Shrewsbury (9 daily; 2hr).

Welshpool to: Aberystwyth (8 daily; 1hr 30min); Birmingham (8 daily; 1hr 30min); Machynlleth (8 daily; 1hr).

⑮

MID-WALES | Travel details

North Wales

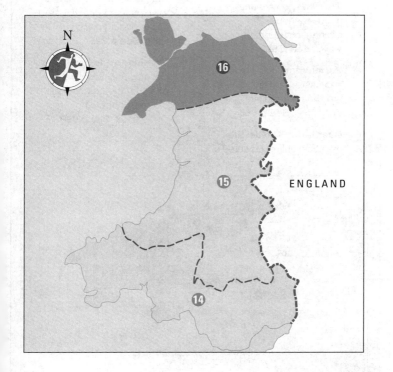

ENGLAND

CHAPTER 16

Highlights

* **Snowdon** Wales' highest mountain is a stunning climb, or a gentle ascent by rack-and-pinion railway. **See p.877**

* **Beddgelert** Impeccably pretty mountain village, filled with flowers and good teashops, and offering lots of great walks. **See p.879**

* **Portmeirion** Hugely impressive fantasy village, the "home for fallen buildings". **See p.885**

* **Caernarfon Castle** The mightiest link in Edward I's chain of Welsh castles. See **See p.887**

* **Beaumaris** A good base for Anglesey's beaches and Neolithic remains. **See p.890**

* **Conwy** Attractive fortified town, with a fantastic castle and intact town walls. **See p.895**

* **Llandudno** The town's classy gentility is nicely offset by the ruggedness of the neighbouring Great Orme peak. **See p.899**

△ Llandudno

16

North Wales

With the advent of the A55 dual carriageway across the width of **North Wales**, the region has become considerably more accessible in recent times. This, however, has not tamed the wilder aspects of this stunningly beautiful area, especially in the western parts of Snowdonia and the Llŷn peninsula. Wales' north coast and its natural offshoot, the isle of Anglesey, not only encompass the geographical extremities of the country, but comprise an area exhibiting the extremes of Welsh life. As you walk around most of the brash seaside towns along the eastern section of the coast, only the street signs give any indication that you are in Wales at all; further west, there are places where English is seldom spoken other than to visitors. Scattered along the coast, dramatically sited castles act as a superb antidote to low-brow fun-seeking.

Without doubt, **Snowdonia** is the crowning glory of North Wales. This tightly packed bundle of soaring cliff faces, jagged peaks and plunging waterfalls measures little more than ten miles by ten, but packs enough mountain paths to keep even the most jaded walking enthusiast happy for weeks. Even if lakeside ambles and rides on antiquated steam trains are more your style, you can't fail to appreciate the natural grandeur of the scenery, occasionally revealing an atmospheric Welsh castle ruin or decaying piece of quarrying equipment. The area's small settlements – well geared up for walking and other outdoor activities – make for lively bases, whether long-standing tourist towns like **Betws-y-Coed** and **Llanberis**, or old mining and quarry towns such as **Beddgelert** and **Blaenau Ffestiniog**.

Snowdonia is the heart – and undisputed highlight – of the massive **Snowdonia National Park** (Parc Cenedlaethol Eryri), an 840-square-mile area which extends north and south, beyond the bounds of Snowdonia and this chapter, to encompass the Rhinogs, Cadair Idris (see p.850) and 23 miles of superb coastal scenery. To the west, this coast is the highlight, in the gentle rockiness of the **Llŷn peninsula**, where Wales ends in a flourish of small coves and seafaring villages, offering almost unlimited rambling potential around the high-hedged lanes. Roads loop back along the Llŷn to the tip of the north coast, where **Caernarfon** sits overshadowed by its stupendous castle, the mightiest link in Edward I's Iron Ring of thirteenth-century fortresses across north Wales.

Across the Menai Strait lies the island of **Anglesey**, a gentle patchwork of beautiful beaches and sites of ancient heritage, well worth exploration. Edward's final castle, a masterpiece of design, is sited in **Beaumaris**, and catamarans and ferries from Anglesey's main town, **Holyhead**, provide the fastest route to Dublin.

16

NORTH WALES

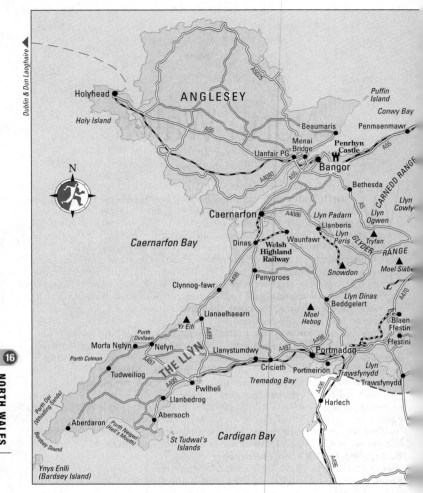

Back on the mainland, the university and cathedral city of **Bangor** is the area's most cosmopolitan haunt, while remaining solidly Welsh in outlook and language. The same could certainly not be said for the string of seaside resorts along the north Wales coast, among which **Conwy** – another walled bastide town built by Edward I – and genteel **Llandudno**, always a cut above the rest, are the mainstay. Further east towards England, faded Victorian resorts are the mainstay. However, a few surprises come embedded into this matrix of bingo halls and caravan sites: the allegedly miraculous waters at **Holywell** have attracted the hopeful since the seventh century, while others come for the National Portrait Gallery's collection at **Bodelwyddan**, and Britain's smallest cathedral at **St Asaph**.

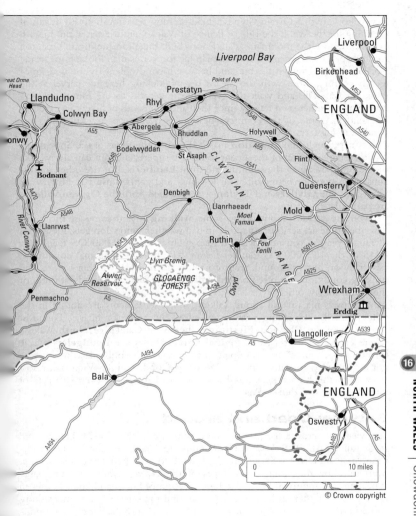

© Crown copyright

Snowdonia

What the coal valleys are to the south of the country, the mountains of **Snowdonia** (Yr Eryri) are to the north – the defining feature, not just in their physical form, but in the way they have shaped the communities within them. To Henry VIII's antiquarian John Leland, the region seemed "horrible with the sight of bare stones"; now it is widely acclaimed as the most dramatic and alluring of all Welsh scenery, a compact, barren land of tortured ridges dividing glacial valleys, whose sheer faces belie the fact that the tallest peaks only just top three thousand feet. It was to this mountain fastness that Llywelyn ap Gruffydd, the last true prince of Wales, retreated in 1277 after his first war with Edward I;

it was also here that Owain Glyndŵr held on most tenaciously to his dream of regaining for the Welsh the title of Prince of Wales. Centuries later, the English came to remove the mountains: slate barons built huge fortunes from Welsh toil and reshaped the patterns of Snowdonian life forever, as men looking for steady work in the quarries left the hills and became town dwellers. By the mid-nineteenth century, those with the means began flocking here to marvel at the plunging waterfalls and walk the ever-widening paths to the mountain tops. Numbers have increased rapidly since then and thousands of hikers arrive every weekend for some of the country's best walks over steep, exacting and constantly varying terrain.

Not surprisingly, the **Snowdon** massif (Eryri) is the focus of the Snowdonia National Park. Several of the ascent routes are superb, and you can always take the cog railway up to the summit café from **Llanberis**. But the other mountains are as good or better, often far less busy and giving unsurpassed views of Snowdon. The **Glyders** and **Tryfan** – best tackled from the **Ogwen Valley** – are particular favourites.

If you are serious about doing some **walking** – and some of the walks described here are serious, especially in bad weather (Snowdon gets 200 inches of rain a year) – you need a good map such as the 1:50,000 OS *Landranger* #115 or the 1:25,000 OS *Outdoor Leisure* #17; bear in mind that conditions, especially on higher ground, are notoriously changeable. Weather reports and walking conditions are often posted on the doors or noticeboards of outdoor shops and tourist offices.

But Snowdonia isn't all about walking. Small settlements are dotted in the valleys, usually coinciding with some enormous mine or quarry. Foremost among these are **Blaenau Ffestiniog**, the "Slate Capital of North Wales", where a mine opens its caverns for underground tours, and **Beddgelert** whose former copper mines are also open to the public. The only place of any size not associated with slate mining is **Betws-y-Coed**, a largely Victorian resort away from the higher peaks, and a springboard for the walkers' hamlets of **Capel Curig** and **Pen-y-Pass**.

Betws-y-Coed and around

Sprawled out across a flat plain at the confluence of the Conwy, Llugwy and Lledr valleys, **BETWS-Y-COED** (pronounced "betoos-er-coyd"), the much-vaunted "Gateway to Snowdonia", is hard to avoid. Its riverside setting, overlooked by the conifer-clad slopes of the Gwydyr forest, is undeniably appealing, and the town boasts the best selection of hotels and guest houses in the region, but after an hour mooching around the outdoor equipment shops and drinking tea you may well be left wondering what to do. For serious mountain walkers, the best advice is to continue on, but for everyone else there are some delightful – and fairly easy – strolls from town into the surrounding hills and river valleys. Particularly good are the two local beauty spots of the **Conwy** and **Swallow** falls, though these can get pretty congested in high summer.

This one-time lead-mining town remained a backwater until 1815 when, as part of his A5 toll road, Telford completed the graceful **Waterloo Bridge** (Y Bont Haearn), speeding access for the leisured classes already alerted to the town's beauty by J.M.W. Turner's landscapes. The arrival of the railway line in 1868 lifted its status from coaching station to genteel resort, an air the town tries to maintain, albeit without much success. By the station, the **Conwy Valley Railway Museum** (daily 10.15am–5pm; Nov–Easter closes 4pm; £1) presents a fairly standard collection of memorabilia and shiny engines, slightly enlivened by the chance of a short ride (£1) on a miniature train or tram. The **Motor Museum** (Easter–Oct daily 10am–6pm; £1.95), a couple of hundred yards away behind the tourist office, is little better, with a half-dozen classic bikes and fifteen cars, including a 1934 Bugatti Straight 8 and a Model T Ford.

Practicalities

The **train station**, for services from Llandudno Junction up the Conwy Valley and on to Blaenau Ffestiniog, is just a few paces across the grass from the **tourist office**, at Royal Oak Stables (daily: Easter–Oct 10am–6pm; Nov–Easter 9.30am–12.30pm & 1.30–4.30pm; ℡01690/710426), and the **bus stop**, outside St Mary's church, on the main street. Whether you're a beginner or intermediate climber, you can arrange **scrambling**, **climbing** and **abseiling** courses with Snowdonia Mountain Guides (℡01690/710554; £30–50 a day). **Mountain bikes** can be rented from Beics Betws (℡01690/710829, ⓦwww.bikewales.com), on Church Hill, at the top of the road beside the post office; permits and information on routes through the Gwydyr Forest are obtainable from the tourist office. The Ultimate Outdoors shop, opposite Pont-y-Pair bridge, is good for all kinds of equipment and information.

The town has plenty of **accommodation**, but has to cope with an ever-larger number of visitors pushing prices up in the summer, when you need to book ahead. The cheapest rooms are above the award-winning *Riverside Restaurant*, Holyhead Road, near the central Pont-y-Pair bridge (℡01690/710650; ❷). *Glan Llugwy*, on the A5, a short way beyond Pont-y-Pair (℡01690/710592; ❶), is another inexpensive option, while *Tŷ Gwyn*, also on the A5 (℡01690/710383, ⓦwww.tygwynhotel.co.uk; ❸), is a prettified old coaching inn half a mile east of the centre, just over Waterloo Bridge. The luxury option is *Tan-y-Foel*, Capel Garmon (℡01690/710507, ⓦwww.tyfhotel.co.uk; ❼), with a heated indoor pool and superb cuisine; take the A470 towards Llanrwst then turn right after about a mile. The nearest **hostel** is at Capel Curig (see p.874); the closest **campsite** is *Riverside* (℡01690/710310; Easter–Oct), right behind the station.

For a town so geared to tourism that you can hardly turn around without knocking someone's cream tea to the floor, there are surprisingly few places to **eat** other than the pubs. The aforementioned *Riverside Restaurant*, with its fresh Mediterranean cuisine, or *Tŷ Gwyn*, on the A5, are the best places to eat in town. The low-cost bar meals at the lively *Royal Oak Hotel*, High Street, are decent value.

The Conwy and Swallow Falls

Nothing in Betws-y-Coed can compete with getting out to the gorges and waterfalls in the vicinity, and **walking** is the ideal way to see them. In the final gorge section of the River Conwy, a couple of miles above Betws-y-Coed, the river plunges fifty feet over the **Conwy Falls** into a deep pool. The *Conwy Falls Café*, reached by bus #49 (4 daily), collects a small fee entitling you to view the falls and a series of rock steps that once formed part of a primitive fish ladder. After carving out a mile or so of what kayakers regard as some of North Wales' toughest white water, the Conwy negotiates a staircase of drops and enters the **Fairy Glen**, a cleft in a small wood which takes its name from the Welsh fairies, the Tylwyth Teg, who are said to be seen hereabouts. The two sights are linked by a mile-long path following a cool green lane giving glimpses of the river through the woods. The path continues a short distance to Beaver Bridge from where you can walk back along the road to Betws-y-Coed – an excellent round trip.

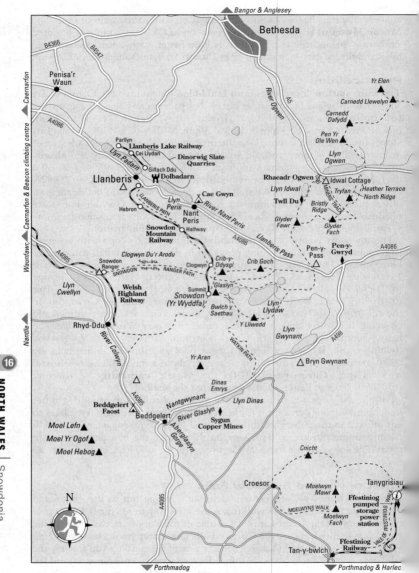

Bangor & Anglesey

Bethesda

B4366

B4547

Penisa'r
Waun

A4086

Caernarfon

Caernarfon & Beacon climbing centre

Waunfawr

Nantlle

Yr Elen

Carnedd Llewelyn

Carnedd
Dafydd

Pen Yr
Ole Wen

River Ogwen

A5

Llyn
Ogwen

Parllyn
Llanberis Lake Railway
Cei Llydan
Dinorwig Slate
Quarries
Llyn Padarn
Gilfach Ddu
Llanberis
Dolbadarn

Hebron

LLANBERIS PATH

Llyn
Peris

Nant
Peris

Snowdon
Mountain
Railway

Halfway

Cae Gwyn

River Nant Peris

A4086

Llanberis Pass

Rhaeadr Ogwen
Idwal Cottage
Llyn Idwal
Twll Du
Tryfan
Heather Terrace
North Ridge
Bristly
Ridge
Glyder
Fawr
Glyder
Fach

MINERS TRACK

Pen-y-
Pass

Pen-y-
Gwryd

A4086

A4085

Snowdon
Ranger

Clogwyn Du'r Arodu
SNOWDON RANGER PATH
Clogwyn

Crib-y-
Ddysgl

Crib Goch

Welsh
Highland
Railway

Llyn
Cwellyn

Summit
Snowdon
(Yr Wyddfa)

Glaslyn

Bwlch y
Saethau

Llyn
Llydaw

Llyn
Gwynant

A498

River Colwyn

Rhyd-Ddu

WATKIN PATH

Y Lliwedd

Yr Aran

Bryn Gwynant

A4085

Nantgwynant

Dinas
Emrys

Llyn Dinas

Beddgelert
Faost
Beddgelert

River Glaslyn

Sygun
Copper Mines

Aberglaslyn Gorge

Moel Lefn
Moel Yr Ogof
Moel Hebog

A4085

Cnicht

Croesor

Moelwyn
Mawr

MOELWYNS WALK

Moelwyn
Fach

Tanygrisiau

Ffestiniog
pumped
storage
power
station

VALE OF FFESTINIOG WALK

Ffestiniog
Railway

Tan-y-bwlch

Porthmadog

Porthmadog & Harlec

N

16

NORTH WALES | Snowdonia

The **Swallow Falls**, two miles west along the A5 towards Capel Curig, is the region's most visited sight, a straightforward, pretty waterfall with the occasional mad kayaker scraping down the precipitous rock. Pay your 50p and you can walk down to a series of viewing platforms. Better still, leave the car park on the north side of Pont-y-Pair, in town, and follow the **Llugwy Valley Walk** (3 miles; 400ft ascent; 1hr 30min), a forested path following the twisting and plunging river upstream towards Capel Curig. Less than a mile from Pont-y-Pair you reach the

872

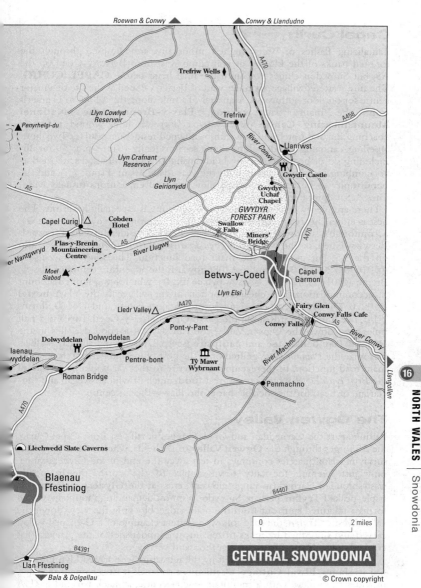

Trefriw Wells ♦

Llyn Cowlyd
Reservoir

Trefriw

● Penyrhelgi-du

A458

River Conwy

● Llanrwst

Llyn Crafnant
Reservoir

♛ ✠
● Gwydir Castle

A5

Llyn
Geirionydd

Gwydir
Uchaf
Chapel

GWYDYR
FOREST PARK

Capel Curig △

Cobden
Hotel ♦

Swallow
Falls

Plas-y-Brenin
Mountaineering
Centre

A5 River Llugwy

Miners'
Bridge

er Nantgwryd

A470

Moel
Siabod

Betws-y-Coed

Capel
Garmon

Llyn Elsi

Fairy Glen ♦
Conwy Falls Cafe

Lledr Valley △   A470

Pont-y-Pant

Conwy Falls   A5

River Conwy

Dolwyddelan ♛   Dolwyddelan

laenau
wyddelan

Pentre-bont

Tŷ Mawr 🏛
Wybrnant

River Machno

Roman Bridge

Penmachno

A470

Llangollen ▶

◖ Llechwedd Slate Caverns

Blaenau
Ffestiniog

B4407

0   2 miles

CENTRAL SNOWDONIA

B4391

● Llan Ffestiniog

▼ Bala & Dolgellau   © Crown copyright

steeply sloping **Miners' Bridge**, which linked miners' homes at Pentre Du, on the south side of the river, to the lead mines in Llanrwst. Just beneath the bridge are a series of idyllic plunge pools, perfect for swimming. The path follows the river on your left for another mile to a slightly obscured view of Swallow Falls. Detailed maps are available from the tourist office showing numerous routes back through the Gwydyr Forest, or you can continue half a mile to the road bridge from where you can wait for the bus back to Betws-y-Coed.

Capel Curig

Tantalizing flashes of Wales' highest mountains are glimpsed through the forested banks of the Llugwy as you climb west from Betws-y-Coed on the A5, but Snowdon eludes you until the final bend before **CAPEL CURIG**. The tiny, scattered village, six miles west of Betws-y-Coed, is the site of a major centre for outdoor enthusiasts. A quarter of a mile along the A4086 to Llanberis from the main road junction, **Plas-y-Brenin: the National Mountaineering Centre** (Ⓦwww.pyb.co.uk) was built around a former coaching inn and hotel, and now runs renowned residential courses. Two-hour abseiling, canoeing and dry-slope skiing sessions (daily 10am–9pm; £9 for 2hr including ski or board rental), are held during July and August, a state-of-the-art climbing wall opens throughout the year (daily 10am–11pm; £3), and the opportunity to hear talks or watch slide shows of expeditions (usually Mon, Tues & Sat 8pm; free).

There are plenty of places to **stay**, though none is especially luxurious. The best is either the *Bron Eryri* (Ⓣ01690/720240, Ⓔbron.eryri@lineone.net; ❸), a comfortable and welcoming B&B half a mile outside the village towards Betws-y-Coed, or the wonderful *Bryn Tyrch Hotel* (Ⓣ01690/720223; ❷), also on the A5, but closer to the main road junction. The *Lluguy Guesthouse* (Ⓣ01690/720218; ❶) is on the A4086 towards the adventure centre of Plas-y-Brenin (Ⓣ01690/720214, Ⓦwww.pyb.co.uk; ❶), which has a limited amount of accommodation. The cheapest option in the village is the YHA **hostel** (Ⓣ0870/770 5746, Ⓔcapelcurig@yha.org.uk; mid-Feb to mid-Dec; ❶, dorms £14), five hundred yards along the A5 towards Betws-y-Coed. Two and a half miles west down the Ogwen Valley you can stay for a good deal less in the *Williams Barn* bunkhouse and **campsite** (see p.876). During the day, walkers patronize the *Pinnacle Café*, grafted onto the post office and general store at the main road junction. In the evening they retire to the warm and lively **bar** of the *Bryn Tyrch Hotel*, which serves great **food**, much of which is vegan and vegetarian, or head for the sociable bar at the Plas-y-Brenin centre.

The Ogwen Valley

Prising apart the Carneddau and Glyder ranges northwest from Capel Curig, the A5 forges through the **Ogwen Valley** to Bethesda, where one of Wales' last surviving slate quarries continues to tear away the end of the Glyders range, only just keeping the tatty town viable. To the north, the frequently mist-shrouded Carneddau range glowers across at the **Glyders** range and its triple-peaked **Tryfan**, perhaps Snowdonia's most demanding mountain, which forms a fractured spur out from the main road, blocking the view down the valley. West of Tryfan, the road follows a perfect example of a U-shaped valley, carved and smoothed by rocks frozen into the undersides of the glaciers that creaked down **Nant Ffrancon** ten thousand years ago.

The time-compacted moraine left by the retreating ice formed Llŷn Ogwen. On its shores, **Idwal Cottage**, a settlement so small it isn't named on maps, provides the valleys with a mountain rescue centre, a snack bar and a YHA hostel, all clustered around the car park. This is the start of some of Wales' most demanding and rewarding hikes (see box), and the easier half-hour walk to the magnificent cirque, **Cwm Idwal**. The cwm's scalloped floor traps the beautifully still **Llŷn Idwal**, which reflects the precipitous grey cliffs behind, split by the jointed cleft of Twll Du, the **Devil's Kitchen**. Down this, a fine watery haze runs off the flanks of **Glyder Fawr**, soaking the crevices where early botanists found rare arctic-alpine plants, the main reason for

Tourists hike up Snowdon, but mountain connoisseurs invariably prefer the sharply angled peaks of **Tryfan and the Glyders**, with their challenging terrain, cantilevered rocks and views back to Snowdon. The sheer number of good walking paths on the Glyders make it almost impossible to choose one definitive circular route. The individual sections of the walk have therefore been defined separately in order to allow the greatest flexibility. All times given are for the ascents: expect to take approximately half the time to get back down. **Maps** are essential for all these walks: the OS *Outdoor Leisure* 1:25,000 "Snowdonia" #17 is by far the best bet.

If you've got the head for it, the **North Ridge of Tryfan**, at 3002ft (1 mile; 2000ft ascent; 1hr–1hr 30min), is one of the most rewarding scrambles in the country. It's never as precarious as Snowdon's Crib Goch, but you get a genuine mountaineering feel as the valley floor drops rapidly. The route starts in the lay-by at the head of Idwal Lake and goes left across rising ground, until you strike a path heading straight up, following the crest of the ridge to the twin monoliths of **Adam and Eve** on the summit. The courageous, or foolhardy, make the jump between them as a point of honour at the end of every ascent. In fact, the leap is trivial, but the consequences of overshooting would be disastrous.

There are two other main routes up Tryfan. The first follows the so-called **Miners' Track** (2 miles; 1350ft ascent; 2hr) from Idwal Cottage, taking the path to Cwm Idwal, then, as it bears sharply to the right, keeping straight ahead and making for the gap on the horizon. This is **Bwlch Tryfan**, the col between Tryfan and Glyder Fach, from where the **South Ridge** of Tryfan (800yd; 650ft ascent; 30min) climbs past the Far South Peak to the summit. This last section is an easy scramble. The second route, which is more often used in descent, follows **Heather Terrace** (1.5 miles; 2000ft ascent; 2hr), which keeps to a fault in the rock running diagonally across the east face.

The assault on **Glyder Fach** (3260ft) begins at Bwlch Tryfan, reached either by the Miners' Track from Idwal Cottage or by the south ridge from Tryfan's summit. The trickier route follows **Bristly Ridge** (1000yd; 900ft ascent; 40min) which isn't marked on OS maps but runs steeply south from the col up past some daunting-looking towers of rock. It isn't that difficult in dry conditions, and saves a long hike southeast along a second section of the *Miners' Track* (1.5 miles; 900ft ascent; 1hr 30min). The summit lies to the west of the ridge, a chaotic jumble of huge grey slabs that many people don't bother climbing up, preferring to be photographed on a massive cantilevered rock a few yards away.

From Glyder Fach, it's an easy enough stroll to **Glyder Fawr** (3280ft), reached by skirting round the tortured rock formations of **Castell y Gwynt** (the Castle of the Winds) then following a cairn-marked path to the dramatic summit of frost-shattered slabs angled like ancient headstones (1 mile; 200ft ascent; 40min). Glyder Fawr is normally approached from Idwal Cottage, following the **Devil's Kitchen Route** (2.5 miles; 2300ft ascent; 3hr) past Idwal Lake, then to the left of the Devil's Kitchen, zigzagging up to a lake-filled plateau. Follow the path to the right of the lake and turn left for the summit where two paths cross.

designating Cwm Idwal as Wales's first **nature reserve** in 1954. An easy, well-groomed path leads up to the reserve from the car park, where the café (daily 8.30am–5pm; later on summer weekends) will give you a nature trail booklet. A five-minute walk down from the car park, the road crosses a bridge over the top of **Rhaeadr Ogwen** (Ogwen Falls), which cascade down a step in the valley floor.

A couple of inconveniently timed **buses** run along the valley daily between Betws-y-Coed and Bangor. **Accommodation** in the valley is limited to a self-catering bunkhouse and campsite at *Williams Barn*, Gwern Gof Isaf Farm, three miles west of Capel Curig (℡01690/720276; £6), the smaller *Gwern Gof Uchaf* campsite, a mile further west, and the *Idwal Cottage* YHA **hostel** (℡0870/770 5874, ℮idwal@yha.org.uk; March–Oct; dorms £11.50), at the western end of Llŷn Ogwen, five miles from Capel Curig. Residents can get meals at the hostel; the valley is otherwise self-catering.

Llanberis and Snowdon

Mention **LLANBERIS** to any mountain enthusiast and they will think of **Snowdon**. The two seem inseparable, and it's not just the five-mile-long umbilical of the **Snowdon Mountain Railway**, Britain's only rack-and-pinion railway, which bonds the town, located ten miles west of Capel Curig, to the summit, nor the popular path running parallel to it (see box, p.878). This is the nearest you'll get to an alpine climbing village in Wales, its single main street thronged with weatherbeaten walkers and climbers decked out in fleeces, high fashion for what is otherwise a dowdy town. At the same time, Llanberis is very much a Welsh rural community, albeit a depleted one now that slate is no longer being torn from the flanks of Elidir Fawr, the mountain across the town's twin lakes. The quarries, which for the best part of two centuries employed up to three thousand men, closed in 1969, making way for the construction of the Dinorwig Pumped Storage Power Station.

Three of the routes up Snowdon start five miles east of Llanberis at the top of the Llanberis Pass, one of the deepest, narrowest and craggiest in Snowdonia. At the summit, a hostel, café and car park comprise the settlement of **PEN-Y-PASS**. Frequent, year-round Sherpa **buses** travel up daily to Pen-y-Pass, and from mid-July to August there is also the #96 Pen-y-Pass shuttle from Llanberis, the recommended approach even if you have a car, since the Pen-y-Pass car park is expensive and almost always full. Use the "Park and Ride" car park at the bottom of the pass, near the *Vaynol Arms*.

The Town

Scattered remains are all that is left of thirteenth-century **Dolbadarn Castle** (free access; CADW), on the road to **Parc Padarn**, where lakeside oak woods are gradually recolonizing the discarded workings of the defunct Dinorwig Slate Quarries. Here, the **Welsh Slate Museum** (Easter–Oct daily 10am–5pm, Nov–Easter Sun–Fri 10am–4pm; free; ⓦwww.nmgw.ac.uk) occupies the former maintenance workshops of what was once one of the largest slate quarries in the world. The line shafts and flapping belts driven by a fifty-foot-diameter waterwheel provide a backdrop to workbenches where former quarry workers demonstrate their skills at turning an inch-thick slab of slate into six, or even eight, perfectly smooth slivers. The craftsmen here operate an ageing foundry, producing pieces for the scattered branches of the National Museum of Wales, as well as repairing the rolling stock belonging to the nearby **Llanberis Lake Railway** (July & Aug daily; March–June & Sept to early Oct Mon–Fri & Sun; £5 return; ⓦwww.lake-railway.co.uk), which formerly transported slate and ore between the Dinorwig quarries and Port Dinorwig on the Menai Strait. It's a tame forty-minute round trip with little to do at the end except come back and explore the old slate workings.

In 1974, five years after the quarry closed, work began on hollowing out the vast underground chambers of the **Dinorwig Pumped Storage Hydro Station**, designed to provide power on demand. If you can bear the thinly disguised electricity industry advertisement that comes before it, you can take an hour-long minibus tour around the enormous pipework in the depths. For this, you need to call at **Electric Mountain** (June–Aug daily 9.30am–5.30pm; April, May, Sept & Oct daily 10.30am–4.30pm; Feb, March, Nov & Dec Wed–Sun 10.30am–4.30pm; £6, or £5 in winter; ⓦwww.fhc.co.uk), by the lake beside the A4086, the town-centre bypass. The museum complex has some tolerably interesting displays on local glaciation, flora and fauna, and an exhibition about mammoths.

Practicalities

All **buses** to Llanberis stop near the **tourist office**, 41b High St (Easter–Oct daily 10am–6pm, Nov–Easter Wed, Fri & Sun 11am–4pm; ☎01286/870765). Adventurous types should contact Blue Peris (☎01286/870853, ⓦwww .blueperis.co.uk) for mountaineering, sea kayaking, mine exploration and coasteering, but with a charge of £150 per day for instructors, you'd best be in a group. Alternatively, High Trek Snowdonia, Tal y Waen, Deiniolen (☎01286/871232, ⓦwww.climbing-wales.co.uk), offers guided walking and courses. Padarn Watersports at Bryn Du, Tydu Road (☎01286/870556), offers organized climbing, abseiling, canoeing and other mountain activities. The Llanberis Path (see box, p.878), Snowdon Ranger Path and Pitt's Head Track to Rhyd-Ddu are open to **cyclists**, although a voluntary agreement exists restricting cycle access to and from the summit between 10am and 5pm (June–Sept).

There's plenty of low-cost **accommodation** in or close to town: *The Heights*, 74 High St (☎01286/871179, ⓦwww.heightshotel.co.uk; ❷, dorms £14), caters to the walking and climbing set, offering B&B and dorms, not to mention a climbing wall, good restaurant and lively bar. Two other options on the High Street are the *Dolafon Hotel* (☎01286/870993, ⓦwww.dolafon.com; ❷), a comfortable B&B in its own grounds, and the family-run *Padarn Lake Hotel* (☎01286/870260; ❸). The only luxurious place is the *Royal Victoria Hotel*, opposite the Mountain Railway (☎01286/870253, ⓦwww .royal-victoria-hotel.co.uk; ❺). Three miles northwest of town in a Victorian farmhouse in Penisarwaun is *Graianfryn* (☎01286/871007, ⓦwww .vegwales.co.uk; ❸), an exclusively vegetarian and vegan wholefood, nonsmoking B&B, also serving three-course evening meals (£16; Fri & Sat only). Llanberis YHA **hostel**, *Llwyn Celyn* (☎0870/770 5928, ⓔllanberis @yha.org.uk; dorms £11.50), is half a mile uphill along Capel Goch Road, signposted off High Street. Four miles east of town is the *Pen-y-Pass* YHA hostel (☎0870/770 5990, ⓔpenypass@yha.org.uk; ❶, dorms £11.50), with the *Pen-y-Gwryd Hotel* (☎01286/870211, ⓦwww.pyg.co.uk; ❷; March–Oct) a mile further east; they're used to muddy boots in the bar. A cheaper option is *Gwastadnant B&B and Bunkhouse*, three miles east of Llanberis in Nant Peris (☎01286/870356; ❶, bed £6), which also has **camping** facilities.

For **food** of gut-splitting proportions, climbers and walkers flock to *Pete's Eats*, 40 High St, while *Y Bistro*, 43–45 High St (☎01286/871278; Sept–May closed Sun), is the best restaurant for miles around. The *Vaynol Arms*, two miles east of Llanberis and the only pub before Pen-y-Gwryd, serves good beer and very tasty food in a convivial atmosphere; it's usually full of campers from across the road.

Snowdon and the Snowdon Mountain Railway

The highest British mountain outside Scotland, the **Snowdon massif** (3560ft) forms a star of shattered ridges with four major peaks: Crib Goch,

Crib-y-ddysgl, Y Lliwedd and the main summit, **Yr Wyddfa**. Snowdon sports some of the finest walking and scrambling in the park and, in winter, the longest season for ice climbers and cramponed walkers. Hardened outdoor enthusiasts dismiss it as overused, and it can certainly be crowded, especially in summer, when a thousand visitors a day can be pressed into the postbox-red carriages of the Snowdon Mountain Railway, while another 1500 pound the well-maintained paths.

Walks on Snowdon

The following are justifiably the most popular of the seven accepted **walking** routes up **Snowdon**. Maps are essential for all these walks: the OS *Outdoor Leisure* 1:25,000 map of "Snowdonia" #17 is highly recommended.

Llanberis Path

The easiest, longest and most derided route up Snowdon, the **Llanberis Path** (5 miles to summit; 3200ft ascent; 3hr) follows the rail line past the *Halfway Station* café (March to late Sept daily; rest of year Sat & Sun only); posted on the wall inside are the barely believable times of the annual Snowdon Race, which passes on the fourth Saturday in July. Continuing up, the path gets steeper to the "Finger Stone" at **Bwlch Glas** (Green Pass), marking the arrival of the Snowdon Ranger Path, and three routes coming up from Pen-y-Pass to join the Llanberis Path for the final ascent to **Yr Wyddfa**, the summit.

The Miners' and Pig tracks

The **Miners' Track** (4 miles to summit; 2400ft ascent; 2hr 30min) is the easiest of the three routes up from Pen-y-Pass, a broad track leading south then west to the dilapidated remains of the former copper mines in Cwm Dyli. Skirting around the right of a lake, the path climbs more steeply to the lake-filled Cwm Glaslyn, then again to Upper Glaslyn, from where the measured steps of those ahead warn of the impending switchback ascent to the junction with the Llanberis Path.

The stonier **Pig Track** (3.5 miles to summit; 2400ft ascent; 2hr 30min) is really just a variation on the Miners' Track, leaving from the western end of the Pen-y-Pass car park and climbing up to **Bwlch y Moch** (the Pass of the Pigs) before meeting the Miners' Track prior to the zigzag up to the Llanberis Path.

Snowdon Horseshoe

Some claim that the **Snowdon Horseshoe** (8 miles round; 3200ft ascent; 5–7hr) is one of the finest ridge walks in Europe. The route makes a full anticlockwise circuit around the three glacier-carved cwms of Upper Glaslyn, Glaslyn and Llydaw. Not to be taken lightly, it includes the knife-edge traverse of **Crib Goch**, which requires a minimum of an ice axe and crampons in winter. The path follows the Pig Track to Bwlch y Moch, then pitches right for the moderate scramble up to Crib Goch. If you balk at any of this, turn back; if not, pick your way along the sensational ridge to **Crib-y-ddysgl** (3494ft) and, on easier ground, to the summit. The return to Llŷn Llydaw and the Miners' Track is via **Bwlch-y-Saethau** (Pass of the Arrows) and **Y Lliwedd** (2930ft).

Watkin Path

The most spectacular of the southern routes up Snowdon, the **Watkin Path** (4 miles to summit; 3350ft ascent; 3hr) begins at Bethania Bridge, three miles northeast of Beddgelert in Nantgwynant. The path starts on a broad track, lined with oaks, which narrows before heading past a disused tramway to a series of cataracts. A natural amphitheatre contains the ruins of a slate works and **Gladstone Rock**, at which, in 1892, the 83-year-old prime minister officially opened the route.

Opprobrium is chiefly levelled at the **Snowdon Mountain Railway** (mid-March to Oct 6–25 trains daily; £20 return; ☎01286/870223, ⓦwww.snowdonrailway.co.uk), completed in 1896, purely for the fact that it exists. Seventy-year-old carriages pushed by equally old steam locos still climb, in just under an hour, from the eastern end of Llanberis opposite the *Royal Victoria Hotel* to the summit café and bar (open when the trains are running to the top). A "Railway Stamp" (10p) affixed to your letter – along with the usual Royal Mail one – entitles you to use the highest postbox in the UK and enchant your friends with a "Summit of Snowdon – Copa'r Wyddfa" postmark. Times, type of locomotive and final destination vary with demand and ice conditions at the top: to avoid disappointment, buy your tickets early on clear summer days. If you walk up by one of the routes detailed in the "Walks on Snowdon" box, you can take the train down, if there is space (£14).

Beddgelert

Almost all of the prodigious quantity of rain which falls on Snowdon spills down either the Glaslyn or Colwyn rivers, which meet at the huddle of grey houses, prodigiously brightened with floral displays in summer, that make up **BEDDGELERT**. A sentimental tale fabricated by a wily local publican to lure punters tells how the town got its name. **Gelert's Grave** (*bedd* means burial place), an enclosure just south of town, is supposedly the final resting place of Prince Llewelyn ap Iorwerth's faithful dog, Gelert, who was left in charge of the prince's infant son while he went hunting. On his return, the child was gone and the hound's muzzle was soaked in blood. Jumping to conclusions, the impetuous Llewelyn slew the dog, only to find the child safely asleep beneath its cot and a dead wolf beside him. Llewelyn hurried to his dog, which licked his hand as it died.

Beyond the "grave", the river crashes down the bony and picturesque **Aberglaslyn Gorge** towards Porthmadog. You can walk along the right bank of the river, past Gelert's Grave, crossing over the bridge onto the Fisherman's Path. This then hugs the left bank for a mile, heading gently down to Pont Aberglaslyn, at the bottom of the gorge, affording a closer look at the river's course through chutes and channels in sculpted rocks. You have to return the same way.

A mile in the opposite direction up Nantgwynant, the **Sygun Copper Mine** (Easter–Sept Mon–Fri 10am–5pm, Sat 10am–4pm, Sun 11am–5pm; Oct, Feb & March Mon–Sat 10.30am–4pm, Sun 11am–4pm; Nov–Jan Sat & Sun 11am–3.30pm; £5.25; ⓦwww.syguncoppermine.co.uk) is the dilapidated remnant of what, until a century ago, had been the valley's prime source of income from Roman times. Restored and made safe, the multiple levels of tunnels and galleries can now be visited on a 45-minute guided tour, accompanied by the disembodied voice of a miner describing his life in the mine.

Buses all stop by the National Trust shop (daily: June–Aug 11am–6pm; April, May, Sept & Oct 11am–5pm), just by the bridge in Tŷ Llywelyn, which houses some interesting exhibits on Snowdonia and the Victorian Romantics. The **tourist office** (Easter–Oct daily 10am–6pm, Nov–Easter Fri–Sun 9.30am–4.30pm; ☎01766/890615) is in Canolfan Hebog, a restored chapel just up the road by the main village car park. The best places to **stay** are the *Beddgelert Bistro & Antiques*, Waterloo House, directly opposite the bridge (☎01766/890543; ❷), with three attractive en-suite rooms above the restaurant; *Plas Tan-y-Graig* (☎01766/890310, ⓦwww.plastanygraig.co.uk; ❷), also near the bridge, a decent budget B&B aimed at walkers and cyclists; and *Sygun*

Fawr Country House, three quarters of a mile away off the A498 (☎01766/890258, ⓦwww.sygunfawr.co.uk; ❸), a sixteenth-century house in its own grounds with a sauna and good, moderately priced evening meals. The excellent *Beddgelert Forest Campsite* (☎01766/890288) is a mile out on the Caernarfon road, four miles before the highly rated *Snowdon Ranger* YHA **hostel** (☎0870/770 6038, ⒺSnowdon@yha.org.uk; mid-Feb to Dec; ❶, dorms £10.25). The *Bryn Gwynant* YHA hostel (☎0870/770 5732, Ⓔbryngwynant@yha.org.uk; Jan–Oct; ❶, dorms £10.25), is beautifully sited in Nantgwynant, four miles northeast of Beddgelert on the A498, and has a **campsite** where you can use the hostel's facilities for half the adult rate.

Blaenau Ffestiniog and around

Every approach to **BLAENAU FFESTINIOG** is dramatic, but none more so than the train journey through the Lledr Valley from Betws-y-Coed. Following the twists of the river, the railway passes through broadleaf woods which give way to the smooth, grassy slopes of the Moel Siabod, where the longest rail tunnel in Wales bores through over two miles of slate to suddenly emerge in

---

The Welsh slate industry

Slate derives its name from the Old French word *esclater*, meaning to split – an apt reflection of its most highly valued quality. The Romans recognized the potential of the substance, roofing the houses of Segontium with it (see p.888), and Edward I used it extensively in his Iron Ring of castles around Snowdonia, but it wasn't until around 1780 that Britain's Industrial Revolution kicked in, leading to greater urbanization and boosting the demand for Welsh roofing slates. Cities grew: Hamburg was reroofed with Welsh slate after its fire of 1842, and it is the same material which still gives that rainy-day sheen to interminable rows of English mill-town houses.

For the 1862 London Exhibition, one skilled craftsman produced a sheet of slate ten feet long, a foot wide and a sixteenth of an inch thick – so thin it could be flexed – firmly establishing Welsh slate as the finest in the world. By 1898, Welsh quarries – largely run, like the coal and steel industries of the south, by the English – were producing half a million tons of dressed slate a year, almost all of it from Snowdonia. At Penrhyn and Dinorwig, mountains were hacked away in terraces, sometimes rising 2000ft above sea level, with the teams of workers negotiating with the foreman for the choicest piece of rock and the selling price for what they produced. They often slept through the week in damp dormitories on the mountain, and tuberculosis was common, exacerbated by the slate dust. At Blaenau Ffestiniog, the seams required mining underground rather than quarrying, but conditions were no better, with miners even having to buy their own candles, the only light they had. In spite of this, thousands left their hillside smallholdings for the burgeoning quarry towns. Few workers were allowed to join Undeb Chwarelwyr Gogledd Cymru (the North Wales Quarrymen's Union), and in 1900 the workers in Lord Penrhyn's quarry at Bethesda went out on strike. They stayed out for three years, but failed to win any concessions. Those who got their jobs back were forced to work for even less money as a recession took hold, and although the two world wars heralded mini-booms as bombed houses were replaced, the industry never recovered its nineteenth-century prosperity, and most quarries and mines closed in the 1970s.

Sadly, what little slate is produced today mostly goes for things besides roofing: floor tiles, road aggregate and an astonishing array of nasty ashtrays and coasters etched with mountainscapes.

the town. Blaenau means "head of the valley", in this case the lush Vale of Ffestiniog, a dramatic contrast to the forbidding town, hemmed in by stark slopes strewn with heaps of splintered slate. When clouds hunker low in this great cwm and rain sheets the grey roofs, grey walls and grey paving slabs, it can be a terrifically gloomy place. Thousands of tons of slate were once hewn from the labyrinth of underground caverns here each year, but these days the town is only kept alive by its extant slate cavern tour, and by tourists who change from the Lledr Valley train line onto the wonderful, narrow-gauge **Ffestiniog Railway** (see p.884), which winds up from Porthmadog.

It's difficult to get a real feeling of what slate means to the town without a visit to the **Llechwedd Slate Caverns** (daily: March–Sept 10am–5.15pm; Oct–Feb 10am–4.15pm; single tour £7.50, both tours £11.50; Ⓦwww .llechwedd-slate-caverns.co.uk), on the edge of town on the road to Betws-y-Coed. There are two tours available. On the **Miners' Tramway Tour**, you are plied with facts about slate mining as a small train takes you a third of a mile along one of the oldest levels to the enormous Cathedral Cave and the open-air Chough's Cavern. The awe-inspiring scale of the place justifies the trip, even without the tableaux of Victorian miners at work. On the more dramatic **Deep Mine Tour**, a steeply inclined railway takes you down to a labyrinth of tunnels through which you are guided by an irksome taped spiel of a Victorian miner. The long caverns angling back into the gloom are increasingly impressive, culminating in one filled by a beautiful opalescent pool.

Practicalities

The **train station** on the High Street serves both the Ffestiniog line to Porthmadog and mainline train services from Betws-y-Coed, and is a short walk up the main drag from the **tourist office** (April–Oct daily 10am–6pm; ☏01766/830360), opposite the *Queen's Hotel*. **Buses** stop either in the car park around the back or outside *Y Commercial* pub, on High Street. A vast number of Blaenau Ffestiniog's visitors ride the train up from Porthmadog, visit a slate mine and leave, and this is reflected in the limited range of **accommodation**. Try the excellent, welcoming cheapie *Afallon*, Manod Road (☏01766/ 830468; ❶), almost a mile south of the tourist office, or, in town itself, the *Queen's Hotel*, 1 High St (☏01766/830055, Ⓦwww.wales-snowdonia.com; ❹).

A walk from Blaenau Ffestiniog

One of the most scenic, and easiest, walks around Blaenau Ffestiniog leads down into the **Vale of Ffestiniog** (4–5 miles; descent only; 2–3hr) following the Ffestiniog Railway past its 360° loop, through sessile oak woods and past several cascades all the way to Tan-y-bwlch. From here, you can return to Blaenau Ffestiniog, or continue on to Porthmadog by train; check the times at the station and buy your ticket to ensure a place on the return train.

The walk can be done from Blaenau Ffestiniog, but it involves a fairly dull first mile easily avoided by catching the train or driving to the reservoir at **Tanygrisiau**. From the station, turn right past the Tanygrisiau information centre then take the second left, not the road beside the reservoir but the next one, following the footpath signs. Cross the train line, then pass a car park on your left before turning left down a track and skirting behind the powerhouse. The path then sticks closely to the train line, occasionally crossing it. Even when there are several paths you can't go far wrong if you keep the train lines in sight. *The Grapes* pub at Maentwrog, half a mile beyond Tan-y-bwlch, is a great place to while away the time until the next train – or the one after that.

A mile or so south on the A470 is *Cae Du*, Manod Road (☎01766/830847; ❷), in a seventeenth-century farmhouse. One of the best in the area is *Bryn Elltyd* (☎01766/831356, ⓦwww.accommodation-snowdonia.com; ❶), a fine B&B about a mile from town overlooking Llyn Ystradau, run by a qualified mountain leader.

Good **food** isn't especially abundant. *Caffi Glen*, south of the tourist office at 36 High St, does decent all-day breakfasts and snacks, but for something more substantial you're limited to the moderate, broad-ranging menu at *Myfanwys*, 4 Market Place (☎01766/830059), or a bar meal at the *Queen's Hotel*. Most locals head for the *Grapes* (☎01766/590208) at Maentwrog, four miles south down the A496, where there's the moderately priced and gamey *Flambard's* restaurant, although the place is also lauded for its gargantuan and inexpensive bar meals.

The Llŷn

The Llŷn takes its name from an Irish word for peninsula – aptly for this most westerly part of North Wales, which, until the fifth century, had a significant Irish population. The cliff- and cove-lined finger of land juts out south and west, separating Cardigan and Caernarfon bays, its hills tapering away along the ancient route to Aberdaron, where pilgrims sailed for Ynys Enlli (Bardsey Island). Today, it's the beaches that lure people to the south coast family resorts of **Cricieth**, **Pwllheli** and **Abersoch**, and unless you want to rent windsurfers or canoes, it's preferable to press on along the narrow roads that dawdle down towards Aberdaron. Not even Snowdonia can match the remoteness of the tip of the Llŷn, and nowhere in Wales is more staunchly Welsh: road signs are still bilingual but the English is frequently obliterated; Stryd Fawr is used instead of High Street, and in most local shops you'll only hear Welsh spoken.

The Llŷn is reached through one of the two gateway towns, Porthmadog and Caernarfon, linked by the A487, an effective boundary between Snowdonia proper and the peninsula's gentler contours. **Porthmadog**, nestling into the crook of the elbow where the Cambrian coast takes a sharp left turn, is of interest for its proximity to the private "dream village" of **Portmeirion**, reached on Wales' finest narrow-gauge train line, the **Ffestiniog Railway**. The Llŷn's northern coast comes to an abrupt end at the mouth of the Menai Strait, guarded by the magnificent fortress which forms the centrepiece of **Caernarfon**, a good base for both the Llŷn and central Snowdonia.

Porthmadog and around

Located right at the point where the Llŷn peninsula turns sharply south down the Cambrian coast, **PORTHMADOG** was once the busiest slate port in North Wales. Nowadays, it's a pleasant enough town to spend a night or two, although it sadly makes little of its situation on the north bank of the vast, mountain-backed estuary. Two things it does make a fuss about are the Italianate folly of Portmeirion, two miles east of town, and the Ffestiniog Railway that originally carried slate down from Blaenau Ffestiniog through verdant mountain scenery. Porthmadog would never have existed at all without the entrepreneurial ventures of a Lincolnshire MP named William Alexander Madocks, who named the town after both himself and the Welsh prince Madog, who some say sailed from the nearby Ynys Fadog (Madog's

883

△ The Ffestiniog Railway

Island) to North America in 1170. Between 1808 and 1812, Madocks fought tides and currents to build the mile-long embankment of The Cob, southeast of present-day Porthmadog, enclosing 7000 acres of the estuary. A wharf was built and, with the completion of the Blaenau Ffestiniog Railway in 1836, the town spread along a waterfront thick with orderly heaps of slate and the masts of merchant ships.

Without a doubt, the **Ffestiniog Railway** (Easter–Oct 4–10 trains daily; Nov–Easter mainly weekends; return to Blaenau Ffestiniog £14, to Tan-y-Bwlch £8.50; ℡01766/512340, ⓦwww.festrail.co.uk) ranks as Wales' finest narrow-gauge rail line, twisting and looping up 650ft from the wharf at Porthmadog to the slate mines at Blaenau Ffestiniog, thirteen miles away. When the line opened in 1836, it carried slate from the mines down to the port with the help of gravity, horses riding with the goods then hauling the empty carriages back up again. Steam had to be introduced to cope with the 100,000 tons of slate a year that Blaenau Ffestiniog was churning out by the late nineteenth century, but the slate roofing market collapsed between the wars and the line was abandoned in 1946. Most of the tracks and sleepers had disappeared by 1954, when a bunch of dedicated volunteers began reconstruction, only completing the entire route in 1982. Leaving Porthmadog, trains cross The Cob and then stop at **Minffordd**, a mile from Portmeirion and a convenient place to change onto the mainline railway. Two stops later is Tan-y-Bwlch, from where it's a short stroll to *The Grapes* pub at Maentwrog and the start of the Vale of Ffestiniog walk (see box, p.881).

Practicalities

Cambrian coast trains pull into Porthmadog mainline **train station** at the north end of the High Street; the **Ffestiniog station** is located down by the harbour, about half a mile to the south. In between the two, National Express **coaches** stop on Avenue Road outside the *Royal Sportsman*; local **bus** services stop outside the *Australia Inn*, on High Street. The helpful **tourist office**, adjoining the community centre on the High Street (Easter–Oct daily 10am–6pm; Nov–Easter daily except Wed 10am–5pm; ℡01766/512981), is over the bridge from the Ffestiniog Railway station.

While limited budgets are well catered for, there's not much really decent **accommodation**, unless you're prepared to splash out for a night at the swanky *Portmeirion Hotel* in Portmeirion (see opposite). The *Royal Sportsman* pub, 131 High St (℡01766/512015, ⓦwww.royalsportsman.co.uk; ❸), is a safe town-centre bet. *Eric Jones's Bunkhouse*, at Prenteg (℡01766/512199), two miles north of Porthmadog on the A498 to Beddgelert, opposite *Eric Jones's Café*, has acceptable dorms for around £4 a night. At the top of High Street, Bank Place forks left, becoming Borth Road, on the way out to numerous family-oriented **campsites** at Black Rock and Morfa Bychan. Along this way, about fifteen minutes' walk from town, you'll come to the pleasant enough *Tyddyn Llwyn* site (℡01766/512205).

For **food** in Porthmadog, there's *Yr Hen Fecus*, Lombard Street (℡01766/514625), an unpretentious restaurant with some good veggie options, or the seafood specialities of the excellent *Harbour Restaurant*, High Street (℡01766/512471; winter Thurs–Sat only), almost opposite the tourist office. If you've got transport or want to walk up an appetite, there's fantastic pub food to be had in nearby Tremadog, less than a mile north, at either the *Union Inn* or the *Golden Fleece*, both on the main square. For **drinking**, make up your own mind as to whether the lively, youthful pub *The Ship & Castle* deserves its local moniker "The Shit & Hassle".

Portmeirion

The area's main lure is the unique, Italianate private village of **PORT-MEIRION** (daily 9.30am–5.30pm; £5.50; ⓦwww.portmeirion-village.com), set on a small rocky peninsula in Tremadog Bay, three miles east near Minffordd. Both the mainline and Ffestiniog trains, as well as buses #1 and #2, stop in Minffordd, from where it's a 25-minute walk to Portmeirion. Perhaps best known as "The Village" in the 1960s cult British TV series *The Prisoner*, Portmeirion was the brainchild of eccentric architect Clough Williams-Ellis, and his dream to build an ideal village which enhances rather than blends in with the surroundings, using a "gay, light-opera sort of approach". The result is certainly theatrical: a stage set with a lucky dip of buildings arranged to distort perspectives and reveal tantalizing glimpses of the seascape behind.

In the 1920s, Williams-Ellis bought the site and turned an existing house into a hotel, the income from this providing funds for his "Home for Fallen Buildings". Endangered buildings from all over Britain and abroad were broken down, transported and rebuilt, every conceivable style being plundered: a Neoclassical colonnade from Bristol, Siamese figures, a Jacobean town hall, and the Italianate touches – a campanile and a pantheon. Williams-Ellis designed his village around a Mediterranean piazza, piecing together a scaled-down nest of loggias, grand porticoes and tiny terracotta-roofed houses and painting them in pastels: turquoise, ochre and buff yellows. Continually surprising, with hidden entrances and cherubs popping out of crevices, the ensemble is eclectic yet never quite inappropriate. A recent addition to the family is the Victorian folly of Castell Deudraeth, opened with a canny eye on the conference trade, but worth a look for other visitors too.

Portmeirion is in need of a lick of paint here and there, but even so, more than three thousand visitors a day come to ogle in summer, when it can be a delight; there are fewer in winter, when it seems just bizarre. In the evening, when the village is closed to the public, patrons at the opulent, waterside *Portmeirion Hotel* (☎01766/770000; ❼) get to see the place at its best – peaceful, even ghostly. Other than walking in the delightful grounds, there's little to actually do, except for viewing a film on the town, popping into the shops selling china and *Prisoner* memorabilia, and eating.

Cricieth and around

When sea-bathing became the Victorian fashion, English families descended on the sweeping sand and shingle beach at **CRICIETH** (sometimes Criccieth), five miles west of Porthmadog, a quiet, amiable resort which curiously abounds with good places to stay and great restaurants, making it a good touring base for the peninsula and Porthmadog. There isn't much here, however, other than the battle-worn remains of **Cricieth Castle** (daily: June–Sept 10am–6pm; April, May & Oct 10am–5pm; other times free access; £2.50; CADW), dominating the coastline with its twin-towered gatehouse. Started by Llywelyn ap Iorwerth in 1230, it was strengthened by Edward I around 1283, and razed by Owain Glyndŵr in 1404, leaving little besides a plan of broken walls. It's a great spot to sit and look over Cardigan Bay to Harlech, but leave time for the ticket office, where there's a workaday exhibition on Welsh castles and a wonderful animated cartoon based on the twelfth-century Cambrian travels of Giraldus Cambrensis as he gathered support for the Third Crusade.

Buses and **trains** along the Cambrian coastline stop a couple of hundred yards west of Y Maes, the open square at the centre of Cricieth. **Accommodation** is plentiful, with the *Moelwyn*, 27–29 Mona Terrace

(T01766/522500, @moelwyn@aol.com; ❸; March–Nov) a smart choice with great sea views. More luxurious places are further afield: *Mynydd Ednyfed*, Caernarfon Road (T01766/523269, Wwww.criccieth.net; ❸), is a classy country hotel a mile north on the B4411, while *Bron Eifion* (T01766/522385, Wwww.broneifion.co.uk; ❺) is a beautiful Victorian country-house hotel set in its own grounds a mile west of town. You'll find the **campsite**, *Mynydd Du*, a mile towards Porthmadog on the A497 (T01766/522533; April–Oct).

For such a small town, good **restaurants** are surprisingly abundant and offer the best range of eating on the peninsula. The two plusher hotels listed above both serve innovative and moderately priced meals. *Tir-a-Môr*, 1–3 Mona Terrace (T01766/523084; closed Sun), isn't strictly Italian, but offers a large range of expensive Italian-influenced dishes, with definite Welsh overtones, in airy surroundings. *Moelwyn* (see above) has a superb sea-facing restaurant; and the *Prince of Wales*, Stryd Fawr, offers a great **pub** atmosphere and decent bar meals.

Llanystumdwy

A mile west of Cricieth, the village of **LLANYSTUMDWY** celebrates its most famous son, the Welsh patriot, social reformer and British prime minister David Lloyd George. He grew up in Highgate House, now part of the **Lloyd George Museum** (July–Sept daily 10.30am–5pm; June Mon–Sat 10.30am–5pm; Easter–May & Oct Mon–Fri 10.30am–4.30pm; £3), comprising a fairly dull collection of gifts, awards and caskets honouring the statesman, displays full of anecdotes and little-known facts, and a couple of short films giving a broad sweep of his life. Lloyd George is buried under a memorial by the River Dwyfor – a boulder and two simple plaques by Portmeirion designer Clough Williams-Ellis. **Bus** #3 from Porthmadog and Cricieth passes through the village on its way to Pwllheli.

Pwllheli and Abersoch

PWLLHELI (pronounced "poolth-heli") is the market town for the peninsula, a role it has maintained since 1355 when it gained its charter, though there's little sign of its history nowadays. The overall tenor is one of low-brow fun-seeking, as holiday-makers flood in from the nearby holiday camp. Pwllheli's one defining feature is its Welshness. Even in the height of summer, you'll hear far more Welsh spoken here than English. Pwllheli is hard to avoid – it's the terminus for National Express **coaches**, which stop on Y Maes, the main square, and is also the final stop for Cambrian coast **trains** – but you should push on if possible. The **tourist office** is bang opposite the station on Sgwar yr Orsaf (daily: April–Oct 10am–6pm; Nov–March Mon–Wed, Fri & Sat 10.30am–4.30pm; T01758/613000). During the summer you can rent **mountain bikes** at Llŷn Cycle Hire, 2 Ala Road (T01758/612414). If you decide to **stay**, try *Bank Place* on Stryd Fawr (T01758/612103; ❶) or, four hundred yards away, *Llys Gwyrfai*, 14 West End Parade (T01758/614877; ❶), a comfortable guest house with sea views and home-cooked meals.

After the distinctly Welsh feel of Pwllheli, **ABERSOCH**, seven miles southwest along the coast, comes as a surprise. This former fishing village pitched in the middle of two golden bays has, over the last century, become a thoroughly anglicized resort, with a distinctly haughty opinion of itself. Such high self-esteem isn't really justified, but at high tide the harbour is attractive, and the long swathe of the beach-hut-backed Town Beach is a fine spot, even if it's barely visible under towels at busy times. A short walk along the beach shakes off most o the crowds, but a better bet is to make for three-mile-long **Porth Neigwl** (Hell's Mouth), two miles to the southwest, which ranks as one of the country's best **surf beaches**; you'll need your own gear, and beware of the undertow if you're swimming. Back in Abersoch, you can get instruction and **rent windsurfers**, surfboards and wetsuits from West Coast Surf Shop, Lôn Pen Cei (☎01758/713067, ⓦwww.westcoastsurf.co.uk), by the harbour. **Buses** from Pwllheli make a loop through the middle of Abersoch, stopping by the privately run **tourist office** on Lôn Pen Cei (daily 10am–5pm; mid-Sept to Easter closes 2pm; ☎01758/712929, ⓦwww.abersochtouristinfo.co.uk). For **accommodation**, try the *Trewen*, Lôn Hawen, just off Lôn Sarn Bach (☎01758/712755; ❷). Two good places on Lôn Sarn Bach itself are *Angorfa Guest House* (☎01758/712967; ❷; Jan–Nov), and the superb *Neigwl Hotel* (☎01758/712363, ⓦwww.neigwl.com; ❸). There are some decent **places to eat**: *Mañana*, on Lôn Pen Cei, serves Mexican and Italian food, or just up the road is *Angelina's* (☎01758/712353), with a broad menu (plus yummy desserts). The *Ship*, out of town in Llanbedrog, near Pwllheli, is excellent.

Aberdaron and Bardsey Island

The small, lime-washed fishing village of **ABERDARON** backs a pebble beach two miles short of the tip of the Llŷn. For a thousand years, from the sixth century onwards, it was the last stop for pilgrims to **Bardsey Island**, or Ynys Enlli (the Island of the Currents), just offshore; three visits were proclaimed equivalent to one pilgrimage to Rome. Many pilgrims came to die there, earning the place its epithet "The Isle of Twenty Thousand Saints". Bardsey is heart-stoppingly beautiful and well worth a visit – there are self-catering cottages available on the island, or you could just go for a day-trip. For details of both, contact the Bardsey Island Trust (☎01758/730740, ⓦwww.bardsey.org). In olden days, the final gathering place before the treacherous crossing was the fourteenth-century Y Gegin Fawr (Great Kitchen), a stone building which still operates as a **café** in the middle of Aberdaron. Today, pilgrims are more likely to be attracted by poetry, as until 1978, **R.S. Thomas** (1913–2000) was the minister at Aberdaron's seafront church of St Hywyn.

Without your own transport, the only way to get to Aberdaron is to catch bus #17 from Pwllheli (Mon–Sat). **Accommodation** is fairly limited; the least expensive option is *Brynmor* (☎01758/760344; ❷), overlooking the bay, just up the road to Porth Oer, the "whistling sands". The *Tŷ Newydd* hotel (☎01758/760207; ❹) is a good bet too; make time for a pint or meal on their beach terrace as the sun sets. The best and quietest **campsite** around is *Mur Melyn* (no phone) just over a mile out from Aberdaron, midway to Porth Oer; take the B4413 west, fork right, then turn left at Pen-y-Bont house.

Caernarfon

It was in **CAERNARFON**, in 1969, that Charles, the current heir to the throne, was invested as prince of Wales, a ceremony which reaffirmed English sovereignty over Wales in this, one of the most nationalist of Welsh-speaking regions. Since 1282, when the English defeated Llywelyn ap Gruffydd, the last Welsh prince of Wales, the title has been bestowed on heirs to the English (and then British) throne, but it wasn't until 1911 that the machinations of David Lloyd George – MP for Caernarfon and future prime minister – brought a theatrical investiture ceremony to the centre of his constituency: an odd move for a proto-nationalist, considering the symbolic implications. Caernarfon's vastly imposing **castle** and near-complete rectangle of town walls make it an appealing place, but apart from the castle, there isn't too much to see: you can only walk a small section of the wall and the rest of the town has been ripped through by a main road and boxed in by modern buildings. That said, it's a spirited and lively town, is well situated on the Menai Strait, between the mainland and Anglesey, and has good bus connections to Llanberis and Snowdonia.

The Town

In 1283, Edward I started work on **Caernarfon Castle** (June–Sept daily 9.30am–6pm; April–May & Oct daily 9.30am–5pm; Nov–March Mon–Sat 9.30am–4pm, Sun 11am–4pm; £4.50; CADW), the strongest link in his Iron Ring, a decisive hammer-blow to any Welsh aspirations to autonomy and the ultimate symbol of Anglo-Norman military might. With the Welsh already smarting from the loss of their prince, Edward is said to have promised "a prince born in Wales who could speak never a word of English" – a vow he fulfilled to the letter by moving his pregnant wife to Caernarfon. The story is almost certainly apocryphal. Instead, Edward attempted to appease the Welsh by paying tribute to aspects of local legend. The Welsh had long associated their town with the eastern capital of the Roman Empire: Caernarfon's old name, Caer Cystennin, was also the name used for Constantinople, and Constantine himself was believed to have been born at Segontium (see below). Edward's architect, James of St George, exploited this connection in the distinctive limestone and sandstone banding and the polygonal towers, both reminiscent of the Theodosian walls in present-day Istanbul.

In military terms, the castle is supreme. It was taken once, before building was complete, but then withstood two sieges by Owain Glyndŵr with a garrison of only 28 men-at-arms. Entering through the **King's Gate**, the castle's strength is immediately apparent. Embrasures and murder holes between the octagonal towers face in on no fewer than five gates and six portcullises, and that's once you have crossed the moat, now bridged by an incongruous modern structure. Inside, the huge lawn gives a misleading impression since both the wall dividing the two original wards and all the buildings that filled them crumbled away long ago. The towers are in a much better state, and linked by an exhausting honeycomb of wall-walks and tunnels. The tallest and most striking is the **King's Tower**, at the western end, whose three slender turrets are adorned with eagle sculptures and give the best views of the town. To the south, the Queen's Tower is entirely taken up by the numbingly thorough **Museum of the Royal Welch Fusiliers**, while the Northeast Tower houses the **Prince of Wales Exhibition**, just outside which is the Dinorwig slate dais used for Charles' investiture.

A ten-minute walk along the A4085 Beddgelert road brings you to the western end of the Roman road from Chester, at **Segontium Roman Fort** (Mon–Sat 10am–5pm, Sun 2–5pm; Nov–March closes 4pm; free; ⓦ www.nmgw.ac.uk). The Romans occupied this five-acre site for three centuries from around 78 AD, though most of the remains are from the final rebuilding after 364. The ground plan is seldom more than shin-high and somewhat baffling, making the museum and displays in the ticket office pretty much essential.

The narrow-gauge **Welsh Highland Railway** (WHR, or Rheilffordd Eryri; ⓦ www.festrail.co.uk) starts in Caernarfon, just near the harbour on St Helen's Road. Ultimately, it will run all the way to Porthmadog via Beddgelert, a route of 25 miles. It currently goes as far as Rhyd-Ddu, starting point for southerly ascents of Snowdon (£14 return), with a stop outside the Snowdon Ranger YHA hostel. Joint tickets with the Ffestiniog Railway are available.

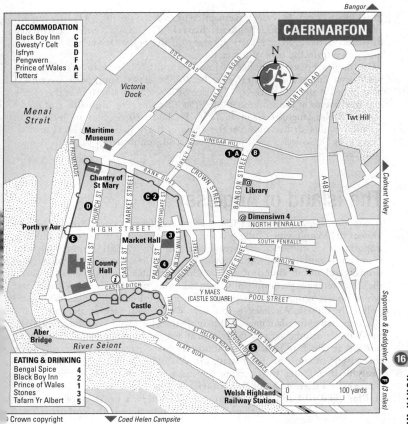

ACCOMMODATION

Black Boy Inn	C
Gwesty'r Celt	B
Isfryn	D
Pengwern	F
Prince of Wales	A
Totters	E

EATING & DRINKING

Bengal Spice	4
Black Boy Inn	2
Prince of Wales	1
Stones	3
Tafarn Yr Albert	5

Crown copyright   Coed Helen Campsite

Practicalities

With no mainline train station, the hub of Caernarfon's public transport system is Y Maes (Castle Square), right under the walls of the castle, where **buses** stop. The **tourist office** is in Oriel Pendeitsh on Castle Street (Easter–Oct daily 10am–6pm; Nov–Easter daily except Wed 10am–4.30pm; ☎01286/672232), just a few steps away. There are a number of **accommodation** options close to the centre: try *Isfryn Guesthouse*, 11 Church St (☎01286/675628; ❷), or the *Prince of Wales* pub on Bangor Street (☎01286/673367; ❷). The characterful *Black Boy Inn*, Northgate Street (☎01286/673023; ❸), is one of the town's oldest buildings, but for more upmarket accommodation, your best bet is the *Gwesty'r Celt* hotel, Bangor Street (☎01286/674477, ⓦwww .celtic-royal.co.uk; ❻), which comes complete with an indoor pool and smart restaurant. Away from town are some excellent country houses, including *Pengwern Farm* in Saron, three miles southwest of Caernarfon (☎01286/831500, ⓔpengwern@talk21.com; ❷; Feb–Nov), which has a lovely rural setting, and serves inexpensive, farm-fresh evening meals. Take the A487 south across the river then turn right towards Saron; Pengwern is just over two miles down on the right. *Totters*, at Plas Porth Yr Aur, 2 High St

(T01286/672963, W www.applemaps.co.uk/totters; dorms £11), is a superb and very friendly independent **hostel**. The *Coed Helen* **campsite** (T01286/676770; March–Oct) sits right on the Seiont River, just across the footbridge from the base of the castle.

Caernarfon boasts a number of low-key and likeable **restaurants**: try the bistro-style fare at *Stone's*, 4 Hole in the Wall St (closed Sun), or the acclaimed balti dishes at the *Bengal Spice*, 11 Palace St. The cheapest option is the excellent **bar meals** at the aforementioned *Black Boy Inn*. For **nightlife**, you might catch a Welsh-language band at *Tafarn Yr Albert*, 10 Segontium Terrace, on Saturday nights, or live music at the *Prince of Wales*, Bangor Street. Thursday's *Caernarfon & Denbigh Herald* newspaper has gig information for both Bangor and Caernarfon.

The island of Anglesey

Across the Menai Strait from Caernarfon, **Anglesey** (Ynys Môn) welcomes visitors to "Mam Cymru", the Mother of Wales, attesting to the island's former importance as the national breadbasket. In the twelfth century Giraldus Cambrensis noted that "when crops have failed in other regions, this island, from its soil and its abundant produce, has been able to supply all Wales," and the land remains predominantly pastoral, with small fields, stone walls and white houses reminiscent of parts of Ireland or England. Linguistically and politically, though, Anglesey is intensely Welsh, with seventy percent of the islanders being first-language Welsh-speakers. The island was the crucible of pre-Roman druidic activity in Britain, and there are still numerous Neolithic remains at which to soak up the atmosphere of a pagan past. Especially since the advent of the A55 main road, many people charge straight through to **Holyhead** and the Irish ferries, missing out on Anglesey's many charms. There's the ancient town of **Beaumaris**, with its fine castle, the Whistler mural at **Plas Newydd** and some superb coastal scenery: a necklace of fine sandy coves and rocky headlands that's a match for anywhere in the country.

Beaumaris

The original inhabitants of **BEAUMARIS** (Biwmares) were evicted by Edward I to make way for the construction of his new castle and bastide town, dubbed "beautiful marsh" in an attempt to attract English settlers. Today the place can still seem like the small English outpost Edward intended, with its elegant Georgian terrace along the front (designed by Joseph Hansom, of cab fame) and more plummy English accents than you'll have heard for a while. Many of their owners belong with the flotilla of yachts, an echo of the port's fleet of merchant ships, which disappeared with the completion of bridges to the mainland and subsequent growth of Holyhead. While Beaumaris repays an afternoon mooching around and enjoying the views across the Strait, it also boasts more sights than the rest of the island put together, inevitably drawing the crowds in summer.

Beaumaris Castle (June–Sept daily 9.30am–6pm; April, May & Oct daily 9.30am–5pm; Nov–March Mon–Sat 9.30am–4pm, Sun 11am–4pm; £3; CADW) might never have been built had Madog ap Llywelyn not captured Caernarfon in 1294. When asked to build the new castle, James of St George abandoned the Caernarfon design in favour of a concentric plan, developing it into a highly evolved symmetrical octagon. Sited on flat land at the edge of town, the castle is denied the domineering majesty of Caernarfon or Harlech, its low outer walls appearing almost welcoming until you begin to appreciate the concentric layout of the defences protected by massive towers, a moat linked to the sea and the Arab-influenced staggered entries through the two gatehouses. Despite more than thirty years' work, the project was never quite finished, leaving most of the inner ward empty and the corbels and fireplaces built into the walls unused. You can explore the internal passages in the walls but the low-parapet wall-walk, from where you get the best idea of the castle's defensive capability, remains off limits. Impressive as they are, none of these defences was able to prevent siege by Owain Glyndŵr, who held the castle for two years from 1403, although they did withhold a Parliamentarian siege during the Civil War.

Almost opposite the castle stands the Jacobean **Beaumaris Courthouse** (Easter–Sept daily 10.30am–5pm; £1.50; joint ticket with gaol £3), built in 1614 and the oldest active court in Britain. It is now used only for the twice-monthly Magistrates Court, but until 1971, when they were moved to Caernarfon, the quarterly Assize Courts were held here. These were traditionally held in English, giving the jury little chance to follow the proceedings and Welsh-speaking defendants no defence against prosecutors renowned for slapping heavy penalties on minor offences. On session days you can watch the trials, but won't be able to take the recorded tour or inspect *The Lawsuit*, a plaque in the magistrates' room depicting two farmers pulling the horns and tail of a cow while a lawyer milks it.

Many citizens were transported from the courthouse to the colonies for their misdemeanours; others only made it a couple of blocks to **Beaumaris Gaol**, Steeple Lane (same hours; £1.50, joint ticket with courthouse £3) which, when it opened in 1829, was considered a model prison, with running water and toilets in each cell, an infirmary and, eventually, heating. Women prisoners did the cooking and were allowed to rock their babies' cradles in the nursery above by means of a pulley system. Advanced perhaps, but nonetheless a gloomy place: witness the windowless punishment cell, the yard for stone-breaking and the treadmill water pump operated by the prisoners. The least fortunate inmates were publicly hanged, the fate of a certain Richard Rowlands, whose disembodied voice leads the recorded tour of the building and various displays on prison life.

After all this gloom, a good way to lift the spirits is aboard one of the **pleasure cruises** (℡01248/810251; £4) on the *Island Princess* out to (but not landing on) Puffin Island. The booking kiosk is at the foot of the pier.

Practicalities

With no trains, long-distance coaches or tourist office, Beaumaris seems poorly served, but it does have a regular **bus** service to Bangor (#53 & #57; infrequent on Sun). The best of the **hotels** is the ancient and luxurious *Ye Olde Bull's Head Inn*, 18 Castle St (℡01248/810329, ⓦwww.bullsheadinn.co.uk; ❻), used as General Mytton's headquarters during the Civil War. The *Bishopsgate House Hotel*, 54 Castle St (℡01248/810302, ⓦwww.bishopsgatehousehotel .co.uk; ❹; mid-Feb to Dec), is only a stone's throw away and almost of the same standard. Cheaper **B&Bs** can be found in the summer, though none are very special – you'd be better off at *Plas Cichle* (℡01248/810488; ❷), an elegant farmhouse a couple of miles north near Llanfaes. *Kingsbridge* is the nearest **campsite**, two miles north in Llanfaes (℡01248/490636). There are plenty of daytime cafés serving snacks, and more substantial **restaurants** are also in good supply, the best being *Ye Olde Bull's Head Inn* and the moderately priced *Bishopsgate House Hotel*, both of which also do great bar meals. For a great pint and good food, there's the wonderfully cosy *Sailor's Return* pub on Church Street. *Y Gragen Cocos / The Cockleshell*, 13 Castle St (℡01248/810623), offers good seafood specialities.

Llanfairpwllgwyngyllgogerychwyrndrobwll llandysiliogogogoch

In the 1880s a local tailor invented the longest place name in Britain in a successful attempt to draw tourists. However, it is an utter disappointment to arrive at **Llanfairpwllgwyngyllgogerychwyrndrobwllllandysilio-gogogoch**, which translates as "St Mary's Church in the hollow of white hazel near a rapid whirlpool and the Church of St Tysilio near the red cave" – commonly shortened to **LLANFAIR PG**. All you'll find here is a train station, a vast car park, a tacky wool shop and a **tourist office** (daily: April–Oct 9.30am–5.30pm; Nov–March 10am–5pm; ℡01248/713177), the only one worth its salt on the island.

The marquises of Anglesey still live at **Plas Newydd** (April–Oct Mon–Wed, Sat & Sun: house noon–5pm, garden 11am–5.30pm; house & garden £4.70, garden only £2.80; NT), a mile and a half south of Llanfair PG, a modest three-storey mansion with incongruous Tudor caps on slender octagonal turrets. Inside, architect James Wyatt was given free stylistic rein, producing a Gothic music room followed by a Neoclassical staircase hall with a cantilevered staircase and deceptively solid-looking Doric columns – actually just painted wood. Endure the slog through corridors of oils and period rooms to the high-light, a 58-foot-long wall consumed by a trompe l'oeil painting by **Rex Whistler**, who spent a couple of years here in the 1930s. Walking along his imaginary seascape, your position appears to shift by over a mile as the mountains of Snowdonia and a whimsical composite of elements, culled from Italy as well as Britain, change perspective. Portmeirion (see p.885) is there, as are the Round Tower from Windsor Castle and the steeple from St Martin-in-the-Fields in London. Whistler himself appears as a gondolier, and again as a gardener in one of the two right-angled panels at either end, which appear to extend the room further. The prize exhibit in the **Cavalry Museum**, a few rooms further on, is the world's first articulated false leg, all wood, leather and springs, designed for the first marquis, who lost his leg at Waterloo.

Holyhead and around

Holy Island (Ynys Gybi) is blessed with Anglesey's best scenery and cursed with its most unattractive town. The spectacular sea cliffs around South Stack, and the Stone Age and Roman remains on Holyhead Mountain are just a couple of miles from workaday Holyhead, whose ferry routes to Ireland and good transport links mean you'll probably find your way there at some stage.

The local council's valiant attempts to brighten up **HOLYHEAD** (Caergybi; pronounced in English as "holly-head") somehow make this town of dilapidated shopfronts and high unemployment even more depressing. In 1727, Swift found it "scurvy, ill provided and comfortless", and little seems to have changed. The town is linked by ferries and catamarans run by Stena Line (℡0870/570 7070, Ⓦwww.stenaline.co.uk) and Irish Ferries (℡0870/517 1717, Ⓦwww.irishferries.com) to both Dublin Port and Dun Laoghaire, six miles south of Dublin. Fortunately, train and ferry timings are reasonably well integrated, so you shouldn't need to spend much time here. If you do have an hour to kill, worth seeing is the **Holyhead Maritime Museum** (Easter–Oct Tues–Fri 1–5pm, Sat & Sun 11am–5pm; £2), down on the Newry Beach seashore in the old lifeboat station. From the combined **train station, bus station** and **ferry terminal**, a pedestrian bridge over London Road, past the A5, leads into the town centre. The **tourist office** (Mon–Sat 8.30am–6pm; ☎01407/762622) is in the ferry terminal.

Shun the bunch of poor **B&Bs** along the A5 into the town in favour of those around Walthew Avenue, most easily reached by turning left just before the tourist office onto the beachfront Prince of Wales Road, then left again into Walthew Avenue. While *Orotavia*, at no. 66 (☎01407/760259; ❷), is simple and cosy, the best of the bunch is *Yr Hendre* (☎01407/762929; ❸), round the corner on Porth-y-Felin Road. Fast **food** is the staple diet in Holyhead, but you can still eat well: *Raja's*, 8 Newry St, serves the tastiest Bengal curries around, and great daytime **pub** food can be found at *The Seventy-Nine* on Market Street, a good start as well for a pub crawl through the many bars of the town centre. Good bets for a pint include the old-fashioned *George Hotel* on Stanley Street.

Holyhead Mountain and South Stack

The northern half of Holy Island is ranged around the skirts of the 700-foot **Holyhead Mountain** (Mynydd Twr), its summit ringed by the seventeen-acre **Caer y Twr** (free access; CADW), one of the largest Iron Age sites in North Wales. The best approach is by car or bus #44 to the car park at **South Stack** (Ynys Lawd), two miles west of Holyhead, from where a path (30min) leads to the top of Holyhead Mountain. Most visitors only walk the few yards to the cliff-top **Ellin's Tower Seabird Centre** (Easter–Sept daily 11am–5pm; free) where, from April until the end of July, binoculars and closed-circuit TV give an unparalleled opportunity to watch up to three thousand birds – razorbills, guillemots and the odd puffin – nesting on the nearby sea cliffs while ravens and peregrines wheel outside the tower's windows. When the birds have gone, rock climbers picking their way up the same cliff face replace them as the main interest. A twisting path leads down from the tower to a suspension bridge over the surging waves, leading over to the now fully automated pepper-pot **lighthouse** (Easter–Sept daily 10.30am–5.30pm; £2.50). Tickets are issued at the *South Stack Kitchen*, a café-cum-interpretative centre a hundred yards back down the lane. Nearby, nineteen low stone circles make up the **Cytiau'r Gwyddelod** or the "Huts of the Irish", a common name for any ancient settlement – in this case late Neolithic or early Bronze Age.

Bangor

After spending a few days in the North Wales rural hinterland, **BANGOR**, across the bridges from Anglesey, makes a welcome change. It's not big, but as the largest town in Gwynedd and home to Bangor University, it passes in these parts for cosmopolitan. The students decamp for the summer, leaving only a trickle of visitors to replace them. Bangor is a hotbed of passionate Welsh nationalism, hardly surprising in such a staunchly Welsh-speaking area, and it's a dramatic change from the largely English-speaking north-coast resorts.

The **university** takes up much of upper Bangor, straddling the hill that separates the town centre from the Menai Strait. The shape of the college's main building is almost an exact replica of the thirteenth- to fifteenth-century **cathedral** (daily 11am–5pm), which boasts the longest continuous use of any cathedral in Britain, easily predating the town. Pop in if only to see the sixteenth-century wooden **Mostyn Christ**, depicted bound and seated on a rock.

Just over the road, the **Bangor Museum and Art Gallery**, Ffordd Gwynedd (Tues–Fri 12.30–4.30pm, Sat 10.30am–4.30pm; free), offers snippets of local history enlivened by a traditional costume section and an archeology room, containing the most complete Roman sword found in Wales. The art gallery concentrates on predominantly Welsh contemporary works. For a good look down the Menai Strait to Telford's graceful bridge (the world's first large iron suspension bridge, completed in 1826), walk along Garth Road to Bangor's rejuvenated and pristine **Victorian Pier** (25p), which reaches halfway across to Anglesey.

Penrhyn Castle

There can hardly be a more vulgar testament to the Anglo-Welsh landowning gentry's oppression of the rural Welsh than the oddly compelling **Penrhyn Castle** (Mon & Wed–Sun: July & Aug 11am–5pm; April–June, Sept & Oct noon–5pm; castle & grounds £6; grounds only £4; NT), two miles east of Bangor, which overlooks Port Penrhyn from its acres of isolating parkland. Built on the backs of slate miners for the benefit of their hated bosses, this monstrous nineteenth-century neo-Norman fancy, with over three hundred rooms dripping with luxurious fittings, was funded by the quarry's huge profits. The sugar and slate fortune built by anti-abolitionist Richard Pennant, first Baron Penrhyn, provided the means for his self-aggrandizing great-great-nephew George Dawkins to hire architect Thomas Hopper, who spent thirteen years from 1827 encasing the neo-Gothic hall in a Norman fortress complete with monumental five-storey keep.

Sour grapes aside, the decoration is glorious, and fairly true to the Romanesque style, with its deeply cut chevrons, billets and double-cone ornamentation. Hopper even looked to Norman architecture for the design of the furniture, but abandoned historical authenticity when it came to installing the central heating system, which piped hot air through ornamental brass ducts at the cost of twenty tons of coal a month. Everything is on a massive scale. Three-foot-thick oak doors separate the rooms, ebony is used to dramatic effect and a slate bed was built for, but declined by, Queen Victoria when she visited. The family amassed Wales' largest private painting collection, including numerous family likenesses, a Gainsborough landscape, Canaletto's *The Thames at Westminster* and a Rembrandt portrait. Also worth a visit are the Victorian kitchen and servants' quarters, something of an antidote to the opulence "above stairs".

Gleaming examples of rolling stock from Richard Pennant's slate railway and the country's other private industrial lines are on display in the **Industrial Railway Museum** (same hours as castle; entry with castle or grounds ticket), including Lord Penrhyn's luxurious coach, linked to a quarrymen's car. Buses #5, #6 and #7 run frequently from Bangor to the gates, from where it is a mile-long walk to the house.

Practicalities

All trains on the North Coast line stop at Bangor **train station**, on Station Road, at the bottom of Holyhead Road. The **tourist office** is in the Town

Hall on Deiniol Road (Easter–Sept daily 10am–6pm; ℡01248/352786). Bangor doesn't have a huge choice of places to **stay**. Most of the cheaper accommodation is bundled at the northern end of Garth Road, about twenty minutes' walk from the train station: try *Dilfan* (℡01248/353030; ❷). *Eryl Môr*, 2 Upper Garth Rd (℡01248/353789, ⓦwww.erylmorhotel.co.uk; ❸), is a quiet and comfortable hotel with views over Bangor's pier and the Menai Strait. Five miles southwest of town on the B4366 is *Tŷ Mawr Farm* (℡01286/670147, ⓦfreespace.virgin.net/jane.pierce), a working farm with good food and a cosy welcome. Bangor's YHA **hostel**, Tan-y-Bryn (℡0870/770 5686, ⓔbangor@yha.org.uk; Jan–Nov; dorms £11.50), is sign-posted off the A56, ten minutes' walk east of the centre (bus #6 or #7 along Garth Road). The nearest **campsite** is the very laid-back *Treborth Hall Farm* (℡01248/364104), fifteen minutes' walk (or bus #5) from Upper Bangor, on the road out towards the Menai Bridge.

With the possible exception of Llandudno, Bangor offers the widest selection of **eating** possibilities in North Wales. Packed out with students and locals, the *Fat Cat Café Bar*, 161 High St, has a menu ranging from huge burgers to salmon and broccoli pasta quills; another good bet is the classy *Greek Taverna Politis*, 12 Holyhead Rd. *Herbs*, 307 High St (℡01248/351249), is a great veggie daytime cafe that's also open for swankier (and meatier) meals on weekend evenings. The expensive restaurant of the *Menai Court Hotel*, Craig-y-Don Road, earns plaudits from foodies for its traditional British and European dishes. If you've tried to learn any of the language you can put it to good use at *Tafarn Y Glôb*, a traditional **pub** on Albert Street, where ordering in Welsh is pretty much a house rule. For "a pint of beer, please" try *un peint o gwrw, os gwelwch chi'n dda* (pronounced "een paint o gooroo, os gweloch un tha"). *Y Castell*, on Glanrafon, a street opposite the cathedral, is a very popular student pub.

Conwy and around

CONWY, twenty miles east of Bangor, has been much prettified since completion of a bypass tunnel under the Conwy River (Afon Conwy), making it one of the highlights of the north coast. Backed by a forested fold of Snowdonia, the town boasts a fine castle, a nearly complete belt of town walls and a wonderful setting on the Conwy estuary. Nowhere in the core of medieval and Victorian buildings is more than two hundred yards from the irregular triangle of protective masonry formed by the town walls. This makes it wonderfully easy to potter around and though you'll get to see everything you want to in a day, you may well want to stay longer.

Conwy Castle

Conwy Castle (June–Sept daily 9.30am–6pm; April, May & Oct daily 9.30am–5pm; Nov–March Mon–Sat 9.30am–4pm, Sun 11am–4pm; £3.50, joint ticket with Plas Mawr Conwy £6.50; CADW), entered through a separate ticket office and over a modern bridge, is the toughest-looking link in Edward I's "Iron Ring" of fortresses. After advancing west of the Conwy River in 1283, Edward decided to maintain a bridgehead by establishing another of his bastide towns. He chose a strategic knoll at the mouth of the river and set James of St George to fashion a castle to fit its contours. With the labour of 1500 men it took only five years.

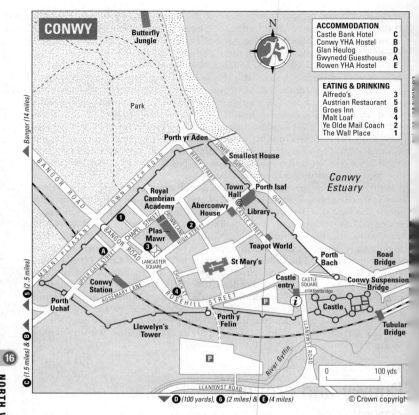

Richard II stayed at the castle on his return from an ill-timed trip to Ireland in 1399, until lured from safety by Bolingbroke's vassal the earl of Northumberland. Northumberland swore in the castle's chapel to grant the king safe passage, but Richard was taken and Bolingbroke became Henry IV. Just two years later, on Good Friday, when the fifteen-strong castle guard were at church, two cousins of Owain Glyndŵr took the castle and razed the town for Glyndŵr's cause. The castle then fell into disuse, and was bought in 1627 for £100 by Charles I's secretary of state, Lord Conway of Ragley, who then had the task of refortifying it for the Civil War. At the restoration of the monarchy, the castle was stripped of all its iron, wood and lead, and was left substantially as it is today.

Being overlooked by a low hill, the castle appears less easily defended than others along the coast, but James constructed eight massive **towers** in a rectangle around the two wards, the inner one separated from the outer by a **drawbridge** and **portcullis**, and further protected by turrets atop the four eastern towers, now the preserve of crows. Strolling along the wall-top gallery, you can look down onto something unique in the Iron Ring fortresses, a roofless but largely intact interior. The outer ward's 130-foot-long **Great Hall** and the **King's Apartments** are both well preserved, but the only part of the castle to have kept its roof is the **Chapel Tower**, named for the small room built into the wall whose semicircular apse still shows some heavily worn carving. On the floor below, there's a small exhibition on religious life in medieval castles which won't detain you long from exploring the passages.

The rest of the town

Anchored to the castle walls as though a drawbridge, Telford's narrow **suspension bridge** (April–Oct daily 10am–5pm; £1.10; joint ticket with Aberconwy House £2.80; NT) was part of the 1826 road improvement scheme, prompted by the need for better communications to Ireland after the Act of Union, and contemporary with his far greater effort spanning the Menai Strait. Restored to its original state, without tarmac, signs or street lighting, it now operates as a footbridge.

The approach to the modern replacement bridge has created the only breach in the thirty-foot high **town walls**, which branch out from the castle into a three-quarter-mile-long circuit, enclosing Conwy's ancient quarter. Inaccessible from the castle they were designed to protect, the walls are punctuated by 21 evenly spaced horseshoe towers, seven of which can be visited on the **wall-walk**, starting from Porth Uchaf on Upper Gate Street and running down to a spur into the estuary. Here, you come down off the walls beside brightly rigged trawlers, mussel boats and the self-proclaimed **smallest house in Britain** (daily: July & Aug 10am–9pm; Easter–June & Sept to mid-Oct 10am–6pm; 50p), only 9ft by 5ft in total. Porth Isaf, the nearby gate in the town walls, leads up Lower High Street to the fourteenth-century timber-and-stone **Aberconwy House**, Castle Street (April–Oct daily except Tues 11am–5pm; £2.20, joint ticket with suspension bridge £2.80; NT), a former merchant's house, its rooms decked out in styles that recall its past. Continue along the High Street to the Dutch-style **Plas Mawr** at no. 20 (Tues–Sun: June–Aug 9.30am–6pm; April, May & Sept 9.30am–5pm; Oct 9.30am–4pm; £4.50, joint ticket with Conwy Castle £6.50; CADW), a beautifully restored Elizabethan townhouse, built in 1576 for Robert Wynn, one of the first Welsh people to live in the town. Much of the dressed stonework was replaced during renovations in the 1940s and 1950s, but the interior sports more original features, in particular the friezes and superb moulded plaster ceilings depicting fleurs-de-lis, griffons, owls and rams. The tour concludes with a wonderfully scatological exhibition on sixteenth- and seventeenth-century ideas about disease and cleanliness.

Light relief from all the worthy history is on hand across the road from Aberconwy House, at **Teapot World**, Castle Street (Easter–Oct Mon–Sat 10am–5.30pm, Sun 11am–5.30pm; £1.50), which has a thousand pots, mostly dating from before the 1950s: Wedgwood and majolica to Bauhaus and Clarice Cliff. If you fancy taking to the water, regular **river cruises** operate from the quay (30min £3.50; 45min £4).

Practicalities

Llandudno Junction, less than a mile across the river to the east, serves as the main **train station**; only slow, regional services stop in Conwy itself. National Express **coaches** pull up outside the town walls on Town Ditch Road, while local **buses** use the stops in the centre, mostly on Lancaster Square or Castle Street. The **tourist office** (April–Oct daily 9.30am–5pm; Nov–March Thurs–Sat 9.30am–4pm; ☎01492/592248) shares the same building as the castle ticket office.

16

NORTH WALES | Conwy and around

Accommodation in the centre of town is a bit thin, so booking ahead is advisable in summer. *Gwynedd Guesthouse*, 10 Upper Gate St (℡01492/596537, ✉abs.conwy@virgin.net; ❶), is the least expensive central B&B and consequently often full. *Glan Heulog*, Llanrwst Road, on the outskirts of town half a mile towards Llanrwst on the B5106 (℡01492/593845, ⓦwww.walesbandb.com; ❶), is about the best B&B within easy walking distance of Conwy. Further afield, there's *Castle Bank Hotel*, Mount Pleasant (℡01492/593888, ⓦwww.castle-bank.co.uk; ❸), a licensed, nonsmoking hotel with country-house atmosphere, ten minutes' walk from the town centre: turn first left outside the town walls on the Bangor road. Take bus #19 to the nearest **campsite**, the family-oriented *Conwy Touring Park*, a mile or so south along the B5106 (℡01492/592856; April–Oct). The YHA **hostel** (℡0870/770 6111, ✉conwy@yha.org.uk; ❶, dorms £13) is on Lark Hill, a ten-minute hike from town up the road to Sychnant Pass, where people staying can also hire bikes. There's another YHA hostel a mile up a steep hill above Rowen village, four miles south of Conwy (℡01492/650089, ℻650700; Easter–Sept; dorms £9); bus #19 connects hourly in summer.

Conwy has relatively few **restaurants**. In town, you're best off going veggie at *The Wall Place*, Bishop's Yard, Chapel Street (℡01492/596326, ⓦwww.wallplace.co.uk), one of Conwy's trendier spots; it even has the occasional night of live folk and Welsh music. Otherwise, you can eat Italian at *Alfredo's*, Lancaster Square (℡01492/592381; closed Sun), or Austrian at the *Austrian Restaurant*, west of town on Old Conwy Road, Capelulo (℡01492/622170; closed Sun eve & Mon). Good **pubs** are easier to find: try *Ye Olde Mail Coach*, 16 High St, for decent beer, food and occasional music, or the scruffy *Malt Loaf*, opposite the station on Rosehill Street, where you'll find regular live folk and other music. The best pub in the area is the fifteenth-century *Groes Inn*, in Tyn-y-Groes, two miles south on the B5106 to Llanrwst, which serves excellent bar meals and good cask ales.

Around Conwy

The best short walk from Conwy is on to **Conwy Mountain** and the 800-foot peaks behind, all giving great views right along the coast. Follow a sign up Cadnant Park off the Bangor road just outside the town walls, then take the road around until Mountain Road heads off on the right towards a hillfort on the summit. This group is separated from the foothills of the Carneddau range by the narrow cleft of **Sychnant Pass**.

Thousands come to Conwy specifically to see **Bodnant Garden** (mid-March to Oct daily 10am–5pm; £5.20; NT), beside the lower reaches of the Conwy, eight miles to the south. During May and June, the Laburnum Arch flourishes and banks of rhododendrons are in full and glorious bloom all over what ranks as one of the finest formal gardens in Britain. Laid out in 1875 around Bodnant Hall (no public access) by its then owner, English industrialist Henry Pochin, the garden spreads out over eighty acres of the eastern Conwy Valley. Facing southwest, the bulk of the gardens – divided into an upper terraced garden and lower pinetum and wild garden – catch the late afternoon sun as it sets over the Carneddau range. Though it's arranged so that shrubs and plants provide a blaze of colour throughout the opening season, autumn is a perfect time to be here, with hydrangeas still in bloom and fruit trees shedding their leaves. Bus #25 runs here from Llandudno (every 2hr), calling at Llandudno Junction, or it's a two-mile walk from the Tal-y-Cafn train station on the Conwy Valley line.

Llandudno

Set on a low isthmus, across the river and a couple of miles north of Conwy, **LLANDUDNO** has an undeniably dignified air. Almost invariably, the wind funnels between the limestone hummocks of the 680-foot **Great Orme** and its southern cousin the **Little Orme**, which flank the gently curving Victorian frontage; but don't let that put you off visiting this archetype of the genteel British seaside town.

Llandudno's early history revolves around the Great Orme, where St Tudno, who brought Christianity to the region in the sixth century, built the monastic cell that gives the town its name. When the early Victorian copper mines looked about to be worked out, in the mid-nineteenth century, local landowner Edward Mostyn exploited the growing craze for sea bathing and set about a speculative venture to create a seaside resort for the upper middle classes. Work got under way around 1854 and the town rapidly gained popularity over the next fifty years, becoming synonymous with the Victorian ideal of a respectable resort.

The town and around

Despite the pavilion being destroyed by fire in early 1994, Llandudno's nineteenth-century **pier** (open all year; free) is one of the few remaining in Wales. It juts out 2220 feet into Llandudno Bay, a leisurely ten-minute stroll along The Promenade from Vaughan Street and the region's premier contemporary art gallery, the **Oriel Mostyn**, 12 Vaughan St (Mon–Sat 10.30am–5.30pm; free; Ⓦ www.mostyn.org), which hosts temporary shows featuring works by artists of international renown, with a particular leaning towards the current Welsh arts scene. Kids are better entertained at the **Alice in Wonderland Visitor Centre**, 3–4 Trinity Square (daily 10am–5pm; Nov–Easter closed Sun; £2.95; Ⓦ www.wonderland.co.uk), where they are guided through the "Rabbit Hole", full of fibre-glass Mad Hatters and March Hares, while a headset treats them to readings of *Jabberwocky* and the like. The Alice books were inspired by Lewis Carroll's meeting with one Alice Liddell, the daughter of friends, here in Llandudno.

The view from the top of the **Great Orme** (Pen y Gogarth) ranks with those from the far loftier summits in Snowdonia, combining the seascapes east towards Rhyl and west over the sands of the Conwy Estuary with the brooding, quarry-chewed northern limit of the Carneddau range where Snowdonia crashes into the sea. This huge lump of carboniferous limestone was subject to some of the same stresses that folded Snowdonia, producing fissures filled by molten mineral-bearing rock. A Bronze Age settlement developed when people began to smelt the contents of the malachite-rich veins, supplying copper throughout Europe. The result of their labour is evident at the **Great Orme Copper Mines** (Feb–Oct daily 10am–5pm; £4.50), accessed via the tramway (see below). What were once considered to be Roman workings have recently revealed 4000-year-old animal bones that had been used as scrapers. Hard hats and miners' lamps are provided for the **guided tour** through just a small portion of the tunnels, enough to get a feel for the cramped working conditions and the dangers of falling rock.

The base of the Great Orme is traditionally circumnavigated on **Marine Drive**, a five-mile anticlockwise circuit from just near Llandudno's pier. To ascend to the dry-ski slope and toboggan run at the **Summit Complex** (daily noon–11pm; Nov–Easter closed Mon–Fri), you can take the road, which runs past the mines, or the San Francisco-style **Great Orme Tramway** (April–Sept 10am–6pm; Oct–March 10am–4pm; £3.95 return; ⓦwww.greatormetramway.com), which creaks up from the bottom of Old Road, much as it has done since 1902. Alternatively, a **Cable Car** (daily: July & Aug 10am–5.30pm; Easter–June, Sept & Oct 10am–1pm & 2–4.20pm; £5) carries you up over the Orme from the Happy Valley formal gardens, at the base of the pier.

Practicalities

Llandudno's central **train station** (not to be confused with the mainline Llandudno Junction, three miles south), is at the corner of Augusta and Vaughan streets, five minutes' walk southeast from the **tourist office**, 1–2 Chapel St (Easter–Sept daily 9.30am–5.30pm; Oct–Easter Mon–Sat 9.30am–4.30pm; ⓣ01492/876413). Chapel Street runs parallel to Mostyn Street, where local **buses** stop. Less than ten minutes' walk south, National Express **coaches** pull in to the coach park on Mostyn Broadway. **Bike rental** is available from West End Cycles, 22 Augusta St (ⓣ01492/876891), across the road from the train station. Snowdonia Cycle Hire (ⓣ01492/878771, ⓦwww.snowdoniacyclehire.co.uk) will deliver and collect bikes within a six-mile radius of Llandudno.

Finding a **place to stay** is not usually a problem, though in high summer and especially on bank holidays, booking ahead is wise. The greatest concentration of budget places is along St David's Road, just west of the station, where you'll find the *Cliffbury Hotel*, 34 St David's Rd (ⓣ01492/877224, ⓦwww.cliffburyhotel.co.uk; ❷). *Fernbank*, 9 Chapel St (ⓣ01492/877251; ❶), is one of the least expensive and best equipped of a string of low-cost hotels just along from the tourist office, while the *Leamore Hotel*, 40 Lloyd St (ⓣ01492/875552; ❶), is family-run, with high standards. Topnotch accommodation is available at *St Tudno Hotel* (ⓣ01492/874411, ⓦwww.st-tudno.co.uk; ❺), a superb, small, seafront hotel at 16 North Parade, just behind the pier. The closest **camping** is at *Dinarth Hall Farm*, Dinarth Hall Road, Rhos-on-Sea (ⓣ01492/548203), three miles east of Llandudno, accessible on buses #13, #14 and #15.

Llandudno has plenty of excellent **restaurants**. The basement bistro at *Richards*, 7 Church Walks, dishes up delicious meals, many based on local seafood, while the *Garden Room* at the *St Tudno Hotel* (see above) is one of Wales' best restaurants, serving French cuisine based on fresh Welsh produce. For substantial, tasty bar food, try the *Cottage Loaf*, Market Street, a flag-floored **pub** built from old ships' timbers on top of an old bakehouse, or the *King's Head*, on Old Road, the oldest pub in town, where Edward Mostyn and his surveyor mapped out the town. For sheer raucous drinking, the bars along Upper Mostyn Street are generally full and extremely lively. Around a century ago all the best music-hall performers clamoured to play Llandudno, but up until recently you were lucky to get anything more than faded stars plying the resorts throughout the summer. However, with the 1500-seat **North Wales Theatre** on the Promenade (Theatr Gogledd Cymru; ⓦwww.nwtheatre.co.uk) and the diverse, week-long **Llandudno Festival** in June (ⓦwww.llandudnofestival.org.uk), things are looking a little rosier these days.

Flintshire and Denbighshire

Making for the coastal resorts or mountains of Snowdonia, you might be tempted to charge headlong through **Flintshire** and **Denbighshire**, two small counties hard up against the English border. No sooner have you cleared the industrial hinterland that spreads over the border from the English market town of Chester (see p.590) than you hit the North Wales coast, a twenty-mile stretch from the end of the Dee estuary to Colwyn Bay which constitutes the ugliest piece of Welsh coastline: almost the entire length is taken up by caravan parks. Inland, however, there are one or two very interesting diversions, notably **St Asaph**, home to Britain's smallest cathedral. Two miles to the north is the second of Edward I's castles at **Rhuddlan**, and a few miles west, the National Portrait Gallery's Welsh outpost at **Bodelwyddan**; all are easily accessed from the brash resort town of Rhyl.

The country flanking the salt marshes of the Dee estuary was once contested by Marcher lords, but skirmishes were quashed by the construction of Flint Castle, the earliest of Edward I's Iron Ring of fortresses and now an insubstantial ruin overlooking the estuary at Flint. Understated **Holywell** has been an important pilgrimage site for the last thirteen hundred years, but now quietly ticks by almost unvisited.

St Asaph and around

ST ASAPH (Llanelwy), some eighteen miles east of Conwy along the A55, ranks as Britain's second-smallest "city" after St David's in Pembrokeshire, and its **cathedral** (daily 8am–dusk) is the country's smallest, no bigger than many village churches. It was founded around 570 by St Kentigern, the patron saint of Glasgow, and takes its name from the succeeding bishop, St Asaph. Both are commemorated in the easternmost window in the north aisle. From 1601 until his death in 1604, the bishopric was held by **William Morgan**, whose grave under the presbytery has gone unmarked since Giles Gilbert Scott's substantial restoration in the 1870s. Morgan was responsible for the translation of the first Welsh-language Bible in 1588, replacing the English ones used up until that time. Over 25 years, he and three other clergymen produced a translation so successful that the Privy Council decreed that a copy of *Y Beibl* should be allocated to every Welsh church, thereby setting a standard for prose and codifying the language. Without his efforts, many claim, Welsh would have died out. A thousand Morgan Bibles were printed, of which only nineteen remain, one of them displayed in the north transept along with notable prayer books and psalters.

Buses stop right outside the cathedral. The best central **rooms** are at the *Kentigern Arms*, towards the bottom of the High Street (☎01745/584157; ❸). The nicely furnished, nonsmoking *Chalet*, The Roe (☎01745/584025; ❷), is a quarter of a mile away – across the river bridge then right. St Asaph's best **food** is served at the moderately priced *Barrow Alms*, High Street (☎01745/582260), followed by the bar meals at the *Kentigern Arms*, which is the most alluring **pub**.

Rhuddlan Castle

RHUDDLAN, two miles north of St Asaph, lies on the banks of a tidal reach of the Clwyd River (Afon Clywedog), which finally meets the sea at Rhyl. The town would be an insignificant suburb of Rhyl but for the diamond-shaped ruin of **Rhuddlan Castle** (Easter–Sept daily 10am–5pm; £2; CADW), built between 1277 and 1282 as a garrison and royal residence for Edward I. The impressive castle commands a canalized section of the river protected by **Gillot's Tower**. Behind, the castle's massive towers were the work of James of

St George, who was responsible for the concentric plan that allowed archers on both outer and inner walls to fire simultaneously. Important though the castle was, Rhuddlan earns its position in history as the place where Edward I signed the **Statute of Rhuddlan** on March 19, 1284, consigning Wales to centuries of subjugation by the English. A large – and somewhat ironic – plaque in Rhuddlan's main street details the terms of the statute.

Bodelwyddan Castle: the National Portrait Gallery

Barrelling west along the A55 towards the coast brings you to the small village of **BODELWYDDAN**. The slender 202-foot limestone spire of Marble Church heralds the finest art showcase in North Wales: an outpost of the National Portrait Gallery at **Bodelwyddan Castle** (mid-April to Sept daily 10.30am–5pm; Oct–mid-April Tues–Thurs, Sat & Sun 10.30am–4pm; £4.50; ⓦwww.bodelwyddan-castle.co.uk), set amidst landscaped gardens on its hill, half a mile south of the village. The opulent Victorian interiors of what is essentially a nineteenth-century mansion were restored in the 1980s to exhibit works contemporary with the castle. As well as the NPG's collection, each summer sees children-oriented temporary exhibitions. Most of the two hundred-odd paintings are on the ground floor, approached through the "Watts Hall of Fame", a long corridor specially decorated in William Morris-style to accommodate a chair by Morris and 26 portraits of eminent Victorians by G.F. Watts, among them Millais, Rossetti, Browning and Walter Crane. In the Ladies' Drawing Room opposite, a beautiful Biedermeier sofa outshines paintings of little-celebrated nineteenth-century women around the walls. Of the three main rooms, it's the Dining Room that stands out. Two sensitive portraits here highlight the Pre-Raphaelite support for social reform: William Holman Hunt's portrayal of the vociferous opponent of slavery and capital punishment, Stephen Lushington; and Ford Madox Brown's double portrait of Henry Farell, prime mover in the passing of the 1867 Reform Bill, and suffragette Millicent Garrett. Works by John Singer Sargent and Hubert von Herkamer also adorn the room, which, like the others, is furnished with pieces from London's Victoria and Albert Museum. Upstairs, nineteenth-century portraiture, portrait photography and works by female artists get generous coverage along with animal painters, Landseer in particular.

Holywell and around

A place of pilgrimage for thirteen hundred years, **HOLYWELL** (Treffynnon), just off the A55 ten miles east of St Asaph, comes billed as "The Lourdes of Wales" – but without the tacky souvenir stalls, it doesn't really warrant such a comparison. **St Winefride's Well** (daily: April–Sept 9am–5.30pm; Oct–March 10am–4pm; 60p) – half a mile from the bus station at the far end of the High Street, then turn right and follow the signs – is the source of all the fuss, a calm pool capacious enough to accommodate the dozens of the faithful who dutifully wade through the waters three times in the hope of curing their ailments, a relic of the Celtic baptism by triple immersion. The existence of the spring was first noted by the Romans, who used the waters to relieve rheumatism and gout. The traditional legend, however, states that in around 660, the virtuous Winefride (Gwenfrewi in Welsh) was decapitated here after resisting the amorous advances of Prince Caradoc; the well is said to have sprung up at the spot where her head fell. Richard I and Henry V provided regal patronage, ensuring a steady flow of believers to what became one of the great shrines of Christendom, and James II came here to pray for a son and heir. Pilgrims formerly spent the night praying in the Perpendicular **St Winefride's Chapel** (key from the ticket office; CADW), built around 1500 to enclose three sides of the well. The site's importance is waning, but pilgrimages do still take place, mainly on St Winefride's Day, the nearest Sunday to June 22, when a couple of thousand pilgrims are led through the streets behind a relic, part of Winefride's thumb-bone.

From St Winefride's Well, a mile-long path runs past the remains of the copper and brass factories which now constitute the **Greenfield Valley Heritage Park** (April–Oct daily 10am–4.30pm; £2), whose moderately interesting farm and museum preserves agricultural and other buildings from around the area. Over the way are the ruined domestic buildings used by the abbot and twelve monks of the Savignac order at **Basingwerk Abbey** (free access; CADW), and there's a good, free exhibition about it in the Greenfield Valley visitor centre (same hours as above).

Holywell has no train station, but frequent **buses** run to Rhyl and Chester from the bus station at the southern end of High Street.

Wrexham and around

Much to the local bigwigs' chagrin, **WREXHAM** (Wrecsam), lost out in the race to be named a city for the Queen's Golden Jubilee in 2002; the honour went to Newport in South Wales instead. Civic pride has taken a dent, but, nonetheless, a curiously boisterous charm survives in Wrexham – the largest town in North Wales – with some fine older buildings surviving amidst the generic shopping streets of the centre. However, there's little reason to stop except to use it as a base for the nearby attractions, which in any case – if you have your own transport – are better visited from Llangollen (see p.842). You might call in at **St Giles' Church** (Easter–Oct Mon–Fri 10am–4pm), its Gothic tower rising gracefully above the kernel of small lanes at the end of Hope Street. Topped off with a steeple in the 1520s, the tower has five distinct levels, stepping up to four hexagonal pinnacles. The same design was used at Yale University, in homage to the ancestral home of the college's benefactor, Elihu Yale, whose tomb can be seen at the base of St Giles' tower.

Wrexham has two **train stations**, half a mile apart, all services stopping at Wrexham General on Mold Road, ten minutes' walk northwest of the centre. Walking into town from here, Mold Street becomes Regent Street and then Hope Street, from which King Street branches off left to the **bus station**, for National Express coaches (tickets from Key Travel, King Street) and frequent local buses serving Chester and Llangollen. The **tourist office**, Lambpit Street (Mon–Sat 10am–5pm; Oct–Easter closes 4pm; ☎01978/292015), is reached by turning left where Hope Street turns to the right. If you need to **stay**, make for *Lyndhurst Guesthouse*, 3 Gerald St, off Grosvenor Road (☎01978/290802; ❶), a short walk from the centre, or the much-refurbished town-centre *Wynnstay Arms* (☎01978/291010; ❸) on Yorke Street, which is also a good place to grab a snack or full meal.

Clywedog Valley and Erddig

The **Clywedog Valley**, which forms an arc around the western and southern suburbs of Wrexham, was the crucible of industrial success in the northern Welsh borders during the eighteenth century. Iron mining and smelting were the principal industries, but as the Industrial Revolution forged ahead, water power harnessed from the Clywedog became less important, and factories moved closer to their raw materials, leaving the valley barely disturbed. A series of former industrial sites – ironworks, lead mines and the like – are now linked by the seven-mile-long **Clywedog Trail**. It's all a bit heavy on packaged heritage, but if you're interested, pick up a leaflet from the Wrexham tourist office.

Despite the closure of the ironworks and the consequent drop in demand, coal continued to be mined in the valley until 1986. After World War II, coal mines were tunnelled under the nearby stately home of **Erddig** (April–Sept Mon–Wed, Sat & Sun: house noon–5pm, gardens 11am–6pm; Oct both close 1hr earlier; £6.60, gardens and outbuildings only £3.40; NT), two miles south of Wrexham, adding subsidence to the troubles of an already decaying seventeenth-century building. The house has now been restored to its 1922 appearance, but it isn't particularly distinguished. While the State Rooms upstairs have their share of fine furniture and portraits – including one by Gainsborough – the real interest lies in the quarters of the servants, whose lives were fully documented by their unusually benevolent masters. Eighteenth- and early nineteenth-century portraits of staff are still on display in the Servants' Hall, and each has a verse written by one of the Yorkes. You can also see the blacksmith's shop, lime yard, stables, laundry, kitchen and still-used bakehouse.

Travel details

Buses

For information on all local and national bus services, contact Traveline ☎ 0870/608 2608, Ⓦ www.traveline.org.uk.

Aberdaron to: Pwllheli (9 daily; 40min).

Abersoch to: Pwllheli (9 daily; 20min).

Bangor to: Beaumaris (at least hourly; 30min); Betws-y-Coed (3 daily; 50min); Caernarfon (every 30min; 30min); Capel Curig (2 daily; 40min); Cardiff (1 daily; 7hr 45min); Chester (2 daily; 2hr 40min); Conwy (every 30min; 45min); Holyhead (every 30min; 1hr); Llanberis (every 30min; 30min); Llandudno (every 30min; 1hr); Llanfair PG (every 30min; 15min).

Beaumaris to: Bangor (at least hourly; 30min).

Beddgelert to: Caernarfon (8 daily; 30min); Llanberis (5 daily; 40min); Porthmadog (8 daily; 30min).

Betws-y-Coed to: Bangor (2 daily; 50min); Blaenau Ffestiniog (1 daily; 30min); Capel Curig (8 daily; 15min); Conwy (6 daily; 55min); Llanberis (3 daily; 40min).

Blaenau Ffestiniog to: Caernarfon (roughly hourly; 1hr 20min); Harlech (4 daily; 35min); Porthmadog (hourly; 30min).

Caernarfon to: Bangor (every 30min; 30min); Beddgelert (6 daily; 30min); Blaenau Ffestiniog (roughly hourly; 1hr 20min); Cricieth (4 daily;

40min); Llanberis (every 30min; 25min); Llandudno (hourly; 1hr 40min); Porthmadog (hourly; 45min); Pwllheli (at least hourly; 45min).

Capel Curig to: Bangor (2 daily; 40min); Betws-y-Coed (8 daily; 15min); Llanberis (3 daily; 30min).

Conwy to: Bangor (every 30min; 45min); Betws-y-Coed (5 daily; 1hr); Llanberis (3 daily; 1hr 30min); Llandudno (every 30min; 20min).

Cricieth to: Caernarfon (4 daily; 40min); Llanystumdwy (hourly; 5min); Porthmadog (hourly; 15min); Pwllheli (hourly; 20min).

Holyhead to: Bangor (every 30min; 1hr); Chester (1 daily; 3hr 30min); Llanfair PG (every 30min; 45min).

Llanberis to: Bangor (7 daily; 40min); Beddgelert (4 daily; 40min); Betws-y-Coed (3 daily; 40min); Caernarfon (every 30min; 25min).

Llandudno to: Bangor (every 30min; 1hr); Betws-y-Coed (5 daily; 1hr 15min); Caernarfon (every 30min; 1hr 40min); Llanberis (4–6 daily in summer only; 2hr).

Llanfair PG to: Bangor (every 30min; 15min); Holyhead (every 30min; 45min).

Porthmadog to: Beddgelert (6 daily; 30min); Blaenau Ffestiniog (hourly; 30min); Caernarfon (hourly; 45min); Cardiff (1 daily; 6hr 40min); Cricieth (hourly; 15min); Dolgellau (6 daily; 50min); Machynlleth (3 daily; 1hr 45min); Pwllheli (hourly; 40min).

Pwllheli to: Aberdaron (7 daily; 40min); Abersoch (9 daily; 15min); Caernarfon (hourly; 45min); Cricieth (hourly; 20min); Porthmadog (hourly; 40min).

Wrexham to: Barmouth (7 daily; 2hr 20min); Chester (every 15min; 40min); Chirk (hourly; 40min); Dolgellau (6 daily; 2hr); Llangollen (at least hourly; 40min).

Trains

For information on all local and national rail services, contact **National Rail Enquiries** ☎ 08457/48 49 50, Ⓦ www.nationalrail.co.uk.

Bangor to: Chester (20 daily; 1hr); Colwyn Bay (20 daily; 30min); Conwy (7 daily; 20min); Holyhead (21 daily; 30–40min); Llandudno Junction (20 daily; 20min); Llanfair PG (7 daily; 10min).

Betws-y-Coed to: Blaenau Ffestiniog (6 daily; 30min); Llandudno Junction (6 daily; 30min).

Blaenau Ffestiniog to: Betws-y-Coed (6 daily 30min); Llandudno Junction (6 daily; 1hr); Porthmadog by Ffestiniog Railway (April–Oct 4–10 daily; 1hr).

Cricieth to: Barmouth (6 daily; 55min); Machynlleth (6 daily; 1hr 45min); Porthmadog (6 daily; 10min); Pwllheli (6 daily; 15min).

Conwy to: Bangor (7 daily; 20min); Holyhead (8 daily; 1hr); Llandudno Junction (8 daily; 5min).

Holyhead to: Bangor (20 daily; 30–40min); Chester (15 daily; 1hr 40min); Llandudno Junction (20 daily; 1hr); Llanfair PG (7 daily; 30min).

Llandudno to: Betws-y-Coed (5 daily; 40min); Blaenau Ffestiniog (5 daily; 1hr 10min); Llandudno Junction (at least hourly; 10min).

Llandudno Junction to: Bangor (20 daily; 20min); Betws-y-Coed (6 daily; 30min); Holyhead (20 daily; 1hr).

Llanfair PG to: Bangor (7 daily; 10min); Holyhead (7 daily; 30min).

Porthmadog to: Barmouth (6 daily; 45min); Blaenau Ffestiniog by Ffestiniog Railway (Easter–Oct 4–10 daily; 1hr); Harlech (6 daily; 20min); Machynlleth (6 daily; 1hr 40min); Pwllheli (6 daily; 25min).

Pwllheli to: Cricieth (6 daily; 15min); Machynlleth (6 daily; 2hr); Porthmadog (6 daily; 25min).

Wrexham to: Chester (every 2hr; 20min); Chirk (every 2hr; 10min); Liverpool (change at Bidston; hourly; 1hr 15min).

Scotland

Scotland

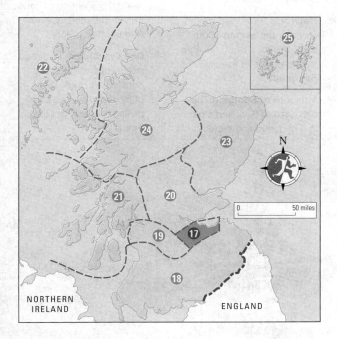

Edinburgh and the Lothians

EDINBURGH AND THE LOTHIANS

NORTHERN IRELAND

ENGLAND

CHAPTER 17 # Highlights

* **Edinburgh Castle** Perched on an imposing volcanic crag, the castle dominates Scotland's capital. **See p.921**

* **The Old Town** The evocative heart of the historic city, with tenements, courtyards, ghosts and catacombs cheek-by-jowl with many of Scotland's most important buildings. **See p.921**

* **Holyrood Park** Wild moors, rocky crags and an 800ft peak (Arthur's Seat), all slap in the middle of the city. **See p.935**

* **Museum of Scotland** The treasures of Scotland's past in a dynamic and superbly conceived building. **See p.937**

* **Café Royal Circle Bar** There are few finer pubs in which to sample a pint of local 80 shilling beer; order six oysters (once the city's staple food) to complete the experience. **See p.952**

* **The Edinburgh Festival** The world's biggest arts festival transforms the city every August. **See p.955**

* **Rosslyn Chapel** With its expressive architecture and detailed carvings, this is one of Scotland's most compelling religious buildings. **See p.965**

△ Edinburgh Castle

Edinburgh and the Lothians

Venerable, dramatic **EDINBURGH**, the showcase capital of Scotland, is a historic, cosmopolitan and cultured city. The setting is wonderfully striking; the city is perched on a series of extinct volcanoes and rocky crags which rise from the generally flat landscape of the Lothians, with the sheltered shoreline of the Firth of Forth to the north. "My own Romantic town", Sir Walter Scott called it, although it was another native author, Robert Louis Stevenson, who perhaps best captured the feel of his "precipitous city", declaring that "No situation could be more commanding for the head of a kingdom; none better chosen for noble prospects."

The centre has two distinct parts, divided by **Princes Street Gardens**, which run roughly east–west under the shadow of **Castle Rock**. To the north, the dignified, Grecian-style **New Town** was immaculately laid out during the Age of Reason, after the announcement of a plan to improve conditions in the city. The **Old Town**, on the other hand, with its tortuous alleys and tightly packed closes, is unrelentingly medieval, associated in popular imagination with the underworld lore of schizophrenic Deacon Brodie, inspiration for Stevenson's *Dr Jekyll and Mr Hyde*, and the body-snatchers Burke and Hare. Edinburgh earned its nickname "Auld Reekie" for the smog and smell generated by the Old Town, which for centuries swam in sewage tipped out of the windows of cramped tenements.

Set on the crag which sweeps down from the towering fairy-tale **Castle** to the royal **Palace of Holyroodhouse**, the Old Town preserves all the key reminders of its role as a capital, plus a brand new **parliament building** rising up opposite the palace. A few hundred yards away a tantalizing glimpse of the wild beauty of Scotland's scenery can be had in **Holyrood Park**, an extensive area of open countryside dominated by **Arthur's Seat**, the largest and most impressive of the volcanoes.

In August and early September, around a million visitors flock to the city for the **Edinburgh Festival**, in fact a series of separate festivals that make up the largest arts extravaganza in the world. While for year-round culture there's a wealth of museums, including the exciting **National Museum of Scotland**, housing 10,000 of Scotland's most precious artefacts, and the **National Gallery of Scotland** and its offshoot, the **Scottish National Gallery of Modern Art**, with two of Britain's finest collections of paintings.

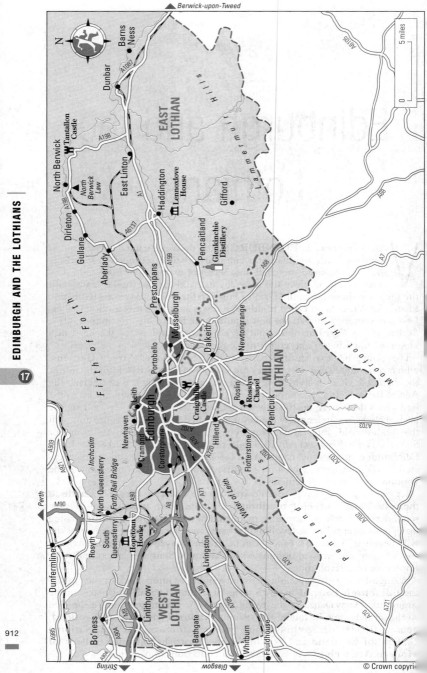

© Crown copyri

On a less elevated level, the city's distinctive *howffs* (pubs), allied to its brewing and distilling traditions, make it a great **drinking** city. The presence of three **universities**, plus several colleges, means that there is a youthful presence for most of the year – a welcome corrective to the stuffiness that is often regarded as Edinburgh's Achilles heel.

Beyond the city centre, the most lively area is **Leith**, the city's medieval port, whose seedy edge is softened by a series of great bars and upmarket seafood restaurants, along with the presence of the former royal yacht **Britannia**, now open to visitors. The wider rural hinterland of Edinburgh, known as the **Lothians**, mixes rolling countryside and attractive country towns with some dramatic historic ruins. In East Lothian, blustery cliff-top paths lead to the romantic battlements of **Tantallon Castle**, while nearby North Berwick, home of the **Scottish Seabird Centre**, looks out to the gannet-covered Bass Rock. The most famous sight in Midlothian is the mysterious fifteenth-century **Rosslyn Chapel**, while West Lothian boasts the towering, roofless **Linlithgow Palace**, thirty minutes from Edinburgh by train. To the northwest of the city, the dramatic curves of the **Forth Rail Bridge** are best seen by walking across the parallel road bridge, starting at **South Queensferry**.

Some history

It was during the **Dark Ages** that the name of Edinburgh – at least in its early forms of Dunedin or Din Eidyn ("fort of Eidyn") – first appeared. Castle Rock, a strategic fort atop one of the volcanoes, served as the nation's **southernmost border post** until 1018, when King Malcolm I established the River Tweed as the permanent frontier. In the reign of Malcolm Canmore, the castle became one of the main seats of the court, and the town, which was given privileged status as a **royal burgh**, began to grow. In 1128 King David established Holyrood Abbey at the foot of the slope, later allowing its monks to found a separate burgh, known as **Canongate**.

Robert the Bruce granted Edinburgh a **new charter** in 1329, giving it jurisdiction over the nearby port of **Leith**, and during the following century the prosperity brought by foreign trade enabled the newly fortified city to establish itself as the permanent **capital of Scotland**. Under King James IV, the city enjoyed a short but brilliant **Renaissance era**, which saw not only the construction of a new palace alongside Holyrood Abbey, but also the granting of a royal charter to the College of Surgeons, the earliest in the city's long line of academic and professional bodies.

This period came to an abrupt end in 1513 with the calamitous defeat by the English at the Battle of Flodden, which led to several decades of political instability. In the 1540s, King Henry VIII's attempt to force a royal union with Scotland led to the sack of Edinburgh, prompting the Scots to turn to France: French troops arrived to defend the city, while the young Queen Mary was dispatched to Paris as the promised bride of the Dauphin. While the French occupiers succeeded in removing the English threat, they themselves antagonized the locals, who had become increasingly sympathetic to the ideals of the **Reformation**. When the radical preacher John Knox returned from exile in 1555, he quickly won over the city to his Calvinist message.

James VI's rule saw the foundation of the University of Edinburgh in 1582, but following the **Union of the Crowns** in 1603 and James's move south, the city was totally upstaged by London: although James promised to visit every three years, it was not until 1617 that he made his only return trip. In 1633 Charles I visited Edinburgh for his coronation, but soon afterwards precipitated a crisis by introducing episcopacy to the Church of Scotland, in the process making Edinburgh a bishopric for the first time. Fifty years of religious turmoil followed, culminating in the triumph of **Presbyterianism**. Despite these vicissitudes, Edinburgh expanded throughout the seventeenth century and, constrained by its walls, was forced to build both upwards and inwards.

The **Union of the Parliaments** of 1707 dealt a further blow to Edinburgh's political prestige, though the guaranteed preservation of the national Church and the legal and educational systems ensured that it was never relegated to a purely provincial role. On the contrary, it was in the second half of the eighteenth century that Edinburgh achieved the height of its intellectual influence, led by an outstanding group, including David Hume and Adam Smith. Around the same time, the city began to expand beyond its medieval boundaries, laying out the **New Town**, a masterpiece of the Neoclassical style. **Industrialization** affected Edinburgh less than any other major city in the nation, and it never lost its white-collar character, but nevertheless, the city underwent an enormous **urban expansion** in the course of the nineteenth century, annexing, among many other small burghs, the large port of Leith.

In 1947 Edinburgh was chosen to host the great **International Festival** which served as a symbol of the new peaceful European order, and, despite some hiccups, it has flourished ever since, in the process helping to make tourism a mainstay of the local economy. While the 1990s saw Glasgow establish a clear lead in driving Scotland's contemporary arts scene, they also marked the return of power and influence to Edinburgh. Following the election of the Labour government in 1997, a referendum in Scotland voted resoundingly in favour of re-establishing its own **parliament** with control over a large part of the domestic agenda. With debates, decisions and demonstrations about crucial aspects of the government of Scotland now taking place in Edinburgh, there has been a notable upturn in the sense of importance of the city, and it has continued to assert itself as a significant centre for finance, research and arts not just in Britain, but also Europe. Though the opening of the new parliament building has been hobbled by spiralling costs and political rows, there's little doubt that the innovative and challenging design of the large new building will quickly make it the emblem of twenty-first century Edinburgh.

Arrival, information and transport

Although Edinburgh occupies a large area relative to its population – less than half a million people – most places worth visiting lie within the compact city centre, which is easily explored on foot. This is divided clearly and unequivocally between the maze-like **Old Town**, which lies on and around the crag linking the castle and the Palace, and the **New Town**, laid out in a symmetrical pattern on the undulating ground to the north.

Edinburgh International Airport (℡0131/333 1000) is at Turnhouse, seven miles west of the city centre, close to the start of the M8 motorway to Glasgow. Regular Airlink shuttle buses (£3.40) connect to Waverley Bridge in the town centre; taxis charge around £15 for the same journey. Conveniently situated at the eastern end of Princes Street in the New Town, **Waverley Station** is the terminus for all mainline trains. The main central exits take you out onto Waverley Bridge, the northern exit leads up a stairway to Princes

Street in the New Town, and the southern exit leads to Market Street, the outer fringe of the Old Town.

There's a second mainline train stop, **Haymarket Station**, just under two miles west on the lines from Waverley to Glasgow, Fife and the Highlands, although this is only really of use if you're staying nearby. The **bus** terminal for local and intercity services is on St Andrew Square, two minutes' walk from Waverley Station, on the opposite side of Princes Street.

Information

Edinburgh's main **tourist office** is found on top of Princes Mall near the northern entrance to the station (April & Oct Mon–Sat 9am–6pm, Sun 10am–6pm; May, June & Sept Mon–Sat 9am–7pm, Sun 10am–7pm; July & Aug Mon–Sat 9am–8pm, Sun 10am–8pm; Nov–March Mon–Wed 9am–5pm, Thurs–Sat 9am–6pm, Sun 10am–5pm; ☎0845/2255121, Ⓦwww.edinburgh.org). Although inevitably flustered at the height of the season, it's efficiently run, with scores of free leaflets and a bank of computers available if you want to search for information on the web. The much smaller **airport branch** is in the main concourse, directly opposite Gate 5 (daily: April–Oct 6.30am–10.30pm; Nov–March 7.30am–9.30pm). For backpacker-related information head to the **Haggis Office** at 60 High St (daily 9am–6pm; ☎0131/557 9393, Ⓦwww.haggisadventures.com). Although their main function is to run minibus tours of Scotland, they're a good source of general information too. For up-to-date maps of the city head for one of the major book stores: Waterstone's, 13–14 Princes St, is the nearest to Waverley Station.

City transport

Most of Edinburgh's **public transport** services terminate on or near Princes Street, the city's main thoroughfare, which divides the Old Town from the New Town.

Edinburgh is well served by **buses**, and most bus stops have a useful diagram indicating which services pass the stop and which routes they take. Most useful are the maroon buses operated by Lothian Buses (Ⓦwww.lothianbuses.co.uk) – all buses referred to in the text are run by them unless otherwise stated. Timetables and passes are available from their ticket centres on Waverley Bridge or 27 Hanover St (enquiry line ☎0131/555 6363). A good investment, especially if you're staying far out or want to explore the suburbs, is the £11 **pass** allowing a week's unlimited travel; you'll need a passport photo. You can also buy a day pass for £2.50 (£1.80 after 9.30am, or £4.20 including the airport bus) or, of course, tickets from the driver, for which you'll need exact change – the most common fare is 80p.

The city is well endowed with **taxi** ranks, and you can also hail black cabs on the street. Phone numbers for local companies are listed on p.959. It is emphatically not a good idea to take a **car** into central Edinburgh: despite the presence of several expensive multistorey car parks, finding somewhere to park involves long and often fruitless searches. In addition, Edinburgh's street parking restrictions are famously draconian, though most ticket and parking-meter regulations cease at 6.30pm Monday to Friday, and at 1.30pm on Saturday.

Edinburgh is a reasonably cycle-friendly city – although hilly – with several **cycle paths**. The local cycling action group, Spokes (☎0131/313 2114, Ⓦwww.spokes.org.uk), publishes an excellent cycle map of the city. For bike rental, see p.958.

Accommodation

As befits its status as a busy tourist city and important commercial centre, Edinburgh has a greater choice of **accommodation** than any other place in Britain outside London. **Hotels** (and large backpacker **hostels**) are essentially the only options you'll find right in the heart of the city, but within relatively easy reach of the centre the selection of **guest houses**, **B&Bs**, **campus accommodation** and even **camping** broadens considerably.

Prices in Edinburgh are significantly higher across all types of accommodation than elsewhere in Scotland, with rates at their highest in August during the Festival – **advance reservations** are very strongly recommended at this time. The **tourist office** (see p.915) sends out accommodation lists for free, and can reserve any type of accommodation in advance for a non-refundable £3 fee: call in personally when you arrive or contact them in advance, stating requirements.

Hotels and guest houses

In the centre of the city, Edinburgh's **hotels** tend to fall into two categories: grand and traditional at the upper end of the market, and budget chain hotels in the middle-to-low price range. Generally offering much better value for money and a far more homely experience than the larger city hotels are Edinburgh's vast range of **guest houses**, **small hotels** and **bed & breakfast** establishments.

Old Town

Bank 1 South Bridge ℡0131/622 6800, ⓦwww.festival-inns.co.uk. Notable location in a 1920s bank at the crossroads of the Royal Mile and South Bridge, with *Logie Baird's* bar downstairs and nine unusual but comfortable rooms upstairs on the theme of famous Scots. ❼

Ibis 6 Hunter Sq ℡0131/240 7000, ⓦwww.accorhotels.com. Best located of many budget chain hotels, right at the heart of the Old Town. ❹

Point 34–59 Bread St ℡0131/221 5555, ⓦwww.point-hotel.co.uk. A former department store and now one of Edinburgh's most stylish and individual modern hotels. There's a popular cocktail bar and a decent restaurant at street level. ❻

The Scotsman 20 Northbridge ℡0131/556 5565, ⓦwww.thescotsmanhotel.co.uk. One of Edinburgh's headline hotels: a plush, smart but unstuffy new occupant of the grand old offices of the *Scotsman* newspaper. It's five-star stuff with modern gadgets and fittings, but the marble staircase and walnut-panelled lobby have been retained, and you can sleep in the editor's office. ❽

Travelodge 33 St Mary St ℡0870/191 1637, ⓦwww.travelodge.co.uk. Another well-placed budget chain hotel, with few frills but a good location just off the Royal Mile. ❸

The Witchery Apartments Castlehill, Royal Mile ℡0131/225 5613, ⓦwww.thewitchery.com.

Seven riotously indulgent suites grouped around the famously spooky *Royal Mile* restaurant. Top of the range, unique and memorable. ❾

New Town

Ardenlee 9 Eyre Place, New Town ℡0131/556 2838, ⓦwww.ardenleeguesthouse.com. Welcoming, nonsmoking guest house near the Royal Botanic Garden, with original Victorian features and spacious rooms. Breakfast includes some vegetarian options, and large family rooms are available. ❸

Balmoral 1 Princes St ℡0131/556 2414, ⓦwww.roccofortehotels.com. Originally known as the *North British*, this elegant landmark is the finest grand hotel in the city, boasting nearly two hundred rooms, full business facilities, a swimming pool and gym, and two highly rated restaurants. ❽

Bonham 35 Drumsheugh Gardens ℡0131/226 6050, ⓦwww.thebonham.com. One of Edinburgh's most stylish modern hotels, cheekily hiding behind a grand West End Victorian facade and with an interesting mix of period and modern furniture. ❽

Davenport House 58 Great King St, New Town ℡0131/558 8495, ⓦwww.davenport-house.com. A grand, regally decorated guest house in an attractive New Town townhouse; a well-priced and intimate alternative to some of the nearby hotels. ❺

Frederick House 42 Frederick St ☎ 0131/226 1999, ⓦ www.townhousehotels.co.uk. A reasonable if slightly plain hotel in a superb location just off George Street in the New Town. ➍

Galloway 22 Dean Park Crescent, Stockbridge ☎ 0131/332 3672, ⓔ galloway_theclarks @hotmail.com. Friendly, family-run option in elegant Stockbridge, within walking distance of the centre. ➌

Gerald's Place 21b Abercromby Place, New Town ☎ 0131/558 7017, ⓦ www.geraldsplace.com. A real taste of New Town life at an upmarket but wonderfully hospitable and comfy basement B&B. ➎

Greenside 9 Royal Terrace, Calton Hill ☎ 0131/557 0022, ⓦ www.townhousehotels.co.uk. One of a number of small hotels on Calton Hill with great views from the top floors – in this case across to Leith and beyond to the Firth of Forth. Value for money considering the location. ➍

Rick's Restaurant with rooms 55a Frederick St, New Town ☎ 0131/622 7800, ⓦ www .ricksedinburgh.co.uk. Ten much sought-after rooms at the back of the popular New Town bar and restaurant. Beautifully styled and fitted with walnut headboards and top quality fabrics, they look out onto a cobbled lane behind. ➏

Six Mary's Place Raeburn Place, Stockbridge ☎ 0131/332 8965, ⓦ www.sixmarysplace.co.uk. Recently refurbished, collectively run "alternative" guest house, with a no-smoking policy and excellent home-cooked vegetarian meals. ➍

Leith and north Edinburgh

Ardmor House 74 Pilrig St, Pilrig ☎ 0131/554 4944, ⓦ www.ardmorhouse.com. Victorian townhouse with some lovely original features combined with smart contemporary decor. Gay-owned, straight-friendly, and located halfway between town and Leith. ➍

Bar Java 48–50 Constitution St, Leith ☎ 0131/553 2020, ⓦ www.hotelbarjava.com. Simple but brightly designed rooms above one of Leith's funkiest bars. Great breakfasts served, and food and drink available till late in the bar itself. ➎

Malmaison 1 Tower Place, Leith ☎ 0131/468 5000, ⓦ www.malmaison.com. Chic modern hotel in a converted harbourside building with bright, bold original designs in each room, as well as CD players and cable TV. Also has gym, room service, Parisian brasserie and café-bar serving lighter meals. ➐

South of the centre

Bruntsfield 69 Bruntsfield Place, Bruntsfield ☎ 0131/229 1393, ⓦ www.thebruntsfield.co.uk. Large, comfortable and peaceful hotel, now part of

the Best Western group, overlooking Bruntsfield Links, a mile south of Princes Street. ➐

Cluaran House 47 Leamington Terrace, Viewforth ☎ 0131/221 0047, ⓦ www .cluaran-house-edinburgh.co.uk. Pleasant B&B in a tastefully decorated, nonsmoking house near Bruntsfield serving wholefood breakfasts. ➍

Edinburgh City Hotel 79 Lauriston Place ☎ 0131/622 7979, ⓦ www .bestwesternedinburghcity.co.uk. Formerly "Simpson's" (after Sir James Young Simpson, pioneer of modern anaesthetics), a reasonably individual and smart medium-sized hotel located in the former maternity hospital near Tollcross and the Meadows. ➏

The Greenhouse 14 Hartington Gardens, Viewforth ☎ 0131/622 7634, ⓦ www.greenhouse-edinburgh .com. A fully vegetarian/vegan guest house, right down to the soaps and duvets, though a relaxed rather than right-on atmosphere prevails. The rooms are neat and tastefully furnished, with fresh fruit and flowers in each. ➎

Hopetoun 15 Mayfield Rd, Mayfield ☎ 0131/667 7691, ⓦ www.hopetoun.com. Bright, friendly non-smoking guest house with just two rooms. Great views of Arthur's Seat and Blackford Hill. ➍

MW Guest House 94 Dalkeith Rd, Newington ☎ 0131/662 9265, ⓔ www.mwguesthouse.co.uk. One of only a few guest houses in town with fresh, contemporary design. The linked *MW Townhouse* just round the corner is equally well presented. ➍

Prestonfield House Priestfield Road, Bruntsfield ☎ 0131/668 3346, ⓦ www.prestonfieldhouse.com. A seventeenth-century mansion set in its own park below Arthur's Seat; recently taken over by James Thomson, the man behind the *Witchery* restaurant and apartments, and tabled to become the city's most lavish and opulent place to stay. ➒

Southside 8 Newington Rd, Newington ☎ 0131/668 4422, ⓦ www.southsideguesthouse.co.uk. Stylish modern decor and a great daytime café make this smart guest house a comfortable if slightly pricey base not far from Holyrood Park. ➎

Sylvern 22 West Mayfield, Mayfield ☎ 0131/667 1241. Lovely large Southside house with original features and comfortable rooms looking onto a large walled garden with conservatory. ➍

West of the centre

The Original Raj Hotel 6 West Coates ☎ 0131/346 1333, ⓦ www.rajempire.com. Imaginatively conceived and lavishly executed, a townhouse hotel with seventeen rooms themed on India and the splendour of the Raj. ➎

EATING & DRINKING

Abbotsford	36	Blonde	66	Café Royal Circle Bar	33	Doric Tavern	
Atrium	53	blue	53	Café Royal Oyster Bar	28	Elephant House	
Bannermans	11	Blue Blazer	60	Candy Bar	40	Favorit	
Barony Bar	19	Blue Parrot Cantina	20	City Café	7	Fishers in the City	
Basement	24	Bow Bar	49	Creelers	5	Glass & Thompson	
Bennets Bar	68	Café Hub	47	David Bann's Vegetarian		Grain Store	
Bert's Bar	15 & 44	Café Marlayne	34	Restaurant	10	Hadrian's	
Black Bo's	8	Café Mediterraneo	21	Dome	35	Hector's	

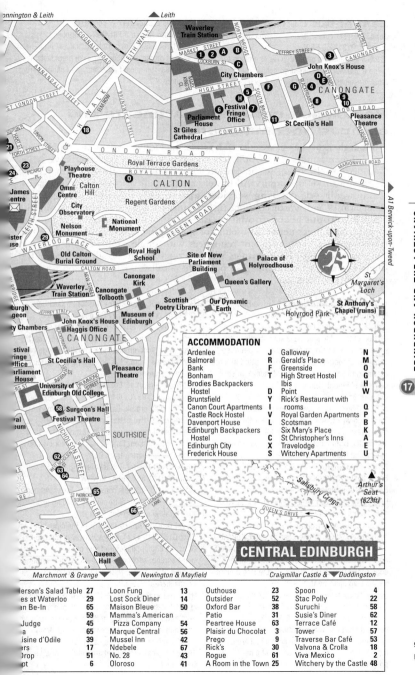

CENTRAL EDINBURGH

ACCOMMODATION

Ardenlee	J
Balmoral	R
Bank	F
Bonham	T
Brodies Backpackers Hostel	D
Bruntsfield	Y
Canon Court Apartments	I
Castle Rock Hostel	V
Davenport House	L
Edinburgh Backpackers Hostel	C
Edinburgh City	X
Frederick House	S
Galloway	N
Gerald's Place	M
Greenside	O
High Street Hostel	G
Ibis	H
Point	W
Rick's Restaurant with rooms	Q
Royal Garden Apartments	P
Scotsman	B
Six Mary's Place	K
St Christopher's Inns	A
Travelodge	E
Witchery Apartments	U

Map labels: Waverley Train Station, Market Street, North Bridge, Jeffrey Street, Canongate, John Knox's House, City Chambers, High Street, Blackfriars St, Canongate, South Bridge, Festival Fringe Office, Parliament House, St Giles Cathedral, Cowgate, St Cecilia's Hall, Holyrood Road, Pleasance Theatre, Pleasance

Leith Walk, McDonald Road, Leith Street, Playhouse Theatre, Omni Centre, Calton Hill, City Observatory, Nelson Monument, National Monument, Old Calton Burial Ground, Royal Terrace Gardens, Royal Terrace, Calton, Regent Gardens, London Road, Regent Road, Old Calton Burial Ground, Waterloo Place, Royal High School, Site of New Parliament Building, Palace of Holyroodhouse, Queen's Gallery, St Margaret's Loch, Holyrood Park, St Anthony's Chapel (ruins)

Waverley Train Station, Canongate Kirk, Canongate Tolbooth, Scottish Poetry Library, Museum of Edinburgh, John Knox's House, Haggis Office, CANONGATE, Our Dynamic Earth, Queen's Drive, St Cecilia's Hall, Pleasance Theatre, University of Edinburgh Old College, Surgeon's Hall, Festival Theatre, SOUTHSIDE, Nicolson Street, St Patrick's Square, Clerk Street, Queens Hall, Salisbury Crags, Arthur's Seat (823ft), Queen's Drive

Bonnington & Leith, Leith, A1 Berwick-upon-Tweed, Marchmont & Grange, Newington & Mayfield, Craigmillar Castle & Duddingston

...erson's Salad Table	27	Loon Fung	13	Outhouse	23	Spoon	4
...es at Waterloo	29	Lost Sock Diner	14	Outsider	52	Stac Polly	22
...an Be-In	65	Maison Bleue	50	Oxford Bar	38	Suruchi	58
	59	Mamma's American		Patio	31	Susie's Diner	62
...Judge	45	Pizza Company	54	Peartree House	63	Terrace Café	12
...a	65	Marque Central	56	Plaisir du Chocolat	3	Tower	57
...isine d'Odile	39	Mussel Inn	42	Prego	9	Traverse Bar Café	53
...rs	17	Ndebele	67	Rick's	30	Valvona & Crolla	18
...rop	51	No. 28	43	Rogue	61	Viva Mexico	2
...t	6	Oloroso	41	A Room in the Town	25	Witchery by the Castle	48

East of the centre

Joppa Turrets Guest House 1 Lower Joppa, Joppa ℡0131/669 5806, ⊛www.joppaturrets.demon.co.uk. The place to come if you want an Edinburgh holiday by the sea: a quiet establishment right by the beach in Joppa,

five miles east of the city centre. ❸

Portobello House 2 Pittville St, Portobello ℡0131/669 6067, ✉portobello.house@virgin.net. Pleasant rooms and good (organic) breakfasts at this family-run guest house, only two minutes from the shore. ❷

Hostel, self-catering apartments and campus accommodation

Edinburgh now has a wealth of **hostels**, including two grand SYHA–run establishments and a cluster of independent outfits on or near the Royal Mile. Competition is fierce, so be prepared for a bit of enthusiastic marketing when you make an enquiry. All hostels are open all year round, unless stated. Custom-built **self-catering serviced apartments** are viable alternatives to guest houses and worth considering for longer stays, for example during the Festival. **Campus accommodation** is available in the city during the summer months, though it's neither as useful nor as cheap as might be expected. SYHA take over three central student residences with single rooms during July and August – one on The Pleasance and two on Cowgate. Both have over 100 single bedrooms for around £20 per night – call ℡0870/155 3255 for their central reservations line.

Argyle Backpackers Hotel 14 Argyle Place, Marchmont ℡0131/667 9991, ⊛www.argyle-backpackers.co.uk. Quieter, less intense version of the typical backpackers' hostel, with small dorms with single beds and a dozen or so double/twin rooms (❶). Pleasantly located in three adjoining townhouses near the Meadows in studenty Marchmont. Dorms from £10.

Brodies Backpackers Hostel 12 High St, Old Town ℡0131/556 6770, ⊛www.brodieshostels.co.uk. Tucked down a typical Old Town close, with four fairly straightforward dorms (from £9.50 per bed) and limited communal areas. Smaller than many others, and a little bit more homely.

Bruntsfield Hostel 7 Bruntsfield Crescent, Bruntsfield ℡0870/004 1114, ⊛www.syha.org.uk. Large SYHA place overlooking Bruntsfield Links a mile south of Princes Street; take bus #11, #15 or #16. Dorms from £12 per person.

Canon Court Apartments 20 Canonmills ℡0131/474 7000, ⊛www.canoncourt.co.uk. All mod cons available in this block of smart, comfortable self-catering apartments on the northern edge of the New Town. Prices start at £74 a night for a studio apartment.

Castle Rock Hostel 15 Johnston Terrace, Old Town ℡0131/225 9666, ⊛www.scotlands-top-hostels.com. Busy 200-bed hostel tucked below the castle ramparts. Dorms are large and bright, and the communal areas include a games room with pool and ping-pong tables.

Edinburgh Backpackers Hostel 65 Cockburn St, Old Town ℡0131/220 1717; booking hotline 0131/220 2200, ⊛www.hoppo.com. Big hostel with a great central location in a side street off the Royal Mile. Accommodation is mostly in large but bright dorms (from £12), although a few doubles (❶) are available.

Eglinton Hostel 18 Eglinton Crescent, Haymarket ℡0870/004 1116, ⊛www.syha.org.uk. Larger but slightly more central of the two main SYHA hostels, in a characterful townhouse west of the centre, near Haymarket Station. Tends to attract more groups and families. Dorms from £12.

High Street Hostel 8 Blackfriars St, Old Town ℡0131/557 3984, ⊛www.scotlands-top-hostels.com. Large, lively and popular hostel in a sixteenth-century building just off the Royal Mile. Dorm bed from £12.

Royal Garden Apartments York Buildings, Queen St ℡0131/625 1234, ⊛www.royal-garden.co.uk. Superbly equipped, comfortable modern one- and two-bedroom serviced apartments very centrally located opposite the National Portrait Gallery. Prices start at £155 per night.

St Christopher's Inns 9–13 Market St, Old Town ℡0131/226 1446, ⊛www.st-christophers.co.uk. Edinburgh's first sighting of the mega-hostels now common in London; 110 beds (all bunks, from £9.50) with smaller rooms as well as dorms. There's a small communal area and a noisy bar for beer and food.

University of Edinburgh Pollock Halls of Residence 18 Holyrood Park Rd, Newington ℡0131/651 2007 or 0800/028 7118, Ⓦwww.edinburghfirst.com. Unquestionably the best setting of any of the campuses, right beside the Royal Commonwealth Pool and Holyrood Park, but relatively expensive (rates are for bed and breakfast). Single rooms and self-catering flats also available. Easter & late June to mid-Sept. ❹

Campsites

Edinburgh Caravan Club Site Marine Drive, Silverknowes ℡0131/312 6874. Caravan-dominated site in a pleasant location close to the shore in the northwestern suburbs, though the stop for city-centre bus #16 is 15min away. Camping May–Sept only.

Drummohr Caravan Park Levenhall, Musselburgh ℡0131/665 6867, Ⓦwww .drummohr.org. A large, pleasant site in this coastal satellite town to the east of Edinburgh, with excellent transport connections to the city, including buses #15, #26, #30 and #44. Open March–Oct.

The Old Town

The **OLD TOWN**, although only about a mile long and 300 yards wide, represents the total extent of the twin burghs of Edinburgh and Canongate for the first 650 years of their existence, and its general appearance and character remain indubitably medieval. Containing as it does the majority of the city's most famous tourist sights, it makes by far the best starting point for your explorations.

In addition to the obvious goals of the **castle**, the **Palace of Holyroodhouse** and **Holyrood Abbey**, you'll find scores of historic buildings along the length of the **Royal Mile**. Inevitably, much of the Old Town is sacrificed to hard-sell tourism, and can be uncomfortably crowded throughout the summer, especially during the Festival. Yet the area remains at the heart of Edinburgh, with daily business of the greatest importance being conducted in **Parliament House**, home of the Scottish Parliament until 1707 and now the location of Scotland's highest Law Courts, and in the **Assembly Hall**, temporary home of the new Scottish Parliament (due to move into its specially designed new home at the foot of the Royal Mile some time in 2004). It's well worth extending your explorations to the area immediately to the south of the Royal Mile, and in particular to the engaging **National Museum of Scotland**. And make sure you spare time for the wonderfully varied scenery and breathtaking vantage points of **Holyrood Park**, an extensive tract of open countryside on the eastern edge of the Old Town which includes Arthur's Seat, the peak which rises so distinctively in the midst of the city.

The Castle

The history of Edinburgh, and indeed of Scotland, is indissolubly bound up with its **castle** (daily: April–Oct 9.30am–6pm; Nov–March 9.30am–5pm; £8.50; HS), which dominates the city from its lofty seat atop an extinct volcanic rock. It requires no great imaginative feat to comprehend the strategic importance that underpinned the castle's, and hence Edinburgh's, importance in Scotland: from Princes Street, the north side rears high above an almost sheer rock face; the southern side is equally formidable; the western, where the rock rises in terraces, only marginally less so. Would-be attackers, like modern tourists, were forced to approach the castle from the crag to the east on which the Royal Mile runs down to Holyrood.

The castle's disparate styles reflect its many changes in usage, as well as advances in military architecture: the oldest surviving part, **St Margaret's Chapel**, is from the twelfth century, while the most recent additions date back to the 1920s. It last saw action in 1745, when the Young Pretender's forces, fresh from their victory at Prestonpans, made a half-hearted attempt to storm it. Subsequently, advances in weapons technology diminished the castle's importance, but under the influence of the Romantic movement it came to be seen as a great national monument.

Though you can easily take in the views and wander round the castle yourself, you might like to join one of the somewhat overheated **guided tours**, with their talk of war, boiling oil and the roar of the cannon. Alternatively, **audioguides** (£3) are available from a booth just inside the gatehouse.

The Esplanade and the lower defences

The castle is entered via the **Esplanade**, a parade ground laid out in the eighteenth century and enclosed a hundred years later by ornamental walls. For most of the year it acts as a coach park, though huge grandstands are erected for the Edinburgh Military Tattoo (see p.957), which takes place every night during August, coinciding with the Edinburgh Festival. A shameless and spectacular pageant of swinging kilts and massed pipe bands, the tattoo makes full use of its dramatic setting.

The **gatehouse** to the castle is a Romantic-style addition of the 1880s, complete with the last drawbridge ever built in Scotland and adorned with appropriately heroic-looking statues of Sir William Wallace and Robert the Bruce. Standing guard by the drawbridge are real-life soldiers, members of the regiment in residence at the castle; while their presence in full dress uniform is always a hit with camera-toting tourists, it's also a reminder that the castle is still a working military garrison.

Rearing up behind is the most distinctive and impressive feature of the castle's silhouette, the sixteenth-century **Half Moon Battery**, which marks the outer limit of the actual defences. Once through the gatehouse, continue uphill along Lower Ward, passing through the **Portcullis Gate**, a handsome Renaissance gateway of the same period as the battery above, marred by the addition of a nineteenth-century upper storey equipped with anachronistic arrow slits rather than gunholes.

Beyond this the wide main path is known as Middle Ward, with the six-gun **Argyle Battery** to the right. Further west on **Mill's Mount Battery**, a well-known Edinburgh ritual takes place – the daily firing of the one o'clock gun. Originally designed for the benefit of ships in the Firth of Forth, these days it's an enjoyable ceremony for visitors to watch and a useful time signal for city-centre office workers. Both batteries offer wonderful panoramic views over Princes Street and the New Town to the coastal towns and hills of Fife across the Forth.

National War Museum of Scotland

Located in the old hospital buildings, down a ramp between the café/restaurant immediately behind the one o'clock gun and the Governor's House, the **National War Museum of Scotland** (free), part of the collection of the National Museums of Scotland, covers the last 400 years of Scottish military history. While the various rooms are packed with uniforms, medals, paintings of heroic actions and plenty of interesting memorabilia, the museum manages to convey a reflective, human tone.

Back on Middle Ward, the **Governor's House** is a 1740s mansion whose masonry and crow-stepped gables are archetypal features of vernacular Scottish architecture. It now serves as the officers' mess for members of the garrison, while the governor himself lives in the northern side wing. Behind stands the largest single construction in the castle complex, the **New Barracks**, built in the 1790s in an austere Neoclassical style. From here a cobbled road then snakes round towards the enclosed citadel at the uppermost point of Castle Rock, entered via **Foog's Gate**.

St Margaret's Chapel

At the eastern end of the citadel, **St Margaret's Chapel** is the oldest surviving building in the castle, and probably also in Edinburgh itself. Used as a powder magazine for 300 years, this tiny Norman church was rediscovered in 1845 and was eventually rededicated in 1934, after sympathetic restoration. Externally, it's plain and severe, but the interior preserves an elaborate zigzag archway dividing the nave from the sanctuary. Although once believed to have been built by the saint herself, and mooted as the site of her death in 1093, its architectural style suggests that it actually dates from about thirty years later, and was thus probably built by King David I as a memorial to his mother.

The battlements in front of the chapel offer the best of all the castle's panoramic views. Here you'll see the famous fifteenth-century siege gun, **Mons Meg**, which could fire a 500-pound stone nearly two miles. Just below the battlements there's a small **cemetery**, the last resting place of the **soldiers' pets**. Continuing eastwards, you skirt the top of the Forewall and Half Moon Batteries, passing the 110-foot **Castle Well** en route to **Crown Square**, the highest, most secure and most important section of the entire complex.

Crown Square

The eastern side of Crown Square is occupied by the **palace**, a surprisingly unassuming edifice built round an octagonal stair turret heightened in the nineteenth century to bear the castle's main flagpole. Begun in the 1430s, the palace owes its Renaissance appearance to King James IV, though it was remodelled for Mary, Queen of Scots and her consort Henry, Lord Darnley, whose entwined initials (MAH), together with the date 1566, can be seen above one of the doorways.

Another section of the palace has recently been refurbished with a detailed audiovisual presentation on the **Honours of Scotland**, the originals of which are housed in the Crown Room at the very end of the display. Though you might be put off by the slow-moving, claustrophobic queues that shuffle past the displays, the interest in them is justified: these magnificent crown jewels – the only pre-Restoration set in the United Kingdom – serve as one of the most potent images of Scotland's nationhood. They were last used for the Scottish-only coronation of Charles II in 1651, an event which provoked the wrath of Oliver Cromwell, who made exhaustive attempts to have the jewels melted down. Having narrowly escaped his clutches by being smuggled out of the castle and hidden in a rural church, the jewels later served as symbols of the absent monarch at sittings of the Scottish Parliament before being locked away in a chest following the Union of 1707. For over a century they were out of sight and eventually presumed lost, before being rediscovered in 1818 as a result of a search initiated by Sir Walter Scott.

Of the three pieces comprising the Honours, the oldest is the **sceptre**, which bears statuettes of the Virgin and Child, St James and St Andrew, rounded off by a polished globe of rock crystal. Even finer is the **sword**, a swaggering

Italian High Renaissance masterpiece by the silversmith Domenico da Sutri, presented to James IV by the great artistic patron Pope Julius II. The jewel-encrusted **crown**, made for James V by the Scottish goldsmith James Mosman, incorporates the gold circlet worn by Robert the Bruce and is surmounted by an enamelled orb and cross.

The glass case containing the Honours was rearranged a few years back to create space for its newest addition, the **Stone of Destiny** (see box), a remarkably plain object that now lies incongruously next to the opulent crown jewels.

The south side of **Crown Square** is occupied by the **Great Hall**, built under James IV as a venue for banquets and other ceremonial occasions. Until 1639 the meeting place of the Scottish Parliament, it later underwent the indignity of conversion and subdivision, firstly into a barracks, then a hospital. During this time, its hammerbeam roof – the earliest of three in the Old Town – was hidden from view. It was restored towards the end of the nineteenth century, when the hall was decked out in the full-blown Romantic manner.

In 1755, the castle church of St Mary on the north side of the square was replaced by a barracks, which in turn was skilfully converted into the quietly reverential **Scottish National War Memorial** in honour of the 150,000 Scots who fell in World War I.

The Royal Mile

The **Royal Mile**, the name given to the ridge linking the castle with Holyrood, was described by Daniel Defoe, in 1724, as "the largest, longest and finest street for Buildings and Number of Inhabitants, not in Britain only, but in the World". Almost exactly a mile in length, it is divided into four separate streets – Castlehill, Lawnmarket, High Street and Canongate. From these, branching out in a herringbone pattern, are a series of tightly packed closes and

The Stone of Destiny

Legend has it that the **Stone of Destiny** (also called the Stone of Scone) was "Jacob's Pillow", on which he dreamed of the ladder of angels from earth to heaven. Its real history is obscure, but it is known that it was moved from Ireland to Dunadd by missionaries, and thence to Dunstaffnage, from where Kenneth MacAlpine, king of the Dalriada Scots, brought it to the abbey at Scone in 838. There it remained for almost five hundred years, used as a coronation throne on which all kings of Scotland were crowned.

In 1296, an over-eager Edward I stole what he believed to be the Stone and installed it at Westminster Abbey, where, apart from a brief interlude in 1950 when it was removed by Scottish nationalists and hidden in Arbroath for several months, it remained for seven hundred years. All this changed in December 1996 when, after an elaborate ceremony-laden journey from London, the Stone returned to Scotland, in one of the doomed attempts by the Conservative government to convince the Scottish people that the Union was a good thing. Much to the annoyance of the people of Perth and the curators of Scone Palace (see p.1082), and to the general indifference of the people of Scotland, the Stone was placed in Edinburgh Castle.

However, speculation surrounds the authenticity of the Stone, for the original is said to have been intricately carved, while the one seen today is a plain block of sandstone. Many believe that the canny monks at Scone palmed this off onto the English king (some say that it's nothing more sacred than the cover for a medieval septic tank), and that the real Stone of Destiny lies hidden in an underground chamber, its whereabouts a mystery to all but the chosen few.

steep lanes entered via archways known as "pends". After the construction of the New Town, much of the housing along the Royal Mile degenerated into a notorious slum, but has since shaken off that reputation, becoming once again a highly desirable place to live. Although marred somewhat by rather too many tacky tourist shops and the odd misjudged new development, it is still among the most evocative parts of the city, and one that particularly rewards detailed exploration.

Castlehill

The narrow uppermost stretch of the Royal Mile is known as **Castlehill**. The first building on the northern side of the street as you leave the castle Esplanade is the former reservoir for the Old Town, which has been converted into the **Edinburgh Old Town Weaving Centre** (daily May–Oct 9am–6.30pm, Nov–April 9am–5.30pm). Very much a commercial enterprise, the centre contains various large shops selling kilts, rugs and other tartan adornments while noisy looms churn the stuff out on the floors below.

On the corner of the wall of the Weaving Centre facing the castle, a pretty Art Nouveau **Witches' Fountain** commemorates the three hundred or more women burnt at the spot on charges of sorcery, the last of whom died in 1722. Rising up behind is **Ramsay Gardens**, surely some of the most picturesque city-centre flats in the world. The oldest part is the octagonal Goose Pie House, home of the eighteenth-century poet Allan Ramsay, author of *The Gentle Shepherd* and father of the better-known portrait painter of the same name.

Opposite the Weaving Centre at the top of the southern side of Castlehill, the so-called **Cannonball House** takes its name from the cannonball embedded in its masonry, which according to legend was the result of a poorly targeted shot fired by the castle garrison at Bonnie Prince Charlie's encampment at Holyrood. The truth is far more prosaic: the ball marks the gravitation height of the city's first piped water supply. Alongside, the **Scotch Whisky Heritage Centre** (daily: June–Sept 9.30am–6.30pm; Oct–May 10am–5.30pm; £7.50; barrel-ride only £3.50) gives the lowdown on all aspects of Scotland's national beverage. The climax of the tour is a gimmicky ride in a moving "barrel" through a series of uninspiring historical tableaux, although all in all there's little on offer here which you won't find done rather better on a tour of a real distillery. For whisky novices, it's worth popping into the shop, whose stock gives an idea of the sheer range and diversity of the drink, with dozens of different brands on sale.

Across the street, the **Outlook Tower** (daily April–Oct 9.30am–6pm, July & Aug open till 7.30pm; Nov–March 10am–5pm; £5.95) has been one of Edinburgh's top tourist attractions since 1853, when the original seventeenth-century tenement was equipped with a **camera obscura**. It makes a good introduction to the city: live images are beamed through a periscope mounted at the highest point of the tower onto a white table in the auditorium, accompanied by a running commentary. For the best views, visit at noon when there are fewer shadows.

A few doors further on is the **Assembly Hall**, normally used as the meeting place of the annual General Assembly of the Church of Scotland but, since May 1999, the home of the **Scottish Parliament** while it awaits more permanent accommodation (see p.934). The Hall is nothing to look at from the Royal Mile side; at its northern entrance, however, on Mound Place, are the twin towers which feature so prominently on vistas of the Old Town skyline from the New Town. It's possible to visit the debating chamber of the Parliament by going to the public entrance in Milne's Court, one of the closes off the Royal Mile just past the Assembly Hall (Mon–Fri 10am–noon & 2–4pm; free). When Parliament is in session, you can sit and watch the **debates** from the large public gallery – tickets are available on an ad hoc basis either from the desk at the public entrance or from the Scottish Parliament **visitor centre** on the corner of George IV Bridge and High Street, although they can also be booked (☏0131/348 5411, ⓦwww .scottish.parliament.uk) up to a week before the date you wish to attend. The best time to see a debate is First Minister's Questions on Thursday afternoon.

The imposing black church building opposite the Assembly Hall at the foot of Castlehill is **The Hub** (daily 9.30am–late; ☏0131/473 2010, ⓦwww .eif.co.uk/thehub), also known as "Edinburgh's Festival Centre", the first permanent home of the Edinburgh International Festival since its inception in 1947. Although the Festival only takes place for three weeks every August and early September, The Hub is open year-round, providing performance, rehearsal and exhibition space, a ticket centre and a café. The building itself was constructed in 1845 to designs by James Gillespie Graham and Augustus Pugin, one of the co-architects of the Houses of Parliament in London – a connection obvious from the superb neo-Gothic detailing and the sheer presence of the building, whose spire is the highest in Edinburgh. On the ground floor level is the *Hub Café* (Tues–Sat 9.30am–9.30pm, Sun & Mon 9.30am–6pm); also worth checking out is the main hall upstairs, where the original neo-Gothic woodwork and high-vaulted ceiling is enlivened with a fabulous fabric design in Rastafarian colours. Permanent works of art have been incorporated into the centre, including over 200 delightful foot-high sculptures by Scottish sculptor Jill Watson, depicting Festival performers and audiences.

Lawnmarket

Below the Tolbooth Kirk, the Royal Mile opens out into the broader expanse of **Lawnmarket**, which, as its name suggests, was once a marketplace. At its northern end is the entry to **Milne's Court**, whose excellently restored tenements now serve as student residences, and immediately beyond, **James Court**, one of Edinburgh's most fashionable addresses prior to the advent of the New Town, with David Hume and James Boswell among those who lived there.

Back on Lawnmarket itself, **Gladstone's Land** (April–Oct Mon–Sat 10am–5pm, Sun 2–5pm; £3.50) takes its name from the merchant Thomas Gledstone who in 1617 acquired a modest dwelling on the site, transforming it into a magnificent six-storey mansion. The Gledstane family are thought to have occupied the third floor, renting out the rest to merchants, in the style of tenement occupation still widespread in the city today. The arcaded ground floor, the only authentic example left of what was once a common feature of Royal Mile houses, has been restored to illustrate its early function as a shopping booth. Several other rooms have been kitted out in authentic period style to give an impression of the lifestyle of a well-to-do household of the late seventeenth century; the Painted Chamber, with its decorated wooden ceiling and wall friezes, is particularly impressive.

A few paces further on, steps lead down to Lady Stair's Close, in which stand the **Writers' Museum** (Mon–Sat 10am–5pm; also Sun 2–5pm during the Festival; free), housed in Lady Stair's House, another fine seventeenth-century residence. Dedicated to the three lions of Scottish literature – Robert Burns

17

Sir Walter Scott and Robert Louis Stevenson, the museum shows off various manuscripts, first editions and portraits, plus personal mementoes (among them locks of hair and walking sticks). Continuing the literary theme, the courtyard outside, called the **Makars' Court** after the Scots word for the "maker" of poetry or prose, has quotations by Scotland's most famous writers and poets inscribed on paving stones.

On the south side of Lawnmarket is **Brodie's Close**, named after the father of one of Edinburgh's most morbid characters, Deacon William Brodie, burglar by night and apparent pillar of society by day. Following his eventual capture, he managed to escape to Holland, but was betrayed, brought back to Edinburgh and hanged in 1788 on gallows of his own design. His ruse of trying to cheat death by secretly wearing an iron collar under his shirt failed. You can visit the popular *Deacon Brodie's Tavern* on the corner of the Lawnmarket and Bank Street and ruminate over a beer on the connections between Brodie, Robert Louis Stevenson's similarly themed tale *Dr Jekyll and Mr Hyde*, and the various split personalities of Edinburgh itself, not least its Old Town and New Town.

Robert Louis Stevenson

Though **Robert Louis Stevenson** (1850–94) is sometimes dismissed for his straight-up writing style, he was undoubtedly one of the best-loved writers of his generation, and one whose travelogues, novels, short stories and essays remain enormously popular more than a century after his death.

Born in Edinburgh into a distinguished family of engineers, Stevenson was a sickly child, with a solitary childhood dominated by his governess, Alison "Cummie" Cunningham, who regaled him with tales drawn from Calvinist folklore. Sent to the University to study engineering, Stevenson rebelled against his upbringing by spending much of his time in the lowlife *howffs* and brothels of the city, and eventually switching to law. Although called to the bar in 1875, by then he had decided to channel his energies into literature: his early successes were two **travelogues**, *An Inland Voyage* and *Travels with a Donkey in the Cevennes*, kaleidoscopic jottings based on his journeys in France, where he went to escape Scotland's weather, which was damaging his health. It was there that he met Fanny Osbourne, an American ten years his senior, who was estranged from her husband and had two children in tow. His voyage to join her in San Francisco formed the basis for his most important factual work, *The Amateur Emigrant*, a vivid first-hand account of the great nineteenth-century European migration to the United States.

Having married the now-divorced Fanny, Stevenson began an elusive search for an agreeable climate that led to Switzerland, the French Riviera and the Scottish Highlands. He belatedly turned to the novel, achieving immediate acclaim in 1881 for **Treasure Island**. In 1886, his most famous short story, **Dr Jekyll and Mr Hyde**, despite its nominal London setting, offered a vivid evocation of Edinburgh's Old Town: an allegory of its dual personality of prosperity and squalor, and an analysis of its Calvinistic preoccupations with guilt and damnation. The same year saw the publication of the historical romance **Kidnapped**, an adventure novel which exemplified Stevenson's view that literature should seek above all to entertain.

In 1887 Stevenson left Britain for good, travelling first to the United States, where he began one of his most ambitious novels, *The Master of Ballantrae*. A year later, he set sail for the South Seas, and eventually settled in **Samoa**; his last works include a number of stories with a local setting, such as the grimly realistic *The Ebb Tide* and *The Beach of Falesà*. He died suddenly from a brain haemorrhage in 1894 and was buried on the top of Mount Vaea overlooking the Pacific Ocean.

The High Kirk of St Giles

Across George IV Bridge is the third section of the Royal Mile, known as the **High Street**, which occupies two blocks either side of the intersection between North Bridge and South Bridge. The dominant building of the southern side of the street is the **High Kirk of St Giles** (May–Sept Mon–Fri 9am–7pm, Sat 9am–5pm, Sun 1–5pm; Oct–April Mon–Sat 9am–5pm, Sun 1–5pm; free) which closes off Parliament Square from High Street. The sole parish church of medieval Edinburgh, where John Knox (see box opposite) launched and directed the Scottish Reformation, the kirk is almost invariably referred to as a cathedral, although it has only been the seat of a bishop on two brief and unhappy occasions in the seventeenth century. According to one of the city's best-known legends, the attempt in 1637 to introduce the English prayer book, and thus episcopal government, so incensed a humble stallholder named Jenny Geddes that she hurled her stool at the preacher, prompting the rest of the congregation to chase the offending clergy out of the building. A tablet in the north aisle marks the spot from where she let rip.

In the early nineteenth century, St Giles received a much-needed but over-drastic restoration, covering most of the Gothic exterior with a smooth stone coating that gives it a certain Georgian dignity while sacrificing its medieval character almost completely. The only part to survive this treatment is the late fifteenth-century tower, whose resplendent crown spire is formed by eight flying buttresses. The **interior** has survived in much better shape. Especially notable are the four massive piers supporting the tower, which date back, at least in part, to the church's twelfth-century Norman predecessor, which itself replaced the very first building on the site, a wooden chapel constructed in 854.

At the southeastern corner of St Giles, the **Thistle Chapel** was built by Sir Robert Lorimer in 1911 as the private chapel of the sixteen knights of the Most Noble Order of the Thistle, the highest chivalric order in Scotland. Self-consciously derivative of St George's Chapel in Windsor, it's an exquisite piece of craftsmanship, with an elaborate ribbed vault, huge drooping bosses, and extravagantly ornate stalls.

Set into the cobblestones of Parliament Square, not far from the main entrance to St Giles, is a stone design known as the **Heart of Midlothian**. Immortalized in Scott's novel of the same name, it marks the site of a demolished tollbooth and prison; you may see passers-by spitting on it for luck.

Parliament Square

The rest of **Parliament Square** is dominated by the continuous Neoclassical facades of the **Law Courts**, originally planned by Robert Adam (1728–92), one of four brothers in a family of architects (their father William Adam designed Hopetoun House; see p.966) whose work helped imbue the New Town with much of its grace and elegance. Because of a shortage of funds, the present exteriors were built to designs by Robert Reid (1776–1856), the designer of the northern part of New Town, who faithfully quoted from Adam's architectural vocabulary without matching his flair.

Around the corner, facing the southern side of St Giles, is **Parliament House**, built in the 1630s for the Scottish Parliament, a role it maintained until the Union, when it passed into the hands of the legal fraternity. To enter the impressive main hall go through the entrance lobby (Mon–Fri 9am–5pm); the most notable feature is the extravagant hammerbeam roof and the delicately carved stone corbels from which it springs – in addition

John Knox

The Protestant reformer **John Knox** has been alternately credited with and blamed for the distinctive national culture that emerged from the Calvinist Reformation, which has cast its shadow over Scottish history and the Scottish character right up to the present.

Little is known about Knox's early years: he was born between 1505 and 1514 in East Lothian, and trained for the priesthood at St Andrews University. Ordained in 1540, Knox then served as a private tutor, in league with Scotland's first significant Protestant leader, **George Wishart**. After Wishart was burnt at the stake for heresy in 1546, Knox became involved with the group who had carried out the revenge murder of the Scottish primate, Cardinal David Beaton, subsequently taking over his castle in St Andrews. The following year this was captured by the French, and Knox was carted off to work as a galley slave.

He was freed in 1548, as a result of the intervention of the English, who invited him to play an evangelizing role in the spread of their own Reformation. Following successful ministries in Berwick-upon-Tweed and Newcastle upon Tyne, Knox turned down the bishopric of Rochester, less from an intrinsic opposition to episcopacy than from a wish to avoid becoming embroiled in the turmoil he guessed would ensue if the Catholic Mary Tudor acceded to the English throne. When this duly happened in 1553, Knox fled to the Continent, ending up as minister to the English-speaking community in Geneva, which was then in the grip of the theocratic government of the Frenchman **Jean Calvin**. Knox was quickly won over to his radical version of Protestantism, declaring Geneva to be "the most perfect school of Christ since the days of the Apostles". In exile, Knox wrote his infamous treatise, *The First Blast of the Trumpet Against the Monstrous Regiment of Women*, a specific attack on the three Catholic women then ruling Scotland, England and France, which has made his name synonymous with misogyny ever since.

When Knox was allowed to return to Scotland in 1555, he took over as spiritual leader of the Reformation, becoming minister of St Giles in Edinburgh, where he established a reputation as a charismatic preacher. However, the establishment of Protestantism as the official religion of Scotland in 1560 was dependent on the forging of an alliance with Elizabeth I, which Knox himself rigorously championed: the swift deployment of English troops against the French garrison in Edinburgh dealt a fatal blow to Franco–Spanish hopes of re-establishing Catholicism in both Scotland and England. Although the return of Mary, Queen of Scots the following year placed a Catholic monarch on the Scottish throne, reputedly Knox was always able to retain the upper hand in his famous disputes with her.

For all his considerable influence, Knox was not responsible for many of the features which have created the popular image of Scottish Presbyterianism – and of Knox himself – as austere and joyless. A man of refined cultural tastes, he did not encourage the iconoclasm that destroyed so many of Scotland's churches and works of art: indeed, much of this was carried out by English hands. Nor did he promote unbending Sabbatarianism, an obsessive work ethic or even the inflexible view of the doctrine of predestination favoured by his far more fanatical successors. Ironically, though, by fostering an irrevocable rift in the "Auld Alliance" with France, he did more than anyone else to ensure that Scotland's future was to be linked with that of England.

⑰

o some vicious grotesques with accurate depictions of several castles, including Edinburgh. In the far corner a small exhibition explains the history of the building and courts, but it's more fun simply to watch the everyday business, with solicitors and bewigged advocates in hushed conferrals. Most of the court rooms have public galleries, which you can sit in if you're interested – ask one of the attendants in the lobby to point you in the right direction.

Upper High Street

The first main building on the northern side of the **High Street** after the intersection of George IV Bridge and Bank Street is the High Court of Justiciary, Scotland's highest criminal court, outside which is a statue of David Hume, the philosopher and one of Edinburgh's greatest sons, who looks decidedly wan and chilly dressed in nothing but a Roman toga. A little further on, opposite the Mercat Cross, the U-shaped **City Chambers** were designed by John Adam, brother of Robert, as the Royal Exchange. Local traders never warmed to the exchange, however, so the town council established its headquarters there instead. Beneath the City Chambers lies **Mary King's Close**, one of Edinburgh's most unusual attractions. When work on the chambers began in 1753, the tops of the existing houses on the site were lopped off as the new building was constructed on top of them. This process left parts of the houses, together with the old streets, or closes, which ran alongside them, intact but entirely enclosed among the basement and cellars of the City Chambers. You can visit this rather spooky subterranean "lost city" on **tours** led by costumed actors (daily April–Oct 10am–9pm, Nov–March 10am–4pm; £7), who lead you round rooms lived in by rich merchants as well as those of whole families afflicted by the plague and even an urban cow byre. The tour ends with a stroll up the remarkably well-preserved Mary King's Close itself.

Across the road you'll find the **Tron Kirk**, a popular focal point for hardy Hogmanay revellers to count down the seconds to the New Year. The church was built in the 1630s and remained in use as a church until 1952. Today the building houses the **Old Town Information Centre** (Easter–May Mon & Thurs–Sun 10am–1pm & 2–5pm; June–Sept daily 10am–7pm), where you can peruse information boards on the buildings of the Old Town and look down from raised walkways on some excavations of further examples of Edinburgh's "lost city".

Lower High Street

Beyond the intersection of North Bridge and South Bridge, **Trinity Apse** in Chalmers Close is a poignant reminder of the fifteenth-century Holy Trinity Collegiate Church, formerly one of Edinburgh's most outstanding buildings. It's now home to a **Brass Rubbing Centre** (Mon–Sat 10am–5pm, Sun noon–5pm during the Festival only; last rubbing sold 1hr before closing; free), where you can rub your own impressions from Pictish crosses and medieval church brasses from around £1.50 upwards.

On the other side of High Street, the noisy **Museum of Childhood** (Mon–Sat 10am–5pm, also Sun noon–5pm July & Aug; free) was, oddly enough, founded by an eccentric local councillor who heartily disliked children. Although he claimed that the museum was a serious social archive for adults – and dedicated it to King Herod – it has always attracted swarms of kids, who delight in the dolls' houses, teddy bears, train sets, marionettes and other paraphernalia.

Almost directly opposite is what's thought to be the city's oldest surviving dwelling, the early sixteenth-century **Moubray House** (closed to the public). The uses of the four-storey house have included tavern, bookshop and even towards the end of the nineteenth century, temperance hotel. Next door lie the picturesque **John Knox's House** (closed for refurbishment until 2005).

built some thirty years later. With its outside stairway, biblical motto, and sundial adorned with a statue of Moses, it gives a good impression of how the Royal Mile must have once looked.

Canongate

For over seven hundred years, the district through which Canongate runs was a burgh in its own right, officially separate from the capital, which was entered through the Netherbow Port. A notorious slum area even into the 1960s, it has been the subject of some of the most ambitious **restoration** programmes in the Old Town, though the lack of harmony between the buildings renovated in different decades can be seen fairly clearly. For such a central district, it's interesting to note that most of the buildings here are residential, and by no means are they all bijou apartments. The development of the Canongate is ongoing, particularly at its lower end around the site of the new Parliament building. This section of the Royal Mile features an eclectic range of shops, from a gallery of historic maps and sea charts to genuine bagpipe-makers.

Near the top of Canongate, a good example of the restoration work can be seen at **Chessel's Court**, a mid-eighteenth-century development with fanciful Rococo chimneys. Over the road the **Morocco Land** is a reasonably faithful reproduction of an old tenement, incorporating the original bust of a Moor from which its name derives.

Dominated by a turreted steeple and an odd external box clock, the late sixteenth-century **Canongate Tolbooth**, a little further down the north side of the street, has served both as the headquarters of the burgh administration and as a prison, and now houses **The People's Story** (Mon–Sat 10am–5pm, also Sun 2–5pm during the Festival; free), a lively museum devoted to the everyday life and work of Edinburgh people down the centuries, with sounds and tableaux on various aspects of city living – including a typical Edinburgh pub. Next door, **Canongate Kirk** was built in the 1680s to house the congregation expelled from Holyrood Abbey when the latter was commandeered by James VII (James II in England) to serve as the chapel for the Order of the Thistle. Its churchyard, one of the city's most exclusive cemeteries, commands a superb view across to Calton Hill. Among those buried here are Adam Smith, Mrs Agnes McLehose (better known as Robert Burns' "Clarinda") and Robert Fergusson, regarded by some as Edinburgh's greatest poet, despite his death at the age of 24; his headstone was donated by Burns, a fervent admirer, who also wrote the inscription.

Opposite the church, the **Museum of Edinburgh** in Huntly House (Mon–Sat 10am–5pm; also Sun 2–5pm during the Festival; free) includes a quirky array of old shop signs, some dating back to the eighteenth century, as well as displays on indigenous industries such as glass, silver, pottery and clock-making, and on the dubious military career of Earl Haig. Also on view is the original version of the National Covenant of 1638; modern science has failed to resolve whether or not some of the signatories signed with their own blood, as tradition has it.

Among the intriguing series of closes and entries on this stretch of Canongate, **Dunbar's Close**, on the north side of the street, has a beautiful seventeenth-century walled garden tucked in behind the tenements. Opposite this is the entry to Crichton's Close, through which you'll find the **Scottish Poetry Library** (Mon–Fri 11am–6pm, Sat noon–4pm; free), a small island of modern architectural eloquence amid a sea of construction work and large-scale developments. Visitors are free to read the books, periodicals and leaflets,

△ Canongate Tolboo

or listen to recordings of poetry in English, Scots and Gaelic. Readings and events are organized through the year.

Holyrood

At the foot of Canongate lies **Holyrood**, for centuries known as Edinburgh's royal quarter. The **legend** of its foundation in 1128 is that King David I, son of Malcolm Canmore and St Margaret, went out hunting one day and was suddenly confronted by a stag who threw him from his horse and seemed ready to gore him. In desperation, the king tried to protect himself by grasping its antlers, but instead found himself holding a crucifix, whereupon the animal ran off. In a dream that night, he heard a voice commanding him to "make a house for Canons devoted to the Cross"; he duly obeyed, naming the abbey Holyrood (rood being an alternative name for a cross). A more prosaic explanation is that David, the most pious of all Scotland's monarchs, simply acquired a relic of the True Cross and decided to build a suitable home for it.

Holyrood soon became a favoured **royal residence**, its situation in a secluded valley making it far more agreeable than the draughty castle. At first, monarchs lodged in the monastic guest house, to which a wing for the exclusive use of the court was added during the reign of James II. This was transformed into a full-blown palace for James IV, which in turn was replaced by a much larger building for Charles II, although he never actually lived there. Indeed, it was something of a white elephant until Queen Victoria started making regular trips to her northern kingdom, a custom that has been maintained by her successors.

The Palace of Holyroodhouse

In its present form, the **Palace of Holyroodhouse** (April–Oct daily 9.30am–6pm; Nov–March daily 9.30am–4.30pm; £7.50) is largely a seventeenth-century creation, planned for Charles II. However, the tower house of the old palace was skilfully incorporated to form the northwestern block, with a virtual mirror image of it erected as a counterbalance at the other end. Inside, the **State Apartments**, as Charles II's palace is known, are decked out with oak panelling, tapestries, portraits and decorative paintings, all overshadowed by the magnificent white stucco **ceilings**, especially in the Morning Drawing Room. The most eye-catching chamber, however, is the **Great Gallery**, which takes up the entire first floor of the northern wing. During the 1745 sojourn of the Young Pretender this was the setting for a banquet, described in detail in Scott's novel *Waverley*, and it is still used for big ceremonial occasions. Along the walls are 89 portraits commissioned from the seventeenth-century Dutch artist Jacob de Wit to illustrate the royal lineage of Scotland from its mythical origins in the fourth century BC; the result is unintentionally hilarious, as it is clear that the artist's imagination was taxed to bursting point by the need to

Admissions to Holyroodhouse

Guided tours of Holyroodhouse take place only from November to March; at other times of the year, visitors are free to move at their own pace. It is worth remembering that Holyroodhouse is still a working palace, so the buildings are closed to the public for long periods during state functions; you won't be able to visit for a fortnight in the middle of May, and during the annual royal visit which usually takes place in the last two weeks of June and the first in July.

paint so many different facial types without having an inkling as to what the subjects actually looked like.

The oldest parts of the palace, the **Historical Apartments**, are mainly of note for their associations with Mary, Queen of Scots and in particular for the brutal murder, organized by her husband, Lord Darnley, of her private secretary, David Rizzio, who was stabbed 56 times and dragged from the small closet, through the Queen's Bedchamber, and into the Outer Chamber. Until a few years ago, visitors were shown apparently indelible bloodstains on the floor of the latter, but these are now admitted to be fakes, and have been covered up. A display cabinet in the same room shows some pieces of **needlework** woven by the deposed queen while in English captivity; another case has an outstanding **miniature portrait** of her by the French court painter, François Clouet.

Holyrood Abbey

In the grounds of the Palace are the wonderfully evocative ruins of **Holyrood Abbey**. Of King David's original Norman church, the only surviving fragment is a doorway in the far southeastern corner. Most of the remainder dates from a late twelfth- and early thirteenth-century rebuilding in the Early Gothic style.

The surviving parts of the **west front**, including one of the twin towers and the elaborately carved entrance portal, show how resplendent the abbey must once have been. Unfortunately, its sacking by the English in 1547, followed by the demolition of the transept and chancel during the Reformation, all but destroyed the building.

The Queen's Gallery

Among the buildings surrounding the palace is the **Queen's Gallery** (April–Oct 9.30am–6pm, Nov–March 9.30am–4.30pm; £4 or £10 joint ticket with Holyroodhouse), entered from Horse Wynd, opposite the Scottish Parliament building. The gallery displays changing exhibitions from the Royal Collection, a vast array of art treasures held by the Queen on behalf of the British nation. Despite this, not much of it is available for public view other than at limited openings of Buckingham Palace and Windsor Castle, so the exhibitions here tend to draw quite a lot of interest.

The Scottish Parliament

Opposite Holyroodhouse at the foot of the Royal Mile stands the massive site of the new **Scottish Parliament**, by far the largest and most controversial public building to be erected in Scotland since World War II. The site, a disused brewery at the foot of the Royal Mile was identified as the location for the new building in the late 1990s, and a competition to design the building was won by Catalan architect **Enric Miralles**, in association with Edinburgh-based architects RMJM. Their concept centres on a series of petal-shaped buildings which have been compared (both favourably and unfavourably) to upturned boats. Miralles died in 2000, causing a few ripples of uncertainty as to whether the famously whimsical designer had in fact set down his final vision. The structure will cost something in the region of £400 million, and is due to be ready by late 2004, until which time the parliament is sitting in the Church of Scotland Assembly Hall on the Mound (see p.925).

While the building is being completed, a temporary **visitor centre** (daily 10am–4pm; free; Ⓦ www.scottish.parliament.uk) has been established in the Tun building on Holyrood Road, where you can view plans, models and computer images of the proposed structure.

Our Dynamic Earth

The New Parliament Building is by no means the only newcomer to this historic area. On the Holyrood Road, beneath a pincushion of white metal struts that make it look like a miniature version of London's Millennium Dome, **Our Dynamic Earth** (April–Oct daily 10am–6pm; Nov–March Wed–Sat 10am–5pm; £8.95), is a high-tech attraction about the natural world aimed mainly at families. Various galleries describe the formation of the earth and continents and the history of life on earth, from primordial swamps to life-size models of some of the odd creatures that once inhabited the earth. The polar regions – complete with a real iceberg – and tropical jungles are imaginatively re-created, with interactive computer screens and special effects at every turn.

Holyrood Park

Holyrood Park – or Queen's Park – a natural wilderness in the very heart of the modern city, is unquestionably one of Edinburgh's main assets, as locals (though relatively few tourists) readily appreciate. Packed into an area no more than five miles in diameter is an amazing variety of landscapes – hills, crags, moorland, marshes, glens, lochs and fields – representing something of a microcosm of Scotland's scenery. The park is a great place for outdoor activities, with toddlers, cyclists and rock climbers all being catered for. A single tarred road, the **Queen's Drive**, circles the park, enabling many of its features to be seen by car, though you really need to stroll around to appreciate it fully. Two of the most rewarding walks begin opposite the southern gates of the Palace: one, a pathway nicknamed the Radical Road, traverses the ridge immediately below the **Salisbury Crags**, one of the main features of the Edinburgh skyline, while you can also walk along the top of the basalt crags, from where there are excellent views of the Palace of Holyroodhouse and Holyrood Abbey.

From the Palace gates, the best way to follow Queen's Drive is in a clockwise direction. Soon you arrive at **St Margaret's Loch**, a nineteenth-century man-made pond, above which stand the scanty ruins of **St Anthony's Chapel**, another fine vantage point. From here, the road's loop is one-way only for vehicular traffic, ascending to **Dunsapie Loch**, again an artificial stretch of water, which makes an excellent foil to the crag behind.

This is the usual starting point for the ascent of **Arthur's Seat**, a majestic extinct volcano rising 823ft above sea level. The Seat is Edinburgh's single most prominent landmark, resembling a huge crouched lion when seen from the west. The climb from Dunsapie, up a grassy slope, followed by a rocky path near the summit, is considerably less arduous than it looks, a fairly straightforward twenty-minute stomp, though there are several other, somewhat longer and more taxing ways up from other points in the park. The views from the top are all you'd expect, covering the entire city and much of the Firth of Forth; on a clear day, you can even see the southernmost mountains of the Highlands.

From Dunsapie Loch, Queen's Drive continues round beneath the summit to meet itself again at a roundabout near the southern point of the Salisbury Crags. At a second roundabout the second exit leads out of the park; the first exit takes you beneath **Samson's Ribs**, a group of basalt pillars strikingly reminiscent of the Hebridean island of Staffa (see p.1106), and onto **Duddingston Loch**, the only natural stretch of water in the park, now a bird sanctuary. Perched above it, just outside the park boundary, **Duddingston Kirk** dates back in part to the twelfth century and is the focus of one of the most unspoilt old villages within modern Edinburgh. In the village, the *Sheep Heid Inn* is a great spot to pull in for a drink or a bar meal, and you can also try your hand at the traditional skittle alley.

Cowgate and the Grassmarket

At the bottom of the valley immediately south of the Royal Mile, and following a roughly parallel course from the Lawnmarket to St Mary's Street, is the **Cowgate**. One of Edinburgh's oldest surviving streets, it was also formerly one of the city's most prestigious addresses. However, the construction of the great **viaducts** of George IV Bridge and South Bridge entombed it below street level, condemning it to decay and neglect. In the last decade or so the Cowgate has experienced something of a revival, with various nightclubs and Festival venues establishing themselves, though few tourists venture here and the contrast with the neighbouring Royal Mile remains stark.

At its western end, Cowgate opens out into the **Grassmarket**, which has played an important role in the murkier aspects of Edinburgh's turbulent history. The public gallows were located here, and it was the scene of numerous riots and other disturbances down the centuries. It was here, in 1736, that Captain Porteous was lynched after he had ordered shots to be fired at the crowd watching a public execution. The notorious duo William Burke and William Hare had their lair in a now-vanished close just off the western end of the Grassmarket, luring to it victims whom they murdered with the intention of selling their bodies to the eminent physician Robert Knox. Eventually, Hare betrayed his partner, who was duly executed in 1829, and Knox's career was finished off as a result.

At the northeastern corner of the Grassmarket are five old tenements of the old **West Bow**, which formerly zigzagged up to the Royal Mile. The rest of this was replaced in the 1840s by curving **Victoria Street**, an unusual two-tier thoroughfare, with arcaded shops below, and a pedestrian terrace above. This sweeps up to **George IV Bridge** and the **National Library of Scotland** which holds a rich collection of illuminated manuscripts, early printed books, historical documents, and the letters and papers of prominent Scottish literary figures, displayed in regularly changing thematic exhibitions (usually Mon–Sat 10am–5pm, Sun 2–5pm; free).

Greyfriars and around

The **statue of Greyfriars Bobby** at the southwestern corner of **George IV Bridge** must rank as Edinburgh's most sentimental tourist attraction. Bobby was a Skye terrier acquired as a working dog by a police constable named John Gray. When John Gray died in 1858, Bobby began a vigil on his grave which he maintained until he died fourteen years later. His statue, originally a fountain, was modelled from life, and erected soon after his death; his story has gained international renown, thanks to a spate of cloying books and tearjerking movies.

The grave Bobby mourned over is in the **Greyfriars Kirkyard**, which among its clutter of grandiose seventeenth- and eighteenth-century funerary monuments boasts the striking mausoleum of the Adam family of architects. Greyfriars is particularly associated with the long struggle to establish Presbyterianism in Scotland: in 1638, it was the setting for the signing of the National Covenant, while in 1679 some 1200 Covenanters were imprisoned in the enclosure at the southwestern end of the yard. Set against the northern wall is the Martyrs' Monument, a defiantly worded memorial commemorating all those who died in pursuit of the eventual victory.

The graveyard rather overshadows **Greyfriars Kirk** itself, completed in 1620 as the first new church in Edinburgh since the Reformation. It's a real oddball in both layout and design, having a nave and aisles but no chancel, and adopting the anachronistic architectural language of the friary that preceded it, complete with medieval-looking windows, arches and buttresses.

At the western end of Greyfriars Kirkyard is one of the most significant surviving portions of the **Flodden Wall**, the city fortifications erected in the wake of Scotland's disastrous military defeat of 1513. When open, the gateway beyond offers a short-cut to **George Heriot's Hospital**, otherwise approached from Lauriston Place to the south. Founded as a home for poor boys by "Jinglin Geordie" Heriot, James VI's goldsmith, it is now one of Edinburgh's most prestigious fee-paying schools; although you can't go inside, you can wander round the quadrangle, whose array of towers, turrets, chimneys, carved doorways and traceried windows is one of the finest achievements of the Scottish Renaissance.

The Museum of Scotland

Immediately opposite Greyfriars Bobby, on the south side of Chambers Street, stands the striking honey-coloured sandstone **Museum of Scotland** (Mon–Sat 10am–5pm, Tues 10am–8pm, Sun noon–5pm; free; Ⓦwww .nms.ac.uk). Opened in 1998 to deserved acclaim, both for its elegant design and for its respectful but imaginative treatment of the nation's treasures, this is undoubtedly Scotland's premier museum. The fresh, open atmosphere of the building is combined with terrific features: specially commissioned art works; the **Discovery Centre**, specifically aimed at 5–14 year olds; the **exhibIT** computer bank with databases of the museum's collections; and the **Tower** restaurant, a sleek, stylish place with fabulous views which is also open in the evenings (for a review, see p.949).

The main entrance to the museum is at the base of the tower (although it's also possible to enter through the neighbouring Royal Museum of Scotland; see p.938). Make your way to the information desk in **Hawthornden Court**, the central atrium of the museum and a useful orientation point; on this level you'll also find the museum shop and access to the Royal Museum café. The glossy **brochure** on sale (£2.50) is more a photographic souvenir than a guidebook, but free guided tours on different themes take place through the day, and audio headsets (free) give detailed information on artefacts and displays.

Level 0

To get to the first section, "**Beginnings**", take the lift or stairs from Hawthornden Court down to Level 0. Here, Scotland's pre-human history is presented with audiovisual displays, artistic re-creations and a selection of rocks and fossils, including some Lewisian gneiss, the oldest rock in Europe, and "Lizzie" (*Westlothiana lizziae*), the oldest known fossil reptile in the world.

The second section, "**Early People**", also on Level 0, covers the period from the arrival of the first people to the end of the first millennium AD. This, in many ways, is the most engrossing section of the entire museum, an eloquent testament to the remarkable craftsmanship, artistry and practicality of Scotland's early people. The best way to approach this section is from the doors of the main lift, where you are confronted by eight giant bronze figures in the distinctive postindustrial style of Edinburgh-born sculptor **Sir Eduardo Paolozzi**. The innovative use of contemporary art is continued with installations by the environmental artist **Andy Goldsworthy**, who shapes natural materials into sinuously beautiful geometrical patterns. Among the artefacts on display, highlights are the **Trappain treasure** hoard, 20kg of silver plates, cutlery and goblets found buried in East Lothian, and the **Cramond Lioness**, a sculpture from a Roman tombstone found recently in the Firth of Forth.

Levels 1–3

The "**Kingdom of the Scots**" on levels 1 and 2 covers the period between Scotland's development as a single independent nation and the union with England in 1707. Many famous Scots are represented here, including Robert the Bruce, Mary, Queen of Scots and her son James VI, under whom the crowns of Scotland and England became united in 1603. Star exhibits include the **Monymusk reliquary**, an intricately decorated box said to have carried the remains of St Columba; the **Lewis chessmen**, exquisitely idiosyncratic twelfth-century pieces carved from walrus ivory; and the "**Maiden**", an early form of the guillotine.

Level 3 shows exhibits under the theme "**Scotland Transformed**", covering the century or so following the Union of Parliaments in 1707. This was the period which saw the last of the Highland uprisings, under Bonnie Prince Charlie (whose silver travelling canteen is on display), yet also witnessed the expansion of trade links with the Americas and developments in industries such as weaving and iron and steel production. Dominating the floor is a reconstructed steam-driven **Newcomen engine**, which was still being used to pump water from a coal mine in Ayrshire in 1901. Alongside it, in contrast, is part of a thatched, cruck-frame house of the 1720s of a type in which many Scots still lived during this time.

Levels 4, 5 and 6

Following the early innovations of steam and mechanical engineering, Scotland went on to pioneer many aspects of heavy engineering, with ship and locomotive production to the fore. Largest of the exhibits in "**Industry and Empire**" on Level 4 is the steam locomotive *Ellesmere*. As well as industrial progress, other fields are covered too, including domestic life, leisure activities and the influence of Scots around the world, both as a result of emigration, and through such luminaries as James Watt, Charles Rennie Mackintosh and Robert Louis Stevenson.

For the **Twentieth Century Gallery** on Level 6, a range of Scots, from schoolchildren to celebrities, were asked to pick a single object to represent the twentieth century. Choices are intriguing, controversial and unexpected, from computers to football strips, cans of Irn Bru to a black Saab convertible. The **roof garden**, accessed by a lift, offers sweeping views to the Firth of Forth, the Pentland hills, and across to the castle and Royal Mile skyline.

The Royal Museum

Interlinked with the National Museum, though also with its own entrance, is the Royal Museum (same hours), a dignified Venetian-style palace with a cast-iron interior containing an extraordinarily eclectic range of exhibits, from exotic stuffed animals to colonial loot. The sculpture in the lofty entrance hall ranges via Classical Greece, Rome and Nubia to Buddhas from Japan and Burma and a totem pole from British Columbia. Also here is the Millennium Clock, a ten-metre tall, Heath-Robinson-style contraption which clicks and whirls into motion every hour and half-hour. On the ground floor are collections of stuffed animals and birds, including the skeleton of a blue whale, suspended from the ceiling. Upstairs there's a fine array of artefacts from Egyptian mummies to stunning French silverware made during the reign of Louis XIV.

The University of Edinburgh

Immediately alongside the Royal Museum is the earliest surviving part of the **University of Edinburgh**, variously referred to as Old College or Old Quad although nowadays it houses only a few University departments; the main campus colonizes the streets and squares to the south. Founded in 1582 by James VI (later James I of England), the university is now the largest in Scotland, with over 13,000 students.

The Old College was designed by Robert Adam, but was built after his death in a considerably modified form by William Playfair (1789–1857), one of Edinburgh's greatest architects. The small **Talbot Rice Art Gallery** (Tues–Sat 10am–5pm, with extended opening during the Festival; free), housed in the southwest corner of the Old College, displays in rather lacklustre fashion some of the University's large art and bronze collection. Touring and temporary avant-garde exhibitions are mounted here on a regular basis – the show held during the Festival is normally of a high standard.

The New Town

The **NEW TOWN**, itself well over two hundred years old, stands in total contrast to the Old Town: the layout is symmetrical, the streets are broad and straight, and most of the buildings are Neoclassical. Originally intended to be residential, the entire area, right down to the names of its streets, is something of a celebration of the Union, which was then generally regarded as a proud development in Scotland's history. Today the New Town is the bustling hub of the city's professional, commercial and business life, dominated by shops, banks and offices.

The existence of the New Town is chiefly due to the vision of **George Drummond**, who made schemes for the expansion of the city soon after becoming Lord Provost in 1725. Work began on the draining of the Nor' Loch below the castle in 1759, a job that was to last some sixty years. The North Bridge, linking the Old Town with the port of Leith, was built between 1763 and 1772 and, in 1766, following a public competition, a plan for the New Town by 22-year-old architect **James Craig** was chosen. Its gridiron pattern was perfectly matched to the site: central George Street, flanked by showpiece squares, was laid out along the main ridge, with parallel Princes Street and Queen Street on either side below, and two smaller streets, Thistle Street and Rose Street in between the three major thoroughfares providing coach houses, artisans' dwellings and shops. Princes and Queen streets were built up on one side only, so as not to block the spectacular views of the Old Town and Fife.

In many ways, the layout of the New Town is its own most remarkable sight, an extraordinary grouping of squares, circuses, terraces, crescents and parks with a few set pieces such as **Register House**, the north frontage of **Charlotte Square** and the assemblage of curiosities on and around **Calton Hill**. However, it also contains assorted Victorian additions, notably the **Scott Monument**, as well as two of the city's most important public collections – the **National Gallery of Scotland** and, further afield, the **Scottish National Gallery of Modern Art**.

Princes Street

Although only allocated a subsidiary role in the original plan of the New Town, Princes Street had developed into Edinburgh's principal thoroughfare by the middle of the nineteenth century, a role it has retained ever since. Its unobstructed views across to the castle and the Old Town are undeniably magnificent. Indeed, without the views, Princes Street would lose much of its appeal; its

17

northern side, dominated by ugly department stores, is almost always crowded with shoppers, and few of the original eighteenth-century buildings remain.

It was the coming of the railway – which follows a parallel course to the south – that ensured Princes Street's rise to prominence. The tracks are well concealed at the far end of the sunken **gardens** that replaced the Nor' Loch, which provide ample space to relax or picnic during the summer. Thomas de Quincey (1785–1859), author of the classic account of drug addiction, *Confessions of an English Opium Eater* (published in 1821), spent the last thirty years of his life in Edinburgh and is buried in the graveyard of St Cuthbert's Church, beneath the castle at the western end of the gardens.

The East End

Register House (Mon–Fri 9am–4.45pm; free), Princes Street's most distinguished building, is at its extreme northeastern corner, framing the perspective down North Bridge, and providing a good visual link between the Old and New Towns. Unfortunately, the majesty of the setting is marred by the **St James Centre** to the rear, a covered shopping arcade now regarded as the city's worst ever planning blunder. Register House was designed in the 1770s by Robert Adam to hold Scotland's historic records, a function it has maintained ever since. Opposite is one of the few buildings on the south side of Princes Street, the **Balmoral Hotel**, formerly known as the *North British*. Among the most luxurious hotels in the city, it has always been associated with the railway, and the timepiece on its bulky clock tower is always kept two minutes fast in order to encourage passengers to hurry to catch their trains.

The Scott Monument and the Royal Scottish Academy

Facing the Victorian shopping emporium Jenners, and set within East Princes Street Gardens, the 200ft-high **Scott Monument** (April–Sept Mon–Sat 9am–6pm, Sun 10am–6pm; Oct–March Mon–Sat 9am–3pm, Sun 10am–3pm; £2.50) was erected in memory of the writer by public subscription within a few years of his death. The largest monument in the world to a man of letters, the elaborate Gothic spire was created by George Meikle Kemp, a carpenter and joiner whose only building this is; underneath the archway is a **statue** of Scott with his deerhound Maida, carved from a thirty-ton block of Carrara marble. Visitors are able to use a tightly winding internal spiral staircase to climb up to a series of platforms which offer some inspiring – if heady – vistas of the city below and hills and firths beyond.

The Princes Street Gardens are bisected by the **Mound**, which provides one of only two direct road links between the Old and New Towns (the other is the Northbridge). At the foot of the Mound on the Princes Street level are two grand sandstone buildings; nearest to Princes Street, Playfair's **Royal Scottish Academy** (opening times and prices vary depending on exhibition) is the more elaborate of the two, a Grecian-style Doric temple topped with a statue of Queen Victoria and four sphinxes. It's used as a partner to the National Gallery next door to show touring and themed exhibitions during the year, a link which is soon to be bolstered by the £26-million Playfair Project, due for completion in 2004, which will provide connecting corridors, exhibition space and a café and restaurant in the space beneath the two galleries.

The National Gallery of Scotland

To the rear of the Royal Scottish Academy, the less elaborate **National Gallery of Scotland** (daily 10am–5pm, with extended opening to 7pm on

Thurs; free, entrance charge for some temporary exhibitions; ⓦwww
.nationalgalleries.org/) is another of Playfair's Athenian constructions, built in
the 1840s and now housing Scotland's premier collection of pre-twentieth-
century European art. Though by no means as vast as national collections
found elsewhere in Europe, the National Gallery of Scotland benefits not just
from a clutch of exquisite Old Masters and Impressionist works, but also from
the fact that it is a manageable gallery enlivened by imaginative displays and a
pleasantly unrushed atmosphere. Elsewhere in the city, the Scottish National
Portrait Gallery (see p.944), the Scottish National Gallery of Modern Art
(p.946) and its neighbour the Dean Gallery (p.946), display other parts of the
National Galleries' collection (all use the same website as the National
Gallery). A free bus service (Mon–Sat 11am–5pm, Sun 12–5pm) connects all
four buildings.

The innovative and often controversial influence of the National Galleries'
flamboyant director, Timothy Clifford, is immediately apparent on the ground
floor, where the rooms have been restored to their 1840s appearance, with the
pictures hung closely together on claret-coloured walls, often on two levels,
and intermingled with sculptures and objets d'art to produce a deliberately
cluttered effect.

Though individual works are frequently rearranged, the layout is broadly
chronological, starting in the upper rooms above the entrance, and continuing
clockwise around the ground floor. The upper part of the rear extension is
devoted to smaller panels of the eighteenth and nineteenth centuries, while the
basement contains the majority of the Scottish collection. The gallery has a
programme of temporary exhibitions, which may mean that some of the paintings described below may not be on display.

Early Netherlandish and German works

Among the gallery's most valuable treasures are the *Trinity Panels*, the remaining parts of the only surviving pre-Reformation altarpiece made for a Scottish
church. Painted by **Hugo van der Goes** in the mid-fifteenth century, they
were commissioned for the Holy Trinity Collegiate Church (which was
demolished to make way for Edinburgh's Waverley Station) by its provost
Edward Bonkil, who appears in the company of organ-playing angels in the
finest and best preserved of the four panels. On the reverse sides are portraits
of James III, his son (the future James IV) and Queen Margaret of Denmark.
Their feebly characterized heads, which stand in jarring contrast to the
superlative figures of the patron saints accompanying them, were modelled
from life by an unknown local painter after the altar had been shipped to
Edinburgh. The panels are turned every half-hour.

Of the later Netherlandish works, **Gerard David** is represented by the
touchingly anecdotal *Three Legends of St Nicholas*, while the *Portrait of a Man* by
Quentin Massys is an excellent early example of northern European assimi-
lation of the forms and techniques of the Italian Renaissance.

Italian Renaissance works

The Italian section includes a wonderful array of **Renaissance** masterpieces,
one of the highlights of which is a superb painting by Botticelli, *The Virgin
Adoring the Sleeping Christ Child*, which was carefully restored and now positively glows with colour and light. Equally graceful are three works by
Raphael, particularly *The Bridgewater Madonna* and the tondo *The Holy Family
with a Palm Tree*, the latter another example of the striking luminosity restoration can reveal.

Of the four mythological scenes by **Titian**, the sensuous *Three Ages of Man*, an allegory of childhood, adulthood and old age, is one of the most accomplished compositions of his early period. The companion pair *Diana and Acteon* and *Diana and Calisto*, painted for Philip II of Spain, show the almost impressionistic freedom of his late style. **Bassano**'s truly regal *Adoration of the Kings*, a dramatic altarpiece *The Deposition of Christ* by **Tintoretto**, and several works by **Veronese** complete a fine Venetian collection.

Seventeenth-century works

Among the seventeenth-century works, **El Greco**'s *A Fable*, painted during his early years in Italy, takes a mysterious subject whose exact meaning is unclear. Indigenous Spanish art is represented by **Velázquez**'s *An Old Woman Cooking Eggs*, an astonishingly assured work for a lad of nineteen, and by **Zurbaran**'s *The Immaculate Conception*, part of his ambitious decorative scheme of the Carthusian monastery in Jerez.

The series of *The Seven Sacraments* by **Poussin** are displayed in their own room, whose floor and central octagonal seat repeat some of the motifs in the paintings. Based on the artist's extensive research into biblical times, the series marks the first attempt to portray scenes from the life of Jesus and the early Christians in an authentic manner and the result is profoundly touching.

Rubens' *The Feast of Herod* is an archetypal example of his grand manner, in which the gory subject matter is overshadowed by the lively depiction of the delights of the table. The trio of large upright canvases by **Van Dyck** date from his early Genoese period; of these, *The Lomellini Family* shows his mastery in creating a definitive dynastic image. Among the four canvases by **Rembrandt** is a poignant *Self-Portrait Aged 51*, and the ripely suggestive *Woman in Bed*, which probably represents the biblical figure of Sarah on her wedding night, waiting for her husband Tobias to put the devil to flight. *Christ in the House of Martha and Mary* is the largest and probably the earliest of the thirty or so surviving paintings by **Vermeer**; as the only one with a religious subject, it inspired a notorious series of forgeries by Han van Meegeren.

Eighteenth and nineteenth-century works

Of the large-scale eighteenth-century works, **Tiepolo**'s *The Finding of Moses*, a gloriously bravura fantasy, stands out. By way of contrast, the gems of the French section are the smaller panels, in particular **Watteau**'s *Fêtes Vénitiennes*, an effervescent Rococo idyll, and **Chardin**'s *Vase of Flowers*, a copybook example of still-life painting. There's also a superb group of early Impressionist works such as Jean Bastien Lepage's beautifully innocent *Pas Meche* and Camille Pissarro's *Kitchen Garden L'Hermitage*. Impressionist masters are also well represented; there's a collection of sketches, painting and bronzes by **Degas**, including the influential *Portrait of Diego Marteli*, as well as Monet's *Haystacks (Snow)* and Renoir's *Woman Nursing Child*. Representing the post-Impressionists are three outstanding examples of **Gauguin**'s work, including *Vision After the Sermon*, set in Brittany; Van Gogh's *Olive Trees*; and **Cézanne**'s *The Big Trees* – a clear forerunner of modern abstraction.

The gallery has relatively few English paintings, but those it does have are impressive. **Hogarth**'s *Sarah Malcolm*, painted in Newgate Prison the day the murderess was executed, once belonged to Horace Walpole. **Gainsborough**'s *The Honourable Mrs Graham* is one of his most memorable society portraits, while **Constable** himself described *Dedham Vale* as being "perhaps my best". The gallery owns a wonderful array of watercolours by **Turner**, faithfully displayed each January when damaging sunlight is at its weakest, though visitors at other times of year can enjoy two of his fine Roman views displayed in one of the darker galleries.

Scottish works

On the face of it, the gallery's Scottish collection is something of an anticlimax. There are, however, some important works displayed within a broad European context; **Gavin Hamilton**'s *Achilles Mourning the Death of Patroclus*, for example, painted in Rome, is an unquestionably arresting image. **Allan Ramsay**, who became court painter to George III, is represented by his *Portrait of a Lady*. The swaggering masculinity of *Sir John Sinclair* in Highland dress is a fine example of **Sir Henry Raeburn**'s technical mastery. He was equally sure when working on a small scale, as shown in one of the gallery's most popular pictures, *The Rev Robert Walker Skating on Duddingston Loch*.

Other Scottish painters represented include the versatile **Sir David Wilkie**, whose huge historical painting, *Sir David Baird Discovering the Body of Sultan Tippo Saib*, is in marked contrast to the genre scenes displayed in the basement, and **Alexander Nasmyth**, whose tendency to gild the lily can be seen in his *View of Tantallon Castle and the Bass Rock*, where the dramatic scenery is further spiced up by the inclusion of a shipwreck.

George Street and around

The street parallel to Princes Street to the north is **George Street**, rapidly changing its role from a thoroughfare of august financial institutions to a highbrow version of Princes Street, where the big deals are these days done in designer-label shops. George Street was designed to be the centrepiece of the First New Town, joining two grand squares. At its eastern end lies **St Andrew Square**, home to Edinburgh's bus station as well as the city's newest shopping mall with Harvey Nichols and other designer outlets. Beside this on the eastern side stands a handsome eighteenth-century town mansion, designed by Sir William Chambers. Headquarters of the Royal Bank of Scotland since 1825, the palatial mid-nineteenth-century banking hall is a symbol of the success of the New Town.

Heading west along George Street, on the north side of the street, the oval-shaped church of **St Andrew** (now known as St Andrew and St George) is chiefly famous as the scene of the 1843 Disruption led by Thomas Chalmers, which split the Church of Scotland in two.

Charlotte Square

At the western end of George Street, **Charlotte Square** was designed by Robert Adam in 1791, a year before his death. Once the most exclusive quarter of the city, when the New Town began to change to commercial use, the square maintained its prestige by attracting the offices of the city's most august law firms. By the 1980s, however, it was becoming more and more difficult for the expanding companies to fit into the space available, and for a period in the 1990s the square was eerily empty. However, the wheel has turned again and the **north side** of the square is once more the city's premier address, with the official residence of the First Minister of the Scottish Parliament at number 6, also the place where the Scottish cabinet meets.

Restored by the NTS, the lower floors of neighbouring number 7 are open to the public under the name of the **Georgian House** (daily: March & Nov–Dec 11am–3pm; April–Oct 10am–5pm; £5), whose contents give a good idea of what the house must have looked like during the period of the first owner, the head of the clan Lamont. The NTS also occupy the south side of the square with their main **headquarters**; the buildings have been superbly restored over the past few years to something approaching their Georgian grandeur. It's well worth paying a visit through the entrance of number 28 to peer at the sumptuous interior. One floor up, a small **gallery** (Mon–Fri 11am–3pm; free) shows a collection of twentieth-century Scottish art. Downstairs there's a pleasant **café**, authentically decked out with severe Georgian family portraits.

Queen Street

Queen Street, the last of the three main streets of the First New Town, is bordered to the north by gardens, and commands sweeping views across to Fife. Occupied mostly by offices, it's the best preserved of the area's three main streets, although it's principally notable for the striking late nineteenth-century home of the National Portrait Gallery.

The Scottish National Portrait Gallery

At the eastern end of Queen Street is the **Scottish National Portrait Gallery** (daily 10am–5pm, Thurs 7pm; free, entrance charge for some temporary exhibitions; ⓦwww.nationalgalleries.org/). The remarkable building is itself a fascinating period piece, its red sandstone exterior, modelled on the Doge's Palace in Venice, encrusted with statues of famous Scots – a theme taken up in the stunning entrance hall, which has a mosaic-like frieze procession by William Hole of great figures from Scotland's past, with heroic murals by the same artist adorning the balcony above.

Temporary exhibitions are displayed in the galleries on the ground floor; elsewhere on this floor are the gallery shop and **café**, a favourite spot with locals. The **permanent collection** is on the two upper floors. Taken as a whole, the gallery offers an engaging procession through Scottish history, with familiar images of Bonnie Prince Charlie, Mary, Queen of Scots and Robert Burns. Twentieth-century portraits occupy the first floor and include royals, inventors, politicians, tycoons and celebrities. Visitors to the café can enjoy the company of Sean Connery, captured by acclaimed Scottish artist John Bellany.

Calton

Of the various extensions to the New Town, the most intriguing is **Calton**, which branches out from the eastern end of Princes Street and encircles a volcanic hill. For years the centre of a thriving **gay** scene, it is an area of extraordinary showpiece architecture, dating from the time of the Napoleonic Wars or just after, and intended as an ostentatious celebration of the British victory.

Waterloo Place forms a ceremonial way from Princes Street to Calton Hill. On its southern side is the sombre and overgrown **Old Calton Burial Ground**, in which you can see Robert Adam's plain, cylindrical memorial to David Hume. Hard up against the cemetery's eastern wall is the only surviving part of the **Calton Gaol**, once Edinburgh's main prison. Next door is the massive **St Andrew's House**, built in the 1930s to house civil servants.

Further on, set majestically in a confined site below Calton Hill, sits one of Edinburgh's greatest buildings, the Grecian **Old Royal High School**, which for many years was assumed to be where Scotland's new parliament would sit. Alma mater to, among others, Robert Adam, Walter Scott and Alexander Graham Bell, the school was built by Thomas Hamilton, himself an old boy. Across the road, Hamilton also built the **Burns Monument**, a circular

Corinthian temple modelled on the Monument to Lysicrates in Athens, as a memorial to the national bard.

Robert Louis Stevenson reckoned that **Calton Hill** was the best place to view Edinburgh, "since you can see the castle, which you lose from the castle, and Arthur's Seat, which you cannot see from Arthur's Seat". Though the panoramas from ground level are spectacular enough, those from the top of the **Nelson Monument** (April–Sept Mon 1–6pm, Tues–Sat 10am–6pm; Oct–March Mon–Sat 10am–3pm; £2.50), perched near the summit of Calton Hill, are even better. Begun just two years after Nelson's death at Trafalgar, this is one of Edinburgh's oddest buildings, resembling a gigantic spyglass. Each day at 1pm a white ball drops down a mast at the top of the monument – together with the one o'clock gun (see p.922), this was a daily check for the mariners of Leith who needed accurate chronometers to ensure reliable navigation at sea.

Alongside, the **National Monument** was begun in 1822 by Playfair to plans by the English architect Charles Cockerell. Had it been completed, it would have been a reasonably accurate replica of the Parthenon, but funds ran out with only twelve columns built. Various later schemes to finish it similarly foundered, earning it the nickname "Edinburgh's Disgrace". Playfair also built the **City Observatory** for his uncle, the mathematician and astronomer John Playfair. At the opposite end of the complex is the **Old Observatory**, one of the few surviving buildings by James Craig, designer of the New Town.

The Royal Botanic Garden

Just beyond the northern boundaries of the New Town, with entrances on Inverleith Row and Arboretum Place, is the seventy-acre site of the **Royal Botanic Garden** (daily: March & Oct 10am–6pm; April–Sept 10am–7pm; Nov–Feb 10am–4pm; free), particularly renowned for the rhododendrons, which blaze out in a glorious patchwork of colours in April and May. In the heart of the grounds a group of hothouses designated the **Glasshouse Experience** displays orchids, giant Amazonian water lilies, and a 200-year-old West Indian palm tree, the latter being in the elegant 1850s glass-topped Palm House. **Guided tours** of the garden (£3) leave from the West Gate on Arboretum Place at 11am and 2pm from April to September.

Dean Village

Work began on the western end of the New Town in 1822, in a small area of land north of Charlotte Square and west of George Street. Instead of the straight lines of the earlier sections, there were now the gracious curves of Randolph Crescent, Ainslie Place and the magnificent twelve-sided Moray Place. Round the corner from Randolph Crescent, the four-arched **Dean Bridge**, a bravura feat of 1830s engineering by Thomas Telford, carries the main road high above Edinburgh's placid little river, the **Water of Leith**. Down to the left lies **Dean Village**, an old milling community that is one of central Edinburgh's most picturesque yet oddest corners, its atmosphere of decay arrested by the conversion of some of the mills into designer flats. There's now a riverside path which runs almost the entire length of the river; though a little gloomy in parts, some stretches are charming and colourful.

The West End and around

The western extension to the New Town was the last part to be built, deviating from the area's overriding Neoclassicism with a number of Victorian

17

additions, including the city's principal Episcopal church, **St Mary's Cathedral**. With its proximity to the city centre the West End is now mostly used for offices, with a decent clutch of bars and restaurants, though there is some elegant terraced housing towards its outer edges. Here, enjoying some green space and a dignified setting are two compelling collections of contemporary art, the well-established **Scottish National Gallery of Modern Art** and its newer neighbour, the **Dean Gallery**, both of which regularly host worthwhile seasonal and touring exhibitions. Further out, Edinburgh's **Zoo**, a popular family attraction, is located on one of the city's prominent rises, Corstorphine Hill.

The Scottish National Gallery of Modern Art

Set in spacious wooded grounds at the far northwestern fringe of the New Town, about ten minutes' walk from either the cathedral or Dean Village, the **Scottish National Gallery of Modern Art** on Belford Road (daily 10am–5pm, till 7pm Thurs; free, entrance charge for some temporary exhibitions; ⓦ www.nationalgalleries.org/), was established as the first collection in Britain devoted solely to twentieth-century painting and sculpture. A **free bus** runs here – and to the Dean Gallery, see below – on the hour (Mon–Sat 11am–5pm, Sun noon–5pm) from outside the National Gallery on the Mound, stopping at the National Portrait Gallery on the way.

The gallery's grounds serve as a sculpture park, featuring works by Jacob Epstein, Henry Moore, Barbara Hepworth and, most strikingly, Charles Jencks, whose swirling mix of ponds and grassy mounds dominates the area in front of the gallery. Inside, the display space is divided between temporary loan exhibitions and selections from the gallery's own holdings. French painters are particularly well represented, beginning with **early twentieth–century** work such as Bonnard's *Lane at Vernonnet* and Vuillard's jewel-like *Two Seamstresses*. There are a few examples of the **Fauves**, notably Matisse's *The Painting Session* and Derain's dazzlingly brilliant *Still Life*, as well as a fine group of late canvases by Leger, notably *The Constructors*. Among some striking examples of **German Expressionism** are Kirchner's *Japanese Theatre*, Feininger's *Gelmeroda III*, and a wonderfully soulful wooden sculpture of a woman by Barlach entitled *The Terrible Year, 1937*. **Cubism** is represented by Picasso's *Soles* and Braque's *The Candlestick*.

Of works by Americans, Roy Lichtenstein's *In the Car* is a fine example of his **Pop Art** style, while Duane Hanson's fibreglass *Tourists* is typically unflinching. English artists on show include Sickert, Nicholson, Spencer, Freud, Hockney and Hirst but, as you'd expect, slightly more space is allocated to Scottish artists. Of particular note are the **Colourists** – S.J. Peploe, J.D. Fergusson, Francis Cadell and George Leslie Hunter – whose works are attracting fancy prices on the art market. Also worth exploring is the vivid realism of the more recent **Edinburgh School**, whose members include Anne Redpath, Sir Robin Philipson and William Gillies, and the distinctive styles of contemporary Scots such as John Bellany, a portraitist of striking originality, and the poet-artist-gardener Ian Hamilton Finlay.

The Dean Gallery

Opposite the Modern Art Gallery on the other side of Belford Road is the latest addition to the National Galleries of Scotland, the **Dean Gallery** (same hours and website; free), housed in an equally impressive Neoclassical building completed in 1833. The interior of the gallery, built as an orphanage and later an education centre, has been dramatically refurbished specifically to make room for the work of Edinburgh-born sculptor **Sir Eduardo Paolozzi**.

Visitors are given an awesome introduction to Paolozzi's work by the huge *Vulcan*, a half-man, half-machine that squeezes into the Great Hall immediately opposite the main entrance. No less persuasive of Paolozzi's dynamic creative talents are the rooms to the right of the main entrance, where his London studio has been expertly re-created, right down to the clutter of half-finished casts, toys and empty pots of glue.

Also on the ground floor is the **Roland Penrose Gallery**, which houses an impressive collection of **Dada** and **Surrealist** art; Penrose was a close friend and patron of many of the movements' leading figures. **Marcel Duchamp**, **Max Ernst** and **Man Ray** are all represented in the gallery. The rooms upstairs are normally given over to special and touring exhibitions, which usually carry an entrance charge.

The Zoo

A couple of miles west of the galleries, **Edinburgh Zoo** (daily: April–Sept 9am–6pm; Oct & March 9am–5pm; Nov–Feb 9am–4.30pm; £8, family from £24; ⓦwww.edinburghzoo.org.uk) is set on an eighty-acre site on the slopes of Corstorphine Hill (buses from town: #12, #26, #31, #100). Here you can see over 1000 animals, including a number of endangered species such as white rhinos, red pandas, pygmy hippos and poison-arrow frogs. Making the most of the space offered by Corstorphine Hill, the **African Plains Experience** has a walkway leading you out over the animals to viewing platforms. The zoo's chief claim to fame is its crowd of penguins (the largest number in captivity anywhere in the world), a legacy of Leith's whaling trade in the South Atlantic. The **penguin parade**, which takes place daily at 2.15pm from April to September, and on sunny March and October days, has gained something of a cult status.

Eating

⑰

Edinburgh has the best range of **restaurants** and places to eat out in Scotland. The country as a whole is beginning to shake off its culinary reputation for – and addiction to – deep-fried stodge, and the last decade has seen an upsurge in style, sophistication and good taste in the capital's dining scene, with the rise of a clutch of original and stylish restaurants, many identifying their cuisine as **contemporary** or **modern Scottish** and championing top-quality meat, game and fish. Below are some of the best eating options the city has to offer.

Cafés, bistros and diners

Café culture has hit the centre of the city in a big way, with tables spilling onto the pavements in the summer and a range of places not even dreamt of a few years ago. For heartier meals, small **diners** and **bistros** predominate, many adopting a casual French style and offering good-value set menus.

Royal Mile and around

Café Hub Lawnmarket ☎0131/473 2067. Colourful, well-run café in the Edinburgh Festival centre, with light modern meals served right through the day and evening. Teas, coffees, snacks and drinks also served. The large terrace is usefully central on sunny days. Inexpensive.

Elephant House 21 George IV Bridge ☎0131/220 5355. A popular café offering a large selection of coffees, teas, sandwiches, light meals and big cakes. The cavernous back room is great for reading newspapers and eavesdropping on philosophical discussions. Open every day 8am–11pm. Inexpensive.

The Outsider 15–16 George IV Bridge
☎ 0131/226 3131. Style-conscious and much-hyped bistro, permanently filled with beautiful young things. The food is fresh, modern and, surprisingly, not overpriced. Open every day noon–11pm. Moderate.

Plaisir du Chocolat 251–253 Canongate
☎ 0131/556 9524. Classy Parisian tearoom serving delicious, if pricey, lunches, luxurious patisserie treats, an array of gourmet teas and real hot chocolate. Open every day 10am–6pm. Moderate.

Spoon 15 Blackfriars St ☎ 0131/556 6922. Just off the Royal Mile, but a world away from modern café blandness. The approach is simple, the menus are short, the food imaginative and delicious. Good coffee and pastries too. Mon–Sat 8am–6pm. Inexpensive.

New Town and the West End

Glass & Thompson 2 Dundas St ☎ 0131/557 0909. An unusually airy deli with huge bowls of olives and an extensive cheese counter; scattered tables and chairs mean you can linger over a made-to-order sandwich, an irresistible cake and coffee. Closed evenings. Inexpensive.

Hadrian's 2 North Bridge ☎ 0131/557 5000. Although it's strictly part of the upmarket *Balmoral Hotel*, this brasserie isn't too overpriced, and the elegance of the design and atmosphere, along with good-quality Modern British cooking, make it worth seeking out. Moderate.

Howies at Waterloo 29 Waterloo Place
☎ 0131/556 5766. Flagship of the small local Howies chain, with a pleasant dining area on the fringe of Calton Hill and reliably well-priced, comforting modern Scottish food. Moderate.

No. 28 28 Charlotte Square ☎ 0131/243 9339. Refined and very pleasant café within the Georgian National Trust for Scotland headquarters, serving porridge with cream for breakfast, classy light lunches and daytime tea and scones. Inexpensive–moderate.

North and west of the New Town

Café Mediterraneo 73 Broughton St ☎ 0131/557 6900. A great little place with a deli counter and a small dining space serving Italian food in unpretentious style. Not a red-checked tablecloth to be seen. Moderate.

The Gallery Café Scottish National Gallery of Modern Art, Belford Road, Dean ☎ 0131/332 8600. Far more than a standard refreshment stop for gallery visitors, the cultured setting and strong

menu attracts reassuring numbers of locals. Open daily 10am–4.30pm. Moderate.

Lost Sock Diner 11 East London St, Broughton
☎ 0131/557 6097. Fill up on burgers, wraps and blackboard specials, all at surprising low prices, while your dirty clothes take a spin in the adjacent laundrette. Try the parsnip chips. Closed Sun & Mon evenings. Inexpensive.

Terrace Café Royal Botanic Garden, Inverleith
☎ 0131/552 0616. Superior spot with outside tables offering stunning views of the city skyline, though the food isn't that exciting. Their changing menu includes hot dishes, sandwiches and cakes. Inexpensive.

Valvona & Crolla 19 Elm Row, Leith Walk
☎ 0131/556 6066. The café at the back of this exquisite Italian deli serves authentic and delicious breakfasts, lunches and snacks. Open Mon–Sat 8am–5pm. Moderate.

South and west of the Old Town

Blonde 75 St Leonards St ☎ 0131/668 2917. Pleasant neighbourhood bistro, serving intriguing global combos such as salmon with black olive noodles and venison with cardamom and bitter chocolate. Moderate.

blue 10 Cambridge St ☎ 0131/221 1222. Long-standing super-stylish café/bistro in the same building as the avant-garde Traverse Theatre. Modern minimalist decor, with tasty modern dishes for under £10. Open till 10.30pm. Closed Sun. Moderate.

Favorit 30–32 Leven St, Bruntsfield ☎ 0131/221 1800. Thoroughly modern café-diner dishing up coffees, fruit shakes, cakes and big sandwiches, as well as drinks, right through to 1am. The branch at 19/20 Teviot Place is open even later.

Ndebele 57 Home St ☎ 0131/221 1141. Colourful African café offering sandwiches with lots of alternative fillings, imaginative salads and biltong for homesick South Africans. Open daily till 10pm. Inexpensive.

Susie's Diner 51 W Nicolson St, Newington
☎ 0131/667 8729. Popular café serving inventive soups, savouries and puddings, and a range of vegan food, to crowds of students. Inexpensive.

Leith and Newhaven

Daniel's 88 Commercial St ☎ 0131/553 5933. Top-grade bistro in an attractive setting on the ground floor of a converted warehouse in Leith. Food is from the Alsace region of France; the *tarte flambée*, one of the specialist dishes, is a sort of pizza with a French name and German ingredients. Moderate.

Restaurants

As with most large cities in Britain, the culinary map of Edinburgh is colourful and **global**, with long-established Chinese, Indian and Mexican places competing with Thai, Japanese, North African and Spanish cuisine. Traditional **Scottish cooking** can still be found at some of the more formal restaurants, and inevitably some tourist-oriented places offer haggis and other classic clichés. Edinburgh excels in **vegetarian** restaurants, including a couple of Indian places, and **seafood** – it's long been a speciality of the **Leith** waterfront, and you'll now also find a number of great seafood places in the centre of town.

Royal Mile and around

David Bann's Vegetarian Restaurant 56–58 St Mary's Street ☎0131/556 5888. Thoroughly modern vegetarian restaurant, with interesting, unconventional dishes, stylish design and not an open-toed sandal in sight. Open 11am–10pm every day, Fri & Sat till midnight. Moderate.

Black Bo's 57 Blackfriars St ☎0131/557 6136. Inventive diner with an earthy atmosphere and friendly service. Long established as a vegetarian favourite, it now offers a short meat menu for unreconstructed carnivores. Open evenings daily and lunch Fri & Sat. Moderate.

Creelers 3 Hunter Square ☎0131/220 4447. The only specialist seafood restaurant in the Old Town, with fresh produce brought in from a sister restaurant/fish shop on Arran. Go for the more relaxed bistro section at the front rather than the lifeless, more expensive restaurant at the back. Moderate–expensive.

The Grain Store 30 Victoria St ☎0131/225 7635. This unpretentious restaurant on eclectic Victoria Street is worth knowing about as a relaxing haven above the tourist bustle of the Old Town. Serves fairly uncomplicated but good-quality modern Scottish food, with reasonable lunchtime and set-price options. Expensive.

Maison Bleue 36 Victoria St ☎0131/226 1900. A contemporary French bistro with an eclectic menu of tapas-style food including sushi or haggis balls in beer batter. Good value at lunch and early evening menus. Moderate.

Mamma's American Pizza Company 30 Grassmarket ☎0131/225 6464. The best pizzas in this part of town, popular with students and big groups, with outside tables in the summer and reasonably priced wine. Open till midnight Sun–Thurs, 1am Fri & Sat. Inexpensive–moderate.

Prego 38 St Mary's St ☎0131/557 5754. A nice little find with freshly cooked, rustic Italian dishes though no pizza. Closed Sun. Moderate.

Le Sept Old Fishmarket Close ☎0131/225 5428. Long-established French brasserie tucked down a cobbled close off the Royal Mile specializing in fish dishes and filling savoury crepes. Moderate.

Suruchi 14a Nicolson St ☎0131/556 6583. Popular establishment serving genuine South Indian dishes – the menu is written in bizarre but entertaining broad Scots. Look out for cross-cultural specials such as tandoori trout. Moderate.

The Tower Museum of Scotland, Chambers Street ☎0131/225 3003. Unique setting on Level 5 of the new Museum of Scotland; at night you are escorted along the empty corridors to the restaurant, where spectacular views to the floodlit castle are revealed. Excellent modern Scottish food in a self-consciously chic setting. Expensive.

Viva Mexico 41 Cockburn Street ☎0131/226 5145. One of Edinburgh's best Mexicans for many years, doing the staples well in a friendly, easy-going atmosphere. Moderate.

The Witchery by the Castle 352 Castlehill, Royal Mile ☎0131/225 5613. The restaurant that only Edinburgh could create, with Gothic panelling, tapestries and heavy stonework only a broomstick-hop from the castle. The superb fish and game dishes are pricey, but you can steal a sense of it all with a pre- or post-theatre set menu (£10). Expensive.

New Town and the West End

Café Marlayne 76 Thistle St ☎0131/226 2230. An intimate venue for French farmhouse cooking, with plenty of hearty dishes. Moderate.

Café Royal Oyster Bar 17a West Register St ☎0131/556 4124. An Edinburgh classic, serving seafood dishes in its splendidly ornate Victorian interior, with stained-glass windows, marble floor and Doulton tiling. Very expensive.

La Cuisine d'Odile 13 Randolph Crescent, West End ☎0131/225 5685. Genuine French home cooking in a West End basement under the French Institute. Lunch only (noon–2pm). Closed Sun, Mon & July. Inexpensive.

Fishers in the City 58 Thistle Street ☎0131/225 5109. New Town incarnation of Leith's best-loved seafood bistro. This one has a sleek modern interior, great service and some stunning seafood. Expensive.

Henderson's Salad Table 94 Hanover St ☎0131/225 2131. A much-loved Edinburgh institution with a self-service basement restaurant offering freshly prepared hot dishes, plus a great choice of salads, soups, sweets and cheeses. The slightly antiquated cafeteria feel can put people off, but the food is rarely short of outstanding. Light jazz every evening. Open Mon–Sat 8am–10.30pm. Inexpensive–moderate.

Loon Fung 2 Warriston Place, Canonmills ☎0131/556 1781. Something of a trailblazer for Cantonese cuisine in Scotland, near the eastern entrance to the Botanic Garden. Moderate.

Mussel Inn 61–65 Rose St ☎0131/225 5979. After feasting on a kilo of mussels and a basket of chips for under £10 you'll realize why there's a demand to get in here. Owned by two west-coast shellfish farmers, which ensures that the time from sea to stomach is minimal. Closed Sun. Moderate.

Oloroso 33 Castle St ☎0131/226 7614. The restaurant of the moment in Edinburgh, with a rooftop location high above the New Town giving views to the castle. Chef Tony Singh's ever-enthusiastic approach makes for classy but interesting eating. Expensive.

The Patio 87 Hanover St ☎0131/226 3653. Best of a bunch of Italian places on Hanover St. Traditional, slightly dated approach but bank on friendly service and filling portions. Closed Sun. Moderate.

A Room in the Town 18 Howe St ☎0131/225 8204. Manages to combine a relaxed atmosphere with decent, Scottish-slanted seasonal food. BYOB keeps the bills down. Sister restaurant *A Room in the West End* is below ground at 26 William St. Moderate.

Stac Polly 29–33 Dublin St ☎0131/556 2231. Teetering on the edge of overbearing Scottishness, *Stac Polly* avoids the kitsch with some classy touches, atmospheric surroundings and a hearty menu of game, fish and meat dishes. Closed lunchtimes Sat & Sun. Expensive.

North and west of the New Town

Lancers 5 Hamilton Place, Stockbridge ☎0131/332 3444. Rich, filling Bengali and Punjabi curries in a slightly dated setting. Non-curry options include steak au poivre and the like. Moderate.

Blue Parrot Cantina 49 St Stephen's St, Stockbridge ☎0131/225 2941. Cosy Stockbridge basement restaurant, with a small, frequently changing menu that deviates from the Mexican clichés. Moderate.

South and west of the Old Town

The Atrium 10 Cambridge St ☎0131/228 8882. One of the most consistently impressive restaurants in the city. Quirky arty design with railway-sleeper tables and innovative *nouvelle* food focusing on high-quality Scottish produce. Closed Sunday. Very expensive.

izzi 119 Lothian Rd ☎0131/466 9888. Set among the bright lights and late-night revelry of Lothian Road, a slick, contemporary restaurant offering both Chinese and Japanese cuisine, including some of the better sushi around. Open daily till midnight. Moderate.

Kalpna 2 St Patrick Square, Newington ☎0131/667 9890. Outstanding vegetarian restaurant serving authentic Gujarati dishes. Four set meals, including a vegan option, stand alongside the main menu. Moderate.

Marque Central 30b Grindlay St ☎0131/229 9859. Sister restaurant to the original Southside venture, moving into the theatreland patch with its great value pre- and post-theatre deals. At any time a place for imaginative modern Scottish food. Closed Sun & Mon. Moderate–expensive.

Rogue Scottish Widows Building, 67 Morrison St ☎0131/228 2700. A typically unconventional venture by Edinburgh's most adventurous restaurateur, David Ramsden. The menu is short but diverse, from a creamy pasta to top-grade fillet steaks, served in a large avant-garde dining area with white linen and smooth service. Moderate–expensive.

Sweet Melinda's 11 Roseneath St, Marchmont ☎0131/229 7953. A smart seafood restaurant in a single, timber-panelled room with a friendly neighbourhood feel. Closed Sun & lunchtimes Mon. Moderate.

Thaisanuk 21 Argyle Place ☎0131/221 1231. Tiny diner with BYOB and some of the best takeaway around. Dishes from Malaysia and Vietnam alongside the Thai classics, but clean, rich, authentic flavours prevail. Open daily 6–11pm. Moderate.

Leith and Newhaven

Britannia Spice 150 Commercial St ☎0131/555 2255. The decor's nautical, the food is prepared by specialist chefs from the subcontinent and the awards for this ambitious Indian restaurant have been piling up. Moderate.

Restaurant Martin Wishart 52 The Shore ☎0131/553 3557. One of only two Michelin-star holders in Edinburgh, this wows the gourmets with highly accomplished, French-influenced Scottish food right by the Water of Leith. The food's incredi-

⑰

ble but the decor is rather beige. Closed Sun & Mon. Very expensive.

The Shore 3 The Shore ☎0131/553 5080. A bar/restaurant with huge mirrors, wood panelling and aproned waiters who serve up good fish dishes and decent wines. Live jazz, folk and hubbub floats through from the adjoining bar. Moderate.

The Vintner's Rooms 87 Giles St ☎0131/554 6767. Splendid restaurant in a seventeenth-cen-tury warehouse; the ornate Rococo dining room is a marvel and the food – from seafood to game – isn't bad either. Expensive.

Waterfront Wine Bar 1c Dock Place ☎0131/554 7427. Housed in the former lock-keeper's cottage, you can eat in the wonderfully characterful wine bar (smoking) or nonsmoking conservatory attached. Fish dishes dominate. Moderate.

Pubs and bars

Many of Edinburgh's **pubs**, especially in the Old Town, have histories that stretch back centuries, while others, particularly in the New Town, are unaltered Victorian or Edwardian period pieces. Add a plentiful supply of trendy modern **bars**, and there's enough to cater for all tastes.

Edinburgh has a long history of brewing beer, though only two principal **breweries** remain: the giant Scottish and Newcastle (who produce McEwan's and Younger's) and the small independent Caledonian Brewery, which uses old techniques and equipment to produce some of the best beers in Britain. Once upon a time Edinburgh's main drinking strip was the near-legendary **Rose Street**, a pedestrianized lane tucked between Princes and George streets in the New Town: the ultimate Edinburgh pub crawl was to take a drink in each of its dozen or so establishments. Things are a bit more sophisticated these days, with **George Street** itself taking a lead: various former financial institutions have been converted into bars, with a predictable invasion of suits by day and style by night. While many of the **Royal Mile**'s pubs aren't ashamed to make the most of local historical connections to draw in the tourists, you don't have to travel far to find some lively places, notably the busy pubs in and around the **Grassmarket**, with a further batch on the studenty **Southside**. **Leith** has a range of bars, from rough spit-and-sawdust places to polished pseudo-Victoriana, while we've also listed a number of characterful places further away from the centre.

17

The Royal Mile and around

Bannermans 212 Cowgate. Once the best pub in the street, now the late-night music can be a bit intrusive. Still atmospheric, though – a former vint-ner's cellar, it has a labyrinthine interior deep under the Old Town and good beer on tap. Open daily till 1am.

Bow Bar 80 West Bow. Wonderful old wood-pan-elled bar that won an award as the best drinkers' pub in Britain a few years back. Choose from among nearly 150 whiskies or a changing selec-tion of first-rate Scottish and English cask beers. Closed Sun afternoons.

City Café 19 Blair St. Longstanding but deter-minedly trendy bar on the street linking the Royal Mile to the clubbers' hub along the Cowgate. The blue pool tables are always popular and you can buy candies behind the American-style bar.

Doric Tavern 15 Market St. Long-established upstairs wine bar (open till 1am) is a favoured watering hole of journalists and artists. The brasserie beside the wine bar serves reliable good-quality Scottish food.

Jolly Judge 7a James Court. Atmospheric, low-ceilinged bar in a close just down from the castle. Cosy in winter and pleasant outside in summer.

Last Drop 74–78 Grassmarket. The "Drop" refers to the Edinburgh gallows, which were located out front, and whose former presence is symbolized by the red paintwork of the exterior. Cheapish pub food and, like its competitors in the same block, patronized mainly by students. Open till 1am.

New Town and West End

Abbotsford 3 Rose St. A large-scale pub whose original Victorian decor, complete with wood pan-elling and island bar, is among the finest in the

951

city. Good range of ales, including a house ale brewed by Broughton.

Café Royal Circle Bar 17 West Register St. As notable as the *Oyster Bar* restaurant next door, the *Café Royal* is worth a visit just for its Victorian decor, notably the huge elliptical "island" counter and the tiled portraits of renowned inventors. Thurs open until midnight, Fri & Sat till 1am. Upstairs, the *Café Royal Bistro Bar* is an unlovely rugby-themed affair.

Candy Bar 113–115 George St. Aimed squarely at the George Street glitterati (including Prince William, it's rumoured) with plasma screens and huge cocktail lists, but small enough to be relatively unintimidating. Daily till 1am.

The Dome 14 George St. Opulent conversion of a massive New Town bank, thronging with well-dressed locals. Probably the most impressive bar interior in Edinburgh, though the ultra-chic atmosphere can be a bit intense. Sun–Thurs open till 11.30pm, Fri & Sat till 1am.

Oxford Bar 8 Young St. Traditional city bar, unpretentious and somewhat of a shrine for rugby fans, off-duty policemen and readers of the books of Ian Rankin. Open until 1am.

Rick's 55a Frederick St. One of the most popular "scene" bars in the city centre, filled with suits after work and glad rags later on. There's good food from their bistro and rooms as well. Open till 1am.

North and west of the New Town

The Barony Bar 81–85 Broughton St. A fine old-fashioned bar, which manages to be big and lively without being spoilt. Real ale and some good food, though there can be a wait to get served. Open till midnight.

The Basement 10a Broughton St. Packed out, especially at the weekends, with a pre-club crowd, this trendy bar is run by young and enthusiastic staff and serves cheap Mexican food till 10pm every day. Open till 1am.

Bert's Bar 2–4 Raeburn Place, Stockbridge and 29 William St, West End. Popular locals' pubs, despite their relatively recent arrival. Both have excellent beer, tasty pies and strive to be authentic, non-theme-oriented venues, though the telly rarely misses any sporting action.

Hector's 47–49 Deanhaugh St. A magnet for trendy Stockbridgers, with chocolate-coloured leather couches and rough-hewn walls. Good place for weekend brunches; food is served all day in a dining area to the rear.

The Outhouse 12a Broughton Street Lane. Busy pre-club bar tucked away down a cobbled lane off Broughton Street, with a lively beer garden and funky music. Open till 1am.

South and west of the Old Town

Bennets Bar 8 Leven St, Tollcross. Edwardian pub with mahogany-framed mirrors and Art Nouveau stained glass; gets packed in the evening, particularly when there's a show at the King's Theatre next door. Mon–Sat serves lunch and opens till midnight.

Blue Blazer 2 Spittal St. Traditional Edinburgh *howff* with oak-clad bar and church pews; serves a good selection of ales. Open till midnight Wed & Thurs, 1am Fri & Sat.

Human Be-In 2–8 West Crosscauseway, Newington. One of the trendiest student bars around, with huge plate glass windows to admire the beautiful people and tables outside for summer posing. Good food too. Open till 1am.

Peartree House 36 W Nicolson St, Newington. Fine bar in an eighteenth-century house with old sofas and a large courtyard – one of central Edinburgh's very few beer gardens. Serves budget bar lunches. Open Mon–Wed & Sun until midnight, Thurs–Sat until 1am.

Traverse Bar Café Traverse Theatre, 10 Cambridge St. Much more than just a theatre bar, attracting a lively, sophisticated crowd which dispels any notion of a quiet interval drink. Good food available in the bar and also at *blue* upstairs. One of *the* places to be during the Festival.

Leith

Bar Java 48–50 Constitution St. Friendly bar in an area where you'd expect all the pubs to have sawdust on the floor. Serves decent food, has a small courtyard beer garden and even B&B rooms upstairs. Open Sun–Wed till midnight; Thurs–Sat till 1am.

Carriers' Quarters 42 Bernard St. Intimate pub that dates back to 1785, with many original features, including a tiny "snug" and blazing log fire. Open till 1am Fri & Sat.

Kings Wark 36 The Shore. Real ale in an atmospheric restored eighteenth-century pub right in the heart of Leith, with bar meals chalked up on the rafters. Open till midnight Fri & Sat.

Elsewhere in the city

Caley Sample Room 58 Angle Park Terrace, Polwarth. Showcase pub for the cask ales of the nearby Caledonian Brewery. Occasionally hosts ceilidhs. Open Mon–Thurs & Sun till midnight, Fri & Sat till 1am.

Cramond Inn Cramond Village ☎0131/336 2035. An authentic old inn by the riverside at Cramond –

the perfect place for a drink or a pub meal after a stroll along the coastal path.

Sheep Heid Inn 43 The Causeway, Duddingston. This eighteenth-century inn with a family atmos-phere makes an ideal refreshment stop at the end of a tramp through Holyrood Park. Decent home-cooked meals are available at the bar, while the old-fashioned skittle alley is popular with students.

Nightlife and entertainment

Inevitably, Edinburgh's **nightlife** is at its best during the Festival (see p.955), which can make the other 49 weeks of the year seem like an anticlimax. However, at any time the city has plenty to offer, especially in the realm of **theatre** and **music**.

The **nightclub** scene is lively, with some excellent venues hosting a changing selection of one-nighters. In the bigger venues, you may find different clubs taking place on each floor. Most of the city-centre clubs stay open till around 3am. While you can normally hear **live jazz**, **folk** and **rock** every evening in one or other of the city's pubs, the city has permanent venues large enough to host large touring **orchestras** and **ballet** companies; elsewhere you can also uncover a lively **comedy** club and a couple of excellent art house **cinemas**.

Edinburgh has a dynamic **gay** culture, for years centred round the top of Leith Walk and Broughton Street, where the first gay and lesbian centre appeared in the 1970s. Since the start of the 1990s, more and more gay enterprises, especially cafés and nightclubs, have moved into this area, now dubbed the "Pink Triangle".

The best way to find out **what's on** is to pick up a copy of *The List*, a fortnightly listings magazine covering both Edinburgh and Glasgow (£2.20). Alternatively, get hold of the *Edinburgh Evening News*, which appears daily except Sunday: its listings column gives details of performances in the city that day, hotels and bars included.

Nightclubs

Ego 14 Picardy Place ✆0131/478 7434. A former casino, this big venue hosts Wiggle, which plays to a gay and mixed crowd monthly on Saturdays, and the epic party night Vegas. The smaller *Cocteau Lounge* downstairs is another popular venue.

Honeycomb 15–17 Niddrie St ✆0131/530 5540. In amongst the vaults and hidden passageways under the Old Town, hosting big drum'n'bass night Manga.

The Liquid Room 9c Victoria St ✆0131/225 2564. One of the best of the larger venues, with nights including hip-hop Jump, indie Evol and Colours, a house/techno club drawing big-name DJs.

Opal Lounge 51 George St ✆0131/226 2275. See and be-seen bar in the New Town with DJs funking things up later on. Always has a quota of suits who didn't make it home.

Gay clubs and bars

Blue Moon Café 1 Barony St ✆0131/556 2788. Coffee, drinks, breakfasts and light meals available at this longstanding friendly café-bar which attracts a mixed crowd. Mon–Fri 11am–11.30pm,

Sat & Sun 9.30am–12.30am.

CC Bloom's 23 Greenside Place ✆0131/556 9331. Big dance floor, stonking rhythms and a young, friendly crowd.

Sala 60 Broughton St ✆0131/478 7069. Fresh food, light snacks and drinks in a relaxed atmosphere at the Edinburgh Gay, Lesbian and Bisexual Centre. Open 11am–11pm. Closed Mon.

Live music pubs and venues

Corn Exchange New Market Rd, Gorgie ✆0131/443 2437. Despite its name, it's actually a former slaughterhouse. With a 3000 capacity it's popular for big name contemporary pop and rock acts, but the location, three miles west of the centre, is a bit off-putting.

Henry's Jazz Bar 8 Morrison St, off Lothian Road ✆0131/467 5200. Edinburgh's premier jazz and hip-hop venue, with live music every night and regular top performers.

The Liquid Room 9c Victoria St ✆0131/225 2528. Good-sized venue frequented by visiting indie and local R&B bands.

Queen's Hall 89 Clerk St ☎0131/668 2019. Medium-sized venue used by touring jazz, blues and folk groups.

Sandy Bell's 25 Forrest Rd ☎0131/225 2751. A friendly bar and a good bet for folk music most nights of the week.

Whistlebinkies 4–6 South Bridge ☎0131/557 5114. One of the most reliable places to find live music every night of the week – often it's rock and pop covers, though there are some folk evenings. Daily till 3am.

Theatre and comedy

Festival Theatre Nicolson Street ☎0131/529 6000. The largest stage in Britain, principally used for Scottish Opera and Scottish Ballet's appearances in the capital, but also for everything from the children's show *Singing Kettle* to Engelbert Humperdinck.

Jongleurs Comedy Club Omni Centre, Greenside Place ☎08707/870707. An Edinburgh link in a national chain located in a huge glass-fronted cinema complex at the foot of Calton Hill. Fairly reliable for a year-round chance to encounter popular Festival stand-up acts and national stars.

King's Theatre 2 Leven St ☎0131/529 6000. Stately Edwardian civic theatre that majors in pantomime, touring West End plays and the occasional drama or opera performance.

Playhouse Theatre 18–22 Greenside Place ☎0870/6063424. The most capacious theatre in Britain – formerly a cinema – and used largely for extended runs of popular musicals and occasional rock concerts.

Royal Lyceum Theatre 30 Grindlay St ☎0131/248 4848. Fine Victorian civic theatre with a compact auditorium. The leading year-round venue for mainstream drama.

The Stand Comedy Club 5 York Place ☎0131/558 7272. The city's top comedy spot, with a different act on every night and some of the UK's top comics headlining at the weekends. The bar is worth a visit in itself.

Traverse Theatre 10 Cambridge St ☎0131/228 1404. Unquestionably one of Britain's premier venues for new plays and avant-garde drama from around the world. Going from strength to strength in its new custom-built home beside the Usher Hall, with a great bar downstairs and the popular *blue* café-bar upstairs.

Concert halls

Queen's Hall 89 Clerk St ☎0131/668 2019. Converted Georgian church with a capacity of around eight hundred, though many seats have little or no view of the stage. Home base of both the Scottish Chamber Orchestra and Scottish Ensemble, and much favoured by jazz, blues and folk groups. Also hosts established comedians.

Usher Hall Corner of Lothian Road and Grindlay Street ☎0131/228 1155. Edinburgh's main civic concert hall, seating over 2500. Excellent for choral and symphony concerts, but less suitable for solo vocalists. The upper circle seats are cheapest and have the best acoustics, but the sound quality overall is much improved after a recent refurbishment.

Cinemas

Cameo 38 Home St, Tollcross ☎0131/228 2800; bookings ☎0131/228 4141. A treasure of an art-house cinema; screens more challenging mainstream releases and cult late-nighters. Tarantino's been here and thinks it's great.

Filmhouse 88 Lothian Rd ☎0131/228 2688. Three screens showing an eclectic programme of independent, art-house and classic films. Their café is a hang-out for the city's dedicated film buffs.

Odeon 118 Lothian Road ☎0131/221 1477; info and credit card bookings ☎0870/505 0007. Central four-screen cinema showing the latest releases.

Warner Village Omni Centre, Greenside Place ☎0870/2406020. Most central of the big new multi-screen venues, tucked under Calton Hill at the top of Leith Walk.

Edinburgh's other festivals

Quite apart from August's Edinburgh Festival, the city is now promoting itself as a year-round festival venue. The **Science Festival** in April (☎0131/220 1882) incorporates hands-on children's events as well as numerous lectures on a vast array of subjects. There is a **Puppet and Animation Festival** in March (☎01786/467155), and a **Children's Festival** in late May (☎0131/225 8050), with readings, magicians and specialist children's drama. The Caledonian Brewery, 42 Slateford Rd, runs its own **beer festival** in early June, showcasing real ales from all over Britain.

Check out ⓦwww.edinburghfestivals.co.uk for links to the official sites of Edinburgh's main festivals.

Hogmanay

Hogmanay is the name Scots give to **New Year's Eve**, a celebration they have made all their own with a unique mix of tradition, hedonism, sentimentality and enthusiasm. The roots of the Hogmanay are in ancient pagan festivities based around the winter solstice, which in most places gradually merged with Christmas. When hardline Scottish Protestant clerics in the sixteenth century abolished Christmas for being a Catholic mass, the Scots, not wanting to miss out on a mid-winter knees-up, instead put their energy into greeting the New Year.

Houses were cleaned from top to bottom, debts were paid and quarrels made up, and, after the bells of midnight were rung, great store was laid by welcoming good luck into your house. This still takes the form of the tradition of "first-footing" – visiting your neighbours and bearing gifts. The ideal first-foot is a tall dark-haired male carrying a bottle of whisky; women or redheads, on the other hand, bring bad luck – though to be honest no one carrying a bottle of whisky tends to be turned away these days, whatever the colour of their hair. All this neighbourly greeting meant that a fair bit of partying went on, of course, and after a while no one was expected to go to work the next day, or, if the party was that good, the day after that either. Even today, January 1 is a public holiday in the rest of the UK, but only in Scotland does the holiday extend to January 2 too. In fact, right up to the 1950s Christmas was a normal working day for many people in Scotland, and Hogmanay was widely regarded as by far the more important celebration.

Over the years, Hogmanay street parties in the middle of towns and cities became popular, often centred around a prominent clockface which would ring out "the bells" at midnight. These days, the largest New Year's Eve street party in Europe takes place in Edinburgh, with around 100,000 people on the streets of the city enjoying the culmination of a week-long series of events. On the night itself, stages are set up in different parts of the city centre, with big name rock groups and local ceilidh bands playing to the increasingly inebriated masses. The high point of the evening is, of course, midnight, when hundreds of tons of fireworks are let off into the night sky above the castle, and Edinburgh joins the rest of the world singing **"Auld Lang Syne"**, an old Scottish tune with lyrics by Robert Burns, Scotland's national poet.

For more details about Hogmanay in Edinburgh, and how to get hold of tickets for the street party, go to Ⓦ www.edinburghshogmanay.org.

17

The Edinburgh Festival

For the best part of August, Scotland's capital is completely transformed by the **Edinburgh Festival**, the world's largest celebration of the arts. Every available performance space – from the city's grandest concert halls to pub courtyards – plays host to a packed programme of cultural entertainment, ranging from high drama to base comedy. The streets fill with buskers, hustlers, circus acts and craft stalls, and the local population swells to twice its normal size as tourists, celebrities, performers, media types and festival-goers throng the city centre. Pubs and restaurants stay open later, posters plaster every vertical space and the atmosphere in town takes on a slightly surreal, vital buzz.

The Edinburgh Festival is actually an umbrella term encompassing different festivals taking place at around the same time in the city. The principal events are the **Edinburgh International Festival** and the much larger **Edinburgh Festival Fringe**, but there are also **Film**, **Book**, **Jazz and Blues** and **Television** festivals, the **Military Tattoo** on the Castle Esplanade and the **Edinburgh Mela**, an Asian festival held over a weekend in late August/early September.

For the visitor, the sheer volume of the Festival's output can be bewildering: virtually every branch of arts and entertainment is represented somewhere. It can be a struggle to find **accommodation**, get hold of the tickets you want, book a table in a restaurant or simply get from one side of town to another; you can end up seeing something truly dire, or something mind-blowing – but then again, if you don't experience these things then you haven't really done the Festival.

Note that dates, venues, names and star acts, change from one year to the next. This unpredictability is one of the Festival's greatest charms, however, so while the following information will help you get to grips with it, be prepared for – indeed, enjoy – the unexpected. If you want up-to-the-minute information at any time of year, ⓦ**www.edinburghfestivals.co.uk** has links to the home pages of most of Edinburgh's main festivals.

In addition to each festival's own programme, various publications give information about what's on day by day during the Festival. Every day the Fringe Office publishes **The Guide**, giving a chronological listing of virtually every Fringe show scheduled for that day. It's available free from the Office and hundreds of other spots around Edinburgh. Of the local newspapers, the best coverage is in **The Scotsman**, which issues a dedicated daily Festival supplement. Their reviews and star-rating system carry a lot of weight.

The Edinburgh International Festival

The **Edinburgh International Festival** (sometimes called the "Official Festival") attracts truly international stars, along with some of the world's finest orchestras and opera, theatre and ballet companies. Performances take place at the city's larger venues such as the Usher Hall and the Festival Theatre and, while ticket prices run to over £40, it is possible to see shows for £10 or less if you're prepared to queue for the handful of tickets kept back until the day. The International Festival's headquarters are located at **The Hub** (see p.926).

The most popular single event in the Festival is the dramatic **Fireworks Concert**, held late at night on the final Saturday of the International Festival: the Scottish Chamber Orchestra belts out pop classics from the Ross Bandstand in Princes Street Gardens, accompanied by a spectacular fireworks display high up above the ramparts of the castle. Hundreds of thousands of people view the display from various vantage points throughout the city, the prime spots being Princes Street, Northbridge and Calton Hill.

The Edinburgh Festival Fringe

Even standing alone from its sister festivals, the **Edinburgh Festival Fringe** is easily the world's largest arts gathering. Each year sees over 15,000 performances from over 700 companies, with 1500 shows every day, round the clock, in 200 venues around the city. The burgeoning of the Fringe began in earnest in the late 1970s as other forms of entertainment established themselves, notably new comedy, which over the next quarter of a century became almost synonymous with the Edinburgh Fringe. Nowadays, the Fringe is *the* place where artists of every conceivable description come to get discovered. Crucially, no artistic control is imposed on those who want to produce a show – anyone who can afford the registration fee can take part. This means that the shows range from the inspired to the diabolical, and ensures a highly competitive atmosphere, in which one bad review in a prominent publication means box-office disaster. Many unknowns rely on self-publicity, taking to the streets

Fringe venues

In addition to the many tiny and unexpected auditoriums, the four **main Fringe venues** are The Assembly Rooms, The Pleasance, The Gilded Balloon and a relative newcomer known as "C". Venue complexes rather than single spaces, the latter three colonize nearby spaces for the duration of the Festival. If you're new to the Fringe, these are all safe bets for decent shows.

The atmosphere at the **Pleasance** is usually less frenetic than at the other venues, with classy drama and whimsical appearances by media stars. The **Assembly Rooms** provide a grand setting for top-of-the-range drama by companies such as the RSC and big-name music and comedy acts. The Fringe's premier comedy venue, **The Gilded Balloon**, runs in various venues around town, as do the "C" venues.

The **Traverse Theatre**, long a champion of new drama, combines the avant-garde with slick presentation. Less glam, but with an excellent line-up of thought-provoking drama, is the **Theatre Workshop**, an intimate venue located in Stockbridge.

to perform highlights from their show, or pressing leaflets into the hands of every passer-by.

The Festival Fringe Office (℡0131/226 0000, 🌐www.edfringe.com) handles postal and telephone **bookings**, while during the Festival, tickets are sold at the Fringe box office (daily 10am–9pm), the venue itself, or through the website. **Ticket** prices for most Fringe shows start at £5, and average from £8 to £12 at the main venues, with the better-known acts going for even more.

The smaller festivals

The **Edinburgh International Film Festival** (🌐www.edfilmfest.org.uk), which runs for the last two weeks of August, is a chance to see some of the year's big cinema hits before they go on general release, along with a varied and exciting bill of reissued movies.

The **Edinburgh International Book Festival** (🌐www.edbookfest.co.uk), which also takes place in the last two weeks of August, is held in a tented village in Charlotte Square, and offers talks, readings and signings by a star-studded line-up of visiting authors, as well as panel discussions and workshops.

The **Edinburgh International Jazz and Blues Festival** (🌐www.jazzmusic.co.uk) runs immediately prior to the Fringe in the first week in August, easing the city into the festival spirit with a full programme of gigs in many different locations. Like all the other festivals, this one has grown over the years, reflecting the panoply of generations and styles that appear under the banner of jazz and blues. Highlights include **Jazz On A Summer's Day**, a musical extravaganza in Princes Street Gardens, and a colourful New Orleans-style **street parade**.

Staged in the spectacular stadium of the Edinburgh Castle Esplanade, the **Military Tattoo** is an unashamed display of pomp and military pride. The programme of choreographed drills, massed pipe bands, historical tableaux, energetic battle re-enactments, national dancing and pyrotechnics has been a feature of the Festival for fifty years, the emotional climax provided by a lone piper on the castle battlements. **Tickets** need to be booked well in advance, and it's advisable to take a cushion and rainwear. Tickets and information are available from the Tattoo Office, 32 Market St, EH1 1QB ℡0131/225 1188, 🌐www.edintattoo.co.uk.

Shopping

Despite the relentless advance of the big chains, it's still possible to track down some characterful and unusual shops in central Edinburgh. **Princes Street**, one of Britain's most famous shopping streets, is all but dominated by standard chain outlets, though no serious shopper should miss out on a visit to Edinburgh's venerable department store, Jenners, at 48 Princes Street, opposite the Scott Monument. More fashionable upmarket shops and boutiques are to be found on parallel **George Street**, while for more original outlets, head for **Cockburn Street**, a hub for trendy clothes and record shops, or **Victoria Street** and in and around the **Grassmarket**, where you'll find an eclectic range of antique and arts and crafts shops plus some antiquarian booksellers.

Books Waterstone's is the major bookselling presence in Edinburgh, with large stores at 128 Princes St (℡0131/226 2666), 13–14 Princes St (℡0131/556 3034) and 83 George St (℡0131/225 3436). Ottakars at 57 George St (℡0131/225 4495) is the main city-centre alternative, with Blackwells' store at 53–59 South Bridge (℡0131/662 8222) providing a strong general/academic presence near the University. There's a good selection of antiquarian and secondhand bookshops in the city: Peter Bell, 68 West Port (℡0131/229 0562); McFeely's, 30 Buccleuch St (℡0131/662 8570); McNaughtan's Bookshop 3a–4a Haddington Place, Leith Walk (℡0131/556 5897); and West Port Books, 147 West Port (℡0131/229 4431).

Haggis Charles MacSween & Son, Dryden Rd, Bilston Glen, Loanhead (℡0131/440 2555), has an international reputation, and also makes a tasty vegetarian version; buy it from the factory or various outlets around Edinburgh, such as the Food Hall in Jenners at 48 Princes St, or Peckhams, 155–159 Bruntsfield Place.

Music Check out Avalanche, 17 West Nicolson St (℡0131/668 2374), 28 Lady Lawson St (℡0131/228 1939) and 63 Cockburn St (℡0131/225 3939) for indie music; Coda,

12 Bank St (℡0131/622 7246) for contemporary Scottish folk and roots music; or Underground Solu'shun, 9 Cockburn St (℡0131/226 2242) for house, garage, techno and drum'n'bass vinyl.

Tartan Kinloch Anderson, on the corner of Commercial and Dock streets, Leith (℡0131/555 1390), has a large showroom; James Pringle Woollen Mill, 70 Bangor Rd, Leith (℡0131/553 5161) has an archive computer which tells you if you're entitled to wear a clan tartan, and gives full historic information; Geoffrey Tailor, 57–59 High St (℡0131/557 0256) is one of the largest and most respected retailers on the Royal Mile – they also have a shop in the Edinburgh Old Town Weaving Co by the Castle Esplanade, where "live" weaving takes place.

Whisky Royal Mile Whiskies, 379–381 High St ℡0131/225 3383; William Cadenhead, 172 Canongate ℡0131/556 5864.

Woollen goods Bill Baber Knitwear, 66 Grassmarket (℡0131/225 3249), has garments designed and made on the premises; Ragamuffin, 2a St Mary's St (℡0131/557 6007), features Skye knitwear; and Shetland Connection, 491 Lawnmarket (℡0131/225 3525) sells Shetland knitting wool, lace and cobweb.

Listings

Banks HBOS (Halifax-Bank of Scotland), The Mound (head office), 38 St Andrew Square; Barclays, 1 St Andrew Square; Clydesdale, 20 Hanover St; HSBC, 76 Hanover St; Lloyds TSB, 120 George St; Royal Bank of Scotland, 42 St Andrew Square.

Bike rental Biketrax, 11 Lochrin Place ℡0131/228 6633; Edinburgh Cycle Hire, 29 Blackfriars St ℡0131/556 5560.

Car rental Arnold Clark, Lochrin Place ℡0131/228 4747; Avis, 5 West Park Place

℡0131/337 6363; Budget, Edinburgh Airport ℡0131/333 1926; Europcar, 24 E London St ℡0131/557 3456; Hertz, 10 Picardy Place ℡0131/556 8311; Thrifty Car Rental, 42 Haymarket Terrace ℡0131/337 1319.

Consulates Australia, 69 George St ℡0131/624 3333; Canada, 30 Lothian Rd ℡0131/220 4333; Germany, 16 Eglinton Crescent ℡0131/337 2323; Italy, 32 Melville St ℡0131/226 3631; Netherlands, 1–2 Thistle St ℡0131/220 3226; USA, 3 Regent Terrace ℡0131/556 8315.

Dentist The National Health Service Helpline ☎0800/224488 will tell you where your nearest surgery is. For emergencies go to Edinburgh Dental Hospital, Lauriston Place (☎0131/536 4900) or the Western General Hospital, Crewe Rd South (☎0131/537 1000).

Exchange Post offices will exchange currency commission-free; Thomas Cook, 28 Frederick St (Mon–Sat 9am–5.30pm; ☎0131/465 7700); currency exchange bureaus in the main tourist office (Mon–Wed 9am–5pm, Thurs–Sat 9am–6pm & Sun 10am–5pm) and beside platform 1 at Waverley Station (Sept–June Mon–Sat 7.30am–9pm, Sun 8.30am–9pm; July–Aug Mon–Sat 7am–10pm, Sun 8am–10pm).

Hospital Royal Infirmary, Little France (☎0131/536 1000), has a 24hr casualty department. There are also casualty departments at the Western General, Crewe Road North (☎0131 537 1000; daytime only), and for children at the Sick Kid's hospital, Sciennes Road (☎0131 536 0000).

Internet easyEverything, 58 Rose St (daily 8am–11pm; ☎0131/220 3580); Internet Cafe, 98 West Bow (daily 10am–11pm; ☎0131/226 5400; Web 13, 13 Bread St (Mon–Fri 9am–5.30pm, Thurs until 7pm, Sat 9am–6pm, Sun 11am–5pm; ☎0131/229 8883, ⓦ www.web13.co.uk).

Laundry Capital Launderette, 208 Dalkeith Rd, Newington (☎0131/667 0825); Sundial Launderette at 7–9 East London St, Broughton (☎0131/556 2743); Tarvit Launderette, 7–9 Tarvit St, Tollcross (☎0131/229 6382).

Left luggage Counter by platform 1 at Waverley Station (daily 7am–11pm; ☎0131/550 2333).

Libraries Central Library, George IV Bridge (Mon–Thurs 10am–8pm, Fri 10am–5pm, Sat 9am–1pm; ☎0131/242 8000). The National Library of Scotland, George IV Bridge is for research purposes only.

Lost property Edinburgh Airport ☎0131/333 1000; Edinburgh Police HQ ☎0131/311 3141; Lothian Buses ☎0131/558 8858; First Bus ☎0131 663 1945; Scotrail ☎0141/335 3276.

Pharmacy Boots, 48 Shandwick Place (Mon–Fri 8am–9pm, Sat 8am–7pm, Sun 10am–5pm; ☎0131/225 6757) has the longest opening hours.

Police In an emergency call 999. Otherwise contact Lothian and Borders Police HQ, Fettes Ave ☎0131/311 3131.

Post office 8–10 St James Centre (Mon 9am–5.30pm, Tues–Fri 8.30am–5.30pm, Sat 8.30am–6pm; ☎0845/722 3344).

Taxis Airport Taxis ☎0131/344 3344; Central Radio Taxis ☎0131/229 2468; and City Cabs ☎0131/228 1211.

Out from the centre

There's a great deal to discover exploring beyond the compact centre of Edinburgh, in particular along the Firth of Forth coastline to the north and the rise of the Pentland Hills to the south. Just over a mile northeast of the city centre is **Leith**, the historic port of Edinburgh, a fascinating mix of cobbled streets and new developments, run-down housing and some of the city's top restaurants. Nearby you can find a flavour of the city's maritime and fishing heritage at the atmospheric harbour of **Newhaven**.

In the southern suburbs of the city, the imposing fifteenth-century **Craigmillar Castle** is incongruously set amid a rather grim housing estate, but there is also a rural aspect to the area, with various hills, parks and, on the southern edge of the city, the range of the **Pentland Hills** which offer some wild walking country and terrific views.

Leith and around

For several hundred years, **LEITH** was separate from Edinburgh. As Scotland's major east coast port, it played a key role in the nation's history, even serving as the seat of government for a time, and in 1833 finally became a burgh in its own right. In 1920, however, it was incorporated into the capital and, in the decades that followed, went into seemingly terminal decline: the population dropped dramatically, and much of its centre was ripped out, to be replaced by grim housing schemes.

The 1980s, however, saw an unexpected turnaround. Against all the odds, a couple of waterfront bistros proved enormously successful; competitors followed apace, and today the port boasts arguably the best concentration of good restaurants (particularly seafood) in Edinburgh (see p.950 for reviews). The surviving historic buildings were spruced up and large blocks of yuppie flats appeared among the crumbling tenements and council housing. Meanwhile the dock areas are being transformed by Europe's largest current waterfront development, most notably the vast building housing civil servants from the Scottish Executive and the new Ocean Terminal, a shopping and entertainment complex beside which the former royal yacht **Britannia** has settled into retirement.

Around the port

While you're most likely to come to Leith for the bars and restaurants, the area itself warrants exploration; though the shipbuilding yards have gone, it remains an active port with a rough-edged character. Most of the showpiece Neoclassical buildings lie on or near **The Shore**, the tenement-lined road along the final stretch of the Water of Leith, just before it disgorges into the Firth of Forth. **Leith Links** is an area of predominantly flat parkland, just east of the police station. Documentary evidence suggests that The Links was a golf course in the fifteenth century, giving rise to Leith's claim to be regarded as the birthplace of the sport: in 1744 its first written rules were drawn up here, ten years before they were formalized in St Andrews.

Britannia

A little to the west of The Shore, moored alongside **Ocean Terminal**, a huge shopping and entertainment centre designed by Terence Conran, is one of the world's most famous ships, **Britannia** (daily: April–Sept 9.30am–4.30pm; Oct–March 10am–3.30pm; £8; ⓦ www.royalyachtbritannia.co.uk). Launched in 1953 at John Brown's shipyard on Clydeside, *Britannia* was used by the royal family for 44 years for state visits, diplomatic functions and royal holidays. Leith acquired her following decommission in 1997, against the wishes of many of the royal family, who felt that scuttling would have been a more dignified end.

Visits to *Britannia* begin in the **visitor centre**, within Ocean Terminal. An audio handset is then handed out and you are allowed to roam around the yacht: the **bridge**, the **admiral's quarters**, the **officers' mess** and a large part of the **state apartments**, including the state dining and drawing rooms and the (separate) cabins used by the Queen and the Duke of Edinburgh, viewed through a glass partition. The ship has been largely kept as she was when she was in service, with a well-preserved 1950s dowdiness that the audioguide loyally attributes to the Queen's good taste and astute frugality in the lean postwar years. Certainly the atmosphere is a far cry from the opulent splendour that many expect.

To get to Ocean Terminal, jump on one of the tour buses that leave from Waverley Bridge; otherwise, make use of buses #1, #11 or #22 from Princes Street.

Newhaven

To the west of Leith lies the village of **NEWHAVEN**, built by James IV at the start of the sixteenth century as an alternative shipbuilding centre to Leith: his massive warship, the *Great Michael*, capable of carrying 120 gunners, 300 mariners and 1000 troops, and said to have used up all the trees in Fife, was built here. Today, the harbour still has a pleasantly salty feel. Among various modern developments, the old fish market remains, housing a couple of fish

17

merchants and the small **Newhaven Heritage Museum** (daily noon–4.45pm; free), a fascinating collection of costumes and other memorabilia staffed by enthusiastic members of local fishing families.

South of the Centre

Craigmillar Castle (April–Sept daily 9.30am–6.30pm; Oct–March Mon–Wed & Sat 9.30am–4.30pm, Thurs 9.30am–12.30pm, closed Fri, Sun 2–4.30pm; HS; £2.20), where the murder of Lord Darnley, second husband of Mary, Queen of Scots was plotted, lies in a green belt five miles southeast of the centre. It's one of the best-preserved medieval fortresses in Scotland, and before Queen Victoria set her heart on Balmoral, it was being considered as her royal castle north of the border, a possibility which seems odd now given its proximity to the ugly council housing scheme of Craigmillar, one of Edinburgh's most deprived districts. That said, it is set among green fields and enjoys splendid views back to Arthur's Seat and the castle. Take bus #30, #33 or #82, or any bus heading for Hawick or Jedburgh, from the city centre to the district called Little France, from where the castle is a ten-minute walk along Craigmillar Castle Road.

The southern hills

The **hills** of Edinburgh's southern suburbs offer good, not overly demanding, walking opportunities, with plenty of sweeping panoramic views. The **Royal Observatory** (open Oct–March for evening talks and public observing; ☎0131/668 8404, ⓦwww.roe.ac.uk) stands at the top of Blackford Hill, just a short walk south of Morningside or Newington. Immediately to the south are the **Braid Hills**, most of whose area is occupied by two golf courses, which are closed on alternate Sundays in order to allow access for walkers.

Further south are the **Pentland Hills**, a chain some eighteen miles long and five wide. Numerous walks, from gentle strolls along well-marked paths to a ten-mile traverse of the hills and moors, are outlined on a pamphlet available from the Regional Park Information Centre at **FLOTTERSTONE**, ten miles south of the city centre on the A702.

⑰

East Lothian

East Lothian consists of the coastal strip and hinterland immediately east of Edinburgh, bounded by the Firth of Forth to the north and the Lammermuir Hills to the south. All of it is within easy day-trip range from the capital though there are places you can stay overnight if you're keen to explore it properly. Often mocked as the "home counties" of Edinburgh, there's no denying its well-ordered feel, with prosperous farms and large estate houses dominating the scenery. The most immediately attractive part of the area is the coastline, extending from **Musselburgh**, all but joined onto Edinburgh, round to **Dunbar**. There's something for most tastes here, including the wide sandy beaches by **Aberlady**, the famous golf courses of **Gullane**, the enjoyable Seabird Centre at **North Berwick** which looks out to the volcanic plug of the Bass Rock, and the dramatic – and romantic – cliff-top ruins at **Tantallon**. The inland region is often ignored in favour of the coast, but it contains the county town of **Haddington**, a pleasant enough place in the Lammermuirs, along with the nearby attractions of Gifford, a neat village deeper into the hills, and Edinburgh's "local" whisky distillery by Pencaitland.

North Berwick and around

NORTH BERWICK has a great deal of charm and a somewhat faded, old-fashioned air, its guest houses and hotels extending along the shore in all their Victorian and Edwardian sobriety. The town's small harbour is set on a headland which cleaves two crescents of sand, providing the town with an appealing coastal setting.

Located in an attractively designed new building by the harbour, the **Scottish Seabird Centre** (April–Oct daily 10am–6pm; Nov–March Mon–Fri 10am–5pm, Sat & Sun 10am–5.30pm; £4.95) opened in 2000 and offers an introduction to all types of sea birds found around the Scottish coast, particularly the 100,000-plus gannets and puffins which nest on the Bass Rock every summer. Thanks to a live link from the centre to cameras mounted on the volcanic island, you're able to view close-up pictures of the birds in their nesting grounds. Elsewhere in the centre, hands-on games and exhibits explain more about different sea birds, and a mock-up of a cliff face has various stuffed birds nesting on it – all the birds, the centre insists, have been ethically gathered.

Resembling a giant molar, the **Bass Rock** rises 350ft above the sea some three miles east of North Berwick. This massive chunk of basalt has had an interesting history, having held out as a Jacobite stronghold for six years longer than anywhere else in the country, then serving as a prison, a fortress and a monastic retreat. The last lighthouse keepers left in 1988, leaving it, quite literally, to the birds – its Scotland's second-largest gannet colony after St Kilda but also hosts razorbills, terns, puffins, guillemots and fulmars.

Tantallon Castle

The melodramatic ruins of **Tantallon Castle** (April–Sept daily 9.30am–6.30pm; Oct–March Mon–Wed & Sat–Sun 9.30am–4.30pm, Thurs 9.30am–noon, closed Fri; £3; HS), three miles east of North Berwick on the A198, stand on the precipitous cliffs facing the Bass Rock. With a sheer drop down to the sea on three sides and a sequence of moats and ditches on the fourth, the castle's desolate invincibility is daunting, especially when the wind howls over the remaining battlements and the surf crashes on the rocks far below. Built at the end of the fourteenth century, the castle was a stronghold of the Douglases, the earls of Angus, one of the most powerful noble families in Scotland.

Besieged several times, the castle was finally destroyed by Cromwell in 1651 after a twelve-day bombardment. The ruins, including a seventeenth-century dovecote left untouched by Cromwell's men, enjoy a wonderfully photogenic setting, with the Bass Rock and the Firth of Forth in the background. You can reach Tantallon Castle from North Berwick by the Dunbar **bus** (Mon–Sat 6 daily, Sun 2 daily), which takes fifteen minutes, or you can walk there from town along the cliffs in around an hour.

Practicalities

North Berwick is served by a regular half-hour **train** from Edinburgh Waverley, with special travel and entry deals available for those heading for the Seabird Centre (ask at Waverley ticket office). **Buses** from Edinburgh (every 30min) run along the coast via Aberlady, Gullane and Dirleton and stop on High Street, while the hourly service from Haddington and Dunbar terminate outside the **tourist office**, on Quality Street (April & May Mon–Sat 9am–6pm; June & Sept Mon–Sat 9am–6pm, Sun 11am–4pm; July Mon–Sat

9am–7pm, Sun 11am–6pm; Aug Mon–Sat 9am–8pm, Sun 11am–6pm; Oct–March Mon–Sat 9am–5pm; ☎01620/892197).

As befits a well-to-do holiday resort, there are several excellent **B&Bs**, including *Chestnut Lodge*, at 2a Ware Rd (☎01620/894256; ❷), a half-timber chalet run by keen golfers, and *Glebe House*, Law Road (☎01620/892608; ❹), a beautiful eighteenth-century manse in secluded grounds overlooking the sea. Of the **guest houses**, *Beach Lodge*, 5 Beach Rd (☎01620/892257, ⓦwww.beachlodge.co.uk; ❸), has wide sea views and serves good vegetarian breakfasts. The nearest **campsite**, *Tantallon Caravan Park* (☎01620/893348, ⓦwww.meadowhead.co.uk/tantallon; closed Feb), occupies a prime cliff-top location a couple of miles east of the centre – take the Dunbar bus (Mon–Sat 6 daily, Sun 2 daily).

One of the best **cafés** in town is at the Seabird Centre, which has panoramic views over the beach. As well as lunches, coffees and cakes, it's also open occasionally as a **bistro** in the evenings (May–Sept Fri & Sat; for bookings call ☎01620/890202). In town, the *Grange* at 35 High St (☎01620/893344; closed Sun) is a pleasant restaurant serving good-quality, moderately priced meals, while both the *Tantallon Inn* on Marine Parade and the *Marine Hotel* on Cromwell Road do decent bar food.

Dunbar

Twelve miles further along the coast lies **DUNBAR**, which bears some resemblance to North Berwick with its wide, recently spruced-up High Street graced by several grand old stone buildings. One of these is the three-storey **John Muir Birthplace**, 126 High St (April–Oct Mon–Sat 9am–5pm, Sun 1–5pm; Nov–March Wed–Sat 9am–5pm, Sun 1–5pm; free), first home of the explorer and naturalist who created the United States national park system. Recently refurbished, the house now acts as an interpretative and education centre inspired by the pioneer's life and legacy. Inspiring though the centre is, a more appropriate tribute, in some respects, is the **country park** in Muir's honour, where an easy three-mile walk west of the harbour takes you along a rugged stretch of coast to the sands of Belhaven Bay.

The **tourist office** is at 143a High St (April & Oct Mon–Sat 9am–5pm, May–June & Sept Mon–Sat 9am–6pm, Sun 11am–4pm; July Mon–Sat 9am–7pm, Sun 11am–6pm; Aug Mon–Sat 9am–8pm, Sun 11am–6pm; ☎01368/863353). For a light **lunch**, the *Food Hamper* and *William Smith's* on the High Street do good sandwiches, while the best evening meal option is the *Creel* (☎01368/863279) by the old harbour, where you can eat excellent seafood and other local produce.

Haddington and around

The East Lothian gentry keep a careful eye on **HADDINGTON**, their favourite country town. Its compact centre preserves an intriguing ensemble of seventeenth- to nineteenth-century architectural styles where everything of any interest has been labelled and plaqued. Haddington's centre is best approached from the west, where tree-trimmed **Court Street** ends suddenly with the soaring spire, stately stonework and dignified Venetian windows of the **Town House**, designed by William Adam in 1748.

Heading east from the town centre along High Street, it's a brief walk down Church Street – past the hooped arches of **Nungate Bridge** – to the hulking mass of **St Mary's Church** (April–Sept Mon–Sat 11am–4pm, Sun 2–4.30pm;

free), Scotland's largest parish church. Built close to the reedy River Tyne, the church dates from the fourteenth century but it's a real hotch-potch of styles, the squat grey tower uneasy above clumsy buttressing and pinkish-ochre stone walls. Inside, on the **Lauderdale Aisle**, a munificent tomb features the best of Elizabethan alabaster carving, moustached knights and their ruffed ladies lying beneath a finely ornamented canopy.

Fast and frequent **buses** connect Haddington with Edinburgh, fifteen miles to the west, and with North Berwick on the east coast, with all services stopping on High Street. There's no **tourist office**, but orientation is easy. For **daytime snacks** and lovely deli lunch platters, the place to seek out is *Jaques & Lawrence* at 37 Court St, opposite the post office. The best place for an **evening meal** is the *Waterside Bistro* (℡01620/825674), on the far side of Nungate Bridge.

Glenkinchie Distillery

Six miles west of Gifford, and about the same distance from Haddington along the A6093, the village of Pencaitland is the closest place to Edinburgh where malt whisky is made. Set in a peaceful dip in the rolling countryside about two miles outside Pencaitland, the **Glenkinchie Distillery** (June–Oct Mon–Sat 10am–5pm, Sun noon–5pm; Nov–Feb Mon–Fri noon–4pm; March–May Mon–Fri 10am–5pm; £4) is one of only a handful found in the Lowlands of Scotland. Here, of course, they emphasize the qualities which set Glenkinchie, a lighter, drier malt, apart from the peaty, smoky whiskies of the north. Also in the tour there's an impressive scale model of a distillery, allowing you to place all the different processes in context, and a room where the art of blending is explained.

Midlothian

Immediately south of Edinburgh lies the old county of **MIDLOTHIAN**, once called Edinburghshire. It's one of the hilliest parts of the Central Lowlands, with the Pentland chain running down its western side, and the Moorfoots defining its boundary with the Borders to the south. Though predominantly rural, it contains a belt of former mining communities, which are struggling to come to terms with the recent decline of the industry. Such charms as it has are mostly low-key, with the exception of the riotously ornate chapel at **Roslin**.

Dalkeith and around

Despite its Victorian demeanour, **DALKEITH**, eight miles southeast of central Edinburgh – to which it is linked by very regular buses (#3/A, #49, or First #86) – grew up in the Middle Ages as a baronial burgh under the successive control of the Douglases and Buccleuchs. Today it's a bustling shopping centre, with an unusually broad High Street at its heart.

A mile or so south is **NEWTONGRANGE**, whose Lady Victoria Colliery is now open to the public as the **Scottish Mining Museum** (daily: Feb–Nov 10am–5pm, Dec–Jan 11am–4pm; £4), with a 1625-foot shaft, and a winding tower powered by Scotland's largest steam engine. A great place for kids, the visitor centre brings the mine and the local community to life with "magic helmets", which enable you to go on shift and experience a virtual-reality tour of life below ground.

Roslin

The tranquil village of **ROSLIN** lies seven miles south of the centre of Edinburgh, from where it can be reached by bus #15A (Mon–Fri) or First #141 (Sat) from St Andrew Square. An otherwise nondescript place, the village has two unusual claims to fame: it was near here, at the Roslin Institute, that the world's first cloned sheep, Dolly, was created in 1997; and it also boasts the mysterious, richly decorated late-Gothic **Rosslyn Chapel** (Mon–Sat 10am–5pm, Sun noon–4.45pm; £4). Only the choir, Lady Chapel and part of the transepts were built of what was intended to be a huge collegiate church dedicated to St Matthew: construction halted soon after the founder's death in 1484, and the vestry built onto the facade nearly four hundred years later is the sole subsequent addition. After a long period of neglect, a massive restoration project has recently been undertaken: a rigid canopy has been constructed over the chapel which will remain in place for several years in order to dry out the saturated ceiling and walls, and other essential repairs are due to be carried out within the chapel.

The outside of the chapel bristles with pinnacles, gargoyles, flying buttresses and canopies, while inside the foliage carving is particularly outstanding, with botanically accurate depictions of over a dozen different leaves and plants. The greatest and most original carving of all is the extraordinary knotted **Apprentice Pillar** at the southeastern corner of the Lady Chapel. According to local legend, the pillar was made by an apprentice during the absence of the master mason, who killed him in a fit of jealousy on seeing the finished work.

The imagery of the carvings, together with the history of the family which owns the chapel, the St Clairs of Rosslyn, leave little doubt about its links to the Knights Templar and freemasonry. A number of books have been written on the subject, which also make tangential connections between the chapel, the Turin Shroud and the regular sightings of UFOs over Midlothian. Conspiracy theories notwithstanding, the chapel is very definitely worth a visit.

17

West Lothian

To many, West Lothian is a poor relative to the rolling, rich farmland of East and Midlothian, with a landscape dominated by motorways, industrial estates and giant hillocks of ochre-coloured mine waste called "bings". However, anywhere this close to the centres of power through Scottish history would find it hard not to have something to show for itself, and in the ruined royal palace at **Linlithgow** the area boasts one of Scotland's more magnificent ruins. The village of **South Queensferry** lies under the considerable shadow of the **Forth rail and road bridges**, while a mile or two beyond South Queensferry is **Hopetoun House**, an impressive stately home.

Linlithgow

Roughly equidistant (fifteen miles) from Falkirk and Edinburgh is the ancient royal burgh of **LINLITHGOW**. The town itself has largely kept its medieval layout, but development since the 1960s has sadly stripped it of some fine buildings, notably close to the **Town Hall** and **Cross** – the former marketplace – on the long High Street.

Though hidden from the main street, **Linlithgow Palace** (April–Sept daily 9.30am–6.30pm; Oct–March Mon–Sat 9.30am–4.30pm, Sun 2–4.30pm; £3;

HS), is a splendid fifteenth-century ruin romantically set on the edge of Linlithgow Loch and associated with some of Scotland's best-known historical figures – including Mary, Queen of Scots, who was born here on December 8 1542 and became queen six days later. A royal manor house is believed to have existed on this site since the time of David I. Fire razed the manor in 1424, after which James I began construction of the present palace, a process that continued through two centuries and the reign of no fewer than eight monarchs.

This is a great place to take children: the rooflessness of the castle creates unexpected vistas and the elegant, bare rooms echo with footsteps and the fluttering of birds flying out through the empty windows. There's a labyrinthine feel to the place with spiral staircases and endless nooks and crannies, while the galleried **Great Hall** and adjoining kitchen, with its truly cavernous fireplace, are magnificent.

Practicalities

Frequent **buses** between Stirling and Edinburgh stop at the Cross, and the town is on the main train routes from Edinburgh to both Glasgow Queen Street and Stirling; the **train station** lies at the southern end of town. The **tourist office** is in the Town Hall building at the Cross (Easter–Oct daily 10am–5pm; ☎01506/844600), between the Palace and the High Street.

There are a few decent places to **eat** in Linlithgow: for good pub food try *The Four Marys*, opposite the Cross on High Street, while *Marynka* (☎01506/840123), on the High Street at number 57, is a modern bistro-style place. Just outside Linlithgow on the way to Blackness is the *Champany Inn* (☎01506/834532), which serves delicious steaks, chops and seafood.

South Queensferry and around

A few miles east along the coast is **SOUTH QUEENSFERRY**, most prominent today for its location at the southern end of the two mighty Forth Bridges. It's a compact little town which earned its name as the crossing point used by St Margaret for her frequent trips between her palaces in Edinburgh and Dunfermline. The small **museum**, 53 High St (Mon & Thurs–Sat 10am–1pm & 2.15–5pm; free), contains relics of the town's history and information on the building of the two bridges which loom over the village. A dedicated museum to the bridge can be found in North Queensferry (see p.1079), while the best way to get a good view of the magnificent Rail Bridge is to walk (or cycle) across the Road Bridge.

Inchcolm

From South Queensferry's Hawes Pier, just west of the rail bridge, the *Maid of the Forth* (April–June Sat & Sun; July to mid-Sept daily; confirm sailing in advance on ☎0131/331 4857; £11) heads out onto the Forth in the direction of the island of **Inchcolm**, whose beautiful ruined **Abbey** was founded in 1123 by King Alexander I in gratitude for the hospitality he received from a hermit. The best-preserved medieval monastic complex in Scotland, the abbey's surviving buildings date from the thirteenth to the fifteenth century, and include a splendid octagonal chapterhouse.

Hopetoun House

Immediately beyond the western edge of South Queensferry, just over the West Lothian border, **Hopetoun House** (April–Sept daily 10am–5.30pm; £ house and grounds, £3 grounds only; ⓦwww.hopetounhouse.com) is one of

Scotland's grandest stately homes. The original house was built at the turn of the eighteenth century for the first earl of Hopetoun by Sir William Bruce, the architect of Holyroodhouse. A couple of decades later, William Adam carried out an enormous extension, engulfing the house in a curvaceous main facade and two projecting wings – superb examples of Roman Baroque pomp and swagger. Among the house's furnishings are seventeenth-century tapestries, Meissen porcelain, and a distinguished collection of paintings. The grounds of Hopetoun House are also open, with magnificent walks along the banks of the Forth.

Travel details

Buses

For information on all local and national bus services, contact Traveline ☎08706/082608 (daily 7am–9pm), ⓦwww.traveline.org.uk.

Edinburgh (St Andrew Square) to: Aberdeen (hourly; 3hr 50min); Birmingham (3 daily; 6hr 50min); Dundee (hourly; 1hr 45min–2hr); Fort William (4 daily direct; 4hr); Glasgow (every 15min; 1hr 10min); Inverness (hourly; 3–4hr); London (6 daily; 7hr 50min); Newcastle upon Tyne (2 daily; 3hr 15min); Oban (3 daily; change at Tyndrum or Perth, 5hr); Perth (hourly; 1hr 20min); York (1 daily; 5hr).

Trains

For information on all local and national rail services, contact National Rail Enquiries

☎08457/484950, ⓦwww.nationalrail.co.uk.

Edinburgh to: Aberdeen (hourly; 2hr 20min); Birmingham (4 daily; 5hr 30min); Dunbar (8 daily; 30min); Dundee (hourly; 1hr 45min); Falkirk (every 15min; 25min); Fort William (change at Glasgow, 3 daily; 4hr 55min); Glasgow (every 15–30min; 50min); Inverness (5 daily; 3hr 50min); London (hourly; 4hr 30min); Manchester (4 daily; 4hr); Newcastle upon Tyne (hourly; 1hr 30min); North Berwick (hourly; 30 min); Oban (change at Glasgow, 3 daily; 4hr 10min); Perth (6 daily; 1hr 15min); Stirling (every 30min; 45min); York (hourly; 2hr 30min).

Flights

Edinburgh to: Kirkwall (Mon–Sat 2 daily, Sun 1 daily; 1hr 55min); Lerwick (1 daily; 1hr 30min); Stornoway (2 daily; 1hr 10 min).

17

Southern Scotland

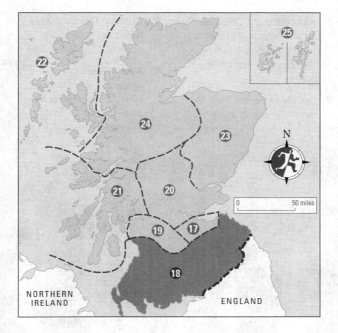

Highlights

CHAPTER 18

* **Melrose Abbey** Border Abbey with the best-preserved sculptural detail, set in a charming town. **See p.974**

* **Caerlaverock** One of Scotland's most photo-genic moated castles. **See p.988**

* **Kirkcudbright** One-time artists' colony, and the best-looking town in the "Scottish Riviera". **See p.991**

* **Galloway Forest Park** Go mountain biking along remote forest tracks, or hiking on the Southern Upland Way. **See p.993**

* **Alloway** The village where poet Robert Burns was born, and the best of many Burns pilgrimage spots in the region. **See p.999**

* **Culzean Castle** Stately home with a fabulous cliff-edge setting. **See p.999**

* **Ailsa Craig** Watch baby gannets learn the art of flying and diving for fish. **See p.1000**

△ Melrose Abbey

18

Southern Scotland

S outhern Scotland divides neatly into three distinct regions: the
Borders, Dumfries and Galloway, and Ayrshire. Although none of the
regions has the highest of tourist profiles, those visitors who whizz past
on their way to Edinburgh, Glasgow or the Highlands are missing out
on a huge swathe of Scotland that is in many ways the very heart of the country. Its inhabitants, particularly in the Borders, bore the brunt of long wars
with the English, its farms have fed Scotland's cities since industrialization, and
two of the country's literary icons, Sir Walter Scott and Robbie Burns, lived
and died here.

Geographically, the region is dominated by the **Southern Uplands**, a chain
of bulging round-topped hills and weather-beaten moorland, punctuated by
narrow glens, fast-flowing rivers and blue-black lochs. This region is at its most
dramatic in the **Galloway Forest Park** to the southwest, with peaks reaching
to over 2000ft, crisscrossed by numerous popular walking trails. Back in the
valleys, and down by the coast, the landscape is fairly lush – farming country
for the most part, with tourism an important, but secondary, industry. On the
coast, you'll find enormous variety: the east coast is fairly bleak, with dramatic
cliffs interspersed with tiny fishing villages; the **Solway coast**, in the southwest, is much gentler, indented by sandy coves and estuaries; while the Ayrshire
coast, by contrast, is much more heavily populated, and in parts an almost continuous stretch of seaside resorts and industrial centres.

Lying north of the inhospitable Cheviot Hills, which separate Scotland
from England, the **Borders** region is dominated by the meanderings of
the **River Tweed**. None of the towns along the Tweed is of any great size,
yet they have provided inspiration for countless folkloric ballads telling of
bloody battles with the English and clashes between the notorious war-
ring families, the Border Reivers. The small but delightful town of
Melrose, in the heart of the Borders, is the most obvious base for exploring the region, and has the most impressive of the four **Border abbeys**
founded by the medieval Canmore kings, all of which are now reduced to
romantic ruins.

Dumfries and Galloway, occupying the southwestern corner of Scotland,
gets even more overlooked than the Borders, though the region remains popular with Lowland Scots and folk from the north of England. If you do make
the effort to get off the main north–south highway to Glasgow, you'll find
several more ruined abbeys, medieval castles, forested hills and dramatic tidal
flats and seacliffs ideal for bird-watching. The key resort is the charming town
of **Kirkcudbright**, halfway along the marshy Solway coast, well placed for
exploring the rest of the county.

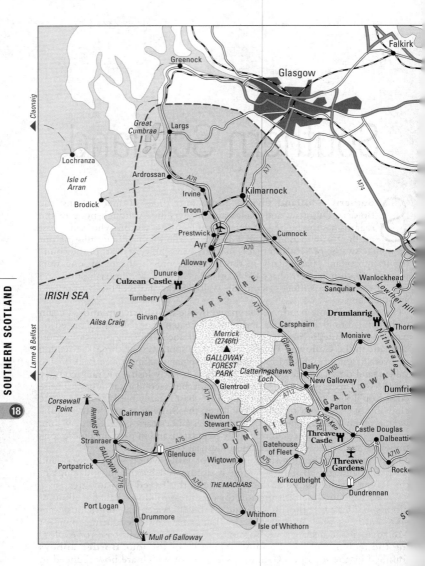

Falkirk

Glasgow

Greenock

◄ Claonaig

Great
Cumbrae — Largs

Lochranza

Isle of
Arran

Ardrossan

Brodick

Irvine

Troon

Kilmarnock

Prestwick

Ayr

Cumnock

Alloway

Dunure

Culzean Castle

Wanlockhead

Turnberry

Sanquhar

IRISH SEA

A Y R S H I R E

◄ Larne & Belfast

Ailsa Craig

Girvan

Carsphairn

Drumlanrig

Thorn

Merrick
(2746ft)
▲
**GALLOWAY
FOREST
PARK**

Moniaive

Glenkens

Lowther Hill

Clatteringshaws
Loch

Dalry

Corsewall
Point

Glentrool

New Galloway

Dumfrie

RHINNS OF GALLOWAY

Cairnryan

Parton

Loch Ken

G A L L O W A Y

Nithsdale

Newton
Stewart

**Threave
Castle**

Castle Douglas

Stranraer

Glenluce

D U M F R I E S &

Dalbeatti

Portpatrick

Wigtown

Gatehouse
of Fleet

**Threave
Gardens**

A710

Rock

Port Logan

THE MACHARS

Kirkcudbright

Dundrennan

Drummore

Whithorn

Isle of Whithorn

S

Mull of Galloway

972

Ayrshire is rich farming country, and not an obvious destination for first-time visitors to Scotland. It has fewer sights than its neighbours, with almost everything of interest confined to the coast. However, the **golf courses** along its gentle coastline are among the finest links courses in the country, and golfers can buy three- and five-day passes from tourist offices allowing free or reduced-fee access to many of the region's golf courses. Fans of **Robert Burns** could happily spend several days exploring the author's old haunts, especially at **Ayr**, the handsome county town, and the nearby village of Alloway, the poet's birthplace.

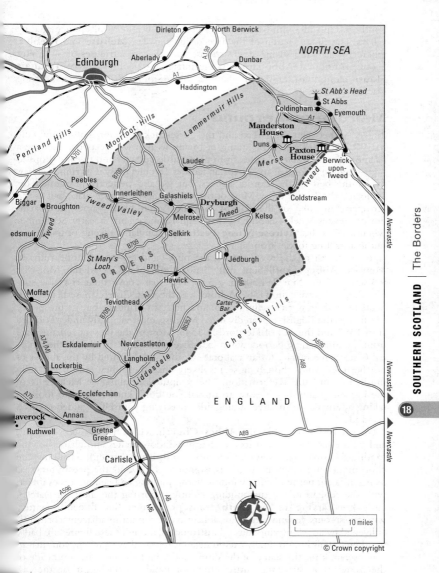

© Crown copyright

The Borders

andwiched between the Cheviot Hills on the English border and the
entland and Moorfoot ranges to the south of Edinburgh, is the **Borders**
gion (Ⓦ www.scot-borders.co.uk). If you've travelled from the south across
e bleak moorland of neighbouring Northumberland, you'll be struck by the
reen lushness of the **Tweed valley**, the pivotal feature of the region's geog-
phy. Yet the Borders also incorporates some of the wildest stretches of the

Southern Uplands, with bare, rounded peaks and heathery hills punctuated by valleys. The finest section of the Tweed lies between **Melrose** and **Peebles**, where you'll find a string of attractions, from the eccentricities of Sir Walter Scott's mansion at **Abbotsford** to the intriguing Jacobite past of **Traquair House**, along with the region's famous abbeys, founded in the reign of King David I (1124–53).

Melrose and around

Tucked in between the Tweed and the gorse-backed Eildon Hills, minuscule **MELROSE** is the most beguiling of towns, its narrow streets trimmed by a harmonious ensemble of styles, from pretty little cottages and tweedy shops to high-standing Georgian and Victorian facades. Its chief draw is its ruined abbey, by far the best of the Border abbeys, but it's also perfectly positioned for exploring the Tweed valley. Most of the year it's a sleepy little place, but as the birthplace in 1883 of the **Rugby Sevens** (seven-a-side games), it swarms during Sevens Week (second week in April), and again in early September when it hosts the **Melrose Music Festival**, a popular weekend of traditional music attracting folkies from afar.

To the north of the town square, the pink- and red-tinted stone ruins of **Melrose Abbey** (April–Sept daily 9.30am–6.30pm; Oct–March Mon–Sat 9.30am–4.30pm, Sun 2–4.30pm; £3.50; HS) soar above their riverside surroundings. Founded in 1136, Melrose was the first Cistercian settlement in Scotland and grew rich selling wool and hides to Flanders, but its prosperity was fragile: the English repeatedly razed Melrose, most viciously under Richard II in 1385 and the earl of Hertford in 1545. Most of the present remains date from the intervening period, when extensive rebuilding abandoned the original Cistercian austerity for an elaborate Gothic style inspired by the abbeys of northern England, though it seems likely that the abbey was never fully finished before the Reformation. The sculptural detailing at Melrose is of the highest quality, but it's easy to miss if you don't know where to look, so taking advantage of the free audioguide, or buying yourself a guidebook, is a good idea.

The site is dominated by the **Abbey Church**, which has lost its west front, and whose nave is reduced to the elegant window arches and chapels of the south aisle. Amazingly, however, the stone **pulpitum** (screen), separating the choir monks from their lay brothers, is preserved. Beyond, the **presbytery** has its magnificent perpendicular window, lierne vaulting and ceiling bosses intact, with the capitals of the surrounding columns sporting the most intricate of curly kale carving. In the **south transept**, another fine fifteenth-century window sprouts yet more delicate, foliate tracery and the adjacent cornice is enlivened by angels playing musical instruments, though these figures are badly weathered. This kind of finely carved detail is repeated everywhere you turn in Melrose: look for the statue of the Virgin and Child, high on the south side of the westernmost surviving buttress, the Coronation of the Virgin on the east end gable, and the numerous mischievous **gargoyles**, from peculiar crouching beasts to the pig playing the bagpipes on the roof on the south side of the nave.

Legend has it that the heart of **Robert the Bruce** is buried here (his body having been buried at Dunfermline Abbey), and in 1997, when a heart cask was publicly exhumed, this theory received an unexpected boost. However, the burial location was not in accordance with Bruce's own wishes. In 1329, the dying king told his friend, Sir James Douglas, to carry his heart on a Crusade to the Holy Land in fulfilment of an old vow: "Seeing therefore, that my body cannot go to achieve what my heart desires, I will send my heart instead of my body, to accomplish my vow." Douglas tried his best, but was killed fighting the Moors in Spain – and Bruce's heart ended up in Melrose. A new commemorative stone marks its current resting place in the chapterhouse, to the north of the sacristy.

The paltry ruins of the old monastic buildings edge the church to the north and lead over the road to the **Commendator's House** (same hours as the abbey), a lovely red sandstone building converted into a private house in 1590 by the abbey's last Commendator, and now housing a modest collection of ecclesiastical bric-a-brac. Beyond the house is the mill-lade, where water used to flow in order to power the abbey's mills, and was also diverted to flush the monks' latrines. Back towards the town, to the south of the abbey, you should pop into the delightful **Priorwood Garden** (April–Sept Mon–Sat 10am–5.30pm, Sun 1.30–5.30pm; Oct–Dec Mon–Sat 10am–4pm, Sun 1.30–4pm; £2.50; NTS), whose compact walled precincts are given over to an orchard and flowers that are suitable for drying; there's a dried flower shop, too.

Practicalities

Buses to Melrose stop in Market Square, from where it's a brief walk north to the abbey ruins and the **tourist office** opposite (Mon–Sat 10am–5pm, Sun 10am–2pm). Melrose has a clutch of **hotels**, with prices generally higher than you might expect. The best of the bunch is *Burt's*, a smartly converted old inn on Market Square (☎01896/822285, ⓦwww.burtshotel.co.uk; ❻); rooms are small, but very comfortable. Across the street is the ten-bedroom *Millars* (☎01896/822645, ⓦwww.millarshotel.co.uk; ❺), recently smartened up and with fewer pretensions than *Burt's*. It's among Melrose's simple **B&Bs**, however, that you'll get the real flavour of the place, most notably at the easy-going and comfortable *Braidwood*, on Buccleuch Street (☎01896/822488; ❷), a stone's throw from the abbey, and the equally agreeable *Dunfermline House* (☎01896/822148, ⓦwww.dunmel.freeserve.co.uk; ❷) opposite – advance booking is recommended at both during the summer. The town also has an SYHA **hostel** (☎0870/004 1141, Ⓔreservations@syha.org.uk; late March to late Oct) in a sprawling Georgian villa overlooking the abbey from beside the access road into the bypass. The *Gibson Caravan Park* **campsite** (☎01896/822969) is in the town centre, just off the High Street, opposite the Greenyards rugby grounds.

Melrose offers a reasonable choice of **eating** options. *Marmion's Brasserie* (☎01896/822245), housed in a spacious Victorian house on Buccleuch Street, serves well-prepared meals from an imaginative, moderately expensive menu. *Burt's* does excellent bar meals, and if you're feeling energetic, walk past the abbey and across the old suspension bridge to Gattonside, where the *Hoebridge Inn* (☎01896/823082; closed Mon), once a bobbin mill and now one of the Borders' best restaurants, serves home-made Scottish food in relaxed, low-key surroundings. If you want a light lunch or snack, head to *Russell's* (closed Thurs out of season), a popular, very traditional tearoom on Market Square; or *Haldane's Fish & Chip Shop* (closed Wed), next door. For **pubs**, try the friendly *King's Arms* on the High Street, or the *Ship Inn*, on East Port at the top of the square, the liveliest in town, especially during the Folk Festival and on Saturday afternoons when the Melrose rugby team have played at home. Be sure to check out what's on at *The Wynd* (☎01896/823854, ⓦwww.thewynd.com), Melrose's very own pint-sized **theatre**, tucked away down the alleyway, north off the main square, which shows films and puts on gigs as well as live drama.

Abbotsford

The stately home of **Abbotsford** (mid-March to May & Oct Mon–Sat 9.30am–5pm; Sun 2–5pm; June-Sept Mon–Sat 9.30am–5pm, Sun 9.30am–5pm; £4), three miles up the Tweed from Melrose, was designed to satisfy the Romantic inclinations of **Sir Walter Scott**, who lived here from 1812 until his death twenty years later. Abbotsford (as Scott chose to call it) took twelve years to evolve, with the fanciful turrets and castellations of the Scots Baronial exterior incorporating copies of medieval originals: the entrance porch imitates that of Linlithgow Palace and the screen wall in the garden echoes Melrose Abbey's cloister. Despite all the exterior pomp, the interior is surprisingly small and poky, with just six rooms open for viewing on the upper floor. Visitors start in the wood-panelled study, with its small writing desk made of salvage from the Spanish Armada, at which Scott banged out the Waverley novels at a furious rate. The heavy wood-panelled library boasts Scott's collection of more than nine thousand rare books and an extraordinary assortment of memorabilia, the centrepiece of which is Napoleon's pen case and blotting book, but which also includes Rob Roy's purse and *skene dhu* (knife), and the inlaid pearl crucifix that accompanied Mary, Queen of Scots to the scaffold. You can also see Henry Raeburn's famous portrait of Scott hanging in the drawing room, and all sorts of weapons – notably Rob Roy's sword, dagger and gun – in the armoury.

The fast and frequent Melrose–Galashiels **bus** provides easy access to Abbotsford: ask for the Tweedbank island on the A6091, from where the house is a ten-minute walk up the road.

Dryburgh Abbey

Hidden away in a U-bend in the Tweed, three or four miles east of Melrose, the remains of **Dryburgh Abbey** (April–Sept daily 9.30am–6.30pm; Oct–March Mon–Sat 9.30am–4.30pm, Sun 2–4.30pm; £3; HS) occupy an idyllic position against a hilly backdrop, with ancient cedars, redwoods, beech and lime trees and wide lawns flattering the pinkish-red hues of the stonework. The Premonstratensians founded the abbey in the twelfth century, but they were never as successful as their Cistercian neighbours in Melrose. The romantic setting is second to none, but the ruins of the **Abbey Church** are much less substantial than, say, at Melrose or Jedburgh. Virtually nothing survives of the nave, but the transepts have fared better, their chapels now serving as private burial grounds for, among others, Sir Walter Scott and Field Marshal Haig, the World War I commander whose ineptitude cost thousands of soldiers' lives. The night stairs, down which the monks stumbled in the early hours of the morning, survive in the south transept, and lead even today to the monks' dormitory. Leaving the church via the east processional door in the south aisle, with its dog-tooth decoration, you enter the cloisters, the highlight of which is the barrel-vaulted **Chapter House**, complete with low stone benches and blind interlaced arcading.

Next door to the abbey is the *Dryburgh Abbey Hotel* (☎01835/822261 ⓦwww.dryburgh.co.uk; ❼), a sprawling red-sandstone **hotel** that's a hunting, shooting, fishing kind of place. You can enjoy the indoor pool, or simply have a cup of tea or a drink in the bar. Dryburgh is not easy to get to by **public transport**, though it's only a mile's walk north from St Boswell's on the A68. Drivers and cyclists should approach the abbey via the much-visited **Scott's View**, to the north on the B6356, overlooking the Tweed Valley, where the writer and his friends often picnicked and where Scott's horse stopped out of habit during the writer's own funeral procession. The scene inspired

Sir Walter Scott

Walter Scott (1771–1832) was born in Edinburgh to a solidly bourgeois family whose roots were in Selkirkshire. As a child he was left disabled by polio and his anxious parents sent him to recuperate at his grandfather's farm in Smailholm, where the boy's imagination was fired by his relatives' tales of derring-do, the violent history of the Borders retold amidst the rugged landscape that he spent long summer days exploring. Scott returned to Edinburgh to resume his education and take up a career in law, but his real interests remained elsewhere. Throughout the 1790s he transcribed hundreds of old Border ballads, publishing a three-volume collection entitled *Minstrelsy of the Scottish Borders* in 1802. An instant success, *Minstrelsy* was followed by Scott's own *Lay of the Last Minstrel*, a narrative poem whose strong story and rose-tinted regionalism proved very popular.

More poetry was to come, most successfully *Marmion* (1808) and *The Lady of the Lake* (1810), not to mention an eighteen-volume edition of the works of John Dryden and nineteen volumes of Jonathan Swift. However, despite having two paid jobs, one as the sheriff-depute of Selkirkshire, the other as clerk to the Court of Session in Edinburgh, his finances remained shaky. He had become a partner in a printing firm, which put him deeply into debt, not helped by the enormous sums he spent on his mansion, Abbotsford. From 1813, Scott was writing to pay the bills and thumped out a veritable flood of historical novels using his extensive knowledge of Scottish history and folklore. He produced his best work within the space of ten years: *Waverley* (1814), *The Antiquary* (1816), *Rob Roy* and *The Heart of Midlothian* (both 1818), as well as two notable novels set in England, *Ivanhoe* (1819) and *Kenilworth* (1821). In 1824 he returned to Scottish tales with *Redgauntlet*, the last of his quality work.

A year later Scott's money problems reached crisis proportions after an economic crash bankrupted his printing business. Attempting to pay his creditors in full, he found the quality of his writing deteriorating with its increased speed and the effort broke his health. His last years were plagued by illness, and in 1832 he died at Abbotsford and was buried within the ruins of Dryburgh Abbey.

Although Scott's interests were diverse, his historical novels mostly focused on the Jacobites, whose loyalty to the Stuarts had riven Scotland since the "Glorious Revolution" of 1688. That the nation was prepared to be entertained by such tales was essentially a matter of timing: by the 1760s it was clear the Jacobite cause was lost for good and Scotland, emerging from its isolated medievalism, had been firmly welded into the United Kingdom. Thus its turbulent history and independent spirit was safely in the past, and ripe for romancing – as shown by the arrival of King George IV in Edinburgh during 1822 decked out in Highland dress. Yet, for Sir Walter the romance was tinged with a genuine sense of loss. Loyal to the Hanoverians, he still grieved for Bonnie Prince Charlie; he welcomed a commercial Scotland but lamented the passing of feudal ties, and so his heroes are transitional, fighting men of action superseded by bourgeois figures searching for a clear identity.

18

oseph Turner's *Melrose 1831*, now on display in the National Gallery of Scotland (see p.940).

Kelso and around

KELSO, ten miles or so downstream from Melrose, at the confluence of the Tweed and Teviot, grew up in the shadow of its now-ruined Benedictine **Abbey** (April–Dec daily; free), once the richest and most powerful of the Border abbeys. Unfortunately, the English savaged Kelso three times in the first half of the sixteenth century: the last (and by far the worst) assault was part of the "Rough Wooing" led by the earl of Hertford when the Scots refused to ratify a marriage treaty between Henry VIII's son and the infant Mary, Queen of Scots. Such was the extent of the devastation – compounded by the Reformation – that less survives of Kelso than any of the Border abbeys. Nevertheless, at first sight, it looks pretty impressive, with the heavy Norman west end of the abbey church almost entirely intact. Beyond, little remains, though it is possible to make out the two transepts and towers which gave the abbey the shape of a double cross, unique in Scotland.

Kelso town managed to rebuild itself and is now centred on **The Square**, an unusually large cobbled expanse presided over by the honey-hued Ionic columns, pediment and oversized clock belltower of the elegant **Town Hall**. To one side stands the imposing *Cross Keys Hotel*, with its distinctive rooftop balustrade, and a supporting chorus of three-storey eighteenth- and nine-teenth-century pastel buildings on every side. Leaving the Square along Roxburgh Street, take the alley down to the **Cobby Riverside Walk**, where a brief stroll leads to Floors Castle (see below). En route, but hidden from view by the islet in the middle of the river, is the spot where the Teviot meets the Tweed. This bit of river, known as The Junction, has long been famous for its **salmon fishing**, with permits – costing thousands – booked years in advance. Permits for fishing other, less expensive reaches of the Tweed and Teviot are available from Tweedside Tackle, 36 Bridge St (℡01573/225306).

Practicalities

Kelso **bus station** on Roxburgh Street is a brief walk from The Square, where you'll find the **tourist office** in the Town Hall (July & Aug Mon–Sat 9am–6pm, Sun 10am–5pm; April–June & Sept Mon–Sat 10am–5pm, Sun 10am–1pm; Oct Mon–Sat 10am–4.30pm, Sun 10am–1pm; ℡01573/223464). **Accommodation** is usually not a problem: one of the best B&Bs in town is *Abbey Bank*, near Kelso Pottery on The Knowes (℡01573/226550, ℮diah@abbeybank.freeserve.co.uk; ❷), a Georgian house with large double beds and a lovely south-facing garden. Another good choice is the *Ednam House Hotel* (℡01573/224168, ⓦwww.ednamhouse.com; ❺), a splendid Georgian mansion set back off Bridge Street, with antique furnishings and fittings and gardens that abut the Tweed; make sure you're not put in the modern extension. Lastly, there's the *Roxburghe Hotel* (℡01573/450331, ⓦwww.roxburghe.net; ❼), a luxury hotel two miles south of Kelso on the A698 at Heiton, owned by the duke and duchess of Roxburghe, which also boasts an eighteen-hole championship golf course.

Most **eating** places are just off The Square: the *Cobbles Inn* restaurant is housed in a former pub just up Bowmont Street – check the specials menu for the best dishes – and the *Cross Keys* in the square specializes in local produce. The moderately expensive *Ednam House Hotel* (see above) restaurant is more upmarket and often features some unusual dishes, while the restaurant at the *Roxburghe Hotel* is even more formal, its top-quality food and service matched by correspondingly high prices. For a snack, try *Le Jardin,* next to Kelso Pottery (closed Mon). If you're looking to pick up picnic food in the area, head for the *Teviot Smokery*, on the A698 five miles south of Kelso, where you can also enjoy a river walk, a stroll through the water gardens or a snack in the café.

Floors Castle

If you stand on Kelso's handsome bridge over the Tweed, you can easily make out the pepperpot turrets and castellations of **Floors Castle** (Easter–Oct daily 10am–4.30pm; £5.75; ⓦwww.floorscastle.com), a vast, pompous mansion mile or so northwest of the town. The bulk of the building was designed by William Adam in the 1720s, and, picking through the Victorian modifications, the interior still demonstrates his uncluttered style. However, you won't see much of it, as just ten rooms and a basement are open to the public. Highlights include Hendrick Danckert's splendid panorama of Horse Guards Parade in London in the entrance hall; the Brussels tapestries in the ante- and drawing rooms; paintings by Augustus John and Henri Matisse in the Needle Room; and all sorts of snuff boxes and cigarette cases in the gallery.

Mellerstain House

Six miles northwest of Kelso off the A6089, **Mellerstain House** (Easter & May–Sept daily except Tues 12.30–5pm; Oct Sat & Sun only; £5.50; Ⓦwww.mellerstain.com) represents the very best of the Adam brothers' work – William designed the wings in 1725, and his son Robert the castellated centre fifty years later. Robert's love of columns, roundels and friezes culminates in a stunning sequence of plaster-moulded, pastel-shaded ceilings, from the looping symmetry of the library ceiling, adorned by medallion oil paintings *Learning* and *Reading* on either side of *Minerva*, to the whimsical griffin and vase pattern in the drawing room. The art collection, which includes works by Constable, Van Dyck, Gainsborough, Ramsay and Veronese, is also noteworthy. It takes an hour to tour the house; afterwards you can wander the formal Edwardian **gardens**, which slope down to the lake.

Smailholm Tower

In marked contrast to Mellerstain is the craggy **Smailholm Tower** (April–Sept daily 9.30am–6.30pm, Oct–March Sat 9.30am–4.30pm, Sun 2–4.30pm; £2; HS), perched on a rocky outcrop a few miles to the south. A remote and evocative fastness recalling Reivers' raids and border skirmishes, the fifteenth-century tower was designed to withstand sudden attack. The rough rubble walls average six feet in thickness and both the entrance – once guarded by a heavy door plus an iron yett (gate) – and the windows are disproportionately small. These were necessary precautions: on both sides of the border, clans were engaged in endless feuds, a violent history that stirred the imagination of Sir Walter Scott, who was but a "wee, sick laddie" when he was brought here to live in 1773. Inside, press on up to the roof, where two narrow **wall-walks**, jammed against the barrel-vaulted roof and the crow-stepped gables, provide panoramic views. On the north side the watchman's seat has also survived, stuck against the chimney stack for warmth and with a recess for a lantern.

Jedburgh

Ten miles south of Melrose, **JEDBURGH** nestles in the lush valley of the Jed Water near its confluence with the Teviot, out on the edge of the wild Cheviot Hills. During the interminable Anglo-Scottish Wars, Jedburgh was the quintessential frontier town, a heavily garrisoned royal burgh incorporating a mighty castle and abbey. Though the castle was destroyed by the Scots in 1409 to keep it out of the hands of the English, its memory has been kept alive by stories: in 1285, for example, King Alexander III was celebrating his wedding feast in the great hall when a ghostly apparition predicted his untimely death and a bloody civil war; sure enough, he died in a hunting accident shortly afterwards and chaos ensued. Today, Jedburgh is the first place of any size that you come to on the A68, having crossed over Carter Bar from England, and as such gets quite a bit of passing tourist trade, most of it heading straight for the town's ruined abbey.

Jedburgh festivals

Jedburgh is at its busiest during the town's two main **festivals**. The **Common Riding**, or Callants' Festival, takes place in late June or early July, when the young people of the town – especially the lads – mount up and ride out to check the burgh boundaries, a reminder of more troubled days when Jedburgh was subject to English raids. In similar spirit, early February sees the day-long **Jedburgh Hand Ba'** game, an all-male affair between the "uppies" (those born above Market Place) and "downies" (those born below). In theory the aim of the game is to get hay-stuffed leather balls – originally representing the heads of English men – from one end of town to the other, but there's more at stake than that: macho reputations are made and lost during the two two-hour games.

Founded in the twelfth century as an Augustinian priory, **Jedburgh Abbey** (May–Sept daily 9.30am–6.30pm; Oct–April Mon–Sat 9.30am–4.30pm, Sun 2–4.30pm; £3.50; HS) is the best-preserved of all the Border abbeys, its vast abbey church towering over a sloping site right in the centre of town, beside the Jed Water. Built in red, yellow and grey sandstone, the abbey church can appear by turns gloomy, calm or richly warm, depending on the weather and the light. The abbey was burned and badly damaged on a number of occasions, but by far the worst destruction was inflicted by the English in the 1540s. Entry is through the bright **visitor centre** at the bottom of the hill, where you can view Jedburgh's most treasured archeological find, the **Jedburgh Comb**, carved around 1100 from walrus ivory and decorated with a griffin and a dragon. All that remains of the conventual buildings where the canons lived are the foundations and basic ground plan, but then Jedburgh's chief glory is really its **Abbey Church**, which remains splendidly preserved. Entering via the west door, the three-storey nave's perfectly proportioned parade of columns and arches lies before you, a fine example of the transition from Romanesque to Gothic design, with pointed window arches surmounted by the round-headed arches of the triforium, which, in turn, support the lancet windows of the clerestory. Be sure you climb up the narrow staircase in the west front to the balcony overlooking the nave, where you can contemplate how the place must have looked all decked out for the marriage of Alexander III to Yolande de Dreux in 1285.

It's a couple of minutes' walk from the abbey round to the small square **Market Place**, up the hill from which, at the top of Castlegate, stands **Jedburgh Castle Jail** (Easter–Oct Mon–Sat 10am–4.30pm, Sun 1–4pm; £2), an impressive castellated nineteenth-century pile built on the site of the old royal castle, with displays on prison life throughout the ages. Back down near the Market Place, signs will guide you to **Mary, Queen of Scots' House** (March–Nov Mon–Sat 10am–4.30pm, Sun 11am–4.30pm; £3). Despite the name, it seems unlikely that Mary ever actually stayed in this particular sixteenth-century house, though she did visit the town during the eventful year of 1566, staying at a place owned by her protector, Sir Thomas Kerr. The attempt to unravel her complex life is cursory, the redeeming features being a copy of Mary's death mask and one of the few surviving portraits of the earl of Bothwell. One curious feature of all Kerr houses is that the staircases spiral to the left for ease of sword-drawing, giving rise to the Scottish term for left-handedness, "kerry haunded" or "kerry fisted".

Practicalities

Buses pick up and drop off at Canongate near the town centre. Yards away on Murray's Green is the **tourist office** (Mon–Sat 9.30am–5pm, Su...

10am–5pm). For **accommodation**, try *Meadhon House*, 48 Castlegate (℡01835/862504; ❷), which has a conservatory round the back overlooking a lovely garden. There's also a Georgian hotel in Castlegate, *Glenbank House Hotel* (℡01835/862258, ⓦwww.glenbankhotel.co.uk; ❸). Another great choice is *Hundalee House* (℡01835/863011, ⓦwww.accommodation-scotland.org; March–Oct; ❷), a seventeenth-century mansion house in open grounds, a mile south of town on the A68. Of the two **campsites** nearby, the *Jedwater Caravan Park* (℡01835/840219; March–Oct) is cheaper and more secluded, in a pleasant riverside site four miles south of town on the A68.

There's a shortage of good **eating** places, but probably the best place is *Simply Scottish*, 6–8 High St (℡01835/864696), a smart but relaxed bistro-style café-restaurant, serving inexpensive Scottish meals, as well as pasta dishes and the usual snacks. Try the local speciality Jethart Snails, sticky boiled sweets invented by a French POW in the 1700s and on sale everywhere. Further out of town, south on the A68 the comfortable *Jedforest Hotel* (℡01835/840222, ⓦwww.jedforesthotel.freeserve.co.uk; ❻) has a restaurant with an excellent reputation.

Selkirk and around

Just south of the River Tweed, some five miles southwest of Melrose, lies the royal burgh of **SELKIRK**. The old town sits high up above Ettrick Water; down in the valley by the riverside, the town's imposing grey-stone woollen mills are mostly boarded up now, an eerie reminder of a once prosperous era. There's precious little reason to linger in Selkirk itself, though the town sits on the edge of some lovely countryside, and serves as the gateway to the picturesque, sparsely populated valleys of Yarrow Water and Ettrick Water, to the west.

At the centre of Selkirk, at one end of the High Street, you'll find the tiny **Market Square**, overlooked by a statue of Sir Walter Scott, behind which stands the former Town House, now dubbed **Sir Walter Scott's Courtroom** (April–Sept Mon–Sat 10am–4pm; July & Aug also Sun 2–4pm; Oct–March Mon–Sat 1–4pm; free), where he served as sheriff for 33 years. At the other end of the High Street is a rather more unusual statue of **Mungo Park**, the renowned explorer and anti-slavery advocate, born in the county in 1771. Just off Market Square to the south is **Halliwell's House Museum** (April–Oct Mon–Sat 10am–5pm, Sun 2–4pm; July & Aug Sun until 6pm; free), an old-style hardware shop and an informative exhibit on the industrialization of the Tweed Valley. Down by the river at the junction of the A7 with the B7014, **Selkirk Glass** (Mon–Fri 9am–4.30pm, Sat 11am–3pm; free) is a thriving craft industry that stands in stark contrast to the neighbouring mills. Visitors arrive by the coachload to sit in the café and watch glass-blowers making intricate paperweights and the like.

The **tourist office** (same hours as Halliwell's House; ℡01750/720054) is in Halliwell's House off Market Square, and can help with **accommodation**. First choice for those with an unlimited budget is the upmarket *Philipburn House Hotel* (℡01750/720747, ⓦwww.philipburnhousehotel.co.uk; ❻), an unusual eighteenth-century house set in its own grounds a mile west of the town centre; the hotel offers expensive, but excellent Scottish cuisine. Slightly more modest in price, but still full of character is the *Heatherlie House Hotel* (℡01750/721200, ⓦwww.heatherlie.freeserve.co.uk; ❺), a Victorian mansion a sharp left turn up from the road to Ettrick at Heatherlie Park.

Bowhill House

Three miles west of Selkirk off the A708, **Bowhill House** (July daily 1–5pm; £4.50) is the property of the duke of Buccleuch and Queensberry, a seriously wealthy man. Beyond the grandiose mid-nineteenth-century mansion's facade of dark whinstone is an outstanding collection of French antiques and European **paintings**: in the dining room, for example, there are portraits by Reynolds and Gainsborough and a Canaletto cityscape, while the drawing room boasts Boulle furniture, Meissen tableware, paintings by Ruysdael, Leandro Bassano and Claude Lorrain, as well as two more family portraits by Reynolds. Look out also for the Scott Room, which features another splendid portrait of Sir Walter by Henry Raeburn, and the Monmouth Room, commemorating James, duke of Monmouth, the illegitimate son of Charles II, who married Anne of the Buccleuchs. After several years in exile, Monmouth returned to England when his father died in 1685, hoping to wrest the crown from James II. He was defeated at the Battle of Sedgemoor in Somerset and subsequently sent to the scaffold; among other items, his execution shirt is on display.

The wooded hills of **Bowhill Country Park** adjoining the house (Easter & June–Aug daily except Fri 11am–5pm; May Sat & Sun only; £2) are criss-crossed by scenic footpaths and cycle trails: you can rent **mountain bikes** from the visitor centre.

Getting to Bowhill by **public transport** is difficult. The Peebles bus, leaving Selkirk daily at 2pm, will drop you at General's Bridge (takes 10min), from where it's a mile or so walk through the grounds to the house.

Peebles and around

Fast, wide, tree-lined and fringed with grassy banks, the Tweed looks at its best at **PEEBLES**, a handsome royal burgh that sits on the north bank, about fif-teen miles northwest of Selkirk. The town itself has a genteel, relaxed air, its wide, handsome High Street bordered by houses in a medley of architectural styles, mostly dating from Victorian times, and ending in the soaring crown spire of the **Old Parish Church** (daily 10am–4pm) at the western end.

Halfway down the High Street is the **Tweedale Museum & Gallery** (Easter–Oct Mon–Fri 10am–noon & 2–5pm, Sat 10am–1pm & 2–4pm; Nov–Easter Mon–Fri 10am–noon & 2–5pm; free), housed in the Chambers Institute, named after a local worthy who presented the building to the town in 1859, complete with an art gallery dedicated to the enlightenment of his neighbours. He stuffed the place with casts of the world's most famous sculp-tures and, although most were lost long ago, today's "Secret Room", once the Museum Room, boasts two handsome friezes: one a copy of the Elgin marbles taken from the Parthenon; the other of the Triumph of Alexander, originally cast in 1812 to honour Napoleon.

Of the various walks through the hills surrounding Peebles, the five-mile **Sware Trail** is one of the easiest and most scenic, weaving west along the north bank of the river and looping back to the south. On the way, it passes **Neidpath Castle** (mid-June to Aug Mon–Sat 10.30am–4.30pm, Sun 12.30–4.30pm; £3) a gaunt medieval tower house perched high above the river on a rocky buff. It' a superb setting, and the interior possesses a pit prison and a great hall bedecked with stunning batik wall hangings depicting the life of Mary, Queen of Scots.

Practicalities

Buses stop outside Peebles' post office, a few doors down from the well-stocke **tourist office** on the High Street (July & Aug Mon–Sat 9am–7pm, Su

10am–6pm; June Mon–Sat 10am–5.30pm, Sun 10am–4pm; Sept Mon–Sat 9.30am–5.30pm, Sun 10am–4pm; April & May Mon–Sat 10am–5pm, Sun 10am–2pm; Oct Mon–Sat 9.30am–5.30pm, Sun 10am–2pm; Nov–March Mon–Sat 9.30am–4.30pm; ℡01721/720138). Peebles boasts a vast number of **B&Bs**; try *Rowanbrae,* a trim, pint-sized Victorian place on a quiet cul-de-sac on Northgate, off the east end of High Street (℡01721/721630, Ⓔjohn@rowanbrae.freeserve.co.uk; ❶); or *Viewfield*, 1 Rosetta Rd (℡01721/721232, Ⓔmmitchell38@yahoo.com; ❶), an attractive detached Victorian house a ten-minute walk west of the bridge, with rooms overlooking a lovely garden. For upmarket **hotels** you have to head out of town: *Castle Venlaw Hotel* (℡01721/720384, Ⓦwww.venlaw.co.uk; ❻) is a Scots baronial house set in its own grounds on the edge of town up the Edinburgh Road; the *Cringletie House Hotel* (℡01721/730233, Ⓦwww.cringletie.com; ❽) is a still more splendid baronial pile a couple of miles further up the Edinburgh Road. Of the two **campsites** on the edge of town, the *Rosetta Caravan Park* (℡01721/720770; April–Oct) is the quieter, set in fields surrounded by mature woods, a fifteen-minute walk north of the High Street.

The best place to **eat** is the *Sunflower* (℡017221/722420), a tiny, brightly coloured restaurant at 4 Bridgegate, just off Northgate, which does sandwiches at lunchtime, and more adventurous (and slightly pricier) evening meals, for which it's advisable to book. The *Tatler Café*, on the High Street, provides basic fare, though it does serve good coffee. As for **pubs**, the *Crown Hotel* on the High Street, is a cosy place to hunker down; the *Tontine Hotel*, opposite, is a grander place with views south over the Tweed, and a standard hotel menu. For really good pub food, try one of the bar meals at the *Castle Venlaw Hotel*, or you could pick up a picnic at *Central Baguette* in the High Street.

Traquair House

Six miles east of Peebles, a mile or so south of the A72, **Traquair House** (daily: June–Aug 10.30am–5.30pm; April, May, Sept & Oct 12.30–5.30pm; £5.60, grounds only £2; Ⓦwww.traquair.co.uk) is the oldest continuously inhabited house in Scotland, with the present owners – the Maxwell Stuarts – having lived here since 1491. Persistently Catholic, the family paid for its principles: the fifth earl got two years in the Tower of London for his support of Bonnie Prince Charlie, Protestant millworkers repeatedly attacked their property, and by 1800 little remained of the family's once enormous estates – certainly not enough to fund any major rebuilding.

Consequently, Traquair's main appeal is its ancient shape and structure. The whitewashed facade is strikingly handsome, with narrow windows and trim turrets surrounding the tiniest of front doors – an organic, homogeneous edifice that's a welcome change from other grandiose stately homes. Inside, the house has kept many of its oldest features. You can see original vaulted cellars, where locals once hid their cattle from raiders; the twisting main staircase as well as the earlier medieval version, later a secret escape route for persecuted Catholics; a carefully camouflaged priest's hole; and even a **priest's room** where a string of resident chaplains lived in hiding until the Catholic Emancipation Act freed things up in 1829. Of the furniture and fittings, it's not any particular piece that impresses, but rather the accumulation of family possessions that give a real insight into the Maxwell Stuarts' revolving-door fortunes and eccentricities. In the **museum room** there is a wealth of treasures, including a fine example of a Jacobite Amen glass, a rosary and crucifix owned by Mary, Queen of Scots, and the cloak worn by the earl of Nithsdale during his dramatic escape from the Tower of London.

It's worth sparing time for the surrounding **gardens**, where you'll find a **hedge maze**, several craft workshops and the **Traquair House Brewery** dating back to 1566, which was revived in 1965, and claims to be the only British brewery that still ferments totally in oak. You can learn about the brewery and taste the ales in the Brewery Shop, as well as buy them. There's an attractive café serving snacks in an estate cottage on the redundant avenue which leads to the locked **Bear Gates**; Bonnie Prince Charlie departed the house through the gates, and the then owner promised to keep them locked till a Stuart should ascend the throne.

If you're really taken by the place, you can stay in one of its three guest **rooms** (T01896/830323; ❽), decked out with antiques and four-posters, on a bed-and-breakfast basis only.

Dumfries and Galloway

The southwest corner of Scotland, now known as **Dumfries and Galloway** (Wwww.dumfriesandgalloway.co.uk), is a region set apart. Some folk heading north from England might pause to explore the Borders region, but few bother to exit the main Carlisle–Glasgow motorway. Yet Dumfries and Galloway have stately homes, deserted hills and ruined abbeys to compete with the best of the Borders. They also have something the Borders don't have, and that's the **Solway coast**, a long, indented coastline of sheltered sandy coves that's been dubbed the "Scottish Riviera" – an exaggeration perhaps, but it's certainly Scotland's warmest, southernmost stretch of coastline.

Dumfries is the obvious gateway to the region, a pleasant enough town that's only really a must for those on the trail of **Robert Burns**, who spent the last part of his life here. Further west, and even more attractive is **Kirkcudbright**, once a bustling port thronged with sailing ships, later an artists' retreat, and now a tranquil, well-preserved little eighteenth- and early nineteenth-century town. Contrasting with the essentially gentle landscape of the Solway coast, is the brooding presence of the **Galloway Hills** to the north, their beautiful moors, mountains, lakes and rivers centred on the 150,000-acre **Galloway Forest Park**, a seriously underused hill-walking and mountain-biking paradise.

Dumfries and around

Situated on the wide banks of the River Nith a short distance inland from the Solway Firth, **DUMFRIES** is by far the largest town in southwest Scotland, with a population of more than thirty thousand. Long known as the "Queen of the South" (as is its football club), the town flourished as a medieval seaport and trading centre, its success attracting the attention of many English armies. The invaders managed to polish off most of the early settlement in 1448, 1536 and again in 1570, but Dumfries survived to prosper with its light industries and port supplying the agricultural hinterland. The town planners of the 1960. badly damaged the town, but enough remains of the warm red-sandstone buildings that distinguish Dumfries from other towns in the southwest to make it worth at least a brief stop. It also acts a convenient base for exploring the Solway coast, to the east and west, and is second only to Ayr for its association with Robbie Burns, who spent the last five years of his life here employed a an exciseman.

△ Dumfries

The Town

Dumfries is characterized by its red-sandstone buildings, which survive in sufficient quantity to distinguish it from other towns in the southwest. Orientation is easy, with the railway to the east, and the River Nith to the north and west. The pedestrianized **High Street** runs roughly parallel to the Nith; at its northern end, presiding over a floral roundabout, is the **Burns Statue**, a sentimental piece of Victorian frippery in white Carrara marble, featuring the great man holding a posy in one hand while the other clutches at his heart. His faithful hound, Luath, lies curled around his feet – though it doesn't look much like a Scots collie (as Luath was). Further down the High Street, Burns' body lay in state at the town's most singular building, the **Midsteeple**, an appealingly wonky hotchpotch of a place, built in 1707 to fulfil the multiple functions of town prison, clocktower, courthouse and arsenal.

If you're on Burns' trail, make sure you duck down the alleyway to the white-washed **Globe Inn**, a little further down the High Street, which was Burns' most famous *howff* (pub). Southeast of the High Street, in Burns Street, stands **Burns' House** (April–Sept Mon–Sat 10am–5pm, Sun 2–5pm; Oct–March Tues–Sat 10am–1pm & 2–5pm; free), a simple sandstone building where the poet died of rheumatic heart disease in 1796, a few days before the birth of his last son, Maxwell. Inside, along with the usual collection of Burns memorabilia, one of the bedroom windows bears his signature, scratched with his diamond ring. As a member of the Dumfries Volunteers, Burns was given a military funeral, before being buried nearby in a simple grave by **St Michael's Church** (Mon–Fri 10am–4pm; free), a large red-sandstone church, built in 1745. In 1815, Burns was dug up and moved across the graveyard to a purpose-built **Mausoleum**, a bright white Neoclassical eyesore, which houses a slightly ludicrous statue of Burns being accosted by the Poetic Muse.

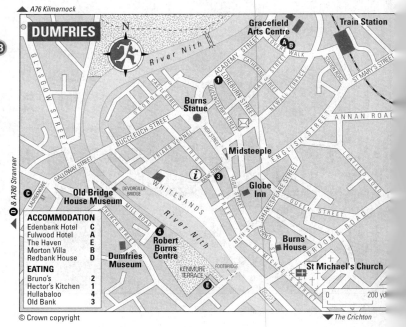

ACCOMMODATION

Edenbank Hotel	C
Fulwood Hotel	A
The Haven	E
Morton Villa	B
Redbank House	D

EATING

Bruno's	2
Hector's Kitchen	1
Hullabaloo	4
Old Bank	3

© Crown copyright

From the church, head down to the shallow and fast-running Nith, and cross over to the old water mill which houses the **Robert Burns Centre**, or RBC (April–Sept Mon–Sat 10am–8pm, Sun 2–5pm; Oct–March Tues–Sat 10am–1pm & 2–5pm; free), with an optional twenty-minute slide show (£1.50) and a simple exhibition on the poet's years in Dumfries upstairs. On the hill above the RBC stands the **Dumfries Museum** (April–Sept Mon–Sat 10am–5pm, Sun 2–5pm; Oct–March Tues–Sat 10am–1pm & 2–5pm; free), from which there are great views over the town. The museum is housed partly in an eighteenth-century windmill, which was converted into the town's observatory in the 1830s, and features a **camera obscura** on its top floor (April–Sept; £1.50), well worth a visit on a clear day.

A little upstream from the RBC is the pedestrian-only **Devorgilla Bridge**, built in 1431 and one of the oldest bridges in Scotland. Attached to its south-western end is the town's oldest house, built in 1660, now housing the tiny **Old Bridge House Museum** (April–Sept Mon–Sat 10am–5pm, Sun 2–5pm; free), stuffed full of Victorian domestic bric-a-brac, including a teeth-chattering range of Victorian dental gear.

Practicalities

Dumfries **train** station is five minutes' walk east of the town centre, while **buses** drop you off at Whitesands beside the River Nith, where you'll also find the **tourist office** (Mon–Sat 10am–5pm; June–Sept Mon–Sat 9.30am–6pm, Sun noon–5pm). Dumfries abounds in **guest houses** and **B&Bs**. For value and convenience, you can't beat *Morton Villa*, 28 Lovers Walk (℡01387/255825; ❷), a large Victorian house with a pleasant garden, or the very welcoming *Fulwood Hotel* (℡01387/252262; ❷), both near the station. For a more distinctive setting, try *The Haven*, 1 Kenmure Terrace (℡01387/251281; ❶), where guests have their own kitchen. If you're looking for a bona fide **hotel**, head for Laurieknowe Street, a five- to ten-minute walk west of Devorgilla Bridge, where you'll find the welcoming, family-run *Edenbank* (℡01387/252759, ⓦwww.edenbank hotel.co.uk; ❹). *Redbank House* (℡01387/247034, ⓦwww.redbankhouse.co.uk; ❸) is a pristine red-brick mansion set within its own wooded garden at the edge of town on the A710, boasting a sauna, snooker room and gym.

By far the best option for **food** is *Hullabaloo* (℡01387/259679; closed Mon & Sun eve), a stylish restaurant on the top floor of the RBC, with a summer terrace overlooking the river. Another good option is *Hector's Kitchen*, a much smaller place at 20 Academy St (closed Sun), which offers toasties, baguettes, nachos and crepes for lunch, and more substantial fare in the evening. The *Old Bank*, a café on Irish Street, has a more predictable menu, plus a wide selection of cream cakes. *Bruno's* is a family-friendly Italian restaurant on Balmoral Road that's become a Dumfries institution, with the equally popular *Balmoral* chippie round the side which justifiably claims to sell the best chips in the southwest.

Two of Burns' favourite drinking places are still in operation: the *Hole in the Wa'* **pub**, down an alley opposite Woolworth's on High Street, serves the usual bar food, but for somewhere with a bit more atmosphere, make for the smoky, oak-panelled *Globe Inn* on the High Street, which is crammed with memorabilia connected with the poet but is otherwise little changed since his time. The *Robert the Bruce* pub, with its Neoclassical portico at the top of Buccleuch Street, is a typical and very popular church conversion by the J.D. Wetherspoons chain. **Films** are regularly shown at the RBC (℡01387/264808, ⓦwww.rbcft.co.uk; Tues–Sat). Grierson and Graham, 10 Academy St (℡01387/259483), offer **bike rental**, useful for reaching the nearby Solway coast.

Drumlanrig Castle

Seventeen miles north of Dumfries, **Drumlanrig Castle** (May–Aug Mon–Fri 11am–4pm, Sat & Sun noon–4pm; £6; ⓦ www.buccleuch.com) is not a castle at all, but the grandiose stately home of the Duke of Buccleuch and Queensberry. Visitors approach via an impressive driveway that sweeps along an avenue of lime trees to the pink-sandstone house with its forest of cupolas, turrets and towers. The highlights of the richly furnished interior are really the paintings in the oak-panelled staircase hall. The castle's most famous trio of works are **Rembrandt**'s *Old Woman Reading*, an extremely sensitive composition dappling the shadow of the subject's hood against her white surplice, **Hans Holbein**'s formal portrait of Sir Nicholas Carew, Master of the Horse to Henry VIII, and the *Madonna with the Yarnwinder* by **Leonardo da Vinci** (yet to be returned after being stolen in 2003). Also be sure to check out the striking 1950s portrait of the present duchess, all debutante coiffure and high-society décolletage, by John Merton in the morning room, and, in the serving room, John Ainslie's *Joseph Florence, Chef*, a sharply observed and dynamic portrait much liked by Walter Scott.

As well as the house, Drumlanrig offers a host of other attractions, including formal **gardens** and a forested **country park** (mid-April to Sept daily 11am–5pm; £3). The old stableyard beside the castle contains a visitor centre, a few shops, the inevitable tearoom, and also a useful **bike rental** outlet, as the park is crisscrossed by footpaths and cycle routes; elsewhere in the grounds, there's an adventure playground. If you're heading here by bus from Dumfries or Ayr, bear in mind it's a one-and-a-half-mile walk from the road to the house.

Caerlaverock

Caerlaverock Castle, eight miles southeast of Dumfries (April–Sept daily 9.30am–6.30pm; Oct–March Mon–Sat 9.30am–4.30pm, Sun 2–4.30pm; £3; HS), eight miles southeast of Dumfries, is a picture-perfect ruined castle. Not only is it moated, it's built from the rich local red sandstone, is triangular in shape and has preserved its mighty double-towered gatehouse. The most surprising addition, however, lies inside, where you're confronted by the ornate Renaissance facade of the **Nithsdale Lodging**, erected in the 1630s by the first earl of Nithsdale. The decorated tympana above the windows feature lively mythological and heraldic scenes in what was clearly the latest style. Sadly, Nithsdale didn't get much value for money: just six years later he and his royal garrison were forced to surrender after a thirteen-week siege and bombardment by the Covenanters, who proceeded to wreck the place. It was never inhabited again.

Three miles further east, at Eastpark, is the **Caerlaverock Wildfowl and Wetlands Trust (WWT) Centre** (daily 10am–5pm; £4; ⓦ www.wwt .org.uk/visit/caerlaverock), more than a thousand acres of protected salt marsh and mud flat edging the Solway Firth. The centre is equipped with screened approaches that link the main observatory to a score of well-situated bird-watchers' hides. It's famous for the 25,000 or so barnacle geese that winter here between September and April. The rest of the year, when the geese are away nesting in Svalbard, there's plenty of other flora and fauna to look out for, as well as the natterjack toad. Throughout the year the wild whooper swans have a daily feeding time and the wardens run free wildlife safaris; call ☏ 01387/770200 for up-to-date details. You can **camp** or stay in one of the **rooms** in the centre's converted farmhouse (❸), which has its own observation tower, plus a kitchen and washing machine for guests' use. Both the castle and the centre are reached along the B725; this is the route the bus takes, mostly terminating at the castle but sometimes continuing to the start of the two-mile lane leading off the B725 to the centre.

Ruthwell

From Caerlaverock, it's about seven miles east along the B725 to the village of **RUTHWELL**, whose modest country church houses the remarkable eighteen-foot **Ruthwell Cross** (the keys are kept at one of the houses at the foot of the lane; look out for the information notice). An extraordinary early Christian monument from the early or mid-eighth century when Galloway was ruled by the Northumbrians, the cross was considered idolatrous during the Reformation, smashed to pieces and buried. Only in the nineteenth century was the cross finally reassembled and given its own purpose-built semicircular apse. The decoration on the cross reveals a strikingly sophisticated style and iconography, probably derived from the eastern Mediterranean. The main inscriptions are in Latin, but running round the edge is a poem written in the Northumbrian dialect in runic figures. However, it's the biblical carvings on the main face that really catch the eye, notably Mary Magdalene washing the feet of Jesus.

New Abbey and Sweetheart Abbey

NEW ABBEY is a tidy little one-street village, eight miles south of Dumfries, that originally evolved in order to service its giant neighbour, **Sweetheart Abbey** (April–Sept daily 9.30am–6.30pm; Oct–March Mon–Wed & Sat 9.30am–4.30pm, Thurs 9.30am–12.30pm, Sun 2–4.30pm; £1.80; HS), which now lies romantically ruined to the east. The abbey takes its unusual name from its founder, Devorgilla de Balliol, lady of Galloway, who carried the embalmed heart of her husband, John Balliol (of Oxford college fame) around with her for the last 22 years of her life – she is buried with the casket, in the presbytery. The last of the Cistercian abbeys to be founded in Scotland – in 1273 – Sweetheart is dominated by the red-sandstone remains of the abbey church, which remains intact, albeit minus its roof. Standing in the grassy nave, flanked by giant compound piers supporting early Gothic arches, and above them a triforium, it's easy to imagine what the completed church must have looked like. The rest of the conventual buildings are revealed only in the outline of the foundations, with the exception of the precinct wall, to the north and east of the abbey. This massive structure – up to ten feet high and four feet wide in places – is made from rough granite boulders, and is the most complete of its kind in the country.

The *Abbey Cottage* **tearoom** is renowned for its good coffee, teas and home-made cakes, and enjoys an unrivalled view over the abbey. At the centre of the village, two **pubs** face one another across a cobbled square: the *Abbey Arms* (℡01387/850489, ✉enquiries@abbeyarms.netlineuk.net; ❸), and the *Criffel Inn* (℡01387/850244, ✉criffel-inn@hotmail.com; ❸); both have seats outside, serve pub food and do B&B.

The Colvend coast and beyond

The **Colvend coast**, twenty miles or so southwest of Dumfries, is probably one of the finest stretches of coastline along the so-called "Scottish Riviera". The best approach is via the A710, which heads south through New Abbey, before cutting across a handsome landscape of rolling farmland to the aptly named Sandyhills, and, beyond, to **ROCKCLIFFE**, a beguiling little place of comfortable villas sheltered beneath wooded hills and nestled around a beautiful rocky, sand and shell bay. Excellent B&B **accommodation** is available at *Millbrae House* (☎01556/630217; March–Oct; ❷), a whitewashed cottage a short stroll from the bay. For **camping**, the *Castle Point Caravan Site* (☎01556/630248; March–Oct) is in a secluded spot, just south of the village, a stone's throw from the seashore. The *Garden House* tearoom (closed Mon & Tues), at the entrance to the village, can give you simple sustenance and has a garden at the back.

For vehicles, Rockcliffe is a dead end, but it's the start of a pleasant half-hour's walk along the Jubilee Path to neighbouring **KIPPFORD**, a tiny, lively yachting centre strung out along the east bank of the Urr estuary. En route, the path passes the Celtic hillfort of the **Mote of Mark**, a useful craggy viewpoint. At low tide you can walk over the Rough Firth causeway from the shore below across the mud flats to **Rough Island**, a humpy twenty-acre bird sanctuary owned by the National Trust for Scotland – it's out of bounds in May and June when the resident terns and oystercatchers are nesting. The reward for your gentle stroll is a drink and a bite to eat at the ever-popular *Anchor Hotel* (☎01556/620205; ❸), on Kippford's waterfront, which serves tasty **bar meals** – be sure to check the specials board. If you need to stay the night, though, you might find it more peaceful at the *Rosemount* (☎01556/620214; Feb–Nov; ❷), an excellent **guest house** close by on the seafront.

Castle Douglas and around

Most folk come to **CASTLE DOUGLAS** (ⓦwww.castledouglas.net), eighteen miles southwest of Dumfries, simply in order to visit the nearby attractions of Threave Garden and Castle.

Threave Garden (daily 9.30am to sunset; £4.50; NTS) is a pleasant walk or cycle of a mile or so south of Castle Douglas, along the shores of Loch Carlingwark. The garden features a magnificent spread of flowers and woodland, sixty acres subdivided into more than a dozen areas, from the bright, old-fashioned blooms of the Rose Garden to the brilliant banks of rhododendrons in the Woodland Garden and the ranks of primula, astilbe and gentian in the Peat Garden. In springtime, thousands of visitors turn up for the flowering of more than two hundred types of daffodil and, from late May onwards, the herbaceous beds are the main attraction, with most of them arranged like islets in a sea of lawn (so that they can be viewed from all sides). The exception is the more formal beds of the Walled Garden which adjoin the greenhouses and the nursery.

The nicest way of reaching **Threave Castle** (April–Sept daily 9.30am–6.30pm; £2.20; HS), a mile or so north of the gardens, is to walk through the estate. However you decide to get there, you should follow the signs to the Open Farm, from where it's a lovely fifteen-minute walk down to the River Dee. Here you ring a brass bell for the boat to take you over to the flat and grassy island on which the stern-looking tower house stands. Built for one of the Black Douglases, Archibald the Grim, in around 1370, the fortress was among the first of its kind, a sturdy, rectangular structure completed shortly after the War of Independence when clan feuding spurred a frenzy of castle-building. The rickety curtain wall to the south and east is all that remains of the artillery fortifications, hurriedly constructed in the 1450s in a desperate – and unsuccessful – attempt to defend the castle against James II's new-fangled cannon. The Covenanters wrecked the place in 1640 after a thirteen-week siege, but enough remains of the interior to make it worth exploring.

Practicalities

Castle Douglas **tourist office** (April–June, Sept & Oct Mon–Sat 10am–4.30pm, Sun 11am–4pm; July & Aug Mon–Sat 10am–6pm, Sun 11am–5pm) is at the top end of King Street. All the old coaching inns on King Street offer **accommodation**, but you're better off trying one of the well-built Victorian guest houses out on Ernespie Road, such as *Albion House* (T01556/502360; March–Oct; ❷), at no. 49, or *Longacre Manor* (T01556/503576, W www.longacremanor.co.uk; ❺); just to the south of Castle Douglas, the *Smithy House* (T01556/503841, W www.smithyhouse.co.uk; ❸) is a nicely converted *smiddy* overlooking Loch Carlinwerk. Campers should make for the *Lochside* **campsite** (T01556/502949; Easter–Oct), beside Loch Carlingwark, a short walk from the bottom of King Street down Marle Street. The best place to grab a bite **to eat** is *Designs* (W www.designsgallery.co.uk), a café at the back of an arts and crafts shop at 179 King Street, with a lovely conservatory and garden and serving great ciabattas and decent coffee. **Bike rental** – useful for getting out to Threave – is available from the Castle Douglas Cycle Centre on Church St (T01556/504542; closed Thurs & Sun).

Kirkcudbright and around

KIRKCUDBRIGHT – pronounced "kir-coo-bree" – hugging the muddy banks of the River Dee ten miles southwest of Castle Douglas, is the only major town along the Solway coast to have retained a working harbour. In addition, it has a ruined castle and the most attractive of town centres, a charming medley of simple two-storey cottages with medieval pends, Georgian villas and Victorian townhouses, all built in a mixture of sandstone, granite and brick, and attractively painted up, with their windows and quoins picked out. It comes as little surprise, then, to find that Kirkcudbright became something of a magnet for Scottish artists from the late nineteenth century onwards. It may no longer live up to the tourist board's "artists' town" label, but it does have a rich artistic heritage that's easy and enjoyable to explore.

The most surprising sight in Kirkcudbright is **MacLellan's Castle** (April–Sept daily 9.30am–12.30pm & 1.30–6pm; Oct Mon–Wed & Sat 9.30am–4.30pm, Thurs 9.30am–12.30pm, Sun 2–4.30pm; £2; HS), a pink-flecked sixteenth-century tower house that sits at one end of the High Street by the harbourside. Part fortified keep and part spacious mansion, the castle was built in the 1570s for the then Provost of Kirkcudbright, Sir Thomas MacLellan of Bombie, when a degree of law and order permitted the aristocracy to relax its former defensive preoccupations and satisfy its increasing desire for comfort and domestic convenience. The interior is well preserved, from the kitchen (complete with bread oven) to the spyhole known as the "**laird's lug**", behind the fireplace of the Great Hall. Sir Thomas MacLellan is buried in the neighbouring **Greyfriars Kirk** (daily 10am–noon & 2–4pm; key from 7 Castle St), where his tomb is an eccentrically crude attempt at Neoclassicism; it even incorporates parts of someone else's gravestone.

Near the castle, on the L-shaped High Street, is **Broughton House** (daily: Easter, July & Aug 11am–5.30pm; April–June, Sept & Oct 1–5.30pm; Nov garden only Mon–Fri 11am–4pm; £3.50; NTS), a smart Georgian town house, former home of the artist **Edward Hornel** (1863–1933), an important member of the late nineteenth-century Scottish art scene, who spent his childhood a few doors down the street, and returned in 1900 to establish an artists' colony in Kirkcudbright with some of the "Glasgow Boys" (see p.1023). At the back of the house Hornel added a studio and a vast, glass-roofed, mahogany-panelled gallery, now filled with the mannered, vibrantly coloured paintings of girls at play, which he churned out in the latter part of his career. Hornel's trip to Japan in 1893 imbued him with a lifelong affection for the country, and his surprisingly large, densely packed, wonderful, rambling **gardens** have a strong Japanese influence.

Before visiting Broughton House, you should really pay a visit to the imposing, church-like **Tolbooth**, with its stone-built clocktower and spire. Built in the 1620s, the building now houses the **Tolbooth Art Centre** (May–Sept Mon–Sat 10am–6pm, Sun 2–5pm; Oct–April Mon–Sat 11am–4pm; £1.50), which has, on the upper floor, a small permanent display of works by some of Kirkcudbright's erstwhile resident artists, including Hornel's striking *Japanese Girl*, and S.J. Peploe's Colourist view of the Tolbooth. The ten-minute video gives you a good, succinct overview of Kirkcudbright's artistic heritage. Don't miss the **Stewartry Museum** on St Mary Street (May–Sept Mon–Sat 10am–6pm, Sun 2–5pm; Oct–April Mon–Sat 11am–4pm; free), an extraordinary collection of local exhibits packed into a purpose-built Victorian building on St Mary Street.

Practicalities

Buses to Kirkcudbright stop by the harbour car park, next to the **tourist office** (July & Aug Mon–Sat 9.30am–6pm, Sun 10am–5pm; April–June, Sept & Oct Mon–Sat 10am–5pm, Sun noon–4pm), where you can get help finding **accommodation**. One of the best options is *14 High St* (☎01557/330766, ℮14highstreet@kirkcudbright.co.uk; April–Sept; ❸), next door to Broughton House, with a garden overlooking the river, followed by *Baytree House*, at no. 110 (☎01557/330824, ⓦwww.baytreehouse.net; ❹), another Georgian house with comfortable rooms, good cooking, and a beautiful garden with sundeck, or *Gladstone House* (☎01557/331734, ℮hilarygladstone@aol.com; ❹), yet another Georgian house set back slightly from the street; cheaper B&B can be had from 1 Gordon Place (☎01557/330472; ❷), at the castle end of the High Street. The *Silvercraigs* caravan and **campsite** (☎01557/330123; Easter to late Oct) is five or ten minutes' walk from the centre down St Mary's Street and Place, on a bluff overlooking town.

Kirkcudbright is strangely limited when it comes to **restaurants**. Top choice is the *Auld Alliance*, 5 Castle St (☎01557/330569), a superior, if pricey, restaurant offering an imaginative mixture of French and Scottish cuisine, where you need to book ahead. Otherwise, there's the usual bar food at the Best–Western-run *Selkirk Arms Hotel* on the High Street, which boasts a large garden out back. There are also several stylish daytime **cafés**: try *Mulberries*, on St Cuthbert Street, or, for more substantial fare, *Harbour Lights*, further up the street (open Fri & Sat eve in season). For a **drink**, the busy *Masonic Arms*, on Castle Street, pulls a reasonable pint of real ale.

Gatehouse of Fleet

Like Castle Douglas, **GATEHOUSE OF FLEET**, ten miles west of Kirkcudbright, has a distinctive long, dead straight main street. However, the quiet streets of Gatehouse have none of the life and bustle of Castle Douglas. By contrast, in the late eighteenth and early nineteenth century, the town was a thriving industrial centre with cotton mills, shipbuilding and a brewery. It's the country setting that sets Gatehouse apart, rather than any particular sight. Ann Street is the most picturesque, at the end of which you can gain access to the wooded grounds of **Cally House** (now the *Cally Palace Hotel*), and it gardens (Easter–Sept Tues–Fri 2–5.30pm, Sat & Sun 10am–5.30pm; wwww.callygardens.co.uk; £1.50). A palatial Neoclassical country mansion, Cally House was built in the 1760s, and is proof positive of the fortune already owned by the Murray family, even before James Murray began his cotton enterprise. Back in town, the **Mill on the Fleet** (April–Oct daily 10.30am–5pm; £1.50), opposite the car park by the river at the bottom of the High Street, traces the economic and social history of Gatehouse and Galloway from inside a restored grey granite bobbin mill. Perched on a hill a mile south-west of Gatehouse stands **Cardoness Castle** (April–Sept daily 9.30am–6.30pm; Oct Mon–Wed & Sat 9.30am–4.30pm, Thurs 9.30am–12.30pm, Sun 2–4.30pm; Nov–March Sat 9.30am–4.30pm, Sun 2–4.30pm; £2.20; HS), a classic late fifteenth-century fortified tower house, which boasts some fashionably decorated fireplaces and plenty of en-suite latrines, plus excellent views out to Fleet Bay in the distance.

Practicalities

The **tourist office** (mid-March–June, Sept & Oct Mon–Sat 10am–4.30pm, Sun 11am–4pm; July & Aug Mon–Sat 10am–5.30pm, Sun 10.30am–4.30pm) is situated by the car park by the river. The place to stay is the sumptuous *Cally Palace* **hotel** (℡01557/814341, Ⓦwww.callypalace.co.uk; ❼; closed Jan), though make sure you're placed in the old house rather than the ugly modern extension, and be sure to take a jacket and tie if you're going to eat there. **B&B** in Gatehouse itself is available at the terraced *Bobbin Guest House*, 36 High St (℡01557/814229; ❷), or at the *Murray Arms Hotel* (℡01557/814207, Ⓦwww.murrayarms.com; ❺), the old coaching inn next to the clocktower, where Robbie Burns wrote *Scots wha hae*. For good **pub food**, head for the bar or the conservatory of the welcoming *Masonic Arms*, just up Ann Street. For the ultimate array of whiskies, head for the *Anwoth Hotel*, at the bottom of the High Street. The *Gatehouse* **tearoom**, inside the original "Gatehouse", the

Galloway Forest Park

Newton Stewart is a popular base for hikers and cyclists heading for the nearby **Galloway Forest Park,** Britain's largest forest park, which stretches all the way from the southern part of Ayrshire right down to Gatehouse of Fleet, laid out on land owned by the Forestry Commission. Many hikers aim for the park's **Glen Trool** by following the A714 north for about ten miles to Bargrennan, where a narrow lane twists the five miles over to the glen's Loch Trool. The Forestry Commission *Caldons* **campsite** (℡01671/840218, Ⓦwww.forestholidays.co.uk; Easter–Sept) sits in the woods close to the western edge of the loch. From here, there's a choice of magnificent **hiking** and **cycling** trails, as well as lesser tracks. Several longer routes curve round the grassy peaks and icy lochs of the Awful Hand and Dungeon ranges, whilst another includes part of the Southern Upland Way, which threads through the Minnigaff Hills to Clatteringshaws Loch.

A twenty-mile stretch of the A712 from Newton Stewart east to New Galloway, known as the **Queen's Way**, cuts through the southern periphery of Galloway Forest Park, a landscape of glassy lochs, wooded hills and bare, rounded peaks. You'll pass all sorts of **hiking trails**, some the gentlest of strolls, others long-distance treks. For a short walk, stop at the **Grey Mare's Tail Bridge**, about seven miles east of Newton Stewart, where the Forestry Commission has laid out various trails, all delving into the pine forests beside the road, crossing gorges, waterfalls and burns. A few miles further on is **Clatteringshaws Loch**, a reservoir surrounded by pine forest, with a fourteen-mile footpath running right round.

oldest (and once the only) house in town, serves snacks washed down with Sulwath ales from Castle Douglas.

Newton Stewart

NEWTON STEWART, famous for its salmon and trout fishing, is an unassuming market town on the west bank of the River Cree. Originally known as Fordhouse of Cree, it was renamed in the seventeenth century by the local laird, William Stewart. A hundred years later, the estate was bought by William Douglas (of Castle Douglas fame), who preferred Newton Douglas, though neither the name, nor the cotton and carpet industry he established lasted long.

Newton Stewart's most intriguing sight is on the eastern riverbank in what used to be the separate village of Minnigaff, where the **Minnigaff parish church** (July & Aug Mon & Fri 2–4.30pm; free) houses three eleventh-century carved grave slabs. Otherwise, the town's attractions are pretty much confined to the local **museum** (Easter–June & Oct Mon–Sat 2–5pm; July & Aug Mon–Fri 10am–12.30pm & 2–5pm, Sat & Sun 2–5pm; Sept daily 2–5pm; £1), housed in the deconsecrated church of St Andrew, to the west of the main street. There's also a remarkable collection of over fifty dolls' houses on display at **Sophie's Puppenstube and Dolls' House Museum** (Easter–Oct Mon–Sat 10am–4pm; Nov, Dec & Feb–Easter Tues–Sat 10am–4pm; £2.75), located at 29 Queen St, on the road heading west from the main square.

On the main square itself, by the bus station, you'll find the local **tourist office** (April & Oct Mon–Sat 10am–4.30pm; May–Sept Mon–Sat 10am–5pm, Sun 10.30am–4pm), which has plenty of helpful literature. *Creebridge House Hotel* (℡01671/402121; ⓦwww.creebridge.co.uk; ❻) is an appealing eighteenth-century hunting lodge near the main bridge. A cheaper option is to go for one of the substantial red-sandstone Victorian villa **B&Bs**, such as *Rowallan House* (℡01671/402520, ⓦwww.rowallan.co.uk; ❸), on Corsbie Road, west of the main street up Church Lane, or *Flowerbank* (℡01671/402629, ⓦwww.flowerbankgh.com; ❷), a lovely house by the river, on the road to Monigaff church. There's also an SYHA **hostel** (℡0870/004 1142, ⓔreservations@syha.org.uk; April–Sept) in an old school in Minnigaff, up Millcroft Road from the bridge.

Whithorn and around

Twenty miles south of Newton Stewart is **WHITHORN** (ⓦwww .whithorn.com), a one-street town which nevertheless occupies an important place in Scottish history, for it is thought that here in 397 **St Ninian** founded the first Christian church north of Hadrian's Wall. According to the Venerable Bede, Ninian built a church in "a manner to which the Britons were not accustomed", and it became known as *Candida Casa*, "a bright and shining place", translated by the southern Picts he had come to convert as "Hwiterne" (White House) – hence Whithorn. No one can be sure where the *Candida Casa* actually stood, and very little is known about Ninian's life, but his tomb at Whithorn soon became a popular place of pilgrimage and, in the twelfth century, a Premonstratensian priory was established to service the shrine. For generations the rich and the royal made the trek here, the last being Mary, Queen of Scots in 1563, but then came the Reformation and the prohibition of pilgrimages in 1581.

These days, it takes a serious leap of the imagination to envisage Whithorn as a medieval pilgrimage centre. For this reason, it's a good idea to start by watching the audiovisual show at the **Whithorn Dig** (**Whithorn Story** (Easter–Oct daily 10.30am–5pm; £2.70; HS members £1.90) on the main street. Heading outside, the dig site is pretty uninspiring, as are the nearby ruins of the nave of **Whithorn Priory**, though the latter does have a couple of finely carved thirteenth-century south-facing doorways. The most compelling early Christian relics found in the vicinity – a series of standing crosses and headstones – are housed in the onsite **Whithorn Museum**.

The pilgrims who crossed the Solway to visit St Ninian's shrine landed at the **ISLE OF WHITHORN**, four miles south of Whithorn, no longer an island, but an antique and picturesque little seaport. If you continue to the end of the harbour, you'll pick up signs to the minuscule remains of the thirteenth-century **St Ninian's Chapel**, which some believe was the site of the original *Candida Casa*. If you want to **stay**, try the unassuming *Steam Packet Inn* (℡01988/500334, @steampacketinn@btconnect.com; ❸), right on the quay in Isle of Whithorn; it does pub food that's above average in quality and price, and has a moderately expensive **restaurant**.

Stranraer

No one could say that **STRANRAER** was beautiful, and if you're heading to (or coming from) Northern Ireland, there's really no reason to linger longer than you have to. If you find yourself with time to kill, head for the town's one specific attraction, the **Castle of St John** (Easter to mid-Sept Mon–Sat 10am–1pm & 2–5pm; free), a ruined four-storey tower house built around 1500, which stands on the main street, one block inland from the harbour front. If you've yet more time on your hands, pop into the local **Stranraer Museum** (Mon–Fri 10am–5pm, Sat 10am–1pm & 2–5pm; free) in the Old Town Hall, a distinctive building in vanilla and pistachio colours a short distance west along George Street.

The **train station** is right by the Stena Line **ferry** terminal (℡0870/570 7070, @www.stenaline.co.uk) on the East Pier, from where boats depart for Belfast. A couple of minutes' walk away, on Port Rodie, is the **bus station**. Stena Line's fast HSS **catamarans** depart for Belfast from the West Pier on the other side of the harbour. P&O Irish Sea ferries (℡0870/2424 777, @www.poirishsea.com) to and from Larne, arrive not in Stranraer, but at the port of **CAIRNRYAN**, some five miles north; note, though, that bus services to Cairnryan are infrequent and aren't integrated with the ferry times.

Stranraer's **tourist office** is at 28 Harbour St (April–Oct 9.30am–5.30pm, Sun 10.30am–4.30pm; Nov–March Mon–Sat 10am–4pm) between the two piers. Should you need **accommodation**, head for the *Harbour Guest House* (℡01776/704626, @www.harbourguesthouse.com; ❸), a decent **B&B** on the seafront on Market Street, just a short stroll from either pier. You'll have few problems **eating out** if you're after fish and chips, pizzas or pub grub, but for something more edifying, aim for the moderately expensive restaurant of the *North West Castle* (℡01776/704413, @www.northwestcastle .co.uk), the vast, whitewashed crenellated pile next to the police station on Port Rodie.

A better bet, if you want to splash out on a posh hotel, is to head out to **Corsewall Point**, eleven miles north of Stranraer, at the northern tip of the Rhinns of Galloway, where the (still functioning) 1815 lighthouse has been incorporated into the luxury *Corsewall Lighthouse Hotel* (℡01776/853220, @www.lighthousehotel.co.uk; ❻). If you don't have your own transport, the owners will collect you from Stranraer, as long as you book in advance.

Portpatrick to the Mull of Galloway

Situated roughly halfway along the west shore of the Rhinns of Galloway, the hilly, hammer-shaped peninsula at the end of the Solway coast, **PORT-PATRICK** has an attractive pastel-painted seafront that wraps itself round a small rocky bay, sheltered by equally rocky cliffs. Until the mid-nineteenth century, when sailing ships were replaced by steamboats, Portpatrick was a thriving seaport, serving as the main embarkation point for Northern Ireland, with coal, cotton and British troops heading in one direction, Ulster cattle and linen in the other.

Portpatrick has several good **hotels** and **guest houses**, the best of which is the lilac-painted *Waterfront Hotel* (℡01776/810800, ⓦwww.waterfronthotel .co.uk; ❹), which has gone for the contemporary look inside. Cheaper choices include the neighbouring *Knowe Guest House* (℡01776/810441, ⓦwww .theknowe.co.uk; ❶), a bright, white B&B which runs a tearoom in its conservatory, and the equally comfortable Victorian *Carlton Guest House*, also on the harbour at 21 South Crescent (℡01776/810253; ❶). It's impossible to miss the *Portpatrick Hotel* (℡01942/824824, ⓦwww.shearingsholidays.com; ❺; Feb–Nov), a grand turreted Edwardian mansion on the hill above the harbour; inside, it's a bit tatty round the edges, but it goes down well with the tour groups, for whom there's live music more or less every night.

There are several caravan and **campsites** in a row on the hill overlooking Portpatrick and Dunskey Castle, quite a distance from town (and the sea), but accessed by a pleasant walk along the disused railway and clifftop trail; *Sunnymeade* (℡01776/810293) has the better facilities, but *Castle Bay* (℡01776/810462) has the more informal atmosphere. For pubs and grub, *The Crown* on the seafront is probably the cosiest, though the adjacent *Harbour Inn* has real ale. For something more formal and slightly pricier, head to the *Waterfront Bistro* next door.

It's twenty miles south from Portpatrick to the **Mull of Galloway** (ⓦwww.mull-of-galloway.co.uk), but it's well worth the ride. This precipitous headland, crowned by a classic whitewashed Stevenson lighthouse, from which you can see the Isle of Man, as well as the coasts of Ireland and England, really feels like the end of the road. It is, in fact, the southernmost point in Scotland, and a favourite nesting spot for guillemots, razorbills and kittiwakes. The headland is also an RSPB reserve with a **visitor centre** (Easter–Sept daily 10am–4pm) in a building near the lighthouse, which can be climbed on summer weekends (April–Sept Sat & Sun 10am–3.30pm; £2).

Ayrshire

The rolling hills and rich soil of **Ayrshire** (ⓦwww.ayrshire-arran.com) make for prime farming country, and as such are not really top of most visitors' Scottish itinerary. **Ayr**, the county town and birthplace of Robert Burns, is handsome enough, but won't distract you for long. Most folk wisely stick to the coastline, attracted by the wide, flat sandy **beaches** and the region's vast number of **golf** courses. South of Ayr, the most obvious points of interest are **Culzean Castle**, with its Robert Adam interior and extensive wooded grounds, and the off-shore islands of **Ailsa Craig**, home to the world's second largest gannetry. North of Ayr, where the towns benefited from the

Robert Burns

The first of seven children, **Robert Burns** (Ⓦ www.robertburns.org), the national poet of Scotland, was born in Alloway on January 25, 1759. His father, William, was employed as a gardener until 1766 when he became a tenant farmer at Mount Oliphant, near Alloway, moving to Lochlie farm, Tarbolton, eleven years later. A series of bad harvests and the demands of the landlord's estate manager bank-rupted the family, and William died almost penniless in 1784. These events had a profound effect on Robert, leaving him with an antipathy towards political authority and a hatred of the land-owning classes.

With the death of his father, Robert became head of the family and they moved again, this time to a farm at Mossgiel, near Mauchline. Burns had already begun writing **poetry** and **prose** at Lochlie, recording incidental thoughts in his *First Commonplace Book*, but it was here at Mossgiel that he began to write in earnest, and his first volume, *Poems Chiefly in the Scottish Dialect*, was published in Kilmarnock in 1786. The book proved immensely popular, celebrated by ordinary Scots and Edinburgh literati alike, with the satirical trilogy *Holy Willie's Prayer*, *The Holy Fair* and *Address to the Devil* attracting particular attention. The object of Burns' poetic scorn was the kirk, whose ministers had obliged him to appear in church to be publicly condemned for fornication – a commonplace punishment in those days.

Burns spent the winter of 1786–87 in the capital, lionized by the literary establish-ment. Despite his success, however, he felt trapped, unable to make enough money from writing to leave farming. He was also in a political snare, fraternizing with the elite, but with radical views and pseudo-Jacobite nationalism that constantly landed him in trouble. His frequent recourse was to play the part of the unlettered plough-man-poet, the noble savage who might be excused his impetuous outbursts and hectic womanizing.

He had, however, made useful contacts in Edinburgh and as a consequence was recruited to collect, write and rearrange two volumes of songs set to traditional Scottish tunes. These volumes, James Johnson's *Scots Musical Museum* and George Thomson's *Select Scottish Airs*, contain the bulk of his **songwriting**, and it's on them that Burns' international reputation rests, with works like *Auld Lang Syne*, *Scots Wha Hae*, *Coming Through the Rye* and *Green Grow the Rushes, O*. At this time, too, though poetry now took second place, he produced two excellent poems: *Tam o' Shanter* and a republican tract, *A Man's a Man for a' That*.

Burns often boasted of his sexual conquests, but in 1788, he eventually married **Jean Armour**, a stonemason's daughter from Mauchline, with whom he already had two children, and moved to Ellisland Farm, near Dumfries. The following year he was appointed excise offi-cer and could at last leave farming, moving to Dumfries in 1791. Burns' years of comfort were short-lived, however. His years of labour on the farm, allied to a rheumatic fever, damaged his heart, and he died in Dumfries on July 21, 1796, aged 37.

Burns' work, inspired by a romantic nationalism and tinged with a wry wit, has made him a potent symbol of "Scottishness". Ignoring the anglophile preferences of the Edinburgh elite, he wrote in Scots vernacular about the country he loved, an exu-berant celebration that filled a need in a nation culturally colonized by England. Today, Burns Clubs all over the world mark every anniversary of the poet's birthday with the Burns' Supper, complete with Scottish totems – haggis, piper and whisky bottle – and a ritual recital of Burns' *Ode to a Haggis*.

ndustrialization of Glasgow, there are even fewer places to detain you, with the xception of **Irvine**, home to several museums including the ever-expanding cottish Maritime Museum.

Ayr and around

With a population of around fifty thousand, **AYR** is by far the largest town on the Firth of Clyde coast. It was an important seaport and trading centre for many centuries, and rivalled Glasgow in size and significance right up until the late seventeenth century. Nowadays, the town won't keep you long, though its prestigious venue for the Scottish Grand National and the Scottish Derby (ⓦwww.ayr-racecourse.co.uk), pulls in huge crowds, and the local tourist industry continues to do steady business out of the fact that Robbie Burns was born in the neighbouring village of **Alloway** (see opposite).

Ayr's busy town centre, wedged between Sandgate and the south bank of the treacly River Ayr, was rebuilt by the Victorians, and is now busy most days with shoppers from all over the county. The most conspicuous landmark is the big, grey, rather ugly castellated **Wallace Tower**, erected in 1828 at the southern end of the High Street. It stands on what is thought to have been the site of Edward I's barracks, which was set alight by Wallace in 1297. At the junction of the High Street and Sandgate stands the rather more impressive Neoclassical **Town Buildings**, completed in 1832, whose spectacular 226ft spire is guarded by griffins, eagles and a Triton.

Ayr's medieval **Auld Brig**, east off the High Street, survived the threat of demolition in the early twentieth century, thanks largely to its featuring in a Burns poem, and is now one of the oldest stone bridges in Scotland, having been built during the reign of James IV (1488–1513). A short stroll upstream from the bridge stands the much-restored **Auld Kirk**, the church funded by Cromwell as recompense for the one he incorporated into the town's fortress. The church's dark and gloomy interior retains the original pulpit (call ℡01292/262580 for access).

All you can see of Cromwell's zigzag **Citadel**, built to the west of the town centre in the 1650s, is a small section of the old walls – the area is still known locally as "the Fort". To the south of the citadel are the wide, gridiron streets of Ayr's main Georgian and Regency residential development. **Wellington Square** is the area's showpiece, its trim gardens and terraces overlooked by the **County Buildings**, a vast, imposing Palladian pile from 1820. The opening of the Glasgow-to-Ayr train line in 1840 brought the first major influx of holiday-makers to the town, but today, only a few hardy visitors and local dog-walkers take a stroll along Ayr's bleak, long **Esplanade** and beach, which look out to the Isle of Arran.

Practicalities

Ayr is the nearest large town to **Glasgow Prestwick airport** (℡01292/511000, ⓦwww.gpia.co.uk), which lies three miles north and has regular trains to Ayr and Glasgow. Ayr **train** station is ten minutes' walk south-east of the town centre; the **bus** station is in the centre at the foot of Sandgate; nearby is the **tourist office**, at 22 Sandgate (July & Aug Mon–Sat 9am–6pm, Sun 10am–5pm; Oct–June Mon–Sat 9am–5pm), which can help with **accommodation**. Of the numerous choices on Queen's Terrace, head for *Craggallan* (℡01292/264998, ⓦwww.craggallan.com; ❷), a friendly little guest house with a dining table that converts into a billiards table, or opt for the *Horizon Hotel* (℡01292/264384, ⓦwww.horizonhotel.com; 3), a purpose-built modern hotel, and the only one (almost) on the seafront. In the leafy streets to the south of the town centre, try *The Crescent*, a lovely spacious Victorian house with a four-poster suite available, at 26 Bellevue Crescent (℡01292/287329, ⓦwww.26crescent.freeserve.co.uk; ❸), or the luxurious *Savoy Park Hotel*

(☎01292/266112, ⓦwww.savoypark.com; ❺), a splendid red-sandstone Scots Baronial building at 16 Racecourse Rd. Campers should head for the *Heads of Ayr* caravan and **campsite** (☎01292/442269; March–Oct), three miles south of town along the A719.

Arguably the town's best **restaurant** is *Fouters*, 2a Academy St, a cellar bistro off Sandgate (☎01292/261391; closed Sun & Mon). On the eastern side of Wellington Square is the *Rupee Room*, a popular Indian restaurant, decked out with modern minimalist furnishings. You can have eat-in or takeaway fish and chips nearby from *Wellington*, a long-established chippie at the corner of Sandgate and Fort Street, next door to which is *Renaldo's*, renowned for its authentic Italian ice cream and Ayr rock. A mixed crowd packs out the *West Kirk*, a **pub** in a converted church on Sandgate, but the most historic drinking den in town is the thatched *Tam o' Shanter*, on the High Street, whose ancient walls sport quotes from Robert Burns.

Alloway

ALLOWAY, formerly a small village but now on the outskirts of Ayr, is the birthplace of Robert Burns (1759–96), Scotland's national poet. The first port of call is the **Burns Cottage and Museum** (daily: April–Oct 9.30am–5.30pm; Nov–March 10am–4pm; £3), the poet's birthplace, a low, whitewashed, thatched cottage where animals and people lived under the same roof. Much altered over the years, you can nevertheless gain an impression of what the place must have been like when Burns, the first of seven children, was born in the box bed in the only room in the house.

Ten minutes' walk down the road from the cottage are the plain, roofless ruins of **Alloway Kirk**, where Robert's father William is buried, and where Burns set much of *Tam o' Shanter*. Down the road from the church, the **Brig o' Doon**, the picturesque thirteenth-century hump-backed bridge over which Tam is forced to flee for his life, still stands, curving gracefully over the river. High above the river and bridge, towers the **Burns Monument** (May–Sept Mon–Sat 9am–5pm; same ticket as Cottage), a striking Neoclassical temple in a small carefully manicured garden and housing yet another museum. For the populist approach to Burns, head for the **Tam o' Shanter Experience** (times as for Burns Cottage; £1.50), on the opposite side of the road from Alloway Kirk, housed in a modern, faceless building that belies a marginally more interesting interior.

True Burns junkies might want to eat, drink and stay at the *Brig o' Doon* **hotel** on the banks of the River Doon (☎01292/442466, ⓦwww.costley-hotels.co.uk; ❺), reputed to be another of Burns' drinking haunts. To reach Alloway from Ayr town centre, **bus** #1 sets off from Sandgate (Mon–Sat hourly) and goes right to the Tam o' Shanter Experience; otherwise, you can catch bus #57, #58 or #60 from the bus station to Alloway.

Culzean Castle

Sitting on the edge of a sheer cliff, looking out over the Firth of Clyde to Arran, **Culzean Castle** (pronounced "Cullane"; daily: April–Oct 11am–4.30pm; £7; NTS), ten miles south of Ayr, couldn't want for a more impressive situation. The current castle is actually a grand, late eighteenth-century stately home, designed by highly successful Scottish Neoclassical architect, **Robert Adam**, for the tenth earl of Cassillis (pronounced "cassles"). Since passing into the hands of the National Trust for Scotland in 1945, Culzean, and in particular its surrounding 560-acre **country park**, has become one of Ayrshire's premier tourist attractions.

The best place to start is at the **visitor centre** (April–Oct daily 10.30am–5.30pm; Nov–March Sat & Sun only) in the modernized Home Farm buildings. Here, you can watch an audiovisual show on the house, and pick up **free maps** – as well as wildlife leaflets – that help you get your bearings, the layout of the place being rather confusing; consult staff about taking a guided walk in the grounds. You can **stay** at Culzean (℡01655/884455, ⓦwww.culzeancastle.net; April–Oct; ➒), on the top floor, where six double bedrooms have been done out in a comfortably genteel style. Another option is the nearby *Culzean Castle* **campsite** (℡01655/760627; March–Oct), located in the woods by the castle entrance.

Irvine

IRVINE, twelve miles north of Ayr, was once the principal port for trade between Glasgow and Ireland, and later for coal from Kilmarnock, its halcyon days recalled by the enjoyable **Scottish Maritime Museum** (April–Oct daily 10am–5pm; £2.50), which is spread across several locations down at the town's beautifully restored old harbour. The best place to start is in the late nineteenth-century **Linthouse Engine Shop**, on Harbour Road, a hangar-like building housing everything from old sailing dinghies and canoes to a giant ship's turbines, and a kids' corner for learning Morse code and semaphore. Free guided tours set off regularly for the nearby **Shipbuilder's Flat**, which has been restored to something like its appearance in 1910, when a family of six to eight would have occupied its two rooms and scullery. Moored at the **pontoons** on Harbour Street is an assortment of craft, which you can board, including a tug, a trawler, a "puffer" boat and the SY *Carola*, the oldest seagoing steam yacht in the country.

Close by, opposite **Magnum** (ⓦwww.themagnum.co.uk), Scotland's largest leisure and swimming complex, a funky retracting footbridge leads visitors to Irvine's newest attraction, the **Big Idea** (daily 10am–6pm; £7.95; ⓦwww.bigidea.org.uk), a half-submerged glass eye of a building with a turf roof. The theme of the place is invention, and it has endless high-tech hands-on exhibits where children can play with robots, check out a toilet flush

Ailsa Craig

If the weather's half decent, it's impossible to miss the views of the island of **Ailsa Craig**, which lies ten miles off the Ayrshire coast in the middle of the Firth of Clyde. The island's name means "Fairy Rock" in Gaelic, though the island looks more like an enormous muffin than a place of enchantment. It would certainly have been less than enchanting for the persecuted Catholics who escaped to the island during the Reformation. The island's granite has long been used for making what many consider to be the finest curling stones – a company in nearby Mauchline still has exclusive rights and sporadically collects a few boulders – and in the late nineteenth century, 29 people lived on the island, either working in the quarry or at the Stevenson lighthouse. With its volcanic, columnar cliffs and 1114ft summit, Ailsa Craig is now a **bird sanctuary** that's home to some 40,000 gannets. The best time to make the trip is at the end of May and in June when the fledglings are trying to fly. Several companies **cruise** round the island, but only Mark McCrindle, who also organizes sea-angling trips, is licensed to land (May to late Sept 1–2 daily; exact timings and prices depend on the length of trip and the tides; ℡01465/713219). It takes about an hour to reach the island, so you've enough time to walk up to the summit of the rock and watch the birds, weather permitting.

system, and get to grips with the scientific principles of cams, rods, levers, gears and valves. There's also a "pink-knuckle" ride called **The History of Explosions**, which is little more than a promotional film for the munitions industry, watched from jolting seats. More informative is the nearby static exhibition telling the story of Nobel's Explosives Company (later to become ICI), which once ran the world's largest explosives factory on the Ardeer peninsula behind the museum.

Arriving at Irvine's adjacent **train** or **bus stations**, you'll find yourself exactly halfway between the harbour, to the west, and the Riverfront shopping complex and old town, to the east. Kilwinning Road, heading north out of Irvine, has several inexpensive **B&Bs** such as *Laurelbank Guest House*, at no. 3 (℡01294/277153, ✉laurelbankguesthouse@hotmail.com; ❶); should you wish to pamper yourself a bit more, head for *Annfield House*, 6 Castle St (℡01294/278903, ⊛www.annfieldhousehotel.co.uk; ❺), a big Victorian mansion overlooking the river at the end of Sandgate, that has spacious bedrooms and its own bar and **restaurant**.

Travel details

Buses

For information on all local and national bus services, contact Traveline ℡08706/082608 (daily 7am–9pm), ⊛www.traveline.org.uk.

Ayr to: Ardrossan (Mon–Sat every 30min, Sun every 2hr; 55min); Culzean Castle (Mon–Sat hourly, Sun every 2hr; 30min); Dumfries (Mon–Sat every 2hr; 2hr 10min); Glasgow (hourly; 55min).

Castle Douglas to: Dumfries (Mon–Sat hourly, Sun every 2hr; 45min); Kirkcudbright (Mon–Sat hourly, 6 on Sun; 20min).

Dumfries to: Ayr (Mon–Sat every 2hr; 2hr 10min); Caerlaverock (Mon–Sat every 2hr, 2 on Sun; 30min); Carlisle (Mon–Sat hourly, Sun every 2hr; 1hr 25min); Castle Douglas (Mon–Sat hourly, 4 on Sun; 30–45min); Gatehouse of Fleet (Mon–Sat 8 daily, 3 on Sun; 55min–1hr 25min); Kirkcudbright (Mon–Sat hourly, 6 on Sun; 1hr 10min); New Abbey (Mon–Sat hourly, 4 on Sun; 15min); Newton Stewart (Mon–Sat 8 daily, 2 on Sun; 1hr 30min); Rockcliffe (5 daily; 1hr); Stranraer (Mon–Sat 8 daily, 2 on Sun; 2hr 10min).

Edinburgh to: Dumfries (Mon–Sat 4 daily, 2 on Sun; 2hr 40min); Jedburgh (3–4 daily; 1hr 50min); Kelso (4–6 daily; 2hr); Melrose (hourly; 2hr 15min); Peebles (hourly; 1hr); Selkirk (hourly; 1hr 40min).

Gatehouse of Fleet to: Kirkcudbright (Mon–Sat –10 daily, 5 on Sun; 20min); Newton Stewart (Mon–Sat 10–12 daily, 3 on Sun; 25min); Stranraer (Mon–Sat every 2hr, 3 on Sun; 1hr 20min).

Jedburgh to: Kelso (Mon–Sat 5–7 daily; 25min);

Melrose (Mon–Sat 1–2 hourly, 7 on Sun; 30min). **Kelso** to: Melrose (Mon–Sat 7–9 daily, 5 on Sun; 30–40min).

Melrose to: Jedburgh (Mon–Sat 1–2 hourly, 7 on Sun; 30min); Kelso (Mon–Sat 8–12 daily, 4 on Sun; 30min); Peebles (Mon–Sat hourly, 6 on Sun; 1hr 10min); Selkirk (Mon–Sat hourly, 2 on Sun; 20min).

Newton Stewart to: Glentrool (Mon–Sat 7 daily, 4 on Sun; 20min); Stranraer (Mon–Sat 15 daily, 5 on Sun; 45min); Whithorn (Mon–Sat hourly, 4 on Sun; 50min); Isle of Whithorn (Mon–Sat hourly, 4 on Sun; 1hr).

Trains

For information on all local and national rail services, contact National Rail Enquiries ℡08457/484950, ⊛www.nationalrail.co.uk.

Ayr to: Glasgow Central (every 30min; 50min); Irvine (every 30min; 15min); Prestwick Airport (every 30min; 7min); Stranraer (Mon–Sat 7 daily, 2 on Sun; 1hr 20min).

Dumfries to: Carlisle (Mon–Sat 14 daily, 5 on Sun; 40min); Glasgow Central (Mon–Sat 8 daily, 2 on Sun; 1hr 50min); Stranraer (Mon–Sat 2 daily; 3hr).

Glasgow Central to: Ayr (every 30min; 55min); Irvine (every 30min; 35min); Dumfries (Mon–Sat 8 daily, 2 on Sun; 1hr 50min); Kilmarnock (hourly; 40min); Prestwick Airport (every 30min; 45min); Stranraer (Mon–Sat 4 daily, Sun 2 daily; 2hr).

Stranraer to: Ayr (Mon–Sat 7 daily, 2 on Sun; 1hr 20min); Dumfries (Mon–Sat 2 daily; 3hr); Glasgow (4 daily; 2hr 10min).

18

Ferries (summer timetable)

Stranraer to: Portpatrick (Mon–Sat 7 daily, 3 on Sun; 25min).
Ardrossan to: Brodick, Isle of Arran (4–6 daily; 55min).

Cairnryan to: Larne (7–9 daily; 1hr–1hr 45min).
Stranraer to: Belfast (7–8 daily; 1hr 45min–3hr 15min).
Troon to: Belfast (3 daily; 2hr 30min); Larne (2 daily; 1hr 50min).

Glasgow and the Clyde

CHAPTER 19 # Highlights

* **Gallery of Modern Art**
Idiosyncratic but populist
collection of contemporary
artworks, bang in the heart
of the city. See p.1015

* **Necropolis** Elegantly
crumbling graveyard on a
city-centre hill behind the
ancient cathedral, with
great views. See p.1021

* **Glasgow School of Art**
Take a student-led tour of
Charles Rennie
Mackintosh's architectural
masterpiece. See p.1023

* **Clydeside** The river that
made Glasgow: walk or
cycle along it, take a boat
on it, cross a bridge over it,
or get a view of it from the
futuristic Science Centre.
See p.1027

* **Burrell Collection** An
inspired and eclectic art
collection displayed in a
purpose-built museum in
Pollok Park. See p.1031

* **"Glaesga nightlife"**
Sample the glamour and
the grit with cocktails at
the *Rogano* followed by a
pint of heavy at the
Horseshoe Bar. See
p.1034 and p.1036

* **New Lanark** Stay for next-
to-nothing at this fascinating nineteenth-century
planned village. See p.1043

△ "The Armadillo", Glasgow

Glasgow and the Clyde

Rejuvenated, upbeat **Glasgow**, Scotland's largest city, has not tradition-ally enjoyed the best of reputations. Set on the banks of the mighty River Clyde, this former industrial giant can still initially seem a grey and depressing place, with the M8 motorway screeching through the centre and dilapidated housing estates on its outskirts. However, the effects of Glasgow's remarkable overhaul, set in motion in the 1980s by the "Glasgow's Miles Better" campaign and crowned by the awarding of the title of European City of Culture in 1990, are still much in evidence, even if the momentum has slowed. Glasgow's image of itself has changed irrevocably and few visitors will be left in any doubt that the city is, in its own idiosyncratic way, a cultured and dynamic place well worth getting to know.

The city has much to offer, including some of the best-financed and most imaginative museums and galleries in Britain – among them the showcase **Burrell Collection** of art and antiquities – nearly all of which are free. Glasgow's **architecture** is some of the most striking in the UK, from the restored eighteenth-century warehouses of the **Merchant City** to the hulking Victorian prosperity of George Square. Most distinctive of all is the work of local luminary Charles Rennie Mackintosh, whose elegantly streamlined Art Nouveau designs appear all over the city, reaching their apotheosis in the stun-ning **School of Art**. Recent development of the old shipyards of the Clyde, notably in the space-age shapes of the new **Glasgow Science Centre**, hint at yet another string to the city's bow: combining design with innovation. The city boasts thriving live-music venues, distinctive places to eat and drink, busy theatres, concert halls and an opera house. Above all, the feature that best defines the individualism and peculiar attraction of the city is its **people**, whether rough-edged comedians on the football terraces or bright young things dressed to the nines in the trendiest of bars.

Despite all the upbeat hype, Glasgow's gentrification has passed by deprived inner-city areas such as the **East End**, home of the **Barras market** and some staunchly change-resistant pubs. This area, along with isolated housing schemes such as Castlemilk and Easterhouse, needs more than a facelift to resolve its complex social and economic problems, and has historically been the breeding ground for the city's much-lauded **socialism**, celebrated in the wonderful **People's Palace** social history museum. Indeed, even in the more stylish

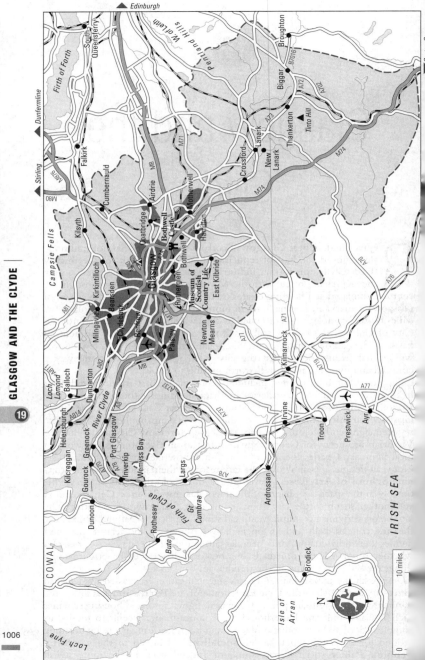

19

© Crown copy

quarters of Glasgow there's a gritty edge that's never far away, reinforcing a peculiar mix of grime and glitz that the city seems to have patented.

Quite apart from its own attractions, Glasgow makes an excellent base from which to explore the **Clyde Valley and coast**, made easily accessible by a reliable train service. Chief among the draws is the remarkable eighteenth-century **New Lanark** mills and workers' village, a World Heritage Site, while other day-trips might take you to the new **National Museum of Scottish Country Life** near East Kilbride or on a boat heading "doon the watter" past the old shipbuilding centres on the Clyde estuary.

History

GLASGOW's earliest history, like so much else in this surprisingly romantic city, is obscured in a swirl of myth. The city's name is said to derive from the Celtic *Glas-cu*, which loosely translates as "the dear, green place" – a tag that the tourist board is keen to exploit as an antidote to the sooty images of popular imagination. It is generally agreed that the first settlers arrived in the sixth century to join Christian missionary **Kentigern** – later to become St Mungo – in his newly founded monastery on the banks of the tiny Molendinar Burn.

William the Lionheart gave the town an official charter in 1175, after which it continued to grow in importance, peaking in the mid-fifteenth century when the **university** was founded on Kentigern's site – the second in Scotland after St Andrews. This led to the establishment of an archbishopric, and hence city status, in 1492, and, due to its situation on a large, navigable river, Glasgow soon expanded into a major industrial **port**. The first cargo of tobacco from Virginia offloaded in Glasgow in 1674, and the 1707 Act of Union between Scotland and England – despite demonstrations against it in Glasgow – led to a boom in trade with the colonies until American independence. Following the **Industrial Revolution** and James Watt's innovations in steam power, coal from the abundant seams of Lanarkshire fuelled the ironworks all around the Clyde, worked by the cheap hands of the Highlanders and, later, those fleeing the Irish potato famine of the 1840s.

The **Victorian** age transformed Glasgow beyond recognition. The population boomed from 77,000 in 1801 to nearly 800,000 at the end of the century, and new tenement blocks swept into the suburbs in an attempt to cope with the choking influxes of people. Two vast and stately **International Exhibitions** were held in 1888 and 1901 to showcase the city and its industries to the outside world, necessitating the construction of huge civic monoliths such as the Kelvingrove Art Gallery and the Council Chambers in George Square. At this time Glasgow became known as the "Second City of the Empire" – a curious epithet for a place that today rarely acknowledges second place in anything.

By the turn of the twentieth century, Glasgow's industries had been honed into one massive **shipbuilding** culture. Everything from tugboats to transatlantic liners were fashioned out of sheet metal in the yards that straddled the Clyde from Gourock to Rutherglen. In the harsh economic climate of the 1930s, however, unemployment spiralled, and Glasgow could do little to counter its popular image as a city dominated by inebriate violence and, having absorbed vast numbers of Irish emigrants, sectarian tensions. The **Gorbals** area in particular became notorious as one of the worst slums in Europe. The city's image has never been helped by the depth of animosity between its two great rival football teams, Catholic **Celtic** and Protestant **Rangers**.

Shipbuilding, and many associated industries, died away almost completely in the 1960s and 1970s, leaving the city depressed, jobless and directionless. Then, in the 1980s, the self-promotion campaign began, snowballing towards the 1988 Garden Festival and year-long party as European City of Culture in 1990. Glasgow then beat off competition from Edinburgh and Liverpool to become **UK City of Architecture and Design** in 1999, an event that strove valiantly to showcase the city's rich architectural heritage and highlight the role of design in modern everyday living. These various titles have helped to reinforce the impression that Glasgow, despite its many problems, has successfully broken the industrial shackles of the past and evolved into a city of stature and confidence.

Arrival, orientation and information

Glasgow International airport (☎0141/887 1111, ⓦwww.glasgow-airport.com) is at Abbotsinch, eight miles southwest of the city – not to be confused with Glasgow Prestwick airport, which is thirty miles south near Ayr. From the international airport, the Glasgow Airport Link bus (£3.30) runs from bus stops 1 or 2 into the central Buchanan Street bus station every fifteen minutes during the day; the journey takes 25 minutes. White airport taxis charge around £17.

From **Glasgow Prestwick** airport (☎01292/511000, ⓦwww.gpia.co.uk), buses to Glasgow depart from directly outside the terminal: there's an express bus #X77 (hourly; £3.30; 50min) to Glasgow's Buchanan Street bus station. The **train** station is by the terminal (alight at the airport not Prestwick Town), with trains taking 45 minutes to reach Glasgow Central station (Mon–Sat every 30min, Sun hourly; £4.90).

Nearly all **trains** from England come into **Central station**, which sits over Argyle Street, one of the city's main shopping thoroughfares. Bus #398 from the front entrance on Gordon Street shuttles every ten minutes to **Queen Street station**, at the corner of George Square, terminus for trains serving Edinburgh and the north. The walk between the two takes about ten minutes. Bus #398 also stops at **Buchanan Street bus station**, arrival point for regional and intercity **coaches**.

Orientation

Glasgow is a sprawling place, built on some punishingly steep hills, and with no obvious focus, although, as most transport services converge on the area around **Argyle Street** and, 200 yards to the north, **George Square**, this pocket is the most obvious candidate for city-centre status. However, with the renovated, upmarket **Merchant City** immediately to the east and the main business and commercial areas to the west, the centre, when the term is used actually refers to a large swathe from **Charing Cross** and the M8 in the west through to **Glasgow Green** in the rundown **East End**.

The **West End** begins just over a mile west of Central station, and covers most of the area beyond the M8 motorway. Today, this is still very much the student quarter of Glasgow, exuding a decorous air, with graceful avenues and parks, and inexpensive, interesting shops and cafés. Parts of the **Southside** have always been very pleasant: the leafy enclaves of **Queen's Park** are home to the national football stadium, Hampden Park, while **Pollok Park** and the **Burrell Collection** are undisputed highlights of the city.

Information

The city's efficient **tourist office**, at 11 George Square (July & Aug Mon–Sat 9am–8pm, Sun 10am–6pm; June & Sept Mon–Sat 10am–7pm, Sun 10am–6pm; April & May Mon–Sat 9am–6pm, Sun 10am–6pm; rest of year Mon–Sat 9am–6pm; ☎0141/204 4400, ⓦwww.seeglasgow.com), provides a wide array of maps and leaflets, and has an accommodation-booking service (fee £2). They also sell travel passes, theatre tickets and organize car rental. Pick up their free *Essential Guide to Glasgow*, a chunky brochure with details of every tourist attraction for miles around.

There's also a branch of the tourist office in the **airport's** international arrivals hall (daily 7.30am–5pm, except Oct–April Sun 8am–3.30pm; ☎0141/848 4440).

City transport

Although it can be tough negotiating Glasgow's steep hills, **walking** is the best way of exploring any one part of the city. The best way to get between the city centre and the West End is to use the **Underground** (Mon–Sat 6.30am–11.30pm, Sun 11am–6pm), whose stations are marked with a large orange U. There's a flat fare of 90p, or you can buy a **day ticket** for £1.70 (Mon–Sat after 9.30am and all day Sun). The main stations are **Buchanan Street**, near George Square and connected to Queen Street train station by a moving walkway, and **St Enoch**, at the junction of Buchanan Street pedestrian precinct and Argyle Street. **Hillhead** station is bang in the heart of the West End, near the university.

The array of different **bus** companies and the various routes they take is perplexing even to locals, and there's no easy guide to using them other than picking up individual timetables at the Travel Centre (see box). The main operator is First Glasgow (ⓦwww.firstgroup.com), which runs the "Overground" buses; Arriva (ⓦwww.arriva.co.uk) also operates many services. Information on relevant services is given at some bus stops.

Transport passes and information

Various **public transport passes** are available if you plan to do lots of travelling on one day or are in the city for more than a few days. For train and underground travel the **Roundabout Glasgow** ticket (£4; available Mon–Fri after 9am, and all day Sat & Sun) gives unlimited travel for a day. The simplest of a complicated system of **Zonecards**, covering train, Underground, buses and ferries, costs £12.10 and gives travel for a week in central Glasgow, including Partick in the west and to the Burrell Collection in the south. Both of the main bus companies offer tickets for all-day travel on their buses, which are cheaper after 9.30am on weekdays.

To help demystify the system, and get detailed information on local public transport, make for the neo-Gothic hut of the **Travel Centre** (Mon–Sat 9.30am–5.30pm), located a couple of hundred yards southwest of the tourist office above St Enoch Underground station, where you can pick up sheaves of maps, leaflets and bus timetables. There are smaller Travel Centres at Buchanan Street bus station and Hillhead Underground station. For information on all transport within the city and further afield, call the fairly efficient national Traveline ☎0870/608 2608 (daily 8am–8pm; ⓦwww.traveline.org.uk).

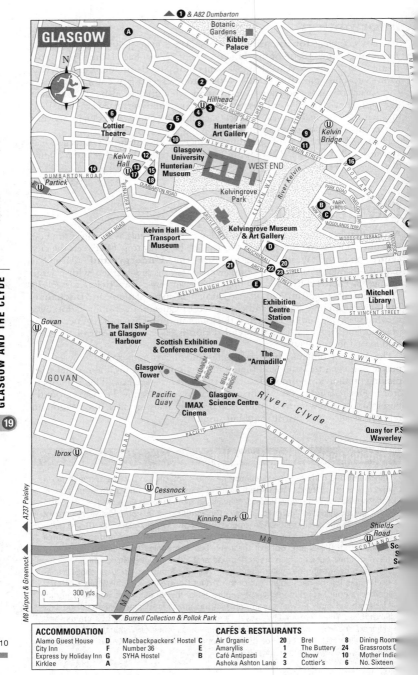

GLASGOW AND THE CLYDE

19

1010

ACCOMMODATION

Alamo Guest House	**D**
City Inn	**F**
Express by Holiday Inn	**G**
Kirklee	**A**
Macbackpackers' Hostel	**C**
Number 36	**E**
SYHA Hostel	**B**

CAFÉS & RESTAURANTS

Air Organic	**20**	Brel	**8**	Dining Room	
Amaryllis	**1**	The Buttery	**24**	Grassroots C	
Café Antipasti	**2**	Chow	**10**	Mother India	
Ashoka Ashton Lane	**3**	Cottier's	**6**	No. Sixteen	

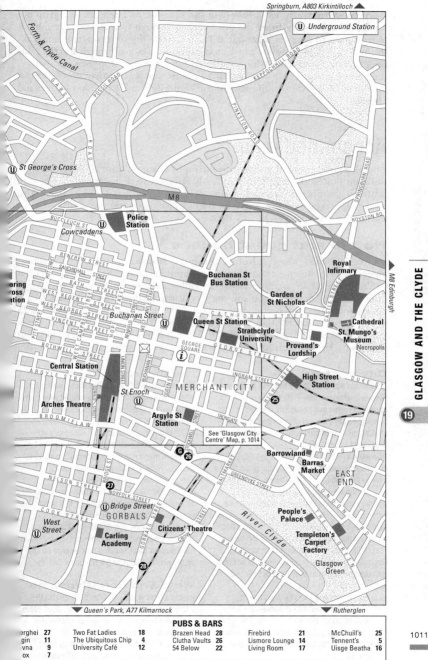

PUBS & BARS

erghei	27	Two Fat Ladies	18	Brazen Head	28	Firebird	21	McChuill's	25
gin	11	The Ubiquitous Chip	4	Clutha Vaults	26	Lismore Lounge	14	Tennent's	5
vna	9	University Café	12	54 Below	22	Living Room	17	Uisge Beatha	16
ox	7						

The suburban **train** network is swift and convenient. There are two grim but functional **cross-city lines**: the one running through Central station connects to southeastern districts as far out as Lanark, while the Queen Street line links to the East End and points east. Trains on both lines go through **Partick** station, near the West End, which is also an Underground stop; beyond Partick, the trains are an excellent way to link to points west and northwest of Glasgow, including Milngavie (for the start of the West Highland Way), Dumbarton and Helensburgh.

Accommodation

There's a good range of **accommodation** in Glasgow, from a couple of large, well-run hostels through to some highly fashionable designer hotels. The city centre is dominated by hotels, many of them fairly bland and characterless, while a few cosier guest houses and B&Bs can be found in the West End or in the southern suburb of Queen's Park.

Hotels and guest houses

It's worth booking ahead at **hotels and guest houses** to ensure a good room, especially in summer – either directly or through the tourist office (£2 fee). If you're prepared to sacrifice character, ambience and home comforts, you'll often find the cheapest rooms in the city at the **budget chain hotels** found throughout the city centre. Big players include Novotel/Ibis (℡0141/225 6000, ⓦwww.accorhotels.com); Travelodge (℡0870/085 0950, ⓦwww.travelodge.co.uk); Travel Inn (℡0870/242 8000, ⓦwww.travelinn.co.uk); and Express by Holiday Inn (℡0800/434040, ⓦwww.hiexpress.com).

City centre

Adelaide's 209 Bath St ℡0141/248 4970, ⓦwww.adelaides.co.uk. Eight simple, well-appointed rooms in a beautifully restored church building, run by pleasant staff as part of a broad-thinking, approachable Baptist community. Breakfast excluded. ❷

Bewley's 110 Bath St ℡0141/353 0800, ⓦwww.bewleyshotels.com. Angular, glass-fronted new central hotel, part of the famous Irish chain, with rooftop views from the upper floors and double, triple and family rooms at a year-round flat rate. ❸

Brunswick 106 Brunswick St ℡0141/552 0001, ⓦwww.brunswickhotel.co.uk. Under the banner "Eat Drink Sleep" in the heart of the Merchant City, a fashionable but good-value designer hotel with minimalist furniture and a smart bar and restaurant. ❸

Express by Holiday Inn 165 West Nile St ℡0141/331 6800 and 122 Stockwell St ℡0141/548 5000, ⓦwww.hiexpress.com. Budget chain hotel with two decent city centre locations, one beside the bus station and the other by the river. ❸

Langs 2 Port Dundas Place ℡0141/333 1500, ⓦwww.langshotels.co.uk. Big, sassy, classy but refreshingly independent modern hotel with a spa, trendy restaurants and lots of mod cons. ❻

Malmaison 278 West George St ℡0141/572 1000, ⓦwww.malmaison.com. Glasgow's version of the sleek, chic mini-chain, an austere Grecian-temple frontage masking a superbly comfortable designer hotel. Breakfast excluded. ❼

The Old School House 194 Renfrew St ℡0141/332 7600. Attractive stand-alone villa with 17 well-equipped rooms right next to a rather gruesome annexe of the School of Art. ❷

Travel Inn 187 George St ℡0870/238 3320, ⓦwww.travelinn.co.uk. Another well-priced budget chain hotel, situated near George Square on the northern edge of the Merchant City. ❷

West End and Clydeside

Alamo Guest House 46 Gray St ℡0141/339 2395, ⓦwww.alamoguesthouse.com. Good-value, family-run boarding house next to Kelvingrove Park. Small but comfortable rooms. ❶

City Inn Finnieston Quay ℡0141/240 1002, ⓦwww.cityinn.com. Chain hotel with stylish rooms and decent rates made interesting by its riverside location right under the Finnieston crane. **⑤**

Kirklee 11 Kensington Gate ☎0141/334 5555, Ⓦwww.scotland2000.com/kirklee. Characterful West End B&B in an Edwardian townhouse, with antique furniture and walls crammed with paintings and etchings. **④**

Number 36 36 St Vincent Crescent ☎0141/248 2086, Ⓦwww.no36.co.uk. Neat, comfortable guest house in a lovely crescent well located for Kelvingrove, the SECC and transport links to the city centre. **③**

Southside

Boswell 27 Mansionhouse Rd ☎0141/632 9812. Informal, relaxing hotel in an old Queen's Park villa with a superb real-ale bar. **③**

Glasgow Guest House 56 Dumbreck Rd ☎0141/427 0129, Ⓦget-me.to/glasgow guesthouse. Pleasant four-room guest house with old furniture, good disabled facilities and handy transport links into the city centre. **②**

Reidholme Guest House 36 Regent Park Square ☎0141/423 1855. Small, friendly guest house in a quiet side street, designed by Alexander "Greek" Thomson (see p.1016). **②**

Hostels, campsites and self-catering

Glasgow doesn't have nearly as many **hostels** as Edinburgh, though it isn't short of bed space, thanks to the bright-pink liveried, seven-storey *Euro Hostel* smack in the centre of the city at 318 Clyde St (☎0141/222 2828, Ⓦwww.euro-hostels.com), which tries to bridge the gap between backpacker hostel and budget hotel. Its 360 beds are all bunks but they're in smart en-suite rooms sleeping two, four, six or more – some of which have great views. Bed and continental breakfast is from £13.75.

The popular SYHA hostel, 7–8 Park Terrace (☎0141/332 3004, Ⓔreservations@syha.org.uk), is located in a large townhouse in one of the West End's grandest terraces. It's a ten-minute walk south of Kelvinbridge underground station; bus #11 or #44 from the city centre leaves you with a short stroll west up Woodlands Road. Following a fire in 2003 the hostel was undergoing modernization and should reopen again in the summer of 2004. A few doors away, at 17 Park Terrace, the Macbackpackers' group also run a townhouse hostel (☎0141/332 9099, Ⓦwww.scotlandstophostels.com)

Campsite

The only **campsite** within a decent distance of Glasgow is *Craigendmuir Park*, Campsie View, Stepps (☎0141/779 4159, Ⓦwww.craigendmuir.co.uk), four miles northeast of the centre, about fifteen minutes' walk from Stepps train station. It has adequate facilities with showers, a laundry and a shop, but there are only ten pitches.

Self-catering

Low-priced **self-catering** rooms and flats are available at the University of Glasgow (☎0800/027 2030, Ⓦwww.gla.ac.uk) from June to mid-September, mostly located in the West End, with prices starting at £14.50 per night. The University of Strathclyde (☎0141/553 4148, Ⓦwww.strath.ac.uk) has B&B in single rooms near the cathedral starting at £25 per person per night.

The City Centre

Glasgow's large **City Centre** is ranged across the north bank of the River Clyde. At its geographical heart is **George Square**, a nineteenth-century municipal showpiece crowned by the enormous **City Chambers** at its eastern end. Behind this lies one of the greatest marketing successes of the

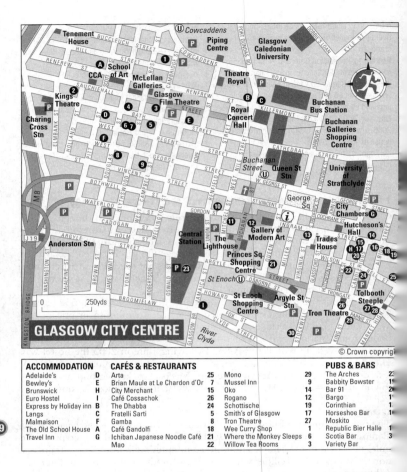

GLASGOW CITY CENTRE

© Crown copyrig

ACCOMMODATION		CAFÉS & RESTAURANTS				PUBS & BARS	
Adelaide's	D	Arta	25	Mono	29	The Arches	2:
Bewley's	E	Brian Maule at Le Chardon d'Or	7	Mussel Inn	9	Babbity Bowster	1!
Brunswick	H	City Merchant	15	Oko	14	Bar 91	2(
Euro Hostel	I	Café Cossachok	26	Rogano	12	Bargo	1:
Express by Holiday inn	B	The Dhabba	24	Schottische	19	Corinthian	1:
Langs	C	Fratelli Sarti	5	Smith's of Glasgow	17	Horseshoe Bar	1(
Malmaison	F	Gamba	8	Tron Theatre	27	Moskito	
The Old School House	A	Café Gandolfi	18	Wee Curry Shop	1	Republic Bier Halle	1:
Travel Inn	G	Ichiban Japanese Noodle Café	21	Where the Monkey Sleeps	6	Scotia Bar	3
		Mao	22	Willow Tea Rooms	3	Variety Bar	

1980s, the **Merchant City**, an area which blends magnificent Victorian architecture with yuppie conversions. The grand buildings and trendy cafés cling to
the borders of the run-down **East End**, a strongly working-class district that
chooses to ignore its rather showy neighbour. The oldest part of Glasgow,
around the **Cathedral**, lies immediately north of the East End.

Called by poet John Betjeman "the greatest Victorian city in the world",
Glasgow's commercial core spreads west of George Square, and is mostly buil
on a large grid system – possibly inspired by Edinburgh's New Town – with
ruler-straight roads soon rising up severe hills to grand, sandblasted buildings
The same style was copied by many North American cities, and indeed part
of Glasgow have been pressed into service as nineteenth-century New Yor
in films such as *House of Mirth*. The main shopping areas here are **Argyl**
Street, running parallel to the river, and **Buchanan Street**, which link
Argyle Street to the pedestrianized shopping thoroughfare, **Sauchieha**
Street. Northwest of here is Charles Rennie Mackintosh's famous **Glasgo**
School of Art.

George Square and around

Now hemmed in by the city's grinding traffic, the imposing architecture of **George Square** reflects the confidence of Glasgow's Victorian age. The wide-open plaza almost has a continental airiness about it, although there isn't much subtlety about the eighty-foot column rising up at its centre. It's topped by a statue of Sir Walter Scott, even though his links with Glasgow are, at best, sketchy. The florid splendour of the **City Chambers**, opened by Queen Victoria in 1888, occupies the entire eastern end of the square. Built from wealth gained by colonial trade and heavy industry, it epitomizes the aspirations and optimism of late-Victorian city elders. You can head inside and wander around the ground floor, where you'll see domed mosaic ceilings and two mighty Italian marble stairwells, but to get any further join in one of the free **guided tours** of the labyrinthine interior (Mon–Fri 10.30am & 2.30pm; booking recommended on ☎0141/287 4018).

The Gallery of Modern Art

Queen Street leads south from George Square to **Royal Exchange Square**, where the focal point is the graceful mansion built in 1775 for tobacco lord William Cunninghame. This was the most ostentatious of the Glasgow merchants' homes and, having served as the city's Royal Exchange and central library, now houses the **Gallery of Modern Art** (Mon–Wed & Sat 10am–5pm, Thurs 10am–8pm, Fri & Sun 11am–5pm; free). Surrounded by controversy from the day it opened in 1996, what it lacks in critical approbation it more than makes up for in popularity, not least with Glaswegians, giving the place a down-to-earth, populist feel lacking in many of the country's grander art collections.

The mirrored reception area leads you straight into the spacious ground-floor gallery, a striking room with elaborate gold leaf fringing its barrelled ceiling, rows of Corinthian pillars and huge windows. It's principally used for temporary exhibitions, though large-scale socially committed works by the "New Glasgow Boys" – Peter Howson, Adrian Wiszniewski, Ken Currie and Steven Campbell – are often included. Look out too for the kinetic sculpture *Titanic* by Russian émigré Eduard Bersudsky, made of scrap metal and old junk, but symbolizing freedom of movement and expression.

Downstairs is an art library and café, while the first floor exhibits items from the gallery's permanent collection, including Andy Goldsworthy's cracked and sun-baked red-clay floor, intricate aboriginal paintings on canvas and bark and a number of paintings by east-coast Scottish artist John Bellany.

Along Buchanan Street

Buchanan Street runs north–south one block west of George Square, defining Glasgow's main shopping district. At the southern end of the street is **Princes Square**, one of the most stylish and imaginative shopping centres in the country, hollowed out of the innards of a soft-sandstone building. The interior, all recherché Art Deco and ornate ironwork, has lots of pricey, highly fashionable shops, the whole place set to a soothing background of classical music.

Glaswegians' voracious appetite for shopping is fed further at the northern end of Buchanan Street, just beyond the Underground station, where the **Buchanan Galleries** is a bewilderingly vast shopping mall stuffed with most of the predictable chain stores. Next door is the anonymous £30-million

Royal Concert Hall, with an excellent auditorium which plays host to world-class musical events, from touring orchestras to rock acts.

The Lighthouse

At 11 Mitchell Lane, an otherwise nondescript alleyway between Buchanan Street and Union Street, is **The Lighthouse** (Mon & Wed–Sat 10.30am–5pm, Tues 11am–5pm, Sun noon–5pm; £3; Ⓦwww.thelighthouse.co.uk), a spectacularly converted Charles Rennie Mackintosh building which has found new life as Scotland's Centre for Architecture, Design and the City. The 1895 building was Mackintosh's first public commission, and housed the offices of the *Glasgow Herald* newspaper; despite glass and sandstone additions by architects Page & Park, it retains many original features, including the distinctive tower from which the building takes its name. The venue mounts temporary exhibitions on design and architecture alongside the permanent **Mackintosh Interpretation Centre**, a great place to learn more about the man and his work.

Glasgow's architecture

Glasgow, founded on religion, built on trade and now well established as a cultural centre, has become recognized for its architectural riches, from the medieval cathedral to the modern glass-lined galleries of the Burrell Collection. Most dominant is the legacy of the **Victorian age**, when booming trade and industry allowed merchants to commission the finest architects of the day. The celebrated work of **Charles Rennie Mackintosh** (see box on p.1025) took Glasgow architecture to the forefront of early twentieth-century design.

The city's expansion: 1750–1850

Glasgow's great expansion was initiated in the eighteenth century by wealthy tobacco merchants who built the grand edifices of public and municipal importance that still make up much of the **Merchant City**. Further west, **Royal Exchange Square** is one of the best examples of a typical Glasgow square: treeless, bare and centred around a building of importance, the 1829 **Royal Exchange**, now housing the Gallery of Modern Art. As workers piled into the centre of Glasgow in the early nineteenth century, filling up the already crowded tenements, wealthy residents began moving west to the gridded streets that line **Blythswood Hill** (mostly developed after 1820) with two- or three-storey terraces, their porches and heavy cornices providing textural relief to the endless sandstone monotony. The dignified proportions and design of **Blythswood Square** are a highlight of this area; at no. 5 the later Art Nouveau doorway designed by Charles Rennie Mackintosh sits incongruously amongst the Georgian solidity. Above all, the long streets provide a beautiful selection of open-ended views, one moment leading into the heart of the city, the next filled with distant hills and sky.

Desiring to surround themselves with trees and fields, the well-to-do continued their migration west; **Woodside Crescent**, leading into Woodside Terrace, is a severe line of buildings with splendid Doric porches and neatly organized gardens. **Park Circus**, on the other hand, is a parade of uninterrupted Georgian magnificence, with delicate detail – such as narrow window slots on either side of the doors – enhancing the dignified crescent.

Greek Thomson and the Victorians

Long since overshadowed by Charles Rennie Mackintosh, the design of **Alexander "Greek" Thomson**, in the latter half of the nineteenth century, though well respected in its time, has been sadly neglected. As his nickname suggests, his work took the principles of Greek architecture, but reprocessed them in a highly unique manner.

The Merchant City

The grid of streets that lies immediately east of the City Chambers is known as the **Merchant City** (ⓦwww.glasgowmerchantcity.net), an area of eighteenth-century warehouses and homes once bustling with cotton, tobacco and sugar traders, which in the last two decades has been sandblasted and swabbed clean with greater enthusiasm and municipal money than any other part of Glasgow in an attempt to bring residents back into the city centre. The expected flood of yuppies, however, was more like a trickle, yet the expensive designer shops, style bars and bijou cafés continue to flock here, giving the area a pervasive air of sophistication and chic.

Around Ingram Street

At the junction of Ingram and John streets, look out for the **Italian Centre**, a revitalized eighteenth-century warehouse now housing lively cafés, outdoor

Energetic and talented, he designed buildings from lowly tenements to grand suburban villas. The 1857 **St Vincent Street Church**, his best work, has a massive simplicity and serenity lightened by the use of exotic Egyptian and Hindu motifs, particularly in the tower with its decorated egg-shaped dome. Most recently, the National Trust has opened his finest domestic dwelling, **Holmwood House**, on the Southside, to the public (see p.1032).

West from Park Circus lies **Glasgow University** (1866–86), its Gothic Revivalism – the work of Sir George Gilbert Scott – representing everything that Greek Thomson despised; he called it "sixteenth-century Scottish architecture clothed in fourteenth-century French details". Scottish features abound, such as crow-stepped gables, round turrets with conical caps and the top-heavy central tower. Inside, cloisters and quadrants sum up a suitably scholastic severity.

Originally conceived as a convenient way to house the influx of workers in the late 1800s, the Glasgow **tenement** design became more refined as the wealthy middle classes began to realize its potential. Mainly constructed between 1860 and 1910, tenements have three to five storeys with two or three apartments per floor. A fascinating example of the style of these buildings, as well as the typical style of life inside them, can be seen at the **Tenement House** (see p.1024).

From World War I to the present

World War I put an end to the glorious century of Glasgow building, and the Depression years did little to enhance the city. However, since World War II bombing was targeted on the shipbuilding district of Clydebank, west of the centre, most of the city's legacy of fine sandstone buildings survived intact.

Glassy office buildings have sprung up in recent years, their mirrored walls basking in the reflected glory of the surrounding buildings to disguise their banality of design. The 1980s onwards have seen the return of the grand public building as inheritor of architectural innovation. Beginning with the imaginative **Burrell Collection**, the theme has been taken up by the titanium-clad behemoths of Clydeside: the unmistakeable Clyde Auditorium, better known as the "**Armadillo**", and the futuristic glass-walled **Science Centre**, flanked by a bubble-like IMAX theatre and the 100-metre-high Glasgow Tower. This is not to ignore the poverty of artistry that went into great works such as the Kingston Bridge and Royal Concert Hall, but few could argue that Glasgow has failed to open itself to innovation and ideas. Above all, the city can be credited with involving its citizens in an awareness that everyone is influenced, as well as represented, by the buildings around them.

△ Statue of Mercury, Merchant City

sculpture and some of the city's most fashionable boutiques – Versace established his first shop in Britain here. Immediately opposite, across John Street, is the delicate white spire of the National Trust for Scotland's regional headquarters, **Hutcheson Hall**, at 158 Ingram St (Mon–Sat 10am–5pm; free). The ground floor houses an exhibition of "Glasgow Style", with some attractive work by contemporary designers and craftsmen on sale, while there's a particularly fine ornately decorated hall upstairs. Here you can pick up a Merchant City Trail leaflet, which guides you around a dozen of the most interesting buildings in the area.

Almost opposite in the other direction, a little way down Glassford Street, the Robert Adam-designed **Trades House** (Mon–Sat 9am–6pm, depending on functions; free) is easily distinguished by its neat, green copper dome. Purpose-built in 1794, it still functions as the headquarters of the Glasgow trade guilds. The former civic pride and status of the guilds is still evident from the rich assortment of carvings and stained-glass windows, with a lively pictorial representation of the different trades in the silk frieze around the walls of the first-floor banqueting hall.

Glasgow Cross

Before 1846, **Glasgow Cross** – the junction of Trongate, Gallowgate and the High Street, at the southeastern corner of the Merchant City – was the city's principal intersection, until the construction of the new train station near George Square shifted the city's emphasis west. The turreted seventeenth-century **Tolbooth Steeple** still stands here, although the rest of the building has long since disappeared, and today the stern tower is little more than a traffic hazard at a busy junction.

Sharmanka Kinetic Gallery

Tucked away on the second floor of 14 King St, an extension of Candleriggs on the south side of the Trongate, is Glasgow's most unusual art gallery. Founded by Russian émigrés Eduard Bersudsky and Tatyana Jakovskaya, the **Sharmanka Kinetic Gallery** (ⓦ www.sharmanka.co.uk) is like a mad inventor's magical workshop, with hundreds of carved figures mounted on moving contraptions made from old wheels, levers, lights and scrap metal. It takes an hour for the sculptures to "perform", so the full programmes are only run a few times during the week (Tues 1pm, Thurs 7pm & Sun 6pm; £3), although special shorter shows can be organized – call ⓣ 0141/5522 7080 to make arrangements.

The East End

East of Glasgow Cross, down Gallowgate beyond the train lines, lies the **East End**, the district that perhaps most closely corresponds to the old perception of Glasgow. The Depression caused the closure of many factories, leaving communities stranded in an industrial wasteland. Today isolated pubs, tatty shops and cafés sit amidst this dereliction, in sharp contrast to the gloss of the Merchant City only a few blocks to the west. Walking around here you definitely get the sense that you're off the tourist trail, but unless you're here after dark it's not as threatening as it may feel, and there's no doubt that the area offers a rich flavour of working-class Glasgow.

Three hundred yards down either London Road or Gallowgate is **The Barras**, Glasgow's largest and most popular weekend market (Sat & Sun 9am–5pm). Red iron gates announce its official entrance, but boundaries are breached as the stalls – selling household goods, bric-a-brac, secondhand clothes and records, none of it of particularly high quality – spill out into the surrounding cobbled streets. The fast-talking traders, lively atmosphere and entertaining vignettes of Glasgow life make it an off-beat diversion from shopping-mall banality.

Between London Road and the River Clyde are the wide and tree-lined spaces of **Glasgow Green**. Reputedly the oldest public park in Britain, the Green has been common land since at least 1178, when it was first mentioned in records. On the northeast side of the Green it's worth taking a look at the extraordinary **Templeton's Carpet Factory**, a massive brick edifice of turrets, arched windows, mosaic-style patterns and castellated grandeur designed in the style of the Doge's Palace in Venice and built in 1892. Subsequent to its days as a carpet factory it has been a small business centre and health centre, but is now disused.

The People's Palace

Opposite the carpet factory on Glasgow Green you can still see some poles erected to hang out washing, recalling the days when the Green was very much a public space in daily use. Beside these, the **People's Palace** (Mon–Thurs & Sat 10am–5pm, Fri & Sun 11am–5pm; free) houses a wonderfully haphazard evocation of the city's history. This squat, red-sandstone Victorian building, with a vast semicircular glasshouse tacked on the back, was purpose-built as a museum back in 1898 – almost a century before the rest of the country caught on to the fashion for social-history collections. While many of the displays are designed to instil a warm glow in the memories of older locals, the museum is refreshingly unpretentious, and visitors are almost always outnumbered by Glaswegian families.

On the **top floor**, glowing murals by local artist Ken Currie powerfully evoke the spirit of radical Glasgow, from the Carlton Weavers' strike in 1787 to the Red Clydesiders of the 1920s. The **west wing** looks at famous Glasgow products through history, with displays of everything from cast-iron railings and biscuit wrappers to a giant portrait of Billy Connolly. In the **East Gallery**, an entertaining sound-and-light show reconstructs a "single-end" or one-roomed house, a typical setting for the daily life of hundreds of thousands of Glasgow people in former years. Downstairs, various themes with a particular resonance in Glasgow are explored, including alcohol, the traditional holiday excursion "doon the watter" by steamer to various Clyde coastal resorts, and some guidance to understanding "the Patter", Glaswegians' idiosyncratic version of the Queen's English. The glasshouse at the back of the palace contains the **Winter Gardens**, with a café, water garden, twittering birds and assorted tropical plants and shrubs.

The cathedral area

Rising north up the hill from the Tolbooth Steeple at Glasgow Cross is Glasgow's **High Street**. In British cities, the name is commonly associated with the busiest central thoroughfare, and it's a surprise to see how forlorn and dilapidated Glasgow's version is, long superseded by the grander thoroughfare further west. The High Street leads up to the **cathedral**, on the site of Glasgow's original settlement.

Glasgow Cathedral

Built in 1136, destroyed in 1192 and rebuilt soon after, stumpy-spired **Glasgow Cathedral** (April–Sept Mon–Sat 9.30am–6pm, Sun 1–4pm; Oct–March

Mon–Sat 9.30am–4pm, Sun 1–4pm; free) was not completed until the late fifteenth century, with the final reconstruction of the chapterhouse and the aisle designed by Robert Blacader, the city's first archbishop. Thanks to the intervention of the city guilds, it is the only Scottish mainland cathedral to have escaped the hands of religious reformers in the sixteenth century. The cathedral is dedicated to the city's patron saint and reputed founder, St Mungo, about whom four popular stories are frequently told – they even make an appearance on the city's coat of arms. These involve a bird that he brought back to life, the bell with which he summoned the faithful to prayer, a tree that he managed to make spontaneously combust and a fish that he caught with a repentant adulterous queen's ring on its tongue.

On entering, you arrive in the impressively lofty nave of the **upper church**, with the lower church entirely hidden from view. Either side of the nave, the narrow **aisles** are illuminated by vivid stained-glass windows, most of which date from the last century. Threadbare Union flags and military pennants hang listlessly beneath them, serving as a reminder that the cathedral is very much a part of the Unionist Protestant tradition. Beyond the nave, the **choir** is hidden from view by the curtained stone pulpit, making the interior feel a great deal smaller than might be expected from the outside.

Two sets of steps from the nave lead down into the **lower church**, where you'll see the dark and musty **chapel** surrounding the tomb of St Mungo. The saint's relics were removed in the late Middle Ages, although the tomb still forms the centrepiece. The chapel itself is one of the most glorious examples of medieval architecture in Scotland, best seen in the delicate fan vaulting rising up from the thicket of cool stone columns.

The Necropolis

Rising up behind the cathedral, the atmospheric **Necropolis** is a grassy mound covered in a fantastic assortment of crumbling and tumbling gravestones, ornate urns, gloomy catacombs and Neoclassical temples. Inspired by the Père Lachaise cemetery in Paris, developer John Strong created a garden of death in 1833, and it quickly became a fitting spot for the great and the good of wealthy nineteenth-century Glasgow to indulge their vanity. Various paths lead through the rows of eroding, neglected graves, and from the summit, next to the column topped with an indignant John Knox, there are superb **views** which capture the city and its trademark mix of grit and grace – the steaming chimneys of the Tennants brewery, the traffic on the M8 motorway, the crowded city-centre offices, the serene cathedral itself, and a wide cityscape of spires and high-rise blocks to the south and west.

Cathedral Square

Back in Cathedral Square, the **St Mungo Museum of Religious Life and Art** (Mon–Thurs & Sat 10am–5pm, Fri & Sun 11am–5pm; free), housed in a late twentieth-century pastiche of a Scots medieval townhouse, focuses on objects, beliefs and art from Christianity, Buddhism, Judaism, Islam, Hinduism and Sikhism. Portrayals of Hindu gods are juxtaposed with the stunning Salvador Dali painting *St John of the Cross*. In addition to the main exhibition there's a small collection of photographs, papers and archive material looking at religion in Glasgow, the power and zealotry of the nineteenth-century temperance movement and Christian missionaries.

Across the square, the oldest house in the city, the **Provand's Lordship** (same times; free) dates from 1471, and has been used, among other things, as an ecclesiastical residence and an inn. Inside, the re-creations of life in the fifteenth century aren't particularly arresting unless you've an interest in period furniture. Behind the Provand's Lordship lies the small **Garden of St Nicholas**, a herb garden contrasting medieval and Renaissance aesthetics and approaches to medicine with muddled clusters of herbs amid stone carvings of the heart and other organs.

Sauchiehall Street and around

Glasgow's most famous street, **Sauchiehall Street**, runs in a straight line west from the northern end of Buchanan Street, past some unexciting shopping malls to a few of the city's most interesting sights. Charles Rennie Mackintosh fans should head for the **Willow Tea Rooms**, not all that easy to spot at first, above Henderson the Jeweller at 217 Sauchiehall St. This is a faithful reconstruction on the site of the 1904 original, which was created for Kate Cranston, one of Rennie Mackintosh's few contemporary supporters in the city, opened in 1980 after more than fifty years of closure. Ask for a table in the Salon de Lux, where everything from the fixtures and fittings right down to the teaspoons and menu cards were designed by Mackintosh. Tea is served here Mon–Sat 9.30am until 4.30pm, and noon–3.30pm on Sundays in summer (for a review, see p.1033).

McLellan Galleries

One block west are the **McLellan Galleries**, 270 Sauchiehall St (daily 10am–5pm, Fri & Sun opens 11am; free), which, despite its inauspicious frontage, is as soothing an example of Neoclassical architecture as anywhere in the city. Until the end of 2005, this is the home of the **Art Treasures of Kelvingrove** exhibition, where a selection of the better-known works from the Kelvingrove Art Gallery and Museum (see p.1026) are on display while the famous West End landmark undergoes a major refurbishment.

The limited space in the McLellan Galleries only serves to highlight the vastness of Kelvingrove, and while there are indeed a number of treasures on display, the exhibition works better as a sampler than as a coherent statement. Of the five rooms used, the most engaging are the "Glasgow Style" room in Gallery 5 and "The Pursuit of Colour" in Gallery 6. The first is dedicated to the era when **Charles Rennie Mackintosh** was in his prime; dominating Gallery 6 are some excellent works by the **Scottish Colourists**: J.D. Fergusson's *Pink Parasol* reveals the influence of Matisse and Cézanne, while Cadell's *Orange Blind*, with its unexpectedly strident blocks of colour contrasting with precise, flat brushwork, is perhaps the best-known Colourist work of all.

The smaller Gallery 9 is dominated by **Rembrandt**'s quiet portrait *The Man in Armour*, while Gallery 8 offers a whistle-stop tour of two centuries of British art, ranging from Sir Henry Raeburn's magnificent *Mr and Mrs Robert N. Campbell of Kailzie* to Turner's radiant *Modern Italy – The Pifferari* and **Whistler**'s subtly expressive portrait of Thomas Carlyle. Finally, Gallery 4 acts as a sampler for the mind-boggling range of Kelvingrove's collection, with items such as Alexander Naysmyth's famous portrait of Robert Burns, found on tins of shortbread around the world, a **televisor** constructed by John Logie Baird, a suit of armour and one or two smaller items from the natural-history collection.

Another artistic space a few blocks further west at no. 350 is the recently remodelled **CCA** (Centre for Contemporary Arts; ☎0141/332 752?

The Glasgow Boys

In the 1870s a group of painters formed a loose association, centred in Glasgow, that was to invest Scottish painting with a fresh approach inspired by contemporary European trends (in particular the *plein air* painting of the Impressionists). They were derisively nicknamed "**The Glasgow Boys**", and only in later years did their work come to be seen as quintessentially Glaswegian and reclaimed with considerable pride. The group was dominated by five men – Guthrie, Lavery, Henry, Hornel and Crawhall – who, despite coming from very different backgrounds, all violently rejected the eighteenth-century conservatism which spawned little other than sentimental, anecdotal renditions of Scottish history peopled by "poor but happy" families, in a detailed, exacting manner. They began to experiment with colour, liberally splashing paint across the canvas. The content and concerns of the paintings, often showing peasant life and work, were as offensive to the art establishment as their style: until then most of Glasgow's public art collections had been accrued by wealthy tobacco lords and merchants, who had a taste for Classical style and noble subjects.

Sir James Guthrie's A Highland Funeral was hugely influential for the rest of the group, who found inspiration in its restrained emotional content, colour and unaffected realism. Seeing it persuaded **Sir John Lavery**, then studying in France, to return to Glasgow. His subtle use of paint reveals his debt to Whistler, but his earlier work, depicting the middle class at play, is filled with fresh colour and figures in motion. Rather than a realistic aesthetic, an interest in colour and decoration united the work of friends **George Henry** and **E.A. Hornel**. Their joint work The Druids (on display in the Art Treasures of Kelvingrove exhibition; see p.1022), in thickly applied impasto, is full of Celtic symbolism. Newcastle-born **Joseph Crawhall** combined superb draughtsmanship and simplicity of line with a photographic memory to create watercolours of an outstanding naturalism and freshness. William Burrell was an important patron, and a good collection of Crawhall's works resides at the Burrell Collection (see p.1031).

The Glasgow Boys school reached its height by 1900, and once its members had achieved the artistic respect – and for some the commercial success – they craved, it began to disintegrate and did not outlast World War I. However, the influence of their work cannot be underestimated, shaking the foundations of the artistic elite and inspiring the next generation of Edinburgh painters, now known as the "Colourists".

19

Ⓦ www.cca-glasgow.com), where eclectically internationalist exhibitions and performances consistently make the centre one of the city's cultural hotspots.

The Glasgow School of Art

Rising above Sauchiehall Street to the north is one of the city centre's steepest hills, where Dalhousie and Scott streets veer up to Renfrew Street, where you'll find Charles Rennie Mackintosh's **Glasgow School of Art**, 167 Renfrew St (guided tours Mon–Fri 11am & 2pm, Sat 10.30 & 11.30am; July & August also Sat 1pm, Sun 10.30, 11.30am & 1pm; booking advised; Ⓣ0141/353 4526, Ⓦwww.gsa.ac.uk; £5). This is one of the most prestigious art schools in the country, with such notable alumni as artists Robert Colquhoun and Robert Macbryde and, more recently, Steven Campbell, Ken Currie and actor Robbie Coltrane. Widely considered to be the pinnacle of Mackintosh's work, the school is a characteristically angular building of warm sandstone which, due to financial constraints, had to be constructed in two sections (1897–99 and 1907–09). There's a clear change in the architect's style from the earlier severity of the mock-baronial east wing to the softer lines of the western half.

The only way to see the school is to take one of the student-led **guided tours**, the extent of which are dependent on curricular activities. You can, however, be sure of seeing key examples of Mackintosh's dynamic and inspired touch and a handful of the most impressive rooms. All over the school, from the roof to the stairwells, Mackintosh's unique touches recur – light Oriental reliefs, tall-backed chairs and stylized Celtic illuminations. Even before entering the building up the gently curving stairway, you cannot fail to be struck by the soaring height of the north-facing windows, which light the art studios and were designed, characteristically, to combine aesthetics with practicality.

The school's most spectacular room is the glorious two-storey **Library**. Designed to give the sense of a clearing in a forest, sombre oak panelling is set against angular lights adorned with primary colours, dangling down in seemingly random clusters. The dark bookcases sit precisely in their fitted alcoves, while, of the furniture, the most unusual feature is the central periodical desk, whose oval central strut displays perfect and quite beautiful symmetry.

The school also puts on various **exhibitions** through the year, which you can view without going on a tour. For details, contact the school or check up-to-date listings.

The Tenement House

Just a few hundred yards north of the School of Art – on the other side of a sheer hill – is the **Tenement House**, 145 Buccleuch Street (March–Oct daily 1–5pm; £3.50; NTS). This is a typical tenement block still lived in on most floors, except for the ground and first floor, where you can see the perfectly preserved home of Agnes Toward, who moved here with her mother in 1911, changing nothing and throwing very little out until she was hospitalized in 1965. On the ground floor, the National Trust for Scotland has constructed a fascinating display on the development of the humble tenement block as the bedrock of urban Scottish housing, with a display of relics – ration books, letters, bills, holiday snaps and so forth – from Miss Toward's life. Upstairs, you have to ring the doorbell to enter the flat, which gives every impression of still being inhabited, with a cluttered hearth and range, kitchen utensils, recess beds, framed religious tracts and sewing machine all untouched.

The Piping Centre

Behind the hulking Royal Scottish Academy for Music and Drama, a short way east of the Tenement House, the **National Piping Centre**, at 30–34 McPhater Street, is a meeting place for fans and performers of the bagpipes from all over the world. For the casual visitor, the single-room **museum** (Mon–Sat 9am–5pm, also Sun 10am–4pm in summer months; £3; Ⓦwww.thepipingcentre.co.uk) is of most interest, with a collection of instruments and related artefacts from the fourteenth century to the present day.

The West End

The urbane **West End** seems a world away from Glasgow's industrial image and the hustle and bustle of the city centre. In the 1800s, the city's wealthy merchants established huge estates away from the soot and grime of city life, and in 1870 the ancient university was moved from its cramped home near the

Charles Rennie Mackintosh

The work of the architect **Charles Rennie Mackintosh** (1868–1928) has come to be synonymous with the image of Glasgow. Historians may disagree over whether his work was a forerunner of the modernist movement or merely a sunset of Victorianism, but he nonetheless undoubtedly created buildings of great beauty, idiosyncratically fusing Scots baronial with Gothic, Art Nouveau and modern design. Though the bulk of his work was conceived at the turn of the twentieth century, since the postwar years Mackintosh's ideas have become particularly fashionable, giving rise to a certain amount of ersatz **"Mockintosh"** in his home city, with his distinctive lettering and small design features used time and again by shops, pubs and businesses. Fortunately, there are also plenty of examples of the genuine article, making the city something of a pilgrimage centre for art and design students from all over the world.

He joined the Glasgow School of Art in 1884, where the vibrant new director, Francis Newberry, encouraged his pupils to create original and individual work. Here he met Herbert MacNair and the sisters Margaret and Frances MacDonald, whose work seemed to be sympathetic with his, fusing the organic forms of nature with a linear, symbolic Art Nouveau style. Nicknamed **"The Spook School"**, the four created a new artistic language, using extended vertical design, stylized abstract organic forms and muted colours, reflecting their interest in Japanese design and the work of Whistler and Beardsley. However, it was architecture that truly challenged Mackintosh, allowing him to use his creative artistic impulse in a three-dimensional and cohesive manner.

His big break came in 1896, when he won the competition to design a new home for the **Glasgow School of Art** (see p.1023). This is his most famous work, but a number of smaller buildings created during his tenure with the architects Honeyman and Keppie, which began in 1889, document the development of his style. One of his earliest commissions was for a new building to house the *Glasgow Herald* on Mitchell Lane, off Argyle Street. A massive tower rises up from the corner, giving the building its popular name of **The Lighthouse**; it now houses the Mackintosh Interpretation Centre (see p.1016).

In the 1890s Glasgow went wild for tearooms, and the imposing Miss Cranston, who dominated the Glasgow teashop scene, gave Mackintosh great freedom of design. Over the next twenty years he designed articles from teaspoons to furniture and, finally, as in the case of the **Willow Tea Rooms** (see p.1022), the structure itself.

Mackintosh designed few **religious buildings**: Queens Cross Church of 1896, still at the junction of Garscube and Maryhill roads in the northwest of the city, is the only completed example standing. It is now home to the **Charles Rennie Mackintosh Society** (Mon–Fri 10am–5pm, Sun 2–5pm; ℡0141/946 6600, ⒲www.crmsociety .com; £2).

The spectre of limited budgets was to haunt Mackintosh throughout his career, and he never had the chance to design and construct with complete freedom. However, these constraints didn't manage to dull his creativity, as demonstrated by the **Scotland Street School** of 1904, just south of the river (see p.1029). Here, the two main stairways that frame the entrance are lit by glass-filled bays that protrude from the building. It is his most symmetrical work, with a whimsical nod to history in the Scots baronial conical tower roofs and sandstone building material. The building which arguably displays Mackintosh at his most flamboyant was one he never saw built, the **House for an Art Lover** (see p.1029), constructed in Bellahouston Park in 1996, 95 years after plans for it were submitted to a German architectural competition.

athedral to a spacious new site overlooking the River Kelvin. Elegant ousing swiftly followed, the Kelvingrove Museum and Art Gallery was built to ouse the 1888 International Exhibition and, in 1896, the Glasgow District

Subway – today's Underground – started its circuitous shuffle from here to the city centre.

The hub of life in this part of Glasgow is **Byres Road**, running between Great Western Road and Dumbarton Road past Hillhead Underground station. Shops, restaurants, cafés, some enticing pubs and hordes of roving young people, including thousands of students, give the area a sense of style and vitality. The main sights straddle the banks of the cleaned-up River Kelvin, which meanders through the gracious acres of the **Botanic Gardens** and the slopes, trees and statues of **Kelvingrove Park**. Overlooked by the Gothic towers and turrets of **Glasgow University**, the latter area is home to the nostalgia-rich **Transport Museum** and the Kelvingrove Museum, off Argyle Street, which is currently undergoing a major refurbishment. While this is taking place, a selection of the collection's more famous pieces are on display at the McLellan Galleries in the city centre (see p.1022).

The Transport Museum

Twin-towered **Kelvin Hall** opposite the Kelvingrove Museum is home to the excellent **Transport Museum**, an enormous collection of trains, cars, trams, circus caravans and prams, along with an array of old Glaswegian ephemera (Mon–Thurs & Sat 10am–5pm, Fri & Sun 11am–5pm; free). "Kelvin Street" is a re-created 1938 cobbled street featuring an old Italian coffee shop and an old-time Underground station. A cinema shows fascinating films – mostly on themes based loosely around transport – of old Glasgow life, with crackly footage of Sauchiehall Street packed solid with trams and shoppers and hordes of pasty-faced Glaswegians setting off for their annual jaunts down the coast. The Clyde Room displays intricate models of ships forged in Glasgow's yards, everything from tiny schooners to ostentatious ocean liners such as the *QE2*.

Glasgow University and the Hunterian bequests

Dominating the West End skyline, the gloomy turreted tower of **Glasgow University**, designed by Sir George Gilbert Scott in the mid-nineteenth century, overlooks the glades edging the River Kelvin. Access to the main buildings and museums is from University Avenue, running east from Byres Road. In the dark neo-Gothic pile under the tower you'll find the **University Visitor Centre** (Mon–Sat 9.30am–5pm, May–Sept also Sun 2–5pm) which, as well as giving information for potential students, distributes leaflets about the various university buildings and the statues around the campus. **Historical tours** of the campus are run from here (May–Sept Mon–Sat 2pm; Oct–April Wed 2pm; ☎0141/330 5511; £2). It's possible to join a tour up the sky-piercing university **tower** (May–Sept Fri 2pm; free), climbing 226 narrow spiral-staircase steps to some heady views; places, though, are limited to twenty people, with tickets available only in person that morning from the Visitor Centre.

Beside the Visitor Centre is the **Hunterian Museum** (Mon–Sat 9.30am–5pm; free), Scotland's oldest public museum, dating back to 1807. The collection was donated to the university by ex-student William Hunter, a pathologist and anatomist whose eclectic tastes form the basis of a fairly diverting zoological and archeological jaunt. Exhibitions include Scotland's only dinosaur, a look at the Romans in Scotland – the furthest outpost of their massive empire – and a vast numismatic collection.

The Hunterian Art Gallery

Opposite the university, across University Avenue, is Hunter's more frequently visited bequest, the **Hunterian Art Gallery** (Mon–Sat 9.30am–5pm; free), best known for its wonderful works by James Abbott McNeill Whistler: only Washington DC has a larger collection. Whistler's more whimsical landscapes are less compelling than his portraits of women, which give his subjects a resolute strength in addition to their fey and occasionally winsome qualities: look out especially for the trio of full-length portraits, *Harmony of Flesh Colour* and *Black, Pink and Gold – the Tulip* and *Red and Black – the Fan*.

A side gallery leads to the **Mackintosh House** (closed 12.30–1.30pm; free), a re-creation of the interior of the now-demolished Glasgow home of Margaret MacDonald and Charles Rennie Mackintosh. Among over sixty pieces of Mackintosh furniture on three floors, the highlights are the studio drawing room, whose cream and white furnishings are bathed in expansive pools of natural light, and the Japanese-influenced guest bedroom in dazzling, monochrome geometrics.

The Botanic Gardens

At the northern, top end of Byres Road, where it meets the Great Western Road, is the main entrance to the **Botanic Gardens** (daily 7am–dusk; free). The best-known glasshouse here, the hulking, domed **Kibble Palace** is closed for restoration until late 2004. Nearby, the **Main Range Glasshouse** (same times) is home to lurid flowers and plants luxuriating in the humidity, including stunning orchids, cacti, ferns and tropical fruit. Between the two in the old curator's house is a small **visitor centre** (daily 11am–4pm; free) with art exhibitions and interactive computer games aimed at younger visitors.

Clydeside

"The **Clyde** made Glasgow and Glasgow made the Clyde" runs an old saying, full of sentimentality for the days when the river was the world's premier shipbuilding centre, and when its industry lent an innovation and confidence which made Glasgow the second city of the British Empire. The last of the great liners to be built on **Clydeside** was the *QE2* in 1967, yet such events are hard to visualize today, with the banks of the river all but devoid of any industry: shipbuilding is now restricted to a couple of barely viable yards, as derelict warehouses, crumbling docks and overgrown wastelands crowd the river's flanks.

The Waverley

One of Glasgow's best-loved treasures is the **Waverley**, the last sea-going paddle steamer in the world, which spends the summer cruising "doon the watter" to various ports on the Firth of Clyde and the Ayrshire coast from its base at Anderson Quay between Finnieston and the Kingston Bridge. Built on Clydeside as recently as 1947, she's an elegant vessel to look at, not least when she's thrashing away at full steam with the hills of Argyll or Arran in the background. Call the booking office on ☎0141/243 2224 or check ⓦwww.waverleyexcursions.co.uk for her sailing times and itinerary.

Glasgow is often accused of failing to capitalize on its river, and it's only in the last few years, with a number of large, striking Clydeside buildings going up, such as the Scottish Exhibition and Conference Centre, or **SECC**, the **Armadillo** and the **Science Centre**, that the river is once again becoming a focus of attention. The easiest way to reach the cluster of Clydeside attractions is to **walk** the mile or so west along the riverside footpath from the city centre. Otherwise, **trains** from Glasgow Central low-level station and half-hourly **bus** #30 from the centre of town run to the Exhibition Centre. Bell's Bridge runs across the river to the Science Centre on the south bank, also served by bus #24 from Renfield Street.

The north bank

On Clydeside immediately south of the West End, just over a mile west of the city centre, is the harshly re-landscaped Scottish Exhibition and Conference Centre, or **SECC**, two vast adjoining red and grey sheds that make a dutifully utilitarian venue for travelling fairs, mega-concerts and anonymous bars and cafés. Although the huge **Finnieston Crane**, retained as an icon of shipbuilding days, stands alongside the SECC, the site was rescued from bland obscurity by the arrival in 1997 of a supplementary concert hall officially entitled the Clyde Auditorium but universally nicknamed "**the Armadillo**" for its rounded exterior of armour-plating. It resembles a poor man's Sydney Opera House but has quickly established itself as one of the city's architectural landmarks.

A few hundred yards downstream on the north bank of the river, the masts and rigging of the huge square-rigger *Glenlee* draw you to an attraction known as the **Tall Ship at Glasgow Harbour** (daily: March–Oct 10am–5pm; Nov–Feb 11am–4pm; £4.50). A 245-foot-long, three-masted barque, the *Glenlee* was launched on the river in 1896 and is now one of only five large sailing vessels built on Clydeside still afloat. The sheer scale of the *Glenlee* is her most impressive feature, though various parts of the ship are imaginatively set up to offer an insight into life aboard when she was a hard-working merchant vessel carrying cargo round Cape Horn.

The Glasgow Science Centre

On the south bank of the river, linked to the SECC by Bell's Bridge, are the three space-age, titanium-clad constructions which make up the **Glasgow Science Centre**, a massive, hands-on collection opened in 2001 (Science Mall £6.95, IMAX £5.95, both £9.95; Ⓦ www.gsc.org.uk). Of the three buildings, the largest is the curvaceous, wedge-shaped **Science Mall** (daily 10am–6pm). Behind the vast glass wall which faces the river are four floors of interactive exhibits ranging from lift-your-own-weight pulleys to high-tech thermograms. The centre covers almost every aspect of science from simple optical illusions to cutting-edge computer technology, including a section on moral and environmental issues – lots of good fun, although weekends and school holidays are busy and noisy. Alongside is the bubble-like **IMAX theatre**, which shows a range of mostly science- and nature-based documentaries on its giant screen, with programmes changing regularly. Also on the site is the 127-metre **Glasgow Tower**, built with an aerofoil-like construction to allow it to rotate to face into the prevailing wind, but it has been dogged with technical difficulties since it opened, preventing visitor access on a reliable schedule.

The Southside

On the Clyde's **Southside**, immediately facing the city centre, are the notoriously deprived districts of the Gorbals and Govan – sprinkled with new developments but still obviously derelict and tatty in many parts. There's little reason to venture here unless you're making your way to the Science Centre (see opposite), the famously innovative Citizen's Theatre (see p.1037), or one of the revived architectural gems of Charles Rennie Mackintosh, the **Scotland Street School** and the **House for an Art Lover**.

Moving further south, inner-city decay fades into altogether gentler and more salubrious suburbs, including Queen's Park, home to Scotland's national football stadium, **Hampden Park**; Pollokshaws and the rural landscape of Pollok Park, which contains two of Glasgow's major museums, the **Burrell Collection** and **Pollok House**; and Cathcart, location of Alexander "Greek" Thomson's **Holmwood House**.

Southside attractions are fairly widely spread. The **Underground** will get you to Scotland Street School and the House for an Art Lover, while a **train** from Central station is best for Hampden Park (Mount Florida station) and Holmwood House (Cathcart station). For Pollok Park either take the train to Pollokshaws West station (not to be confused with Pollokshields West), or **bus** #45, #47, #48 or #57 to Pollokshaws Road, or a **taxi** (£8–10 from the centre). From the park gates a **free minibus** runs every half-hour between 10am and 4.30pm to both the Burrell Collection and Pollok House.

Scotland Street School Museum of Education

Opposite Shields Road Underground station is the **Scotland Street School Museum of Education** (Mon–Thurs & Sat 10am–5pm, Fri & Sun 11am–5pm; free), another of the city's Charles Rennie Mackintosh treasures. Opened as a school in 1906 to Mackintosh's distinctively angular design, it closed in 1979, since when it has been entertainingly refurbished to house a fascinating collection of memorabilia related to classroom life. There are reconstructed classrooms from the Victorian and Edwardian eras, World War II and the 1960s, as well as changing rooms, a primitive domestic science room and re-creations of the school matron's sanatorium and a janitor's lair.

House for an Art Lover

West of Scotland Street School, tucked just inside Bellahouston Park, is Charles Rennie Mackintosh's **House for an Art Lover** (April–Sept daily except Fri 10am–4pm; Oct–March Sat & Sun 10am–4pm but closed occasionally for functions; ☎0141/353 4449; £3.50). Designed in 1901 for a German competition, it was not until 1996, after years of detailed research and painstaking work, that the building was actually constructed and opened as a centre for Glasgow School of Art postgraduate students, with a limited number of rooms open to the public.

It's all quintessential Mackintosh, almost unimaginable as a living space but exquisitely stylish and original at the same time. On the upper floor is the main **hallway**, where massive windows cast a cool light upon an area designed for large parties. In direct contrast, the dazzling white **Music Room** has bow windows opening out to a large balcony. The **Dining Room** is decorated with

19

darkened stained wood and enhanced by some beautiful gesso tiles. On the ground floor, the **café** (℡0141/353 4779) is particularly popular with locals on Sunday mornings; there's an attractive menu, and it's open through the day and sometimes also in the evenings.

Hampden Park and the Scottish Football Museum

Two and a half miles due south of the city centre, just to the west of the tree-filled Queen's Park, the floodlights and giant stands of Scotland's national football stadium, **Hampden Park**, loom over the surrounding sub-urban tenements and terraces. Home of Queen's Park Football Club, the fact that it's the venue for Scotland's international fixtures and major cup finals makes it a place of pilgrimage for the country's football fans. Regular **guided tours** (daily 10.30am–3.30pm; £2.50; ⓦwww.hampdenpark.co.uk) offer the chance to see the changing rooms, warm-up areas and inside the stadium itself. Also here is the engaging **Scottish Football Museum** (Mon–Sat 10am–5pm, Sun 11am–5pm; £5), with extensive collections of memorabilia, video clips and displays covering almost every aspect of the game.

Football in Glasgow

Football, or *fitba'* as it's pronounced locally, is one of Glasgow's great passions – and one of its great blights. While the city can claim to be one of Europe's premier footballing centres, it's known above all for one of the most bitter rivalries in any sport, that between **Celtic** and **Rangers**. Two of the largest clubs in Britain, with weekly crowds regularly topping 60,000, the Old Firm, as they're collectively known, have dominated Scottish football for a century, most notably in the last fifteen years as they have lavished vast sums of money on foreign talent in an often frantic effort both to out-do each other and to stay in touch with the standards of the top English and European teams.

The roots of Celtic, who play at Celtic Park in the eastern district of Parkhead (℡0141/551 8653), lie in the city's immigrant Irish and **Catholic** population, while Rangers, based at Ibrox Park in Govan on the Southside (℡0870/600 1993), have traditionally drawn support from local **Protestants**. As a result, sporting rivalries have been enmeshed in a sectarian divide which many argue would not have remained so long, nor so deep, had it been divorced from the footballing scene: although Catholics do play for Rangers, and Protestants for Celtic, sections of supporters of both clubs seem intent on perpetuating the feud. While large-scale violence on the terraces and streets has not been seen for some time – thanks in large measure to canny policing – Old Firm matches often seethe with bitter passions, and sectarian-related assaults do still occur in parts of the city.

However, there is a less intense side to the game, found not just in the fun-loving "Tartan Army" which follows the (often rollercoaster) fortunes of the Scottish national team, but also in Glasgow's smaller clubs, who actively distance themselves from the distasteful aspects of the Old Firm and plod along with home-grown talent in the lower reaches of the Scottish league. **Queen's Park**, residents of Hampden (℡0141/632 1275), **St Mirren**, the Paisley team (℡0141/889 2558), and the much-maligned **Partick Thistle**, who play at Firhill Stadium in the West End (℡0141/579 1971), offer the best chances of experiencing the more down-to-earth side of Glaswegian football – along with all-important reminders that it is, in the end, only a game.

The Burrell Collection

Located in Pollok Park some six miles southwest of the city centre, the outstanding **Burrell Collection** (Mon–Thurs & Sat 10am–5pm, Fri & Sun 11am–5pm; free), the lifetime collection of shipping magnate Sir William Burrell (1861–1958), is, for some, the principal reason for visiting Glasgow. Unlike many other art collectors, Sir William's only real criterion for buying a piece was whether he liked it or not, enabling him to buy many "unfashionable" works, which cost comparatively little but subsequently proved their worth. He wanted to leave his collection of art, sculpture and antiquities for public display, but stipulated in 1943 that they should be housed "in a rural setting far removed from the atmospheric pollution of urban conurbations, not less than sixteen miles from the Royal Exchange". For decades, these conditions proved too difficult to meet, with few open spaces available and a pall of industrial smoke ruling out any city site. However, by the late 1960s, after the nationwide Clean Air Act had reduced pollution, and vast **Pollok Park** had been donated to the city, plans began for a new, purpose-built gallery, which finally opened in 1983. Today the simplicity and clean lines of the Burrell building are its greatest assets, with large picture windows giving sweeping views over woodland and serving as a tranquil backdrop to the objects inside.

The courtyard

On entering the building, head past the information desk and shop to an airy covered **courtyard** where the most striking piece, by virtue of sheer size, is the **Warwick Vase**, a huge bowl containing fragments of a second-century AD vase from Emperor Hadrian's villa in Tivoli. Next to it is a series of sinewy and naturalistic bronze casts of **Rodin sculptures**, among them *The Age of Bronze*, *A Call to Arms* and the famous *Thinker*. On three sides of the courtyard, a trio of dark and sombre panelled rooms have been re-erected in faithful detail from the Burrells' Hutton Castle home, their heavy tapestries, antique furniture and fireplaces displaying the same eclectic taste as the rest of the museum.

The ground floor

From the courtyard, go through the massive sandstone portal and door from Hornby Castle to the start of the **Ancient Civilizations** collection – a catch-all title for Greek, Roman and earlier artefacts – which includes an exquisite mosaic Roman cockerel from the first century BC and a 4000-year-old Mesopotamian lion's head. Nearby, also illuminated by enormous windows, the **Oriental Art** collection forms nearly one-quarter of the whole display, ranging from Neolithic jades through bronze vessels and Tang funerary horses to cloisonné. The most dominant piece is the serene fifteenth-century *Lohan* (disciple of Buddha), who sits cross-legged and contemplative up against the window and the trees of Pollok Park.

Burrell considered his **Medieval and Post-Medieval European Art**, which encompasses silverware, glass, textiles and sculpture, to be the most valuable part of his collection. Among the church art are simple thirteenth-century Spanish wooden images and cool fifteenth-century English alabaster, while a trio of period interiors span the period from the Gothic era to the eighteenth century. This is interrupted by a selection from Burrell's vast art collection, the highlight of which is one of Rembrandt's evocative early self-portraits.

The mezzanine

Upstairs, the cramped and comparatively gloomy **mezzanine** is probably the least satisfactory section of the gallery, not the best setting for its sparkling array of paintings. The selection incongruously leaps from a small gathering of fifteenth-century religious works to Géricault's darkly dynamic *Prancing Grey Horse* and Degas's thoughtful and perceptive *Portrait of Émile Duranty*. Pissarro, Manet and Boudin are also represented, along with some exquisite watercolours by Glasgow Boy Joseph Crawhall, revealing his accurate and tender observations of the animal world.

Pollok House

Within Pollok Park, a quarter of a mile down rutted tracks west of the Burrell Collection, lies the lovely eighteenth-century **Pollok House** (daily 10am–5pm; April–Oct £5, rest of year free; café and gardens free year-round; NTS), the manor of the Pollok Park estate and once home of the Maxwell family, local lords and owners of most of southern Glasgow until well into the nineteenth century. Designed by William Adam in the mid-1700s, the house is typical of its age: graciously light and sturdily built, looking out onto the pristine raked and parterre gardens.

The **paintings** range from Spanish masterpieces in the morning room and some splendid Dutch hunting scenes in the dining room to Sir John Maxwell's own worthy but noticeably amateur efforts that line the upstairs corridors. Generally, the rooms have the flavour of a well-to-do but unstuffy country house, with the odd piece of attractive furniture and some pleasant rooms, but little that can be described as outstanding. The servants' quarters downstairs, however, do capture the imagination – the virtually untouched labyrinth of tiled Victorian parlours and corridors includes a good **tearoom** in the old kitchen.

Holmwood House

Four miles south of the city centre in the suburb of Cathcart, **Holmwood House** (April–Oct daily noon–5pm; £3.50; NTS) is the finest domestic design by rediscovered Glasgow architect Alexander "Greek" Thomson. The house shows off Thomson's bold Classical concepts, with exterior pillars on two levels and a raised main door, as well as his detailed and highly imaginative interiors. One room upstairs is given over to a series of displays about Thomson and the history of the house. Also on the upper floor is the **drawing room** – look for the white marble fireplace and the night-time star decorations on the ceiling, which contrast with a black marble fireplace and sunburst decorations in the room immediately underneath on the downstairs level, the **parlour**, which also boasts a delightful round bay window.

Eating

Fuelled by a lively social scene, an ethnically mixed (by Scottish standards) population, just enough slick business types and suburbanites as well as tourists Glasgow's **restaurants**, bistros and diners offer a pretty varied selection, from fine dining at the hands of celebrity chefs to the curries available at the city's renowned Indian restaurants. Contemporary Scottish cuisine – featuring fresh west-coast produce with French and other international influences – is a particular strength of Glasgow.

Cafés, diners and café-bars

City centre

Café Gandolfi 64 Albion St ☎0141/552 6813. This bona fide landmark (now with a cool bar in its attic space) was one of the first to test the waters in the Merchant City. Designed with distinctive wooden furniture, it serves up healthy and hearty portions of staples (including great black pudding), soups, salads, fish dishes and more. Moderate.

Grassroots Café 93 St Georges Rd ☎0141/333 0534. Although the competition is not especially stiff, this vegetarian outlet (just cross the M8 motorway from the city centre) has the best reputation in Glasgow. Fresh, creative cooking and a relaxed atmosphere. Inexpensive.

Mono 12 King's Court ☎0141/553 2400. Opened in late 2002, this is a combination vegan restaurant, fair trade food shop, bar and indie CD shop. Lots of space and home-made organic beers. Inexpensive.

Tron Theatre Chisholm St off the Trongate ☎0141/552 8587. Another arty hangout, this time for writers and theatrical types in either the modern-design street-side pub/café or the more traditional Victorian bar inside. One all-day menu serves both spaces, with pre-theatre specials most evenings. Moderate.

Where the Monkey Sleeps 182 West Regent St ☎0141/226 3406. Owned by gregarious art graduates who acquired their barista skills while studying, this hip home-grown café doubles as a gallery. Food options focus on soups and sandwiches and the espresso is superb. Usually closes at 7pm. Inexpensive.

Willow Tea Rooms 217 Sauchiehall St ☎0141/332 0521. A well-kept and genuinely authentic landmark on the Charles Rennie Mackintosh trail, serving high tea with scones. A similarly themed branch at 97 Buchanan Street is less authentic. Closes late afternoon. Inexpensive–moderate.

West End

Air Organic 36 Kelvingrove St ☎0141/564 5200. This stylish post-*2001 A Space Odyssey* bistro (and pre-club bar downstairs) boasts design awards as well as excellent, mostly organic Asian-influenced food. Recommended for Sunday brunch. Moderate.

Brel 39–43 Ashton Lane ☎0141/342 4966. Popular with students, post-grads and profs, offering a smattering of Belgian food (*moules et frites*) and beers. A rear conservatory opens onto a secluded grassy knoll. Frequent live music and ambient DJs. Moderate.

Stravaigin 2 8 Ruthven Lane ☎0141/334 7165. A popular diner (formerly known as the *Back Alley*) that serves excellent burgers alongside an innovative menu similar to the award-winning modern Scottish *Stravaigin* restaurant (see p.1035). Moderate.

Tchai Ovna 42 Otago Lane ☎0141/357 4524. A low-key bohemian hangout near the Kelvin River with cakes, snacks and a selection of teas from around the world. Tobacco is forbidden but the house water-pipe with dried fruit in the bowl serves as a substitute. Inexpensive.

Tinderbox 189 Byres Rd ☎0141/339 3108. A modern espresso café-bar offering an array of lattes, cappuccinos and the like as well as designer looks. Even in trendy Glasgow, it remains amazingly successful. Inexpensive.

University Café 87 Byres Rd ☎0141/339 5217. A Glasgow institution adored by generations of students and West End residents. Formica tables in snug booths, glass counters and original Art Deco features, where the favourites are fish'n'chips or mince'n'tatties rounded off with an ice-cream cone. Sometimes closes in afternoon. Inexpensive.

Southside

The Granary 10–16 Kilmarnock Rd ☎0141/649 0594. At Shawlands Cross, in the commercial heart of the Southside, this bar/bistro serves an international selection of food and rich, satisfying desserts. Moderate.

1901 1534 Pollokshaws Rd ☎0141/632 0161. Once known as the *Stoat & Ferret*, this French-influenced bistro/pub near Pollok Country Park is a lesser-known gem serving hearty Mediterranean food. Moderate.

Restaurants

City centre

Arta Old Cheese Market, 13–19 Walls St ☎0141/552 2101. The OTT ground-floor bar is decked out like a Spanish townhouse, while the restaurant upstairs is minimalist. Good, freshly prepared tapas. Late licence plus basement club. Closed Mon & Tues. Moderate.

Brian Maule at Le Chardon d'Or 176 West

Regent St ☎0141/248 3801. Owner/chef Maule once worked with the Roux brothers at *Le Gavroche* restaurant in London. Fancy but not pretentious French-influenced food. Closed Sun (and bank holidays). Expensive.

The Buttery 652 Argyle St ☎0141/221 8188. Located in no-man's land in the shadow of the sleepless M8, this atmospheric Victorian-era dining space rose from the dead in 2002. Once one of the city's best, it's regaining its stature with complex dishes handled deftly. Book ahead, and don't be surprised if the cabbie insists the place is long gone. Closed Sun & Mon. Expensive.

Café Cossachok 10 King St ☎0141/553 0733. Hearty Slavic style dishes accompanied by Russian musicians and plenty of chilled vodka. There's a gallery on the mezzanine. Closed Mon. Moderate.

City Merchant 97 Candleriggs ☎0141/553 1577. Popular brasserie that blazed the Merchant City trail that plenty of others have followed. Fresh Scottish produce from Ayrshire lamb to the house speciality – west-coast seafood. Expensive.

The Dhabba 44 Candleriggs ☎0141/553 1249. Not your typical Glasgow curry house – prices are higher, portions smaller – but the menu has some truly interesting options. Moderate.

Fratelli Sarti 133 Wellington St or 121 Bath St ☎0141/204 0440. The Sarti brothers' flagship Italian café and restaurant: fairly authentic and very popular. The formal dining space is accessed from the Bath Street entrance; the more atmospheric café round the corner opens 8am Mon–Sat. Moderate.

Gamba 225a West George St ☎0141/572 0899. This modern basement restaurant is arguably the best in Glasgow – but you have to like fish. Continental contemporary sophistication prevails, with dishes such as turbot and sea bass with puy lentils or sun-blushed tomatoes. Closed Sun. Expensive.

Ichiban Japanese Noodle Café 50 Queen St ☎0141/204 4200. Japanese-style informal eating, with long benches and tables shared by diners. Bowls of noodles (dry or soupy) and sushi are the staples here; service is efficient. Completely nonsmoking. Inexpensive.

Mao 84 Brunswick St ☎0141/564 5161. Bright café-bar in the Merchant City with a range of Asian cuisine, including spicy Korean and Indonesian specialities, and a bustling pre-club feel most nights. Moderate.

Mussel Inn 157 Hope St ☎0141/572 1405. Like the Edinburgh flagship, this branch concentrates on simply prepared pots of fresh mussels, grilled scallops and other delights from the sea in

relaxed, buzzy environs. Moderate.

Oko 68 Ingram St ☎0141/572 1500. Locally owned restaurant bringing freshly prepared sushi on colour-coded plates and a conveyor belt to the Merchant City. Closed Mon. Moderate.

Rogano 11 Exchange Place ☎0141/248 4055. An Art Deco fish restaurant and Glasgow institution, decked out in 1935 in the style of the *Queen Mary*. *Café Rogano*, in the basement, is cheaper. Or just have some oysters at the bar. Expensive.

Schottische 16 Blackfriars St ☎0141/552 7774. Relaxed, cosy restaurant with French/Mediterranean bistro fare above the popular *Babbity Bowster* pub (see p.1035) Closed Sun & Mon. Moderate.

Smith's of Glasgow 109 Candleriggs ☎0141/552 6539. Owner/chef Michael Smith re-creates Parisian brasserie style in the Merchant City, with seasonally changing menus and complimentary apéritifs. Moderate.

Wee Curry Shop 7 Buccleuch St ☎0141/353 0777. Tiny café near the Glasgow Film Theatre and Sauchiehall Street shops, serving homemade bargain meals to compete with the best in town. BYOB. Closed Sun. Inexpensive.

West End

Amaryllis 1 Devonshire Gardens, corner of Great Western and Hyndland roads ☎0141/337 3434. Gordon Ramsay, the Glasgow-raised celebrity chef who made it big in London, opened this critically acclaimed French restaurant in 2001. Not as expensive as you'd expect, especially in the brasserie half, though that might reflect the fact that the main man still spends most of his time down south. Closed Mon & Tues. Expensive.

Café Antipasti 337 Byres Rd ☎0141/337 2737. A busy Italian bistro near the Botanic Gardens serving tasty and well-priced pastas and salads. No bookings are taken, so expect a queue on busy nights. Second branch in town at 305 Sauchiehall Street. Inexpensive.

Ashoka Ashton Lane 19 Ashton Lane ☎0141/337 1115. Lively curry house in the Harlequin chain, which dominates the Indian restaurant community throughout the west of Scotland; all have consistent quality and this branch is particularly popular with students. Branches at 1284 Argyle St, and on the Southside at 268 Clarkston Rd. Moderate.

Chow 98 Byres Rd ☎0141/334 9818. Proof that Chinese restaurants can be modern and non-kitsch. This bijou diner with extra tables upstairs offers excellent value-for-money meals. No smoking. Moderate.

19

Cottier's 93–95 Hyndland St ☎0141/357 5825. Not pure Mexican, as it takes in Latin American and Caribbean. With a welcoming West End vibe, it's located on the top floor of a church annexe adjacent to Cottier's Theatre. Moderate.

Dining Room 41 Byres Rd ☎0141/339 3666. A promising newcomer, with adventurous but unfussy modern Scottish cooking. Excellent wine list. Closed Mon; lunches Thurs & Fri only. Expensive.

Mother India 28 Westminster Terrace, off Sauchiehall St ☎0141/221 1663. This is one of the best Indian restaurants in Glasgow. Home cooking with some original Goan specials as well as the old favourites at affordable prices in refreshingly laid-back surroundings. BYOB; small corkage fee. Moderate.

No. Sixteen 16 Byres Rd ☎0141/339 2544. A local favourite with daily changing menus of Scottish produce, from pigeon to fillet of sea bream. Moderate.

Stravaigin 28–30 Gibson St ☎0141/334 2665. Local meats and fish are given an international make-over using a host of unexpected ingredients, with combinations such as avocado and coriander sorbet or harissa marinated venison. Adventurous fine dining in the basement restaurant and an exceptional-value menu in the street-level bar/café. Moderate upstairs, expensive downstairs.

Two Fat Ladies 88 Dumbarton Rd ☎0141/339 1944. The second-best fish restaurant in Glasgow, after *Gamba* (see p.1034). Intimate space with the kitchen right up front. Moderate–expensive.

The Ubiquitous Chip 12 Ashton Lane ☎0141/334 5007. Opened in 1971, *The Chip* led the way in headlining Scotland's quality fresh produce at the heart of a contemporary, upmarket dining experience. Some say it's living on its well-deserved reputation, but it's still up there. Expensive.

Southside

Arigo 67 Kilmarnock Rd ☎0141/636 6616. A charming local favourite that has a claim to be the best Italian restaurant in the city. Everything is made fresh to order. There's a city centre branch too at 85 Renfield St. Moderate.

Art Lovers' Café In House for an Art Lover, Bellahouston Park, 10 Dumbreck Rd ☎0141/353 4779. This showcase house based on unfinished Mackintosh designs offers sublime lunches looking onto a charming garden. Moderate.

Greek Golden Kebab 34 Sinclair Drive ☎0141/649 7581. The longest-running Greek restaurant in Glasgow hasn't changed its rustic cooking in probably thirty years. Worth seeking out. Closed Mon–Wed. Moderate.

Café Serghei 67 Bridge St ☎0141/429 1547. In a converted bank near the Clyde (easy walking distance from the city centre), this place looks formal but is quite relaxed, serving hearty Greek dishes. Inexpensive–moderate.

Drinking

Glasgow's notorious tough image has been linked with its **pubs**, mistakenly thought of as no-go areas for visitors. Today, many of the traditionally windowless, nicotine-stained working men's pubs have been converted into airy modern bars, though – in truth – almost any drinking spot is a great place for real Glaswegian bonhomie.

If you tire of the trendier pre-club bars in the **city centre** and its buzzing Merchant City, the liveliest area is the **West End**, with students mixing with locals around Byres Road. Decent pubs are more widely scattered in the **Southside**, but you'll find a handful of pleasant spots, ranging from stylish hangouts to historic locals.

As for **opening hours**, Glasgow's licensing regulations have been in flux. Many pubs and bars often keep serving until midnight, although some outside the centre close at 11pm during the week. But then again in certain areas you'll find bars open at the weekend until 1am. After closing time, your option is to head to a nightclub (see p.1037).

City centre

The Arches 253 Argyle St. The basement bar is a local point in this contemporary arts centre under central station. Happy-hour bargains and arty clientele.

Babbity Bowster 16–18 Blackfriars St, off the High Street. Lively place with an unforced and kitsch-free Scottish feel that's great for spontaneous folk sessions at the weekend. Excellent beer, good basic food and outdoor seating.

Bar 91 91 Candleriggs. This Merchant City style bar tends to be friendlier, less pretentious and draws a more diverse crowd than some others.

Bargo 80 Albion St. Design-award winner with a spacious wood and stainless-steel interior that opens onto the pavement. Popular with students who appreciate the scene and the cheap eats.

Corinthian 191 Ingram St. A remarkable renovation of a florid early Victorian Italianate bank. Three distinct bars, one restaurant and a private club: dress smartly.

Horseshoe Bar 17 Drury St. A must for pub aficionados. Original "Gin Palace" with the longest continuous bar in the UK, this is reputedly Glasgow's busiest drinking hole; karaoke upstairs.

Moskito 200 Bath St. Newer arrival, less full of posing youth than nonetheless hip and stylish, with inexpensive food and ambient tunes.

Republic Bier Halle 9 Gordon St. Chunky modern industrial design using shuttered concrete and blocks of stone. Serves 130 different beers and hearty Eastern European grub, from sausages to goulash.

Variety Bar 401 Sauchiehall St. Featuring faded faux Art Nouveau decor, this place is frequented by nearby Glasgow Art School students. Located near clubs.

East End and Saltmarket

Clutha Vaults 167 Stockwell St. Slightly more scrubbed and less atmospheric than the *Scotia* (see below) but host to a similar line-up of free live music.

McChuill's 40 High St. Just skirting the Merchant City, this converted railway shed with vaulted brick ceilings manages to be neither style bar nor traditional pub. Popular for music, ranging from hip-hop DJ nights to salsa and jazz.

Scotia Bar 112 Stockwell St. The management says this is the oldest pub in the city – and it looks the part, with low, exposed timber ceilings. Still the place for live blues, folk and skiffle sessions; Billy Connolly began his career here, telling jokes between singing folk songs.

West End

54 Below 3 Kelvingrove St, corner of Argyle St. One of the more recent bars converted from gloom to glam – but not too much of the latter.

Firebird 1321 Argyle St. Airy modern drinking spot near the Kelvingrove Art Gallery, with a wood-stoked pizza oven producing some tasty snacks plus DJs to keep the pre-clubbing crowd entertained.

Lismore Lounge 206 Dumbarton Rd. One-time working man's pub, tastefully redecorated with specially commissioned stained-glass panels depicting the Highland Clearances, this bar is a meeting point for the local Gaels, who come here to chat, relax and listen to the impromptu music sessions.

Living Room 5–9 Byres Rd. Hotbed for the young and hip, at the lower end of Byres Road. Wrought iron and candles enhance the pre-club atmosphere.

Tennent's 191 Byres Rd. No-nonsense, beery pub that offers a refreshing antidote to designer-driven bars nearby. Large and popular, with real ale and a no-music policy.

Uisge Beatha 232 Woodlands Rd. An unexceptional frontage belies an eclectic interior, with lots of sofas and ironic Scots kitsch. Barmen wear kilts and keep the atmosphere lively. The name is Gaelic for "the water of life" – that is, whisky.

Southside

Brazen Head 1–3 Cathcart Rd. Local Irish-Italian bar close to the Citizens' Theatre and decorated with football strips.

Heraghty's Free House 708 Pollokshaws Rd. Authentic Irish pub that prides itself on pouring the perfect pint of Guinness. Still living down its history of not having a women's loo: one's been installed for several years now.

The Taverna 778 Pollokshaws Rd. A favourite of many who stay in this neck of the Southside; in a bright, light corner location with potted palms and a selection of real ales.

Nightlife and entertainment

The **clubbing scene** in Glasgow has long been highly rated, with the city attracting top DJs from around the world and also breeding a good deal of local talent. Opening hours hover between 11pm and 3am, though some stay open until 5am. Cover charges are variable: expect to pay around £4 during the week and up to £15 at the weekend. Drinks are usually about thirty percent more expensive than in the pubs.

Glasgow is home to Scottish Opera, Scottish Ballet and the Royal Scottish National Orchestra, and the city's cultural programme offers a range of **music**, from contemporary to heavyweight classical, plus **dance**, **theatre**, **film** and performance art. For detailed **listings**, pick up the comprehensive fortnightly magazine *The List* (£2.20), which also covers Edinburgh, or consult Glasgow's *Herald* or *Evening Times* newspapers. To book **tickets** for theatre productions or big concerts, try Tickets Scotland, 239 Argyle St, under Central Station (Mon–Wed, Fri & Sat 9am–6pm, Thurs 9am–7pm, Sun 11.30am–5.30pm; ☎0141/204 5151), or Way Ahead (☎0141/339 8383).

Clubs

Archaos 25 Queen St ☎0141/204 3189. Massive, multi-level place with designer decor and a mainstream music policy.

The Arches 30 Midland St, off Jamaica St ☎0141/221 4001. In converted railway arches under Central station, the club portion of this arts venue offers an eclectic array of music: hard house, trance, techno and funk.

Sub Club 22 Jamaica St ☎0141/248 4600. Near-legendary venue reopened after a fire and base to the noteworthy Subculture, the home of house and techno in Scotland.

The Tunnel 84 Mitchell St ☎0141/204 1000. Contemporary and progressive house music club with arty decor (dig the gents' cascading waterfall walls) and fairly strict dress codes.

The Velvet Rooms 520 Sauchiehall St ☎0141/332 0755. Consists of a small bar with postage-stamp dance area for mainstream dance, garage and soul.

Gay clubs and bars

Delmonica's 68 Virginia St ☎0141/552 4803. One of Glasgow's liveliest gay bars, in a popular area, with a mixed, hedonistic crowd and some kind of entertainment or event nightly.

LGBT Centre 11 Dixon St ☎0141/221 7203, ⓦglgbt.org.uk/. Licensed café in addition to more institutional support such as information and reading rooms.

Polo Lounge 84 Wilson St, off Glassford St ☎0141/553 1221. Original decor – marble tiles and open fires – and gentleman's club atmosphere upstairs, with dark, pounding nightclubs underneath which attract a gay and gay-friendly crowd.

Live music venues

Barrowland 244 Gallowgate ☎0141/552 4601. Legendary East End ballroom that hosts some of the sweatiest and best gigs you may ever encounter. With room for a couple of thousand, it mostly books bands securely on the rise but still hosts some big-time acts who return to it as their favourite venue in Scotland.

Carling Academy Eglington St. Owned by same people behind the famous Brixton and other Academies and only opened in 2002, this renovated theatre on the south side of the Clyde has stolen some of the *Barrowland*'s thunder.

King Tut's Wah Wah Hut 272a St Vincent St ☎0141/221 5279. Famous as the place where Oasis were discovered, and still presenting one of the city's best live music programmes. Also has a good downstairs bar, with an excellent jukebox.

Scotia Bar 112 Stockwell St ☎0141/552 8681. The folkies' favourite, a mellow musical pub with regular live gigs and jam sessions. Free.

The 13th Note 50–60 King St ☎0141/553 1638. The basement of this relaxed bar and vegetarian restaurant is the place to sample local and cutting-edge musical talent, including jazz and R&B.

Theatres and comedy venues

Arches Theatre 253 Argyle St ☎0901/022 0300. Andy Arnold runs the Arches theatre company, reviving old classics and introducing new talent in this hip venue.

Citizens' Theatre 119 Gorbals St ☎0141/429 0022. The "Citz" has evolved from its 1960s working-class roots into one of the most respected and innovative contemporary theatres in Britain. Their Christmas shows are legendary. Three stages, concession rates for students and free preview nights.

Cottier Theatre 935 Hyndland St ☎0141/357 3868. This performance space in the old Dowanhill church hosts touring shows, dance and music gigs. An adjoining bar with beer garden is a favourite on summer evenings.

The Stand 333 Woodlands Rd ☎0870/600 6055. Sister of the first-rate comedy club in Edinburgh, booking national and international acts.

Tron Theatre 63 Trongate ☎0141/552 4267. Varied repertoire of mainstream and more challenging productions from itinerant companies, such as Glasgow's Vanishing Point.

Concert halls

Glasgow Royal Concert Hall 2 Sauchiehall St ☎0141/287 5511. One of Glasgow's less memorable modern buildings, this is the venue for big-name touring orchestras and the home of the Royal Scottish National Orchestra. Also features major rock and R&B stars, and middle-of-the-road music hall acts.

Scottish Exhibition and Conference Centre, and Clyde Auditorium Finnieston Quay ☎0870/040 4000. The SECC is a gigantic aircraft hangar-like space with dreadful acoustics that, unfortunately, is the only indoor venue in Scotland for world-touring megastars from Tom Jones to Eminem. The adjacent Clyde Auditorium − better known as the Armadillo − is smaller but more melodic.

Theatre Royal 282 Hope St ☎0141/332 9000. This late nineteenth-century theatre was revived in the mid-1970s as the opulent home of Scottish Opera, whose recent productions include an acclaimed *Ring* cycle. It also plays regular host to visiting orchestras, opera and theatre groups, including the Royal Shakespeare Company.

Cinemas

Glasgow Film Theatre 12 Rose St ☎0141/332 8128. Dedicated art, independent and repertory cinema house. Its in-house *Café Cosmo* is an excellent place for pre-show drinks.

Imax Theatre Glasgow Science Centre, 50 Pacific Quay ☎0141/420 5000. 3D and super-screen documentaries and features.

Odeon City Centre 56 Renfield St ☎0141/332 3413. Multi-screen cinema with the latest releases.

UGC Renfrew Street 7 Renfrew Street ☎0870/907 0789. Gigantic multistorey cinema with first-run Hollywood and a few art films as well.

Listings

Bike rental Dales, 150 Dobbies Loan (☎0141/332 2705), a block north of the Buchanan Street bus station. A larger selection is at West End Cycles, 16 Chancellor St (☎0141/357 1344), which is placed close to the start of the Glasgow to Loch Lomond route, one of a number of cycle routes that radiate out from the city. For further details, check ⊛www.sustrans.co.uk.

Books Borders, 98 Buchanan St; Waterstone's 153 Sauchiehall St. For secondhand try Caledonian Bookshop, 483 Great Western Rd; Voltaire & Rousseau, 12−14 Otago Lane; or Oxfam Second-Hand Bookshop, 330 Byres Rd.

Car rental Arnold Clark, multiple branches ☎0845/607 4500; Avis ☎0141/221 2827; Budget ☎0141/221 9241; Europcar ☎0141/248 8788.

Dentist National Health Service line (☎0800/224488) lists local and emergency dentists. Glasgow Dental Hospital, 378 Sauchiehall St ☎0141/211 9600.

Hospital 24hr casualty department at the Royal Infirmary, 84 Castle St ☎0141/211 4000.

Internet EasyEverything is open 24hr at 57−61 St Vincent St (☎0141/222 2365). Many local libraries also offer access.

Laundry Harvey's, 161 Great Western Rd; Majestic Laundrette, 1110 Argyle St.

Police Strathclyde Police HQ, Pitt Street (☎0141/532 2000).

Post office General information (☎0845/722 3344). Main office at 47 St Vincent St (Mon−Fri 8.30am−5.45pm, Sat 9am−5.30pm); other city centre offices at 87−91 Bothwell St and 228 Hope St.

Swimming pools At city-run leisure centres in the Gorbals (☎0141/418 6400); Scotstoun (☎0141/959 4000); Tollcross (Olympic size; ☎0141/763 2345).

Taxis Glasgow Wide TOA (☎0141/429 7070); Glasgow Private Hire (☎0141/774 3000).

The Clyde

The **River Clyde** is the dominant physical feature of Glasgow and its environs, an area which comprises the largest urban concentration in Scotland, with almost two million people living in the city and satellite towns. Little of this immediate hinterland can be described as beautiful, with crisscrossin motorways and relentlessly grim housing estates dominating much of the landscape. However, there are pockets of interest, many related to the river itself or the industries that grew up from it.

West of the city is **Paisley**, where the distinctive cloth pattern gained its name, and the former ship-building towns of **Port Glasgow**, **Greenock** and **Gourock**. On the north bank of the firth – the ancient Strathclyde capital of **Dumbarton**, and **Helensburgh**, birthplace of architect Charles Rennie Mackintosh and television pioneer John Logie Baird.

Heading southeast out of Glasgow, the industrial landscape of the **Clyde Valley** eventually gives way to a far more attractive scenery of gorges and towering castles. Here, eighteenth-century philanthropists built their model workers' community around the mills of **New Lanark**, while deep into the rolling countryside of South Lanarkshire the market town of **Biggar** serves as a useful orientation point to the hill-farming country of the Scottish Borders beyond.

The Firth of Clyde – south bank

The swift journey from Glasgow along the M8, coupled with the proximity of the international airport, can belie the fact that **Paisley** is not a suburb of Glasgow but a town in its own right, with a long and distinctive history, particularly in the textile trade. Further west, the former shipbuilding centres of Port Glasgow and **Greenock** crowd the riverbank, followed by the old-fashioned seaside resort of **Gourock**, and eventually **Wemyss Bay**, jumping-off point for the ferry to Rothesay on Bute.

Paisley

Founded in the twelfth century as a monastic settlement around an abbey, **PAISLEY** expanded rapidly after the eighteenth century as a linen manufacturing town, specializing in the production of highly fashionable imitation Kashmiri shawls. Paisley quickly eclipsed other British centres producing the cloth, eventually lending its name to the swirling pine-cone design.

South of the train station, down Gilmour or Smithills streets, the **Abbey** (Mon–Sat 10am–3.30pm; free) was built on the site of the town's original settlement and was massively overhauled in the Victorian age. The unattractive, fat grey facade of the church does little justice to the renovated interior, which is tall, spacious and elaborately decorated; the elongated choir, rebuilt extensively throughout the last two centuries, is illuminated by jewel-coloured stained glass from a variety of ages and styles.

The bland pedestrianized **High Street** leads from the abbey to Paisley's civic **Museum and Art Gallery** (Tues–Sat 10am–5pm, Sun 2–5pm; free), where the Shawl Gallery deals with the growth and development of the Paisley pattern, from its simple beginnings to elaborate later incarnations. Paisley's identity as a centre for craftsmanship is also celebrated in displays of the work of contemporary local artisans, alongside a number of working looms looked after by a weaver-in-residence. The Upper Gallery houses a small art collection including works by Glasgow Boys Hornel, Guthrie and Lavery (see box on p.1023), as well as one or two paintings by local boy John Byrne, artist and playwright best known for his plays *The Slab Boys* and *Tutti Frutti*.

Regular **trains** from Glasgow Central connect with Paisley's Gilmour Street station in the centre of town. Buses leave Paisley's Gilmour Street forecourt every ten minutes for Glasgow International Airport, two miles north of the town. The **tourist office** is right in the centre at 9a Gilmour Street

(April–Sept Mon–Sat 9.30am–5.30pm, Sun noon–5pm; Oct–March Mon–Sat 10am–5pm; ☎0141/889 0711).

For **food** the Paisley Arts Centre has a small bar, daytime café and outside seating, while most of the pubs in the centre, including the *Last Post* pub in the old Post Office building in County Square, serve a range of bar meals. *Aroma Room* is a more modern spot right opposite the Museum and Art Gallery, which serves coffees, snacks and lunches; not far away, both *Cardosi's* on Storie Street and *Raeburn's Bistro and Grill* on New Street have decent evening menus.

Greenock

GREENOCK, west of Glasgow, was the site of the first dock on the Clyde, founded in 1711, and the community has grown on the back of shipping ever since. Despite its ranks of anonymous tower blocks and sterile shopping centres, the town still retains a few features of interest. From the Central train station in Greenock (also served by hourly Citylink buses from Glasgow's Buchanan Street station), it's a short walk to the dockside, reached by crossing the dual carriageway, where the Neoclassical **Custom House** is Greenock's finest building, splendidly located looking out over the river. Now the principal office for HM Customs & Excise in Scotland, there's an informative **museum** (Mon–Fri 10am–4pm; free) inside, which covers the work of the Customs and Excise departments, with a display on illicit whisky distilleries as well as more modern contraband. From the dock in front, tens of thousands of nineteenth-century emigrants departed for the New World.

Greenock's town centre has been disfigured by astonishingly unsympathetic developments. More attractive, and indicative of the town's wealthy past, is the western side of town, with its mock-baronial houses, graceful churches and quiet, tree-lined avenues. A hundred yards from the well-proportioned **George Square**, close to Greenock West station, the **McLean Museum and Art Gallery** in Union Street (Mon–Sat 10am–5pm; free) contains pictures and contemporary records of the life and achievements of Greenock-born James Watt, prominent eighteenth-century industrialist and pioneer of steam power, as well as featuring exhibits on the shipbuilding industry and other local trades. The small art gallery on the ground floor contains work by Glasgow Boys Hornel and Guthrie plus Colourists Fergusson, Cadell and Peploe.

Greenock's eating options are restricted to predictable high-street cafés and takeaways; neighbouring Gourock has a better selection all round, including *Sette Odori*, a smart deli serving daytime snacks, near the outdoor swimming pool at 81 Kempock Street, and *Café Continental*, also on Kempock Street, serving bar/bistro food with views across the Clyde.

Gourock

On the train line west of Greenock, the dowdy old resort of **GOUROCK** was once a holiday destination for generations of Glaswegians, but today is only of significance as a **ferry** terminal: both CalMac (enquiries ☎01475/650100, sales ☎0870/565 0000, ⓦwww.calmac.co.uk) and the more frequent Western Ferries (☎01369/704452, ⓦwww.western-ferries.co.uk) ply the twenty-minute route across the Firth of Clyde to Dunoon on the Cowal peninsula (see p.1097).

Wemyss Bay

There's not much south of Gourock until you reach **WEMYSS BAY** and its breathtaking railway station, a startling wrought-iron and glass palace which serves as a reminder of the great glory days when thousands of Glaswegian would alight for their steamer trip "doon the watter". Today the only steamer connection is the rather prosaic CalMac **ferry** over to Rothesay, capital of the Isle of Bute (see p.1098).

The Firth of Clyde – north bank

Heading west out of Glasgow, the A82 road and the train tracks both follow the north bank of the river, passing through Clydebank, another ex-shipbuilding centre, and Bowling, the western entry point of the newly reopened Forth & Clyde canal. At **Dumbarton**, an ancient regional capital, the main road swings north towards Loch Lomond (see p.1061), while the railway and A814 carry on along the shores of the Firth of Clyde to wealthy **Helensburgh**, before themselves turning north along the shores of Gare Loch and Loch Long to Arrochar, which marks the beginning of Argyll (see p.1093).

Dumbarton

Founded in the fifth century, today the town of **DUMBARTON** is for the most part a brutal concrete sprawl, fulfilling every last cliché about postwar planning and architecture. **Dumbarton Castle** (April–Sept Mon–Sun 9.30am–6.30pm; Oct–March Mon–Wed & Sat 9.30–4.30pm, Thurs 9.30am–12.30pm, Sun 2–4.30pm; £2.20), which sits atop a twin outcrop of volcanic rock surrounded by water on three sides, was Strathclyde's capital until its absorption into the greater kingdom of Scotland in 1034. Vertiginous steps ascend to each peak: to see both you must climb more than five hundred steps. The **eastern rock** is the higher, with a windy summit that affords excellent views over the lochs and mountains of the Firth of Clyde.

Regular **trains** run from Glasgow's Queen Street station to Dumbarton East and Dumbarton Central stations; the former gives best access to the castle and accommodation. The **tourist office** (daily: July & Aug 9.30am–6.30pm; June & Sept 10am–6pm; April, May & Oct 10am–5pm; ☎01389/742306) is situated a couple of miles east of town on the A82 and mainly caters for the vast number of car-bound tourists on their way to the Highlands.

Helensburgh

HELENSBURGH, twenty miles or so northwest of Glasgow, is a smart, Georgian grid-plan settlement laid out in an imitation of Edinburgh's New Town and overlooking the Clyde estuary. The inventor of TV, John Logie Baird, was born here, as was Charles Rennie Mackintosh, who in 1902 was commissioned by the Glaswegian publisher Walter Blackie to design **Hill House** on Upper Colquhoun Street (April–Oct daily 1.30–5.30pm; £7; NTS). Without doubt the best surviving example of Mackintosh's domestic architecture, the house is stamped with his very personal, elegant interpretation of Art Nouveau – right down to the light fittings and fire irons – characterized by his sparing use of colour and stylized floral patterns. The effect is occasionally overwhelming – it's difficult to imagine actually living in such an environment – yet it is precisely Mackintosh's attention to detail that makes the place so special.

Hill House is a good twenty-minute walk up Sinclair Street from Helensburgh Central **train** station, or just five minutes from Helensburgh Upper train station (where trains to and from Oban and Fort William stop). The local **tourist office** is on the ground floor of the old Italianate church tower by the Clyde (June–Sept daily 9.30am–6pm; April & May daily 10am–5pm; Oct Mon–Thurs 10am–4.30pm, Fri–Sun 10am–5pm; ☎01436/672642).

The Clyde valley

The journey southeast of Glasgow into Lanarkshire, while mostly following the course of the Clyde upstream, is dominated by endless suburbs, industrial parks and wide strips of concrete highway. The principal road here is the M74, though you'll have to get off the motorway to find the main points of interest, which tend to lie on or near the banks of the river. Less than ten miles from central Glasgow, **Bothwell Castle** lies about a mile northeast of the **Blantyre** millworkers' tenement in which the explorer David Livingstone was born. Five miles west of Blantyre, on the outskirts of the new town of East Kilbride, the **National Museum of Scottish Country Life**, set on a historic farm, offers an in-depth look at the history of agriculture in Scotland.

South of here, the Clyde winds past the sturdy little town of **Lanark**, probably the best base from which to explore the valley. **New Lanark**, on the riverbank, is a remarkable eighteenth-century planned village. Ten miles further upstream, the country town of **Biggar** is a pleasant spot with a surprising number of rather quirky museums, and marks the transition from the industrial central belt to rolling Border country.

Blantyre

BLANTYRE, now a colourless suburb of Hamilton, was a remote hamlet based around a mill on the banks of the Clyde when explorer and missionary David Livingstone was born there in 1813. First Bus's **bus** #267 from Glasgow (Buchanan St) to Hamilton runs via Blantyre, or there are frequent **trains** from Glasgow Central's lower level.

From Blantyre station, a right turn brings you through suburban housing to a quiet country park. The separate tenement block near the river, now painted a brilliant white, has been taken over by the **David Livingstone Centre** (April–Dec Mon–Sat 10am–5.30pm, Sun 12.30–5pm; £3.50; NTS), exploring his life, from his boyhood until his death in 1873 when he was searching for the source of the Nile. In 1813, the block consisted of 24 one-room tenements, each occupied by an entire family of millworkers. Today, the Livingstone family room shows the claustrophobic conditions under which he was brought up; all the others feature slightly defensive exhibitions on the missionary movement, with tableaux of scenes from his life in Africa, including his "discovery" of the Victoria Falls and the famous meeting of November 10, 1871, with Henry Stanley.

A mile or so north of Blantyre, **Bothwell Castle** (April–Sept daily 9.30am–6.30pm; Oct–March Mon–Wed & Sat 9.30am–4.30pm, Thurs 9.30am–12.30pm, Sun 2–4.30pm; £2.20; HS) is one of Scotland's most dramatic citadels, its great red-sandstone bulk looming high above a loop in the river. The oldest section is the solid donjon, or circular tower, at the western end, built by the Moray family in the late thirteenth century. Over the next two centuries, the castle changed hands numerous times and was added to by each successive owner, with the last section, the Great Hall, overlooking the grassy inner courtyard. Despite its jigsaw construction, today the overwhelming impression is of the near-impenetrable strength of the castle. First Bus operates **bus** #255 from Glasgow (Buchanan Street) to Hamilton, which will drop you off on the Bothwell Road near the castle entrance. By car, it's best approached from the B7071 Bothwell–Uddingston road.

National Museum of Scottish Country Life

On the edge of **EAST KILBRIDE** new town, five miles west of Blantyre and seven miles southeast of Glasgow centre, the **National Museum of Scottish**

Country Life (daily 10am–5pm; £3; NTS) is a slightly unexpected union of historic farm and modern museum. The site of the museum, **Kittochside**, is a 170-acre farm where traditional methods of farming can be observed. The custom-built, £6-million museum building on the edge of the farm has three principal sections: the **Land Gallery** is concerned with how Scots have used the land over centuries, and how the landscape has changed as a result; the **People Gallery** looks at the way of life for farmers and their families; and the **Tools Gallery**, occupying the large central hall, displays all kinds of farm equipment from early ploughs to a combine harvester. What really makes the museum, however, is its contextual setting. A tractor and trailer shuttles visitors the half-mile up to the eighteenth-century **farmhouse**. There are **paths** leading from here through the surrounding fields, and you're encouraged to wander, not just to get a sense of the wider farm, but also to see and experience the farm in use.

Transport isn't straightforward. If you don't have your own vehicle, **bus** #31 from Glasgow's St Enoch Centre to East Kilbride takes you past the museum, or you can get the **train** from Glasgow Central, and then take a taxi for the final three miles to the museum.

Lanark and New Lanark

The neat little market town of **LANARK** is an old and distinguished burgh, sitting in the purple hills high above the River Clyde, its rooftops and spires visible for miles around. Most people head straight on to the village of **NEW LANARK** (Ⓦ www.newlanark.org), a mile below the main town on Braxfield Road, whose importance as a centre of social and industrial innovation has recently been recognized by UNESCO, who include it on their list of World Heritage Sites.

Although New Lanark is served by an hourly **bus** from Lanark train station, it's well worth the steep downhill walk to get there. The first sight of the village, hidden away down in the gorge, is unforgettable: large broken curving walls of honeyed warehouses and tenements, built in Palladian style, are lined up along the turbulent river's edge. The community was founded by David Dale and Richard Arkwright in 1785 to harness the power of the Clyde waterfalls in their cotton-spinning industry, but it was Dale's son-in-law, Robert Owen, who revolutionized the social side of the experiment in 1798, creating a "village of unity". Believing the welfare of the workers to be crucial to industrial success, Owen built adult educational facilities, the world's first day nursery and playground, and schools in which dancing and music were obligatory and there was no punishment or reward.

While you're free to wander around the village, which rather unexpectedly for such a historic site is still partially residential, to get into any of the **exhibitions** (all daily 11am–5pm) you need to buy a passport ticket (£5.75; various discount tickets are available, including an all-in ticket covering admission and the return train and bus trip from Glasgow). The Neoclassical building now housing the visitor reception was opened by Owen in 1816 under the utopian title of **The Institute for the Formation of Character**. These days, it houses the **New Millennium Experience**, which whisks visitors on a chairlift through a social history of the village, conveying Robert Owen's vision not just for the idealized life at New Lanark, but also what he predicted for the year 2000.

Other parts of New Lanark village prove just as fascinating: everything, from the cooperative store to the workers' tenements and workshops, was built in an attempt to prove that industrialism need not be unaesthetic. You can wander through the 1820s shop, and find out how the workers lived in the **New Buildings**, then poke around the domestic kitchen, study and living areas of **Robert Owen's House**. In the **School for Children** there's a clever cinematic show giving an unsentimental picture of village life through the imaginary perspective of a young mill girl. Situated in the Old Dyeworks, the **Scottish Wildlife Trust Visitor Centre** (daily March–Dec 11am–5pm; Jan & Feb daily noon–4pm; free) provides information about the history and wildlife of the area. Beyond the visitor centre, a riverside path leads you the mile or so to the major **Falls of the Clyde**, where at the stunning tree-fringed Cora Linn, the river plunges 90ft in three tumultuous stages.

Practicalities

Lanark is the terminus of **trains** from Glasgow Central. The town's **tourist office** (May–Sept daily 10am–5pm; Oct–April Mon–Sat 10am–5pm; ☏01555/661661) is housed in the Horsemarket, next to Somerfields supermarket, 100 yards west of the station.

By far the most original **accommodation** options in the area, at both ends of the market, make use of reconstructed mill buildings in New Lanark: the SYHA **hostel** (☏01555/666710, ✉reservations@syha.org.uk) has two-, four- and five-bed rooms in the cutely named Wee Row on Rosedale Street, while the *New Lanark Mill* (☏01555/667200, ⓦwww.newlanark.org; ❻) is a four-star **hotel** with good views and lots of character.

Biggar and around

On the journey upstream, you leave industrial Lanarkshire behind and come instead into the gentle undulations of the Border hills. **BIGGAR**, twelve miles from Lanark, has the sense of being slightly adrift, formally in Lanarkshire but more a Border town, as close to Edinburgh as it is to Glasgow but with no strong connection to either. An old market town, Biggar has an inordinate number of museums; none could be described as essential, though each has its own quirky appeal. The most general is the **Moat Park Heritage Centre** (Easter to mid-Oct Mon–Sat 11am–4.30pm, Sun 2–4.30pm; £2), where the geological and archeological history of Upper Clydesdale is traced. Tucked in behind the High Street, the **Gladstone Court Museum** (Easter–Oct Mon–Sat 10.30am–5pm, Sun 2–5pm; £2) has a re-created street of Victorian shops, including a telephone exchange, bank and cobbler. Beside Biggar burn, **Biggar Gasworks Museum** (June–Sept daily 2–5pm; £1) has the appearance of a Lilliputian power station. Built in 1839, it is the only coal-based gasworks still standing; most were demolished in the 1970s when the North Sea gas grid was developed. Finally, on Broughton Road near the country park, is the bizarre **Puppet Museum** (Easter–Sept Tues–Sat 10am–4.30pm and also open on performance days; £2.50; call ☏01899/220631 or go to ⓦwww.purvespuppets.com for details of shows), which features marionettes from around the world, and stages regular workshops and shows in the Victorian theatre.

Regular **bus** services to Biggar arrive from a wide range of towns; from Lanark, take bus #191, but there are also services from Edinburgh, Peebles, Moffat, Dumfries and more. They stop on High Street, near the **tourist office** (May–Aug daily 10am–5pm, April & Sept Mon–Sat 10am–5pm; ☏01899/221066). There's a **B&B**, *Daleside*, a few doors down at 165 High St (☏01899/220097, ❷), and **camping** at *Biggar Caravan Park* on Broughton Road (☏01899/220319). For **food**, both the *Elphinstone Hotel* and the *Crown*, on High Street, serve up hearty pub grub.

Six miles west of Biggar along the A72/73, near the village of Thankerton, the solitary peak of **Tinto Hill**, or "hill of fire" was the site of Druidic festivals in honour of the sun-god Baal, or Bel. It's relatively easy to walk the footpath up to the 2320ft summit, from where the views are splendid – you'll also see a Druidic circle and a Bronze Age burial cairn on the summit. Regular **buses** between Biggar and Lanark stop at Thankerton.

Travel details

Buses

For information on all local and national bus services, contact Traveline ⓣ 0870/608 2608, ⓦ www.traveline.org.uk.

Glasgow Buchanan St to: Aberdeen (every 2hr; 3hr 20min); Aviemore (every 2hr; 3hr 30min); Campbeltown (3 daily; 4hr 20min); Dundee (hourly; 2hr 15min); Edinburgh (every 15min; 1hr 10min); Fort William (4 daily; 3hr); Glen Coe (4 daily; 2hr 30min); Inverness (every 2hr; 4–5hr); Kyle of Lochalsh (3 daily; 5hr); Lochgilphead (3 daily; 2hr 40min); Loch Lomond (hourly; 45min); London (5 daily; 7hr 30min); Newcastle upon Tyne (1 daily; 4hr); Oban (4 daily; 3hr); Perth (hourly; 1hr 35min); Pitlochry (every 2hr; 2hr 20min); Portree (3 daily; 6hr); Stirling (hourly; 45min); York (1 daily; 6hr 30min).

Trains

For information on all local and national rail services, contact National Rail Enquiries ⓣ 08457/484950, ⓦ www.nationalrail.co.uk.

Glasgow Central to: Ardrossan for Arran ferry (every 30min; 45min); Ayr (every 30min; 50min); Birmingham (5 daily; 3hr 50min); Blantyre (every 30min; 20min); Carlisle (hourly; 2hr 25min); Crewe (6 daily; 3hr 35min); East Kilbride (Mon–Sat every 30min; 30min); Gourock (every 30min; 50min); Greenock (every 30min; 40min); Hamilton (every 30min; 25min); Lanark (Mon–Sat hourly; 50min); Largs (hourly; 1hr); London (10 daily; 5hr 45min); Manchester (1 daily; 3hr 50min); Motherwell (every 20min; 30min); Paisley (every 15min; 10min); Queen's Park (every 15min; 6min); Stranraer (6 daily; 2hr 10min); Wemyss Bay (hourly; 55min); York (7 daily; 3hr 30min).

Glasgow Queen St to: Aberdeen (hourly; 2hr 35min); Aviemore (3 daily; 2hr 40min); Balloch (every 30min; 45min); Dumbarton (every 20min; 25min); Dundee (hourly; 1hr 20min); Edinburgh (every 15min; 50min); Fort William (Mon–Sat 3 daily, Sun 2 daily; 3hr 40min); Helensburgh (every 30min; 45min); Inverness (3 daily; 3hr 25min); Mallaig (Mon–Sat 3 daily, Sun 2 daily; 5hr 15min); Milngavie (every 30min; 22min); Oban (Mon–Fri 3 daily, Sat 4 daily, Sun 3 daily; 3hr); Perth (hourly; 1hr); Stirling (hourly; 30min).

Flights

Glasgow International to: Barra (Mon–Fri 2 daily; 1hr 5min); Islay (Mon–Fri 2 daily; 45min); Kirkwall (1 daily; 2hr); Lerwick (Mon–Fri 2 daily, Sat & Sun 1 daily; 2hr 30min); Tiree (Mon–Sat 1 daily; 50min); Stornoway (Mon–Sat 2 daily; 1hr 10min).

Central Scotland

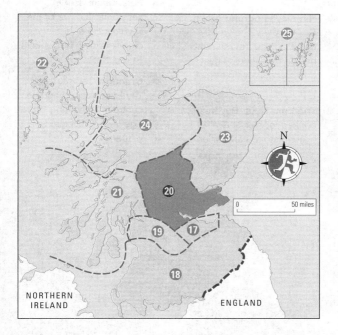

CHAPTER 20 **Highlights**

* **Stirling Castle** Scotland's finest castle – impregnable and highly explorable. See p.1055

* **The Trossachs** Pocket Highlands with shining lochs, wooded glens and noble peaks. See p.1064

* **Himalayas putting green, St Andrew's** The world's finest putting course right beside the world's finest golf course; a snip at just 80p to play. See p.1073

* **The East Neuk** Buy freshly cooked lobster at Crail's historic stone harbour or dine in style at the *Cellar* restaurant in Anstruther. See p.1074

* **Forth Rail Bridge** An icon of Victorian engineering spanning the Firth of Forth, stunningly floodlit at night. See p.1079

* **Folk music** Join in a session at the bar of the *Taybank Hotel* in the dignified town of Dunkeld. See p.1084

* **Crannog Centre, Loch Tay** Fascinating heritage centre investigating Bronze Age lake dwellings. See p.1086

△ Stirling Castle

20

Central Scotland

Central Scotland, the strip of mainland north of the densely populated Glasgow–Edinburgh axis and south of the main swathe of Highlands, is an accessible, popular and richly varied region. The Highland Boundary Fault, running southwest to northeast across the region, has rendered central Scotland the main stage for some of the most important events in Scottish history. Today the landscape is not only littered with remnants of the past – well-preserved medieval towns and castles, royal residences and battle sites – but also coloured by the many romantic myths and legends that have grown up around it.

Stirling, its imposing castle perched high above the town, was historically the most important bridging point across the River Forth, and from the castle battlements you can see the site of two of Scotland's most famous battlefield victories. Beyond Stirling are the fabled mountains, glens, lochs and forests of the **Trossachs**, often conveniently described as the Highlands-in-miniature for its taste of archetypal Scottish scenery. Popular for walking and, in particular, cycling, much of the Trossachs, together with the attractive islands and "bonnie banks" of **Loch Lomond**, form part of Scotland's first National Park, established in 2002.

In the eastern part of this central region, between the firths of Forth and Tay, lies the county of **Fife**, a Pictish kingdom which boasts a fascinating coastline sprinkled with historic fishing villages and sandy beaches, while on the North Sea fringe lies the historic university town of **St Andrews**, famous worldwide for its venerable golf courses and as the home of the game's governing body.

Occupying the same strategic position at the mouth of the River Tay as Stirling holds on the Forth, the ancient town of **Perth** has as much claim as anywhere to be the gateway to the Highlands. At nearby **Scone**, Kenneth Mcalpine established the capital of the kingdom of the Scots and the Picts in 846. When this settlement was washed away by floods in 1210, William the Lion founded Perth as a royal burgh and it stood as Scotland's capital until 1452. North and west of Perth, **Highland Perthshire** begins to show its charms: mighty woodlands blend with gorgeously rich scenery, particularly along the banks of the River Tay, leading to **Loch Tay**, overlooked by **Ben Lawers**, the area's tallest peak. Further north, the countryside becomes more sparsely populated and more spectacular, with some wonderful walking country, especially around **Pitlochry, Blair Atholl** and the wild expanses of **Rannoch Moor** to the west.

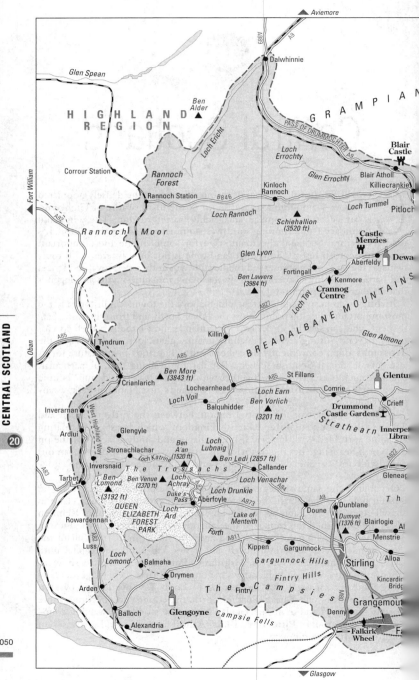

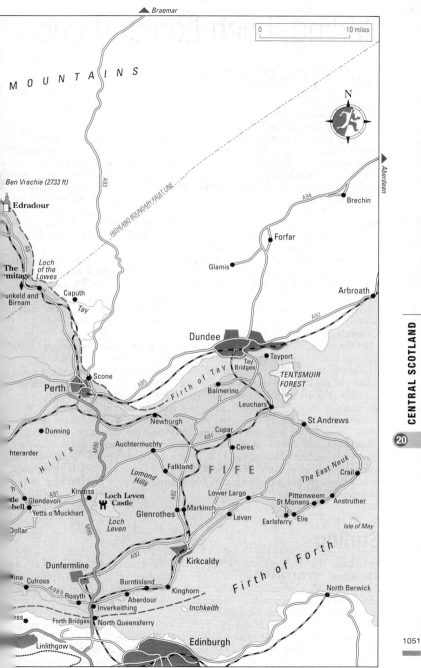

© Crown copyright

Stirling, Loch Lomond and the Trossachs

The central lowlands of Scotland, were, for several centuries, the most strategically important area in Scotland. In 1250, a map of Britain was compiled by Matthew Paris, a monk of St Albans, which depicted Scotland as two separate land masses connected only by the thin band of Stirling Bridge; although this was a figurative interpretation, Stirling was once the only gateway from the fertile central belt to the rugged, mountainous north. For long periods of Scotland's history, kings, queens, nobles, clan chiefs and soldiers wrestled for control of the area, and it's no surprise that today the landscape is not only littered with remnants of the past – preserved medieval towns and castles, royal residences and battle sites – but also coloured by the many romantic myths and legends that have grown up around it.

Lying at the heart of Scotland, **Stirling** and its fine castle, from where you can see both snowcapped Highland peaks and Edinburgh, is unmissable for anyone wanting to grasp the complexities of Scottish history. To the south of the city on the road to Edinburgh lies **Falkirk**, its industrial heritage now enlivened by the extraordinary Falkirk Wheel, while to the north are the fabled mountains, glens, lochs and forests of the **Trossachs**, stretching west from **Callander**.

On the western side of the region, **Loch Lomond** is the largest – and most romanticized – stretch of fresh water in Scotland. Now at the heart of the recently created Loch Lomond and the Trossachs **National Park**, the peerless scenery of the loch and its famously "bonnie banks" can be tainted by the sheer numbers of tourists and day-trippers who stream towards it in summer. It can get similarly clogged in the neighbouring Trossachs region, although, as with much of this area, there's plenty in the way of trips and attractions for families, as well as for those keen on **outdoor activities**: the area is traversed by the **Glasgow–Loch Lomond–Killin cycleway**; well managed forest tracks are ideal for mountain biking; the hills of the Trossachs provide great walking country; while the **West Highland Way**, Scotland's premier long-distance footpath, winds along the length of Loch Lomond up to Fort William in the Highlands.

Stirling

Straddling the River Forth a few miles upstream from the estuary at Kincardine, **STIRLING** appears at first glance like a smaller version of Edinburgh. With its crag-top castle, steep, cobbled streets and mixed community of locals, students and tourists, it's an appealing place, though it lacks the cosmopolitan edge of its larger neighbours.

Stirling was the scene of some of the most significant developments in the evolution of the Scottish nation. It was here that the Scots under William Wallace defeated the English at the **Battle of Stirling Bridge** in 1297, only to fight – and win again – under Robert the Bruce just a couple of miles away at the **Battle of Bannockburn** in 1314. Stirling enjoyed its golden age in the fifteenth to seventeenth centuries, most notably when its castle was the favoured residence of the Stuart monarchy and the setting for the coronation in 1543 of the young Mary, future Queen of Scots. By the early eighteenth century the town was again besieged, its location being of strategic importance during the Jacobite rebellions of 1715 and 1745.

Today Stirling is known for its **castle** – arguably the best in Scotland, and certainly as atmospheric and explorable as Edinburgh's – and the lofty **Wallace Monument**, a mammoth Victorian monolith high on Abbey Craig to the northeast which has become a place of pilgrimage for admirers both of William Wallace and of Mel Gibson's Oscar-winning film epic *Braveheart*, based loosely on Wallace's life.

Arrival and information

The **train station** is near the centre of town on Station Road, near the **bus station** on Goosecroft Road. Stirling's **tourist office** is very near the town centre at 41 Dumbarton Rd (July & Aug Mon–Sat 9am–7.30pm, Sun 9.30am–6.30pm; June & Sept Mon–Sat 9am–6pm, Sun 10am–4pm; April & May Mon–Sat 9am–5pm; Oct Mon–Sat 9.30am–5pm; Nov–March Mon–Fri 10am–5pm, Sat 10am–4pm; ☎01786/475019, ⓦwww.scottish.heartlands.org). Because of Stirling's compact size – barely five miles from the centre to the outermost fringes – sightseeing in the Old Town is best done **on foot**, though to avoid the steep hills or to reach the more distant attractions you can take the hop-on hop-off City Sightseeing **bus tours** (every half-hour April–Oct 9.30am–4.30pm; £7.50) which take a circular route around the bus and train stations, Bannockburn, the castle, Bridge of Allan, the university and Wallace Monument.

Accommodation

Between May and October, it's worth booking **accommodation** as far in advance as possible. Stirling has good options in most categories, from backpacker hostels to large hotels, and is understandably popular both as a lower-key alternative to Glasgow or Edinburgh, and as a base for exploring central Scotland. For a fee, the tourist office will help you find somewhere to stay.

Hotels and B&Bs

Castlecroft Ballengeich Road ☎01786/474933, ⓦwww.castlecroft.uk.com. Modern guest house with six en-suite rooms on the site of the King's Stables just beneath the castle rock, with terrific views north and west. ➋

No. 10 10 Gladstone Place ☎01786/472681, ⓦwww.cameron-10.co.uk. Modernized Victorian home with neat, uncluttered decor providing friendly and pleasant B&B accommodation close to the city centre. ➋

The Portcullis Castle Wynd ☎01786/472290, ⓦwww.theportcullishotel.com. Traditional hotel with rooms in an imposing two-hundred-year-old building with a dramatic Old Town location adjacent the castle. Cosy bar and beer garden. ➎

Victoria Square 11 Victoria Square 01786/475545, ⓦwww.xivictoriasquare.com.

The most stylish B&B in town with designer rooms, upmarket breakfasts and great views of the old town. ➎

Hostels and campsite

Willy Wallace Independent Hostel, 77 Murray Place ☎01786/446773, ⓦwww.willywallacehostel.com. Welcoming, friendly place with a big, bright common room, six dorms, a double and a twin (both ➊).

SYHA hostel St John Street ☎0870/004 1149, ⓔreservations@syha.org.uk. Housed in a converted church with an impressive 1824 Palladian facade, this place is modern and a little lacking in character, but all rooms have showers and toilets en suite.

Witches Craig Campsite Blairlogie, three miles east off the A91 road to St Andrews ☎01786/474947. Open April–Oct.

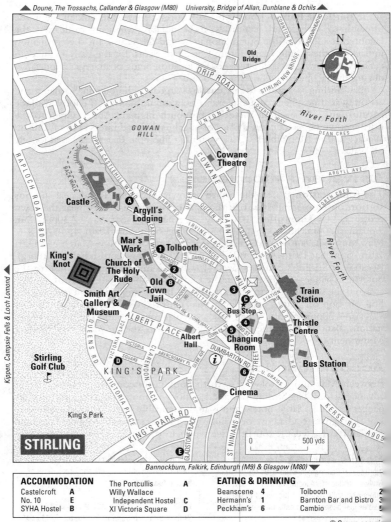

ACCOMMODATION				EATING & DRINKING			
Castelcroft	A	The Portcullis	A	Beanscene	4	Tolbooth	2
No. 10	E	Willy Wallace		Hermann's	1	Barnton Bar and Bistro	3
SYHA Hostel	B	Independent Hostel	C	Peckham's	6	Cambio	5
		XI Victoria Square	D				

© Crown copyright

The Town

Stirling evolved from the top down, starting with its castle and gradually spreading south and east onto the low-lying flood plain. At the centre of the original **Old Town**, Broad Street was the main thoroughfare, with St John Street running more or less parallel, and St Mary's Wynd forming part of the original route to Stirling Bridge below. In the eighteenth and nineteenth centuries, as the threat of attack decreased, the centre of commercial life crept down towards the River Forth, with the modern town growing on the edge of the plain over which the castle has traditionally stood guard.

Stirling Castle

Stirling Castle (daily 9.30am–6pm; Oct–March closes 5pm; £7.50, includes entry to Argyll's Lodging; HS) must have presented would-be invaders with a formidable challenge. Its impregnability is most daunting when you approach the town from the west, from where the sheer 250ft drop down the side of the crag is most obvious. The rock was first fortified during the Iron Age, though what you see now dates largely from the fifteenth and sixteenth centuries. Built on many levels, the main buildings are interspersed with delightful gardens and patches of lawn, while endless battlements, cannon ports, hidden staircases and other nooks and crannies make it thoroughly explorable and inspiring.

From the Esplanade, cross a bridge over the grassy moat to Guardroom Square, where you can join a **guided tour** (free), which leaves every hour on the hour. From here, head up through the much-modified but still imposing **Forework**, designed by James IV to underline his romantic view of royal authority. Through the archway is the **Outer Close**, the first of two main courtyard areas. Looming over it is the magnificently restored **Great Hall**, dating from 1501–3 and used as a barracks by the British army until 1964. The building stands out not just in the courtyard but across Stirling for its controversially bright, creamy yellow cladding. Inside, the hall has been restored to its original state as the finest medieval secular building in Scotland, complete with five gaping fireplaces and an impressive hammerbeam ceiling of rough-hewn wood. To one side of the Great Hall, displays in the restored castle **kitchens** make a lively attempt to re-create the preparations for the spectacular Renaissance banquet given by Mary, Queen of Scots for the baptism of her son, the future James VI.

The exterior of the **Palace**, the largest building in the castle, dates from 1540–42 and is richly decorated with grotesque carved figures and Renaissance sculpture, including, in the left-hand corner, the glaring bearded figure of James V in the dress of a commoner. Inside in the royal apartments are the **Stirling Heads**, 56 elegantly carved oak medallions which once comprised the ceiling of the Presence Chamber, where visitors were presented to royalty. Otherwise the royal apartments are mostly bare, their emptiness emphasizing the fine dimensions and wonderful views.

On the opposite side of the Inner Close, the sloping upper courtyard of the castle, the **Chapel Royal** was built in 1594 by James VI for the baptism of his son, to replace an earlier chapel that was deemed insufficiently impressive. The interior is lovely, with a seventeenth-century fresco of elaborate scrolls and patterns. Alongside, the **King's Old Building**, at the highest point in the castle, now houses the museum of the Argyll and Sutherland Highlanders regiment, with its collection of well-polished silver and memorabilia. Go through a narrow passageway between the King's Old Building and the Chapel Royal to get to the **Douglas Gardens**, reputedly the place where the eighth earl of Douglas, suspected of treachery, was thrown to his death by James II in 1452. It's a lovely, quiet corner of the castle, with mature trees and battlements over which there are splendid views of the rising Highlands beyond, as well as a bird's-eye view down to the **King's Knot**, a series of grassed octagonal mounds which in the seventeenth century were planted with box trees and ornamental hedges.

The Old Town

Leaving the castle, head downhill into the old centre of Stirling, fortified behind the massive, whinstone boulders of the **town walls**, built in the first half of the sixteenth century and intended to ward off the advances of Henry

CENTRAL SCOTLAND | Stirling

20

VIII, who had set his sights on the young Mary, Queen of Scots as a wife for his son, Edward. The walls now constitute some of the best-preserved town defences in Scotland, and can be traced by following the path known as **Back Walk**. This circular walkway was built in the eighteenth century and in the upper reaches encircles the castle, taut along the edge of the crag. Though a little overgrown in places, it's a great way to take in the castle's setting, and in various places you'll catch panoramic views of the surrounding countryside.

At the top of Castle Wynd, **Argyll's Lodging** (daily: April–Sept 9.30am–6pm; Oct–March 9.30am–5pm; £7.50 includes entry to Stirling Castle; HS) is a romantic Renaissance mansion built by Sir William Alexander of Menstrie. The oldest part of the building, marked by low ceilings and tiny windows, is the Great Kitchen, whose enormous fireplace comes complete with a special recess for salt, while the Drawing Room, hung with lavishly decorated purple tapestries, contains the ninth earl's imposing chair of state.

Further down Castle Wynd at the top of Broad Street, a richly decorated facade hides the dilapidated **Mar's Wark**, a would-be palace which the first earl of Mar, regent of Scotland and hereditary Keeper of Stirling Castle, started in 1570. Behind here is the **Church of the Holy Rude** (May–Sept Mon–Sat 10am–5pm), a fine medieval structure, the oldest parts of which, including the impressive oak hammerbeam ceiling, date from the early fifteenth century. A short walk down St John Street, a sweeping driveway leads up to the impressive **Old Town Jail** (April–Sept actor-led tours daily 10am–5pm; Oct–March self-guided tours Mon–Fri 10am–5pm, actor-led tours Sat & Sun 11.30am–3pm; £5), built by Victorian prison reformers as an alternative to the depravity of the medieval Tolbooth. Telling the history of the building and prisons in general, tours are brought to life by enthusiastic actors who change costumes and character a number of times. Take the glass lift up to the prison roof to admire spectacular views across Stirling and the Forth Valley.

Directly opposite the Old Town Jail, between St John Street and Broad Street, is the original medieval prison, the **Tolbooth**, itself brought back from dereliction in the form of the city's brand-new arts centre (℡01786/274000, Ⓦwww.stirling.gov.uk). Originally built in 1705, the striking modern redevelopment incorporates three separate medieval buildings, and incorporates an airy café-bar, a restaurant for evening dining (see opposite), a top-floor viewing platform looking out over the Old Town rooftops, and a box office where you can find out about the centre's diverse programme incorporating comedy, theatre, touring bands and the occasional festival.

The Lower Town

The further downhill you go in Stirling's Lower Town, the more recent the buildings become. Stirling's main **shopping** area is down here, along Port Street and Murray Place. The only other sight of note in the centre is the **Smith Art Gallery and Museum** (Tues–Sat 10.30am–5pm, Sun 2–5pm; free), a short walk west up Dumbarton Road near the King's Knot. It houses "The Stirling Story", a reasonably entertaining whirl through the history of the town, balancing out the stories of kings and queens with more social and domestic history.

The National Wallace Monument

Located to the north of Stirling, near the university and on the road to the village of Bridge of Allan, the prominent **National Wallace Monument** (daily: March–May 10am–5pm; June 10am–6pm; July & Aug 9.30am–6.30pm; Sept 9.30am–5pm; Oct 10am–5pm; Nov–Feb 10.30am–4pm; £5) is a free-standing, five-storey tower built in the 1860s as a tribute to Sir William Wallace, the freedom fighter who led Scottish resistance to Edward I, the "Hammer of the Scots", in the late thirteenth century. A hero to generations of Scots, Wallace shot to international fame on the back of his depiction by Mel Gibson in the epic movie *Braveheart*. Though derided for its historical inaccuracies, the film was hugely popular not just in Scotland but around the world, and with the general lack of historic buildings closely associated with Wallace, the monument has become a focus for Wallace (and *Braveheart*) fans. The crag on which it is set was the scene of Wallace's greatest victory, when he sent his troops charging down the hillside onto the plain to defeat the English at the Battle of Stirling Bridge in 1297. Exhibits inside the tower include Wallace's long steel sword and a life-size "talking" model of the hero. If you can manage the climb – up 246 spiral steps – there are superb views across to Fife and Ben Lomond from the top of the 220ft tower.

Bannockburn

A couple of miles south of Stirling centre, all but surrounded by suburban housing, the **Bannockburn Heritage Centre** (daily: April–Oct 10am–5.30pm; Feb–March & Nov–Dec 10.30am–4pm; £3.50; NTS) commemorates the most famous battle in Scottish history, when King Robert the Bruce won his mighty victory over the English at the **Battle of Bannockburn** on June 24, 1314. It was this battle, the climax of the Wars of Independence, which united the Scots under Bruce and led to independence from England sealed by the Declaration of Arbroath (1320) and the Treaty of Northampton (1328).

The now slightly dated centre shows an audiovisual presentation on the battle and the background to it, highlighting the brilliantly innovative tactics Bruce employed in mustering his army to defeat a much larger English force. Outside is a stirring equestrian **statue** of Bruce, set against the skyline of Stirling Castle. The actual site of the main battle is, oddly, still a matter of debate. Most agree that it didn't take place near the present visitor centre; the most cogent theory argues that it took place on a boggy carse a mile or so to the west. Bus #52 leaves for Bannockburn from Murray Place every half-hour.

Eating

Stirling doesn't have a strong reputation for its **restaurants**, with venues struggling to hang around long enough to earn a good name. In the neighbouring village of **Bridge of Allan**, knowledgeable foodies head straight for *Clive Ramsay* delicatessen at 28 Henderson Street (the main street), one of the best delis in Scotland which also has a great **café** (daily 8am–late) serving everything from breakfast through to table d'hôte dinners at night.

Barnton Bar and Bistro Barnton St. Popular local bar with a hearty menu of pub staples and an upbeat attitude. Moderate.

Beanscene 40 King St. Open daily 8am–11pm for relaxed coffees, pastries and tapas snacks. Inexpensive.

Hermann's Broad St ☎01786/450632. Set in the historic Mar Place House towards the top of the Old Town, with a downstairs brasserie open at lunchtime and upmarket Austrian-Scottish dining in the evening. Expensive.

Peckham's 52 Port St ☎01786/463222. Accomplished bistro, attached to a late-opening deli, serving a good range of pleasant modern dishes.

Tolbooth Tolbooth Arts Centre, Jail Wynd, ☎01786/274010. A beautiful panelled dining room in the arts hub serving stylish contemporary dishes with decent early dining deals. Moderate.

Nightlife and entertainment

Nightlife in Stirling revolves around **pubs** and **bars** and is dominated by the student population. The lively *Barnton Bar and Bistro* serves a good selection of beers and food in a setting of wrought-iron and marble tables. The hipper modern bars in town include *Cambio*, located in an old bank at 1 Corn Exchange Place. If you're looking for **live music**, the Tolbooth (☎01786/274000) is the venue for gigs by local and touring folk, rock and jazz acts. The main venue for **theatre** and **film** is the excellent MacRobert Arts Centre (☎01786/466666, ⊛www.macrobert.org) on the university campus, which shows a good selection of drama plus mainstream and art-house films.

Around Stirling

Stirling's strategic position between the Highlands and Lowlands was not only important in medieval times, but as the Industrial Revolution grew across Scotland's central belt so the town's proximity to the Forth gave it renewed significance. To the north and west of Stirling, the historic aspect of the region is reflected in the cathedral at **Dunblane**, the imposing castle at **Doune** and the sedate settlements of the **Carse of Stirling**, while to the east and south, on either side of the Forth, the **Clackmannanshire** mill towns and the area around **Falkirk** tell of a rich industrial heritage. An undoubted highlight of this hinterland is the massive **Falkirk Wheel**, a spectacular feat of modern engineering that transfers canal boats up and down a 100-foot drop at the interchange of the newly restored Forth and Clyde and Union canals.

Dunblane and Doune

Frequent trains, bus #58 (and bus #358 in school term-time) make the journey four miles north of Stirling to **DUNBLANE**, a small, attractive place which has been an important ecclesiastical centre since the seventh century, when the Celts founded the church of St Blane here. The town prefers to put the more recent past gently to one side, Dunblane having witnessed a horrific massacre in March 1996 when Thomas Hamilton entered a local primary school and shot dead fifteen children and their teacher before turning the gun on himself. Scene of an intensely moving memorial service following the killings, **Dunblane Cathedral** (April–Sept Mon–Sat 9.30am–6.30pm, Sun 1–6.30pm; Oct–March Mon–Sat 9.30am–4.30pm, Sun 2–4.30pm; free; HS) dates mainly from the thirteenth century, and restoration work carried out a century ago has returned it to its Gothic splendour. Inside, note the delicate blue-purple stained glass, and the exquisitely carved pews, screen and choir stalls, all crafted in the early twentieth century. The cathedral stands serenely amid a clutch of old buildings, among them the seventeenth-century Dean's House, which houses the small **Dunblane Museum** (May to early Oct Mon–Sat 10.30am–4.30pm; free) with exhibits on local history.

DOUNE, eight miles northwest of Stirling and three miles due west of Dunblane, is a sleepy village with a violent past. The fourteenth-century **castle** (April–Sept daily 9.30am–6.30pm; Oct–March Mon–Wed & Sat 9.30am–4.30pm, Thurs 9.30am–1pm, Fri & Sun 2–4.30pm; £2.80; HS) is marvellous semi-ruin standing on a small hill in a bend of the River Teith. The castle's greatest claim to fame today, however, is as the setting for the 1970 movie *Monty Python and the Holy Grail*. Close to the castle, **accommodatio**

is available at the excellent *Glenardoch House*, Castle Road (℡01786/841489; ❸), an eighteenth-century country-house B&B with two comfortable en-suite rooms and a beautiful riverside garden.

Falkirk and around

Southeast of Stirling along the south bank of the widening Forth Estuary, farmland gives way to industry, notably BP's gargantuan petrochemical plant nearby at Grangemouth. The lights and fires of the refineries are spectacular at night, and inspired Bertrand Tavernier to make his dour 1979 sci-fi film *Death Watch* in Scotland. Strangely, given its nondescript industrial surroundings, **FALKIRK** – located about halfway between Stirling and Edinburgh on the M9 motorway – has a good deal of visible history, going right back to the remains of the Roman Antonine Wall. It was also the site of two major battles, one in 1298, when William Wallace's army fell victim to the English under Edward I, and the other in 1746, when Bonnie Prince Charlie's disintegrating force, retreating northwards, sent the Hanoverians packing in one of its last victories. Traditionally a livestock centre, Falkirk became better known for its industry, with the founding in 1759 of the now-redundant Carron Ironworks which manufactured "carronades" (small cannons) for Nelson's fleet. The town was further transformed later in the eighteenth century by the construction of first the Forth and Clyde Canal, allowing easy access to Glasgow and the west coast, and then the Union Canal, which continued the route through to Edinburgh. Just twenty years later, the trains arrived, and the canals gradually fell into disuse.

The icon of British Waterways' £84.5 million **Millennium Link** project to restore the canals and re-establish a navigable link between east and west coasts is the remarkable **Falkirk Wheel** (Ⓦwww.thefalkirkwheel.co.uk), two miles west of Falkirk town centre. Opened in 2002, the giant grey wheel, the world's first rotating boat lift, scoops boats in two giant buckets, or caissons, the 115 feet between the level of the two canals. Previously, boats transferring between the Union and Forth and Clyde canals had to negotiate an exhausting flight of eleven locks, which could take a full day to complete. The modern solution was this unique structure, built in concrete and steel and capable of lifting some 600 tonnes of water extremely efficiently. A **visitor centre** (daily 9am–5pm; free) is located right underneath the wheel, and this is where to head for background information and to buy tickets for a **boat trip** (£8), which involves a 40-minute journey from the lower basin into the wheel, along the Union Canal for a short distance, then back down to the basin again via the wheel.

Practicalities

Falkirk's centrally located **bus** station is at Callender Riggs. Regular **trains** run from Edinburgh to Stirling via Falkirk **Grahamston Station**, while Falkirk **High Station**, which is further from the centre, is a stop on the Edinburgh–Glasgow line. From Grahamston Station it's a five-minute walk to the **tourist office**, 2–4 Glebe St (June–Oct daily 9.30am–6pm; April & May daily 9.30am–5pm; Nov–March Mon–Sat 10am–4pm; ℡01324/620244). The town has a good selection of decent places to **eat** and **drink**. *Comma Bar Café*, 4 Lint Riggs, is a brasserie-style café and trendy bar, while *Behind the Wall*, 14 Melville St, serves real ales and Tex-Mex-style food.

Around Falkirk

Unlikely as it might seem, **BONNYBRIDGE**, a largely nondescript settlement five miles west of Falkirk, claims more UFO sightings than anywhere else in

Britain. Quite what attracts aliens to the area is a puzzle, as the only notable draw hereabouts is **Rough Castle**, one of the forts set up, at two-mile intervals, to defend the entire length of the Roman **Antonine Wall**. The most northerly frontier of the Roman Empire, it was built in 142 AD of turf rather than stone, stretching for 37 miles right across the country from the Forth to the Clyde. The signposted site lies along a pot-holed back road, and though little more than a large grassy mound interpreted by a couple of information boards, the remains at Rough Castle are the best-preserved part of the Antonine Wall. If you're interested in tracking down further parts of the wall, pick up the factsheet available at Falkirk tourist office.

The Ochil Hills

The rugged **Ochil Hills** stretch for roughly forty miles northeast of Stirling, forming a steep-faced range which drops down to the flood plain of the Forth Valley and is sliced by a series of deep-cut, richly wooded glens. Tucked up against the southern slopes of the Ochils is a string of settlements known as the **Hillfoot villages**, which have been at the centre of Scotland's wool production for centuries, rivalled only by the Borders. By the mid-nineteenth century there were more than thirty mills in the tiny county of **Clackmannanshire**, a fifteen-mile stretch between the Ochils and the banks of the Forth, though recent times have seen the old family firms and hand-knitters unable to compete with modern technology. The main highlights here are **Castle Campbell** at Dollar, an atmospheric spot with some great walks nearby, and **Kinross**, on the shores of Loch Leven, where you can take a boat out to wander round the ruins of a castle in which Mary, Queen of Scots was once imprisoned.

Dollar and around

Nestling in a fold of the Ochils on the northern bank of the small River Devon, affluent **DOLLAR** is known for its Academy, founded in 1820 and now one of Scotland's most respected private schools. Above the town, the dramatic chasm of **Dollar Glen** is commanded by **Castle Campbell** (April–Sept daily 9.30am–6.30pm; Oct–March Mon–Wed & Sat 9.30am–4.30pm, Thurs 9.30am–noon, Sun 2–4.30pm; £3; HS), formerly, and still unofficially, known as Castle Gloom – a fine and evocative tag but, prosaically, a derivation of "Gloume", an old Gaelic name. There are a series of marked **walks** around the glen, taking in mossy crags, rushing streams and, if you strike out on the three-hour hike to the top of Dollar Hill, great views.

The castle came into the hands of the Campbells in 1481, who changed its name from Castle Gloom in 1489. In 1654 the castle was burnt by Cromwell's troops; the remains of a graceful seventeenth-century loggia and a roofless hall bear witness to the destruction. You can also walk round the roof of the tower, where there's a wonderful vista of the hills behind the castle, and down the glen to Dollar.

Kinross and Loch Leven

Although by no means a large place, **KINROSS**, ten miles east of Dollar, ha been transformed in the last couple of decades by the construction of the nearby M90 Edinburgh–Perth motorway. The old village is still there, at the southern end of the main street, but apart from the views of Loch Leven it charm has been eroded by amorphous splodges of modern housing, which threaten to nudge it into the loch itself.

Without doubt the most attractive part of Kinross is by the shores of trout-filled **Loch Leven**, signposted from the main street. In recent years the loch has become a National Nature Reserve and as well as some interesting birds, including visiting geese and various types of duck, you'll almost always find a number of fishermen casting from small boats. From the shore a small ferry chugs over to an island on which stands the ruined fourteenth-century **Loch Leven Castle** (April–Sept daily 9.30am–last ferry 5.15pm; Oct Mon, Wed, Thurs, Sat & Sun 9.30am–last ferry 3.15pm; £3.50; HS), where Mary, Queen of Scots was imprisoned for eleven months in 1567–68. This isn't the only island fortress Mary spent time in, and it's easy to imagine the isolation of the tragic queen, who is believed to have miscarried twins while here. She managed to charm the 18-year-old son of Lady Douglas into helping her escape: he stole the castle keys, secured a boat in which to row ashore, locked the castle gates behind them and threw the keys into the loch – from where they were retrieved three centuries later.

Loch Lomond

The largest stretch of fresh water in Britain (23 miles long and up to five miles wide), **Loch Lomond** is the epitome of Scottish scenic splendour, thanks in large part to the ballad that fondly recalls its "bonnie, bonnie banks". The song was said to be have been written by a Jacobite prisoner captured by the English, who, sure of his fate, wrote that his spirit would return to Scotland on the low road much faster than his living compatriots on the high road. However, all is not so bonnie at the loch nowadays, especially on its busy western banks around **Balloch** and **Luss**, which are mobbed by tour coaches and day-trippers from Glasgow, just twenty or so miles away. The upgraded A82 no longer meanders along the lochside, but speeds traffic past giving only the occasional glimpse across the water. Very different in tone, the eastern side of the loch operates at a different pace with wooden ferryboats pottering out to a scattering of tree-covered islands off the village of **Balmaha**.

Balloch

The main settlement on Loch Lomond is **BALLOCH**, at the southwestern corner of the loch, where the water channels into the River Leven for its short journey south to the sea in the Firth of Clyde. Surrounded by housing estates and overstuffed with undistinguished guest houses, Balloch has few redeeming features, but its accessibility from Glasgow by both car and train ensured that it was chosen as the focal point of the new national park with the siting of a huge multifaceted development, **Loch Lomond Shores** (Ⓦwww.lomondshores.com). Signposted from miles around, the complex contains the **National Park Gateway Centre** (daily 10am–5pm, extended hours in the summer; ☎01389/722199), which has background on the park and other tourist information, a "retail crescent" of shops including a branch of Edinburgh's venerable department store *Jenners*, and the **Drumkinnon Tower** (daily: April–Oct 10am–6pm; Nov–March 11am–4pm; free), a striking, stone-built, cylindrical building which houses a giant-screen auditorium where films about the natural and cultural history of the area are shown (£4.95). The tower's top-floor lookout post (£2) and viewing gallery café gaze out over the loch to Ben Lomond.

20

Balloch's **train station** is in the town centre, right beside the river. Opposite is a small **tourist office** (daily: July & Aug 9.30am–6pm; June & Sept 9.30am–5.30pm; April, May & Oct 10am–5pm; ☎01389/753533) – a larger office can be found at the Loch Lomond Shores Gateway Centre (see above). There's really little point in basing yourself in Balloch, although there are one or two more appealing options on the outskirts, including one of Scotland's most impressive SYHA **hostels** (☎0870/004 1136, ✉reservation @syha.org.uk; April–Oct): the grand country house with turrets, stained-glass windows and walled gardens lies two miles northwest of Balloch train station, just off the A82; you can either walk there from Balloch, or if you're travelling by bus, ask the driver to drop you off close by. Also on the western side of Balloch is *Sheildaig Farm* (☎01389/752459, Ⓦwww.sheildaigfarm.co.uk; ❸), a pleasant **B&B** with a good restaurant. In Balloch itself there's the year-round *Lomond Woods Holiday Park*, beside Lomond Shores (☎01389/755000, Ⓦwww.holiday-parks.co.uk), an excellent campsite that also rents out **bikes**.

At Loch Lomond Shores there are various daytime **eating** options, including the viewing gallery café at the top of Drumkinnon Tower; in the evening, a restaurant operates in the Great Hall of the tower on Fri & Sat night only (bookings required ☎01389/722416), while *Mesón del Lago*, situated above in the retail crescent with a balcony overlooking the loch, serves drinks and tapas. In Balloch itself, the *Tullie Inn*, next to the train station, is a reliable bet for pub grub.

The eastern shore

The tranquil **eastern shore** is far better for walking and appreciating the loch's natural beauty than the overcrowded western side. The dead-end B837 from Drymen will take you halfway up the east bank, as far as you can get by car or bus, while the West Highland Way sticks close to the shore for the entire length of the loch, beginning at the tiny lochside settlement of **BALMAHA**, which stands on the Highland Boundary Fault, the geological fault that separates the Highlands from the Lowlands. If you stand on the viewpoint above the pier, you can see the fault line clearly marked by the series of woody islands that form giant stepping stones across the loch. Many of the loch's 37 islands are privately owned, and rather quaintly an old wooden mail boat still delivers post to four of them. It's possible to join the mail boat cruise, which is run by MacFarlane & Son from the jetty at Balmaha (May, June & Sept Mon, Thurs & Sat; July & Aug Mon–Sat 11.30am, returns 2pm; Oct–April Mon & Thurs 10.50am, return noon; £7; ☎01360/870214; Ⓦwww.balmahaboatyard.co.uk). The same company offers boat hire and fishing, and runs a ferry service to Inchcailleach, where you can walk the length of the island on a Nature Trail.

Beside Balmaha's large car park is a **National Park Centre** (daily April–May & Oct 10am–5pm; June & Sept 10am–6pm; July & Aug 10am–7pm), where you can find out about local forest walks. You can **stay** at the well-run *Oak Tree Inn* (☎01360/870357, Ⓦwww.oak-tree-inn.co.uk; ❸) there's also a convivial pub and all-day food served here.

Public transport ends at Balmaha, but another seven miles north through the woods brings you to the end of the road at **ROWARDENNAN**, a scattered settlement, below Ben Lomond. Passenger ferries (Easter–Sept 2 daily) cross between Inverbeg and Rowardennan, where **accommodation** is available at the *Rowardennan Hotel* (☎01360/870273, Ⓦwww.rowardennanhotel.com; ❺) and, half a mile beyond, at a wonderfully situated SYHA **hostel** (☎0870/00 1148, ✉reservations@syha.org.uk; March–Oct), a classic Scottish stone-built lodge with lawns running down to the loch shore.

Opened in 1980, the spectacular **West Highland Way** was Scotland's first long-distance footpath, stretching some 95 miles from Milngavie (pronounced "mill-guy"), six miles north of central Glasgow, to Fort William, where it reaches the foot of Ben Nevis, Britain's highest mountain. Today, it is by far the most popular such footpath in Scotland, and while for many the range of scenery, relative ease of walking and nearby facilities make it a classic route, others find it a little too busy in high season, particularly in comparison with the relative isolation which can be found in many other parts of the Highlands.

The route follows a combination of ancient **drove roads**, along which Highlanders herded their cattle and sheep to market in the lowlands, military roads built by troops to control the Jacobite insurgence in the eighteenth century, old coaching roads and disused railway lines. In addition to the stunning scenery, which is increasingly dramatic as the path heads north, walkers may see some of Scotland's rarer **wildlife**, including red deer and, soaring over the highest peaks, golden eagles.

Passing through the lowlands north of Glasgow, the route runs along the eastern shores of Loch Lomond, over the Highland Boundary Fault Line, then round Crianlarich, crossing open heather moorland across the **Rannoch Moor** wilderness area. It passes close to **Glen Coe**, notorious for the massacre of the MacDonald clan, before reaching **Fort William**. Apart from a stretch between Loch Lomond and Bridge of Orchy, when the path is within earshot of the main road, this is wild, remote country: north of Rowardennan on Loch Lomond, the landscape is increasingly exposed, and you should be well prepared for sudden and extreme weather changes.

Though this is emphatically not the most strenuous of Britain's long-distance walks – it passes between lofty mountain peaks, rather than over them – a moderate degree of fitness is required as there are some steep ascents. If you're looking for an added challenge, you could work a climb of Ben Lomond or Ben Nevis into your schedule. You might choose to walk individual sections of the Way (the eight-mile climb from Glen Coe up the Devil's Staircase is particularly spectacular), but to tackle the whole thing you need to set aside at least seven days; avoid a Saturday start from Milngavie and you'll be less likely to be walking with hordes of people, and there'll be less pressure on accommodation. Most walkers tackle the route from south to north, and manage between ten and fourteen miles a day, staying at hotels, B&Bs and bunkhouses en route. Camping is permitted at recognized sites.

Although the path is clearly waymarked, you may want to check one of the many maps or guidebooks published: the **official guide**, published by Mercat Press (£14.99), includes a fold-out map as well as descriptions of the route, with detailed cultural, historical, archeological and wildlife information. Further details about the Way, including an accommodation list, can be found at ⓦwww.west-highland-way.co.uk, which has comprehensive accommodation listings as well as links to tour companies and transport providers, who can take your luggage from one stopping point to the next.

The western shore of Loch Lomond

Despite the roar of traffic hurtling along the A82, the **west bank** of Loch Lomond is an undeniably beautiful stretch of water and gives better views of the loch's wooded islands and surrounding peaks than the heavily wooded east side. **LUSS**, setting for the Scottish TV soap *High Road*, is without doubt the prettiest village in the region, with its prim, identical sandstone and slate cottages garlanded in rambling roses, and its narrow sandy, pebbly strand. However, its charms are no secret, and its streets and beach can become unbearably crowded in summer. There's a **National Park Centre** (April–May & Oct daily 10am–5pm; June & Sept daily 10am–6pm; July & Aug daily 10am–7pm; Oct–Dec Sat & Sun 10am–5pm) adjacent to the massive village car park, which is often choked with coaches, busking bagpipers and souvenir stalls.

Seventeen miles north at **TARBET**, the West Highland **train** – the line from Glasgow to Fort William and Mallaig, with a branch line to Oban – reaches the shoreline at the point where the A83 heads off west into Argyll; the A82 continues north along the banks of the loch towards Crianlarich. Tarbet has a small **tourist office** (July & Aug 9.30am–6pm; April–June & Sept–Oct 10am–5pm; ☎01301/702260), situated opposite the *Tarbet Hotel*, but there's no other reason for stopping, unless you want to join one of the **loch cruises**, run by *Cruise Loch Lomond* (☎01301/702356) that depart from the pier.

North of Tarbet, the A82 turns back into the narrow, winding road of old, making for slower but much more interesting driving. There's one more **train station** on Loch Lomond at Ardlui, while a couple of miles further north at **Inverarnan**, there's a bridge over the river beside the *Drover's Inn* (☎01301/704234, ⓦ www.droversinn.co.uk; ➌), one of the most idiosyncratic **hotels** in Scotland: typically, the bar has a roaring fire, barmen dressed in kilts, weary hillwalkers sipping pints and bearded musicians banging out folk songs.

Crianlarich and Tyndrum

CRIANLARICH, some eight miles north of the head of Loch Lomond, is an important staging post on various transport routes. The West Highland Way long-distance footpath (see p.1063) also trogs past. Otherwise there's little reason to stop here, unless you're keen on tackling some of the steep-sided hills that rise up from the glen.

Five miles further north from here on the A82/A85, the village of **TYNDRUM** owes its existence to a minor (and very short-lived) nineteenth-century gold rush, but today is dotted with some rather ugly hotels and service stations. At Tyndrum the road divides, with the A85 heading west to Oban, and the A82 heading for Fort William via Glen Coe.

The Trossachs

Often described as the Highlands in miniature, the **Trossachs** area boasts a magnificent diversity of scenery, with dramatic peaks and forest-covered slopes that live up to all the images ever produced of Scotland's wild land. It is country ripe for stirring tales of brave kilted clansmen, a role fulfilled by Rob Roy Macgregor, the seventeenth-century outlaw whose name seems attached to every second waterfall, cave and barely discernible path. Strictly speaking, the name "Trossachs", normally translated as either "bristly country" or "crossing place", originally referred only to the wooded glen between **Loch Katrine** and Loch Achray, but today it is usually taken as being the whole area from **Callander** right up to the eastern banks of Loch Lomond, with which it has been grouped as part of Scotland's first national park.

The Trossachs' high tourist profile was largely attributable in the early days to Sir Walter Scott, whose novels *Lady of the Lake* and *Rob Roy* were set in and around the area. Since then, neither the popularity nor beauty of the region have waned, and in high season the place is jam-packed with coaches full of tourists as well as walkers and mountain-bikers taking advantage of the easi

Rob Roy

A member of the outlawed Macgregor clan, **Rob Roy** (meaning "Red Robert" in Gaelic) was born in 1671 in Glengyle, just north of Loch Katrine, and lived for some time as a respectable cattle farmer and trader, supported by the powerful duke of Montrose. In 1712, finding himself in a tight spot when a cattle deal fell through, Rob Roy absconded with £1000, some of it belonging to the duke. He took to the hills to live as a brigand, his feud with Montrose escalating after the duke repossessed Rob Roy's land and drove his wife from their house. He was present at the Battle of Sheriffmuir during the earlier Jacobite uprising of 1715, ostensibly supporting the Jacobites but probably as an opportunist: the chaos would have made cattle-raiding easier. Eventually captured and sentenced to transportation, Rob Roy was pardoned and returned to **Balquhidder**, where he remained until his death in 1734.

Rob Roy's status as a local hero in the mould of Robin Hood should be tempered with the fact that he was without doubt a notorious bandit and blackmailer. His life has been much romanticized, from Sir Walter Scott's 1818 novel *Rob Roy* to the 1995 film starring Liam Neeson, although the tale does serve well to dramatize the clash between the doomed clan culture of the Gaelic-speaking Highlanders and the organized feudal culture of lowland Scots, which effectively ended with the defeat of the Jacobites at Culloden in 1746. His **grave** in Balquhidder, a simple affair behind the ruined church, is one of the principal sights on the unofficial Rob Roy trail, though the peaceful graveyard is mercifully underdeveloped and free of the tartan trappings that have seen the Trossachs dubbed "Rob Roy Country".

accessed richness of the scenery. Autumn is a better time to come, when the hills are blanketed in rich, rusty colours and the crowds are thinner. In terms of where to stay, **Aberfoyle** has a rather dowdy air while **Callander** feels rather overrun, and you're often better seeking out one of the guest houses or B&Bs tucked away in secluded corners of the region.

If you don't have your own transport, the **Trossachs Trundler** is a useful minibus service which loops round Callander, Loch Katrine and Aberfoyle four times a day from late May to early Oct (not Wed); helpfully for walkers, it stops on demand and can also cope with bikes and wheelchairs. The bus is timed to connect with sailings of the *SS Sir Walter Scott* on Loch Katrine (see p.1068), and costs £5.50 for a day pass or £8 including the connection (on bus #59) from Stirling to Callander.

Aberfoyle and the Lake of Menteith

Each summer the sleepy little town of **ABERFOYLE**, twenty miles west of Stirling, dusts itself down for its annual influx of tourists. Though of little appeal itself, Aberfoyle's position in the heart of the Trossachs is ideal, with **Loch Ard Forest** and **Queen Elizabeth Forest Park** stretching across to Ben Lomond and Loch Lomond to the west, the long curve of Loch Katrine and Ben Venue to the northwest, and Ben Ledi to the northeast.

Regular **buses** from Stirling pull into the car park on Aberfoyle's Main Street. The **tourist office** next door (daily: July & Aug 9.30am–6pm; April–June, Sept & Oct 10am–5pm; Nov–March Sat & Sun 10am–4pm; ☎01877/382352) has full details of local accommodation, sights and activities. Best of the **B&Bs** is *Creag-Ard House* (☎01877/382297, www.creag-ard.co.uk; ❹; March–Oct) in the pretty village of Milton, two miles west of Aberfoyle. For **camping**, a couple of miles south of Aberfoyle on the edge of Queen Elizabeth Forest Park is *Cobleland* (☎01877/382392, stream here). Further south, the excellent family-run *Trossachs Holiday Park* (℡01877/382614, W www.trossachsholidays.co.uk; March–Oct), is twice the size and has **bikes** for rent.

For **food** in Aberfoyle, your best bet is to stick with the local hotels: the *Forth Inn* on the main street or the *Covenanters Inn* at the large, turreted *Inchrie Castle Hotel*, five minutes' walk from the centre; both serve bar food and smarter restaurant meals.

The Lake of Menteith

About four miles east of Aberfoyle towards Doune, the **Lake of Menteith** is a superb fly-fishing centre and Scotland's only lake (as opposed to loch), so named due to a historic mix-up with the word *laigh*, Scots for "low-lying ground", which applied to the whole area. To rent a **fishing boat**, contact the Lake of Menteith Fisheries (℡01877/385664; April–Oct).

From the northern shore of the lake, you can take a little ferry (April–Sept daily 9.30am–6.30pm; £3.50; HS) out to the **Island of Inchmahome** in order to explore the lovely Augustinian abbey. Founded in 1238, the ruined **Inchmahome Priory** is the most beautiful island monastery in Scotland, its remains rising tall and graceful above the trees. Five-year-old Mary, Queen of Scots was hidden at Inchmahome in 1547 before being taken to France, and there's a formal garden in the west of the island, known as Queen Mary's bower, where legend has it she played.

Aberfoyle to Callander

North of Aberfoyle, the A821 road to Loch Katrine winds its way into the Queen Elizabeth Forest, snaking its way up **Duke's Pass** (so called because it

---

Hiking and biking in the Trossachs

Despite the steady flow of coach tours taking in the scenic highlights of the area, the Trossachs is seen at its best **on foot** or on a **mountain bike**. This is partly because the terrain is slightly more benign that the Highlands proper, but much is due to the excellent management of the **Queen Elizabeth Forest Park**, a huge chunk of the National Park between Loch Lomond and Loch Lubnaig. The main visitor centre for the area, David Marshall Lodge, is just outside Aberfoyle, and is well worth a visit if you want to get some orientation on the region and learn about the local trees, geology and wildlife, which includes roe deer and birds of prey.

For **hillwalkers**, the prize peak is Ben Lomond (3192ft), best accessed from Rowardennan (see p.1062). Other highlights include Ben Venue and Ben A'an on the shores of Loch Katrine, as well as Ben Ledi, just northwest of Callander, which all offer relatively straightforward but very rewarding climbs and, on clear days, stunning views. Walkers can also choose from any number of waymarked routes through the forests and along lochsides; pick up a map of these at the visitor centre.

The area is also a popular spot for **mountain biking**, with a number of useful rental shops, a network of forest paths and one of the more impressive stretches of the National Cycle Network cutting through the region from Loch Lomond to Killin. If you don't have your own bike, Wheels Cycling Centre, next to *Trossachs Backpackers* a mile and a half southwest of Callander (℡01877/331100), is the best place in the area to **rent**, with front- or full-suspension models available, as well as baby seats and children's cycles. Also well set up is Trossachs Cycles, at the *Trossachs Holiday Park* on the A81 two miles south of Aberfoyle (℡01877/382614).

20

△ Lake of Menteith

once belonged to the Duke of Montrose). You can walk or drive the short distance to the park's excellent **visitor centre** at David Marshall Lodge (daily 10am–5pm; Nov–March closes 4pm; ☎01877/382258; car park £1), where you can pick up maps of the walks and cycle routes in the forest, get background information on the flora and fauna of the area (there's a video relay to the nests of local peregrine falcons or ospreys), or settle into the café with its splendid views out over the tree tops. From the centre, various marked paths wind through the forest, giving glimpses of the lowlands and surrounding hills. The only road in the forest open to cars is the **Achray Forest Drive**, just under two miles further on, which leads through the forest and along the western shore of **Loch Drunkie** before rejoining the main road.

Loch Katrine

Heading down the northern side of the Duke's Pass you come first to **Loch Achray**, tucked under Ben A'an. At the head of the loch a road branches the short distance through to the southern end of **Loch Katrine** at the foot of Ben Venue (2370ft), from where the elegant Victorian passenger **steamer**, the *SS Sir Walter Scott*, chugs up the loch to the wild country of Glengyle. It does two runs from the pier each day, the first departing at 11am and stopping off at Stronachlachar before returning (April–Oct daily except Wed; £4.50 single, £6.80 return); the afternoon cruise leaves at 1.45pm but doesn't make any stops (April–Oct daily; £5.80). A popular combination is to rent a bike from the Katrinewheels hut by the pier (☎01877/376284), take the steamer up to Stronachlachar, then cycle back by way of the road around the north side of the loch.

From Loch Katrine the A821 heads due east, along the north side of Loch Achray, past the tiny village of **Brig o'Turk**, where it's worth looking in on the *Byre Inn*, a tiny pub and restaurant set in an old stone barn with wooden pews and a welcoming open fire.

Callander and around

CALLANDER, on the eastern edge of the Trossachs, sits at the southern end of the **Pass of Leny**, one of the key routes into the Highlands. Significantly larger than Aberfoyle, it is a popular summer holiday base and suffers in high season for being right on the main tourist trail from Stirling through to the west Highlands.

The chief attraction in town is the **Rob Roy and Trossachs Visitor Centre** in a converted church at Ancaster Square on the main street (Jan & Feb Mon–Fri 11am–3pm, Sat & Sun 11am–4pm; March–May & Oct–Dec daily 10am–5pm; June daily 9.30am–6pm; July & Aug daily 9am–6pm; Sept daily 10am–6pm; £3.25). Downstairs is the tourist office and bookshop; upstairs a hammed-up audiovisual display offers an entertaining and partisan account o the life and times of Rob Roy and those who have portrayed him in film and fiction.

Callander's **tourist office** is in the Rob Roy and Trossachs Visitor Centr (same times as above; ☎01877/330342), and can book accommodatior Wheels Cycling Centre (☎01877/331100, ⓦwww.scottish-cycling.co.uk part of *Trossachs Backpackers* (see below), offers excellent **bike rental** as well a advice on the best local routes. For **accommodation** there's **Arden Hous** on Bracklinn Road (☎01877/330235, ⓦwww.ardenhouse.org.uk; ❹), a gran Victorian guest house in its own gardens with good views and woodland wall from the back door. Alternatively, there's the slightly cheaper **Conservatory**

Ballachallan, two miles southeast of town (☎01877/339190, ⓦwww
.ballachallan.co.uk; ❸), a restaurant with pleasant, well-presented rooms in the
farmhouse alongside. For those on a budget, **Trossachs Backpackers** on
Invertrossachs Road (☎01877/331200, ⓦwww.scottish-hostel.co.uk; ❶) is a
friendly and comfortable 32-bed hostel and activity centre with self-catering
dorms and family rooms, located a couple of miles southwest of town down a
turn-off from the A81 to Port of Menteith.

Fife

The ancient Kingdom of **Fife**, designated as such by the Picts in the fourth
century, is a small area barely fifty miles at its widest point, but one which has
a definite identity, inextricably linked with the waters which surround it on
three sides – the Tay to the north, the Forth to the south, and the cold North
Sea to the east. Despite its small size, Fife encompasses several different regions,
with a marked difference between the rural north and the semi-industrial
south. Tourism and agriculture are the economic mainstays of the **northeast**
corner of Fife, but ultimately it is to **St Andrews**, Scotland's oldest university
town and the home of the world-famous Royal and Ancient Golf Club, that
most visitors are drawn. Development here has been cautious, and both the
town itself and the surrounding area retain an old-fashioned feel. South of St
Andrews, the tiny stone harbours of the fishing villages of the **East Neuk** are
an appealing extension to any visit to this part of Fife.

The unremarkable new town of **Glenrothes** in central Fife is overshadowed
by the absorbing village of **Falkland** with its impressive ruined palace. In the
south, the perfectly preserved town of **Culross** is the most notable draw, with
its cobbled streets and collection of historic buildings. Otherwise, southern Fife
is dominated by the town of **Dunfermline**, a former capital of Scotland, with
the **Forth Rail Bridge** and Road Bridge the most memorable sights.

The main **road** into the region is the M90, which links the Forth Road
Bridge northwest of Edinburgh with Perth, fringing Fife's western boundary.
The A92 road cuts a swathe across the county, linking Dunfermline, Glenrothes
and the Tay Road Bridge in the north. The **train** line follows the coast as far
north as Kirkcaldy and then cuts inland towards Dundee, stopping on the way
at Cupar and Leuchars (from where buses run to St Andrews).

St Andrews and the East Neuk

Confident, poised and well groomed if a little snooty, **ST ANDREWS**,
Scotland's oldest **university town** and a pilgrimage centre for **golfers** from
all over the world, is situated on a wide bay on the northeastern coast of Fife.
Of all Scotland's universities, St Andrews is most often compared to Oxford
or Cambridge both for the dominance of gown over town, and for the intimate, collegiate feel of the place. Accentuating the comparison is the fact that

the student population has a significant proportion of English undergraduates, among them, famously, Prince William, who was responsible for a substantial increase in the intake of female art history students during his time here.

According to legend, the town was founded, pretty much by accident, in the fourth century. **St Rule** – or Regulus – a custodian of the bones of St Andrew in Patras in southern Greece, had a vision in which an angel ordered him to carry five of the saint's bones to the western edge of the world, where he was to build a city in his honour. The conscientious courier set off, but was shipwrecked on the rocks close to the present harbour. Struggling ashore with his precious burden, he built a shrine to the saint on what subsequently became the site of the **cathedral**; St Andrew became Scotland's patron saint and the town its ecclesiastical capital.

St Andrews isn't a large place, with only three main streets and an open, airy feel encouraged by the long stretches of sand on either side of town and the acreage of golf links all around. Local residents are proud of their town, with its refined old-fashioned ambience. Thanks to a strong and well-informed local conservation lobby, many of the original buildings have survived. Almost the entire centre consists of listed buildings, while the ruined castle and cathedral have all but been rebuilt in the efforts to preserve their remains.

From St Andrews, the attractive beaches and little fishing villages of the **East Neuk** (*neuk* is Scots for "corner") are within easy reach, although the area can also be approached from the Kirkcaldy side. Though golf and coastal walks are a shared characteristic, the East Neuk villages have few of the grand buildings and important bustle of St Andrews, with old cottages and merchants' houses huddling round stone-built harbours in scenes fallen upon with joy by artists and photographers.

Arrival and information

The nearest **train station** to St Andrews is on the Edinburgh–Dundee line at Leuchars, five miles northwest across the River Eden, from where regular buses make the fifteen-minute trip into town – when you buy your rail ticket to Leuchars, ask for a St Andrews rail-bus ticket which includes the bus fare. Frequent **buses** from Edinburgh and Dundee terminate at the bus station on City Road at the west end of Market Street. The **tourist office**, 70 Market St (May & June Mon–Sat 9.30am–5.30pm, Sun 11am–4pm; July & Aug Mon–Sat 9.30am–7pm, Sun 10.30am–5pm; Sept Mon–Sat 9.30am–6pm, Sun 11am–4pm; April Mon–Sat 9.30am–5pm, Sun 11am–4pm; Oct–March Mon–Sat 9.30am–5pm; ℡01334/472021, ⓦwww.standrews.com), holds comprehensive information about St Andrews and northeast Fife.

The town's fiendish **parking** system requires vouchers (Mon–Sat 9am–5pm, 50p an hour) that you can get from the tourist office and some local shops - you may find it easier leaving your car in one of the free car parks fringing the centre. Spokes at 37 South St (℡01334/477835) offers **bike hire**.

Accommodation

With St Andrews' wide-ranging appeal to visitors there's no shortage of **accommodation** both in town and around, although average prices in all categories vie with Edinburgh's as the highest in Scotland. Upmarket **hotels** are thick on the ground, notably around the golf courses, and there are plenty of **guest houses** in a central location, though rooms often get booked up in the summer, when you should definitely book in advance.

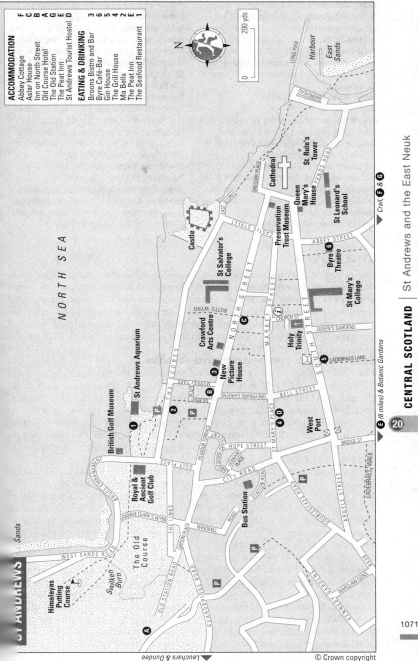

ST ANDREWS

Sands

NORTH SEA

ACCOMMODATION

Abbey Cottage	F
Aslar House	C
Inn on North Street	B
Old Course Hotel	A
The Old Station	G
The Peat Inn	E
St Andrews Tourist Hostel	D

EATING & DRINKING

Broons Bistro and Bar	3
Byre Café-Bar	6
Gin House	5
The Grill House	4
Ma Bells	2
The Peat Inn	E
The Seafood Restaurant	1

N

0   200 yds

Himalayas Putting Course

The Old Course

Swilken Burn

British Golf Museum

Royal & Ancient Golf Club

St Andrews Aquarium

Crawford Arts Centre

New Picture House

St Salvator's College

Castle

Cathedral

St Rule's Tower

Preservation Trust Museum

Queen Mary's House

St Leonard's School

Byre Theatre

St Mary's College

Holy Trinity

West Port

Bus Station

Harbour

East Sands

Long Pier

WEST SANDS ROAD

GOLF PLACE

THE LINKS

GRANNIE CLARK'S WYND

BRUCE EMBANKMENT

THE SCORES

EAST SCORES

GREGORY PLACE

SHOREHEAD

FEDS ROAD

GIBSON PLACE

OLD STATION ROAD

GUARDBRIDGE ROAD

WINDMILL

CITY ROAD

HOPE STREET

PILMOUR TERRACE

PILMOUR LINKS

ABBOTSFORD CRES

HOWARD PLACE

MURRAY PARK

MURRAY PLACE

BUTTS WYND

NORTH STREET

THE SCORES

GREYFRIARS GARDENS

BELL STREET

MARKET STREET

CHURCH ST

SOUTH STREET

CASTLE STREET

ABBEY STREET

QUEEN'S GARDENS

LADEBRAES LANE

ST MARY'S PLACE

BRIDGE ST

STATION ROAD

DOUBLEDYKES ROAD

ARGYLE STREET

LADEBRAES WALK

KENNEDY GARDENS

WARDLAW GARDENS

A918

▲ *Leuchars & Dundee*

▼ **E** *(6 miles) & Botanic Gardens*

▼ *Crail,* **F** & **G**

CENTRAL SCOTLAND St Andrews and the East Neuk

20

© Crown copyright

Abbey Cottage Abbey Walk ℡ 01334/473727, Ⓦ www.abbeycottage.co.uk. Pleasant B&B in a cottage with a pretty garden near the cathedral and harbour. ❷

Aslar House 120 North St ℡ 01334/473460, Ⓦ www.aslar.com. A smart guest house in a three-storey townhouse with an unusual round tower at the back. ❹

Inn on North Street 127 North St ℡ 01334/473387, Ⓦ www.theinnonnorthstreet.com. Appealing mid-range option with a youthful feel and modern Gaelic style: tasteful rooms, wooden floors, and a lively bar and restaurant area. ❻

Old Course Hotel ℡ 01334 474371, Ⓦ www .oldcoursehotel.co.uk. The best-known hotel in St Andrews, located just a sliced two-iron from the 17th tee. A large, luxurious resort complex with all facilities including a spa. ❾

The Old Station Stravithie Bridge ℡ 01334/880505, Ⓦ www.theoldstation.co.uk. A couple of miles south of St Andrews on the B9131 to Anstruther, you can stay in tasteful rooms in the main house (based around a former station waiting room) or in an imaginatively designed suite in an old railway carriage parked alongside. Main house ❺, carriage ❼

The Peat Inn Peat Inn ℡ 01334/840206, Ⓦ www.thepeatinn.co.uk. Five miles south of town on the A915 and then one mile west on the B940 in a village named after it, this old coaching inn has eight plush if pricey suites in a modern build-ing tucked behind, and is renowned for its won-derful restaurant (see p.1074). ❼

St Andrews Tourist Hostel St Mary's Place ℡ 01334/479911, Ⓦ www .hostelsaccommodation.com. Superbly located backpacker hostel in a pleasantly converted town-house right above *The Grill House* restaurant with plenty of dorm beds but no doubles.

The Town

The centre of St Andrews still follows its medieval layout. On the three main thoroughfares, **North Street**, **Market Street** and **South Street**, which run west to east towards the ruined Gothic cathedral, are several of the original university buildings from the fifteenth century. Narrow alleys connect the cobbled streets, attic windows and gable ends shape the rooftops, and here and there you'll see old wooden doors with heavy knockers and black iron hinges.

St Andrews Cathedral and Castle

The ruin of the great **cathedral** (visitor centre: April–Sept daily 9.30am–6.30pm; Oct–March 9.30am–4.30pm; £2.50, joint ticket with castle £4; grounds: year-round Sun 9am–6.30pm; free; HS), at the east end of town, gives only an idea of the importance of what was the largest cathedral in Scotland. Though founded in 1160, it was not finished and consecrated until 1318, in the presence of Robert the Bruce. On June 5, 1559, the Reformation took its toll, and supporters of John Knox, fresh from a rousing meeting, plun-dered the cathedral and left it to ruin.

The cathedral site, above the harbour where the land drops to the sea, can be a blustery place, with the wind whistling through the great east window and down the stretch of turf that was once the central aisle. In front of the window a slab is all that remains of the high altar, where the relics of St Andrew were once enshrined. Previously, it was believed that they were kept in **St Rule's Tower**, the austere Romanesque monolith next to the cathedral, which was built as part of an abbey in 1130. From the top of the tower (a climb of 15? steps), there's a good view of the town and surroundings.

Not far north of the cathedral, the rocky coastline curves inland to the ruined **castle** (same hours as cathedral; £2.50, joint ticket with cathedral £4; HS with a drop to the sea on two sides and a moat on the inland side. Founded around 1200 and extended over the centuries, it was built as part of the Palace of the Bishops and Archbishops of St Andrews and was consequently the scene of some fairly grim incidents at the time of the Reformation. There's not a great deal left of the castle, since it fell into ruin in the seventeenth century, and most of what can be seen dates from the sixteenth century, apart from the fourteenth-century Fore Tower.

Around the university

A little way down North Street from the cathedral, housed in a picturesque sixteenth-century cottage with a low wooden door, the **St Andrews Preservation Trust Museum and Garden** (June–Sept daily 2–5pm; free) presents an intimate picture of the town's history and glamorous golf connections. As you progress towards the centre of town, it's clear that you're in amongst the buildings of St Andrews University, the oldest in Scotland, founded in 1410 by Bishop Henry Wardlaw, although James I, to whom the bishop was tutor, is the nominal founder (and was a great benefactor of the university). A **guided tour** of the university buildings starts from St Salvator's College, or you can wander freely around the buildings at your own pace.

The beaches

St Andrews has two great **beaches**, the West Sands which stretch for two miles from just below the R&A Clubhouse, and the shorter more compact East

---

Golf in St Andrews

St Andrews **Royal and Ancient Golf Club** (or "R&A") is the international governing body for golf, and dates back to a meeting of 22 of the local gentry in 1754, who founded the Society of St Andrews Golfers, being "admirers of the ancient and healthful exercise of golf". The game itself has been played here since the fifteenth century. Those early days were instrumental in establishing Scotland as the home of golf, for the rules were distinguished from those of the French game by the fact that participants had to manoeuvre the ball into a hole, rather than hit an above-ground target.

The approach to St Andrews from the west runs adjacent to the famous **Old Course**, one of seven courses in the immediate vicinity of the town. The Old Course's strictly private **clubhouse**, a stolid, square building dating from 1854, is at the eastern end of the course overlooking both the eighteenth green and the long strand of the West Sands. The British Open Championship was first held here in 1873, having been inaugurated in 1860 at Prestwick in Ayrshire, and since then it has been held at St Andrews regularly, pulling in enormous crowds. Pictures of golfing greats from Tom Morris to Tiger Woods, along with clubs and a variety of memorabilia donated by famous players, are displayed in the admirable **British Golf Museum** on Bruce Embankment, along the waterfront below the clubhouse (April to mid-Oct daily 9.30am–5.30pm; mid-Oct to March Thurs–Mon 11am–3pm; £4).

Where to play

It's possible to **play** any of the town's courses, ranging from the nine-hole Balgove course (£10 per round) to the venerated Old Course itself – though for the latter you'll need a valid handicap certificate and must enter a daily ballot for tee times; if you're successful the green fees are £105 in summer. All this and more is explained at the clubhouse of the **St Andrews Links Trust** (Ⓦ www.standrews.org.uk), the organization which looks after all the courses in town, located alongside the fairway of the first hole of the Old Course.

Arguably the best golfing experience in St Andrews, even if you can't tell a birdie from a bogey, is the **Himalayas**, a fantastically lumpy eighteen-hole putting course in an ideal setting right next to the Old Course and the sea. Officially the Ladies Putting Club, founded in 1867, with its own clubhouse, the grass is as perfectly manicured as the championship course, and you can have all the thrill of sinking a six-footer in the most famous location in golf, all for less than £1 per round.

Sands which curve round from the harbour. The West Sands are best known from the opening sequences of the Oscar-winning film *Chariots of Fire*; the blustery winds which are the scourge of golfers and walkers alike do at least make the beach a great place to fly a kite – if you're keen to try contact Wind and Water, who have a shop just off South St (☎01334/460600, ⓦwww.wind-and-water.co.uk).

Eating and drinking

St Andrews has no shortage of **restaurants** and **cafés**, and given the local student population, there's also plenty of choice at the cheaper end of the market, as well as lots of good **pubs**.

Restaurants

Byre Café-Bar Abbey St ☎01334/468720. One of the nicer spots in town for a leisurely coffee or light meal; interesting contemporary dishes include red snapper and venison steak. Moderate.

The Grill House Inchcape House, St Mary's Place. Located opposite the student union, this is a lively steak'n'burger place with a bit more to it than the imported chains. Moderate.

The Peat Inn Five miles southwest of town ☎01334/840206. One of Britain's top restaurants, serving a varied menu of local specialities. The dining area is intimate without being cramped, and a three-course meal – perhaps featuring lobster broth, venison or roast monkfish – will set you back at least £40 per head. Very expensive.

The Seafood Restaurant The Scores ☎01334/479475. Sister to its acclaimed name-sake in St Monans (see p.1075), this restaurant has an amazing location in a custom-built glass building on the beach between the Aquarium and the Old Course. Lots of wow on the fish-dominated menu as well as in the venue. Very expensive.

Pubs and bars

Broons Bistro and Bar North Street. Right beside the classic New Picture House cinema, a comfortable yet still young and fun café-bar-bistro with regular live music sessions.

Gin House 116 South St. Raucous spot and a current student favourite. Full of chrome and wood, with regular DJs and food served all day.

Ma Bells 40 The Scores. In the basement of the *St Andrews Golf Hotel*, a lively pub serving cheap food which is often thronged with students.

The East Neuk

Extending south of St Andrews as far as Largo Bay, the **East Neuk** is famous for its series of quaint fishing villages, all crow-stepped gables and tiled roofs, the Flemish influence in the architecture indicating a history of strong trading links with the Low Countries. Inland, gently rolling hills provide some of the best farmland in Scotland, with quiet country lanes more redolent of parts of southern England than north of the border. Not surprisingly the area is dotted with windy **golf courses**, though if you prefer your walk unspoilt there are plenty of bracing coastal paths, including one out to Fife Ness, the "nose" of Fife sticking out into the North Sea, or along the waymarked **Fife Coastal Path**, which traces the shoreline all the way between St Andrews and the Forth Rail Bridge, and is at its most scenic in the East Neuk stretch. **Bus** #95 runs from Leven around the coast to Dundee.

Well patronized by holidaymakers and weekenders from the Central Belt, the various **restaurants** of the East Neuk are one of the highlights of the area, with fresh seafood a speciality, but often complemented by produce gleaned from the fertile Fife farmland.

Crail

CRAIL is the archetypally charming East Neuk fishing village, its maze of rough cobbled streets leading down to a tiny stone-built harbour surrounded by piles of lobster creels, and with fishermen's cottages tucked into every nook and cranny in the cliff. Though often populated by artists at their easels and camera-toting tourists, it is still a working harbour, and if the boats have been out you can often buy fresh lobster and crab cooked to order from a small wooden shack right on the harbour edge. You can trace the history of the town at the **Crail Museum and Heritage Centre**, 62 Marketgate (Easter–Sept daily 10am–1pm & 2–5pm, Sun 2–5pm; free), which also doubles up as the town's **tourist office**. **Crail Pottery**, 75 Nethergate (Mon–Fri 9am–5pm, weekends 10am–5pm), is worth a visit for its wide range of locally made pottery, while the **Jerdan Gallery**, 42 Marketgate South (daily 11am–5pm, closed Tues), displays an array of contemporary painting, sculpture and ceramics by top Scottish artists.

Anstruther and around

ANSTRUTHER is the largest of the East Neuk fishing harbours, but it too has an attractively old-fashioned air and no shortage of character in its houses and narrow streets. It's home to the wonderfully unpretentious **Scottish Fisheries Museum** (April–Oct Mon–Sat 10am–5.30pm, Sun 11am–5pm; Nov–March Mon–Sat 10am–4.30pm, Sun noon–4.30pm; £3.50), quite in keeping with the no-frills integrity of the area in general. Set in an atmospheric complex of sixteenth- to nineteenth-century buildings with timber ceilings and wooden floors, it chronicles the history of the Scottish fishing and whaling industries. Anstruther's helpful **tourist office** (Easter–Aug Mon–Sat 10am–5pm, Sun 11am–4pm; Sept to mid-Oct Mon–Sat 10am–4.30pm, Sun 11am–4pm; ℡01333/311073) is next to the museum.

Anstruther has a fine fish **restaurant**, the *Cellar*, at 24 East Green (℡01333/310378), in one of the village's oldest buildings, once a cooperage and smokehouse. For decent fish and chips, head for the *Anstruther Fish Bar*, 44 The Shore.

Pittenweem, St Monans and Elie

West of Anstruther are more fishing villages, all undeniably attractive and rewarding if you have the time to stroll around, take in some of the coastline, or seek out one or two of the fine places to eat and drink. Two miles from Anstruther, **PITTENWEEM** has a busy harbour and fish market, as well as a number of small art galleries. Pittenweem almost merges into **ST MONANS**, the smallest of the East Neuk fishing villages, and worth a visit for its splendid *Seafood Restaurant*, at the far end of the harbour (℡01333/730327), a smart restaurant perched right on the sea's edge with panoramic views out to sea.

Three miles on from St Monans is **ELIE**, a popular escape for middle-class Edinburgh families who come for the bracing air and golf courses. The essential stop in Elie is the relaxed and convivial *Ship Inn*, overlooking the beach near the harbour, where you'll find great **bar food** and, come summer, lots of lively local banter in the beer garden.

Central Fife

The main A92 road cuts right through **Central Fife**, ultimately connecting the Forth Road Bridge on the southern coast of Fife with the Tay Road Bridge on the northern coast. The main settlement of this inland region is Glenrothes, a new town created after World War II in old coal-mining territory. Generally the scenery in this part of the county is pleasant rather than startling, though it's worth diverting off the road to seek out **Falkland** and its magnificent ruined palace.

Falkland

The **Howe of Fife**, north of Glenrothes, is a low-lying stretch of ground (or "howe") at the foot of the twin peaks of the heather-swathed **Lomond Hills** – West Lomond (1696ft) and East Lomond (1378ft). Nestling in the lower slopes of East Lomond, the narrow streets of **FALKLAND** are lined with fine and well-preserved seventeenth- and eighteenth-century buildings. The village grew up around **Falkland Palace** (March–Oct Mon–Sat 10am–6pm, Sun 1–5pm; £7, gardens only £3.50; NTS), which stands on the site of an earlier castle, home to the Macduffs, the earls of Fife. James IV began the construction of the present palace in 1500; it was completed and embellished by James V, and became a favoured country retreat for the royal court. Charles II stayed here in 1650, when he was in Scotland for his coronation, but after the Jacobite rising of 1715 and temporary occupation by Rob Roy the palace was abandoned, remaining so until the late nineteenth century when the keepership was acquired by the third marquess of Bute. He completely restored the palace, and today it's a stunning example of Early Renaissance architecture, complete with corbelled parapet, mullioned windows, round towers and massive walls. A **guided tour** (40min) takes in a cross section of public and private rooms in the south and east wings. Outside, the **gardens** are also worth a look, their well-stocked herbaceous borders lining a pristine lawn. Don't miss the high walls of the oldest real (or Royal) tennis court in Britain – built in 1539 for James V and still used.

The concentration of charming old cottages and historic buildings in the heart of Falkland makes it a particularly pleasant place to wander around. **Accommodation** includes the *Burgh Lodge*, a newly renovated independent **hostel** on Back Wynd (℡01337/857710) which has facilities for families and people with disabilities. Both the *Hunting Lodge Hotel*, on High Street, directly opposite the palace (℡01337/857226; ❷), and the *Covenanter Hotel* (℡01337/857224, ⓦwww.covenanterhotel.com; ❷ in separate cottage; ❸ in hotel), just up the road, are comfortable traditional inns, with great pubs as well as a couple of rooms upstairs. *The Greenhouse* (℡01337/858400; closed Mon & Tues), also on the High Street, is a small modern restaurant serving local organic food.

Southern Fife

Although the coast of **southern Fife** is predominantly industrial – with everything from cottage industries to the refitting of nuclear submarines – thankfully only a small part has been blighted by insensitive development. Even in the old coal-mining areas, disused pits and left-over slag heaps have either been well camouflaged through landscaping or put to alternative use as recreatio areas. Thanks to its proximity to the early coal-mines, the charming village of **Culross** was once a lively port that enjoyed a thriving trade with Holland, the Dutch influence obvious in its lovely gabled houses. It was from nearby **Dunfermline** that Queen Margaret ousted the Celtic Church from Scotland in the eleventh century; her son, David I, founded an abbey here in the twelfth century, and Dunfermline remains the chief town and focus of the are

Southern Fife is linked to Edinburgh by the two **Forth bridges**, the red-painted girders of the Rail Bridge representing one of Britain's great engineering spectacles.

Culross

The A985 crosses the Forth Road Bridge, with unattractive views of the shipyard at Inverkeithing and the naval dock at Rosyth (now used as a port for ferry crossings to Zeebrugge in Belgium), before heading west along the Forth estuary to **CULROSS** (pronounced "Coorus"), one of Scotland's most picturesque settlements, all cobbled streets and squat cottages with crow-stepped gables. The town's development began in the fifth century with the arrival of St Serf on the northern side of the Forth at Cuileann Ros ("point where holly grows"), and is also said to have been the birthplace of St Mungo, founder of Glasgow cathedral. Culross today is the best-preserved seventeenth-century town in Scotland, thanks in large part to the work of the National Trust for Scotland, which has been renovating its whitewashed, pan-tiled buildings since 1932. **Bus** #14/a between Dunfermline and Stirling passes through hourly.

For an excellent introduction to the burgh's history, head to the **National Trust Visitor Centre** (Easter–Sept daily noon–5pm; joint ticket for Town House, Palace and Study; £5; NTS), located in the **Town House** facing Sandhaven, where goods were once unloaded from ships. The most impressive building in the village is the nearby ochre-coloured **Culross Palace** (same hours), built by wealthy coal merchant George Bruce in the late sixteenth century; it's not a palace at all – its name comes from the Latin *palatium*, or "hall" – but a grand and impressive house, with lots of small rooms and connecting passageways.

The charm of Culross is evident simply by wandering through its narrow streets looking for old inscriptions above windows or investigating crooked passageways with names such as "Wee Causeway" and "Stinking Wynd". Further uphill lie the remains of **Culross Abbey**, founded by Cistercian monks on land given to the Church in 1217 by the earl of Fife. The nave of the original building is a ruin, a lawn studded with great stumps of columns. Although it's difficult to get a sense of what the abbey would have looked like, the overall effect is of grace and grandeur. It adjoins the fine seventeenth-century **manse** and the choir of the abbey, which became the **parish church** in 1633. Inside, alabaster figures of Sir George Bruce, his lady, three sons and five daughters decorate a splendid family tomb.

The **graveyard** of the church is fascinating. Many of the graves are eighteenth century, with symbols depicting the occupation of the person who is buried; the gravestone of a gardener has a crossed spade and rake as well as an hourglass with the sand run out. Note the Scottish custom, still continued, of marking women's graves with maiden names, even when they are buried with their husbands.

Dunfermline

Scotland's capital until the Union of the Crowns in 1603, **DUNFERMLINE** lies inland seven miles east of Culross, north of the Forth bridges. This "auld, grey toun" is built on a hill, dominated by the **abbey** and ruined **palace** at the top. In the eleventh century, Malcolm III (Malcolm Canmore) offered refuge here to Edgar Atheling, heir to the English throne, and his family, who were shipwrecked in the Forth while fleeing the Norman Conquest. Malcolm married Edgar's Catholic sister Margaret in 1067, and in so doing started a process of reformation that ultimately supplanted the Celtic Church. Until the late nineteenth century, Dunfermline was one of Scotland's foremost linen producers, as well as a major coal-mining centre, and today the town is a busy place, its ever-increasing sprawl attesting to a growing economy.

The Town

Dunfermline's appealing **centre**, at the top of the hill around the abbey and palace, features narrow, cobbled streets, pedestrianized shopping areas and gargoyle-adorned buildings. The oldest part of **Dunfermline Abbey** (April–Sept daily 9.30am–6.30pm; Oct–March Mon–Wed & Sat 9.30am–4.30pm, Thurs 9.30am–12.30pm, Sun 2–4.30pm, closed Fri; £2.20; HS) is attributable to Queen Margaret, who began building a Benedictine priory in 1072. In 1303, during the first of the **Wars of Independence**, the English king Edward I occupied the palace, had the church roof stripped of lead to provide ammunition for his army's catapults, and also appears to have ordered the destruction of most of the monastery buildings. **Robert the Bruce** helped rebuild the abbey, and when he died of leprosy was buried here 25 years later, although his body went undiscovered until building began on a new parish church in 1821. The enormous stonework graffiti, "King Robert the Bruce", at the top of the tower is attributable to an overexcited architect thrilled by the discovery of Bruce's remains.

The guest house of Margaret's Benedictine monastery, south of the abbey, became the **palace** in the sixteenth century under James VI, who gave both it and the abbey to his consort, Queen Anne of Denmark. Charles I, the last monarch to be born in Scotland, entered the world here in 1600. All that is left of it today is a long, sandstone facade, especially impressive when silhouetted against the evening sky.

Pittencrieff Park, known to locals as "the Glen", covers a huge area in the centre of Dunfermline. Bordering the ruined palace, the 76-acre park used to be owned by the lairds of Pittencrieff. In 1902, however, the entire plot was purchased by the local rags-to-riches industrialist and philanthropist Andrew Carnegie, who donated it to his home town. Just beyond the southeast corner of the park, the modest little cottage at the bottom of St Margaret Street is **Andrew Carnegie's Birthplace** (April–Oct Mon–Sat 11am–5pm, Sun 2–5pm; £2). The son of a weaver, Carnegie (1835–1919) lived as a child upstairs with his family, while the room below housed his father's loom shop. After the family emigrated to America in 1848, Carnegie began acquiring steel-production firms in the 1870s and was so successful that by the time he retired in 1901 he was a multimillionaire – one of the richest men in the world. For the next 18 years he devoted himself to giving the money away, endowing educational establishments and free libraries around the world including some 600 in Britain.

Practicalities

Trains from Edinburgh stop at Dunfermline Town **train station**, halfway down the long hill of St Margaret's Drive, southeast of the centre. It's a fifteen-minute walk up the hill from here to the **tourist office** at 1 High St, immediately opposite the City Chambers (April–June Mon–Sat 9.30am–5pm; July to mid-Sept Mon–Sat 9.30am–5.30pm, Sun 11am–4pm; mid-Sept to March Mon–Sat 9.30am–5pm; ☎01383/720999). An hourly bus from Edinburgh comes in at the **bus station**, in the Kingsgate Centre, on the north side of town. There are some good, well-priced **places to eat** including the idiosyncratic modern Town House Restaurant and Bistro at 4

20

East Port (☎01383/432382); the stylish *Bar Café Brio* on the corner of Canmore and Guildhall streets; and the *Old Inn*, just down Kirkgate, which serves bar meals and has *The Creepy Wee Pub* right next door.

Good **accommodation** options locally are limited: try *St Mungo's Cottage* (☎01383/882102; ❶) in Culross, which offers B&B and has views out to the Forth, or, in Dunfermline, *Hillview House*, 9 Aberdour Rd (☎01383/726278; Ⓦwww.hillviewhousedunfermline.co.uk; ❷).

The Forth bridges to Kirkcaldy

Cowering beneath the Forth bridges, **NORTH QUEENSFERRY** is a small fishing village which, until the opening of the road bridge, was the northern landing point of the ferry from South Queensferry (see p.956). The cantilevered **Forth Rail Bridge**, built from 1883 to 1890 by Sir John Fowler and Benjamin Baker, ranks among the supreme achievements of Victorian engineering. Some 50,000 tons of steel were used in the construction of a design that manages to express grace as well as might. Derived from American models, the suspension format chosen for the **Forth Road Bridge** alongside makes an interesting modern complement to the older structure. Erected between 1958 and 1964, it finally killed off the 900-year-old ferry, and now attracts a heavy volume of traffic.

The only way to cross the rail bridge is aboard a train heading to or from Edinburgh, though inevitably this doesn't allow much of a perspective of the spectacle itself. For the best **panorama** make use of the pedestrian and cycle lane on the east side of the road bridge. For some background to the construction of the bridges, head to the **Forth Bridges Exhibition** (daily 9am–9pm; free), occupying a couple of rooms tacked onto the modern *Queensferry Lodge Hotel*, which has a series of storyboards, photographs, models and displays. Here you can contemplate various mind-boggling statistics such as the fact that there are six and a half million rivets in the rail bridge, and that a shower of rain adds around 100 tons to its weight.

Tucked underneath the mighty geometry of the rail bridge is **Deep-Sea World** (April–Oct daily 10am–6pm; Nov–March daily 11am–5pm; Ⓦwww.deepseaworld.com, ☎01383/411880; £8.95), one of Scotland's most popular family attractions. Full of weird and wonderful creatures from sea horses to piranhas, the highlight is a huge aquarium that boasts the world's largest underwater viewing tunnel, through which you glide on a moving walkway while sharks, conger eels and all manner of fish from the deep swim nonchalantly past.

The coast

Fife's **south coast** curves sharply north at the mouth of the Firth of Forth, exposing the towns and villages to an icy east wind that somewhat undermines the sunshine image of the beaches. East from the bridges are a straggle of Fife fishing communities such as **Aberdour**, **Burntisland** and **Kinghorn** which have depended on the sea for centuries, and now make popular, although not especially attractive, holiday spots as well as a commuter belt for Edinburgh. The fast route from the Forth Road Bridge to Kirkcaldy and the rest of Fife is along the inland A92 dual carriageway; a pleasant but more time-consuming alternative route is along the A921 that follows the northern shore of the firth. Both the **train** line from Inverkeithing and twice-hourly **buses** #7 and #7a from Dunfermline stop at all towns, making it quite possible to take on a section of the **Fife Coastal Path** (Ⓦwww.fifecoastalpath.com), a waymarked walking trail

20

which begins underneath the Forth Rail Bridge at North Queensferry and finishes up at the Tay Road Bridge at Newport-on-Tay.

Kirkcaldy

KIRKCALDY (pronounced "kir-coddy") doesn't hold a great deal of interest for the visitor, its charms largely obliterated by overdevelopment. The esplanade was built in 1923 – not just to hold back the sea, but also to alleviate unemployment – and runs parallel for part of the way with the shorter High Street. The town's history is chronicled in its **Museum and Art Gallery** (Mon–Sat 10.30am–5pm, Sun 2–5pm; free) in the colourful War Memorial Gardens between the train and bus stations. The museum covers everything from archeological discoveries to the tradition of the local Wemyss Ware pottery and the evolution of the present town. Since its inception in 1925, the gallery has built up its collection to around three hundred works by some of Scotland's finest painters from the late eighteenth century onwards, including works by the portraitist Sir Henry Raeburn, the Scottish Colourists, the Glasgow Boys and William McTaggart. For a town known primarily for linoleum production and with a reputation firmly rooted in the prosaic, the art gallery is an unexpected draw.

Kirkcaldy's **train** and **bus stations** are in the upper part of town – keep heading downhill to get to the centre. For the **tourist office**, 19 Whytescauseway (Mon–Sat 10am–5pm; ☎01592/267775), follow the road for about ten minutes round to the right from the bus station. There are few places **to stay** in the centre, and the layout of the rest of the town is not easy to follow because of the way it falls across the hillside. In the town centre the refined *Dunnikier House Hotel*, Dunnikier Park, Dunnikier Way (☎01592/268393, ⓦwww.dunnikier-house-hotel.co.uk; ❻), serves fine local food and is set in pleasant grounds. Otherwise, *Dunedin House*, 25 Townsend Place (☎01592/203874, ⓦwww.dunedinhouse.com; ❷) offers decent B&B in a relatively central location.

Perthshire

Genteel, attractive **Perthshire** is, in many ways, the epitome of well-groomed rural Scotland. An area of gentle glens, mature woodland, rushing rivers and peaceful lochs, it's the long-established domain of Scotland' country-club set. First settled over eight thousand years ago, it was taken by the Romans and then the Picts before Celtic missionaries established themselves, enjoying the amenable climate, fertile soil and ideal defensive and trading location.

Occupying a strategic position at the mouth of the River Tay as Stirling hold on the Forth, the ancient town of **Perth** has as much claim as anywhere to be the gateway to the Highlands. Salmon, wool and, by the sixteenth century whisky – Bell's, Dewar's and the Famous Grouse brands all hail from this are – were exported, while a major import was Bordeaux claret. At nearby **Scon** Kenneth Macalpine established the capital of the kingdom of the Scots and th

Out and about in Perthshire

To many, Perthshire is an extended celebration of the great outdoors, with **activities** ranging from gentle strolls through ancient oak forests to river-rafting down the rapids of the River Tay. The variety of landscapes and their relative accessibility from the Central Belt also mean that there are a significant number of operators based in the area. Many of these are linked to the tourist board's Activity Line (℡01577/861186, ⓦwww.adventureperthshire.co.uk), which can give advice and contacts for over thirty different outdoor activities and sports. For canyoning, cliff-jumping, white-water kayaking and an "activity" which involves tumbling down a hill-side inside a giant plastic ball, get in touch with adrenalin junkies Nae Limits (℡01250/876310, ⓦwww.naelimits.co.uk); while for rafting on larger craft through the best rapids on the Tay at Grandtully try Splash (℡01887/829706, ⓦwww .rafting.co.uk) or Freespirits (℡01887/829280, ⓦwww.freespirits-online.co.uk), both based in Aberfeldy. Also near Aberfeldy are Highland Adventure Safaris (℡01887/820071, ⓦwww.highlandadventuresafaris.co.uk), giving an inspiring introduction to wild Scotland in which you're taken by four-wheel-drive vehicle to search for golden eagle eyries, stags and pine martens.

Picts in 846. When this settlement was washed away by floods in 1210, William the Lion founded Perth as a royal burgh and it stood as Scotland's capital until 1452.

North and west of Perth, **Highland Perthshire** begins to weave its charms: mighty woodlands blend with gorgeously rich scenery, particularly along the banks of the River Tay. The area is dotted with neat, confident towns and villages like **Dunkeld** with its lovely ruined cathedral and **Aberfeldy** at the eastern tip of Loch Tay. Further north, the countryside becomes more sparsely populated and more spectacular, with some wonderful walking country, especially around **Pitlochry**, **Blair Atholl** and the wild expanses of **Rannoch Moor** to the west.

Transport connections in the region are at their best if you head straight north from Perth, along the main A9 road and train line to Inverness, but buses – albeit often infrequent – also serve the more remote areas. Keep asking at bus stations for details of services, as the further you get from the main villages the less definitive timetables become.

Perth and around

Surrounded by fertile agricultural land and beautiful scenery, the bustling market town of **PERTH** was for several centuries Scotland's capital. During the reign of James I, Parliament met here on several occasions, but its glory was short-lived: the king was murdered in the town's Dominican priory in 1437 by the traitorous Sir Robert Graham. Despite decline in the seventeenth century, the community expanded in the eighteenth and has prospered ever since; today the whisky and insurance trades employ significant numbers, and Perth remains an important town.

The Town and around

Perth's compact **centre** occupies a small area on the west bank of the Tay. Two large areas of green parkland, known as the North and South Inch, flank the

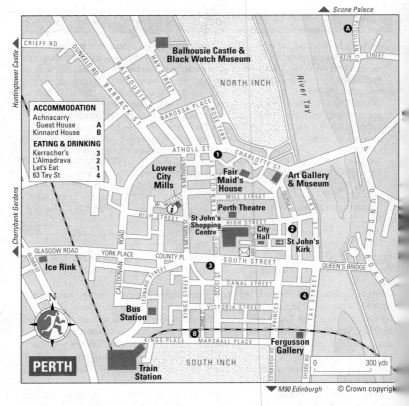

ACCOMMODATION
Achnacarry
  Guest House   A
  Kinnaird House   B

EATING & DRINKING
Kerracher's   3
L'Almadrava   2
Let's Eat   1
63 Tay St   4

M90 Edinburgh   © Crown copyright

centre. The **North Inch** was the site of the Battle of the Clans in 1396, in which thirty men from each of the clans Chattan and Quhele (pronounced "kay") clashed, while the **South Inch** was the public meeting-place for witch-burning in the seventeenth century. Both are now used for more civilized public recreation, with sports matches to the north, and boating and putting to the south.

High-street chain stores line **High Street** and **South Street**, as well as filling St John's shopping centre on King Edward Street. Behind here lies the solid and attractive **St John's Kirk** (Mon–Sat 10am–4pm, Sun 12.30–2pm, except during services; free), surrounded by cobbled lanes and cafés. The town's **Art Gallery and Museum**, 78 George St (Mon–Sat 10am–5pm; July–Sept also open Thurs till 7pm; Sun 1–4.30pm; free), another of Perth's grand buildings, has exhibits on local history, art, natural history, archeology and whisky, and gives a good overview of local life through the centuries.

Perth Ice Rink, in the Dewar's Centre, Glasgow Road, is one of the best places in the country to watch a game of **curling**, a winter sport popular in Scotland, Canada and northern Europe but little known elsewhere.

Scone Palace

Just a couple of miles north of Perth on the A93 (catch the Guide Friday tour bus, or bus #3) is **Scone Palace** (pronounced "skoon"; April–Oct dail

9.30am–5.15pm; £6.35, grounds only £3.25), one of Scotland's finest histori-cal country homes. Owned and occupied by the earl and countess of Mansfield, whose family has held it for almost four centuries, the two-storey building on the eastern side of the Tay is stately but not overpowering, far more a home than an untouchable monument: the rooms, although full of priceless antiques and lavish furnishings, feel lived-in and used.

Restored in the nineteenth century, the palace today consists of a sixteenth-century core surrounded by earlier buildings, most built of red sandstone, com-plete with battlements and the original gateway. Long before that, Scone was the capital of Pictavia, and it was here that Kenneth Macalpine brought the famous Coronation **Stone of Destiny**, or Stone of Scone, now to be found in Edinburgh Castle (see p.924) and ruled as the first king of a united Scotland. A replica of the (surprisingly small) stone can be found on Moot Hill, imme-diately opposite the palace.

Practicalities

Perth's **tourist office** is a five-minute walk away from both train and bus stations on West Mill Street (July & Aug Mon–Sat 9.30am–6.30pm, Sun 11am–5pm; April–June, Sept & Oct Mon–Sat 9.30am–5.30pm, Sun 11am–4pm; Nov–March Mon–Sat 9am–5pm; ☎01738/450600, Ⓦwww.perthshire.co.uk). While it's easy to walk to all the main attractions in the centre of Perth, an open-topped Guide Friday **tour bus** (June–Aug; not Sun) loops around town stopping off at the sights on the outskirts, including Scone Palace.

There are **B&Bs** and guest houses on most of the approach roads into town. Marshall Place, overlooking the South Inch, is a good place to look right in the centre; of the many possibilities along here *Kinnaird House*, 5 Marshall Place (☎01738/628021, Ⓦwww.kinnaird-guesthouse.co.uk; ❸), offers a warm welcome in a lovely townhouse with well-equipped en-suite rooms. Along Pitcullen Crescent, on the east bank of the Tay, *Achnacarry Guest House*, at number 3 (☎01738/621421, Ⓦwww.achnacarry.co.uk; ❷), is a reasonable if plain, alternative within walking distance of town. You can **camp** in pleasant surroundings by Scone Palace (☎01738/552323) on the outskirts of town, from where there are regular bus connections to Perth town centre.

Perth has an excellent range of **restaurants**. At the top end of the market are places such as *63, Tay Street* (☎01738/441451), in a designer setting serving classy and expensive modern Scottish fare; *Kerracher's*, 168 South St (☎01738/449777), a lovely fish restaurant with a downstairs wine bar and coffee shop; and the award-winning *Let's Eat* restaurant at 77 Kinnoull St (☎01738/643377) which serves innovative, top-notch and reasonably priced food. Alternatively, *L'Almadrava* at 24 St John St, one of a number of pubs and cafés in the streets around St John's Kirk and City Hall, is a lively Spanish tapas bar.

Strath Tay to Loch Tay

From Perth both the railway and main A9 trunk road carry much of the traffic heading into the Highlands, often speeding straight through some of Perthshire's most attractive countryside in its eagerness to get to the bleaker country to the north. Perthshire has been dubbed "**Big Tree Country**" by the tourist board in recognition of some magnificent woodland in the area, including a number of individual trees which rank among Europe's oldest, tallest and certainly most handsome specimens. Many of these are found around the valley – or "strath" – of the River Tay as it heads towards the sea from attractive Loch Tay, set up among the high Breadalbane mountains. Near the eastern end of the loch is the prosperous small town of **Aberfeldy**; from here the Tay drifts southeast between the unspoilt twin villages of **Dunkeld** and **Birnam** before meandering its way past Perth.

Dunkeld and Birnam

DUNKELD, twelve miles north of Perth on the A9, also served by trains between Perth and Inverness and buses #23 and #27, was proclaimed Scotland's ecclesiastical capital by Kenneth Macalpine in 850. The town is one of the area's most pleasant communities, with handsome whitewashed houses, appealing arts and crafts shops and a lovely cathedral. The **tourist office** is at The Cross in the town centre (July & Aug Mon–Sat 9.30am–6.30pm, Sun 11am–5pm; April–June, Sept & Oct Mon–Sat 9.30am–5.30pm, Sun 11am–4pm; Nov–March Fri–Tues 10am–4pm; ☎01350/727688).

Dunkeld's partly ruined **cathedral** is on the northern side of town, in an idyllic setting amid lawns and trees on the east bank of the Tay. The present structure consists of the fourteenth-century choir and the fifteenth-century nave; the choir, restored in 1600 (and several times since), now serves as the parish church, while the nave remains roofless apart from the clock tower.

Dunkeld is linked to its sister community, **BIRNAM**, by Thomas Telford's seven-arched bridge of 1809. This little village has a place in history thanks to Shakespeare, for it was on Dunsinane Hill, to the southeast of the village, that Macbeth declared: "I will not be afraid of death and bane/Till Birnam Forest come to Dunsinane", only to be told later by a messenger " I look'd toward Birnam, and anon me thought/The Wood began to move . . ."

The **Birnam Oak**, a gnarly old character propped up by crutches just on the edge of the village, is inevitably claimed to be a survivor of the infamous mobile forest. Several centuries after Shakespeare, another literary personality, Beatrix Potter, drew inspiration from the area, recalling her childhood holidays here when penning the Peter Rabbit stories. An exhibition on Potter, directed both at children and parents, can be found on the main road in the impressive barrel-fronted **Birnam Institute** (daily 10am–5pm; free), a brand-new theatre, arts and community centre. It incorporates the **Beatrix Potter Garden**, where various characters from the books are hidden amongst the bushes.

Practicalities

Of the **hotels** in Dunkeld and Birnam, the *Taybank Hotel* (☎01350/727340, ⓦwww.taybank.com; ❷), is a real beacon for music fans with regular live sessions in the convivial, TV-free bar. The rooms are simple and inexpensive and the rate includes a continental breakfast. Local **B&Bs** include *Waterbury Guest House* (☎01350/727324, ⓦwww.waterbury-guesthouse.co.uk; ❸) or Murthly Terrace in Birnam, or the more luxurious *The Pend* (☎01350/727586, ⓦwww.thepend.com; ❹).

Around Dunkeld

Dunkeld and Birnam are surrounded by some lovely countryside, both along the banks of the Tay and into the deep forests that seem to close in on th settlement. A good way to explore the area is by **bike** – you can rent good quality mountain bikes, as well as tandems, child seats and maps of local route from Dunkeld Bike Hire (☎01350/728744), based in the Old Police Station on the Perth Road in Birnam.

On the other side of the busy A9 from Birnam, paths lead the mile and a half to **The Hermitage**, set in a grandly wooded gorge of the plunging River Braan. Here you'll find a pretty eighteenth-century folly, also known as Ossian's Hall, which was once mirrored to reflect the water – the mirrors were smashed by Victorian vandals and the folly was more tamely restored. Two miles east of Dunkeld, the **Loch of the Lowes** is a nature reserve which offers a rare chance to see breeding ospreys and other wildfowl; the visitor centre (April–Sept 10am–5pm; £2) has video relay screens and will point you in the direction of the best vantage points.

Aberfeldy and around

From Dunkeld the A9 runs north alongside the Tay for eight miles before the road leaves the river near Ballinluig, a little place which marks the turn-off along the A827 to **ABERFELDY**, a prosperous settlement of large stone houses and four-wheel-drive vehicles which acts as a service centre for the wider Loch Tay area. The **tourist office** at The Square in the town centre (July & Aug Mon–Sat 9.30am–6.30pm, Sun 11am–5pm; April–June, Sept & Oct Mon–Sat 9.30am–5.30pm, Sun 11am–4pm; Nov–March Mon–Fri 9.30am–5pm, Sat 10am–2pm; ☎01887/820276) gives details of local trails to take in all the main sights.

Aberfeldy sits at the point where the Urlar Burn – lined by the silver birch trees celebrated by Robert Burns in his poem *The Birks of Aberfeldy* – flows into the River Tay. The Tay is spanned by the humpbacked, four-arch **Wade's Bridge**, built by General Wade in 1733 during his efforts to control the unrest in the Highlands, and one of the general's more impressive pieces of work. The main set-piece attraction in town is **Dewar's World of Whisky** at the Aberfeldy Distillery (April–Oct Mon–Sat 10am–6pm, Sun noon–4pm; Nov–March Mon–Sat 10am–4pm; £5), which puts on an impressive show describing the making of whisky – worthwhile if you haven't been given a similar lowdown at distilleries elsewhere.

One mile west of Aberfeldy, across Wade's Bridge, **Castle Menzies** (April to mid-Oct Mon–Sat 10.30am–5pm, Sun 2–5pm; £3.50) is an imposing, Z-shaped, sixteenth-century tower house run by the Menzies Clan Society, which since 1971 has been involved in the lengthy process of restoring it. The majority of the interior is on view, most of it refreshingly free of fixtures and fittings, displaying an austerity which is much more realistic to medieval life than many grander castles elsewhere in the country.

Accommodation in Aberfeldy includes *Balnearn House* (☎01887/820431, ❼www.balnearnhouse.com; ❷), or *Mavisbank*, Taybridge Drive (☎01887/820223, ✉nancynunn@onetel.net; ❶; April–Oct), both attractive stone houses in town. Up on the hillside above Weem, about two and a half miles from the centre of Aberfeldy, *Glassie Farm* (☎01887/820265, ❼www.thebunkhouse.co.uk) has a **bunkhouse** which is popular with those taking part in outdoor activities locally.

Decent bar **meals** can be found over the Wade Bridge in Weem at the *Ailean Chraggan Inn*, while beside Castle Menzies, an imaginative and impressive modern conversion has turned an old cow byre into the *House of Menzies* (May–Oct Mon–Sat 10am–5pm, Sun 11am–5pm; Oct–Dec closed Mon & Tues, ❾www.houseofmenzies.com), which combines a specialist New World wine shop, a tasteful modern café, a deli and an arts and crafts showroom.

Loch Tay

Aberfeldy grew up around a crossing point on the River Tay, six miles short of Loch Tay, a fourteen-mile-long stretch of freshwater that all but hooks together the western and eastern Highlands. Guarding the northern end of the loch is **KENMORE**, a cluster of whitewashed estate houses and well-tended gardens. The main attraction here is the **Scottish Crannog Centre** (Ⓦ www.crannog.co.uk; mid-March to Oct daily 10am–5.30pm, Nov daily 10am–4pm; £4.25), one of the best heritage museums in the country. Crannogs are loch dwellings dating from the Iron Age which were built on stilts over the water, with a gangway to the shore which could be lifted up to defy a hostile intruder, whether animal or human. Following extensive underwater archeological excavations in Loch Tay, the team here has superbly reconstructed a crannog, and visitors can now walk out over the loch to the thatched wooden dwelling, complete with sheepskin rugs, wooden bowls and other evidence of the way life was lived 2500 years ago.

Dominating the northern side of Loch Tay is moody **Ben Lawers** (3984ft), Perthshire's highest mountain; the ascent – which should not be tackled unless you're properly equipped for Scottish hillwalking (see p.54) – takes around three hours from the NTS visitor centre (April–Sept daily 10am–5pm; ☎01567/820397), located at 1300ft and reached by a track off the A827.

Glen Lyon

North of Loch Tay, the mountains tumble down into **Glen Lyon** – at 34 miles, the longest enclosed glen in Scotland – where, legend has it, the Celtic warrior Fingal built twelve castles. The narrow single track road down the glen starts at **Keltneyburn**, near Kenmore at the northern end of the loch. A few miles on, the village of **FORTINGALL** is little more than a handful of pretty thatched cottages, although locals make much of their 5000-year-old yew tree – believed (by them at least) to be the oldest living thing in Europe. The venerable tree can be found in the churchyard, showing its age a little but well looked after, with a timeline nearby listing some of the events the yew has lived through. One of these, bizarrely, is the birth of Pontius Pilate, reputedly the son of a Roman officer who came to the area in the last years BC.

Highland Perthshire

North of the Tay valley, Perthshire doesn't discard its lush richness immediately but there are clear indications of the more rugged, barren influences of the Highlands proper. The principal settlements of **Pitlochry** and **Blair Atholl**, both just off the A9, are separated by the narrow gorge of Killiecrankie, a crucial strategic spot in times past for anyone seeking to control movement o cattle or armies from the Highlands to the Lowlands. Though there are reason to stop in both places, inevitably the greater rewards are to be found furthe from the main drag, and are often best explored on foot.

Pitlochry

PITLOCHRY has, on the face of it, a lot going for it, not least the backdro of Ben Vrackie (see box) and the River Tummel slipping by. However, there little charm to be found on the main street, filled with crawling traffic an

Pitlochry is surrounded by good walking country, for which the most helpful map is *Ordnance Survey Explorer Map no. 386*. The biggest lure has to be **Ben Vrackie** (2733ft), which provides a stunning backdrop for the town and deserves better than a straight up-and-down walk; however, the climb should only be attempted in settled weather conditions, with the right equipment and following the necessary safety precautions (see p.54).

The direct route up the hill follows the course of the Moulin burn past the inn of the same name. Alternatively, a longer but much more rewarding circular route heads north out of Pitlochry, along the edge of attractive Loch Faskally, then up the River Garry to go through the **Pass of Killiecrankie**. This is looked after by the NTS, which has a visitor centre detailing the famous battle here as well as the abundant natural history of the gorge. From the NTS centre walk north up the old A9 and branch off on the small road signposted **Old Faskally**, which twists up under the new A9. The route from here is signposted: continue up the hillside until you finally leave the cultivated land and join a track which zigzags up heathery pasture and then heads across open hillside to reach a saddle by **Loch a'Choire**. Here you join the track from Pitlochry/Moulin which crosses below the dam on the loch and heads directly up the peak. To get back to Pitlochry take the Moulin path back from the loch.

Other worthwhile walks in the area include the trip right round **Loch Faskally**, or you could follow the walk above but turn back from Killiecrankie. A lovely short hill walk from the south end of Pitlochry follows a path through oak forests along the banks of the **Black Spout** burn; when you emerge from the woods it's a few hundred yards further uphill to the lovely Edradour Distillery (see below).

seemingly endless shops selling cut-price woollens, knobbly walking sticks and glass baubles. The one attraction with some distinction in the immediate vicinity is the **Edradour Distillery** (March–Oct Mon–Sat 9.30am–6pm, Sun 11.30am–5pm; Nov & Dec Mon–Sat 9.30am–5pm, Sun noon–5pm; Jan & Feb Mon–Sat 10am–4pm, Sun noon–4pm; free), Scotland's smallest, set in an idyllic position tucked into the hills a couple of miles east of Pitlochry on the A924. Although the whistle-stop audiovisual presentation and tour of the distillery itself isn't out of the ordinary, the lack of industralization and the fact that the whole traditional process is done on site gives Edradour more personality than many of its rivals.

On the western edge of Pitlochry, just across the river, lies Scotland's renowned "Theatre in the Hills", the **Pitlochry Festival Theatre** (℡01796/484626, ⓦwww.pitlochry.org.uk). By day it's worth coming here to wander around the **Scottish Plant Collectors' Garden** (daily April–Oct 10am–5pm; £3), an extended garden and forest area set up in association with the Royal Botanic Garden in Edinburgh to pay tribute to the local botanists and collectors who roamed the world in search of new plant species.

Pitlochry is on the main **train** line to Inverness, and has regular **buses** running from Perth which stop near the train station on Station Road, at the north end of town, ten minutes' walk from the centre and the **tourist office**, 22 Atholl Rd (mid-May to Sept daily 9am–7pm, Sun closes 6pm; Easter to mid-May & Oct Mon–Sat 9am–6pm, Sun 11am–5pm; Nov–Easter Mon–Fri 9am–5pm, Sat 10am–2pm; ℡01796/472215). The office can sell you a guide to walks in the surrounding area (50p), and also offers an accommodation booking service.

As a well-established holiday town, Pitlochry is packed with grand houses converted into large- and medium-sized **hotels**. The *Moulin Hotel*

(☎01796/472196, ⓦwww.moulinhotel.co.uk; ❸), at Moulin on the outskirts, is a popular travellers' inn with a great bar and its own brewery. Of the many guest houses and **B&Bs**, try *Ferryman's Cottage*, Port-na-Craig (☎01796/473681, ⓔkath@ferrymanscottage.fsnet.co.uk; ❸), in a beautiful position next to the River Tummel. The SYHA **hostel** (☎0870/004 1145, ⓔreservation@syha.org.uk) is in a fine stone mansion on Knockard Road at the top of town, while right in the centre *Pitlochry Backpackers Hotel*, 134 Atholl Rd (☎01796/470044, ⓦwww.scotlands-top-hostels.com), is based in a former hotel and offers mainly twin and double rooms.

Pitlochry is the domain of the tearoom and you have to hunt to find the decent **restaurants** and pubs; in town, try the impressive *Port-na-craig Inn* (☎01796/472777), which serves upmarket meals based on local produce from a beautiful riverside location near the theatre, while *the* best bet for good **pub grub** is the *Moulin Inn*, handily placed at the foot of Ben Vrackie.

Loch Tummel and Loch Rannoch

West of Pitlochry, the B8019/B846 makes a memorably scenic traverse of the shores of **Loch Tummel** and then **Loch Rannoch**. This is a spectacular stretch of countryside and one that deserves leisurely exploration. **Queen's View** at the eastern end of Loch Tummel is a fabulous vantage point, looking down the loch across the hills to the misty peak of **Schiehallion** (3520ft) or the "Fairy Mountain", one of the few free-standing hills in Scotland. It's a popular and inspiring mountain to climb, with views on a good day to both sides of Scotland; the path up starts at Braes of Foss, just off the B846 which links Aberfeldy with Kinloch Rannoch.

Beyond Loch Tummel, marking the eastern end of Loch Rannoch, the small community of **KINLOCH RANNOCH** doesn't see a lot of passing trade – fishermen and hill-walkers are the most common visitors. Otherwise, the only real destination here is Rannoch Station, a lonely outpost on the Glasgow–Fort William West Highland train (see p.1204), six miles or so beyond the western end of Loch Rannoch. The road goes no further. Here you can contemplate the bleakness of **Rannoch Moor**, a wide expanse of bog, heather and

⑳

Rannoch Moor

Rannoch Moor occupies roughly 150 square miles of uninhabited and uninhabitable peat bogs, lochs, heather hillocks, strewn lumps of granite and a few gnarled Caledonian pine, all of it over 1000 feet above sea level. Perhaps the most striking thing about the moor is its inaccessibility: one road, between Crianlarich and Glen Coe, skirts its western side, while another struggles west from Pitlochry to reach its eastern edge at Rannoch Station. The only regular form of transport is the West Highland railway, which stops at Rannoch and, a little to the north, Corrour Station, which has no road access at all. Corrour stole an unlikely scene in *Trainspotting* when the four heroes headed here for a taste of the great outdoors; there's now a bunkhouse and café on the station platform (☎01397/732236, ⓦwww.corrour.co.uk), as well as a SYHA hostel a mile away on the shores of Loch Ossian (☎0870/004 1139, ⓔreservations@syha.org.uk; April–Oct), making the area a great place for hikers seeking somewhere genuinely off the beaten track. From Rannoch Station it's possible to catch the train to Corrour and walk the nine miles back; it's a longer slog west to the *King's House Hotel* (see p.1227) at the eastern end of Glen Coe, while hill-walkers will find a clutch of munros around Corrour, including remote Ben Alder (3700ft), high above the forbidding shores of Loch Ericht.

wind-blown pine tree that stretches right across to the imposing entrance to Glen Coe (see p.1225). There is a tearoom and hotel here, but even these struggle to diminish the feeling of isolation.

North of Pitlochry

Four miles north of Pitlochry, the A9 cuts through the **Pass of Killiecrankie**, a breathtaking wooded gorge which falls away to the River Garry below. This dramatic setting was the site of the **Battle of Killiecrankie** in 1689, when the Jacobites beat the forces of General Mackay. Exhibits at the slick NTS **visitor centre** (daily: April–June & Sept–Oct 10am–5.30pm; July & Aug 9.30am–6pm; ☏01796/473233; parking £2) recall the battle and examine the gorge in detail. The surroundings here are thick, mature forest, full of interesting plants and creatures – the local ranger often sets off on **guided walks** which are well worth joining if you're around at the right time. Walks leave from the visitor centre and they'll let you know what's scheduled when.

Blair Atholl

Three miles north of Killiecrankie, the village of **BLAIR ATHOLL** makes for a much quieter and more idiosyncratic stop than Pitlochry. At the **Atholl Estates Information Centre** (April–Oct daily 9am–4.45pm; ☏01796/481355) you can get details of the extensive network of local walks and bike rides; alongside is Atholl Mountain Bike Hire.

  Blair Castle (April–Oct daily 9.30am–5pm; Nov–March Tues only 9.30am–1pm; £6.50, grounds only £2), reached by a driveway leading from the centre of Blair Atholl village, is the seat of the Atholl dukedom, a whitewashed, turreted castle, surrounded by parkland and dating from 1269. Highlights are the soaring **entrance hall**, with every spare inch of wood panelling covered in weapons; the **Tapestry Room**, hung with Brussels tapestries; and the vast **ballroom**, with its timber roof, antlers and mixture of portraits.

Travel details

Buses

For information on all local and national bus services, contact Traveline ☏ 0870/608 2608 (daily 7am–9pm; Ⓦ www.traveline.org.uk.

Aberfeldy to Pitlochry (3 daily; 30min); Killin (5 daily; 1hr).

Aberfoyle to: Callander (June–Sept 4 daily; 25min); Port of Menteith (June–Sept 4 daily; 10min).

Balloch to: Balmaha (every 2hr; 30min); Luss (every 2hr; 30min).

Callander to: Loch Katrine (June–Sept 4 daily; 55min).

Dumfermline to: Culross (hourly; 20min); Glasgow (hourly; 1hr 15min); Edinburgh (hourly; 1hr 20min); Kirkcaldy (hourly; 30min); Stirling (hourly; 1hr 5min).

Kinloch Rannoch to Pitlochry (4 daily; 1hr); Rannoch Station (3 daily; 40min)

Kirkcaldy to: Anstruther (hourly; 1hr 20min); Glasgow (hourly; 1hr 45min); Edinburgh (every 30min; 1hr 5min); St Andrews (twice hourly; 1hr).

Luss to: Tarbet (Mon–Sat 2–3 daily; 10min).

Perth to: Aberfeldy (10 daily; 1hr 15min); Crieff (hourly; 45min); Dundee (hourly; 45min); Dunkeld (hourly; 30min); Edinburgh (hourly; 1hr 20min); Glasgow (hourly; 1hr 35min); Gleneagles (hourly; 25min); Inverness (hourly; 2hr 45min); Oban (2 daily; 3hr); Pitlochry (hourly; 45min); Stirling (hourly; 50min).

Stirling to: Aberfoyle (4 daily; 45min); Callander (hourly; 45min); Dollar (6 daily; 35min); Doune (hourly; 25min); Dunblane (hourly; 25min); Dundee (hourly; 1hr 30min); Edinburgh (hourly; 1hr 10min); Falkirk (every 45min; 30min); Glasgow (hourly; 1hr 10min); Inverness (every 2hr; 3hr 30min); Killin (6 daily; 1hr 30min); Perth (hourly; 50min); St Andrews (6 daily; 2hr).

St Andrews to: Dundee (every 20min; 40min); Dunfermline (hourly; 1hr 30min); Edinburgh (twice hourly; 2hr 10min); Glasgow (hourly; 2hr 30min); Glenrothes (hourly; 45min); Kirkcaldy (twice hourly; 1hr); Stirling (every 2hr; 2hr).

Trains

For information on all local and national rail services, contact National Rail Enquiries ☏ 08457/48 49 50, Ⓦ www.nationalrail.co.uk.

Balloch to: Glasgow (every 30min; 40min).
Crianlarich to: Fort William (3–4 daily; 1hr 50min); Glasgow Queen Street (3–4 daily; 1hr 50min); Oban (3–4 daily; 1hr 10min).
Dunfermline to: Edinburgh (every 30min; 30min); Kirkcaldy (hourly; 40min).
Falkirk to: Edinburgh (every 30min; 35min); Glasgow Queen Street (every 30min; 25min); Stirling (every 30min; 15min).

Kirkcaldy to: Aberdeen (hourly; 2hr); Dundee (hourly; 40min–1hr); Edinburgh (every 30min; 50min); Perth (every 2–4hr; 45min).
Leuchars (for St Andrews) to: Aberdeen (1–2 hourly; 1hr 30min); Dundee (1–2 hourly; 15min); Edinburgh (1–2 hourly; 1hr).
Perth to: Aberdeen (hourly; 1hr 40min); Dundee (hourly; 25min); Edinburgh (9 daily; 1hr 25min); Glasgow Queen Street (hourly; 1hr 5min); Inverness (4–9 daily; 2hr); Stirling (hourly; 30min); Dunkeld (3–7 daily; 20min); Pitlochry (4–9 daily; 30min); Blair Atholl (3–7 daily; 40min).
Rannoch to: Corrour (2–4 daily; 12min); Fort William (2–4 daily; 1hr); Glasgow Queen Street (2–4 daily; 2hr 45min).
Stirling to: Aberdeen (hourly; 2hr 15min); Dundee (hourly; 1hr); Edinburgh (hourly; 1hr); Falkirk Grahamston (hourly; 30min); Glasgow Queen Street (hourly; 30min); Inverness (3–5 daily; 2hr 30min); Linlithgow (hourly; 35min); Perth (hourly; 30min).

Argyll

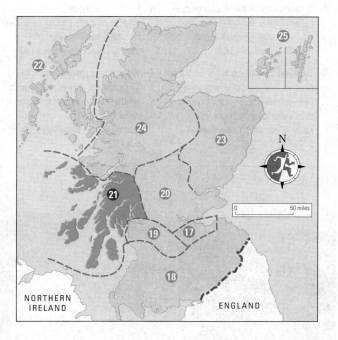

* **Loch Fyne Oyster Bar, Cairndow** Scotland's finest smokehouse and seafood outlet. See p.1097

* **Mount Stuart, Bute** Overblown aristocratic mansion, set in beautiful grounds. See p.1098

* **Tobermory, Mull** Picturesque fishing village, with colourful houses along a sheltered harbour. See p.1103

* **Golden beaches** Kiloran Bay on the Isle of Colonsay is a perfect sandy beach, but there are plenty more on Islay, Coll and Tiree. See p.1111

* **Isle of Gigha** The perfect island escape: sandy beaches, friendly folk, decent hotel and lovely gardens. See p.1114

* **Goat Fell, Arran** Spectacular views over north Arran's craggy mountain range and the Firth of Clyde. See p.1119

* **Port Charlotte, Islay** Idyllic village of pretty whitewashed houses, looking out over a sandy beach. See p.1122

* **Wintering geese on Islay** Thousands of barnacle and white-fronted geese winter here before flying off each summer to Greenland. See p.1122

△ Geese on Islay

Argyll

C ut off for centuries from the rest of Scotland by the mountains and sea lochs that characterize the region, **Argyll** remains remote, its scatter of offshore islands forming part of the Inner Hebridean archipelago (the remaining Hebrides are dealt with in the next chapter). Geographically as well as culturally, this is a transitional area between Highland and Lowland, boasting a rich variety of scenery, from lush, subtropical gardens warmed by the Gulf Stream to flat and treeless islands on the edge of the Atlantic. It's in the folds and twists of the countryside, the interplay of land and water and the views out to the islands that the strengths and beauties of mainland Argyll lie. The one area of man-made sights you shouldn't miss, however, is the cluster of **Celtic** and **prehistoric sites** near Kilmartin. Overall, the population is tiny; even **Oban**, Argyll's chief ferry port, has just seven thousand inhabitants, while the prettiest town, **Inveraray**, boasts less than eight hundred.

The eastern duo of **Bute** and **Arran** are the most popular of Scotland's more southerly islands, the latter – now, strictly speaking, part of Ayrshire – justifiably so, with spectacular scenery ranging from the granite peaks of the north to the Lowland pasture of the south. Of the Hebridean islands covered in this chapter, mountainous **Mull** is the most visited, though it is large enough to absorb the crowds, many of whom are only passing through en route to the tiny isle of **Iona**, a centre of Christian culture since the sixth century. **Islay**, best known for its distinctive malt whiskies, is fairly quiet even in the height of summer, as is neighbouring **Jura**, which offers excellent walking opportunities. And, for those seeking further solitude, there are the more remote islands of **Tiree** and **Coll**, which, although swept with fierce winds, boast more sunny days than anywhere else in Scotland.

The region's name derives from *Aragaidheal*, which translates as "Boundary of the Gaels", the Irish Celts who settled here in the fifth century AD, and whose **kingdom of Dalriada** embraced much of what is now Argyll. Known to the Romans as *Scotti* – hence "Scotland" – it was the Irish Celts who promoted Celtic Christianity, and whose Gaelic language eventually became the national tongue. In the twelfth century, the immensely powerful Somerled became king of the Hebrides and lord of Argyll. His successors, the MacDonalds, established Islay as their headquarters in the 1200s, but were in turn dislodged by Robert the Bruce, whose allies, the **Campbells**, eventually gained control of the entire area as the dukes of Argyll; even today, they remain one of the largest landowners in the region.

In the aftermath of the Jacobite uprisings, Argyll, like the rest of the Highlands, was devastated by the **Clearances**, with thousands of crofters

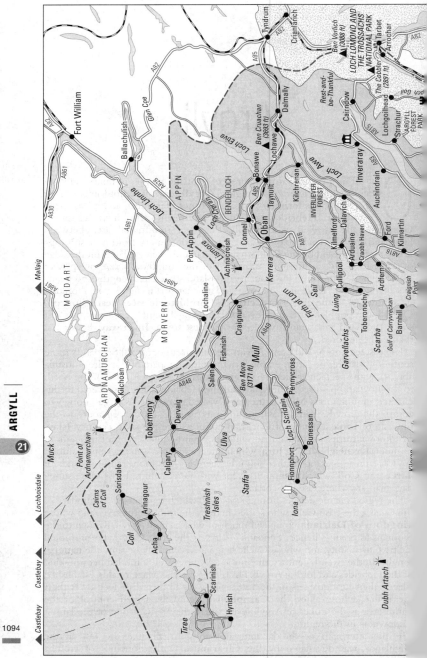

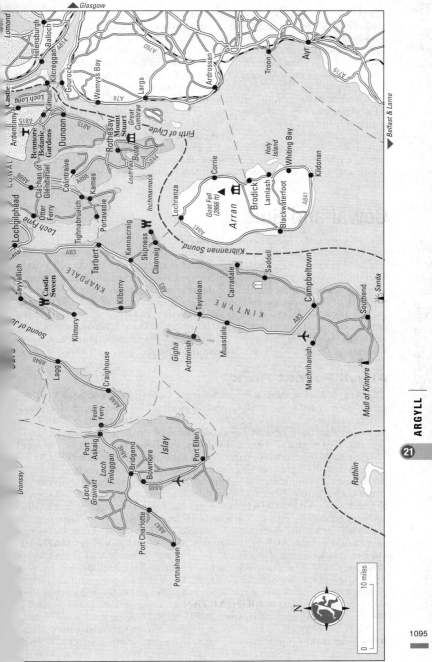

© Crown copyright

evicted to make room for profitable sheep farming – "the white plague" – and cattle-rearing. More recently forestry plantations have dramatically altered the landscape, while purpose-built marinas have sprouted all around the heavily indented coastline. Today the traditional industries of fishing and farming are in deep crisis, as is the modern industry of fish-farming, leaving the region ever more dependent on tourism, EU grants and a steady influx of new settlers to keep things going. Gaelic, once the language of the majority in Argyll, retains only a tenuous hold on the outlying islands of Islay, Coll and Tiree.

Public transport throughout Argyll is minimal, though buses do serve most major settlements, and the train line reaches all the way to Oban. In the remoter parts of the region and on the islands, you'll have to rely on a combination of walking, shared taxis and the postbus. If you're planning to take a **car** across to one of the islands, it's essential that you book both your outward and return journeys as early as possible, as the ferries get very booked up.

Cowal and Bute

The claw-shaped **Cowal peninsula**, formed by Loch Fyne and Loch Long, is the most-visited part of Argyll, largely due to its proximity to Glasgow. The landscape is extremely varied, ranging from the Munros of the **Argyll Forest Park** in the north (part of the Loch Lomond and the Trossachs National Park), to the gentle low-lying coastline of the southwest, but most visitors – and the majority of the population – confine themselves to the area around **Dunoon** (which has Cowal's chief tourist office) in the east, leaving the rest of the countryside relatively undisturbed. The island of **Bute** is separated from the peninsula by the merest sliver of water; its chief town, **Rothesay**, rivals Dunoon as the major seaside resort on the Clyde.

Argyll Forest Park

The **Argyll Forest Park** stretches from the western shores of Loch Lomond south as far as Kilmun, on Holy Loch, providing the most grandiose scenery on the peninsula. The park includes the **Arrochar Alps**, north of Glen Croe and Glen Kinglas, whose Munros offer some of the best climbing in Argyll: Ben Ime (3318ft) is the tallest of the range, and Ben Arthur or "The Cobbler" (2891ft) easily the most distinctive. All are for experienced walkers only. At the other end of the scale, there are several gentle forest walks clearly laid out by the Forestry Commission and helpful leaflets available from tourist offices.

Approaching from Glasgow along the A82, followed by the A83, you enter the park from **ARROCHAR**, at the head of Loch Long. The village itself is ordinary enough, but the setting is dramatic, and it makes a convenient base for exploring the northern section of the park. There's a **train station** a mile or so east, just off the A83 to Tarbert (see p.1114), and numerous **hotels** and **B&Bs**; try the very friendly *Lochside Guest House* on the main road (℡01301/702467, ⊛www.stayatlochlomond.com/lochside; ❷), or *Fascadail* (℡01301/702344, ⊛www.fascadail.com; ❷), a guest house with a glorious garden, situated a little to the south on the quieter A814 to Garelochhead. Two miles west of Arrochar at **ARDGARTAN**, there's a well-maintained lochside Forestry Commission **campsite** (℡01301/702293, ⊛www.forestholiday .co.uk; April–Oct), and, a little further down the road, a **tourist office** (daily July & Aug 10am–6pm; April–June, Sept & Oct 10am–5pm; ℡01301/702432) which doubles as a forestry office and has occasional organized walks. There ar also waymarked **walks** starting from the tourist office, and a bike rental place called South Peak (℡01301/702288).

Approaching Cowal from the east, you're forced to climb **Glen Croe**, a strategic hill pass whose saddle is called Rest-and-be-Thankful, for obvious reasons. From here, continue along the A83 down the grand Highland sweep of **Glen Kinglas** to **CAIRNDOW**, at the head of Loch Fyne. A mile or so around the head of the loch on the main road is famous **Loch Fyne Oyster Bar** (℡01499/600264, ⓦwww.loch-fyne.com), which sells more oysters than anywhere else in the country, plus lots of other fish and seafood treats. You can easily assemble a gourmet picnic here or stock up on provisions for the week, and the moderately expensive **restaurant** is excellent, though booking is advisable at busy times.

To delve further into Cowal, take the A815 southwest to Strachur before heading inland to **Loch Eck**, an exceptionally narrow freshwater loch, squeezed between steeply banked woods, and a favourite spot for trout fishing. At the loch's southern tip are the beautifully laid-out **Benmore Botanic Gardens** (daily: March & Oct 10am–5pm; April–Sept 10am–6pm; £3), an offshoot of Edinburgh's Royal Botanic Gardens, famed for their rhododendrons and especially striking for their avenue of Great Redwoods, planted in 1863 and now over 100ft high. There's an excellent, inexpensive **café** by the entrance, open in season, with an imaginative menu; you can eat there without visiting the gardens if trees aren't your thing.

Dunoon

In the nineteenth century, **DUNOON**, Cowal's capital, grew from a mere village to a major Clyde seaside resort and favourite holiday spot for Glaswegians. Nowadays, tourists tend to arrive by ferry from Gourock and, though their numbers are smaller, Dunoon remains by far the largest town in Argyll, with 13,000 inhabitants. Apart from its practical uses and its fine pier, however, there's little to tempt you to linger.

The **Castle House Museum** (Easter–Oct Mon–Sat 10.30am–4.30pm, Sun 2–4.30pm; ⓦwww.castlehousemuseum.org.uk; £1.50) has some good hands-on nature stuff for kids, an excellent section on the Clyde steamers as well as details of "Highland Mary", betrothed to Robbie Burns (despite the fact that he already had a pregnant wife), who nursed the poet through typhus while they planned to elope to the West Indies, only to die from the disease herself. A statue of her is in the grounds. With an hour or so to spare, you could visit the **Cowal Bird Garden** (April–Oct daily 10.30am–6pm; £4), one mile northwest along the A885 to Sandbank, and wander through its woodland amid exotic caged birds as well as free-roaming peacocks, macaws and pot-bellied pigs. If the weather's fine, take the **Ardnadam Heritage Trail**, a mile further up the road, to the wonderful Dunan viewpoint looking out to the Firth of Clyde.

It's a good idea to take advantage of Dunoon's **tourist office**, the principal one in Cowal, located on Alexandra Parade (Mon–Fri 9am–5.30pm, Sat & Sun 10am–5pm). There are two **ferry crossings** across the Clyde from Gourock to Dunoon; the shorter, more frequent service is half-hourly on Western Ferries to Hunter's Quay, a mile north of the town centre; CalMac's boats, though, arrive at the main pier, and have better transport connections if you're on foot. There's an enormous choice of **B&Bs**, none of them outstanding. You're better off heading out of town or persuading the tourist office to help you out, since availability is the biggest problem. Worth considering are the

21

welcoming *Abbot's Brae* above West Bay (☎01369/705021, ⓦwww
.abbotsbrae.co.uk; ❺); the smart Dhailling Lodge (☎01369/701253,
ⓦwww.dhaillinglodge.com; ❹), closer to town on Alexandra Parade; or,
topping the lot, the luxurious *Enmore Hotel* (☎01369/702230,
ⓦwww.enmorehotel.co.uk; ❺), an eighteenth-century villa on Marine Parade
near Hunter's Quay.

Chatters, 58 John St (☎01369/706402; Wed–Sat only; closed Jan & Feb), is
Dunoon's best **restaurant**, offering delicious Loch Fyne seafood and Scottish
beef. For something a bit less pricey, you could do worse than the simple café
serving soups, sandwiches and light meals run by the Baptist Church right next
door to the tourist office; there's also a vast Italian menu at *Di Marco's Café Bar*
in Argyll Street (closed Mon). Dunoon boasts a two-screen **cinema** (a rarity
in Argyll) on John Street, but the town's most famous entertainment is the
Cowal Highland Gathering (ⓦwww.cowalgathering.com), the largest of its
kind in the world, held here on the last weekend in August, and culminating
in the awesome spectacle of the massed pipes and drums of more than 150
bands marching through the streets.

The Isle of Bute

Thanks to its consistently mild climate and its ferry link with Wemyss Bay (see
p.1040), the island of **Bute** (ⓦwww.visitbute.com) has been a popular holiday
and convalescence spot for Clydesiders – particularly the elderly – for over a
century. Even considering the island's small size (fifteen miles long and five
miles wide) you can find peace and quiet; most of its inhabitants are centred
on the two wide bays on the east coast of the island.

Bute's only town, **ROTHESAY**, is a handsome Victorian resort set in a wide
sweeping bay, backed by green hills, with a classic palm-tree promenade and
1920s pagoda-style Winter Gardens. It creates a much better general impression than Dunoon, with its period architecture and the occasional flourishes of
wrought-ironwork. Even if you're just passing through, you should pay a visit
to the ornate **Victorian toilets** (daily: Easter–Sept 8am–9pm; Oct–Easter
9am–5pm; 15p) on the pier, which were built by Twyfords in 1899 and have
since been declared a national treasure. Men have the best time, since the
porcelain urinals steal the show, but women can ask for a guided tour.

Rothesay also boasts the militarily useless, but architecturally impressive,
moated ruins of **Rothesay Castle** (April–Sept daily 9.30am–6.30pm;
Oct–March Mon–Wed 9.30am–4.30pm, Thurs 9.30am–noon, Sat
9.30am–4.30pm, Sun 2–4.30pm; £2.20; HS), hidden amid the town's backstreets but signposted from the pier. Built around the twelfth century, it was
twice captured by the Vikings in the 1200s; such vulnerability was the reason-
ing behind the unusual, almost circular curtain wall, with its four big drum
towers, only one of which remains fully intact.

A very good reason for coming to Bute is to visit **Mount Stuart** (May–Aug
Mon, Wed & Fri–Sun 11am–5pm; £7, gardens only £3.50; ⓦwww
.mountstuart.com), three miles south of Rothesay. Seat of the fantastically
wealthy seventh marquis of Bute (aka former racing driver Johnny Dumfries),
the mansion was built for the third marquis between 1879 and World War I,
as an incredible High Gothic fancy, drawing architectural inspiration from all
over Europe. The sumptuous interior was decked out by craftsmen who
worked with William Burges on the marquis's earlier medieval concoctions a
Cardiff Castle. The gardens, established in the eighteenth century by the third
earl of Bute, who had a hand in London's Kew Gardens, are equally lovely.

For the best overall view of the island, take a walk up **Canada Hill** above the freshwater Loch Fad, which all but divides Bute in two. The northern half of the island is hilly, uninhabited and little visited, while the southern half is made up of Lowland-style farmland. The early monastic history of the island is recalled at **St Blane's Chapel**, a twelfth-century ruin beautifully situated in open countryside on the west coast, close to the very southernmost tip. Bute's finest sandy beach is **Scalpsie Bay**, further up the west coast, beyond which lies **St Ninian's Point**, where the ruins of a sixth-century chapel overlook another fine sandy strand and the deserted island of **Inchmarnock**.

Practicalities

Rothesay's **tourist office** is opposite the pier at 15 Victoria St (Mon–Fri 9am–5pm, Sat & Sun 10am–4pm; longer hours in peak season). There's no shortage of modest places to **stay** along the seafront, but one of the most attractive is *Cannon House* (℡01700/502819, ⓦwww.cannonhousehotel .co.uk; ❹), a Georgian house close to the pier on Battery Place, while the nearby *Commodore* (℡01700/502178, ⓦwww.commodorebute.com; ❶) is a more modest guest house, but equally accommodating. Further out in Ascog, the B&B at *Ascog Farm* (℡01700/503372; ❷) is exceptionally good value. The best **food** options are *The Bistro* in the Winter Garden, which offers a good-value restaurant menu and a superb view of the bay, or the highly original and engaging *Port Royal Hotel* in Port Bannatyne, which describes itself as a "Waterfront Russian Tavern" and serves fresh local seafood alongside dishes such as blini, as well as a terrific array of real ales. For Rothesay's finest fish and chips, head for the *West End Café* on Gallowgate. Rothesay's **cinema** is in the Winter Gardens. Bute holds its own **Highland Games** on the second-to-last weekend in August – Prince Charles, the duke of Rothesay, occasionally attends.

Inveraray

A classic example of an eighteenth-century planned town, **INVERARAY** was built on the site of a ruined fishing village in 1745 by the third duke of Argyll, head of the powerful Campbell clan, in order to distance his newly rebuilt castle from the hoi polloi in the town and to establish a commercial and legal centre for the region. Today Inveraray, an absolute set piece of Scottish Georgian architecture, has a truly memorable setting, the brilliant white arches of Front Street reflected in the still waters of **Loch Fyne**, which separate it from the Cowal peninsula.

Squeezed onto a promontory some distance from the duke's new castle, there's not much more to Inveraray's "New Town" than its distinctive **Main Street** (set at a right angle to Front Street), flanked by whitewashed terraces, whose window casements are picked out in black. At the top of the street, the road divides to circumnavigate the town's Neoclassical church, originally built in two parts: the southern half served the Gaelic-speaking community, while the northern half served those who spoke English.

East of the church is **Inveraray Jail** (daily: April–Oct 9.30am–6pm; Nov–March 10am–5pm; £5.75), whose attractive Georgian courthouse and grim prison blocks ceased to function in the 1930s. The jail is now an imaginative and thoroughly enjoyable museum, which graphically recounts prison conditions from medieval times. You can also sit in the beautiful semicircular courthouse and listen to the trial of a farmer accused of fraud.

21

A ten-minute walk north of the New Town, the neo-Gothic **Inveraray Castle** (June–Sept Mon–Sat 10am–5.45pm, Sun 1–5.45pm; April–May & Oct Mon–Thurs & Sat 10am–1pm & 2–5.45pm, Sun 1–5.45pm; £5.50) remains the family home of the Duke of Argyll. Built in 1745 by the third duke, it was given a touch of the Loire in the nineteenth century with the addition of dormer windows and conical roofs. Inside, the most startling feature is the armoury hall, whose displays of weaponry – supplied to the Campbells by the British government to put down the Jacobites – rise through several storeys; look out for Rob Roy's rather sad-looking sporran and dirk handle (a "dirk" being a dagger, traditionally worn in Highland dress).

Practicalities

Inveraray's **tourist office** is on Front Street (April–Oct Mon–Sat 9am–5pm, Sun noon–5pm; Nov–March Mon–Fri 10am–3pm, Sat & Sun 11am–3pm), as is the town's chief **hotel**, the historic *Argyll* (℡01499/302466, Ⓦwww.the-argyll-hotel.co.uk; ❺), now part of the Best Western chain. A cheaper, but equally well-appointed alternative is the Georgian *Fernpoint Hotel* (℡01499/302170; ❷), round by the pier, which has a nice pub garden. The SYHA **hostel** (℡0870/004 1125, Ⓔreservations@syha.org.uk; April–Oct) is in a modern building a short distance north on the A819 Dalmally road. The **bar** of the central *George Hotel* is the town's liveliest spot. The best place to sample Loch Fyne's delicious fresh fish and seafood is the superb, moderately priced restaurant of the *Loch Fyne Oyster Bar* (see p.1097), six miles northeast back up the A83 towards Glasgow.

Oban

The solidly Victorian resort of **OBAN** enjoys a superb setting – the island of Kerrera providing its bay with a natural shelter – distinguished by a bizarre granite amphitheatre, dramatically lit at night, on the hilltop above the town. Despite a population of just eight thousand, it's by far the largest port in northwest Scotland, the second-largest town in Argyll, and the main departure point for ferries to the Hebrides. If you arrive late, or are catching an early boat, you may have to spend the night here (there's no real need otherwise); if you're staying elsewhere, it's a useful base for wet-weather activities and shopping, although it does get uncomfortably crowded in the summer.

The only truly remarkable sight in Oban is the town's landmark, **McCaig's Tower**, a stiff ten-minute climb from the quayside. Built in imitation of Rome's Colosseum, it was the brainchild of a local businessman a century ago, who had the twin aims of alleviating off-season unemployment among the local stonemasons and creating a museum, art gallery and chapel. In his will, McCaig gave instructions for the lancet windows to be filled with bronze statues of the family, though no such work was ever undertaken. Instead, the folly has been turned into a sort of walled garden, and simply provides a wonderful seaward panorama, particularly at sunset.

Down in the centre of town, you can pass a few hours admiring the boats in the harbour and looking out for scavenging seals in the bay. If the weather's bad, the best option is to sign up for one of the excellent guided tours around **Oban Distillery** (Easter–Oct Mon–Sat 9.30am–5pm, July–Sept also open until 7.30pm Mon–Fri & Sun noon–5pm; Nov & March Mon–Fri 10am–5pm; Dec–Feb Mon–Fri 12.30–4pm; £4), in the centre of town or

George Street. The tour ends with a generous dram of Oban's lightly peaty malt (and a partial refund of the admission fee if you buy a bottle).

Practicalities

The CalMac **ferry terminal** (☎01631/566688, ⓦ www.calmac.co.uk) for the islands is on Railway Pier, a stone's throw from the **train station**, which is itself adjacent to the **bus station** on Station Square. The **tourist office** (April–Oct Mon–Sat 9am–5.30pm, Sun 10am–4pm; longer hours in peak season; Nov–March Mon–Fri 9.30am–5pm, Sat & Sun noon–4pm) is housed in a converted church on Argyll Square.

Oban is positively heaving with **hotels** and **B&B**s. Top choices include the *Glenbervie Guest House* (☎01631/564770, ⓔ glenbervie@lineone.net; ❷), a superior Victorian guest house set slightly above the town on Dalriach Road; the *Kilchrenan House* (☎01631/562663, ⓦ www.kilchrenanhouse.co.uk; ❹), a tasteful hospitable place on the quieter northern section of the Corran Esplanade; and the *Caledonian Hotel*, on Station Square (☎0871/2223415, ⓦ www.go2oban.co.uk; ❸), the best of Oban's big central hotels. There are also three **hostels**, the friendliest, cheapest and most central of which is the *Oban Backpackers*, on Breadalbane Street (☎01631/562107, ⓦ www .scotlands-top-hostels.com; March–Oct). **Campers** should head for *Oban Caravan & Camping Park*, Gallanachmore Farm, Gallanach Road (☎01631/562425, ⓦ www.obancaravanpark.co.uk; April to mid-Oct), two miles southwest of Oban along the Gallanach Road.

For sit-down snacks, there's a **café** on the mezzanine above the impressive *Kitchen Garden* deli on George Street, or *F'Eats*, a modern café on John Street offering delicious toasted panini and good cappuccino. On the North Pier the swanky designer *Ee-usk* serves glistening seafood platters and fresh fish dishes, while in the old seaman's mission on the CalMac pier, *The Waterfront* rustles up impressive dishes using the best of the daily catch. Of course, there's always fish and chips from *Oban Fish & Chip Shop & Restaurant*, 116 George St. Oban's only half-decent **pub** is the *Oban Inn* opposite the North Pier, with a classic dark-wood-flagstone-and-brass bar downstairs and lounge bar with stained glass upstairs. It's worth noting, however, that Oban is one of the few places in Argyll with a **cinema**, confusingly known as the Highland Theatre (☎01631/562444), at the north end of George Street. The annual **Argyllshire Gathering** takes place on the last Thursday in August, featuring piping competitions and Highland Games.

The Isle of Mull

The second largest of the Inner Hebrides, **Mull** (ⓦ www.holidaymull.org.uk) is by far the most accessible: just forty minutes from Oban by ferry. As so often, first impressions largely depend on the weather – it's the wettest of the Hebrides (and that's saying something) – as without the sun the large tracts of moorland, particularly around the island's highest peak, Ben More (3196ft), can appear bleak and unwelcoming. There are, however, areas of more gentle pastoral scenery around **Dervaig** in the north and the indented west coast varies from the sandy beaches around **Calgary** to the cliffs of Loch na Keal. The most common mistake is to try and "do" the island in a day or two: flogging up the main road to the picturesque capital of **Tobermory**, then covering the fifty-odd miles between there and Fionnphort, in order to visit **Iona**.

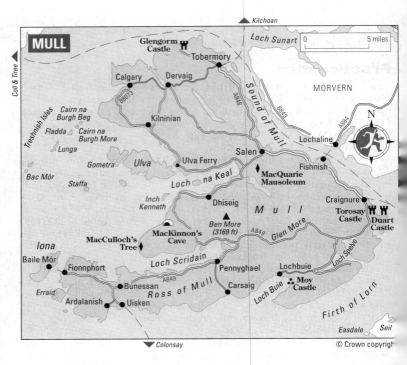

MULL

Kilchoan

Loch Sunart

0   5 miles

Coll & Tiree

Glengorm Castle

Tobermory

Calgary   Dervaig

B8073

Kilninian

Cairn na Burgh Beg

Treshnish Isles

Fladda   Cairn na Burgh More

Lunga

Gometra   Ulva

Bac Mór   Ulva Ferry

Staffa

Loch na Keal

Inch Kenneth

Dhiseig

MORVERN

A848

Sound of Mull

B849

A884

N

Lochaline

Salen   Fishnish

MacQuarie Mausoleum

Craignure

Ben More (3169 ft)

MacKinnon's Cave

MacCulloch's Tree

Mull

Torosay Castle   Duart Castle

A849   Glen More

Loch Spelve

Iona

Baile Mór   Fionnphort

Loch Scridain

A849

Pennyghael

Lochbuie

Moy Castle

Loch Buie

Firth of Lorn

Erraid   Bunessan

Ardalanish   Uisken

Ross of Mull   Carsaig

Easdale   Seil

Colonsay   © Crown copyright

Mull is a place that will grow on you only if you have the time and patience to explore.

Historically, crofting, whisky distilling and fishing supported the islanders (*Muileachs*), but the population – which peaked at 10,000 – decreased dramatically in the late nineteenth century due to the Clearances and the 1846 potato famine. On Mull, it's a trend that has been reversed, mostly due to the large influx of settlers from elsewhere in the country which has brought the current population up to over 2500. One of the main reasons for this resurgence is, of course, tourism – more than half a million visitors come here each year – although, oddly enough, there are very few large hotels or campsites.

Craignure is the main arrival point, with a frequent daily **car ferry** link with Oban (booking advised). Two much smaller car ferries operate on a first-come, first-served basis: from Lochaline on the Morvern peninsula to the slipway at Fishnish, six miles northwest of Craignure; and from Kilchoan on the Ardnamurchan peninsula to Tobermory, 24 miles northwest of Craignure. **Public transport** on Mull is not too bad on the main A849, but there's more or less no service along the west coast (for more information, visit Ⓦ www.mict.co.uk/travel).

Craignure and around

CRAIGNURE is little more than a scattering of cottages with a small shop, a bar, some toilets and a CalMac and **tourist office** – the only one on the island, open all year round – situated opposite the pier (April–June & Sept Mon–F 8.30am–5pm, Sat 9am–5pm, Sun 10am–5pm; July & Aug Mon–F

8.30am–7.30pm, Sat 9am–6.30pm, Sun 10am–7pm; Oct–March Mon–Sat 9am–5pm, Sun 11am–5pm). The *Craignure Inn* (℡01680/812305, ⓦwww.craignure-inn.co.uk; ❺), just a minute's stroll up the road towards Fionnphort, is a snug **pub** to hole up in. There's also a well-equipped **campsite** (℡01680/812496, ⓦwww.shielingholidays.co.uk; April–Oct) on the south side of Craignure Bay, behind the new village hall.

Two castles lie immediately southeast of Craignure. **Torosay Castle** (April to mid-Oct daily 10.30am–5.30pm; £5), a full-blown Scots baronial creation, is linked to Craignure by the narrow-gauge **Mull Rail** (Easter to mid-Oct; ℡01680/812494; £3.75 return). The magnificent **gardens** (open all year daily 10.30am–5.30pm; gardens only £4) include an avenue of eighteenth-century Venetian statues, Japanese section and views over to neighbouring Duart. The house itself, in the mid-nineteenth-century style, is stuffed with junk relating to the present owners, the little-known Guthries.

Lacking the gardens, but perched on a picturesque spit of rock a couple of miles east of Torosay, **Duart Castle** (April to mid-Oct daily 10.30am–6pm; ⓦwww.duartcastle.com; £4) is clearly visible from the Oban–Craignure ferry. Headquarters of the once-powerful MacLean clan from the thirteenth century, it was burnt down by the Campbells and confiscated after the 1745 rebellion. Finally in 1911, the 26th clan chief, Fitzroy MacLean (1835–1936) managed to buy it back and restore it. You can peek at the dungeons, climb up to the ramparts, study the family photos, and learn about the world scout movement – the 27th clan chief became chief scout in 1959. After your visit, you can enjoy homemade cakes and tea at the castle's excellent tearoom.

Tobermory

Mull's chief town, **TOBERMORY** (ⓦwww.tobermory.co.uk), at the northern tip of the island, is easily the most attractive fishing port on the west coast of Scotland, its clusters of brightly coloured houses and boats sheltering in a bay backed by a steep bluff. Founded in 1788 by the British Society for Encouraging Fisheries, it never really took off as a fishing port and only survived due to the steady influx of crofters evicted from other parts of the island during the Clearances. With a population of more than 800, it's the most important settlement on Mull, and if you're staying any length of time on the island you're bound to end up here, not least because it has a Womble named after it (or, if you're under 10, because it's the setting for another children's TV show *Balamory*).

Practicalities aside, the harbour's shops are good for browsing, and you could pay a visit to the **Hebridean Whale and Dolphin Trust** (April–Oct daily 10am–5pm; Nov–March Mon–Fri 11am–5pm; free; ⓦwww.hwdt.org), run by a welcoming bunch of enthusiasts. The small office has lots of information on how to identify marine mammals, and on recent sightings. They're very child-friendly, with computer marine games, word searches and a bit of artwork. Note that you can't book whale-watching trips here – head instead to Mull & Iona Trips and Tours (Easter–Oct daily 9am–6pm; ℡01688/302808) beside MacGochan's pub (near the distillery).

Another good wet-weather retreat is the **Mull Museum** (Easter to mid-Oct Mon–Fri 10am–4pm, Sat 10am–1pm; £1), further along Main Street, which packs a great deal of information and artefacts – including a few objects salvaged from the sixteenth-century wreck of the *San Juan* – into one tiny room. A stiff climb up Back Brae will bring you to the island's main arts centre, An Tobar (March–Dec Mon–Sat 10am–5pm; June–Aug also Sun 1–4pm; free;

△ Tobermory Harbour, M

@www.antobar.co.uk), housed in a converted Victorian schoolhouse. The small but attractive centre hosts exhibitions, a variety of live events, and contains a café with comfy sofas set before a real fire. The rest of the upper town is laid out on a classic grid plan, and merits a stroll, if only for the great views over the bay.

Practicalities

The **tourist office** (April–Oct Mon–Fri 10am–5pm, Sat & Sun noon–5pm; longer hours in peak season) is in the same building as the CalMac ticket office at the far end of Main Street. There are several **accommodation** options on Main Street: try the excellent *Fàilte* (T01688/302495; ❷), the *Harbour Guest House* (T01688/302209; March–Oct; ❶), or the small, friendly SYHA **hostel** (T0870/004 1151, @reservations@syha.org.uk; March–Oct). *Ach-na-Craiboh* (T01688/302301, @plogan7934@aol.com; ❷) is a lovely house up the hill near the golf course with guest rooms in a garden "bothy". The nearest **campsite** is *Newdale* (T01688/302525; April–Oct), nicely situated one a half miles outside Tobermory on the B8073 to Dervaig.

Main Street is heaving with **places to eat**, including a highly rated fish-and-chip van on the old pier which serves scallops and chips alongside more traditional fish suppers. You can get reasonable, filling meals at *The Anchorage* as well as bar food in the lounge bar at the *Mishnish*. A good option for more sophisticated meals using local produce is the pleasant surroundings of the upstairs café/bistro at the Mull Pottery at Ballinsgate, just on the edge of town (closed Mon evenings; T01688/302347). The *Mishnish* has been the most popular local **pub** for many years, and features live music at the weekend. It's also the focus of Mull's annual **Traditional Music Festival**, a feast of Gaelic folk music held on the last weekend in April. Mull's other major musical event, after the folk festival, is the annual **Mendelssohn on Mull Festival**, held over ten days in early July, which commemorates the composer's visit here in 1829.

Dervaig and Calgary

The gently undulating countryside west of Tobermory, beyond the freshwater Mishnish lochs, provides some of the most beguiling scenery on the island. Added to this, the road out west, the B8073, is exceptionally dramatic, with fiendish switchbacks much appreciated during the annual Mull Rally, which takes place each October. The only village of any size is **DERVAIG**, which nestles beside narrow Loch Chumhainn, just eight miles southwest of Tobermory, distinguished by its unusual pencil-shaped church spire and dinky whitewashed cottages set in twos along its main street. Dervaig is best known as the home of **Mull Theatre**, one of the smallest professional theatres in the world, which puts on an adventurous season of plays adapted for a handful of resident actors (April–Sept; T01688/302828, @www.mulltheatre.org.uk); booking is recommended. There's a box office for the theatre on the main street in Tobermory, while the theatre itself lies within the grounds of the Victorian *Druimard Country House* (T01688/400345, @www.druimard.co.uk; ❹ for dinner, B&B; late March–Oct), on the fringe of Dervaig along the Salen road. Dervaig has a wide choice of **places to stay**: the *Druimnacroish Hotel* (T01688/400274, @www.druimnacroish.co.uk; ❺), a lovely country house two miles out on the Salen road, and several good B&Bs ranging from the vegetarian-friendly *Glen Bellart House* (T01688/400282; ❶; Easter–Oct), on the main street, to *Glenview* (T01688/400239; ❷; April–Oct), a really lovely 1890s house on the edge of the village. There's also a **bunkhouse**

(T01688/400492) right in the centre of the village, with bedding provided and disabled facilities.

The road continues cross-country to **CALGARY**, once a thriving crofting community, now an idyllic holiday spot boasting Mull's finest sandy bay, backed by low-lying dunes and machair, with wonderful views over to Coll and Tiree. There's just one hotel, the delightful *Calgary Farmhouse* (T01688/400256, W www.calgary.co.uk; ❺; March–Nov), whose excellent, moderately priced *Dovecote* restaurant (closed Mon) is (unsurprisingly) housed in a converted dovecote. The south side of the beach is a favourite spot for **camping** rough, though the only facilities are the public toilets.

The Isle of Staffa

Seven miles off the west coast of Mull, **Staffa** is the most romantic and dramatic of Scotland's many uninhabited islands. On its south side, the perpendicular rockface features an imposing series of black basalt columns, known as the Colonnade, which have been cut by the sea into cathedralesque caverns, most notably **Fingal's Cave**. The Vikings knew about the island – the name derives from their word for "Island of Pillars" – but it wasn't until 1772 that it was "discovered" by the world. Turner painted it, Wordsworth explored it, but Mendelssohn's *Die Fingalshöhle*, inspired by the sounds of the sea-wracked caves he heard on a visit here in 1829, did most to popularize the place – after which Queen Victoria gave her blessing, too. The geological explanation for these polygonal basalt organ pipes is that they were created by a massive subterranean explosion some sixty million years ago. A huge mass of molten basalt burst forth onto land and, as it cooled, solidified into what are, essentially, crystals. To **get to Staffa**, you can join one of the many boat trips from Fionnphort, Iona, Ulva Ferry, Dervaig or even Oban. Staffa-only trips run from April to October and cost £14 per person on the *Iolaire* (T01681/700358, W www.staffatrips .f9.co.uk), which sails out of Fionnphort and Iona twice daily; Turus Mara (T0800/085 8786, W www.turusmara.com), which operates out of Ulva Ferry, on Mull's west coast, costs a bit more, as do Inter-Island Cruises (T01688/400264, W www.jenny.mull.com), which run from Dervaig.

Ben More and the Ross of Mull

From the southern shores of Loch na Keal, which almost splits Mull in two, rise the terraced slopes of **Ben More** (3169ft) – literally "big mountain" – a mighty extinct volcano, and the only Munro in the Hebrides outside of Skye. Stretching for twenty miles west of Ben More as far as Iona is Mull's rocky southernmost peninsula, the **Ross of Mull**, which, like much of Scotland, appears blissfully tranquil in good weather, and desolate and bleak in bad.

The road ends at **FIONNPHORT**, facing Iona, probably the least attractive place to stay on the Ross, though it has a nice sandy bay backed by pink granite rocks to the north of the ferry slipway. Partly to ease congestion on Iona, and to give their neighbours a slice of the tourist pound, Fionnphort was chosen as the site for the **St Columba Centre** (Easter–Sept daily 10.30am–1pm & 2–5.30pm; free); inside, a small exhibition outlines Iona's history, tells a little of Columba's life (for more on which, see p.1108) and has a few facsimiles of the illuminated manuscripts produced by the island's monks.

If you're in need of a **B&B** in Fionnphort, try the granite *Seaview* (T01681/700235, W www.iona.bed.breakfast.mull.com; ❷), or the white-washed *Staffa House* (T01681/700677, W www.iona-staffahouse-mull.co.u

❸; March–Oct), both of which are close to the ferry and the local pub, the *Keel Row*, which serves reasonable meals. Just out of Fionnphort (no bad thing), there's also *Achaban House* (☎01681/700205, ⓦ www.achabanhouse.co.uk; ❸), an old manse with some character overlooking Loch Pottie. The basic *Fidden Farm* campsite (☎01681/700427; April–Sept), a mile south along the Knockvologan road by Fidden beach, is the nearest to Iona.

The Isle of Iona

Less than a mile off the southwest tip of Mull, **IONA** – just three miles long and not much more than a mile wide – has been a place of pilgrimage for several centuries, and a place of Christian worship for more than 1400 years. It was to this flat Hebridean island that St Columba fled from Ireland in 563 and established a monastery which was responsible for the conversion of more or less all of pagan Scotland as well as much of northern England. This history and the island's splendid isolation have lent it a peculiar religiosity; in the much-quoted words of Dr Johnson, who visited in 1773, "that man is little to be envied . . . whose piety would not grow warmer among the ruins of Iona". Today, however, the island can barely cope with the constant flood of day-trippers, and charges visitors entry to its abbey, so to appreciate the special atmosphere and to have time to see the whole island, including the often-overlooked west coast, you should plan on staying at least one night.

The passenger ferry from Fionnphort drops you off at the island's main village, **BAILE MÓR** (literally "large village"), which is in fact little more than a single terrace of cottages facing the sea. Just inland lie the extensive pink-granite ruins of the **Augustinian nunnery**, built around 1200 but disused since the Reformation – if nothing else, it gives you an idea of the state of the present-day abbey before it was restored. Across the road to the north is the **Iona Heritage Centre** (Easter–Oct Mon–Sat 10.30am–4.30pm; £2), with displays on the social history of the island over the last 200 years, including the Clearances, which nearly halved the island's population of 500 in the mid-nineteenth century. At a bend in the road, just south of the manse and church, stands the fifteenth-century **MacLean's Cross**, a fine late medieval example of the distinctive, flowing, three-leaved foliage of the Iona school.

No buildings remain from Columba's time: the present **abbey** (daily: April–Sept 9.30am–6.30pm; Oct–March 9.30am–4.30pm; £3; HS) dates from the arrival of the Benedictines in around 1200, was extensively rebuilt in the fifteenth and sixteenth centuries, and was restored virtually wholesale early last century. Adjoining the facade is a small steep-roofed chamber, believed to be St Columba's grave, now a small chapel. The three high crosses in front of the abbey date from the eighth to tenth centuries, and are decorated with the Pictish serpent and boss and Celtic spirals for which Iona's early Christian masons were renowned. For reasons of sanitation, the cloisters were placed, contrary to the norm, on the north side of the church (where running water was available); entirely reconstructed in the late 1950s, they now shelter a useful historical account of the abbey's development.

Iona's oldest building, the plain-looking **St Oran's Chapel**, lies south of the abbey, and boasts an eleventh-century door. Oran's Chapel stands at the centre of Iona's sacred burial ground, **Reilig Odhráin** (Oran's Cemetery), which is said to contain the graves of sixty kings of Norway, Ireland, France and Scotland, including Duncan and Macbeth. The best of the early Christian

A brief history of Iona

Legend has it that **St Columba** (Colum Cille), born in Donegal in northwestern Ireland some time around 521, was a direct descendant of the semi-legendary Irish king, Niall of the Nine Hostages. A scholar and soldier priest, who founded numerous monasteries in Ireland, he is thought to have become involved in a bloody dispute with the king when he refused to hand over a copy of *St Jerome's Psalter*, copied illegally from the original owned by St Finian of Moville. This, in turn, provoked the Battle of Cúl Drebene (Cooldrumman) – also known as the **Battle of the Book** – at which Columba's forces won, though with the loss of over 3000 lives. The story goes that, repenting this bloodshed, Columba went into exile with twelve other monks, eventually settling on Iona in 563. The bottom line, however, is that we know very little about Columba, though he undoubtedly became something of a cult figure after his death in 597. He was posthumously credited with miraculous feats such as defeating the Loch Ness monster and banishing snakes (and, some say, frogs) from the island.

Whatever the truth about Columba's life, in the sixth and seventh centuries, Iona enjoyed a great deal of autonomy from Rome, establishing a specifically **Celtic Christian** tradition. Missionaries were sent out to the rest of Scotland and parts of England, and Iona quickly became a respected seat of learning and artistry; the monks compiled a vast library of intricately **illuminated manuscripts** – most famously the *Book of Kells* (now on display in Trinity College, Dublin) – while the masons excelled in carving peculiarly intricate crosses. Two factors were instrumental in the demise of the Celtic tradition: a series of Viking raids, the worst of which was the massacre of 68 monks on the sands of Martyrs' Bay in 806; and relentless pressure from the established Church, beginning with the Synod of Whitby in 664, which chose Rome over the Celtic Church, and culminated in the suppression of the Celtic Church by King David I in 1144.

In 1203, Iona became part of the mainstream Church with the establishment of an **Augustinian nunnery** and a **Benedictine monastery** by Reginald, son of Somerled, lord of the Isles. During the Reformation, the entire complex was ransacked, the contents of the library burnt and all but three of the island's 360 crosses destroyed. Although plans were drawn up at various times to turn the abbey into a Cathedral of the Isles, nothing came of them until in 1899, when the then owner, the eighth duke of Argyll, donated the abbey buildings to the **Church of Scotland**, which restored the abbey church for worship over the course of the next decade. Iona's modern resurgence began in 1938, when **George MacLeod**, a minister from Glasgow, established a group of ministers, students and artisans to begin rebuilding the remainder of the monastic buildings. What began as a mostly male, Gaelic-speaking, strictly Presbyterian community is today a lay, mixed and ecumenical retreat. The entire abbey complex has been successfully restored, and is now looked after by Historic Scotland, while the island, apart from the church land and a few crofts, is in the care of the National Trust for Scotland.

gravestones and medieval effigies that once lay in the Reilig Odhráin have unfortunately been removed to the Infirmary Museum, behind the abbey.

Practicalities

There's no **tourist office** on Iona, and as demand far exceeds supply you should organize **accommodation** well in advance. Of the island's two **hotels**, the stone-built *Argyll* (℡01681/700334, ℗www.argyllhoteliona.co.uk; ❹ April–Oct), in the terrace of cottages overlooking the Sound of Iona, is by far the nicer. As for **B&Bs**, try *Iona Cottage* (℡01681/700579, ℗© @ionacottage.freeserve.co.uk; ❷), which overlooks the jetty. **Camping** is no permitted on Iona, but there is a terrific **hostel** (℡01681/700781, Ⓦwww.ionahostel.co.uk) at the north of the island looking out to the Treshnish Islands. If you want to stay with the **Iona Community**, contact the *MacLeod Centre* (℡01681/700404, Ⓦwww.iona.org.uk), popularly known as the "Mac". The **restaurant** at the *Argyll* isn't bad, and the grub at the *Martyr's Bay Restaurant* by the jetty is reasonable too; for even more convivial surroundings you can eat from the same menu in the adjoining bar. For something lighter during the day, head for the tearoom beside the Heritage Centre, which serves homemade soup and delicious cakes.

Coll, Tiree and Colonsay

Coll and **Tiree** are among the most isolated of the Inner Hebrides, and if anything have more in common with the outlying Western Isles than with their closest neighbour, Mull. Each is roughly twelve miles long and three miles wide, both are low-lying, treeless and exceptionally windy, with white sandy beaches and the highest sunshine records in Scotland. Isolated between Mull and Islay, **Colonsay** – eight miles by three at its widest – is nothing like as bleak and windswept as Coll or Tiree. All the islands have strong Gaelic roots, but the percentage of English-speaking newcomers is rising steadily.

The Isle of Coll

The fish-shaped rocky island of **Coll** (Ⓦwww.isleofcoll.org), with a population of around 180, lies less than seven miles off the coast of Mull. The CalMac ferry drops off at Coll's only real village, **ARINAGOUR**, whose whitewashed cottages dot the western shore of Loch Eatharna. Half the island's population lives in the village, and it's here you'll find the hotel and pub, post office, churches and a couple of shops.

On the southwest coast there are two edifices, both confusingly known as **Breachacha Castle**, and both built by the MacLeans. The older, at the head of Loch Breachacha, is a fifteenth-century tower house with an additional curtain wall, recently restored, and is now a training centre for Project Trust overseas aid volunteers. The less attractive "new castle", to the northwest, is made up of a central block built around 1750 and two side pavilions added a century later, and is currently being restored. It was here that Dr Johnson and Boswell stayed in 1773 after a storm forced them to take refuge en route to Mull; they considered the place to be "a mere tradesman's box". Much of the area around the castles is now owned by the RSPB, in the hope of protecting the island's precious corncrake population. A vast area of **giant sand dunes** lies to the west of the castles, with two glorious golden sandy bays stretching for over a mile on either side. At the far western end is *Caolas*, where you can get a cup of tea and home-baked goodies, and where you can book ahead to stay (℡01879/230438; ❶).

The CalMac **ferry** from Oban calls at Coll daily except Thursdays. In Arinagour, the small, family-run *Coll Hotel* (℡01879/230334, Ⓦwww.collhotel.com; ❸) can provide **accommodation**. Otherwise, there are a couple of B&Bs to choose from: *First Port of Coll* (℡01879/230262, Ⓦwww.firstportofcoll.com; ❸), with smartly furnished rooms and a residents' lounge overlooking the bay, and *Tigh-na-Mara* (℡01879/230354; ❷), a purpose-built guest house near the pier. At *Caolas* (℡01879/230438,

@ www.caolas.net; full board ❺), a restored farmhouse on the remote western side of the island, there's a **self-catering bothy** that can be rented by the day (❸). The *Coll Hotel* doubles as the island's social centre, does excellent **meals** and has a dining room overflow. Another good eating option is the *First Port of Coll* restaurant, which offers breakfast and tea to nonresidents, as well as full-blown meals. For **bike rental**, go to Taigh Solas (℡01879 230216) opposite the post office; for whale-watching trips, phone Roy Barrie (℡01879/230333).

The Isle of Tiree

Tiree (@ www.isleoftiree.com), as its Gaelic name *tir-iodh* ("land of corn") suggests, was once known as the breadbasket of the Inner Hebrides, thanks to its acres of rich machair (sandy, grassy, lime-rich land). Nowadays crofting and tourism are the main sources of income for the resident population of around 800. One of the most distinctive features of Tiree is its architecture, in particular the large numbers of "pudding" or "spotty" houses, where only the mortar is painted white. Tiree's sandy beaches also attract large numbers of windsurfers for the Tiree Wave Classic (@ www.tireewaveclassic.com) every October.

The CalMac ferry calls at Gott Bay Pier, now best known for **An Turas** (The Journey), Tiree's award-winning "shelter". Just up the road from the pier is the village of **SCARINISH**, home to a post office, some public toilets, a supermarket, a butcher's and a bank, with a petrol pump back at the pier. Also in Scarinish you'll find **An Iodhlann** (Mon, Wed & Thurs 10am–4pm, Tues & Fri 2–5pm; @ www.tireearchive.com; £3) – meaning "haystack" in Gaelic – the island's two-roomed archive which puts on occasional exhibitions. To the east of Scarinish, **Gott Bay** is backed by a two-mile stretch of sand, and just one mile to the north is Vaul Bay, on the north coast, where the well-preserved remains of a dry-stone broch, **Dun Mor** – dating from the first century BC – lie hidden in the rocks to the west of the bay. From here it's another two miles west along the coast to the *Clach a'Choire* or **Ringing Stone**, a huge glacial boulder decorated with mysterious prehistoric markings, which when struck with a stone gives out a metallic sound. The story goes that, should the Ringing Stone ever be broken in two, Tiree will sink beneath the waves. A mile further west you come to the lovely **Balephetrish Bay**, where you can watch waders feeding in the breakers, and look over the sea to Skye and the Western Isles.

The most intriguing sights, however, lie in the bulging western half of the island, where Tiree's two landmark hills rise up. The highest of the two, **Ben Hynish** (463ft), is unfortunately occupied by a "golf-ball" radar station, which tracks incoming transatlantic flights; the views from the top, though, are great. Below Ben Hynish to the east is **HYNISH**, with its recently restored **harbour**, designed by Alan Stevenson in the 1830s to transport building materials for the magnificent 140-foot-tall **Skerryvore Lighthouse**, which lies on a sea-swept reef some twelve miles southwest of Tiree. Up on the hill behind the harbour, a stumpy granite signal tower, whose signals used to be the only contact the lighthouse keepers had with civilization, now houses **museum** telling the history of the Herculean effort required to erect the lighthouse; weather permitting, you can see the lighthouse from the tower viewing platform.

The CalMac **ferry** from Oban calls at Tiree daily (3hr 40min). Tiree also has an **airport** with flights (Mon–Sat) to and from Glasgow. Of the island's two

hotels, the *Tiree Lodge Hotel* (☎01879/220368; ❷), a mile or so east of Scarinish along Gott Bay, is preferable to the *Scarinish*. Better still is *Kirkapol House* (☎01879/220729; ❸), just beyond *Skerryvore House*, a great B&B in a converted kirk. **Budget accommodation** is available at *The Millhouse* (☎01879/220435, ⓦwww.tireemillhouse.co.uk; ❶), in the northwest of the island, either in bunks or twins. There's no official campsite, but **camping** is allowed with the local crofter's permission. As for **eating**, bar snacks and a la carte at the *Tiree Lodge Hotel* are perfectly acceptable; unpretentious snacks and meals are available at the pine-clad *Rural Centre* café by the airport.

The Isle of Colonsay

Isolated between Mull and Islay, **Colonsay** (ⓦwww.colonsay.org.uk) is not as bleak and windswept as Coll or Tiree. Its craggy, heather-backed hills even support the occasional patch of woodland, plus a bewildering array of plant and bird life, wild goats and rabbits, and one of the finest quasi-tropical gardens in Scotland. The population is currently around 200, down from a pre-Clearance peak of just under 1000. CalMac **ferries** call daily except Tuesday and Saturday from Oban (2hr 15min); one a week from Kennacraig via Islay (Wed; 3hr 35min), when a day-trip is possible, giving you around six hours on the island. There are a large number of self-catering cottages, but, with no camping and just one hotel, a couple of B&Bs and a bunkhouse, there's no fear of mass tourism taking over.

The CalMac ferry terminal is at **SCALASAIG**, on the east coast, where there's a post office/shop, a petrol pump, a restaurant and the island's hotel. Right by the pier, the old waiting room now serves as the island's heritage centre and is usually open when the ferry docks. Two miles north of Scalasaig is **Colonsay House**, built in 1722 by Malcolm MacNeil. In 1904, the island and house were bought by Lord Strathcona, who made his fortune building the Canadian Pacific Railway (and whose descendants still own the island).

To the north of Colonsay House, where the road ends, you'll find the island's finest sandy beach, the breathtaking **Kiloran Bay**, where the breakers roll in from the Atlantic. There's another unspoilt sandy beach backed by dunes at Balnahard, two miles northeast along a rough track; en route, you might spot wild goats, choughs and even a golden eagle.

The **Isle of Oronsay**, half a mile to the south, is only an island when the tide is in, and, as you can't stay overnight, it can only be visited as a day-trip from Colonsay. The two are separated by "The Strand", a mile of tidal mud flats which act as a causeway for two hours either side of low tide; check locally for current timings. Although legends (and etymology) link saints Columba and Oran with both Colonsay and Oronsay, the ruins of the **Oronsay Priory** only date back to the fourteenth century. Abandoned since the Reformation, it still has the original church and cloisters, but the highlight is the Oronsay Cross, a superb example of late medieval artistry from Iona, and the numerous finely carved grave slabs that lie within the Prior's House.

Colonsay's only **hotel**, the *Isle of Colonsay* (☎01951/200316; ❻), is within easy walking distance of the pier in Scalasaig and serves very decent bar snacks. The best alternative is to stay at the superb *Seaview* **B&B** (☎01951/200315; ❸; April–Oct), and the budget option is the *Keepers' Lodge*, in Kiloran (☎01951/200312), a very comfortable **hostel** with a real fire. An alternative to **eating out** at the hotel bar is the *Pantry*, above the pier in Scalasaig, which offers simple home-cooking as well as teas and cakes (ring ahead if you want to eat in the evening; ☎01951/200325).

Mid-Argyll

Mid-Argyll is a vague term that loosely describes the central wedge of land south of Oban and north of Kintyre. The highlights of this gently undulating scenery lie along the sharply indented west coast, in particular the rich Bronze Age and Neolithic remains in the **Kilmartin** valley, one of the most important prehistoric sites in Scotland.

LOCHGILPHEAD, on the shores of Loch Fyne, is the chief town in the area, though it has little to offer beyond its practical use: it has a supermarket, several banks and a **tourist office** at 27 Lochnell St (April–Oct Mon–Sat 10am–5pm, Sun noon–5pm; longer hours in summer). It also has an excellent modern veggie **restaurant** called *Pinto's* (℡01546/602547; Tues–Sat), on the main street.

Kilmartin Glen

The **Kilmartin Glen** is the most important prehistoric site on the Scottish mainland. The most remarkable relic is the **linear cemetery**, where several cairns are aligned for more than two miles, to the south of the village of Kilmartin. These are thought to represent the successive burials of a ruling family or chieftains, but nobody can be sure. The best view of the cemetery's configuration is from the Bronze Age **Mid-Cairn**, but the Neolithic **South Cairn**, dating from around 3000 BC, is by far the oldest and the most impressive, with its large chambered tomb roofed by giant slabs.

Close to the Mid-Cairn, the two **Temple Wood stone circles** appear to have been the architectural focus of burials in the area from Neolithic times to the Bronze Age. Visible to the south are the impressively cup-marked **Nether Largie standing stones** (no public access), the largest of which looms over 10ft high. **Cup- and ring-marked rocks** are a recurrent feature of prehistoric sites in the Kilmartin Glen and elsewhere in Argyll. There are many theories as to their origin: some see them as Pictish symbols, others as primitive solar calendars. The most extensive markings in the entire country are at **Achnabreck**, off the A816 towards Lochgilphead.

Situated on high ground to the north of the cairns is the tiny village of **KILMARTIN**, where the old manse adjacent to the village church now houses a **Museum of Ancient Culture** (daily 10am–5.30pm; ⓦwww .kilmartin.org; £3.90), which is both enlightening and entertaining. Not only can you learn about the various theories concerning prehistoric crannogs henges and cairns, but you can practise polishing an axe, examine different types of wood and fur, and listen to a variety of weird and wonderful sound (check out the Gaelic bird imitations). The **café** is equally enticing, with loca produce on offer, which you can wash down with heather beer. The nearby church is worth a brief reconnoitre, as it shelters the badly damaged and weathered **Kilmartin crosses**, while a separate enclosure in the graveyard houses large collection of medieval grave slabs of the Malcolms of Poltalloch.

To the south of Kilmartin, beyond the linear cemetery, lies the raised peat bo of Mòine Mhór (Great Moss), best known as home to the Iron Age fort o **Dunadd**, one of Scotland's most important Celtic sites, occupying a distinc tive 176-foot-high rocky knoll once surrounded by the sea but currentl stranded beside the winding River Add. It was here that Fergus, the first kin of Dalriada, established his royal seat, having arrived from Ireland in around 50 AD. Its strategic position, the craggy defences and the view from the top are a impressive, but it's the **stone carvings** between the twin summits which mak

Dunadd so remarkable: several lines of inscription in ogam (an ancient alphabet of Irish origin), the faint outline of a boar, a hollowed-out footprint and a small basin. The boar and the inscriptions are probably Pictish, since the fort was clearly occupied long before Fergus got there, but the footprint and basin have been interpreted as being part of the royal coronation rituals of the kings of Dalriada. It's thought that the Stone of Destiny was used at Dunadd before being moved to Scone Palace (see p.1082), then to Westminster Abbey in London, where it languished until it was returned to Edinburgh in 1996.

B&B is available at *Dunchraigaig House* (℡01546/605209, ⓔdunchraig @aol.com; ❸), a large detached Victorian house situated opposite the Ballymeanoch standing stones, or the supremely isolated *Ardifuir* (℡01546/510271, ⓔduntrune@msn.com; ❸), a farmhouse in the grounds of Duntrune Castle, very close to the sea. Alternatively, you could hole up in Crinan or Cairnbaan (see below). The aforementioned café/restaurant at Kilmartin House is a great lunchtime **eating** option; alternatively, *The Cairn* (℡01546/510254; March–Oct), opposite the church in Kilmartin, is open in the evening, and features moderately expensive Scottish and Mediterranean dishes.

Crinan Canal

In 1801 the nine-mile-long **Crinan Canal** opened, linking Loch Fyne, at Ardrishaig south of Lochgilphead, with the Sound of Jura, thus cutting out the long and treacherous journey around the Mull of Kintyre. John Rennie's original design, although an impressive engineering feat, had numerous faults, and by 1816 Thomas Telford was called in to take charge of the renovations. The canal runs parallel to the sea for quite some way before cutting across the bottom of Mòine Mhór and hitting a flight of locks either side of **CAIRNBAAN** (there are fifteen in total); a walk along the towpath is both picturesque and pleasantly unstrenuous. A useful pit stop can be made at the *Cairnbaan Hotel* (℡01546/603668; ❻), an eighteenth-century coaching inn overlooking the canal, with a decent restaurant and bar meals featuring locally caught seafood.

There are usually one or two yachts passing through the locks, but the most relaxing place from which to view the canal in action is **CRINAN**, a pretty little fishing port at its western end. Crinan's tiny harbour is, for the moment at least, still home to a small fishing fleet. Every room in the *Crinan Hotel* (℡01546/830261, ⓦwww.crinanhotel.com; ❾) looks across Loch Crinan to the Sound of Jura. If the *Crinan* is beyond your means, try the secluded **B&B** *Tigh-na-Glaic* (℡01546/830245, ⓔmairi@mcanderson.freeserve.co.uk; ❸), perched above the harbour, also with views out to sea, or the superb *Bellanoch House* (℡01546/830149, ⓦwww.bellanochhouse.co.uk; ❸), a grand, old schoolhouse right on the canal, a mile or so before Crinan. Bar **meals** at the *Crinan* are expensive, but fairly reliable. Down on the lockside is a cheaper, cheerful **café** called the *Coffee Shop* (Easter–Oct), serving mouthwatering homemade cakes and wonderful dumplings.

Kintyre

ut for the mile-long isthmus between West Loch Tarbert and the much smaller East Loch Tarbert, the little-visited peninsula of **KINTYRE** (ⓦwww.kintyre.org) – from the Gaelic *ceann tire*, "land's end" – would be an island. Indeed, in the eleventh century, when the Scottish king, Malcolm Canmore, allowed Magnus Barefoot, king of Norway, to lay claim to any island he could circumnavigate by boat, Magnus succeeded in dragging his boat across the Tarbert isthmus and added the peninsula to his Hebridean kingdom. During the Wars of the Covenant, the vast majority of the population and property were wiped out by a combination of the 1646 potato blight and the destructive attentions of the earl of Argyll. Kintyre remained a virtual desert until the earl began his policy of transplanting Gaelic-speaking Lowlanders to the region. They probably felt quite at home here, as the southern half of the peninsula lies on the Lowland side of the Highland Boundary Fault.

Tarbert

A distinctive rocket-like church steeple heralds the fishing village of **TAR-BERT** (in Gaelic *An Tairbeart*, meaning "isthmus"), sheltering an attractive little bay backed by rugged hills. Tarbert's herring industry was mentioned in the Annals of Ulster as far back as 836 AD, though right now the local fishing industry is down to its lowest level ever, due to the strict EU quota system. Tourism is now an increasingly important source of income, as is the money that flows through the town during the last week in May, when the yacht races of the famous Scottish Series take place. Tarbert's harbourfront is pretty, and is best appreciated from the rubble of Robert the Bruce's fourteenth-century **castle** above the town to the south.

Tarbert's **tourist office** (April–Oct Mon–Sat 10am–5pm, Sun noon–5pm; longer hours in summer) is on the harbour. If you need to **stay**, there's no shortage of B&Bs, though none are outstanding – try *Springside* on Pier Road (☎01880/820413, ✉arshall.springside@virgin.net; ❷), which overlooks the harbour. One place that can be recommended, however, is the *Victoria Hotel* (☎01880/820236, ⓦwww.victarbert.com; ❹), the comfortable bright yellow pub on the opposite side of the harbour. The best bar **food** is to be had at the *Victoria*, where you can sit in the conservatory and look out across the harbour. For some excellent local meat, fish and seafood dishes, head for the expensive, evening-only *Anchorage* (☎01880/820881; Wed–Sat), on the opposite side of the harbour.

The Isle of Gigha

Gigha (ⓦwww.isle-of-gigha.co.uk) – pronounced "gheeya" – is a low-lying, fertile island three miles off the west coast of Kintyre, reputedly occupied for 5000 years. The island's Ayrshire cattle produce over a quarter of a million gallons of milk a year, though since the closure of Gigha's creamery in the 1980s, the island's distinctive fruit-shaped cheese has been produced on the mainland. Like many of the smaller Hebrides, Gigha was bought and sold numerous times after its original lairds, the MacNeils, sold up, and was finally bought by the 140 or so inhabitants themselves in 2001.

The ferry from Tayinloan, 23 miles south of Tarbert, deposits you at the island's only village, **ARDMINISH**, where you'll find the post office and shop. The main attraction on the island is the **Achamore Gardens** (daily 9am–dusk; donation requested), a mile and a half south of Ardminish. Established by the first postwar owner, Sir James Horlick of hot drink fame, their spectacularly colourful display of azaleas are best seen in early summer. The real draw of Gigha, however, apart from the peace and quiet, is the white sandy beaches – including one at Ardminish itself – that dot the coastline.

Gigha is so small – six miles by one mile – that most visitors come here just for the day. It is, however, possible **to stay** either at the *Post Office House* (℡01583/505251, Ⓦwww.gigha.net; ❷) or the *Gigha Hotel* (℡01583/505254; ❻; March–Oct), the very pleasant social centre of the island and also the place to go for tea and cakes, and bar meals. **Bike rental** is available from the shop (open daily).

Campbeltown

CAMPBELTOWN's best feature is its setting, in a deep bay sheltered by Davaar Island and the surrounding hills. With a population of 6000, it's also one of the largest towns in Argyll and, if you're staying in the southern half of Kintyre, its shops are by far the best place to stock up on supplies. As is evident from the architecture, Campbeltown's heyday was the Victorian era, when shipbuilding was going strong, coal was shipped by canal from Drumlemble, the fishing fleet was vast and Campbeltown Loch was said to be made of whisky. The decline of all its old industries has left the town permanently depressed, and unemployment and under-employment remain a persistent problem.

Nineteenth-century visitors to Campbeltown frequently found the place engulfed in a thick fog of pungent peat smoke from the town's 34 **whisky distilleries** – today, only two remain. The deeply traditional, family-owned Springbank, off Longrow, is the only distillery in Scotland that does absolutely everything from malting to bottling, on its own premises. There are regular no-nonsense guided tours (Easter–Sept Mon–Thurs by appointment; ℡01586/552085, Ⓦwww.springbankdistillers.com; £3). At the end, you get a voucher to exchange for a miniature at Eaglesomes, on Longrow South, whose range of whiskies is awesome.

On the town's palm-tree-dotted waterfront you'll find the **Wee Pictures**, a little Art Deco cinema on Hall Street, built in 1913 and still going strong (daily except Fri; ℡01586/533657, Ⓦwww.weepictures.co.uk). Next door is the equally delightful **Campbeltown Museum and Library** (Tues–Sat 10am–1pm & 2–5pm, Tues & Thurs 5.30–7.30pm; free), built in 1897 in the local sandstone, crowned by a distinctive lantern, and decorated on its harbourside wall with four relief panels depicting each of the town's main industries at the time. The library also hides one new, but little-known sight: the **Lady Linda McCartney Memorial Gardens**, which feature a slightly ludicrous bronze statue of Linda holding a lamb. For a better rundown on local history head for **Campbeltown Heritage Centre** on the Machrihanish road (April–Oct Mon–Sat noon–5pm, Sun 2–5pm; £2), housed in the church known locally as the "Tartan Kirk", partly due to its Gaelic associations, but mainly for its stripy bellcote and pinnacles.

Campbeltown's **tourist office** is currently on the Old Quay (April–Oct Mon–Fri 10am–5pm, Sun noon–4pm; Nov–March Mon–Fri 9am–4pm), and will happily hand out a free map of the town. The best centrally located **accommodation** is the delightful family-run *Ardshiel Hotel*, on Kilkerran Road (℡01586/552133, Ⓦwww.ardshiel.co.uk; ❹), situated on a lovely leafy square, just a block or so back from the ferry terminal. On the north side of the bay, *Craigard House* (℡01586/554242, Ⓦwww.craigard-house.co.uk; ❻), a former whisky distiller's sandstone mansion is even more palatial. For an inexpensive, central B&B, head for *Westbank Guest House*, on Dell Road (℡01586/553660; ❷), off the B842 to Southend. The best bar **food** is to be found at the *Ardshiel Hotel*.

Southend and the Mull of Kintyre

The bulbous, hilly end of Kintyre, to the south of Campbeltown, features some of the most spectacular scenery on the whole peninsula, mixed with large swathes of Lowland-style farmland. **SOUTHEND** itself, a bleak, blustery spot, comes as something of a disappointment, though it does have a golden sandy beach. Below the cliffs to the west of the beach, a ruined thirteenth-century chapel marks the alleged arrival point of St Columba prior to his trip to Iona, and on a rocky knoll nearby a pair of footprints carved into the rock are known as **Columba's footprints**, though only one is actually of ancient origin.

Most people venture west of Campbeltown to make a pilgrimage to the **Mull of Kintyre** – the nearest Britain gets to Ireland, whose coastline, just twelve miles away, appears remarkably close on fine days. Although the Mull was made famous by the mawkish number-one hit by sometime local resident Paul McCartney, with the help of the Campbeltown Pipe Band, there's nothing specifically to see in this godforsaken storm-racked spot but the view. The roads up to the "**Gap**" (1150ft) – where you must leave your car – and particularly down to the lighthouse, itself 300ft above the ocean waves, are terrifyingly tortuous.

Southend still has a **pub**, the *Argyll Arms*, unremarkable except for the fact that it has a post office inside it. The only hotel has been closed for a long time now and cuts a forlorn figure, set back from the bay, but there are a couple of excellent **B&Bs**: *Ormsary Farm* (☏01586/830665; ❶; April–Sept), a small dairy farm up Glen Breakerie, and the nearby picturesque croft of *Low Cattadale* (☏01586/830205; ❶; March–Nov). **Camping** is possible in the field right by the beach, run by *Machribeg Farm* (☏01586/830249; Easter–Sept).

The Isle of Arran

Shaped like a kidney bean and occupying centre stage in the Firth of Clyde, **Arran** is the most southerly (and therefore the most accessible) of all the Scottish islands. The Highland–Lowland dividing line passes right through its centre – hence the cliché about it being like "Scotland in miniature" – leaving the northern half sparsely populated, mountainous and bleak, while the lush southern half enjoys a much milder climate. Despite its immense popularity, the tourists, like the population of around five thousand – many of whom are incomers – tend to stick to the southeastern quarter of the island, leaving the west and the north relatively undisturbed.

Although tourism is now by far its most important industry, Arran, at twenty miles in length, is large enough to have a life of its own. While the island's post-1745 history and the Clearances (set in motion by the local lairds, the dukes of Hamilton) are as depressing as elsewhere in the Highlands, in recent years Arran has not suffered from the depopulation which has plagued other, more remote islands. Once a county in its own right (along with Bute), Arran has been left out of the new Argyll and Bute district in the latest county boundary shake-up, and is coupled instead with mainland North Ayrshire, with which it enjoys year-round transport links, but little else.

Transport on Arran itself is pretty good: daily **buses** circle the island (Brodick tourist office has timetables and an Arran Rural Rover day ticket costs just £3.50)

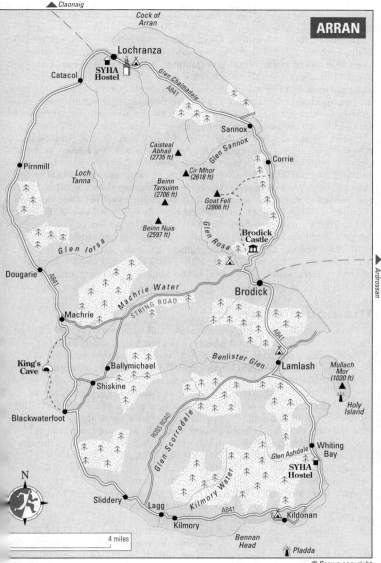

ARRAN

© Crown copyright

Brodick

Although the resort of **BRODICK** (from the Norse *breidr vik*, "broad bay") is a place of only moderate charm, it does at least have a grand setting in a wide, sandy bay set against a backdrop of granite mountains. Its development as a tourist resort was held back for a long time by its elitist owners, the dukes of

Hamilton, though nowadays, as the island's capital and main communication hub, Brodick is by far the busiest town on Arran.

The dukes lived at **Brodick Castle** (daily: April–Sept 11am–4.30pm; Oct 11am–3.30pm; £7; NTS), on a steep bank on the north side of the bay. The interior is comfortable if undistinguished, but the walled **gardens** (daily 9.30am–dusk; gardens and country park only: £3.50) and extensive grounds, contain a treasury of exotic plants and trees and command a superb view across the bay. Hidden in the grounds is a bizarre Bavarian-style summerhouse lined entirely with pine cones, one of three built by the eleventh duke to make his wife, Princess Marie of Baden, feel at home.

Brodick's **tourist office** (May–Sept Mon–Thurs & Sat 9am–5pm, Fri 9am–7.30pm, Sun 10am–5pm; Oct–April Mon–Sat 9am–5pm) is by the CalMac pier, and has reams of information on every activity from pony trekking to paragliding. Unless you've got to catch an early-morning ferry, however, there's little reason to stay in Brodick, though should you need to, the best **rooms** close to the ferry terminal are at the excellent *Dunvegan House Hotel* (☎01770/302811; ❹) or *Carrick Lodge* (☎01770/302550; ❷; Feb–Oct). The nearest **campsite** is *Glenrosa* (☎01770/302380), a lovely, but very basic farm site (cold water only and no showers), two miles from town off the B880 to Blackwaterfoot. For **food**, the only place that really stands out is the expensive seafood restaurant *Creelers* (☎01770/302797; mid-March to Oct; ⓦwww.creelers.co.uk), on the road to the castle. The *Wineport*, near the castle, does above-average bar meals.

The south of Arran

The southern half of Arran is less spectacular and less forbidding than the north; it's more heavily forested and the land is more fertile, and for that reason the vast majority of the population lives here. With its distinctive Edwardian architecture and mild climate, **LAMLASH** epitomizes the sedate charm of southeast Arran. Its major drawback is its bay, which is made not of sand but of boulder-strewn mud flats. You can take a boat out to the slug-shaped hump of **Holy Island**, which shelters the bay, and is now owned by a group of Tibetan Buddhists – providing you don't dawdle, it's possible to scramble up to the top of Mullach Mór (1030ft), the island's highest point, and still catch the last ferry back. The Holy Island ferry runs more or less hourly (☎01770/600998; £8 return), and you can stay at the Buddhist centre (☎01387/373232, ⓦwww.holyisland.org) To **stay** in style, head for the comfortable *Lilybank* (☎01770/600230; ❸), which does good homemade food. You can **camp** at the fully equipped *Middleton Camping Park* (☎01770/600255; April–Oct), just five minutes' walk south of the centre. The best food option is the **bar meals** at the *Pier Head Tavern*, or at the friendly *Drift Inn*, which has tables by the shore.

An established Clydeside resort for over a century now, **WHITING BAY**, four miles south of Lamlash, is spread out along a very pleasant bay, though doesn't have quite the distinctive architecture of Lamlash. However, there are some excellent places to **stay**, including the *Royal* (☎01770/700280, ⓦwww.royalarran.co.uk; March–Oct; ❸) and the *Argentine House Hotel*, run (confusingly) by a multilingual Swiss couple (☎01770/700662, ⓦwww.argentinearran.co.uk; ❷), both on Shore Road. Whiting Bay also boasts a SYHA **hostel** (☎0870/004 1158; April–Oct), at the southern end of the bay. The **food** is very good (and expensive) at both hotels; otherwise, it's snacks at the *Coffee Pot*, or simple bistro fare at the *Pantry* (closed Sun eve) opposite the post office.

The north of Arran

The desolate north half of Arran – effectively the Highland part – features bare granite peaks, the occasional golden eagle and miles of unspoilt scenery, within reach only to those prepared to do some serious hiking. Arran's most accessible peak is also the island's highest, **Goat Fell** (2866ft) – take your pick from the Gaelic, *goath*, meaning "windy", or the Norse, *geit-fjall*, "goat mountain" – which can be ascended in just three hours from Brodick (or from Corrie, see below; return journey 5hr), though it's a strenuous hike.

Another good base for hiking is **CORRIE**, Arran's prettiest little seaside village, six miles north of Brodick, where a procession of pristine cottages lines the road to Lochranza and wraps itself around an exquisite little harbour and pier. *Blackrock* (℡01770/810282, ⓦwww.arran.net/corrie/blackrock; ❶) is a large, traditional seafront **guest house** on the edge of the village, while a good budget option is the *North High Corrie Croft*, a **bunkhouse** (℡01770/302310), ten minutes' steep climb above the village on a raised beach; it has one large room for group bookings, and an annexe with eight beds (advance booking advisable). The red sandstone *Corrie Hotel*, at the centre of the village, does bar **meals**, and *Corrie Golf Club*, confusingly in Sannox, offers good-value food all day in summer.

The ruined castle which occupies the mud flats of the bay, and the brooding north-facing slopes of the mountains which frame it, make for one of the most spectacular settings on the island – yet **LOCHRANZA**, despite being the only place of any size in this sparsely populated area, attracts far fewer visitors than Arran's southern resorts. The castle is worth a brief look inside (get the key from the post office), but Lochranza's main sight now is the brand new whisky **distillery** (April–Oct daily 10am–5pm; Nov–March phone ℡01770/830264, ⓦwww.arranwhisky.com; £3.50), a pristine complex distinguished by its pagoda-style roofs at the south end of the village. The tours are entertaining and slick, and end with a free sample of the island's newly emerging single malt. The finest **accommodation** is to be had at the superb *Apple Lodge* (℡01770/830229; ❹), the old village manse where you'll get excellent home cooking, or at the *Lochranza Hotel* (℡01770/830233, ⓦwww.lochranza.co.uk; ❷), whose bar is the centre of the local social scene. Lochranza also has an SYHA **hostel** (℡0870/004 1140; March–Oct), situated halfway between the distillery and the castle, and a well-equipped **campsite** (℡01770/830273, ⓦwww.arran.net/lochranza; April-Oct) beautifully placed by the golf course on the Brodick Road, where deer come to graze in the early evening. The distillery café offers salads, pasta dishes, baguettes and Scottish specialities during the day; in the evening, your only option is bar meals at the *Lochranza*.

Islay and Jura

The fertile, largely treeless island of **ISLAY** (pronounced "eye-la") is famous for one thing – single malt **whisky**. The smoky, peaty, pungent quality of Islay whisky is unique, recognizable even to the untutored palate, and all seven of the island's distilleries will happily take visitors on a guided tour, ending with the customary complimentary tipple. Yet, despite the fame of its whiskies, Islay remains relatively undiscovered, much as Skye and Mull were some 25 years ago. Part of the reason may be the expense of the two-hour ferry journey from Kennacraig on Kintyre, or perhaps the relative paucity of luxury hotels or fancy restaurants. If you do make the effort, however, you'll be rewarded with a genuinely friendly welcome from islanders proud of their history, landscape and Gaelic culture. The long whale-shaped island of **Jura** is one of the wildest and most mountainous of the Inner Hebrides, its entire west coast uninhabited and inaccessible except to the dedicated walker.

In medieval times, Islay was the political centre of the Hebrides, with **Finlaggan**, near Port Askaig, the seat of the MacDonalds, lords of the Isles. The picturesque, whitewashed villages you see on Islay today, however, date from the planned settlements founded by the Campbells in the late eighteenth and early nineteenth centuries. Apart from whisky and solitude, the other great draw is the **bird life** – there's a real possibility of spotting a golden eagle, or the rare crow-like chough, and no possibility at all of missing the scores of

Islay whisky

Islay has slowly woken up to the fact that its whisky distilleries are a major tourist attraction. Nowadays, each distillery offers guided tours, traditionally ending with a generous dram, and a refund for your entrance fee if you buy a bottle in the shop – be warned, however, that a bottle of single malt is no cheaper at source, so expect to pay over £20 for the privilege. Pick up the tourist board's *Islay and Jura Whisky Trail* leaflet or visit ⊛www.islaywhiskysociety.com, and phone ahead to make sure there's a tour running, as times do change frequently.

Ardbeg ☏01496/302244, ⊛www.ardbeg.com. The ten-year-old Ardbeg is tradition-ally considered the saltiest, peatiest malt on Islay (and that's saying something). Bought by Glenmorangie in 1997, the distillery has been thoroughly overhauled and restored, yet it still has bags of character inside. The *Old Kiln Café* is excellent (Mon–Fri 10am–4pm; June–Aug daily 10am–5pm). Guided tours regularly from 10.30am–3.30pm; £2.

Bowmore ☏01496/810441, ⊛www.morrisonbowmore.com. Bowmore is the most touristy of the Islay distilleries, too much so for some. However, it's by far the most central distillery (with unrivalled disabled access), and also one of the few still doing its own malting and kilning. Guided tours Easter–Sept Mon–Fri 10.30am, 11.30am, 2pm & 3pm, Sat 10.30am; Oct–Easter Mon–Fri 10.30am & 2pm; £2.

Bruichladdich ☏01496/850221. Bruichladdich only came back into production in 2001, and is the only independent distillery left on Islay. Regular guided tours have only just started again (Mon–Fri 10.30am, 11.30am & 2.30pm, Sat 10.30am & 2.30pm; £3).

Bunnahabhainn ☏01496/840646. A visit to Bunnahabhain (pronounced "Bunna-have-in") is really only for whisky obsessives. The road from Port Askaig is windy, the whisky is the least characteristically Islay, and the distillery itself is only in pro-duction for a few months each year. Guided tours Mon–Fri 10.30am, 1 & 3pm; free).

Caol Ila ☏01496/840207. Caol Ila (pronounced "Cul-eela"), just north of Port Askaig, is a modern distillery, the majority of whose lightly peaty malt goes into blended whiskies. No-frills guided tours are by appointment (April–Oct; £3).

Lagavulin ☏01496/302400, ⊛www.scotch.com. Lagavulin is probably the classic, all-round Islay malt, with lots of smoke and peat. The distillery enjoys a fabulous set-ting and is extremely busy all year round. Phone ahead for details of the guided tours (Mon–Fri 10am, 11.30am & 2pm; £3), at the end of which you'll get a taste of the best-selling 16-year-old.

Laphroaig ☏01496/302418, ⊛www.laphroaig.com. Another classic smoky, peaty Islay malt, and another great setting. One bonus at Laphroaig is that you get to see the malting and see and smell the peat kilns. There are regular guided tours (Mon–Fri 10.15am & 2.15pm; free), but phone ahead to book.

white-fronted and barnacle geese who winter here in their thousands. A good time to visit is in late May/early June, when the **Feis Ile** (ⓦ www.ileach.co.uk /festival) takes place, with whisky tasting, piping recitals, folk dancing and other events celebrating the island's Gaelic roots.

Port Ellen and around

Laid out as a planned village in 1821 by Walter Frederick Campbell, and named after his wife, **PORT ELLEN** is the chief port on Islay, with the island's largest fishing fleet, and main CalMac ferry terminal. The neat whitewashed terraces of Frederick Crescent, which overlook the town's bay of golden sand, are pretty enough, but the strand to the north, up Charlotte Street, is dominated by the modern maltings, on the Bowmore road, whose powerful odours waft across the town. For **accommodation** in Port Ellen itself, the best place is *Caladh Sona* (ⓣ01496/302694, ⓔhamish.scott@lineone.net; ❷), a detached house at 53 Frederick Crescent, followed by the artistic *Carraig Fhada* B&B by the lighthouse (ⓣ01496/302114; ❶). However, you'd be better off heading up the A846 towards the airport, to the excellent *Glenmachrie Farmhouse* (ⓣ01496/302560, ⓦwww.glenmachrie.com; ❺), a whitewashed, family-run guest house, which does superb home-cooking. Alternatively, there's a **campsite** at the stone-built *Kintra Farm* B&B (ⓣ01496/302051, ⓦwww .kintrafarm.freereserve.co.uk; April–Sept; ❶), three miles northwest of Port Ellen, at the southern tip of Laggan Bay.

From Port Ellen, a dead-end road heads off east along the coastline, passing three distilleries in as many miles. First comes **Laphroaig**, which, as every bottle tells you, is Gaelic for "the beautiful hollow by the broad bay", and, true enough, the whitewashed distillery is indeed in a gorgeous setting by the sea. A mile down the road lies **Lagavulin** distillery, beyond which stands **Dunyvaig Castle** (*Dún Naomhaig*), a romantic ruin on a promontory looking out to the tiny isle of Texa. Another mile further on is **Ardbeg** distillery, whose *Old Kiln Café* is the best place to grab a bite to eat in the area. In common with all Islay's distilleries, the above three offer guided tours (see box). There are a few **B&Bs** along the rapidly deteriorating road – *Tigh-na-Suil* (ⓣ01496/ 302483; ❷) has a lovely secluded position. A mile beyond this, slightly off the road, the simple thirteenth-century **Kildalton Chapel** boasts a wonderful eighth-century Celtic ringed cross made from the local "bluestone", which is a rich blue-grey. The quality of the scenes matches any to be found on the crosses carved by the monks in Iona.

Bowmore

At the northern end of the seven-mile-long Laggan Bay, across the monotonous peat bog of Duich Moss, lies **BOWMORE**, Islay's administrative capital, with a population of around 800. It's a striking place, laid out in a grid plan rather like Inveraray, with the whitewashed terraces of Main Street climbing up the hill in a straight line from the pier on Loch Indaal to the town's crowning landmark, the **Round Church**, whose central tower looks uncannily like a lighthouse. Built in the round, so that the devil would have no corners in which to hide, it has a plain, wood-panelled interior, with a lovely tiered balcony and a big central mushroom pillar. A little to the west of Main Street is **Bowmore distillery** (see box), the first of the legal Islay distilleries, founded in 1779, and still occupying its original whitewashed buildings by the loch.

Islay's only official **tourist office** is in Bowmore (April–Oct Mon–Sat 9am–5pm; May–Aug also Sun 2–5pm; Nov–March Mon–Fri noon–4pm);

21

it can help find **accommodation** anywhere on Islay or Jura. Like Port Ellen, Bowmore itself is, in fact, not necessarily the best place to stay on the island. If you choose to, however, the *Harbour Inn* (℡01496/810330, ⓦwww .harbour-inn.com; ❺) on Main Street, is Bowmore's cosiest and most central pub, or you could stay in one of the town's better B&Bs, such as *Lambeth House* (℡01496/810597; ❷), centrally located on Jamieson Street.

If you're visiting Islay between mid-September and the third week of April, it's impossible to miss the island's staggeringly large wintering population of **barnacle** and **white-fronted geese**. During this period, the geese dominate the landscape, feeding incessantly off the rich pasture, strolling by the shores, and flying in formation across the winter skies. You can see the geese just about anywhere on the island – there are an estimated 15,000 white-fronted and 40,000 barnacles here (and rising) – though in the evening, they tend to congregate in the tidal mud flats and fields around **Loch Gruinart**, which is now an **RSPB nature reserve**.

Port Charlotte

PORT CHARLOTTE, named after the founder's mother, is generally agreed to be Islay's prettiest village, its immaculate whitewashed cottages cluster around a sandy cove overlooking Loch Indaal. On the northern fringe of the village, in a whitewashed former chapel, the imaginative **Museum of Islay Life** (Easter–Oct Mon–Sat 10am–5pm, Sun 2–5pm; Nov–Easter Mon–Fri 10am–4pm, Sat 10am–4pm; £2), has a children's corner, quizzes, a good library of books about the island, and tantalizing snippets about eighteenth-century illegal whisky distillers. The **Wildlife Information Centre** (Easter–Oct daily except Sat 10am–3pm; July & Aug daily 10am–5pm; £2.50), housed in the former distillery warehouse, is also worth a visit for anyone interested in the island's fauna and flora. As well as an extensive library to browse, there's lots of hands-on stuff for kids: microscopes, a touch table full of natural goodies, a seawater aquarium, a bug world, and owl pellets to examine.

Port Charlotte is the perfect place in which to base yourself on Islay. The welcoming *Port Charlotte Hotel* (℡01496/850360, ⓦwww.portcharlottehotel .co.uk; ❺) has the best **accommodation** – the seafood lunches served in the bar are very popular, and there's a good (though expensive) restaurant. For B&B, you're better off going for *Octofad Farm* (℡01496/850225; ❶; April–Oct), a dairy farm a few miles down the road beyond Nerabus. Port Charlotte itself is also home to Islay's SYHA **hostel** (℡0870/004 1128 ⓔreservations@syha.org.uk; April–Sept), housed in an old bonded warehouse next door to the Wildlife Information Centre. The *Croft Kitchen* (℡01496/850230; April–Oct), opposite the museum, serves simple **food**, such as sandwiches and cakes, as well as inexpensive seafood during the day and more adventurous fare in the evenings (except Wed). The **bar** of the *Port Charlotte* is very easy-going, while the local craic (and occasional live music) goes on at the *Lochindaal Inn*, down the road, where you can also tuck into very good local-bred steak.

Finlaggan and Port Askaig

Just beyond Ballygrant, on the road to Port Askaig, a narrow road leads off north to **Loch Finlaggan**, site of a number of prehistoric crannogs (artificial islands) and, for four hundred years from the twelfth century, headquarters of the lords of the Isles, semi-autonomous rulers over the Hebrides and Kintyre. Unless you need shelter from the rain, or are desperate to see the head of the commemorative medieval cross found here, you can happily skip the **information centre** (Easter & Oct Tues, Thurs & Sun 2–4pm; May–Sept daily except Sat 2.30–5pm; £1.50), to the northeast of the loch, and simply head on down to the site itself (access at any time), which is dotted with interpretive panels. Duckboards allow you to walk out across the reed beds of the loch and explore the main crannog, **Eilean Mor**, where several carved gravestones are displayed under cover in the chapel, which seem to support the theory that the lords of the Isles buried their wives and children here, while having themselves interred on Iona.

Islay's other ferry connection with the mainland, and its sole link with Colonsay and Jura, is from **PORT ASKAIG**, a scattering of buildings that tumble down a little cove by the narrowest section of the Sound of Islay (*Caol Ila*). Easily the most comfortable **place to stay** nearby is the lovely white-washed *Kilmeny Farmhouse* (℡01496/840668, ⓦwww.kilmeny.com; ❺), south-west of Ballygrant, a place that richly deserves all the superlatives it regularly receives. The *Ballygrant Inn* is a good **pub** in which to grab a pint, as is the bar of the *Port Askaig Hotel*, which enjoys a wonderful position by the pier at Port Askaig, with views over to the Paps of Jura.

The Isle of Jura

Jura's distinctive Paps – so called because of their smooth breast-like shape, though there are in fact three of them – seem to dominate every view off the west coast of Argyll, their glacial rounded tops covered in a light dusting of quartzite scree. The island's name is commonly thought to derive from the Norse *dyr-oe* (deer island) and, appropriately enough, the current deer population of 6000 outnumbers the 180 humans by 33-to-one. With just one road, which sticks to the more sheltered eastern coast of the island, and only one hotel and a smattering of B&Bs, Jura is an ideal place to go for peace and quiet and some great walking.

If you're just coming over for the day from Islay, and don't fancy climbing the Paps, you could happily spend the day in the lovely wooded grounds of **Jura House** (daily 9am–5pm; £2), five miles up the road from Feolin Ferry, where the car ferry from Port Askaig arrives. Pick up a booklet at the entrance to the grounds, and follow the path down to the sandy shore, a perfect picnic spot in fine weather. Closer to the house itself, there's an idyllic **walled garden**, divided in two by a natural rushing burn that tumbles down in steps. The garden specializes in Antipodean plants, which flourish in the frost-free climate; in season, you can buy some of the garden's organic produce or take tea in the tea tent.

Anything that happens on Jura happens in the island's only real village, **CRAIGHOUSE**, eight miles up the road from Feolin Ferry. The village enjoys a sheltered setting, overlooking Knapdale on the mainland – so sheltered, in fact, that there are even a few palm trees thriving on the seafront. There's a shop/post office, the island hotel and a tearoom, plus the tiny **Isle of Jura distillery** (℡01496/820240; Mon–Fri 10am–4pm), which is very welcoming to visitors.

The family-run *Jura Hotel* in Craighouse is the island's one and only **hotel** (℡01496/820243; ❹), not much to look at from the outside, but warm and friendly within, and centre of the island's social scene. The hotel does moderately expensive bar meals, and has a shower block and laundry facilities round the back for those who wish to camp in the hotel gardens. For **B&B**, look no further than Mrs Boardman at 7 Woodside (℡01496/820379; ❶; April–Sept).

There's an infrequent **minibus service** on the island (phone ☎01496/820314 to find out when it's running). The **ferry** from Port Askaig occasionally fails to run if there's a strong northerly or southerly wind, so bring your toothbrush if you're coming for a day-trip.

In April 1946, Eric Blair (better known by his pen name of **George Orwell**), suffering badly from TB and intending to give himself "six months' quiet" in which to write his novel *1984*, moved to a remote farmhouse called Barnhill, on the northern tip of Jura. He lived out a spartan existence there for two years but was forced to return to London shortly before his death. The house, 23 miles north of Craighouse up an increasingly poor road, is as remote today as it was in Orwell's day, and sadly there is no access to the interior.

Travel details

Mainland buses (excluding postbuses)

Arrochar to: Inveraray (Mon–Sat 5 daily, Sun 2 daily; 35min); Lochgilphead (Mon–Sat 3 daily, Sun 2 daily; 1hr 30min).

Campbeltown to: Campbeltown airport (Mon–Fri 2 daily; 10min); Southend (Mon–Sat 5–6 daily, Sun 2 daily; 23min).

Dunoon to: Inveraray (Mon–Fri 5 daily, Sat 3 daily; 1hr 15min).

Glasgow to: Arrochar (Mon–Sat 6 daily, Sun 3 daily; 1hr 10min); Campbeltown (Mon–Sat 3 daily, Sun 2 daily; 4hr 25min); Inveraray (Mon–Sat 6 daily, Sun 3 daily; 1hr 45min); Kennacraig (Mon–Sat 2 daily, Sun 1 daily; 3hr 30min); Lochgilphead (Mon–Sat 3 daily, Sun 2 daily; 2hr 40min); Oban (Mon–Sat 4 daily, Sun 2 daily; 3hr); Tarbert (Mon–Sat 3 daily, Sun 2 daily; 3hr 15min).

Inveraray to: Dunoon (Mon–Fri 5 daily, Sat 3 daily; 1hr 15min); Lochgilphead (Mon–Sat 3 daily, Sun 2 daily; 40min); Oban (Mon–Sat 3 daily, Sun 1 daily; 1hr 5min); Tarbert (Mon–Sat 3 daily, Sun 2 daily; 1hr 10min).

Kennacraig to: Claonaig (Mon–Sat 3 daily; 15min).

Lochgilphead to: Campbeltown (3–4 daily; 1hr 45min); Crinan (Mon–Sat 3–4 daily; 20min); Inveraray (3–4 daily; 40min); Kilmartin (Mon–Sat 2–5 daily; 15min); Oban (Mon–Sat 2–4 daily; 1hr 30min); Tarbert (3–4 daily; 30min).

Oban to: Kilmartin (Mon–Sat 2–4 daily; 1hr 20min); Lochgilphead (Mon–Sat 2–4 daily; 1hr 30min).

Tarbert to: Campbeltown (Mon–Sat 4 daily, Sun 2 daily; 1hr 15min); Claonaig (Mon–Sat 3 daily; 30min); Kennacraig (Mon–Sat 5 daily, Sun 1 daily; 15min).

Island buses

Arran

Brodick to: Blackwaterfoot (Mon–Sat 18–22 daily, Sun 12 daily; 30min–1hr 20min); Corrie (4–6 daily; 20min); Lamlash (Mon–Sat 14–16 daily, Sun 4 daily; 10–15min); Lochranza (4–6 daily; 45min); Pirnmill (4–6 daily; 1hr); Whiting Bay (Mon–Sat 14–16 daily, Sun 4 daily; 25min).

Bute

Rothesay to: Kilchattan Bay (Mon–Sat 4 daily, Sun 3 daily; 30min); Mount Stuart (1 daily except Tues & Thurs every 45min; 15min); Rhubodach (Mon–Sat 1–2 daily; 20min).

Colonsay

Scalasaig to: Kilchattan (Mon–Fri 2–4 daily; 30min); Kiloran Bay (Mon–Fri 2–3 daily; 12min); The Strand (Mon–Fri 1 daily).

Islay

Bowmore to: Port Askaig (Mon–Sat 8–10 daily, Sun 1 daily; 30–40min); Port Charlotte (Mon–Sat 5–6 daily; 25min); Port Ellen (Mon–Sat 9–12 daily, Sun 1 daily; 20–30min); Portnahaven (Mon–Sat 5–7 daily; 50min).

Mull

Craignure to: Fionnphort (Mon–Sat 3–4 daily, Sun 1 daily; 1hr 15min); Fishnish (Mon–Sat 4 daily, Sun 3 daily; 10min); Tobermory (Mon–Sat 4–5 daily, Sun 2 daily; 50min).

Tobermory to: Calgary (Mon–Fri 3–6 daily, Sat 2 daily; 45min); Dervaig (Mon–Fri 3–6 daily, Sat 2 daily; 30min); Fishnish (Mon–Sat 4 daily, Sun 3 daily; 40min).

Trains

For information on all local and national rail services, contact **National Rail Enquiries** ☎08457/48 49 50, ⓦwww.nationalrail.co.uk.
Glasgow (Queen St) to: Arrochar and Tarbert (Mon–Sat 3–4 daily, 1–2 on Sun; 1hr 15min); Oban (Mon–Sat 3–4 daily, 1–2 on Sun; 3hr).

Car ferries (summer timetable)

To Arran: Ardrossan–Brodick (4–6 daily; 55min); Claonaig–Lochranza (8–9 daily; 30min).
To Bute: Colintraive–Rhubodach (frequently; 5min); Wemyss Bay–Rothesay (every 45min; 30min).
To Coll: Oban–Coll (daily except Thurs; 2hr 40min).
To Colonsay: Kennacraig–Colonsay (Wed 1 daily; 3hr 35min); Oban–Colonsay (daily except Tues & Sat; 2hr 15min); Port Askaig–Colonsay (Wed 2 daily; 1hr 15min).
To Dunoon: Gourock–Dunoon (hourly; 20min); McInroy's Point–Hunter's Quay (every 30min; 20min).
To Gigha: Tayinloan–Gigha (hourly; 20min).

To Islay: Colonsay–Port Askaig (Wed 2 daily; 1hr 15min); Kennacraig–Port Askaig (1–3 daily; 2hr); Kennacraig–Port Ellen (1–3 daily; 2hr 10min).
To Jura: Port Askaig–Feolin Ferry (Mon–Sat 14–18 daily, Sun 6 daily; 10min).
To Kintyre: Portavadie–Tarbert (hourly; 25min).
To Mull: Kilchoan–Tobermory (Mon–Sat 7 daily; June–Aug also Sun 5 daily; 35min); Lochaline–Fishnish (Mon–Sat every 50min, Sun hourly; 15min); Oban–Craignure (Mon–Sat 6–7 daily, Sun 4–5 daily; 45min).
To Tiree: Barra–Tiree (Wed 1 daily; 3hr 5min); Oban–Tiree (daily; 3hr 40min).

Passenger-only ferries (summer timetable)

To Iona: Fionnphort–Iona (Mon–Sat frequently, Sun hourly; 5min).

Flights

Glasgow to: Campbeltown (Mon–Fri 2 daily; 35min); Islay (Mon–Fri 2 daily, Sat 1 daily; 40min); Tiree (Mon–Sat 1 daily; 45min).

ARGYLL | Travel details

㉑

Skye and the
Western Isles

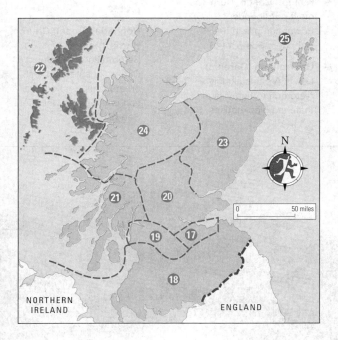

CHAPTER 22

Highlights

* **Loch Coruisk boat trip, Skye** Take the boat from Elgol to the beautiful remote glacial Loch Coruisk in the midst of the Skye Cuillin, and walk back. See p.1135

* **Skye Cuillin** These jagged peaks make Skye a great place to visit. See p.1135

* **Kinloch Castle, Rùm** The most outrageous Edwardian pile in the Hebrides. See p.1143

* **Gearrannan (Garenin), Lewis** A painstakingly restored crofting village of thatched blackhouses. See p.1149

* **Calanais (Callanish), Lewis** Scotland's finest standing stones are set in a serene lochside setting. See p.1150

* **Golden sandy beaches** South Harris and the Uists have some stunning, mostly deserted, golden beaches, backed by flower-strewn machair. See p.1152

* **Roghadal (Rodel) Church, Harris** The pre-Reformation St Clement's Church boasts the most ornate sculptural decoration in the Outer Hebrides. See p.1153

△ Skye Cuillin

Skye and the Western Isles

A procession of Hebridean islands, islets and reefs off the northwest shore of Scotland, **Skye and the Western Isles** between them boast some of the country's most alluring scenery. It's here that the turbulent seas of the Atlantic smash up against an extravagant shoreline hundreds of miles long, a geologically complex terrain whose rough rocks and mighty sea cliffs are interrupted by a thousand sheltered bays and, in the far west, a long line of sweeping sandy beaches. The islands' interiors are equally dramatic, a series of formidable mountain ranges soaring high above great chunks of boggy peat moor, a barren wilderness enclosing a host of lochans, or tiny lakes.

Each island has its own distinct character, though the grouping splits quite neatly into two. **Skye** and the so-called **Small Isles** – the improbably named **Rùm**, **Eigg**, **Muck** and **Canna** – are part of the Inner Hebrides, which also include the islands of Argyll (see p.1093). Beyond Skye, across the unpredictable waters of the Minch, lie the Outer Hebrides or Outer Isles, nowadays known as the **Western Isles**, a 130-mile-long archipelago stretching from **Lewis** and **Harris** in the north to **Barra** in the south.

Although this area is one of the most popular holiday spots in Scotland, the crowds only become oppressive on Skye, and even there most visitors stick to a well-trodden sequence of roadside sights that leaves the rest of the island unaffected. The main attraction, the spectacular scenery, is best explored on foot, following the scores of paths that range from the simplest of cross-country strolls to arduous treks. There are four obvious areas of outstanding natural beauty to aim for: on Skye, the harsh peaks of the **Cuillin** and the bizarre rock formations of the **Trotternish** peninsula; on the Western Isles, the mountains of **North Harris** and the splendid sandy beaches that string along the Atlantic seaboard of **South Harris** and the **Uists**.

Skye and the Western Isles were first settled by Neolithic farming peoples in around 4000 BC. They lived along the coast, where they are remembered by scores of remains, from passage graves through to stone circles, most famously at **Calanais** (Callanish) on Lewis. Viking colonization gathered pace from 700 AD onwards – on Lewis four out of every five place-names is of Norse origin and it was only in 1266 that the islands were returned to the Scottish crown. James VI (James I of England), a Stuart and a Scot, though no Gaelic-speaker,

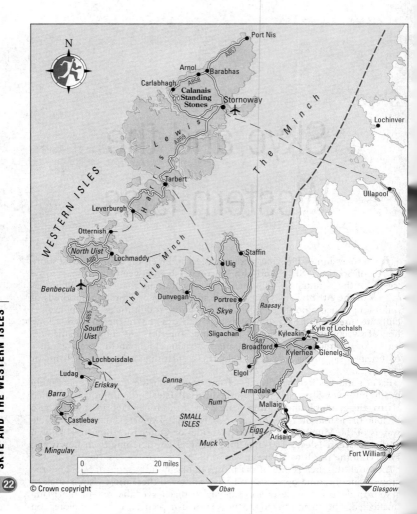

© Crown copyright

▼ Oban   ▼ Glasgow

was the first to put forward the idea of clearing the Hebrides, though it wasn't until after the Jacobite uprisings, in which many Highland clans disastrously backed the wrong side, that the **Clearances** began in earnest.

The isolation of the Hebrides exposed them to the whims and fancies of the various merchants and aristocrats who bought them up. Time and again from the mid-eighteenth century to the present day, both the land and its people were sold to the highest bidder. Some proprietors were well-meaning but insensitive, like Lord Leverhulme, who wanted to turn Lewis into a centre of the fishing industry in the 1920s – while others were simply autocratic, such as **Colonel Gordon of Cluny**, who bought Benbecula, South Uist, Eriskay and Barra, and forced the inhabitants onto ships bound for North America at gunpoint. Always the islanders were powerless and almost everywhere they were driven from their ancestral homes. However, the language survived, ensuring a degree of cultural continuity, especially in the Western Isles, where even today the first language of the vast majority is **Gaelic** (pronounced "gallic").

Skye

Jutting out from the mainland like a giant butterfly, the bare and bony promontories of **Skye** (Ⓦ www.skye.co.uk) fringe a deeply indented coastline. Justifiably, Skye was named after the Norse word for "cloud" (*skuy*), earning itself the Gaelic moniker, *Eilean a Cheo* (Island of Mist). Yet, despite the unpredictability of the weather, **tourism** has been an important part of the island's economy for a hundred years, since the train line pushed through to **Kyle of Lochalsh** in the western Highlands in 1897. From Kyle, it was the briefest of boat trips across to Skye, and the Edwardian bourgeoisie was soon swarming over to walk its mountains, whose beauty had been proclaimed by an earlier generation of Victorian climbers.

Though some estimate that only half the island's population are indigenous *Sgiathanachs* (pronounced "Ski-anaks"), Skye remains the most important centre for **Gaelic culture** and language outside of the Western Isles. Despite the Clearances, which saw an estimated 30,000 emigrate in the mid-nineteenth century, around a third of the population is fluent in Gaelic, the Gaelic college on Sleat is the most important in Scotland, and the Free Church maintains a strong presence. As an English-speaking visitor, it's as well to be aware of the tensions that exist within this idyllic island, even if you never experience them first-hand. For a taste of the resurgence of Gaelic culture, try and get here in time for the Skye and Lochalsh Festival, *Feis an Eilein* (Ⓦ www.feisaneilein.com), which takes place over two weeks in mid-July.

The island's most popular destination is the **Cuillin** ridge, whose jagged peaks dominate the island during clear weather; to explore them at close quarters you'll need to be a fairly experienced and determined walker. More accessible and equally dramatic in their own way are the rock formations of the **Trotternish** peninsula, in the north, from which there are inspirational views across to the Western Isles. If you want to escape the summer crush, shuffle off to **Glendale** and the cliffs of Neist Point or head for the **Isle of Raasay**, off Skye's east coast. Of the two main settlements, **Portree** is the only one with any charm, and a useful base for exploring the Trotternish; however, neither Portree nor Broadford are practical as jumping-off points for the Cuillin, for which you need to head for Glenbrittle or Sligachan.

Transport practicalities

Most visitors still reach Skye via **Kyle of Lochalsh**, which is linked to Inverness by train and to Kyleakin, on the eastern tip of the island, by the controversial **Skye Bridge**. The more scenic approach is by **ferry** from Mallaig, further south, crossing to Armadale. A third option is the privately operated summer-only car ferry that leaves the mainland at **Glenelg**, south of Kyle of Lochalsh, to arrive at **Kylerhea**. Most visitors arrive by car, as the **bus** services, while adequate between the villages, virtually close down on Sundays.

Sleat

Ferry services (Mon–Sat 7–8 daily; mid-May to mid-Sept also Sun; 30min) from Mallaig connect with the **Sleat** (pronounced "Slate") **peninsula**, Skye's southern tip, an uncharacteristically fertile area that has earned it the sobriquet "The Garden of Skye". The CalMac ferry terminal is at **ARMADALE** (Armadal), an elongated hamlet stretching along the wooded shoreline. If you're leaving Skye on the early-morning ferry and you need **accommodation** near Armadale, head a mile southwest to neighbouring Ardvasar, where the traditional, whitewashed *Ardvasar Hotel* (☎01471/844223, ⓦwww.ardvasarhotel.com; ❷; March–Dec) has a good restaurant specializing in local seafood and a lively bar; or for **B&B** try *Holme Leigh* (☎01599/534011, ⓔholmeleigh@eyeconvista.co.uk; ❶). There are two **hostels** on the peninsula: Armadale SYHA **hostel** (☎0870/004 1103; mid-March to Sept) is a conven-

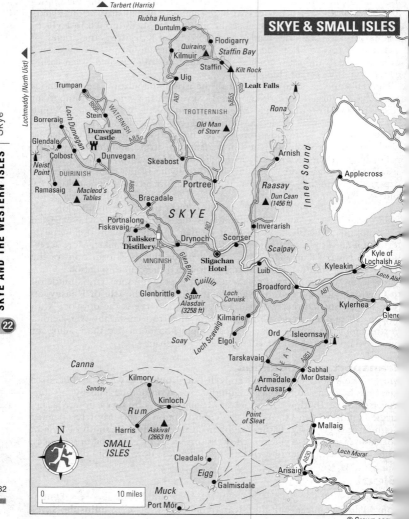

SKYE & SMALL ISLES

Tarbert (Harris)

Rubha Hunish
Duntulm
Quiraing
Flodigarry
Kilmuir
Staffin Bay
Staffin
Uig
Kilt Rock
Lealt Falls
Trumpan
Rona
TROTTERNISH
Stein
Old Man
of Storr
Borreraig
Loch Dunvegan
WATERNISH
Dunvegan Castle
Glendale
A850
Arnish
Neist Point
Colbost
Dunvegan
Skeabost
Applecross
DUIRINISH
Ramasaig
Macleod's Tables
Bracadale
Portree
Raasay
Dun Caan (1456 ft)
Inner Sound
S K Y E
Portnalong
Fiskavaig
Inverarish
Talisker Distillery
Drynoch
Sconser
Scalpay
MINGINISH
Glen Brittle
Sligachan Hotel
Luib
Kyle of Lochalsh
Kyleakin
Loch Alsh
Cuillin
Broadford
Glenbrittle
Sgurr Alasdair (3258 ft)
Loch Coruisk
Kylerhea
Glene
Kilmarie
Soay
Loch Scavaig
Elgol
Ord
Isleornsay
Tarskavaig
S L E A T
A851
Canna
Kilmory
Sabhal Mor Ostaig
Armadale
Sanday
Kinloch
Ardvasar
R u m
Point of Sleat
Mallaig
Harris
Askival (2663 ft)
SMALL ISLES
Cleadale
Arisaig
Loch Morar
N
Eigg
Galmisdale
Muck
Port Mór
A8

0   10 miles

ient ten-minute walk up the A851 towards Broadford and has a good position overlooking the bay; the *Flora MacDonald Hostel* (℡01471/844440, 🅦www.isle-of-skye-tour-guide.co.uk), two miles further up the same road, is a newly converted barn with two large dormitories; they will fetch you from the ferry. **Bike rental** is available from the SYHA hostel or the local petrol station (℡01471/844249), close to the pier.

A little further along the A851, past the SYHA hostel, you'll find the **Armadale Castle Gardens & Museum of the Isles** (April–Oct daily 9am–5.30pm; £4.50; 🅦www.highlandconnection.org/clandonaldcentre.htm), housed in a striking, purpose-built new home entered through a stone circle to the sound of Gaelic music. There's a wealth of imaginatively displayed information about the MacDonald clan's descent from the Lord of the Isles, through the Clearances to the present day, including an account of the attack by HMS Dartmouth, sent by William and Mary to shell the castle, which "sent them scampering to the hills"; those who surrendered were hanged. The handsome forty-acre **gardens**, within which lie the ruins of the MacDonalds' neo-Gothic castle, are also well worth a visit. There's a café and a library for those who want to chase up their ancestral Donald connections.

Continuing northeast, it's another eight miles to **ISLEORNSAY** (Eilean Iarmain), a secluded little village of whitewashed cottages that was once Skye's main fishing port. With the mountains of the mainland on the horizon, the views out across the bay are wonderful, overlooking a necklace of seaweed-encrusted rocks and the tidal **Isle of Ornsay**, which sports a trim lighthouse built by Robert Louis Stevenson's father. You can **stay** at the mid-nineteenth-century *Isleornsay Hotel* – also known by its Gaelic name *Hotel Eilean Iarmain* – a pricey place with excellent service, whose **restaurant** serves great seafood (℡01471/833332, 🅦www.eilean-iarmain.com; ❼). Another couple of miles brings you to the turning for *Kinloch Lodge Hotel* (℡01471/833333, 🅦www.kinloch-lodge.co.uk; ❼), centred on an old hunting lodge still in the possession of Lord Macdonald of Macdonald, with excellent food guaranteed by wife Claire whose cookery books are internationally famous.

Kyleakin and Kylerhea

The privately financed **Skye Bridge** links the tidy hamlet of **KYLEAKIN** (Caol Acain – pronounced "Ka*la*kin") with the Kyle of Lochalsh on the mainland. The bridge itself was welcomed by the vast majority of islanders, but the exorbitant tolls were not and it now looks likely that the Scottish Executive will have to buy out the firm in order to abolish them. Strictly speaking there are two bridges, resting on an island in the middle, **Eilean Ban**, once the home of author and naturalist Gavin Maxwell, and now a wildlife sanctuary with the emphasis on otters. Visitors, limited to twelve, have to assemble on the bridge and must book in advance through the **Bright Water Visitor Centre** in Kyleakin (April–Oct Mon–Fri 10am–5pm; ℡01599/530040; £8) for an hour-long guided tour. The centre itself is well worth a visit as it's full of hands-on things for kids of all ages and it's free.

With its ferry now defunct, Kyleakin has reinvented itself as something of a backpackers' hangout – in summer, the population more than doubles – to the consternation of many villagers. If you're intent on joining the throng, the SYHA **hostel** (℡01599/534585, 🅔reservations@syha.org.uk) is an ugly, modern building a couple of hundred yards from the old pier; nearby *Skye Backpackers* (℡01599/534510, 🅦www.scotlands-top-hostels.com) is a more laid-back option, as is *Dun Caan Hostel* (℡01599/534087, 🅦www.skyerover

.co.uk). **Bike rental** is available from *Dun Caan Hostel* and Skye Bikes (℡01599/534795) on the pier.

You can still avoid crossing the Skye Bridge by taking the small car ferry (mid–March to mid–May & Sept to mid-Oct Mon–Sat 9am–5.45pm, Sun 10am–5.45pm; mid–May to Aug Mon–Sat 9am–7.45pm, Sun 10am–5.45pm; 15min) from Glenelg to **KYLERHEA** (pronounced "Kile-ray"), a peaceful little place some four miles down the coast from Kyleakin. From here you can walk half an hour up the coast to the Forestry Commission **Otter Hide**, where, if you're lucky, you may be able to spot one of the elusive creatures.

Broadford

Heading west out of Kyleakin or Kylerhea brings you eventually to Skye's second-largest village, charmless **BROADFORD** (An t-Ath Leathann), whose mile-long main street curves round a wide bay. Despite its rather unlovely appearance, Broadford makes a useful base for exploring the southern half of Skye. At the west end of the village there's a bank, a bakery, a tearoom and a post office. The SYHA **hostel** is on the west shore of Broadford Bay (℡01471/822442, ℮reservations@syha.org.uk; March–Oct). Two **B&Bs** which stand out are the delightful old croft-house *Lime Stone Cottage*, 4 Lime Park (℡01471/822142, ℮kathielimepark@btinternet.com; ❷), and the modern, comfortable *Ptarmigan* (℡01471/822744, ⓦwww.ptarmigan-cottage.com; ❸), on the main road, with views over the bay. If you want a bite **to eat**, try the popular *Creelers Seafood Restaurant* at the south end of the bay, with a more standard takeaway at the back. Pricey, real chef cooking is to be found at award-winning *The Rendezvous* on the main road at Breakish (booking advisable; ℡01471/822001), a mile or so east of Broadford. **Bike rental** is available from the SYHA hostel or from *Fairwinds*, another good place to stay (℡01471/822270; ❷; March–Oct), just past the *Broadford Hotel*.

Isle of Raasay

Travelling west from Broadford, with the Skye Cuillin to your left and the sea to your right, it's thirteen miles to Sconsor, where a CalMac car ferry leaves for the lovely **Isle of Raasay** (Mon–Sat 8–10 daily; 15min), which, with its bleak and barren hills, remains well off the tourist trail. Raasay's population stands between 150 and 200. The Free Presbyterian Church has a strong following and the island keeps a strict observance of the Sabbath – no work or play on Sundays.

The ferry docks at the southern tip of the island, an easy fifteen-minute walk from **INVERARISH**, a tiny village set within thick woods on the island's southwest coast. The grand Georgian mansion of **Raasay House,** built by the MacLeods in the late 1740s, is now the *Raasay Outdoor Centre*, offering comfortable **accommodation** in pleasantly casual rooms (℡01478/660266 ⓦwww.raasayoutdoorcentre.co.uk; ❶; March to mid-Oct). You can also **camp** in the grounds or stay in the bunkhouse, and, for a daily cost of around £40, join in the centre's activity programme: anything from sailing, windsurfing and canoeing, to climbing and hillwalking. Close by is the welcoming *Isle of Raasay Hotel* (℡01478/660222, ⓦwww.isleofraasayhotel.co.uk; ❸), which serves traditional Scottish food and where the view of the Cuillin surpasses any other. In the village is a pleasant Victorian guest house, *Churchton House* (℡01478/660260; ❶).

A rough track cuts up the steep hillside from the village to Raasay's isolated but beautifully placed SYHA **hostel** (℡0870/004 1146; mid-March to Sept

Most of the rest of Raasay is starkly barren, a rugged and rocky terrain of sand-stone in the south and gneiss in the north, with the most obvious feature being the curiously truncated basalt cap on top of **Dun Caan** (1456ft), where Boswell "danced a Highland dance" on his visit to the island with Dr Johnson in 1773.

The Cuillin and the Red Hills

For many people, the **Cuillin**, whose sharp snowcapped peaks rise mirage-like from the flatness of the surrounding terrain, are the *raison d'être* for a visit to Skye. When the clouds finally disperse, they are the dominating feature of the island, visible from every other peninsula. There are basically three approaches to the Cuillin: from the south, by foot or by boat from Elgol; from the *Sligachan Hotel* to the north; or from Glen Brittle to the west of the mountains. Glen Sligachan is one of the most popular routes, dividing as it does the granite of the round-topped **Red Hills** (sometimes known as the Red Cuillin) to the east from the dark, coarse-grained jagged-edged gabbro of the real Cuillin (also known as the Black Cuillin) to the west. With some twenty Munros between them, these are mountains to be taken seriously, and many routes through the Cuillin are for experienced climbers only.

Elgol and Loch Coruisk

The road to **ELGOL** (Ealaghol), fourteen miles southwest of Broadford at the tip of the Strathaird peninsula, is one of the most dramatic on the island, lead-ing right into the heart of the Red Hills and then down a precipitous slope, with a stunning view from the top down to Elgol pier. The chief reason for visiting Elgol is, weather permitting, to take a boat across Loch Scavaig (March–Sept 2–4 daily), past a seal colony, to a jetty near the entrance of **Loch Coruisk** (from *coire uish*, "cauldron of water"). An isolated, glacial loch, this needle-like shaft of water, nearly two miles long but only a couple of hundred yards wide, lies in the shadow of the highest peaks of the Black Cuillin, a won-derfully overpowering landscape.

The journey by sea takes 45 minutes and passengers are dropped to spend about one and a half hours ashore; for booking (essential) and details of sailing times, ring the *Bella Jane* (☎0800/731 3089 before 10am and after 7.30pm). Walkers can use the boat on a one-way trip simply to get to Loch Coruisk, from where there are numerous possibilities for hiking amidst the Red Hills, the most popular (and gentle) of which is the eight-mile trek north over the pass into **Glen Sligachan**. Alternatively, you could walk round the coast to the sandy bay of **Camasunary**, over two miles to the east – a difficult walk that involves a tricky river crossing and negotiating "The Bad Step", an overhang-ing rock with a thirty-foot drop to the sea – and either head north to Glen Sligachan or continue south three miles along the coast to Elgol.

The only public transport is the morning **postbus** from Broadford (Mon–Fri daily, Sat 1 daily; 2hr; check in Broadford post office). If you're fond of seafood, then *Coruisk House* is the **place to stay** (☎01471/866330, Ⓦwww.coruisk-skye-bb.demon.co.uk; ❷). If you don't want to stay in Elgol, head for *Rowan Cottage* (☎01471/866287, Ⓦwww.rowancottage-skye.co.uk; ❶; March–Nov), a lovely **B&B** a mile or so east in Glasnakille. By far the most popular place to stay, though, is the **campsite** (April–Oct) by the *Sligachan Hotel* (☎01478/650204, Ⓦwww.sligachan.co.uk; ❺) on the A87, at the north-ern end of Glen Sligachan; the hotel also has a **bunkhouse**. Its huge *Seamus Bar* serves food for weary walkers until 10pm, and quenches their thirst with the full range of real ales produced by Skye's very own microbrewery in Uig and there are often live bands; there's also a more formal restaurant with splendid food.

Glen Brittle

Six miles along the A863 to Dunvegan from the *Sligachan Hotel*, a turning signed "Carbost and Portnalong" quickly leads to the entrance to stony **Glen Brittle**, edging the most spectacular peaks of the Cuillin; at the end of the glen, idyllically situated by the sea, is the village of **GLENBRITTLE**. Climbers and serious walkers tend to congregate at the SYHA **hostel** (℡0870/004 1121, ⒺReservations@syha.org.uk; March–Sept) or the beautifully situated **campsite** (℡01478/640404; April–Oct), a mile or so further south behind the wide sandy beach at the foot of the glen. From mid-May to September two buses a day (Mon–Sat only) from Portree make it to Glenbrittle; both the hostel and the campsite have grocery stores, the only ones for miles.

From the valley a score of difficult and strenuous trails lead east into the **Black Cuillin**, a rough semicircle of peaks rising to about 3000ft, which surround Loch Coruisk. One of the easiest walks is the five-mile round-trip from the campsite up **Coire Lagan**, to a crystal-cold lochan squeezed in among the sternest of rock faces. Above the lochan is Skye's highest peak, **Sgurr Alasdair** (3258ft), one of the more difficult Munros, while Sgurr na Banachdich (3166ft) is considered the most easily accessible Munro in the Cuillin. The Mountain Rescue Service has produced a book of walks for those who are not climbers, available locally.

Dunvegan and Duirinish

After the Portnalong and Glen Brittle turning, the A863 slips across bare rounded hills to skirt the bony sea cliffs and stacks of the west coast twenty miles or so north to **DUNVEGAN** (Dùn Bheagain). It's an unimpressive place, strung out along the east shore of the sea loch of the same name, though it does make quite a good base for exploring the interesting peninsula of Duirinish.

The main tourist trap in the village is **Dunvegan Castle** (daily: mid-March to Nov 10am–5.30pm; Dec to mid-March 11am–4pm; £6.50, gardens only £4.50; ⓦwww.dunvegancastle.com) which sprawls on top of a rocky outcrop, sandwiched between the sea and several acres of beautifully maintained gardens. It's been the seat of the Clan MacLeod since the thirteenth century, but the present greying, rectangular fortress, with its uniform battlements and dummy pepper pots, dates from the 1840s. Inside, you don't get a lot of castle for your money and the contents are far from stunning, the most intriguing being the battered remnants of the **Fairy Flag** which was allegedly carried back to Skye by Norwegian King Harald Hardrada's Gaelic boatmen after the Battle of Stamford Bridge in 1066.

The hammerhead **Duirinish peninsula** lies to the west of Dunvegan, much of it inaccessible to all except walkers prepared to scale or skirt the area's twin flat-topped basalt peaks: Healabhal Bheag (1600ft) and Healabhal Mhòr (1538ft). The mountains are better known as **MacLeod's Tables**, for legend has it that the MacLeod chief held an open-air royal feast on the lower of the two for James V. The main areas of habitation lie to the north, along the western shores of Loch Dunegon, and in the broad green sweep of **Glen Dal** attractively dotted with white farmhouses and dubbed "Little England" b the locals, due to its high percentage of "white settlers": English incomers searching for a better life.

Glendale's turbulent history, and a great deal about nineteenth-century crofting, is told through fascinating contemporary news cuttings at **Colbost Folk Museum** (Easter–Oct daily 9am–6pm; £1.50), situated in a restored blackhouse, four miles up the road from Dunvegan. A guide is usually on hand to answer questions, the peat fire smokes all day, and there's a restored illegal whisky still round the back.

Beyond the village of Glendale itself, blustery but easy footpaths lead to the dramatically sited lighthouse on **Neist Point**, Skye's most westerly spot, which features some fearsome sea cliffs, and wonderful views across the sea to the Western Isles. Despite the fact that the present owner has put up "Keep Out!" notices, the locals continue to exert their right to roam right up to the lighthouse.

Practicalities

Dunvegan is a useful base, with a **tourist office** (Mon–Sat 9am–5.30pm) and several excellent **hotels** and **B&Bs** dotted along the main road, such as the converted traditional croft *Roskhill House* (℡01470/521317, Ⓔstay@roskhill .demon.co.uk; ❸). Other possibilities include the *Silverdale* (℡01470/521251; ❶), just before you get to Colbost, which also has a self-catering cottage, or the luxurious *Harlosh House* (℡01470/521367, harlosh.house@virgin.net; ❻; April–Oct), four miles south of Dunvegan. There's an excellent lochside **campsite** at Loch Greshornish, a mile north of Edinbane on the A850, (℡01470/582230, Ⓦwww.skyecamp.com; April–Sept; bike and canoe rental available).

The culinary mecca in the area is the expensive *Three Chimneys* **restaurant** (℡01470/511258, Ⓦwww.threechimneys.co.uk; closed Sun), located beside Colbost Folk Museum; if you want to stay for bed and breakfast as well, there are six fabulous rooms at the restaurant's adjacent *House Over-By* (❽). A good place to stay, with welcoming fires and good food is the sixteenth-century *Stein Inn* (℡01470/592362, Ⓦwww.steininn.co.uk; ❸), in Stein, and outstanding seafood at the *Lochbay Seafood Restaurant* (℡01470/592235; Easter–Oct closed Sat & Sun; Aug closed Sun). Without doubt, the best place to eat in Dunvegan is *The Old Schoolhouse* (℡01470/521421) whose excellent food belies its appearance from outside. Otherwise, all the hotels do dinner and, on a more modest scale, there's a snug **café** (April–Oct) attached to *Dunvegan Bakery*, where you can also pick up sandwich components and homemade carrot cake.

Portree

Although referred to by the locals as "the village", **PORTREE** is the only real town on Skye. It's also one of the most attractive fishing ports in northwest Scotland, its deep, cliff-edged harbour filled with fishing boats and circled by multicoloured restaurants and guest houses. The attractive harbour is overlooked by **The Lump**, a steep and stumpy peninsula with a flagpole on it that was once the site of public hangings on the island, attracting crowds of up to five thousand; it also sports a folly built by the celebrated Dr Ban, a visionary who wanted to make Portree into a second Oban. Up above the harbour is the spick-and-span town centre, spreading out from **Somerled Square**, built in the late eighteenth century as the island's administrative and commercial centre, and now housing the bus station and car park. The **Royal Hotel** on

22

Bank Street occupies the site of *McNab's Inn* where Bonnie Prince Charlie took leave of Flora MacDonald (see p.1140), and where, 27 years later, Boswell and Johnson had "a very good dinner, porter, port and punch".

A mile or so out of town on the Sligachan road is the **Aros Centre** (daily 9am–6pm; open later in summer; Ⓦwww.scotlandcreates.com/aros), one of Skye's most successful tourist attractions despite the fact that it's little more than one enormous souvenir shop. Aros's best feature is that it hosts gigs and contains a **cinema**, a modern exhibition space, a licensed bar and a popular café, plus a special play area for small kids. For a view of the contemporary visual arts scene, it's well worth seeking out **An Tuireann Arts Centre**, housed in a converted fever hospital on the Struan road (Mon–Sat 10am–5pm; free; closed Mon in winter; Ⓦwww.antuireann.org.uk), which puts on exhibitions, stages concerts, and has an excellent small licensed café where even the counter is a work of art, with an imaginative range of food on offer.

Practicalities

Hours vary enormously at Portree's **tourist office**, just off Bridge Street, so the ones here are just a guideline (April–Oct Mon–Sat 9am–8pm, Sun 10am–4pm; Nov–March 9am–5.30pm, closed Sun). Probably the best **hotel** is the comfortable *Cuillin Hills* (Ⓣ01478/612003, Ⓦwww.cuillinhills.demon .co.uk; ❼), ten minutes' walk out of town along the northern shore of the bay. *Viewfield House Hotel* (Ⓣ01478/612217, Ⓦwww.viewfieldhouse.com; ❻; mid-April to mid-Oct), on the southern outskirts of town, is worth investigating for the Victorian atmosphere, stuffed polecats and antiques. In the lower price range Portree is stuffed with B&Bs, although they may all be full in the season: try *Conusg*, a B&B in a quiet spot by the *Cuillin Hills Hotel*, originally built for the coachman in the 1880s (Ⓣ01478/612426, ❶; Easter–Sept), or *Balloch* in Viewfield Road (Ⓣ01478/612093; ❷; Easter–Oct). The only **hostel** in Portree is the smart *Portree Independent Hostel* (Ⓣ01478/613737, Ⓔhostel@beeb.net) housed in the Old Post Office on the Green. Torvaig **campsite** (Ⓣ01478/612209; April–Oct) lies a mile and a half north of town off the A855 Staffin road.

The best **food** in town is on Bosville Terrace, but it's pricey: the *Bosville Hotel*'s *Chandlery* restaurant serves excellent meals, with its sister *Bosville* restaurant being much cheaper; *Harbour View* has a seafood **restaurant** with candlelit ambience. The popular *Lower Deck Seafood Restaurant* (Ⓣ01478/613611) on the harbour has a wood-panelled warmth to it, and is reasonably priced at lunchtime (less so in the evenings when booking is essential); for good **fish and chips**, pop next door to their excellent chippy. As for **pubs**, the bar of the *Pier Hotel* on the quayside is the fishermen's drinking hole, and the *Tongadale* on Wentworth Street is lively. Currently the most popular evening venue by far is the *Isles Inn* on Somerled Square, with excellent bar meals as well as live music.

Trotternish

Protruding twenty miles north from Portree, the **Trotternish peninsula** boasts some of the island's most bizarre scenery, particularly on the east coast where volcanic basalt has pressed down on the softer sandstone and limestone underneath, causing massive landslides. These, in turn, have created sheer cliffs peppered with outcrops of hard, wizened basalt, which run the full length of the peninsula. These pinnacles and pillars are at their most eccentric in the Quiraing, above Staffin Bay, on the east coast. Trotternish is best explored with your own transport, but an occasional bus service (Mon–Sat 2–4 daily) along the road encircling the peninsula gives access to almost all the coast.

The east coast

The first geological eccentricity on the **Trotternish** peninsula, six miles north of Portree along the A855, is the **Old Man of Storr**, a distinctive column of rock, shaped like a willow leaf, which, along with its neighbours, is part of a massive land-slip. Huge blocks of stone still occasionally break off the cliff face of the Storr (2358ft) above and slide downhill. At 165ft, the Old Man is a real challenge for climbers; less difficult is the half-hour trek up the new footpath to the foot of the column from the woods beside the car park. Further north, **Staffin Bay** is spread out before you, dotted with whitewashed and "spotty" houses; **STAFFIN** itself is a lively, largely Gaelic-speaking community where crofts have been handed down the generations. A single-track road cuts across the peninsula from the north end of the bay, allowing access to the **Quiraing**, a spectacular forest of mighty pinnacles and savage rock formations. There are two car parks: from the first, beside a cemetery, it's a steep half-hour climb to the rocks; from the second, on the saddle, it's a longer but more gentle traverse.

The **accommodation** on the east coast is among the best on Skye, with most places enjoying fantastic views out over the sea. Just beyond the Lealt Falls there's the very welcoming and comfortable *Glenview Inn* (☎01470/562248, Ⓦ www.glenview-skye.co.uk; ❸; March–Oct), with an excellent restaurant, and a **campsite** (☎01470/562213; April–Sept) south of Staffin Bay. In fine weather, you can enjoy good bar snacks on the castellated terrace of the stylish, award-winning *Flodigarry Country House Hotel* (☎01470/552203, Ⓦ www.flodigarry.co.uk; ❻), three miles up the coast from Staffin. Behind the hotel (and now part of it) is the cottage where local heroine Flora MacDonald lived, and had six of her seven children, from 1751 to 1759. If the hotel's rooms are beyond your means, try the neat and attractive *Dun Flodigarry Backpackers' Hostel* (☎01470/552212, Ⓦ www.flodigarry.f9.co.uk; £9 per bed), a couple of minutes' walk away – you can ring the hostel to arrange transport or catch the local bus.

The west coast

Beyond Flodigarry, at the tip of the Trotternish peninsula, by the road to Shulista, a public footpath leads past the ruins of a cleared hamlet to the spectacular sea stacks of **Rubha Hunish**, the most northerly point on Skye. A couple of miles further along the A855 lies **DUNTULM** (Duntuilm), whose heyday as a major MacDonald power base is recalled by the shattered remains of a headland fortress. The imposing *Duntulm Castle Hotel* (☎01470/552213, Ⓦ www.duntulmcastle.co.uk; ❷; April–Nov) is close by, and provides good bar meals as well as wonderful views across the Minch to the Western Isles.

Heading down the west shore of the Trotternish, it's two miles to the **Skye Museum of Island Life** (Easter–Oct Mon–Sat 9.30am–5.30pm; £1.75), an impressive cluster of thatched blackhouses on an exposed hill overlooking Harris. The museum, run by locals, gives a fascinating insight into a way of life that was commonplace on Skye a hundred years ago. The blackhouse, now home to the ticket office, is much as it was when it was last inhabited in 1957, while the two houses to the east contain interesting snippets of local history. Behind the museum in the cemetery up the hill are the graves of **Flora MacDonald** and her husband. Thousands turned out for her funeral in 1790, creating a funeral procession a mile long – indeed, so widespread was her fame that the original family mausoleum fell victim to souvenir hunters and had to

Bonnie Prince Charlie

Prince Charles Edward Stewart – better known as **Bonnie Prince Charlie** or "The Young Pretender" – was born in Rome in 1720, where his father, "The Old Pretender", claimant to the British throne, was living in exile. At the age of 25, having little military experience, no knowledge of Gaelic, an imperfect grasp of English and a strong attachment to the Catholic faith, the prince set out for Scotland on a French ship, disguised as a seminarist from the Scots College in Paris. He arrived on the Outer Hebridean island of Eriskay on July 23, 1745, and was immediately implored to return to France by the clan chiefs, who were singularly unimpressed by his lack of army. Charles was unmoved and went on to raise the royal standard at Glenfinnan, gather together a Highland army, win the Battle of Prestonpans, march south into England and reach Derby before finally (and foolishly) agreeing to retreat. Back in Scotland, he won one last victory, at Falkirk, before the final disaster at Culloden in April 1746.

The prince spent the following five months in hiding, with a price of £30,000 on his head, and literally thousands of government troops searching for him. He certainly endured his fair share of cold and hunger whilst on the run, but the real price was paid by the Highlanders themselves, who risked and sometimes lost their lives by aiding and abetting the prince. The most famous of these was, of course, 23-year-old **Flora MacDonald**, whom Charles met on South Uist in June 1746. Flora was persuaded – either by his beauty or her relatives, depending on which account you believe – to convey Charles "over the sea to Skye", disguised as an Irish servant girl by the name of Betty Burke. She was arrested just seven days after parting with the prince in Portree, and held in the Tower of London until July 1747. She went on to marry a local man, had seven children, and in 1774 emigrated to America, where her husband was taken prisoner during the American War of Independence. Flora returned to Scotland and was reunited with her husband on his release; they resettled in Skye and she died at the age of 68.

Charles eventually boarded a ship back to France in September 1746, but, despite his promises – "for all that has happened, Madam, I hope we shall meet in St James's yet" – never returned to Scotland, nor did he ever see Flora again. After mistreating a string of mistresses, he eventually got married at the age of 52 to the 19-year-old princess of Stolberg, in an effort to produce a Stewart heir. They had no children, and she eventually fled from his violent drunkenness; in 1788, a none-too-"bonnie" Prince Charles died in the arms of his illegitimate daughter in Rome. Bonnie Prince Charlie became a legend in his own lifetime, but it was the Victorians who really milked the myth for all its sentimentality, conveniently overlooking the fact that the real consequence of 1745 was the virtual annihilation of the Highland way of life.

be replaced. The Celtic cross headstone is inscribed with a simple tribute by Dr Johnson, who visited her in 1773: "Her name will be mentioned in history, if courage and fidelity be virtues, mentioned with honour."

A further five miles south is the ferry port of **UIG** (Uige), which curves its way round a dramatic, horseshoe-shaped bay, and is the arrival point for CalMac ferries from Tarbert (Harris) and Lochmaddy (North Uist); if you've time to spare while waiting for a ferry, pop into Uig Pottery. Most folk come to Uig to take the ferry to the Western Isles, but if you need to stay near the ferry terminal, try the inexpensive **B&B**, *Orasay*, 14 Idrigill (☎01470/542316, ⓔbarbara@orasay.freeserve.co.uk; ❶), or the **campsite** just behind (☎01470/542714), which also offers **bike rental**. By contrast, the SYHA **hostel** (☎0870/004 1155, ⓔreservations@syha.org.uk; April–Oct) is high up on the south side of the village, with exhilarating views over the bay. The *Pu*

1141

△ Quiraing, Skye

at the Pier offers filling meals, and serves the local Skye beers, which are also on sale in the shop of the nearby brewery (Mon–Fri tours by appointment; ℡01470/542477, ⓦwww.skyebrewery.demon.co.uk).

The Small Isles

The history of the **Small Isles**, which lie to the south of Skye, is typical of the Hebrides: early Christianization, followed by a period of Norwegian rule that ended in 1266 when the islands fell into Scottish hands. Their support for the Jacobite cause resulted in hard times after the failed rebellion of 1745, but the biggest problems came with the introduction of the **potato** in the mid-eighteenth century. The consequences were as dramatic as they were unforeseen: the success of the crop and its nutritional value – when grown in conjunction with traditional cereals – eliminated famine at a stroke, prompting a population explosion. In 1750, there were just a thousand islanders, but by 1800 their numbers had almost doubled.

At first, the problem of overcrowding was camouflaged by the **kelp** boom, in which the islanders were employed, and the islands' owners made a fortune, gathering and burning local seaweed to sell for use in the manufacture of gunpowder, soap and glass. But the economic bubble burst with the end of the Napoleonic Wars and, to maintain their profit margins, the owners resorted to drastic action. The first to sell up was Alexander MacLean, who sold Rùm as grazing land for **sheep**, got quotations for shipping its people to Nova Scotia, and gave them a year's notice to quit. He also cleared Muck to graze cattle, as did the MacNeills on Canna. Only on Eigg was some compassion shown: the new owner, a certain Hugh MacPherson, who bought the island from the Clanranalds in 1827, actually gave some of his tenants extended leases.

Since the Clearances, each of the islands has been bought and sold several times, though only **Muck** is now privately owned by the benevolent laird, Lawrence MacEwen. **Eigg** hit the headlines in 1997, when the islanders finally managed to buy the island themselves and put an end to more than 150 years of property speculation. The other islands were bequeathed to national agencies: **Rùm**, by far the largest and most-visited of the group, possessing a cluster of formidable volcanic peaks and the architecturally remarkable Kinloch Castle, passed to the Nature Conservancy Council (now Scottish Natural Heritage) in 1957; and **Canna**, in many ways the prettiest of the isles with its high basalt cliffs, has been in the hands of the National Trust for Scotland since 1981.

Accommodation on the Small Isles is limited and requires **forward planning** at all times of year; formal public transport is nonexistent, but the local will usually oblige if you have heavy baggage to shift.

Getting to the islands

CalMac run passenger-only ferries to the Small Isles every day except Sunday from Mallaig (℡01687/462403, ⓦwww.calmac.co.uk). Day-trips are possible to each of the islands on certain days, and to all four islands on Saturdays, if you catch the 6.30am ferry. From May to September, you can also reach Rùm, Eigg and Muck from Arisaig with **Arisaig Marine**, run by Murdo Grant (℡01687/450224, ⓦwww.arisaig.co.uk). This is a much more pleasant way to get there, as the boat is licensed, and, if any marine mammals are spotted en route, the boat will pause for a bit of whale-watching. Day-trips are possible

Eigg on most days, allowing four to five hours ashore, and to Rùm and Muck on a few days, allowing two to three hours ashore. With careful studying of both CalMac and Murdo Grant timetables, you should be able to organize a visit to suit you, especially as Arisaig and Mallaig are linked by railway. Be warned, however, that boats to the Small Isles are frequently cancelled in bad weather, so be prepared to holiday for longer than you planned.

Rùm

Like Skye, **Rùm** is dominated by its Cuillin, which, though only reaching a height of 2663ft at the summit of Askival, rises up with comparable drama straight up from the sea in the south of the island. Rùm's chief formal attraction is **Kinloch Castle** (guided tours most days at 2pm; £4), a squat red sandstone edifice fronted by colonnades and topped by crenellations and turrets, that dominates the village of Kinloch. Completed at enormous expense in 1900 – the red sandstone was shipped in from Arran and the soil for the gardens from Ayrshire – its interior is a perfectly preserved example of Edwardian decadence, "a living memorial of the stalking, the fishing and the sailing, the tenantry and plenty of the days before 1914". From the galleried hall, with its tiger rugs, stags' heads and giant Japanese incense-burners, to the "Extra Low Fast Cushion" of the Soho snooker table in the Billiard Room, the interior is packed with knick-knacks and technical gizmos accumulated by **Sir George Bullough** (1870–1939), the spendthrift son of self-made millionaire Sir John Bullough, who bought the island as a sporting estate in 1888. As such, it was only really used for a few weeks each autumn, during the "season", yet employed an island workforce of one hundred all year round. Bullough's guests were woken at eight each morning by a piper; later on, an orchestrion, an electrically driven barrel organ (originally destined for Balmoral) crammed in under the stairs, would grind out an eccentric mixture of pre-dinner tunes – *The Ride of the Valkyries* and *Ma Blushin' Rosie* among others; a demo is included in the tour. The ballroom has a sprung floor, the library features a gruesome photographic collection from the Bulloughs' world tours, but the *pièce de résistance* has to be Bullough's **Edwardian bathrooms**, whose baths have hooded walnut shower cabinets, fitted with two taps and four dials, which allow the bather to fire high-pressure water at their body from every angle.

For those with limited time or energy, there are two gentle waymarked **heritage trails**, both of which start from Kinloch and take around two hours to complete. For longer walks, you must fill in route cards and pop them into the White House (Mon–Fri 9am–12.30pm), where the reserve manager can give useful advice. The island's best beach is at **KILMORY**, to the north (5hr return), though this part of the island is only open to the public at the weekend as it's given over to the study of red deer; it's also closed completely in June, during calving, and October, during rutting. When the island's human head count peaked at 450 in 1791, the hamlet of **HARRIS** on the southwest coast (6hr return) housed a large crofting community; all that remains now are several ruined blackhouses and the extravagant **Bullough Mausoleum**, built by Sir George to house the remains of his father in the style of a Greek Doric temple, overlooking the sea.

You need to book **accommodation** in advance. There's just one **B&B**, *Bay View* (☎01687/462023; ❶), in Kinloch. Kinloch Castle lets a few of its four-poster rooms (❹), but it's basically run as an independent **hostel** (☎01687/462037), with dormitories in the old servants' quarters. There are also two simple mountain **bothies** (maximum stay three nights), in Dibidil and

Guirdil, and basic **camping** near the old pier – book ahead for both with the White House (℡01687/462026). Wherever you're staying, you can either do self-catering – hostellers can use the hostel kitchen – or eat the unpretentious **food** offered in the hostel's licensed bistro, which serves full breakfasts, offers packed lunches and charges just over £10 a head for a three-course evening meal. There is also a small shop/off-licence/post office in Kinloch. Bear in mind that Rùm is the wettest of the Small Isles, and is known for having some of the worst **midges** in Scotland – come prepared for both.

Eigg

Eigg (ⓦwww.isleofeigg.org) is without doubt the most easily distinguishable of the Small Isles from a distance, since the island is mostly made up of a basalt plateau 1000ft above sea level, and a great stump of columnar pitchstone lava, known as An Sgurr, rising out of the plateau another 290ft. It's also by far the most vibrant, populous and welcoming of the Small Isles, with a strong sense of community.

Ferries now arrive at the new causeway, which juts out into **Galmisdale Bay** at the southeast corner of the island where **An Laimhrig** (The Anchorage), the island's community centre, stands, housing a shop, post office, tearoom and information centre. The island minibus meets incoming ferries, and will take you to wherever you need to go on the island. If time is limited, you could simply head for the nearby **Lodge**, the former laird's house and gardens which the islanders plan to renovate in the future. With the island's great landmark, **An Sgurr** (1292ft), watching over you wherever you go, many folk feel duty bound to climb it, and enjoy the wonderful views over to Muck and Rùm (3–4hr return).

The nicest place **to stay** on Eigg is *Kildonan House* (℡01687/482446; full board ➍), a beautiful eighteenth-century wood-panelled house where the cooking is superb. The island boasts a comfortable new **bunkhouse**, *Glebe Barn* (℡01687/482417, ⓔsimon@glebebarn.co.uk), where you must book ahead; basic **camping** is possible at Galmisdale Bay and with Sue Holland in Cleadale (℡01687/482480, ⓔsueholland@talk21.com). **Bike rental** is available from Eigg Bikes (℡01687/482469) by the pier.

Muck

Smallest and most southerly of the Small Isles, **Muck** (ⓦwww.islemuck.com) is low-lying, mostly treeless and extremely fertile, and as such shares more characteristics with the likes of Coll and Tiree than its nearest neighbours. **PORT MÓR**, the village on the southeast corner of the island, is where visitors arrive. A road, just over a mile in length, connects Port Mór with the island's main farm, **GALLANACH**, which overlooks the rocky seal-strewn skerries on the north side of the island. The nicest sandy beach is Camas na Cairidh, to the east of Gallanach. Despite being only 452ft above sea level, it really is worth climbing **Beinn Airein**, in the southwest corner of the island, for the 360-degree panoramic view of the surrounding islands; the return journey from Port Mór takes around two hours.

You can **stay** with one of the MacEwen family, who have owned the island since 1896, at *Port Mór House* (℡01687/462365; full board ➍); the rooms are pine-clad and enjoy great views, and the food is delicious. Alternatively, you can stay at the island's **bunkhouse** (℡01687/462362), a characterful, wood-panelled bothy. With permission from the landowner you may also **camp rough**, but bring supplies with you as there's no shop. The craftshop in Po

22

Mór springs into life when day-trippers arrive, and doubles as a licensed **restaurant**.

Canna

Measuring a mere five miles by one, and with a population of less than twenty, **Canna** is run as a single farm and bird sanctuary by the National Trust for Scotland. For visitors, the chief pastime is walking: from the dock it's about a mile across a grassy basalt plateau to the bony sea cliffs of the north shore, which rise to a peak around **Compass Hill** (458ft) – so called because its high metal content distorts compasses – in the northeastern corner of the island, from where you get great views across to Rùm and Skye. The cliffs of the buffeted western half of the island are a breeding ground for both Manx shearwater and puffin. Some seven miles offshore stands the **Heiskeir of Canna**, a curious mass of stone columns sticking up thirty feet above the water.

Accommodation is virtually nonexistent, but with permission from the NTS you may **camp rough**. The NTS rep on Canna is Winnie MacKinnon, who can help answer most queries (☏01687/462466). Remember, however, that there are no shops on Canna (bar the post office), so you must bring your own supplies, or order them to be delivered from Mallaig.

The Western Isles

Beyond Skye, across the unpredictable waters of the Minch, lie the wild and windy Outer Hebrides or Outer Isles, nowadays known as the **Western Isles** (ⓦ www.visithebrides.com/), a 130-mile-long archipelago stretching from Lewis and Harris in the north to the Uists and Barra in the south. An elemental beauty pervades each of the more than two hundred islands that make up the Long Isle, as it's sometimes known, though only a handful are inhabited, by a total population of just under 27,000 people. This is truly a land on the edge, where the turbulent seas of the Atlantic smash up against a geologically complex terrain whose rough rocks and mighty sea cliffs are interrupted by a thousand sheltered bays and, in the far west, a long line of sweeping sandy beaches. The islands' interiors are equally dramatic, a series of formidable mountain ranges soaring high above great chunks of boggy peat moor, a barren wilderness enclosing a host of tiny lakes, or lochans.

The most significant difference from Skye is that tourism on the Western Isles is much less important to the fragile economy, which is still mainly

㉒

Gaelic in the Western Isles

Except in Stornoway, and Balivanich on North Uist, **road signs** in the Western Isles are now almost exclusively in **Gaelic**, a difficult language to the English-speaker's eye, with complex pronunciation, though as a (very) general rule, the English names often provide a rough pronunciation guide. Particularly if you're driving, it's a good idea to buy the bilingual Western Isles **map**, produced by the local tourist board, Bord Turasachd nan Eilean, and available at most tourist offices. To reflect the signposting, we've put the Gaelic first in the text, with the English equivalent in brackets. Thereafter we've stuck to the Gaelic names, to try to familiarize readers with their (albeit variable) spellings – the only exceptions are in the names of islands and ferry terminals, where we've stuck to the English names (with the Gaelic in brackets) partly to reflect the ferry company CalMac's own policy.

concentrated around crofting, fishing and weaving; the percentage of "white settlers" is also a lot lower. The Outer Hebrides remain the heartland of **Gaelic** culture, with the language spoken by the vast majority of islanders, though its everyday usage remains under constant threat from the national dominance of English. Its survival is due, in no small part, to the all-pervading influence of the Free Church and its offshoots, whose strict Calvinism is the creed of the vast majority of the population, with the sparsely populated South Uist, Barra and parts of Benbecula adhering to the more relaxed demands of Catholicism.

The interior of the northernmost island, **Lewis**, is mostly peat moor, a barren and marshy tract that gives way abruptly to the bare peaks of **North Harris**. Across a narrow isthmus lies **South Harris**, presenting some of the finest scenery in Scotland, with wide beaches of golden sand trimming the Atlantic in full view of the mountains and a rough boulder-strewn interior lying to the east. Across the Sound of Harris, to the south, a string of tiny, flatter isles – **North Uist**, **Benbecula**, **South Uist** – linked by causeways, offer breezy beaches, whose fine sands front a narrow band of boggy farmland, which, in turn, is mostly bordered by a lower range of hills to the east. Finally, tiny **Barra** contains all these landscapes in one small Hebridean package, and is a great introduction to the region.

In direct contrast to their wonderful landscapes, villages in the Western Isles are rarely very picturesque in themselves, and are usually made up of scattered, relatively modern croft houses dotted about the elementary road system. **Stornoway**, the only real town in the Outer Hebrides, is eminently unappealing. Many visitors, walkers and nature watchers forsake the settlements altogether and retreat to secluded cottages and B&Bs.

Transport practicalities

Several airlines operate fast and frequent **flights** from Glasgow, Edinburgh and Inverness to Stornoway on Lewis, and from Glasgow to Barra and Benbecula (Mon–Sat only). But be warned: the weather conditions on the islands are notoriously changeable, making flights prone to cancellation, delay and stomach-churning bumpiness. On Barra, the other complication is that you land on the beach, so the timetable is adjusted with the tides. CalMac **car ferries** run from Ullapool in the Highlands to Stornoway (Mon–Sat only); from Uig, on Skye, to Tarbert and Lochmaddy (Mon–Sat only); and from Oban to South Uist and Barra (daily), via Tiree (Thurs only). There's also an **inter-island ferry** from Leverburgh, on Harris, to Berneray, and thence to the Uists, and between Eriskay, at the foot of the Uists, and Barra. For more on ferry services, see "Travel details" on p.1159.

Lewis (Leodhas)

Lewis is the largest and most populous of the Western Isles and the northernmost island in the Hebridean archipelago. After Viking rule ended in 1266, the island was fought over by the MacLeods and MacKenzies, until eventually being sold by the latter in 1844. The new owner, Sir James Matheson, invested heavily in new industries, as did **Lord Leverhulme** with the fishing industry when he acquired the island (along with Harris) in 1918. Though undoubtedly a benevolent despot, Leverhulme's unpopularity with crofters on Lewis, and his financial difficulties, forced him to give up his grandiose plans in 1923, when he gave the island to its inhabitants. His departure, however, left a big gap in the economy, and between the wars thousands more emigrated.

Most of the island's 20,000 inhabitants – more than two-thirds of the Western Isles' total population – now live in the crofting and fishing villages strung out along the northwest coast, between **Calanais** and **Port Nis**, in one of the most densely populated rural areas in the country. On this coast you'll also find the islands' best-preserved **prehistoric remains** – Dùn Charlabhaigh broch and Calanais standing stones – as well as a smattering of ancient crofters' houses in various stages of abandonment. The landscape is mostly flat peat bog – hence the island's name, derived from the Gaelic *leogach* (marshy) – with a gentle shoreline that only gets really dramatic around Rubha Robhanais (Butt of Lewis), a group of rough rocks on the island's northernmost tip, near Port Nis. To the south, where Lewis is physically joined with Harris, the land rises to just over 1800ft, providing a more exhilarating backdrop for the excellent beaches that pepper the isolated coastline of **Uig**, to the west of Calanais.

Stornoway, on the east coast, is the only substantial town in the Western Isles, but it's really only useful for stocking up on provisions or catching the bus: there are regular services to all parts of the island, and most usefully to Port Nis and Tarbert, and along the 45-mile round trip from Stornoway to Calanais, Carlabhagh, Arnol and back (for which there's a rover ticket available).

Stornoway (Steornabhagh)

In these parts, **STORNOWAY** is a buzzing metropolis, with some 8000 inhabitants, a one-way system, pedestrian precinct with CCTV and all the trappings of a large town. It's a centre for employment, a social hub for the island and, perhaps most importantly of all, home to the Western Isles Council or **Comhairle nan Eilean Siar** (ⓦ www.cne-siar.gov.uk), set up in 1974, which has done so much to promote Gaelic language and culture, and try to stem the tide of anglicization. For the visitor, however, the town is unlikely to win any great praise – aesthetics are not its strong point, and the urban pleasures on offer are limited.

Stornoway's Scots baronial Town Hall on South Beach houses the **An Lanntair Art Gallery** (Mon–Sat 10am–5.30pm; free; ⓦ www.lanntair.com) on the first floor, with exhibitions featuring the work of local artists plus a very pleasant café. Anyone remotely interested in Harris Tweed should head for the **Lewis Loom Centre** (Mon–Sat 9am–6pm; £1; ⓦ www.lewisloomcentre .co.uk), run by an eccentric and engaging man and located at the far end of Cromwell Street, in the Old Grainstore off Bayhead. Continuing up the pedestrian precinct into Francis Street, you'll eventually reach the **Museum nan Eilean** (April–Sept Mon–Sat 10am–5.30pm; Oct–March Tues–Fri 10am–5pm, Sat 10am–1pm; free; ⓦ www.cne-siar.gov.uk), with lots of information about the island's history and its herring and weaving industries.

To the northwest of the town centre stands **Lews Castle** (ⓦ www lewscastlegrounds.org.uk), a nineteenth-century Gothic pomposity built by Sir James Matheson in 1863 after resettling the crofters who used to live here. As the former laird's pad, it's seen as a symbol of old oppression by many. Its chief attraction is its mature wooded grounds, a unique sight on the Western Isles, and its **Woodland Centre** (Mon–Sat 10am–5pm; free), which has a straightforward exhibition on the history of the castle and the island upstairs, with a live CCTV link to a nearby nest box, and a decent **café** serving soup, salads and cakes downstairs.

Practicalities

The best thing about Stornoway is the convenience of its services. The island's **airport** is four miles east of the town centre (£5 by taxi); the swanky octagonal

CalMac **ferry terminal** is on South Beach, close to the **bus station**. You can get bus timetables, a map of the town and other useful information from the **tourist office**, near North Beach at 26 Cromwell St (April to mid-Oct Mon–Fri 9am–6pm, Sat 9am–5pm, plus open for an hour to meet the evening ferry; mid-Oct to March Mon–Fri 9am–5pm).

Of the **hotels**, the *Royal Hotel* on Cromwell Street (℡01851/702109, ⓦwww.calahotels.com; ❺) is your best bet. Better value by far, though, is the *Park Guest House* (℡01851/702485; ❷) on James Street where the public areas have bags of lugubrious late-Victorian character, the bedrooms significantly less. Of the **B&Bs** try *Fernlea*, a listed Victorian house, along leafy Matheson Road, at no. 9 (℡01851/702125, Ⓔmaureenmacmillan@amserve.com; ❷) or *Hal O The Wynd*, 2 Newton St (℡01851/706073; ❷), opposite the ferry terminal. The *Stornoway Backpackers'* **hostel** is a basic affair about five minutes' walk from the ferry at 47 Keith St (℡01851/703628, ⓦwww.stornoway -hostel.co.uk), while *Fairhaven*, 28 Francis St (℡01851/705862, ⓦwww.hebrideansurf.co.uk; ❶) is primarily a centre for surfers, but welcomes all; accommodation consists of bunkhouse, family rooms and single rooms. The nearest **campsite**, *Laxdale Holiday Park* (℡01851/703234, ⓦwww .laxdaleholidaypark.force9.co.uk; open all year), lies a mile or so along the road to Barabhas, on Laxdale Lane; it has a self-catering bungalow and a purpose-built **bunkhouse**.

Decent **food** options are disappointingly limited in Stornoway, especially in the evening. The best option is the *Thai Café*, 27 Church St (℡01851/701811; closed Sun), which serves inexpensive but authentic Thai food – as a consequence it's very popular, so book ahead. The new café-bar *HS-1*, in the *Royal Hotel*, is the first really stylish, modern place to open in Stornoway; the menu ranges from simple fare like baked potatoes to stir-fries and curry. There are excellent light lunches to be had from the *An Lanntair* tearoom (closed Sun). The restaurant of the *Park Guest House*, on James Street (closed Mon & Sun), serves good local food, but it's expensive, unless you go for the "early bird" option. *MacNeills* on Cromwell Street is the liveliest central **pub**, with a mixed clientele of keen drinkers. *The Criterion*, a tiny wee pub on Point Street, is another option. There's sometimes **live music** at the Royal British Legion, opposite the ferry terminal, or the Sea Angling Club, a little further along Shell Street – look out for notices on the library notice board, or in the *Stornoway Gazette*.

The road to Port Nis (Port of Ness)

Northwest of Stornoway, the A857 crosses the vast, barren **peat bog** of the interior, an empty undulating wilderness riddled with stretchmarks formed by peat cuttings and pockmarked with freshwater lochans. The whole area was once covered by forests, but these disappeared long ago, leaving a smothering deposit of peat that is, on average, six feet thick, and is still being formed in certain places. For the people of Lewis the peat continues to serve as a valuable energy resource, its pungent smoke one of the most characteristic smells of the Western Isles. Tourists tend to cross this barren, almost intimidating, landscape at speed – even the locals spend little time on the moor except to gather peat. Yet these natural wetlands have been identified as important "carbon sinks", which soak up greenhouse gases, and as a vital breeding ground for species such as golden plover, dunlin and greenshank. In a tricky little clash of ecological interests, however, there are plans afoot to build Europe's largest **wind farm** (ⓦwww.lewiswind.com) here to harness a renewable resource that the Western Isles has in vast quantities.

Twelve miles across the peat bog the road approaches the west coast of Lewis and divides, heading southwest towards Calanais (see p.1150), or northeast through **BARABHAS** (Barvas), and a whole string of bleak and fervently Free Church crofting and weaving villages. These scattered settlements have none of the photogenic qualities of Skye's whitewashed villages: the churches are plain and unadorned; the crofters' houses are relatively modern and smothered in grey, pebble-dash rendering or harling; the stone cottages and enclosures of their forebears often lie half-abandoned in the front garden; while a rusting assortment of discarded cars and vans store peat bags and the like.

The road eventually terminates at the fishing village of **PORT NIS** (Port of Ness), with a tiny harbour and lovely golden beach. Shortly before you reach Port Nis, a minor road heads two miles northwest to the hamlet of **EOROPAIDH** (Europie) – pronounced "yor-erpee". Here, by the road junction that leads to the Butt of Lewis, stands the simple stone structure of **Teampull Mholuaidh** (St Moluag's Church), thought to date from the twelfth century. From Eoropaidh, a narrow road twists to the bleak and blustery northern tip of the island, Rubha Robhanais – well known to devotees of the BBC shipping forecast as the **Butt of Lewis** – where a lighthouse sticks up above a series of sheer cliffs and stacks, alive with sea birds and a great place for marine mammal-spotting.

There are between six and eight buses a day from Stornoway to Port Nis, Sundays excepted, and one or two **accommodation** possibilities. The best place to stay is *Galson Farm Guest House* (℡01851/850492, ⓦwww.galsonfarm.freeserve.co.uk; ❹), an eighteenth-century farmhouse in Gabhsann Bho Dheas (South Galson), halfway between Barabhas and Port Nis, with a **bunkhouse** close by (phone number as above). The only tearoom is *Harbour View* in Port Nis, and there are only a few shops (supplemented by mobile ones) in these parts, so it's as well to stock up in Stornoway before you set out. The *Cross Inn* in Cros is about the only **pub** in the area, but look out for any **live music** or other events going on at *Taigh Dhonnchaidh* (ⓦwww.taighdhonnchaidh.com), a new arts and music centre in Tabost.

Arnol and around

Heading southwest from the crossroads near Barabhas brings you to several villages that meander down towards the sea. In **ARNOL**, the remains of numerous blackhouses lie abandoned by the roadside; at the north end of the village, no. 42 has been preserved as the **Arnol Blackhouse** (Mon–Sat: May–Sept 9.30am–6.30pm; Oct–March 9.30am–4.30pm; £3; HS) to show exactly how a true blackhouse or *taigh dubh* would have been. The dark interior is lit and heated by a small peat fire, which is kept alight in the central hearth of bare earth, and is usually fairly smoky as there's no chimney; instead, smoke drifts through the thatch, helping to kill any creepy-crawlies, keep out the midges and turn the heathery sods and oat-straw thatch itself into next year's fertilizer. The animals slept in the byre, separated from the living quarters only by a low partition, while potatoes and grain were stored in the adjacent barn. The old woman who lived here moved out only very reluctantly in 1964. There's a great **B&B** in Siabost Bho Deas (South Shawbost) at *Airigh* (℡01851/710478, ⒺEileenmaclean@lineone.net; ❶; March–Nov) and behind the church is the *Eilean Fraoich* **campsite** (℡01851/710504; May–Oct). You can grab a bite to eat at the *Shawbost Inn*.

Five miles on at Carlabhagh (Carloway), a mile-long road leads off north to the beautifully remote coastal settlement of **GEARRANNAN** (Garenin),

22

where nine thatched crofters' houses – the last of which was abandoned in 1974 – have been restored. One of the houses has simple information boards telling the history of the village and the folk who lived there. Another building is now a **café** (closed Sun), serving cheap and cheerful fare during the day; a meal is £25 a head in the evening (Wed–Sat only; phone ahead Ⓣ01851/643416). One blackhouse now serves as the GHHT **hostel** (Ⓦwww.gatliff.org.uk), four are **self-catering** houses, (Ⓦwww.gearrannan.com), while another contains public toilets.

Just beyond Carlabhagh, about 400 yards from the road, the two-thousand-year-old **Dùn Charlabhaigh Broch** perches on top of a conspicuous rocky outcrop overlooking the sea. Scotland's Atlantic coast is strewn with the remains of over 500 brochs, or fortified towers, but this is one of the best preserved, its dry-stone circular walls reaching a height of more than 30ft on one side. The broch consists of two concentric walls, the inner one perpendicular, the outer one slanting inwards, the two originally fastened together by roughly hewn flagstones, which also served as lookout galleries reached via a narrow stairwell. The only entrance to the roofless inner yard is through a low doorway set beside a crude and cramped guard cell. Dùn Charlabhaigh now has its very own **Doune Broch Centre** (June–Sept Mon–Sat 10am–6pm; free), situated at a discreet distance, stone-built and sporting a turf roof. It's a good wet-weather retreat, and fun for kids, who can walk through the hay-strewn mock-up of the broch as it might have been. A mile or so beyond the broch, beside a lochan, is the *Doune Braes Hotel* (Ⓣ01851/643252, Ⓦwww.doune-braes.co.uk; ❸), a friendly, unpretentious place whose bar serves up the same tasty seafood dishes as its restaurant, only cheaper.

Calanais (Callanish)

Five miles south of Carlabhagh lies the village of **CALANAIS** (Callanish), site of the islands' most dramatic prehistoric ruins, the **Calanais Standing Stones**, whose monoliths – nearly fifty of them – occupy a serene lochside setting. There have been years of heated debate about the origin and function of the stones – slabs of gnarled and finely grained gneiss up to 15ft high – though almost everyone agrees that they were lugged here by Neolithic peoples between 3000 and 1500 BC. It's also obvious that the planning and construction of the site – as well as several other lesser circles nearby – was spread over many generations. Such an endeavour could, it's been argued, only be prompted by the desire to predict the seasonal cycle upon which these early farmers were entirely dependent, and indeed many of the stones are aligned with the position of the sun and the stars. This rational explanation, based on clear evidence that this part of Lewis was once a fertile farming area, dismisses as coincidence the ground plan of the site, which resembles a colossal Celtic cross, and explains away the central burial chamber as a later addition of no special significance. These two features have, however, fuelled all sorts of theories ranging from alien intervention to human sacrifice.

A blackhouse adjacent to the main stone circle has been refurbished as **tearoom** and shop, and it's to this you should head for refreshment rather than the superfluous **Calanais Visitor Centre** (Mon–Sat: April–Sept 10am–6pm; Oct–March 10am–4pm; museum £1.75) on the other side of the stones (and thankfully out of view), to which all the signs direct you from the road. The centre runs a decent restaurant and a small museum on the site, but with so much information on the panels beside the stones there's little reason to visit. You're politely asked not to walk between the stones, only along the path that surrounds them, so if you want to commune with standing stones solitude, head for the smaller circles in more natural surroundings a mile or two southeast of Calanais, around Gearraidh na h-Aibhne (Garynahine).

For a **place to stay**, Mrs Catherine Morrison, 27 Calanais (℡01851/621392; ❷; March–Sept) runs an inexpensive B&B in Calanais itself, and there's a modern guest house close by, the *Eshcol Guest House* (℡01851/621357, ⓦwww.eshcol.com; ❹) – no beauty from the outside, but very well run and comfortable within. If it's just **food** you want, *Tigh Mealros* (℡01851/621333; closed Sun), in Gearraidh na h-Aibhne, serves good, inexpensive lunches and evening meals, featuring local seafood.

Harris (Na Hearadh)

Harris, to the south of Lewis, is much hillier, more dramatic and much more appealing, its boulder-strewn slopes descending to aquamarine bays of dazzling, white sand. The shift from Lewis to Harris is almost imperceptible, as the two are, in fact, one island, the "division" between them embedded in a historical split in the MacLeod clan, lost in the mists of time. Harris itself is more clearly divided by a minuscule isthmus, into the wild, inhospitable mountains of **North Harris** and the gentler landscape and sandy shores of **South Harris**.

Along with Lewis, Harris was purchased in 1918 by Lord Leverhulme, and after 1923, when he pulled out of Lewis, all his efforts were concentrated here.

Harris Tweed

Far from being a picturesque cottage industry, as it's sometimes presented, the production of **Harris Tweed** is vital to the local economy, with a well-organized and unionized workforce. Traditionally, the tweed was made by women from the wool of their own sheep, to provide clothing for their families, using a 2500-year-old process. Each woman was responsible for plucking the wool by hand, washing and scouring it, dyeing it with lichen, heather flowers or ragwort, carding (smoothing and straightening the wool, often adding butter to grease it), spinning and weaving. Finally the cloth was dipped in urine and "waulked" by a group of women, who beat the cloth on a table to soften and shrink it whilst singing Gaelic waulking songs. Harris Tweed was originally made all over the islands, and was known simply as *clò mór* (big cloth).

In the mid-nineteenth century, the countess of Dunmore, who owned a large part of Harris, started to sell surplus cloth to her aristocratic friends; she then sent two sisters from Srannda (Strond) to Paisley to learn the trade. On their return, they formed the genesis of the modern industry, which serves as a vital source of employment, though demand (and therefore employment levels) can fluctuate wildly as fashions change. To earn the official Harris Tweed Association trademark of the Orb and the Maltese Cross – taken from the Countess of Dunmore's coat of arms – the fabric has to be hand-woven on the Outer Hebrides from 100 percent pure new Scottish wool, while the other parts of the manufacturing process must take place only in the local mills.

The main centre of production is now Lewis, where the wool is dyed, carded and spun; you can see all these processes by visiting the **Lewis Loom Centre** in Stornoway (see p.1147). In the last few decades there has been a revival of traditional tweed-making techniques, with several small producers following old methods. Soay Studio in West Tarbert (℡01859/502361) is one such place that uses indigenous plants and bushes to dye the cloth: yellow comes from rocket and broom, green from heather, grey and black from iris and oak, and, most popular of all, reddish brown from crotal, a flat grey lichen scraped off rocks.

In contrast to Lewis, though, Leverhulme and his ambitious projects were broadly welcomed by the people of Harris. However, when he died in 1925 the plug was pulled on all of them by his executors. Since then, **unemployment** has been a constant problem in Harris. Crofting continues on a small scale, supplemented by the tweed industry, though the main focus of this has shifted to Lewis. Shellfish fishing continues on Scalpay, while the rest of the population gets by on whatever employment is available: roadworks, crafts and, of course, tourism. There's a regular **bus** connection between Stornoway and **Tarbert**, and an occasional service that circumnavigates South Harris.

Tarbert (An Tairbeart)

The largest place on Harris is the ferry port of **TARBERT**, sheltered in a green valley on the narrow isthmus that marks the border between North and South Harris. The town's mountainous backdrop is impressive, and the town is attractively laid out on steep terraces sloping up from the dock. It boasts Harris's only **tourist office** (April–Oct Mon–Fri 9am–5pm, Sat 9am–1pm & 2–5pm, also open to greet the evening ferry; winter hours variable), close to the ferry terminal. The office can arrange modest, inexpensive B&B **accommodation** and has a full set of bus timetables, but its real value is as a source of information on local walks.

In Tarbert there's an excellent **hostel** called the *Rockview Bunkhouse* (℡01859/502626), on Main Street, which also offers **bike rental**. Close to the ferry terminal, there's a very good **B&B**, *Tigh na Mara* (℡01859/502270, ⊛www.tigh-na-mara.co.uk; ❶), or the old-fashioned *Harris Hotel* (℡01859/502154, ⊛www.harrishotel.com; ❹), five minutes' walk away. You'll need to book ahead to stay in Tarbert's popular **guest houses**: *Leachin House* (℡01859/502157, ⊛www.leachin-house.com; ❻), which looks out west to the sea, just off the road to Stornoway, and *Ardhasaig House* (℡01859/502066, ⊛www.ardhasaig.co.uk; ❻), further up the Stornoway road, looking out over North Harris. The lounge and bar of the *Harris Hotel* act as the local social centre, but the best **fish and chips** are dispensed by *Ad's Take-Away* (April–Oct; closed Sun), next to the hostel. During the day, you're best off heading for the very pleasant *First Fruits* **tearoom** (April–Sept; closed Sun), behind the tourist office, serving real coffee, homemade cakes, toasties and so forth.

North Harris (Ceann a Tuath na Hearadh)

The A859 north to Stornoway takes you over a boulder-strewn saddle between mighty **Sgaoth Aird** (1829ft) and An Cliseam or the **Clisham** (2619ft), the highest peak in the Western Isles. This bitter terrain, littered with debris left behind by retreating glaciers, offers but the barest of vegetation, with an occasional cluster of crofters' houses sitting in the shadow of a host of pointed peaks, anywhere between 1000ft and 2500ft high. These bulging, pyramidal mountains reach their climax around the dramatic shores of the fjord-like **Loch Seaforth**. The only place to stay in this area is the GHHT **hostel** (⊛www.gatliff.org.uk; £8) in the lonely coastal hamlet of **REINIGEADAL** (Rhenigdale). To reach the hostel on foot from Tarbert (3hr one-way), take the path from Caolas Scalpaigh (Kyles Scalpay), which threads its way through the peaks of the craggy promontory that lies trapped between Loch Shìphoirt and Loch an Tairbeart.

South Harris (Ceann a Deas na Hearadh)

The mountains of **South Harris** are less dramatic than in the north, but the scenery is equally breathtaking. There's a choice of routes from Tarbert to the ferry port of **Leverburgh**, which connects with North Uist: the east coast, known as Na Baigh (The Bays), is rugged and seemingly inhospitable, while the **west coast** is endowed with some of the finest stretches of golden sand in the whole of the archipelago, buffeted by the Atlantic winds. Paradoxically, most people on South Harris live along the harsh eastern coastline of **Bays** rather than the more fertile west side. But not by choice – they were evicted from their original crofts to make way for sheep-grazing.

The main road from Tarbert into South Harris snakes its way west for ten miles across the boulder-strewn interior to reach the coast. Once there, you get a view of the most stunning **beach**, the vast golden strand of **Tràigh Losgaintir**. The road continues to ride above a chain of sweeping sands, backed by rich **machair**, that stretches for nine miles along the Atlantic coast. In good weather, the scenery is particularly impressive, foaming breakers rolling along the golden sands set against the rounded peaks of the mountains to the north and the islet-studded turquoise sea to the west – and even on the dullest day the sand manages to glow beneath the waves. A short distance out to sea is the large island of **Taransay** (Tarasaigh), which once held a population of nearly a hundred, but was abandoned as recently as 1974. In 2000 it was the setting of the BBC series *Castaway*, in which thirty-odd contestants were filmed living on the island for the best part of a year; you can now take day-trips to, or book self-catering on, the island (℡01859/550260, Ⓦwww.visit-taransay.com). There are two very good **B&Bs** overlooking the sands: *Moravia* (℡01859/550262; ❶; March–Oct), at Losgaintir (Luskentyre), and *Beul-na-Mara* at Seilebost (℡01859/550205, Ⓔmorrisoncl@talk21.com; ❷). The most luxurious **guest house**, though, is five miles further south in Sgarasta (Scarista), where one of the first of the Hebridean Clearances took place in 1828, when thirty families were evicted and their homes burnt. Here, the Georgian former manse of *Scarista House* (℡01859/550238, Ⓦwww.scaristahouse.com; ❼) overlooks the nearby golden sands; if you can't afford to stay, it's worth splashing out and booking for dinner, as the meat and seafood served here is among the freshest and finest on the Western Isles.

From Taobh Tuath the road veers to the southeast to trim the island's south shore, eventually reaching the sprawling settlement of **LEVERBURGH** (An t-Ob), named after Lord Leverhulme, who planned to turn the place into the largest fishing port on the west coast of Scotland. It's a place that has languished for quite some time, but has picked up quite a bit since the establishment of the CalMac **car ferry** service to Berneray and the Uists. There are several B&Bs strung out within a two-mile radius of Leverburgh: try *Caberfeidh House* ℡01859/520276; ❶), a lovely stone-built Victorian building by the turn-off to the ferry, or *Sorrel Cottage* (℡01859/520319, Ⓔsorrelcottage@virgin.net; ❷), which specializes in vegetarian and seafood cooking and offers **bike rental**. A cheaper alternative is the quirky, purpose-built, timber-clad *Am Bothan* **bunkhouse** (℡01859/520251, Ⓦwww.ambothan.com), which is very welcoming, has great facilities, and is only a few minutes' walk from the ferry. On the north side of the bay, *An Clachan* coop store has a **café** (closed Sun) upstairs, and houses the small **tourist office**.

Three miles southeast of Leverburgh and a mile or so from Renish Point, the southern tip of Harris, is the old port of **ROGHADAL** (Rodel), where a smattering of ancient stone houses lies among the hillocks surrounding the dilapidated harbour where the ferry from Skye used to arrive. On top of one of these grassy humps, with sheep grazing in the graveyard, is **St Clement's church** (Tur Chliamainn), burial place of the MacLeods of Harris and

Dunvegan in Skye. Dating from the 1520s, the church's bare interior is distinguished by its wall tombs, notably that of the founder, Alasdair Crotach (also known as Alexander MacLeod), whose heavily weathered effigy lies beneath an intriguing backdrop and canopy of sculpted reliefs depicting vernacular and religious scenes – elemental representations of, among others, a stag hunt, the Holy Trinity, St Michael, and the devil and an angel weighing the souls of the dead. Look out, too, for the *sheila-na-gig* (a naked pre-Christian fertility goddess) halfway up the south side of the church tower; unusually, she has a brother displaying his genitalia too, below a carving of St Clement on the west face. Beyond the church, tucked away by a quiet harbour, the *Rodel* **hotel** (℡01859/520210, ⑩www.rodelhotel.co.uk; ❻) has been totally refurbished inside and serves decent bar **meals.**

North Uist (Uibhist a Tuath)

Compared to the mountainous scenery of Harris, **North Uist** – seventeen miles long and thirteen miles wide – is much flatter and for some comes as something of an anticlimax. Over half the surface area is covered by water, creating a distinctive peaty-brown lochan-studded "drowned landscape". Most visitors come here for the trout and salmon fishing and the deerstalking, both of which (along with poaching) are critical to the survival of the island's economy. Others come for the smattering of prehistoric sites, the birds, or the sheer peace of this windy isle, and the solitude of North Uist's vast sandy beaches, which extend – almost without interruption – along the north and west coast.

Despite being situated on the east coast, some distance away from any beach, the ferry port of **LOCHMADDY** (Loch nam Madadh, or "Loch of the Dogs") makes a good base for exploring the island. The village itself, occupying a narrow, bumpy promontory, is nothing special, though, one place that's well worth visiting is **Taigh Chearsabhagh** (Mon–Sat 10am–5pm; ⑩www.taigh-chearsabhagh.org), a converted eighteenth-century merchant's house, now home to a community arts centre, with a simple airy café, post office, shop and excellent museum (£1) which puts on changing long-term exhibitions. Taigh Chearsabhagh was one of the prime movers behind the **Uist Sculpture Trail** that starts outside the arts centre on the shore, and takes visitors to some remote corners of the Uists – pick up a leaflet from the centre. The first and most popular of the sculptures, **Both nam Faileas** (Hut of the Shadow), is a short walk past the Uist Outdoor Centre, and across the footbridge that leads to the derelict Sponish House. The **tourist office** (April to mid-Oct Mon–Sat 9am–5pm; also open for an hour to greet the evening ferry), near the quayside, has local bus and ferry timetables, and can help with **accommodation**. Lochmaddy itself doesn't have the best options: th *Lochmaddy Hotel* (℡01876/500331; ❺) is the anglers' HQ, and is perfectly fine but it's not cheap; the *Old Courthouse* (℡01876/500358, ✉mjohnso @oldcourthouse.fsnet.co.uk; ❷), a Georgian former gaol, is half the price, an at least retains some character. A little further north lies the *Uist Outdoor Cent* (℡01876/500480, ⑩www.uistoutdoorcentre.co.uk), which has **hostel** accom modation in four-person bunk rooms, and offers a wide range of outdo activities, from canoeing round the indented coastline to "rubber tubing The **bar** in the *Lochmaddy Hotel* is the lively local pub and serves the usu bar meals.

Several prehistoric sights lie within easy cycling distance of Lochmaddy (even walking distance if you use the postbus for the outward journey). Th most significant is the **Barpa Langass**, a large, mostly intact, chambered cai seven barren miles to the southwest along the A867; a mile to the southeast is the small stone circle of **Pobull Fhinn**. Three miles northwest of Lochmaddy along the A865 is **Na Fir Bhreige** (The Three False Men), three standing stones which, depending on your legend, mark the graves of three spies buried alive, or three men who deserted their wives and were turned to stone by a proto-feminist witch.

North Uist's other main draw is the **Balranald RSPB Reserve**, best known for its population of corncrakes, once common throughout the British countryside but now one of the country's rarest birds. Unfortunately, the birds are very good at hiding in long grass, so you're unlikely to see one; however, the males' loud "craking" is relatively easy to hear from May to July throughout the Uists and Barra: there are usually one or two making a loud noise right outside the RSPB **visitor centre**, from which you can pick up a leaflet outlining a two-hour walk along the headland, marked by posts. A wonderful carpet of flowers covers the machair in summer, and there are usually corn buntings and arctic terns inland, and gannets, Manx shearwater and skuas out to sea – guided walks take place throughout the summer (May–Aug Tues 2pm; £3; ☎01878/602188). On a clear day you can see the unmistakeable shape of St Kilda, seeming miraculously near. Another **hostel** worth noting is *Taigh mo Sheanair* (☎01876/580246), a very welcoming, family-run place, where you can also **camp**; it's a clearly signposted fifteen-minute walk from the main road, south of the crossroads at Clachan.

Bhearnaraigh (Berneray)

For those in search of still more seclusion, there's the low-lying island of **Berneray** immediately to the north of North Uist and connected to the latter

---

St Kilda

Britain's westernmost island chain is the NTS-owned **St Kilda** archipelago (ⓦwww.kilda.org.uk), roughly a hundred miles west-south-west of the Butt of Lewis and over forty miles from its nearest landfall, Griminish Point on North Uist. Dominated by the highest cliffs and sea stacks in Britain, Hirta, St Kilda's main island, was occupied on and off for some two thousand years, with the last 36 Gaelic-speaking inhabitants evacuated at their own request in 1930. Immediately after evacuation, the island was bought by the marquess of Bute, who was keen to protect the island's population of between one and two million puffins, gannets, petrels and other sea birds. In 1957, having agreed to allow the army to build a missile-tracking radar station here linked to South Uist, the marquess bequeathed the island to the NTS (☎01463/232034, ⓦwww.nts.org.uk) and in 1987 St Kilda was declared a UNESCO World Heritage Site. Despite its inaccessibility, around 2000 visitors make it out to St Kilda each year; the resident NTS ranger usually gives a little talk, you get to see the museum, send a postcard and enjoy a drink at the army's pub, the *Puff Inn*. If you have your own yacht, you must have permission in order to land; several boat companies also offer **day-trips** to St Kilda in a rigid inflatable for around £125 per person. Between mid-May and mid-August, the NTS organize volunteer **work parties** who either restore and maintain the old buildings or take part in archeological digs. Volunteers are expected to work 24–36 hours a week for two weeks, for which they must pay around £500 per person, though with only twelve people in each party, and more applications than there are places, there's no guarantee you'll get on one. Volunteers meet at Oban, and should be prepared for a rough, fifteen-hour overnight crossing. For the armchair traveller, the best general book on St Kilda is Tom Steel's *The Life and Death of St Kilda*.

via a causeway. Two miles by three, with a population of just over a hundred, the island has a superb three-mile-long sandy beach on the west and north coast, backed by rabbit-free dunes and machair. Prince Charles, lover of Gaelic culture, was a frequent visitor at one time, and was memorably filmed helping local crofter "Splash" MacKillop pick potatoes. The other great draw is the wonderful GHHT **hostel** (ⓦwww.gatliff.org.uk), which occupies a pair of thatched blackhouses in a lovely spot by a beach, beyond Loch a Bhàigh and the main village. Alternatively you can follow in the prince's footsteps and stay (and help out) at "Splash" MacKillop's *Burnside Croft* **B&B** (ⓣ01876/540235, ⓦwww.burnsidecroft.fsnet.co.uk; ❷; Feb–Nov), and enjoy "story telling evenings"; bike rental is also available. There are several **tearooms** currently functioning along the main road, including one in the community centre at the end of the road to **Borgh** (Borve), all of which serve simple refreshments, and there's now a **bus** connection with Lochmaddy.

Benbecula (Beinn na Faoghla)

Blink and you could miss the pancake-flat island of **Benbecula** (put the stress on the second syllable), sandwiched between Protestant North Uist and Catholic South Uist. Most visitors simply trundle along the main road that cuts across the middle of the island in less than five miles – not such a bad idea, since the island is scarred from the postwar presence of the Royal Artillery who until recently used to make up half the local population. Economically, of course, the area benefited enormously from the military presence, though the impact on the environment and Gaelic culture (with so many English-speakers around) has been less positive.

The legacy of Benbecula's military past is only too evident in the depressing, barracks-like housing developments of **BALIVANICH** (Baile a Mhanaich), the grim, grey capital of Benbecula in the northwest. The only reason to come here at all is if you happen to be flying into or out of **Benbecula airport** (direct flights to Glasgow, Barra and Stornoway), need to take money out of the Bank of Scotland ATM (the only one on Benbecula and South Uist), do some laundry (the laundrette is opposite the post office). There's no tourist office and no need **to stay** here, but if you have to, try the modern **Balivanich hostel** *Taigh-na-Cille* (ⓣ01870/602522), within easy walking distance of the airport, on the road to North Uist or the **campsite** (ⓣ01870/602447; April–Oct), in Lionacleit (Liniclate), adjacent to the secondary school. If you need a bite to eat, *Stepping Stone* (closed Mon eve), the purpose-built **café/restaurant**, is divided into the *Food Base* café which serves up cheap filled rolls, hot meals and chips with everything, and the rather underwhelming £20-a-head *Sinteag* restaurant (evenings only), up the steps.

South Uist (Uibhist a Deas)

To the south of Benbecula, the island of **South Uist** is arguably the most appealing of the southern chain of islands. The west coast boasts some of the region's finest machair and beaches – a necklace of gold and grey sand strung twenty miles from one end to the other – while the east coast features a ridge of high mountains rising to 2034ft at the summit of Beinn Mhor. The only blot on South Uist's landscape is the old Royal Artillery missile range, which occupies the northwest corner of the island.

One of the best places to gain access to the sandy shoreline is at **TOBHA MÒR** (Howmore), a pretty little crofting settlement with a fair number of restored houses, many still thatched, including one distinctively roofed brown heather. A GHHT **hostel** (Ⓦ www.gatliff.org.uk) occupies one such house near the village church, from where it's an easy walk across the flower-infested machair to the gorgeous beach. Close by the hostel are the shattered, lichen-encrusted remains of no fewer than four medieval churches and chapels, and a burial ground now harbouring just a few scattered graves.

Five miles south of Tobha Mòr, on the main road, the Kildonan Museum or **Taigh-tasgaidh Chill Donnain** (April & May Mon–Sat 11am–4pm; June–Sept Mon–Sat 10am–5pm, Sun 2–5pm; £1.50), includes mock-ups of Hebridean kitchens through the ages, two lovely box beds and an impressive selection of old photos, accompanied by a firmly unsentimental yet poetic written text on crofting life in the last two centuries. Among the more unusual exhibits is a pair of ornamental shoes made of deer hooves. Pride of place goes to the sixteenth-century **Clanranald Stone**, carved with the arms of the clan who ruled over South Uist from 1370 to 1839, which used to lie in the church at Tobha Mòr. The museum also runs a café serving sandwiches and homemade cakes, and has a choice of historical videos for those really wet and windy days.

Without doubt, the best **hotel** on the Uists is the *Orasay Inn* (Ⓣ01870/610298, Ⓔorasayinn@btinternet.com; ❸), located in a peaceful spot off the road to Loch a Charnain (Lochcarnan), in the northeastern corner of the island. South Uist's chief settlement and ferry port, **LOCHBOIS-DALE**, occupying a narrow, bumpy promontory on the east coast, has much less to offer than Lochmaddy. There's a **tourist office** (Easter to mid-Oct Mon–Sat 9am–5pm; open for an hour to meet the ferry), the *Past & Present Tea House* by the pier and a few small, friendly **B&Bs** within comfortable walking distance of the dock, one of the best (and nearest) being *Brae Lea House* (Ⓣ01878/700497, Ⓔbraelea@supanet.com; ❸). Perhaps the best place to hole up in this part of South Uist is the *Polochar Inn* (Ⓣ01878/700215, Ⓔpolocharinn@btinternet.com; ❺), eight miles from Lochboisdale, right on the south coast overlooking the Sound of Barra, with its own sandy beach close by.

Eriskay (Eiriosgaigh)

Connected to the south of South Uist by a causeway is the barren, hilly island of **Eriskay**, famous for its patterned jerseys (on sale at the community centre), and a peculiar breed of pony, originally used for carrying peat and seaweed. The island, which measures just over two miles by one, and shelters a small fishing community of about 150, makes a great day-trip from South Uist. The walk up to the island's highest point, **Ben Scrien** (607ft), is well worth the effort on a clear day, as you can see the whole island, plus Barra, South Uist, and across the sea to Skye, Rùm, Coll and Tiree (2hr return from the village). On the way up or down, look out for the diminutive Eriskay ponies, who roam free on the hills but tend to graze around Loch Crakavaig, the island's freshwater source. You can **camp rough** with permission, or stay at the **self-catering** apartment run by Mrs Campbell (four people; £180 per week; Ⓣ01878/720274). CalMac runs a **car ferry to Barra** (4–5 daily; 40min) from a new harbour on the southwest coast of Eriskay.

For a small island, Eriskay has had more than its fair share of historical head-lines. The island's main beach on the west coast, Coilleag a Phrionnsa (Prince's Cockle Strand), was where **Bonnie Prince Charlie** landed on Scottish soil on July 23, 1745 – the sea bindweed that grows there to this day is said to have sprung from the seeds Charles brought with him from France. Eriskay's other claim to fame came in 1941 when the 8000-ton **SS Politician** or *Polly* as it's fondly known, sank on its way from Liverpool to Jamaica, along with its cargo of bicycle parts, £3 million in Jamaican currency and 264,000 bottles of whisky, inspiring Compton MacKenzie's book – and the Ealing comedy (filmed here in 1948) – *Whisky Galore!* (released in the US as *Tight Little Island*). The ship's stern can still be seen to the northwest of the Isle of Calvey at low tide, and one of the original bottles (and lots of other related memorabilia) is on show in the island's purpose-built pub, *Am Politician*, on the west coast.

Barra (Barraigh)

Just four miles wide and eight miles long, **Barra** has a well-deserved reputation for being the Western Isles in miniature. It has sandy beaches, backed by machair, glacial mountains, prehistoric ruins, Gaelic culture, and a welcoming Catholic population of just over 1300. The only settlement of any size is **CASTLEBAY** (Bàgh a Chaisteil), which curves around the barren rocky hills of a wide bay on the south side of the island. It's difficult to imagine it now, but Castlebay was a herring port of some significance back in the nineteenth century, with up to 400 boats in the harbour and curing and packing factories ashore. Barra's religious allegiance is immediately announced by the large Catholic church, Our Lady, Star of the Sea, which overlooks the bay; to underline the point, there's a Madonna and Child on the slopes of **Sheabhal** (1260ft), the largest peak on Barra, and a fairly easy hike from the bay.

As its name suggests, Castlebay has a castle in its bay, the medieval islet-fortress of Caisteal Chiosmuil or **Kisimul Castle** (April–Sept daily 9.30am–12.30pm & 1.30–6.30pm; £3.30; HS), ancestral home of the MacNeil clan. The castle burnt down in the eighteenth century, but when the 45th MacNeil chief – conveniently enough a wealthy American and trained architect – bought the island back in 1937, he set about restoring the castle. There's nothing much to see inside, but the whole experience is fun – head down to the slipway at the bottom of Main Street, where the HS ferryman will take you over (weather permitting; ☎01871/810313). To learn more about the history of the island, and about the postal system of the Western Isles, it's worth paying a visit to Barra Heritage Centre, known as **Dualchas** (Mon–Sat 11am–5pm; £1) housed in an unprepossessing block on the road that leads west out of town.

One of Barra's most fascinating sights is its **airport**, on the north side of the island, where planes land and take off from the crunchy shell sands of Tràigh Mhór, better known as **Cockle Strand**; the exact timing of the flights depends on the tides, since at high tide the beach (and therefore the runway) is covered in water. As its name suggests, the strand is also famous for its cockles and cockleshells, the latter being used to make harling (the rendering used on most Scottish houses). Traditional hand-raking is permitted, but mechanical cockle extraction using tractors is banned as it would decimate the cockle stocks and threaten the beach's use as an airport. The popular airport **café**, *Cafaidh Fosgailte*, is open daily and serves homemade soup, sandwiches and cakes.

There are two **ferry terminals** on Barra: from Eriskay, you arrive at an uninhabited spot on the northeast of the island; from Oban, Lochboisdale or Tiree you arrive at the main terminal in Castlebay itself. Barra Car Hire (☎01871/810243) will deliver **cars** to either terminal, and Barra Cycle Hire (☎01871/810438) will do the same with **bikes.** Barra's **tourist office** (April–Oct Mon–Sat 9am–1pm & 2–5pm; also open to greet the Oban ferry) is situated on Main Street in Castlebay just round from the pier. In Castlebay itself, the *Castlebay Hotel* (☎01871/810223, ⓦwww.castlebay-hotel.co.uk; ❺) is the more welcoming of the town's two hotels, followed by *Tigh-na-Mara* (☎01871/810304, ⓔtighnamara@aol.com; ❶), a Victorian guest house a couple of minutes' walk from the pier, overlooking the sea. However, the best option outside Castlebay is *Northbay House* (☎01871/890255, ⓦwww.witb .co.uk/links/savory.htm; ❸), which is in a converted school in Buaile nam Bodach (Balnabodach). Lastly, there's *Dunard Hostel* (☎01871/810443, ⓦwww.isleofbarrahostel.com), a relaxed, family-run place just 200m west of the ferry terminal in Castlebay. Places to eat include the *Kisimul Galley* **café** (closed Sun) that specializes in cheap-and-cheerful Scottish fry-ups. For more fancy fare, head to the *Castlebay Hotel*'s cosy **bar**, which regularly has cockles, crabs and scallops on its menu, and good views out over the bay.

Travel details

Trains

Aberdeen to: Kyle of Lochalsh (Mon–Sat 3 daily, 1 on Sun; 5hr).
Fort William to: Mallaig (4–5 daily; 1hr 25min).
Glasgow (Queen Street) to: Mallaig (Mon–Sat 4 daily, 2 on Sun; 5hr 20min).
Inverness to: Kyle of Lochalsh (Mon–Sat 3–4 daily, 1–2 on Sun; 2hr 30min).

Buses

Mainland
Glasgow to: Broadford (3–4 daily; 5hr 25min); Portree (3–4 daily; 6hr–6hr 30min); Uig (Mon–Sat 3–4 daily; 7hr 40min).
Inverness to: Broadford (2 daily; 2hr 50min); Portree (2 daily; 3hr 15min).
Kyle of Lochalsh to: Kyleakin (every 30min; 10min).

Skye
Armadale to: Broadford (Mon–Sat 3–10 daily; 25min); Portree (Mon–Sat 3–10 daily; 1hr 20min); Sligachan (Mon–Sat 3–10 daily; 1hr 10min).
Broadford to: Portree (Mon–Sat 5–10 daily; 40min).
Dunvegan to: Glendale (Mon–Sat 1–2 daily; 30min).
Kyleakin to: Broadford (Mon–Sat 4–10 daily, 3–5 on Sun; 15min); Portree (Mon–Sat 4 daily, 3–5 on Sun; 1hr); Sligachan (Mon–Sat 7–8 daily, 5 on Sun; 45min); Uig (Mon–Sat 2 daily; 1hr 20min).
Portree to: Carbost (Mon–Fri 4–5 daily, 1 on Sat; 45min); Duntulm (Mon–Sat 2–4 daily; 1hr); Dunvegan (Mon–Sat 2–4 daily; 50min); Glenbrittle (April–Sept Mon–Sat 2 daily; 1hr); Staffin (Mon–Sat 2–4 daily; 40min); Uig (Mon–Sat 4–5 daily; 30min).

Lewis/Harris
Stornoway to: Barabhas (Mon–Sat 8–12 daily; 25min); Calanais (Mon–Sat 4–8 daily; 40min); Carlabhagh (Mon–Sat 4–8 daily; 1hr); Great Bernera (Mon–Sat 4–5 daily; 1hr); Leverburgh (Mon–Sat 3–6 daily; 1hr 55min); Port Nis (Mon–Sat 8 daily; 1hr); Siabost (Mon–Sat 4–8 daily; 45min); Tarbert (Mon–Sat 3–6 daily; 1hr 5min); Uig (Mon–Sat 3 daily; 1hr–1hr 30min).
Tarbert to: Huisinis (Mon–Fri schooldays 2–4 daily; school holidays Tues & Fri 3 daily; 45min); Leverburgh (Mon–Sat 7 daily; 45min); Leverburgh via the Bays (Mon–Sat 3 daily; 1hr 10min); Rhenigadale (Mon–Sat 2 daily; 30min); Scalpay (Mon–Sat 2–5 daily; 20min).

The Uists and Benbecula
Lochboisdale to: Eriskay (Mon–Fri 8 daily, 6 on Sat; 35min).
Lochmaddy to: Balivanich (Mon–Sat 4–7 daily; 45min–2hr); Balranald (Mon–Sat 3 daily; 50min); Berneray (Mon–Sat 4–7 daily; 30min); Lochboisdale (Mon–Sat 4–7 daily; 2hr).
Berneray to: Balivanich (Mon–Sat 4–7 daily; 1hr–2hr 20min); Lochmaddy (Mon–Sat 4–7 daily; 20–50min).

Barra
Castlebay to: Airport/Ferry for Eriskay (Mon–Sat 5–8 daily; 35–45min).

CalMac ferries (summer timetable)

To Barra: Lochboisdale–Castlebay (daily except Sat; 1hr 35min); Oban–Castlebay (daily except Wed; 5hr); Tiree–Castlebay (Thurs; 3hr).
To Canna: Eigg–Canna (Mon & Sat; 2hr 10min–3hr); Mallaig–Canna (Mon, Wed, Fri & Sat;

2hr–4hr 10min); Muck–Canna (Sat; 2hr 15min);
Rùm–Canna (Mon, Wed, Fri & Sat; 1hr 10min).

To Eigg: Canna–Eigg (Mon & Sat; 2hr 5min–3hr);
Mallaig–Eigg (Mon, Tues & Thurs–Sat; 1hr
10min–2hr 20min); Muck–Eigg (Tues & Thurs–Sat;
45–50min); Rùm–Eigg (Mon & Sat; 55min–2hr).

To Harris: Berneray–Leverburgh (Mon–Sat 3–4
daily; 1hr 10min); Uig–Tarbert (Mon–Sat 1–2 daily;
1hr 35min).

To Lewis: Ullapool–Stornoway (Mon–Sat 2–3
daily; 2hr 40min).

To Muck: Canna–Muck (Sat; 2hr 25min);
Eigg–Muck (Tues, Thurs & Sat; 30min–1hr);
Mallaig–Muck (Tues, Thurs, Fri & Sat; 1hr
30min–4hr 30min); Rùm–Muck (Sat; 1hr 10min).

To North Uist: Leverburgh–Berneray (Mon–Sat 4
daily; 1hr 10min); Uig–Lochmaddy (1–2 daily; 1hr
40min).

To Raasay: Sconser–Raasay (Mon–Sat 8–10 daily;
15min).

To Rùm: Canna–Rùm (Mon, Wed, Fri & Sat;
1hr–1hr 15min); Eigg–Rùm (Mon & Sat; 1hr
5min–1hr 45min); Mallaig–Rùm (Mon, Wed, Fri &
Sat; 1hr 10min–3hr 15min); Muck–Rùm (Sat; 1hr
10min).

To Skye: Glenelg–Kylerhea (daily frequently;
15min); Mallaig–Armadale (Mon–Sat 8–9 daily;
mid-May to mid-Sept also Sun; 30min).

To South Uist: Castlebay–Lochboisdale (Mon,
Tues & Fri–Sun; 1hr 40min); Oban–Lochboisdale
(daily except Wed; 4hr 50min–6hr 40min).

Flights

Benbecula to: Barra (Mon–Fri 1 daily; 20min);
Stornoway (Mon–Fri 2 daily; 30min).
Edinburgh to: Stornoway (1–2 daily; 55min).
Glasgow to: Barra (Mon–Sat 1 daily; 1hr 5min);
Benbecula (Mon–Sat 1 daily; 1hr); Stornoway
(Mon–Sat 2 daily; 1hr).

Northeast Scotland

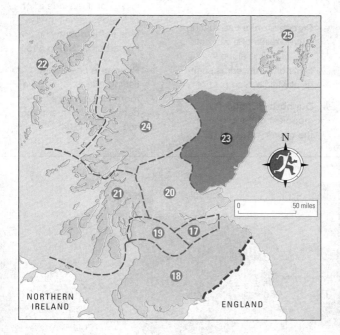

CHAPTER 23

Highlights

* **DCA** Arts centre-cinema-café at the hip new heart of Dundee's up-and-coming cultural scene. See p.1169

* **Arbroath smokie** A true Scottish delicacy: succulent haddock still warm from the oak smoker. See p.1172

* **Pictish stones** Fascinating carved relics of a lost culture, standing alone in fields or in museums such as at Meigle. See p.1174

* **Dunnottar Castle** The moodiest cliff-top ruin in the country. See p1187

* **Speyside Way** Walking route taking in Glenfiddich, Glenlivet and Glen Grant, with the chance to drop in and taste their whiskies too. See p.1191

* **Museum of Scottish Lighthouses** Lights, lenses and legends at one of the best small museums in the country, in Fraserburgh. See p.1194

* **Pennan** A one-street fishing village: there's no room for any more between the cliff and the sea. See p.1194

△ Dunnottar Castle

23

Northeast Scotland

A large triangle of land thrusting into the North Sea, **northeast Scotland** comprises the area east of a line drawn roughly from Perth north to the fringe of the Moray Firth at Forres. The area takes in the county of Angus and the city of Dundee to the south and, beyond the Grampian Mountains, the counties of Aberdeenshire and Moray and the city of Aberdeen. Geographically diverse, the landscape in the south of the region is made up predominantly of undulating farmland, but, as you get further north of the Firth of Tay, this gives way to wooded glens, mountains and increasingly harsh land fringed by a dramatic coast of cliffs and long sandy beaches.

The northeast was the southern kingdom of the **Picts**, reminders of whom are scattered throughout the region in the form of numerous symbolic and beautifully carved stones found in fields, churchyards and museums (such as the one at **Meigle**). Remote, self-contained and cut off from the centres of major power in the south, the area never grew particularly prosperous, and a handful of feuding and intermarrying families, such as the Gordons, the Keiths and the Irvines, grew to wield disproportionate influence, building many of the region's **castles** and religious buildings and developing and planning its towns.

Many of the most appealing settlements are along the coast, but while the fishing industry is but a fondly held memory in many parts, a number of the northeast's ports have been transformed by the discovery of **oil** in the North Sea in the 1960s – particularly **Aberdeen**, Scotland's third-largest city. Despite its relative isolation in the Scottish context, Aberdeen remains a sophisticated city which, for the time being, still rides a diminishing wave of oil-based prosperity. At the same time, **Dundee**, the northeast's next-largest metropolis, is fast losing its depressed postindustrial image with a reinvigorated cultural scene and some heavily marketed tourist attractions, including *Discovery*, the ship of Captain Scott ("of the Antarctic"). A little way up the Angus coast lie the historically important towns of **Arbroath** and **Montrose** while, inland, the picturesque **Angus glens** cut into the Grampian mountains, offering a readily accessible taste of wild Highland scenery to both hikers and skiers.

North of the glens and west of Aberdeen, **Deeside** is a fertile yet ruggedly attractive area made famous by the Royal Family, who have favoured the estate at **Balmoral** as a summer holiday retreat ever since Queen Victoria fell in love with it back in the 1840s. Beyond, the **Don Valley** is similarly endowed though less visited, while tranquil **Speyside**, a little way northwest, is best known as Scotland's premier whisky-producing region, where **malt whisky** trails, both official and unofficial, can be followed. The northeast coast offers yet another aspect of a diverse region, with rugged cliffs, empty beaches and historic fishing villages tucked into coves and bays.

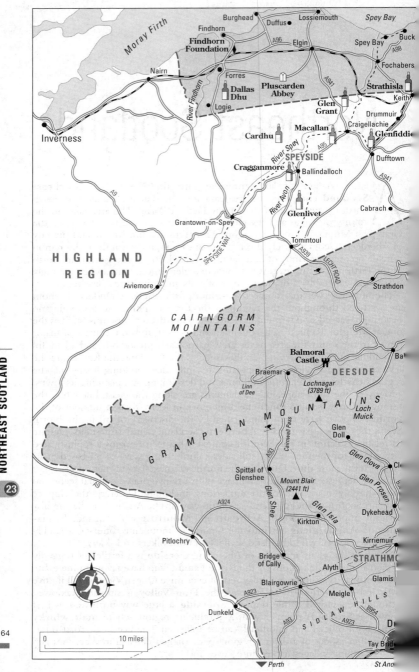

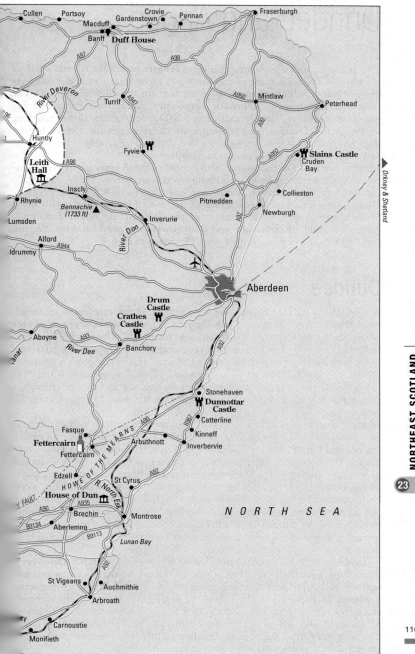

© Crown copyright

Dundee and Angus

The predominantly agricultural county of **Angus**, east of the A9 and north of the Firth of Tay, holds some of the northeast's greatest scenery and is relatively free of tourists, who tend to head further west for the Highlands proper. The coast from **Montrose** to **Arbroath** is especially inviting, with scarlet cliffs and sweeping bays, then, further south towards Dundee, gentler dunes and long sandy beaches. **Dundee** itself, although not the most obvious tourist destination, has in recent years become a more dynamic and progressive city, and makes for a less snooty alternative to Aberdeen.

In the north of the county, the long fingers of the **Angus glens** – heather-covered hills tumbling down to rushing rivers – are overlooked by the southern peaks of the Grampian Mountains. Each has its own feel and devotees, **Glen Clova** being, deservedly, one of the most popular, along with **Glen Shee**, which attracts large numbers of people to its ski slopes. Handsome market towns like **Kirriemuir** and **Blairgowrie** are good bases for the area, and Angus is also liberally dotted with **Pictish remains**.

Dundee

At first sight, **DUNDEE** can seem a grim place. In the nineteenth century it was Britain's main processor of jute, the world's most important vegetable fibre after cotton, which earned the city the tag "Juteopolis". The decline of manufacturing wasn't kind to Dundee, but regeneration is very much the buzzword today, with some commentators drawing comparisons to Glasgow's reinvention of itself as a city of culture in the 1980s and 1990s. Less apparent is the city's international reputation as a centre of biotechnology and cancer research, a theme recently given a notable monument in the new Maggie Centre for cancer care.

Even prior to its Victorian heyday, Dundee was a town of considerable importance. It was here in 1309 that **Robert the Bruce** was proclaimed the lawful king of Scots, and during the Reformation it earned itself a reputation for tolerance, sheltering leading figures such as George Wishart and John Knox. In the 1800s, Dundee's train and harbour links made it a major centre for shipbuilding, whaling and the manufacture of **jute**. This, along with jam and journalism – the three Js which famously defined the city – has all but disappeared, with only local publishing giant D.C. Thomson, publisher of the timelessly popular *Beano* and *Dandy* comics, as well as a spread of other comics and newspapers, still playing a meaningful role in the city.

The major sight is Captain Scott's Antarctic explorer ship, **RRS Discovery**, docked underneath the Tay Road Bridge. **Verdant Works** is a re-created jute mill which has picked up tourism awards for its take on the city's distinctive industrial heritage, while the suburb of **Broughty Ferry** offers a distinct change of tone, particularly if you're looking for somewhere to eat or drink. You should also try to spend some time at the upbeat **DCA** (Dundee Contemporary Arts), the totemic building of the developing cultural quarter around which most of the city's lively artistic and social life revolves.

Arrival, information and city transport

By **train**, you'll arrive in Dundee at Taybridge Station on South Union Street (enquiries ☎0845/748 4950), about 300 yards south of the city centre near the river. Long-distance **buses** arrive at the Seagate bus station, a couple of hundred yards east of the centre.

The very helpful **tourist office** is right in the centre of things at 21 Castle St (June–Sept Mon–Sat 9am–6pm, Sun noon–4pm; Oct–May Mon–Sat 9am–5pm; ☎01382/527527, Ⓦwww.angusanddundee.co.uk or Ⓦwww.dundeecity.gov.uk). They have the free *Accent* listings magazine, detailing local theatre, music and exhibitions; Ⓦwww.dundee.com has local listings online. The city's two daily newspapers are the morning *Courier & Advertiser* and the *Evening Telegraph & Post*.

Dundee's centre is reasonably compact and you can walk to most sights; **local buses** leave from the High Street or from Albert Square, one block to the north; for bus information, call ☎01382/201121, check Ⓦwww.traveldundee.co.uk or go to the Travel Dundee Travel Centre, in the Forum Centre at 92 Commercial St. A Daysaver ticket, with unlimited bus travel for a day, costs £2.

Accommodation

Dundee has no recommended hostel or backpacker accommodation – the cheaper **B&B**s on the fringes of the city centre are the most reasonable alternative. You'll find plenty of rooms out by the suburb of Broughty Ferry, a twenty-minute bus ride (£1) into the city on Travel Dundee buses #7, #8 or #9, or Strathtay buses #73 and #76 (all leave from either Commercial Street or Seagate in the town centre).

Hotels, guest houses and B&Bs

Apex City Quay Hotel West Victoria Dock Rd ☎01382/202404, Ⓦwww.apexhotels.co.uk. Large, sleek and modern hotel in the redeveloping dockland area, incorporating a spa, pool and restaurant. ❼

Discovery Quay Travel Inn Riverside Drive ☎01382/203240, Ⓦwww.travelinn.co.uk. Bland, modern chain hotel well positioned right beside Discovery Point and the railway station. ❸

Howies 25 Tay St ☎01382/200399, Ⓦwww.howies.uk.com. Right beside the action in the Cultural Quarter, with four designer rooms above the restaurant (see p.1170). ❹

Errolbank 9 Dalgleish Rd ☎01382/462118.

No-smoking Victorian villa with good views of the Tay; all rooms are en suite. ❷

Fisherman's Tavern 12 Fort St, Broughty Ferry ☎01382/775941, Ⓦwww.fishermans-tavern-hotel .co.uk. Refurbished en-suite rooms above a cosy traditional pub with decent food, great real ales and malt whiskies. ❹

Nelson Guest House 8 Nelson Terrace ☎01382/225354. Inexpensive B&B with three twin rooms, located up the hill from the downtown area. ❶

Campsite

Riverview Caravan Park Marine Drive, Monifieth ☎01382/535471. Well-run camping park in a suburb beyond Broughty Ferry, with an easy train link to Dundee. March–Oct.

The City and around

The best approach to Dundee is across the mile-and-a-half-long **Tay Road Bridge** from Fife. While the Tay bridges aren't nearly as spectacular as the bridges over the Forth near Edinburgh, they do offer a magnificent panorama of the city on the northern bank of the firth. The bridge, opened in 1966, has a central walkway for pedestrians. Running parallel half a mile upstream is the **Tay Rail Bridge**, opened in 1887 to replace the spindly structure which

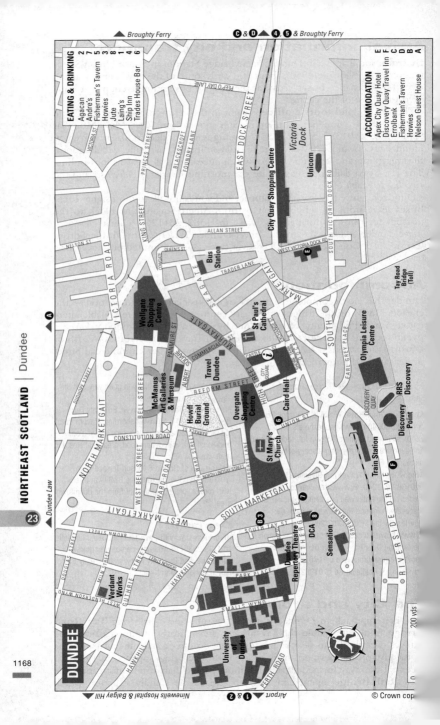

DUNDEE

EATING & DRINKING

Agacan	2
Andre's	7
Fisherman's Tavern	5
Howies	3
Jute	8
Laing's	1
Ship Inn	4
Trades House Bar	6

ACCOMMODATION

Apex City Quay Hotel	E
Discovery Quay Travel Inn	F
Errolbank	C
Fisherman's Tavern	D
Howies	B
Nelson Guest House	A

Broughty Ferry

C & D ▲ 4 5 & Broughty Ferry

PEEP O' DAY LANE

VICTORIA ST

PRINCES STREET

BLACKSCROFT

FOUNDRY LANE

EAST DOCK STREET

Victoria Dock

City Quay Shopping Centre

Unicorn

SOUTH VICTORIA DOCK RD

WEST VICTORIA DOCK RD

E

ALLAN STREET

QUEEN'S ST.

Bus Station

TRADER LANE

SEAGATE

NELSON ST

VICTORIA ROAD

KING STREET

COWGATE

Wellgate Shopping Centre

PANMURE ST

MURRAYGATE

St Paul's Cathedral

i

MARKETGAIT

Tay Road Bridge (Toll)

Olympia Leisure Centre

SOUTH

EARL GREY PLACE

DUNDEE LAW

DUNDEE STREET

BELL STREET

McManus Art Galleries & Museum

Howff Burial Ground

Travel Dundee

ALBERT SQUARE

COMMERCIAL ST

REFORM STREET

CASTLE ST

CITY SQUARE

HIGH STREET

Caird Hall

6

UNION ST

Discovery Quay

RRS Discovery

Discovery Point

NORTH MARKETGAIT

CONSTITUTION ROAD

WEST BELL STREET

WARD ROAD

BARRACK ST

SOUTH WARD STREET

NORTH LINDSAY STREET

OVERGATE LANE

Overgate Shopping Centre

St Mary's Church

Train Station

F

RIVERSIDE DRIVE

Dundee Law

BROWN STREET

MILN STREET

DOUGLAS STREET

SOUTH MARKETGAIT

WEST MARKETGAIT

HAWKHILL

W.S. BURN

PARK PLACE

7

SOUTH TAY ST

NETHERGATE

B 3

DCA 8

Sensation

GREENMARKET

University of Dundee

PERTH ROAD

Verdant Works

WEST HENDERSON WYND

GUTHRIE

HAWKHILL

SMALLS WYND

Dundee Repertory Theatre

N

200 yds

Niewewells Hospital & Balgay Hill

Airport

1 & 2

0

collapsed in a storm in May 1878 only eighteen months after it was built, killing the crew and 75 passengers on a train passing over the bridge at the time.

Dundee's city centre, dominated by large shopping malls filled with mundane chain stores, is focused on **City Square**, a couple of hundred yards north of the Tay. The attractive square, set in front of the city's imposing Caird Hall, has been much spruced up in recent years, with fountains, benches and extensive pedestrianization making for a relaxing environment. Where Reform Street meets City Square, look out for a couple of other statues to Dundee heroes: **Desperate Dan** and **Minnie the Minx**, both from the *Dandy* and *Beano* comics, which are produced a few hundred yards away in the D.C. Thomson building on Albert Square.

Also fringing Albert Square are Dundee High School and, on its eastern side, the **McManus Art Galleries and Museum** (Mon–Sat 10.30am–5pm, plus Thurs until 7pm, Sun 12.30–4pm; free). Designed by Gilbert Scott, the museum is Dundee's most impressive Victorian structure, with a delightful sweep of outside curved stone staircases and elaborate Gothic touches. Inside, there's an excellent overview of the city's past, with displays ranging from Pictish stones to the Tay Bridge disaster. On the ground floor, the most impressive exhibit is the skeleton of a whale, washed up on a nearby beach in 1883 and eulogized in a poem by William McGonagall, a strong contender for the title of the world's worst poet ("'Twas in the month of December, and in the year 1883/That a monster whale came to Dundee"). Upstairs, the magnificent **Albert Hall** – crowned by a roof of 480 pitch-pine panels in a Gothic arch – houses antique musical instruments, decorative glass, gold, silver, sculpture and some exquisite furniture. On the same floor, the barrel-roofed **Victoria Gallery**'s red walls are packed with nineteenth- and twentieth-century paintings, including some notable Pre-Raphaelite and Scottish works, William McTaggart's seascapes being a particular highlight.

Across Ward Road from the museum, the **Howff Burial Ground** (daily 9am–dusk) has some great carved tombstones dating from the sixteenth to nineteenth centuries. Five minutes' walk west of here, on West Henderson Wynd in Blackness, an award-winning museum, **Verdant Works**, tells the story of jute from its harvesting in India to its arrival in Dundee on clipper ships (April–Oct Mon–Sat 10am–6pm, Sun 11am–6pm; Nov–March Wed–Sat 10.30am–4.30pm, Sun 11am–4.30pm; £5.95, joint ticket with Discovery Point £10.95; @www.verdant-works.co.uk). The museum, set in an old jute mill, makes a lively attempt to re-create the turn-of-the-twentieth-century factory floor, the highlight being the chance to watch jute being processed on fully operational quarter-size machines originally used for training workers.

The Cultural Quarter

Immediately west of the city centre, High Street becomes Nethergate and passes into what is now being dubbed, with a fair amount of justification, Dundee's "Cultural Quarter". As well as the university and the highly respected Rep theatre, the area is also home to the best concentration of pubs and cafés in the city. Principal among the area's many arts venues is the hip and exciting **DCA**, or Dundee Contemporary Arts, at 152 Nethergate (Mon–Sat 10.30am–midnight, Sun noon–midnight; galleries Tues–Sun 10.30am–5.30pm, until 8.30pm Thurs, Sun noon–5.30pm; T01382/909900, @www.dca.org.uk), a stunningly designed complex that incorporates galleries, a print studio and an airy café-bar (see p.1170). The centre is worth visiting for its simulating temporary and touring exhibitions of contemporary art, and eclectic programme of art-house films and cult classics.

The waterfront

Just south of the city centre, at the water's edge alongside the Tay Road Bridge, the domed **Discovery Point** is an impressive development centring on the Royal Research Ship *Discovery* (April–Oct Mon–Sat 10am–6pm, Sun 11am–5pm; Nov–March Mon–Sat 10am–5pm, Sun 11am–5pm; £6.25, joint ticket with Verdant Works £10.95; ⓦ www.rrs-discovery.co.uk). Something of an icon for Dundee's renaissance, *Discovery* is a three-mast steam-assisted vessel built in Dundee in 1901 to take Captain Robert Falcon Scott on his polar expeditions. A combination of brute strength and elegance, she has been beautifully restored, with polished wood panels and brass trimmings giving scant indication of the privations suffered by the crew. You're led through a series of displays including the chill-inducing "Polarama" about life in Antarctica and a compelling, if overhyped, audiovisual spectacular involving a model ship bursting through the screen and lots of dry ice.

In total contrast is the endearingly simple wooden frigate **Unicorn** (April–Oct daily 10am–5pm; Nov–March Wed–Fri noon–4pm, Sat & Sun 10am–4pm; £3.50), moored amidst some new dockland redevelopments in Victoria Dock on the other side of the road bridge (a footpath connects the two ships). Built in 1824, it's the oldest British warship still afloat; although the interior is sparse, the cannons, the splendid figureheads and the wonderful model of the ship in its fully rigged glory (the real thing would have featured over 23 miles of rope) are fascinating.

Out from the centre

Two miles west from the centre is the sprawling Ninewells Hospital, not an obvious draw for fans of modern architecture. In the grounds of the hospital, however, is **Maggie's Centre**, designed by US architect Frank Gehry, best known for Bilbao's Guggenheim Museum. Gehry's first public commission in the UK, the building is a cancer-support centre and features a distinctively free-form style with a wavy roof constructed from timber, clad with stainless steel. The building is not open to the general public, and is operational through the week, but for anyone interested in seeing one of Gehry's visionary constructions up close it is possible to walk up to and around it at weekends. Buses #22 and #9 go to the hospital; if you're travelling by car use the main hospital car park.

Eating, drinking and nightlife

The west end of Dundee, around the main university campus and Perth Road, is the best area for **eating and drinking**; the city centre, though good for a few pubs, is a bit of a nonstarter for decent food. Broughty Ferry is a pleasant alternative, with a good selection of pubs and restaurants that get particularly busy on summer evenings.

Restaurants and cafés

Agacan 113 Perth Rd ☎01382/644227. Tiny Turkish restaurant with an unmistakeable colourful exterior, and rough-hewn walls inside; they serve up decent kebabs and stuffed pittas, and also do takeaways. Closed lunchtimes & all day Mon. Moderate.

Andre's 134a Nethergate ☎01382/224455. A cosy, endearing bastion of traditional French dining – expect *coq au vin* or *moules marinière* done just the way they should be. Closed Mon. Moderate.

Howies 25 Tay St ☎01382/200399. Large, smartly contemporary but friendly restaurant serving modern Scottish dishes, with *The Basement* café-bar on the lower ground floor for cocktails and light snacks. Moderate.

Jute Dundee Contemporary Arts (DCA), 152 Nethergate. Trendy spot occupying a large openplan space on the lower level of this arts centre, with large windows looking out over the industrial wasteland and railway tracks that line the Tay.

Table service for the decent range of sandwiches and light meals, served until 9.30pm. Inexpensive. **Ship Inn** 121 Fisher St, Broughty Ferry. A narrow pub with a warm atmosphere right on the waterfront. The bistro upstairs has views over the Tay and serves big platefuls of great seafood. Moderate.

Pubs

Fisherman's Tavern 12 Fort St, Broughty Ferry.

Best real-ale pub around, and plenty of seafood on the menu. Not quite on the sea, but tucked away in a low-ceilinged cottage.

Laing's 8 Roseangle, off Perth Rd. Usually packed on warm summer nights, thanks to its beer garden and great river views.

Trades House Bar 40 Nethergate. Probably the best pub in the centre of town, with nice wood fittings, stained-glass windows and some decent ales.

Nightlife

Right at the heart of the Cultural Quarter on Tay Square, north of Nethergate, is the prodigious Dundee Repertory Theatre (☏01382/223530, ⓦwww .dundeereptheatre.co.uk), an excellent place for indigenously produced contemporary **theatre**. For **movies**, DCA (☏01382/909900, ⓦwww.dca .org.uk) has two comfy auditoriums showing an appealing range of foreign and art-house movies alongside more mainstream releases; otherwise you have to head a fair way out of the centre to the UGC multiplex at Camperdown Leisure park (☏0870/902 0407; bus #4A/4B) or the Odeon at Douglasfield, east of the city (☏0870/5050007; bus #28 or #29).

Listings

Bike rental Easy Ride Cycles, off Wm Fitzgerald Way, Barns of Claverhouse ☏01382/505683; Just Bikes, 57 Grey St, Broughty Ferry ☏01382/732100.

Books Ottakars, 7 High St; Waterstone's, 34 Commercial St.

Bus information Scottish Citylink ☏0870/550 5050; Strathtay Scottish for regional buses ☏01382/228345; Traveline Scotland ☏0870/608 2608.

Car rental Arnold Clark ☏01382/225382; Alamo National ☏01382/224037; Hertz ☏01382/223711.

Internet Webgate Internet, Central Library, Wellgate Shopping Centre (Mon–Fri

9.30am–8.30pm, Sat 9.30am–4.30pm). The tourist office also has Internet access.

Medical facilities Ninewells Hospital in the west of the city has an Accident and Emergency department ☏01382/660111. NHS Helpline ☏0800/224488. Boots pharmacy is at 49–53 High St (Mon–Sat 8.30am–5.45pm, Thurs until 7pm, Sun 12.30–5pm).

Police Tayside Police HQ, West Bell St ☏01382/223200.

Post office 4 Meadowside (Mon–Fri 9am–5.30pm, Sat 9am–12.30pm).

Taxis There are taxi ranks on Nethergate, or call City Cabs ☏01382/566666; Handy Taxis ☏01382/225825; or, in Broughty Ferry, Discovery Taxis ☏01382/732111.

㉓

The Angus coast

Two roads link Dundee to Aberdeen and the northeast coast of Scotland. By far the more pleasant option is the slightly longer A92 coast road, which joins the inland A90 at Stonehaven, just south of Aberdeen. Intercity **buses** follow both roads, while the coast-hugging train line from Dundee is one of the most picturesque in Scotland, passing attractive beaches and impressive cliffs, and stopping in the old seaports of **Arbroath** and **Montrose**.

Arbroath

Since it was settled in the twelfth century, local fishermen have been landing their catches at **ARBROATH**, situated on the Angus coast where it starts to curve in from the North Sea towards the Firth of Tay, about fifteen miles northeast of Dundee. The town's most famous product is the **Arbroath smokie** – line-caught haddock, smoke-cured over smouldering oak chips, and still made here in a number of family-run smokehouses tucked in around the harbour. One of the most approachable and atmospheric is M&M Spink's tiny whitewashed premises at 10 Marketgate; chef and cookery writer Rick Stein described the fish here, warm from the smoke, as "a world-class delicacy".

By the late eighteenth century, chiefly due to its harbour, Arbroath had become a trading and manufacturing centre, famed for boot-making and sail-making (the *Cutty Sark*'s sails were made here). The town's real glory days, however, came much earlier in the thirteenth century with the completion in 1233 of **Arbroath Abbey** (daily April–Sept 9.30am–6.30pm; Oct–March 9.30am–4.30pm; £3; HS), whose rose-pink sandstone ruins, described by Dr Johnson as "fragments of magnificence", stand on Abbey Street. It was the scene of one of the most significant events in Scotland's history when, on April 6, 1320, a group of Scottish barons drew up the **Declaration of Arbroath**, asking the pope to reverse his excommunication of Robert the Bruce and recognize him as king of a Scottish nation independent from England. The wonderfully resonant language of the document still makes for a stirring expression of Scottish nationhood: "For so long as one hundred of us remain alive, we will never in any degree be subject to the dominion of the English, since it is not for glory, riches or honour that we do fight, but for freedom alone, which no honest man loses but with his life." It was duly despatched to Pope John XXII in Avignon, who in 1324 agreed to Robert's claim. A radically designed new **visitor centre** at the Abbey Street entrance offers some in-depth background on these events and other aspects of the history of the building.

Practicalities

Arbroath's helpful **tourist office** is at Market Place right in the middle of town (June–Aug Mon–Sat 9.30am–5.30pm, Sun 10am–3pm; April, May & Sept Mon–Fri 9am–5pm, Sat 10am–5pm; Oct–March Mon–Fri 9am–5pm, Sat 10am–3pm; ☎01241/872609). For somewhere **to stay**, the *Five Gables House* (☎01241/871632, ⓦwww.fivegableshouse.co.uk; ❶) is a mile south of Arbroath on the A92; formerly a golf clubhouse, it has a great position overlooking the sea. Alternatively, try the *Harbour Nights Guest House* (☎01241/434343; ❸), down by the harbour at 4 The Shore, which is also where you'll find the best **restaurants** and **pubs**. The best way to sample Arbroath smokies is while they're still warm, straight from one of the smokehouses. *The Old Brewhouse* (☎01241/879945) is a convivial and moderately priced restaurant-cum-pub by the harbour wall at the end of High Street. A little north of town in the village of Auchmithie, the *But'n'Ben* **restaurant** (☎01241/877223; closed Tues) specializes in delicious, moderately priced Scottish dishes and seafood.

Montrose and around

Here's the Basin, there's Montrose, shut your een and haud your nose.

As the old rhyme indicates, **MONTROSE**, a seaport and market town since the thirteenth century, can sometimes smell a little rich, mostly because of its position on the edge of a virtually landlocked two-mile-square lagoon of mud known as the Basin. On the south side of the Basin, a mile out of Montrose along the A92, the **Montrose Basin Wildlife Centre** (daily 10.30am–5pm

Nov–March closes 4pm; £2.50; ⓦ www.montrosebasin.org.uk) has binoculars, high-powered telescopes, bird hides and remote-control video cameras. In addition, the centre's resident ranger leads regular guided walks around the reserve.

Montrose locals are known as "Gable Endies", because of the unusual way in which the town's eighteenth- and nineteenth-century merchants, influenced by architectural styles they had seen on the continent, built their houses gable-end to the street. The few remaining original gabled houses line the wide **High Street**, off which are numerous tiny alleyways and quiet courtyards.

Two blocks behind the soaring kirk steeple at the lower end of High Street, the **Montrose Museum and Art Gallery** (Mon–Sat 10am–5pm; free), on Panmure Place on the western side of Mid Links Park, is one of Scotland's oldest museums, dating from 1842. For a small-town museum, it has some particularly unusual exhibits, among them the so-called Samson Stone, a Pictish relic dating from 900 AD bearing a carving of Samson slaying the Philistines. In the local history section, look out for the mechanical paper sculpture of the town of Montrose, with a green train running along the top and yachts sailing by.

Outside the museum entrance stands a winsome study of a boy by local sculptor William Lamb (1893–1951). More of his work can be seen in the moving **William Lamb Memorial Studio** on Market Street (July to mid-Sept daily 2–5pm; at other times, ask at the museum; free), including bronze heads of the Queen, Princess Margaret and the Queen Mother. Finally, don't ignore the town's fabulous golden **seashore**. The beach road, Marine Avenue, across from the town museum, heads down through sand dunes and golf links to car parks fringing the fine, wide beach overlooked by a slender white lighthouse.

The House of Dun

Across the Basin, four miles west of Montrose, is the Palladian **House of Dun** (July & Aug daily noon–5pm; April–June & Sept Fri–Tue noon–5pm; £7, grounds only £1; NTS), accessible on the regular Montrose–Brechin bus #30; ask the driver to let you off outside. Built in 1730 for David Erskine, laird of Dun, to designs by William Adam, the house was opened to the public in 1989 after extensive restoration, and is crammed full of period furniture and objets d'art. Inside, the ornate relief plasterwork is the most impressive feature, extravagantly emblazoned with Jacobite symbolism.

Practicalities

Montrose **tourist office** is squeezed into a former public toilet next to the library, at the point where Bridge Street merges into the lower end of High Street (July & Aug Mon–Sat 9.30am–5.30pm; April–June & Sept Mon–Sat 10am–5pm; ☎01674/672000). Most **buses** stop in the High Street, while the train station lies a block back on Western Road. For B&B **accommodation**, try *Oaklands*, over the river bridge at 10 Rossie Island Rd (☎01674/672018, ⓦ www.nebsnow.com/oaklands; ❷), or if you don't mind heading out of Montrose, make for *Woodston Fishing Station* (☎01674/850226, ⓦwww.woodstonfishingstation.co.uk; ❸), a neat, antique-filled house on the cliff top at St Cyrus, a couple of miles north of town. For **eating**, the liveliest place in town is unquestionably *Roo's Leap*, a sports bar and restaurant by the golf club at the northern end of Trail Drive, with an unlikely, but decent mix of moderately priced Scottish, American and Australian cuisine.

Strathmore and the Angus glens

Immediately north of Dundee, the low-lying Sidlaw Hills divide the city from the rich agricultural region of **Strathmore**, whose string of tidy market towns lies on a fertile strip along the southernmost edge of the heather-covered lower slopes of the Grampian Mountains. These towns act as gateways to the **Angus glens**, a series of tranquil valleys penetrated by single-track roads and offering some of the most rugged and majestic landscapes in northeast Scotland. It's a rain-swept, wind-blown, sparsely populated area, whose roads become impassable with the first snows, sometimes as early as October, and where the summers see clouds of ferocious midges. The most useful road through the glens is the A93, which cuts through **Glen Shee**, linking Blairgowrie to Braemar on Deeside (see p.1189). It's pretty dramatic stuff, threading its way over Britain's highest main-road pass, the **Cairnwell Pass** (2199ft).

Blairgowrie and Glen Shee

The upper reaches of **Glen Shee**, the most dramatic and best known of the Angus glens, are dominated by its **ski fields**, ranged over four mountains above the Cairnwell mountain pass. To get to Glen Shee from the south you'll pass through the well-heeled town of **BLAIRGOWRIE**, little more than one main road set among raspberry fields on the glen's southernmost tip, but a good place to pick up information and plan your activities. Blairgowrie **tourist office** (July & Aug Mon–Sat 9.30am–6.30pm, Sun 11am–5pm; April–June & Sept–Oct Mon–Sat 9.30am–5.30pm, Sun 11am–4pm; Nov–March Mon–Sat 9.30am–4.30pm; ☎01250/872960, ⓦwww.perthshire.co.uk), on the high side of the Wellmeadow, can help with **accommodation**. A number of Blairgowrie's grand houses offer B&B, among them the attractive *Duncraggan* (☎01250/872082; ❶) on Perth Road. **Camping** is available at the year-round *Blairgowrie Holiday Park* on Rattray's Hatton Road (☎01250/876666), within walking distance from the Wellmeadow. Blairgowrie boasts plenty of places to **eat**: *Cargills* by the river on Lower Mill Street (☎01250/876735; closed Tues) is the best bet for a moderately priced formal meal; for good **pub** grub try the youthful *Driftwood*, just off the Wellmeadow, which has a terrace overlooking the river, or head six miles north of town on the A93 to the delightfully situated *Bridge of Cally Hotel* (☎01250/886231, ⓦwww.bridgeofcallyhotel.com ❺). Back in Blairgowrie you can rent **bikes** from Crichton's Cycle Hire, 87 Perth St (☎01250/876100).

Nearly twenty miles north of Blairgowrie, the small settlement of **SPITTAL OF GLENSHEE** (the names derives from the same root as 'hospital', indicating a refuge), though ideally situated for skiing, has little to commend it other than the busy *Gulabin Bunkhouse* on the A93, run by Cairnwell Mountain Sport (see box opposite), which rents out skis and bikes and offers hang-gliding lessons.

Meigle and Glen Isla

Fifteen miles north of Dundee on the B954 lies the tiny settlement of **MEIGLE**, home to Scotland's most important collection of early Christian and Pictish inscribed stones. Housed in a modest former schoolhouse, the **Meigle Museum** (April–Sept daily 9.30am–6.30pm; Oct Mon–Sat 9.30am–4.30pm Sun 2–4.30pm; £2; HS) displays some thirty pieces dating from the seventh to the tenth centuries, all found in and around the nearby churchyard. The majority are either gravestones that would have lain flat, or cross slabs inscribed with the sign of the cross, usually standing. Most impressive is the 7ft-tall great cross

Skiing at Glenshee

Glenshee is the most accessible of Scotland's **ski** areas, just over two hours from both Glasgow and Edinburgh; for information, contact Ski Glenshee (℡013397/41320, 🅦 www.ski-glenshee.co.uk), who also offer ski rental and lessons. In addition, lessons, skis and boards are available from Cairnwell Mountain Sports (℡01250/885255, 🅦 www.cairnwellmountainsports.co.uk), at the Spittal of Glenshee. **Ski rental** starts at around £12 a day, while lessons are around £12 per half-day. **Lift passes** cost £20 per day or £75 for a five-day (Mon–Fri) ticket. For the latest snow and **weather conditions**, phone the centre itself or check out the Ski Scotland website (🅦 ski.visitscotland.com). Should you be more interested in **cross-country** skiing, there are some good touring areas in the vicinity; contact Cairnwell Mountain Sports (see above) or Braemar Mountain Sports (℡013397/41242) for information and equipment rental.

slab, said to be the gravestone of Guinevere, wife of King Arthur, carved on one side with a portrayal of Daniel surrounded by lions, a beautifully executed equestrian group, and mythological creatures including a dragon and a centaur.

Three miles north of Meigle is **Alyth**, near which, legend has it, Guinevere was held captive by Mordred. The sleepy village lies at the south end of **Glen Isla**, which runs parallel to Glen Shee and is linked to it by the A926. The tiny hamlet of **KIRKTON OF GLENISLA** is ten miles or so up the glen. Here, the cosy *Glenisla Hotel* (℡01575/582223, 🅦 www.glenisla-hotel.com; ❸) is great for classy homemade bar food and convivial drinking. There are some relatively easy **hiking** trails in the nearby Glenisla forest, while just before Kirkton, a turn-off on the right-hand side leads northeast up a long bumpy road to the unexpected *Glenmarkie Guesthouse Health Spa and Riding Centre* (℡01575/582295 🅦 www.glenmarkie.co.uk; ❸), which offers both pedicures and pony trekking.

Forfar and around

Around fifteen miles north of Dundee on the main A90 lies **FORFAR**, Angus's county town and the ancient capital of the Picts. Midway along the wide High Street, framed by some impressive Victorian architecture and small old-fashioned shops, the **Meffen Institute Museum and Art Gallery**, 20 West High St (Mon–Sat 10am–5pm; free), exhibits Neolithic, Pictish and Celtic remains and a thoroughly enjoyable collection of re-created historical street scenes. There's also a comprehensive interactive computer catalogue of all the Pictish stones in Angus, and an art gallery with good changing exhibitions. Forfar's small **tourist office** (July & Aug Mon–Sat 9.30am–5.30pm; April–June & Sept Mon–Sat 10am–5pm; ℡01307/467876) is at 45 East High St, opposite the soaring steeple of the parish church. Numerous shops and bakers stock the famous **Forfar Bridie**, a semicircular folded pastry-case of mince, onion and seasonings, including Saddlers, a few doors down from the tourist office, and McLarens (the locals' favourite), at 8 West High St.

Glamis Castle

Bus #22 from Forfar runs regularly to Dundee via the pink-sandstone **Glamis Castle** (April–Oct daily 10.30am–5.30pm, last tour 4.45pm; £6.70, grounds only £3.50; 🅦 www.glamis-castle.co.uk), located a mile north of the picturesque village of **GLAMIS** (pronounced "glahms"). A wondrously over-the-top, L-shaped five-storey pile set in an extensive landscaped park complete with deer

❷❸

and pheasants, this is one of the most famous Scottish castles. Shakespeare chose it as a central location in *Macbeth*, and its **royal connections** (as the childhood home of the late Queen Mother and birthplace of Princess Margaret) make it one of the essential stops on every coach tour of Scotland, though for many visitors the Queen Mum gloss is laid on rather thick.

Obligatory guided tours take visitors through the Victorian **Dining Room**, notable for its fine rose-and-thistle ceiling, then through a door in the wood panelling to the fifteenth-century **Crypt**, where the atmosphere changes dramatically. As the Lower Hall of the original tower house, the crypt's 12ft-thick walls enclose a haunted "lost" room, reputed to be have been sealed with the red-bearded lord of Glamis and Crawford (also known as Beardie Crawford) inside, after he dared to play cards with the Devil one Sabbath. From here, the tour passes up a seventeenth-century staircase, whose hollow central pillar provided a primitive system of central heating, into the arch-roofed **Drawing Room**, with delightful wedding-cake plasterwork (dated 1621), and then to the family **Chapel**, completed in 1688. **King Malcolm's Room**, so called because it is believed he died nearby in 1034, is most notable for its carved wooden chimneypiece, on which many of its most decorative panels are made from highly polished leather.

Glamis' **grounds** are worth a few hours in their own right, holding lead statues of James VI and Charles I at the top of the main drive, a seventeenth-century Baroque sundial, a formal Italian Garden and verdant walks out to Earl John's Bridge and through the woodland.

Kirriemuir and glens Clova and Doll

The sandstone town of **KIRRIEMUIR**, known locally as Kirrie, is set on a hill six miles northwest of Forfar on the cusp of glens Clova and Prosen. The main cluster of streets have all the appeal of an old film set, with their old-fashioned bars, tiled butcher's shop, tartan outlets and haberdasheries somehow managing to avoid being contrived and quaint – although the recent recobbling of the town centre around a twee statue of Peter Pan undermines this somewhat. Peter Pan's presence is justified, however, since Kirrie was the birthplace of his creator, **J.M. Barrie**. A local handloom-weaver's son, Barrie first came to notice with his series of novels about "Thrums", a village based on his hometown, in particular *A Window in Thrums* and his third novel, *The Little Minister*. The story of Peter Pan, the little boy who never grew up, was penned by Barrie in 1904 – some say as a response to a strange upbringing dominated by the memory of his older brother, who died as a child. **Barrie's birthplace** a plain little whitewashed cottage at 9 Brechin Rd (April–June & Sept Fri–Tues noon–5pm; July & Aug daily noon–5pm; £5, includes entrance to the camera obscura; NTS), has been opened up as a visitor attraction, with a serie of small rooms decorated as they would have been during Barrie's childhood as well as displays about his life and works.

The **Kirriemuir Museum** (Mon–Wed, Fri & Sat 10am–5pm, Sun 2–5pm free), in the old Town House on the main square, has seen service as a toll booth, court, jail, post office, police station and chemist; these days you can fin two floors of information and exhibits on the town and the Angus Glen Kirrie's helpful **tourist office** is in Cumberland Close (July & Aug Mon–S 9.30am–5.30pm; April–June & Sept Mon–Sat 10am–5pm; ☎01575/574097 in the new development behind *Visocchi's* in the main squar **Accommodation** is available at the respectable *Airlie Arms*, St Malcoln Wynd (☎01575/572487, ⓦwww.airliearms-hotel.co.uk; ❹), while on th

23

edge of town, and offering a taste of the rolling countryside, is the working *Muirhouses Farm* (℡01575/573128, Ⓦwww.muirhousesfarm.co.uk; ❷).

Glen Clova and Glen Doll

With its stunning cliffs, heather slopes and valley meadows, **Glen Clova** – which in the north becomes **Glen Doll** – is firm favourite amongst the Angus glens. Although it can get unpleasantly congested in peak season, the area is still remote enough to enable you to leave the crowds with little effort. Wildlife is abundant, with deer on the mountains, wild hares and even grouse and the occasional buzzard. The meadow flowers on the valley floor and arctic plants (including great splashes of white and purple saxifrage) on the rocks also make it something of a botanist's paradise.

The hamlet of **CLOVA** consists of little more than the hearty *Glen Clova Hotel* (℡01575/550350, Ⓦwww.clova.com; ❺), which also has a refurbished bunkhouse (£10 per night) and a private fishing loch. Meals and real ale are available in the lively *Climbers' Bar* at the side of the hotel. Also pleasant, though slightly less susceptible to the high jinks of university climbing clubs, is *Brandy Burn House* (℡01575/550203, Ⓦwww.glenclova.co.uk; ❷), with a bar and coffee shop in its stables, a beer garden and comfortable B&B. An excellent, if fairly strenuous, four-hour walk from behind the old school at the back of the hotel leads up into the mountains and around the lip of **Loch Brandy**, which legend predicts will one day flood and drown the valley below.

Aberdeenshire and Moray

Aberdeenshire and Moray cover some 3500 square miles of open and varied country dotted with historic and archeological sights, from neat NTS properties and eerie prehistoric rings of standing stones to quiet kirkyards, serene abbeys and a rash of dramatic castles. Geographically, the counties break down into two distinct areas: the **hinterland**, once barren and now a patchwork of fertile farms, rising towards high mountains, sparkling rivers and gentle valleys; and the **coast**, a classic stretch of rocky cliff, remote fishing villages and long, sandy beaches.

For visitors, the large city of **Aberdeen** is the obvious focal point of the region, and while it's not a place to keep you engrossed for long, it does boast some intriguing architecture, attractive museums and a lively social scene. From here, it's a short hop west to **Deeside**, annually visited by the Royal Family and an easily accessed gateway to some spectacular mountain scenery. To the north lies the **Don Valley**, a quiet area notable for its castles and increasingly remote scenery. Further north, the **coast** offers some dramatic seascapes, punctuated by picturesque villages left almost unchanged by the centuries.

Aberdeen

The third-largest city in Scotland, **ABERDEEN**, commonly known as the Granite City, lies 120 miles northeast of Edinburgh on the banks of the rivers

Dee and Don, smack in the middle of the northeast coast. Based around a working harbour, it's a place that people either love or hate. Certainly, while some extol the many tones and colours of Aberdeen's **granite** buildings, others see only uniform grey and find the city grim, cold and unwelcoming. The weather doesn't help: Aberdeen lies on a latitude north of Moscow and the cutting wind and driving rain (even if it does transform the buildings into sparkling silver) can be tiresome.

Since the 1970s, **oil** has made Aberdeen a hugely wealthy and self-confident place: only four percent of Scotland's population live in the city, yet it has eight percent of the country's spending power. Despite (or perhaps because of) this, it can seem a soulless city; there's a feeling of corporate sterility and sometimes, despite its long history, Aberdeen seems to exist only as a departure point and service station for the transient population of some ten to fifteen thousand who live on the 130 oil platforms out to sea.

Staying in such a prosperous place has its advantages. There are plenty of good restaurants and hotels, local transport is efficient and certain sights, including Aberdeen's splendid **Art Gallery** and the excellent **Maritime Museum**, are free. Furthermore, the fact that the city is the bright light in a wide hinterland helps it to sustain a lively **nightlife**, with some decent pubs and a colourful arts and cultural scene.

Some history

In the twelfth century, Alexander I noted "Aberdon" as one of his principal towns, and by the thirteenth century it had become a centre for **trade and fishing**, a jumble of timber and wattle houses perched on three small hills, with the castle to the east and St Nicholas's Kirk outside the gates to the west.

It was here that **Robert the Bruce** sought refuge during the Scottish Wars of Independence, leading to the garrison of the castle by Edward I and Balliol's supporters. In a night-time raid in 1306, the townspeople attacked the garrison and killed them all, an event commemorated by the city's motto "Bon Accord", the watchword for the night. The victory was not to last, however,

Oil and Aberdeen

When **oil** was discovered in BP's Forties Field in 1970, Aberdonians rightly viewed it as a massive financial opportunity, and – despite fierce competition from other east coast British ports, Scandinavia and Germany – the city succeeded in persuading the oil companies to base their headquarters here. The city's **population** swelled by sixty thousand, and earnings escalated from fifteen percent below the national average to a figure well above it. At the peak of production in the **mid-1980s**, 2.6 million barrels a day were being turned out, and the price had reached $80 a barrel. The effect of the slump of 1986 – when oil prices dropped to $10 a barrel – was devastating: jobs vanished at the rate of a thousand a month, house prices dropped and Aberdeen soon discovered just how dependent on oil it was. The moment oil prices began to rise, crisis struck again with the loss of 167 lives when the **Piper Alpha oil rig** exploded, precipitating an array of much-needed but very expensive safety measures.

Oil remains the cornerstone of Aberdeen's economy, keeping unemployment down to one of the lowest levels in Britain and driving up house prices not just in the city itself but in an increasingly wide area of its rural hinterland. Predictions of the imminent decline in oil reserves and the end of Aberdeen's economic boom are heard frequently, as they have been since 1970, but reliable indicators suggest that the black gold will be flowing well into the new millennium.

and in 1337 Edward III stormed the city, forcing its rebuilding on a grander scale. A century later Bishop Elphinstone founded the Catholic university in the area north of town known today as **Old Aberdeen**, while the rest of the city developed as a mercantile centre and important port.

By the mid-twentieth century, Aberdeen's traditional industries were in decline, but the discovery of **oil** in the North Sea transformed the place from a depressed port into a boomtown (see box on p.1178). The oil-borne prosperity may have served to mask the thinness of the region's other wealth creators, but it has nonetheless allowed Aberdeen to hold its own as a cultural and academic centre and as a focus of the northeast's identity.

Arrival, information and city transport

Aberdeen's Dyce **airport**, seven miles northwest of town, is served by airport bus #27 and Aberdeen–Inverness bus #10, which both run to the city centre; a taxi costs approximately £13. The main **train station** is on Guild Street, in the centre of the city, with the **bus** terminal for intercity and regional services right beside it. Aberdeen is also linked to Lerwick in Shetland and Stromness in Orkney by **ferry**, with regular crossings provided by Northlink.

From the train and bus station it's a two-minute walk up the hill to Union Street, Aberdeen's main thoroughfare. The **tourist office**, 23 Union Street, is at the north end (July–Aug Mon–Sat 9am–7pm, Sun 10am–4pm; June & Sept Mon–Sat 9.30am–5pm; rest of year Mon–Sat 9am–5.30pm; ☎01224/288828, ⓦwww.agtb.org).

Aberdeen's centre is best explored on foot, but you might need to use **local buses**, almost all of which pass along Union Street. An all-day ticket covering all city bus routes costs £2.50 (£2.20 after 9.30am on weekdays). An open-topped **bus tour** passing by the main sights runs regularly throughout the summer (July–Sept). It leaves from outside the Town House on Union Street and costs £4 for a standard ticket or £6 for an "explorer" ticket, which includes all other local buses for the rest of the day.

Accommodation

As befits a high-flying business city, Aberdeen has a large choice of **accommodation** – much of it is characterless and expensive. Predictably, the best budget options are the **B&Bs** and **guest houses**, many of which are strung along Bon Accord and Crown streets (served by buses #6 and #17 to and from Union Street) and the Great Western Road (buses #18, #19 and #24).

Aberdeen Youth Hostel 8 Queens Rd ☎0870/004 1100, ⓔreservations@syha.org.uk. Rather soulless SYHA hostel with dorms for four to sixteen, and a 2am curfew. Bus #14 or #15 from Union St.

Allan Guest House 56 Polmuir Rd ☎01224 584484, ⓦwww.theallan.co.uk. Unexpectedly tasteful and enthusiastically run guest house not far from Duthie Park. Filling meals or a light supper available if arranged in advance. ❸

Braeside Guest House 68 Bon Accord St ☎01224/571471, ⓔcheynemcmenal@amserve.net. Standard but inexpensive B&B within easy walking distance of the station and city centre. ❶

Campbell's Guest House 444 King St ☎01224/625444, ⓦwww .campbellsguesthouse.com. Standard guest-house rooms but highly recommended breakfasts. One mile from the city centre and handy for the beach and Old Aberdeen. ❷

Ferryhill House 169 Bon Accord St ☎01224/590867. A mansion set apart in its own grounds within walking distance of Union St. Its historic pub has real ale, a beer garden and decent food. ❺

Globe Inn 13–15 North Silver St ☎01224/624258, ⓔinfo@the-globe-inn.com. Easy-going, traditional-style city-centre inn with seven en-suite rooms above a bar that regularly

23

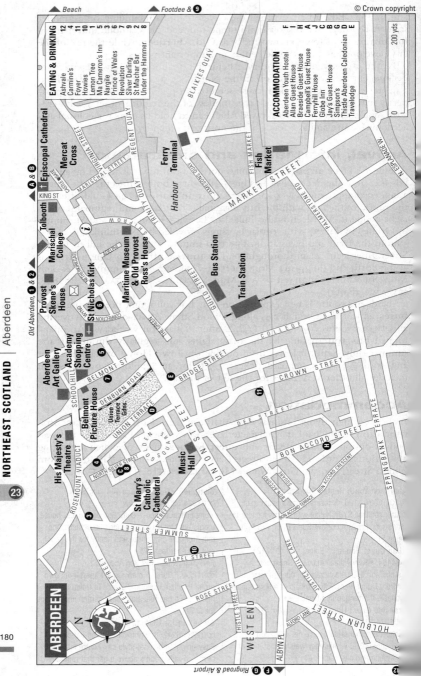

ABERDEEN

N

© Crown copyright

▲ Beach   ▲ Footdee & ❾

Old Aberdeen, ❶ & ❷

A & B

EATING & DRINKING
Ashvale	12
Carmine's	4
Foyer	11
Howies	10
Lemon Tree	1
Ma Cameron's Inn	5
Nargile	3
Prince of Wales	6
Revolution	7
Silver Darling	9
St Machar Bar	2
Under the Hammer	8

ACCOMMODATION
Aberdeen Youth Hostel	F
Allan Guest House	I
Braeside Guest House	H
Campbell's Guest House	A
Ferryhill Guest House	J
Globe Inn	C
Jay's Guest House	B
Simpson's	G
Thistle Aberdeen Caledonian	D
Travelodge	E

0   200 yds

Ringroad & Airport   ▲ ❻ ❼ ▲

Episcopal Cathedral

Mercat Cross

Tolbooth

Marischal College

Provost Skene's House

Maritime Museum & Old Provost Ross's House

St Nicholas Kirk

Aberdeen Art Gallery

Academy Shopping Centre

Belmont Picture House

His Majesty's Theatre

St Mary's Catholic Cathedral

Music Hall

Union Terrace Gdns.

Ferry Terminal

Harbour

Fish Market

Bus Station

Train Station

BLAIKIES QUAY

MARKET STREET

REGENT QUAY

CASTLE ST

KING ST

MARISCHAL STREET

VIRGINIA STREET

TRINITY QUAY

THE GREEN

GUILD STREET

COLLEGE STREET

BRIDGE STREET

UNION STREET

CROWN STREET

DEE STREET

BON ACCORD STREET

SPRINGBANK TERRACE

PALMERSTON ROAD

N ESPLANADE

M ESPLANADE

COLLEGE STREET

CORRECTION WYND

SCHOOLHILL

BELMONT ST

DENBURN ROAD

UNION TERRACE

GOLDEN SQUARE

N SILVER STREET

SUMMER STREET

ROSE STREET

SKENE STREET

ROSEMOUNT VIADUCT

THISTLE STREET

ALBYN PL

ALFORD LANE

JUSTICE MILL LANE

HOLBURN STREET

WEST END

CHAPEL STREET

HUNTLY STREET

BON ACCORD TERRACE

BON ACCORD CRESCENT

SQUARE

i

features live jazz. Rate includes continental breakfast. ❷

Jay's Guest House 422 King St ☎01224/638295, Ⓦwww.jaysguesthouse.co.uk. Well-run, nonsmoking place in Old Aberdeen, near the university. ❸

Simpson's 59–63 Queens Rd ☎01224/327777, Ⓦwww.simpsonshotel.co.uk. Highly style-conscious, terracotta-coloured modern interior to this large granite terraced house, with an excellent brasserie and good weekend rates. ❼

Thistle Aberdeen Caledonian 10–14 Union Terrace ☎01224/640233, Ⓦwww.thistlehotels.com. The best of the posh hotels, in an impressive Victorian edifice just off Union St. ❼

Travelodge 9 Bridge St ☎01224/584555, Ⓦwww.travelodge.co.uk. Typically bland budget hotel – but you can't beat the convenient location, right on Union St and minutes from the station. ❷

The City

Aberdeen divides neatly into five main areas. The **city centre** – roughly bounded by Broad Street, Union Street, Schoolhill and Union Terrace – features the opulent **Marischal College**, the colonnaded **Art Gallery** with its fine collection, the burgeoning nightlife of Belmont Street, and homes that predate Aberdeen's nineteenth-century town planning and have been preserved as **museums**. Union Street continues west to the tall grey townhouses of the comparatively cosmopolitan **West End**. To the south, the **harbour** still heaves with boats serving the fishing and oil industries, while north of the centre lies attractive **Old Aberdeen**, a village neighbourhood presided over by **King's College** and **St Machar Cathedral** and influenced by the large student population. The long sandy **beach** with its esplanade development, only a mile or so from the heart of the city, marks Aberdeen's eastern border.

The city centre

The centre of Aberdeen is dominated by mile-long **Union Street**, still the grandest and most ambitious single thoroughfare in Scotland – although these days its impressive architecture is sometimes lost among the shoppers and chain stores. The key for the early nineteenth-century city planners who conceived the street was the building of the ambitious **Union Street Bridge**, spanning two hills and the Denburn gorge. The famous Thomas Telford, called in as an adviser, proposed a single-arch structure which, when completed, became one of the engineering wonders of its age.

Castlegate and around

Any exploration of the **city centre** should begin at the open, cobbled **Castlegate**, where Aberdeen's long-gone castle once stood. At its centre is the late seventeenth-century **Mercat Cross**, carved with a unique gallery of Stewart sovereigns alongside some fierce gargoyles. Castlegate was once the focus of city life but nowadays is rather lifeless, with litter swirling around and pigeons easily outnumbering shoppers. However, the view up gently rising Union Street – a jumble of grey spires, turrets and jostling double-decker buses – is quintessential Aberdeen and well worth taking a moment or two to savour. Nearby, on King Street, the sandstone **St Andrew's Episcopal Cathedral** (mid-May to mid-Sept Mon–Sat 11am–4pm; free), offers a welcome relief from the uniform granite. Originally built in 1817, there have been a number of additions over the years, including various memorials to Samuel Seabury, who was ordained in Aberdeen in 1784 as the first bishop of America's Episcopal Church. Built between 1934 and 1943, the striking Seabury memorial restoration of the north and south aisles incorporates florid gold ceiling bosses that show the crests of the (then) 48 states of the USA.

△ Union Street, Aberde

Heading west, Union Street brings you to Broad Street where, at 45 Guestrow, **Provost Skene's House** (Mon–Sat 10am–5pm, Sun 1–4pm; free) is Aberdeen's oldest-surviving private house, dating from 1545; it's now a museum, with a costume gallery, archeological exhibits and a Painted Gallery, where a cycle of beautiful religious tempera paintings from the mid-seventeenth century show scenes from the life of Christ.

Marischal College and museum

On Broad Street itself stands Aberdeen's most imposing edifice, and the world's second-largest granite building after the Escorial in Madrid – the exuberant **Marischal College**, whose tall, steely-grey pinnacled neo-Gothic facade is in absolute contrast to the hideously utilitarian concrete office blocks which face it. This spectacular building, with all its soaring, surging lines, has been painted and sketched more than any other in Aberdeen, and though not to everyone's taste – it was once described by a minor art historian as "a wedding cake covered in indigestible grey icing" – there's no escaping the fact that it is a most extraordinary feat of sculpture. The facade was a 1906 addition to Archibald Simpson's marginally more modest 1837 construction, though the college itself was founded in 1593 by the fourth earl Marischal, and coexisted as a separate Protestant university from Catholic King's, just up the road, for over two centuries. It was long Aberdeen's boast that their city had as many universities as the whole of England, and it wasn't until 1860 that the two were united as the University of Aberdeen. The **Marischal Museum** (Mon–Fri 10am–5pm, Sun 2–5pm; free) is made up of two large rooms that contain a wealth of weird exhibits, many gathered by Victorian anthropologists and other collectors who roamed the world filling their luggage with objects. Sensitive to the cultural crassness this represents to the modern world, the museum concentrates as much on the phenomenon of these collectors as the objects they brought back.

The Aberdeen Art Gallery and around

A little further west, up Schoolhill, Aberdeen's engrossing **Art Gallery** (Mon–Sat 10am–5pm, Sun 2–5pm; free) was purpose-built in 1884 to a Neoclassical design by Mackenzie. You enter via the airy **Centre Court**, dominated by Barbara Hepworth's central fountain and the thick pillars running down from the upper balcony, each hewn from a different local marble. The walls here highlight the gallery's policy of acquiring contemporary art, with British work to the fore, including one of Francis Bacon's *Pope* paintings – the artist was obsessed with this subject for some thirty years and the series is considered his most important work. From here, the **Side Court** contains selected work by YBAs (Young British Artists) gifted by the Saatchi Collection in 2000, including Jordan Baseman's extraordinary *I Love You Still*, made from tree limbs and human hair.

The **upstairs** rooms house the main body of the gallery's painting collection. The permanent collection is occasionally moved around, and some of the rooms are given over to temporary and touring exhibitions: you'll find these advertised downstairs as well as in the local press.

Starting at the top of the staircase, the sheer number of landscapes crowding the walls of **Room One** can be disconcerting at first, but closer inspection reveals a superb collection of Victorian narrative art. **Room Two** takes a step back in history, concentrating on eighteenth-century painters such as landscape artist Alexander Nasmyth and Scotland's famous portraitists, Henry Raeburn and Alan Ramsay. **Room Three** is predictably popular for its Impressionist collection, including a deliciously bright Renoir, *La Roche Guyon*. The strong connections between the French schools and the development of modernism in Scottish painting saw the emergence of the "Glasgow Boys" in the 1880s (see p.1023), exemplified here by John Lavery's *The Tennis Party*. Inheritors of the Glasgow Boys' mantle, the now much-in-vogue Scottish Colourists, can be found in **Room Four**. Here, Peploe's *Landscape, Cassis* shows off his instinct for colour, with daringly angled foreground tree trunks in rich blue, chocolate and purple shadows. In **Room Six** and on the balcony overlooking the Central Court you'll find some superb works by British Impressionists and Modernists.

The harbour

The old cobbled road of Shiprow winds down from Castlegate at the east end of Union Street to the north side of the **harbour**. Just off this steep road, peering out at the harbour through a striking modern glass facade, is the **Maritime Museum** (Mon–Sat 10am–5pm, Sun noon–3pm; free), which combines a thoroughly modern, airy museum with Aberdeen's oldest-surviving building, **Old Provost Ross's House**, laced with labyrinthine corridors, low doorways and small rooms. The marriage has been successful, and the museum is a thoroughly engrossing, imaginatively designed tribute to Aberdeen's maritime traditions.

Suspended above the foyer and visible from five different levels is a spectacular 27ft-high model of an oil rig, which, along with terrific views over the bustling harbour, serves as a constant reminder that Aberdeen's maritime links are very much alive today. While large sections of the museum are devoted to telling the story of North Sea oil and gas production, the older industries of herring-fishing, whaling, shipbuilding and lighthouses also have their place, with well-designed displays and audiovisual presentations, many of which draw heavily on personal reminiscences. Passages lead from various levels of the museum into Provost Ross's House, where intricate ship's models and a variety of nautical paintings and drawings are on display.

At the bottom of Shiprow, the cobbles meet Market Street, which runs the length of the **harbour**. Here, brightly painted oil-supply ships, sleek cruise ships and peeling fishing boats jostle for position to an ever-constant clatter and the screech of well-fed seagulls. With high fences, rushing traffic and a series of drab office blocks, it's not the most attractive part of the city, but you'll encounter plenty of life and colour if you follow your nose down the road to the **fish market**, at Blaikies Quay, best visited early (7–8am) when the place is in full swing.

Back at the north end of Market Street, Trinity Quay runs to the shipbuilding yards and down York Street to the east corner of the harbour. Here you'll come to Aberdeen's **Footdee** or Fittie (an easy walk or bus #14 or #15 from Union Street), a quaint nineteenth-century fishermen's village of higgledy-piggledy cottages. Here, in a great setting beside the lighthouse which marks the channel into the harbour, you'll find the *Silver Darling* (see opposite), one of the finest seafood restaurants in the Northeast.

Old Aberdeen

An independent burgh until 1891, the tranquil district of **Old Aberdeen**, twenty-minute ride north of the city centre on bus #20 from Marischal College at Littlejohn Street, has always maintained a separate village-like identity, and its medieval cobbled streets, tiny wynds and little lanes are beautifully preserved. The southern half of High Street is overlooked by **King's College Chapel** (Mon–Fri 8am–4pm; free), the first and finest of the college buildings completed in 1495, with a chunky Renaissance spire. Named in honour of James IV, the chapel's west door is flanked by his coat of arms and those of his queen. The highlight of the interior, which unusually has no central aisle, are the ribbed arched wooden ceiling and the rare and beautiful examples of medieval Scottish woodcarving seen in the screen and the stalls.

From the college, the cobbled High Street leads a short way north to **St Machar Cathedral** on the leafy Chanonry (daily 9am–5pm, except during services; free), overlooking Seaton Park and the River Don. The site was reputedly founded in 580 by Machar, a follower of Columba, when he was sent by the latter to find a grassy platform near the sea, overlooking a river shaped like the crook on a bishop's crozier. This setting fitted the bill perfectly, and the cathedral, a huge fifteenth-century fortified building, became one of the city's first great granite edifices.

The beach

Aberdeen can surely claim to have the best **beach** of all Britain's large cities. Less than a mile east of Union Street is a great two-mile sweep of clean sand, broken by groynes and lined all along with an esplanade, where most of the city's population seems to gather on a sunny day. Towards the southern end of the beach is a burgeoning concrete expanse of cinemas and fast-food outlets, a couple of fairly tatty amusement parks and a vast leisure centre. As you head further north, most of the beach's hinterland is devoted to successive golf links. Bus #14 goes along the southern esplanade.

A few hundred yards inland, the city's old tram depot at 179 Constitution Street, just across from the *Patio Hotel*, houses **Satrosphere** (Mon–Sat 10am–5pm, Sun 11.30am–5pm; £5.25; Ⓦ www.satrosphere.net), Aberdeen's thoroughly entertaining hands-on science exhibition.

Eating, drinking and nightlife

You'll find most of the more attractive **cafés** and **restaurants** on Union Street and its surrounds. Like most ports Aberdeen caters for a transient population with a lot of disposable income and a desire to get drunk as quickly as possible. Although you'll find no shortage of loud, flashy **bars** catering to such needs, there are still a number of more traditional old **pubs** which, though usually packed, are well worth a visit.

Cafés and restaurants

Ashvale 46 Great Western Rd. One of Scotland's finest, and biggest, fish-and-chip shops, with seating for 300. Restaurant open daily until 11pm; takeaway until 1am. Inexpensive.

Carmine's 32 Union Terrace ☏ 01224/624145. An Aberdeen institution, featuring an amazing three-course lunchtime menu of Italian staples for less than a fiver. Also open early evening. Inexpensive.

Foyer 82a Crown St ☏ 01224/582277. A top-notch contemporary bistro in a tastefully converted church, acting as the commercial arm of a charity for the disadvantaged young people and the homeless. Moderate.

Lowies 50 Chapel St ☏ 01224/639500. The Aberdeen outpost of an Edinburgh institution, serving modern Scottish cooking in a very accessible environment. Good-price set-meal deals and cheap house wine. Moderate.

Lemon Tree 5 West North St. Easy-going café inside the arts centre, serving good vegetarian and vegan snacks and meals. Inexpensive.

Nargile Corner of Skene & Summer streets ☏ 01224/636093. Much loved and highly regarded family-run Turkish restaurant. The smaller, more casual *Nargile Meze Bar* is on Rose St. Moderate.

Silver Darling Pocra Quay, North Pier ☏ 01224/576229. Attractively located right at the mouth of the Dee in Footdee, this impressive restaurant majors in sophisticated French seafood dishes. Closed Sat lunch & Sun. Expensive.

Pubs and bars

Ma Cameron's Inn 6 Little Belmont St.

23

Aberdeen's oldest pub, though only a section of the original building remains. Serves food.

Prince of Wales 7 St Nicholas Lane. The quintessential Aberdeen pub with a long bar and flagstone floor. With fine pub grub, renowned real ales and a Sunday evening folk session, it's little wonder that it's often crowded.

Revolution 25 Belmont St. Stylish bar with explosive cocktails and a perfect understanding of the vagaries of Scottish weather – there's a fire and comfy sofas as you go in, and rooftop alfresco drinking out back.

St Machar Bar 97 High St, Old Aberdeen. The medieval quarter's only pub, a poky, old-fashioned bar attracting an intriguing mix of King's College students and workers.

Under the Hammer 11 North Silver St. This snug little basement wine bar with a continental vibe is a popular refuge when icy winter winds hit the city.

Clubs and live music venues

The Blue Lamp 121 Gallowgate. A big bar featuring live bands (Fri & Sat) and a folk session (Mon); there's also a much smaller snug for relative peace and quiet.

Drummonds 1 Belmont St. Unapologetically murky bar, providing a welcome contrast to more glossy neighbours, that has undergone a renaissance since putting the emphasis back onto live music; the intimate stage area attracts plenty of upcoming talent and the occasional big name.

The Globe Inn 13–15 North Silver St. Pleasant city-centre inn with jamming sessions on Tuesdays and live jazz, blues and covers bands on Thurs, Fri, Sat & Sun.

Lemon Tree 5 West North St ☎01224/642230, ⓦ www.lemontree.org. The fulcrum of the city's arts scene, with a great buzz and regular live music, comedy and folk.

The Priory St Nicholas Hall, 33 Belmont St ☎01224/625555. Converted two-tier church building pumping out chart sounds onto increasingly flash Belmont St; often packed to the rafters with a young crowd.

Theatres and cinemas

Belmont Picture House 9 Belmont St ☎01224/343536, ⓦ www.picturehouses.co.uk. Art-house cinema showing the more cultured new releases and a back-list of classic, cult and foreign-language films. There's a decent café inside and some good places nearby for a bite before or after.

Lemon Tree 5 West North St ☎01224/642230, ⓦ www.lemontree.org. Avant-garde events with off-the-wall comedians and plays, many coming hotfoot from the Edinburgh festivals.

UGC Beach Esplanade ☎0870/155 0502. Huge multiplex cinema in a beachside development, showing all the mainstream releases.

Listings

Airport ☎01224/722331.

Bike rental Alpine Bikes, 66–70 Holburn St ☎01224/211455; Cycling World, 460 George St ☎01224/632994.

Bookshops The largest are Waterstone's, 269–271 Union St, and Ottakar's, in Trinity Shopping Centre, Union Bridge. Bon Accord Books, 69–75 Spital, is the best for secondhand.

Bus information Grampian Transport Busline ☎01224/650065.

Car rental Arnold Clark ☎01224/249159, airport ☎01224/663723; Budget ☎01224/793333, airport ☎01224/771777; National ☎0870/400 4502.

Exchange Thomas Cook in the Bon Accord Centre (Mon, Wed, Fri, Sat 9am–5.30pm, Tues 10am–5.30pm, Thurs 9am–8pm, Sun noon–5pm; ☎01224/807100).

Ferry information ☎0845/600 0449, ⓦ www.northlinkferries.co.uk.

Internet There's free access in the Reference section of the main library on Rosemount Viaduct (Mon–Thurs 9am–8pm, Fri & Sat 9am–5pm). Otherwise, try the tourist office, 23 Union St, and Costa Coffee on Loch St, at the back of the Bon Accord Centre.

Left luggage Small 24hr lockers at the train station cost £2–4.

Medical facilities The Royal Infirmary, on Foresterhill, northeast of the town centre, has a 24hr casualty department (☎01224/681818). Boots pharmacy is at 161 Union St (Mon–Sat 8am–6pm; ☎01224/211592). Late-night pharmacies are listed each day in the Evening Express.

Police Main station is on Queen St ☎01224/386000.

Post office The central post office is in the St Nicholas Centre, between Union St and Upperkirkgate (Mon–Sat 9am–5.30pm), with a branch at 489 Union St (Mon–Fri 9am–5.30pm, Sat 9am–12.30pm).

Taxis ComCab ☎01224/353535.

Stonehaven and the Mearns

South of Aberdeen, the A92 and the main train line follow the coast to the busy, pebble-dashed town, **STONEHAVEN**, which attracts hordes of holiday-makers in the summer due to its sheltered Kincardine coastline, and in mid-July in particular because of its respected **folk festival**. The town itself is split into two parts, the picturesque working harbour area being most likely to detain you. The old High Street, lined with some fine townhouses and civic buildings, connects the harbour and its surrounding old town with the late eighteenth-century planned centre on the other side of the River Carron. On New Year's Eve, High Street is the location for the ancient ceremony of **Fireballs**, when locals parade its length swinging metal cages full of burning debris around their heads to ward off evil spirits for the year ahead. In the northern part of the town is Stonehaven's wonderful open-air Art Deco **swimming pool** (June Mon–Fri 1–7.30pm, Sat & Sun 10am–6pm; July–Aug Mon–Fri 10am–7.30pm, Sat & Sun 10am–6pm; £3.20), opened in 1934 and always packed with locals on a sunny day. As well as regular daytime hours, it's open for midnight swims on Wednesday evenings (July & Aug 10pm–midnight).

The **tourist office** is at 66 Allardice St, the main street past the square (July & Aug Mon–Sat 10am–7pm, Sun 1–6pm; April–June, Sept & Oct Mon–Sat 10am–5pm; ℡01569/762806). For **B&B** accommodation, try *Arduthie House* on Ann Street (℡01569/762381, ℮arduthie@talk21.com; ❸) or, a few miles south of town on the A92, *Dunnottar Mains Farm* (℡01569/762621, ⓦwww.dunnottarmains.co.uk; ❷). For **food**, the *Tolbooth Seafood Restaurant* (℡01569/762287; closed Mon), above the museum on the harbour, is the place to go; for cheaper **pub** food or just a drink, try the entertaining *Marine Hotel* or the attractive *Ship Inn*, both on the harbour.

Dunnottar Castle and Arbuthnott

Two miles south of Stonehaven (the tourist office sells a walking guide for the scenic amble), **Dunnottar Castle** (Easter–Oct Mon–Sat 9am–6pm, Sun 2–5pm; Nov–Easter Fri–Mon 9am–4pm, Dec & Jan closes 3pm; £3.50) is one of the finest of Scotland's ruined castles, a huge ninth-century fortress set on a three-sided sheer cliff jutting into the sea – a setting striking enough to be chosen as the backdrop for Zeffirelli's movie version of *Hamlet*. Once the principal fortress of the northeast, the ruins are worth a good root around, and there are any number of dramatic views out to the crashing sea. Siege and bloodstained drama splatter the castle's past: in 1297 the whole English Plantagenet garrison were burnt alive here by William Wallace, while one of the more gruesome tales from the castle's history tells of the imprisonment and torture of 122 men and 45 women Covenanters in 1685 – an event, as it says on the Covenanters' Stone in the churchyard, "whose dark shadow is for ever-more flung athwart the Castled Rock".

Inland from here is the **Mearns**, an agricultural district of scattered popula-tion and gathering hills. The straggling village of **ARBUTHNOTT** was the home of prolific local author, Lewis Grassic Gibbon (1901–35), whose roman-ticized realism perfectly encapsulates the spirit of the agricultural Mearns area. *Sunset Song*, his most famous work, is an essential read for those travelling in this area. The community-run **Grassic Gibbon Centre** (April–Oct daily 10am–4.30pm; £2.50), on the B967 through the village, is a great introduction to this fascinating and self-assured man who died so young. He is buried (under his real name of James Leslie Mitchell) in the corner of the little village grave-yard, overlooking the forested banks of the Bervie Water off the main road.

Deeside

More commonly known as **Royal Deeside**, the land stretching west from Aberdeen along the River Dee revels in its connections with the royal family, who have regularly holidayed here, at **Balmoral**, since Queen Victoria bought the estate. Eighty thousand Scots turned out to welcome her on her first visit in 1848, but some weren't so charmed: one local journalist remarked that the area was about to be "desolated by cockneys and other horrible reptiles". Today, most locals are fiercely protective of the royal connection.

Many of Victoria's guests weren't as enthusiastic about Deeside as she was: Count von Moltke, then aide-de-camp to Prince Frederick William of Prussia, observed, "It is very astonishing that the Royal Power of England should reside amid this lonesome, desolate, cold mountain scenery", while Tsar Nicholas II whined, "The weather is awful, rain and wind every day and on top of it no luck at all – I haven't killed a stag yet." However, Victoria adored the place, and the woods were said to remind Prince Albert of Thuringia, his homeland.

Deeside is undoubtedly handsome in a fierce, craggy, Scottish way, and the royal presence has helped keep a lid on any unattractive mass development. The villages strung along the A93, the main route through the area, are well heeled and have something of an old-fashioned air. Facilities for visitors hereabouts are first-class, with a number of bunkhouses and hostels, some outstanding hotels and plenty of castles and grounds to snoop around. It's also an excellent area for **outdoor activities**, with hiking routes into both the Grampian and Cairngorm mountains, and good mountain biking, horse riding and skiing.

Stagecoach Bluebird **bus** #201 from Aberdeen regularly chugs along the A93, serving most of the towns on the way to Braemar.

West of Aberdeen

Ten miles west of Aberdeen on the A93, **Drum Castle** (daily: June–Aug 10am–5.30pm; April, May & Sept 12.30–5.30pm; grounds 9.30am–sunset all year; £7, grounds only £2.50; NTS) stands in a clearing in the ancient **woods of Drum**, made up of the splendid pines and oaks that covered this whole area before the shipbuilding industry precipitated mass forest clearance. The castle itself combines a 1619 Jacobean mansion with Victorian extensions and the original, huge thirteenth-century keep, which has been restored and reopened.

Four miles west of Drum Castle, **Crathes Castle** (daily: April–Sept 10am–5.30pm; Oct 10am–4.30pm; £7; NTS) is a splendid sixteenth-century granite tower house adorned with flourishes such as overhanging turrets, gargoyles and conical roofs. Its thick walls, narrow windows and tiny rooms loaded with heavy old furniture make Crathes rather claustrophobic, but it's still worth visiting for some wonderful painted ceilings, either still in their original form or sensitively restored; the earliest dates from 1602. The grounds include an impressive walled garden complete with yew hedges clipped into various shapes.

Twelve miles further west on the A93, **ABOYNE** is a typically well-mannered Deeside village at the mouth of **Glen Tanar**, which runs southwest from here for ten miles or so deep into the Grampian hills. The glen, with few steep gradients and some glorious stands of mature Caledonian pine, is ideal for walking, mountain biking or horse riding; the ranger information point two miles int the glen off the B976 has details of suitable routes, while the Glen Tanar Equestrian Centre (℡01339/886448) offers one- and two-hour horse rides.

Ballater and Balmoral

Ten miles west of Aboyne is the neat and ordered town of **BALLATER**, attractively hemmed in by the river and fir-covered mountains. It was in Ballater that Queen Victoria first arrived in Deeside by train from Aberdeen back in 1848; she wouldn't allow a station to be built any closer to Balmoral, eight miles further west. Although the line has long been closed, the town's rather self-important royalism is much in evidence at the restored **train station** in the centre (daily June–Sept 9am–6pm, Oct–May 10am–5pm), where various video presentations and life-sized models relive the comings and goings of generations of royals. The local shops, having provided Balmoral with groceries and household basics, also flaunt their connections, with oversized "By Appointment" crests sported above the doorways of most businesses from the butcher to the newsagent.

If you prefer to discover the fresh air and natural beauty that Victoria came to love so much, Ballater is an excellent base for local **walks and outdoor activities**. There are numerous hikes from Loch Muik (pronounced "mick"), nine miles southwest of town, including the strenuous all-day trek up and around Lochnagar (3789ft), the mountain much painted and written about by the current prince of Wales. Good-quality **bikes** can be rented from Wheelin' Around (℡013397/55864), based in the Pavilion, Victoria Road (opposite the *Lauriston Hotel*).

Practicalities

The **tourist office** is in the renovated train station (daily June–Sept 9am–6pm, Oct–March 10am–5pm; ℡013397/55306). There are plenty of reasonable **B&Bs** in town, including the nonsmoking *Inverdeen House*, on Bridge Square (℡013397/55759, ⓦwww.inverdeen.com; ❸), which offers a wide choice of breakfasts, most involving local produce and home baking. A few miles north of town on the road to Tomintoul is *Gairnshiel Lodge* (℡013397/55582, ⓦwww.gairnshiellodge.co.uk; ❸). In a remote but beautiful setting, it's a particularly child-friendly place and a great base for walking or cycling. For **camping**, head for *Anderson Road Caravan Park* (℡013397/55727; Easter–Oct) down towards the river.

Balmoral Estate

Originally a sixteenth-century tower house built for the powerful Gordon family, **Balmoral Castle** (April–July daily 10am–5pm; £5; ⓦwww. balmoralcastle.com) has been a royal residence since 1852, when it was converted to the Scots baronial mansion that stands today. The Royal Family traditionally spend their summer holidays here each August, but despite its fame can be something of a disappointment even for a dedicated royalist. For the four months when the doors are nudged open, the general riffraff are permitted to view only the ballroom, an exhibition room and the grounds; for the rest of the year it's not even visible to the paparazzi who have been known to snoop around with their long lenses.

Braemar

Continuing westwards for another few miles, the road rises to 1100ft above sea level in the upper part of Deeside and the village of **BRAEMAR**, situated where three passes meet and overlooked by an unremarkable **castle** (July & Aug daily 10am–6pm; Easter–June & Sept–Oct closed Fri; £3.50). Signs as you enter Braemar boast that it's an "Award-Winning Tourist Village", which just about sums it up, as everything seems to have been prettified to within an inch of its life. That said, it's an invigorating, outdoor kind of place, well patronized by committed hikers, but probably best known for its Highland Games, the annual **Braemar Gathering**, on the first Saturday of September (Ⓦ www.braemargathering.org). Since Queen Victoria's day, successive generations of royals have attended, and the world's most famous Highland Games have become rather an overcrowded, overblown event. You're not guaranteed to get in if you just turn up; the website has details of how to book tickets in advance.

Braemar's **tourist office** is in the modern building known as the Mews, in the middle of the village on Mar Road (July & Aug daily 9am–7pm; June & Sept daily 10am–6pm; Oct–May Mon–Sat 10am–1.30pm & 2–4.30pm, Sun noon–4.30pm; ☏013397/41600). *Clunie Lodge Guest House*, Clunie Bank Road (☏013397/41330, Ⓔ clunielodge@msn.com; ❷), on the edge of town, is a good **B&B** with lovely views up Clunie Glen. The cheery *Rucksacks*, an easy-going bunkhouse well equipped for walkers and backpackers, is just behind the Mews complex (☏013397/41517), while the *Invercauld Caravan Club Park* (☏013397/41373), just south of the village off Glenshee Road, has fifteen **camping** pitches.

For **food**, try either *Taste*, a coffee shop and moderately priced, contemporary restaurant on the road out to the Linn of Dee, or *The Gathering Place*, a pleasant bistro with reasonably priced meat and game dishes in the heart of the village.

Speyside

Strictly speaking, the term "**Speyside**" should refer to the entire region surrounding the Spey River, but to most people the name is synonymous with the **whisky triangle**, stretching from just north of Craigellachie down towards Tomintoul in the south, and east to Huntly. Indeed, there are more whisky distilleries and famous brands concentrated in this small area (including Glenfiddich and Glenlivet) than in any other part of the country. Running through the heart of the region is the River Spey, whose clean, clear, fast-running waters not only play such a vital part in the whisky industry, but are also home to thousands of salmon, making it one of Scotland's finest angling locations. At the centre of Speyside is the quiet market town of **Dufftown**, full of solid, stone-built workers' houses and dotted with no fewer than nine whisky distilleries. Along with the well-kept nearby village of **Craigellachie** and **Aberlour**, it makes the best base for a tour of whisky country, whether on the official Malt Whisky Trail or more independent explorations.

Dufftown

The cheery community of **DUFFTOWN**, founded in 1817 by James Duff, the fourth earl of Fife, proudly proclaims itself "Malt Whisky Capital of the World" – it exports more of the stuff than anywhere else in Britain. There isn't a great deal to do in the town, but it's a useful starting point for orienting yourself towards the whisky trail. On the edge of town along the

The Speyside Way

The **Speyside Way**, with its beguiling mix of mountain, river, wildlife and whisky, is fast establishing itself as an appealing alternative to the popular West Highland and Southern Upland long-distance footpaths. Starting at **Buckie** on the Moray Firth coast (see p.1195), it follows the fast-flowing River Spey from its mouth at Spey Bay south to **Aviemore** (see p.1213), with branches linking it to **Dufftown**, Scotland's malt whisky capital, and **Tomintoul** on the remote edge of the Cairngorm mountains. Some 65 miles long without taking on the branch routes, the whole thing is a five- to seven-day expedition, but its proximity to main roads and small villages means that it is excellent for shorter walks or even bicycle trips, especially in the heart of **distillery** country between Craigellachie and Glenlivet: Glenfiddich, Glenlivet, Macallan and Cardhu distilleries, as well as the Speyside Cooperage, lie directly on or a short distance off the route. Other highlights include the chance to encounter an array of **wildlife**, from dolphins at Spey Bey to ospreys at Loch Garten, as well as the restored **railway** trips on offer at Dufftown and Aviemore. The path uses disused railway lines for much of its length, and there are simple campsites and good B&Bs at strategic points along the route. For more details contact the Speyside Way Visitor Centre at Craigellachie (℡01340/881266, ⓦwww.speysideway.org).

A941 is the town's largest working distillery, **Glenfiddich** (see p.1192), as well as the old Dufftown train station, which has been restored by enthusiasts in recent years.

Dufftown's four main streets converge on Main Square. The official **tourist office** is located inside the handsome clocktower at the centre of the square (July & Aug Mon–Sat 10am–6pm, Sun 1–6pm; April–June, Sept & Oct Mon–Sat 10am–1pm & 2–5pm; ℡01340/820501), though an informal information and accommodation booking service has developed at *The Whisky Shop* (℡01340/821097) across the road.

There's a handful of **places to stay** in Dufftown itself, although you may choose to look elsewhere on Speyside where you'll feel a bit closer to the attractive countryside. The only **hostel** accommodation nearby is the small self-catering *Swan Bunkhouse* (℡01542/810334), located at Drummuir, three miles northeast of Dufftown. In town, *Tannochbrae*, 22 Fife St (℡01340/820541, ⓦwww.tannochbrae.co.uk; ❷) is a pleasant, enthusiastically run place with a small restaurant, *Scott's*, on the ground floor.

Craigellachie

Four miles north of Dufftown, and linked by a spur of the Speyside Way which follows the disused railway track, the small settlement of **CRAIGELLACHIE** (pronounced "Craig-*ell*-ach-ee") sits above the confluence of the sparkling waters of the Fiddich and the Spey. For an unusual alternative to a distillery tour, the **Speyside Cooperage** (Mon–Fri 9.30am–4.30pm; £3.10) is well worth a visit. After a short exhibition explaining the ancient and skilled art of cooperage, you're shown onto a balcony overlooking the large workshop where the oak casks for whisky are made and repaired by fast-working, highly skilled coopers.

On the edge of Craigellachie, by the River Fiddich on the A95 Huntly road, there's a **visitor centre** for the Speyside Way (Easter–Oct generally daily 9am–5pm; ℡01340/881266), which sells maps of the route and gives advice on what to look for along the way. For somewhere to **stay** in the village there's an extremely welcoming and tasteful B&B attached to the *Green Hall Gallery*

Touring malt whisky country

It sometimes comes as a surprise to visitors that a lot of whisky distilleries are unglamorous industrial units, and by no means all are open to the public. Having said that, there are plenty located in attractive historic buildings which now go to some lengths to provide an engaging experience for visitors. Mostly this involves a tour around the essential stages in the whisky-making process, though if you're a real enthusiast a number of distilleries now offer pricier connoisseur tours with a tutored tasting (or **nosing**, as it's properly called) and in-depth studies of the distiller's art.

There are eight distilleries on the official **Malt Whisky Trail**, a clearly signposted seventy-mile meander around the region. Unless you're seriously interested in whisky, it's best to just pick out a couple that appeal. The following are selected highlights:

Cardhu, on the B9102 at Knockando (Easter–June Mon–Fri 10am–5pm; July–Sept Mon–Sat 10am–5pm, Sun noon–4pm; Oct Mon–Fri 11am–4pm; Nov–Easter Mon–Fri tours at 11am, 1pm & 2pm; £4 including voucher). This distillery was established over a century ago when the founder's wife was kind enough to raise a red flag to warn local crofters if the authorities were on the lookout for their illegal stills. Attractive, pagoda-topped buildings in a nice location, which sells rich, full-bodied whisky which has distinctive peaty flavours and comes in an attractive bulbous bottle.

Glen Grant, Rothes (April–Oct Mon–Sat 10am–4pm, Sun 12.30–4pm; free). A well-known, floral whisky aggressively marketed to a younger market. A regular, well-informed tour, but the highlight here is the attractive Victorian gardens, a mix of well-tended lawns and mature trees, which include a tumbling waterfall and a hidden whisky safe.

Glenfiddich, on the A941 just north of Dufftown (April to mid-Oct Mon–Sat 9.30am–4.30pm, Sun noon–4.30pm; mid-Oct to March Mon–Fri 9.30am–4.30pm; free). Probably the best known of the malt whiskies, and the biggest and slickest of all the distilleries, despite the fact that it's still owned by the same Grant family that founded it in 1887. It's a light, sweet whisky which comes in triangular shaped bottles. Uniquely, the whisky is bottled on the premises – an interesting process to watch. The tours (available in various languages) are informative, though the place is thronged with tourists. Connoisseurs' Tour available (£12).

Glenlivet, on the B9008 to Tomintoul (April–Oct Mon–Sat 10am–4pm, Sun 12.30–4pm; free). A famous name in a lonely hillside setting. A stretch of the

on Victoria Street (℡01340/871010, ⓦ www.greenhall-gallery.co.uk; ❷); in Archiestown, a few miles west of Craigellachie, the pleasant, traditional *Archiestown Hotel* (℡01340/810218, ⓦ www.archiestownhotel.co.uk; ❺) caters for fishermen and outdoor types, and serves good evening **meals**.

The coast

The **coast** of northeast Scotland from Aberdeen to Inverness is a rugged, often bleak, landscape. Still, if the weather is good, it's well worth spending a couple of days meandering through the various little fishing villages and along the miles of deserted, unspoilt beaches. Keen walkers have the best run of the area: some of the cliffs are so steep that you have to hike considerable distances to get the optimum views of the coast.

The largest coastal towns are **Peterhead** and **Fraserburgh**, both dominated by sizeable fishing fleets; while neither has much to offer, the latter's Museum

Speyside Way passes through the distillery grounds. This was the first licensed distillery in the Highlands, following the 1823 Act of Parliament which aimed to reduce illicit distilling and smuggling. The Glenlivet twelve-year-old malt is a floral, fragrant medium-bodied whisky.

Strathisla, Keith (April–Oct Mon–Sat 10am–4pm, Sun 12.30–4pm; £5). A small old-fashioned distillery claiming to be Scotland's oldest (1786); it's certainly one of the most attractive, with classic pagoda-shaped buildings and the Isla River rushing by. Inside there are some impressive and interesting bits of equipment such as an old-fashioned mashtun and brass-bound spirit safes. The malt itself has a rich almost fruity taste and is pretty rare, but is used as the heart of the better-known Chivas Regal blend.

In addition, the **Speyside Cooperage** at Craigellachie (see p.1191) is part of the official trail but offers an alternative to a distillery tour.

There are also a number of other distilleries, not on the official trail, that you can visit:

Macallan, near Craigellachie (April–Oct Mon–Sat 9.30am–5pm, Nov–March Mon–Fri 11am–3pm; ☎01340/872280) can only take ten people on its tours, and therefore doesn't get the coaches pulling in. It has a modern visitor centre and three different tours: the half-hour "Macallan experience" (free), a one-hour, in-depth "Spirit of Macallan" tour (£8), and the "Macallan Precious Whisky Tour" which includes a tutored nosing of four different Macallan whiskies. Bookings are essential for both the latter two tours.

Cragganmore, at Ballindalloch (tours June–Sept Mon–Fri 10am, 1pm & 3pm; booking essential ☎01479/874700; £5 including discount voucher), also offers a personalized, exclusive tour that includes a tasting.

Aberlour, on the outskirts of the village (April–Oct; £7.50; booking essential ☎01340/881249). The twice-daily tours are also quite specialized, with a tutored nosing and the chance to buy and fill your own bottle of cask-strength single malt.

Glendronach, eight miles northeast of Huntly (tours Mon–Fri 10am & 2pm; free). An isolated distillery that makes much of its malt's place at the heart of the well-known *Teacher's* blend, as well as the fact that, uniquely, the stills are heated in the traditional method by coal fires.

of Scottish Lighthouses is one of the most attractive small museums in Scotland. More appealing to most visitors are the quieter spots along the Moray coast, including the charming villages of **Pennan**, **Portsoy** and nearby Cullen. The other main attractions are **Duff House** in Banff, a branch of the National Gallery of Scotland; the working abbey at **Pluscarden** by Elgin; and the **Findhorn Foundation**, near Forres.

The main towns and larger villages are fairly well served by **buses**, while **trains** from Aberdeen and Inverness stop at Elgin, Forres and Nairn. Even so, it's preferable to have your own transport for reaching some of the far-flung places.

Peterhead

PETERHEAD, the easternmost mainland town in Scotland, stands in sharp contrast to the picturesque fishing villages on this stretch of coast. As notable for its high-security prison and ugly power station as its busy harbour, it's an unashamedly functional place. Although in recent years the oil industry has created a surge in wealth and population, Peterhead's *raison d'être* is **fishing**, and it was for many years the busiest white-fish port in Europe. The oldest building in town is the 400-year-old **Ugie Salmon Fish House** on Golf Road at the mouth of the River Ugie, at the north end of town (Mon–Fri 9am–5pm, Sat 9am–noon; free), where you can watch the traditional methods of oak-smoking salmon and trout in Scotland's oldest smokehouse; the finished product is for sale at reasonable prices. On the beach just off the main road, one of the town's newest buildings houses the **Peterhead Maritime Heritage**, a combined college and museum (June–Aug Mon–Sat 10.30am–5pm, Sun 11.30am–5pm; £3) that tells the story of the town's fishing industry from the old herring fleet to the modern day.

Fraserburgh and the north coast

FRASERBURGH is a large and fairly severe-looking place in the same vein as Peterhead, although its economy still relies on fishing alone. At the northern tip of the town, an eighteenth-century lighthouse protrudes from the top of sixteenth-century **Fraserburgh Castle**, where the highest wind speeds on mainland Britain were recorded in 1989 (they reached 140mph). The lighthouse was one of the first to be built in Scotland and is now part of the excellent **Museum of Scottish Lighthouses** (April–Oct Mon–Sat 10am–5pm, Sun noon–5pm, plus July & Aug open till 6pm; Nov–March Mon–Sat 11am–4pm, Sun noon–4pm; £3.50), where you can see a collection of huge lenses and prisms gathered from decommissioned lighthouses, and a display on various members of the famous "Lighthouse" Stevenson family, who designed many of them (including the father and grandfather of author Robert Louis Stevenson). Highlight of the museum is the tour of Kinnaird Head light itself, preserved as it was when the last keeper left in 1991, with its century-old equipment still in perfect working order.

Next door, and also well worth a visit, is the **Fraserburgh Heritage Centre** (April–Oct Mon–Sat 11am–5pm, Sun 1–5pm; £2.50), a wide-ranging exhibition on the history of the town with small boats, audiovisual presentations, and details of some experiments in wireless communication performed in town by Marconi in 1904.

West of Fraserburgh

The coast road between Fraserburgh and Pennan, twelve miles west, is particularly attractive: it's lined with pretty churches and cottages, while countless paths lead off it to ruined castles, cliff-top walks and lonely beaches. **PENNAN** itself, a tiny fishing hamlet, lies just off the road, down a steep and hazardous hill. Consisting of little more than a single row of whitewashed stone cottages tucked between a cliff and the sea, the village leapt into the limelight when the British movie *Local Hero* was filmed here in 1982. You can stay at one of the identifiable landmarks from the film, the *Pennan Inn* (℡01346/561201, Ⓦwww.thepennaninn.com; ❸), a convivial, lively spot with an excellent, moderately priced seafood **restaurant** and a cosy bar, whose customers spill out onto the sea wall on summer evenings. The tiny village of **CROVIE** (pronounced "crivie", where locals frequently have their doorsteps washed by the sea, is just as appealing. Tucked against the steep cliffs, it's so narrow that its residents have to park at one end of the village and continue to their houses on foot. **GARDEN STOWN**, another village of the same style on the other side of Troup Head from Pennan, is a little larger and slightly down-at-heel, but has a nice beach.

Macduff and Banff

Heading west along the coast from Pennan brings you, after ten miles,

MACDUFF and its neighbour **BANFF**, separated by little more than the beautiful seven-arch bridge over the River Deveron. Banff's **tourist office** (July & Aug Mon–Sat 10am–1pm & 2–6pm, Sun 1–6pm; April–June & Sept Mon–Sat closes 5pm; ☎01261/812419) is housed in the old gatehouse of Duff House in St Mary Square.

Banff's undoubted highlight is the extravagant **Duff House** (generally April–Oct daily 10am–5pm; Nov–March Thurs–Sun 10am–4pm; £4.50; HS). Built to William Adam's design in 1730, this elegant four-floor Georgian Baroque house was originally intended for one of the Northeast's richest men, William Braco, who became earl of Fife in 1759. The house has been painstakingly restored and reopened as an outpost of the **National Gallery of Scotland**'s extensive collection, and while the emphasis is to display original artwork rather than any broader selection of the Gallery's paintings, temporary exhibitions of work from the collections are mounted regularly. The downstairs rooms set the tone, principally the Rococo vestibule and the **dining room**, hung with ponderous eighteenth-century portraits, among which Allan Ramsay's *Elizabeth, Mrs Daniel Cunyngham* leaps out for its delightfully cool composition. On the other side of the ground floor, **Countess Agnes' Boudoir**, formerly Lord Macduff's dressing room, contains a riotous gilded Rococo mirror and El Greco's heartfelt *St Jerome in Penitence*. Ascending the **Great Staircase**, all eyes are drawn to the enormous copy of Raphael's *Transfiguration* by Inverness's Grigor Urquhart (1797–1846). Upstairs, the **North Drawing Room** contains the only piece of furniture original to the house, a 1760s mirror, but more obvious is the bewilderingly bold gold and cherry-red ceiling, a not entirely successful Victorian pastiche of Adam's style. Beyond the house there are extensive **grounds** with some pleasant parkland walks, notably along the River Deveron to a local beauty spot, the **Bridge of Alvah**, a couple of miles south.

Cullen to Spey Bay

Twelve miles west of Banff is **CULLEN**, strikingly situated beneath a superb series of arched viaducts. There's a lovely stretch of sheltered sand by Seatown, where the colourful houses – confusingly numbered according to the order in which they were built – huddle end-on to the sea. The local delicacy, Cullen skink – a soup made from milk (or cream), potato and smoked haddock – is available at the *Seafield* and elsewhere, including the bar of the *Royal Oak Hotel* at 43–45 Castle Terrace, and the *Three Kings* **pub** on North Castle Street, both tucked in under the towering viaducts of the now disused railway.

Six miles east is the quiet village of **PORTSOY**, renowned for its green marble once shipped to Versailles, and its annual traditional boat festival in early July. The *Shore Inn* by its atmospheric old stone harbour is a top spot for a beer or a meal on a sunny day.

West of Cullen, the dull fishing and service town of **BUCKIE** is home to the **Buckie Drifter** heritage museum (April–June & Sept–Oct Mon–Sat 10am–5pm, Sun noon–5pm; July & Aug daily 10am–5pm; £2.75), a hands-on exhibition telling the history of the area's fishing industry. It's well geared to families, though inevitably – given the dominance of fishing a century and more ago – it's only one of half-a-dozen maritime heritage museums found up and down this coast.

Buckie also marks one end of the **Speyside Way** long distance footpath (see p.191). This follows the coast west for five miles to windy **Spey Bay**, at the mouth of the river of the same name and also reached by a small coastal road from Buckie. It's a remote spot bounded by sea and river and sky; interpretation

23

is offered by a small **wildlife centre** (April–Oct daily 10.30am–5pm; Nov–Dec & Feb–March Sat & Sun 10.30am–5pm; ⓦwww.mfwc.co.uk; free), whose main mission is research of the Moray Firth dolphin population (for more on which, see p.1211).

Elgin and around

The lively market town of **ELGIN**, inland about fifteen miles west of Cullen, grew up in the thirteenth century around the River Lossie. The centre has mostly kept its medieval street plan, and while the busy main street is choked with chain stores, it does open out onto an old cobbled marketplace with a tangle of wynds and pends on either side.

On North College Street, a few blocks from the tourist office and clearly signposted, is the lovely ruin of **Elgin Cathedral** (April–Sept daily 9.30am–6.30pm; Oct–March Mon–Wed & Sat 9.30am–4.30pm, Thurs 9.30am–12.30pm, Sun 2–4.30pm; £3; HS). Once considered Scotland's most beautiful cathedral, rivalling St Andrews in importance, it's little more than a shell today, though it does retain its original facade. Founded in 1224, the three-towered building was extensively rebuilt after a fire in 1270, and stood as the region's highest religious house until 1390 when the inimical Wolf of Badenoch (Alexander Stewart, earl of Buchan and illegitimate son of Robert II) burned the place down, along with the rest of the town, in retaliation for having been excommunicated by the bishop of Moray when he left his wife. The cathedral suffered further during the post-Reformation, when all its valuables were stripped and the building was reduced to common quarry for the locals. Unusual features include the Pictish cross slab in the middle of the ruins and the cracked gravestones with their *memento mori* of skulls and crossbones.

Elgin is on the edge of whisky country, and while the local **distillery, Glen Moray** (Mon–Fri 9.30am–3.30pm, plus June to mid-Sept Sat 10.30am–2.30pm; £2; ⓦwww.glenmoray.com) isn't part of the official Malt Whisky Trail (see p.1192), tours are still available – the distinctive thing here is that your guide is quite likely to be the stillman, mashman or one of the other workers from the distillery floor.

Practicalities

Elgin is well served by public transport, with the Aberdeen–Inverness train stopping here several times a day. The **bus station** is on Alexandra Road (☎01343/544222), a block from the prominent and central St Giles Church while the **train station** is slightly less convenient, on the south side of town on Station Road (turn right out of the station, left at the island and up Moss Street to reach the centre).

The **tourist office** is at 17 High St (July & Aug Mon–Sat 9am–6pm, Sun 11am–4pm; April–June & Sept Mon–Sat 10am–5pm, Sun 11am–3pm; Oct–March Mon–Sat 10am–4pm; ☎01343/542666). *The Lodge*, 20 Duff Av (☎01343/549981, ⓦwww.beeandbee.com; ❷), is a good-quality **B&B** in house built for a former tea-plantation owner; while *Carrick House*, 13 South Guildry St (☎01343/569321, ⓦwww.scotbandb.co.uk; ❷), is small, tasteful and well priced. Five miles east of town, the *Old Church of Urquhart* (☎01343/843063, ⓦwww.oldkirk.co.uk; ❷) is the most appealing place to stay in the area, an unusual and comfortable B&B in an imaginatively converted church on Meft Road.

For **food**, *Toscana* (☎01343/551066) on Thunderton Place is good for pizza and pasta, or there's the *Ashvale* on Moss Street for sit-down or takeaway fish and chips. For great **picnic** foods, head to the old-fashioned high-street store Gordon & McPhail, 58–60 South St, an Aladdin's cave of aromas, colours and delicacies, which sells one of the widest ranges of malt whiskies in the world.

Pluscarden Abbey

Set in an attractive verdant valley seven miles southwest of Elgin, **Pluscarden Abbey** (daily 9am–5pm; ⓦwww.pluscardenabbey.org; free), looms impressively large in a peaceful clearing off an unmarked road. One of only two abbeys in Scotland with a permanent community of monks, it was founded in 1230 for a French order and, in 1390, became another of the properties burnt by the Wolf of Badenoch; recovering from this, it became a priory of the Benedictine Abbey of Dunfermline in 1454 and continued as such until monastic life was suppressed in Scotland in 1560. The abbey's revival began in 1897 when the Catholic antiquarian, John, third marquis of Bute, started to repair the building. In 1948 his son donated it to a small group of Benedictine monks from Gloucester, who established the present community. They are an active bunch, running stained-glass workshops, making honey and even recording Gregorian chants on CDs, all of which is detailed on their website. The abbey itself is airy and tranquil, with the monks' singing often eerily floating through from the connecting chapel. It's possible to **stay** here on retreat for a few days; see the website for details.

The Findhorn Foundation

In 1962, with little money and no employment, Eileen and Peter Caddy, their three children and friend Dorothy Maclean, settled on a caravan site at Findhorn. Dorothy believed she had a special relationship with what she called the "devas... the archetypal formative forces of light or energy that underlie all forms in nature – plants, trees, rivers", and from the uncompromising sandy soil they built a remarkable garden filled with plants and vegetables, far larger than had ever been seen in the area.

A few of those who came to see the phenomenon stayed to help out and tune into the spiritual aspect of the daily life of the nascent community. With its emphasis on inner discovery and development, but unattached to any particular doctrine or creed, the **Findhorn Foundation** has today blossomed into a permanent community of a couple of hundred people, with a well-developed series of courses and retreats on subjects ranging from astroshamanic healing to organic gardening drawing another 8000 or so visitors each year. The original caravan still stands, surrounded by a whole host of newer timber buildings and other caravans employing solar power, earth roofs and other green initiatives. The most intriguing of these are a group of round houses made from huge barrels reclaimed from a Speyside whisky distillery, while elsewhere you can see an ecological sewage treatment centre, a huge wind generator and various community businesses including a pottery and weaving studio.

The foundation is not without controversy: one community leader declared that "behind the benign and apparently religious front lies a hard core of New Agers experimenting with hallucinatory techniques marketed as spirituality". Findhorn, now a public company, is also accused of being overly well heeled: a glance into the shop or a tally of the smart cars parked outside the well-appointed eco-houses does give some substance to such ideas. However, there's little doubt that the community appeals to large numbers of people, and it's well known around the world. The reputation of the place is such that it attracts visitors both sympathetic and cynical – and both find something to feed their impressions.

Findhorn

A wide sweep of sandy beach stretches five miles around Burghead Bay to **FINDHORN**, a tidy village with a magnificent beach, a delightful harbour dotted with moored yachts, a small **Heritage Centre** (June–Aug Mon & Wed–Sat 2–5pm; May & Sept Sat & Sun 2–5pm; free), and a couple of good pubs: on a sunny day, a pint or some seafood on the terrace at the *Kimberbey Inn* is hard to beat. Findhorn is best known, however, for the controversial **Findhorn Foundation** (see box on p.1198), based beside the town's caravan park about a mile before you reach the village itself. Visitors are generally free to stroll around the community, but it's worth trying to take a more informed look at the different activities and projects by means of a **guided tour** (Mon, Wed, Fri & Sat 2pm; £3); you can also guide yourself via a booklet (£3) available from the shop or visitor centre.

Travel details

Buses

For more information on all local and national bus services, contact Traveline ☎0870/608 2608, ⓦwww.traveline.org.uk.

Aberdeen to: Ballater (hourly; 1hr 45min); Banchory (every 30min; 55min); Banff (hourly; 1hr 55min); Braemar (hourly; 2hr 10min); Crathie (for Balmoral) (hourly; 1hr 55min); Cullen (hourly; 2hr 30min); Dundee (hourly; 2hr); Elgin (hourly; 2hr 35min); Forfar (1 daily; 1hr 20min); Forres (hourly; 2hr 35min); Fraserburgh (hourly; 1hr 20min); Macduff (hourly; 1hr 50min); Peterhead (every 30min; 1hr 15min); Stonehaven (every 30min; 25min).

Dufftown to: Craigellachie (Mon–Sat hourly; 10min); Elgin (Mon–Sat hourly; 50min).

Dundee to: Aberdeen (hourly; 2hr); Arbroath (hourly; 40min–1hr); Blairgowrie (hourly; 1hr); Forfar (hourly; 30min); Glamis (2 daily; 40min); Kirriemuir (hourly; 1hr 10min); Meigle (hourly; 40min); Montrose (hourly; 1hr 15min).

Elgin to: Aberdeen (hourly; 2hr 35min); Forres (hourly; 25min); Nairn (hourly; 40min); Pluscarden (1 daily; 20min).

Forres to: Elgin (hourly; 25min); Findhorn (1–2 daily; 20min).

Fraserburgh to: Banff (2 daily; 55min); Macduff (2 daily; 45min).

Trains

For information on all local and national rail services, contact National Rail Enquiries: ☎08457/484950, ⓦwww.rail.co.uk.

Aberdeen to: Arbroath (every 30min; 1hr); Dundee (every 30min; 1hr 15min); Edinburgh (1–2 hourly; 2hr 35min); Elgin (Mon–Sat 10 daily, Sun 5 daily; 1hr 30min); Forres (Mon–Sat 10 daily, Sun 5 daily; 1hr 45min); Glasgow (hourly; 2hr 35min); London (5 daily; 7hr); Montrose (every 30min; 45min); Nairn (Mon–Sat 10 daily, Sun 5 daily; 2hr); Stonehaven (every 30min; 15min).

Dundee to: Aberdeen (every 30min; 1hr 15min); Arbroath (hourly; 20min); Edinburgh (1–2 hourly; 1hr 15min); Glasgow (hourly; 1hr 15min); Montrose (hourly; 15min).

Elgin to: Forres (hourly; 15min); Nairn (hourly; 25min).

Ferries

Aberdeen to: Lerwick, Shetland (daily; 10–12hr overnight); Kirkwall, Orkney (Tues, Thurs, Sat & Sun; 6hr).

Flights

Aberdeen to: Kirkwall, Orkney (2 daily; 55min); Sumburgh, Shetland (Mon–Fri 3 daily, Sat & Sun daily; 1hr).

The Highland region

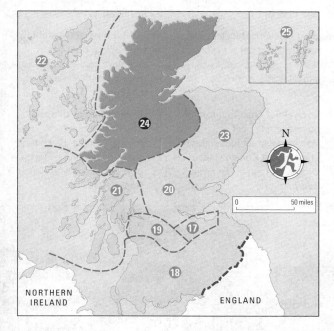

NORTHERN
IRELAND

ENGLAND

CHAPTER 24

Highlights

* **West Highland Railway**
  From Glasgow to Mallaig via
  Fort William; the further north
  it travels, the more spectacular it gets. **See p.1204**

* **The Cairngorms** Scotland's
  grandest mountain massif, a
  place of rare plants, wild animals, inspiring vistas – and
  challenging outdoor activities.
  See p.1212

* **Glen Coe** Spectacular,
  moody, poignant – a glorious
  place for hiking, history or
  simple admiration. **See
  p.1225**

* **Loch Shiel** The most roman-
  tic and least spoilt of
  Scotland's great lochs, the
  place where Bonnie Prince
  Charlie first raised an army.
  See p.1230

* **Knoydart** – Only reached by
  boat or a two-day hike over
  the mountains, this peninsula
  also boasts mainland Britain's
  most isolated pub, the welcoming Old Forge. **See p.1232**

* **Wester Ross** Scotland's
  finest scenery, a heady mix of
  dramatic mountains, rugged
  sea lochs, sweeping bays and
  scattered islands. **See p.1235**

* **Gairloch whale-watching
  trips** Join a boat trip in
  search of seals, porpoises,
  dolphins and whales. **See
  p.1238**

* **Ceilidh Place, Ullapool**
  The best venue for
  modern Highlands culture,
  regularly hosting evenings
  of music, song and dance.
  See p.1240

△ West Highlands Railway

24

The Highland region

The **Highland region** of Scotland, covering the northern two-thirds of the country, holds much of the mainland's most spectacular scenery: a classic combination of mountains, glens, lochs and rivers surrounded on three sides by a magnificently pitted and rugged coastline. The inspiring landscape and the tranquillity and space which it offers are without doubt the main attractions of the region. You may be surprised at just how remote much of it still is: the vast peat bogs in the north, for example, are among the most extensive and unspoilt wilderness areas in Europe, while a handful of the west coast's isolated crofting villages can still be reached only by boat.

Capital of the Highlands and the only major urban centre in the region, **Inverness** is an obvious springboard for more remote areas, with good transport links and facilities, and while there are some engaging historic sites nearby, the city itself is of limited appeal. South of Inverness, the **Strathspey** region, with a string of villages lying along the River Spey, is dominated by the dramatic **Cairngorm mountains**, an area brimming with attractive scenery and opportunities for outdoor activity.

The Monadhliath mountains lie between Strathspey and **Loch Ness**, the largest and most famous of the necklace of lochs which make up the **Great Glen**, an ancient geological fault-line which cuts southwest across the region from Inverness to the town of **Fort William**. From Fort William, located beneath Scotland's highest peak, Ben Nevis, it's possible to branch out to some fine scenery – most conveniently the beautiful expanses of **Glen Coe**, but also in the direction of the appealing **west coast**, notably the remote and tranquil **Ardnamurchan peninsula**, the "Road to the Isles" to **Mallaig**, and the lochs and glens that lead to **Kyle of Lochalsh** on the most direct route to Skye. Between Kyle of Lochalsh and **Ullapool**, the main settlement in the northwest, lies **Wester Ross**, home to quintessentially west-coast scenes of sparkling sea lochs, rocky headlands and sandy beaches set against some of Scotland's most dramatic mountains, with Skye and the Western Isles on the horizon.

The little-visited **north coast** stretching from wind-lashed **Cape Wrath**, at the very northwest tip of the mainland, east to **John O'Groats** is yet more rugged, with sheer cliffs and sand-filled bays bearing the brunt of frequently fierce Atlantic storms. The main settlement on this coast is **Thurso**, jumping-off point for the main ferry service to Orkney.

On the fertile **east coast**, stretching north from Inverness to the old herring port of **Wick**, green fields and woodland run down to the sweeping sandy beaches of the **Black Isle** and the **Cromarty** and **Dornoch firths**. This region is rich with historical sites, including the **Sutherland Monument** by Golspie, **Dornoch**'s fourteenth-century sandstone cathedral, and a number of

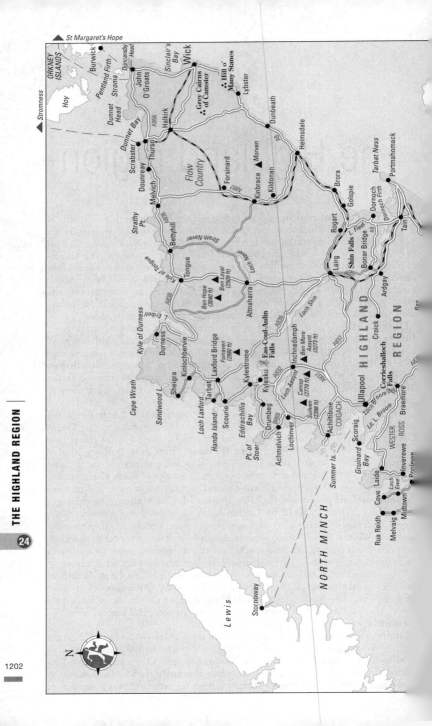

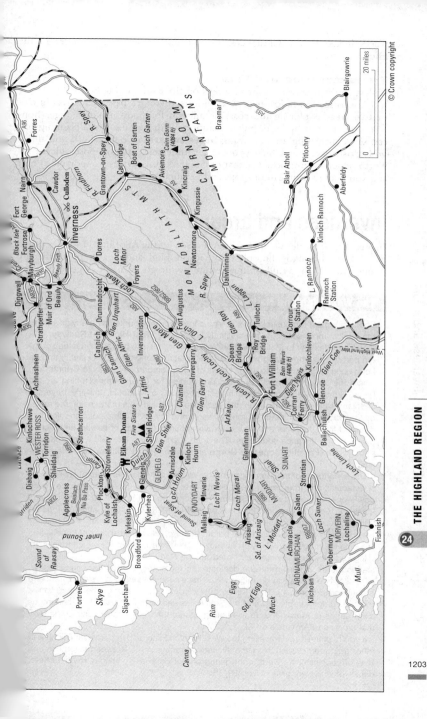

THE HIGHLAND REGION

24

1203

places linked to the Clearances, a poignantly remembered chapter in the Highland story.

Transport practicalities

Unless you're prepared to spend weeks on the road, the Highlands are simply too vast to see in a single trip. Most visitors, therefore, base themselves in one or two areas, exploring the coast or hills on foot, and making longer hops across the interior by car or public transport. With a little forward planning you can see a surprising amount using **buses** and **trains**, especially if you fill in with **postbuses** (for which you can get timetables at most post offices). It's worth remembering, however, that on Sundays bus services are sporadic at best and you may well find most shops and restaurants closed.

Inverness and around

Inverness, 105 miles northwest of Aberdeen by the A96, and 114 miles north of Perth by the A9, is the only "city" in the Highlands – a status it officially attained in 2000 as a millennium gesture by the government. A good base for

The West Highland Railway

Scotland's most famous railway line, and a train journey counted by many as among the world's most scenic, is the brilliantly engineered **West Highland Railway**, running from Glasgow to Mallaig via Fort William. The line is in two sections: the southern part travels from **Glasgow** Queen Street station along the Clyde estuary and up Loch Long before switching to the banks of Loch Lomond on its way to **Crianlarich**, where the train divides with one section heading for Oban. After climbing around Beinn Odhar on a unique horseshoe-shaped loop of viaducts, the line traverses desolate **Rannoch Moor**, where the track had to be laid on a mattress of tree roots, brushwood and thousands of tons of earth and ashes. By this point the line has diverged from the road, and travels through country that can otherwise be reached only by long-distance footpaths. The train then swings into Glen Roy, passing through the dramatic **Monessie Gorge** and entering **Fort William** from the northeast.

The second leg of the journey, from Fort William to Mallaig, is arguably even more spectacular, and from mid-June to September one of the scheduled services each day is pulled by the **Jacobite Steam Train** (departs Fort William 10.20am, departs Mallaig 2.10pm; day-return £25; book on ☎01463/239026). Shortly after leaving Fort William the railway crosses the Caledonian Canal beside Neptune's Staircase by way of a swing bridge at **Benavie**, before travelling along the shores of Locheil and crossing the magnificent 21-arch viaduct at **Glenfinnan**, where the steam train, in its "Hogwarts Express" livery, was filmed for the *Harry Potter* movies. At Glenfinnan station there's a small **museum** dedicated to the history of the West Highland line, as well as two old railway carriages which have been converted into a restaurant and a bunkhouse (see p.1231). Not long afterwards the line reaches the coast, where there are unforgettable views of the Small Isles and Skye as it runs past the famous silver sands of **Morar** and up to **Mallaig**, where there are connections to the ferry that crosses to Armadale on Skye.

If you're planning on travelling the West Highland line, and in particular linking it to other train journeys (such as the similarly attractive route between Inverness and Kyle of Lochalsh), it's worth considering one of ScotRail's multiday **rover tickets**, details of which are given on pp.29–35.

day-trips and a jumping-off point for many of the more remote parts of the region, it's not a compelling place to stay for long. The approach to the city on the A9 over the barren Monadhliath Mountains provides a spectacular introduction to the district, with the **Great Glen** to the left, stretching southwestwards towards Fort William and, beyond, the massed peaks of Glen Affric. To the north is the huge, rounded form of Ben Wyvis, whilst to the east lies the **Moray Firth**, to some extent a commuter belt for Inverness, but also boasting a lovely coastline and some of the region's best castles and historic sites. The gentle, undulating green landscape is well tended and tranquil, a fertile contrast to the windswept moorland and mountains that almost surround it.

A string of worthwhile sights punctuates the approaches to Inverness along the main route from Aberdeen. The low-key holiday resort of **Nairn**, with its long white-sand beaches and championship golf course, stands within striking distance of several monuments, including the whimsical **Cawdor Castle**, featured in Shakespeare's *Macbeth*, and **Fort George**, one of several impressive Hanoverian bastions erected in the wake of the Jacobite rebellion. The infamous battle and ensuing massacre that ended Bonnie Prince Charlie's uprising took place on the outskirts of Inverness at **Culloden**, where a small visitor centre and memorial stones beside a heather-clad moor recall the gruesome events of 1746.

Inverness

Straddling a nexus of major road and rail routes, **INVERNESS** is the busy and prosperous hub of the Highlands, and an inevitable port of call if you're exploring the region by public transport. **Buses** and **trains** leave for communities right across the far north of Scotland, and it isn't uncommon for people from

---

Tours and cruises from Inverness

Inverness is the departure point for a range of day **tours** and **cruises** to nearby attractions. City Sightseeing run an open-topped double-decker **city tour** of **Inverness** (May–Sept daily every 30min; 45min; £5), which you can hop on and off all day; their buses also offer a hop-on-hop-off **country tour** to **Culloden**, Cawdor Castle and Fort George (1hr 20min; £8.50). You can buy tickets on the buses, which leave from Bridge Street near the tourist office, or at their office in the train station (May–Sept daily 9am–6pm). An entertaining if slightly bizarre **Terror Tour** takes groups on foot around Inverness town centre (daily 7pm from the tourist office; £5.50), with grisly tales told along the way of ghosts, torture and witches. There are various **Loch Ness** tours leaving from the tourist office: try Jacobite Cruises (☎01463/233999, ⓦwww.jacobite.co.uk). Far more original and personal are Tony Harmsworth's **Discover Loch Ness** tours (☎01456/450168 or 0800/731 5564, ⓦwww.discoverlochness.com).

To explore the northwest, Dearman Coaches have a daily service to **Ullapool**, **Lochinver**, **Durness**, **Smoo Cave** and back which stops at several hostels en route (May–Sept Mon–Sat; £17.50; or you can buy a £28 rover ticket valid for six days).

Enjoyable trips to **John O'Groats** and back in a day, with the chance to see puffins and visit prehistoric sites, are run by Puffin Express (☎01463/717181, ⓦwww.puffinexpress.co.uk), who also put together a package which includes an overnight stop on **Orkney**. You can get to the islands and back with a gruelling full-day whistle-stop tour on the Orkney Bus, which leaves Inverness bus station every day during the summer (£45; advance bookings may be made at the tourist office or on ☎01955/611353, ⓦwww.jogferry.co.uk/orkexp.htm).

See p.1211 for details of **dolphin**-spotting cruises on the Moray Firth.

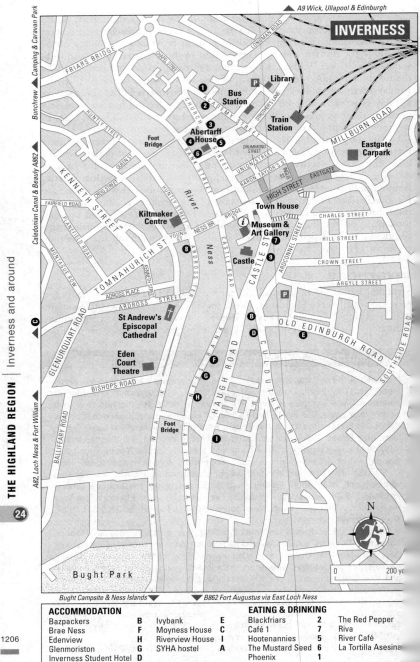

A9 Wick, Ullapool & Edinburgh

INVERNESS

Bunchrew ◄ Camping & Caravan Park

Caledonian Canal & Beauly A862 ◄

A82, Loch Ness & Fort William ◄

FRIARS BRIDGE

CHARLES STREET

ACADEMY STREET

CHURCH STREET

Library

Bus Station

SPROHER'S LANE

LONGMAN ROAD

Train Station

MILLBURN ROAD

Eastgate Carpark

1

2

3

Abertarff House

4 **5**

6

Foot Bridge

BANK STREET

DRUMMOND STREET

UNION STREET

BARON TAYLOR'S ST.

EASTGATE

HIGH STREET

Town House

Museum & Art Gallery

7

Castle

9

CHARLES STREET

HILL STREET

CROWN STREET

ARGYLE STREET

ARDCONNEL STREET

HUNTLY STREET

QUEEN ST.

CREIG STREET

FAIRFIELD ROAD

KENNETH STREET

PLANEFIELD ROAD

MONTAGUE ROW

Kiltmaker Centre

YOUNG ST.

ARDROSS TER.

ARDROSS STREET

TOMNAHURICH ST.

FRENCH STREET

River Ness

Ness BR.

CASTLE ROAD

CASTLE STREET

8

ARDROSS PLACE

GLENURQUHART ROAD

St Andrew's Episcopal Cathedral

Eden Court Theatre

BISHOPS ROAD

BALLIFEARY ROAD

NESS WALK

Foot Bridge

LADIES WALK

B

D

F

G

H

I

OLD EDINBURGH ROAD

E

SOUTHSIDE ROAD

CULDUTHEL RD.

HAUGH ROAD

Bught Park

N

0   200 yards

Bught Campsite & Ness Islands ▼   ▼ B862 Fort Augustus via East Loch Ness

ACCOMMODATION

Bazpackers	**B**
Brae Ness	**F**
Edenview	**H**
Glenmoriston	**G**
Inverness Student Hotel	**D**
Ivybank	**E**
Moyness House	**C**
Riverview House	**I**
SYHA hostel	**A**

EATING & DRINKING

Blackfriars	**2**
Café 1	**7**
Hootenannies	**5**
The Mustard Seed	**6**
Phoenix	**1**

The Red Pepper
Riva
River Café
La Tortilla Asesina

as far afield as Thurso, Durness and Kyle of Lochalsh to travel down for a day's shopping here – Britain's most northerly chain-store centre. Though boasting few conventional sights, the city's setting on the banks of the River Ness is appealing.

Arrival, information and accommodation

Inverness **airport** (℡01667/464000) is at Dalcross, seven miles east of the city; from here, bus #11 (Mon–Sat every 1hr–1hr 30min; 20min; £2.50) goes into town, while a taxi costs around £10. The **bus station** (℡01463/233371) and **train station** (℡0845/748 4950) both lie just off Academy Street to the east of the centre. The **tourist office** (June–Aug Mon–Fri 9am–6pm, Sat & Sun 9.30am–5pm; mid-July to Aug Mon–Fri until 8pm; rest of year Mon–Fri 9am–5pm, Sat 10am–4pm; ℡01463/234353) is in a 1960s block on Castle Wynd, just five minutes' walk from the station. It stocks a wide range of literature on the area, including useful free maps of the city and environs, and the friendly staff can book local accommodation for a £3 fee.

Inverness is one of the few places in the Highlands where you're unlikely to have problems finding **accommodation**, although in July and August you'll have to book ahead. Good places to look include both banks of the river south of the Ness Bridge, and Kenneth Street and its offshoots on the west side of the river.

Hotels and B&Bs

Brae Ness Ness Bank ℡01463/712266, ⓦwww.braenesshotel.co.uk. A homely Georgian hotel with only ten rooms (all nonsmoking) overlooking the river and St Andrews Cathedral. May–Oct. ❺

Glenmoriston Town House Hotel 20 Ness Bank ℡01463/223777, ⓦwww.glenmoriston.com. Very classy and comfortable hotel slap on the riverside with well-appointed rooms and a top-notch Italian restaurant. ❻

Edenview 26 Ness Bank ℡01463/234397, ⓔedenview@clara.co.uk. Very pleasant B&B in a riverside location as good as the more expensive hotels, five minutes' walk from the centre. Nonsmoking. March–Oct. ❸

Ivybank Guest House 28 Old Edinburgh Rd ℡01463/232796, ⓦwww.ivybankguesthouse.com. A grand Georgian home just up the hill from the castle, with open fires and a lovely wooden interior. ❷

Moyness House 6 Bruce Gardens ℡01463/233836, ⓦwww.moyness.co.uk. Warm, welcoming, upmarket B&B with original Victorian features and a nice walled garden on the west side of Inverness. ❺

Riverview House 2 Moray Park, Island Bank Rd ℡01463/235557. A welcoming B&B in a characterful old house a little further down the river than some pricier guest houses, but still an easy stroll from the centre. ❸

Hostels

Bazpackers Top of Castle St ℡01463/717663. The most cosy and relaxed of the city's hostels, with thirty beds including two double rooms and a twin; some dorms are mixed. It has good views and a garden, which is used for barbecues, as well as the usual cooking facilities. Nonsmoking.

Inverness Student Hotel 8 Culduthel Rd ℡01463/236556, ⓦwww.scotlands -top-hostels.com. A busy fifty-bed hostel with the usual facilities and fine views over the river. Part of the Macbackpackers group, so expect minibus tours to pull in most days.

SYHA hostel Victoria Drive, off Millburn Rd, about three-quarters of a mile east of the centre ℡01463/231771, ⓔreservations@syha.org.uk. One of SYHA's flagship hostels, fully equipped with large kitchens and communal areas, ecofriendly facilities and ten four-bed family rooms among the 166-bed total, but all rather soulless.

The Town

The logical place to begin a tour of Inverness is the central **Town House** on the High Street. Built in 1878, this Gothic pile hosted Prime Minister Lloyd George's emergency meeting to discuss the Irish crisis in September 1921, and now accommodates council offices.

24

Looming above the Town House and dominating the horizon is **Inverness Castle**, a predominantly nineteenth-century red-sandstone edifice perched picturesquely above the river. It houses the Sheriff Court and, in summer, the **Castle Garrison Encounter** (March–Oct Mon–Sat 10am–5pm; £4.50), an entertaining and noisy interactive exhibition in which the visitor plays the role of a new recruit in the eighteenth-century Hanoverian army. Around 7pm during the summer, a lone piper clad in full Highland garb performs for tourists on the castle esplanade.

Below the castle, the **Inverness Museum and Art Gallery** on Castle Wynd (Mon–Sat 9am–5pm; free) gives a good general overview of the development of the Highlands. Informative sections on geology, geography and history cover the ground floor, while upstairs you'll find a muddled selection of silver, taxidermy, weapons and bagpipes, alongside an art gallery which occasionally attracts worthwhile touring exhibitions.

The truth about tartan

To much of the world, **tartan** is synonymous with Scotland. It's the natural choice of packaging for Scottish exports from shortbread to Sean Connery, and when the Scottish football team travels abroad to play a fixture, the high-spirited "Tartan Army" of fans are never far behind. Not surprisingly, tartan is big business for the tourist industry, yet the truth is that romantic fiction and commercial interest have enclosed this ancient Highland art form within an almost insurmountable wall of myth.

The original form of tartan, the kind that long ago was called "**Helande**", was a fine, hard and almost showerproof cloth spun in Highland villages from the wool of the native sheep, dyed with preparations of local plants and with patterns woven by artist-weavers. It was worn as a huge single piece of cloth, or **plaid**, which was belted around the waist and draped over the upper body, rather like a knee-length toga. The natural colours of old tartans were clear but soft, and the broken pattern gave superb camouflage, unlike modern versions, where garish, clashing colours are often used to create impact.

After Culloden, a ban on the wearing of tartan in the Highlands lasted some 25 years; in that time it became a fondly held emblem for emigrant Highlanders in the colonies and was incorporated into the uniforms of the new Highland regiments in the British Army. Then Sir Walter Scott set to work glamorizing the clans, dressing George IV in a kilt for his visit to Edinburgh in 1822. By the time Queen Victoria set the royal seal of approval on both the Highlands and tartan with her extended annual holidays at Balmoral, the concept of tartan as formal dress rather than rough Highland wear was assured.

Hand in hand with the gentrification of the kilt came "rules" about the correct form of attire and the idea that every clan had its own distinguishing tartan. To have the right to wear tartan, one had to belong, albeit remotely, to a clan, and so the way was paved for the "what's-my-tartan?" lists that appear in tartan picture books and souvenir shops.

Scotsmen today will commonly wear the **kilt** for weddings and other formal occasions; properly made kilts, however – comprising some four yards of 100-percent wool – are likely to set you back £300 or more, with the rest of the regalia at least doubling that figure. If the contents of your sporran don't stretch that far, most places selling kilts will rent outfits on a daily basis. The best place to find better quality material is a recognized Highland outfitter rather than a souvenir shop: in Inverness, try the Scottish Kiltmaker Centre at Hector Russell's (see opposite page) or Chisholms Highland Dress at 47–49 Castle St.

Just across Ness Bridge from Bridge Street is the **Kiltmaker Centre** in the Hector Russell shop (mid–May to Sept Mon–Sat 9am–10pm, Sun 10am–5pm; Oct to mid–May Mon–Sat 9am–5.30pm; £2). Entered through the factory shop, a small visitor centre sets out everything you ever wanted to know about tartan, and on weekdays you can watch various tartan products being made in the workshop. The finished products are, of course, on sale in the showroom downstairs, along with all manner of Highland knitwear, woven woollies and Harris tweed.

Rising from the west bank directly opposite the castle, **St Andrews Episcopal Cathedral** was intended by its architects to be one of the grandest buildings in Scotland. However, funds ran out before the giant twin spires of the original design could be completed. From here, you can wander a mile or so upriver to the peaceful **Ness Islands**, an attractive, informal public park reached and linked by footbridges.

Eating

Inverness has lots of **eating** places, including a few excellent–quality gourmet options. The best place for **picnic food** is The Gourmet's Lair, a well-stocked deli at 8 Union St.

Cafés and restaurants

Café 1 75 Castle St ☎01463/226200. Impressive contemporary Scottish cooking using good local ingredients in a bistro-style setting. Closed Sun. Moderate to expensive.

The Mustard Seed 16 Fraser St ☎01463/220220. The most stylish place in town to eat out – an airy converted church with stone walls, smart table settings and an upbeat approach, serving modern Scottish cuisine and a range of light, bistro-style dishes. Despite the wow factor it's still reasonably priced. Moderate.

The Red Pepper 74 Church St ☎01463/237111. Linked to the *Mustard Seed*, this is the city's hip coffee-bar hangout, but there's lots of good food and takeaway too.

Riva 4–6 Ness Walk ☎01463/237377. Reasonably authentic modern Italian bistro/café beside the river with antipasta, decent mains and good coffee and cakes. Moderate. Upstairs, inexpensive pasta dishes can be had at *Pazzo's Pasta Bar* (evenings only; closed Sun & Mon).

River Café and Restaurant 10 Bank St ☎01463/714884. Healthy wholefood lunches and evening meals, with a great selection of freshly baked cakes and good coffee. Inexpensive to moderate.

La Tortilla Asesina 99 Castle St ☎01463/709809. Simple but lively tapas restaurant, serving all the old favourites as well as some "tartan tapas" majoring on local ingredients. Moderate.

Drinking & nightlife

The liveliest **nightlife** in Inverness revolves around the pubs and, on Friday and Saturday nights, the city's main nightclub. The far end of Academy Street has a cluster of good **pubs**; the public bar of the *Phoenix* is the most original town-centre place, though *Blackfriars* across the street has a bit more going for it with entertainment seven nights a week. *Hootenanny* is a bright, youthful place to drink which also hosts lots of live gigs and ceilidhs.

Listings

Bike rental Barney's, 35 Castle St ☎01463/232249.

Bookshops Leakey's is a huge former church, Greyfriars' Hall, on Church St, filled with books, and is a great spot to browse for secondhand books. There's also Ottakars in the Eastgate Centre and Waterstones at 50–52 High St.

Car rental Budget ☎01463/713333; Europcar ☎01463/235337; Arnold Clark ☎01463/236200; Thrifty ☎01463/224466; Sharps Reliable Wrecks ☎01463/236694.

Cinemas The Eden Court Theatre and the attached Riverside Screen, on the banks of the Ness, host touring theatre productions, concerts

and films; La Scala (☎01463/233302) on
Strother's Lane, just off Academy St, has three
screens; Warner Village (☎0870/240 6020), on the
A96 Nairn road about two miles from the town
centre, boasts seven screens.
Exchange American Express agents Alba Travel are
at 43 Church St (Mon–Sat 9am–5pm; ☎01463/
239188). The tourist office's *bureau de change*
changes cash and currency for a small commission.

Hospital Raigmore Hospital (☎01463/704000)
on the southeastern outskirts of town close to
the A9.
Internet MTC, 2 Grant St (Mon–Thurs 9am–5pm,
Fri 9am–4.30pm). There are also terminals in the
tourist office and library.
Post office 14–16 Queensgate (Mon–Thurs
9am–5.30pm, Fri 9.30am–5.30pm, Sat 9am–6pm;
☎0845/722 3344).

East of Inverness

East of Inverness lies the fertile, sheltered coastal strip of the **Moray Firth** and
its hinterland, the pastoral countryside contrasting with the scenic splendours
you'll encounter once you head further north into the Highlands. Primary
among the sites is **Culloden**, the most poignant battlefield site in Scotland,
where Bonnie Prince Charlie's Jacobites were routed in 1746. Further east are
Cawdor Castle and **Fort George**, two of the best-preserved fortified structures in the Highlands. **Nairn**, the main town of the district, has a pretty
harbour as well as appealing walks and cycle routes.

The overloaded A96 traverses this stretch and the region is well served by
public transport, with all the historic sites and castles accessible on day-trips from
Inverness, or en route to Aberdeen. To get to Fort George, Cawdor Castle and
Culloden you can juggle the Highland County Tourist Trail buses (#11, #12 and
#13; £6 for a day-rover ticket) that depart from Queensgate in Inverness.

Culloden

The windswept moorland of **CULLODEN** (site open all year; free), five miles
east of Inverness, witnessed the last-ever battle on British soil when, on April
16, 1746, the Jacobite cause was finally subdued – a turning point in the
history of the Scottish nation.

The second Jacobite rebellion had begun on August 19, 1745, with the raising of the Stuarts' standard at **Glenfinnan** on the west coast (see p.1230).
Shortly after, Edinburgh fell into Jacobite hands, and Bonnie Prince Charlie
began his march on London. The English had appointed the ambitious young
duke of Cumberland to command their forces, and his pursuit, together with
bad weather and lack of funds, eventually forced the Jacobites to retreat north.
They ended up at Culloden, where, ill-fed and exhausted after a pointless night
march, they were hopelessly outnumbered by the English. The open, flat
ground of Culloden Moor was totally unsuitable for the Highlanders' style of
courageous but undisciplined fighting, which needed steep hills and lots of
cover to provide the element of surprise, and they were routed. After the battle
in which 1500 Highlanders were slaughtered (many of them as they lay
wounded on the battlefield), Bonnie Prince Charlie fled west to the hills and
islands, where loyal Highlanders sheltered and protected him. He eventually
escaped to France, leaving his erstwhile supporters to their fate – and, in effect,
ushering in the end of the clan system. The clans were disarmed, the wearing
of tartan and playing of bagpipes forbidden, and the chiefs became landlords
greedy for higher and higher rents.

Today you can walk freely around the battle site; flags show the positions of
the two armies, and **clan graves** are marked by simple headstones. The **visitor centre** itself (daily: July & Aug 9am–7pm; April–June & Sept–Oct
9am–6pm; Nov–March 10am–4pm; closed Jan; £5; NTS) provides

The dolphins of the Moray Firth

The **Moray Firth**, a great wedge-shaped bay forming the eastern coastline of the Highlands, is one of only three areas of UK waters that supports a resident population of **dolphins**. Over a hundred live in the estuary, the most northerly breeding ground for this particular species – the bottle-nosed dolphin (*Tursiops truncatus*) – in Europe, and you stand a good chance of spotting a few.

One of the best places to look for them is **Chanonry Point**, on the Black Isle (see p.1249) – a spit of sand protruding into a narrow, deep channel, where converging currents bring fish close to the surface, and thus the dolphins close to shore; the hour or so before high tide is the most likely time to see them. **Kessock Bridge**, one mile north of Inverness, is another prime dolphin-spotting location. You can go all the way down to the beach at the small village of North Kessock, underneath the road bridge, where there's a decent place to have a drink at the pub in the *North Kessock Hotel*, or you can stop above the village in a car park just off the A9 at the visitor centre and listening post (see p.1250) set up by a team of zoologists from Aberdeen University studying the dolphins, where hydrophones allow you to eavesdrop on the underwater conversations.

In addition, several companies run dolphin-spotting **boat trips** around the Moray Firth. Operators currently accredited to the Dolphin Space Programme's Accreditation Scheme (Ⓦwww.greentourism.org.uk/DSP) include Phoenix, based in Nairn (Ⓣ01667/456078); Moray Firth Cruises, Inverness (Ⓣ01463/717900); the Moray Firth Wildlife Centre, Spey Bay (Ⓣ01343/820339; see p.1196), and Benbola Tours, Buckie (Ⓣ01542/832289). In addition, Dolphin Trips Avoch (Ⓣ01381/620958; Ⓦwww.dolphintripsavoch.co.uk); and Dolphin Écosse, Cromarty (Ⓣ01381/600323) are based on the Black Isle, on the northern side of the firth. Half-day trips cost around £20.

background information through detailed displays and a film show, as well as a short play set on the day of the battle presented by local actors (June–Sept only; included in admission fee), or you can take the evocative hour-long guided **walking tour** (June–Sept daily; £3).

The site is served by City Sightseeing's hop-on-hop-off country tour **buses** from Bridge Street in Inverness (daily, May–Sept) and Highland Country bus #12 from Queensgate in Inverness (Mon–Sat 8 daily).

The Clava Cairns

If you're visiting Culloden with your own transport, a short detour is worthwhile to the **Clava Cairns**, an impressive collection of prehistoric burial chambers clustered around the south bank of the River Nairn, a mile southeast of the battlefield. Erected some time before 2000 BC, the cairns, which are encircled by standing stones in a spinney of mature beech trees, are of two different kinds: one large and one very small **ring-cairn**, and two **passage graves**, which have a narrow passageway from edge to centre.

Cawdor Castle

The pretty, if slightly self-satisfied, village of **CAWDOR**, eight miles east of Culloden, is the site of **Cawdor Castle** (May to mid-Oct daily 10am–5.30pm; £6.30; gardens only £3.50), a setting intimately linked to Shakespeare's *Macbeth*: the fulfilment of the witches' prediction that Macbeth was to become thane of Cawdor sets off his tragic desire to be king. The castle, which dates from the early fourteenth century, could not possibly have witnessed the grisly historical events on which the Bard's drama was based. However, the immaculately restored monument – a fairy-tale affair of towers, turrets, hidden passageways, dungeons, gargoyles and crenellations whimsically shooting off from the original keep – is still well worth a visit.

As you explore, look out for the **Thorn Tree Room**, a vaulted chamber complete with the remains of an ancient holly tree carbon-dated to 1372 – an ancient pagan fertility symbol believed to ward off fairies and evil spirits. The **grounds** of the castle are impressive, with an attractive walled garden, a topiarian maze, a small golf course, a putting green and nature trails. It's also worth visiting the village for a drink or meal at the traditional *Cawdor Tavern*, an old inn serving beautifully prepared local food.

Fort George

Eight miles of undulating coastal farmland separate Cawdor Castle from **Fort George** (daily: April–Sept 9.30am–6.30pm; Oct–March 9.30am–4.30pm; £5.50; HS), an old Hanoverian bastion with walls a mile long, considered by military architectural historians to be one of the finest fortifications in Europe. Crowning a sandy spit that juts into the middle of the Moray Firth, it was built between 1747 and 1769 as a base for George II's army, in case the Highlanders should attempt to rekindle the Jacobite flame.

Apart from the sweeping panoramic views across the firth from its ramparts, the main incentive to visit Fort George is the **Regimental Museum** of the Queen's Own Highlanders. Displayed in polished glass cases is a predictable array of regimental silver, coins, moth-eaten uniforms and medals, along with some macabre war trophies, ranging from blood-stained nineteenth-century Sudanese battle robes to Iraqi gas masks gleaned in the first Gulf War. The **chapel** is also worth a look – squat and solid outside, and all light and grace within.

Nairn and around

One of the driest and sunniest places in the whole of Scotland, **NAIRN**, sixteen miles east of Inverness, began its days as a peaceful community of fishermen and farmers. The former spoke Gaelic, the latter English, allowing James VI to boast that a town in his kingdom was so large that people at one end of the main street could not understand those at the other end. It boasts two championship golf courses, and Thomas Telford's **harbour** is filled with leisure craft rather than fishing boats. Nearby, amid the huddled streets of old Fishertown – the town centre is known as new Fishertown – is the tiny **Fishertown Museum** (June–Sept Mon–Sat 10.30am–12.30pm; free).

Nairn no longer has a tourist office. For **accommodation**, try *Greenlawns*, 13 Seafield St (☎01667/452738, ⓦwww.greenlawns.uk.com; ❷), a spacious and friendly B&B with most rooms en suite. The *Golf View Hotel* (☎01667/452301, ⓦwww.morton-hotels.com; ❽), overlooks the sea (and unsurprisingly, the golf course) and serves meals in its restaurant and conservatory. The more down-to-earth *Longhouse Restaurant* (☎01667/455532) on the corner of Harbour Street and Watson's Place, serves big portions of appetizing seafood and many other dishes.

Strathspey and the Cairngorms

Rising high in the heather-clad hills above remote Loch Laggan, forty miles due south of Inverness, the **River Spey**, Scotland's second longest river, drains northeast towards the Moray Firth through one of the Highlands' most spell-binding valleys. Famous for its ancient forests, salmon fishing and ospreys, the area around the upper section of the river, known as **Strathspey**, is dominated by the sculpted **Cairngorms**, Britain's most extensive mountain massif, unique in supporting subarctic tundra on its high plateau. Though the area has been admired and treasured for many years as one of Scotland's prime natural assets, the Cairngorms National Park was declared only in 2004, and even then with grumblings from conservationists about inadequate planning regulations and unnatural boundaries. Even so, outdoor enthusiasts flock to the area to take advantage of the superb hiking, water sports and winter snows, aided by the fact that the area is easily accessible by road and rail from both the central belt and Inverness.

Of Strathspey's scattered settlements, **Aviemore** absorbs the largest number of visitors, particularly in midwinter when it metamorphoses into the UK's busiest ski resort. The village itself isn't up to much, but it's a good first stop for information, to sort out somewhere to stay or to find out about nearby outdoor activities, which suddenly seem a lot more enticing after a glimpse of the stunning mountain scenery provided by the 4000ft summit plateau of the Cairngorms. The planned Georgian town of **Grantown-on-Spey** makes a good alternative base for summer visitors, though while it has more charm than Aviemore, there are fewer facilities. Further upriver, the sedate villages of **Kingussie** and **Newtonmore** are older-established holiday centres, popular more with anglers and grouse hunters than canoeists and climbers. Rather unusually for Scotland, the area boasts a wide choice of good-quality accommodation, particularly in the budget market, with various easy-going hostels run by and for outdoor enthusiasts.

Note that Strathspey is distinct from Speyside, located further downstream to the north and famous for its whiskies, which is described on p.1190.

Aviemore and around

The once-sleepy village of **AVIEMORE** was first developed as a ski and tourism resort in the mid-1960s and, over the years, it fell victim to profiteering developers with scant regard for the needs of the local community. Although a large-scale face-lift has removed some of the architectural eyesores of that era, the settlement remains dominated by a string of soulless shopping centres and sprawling housing estates surrounding an attractive Victorian railway station. That said, Aviemore is well equipped with services and facilities for visitors to the area and is the most convenient base for the Cairngorms, benefits which for most folk far outweigh its lack of aesthetic appeal.

The main attractions of Aviemore are its **outdoor pursuits**, though train enthusiasts are drawn to the restored **Strathspey Steam Railway**, which hugs the short distance between Aviemore and Broomhill, just beyond Boat of Garten village, five times daily through the summer (June–Sept; less regular service at other times; call ☎01479/810725 or go to ⓦwww.strathspeyrailway.co.uk for details).

Summer activities

In summer, the main activities around Aviemore are **walking** (see box, p.1216) and **water sports**, though there are great opportunities to do most things from mountain biking to fly-fishing. There are two centres that offer sailing, windsurfing and canoeing: the Loch Morlich Watersports Centre (☎01479/861221, ⓦwww.lochmorlich.com), at the east end of the loch five miles or so east of Aviemore on the way to Cairn Gorm mountain, rents equipment and offers tuition in a lovely setting with a sandy beach, while six miles up-valley near Kincraig, the Loch Insh Watersports Centre (see p.1217) offers the same facilities in equally beautiful surroundings. It also rents mountain bikes and boats for loch fishing, and gives ski instruction on a short dry slope.

Riding and **pony trekking** are on offer up and down the valley: try Ingrid at Alvie Stables near Kincraig (℡01540/651409), or the Carrbridge Trekking Centre, Station Road, Carrbridge, a few miles north of Aviemore (℡01479/841602).

Fishing is very much part of the local scene; you can fish for trout and salmon on the River Spey, and the Rothiemurchus Estate has a stocked trout-fishing loch at **Inverdruie**, where success is virtually guaranteed. Instruction and rod rental is available from the centre beside the loch.

The area is also great for **mountain biking**, with both Rothiemurchus and Glenmore estates more progressive in their attitude to the sport than many. The Rothiemurchus visitor centre at Inverdruie has route maps, and you can also rent bikes here, while Bothy Bikes (℡01479/810111), in the Aviemore Shopping Centre beside the train station on Grampian Road, rents out good-quality mountain bikes with front suspension, as well as offering advice and guided bike tours. For other outdoor equipment, in particular **climbing** and **hill-walking** gear, try Mountain Supplies in Aviemore (℡01479/810903).

Winter activities

Scottish **skiing** on a commercial level first really took off in Aviemore. By continental European and North American standards it's all on a tiny scale, but occasionally snow, sun and lack of crowds coincide and you can have a great day. February and March are usually the best times, but there's a chance of decent snow at any time between mid-November and April. Lots of places – not just in Aviemore itself – sell or rent equipment; for a rundown of ski schools and rental facilities in the area, check out the tourist office's *Ski Scotland* brochure or ⓦski.visitscotland.com.

The **Cairngorm Ski Area**, about eight miles southeast of Aviemore, above Loch Morlich in Glenmore Forest Park, is well served during winter by buses from Aviemore. You can rent skis, boards and other equipment from the Day Lodge at the foot of the ski area (℡01479/861261, ⓦwww .cairngormmountain.com), which also has a shop, a bar and restaurant, as well as the base station for the **funicular railway**, the principal means of getting to the top of the ski slopes. Various types of ski pass are available from here – in person, by phone or online. The facilities include a ski school, cafes at three different levels and a separate terrain park for skier and boarders. If there's lots of snow, the area around **Loch Morlich** and into the **Rothiemurchus Estate** provides enjoyable cross-country skiing through lovely woods, beside rushing burns and even over frozen lochs.

To add to the winter scene, there's a herd of reindeer at the **Cairngorm Reindeer Centre** by Loch Morlich (daily 10am–5pm; guided excursions to the main herd 11am), while between Loch Morlich and Inverdruie the **Cairngorm Sleddog Adventure Centre**, home of the UK's only sled dog team, offers daily tours of the kennels and a small museum (10am & 2pm; £7.50), as well as three-hour trips on a wheeled or ski-based sled pulled by the dogs (Oct–April only; £45 per person).

Practicalities

Aviemore's businesslike **tourist office** is just south of the train station on the main drag, Grampian Road (April–Oct Mon–Sat 9am–5pm, Sun 10am–4pm

Nov–March Mon–Fri 9am–5pm, Sat 10am–4pm; ☎01479/810363). It offers an accommodation booking service and reams of leaflets on local attractions.

There's no shortage of **accommodation** locally. On Grampian Road in Aviemore, *MacKenzies Hotel* (☎01479/810672, ⓔmackhotel@aol.com; ❷) is welcoming and family-friendly, while *Ravenscraig Guest House* (☎01479/810278, ⓦwww.aviemoreonline.com; ❷) offers similarly good value. The grandest place in the area is *Corrour House Hotel* at Inverdruie, two miles southeast of Aviemore (☎01479/810220, ⓦwww.corrourhousehotel.com; ❺). Aviemore's large SYHA **hostel** (☎0870/004 1104, ⓔreservations@syha .org.uk), is close to the tourist office, while the Aviemore Bunkhouse (☎01479/811181, ⓦwww.aviemore-bunkhouse.com) is a large, modern place beside the Old Bridge Inn on Dalfaber Road, within walking distance from the station. Towards the Cairngorms, there's another SYHA hostel at Loch Morlich (☎0870/004 1137; Christmas–Oct), as well as excellent accommodation in twin rooms (with shared facilities) at *Glenmore Lodge* (☎01479/861256, ⓦwww.glenmorelodge.org.uk; ❶) – full use of their superb facilities, which include a pool, weights room and indoor climbing wall is included. There's no shortage of **campsites** either: two of the best are Rothiemurchus Caravan Park at Coylumbridge (☎01479/812800) and the Forestry Enterprise site at Glenmore (☎01479/861271).

All along Aviemore's main drag are bistros, hotels and takeaways serving fairly predictable, run-of-the-mill **food**, but for a more interesting option head to *The Old Bridge Inn* on the east side of the railway on Dalfaber Road, which serves delicious meals and real ales in a mellow, cosy setting.

Cairn Gorm mountain

From Aviemore, a road leads past Rothiemurchus and Loch Morlich and winds its way up into the Cairngorms, reaching the Coire Cas car park at a height of 2150ft. Here there's the base station for the ski area and the departure point for the **Cairn Gorm Mountain Railway** (daily 10am–5.15pm; last train up 4.30pm; trains run every 15min; £8), a two-car funicular system which in 2001 replaced the main chairlift as the principal means of transportation to the top of the ski area. A highly controversial, £15 million scheme, it whisks skiers in winter, and tourists at any time of year, along a mile and a half of track to the top station at an altitude of 3600 feet, not far from the summit of Cairn Gorm mountain. The top station incorporates an exhibition/interpretation area and a café/restaurant from which spectacular views can be had on clear days.

At the base station there's a **ranger office** (daily: April–Oct 9am–5pm; Nov–March 8.30am–4.30pm) where you can find out about various trails leading out from the base station. If you're aiming to head to the summits, check here for the latest weather report.

Loch Garten and around

The **Abernethy Forest RSPB Reserve** on the shore of **LOCH GARTEN**, seven miles northeast of Aviemore and eight miles south of Grantown-on-Spey, is famous as the nesting site of one of Britain's rarest birds. A little over fifty years ago, the **osprey**, known in North America as the fish hawk, had completely disappeared from the British Isles. Then, in 1954, a single pair of these exquisite white-and-brown raptors mysteriously reappeared and built a nest in a tree half a mile or so from the loch. Now well established not only here but elsewhere, there are believed to be up to 150 pairs nesting across the Highlands. The best time to visit is between April and August, when the ospreys return from West Africa to nest and the RSPB opens an **observation**

24

Walks around Aviemore

Ordnance Survey Explorer map no. 403.

Walking of all grades is a highlight of the Aviemore area, though before setting out you should heed the usual safety guidelines. These are particularly important if you want to climb to the high tops, which include a number of Scotland's loftiest peaks. However, as well as the high mountain trails, there are some lovely and well-signposted **low-level walks** in the area. It takes an hour or so to complete the gentle circular walk around pretty **Loch an Eilean** (with its ruined castle) in the Rothiemurchus Estate, beginning at the end of the back road that turns east off the B970 two miles south of Aviemore. The helpful estate **visitor centres** at the lochside and by the roadside at Inverdruie provide more information on the many woodland trails that crisscross this area. A longer walk through this estate, famous for its atmospheric native woodland of gnarled Caledonian pines and shimmering birch trees, starts at the near end of **Loch Morlich**. Cross the river by the bridge and follow the dirt road, turning off after about twenty minutes to follow the signs to Aviemore. The path goes through beautiful pine woods and past tumbling burns, and you can branch off to Coylumbridge and Loch an Eilean. Unless you're properly prepared for a 25-mile hike, don't take the track to the **Lairig Ghru**, a famous old cattle drovers' route through a dramatic cleft in the mountain range which eventually brings you out near Braemar on the far side of the Cairngorm range.

Another good shortish (half-day) walk leads along a well-surfaced forestry track from Glenmore Lodge up towards the **Ryvoan Pass**, taking in An Lochan Uaine, known as the "Green Loch" and living up to its name, with amazing colours that range from turquoise to slate grey depending on the weather. The track narrows once past the loch and leads east towards Deeside, so retrace your steps if you don't want a major trek. The **Glenmore Forest Park Visitor Centre** by the roadside at the turn-off to Glenmore Lodge is the starting point for the three-hour round trip climb of Meall a' Bhuachaillie (2654ft), which offers excellent views and is usually accessible year-round. The centre has information on other trails in this section of the forest.

The **Speyside Way** (see p.1191), the long-distance footpath which begins on the Moray Firth coast at Buckie and follows the course of the Spey through the heart of whisky country, has recently been extended to Aviemore. A pleasant day-trip involves walking from Aviemore to Boat of Garten, on to the RSPB osprey sanctuary at Loch Garten, and return on the Strathspey Steam Railway.

---

centre (daily 10am–6pm; £2.50), complete with powerful telescopes and CCTV monitoring of the nest. This is the place to come to get a glimpse of osprey chicks in their nest; you'll be luckier to see the birds perform their trademark swoop over water to pluck a fish out with their talons. The reserve is also home to several other species of rare birds and animals, including the Scottish crossbill, capercaillie, whooper swan and red squirrel; once-weekly **guided walks** leave from the observation centre (Wed 9.30am).

Loch Garten is about a mile and a half east of **BOAT OF GARTEN** village: from the village, if you cross the Spey then take the Grantown road, the reserve is signposted to the right. An attractive wee place, Boat of Garten has a number of good **accommodation** options: *Fraoch Lodge*, 15 Deshar Rd (☎01479/831331, ✆www.scotmountain.co.uk) is an excellent hostel with bunkhouse and twin rooms (❶); alternatively, the *Old Ferryman's House* (☎01479/831370; ❷), just across the Spey, is a wonderfully homely, hospitable B&B, with no TVs, lots of books and delicious evening meals and breakfasts.

Kincraig

At **KINCRAIG**, six miles southwest of Aviemore on the B9152 towards Kingussie, there are a couple of unusual encounters with animals which offer a memorable diversion if you're not setting off on outdoor pursuits. While the style of the **Highland Wildlife Park** (daily: June–Aug 10am–7pm; April, May, Sept & Oct closes 6pm; Nov–March closes 4pm; last entry 2hr before closing; in snowy conditions call in advance; ☏01540/651270; £7.50), with its various captive animals, may not appeal to everyone, it is accredited to the Royal Zoological Society of Scotland and offers a chance to see exotic foreigners such as wolves and bison, as well as many rarely seen natives, including pine martens, capercaillie, wildcat and eagles. Nearby, the engrossing **Working Sheepdogs** at Leault Farm has demonstrations (May–June & Sept–Oct Sun–Fri noon & 4pm; July & Aug also 2pm; Nov–April call ☏01540/651310 to arrange visit; £4) which offers the rare opportunity to see a champion shepherd herd a flock of sheep with up to eight dogs.

The Loch Insh Watersports Centre (☏01540/651272, ⓦwww.lochinsh.com), beautifully sited beside the loch, has en-suite B&B and self-catering chalets (❶) as well as a decent waterfront café/restaurant (daily 10am–10pm).

Grantown-on-Spey

Buses run from Aviemore and Inverness to the small town of **GRANTOWN-ON-SPEY**, about fifteen miles northeast of Aviemore, which makes a relaxing alternative base for exploring the Strathspey area. Life is concentrated around the central square, with its attractive Georgian architecture, including a small **museum** and resource centre on Burnfield Avenue (Mon–Sat 10am–4pm; £2; ⓦwww.grantown-on-spey.co.uk). The **tourist office** is on the High Street (March–Oct Mon–Sat 9am–5pm, Sun 10am–4pm; ☏01479/872773).

As with much of Speyside, there's a decent choice of **accommodation**. For B&B, *Parkburn Guest House* (☏01479/873116, ⓦwww.parkburn.btinternet.co.uk; ❷) is welcoming, while if you're after something more upmarket, head for the large seventeenth-century *Garth Hotel*, at the north end of the square (☏01479/872836, ⓦwww.garthhotel.com; ❹). In the budget range, there's a bunkhouse at *Ardenbeg Outdoor Centre* (☏01479/872824, ⓦwww.ardenbeg.co.uk), on Grant Road, parallel to the High Street.

Newtonmore and Kingussie

Twelve miles southwest of Aviemore, close neighbours **NEWTONMORE** and **KINGUSSIE** (pronounced "king-*yoos*-ee") are pleasant villages at the head of the Strathspey Valley separated by a couple of miles of farmland. On the **shinty** field, however, their peaceful coexistence is forgotten and the two become bitter rivals; in recent years Kingussie have been the dominant force in the game, a fierce, home-grown relative of hockey (ⓦwww.shinty.com). The chief attraction is the excellent **Highland Folk Museum** (☏01540/661307), split between complementary sites in the two towns. The Kingussie section (April–Sept Mon–Sat 9.30am–5.30pm, Oct Mon–Fri 9.30am–4.30pm; winter by appointment; £2.50) contains an absorbing collection of artefacts typical to traditional Highland ways of life, as well as a farming museum, an old smokehouse, a mill, a Hebridean "blackhouse", and a traditional herb and flower garden; most days in summer there's a demonstration of various traditional crafts. The larger outdoor site at Newtonmore (April–Aug daily

10.30am–5.30pm; Sept daily 11am–4.30pm; Oct Mon–Fri 11am–4.30pm; £5, or £6 for a joint ticket for both sites), tries to create more of a living history museum, with an old vintage bus offering a hop-on-hop-off tour round reconstructions of a working croft, a water-powered sawmill, a church where recitals on traditional Highland instruments are given, and a small village of blackhouses constructed using only authentic tools and materials.

Kingussie is also notable for the ruins of **Ruthven Barracks** (free access), standing east across the river on a hillock. The best-preserved garrison built to pacify the Highlands after the 1715 rebellion, it makes for great exploring by day and is impressively floodlit at night.

Kingussie's friendly **tourist office** is in the same building as the entrance to the Highland Folk Museum, on Duke Street (same hours as museum; ☎01540/661307). The Wildcat Centre in Newtonmore (varied hours, generally Mon–Fri 9.30am–12.30pm & 2.15–5.15pm, Sat 9.30am–12.30pm; call ☎01540/673131 to confirm) also offers local information and details of some well-organized walking trails in the area. The *Auld Poor House* (☎01540/661558, ⓦ www.yates128.freeserve.co.uk; ❶), on the road to Kincraig, is a comfortable **B&B** with a resident qualified masseuse, while *Ruthven Steadings* (☎01540/662328, ⓦ www.ruthvensteadings.co.uk; ❷) is just along the road from the striking ruined barracks. The best of a number of local **hostels** are the *Newtonmore Independent Hostel* (☎01540/673360, ⓦ www.highlandhostel.co.uk) and the *Strathspey Mountain Hostel* (☎01540/673694). Of the **hotels**, the *Scot House* in Kingussie (☎01540/661351, ⓦ www.scothouse.com; ❹) is known for its hospitality and restaurant, while the nine rooms at *The Cross* restaurant (see below) are pricier but individual and luxurious (March–Dec; ❺).

The most ambitious **food** in the area is served at *The Cross* restaurant, in a converted tweed mill on Tweed Mill Brae in Kingussie (☎01540/661166, ⓦ www.thecross.co.uk; closed Sun/Mon & Dec–Feb). Its pricey meals make interesting use of local ingredients and there's a vast wine list. Cheaper food is available at several cafés and pubs in both towns – *The Glen* or the *Braeriach* in Newtonmore, or the *Royal Hotel* or *Tipsy Laird* in Kingussie.

The Great Glen

The **Great Glen**, a major geological fault line cutting diagonally across the Highlands from Fort William to Inverness, is the defining geographic feature of the north of Scotland. A huge rift valley was formed when the northwestern and southeastern sides of the fault slid in opposite directions for more than sixty miles, while the present landscape was shaped by glaciers that retreated only around 8000 BC. The glen is impressive more for its sheer scale than its beauty, but the imposing barrier of loch and mountain means that no one can travel into the northern Highlands without passing through it. With the two major service centres of the Highlands at either end it makes an obvious and rewarding route between the west and east coasts.

Of the Great Glen's four elongated lochs, the most famous is **Loch Ness**, home to the mythical monster; lochs **Oich**, **Lochy** and **Linnhe** (the last of these a sea loch) are less renowned though no less attractive. All four are linked by the Caledonian Canal. The southwestern end of the Great Glen is dominated by **Fort William**, the second-largest town in the Highland region – a useful base, with plenty of places to stay, eat and get hold of information on nearby activities, but not one of the more charming places you'll encounter

Scotland. The countryside around the town, however, is a blend of rugged mountain terrain and tranquil sea loch.

The main **A82** road runs the length of the Great Glen, although relatively high traffic levels means that it's not a fast or particularly easy route to drive. The area is reasonably well served by **buses**, with several daily services between Inverness and Fort William, and a couple of extra buses covering the section between Fort William and Invergarry during school terms. However, the traditional and most rewarding way to travel through the Glen itself is by **boat**. A flotilla of kayaks, small yachts and pleasure vessels take advantage of the canal and its old wooden locks during the summer. Alternatively, an excellent **cycle path** traverses the Glen, as well as a long-distance footpath, the seventy-mile **Great Glen Way** (ⓦ www.greatglenway.com), a relatively undemanding five-day hike that uses a combination of canal towpath and forest and hill tracks.

Loch Ness and around

Twenty-three miles long, unfathomably deep, cold and often moody, **Loch Ness** is bounded by rugged heather–clad mountains rising steeply from a wooded shoreline and attractive valleys opening up on either side. Its fame,

---

Nessie

The world-famous **Loch Ness monster**, affectionately known as **"Nessie"** (and by serious aficionados as *Nessiteras rhombopteryx*), has been a local celebrity for some time. The first mention of a mystery creature crops up in St Adamnan's seventh-century biography of **St Columba**, who allegedly calmed an aquatic animal that had attacked one of his monks. Present-day interest, however, is probably greater outside Scotland than within the country, and dates from the building of the road along the loch's western shore in the early 1930s. In 1934, the *Daily Mail* published London surgeon R.K. Wilson's sensational photograph of the head and neck of the monster peering up out of the loch, and the hype has hardly diminished since. Recent encounters range from glimpses of ripples by anglers to the famous occasion in 1961 when thirty hotel guests saw a pair of humps break the water's surface and cruise for about half a mile before submerging.

Photographic evidence is showcased in the two "Monster Exhibitions" at Drumnadrochit, but the most impressive of these exhibits – including the renowned black-and-white movie footage of Nessie's humps moving across the water, and Wilson's original head and shoulders shot – have now been exposed as fakes. Indeed, in few other places on earth has watching a rather lifeless and often grey expanse of water seemed so compelling, or have floating logs, otters and boat wakes been photographed so often and with such excitement. Yet while even high-tech sonar surveys carried out over the past two decades have failed to come up with conclusive evidence, it's hard to dismiss Nessie as pure myth. After all, no one yet knows where the unknown layers of silt and mud at the bottom of the loch begin and end: best estimates say the loch is over 750 feet deep, deeper than much of the North Sea, while others point to the possibilities of underwater caves and undiscovered channels connected to the sea. What scientists have found in the cold, murky depths, including pure white eels and rare Arctic char, offer fertile grounds for speculation, with different theories declaring Nessie to be a remnant from the dinosaur age, a giant newt or a huge visiting Baltic sturgeon. With the possibility of a definitive answer sending shivers through the local tourist industry, monster-hunters are these days recruited over the web, with the site ⓦ www.lochnessproject.org offering round-the-clock **webcams** with views both across the loch and underwater.

however, is based overwhelmingly on its legendary inhabitant Nessie, the "Loch Ness monster", whose fame ensures a steady flow of hopeful visitors to the settlements dotted along the loch, in particular **Drumnadrochit**. Nearby, the impressive ruins of **Castle Urquhart** – a favourite monster-spotting location – perch atop a rock on the lochside and attract a deluge of bus parties during the summer. Almost as busy in high season is the village of **Fort Augustus**, at the more scenic southwest tip of Loch Ness, where you can watch queues of boats tackling one of the Caledonian Canal's longest flight of locks.

Away from the lochside, and seeing a fraction of Loch Ness's visitor numbers, the remote glens of **Urquhart** and **Affric** make an appealing contrast, with Affric in particular boasting narrow, winding roads, gushing streams and hillsides dotted in ancient Caledonian pine forests. More commonly encountered is the often bleak high country of **Glen Moriston**, a little to the southwest of Glen Affric, which holds the main road between Inverness and Skye.

Although most visitors use the tree-lined A82 road, which runs along the western shore of Loch Ness, the sinuous single-track B862/B852 (originally a military road built to link Fort Augustus and Fort George) that skirts the eastern shore is quieter and affords far more spectacular views. You'll need your own transport to complete the whole loop around the loch.

Drumnadrochit and around

Situated above a verdant, sheltered bay of Loch Ness fifteen miles southwest of Inverness, **DRUMNADROCHIT** is the epicentre of Nessie hype, sporting a rash of tacky souvenir shops and two rival monster exhibitions whose head-to-head scramble for punters occasionally erupts into acrimonious exchanges, detailed with relish by the local press. Of the pair, the **Loch Ness 2000 Exhibition** (daily: July & Aug 9am–8pm; June & Sept 9am–6pm; Easter–May 9.30am–5pm; Oct–Easter 10am–3.30pm; £5.95), though more expensive, is the better bet, offering an in-depth rundown of eyewitness accounts through the ages and various research projects carried out in the loch. A recent upgrade has attempted to offer something to sceptics as well as believers by outlining more of the scientific background to set against the various myths. The **Original Loch Ness Monster Exhibition** (daily: July & Aug 9am–9pm; rest of year 9am–5pm; Dec–March closes 4pm; £4.75) is less worthwhile – basically a gift shop with a shoddy audiovisual show tacked on the side.

Cruises on the loch aboard the *Nessie Hunter* (Easter–Oct hourly 9.30am–6pm; rest of year phone ☎01456/450395; 50min; £9) can be booked at the Original Loch Ness Visitor Centre, though a more relaxing alternative i to head out **fishing** with a local gillie – the boat can take 5–8 people and cost around £30 for two hours; contact Bruce on ☎01456/450279 to book.

Most photographs allegedly showing the monster have been taken a coupl of miles east of Drumnadrochit, around the fourteenth-century ruine lochside **Castle Urquhart** (daily: April–Sept 9.30am–6.30pm; Oct–Marc 9.30am–4.30pm; £5.50; HS). Built as a strategic base to guard the Great Gler the castle was taken by Edward I of England and later held by Robert th Bruce against Edward III, only to be blown up in 1692 to prevent it fror falling to the Jacobites. Today it's one of Scotland's classic picture-postca ruins, crawling with tourists by day but particularly splendid floodlit at nigł when all the crowds have gone.

Practicalities

Drumnadrochit's **tourist office** (April–June & Oct Mon–Sat 9am–5pm; Ju & Aug Mon–Sat 9am–6pm, Sun 10am–4pm; Sept Mon–Sat 9am–5pm, St

10am–4pm; Nov–March Mon–Fri 10am–1.30pm; ☎01456/459076) shares space with a Highland Council service point in the middle of the main car park in the village. Two very welcoming **B&Bs** are *Gillyflowers* (☎01456/450641, ⓦwww.cali.co.uk/freeway/gillyflowers; ❶), a renovated farmhouse tucked away down a country lane in Lewiston, or the modern *Drumbuie* (☎01456/450634, ⓔdrumbuie@amserve.net; ❶), on the northern approach to Drumnadrochit. For **hostel** beds, head to the immaculate and friendly *Loch Ness Backpackers Lodge* (☎01456/450807, ⓦwww.lochness -backpackers.com), at Coiltie Farmhouse in Lewiston; follow the signs to the left when coming from Drumnadrochit.

Most of the hotels in the area – the *Benleva* in particular – serve good bar **food**; in Drumnadrochit the *Glen Café* has a short and simple menu with basic grills, while the slightly more upmarket *Fiddlers' Café Bar*, next door to the *Glen* on the village green, offers local steaks, salmon and appetizing home-baked pizza; it also rents good-quality **mountain bikes** (☎01456/450678), and provides maps and rain capes.

Glen Affric

Due west of Drumnadrochit is a vast area of high peaks, remote glens and few roads. The reason most folk head this way is to explore the native forests and grand mountains of **Glen Affric**, generally held as one of Scotland's most beautiful landscapes. The approach to the glen is through the small settlement of **CANNICH**, fourteen miles west of Drumnadrochit on the A831. Hemmed in by a string of Munros, the Glen Affric is great for picnics and pottering, particularly on a calm and sunny day, when the still water reflects the islands and surrounding hills. From the car park at the head of the single-track road along the glen, ten miles southwest of Cannich, there's a selection of **walks**: the trip round Loch Affric will take you a good five hours but captures the glen, its wildlife and Caledonian pine and birch woods in all their remote splendour.

Fort Augustus

FORT AUGUSTUS, a tiny village at the scenic southwestern tip of Loch Ness, was named after George II's son, the chubby lad who later became the 'Butcher' duke of Cumberland of Culloden fame; it was built as a barracks after the 1715 Jacobite rebellion. Today, it's dominated by comings and goings along the Caledonian Canal, which leaves Loch Ness here, and by its large former **Benedictine Abbey**, a campus of grey Victorian buildings founded on the site of the original fort in 1876. The abbey formerly housed a Catholic boys school and was subsequently home to a small but active community of monks. More recently it has been bought and sold by a series of developers, but its future use remains uncertain. Traditional Highland culture is the subject of the lively and informative exhibition at the **Clansmen Centre** (Easter to mid-Oct daily 10am–6pm; £3), on the banks of the canal. Guides sporting sporrans and rough woollen plaids talk you through the daily life of the region's seventeenth-century inhabitants inside a mock-up of a turf-roofed stone croft, followed by demonstrations of weaponry in the back garden. Rather more sedate is the small **Caledonian Canal Heritage Centre** (July–Sept daily 10am–5pm; Easter–June & Oct Mon–Thurs & Sun 10am–5pm; free), in Ardchattan House on the northern bank of the canal, where you can view old photographs and records about the history of the canal and watch a black-and-white film of the days when paddle boats and large barges passed through the locks every day.

Fort Augustus's small **tourist office** (daily: July & Aug 9am–6pm; April–June, Sept & Oct 9am–5pm; ☎01320/366779) hands out useful free maps detailing popular walks in the area. They'll also help sort out fishing permits for the loch or nearby river. There's **hostel** accommodation at *Morag's Lodge* (☎01320/366289) and at *Stravaigers Lodge* (☎01320/366257; ⓦwww .highlandbunkhouse.com), which has 15 twin rooms (❶) and good facilities. The *Old Pier* (☎01320/366418, ⓔjenny@oldpierhouse.com; min. stay two nights; ❸) is a particularly appealing **B&B** right on the loch. For **food**, your best bet is to head to the lively local pub, the *Lock Inn*, which has regular music and draws a mixed clientele of locals, yachties and backpackers, as does *Poachers* on the main road.

Fort William and around

With its stunning position on Loch Linnhe, tucked in below the snow-streaked bulk of Ben Nevis, **FORT WILLIAM** (known by the many walkers and climbers that come here as "Fort Bill"), should be a gem. Sadly, the same lack of taste that nearly saw the town renamed "Abernevis" in the 1950s is evident in the ribbon bungalow development and ill-advised dual carriageway – complete with grubby pedestrian underpass – which have wrecked the waterfront. The main street and the little squares off it are more appealing, though occupied by some decidedly tacky tourist gift shops. Ultimately, however, Fort William is an important regional centre, and the useful facilities here include a cinema, swimming pool and a couple of large supermarkets.

Any disappointment you harbour about the dispiriting flavour of Fort William itself should be offset against the wealth of scenery and activities in its immediate vicinity. Dominating the scene is **Ben Nevis**, Britain's highest peak, best approached from scenic Glen Nevis. The most famous glen of all, **Glen Coe**, lies on the main A82 road half an hour's drive south of Fort William. Nowadays the whole area is unashamedly given over to tourism, and Fort

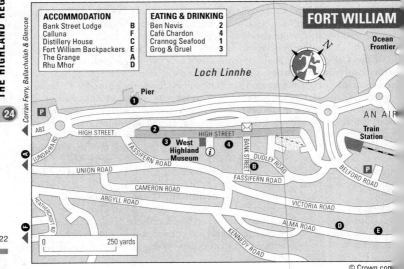

24

Corran Ferry, Ballachulish & Glencoe

ACCOMMODATION
Bank Street Lodge	B
Calluna	F
Distillery House	C
Fort William Backpackers	E
The Grange	A
Rhu Mhor	D

EATING & DRINKING
Ben Nevis	2
Café Chardon	4
Crannog Seafood	1
Grog & Gruel	3

FORT WILLIAM

Ocean Frontier

Loch Linnhe

Pier

AN AIR

Train Station

HIGH STREET · HIGH STREET

West Highland Museum ⓘ

A82

LUNDAVRA RD

FASSIFERN ROAD

BANK STREET

DUDLEY ROAD

FASSIFERN ROAD

BELFORD ROAD

UNION ROAD

CAMERON ROAD

ARGYLL ROAD

VICTORIA ROAD

HEATHERCROFT RD

KENNEDY ROAD

ALMA ROAD

0 · 250 yards

© Crown cop

William is swamped by bus tours throughout the summer, but, as ever in the Highlands, within a thirty-minute drive you can be totally alone.

The Town

Fort William's downfall started in the nineteenth century, when the original fort, which gave the town its name, was demolished to make way for the train line. Today, the town is a sprawl of dual carriageways, and there's little to detain you except the splendid and idiosyncratic **West Highland Museum**, on Cameron Square, just off the High Street (June–Sept Mon–Sat 10am–5pm; July & Aug also Sun 2–5pm; Oct–May Mon–Sat 10am–4pm; £2). Its collections cover virtually every aspect of Highland life and the presentation is traditional, but very well done, making a refreshing change from state-of-the-art heritage centres. On the loch side of the railway station, **Ocean Frontier** (daily 10am–6pm) is an undersea centre with a difference, devoted to various forms of underwater exploration from old copper-helmeted diving suits to remote control submarines.

Excursions from town include the popular day-trip to Mallaig (see p.1231) on the **Jacobite Steam Train** (mid-June to Sept Mon–Fri; Aug also Sun; depart Fort William 10.20am, depart Mallaig 2.10pm; day-return £24; bookings ☎01463/239026), enjoying star status these days as the locomotive used in the *Harry Potter* films. Heading to the west coast via historic Glenfinnan (see p.1230), the journey takes in some of the region's most spectacular scenery.

Practicalities

Next to each other at the north end of the High Street are the **bus station** (with services from Inverness) and the **train station** (a stop on the scenic West Highland Railway direct from Glasgow; see p.1204). The busy **tourist office** is on Cameron Square, just off High Street (April–May & Oct Mon–Sat 9am–5pm, Sun 10am–4pm; June & Sept Mon–Sat 9am–6pm, Sun 10am–6pm; July Mon–Sat 9am–7pm, Sun 10am–6pm; Aug Mon–Sat 9am–8pm, Sun 10am–6pm; Nov–March Mon–Fri 10am–5pm, Sat 10am–4pm; ☎01397/703781).

The Nevis Range

Seven miles northeast of Fort William by the A82, on the slopes of **Aonach Mhor**, one of the high mountains abutting Ben Nevis, the **Nevis Range** (☎01397/705825, ⓦwww.nevis-range.co.uk) is, in winter, Scotland's highest ski area. All year round, however, Highland County bus #41 runs from Fort William five times a day (Mon–Fri) to the base station of the country's only **gondola** system (July & Aug daily 9.30am–6pm, Thurs & Fri until 9pm; rest of year daily 10am–5pm; closed mid-Nov–mid-Dec for maintenance; £7.50 return). The one-and-a-half mile gondola trip (15min), rising 2000ft, gives an easy approach to some high-level walking as well as spectacular views from the terrace of the self-service restaurant at the top station. Active Highs (☎01397/712188, ⓦwww.active-highs.co.uk) offer dual **paragliding** flights off the mountain, while Britain's only championship-grade **downhill mountain bike course** (mid-May–mid-Sept 11am–3pm; £9.75 includes gondola one-way), a hair-raising 3km route, starts at the gondola top station. There's also 25 miles of waymarked off-road bike routes on the mountainside and in the Leanachan Forest, ranging from gentle paths to cross-country scrambles. Off Beat Bikes (☎01397/704008, ⓦwww.offbeatbikes.co.uk) rent general mountain bikes as well as full-suspension bikes for the downhill course from their shops in Fort William and at the gondola base station (mid-May–mid-Sept).

Numerous B&Bs are also scattered across the town, many of them in the suburb of Corpach on the other side of Loch Linnhe, three miles along the Mallaig road (served by regular buses), where you'll also find a couple of good hostels.

In town

Bank Street Lodge Bank St ☏01397/700730, ⓦwww.accommodation-fortwilliam.com. New and slightly characterless lodge with neat doubles, twin and family rooms, all with TVs, and a very central location. Also has a couple of rooms used as four- or eight-bed dorms (£11 per person). ❶

Calluna Heathcroft ☏01397/700451, ⓦwww .westcoast-mountainguides.co.uk/accommodation .htm. Family-run budget self-catering flats with twin and four-person rooms and standard facilities. It can be tricky to find – though a free pick-up from town is available. The owner is one of the area's top mountain guides, so there's plenty of good outdoor advice available.

Distillery House North Rd, just north of the town centre near the junction for Glen Nevis ☏01397/700103, ⓦwww.visit-fortwilliam .co.uk/distillery-house. Very comfortable and well-equipped upper-range B&B. ❸

Fort William Backpackers Alma Rd ☏01397/700711, ⓦwww.scotlandstophostels.com. A big, rambling, archetypal backpacker hostel five-minutes' walk up the hill from town, with great views and large communal areas. Part of the Macbackpackers chain, so minibus tours pull in at regular intervals.

The Grange Grange Rd ☏01397/705516, ⓦwww.thegrange-scotland.co.uk. Top-grade accommodation in a striking old stone house, with four luxurious en-suite doubles and a spacious garden. Vegetarian breakfasts on request. Non-smoking. April–Oct. ❺

Rhu Mhor 42 Alma Rd ☏01397/702213, ⓦwww.rhumhor.co.uk. Congenial B&B ten minutes' walk from the town centre, offering good breakfasts; vegetarians and vegans are catered for by arrangement. ❶

Out of town

Achintee Farm Guest House Glen Nevis ☏01397/702240, ⓦwww.glennevis.com. Pleasant B&B run by the same folk as Ben Nevis Bunkhouse (see below) right at the start of the Ben Nevis footpath. ❹

Ben Nevis Bunkhouse Achintee Farm, Glen Nevis ☏01397/702240, ⓦwww.glennevis.com. A more civilized option than the nearby SYHA place, with hot showers, self-catering kitchen and a small licensed restaurant, as well as quite smart B&B (see above). Located just over the river from the Ben Nevis Visitor Centre – get to it by following the Ben path across the river or by taking Achintee Rd along the north side of the River Nevis from Claggan.

Farr Cottage On the main A830 in Corpach ☏01397/772315, ⓦwww.farrcottage.co.uk. One of the liveliest of the local backpacker hostels, with everything from pizza feasts to whisky tastings going on in the evenings. Accommodation is in medium-size dorms with three rooms with double bunks available as twins or doubles. ❶

Glen Nevis SYHA hostel Two and a half miles up the Glen Nevis road ☏01397/702336, ⓔreservations@syha.org.uk. Large, but best avoided in midsummer, when it's chock-full of teenagers. Handy for the Ben Nevis path but a long walk from town.

Eating and drinking

Fort William has a reasonable range of places **to eat**. The pick of the bunch i the *Crannog Seafood Restaurant*, an elegantly converted bait store on the pier where oysters, langoustines, prawns and salmon are cooked with flair. On th High Street, the *Grog and Gruel* serves an eclectic mix of pizzas, pasta an Mexican dishes with real ale, while the *Ben Nevis Inn* opposite has tradition pub grub as well as live music a couple of times a week. Your best chance of decent coffee is at *Fired Art*, a "paint-your-own-pottery" studio with its ow café at 147 High Street. A good place for **picnic food** as well as a snack is th *Café Chardon*, up a lane off High Street; they do excellent baguettes, croissan and pastries to eat in or take away.

Glen Nevis and Ben Nevis

A ten-minute drive south of Fort William, **GLEN NEVIS** is indisputab among the Highlands' most impressive glens: a classic U-shaped glacial vall

24

hemmed in by steep bracken-covered slopes and swathes of blue-grey scree. Herds of shaggy Highland cattle graze the valley floor, where a sparkling river gushes through glades of trees. Highland County **bus** #42 runs from An Aird, beside the Safeway supermarket and the railway station, Fort William (roughly hourly) as far as the SYHA hostel, two and a half miles up the Glen Nevis road; some buses carry on another two and a half miles up the glen to the car park by the Lower Falls (late-May to Sept only; 10–20min beyond the hostel).

Of all the walks in and around Glen Nevis, the **ascent of Ben Nevis** (4406ft), Britain's highest summit, inevitably attracts the most attention. Despite the fact that it's quite a slog up to the summit, and that it is by no means the most attractive mountain in Scotland, in high summer the trail is teeming with hikers, whatever the weather. However, this doesn't mean the mountain should be treated casually. It can snow round the summit any day of the year and more people perish here annually than on Everest, so take the necessary precautions; in winter, of course, the mountain should be left to the experts. The most obvious **route** to the top, a Victorian pony path up the whaleback south side of the mountain, built to service the observatory that once stood on the top, starts from the helpful Glen Nevis visitor centre (daily June–Sept 9am–6pm; Easter–mid-May & Oct 9am–5pm), a mile and a half southeast of Fort William along the Glen Nevis road (bus #42 from An Aird in Fort William). Allow a full day for the climb (8hr).

Spean Bridge

Ten miles northeast of Fort William, the village of **SPEAN BRIDGE** marks the junction of the A82 with the A86 from Dalwhinnie and Kingussie (see p.1217). If you're here, its well worth heading a mile out of the village on the A82 towards Inverness to the **Commando Memorial**, a group of bronze soldiers commemorating the men who trained in the area during World War II. The statue looks out on an awesome sweep of moor and mountain that takes in Lochaber and the Ben Nevis massif. A few hundred yards from the memorial, on the minor B8004 which heads towards **Gairlochy**, is one of the Highland's great foodie havens, the *Old Pines* "restaurant with rooms" (℡01397/712324, �W www.oldpines.co.uk; half-board ❽).

Glen Coe

Breathtakingly beautiful **Glen Coe** (literally "Valley of Weeping"), sixteen miles south of Fort William on the A82, is one of the best-known Highland glens: a spectacular mountain valley between velvety-green conical peaks, their tops often wreathed in cloud, and cascades of rock and scree. In 1692 it was the site of a notorious massacre, in which the MacDonalds were victims of a long-standing government desire to suppress the clans. Fed up with what they regarded as unacceptable lawlessness, and a groundswell of Jacobitism and Catholicism, the government offered a general pardon to all those who signed an oath of allegiance to William III by January 1, 1692. When clan chief **Alastair MacDonald** missed the deadline, a plot was hatched to make an example of "that damnable sept", and **Campbell of Glenlyon** was ordered to billet his soldiers in the homes of the MacDonalds, who for ten days entertained them with traditional Highland hospitality. In the early morning of February 13, the soldiers turned on their hosts, slaying between 38 and 45 and causing more than 300 to flee in a blizzard, some to die of exposure.

Beyond the small village of **GLENCOE** at the western end of the glen, the glen itself, a property of the National Trust for Scotland since the 1930s, is virtually uninhabited, and provides outstanding climbing and walking. The

Walks around Glen Coe

Ordnance Survey Explorer map no. 384.

A good introduction to the splendours of Glen Coe is the half-day hike over the **Devil's Staircase**, which follows part of the old military road that once ran between Fort William and Stirling. The trail, part of the West Highland Way and a good option for families and less experienced hikers, starts at the village of **Kinlochleven** and is marked by thistle signs, which lead uphill to the 1804ft pass and down the other side into Glen Coe. The Devil's Staircase was named by 400 soldiers who endured severe hardship to build it in the seventeenth century, but in fine settled weather the trail is safe and affords stunning views of Loch Eilde and Buachaille Etive Mhor.

Set right in the heart of the glen, the half-day **Allt Coire Gabhail** hike starts at the car park opposite the distinctive Three Sisters massif on the main A82. From the road, drop down to the floor of the glen and cross the River Coe via the wooden bridge, where the path heads straight up the Allt Coire Gabhail for a couple of miles to a false summit directly ahead – actually the rim of the so-called "Lost Valley" which the Clan MacDonald used to flee to and hide their cattle in when attacked. Once in the valley, there are superb views of Bidean nan Bian, Gearr Aonach and Beinn Fhada. Undoubtedly one of the finest walks in the Glen Coe area not entailing the ascent of a Munro is the **Buachaille Etive Beag** circuit, which follows the textbook glacial valleys of Lairig Eilde and Lairig Gartain, ascending 1968ft in only nine miles of rough trail. Park near the waterfall at **The Study** – the gorge part of the A82 through Glen Coe – and walk up the road until you see a sign pointing south to "Loch Etiveside". The path angles up from here to the top of the pass, a rise of 787ft from the road. From here, follow the burn until you can pick up the trail heading up the eastern side of Stob Dubh (the "black peat"), which leads to the col of the Lairig Gartain, and onwards to the top of the pass. Drop down the other side to the main road, where the roughly parallel route of the old military road offers a gentler and safer return to the Study with superb views of the Three Sisters – finer than those ever seen by drivers.

NTS **visitor centre** (April–Aug daily 9.30am–5.30pm, Sept & Oct daily 10am–5pm, Nov–Feb Fri–Mon 10am–4pm, March daily 10am–4pm; £3.50; NTS), on the main road near the village, is an interesting ecofriendly building where you'll find a good exhibition with a balanced account of the massacre alongside some entertaining material on climbing down the years and the conservation challenges faced by the glen. There's also a café here, but to work off the cakes, informative ranger-led **guided walks** (June–Aug) leave from the centre: on different days of the week a high-level hike and a low-level walk are offered.

Practicalities

To get to the heart of Glen Coe from Fort William by **public transport** the best option is to hop on the Glasgow-bound Scottish Citylink coach service. The Highland County bus #44 from Fort William to Kinlochleven also stops at Glencoe village.

There's a good selection of **accommodation** in Glen Coe and the surrounding area. Basic options include an SYHA **hostel** (T01855/811219, Ⓔreservations@syha.org.uk) on a back road halfway between Glencoe village and the *Clachaig Inn*; the year-round *Red Squirrel* **campsite** (T01855/811256) nearby; and a grassier NTS campsite (T01855/811397; April–Oct) on the main road. Glencoe village has a few comfortable **B&Bs**, such as the secluded *Scorry Breac* (T01855/811354, Ⓦwww.scorrybreac.co.uk; ❷), and the *Glen C*

Guest House (☎01855/811244; ⓦwww.theglencoeguesthouse.com; ❷), while the best-known **hotel** in the area is the stark *Clachaig Inn* (☎01855/811252, ⓦwww.clachaig.com; ❸), a great place to swap stories with fellow climbers and to reward your exertions with pints of beer and heaped platefuls of food; it's three miles up Glen Coe, on the minor road from Glencoe village. At the other, eastern end of the glen, close to the Glen Coe ski area, is another well-established climber's watering hole, the *Kingshouse Hotel* (☎01855/851259; ⓦwww.kingy.com; ❸ excludes breakfast), a classic wayfarers' inn which always proves a welcome sight after the wide emptiness of Rannoch Moor.

The west coast

For many people, the Highlands' starkly beautiful **west coast** – stretching from the **Morvern peninsula** (opposite Mull) in the south to wind-lashed **Cape Wrath** in the far north – is the finest part of Scotland. Serrated by fjord-like sea lochs, the long coastline is scattered with windswept white-sand beaches, cliff-girt headlands, and rugged mountains sweeping up from the shoreline. The fast-changing weather rolling off the North Atlantic can be harsh, but it can also often create memorable plays of light, mood and landscape. When the sun shines, the sparkle of the sea, the richness of colour and the clarity of the views out to the scattered Hebrides are simply irresistible. This also is the least populated part of Britain, with just two small towns, and yawning tracts of moorland and desolate peat bog between crofting settlements.

The **Vikings**, who ruled the region in the ninth century, called it the "South Land", from which the modern district of Sutherland takes its name. After Culloden, the Clearances (see p.1250) emptied most of the inland glens of the far north, however, and left the population clinging to the coastline, where a herring-fishing industry developed. Today, tourism, crofting, fishing and salmon farming are the mainstay of the local economy, supplemented by EU construction grants and subsidies to farm the sheep you'll encounter everywhere.

For visitors, **cycling** and **walking** are the obvious ways to make the most of the superb scenery, and countless lochans and crystal-clear rivers offer superlative trout and salmon **fishing**. The shattered cliffs of the far northwest are an ornithologist's dream, harbouring some of Europe's largest and most diverse **seabird colonies**, while the area's craggy mountaintops are the haunt of the elusive golden eagle.

The most visited part of the west coast is the stretch between Kyle of Lochalsh and Ullapool. Lying within easy reach of Inverness, this sector boasts the region's more obvious highlights: the awesome mountainscape of **Torridon**, **Gairloch**'s sandy beaches, the famous botanic gardens at **Inverewe**, and **Ullapool** itself, a picturesque and bustling fishing town from where ferries leave for the Outer Hebrides. However, press on further north, or south, and you'll get a truer sense of the isolation that makes the west coast so special. Traversed by few roads, the remote northwest corner of Scotland is wild and bleak, receiving the full force of the North Atlantic's frequently ferocious weather. The scattered settlements of the far southwest, meanwhile, tend to be more sheltered, but they are separated by some of the most extensive wilderness areas in Britain – lonely peninsulas with evocative Gaelic names like **Ardnamurchan**, **Knoydart** and **Glenelg**.

24

Without your own vehicle, **transport** can be a problem. There's a reasonable **train** service from Inverness to Kyle of Lochalsh and from Fort William to Mallaig, and a useful **summer bus** service connects Inverness to Ullapool and Durness. **Driving** is a much simpler option: the roads aren't busy, though they are frequently single-track and scattered with sheep.

Morvern to Knoydart: the "Rough Bounds"

The remote and sparsely-populated southwest corner of the Highlands, from the empty district of **Morvern** to the isolated peninsula of **Knoydart**, is a dramatic, lonely region of mountain, moorland and almost deserted glens fringed by a coast of stunning white beaches, with wonderful views to Mull and Skye. Its Gaelic name, *Garbh-chiochan*, translates as the **Rough Bounds**, implying a region geographically and spiritually apart. Even if you have a car, you should spend a few days here exploring on foot; there are so few roads that some determined hiking is almost inevitable.

The southwest Highlands' main road is the A830, often described as "the Road to the Isles", which winds in tandem with the rail line through the glens from Fort William to the road- and railhead at **Mallaig**, a busy fishing port with ferry connections to Skye. Along the way, the road passes **Glenfinnan**, the much-photographed spot at the head of stunning **Loch Shiel** where Bonnie Prince Charlie gathered the clans to start the doomed Jacobite uprising of 1745. There are regular buses and trains along the main road; elsewhere in the region you'll usually have to rely on daily post- or schoolbuses. If you have your own transport, the five-minute ferry crossing at **Corran Ferry** (every 15min daily summer 7am–9pm; winter 7am–8pm; car and passengers £5.20; foot passengers and bicycles go free), a nine-mile drive south of Fort William down Loch Linnhe, provides a more direct point of entry for Morvern and the rugged **Ardnamurchan** peninsula.

The Ardnamurchan peninsula

The tortuous single-track B8007 road winds west from Salen along the northern shore of Loch Sunart to the wild **Ardnamurchan peninsula**, the most westerly point on the British mainland. The unspoilt landscape is relatively gentle and wooded at the eastern end, with much of the coastline of long Loch Sunart fringed by ancient oakwoods, protected as among the last remnants of the extensive temperate rainforests once common along the Atlantic coast of Europe. The peninsula, which lost most of its inhabitants during the infamous Clearances (see p.1250), has only a handful of tiny crofting settlements clinging to its jagged coastline and is sparsely populated – all the more so when you realize that many of the houses are seldom-used holiday cottages. Ardnamurchan, however, can be an inspiring place for its pristine, empty beaches, wonderful vistas of sea and island, and the sense of nature all around. With its variety of undisturbed habitat the peninsula harbours a huge variety of birds, animals and wildflowers such as thrift and wild iris, making **walking** an obvious attraction. A variety of routes, from hill-climbs to coastal scrambles, are detailed in a comprehensive guide to the peninsula produced annually by the local community (available from tourist offices and most shops on the peninsula, priced around £4).

The Glenmore Natural History Centre

An inspiring introduction to the diverse flora, fauna and geology of Ardnamurchan is the superb **Glenmore Natural History Centre** (April–Oct Mon–Sat 10.30am–5.30pm, Sun noon–5.30pm; £2.50), nestled

24

near the shore just west of the hamlet of **GLENBORRODALE**. Originally set up by local photographer Michael MacGregor (whose stunning work enlivens postcard stands along the west coast), the centre is housed in a sensitively designed timber building called "The Living Building", complete with turf roof and wildlife ponds. CCTV cameras relay live pictures of the comings and goings of the surrounding wildlife, from a pine marten's nest, a heronry and from underwater pools in the nearby river. The small **café** serves sandwiches and good home-baked cakes and there's a useful bookshop.

Kilchoan and Ardnamurchan Point

KILCHOAN, nine miles west of the Glenmore Centre, is Ardnamurchan's main village – a straggling but appealing crofting township overlooking the Sound of Mull. A **car ferry** runs from here to Tobermory (7 daily; 35min). The community centre in the village houses a **tourist office** (Easter–Oct daily 9am–5pm; ☏01972/510222, ⓦwww.ardnamurchan.com), who will help with and book accommodation, though year-round the community centre will act as an informal source of local advice and assistance. For **boat trips** out of Kilchoan – either wildlife-spotting or fishing – contact Nick Peake (☏01972/510212), who also leads guided walks to look for land-based wildlife such as eagles, pine martens and badgers. The only direct **bus** to Kilchoan leaves from Fort William at 12.55pm (Mon–Sat), travelling via the Corran Ferry and arriving two hours later.

The road continues beyond Kilchoan to the rocky, windy **Ardnamurchan Point**, with its famous **lighthouse** and spectacular views of the Hebrides north and south. The lighthouse buildings house a decent café and an enthusiastically run **visitor centre** (daily April–Oct 10am–5pm; £2.50; ☏01972/510210), with well-assembled displays about lighthouses in general, their construction and the people who lived in them. Best of all is the chance to admire the Egyptian-style lighthouse tower, and find a sheltered spot on the nearby cliff to sit peering out to sea.

Also worth exploring around the peninsula are the myriad coves, beaches and headlands along the long coastline. The finest of the sandy beaches is about three miles north of the lighthouse at **Sanna Bay**, a shell-strewn strand and series of dunes which offer truly unforgettable vistas of the Small Isles to the north, circled by gulls, terns and guillemots.

Practicalities

Accommodation isn't plentiful in Kilchoan, and in summer you're well advised to book well ahead. You can normally camp in the gardens of the Kilchoan House Hotel, though wild camping elsewhere on the peninsula is also possible. For B&B, try *Doirlinn House* (☏01972/510209, ⓔdorlinnhouse@yahoo.co.uk; ❷; March–Oct), or *Tigh a'Ghobhainn* (☏01972/510771, ⓔmairihunter.kilchoan@virgin.net; ❷; March–Oct), both with lovely views over the Sound of Mull. Most of the local hotels offer **food** to nonresidents, among them the *Kilchoan House Hotel* (☏01972/510200; ❸) and the *Sonachan Hotel* (☏01972/510211; ❷), which despite being hailed as the most westerly hotel on the British mainland is tucked inland away from the coast, halfway between Kilchoan and Ardnamurchan Point. The Ferry Stores in Kilchoan, the only **shop** west of Salen, makes an impressive effort to carry fresh food and local produce when it's available.

Acharacle and Castle Tioram

At the eastern end of Ardnamurchan, just north of Salen where the A861 heads north towards the district of Moidart, the main settlement is **ACHARACLE**,

24

an ancient crofting village set back a few hundred yards from the seaward end of freshwater **Loch Shiel**. Surrounded by gentle hills, it's an attractive place, and being a couple of miles from the sea has a different feel to many of the area's other main villages.

A mile north of Acharacle, a side road running north off the A861 winds for three miles or so past a secluded estuary lined with rhododendron thickets and fishing platforms to **Loch Moidart**, a calm and sheltered sea loch. Perched atop a rocky promontory in the middle of the loch is **Castle Tioram** (pronounced "cheerum"), one of Scotland's most atmospheric historic monuments. Reached via a sandy causeway, the thirteenth-century fortress, whose Gaelic name means "dry land", was the seat of the MacDonalds of Clanranald until it was destroyed by their chief in 1715 to prevent it from falling into Hanoverian hands while he was away fighting for the Jacobites. Today, a certain amount of controversy surrounds the upkeep of the castle: while the setting and approach to the castle are undoubtedly stunning, large notices and fences keep you from getting too close due to the danger of falling masonry.

The Road to the Isles

The "**Road to the Isles**" from Fort William to Mallaig, followed by the West Highland Railway and the narrow, winding A830, traverses the mountains and glens of the Rough Bounds before breaking out near **Arisaig** onto a spectacularly scenic coast of sheltered inlets, stunning white beaches and wonderful views to the islands of Rùm, Eigg, Muck and Skye. This is country commonly associated with **Bonnie Prince Charlie**, whose adventures of 1745–46 began and ended on this stretch of coast, with his first, defiant raising of the standard at **Glenfinnan** at the head of lovely **Loch Shiel**.

Glenfinnan

GLENFINNAN, nineteen miles west of Fort William at the head of Loch Shiel, was where Bonnie Prince Charlie raised his standard to signal the start of the Jacobite uprising of 1745. Surrounded by no more than 200 loyal clansmen, the young rebel prince waited to see if the Cameron of Loch Shiel would join his army. Despite strong misgivings, Cameron did decide to support the uprising, and arrived at Glenfinnan on a sunny August 19 with 800 men, thereby encouraging other, wavering clan leaders to follow suit. Assured of adequate backing, the prince raised his red-and-white silk colour, proclaimed his father King James III of England, and set off on the long march to London – from which only a handful of the soldiers gathered at Glenfinnan would return. The spot is marked by a column (now a little lop-sided, Pisa-like) crowned with a clansman in full battle dress, erected as a tribute by Alexander Macdonald of Glenaladale in 1815.

Glenfinnan is a poignant place, a beautiful stage for the opening scene in brutal drama that was to change the Highlands forever. The **visitor centre** and café (daily: June–Aug 9.30am–5.30pm; April, May, Sept & Oct 10am–5pm; £2; NTS), opposite the monument, gives an account of the '45 uprising through to the rout at **Culloden** eight months later (see p.1210). A **boat trip** on the loch with Loch Shiel Cruises (April–mid-Oct ☏01687/470322) is highly recommended.

Glenfinnan is one of the most spectacular parts of the **West Highland Railway** line (see box on p.1204), not only for the glimpse it offers of the monument and graceful Loch Shiel, but also the mighty 21-arched Loch nan Uamh **viaduct** built in 1901 and one of the first-ever large constructions made out concrete. You can learn more of the history of this section of the railway at the **Glenfinnan Station Museum** (June–Sept daily 9.30am–4.30pm; 50p), set in the old booking office of the station. Right beside the station, two old railway carriages have been pressed into use as a highly original **restaurant** and **bunkhouse**; the *Dining Car* (June–Sept daily 10am–5pm; ☎01397/722300) is open for light lunches, home baking and evening meals if you phone ahead to make arrangements, while the *Sleeping Car* (☎01397/722295; year-round), a converted 1958 camping coach, sleeps ten in bunk beds.

Arisaig and around

West of Glenfinnan, the A830 runs alongside captivating Loch Eilt in the district of **Morar**, through Lochailort – where it meets the road from Acharacle – and onto a coast marked by acres of white sands, turquoise seas and rocky islets draped with orange seaweed. **ARISAIG**, scattered round a sandy bay at the west end of the Morar peninsula, makes a good base for exploring this area. A recently constructed **bypass** now whizzes cars (and, more importantly, fish lorries) on their way to Mallaig, but you shouldn't miss out on the slower coast road, which enjoys all the best of the scenery.

The only specific attraction in Arisaig village is the **Land, Sea and Islands Centre** (Easter–mid-Oct Mon–Sat 10am–3pm, Sun noon–4pm; £2), a small, volunteer-run community project relating the social and natural history of the area. A **boat** also leaves from here daily during the summer for the Small Isles (see p.1142), operated by Arisaig Marine (☎01687/450224, ⓦwww .arisaig.co.uk). **Accommodation** in the village is plentiful. *Kinloid Farm House* (☎01687/450366; ❸; March–Oct) is one of several pleasant B&Bs with sea views, while the more upmarket *Old Library Lodge* (☎01687/450651, ⓦwww.oldlibrary.co.uk; ❺; April–Oct) has a handful of well-appointed rooms, though only two overlook the seafront. For **food**, the restaurant at the *Old Library* is quite upmarket, while there's bar food available at the *Arisaig Hotel*, just along the road.

Stretching for eight miles or so north of Arisaig is a string of stunning whitesand **beaches** backed by flowery machair, with barren granite hills and moorland rising up behind and wonderful seaward views of Eigg and Rùm. The next settlement of any significance is **MORAR**, where the famous beach scenes from *Local Hero* were shot. Since then, however, a bypass has been built around the village, and the white sands are no longer an unspoilt idyll. Of the string of **campsites** along the coast road try *Camusdarach* (☎01687/450221, ⓦwww.road-to-the-isles.org.uk/camusdarach), which isn't quite on the beach but is quieter and less officious than others nearby.

Mallaig

A cluttered, noisy port whose pebble-dashed houses struggle for space with great lumps of granite tumbling down to the sea, **MALLAIG**, 47 miles west of Fort William along the A830 (regular buses and trains run this route), is not pretty. Before the railway reached here in 1901, it consisted of only a few cottages, but now it's a busy, bustling place and, as the main ferry stop for Skye and the Small Isles (see p.1142), is always full of visitors. The continuing source of the village's wealth is its thriving **fishing** industry: on the quayside, piles of nets, tackle and ice crates lie scattered around a bustling modern market. Apart from the daily bustle of Mallaig's harbour, the main attraction in town is **Mallaig Marine World**, north of the train station near the harbour (March–Oct Mon–Sat 9am–6pm, Sun 11am–6pm; July & Aug Mon–Sat until 9pm; Nov–Feb Mon–Sat 9am–6pm; £2.75), where tanks of local sea creatures and informative exhibits about the port provide an unpretentious introduction to the local waters.

Mallaig is a compact place, concentrated around the harbour, where you'll find the **tourist office** (April–Oct Mon–Sat 10am–5pm; Nov–March Mon, Tues & Fri 11am–3pm; ☎01687/462170), which will book accommodation for you, and the **bus** and **train stations**. The CalMac ticket office (☎01687/462403), serving passengers for Skye and the Small Isles, is also nearby, and you can arrange transport to Knoydart by calling Bruce Watt Cruises (☎01687/462320, ⓦwww.knoydart-ferry.co.uk), which sails to Inverie, on the Knoydart peninsula, every morning and afternoon (mid-May to mid-Sept Mon–Fri; otherwise Mon, Wed & Fri), the later cruise continuing east along Loch Nevis to Tarbet; the loch is sheltered, so crossings are rarely cancelled.

For **B&B**, head around the harbour to East Bay, where you'll find the immaculate *Western Isles Guest House* (☎01687/462320, ⓔwesternisles@aol.com; ❶). *Sheena's Backpackers' Lodge* (☎01687/462764), a refreshingly laid-back independent **hostel** overlooking the harbour, has mixed dorms, self-catering facilities and a sitting room. For **eating**, the *Fishmarket Restaurant* features lots of fresh seafood. During the day, the *Tea Garden* at *Sheena's Lodge* is a great place to watch the world go by while you tuck into a bowl of cullen skink (soup made from smoked haddock), a pint of prawns or home-made scones. Also worth seeking out are the freshest of fish and chips – or a portion of scallops and chips if you're feeling decadent – served at the *Cornerstone*, just across the road from the tourist office.

The Knoydart peninsula

Many people regard the **Knoydart peninsula** as Britain's most dramatic and unspoilt wilderness area. Flanked by **Loch Nevis** ("Loch of Heaven") in the south and the fjord-like inlet of **Loch Hourn** ("Loch of Hell") to the north, Knoydart's knobbly green peaks – three of them Munros – sweep straight out of the sea, shrouded for much of the time in a pall of grey mist. To get to the heart of the peninsula, you must catch a **boat** from Mallaig or Glenelg, or else **hike** for a couple of days across rugged moorland and mountains and sleep rough in old stone bothies (most of which are marked on Ordnance Survey maps). Unsurprisingly, the peninsula tends to attract walkers, lured by the network of well-maintained trails that wind east into the wild interior, where Bonnie Prince Charlie is rumoured to have hidden out after Culloden.

At the end of the eighteenth century, around a thousand people eked out a living from this inhospitable terrain through crofting and fishing. These days the peninsula supports around seventy people, most of whom live in the hamlet of **INVERIE**. Nestled beside a sheltered bay on the south side of the peninsula, it has a pint-sized post office, a shop and mainland Britain's most remote pub, the *Old Forge*. Bruce Watt Cruises' **boat** chugs into Inverie from Mallaig (see p.1231). To arrange for a boat crossing from Arnisdale on the Glenelg peninsula to the north coast of Knoydart or Kinloch Hourn, contact Len Morrison (☎01599/522352; £8–25, depending on passenger numbers).

Torrie Shieling (☎01687/462669, ⓔtorriedh@aol.com; £16 per person), an upmarket independent **hostel** located three-quarters of a mile east of the village on the side of the mountain, is popular with hikers and families. The Knoydart Community also run a bunkhouse, with simple but adequate facilities, in some old steadings not far from Torrie Shieling. To book this call the foundation office ☎01687/462242. In Inverie itself there's just one gue house, the *Pier House* (☎01687/462347, Ⓦwww.thepierhouseknoydart.co.uk; half-board ❺), a great place to stay: they have their own **restaurant** serving a la carte evening meals, including some good veggie options. Dinner is available to nonresidents (three courses for around £15). The *Old Forge* is one of Scotland's finer pubs, with a convivial atmosphere where visitors and locals mix, generous bar meals often featuring recently caught seafood, real ales, an open fire, and a good chance of live music of an evening. You can rent **mountain bikes** from *Pier House*.

Kyle of Lochalsh and around

As the main gateway to Skye, **Kyle of Lochalsh** used to be an important transit point for tourists, locals and services. However, with the building of the Skye Bridge in 1995, Kyle was left as merely the terminus for the train route from Inverness, with little else to offer. Of much more interest to most visitors is nearby **Eilean Donan Castle**, one of Scotland's most famous and popular sights, perched at the end of a stone causeway on the shores of **Loch Duich**. It's not hard, however, to step off the tourist trail, with the **Glenelg** peninsula on the south side of Loch Duich testimony to how quickly the west coast can seem remote and undiscovered. A few miles north of Kyle of Lochalsh, the delightful village of **Plockton** is a refreshing alternative to its utilitarian neighbour, with cottages grouped around a yacht-filled bay and Highland cattle wandering the streets.

Kyle of Lochalsh

KYLE OF LOCHALSH is not particularly attractive – concrete buildings, rail junk and myriad signs of the once thriving fishing industry abound – and is ideally somewhere to pass through rather than linger in. With the building of the **Skye Road Bridge**, traffic has little reason to stop before rumbling over the channel a mile to the west, leaving Kyle's shopkeepers bereft of the passing trade they used to enjoy. The bridge, built with private-sector money, has also sparked controversy over its high tolls.

Buses run to Kyle of Lochalsh from Glasgow via Fort William and Invergarry and from Inverness via Invermoriston. Book in advance for all of them – all continue at least as far as Portree on Skye. **Trains** run to Kyle of Lochalsh from Inverness; curving north through Achnasheen and Glen Carron, the train line is a rail enthusiast's dream, even if scenically it doesn't quite match the West Highland line to Mallaig.

Kyle's **tourist office** (July & Aug Mon–Sat 9am–6pm, Sun 10am–4pm; April–June, Sept & Oct Mon–Sat 9am–5pm), on top of the small hill near the old ferry jetty, can book **accommodation** – a useful service as there are surprisingly few options. The best hotel is probably the welcoming *Kyle Hotel* in Main Street, recently refurbished and with a reputation for good food (☎01599/534204; Ⓦwww.kylehotel.co.uk; ❺). One of the most pleasant **B&Bs** in the area is the *Old Schoolhouse* at Erbusaig, between Kyle and Plockton (☎01599/534369; Ⓔcuminecand@lineone.net; ❸). There's a simple, clean hostel in town, *Cúchulainn's* (☎01599/534492), above a pub across the main street from the tourist office. **Eating** is a problem – apart from hotels, the best place is *The Seafood Restaurant* at the train station.

Eilean Donan Castle

Skirted on its northern shore by the A87, **Loch Duich**, the boot-shaped inlet just to the south of Kyle of Lochalsh, features prominently on the tourist trail,

24

with buses from all over Europe thundering down the sixteen miles from **SHIEL BRIDGE** to Kyle of Lochalsh on their way to Skye.

After Edinburgh's hilltop fortress, **Eilean Donan Castle** (April–Oct daily 10am–5.30pm; £3.95), ten miles north of Shiel Bridge on the A87, has to be Scotland's most photographed monument. Presiding over the once strategically important confluence of lochs Alsh, Long and Duich, the forbidding crenellated tower rises from the water's edge, joined to the shore by a narrow stone bridge and with sheer mountains as a backdrop. The original castle was established in 1230 by Alexander II to protect the area from the Vikings. It lay in ruins until John Macrae-Gilstrap had it rebuilt between 1912 and 1932. Eilean Donan has also featured in several major **films**, including *Highlander*, *Entrapment* and the James Bond adventure *The World is Not Enough*. Three floors, including the banqueting hall, the bedrooms and the troops' quarters are open to the public, with various Jacobite and clan relics also on display, though like many of the region's most popular castles, the large numbers of people passing through make it hard to appreciate the real charm of the place.

The Glenelg peninsula

South of Loch Duich, the **Glenelg peninsula**, jutting out into the Sound of Sleat, is the isolated and little-known crofting area featured in Gavin Maxwell's otter novel *Ring of Bright Water*. Maxwell disguised the identity of this pristine stretch of coast by calling it "Camusfearnà", and it has remained a tranquil backwater. The landward approach to the peninsula is from the east by turning off the fast A87 at Shiel Bridge on Loch Duich. The main settlement is **GLENELG**, strewn along a pebbly bay on the Sound of Sleat. A row of little whitewashed houses surrounded by trees, the village is dominated by the rambling, weed-choked ruins of the **Bernera Barracks**, an eighteenth-century garrison for English government troops, now little more than a shell. The *Glenelg Inn* (☎01599/522273, ⓦwww.glenelg-inn.com; ❺) is a wonderful spot to discover at the end of so remote a road, with its luxurious, cosy **rooms** overlooking the bay, tasty food served all day and a good chance of live music from any local musicians who happen to be in the **pub**.

The frequent six-car **Glenelg–Kylerhea ferry** (5min; information ☎01599/511302; April–Oct) shuttles across the Sound of Sleat from a jetty northwest of the village. In former times, this choppy channel used to be an important drovers' crossing: 8000 cattle each year were herded head to tail across from Skye to the mainland.

Plockton

A fifteen-minute train ride north of Kyle at the seaward end of islet-studded Loch Carron lies the unbelievably picturesque village of **PLOCKTON**: a chocolate-box row of neatly painted cottages ranged around the curve of a tiny harbour and backed by a craggy landscape of heather and pine. Its fifteen minutes of fame came in the mid-1990s, when the BBC chose the village as the setting for the TV drama *Hamish Macbeth*. Though the resulting spin-off has since quietened, in high season it's still packed full of tourists, yachties and second-home owners. The unique brilliance of Plockton's light has also made it something of an artists' hangout, and during the summer the waterfront, with its row of shaggy palm trees, even shaggier Highland cattle, flower gardens and pleasure boats, is invariably dotted with painters dabbing at their easels.

The friendly, cosy *Haven Hotel*, on Innes Street (☎01599/544223; ❺), renowned for its excellent food, while the *Plockton Inn*, also on Innes Street (☎01599/544222, ⓦwww.plocktoninn.co.uk; ❸), makes an informal an comfortable alternative. Of the fifteen or so **B&Bs**, *The Shieling* (☎01599/544282; ❷) has a great location on a tiny headland at the top of the harbour, and at *An Caladh* (☎01599/544356; ❶), on the main street, guests have the free use of a wooden sailing dinghy. There's also the attractive new *Station Bunkhouse* (☎01599/544235, ✉mickcoe@btinternet.com), built in the shape of a signal box next to the railway station, which has four- and six-person dorms and a cosy open-plan kitchen and living area.

There's a wealth of good places to **eat**: *The Haven,* the *Plockton Inn* and *The Plockton Hotel* all have excellent seafood **restaurants**, while *Off the Rails*, in the train station, serves good-value, imaginative snacks by day and evening meals. *The Buttery*, part of Plockton Stores on the seafront, is also open all day for snacks and inexpensive meals. For **fishing** or **seal-spotting** boat trips from Plockton, try Leisure Marine (☎01599/544306) or Plockton Activity Holidays (☎01599/544356); **bike rental** from Plockton Craft Shop on the seafront.

Wester Ross

Wester Ross, the western seaboard of the old county of Ross-shire, is widely regarded as the most glamorous stretch of this coast. Here all the classic elements of Scotland's **coastal scenery** – dramatic mountains, sandy beaches, whitewashed crofting cottages and shimmering island views – come together in spectacular fashion. Though popular with generations of adventurous Scottish holidaymakers, only one or two places feel blighted by tourist numbers, with others such as **Applecross** and the peninsulas north and south of **Gairloch** maintaining an endearing simplicity and sense of isolation. There is some tough but wonderful **hiking** to be had in the mountains around **Torridon** and **Coigach**, while **boat trips** out among the islands and the prolific sea and bird life of the coast are another draw. The main settlement is the attractive fishing town of **Ullapool**, port for ferry services to Stornoway in the Western Isles, but a pleasant enough place to use as a base, not least for its active social and cultural scene.

The Applecross peninsula

The most dramatic approach to the **Applecross peninsula** (the English-sounding name is a corruption of the Gaelic *Apor Crosan*, meaning "estuary") is from the south, up a classic, glacial U-shaped valley and over the infamous **Bealach na Bà** (literally "Pass of the Cattle"). Crossing the forbidding hills behind Kishorn and rising to 2053ft, with a gradient and switchback bends worthy of the Alps, this route – a popular cycling piste – is hair-raising in places, but the panoramic views across the Minch to Raasay and Skye more than compensate.

The sheltered, fertile coast around **APPLECROSS** village, where the Irish missionary monk Maelrhuba founded a monastery in 673 AD, comes as a surprise after the bleakness of the moorland approach. Maybe it's the journey, but Applecross feels like an idyllic place: you can wander along lanes banked with wild iris and orchids, and explore beaches and rock pools on the shore. There's small **Heritage Centre** (April–Oct Mon–Sat noon–4pm; ⊛www.applecrossheritage.org.uk) overlooking Clachan church and graveyard, and a number of short **waymarked trails** along the shore – great for walking off a pub lunch. The old *Applecross Inn* (☎01520/744262, ⊛www.applecross.net; ●), right beside the sea, is the focal point of the community, with **rooms** upstairs and a lively bar serving snacks and tasty platefuls of local seafood. The Inn is the first stop for most folk coming here; if their rooms are full they'll happily recommend any houses locally offering B&B. **Camping** (☎01520/744268) is provided at the *Flower Tunnel*, as you come into the village from the pass.

Loch Torridon

Loch Torridon marks the northern boundary of the Applecross peninsula, its awe-inspiring setting backed by the appealingly rugged mountains of **Liathach** and **Beinn Eighe**, tipped by streaks of white quartzite. The greater part of this area is composed of the reddish 750-million-year-old Torridonian sandstone, and some 15,000 acres of the massif are under the protection of the National Trust for Scotland. They run a **Countryside Centre** (May–Sept Mon–Sat 10am–5pm, Sun 2–5pm; £2), where you can call in and learn a bit more about the local geology, flora and fauna. On the south side of the loch stands one of the area's grandest **hotels**, the smart, rambling Victorian *Loch Torridon Hotel* (☎01445/791242, ⓦ www.lochtorridonhotel.com; ❽), set amid well-tended lochside grounds. The hotel also runs the adjacent *Ben Damph Lodge* (March–Oct), a modern conversion of an old farmstead, with neat if characterless twins and doubles (❸), a dorm and a large climber's bar. It's also worth asking about some of the **outdoor activities** the hotel offers to residents and nonresidents alike, from archery to sea kayaking. Close to the Countryside Centre is a rather unsightly SYHA **hostel** (☎0870/004 1154, ⓔ reservations@syha.org.uk; March–Oct & New Year) and adjacent **campsite**; three miles beyond Diabaig is the much more picturesque, but spartan SYHA hostel *Craig* (no phone; May–Aug), a stone cottage by the shore with access only on foot.

Loch Maree

About eight miles north of Loch Torridon, **Loch Maree**, dotted with Caledonian pine-covered islands, is one of the west's scenic highlights, best viewed from the A832 road that drops down to its southeastern tip through Glen Docherty. At the southeastern end of the loch, the A896 from Torridon meets the A832 from Achnasheen at the small settlement of **KINLOCHEWE** (ⓦ www.torridon-mountains.co.uk), a good base if you're heading into the

---

Walks around Torridon

Ordnance Survey Outdoor Explorer Map no. 433.
There can be difficult conditions on virtually all hiking routes around Torridon, and the weather can change very rapidly. If you're relatively inexperienced but want to do the magnificent ridge walk along the **Liathach** (pronounced "lee-ach") massif, or the strenuous traverse of **Beinn Eighe** (pronounced "ben ay"), you can join a National Trust Ranger Service guided hike (details from the Torridon Countryside Centre; ☎01445/791221).

For those confident to go it alone, one of many possible routes takes you behind Liathach and down the pass, **Coire Dubh**, to the main road in Glen Torridon. This is a great, straightforward walk if you're properly equipped, covering thirteen miles and taking in superb landscapes. Allow yourself the whole day. A rewarding walk even in rough weather is the seven-mile hike up the coast from **Lower Diabaig**, ten miles northwest of Torridon village, to **Redpoint**. On a clear day, the views across to Raasay and Applecross from this gentle undulating path are superlative, but you'll have to return along the same trail, or else make your way back via Loch Maree on the A832. If you're staying in Shieldaig, the track that winds up the peninsula running north from the village makes a pleasant ninety-minute round walk.

hills. *Cromasaig* B&B (☎01455/760234, ✉cromasaig@msn.com; ❷) is a great place for hillwalkers set in the forest right at the foot of the track up Beinn Eighe. The *Cromasaig* folk also run the Moru outdoor shop at the old petrol station opposite the hotel and will furnish you with maps and guidebooks, as well as equipment and sound local advice.

The A832 skirts the southern shore of Loch Maree, passing the **Beinn Eighe Nature Reserve**, the UK's oldest wildlife sanctuary. Parts of the Beinn Eighe reserve are forested with Caledonian pinewood, and a mile north of Kinlochewe, the **Beinn Eighe Visitor Centre** (Easter & May–Sept daily 10am–5pm) on the A832, gives details of the area's rare species and marks the beginning of a couple of very easy walks through the surrounding, newly planted Caledonian pine forest. Several other interesting **walks** start from the car park, a mile north of the visitor centre.

Loch Maree is surrounded by some of Scotland's finest **deerstalking** country: the remote, privately owned *Letterewe Lodge* on the north shore, accessible only by helicopter or boat, lies at the heart of a famous deer forest. In 1877, Queen Victoria stayed for a few days at the wonderfully sited *Loch Maree Hotel* (☎01445/760288, ⓦwww.lochmareehotel.co.uk; ❺), halfway along the southern shore; it's but tumbledown these days but not a bad spot for a bar meal, particularly on a nice day when you can sit outside on the lochside lawn. An even better place **to stay** nearby is *The Old Mill* (☎01445/760271; ❻), a beautiful Highland lodge where all rates include an absolutely fabulous dinner, bed and breakfast.

Gairloch and around

GAIRLOCH spreads itself around the northeastern corner of the wide sheltered bay of Loch Gairloch, with its sometimes sandy, sometimes rocky shores. During the summer, Gairloch thrives as a low-key holiday resort with several tempting sandy beaches and some excellent coastal walks within easy reach. The main supermarket and **tourist office** (April–June & mid-Sept to Oct Mon–Sat 10am–1pm & 1.30–5pm; July to mid-Sept Mon–Sat 9am–6pm, Sun noon–5pm) are in Achtercairn, right by the **Gairloch Heritage Museum** (April–Sept Mon–Sat 10am–5pm, Oct Mon–Fri 10am–1.30pm; call for winter hours; ☎01445/712287; £2.50), which has eclectic, appealing displays covering geology, archeology, fishing and farming that range from a mock-up of a croft house to an early knitting machine.

Gairloch has a good choice of **accommodation**, but you might prefer to stay out along the road north to Melvaig or south to Redpoint (see below). In Achtercairn, opposite the post office, the *Mountain Lodge & Restaurant* (☎01445/712316; March–Dec; ❷) offers a refreshingly alternative experience – run by enthusiastic, young outdoor types the ground floor has a shop crammed with wind chimes and travel books, a café and a conservatory and deck with great views over the bay, while upstairs are three comfortable rooms. There are also some very good **B&Bs**: in Strath, try Gaelic-speaking Miss Mackenzie's *Duisary* (☎01445/712252, ⓦwww.duisary.freeserve.co.uk; April–Oct; ❶); near the pier, head for *Heatherdale* (☎01445/712388, ✉ebrochodi@aol.com; ❷); further south still, just before the turn-off to Badachro, there's the tastefully furnished *Kerrysdale House* (☎01445/712292, ⓦwww.kerrysdalehouse.co.uk; ❷) set back in its own lovely gardens.

For **food**, head for the harbour, where you'll find *The Corrie* (April–Sept) serving up the local catch, and the nearby *Old Inn* (ⓦwww.theoldinn.co.uk) also offering seafood on its bar menu and a very good range of Scottish real ales.

One leisurely way to explore the coast is on a wildlife-spotting **cruise**: Gairloch Marine Life Centre & Cruises (Easter–Oct; ☎01445/712636), at the pier, run informative and enjoyable boat trips across the bay in search of dolphins, porpoises, seals and even the odd whale.

Around Gairloch

The area's real attraction, however, is its beautiful **coastline**. To get to one of the most impressive stretches, head around the north side of the bay and follow the single-track B8021 to **BIG SAND**, which has a cleaner and quieter **beach** than the one in Gairloch. The B8021, and the postbus from Gairloch, terminate at the tiny crofting hamlet of Melvaig, from where a narrow surfaced track winds out to **Rubha Reidh** (pronounced "roo-a-ray"). You can stay at the headland's Stevenson-designed *Rua Reidh Lighthouse* (☎01445/771263, ⓦ www.ruareidh.co.uk; ❸), which looks straight out to the Outer Hebrides, either in one of the double rooms or in the comfortable and relaxed **bunkhouse** (book ahead in high season); they also serve slap-up **afternoon teas** and homemade cakes (Tues & Thurs afternoons only), pre-booked evening meals and organize popular walking or activity holidays.

Three miles south of Gairloch, a narrow single-track lane winds west from the main A832, past wooded coves and inlets on its way south of the loch to **BADACHRO**, a sleepy former fishing village in a very attractive setting with a wonderful pub, the *Badachro Inn*, right by the water's edge, where you can sit in the beer garden watching the boats come and go and tuck into some lovely food. Beyond Badachro, the road winds for five more miles along the shore to **REDPOINT**, a straggling hamlet with beautiful beaches of peach-coloured sand and great views to Raasay, Skye and the Western Isles.

Poolewe and around

It's a fifteen-minute hop by bus over the headland from Gairloch to the trim little village of **POOLEWE** which sits by a small bay at the sheltered southern end of Loch Ewe, where the (very short) River Ewe rushes down from Loch Maree. Half a mile across the bay from Poolewe on the A832, **Inverewe Gardens** (daily: April–Oct 9.30am–9pm or dusk; Nov–March 9.30am–4pm £7; NTS), a verdant oasis of foliage and riotously colourful flower collections forms a vivid contrast to the wild, heathery crags of the adjoining coast. The gardens were the brainchild of **Osgood MacKenzie**, who inherited the surrounding 12,000-acre estate from his stepfather, the laird of Gairloch, in 1862. Taking advantage of the area's famously temperate climate (a consequence of the Gulf Stream, which draws a warm sea current from Mexico to within a stone's throw of these shores), Mackenzie collected plants from all over the world for his walled garden, which still forms the nucleus of the complex. Protected from Loch Ewe's corrosive salt breezes by a dense brake of Scots pine, rowan, oak, beech and birch trees, the fragile plants flourished on rich soil brought here as ballast on Irish ships to overlay the previously infertile beach gravel and sea grass. By the time Mackenzie died in 1922, his garden sprawled over the whole peninsula, surrounded by 100 acres of woodland. Today the National Trust for Scotland strives to develop the place along the lines envisaged by its founder.

Around 200,000 visitors pour through here annually, but the place rarely feels overcrowded. Interconnected by a labyrinthine network of twisting paths and walkways, more than a dozen gardens feature exotic plant collections from far afield as Chile, China, Tasmania and the Himalayas. You'll need at least a couple of hours to do the whole lot justice, and leave time for the **visit** centre (April–Sept daily 9.30am–5pm), which houses an informative display on the history of the garden and is the starting point for **guided walks** (May–Aug). The **restaurant** at the top of the car park does good snacks and lunches.

Ullapool

ULLAPOOL (ⓦ www.ullapool.co.uk), the northwest's principal centre of population, was founded at the height of the herring boom in 1788 by the British Fisheries Society, on a sheltered arm of land jutting into Loch Broom. The grid-plan town is still an important fishing centre, though the **ferry** link to Stornoway on Lewis (see p.1147) means that in high season its personality is practically swamped by visitors. Even so, it's still a hugely appealing place and a good base for exploring the northwest Highlands. Regular **buses** run from here to Inverness and Durness, while there's an early-morning run through to the remote train station at Lairg. Accommodation is plentiful and Ullapool is an obvious hideaway if the weather is bad, with cosy pubs, a new swimming pool and a lively arts centre, the *Ceilidh Place*.

Information and accommodation

The well-run **tourist office** (June–Aug Mon–Sat 9am–5.30pm, Sun noon–5pm; April, May & Sept, Mon–Sat 9am–5pm, Sun noon–4pm; Oct Mon–Fri 10am–5pm, Sat noon–4pm; Nov & Dec Mon–Fri 2–5.30pm), on Argyle Street, offers an accommodation booking service.

Accommodation

The Ceilidh Place West Argyle St ☎01854/612103, ⓦ www.theceilidhplace.com. Tasteful and popular hotel, with the west coast's best bookshop, a relaxing first-floor lounge, a great bar-restaurant, sea views and a laid-back atmosphere. Also has a good-value bunkhouse (May–Oct), at £12 per person in family rooms. ❻

Ferry Boat Inn Shore St ☎01854/612366, ⓦ www.ferryboat-inn.com. Traditional inn right on the waterfront with a friendly atmosphere and reasonable food. ❺

The Shieling Garve Rd ☎01854/612947, ⓦ www.theshielingullapool.co.uk. Outstandingly comfortable guest house overlooking the loch, with immaculate, spacious rooms (nos. 4 and 5

have the best views), superb breakfasts (try their homemade venison and leek sausages) and a sauna. ❸

Waterside House 6 West Shore St ☎01854/612140, ⓦ www.waterside.uk.net. Very appealing rooms in a very pleasant, friendly B&B on the seafront. ❷

SYHA hostel Shore St ☎0870/004 1156, ⓦ www.syha.org.uk. Busy hostel on the front, with Internet access and lots of good information about local walks. March–Oct.

West House West Argyle St ☎01854/613126, ⓦ www.scotpackers-hostels.co.uk. Lively, welcoming hostel with four- to six-bed dorms and more civilized B&B on offer in a nearby house. Minibus day-tours organized and bike rental available.

The Town

Day or night, most of the action in Ullapool centres on the **harbour**, which has an authentic and salty air, especially when the boats are in. By day, attention focuses on the comings and goings of the ferry, fishing boats and smaller craft, while in the evening, yachts swing on the current, the shops stay open late, and customers from the *Ferry Boat Inn* line the sea wall. During summer, booths advertise trips to the **Summer Isles** – a cluster of uninhabited islets two to three miles offshore – to view sea-bird colonies, dolphins and porpoises, but if you're lucky you'll spot marine life from the waterfront. Otters occasionally nose around the rocks near the *Ferry Boat Inn*, and seals swim past, begging scraps from the boats moored in the middle of the loch.

The only conventional attraction in town is the **museum**, in the old parish church on West Argyle Street (April–Oct Mon–Sat 9.30am–5.30pm; March Mon–Sat 11am–3pm; Nov–Feb Wed, Thurs & Sat 11am–3pm; £3), with displays on crofting, fishing, local religion and emigration. During the Clearances, Ullapool was one of the ports through which evicted crofters left to start new lives in Canada, Australia and New Zealand.

Eating, drinking and entertainment

The two best **pubs** in Ullapool are the *Arch Inn*, home of the Ullapool football team, and the *Ferry Boat Inn* (known as the "FBI"), where you can enjoy a pint of real ale at the lochside – midges permitting. **Live folk music** is a regular occurrence at *The Ceilidh Place* or on Thursday nights at the *FBI*. *The Ceilidh Place* is one of the happening places in the Highlands, with a decent-quality line-up of touring plays, music festivals, poetry-readings and live entertainment.

The Ceilidh Place is also one of the best places in town to find something to **eat**, with a coffee shop, a pleasant bar serving filling snacks and a spacious restaurant offering a selection of imaginative seafood and vegetarian dishes. All three pubs also serve bar meals – the *FBI* is probably the pick of the bunch. If you're looking for **picnic fare**, try John MacLean's wholefood shop and deli on West Argyle Street, or the Ullapool Catering Company who operate out of *The Frigate*, on Shore St, where you can pick up organic vegetables, fresh seafood, soup and sandwiches.

Assynt

If you've come as far as Ullapool it really is worth continuing just that bit further north into the highly distinctive hills of **Assynt** (Ⓦ www.assynt.co.uk), which marks the transition from Wester Ross into Sutherland. This is a landscape not of mountain ranges but of extraordinary peaks rising individually from the moorland. It's an area of peaceful, slow, back roads, which, after twisting through idyllic crofts, invariably end up at a deserted beach or windswept headland with superb clear-day views west to the Outer Hebrides. **Lochinver**, midway along the west coast, is the main settlement, though you're unlikely to want to stay there. Head, instead, for one of the crofting villages along the coast, like those around **Achiltibuie**, or – if you're keen to climb the mountains – head for **Inchnadamph**, which sits below the region's two Munros.

Coigach

Coigach is the peninsula immediately to the north of Loch Broom, accessible via a slow, winding single-track road that leaves the A835 ten miles north of Ullapool, squeezing between the northern shore of Loch Lurgainn and the lower slopes of **Cul Beag** (2523ft) and craggy Stac Pollaidh (2012ft). Coigach's main settlement is **ACHILTIBUIE**, an old crofting village scattered across the hillside above a series of white-sand coves and rocks tapering into the Atlantic, from where a fleet of small fishing boats carries sheep, and tourists, to the enticing pastures of the **Summer Isles** which lie a little way offshore. For **boat** trips round the isles, including some time ashore on the largest, Tanera Mor, Ian Macleod's boat *Hectoria* (☎01854/622200) runs twice a day from the pier.

The village attracts gardening enthusiasts, thanks to the unlikely presence of the **Hydroponicum** (April–Sept daily 10am–6pm; Oct Mon–

11.30am–3pm; @ www.thehydroponicum.com; £4.75; tours on the hour), a cross between a giant greenhouse and a futuristic scientific research station, and, it has to be said, something of an eyesore. Dubbed "The Garden of the Future", all kinds of flowers, fruits and vegetables are grown without using soil in conditions that concentrate the sun's heat while protecting the plants from winter (and summer) chill. You can taste whatever's being harvested in the subtropical setting of the *Lilypond Café*, which serves meals, desserts and snacks and is open in the evening (Thurs–Sun only).

For **accommodation**, the wonderfully understated *Summer Isles Hotel* (℡01854/622282, @ www.summerislehotel.co.uk; ❻; Easter–Oct), just up the road from the Hydroponicum, enjoys a near-perfect setting with views over the islands, and is virtually self-sufficient. A set dinner costs a pricey £40, although superb bar snacks and lunches feature crab, langoustines and smoked mackerel starting from £5. Of Achiltibuie's several **B&Bs**, *Dornie House* (℡01854/622271, @ dorniehousebandb@aol.com; ❶; Easter–Nov), halfway to Altandhu, is welcoming. There's also a beautifully situated twenty-bed SYHA **hostel** (℡0870/004 1101, @ reservations@syha.org.uk; May–Sept), three miles southeast of Achiltibuie down the coast at **Achininver**.

Also worth a visit is the **Achiltibuie Smokehouse** (April–Sept Mon–Sat 9.30am–5pm; free), five miles northwest of the Hydroponicum at **ALTANDHU**, where you can see meat, fish and game being cured in the traditional way and can buy some afterwards. Next to this, the *Am Fuaran* bar serves evening meals, including fresh shellfish, and, like everywhere else along this stretch, enjoys terrific views over to the Summer Isles.

Lochinver and around

The potholed and narrow road north from Achiltibuie through Inverkirkaig is unremittingly spectacular, threading its way through a tumultuous landscape of secret valleys, moorland and bare rock, past the startling shapes of Cul Beag (2523ft), Cul Mor (2785ft) and the distinctive sugar-loaf **Suilven** (2398ft). A scattering of pebble-dashed bungalows around a sheltered bay heralds your arrival at **LOCHINVER**, sixteen miles due north of Ullapool (although more than twice that by road). It's a workaday place, with a huge fish market, from where large trucks head off around Britain. The **tourist office** (April–June, Sept & Oct Mon–Sat 10am–5pm; July & Aug Mon–Sat 9am–6pm, Sun 10am–4pm), within the excellent **Assynt Visitor Centre**, gives an interesting rundown on the area's geology, wildlife and history and has a CCTV link to a nearby heronry.

Heading **north** from Lochinver, there are two possible routes: the fast A837, which runs eastwards along the shore of Loch Assynt (see p.1242) to join the northbound A894, or the narrow, more scenic B869 **coast road** that locals dub "The Breakdown Zone", because its ups and downs claim so many victims during summer. Hugging the indented shoreline, this route offers superb views of the Summer Isles, as well as a number of rewarding side-trips to beaches and dramatic cliffs. Post- and schoolbuses from Lochinver cover the route as far as Drdvar or Drumbeg (Mon–Sat).

The first village worthy of a detour is **ACHMELVICH**, a couple of miles long a side road, whose tiny bay cradles a stunning white-sand beach lapped by startlingly turquoise water. There's a noisy **campsite** and a basic forty-bed SYHA **hostel** (℡0870/004 1102, @ reservations@syha.org.uk; April–Sept) just behind the largest beach. However, for total peace and quiet, head to other, equally seductive beaches beyond the headlands.

The side road that branches north off the B869 between **STOER** and **CLASHNESSIE**, both of which have sandy beaches, ends abruptly by the automatic lighthouse at **Raffin**, Stevenson-built in 1870. You can continue for two miles along a boggy, slightly tricky track to the Point of Stoer, named after the colossal rock pillar that stands offshore known as "**The Old Man of Stoer**", surrounded by sheer cliffs and splashed with guano from the seabird colonies that nest on its 200ft sides.

East of Lochinver

The area east of Lochinver, traversed by the A837, centred on **Loch Assynt**, and bounded by the gnarled peaks of the Ben More Assynt massif, is a wilderness of mountains, moorland, mist and scree. Dotted with lochs and lochans, it's also an angler's paradise, home to the only non-migratory fish in northern Scotland, the brown trout, and numerous other sought-after species, including the Atlantic salmon, sea trout and Arctic char.

The *Inchnadamph Hotel* (℡01571/822202, Ⓦwww.inchnadamphhotel.co.uk; ❺), at **INCHNADAMPH** in the southeastern tip of Loch Assynt, is a wonderfully traditional Highland retreat. It's popular with anglers, who get free fishing rights to Loch Assynt, as well as several hill lochs backing onto Ben More, haunts of the infamous ferox trout. Just along the road, the Assynt Field Centre or *Inchnadamph Lodge* (℡01571/822218, Ⓦwww.inch-lodge.co.uk; ❶) has basic but comfortable bunk rooms, some doubles, twins and triples as well as more spacious B&B accommodation. Through the year, the centre offers a variety of outdoor activity breaks and holidays, ranging from hill walking to dry-stone dyke building and cookery courses focusing on local products.

Kylesku to Sandwood Bay

KYLESKU, 33 miles north of Ullapool on the main A894 road, is the point where a curvaceous road bridge sweeps over the mouth of lochs Glencoul and Glendhu. There's very little to the place, though the congenial *Kylesku Hotel* (℡01971/502231; ❹; March–Oct) by the water's edge above the old ferry slipway has en-suite rooms, a welcoming bar popular with locals, and serving **fresh seafood**, including lobster, langoustines, crab, mussels and local salmon (you can watch the fish being landed on the pier). Statesman Cruises run entertaining **boat trips** (March–Oct twice daily except Sat; round trip 2hr £10; ℡01571/844446) from the jetty below the *Kylesku Hotel* to the 650ft **Eas-Coul-Aulin**, Britain's highest waterfall, located at the head of Loch Glencoul; otters, seals, porpoises and minke whales can occasionally be spotted along the way.

The far northwest coast

The Sutherland coastline north of Kylesku is a bridge too far for some, yet for others the stark, elemental beauty of the Highlands is to be found on the **far northwest coast** as nowhere else. Here, the peaks become more widely spaced and settlements smaller and fewer, linked by twisting single-track roads and shoreside footpaths that make excellent hiking trails. From the Kylesku Bridge to the beautiful strip of sand at **Sandwood Bay**, a day's hike from Cape Wrath, the area retains an exhilarating essence of wildness. One of the few conventional tourist attractions is the simple ferry that takes you to see the puffins of the island wildlife reserve of **Handa**. Places to stay and eat can be thin on the ground, particularly out of season, but the very la of infrastructure is testimony to the isolation that this corner of Scotland delivers in such sweeping style.

Scourie, Tarbet and Handa Island

Ten miles north of Kylesku, the widely scattered crofting community of **SCOURIE**, on a bluff above the main road, surrounds a beautiful sandy beach. Visible just offshore to the north of Scourie is **Handa Island**, a huge chunk of red Torridon sandstone surrounded by sheer cliffs, carpeted with machair and purple-tinged moorland, and teeming with sea birds. It's private property, but is administered as an internationally important **wildlife reserve** by the Scottish Wildlife Trust (@ www.swt.org.uk) and is a real treat for ornithologists, with vast colonies of razorbills and guillemots breeding on its guano-splashed cliffs during summer. From late May to mid-July, large numbers of puffins waddle comically over the turf-covered clifftops where they dig their burrows.

Weather permitting, **boats** (@01971/502347) leave for Handa throughout the day (April–Sept Mon–Sat; £7) from the tiny cove of **TARBET**, three miles northwest of the main road and accessible by postbus from Scourie, where there's a small car park and jetty. You're encouraged to make a donation towards Handa's upkeep. You'll need about three hours to follow the **footpath** around the island – an easy and enjoyable walk taking in the north shore's Great Stack rock pillar and some fine views across the Minch: a detailed route guide is featured in the SWT's free leaflet, available from the warden's office when you arrive. Camping is not allowed on the island, but the SWT maintains a **bothy** for bird-watchers (reservations essential on @01463/714746). In Tarbet, the *Croft House* (@01971/502098; ❶) is a comfortable little **B&B** overlooking the bay. For **food**, Tarbet's unexpected *Seafood Restaurant* (Mon–Sat noon–8pm) serves delicious, moderately priced fish and vegetarian dishes, and a good selection of homemade cakes and desserts, in its airy conservatory just above the jetty.

Loch Laxford to Sandwood Bay

North of Scourie, the road sweeps inland through the starkest part of the Highlands; rocks piled on rocks, bog and water create an almost alien landscape, and the astonishingly bare, stony coastline looks increasingly inhospitable. At **RHICHONICH**, the B801 side road branches off to **KINLOCHBERVIE**, which for all the world seems to be a typical, straggling West Highland crofting community until you turn a corner and encounter an incongruously huge fish-processing plant and modern concrete harbour. Trucks from all over Europe pick up cod and shellfish from the trawlers here, crewed mainly by east-coast fishermen. If you're in need of sustenance, try the **fish and chips** at the *Fishermen's Mission* (closed Sat & Sun); otherwise Kinlochbervie is not a place to linger.

A single-track road continues northwest of Kinlochbervie through isolated **OLDSHOREMORE**, a working crofters' village scattered above a stunning white-sand beach, to **BLAIRMORE**, where you can park for the four-mile walk across peaty moorland to **Sandwood Bay**. Few visitors make this half-day detour north, but the **beach** at the end of the rough track is one of the most beautiful in Scotland. Flanked by rolling dunes and lashed by fierce gales for much of the year, the shell-white sands and the dramatic leaning rock stack are said to be haunted by a bearded mariner. There's a well-equipped **campsite** at Oldshoremore (@01971/521281), or you can continue through Blairmore to **SHEIGRA**, where the road ends, for informal camping behind the beach.

24

The north coast

Though a constant stream of sponsored walkers, caravans and tour groups makes it to the dull town of **John O'Groats**, surprisingly few visitors travel the whole length of the Highlands' wild **north coast**. Those that do, however, rarely return disappointed. Pounded by one of the world's most ferocious seaways, Scotland's rugged northern shore is backed by barren mountains in the west, and in the east by lochs and open rolling grasslands. Between its far ends, mile upon mile of crumbling cliffs and sheer rocky headlands shelter bays whose perfect white beaches are nearly always deserted, even in the height of summer – though, somewhat incongruously, they're also home to Scotland's best surfing waves.

Though only a wee place, **Durness** is a good jumping-off point for nearby Balnakiel beach, one of the area's most beautiful sandy strands, and for rugged **Cape Wrath**, the windswept promontory at Scotland's northwest tip, which has retained an end-of-the-world mystique lost long ago by John O'Groats. **Tongue** is the most picturesque of the small crofting villages, while **Thurso**, the largest town on the north coast, is really only visited by those en route to Orkney. More enticing are the huge sea-bird colonies clustered in clefts and on remote stacks at **Dunnet Head** and **Duncansby Head**, to the east of Thurso.

Public transport around this stretch of coast can be a slow and frustrating business: Thurso, the area's main town and springboard for Orkney, is well connected by **bus** and **train** with Inverness, but further west, after the main A836 peters out into a single-track road, you have to rely on **postbus** connections.

Durness and around

Scattered around a string of sheltered sandy coves and grassy clifftops, **DURNESS** (Ⓦwww.durness.org), the most northwesterly village on the British mainland, straddles the turning point on the main A838 road as it swings east. Durness village sits above its own sandy bay, Sango Sands, while half a mile to the east is **SMOO**, which used to be an RAF station. In between Durness and Smoo is the millennial village hall, which features a windblown and rather forlorn community garden that harbours a memorial commemorating the Beatle **John Lennon**, who used to come to Durness on family holidays as a kid (and even revisited the place in the 1960s with Yoko). It's worth pausing at Smoo to see the 200ft-long **Smoo Cave** (April & May 11am–4pm; June–Sep 10am–5pm; £3), a gaping hole in a sheer limestone cliff formed partly by the action of the sea and partly by the small burn that flows through it. **Boat trips** (May–Sept daily; 1hr 30min; £7; call Ⓣ01971/511365 or 511284 for schedule) also leave from Smoo Cave on a wildlife tour of the coast around Durness, taking in sea-bird colonies and stretches of the shoreline that are only accessible by sea; sightings of seals, puffins and porpoises are common.

A narrow road winds a mile or so northwest of Durness to **BALNAKIEL**, passing **Balnakiel Craft Village** en route. Disabuse yourself of any notion of quaint cottages, as the craft village is housed in a grim 1940s military base transformed in the 1960s into a sort of industrial estate for arts and crafts thanks to the carrot of cheap rents for studio and living quarters. It's come a long way since those idealistic days, but a dozen or so workshops continue to function where you can watch painters, potters, leather workers, candle makers, woodworkers, stone carvers, knitters and weavers in action – there's also the friendly *Loch Croispol* bookshop with an excellent **café-restaurant** (Ⓣ01971/511777, Ⓦwww.scottish-books.org).

Balnakiel is also known for its **golf course**, whose ninth and final hole involves a well-judged drive over the Atlantic; you can rent equipment from the clubhouse. The white-sand beach on the east side of **Balnakiel Bay** is a stunning sight in any weather, but most spectacular on sunny days when the water turns to brilliant turquoise. For the best views, walk along the path that winds north through the dunes (pockmarked from occasional naval bombing exercises) behind it; this eventually leads to **Faraid Head** – from the Gaelic *Fear Ard* (High Fellow) – where there's a very small colony of nesting puffins (ask the tourist office for directions). The fine views east to the mouth of Loch Eriboll and west to Cape Wrath make this round walk (3–4hr) the best in the Durness area.

Practicalities

Public transport is sparse; the key service is the Dearman Coaches link (May–Sept Mon–Sat 1 daily) from Inverness via Ullapool and Lochinver. Postbuses provide a more complicated year-round alternative and meet trains at Lairg; check schedules at the post office or tourist office. Durness **tourist office** (April–Oct Mon–Sat 10am–5pm; July & Aug also Sun 11am–4pm; Oct–March Mon–Fri 10am–1.30pm) has a small **visitor centre** that features excellent interpretive panels detailing the area's history, geology, flora and fauna, with some good insights into the day-to-day life of the community.

There is some good **accommodation**: the excellent *Lazy Crofter Bunkhouse* (℡01971/511209 or 511366, ⓦwww.durnesshostel.com) is open all year and has good facilities including a drying room. The basic SYHA **hostel** (℡0870/004 1113, ⓔreservations@syha.org.uk; April–Sept), beside the Smoo Cave car park half a mile east of the village, also rents out mountain bikes. Of the **B&Bs**, *Puffin Cottage* (℡01971/511208, ⓦwww.puffincottage.com; ❶. April–Sept) is small but very pleasant

Cape Wrath

An excellent day-trip from Durness begins two miles southwest of Durness at **KEOLDALE**, where (tides and weather permitting) a foot-passenger **ferry** (June–Aug hourly 9.30am–4.30pm; May & Sept 4 daily; ℡01971/511376) crosses the spectacular Kyle of Durness estuary to link up with a **minibus** (℡01971/511287; May–Sept) that runs the eleven miles out to **Cape Wrath**, the British mainland's most northwesterly point. Note that Garvie Island (An Garbh-eilean) is an air bombing range, and the military regularly close the road to Cape Wrath, so check with Durness tourist office before you set off. The headland takes its name not from the stormy seas that crash against it for most of the year, but from the Norse word *hvarf*, meaning "turning place" – a throwback to the days when Viking warships used it as a navigation point during raids on the Scottish coast.

Tongue to Thurso

There's great drama in the landscape between Tongue and Thurso, as the A836 wends its way over bleak and often totally uninhabited rocky moorland, interspersed with sandy sea lochs. Tiny little **Tongue** is pleasant enough, as is the equally small settlement of **Bettyhill**, to the east, but the real reason to venture this far is to explore the countryside: **Ben Hope** (3040ft), the most northerly Munro, and the fascinating blanket bog of the **Flow Country** even further inland.

Tongue and around

The road takes a wonderfully slow and circuitous route around Loch Eriboll and east over the top of A' Mhoine moor to the pretty crofting township of **TONGUE**. Dominated by the ruins of **Castle Varrich** (Caisteal Bharraich), an eleventh-century Norse stronghold, the village is strewn above the east shore of the **Kyle of Tongue**. When the tide recedes, this shallow estuary becomes a mass of golden sand flats, superb on sunny days, with the sharp profiles of **Ben Hope** (3040ft) and **Ben Loyal** (2509ft) looming like twin sentinels to the south, and the Rabbit Islands a short way out to sea.

The best **accommodation** in Tongue is the *Tongue Hotel* (☎01847/611206, ⓦwww.scottish-selection.co.uk/tongue; ❻; April to mid-Nov), the plush, former hunting lodge of the Duke of Sutherland, which does excellent food, and has a cosy downstairs bar. There's also a well-situated SYHA **hostel** (☎0870/004 1153, ⓔreservations@syha.org.uk; April–Sept), in an old Victorian building right beside the causeway a mile north of the village centre on the east shore of the Kyle, and the *Kincraig* **campsite** (☎01847/611218), just south of Tongue post office.

Bettyhill and around

Twelve miles east of Tongue, **BETTYHILL** is a major crofting village, set among rocky green hills. In Gaelic, it was known as *Am Blàran Odhar* (Little Dun-coloured Field), but the origins of the English name are unknown; however, it was definitely not named after Elizabeth, countess of Sutherland, who presided over the Strathnaver Clearances. The story of those terrible times is told by local schoolchildren at the delightful and loyally maintained **Strathnaver Museum** (April–Oct Mon–Sat 10am–1pm & 2–5pm; £2), housed in the old Farr church, set apart from the main village. Inside, you can also see some Pictish stones and a 3800-year-old, early Bronze Age beaker found in Strathnaver, the river valley south of the village, whose numerous prehistoric sites are dotted about the area. In the churchyard itself, to the west of the church, stands the mysterious **Farr Stone**, a 6ft-high Pictish cross decorated with intricate interlacing and dating from around 800.

As you move east from Bettyhill, the north coast changes dramatically as the hills on the horizon recede to be replaced by fields fringed with flagstone walls. At the hamlet of **MELVICH**, twelve miles east of Bettyhill, the A897 cut south through Strath Halladale, the Flow Country (see below) and the Strath of Kildonan to Helmsdale on the east coast (see p.1256). Five miles further eas of Melvich the A836 passes **Dounreay Nuclear Power Station** (ⓦwww.ukaea.org.uk), a surreal collection of chimney stacks and box-lik buildings, plus the famous golf-ball-shaped DLR (Dounreay Fast Reactor Established back in 1955, Dounreay pioneered the development of fast reacto technology and was the first reactor in the world to provide mains electricit The reactors themselves have long since closed, though Dounreay remains b the far the biggest employer on the north coast, with decommissionin estimated to take over fifty years at a cost over £4 billion. A **visitor centr** (May–Oct daily 10am–4pm; free) details the processes (and, unsurprisingly, th benefits) of nuclear power, and gives the nuclear industry gloss on issues suc as the area's "leukaemia cluster" (allegedly not connected with radiation), ar the radioactive particles that continue to be found on the nearby beaches.

The Flow Country

From Melvich, you can head forty miles or so south towards Helmsdale on t A897, through the **Flow Country**, whose name comes from *flói*, an O Norse word meaning "marshy ground". This huge expanse of "blanket bog a valuable "carbon sink" and home to a wide variety of wildlife. At the tr station at **FORSINARD**, fifteen miles south of Melvich and easily accessible from Thurso, Wick and the south by train, there's an RSPB **visitor centre** (April–Oct daily 9am–6pm; ☎01641/571225), with CCTV coverage of hen harriers nesting, and also a **Peatland Centre**, which explains the wonders of peat. To get to grips with the whole concept of blanket bog, take a leaflet and follow the short **Dubh Lochan Trail** that's been laid out over the flagstones and peat banks to some nearby black lochans.

Thurso

Approached from the isolation of the west, **THURSO** feels like a metropolis. In reality, it's a relatively small service centre visited mostly by people passing through to the adjoining port of **Scrabster** to catch the ferry to Orkney. Thurso's grid-plan streets boast some rather handsome Victorian architecture in the local, greyish sandstone, though there's nothing really specific to detain you. **Traill Street** is the main drag, turning into the pedestrianized Rotterdam Street and High Street precinct at its northern end. On the High Street, by the side of the old Victorian town hall, is **Thurso Heritage Museum** (June–Sept Mon–Sat 10am–1pm, 2–5pm; £1) whose most intriguing exhibits are the Ulbster Stone in the entrance, which features elephants, fish and other beasts, the Skinnet Stone, intricately carved with enigmatic symbols, and a runic cross.

Trains from Inverness (all of which go on to Wick) arrive at Thurso **train station**, adjacent to the **bus station**, both a ten-minute walk down Princes Street and Sir George's Street to the riverside **tourist office** (April–May & Oct Mon–Sat 10am–5pm; June–Sept Mon–Sat 10am–5pm, Sun 10am–4pm). The **Scrabster ferry terminal** is a mile or so northwest of town, with regular buses from the train station in the morning, and from Olrig St in the afternoon. For more on **ferries to Orkney** from Scrabster, Gill's Bay and John O' Groats, see p.1248.

Thurso is well stocked with **accommodation**, including several hostels, best of which is *Sandra's*, 24 Princes St (☎01847/894575, Ⓦwww sandras-backpackers.ukf.net), a cramped but very welcoming **hostel** above a lively local chippie, with dorm beds and doubles (❶); they also offer **bike rental** and **Internet** access. The most comfortable **hotel** is the smart and central *Royal Hotel* (☎01847/893191, Ⓦwww.british-trust-hotels.com; ❻), on Traill St. Of the **B&Bs**, *Murray House*, 1 Campbell St (☎01847/895759, Ⓦwww.murrayhousebb.com; ❷), is central, comfortable and friendly; there's also *Tigh na Abhainn*, an old house by the river (☎01847/893443; ❶), or the long-established *Orcadia*, 27 Olrig St (☎01847/894395; ❶). The nearest **campsite** (☎01847/805503) is out towards Scrabster alongside the main road, though there's a much nicer one at Dunnet Bay, a few miles east (see below).

By far the best place **to eat** in Thurso is *Le Bistro*, 2 Traill St (☎01847/893737; Tues–Sat), with a moderately priced menu featuring lots of local seafood and veggie dishes. If you're coming to **surf**, it's best to bring your own gear, though Harper's fishing shop, 57 High St (☎01847/893179) does rent and sell wetsuits or boards.

Dunnet Head and the Castle of Mey

Thurso doesn't have much of a beach, so if you want to sink your toes into sand, head five miles east along the A836 to **Dunnet Bay**, a vast golden beach backed by huge dunes. The bay is popular with surfers, and even in the winter you can usually spot intrepid figures far out in the Pentland Firth's breakers. At the northeast end of the bay, there's a **Ranger Centre** (April–Sept Tues–Fri &

Sun 2–5pm) beside the excellent campsite, where you can pick up information on good local history and nature walks, including a short self-guided trail into nearby **Dunnet Forest**, a failed plantation which has been left to go – literally – to seed, allowing a rich range of plant and animal life to thrive. To the north of the bay is the small village of **Dunnet**, where it's worth stopping in at **Mary-Ann's Cottage** (June–Sept Tues–Sun 2–4.30pm; £1), a farming croft vacated in 1990 by 93-year-old Mary-Ann Calder, whose grandfather had built the cottage, and maintained just as she left it, full of reminders of the three generations who lived and worked there over the last 150 years.

Despite the publicity that John O'Groats customarily receives, mainland Britain's most northerly point is in fact **Dunnet Head**, north of Dunnet along the B855, which runs for four miles over windy heather and bog to the tip of the headland, crowned with a Stevenson lighthouse. The red cliffs below are startling, with weirdly eroded rock stacks and a huge variety of sea birds; on a clear day you can see the whole northern coastline from Cape Wrath to Duncansby Head, and across the treacherous Pentland Firth to Orkney.

Roughly fifteen miles east of Thurso, just off the A836, is the Queen Mum's former Scottish home, the **Castle of Mey** (April to mid-May & mid-August to mid-Oct Tues–Sat 11am–4.30pm, Sun 2–5pm; ⓦ www.castleofmey.org.uk; £5), now easily the most popular tourist attraction in Caithness. It's a modest little place, hidden behind high flagstone walls, with great views north to Orkney, and a herd of the Queen Mum's beloved Aberdeen Angus grazing out front. The Queen Mum used to spend every August here, and unusually for a royal palace, it's remarkably unstuffy inside, the walls hung with works by local amateur artists (and watercolours by Prince Charles), the sideboards cluttered with tacky joke ornaments and the video library well stocked with videos of Fawlty Towers and Dad's Army.

John O'Groats and around

Romantics expecting to find a magical meeting of land and water at **JOHN O'GROATS** (ⓦ www.visitjohnogroats.com) are invariably disappointed – sadly, but all too predictably, it's a seedy little tourist trap. The views north to Orkney are fine enough, but the village is little more than a string of over-priced souvenir shops thronged with coach parties. The village gets its name from the Dutchman, Jan de Groot, who obtained the ferry contract for the hazardous crossing to Orkney in 1496. The eight-sided house he built for his eight quarrelling sons (so that each one could enter by his own door) is echoed in the octagonal tower of the much-photographed *John O'Groats Hotel*, which is fast falling into disrepair but remains a good stop-off for a drink. Aside from regular **buses** to Wick and Thurso, there are frequent if irregular links with Land's End (the far southwest tip of England), maintained by a succession of walkers, cyclists, vintage-car drivers and pushers of baths.

There are several **boat trips** to be had: John O'Groats Ferries (ⓣ01955/611353, ⓦ www.jogferry.co.uk) offers a leisurely afternoon cruise which will take you round the sea-bird colonies and stacks of Duncansby Head or the seal colonies of Stroma (mid-June to Aug daily; 1hr 30min; £14); North Coast Marine Adventures (ⓣ0786/766 6273, ⓦ www.northcoast-marine-adventures.co.uk) offer rather more high-adrenalin trips in a rigid inflatable, and Mr Simpson (ⓣ01955/611252) periodically takes groups across to the nearby island of Stroma in his boat.

If you're disappointed by John O'Groats, press on a couple of miles further east to **Duncansby Head**, which, with its lighthouse, dramatic cliffs a well-worn coastal path, has a lot more to offer. The bird life here is prolific, and south of the headland lie some spectacular 200ft cliffs, cut by sheer-sided clefts known locally as *geos*, and several impressive sea stacks, including a very photogenic triangular one.

The east coast

The **east coast** of the Highlands, between Inverness and Wick, is nowhere near as spectacular as the west, with gently undulating moors, grassland and low cliffs where you might otherwise expect to find sea lochs and mountains. While many visitors bypass this region in a headlong rush to the Orkneys, those who choose to dally will find equally impressive prehistoric and historic sites and reminders here. The area around the Black Isle and the Tain Peninsula was a Pictish heartland, while further north, from around the ninth century AD onwards, the **Norse** influence was more keenly felt than in any other part of mainland Britain. The whole area is studded with prehistoric brochs, cairns and standing stones, many in remarkable condition.

Culturally and scenically, much of the east coast is more lowland than highland, and Caithness in particular evolved more or less separately from the Highlands, avoiding the bloody tribal feuds that wreaked such havoc further south and west. Later, however, the nineteenth-century **Clearances** hit the region hard, as countless ruined cottages and empty glens show (see box, p.1250). Hundreds of thousands of crofters were evicted and forced to emigrate to New Zealand, Canada and Australia, or else take up fishing in one of the numerous herring ports established on the coast. The oil boom has brought a transient prosperity to one or two places over the past few decades, but this has been countered by the downturn in the North Sea fishing industry.

The one stretch of the east coast that's always been relatively rich is the **Black Isle** just over the Kessock Bridge heading north out of Inverness, whose main village, **Cromarty**, is the region's undisputed highlight, with a crop of elegant mansions and appealing fishermen's cottages clustered near the entrance to the Cromarty Firth. Beyond **Dornoch**, a golfing resort made famous as the site of Madonna's wedding, the ersatz-Loire château **Dunrobin Castle** is the main tourist attraction, a monument as much to the iniquities of the Clearances as to the eccentricity of Victorian taste. **Wick**, the largest town on this section of coast, has an interesting past inevitably entwined with the fishing industry, whose story is told in another good heritage centre, but is otherwise uninspiring. The relatively flat landscapes of this northeast corner – windswept peat bog and farmland dotted with lochans and grey-and-white crofts – are a surprising contrast to the more rugged country south and west of here.

The Black Isle and around

Sandwiched between the Cromarty Firth to the north and, to the south, the Moray and Beauly firths which separate it from Inverness, the **Black Isle** is not an island at all, but a fertile peninsula whose rolling hills, prosperous farms and stands of deciduous woodland make it more reminiscent of Dorset or Sussex than the Highlands. It probably gained its name because of its mild climate: there's rarely frost, which leaves the fields "black" all winter; another explanation is that the name derives from the Gaelic word for black, *dubh* – a possible corruption of St Duthus.

The Highland Clearances

Once the clan chiefs had been forbidden their own armies after the defeat at Culloden, they had no need of the large tenantry that had previously been a vital military asset – and yet the second half of the eighteenth century saw the Highland population double after the introduction of the easy-to-grow and nutritious potato. The clan chiefs adopted different policies to deal with the new situation. Some encouraged emigration, and as many as six thousand Highlanders left for the Americas between 1800 and 1803 alone. Other landowners developed alternative forms of employment for their tenants, mainly fishing and the gathering of kelp. This brown seaweed was burnt to produce soda ash, which was used in the manufacture of soap, glass and explosives. Other landowners developed sheep runs on the Highland pastures, introducing hardy breeds like the black-faced Linton and the Cheviot. But extensive sheep farming proved incompatible with a high peasant population, and many landowners decided to clear their estates of tenants, some of whom were forcibly moved to tiny plots of marginal land, where they were to farm as crofters.

The pace of these **Highland Clearances** accelerated after the end of the Napoleonic Wars in 1815, when the market price for kelp, fish and cattle declined, leaving sheep as the only profitable Highland product. As the dispossessed Highlanders scratched a living from the acid soils of some tiny croft, they learnt through bitter experience the limitations of the clan. Famine followed, forcing large-scale emigration and leaving the huge uninhabited areas found in the region today. The crofters eked out a precarious existence, but they hung on throughout the nineteenth century, often by taking seasonal employment away from home.

In the 1880s, however, a sharp downturn in agricultural prices made it difficult for many crofters to pay their rent. This time, inspired by the example of the Irish Land League, they resisted eviction, forming the **Highland Land Reform Association** and the **Crofters' Party**. In 1886, in response to the social unrest, Gladstone's Liberal government passed the **Crofters' Holdings Act**, which conceded three of the crofters' demands: security of tenure, fair rents to be decided independently, and the right to pass on crofts by inheritance. But Gladstone did not attempt to increase the amount of land available for crofting and shortage of land remained a major problem until the **Land Settlement Act** of 1919 made provision for the creation of new crofts. Nevertheless, the population of the Highlands continued to decline during the twentieth century, with many of the region's young people finding city life more appealing.

The Black Isle is littered with dozens of **prehistoric sites**, but the main incentive to make the detour east from the A9 is to visit the picturesque eighteenth-century town of **Cromarty**, huddled at the northeast tip of the peninsula. A string of villages along the south coast is also worth stopping in en route, and one of them, Rosemarkie, has an outstanding small **museum** devoted to Pictish culture. Nearby Chanonry Point is among the best **dolphin-spotting** sites in Europe.

Fortrose and Rosemarkie

Just across the Kessock Bridge from Inverness is a roadside complex with **tourist office** (Easter–Oct Mon–Sat 10am–5pm, Sun 11am–4pm; July & Au Mon–Sat until 6pm; ☎01463/731505), as well as two wildlife centres. Th **dolphin and seal centre** (June–Sept daily 9.30am–4.30pm; £1) offers t chance to see (and listen to) these popular creatures, while the RSPB have s up an observation post for the **red kite**, a bird of prey successfully reintroduc to Scotland in 1992.

FORTROSE, a few miles east of Avoch, is a quietly elegant village dominated by the beautiful ruins of an early thirteenth-century **cathedral** (daily 8am–8pm). Founded by King David I, it now languishes on a lovely green bordered by red-sandstone and colourwashed houses, where a horde of gold coins dating from the time of Robert III was unearthed in 1880. There's also a memorial to the Seaforth family, whose demise the Brahan Seer famously predicted (see box). There's a memorial plaque to the seer at nearby **Chanonry Point**, reached by a back road from the north end of Fortrose; the thirteenth hole of the golf course here marks the spot where he met his death. Jutting into a narrow channel in the Moray Firth (deepened to allow warships into the estuary during World War II), the point, fringed on one side by a beach of golden sand and shingle, is an excellent place to look for **dolphins**. Come here around high tide, and you stand a good chance of spotting a couple leaping through the surf in search of fish brought to the surface by converging currents.

ROSEMARKIE, a lovely one-street village a mile north of Fortrose at the opposite (northwest) end of the beach, is thought to have been evangelized by St Boniface in the early eighth century. The cosy **Groam House Museum** (May–Sept Mon–Sat 10am–5pm, Sun 2–4.30pm; Oct–April Sat & Sun 2–4pm; free), at the bottom of the village, displays a bumper crop of intricately carved Pictish standing stones (among them the famous Rosemarkie Cross Slab), and shows an informative video highlighting Pictish sites in the region. A lovely mile-and-a-half **woodland walk**, along the banks of a sparkling burn to Fairy Glen, begins at the car park just beyond the village on the road to Cromarty. Quality bar food (as well as beer from the Black Isle Brewery) is available at the wonderfully old-fashioned *Plough Inn*, just down the main street from the museum.

Cromarty

An ancient legend recalls that the twin headlands flanking the entrance to the **Cromarty Firth**, known as The Sutors (from the Gaelic word for shoemaker), were once a pair of giant cobblers who used to protect the Black Isle from pirates. Nowadays, however, the only giants in the area are Nigg and Invergordon's colossal oil rigs, marooned in the estuary like metal monsters marching out to sea. **CROMARTY**, the Black Isle's main settlement, was an ancient ferry crossing-point on the pilgrimage trail to St Duthus's shrine in Tain. Although a royal burgh since the fourth century, Cromarty didn't become a prominent port until 1772 when the entrepreneurial local landlord, George Ross, founded a hemp mill here, fuelling a period of prosperity during which Cromarty acquired some of Scotland's finest Georgian houses; these, together with the terraced fishers' cottages of the nineteenth-century herring boom, have left the town with a wonderfully well-preserved concentration of Scottish domestic architecture.

To get a sense of Cromarty's past, head straight for the award-winning **museum** housed in the old **Courthouse** on Church Street (daily: April–Oct 10am–5pm; Nov–Dec & March noon–4pm; £3), which tells the history of the town using audiovisuals and animated figures. **Hugh Miller**, a nineteenth-century stonemason turned author, geologist, folklorist and Free Church campaigner, was born in Cromarty, and his **birthplace** (Easter–Sept daily noon–5pm; Oct Sun–Wed noon–5pm; £2.50; NTS), a modest thatched cottage on Church Street, has been restored to give an idea of what Cromarty must have been like in his day.

The widely respected Dolphin Écosse (℡01381/600323, Ⓦwww .dolphinecosse.co.uk) runs half- or full-day **boat trips** to see seals, porpoises, bottle-nosed dolphins and occasionally minke whales from their Dolphin Centre by the harbour behind the *Royal Hotel*. At the centre is background information on dolphins and whales, along with some spectacular photographs of the animals taken by clients while out on the boat. The tiny two-car Nigg–Cromarty **ferry** (June–Oct daily 8am–6.15pm), Scotland's smallest, also doubles up as a cruiser on summer evenings; you can catch it from the jetty near the lighthouse.

Nine **buses** a day run to Cromarty from Inverness (55min), returning from the car park at the bottom of Forsyth Place. For **B&B**, try one of the attractive old houses on Church Street, such as Mrs Robertson's at no. 7 (℡01381/600488; ❶), where you can also **rent bikes**. Above the town *Beechfield House* (℡01381/600308; ❷) offers modern rooms and good views. The most down-to-earth place **to eat** is the *Cromarty Arms*, which has a beer garden and serves basic, inexpensive bar meals – it also has occasiona live music.

Dingwall and Strathpeffer

Most traffic nowadays takes the upgraded A9 north from Inverness, bypassin the small market town of **DINGWALL** (from the Norse *thing*, "parliament" and *vollr*, "field"), a royal burgh since 1226 and former port that was left hig and dry when the river receded during the nineteenth century. Today, it ha succumbed to the curse of British provincial towns and acquired an ugly busi ness park and characterless pedestrian shopping street. Dingwall's only re claim to fame is that it was the birthplace of Macbeth, whose family occupie the now ruined castle on Castle Street. You're unlikely to want to hang arou here for long – for somewhere pleasant to stay move onto Strathpeffer or pu on north.

STRATHPEFFER, a mannered and leafy Victorian spa town surround by wooded hills four miles west of Dingwall, is pleasant enough but does suf from a high density of coach parties. During its heyday, this was a renown European **health resort** reached by the tongue-twisting Strathpeffer S

Express train from Aviemore. Strathpeffer is within striking distance of the bleak **Ben Wyvis**, and so is also a popular base for walkers. One of the best hikes in the area is up the hill of Cnoc Mor, where the vitrified Iron Age hill fort of **Knock Farril** affords superb panoramic views to the Cromarty Firth and the surrounding mountains.

Buses run regularly between Dingwall and Strathpeffer (11 daily Mon–Sat), dropping passengers in the square, where you'll find a small **tourist office** (July & Aug Mon–Sat 9am–5.30pm, Sun 10am–5.30pm; June & Sept to mid-Oct Mon–Sat 10am–5pm, Sun 11am–4pm; April & May Mon–Sat 10am–5pm; ☎01997/421415) with information on points west as well as local areas. The large **hotels** in the village are very popular with bus tours, so try one of the smaller places such as *Brunstane Lodge* (☎01997/421261, ⓦwww .brunstanelodge.com; ❹); there's also **B&B** at the upmarket *Craigvar* (☎01997/421622, ⓦwww.craigvar.com; ❸), which overlooks the square, or *Inver Lodge*, west of the main square (☎01997/421392; ❶; March–Dec).

The Dornoch Firth and around

North of the Cromarty Firth, the hammer-shaped **Tain peninsula** can still be approached from the south by the ancient ferry crossing from Cromarty to Nigg, though to the north the link is a more recent causeway over the **Dornoch Firth**, the inlet which marks the northern boundary of the peninsula. On the southern edge of the Dornoch Firth the A9 bypasses the quiet town of **Tain**, probably best known as the home of Glenmorangie whisky. Inland, at the head of the firth, there's not much to the village of **Bonar Bridge**, but fans of unusual hostels travel from far and wide to spend a night at **Carbisdale Castle**. On the north side of the Dornoch Firth, the neat town of **Dornoch** itself, long known for its impressive cathedral and well-manicured golf courses, found renewed fame in 2000 as the venue for Madonna's wedding.

Tain

The peninsula's largest settlement is **TAIN**, an attractive and pleasant small town of grand whisky-coloured sandstone buildings. A good place to get to grips with the peninsula's past is the **Tain Through Time** exhibition (April–Oct Mon–Sat 10am–5pm; £3.50), which makes creative use of three old buildings around the church and graveyard, leading you round using an audioguide. Tain's other main attraction is the **Glenmorangie whisky distillery** where the highly rated malt is produced (☎01862/892477; shop Mon–Fri 9am–5pm, June–Aug also Sat 10am–4pm, Sun noon–4pm; tours Mon–Fri 10.30am–3.30pm, Sat 10.30am–2.30pm, Sun 12.30–2.30pm; £2 including discount voucher); it lies just off the A9 on the north side of town. Booking is recommended for the tours.

Bonar Bridge and Carbisdale Castle

Before the causeway was built across the Dornoch Firth, traffic heading along the coast used to skirt west around the estuary, crossing the Kyle of Sutherland the village of **BONAR BRIDGE**. Bonar Bridge has struggled since it was bypassed: there's little of note here other than the **bridge** itself, which has had three incarnations up to the present steel construction of 1973, all recalled on a stone plinth on the north side.

Towering high above the River Shin, three miles northwest of Bonar Bridge, the daunting neo-Gothic profile of **Carbisdale Castle** overlooks the Kyle of

Sutherland. The castle was erected between 1906 and 1917 for the dowager duchess of Sutherland, following a protracted family feud, during which the duchess was found in contempt of court for destroying important documents pertinent to a legal case, and locked up in London's Holloway prison for six weeks. However, by way of compensation, a castle was built for the duchess worthy of her rank. Carbisdale was eventually acquired by a Norwegian shipping magnate in 1933, and finally gifted, along with its entire contents and estate, to the Scottish Youth Hostels Association, which has turned it into what must be one of the most opulent **hostels** in the world, full of white Italian marble sculptures, huge gilt-framed portraits, sweeping staircases and magnificent drawing rooms alongside standard facilities such as self-catering kitchens, games rooms, TV rooms and thirty dorms, including some recently upgraded four-bed family rooms (T0870/004 1109, Wwww.carbisdale.org; March–Oct; £13.50), often booked out by groups. The best way to get here by public transport is to take a **train** to nearby Culrain station, which lies within easy walking distance of the castle. **Buses** from Inverness (3 daily; 1hr 30min) and Tain (4 daily; 25min) only stop at **Ardgay**, three miles south.

Dornoch

DORNOCH, a genteel and appealing town eight miles north of Tain, lies on a flattish headland overlooking the **Dornoch Firth**. Surrounded by sand dunes and blessed with an exceptionally sunny climate by Scottish standards, it's something of a middle-class holiday resort, with solid Edwardian hotels, trees and flowers in profusion, and miles of sandy beaches giving good views across the estuary to the Tain peninsula. The town is also renowned for its championship **golf course**, ranked among the top twenty in the world and the most northerly first-class course. In 2000 Dornoch was the scene for Scotland's most prestigious rock'n'roll wedding of recent times, when Madonna married Guy Ritchie at nearby Skibo Castle and had her son baptized in Dornoch Cathedral.

Dating from the twelfth century, Dornoch became a royal burgh in 1628. Among its oldest buildings, which are all grouped round the spacious square, the exquisite **cathedral** was founded in 1224 and built of local sandstone. The original building was horribly damaged by marauding Mackays in 1570, and much of what you see today was restored by the countess of Sutherland in 1835, though her worst excesses were removed in the twentieth century, when the interior stonework was returned to its original state.

Local **tourist information** can be found alongside the arts and crafts at *Jail Dornoch* (April–Sept Mon–Sat 9am–6pm, Sun 10am–4pm; Oct–March Mon–Sat 9am–5pm; sun 10am–4pm; T01862/810916), where there's also a coffee shop and bike hire available. There's no shortage of **accommodation**. *Tordarroch B&B* (T01862/810855; ❷; March–Oct) has a great location opposite the cathedral, as does the *Trevose* (T01862/810269; ❷; March–Sept) which is swathed in roses. Expensive gourmet **meals** are available at the *2 Quail* restaurant (T01862/811811; Tues–Sat) on Castle Street, which also has tasteful rooms (❺), while both the hotels do good bar and restaurant meals.

North to Wick

North of Dornoch, the A9 hugs the coastline for most of the sixty or so miles to **Wick**, the principal settlement in the far north of the mainland. Perhaps the most important landmark in the whole stretch is the **Sutherland Monument** near Golspie, erected in memory of the first duke of Sutherland, known as the landowner who oversaw the eviction of thousands of his tenants in a process known as the Clearances. The bitter memory of those times resonates through most of the small towns and villages on this stretch, including **Brora**, the gold-prospecting village of **Helmsdale**, **Dunbeath** and **Lybster**. With sites dotted around recalling Iron-Age settlers and Viking rule, many of these settlements also hark back to the days of a thriving fishing trade, none more so than the main town of Wick, once the busiest herring port in Europe.

Golspie and around

Ten miles north of Dornoch on the A9 lies the straggling red-sandstone town of **GOLSPIE**, whose status as an administrative centre does little to relieve its dullness. The main reason to stop in Golspie is to look around **Dunrobin Castle** (April–mid-Oct Mon–Sat 10.30am–4.30pm, Sun noon–4.30pm; June–Sept daily 10.30am–5.30pm; £6.70), overlooking the sea a mile north of town. Approached via a long tree-lined drive, this fairy-tale confection of turrets and pointed roofs – modelled by the architect Sir Charles Barry (responsible for the Houses of Parliament) on a Loire château – is the seat of the infamous Sutherland family, at one time Europe's biggest landowners, with a staggering 1.3 million acres, and the principal driving force behind the Clearances in this area. The castle is on a correspondingly vast scale, boasting 189 furnished rooms, of which the tour takes in only seventeen. Staring up at the pile from the midst of its elaborate **formal gardens**, it's worth remembering that such extravagance was paid for by uprooting literally thousands of crofters from the surrounding glens.

Set aside at least an hour for Dunrobin's amazing **museum**, housed in an eighteenth-century building at the edge of the garden. Inside, hundreds of disembodied animals' heads and horns peer down from the walls, alongside other more macabre appendages, from elephants' toes to rhinos' tails. Bagged mainly by the fifth duke and duchess of Sutherland, the trophies vie for space with other fascinating family memorabilia, including one of John O'Groat's bones, Chinese opium pipes, and such curiosities as a "picnic gong from the South Pacific". There's also an impressive collection of ethnographic artefacts acquired by the Sutherlands on their frequent hunting jaunts, ranging from an Egyptian sarcophagus to some finely carved Pictish stones. The admission price to the castle includes a falconry display (three daily).

The Sutherland Monument

A mile northwest of Golspie, you can't miss the 100ft **monument** to the first duke of Sutherland, which peers down from the summit of the 1293ft **Beinn a'Bhragaidh** (Ben Bhraggie). An inscription cut into its base recalls that the statue was erected in 1834 by "a mourning and grateful tenantry [to] a judicious, kind and liberal landlord [who would] open his hands to the distress of the widow, the sick and the traveller". Unsurprisingly, there's no reference to the fact that the duke, widely regarded as Scotland's own Josef Stalin, forcibly evicted 15,000 crofters from his million-acre estate – a fact that, in the words of one local historian, makes the monument "a grotesque representation of the many forces that destroyed the Highlands". The campaign to have the statue smashed and scattered over the hillside has largely died down; the general attitude now seems to be that the statue stands as a useful reminder of the duke's infamy as much as his achievements.

It's worth the wet, rocky **climb** to the top of the hill (round trip 1hr 30min) for the wonderful views south along the coast past Dornoch to the Moray Firth and west towards Lairg and Loch Shin. It's steep and strenuous, however, and there's no view until you're out of the trees, about ten minutes from the top. Take the road opposite Munro's TV Rentals in Golspie's main street; after a farmyard, follow the Beinn a'Bhragaidh footpath (BBFP) signs along the path into the woods.

Rogart

Just to the south of Golspie on the A839 to Lairg is one of Scotland's most unusual and imaginative **hostels**, *Sleeperzzz.com* (☏01408/641343, Ⓦwww.sleeperzzz.com), where you can stay in one of two first-class railway carriages parked in a siding beside the station on the Inverness–Thurso line in the tiny settlement of **ROGART**. Each of the comfortable compartments has a bunk bed on one side and the original seats on the other, while the two end compartments are used as a kitchen and common room. The owners have free **mountain bikes** available to let you explore the local countryside, and the place stands 100 yards from a convivial local **pub**, the *Pittentrail Inn*, that serves warming evening meals. A small reduction is even offered to those arriving by train or bicycle.

Helmsdale and around

Eleven scenic miles north along the A9 from Golspie, **HELMSDALE** is an old herring port, founded in the nineteenth century to house the evicted inhabitants of Strath Kildonan, which lies behind it. Today, the sleepy-looking grey village attracts thousands of tourists, most of them coming to see the attractively designed **Timespan Heritage Centre** beside the river (April–Oct Mon–Sat 9.30am–5pm, Sun noon–5pm; £4). It's a remarkable venture for a place of this size, telling the local story of Viking raids, witch burning, Clearances, fishing and gold prospecting through high-tech displays, sound effects and an audiovisual programme. The centre also has an art gallery, which often has a decent show of works by Scottish artists, as well as a café.

There's no official tourism office in town, but you'll pick up lots of local information at *Strath Ullie Crafts* on the harbour. **Eating** options abound in Helmsdale. On the main street, local fish wars have been known to break out between the *Mirage* restaurant and the *Bunillidh* opposite; however, the happy fact is that both places serve excellent meals (especially seafood) at decent prices. Meals are also available at the friendly *Belgrave Arms* pub, as well as the *Bannockburn* opposite.

Baile an Or

From Helmsdale the single-track A897 runs up Strath Kildonan and across the Flow Country (see p.1246) to the north coast, at first following the River Helmsdale, a strictly controlled and exclusive salmon river frequented by the Royal Family. Some eight miles up the Strath at **BAILE AN OR** (Gaelic for "goldfield"), gold was discovered in the bed of the Kildonan Burn in 1869; **gold rush** ensued, hardly on the scale of the Yukon, but quite bizarre in the Scottish Highlands. A tiny amount of gold is still found by some hardy prospectors every year: should you fancy **gold panning** yourself, you can rent the relevant equipment for £2.50 from *Strath Ullie Crafts*, which also sells a booklet with a few basic tips.

Lybster and around

The planned village of **LYBSTER** (pronounced "libe-ster"), established at the height of the nineteenth-century herring boom, once had 200-odd boats working out of its harbour. The new **Water Lines** heritage centre on the harbour (April–Sept daily 11am–5pm; £2) is an attractive modern disp about the "silver darlings" and the fishermen that pursued them; there's a snug café downstairs. There's not much else to see here apart from the harbour area; the upper town is a grim collection of grey pebble-dashed bungalows centred on a broad main street.

The **Grey Cairns of Camster**, seven miles due north and one of the most memorable sights on the northeast coast, are a different story. Surrounded by bleak moorland, these two enormous reconstructed prehistoric burial chambers, originally built four or five thousand years ago, were immaculately designed, with corbelled dry-stone roofs in their hidden chambers, which you can crawl into through narrow passageways. More extraordinary ancient remains lie at **East Clyth**, two miles north of Lybster on the A99, where a path leads to the "**Hill o'Many Stanes**". Some 200 boulders stand in the ground here, forming 22 parallel rows that run north to south; no one has yet worked out what they were used for, although archeological studies have shown there were once 600 stones in place.

Wick and beyond

Originally a Viking settlement named *Vik* (meaning "bay"), **WICK** has been a royal burgh since 1589. It's actually two towns: Wick proper, and **Pultneytown**, immediately south across the river, a messy, rather run-down community planned by Thomas Telford in 1806 for the British Fisheries Society, to encourage evicted crofters to take up fishing. Wick's heyday was in the mid-nineteenth century, when it was the busiest herring port in Europe, with a fleet of over 1100 boats, exporting tons of fish to Russia, Scandinavia and the West Indian slave plantations. Pultneytown, lined with rows of fishermen's cottages, is the area most worth a wander, with the acres of largely derelict net-mending sheds, stores and cooperages around the harbour giving some idea of the former scale of the fishing trade. The town's story is told in the excellent **Wick Heritage Centre** in Bank Row, Pultneytown (Easter–Oct Mon–Sat 10am–5pm; £2), which contains a fascinating array of artefacts from the old fishing days, including fully rigged boats, original boat models, the old Noss Head lighthouse light and a great photographic collection dating from the 1880s. Interestingly, Wick was a dry town for a quarter of a century until 1947, although that didn't stop some of the locals heading off to Lybster or Thurso for a quiet beer or two.

The **train** station and **bus** stops are next to each other behind the hospital. Frequent local buses run to Thurso and up the coast to John O'Groats. Wick also has an **airport** (☎01955/602215), a couple of miles north of the town, with direct flights from Edinburgh and Aberdeen, and connections further south. From the train station, head across the river down Bridge Street to the cheerful **tourist office**, just off the High Street (April–Oct Mon–Sat 10am–5pm; July–Sept also Sun 10am–4pm; ☎01955/602596). Among the **B&B** options are the low-priced *Quayside*, 25 Harbour Quay (☎01955/603229, ⓦwww.quaysidewick.co.uk; ●), and *Mt Pleasant House*, North Road (☎01955/605716; Easter–Sept; ●), on the north side of town. Five miles towards Thurso is the lovely *Bilbster House* (☎01955/621212, ⓦwww.accommodationbilbster.com; ●; April-Oct, in winter by arrangement).

The north bank of the river, at the east end of High Street, is the best spot for **eating and drinking**. On Market Street, the *Bord de l'Eau* (☎01955/604400; Tues–Sun) produces gourmet French cuisine at excellent prices, while round the corner *Cabrelli's* may be trapped in a time warp but it serves piles of fish and chips, along with authentic pizza.

24

Travel details

Buses

For information on all local and national bus services, contact Traveline ☎ 0870/608 2608 (daily 7am–9pm), ⊛ www.traveline.org.uk.
Aviemore to: Edinburgh (3 daily direct; 2hr 30min–3hr 30min); Glasgow (5 daily direct; 3hr 30min); Grantown-on-Spey (Mon–Sat 6–8 daily; 40min); Inverness (10 daily; 45min).
Fort William to: Acharacle (Mon–Sat 2–3 daily; 1hr 30min); Drumnadrochit (6 daily; 1hr 30min); Edinburgh (1 direct daily; 4hr); Fort Augustus (6 daily; 1hr); Glasgow (4 daily; 3hr); Inverness (6 daily; 2hr); Kilchoan (1–2 daily; 3hr 35min); Mallaig (Mon–Fri 1 daily; 1hr 30min); Oban (Mon–Sat 4 daily; 1hr 30min); Portree, Skye (3 daily; 3hr).
Gairloch to: Dingwall (3 weekly; 2hr); Inverness (Mon–Sat 1 daily; 2hr 20min); Redpoint (1–3 daily; 1hr 35min); Ullapool (1 weekly; 1hr 45min).
Inverness to: Aberdeen (hourly; 3hr 40min); Aviemore (10 daily; 45min); Drumnadrochit (6 daily; 25min); Durness (Mon–Sat 1 daily, May–Sept only; 5hr); Fort Augustus (6 daily; 1hr); Fort William (6 daily; 2hr); Glasgow (7 daily direct; 3hr 35min–4hr 25min); Kyle of Lochalsh (2 daily; 2hr); Nairn (Mon –Sat hourly; 35min); Perth (10 daily; 2hr 35min); Portree (2 daily; 3hr 20min); Thurso (Mon–Sat 5 daily, Sun 3 daily; 3hr 30min); Ullapool (4–6 daily; 1hr 30min); Wick (Mon–Sat 4 daily, Sun 3 daily; 3hr).
Kyle of Lochalsh to: Fort William (3 daily; 1hr 50min); Glasgow (3 daily; 5hr); Inverness (2 daily; 2hr).
Lochinver to: Inverness (June–Sept 1 daily; 3hr 10min); Ullapool (Mon–Sat 1 daily; 1hr).
Thurso to: Inverness (4 daily; 3hr 30min); John O' Groats (Mon–Fri 5 daily, 2 on Sat; 1hr); Wick (Mon–Fri hourly, Sat & Sun 6 daily; 35min).
Ullapool to: Durness (Mon–Sat 1 daily; 3hr); Inverness (Mon–Sat 10 daily; 1hr 30min).
Wick to: John O' Groats (7 daily Mon–Sat; 50min).

Trains

For information on all local and national rail services, contact National Rail Enquiries ☎ 08457/484950, ⊛ www.nationalrail.co.uk.
Aviemore to: Edinburgh (Mon–Sat 4 daily, 3 on Sun; 2hr 30min); Glasgow (2 daily; 2hr 30min);

Inverness (Mon–Sat 6 daily, 3 on Sun; 1hr).
Inverness to: Aberdeen (Mon–Sat 10 daily; Sun 5 daily; 2hr 15min); Aviemore (Mon–Sat 8–9 daily, 3–4 on Sun; 40min); Dingwall (Mon–Sat 6–7 daily, 4 on Sun; 25min); Edinburgh (Mon–Sat 5–6 daily, 2–3 on Sun; 3hr 30min); Helmsdale (Mon–Sat 3 daily, 1 on Sun; 2hr 20min); Kyle of Lochalsh (Mon–Sat 3 daily, 1 on Sun; 2hr 40min); Lairg (Mon–Sat 3 daily, 1 on Sun; 1hr 40min); Plockton (Mon–Sat 3 daily, 1 on Sun; 2hr 15min); Thurso (Mon–Sat 3 daily, 1 on Sun; 3hr 25min); Wick (Mon–Sat 3 daily, 1 on Sun; 3hr 45min).
Fort William to: Arisaig (Mon–Sat 4 daily, 1 on Sun; 1hr 10min); Crianlarich (Mon–Sat 3–4 daily, 2 on Sun; 1hr 50min); Glasgow (Mon–Sat 3–4 daily, 1–2 on Sun; 3hr 45min); Glenfinnan (Mon–Sat 4 daily, 1 on Sun; 35min); Mallaig (Mon–Sat 4 daily, 1 on Sun; 1hr 25min).
Kyle of Lochalsh to: Dingwall (Mon–Sat 3–4 daily, plus 2 on Sun in summer; 2hr); Inverness (Mon–Sat 3–4 daily, plus 2 on Sun in summer; 2hr 40min); Plockton (Mon–Sat 3–4 daily, plus 2 on Sun in summer; 20min).
Thurso to: Dingwall (Mon–Sat 3 daily, 1 on Sun; 3hr); Inverness (Mon–Sat 3 daily, 1 on Sun; 3hr 20min); Lairg (Mon–Sat 3 daily, 1 on Sun; 1hr 50min); Wick (Mon–Sat 3 daily, 1 on Sun; 20min).
Wick to: Dingwall (Mon–Sat 3 daily, 1 on Sun; 3hr 30min); Inverness (Mon–Sat 3 daily, 1 on Sun; 4hr); Lairg (Mon–Sat 3 daily, 1 on Sun; 2hr 20min).

Ferries

To Lewis: Ullapool–Stornoway (Mon–Sat 2–3 daily; 2hr 40min).
To Mull: Kilchoan–Tobermory (Mon–Sat 7 daily; June–Aug also Sun 5 daily; 35min); Lochaline–Fishnish (Mon–Sat every 50min, Sun hourly; 15min).
To Orkney: Gill's Bay–St Margaret's Hope (3 daily 1hr); John O'Groats–Burwick (passengers only; 2-daily; 40min); Scrabster–Stromness (2–3 daily; 2hr).
To Skye: Glenelg–Kylerhea (daily frequently; 15min); Mallaig–Armadale (Mon–Sat 8–9 daily; mid-May to mid-Sept also Sun; 30min).
To the Small Isles: Mallaig to Eigg, Rùm, Muck and Canna, see p.1145.

Flights

Inverness to: Edinburgh (Mon–Fri 2 daily, Sat & Sun 1 daily; 50min); Glasgow (Mon–Fri 3 daily, Sat & Sun 1 daily; 50min); Kirkwall (Mon–Sat 2 daily; 45min); London (Gatwick 4 daily; Luton 1–2 daily; 1hr 45min); Shetland (Mon–Sat 1 daily; 1hr 45min); Stornoway (Mon–Fri 2 daily, 1 on Sat & Sun; 40min).

Wick to: Inverness (Mon–Fri 2 daily; 35min); Edinburgh (Mon–Sat 1 daily; 1hr 10min); Kirkwall (Mon–Sat 1 daily; 25min).

25

Orkney
and Shetland

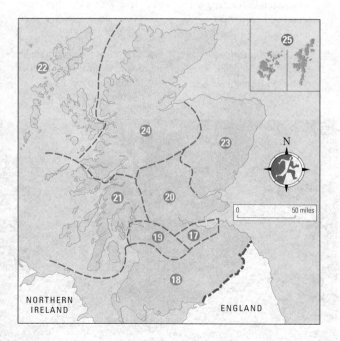

25

Highlights

* **Skara Brae** Neolithic village giving a fascinating insight into prehistoric life. See p.1268

* **Woodwick House** Beautiful guest house hideaway, producing simple but superb food. See p.1269

* **St Magnus Cathedral, Kirkwall** Beautiful red-stone cathedral built by the Vikings. See p.1270

* **Tomb of the Eagles** Fascinating Neolithic site on South Ronaldsay. See p.1272

* **Sanday** A coastline made up almost entirely of glorious sandy beaches, backed by sand dunes. See p.1278

* **Isle of Noss** Guaranteed seals, puffins and dive-bombing "bonxies". See p.1284

* **Mousa** Remote Shetland islet with a two-thousand-year-old broch. See p.1284

* **Jarlshof** Site mingling Iron Age, Bronze Age, Pictish, Viking and medieval settlements. See p.1285

△ St Magnus Cathedral, Orkney

Orkney
and Shetland

Reaching up towards the Arctic Circle, and totally exposed to turbulent Atlantic weather systems, the **Orkney** and **Shetland** islands gather neatly into two distinct and very different clusters. Often referring to themselves first as Orcadians or Shetlanders, and with unofficial but widely displayed flags, their inhabitants regard Scotland as a separate entity; the mainland to them is the one in their own archipelago, not the Scottish mainland. This feeling of detachment arises from their distinctive geography, history and culture, in which they differ not only from Scotland but also from each other.

To the south, just a short step from the Scottish mainland, are the seventy or so **Orkney Islands**. With the major exception of **Hoy**, which is high and rugged, these islands are mostly low-lying, gently sloping and richly fertile, and for centuries have provided a reasonably secure living for their inhabitants from farming and, to a much lesser extent, fishing. In spring and summer the days are long, the skies enormous, the sandy beaches dazzling and the meadows thick with wild flowers. There's a peaceful continuity to Orcadian life reflected not only in the well-preserved treasury of Stone Age settlements, such as **Skara Brae**, and standing stones, most notably the **Stones of Stenness**, but also in the rather conservative nature of society here today.

Another sixty miles north, the **Shetland Islands** are in nearly all respects a complete contrast. Dramatic cliffs, teeming with thousands of seabirds, rise straight out of the water to rugged, heather-coated hills, while ice-sculpted sea inlets cut deep into the land, offering memorable coastal walks in Shetland's endless summer evenings. With little fertile ground, Shetlanders have traditionally been crofters rather than farmers, often looking to the sea for an uncertain living in fishing and whaling or the naval and merchant services. Today islanders enthusiastically embrace new opportunities such as fish farming and computing. Nevertheless, the past isn't forgotten; the Norse heritage is clear in every road sign and there are many well-preserved prehistoric sites, such as **Mousa Broch** and **Jarlshof**.

Since people first began to explore the North Atlantic, Orkney and Shetland have been stepping stones on routes between Britain, Ireland and Scandinavia, and both groups have a long history of settlement, certainly from around 4000–3500 BC. The **Norse settlers**, who began to arrive from about 800 AD, left the islands with a unique cultural character. Orkney was a powerful Norse earldom, and Shetland (at first part of the same earldom) was ruled directly from Norway for nearly three hundred years after 1195. The Norse legacy is clearly evident today in place names and in dialect words; neither group was ever part of the Gaelic-speaking culture of Highland Scotland, and the later Scottish influence is essentially a Lowland one.

It's impossible to underestimate the influence of the **weather**. More often than not, it will be windy and rainy, though you can have all four seasons in one day. The wind-chill factor is not to be taken lightly, and there's often a dampness or drizzle in the air, even when it's not actually raining. Even in late spring and summer, when there can be long dry spells with lots of sunshine, you still need to come prepared for wind, rain and, most frustrating of all, the occasional sea fog. The one good thing is that midges are less of a problem, except on Hoy.

Orkney

Just a short step from John O'Groats, the **Orkney Islands** are a unique and fiercely independent archipelago. In spring and summer, the meadows and cliff tops are a brilliant green, shining with wild flowers, while long days pour light onto the land and sea. In autumn and winter, the islands are often battered by gale-force winds and daylight is scarce, but the temperature stays remarkably mild thanks to the ameliorating effect of the Gulf Stream. For an Orcadian, the "Mainland" invariably means the largest island in Orkney rather than the rest of Scotland, and throughout their history they've been linked to lands much further afield, principally Scandinavia.

Small communities began to settle in the islands around 4000 BC, and the village at **Skara Brae** on the Mainland is one of the best-preserved Stone Age settlements in Europe. This and many of the other older archeological sites including the **Stones of Stenness** and **Maes Howe**, are concentrated in West Mainland. Elsewhere the islands are scattered with chambered tombs and stone circles, a tribute to the religious and ceremonial practices taking place here from around 2000 BC. More sophisticated **Iron Age** inhabitants built fortified villages incorporating stone towers known as brochs, protected by walls and ramparts, the finest being the **Broch of Gurness**. Later, **Pictish** culture spread to Orkney and the remains of several of their early Christian settlements can still be seen, the best at the **Brough of Birsay**, where a group of small houses cluster around the remains of a church. Around the ninth century, **Norse** settlers arrived and the islands became Norse earldoms, forming an outpost of a powerful, expansive culture which was gradually forcing its way south. The last of the Norse earls was killed in 1231, but they had a lasting impact on the islands, leaving behind not only their language but also the outstanding **St Magnus Cathedral** in Kirkwall.

With the end of Norse rule, the islands became the preserve of **Scottish earls**, who exploited and abused the islanders, although a steady increase in sea trade did offer some chance of escape. French and Spanish ships sheltered here in the sixteenth century, and the ships of the **Hudson Bay Company** recruited hundreds of Orcadians to work in the Canadian fur trade. The islands were also an important staging post in the **whaling industry** and the herring boom, which drew great numbers of small Dutch, French and Scottish boats. More recently, the choice of **Scapa Flow**, Orkney's natural harbour, as the Royal Navy's main base brought plenty of money and activity during both

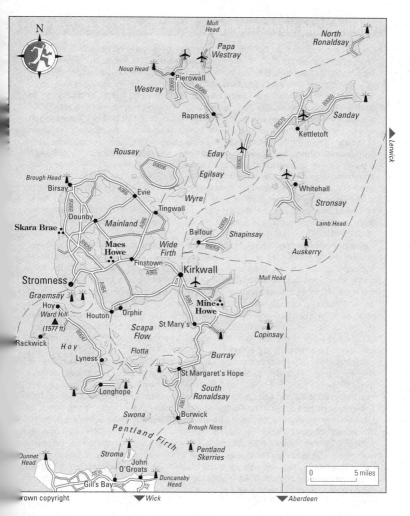

world wars, and left the clifftops dotted with gun emplacements and the seabed scattered with wrecks – which these days make for wonderful diving opportunities. Since the war, things have quietened down, although since the mid-1970s the large **oil terminal** on the island of Flotta, combined with EU development grants, have brought surprise windfalls, stemming the exodus of young people. Meanwhile, disenchanted southerners have become "ferryloupers" (incomers), moving to Orkney in search of the apparent simplicity of island life.

Stromness

STROMNESS has to be one of the most enchanting ports at which to arrive by boat, its picturesque waterfront a procession of tiny sandstone

Getting to and around Orkney

Orkney is connected to the Scottish mainland by several **ferry** routes. Pentland Ferries (℡01856/831226, ⓦwww.pentlandferries.com) operates the shortest car ferry crossing, from **Gills Bay**, on the north coast near John O'Groats (and linked by bus to Wick and Thurso) to **St Margaret's Hope** on South Ronaldsay (3 daily; 1hr). Services to **Stromness** from **Scrabster** (2–3 daily; 2hr), which is connected to nearby Thurso by a shuttle bus, are run by Northlink Ferries (℡0845/600 0449, ⓦwww.northlinkferries.co.uk), who also run ferries to **Kirkwall** from **Aberdeen** (4 weekly; 5hr 45min) and from **Lerwick** in Shetland (3 weekly; 4hr 30min). John O'Groats Ferries (℡01955/611353, ⓦwww.jogferry.co.uk) runs a passenger ferry from **John O'Groats** to **Burwick** on South Ronaldsay (May & Sept 2 daily; June–Aug 4 daily; 40min), its departure timed to connect with the arrival of the Orkney Bus from Inverness; there's also a free taxi service from Thurso train station. The ferry is small and, except in fine weather, is recommended only for those with strong stomachs. Direct **flights** serve Kirkwall airport from Sumburgh in Shetland, Wick, Inverness and Aberdeen, and there are good connections from Edinburgh, Glasgow, Manchester, Birmingham and London. All can be booked through British Airways (℡0870/850 9850, ⓦwww.ba.com).

Bus services on the Orkney Mainland are infrequent, and skeletal on Sundays, making a Day Rover (£6) or Three-Day Rover (£15) of limited value (see ⓦwww.rapsons.co.uk for more). On the smaller islands, a minibus usually meets the ferry and will take you to your destination; in addition, folk are very friendly and it's easy enough to hitch a lift. **Cycling** is not a bad option, though the wind can make it hard going. **Renting a car** will save you the steep ferry fares. If your time is limited, you may want to consider one of the informative bus or minibus **tours** on offer: Wildabout Orkney Tours (℡01856/851011, ⓦwww.orknet.co.uk/wildabout) have good-value tours of the chief sights on the Mainland and Hoy; other tours for specific islands are detailed in the text.

Getting to the other islands from the Mainland isn't difficult, though it is expensive: Orkney Ferries (℡01856/872044, ⓦwww.orkneyferries.co.uk) operates several **ferries** daily to Hoy, Shapinsay and Rousay, and between one and three a day, depending on route and season, to all the others except North Ronaldsay, which has a weekly boat on Fridays. If you're taking a car on any of the ferries, it's essential to book your ticket well in advance. There are also **flights** from Kirkwall to Eday, North Ronaldsay, Westray, Papa Westray, Sanday and Stronsay, operated by Loganair (℡01856/872494, ⓦwww.loganair.co.uk), using a tiny eight-seater plane. Loganair also offers **sightseeing flights** over Orkney, which are spectacular in fine weather (but cancelled in bad), as well as a discounted Orkney Adventure Ticket, which allows you return tickets to three islands for around £70, and a special £10 offer on return flights to North Ronaldsay if you stay over.

jetties and slate roofs nestling below the green hill of Brinkies Brae. As Orkney's main point of arrival, Stromness is a great introduction, and one that's well worth spending a day exploring, or using as a base in preference to Kirkwall. Its natural sheltered harbour (known as Hamnavoe) must have been used in Viking times, but the town itself only really took off in the eighteenth century when the Hudson's Bay Company made Stromness its main base from which to make the long journey across the North Atlantic and crews from Stromness were also hired for herring and whaling expeditions – and, of course, press-ganged into the Royal Navy. Today Stromness remains an important harbour town and fishing port, serving as Orkney's main ferry terminal and is the focus of the popular four-day **Orkney Folk Festival** (ⓦwww.orkneyfolkfestival.com), held in May.

The Town

Unlike Kirkwall, Orkney's capital, the old town of Stromness still hugs the shoreline, its one and only street, a narrow winding affair, built long before the advent of the motor car, still paved with great flagstones and fed by a tight network of alleyways or closes. The central section, which begins at the *Stromness Hotel*, is known as **Victoria Street**, though it has several other names – Graham Place, Dundas Street, Alfred Street and South End – as it heads southwards. On the east side the houses are gable-end-on to the waterfront, and originally each would have had its own pier, from which merchants would trade with passing ships.

The first of the old jetties, south of the modern harbour, houses the **Pier Arts Centre** (Tues–Sat 10.30am–12.30pm & 1.30–5pm; free). The art gallery is spread over two buildings, the first often featuring painting and sculpture by local artists, the warehouse housing a remarkable display of twentieth-century British art.

At the junction of Alfred Street and South End, is the **Stromness Museum** (April–Sept daily 10am–5pm; Oct–March Mon–Sat 11am–3.30pm; £2.50), built in 1858, partly to house the collections of the local natural history society. On the ground floor, there's a Halkett cloth boat, an early inflatable like the one used by John Rae, the Stromness-born Arctic explorer, whose fiddle, octant and shotgun are also on display. There are also numerous salty artefacts gathered from shipwrecks, including some barnacle-encrusted crockery from the German High Seas Fleet that sank in Scapa Flow.

Practicalities

Arriving by ferry, you disembark at the modern ferry terminal, which also houses the **tourist office** (April–Oct Mon–Fri 8am–5pm, Sat 9am–4pm & Sun 10am–3pm; Nov–March Mon–Fri 9am–5pm). As far as **hotels** go, the venerable Victorian *Stromness Hotel* (℡01856/850298, ⓦwww.stromnesshotel.com; ❺) – the town's first – is probably your best bet. As for **B&Bs**, there's a traditional end-on waterfront house next to the museum at 2 South End (℡01856/850215; ❷; April–Oct); if you've got your own transport, you might prefer to head to the modern *Thira* (℡01856/851181; ❸), up on the hill above the town, boasting great views overlooking Hoy. Stromness has an SYHA **hostel** with single-sex dorms in a converted school on Hellihole Road (℡0870/004 1150, Ⓔreservations@syha.org.uk; May–Sept), signposted off the main street. More laid-back is the family-run *Brown's Hostel*, 45–47 Victoria St (℡01856/850661), with bunk beds in very small, shared rooms and kitchen facilities; it's open all year, and there's no daytime closing or late-night curfew. There's also a **campsite** (℡01856/873535; May to mid-Sept) in a superb setting a mile south of the ferry terminal at Point of Ness, with views out to Hoy; it's well equipped and even has its own lounge, but is extremely exposed, especially if a southwesterly is blowing. **Bike rental** is available from Stromness Cycle Hire, opposite the ferry terminal (℡01856/850750), and from Orkney Cycle Hire, near the museum (℡01856/850255).

Stromness has a couple of decent **places to eat**, starting with *Julia's Café and Bistro* (lunchtime only except in high summer), opposite the ferry terminal. The moderately expensive *Hamnavoe Restaurant* at 35 Graham Place (℡01856/850606; April–Sept; closed Mon) offers the town's most ambitious cooking in a very pleasant setting. For traditional hotel fare, head for the downstairs bar of the *Stromness Hotel*, which does good bar meals – go for their specials.

West Mainland

The great bulk of the **West Mainland** is fertile, productive farmland, fenced off into a patchwork of fields used either to produce crops or for cattle grazing. It is, however, fringed by some spectacular coastline, particularly in the west, and littered with some of the island's most impressive prehistoric sites, such as the village of **Skara Brae**, the standing **Stones of Stenness** and the chambered tomb of **Maes Howe**.

The Stones of Stenness and Maes Howe

The parish of **STENNESS** lies along the main road from Stromness to Kirkwall, south of the twin lochs of Stenness and Harray, which are separated by a couple of promontories, that once stood at the heart of Orkney's most important Neolithic ceremonial complex. The most visible part of the complex are the **Stones of Stenness**, originally a circle of twelve rock slabs, now just four, the tallest of which is over 16ft and remarkable for its incredible thinness. A broken table-top lies within the circle, which is surrounded by a much-diminished henge (a circular bank of earth and a ditch) with a couple of entrance causeways. Less than a mile to the northwest, you reach another stone circle, the **Ring of Brodgar**, a much wider circle dramatically sited on raised ground. Here there were originally sixty stones, 27 of which now stand; of the henge, only the ditch survives.

There are several quite large burial mounds visible to the south of the Ring of Brodgar, but these are entirely eclipsed by one of the most impressive Neolithic burial chambers in the whole of Europe, **Maes Howe** (April–Sept daily 9.30am–6.30pm; Oct–March Mon–Sat 9.30am–4.30pm, Sun 2–4.30pm; £3; HS), which lies less than a mile northeast of the Stones of Stenness. Dating from around 3000 BC, its excellent state of preservation is partly due to the massive slabs of sandstone it was constructed from, the largest of which weighs over thirty tons. Perhaps the most remarkable aspect of Maes Howe is that the tomb is aligned so that the rays of the winter solstice sun reach right down the passage to the ledge of one of the three cells built into the walls of the tomb. When Maes Howe was opened in 1861, it was found to be virtually empty, thanks to the work of generations of grave-robbers who had left behind only a handful of human bones. The Vikings entered in the twelfth century, leaving large amounts of runic graffiti, cut into the walls of the main chamber and still clearly visible today.

Skara Brae

Around seven miles north of Stromness, the beautiful white curve of the Bay of Skaill is home to **Skara Brae** (April–Sept daily 9.30am–6.30pm; Oct–March Mon–Sat 9.30am–4.30pm, Sun 2–4.30pm; £5 in summer, £4 in winter), where the extensive remains of a small Neolithic fishing and farming village, dating back to 3000 BC, were discovered in 1850 after a fierce storm. The village is very well preserved, its houses huddled together and connected by narrow passages which would originally have been covered over with turf. The houses themselves consist of a single, spacious living room, filled with domestic detail, including fireplaces, cupboards, beds and boxes, all ingeniously constructed from slabs of stone.

Unfortunately, the sheer numbers now visiting Skara Brae mean that you can no longer explore the site itself properly, but only look down from the outer walls. Before you reach the site you must buy a ticket from the new **visitor centre**, which houses an excellent **café–restaurant**. After a short video, you pass through a small introductory **exhibition**, with a few replica finds, before proceeding to a full-scale replica of House 7 (the best-preserved house); it's all a tad neat and tidy, but it'll give you the general idea.

In the summer months, your ticket to Skara Brae also covers entry to nearby **Skaill House**, an extensive range of buildings 300 yards inland, home of the laird of Skaill. The original house was a simple two-storey block with a small courtyard, built for Bishop George Graham in the 1620s, but it has since been much extended. The last occupant of the house was Mrs Kathleen Scarth, who died in 1991; her bedroom has been left as it was, and is filled with old frocks, an ostrich-feather fan and a "twist and slim exerciser".

Birsay and Evie

Occupying the northwest corner of the Mainland, the parish of **BIRSAY** was the centre of Norse power in Orkney for several centuries before the earls moved to Kirkwall, some time after the construction of its cathedral. Today a tiny cluster of homes is gathered around the sandstone ruins of the **Earl's Palace**, which was built in the second half of the sixteenth century by Robert Stewart, Earl of Orkney, using the forced labour of the islanders. The palace appears to have lasted barely a century before falling into rack and ruin; the crumbling walls and turrets retain much of their grandeur, although inside there's little remaining domestic detail.

Just over half a mile northwest of the palace is the **Brough of Birsay**, a substantial Pictish settlement on a small tidal island that is only accessible during the two hours each side of low tide. The focus of the village was – and still is – the sandstone-built twelfth-century **St Peter's Church**, which is thought to have stood at the centre of a monastic complex of some sort – the foundations of a courtyard and outer buildings can be made out to the west. Close by is a large complex of Viking-era buildings, including several houses, a sauna and some sophisticated stone drains.

Overshadowed by the great wind turbine on Burgar Hill, the village and parish of **EVIE**, on the north coast, looks out across the turbulent waters of Eynhallow Sound towards the island of Rousay. Its chief draw is the **Broch of Gurness** (April–Sept daily 9.30am–6.30pm; £3; HS), the best-preserved broch on an archipelago replete with them, and one which is still surrounded by a remarkable complex of later buildings. As at Birsay, the sea has eaten away half the site, but the broch itself, dating from around 100 BC, still stands, its walls reaching a height of 12ft in places, its inner cells still intact. The compact group of homes clustered around the broch have also survived amazingly well, with much of their original and ingenious stone shelving and fireplaces still in place.

Practicalities

The best **B&B** in the West Mainland is the carefully converted *Mill of Eyrland* (☎01856/850136, ⓦ www.millofeyrland.com; ❸), in a delightful setting on the 964 to Orphir. Also worth recommending is the artistically-inclined *Woodwick House* (☎01856/751330, ⓦ www.woodwickhouse.co.uk; ❸), situated in a beautiful, secluded position southeast of Evie. You can also stay in Evie's nicely modernized *Eviedale* **bothy and campsite**, run by Dale Farm (☎01856/751270, ⓦ www.orknet.co.uk/eviedale; April–Oct) and found by the junction of the road to Dounby.

Kirkwall

Initial impressions of **KIRKWALL**, Orkney's capital, are not always favourable. However, it does have one great redeeming feature – its sandstone **cathedral**,

25

without doubt the finest medieval building in the north of Scotland. Nowadays, the town is very much divided into two main focal points: the busy **harbour**, at the north end of the town, where ferries come and go all year round, and the flagstoned **main street**, which changes its name four times as it twists its way south from the harbour past the cathedral.

The Town

Standing at the very heart of Kirkwall, **St Magnus Cathedral** (Mon–Sat 8.30am–6.30pm, Sun 1.30–6.30pm) is the town's most compelling sight. This beautiful red sandstone building was begun in 1137 by the Orkney Earl Rognvald, who decided to make full use of a growing cult surrounding the figure of his uncle Magnus, killed on the orders of his cousin Haakon in 1117. When Magnus's body was buried in Birsay a heavenly light was said to have shone overhead, and his grave soon became a place of pilgrimage attributed with miraculous powers that drew pilgrims from far afield. When Rognvald finally took over the earldom he built the cathedral in his uncle's honour, moving the centre of religious and secular power from Birsay to Kirkwall.

The first version of the cathedral, built using yellow sandstone from Eday and red sandstone from the Mainland, was somewhat smaller than today's structure, which has been added to over the centuries, with a new east window in the thirteenth century, the extension of the nave in the fifteenth century and a new west window to mark the building's 850th anniversary in 1987. Today much of the detail in the soft sandstone has worn away – the capitals around the main doors are reduced to gnarled stumps – but it's still an immensely impressive building, its shape and style echoing the great cathedrals of Europe. Inside, the atmosphere is surprisingly intimate, the bulky sandstone columns drawing your eye up to the exposed brickwork arches, while around the walls is a series of mostly seventeenth-century tombstones, many carved with a skull and cross-bones and other emblems of mortality.

To the south of the cathedral are the ruined remains of the **Bishop's Palace** (April–Sept daily 9.30am–6.30pm; Oct & Nov Mon–Sat 9.30am–4.30pm, Sun 2–4.30pm; £2; HS), residence of the Bishop of Orkney since the twelfth century. Most of what you see now, however, dates from the time of Bishop Robert Reid, the founder of Edinburgh University, in the mid-sixteenth century. The walls still stand, as does the tall round tower in which the bishop had his private chambers; a narrow spiral staircase takes you to the top for good view of the cathedral and across Kirkwall's rooftops.

The ticket for the Bishop's Palace also covers entry to the neighbouring **Earl's Palace**, built by the infamous Earl Patrick Stewart around 1600 using forced labour. With its grand entrance, fancy oriel windows, dank dungeon, massive fireplaces and magnificent central hall, it has a confident solidity, and reckoned to be one of the finest examples of Renaissance architecture i Scotland. The roof may be missing, but many domestic details remain, including a set of toilets and the stone shelves used by the clerk to do his filing. Ea Patrick enjoyed his palace for only a very short time before he was imprisoned.

Opposite the cathedral stands the sixteenth-century Tankerness House, no home to the **Orkney Museum** (Mon–Sat 10.30am–5pm; May–Sept also S 2–5pm; free). Among the more unusual artefacts to look out for are a witch spell box, and a lovely whalebone plaque from a Viking boat grave discovered on Sunday. Further afield, a mile or so south of the town centre on the A9 to South Ronaldsay, is the **Highland Park distillery** (April–Oct Mon–F 10am–5pm; July–Sept also Sat & Sun noon–5pm; Nov–March Mon–Fri to at 2pm; ☎01856/874619, ⓦwww.highlandpark.co.uk; £3), billed as "the most northerly legal distillery in Scotland".

Practicalities

Northlink **ferries** from Shetland and Aberdeen (and all cruise ships) dock at the new Hatston terminal, a mile or so northwest of town; the buses waiting at Hatston will take you to Stromness, but to get into the centre of Kirkwall, you have to get a taxi (£2.50). Kirkwall **airport** is about three miles southeast of town on the A960; an hourly bus service will take you to Broad Street in the town centre, before terminating at the **bus station**, five minutes' walk west of the centre. For **bike rental** head for Bobby's Cycle Hire, Tankerness Lane (☎01856/875777). The helpful **tourist office** is on Broad Street beside the cathedral graveyard (April–Sept daily 8.30am–8pm; Oct–March Mon–Sat 9.30am–5pm). Most events are advertised in *The Orcadian*, which comes out on Thursdays (ⓦwww.orcadian.co.uk), and there's a news programme called *About Orkney* on BBC Radio Orkney (93.7 FM; Mon–Fri 7.30–8am).

The friendly, waterfront *Ayre Hotel* on Ayre Road (☎01856/873001, ⓦwww.ayrehotel.co.uk; ⑥) offers the smartest **accommodation** in town; equally central is the *Albert* on Mounthoolie Lane (☎01856/876000, ⓦwww.alberthotel.co.uk; ❸). The *Lav'rockha* (☎01856/876103, ⓦwww .lavrockha.co.uk; ❷) is a good, modern guest house on Inganess Road, near the Highland Park distillery. The SYHA **hostel** (☎0870/004 1133; April–Sept) is ten minutes' walk out of the centre on the road to Orphir. The small, privately run *Peedie Hostel* (☎01856/875477) is on the waterfront beside the *Ayre Hotel*. There's also a **campsite** (☎01856/879900; mid-May to mid-Sept) behind the Pickaquoy Leisure Centre, five minutes' walk west of the bus station.

The nicest **café** for lunch is the *Mustard Seed*, which serves imaginative, inexpensive food at two separate locations on Victoria Street: no. 86 is small and quiet and doubles as a Christian bookshop; no. 65 is larger and has a more traditional café menu. In the evening, the *Kirkwall Hotel*, on Harbour Street, is probably the best option, as it offers both **bar meals** and reasonable a la carte, though the bar meals at the *Albert* are decent too. The liveliest **pub** is the *Torvhaug Inn* at the harbour end of Bridge Street; another good place to try is the *Bothy Bar* in the *Albert Hotel*, which sometimes has live music. *Fusion* (ⓦwww.fusionclub.co.uk), on Ayre Road, is Kirkwall's very own state-of-the-art **nightclub** (Thurs–Sat), which also puts on occasional live gigs. The Pickaquoy Leisure Centre (ⓦwww.pickaquoy.com) – known locally as the "Picky" – contains the New Phoenix **cinema** (☎01856/879900). Kirkwall's chief cultural bash is the week-long **St Magnus Festival** (ⓦwww.stmagnusfestival.com), a superb arts festival based in Kirkwall.

East Mainland and South Ronaldsay

Southeast from Kirkwall, the narrow spur of the **East Mainland** juts out into the North Sea and is joined, thanks to the remarkable Churchill Barriers (see box, p.1272), to several smaller islands, the largest of which are Burray and South Ronaldsay. As with the West Mainland, the land here is relatively densely populated and heavily farmed. However, there's one sight you should pay a quick visit to, the Iron Age mound of **Mine Howe** (May Wed & Sun 11am–3pm; June–Aug daily 11am–5pm; Sept Wed & Sun 11am–2pm; £2), just off the A960 beyond the airport. Originally Mine Howe would have been a large mound surrounded by a deep ditch, but only a small section has

Scapa Flow and the Churchill Barriers

The presence of the huge naval base in **Scapa Flow** during both world wars presented an irresistible target to the Germans, and protecting the fleet was always a nagging problem for the Allies. During World War I, blockships were sunk to guard the eastern approaches, but in October 1939, just weeks after the outbreak of World War II, a German U-boat managed to manoeuvre past the blockships and torpedo the battleship HMS *Royal Oak*, which sank with the loss of 833 lives. The U-boat captain claimed to have acquired local knowledge while fishing in the islands before the war. Today the wreck of the *Royal Oak*, marked by a green buoy off the Gaitnip Cliffs, is an official war grave.

The sinking of the *Royal Oak* convinced the First Lord of the Admiralty, Winston Churchill, that Scapa Flow needed better protection, and in 1940 work began on a series of barriers – known as the **Churchill Barriers** – to seal the waters between the Mainland and the string of islands to the south. Special camps were built to accommodate the 1700 men involved in the project; their numbers were boosted by the surrender of Italy in 1942, when Italian prisoners of war were sent to work here. Besides the barriers, which are an astonishing feat of engineering when you bear in mind the strength of Orkney tides, the Italians also left behind the beautiful **Italian Chapel** (daily: April–Sept 9am–10pm; Oct–March 9am–4.30pm; free) on the first of the islands, Lamb Holm. This, the so-called "miracle of Camp 60", must be one of the greatest adaptations ever, made from two Nissen huts, concrete, barbed wire and parts of a rusting blockship. It has a great false facade, and colourful trompe l'oeil decor, lovingly restored by the chapel's principal architect, Domenico Chiocchetti.

been excavated. At the top of the mound a series of steps leads steeply down to a half-landing, and then plunges even deeper to a small chamber some twenty feet below the surface. The whole layout is unique and has left archeologists totally baffled, though, naturally, numerous theories as to its purpose abound, from execution by ritual drowning to a temple to the god of the underground.

At the southern end of the Churchill barriers is low-lying **South Ronaldsay**, the largest of the islands linked to the Mainland and, like the latter, rich farming country. The main settlement is **ST MARGARET'S HOPE** – or "The Hope", as it's known locally – a pleasing little gathering of stone-built houses overlooking a sheltered bay. As is obvious from the architecture, and the piers, The Hope was once a thriving port. Nowadays, despite the presence of the Pentland Ferries terminal, it remains a very peaceful place.

One of the most enjoyable archeological sights on Orkney is the ancient chambered burial cairn at the southeastern corner of South Ronaldsay, known as the **Tomb of the Eagles** (daily: April–Oct 9.30am–6pm; Nov–March 10am–noon; £3.50). Discovered, excavated and still owned by local farmer Ronald Simpson, a visit here makes a refreshing change from the usual interpretative centre. First off, you get to look round the family's private museum of prehistoric artefacts; then, you get a brief guided tour of a nearby Bronze Age **burnt mound**, which is basically a Neolithic rubbish dump; and finally you get to walk out to the **chambered cairn**, by the cliff's edge, where human remains were found alongside talons and carcasses of sea eagles. To enter the cairn, you must lie on a trolley and pull yourself in using an overhead rope.

First **accommodation** choice is the comfortable *Creel* on the harbourfront (℡01856/831311, ⓦwww.thecreel.co.uk; ❹), also one of the best **restaurants** in Scotland; at £25 for two courses, it's expensive, but friendly and relaxed

More modest meals are available from the *Murray Arms Hotel* (℡01856/831205, Ⓦwww.murrayarmshotel.com; ❷), on Back Road, which has rooms above the pub and a backpackers' dorm round the side. The best B&B option is *Roeberry House* (℡01856/831838, Ⓦwww.roeberry.com; ❸), an imposing country house with fine views. For a **hostel** with some character, head for *Wheems* (℡01856/831537; April–Oct), a mile and a half from the war memorial on the main road outside The Hope.

Hoy

Hoy, Orkney's second-largest island, rises sharply out of the sea to the southwest of the Mainland. The least typical of the islands, but certainly the most dramatic, its north and west sides are made up of great glacial valleys and mountainous moorland rising to over 1500ft, dropping into the sea off the red sandstone cliffs of St John's Head.

Walkers arriving by passenger ferry from Stromness at Moaness Pier, near the tiny village of **HOY**, and heading for Rackwick (four miles southwest), can either take the well-marked footpath that passes Sandy Loch or catch the minibus via the single-track road. En route, duckboards head across the heather to the **Dwarfie Stane**, Orkney's most unusual chambered tomb, cut from a solid block of sandstone and dating back to 3000 BC.

RACKWICK is an old crofting and fishing village squeezed between towering sandstone cliffs on the west coast. A small farm building beside the hostel serves as a tiny **museum** (open any time; free), with a few old photos and a brief rundown of Rackwick's rough history. Despite its isolation, Rackwick has a steady stream of walkers and climbers passing through it en route to the **Old Man of Hoy**, a great sandstone column some 450ft high, perched on an old lava flow which protects it from the erosive power of the sea. The well-trodden footpath from Rackwick is an easy three-mile walk (3hr return) – the great skuas will divebomb you only during the nesting season – and gives the reward of a great view of the stack. Continuing north along the cliff tops, the path peters out before **St John's Head** which, at 1136ft, is one of the highest sea cliffs in the country and mostly too sheer even for nesting seabirds.

Lyness

Along the sheltered eastern shore of Hoy, high moorland gives way to a gentler environment similar to that on the rest of Orkney. Hoy defines the western boundary of Scapa Flow, and **LYNESS** played a major role for the Royal Navy during both world wars. Many of the old wartime buildings have been cleared away over the last few decades, but the harbour and hills around Lyness are still scarred with the scattered remains of concrete structures which once served as hangars and storehouses during World War II, and are now used as barns and cowsheds. The old oil pump house, which still stands opposite the new Lyness ferry terminal, has been turned into the **Scapa Flow Visitor Centre & Museum** (Mon–Fri 9am–4.30pm, Sat & Sun 9.30am–4.30pm; free), a fascinating insight into wartime Orkney. The pump house itself retains much of its old equipment – you can even ask for a working demo of one of the oil-fired boilers – used to pump oil off tankers moored at Lyness into sixteen tanks, and from there into underground reservoirs cut into the neighbouring hillside. On request, an audiovisual show on the history of Scapa Flow is screened in the sole surviving tank, which has incredible acoustics. Even the café has an old NAAFI feel about it.

Practicalities

Two **ferry services** run to Hoy: a passenger ferry from Stromness to the village of Hoy (Mon–Fri 4–5 daily, Sat & Sun 2 daily; 25min; ☎01856/850624), which also serves the small island of Graemsay; and the roll-on/roll-off car ferry from Houton on the Mainland to Lyness (Mon–Fri 6 daily, Sat & Sun 2–4 daily; 30min–1hr; ☎01856/811397), which sometimes calls in at the oil terminal island of Flotta, and begins and ends its daily schedule at Longhope. There's no bus service on Hoy, but those arriving on the passenger ferry from Stromness should find a **minibus** waiting to take them to Rackwick. **Bike rental** is available from Moaness Pier (☎01856/791225).

There are two council-run, SYHA-affiliated **hostels** in North Hoy: the *North Hoy Hostel* (May to mid-Sept) in Hoy village and the much smaller *Rackwick Hostel* (mid-March to mid-Sept); to book ahead, you must contact the council (☎01856/873535). You can also **camp** in Rackwick, either behind the hostel, down by the unusually attractive public toilets, or beside *Burnside Cottage* (☎01856/791316), the heather-thatched **bothy**. South Hoy has a handful of very good, friendly **B&Bs**, including *Stonequoy Farm* (☎01856/791234, ⊛www.visithoy.com; ❶), a lovely 200-acre stone-built farm south of Lyness, overlooking Longhope, and welcoming *Stromabank Hotel*, a delightfully converted old schoolhouse (☎01856/701494, ⊛www.stromabank .co.uk; ❸) which also does good bar meals (closed Thurs). The *Hoy Inn* (closed Mon), near the post office in Hoy village, also serves very good **bar meals** in season.

Shapinsay

Just a few miles northeast of Kirkwall, **Shapinsay** is the most accessible of Orkney's northern isles. A gently undulating grid-plan patchwork of rich farmland, it's a bit like an island suburb of Kirkwall, which is clearly visible across the bay. Its chief attraction for visitors is **Balfour Castle** (May–Sept guided tours Sun 3pm; see below for details of the all-inclusive ticket), the imposing Baronial pile designed by David Bryce and completed in 1848 by the Balfour family of Westray, who had made a small fortune in India the previous century. The Balfours died out in 1960 and the castle was bought by a Polish cavalry officer, Captain Tadeusz Zawadski, whose family now run the place as a hotel. The guided tours are great fun, finishing off with complimentary tea and cakes in the servants' quarters.

Less than thirty minutes from Kirkwall by **ferry** (Mon–Fri 5 daily, Sat & Sun 3–4 daily), Shapinsay is an easy day-trip. If you want to visit the castle, before you set out you must buy an **all-inclusive ticket** from Balfour Castle (£16) which includes a return ferry ticket. The ferry for the guided tour leaves at 2.15pm, but you can catch an earlier ferry if you want to have some time to explore the rest of the island. It's also possible **to stay** in lord-of-the-manor style at *Balfour Castle* (☎01856/711282, ⊛www.balfourcastle.co.uk; ❻). More modest **B&B** is available at *Girnigoe* (☎01856/711256, ⊜jea⟩ @girnigoe.f9.co.uk; ❷), a very comfortable Orcadian croft close to the nort⟩ shore of Veantro Bay.

Rousay

Just over half a mile from the Mainland's northern shore, the hilly island ⟨ **Rousay** is home to a number of intriguing prehistoric sites. The group of dozen or so houses above the ferry terminal is the only settlement of any siz⟨ but a single road runs around the edge of the island, connecting a string ⟨

small farms which make use of the more cultivable coastal fringes. It's easy enough to reach the main points of interest on the south coast by foot or bike from the ferry terminal.

The first trio of archeological sights is spread out over a couple of miles, on and off the road that leads west from the ferry terminal. **Taversoe Tuick**, the nearest chambered cairn, is unusual in that it exploits its sloping site by having two storeys, one entered from the upper side and one from the lower. A little further west is the **Blackhammar Cairn**, which is divided into "stalls" by large flagstones, rather like the more famous cairn at Midhowe (see below). Finally, there's the **Knowe of Yarso**, another stalled cairn dating from the same period that's a stiff climb up the hill from the road, worth it if only for the magnificent view.

The southwestern side of Rousay is home to the most significant of the island's archeological remains. Most lie on the **Westness Walk**, a mile-long heritage trail that begins at Westness Farm, four miles west of the ferry terminal. **Midhowe Cairn**, about a mile on from the farm, comes as something of a surprise, both for its immense size – it's known as "the great ship of death", and measures nearly 100ft in length – and for the fact that it's now entirely surrounded by a stone-walled barn with a corrugated roof. Unfortunately, you can't actually explore the roofless communal burial chamber, dating back to 3500 BC, but only look down from the overhead walkway. A couple of hundred yards beyond Midhowe Cairn is **Midhowe Broch**, built as a sort of fortified family house, surrounded by a complex series of ditches and ramparts. The interior of the broch is divided into two separate rooms, each with their own hearth, water tank and quernstone, all of which date from the final phase of occupation around the second century AD.

Practicalities

Rousay makes a good day-trip from the Mainland, with regular **car ferry** sailings from Tingwall (30min), linked to Kirkwall by buses. **Bike rental** is available from Arts, Bikes & Crafts, near the pier (℡01856/821398). **Accommodation** on Rousay is limited to a couple of B&Bs: try the Victorian croft *Blackhamar* (℡01856/821333, ⓦwww.orknet.co.uk/blackhamar; ❶). Another option is the hostel at *Trumland Farm* (℡01856/821252), half a mile or so west of the terminal. As well as a couple of dorms, you can also camp, and there's a self-catering cottage, sleeping four. The *Taversoe Inn*, further along the road, offers unpretentious accommodation (℡01856/821325, ⒺTaversoehotel@aol.com; ❶) and does good bar meals. The *Pier Restaurant* (℡01856/821359), right beside the terminal, serves bar meals at lunchtime and functions as a pub in the evenings; if you phone in advance, they can pack you a delicious **picnic** of crab, cheese, fruit and bannock bread.

Westray and Papa Westray

Although exposed to the full force of the Atlantic weather in the far northwest of Orkney, **Westray** shelters one of the most tightly knit and prosperous island communities. It has a fairly stable population of 600 or so, producing superb beef, scallops, shellfish and a large catch of white fish, with its own small fish-processing factory and an organic salmon farm. Old Orcadian families still dominate every aspect of life, giving the island a strong individual character.

The main village and harbour is **PIEROWALL** in the north, a good eight miles from the Rapness ferry terminal on the southernmost tip of the island.

25

Pierowall houses the excellent **Westray Heritage Centre** (mid-May to mid-Sept Tues–Sat 9.30am–12.30pm & 2–5pm; £2), a very welcoming wet-weather retreat. The island's most impressive ruin is the colossal sandstone hulk of **Noltland Castle**, which stands above the village half a mile west up the road to Noup Head. This Z-plan castle, which is pockmarked with over seventy gun loops, was begun around 1560 by Gilbert Balfour, a shady character from Fife, who was Master of the Household to Mary, Queen of Scots, and was implicated in the murder of her husband Lord Darnley. To explore the castle, you must first pick up the key from the nearby farm.

The northwestern tip of Westray rises up sharply, culminating in the dramatic sea cliffs of **Noup Head**. The whole area is an RSPB reserve, and during the summer months the guano-covered rock ledges are packed with over 100,000 nesting seabirds, primarily guillemots, razorbills, kittiwakes and fulmars, with puffins as well: a truly awesome sight, sound and smell. The sea cliffs in the southeast of the island around **Stanger Head** are not quite as spectacular as at Noup Head, but it's here that you'll find **Castle o'Burrian**, a sea stack that was once an early Christian hermitage. It's now the best place on Westray at which to see **puffins** nesting.

Practicalities

Westray is served by car **ferry** from Kirkwall (2–3 daily; takes 1hr 25min; ☏01856/872044), or you can **fly** from Kirkwall (Mon–Sat 2 daily; 12min). **Minibus tours** of the island can be arranged with Island Explorer (☏01857/677355), which connects with ferries. J&M Harcus of Pierowall (☏01857/677450) runs a **bus service** which will take you from Rapness to Pierowall, though you should phone ahead to check it's running. For **bike rental**, contact either of the hostels (see below).

Westray's finest **accommodation** is at the *Cleaton House Hotel* (☏01857/677508, ⓦwww.cleatonhouse.com; ❺), a whitewashed Victorian manse about two miles southeast of Pierowall, with great views. This is also the best place on the island at which to sample Westray's organic salmon, either in the expensive **restaurant** or the congenial **bar**. The *Pierowall Hotel* (☏01857/677472, ⓦwww.orknet.co.uk/pierowall; ❷), in Pierowall itself, is less stylish but nevertheless welcoming, with a popular bar and a well-justified reputation for excellent fish and chips, fresh off the boats. **B&B** is available at *Sand O'Gill* (☏01857/677374; ❶), where you can also **camp**. Westray is positively spoilt for **hostels**: *Bis Geos* (☏01857/677420, ⓦwww.bisgeos.co.uk May–Sept), on the road to Noup Head, has unbeatable views along the cliff and out to sea; inside, it's beautifully furnished. *The Barn* (☏01857/677214 ⓦwww.orkneyisles.co.uk/thebarn) is in Pierowall; it's luxurious inside, easier to get to, has a small **campsite** adjacent to it, a games room and genuinely friendly hosts.

Papa Westray

Across the short Papa Sound from Westray is the island of **Papa Westray**, known locally as "Papay" (ⓦwww.papawestray.co.uk). With a population hovering precariously around seventy, Papay has had to fight hard to keep itself viable over the last couple of decades, helped by a hefty influx of outsiders. To get an idea how life used to be when the Traill family ruled over the island, visit the small **museum** (free access) in an old bothy opposite Holland House at the centre of the island.

A road leads down from Holland House to the western shore, where the **Knap of Howar** stands. Dating from around 3500 BC, this Neolithic farm building makes a fair claim to being the oldest standing house in Europe. Half a mile north along the coast is **St Boniface Kirk**, a restored pre-Reformation church, with a bare flagstone floor, dry-stone walls, a little wooden gallery and just a couple of surviving box pews. In the surrounding graveyard there's a Viking hogback grave, decorated with carvings in imitation of the wooden shingles on the roof of a Viking longhouse.

Papay is an easy day-trip from Westray, with a regular **passenger ferry** service from Pierowall (3–6 daily; 25min). On Tuesdays and Fridays, the **car ferry** from Kirkwall to Westray continues on to Papa Westray; at other times, a bus (which accepts a limited number of bicycles) from Rapness connects with the Pierowall passenger ferry. Papay is also connected to Westray by the **world's shortest scheduled flight** (2min; £15 one-way). You can also fly direct from Kirkwall to Papa Westray (Mon–Sat 2–3 daily). Papay's Community Co-operative (℡01857/644267) has a **minibus** that will take you from the pier to anywhere on the island, and can arrange a "package tour" (mid-May to mid-Sept Tues, Thurs & Sat; £30; ℡01857/644321). It also runs a shop, a sixteen-bed SYHA-affiliated **hostel** and the *Beltane House* **B&B** (❷), all housed within the old estate workers' cottages at Beltane, east of Holland House.

Eday

A long, thin island at the centre of Orkney's northern isles, **Eday** shares more characteristics with Rousay and Hoy than with its immediate neighbours, dominated as it is by a great block of heather-covered upland, with farmland confined to a narrow strip of coastal ground. The chief points of interest are all in the northern half of the island, beyond the post office, petrol pump and community shop on the main road. This marks the beginning of the signposted **Eday Heritage Walk**, which covers all the main sights (about 3hr). The walk initially follows the road heading northwest, past the RSPB bird hide overlooking **Mill Loch**, where several pairs of red-throated divers regularly breed. Clearly visible to the north of the road is the fifteen-foot **Stone of Setter**, weathered into three thick, lichen-encrusted fingers. From here, you can climb the hill to reach the **Vinquoy Chambered Cairn**, which has a similar structure to that of Maes Howe. You can crawl into the tomb through the narrow entrance: a skylight inside lets light into the main, beehive chamber, but not into the four side-cells.

Eday's terminal for **ferries** (2 daily; takes 1hr 15min–2hr) is at Backaland pier in the south. Car rental and taxis can be organized through Mr A. Stewart by the pier (℡01857/622206); he also runs tailor-made two-hour minibus tours May–Aug Mon, Wed & Fri). It's also possible to do a day-trip **flight** on Wednesdays from Kirkwall to Eday and back (℡01856/872494 or 873457). **Bike rental** is available from Martin Burkett at Hamarr, in the valley below the post office (℡01857/622331). Friendly **B&B** with full board is available at *Skaill Farm*, a traditional farmhouse just south of the airport (℡01857/622271; ❷; closed April & May). The basic SYHA-affiliated **hostel** occupies an exposed spot just north of the airport; it's run by Eday Community Association (℡01857/622206; April–Sept), who will also advise on **camping**.

Stronsay

A beguiling combination of green pastures, white sands and clear turquoise bays, **Stronsay** has seen two economic booms in the last three hundred years. The first was built on collecting vast quantities of seaweed and exporting the kelp for use in the chemical industry, particularly in making iodine, soap and glass. Later, **fishing** on a grand scale came to dominate life here, as Whitehall, in the north of the island, became one of the main Scottish centres for the curing of herring. By the 1840s, up to four hundred boats were working out of the port, attracting hundreds of women herring-gutters. By the 1930s, however, the herring stocks had been severely depleted and the industry began a long decline.

WHITEHALL remains the only real village, made up of rows of stone-built fishermen's cottages set between two large piers. Wandering along the tranquil, rather forlorn harbourfront today, you'll find it hard to believe that the village once supported five thousand people in the fishing industry during the summer season, as well as a small army of coopers, coal merchants, butchers, bakers, several Italian ice-cream parlours and a cinema. It was said that, on a Sunday, you could walk across the decks of the boats all the way to **Papa Stronsay**, the tiny island that shelters Whitehall from the north, on which a new monastery has been built by the Order of Transalpine Redemptorists. The old fish market by the pier houses a **museum**, with a few photos and artefacts from the herring days; ask at the adjacent café.

Stronsay is served by a regular car **ferry** service from Kirkwall to Whitehall (2 daily; takes 1hr 40min–2hr), and weekday **flights**, also from Kirkwall (Mon–Sat 2 daily; 25min). There's no bus service, but D.S. Peace (℡01857/616335) operates taxis and **rents cars**. Of the few **accommodation** options, a good choice is the *Stronsay Fish Mart* **hostel** (℡01857/616346) in the old fish market by the pier, or the refurbished *Stronsay Hotel* (℡01857/616213, ⊛www.stronsayhotel.com; ❸) opposite. A cheaper alternative is the *Stronsay Bird Reserve* (℡01857/616363; ❷), a nicely positioned **B&B** in a lovely old crofthouse, which also tolerates camping on the shores of Mill Bay. The *Stronsay Hotel* does good pub **food**.

Sanday

Sanday (⊛www.sanday.co.uk), though the largest of the northern isles, is also the most insubstantial, a great low-lying, drifting dune strung out between several rocky points. The island's sweeping aquamarine bays and vast stretches of clean white sand are the finest in Orkney, and in dry, clear weather it's a superb place to spend a day or two. The island has a long history as a shipping hazard, with many wrecks smashed against its shores, although the construction of the **Start Point Lighthouse** in 1802 on the island's exposed eastern tip reduced the risk for seafarers. Today the islanders still survive largely from farming and fishing.

The shoreline supports a healthy seal, otter and wading bird population, and behind the splendid sandy beaches are stretches of beautiful open machair and grassland, thick with wild flowers during the spring and summer. The entire coastline presents the opportunity for superb walks, with particularly spectacular sand dunes to the south of Cata Sand. Sanday is also rich in archeology, with hundreds of mostly unexcavated sites including cairns, brochs and burnt mounds. The most impressive is **Quoyness Chambered Cairn**, on the fertile farmland of Els Ness peninsula, dating from before 2000 BC, and partially reconstructed to a height of around 13ft.

Ferries arrive at the new terminal at the southern tip of the island and are met by the **minibus** (book on ℡01857/600467), which will take you to most points. The airfield is in the centre of the island and there are regular **flights** to Kirkwall (Mon–Sat 2 daily; 10–20min). The fishing port of **KETTLETOFT**

is where the ferry used to dock, and where you'll find the island's two **hotels**. Of the two, *The Belsair* (℡01857/600206, ℮orkneyretreat@hotmail.com; ❶) now advertises itself as a "healing retreat", and has a fairly adventurous restaurant menu; the *Kettletoft* has a lively bar that's popular with the locals. Of the numerous **B&Bs**, try the *Marygarth Manse* (℡01857/600467; ❶), in Broughtown, who can also organize car and bike rental. If you're on a budget, head for nearby *Ayre's Rock* (℡01857/600410), a well-equipped **hostel** and **campsite** by the Bay of Brough, with washing and laundry facilities and bike rental available.

North Ronaldsay

North Ronaldsay – or "North Ron" as it's fondly known – has a unique outpost atmosphere, brought about by its extreme isolation. Measuring just three miles by one and rising only 66ft above sea level, the island is almost overwhelmed by the enormity of the sky, the strength of wind and the ferocity of the sea – so much so that its very existence seems an act of tenacious defiance. Despite these adverse conditions, North Ronaldsay has been inhabited for centuries, and continues to be heavily farmed, from old-style crofts whose roofs are made from huge local flagstones.

The island's **sheep** are a unique, tough, goat-like breed, who feed mostly on seaweed, giving their flesh a dark tone and a rich, gamey taste, and making their thick wool highly prized. A high **drystone dyke**, completed in the mid-nineteenth century and running the thirteen miles around the edge of the island, keeps them off the farmland, except during lambing season. The most frequent visitors are ornithologists, who come to catch a glimpse of the rare migrants who land here briefly on their spring and autumn migrations: there's a permanent **Bird Observatory**, established in 1987 by adapting a croft situated in the southwest corner of the island to wind and solar power; they can give advice as to what birds have recently been sighted.

Holland House – built by the Traill family who bought the island in 1727 – and the two lighthouses at Dennis Head, are the only features to interrupt the island's flat horizon. The attractive, stone-built **Old Beacon** was first lit in 1789, but the lantern was replaced by the huge bauble of masonry you now see as long ago as 1809. The **New Lighthouse** (May–Sept Sun noon–5.30pm; at other times by appointment; ℡01857/633257; £3), designed by Alan Stevenson in 1854 half a mile to the north, is the tallest land-based lighthouse in Britain, rising to a height of over 100ft.

The **ferry** from Kirkwall runs only once a week (usually Fri; takes 2hr 40min–3hr), though day-trips are possible on occasional summer Sundays phone ℡01856/872044 for details). Your best bet is to catch a **flight** from Kirkwall (Mon–Sat 2–3 daily, plus summer Sun; 15min): if you stay the night on the island, you're eligible for a bargain £10 return fare. A **minibus** usually meets the ferries and planes (phone ℡01857/633244) and will take you to the lighthouse. You can **stay** at the *Bird Observatory* (℡01857/633200, ℮www.nrbo.f2s.com; ❸), which offers full board either in private guest rooms or in dorms; the observatory's *Obscafé* is a sort of pub-restaurant and serves decent meals. Full-board accommodation is also available at *Garso*, in the northeast (℡01857/633244, ℮christine.muir@virgin.net; ❸). The *Burrian Inn*, to the southeast of the war memorial, is the island's small **pub**, and does hot food. **Camping** is possible; for further information, phone Mr Scott on 01857/633222.

Shetland

Many maps plonk the **Shetland Islands** in a box somewhere off Aberdeen, but in fact they're a lot closer to Bergen in Norway than Edinburgh. The Shetland **landscape** is a product of the struggle between rock and the forces of water and ice that have, over millennia, tried to break it to pieces. Smoothed by the last glaciation, the surviving land has been exposed to the most violent weather experienced in the British Isles. In winter, gales are routine and Shetlanders take even the occasional hurricane in their stride, marking a calm fine day as "a day atween weathers". There are some good spells of dry, sunny weather from May to September, but it's the **"simmer dim"**, the twilight which lingers through the small hours at this latitude, which makes Shetland summers so memorable; in June especially, the northern sky is an unfinished sunset of blue and burnished copper.

People have lived in Shetland since **prehistoric times**, certainly from about 3500 BC, and the islands display spectacular remains. For six centuries they were part of the **Norse empire** which brought together Sweden, Denmark and Norway. In 1469, Shetland followed Orkney in being mortgaged to Scotland, King Christian I of Norway being unable to raise the dowry for the marriage of his daughter, Margaret, to King James III. The Scottish king annexed Shetland in 1472 and the mortgage was never redeemed. Though Shetland retained links with other North Sea communities, religious and administrative practice gradually became Scottish, and **mainland lairds** set about grabbing what land and power they could. Later, especially in rural Shetland, the economy fell increasingly into the hands of **merchant lairds**, who controlled the fish trade and the tenants who supplied it through a system of truck, or forced barter.

During the two world wars, Shetland's role as gatekeeper between the North Sea and North Atlantic meant that the defence of the islands and control of the seas around them were critical. With a rebirth of the local economy in the 1960s, Shetland was able to claim, in the following decade, that the **oil industry** needed the islands more than they needed it. Careful negotiation, backed up by pioneering local legislation, produced a substantial income from oil which has been reinvested in the community. However, it's clear that the boom days are over, and the islanders are having to think afresh how to carve out a living in the new millennium.

Lerwick

For Shetlanders, there's only one place to stop, meet and do business, and that "da toon", **LERWICK**. It's home to about 7500 people – roughly a third o

Getting to Shetland

NorthLink Ferries (☎0845/600 0449, ⊛www.northlinkferries.co.uk) operates a daily overnight **car ferry** to Lerwick **from Aberdeen**, either direct (11hr) or via Kirkwall (13hr). British Airways (☎0870/850 9850) has **flights** nonstop to Shetland from Aberdeen, Inverness, Kirkwall and Wick, with connections into those airports from Edinburgh, Glasgow, Birmingham, Manchester and London. Highland Airways (☎01667/464141) also operates a daily Inverness to Shetland flight, and twice-weekly flights from Glasgow. Shetland's main airport is at **Sumburgh** (☎01950/461000), from where buses make short work of the 25-mile journey north to Lerwick. Standard airfares are high, but various cheaper tickets and special offers are sometimes available.

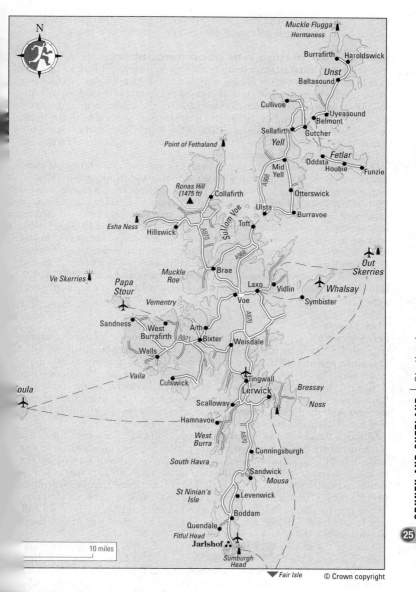

© Crown copyright

ne islands' population – and all year its sheltered **harbour** at the heart of the
wn is busy with ferries, fishing boats, oil-rig supply vessels and a variety of
ore specialized craft, including seismic survey and naval vessels from all round
e North Sea. In summer, the quaysides come alive with local pleasure craft,
siting yachts, cruise liners, historic vessels such as the restored *Swan*, and the
casional tall sailing ship. Behind the old harbour is the compact town centre,

made up of one long main street, Commercial Street; from here, narrow lanes, known as "**closses**", rise westwards to the late-Victorian new town.

Arrival, information and accommodation

The **ferry terminal** is situated in the unprepossessing north harbour, about a mile from the town centre. **Flying** into Sumburgh Airport, you can take one of the regular buses to Lerwick; taxis (around £25) and car rental are also available. Buses stop on the Esplanade, very close to the old harbour and Market Cross, or at the Viking bus station on Commercial Road a little to the north of the town centre. The **tourist office** (May–Sept Mon–Sat 8am–6pm, Sun 10am–1pm; Oct–April Mon–Fri 9am–5pm; Ⓦ www.visitshetland.com) is at the Market Cross on Commercial Street.

The *Kvelsdro House Hotel*, Greenfield Place (℡01595/692195, Ⓦ www .kgqhotels.co.uk; ❼), is Lerwick's luxury **accommodation** option, followed by the venerable *Queen's Hotel* right on the waterfront on Commercial Street (℡01595/692826, Ⓦ www.kgqhotels.co.uk; ❼). *Alder Lodge Guest House*, 6 Clairmont Place (℡01595/695705; ❸), is the best middle-range option, followed by *Carradale Guest House*, 36 King Harald St (℡01595/692251; ❷), situated in a large, comfortable Victorian family home. The SYHA **hostel** (℡01595/692114, Ⓔreservations@syha.org.uk; April–Sept) at Islesburgh House on King Harald Street, offers unusually comfortable surroundings, and has useful laundry facilities. The *Clickimin* **campsite** (℡01595/741000, Ⓔmail@srt.org.uk; May–Sept) enjoys the excellent facilities of the neighbouring Clickimin leisure centre.

The Town

Lerwick's attractive, flagstone-clad **Commercial Street** is still very much the core of the town. Its narrow, winding form, set back one block from the Esplanade, provides shelter from the elements even on the worst days, and is where locals meet, shop, exchange news and gossip. The Street's northern end is marked by the towering walls of **Fort Charlotte** (daily: June–Sept 9am–10pm; Oct–May 9am–4pm; free), begun for Charles II in 1665 during the wars with the Dutch, burnt down by the Dutch fleet in August 1673, and in the 1780s repaired and named in honour of George III's queen.

Although the closses that connect the Street to Hillhead are now a desirable place to live, it's not so long ago that they were regarded as slum-like dens of iniquity, from which the better-off escaped to the Victorian new town laid out to the west on a grid plan. **Hillhead**, up in the Victorian new town, is dominated by the splendid **Town Hall** (Mon–Thurs 9am–5pm, Fri 9am–4pm free), a Scottish Baronial monument to civic pride, built by public subscription. You're free to admire the wonderful stained-glass windows in the main hall which celebrate Shetland's history, and to climb the castellated central tower which occupies the town's highest point.

Opposite the town hall, housed on the first floor of the desperately ugly municipal library, the **Shetland Museum** (Mon, Wed & Fri 10am–7pm, Tues, Thurs & Sat 10am–5pm; Ⓦ www.shetland-museum.org.uk; free) is full to the brim with nauticalia. More unusual exhibits include Shetland's oldest telephone, fitted with a ceramic mouthpiece, and a carved head of Goliath by Adam Christie (1869–1950), a Shetlander who spent much of his life in Montrose Asylum, and who is perhaps best known for his application to patent a submarine built of glass, which would thus be invisible to enemies.

A mile or so southwest of the town centre on the road leading to Sumburgh, the much-restored **Clickimin Broch** stands on what was once a small island

On the last Tuesday in January, whatever the weather, Lerwick's new town is the setting for the most spectacular part of the **Up Helly-Aa**, a huge fire festival, the largest of several held in Shetland from January to March. Around nine hundred torchbearing participants, all male and all in extraordinary costumes, march in procession behind a grand Viking longship. The annually appointed Guizer Jarl and his "squad" appear as Vikings with shields and silver axes; each of the forty or so other squads is dressed for their part in the subsequent entertainment, perhaps as giant insects, space invaders or ballet dancers. Their circuitous route leads to the King George V Playing Field where, after due ceremony, all the torches are thrown into the longship, creating an enormous bonfire. A firework display follows, then the participants, known as "guizers", set off in their squads to do the rounds of more than a dozen "halls" (which usually include at least one hotel and the Town Hall) from around 8.30pm in the evening until 8am the next morning, performing some kind of act – usually a comedy routine – at each.

Up Helly-Aa itself is not that ancient, dating only from Victorian times, when it was introduced to replace the much older Christmas tradition of rolling burning tar barrels through the streets, which was banned in 1874. Seven years later a torch-light procession took place, which eventually developed into a full-blown Viking celebration, known as "Up Helly-Aa". Although this is essentially a community event with entry to halls by invitation only, visitors are welcome at the Town Hall, for which tickets are sold in early January; contact the tourist office well in advance. To catch some of the atmosphere of the event, check out the annual Up Helly-Aa exhibition in the **Galley Shed** on St Sunniva Street (mid-May to mid-Sept Tues 2–4pm & 7–9pm, Fri 7–9pm, Sat 2–4pm; £3), where you can see a full-size longship, costumes, shields and photographs.

in Loch Clickimin. The settlement here began as a small farmstead around 700 BC and was later enclosed by a defensive wall. The main tower served as a castle and probably rose to around 40ft, as at Mousa (see p.1284), though the remains are now not much more than 10ft high.

In earlier times the seasonal nature of the Shetland fishing industry led to the establishment of small stores, known as **böds**, often incorporating sleeping accommodation, beside the beaches where fish were landed and dried. Just beyond Lerwick's main ferry terminal, a mile and a half north of the town centre, stands the **Böd of Gremista** (June to mid-Sept Wed–Sun 10am–1pm & 2–5pm; Ⓦ www.shetland-museum.org.uk; free), the birthplace of **Arthur Anderson** (1792–1868). The displays explore Anderson's life as beach boy (helping to cure and dry fish), naval seaman, businessman, philanthropist, Shetland's first native MP and founder of Shetland's first newspaper, the *Shetland Journal*.

Eating, drinking and entertainment

Lerwick's best **restaurant** is *Monty's Bistro* on Mounthooly Street (closed Mon & Sun), serving inexpensive and delicious meals and snacks at lunchtimes, and accomplished contemporary cooking in the evening. Other places to try include the very good Indian *Raba*, 26 Commercial Rd, and the Chinese/Thai *Great Wall*, located above the Viking Bus Station. The *Peerie Café* (closed Sun), on the Esplanade, is a great café, with imaginative cakes, soup and sandwiches. The *Fort Café*, situated below Fort Charlotte at 2 Commercial St, is Lerwick's best fish-and-chip shop.

The friendliest **pub** in town is the upstairs bar in the *Lounge*, up Mounthooly Street, where local musicians often do sessions. The Garrison Theatre

25

(℡ 01595/692114, Ⓦ www.islesburgh.org.uk), by the Town Hall, shows **films** as well as putting on occasional theatre productions, comedy acts and live gigs. The Islesburgh Community Centre has introduced regular crafts and culture evenings (mid–May to mid–Sept Wed & Fri), where you can buy local knitwear and listen to traditional **music**.

In late April or early May, musicians from all over the world converge on Shetland for the excellent **Shetland Folk Festival**, which embraces a wider range of musical styles than the title might suggest; there are concerts and dances in every corner of the islands. For details, contact the Folk Festival Society (℡ 01595/694757, Ⓦ www.sffs.shetland.co.uk). In mid–October, there's an **Accordion and Fiddle Festival**: similar format, same coordinating office, but a different musical focus. Listen to *Evening Shetland* on BBC Radio Shetland, 92.7 FM (Mon–Fri 5.30pm), buy the *Shetland Times* on Fridays, or consult Ⓦ www.shetlandtoday.co.uk. Some events are also advertised on Shetland's independent radio station SIBC, 96.2 FM.

Bressay and Noss

Shielding Lerwick from the full force of the North Sea is the island of **Bressay**, dominated at its southern end by the conical Ward Hill (744ft) – "da Wart" – and accessible on an hourly car and passenger ferry from Lerwick (takes 5min). The chief reason most visitors pass through Bressay is in order to visit the tiny but spectacular island of **Noss** – the name means "a point of rock" – just off Bressay's eastern shore. The island was inhabited until World War II but is now given over to sheep farming and is also a National Nature Reserve. Scottish Natural Heritage operates an inflatable as a ferry from the landing stage below the car park at the east side of Bressay (mid–May to Aug only; phone ℡ 01595/693345 for times; £3 return). On the island, the old farmhouse of Gungstie contains a small **visitor centre** where the warden will give you a free map and guide. Behind the house is an old stud farm for **Shetland ponies**, which were sent to work in the mines of County Durham in northeast England. The most memorable feature of Noss is its cliffed coastline rising to a peak at the massive 500-foot **Noup**, home to vast colonies of cliff-nesting gannets, puffins, guillemots, shags, razorbills and fulmars. Be warned: if you stray off the marked path, the great skuas will do their best to intimidate with dive-bombing raids that may hit you hard.

South Mainland

Shetland's **South Mainland** is a long, thin finger of land, only three or four miles wide, but 25 miles long, ending in the cliffs of Sumburgh Head and Fitful Head. It's a beautiful area with wild landscapes but also good farmland, and has yielded some of Shetland's most impressive archeological treasures – in particular, Jarlshof.

From Leebitton, in the district of Sandwick, halfway to Sumburgh Head, you can take the small passenger **ferry** (mid–April to mid–Sept 2 daily; take 15min; £8 return; ℡ 01950/431367, Ⓦ www.mousaboattrips.co.uk) to the small **Isle of Mousa**, on which stands the best-preserved broch in the whole of Scotland. Rising to more than 40ft, and looking rather like a Stone Age cooling tower, **Mousa Broch** has a remarkable presence, and features in both *Egil's Saga* and the *Orkneyinga Saga*, contemporary chronicles of Norse exploration and settlement. The low entrance passage leads through two concentric walls to a central courtyard, divided into separate beehive chambers. Between the walls, a rough (very dark) staircase leads to the top parapet (torch provided

From late May to late July, a large colony of around five thousand **storm petrels** breeds in and around the broch walls, fishing out at sea during the day, and only returning to the nests after dark. The ferry also runs special late-night trips (Wed & Sat weather permitting), setting off in the "simmer dim" twilight around 11pm.

The main road leads eventually to **Sumburgh airport**, beyond which excavations are currently underway at **Old Scatness** (July & Aug daily except Fri 10am–5.30pm; £2), where a broch, and possibly the best-preserved Iron Age house in Europe, have recently been discovered. A little further along the road lies **Jarlshof** (April–Sept daily 9.30am–6.30pm; £3; HS; Oct–March open access to grounds; free), the largest and most impressive of Shetland's archeological sites. There's evidence of more than four thousand years of continuous occupation, with buildings dating from the Stone Age to the early seventeenth century. The best-preserved buildings are the Pictish wheelhouses surrounding a Neolithic broch, and also the Norse longhouses. Sir Walter Scott was responsible for the name: while visiting Shetland in 1814 he decided to use part of the ruins in his novel *The Pirate*. Towering over the whole complex is the laird's house, originally built by Robert Stewart, Earl of Orkney and Lord of Shetland, in the late sixteenth century. Beside Jarlshof is the Scots Baronial *Sumburgh Hotel*, where the bar **food** is surprisingly good.

The Mainland comes to a dramatic end at **Sumburgh Head**, about two miles from Jarlshof. The lighthouse, designed by Robert Stevenson, was built in 1821; although not open to the public its grounds offer great views to Noss in the north and Fair Isle to the south. This is also the easiest place in Shetland to get close to **puffins**. During the nesting season, you simply need to look over the western wall by the lighthouse gate to see them arriving at their burrows with beakfuls of fish or giving flying lessons to their offspring; on no account should you try to climb over the wall.

Fair Isle

Tiny **Fair Isle** (Ⓦ www.fairisle.org.uk) is marooned in the sea halfway between Shetland and Orkney and very different from both. The weather reflects its isolated position: you can almost guarantee that it'll be windy, though if you're lucky your visit might coincide with fine weather – what the islanders call "a given day". At one time Fair Isle's population was not far short of four hundred, but by the 1950s, the population had shrunk to just 44, a point at which evacuation and abandonment of the island was seriously considered. George Waterston, who'd bought the island and set up a bird observatory in 1948, passed it into the care of the National Trust for Scotland in 1954 and rejuvenation began.

The croft land and the island's scattered houses are concentrated in the south, but the focus for many visitors is the **Bird Observatory**, built just above the sandy bay of North Haven where the ferry from Shetland Mainland arrives. It's one of the major European centres for ornithology and its work in watching, trapping, recording and ringing birds goes on all year. Fair Isle is a landfall for a huge number and range of migrant birds during the spring and autumn passages. Migration routes converge here and more than 345 species, including many rarities, have been noted. Fair Isle is, of course, even better known for its **knitting** patterns, still produced with great skill by the local knitwear cooperative. There are a few samples on display at the island's museum (Mon 2–5pm, Wed 10am–noon, Fri 2–4.30pm; ☎01595/760244; free), situated next door to the island's Methodist Chapel.

The passenger **ferry** (☎01595/760222) connects Fair Isle with either Lerwick (on alternate Thurs; takes 4hr 30min) or Grutness in Sumburgh (Tues, Sat & alternate Thurs; takes 3hr). **Flights** go from Tingwall (Mon, Wed, Fri & Sat) or Sumburgh (Sat); a one-way ticket costs £38, and day-trips are possible (Mon, Wed & Fri). Camping is not permitted, but there is full-board **accommodation** at the *Fair Isle Lodge & Bird Observatory* (☎01595/760258, ⓦwww.fairislebirdobs.co.uk; full board ❺) in twins and singles or hostel-style dorms. A good **B&B** option is *Upper Leogh* in the south of the island (☎01595/760248, ⓔkathleen.coull@ lineone.net; ❷).

Scalloway

Approaching **SCALLOWAY**, six miles west of Lerwick, from the shoulder of the steep hill to the east known as the **Scord**, there's a dramatic view over the town and the islands to the south and west. Once the capital of Shetland, Scalloway's importance waned through the eighteenth century as Lerwick grew in trading success and status. Nowadays, Scalloway is fairly sleepy, though its prosperity, always closely linked to the fluctuations of the fishing industry, has been given a boost with investment in new fish-processing factories and in the impressive North Atlantic Fisheries College on the west side of the busy harbour.

In spite of modern developments nearby, Scalloway is dominated by the imposing shell of **Scalloway Castle**, a classic fortified tower house built with forced labour in 1600 by the infamous Earl Patrick Stewart, who held court in the castle and gained a reputation for enhancing his own power and wealth through the calculated use of harsh justice. He was eventually arrested and imprisoned in 1609 for his aggressive behaviour towards his fellow landowners; his son, Robert, attempted an insurrection and both were executed in Edinburgh in 1615. On Main Street, the small **Scalloway Museum** (May–Sept Mon 9.30–11.30am & 2–4.30pm, Tues–Fri 10am–noon & 2–4.30pm, Sat 10am–12.30pm & 2–4.30pm; free), run by volunteers, attempts to tell the story of the Shetland Bus, the link between Shetland and Norway which helped to sustain the Norwegian resistance in World War II.

Scalloway's best accommodation is at the very comfortable and welcoming *Hildasay Guest House* (☎01595/880822; ❷), a Hansel-and-Gretel weatherboarded house on the top of the hill above Scalloway, behind the swimming pool. For food, head for *Da Haaf* (closed Sat & Sun), the unpretentious licensed restaurant in the North Atlantic Fisheries College, which serves fresh fish, simply prepared.

The Westside

The **Westside**'s rolling brown and purple moorland is scattered with dozens of small picturesque lochs gleaming blue or silver and patches of bright green, where cultivation and reseeding have taken place. The coast, cut by several deep voe (fjord-like sea loch) is very varied; aside from dramatic cliffs, there are intimate coves and some fine beaches. The crossroads for the area is effectively Bixter, southwest of which lies the finest Neolithic structure in the Westside, dubbed the **Staneydale Temple** by the archeologist who excavated it because it resembled one on Malta. Whatever its true function, it was twice as large as the surrounding oval-shaped houses (now in ruins) and was certainly of great importance, perhaps as some kind of community centre. The foundations measure more than 40ft by 20ft internally with immensely thick walls, still around 4ft high, whose roof would have been supported by spruce posts (two postholes can still be clearly seen).

The best **accommodation** and **eating** options on the Westside are in and around Walls, 24 miles northwest of Lerwick. Pick of the B&Bs is the wonderfully welcoming *Skeoverick* (℡01595/809349; ❶), a lovely modern crofthouse which lies a mile or so north of Walls. The only hotel is *Burrastow House* (℡01595/809307, ⓦ www.users.zetnet.co.uk/burrastow-house-hotel; ❺), beautifully situated about three miles southwest of Walls; dinner is available for residents only and, though expensive, the meals are superb.

Papa Stour

A mile offshore from Sandness is the quintessentially peaceful island of **Papa Stour** (ⓦ www.papastour.shetland.co.uk); apart from early Christian connections, it was home, in the eighteenth century, to people who were mistakenly believed to have been lepers. The sea has eroded its volcanic rocks to produce some of the most impressive coastal scenery in Shetland, with **stacks, caves** and **natural arches**. The east side is the most fecund area, partly because much of the soil from the western side was painstakingly transported here. In the nineteenth century, Papa Stour supported around three hundred inhabitants; today there's only thirty or so. In summer, the passenger **ferry** runs from West Burrafirth to Papa Stour (Mon, Wed & Fri–Sun). Always book in advance, and reconfirm the day before departure (℡01595/810460); day-trips are only possible Friday to Sunday. There's also a **flight** from Tingwall every Tuesday, and again a day-trip is feasible (£17 one-way). Papa Stour's airstrip is southwest of Biggings, by the school. There's just one **B&B** on the island, *North House* (℡01595/873238, ⓔ andyholt48@hotmail.com; ❷), a crofthouse overlooking Housa Voe (camping possible, too), and a small, clean, friendly **bunkhouse** (℡01595/873229, ⓔ fay@hurdiback.shetland.co.uk; April–Sept) at Hurdiback, near the pier and beside the island's only phone box.

Foula

Southwest of Walls, at "the edge of the world", **Foula** is without a doubt the most isolated inhabited island in the British Isles, separated from the nearest point on Mainland Shetland by about fourteen miles of often turbulent ocean. Seen from the Mainland, its distinctive mountainous form changes subtly, depending upon the vantage point, but the outline is unforgettable. Its western **cliffs**, the second highest in Britain after those of St Kilda, rise at **The Kame** to some 1220ft above sea level; a clear day at The Kame offers a magnificent panorama stretching from Unst to Fair Isle. On a bad day, the exposure is complete and the cliffs generate turbulent blasts of wind known in Shetland as "flans", which rip through the hills with tremendous force.

Arriving on Foula, you can't help but be amazed by the sheer size of the island's immense, bare mountain summits. As well as having forty human inhabitants, the island, whose name is derived from the Old Norse for "bird land", also provides a home for a quarter of a million **birds**. Arctic terns wheel overhead at the airstrip, red-throated divers can usually be seen on Mill Loch, while fulmars, guillemots and gannets cling to the rock ledges, but it is the island's colony of **great skuas** or "bonxies" which you can't fail to notice. It's essential to book and reconfirm the summer passenger **ferry** from Walls (Tues, Thurs & Sat; 2hr 30min; ℡01595/810460). The boat arrives at Ham, in the middle of Foula's east coast, and has to be winched up onto the pier to protect it. However, there are regular **flights** from Tingwall (Mon–Wed & Fri; ℡01595/753226); tickets cost around £22 one way and day-trips are possible Wednesdays (summer only) and Fridays all year. Foula's only **B&B** is *Laraback* (℡01595/753226, ⓦ www.originart2.shetland.co.uk; ❸), near Ham, which does full board only.

△ Papa S

North Mainland

The **North Mainland**, stretching more than thirty miles north from the central belt around Lerwick, is wilder than much of Shetland, with almost relentlessly bleak moorland and some rugged and dramatic coastal scenery. You're bound to pass by **VOE**, as it sits at the main crossroads of the area, but it's easy to miss the picturesque old village, a tight huddle of homes and workshops down below the road around the pier. Set at the head of a deep, sheltered, sea loch, Voe has a Scandinavian appearance, helped by the presence of the **Sail Loft**, painted in a rich, deep red. The building has been converted into a large **hostel** (book through Lerwick tourist office; April–Sept); it has hot showers, a kitchen, and a solid-fuel heater in the smaller of the bedrooms. Across the road, the *Pierhead Restaurant & Bar* is a cosy wood-panelled **pub** with a real fire, occasional live music, a good bar menu and an upstairs restaurant.

From Voe the main road divides; the northern leg leads to Toft, the ferry terminal for the island of Yell (see p.1290), while the other branch cuts northwest to **BRAE**, a sprawling settlement expanded in some haste in the 1970s to accommodate the workforce for the huge **Sullom Voe Oil Terminal** nearby. Brae boasts one of Shetland's finest **hotels**, *Busta House* (℡01806/522506, ⓦ www.bustahouse.com; ⓺), a lovely laird's house which sits across the bay of Busta Voe from the modern sprawl of Brae. It's worth coming here for a drink or an excellent meal in the hotel's pub-like bar.

Northmavine, the northwest peninsula of North Mainland, is unquestionably one of the most picturesque areas of Shetland, with its often rugged scenery, magnificent coastline and wide open spaces. The peninsula begins a mile west of Brae at **Mavis Grind**, a narrow isthmus at which it's said you can throw a stone from the Atlantic to the North Sea, or at least to Sullom Voe. **HILLSWICK**, the main settlement, was once served by the steamers of the North of Scotland, Orkney & Shetland Steam Navigation Company and in the early twentieth century the firm also built the **Magnus Bay Hotel**, importing it in the form of a timber kit from Norway; it still stands, albeit somewhat altered. Nearer the shore is the much older Hillswick House and, attached to it, **Da Böd**, once the oldest pub in Shetland, said to have been founded by a German merchant in 1684, now an alternative veggie café and wildlife sanctuary called *The Booth* (℡01806/503348; May–Sept).

Just outside Hillswick, a sideroad leads west to the exposed headland of **Esha Ness** (pronounced "*Ay*sha Ness"), celebrated for its splendid coastline views. Spectacular eroded red granite **cliffs** are spread out before you as the road climbs away from Hillswick: in the foreground are the stacks known as **The Drongs** off the Ness of Hillswick. A mile or so south off the main road is the **Tangwick Haa Museum** (May–Sept Mon–Fri 1–5pm, Sat & Sun 11am–7pm; free), which tells the often moving story of this remote corner of Shetland and its role in the dangerous trade of deep-sea fishing and whaling. To the north the road ends at the **Esha Ness Lighthouse**, a great place to view the cliffs, stacks and, in rough weather, blowholes of this stretch of coast, and the starting point for an excellent three-hour walk. One of the few places to stay in Esha Ness is *Johnnie Notions* **hostel** (April–Sept; book through Lerwick tourist office; no electricity), up a turning north off the main road, in **Hamnavoe**.

The North Isles

Many visitors never make it out to Shetland's trio of remote **North Isles**, which is a shame, as the ferry links are frequent and inexpensive, and the roads fast. Certainly, there is no dramatic shift in scenery: much of what awaits you is the familiar Shetland landscape of undulating peat moorland, dramatic coastal cliffs and silent glacial voes. However, with Lerwick that much further away, the spirit of independence and self-sufficiency in the North Isles is much more keenly felt. **Yell**, the largest of the three, is best known for its vast otter population. **Fetlar**, the smallest, is home to the rare red-necked phalarope. **Unst**, though, probably has the widest appeal, partly as the most northerly land mass in the British Isles, but also for its nesting seabird population.

Yell

Historically, **Yell** (Ⓦ www.yell-tourism.shetland.co.uk) hasn't had good write-ups. The writer Eric Linklater described it as "dull and dark", while the Scottish historian Buchanan claimed it was "so uncouth a place that no creature can live therein, except such as are born there". Certainly, if you keep to the fast main road, which links the island's two ferry terminals of Ulsta and Gutcher, you'll pass a lot of uninspiring peat moorland, but the landscape is relieved by several voes which cut deeply into it, providing superb natural harbours. Yell's coastline, too, is gentler and greener than the interior and provides an ideal habitat for a large population of **otters**.

At **BURRAVOE**, in the southeast corner, there's a lovely whitewashed laird's house that now houses the **Old Haa Museum** (late April to Sept Tues–Thurs & Sat 10am–4pm, Sun 2–5pm; free), which is stuffed with artefacts, and has lots of material on the history of the local herring and whaling industry; there's a very pleasant wood-panelled café on the ground floor. In the north, the area around **CULLIVOE** has relatively gentle, but attractive, coastal scenery. The **Sands of Brekken** are made from crushed shells, and are beautifully sheltered in a cove a mile or two north of Cullivoe. A couple of miles to the west, the road ends at **GLOUP**, with its secretive, narrow voe. This area provides some excellent walking, as does the coast further west, where there's an Iron Age fort and field system at **Burgi Geos**.

Ferries from Toft on the Mainland are frequent and inexpensive, and taking a car over is easy, too (1–2 hourly; takes 20min). One of the best **B&Bs** is *Hillhead* (Ⓣ01957/722274, Ⓔrita.leask@btopenworld.com; ❶), a comfortable modern house halfway between Ulsta and Burravoe; you can also stay with the very welcoming Tullochs at *Gutcher Post Office* (Ⓣ01957/744201; ❶) overlooking the ferry terminal. A cheaper alternative is to stay in the **hostel** at *Windhouse Lodge* (April–Sept; book through Lerwick tourist office), the gatehouse on the main road near Mid Yell. The functional *Hilltop Bar* in Mid Yell offers standard bar meals, while the funky *Wind Dog Café* (Ⓦwww .winddogcafe.co.uk), opposite the post office at Gutcher, provides a welcom shelter, Internet access, as well as snacks.

Fetlar

Fetlar is the most fertile of the North Isles, much of it grassy moorland and lus green meadows with masses of summer flowers. At the main settlemen **HOUBIE**, you can learn more about the island from the nearby welcomin **Fetlar Interpretive Centre** (May–Sept Tues–Sun 12.30–5.30pr Ⓦwww.fetlar.com; free). Fetlar is also one of the very few places in the UK whe you'll see graceful **red-necked phalarope** (late May to early Aug): the islar boasts ninety percent of the UK's phalarope population, and an RSPB hide h been provided overlooking the marshes (or mires) to the east of the **Lo of Funzie** (pronounced "finny"). **Ferries** (6–8 daily; takes 25–40min) dep from both Gutcher on Yell and Belmont on Unst, docking at Oddsta, three mi northwest of Houbie. The only public transport is an infrequent postcar (Mon–Fri 2 daily). **Accommodation** boils down to *Gord* (℡01957/733227, ©lynboxall @zetnet.co.uk; ❸), a comfortable modern house attached to the island shop in Houbie, and the *Glebe* (℡01957/733242, ©theglebe@zetnet.co.uk; ❸), a characterful old manse near Papil Water. *Garths* **campsite** (℡01957/733227; May–Sept) is a simple field just to the west of Houbie.

Unst

Much of **Unst** (⊕www.unst.shetland.co.uk) is rolling grassland – a blessed relief for some after the peaty moorland of Yell – but the coast is more dramatic: a fringe of cliffs relieved by some beautiful sandy beaches. As Britain's most northerly inhabited island, there is a surfeit of "most northerly" sights, which is fair enough, given that many visitors only come here in order to head straight for Hermaness, to see the seabirds and look out over Muckle Flugga and the northernmost tip of Britain, to the North Pole beyond. The island has been badly affected by the drastic downsizing of the local RAF radar base at Saxa Vord, which until recently employed a third of the island's population.

On the south coast, not far from the ferry terminal, is **UYEASOUND**, east of which lie the ruins of **Muness Castle**, a diminutive defensive structure, built in 1598 with matching bulging bastions and corbelled turrets at opposite corners (keys and torch from the house nearby). Unst's main settlement is **BALTASOUND**, five miles north, whose herring industry used to boost the local population of around five hundred to as much as ten thousand during the fishing season. The excellent **Unst Heritage Centre** (May–Sept daily 2–5pm; free) occupies the old school building by the main crossroads. From Baltasound, the main road crosses a giant boulder field of serpentine, a greyish green, occasionally turquoise rock that weathers to a rusty orange. The **Keen of Hamar**, east of Baltasound, and clearly signposted from the main road, is one of the largest expanses of serpentine debris in Europe, and is home to an extraordinary array of plantlife.

Beyond the Keen of Hamar, the road drops down into **HAROLDSWICK**, where near the shore you'll find the **Unst Boat Haven** (May–Sept daily 2–5pm; otherwise a key is available from the adjacent shop; free), displaying a beautifully presented collection of historic boats with many tools of the trade and information on fishing. The road that heads off northwest leads to the bleak headland of **Hermaness**, now a National Nature Reserve and home to more than 100,000 nesting seabirds. There's an excellent **visitor centre** in the former lighthouse-keepers' shore station, where you can pick up a leaflet showing the marked routes across the heather to the view over to **Muckle Flugga** lighthouse and **Out Stack**, the most northerly bit of Britain. The views from here are inevitably marvellous, as is the birdlife; there's a huge gantry on one of the stacks, and puffins burrow all along the cliff tops.

Book in advance for the regular **ferries** that shuttle from Gutcher on Yell over to **BELMONT** on Unst (1–2 hourly; 10min; ℡01957/722259). The best and most unusual **accommodation** is the family-owned *Buness House* (℡01957/711315, ⊕www.users.zetnet.co.uk/buness-house; ❺), a seventeenth-century Haa in Baltasound. Another very good bet is *Prestegaard* (℡01957/755234, ©prestegaard@postmaster.co.uk; ❶), a more modest Victorian B&B in Uyeasound, where there's also the clean and modern *Gardiesfauld Hostel* (℡01957/755259, ⊕www.gardiesfauld.shetland.co.uk; April–Sept) near the pier, which allows **camping** and offers **bike rental**.

Travel details

Orkney

Ferries to Orkney (summer only)

Aberdeen to: Kirkwall (4 weekly; 5hr 45min).
Gill's Bay to: St Margaret's Hope (3 daily; 1hr).
John O'Groats to: Burwick (passengers only; 2–4 daily; 40min).
Lerwick to: Kirkwall (3 weekly; 4hr 30min).
Scrabster to: Stromness (2–3 daily; 2hr).

Inter-island ferries (summer only)

To Eday: Kirkwall–Eday (2 daily; 1hr 15min–2hr).
To Hoy: Houton–Lyness (Mon–Fri 6 daily, Sat & Sun 2–4 daily; 30min–1hr); Stromness–Hoy (passengers only; Mon–Fri 4–5 daily, Sat & Sun 2 daily; 25min).
To North Ronaldsay: Kirkwall–North Ronaldsay (1 weekly, usually Fri; 2hr 40min–3hr).
To Papa Westray: Kirkwall–Papa Westray (Tues & Fri; 2hr 15min); Pierowall (Westray)–Papa Westray (passengers only; 3–6 daily; 25min).
To Rousay: Tingwall–Rousay (6 daily; 30min).
To Sanday: Kirkwall–Sanday (2 daily; 1hr 25min).
To Shapinsay: Kirkwall–Shapinsay (Mon–Fri 5 daily, Sat & Sun 3–4 daily; 45min).
To Stronsay: Kirkwall–Whitehall (2 daily; 1hr 35min–2hr).
To Westray: Kirkwall–Westray (2–3 daily; 1hr 25min).

Inter-island flights (Mon–Sat only)

Kirkwall to: Eday (Wed; 8–36min); North Ronaldsay (2 daily; 15min); Papa Westray (Mon–Sat 2 daily; 12min); Sanday (Mon–Sat 2 daily; 10–20min); Stronsay (Mon–Sat 2 daily; 25min); Westray (Mon–Sat 2 daily; 12min).

Buses on Orkney Mainland

Kirkwall to: Burwick (4 daily; 50min); Birsay (Mon–Fri 2 daily; 45min); Evie (Mon–Sat 4 daily; 30min); Houton (Mon–Fri 5 daily, 3 on Sat; 30min); St Margaret's Hope (Mon–Sat 3–4 daily; 40min); Skara Brae (Mon–Fri 2 daily; 1hr 15min); Stromness (Mon–Fri 10–12 daily, 7 on Sat, 4 on Sun; 30min); Tingwall (Mon–Fri 4 daily, Sat 2 daily; 35min).
Stromness to: Skara Brae (3–4 daily; 20min).

Shetland

Ferries to Shetland (summer only)

Aberdeen to: Lerwick (daily; 12–14hr).

Kirkwall (Orkney) to: Lerwick (3–4 weekly; 5–7hr).

Inter-island ferries (summer only)

To Bressay: Lerwick–Bressay (every 30min–1hr; 5min).
To Fair Isle: Lerwick–Fair Isle (alternate Thurs; 4hr 30min); Grutness–Fair Isle (Tues, Sat & alternate Thurs; 3hr).
To Fetlar: Belmont (Unst) and Gutcher (Yell)–Oddsta (5–8 daily; 25min).
To Foula: Scalloway–Foula (alternate Thurs; 3hr); Walls–Foula (Tues, Sat & alternate Thurs; 2hr 30min).
To Papa Stour: West Burrafirth–Papa Stour (Mon, Wed & Sun 1 daily, Fri & Sat 2 daily; 45min).
To Unst: Gutcher (Yell)–Belmont (every 30min; 10min).
To Yell: Toft–Ulsta (1–2 hourly; 20min).

Inter-island flights (summer only)

Sumburgh to: Fair Isle (Sat; 25min).
Tingwall to: Fair Isle (Mon, Wed & Fri 2 daily; 25min); Foula (Mon & Tues 1 daily, Wed & Fri 2 daily, 15min); Papa Stour (Tues 2 daily; 10min).

Buses on Shetland Mainland

Lerwick to: Brae (Mon–Sat 5–7 daily, 1 on Sun in school term; 45min); Hamnavoe (Mon–Sat 3–7 daily; 30min); Hillswick (Mon–Sat 2 daily; 1hr 15min); Sandwick (Mon–Sat 7–11 daily, 3 on Sun; 25min); Scalloway (Mon–Sat hourly; 15min); Sumburgh (7–11 daily; 45min); Toft (Mon–Fri 5 daily, 2 on Sat, 1 on Sun in school term; 50min); Voe (Mon–Sat 4–7 daily, 1 on Sun in school term; 30min); Walls (Mon–Sat 1–3 daily; 45min).

Buses on Unst

Baltasound to: Haroldswick (Mon–Sat 2–3 daily; 10min).
Belmont to: Baltasound (Mon–Sat 2–3 daily; 20–45min); Uyeasound (Mon–Sat 1–3 daily; 5min).

Buses on Yell

Mid Yell to: Gutcher (Mon–Sat 2–3 daily, 1 on Sun in school term; 20min).
Ulsta to: Burravoe (Mon–Sat 1 daily; 15min); Gutcher (Mon–Sat 2 daily, 1 on Sun in school term; 30min).

Contexts

Contexts

History

O ff and on, people have probably lived in **Britain** for the best part of half a million years, though the earliest evidence of human life dates from about 250,000 BC. These meagre remains, found near Swanscombe, east of London across the Thames from Tilbury, belong to one of the migrant communities whose comings and goings depended on the fluctuations of the Ice Ages. Renewed glaciation then made the area unin-habitable once more, and the next traces – mainly roughly worked flint imple-ments – were left around 40,000 BC by cave-dwellers at Creswell Crags in Derbyshire, Kent's Cavern near Torquay and Cheddar Cave in Somerset. The last spell of intense cold began about 17,000 years ago, and it was the final thawing of this last **Ice Age** around 5000 BC that caused the British Isles to separate from the European mainland.

The sea barrier did nothing to stop further migrations of nomadic hunting communities, drawn by the rich forests that covered ancient Britain. In about 3500 BC a new wave of colonists arrived from the continent, probably via Ireland, bringing with them a **Neolithic** culture based on farming and the rearing of livestock. These tribes were the first to make some impact on their environment, clearing forests, enclosing fields, constructing defensive ditches around their villages and digging mines to obtain flint used for tools and weapons. Fragments of Neolithic pottery have been found near Peterborough and at Windmill Hill, near Avebury in Wiltshire; other settlements – like the well-preserved village of Skara Brae in Orkney – were near the sea, enabling them to supplement their diet by fishing and to develop their skills as boat builders. The most profuse relics of this culture are their graves, usually stone-chambered, turf-covered mounds (called long barrows, cairns or cromlechs), which are scattered throughout the country; the most impressive ones are at Belas Knap in Gloucestershire, Barclodiad y Gawres in Anglesey, and Maes Howe on Orkney.

The transition from the Neolithic to the Bronze Age began around 2000 BC, with the immigration from northern Europe of the so-called **Beaker Folk** – named from the distinctive cups found at their burial sites. Originating in the Iberian Peninsula and bringing with them bronze-workers from the Rhineland, these newcomers had a well-organized social structure with an established aristocracy, and quickly intermixed with the native tribes. Many of Britain's **stone circles** were completed at this time, including Stonehenge in Wiltshire, and Calanais on the Isle of Lewis, while many others belong entirely to the Bronze Age – for example, the Hurlers and the Nine Maidens on Cornwall's Bodmin Moor. Large numbers of earthwork forts were also built in this period, suggesting a high level of tribal warfare, but none of these were able to withstand the waves of Celtic invaders who, spreading from a homeland in central Europe, began settling in Britain around 600 BC.

The Celts

Highly skilled in battle, the **Celts** soon displaced the local inhabitants all over Britain, establishing a sophisticated farming economy and a social hierarchy that was headed by **Druids**, a priesthood with attendant poets, seers and warriors. Through a deep knowledge of ritual, legend and the mechanics of the heavens, the Druids maintained their position between the people and a pantheon of over four thousand gods. Familiar with Mediterranean artefacts through their far-flung trade routes, they introduced superior methods of metalworking that favoured iron rather than bronze, from which they forged not just weapons but also coins. Gold was used for ornamental works – the first recognizable British art – heavily influenced by the symbolic, patterned **La Tène** style still thought of as quintessentially Celtic.

The principal Celtic contribution to the landscape was a network of hill forts or brochs, and other defensive works stretching over the entire country, the greatest of them at **Maiden Castle** in Dorset, a site first fortified almost 3000 years earlier, and **Mousa** in the Shetland islands. The original Celtic tongue – the basis of modern Welsh and Scottish Gaelic – was spoken over a wide area, gradually dividing into Goidelic (or Q-Celtic) now spoken in Ireland and Scotland, and Brythonic (P-Celtic) spoken in Wales and Cornwall, and later exported to Brittany in France. Great though the Celtic technological and artistic achievements were, the people and their pan-European cousins were unable to maintain an organized civic society to match that of their successors, the Romans.

The Romans

The **Roman** invasion began hesitantly, with small cross-Channel incursions by **Julius Caesar** in 55 and 54 BC. Britain's rumoured mineral wealth was a primary motive behind these raids, but the immediate spur to the eventual conquest nearly a century later was the dangerous collaboration between British Celts and the fiercely anti-Roman tribesmen in France, and the need of the emperor **Claudius**, who owed his power to the army, for a great military triumph. The death of the British king Cunobelin, who ruled all southeast England and was the original of Shakespeare's Cymbeline, offered the opportunity Claudius required, and in August 43 AD, a substantial force landed in Kent, from where it fanned out, soon establishing a base along the estuary of the Thames. Joined by Claudius and a menagerie of elephants and camels for the major battle of the campaign, the Romans soon reached Camulodunum (Colchester), and within four years were dug in on the frontier of south Wales.

The Catuvellauni chief, **Caratacus**, continued to conduct a guerrilla campaign from Wales until his eventual betrayal and capture in about 50 AD. About ten years later, a more serious challenge to the Romans arose when the East Anglian Iceni, under their queen **Boudicca** (or Boadicea), sacked Camulodunum and Verulamium (St Albans), and even reached the undefended port of Londinium, precursor of London. The uprising was soon quashed, and turned out to be an isolated act of resistance, with many of the already Romanized southeastern tribes of England probably welcoming absorption into the empire. However, it was not until 79 AD that Wales and the north of England were subdued.

By 80 AD the Roman governor, Agricola, felt secure enough in the south of Britain to begin an invasion of the north, building a string of forts across the Clyde–Forth line and defeating a large force of Scottish tribes at Mons Graupius. The long-term effect of his campaign, however, was slight. In 123 AD the emperor Hadrian decided to seal the frontier against the northern tribes and built **Hadrian's Wall**, which stretched from the Solway Firth to the Tyne and was the first formal division of the island of Britain. Twenty years later, the Romans again ventured north and built the **Antonine Wall** between the Clyde and the Forth. This was occupied for about forty years, but thereafter the Romans, frustrated by the inhospitable terrain of the Highlands, largely gave up their attempt to subjugate the north, and instead adopted a policy of containment.

The written history of Britain begins with the Romans, whose rule lasted nearly four centuries. For the first time most of England was absorbed into a unified and peaceful political structure, in which commerce flourished and cities prospered, particularly **Londinium**, which immediately assumed a pivotal role in the commercial and administrative life of the province. Although Latin became the language of the Romano–British ruling elite, local traditions were allowed to coexist with imported customs, so that Celtic gods were often worshipped at the same time as the Roman, and sometimes merged with them. Perhaps the most important legacy of the Roman occupation, however, was the introduction of **Christianity** from the third century on, becoming firmly entrenched after its official recognition by the emperor Constantine in 313.

The Anglo-Saxon period: 410–1066

As early as the reign of Constantine, Roman England was being raided by Germanic Saxon pirates. As economic life declined and rural areas became depopulated, individual military leaders began to usurp local authority, so that by the start of the fifth century England had become irrevocably detached from what remained of the Roman Empire. Within fifty years the **Saxons** were settling on the island, the start of a gradual conquest that – despite bitter resistance led by such semi-mythical figures as King Arthur, who is alleged to have held court at Caerleon in Wales – culminated in the defeat of the native Britons in 577 at the **Battle of Dyrham** (near Bath), at which three British kings were killed. Driving the few recalcitrant Celtic tribes deep into Cumbria, Wales and England's West Country, the invaders eliminated the Romano-British culture and by the end of the sixth century the rest of England was divided into the Anglo-Saxon kingdoms of Northumbria, Mercia, East Anglia, Kent and Wessex. Only in Scotland, Wales and the far southwest of England did the ancient Celtic traditions survive. In the fifth century, Irish-Celtic invaders formed distinct colonies in parts of Wales and in the northwest of Scotland. Between the fifth and the eighth centuries the Celtic saints, ascetic evangelical missionaries, spread the gospel around Ireland and western Britain, promoting the eremitical tradition of living a reclusive life. In south Wales, **St David** was the most popular (and subsequently Wales' patron saint), while in northwest Scotland, **St Columba** founded several Christian outposts, the most famous of which was on the island of Iona.

The revival of Christianity in England was driven mainly by the arrival of **St Augustine**, who was dispatched by Pope Gregory I and landed on the Kent coast in 597, accompanied by forty monks. The missionaries were received by Ethelbert, who gave Augustine permission to found a monastery at Canterbury, where the king himself was then baptized, followed by ten thousand of his subjects at a grand Christmas ceremony. Despite some reversals in the years that followed, the Christianization of England proceeded quickly, so that by the middle of the seventh century all of the Anglo-Saxon kings had at last nominally adopted the faith. Tensions and clashes between the Augustinian missionaries and the more freebooting Celtic monks inevitably arose, to be resolved by the **Synod of Whitby** in 663, when it was settled that the English church should follow the rule of Rome, thereby ensuring a realignment with the European cultural mainstream.

The central English region of **Mercia** became the dominant Anglo-Saxon kingdom in the eighth century under kings Ethelbald and Offa, the latter being responsible for the greatest public work of the Anglo-Saxon period, **Offa's Dyke**, an earthwork stretching from the River Dee to the Severn, marking the border with Wales. After Offa's death **Wessex** gained the upper hand, and by 825 King Egbert had conquered or taken allegiance from all the other English kingdoms. The supremacy of Wessex coincided with the first large-scale Norse or **Danish** Viking invasions, which began with coastal pirate raids, such as the one that destroyed the great monastery of Lindisfarne in 793, but gradually grew into a migration, chiefly in the Scottish islands of Orkney, Shetland and the Hebrides.

In 865 a substantial Danish army landed in East Anglia, and within six years they had conquered Northumbria, Mercia and East Anglia, and were attacking Wessex. At about the same time, the leadership of Wessex was assumed by **Alfred the Great**, a warrior whose dogged resistance and acceptance of the need to coexist with the Danes ensured the survival of his kingdom. Having established a border demarcating his domain from the northern **Danelaw**, the part of England in which the rule of the now Christianized Danes was accepted (a border roughly coinciding with the Roman Watling Street), Alfred directed his resources into internal reforms and the strengthening of his defences.

Although Danish attacks had recommenced before the end of Alfred's reign in 899, his successor, Edward the Elder, established supremacy over the Danelaw and was thus the de facto overlord of all England, acknowledged even by Scottish and Welsh chieftains. In 973, **Edgar**, king of Mercia and Northumberland, became the first ruler to be crowned king of England, but the aggression from the Danes was unrelenting, and in 1016 Ethelred the Unready, having failed to buy off the enemy, fled to Normandy, establishing links there which were to have a far-reaching effect on future events.

The first and best king of the short-lived Danish dynasty was **Canute**, who was followed by his two unexceptional and disreputable sons, after whom the Saxons were restored under Ethelred's son, **Edward the Confessor**. It was said of Edward that he was better suited to have been a priest than a king, and most of his reign was dominated by Godwin, Earl of Wessex, and by Godwin's son Harold. On Edward's death, the Witan – a sort of council of elders – confirmed **Harold** as king, despite the claim of William, duke of Normandy, that the exiled and childless Edward had promised him the succession. Harold's brief reign was overshadowed by the events in the last two of its ten months when he first marched north to fend off an invasion attempt by his brother Tostig (who had been deprived of his earldom of Northumbria) in league with King Harald of Norway. Having defeated their combined forces at Stamford Bridge in Yorkshire, Harold was immediately forced to return south to meet the invading William, who routed his forces at the **Battle of Hastings in 1066**. Harold was killed, and on Christmas Day of that year William the Conqueror was installed as king in Westminster Abbey.

England: Normans and Plantagenets: 1066–1307

Making little attempt to reach any understanding with the indigenous Saxon culture, **William I** imposed a new military aristocracy on his subjects, enforcing his rule with a series of strongholds all over England, the grandest of which was the Tower of London. The sporadic rebellions that broke out during the early years of his reign were ruthlessly suppressed by a scorched earth policy, especially in Yorkshire and north of the River Tees, but perhaps the single most effective controlling measure was the compilation of the **Domesday Book** between 1085 and 1086. Recording land ownership, type of cultivation, the number of inhabitants and their social status, it afforded William an unprecedented body information about his subjects, providing the framework for the administration of taxation, the judicial structure and feudal obligations.

William was succeeded in 1087 by his son **William Rufus**, an ineffectual ruler but a notable benefactor of the religious foundations that were springing up throughout the realm. Killed by an arrow while hunting in the New Forest, William was in turn followed by William I's youngest son, **Henry I**, who spent much of his reign in tussles with the country's barons, but at least was the first Norman king to encourage intermarriage, himself marrying a Saxon princess. On his death in 1135, William I's grandson **Stephen** of Blois contested the accession of Henry's daughter Mathilda, with the consequence that the nineteen years of his reign were spent in civil war. Mathilda's son was eventually recognized as Stephen's heir, and the reign of **Henry II** (1154–89), the first of the **Plantagenet** branch of the Norman line, provided a welcome respite from baronial brawling. Asserting his authority throughout a domain that reached from the Cheviots to the Pyrenees, Henry presided over immense administrative reforms, including the introduction of trial by jury. His attempts to subordinate ecclesiastical authority to the Crown went terribly awry in 1170, with the murder in Canterbury Cathedral of his erstwhile drinking companion **Thomas à Becket**, whose canonization just three years later created an enduring Europe-wide cult.

The last years of Henry's reign were riven by quarrels with his sons, the eldest of whom, **Richard I** (the Lionheart), spent most of his ten-year reign crusading in the Holy Land. Alienated by the king's rift with the Church in Rome, and by his loss of Henry II's huge legacy of French territory, the barons eventually forced Richard's brother **King John** to consent to a charter guaranteeing their rights and privileges, the **Magna Carta**, which was signed in 1215 at Runnymede, on the Thames. The power struggle with the barons continued into the reign of **Henry III**, who was defeated by their leader Simon de Montfort at Lewes in 1265, when both Henry and Prince Edward were taken prisoner. Edward escaped, defeated the barons' army at the battle of Evesham and killed de Montfort, ascending the throne in 1272 as **Edward I**. A great law-maker in the mould of William I and Henry II, Edward presided over the Model Parliament of 1295, a significant step in the evolution of consensual politics, though he was mostly absorbed in extending his kingdom within the island, annexing Wales and imposing English jurisdiction in Scotland.

The conquest of Wales: 1272–1408

Though Wales was unable to present a unified opposition to the Norman invaders, William the Conqueror didn't attempt to annex the country. Instead, he installed a huge retinue of barons, the **Lords Marcher**, along the border to bring as much Welsh territory under their own jurisdiction as possible. Despite generations of squabbling, the barons managed to hold onto their privileges until Henry VIII's Act of Union over four hundred years later.

The status quo between Wales and England changed irrevocably, however, when **Edward I** succeeded Henry III and began a crusade to unify Britain. The Welsh chief, Llywelyn the Last, had failed to attend Edward's coronation, and refused to pay him homage. With effective use of sea power, Edward had little trouble forcing Llywelyn into Snowdonia. Peace was restored with the **Treaty of Aberconwy**, which deprived Llywelyn of almost all his land and stripped him of his financial tributes from the other Welsh princes, but left him with the hollow title of "Prince of Wales". After a relatively cordial four-year period, Llywelyn's brother Dafydd rose against Edward, inevitably dragging

Llewelyn along with him. Edward crushed the revolt, captured Llewelyn, and executed him. The **Treaty of Rhuddlan** in 1284 set down the terms by which the English monarch was to rule Wales: much of it was given to the Marcher lords who had helped Edward, the rest was divided into administrative and legal districts similar to those in England. Though the treaty is often seen as a symbol of English subjugation, it respected much of Welsh law and provided a basis for civil rights and privileges. Many Welsh were content to accept and exploit Edward's rule for their own benefit, but in 1294 a rebellion led by **Madog ap Llywelyn** gripped Wales and was only halted by Edward's swift and devastating response. Most of the privileges enshrined in the Treaty of Rhuddlan were now rescinded and the Welsh seemed crushed for a century.

Pent-up resentment towards the English sowed seeds of a rebellion led by the tyrannical but charismatic Welsh hero **Owain Glyndŵr**, who declared himself "Prince of Wales" in 1400, and with a crew of local supporters attacked the lands of nearby barons, slaughtering the English. **Henry IV** misjudged the political climate and imposed restrictions on Welsh land ownership, swelling the general support Glyndŵr needed to take Conwy Castle the following year. In 1404 Glyndŵr summoned a parliament in Machynlleth, and had himself crowned Prince of Wales, with envoys of France, Scotland and Castile in attendance. He then demanded independence for the Welsh Church from Canterbury and set about securing alliances with English noblemen who had grievances with Henry IV. This last ambitious move heralded Glyndŵr's downfall. A succession of defeats saw his allies desert him and by 1408, when the castles at Harlech and Aberystwyth were retaken for the Crown, this last protest against Edward I's English conquest had lost its momentum.

Scotland in the Middle Ages: 1057–1320

In the post-Roman period, **Picts** and **Scotti** – followed later by Viking invaders – battled over Scotland's territory, but by the ninth century **Kenneth MacAlpine**, king of the Scotti and son of a Pictish princess, was able to create a united kingdom of Alba (later known as Scotia). His successors extended the frontiers by marriage and conquest until, by 1034, almost all of modern Scotland was under their rule.

The victory of the Scottish king, **Malcolm III**, known as Canmore ("Bighead"), over **Macbeth** in 1057 marked the beginning of a period of fundamental change in Scottish society. Having avenged his father Duncan, Malcolm III, who had spent the previous seventeen years at the English court, sought to apply to Scotland a range of ideas he had brought back with him. He and his heirs established a secure dynasty based on succession through the male line and introduced **feudalism** into Scotland, a system that was diametrically opposed to the Gaelic system, which rested on blood ties: the followers of a Gaelic king were his kindred, whereas the followers of a feudal king were vassals bought with land. The Canmores successfully feudalized much of southern and eastern Scotland by making grants to their Norman, Breton and Flemish followers, but beyond that, traditional clan-based forms of social relations persisted.

The Canmores, independent of the local nobility, who remained a military threat, also began to reform the **Church**. This development started with the efforts of **Margaret**, Malcolm III's English wife, who brought Scottish religious practices into line with those of the rest of Europe and was eventually canonized. **David I** (1124–53) continued the process by importing monks, found a series of monasteries, principally along the border at Kelso, Melrose

Jedburgh and Dryburgh. By 1200 the entire country was covered by a network of eleven bishoprics, although church organization remained weak within the Highlands. Similarly, the dynasty founded a series of **royal burghs**, towns such as Edinburgh, Stirling and Berwick, and bestowed upon them charters recognizing them as centres of trade. The charters usually granted a measure of self-government, vested in the town corporation or guild, and the monarchy hoped this liberality would both encourage loyalty and increase the prosperity of the kingdom. Scotland's Gaelic-speaking clans had little influence within the burghs, and by 1550 Scots – a northern version of Anglo-Saxon – had become the main language throughout the Lowlands.

The policies of the Canmores laid the basis for a cultural rift in Scotland between the Highland and Lowland communities. Before that became an issue, however, the Scots had to face a major threat from the south. In 1286 **Alexander III** died, and a hotly disputed succession gave Edward I, the king of England, an opportunity to subjugate Scotland. In 1291 Edward presided over a conference where the rival claimants to the Scottish throne presented their cases. Edward chose John Balliol, in preference to **Robert the Bruce**, and obliged John to pay him homage, thus turning Scotland into a vassal kingdom. Bruce refused to accept the decision, thereby continuing the conflict, and in 1295 Balliol renounced his allegiance to Edward and formed an alliance with **France** – the beginning of what is known as the "Auld Alliance". In the conflict that followed, Balliol was defeated and imprisoned, and Edward seized control of almost all of Scotland.

Edward had shown little mercy during his conquest of Scotland and his cruelty seems to have provoked a truly national resistance. This focused on **William Wallace**, a man of relatively lowly origins who forged an army of peasants, lesser knights and townsmen that was fundamentally different from the armies raised by the nobility. Figures like Balliol, holding lands in England, France and Scotland, were part of an international aristocracy for whom warfare was merely the means by which they struggled for power. Wallace, by contrast, led proto-nationalist forces determined to expel the English from their country. Probably for that very reason Wallace never received the support of the nobility, and, after a bitter ten-year campaign, he was betrayed and executed in London in 1305.

With Wallace out of the way, feudal intrigue resumed. In 1306 **Robert the Bruce**, the erstwhile ally of the English, defied Edward and had himself crowned king of Scotland. Edward died the following year, but the unrest dragged on until 1314, when Bruce decisively defeated a huge English army under Edward II at the battle of **Bannockburn**. At last Bruce was firmly in control of his kingdom, and in 1320 the Scots asserted their right to independence in a successful petition to the pope, now known as the **Arbroath Declaration**.

rom Bannockburn to Bosworth: 1314–1485

he defeat at Bannockburn added to the unpopularity of **Edward II**, and the ng was eventually overthrown by his wife Isabella and her lover Roger ortimer, by whom he was horribly put to death in Berkeley Castle, Gloucesshire. Although **Edward III** was initially preoccupied by Scottish wars, his gn is chiefly remembered for his claim to the French throne, a feeble tence – he had earlier recognized the king of France and done homage to – but one that launched the **Hundred Years' War** in 1337. Early English ories such as the Battle of Crécy in 1346, and the capture of Calais the following year, were interrupted by the outbreak of the **Black Death** in 1349, a plague that claimed about a third of the English population. The resulting scarcity of labour produced economic turmoil in the land, and attempts to restrict the rise of wages and to levy a poll tax (a tax on each person irrespective of wealth) provoked widespread riots, which peaked with the **Peasants' Revolt** of 1381. After seizing Rochester Castle and sacking Canterbury, the rebels marched on London, where the boy king **Richard II** met Wat Tyler, the leader of the revolt, at Smithfield. The resulting scuffle led to Tyler's murder and the dispersal of the mob, and soon afterwards the Bishop of Norwich routed the Norfolk rebels, the prelude to a wave of repression and terrible retribution.

Parallel with this social unrest were the clerical reforms demanded by the scholar **John Wycliffe**, whose followers made the first translation of the Bible into English in 1380. Another sign of the elevation of the language was the success enjoyed by **Geoffrey Chaucer** (c.1340–1400), a wine merchant's son, whose *Canterbury Tales* was the first major work written in the vernacular and one of the first English books to be printed.

During the later years of Edward III's reign England had in effect been ruled by his son, **John of Gaunt**, duke of Lancaster, whose influence remained paramount during the minority of Richard II. In 1399 the vacillating Richard II was overthrown by John of Gaunt's son, who took the title **Henry IV** and founded the **Lancastrian** dynasty. Fourteen years later, he in turn was succeeded by his son, **Henry V**, who promptly renewed the war with France, which had been limping along ingloriously since the victory at Poitiers in 1356. After the much-celebrated triumph at **Agincourt**, Henry forced the French king to sign the Treaty of Troyes in 1420, making the English king the heir to the French throne, but on Henry's death just two years later his son was still an infant, which left regents governing the country on behalf of the monarch. Settling their differences, the French rallied under **Joan of Arc** to beat back the English, and by 1454 only Calais was left in English hands.

Meanwhile **Henry VI**, who was temperamentally more inclined to the creation of such architectural coups as King's College Chapel in Cambridge and Eton College Chapel than to warfare, had suffered lapses into insanity. Strongest of the rival contenders for the throne was Richard, duke of York, by virtue of his direct descent from Edward III. It was no accident that the **War of the Roses** – named from the red rose that symbolized the Lancastrian cause and the white Yorkist rose – broke out just a year after the return of the last English garrisons from France, filling the country with footloose knights and archers accustomed to a life of plunder and war. The instability of the time was signalled by **Jack Cade's Rebellion** of 1450, when a disorganized rabble – though with more participation by dissatisfied gentry than had been the case in the 1381 Peasants' Revolt – challenged the king's authority, winning a battle at Sevenoaks before being scattered. Political disputes within the circle surrounding the mad king were to prove more threatening to the regime. The Duke of York's authority over Henry was challenged by the king's accomplished and ambitious wife, Margaret of Anjou, whose forces defeated and slew Richard at Wakefield in 1460. She and Henry were in turn overwhelmed by Richard's son, who was crowned **Edward IV** in 1461 – the first king of the **Yorkist** line.

The civil strife entered a new stage when Edward attempted to shrug off the overbearing influence of Richard Neville, earl of Warwick and Salisbury, or "Warwick the Kingmaker", as he became known. Warwick then performed a dramatic *volte-face* by allying himself with his old enemy Margaret of Anjou forcing Edward into exile and proclaiming Henry king once more. Henry VI's second term was soon interrupted by Edward's unexpected return in 1471, when Warwick was defeated and killed at the Battle of Barnet and the rest of the Lancastrians were crushed at Tewkesbury three months later. Margaret was captured, Henry's heir was killed and Henry himself was soon afterwards dispatched in the Tower.

Edward IV proved to be a precursor of the great Tudor princes – licentious, cruel and despotic, but also a patron of Renaissance learning. In 1483, his twelve-year-old son succeeded as **Edward V**, but his reign was cut short after only two months, when he and his younger brother were murdered in the Tower of London – probably by their uncle, the Duke of Gloucester, who was crowned **Richard III**. Increasingly unpopular as rumours circulated of his part in the fate of the princes in the Tower, Richard was toppled at Bosworth Field in 1485 by **Henry Tudor**, Earl of Richmond, who took the throne as **Henry VII**.

The Tudors: 1485–1603

The opening of the **Tudor period** brought radical transformations. A Lancastrian through his mother's descent from John of Gaunt, Henry VII reconciled the Yorkist faction by marrying Edward IV's daughter Elizabeth, putting an end to the internecine squabbling among the discredited gentry. The growth of the wool and cloth trades and the rise of a powerful merchant class brought a general increase in wealth, while England began to assume the status of a major European power partly as a result of Henry's alliances and political marriages – his daughter to James IV of Scotland and his son to Catherine, daughter of Ferdinand and Isabella of Spain.

The relatively easy suppression of the rebellions of Yorkist pretenders Lambert Simnel and Perkin Warbeck ensured a smooth succession for **Henry VIII** in 1509. Although Henry was himself not a Protestant and even received from the pope the title of "Defender of the Faith" for a book he published criticizing Luther's doctrine, this tumultuous king is chiefly noted for the separation of the English Church from Rome. The schism was triggered not by doctrinal issues but by the failure of his wife Catherine of Aragon – widow of his elder brother – to provide Henry with male offspring. Failing to obtain a decree of nullity from Pope Clement VII, he dismissed his long-time chancellor Thomas Wolsey and followed the advice of Thomas Cromwell, forcing the English Church to recognize him as its head. The most far-reaching consequence of this step was the **Dissolution of the Monasteries**, a decision taken mainly to enjoy the profits of the ensuing land sales. The first phase of the Dissolution in 1536, involving the smaller religious houses, was a factor in the only significant rebellion of the reign, the **Pilgrimage of Grace**, a protest largely in the north of the country, which Henry put down with great cruelty, preparing the ground for the closure of the larger foundations in 1539.

In his later years Henry became a corpulent tyrant, six times married but at last furnished with an heir, **Edward VI**, who was only nine years old when he ascended the throne in 1547. His short reign saw Protestantism established on a firm footing, with churches stripped of their images and Catholic services banned, yet on Edward's death most of the country recognized his half-sister **Mary**, daughter of Catherine of Aragon and a fervent Catholic. She restored England to the papacy and married the future Philip II of Spain, forging an alliance whose immediate consequence was war with France and the loss of Calais, last of England's French possessions. Mary's unpopularity increased when she began a savage persecution of Protestants, executing the leading lights of the English Reformation, Hugh Latimer, Nicholas Ridley and Thomas Cranmer, the Archbishop of Canterbury who was largely responsible for the first English Prayer Book, published in 1549.

The accession of the Protestant **Elizabeth I** in 1558 took place in a highly volatile atmosphere, with the country riven between opposing religious loyalties and threatened abroad by Philip II. Heresy and treason were the twin preoccupations of the Elizabethan state, a society in which a sense of English nationhood was evolving on an almost mystical level in the vacuum created by the break with Rome. Aided by a team of exceptionally able ministers, the "Virgin Queen" provided a focal point for national feeling, enthusiastically supported by a mercantile class that was opposed to foreign entanglements or clerical restrictions, and was represented in a parliament made stronger by the constitutional decisions of the preceding fifty years.

The 45 years of Elizabeth's reign saw the efflorescence of a specifically English Renaissance, especially in the field of literature, which reached its pinnacle in the brilliant career of **William Shakespeare** (1564–1616). It was also the age of the **seafarers** Walter Raleigh, Francis Drake, Martin Frobisher and John Hawkins, whose piratical exploits helped to map out the world for English commerce. English navigational skills – as demonstrated by Drake's voyage round the world (1577–80) – and the country's growing naval strength triumphed with the defeat of the **Spanish Armada** in 1588. The commander of the English fleet, Lord Howard of Effingham, was a practising Catholic, a fact that dashed Philip's hope of a Catholic insurrection in England – a hope in part founded on the widespread sympathy for Elizabeth's cousin Mary, Queen of Scots, whose twenty-year imprisonment in England had ended with her beheading in 1587.

Wales under the Tudors

Welsh allegiance during the Wars of the Roses lay broadly with the Lancastrians, who had the support of the ascendant north Welsh Tewdwr (or Tudor) family. Welsh expectations of the first Tudor monarch, Henry VII, were high and though Henry lived up to some of them – removing many of the restrictions on land ownership imposed at the start of Glyndŵr's uprising and promoting many Welshmen to high office – administration remained piecemeal. Control was still shared between the Crown and largely independent Marcher lords until a uniform administrative structure was achieved under Henry VIII.

Wales had been largely controlled by the English monarch since the Treaty of Rhuddlan in 1284, but the **Acts of Union** in 1536 and 1543 fixed English sovereignty over the country. At the same time the Marches were replaced by shires (the equivalent of modern counties), the Welsh laws codified by Hywel Dda were made void and partible inheritance gave way to primogeniture, the eldest son becoming the sole heir. For the first time the Welsh and English enjoyed legal equality, but the break with native traditions wasn't well received. Most of the people remained poor, the gentry became increasingly anglicized, the use of Welsh was proscribed, and legal proceedings were held in English language few peasants understood).

Since Christianity had always been a ritual way of life rather than a philosophical code in Wales, Catholicism was easily replaced by Protestantism during the religious upheavals of Henry VIII's reign. What the Reformation did promote was a more studied approach to religion and learning in general. Under the reign of Elizabeth I, Jesus College was founded in Oxford for Wel scholars, and the Bible was translated into Welsh for the first time by a team led by Bishop **William Morgan**.

With new land-ownership laws enshrined in the Acts of Union, the stimulus provided by the Dissolution hastened the emergence of the Anglo-Welsh gentry, a group eager to claim a Welsh pedigree while promoting the English language and the legal system, helping to perpetuate their grasp. Meanwhile, landless peasants continued in poverty, only gaining slightly from the increase in cattle trade with England and the slow development of mining and ore smelting.

The Stewarts in Scotland: 1371–1625

In the years following Bruce's death in 1329, the Scottish monarchy gradually declined in influence. The last of the Bruce dynasty died in 1371, to be succeeded by the "Stewards", hence **Stewarts** (known as Stuarts in England), but thereafter a succession of Scottish rulers, culminating with James VI in 1567, came to the throne while still children. The power vacuum was filled by the nobility, whose key members exercised control as Scotland's regents while carving out territories where they ruled with the power, if not the title, of kings. **James IV** (1488–1513), the most talented of the early Stewarts, might have restored the authority of the Crown, but his invasion of England ended in a terrible defeat for the Scots – and his own death – at the **Battle of Flodden Field**.

The reign of **Mary, Queen of Scots** (1542–87) typified the problems of the Scottish monarchy. Mary came to the throne when just one week old, and immediately caught the attention of the English king, Henry VIII, who sought, first by persuasion and then by military might, to secure her hand in marriage for his five-year-old son, Edward. Beginning in 1544, the English launched a series of devastating attacks on Scotland, an episode Sir Walter Scott later called the "Rough Wooing", until, in the face of another English invasion in 1548, the Scots – or at least those not supporting Henry – turned to the "Auld Alliance". The French king proposed marriage between Mary and the Dauphin Francis, promising in return military assistance against the English. The six-year-old queen sailed for France in 1548, leaving her loyal nobles and their French allies in control, and her husband succeeded to the French throne in 1559. When she returned thirteen years later, following the death of Francis, she had to pick her way through the rival ambitions of her nobility and deal with something entirely new – the religious Reformation.

The **Reformation** in Scotland was a complex social process, whose threads are often hard to unravel. Nevertheless, it's quite clear that, by the end of the sixteenth century, the established Church was held in general contempt. Another spur to the Scottish Reformation was the identification of Protestantism with anti-French feeling. In 1554 Mary of Guise, the French mother of the absent Queen Mary, had become regent, and her habit of appointing Frenchmen to high office caused considerable resentment. In 1557, a group of nobles banded together to form the **Lords of the Congregation**, whose dual purpose was to oppose French influence and promote the reformed religion. With English military backing, the Protestant lords succeeded in deposing the French regent in 1560, and, when the Scottish parliament assembled shortly afterwards, it asserted the primacy of Protestantism by prohibiting Mass and abolishing the authority of the pope. The nobility proceeded to confiscate two thirds of Church lands, a huge prize that did much to bolster their new beliefs.

Even without the economic incentives, Protestantism was a highly charged political doctrine. As the Protestant reformer **John Knox** told Queen Mary at their first meeting in 1561, subjects are not bound to obey an ungodly monarch. Mary ducked and wove, trying to avoid an open breach with her Protestant subjects. Her difficulties were exacerbated by her disastrous second marriage to **Lord Darnley**, a cruel and politically inept character, whose jealousy led to his involvement in the murder of Mary's favourite, David Rizzio, who was dragged from the queen's supper room at Holyrood and stabbed 56 times. The incident caused the Scottish Protestants more than a little unease, but they were entirely scandalized in 1567, when Darnley himself was murdered and Mary promptly married the **Earl of Bothwell**, widely believed to be the murderer. This was too much to bear, and the Scots rose in rebellion, driving Mary into exile in England at the age of just 25. The queen's illegitimate half-brother, the Earl of Moray, became regent and her son, the infant James, was left behind to be raised a Protestant prince. Mary, meanwhile, became perceived as such a threat to the English throne that, after twenty years' imprisonment in England, Queen Elizabeth I had her executed in 1587.

Knox could now concentrate on the organization of the reformed Church, or **Kirk**, which he envisaged as a body empowered to intervene in the daily lives of the people. Andrew Melville, another leading reformer, proposed the abolition of all traces of episcopacy – the rule of the bishops in the Church – and that the Kirk should adopt a **presbyterian** structure, administered by a hierarchy of assemblies, part elected and part appointed. At the bottom of the chain, beneath the General Assembly, Synod and Presbytery, would be the Kirk session, responsible for church affairs, the performance of the minister and the morals of the parish. In 1592, the Melvillian party achieved a measure of success when presbyteries and synods were accepted as legal church courts and the office of bishop was suspended.

James VI (1567–1625) disliked Presbyterianism because its quasi-democratic structure – particularly the lack of royally appointed bishops – appeared to threaten his authority. He was, however, unable to resist the reformers until 1610, when, strengthened by his installation as king of England, he restored the Scottish bishops. The argument about the nature of Kirk organization would lead to bloody conflict in the years after James's death.

United Kingdom: 1603–1660

On Elizabeth's death in 1603, James VI of Scotland also became **James I** of England, thereby uniting the English and Scottish crowns. He quickly moved to end hostilities with Spain – a move resented by the increasingly powerful English Puritans, an extreme Protestant group – but his intention to exercise tolerance towards the country's Catholics was thwarted by the outcry in the wake of the **Gunpowder Plot** of 1605, when Guy Fawkes and a group of Catholic conspirators were discovered preparing to blow up king and Parliament. Puritan fundamentalism and commercial interests converged in the foundation of Virginia in 1608, the first permanent **colony in North America**, followed in 1620 by the landing in New England of the Pilgrim Fathers, the nucleus of a colony that would absorb about 100,000 mainly Puritan immigrants by the middle of the century.

A split was inevitable between James, who clung to the medieval notion of the divine right of kings, and the landed gentry who dominated the increasingly powerful Parliament, a situation exacerbated by the persecution of the Puritans. Recoiling from the demands of the Parliamentarians, the king relied heavily on court favourites, progressing from the skilful Robert Cecil, earl of Salisbury, and the philosopher Francis Bacon, to the rash and unpopular George Villiers, duke of Buckingham, who also had a close influence on the second Stuart king, **Charles I** (1625–49).

Raised in Episcopalian England, Charles had little understanding of Scottish reformism and, like his father, he believed in the divine right of kings. In 1637, Charles attempted to impose a new prayer book on the Scottish Kirk, laying down forms of worship in line with those favoured by the High Anglican Church. The reformers denounced these changes as "popery" and organized the **National Covenant**, a religious pledge that committed the signatories to "Labour by all means lawful to recover the purity and liberty of the Gospel as it was established and professed". Charles declared all the "Covenanters" to be rebels, a proclamation endorsed by his Scottish bishops. Consequently, when the king backed down from military action and called a General Assembly of the Kirk, the assembly promptly abolished the episcopacy. Charles pronounced the proceedings illegal, but lack of finance stopped him from mounting an effective military campaign – whereas the Covenanters, well financed by the Kirk, assembled a proficient army under Alexander Leslie.

In desperation, Charles summoned the English Parliament, the first for eleven years, hoping it would pay for an army. But, like the calling of the General Assembly, the decision was a disaster and Parliament was much keener to criticize his policies than to raise taxes. In 1642, facing the concerted hostility of Parliament, the king withdrew to Nottingham where he raised his standard, the opening military act of the **Civil War**. The Royalist forces were initially successful against the Parliamentarian army, gaining an advantage after the first battle of the war, **Edgehill**, at which Charles's nephew, the dashing cavalry officer Prince Rupert, displayed the reckless valour that was to distinguish his participation in subsequent engagements. After Edgehill, the Parliamentarian army was completely overhauled by **Oliver Cromwell** as the New Model Army, and won victories at Marston Moor and Naseby. Charles was captured by the Scots at Newark in Nottinghamshire in 1646 and was finally handed over to the English, by whom, after prolonged negotiations and more fighting, he was executed in January 1649.

The following year, at the invitation of the Earl of Argyll, Charles's son, the future Charles II, came to Scotland. To regain his Scottish kingdom, Charles was obliged to renounce his father and sign the Covenant, two bitter pills taken to impress the population. In the event, the "presbyterian restoration" was short-lived. Cromwell invaded, defeated the Scots at Dunbar and forced Charles into exile. For the next eleven years the whole country was a **Commonwealth** – at first a true republic, then, after 1653, a Protectorate under Cromwell, who was ultimately as impatient of Parliament and as arbitrary as Charles had been. Cromwell's policies were especially savage in Ireland, where his depredations are remembered to this day. At his death in 1658 his son Richard ruled briefly and ineffectually, and in 1660 Parliament voted to restore the monarchy in the person of **Charles II** (1660–85), the exiled son of the previous king.

The Restoration and the Glorious Revolution: 1660–1714

The turmoil of the previous twenty years had unleashed a furious debate on every strand of legalistic, theological and political thought, an environment that spawned a host of fringe sects – such as the Levellers, who demanded constitutional reform, and the more radical Ranters, who proposed common ownership of all land. Nonconformist religious groups flourished, prominent among them the pacifist **Quakers**, led by George Fox (1624–91), and the Dissenters, to whom the most famous writers of the day, John Milton (1608–74) and John Bunyan (1628–88), both belonged. With the **Restoration**, however, these philosophical eddies gave way to a new exuberance in the fields of art, literature and the theatre, a remarkable transition from the sombreness of the Puritan era, when secular drama and other such fripperies were banned outright. In the scientific arena, just six months after his accession, Charles founded the **Royal Society**, which numbered Isaac Newton (1642–1727) among its first fellows.

The low points of Charles II's reign came with the **Great Plague** of 1665 and the **Great Fire of London** the following year, though the latter had the positive consequence of allowing Christopher Wren (1632–1723) and other great architects to redesign the capital along more contemporary classical lines. Moreover, the political scene was not entirely tranquil: tensions still existed between king and Parliament, where the traditional divisions of court and country began to coalesce into **Whig** and **Tory** parties, respectively representing the Low Church gentry and the High Church aristocracy. A measure of vengeance was also wreaked on the regicides and other leading parliamentarians, though its intensity was nothing like that of the anti-Catholic hysteria sparked off by the Popish Plot of 1678, the fabrication of the trickster Titus Oates.

The succession in 1685 of the Catholic **James II** (James VII of Scotland), brother of Charles II, provoked much opposition, though – as one might expect from a country recently racked by civil war – there was an indifferent response when the Duke of Monmouth, favourite of Charles II's illegitimate sons, landed at Lyme Regis to mount a challenge to the new king. His undisciplined forces were routed at Sedgemoor in Somerset, in July 1685; nine days later Monmouth was beheaded at Tower Hill, and in the subsequent **Bloody Assizes** of Judge Jeffreys, hundreds of rebels and suspected sympathizers – mainly in Somerset and Devon – were executed or deported.

When seven bishops protested against James's **Declaration of Indulgence** of 1687, removing anti-Catholic restrictions, the king showed something of his father's obstinacy by having them tried for seditious libel, though he was quickly forced to acquit them. When James's son and heir was born, a child destined to be brought up in the Catholic faith, messengers were dispatched to William of Orange, the Dutch husband of Mary, the Protestant daughter of James II. William landed in Brixham in Devon, proceeding to London where he was acclaimed king in the so-called **Glorious Revolution** of 1688, the final postscript to the Civil War, while James fled to France with his new-born son.

William and Mary were made joint sovereigns, having agreed to a **Bill of Rights** defining the limitations of the monarch's power and the rights of his or her subjects. This, together with the **Act of Settlement** of 1701 – among other things, barring Catholics or anyone married to one from succession to the English throne – made Britain the first country to be governed by **constitutional monarchy**, in which the roles of legislature and executive were separate and interdependent, a model broadly consistent with that outlined by the philosopher and political thinker John Locke (1632–1704), whose essentially Whig doctrines of toleration and social contract were gradually embraced as the new orthodoxy.

Ruling alone after Mary's death in 1694, William regarded England as a prop in his defence of Holland against France, a stance that defined England's political alignment in Europe for the next sixty years. Mary died without leaving an heir and, on William's death in 1702, the Crown passed to her sister **Anne**, who had no surviving children. In response, the English Parliament secured the Protestant succession through the Act of Settlement, naming the Electress Sophia of Hanover as the next in line to the throne. The Act did not, however, apply in Scotland, and the English feared that the Scots would invite James II's son, James Edward Stuart, back from France to be their king. Nevertheless, despite the strength of anti-English feeling, the Scottish Parliament passed the **Act of Union** by 110 votes to 69 in 1707. Some historians have explained the vote purely in terms of bribery and corruption, but there were other factors. Scottish politicians were divided between the Cavaliers – Jacobites (supporters of the Stuarts) and Episcopalians – and the Country party, whose presbyterian members dreaded the return of the Stuarts more than they disliked the Hanoverians. There were commercial considerations too. In 1705, the English Parliament had passed the Alien Act, which threatened to impose severe penalties on cross-border trade, whereas the Union gave merchants of both countries free access to each other's markets. The Act of Union also guaranteed the Scottish legal system and the Presbyterian Kirk, though it replaced the two separate parliaments with a new British Parliament based in London.

The Hanoverians: 1714–1815

When Anne died in 1714, the succession passed – in accordance with the terms of the Act of Settlement – to a non-English-speaking German, the Elector of Hanover, who became **George I** of England. This prompted the first major **Jacobite uprising** in support of James Edward Stuart, the "Old Pretender" (Pretender in the sense of having pretensions to the throne, Old to distinguish him from his son Charles, the "Young Pretender"). Its timing appeared perfect. Scottish opinion was moving against the Union, which had failed to bring Scotland any tangible economic benefits. Neither were Jacobite sentiments confined to Scotland. There were many in England who toasted the "king across the water" and showed no enthusiasm for the new German ruler. In 1715, the fiercely Jacobite John Erskine, Earl of Mar, raised the Stuart standard at Braemar Castle. Just eight days later, he captured Perth, where he gathered an army of over 10,000 men, drawn mostly from the Episcopalians of northeast Scotland and from the Highlands. Mar's rebellion took the government by surprise. They had only 4000 soldiers in Scotland, under the command of the Duke of Argyll, but Mar dithered until he lost the military advantage. There was an indecisive battle at Sheriffmuir, but by the time the Old Pretender arrived in December 1715, 6000 veteran Dutch troops had reinforced Argyll. The rebellion disintegrated rapidly and James sank back to exile in France.

As power leaked away from the monarchy into the hands of the Whig oligarchy – many Tories having been discredited for suspected Jacobite sympathies – the king ceased to attend cabinet meetings, his place being taken by his chief minister. Most prominent of these ministers was **Robert Walpole**, regarded as Britain's **first prime minister**, who effectively ruled the country in the period 1721–42. This was a tranquil period politically, with the country standing aloof from foreign affrays, but the financial world was prey to a mania for speculation. Of the numerous fraudulent or ill-conceived financial ventures of the time, the greatest was the fiasco of the **South Sea Company**, which in

1720 sold shares in its monopoly of trade in the Pacific and along the east coast of South America. The "bubble" burst when the shareholders took fright at the extent of their own investments and the value of the shares dropped to nothing, reducing many to penury, and almost wrecking the government, which was saved only by the astute intervention of Walpole.

Peace ended in the reign of **George II**, when in 1739 England declared war on Spain, the prelude to the eight-year War of the Austrian Succession. Then in 1745 the country was invaded by the **Young Pretender**, Charles Edward Stuart ("Bonnie Prince Charlie"), the Old Pretender's dashing son, in the **Jacobite uprising** of 1745. This second rebellion had little chance of success: the Hanoverians had consolidated their hold on the English throne, Lowland society was uniformly loyalist, and even among the Highlanders Charles only attracted just over half of the 20,000 clansmen who could have marched with him. Nevertheless, after a decisive victory over government forces at Prestonpans, Charles made a spectacular advance into England, getting as far as Derby. London was in a state of panic: its shops were closed and the Bank of England, fearing a run on sterling, slowed withdrawals by paying out in sixpences. But Derby was as far south as Charles got. Threatened by superior forces, the Jacobites retreated to Scotland. The Duke of Cumberland was sent in pursuit and the two armies met on **Culloden Moor**, near Inverness, in April 1746. Outnumbered and outgunned, the Jacobites were swept from the field, losing over 1200 men compared to Cumberland's 300. After the battle, many of the wounded Jacobites were slaughtered, an atrocity that earned Cumberland the nickname "Butcher". Jacobite hopes died at Culloden and the prince lived out the rest of his life in drunken exile. In the aftermath of the uprising, the wearing of tartan, the bearing of arms and the playing of bagpipes were all banned. Rebel chiefs lost their land and the Highlands were placed under military occupation. Most significantly, the government prohibited the private armies of the chiefs, thereby effectively destroying the clan system.

Meanwhile, the **Seven Years' War** brought yet more overseas territory, as English armies wrested control of India and Canada from France, then in 1768 **Captain James Cook** departed from Plymouth on his voyage to New Zealand and Australia, further widening the scope of the colonial empire.

In 1760, George II had been succeeded by **George III**, the first native English Hanoverian. The early years of his sixty-year reign saw a revived struggle between king and Parliament, enlivened by the intervention of John Wilkes, first of a long and increasingly vociferous line of parliamentary radicals. The contest was exacerbated by the deteriorating relationship with the thirteen colonies of North America, a situation brought to a head by the American **Declaration of Independence** and Britain's defeat in the Revolutionary War. Chastened by this disaster, Britain chose not to interfere in the momentous events taking place across the Channel, where France, its most consistent foe in the eighteenth century, was convulsed by revolution. Out of the turmoil emerged the country's most daunting enemy yet, **Napoleon**, whose progress was interrupted by Nelson at Trafalgar in 1805, and finally stopped ten years later by the Duke of Wellington at Waterloo.

The Industrial Revolution

Britain's triumph was largely due to its financial strength, itself largely due to the gradual switch from an agricultural to a manufacturing economy, a process generally referred to as the **Industrial Revolution**. The earliest mechanized production lines were constructed in the Lancashire cotton mills where cotton-spinning was transformed from a cottage industry into a highly productive factory-based system. Water power became a thing of the past after James Watt patented his **steam engine** in 1781, and the utilization of coal as an engine fuel made it convenient to locate mills and factories near coal mines, a tendency that was accelerated as **ironworkers** took up coal as a smelting fuel, vastly increasing the output from their furnaces. Accordingly there was a shift of population towards the Midlands and north of England, where the great coal reserves were located, resulting in the rapid growth of the industrial towns and the expansion of Liverpool as a commercial port, importing raw materials from India and the Americas and exporting manufactured goods. Commerce and industry were served by steadily improving transport facilities, such as the building of a network of **canals** in the wake of the success of the Bridgewater Canal in 1765, which linked coalmines at Worsley with Manchester and the River Mersey. But the great leap forward occurred with the arrival of the **railway** age, heralded by the opening of the Stockton–Darlington line in 1825, with power provided by George Stephenson's steam-driven "Locomotion".

Boosted by influxes of Jewish, Irish, French and Dutch immigrants, many of whom introduced new manufacturing techniques, the country's population rose from about seven and a half million at the beginning of George III's reign to more than fourteen million at its end. But while factories and their attendant towns expanded, the rural settlements of England suffered, inspiring the elegiac pastoral yearnings of Samuel Taylor Coleridge and William Wordsworth, the first great names of the **Romantic** movement in English literature. Later Romantic poets such as Percy Bysshe Shelley and Lord Byron took a more socially engaged stance, inveighing against social injustices that were aggravated by the expenses of the Napoleonic Wars and by its aftermath, when many returning soldiers found their jobs had been taken by machines. Discontent emerged in demands for parliamentary reform, and in 1819 demonstrators in Manchester – centre of the cotton industry and most important of the industrial boom towns still unrepresented in Parliament – were mown down by troops in what became known as the **Peterloo Massacre**.

The following year George III, by now weak, old, blind and insane, died and was succeeded by his son **George IV**. During his reign religious toleration became a reality, as Catholics and Nonconformists were permitted to enter Parliament, workers' associations were legalized, and a civilian police force was created, largely the work of **Robert Peel**, a reforming Tory who outlined the basic ideology of modern Conservatism. More far-reaching changes came under **William IV**, with the passing of the **Reform Act** of 1832, whereby the principle of popular representation was acknowledged (though most adult males still had no vote); two years later, the revised **Poor Law** alleviated the condition of the destitute. Significant sections of the middle classes wanted far swifter democratic reform, as was expressed in public indignation over the **Tolpuddle Martyrs** – the Dorset labourers transported to Australia in 1834 for joining an agricultural trade union – and support for **Chartism**, a working-class movement demanding universal male suffrage. Poverty and injustice were the dominant theme of the novels of **Charles Dickens** (1812–70) and the preoccupation of the paternalistic reform movements that were a feature of the nineteenth century. This social concern had been anticipated in the previous century by the **Methodism** of John Wesley (1703–91) and the **anti-slavery** campaign promoted by evangelical Christians such as the Quakers and William Wilberforce. As a result of their efforts, slavery was banned in Britain in 1772 and throughout the colonies in 1833 – putting an end to what had been a major factor in the prosperity of ports such as Bristol and Liverpool.

Victorian and Edwardian Britain: 1837–1910

In 1837 William IV was succeeded by his niece **Victoria**, who, living through a period in which Britain's international standing reached unprecedented heights, came to be as much a national icon as Elizabeth I had been. Though the intellectual achievements of the Victorian age were immense – as typified by the publication of Charles Darwin's *The Origin of Species* in 1859 – the country saw itself primarily as an imperial power founded on industrial and commercial prowess, its spirit perhaps best embodied by the great engineering feats of Isambard Kingdom Brunel and by the **Great Exhibition** of 1851, a display of manufacturing achievements from all over the world. With trade at the forefront of the agenda, much of the political debate during this period crystallized into a conflict between the **Free Traders** – represented by an alliance of the Peelites and the Whigs, forming the Liberal Party – and the **Protectionists** under Bentinck and **Disraeli**, guiding light of the Tories. During the last third of the century, Parliament was dominated by the duel between Disraeli and the Liberal leader **Gladstone**. Although it was Disraeli who eventually passed the Second Reform Bill in 1867, further extending the electoral franchise, it was Gladstone who had first proposed it, and it was Gladstone's first ministry of 1868–74 that passed some of the century's most far-reaching legislation, including compulsory education, the full legalization of trade unions and an Irish Land Act.

In 1854 troops were sent to protect the Turkish empire against the Russians in the **Crimea**, an inglorious debacle whose horrors were relayed to the public by the first-ever press coverage of a military campaign and by the shocking revelations of **Florence Nightingale**. The fragility of Britain's empire was further exposed by the **Indian Mutiny** of 1857, though the country's prestige was not sufficiently dented to prevent Victoria from taking the title Empress of India after 1876. Apart from the Chinese Opium War of 1839–42 and some colonial skirmishes in Asia and Africa, the only other serious conflict to occur in Victoria's reign was the **Boer War** against the Dutch settlers in South Africa (1899–1902), another mishandled affair leading to the establishment of self-government there in 1906 and a military shake-up at home that was to be of significance in the coming European war.

Victoria died in the first month of 1901, to be succeeded by her son, **Edward VII**, whose leisurely and dissolute life could be seen as the epitome of the complacent era to which he gave his name. This complacency came to an end on August 4, 1914, when the Liberal government, honouring its committment to Belgian independence, declared war on Germany.

The two World Wars: 1914–1945

World War I was a futile massacre that destroyed millions of lives and eradicated whatever remained of the majority's respect for the ruling classes, whose officers had treated their conscripts as mere cannon fodder. At the war's end in 1918 the social fabric of Britain was changed drastically as the **voting** franchise was extended to all men aged 21 or over and to women of 30 or over. This tardy liberalization of women's rights – largely due to the radical **Suffragettes** led by Emmeline Pankhurst and her daughters Sylvia and Christabel – was not completed until 1929, a year after Emmeline's death, when women were at last granted the vote on equal terms with men.

At around this time the progressive wing of British politics, formerly occupied by the Liberal Party, was taken over by the **Labour Party**, the fruit of alliance between trade-union interests and middle-class radicals. Labour formed its first government in 1923 under Ramsay MacDonald, but following the publication of the **Zinoviev Letter**, a forged document purportedly showing Soviet encouragement of British socialist subversion, the Conservatives were returned with a large majority. In 1926, the tensions that had been building up since the end of the war, produced by severe decline in manufacturing and attendant escalating unemployment, erupted with the **General Strike**. Spreading instantly from the coal mines to the railways, the newspapers and the iron and steel industries, the strike lasted nine days and involved half a million workers, provoking the government into draconian action: the army was called in, and the strikers were forced to surrender. The economic situation deteriorated even further with the **Depression** after the crash of the New York Stock Exchange in 1929, with unemployment reaching over 2.8 million in 1931, generating a series of mass demonstrations that reached a peak with the **Jarrow March** of 1936. The same year, economist John Maynard Keynes argued in his General Theory of Employment, Interest and Money for a greater degree of state intervention in the management of the economy, though the whole question was soon overshadowed by international events.

Abroad, the structure of the British Empire had undergone profound changes since World War I. The status of Ireland had been partly resolved after the electoral gains of the nationalist party Sinn Fein in 1918 led to the establishment of the Irish Free State in 1922, from which the six counties of the mainly Protestant North "contracted out". Four years later, the **Imperial Conference** recognized the autonomy of the British dominions, an agreement formalized in the 1931 Statute of Westminster, whereby each dominion was given an equal footing in a Commonwealth of Nations, though each still recognized the British monarch. The royal family itself was shaken in 1936 by the **abdication of Edward VIII**, following his decision to marry a twice-divorced American, Wallis Simpson. Although the succession passed smoothly to his brother **George VI**, the scandal further reduced the standing of the royals.

Non-intervention in the Spanish Civil War and the Sino–Japanese War was paralleled by a policy of appeasement towards **Adolf Hitler**, who had massively rearmed Germany in pursuit of his territorial ambitions. In 1938 Prime Minister Neville Chamberlain returned from meeting Hitler and Mussolini at Munich with an assurance of good intentions from the two fascist leaders, and when **World War II** broke out in September 1939, Britain was still seriously unprepared. In May 1940 the discredited Chamberlain stepped down in favour of a national coalition government headed by the charismatic **Winston Churchill**, whose bulldog persistence and heroic speeches provided the inspiration needed in the backs-against-the-wall mood of the time. Partly through Churchill's manoeuvres, the United States became a supplier of food and munitions to Britain. The Japanese bombing of Pearl Harbor on December 7, 1941 precipitated the US's entry into the war as a combatant, and this, combined with the bloody resistance of the Russian Red Army, swung the balance. In terms of the number of casualties it caused, World War II was not as calamitous as World War I, but its impact upon the civilian population was much more terrible. In its first wave of **bombing**, the Luftwaffe caused massive damage to industrial and supply centres such as London, Glasgow, Swansea, Coventry and Plymouth; in later raids, intended to shatter morale rather than factories and docks, the cathedral cities of Canterbury, Exeter, Bath, Norwich and York were targeted. At the end of the fighting, nearly one in three of all the houses in the nation had been destroyed or damaged, nearly a quarter of a million members of the British armed forces had lost their lives and over 58,000 civilians were dead.

From Attlee to Thatcher: 1945–1990

The end of the war in 1945 was quickly followed by a general election. Hungry for change, the electorate displaced Churchill in favour of the Labour Party under **Clement Attlee**, who, with a large parliamentary majority, set about a radical programme to nationalize the coal, gas, electricity, iron and steel industries, as well as the inland transport services. Building on the plans for a social security system presented in Sir William Beveridge's report of 1943, the National Insurance Act and the National Health Service Act were both passed early in the Labour administration, giving birth to what became known as the **welfare state**. But despite substantial American aid, the huge problems of rebuilding the economy made austerity the keynote, with the rationing of food and fuel remaining in force long after they had ended in most other European countries.

In 1949 Britain, the United States, Canada, France and the Benelux countries signed the **North Atlantic Treaty** as a counterbalance to Soviet power in eastern Europe, defining the country's postwar international commitments. Yet confusion regarding Britain's post-imperial role was shown up by the Suez Crisis of 1956, when Anglo-French forces invaded Egypt, only to be hastily recalled following international condemnation. Revealing severe limitations on the country's capacity for independent action, the Suez incident resulted in the resignation of Conservative prime minister Anthony Eden and his replacement by the more pragmatic **Harold Macmillan**. Nonetheless, Macmillan maintained a nuclear policy that suggested a continued desire for an international role, and nuclear testing went on against a background of widespread marches under the auspices of the pacifist Campaign for Nuclear Disarmament.

The 1960s, dominated by the Labour premiership of **Harold Wilson**, saw a revival of consumer spending and a corresponding cultural upswing, with London becoming the hippest city on the planet. The good times lasted barely a decade. Though Tory prime minister Edward Heath led Britain into the European Economic Community (forerunner of the European Union), the 1970s was a decade of recession and industrial strife. A succession of public-sector strikes and mistimed decisions by James Callaghan's Labour government handed the 1979 general election to **Margaret Thatcher**, who four years earlier had ousted Heath to become the first woman to lead a major political party in Britain.

Thatcher went on to win three general elections, steering the country into a period of ever-greater social polarization. While taxation policies and easy credit fuelled a consumer boom for the professional classes, the erosion of manufacturing industry and the weakening of the welfare state created a calamitous number of people trapped in long-term impoverished unemployment. Social tensions surfaced in sporadic urban rioting and the year-long **miners' strike** against pit closures (1984–85), while violence in Northern Ireland also intensified and the IRA came close to killing the entire Cabinet when it blew up the Brighton hotel in which the Conservatives were staying for their 1984 annual conference.

The 1990s to the present

The divisive politics of Thatcherism reached their apogee with the introduction of the Poll Tax, a lunatic scheme that led ultimately to Thatcher overthrow in 1990 by colleagues who feared annihilation should she lead them into another general election. The uninspiring new Tory leader, **John Major**, unexpectedly won the Conservatives a fourth term of office in 1992, albeit with a much-reduced majority in Parliament. While his government presided over steady economic growth, this was overshadowed by mismanagement, feckless leadership and scandals involving Conservative MPs. Furthermore, the party was in increasing disarray over Europe with vocal right-wing **Eurosceptics** calling for Britain to dissociate itself from the planned integration of the economies of the European Union and the introduction of a single European currency.

Relations with Britain's European partners plummeted further when it was revealed that a brain-wasting disease in cattle (bovine spongiform encephalopathy or BSE, dubbed "mad cow disease") was widespread in British beef. The result was an EU ban on exports of British beef. The embargo was only lifted after the slaughter of millions of livestock, though concerns remain to this day regarding the links between **BSE** and the human degenerative condition Creutzfeldt-Jacob disease (**CJD**).

Meanwhile, the early 1990s saw the credibility of the **Royal Family** undermined with the break-up of the marriages of Charles and Diana, and Charles's brother Andrew (Duke of York) and Sarah Ferguson, along with a growing sense that the monarchy had become an anachronistic institution incapable of relating effectively with its subjects. **Diana**, who formally divorced from Charles in 1996, was championed, in some quarters, as an example of the humanity and glamour lacking in the other royals, and her death in a car accident in Paris in 1997 had a profound impact on the British people, many of whom joined in spontaneous public mourning unprecedented in recent history. The reaction to her death, as much as her death itself, marked a watershed in the Royal Family's relationship with both the public and the media.

The Labour Party, in disarray through the 1980s, had begun to regroup under a dynamic young leader, **Tony Blair**, who persuaded the party to distance itself from traditional left-wing socialism and take on a mantle of idealistic, media-friendly populism under the brand "New Labour". The transformation worked to devastating effect, sweeping Blair to power in the general election of 1997 on a surge of optimism that was immediately reflected in enhanced relations with Europe and progress in the Irish peace talks. Blair's electoral touch was repeated in Labour-sponsored votes in both Scotland and Wales in favour of devolved regional government, leading to the establishment of a **Scottish Parliament** in Edinburgh and a **Welsh Assembly** in Cardiff (the difference in title indicating that the former has stronger powers). While the Scottish Parliament has already made an impact, both it and the Assembly have been bedevilled by leadership issues and have yet to gain the full confidence of their nations.

These changes undoubtedly set the tone for a period of re-evaluation and modernism in British affairs. There was also much Labourite tub-thumping about the need to improve **public services**, but Blair only set about the task in earnest after the **general election** of June 2001, which Labour won with another parliamentary landslide. This second victory was, however, qualitatively different from the first. There remained little of the optimism of before and voter turnout was lower than at any time since World War II. Government manipulation of the media – dubbed "**spin**" – was blamed, as was the electorate's belief that public services were not improving despite Blair's fond words.

Media cynicism and internal dissent overshadowed the government's genuine achievements – introduction of a minimum wage, reform of the House of Lords – but did little to bolster the ailing Conservative Party, leaving Blair streets ahead of his political rivals in the opinion polls when the hijacked planes hit New York's World Trade Center on **September 11, 2001**. Blair rushed to support President Bush, joining in the attack on Afghanistan and then, much to the horror of many in the Labour Party and the country as a whole, sending British forces into **Iraq** alongside the Americans in 2003. Saddam Hussein was deposed with relative ease, but neither Bush nor Blair seemed to have a coherent exit strategy, and back home Blair's government was widely seen as having spun Britain into the war by exaggerating the danger the Iraqi dictator presented. With no "weapons of mass destruction" found in Iraq, and the Conservatives and Liberal Democrats gaining ground in the opinion polls, British politics is the most finely balanced it has been in decades. The Labour government faces considerable challenges if it is to regain the popular appeal it once had.

Books

Britain has an enviable wealth of fiction and poetry, and the selection below is intended only as a very general guide that is, by its nature, partial and partisan. Most of the books listed below are in print in paperback – those that are out of print (o/p) should be easy to track down secondhand. Finally, while we recommend all those we've listed below, we've indicated particular favourites with a ★

Travel and journals

★ **Bill Bryson** *Notes from a Small Island*. Bryson's best-selling and highly amusing account of a journey round Britain.

Giraldus Cambrensis *The Journey through Wales* and *The Description of Wales*. Two witty and frank books in one volume, written in Latin by the quarter-Welsh clergyman after his 1188 tour around Wales recruiting for the Third Crusade.

James Campbell *Invisible Country: a Journey through Scotland*. Insightful tour of a country seeking to develop a modern outlook while failing to come to terms with its past.

William Cobbett *Rural Rides*. First published in 1830, Cobbett's account of his various fact-finding tours bemoaned the death of the old rural England and its ways while decrying both the growth of cities and the iniquities suffered by the exploited urban poor.

David Craig *On the Crofter's Trail*. Using anecdotes and interviews with descendants, Craig conveys the hardship and tragedy of the Highland Clearances without being mawkish.

Nick Danziger *Danziger's Britain*. A well-timed journey through the "other Britain" of counter-estates and poverty that captures the mood of post-Thatcherite Britain.

Daniel Defoe *Tour through the Whole Island of Great Britain* (o/p). Defoe, the son of a London butcher, was a novelist, pamphleteer, journalist and sometime spy. This classic travelogue opens a fascinating window onto 1720s Britain.

Charles Jennings *Up North*. A provocative, but very readable account of a journey round the north of England, by a self-confessed southerner.

Jan Morris *The Matter of Wales* (o/p). Prolific half-Welsh travel writer Jan Morris immerses herself in the country that she evidently loves. Highly partisan and fiercely nationalistic, the book combs over the origins of the Welsh character, and describes the people and places of Wales with precision and affection.

Samuel Pepys *The Diary of Samuel Pepys*. Pepys kept a voluminous diary from 1660 until 1669, recording the fall of the Commonwealth, the Restoration, the Great Plague and the Great Fire, as well as describing the daily life of the nation's capital. The unabridged version is published in eleven weighty tomes; there's also an abridged version.

Paul Theroux *The Kingdom by the Sea*. Thoroughly bad-tempered critique of a depressed and drizzly nation.

Dorothy Wordsworth *Journals*. The engaging diaries of William's sister, with whom he shared Dove Cottage in the Lake District, provide a vivid account of walks and visits, and reflect Dorothy's fascination with the natural world.

History and society

Venerable Bede *Ecclesiastical History of the English People*. First-ever English history, written in seventh-century Northumbria.

★ **Asa Briggs** *Social History of England*. Immensely accessible overview of English life from Roman times to the 1980s.

Vera Brittain *Testament of Youth*. Vera Brittain was an exemplar of a golden generation – young, gifted and ideal-istic – whose lives were shattered by the Great War. She lost her fiancé, brother and two close friends to the trenches, and this book stands testa-ment to the dead, to her own pain, and to the burgeoning pacifism which was to shape her brilliant career as an activist and writer.

Beatrix Campbell *Diana, Princess of Wales: How sexual politics shook the monarchy*. A little hastily written per-haps, but still the most penetrating insight into the life and times of Diana – and the appalling callousness of her in-laws. Read this and you'll never want Charles to be king (if you ever did).

★ **David Daiches** (ed) *The New Companion to Scottish Culture*. More than 300 articles interpreting Scottish culture in its widest sense, from eating to marriage customs, the Scottish Enlightenment to children's street games.

Friedrich Engels *The Conditions of the Working Class in England*. Portrait of life in England's hellish industrial towns, written in 1844 when Engels was only 24.

Christopher Hill *The English Revolution* and *The World Turned Upside-Down*. Britain's foremost Marxist historian, Hill is without doubt the most interesting writer on the Civil War and Commonwealth period.

★ **Eric Hobsbawm** *Industry and Empire*. Ostensibly an economic history of Britain from 1750 to the late 1960s charting Britain's decline and fall as a world power, but Hobsbawm's book also offers detailed analysis of the effects on ordinary people.

Will Hutton *The State We're In*. Widely regarded economic and political survey of Major's Britain by the former editor of the *Observer* newspaper; spoken of as the text-book for Blair's New Labour.

Philip Jenkins *A History of Modern Wales 1536–1990*. Magnificently thorough book, placing Welsh his-tory in its British and European contexts. Unbiased and rational appraisal of events and the struggle to preserve Welsh consciousness.

Michael Lynch (ed) *The Oxford Companion to Scottish History*. A copi-ous collection, covering two thou-sand years and subjects as varied as climate, archeology, folklore and national identity.

★ **Andrew O'Hagan** *The Missing*. A part-autobiographical journey through Britain's modern underbelly, focusing on missing per-sons from bygone Glasgow to the secrets of a Gloucester cellar.

★ **George Orwell** *The Road to Wigan Pier* and *Down and Out in Paris and London*. The former depicts the effects of the Great Depression on the industrial communities of Lancashire and Yorkshire; the latter is Orwell's tramp's-eye view of the world, written with first-hand experience – the London section is particularly harrowing.

Wynford Vaughan-Thomas *Wales – a History* (o/p). One of the country's most missed broadcasters and writers, Vaughan-Thomas's masterpiece is this warm and spirited his-

tory of Wales. Working chronologically from the pre-Celtic dawn to the aftermath of the 1979 devolution vote, the book offers perhaps the clearest explanation of the evolution of Welsh culture.

Jennifer Westwood *Albion: a Guide to Legendary Britain* (o/p). Highly readable volume on the development of myth in literature, with a section on Scottish legends.

Regional guides

Daphne Du Maurier *Vanishing Cornwall*. Good overall account of Cornwall from an author who lived most of her life there.

★ **Joe Fisher** *The Glasgow Encyclopedia* (o/p). The essential Glasgow reference book, covering nearly every facet of this complex urban society.

Christopher Hibbert (ed) *Pimlico County History Guides* (o/p). An informative series giving a detailed history of selected English counties. Currently available are guides to Bedfordshire, Cambridgeshire, Dorset, Lincolnshire, Norfolk, Oxfordshire, Somerset (with Bath and Bristol), Suffolk and Sussex.

Pathfinder Guides With more than forty titles covering England, Scotland and Wales, these user-friendly walking guides feature

Ordnance Survey maps and clear route details.

Richard Sale *Collins Ramblers Guide: Snowdonia and North Wales*. Describes thirty walks with information on major landmarks and the region's natural history.

★ **A. Wainwright** *A Coast to Coast Walk*. Beautiful palm-sized guide by acclaimed English hiker and Lake District expert. Printed from his handwritten notes and sketched maps. Also in the series are seven authoritative books covering a variety of walks and climbs in the Lake District. Not all are available in the US.

Ben Weinreb and Christopher Hibbert *The London Encyclopaedia*. More than one thousand pages of concisely presented and well-illustrated information on London past and present – the most fascinating single book on the capital.

Art, architecture and archeology

Nicholas Best and Jason Hawkes *Historic Britain from the Air*. Beautiful aerial photos illustrate this geographical overview of Britain from Roman times to the aftermath of the Blitz.

Alan Crawford *Charles Rennie Mackintosh*. Part of Thames &

Hudson's World of Art series, describing the major contribution of Scotland's premier architect.

Samantha Hardingham *London: a Guide to Recent Architecture*. A handy pocket-sized book detailing the best of the capital's modern buildings.

★ **Duncan MacMillan** *Scottish Art 1460–2000* and *Scottish Art in the Twentieth Century*. The former is a lavish overview of Scottish painting with good sections on landscape, portraiture and the Glasgow Boys while the latter covers the last hundred years in splendid detail.

Nikolaus Pevsner *The Englishness of English Art*. Wide-ranging romp through English art, concentrating on Hogarth, Reynolds, Blake and Constable, including a section on the Perpendicular style and landscape gardening.

★ **Nikolaus Pevsner and others** *The Buildings of England & Wales*. Magisterial series, at least one volume per county, covering just about every inhabitable structure in the country. This project was initially a one-man show, but later authors have revised Pevsner's text, inserting newer buildings but generally respecting the founder's personal tone.

Fiction before 1900

★ **Jane Austen** *Pride and Prejudice*. Austen wrote with wit and vigour on manners, society and the pursuit of happiness, never more enjoyably than in *Pride and Prejudice*. Her amusing sense of irony, especially when delineating acquisitive and socially pretentious characters, is never far from the surface.

R.D. Blackmore *Lorna Doone*. Blackmore's swashbuckling, melodramatic romance, set on Exmoor, has done more for West Country tourism than anything else since.

Charlotte Brontë *Jane Eyre*. A wonderful Victorian "progress" story, following Jane from her pinched, unhappy childhood and schooling to her romance with Mr Rochester. The novel features scenes of quintessential Gothic melodrama – the mad woman in the attic wreaking revenge – and also functions as a deep psychological study of emotional repression.

★ **Emily Brontë** *Wuthering Heights*. One of the best, and strangest, novels in the English language. Often falsely claimed as a romance, it is more accurately a work about obsession, and still has the power to disturb. The complex intertwining of the narrative voices in the novel is just one aspect of its genius.

Thomas De Quincey *Confessions of an English Opium Eater*. Trip out with one of the most famous literary drug-takers. The opium visions only come at the end of the book; the rest is a digressive but entertaining account of the author's childhood and struggles.

★ **Charles Dickens** Many of Dickens' novels are located in London, including *Bleak House*, *Oliver Twist* and *Little Dorrit*, and contain some of his most trenchant passages of social analysis; *Hard Times* is set in a Lancashire mill town; while *David Copperfield* draws on Dickens' own unhappy experiences as a boy, with much of the action taking place in Kent and Norfolk.

George Eliot (real name Mary Ann Evans) wrote mostly about the county of her birth, Warwickshire, the setting for the three tales from her fictional debut, *Scenes of Clerical Life*. *Middlemarch* is a gargantuan portrayal of English provincial life prior to the Reform Act of 1832, while *The Mill on the Floss* is based on her own childhood experiences.

Henry Fielding *Tom Jones*. Mock-epic comic novel detailing the exploits of its lusty orphan hero, set in Somerset and London.

Thomas Hardy *Far from the Madding Crowd; The Mayor of Casterbridge; Tess of the D'Urbervilles; Jude the Obscure.* Hardy's novels contain some famously evocative descriptions of his native Dorset, but at the time of their publication it was Hardy's defiance of conventional pieties that attracted most attention: *Tess*, in which the heroine has a baby out of wedlock and commits murder, shocked his contemporaries, while his bleakest novel, the Oxford-set *Jude the Obscure*, provoked such a violent response that Hardy gave up novel-writing altogether.

Rudyard Kipling *Stalky & Co.* Nine stories about a mischievous trio of schoolboys, drawn from Kipling's experiences of public school in Devon.

Sir Thomas Malory *La Morte d'Arthur.* Fifteenth-century tales of King Arthur and the Knights of the Round Table, written while the author was in London's Newgate Prison.

Sir Walter Scott *Waverley.* The first of the books that did much to create the romanticized version of Scottish life and history. Others include *Rob Roy*, a rich and ripping yarn that transformed the diminutive brigand into a national hero.

Lawrence Sterne *Tristram Shandy.* Anarchic, picaresque eighteenth-century ramblings based on life in a small English village, and full of bizarre textual devices – like an all-black page in mourning for one of the characters.

★ **Robert Louis Stevenson** *Dr Jekyll and Mr Hyde; Kidnapped; The Master of Ballantrae; Treasure Island; Weir of Hermiston.* Superbly imagined and pacily written nineteenth-century tales of intrigue and adventure.

William Makepeace Thackeray *Vanity Fair.* A sceptical but compassionate overview of English capitalist society by one of the leading realists of the mid-nineteenth century.

Anthony Trollope *The Warden; The Small House at Allington.* Trollope was an astonishingly prolific novelist who also, in his capacity as a postal surveyor, found time to invent the letter box. His best-known book, *The Warden*, tells of a collision of family and moral duties in an English cathedral city, while *The Small House at Allington* is a tender story of a failed love affair.

Fiction since 1900

Peter Ackroyd *English Music.* A novel constructing parallels between interwar London and distant epochs to conjure a kaleidoscopic vision of English culture.

Martin Amis *London Fields.* A gleefully satirical novel that follows its seedy anti-hero, minor crook Keith Talent, through the mean streets of inner-city London. The rusticity suggested by the title is emphatically ironic.

Iain Banks An amazingly prolific author, who also writes sci-fi as Iain M. Banks. *The Wasp Factory* was one of the most startling debut novels, chronicling a dysfunctional Scottish childhood.

Julian Barnes *England England.* A satire of the all-pervasive "heritage industry"; a tycoon builds replicas of England's greatest monuments on the Isle of Wight, which gradually come to possess a greater power and importance than the originals.

Arnold Bennett Bennett's first novel, *Anna of the Five Towns*, is the story of a miser's daughter and – like

C

the later *Clayhanger* trilogy – is set in the English Potteries region.

George Mackay Brown *Beside the Ocean of Time*. A child's journey through the history of an Orkney island, and an adult's effort to make sense of the place's secrets in the late twentieth century.

John Buchan *The Complete Richard Hannay*. This one volume includes *The 39 Steps, Greenmantle, Mr Standfast, The Three Hostages* and *The Island of Sheep*. Good gung-ho stories with a great feel for Scottish landscape.

Joseph Conrad *The Secret Agent*. Spy story based on the 1906 Anarchist bombing of London's Greenwich Observatory, exposing the hypocrisies of both the police and the Anarchists.

Isla Dewar *Women Talking Dirty*. The outrageous, funny and poignant soul-bearing of two women in suburban Edinburgh who become friends over a bottle of vodka.

Daphne Du Maurier *Frenchman's Creek* and *Jamaica Inn* are nail-biting, swashbuckling romantic novels set in the author's adopted home of Cornwall; but *Rebecca* – in which an unnamed and anonymous bride narrates in terrified thrall the story of her predecessor, the shadowy "first Mrs de Winter" – is Du Maurier's best-known novel.

E.M. Forster *Howard's End*. Bourgeois angst in Hertfordshire and Shropshire; this is the best book by one of the country's most affectionately regarded modern novelists.

John Fowles *The Collector; The French Lieutenant's Woman; Daniel Martin*. *The Collector*, Fowles's first, is a psychological thriller in which the heroine is kidnapped by a psychotic lottery winner, the story told once by each character. *The French Lieutenant's Woman*, set in Lyme Regis on the Dorset coast, is a

tricksy neo-Victorian novel with a famous DIY ending. *Daniel Martin*, a dense, realistic novel, is set in postwar Britain.

Lewis Grassic Gibbon *A Scots Quair*. A landmark trilogy, set in northeast Scotland during and after World War I, the events are seen through the eyes of Chris Guthrie, "torn between her love for the land and her desire to escape a peasant culture". Strong, seminal work.

William Golding *The Spire*. An atmospheric novel centred on the building of a cathedral spire, taking place in a thinly disguised medieval Salisbury.

Robert Graves *Goodbye to All That*. Horrific and humorous memoirs of public school and World War I trenches, followed by postwar trauma and life in Wales, Oxford and Egypt.

Alasdair Gray *Lanark*. Gray's extraordinary first novel is a postmodern blend of social realism and labyrinthine fantasy featuring his own allegorical illustrations; it takes invention and comprehension to their limits.

Graham Greene *Brighton Rock; The Human Factor*. *Brighton Rock* is an action-packed thriller with heavy Catholic overtones, set in the criminal underworld of a seaside resort; *The Human Factor*, written some forty years later, probes the underworld of London's spies.

Nick Hornby *Fever Pitch; High Fidelity*. Hornby, one of Britain's most popular current writers, made his name with *Fever Pitch*, an autobiographical account of his obsession with football. *High Fidelity* is a fictionalized account of another obsession – records and record collecting – and examines the modern male with caustic incision.

Kazuo Ishiguro *The Remains the Day*. An intelligent novel, beautifully economical in style. It tells of an ageing butler who comes to realize that the master to whom he has devoted himself has Nazi sympathies; it is also a restrained and poignant love story.

Jackie Kay *The Trumpet.* The poet's debut novel, the powerful tale of a mixed-race Scottish jazz trumpeter whose death brings the discovery that "he" was actually a woman.

James Kelman *The Busconductor Hines*; *How Late It Was.* The first is a wildly funny story of a young Glasgow bus conductor with an intensely boring job and a limitless imagination. *How Late It Was* is Kelman's award-winning and controversial look at life from the perspective of a blind Glaswegian drunk. A disturbing study of personal and political violence, with language to match.

D.H. Lawrence *Sons and Lovers*; *Lady Chatterley's Lover.* Lawrence wrote magnificently on the social and emotional aspirations of the working class in Nottinghamshire's pit villages. His early short stories contain some of his finest writing, as does *Sons and Lovers*, a rich semi-autobiographical novel, and the infamous *Lady Chatterley's Lover.*

Laurie Lee *Cider with Rosie.* Reminiscences of adolescent bucolic frolics in the Cotswolds during the 1920s.

Richard Llewellyn *How Green Was My Valley*; *Up into the Singing Mountain* (o/p); *Down Where the Moon is Small* (o/p); *Green, Green My Valley Now* (o/p). Vital tetralogy in eloquent and passionate prose, following the life of Huw Morgan from his youth in a South Wales mining valley through emigration to the Welsh community in Patagonia and back to 1970s Wales. A bestseller during World War II and still the best introduction to the vast canon of "valleys novels", *How Green was*

my Valley captured a longing for a simple if tough life, steering clear of cloying sentimentality.

Compton Mackenzie *Whisky Galore.* Comic novel based on a true story of the wartime wreck of a cargo of whisky on a Hebridean island. Full of predictable stereotypes but still funny.

★ **Ian McEwan** *Atonement.* McEwan's ninth novel and possibly his most masterful yet, tracing the course of three lives from a sweltering country garden in 1935 to seeking absolution in the new century.

Timothy Mo *Sour Sweet.* A dense comic novel set in London's Chinatown in the 1960s, which follows the fortunes of the Chen family as they attempt to set up a restaurant, their malevolent rivals posing an increasingly sinister threat.

★ **Ian Rankin** *The Falls.* Astonishingly prolific and politically astute Scottish writer whose long-running series chronicles the vicissitudes of the dysfunctional Detective Inspector John Rebus, whose latest venture concerns the disappearance of the daughter of rich bankers.

Graham Swift *Waterland*; *Last Orders.* *Waterland* is a postmodern family saga set in East Anglia's fenlands – excellent on the strange history of this landscape. *Last Orders* is a bizarre and deceptively simple tale, which follows four men as they take the ashes of their friend, London butcher Jack Dodds, to the sea.

Dylan Thomas *Under Milk Wood*; *Collected Stories.* *Under Milk Wood* is Thomas's most popular play, telling the story of a microcosmic Welsh seaside town over a 24-hour period. *Collected Stories* contains all of Thomas's classic prose pieces: *Quite Early One Morning*, which metamorphosed into *Under Milk Wood*, the magical *A Child's Christmas in Wales* and the compulsive, crackling auto-biography, *Portrait of the Artist as a Young Dog*.

Evelyn Waugh The *Sword of Honour Trilogy* is a brilliant satire of the World War I officer class laced with some of Waugh's funniest set-pieces. The best-selling *Brideshead Revisited* is possibly his worst book, rank with snobbery, nostalgia and money-worship.

★ **Irvine Welsh** *Trainspotting*. A contemporary trawl through the horrors of drug addiction, sexual

fantasy, urban decay and hopeless youth. Still Welsh's most famous book, though (thankfully) his unflinching attention is not without humour.

★ **Virginia Woolf** *Orlando*; *Mrs Dalloway*. Woolf's lover, Vita Sackville-West, was the inspiration for the mesmeric *Orlando*, the life of the eponymous protagonist spanning four centuries and both genders. *Mrs Dalloway*, which relates the thoughts of a London society hostess and a shell-shocked war veteran, is a compelling example of her stream-of-consciousness style.

Poetry

★ **The New Penguin Book of English Verse** ed. Paul Keegan. Seven hundred years of English poetry, listed chronologically rather than by author.

Poetry before 1900

Beowulf trans. Seamus Heaney. A wonderful verse translation of the tenth-century Anglo-Saxon poem, which relates the epic progress of the warrior Beowulf.

★ **William Blake** *The Complete Poems*. Blake ranges from the limpid wisdom of *Songs of Innocence and Experience* to the mystical complexities of the prophetic books. He is unique among major poets in illustrating his own work, most of which is set in, or has a significant relationship to, London.

★ **Robert Burns** *Selected Poems*. Comprises the best-known work of Scotland's most famous bard, who employed vigorous vernacular language. Immensely popular all over the world, his famous early poems include *Auld Lang Syne* and *My Love Is Like A Red, Red Rose*.

Lord Byron *Selected Poems*. Byron was a best-seller in his day for exotic

poems of adventure such as *The Corsair*, and he is also a master of the Romantic lyric, but the core of his achievement lies in his unfailingly inventive and hilarious satire on all aspects of early nineteenth-century life, *Don Juan*.

Geoffrey Chaucer *The Canterbury Tales*. Fourteenth-century collection of bawdy verse tales that follows a pilgrimage to Becket's shrine at Canterbury; translated into modern English blank verse.

★ **Samuel Taylor Coleridge** wrote little, but to the highest quality. *Kubla Khan* and *The Rime Of The Ancient Mariner* are amongst the strangest productions of the Romantic period, but equally noteworthy are the quieter "conversation" poems such as *Frost at Midnight*.

★ **John Donne** *The Complete English Poems*. Donne (1572–1631), the greatest of the "metaphysical poets", brought passionate physicality and brilliant intellectual rigour to both his love poetry and religious verse.

Thomas Gray A minor talent who produced one great poem, *Elegy*

Written in a Country Churchyard, a powerful meditation on changes in an apparently changeless English countryside.

★ **John Keats** *Selected Poems*. Keats was potentially one of the greatest writers who ever lived. Even given his early death – he was only 25 – his achievements in poems such as the *Ode to Autumn* are extraordinary.

Christina Rossetti *The Complete Poems*. Like the American Emily Dickinson, Rossetti is an utterly unpredictable original, capable of producing lyric poems of piercing intensity in addition to the uncanny and gripping long work, *Goblin Market*.

William Shakespeare There are many one-volume editions of Shakespeare's entire output at a bargain price. For individual plays, you can't beat the Arden series, each volume containing illuminating notes and good introductory essays on the bard.

Percy Bysshe Shelley *Selected Poems*. Shelley's poetry moves from swooning romantic intensity to rigorously expressed hatred of the establishment of his day. He is a seminal figure in the pantheon of English radical dissent.

Alfred Tennyson *Selected Poems*. Tennyson's is perhaps the most purely beautiful and musical poetry in English, filled with sensuous detail and dreamy evocations of natural beauty and the past. *In Memoriam* shows him to be the great poet of Victorian doubt and faith.

William Wordsworth *Selected Poetry*. It's impossible to exaggerate Wordsworth's originality and his influence on the future direction of English culture; his presence is clearly felt in the novels of Dickens and George Eliot as well as in later poets. His understanding of what it means to be human can only be described as profound.

Poetry since 1900

The New Poetry ed. Hulse, Kennedy & Morley. Over fifty poets, all born since 1945.

Simon Armitage *All Points North*. An engaging and funny poetic travelogue, moving out from Armitage's home town of Marsden in West Yorkshire and taking in Leeds Airport, Huddersfield Town football ground on a Saturday afternoon, amateur dramatics and nights on the town.

★ **W.H. Auden** *Collected Poems*. Auden combines the themes of history, politics and love in poems that are definitive expressions of his times. The politically committed work of the 1930s gives way to a later religious commitment, but all his work is marked by stylistic virtuosity.

John Betjeman *Collected Poems*. Betjeman was the English poet laureate; his humorous and often nostalgic work was profoundly concerned with England and the English.

Carol Ann Duffy *Meeting Midnight*. That rarest of collections – unpretentious poetry for children which actually works. *Selected Poems* shows exactly the reason with its refreshing range of subverted stereotypes.

★ **T.S. Eliot** *The Waste Land*. Published in 1922, this is considered one of the cornerstones of Modernist writing, offering a revolutionary vision of Western civilization imbued with resonant images of contemporary and ancient London.

★ **Tony Harrison** One of the most prodigious poets to have emerged over the last thirty years, Harrison's longest work, *V*, explores his feelings at discovering the vandalisation of his parents' grave, while *Selected Poems* sweeps across a broad canvas of sex, politics and the lives of his native Northern English working class.

A.E. Housman *A Shropshire Lad.* Housman's poem is a richly detailed evocation of English pastoralism shot through with a strong, if suppressed, vein of homoeroticism.

Ted Hughes Soon before he died, Hughes published *Birthday Letters*, a moving account of his relationship with the poet Sylvia Plath, and his response to her suicide. *New Selected Poems 1957–1994* is the most comprehensive collection of Hughes's work available.

★ **Jackie Kay** *The Adoption Papers*; *Other Lovers.* Kay's poetry explores being black, Scottish and gay, and deals with personal relationships in an accessibly intimate way.

Philip Larkin *Collected Poems.* Larkin used plain language in his work, the subject of which is often the insignificance of human life. Many of the poems achieve an apparently unstudied beauty, though in fact Larkin published very little, preferring to refine his verse to its basic elements.

★ **Hugh MacDiarmid** *Selected Poems.* A poet and nationalist who sought, through his fine lyrical verse, to reinvigorate the use of Scottish literary language.

★ **Roger McGough** *Blazing Fruit: Selected Poems.* A contemporary Liverpool poet, whose witty rhetorical verse is instantly recognizable. Some of McGough's earlier work, alongside Adrien Henri and Brian Patten, can be found in the influential collection *The Mersey Sound.*

Edwin Muir *Collected Poems.* Muir's childhood on Orkney remained with him as a dream of paradise from which he was banished to Glasgow. His poems are passionately concerned with Scotland.

Wilfred Owen *The Poems of Wilfred Owen.* As with Keats, Owen's early death was a tragedy for English literature. His war poetry is at its best in *Strange Meeting*, with its strikingly original use of half-rhymes.

★ **Stevie Smith** *Selected Poems.* Smith's best-known poem is *Not Waving But Drowning* (1957), which uses the format of the comic poem but is loaded with economically expressed tragedy.

★ **Dylan Thomas** *Collected Poems: 1934–1953.* Thomas's beautifully wrought and inventive verse carried a deep, pained concern with mortality and the nature of humanity.

R.S. Thomas *Collected Poems: 1945–1990.* Welsh poet R.S. Thomas takes as his theme the enduring nature of Christianity, juxtaposed with the fleeting superficialities of contemporary culture. His finest poems have a strong visionary element, distilled in wonderfully still language.

Benjamin Zephaniah *Too Black, Too Strong.* Born in Jamaica but brought up in Britain, Zephaniah is an accomplished dub-poet, and a great performer of his own work.

Film

For much of its history the British **film** industry has largely been an English affair, with its major studios (Ealing, Pinewood and Shepperton) not far from central London and its stars drawn from the ranks of the capital's stage. However, unlike the Hollywood star system, the English film industry tended towards – and still significantly relies on – strong ensemble playing. While Ealing's films were a byword for social comedy, other significant elements have included the **Hammer horror** series (usually featuring one or both of Christopher Lee and Peter Cushing), costume dramas (typified by the **Gainsborough** company's productions) and the **James Bond** films, while the **Carry On** series kept a generation of comedy actors in work long past their sell-by date. In the 1960s, English films developed a justifiable reputation for social realism, which has been maintained in more recent times by directors such as **Ken Loach** and **Mike Leigh**.

Over the last twenty years and more, the television company **Channel 4** has commissioned a wide range of independently made films, single-handedly sparking small-scale film industries in both Wales and Scotland. Apart from *Gregory's Girl*, success remained relative, however, until the worldwide acclaim received by 1995's *Trainspotting*. Today's British film industry is in a healthier state now than perhaps at any point since the 1930s, with a diversity and vitality that reflects the dominance of independent productions. Some film fans might argue that the influence of television means that many such productions are essentially small-screen ventures, but within the last ten years a host of English pictures – *The Full Monty* and *Four Weddings and a Funeral* are just two examples – have enjoyed great success internationally.

The films listed below are all set in England, Scotland or Wales. They are not exclusively greats – though some rank amongst the best movies ever made – but all depict a particular aspect of British life, whether reflecting the experience of immigrant communities, exploring the country's history, or depicting its richly varied landscapes.

The 1930s and 1940s

Brief Encounter (David Lean, 1945). Extramarital attraction at a railway station is the theme of this mysteriously popular classic. Noël Coward is responsible for the clipped dialogue, Rachmaninov for the creepy score, Trevor Howard keeps his upper lip stiff and Celia Johnson wears an improbable hat.

Brighton Rock (John Boulting, 1947). A fine adaptation of Graham Greene's novel, featuring a young, genuinely scary Richard Attenborough as the psychopathic hood Pinkie, who marries a witness to one of his crimes to ensure her silence. Beautiful cinematography and good performances, with a real sense of *film noir* menace.

A Canterbury Tale (Michael Powell and Emeric Pressburger, 1944). Set in a wartime Kent village, where a plucky land girl, a small-town GI and a sardonic English sergeant are billeted. Overseen by a mysterious local magistrate, they make their own pilgrimage to Canterbury, the cathedral glowing high over bomb-damaged streets. A mystical vision of English history is fused with bucolic images of rural life, a restrained exploration of the characters' personal suffering underlying a truly magical masterpiece.

Fires Were Started (Humphrey Jennings, 1943). One of the best films to come out of the documentary tradition, this is the story of the experiences of a group of firemen through one night of bombing during the Blitz. The use of real firemen as performers rather than professional actors, and the avoidance of formulaic heroics, gives the film great power as an account of the courage of ordinary people who fought, often uncelebrated, on the home front.

Great Expectations (David Lean, 1946). Early film by one of England's finest directors – *Lawrence of Arabia*, *Bridge on the River Kwai* – this superb rendition of the Dickens novel features magnificent performances by John Mills (as Pip) and Finlay Currie (as Abel Magwitch). The scene in the graveyard is nothing short of wonderful.

Henry V (Laurence Olivier, 1944). Featuring glowing Technicolor backdrops, this wonderful piece of wartime propaganda is emphatically "theatrical", the action spiralling out from the Globe Theatre itself. Olivier is a brilliantly charismatic king, the pre-battle scene where he goes disguised amongst his men being delicately muted and atmospheric.

Jane Eyre (Robert Stevenson, 1943). Joan Fontaine does a fine job of portraying Jane, and Orson Welles is a suavely sardonic Rochester – the scene where he is thrown from his horse in the mist hits the perfect melodramatic pitch. With the unlikely tagline "A Love Story Every Woman Would Die a Thousand Deaths to Live!", it briefly features a young Elizabeth Taylor as dying Helen Burns.

Kind Hearts and Coronets (Robert Hamer, 1949). As with the best of the Ealing movies, this is a totally savage comedy on the cruel absurdities of the British class system. With increasing ingenuity, Dennis Price's suave and ruthless anti-hero murders his way through the d'Ascoyne clan (all brilliantly played by Alec Guinness) to claim the family title.

The Life and Death of Colonel Blimp (Michael Powell and Emeric Pressburger, 1943). An epic celebration of the oft-ridiculed romantic spirit of the English, personified by the wonderful Roger Livesey. We follow him through the actual and emotional duels of his youth, against his equally dashing German foe, to crusty old age in World War II. A daring and visually stunning story of love and friendship, it was hated by Churchill for supposedly being unpatriotic, which is surely recommendation enough.

A Matter of Life and Death (Michael Powell and Emeric Pressburger, 1946). Remarkable fantasy, opening with David Niven's airman miraculously surviving a fall from his stricken bomber. There follows a tussle between the monochrome bureaucracy of Heaven, who seek to reclaim him, and his fast-evolving Earth-bound love affair. Great performances and beautiful Technicolor images in another of Powell and Pressburger's enchanting romances.

Rebecca (Alfred Hitchcock, 1940). Hitchcock does Du Maurier: Laurence Olivier is wonderfully enigmatic as Maxim de Winter, and Joan Fontaine glows as his meek second wife, living in the shadow of her mysterious predecessor. Perfectly paced and beautifully shot, Hitch's first Hollywood picture is a true classic.

The Thirty-Nine Steps (Alfred Hitchcock, 1935). Hitchcock's best-loved British movie, full of wit and bold acts of derring-do. Robert Donat stars as innocent Richard

Hannay, inadvertently caught up in a mysterious spy ring and forced to flee both the spies and the agents of Scotland Yard. In a typically perverse Hitchcock touch, he spends a generous amount of time handcuffed to Madeleine Carroll, fleeing across the Scottish countryside, before the action returns to London for the film's great music-hall conclusion.

The Wicked Lady (Leslie Arliss, 1945). One of the best of Gainsborough Studios' series of escapist romances, this features a magnificently amoral and headstrong Margaret Lockwood, wooed into a criminal double life by James Mason's quintessentially dashing

highwayman. Its opulent re-creation of eighteenth-century England is terribly appealing, as are the tempestuous entanglements of its two wayward stars.

Whisky Galore! (Alexander Mackendrick, 1949). When a shipwrecked stock of the water of life is washed ashore on a remote Scottish island, the locals contrive all manner of cunning ruses to conceal its presence from the pursuing authorities. A beautiful Ealing comedy, with real sympathy for its eccentric little community as they battle the forces of dull authority in the entirely laudable ambition of having a good time at no expense.

1950 to 1970

Billy Liar! (John Schlesinger, 1963). Tom Courtenay is stuck in a dire job as an undertaker's clerk in a northern town, and spends his time creating extravagant fantasies. His life is lit up by the appearance of Julie Christie, who holds out the glamour and promise of swinging London. Touching and amusing.

Brigadoon (Vincente Minnelli, 1954). Gene Kelly escapes brash New York for the Highland glens, discovering love in the agreeable shape of local lass Cyd Charisse in the eponymous mythical village, which appears from the gloaming only once a century. Despite the slightly awkward studio landscapes, this is a delightful escapist fantasy, with some great Lerner and Loewe tunes.

Carry On Screaming (Gerald Thomas, 1966). One of the better efforts from the Carry On crew, with most of the usual suspects (Kenneth Williams, Charles Hawtrey, Jan Sims) hamming it up in a Hammer Horror spoof and serving up a few scares along with the usual single-entendre jokes.

Dracula (Terence Fisher, 1958). Classic Hammer Horror flick, loosely based on Bram Stoker's original book, and pairing Christopher Lee as the blood-sucking count with Peter Cushing's vampire-staking Van Helsing.

Far From the Madding Crowd (John Schlesinger, 1967). A largely successful and imaginative adaptation of Hardy's doom-laden tale of the desires and ambitions of wilful Bathsheba Everdene. Julie Christie is a radiant and spirited Bathsheba, Terence Stamp flashes his blade to dynamic effect, Alan Bates is quietly charismatic as dependable Gabriel Oak, and the West Country setting is sparsely beautiful.

If... (Lindsay Anderson, 1968). The stifling world of the English public school as a rather inadequate microcosm of society. Malcolm McDowell plays our iconoclastic hero, leading his little cell in revolution against the arbitrary discipline and cruelty of the school hierarchy. Although beautifully shot and well realized in its own caricatural terms, it seems dated now and rather too narrowly of its time.

I'm All Right, Jack (John and Roy Boulting, 1959). The best of The Boulting Brothers' comic explorations of English social mores explores the class system in the context of industrial unrest. Peter Sellers is on top form as the shop steward, while management is represented by a hapless Ian Carmichael (brought in to cause disruption through his own ineptitude) who, naturally, falls in love with Sellers' daughter.

Kes (Ken Loach, 1969). This is the unforgettable story of a neglected Yorkshire schoolboy who finds solace and liberation in training his kestrel. As a still-pertinent commentary on poverty and an impoverished school system, it's bleak but idealistic, and pale and pinched David Bradley, who plays Billy Casper, is hugely affecting.

The Ladykillers (Alexander Mackendrick, 1955). Alec Guinness is fabulously toothy and malevolent as "Professor Marcus", a murderous conman who lodges with a sweet little old lady, Mrs Wilberforce. The professor and his ragbag of criminal accomplices – their sinister intent a hilarious counterpoint to Mrs Wilberforce's genteel tea parties – try to pass themselves off as musicians, while, thanks to her innocent interventions, the body count inexorably mounts.

A Man for All Seasons (Fred Zinnemann, 1966). Sir Thomas More versus Henry VIII: one of British history's great moral confrontations made skilfully tedious by this film's stage-bound, talky origins in Robert Bolt's play. Despite muted, atmospheric visuals and a heavenly host of theatrical talent (including a cheering appearance by Orson Welles as Cardinal Wolsey), nothing can save this from paralysing dullness.

Night and the City (Jules Dassin, 1950). Great *film noir*, with Richard Widmark as an anxious nightclub hustler on the run. Gripping and convincingly sleazy, the London streetscapes have an expressionist edge of horror.

Only Two Can Play (Sidney Gilliat, 1961). Drily funny if faintly depressing adaptation of Kinsley Amis's farce *That Uncertain Feeling*, with Peter Sellers in convincingly seedy mode as an adulterous Welsh librarian.

Performance (Nicolas Roeg/Donald Cammell, 1970). Credited with precipitating James Fox's breakdown and subsequent retirement from the movies, this shape-shifting tale of gangsters and pop culture is the best account of the hedonistic end to Britain's psychedelic 1960s. Well known for its strange drug-hazed second half, the film is also brilliantly funny in parts and should be cherished for its hilarious destruction of the myth of Kray-style criminals.

This Sporting Life (Lindsay Anderson, 1963). One of the key British films of the 1960s, *This Sporting Life* tells the story of a northern miner turned star player for his local rugby team. The young Richard Harris gives a great performance as the inarticulate anti-hero, able only to express himself through physical violence, and the film is one of the best examples of the gritty "kitchen sink" genre it helped to usher in.

The 1970s and 1980s

Akenfield (Peter Hall, 1974). A powerfully involving evocation of English rural life whose ingredients include glowing cinematography and Michael Tippett's wonderful music. Past and present are skilfully contrasted, but the heart of the film lies in its sometimes ecstatic, but also harsh, rendering of the past.

Babylon (Franco Rosso, 1980). A moving account of black working-class London life. We follow the experiences of young Blue through a series of encounters that reveal the insidious forces of racism at work in Britain. Good performances and a great reggae soundtrack: an all too rare example of Black Britain taking centre stage in British movies.

Chariots of Fire (Hugh Hudson, 1981). This hugely successful movie prompted writer Colin Welland to bombastically – and optimistically – proclaim, "The British are coming." Based around the 1924 Olympics, it tells the true story of Scottish missionary Eric Liddell (Ian Charleson) and repressed Cambridge student Harold Abrahams (Ben Cross). Oscar-winning and overblown, it is distinguished only by Charleson's quiet performance, and some great locations.

A Clockwork Orange (Stanley Kubrick, 1971). Famously banned in the UK by director Kubrick, this is a genuinely disturbing, if now slightly dated, depiction of violence and society's reaction to it, in which young droog Alex – played with charm and menace by Malcolm McDowell – finds himself first the perpetrator and then the victim to a rousing soundtrack of Beethoven classics.

Comrades (Bill Douglas, 1986). In 1830s England, a group of farm workers decide to stand up to the exploitative tactics of the local landowner, and find themselves prosecuted and transported to Australia. Based on the true story of the Tolpuddle Martyrs, this combines political education (the founding of the modern union movement) with a moving and visually stunning celebration of working lives.

Distant Voices, Still Lives (Terence Davies, 1988). Beautifully realized autobiographical tale of growing up in Forties and Fifties Liverpool. The mesmeric pace is punctuated by astonishing moments of drama, and the whole is a very moving account of how a family survives and triumphs, in small ways, against the odds.

Frenzy (Alfred Hitchcock, 1972). Hitchcock comes back to Blighty in top form, with the story of a man on the run, under suspicion for the vicious "necktie" murders carried out in Covent Garden. Trademark sly black humour combines with a disturbing exploration of sexual immaturity.

Get Carter (Mike Hodges, 1971). Although not the masterpiece some claim, this is still one of the most vivid and interesting British gangster movies, featuring a monumentally evil outing for Michael Caine as the eponymous villain, returning to his native Newcastle to avenge his brother's death. Great use of its northeast locations and a fine turn by playwright John Osborne as the local godfather don't quite, however, compensate for its now faintly ridiculous misogyny.

Gregory's Girl (Bill Forsyth, 1981). John Gordon Sinclair is engaging and gangly as Gregory, whose adolescent dreams are filled with football-playing schoolgirl siren Dorothy. Gregory's gauche attempts to woo her keep the gentle plot tripping along nicely, his teachers making sardonic asides and his little sister proffering grave advice.

Hope and Glory (John Boorman, 1987). A glorious autobiographical feature about the Blitz seen through the eyes of 9-year-old Bill, who revels in the liberating chaos of bomb-site playgrounds, tumbling barrage balloons and shrapnel collections. His older sister's unfettered romps with a Canadian soldier and the adults' privation and occasional despair are an additional source of amusement for Bill and his tiny sister.

The Last of England (Derek Jarman, 1987). Derek Jarman was a genuine maverick presence in Eighties Britain; this is his most abstract account of the state of the nation. Composed of apparently unrelated shots of decaying London landscapes, rent boys and references to emblematic national events such as the Falklands War, this may not be to all tastes, but it is a fitting testament to a unique talent in British film-making.

Letter to Brezhnev (Chris Bernard, 1986). Frank Clarke's screenplay about chicken factories, Russian sailors, drink, love and idealism proved a marvellous vehicle for his larger-than-life sister, Margi, and the more considered Alexandra Pigg.

Made in Britain (Alan Clarke, 1982). One of Alan Clarke's series of savage dissections of Eighties Britain, featuring a 17-year-old Tim Roth as skinhead Trevor on a downbeat odyssey of job-centre visits, drug-taking and racist explosions. The energy of the central performance delivers a film of real force, and a very powerful indictment of Thatcher's Britain.

The Madness of King George (Nicholas Hytner, 1994). Adapted from an Alan Bennett play, this eighteenth-century royal romp has an irritating staginess, with the king's loopy antics played against a cartoon-like court and an England apparently devoid of real people.

Mona Lisa (Neil Jordan, 1986). This fine London-based thriller has powerful performances from Bob Hoskins, Michael Caine and then-newcomer Cathy Tyson, the latter playing a high-class prostitute who recruits Hoskins to help find her lost friend. This takes him, and us, on a nightmarish exploration of the dark side of Eighties London, lightened only slightly by an utterly convincing, poignant love story, as Bob begins to fall for his beautiful employer.

My Beautiful Laundrette (Stephen Frears, 1985). A slice of Thatcher's Britain, with a young Asian, Omar, on the make, opening a ritzy laundrette. His lover, Johnny (Daniel Day-Lewis), is an ex-National Front glamour boy, angry and inarticulate when forced by the acquisitive Omar into a menial role in the laundrette. The racial, sexual and class dynamics of their relationship are closely observed, and mirror the tensions engendered by the Asian presence in a hostile London.

On the Black Hill (Andrew Grieve, 1987). A visually absorbing adaptation of Bruce Chatwin's rather slight novel of Welsh farming folk. Hardyesque characterization and a similar predilection for doom, with a strong performance by Bob Peck as stubborn Amos Jones, trapped in an unhappy marriage to a middle-class woman.

The Wicker Man (Robin Hardy, 1973). A classic more by virtue of its unutterable weirdness than any great achievements of film-making. Edward Woodward plays a detective investigating the mysterious disappearance of a local girl on an isolated Scottish island, and finds himself drawn into a strange world of maypole-dancing and inadvertently hilarious pagan rites. Christopher Lee manages to keep a straight face throughout.

Withnail and I (Bruce Robinson, 1986). Richard E. Grant is superb as the raddled, drunken Withnail, an out-of-work actor with a penchant for drinking lighter fluid. Paul McGann is the "I" of the title – a

C

bemused and beautiful spectator of Withnail's wild excesses, as they abandon an astonishingly grotty London flat for the wilds of a remote cottage, and the attentions of Withnail's randy uncle Monty. A rare look at the Sixties that avoids nostalgia, and opts instead for emotional truth.

The 1990s to the present

Bend It like Beckham (Gurinder Chadha, 2003). Immensely successful film focusing on the coming of age of a football-loving Punjabi girl in a suburb of London. Both socially acute and comic.

Bhaji on the Beach (Gurinder Chadha, 1993). An Asian women's group takes a day-trip to Blackpool in this issue-laden but enjoyable picture. A lot of fun is had contrasting the seamier side of British life with the mores of the Asian aunties, though the male characters are cartoon villains all.

Billy Elliot (Stephen Daldry, 2000). Set against the depressing backdrop of the turbulent miners' strike of 1984, this ultimately feel-good film tells the story of a young boy (Jamie Bell), torn between his unexpected love of dance and the disintegration of his family.

Brassed Off (Mark Herman, 1996). A pacy film about British working-class life that eschews pathos, opting instead for uncompromising anger, underscored by robust black humour. With the imminent demise of the town's coal pit, the future for the Grimley Colliery Brass Band looks hopeless. Danny (Pete Postlethwaite) valiantly attempts to keep the band alive as the emotional lives of the musicians collapse.

Braveheart (Mel Gibson, 1995). Cod-Highland high camp, with a shaggy-haired Mel Gibson wielding his claymore as thirteenth-century independence hero William Wallace. The English are thieving effete scum, the Scots all warm-blooded noble savages, and history takes a firm back seat. Filmed largely in Ireland.

Breaking the Waves (Lars von Trier, 1996). A lyrical, moving drama set in a devout community in the north of Scotland. An innocent young woman, Bess (Emily Watson), falls in love with Danish oil-rig worker Jan (Stellan Skarsgaard). Blaming herself for the injury which cripples him, she embarks on a masochistic sexual odyssey, which rapidly takes her into dark and uncharted waters.

Bridget Jones's Diary (Sharon Maguire, 2001). American Renée Zellweger put on a plummy English accent and several pounds to play the lead in this *Pride and Prejudice* for the new millennium. Ably assisted by deliciously nasty love-interest Hugh Grant, the film stands out as one of the better British romantic comedies of the last few years.

Dirty, Pretty Things (Stephen Frears, 2003). A tumbling mix of melodrama, social criticism and black comedy, this forceful, thought-provoking film explores the world of Britain's illegal migrants.

East is East (Damien O'Donnell, 1999). Seventies Salford is the setting for this lively comedy, with a Pakistani chip-shop owner struggling to keep control of his seven children as they rail against the strictures of Islam and arranged marriages. Inventively made, and with some pleasing performances.

Elizabeth (Shekhar Kapur, 1998). Charismatic Cate Blanchett is, thankfully, the still heart of this history-lite and madly overblown production, where all political and emotional nuance is lost in an orgy of decapitations, swirling cloaks and stagy thunderstorms.

C

Enigma (Michael Apted, 2001). This blockbuster, scripted by playwright Tom Stoppard, is a fictional tale depicting Britain's wartime efforts to crack the Germans' Enigma encrypting machine, with Kate Winslet excelling amongst a generally fine cast.

Four Weddings and a Funeral (Mike Newell, 1994). Standard rom-com that used an American actress and gags based on English eccentricities to pull in big audiences worldwide. Unrepresentative of contemporary England with its Hugh Grant–led cast of middle-class whites, it still manages some very funny – and quite moving – set-pieces.

The Full Monty (Peter Cattaneo, 1997). Six Sheffield ex-steel workers throw caution to the wind and become male strippers, their boast being that all will be revealed: the "full monty". Unpromising physical specimens all, they score an unlikely hit with the local lasses. The film was itself an unlikely hit worldwide: the theme of manhood in crisis is sensitively explored, and the long-awaited striptease is a joy to behold.

Gosford Park (Robert Altman, 2001). Astutely observed upstairs-downstairs murder mystery set in class-ridden 1930s England. The multilayered plot is typical of the director, while the who's who of great British actors is led by the superb Maggie Smith – and only let down by Stephen Fry's bumbling police inspector who looks like he's wandered in from an entirely different film.

Harry Potter and the Philosopher's Stone (Chris Columbus, 2001). Though this overly-faithful-to-the-original-book adaptation crams in too much and feels rushed, this film about hero Harry's first year at wizards' school did wonders for the English tourist

industry with its use of places such as Alnwick Castle as locations. The second outing, *Harry Potter and the Chamber of Secrets* proved better-paced and more darkly enjoyable.

Howards End (James Ivory, 1991). E.M. Forster's tale of the forward-thinking Schlegel sisters, and their relationship with the conventional, domineering Wilcoxes. One of many immaculate British costume dramas, with precise performances from Vanessa Redgrave, Helena Bonham Carter and, most notably, Emma Thompson as Margaret Schlegel.

Little Voice (Mark Herman, 1998). Entertaining screen adaptation of Jim Cartwright's hit play about reclusive "Little Voice" (Jane Horrocks), who comes miraculously to life only on stage, brilliantly impersonating Fifties stars such as Marilyn Monroe. It features a great performance from Michael Caine as the impossibly seedy agent who seeks to exploit her bizarre talent, and offers a great glimpse of seaside England, with all its eccentric charm.

Lock, Stock and Two Smoking Barrels (Guy Ritchie, 1998). Four lads attempt to pay off gambling debts by making a drug deal in this over-stylized and rather shallow picture, which, though it has a modern setting, pays dubious homage to the London of the Kray twins. However, the suits are sharp, the production is slick and football's hardman-turned-actor Vinnie Jones turns in a surprisingly solid debut performance.

Nil by Mouth (Gary Oldman, 1997). With strong performances by Ray Winstone (Ray) as a boorish south Londoner and Kathy Burke (Valery) as his battered wife, this brave and bleak realist picture depic Ray as a victim of his own violenc as well as the devastatingly vulnerable Valery. Brace yourself.

Notting Hill (Roger Michell, 1999). After their huge hit with *Four Weddings*, writer Richard Curtis and actor Hugh Grant returned with more middle-class jollity. Grant reprises his bumbling floppy-haired Englishman role and falls for a glamorous American (Julia Roberts) – again. Spanning a year in the life of Notting Hill, it perversely fails to feature the event for which this part of London is best known: the biggest and best street carnival in Europe.

Orlando (Sally Potter, 1992). Vivid and visually beautiful adaptation of Virginia Woolf's novel, following its hero/heroine through 400 years of British history. Tilda Swinton is perfectly cast as the androgynous immortal, and choice moments spanning Elizabethan England to the present day (through the Civil War and Victoria's reign, for example) are perfectly and mysteriously realized.

Ratcatcher (Lynne Ramsay, 1999). Set in 1970s Glasgow during a refuse-workers' strike, Ramsay's striking first feature follows 12-year-old James, who accidentally drowns his friend as the rubbish around the tenement blocks mounts. Weaving rich humour into the gloomy narrative, Ramsay layers poetic images of the city, rejecting realism for a lyrical, symbolic approach.

The Remains of the Day (James Ivory, 1993). Kazuo Ishiguro's masterly study of social and personal repression translates beautifully to the big screen. Anthony Hopkins is the overly decorous butler who gradually becomes aware of his master's fascist connections, Emma Thompson the housekeeper who struggles to bring his real, deeply oppressed feelings to the surface.

Richard III (Richard Loncraine, 1995). A splendid film version of a renowned National Theatre production, which brilliantly transposed the action to a fascist state in the 1930s.

The infernal political machinations of a snarling Ian McKellen as Richard are heightened by Nazi associations, and the style of the period imbues the film with the requisite glamour, as does languorously drugged Kristin Scott-Thomas as Lady Anne.

Secrets and Lies (Mike Leigh, 1995). Much-loved Mike Leigh slice-of-life drama, with wonderful Timothy Spall at the head of a spectacularly dysfunctional London family. His sister Cynthia (Brenda Blethyn), her heart of gold buried in boozy, cloying unhappiness, is reunited with the black daughter she gave up for adoption at birth. Over-long improvised sequences and a depiction of suburban vulgarity which comes close to parody, are lifted by stunning ensemble performances and sustained by the simple strength of its central tenet: that secrets and lies in a family will only cause unnecessary pain.

Sense and Sensibility (Ang Lee, 1995). Jane Austen's sprightly essay on the merits of well-modified behaviour is nicely realized by Lee, and neatly scripted by Emma Thompson. Thompson and Kate Winslet are charming as the downtrodden Dashwood sisters: Winslet is a brilliantly over-wrought, romantic Marianne, while Thompson turns in another perfect performance as prudent Elinor.

Shakespeare in Love (John Madden, 1998). An irresistible homage to life, love and Shakespeare has an energetic Joseph Fiennes as the quill-chewing bard and Gwyneth Paltrow as his sparky love interest. Sharply scripted by Tom Stoppard, it skips a dainty line between parody and over-reverence, and has fun sending up the British fondness for cameos, with Rupert Everett as melancholy Kit Marlowe, off on a one-way trip for a drink in Deptford.

Film

CONTEXTS

C

Small Faces (Gillies MacKinnon, 1995). A moving little saga about the lives of three brothers growing up in 1960s Glasgow amid feuding gangs of local teenagers. We follow the rough education of young Lex, torn between the excitement and real danger of a life of fighting, and the alternative artistic ambitions of his older brother. A convincing and occasionally very funny re-creation of the period.

Trainspotting (Danny Boyle, 1995). An innovative, energetic adaptation of Irvine Welsh's novel, featuring a sensational soundtrack for a head-long dive into the drug-fuelled dark side of Edinburgh. Exciting and disturbing in equal measure, with almost insolently superb performances from McGregor, Ewen Bremner and Robert Carlyle.

Glossaries

Architectural terms

Aisle Clear space parallel to the nave, usually with lower ceiling than the nave.

Altar Table at which the Eucharist is celebrated, at the east end of the church. (When church is not aligned to the geographical east, the altar end is still referred to as the "east" end.)

Ambulatory Passage behind the chancel.

Apse The curved or polygonal east end of a church.

Arcade Row of arches on top of columns or piers, supporting a wall.

Bailey Area enclosed by castle walls.

Barbican Defensive structure built in front of main gate.

Barrel vault Continuous rounded vault, like a semi-cylinder.

Boss A decorative carving at the meeting point of the lines of a vault.

Box pew Form of church seating in which each row is enclosed by high, thin wooden panels.

Broach spire Octagonal spire rising straight out of a square tower.

Buttress Stone support for a wall; some buttresses are wholly attached to the wall, others take the form of an outer support with a connecting half-arch, known as a "flying buttress".

Capital Upper section of a column, usually carved.

Chancel Section of the church where the altar is located.

Chantry Small chapel in which masses were said for the soul of the person who financed its construction; none built after the reign of Henry VIII.

Choir Area in which the church service is conducted; next to or same as chancel.

Clerestory Upper storey of nave, containing a line of windows.

Coffering Regular recessed spaces set into a ceiling.

Crenellations Battlements with square indentations.

Decorated Middle Gothic style, about 1280–1380.

Dogtooth Form of early Gothic decorative stonework, looking like raised "X"s.

Early English First phase of Gothic architecture in England, about 1150–1280.

Fan vault Late Gothic form of vaulting, in which the area between walls and ceiling is covered with stone ribs in the shape of an open fan.

Finial Any decorated tip of an architectural feature.

Flushwork Kind of surface decoration in which tablets of white stone alternate with pieces of flint; very common in East Anglia.

Gargoyle Grotesque exterior carving, usually a decorative form of water spout.

Hammer beam Type of ceiling in which horizontal brackets support vertical struts that connect to the roof timbers.

Keep Main structure of a castle.

Lady Chapel Chapel dedicated to the Virgin, often found at the east end of major churches.

Lancet Tall, narrow and plain window.

Lantern Upper part of a dome or tower, often glazed.

Misericord Carved ledge below a tip-up seat, usually in choir stalls, as support when occupant stands.

Motte Mound on which a castle keep stands.

Mullion Vertical post between the panes of a window.

Nave The main part of the church to the west of the crossing.

Ogee Double curve; distinctive feature of Decorated style.

Oriel Projecting window.

Palladian Seventeenth- and eighteenth-century classical style adhering to the principles of Andrea Palladio.

Pediment Triangular space above a window or doorway.

Perpendicular Late Gothic style, about 1380–1550.

Pilaster Flat column set against a wall.

Reredos Painted or carved panel behind an altar.

Rood screen Wooden screen supporting a crucifix (or rood), separating the choir from the nave; few survived the Reformation.

Rose window Large circular window, divided into vaguely petal-shaped sections.

Stalls Seating for clergy in the choir area of a church.

Tracery Pattern formed by narrow bands of stone in a window or on a wall surface.

Transept Section of the main body of the church at right angles to the choir and nave.

Triforium Arcade above the nave or transept in a church.

Tympanum Panel over a doorway, often carved in medieval churches.

Vault Arched ceiling.

British terminology

Bill Restaurant check

Biscuit Cookie or cracker

Bonnet Car hood

Boot Car trunk

Brummies People born in Birmingham

Caravan Trailer

Car park Parking lot

Cheap Inexpensive

Chemist Pharmacist

Chips French fries

Coach Bus

Crisps Potato chips

Dual Carriageway Divided highway

Dustbin Trash can

First floor Second floor

Fiver Five pounds (money)

Flat Apartment

Fortnight Two weeks

Geordie Person from Newcastle upon Tyne

Ground floor First floor

High Street Main Street

Hire Rent

Jam Jelly

Jelly Jell-O

Jumble sale Yard sale

Jumper Sweater

Lay-by Road shoulder

Leaflet Pamphlet

Lift Elevator

Lorry Truck

Motorway Highway

Off-licence Liquor store

Pants Underwear

Petrol Gasoline

Pudding Dessert

Queue Line

Return ticket Round-trip ticket

Roundabout Rotary interchange

Scouser Person from Liverpool

Single carriageway Non-divided highway

Single ticket One-way ticket

Snug Small, intimate section of a pub

Stalls Orchestra seats

Stone Fourteen pounds (weight)

Subway Pedestrian passageway

Sweets Candy

Tap Faucet

Tenner Ten pounds (money)

Tights Pantyhose

Torch Flashlight

Trainers Sneakers

Trousers Pants

Tube/Underground Subway (train)

Vest Undershirt

Rough Guides travel...

Rough Guides are available from good bookstores worldwide. New title
published every month. Check www.roughguides.com for the latest ne